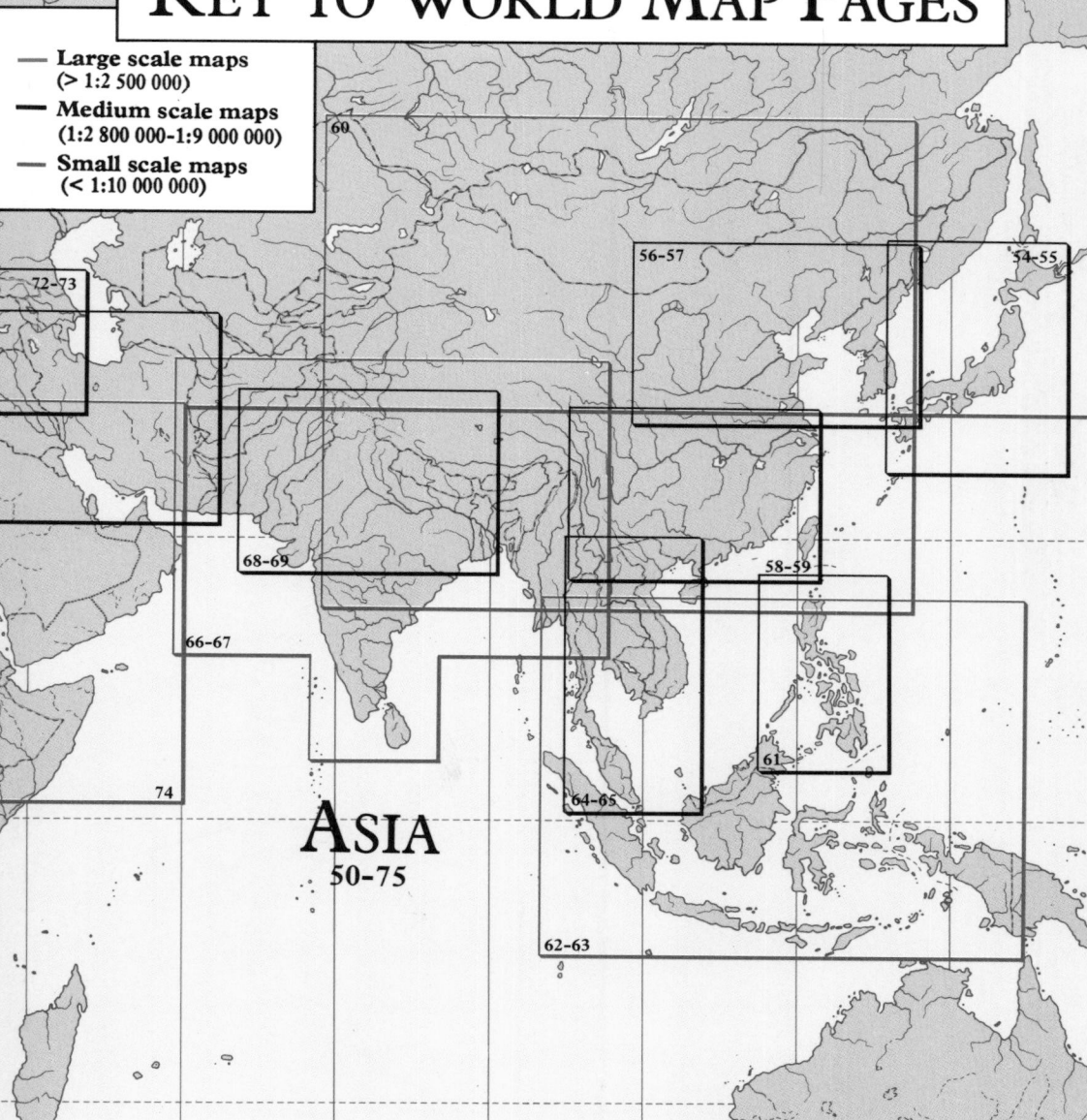

KEY TO WORLD MAP PAGES

— **Large scale maps**
  (> 1:2 500 000)
— **Medium scale maps**
  (1:2 800 000–1:9 000 000)
— **Small scale maps**
  (< 1:10 000 000)

ASIA
50–75

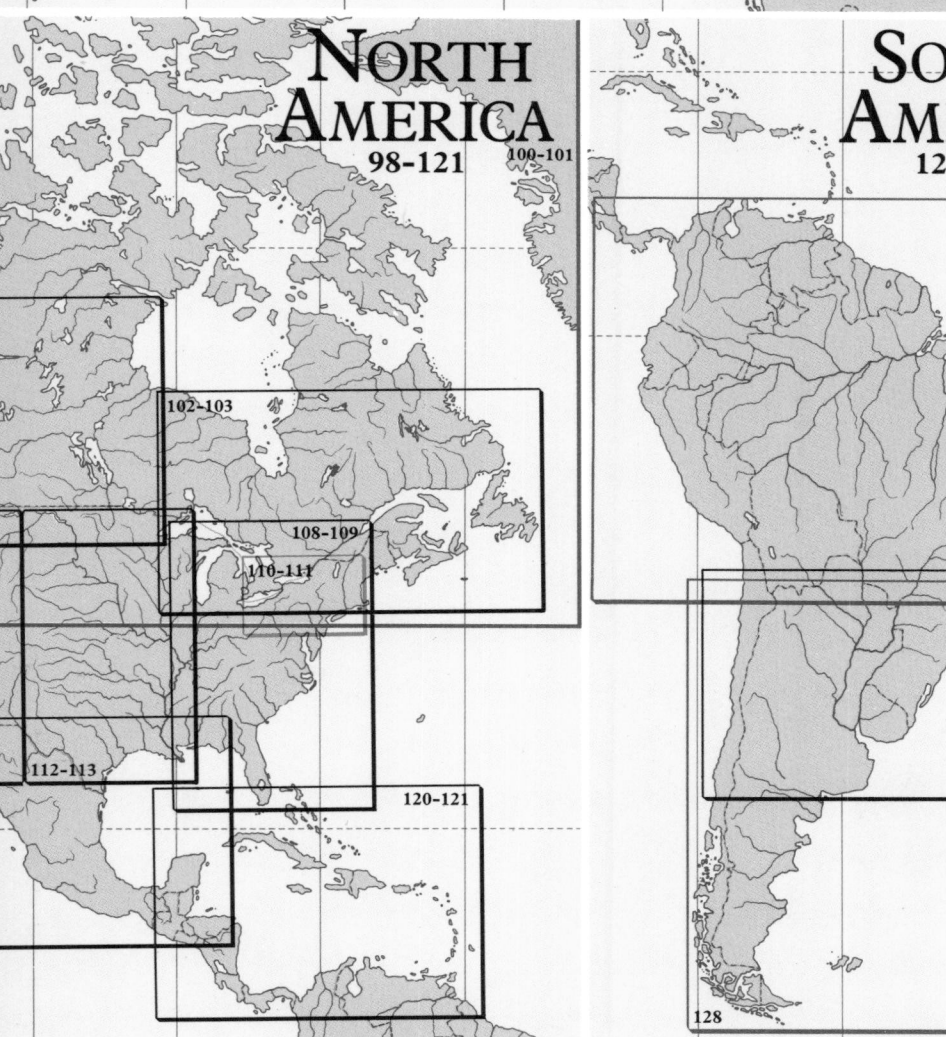

NORTH AMERICA
98–121

SOUTH AMERICA
122–128

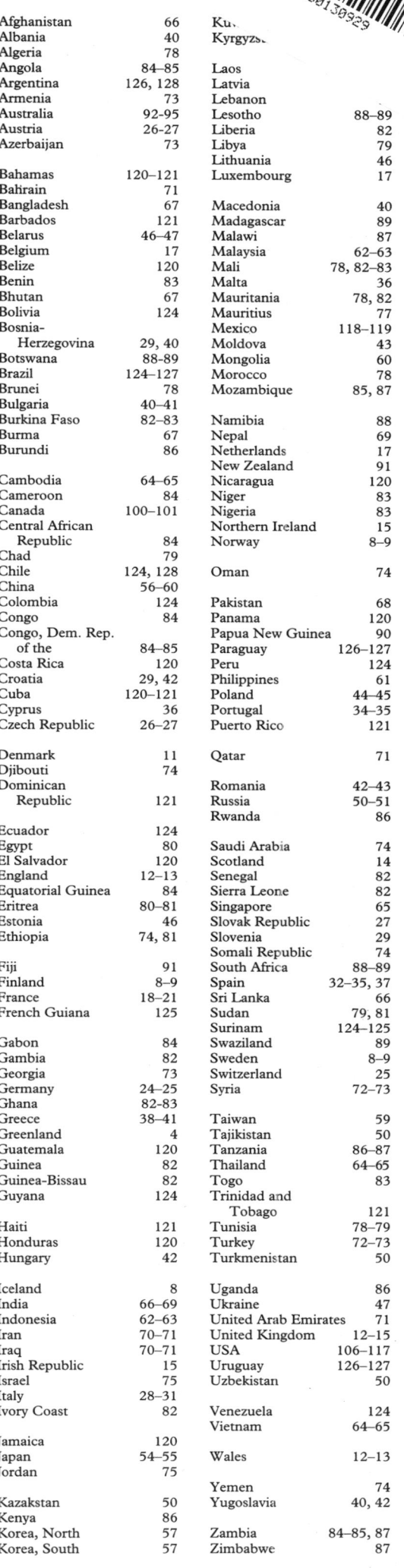

COUNT...

Afghanistan	66	Ku...	
Albania	40	Kyrgyz...	
Algeria	78		
Angola	84–85	Laos	
Argentina	126, 128	Latvia	
Armenia	73	Lebanon	
Australia	92–95	Lesotho	88–89
Austria	26–27	Liberia	82
Azerbaijan	73	Libya	79
		Lithuania	46
Bahamas	120–121	Luxembourg	17
Bahrain	71		
Bangladesh	67	Macedonia	40
Barbados	121	Madagascar	89
Belarus	46–47	Malawi	87
Belgium	17	Malaysia	62–63
Belize	120	Mali	78, 82–83
Benin	83	Malta	36
Bhutan	67	Mauritania	78, 82
Bolivia	124	Mauritius	77
Bosnia-		Mexico	118–119
Herzegovina	29, 40	Moldova	43
Botswana	88–89	Mongolia	60
Brazil	124–127	Morocco	78
Brunei	78	Mozambique	85, 87
Bulgaria	40–41		
Burkina Faso	82–83	Namibia	88
Burma	67	Nepal	69
Burundi	86	Netherlands	17
		New Zealand	91
Cambodia	64–65	Nicaragua	120
Cameroon	84	Niger	83
Canada	100–101	Nigeria	83
Central African		Northern Ireland	15
Republic	84	Norway	8–9
Chad	79		
Chile	124, 128	Oman	74
China	56–60		
Colombia	124	Pakistan	68
Congo	84	Panama	120
Congo, Dem. Rep.		Papua New Guinea	90
of the	84–85	Paraguay	126–127
Costa Rica	120	Peru	124
Croatia	29, 42	Philippines	61
Cuba	120–121	Poland	44–45
Cyprus	36	Portugal	34–35
Czech Republic	26–27	Puerto Rico	121
Denmark	11	Qatar	71
Djibouti	74		
Dominican		Romania	42–43
Republic	121	Russia	50–51
		Rwanda	86
Ecuador	124		
Egypt	80	Saudi Arabia	74
El Salvador	120	Scotland	14
England	12–13	Senegal	82
Equatorial Guinea	84	Sierra Leone	82
Eritrea	80–81	Singapore	65
Estonia	46	Slovak Republic	27
Ethiopia	74, 81	Slovenia	29
		Somali Republic	74
Fiji	91	South Africa	88–89
Finland	8–9	Spain	32–35, 37
France	18–21	Sri Lanka	66
French Guiana	125	Sudan	79, 81
		Surinam	124–125
Gabon	84	Swaziland	89
Gambia	82	Sweden	8–9
Georgia	73	Switzerland	25
Germany	24–25	Syria	72–73
Ghana	82–83		
Greece	38–41	Taiwan	59
Greenland	4	Tajikistan	50
Guatemala	120	Tanzania	86–87
Guinea	82	Thailand	64–65
Guinea-Bissau	82	Togo	83
Guyana	124	Trinidad and	
		Tobago	121
Haiti	121	Tunisia	78–79
Honduras	120	Turkey	72–73
Hungary	42	Turkmenistan	50
Iceland	8	Uganda	86
India	66–69	Ukraine	47
Indonesia	62–63	United Arab Emirates	71
Iran	70–71	United Kingdom	12–15
Iraq	70–71	USA	106–117
Irish Republic	15	Uruguay	126–127
Israel	75	Uzbekistan	50
Italy	28–31		
Ivory Coast	82	Venezuela	124
		Vietnam	64–65
Jamaica	120		
Japan	54–55	Wales	12–13
Jordan	75		
		Yemen	74
Kazakstan	50	Yugoslavia	40, 42
Kenya	86		
Korea, North	57	Zambia	84–85, 87
Korea, South	57	Zimbabwe	87

PHILIP'S

WORLD TRAVELLER'S ATLAS

PHILIP'S

WORLD TRAVELLER'S ATLAS

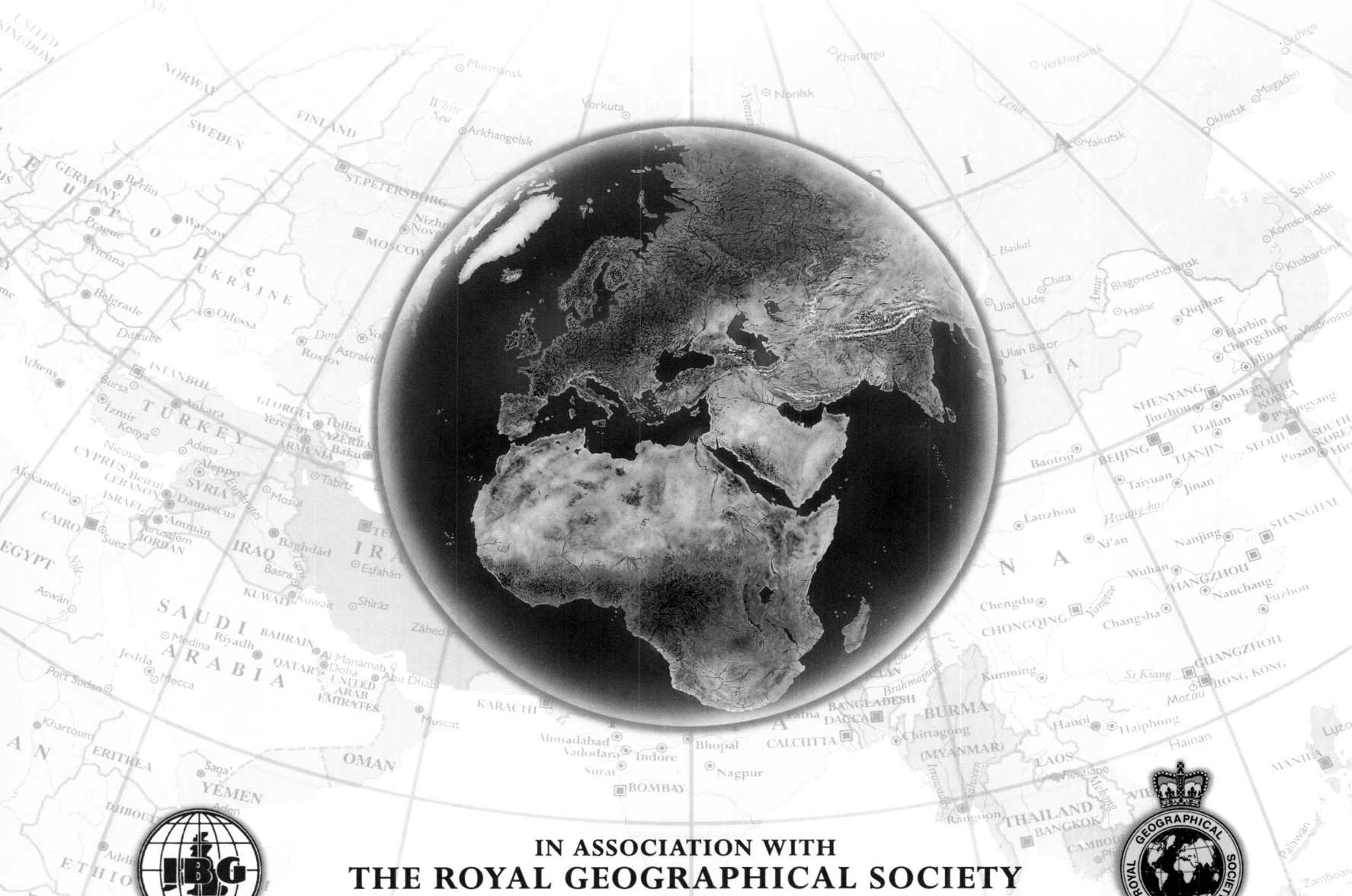

IN ASSOCIATION WITH
THE ROYAL GEOGRAPHICAL SOCIETY
WITH THE INSTITUTE OF BRITISH GEOGRAPHERS

PICTURE ACKNOWLEDGEMENTS

WORLD EXPLORER:
© CORBIS 26 bottom, 27 bottom, /Adam Woolfitt 5 centre right, 30 centre left, /AFP 24 top, 25 bottom, /Angelo Hornak 29 centre left, /Australian Picture Library 13 top, /Bob Krist 14 top, /Bob Winsett 20 top, /Brandon D. Cole 11 bottom, /Buddy Mays 26 centre, 22 bottom, /Catherine Karnow 19 bottom, /Charles and Josette Lenars 30 bottom right, /Charles O'Rear 23 left, /Clem Haagner; Gallo Images 10 centre, /Dave G. Houser 30 top, /David Muench 4 left, /Dean Conger 15 bottom, /Derek Hall; Frank Lane Picture Agency 3 centre, /Douglas Peebles 32 bottom, /Duomo 20 right, /Enzo and Paolo Ragazzini 16 bottom, /Galen Rowell 2 left, 9 bottom, 21 top, /George H. H. Huey 4 top, /George Lepp 12 bottom, /Hans Georg Roth 5 top, /Inge Yspeert 10 bottom right, /James Marshall 6 centre right, /John Dakers; Eye Ubiquitous 25 right, /Kevin Schafer 13 bottom, /Marc Muench 20 left, /Michael and Patricia Fogden 8 /Michael Busselle 3 top, /Michael S. Yamashita 22 top, /Milepost 92½ 15 top, /Mimmo Jodice 29 bottom, /Morton Beebe, S. F. 24 centre right, /Nik Wheeler 19 top, /O. Alamany and E. Vicens 5 bottom, /Patrick Ward 7 bottom, 16 centre right, /Peter Johnson 10 top, /Peter Wilson 28 bottom, /Premium Stock 28 top, /Quadrillion 31 bottom, /Raymond Gehman 2 top, 6 top, /Rick Doyle 23 bottom, /Robert Holmes 16 top, /Roger Ressmeyer 3 bottom, /Roger Tidman 9 left, /Stephanie Maze 24 bottom, /Stephen Frink 12 top, 13 centre, /Steve Kaufman 6 bottom, /Tim Thompson 14 centre right, 14 bottom, /Tiziana and Gianni Baldizzone 7 centre right, /Tom Bean 8 bottom, /Tom Brakefield 11 top, /Tom Nebbia 17 right, /Tony Arruza 23 top, /Vanni Archive 29 top, /W. Cody 18 right, 27 top, /Wild Country 26 top, /Wolfgang Kaehler 17 top, 18 top and bottom, 8 top.
© ALTON TOWERS 32 left.

CITY GAZETTEER:
© CORBIS /Bettmann 41 bottom right, /Carmen Redondo 44 centre left, /Charles E. Rotkin 40 top right, /Chris Lisle 47 centre top, /Hubert Stadler 41 centre top, /John Heseltine 42 top right, /Larry Lee 46 bottom right, /Lindsay Hebberd 42 left, /Patrick Ward 44 bottom right, /Paul A. Souders 47 bottom right, /Richard T. Nowitz 43 bottom centre, /Tim Thompson 41 left, /Todd Gipstein 44 centre top, /Wolfgang Kaehler 45 top right, /Yann Arthus-Bertrand 46 top left.
© MIKE MOULE 40 left, 43 top left and centre right, 45 left, 46 centre, 48 centre and right.

CITY MAPS

PAGE 15, LONDON. Based upon the Ordnance Survey Maps with the permission of the Controller of Her Majesty's Stationery Office. © Crown copyright 2000. All rights reserved. Licence No. 339817.

PAGE 11, DUBLIN. Based on Ordnance Survey Ireland by permission of the Government Permit No. 7183. © Government of Ireland

VECTOR DATA: Courtesy of Gräfe and Unser Verlag GmbH, München, Germany (city centre maps of Bangkok, Beijing, Cape Town, Jerusalem, Mexico City, Moscow, Singapore, Sydney, Tokyo and Washington D.C.)

> **NOTE:**
> For reasons of safety or politics, there may be times when it is not advisable, or desirable, to visit one or more of the places described in the World Explorer and City Gazetteer sections. If in doubt, please check with the Foreign Office.

Published in Great Britain in 2001 by George Philip Limited,
a division of Octopus Publishing Group Limited,
2–4 Heron Quays, London E14 4JP

Copyright © 2001 George Philip Limited

Cartography by Philip's

ISBN 0–540–07711–9

A CIP catalogue record for this book is available from the British Library.

All rights reserved. Apart from any fair dealing for the purpose of private study, research, criticism or review, as permitted under the Copyright, Designs and Patents Act, 1988, no part of this publication may be reproduced, stored in a retrieval system, or transmitted in any form or by any means, electronic, electrical, chemical, mechanical, optical, photocopying, recording, or otherwise, without prior written permission. All enquiries should be addressed to the Publisher.

Printed in China

Details of other Philip's titles and services can be found on our website at: www.philips-maps.co.uk

Philip's is proud to announce that its World Atlases are now published in association with The Royal Geographical Society (with The Institute of British Geographers).

The Society was founded in 1830 and given a Royal Charter in 1859 for 'the advancement of geographical science'. It holds historical collections of national and international importance, many of which relate to the Society's association with and support for scientific exploration and research from the 19th century onwards. It was pivotal in establishing geography as a teaching and research discipline in British universities close to the turn of the century, and has played a key role in geographical and environmental education ever since.

Today the Society is a leading world centre for geographical learning – supporting education, teaching, research and expeditions, and promoting public understanding of the subject.

The Society welcomes those interested in geography as members. For further information, please visit the website at: www.rgs.org

Philip's World Maps

The reference maps which form the main body of this atlas have been prepared in accordance with the highest standards of international cartography to provide an accurate and detailed representation of the Earth. The scales and projections used have been carefully chosen to give balanced coverage of the world, while emphasizing the most densely populated and economically significant regions. A hallmark of Philip's mapping is the use of hill shading and relief colouring to create a graphic impression of landforms: this makes the maps exceptionally easy to read. However, knowledge of the key features employed in the construction and presentation of the maps will enable the reader to derive the fullest benefit from the atlas.

MAP SEQUENCE

The atlas covers the Earth continent by continent: first Europe; then its land neighbour Asia (mapped north before south, in a clockwise sequence), then Africa, Australia and Oceania, North America and South America. This is the classic arrangement adopted by most cartographers since the 16th century. For each continent, there are maps at a variety of scales. First, physical relief and political maps of the whole continent; then a series of larger-scale maps

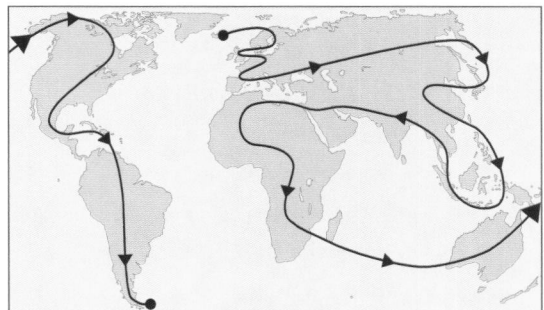

of the regions within the continent, each followed, where required, by still larger-scale maps of the most important or densely populated areas. The governing principle is that by turning the pages of the atlas, the reader moves steadily from north to south through each continent, with each map overlapping its neighbours. A key map showing this sequence, and the area covered by each map, can be found on the endpapers of the atlas.

MAP PRESENTATION

With very few exceptions (e.g. for the Arctic and Antarctic), the maps are drawn with north at the top, regardless of whether they are presented upright or sideways on the page. In the borders will be found the map title; a locator diagram showing the area covered and the page numbers for maps of adjacent areas; the scale; the projection used; the degrees of latitude and longitude; and the letters and figures used in the index for locating place names and geographical features. Physical relief maps also have a height reference panel identifying the colours used for each layer of contouring.

MAP SYMBOLS

Each map contains a vast amount of detail which can only be conveyed clearly and accurately by the use of symbols. Points and circles of varying sizes locate and identify the relative importance of towns and cities; different styles of type are employed for administrative, geographical and regional place names to aid identification. A variety of pictorial symbols denote landscape features such as glaciers, marshes and coral reefs, and man-made structures including roads, railways, airports, canals and dams. International borders are shown by red lines. Where neighbouring countries are in dispute, for example in parts of the Middle East, the maps show the *de facto* boundary between nations, regardless of the legal or historical situation. The symbols are explained on the first page of the World Maps section of the atlas.

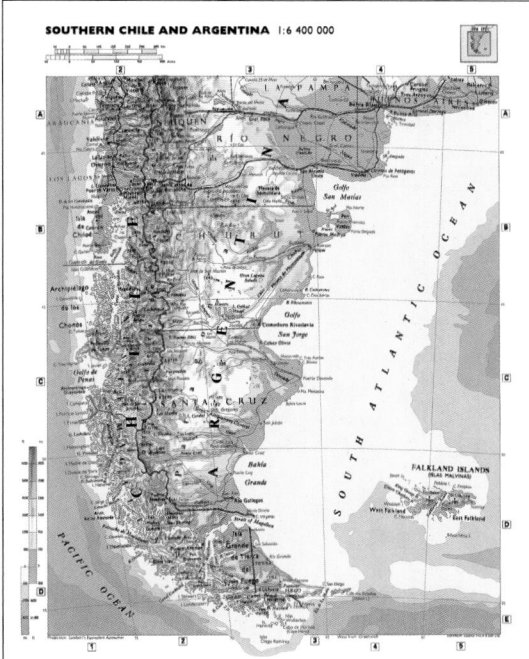

SOUTHERN CHILE AND ARGENTINA 1:6 400 000

MAP SCALES

1:16 000 000
1 inch = 252 statute miles

The scale of each map is given in the numerical form known as the 'representative fraction'. The first figure is always one, signifying one unit of distance on the map; the second figure, usually in millions, is the number by which the map unit must be multiplied to give the equivalent distance on the Earth's surface. Calculations can easily be made in centimetres and kilometres, by dividing the Earth units figure by 100 000 (i.e. deleting the last five 0s). Thus 1:1 000 000 means 1 cm = 10 km. The calculation for inches and miles is more laborious, but 1 000 000 divided by 63 360 (the number of inches in a mile) shows that 1:1 000 000 means approximately 1 inch = 16 miles. The table below provides distance equivalents for scales down to 1:50 000 000.

LARGE SCALE		
1:1 000 000	1 cm = 10 km	1 inch = 16 miles
1:2 500 000	1 cm = 25 km	1 inch = 39.5 miles
1:5 000 000	1 cm = 50 km	1 inch = 79 miles
1:6 000 000	1 cm = 60 km	1 inch = 95 miles
1:8 000 000	1 cm = 80 km	1 inch = 126 miles
1:10 000 000	1 cm = 100 km	1 inch = 158 miles
1:15 000 000	1 cm = 150 km	1 inch = 237 miles
1:20 000 000	1 cm = 200 km	1 inch = 316 miles
1:50 000 000	1 cm = 500 km	1 inch = 790 miles
SMALL SCALE		

MEASURING DISTANCES

Although each map is accompanied by a scale bar, distances cannot always be measured with confidence because of the distortions involved in portraying the curved surface of the Earth on a flat page. As a general rule, the larger the map scale (i.e. the lower the number of Earth units in the representative fraction), the more accurate and reliable will be the distance measured. On small-scale maps such as those of the world and of entire continents, measurement may only

be accurate along the 'standard parallels', or central axes, and should not be attempted without considering the map projection.

MAP PROJECTIONS

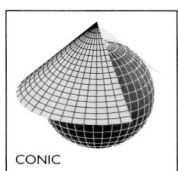  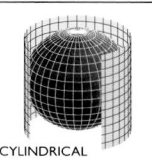

CONIC   AZIMUTHAL   CYLINDRICAL

Unlike a globe, no flat map can give a true scale representation of the world in terms of area, shape and position of every region. Each of the numerous systems that have been devised for projecting the curved surface of the Earth on to a flat page involves the sacrifice of accuracy in one or more of these elements. The variations in shape and position of landmasses such as Alaska, Greenland and Australia, for example, can be quite dramatic when different projections are compared.

For this atlas, the guiding principle has been to select projections that involve the least distortion of size and distance. The projection used for each map is noted in the border. Most fall into one of three categories – conic, cylindrical or azimuthal – whose basic concepts are shown above. Each involves plotting the forms of the Earth's surface on a grid of latitude and longitude lines, which may be shown as parallels, curves or radiating spokes.

LATITUDE AND LONGITUDE

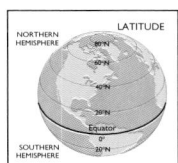 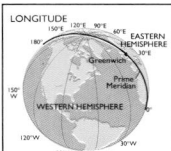 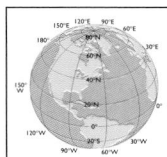

Accurate positioning of individual points on the Earth's surface is made possible by reference to the geometrical system of latitude and longitude. Latitude *parallels* are drawn west–east around the Earth and numbered by degrees north and south of the Equator, which is designated 0° of latitude. Longitude *meridians* are drawn north–south and numbered by degrees east and west of the *prime meridian*, 0° of longitude, which passes through Greenwich in England. By referring to these co-ordinates and their subdivisions of minutes (1/60th of a degree) and seconds (1/60th of a minute), any place on Earth can be located to within a few hundred yards. Latitude and longitude are indicated by blue lines on the maps; they are straight or curved according to the projection employed. Reference to these lines is the easiest way of determining the relative positions of places on different maps, and for plotting compass directions.

NAME FORMS

For ease of reference, both English and local name forms appear in the atlas. Oceans, seas and countries are shown in English throughout the atlas; country names may be abbreviated to their commonly accepted form (e.g. Germany, not The Federal Republic of Germany). Conventional English forms are also used for place names on the smaller-scale maps of the continents. However, local name forms are used on all large-scale and regional maps, with the English form given in brackets only for important cities – the large-scale map of Russia and Central Asia thus shows Moskva (Moscow). For countries which do not use a Roman script, place names have been transcribed according to the systems adopted by the British and US Geographic Names Authorities. For China, the Pin Yin system has been used, with some more widely known forms appearing in brackets, as with Beijing (Peking). Both English and local names appear in the index, the English form being cross-referenced to the local form.

Contents

WORLD STATISTICS

Countries	x
Cities	xi
Distances	xii
Climate	xiii
Physical Dimensions	xiv–xv
Regions in the News	xvi

WORLD EXPLORER

Mountains and volcanoes	2–3
Deserts and canyons	4–5
Lakes and waterfalls	6–7
Wildlife in the Americas and Europe	8–9
Wildlife in Africa, Asia and Australasia	10–11
Marine wildlife	12–13
Great railway journeys	14–15
River and canal journeys	16–17
Sea and ocean cruises	18–19
Winter sports	20–21
Great beaches	22–23
Festivals	24–25
Historic sites in the Americas	26–27
Historic sites in Europe	28–29
Historic sites in Africa, Asia and Australasia	30–31
Theme parks	32

CITY MAPS

Amsterdam	2
Athens	2
Atlanta	3
Baghdad	3
Bangkok	3
Barcelona	4
Beijing	4
Berlin	5
Boston	6
Brussels	6
Budapest	7
Buenos Aires	7
Cairo	7
Calcutta (Kolkata)	8
Canton (Guangzhou)	8
Cape Town	8
Chicago	9
Copenhagen	10
Delhi	10
Dublin	11
Edinburgh	11
Helsinki	12
Hong Kong	12
Istanbul	12
Jakarta	13
Jerusalem	13
Johannesburg	13
Karachi	14
Lagos	14
Lisbon	14
London	15
Lima	16
Los Angeles	16
Madrid	17
Manila	17
Melbourne	17
Mexico City	18
Miami	18
Milan	18
Montréal	19
Moscow	19
Mumbai (Bombay)	20
Munich	20
New York	21
Osaka	22
Oslo	22
Paris	23
Prague	24
Rio de Janeiro	24
Rome	25
San Francisco	25
St Petersburg	26
Santiago	26
São Paulo	26
Seoul	26
Shanghai	27
Singapore	27
Stockholm	28
Sydney	28
Tokyo	29
Tehran	30
Tianjin	30
Toronto	30
Vienna	31
Warsaw	31
Washington	32
Wellington	32

INDEX TO CITY MAPS 33–39

CITY GAZETTEER

Accra, Ghana	40
Agra, India	40
Amsterdam, The Netherlands	40
Athens, Greece	40
Atlanta, Georgia, USA	40
Auckland, New Zealand	40
Baghdad, Iraq	40
Bangkok, Thailand	40
Barcelona, Spain	40
Beijing, China	40
Berlin, Germany	40
Boston, Massachusetts, USA	41
Brisbane, Queensland, Australia	41
Brussels, Belgium	41
Budapest, Hungary	41
Buenos Aires, Argentina	41
Cairo, Egypt	41
Calcutta, India	41
Canton (Guangzhou), China	41
Cape Town, South Africa	41
Cartagena, Colombia	41
Chicago, Illinois, USA	41
Cologne, Germany	42
Copenhagen, Denmark	42
Delhi, India	42
Dublin, Ireland	42
Edinburgh, Scotland	42
Esfahan, Iran	42
Fès, Morocco	42
Florence, Italy	42
Geneva, Switzerland	42
Hamburg, Germany	42
Hanoi, Vietnam	42
Havana, Cuba	42
Helsinki, Finland	43
Hong Kong, China	43
Istanbul, Turkey	43
Jaipur, India	43
Jakarta, Indonesia	43
Jerusalem, Israel	43
Johannesburg, South Africa	43
Kairouan, Tunisia	43
Karachi, Pakistan	43
Katmandu, Nepal	43
Kraków, Poland	43
Kuala Lumpur, Malaysia	44
Kyoto, Japan	44
Lagos, Nigeria	44
Lahore, Pakistan	44
Las Vegas, Nevada, USA	44
Lima, Peru	44
Lisbon, Portugal	44
London, England	44
Los Angeles, California, USA	44
Luxembourg City, Luxembourg	44
Madrid, Spain	44
Manila, Philippines	45
Marrakech, Morocco	45
Melbourne, Victoria, Australia	45
Mexico City, Mexico	45
Miami, Florida, USA	45
Milan, Italy	45
Montréal, Québec, Canada	45
Moscow, Russia	45
Mumbai (Bombay), India	45
Munich, Germany	45
Nairobi, Kenya	45
New Orleans, Louisiana, USA	45
New York, NY, USA	46
Osaka, Japan	46
Oslo, Norway	46
Panama City, Panama	46
Paris, France	46
Perth, Western Australia, Australia	46
Prague, Czech Republic	46
Quito, Ecuador	46
Reykjavik, Iceland	46
Riga, Latvia	46
Rio de Janeiro, Brazil	46
Rome, Italy	46
St Petersburg, Russia	47
San Francisco, California, USA	47
Santiago, Chile	47
São Paulo, Brazil	47
Seattle, Washington, USA	47
Seoul, South Korea	47
Shanghai, China	47
Singapore City, Singapore	47
Stockholm, Sweden	47
Sydney, New South Wales, Australia	47
Tehran, Iran	47
Tianjin, China	48
Tokyo, Japan	48
Toronto, Ontario, Canada	48
Vancouver, British Columbia, Canada	48
Varanasi, India	48
Venice, Italy	48
Vienna, Austria	48
Warsaw, Poland	48
Washington DC, USA	48
Wellington, New Zealand	48
Xi'ian, China	48
Yangon (Rangoon), Burma (Myanmar)	48

WORLD MAPS

Map Symbols   1

The World: Political
1:71 100 000   2–3

Arctic Ocean
1:31 100 000   4

Antarctica
1:31 100 000   5

Europe

Europe: Physical
1:17 800 000   6

Europe: Political
1:17 800 000   7

Scandinavia
1:4 400 000   8–9

Denmark and Southern Sweden
1:2 200 000   10–11

England and Wales
1:1 800 000   12–13

Scotland
1:1 800 000   14

Ireland
1:1 800 000   15

British Isles
1:4 400 000   16

Netherlands, Belgium and Luxembourg
1:2 200 000   17

Northern France
1:2 200 000   18–19

Southern France
1:2 200 000   20–21

Middle Europe
1:4 400 000   22–23

Germany and Switzerland
1:2 200 000   24–25

**Austria, Czech Republic
and Slovak Republic**
1:2 200 000   26–27

Northern Italy, Slovenia and Croatia
1:2 200 000   28–29

Southern Italy
1:2 200 000   30–31

Eastern Spain
1:2 200 000   32–33

Western Spain and Portugal
1:2 200 000   34–35

Malta, Crete, Corfu, Rhodes and Cyprus
1:900 000 / 1:1 200 000   36

The Balearics, the Canaries and Madeira
1:900 000 / 1:1 800 000   37

Southern Greece and Western Turkey
1:2 200 000   38–39

Northern Greece, Bulgaria and Yugoslavia
1:2 200 000   40–41

Hungary, Romania and the Lower Danube
1:2 200 000   42–43

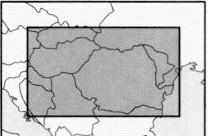

Poland and the Southern Baltic
1:2 200 000

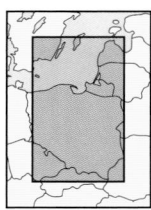

44–45

Baltic States, Belarus and Ukraine
1:4 400 000

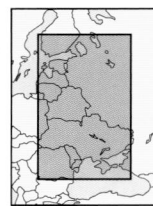

46–47

The Volga Basin and the Caucasus
1:4 400 000

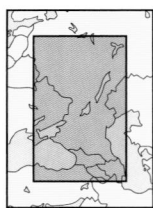

48–49

Asia

Russia and Central Asia
1:17 800 000

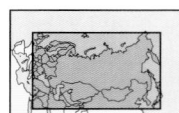

50–51

Asia: Physical
1:44 400 000   52

Asia: Political
1:44 400 000   53

Japan
1:4 400 000

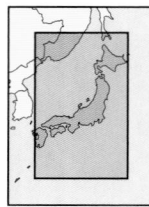

54–55

Northern China and Korea
1:5 300 000

56–57

Southern China
1:5 300 000

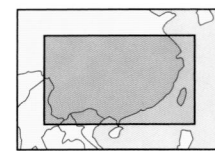

58–59

China
1:17 800 000

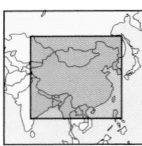

60

The Philippines
1:6 700 000

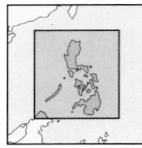

61

Indonesia and the Philippines
1:11 100 000

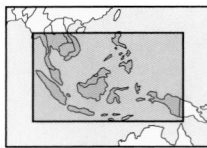

62–63

Mainland South-east Asia
1:5 300 000

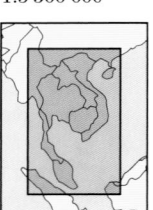

64–65

South Asia
1:8 900 000

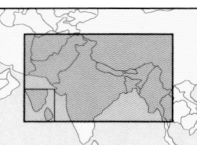

66–67

The Indo-Gangetic Plain
1:5 300 000

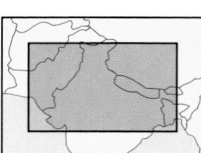

68–69

The Middle East
1:6 200 000

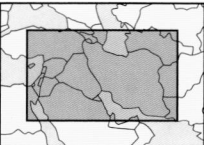

70–71

Turkey and Transcaucasia
1:4 400 000

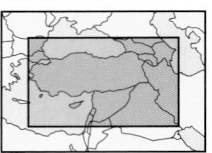

72–73

Arabia and the Horn of Africa
1:13 300 000

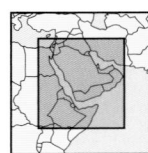

74

The Near East
1:2 200 000

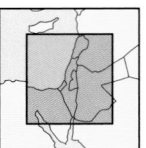

75

Africa

Africa: Physical
1:37 300 000   76

Africa: Political
1: 37 300 000   77

Northern Africa
1:13 300 000

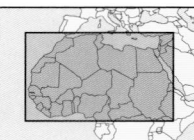

78–79

The Nile Valley and the Nile Delta
1:7 100 000 / 1:3 600 000

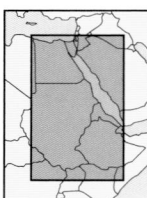

80–81

West Africa
1:7 100 000

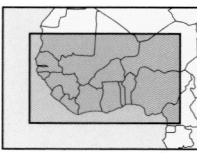

82–83

Central and Southern Africa
1:13 300 000

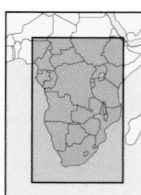

84–85

East Africa
1:7 100 000

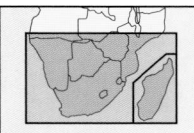

86–87

Southern Africa
1:7 100 000 / 1:7 100 000

88–89

Australia and Oceania

**Australia and Oceania:
Physical and Political**
1:44 400 000   90

New Zealand and Samoa, Fiji and Tonga
1:5 300 000 / 1:10 700 000

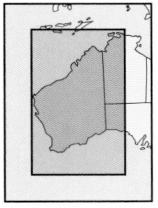

91

Western Australia
1:7 100 000

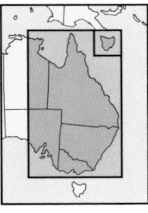

92–93

Eastern Australia
1:7 100 000

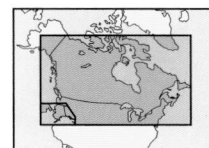

94–95

Pacific Ocean
1:48 000 000   96–97

North America

North America: Physical
1:31 100 000   98

North America: Political
1:31 100 000   99

Canada and Alaska
1:13 300 000 / 1:26 700 000

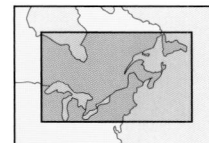

100–101

Eastern Canada
1:6 200 000

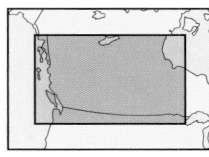

102–103

Western Canada
1:6 200 000

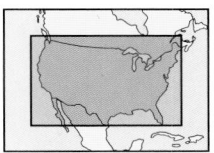

104–105

United States and Hawaii
1:10 700 000 / 1:8 900 000

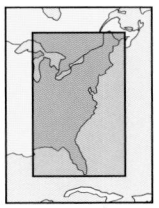

106–107

Eastern United States
1:5 300 000

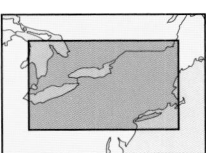

108–109

North-eastern United States
1:2 200 000

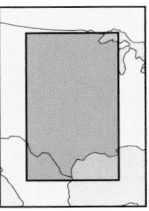

110–111

Middle United States
1:5 300 000

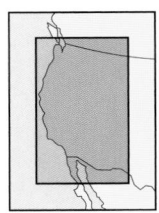

112–113

Western United States
1:5 300 000

114–115

**Central and Southern California
and Western Washington**
1:2 200 000

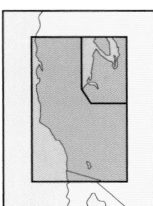

116–117

Mexico
1:7 100 000

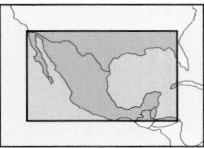

118–119

Central America and the West Indies
1:7 100 000

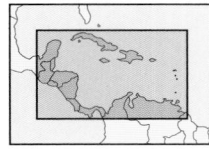

120–121

South America

South America: Physical
1:31 100 000   122

South America: Political
1:31 100 000   123

South America – North
1:14 200 000

124–125

Central South America
1:7 100 000

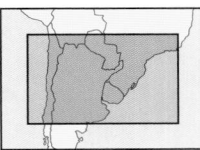

126–127

South America – South
1:14 200 000

128

INDEX TO WORLD MAPS

129–224

World Statistics: Countries

This alphabetical list includes all the countries and territories of the world. If a territory is not completely independent, then the country it is associated with is named. The area figures give the total area of land, inland water and ice. Units for areas and populations are thousands. The population figures are 2000 estimates. The annual income is the Gross National Product per capita in US dollars. The figures are the latest available, usually 1998.

Country/Territory	Area km^2 Thousands	Area $miles^2$ Thousands	Population Thousands	Capital	Annual Income US $
Afghanistan	652	252	26,511	Kabul	800
Albania	28.8	11.1	3,795	Tirana	810
Algeria	2,382	920	32,904	Algiers	1,550
American Samoa (US)	0.20	0.08	39	Pago Pago	2,600
Andorra	0.45	0.17	49	Andorra La Vella	18,000
Angola	1,247	481	13,295	Luanda	340
Anguilla (UK)	0.1	0.04	8	The Valley	6,800
Antigua & Barbuda	0.44	0.17	79	St John's	8,300
Argentina	2,767	1,068	36,238	Buenos Aires	8,970
Armenia	29.8	11.5	3,968	Yerevan	480
Aruba (Netherlands)	0.19	0.07	58	Oranjestad	22,000
Australia	7,687	2,968	18,855	Canberra	20,300
Austria	83.9	32.4	7,613	Vienna	26,850
Azerbaijan	86.6	33.4	8,324	Baku	490
Azores (Portugal)	2.2	0.87	238	Ponta Delgada	–
Bahamas	13.9	5.4	295	Nassau	20,100
Bahrain	0.68	0.26	683	Manama	7,660
Bangladesh	144	56	150,589	Dhaka	350
Barbados	0.43	0.17	265	Bridgetown	7,890
Belarus	207.6	80.1	10,697	Minsk	2,200
Belgium	30.5	11.8	9,832	Brussels	25,380
Belize	23	8.9	230	Belmopan	2,610
Benin	113	43	6,369	Porto-Novo	380
Bermuda (UK)	0.05	0.02	62	Hamilton	34,000
Bhutan	47	18.1	1,906	Thimphu	1,000
Bolivia	1,099	424	9,724	La Paz/Sucre	1,000
Bosnia-Herzegovina	51	20	4,601	Sarajevo	1,720
Botswana	582	225	1,822	Gaborone	3,600
Brazil	8,512	3,286	179,487	Brasília	4,570
Brunei	5.8	2.2	333	Bandar Seri Begawan	24,000
Bulgaria	111	43	9,071	Sofia	1,230
Burkina Faso	274	106	12,092	Ouagadougou	240
Burma (= Myanmar)	677	261	51,129	Rangoon (Yangon)	1,200
Burundi	27.8	10.7	7,358	Bujumbura	140
Cambodia	181	70	10,046	Phnom Penh	280
Cameroon	475	184	16,701	Yaoundé	610
Canada	9,976	3,852	28,488	Ottawa	20,020
Canary Is. (Spain)	7.3	2.8	1,494	Las Palmas/Santa Cruz	–
Cape Verde Is.	4	1.6	515	Praia	1,060
Cayman Is. (UK)	0.26	0.10	35	George Town	20,000
Central African Republic	623	241	4,074	Bangui	300
Chad	1,284	496	7,337	Ndjaména	230
Chile	757	292	15,272	Santiago	4,810
China	9,597	3,705	1,299,180	Beijing	750
Colombia	1,139	440	39,397	Bogotá	2,600
Comoros	2.2	0.86	670	Moroni	370
Congo	342	132	3,167	Brazzaville	690
Congo (Dem. Rep. of the)	2,345	905	49,190	Kinshasa	110
Cook Is. (NZ)	0.24	0.09	17	Avarua	900
Costa Rica	51.1	19.7	3,711	San José	2,780
Croatia	56.5	21.8	4,960	Zagreb	4,520
Cuba	111	43	11,504	Havana	1,560
Cyprus	9.3	3.6	762	Nicosia	13,000
Czech Republic	78.9	30.4	10,500	Prague	5,040
Denmark	43.1	16.6	5,153	Copenhagen	33,260
Djibouti	23.2	9	552	Djibouti	1,200
Dominica	0.75	0.29	87	Roseau	3,010
Dominican Republic	48.7	18.8	8,621	Santo Domingo	1,770
Ecuador	284	109	13,319	Quito	1,530
Egypt	1,001	387	64,210	Cairo	1,290
El Salvador	21	8.1	6,739	San Salvador	1,850
Equatorial Guinea	28.1	10.8	455	Malabo	1,500
Eritrea	94	36	4,523	Asmara	200
Estonia	44.7	17.3	1,647	Tallinn	3,390
Ethiopia	1,128	436	61,841	Addis Ababa	100
Faroe Is. (Denmark)	1.4	0.54	49	Tórshavn	16,000
Fiji	18.3	7.1	883	Suva	2,110
Finland	338	131	5,077	Helsinki	24,110
France	552	213	58,145	Paris	24,940
French Guiana (France)	90	34.7	130	Cayenne	6,000
French Polynesia (France)	4	1.5	268	Papeete	10,800
Gabon	268	103	1,612	Libreville	3,950
Gambia, The	11.3	4.4	1,119	Banjul	340
Georgia	69.7	26.9	5,777	Tbilisi	930
Germany	357	138	76,962	Berlin	25,850
Ghana	239	92	20,564	Accra	390
Gibraltar (UK)	0.007	0.003	32	Gibraltar Town	5,000
Greece	132	51	10,193	Athens	11,650
Greenland (Denmark)	2,176	840	60	Nuuk (Godthåb)	16,100
Grenada	0.34	0.13	83	St George's	3,170
Guadeloupe (France)	1.7	0.66	365	Basse-Terre	9,200
Guam (US)	0.55	0.21	128	Agana	19,000
Guatemala	109	42	12,222	Guatemala City	1,640
Guinea	246	95	7,830	Conakry	540
Guinea-Bissau	36.1	13.9	1,197	Bissau	160
Guyana	215	83	891	Georgetown	770
Haiti	27.8	10.7	8,003	Port-au-Prince	410
Honduras	112	43	6,846	Tegucigalpa	730
Hong Kong (China)	1.1	0.40	6,336	–	23,670
Hungary	93	35.9	10,531	Budapest	4,510
Iceland	103	40	274	Reykjavik	28,010
India	3,288	1,269	1,041,543	New Delhi	430
Indonesia	1,905	735	218,661	Jakarta	680
Iran	1,648	636	68,759	Tehran	1,770
Iraq	438	169	26,339	Baghdad	2,400
Ireland	70.3	27.1	4,086	Dublin	18,340
Israel	27	10.3	5,321	Jerusalem	15,940
Italy	301	116	57,195	Rome	20,250
Ivory Coast (Côte d'Ivoire)	322	125	17,600	Yamoussoukro	700
Jamaica	11	4.2	2,735	Kingston	1,680
Japan	378	146	128,470	Tokyo	32,380
Jordan	89.2	34.4	5,558	Amman	1,520
Kazakstan	2,717	1,049	19,006	Astana	1,310
Kenya	580	224	35,060	Nairobi	330
Kiribati	0.72	0.28	72	Tarawa	1,180
Korea, North	121	47	26,117	Pyŏngyang	1,000
Korea, South	99	38.2	46,403	Seoul	7,970
Kuwait	17.8	6.9	2,639	Kuwait City	22,700
Kyrgyzstan	198.5	76.6	5,403	Bishkek	350
Laos	237	91	5,463	Vientiane	330
Latvia	65	25	2,768	Riga	2,430
Lebanon	10.4	4	3,327	Beirut	3,360
Lesotho	30.4	11.7	2,370	Maseru	570
Liberia	111	43	3,575	Monrovia	1,000
Libya	1,760	679	6,500	Tripoli	6,700
Liechtenstein	0.16	0.06	28	Vaduz	50,000
Lithuania	65.2	25.2	3,935	Vilnius	2,440
Luxembourg	2.6	1	377	Luxembourg	43,570
Macau (China)	0.02	0.006	656	Macau	16,000
Macedonia (F.Y.R.O.M.)	25.7	9.9	2,157	Skopje	1,290
Madagascar	587	227	16,627	Antananarivo	260
Madeira (Portugal)	0.81	0.31	253	Funchal	–
Malawi	118	46	12,458	Lilongwe	200
Malaysia	330	127	21,983	Kuala Lumpur	3,600
Maldives	0.30	0.12	283	Malé	1,230
Mali	1,240	479	12,685	Bamako	250
Malta	0.32	0.12	366	Valletta	9,440
Marshall Is.	0.18	0.07	70	Dalap-Uliga-Darrit	1,540
Martinique (France)	1.1	0.42	362	Fort-de-France	10,700
Mauritania	1,030	412	2,702	Nouakchott	410
Mauritius	2.0	0.72	1,201	Port Louis	3,700
Mayotte (France)	0.37	0.14	141	Mamoundzou	1,430
Mexico	1,958	756	107,233	Mexico City	3,970
Micronesia, Fed. States of	0.70	0.27	110	Palikir	1,800
Moldova	33.7	13	4,707	Chişinău	410
Monaco	0.002	0.0001	30	Monaco	25,000
Mongolia	1,567	605	2,847	Ulan Bator	400
Montserrat (UK)	0.10	0.04	13	Plymouth	4,500
Morocco	447	172	31,559	Rabat	1,250
Mozambique	802	309	20,493	Maputo	210
Namibia	825	318	2,437	Windhoek	1,940
Nauru	0.02	0.008	10	Yaren District	10,000
Nepal	141	54	24,084	Katmandu	210
Netherlands	41.5	16	15,829	Amsterdam/The Hague	24,760
Netherlands Antilles (Neths)	0.99	0.38	203	Willemstad	11,500
New Caledonia (France)	18.6	7.2	195	Nouméa	11,400
New Zealand	269	104	3,662	Wellington	14,700
Nicaragua	130	50	5,261	Managua	390
Niger	1,267	489	10,752	Niamey	190
Nigeria	924	357	105,000	Abuja	300
Northern Mariana Is. (US)	0.48	0.18	50	Saipan	11,500
Norway	324	125	4,331	Oslo	34,330
Oman	212	82	2,176	Muscat	7,900
Pakistan	796	307	162,409	Islamabad	480
Palau	0.46	0.18	18	Koror	5,000
Panama	77.1	29.8	2,893	Panama City	3,080
Papua New Guinea	463	179	4,845	Port Moresby	890
Paraguay	407	157	5,538	Asunción	1,760
Peru	1,285	496	26,276	Lima	2,460
Philippines	300	116	77,473	Manila	1,050
Poland	313	121	40,366	Warsaw	3,900
Portugal	92.4	35.7	10,587	Lisbon	10,690
Puerto Rico (US)	9	3.5	3,836	San Juan	9,000
Qatar	11	4.2	499	Doha	17,100
Réunion (France)	2.5	0.97	692	Saint-Denis	4,800
Romania	238	92	24,000	Bucharest	1,390
Russia	17,075	6,592	155,096	Moscow	2,300
Rwanda	26.3	10.2	10,200	Kigali	230
St Kitts & Nevis	0.36	0.14	44	Basseterre	6,130
St Lucia	0.62	0.24	177	Castries	3,410
St Vincent & Grenadines	0.39	0.15	128	Kingstown	2,420
San Marino	0.06	0.02	25	San Marino	20,000
São Tomé & Príncipe	0.96	0.37	151	São Tomé	280
Saudi Arabia	2,150	830	20,697	Riyadh	9,000
Senegal	197	76	8,716	Dakar	530
Seychelles	0.46	0.18	75	Victoria	6,450
Sierra Leone	71.7	27.7	5,437	Freetown	140
Singapore	0.62	0.24	3,000	Singapore	30,060
Slovak Republic	49	18.9	5,500	Bratislava	3,700
Slovenia	20.3	7.8	2,055	Ljubljana	9,760
Solomon Is.	28.9	11.2	429	Honiara	750
Somalia	638	246	9,736	Mogadishu	600
South Africa	1,220	471	43,666	C. Town/Pretoria/Bloem.	2,880
Spain	505	195	40,667	Madrid	14,080
Sri Lanka	65.6	25.3	19,416	Colombo	810
Sudan	2,506	967	33,625	Khartoum	290
Surinam	163	63	497	Paramaribo	1,660
Swaziland	17.4	6.7	1,121	Mbabane	1,400
Sweden	450	174	8,560	Stockholm	25,620
Switzerland	41.3	15.9	6,762	Bern	40,080
Syria	185	71	17,826	Damascus	1,020
Taiwan	36	13.9	22,000	Taipei	12,400
Tajikistan	143.1	55.2	7,041	Dushanbe	350
Tanzania	945	365	39,639	Dodoma	210
Thailand	513	198	63,670	Bangkok	2,200
Togo	56.8	21.9	4,861	Lomé	330
Tonga	0.75	0.29	92	Nuku'alofa	1,690
Trinidad & Tobago	5.1	2	1,484	Port of Spain	4,430
Tunisia	164	63	9,924	Tunis	2,050
Turkey	779	301	66,789	Ankara	3,160
Turkmenistan	488.1	188.5	4,585	Ashkhabad	1,630
Turks & Caicos Is. (UK)	0.43	0.17	12	Cockburn Town	5,000
Tuvalu	0.03	0.01	11	Fongafale	600
Uganda	236	91	26,958	Kampala	320
Ukraine	603.7	233.1	52,558	Kiev	850
United Arab Emirates	83.6	32.3	1,951	Abu Dhabi	18,220
United Kingdom	243.3	94	58,393	London	21,400
United States of America	9,373	3,619	266,096	Washington, DC	29,340
Uruguay	177	68	3,274	Montevideo	6,180
Uzbekistan	447.4	172.7	26,044	Tashkent	870
Vanuatu	12.2	4.7	206	Port-Vila	1,270
Venezuela	912	352	24,715	Caracas	350
Vietnam	332	127	82,427	Hanoi	330
Virgin Is. (UK)	0.15	0.06	15	Road Town	–
Virgin Is. (US)	0.34	0.13	135	Charlotte Amalie	12,500
Wallis & Futuna Is. (France)	0.20	0.08	26	Mata-Utu	–
Western Sahara	266	103	228	El Aaiún	300
Western Samoa	2.8	1.1	171	Apia	1,020
Yemen	528	204	13,219	Sana	300
Yugoslavia	102.3	39.5	10,761	Belgrade	2,300
Zambia	753	291	12,267	Lusaka	330
Zimbabwe	391	151	13,123	Harare	610

World Statistics: Cities

This list shows the principal cities with more than 500,000 inhabitants (for Brazil, China and India only cities with more than 1 million inhabitants are included). The figures are taken from the most recent census or population estimate available, and as far as possible are the population of the metropolitan area, e.g. greater New York, Mexico or Paris. All the figures are in thousands. Local name forms have been used for the smaller cities (e.g. Kraków).

City	Population
AFGHANISTAN	
Kabul	1,565
ALGERIA	
Algiers	2,168
Oran	916
ANGOLA	
Luanda	2,418
ARGENTINA	
Buenos Aires	11,256
Córdoba	1,208
Rosario	1,118
Mendoza	773
La Plata	642
San Miguel de Tucumán	622
Mar del Plata	512
ARMENIA	
Yerevan	1,248
AUSTRALIA	
Sydney	3,770
Melbourne	3,217
Brisbane	1,489
Perth	1,262
Adelaide	1,080
AUSTRIA	
Vienna	1,595
AZERBAIJAN	
Baku	1,720
BANGLADESH	
Dhaka	6,105
Chittagong	2,041
Khulna	877
Rajshahi	517
BELARUS	
Minsk	1,700
Homyel	512
BELGIUM	
Brussels	948
BENIN	
Cotonou	537
BOLIVIA	
La Paz	1,126
Santa Cruz	767
BOSNIA-HERZEGOVINA	
Sarajevo	526
BRAZIL	
São Paulo	16,417
Rio de Janeiro	9,888
Salvador	2,211
Belo Horizonte	2,091
Fortaleza	1,965
Brasília	1,821
Curitiba	1,476
Recife	1,346
Pôrto Alegre	1,288
Manaus	1,157
Belém	1,144
Goiânia	1,004
BULGARIA	
Sofia	1,116
BURKINA FASO	
Ouagadougou	690
BURMA (MYANMAR)	
Rangoon (Yangon)	2,513
Mandalay	533
CAMBODIA	
Phnom Penh	920
CAMEROON	
Douala	1,200
Yaoundé	800
CANADA	
Toronto	4,344
Montréal	3,337
Vancouver	1,831
Ottawa–Hull	1,022
Edmonton	885
Calgary	831
Québec	693
Winnipeg	677
Hamilton	643
CENTRAL AFRICAN REP.	
Bangui	553
CHAD	
Ndjaména	530
CHILE	
Santiago	5,067
CHINA	
Shanghai	15,082
Beijing	12,362
Tianjin	10,687
Hong Kong (SAR)*	6,502
Chongqing	3,870
Shenyang	3,860
Wuhan	3,520
Guangzhou	3,114
Harbin	2,505
Nanjing	2,211
Xi'an	2,115
Chengdu	1,933
Dalian	1,855
Changchun	1,810
Jinan	1,660
Taiyuan	1,642
Qingdao	1,584
Fuzhou, Fujian	1,380
Zibo	1,346
Zhengzhou	1,324
Lanzhou	1,296
Anshan	1,252
Fushun	1,246
Kunming	1,242
Changsha	1,198
Hangzhou	1,185
Nanchang	1,169
Shijiazhuang	1,159
Guiyang	1,131
Ürümqi	1,130
Jilin	1,118
Tangshan	1,110
Qiqihar	1,104
Baotou	1,033
Hefei	1,000
COLOMBIA	
Bogotá	6,004
Cali	1,985
Medellín	1,970
Barranquilla	1,157
Cartagena	812
CONGO	
Brazzaville	937
Pointe-Noire	576
CONGO (DEM. REP.)	
Kinshasa	1,655
Lubumbashi	851
Mbuji-Mayi	806
COSTA RICA	
San José	1,220
CROATIA	
Zagreb	931
CUBA	
Havana	2,241
CZECH REPUBLIC	
Prague	1,209
DENMARK	
Copenhagen	1,362
DOMINICAN REPUBLIC	
Santo Domingo	2,135
Santiago	691
ECUADOR	
Guayaquil	1,973
Quito	1,487
EGYPT	
Cairo	9,900
Alexandria	3,431
El Gîza	2,144
Shubra el Kheima	834
EL SALVADOR	
San Salvador	1,522
ETHIOPIA	
Addis Ababa	2,112
FINLAND	
Helsinki	532
FRANCE	
Paris	9,319
Lyon	1,262
Marseille	1,087
Lille	959
Bordeaux	696
Toulouse	650
Nice	516
GEORGIA	
Tbilisi	1,300
GERMANY	
Berlin	3,470
Hamburg	1,706
Munich	1,240
Cologne	964
Frankfurt	651
Essen	616
Dortmund	600
Stuttgart	587
Düsseldorf	571
Bremen	549
Duisburg	535
Hanover	524
GHANA	
Accra	949
GREECE	
Athens	3,097
GUATEMALA	
Guatemala	1,167
GUINEA	
Conakry	1,508
HAITI	
Port-au-Prince	1,255
HONDURAS	
Tegucigalpa	813
HUNGARY	
Budapest	1,885
INDIA	
Bombay (Mumbai)	12,572
Calcutta (Kolkata)	10,916
Delhi	7,207
Madras (Chennai)	5,361
Hyderabad	4,280
Bangalore	4,087
Ahmadabad	3,298
Pune	2,485
Kanpur	2,111
Nagpur	1,661
Lucknow	1,642
Surat	1,517
Jaipur	1,514
Coimbatore	1,136
Vadodara	1,115
Indore	1,104
Patna	1,099
Madurai	1,094
Bhopal	1,064
Vishakhapatnam	1,052
Varanasi	1,026
Ludhiana	1,012
INDONESIA	
Jakarta	11,500
Surabaya	2,701
Bandung	2,368
Medan	1,910
Semarang	1,366
Palembang	1,352
Tangerang	1,198
Ujung Pandang	1,092
Bandar Lampung	832
Malang	763
Padang	721
Pakanbaru	558
Samarinda	536
Banjarmasin	535
Surakarta	516
IRAN	
Tehran	6,750
Mashhad	1,964
Esfahan	1,221
Tabriz	1,166
Shiraz	1,043
Ahvaz	828
Qom	780
Bakhtaran	666
Karaj	588
IRAQ	
Baghdad	3,841
Diyala	961
As Sulaymaniyah	952
Arbil	770
Al Mawsil	664
Kadhimain	521
IRELAND	
Dublin	952
ISRAEL	
Tel Aviv-Yafo	1,502
Jerusalem	591
ITALY	
Rome	2,775
Milan	1,369
Naples	1,067
Turin	962
Palermo	698
Genoa	678
IVORY COAST	
Abidjan	2,500
JAMAICA	
Kingston	644
JAPAN	
Tokyo–Yokohama	26,836
Osaka	10,601
Nagoya	2,152
Sapporo	1,757
Kyoto	1,464
Kobe	1,424
Fukuoka	1,285
Kawasaki	1,203
Hiroshima	1,109
Kitakyushu	1,020
Sendai	971
Chiba	857
Sakai	803
Kumamoto	650
Okayama	616
Sagamihara	571
Hamamatsu	562
Kagoshima	546
Funabashi	541
Higashiosaka	517
Hachioji	503
JORDAN	
Amman	1,300
Az-Zarqā	609
KAZAKSTAN	
Almaty	1,150
Qaraghandy	573
KENYA	
Nairobi	2,000
Mombasa	600
KOREA, NORTH	
Pyŏngyang	2,639
Hamhung	775
Chŏngjin	754
Chinnampo	691
Sinŭiju	500
KOREA, SOUTH	
Seoul	11,641
Pusan	3,814
Taegu	2,449
Inchon	2,308
Taejŏn	1,272
Kwangju	1,258
Ulsan	967
Sŏngnam	869
Puch'on	779
Suwŏn	756
Anyang	590
Chŏnju	563
Chŏngju	531
Ansan	510
P'ohang	509
KYRGYZSTAN	
Bishkek	584
LATVIA	
Riga	846
LEBANON	
Beirut	1,900
Tripoli	500
LIBYA	
Tripoli	1,083
LITHUANIA	
Vilnius	580
MACEDONIA	
Skopje	541
MADAGASCAR	
Antananarivo	1,053
MALAYSIA	
Kuala Lumpur	1,145
MALI	
Bamako	800
MAURITANIA	
Nouakchott	735
MEXICO	
Mexico City	15,048
Guadalajara	2,847
Monterrey	2,522
Puebla	1,055
León	872
Ciudad Juárez	798
Tijuana	743
Culiacán Rosales	602
Mexicali	602
Acapulco de Juárez	592
Mérida	557
Chihuahua	530
San Luis Potosí	526
Aguascalientés	506
MOLDOVA	
Chişinău	700
MONGOLIA	
Ulan Bator	627
MOROCCO	
Casablanca	3,079
Rabat-Salé	1,344
Fès	735
Marrakesh	621
MOZAMBIQUE	
Maputo	2,000
NEPAL	
Katmandu	535
NETHERLANDS	
Amsterdam	1,101
Rotterdam	1,076
The Hague	694
Utrecht	548
NEW ZEALAND	
Auckland	997
NICARAGUA	
Managua	864
NIGERIA	
Lagos	10,287
Ibadan	1,365
Ogbomosho	712
Kano	657
NORWAY	
Oslo	714
PAKISTAN	
Karachi	9,863
Lahore	5,085
Faisalabad	1,875
Peshawar	1,676
Gujranwala	1,663
Rawalpindi	1,290
Multan	1,257
Hyderabad	1,107
PARAGUAY	
Asunción	945
PERU	
Lima–Callao	6,601
Callao	638
Arequipa	620
Trujillo	509
PHILIPPINES	
Manila	9,280
Quezon City	1,989
Davao	1,191
Caloocan	1,023
Cebu	662
Zamboanga	511
POLAND	
Warsaw	1,638
Lódz	825
Kraków	745
Wroclaw	642
Poznań	581
PORTUGAL	
Lisbon	2,561
Oporto	1,174
ROMANIA	
Bucharest	2,060
RUSSIA	
Moscow	9,233
Petersburg	4,883
Nizhniy Novgorod	1,425
Novosibirsk	1,400
Yekaterinburg	1,300
Samara	1,200
Omsk	1,200
Chelyabinsk	1,100
Kazan	1,100
Ufa	1,100
Volgograd	1,003
Perm	1,000
Rostov	1,000
Voronezh	908
Saratov	895
Krasnoyarsk	869
Togliatti	689
Simbirsk	678
Izhevsk	654
Krasnodar	645
Vladivostok	632
Yaroslavl	629
Khabarovsk	618
Barnaul	596
Irkutsk	585
Novokuznetsk	572
Ryazan	536
Penza	534
Orenburg	532
Tula	532
Naberezhnyye-Chelny	526
Kemerovo	503
SAUDI ARABIA	
Riyadh	1,800
Jedda	1,500
Mecca	630
SENEGAL	
Dakar	1,571
SIERRA LEONE	
Freetown	505
SINGAPORE	
Singapore	3,104
SOMALIA	
Mogadishu	1,000
SOUTH AFRICA	
Cape Town	2,350
East Rand	1,379
Johannesburg	1,196
Durban	1,137
Pretoria	1,080
West Rand	870
Port Elizabeth	853
Vanderbijlpark–Vereeniging	774
Soweto	597
Sasolburg	540
SPAIN	
Madrid	3,029
Barcelona	1,614
Valencia	763
Sevilla	719
Zaragoza	607
Málaga	532
SRI LANKA	
Colombo	1,863
SUDAN	
Omdurman	1,267
Khartoum	925
Khartoum North	879
SWEDEN	
Stockholm	1,744
Göteborg	775
SWITZERLAND	
Zürich	1,175
Bern	942
SYRIA	
Aleppo	1,591
Damascus	1,549
Homs	644
TAIWAN	
Taipei	2,653
Kaohsiung	1,405
Taichung	817
Tainan	700
Panchiao	544
TAJIKISTAN	
Dushanbe	524
TANZANIA	
Dar-es-Salaam	1,361
THAILAND	
Bangkok	5,572
TOGO	
Lomé	590
Tunisia	
Tunis	1,827
TURKEY	
Istanbul	7,490
Ankara	3,028
Izmir	2,333
Adana	1,472
Bursa	1,317
Konya	1,040
Gaziantep	930
Icel	908
Antalya	734
Diyarbakir	677
Kocaeli	661
Urfa	649
Kayseri	648
Manisa	641
Hatay	561
Samsun	557
Eskisehir	508
Balikesir	501
TURKMENISTAN	
Ashkhabad	536
UGANDA	
Kampala	773
UKRAINE	
Kiev	2,630
Kharkiv	1,555
Dnipropetrovsk	1,147
Donetsk	1,088
Odesa	1,046
Zaporizhzhya	887
Lviv	802
Kryvyy Rih	720
Mariupol	510
Mykolayiv	508
UNITED KINGDOM	
London	8,089
Birmingham	2,373
Manchester	2,353
Liverpool	852
Glasgow	832
Sheffield	661
Nottingham	649
Newcastle	617
Bristol	552
Leeds	529
UNITED STATES	
New York	16,329
Los Angeles	12,410
Chicago	7,668
Philadelphia	4,949
Washington, DC	4,466
Detroit	4,307
Houston	3,653
Atlanta	3,331
Boston	3,240
Dallas	2,898
Minneapolis–St Paul	2,688
San Diego	2,632
St Louis	2,536
Phoenix	2,473
Baltimore	2,458
Pittsburgh	2,402
Cleveland	2,222
San Francisco	2,182
Seattle	2,180
Tampa	2,157
Miami	2,025
Newark	1,934
Denver	1,796
Portland (Or.)	1,676
Kansas City (Mo.)	1,647
Cincinnati	1,581
San Jose	1,557
Norfolk	1,529
Indianapolis	1,462
Milwaukee	1,456
Sacramento	1,441
San Antonio	1,437
Columbus (Oh.)	1,423
New Orleans	1,309
Charlotte	1,260
Buffalo	1,189
Salt Lake City	1,178
Hartford	1,151
Oklahoma	1,007
Jacksonville (Fl.)	665
Omaha	663
Memphis	614
El Paso	579
Austin	514
Nashville	505
URUGUAY	
Montevideo	1,378
UZBEKISTAN	
Tashkent	2,107
VENEZUELA	
Caracas	2,784
Maracaibo	1,364
Valencia	1,032
Maracay	800
Barquisimeto	745
Ciudad Guayana	524
VIETNAM	
Ho Chi Minh City	4,322
Hanoi	3,056
Haiphong	783
YEMEN	
Sana	972
Aden	562
YUGOSLAVIA	
Belgrade	1,137
ZAMBIA	
Lusaka	982
ZIMBABWE	
Harare	1,189
Bulawayo	622

* SAR = Special Administrative Region of China

World Statistics: Distances

The table shows air distances in miles and kilometres between 30 major cities. Known as 'Great Circle' distances, these measure the shortest routes between the cities, which aircraft use wherever possible. The maps show the world centred on six cities, and illustrate, for example, why direct flights from Japan to northern America and Europe are across the Arctic regions. The maps have been constructed on an Azimuthal Equidistant projection, on which all distances measured through the centre point are true to scale. The red lines are drawn at 5,000, 10,000 and 15,000 km from the central city.

Upper-right values are in Miles; lower-left values are in Kms. Diagonal cells are left blank.

	Beijing	Bombay	Buenos Aires	Cairo	Calcutta	Caracas	Chicago	Hong Kong	Honolulu	Johannesburg	Lagos	London	Los Angeles	Mexico City	Moscow	Nairobi	New York	Paris	Rio de Janeiro	Rome	Singapore	Sydney	Tokyo	Wellington
Beijing		2956	11972	4688	2031	8947	6588	1220	5070	7276	7119	5057	6251	7742	3600	5727	6828	5106	10773	5049	2783	5561	1304	6700
Bombay	4757		9275	2706	1034	9024	8048	2683	8024	4334	4730	4467	8700	9728	3126	2816	7793	4356	8332	3837	2432	6313	4189	7686
Buenos Aires	19268	14925		7341	10268	3167	5599	11481	7558	5025	4919	6917	6122	4591	8374	6463	5298	6867	1214	6929	9867	7332	11410	6202
Cairo	7544	4355	11814		3541	6340	6127	5064	8838	3894	2432	2180	7580	7687	1803	2197	5605	1994	6149	1325	5137	8959	5947	10268
Calcutta	3269	1664	16524	5699		9609	7978	1653	7048	5256	5727	4946	8152	9494	3438	3839	7921	4883	9366	4486	1800	5678	3195	7055
Caracas	14399	14522	5096	10203	15464		2502	10166	6009	6847	4810	4664	3612	2228	6175	7173	2131	4738	2825	5196	11407	9534	8801	8154
Chicago	10603	12953	9011	3206	12839	4027		7783	4247	8689	5973	3949	1742	1694	4971	8005	711	4132	5311	4809	9369	9243	6299	8358
Hong Kong	1963	4317	18478	8150	2659	16360	12526		5543	6669	7360	5980	7232	8775	4439	5453	8047	5984	11001	5769	1615	4582	1786	5857
Honolulu	8160	12914	12164	14223	11343	9670	6836	8921		11934	10133	7228	2558	3781	7036	10739	4958	7437	8290	8026	6721	5075	3854	4669
Johannesburg	11710	6974	8088	6267	8459	11019	13984	10732	19206		2799	5637	10362	9063	5692	1818	7979	5426	4420	4811	5381	6860	8418	7308
Lagos	11457	7612	7916	3915	9216	7741	9612	11845	16308	4505		3118	7713	6879	3886	2366	5268	2929	3750	2510	6925	9643	8376	9973
London	8138	7190	11131	3508	7961	7507	6356	9623	11632	9071	5017		5442	5552	1552	4237	3463	212	5778	889	6743	10558	5942	11691
Los Angeles	10060	14000	9852	12200	13120	5812	2804	11639	4117	16676	12414	8758		1549	6070	9659	2446	5645	6310	6331	8776	7502	5475	6719
Mexico City	12460	15656	7389	12372	15280	3586	2726	14122	6085	14585	11071	8936	2493		6664	9207	2090	5717	4780	6365	10321	8058	7024	6897
Moscow	5794	5031	13477	2902	5534	9938	8000	7144	11323	9161	6254	2498	9769	10724		3942	4666	1545	7184	1477	5237	9008	4651	10283
Nairobi	9216	4532	10402	3536	6179	11544	12883	8776	17282	2927	3807	6819	15544	14818	6344		7358	4029	5548	3350	4635	7552	6996	8490
New York	10988	12541	8526	9020	12747	3430	1145	12950	7980	12841	8477	5572	3936	3264	7510	11842		3626	4832	4280	9531	9935	6741	8951
Paris	8217	7010	11051	3210	7858	7625	6650	9630	11968	8732	4714	342	9085	9200	2486	6485	5836		5708	687	6671	10539	6038	11798
Rio de Janeiro	17338	13409	1953	9896	15073	4546	8547	17704	13342	7113	6035	9299	10155	7693	11562	8928	7777	9187		5725	9763	8389	11551	7367
Rome	8126	6175	11151	2133	7219	8363	7739	9284	12916	7743	4039	1431	10188	10243	2376	5391	6888	1105	9214		6229	10143	6127	11523
Singapore	4478	3914	15879	8267	2897	18359	15078	2599	10816	8660	11145	10852	14123	16610	8428	7460	15339	10737	15712	10025		3915	3306	5298
Sydney	8949	10160	11800	14418	9138	15343	14875	7374	8168	11040	15519	16992	12073	12969	14497	12153	15989	16962	13501	16324	6300		4861	1383
Tokyo	2099	6742	18362	9571	5141	14164	10137	2874	6202	13547	13480	9562	8811	11304	7485	11260	10849	9718	18589	9861	5321	7823		5762
Wellington	10782	12370	9981	16524	11354	13122	13451	9427	7513	11761	16050	18814	10814	11100	16549	13664	14405	18987	11855	18545	8526	2226	9273	

Northern Hemisphere

MEXICO CITY
19 26°N 99 4°W

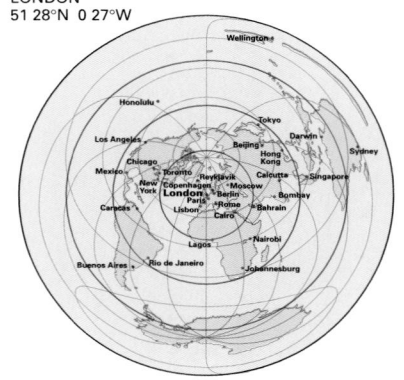

LONDON
51 28°N 0 27°W

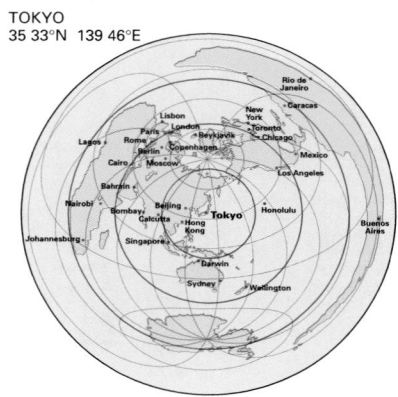

TOKYO
35 33°N 139 46°E

Southern Hemisphere

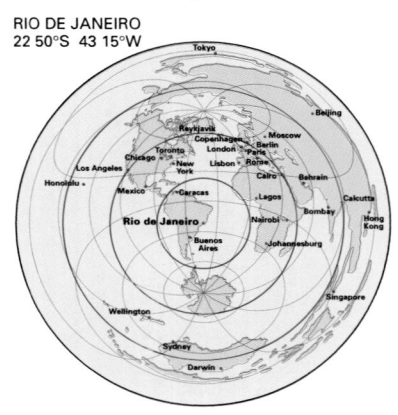

RIO DE JANEIRO
22 50°S 43 15°W

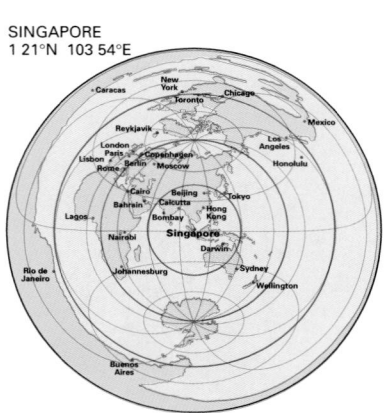

SINGAPORE
1 21°N 103 54°E

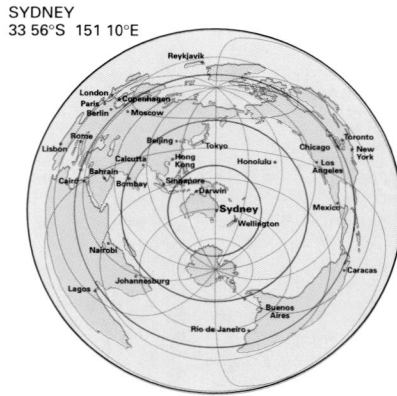

SYDNEY
33 56°S 151 10°E

World Statistics: Climate

R ainfall and temperature figures are provided for more than 70 cities around the world. As climate is affected by altitude, the height of each city is shown in metres beneath its name. For each month, the figures in blue show the total rainfall or snow in millimetres, and in red the average temperature in degrees Celsius; the total annual rainfall and average annual temperature are at the end of the rows.

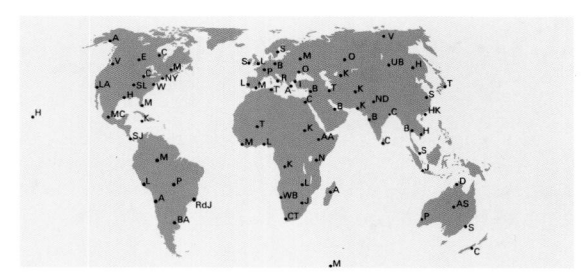

EUROPE

City	Jan.	Feb.	Mar.	Apr.	May	June	July	Aug.	Sept.	Oct.	Nov.	Dec.	Year
Athens, Greece 107 m	62	37	37	23	23	14	6	7	15	51	56	71	402
	10	10	12	16	20	25	28	28	24	20	15	11	18
Berlin, Germany 55 m	46	40	33	42	49	65	73	69	48	49	46	43	603
	−1	0	4	9	14	17	19	18	15	9	5	1	9
Istanbul, Turkey 14 m	109	92	72	46	38	34	34	30	58	81	103	119	816
	5	6	7	11	16	20	23	23	20	16	12	8	14
Lisbon, Portugal 77 m	111	76	109	54	44	16	3	4	33	62	93	103	708
	11	12	14	16	17	20	22	23	21	18	14	12	17
London, UK 5 m	54	40	37	37	46	45	57	59	49	57	64	48	593
	4	5	7	9	12	16	18	17	15	11	8	5	11
Málaga, Spain 33 m	61	51	62	46	26	5	1	3	29	64	64	62	474
	12	13	16	17	19	29	25	26	23	20	16	13	18
Moscow, Russia 156 m	39	38	36	37	53	58	88	71	58	45	47	54	624
	−13	−10	−4	6	13	16	18	17	12	6	−1	−7	4
Odesa, Ukraine 64 m	57	62	30	21	34	34	42	37	37	13	35	71	473
	−3	−1	2	9	15	20	22	22	18	12	9	1	10
Paris, France 75 m	56	46	35	42	57	54	59	64	55	50	51	50	619
	3	4	8	11	15	18	20	19	17	12	7	4	12
Rome, Italy 17 m	71	62	57	51	46	37	15	21	63	99	129	93	744
	8	9	11	14	18	22	25	25	22	17	13	10	16
Shannon, Irish Republic 2 m	94	67	56	53	61	57	77	79	86	86	96	117	929
	5	5	7	9	12	14	16	16	14	11	8	6	10
Stockholm, Sweden 44 m	43	30	25	31	34	45	61	76	60	48	53	48	554
	−3	−3	−1	5	10	15	18	17	12	7	3	0	7

ASIA

City	Jan.	Feb.	Mar.	Apr.	May	June	July	Aug.	Sept.	Oct.	Nov.	Dec.	Year
Bahrain 5 m	8	18	13	8	<3	0	0	0	0	0	18	18	81
	17	18	21	25	29	32	33	34	31	28	24	19	26
Bangkok, Thailand 2 m	8	20	36	58	198	160	160	175	305	206	66	5	1,397
	26	28	29	30	29	29	28	28	28	28	26	25	28
Beirut, Lebanon 34 m	191	158	94	53	18	3	<3	<3	5	51	132	185	892
	14	14	16	18	22	24	27	28	26	24	19	16	21
Bombay, India 11 m	3	3	3	<3	18	485	617	340	264	64	13	3	1,809
	24	24	26	28	30	29	27	27	27	28	27	26	27
Calcutta, India 6 m	10	31	36	43	140	297	325	328	252	114	20	5	1,600
	20	22	27	30	30	30	29	29	29	28	23	19	26
Colombo, Sri Lanka 7 m	89	69	147	231	371	224	135	109	160	348	315	147	2,365
	26	26	27	28	28	27	27	27	27	27	26	26	27
Harbin, China 160 m	6	5	10	23	43	94	112	104	46	33	8	5	488
	−18	−15	−5	6	13	19	22	21	14	4	−6	−16	3
Ho Chi Minh, Vietnam 9 m	15	3	13	43	221	330	315	269	335	269	114	56	1,984
	26	27	29	30	29	28	28	28	27	27	27	26	28
Hong Kong, China 33 m	33	46	74	137	292	394	381	361	257	114	43	31	2,162
	16	15	18	22	26	28	28	28	27	25	21	18	23
Jakarta, Indonesia 8 m	300	300	211	147	114	97	64	43	66	112	142	203	1,798
	26	26	27	27	27	27	27	27	27	27	27	26	27
Kabul, Afghanistan 1,815 m	31	36	94	102	20	5	3	3	<3	15	20	10	338
	−3	−1	6	13	18	22	25	24	20	14	7	3	12
Karachi, Pakistan 4 m	13	10	8	3	3	18	81	41	13	<3	3	5	196
	19	20	24	28	30	31	30	29	28	28	24	20	26
Kazalinsk, Kazakstan 63 m	10	10	13	13	15	5	5	8	8	10	13	15	125
	−12	−11	−3	6	18	23	25	23	16	8	−1	−7	7
New Delhi, India 218 m	23	18	13	8	13	74	180	172	117	10	3	10	640
	14	17	23	28	33	34	31	30	29	26	20	15	25
Omsk, Russia 85 m	15	8	8	13	31	51	51	51	28	25	18	20	318
	−22	−19	−12	−1	10	16	18	16	10	1	−11	−18	−1
Shanghai, China 7 m	48	58	84	94	94	180	147	142	130	71	51	36	1,135
	4	5	9	14	20	24	28	28	23	19	12	7	16
Singapore 10 m	252	173	193	188	173	173	170	196	178	208	254	257	2,413
	26	27	28	28	28	28	28	27	27	27	27	27	27
Tehran, Iran 1,220 m	46	38	46	36	13	3	3	3	3	8	20	31	246
	2	5	9	16	21	26	30	29	25	18	12	6	17
Tokyo, Japan 6 m	48	74	107	135	147	165	142	152	234	208	97	56	1,565
	3	4	7	13	17	21	25	26	23	17	11	6	14
Ulan Bator, Mongolia 1,325 m	<3	<3	3	5	10	28	76	51	23	5	5	3	208
	−26	−21	−13	−1	6	14	16	14	8	−1	−13	−22	−3
Verkhoyansk, Russia 100 m	5	5	3	5	8	23	28	25	13	8	8	5	134
	−50	−45	−32	−15	0	14	14	9	2	−15	−38	−48	−17

AFRICA

City	Jan.	Feb.	Mar.	Apr.	May	June	July	Aug.	Sept.	Oct.	Nov.	Dec.	Year
Addis Ababa, Ethiopia 2,450 m	<3	3	25	135	213	201	206	239	102	28	<3	0	1,151
	19	20	20	20	19	18	18	18	19	21	22	21	20
Antananarivo, Madagas. 1,372 m	300	279	178	53	18	8	8	10	18	61	135	287	1,356
	21	21	21	19	18	15	14	15	17	19	21	21	19
Cairo, Egypt 116 m	5	5	5	3	3	<3	0	0	<3	<3	3	5	28
	13	15	18	21	25	28	28	28	26	24	20	15	22
Cape Town, South Africa 17 m	15	8	18	48	79	84	89	66	43	31	18	10	508
	21	21	20	17	14	13	12	13	14	16	18	19	17
Johannesburg, S. Africa 1,665 m	114	109	89	38	25	8	8	8	23	56	107	125	709
	20	20	18	16	13	10	11	13	16	18	19	20	16
Khartoum, Sudan 390 m	<3	<3	<3	<3	3	8	53	71	18	5	<3	0	158
	24	25	28	31	33	34	32	31	32	32	28	25	29
Kinshasa, Congo (D.R.) 325 m	135	145	196	196	158	8	3	3	31	119	221	142	1,354
	26	26	27	27	26	24	23	24	25	26	26	26	25
Lagos, Nigeria 3 m	28	46	102	150	269	460	279	64	140	206	69	25	1,836
	27	28	29	28	28	26	26	25	26	26	28	28	27
Lusaka, Zambia 1,277 m	231	191	142	18	3	<3	<3	0	<3	10	91	150	836
	21	22	21	21	19	16	16	18	22	24	23	22	21
Monrovia, Liberia 23 m	31	56	97	216	516	973	996	373	744	772	236	130	5,138
	26	26	27	27	26	25	24	25	25	25	26	26	26
Nairobi, Kenya 1,820 m	38	64	125	211	158	46	15	23	31	53	109	86	958
	19	19	19	19	18	16	16	16	18	19	18	18	18
Timbuktu, Mali 301 m	<3	<3	3	<3	5	23	79	81	38	3	<3	<3	231
	22	24	28	32	34	35	32	30	32	31	28	23	29
Tunis, Tunisia 66 m	64	51	41	36	18	8	3	8	33	51	48	61	419
	10	11	13	16	19	23	26	27	25	20	16	11	18
Walvis Bay, Namibia 7 m	<3	5	8	3	3	<3	<3	3	<3	<3	<3	<3	23
	19	19	19	18	17	16	15	14	14	15	17	18	18

AUSTRALIA, NEW ZEALAND AND ANTARCTICA

City	Jan.	Feb.	Mar.	Apr.	May	June	July	Aug.	Sept.	Oct.	Nov.	Dec.	Year
Alice Springs, Australia 579 m	43	33	28	10	15	13	8	8	8	18	31	38	252
	29	28	25	20	15	12	12	14	18	23	26	28	21
Christchurch, N. Zealand 10 m	56	43	48	48	66	66	69	48	46	43	48	56	638
	16	16	14	12	9	6	6	7	9	12	14	16	11
Darwin, Australia 30 m	386	312	254	97	15	3	<3	3	13	51	119	239	1,491
	29	29	29	29	28	26	25	26	28	29	30	29	28
Mawson, Antarctica 14 m	11	30	20	10	44	180	4	40	3	20	0	0	362
	0	−5	−10	−14	−15	−16	−18	−18	−19	−13	−5	−1	−11
Perth, Australia 60 m	8	10	20	43	130	180	170	149	86	56	20	13	881
	23	23	22	19	16	14	13	13	15	16	19	22	18
Sydney, Australia 42 m	89	102	127	135	127	117	117	76	73	71	73	73	1,181
	22	22	21	18	15	13	12	13	15	18	19	21	17

NORTH AMERICA

City	Jan.	Feb.	Mar.	Apr.	May	June	July	Aug.	Sept.	Oct.	Nov.	Dec.	Year
Anchorage, Alaska, USA 40 m	20	18	15	10	13	18	41	66	66	56	25	23	371
	−11	−8	−5	2	7	12	14	13	9	2	−5	−11	2
Chicago, Illinois, USA 251 m	51	51	66	71	86	89	84	81	79	66	61	51	836
	−4	−3	2	9	14	20	23	22	19	12	5	−1	10
Churchill, Man., Canada 13 m	15	13	18	23	32	44	46	58	51	43	39	21	402
	−28	−26	−20	−10	−2	6	12	11	5	−2	−12	−22	−7
Edmonton, Alta., Canada 676 m	25	19	19	22	43	77	89	78	39	17	16	25	466
	−15	−10	−5	4	11	15	17	16	11	6	−4	−10	3
Honolulu, Hawaii, USA 12 m	104	66	79	48	25	18	23	28	36	48	64	104	643
	23	18	19	20	22	24	25	26	26	24	22	19	22
Houston, Texas, USA 12 m	89	76	84	91	119	117	99	99	104	94	89	109	1,171
	12	13	17	21	24	27	28	29	26	22	16	12	21
Kingston, Jamaica 34 m	23	15	23	31	102	89	38	91	99	180	74	36	800
	25	25	25	26	26	28	28	28	27	27	26	26	26
Los Angeles, Calif., USA 95 m	79	76	71	25	10	3	<3	<3	5	10	31	66	381
	13	14	14	16	17	19	21	22	21	18	16	14	17
Mexico City, Mexico 2,309 m	13	5	10	20	53	119	170	152	130	51	18	8	747
	12	13	16	18	19	19	17	18	18	16	14	13	16
Miami, Florida, USA 8 m	71	53	64	81	173	178	155	160	203	234	71	51	1,516
	20	20	22	23	25	27	28	28	27	25	22	21	24
Montréal, Que., Canada 57 m	72	65	74	74	66	82	90	92	88	76	81	87	946
	−10	−9	−3	6	13	18	21	20	15	9	2	−7	6
New York City, N.Y., USA 96 m	94	97	91	81	81	84	107	109	86	89	76	91	1,092
	−1	−1	3	10	16	20	23	23	21	15	7	2	11
St Louis, Mo., USA 173 m	58	64	89	97	114	114	89	86	81	74	71	64	1,001
	0	1	7	13	19	24	26	26	22	15	8	2	14
San José, Costa Rica 1,146 m	15	5	20	46	229	241	211	241	305	300	145	41	1,798
	19	19	21	21	22	21	21	21	21	20	20	19	20
Vancouver, B.C., Canada 14 m	154	115	101	60	52	45	32	41	67	114	150	182	1,113
	3	5	6	9	12	15	17	17	14	10	6	4	10
Washington, D.C., USA 22 m	86	76	91	84	94	99	112	109	94	74	66	79	1,064
	1	2	7	12	18	23	25	24	20	14	8	3	13

SOUTH AMERICA

City	Jan.	Feb.	Mar.	Apr.	May	June	July	Aug.	Sept.	Oct.	Nov.	Dec.	Year
Antofagasta, Chile 94 m	0	0	0	<3	<3	3	5	3	<3	3	<3	0	13
	21	21	20	18	16	15	14	14	15	16	18	19	17
Buenos Aires, Argentina 27 m	79	71	109	89	76	61	56	61	79	86	84	99	950
	23	23	21	17	13	9	10	11	13	15	19	22	16
Lima, Peru 120 m	3	<3	<3	<3	5	5	8	8	8	3	3	<3	41
	23	24	24	22	19	17	16	16	17	18	19	21	20
Manaus, Brazil 44 m	249	231	262	221	170	84	58	38	46	107	142	203	1,811
	28	28	28	27	28	28	28	29	29	29	29	28	28
Paraná, Brazil 260 m	287	236	239	102	13	<3	3	5	28	127	231	310	1,582
	23	23	23	23	21	21	21	22	24	24	24	23	23
Rio de Janeiro, Brazil 61 m	125	122	130	107	79	53	41	43	66	79	104	137	1,082
	26	26	25	24	22	21	21	21	22	23	22	23	23

World Statistics: Physical Dimensions

Each topic list is divided into continents and within a continent the items are listed in order of size. The order of the continents is as in the atlas, Europe through to South America. The lists down to this mark > are complete; below they are selective. The world top ten are shown in square brackets; in the case of mountains this has not been done because the world top 30 are all in Asia. The figures are rounded as appropriate.

WORLD, CONTINENTS, OCEANS

THE WORLD	km²	miles²	%
The World	509,450,000	196,672,000	–
Land	149,450,000	57,688,000	29.3
Water	360,000,000	138,984,000	70.7
Asia	44,500,000	17,177,000	29.8
Africa	30,302,000	11,697,000	20.3
North America	24,241,000	9,357,000	16.2
South America	17,793,000	6,868,000	11.9
Antarctica	14,100,000	5,443,000	9.4
Europe	9,957,000	3,843,000	6.7
Australia & Oceania	8,557,000	3,303,000	5.7
Pacific Ocean	179,679,000	69,356,000	49.9
Atlantic Ocean	92,373,000	35,657,000	25.7
Indian Ocean	73,917,000	28,532,000	20.5
Arctic Ocean	14,090,000	5,439,000	3.9

SEAS

PACIFIC	km²	miles²
South China Sea	2,974,600	1,148,500
Bering Sea	2,268,000	875,000
Sea of Okhotsk	1,528,000	590,000
East China & Yellow	1,249,000	482,000
Sea of Japan	1,008,000	389,000
Gulf of California	162,000	62,500
Bass Strait	75,000	29,000

ATLANTIC	km²	miles²
Caribbean Sea	2,766,000	1,068,000
Mediterranean Sea	2,516,000	971,000
Gulf of Mexico	1,543,000	596,000
Hudson Bay	1,232,000	476,000
North Sea	575,000	223,000
Black Sea	462,000	178,000
Baltic Sea	422,170	163,000
Gulf of St Lawrence	238,000	92,000

INDIAN	km²	miles²
Red Sea	438,000	169,000
The Gulf	239,000	92,000

MOUNTAINS

EUROPE		m	ft
Elbrus	Russia	5,642	18,510
Mont Blanc	France/Italy	4,807	15,771
Monte Rosa	Italy/Switzerland	4,634	15,203
Dom	Switzerland	4,545	14,911
Liskamm	Switzerland	4,527	14,852
Weisshorn	Switzerland	4,505	14,780
Taschorn	Switzerland	4,490	14,730
Matterhorn/Cervino	Italy/Switz.	4,478	14,691
Mont Maudit	France/Italy	4,465	14,649
Dent Blanche	Switzerland	4,356	14,291
Nadelhorn	Switzerland	4,327	14,196
> Grandes Jorasses	France/Italy	4,208	13,806
Jungfrau	Switzerland	4,158	13,642
Barre des Ecrins	France	4,103	13,461
Gran Paradiso	Italy	4,061	13,323
Piz Bernina	Italy/Switzerland	4,049	13,284
Eiger	Switzerland	3,970	13,025
Monte Viso	Italy	3,841	12,602
Grossglockner	Austria	3,797	12,457
Wildspitze	Austria	3,772	12,382
Monte Disgrazia	Italy	3,678	12,066
Mulhacén	Spain	3,478	11,411
Pico de Aneto	Spain	3,404	11,168
Marmolada	Italy	3,342	10,964
Etna	Italy	3,340	10,958
Zugspitze	Germany	2,962	9,718
Musala	Bulgaria	2,925	9,596
Olympus	Greece	2,917	9,570
Triglav	Slovenia	2,863	9,393
Monte Cinto	France (Corsica)	2,710	8,891
Gerlachovka	Slovak Republic	2,655	8,711
Ben Nevis	UK	1,343	4,406

ASIA		m	ft
Everest	China/Nepal	8,850	29,035
K2 (Godwin Austen)	China/Kashmir	8,611	28,251
Kanchenjunga	India/Nepal	8,598	28,208
Lhotse	China/Nepal	8,516	27,939
Makalu	China/Nepal	8,481	27,824
Cho Oyu	China/Nepal	8,201	26,906
Dhaulagiri	Nepal	8,172	26,811
Manaslu	Nepal	8,156	26,758
Nanga Parbat	Kashmir	8,126	26,660
Annapurna	Nepal	8,078	26,502
Gasherbrum	China/Kashmir	8,068	26,469
Broad Peak	China/Kashmir	8,051	26,414
Xixabangma	China	8,012	26,286
Kangbachen	India/Nepal	7,902	25,925
Jannu	India/Nepal	7,902	25,925
Gayachung Kang	Nepal	7,897	25,909
Himalchuli	Nepal	7,893	25,896
Disteghil Sar	Kashmir	7,885	25,869
Nuptse	Nepal	7,879	25,849
Khunyang Chhish	Kashmir	7,852	25,761
Masherbrum	Kashmir	7,821	25,659
Nanda Devi	India	7,817	25,646
Rakaposhi	Kashmir	7,788	25,551
Batura	Kashmir	7,785	25,541
Namche Barwa	China	7,756	25,446
Kamet	India	7,756	25,446
Soltoro Kangri	Kashmir	7,742	25,400
Gurla Mandhata	China	7,728	25,354
Trivor	Pakistan	7,720	25,328
> Kongur Shan	China	7,719	25,324
Tirich Mir	Pakistan	7,690	25,229
K'ula Shan	Bhutan/China	7,543	24,747
Pik Kommunizma	Tajikistan	7,495	24,590
Demavend	Iran	5,604	18,386
Ararat	Turkey	5,165	16,945
Gunong Kinabalu	Malaysia (Borneo)	4,101	13,455
Yu Shan	Taiwan	3,997	13,113
Fuji-San	Japan	3,776	12,388

AFRICA		m	ft
Kilimanjaro	Tanzania	5,895	19,340
Mt Kenya	Kenya	5,199	17,057
Ruwenzori (Margherita)	Uganda/Congo (D.R.)	5,109	16,762
Ras Dashan	Ethiopia	4,620	15,157
Meru	Tanzania	4,565	14,977
Karisimbi	Rwanda/Congo (D.R.)	4,507	14,787
Mt Elgon	Kenya/Uganda	4,321	14,176
Batu	Ethiopia	4,307	14,130
Guna	Ethiopia	4,231	13,882
Toubkal	Morocco	4,165	13,665
Irhil Mgoun	Morocco	4,071	13,356
Mt Cameroon	Cameroon	4,070	13,353
Amba Ferit	Ethiopia	3,875	13,042
Pico del Teide	Spain (Tenerife)	3,718	12,198
Thabana Ntlenyana	Lesotho	3,482	11,424
Emi Koussi	Chad	3,415	11,204
> Mt aux Sources	Lesotho/S. Africa	3,282	10,768
Mt Piton	Réunion	3,069	10,069

OCEANIA		m	ft
Puncak Jaya	Indonesia	5,029	16,499
Puncak Trikora	Indonesia	4,750	15,584
Puncak Mandala	Indonesia	4,702	15,427
Mt Wilhelm	Papua NG	4,508	14,790
> Mauna Kea	USA (Hawaii)	4,205	13,796
Mauna Loa	USA (Hawaii)	4,169	13,681
Mt Cook (Aoraki)	New Zealand	3,753	12,313
Mt Balbi	Solomon Is.	2,439	8,002
Orohena	Tahiti	2,241	7,352
Mt Kosciuszko	Australia	2,237	7,339

NORTH AMERICA		m	ft
Mt McKinley (Denali)	USA (Alaska)	6,194	20,321
Mt Logan	Canada	5,959	19,551
Citlaltepetl	Mexico	5,700	18,701
Mt St Elias	USA/Canada	5,489	18,008
Popocatepetl	Mexico	5,452	17,887
Mt Foraker	USA (Alaska)	5,304	17,401
Ixtaccihuatl	Mexico	5,286	17,342
Lucania	Canada	5,227	17,149
Mt Steele	Canada	5,073	16,644
Mt Bona	USA (Alaska)	5,005	16,420
Mt Blackburn	USA (Alaska)	4,996	16,391
Mt Sanford	USA (Alaska)	4,940	16,207
Mt Wood	Canada	4,848	15,905
Nevado de Toluca	Mexico	4,670	15,321
Mt Fairweather	USA (Alaska)	4,663	15,298
Mt Hunter	USA (Alaska)	4,442	14,573
Mt Whitney	USA	4,418	14,495
Mt Elbert	USA	4,399	14,432
Mt Harvard	USA	4,395	14,419
Mt Rainier	USA	4,392	14,409
Blanca Peak	USA	4,372	14,344
> Longs Peak	USA	4,345	14,255
Tajumulco	Guatemala	4,220	13,845
Grand Teton	USA	4,197	13,770
Mt Waddington	Canada	3,994	13,104
Mt Robson	Canada	3,954	12,972
Chirripó Grande	Costa Rica	3,837	12,589
Pico Duarte	Dominican Rep.	3,175	10,417

SOUTH AMERICA		m	ft
Aconcagua	Argentina	6,960	22,834
Bonete	Argentina	6,872	22,546
Ojos del Salado	Argentina/Chile	6,863	22,516
Pissis	Argentina	6,779	22,241
Mercedario	Argentina/Chile	6,770	22,211
Huascaran	Peru	6,768	22,204
Llullaillaco	Argentina/Chile	6,723	22,057
Nudo de Cachi	Argentina	6,720	22,047
Yerupaja	Peru	6,632	21,758
N. de Tres Cruces	Argentina/Chile	6,620	21,719
Incahuasi	Argentina/Chile	6,601	21,654
Cerro Galan	Argentina	6,600	21,654
Tupungato	Argentina/Chile	6,570	21,555
> Sajama	Bolivia	6,542	21,463
Illimani	Bolivia	6,485	21,276
Coropuna	Peru	6,425	21,079
Ausangate	Peru	6,384	20,945
Cerro del Toro	Argentina	6,380	20,932
Siula Grande	Peru	6,356	20,853
Chimborazo	Ecuador	6,267	20,561
Alpamayo	Peru	5,947	19,511
Cotapaxi	Ecuador	5,896	19,344
Pico Colon	Colombia	5,800	19,029
Pico Bolivar	Venezuela	5,007	16,427

ANTARCTICA		m	ft
Vinson Massif		4,897	16,066
Mt Kirkpatrick		4,528	14,855
Mt Markham		4,349	14,268

OCEAN DEPTHS

ATLANTIC OCEAN	m	ft	
Puerto Rico (Milwaukee) Deep	9,220	30,249	[7]
Cayman Trench	7,680	25,197	[10]
Gulf of Mexico	5,203	17,070	
Mediterranean Sea	5,121	16,801	
Black Sea	2,211	7,254	
North Sea	660	2,165	
Baltic Sea	463	1,519	
Hudson Bay	258	846	

INDIAN OCEAN	m	ft
Java Trench	7,450	24,442
Red Sea	2,635	8,454
Persian Gulf	73	239

PACIFIC OCEAN	m	ft	
Mariana Trench	11,022	36,161	[1]
Tonga Trench	10,882	35,702	[2]
Japan Trench	10,554	34,626	[3]
Kuril Trench	10,542	34,587	[4]
Mindanao Trench	10,497	34,439	[5]
Kermadec Trench	10,047	32,962	[6]

PACIFIC OCEAN (continued)

	m	ft	
Peru–Chile Trench	8,050	26,410	[8]
Aleutian Trench	7,822	25,662	[9]

ARCTIC OCEAN

	m	ft
Molloy Deep	5,608	18,399

LAND LOWS

		m	ft
Dead Sea	Asia	−403	−1,322
Lake Assal	Africa	−156	−512
Death Valley	N. America	−86	−282
Valdés Peninsula	S. America	−40	−131
Caspian Sea	Europe	−28	−92
Lake Eyre North	Oceania	−16	−52

RIVERS

EUROPE

		km	miles	
Volga	Caspian Sea	3,700	2,300	
Danube	Black Sea	2,850	1,770	
Ural	Caspian Sea	2,535	1,575	
Dnepr (Dnipro)	Black Sea	2,285	1,420	
Kama	Volga	2,030	1,260	
Don	Black Sea	1,990	1,240	
Petchora	Arctic Ocean	1,790	1,110	
Oka	Volga	1,480	920	
Belaya	Kama	1,420	880	
Dnister (Dniester)	Black Sea	1,400	870	
Vyatka	Kama	1,370	850	
Rhine	North Sea	1,320	820	
N. Dvina	Arctic Ocean	1,290	800	
Desna	Dnepr (Dnipro)	1,190	740	
Elbe	North Sea	1,145	710	
Wisla	Baltic Sea	1,090	675	
Loire	Atlantic Ocean	1,020	635	

ASIA

		km	miles	
Yangtze	Pacific Ocean	6,380	3,960	[3]
Yenisey–Angara	Arctic Ocean	5,550	3,445	[5]
Huang He	Pacific Ocean	5,464	3,395	[6]
Ob–Irtysh	Arctic Ocean	5,410	3,360	[7]
Mekong	Pacific Ocean	4,500	2,795	[9]
Amur	Pacific Ocean	4,400	2,730	[10]
Lena	Arctic Ocean	4,400	2,730	
Irtysh	Ob	4,250	2,640	
Yenisey	Arctic Ocean	4,090	2,540	
Ob	Arctic Ocean	3,680	2,285	
Indus	Indian Ocean	3,100	1,925	
Brahmaputra	Indian Ocean	2,900	1,800	
Syrdarya	Aral Sea	2,860	1,775	
Salween	Indian Ocean	2,800	1,740	
Euphrates	Indian Ocean	2,700	1,675	
Vilyuy	Lena	2,650	1,645	
Kolyma	Arctic Ocean	2,600	1,615	
Amudarya	Aral Sea	2,540	1,575	
Ural	Caspian Sea	2,535	1,575	
Ganges	Indian Ocean	2,510	1,560	
Si Kiang	Pacific Ocean	2,100	1,305	
Irrawaddy	Indian Ocean	2,010	1,250	
Tarim–Yarkand	Lop Nor	2,000	1,240	
Tigris	Indian Ocean	1,900	1,180	

AFRICA

		km	miles	
Nile	Mediterranean	6,670	4,140	[1]
Congo	Atlantic Ocean	4,670	2,900	[8]
Niger	Atlantic Ocean	4,180	2,595	
Zambezi	Indian Ocean	3,540	2,200	
Oubangi/Uele	Congo (D.R.)	2,250	1,400	
Kasai	Congo (D.R.)	1,950	1,210	
Shaballe	Indian Ocean	1,930	1,200	
Orange	Atlantic Ocean	1,860	1,155	
Cubango	Okavango Swamps	1,800	1,120	
Limpopo	Indian Ocean	1,600	995	
Senegal	Atlantic Ocean	1,600	995	
Volta	Atlantic Ocean	1,500	930	

AUSTRALIA

		km	miles
Murray–Darling	Indian Ocean	3,750	2,330
Darling	Murray	3,070	1,905
Murray	Indian Ocean	2,575	1,600
Murrumbidgee	Murray	1,690	1,050

NORTH AMERICA

		km	miles	
Mississippi–Missouri	Gulf of Mexico	6,020	3,740	[4]
Mackenzie	Arctic Ocean	4,240	2,630	
Mississippi	Gulf of Mexico	3,780	2,350	
Missouri	Mississippi	3,780	2,350	
Yukon	Pacific Ocean	3,185	1,980	
Rio Grande	Gulf of Mexico	3,030	1,880	

NORTH AMERICA (continued)

		km	miles
Arkansas	Mississippi	2,340	1,450
Colorado	Pacific Ocean	2,330	1,445
Red	Mississippi	2,040	1,270
Columbia	Pacific Ocean	1,950	1,210
Saskatchewan	Lake Winnipeg	1,940	1,205
Snake	Columbia	1,670	1,040
Churchill	Hudson Bay	1,600	990
Ohio	Mississippi	1,580	980
Brazos	Gulf of Mexico	1,400	870
St Lawrence	Atlantic Ocean	1,170	730

SOUTH AMERICA

		km	miles	
Amazon	Atlantic Ocean	6,450	4,010	[2]
Paraná–Plate	Atlantic Ocean	4,500	2,800	
Purus	Amazon	3,350	2,080	
Madeira	Amazon	3,200	1,990	
São Francisco	Atlantic Ocean	2,900	1,800	
Paraná	Plate	2,800	1,740	
Tocantins	Atlantic Ocean	2,750	1,710	
Paraguay	Paraná	2,550	1,580	
Orinoco	Atlantic Ocean	2,500	1,550	
Pilcomayo	Paraná	2,500	1,550	
Araguaia	Tocantins	2,250	1,400	
Juruá	Amazon	2,000	1,240	
Xingu	Amazon	1,980	1,230	
Ucayali	Amazon	1,900	1,180	
Maranón	Amazon	1,600	990	
Uruguay	Plate	1,600	990	

LAKES

EUROPE

		km²	miles²
Lake Ladoga	Russia	17,700	6,800
Lake Onega	Russia	9,700	3,700
Saimaa system	Finland	8,000	3,100
Vänern	Sweden	5,500	2,100
Rybinskoye Res.	Russia	4,700	1,800

ASIA

		km²	miles²	
Caspian Sea	Asia	371,800	143,550	[1]
Lake Baykal	Russia	30,500	11,780	[8]
Aral Sea	Kazakhstan/Uzbekistan	28,687	11,086	[10]
Tonlé Sap	Cambodia	20,000	7,700	
Lake Balqash	Kazakhstan	18,500	7,100	
Lake Dongting	China	12,000	4,600	
Lake Ysyk	Kyrgyzstan	6,200	2,400	
Lake Orumiyeh	Iran	5,900	2,300	
Lake Koko	China	5,700	2,200	
Lake Poyang	China	5,000	1,900	
Lake Khanka	China/Russia	4,400	1,700	
Lake Van	Turkey	3,500	1,400	

AFRICA

		km²	miles²	
Lake Victoria	E. Africa	68,000	26,000	[3]
Lake Tanganyika	C. Africa	33,000	13,000	[6]
Lake Malawi/Nyasa	E. Africa	29,600	11,430	[9]
Lake Chad	C. Africa	25,000	9,700	
Lake Turkana	Ethiopia/Kenya	8,500	3,300	
Lake Volta	Ghana	8,500	3,300	
Lake Bangweulu	Zambia	8,000	3,100	
Lake Rukwa	Tanzania	7,000	2,700	
Lake Mai-Ndombe	Congo (D.R.)	6,500	2,500	
Lake Kariba	Zambia/Zimbabwe	5,300	2,000	
Lake Albert	Uganda/Congo (D.R.)	5,300	2,000	
Lake Nasser	Egypt/Sudan	5,200	2,000	
Lake Mweru	Zambia/Congo (D.R.)	4,900	1,900	
Lake Cabora Bassa	Mozambique	4,500	1,700	
Lake Kyoga	Uganda	4,400	1,700	
Lake Tana	Ethiopia	3,630	1,400	

AUSTRALIA

		km²	miles²
Lake Eyre	Australia	8,900	3,400
Lake Torrens	Australia	5,800	2,200
Lake Gairdner	Australia	4,800	1,900

NORTH AMERICA

		km²	miles²	
Lake Superior	Canada/USA	82,350	31,800	[2]
Lake Huron	Canada/USA	59,600	23,010	[4]
Lake Michigan	USA	58,000	22,400	[5]
Great Bear Lake	Canada	31,800	12,280	[7]
Great Slave Lake	Canada	28,500	11,000	
Lake Erie	Canada/USA	25,700	9,900	
Lake Winnipeg	Canada	24,400	9,400	
Lake Ontario	Canada/USA	19,500	7,500	
Lake Nicaragua	Nicaragua	8,200	3,200	
Lake Athabasca	Canada	8,100	3,100	
Smallwood Reservoir	Canada	6,530	2,520	
Reindeer Lake	Canada	6,400	2,500	
Nettilling Lake	Canada	5,500	2,100	
Lake Winnipegosis	Canada	5,400	2,100	

SOUTH AMERICA

		km²	miles²
Lake Titicaca	Bolivia/Peru	8,300	3,200
Lake Poopo	Peru	2,800	1,100

ISLANDS

EUROPE

		km²	miles²	
Great Britain	UK	229,880	88,700	[8]
Iceland	Atlantic Ocean	103,000	39,800	
Ireland	Ireland/UK	84,400	32,600	
Novaya Zemlya (N.)	Russia	48,200	18,600	
W. Spitzbergen	Norway	39,000	15,100	
Novaya Zemlya (S.)	Russia	33,200	12,800	
Sicily	Italy	25,500	9,800	
Sardinia	Italy	24,000	9,300	
N.E. Spitzbergen	Norway	15,000	5,600	
Corsica	France	8,700	3,400	
Crete	Greece	8,350	3,200	
Zealand	Denmark	6,850	2,600	

ASIA

		km²	miles²	
Borneo	S. E. Asia	744,360	287,400	[3]
Sumatra	Indonesia	473,600	182,860	[6]
Honshu	Japan	230,500	88,980	[7]
Sulawesi (Celebes)	Indonesia	189,000	73,000	
Java	Indonesia	126,700	48,900	
Luzon	Philippines	104,700	40,400	
Mindanao	Philippines	101,500	39,200	
Hokkaido	Japan	78,400	30,300	
Sakhalin	Russia	74,060	28,600	
Sri Lanka	Indian Ocean	65,600	25,300	
Taiwan	Pacific Ocean	36,000	13,900	
Kyushu	Japan	35,700	13,800	
Hainan	China	34,000	13,100	
Timor	Indonesia	33,600	13,000	
Shikoku	Japan	18,800	7,300	
Halmahera	Indonesia	18,000	6,900	
Ceram	Indonesia	17,150	6,600	
Sumbawa	Indonesia	15,450	6,000	
Flores	Indonesia	15,200	5,900	
Samar	Philippines	13,100	5,100	
Negros	Philippines	12,700	4,900	
Bangka	Indonesia	12,000	4,600	
Palawan	Philippines	12,000	4,600	
Panay	Philippines	11,500	4,400	
Sumba	Indonesia	11,100	4,300	
Mindoro	Philippines	9,750	3,800	

AFRICA

		km²	miles²	
Madagascar	Indian Ocean	587,040	226,660	[4]
Socotra	Indian Ocean	3,600	1,400	
Réunion	Indian Ocean	2,500	965	
Tenerife	Atlantic Ocean	2,350	900	
Mauritius	Indian Ocean	1,865	720	

OCEANIA

		km²	miles²	
New Guinea	Indon./Papua NG	821,030	317,000	[2]
New Zealand (S.)	Pacific Ocean	150,500	58,100	
New Zealand (N.)	Pacific Ocean	114,700	44,300	
Tasmania	Australia	67,800	26,200	
New Britain	Papua NG	37,800	14,600	
New Caledonia	Pacific Ocean	19,100	7,400	
Viti Levu	Fiji	10,500	4,100	
Hawaii	Pacific Ocean	10,450	4,000	
Bougainville	Papua NG	9,600	3,700	
Guadalcanal	Solomon Is.	6,500	2,500	
Vanua Levu	Fiji	5,550	2,100	
New Ireland	Papua NG	3,200	1,200	

NORTH AMERICA

		km²	miles²	
Greenland	Atlantic Ocean	2,175,600	839,800	[1]
Baffin Is.	Canada	508,000	196,100	[5]
Victoria Is.	Canada	212,200	81,900	[9]
Ellesmere Is.	Canada	212,000	81,800	[10]
Cuba	Caribbean Sea	110,860	42,800	
Newfoundland	Canada	110,680	42,700	
Hispaniola	Dom. Rep./Haiti	76,200	29,400	
Banks Is.	Canada	67,000	25,900	
Devon Is.	Canada	54,500	21,000	
Melville Is.	Canada	42,400	16,400	
Vancouver Is.	Canada	32,150	12,400	
Somerset Is.	Canada	24,300	9,400	
Jamaica	Caribbean Sea	11,400	4,400	
Puerto Rico	Atlantic Ocean	8,900	3,400	
Cape Breton Is.	Canada	4,000	1,500	

SOUTH AMERICA

		km²	miles²	
Tierra del Fuego	Argentina/Chile	47,000	18,100	
Falkland Is. (East)	Atlantic Ocean	6,800	2,600	
South Georgia	Atlantic Ocean	4,200	1,600	
Galapagos (Isabela)	Pacific Ocean	2,250	870	

World: Regions in the News

YUGOSLAVIA
Population 10,761,000
(Serb 62.6%, Albanian 16.5%,
Montenegrin 5%, Hungarian 3.3%,
Muslim 3.2%)
Serbia Population: 5,799,800
(Serb 87.7%, excluding the
provinces of Kosovo and
Vojvodina)
Kosovo Population: 2,084,4000
(Albanian 81.6%, Serb 9.9%)
Vojvodena Population: 1,980,800
(Serb 56.8%, Hungarian 16.9%)
Montenegro Population: 635,000
(Montenegrin 61.9%, Muslim
14.6%, Albanian 7%)

CROATIA
Population: 4,960,000
(Croat 78.1%, Serb 12.2%)

SLOVENIA
Population: 2,055,000
(Slovene 88%, Croat 3%, Serb 2%)

MACEDONIA (F. Y. R. O. M.)
Population: 2,157,000
(Macedonian 64%, Albanian 21.7%,
Turkish 5%, Romanian 3%,
Serb 2%)

BOSNIA-HERZEGOVINA
Population: 4,601,000
(Muslim 49%, Serb 31.2%,
Croat 17.2%)

Legend:
- — · — International boundaries
- — · · — Republic boundaries
- — — — Province boundaries
- ■ Capital cities
- ——— Dayton Peace Agreement Boundary
- Muslim–Croat Federation
- Bosnian Serb Republic

FORMER YUGOSLAVIA AND KOSOVO

The former Yugoslavia, a federation of six republics, split apart in 1991–2. Fearing Serb domination, Croatia, Slovenia, Macedonia and Bosnia-Herzegovina declared themselves independent. This left two states, Serbia and Montenegro, to continue as Yugoslavia. The presence in Croatia and Bosnia-Herzegovina of Orthodox Christian Serbs, Roman Catholic Croats, and Muslims led to civil war and 'ethnic cleansing'. In 1995, the war ended when the Dayton Peace Accord affirmed Bosnia-Herzegovina as a single state partitioned into a Muslim-Croat Federation and a Serbian Republic.

But the status of Kosovo, a former autonomous Yugoslav region, remained unresolved. Kosovo's autonomy had been abolished in 1989 and the Albanian-speaking, Muslim Kosovars were forced to accept direct Serbian rule. After 1995, support grew for the rebel Kosovo Liberation Army. The Serbs hit back and thousands of Kosovars were forced to flee their homes. In March 1999, NATO launched an aerial offensive in an attempt to halt the 'ethnic cleansing'. A Serb military withdrawal from Kosovo was finally agreed in June 1999.

KOSOVO
Scale: 0 20 40 km
- ■ Capital city
- ● Other towns
- — · — International boundaries

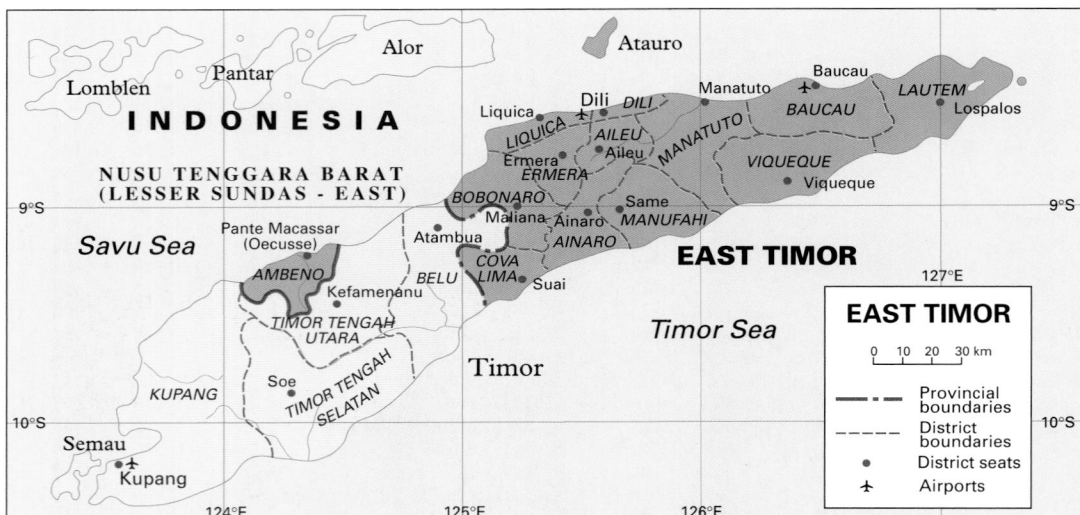

EAST TIMOR
Scale: 0 10 20 30 km
- — · — Provincial boundaries
- — — — District boundaries
- ● District seats
- ✈ Airports

THE NEAR EAST
Scale: 0 25 50 km
- — · · — 1949 Armistice Line
- — — — 1974 Cease-fire Line
- *Efrata* ● Main Jewish settlements in the West Bank and Gaza Strip
- *Halhul* ● Main Palestinian Arab towns in the West Bank and Gaza Strip
- ■ Capital cities

ISRAEL
Population: 5,321,000 (inc. East Jerusalem and Jewish settlers in the areas under Israeli administration. Jewish 82%, Arab Muslim 13.8%, Arab Christian 2.5%, Druze 1.7%)

West Bank
Population: 1,122,900 (Palestinian Arabs 97% [of whom Arab Muslim 85%, Jewish 7%, Christian 8%])

Gaza Strip
Population: 748,400 (Arab 98%)

JORDAN
Population: 5,558,000 (Arab 99% [of whom about 50% are Palestinian Arab])

LEBANON
Population: 3,327,000 (Arab 93% [of whom 83% are Lebanese Arab and 10% Palestinian Arab])

COUNTRIES AND REPUBLICS OF THE CAUCASUS REGION

RUSSIAN REPUBLICS IN THE NEWS
North Ossetia (Alania)
Population: 695,000
(Ossetian 53%, Russian 29%,
Chechen 5.2%, Armenian 1.9%)
Chechenia Population: 1,308,000
(Chechen and Ingush 70.7%,
Russian 23.1%, Armenian 1.2%)
Ingushetia (Split from Chechenia
in June 1993) Population: 250,000

GEORGIA
Population: 5,777,000
(Georgian 70.1%, Armenian 8.1%,
Russian 6.3%, Azerbaijani 5.7%,
Ossetian 3%, Greek 2%,
Abkhazian 2%)
Abkhazia Population: 537,500
(Georgian 45.7%, Abkhazian 17.8%,
Armenian 14.6%, Russian 14.3%)
Ajaria Population: 382,000
(Georgian 82.8%, Russian 7.7%,
Armenian 4%)

ARMENIA
Population: 3,968,000
(Armenian 93%, Azerbaijani 3%)
Nagorno-Karabakh
Population: 192,400 (Armenian
76.9%, Azerbaijani 21.5%)

AZERBAIJAN
Population: 8,324,000
(Azerbaijani 83%, Russian 6%,
Armenian 6%, Lezgin 2%)
Naxçivan Population: 300,400

THE CAUCASUS
Scale: 0 100 200 km
- — · — International boundaries
- — — — Republic boundaries

Georgia, Armenia and Azerbaijan achieved independence in 1991. Abkhazia, Ajaria and South Ossetia seek independence from Georgia. Chechenia has been trying to break away from Russia since 1991, but Russia has resisted with military force. Hostility also continues between Armenia and Azerbaijan over the enclave of Nagorno-Karabakh.

WORLD EXPLORER

CONTENTS

Mountains and volcanoes	2–3	Sea and ocean cruises	18–19
Deserts and canyons	4–5	Winter sports	20–21
Lakes and waterfalls	6–7	Great beaches	22–23
Wildlife in the Americas and Europe	8–9	Festivals	24–25
Wildlife in Africa, Asia and Australasia	10–11	Historic sites in the Americas	26–27
Marine wildlife	12–13	Historic sites in Europe	28–29
Great railway journeys	14–15	Historic sites in Africa, Asia and Australasia	30–31
River and canal journeys	16–17	Theme parks	32

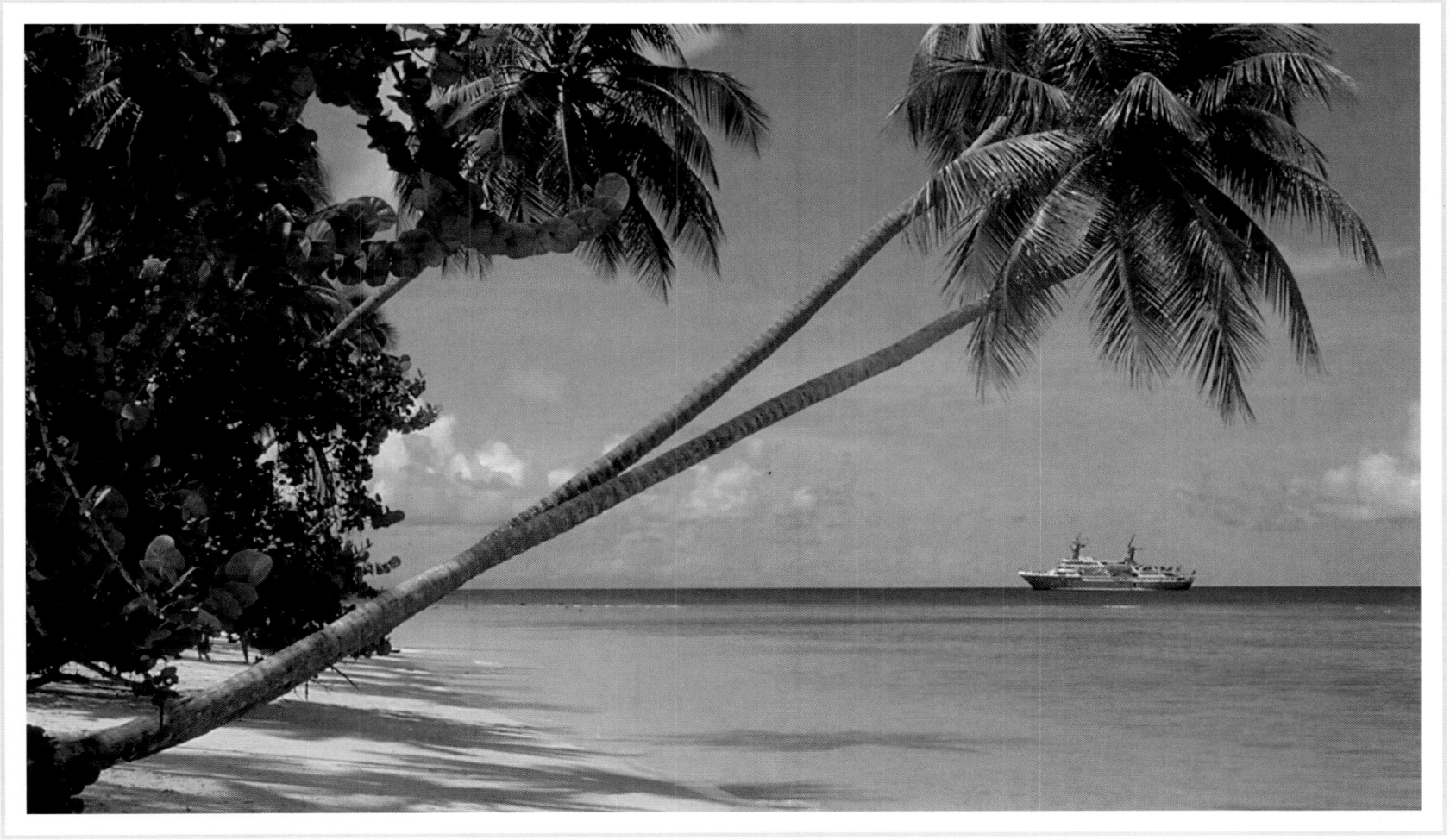

Mountains and volcanoes

The world's mountains provide a huge variety of magnificent scenery, ranging from the tree-covered Blue Mountains of Australia, little more than 1,070 m (3,500 ft) high, to the towering snow-covered Himalayan peaks of Nepal and China, several of which are over 8,000 m (26,000 ft) high. Many are accessible by road, or sometimes by train or cable car, but walking, even if only a short distance, is usually the best way to experience the breathtaking views that they offer.

◄ **Rocky Mountains, Banff National Park, Canada**
Pointed peaks and sheer cliffs contribute to a magnificent land-scape. Over 1,600 km (1,000 miles) of trails pass by glaciers, turquoise lakes and forests of pine, fir and spruce. In the town of Banff a cable car rises to the top of Sulfur Mountain, 2,263 m (7,440 ft) high.
Best time to visit: June–September

THE AMERICAS

Mount McKinley, Denali National Park, Alaska, USA
The USA's highest mountain at 6,194 m (20,321 ft) is in a spectacular wilderness of snow-covered peaks and glaciers with wildlife that includes brown bears, caribou, moose and marmots. Activities include river rafting and sightseeing by plane.
Best time to visit: June–August

Popocatepetl Volcano ('Smoking Mountain'), Sierra Nevada, Mexico
A cloud of smoke often hovers above the massive crater of Popocatepetl, which is 5,452 m (17,887 ft) high. It is possible to climb and descend the mountain in one very long day with the aid of a guide.
Best time to climb: November–March

Cotopaxi and Chimborazo Volcanoes, Ecuador
The two highest active volcanoes in the world are in a country where the main road is known as the 'Avenue of the Volcanoes'. Non-mountaineers can climb Cotopaxi (5,896 m/19,344 ft) and get near to the top of Chimborazo (6,267 m/20,561 ft).
Best time to climb: January–April

Cordillera Blanca, Huascaran National Park, Peru
With 663 glaciers, the peaks of the Cordillera Blanca, more than 50 of which rise to heights of between 5,000 and 6,000 m (16,500 and 19,700 ft), are a great attraction for ice climbers. Huarez is the main climbing centre. An alternative for those who prefer to trek is the richly glaciated Huayhuash range.
Best time to visit: July–September

EUROPE

Landmannalaugar, Iceland
A combination of volcanic and geothermal activity has produced a unique landscape in Landmannalaugar, where mountain peaks (little more than 1,070 m/3,500 ft high) rise above a landscape of convoluted lava fields and blue mountain lakes, and hot springs provide open-air baths.
Best time to visit: July–early September

Mount Vesuvius, Italy
The volcano of Vesuvius dominates the landscape around Naples. Although it lost its plume of smoke after erupting in 1944, it is still active. A bus from Pompeii goes to within 1.5 km (1 mile) of the summit (1,277 m/4,189 ft).
Time to visit: All seasons

AFRICA

Atlas Mountains, Morocco
Canyons with dramatic rock formations are to be found in these rugged mountains that rise to a height of over 3,900 m (13,000 ft). Organized treks pass by numerous isolated Berber villages, far from the road from Marrakech, which winds up to a mountain pass 2,275 m (7,467 ft) high.
Best time to visit: June–October

Mount Kilimanjaro, Tanzania
Africa's highest mountain rises majestically to 5,895 m (19,340 ft) above the plains of Amboseli National Park. It is possible to trek to the top for stunning views over Kenya and Tanzania, along

▲ **Sierra Nevada, Yosemite National Park, USA**
The Californian Yosemite National Park is famous for its sheer-sided granite domes, such as the Half Dome and the 1,066 m (3,500 ft) high El Capitan, which rise above forests and emerald lakes. Among the many species of flowers and trees to be found in the park are ancient giant sequoias over 60 m (200 ft) high, one of which is estimated to be 2,700 years old. An added attraction are the Yosemite Falls which, with a drop of 739 m (2,425 ft), are the highest in North America. Walkers can escape the summer crowds by using the 1,280 km (800 miles) of trails.
Best time to visit: May–September

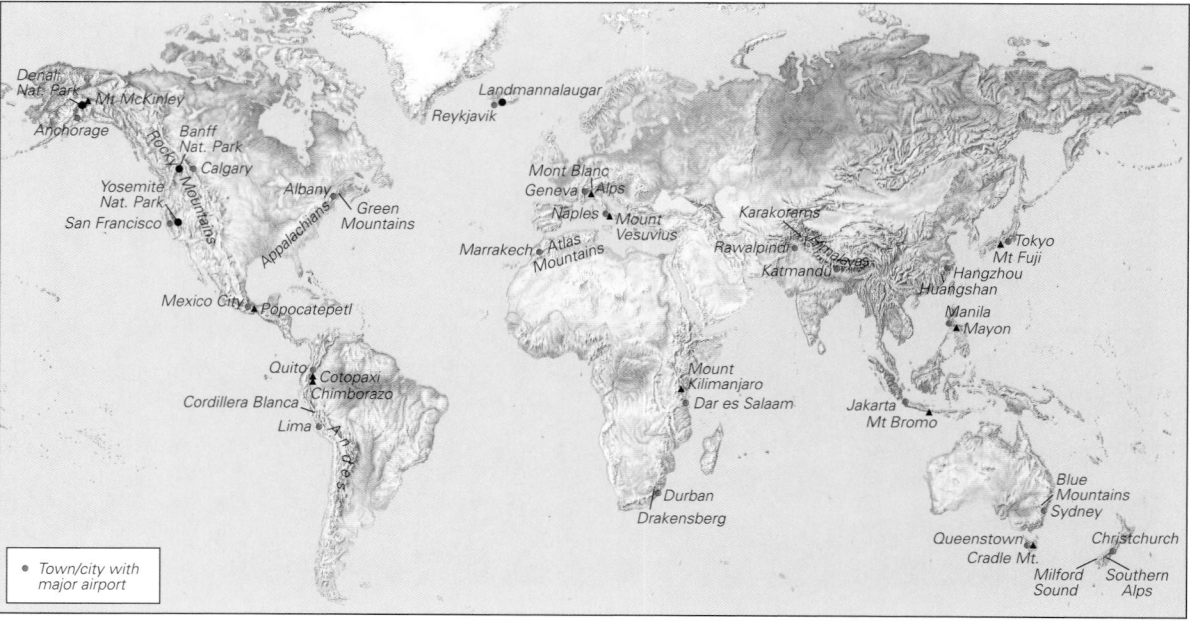

Town/city with major airport

▲ Mont Blanc, Alps, France
Europe's highest mountain rises to a height of 4,807 m (15,760 ft). A splendid view of it can be had from the peak of the Aiguille de Midi, a granite spear 3,840 m (12,600 ft) high, that is reached by a steep 3 km (2-mile) ascent in a cable car from Chamonix. Below Mont Blanc is the start of a long-distance ski and walking route, which passes ten of the 12 highest peaks in the Alps on its way to the Matterhorn in Switzerland and Italy.
Best time for walking: May–September

▼ Mt Bromo, Java
A crater within a vast outer crater, Bromo emits white smoke, as does Mount Semeru, seen here in the distance. Visitors usually stay over-night in a village at the rim of the outer crater, from where it is possible to walk to Bromo at dawn to watch the sun rise up over the outer crater.
Best time to visit: April–October

routes that pass through farmland and lush forest before reaching alpine-like vegetation and snow-covered rock.
Best time to climb: mid January–late February and late August–September

Drakensberg Mountains, South Africa
Vast pinnacles and blocks of basalt rise to a height of over 3,475 m (11,400 ft) in this range of mountains that also runs through Lesotho. Snowcapped in winter, many of the peaks are an enormous challenge for mountaineers. The Royal Natal National Park has numerous hiking trails.
Best time to visit: April–October

ASIA

Himalayas, Nepal
Within the Himalayas in Nepal are ten of the world's 14 peaks with a height of over 8,000 m (26,000 ft), including Everest (8,850 m/29,035 ft). Far below the snow-capped peaks are terraced hillsides dotted with villages, while above a height of about 2,700 m (9,000 ft) are forests in which rhododendrons bloom between February and April. The most popular base for exploring the mountains is Pokhara. The famous ten-day trek to the mountain town of Jomsom begins here, as does the three-to four-day Annapurna Skyline Trek which provides superb views while being easy enough to be undertaken with children.
Best time to visit: October–April

Karakorams, Pakistan
The jagged peaks of the Karakorams include K2, the world's second highest mountain (8,611 m/28,400 ft). A journey along the Karakoram Highway follows the route of the old Silk Road along the Indus Valley from Rawalpindi to Kashgar in China, sometimes clinging to cliff faces as it winds its way through the mountains up to the Khunjerab Pass at 4,934 m (16,280 ft).
Best time to visit: May–August

Great mountain treks
The following is a selection of great mountain treks that take four or more days. The months given are those in which it is best to undertake each trek.

Long Trail, Vermont, USA (424 km/265 miles; 16–21 days; May–Sept) Easily reached by road, the trail through Vermont's Green Mountains can be walked in sections. It is part of the 3,456 km (2,160-mile) long Appalachian Trail, whose most demanding section is through New Hampshire's White Mountains.
Inca Trail, Peru (4–5 days; April–Sept) By far the best way to approach the spectacular Inca site of Machu Picchu (see *Historic Sites of the Americas*), the Inca Trail begins some distance from Cuzco.
Mont Blanc Circuit, France and Switzerland (10 days; July–Sept) Possibly the finest walk in Europe, it usually starts from Chamonix. With an average altitude of 1,525 m (5,000 ft), it links the seven valleys surrounding Mont Blanc.

Annapurna Circuit, Nepal (17 days; Oct–Nov and March–April) Regarded as Nepal's classic trek, it goes through many types of landscape *(see picture below)*, and reaches a height of 5,416 m (17,765 ft), as well as providing superb views of Annapurna and Dhaulagiri.
Everest Trek, Nepal (14–16 days; Oct–Nov and March–April) A trek from Jiri to the Everest Base Camp on the Khumbu Glacier provides wonderful views of Everest. It is possible to fly back to Katmandu from Lukla, three days' walk away.
Milford Track, New Zealand (54 km/34 miles; 4 days; Oct–April) A walk that is regarded as a must by most New Zealanders ends at the breathtaking Milford Sound (see *Sea and ocean cruises*). The number of walkers is limited and booking well ahead is necessary.

Mayon Volcano, Philippines
Often described as the world's most perfect volcano cone, Mayon (2,462 m/8,075 ft) is still very active. An eruption in 1993 killed 70 people. It can be climbed in two days but it is essential to do so with a guide.
Best time to climb: December–May

Mt Kinabalu, Borneo, Malaysia
It is possible to walk rather than climb to the top of the highest mountain in South-east Asia (4,010 m/13,455 ft). It does, however, take two days and hiring a guide is compulsory. The view from the top some-times stretches to the Philippines.
Best time to climb: April–September

Huangshan, China
The Chinese regard the 72-peak Huang-shan range as one of the great natural attractions of their country. Some 30 peaks rise to over 1,500 m (4,900 ft). There are two main walking routes up the side of the range, and an eight-minute cable car ride from Yungusi to the top.
Best time to visit: spring and autumn

Mt Fuji, Japan
The perfectly symmetrical cone of Japan's highest mountain (3,776 m/12,388 ft), which last erupted in 1707, is climbed by people of all ages in the summer. A road goes to the fourth and fifth 'stations', from where it takes four or five hours to climb to the crater. This is best reached at dawn, before the clouds gather.
Best time to climb: July–August

AUSTRALASIA

Blue Mountains, New South Wales, Australia
Reaching a height of just over 1,070 m (3,500 ft), the Blue Mountains – with their densely forested slopes, sandstone chasms, dramatic rock formations and waterfalls – provide a beautiful environment in which to drive and walk. As well as a network of trails there are a number of interesting villages and towns, of which the largest, Katoomba, is served by a railway from Sydney just 80 km (50 miles) away.
Time to visit: All seasons

Cradle Mountain/Lake St Clair National Park, Tasmania, Australia
Australia's best mountain trails and rugged alpine scenery are to be found around Cradle Mountain. Jagged peaks, the highest of which is Mt Ossa (1,617 m/5,300 ft), rise above tarns and lakes in deep valleys.
Best time to visit: November–March

Deserts and canyons

For the adventurous traveller, the stunning landscapes of rock and sand which make up some of the world's most inhospitable environments offer a challenge not to be missed. From the vast sand seas of the Sahara Desert to the deep canyons and distinctive rock formations of the south-western United States, there is an extraordinary range of landforms to explore.

NORTH AMERICA

Bryce Canyon, Utah, USA
On a more human scale than the Grand Canyon, Bryce Canyon is not really a canyon at all but a natural amphitheatre filled with dazzling orange, red and pink rock pinnacles – known as 'hoodoos' – overlooking spectacularly colourful ravines. This surreal landscape can be explored on foot along a network of marked trails, or simply enjoyed from one of the viewpoints along the rim of the amphitheatre.

Monument Valley, Arizona, USA
With its majestic rock pillars towering over a barren, desert landscape, Monument Valley is an awe-inspiring sight. It has been made famous as a backdrop to numerous Hollywood westerns and is now part of the Navajo Reservation. A 27 km (17-mile) road tour of the valley takes two to three hours and offers stunning views of this unforgettable place.

Zion Canyon, Utah, USA
The road through the steep-sided Zion Canyon can become crowded in summer, and it is worth leaving the car to follow one of the short trails to the Emerald Pools or the hanging gardens at Weeping Rock. Longer trails lead from the canyon to the desert plateau above and offer spectacular views of the contrasting landscapes.

SOUTH AMERICA

Colca Canyon, Peru
High in the Andes the River Colca runs through a gorge which is twice the depth of the Grand Canyon, past ancient Inca granaries cut into the rock and green slopes covered by pre-Inca terracing. This astonishingly beautiful landscape, complete with smoking volcano in the background, is home to the Collagua and Cabana people, whose traditional way of life is punctuated with lively festivals.

Atacama Desert, Chile
Overlooked by a ruined pre-Inca fortress, the picturesque oasis village of San Pedro de Atacama, with its adobe buildings and excellent archeological museum, makes a good base for exploring the canyons, saltpans and stark landscapes of the surrounding desert. One of the most beautiful places to visit is the Valle de la Luna, where the multi-coloured desert formations are a magnet for photographers and filmmakers.

EUROPE

Almerían Desert, Spain
The setting for the film *Lawrence of Arabia* as well as many 'spaghetti westerns', the Almerían Desert is an extraordinary, almost lunar landscape of sand dunes dissected by dried-up river beds and littered with sandstone cones. Film sets are open to the public at Mini-Hollywood.

Timanfaya National Park, Lanzarote, Canary Islands
On an island where it rarely rains, a series of volcanic eruptions in the 1730s created an extraordinary apocalyptic landscape. Guided tours go to an area of solidified lava and volcanic cones, aptly called the Mountains of Fire, where a dry bush dropped into a crevice will burst into flames and meals at a solitary restaurant are barbecued on a volcano.

AFRICA

Draa Valley, the Sahara, Morocco
From the town of Ouarzazate, with its dramatic kasbah, the Draa river runs south-east through a rich landscape of dramatic gorges, agricultural land and kasbahs towards the Sahara. After around 160 km (100 miles), the river reaches the former frontier fort of Zagora, which makes a good base for exploring the desert.

▲ **Grand Canyon, Arizona, USA**
Carved by the Colorado River out of the multi-coloured rock of the Arizona Desert, the Grand Canyon is one of North America's most awe-inspiring natural features. Drives and trails around its rim – 443 km (277 miles) in length – provide stunning views. Visitors can walk or ride mules down one of the vertiginous trails to the valley floor, 1.7 km (1 mile) below, or try rafting on the river.

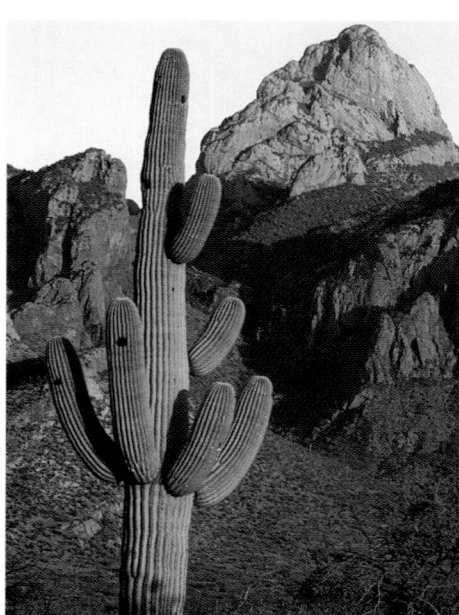

▲ **Sonoran Desert, USA/Mexico**
Almost encircling the Gulf of California and covering 310,000 sq km (120,00 sq miles), the Sonoran Desert is the hottest of North America's deserts. Tucson, Arizona, serves as a base for tours into the desert, including archaeological tours. Nearby are the excellent Arizona-Sonora Desert Museum and the protected desert habitat of Organ Pipe Cactus National Monument where visitors can see the giant saguaro and organ pipe cacti which have come to symbolize the area. There are good trails and scenic drives around the park, and plenty of desert wildlife to watch.

Bryce Canyon
Zion Canyon
Las Vegas
Phoenix
Monument Valley
Grand Canyon
Sonoran Desert
Almerian Desert
Granada
Tunis
Lanzarote
Agadir
Arrecife
Draa Valley
Sahara
Desert
Agadez
Ténéré
Desert
Cairo
Amman
Wadi Rum
Sinai
Desert
Ulaanbaatar
Gobi Desert
Delhi
Thar
Desert
Nairobi
North Kenyan
Desert
Lima
Colca Canyon
Atacama
Desert
Santiago
Namib
Desert
Windhoek
Durban
Blyde River
Canyon
Uluru-Kata Tjuta
National Park
Alice Springs

• Town/city with major airport

Saharan oases, Tunisia

The shifting sand dunes around the town of Douz are an excellent example of the landscape popularly associated with the Sahara Desert. In fact the desert, which covers an area of 8,600,000 sq km (3,320,000 sq miles), has extensive stony plains, rock-strewn plateaux, mountains and large oasis depressions as well as seas of sand. Douz is a good base for camel safaris and for exploring the more isolated southern oases. To the north-west the town of Tozeur, with its beautiful 12th-century mosque, is set beside a vast oasis fed by over 200 springs. It serves as an excellent starting point for four-wheel-drive tours into the desert and to the nearby beautiful mountain oases, such as Tamerza, Mides and Chebika.

Guided expeditions of up to a week can include camel riding and stargazing under the immense Saharan sky.

Ténéré Desert, Niger

For desert purists the seemingly endless sea of sand that is the Ténéré Desert is perhaps the most beautiful part of the Sahara. A two-week round trip from the desert city of Agadez might pass through a massive dinosaur cemetery on the way to the classic oasis town of Bilma and the prehistoric cave paintings of the Djado Plateau. Crossing the Ténéré is notoriously challenging and often dangerous, but the experience is unforgettable.

Sinai Desert, Egypt

Inland from the coastal resorts of the Sinai Peninsula is a hot, desolate wilderness sprinkled with oases and ancient settlements. They include the 6th-century monastery of St Catherine, which stands at the foot of Mount Sinai, where Moses is said to have received the Ten Command-ments from God. Camel treks and jeep safaris take visitors into the aptly-named Wilderness of Wanderings, in the centre of the peninsula.

North Kenyan Desert

In sharp contrast to the developed south of Kenya, the North Kenyan Desert is a vast tract of scrubland inhabited by ancient nomadic tribes whose way of life has changed little over the centuries. A rich diversity of desert landscapes here includes scrub desert – which bursts into colour after rainfall – and lunar, volcanic areas. There are lush oases and river-cut canyons too, but the reason most people come here is to see the 'Jade Sea', Lake Turkana, with its profusion of birdlife, hippos and Nile crocodiles.

Namib Desert, Namibia

Stretching for 1,930 km (1,200 miles) down the length of the Namibian coastline to the mouth of the Orange River in South Africa, the Namib is a strip of desert with an average width of 110 km (70 miles). The highest sand dunes in the world – sometimes exceeding 244 m (800 ft) – are to be found at Sossus Vlei, in the Namib-Naukluft National Park. The northern section is known as Skeleton Coast because of the many shipwrecks that lie on the ocean bed nearby.

Blyde River Canyon, South Africa

The view over the canyon from the spot known as God's Window is one of the highlights of any visit to the beautiful Blyde River Nature Reserve, in the Drakensberg. There are two trails down into the canyon – which in some places is over 700 m (2,300 ft) deep – from Bourke's Luck Portholes, where strange natural rock formations can be seen.

ASIA AND AUSTRALASIA

Thar Desert, Rajasthan, India

Within the Rajasthan Desert National Park two areas of interest to tourists can be reached easily from the attractive city of Jaisalmer with its 12th-century fort. One is the Akal Fossil Park where the petrified trunks of 25 trees once covered by the sea lie on a bare hillside. The second is the 3 km (2-mile) long Sam Dunes, just 40 km (25 miles) from Jaisalmer. The dunes are usually crowded with tourists taking camel rides, but it is possible to escape the crowds and go on safaris of several days, by either jeep or camel.

Gobi Desert, Mongolia

For 70 years part of the Soviet Union, the Gobi Desert has only recently become accessible to western travellers. Its greatest attraction is the red sandstone Flaming Cliffs, 80 km (50 miles) north-west of Dalandzadgad, which became famous in the 1920s when the explorer and scientist Roy Chapman Andrews (on whom the character of Indiana Jones was based) discovered fossilized dinosaur remains there. Still rich in dinosaur fossils, the cliffs are just north of the vast Three Beauties National Park with a landscape of mountains, canyons, gravel and sand.

▼ **Wadi Rum, Jordan**
Soaring vertically from the desert floor of Wadi Rum are the massive rock form-ations known as jebels for which the area is famous. Vehicles and camels can be hired in the Bedouin settlement of Rum, but it is hard to beat the experience of walking through this extraordinary, silent landscape and sleeping out in the desert under the stars.

◀ **Uluru National Park, Northern Territory, Australia**
The largest sand-stone monolith in the world, Uluru (Ayers Rock) is a magnificent sight, particularly at sunset when it appears to burn from within. Some 40 km (25 miles) to the west are the Olgas – 36 enormous granite domes – which, like Uluru, are an important Aboriginal site. Access is restricted, but visitors can exper-ience their haunting beauty by following the trail through the Valley of the Winds.

Lakes and waterfalls

From the azure tranquillity of Lake Garda in Italy to the thundering roar of Zimbabwe's Victoria Falls, the great lakes and waterfalls of the world are set amidst dramatically beautiful scenery. Many resorts offer watersports as well as long-distance trails for ramblers and horse-riders.

▶ Lake Maligne, Jasper National Park, Canada
The glacier-fed Lake Maligne – shown here at dawn – is set among the snow-covered peaks of Jasper National Park, the biggest and wildest of Canada's four Rocky Mountain national parks at 10,400 sq km (4,000 sq miles). Boat and hiking tours, fishing, rafting and riding are available, while the independent explorer can hire a boat or walk along the excellent network of trails.

▼ Lake Argentino, Argentina
The south-western arm of Lake Argentino is periodically dammed by the Moreno Glacier, from which icebergs regularly break off and crash into the channel below. Visitors can see, hear and photograph the glacier in safety from a series of platforms and viewing points. The massive Upsala Glacier on the northern arm of the lake can be reached by boat from Puerto Bandera.

NORTH AMERICA

Niagara Falls, Canada/USA
The most-visited waterfall in the world, Niagara Falls has been developed as a tourist attraction offering every possible viewing experience, including cable cars, helicopter rides, viewing towers, boats and even tunnels in the rockface. Despite the commercialization, this massive, perpetual curtain of falling water lives up to its reputation as one of the wonders of the natural world.

Waterton-Glacier Park, Montana and Alberta, Canada/USA
Silver lakes are a major feature of the landscape of mountain peaks, waterfalls and hanging valleys, carved by glaciers 10,000 years ago, in the Waterton-Glacier Park. There are spectacular trails for walkers of all levels, and the Going-to-the-Sun Road through the park is considered to be one of the USA's driving highlights.

Lake Tahoe, California, USA
High in the Sierra Nevada mountains on the border between California and Nevada, Lake Tahoe is a popular year-round holiday destination. In winter the area is packed with skiers (see *Winter sports*) while summer brings people seeking the cooler temperatures of the mountains and the crystal waters and sandy beaches of the lake. On the California side, there is swimming, boating, fishing and walking, while the Nevada side offers a glittering nightlife of restaurants and casinos.

SOUTH AMERICA

Iguaçu Falls, Brazil
The torrential waters of the Iguaçu River plunge more than 75 m (250 ft) over a huge, crescent-shaped cliff into the gorge below in a series of some 275 separate waterfalls. Surrounded by lush rainforest, the 4 km (2.5-mile) wide cascades can be viewed from platforms and paths on both sides of the Falls.

Lake Titicaca, Bolivia
High in the Altiplano the clear blue waters of Lake Titicaca bring an oasis of life and colour to the parched landscape. At 8,340 sq km (3,220 sq miles), it is the largest lake in South America, with many lakeside settlements. Boat trips can be made to the floating reed islands inhabited by the Uros, and to ancient Inca ruins on the sacred islands of the Sun and Moon.

Lake Llanquihue, Chile
A reflection of the perfect cone of Volcano Orsono can be seen in this immense lake which lies amid gently rolling pastureland. Towns on the shore include Frutillar Bajo, a popular summer resort with black-sand beaches, and Puerto Varas, a centre for 'adventure' activities such as rafting, riding, hiking and climbing.

EUROPE

Lake Siljan, Sweden
In a land of around 96,000 lakes, Siljan is noted as a centre of Swedish folk tradition

▼ Angel Falls, Venezuela
The world's highest waterfall with an uninterrupted drop of 2,650 ft (807 m), Angel Falls are 16 times the height of Niagara Falls. Although often shrouded in mist, the Falls are at their most spectacular during the rainy season (June–November) when the volume of water is greatest and when visitors can travel by motorized canoe along the river to Devil's Canyon at the foot of the Falls.

and art. Locals and visitors arrive in boats reminiscent of Viking longships during midsummer celebrations at the lakeside church of Rättvik, and traditional mystery plays are performed annually in the open-air theatre at Leksand. Visitors can watch traditional painted wooden horses being made at Nusnäs, and visit the studio of the painter Anders Zorn, who lived in the lakeside town of Mora.

Lake District, England
Famous as the haunt of the Romantic Poets, the Lake District is a beautiful and varied landscape of hills, mountains, lakes and rivers, encompassing a wide range of scenery within a relatively small area. The southern lakes – including Windermere, Coniston and Grasmere – are surrounded by gentle green slopes and attract enormous numbers of visitors in summer.

The wilder north, with its sheer, forbidding crags is more spectacular and much less crowded. Boating is popular on the larger lakes, and a network of paths makes the area a haven for walkers and climbers.

Lake Lucerne, Switzerland
The picturesque medieval town of Lucerne with its famous Kapellbrücke bridge makes an excellent base for exploring this beautiful lake and its mountain surroundings. Visitors can go on a lake cruise and stop off at some of the peaceful villages along the shore, or take the oldest mountain railway in Europe to Mount Rigi for wonderful views of the Alpine scenery.

Lake Garda, Italy
The largest of Italy's lakes, Lake Garda is certainly one of its most beautiful. Sheltered from the north-east by the Dolomites, its climate is particularly gentle, with orange and lemon groves flourishing on its banks. Dotted around the lake are many attractive and historic resort towns – some dating back to Roman times – and romantic hillside villas.

AFRICA

Lake Bosumtwi, Ghana
Sacred to the Asante people, the crater lake of Bosumtwi is the deepest natural lake in Ghana, and its waters are still rising. Its beautiful setting among thickly wooded crater walls makes it a relaxing place to go fishing, boating and swimming. Motorboat trips across the lake are available, and walks around the shore can include visits to lakeside villages.

Murchison Falls, Uganda
The sheer force of the Nile as it shoots through a narrow cleft in the rocks and crashes over a 30 m (100 ft) precipice is what makes Murchison Falls so spectacular. A journey up the river from Paraa Camp to the base of the falls is also an excellent way to see some of the wildlife of the Murchison Falls National Park, including crocodiles, elephants, hippos, giraffes, buffalo, waterbucks and many bird species.

Lake Baringo, Kenya
Encircled by mountains and rich in bird and animal life, Lake Baringo is a fascinating and beautiful place to visit. The shoreline is home to crocodiles and herds of hippos and the area is famous for its hundreds of bird species, attracting birdwatchers from all over the world. A resident ornithologist offers guided walks, and there are also horse rides, camel rides and boat trips to the lake's islands.

ASIA

Lake Toba, Sumatra
Encircled by steep crags – once the rim of an enormous ancient volcano – Lake Toba is the largest crater lake in the world. The area is home to the Toba Batak people, whose brightly painted houses with distinctive crescent-shaped roofs can be seen around the lake. The beautiful island of Samosir is a popular tourist destination

with excellent trekking and rafting as well as interesting megalithic tombs to visit.

Lake Batur, Bali
The largest lake in Bali, Lake Batur is a crater lake and is sacred to the Balinese as the home of the goddess Dewi Danu. The hot springs at Toya Bungkah are said to have healing properties, and the lakeside temple of Pura Jati presides over a holy bathing place. From Toyah Bungkah there are trekking routes up to the summit of Gunung Batur, the soaring 1,717 m (5,630 ft) high volcano which dominates the lake.

Lake Karakul, Tajikistan
At a height of 3,600 m (11,800 ft) in the foothills of the Pamir mountains, Lake Karakul's setting is remote and beautiful. Flanked by the massive Mount Kongur to the north and the magnificent Mount Muztaghata to the south, Karakul is the home of the Kirgiz people and their herds of sheep, goats, horses and camels. It takes a day to walk around the lake, after which walkers can stay overnight in a traditional felt-covered *yurt* at the visitors' camp.

Lake Chuzenji-ko and Kegon Waterfall, Japan
Visitors to Lake Chuzenji-ko and the dramatic Kegon Waterfall are well provided for with cable cars and platforms from which to gaze at the spectacular view, especially popular in autumn when the

leaves are changing colour. Beside the lake is a colourful shrine after which both the town and lake are named.

AUSTRALASIA

Lake Rotorua, New Zealand
Bubbling hot springs, vertical jets of steam and scalding geysers make Rotorua an exciting place to visit. There are lakeside bath houses where visitors can sample the waters, as well as cruises and facilities for a wide range of watersports on the lake and nearby rivers. Maoris have lived beside the lake for around 700 years, and there are many cultural attractions on offer, some more authentic than others.

▲ **Keli Mutu, Flores, Indonesia**
An extinct volcano, Keli Mutu has three extraordinary crater lakes. Not only is each lake a different colour, but the colours change over decades from vivid green through to deep red and intense turquoise as mineral layers dissolve.

◄ **Victoria Falls, Zimbabwe**
The 1.7 km (1-mile) wide Victoria Falls are made up of five separate waterfalls which plummet more than 100 m (320 ft) into the gorge below. The Falls are a popular base for adrenaline-boosting activities, such as bungee jumping, white-water rafting and riverboarding, and tours of every description can be taken from operators based in Victoria Falls town.

The following map labels appear on image 1:
Lake Siljan, Stockholm, Lake District, Manchester, Lake Maligne, Edmonton, Calgary, Waterton-Glacier Park, Zurich, Verona, Hamilton, Lake Luzern, Lake Garda, Lake Karakul, Kashi, Lake Chuzenji-ko and Kegon Waterfall, Tokyo, Niagara Falls, Buffalo, San Francisco, Lake Tahoe, Caracas, Angel Falls, Lake Bosumtwi, Accra, Murchison Falls, Lake Baringo, Entebbe, Nairobi, Medan, Lake Toba, Lake Batur, Keli Mutu, Denpasar, Ende, La Paz, Lake Titicaca, São Paulo, Iguaçu Falls, Victoria Falls, Lusaka, Harare, Santiago, Buenos Aires, Lake Llanquihue, Auckland, Lake Rotorua, Lake Argentino
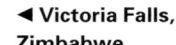
● Town/city with major airport

Wildlife in the Americas and Europe

From the bears and moose of the Alaskan wilderness, to the jaguars and toucans of the Central American forests, to the condors and rheas of Patagonia, the Americas have an amazing variety of wildlife. Europe by contrast is famed for its seabirds, and the vast flocks of migrant wildfowl that gather in its wetlands.

▶ **Torres del Paine National Park, Chile**
An awe-inspiring landscape of forests, glaciers, shimmering lakes, thundering cascades and soaring granite pillars, Torres del Paine National Park in Patagonia is a haven for wildlife, including guanacos, rheas, flamingos, condors and the shy huemul (Chilean deer). There is an excellent network of short- and long-distance trails through the park.

▼ **Wrangell-St Elias National Park, Alaska, USA**
Of all the Alaskan national parks, Wrangell-St Elias is the best for wildlife watching. This vast landscape of mountains and glaciers is home to moose, wolves, wolverines, bears, beavers and herds of caribou. There are several campsites but few other facilities for visitors in this true wilderness park.

NORTH AMERICA

Wood Buffalo National Park, Alberta/NW Territories, Canada
Canada's largest national park, Wood Buffalo is famous for its free-roaming buffalo herd. Among other inhabitants are lynx, bears and hundreds of bird species, including a river rookery of rare white pelicans and the few remaining whooping cranes in the world. Fort Smith has some accommodation, but canoeing along the rivers and camping are perhaps the best ways to explore this wilderness of forest, marsh and grassland.

Yellowstone National Park, Wyoming, USA
Famous for its many geothermal geysers and hot springs, Yellowstone Park is also home to one of the largest and most diverse populations of mammals in North America. Inhabitants include bison, moose, elks, Bighorn sheep, beavers and marmots as well as lynx, bobcats, wolves and coyotes. Millions of visitors flock to Yellowstone every year, but despite the inevitable tourist development, most of the park is still a true wilderness.

Everglades National Park, Florida, USA
The largest sub-tropical wilderness on the North American mainland, Everglades National Park is a vast area of swamps, mangrove forests and grasslands. It is the only place in the world where alligators and crocodiles live side by side, and there are still a few panthers and black bears. Canoe trails and boat tours are the best way to view the abundant wildlife, which includes a huge variety of bird species.

CENTRAL AMERICA

Braulio Carrillo Park, Costa Rica
Many different habitats exist in Braulio Carrillo, a large area of rainforest covering a range of altitudes from just above sea level to 3,000 m (9,850 ft). Each has its own distinct flora and fauna, although the astonishingly lush vegetation can make spotting animals such as tapirs, sloths, ocelots, jaguars and pumas difficult. The park's abundant birdlife includes toucans, quetzels, umbrella birds, guans and eagles.

Corcovado National Park, Costa Rica
Set on the remote Osa peninsula, Corcovado National Park encompasses coastal mangrove swamps, pristine cloud forests and rocky canyons. Many of Costa Rica's endangered species live here, including tapirs, caymans and jaguars, while crocodiles swim in its waters and turtles lay their eggs on the park's deserted beaches. Ranger stations provide simple accommodation and advice.

Darién National Park, Panama
More than 500 bird species have been seen in the pristine rainforest of Darién National Park, among them many endangered species such as the harpy eagle. Indeed, Cerro Pirre mountain is considered by many birdwatchers to be one of the best sites in the world. Boat trips and forest walks are ideal ways to view the abundant wildlife, although visitors should seek advice on when it is safe to travel because of possible paramilitary activity.

Cockscomb Basin Wildlife Sanctuary, Belize
Beneath the peaks of the Cockscomb mountain range, the dense rainforest of the Cockscomb Basin is home to around 600 jaguars as well as tapirs, anteaters, armadillos and otters. Nearly 300 bird species have been reported in this lush jungle, and a wide variety of reptiles and amphibians are readily visible. Excellent forest trails make this a very rewarding place for wildlife watchers.

SOUTH AMERICA

Podocarpus National Park, Ecuador
Encompassing a wide range of habitats at different altitudes, Podocarpus (near Loja) has many rare plant and animal species, such as the Andean fox, the Andean speckled bear and the mountain tapir. Birdlife is abundant, and it is easy to see many fascinating species. This is, however, a park in peril, with the authorities struggling to protect the environment from poachers, loggers and others. For visitors prepared to rough it, there is much to enjoy in this landscape of lakes, mountains and rainforest.

Manu Biosphere Reserve, Peru
Altitudes range from 200 m (650 ft) to over 4,000 m (13,000 ft) in this area of rainforest near Cuzco. An astonishing 850 bird species are found here, and mammals include jaguars, ocelots, otters and many primate species. The reserve is divided into zones, with restricted visitor access in some areas. A stay in the Reserved Zone, which is set aside for ecotourism and research, must be arranged in advance, but offers the best jungle experience.

▲ **Monteverde Cloud Forest Reserve, Costa Rica**
Festooned with bromeliads and orchids, the towering rainforest trees of Monteverde Cloud Forest provide shelter for an enormous variety of wildlife including tapirs, monkeys, coatimundis and armadillos, as well as more than 400 bird species. The reserve was established in 1950 by a group of Quakers, who have developed a range of unobtrusive facilities for visitors, including simple accommodation and excellent guided walks.

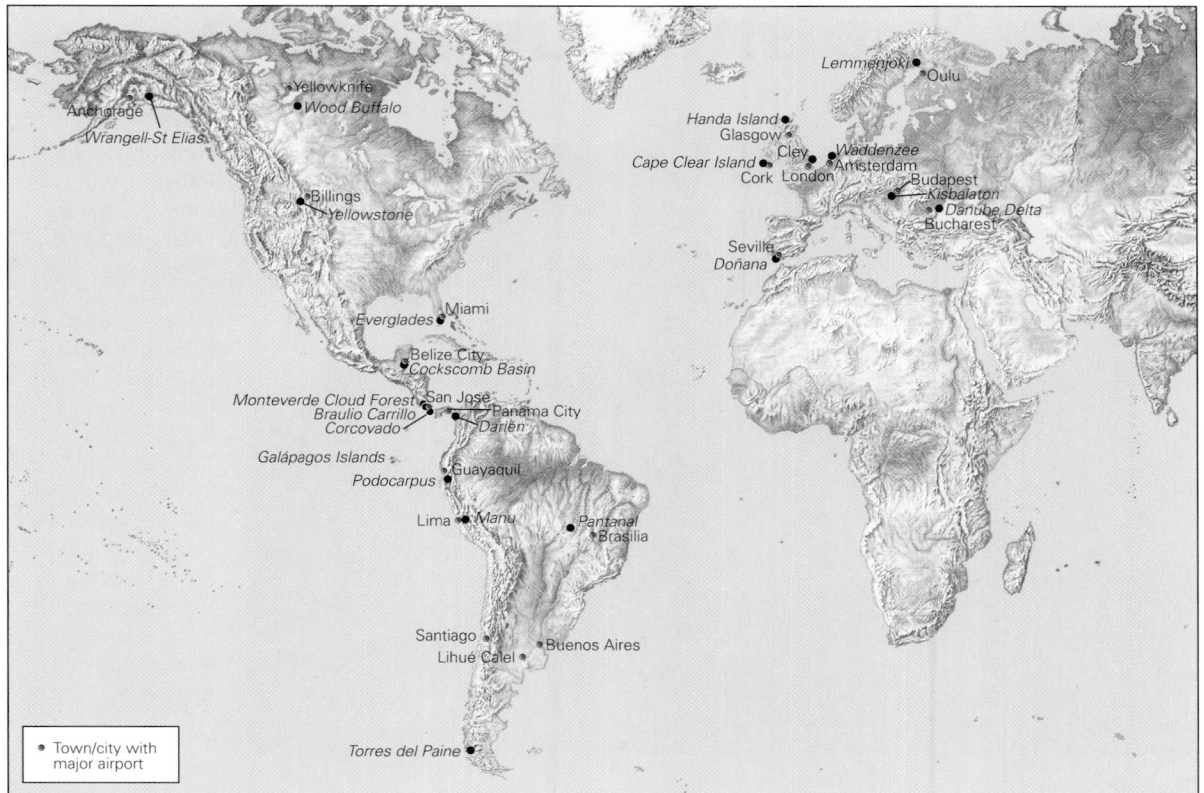

The map shows various locations worldwide with town/city markers.

Town/city with major airport

▶ Handa Island, Scotland

The sea cliffs of Handa Island are one of north-west Europe's largest seabird nesting sites, with the high cliff ledges attracting guillemots, razorbills and kittiwakes in enormous numbers. Fulmars, puffins and shags also nest here, while the island's moorland is home to great and Arctic skuas, red-throated divers, shelducks, ringed plovers, wheatears, meadow pipits and skylarks. The island can be visited for the day by boat from the mainland village of Tarbet, near Loch Laxford.

Pantanal, Brazil

A vast swamp covering an area the size of Great Britain, the Pantanal is perhaps the best place to see wildlife in the Americas. Animals wander freely around the wide open spaces, making it relatively easy for visitors to spot such creatures as alligators, jaguars and anacondas, and birds such as the giant red-necked stork. There are organized tours by boat or jeep and on horseback, with overnight accommodation at converted ranch houses.

Lihué Calel National Park, Argentina

An arid landscape of low, pink granite mountains and scrub forest, Lihué Calel (south-west of Santa Rosa) is home to several wild cat species and other mammals such as guanacos, Patagonian foxes, Patagonian hares and chinchillas. Birdlife is plentiful, too, and includes many species of birds of prey. The park has an excellent campsite and visitor centre.

EUROPE

Lemmenjoki National Park, Lappland, Finland

Lemmenjoki (near Inarijärvi) is one of the most extensive areas of uninhabited, forested wilderness in Europe (2,855 sq km/1,102 sq miles). Wide rivers flow through a landscape of peatland and spruce- and birch-forested hills, home to brown bears, golden eagles, foxes, lynx, wolverines and moose. There are also plenty of semi-domesticated reindeer.

Cape Clear Island, Ireland

Ireland's southernmost inhabited island, tiny Cape Clear is famous for its birds. It has breeding populations of chough, black guillemot and rock dove and is visited by many migrant species in August–October, including the rare bee-eater, little bittern, night and purple herons, and great reed warbler, as well as many seabirds. The Bird Observatory has a full-time bird-warden and offers simple accommodation.

Cley Marshes, Norfolk, England

One of Britain's leading birdwatching reserves, Cley Marshes (near Sheringham) has many thatched hides offering excellent views of thousands of water birds. Migrating waders stop in the area on their way to and from their Arctic breeding grounds, and in summer bitterns and avocets breed here. Wildfowl such as teals, widgeons and shovelers are plentiful in winter.

Waddenzee, The Netherlands

Regarded by birdwatchers as the most important intertidal area in Europe, Waddenzee has huge populations of waders and wildfowl. One of the best areas to see the birds is around Schiermonnikoog, particularly at high tide. Among the birds present in summer are avocets, godwits and ruffs, while in winter they include Bewick's swans, barnacle geese, marsh and hen harriers and white-tailed eagles.

Kisbalaton Reserve, Lake Balaton, Hungary

With its reed beds, the Kisbalaton Reserve provides the perfect environment for marsh birds to breed. Night, purple and squacco herons are all to be found here along with little and great white egrets, spoonbills, marsh harriers and several warblers. From October huge flocks of migrating ducks and geese stop in the reserve on their journey south.

Danube Delta, Romania

One of Europe's last unspoiled ecosystems, consisting of forest, lakes, reed beds and marshland, the Danube Delta is home to huge numbers of birds. Due to the lack of tourist facilities, it is probably best-visited in an organized group, ideally from late May–June. Species include bitterns, pygmy cormorants, white pelicans, night, purple and squacco herons, spoonbills, ruddy shelducks, honey buzzards, bee-eaters and white-tailed eagles.

Doñana National Park, Spain

Huge sand dunes and the seasonally flooded plains (*marismas*) behind them provide ideal conditions for a great variety of birdlife in one of Europe's most important wildlife habitats. Peregrines, stone-curlews and short-toed eagles are to be seen in the dunes, while the marismas are feeding grounds for white storks, spoonbills, night and purple herons and colonies of little and cattle egrets.

Galápagos Islands and ecotourism

Lying 960 km (600 miles) off the coast of Ecuador, the fragile wilderness of the Galápagos Islands provides a habitat for a surprising combination of penguins and corals as well as giant tortoises, land and marine iguanas, sperm whales, sea lions, fur seals, orca whales, sharks and a variety of tropical fish. Many of the species living here are found nowhere else in the world, making the Galápagos a vital laboratory for the study of animal and plant life. Access to the islands is strictly controlled and limited to 50 designated visitor sites. The development of ecotourism in the Galápagos Islands aims to ensure the preservation of the habitats and wildlife while enabling tourists to visit and learn about this unique environment.

Wildlife in Africa, Asia and Australasia

An African safari is one of the world's great wildlife-watching experiences. Vast stretches of open savanna are home to the 'big five' – lion, leopard, elephant, rhinoceros and buffalo – as well as herds of zebra and gazelle. The endangered Indian tiger and exotic komodo dragon are just two of the animals that attract visitors to Asia, while Australia has its own unique fauna, including kangaroo, koala and duck-billed platypus.

◀ **Masai Mara National Reserve, Kenya**
Kenya's greatest concentration of wildlife can be seen in Masai Mara, where cheetahs, hyenas, zebras, hartebeest, hippos and crocodiles share the territory with the 'big five'. During the summer enormous herds of wildebeest, zebras and gazelles arrive from the Serengeti on the first stage of their dramatic annual migration.

AFRICA

Abuko Nature Reserve, Gambia
In this small reserve, mangroves, gallery forest and savanna combine to attract over 270 bird species – including the world's largest and smallest kingfishers – making it one of the best birdwatching sites in West Africa. Abuko is also known for its troops of colobus, patas and vervet monkeys.

Niokolo-Koba National Park, Senegal
Some 80 mammal species, including lions, leopards, elephants, waterbucks, bushbucks, baboons and chimpanzees live in Niokolo-Koba, along with around 350 bird species. The best time to see the animals is when they gather at waterholes during the hot season in April and May.

Tsavo (East and West), Kenya
Tsavo East and Tsavo West combine to make one of the world's biggest national parks, covering an area of 21,000 sq km (8,000 sq miles). As well as the 'big five', the animals include cheetahs, giraffes, zebras, crocodiles, hippos, porcupines and mongooses. Tsavo East is a popular safari destination while at Tsavo West the excellent facilities include underwater hides for hippo watching.

Ngorongoro Crater, Tanzania
Protected within a circle of thickly-forested crater walls, Ngorongoro Crater is an expanse of grassland and forest measuring 14 km (9 miles) across and teeming with wildlife. Elephants, leopards, hyenas, bushbucks, buffalo, wildebeest, elands, warthogs, gazelles and ostriches live alongside the rare black rhinoceros and the handsome black-maned lion, while Lake Makat is home to flocks of flamingos and other water birds.

Jozani Reserve, Zanzibar, Tanzania
The largest remaining area of indigenous forest on Zanzibar, Jozani Reserve is home to a variety of birds and butterflies, as well as a number of rare mammals, including the red colobus monkey, which can only be found here.

Bwindi National Park, Uganda
Half of all the world's endangered mountain gorillas live in Bwindi National Park, an area of hilly rainforest. The park supports a rich variety of animal life including chimpanzees, golden cats, civets, leopards, bushpigs and giant forest hogs. Small groups of visitors who have booked several months in advance can go on guided gorilla-tracking expeditions.

Chobe National Park, Botswana
Encompassing habitats that range from marshland to forest, Chobe is home to a great variety of wildlife, including the rare puku and red lechwe antelope. Other inhabitants include lions, cheetahs, buffalo, giraffes, elephants, zebras, jackals, warthogs, hippos, crocodiles, hyenas, antelopes and wildebeest, as well as an abundance of birdlife. The animals can be viewed from boats on the Chobe River.

Kruger National Park, South Africa
A vast game reserve covering almost 20,000 sq km (7,400 sq miles), Kruger Park is home to around 137 mammal species, including lions, elephants, rhinoceros, leopards, buffalo, zebras, giraffes, impalas, wildebeest, hippos and crocodiles, as well as the rare roan and sable antelopes and oribi. The northern part is especially noted for its birdlife, including the highest density of birds of prey anywhere in the world.

Bird Island, Seychelles
Huge colonies of seabirds nest on the tiny, coral Bird Island. The sooty tern, fairy tern and common noddy are everywhere, while passing migrants add to the interest for birdwatchers. The island is also home to large numbers of giant turtles.

▼ **Serengeti National Park, Tanzania**
Covering 14,763 sq km (5,700 sq miles) and including woodland and mountains, as well as huge tracts of open grassland, the Serengeti is home to the 'big five' plus cheetahs, hyenas, zebras, giraffes, gazelles and many others. It also has around 500 bird species. It is most famous for the spectacular summer migration of gazelles, wildebeest and zebras, when around 2 million animals set off on a 800 km (500-mile) trek to fresh feeding grounds.

▲ **Etosha National Park, Namibia**
One of the most important game reserves in Africa, Etosha covers a vast 20,000 sq km (7,720 sq miles) of woodland and grassland surrounding the Etosha Pan – an immense saline desert. Animals living here include springboks, impalas, kudu, wildebeest, hartebeest, roan antelopes, elands, zebras, elephants and the rare white rhinoceros, as well as predators such as lions, leopards, cheetahs, caracals, jackals and hyenas. There are around 340 bird species, including eagles, ostriches and secretary birds. Accommodation to suit all budgets is available.

ASIA

Kaziranga National Park, Assam, India

Famous as the home of the rare one-horned Great Indian Rhinoceros – most of the surviving 1,500 are here – Kaziranga (east of Gauhati) also has tigers, bears, elephants, bison and many bird species. A good way to travel around the tall-grass and swampy terrain is on an elephant. The park is only open from November to April.

Keoladeo Ghana National Park, Rajasthan, India

Formerly known as the Bharatpur Bird Sanctuary, Keoladeo is famous for its breeding populations of native water birds as well as its thousands of migrating birds which arrive every year from China and Siberia, including herons, storks, snake birds and the rare Siberian crane. The best time to visit is from October to February, when the migratory birds are in residence.

Sundarbans Wildlife Sanctuary, India/Bangladesh

Home to one of the largest remaining tiger populations in India, the Sundarbans Wildlife Sanctuary covers 6,695 sq km (2,585 sq miles) of mangrove swamp in the vast Ganges delta. Tigers are not often spotted by visitors, but a boat excursion through the peaceful mangroves will reveal many other animals – monkeys, wild pigs, spotted deer, crocodiles and fishing cats, as well as a profusion of birdlife.

Kanha National Park, Madhya Pradesh, India

Kipling set his *Jungle Book* in this beautiful landscape of forests, rivers and grasslands (near Mandla). Kanha is the only home of the barasingha (swamp deer) and it also plays an important role in the preservation of the tiger, leopard, chital, sambar and gaur (Indian bison). The park is open November–May, with sightings increasing from March onwards as the hot weather brings out the animals in search of water. Excursions are available.

Khao Yai National Park, Thailand

Encompassing a variety of habitats, from mountains clad in evergreen forest to lowland scrub and grassland, Khao Yai

(north-east of Bangkok) has an abundance of wildlife, including elephants, gibbons, porcupines, tigers, leopards, Indian munjaks, Malaysian sun bears and several species of deer and monkey. There are over 250 bird species here, too, including the great hornbill and many colourful parrots and parakeets. Visitors can venture deep into the forest on several excellent trails, some of which require guides.

Taman Negara, Malaysia

Covering 4,340 sq km (1,676 sq miles) of ancient tropical rainforest, Taman Negara is a haven for hundreds of species of birds and animals, while its vegetation includes some of the world's rarest orchids. Inhabitants include tapirs, bears, elephants and gibbons. The park, which is the most visited in Pahang, has an elevated canopy walkway, and jungle hides in the trees, where visitors can spend the night.

Komodo National Park, Indonesia

The world's largest lizard, the astonishing 3 m (10 ft) long Komodo dragon, is found only on Komodo and a few neighbouring small islands. Guided treks usually include visits to dragon feeding places, and allow visitors to see some of the other wildlife of the park, such as wild pigs, deer, monkeys, water buffalo and eagles.

Ujung Kulon National Park, Indonesia

The last remaining low-relief forest on Java, in the far west, Ujung Kulon National Park is the only home of the one-horned Javan rhinoceros. Other inhabitants include the Javan gibbon, Javan tiger, muntjac (barking deer), chevrotain (mouse deer), green sea turtle and crocodile.

AUSTRALASIA

Eungella National Park, Queensland, Australia

With its tall, ancient rainforest trees, rocky creeks and spectacular waterfalls, Eungella is an extraordinarily beautiful place to watch wildlife. Among its inhabitants are kangaroos, possums, feathertail gliders, pythons and the native Eungella honey-eater, but the star attraction is the shy duck-billed platypus, which can be seen around the riverbanks at dawn and dusk.

Otago Peninsula, New Zealand

A remarkable variety of wildlife is concentrated on the Otago Peninsula. Seals and other marine life can be seen along the rocky coastline, while the inlets and beaches shelter numerous waders and waterfowl. A protected albatross nesting-site at Taiaroa Head is open to the public once the eggs are laid, and yellow-eyed penguins can be seen at close quarters from an excellent conservation reserve.

Catlins Forest Park, New Zealand

Ancient rainforest runs down to the rocky inlets and estuaries of the coast, offering a variety of habitats for some of New Zealand's rarest plants and animals. There are colonies of Hooker's sea lion and yellow-eyed penguin, and much birdlife. Two- and four-day ecotours are available.

◄ **Royal Chitwan National Park, Nepal**
With its lush sub-tropical jungle and floodplain swamp, Chitwan National Park is a natural habitat for animals such as the tiger, Indian rhinoceros and leopard. Tours on foot, by jeep or on the back of an elephant are best undertaken between October and March.

▼ **Kakadu National Park, Northern Territory, Australia**
Australia's largest national park, Kakadu encompasses a spectacular collection of rainforest, ravines and wetlands along the South Alligator River. These varied habitats shelter a vast array of wildlife, including 1,500 species of butterflies and moths, 75 reptile species, including crocodiles, 25 species of frog and one third of all Australia's bird species. Mammals include kangaroos, wallabies, walleroos, dingoes and many species of bat.

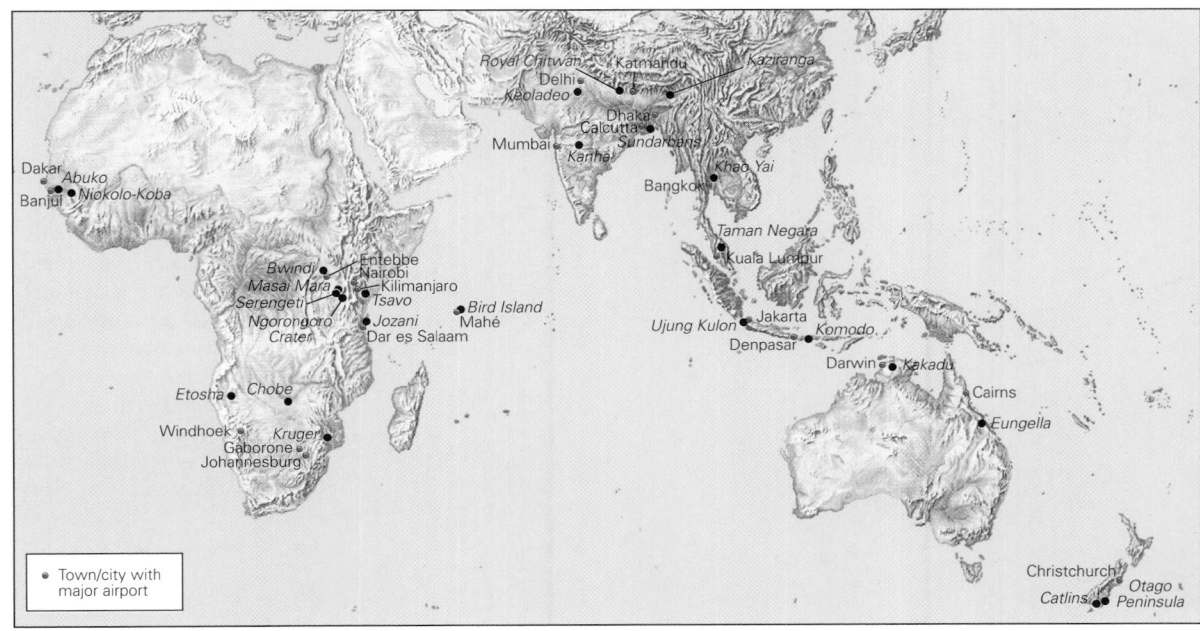

■ Town/city with major airport

Marine wildlife

With whale numbers recovering strongly following the world ban on hunting, many seaports in North America, South Africa and Australasia offer boat trips to watch whales and other large fish and mammals. In the warm waters of the tropics, coral reefs teeming with vividly coloured sealife can be explored by scuba divers and snorkellers or viewed from the comfort of a glass-bottomed boat.

◀ **Florida Keys, USA**
Among many places in the Caribbean that serve as a base for viewing or swimming with dolphins is Florida Keys. Consisting of 45 islands surrounded by spectacular corals, Florida Keys also provides a perfect environment for scuba diving.

THE AMERICAS

Johnstone Strait, Canada
The sea between Vancouver Island and the mainland is one of the best places in the world to see orcas (killer whales), the largest and most powerful predators on earth, and minke whales.

Hudson Bay, Canada
Beluga whales can be seen in June, July and August in the bay's Arctic waters. Particularly large numbers spend these months in the Churchill River estuary, an area famous for its polar bears.

Cape Breton and Grand Manan Islands, Canada
Whale-watching boat trips take place around both islands. Off Grand Manan, in the Bay of Fundy, up to 20 whale species, including the rare northern right whale and the finback, can be seen.

Massachusetts Bay, USA
Stellwagen Bank in Massachusetts Bay is a feeding ground for humpback, finback and minke whales from April to October. It is a world-renowned whale-watching area, attracting around 1.5 million whale watchers a year. The coastal towns of New England offer a range of boat trips.

Caribbean Sea, Cayman Islands
The islands are famous among scuba divers for their exceptionally clear waters and deep diving with spectacular sponge colonies and a wide range of reef fish. Those interested in larger species can see dolphins, barracudas and sharks – including silky sharks – here.

Caribbean Sea, Belize
The barrier reef of Belize is the largest in the western hemisphere, and second only to Australia's in the world. Between the reef and the mainland lie more than 175 cays and atolls (coral islands and rings) offering some of the best diving opportunities in the world. The extraordinary Blue Hole at the centre of Lighthouse Reef is a circular shaft over 120 m (395 ft) deep which was once a cavern underneath the sea bed. Half Moon Caye offers one of Belize's most spectacular wall dives, with an almost sheer drop overhung with wonderful coral spurs, rich in marine life.

Caribbean Sea, Venezuela
There is good diving to be had around the offshore islands of Venezuela, especially in the archipelago of Los Roques with its white sand beaches and beautiful coral reefs. The Parque Nacional Morrocoy on the north-west coast of Venezuela is very popular for snorkelling.

Paracas National Park, Peru
A boat trip around the offshore islands within this national park provides an opportunity to see dolphins, seals and sea lions, as well as pelicans and the great Andean condors that inhabit the cliffs.

AFRICA AND THE INDIAN OCEAN

Canary Islands
The waters around the islands provide sheltered feeding grounds for pilot whales, not usually seen so close to shore, and there are many boat trips available from Tenerife. Unfortunately, whale watching is not properly regulated here and whales have been injured by the boats.

Red Sea, Egypt
Hurghada is a good base for snorkelling and diving around the coral reefs of the Red Sea. Jolanda Reef, at the tip of the Sinai Peninsula in the Ras Muhammad National Park, is a spectacular column of coral 800 m (2,625 ft) high. The park is best approached from the Sharm el Sheikh resort.

▲ **Point Reyes, California, USA**
Grey whales can be seen from Point Reyes, north of San Francisco, between October and January as they migrate down the coast of Canada and the USA to the Gulf of California. Between December and March they can be found at Guerrero Negro in Mexico, where they gather to calve.

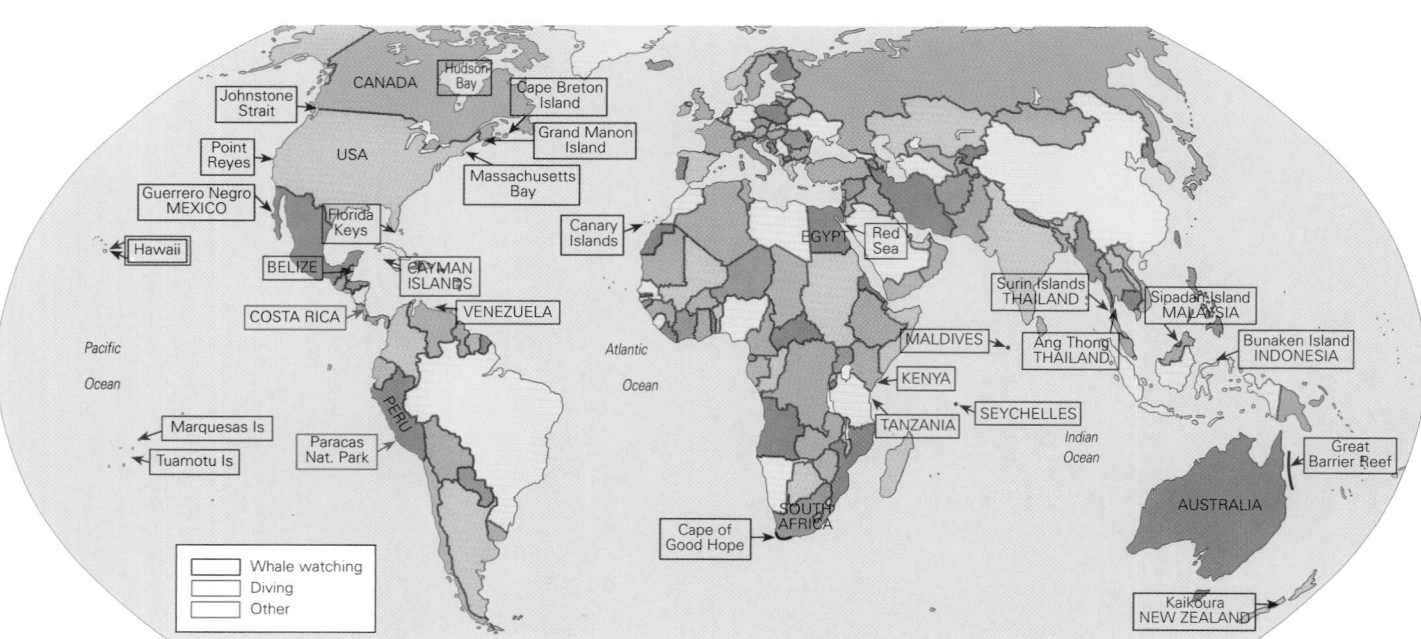

Whale watching
Diving
Other

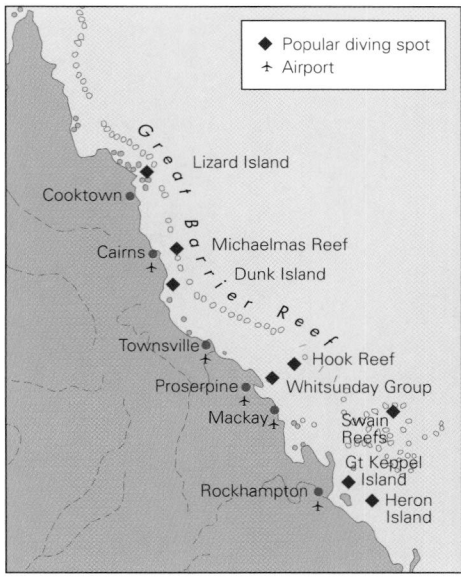

Popular diving spot
Airport

Pemba, Zanzibar and Mafia, Tanzania

The three main islands off the Tanzanian coast are surrounded by spectacular coral reefs which are home to a wide variety of marine species including bat fish, lion fish, turtles and rays. They offer some of the best diving opportunities in the world from August to December. Mafia Island is also a favourite breeding ground for giant turtles.

Cape of Good Hope, South Africa

In a country which has the strictest whale protection laws in the world, most whale watching takes place from the shore. The 'Whale Route' is a spectacularly scenic road along the coast from Cape Town, around the Cape of Good Hope, to the Indian Ocean, with many official whale-viewing sites. The town of Hermanus (the self-proclaimed 'whale capital' of South Africa) makes a good base. From June to October southern right whales, once hunted to near-extinction, can be seen swimming in these waters.

Seychelles

The outlying islands in particular offer world-class diving. The reef-ringed shores are a paradise for snorkellers, with over 150 species of tropical reef fish and 30 species of coral. Dolphins, porpoises, sharks and barracudas can also be seen. There are four marine national parks and diving schools with good facilities.

Maldives

Without doubt the Maldives are the best place in the Indian Ocean for diving. There are hundreds of diving sites, with something for everyone from beginners to experts. The more adventurous can explore shipwrecks as well as spectacular caves and terraces of coral. There is also plenty of scope for snorkellers.

▶ Tortuguero Park, Costa Rica

In the company of a guide, limited numbers of visitors can watch green turtles at their largest nesting site in the western hemisphere. The turtles lay their eggs on the beach between July and October, the peak time being late August.

Australia's Great Barrier Reef

The Great Barrier Reef is the largest structure on earth made by living organisms. It is a chain of coral reefs 2,000 km (1,200 miles) long, encompassing more than 600 islands and cays. About 20 of these islands have resort facilities, with Heron Island and Lizard Island both especially popular with divers. There are around 2,000 species of fish living on the reef and the area is home to many marine mammals, including the rare dugong and several species of whale. The best time to visit the reef is between April and December. Cairns is the mainland base for most reef activities and offers all kinds of tours.

ASIA

Ang Thong National Marine Park, Thailand

Boat trips around 42 limestone islands, many eroded into fantastic shapes, provide opportunities for seeing a variety of wildlife – including dolphins, turtles and sea otters – and for snorkelling and diving.

Surin Islands, Thailand

The Surin Islands are noted for diving in moonlight. The wildlife that may be encountered includes wahoo turtles, moray eels, black tip sharks and bat fish.

Sipadan Island, Sabah, Malaysia

An amazing undersea 'wall', teeming with marine life that includes whale sharks, manta rays, turtles and tuna, makes Sipadan one of the world's great diving destinations. The island is the tip of an underwater mountain, making it possible to dive from the beach.

Bunaken Island, Sulawesi, Indonesia

Perhaps the most famous marine destination in Indonesia, Bunaken Island near Manado serves as the main base for exploring the stunning coral reefs known as the 'sea gardens of Sulawesi'.

AUSTRALASIA AND THE PACIFIC

Kaikoura, New Zealand

A world-famous whale-watching centre, Kaikoura caters for 30,000 whale watchers

a year. The deepwater canyons near the shore are home to sperm whales.

Hawaii, USA

The extraordinary song of the humpback whale can be heard in the waters around Hawaii from November to May, after which these rare animals return to their summer feeding grounds in the near-polar waters of the north Pacific. Whale watching is strictly regulated, but there are plenty of boat trips on offer. Hawaii also has coral reefs, though with fewer species than on other Indo-Pacific reefs. Diving is popular, with lessons being provided in the crater lake of the extinct Molokini volcano. Excursions in submarines down to a depth of 50 m (160 ft) offer superb views of the underwater world through portholes.

Rangiroa, Tuamotu Islands

Among many excellent diving sites in French Polynesia, this is possibly the best, with outstanding coral, sharks, dolphins, barracudas and rays.

Marquesas Islands

The oxygen-rich water around the islands, which is thick with plankton, supports a variety of marine creatures, including hammerhead and white-tipped sharks, leopard and manta rays, tuna and barracudas. There are around 20 dive sites, including some impressive caves.

▲ Malindi and Wasini Island, Kenya

One of a number of good diving and snorkelling spots in Kenya, Malindi also offers excursions in glass-bottomed boats to the nearby coral reef. The Kisite Marine National Park on Wasini Island, in the far south, provides spectacular diving safaris.

Great railway journeys

From the luxury of the Orient-Express to the spartan rigours of the Trans-Siberian Railway, the world's great train journeys exert an irresistible lure for many travellers, passing through spectacular landscapes. Journeys vary in length from a few hours to a fortnight, and the more sought-after trains must be booked well in advance.

NORTH AMERICA

Green Mountain Flyer, Vermont, USA
Distance: 21 km (13 miles)
A vintage train takes passengers through the beautiful Vermont countryside, running alongside the Connecticut River for part of the way. Largely a tourist service, the peak period is during October when the autumn colours are at their best.

Coast Starlight, USA
Distance: 2,235 km (1,389 miles)
A journey from Seattle to Los Angeles, through the magnificent landscapes of the west coast of the USA, includes amongst its highlights the mountains of the Oregon Cascades and the Californian Coast Range. South of Oakland the track runs along the edge of the Pacific Ocean, passing several of California's most popular beaches.

Los Mochis to Chihuahua, Mexico
Distance: 655 km (407 miles)
This 14-hour journey is one of contrasting landscapes, from the tropical Pacific coastlands to the high northern plateau by way of the magnificent Copper Canyon (Barranca del Cobre). Longer and deeper than Arizona's Grand Canyon, this is an area of steeply wooded gorges and spectacular mountain peaks.

SOUTH AMERICA

Guayaquil to Quito, Ecuador
Distance: 463 km (288 miles)
For those who relish danger as well as breathtaking scenery, this line – which has been called 'the world's greatest roller-

▶ Palace on Wheels
India's most luxurious train, originally hauled by the *Desert Queen*, takes passengers on an eight-day tour that begins and ends in Delhi. It includes Jaipur and the other major cities of Rajasthan, and Agra.

coaster' – is a must. It climbs high into the Andes, zigzagging perilously to an altitude of 3,609 m (11,840 ft) and passing directly under a waterfall. Trains are erratic and often break down.

Central Railway, Peru
Distance: 335 km (208 miles)
The highest railway in the world, this takes passengers on an eight- to nine-hour journey across the Andes, from Lima to Huancayo. Dizzy heights, sheer drops, zigzags, loops and tunnels abound.

EUROPE

Flåm Railway, Norway
Distance: 20 km (12 miles)
Dropping 865 m (2,838 ft) in just 20 km (12 miles), this is one of the steepest non-rack railways in the world. Beginning with a view over the Kjosfossen lake and waterfall, the train weaves its way from Myrdal towards Aurlands Fjord and Flåm through a series of tunnels, with spectacular views between tunnels and snow shelters.

West Highland Line, Scotland
Distance: 264 km (164 miles)
Running between Glasgow and Mallaig, this line provides one of the most spectacular railway journeys in Britain. The route is particularly dramatic between Fort William and Mallaig, with a series of viaducts and tunnels through the mountains high above the Atlantic coast.

Venice Simplon-Orient-Express, Europe
Distance: 1,714 km (1,065 miles)
Passengers travel in style on a train that re-creates the romance of the golden age of rail as it crosses Europe from London to Venice, via Paris, Zürich, Innsbruck and Verona, in 32 hours. Orient-Express trains also run to Rome and Istanbul on a variety of routes that go through Venice, Florence, Lucerne, Budapest and Bucharest.

Andalusian Express, Spain
Distance: 740 km (460 miles)
The luxurious *Al Andalus* follows a circular route from Seville through the beautiful Andalusian countryside, with its citrus and olive groves, vineyards and hilltop villages. There are opportunities to stop off and see the sites at Córdoba, Granada, Antequera and Ronda.

◀ Glacier Express, Switzerland
Distance: 290 km (180 miles)
An exhilarating seven-and-a-half hour journey in the Swiss Alps, between the ski resorts of St Moritz and Zermatt, is provided by this train. Extraordinary feats of engineering are displayed as it weaves its way through the mountains, travelling through 91 tunnels, crossing 291 bridges and negotiating hairpin bends and steep ascents.

▲ Canadian, Canada
Distance: 2,776 miles (4,4467 km)
On a 69-hour journey that begins in Toronto, this train passes through some of the most beautiful scenery on earth. The prairie lands of Manitoba and Saskatchewan give way to the cattle ranches of Alberta, from where the train climbs into the Rockies. Here it passes lakes, glaciers and the dramatic Fraser Canyon before reaching Vancouver.

Useful web addresses
all preceded by www.

Canadian trains:
cwrr.com
viarail.ca

US trains:
amtrak.com

European trains:
raileurope.com

Orient-Express:
orient-expresstrains.com

Pride of Africa:
rovos.co.za

Palace on Wheels:
palaceonwheels.net

Eastern and Oriental Express:
diethelm-travel.com/eastern.htm

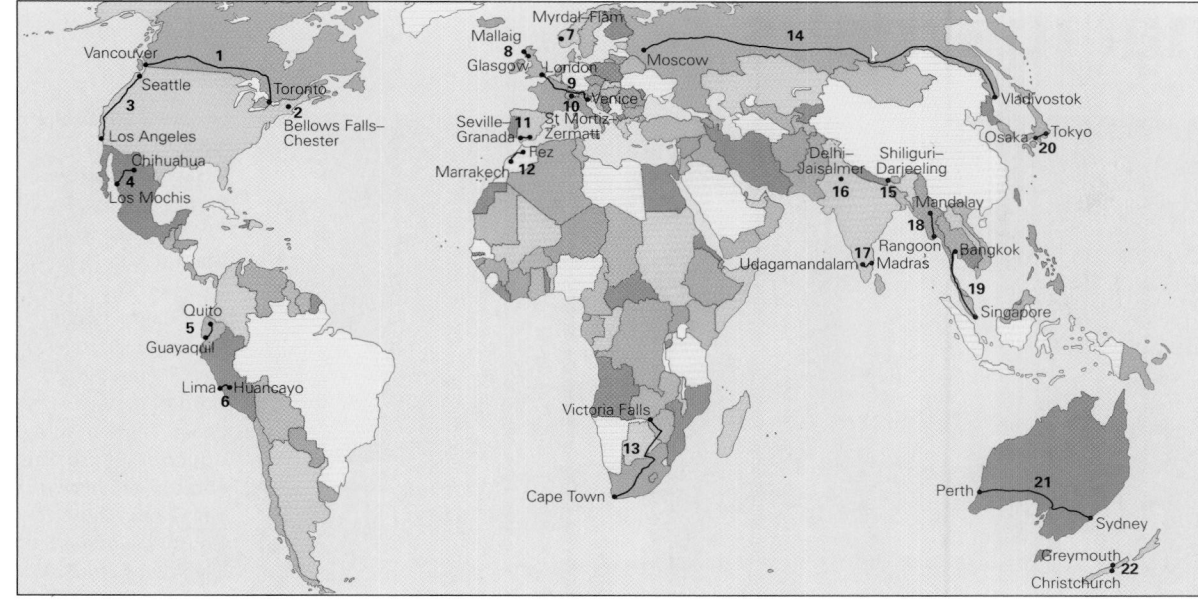

1	Canadian, Canada
2	Green Mountain Flyer, USA
3	Coast Starlight, USA
4	Los Mochis to Chihuahua, Mexico
5	Guayaquil to Quito, Ecuador
6	Central Railway, Peru
7	Flåm Railway, Norway
8	West Highland Line, Scotland
9	Venice Simplon-Orient-Express, Europe
10	Glacier Express, Switzerland
11	Andalusian Express, Spain
12	Marrakech Express, Morocco
13	Pride of Africa, Southern Africa
14	Trans-Siberian Railway, Russia
15	Darjeeling Himalayan Railway, India
16	Palace on Wheels, India
17	Madras to Udagamandalam, India
18	Mandalay Express, Burma (Myanmar)
19	Eastern Oriental Express, Thailand and Malaysia
20	Tokyo to Osaka, Japan
21	Indian–Pacific, Australia
22	TranzAlpine Express, New Zealand

AFRICA

Marrakech Express, Morocco
Distance: 583 km (362 miles)

Passing through Morocco's four imperial cities, this nine-hour journey begins in Marrakech, near the foot of the High Atlas Mountains, and travels north through the desert to Casablanca. From here the line follows the Atlantic coast to Rabat then gradually heads back inland through orchards and olive groves to Meknès and on to Fès.

Pride of Africa, Southern Africa
Distance: 3,2000 km (2,000 miles)

The journey from Cape Town in this luxurious train is full of romance and drama. In the early stages the train travels through a landscape of vineyards and farmland and across the Karoo Desert to Pretoria. Passengers can enjoy watching wildlife as the journey continues through the African bush across Botswana and Zimbabwe to the spectacular Victoria Falls on the Zambian border.

ASIA

Madras to Udagamandalam, India
Distance: 640 km (400 miles)

This 16-hour journey takes travellers from the plains of Madras through a colourful rural landscape and up into the beautiful Nilgiri hills to the famous hill station of Udagamandalam, formerly known as Ootacamund, or Ooty. The train passes through some of the most dramatic scenery India has to offer, climbing steeply on India's only rack railway to the gentler landscapes of the Deccan Plateau.

Darjeeling Himalayan Railway, India
Distance: 88 km (55 miles)

The tiny engine used on this railway, which is a UNESCO heritage site, takes passengers from Shiliguri on the hot Bengal plains to the mountain climate of Darjeeling in the Himalayas. The journey involves steep ascents and precipitous curves, climbing 2,164 m (7,100 ft). On the way the train passes through Ghoom, which is the second highest station in the world at 2,258 m (7,408 ft) above sea level.

Mandalay Express, Burma (Myanmar)
Distance: 616 km (385 miles)

By no means a tourist train, the Express offers the traveller a truly local experience as it makes its way slowly north from Yangon (formerly Rangoon) through a landscape of rice fields and golden-spired pagodas. The crowded train makes numerous – often unscheduled – stops along the way, making it an unpredictable and colourful journey. Best undertaken between November and February, the journey takes around 16 hours.

Eastern and Oriental Express, Thailand and Malaysia
Distance: 1,943 km (1,207 miles)

Starting in Bangkok, this train takes 52 hours to travel south through the terraced farmlands of Thailand and the rubber plantations and jungles of Malaysia to Singapore. It represents the height of luxury in train travel, while International Express trains that follow the same route provide a more down-to-earth experience.

AUSTRALASIA

Indian–Pacific, Australia
Distance: 3,960 km (2,461 miles)

This three-day transcontinental service from Perth to Sydney includes the longest stretch of straight railway track in the world (462 km/287 miles) across the vast expanse of the Nullarbor Plain, offering the traveller a rare sense of space and distance. The mountains of the Flinders and Gawler ranges provide a stunning contrast, while the Blue Mountains (see *Mountains and volcanoes*) offer a spectacular finale.

TranzAlpine Express, New Zealand
Distance: 233 km (154 miles)

Travelling from Christchurch on the South Island's east coast to Greymouth on the west coast, the Express takes passengers on a four-and-a-half hour journey through a variety of landscapes. After crossing the farmlands of the Canterbury Plains it follows the Waimakariri River gorge into the mountainous Arthur's Pass National Park, where it enters the long Otira tunnel. From here the line descends through lush rainforest, passing lakes Poerua and Brunner, to Greymouth.

◄ **Tokyo to Osaka, Japan**
Distance: 518 km (322 miles)
The Nozomi Express – the fastest scheduled train service in the world – travels at speeds of up to 300 km/h (186 mph) along this line. Not quite as fast, the Hikari Express completes the journey in just over three hours. However, the scenery, which includes Mount Fuji, can best be appreciated from the slower 'bullet' trains.

Trans-Siberian Railway, Russia
Distance: 9,297 km (5,776 miles)
The southern shore of Lake Baikal is on the route of the Trans-Siberian Railway, the world's longest, and possibly most famous, railway. The eight-day journey takes passengers from Moscow to Vladivostok via the Urals, the forested wilderness of Siberia, and the Transbaikalian Mountains.

In the early days of the railway, built between 1891 and 1916, a ferry was used in summer to carry the train across Lake Baikal, while in winter, when the lake froze, temporary rails were laid over the ice. The Siberian landscape is particularly beautiful in winter when it is covered with snow. In the spring there are carpets of wild flowers while in autumn there are the golden colours of the birch forests.

River and canal journeys

The world's great boat journeys give travellers a unique perspective on the countries through which they pass: rivers and canals were the highways of the past, and there are often opportunities to visit historic sites or natural habitats. Whether you are steaming down the Mississippi in a paddleboat, gliding through the French countryside past castles and vineyards or exploring the tributaries of the Amazon, the pace of the journey gives ample time to enjoy the beauty of the surroundings.

NORTH AMERICA

St Lawrence, Canada

From Kingston, where Lake Ontario flows into the majestic St Lawrence River, a six-night journey can be made on a replica steamboat to Montréal (see *World Cities*) and Québec (see *Historic sites in the Americas*). Just east of Kingston the river is dotted with literally a Thousand Islands, many of which have summer houses and opulent mansions set amid forests of yellow birch, silver maple and red and white trillium. In the spring the trillium trees are covered by white blossom.

Upper Mississippi, USA

In the summer months, seven-day cruises by paddleboat run between Minneapolis/St Paul and St Louis. There are also three-day cruises between St Louis and Memphis. The upper river, flowing through relatively flat countryside, is wide, slow moving and dotted with islands, but the stretch immediately below St Louis flows between rocky bluffs. Days spent cruising are alternated with sightseeing tours of such places as the boyhood home of Mark Twain, in Hannibal, Memphis, and a historic Native American site in Burlington, Iowa.

▶ St Petersburg to Moscow, Russia

This seven-day cruise passes through a network of rivers, lakes and canals in the richly wooded region of Southern Karelia, and down the upper reaches of the Volga River. Ports of call include the ancient town of Yaroslavl, the attractive Karelian capital of Petrozavodsk, and the Church of the Transfiguration on the island of Kizhi in Lake Onega, with its 22 wooden domes, constructed without a single nail.

CENTRAL AND SOUTH AMERICA

Amazon, Peru and Brazil

Cruises of between three and ten days along the Amazon River, starting from the remote but elegant Peruvian town of Iquitos, or from the brash and bustling Manaus in Brazil, are a relatively comfortable way to see the abundant wildlife of the rainforest. Many companies adopt an educational approach and include lectures on the local flora and fauna. Some include an opportunity to explore smaller tributaries by canoe. For the adventurous independent traveller who is prepared to rough it, a six-day journey by local riverboat from the Atlantic port of Belém to Manaus offers an unforgettable experience of local life and culture.

Orinoco Delta, Venezuela

The vast Orinoco Delta – a maze of channels running between countless forested islands – is one of Venezuela's wildest regions. The area is home to the indigenous Warao people, known for their skilled carving and basketwork, whose houses on stilts can be seen on the riverbanks. Boat tours into the delta can be arranged from the town of Tucupita, and usually last for between two and four days.

EUROPE

Shropshire Union Canal, UK

From Autherley, a 100 km (60-mile) journey can be taken on a slow-moving barge along the Shropshire Union Canal. Deep wooded cuttings, peaceful rural landscapes, medieval market towns and quiet villages are all passed at little more than walking pace. The ancient city of Chester, with its Roman ruins and medieval city walls, is a highlight of the journey. The canal ends at Ellesmere Port on the River Mersey, where there is an excellent boating museum.

Rhine, Switzerland, Germany and the Netherlands

A ten-day journey down the Rhine from Basel to Arnhem combines stunning scenery with a chance to visit the historic towns and cities along its banks. After flowing through the German Black Forest, the river passes romantic clifftop castles, sloping vineyards and picturesque villages on its way to the cities of the north: Bonn, Cologne and Düsseldorf. A detour up the River Neckar to the historic town of Heidelberg is often included.

◀ **Lower Mississippi, USA**
A seven-day cruise by paddleboat can be taken from Memphis to New Orleans. The Mississippi twists and turns on its way to the marshlands bordering the coast. There are opportunities to visit some of the historic sites of the Deep South, including the Civil War battlefields of Vicksburg, and the elegant mansion at Oak Alley Plantation, and to sample some of the local Creole and Cajun cuisine.

▲ **The Burgundy Canal, France**
Passing through a landscape of wooded valleys and sleepy villages, the six-day journey on a barge from Tonnere to Dijon along the Burgundy Canal provides an opportunity to see the beautiful 16th-century chateaux of Tanlay and Ancy le Franc and the 12th-century Cistercian Abbey of Fontenay. The region is famous for its *grand cru* vineyards and its robust cuisine, and there are plenty of opportunities to enjoy both along the way.

Douro, Portugal

Most cruises on the Douro are round trips of seven to nine days, beginning and ending in Porto. Once the boat leaves the coastal plain, it passes between spectacularly terraced vineyards, in an area unspoilt by major roads. Ports of call include the picturesque towns of Lamego and Vila Real. The region is the centre of Portugal's port wine production, and all cruises include a visit to a vineyard to sample the local produce.

Danube, Hungary, Slovak Republic, Austria and Germany

A Danube cruise of around eight days combines sightseeing tours of some of Central Europe's most historic towns and cities with an opportunity to relax on board, watching rich farmland and terraced slopes slip past. A cruise up-river from Budapest to Regensburg includes frequent stops, enabling passengers to explore Bratislava, Vienna, Linz and Passau, and to visit the sumptuous Baroque palace of Schönbrunn and the Benedictine Abbey in Melk. Since the boat berths overnight, passengers can also enjoy some nightlife ashore, and attend specially organized classical concerts.

AFRICA

River Gambia National Park, Gambia

A day trip on the river from Janjanbureh (Georgetown) or Kuntaur provides an opportunity to view crocodiles and hippos at close range. As the rice fields and coconut trees on the banks give way to dense forest, it may also be possible to glimpse monkeys, baboons and many species of birds.

Niger, Mali

A journey along the River Niger as it curves through the semi-desert of the Sahel is the classic way to see and experience the life of this area. Local passenger boats are scheduled to take seven days, but can take as long as 14 to travel between Gao and Koulikoro. The most popular section is the two days or so between Mopti and Korioumé, the stopping point for visits to the ancient desert city of Timbuktu. Also highly recommended is a detour up the River Bani to the beautiful old town of Djenné, where the mosque is a stunning example of construction using mud bricks and render.

ASIA AND AUSTRALASIA

Backwaters of Kerala, India

The eight-hour journey through the backwaters of Kerala, from Kollam (Quilon) to Alappuzha, is popular with tourists. Passengers are transported along a network of rivers, canals and lagoons, overhung with dense tropical foliage that every so often gives way to open paddy fields. Brightly coloured birds and ancient buildings can be glimpsed on the banks, and the Keralan people can be seen going about their daily lives.

Gorges of the Yangtze, China

Time is running out for those who want to experience the ferocious pounding of the Yangtze River as it passes between the rocky pinnacles of the Three Gorges. In 2008 the controversial Three Gorges Dam is due to be completed, creating the world's largest reservoir. Until then it is still possible to travel by steamship from Chongqing to Shanghai in a week, passing through the Qutang, Wuhang, and Xiling gorges, stopping off at the small town of Badong, perched precariously on the cliffs, and out into the wider, slower-moving lower reaches of the river.

Sepik, Papua New Guinea

The Sepik River twists and turns its way from the central mountains of Papua New Guinea through jungles, swamps and grasslands to the sea. Most cruises start from a remote inland location, to which passengers are transferred from Port Moresby by small plane. There is then a leisurely journey through the rainforest, with stops at riverside villages, some of which are on stilts. The people of the region are renowned for their woodcarving and traditional art, each village having its own distinctive style.

Murray, South Australia

A six-day cruise on a paddelboat, beginning and ending at Mannum, passes through colourful scenery, including verdant wetlands, brick-red plains, sandstone cliffs and deep blue lagoons. The cruise may also include a visit to the old river port of Morgan and an opportunity to hear about Aboriginal customs from elders at the Ngaut Ngaut Conservation Park.

◄ **Nile, Egypt**
A week-long cruise up the Nile from Luxor to Aswan and back combines visits to magnificent historic sites – such as the huge temple of Karnak and the tombs in the Valley of the Kings at Luxor – with periods of relaxation on board an air-conditioned riverboat. There are also opportunities to take camel rides into the desert that lies beyond the narrow fertile strip on either side of the river. From Aswan, where it is possible to sail on the river in a *felucca* (pictured here), a short flight takes passengers to the splendid temple of Abu Simbel, above the shores of Lake Nasser. Abu Simbel can also be reached by taking a luxury three-day cruise on the lake. Created by the building of the Aswan Dam, the lake itself is an impressive sight.

Useful web addresses
all preceded by www.

fieldingtravel.com
cruise-tours.com
goway.com/cruises
burgundy-canal.com
cruiselocator.com

▼ **Li, China**
The 80 km (50-mile) journey down the Li River from Guilin to the beautiful town of Yangshuo passes through a landscape of precipitous peaks, with names such as Paint Brush Hill and Five Tigers Catch a Goat Hill. Gliding past bamboo-lined riverbanks and picturesque villages, the trip and a bus-ride back to Guilin takes one day.

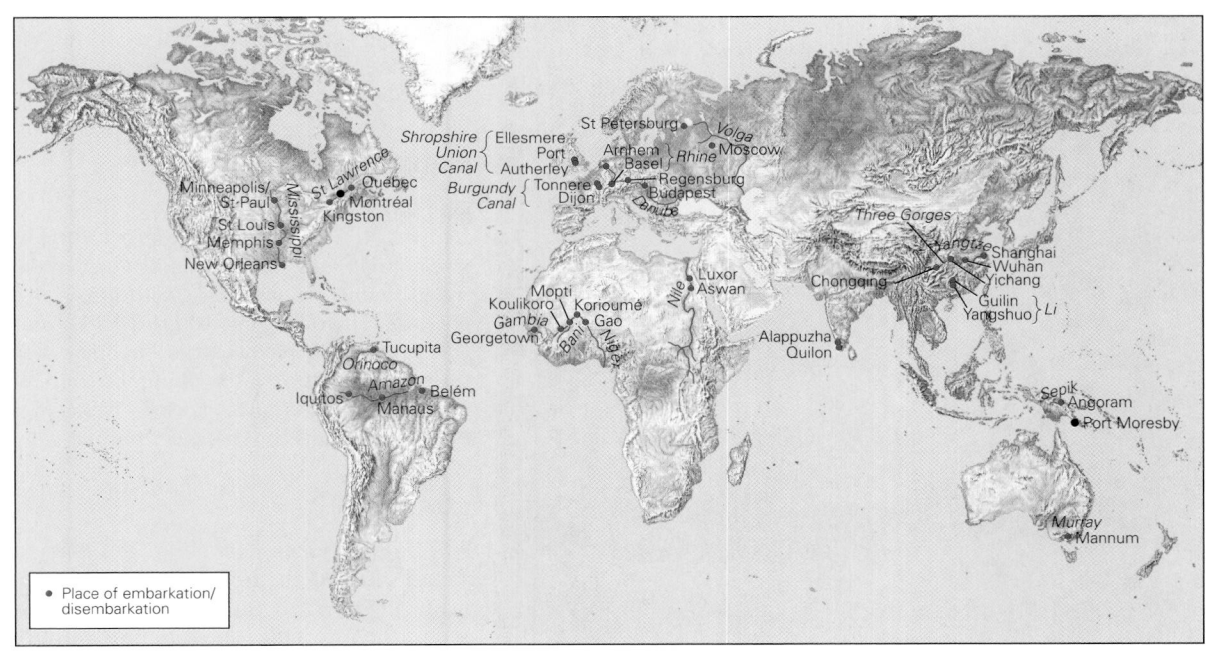

• Place of embarkation/
disembarkation

Sea and ocean cruises

Cruises attract all kinds of travellers and cater for an increasingly wide range of tastes. The steep-sided inlets of Alaska, Chile, Norway and New Zealand allow cruise liners to hug the coast, providing matchless views of these dramatic landscapes. Caribbean cruises allow almost daily shore visits, for shopping and exploring. Transatlantic cruises provide lavish on-board entertainment during the long sea passages. Cruise companies also vary in their appeal: some include lectures on the places they visit; others take a far less serious approach!

◄ **The Caribbean**
There are numerous variations on the Caribbean cruise, but virtually all have relatively short sea passages and a visit to a different island almost every day. There are organized trips to the rain-forests of Puerto Rico and sites of European colonial history. Some passengers, however, prefer to spend their time simply enjoying the islands' magnificent beaches.

NORTH AMERICA AND THE ATLANTIC

Alaska/British Columbia
The main attractions of a cruise in this area are the spectacular mountain scenery and the opportunity to see whales and seals, bears and birds of prey at close hand. Ships hug the coastline, entering steep-sided fjords and sailing close to the mouths of glaciers. Ports of call include Juneau, Alaska's capital, the 'gold rush' town of Skagway, and the Russian settlement of Sitka, with its onion domes.

Mexican Riviera
Mexico's west coast is becoming an increasingly popular area for relatively short cruises to catch the late-summer sunshine. For some tourists, the attractions are miles of unspoilt beaches fringed by jungle, such as those at Manzanillo and Zihuatanejo, and being able to go marlin fishing. For others they are the opportunities to experience Mexican culture and to visit the chic resort of Puerto Vallarta.

▼ **Antarctic**
Many of the 'expedition cruises' to the Antarctic use converted research ships or ice breakers, which offer less luxurious accommodation than other cruise ships. Passengers are taken ashore in small inflatable craft, and are thus able to get close to the teeming wildlife. There is always the chance of encountering whales in the surrounding seas, as well as sighting beautifully sculpted icebergs.

Atlantic Isles (Canaries, Madeira)
The Atlantic Isles are a popular cruise destination, particularly in winter and spring, when the lower mountain slopes are brilliant with flowers. Shore visits in Madeira usually include the novelty of a ride in a bullock cart or wicker sled on the mountain roads, while a trip to the summit of Tenerife's Mount Teide (3,718 m/12,000 ft) provides spectacular views of the surrounding islands.

Transatlantic cruises
Cruises link Europe with New York or Boston, with ports further south, such as Miami, and also with various Caribbean islands. The most direct, more northerly, route is for those wishing to enjoy the elaborate onboard entertainment, high standard of cuisine, and formal social life that are typical of the transatlantic liner. On ships plying more southerly waters, passengers can combine a luxury lifestyle with sunbathing, swimming and other deck activities.

SOUTH AMERICA

Chilean fjords
Cruises along the most southern 1,000 km (625 miles) of Chile's coastline provide magnificent views of mountains and glaciers. The further south, the colder and less predictable the weather becomes, but for many the thrill of travelling the route of Darwin's *Beagle* and visiting Tierra del Fuego outweighs the risk of storms.

EUROPE

Norwegian fjords
Those cruising the fjords of Norway do so primarily to enjoy the majestic mountain scenery. Waterfalls, glaciers and wildlife can all be viewed from the comfort of the ship, while shore visits include a ride on a spectacular mountain railway from Flåm (see *Great railway journeys*). Some cruises extend as far as Europe's most northern point, where passengers can experience the midnight sun.

Western Mediterranean
One of the joys of a cruise in the Western Mediterranean is the opportunity to sample the local cuisine and wines. Most cruises include a day in the vibrant Spanish city of Barcelona. In Italy, there are brief organized trips to view the art treasures of Pisa and Florence, and the Roman remains of Pompeii (see *Historic sites in Europe*). There are also opportunities to enjoy the high-life in some of the fashionable resorts of the French Riviera, such as St Tropez, to visit the casinos of Monte Carlo, and to watch the Spanish flamenco dancers in Cartagena. Some cruises extend as far as the Adriatic, call in at the fortress town of Dubrovnik and include a day's sightseeing in Venice.

Eastern Mediterranean
A region rich in the remains of earlier civilizations, the Eastern Mediterranean provides much of historic interest, and many cruises have on-board experts to give background lectures. Some of the main sites visited include the Roman town of Ephesus in Turkey, the Ancient Greek ruins of Delos, the Crusader castle of Krak des Chevaliers in Syria, and the pyramids in Egypt (see *Historic sites in Africa*). Most cruises also include opportunities for swimming, snorkelling and sunbathing.

▲ **North-east America**
The north-eastern seaboard of America offers areas of great natural beauty such as Acadia National Park in Maine, whose fall colours are the focus of October cruises. There is also an opportunity to see the whales that frequent the waters of Stellwagen Bank off the coast of Massachusetts. Included in a wide variety of shore visits are the Canadian fishing town of Lunenburg, the popular US resort of Martha's Vineyard, and the cities of Boston and New York.

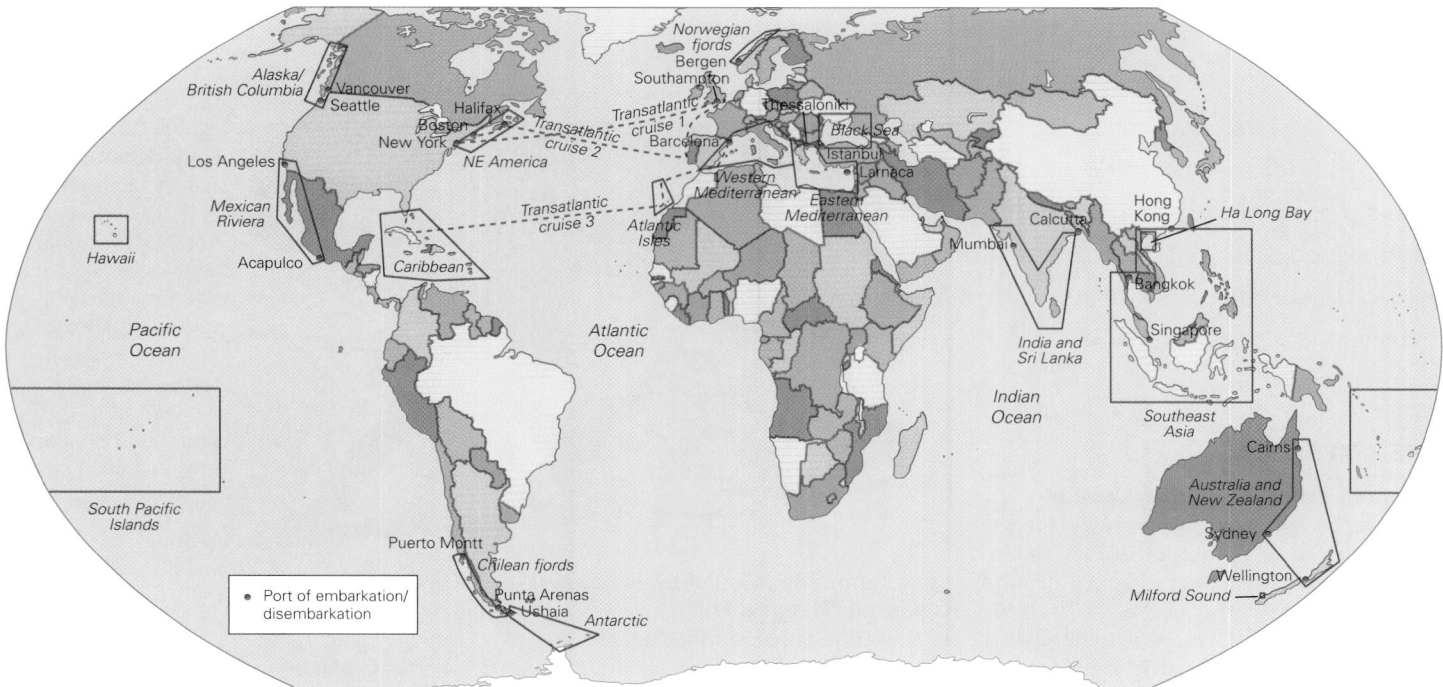

▼ **Black Sea**
A day in Istanbul (see *World Cities*) is included in most cruises of the Black Sea. The countries bordering the Black Sea provide a rich variety of historic sites, from the medieval churches of Nesebúr in Bulgaria, to the 19th-century opera house in Ukrainian Odessa, the 18th-century palace of Tsar Alexander II on the Crimean peninsula, and the abandoned Byzantine monastery of Sumela, high above the Turkish port of Trabzon.

AFRICA, ASIA AND THE INDIAN OCEAN

India and Sri Lanka

Cruises around the Indian subcontinent provide an opportunity to visit a number of historic sites without the strain of overland travel. A day's sightseeing is followed by a day's relaxation in the relatively cool sea breezes. Many of the sites visited are from India's colonial past – the Dutch fort at Cochin, the former Portuguese colony of Goa, remnants of the British Raj in Madras – but there are also trips to some indigenous sites, such as the Hindu cave temples of Mumbai (Bombay).

South-east Asia

With such a wealth of possible sights and exciting ports of call, there are many varieties of the South-east Asian cruise, which is a popular option for the Christmas break. Most shore visits consist of whistle-stop tours of the port of call, but there are also more adventurous expeditions, such as a visit to an orang-utan sanctuary in Sarawak, or a trek to catch a glimpse of the famous 'Komodo dragon' (see *Wildlife in Asia*). Many of the cruises visit Bali, with its sandy beaches, terraced rice fields and ornate Hindu temples.

AUSTRALASIA AND THE PACIFIC

Australia and New Zealand

Most cruises of Australia's east coast provide more than one opportunity to stop on the 2,000 km (1,250-mile) long Great Barrier Reef (see *Marine wildlife*). By way of contrast, the natural wonders of New Zealand include the spouting geysers and boiling mud of Rotorua (see *Lakes and waterfalls*), and the dolphins, whales and penguins of the verdant Bay of Islands.

Milford Sound, New Zealand

Milford Sound is perfect for a cruise of just a few hours. It is possible to enjoy lunch while gazing out at towering granite peaks and glaciers, and, on the lower slopes, thick beech forests and waterfalls. There is always the chance of sighting the dolphins, seals, penguins and other sea birds that inhabit the sheltered inlet.

Hawaii, USA

The mountainous Hawaiian island chain was formed by a series of volcanoes, many

of which are still active. Trips to Volcanoes National Park and the world's most active volcano usually include the memorable experience of getting as close as is safe to the actual lava flow. The lower slopes of the mountains are covered in rainforest, home to 20,000 species of orchid and echoing to the sound of waterfalls. Hawaii is a port of call for most Pacific cruises, but it is also possible to take a cruise exclusively of the islands, and so be able to enjoy some of the dramatic beaches and the local culture.

Useful web addresses
all preceded by www.

travelshop.de/english/
cruises.html

cruises.about.com/travel
/cruises/mbody.htm

fieldingtravel.com

cruiselocator.com

cruiseweb.com

cruiseinformationservice
.co.uk

◄ **Ha Long Bay, Gulf of Tonkin, Vietnam**
'Ha Long' means 'where the dragon plunged into the sea', and the bay contains around 3,000 islands, famous for their sheer, limestone cliffs with honeycombs of caves. A day trip from Haiphong (by motorboat or slower junk) is included in the itineraries of long-distance cruises as well as being available to the independent traveller.

Where, when and for how long?

	Main season	Duration of cruise (in days)
Alaska	May–Sept	7–14
NE America	Aug–Oct	7–14
Mexican Riviera	Sept–Oct	7–10
Atlantic Islands	Apr–Dec	9–14
Transatlantic	April and Sep–Nov	14
Caribbean	Oct–Dec	3–23
Chilean fjords	Oct–May	3–7
Antarctica	mid-Oct–early March	9–12
Norwegian fjords	May–July	7–14
Western Mediterranean	Apr–Nov	12–14
Eastern Mediterranean	Aug–Dec	10–14
Black Sea	Aug–Oct	14
India/Sri Lanka	Dec–Feb	14
Southeast Asia	Dec–Feb	8–17
Ha Long, Vietnam	All year	1
Australia/New Zealand	Nov–Apr	14
Milford Sound	Nov–Apr	half day
Hawaii	Sept–Oct	7–14

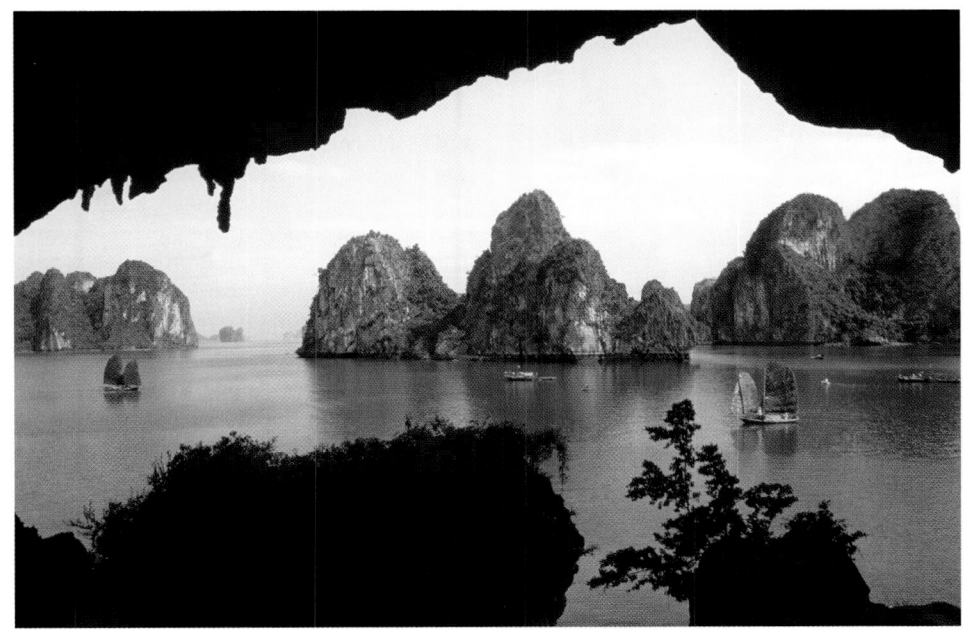

Winter sports

Mountain resorts all over the world are upgrading their facilities: constructing 'ski parks' for snowboarders, installing faster ski-lifts to cut queuing times, and using snow cannons to guarantee good conditions. Now that many of the top resorts can be reached by long-haul flights from either hemisphere, it is possible to enjoy 'winter sports' at any time of year.

◀ **Vail, Colorado, United States**
Vail has runs for all abilities and a special family skiing area. Snowboarders are provided with dedicated pistes, a half-pipe and two fun parks. Numerous winter sports are possible, including dog sledding and snowmobiling.

THE AMERICAS

Whistler, British Columbia, Canada
Considered one of the top ski resorts in the world, the resort provides access to two mountains with vertical drops of around 1,500 m (5,000 ft). As well as a wide variety of runs, Whistler's crowning glory is its five bowls, which provide plenty of scope for expert skiers and boarders, the latter being well catered for. The base village, which is pedestrian-only, has over 100 restaurants.

Banff, Alberta, Canada
The city of Banff is the gateway to three resorts that are linked by a shuttle bus and share a lift pass. **Lake Louise**, a particularly beautiful resort, is a good choice for families of mixed ability, with a beginners' run from the top of every chair lift. **Sunshine Village** includes 'Delirium Dive', one of the most challenging runs in North America. **Mt Norquay/Mystic Ridge** has a number of runs for the very best skiers and also offers night skiing.

Killington, Vermont, USA
The largest ski area in the eastern USA, Killington spreads over seven mountains. It caters for every level of skier, but is especially suitable for beginners, who have their own network of pistes, and for snowboarders who are provided with their own trail map. Snow cannons ensure good coverage throughout an extended season.

▼ **Jackson Hole, Wyoming, USA**
One of the most spectacular mountain resorts in the United States, Jackson Hole is most suited to the experienced skier or snowboarder. A 60-person cable car transports skiers from Teton Village to Mount Rendezvous, from where the skilled and intrepid can experience some of the most difficult piste skiing in the world. Other attractions include trips into Yellowstone Park, a swim at 2,460 m (8,000 ft) in the Granite Hot Springs, and sleigh rides to view a huge elk herd.

Lake Tahoe (Squaw Valley, Heavenly) California/Nevada, USA
Lake Tahoe is surrounded by ski resorts. **Squaw Valley** comprises six inter-linked mountain areas, some of which are still open in June. It has excellent facilities for children, including a family fun snow park. **Heavenly** has a spectacular setting, with something to suit skiers and snowboarders of all abilities. Snowboarders are further catered for by specially constructed mountainside features and by a dedicated fun park. A single ski pass is available for all resorts in the area.

Aspen, Colorado, USA
Long considered the smartest ski resort in the United States, Aspen provides an enormous range of facilities and entertainment, including opera. A linked ticket gives access to four mountains. Aspen Mountain and Aspen Highlands are most suitable for intermediates and experts, Buttermilk for beginners, and Snowmass for all levels. Snowboarding is allowed on all but Aspen Mountain.

Valle Nevado, Chile
A purpose-built resort in the Andes, at an altitude of 2,900 m (9,500 ft), Valle Nevado has wide, open pistes and spectacular views. It is also possible to heli-ski.

Gran Catedral (Bariloche), Argentina
Perched on Catedral Mountain, overlooking Lake Nahuel Huapi, Gran Catedral (formerly Bariloche) is Argentina's best-known and most extensive resort. Many visitors are attracted to the area in August for the National Snow Party.

EUROPE

Geilo, Norway
On the edge of the Hardanger plateau, Geilo provides uncomplicated downhill skiing as well as extensive cross-country trails. It is an excellent family resort, with ski schools giving tuition (in English) in snowboarding and cross-country skiing, as well as alpine skiing.

Soldeu/El Tarter, Andorra
For those on a budget, Andorra is a good option, and Soldeu/El Tarter the best of its resorts. Its reputable ski school and gentle slopes make it ideal for the beginner. A drag lift linking it with the neighbouring resorts of Pas de la Casa/Grau Roig has expanded the quality and quantity of runs available for the more experienced skier.

Three Valleys, France
The vast inter-linked ski area of the Three Valleys can be accessed from several resorts. **Courchevel** provides varied skiing, including wooded slopes, but intrepid skiers can also make their way across the whole Three Valleys system. **Méribel** is conveniently placed in the centre of the system. **Val Thorens**, which at 2,320 m (7,544 ft) is Europe's highest ski resort, has three lifts still open in summer.

Chamonix, France
Chamonix is an attractive town set in a steep-sided valley and dominated by Mont Blanc (see *Mountains and volcanoes*). There is extensive, varied skiing on both sides of the valley, linked by bus services. The most famous run, the Vallée Blanche, involves a cable-car ride up to the Aiguille du Midi, followed by a tough walk to the top of the glacier, and a 20 km (13-mile) run down to the valley. The Mont Blanc Ski Pass includes other resorts, giving access to 1,000 km (625 miles) of piste.

▲ **Val d'Isère/Tignes, France**
Snowboarders and off-piste skiiers are among those well catered for by the huge inter-linked system of L'Espace Killy. The system is served by a number of modern resorts. The largest is **Val d'Isère**, which is better suited to more advanced skiers than to beginners, since its easiest skiing is inconveniently located on the upper slopes. **Tignes**, a collection of villages clustered around a mountain lake, offers skiing all year round. The lift pass provides access to the whole Espace Killy, as well as a day's skiing at nearby Les Arcs or La Plagne.

Skiing and snowboarding resorts

Level: B = Beginner I = Intermediate A = Advanced Sb = Snowboarding

Resort	Main season	Skiable area or distance	Best-suited level(s)
NORTH AMERICA			
Whistler	Nov–Apr	2,863 ha (7,071 acres)	I/A/Sb
Banff	Dec–Apr	100 km (62 miles)	I
Killington	Oct–Apr	152 km (95 miles)	B/Sb
Squaw Valley	Nov–May	1,600 ha (4,000 acres)	I/A/Sb
Heavenly	Nov–May	1,942 ha (4,800 acres)	I/A
Jackson Hole	Dec–Apr	1,011 ha (2,500 acres)	A
Aspen	late Nov–Apr	1,936 ha (4,785 acres)	all
Vail	early Nov–late May	1,879 ha (4,644 acres)	all
Valle Nevado	mid-June–mid-Oct	64 km (40 miles)	I/A
Gran Catedral	mid-June–end Sept	640 ha (1,600 acres)	I
EUROPE			
Geilo	Nov–May	25 km (16 miles) 250 km (156 miles) cross-country	B/I
Soldeu/El Tarter	Dec–Mar	74 km (46 miles)	B/I
Three Valleys	Dec–Apr	300 km (187 miles)	all/Sb
Val d'Isère/Tignes	Dec–Apr	300 km (187 miles)	I/A/Sb
Chamonix	Dec–Apr	140 km (87 miles)	A/Sb
Zermatt	Dec–Apr	150 km (93 miles)	I/A
Cervinia	Dec–Mar	80 km (50 miles)	B/I
Wengen/Grindelwald	Dec–Mar	195 km (121 miles)	B/I
St Moritz	Dec–Apr	80 km (50 miles)	I
St Anton	Dec–Apr	170 km (106 miles)	I/A
Söll, Ski-Welt	Dec–Mar	250 km (156 miles)	B/I
Cortina	Dec–Mar	140 km (87 miles)	all
ASIA AND AUSTRALASIA			
Hakuba	Dec–Apr	c. 500 ha (1,250 acres)	all
Perisher Blue	June–Oct	1,250 ha (3,100 acres)	I
The Remarkables	June–Oct	220 ha (550 acres)	I
Coronet Peak	June–Oct	280 ha (700 acres)	I

◄ **Matterhorn (Zermatt, Cervinia), Switzerland/Italy**
The visitor to the Matterhorn area has the choice of staying in the expensive, car-free, Swiss resort of **Zermatt**, or the cheaper, more lively, Italian resort of **Cervinia**. The lift systems of the two resorts are linked. Zermatt provides a huge variety of skiing, from the wooded slopes immediately above the town to the steep runs below the Kleine Matterhorn. The sunny, south-facing slopes of Cervinia provide plenty of runs of intermediate standard. Summer skiing is possible on the highest slopes.

Jungfrau (Wengen, Grindelwald), Switzerland
The slopes of this famous mountain are served by two of Switzerland's best-known resorts. **Wengen**, which considers itself the 'birthplace of Alpine skiing', is an attractive town whose charm is enhanced by a lack of cars (a mountain railway providing the only access). **Grindelwald** is a larger, livelier town. The two are linked by a lift system that provides access to wonderfully varied skiing.

St Moritz, Switzerland
Famous in particular for its glamorous nightlife, St Moritz serves as a gateway to two major lift systems. Corvatsch/Furtshellas provides an opportunity for glacier skiing in both winter and summer. Corviglia provides varied skiing, interspersed by numerous restaurants in spectacular locations.

St Anton, Austria
St Anton attracts skiers from all over the world to its challenging ski runs, with cannon ensuring a good snow coverage. Dramatic off-piste skiing adds to its attraction for the experienced skier and boarder, but there is little for the beginner.

Söll, Ski-Welt, Austria
Söll provides good family skiing. It is ideal for the beginner and intermediate skier, but is not for the adventurous. Its low altitude results in a short season, although snow cannons have been installed.

Cortina, Italy
Surrounded by the distinctive rocky outcrops of the Dolomites, Cortina provides skiing in five main areas. There are runs for a range of skills, including a difficult descent from the Tofana bowl, and the gentle runs of the Socrepes–Pocol area. Cortina is the smartest of the Italian resorts, with a lively nightlife. Activities off the slopes include ice-skating.

ASIA AND AUSTRALASIA

Hakuba, Japan
The village of Hakuba (near Nagano) is the gateway to seven ski areas, providing runs for different standards of skiers, with beginners and intermediates best served by **Hakuba Goryu-Toomi**, and more advanced skiers by Happo'one (where night skiing is possible) and **Hakuba 47**.

Perisher Blue, Australia
This winter sports area comprises four resorts, spread over seven mountain peaks, accessed by an underground alpine railway and covered by one ski pass. There is a Nordic Ski Centre at Guthega, and 90 km (55 miles) of cross-country skiing. The main resort town is Jindabyne.

Queenstown (Coronet Peak, The Remarkables), New Zealand
Queenstown provides a residential base for two winter sports areas, The Remarkables and Coronet Peak, with shuttles operating between them. As well as good skiing, both areas offer facilities for snowboarders, including pipes and a terrain park. Families are well catered for, with good ski schools. Heli-skiing is also available.

21

Great beaches

► Negril, Jamaica
Negril beach is 11 km (7 miles) long and fringed by trees that hide low-rise hotels and restaurants. While definitely a tourist resort, it still retains a laid-back Jamaican character. Growing environmentalism has led to planning restrictions and active preservation of the surrounding area, including the creation of the Negril Marine Park. This encompasses the Great Morass swamp behind the beach, and the coral reef, cliffs and grottoes that make Negril so popular with scuba divers and snorkellers.

From California to the Caribbean to Australia, the lure of the beach still has a part in most holiday plans. The range is endless – chic and cosmopolitan in the Mediterranean, wild and rugged along the Atlantic shores or palm-fringed coral in the South Pacific. This small selection highlights some of the great beaches that can be linked into a round-the-world trip – whether for the exhilaration of surfing or sailing, or just to do absolutely nothing.

NORTH AMERICA

Venice Beach, Los Angeles, USA

Venice Beach is famous not so much for its wide stretch of sand as for its curving 'boardwalk'. Here, some of LA's more flamboyant citizens display themselves – on foot, skateboard, rollerblade and cycle. The area was originally developed to imitate its European namesake and, although there is no comparison, it is pleasant to stroll along its canals.

Assateague Island, Maryland/Virginia, USA

Assateague Island National Seashore on the Atlantic coast of the Chesapeake Peninsula consists of 60 km (37 miles) of pristine sandy beach, fringed by pine forest and salt marsh. Only a small area of it is accessible by car and the rest of the beach is deserted, except for the more intrepid campers, many of whom come for the fishing and birdwatching. Herds of wild ponies roam the island.

Sanibel Island, Florida, USA

Sanibel's 19 km (12 miles) of beaches are famous for their seashells. Visitors can be seen scouring the seashore or taking boat trips to more remote locations to find the best shells. Around 40% of the island, which can be toured on rented bicycles, is a wildlife preserve and it is also within striking distance of the Florida Everglades (see *Wildlife in the Americas*).

Puerto Escondido, Mexico

The resort of Puerto Escondido has a beach to suit every taste. 'Playa Zicatela' is considered one of the best surfing beaches in North America, but is suitable only for the strongest swimmers. 'Playa Principal' is a more urban beach, with pleasure craft and waterfront restaurants, while the small coves just out of town provide perfect swimming conditions.

THE CARIBBEAN AND SOUTH AMERICA

Magens Bay, St Thomas, US Virgin Islands

The heart-shaped Magens Bay contains a gently sloping sandy beach, surrounded by overhanging trees that provide welcome shade. Protected from the winds and currents, the bay is safe for bathing. Although nude bathing is not allowed on the main beach, it is permitted on the nearby Little Magens Beach. Interesting rock formations on the fringes of the bay are good for snorkelling. The beach is well served by restaurants and bars, carefully hidden among the trees.

Copacabana Beach, Rio de Janeiro, Brazil

Copacabana's 4 km (2.5 miles) of sand is fringed by a wavy black and white mosaic walkway. The beach is provided with modern amenities, such as public showers, kiosks and restaurants, and the shopping centre is only a short walk away. As well as attracting tourists, the beach is a meeting place for the citizens of Rio, and is the focus of the New Year celebrations. It is framed on one side by a huge granite headland and on the other by an imposing World War I fort, below which is an area from which local fishermen still operate.

Viña del Mar, Chile

Known as 'the Garden City' because of the luscious, tropical foliage that lines its boulevards, Viña del Mar also has a beautiful beach. Visitors who tire of the soft white sand and rolling surf can enjoy a tour of the town by horse-drawn carriage, visit the art museum and the extensive botanical gardens. Evening entertainment comes in the form of gourmet restaurants, casinos, discos and concerts.

▲ Oahu, Hawaiian Islands, USA
Most visitors to the island of Oahu flock to the string of connected beaches in the resort of Waikiki, just to the east of Honolulu, where the curving sand, studded with palm trees, is backed by a towering wall of high-rise hotels. Those looking for a more peaceful holiday, however, head further around the coast and seek out Waimanalo Beach (above), with its gently shelving, near-white sand and mountain backdrop. On the north coast the calm waters of Waimea Bay in summer also provide excellent swimming, but in winter months it is the centre of the surfing scene, as 10 m (30 ft) waves roll in across the Pacific.

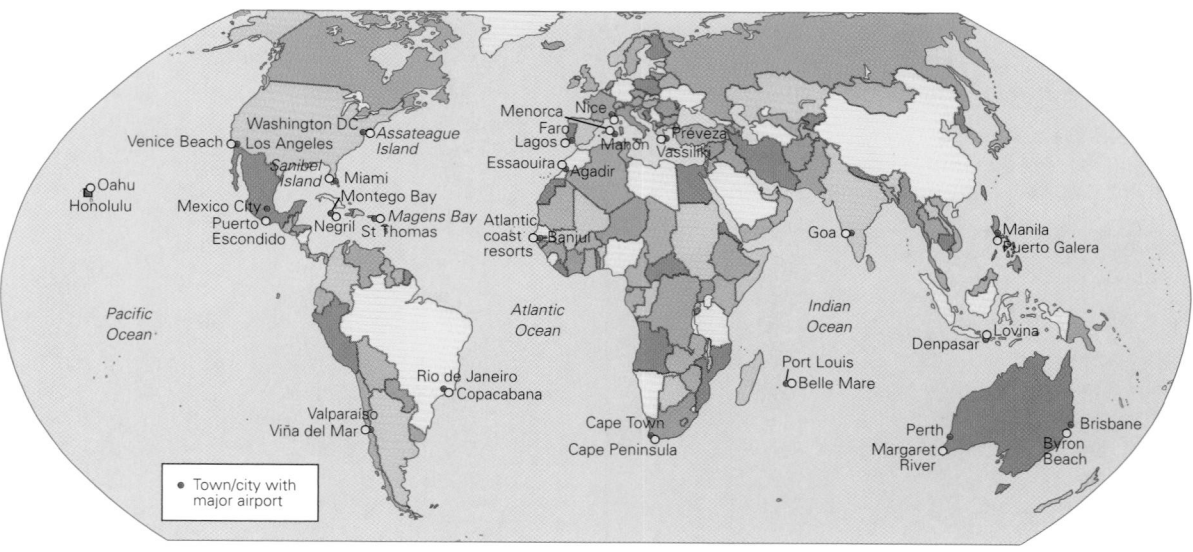

EUROPE

Nice, France

Nice is the largest town on the Côte d'Azur, renowned for the clarity of its light and the colour of its sea. Many famous artists have been inspired by the region, and some are represented in the town's art gallery. The long curved beach is rather pebbly, but its surroundings are attractive, with a wide esplanade on which 'to see and be seen'.

Santa Galdana, Menorca

The Balearic Island least affected by tourism, Menorca is famous for its beaches. The main beach at Santa Galdana can be very crowded in summer, but it is still possible to find relatively unspoilt coves nearby. Just a 1 km (0.5-mile) walk east is the wood-lined sandy beach of Cala Mirjana, where the favourite sport is to jump from rocks into crystal-clear water.

Vassiliki, Levkás, Greece

The small resort of Vassiliki is one of the foremost windsurfing and dinghy sailing centres in the eastern Mediterranean. Set in a bay that provides some shelter for the beginner, it is blessed with reliable winds. The lighter breezes of the morning are followed, after a brief lunchtime lull, by winds strong enough to delight the expert.

AFRICA AND THE INDIAN OCEAN

Essaouira, Morocco

The ancient town of Essaouira provides a fascinating backdrop to 3 km (2 miles) of

▲ **Cape Peninsula, South Africa**
Among the many beaches on the narrow peninsula south of Cape Town is Boulders Beach, so named because of the huge rocks that provide shelter from the wind. Here, visitors share the sands with a colony of jack-ass penguins. Other resorts on the peninsula, where the ocean water to the west is considerably colder than that of False Bay to the east, include some, such as Fish Hoek, which cater specifically for families, and some, such as the fashionable Clifton area, which attract the young and wealthy. Surfers head for the remote Long Beach at Kommetjie.

sandy shoreline. The commercial life of the town tends to spill over on to the beach, with fishermen offering to cook their catch and camel drivers selling rides, although it is possible to find more secluded areas. The town is the centre of the craft of wood inlay, the local Thuya trees providing the raw material.

Atlantic coast resorts, Gambia

The resorts of Kololi, Kotu, Fajara and Bakau, strung out along a 10 km (6-mile) coastal strip, provide a full range of amenities, including golf courses, equipment for water sports, and swimming pools. Although the sea is relatively safe, there are times when the conditions are unsuitable for all but the strongest swimmer. For those seeking a more authentic African experience, the market town of Serekunda is nearby.

Belle Mare, Mauritius

The coral reef that surrounds much of the island of Mauritius provides a natural breakwater, ensuring calm inshore waters. The beaches are all beautiful, although some have been over-developed or have areas cordoned off by hotels. However, Belle Mare, on the less-developed east coast, still has plenty of public areas. There are also the attractions of a mixed French, Indian and Chinese culture, evident in the island's architecture and cuisine.

ASIA

Goa, India

The dozens of beaches on Goa's 100 km (62-mile) coastline provide plenty of choice. Calangute and Colva, to which young people flocked in the 1970s, are now tourist resorts. However, at both the northern and southern ends of the Goan coast are many relatively unspoilt beaches, including Arambol and Palolem, where beach huts and tree houses provide the main accommodation. At Palolem visitors can take dolphin-watching boat trips.

Puerto Galera, Mindoro, Philippines

A resort area comprising 12 separate coastal districts, Puerto Galera is renowned for its pristine sandy coves, sheltered by a rugged, jungle-covered coastline. Accommodation ranges from

bamboo beach huts to air-conditioned bungalows and family-run hotels. The rich marine life of the area attracts scuba-divers, and equipment for underwater and other marine activities is available for hire.

Lovina, Bali

Although second in size only to Kuta, famous for its surf, Lovina manages to retain the relaxed atmosphere its larger rival has long since lost. Situated on Bali's rugged northern coast, the resort comprises six villages, dotted along 8 km (5 miles) of black-sand beach. Those who enjoy some lively nightlife make for the village of Kalibukbuk. Beach-centred activities include snorkelling and dolphin watching. Excursions can be made inland to nearby hot springs and a Buddhist temple, or further afield to the volcanic regions of Bedugul and Batur.

AUSTRALASIA

Byron Beach, New South Wales, Australia

Byron Beach offers a wide range of beaches. Main Beach is ideal for families, with a life-guard patrol and play equipment shaded by trees, while those wishing for more seclusion head for the smaller coves out on Cape Byron. The area also provides some good surfing and the opportunity to watch passing whales and dolphins. The town itself is less commercial, and better suited to those seeking an alternative lifestyle, than the popular resort of Gold Coast, 50 km (30 miles) to the north.

◀ **Lagos, Portugal**
Lagos is a busy fishing port and one of the Algarve's oldest settlements, with a long maritime tradition. To the east lie miles of sand dunes and the gently sloping Meia beach. West of the town, the dramatically eroded sandstone cliffs typical of the region form numerous small coves, some of which are only accessible from the sea. Lagos is an excellent base for surfers, who can travel the short distance to Portugal's west-facing beaches if local surf fails. The town provides plenty of interest, from seafood restaurants and bars to the curiosities of the local museum.

▼ **Margaret River, Western Australia**
Margaret River is among the best surfing areas in Australia, providing conditions to suit both beginners and experts. It also has much for the non-surfer to enjoy, including swimming beaches, river canoeing trips, and visits to local vineyards to taste some of Australia's best wines.

Festivals

Whether sacred or profane, festivals throughout the world bring thousands of participants and spectators out on to the streets with grand processions and dazzling displays of music and dance, drama and sporting prowess.

◀ **Palio, Siena, Italy** Celebrated every year on 2 July and 16 August, the Palio is a bare-back horserace that dates from the 16th century. Ten horses, each representing one of Siena's *contrade*, or districts, race three times around the crowded central piazza, sometimes barging into each other and unseating their riders. Before the race there is a procession in which men dressed in medieval clothes whirl and twist the *palio*, or flag, of their *contrada*, to the accompaniment of drummers.

THE AMERICAS

▼ **Chinese New Year, San Francisco, California, USA**
For Chinese communities everywhere, the New Year is a week-long festival. Many celebrations are family-based, but they lead up to a very public grand finale. Chinatown in San Francisco is taken over by the Golden Dragon Parade when hundreds of people, including drummers and other musicians, accompany a 23 m (75 ft) dragon through the streets. The Chinese follow a lunar calendar, which means that their New Year occurs in late January or early February.

Corn Dance Festival, Santa Domingo, New Mexico, USA
At Santa Domingo (near Albuquerque) the Pueblo people honour the harvest goddess, Iyatiko, in the Corn Dance Festival. Celebrants, known as the *koshare*, dress in cornhusks and animal skins to enact the history of their people on a day that is filled with drumming, dancing and feasting. The festival which, unlike many Pueblo ceremonies, is a public event, is always held on 4 August.

Heritage and Jazz Festival, New Orleans, Louisiana, USA
Jazz evolved in New Orleans during the late 19th and early 20th centuries, but the first jazz festival was not until 1968. A major event in the musical calendar and organized by the Heritage and Jazz Festival, it runs over two weekends in April or May. Musicians from all over the world perform in large tents at the Fair Grounds and in smaller venues – clubs, theatres and halls – throughout the city.

Fisherman's Festival, Jamaica
29 June is Saint Peter's day. He is the patron saint of fishermen, and in the fishing ports of Jamaica boats are drawn up to the beach where the owners decorate them with shells and flowers. Long processions follow priests to the edge of the sea where they bless the boats, and the beaches become crowded with steel bands, dancers and family picnics.

Urkupina, Calvario Hill, Bolivia
Early in the 20th century a girl tending her sheep on Calvario Hill had a vision of the Virgin Mary. Now, on 15 August, thousands of pilgrims carrying candles and flowers, and accompanied by musicians, performers and vendors, climb the hill to pay homage to the Virgin. The festivities that follow last for three days.

National Rodeo Festival, Rancagua, Chile
Rodeos take place all over the country and, in late March, the best competitors go to the National Rodeo in Rancagua. This event celebrates the Chilean *huaso* or cowboy. Thousands come to watch as huasos, wearing traditional costume and the heavy spurs unique to Chile, provide exhibitions of horsemanship. The town is given over to feasts of cowboy food and *la cueca*, the erotic folk dance of Chile.

Mardi Gras Carnaval, Rio de Janeiro, Brazil
All over the Catholic Christian world, there are festivals at Mardi Gras, the last day before the 40 days of Lenten fasting. The Mardi Gras Carnaval in Rio de Janeiro is the most famous. Over the course of two nights the city's 14 main samba schools compete with each other by dancing and parading down the 1 km (0.5-mile) long Sambadrome, watched by thousands of spectators. Each school's parade consists of around 4,000 people in lavish, often extravagant, costumes, accompanied by enormous and elaborate floats, and a band of over 500 drummers. The judging takes place a few days later. Broadcast live on television, it is followed by great celebrations.

EUROPE

Puck Fair, Killorglin, Ireland
A billygoat, King Puck – adorned with ribbons and a crown – opens the three-day Puck Fair every year on 2 August. Musicians from all over Europe perform, and Romanies are among those who entertain the crowds with Irish jigs and stories. The billy is honoured because in the 17th century a herd of goats warned the village of an impending English attack.

Oktober Bierfest, Munich, Germany
The Oktober Bierfest has been an annual event since 1835. It is an important festival for most young visitors to the city and is a huge celebration in honour of beer. It lasts for 16 days from 17 October, and vast beer tents that each house 5,000 drinkers are erected. Food stalls and funfairs add to the festive atmosphere.

Lajkonic, Kraków, Poland
Every year, usually in June, a man dressed as a Tartar rides a mock horse through the streets, accompanied by trumpeters and citizens dressed in medieval costume. He does so in memory of Lajkonic, who in the 13th century killed a Tartar and put on the dead man's clothing before riding into the city to warn that the Tartars were about to attack. The resulting defeat of the Tartars is now celebrated with much pageantry.

San Fermin, Pamplona, Spain
Starting on 6 July and running for eight days, the festival is held in honour of Fermin, patron saint of bullfighters. Each day starts with the playing of drums and pipes, and an effigy of the saint is followed by a procession of matadors and horses, dressed and decorated for the occasion. A rocket signals the release of the bulls from their pen to race through the streets to the bullring. Men run and leap ahead of them, a practice that more than once has resulted in someone being killed. Bull fights and parties fill the evenings.

Aksu Black Sea Festival, Turkey

The origins of this July festival are very old, dating back to pre-Christian fertility rites. Cybele, the fertility goddess, wore a pebble in her crown and women still throw pebbles into the Black Sea in the hope that this will help them conceive. The highlight of the festival is a performance by male dancers dressed in black and silver, and other artists – musicians, potters, painters and weavers – flock to the site where they perform or sell their work.

AFRICA

Odwira, Ghana

The Asante calendar is filled with religious days and ceremonies, of which the Odwira, usually in August or September, is one of the most important. The high chiefs and priests are involved for some days in secret and sacred rituals, and then the roll of drums announces the start of feasting. It all ends with a grand procession, in which the chiefs are carried in splendid palanquins.

Abu El-Haggag, Luxor, Egypt

Among the ancient ruins of Luxor is a small mosque dedicated to a 12th-century Muslim saint, El-Haggag. Each year, in October or November, thousands of people crowd into Luxor for the saint's *mulid*, or festival, during which Sufis and floats parade the streets. Three model boats are carried about by groups of men, though whether this is in memory of the Ancient Egyptian journey into the Underworld, or of the time when the pilgrimage to Mecca involved a sea crossing, is uncertain.

Timket, Ethiopia

Ethiopian Christians celebrate the baptism of Christ for three days starting on 19 January. The priests, after all-night prayers, emerge from churches carrying holy tabots – caskets holding sacred texts – followed by singing children. Multi-coloured umbrellas, signifying high office and authority, are held above the priests. After this religious ceremony, a party mood takes over and there are huge communal meals, music, and excited horse races which sometimes lurch into the spectators.

▶ **Ganesh Festival, Mumbai, India**
Chowpatty Beach is crowded for ten days in August through to September. Families exchange gifts and women decorate shrines to Shiva, mother of the Hindu elephant-headed god Ganesh. On the tenth day a huge effigy of Ganesh is carried through the streets to be cast into the sea. Drummers and pipers announce its passage, which is followed by a large procession of people dancing and singing.

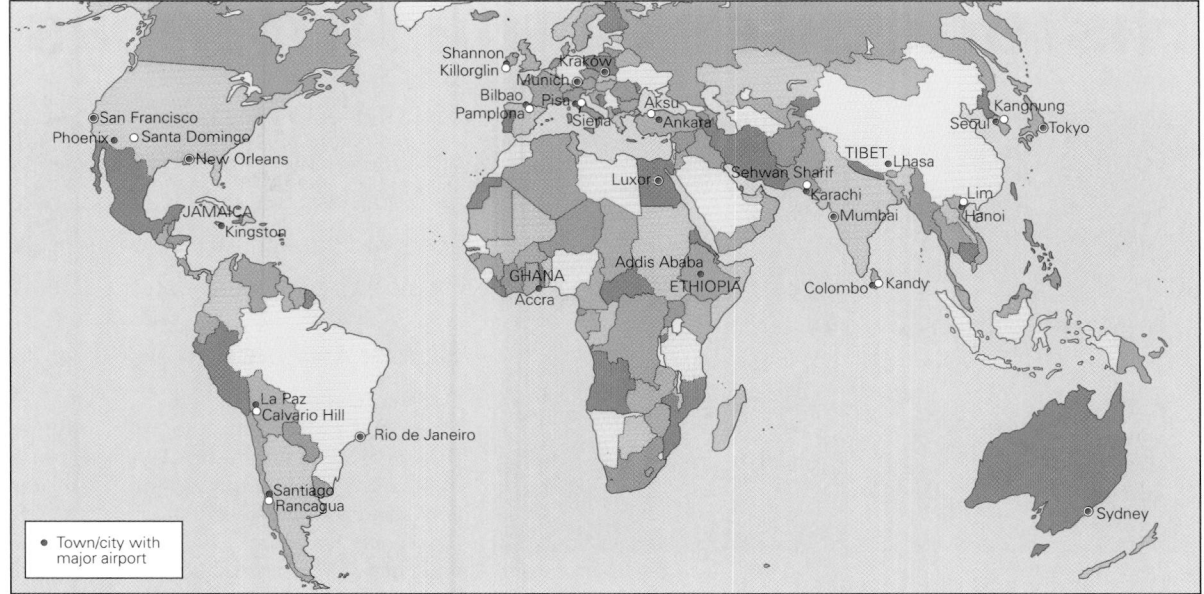

ASIA AND AUSTRALIA

Urs to Lal Shahbaz Qalandar, Sehwan Sharif, Pakistan

All over Pakistan, Muslims celebrate holy men with *urs*, or saints' days. One of the most popular, attracting many thousands of pilgrims, is held in Sehwan Sharif, around the tomb of the 12th-century Iranian scholar-poet Lal Shahbaz Qalandar. For three days, in October or November, Sufis perform their holy, trance-like dances, while drums and gongs beat hour after hour. The entire crowd dances and chants, and many offer votive offerings to the tomb.

Festival of the Tooth, Kandy, Sri Lanka

In the Esala Perhera temple in Kandy is the Tooth Relic of the Buddha. Usually in July, but occasionally in August, there is a spectacular festival in which there are festive meals and dances to celebrate the relic and Buddha. At the festival's climax a great procession of dancers, drummers, temple chieftains, and over 50 elephants in ceremonial attire, goes to the temple, followed by huge crowds of pilgrims.

Ho Lim, Lim, Vietnam

Singers from all over Vietnam pour into the village of Lim (near Bac Ninh) seven days after Tet, the Chinese New Year, in January or February. They participate in a folk-singing contest, and competition is fierce. The crowds who come to listen are also

entertained by a circus, street performers, wrestling competitions, and chess games in which people play the parts of the pieces.

Losar, Tibet

The calendar in Tibet follows the lunar cycle. There are two 'New Year' days, but the significant one is Gyalpo Losar, the King's New Year, which is usually in April. People wear new, decorative clothing; the priests fill the temples with chanting, the beating of gongs and the ringing of bells, and new prayer flags are lifted above the temple roofs. Throughout the city, street theatres and musicians perform while people party and play dice in the parks.

Tano, Kangnung, South Korea

This spring festival, usually in April or May, traditionally involved displays of the Korean form of wrestling, *ssirum*, even in the most remote villages. Now, many Koreans spend the holiday watching *ssirum* on television, except in the village of Kangnung. Here they celebrate for five days, not only with wrestling matches but also with performances of the traditional dance called *nong-ak*. The huge crowds also enjoy a spring drink, *chehotang*.

Gay and Lesbian Mardi Gras, Sydney, Australia

Participants pride themselves on outrageous displays and flamboyant costumes during the annual Mardi Gras parade. The street procession ends in a huge party at the RAS Show Ground in Moore Park, which is restricted to ticket holders. However, revellers throughout the city regard this as an opportunity to party until dawn and beyond.

▲ **Sanja Matsuri, Tokyo, Japan**
Matsuri – festivals where shrines, or *mikoshi*, believed to contain a god-spirit, are carried through towns and villages – take place all over Japan. However, the biggest event is in Tokyo in April or May. Here the *mikoshi* weigh about 1 tonne each, and 50 men are needed to hoist one through the streets to the Asakusa Temple. Groups of costumed figures, and musicians playing flutes and beating drums, accompany the *mikoshi* on its journey.

Historic sites in the Americas

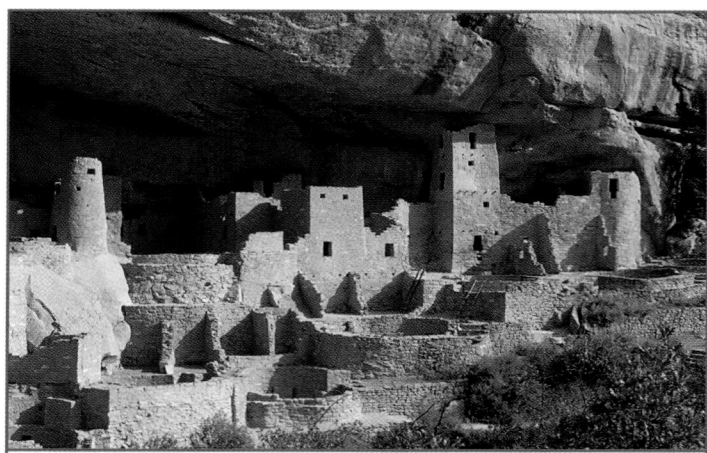

Amid the rocky canyons of New Mexico, Arizona and Colorado, the dense jungle of Central America and the towering peaks of the Andes lie the spectacular ruins of civilizations that flourished long before 1500 and the arrival of the Europeans. Scattered throughout the continent are the mansions, churches, cathedrals and forts built by European settlers and their descendants since the 16th century.

Mesa Verde and the Anasazi

Mesa Verde National Park in Colorado, USA, contains the ruins of spectacular Anasazi complexes of multi-storey apartments constructed on natural or artificial platforms on the face of canyon cliffs. They are among the remains of hundreds of villages that were built by the Anasazi from the 8th century onwards in south-western USA. Called pueblos by the Spanish, they took various forms. In Chaco Canyon, for example, elaborate complexes of adjoining rooms surrounded circular subterranean ceremonial structures known as *kivas*. The Anasazi began to abandon their pueblos in the 15th century, eventually settling along the Rio Grande. There are many impressive sites worth visiting, but they are usually in remote locations.
Peak season: May–October
Nearest airports: Albuquerque, Santa Fe

NORTH AMERICA

Québec, Canada

Founded by the French in 1608 and now the only walled city in the Americas north of Mexico, Québec has several 17th- and 18th-century buildings. The area by the St Lawrence River has the general appearance of 1759, when the city was captured by the British. On the cliff-top above is the citadel of Cap Diamant, dating from 1820.

Plymouth Plantation, Massachusetts, USA

Costumed actors re-create the life and times of the first permanent colony and a Native American encampment in New England at Plymouth Plantation, a historical theme park. Visitors can go aboard the *Mayflower II*, a reconstruction of the ship that brought the original settlers from England in 1620.

Historic Triangle, Virginia, USA

The colonial towns of Williamsburg, Jamestown and Yorktown comprise the Historic Triangle. **Williamsburg**, Virginia's capital 1699–1780, has a large restored historic district of 17th- and 18th-century buildings with tours led by costumed guides. **Jamestown**, founded in 1607, has some 17th-century ruins, a reconstruction of the 1607 James Fort and full-scale replicas of 17th-century ships. **Yorktown**, the site of the last major battle (1781) in the American Revolution, and besieged during the Civil War, contains fortifications dating from both wars. Other historic sites in Virginia include Thomas Jefferson's house, **Monticello**, George Washington's house, **Mount Vernon**, the plantation house, **Shirley Plantation**, built in the 1660s, and Civil War sites in **Richmond**.

Pueblo de Taos, New Mexico, USA

The largest, multi-storied, adobe (sun-dried brick) structure in the USA, Pueblo de Taos dates from around 1450 and is still inhabited by 1,500 Native Americans. In the town of Taos is the home of Kit Carson, the famous 19th-century mountain man.

Chaco Culture National Historic Park, New Mexico, USA

Impressive Anasazi ruins are to be found in this remote park. Among them is the site of Pueblo Bonito, with remains of a massive plaza surrounded by a semi-circular, five-storey tiered complex of some 200 rooms which once housed up to 1,200 people.

Charleston, USA

A historic centre of Southern culture, Charleston has many colonial buildings. The military relics of the Battery overlook the harbour, while 5 km (3 miles) away is Fort Sumter where the first shot of the Civil War was fired.

San Miguel de Allende, Mexico

An almost totally colonial town, San Miguel de Allende has many attractive houses and churches dating from the 18th century. It is also an important artistic centre, where painting, pottery, sculpture, drama, music and literature all flourish.

Guanajuato, Mexico

A former silver-mining town, founded in the 16th century, Guanajuato has colonial buildings dating from the 17th and 18th centuries among its narrow streets with houses painted in bright colours.

Teotíhuacán, Mexico

Impressive ruins are all that remain of a city which in AD 500 was the sixth largest in the world, with a population of around

▲ Savannah, Georgia, USA
The Cotton Exchange is just one of over 1,000 splendid 18th- and 19th-century buildings that have been restored in the historic downtown district of Savannah. Others include the US Customs House and the gold-domed City Hall. Near the city are the Civil War forts of Old Fort Jackson and Fort Pulaski.

Chichén-Itzá and the Maya

Chichén-Itzá in Mexico is a particularly impressive Mayan site that is unique because it displays many features of the Toltecs who occupied the city in the 10th century. Among them is the reclining sculpture of the Toltec rain god. The magnificent remains of the literate Mayan civilization are scattered throughout southern Mexico, Guatemala, Belize and Honduras. Mayan cities expanded rapidly in the 7th and 8th centuries but were then abandoned between the 9th and 13th centuries. Their ruins often include stone-built pyramids crowned by temples and palaces, and courts used in a ritual ball game that involved the sacrifice of the losing team.

There are numerous Mayan sites worth visiting, and it is possible to spend two to three weeks following a route that links the most important in Mexico, Guatemala and Belize.
Peak season: November–April
Nearest airports: See map of 'Mayan Route'

- Pre-AD1500 site
- Post-AD1500 site
- Major city with historic sites (described in *World Cities*)

'Mayan Route' sites
- Mayan site
+ Airport

▲ **Gettysburg National Cemetery, Pennsylvania, USA**
The burial place of 979 Union soldiers killed in the Civil War battle of 1863 is also the site of President Lincoln's famous Gettysburg Address. Tours include the 91 m (300 ft) National Tower and the Cyclorama Center, where a film about the battle is shown.

200,000. Once a centre of pilgrimage, Teotíhuacán includes the remains of hundreds of temples, among them the 70 m (230 ft) high Pyramid of the Sun, built in the 1st century AD and one of the largest buildings in the New World before 1500.

Oaxaca and Monte Albán, Mexico
Oaxaca is a well-preserved colonial town with a cathedral and many other buildings dating from the 16th century onwards. Just 10 km (6 miles) away are the impressive ruins of Monte Albán, which from the 7th century BC served as a centre of worship for many different peoples, including the Maya. Surrounding a huge man-made plateau are the remains of pyramids, a ball court, burial chambers with beautiful murals, and carvings of dancers.

Palenque, Mexico
A Mayan site in a clearing in the jungle, Palenque has numerous buildings with particularly beautiful decoration. They include the Temple of Inscriptions, a stepped pyramid with a 25 m (80 ft) tunnel that leads to a crypt containing the sarcophagus of a 7th-century Mayan king.

Uxmal, Mexico
One of the most beautiful pre-1500 sites in Mexico, Uxmal has Classical Maya architecture. The chief building is the smooth-sided El Adivino, or Pyramid of the Soothsayer, up which there is an almost vertical climb to the 35 m (115 ft) high summit that is crowned by a temple. Nearby is the Governor's Palace, which features a frieze with 103 masks.

CENTRAL AMERICA AND THE CARIBBEAN

Caracol, Belize
An amazing Mayan site deep in the rainforest, Caracol is still being excavated. The ruins, whose full extent has only recently become apparent, include a pyramid 42 m (140 ft) high.

Tikal, Guatemala
Possibly the greatest Mayan site, Tikal is surrounded on all sides by jungle. The remains of 3,000 buildings can be seen, some with painted carvings. The pyramid-like Temple of the Great Jaguar, built in AD 700, is considered the world's best example of Mayan temple construction.

Trinidad, Cuba
Cuba's best-preserved colonial town, Trinidad has many buildings that reflect the town's prosperity as a centre of the sugar trade in the 18th and 19th centuries.

SOUTH AMERICA

Cuzco and the Urubumba Valley, Peru
Former capital of the Incas high in the Andes, Cuzco contains extensive Inca ruins mixed with colonial churches, palaces, houses and a 17th-century cathedral. An attractive and lively town, it is the main starting point for people visiting Machu Picchu (by train or a four-day trek) and other Inca ruins in the Urubumba Valley.

Nazca Lines, Peru
People of the Nazca culture (375 BC–AD 650) created gigantic lines by removing stones to expose the desert soil beneath. The lines, which depict geometrical shapes, birds – one with a wing-span of over 100 m (328 ft) – and animals, are best seen from the air, in a local plane.

Potosí, Bolivia
Founded in 1545 as a silver-mining town, Potosí was the largest city in the Americas in the early 17th century. Today it has over 2,000 colonial buildings, including several 18th-century Baroque churches.

Machu Picchu and the Incas
Machu Picchu in Peru is the most spectacular of many Inca sites in the Andes. Tier upon tier of houses, palaces, temples and defensive walls rise up the side of a high mountain ridge overlooked by the granite pinnacle of Huayana Picchu. The Spaniards failed to find the site in the 16th century, and it was mysteriously abandoned and forgotten until the early 20th century. The Incas developed an enormous empire between the 14th and 15th centuries that extended from modern Ecuador, through Peru to southern Chile. It was conquered by the Spaniards in the 1530s.
Peak season: April–October
Nearest airport: Lima

Olinda, Brazil
One of the best-preserved colonial cities in Brazil, on a hill overlooking the Atlantic, Olinda has many 16th- to 18th-century buildings. It is a major cultural centre, with art galleries, music and festivals.

Ouro Prêto, Brazil
A beautiful colonial town founded in 1711, Ouro Prêto has cobblestone roads, statues, fountains, churches, a palace and a theatre. It also serves as a base for exploring other colonial towns in Minas Gerais province, such as Diamantina.

San Ignacio Mini, Argentina
The most impressive of the ruins of Jesuit mission villages in the Misiones region, San Ignacio Mini had 4,356 Guarani inhabitants before the Jesuits were expelled from Spanish territory in 1767. The ruins of only three other missions indicate their former splendour: Sao Miguel in Brazil, and Jesús and Trinidad in Paraguay.

Major cities with historic sites
(see *World Cities*)
- Boston
- Buenos Aires
- Cartagena
- Chicago
- Havana
- Lima
- Los Angeles
- Miami
- Mexico City
- Montréal
- New Orleans
- New York
- Panama
- Quito
- Rio de Janeiro
- San Francisco
- Sucre
- Washington

Historic sites in Europe

There is a huge variety of historic sites in Europe, ranging from prehistoric monuments over 5,000 years old to 19th-century castles. Ruins of the architectural achievements of the Classical Greek and Roman civilizations contrast with what are often perfectly preserved cathedrals, churches, monasteries, castles, palaces and civic buildings dating from the 11th century onwards.

◀ **Neuschwanstein Castle, Germany**
The ultimate fairytale castle, Neuschwanstein (near Fussen) was built in 1869–86 and is the most famous of Ludwig II's castles inspired by Wagner's vision of medieval Germany. It has a wide range of architectural styles, and its tall white marble towers topped by cone-shaped pinnacles, which have been copied by Disneyworld, are instantly recognizable.

Rock of Cashel, Ireland

Poised dramatically above the town of Cashel in County Tipparary stands a limestone outcrop, 109 m (358 ft) high, known as the Rock of Cashel. It is topped by a group of medieval ecclesiastical ruins, which include a bishop's palace, the 13th-century St Patrick's Cathedral, and the adjoining 12th-century Romanesque St Cormac's chapel.

Caernarfon Castle, Wales

Considered to be the finest of the castles built by Edward I of England after his conquest of Wales in 1283, Caernarfon Castle is exceptionally well preserved. Constructed as a royal palace as well as a military stronghold, it dominates the surrounding walled town, which was also founded by Edward.

Stonehenge, England

The most famous prehistoric monument in Europe, Stonehenge is a circular arrangement of massive standing stones, surrounded by earthworks, whose function is a subject of controversy. Built in stages between c. 3100 BC and c. 1000 BC, it may have been an astronomical observatory, a temple or a secular ceremonial centre. Its distinctive stone trilithons – pairs of uprights topped with horizontal lintels – are an impressive landmark on the Salisbury Plain.

Bruges, Belgium

Once one of Europe's greatest trading centres, Bruges is a well-preserved medieval city with narrow streets and canals spanned by picturesque bridges. Within its 13th-century walls are many historic buildings, including the magnificent Gothic Town Hall and the medieval Cloth Hall. The Groeninge Museum contains paintings by the 15th-century Flemish masters.

Mont-St-Michel, France

Rising dramatically out of the Bay of St-Michel is a steep, rocky island with a medieval abbey on its summit. Buildings and fortifications have been added since the 11th century, resulting in a mixture of styles and shapes which culminate in the 19th-century spire of the church.

Versailles, France

Built for Louis XIV, the 'Sun King', the vast Baroque palace of Versailles was the envy of all Europe in the 17th century. Today, visitors flock to see the Hall of Mirrors – where the Treaty of Versailles was signed at the end of World War I – and to wander between the elaborate fountains in the magnificent formal gardens.

Heidelberg, Germany

Majestically set on the banks of the River Neckar and dominated by the romantic ruins of the castle, Heidelberg is one of Germany's most beautiful and best preserved historic towns, with many fascinating buildings. Its 600-year-old university provides a youthful atmosphere on the streets, especially in the evenings.

Petrodvorets, Russia

An imperial palace in the Baroque style, Petrodvorets was built by Peter the Great after he had visited Versailles. It is set in beautiful parkland interwoven by a system of fountains, cascades and waterways connected to the sea.

▼ **Meteora, Greece**
Perched on top of natural rock pinnacles which rise hundreds of metres from the flat plain of Thessaly, near Tríkkala, is a group of Greek orthodox monasteries, some of which are still inhabited today. The highest of these – at 533 m (1,749 ft) is Great Meteoron, which was built from 1356 with a domed church added in the 16th century.

Pre-AD 500 site
Post-AD 500 site
Major city with historic sites (described in World Cities)

Salzburg, Austria

Set in a magnificent subalpine landscape, Salzburg is a picturesque city with many fine Baroque churches and a grand Italianate cathedral, the first of its kind to be built north of the Alps. The simple apartment where Mozart was born is a place of pilgrimage for music lovers.

Český Krumlov, Czech Republic

One of Europe's most picturesque towns, Český Krumlov has hardly changed since the 18th century. Its beautiful medieval and Renaissance buildings are almost

▲ **Chartres Cathedral, France**
Built in the middle of the 13th century, and almost unaltered since, the great cathedral of Notre Dame at Chartres is an exceptionally fine example of high Gothic architecture, with its flying buttresses, vaulted ceilings, intricate stonework and beautifully detailed stained glass. A rare 13th-century labyrinth design on the floor, a Renaissance choir screen and the glowing stained glass of the rose window all add to the beauty and impact of the building.

encircled by the Vltava River and overlooked by a magnificent castle. Originally a Gothic fortress, Krumlov Castle was rebuilt in the 16th century as a fortified palace.

Évora, Portugal

An attractive city with a history dating back to Roman times, Évora has a walled medieval centre with a distinctly Moorish atmosphere, and many fine Renaissance buildings from its time as a royal residence. The church of São Francisco is a good example of the Portuguese Manueline style of architecture, combining Gothic and Moorish influences.

Toledo, Spain

An ancient city of steep, winding streets lined with elegant if sombre buildings, Toledo is a splendid monument to the many cultures that have flourished here in the past. Moorish, Jewish and Christian traditions are all represented, and parts of the city walls date from the 6th century, when the Visigoths made Toledo their capital. The cathedral is a particularly fine example of the Spanish Gothic.

Segovia, Spain

Set on a rock, Segovia is a delightful old town with a fairytale castle and a 1st-century Roman aqueduct. Other notable buildings include the palace of La Granja, the 16th-century Gothic cathedral and the 12-sided, 13th-century Templar church of Vera Cruz.

Pisa, Italy

The famous Leaning Tower of Pisa is just one of a quartet of ecclesiastical buildings which make up the beautiful Campo dei

Pompeii and the Romans

Pompeii is an exceptional historic site because, when the eruption of Vesuvius in AD 79 engulfed the city in volcanic debris, the life of the people, their homes and streets, public spaces and palaces were preserved as if frozen in time. Excavations have revealed a wealth of detailed information about the everyday life of citizens of the Roman Empire, including their public notices, graffiti, brothels, latrines, furnishings and food. At its greatest extent, in the 1st–4th centuries AD, the Roman Empire encircled the Mediterranean Sea, reaching north as far as Britain and south into Egypt. Remains of Roman theatres, temples, baths, arenas, villas and other buildings can be found at sites throughout Europe and north Africa.

Miracoli (Field of Miracles) in this medieval walled city. The black and white marble facades of the Duomo and Baptistery, decorated by a succession of distinguished sculptors, are perfect examples of the Pisan Romanesque style, while the cloistered cemetery of Camposanto contains 14th-century frescoes.

Siena, Italy

Surrounded by city walls, Siena's medieval centre, with its narrow, winding streets, fine buildings and palaces, is wonderfully preserved. It is dominated by the Piazza del Campo, a large, shell-shaped square where the spectacular horserace known as the Corsa del Palio is held (see *Festivals*).

Delphi, Greece

In a stunning location, at the foot of Mount Parnassós, lie the impressive ruins of a sanctuary dedicated to Apollo, whose oracle was the most important in Classical Greece. The ruins include the 4th-century BC Temple of Apollo, the Doric Treasury of Athens, a theatre restored by the Romans, and a well-preserved stadium where the Pythian games were held.

Knossós, Crete

The ruined palace of Knossós is one of the few remains of the Minoan civilization, which flourished c. 3000–1100 BC. The first palace at Knossós was built around 2000 BC, and was rebuilt after an earthquake in c. 1720 BC. Excavations have revealed workshops, storerooms, dwellings and ceremonial rooms, one of which contains a gypsum throne.

Dubrovnik, Croatia

The fortifications of the ancient port of Dubrovnik rise straight from the Adriatic, and the double line of city walls encompass two palaces, two monasteries and many churches and other historic buildings, mostly dating from the 15th and 16th centuries. The narrow, winding streets of the old city are free from motor vehicles.

Ephesus, Turkey

The extensive and well-preserved ruins of the ancient city of Ephesus are one of Turkey's most popular historic sites, containing buildings from ancient Greek, Roman and Byzantine times. Among those dating from the Roman period are several temples, a theatre, a library, terraced houses, public baths and latrines, as well as some fine mosaics and wall paintings.

▲ **The Alhambra, Granada, Spain**
The most splendid example of Moorish architecture in Spain is the hilltop Alhambra palace, which was built in the 13th–14th centuries. The unassuming fortress walls contain a richly decorated interior made up of many halls and courtyards, with fountains and pools throughout.

Major cities with historic sites
(see *World Cities*)
- Amsterdam
- Athens
- Barcelona
- Berlin
- Brussels
- Budapest
- Copenhagen
- Dublin
- Edinburgh
- Florence
- Geneva
- Hamburg
- Helsinki
- Istanbul
- Kraków
- Lisbon
- London
- Luxembourg
- Madrid
- Milan
- Moscow
- Munich
- Oslo
- Paris
- Prague
- Reykjavik
- Riga
- Rome
- St Petersburg
- Stockholm
- Vienna
- Warsaw
- Venice

Historic sites in Africa, Asia and Australasia

Africa is the home of the imposing ruins of ancient Egypt – one of the world's first civilizations. With the Middle East, it also has historic sites that reflect the competing influences of Christianity and Islam. In Asia, vast temple complexes, often adorned with wonderful sculptures, are among the remains of great empires, while in Australia, Aboriginal rock paintings are evidence of a culture that flourished long before the Europeans arrived.

AFRICA AND THE MIDDLE EAST

Dogon cliffside villages, Mali
Built among the rocks at the foot of the Bandiagara escarpment are the picturesque traditional houses, temples, granaries and meeting places of the Dogon people, whose culture has survived since the 14th century. The area can be reached only on foot and conditions can be gruelling. The best time to visit is December, for the harvest celebrations.

Rock churches of Lalibela, Ethiopia
Carved out of the red volcanic rock of the central highlands are 11 extraordinary medieval churches containing rare and beautiful frescoes, elaborate carvings and bas-reliefs. A complex network of tunnels and passageways connects the churches, some of which are hidden in deep trenches while others have been cut into the cliff face. The best time to visit is the Ethiopian Christmas (7 January) and Easter.

Kilwa Kisiwani, Tanzania
Once an Islamic city-state, the island of Kilwa Kisiwani has extensive ruins, which include a 12th-century mosque, several palaces and grand houses, and a 15th-century Portuguese fort. The impressive 14th-century cliff-top palace of Husuni Kubwa has a 30 m (98 ft) high dome and over 100 rooms.

Zanzibar, Tanzania
The buildings of Zanzibar Town's 'old quarter', Stone Town, reflect its colourful history as an important trading centre, particularly in the 19th century. A maze of narrow streets contain a sultan's palace, an ochre-coloured Arab fort, and the home of the notorious slave trader Tippu Tip, as well as numerous bazaars.

Great Zimbabwe, Zimbabwe
The extensive ruins of a major medieval city dating from the 10th century onwards, Great Zimbabwe is made up of curved stone walls and enclosures which incorporate features of the landscape into their design. The Elliptical Building, with an unusual conical tower and a diameter of almost 100 m (328 ft), is the largest ancient structure in sub-Saharan Africa.

Akko, Israel
The ancient walled port of Akko contains many relics of its long and distinguished history, including the underground 12th-century Crusader vaults and halls, the Ottoman Turkish citadel, and the beautiful 18th-century El Jazzar mosque. A remarkable 18th-century Turkish bathhouse has been sensitively restored.

Petra, Jordan
Carved out of red sandstone mountains, the majestic remains of the desert city of Petra include two theatres, the High Place of Sacrifice, a temple and many elaborate tombs. The majority date from the period c. 100 BC –AD 150, when Petra was at the height of its prosperity as an important centre of trade. It had strong links with the Greek Hellenistic world, which are reflected in the Classical facades of its tombs.

ASIA

Mohenjodaro, Pakistan
The excavated remains of a city, Mohenjodaro is the most impressive of all the sites relating to the civilization that flourished in the Indus Valley c. 2600–1800 BC. The site consists of a raised citadel, with public buildings that include an assembly hall and a Great Bath, and a lower town containing residential and industrial areas.

◄ **Angkor, Cambodia**
The magnificent ruins at Angkor, capital of the Khmer empire, merit more than one day of sight-seeing. The best-preserved of the buildings is the 12th-century sandstone temple of Angkor Wat, which symbolizes the Hindu universe. Surrounded by pools, it is lavishly decorated with statues and bas-reliefs that are the longest in the world. Around 1.5 km (1 mile) away is the temple complex of Angkor Thom, within which is the Buddhist temple of Bayon with reliefs depicting everyday life.

▼ **Ajanta and Ellora Caves, near Aurangabad, India**
Cut into a spectacular horseshoe-shaped cliff, the Buddhist temples and monasteries of Ajanta are decorated with wall-paintings which are among the greatest examples of early Indian art. The series of rock-cut temples at Ellora includes the 8th-century Hindu Kailasa temple which is renowned for its exceptional sculptures of gods and mythological figures.

The Pyramids and Ancient Egypt
Khafre's Sphinx, 73 m (240 ft) in length and carved from a limestone outcrop, stands near the three pyramids at Giza. The most famous of the Egyptian pyramids, they were built as spectacular royal tombs over 4,500 years ago, during the period of the Old Kingdom. The largest at Giza is nearly 150 m (500 ft) high. The last of the Old Kingdom dynasties collapsed c. 2180 BC, but central government was restored by the dynasties of the Middle Kingdom (c. 2055–1650 BC) and New Kingdom (c. 1550–1070 BC). In the era of the New Kingdom, vast temples and lavishly painted royal tombs were constructed, most notably those either side of the River Nile at Luxor and overlooking Lake Nasser at Abu Simbel (see *River and canal journeys*).

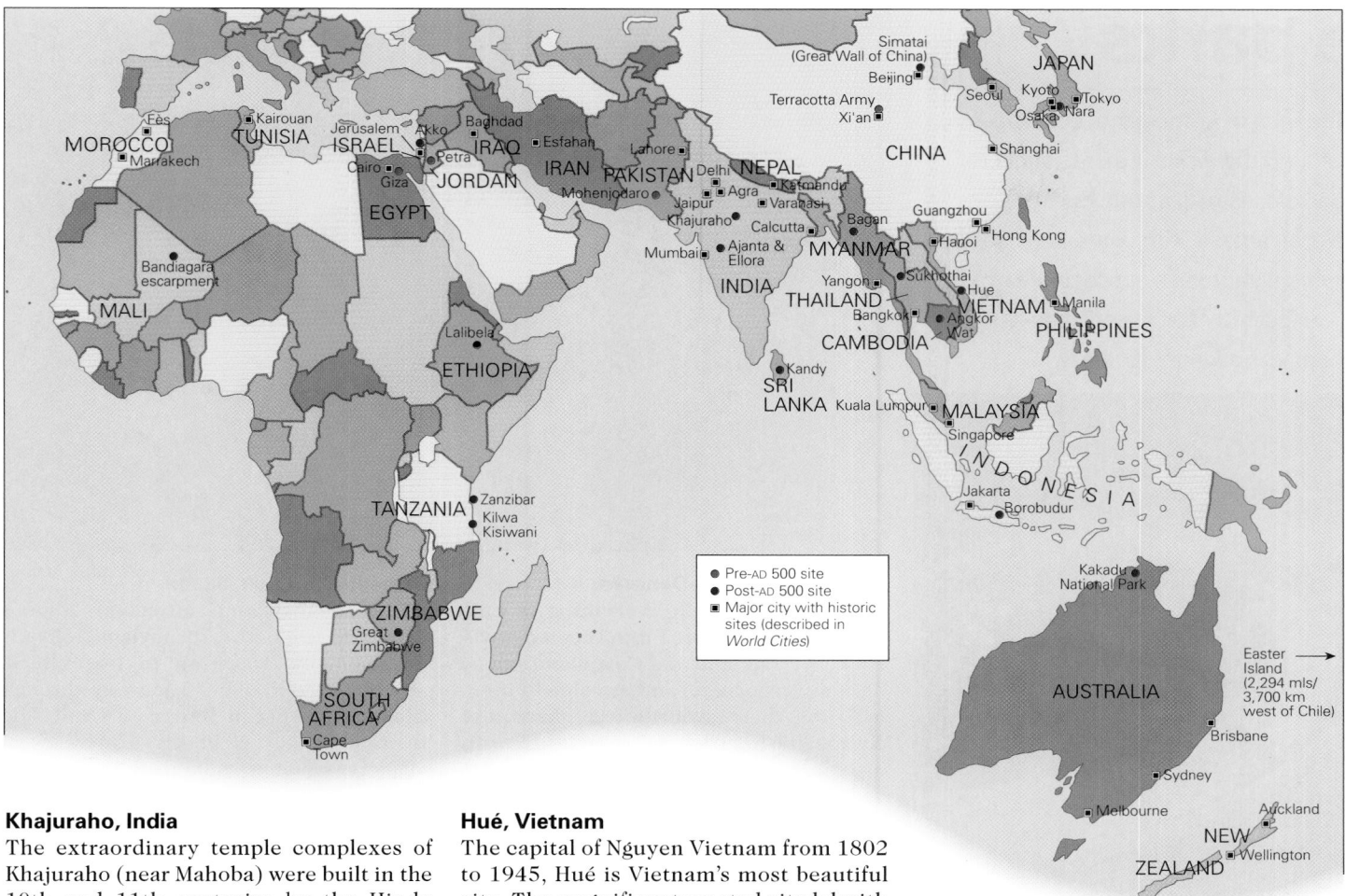

Major cities with historic sites
(see *World Cities*)
AFRICA
• Cairo
• Cape Town
• Fès
• Kairouan
• Marrakech
ASIA
• Agra
• Baghdad
• Bangkok
• Beijing
• Calcutta
• Delhi
• Esfahan
• Guangzhou
  (Canton)
• Hanoi
• Hong Kong
• Jaipur
• Jakarta
• Jerusalem
• Katmandu
• Kuala Lumpur
• Kyoto
• Lahore
• Manila
• Mumbai
• Osaka
• Seoul
• Singapore
• Tokyo
• Varanasi
• Xi'an
• Yangon
AUSTRALASIA
• Auckland
• Brisbane
• Melbourne
• Sydney
• Wellington

Map legend:
● Pre-AD 500 site
● Post-AD 500 site
■ Major city with historic sites (described in *World Cities*)

Khajuraho, India

The extraordinary temple complexes of Khajuraho (near Mahoba) were built in the 10th and 11th centuries by the Hindu Chandela dynasty, but were abandoned in the 14th century. Rediscovered in the jungle in 1838, they were carefully restored and are now famous for their sensual and erotic sculptures depicting human, divine, animal and mythological subjects.

Kandy and the Cultural Triangle, Sri Lanka

Famous for its temple and Festival of the Tooth (see *Festivals*), Kandy is one of three former Sinhalese capitals that together form a 'Cultural Triangle'. The other two are Anuradhapura, a huge site with the remains of palaces and temples dating back to the 3rd century BC, and the more compact and better-preserved Polonnaruwa, around 1,000 years old. Within the triangle is the 1st-century BC cave-temple of Dambulla, with 150 Buddha images, and the impressive 6th-century palace-fortress of Sigiriya. Built on top of 'Lion Rock', this is decorated with frescoes and includes a water garden.

Bagan, Burma (Myanmar)

Built between the 11th and the 13th centuries, Bagan (Pagan, near Pakkoku) became known as 'the city of 4 million pagodas', and was the capital of a vast realm. Today it is an important archeological site covering about 40 sq km (15 sq miles) with over 2,000 structures still standing. Among the most impressive are the Temple of Ananda and the Shwezigon Pagoda, with glazed plaques showing scenes from the life of Buddha.

Old Sukhothai, Thailand

The ruins of the 13th-century capital of the Sukhothai empire have been preserved as a 70 sq km (27 sq mile) historical park. They contain numerous temples set in a landscape of lakes, trees and lawns. The most impressive is Wat Mahathat, with fine stucco work and carved Buddhas.

Hué, Vietnam

The capital of Nguyen Vietnam from 1802 to 1945, Hué is Vietnam's most beautiful city. The magnificent moated citadel with its ten fortified gates contains a palace, a mandarin hall and a museum. In the hills to the south of the city there are seven elaborate royal tombs.

Borobudur, Java, Indonesia

Rising like a squat pyramid from the Kedu Plain, Borobudur (near Yogyakarta) is a colossal 9th-century Buddhist stupa (temple) built by the Sailendra dynasty. The largest monument in the southern hemisphere, it covers 200 sq m (2,153 sq ft) and includes over 500 shrines with seated Buddhas. The walls of the stupa, which has five square and four circular terraces, are decorated with bas-reliefs.

Great Wall of China, Simatai, China

Stretching from the Central Asian desert to the Yellow Sea, the Great Wall is over 2,240 km (1,400 miles) long, averages over 6 m (20 ft) in height, and has a central walkway nearly 4 m (13 ft) wide. Much of what exists today dates from the 14th–16th centuries. The Wall can be visited at Badaling, just 70 km (45 miles) from Beijing. However, a less crowded section is at Simatai, 110 km (68 miles) from Beijing, where there are wonderful views to the distant mountains.

Nara, Japan

The ancient city of Nara has many beautiful pagodas, shrines, gardens and temples, the most famous of which is the 8th-century Eastern Great Temple, the Tadai-Ji. Its Great Buddha Hall houses Japan's largest bronze statue of Buddha; the hall itself is the largest wooden building in the world.

AUSTRALASIA AND THE PACIFIC

Kakadu National Park, Australia

Thousands of Aboriginal rock paintings cover the walls of the caves and cliffs of the ancient Aboriginal lands in Kakadu National Park (see also *Wildlife in Australasia*). The paintings, some of which are estimated to be over 20,000 years old, provide a continuous link with the past for the several hundred Aboriginal people who still live there today.

Easter Island statues, Polynesia

The extraordinary stone statues of Easter Island are the legacy of a lost culture which flourished on the island between around AD 400 and 1600. More than 800 colossal stone heads were erected all around the island's coast. The volcanic crater from which the stone was quarried still contains hundreds of unfinished statues, including the 20 m (65 ft) high El Gigante.

◄ **Army of Terracotta Warriors, near Xi'an, China**
The massive underground mausoleum of China's first emperor, Shi Huang Di, who died in 210 BC, contains an army of around 7,500 life-size terracotta soldiers. Standing in military formation, they are a unique sight.

Theme parks

Inspired by the phenomenon of Disneyland, Los Angeles, the top theme parks around the world are irresistible to children both young and old, as well as adults. The combination of charm and fantasy with white-knuckle rides and superb service guarantees a successful family visit, and since most are located near major cities it is easy to incorporate them into a longer itinerary.

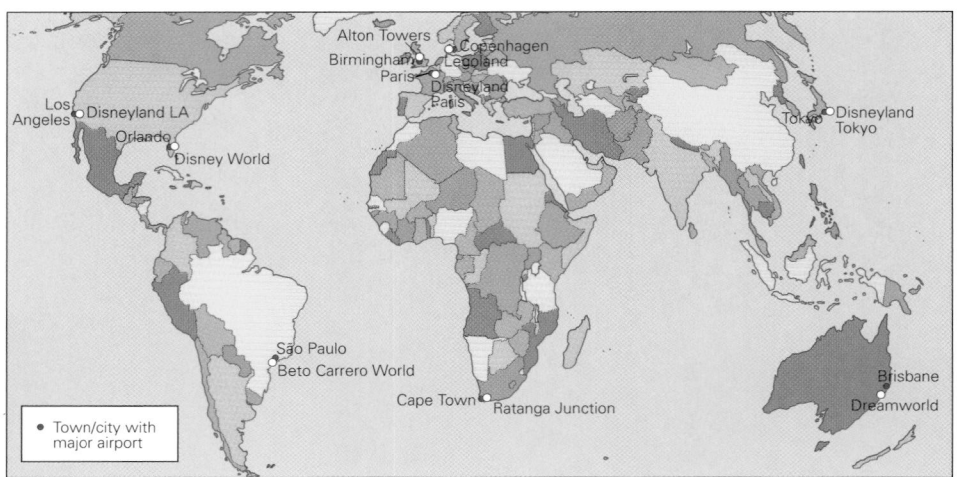

Town/city with major airport

▲ Alton Towers, England

The combination of a ruined stately home, wooded parkland and over 100 rides means that Alton Towers (in Staffordshire) provides entertainment for all tastes. For the benefit of its younger visitors it puts on shows featuring characters from storybooks and songs, such as 'Peter Rabbit and Friends on Ice'. Its more challenging rides have a much darker theme, with names such as Nemesis and Oblivion.

Useful web addresses
preceded by www.
themeparks.about.com
funguide.com/country
disney.com

Disneyland, Los Angeles, USA

Disneyland, founded in 1955, is the original Disney theme park, and Mainstreet, Frontierland and Fantasyland – representations of American life and its dreams – have been duplicated in Disney theme parks around the world. Visitors are attracted not only by rides like the runaway train of Big Thunder Mountain, the parade of Disney characters and the famous nightly firework show, but also out of nostalgia and a desire to experience what is itself now a historic site.

Beto Carrero World, Santa Catarina, Brazil

The most extensive theme park in Brazil, Beto Carrero World (near Itajai) combines thrilling rides, shows and a zoo. Its themed areas cover a range of cultures, including a German House complete with beer cellar, a Viking longboat and a Wild West area. Its shows are similarly wide-ranging and feature the legend of Excalibur. Its white-knuckle rides include the free-falling Tower of Terror, and Star World Mountain, with two 360-degree loops. The animal park includes African wildlife and a large collection of cobras.

Disneyland Paris, France

Although based on the same formula as the Los Angeles theme park, the marketing for Disneyland Paris emphasizes the educational element. There are 'Discovery rides', such as the 'Mississippi Steamboat' which provides information about life in frontier towns, while the Swiss Family Robinson tree-house demonstrates practical survival tips. Most visitors, however, go for the glamour of the shows and parades, and the thrill of the rides. These include being catapulted 'From the Earth to the Moon' on a Jules Verne style rocket.

Legoland, Billund, Denmark

Legoland, in which everything is built out of lego, is divided into themed areas, such as Pirateland and Castleland, where children recognize, and are able to interact with, their favourite lego characters. Although the park is aimed primarily at children, providing them with opportunities to play creatively, adults are also charmed by the intricate scale models of real, if somewhat idealized, scenes.

Ratanga Junction, Cape Town, South Africa

Africa's first theme park opened in the late 1990s. It takes as its theme the wildlife of Africa, with rides such as The Cobra, Monkey Falls, and Crocodile Gorge, in which visitors can experience white-water rafting in controlled conditions. A diamond mine is featured, with an underground runaway mine train providing the thrills. There are also less alarming rides for all the family, and 'interactive play areas' for young children.

Disneyland Tokyo, Japan

With many of the same attractions as other Disney theme parks, Disneyland Tokyo is unashamedly American in its culture, although it also offers a journey through Japanese history in Tomorrow Land. The Disney Parade celebrates '100 years of magic', with characters from the earliest cartoons through to the present day, and attempts to predict those of the future.

Dreamworld, Queensland, Australia

Thrilling rides and shows are combined with a wildlife park and conservation zone in Dreamworld (near Gold Coast). The Tower of Terror roller coaster reaches speeds of 160 km (100 miles) per hour as it descends from a height of 115 m (375 ft). The Giant Drop uses the same structure to release passengers vertically so that they experience momentary weightlessness. In an 'interactive tiger exhibition' tigers swim with their trainers, while in the Koala Park visitors can handle koalas and watch other native Australian animals.

Walt Disney World, Orlando, Florida, USA

The massive Walt Disney World in Florida encompasses four separate theme parks. At Magic Kingdom there are rides graded for every taste, from those in Fantasyland aimed specifically at younger children, to the Space Mountain rocket trip, which is not for the faint-hearted. The Epcot Centre aims to re-create the atmosphere and architecture of different countries, including Norway, China and Italy. Visitors can eat food typical of the region, and enjoy themed rides, shows and videos. Disney MGM re-creates urban areas, such as New York Street and Hollywood Boulevard, and uses computer technology to enable visitors to come face to face with characters from recent films. The newest of the parks, Animal Kingdom, combines a safari park with typical Disney features, including thrilling rides, exhibitions and shows.

WORLD CITIES

CITY MAPS

Amsterdam	2	Canton	8	Lagos	14	Munich	20	Singapore	27
Athens	2	Cape Town	8	Lisbon	14	New York	21	Stockholm	28
Atlanta	3	Chicago	9	London	15	Osaka	22	Sydney	28
Baghdad	3	Copenhagen	10	Lima	16	Oslo	22	Tokyo	29
Bangkok	3	Delhi	10	Los Angeles	16	Paris	23	Tehran	30
Barcelona	4	Dublin	11	Madrid	17	Prague	24	Tianjin	30
Beijing	4	Edinburgh	11	Manila	17	Rio de Janeiro	24	Toronto	30
Berlin	5	Helsinki	12	Melbourne	17	Rome	25	Vienna	31
Boston	6	Hong Kong	12	Mexico City	18	San Francisco	25	Warsaw	31
Brussels	6	Istanbul	12	Miami	18	St Petersburg	26	Washington	32
Budapest	7	Jakarta	13	Milan	18	Santiago	26	Wellington	32
Buenos Aires	7	Jerusalem	13	Montréal	19	São Paulo	26		
Cairo	7	Johannesburg	13	Moscow	19	Seoul	26		
Calcutta	8	Karachi	14	Mumbai	20	Shanghai	27	INDEX	33–39

CITY GAZETTEER 40–48

City Maps

Motorway, freeway, expressway with toll – with road number   A10

Motorway, freeway, expressway – with European road number   E51

Road junction

Under construction

Tunnel

Primary road – with road number
dual carriageway   14
single carriageway   14

Secondary road – with road number
dual carriageway   96
single carriageway   96

Other road

Ferry

Railroad

Principal station   Estación Central

Height above sea level (m)   234

Airport

Airfield

Central area coverage

Urban area

Woodlands and parks

Central Area Maps

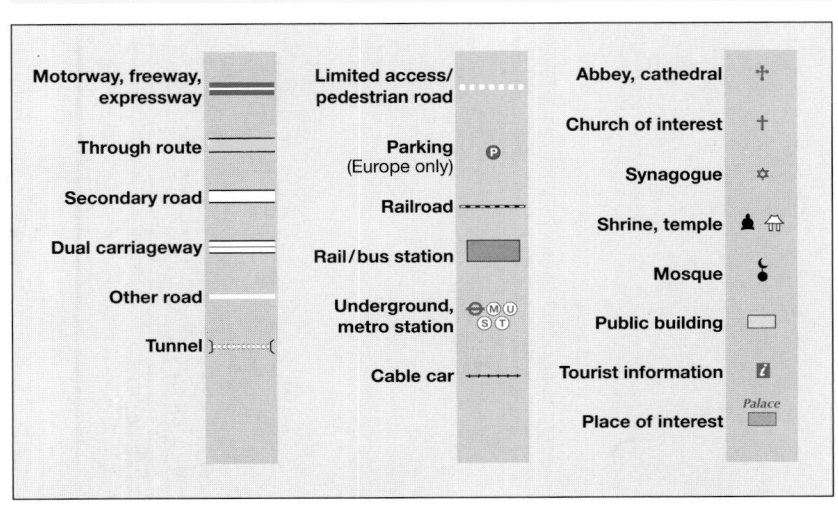

Motorway, freeway, expressway

Through route

Secondary road

Dual carriageway

Other road

Tunnel

Limited access/ pedestrian road

Parking (Europe only)   P

Railroad

Rail/bus station

Underground, metro station   M U S T

Cable car

Abbey, cathedral   †

Church of interest   †

Synagogue   ✡

Shrine, temple

Mosque

Public building

Tourist information   i

Place of interest   Palace

Amsterdam

km 5
miles 3

Assendelft · N8 · Westzaan · A8 · E22 · A7 · Zaandijk · Zaanstad · Wijde Wormer · Ilpendam · Monnickendam · N247 · N235 · Waterland · Gouw zee · Zaandam · E35 · Oostzaan · Den Ilp · Broek in Waterland · Landsmeer · Zuiderwoude · N203 · Tuindorp Oostzaan · A10 · Buiksloot · Zunderdorp · Holysloot · N202 · N5 · S101 · S116 · Nieuwendam · Ransdorp · Zwanenburg · AMSTERDAM · Het IJ · IJ-meer · Sloterpark · Rembrandt-Park · S100 · Zoo · Vondelpark · Stedelijk Mus. · Van Goghmus. · S112 · Watergraafsmeer · Osdorp · A10 · Sloten · Diemen · Bådhoevedorp · A4 · A10 · A2 · Muiden · A1 E231 · Buitenveldert · E35 · Amsterdamse Bos · N232 · Amstelveen · Amsterdam Zuidoost · A9 · Weesp · LUCHTHAVEN SCHIPHOL · E19 · A9 · Ouderkerk · A9 · N236 · Bovenkerk · Abcoude · Aalsmeer · Bovenkerker Polder · Amstel-Drecht-Kanaal · Nederhorst · E35 A2 · Uithoorn · N201 · Westeinder Plassen · Vinkeveense Plassen · Ankeveense Plassen · Baambrugge

East from Greenwich

Central Amsterdam

km 2
miles 1

HAARLEMMERWEG · Westerpark · HET IJ · NOORD · HAARLEMMER DIJK · Noorder Kerk · Central Station · DE RUIJTERKADE · IJ TUNNEL · IJ Haven · PIET HEINKADE · NASSAUKADE · ROZENGRACHT · Anne Frankhuis · Wester Kerk · Koninklijk Paleis · St. Nicolaas · Oude Kerk · DAM RAK · PRINS HENDRIK KADE · Scheepvaart-museum · KATTEN-B. GRACHT · OOSTEN-B. GRACHT · Universiteit · Rembrandt huis · VALKEN BURGERSTR · Planetarium · Zoo · Cruquiuskade · Univ. Bibl. · Allard Pierson Museum · AMSTEL · Muziek theater · Artis · MAURITSKADE · OVERTOOM · Rembrandt plein · Waterlooplein · Tropenmuseum · OOST · Filmmuseum · Rijksmus. · Theater Carré · Weesperplein · Sarphatistraat · Muiderpoort Station · Vondelpark · Stedelijk Mus. · Van Goghmus. · OUD ZUID · STADHOUDERS KADE · Onze Lieve Vrouwe Gasthuis · Oosterpark · HOBBEMAKADE · Concertgebouw · Albert Cuypstr · WIBAUT STRAAT · WATERGRAAFSMEER · NIEUW ZUID · FERDINAND BOLSTRAAT · AMSTEL DIJK · Amstel · HUGO · STADIONWEG · CHURCHILLAAN · Amstel Station · GOOISEWEG · DE VRIES LAAN · Juliana plein

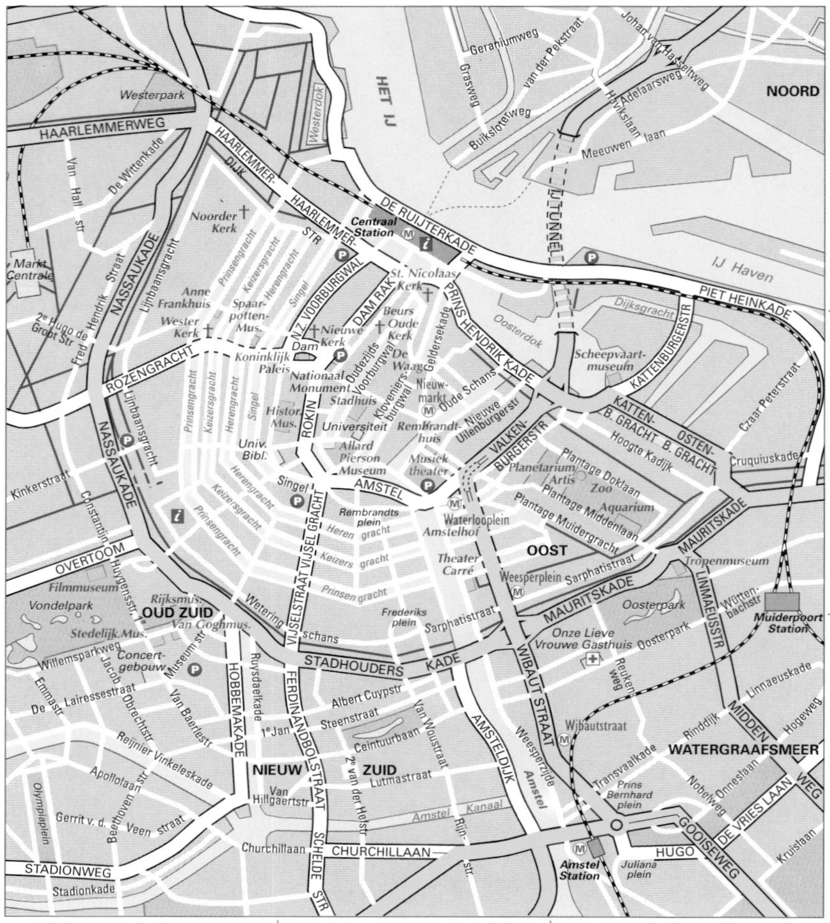

Athens

km 5
miles 3

Diflistiria · Néa Liósia · Néa Ionía · Petroúpolis · Verdi · Patisia · Filothei · Khalándrion · Khaidhárion · Filadhélfia · Psikhikón · Dháfni · Sepolia · Galátsion · Ay. Paraskevi · Skaramangas · Peristérion · Attiki · Óros Aiyáleo · 468 · Lioumi · Kolokinthóu · Kolonos · Larisa · Kipséli · Kholargós · Glika Nera · Koridhallós · Aiyáleo · ATHÍNAI · Ampelokipi · Néapolis · Zografos · Koupónia · Néapolis · Dhamarakia · Tavros · Akropoli · Stadion · Kaisariani · Gargáreta · Pangrati · Ay. I. Rendis · Ay. Gheorghios · Nikaia · Kallithéa · Víron · Dráphni · Imittós · Dhrapetsón · Moskháton · N. Smírni · Ilioúpolis · 1026 Évzonos · Ay. Dhimitrios · Óros Imittós · Piraiévs · N. Fáliron · P. Fáliron · N. Alexandhria · 765 · Peania · Saronikós Kólpos · Ormos Fáliron · Alimos · Aryiróupolis · Elliniko · Kalamákion · Iráklion, Khania, Kithnos, Kos, Mikonos, Milos, Náxos, Paros, Ródhos, Sámos · ATHÍNAI ELLINIKÓN · Glifádha · Idrousa · Vari · Barako 230 · Voúla · 91 · Kitsi · Vouliagmeni · C. Kavouri · Varkiza · Ayía Marina

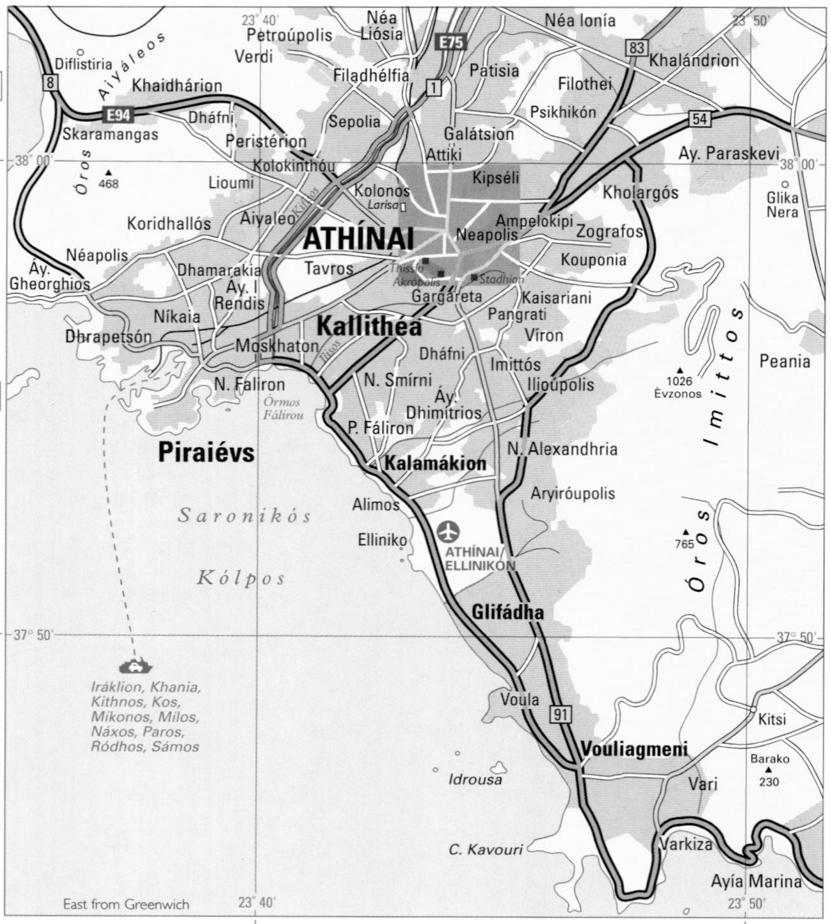

East from Greenwich

Central Athens

km 1
miles 0.5

KODRICTONOS · EVELPIDON · Vergovitsis · Pedion Areos · PATISSION · ALEXANDRAS · ACHARNON · LEOFOROS · Victorias · IPPOKRATOUS · Larisa · Likavitos · Ethnikó Arheologikó Moussío · Ayios Georgios · CHALKOKONDILI · Omonia · Opera · AG. KONSTANTINOU · Ethnikó Viliothiki · Panepistimio · Ethniko Kipos · Evangelismos · PIREOS · ATHINAS · EOLOU · Kendriki Agorá · Akadimia · Panepistimio · VASILISSIS · SOFIAS · Moussio Benaki · Keramikós · ERMOU · Syntagma · Vouli · VASILEOS KONSTANTINOU · Monastiráki · Mitrópolis · FILELLINON · PLAKA · Ethnikos Kipos · Zappeio · LEOFOROS OLGAS · Thissio · Arhéa Agora · Ários Págos · Akrópolis · Parthenon · Naós Olimpíou Diós · ARDITOS · DIONISIOU AREOPAGITOU · Lófos Nimfón · Pnika · Lófos Filópapou · Dora Stratou Théatro

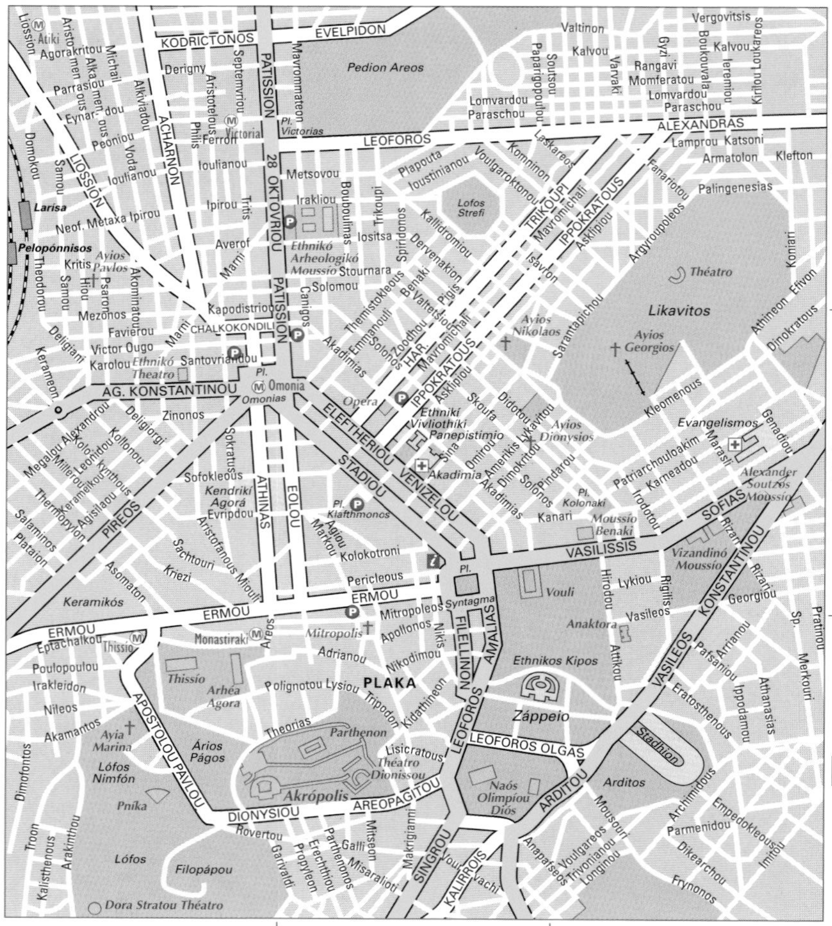

COPYRIGHT GEORGE PHILIP LTD.

Atlanta

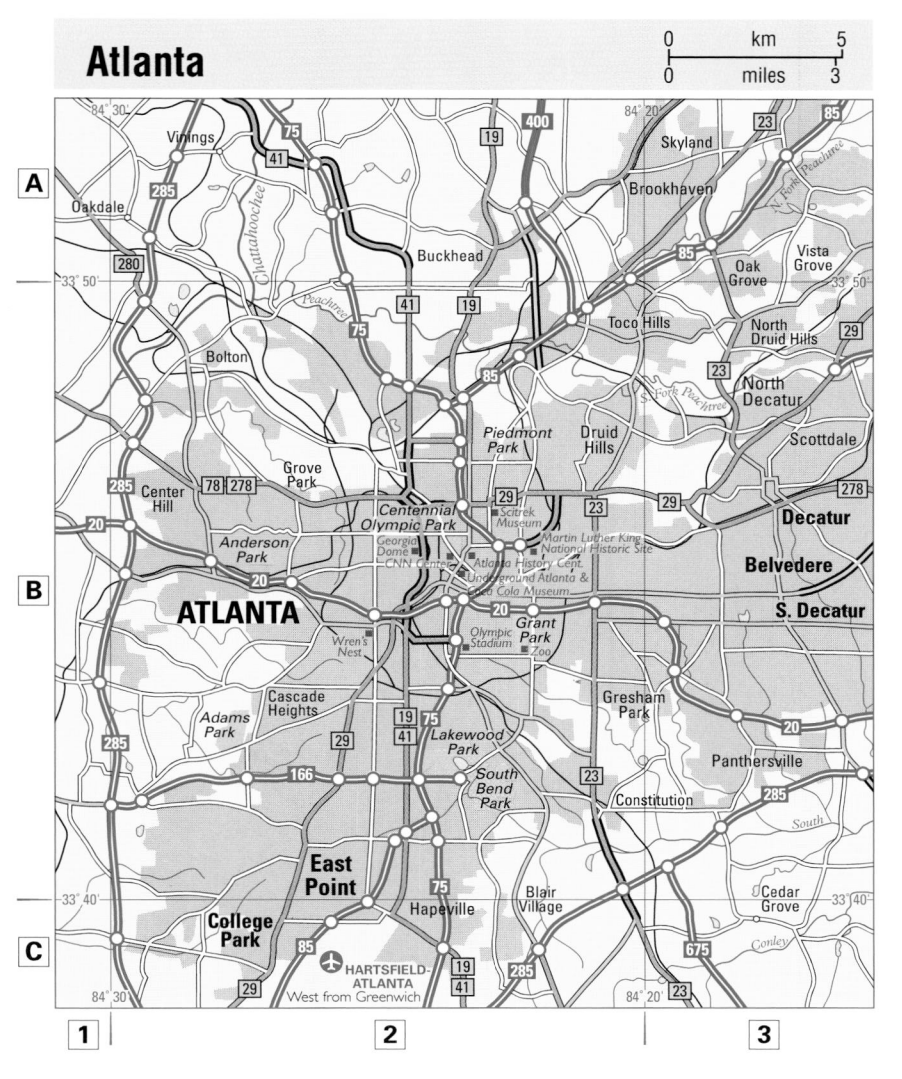

Baghdad

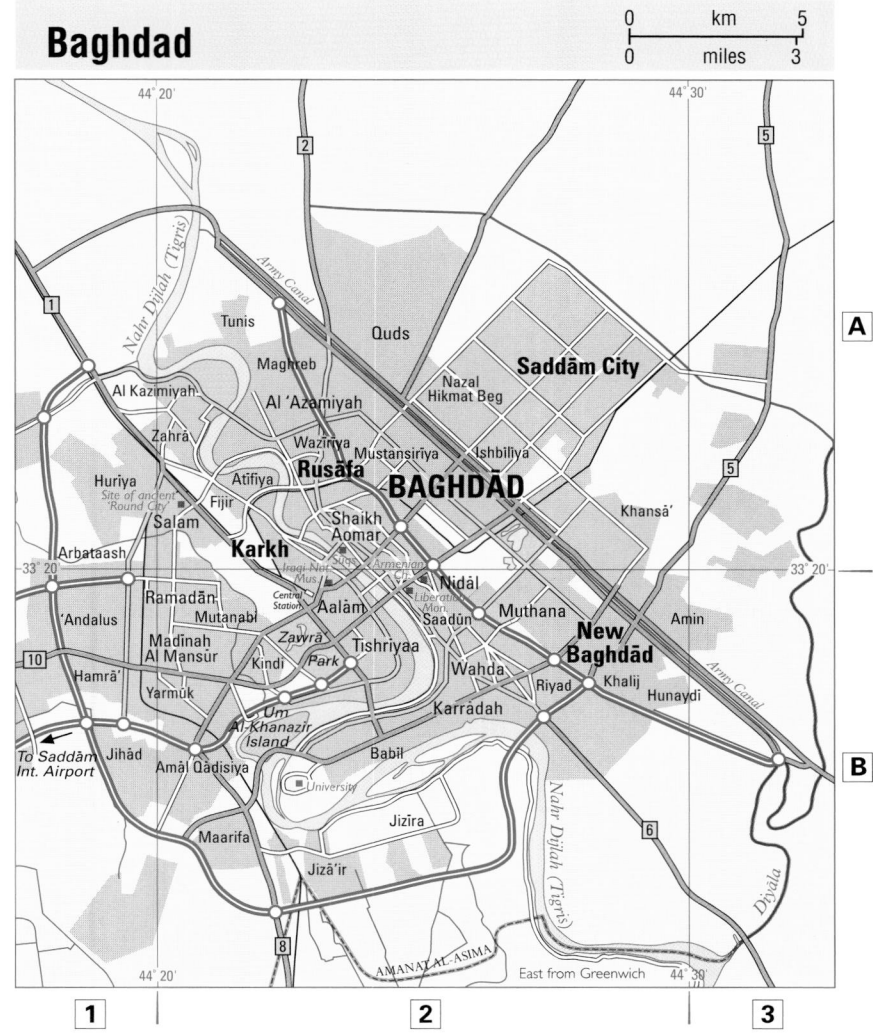

Bangkok

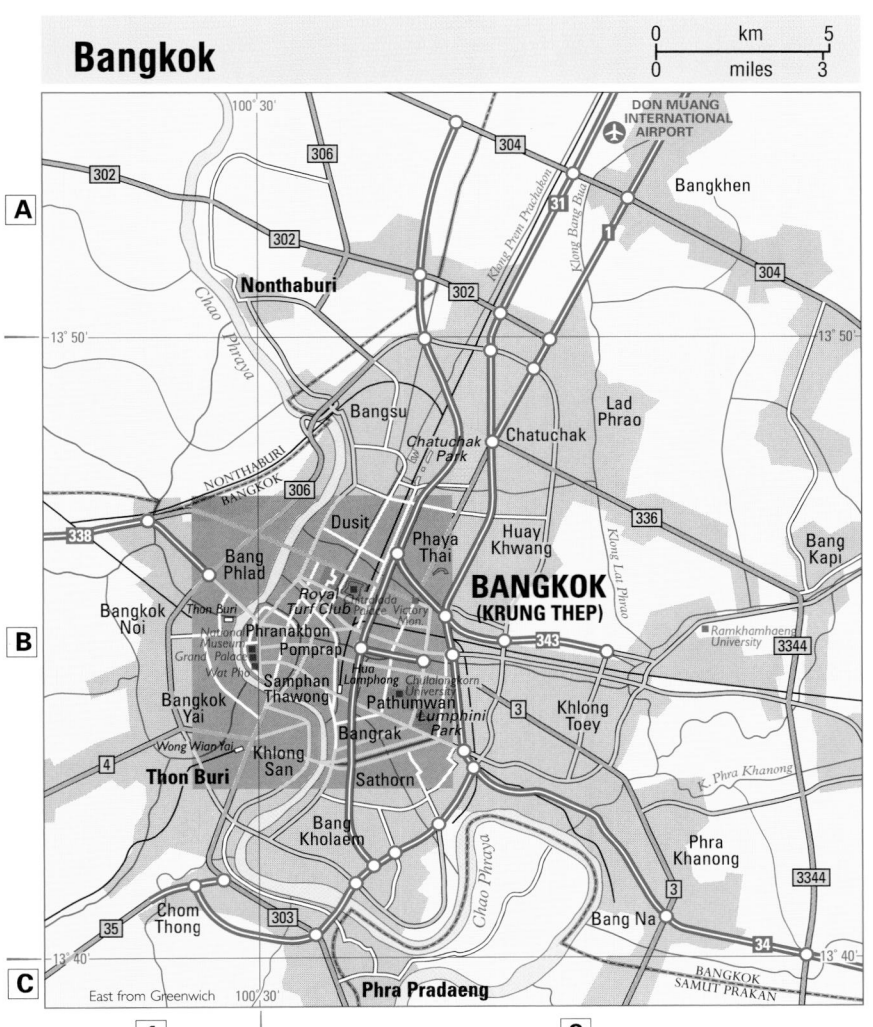

Central Bangkok

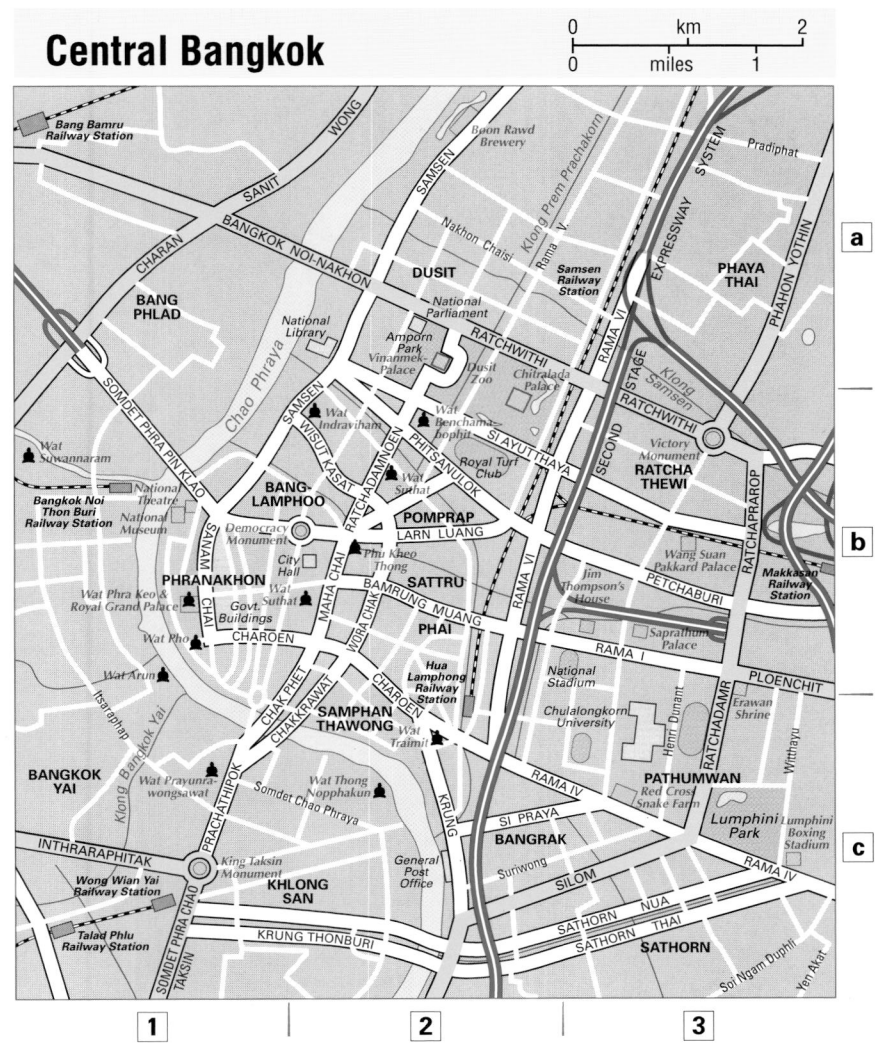

COPYRIGHT GEORGE PHILIP LTD.

Barcelona

km 5
miles 3

Turo de Galceran ▲477
Cerdanyola del Vallès
Ripollet
Sant Cugat del Vallès
C'an Sant Joan
Llano de Can Gineu 327
La Puntigala 151▲
E90 Valldoreix
E15
Madrona
La Floresta
Sant Andreu
S. Andreu
Sta. Coloma de Gramanet
Sta. Eulalia
Badalona
Vallcarca
La Taxonera
La Sagrera
Sant Adrià de Besós
El Papiol
Tibidabo 512▲
Santa Cruz de Olorde
Valldvidrera
Guinardó
La Llacuna
San Martin
Molins de Rei
▲435
387
Putxet Gracia
Pueblo Nuevo
Sant Vicenç dels Horts
San Pedro Martir 389▲
Sarrià
Universitat
Las Corts
La Fransa
BARCELONA
Sant Just Desvern
Pedralbes
Est. de França
Barceloneta
Sant Feliu de Llobregat
Colonia Güell
Esplugas
Sans
Moll Maritim
Beri
Hostafranchs
La Ribera
L'Hospitalet de Llobregat
Castillo
Cornella
Sant Joan Despi
Sant Boi de Llobregat
Rio Llobregat
Mahón, Palma, Ibiza
Génova
Viladecáns
El Prat de Llobregat
Gavá
AEROPUERTO DE BARCELONA PRAT
Laguna de la Ricarda
MEDITERRANEAN SEA
La Pineda
Laguna del Rémola

East from Greenwich

Central Barcelona

km 1
miles 0.5

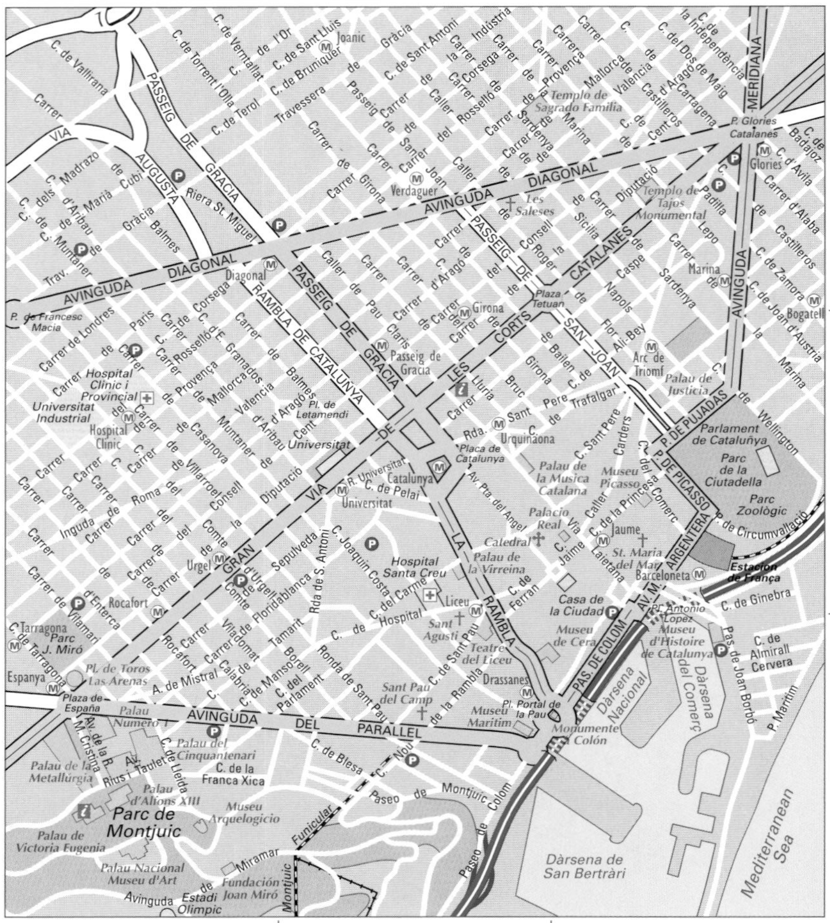

AVINGUDA DIAGONAL
PASSEIG DE GRACIA
RAMBLA DE CATALUNYA
Templo de Tajó Monumental
Plaza de Francesc Macia
Hospital Clinic i Provincial
Universitat Industrial
Hospital Clinic
Universitat
Plaza de Catalunya
Palau de la Musica Catalana
Museu Picasso
Parc de la Ciutadella
Parc Zoològic
GRAN
Hospital Santa Creu
Palau de la Virreina
Catedral
Palau de la Generalitat
St. Maria del Mar
Casa de la Ciudad
Teatro del Liceu
Museu de Cera
Parlament de Catalunya
PL. de Toros Las Arenas
Sant Pau del Camp
Drassanes
Museu Maritim
Monumente Colón
AVINGUDA DEL PARALLEL
Palau del Cinquantenari
Palau de Metallúrgia
Museu Arqueológico
Parc de Montjuic
Palau de Victoria Eugenia
Palau Nacional Museu d'Art
Fundació Joan Miró
Avinguda Estadi Olimpic
Miramar
Dàrsena de San Bertrari
MEDITERRANEAN SEA

Beijing

km 5
miles 3

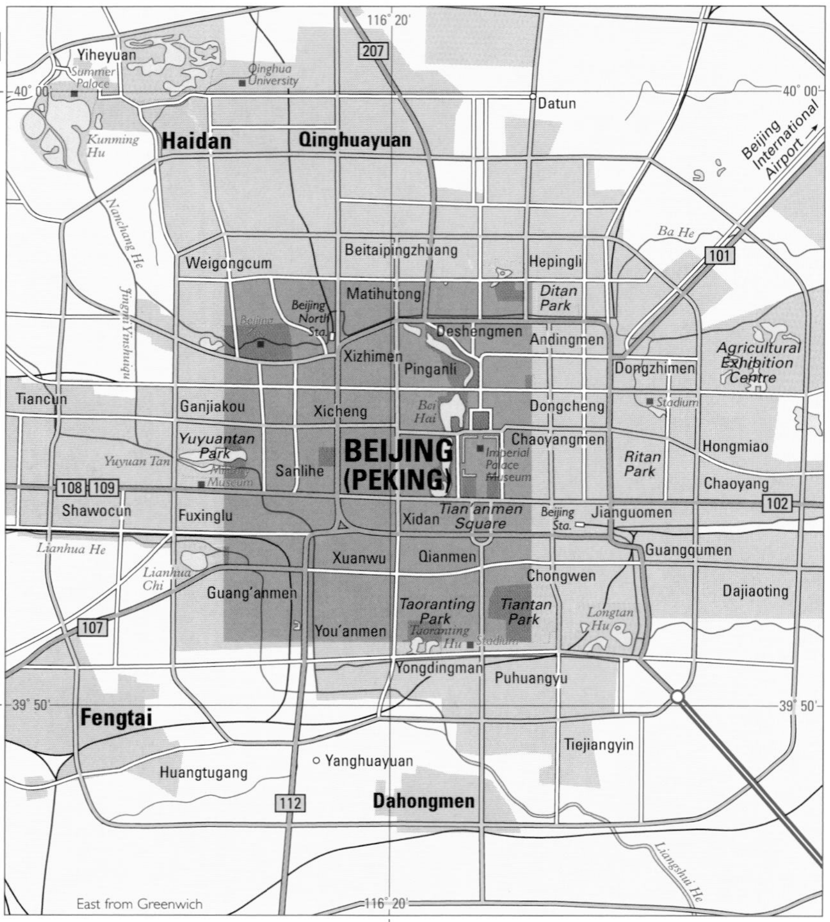

Yiheyuan Summer Palace
Qinghua University
207
Datun
Haidan
Qinghuayuan
Beijing International Airport
Kunming Hu
Weigongcum
Beitaipingzhuang
Hepingli
101
Matihutong
Ba He
Ditan Park
Beijing North Sta.
Deshéngmen
Andingmen
Dongzhimen
Tiancun
Xizhimen
Pinganli
Ganjiakou
Xicheng
Bei Hai
Dongcheng
Dongzhimen
Agricultural Exhibition Centre
Yuyuantan Park
Sanlihe
Imperial Palace Museum
Chaoyangmen
Ritan Park
Hongmiao
108 109
Shawocun
Museum
BEIJING (PEKING)
Chaoyang
Fuxinglu
Xidan
Tian'anmen Square
Beijing Sta.
Jianguomen
102
Guang'anmen
Xuanwu
Qianmen
Chongwen
Guangqumen
Dajiaoting
107
Taoranting Park
Tiantan Park
Longtan Hu
You'anmen
Yongdingman
Puhuangyu
Fengtai
Huangtugang
Yanghuayuan
112
Dahongmen
Tiejiangyin

East from Greenwich

Central Beijing

km 2
miles 1

Chinese Opera House
Xueyuannan Lu
Réndinghu Park
Ditan Park (Temple of Earth)
Bashihuqiao Lu
Jishuitan
Ande Lu
Gulou
Qingnianhu Park
Beijing Library
Beijing North Sta.
Xizhimen
Gaoliangqiao Lu
Bell Tower
Capital Library and Mus.
Xu Beihong Mem. Hall
Beijing Zoo
Xizhimennei Dajie
Drum Tower
XIZHIMENWAI DAJIE
Xizhimennan lu
Planetarium
Pantheon of Mei Lanfang
Qianhai
Houhai
Chegongzhuang
Chegongzhuang Dajie
Beihai
SANLIHI LU
Lu Xun Museum
People's Theatre
Di'anmenxi Dajie
Di'anmendong Dajie
Fuchengmen
Beihai Park
Chinese Art Gallery
FUCHENMENWAI DAJIE
FUCHENGMENNEI DAJIE
XI'ANMEM DAJIE
Jingshan Park
WUSI DAJIE
Song Chingling Children's Science Park
Yuetan Park
Imperial Palace Mus.
Capital Theatre
Yuyuantan Park
Erqi Theatre
Cultural Palace for Nationalities
Zhongnanhai
Nanhai
Zhongshan Park
Beijing Children's Art Th.
Military Museum
FUXINGMENWAI DAJIE
FUXINGMENNEI DAJIE
XICHANG'AN JIE
Working People's Cult. Pal.
DONGCHANG'AN JIE
Junshibowuguan
Muxidi
Fuxingmen
Great Hall of the People
Tian'anmen Square
Mus. of Chinese Revolution and Chinese History
Xidan
Southern Cathedral
Xuanwumen
Hepingmen
Mao Mausoleum
Xibianmen Station
Lianhuachidong Lu
XUANWUMEN
QIANMEN
DONG DAJIE
XI DAJIE
Qianmen
Liulichang Jie
Xinlong Jie
GUANG'ANMENWAI DAJIE
Guang'anmennei Dajie
Luomashi Dajie
Zhushikouxi Dajie
Liyuan Theatre
Yong'an Lu
Zhushikoudong Dajie
Tiantan Lu
Guang'anmen Station
Baiguang Lu
Nanheng Jie
Beiwei Lu
Natural History Museum
Tiantan Park (Temple of Heaven)
Peking Opera
Taoranting Lu
Baizhifang Lu
Wanshou Park
Fasting Palace
Taoranting Park

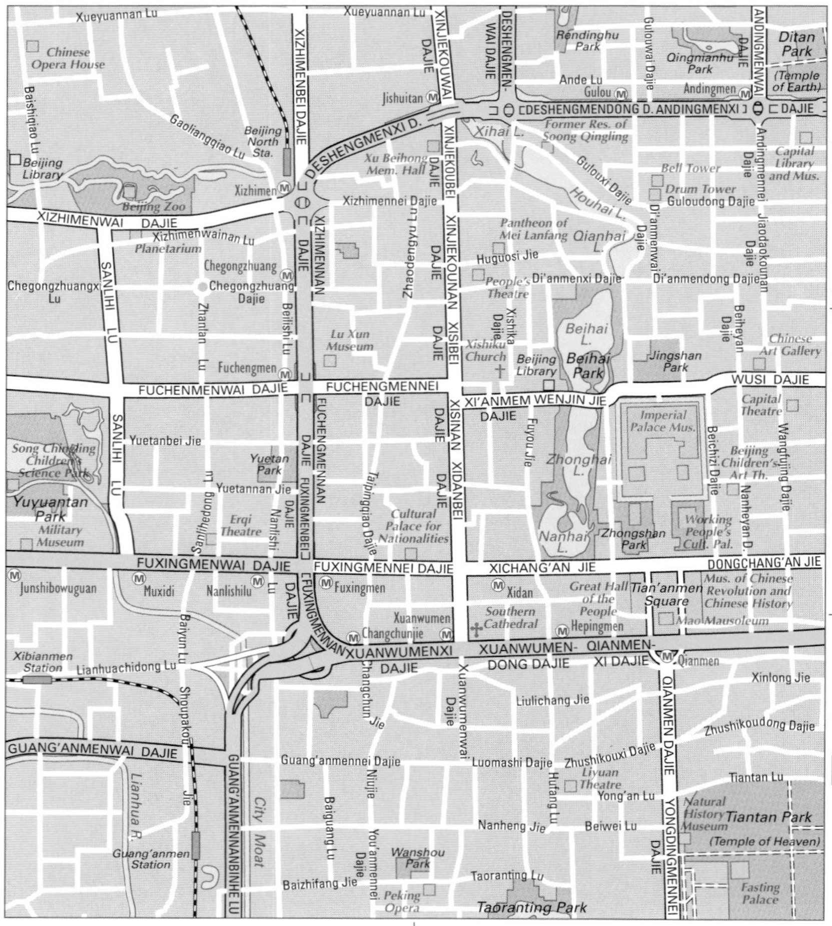

COPYRIGHT GEORGE PHILIP LTD.

Berlin

0 km 5
0 miles 3

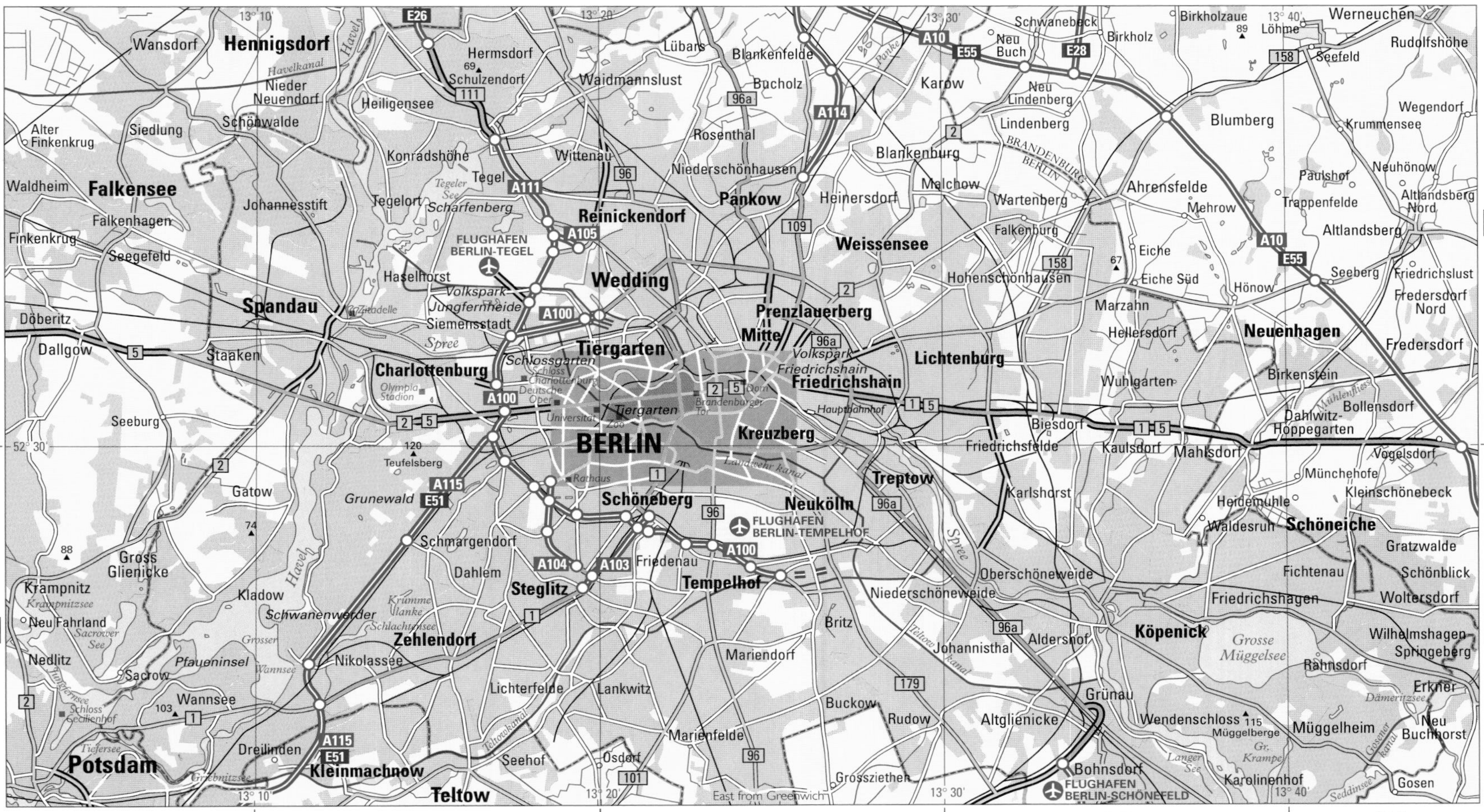

Wansdorf · Hennigsdorf · Hermsdorf · Schulzendorf · Lübars · Blankenfelde · Schwanebeck · Birkholzaue · Löhme · Werneuchen · Rudolfshöhe
Alter Finkenkrug · Nieder Neuendorf · Heiligensee · Waidmannslust · Buchholz · Karow · Neu Buch · Birkholz · Seefeld
Waldheim · Falkensee · Siedlung · Schönwalde · Tegelort · Tegel · Wittenau · Niederschönhausen · Rosenthal · Lindenberg · Neu Lindenberg · Blumberg · Krummensee · Wegendorf
Falkenhagen · Johannesstift · Scharfenberg · Pankow · Heinersdorf · Melchow · Wartenberg · Ahrensfelde · Mehrow · Paulshof · Neuhönow · Altlandsberg Nord
Finkenkrug · Reinickendorf · Weissensee · Falkenberg · Hohenschönhausen · Eiche · Eiche Süd · Hönow · Seeberg · Fredersdorf · Altlandsberg

A

Seegefeld · FLUGHAFEN BERLIN-TEGEL · Hasellhorst · Wedding · Marzahn · Hellersdorf · Trappenfelde · Fredersdorf Nord
Spandau · Volkspark Jungfernheide · Siemensstadt · Prenzlauerberg · Mitte · Lichtenburg · Wuhlgarten · Birkenstein · Neuenhagen · Fredersdorf
Döberitz · Charlottenburg · Schlossgarten · Tiergarten · Volkspark Friedrichshain · Friedrichshain · Bollensdorf
Dallgow · Staaken · Spree · Olympia Stadion · BERLIN · Kreuzberg · Hauptbahnhof · Biesdorf · Kaulsdorf · Mahlsdorf · Dahlwitz-Hoppegarten
Seeburg · Teufelsberg · Grunewald · Schöneberg · Neukölln · Friedrichsfelde · Vogelsdorf · Münchehofe

B

Krampnitz · Gross Glienicke · Kladow · Dahlem · Schmargendorf · Friedenau · Steglitz · FLUGHAFEN BERLIN-TEMPELHOF · Treptow · Karlshorst · Oberschöneweide · Kleinschönebeck · Schöneiche
Neu Fahrland · Schwanenwerder · Zehlendorf · Tempelhof · Niederschöneweide · Heidemühle · Waldesruh · Gratzwalde
Nedlitz · Sacrow · Pfaueninsel · Wannsee · Nikolassee · Lichterfelde · Lankwitz · Britz · Johannisthal · Adlershof · Köpenick · Grosse Müggelsee · Fichtenau · Schönblick · Friedrichshagen · Wilhelmshagen · Springeberg
Dreilinden · Kleinmachnow · Seehof · Buckow · Rudow · Altglienicke · Grünau · Rahnsdorf · Wendenschloss · Müggelberge · Müggelheim · Erkner · Neu Buchhorst
Potsdam · Teltow · Osdorf · Marienfelde · Grossziethen · Bohnsdorf · FLUGHAFEN BERLIN-SCHÖNEFELD · Karolinenhof · Gosen

Central Berlin

0 km 1
0 miles 0.5

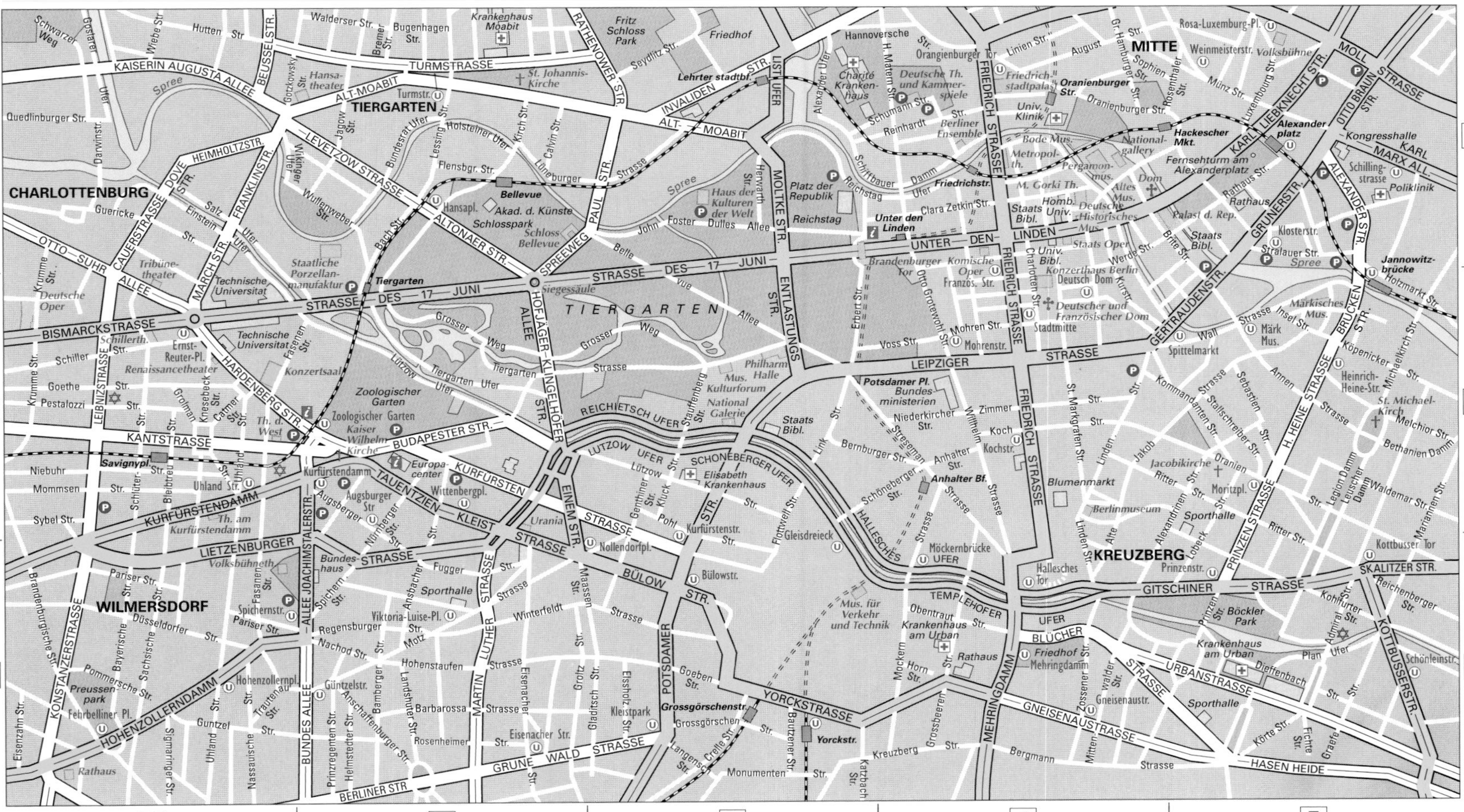

TIERGARTEN · CHARLOTTENBURG · MITTE · KREUZBERG · WILMERSDORF

COPYRIGHT GEORGE PHILIP LTD.

Boston

0 km 5
0 miles 3

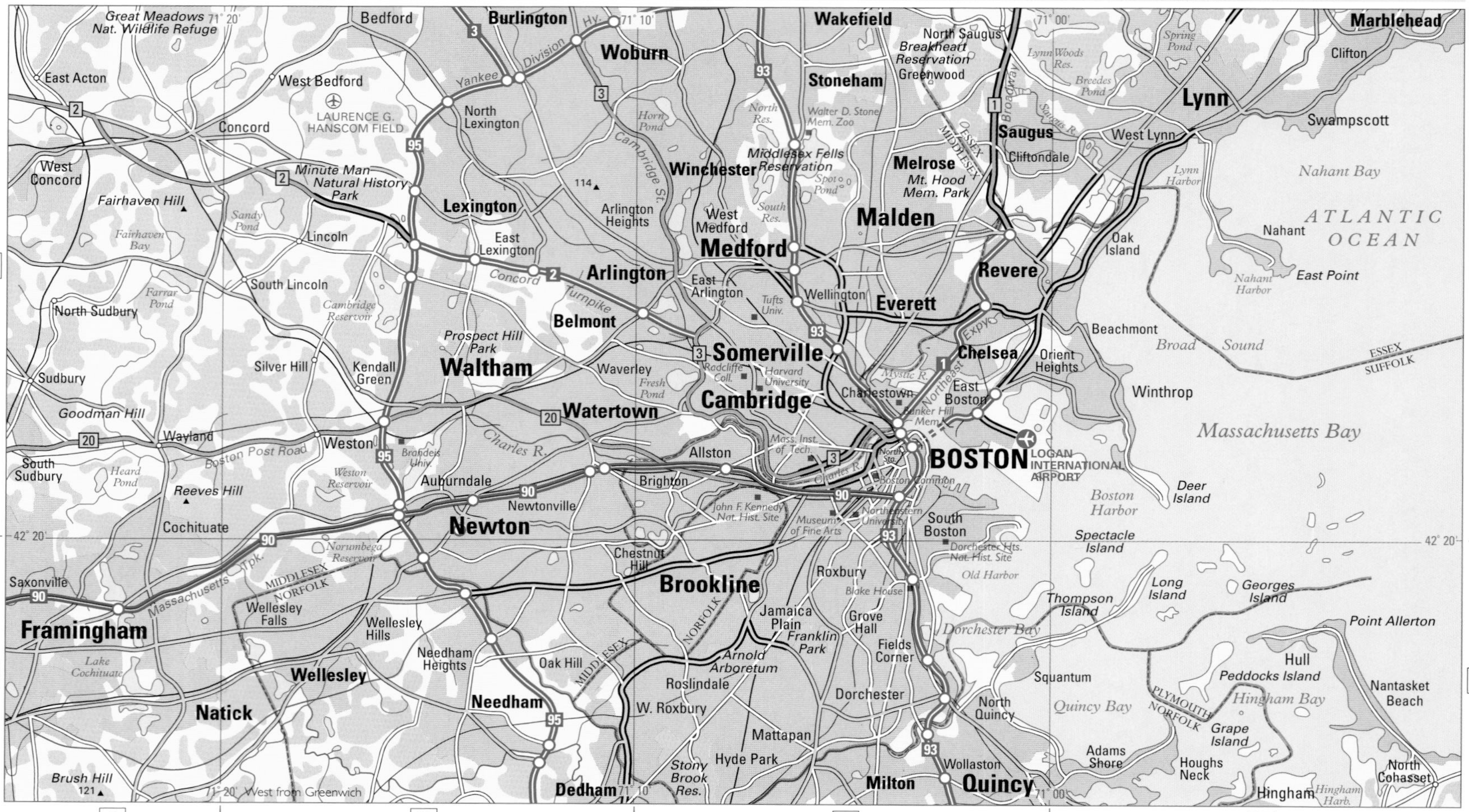

Great Meadows Nat. Wildlife Refuge · Bedford · Burlington · Woburn · Wakefield · Marblehead · East Acton · West Bedford · Stoneham · North Saugus Breakheart Reservation Greenwood · Clifton · Concord · LAURENCE G. HANSCOM FIELD · North Lexington · Lynn · Swampscott · West Concord · Minute Man Natural History Park · Winchester · Saugus · West Lynn · Nahant Bay · Fairhaven Hill · Lexington · Middlesex Fells Reservation · Melrose Mt. Hood Mem. Park · Cliftondale · ATLANTIC OCEAN · Fairhaven Bay · Lincoln · East Lexington · West Medford · Malden · Nahant · North Sudbury · South Lincoln · Arlington Heights · Medford · Revere · East Point · Belmont · Arlington · East Arlington · Everett · Beachmont · Nahant Harbor · Silver Hill · Waverley · Somerville · Chelsea · Orient Heights · Broad Sound · Sudbury · Goodman Hill · Prospect Hill Park · Waltham · Cambridge · East Boston · Winthrop · ESSEX SUFFOLK · Wayland · Weston · Watertown · Allston · Charlestown · LOGAN INTERNATIONAL AIRPORT · Massachusetts Bay · Boston Post Road · Weston Reservoir · Auburndale · Brighton · BOSTON · Deer Island · Cochituate · Newtonville · Boston Harbor · Newton · Chestnut Hill · Museum of Fine Arts · South Boston · Spectacle Island · Saxonville · Wellesley Falls · Brookline · Roxbury · Old Harbor · Long Island · Georges Island · Framingham · Wellesley Hills · Jamaica Plain · Franklin Park · Grove Hall · Dorchester Bay · Thompson Island · Point Allerton · Wellesley · Needham Heights · Oak Hill · Arnold Arboretum · Fields Corner · Squantum · Hull · Peddocks Island · Nantasket Beach · Natick · Needham · Roslindale · Dorchester · Quincy Bay · Hingham Bay · W. Roxbury · North Quincy · Adams Shore · Grape Island · Brush Hill · Mattapan · Hyde Park · Wollaston · Houghs Neck · North Cohasset · Stony Brook Res. · Dedham · Milton · Quincy · Hingham

West from Greenwich

A B · 1 2 3 4

Brussels

0 km 5
0 miles 3

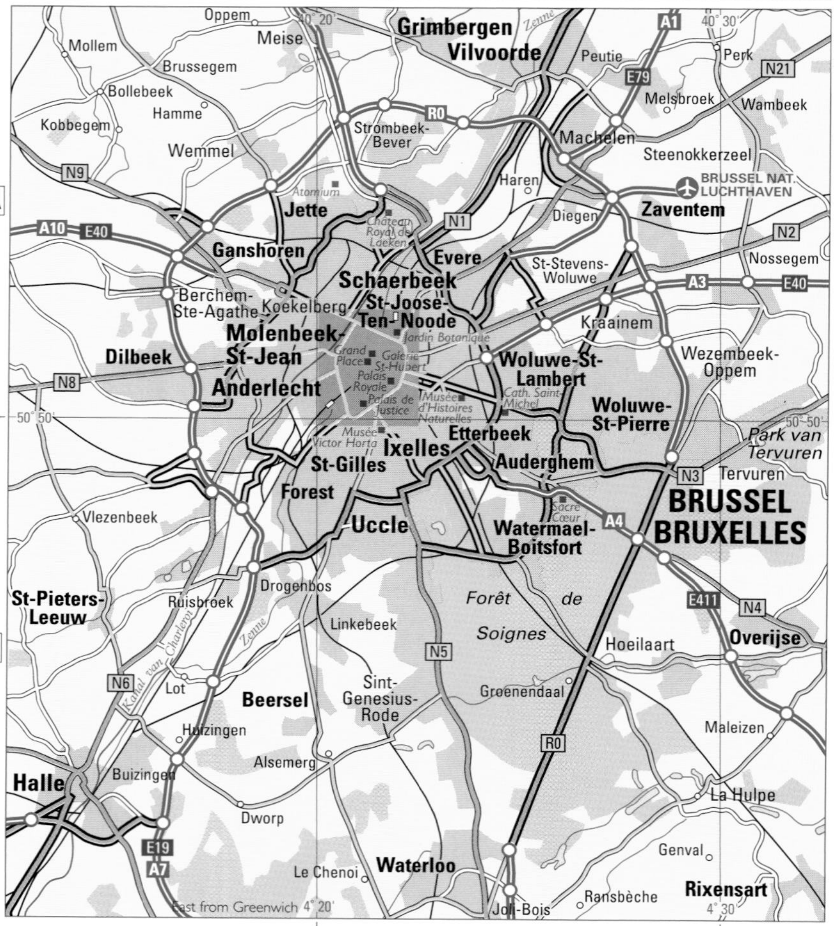

Oppem · Grimbergen · Vilvoorde · Mollem · Meise · Peutie · Perk · Brussegem · Bollebeek · Strombeek-Bever · Machelen · Wambeek · Kobbegem · Wemmel · BRUSSEL NAT. LUCHTHAVEN · Jette · Haren · Diegem · Zaventem · Ganshoren · Evere · St-Stevens-Woluwe · Nossegem · Berchem-Ste-Agathe · Schaerbeek · St-Joose-Ten-Noode · Kraainem · Dilbeek · Koekelberg · Molenbeek-St-Jean · Woluwe-St-Lambert · Wezembeek-Oppem · Anderlecht · Ixelles · Woluwe-St-Pierre · Etterbeek · Auderghem · Park van Tervuren · St-Gilles · Tervuren · Forest · BRUSSEL BRUXELLES · Uccle · Watermael-Boitsfort · St-Pieters-Leeuw · Vlezenbeek · Drogenbos · Forêt de Soignes · Overijse · Roosbroek · Linkebeek · Hoeilaart · Lot · Beersel · Sint-Genesius-Rode · Groenendaal · Maleizen · Halle · Buizingen · Holzingen · Alsemberg · Dworp · La Hulpe · Rixensart · Waterloo · Le Chenoi · Jon-Bois · Ransbèche · Genval

East from Greenwich

A B · 1 2 3

Central Brussels

0 km 1
0 miles 0.5

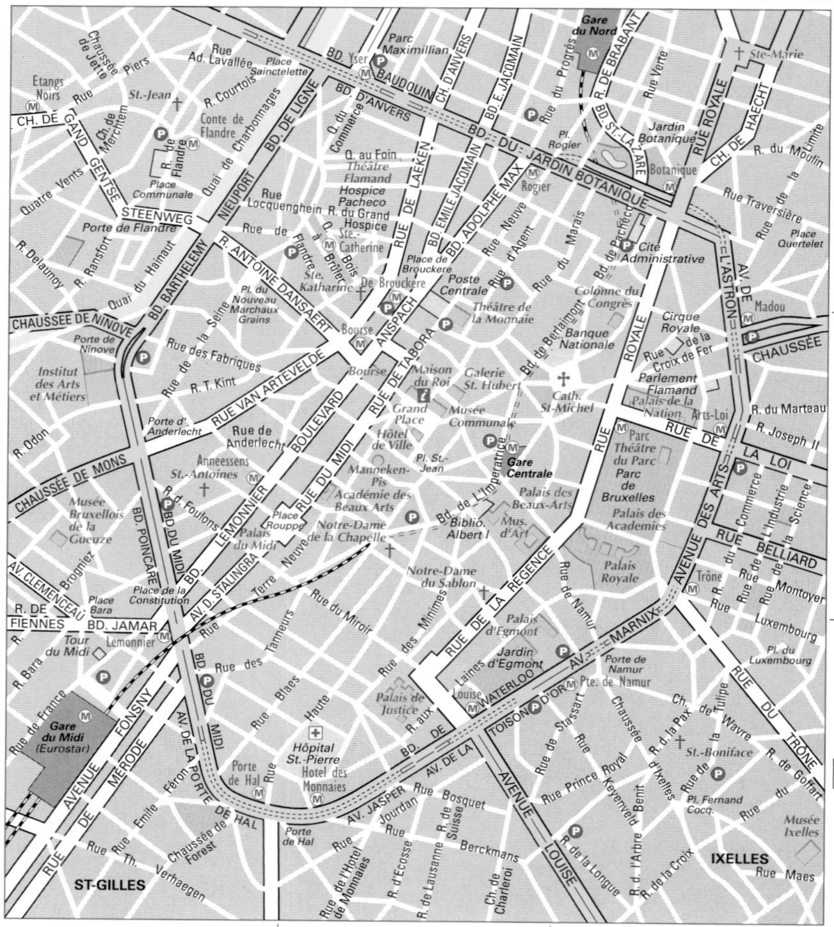

Gare du Nord · Ste-Marie · Parc Maximilien · Jardin Botanique · St-Jean · BD BAUDOUIN · Rue Traversière · Place Quertelet · Cité Administrative · Porte de Flandre · Théâtre Flamand · Poste Centrale · Colonne du Congrès · Banque Nationale · Institut des Arts et Métiers · Bourse · Galerie St. Hubert · Parlement Flamand Palais de la Nation · Grand Place · Hôtel de Ville · Musée Communal · Palais des Beaux-Arts · Parc de Bruxelles · Palais Royal · Manneken Pis · Notre-Dame de la Chapelle · Notre-Dame du Sablon · Palais de Justice · Place Fernand Cocq · Musée Ixelles · Gare du Midi (Eurostar) · Hôpital St-Pierre · Porte de Hal · ST-GILLES · IXELLES

a b c · 1 2 3

COPYRIGHT GEORGE PHILIP LTD.

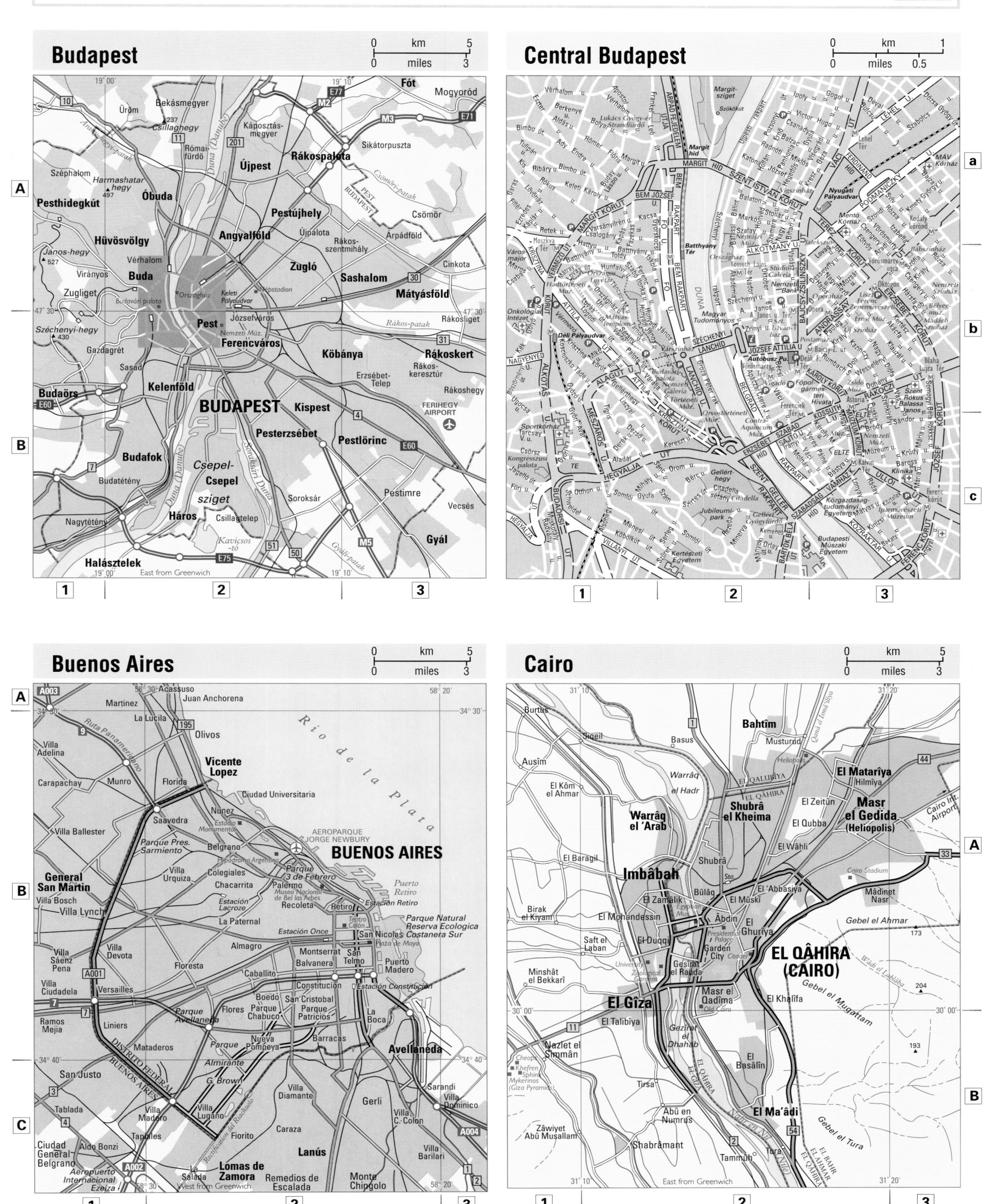

Budapest

km 0—5
miles 0—3

Central Budapest

km 0—1
miles 0—0.5

Buenos Aires

km 0—5
miles 0—3

Cairo

km 0—5
miles 0—3

COPYRIGHT GEORGE PHILIP LTD.

Calcutta

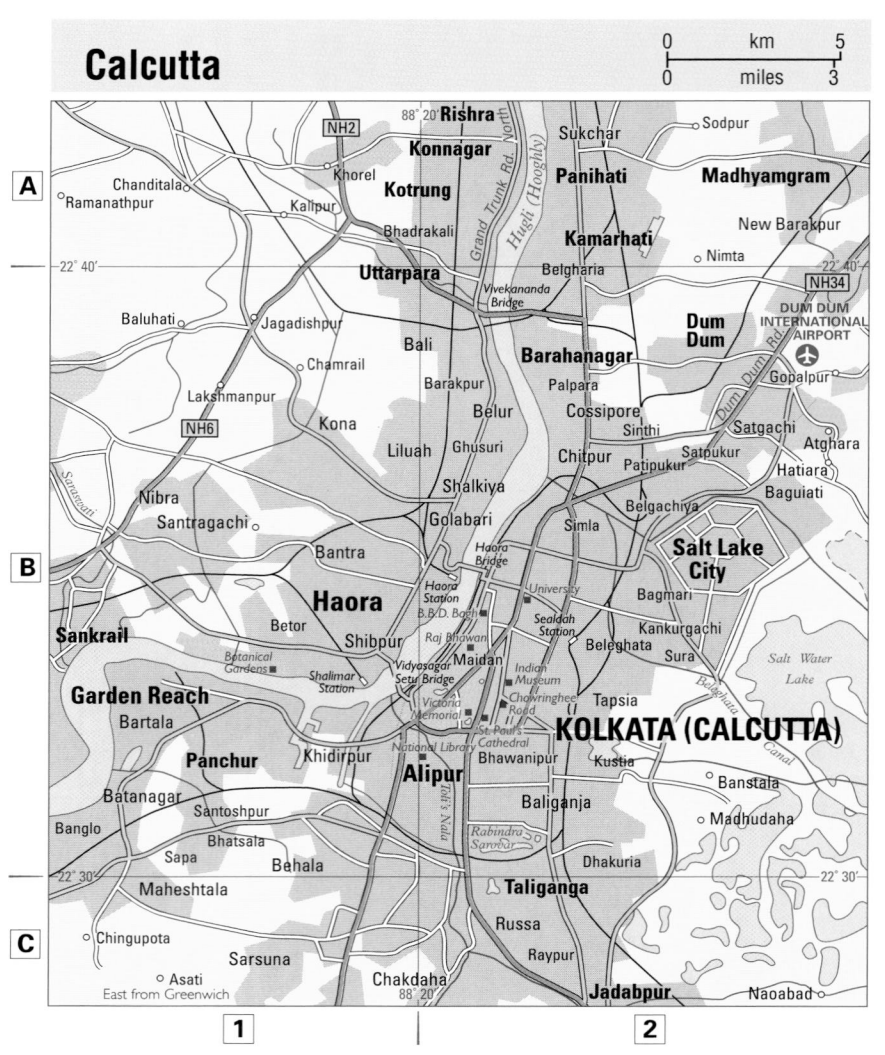

Canton

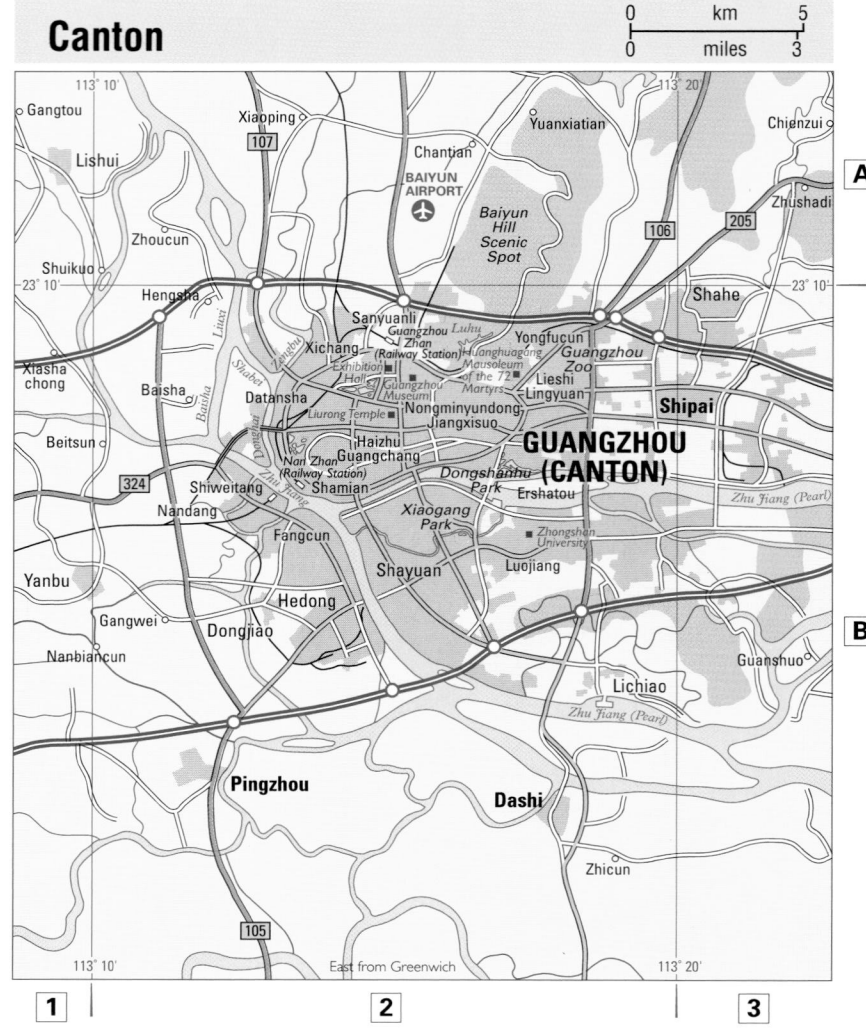

Cape Town

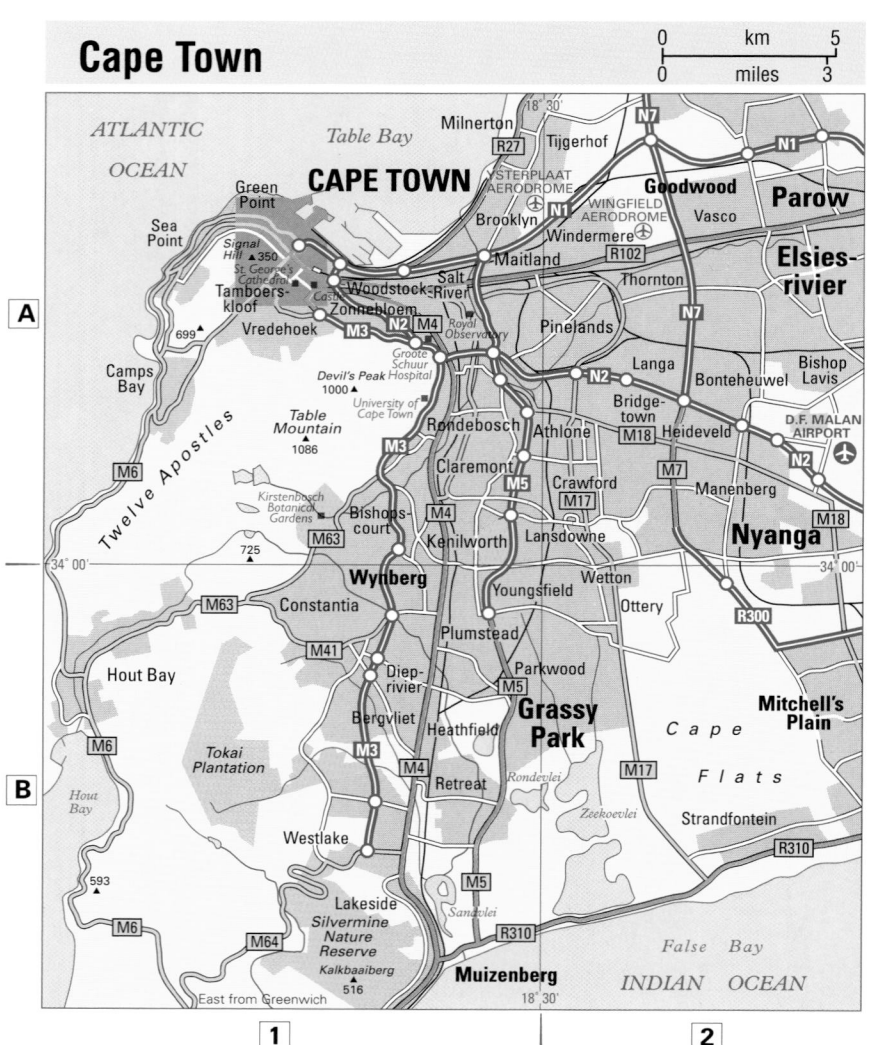

Central Cape Town

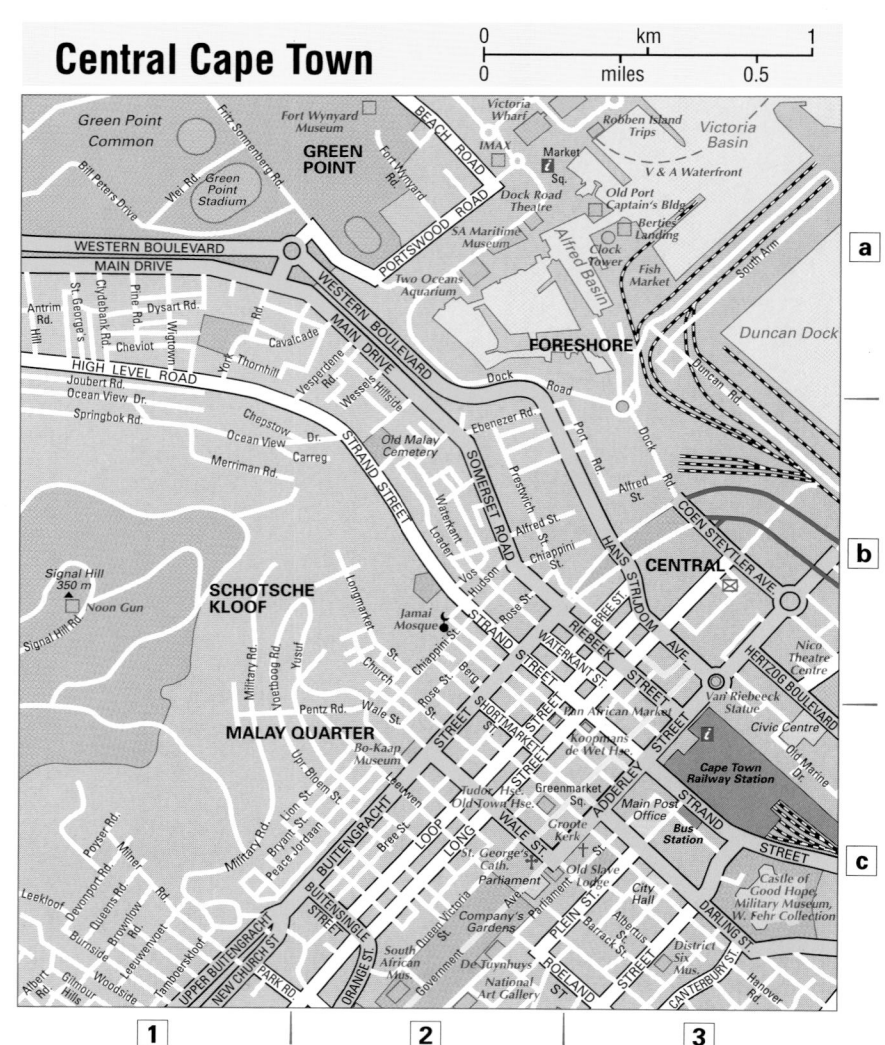

COPYRIGHT GEORGE PHILIP LTD.

Chicago

km 0 5
miles 0 3

LAKE MICHIGAN

CHICAGO

Evanston · Wilmette · Skokie · Niles · Glenview · Morton Grove · Park Ridge · Des Plaines · Glenview Countryside

Northwestern University · Baha'i Temple · Rogers Park · Loyola University · Uptown · Lakeview · Lincoln Park · Lincoln Park Zoo · Gold Coast · Near North · The Loop · Navy Pier · John Hancock Center · Water Tower · Chicago Harbor · Grant Park · Adler Planetarium · Field Museum · Soldier Field · Burnham Park · Burnham Harbor

Lincolnwood · Irving Park · Portage Park · Belmont Cragin · Austin · Avondale · Logan Square · Humboldt Park · West Town · Wrigley Field · Old Town

Edison Park · Norridge · Norwood Park · Harwood Heights · Dunning · Elmwood Park · River Forest · Oak Park · Cicero · Berwyn · Garfield Park · Douglas Park · Lawndale · United Center

Schiller Park · Schiller Woods · Franklin Park · Northlake · River Grove · Melrose Park · Stone Park · Maywood · Bellwood · Broadview · Miller Meadow · Forest Park · North Riverside · Riverside · Brookfield

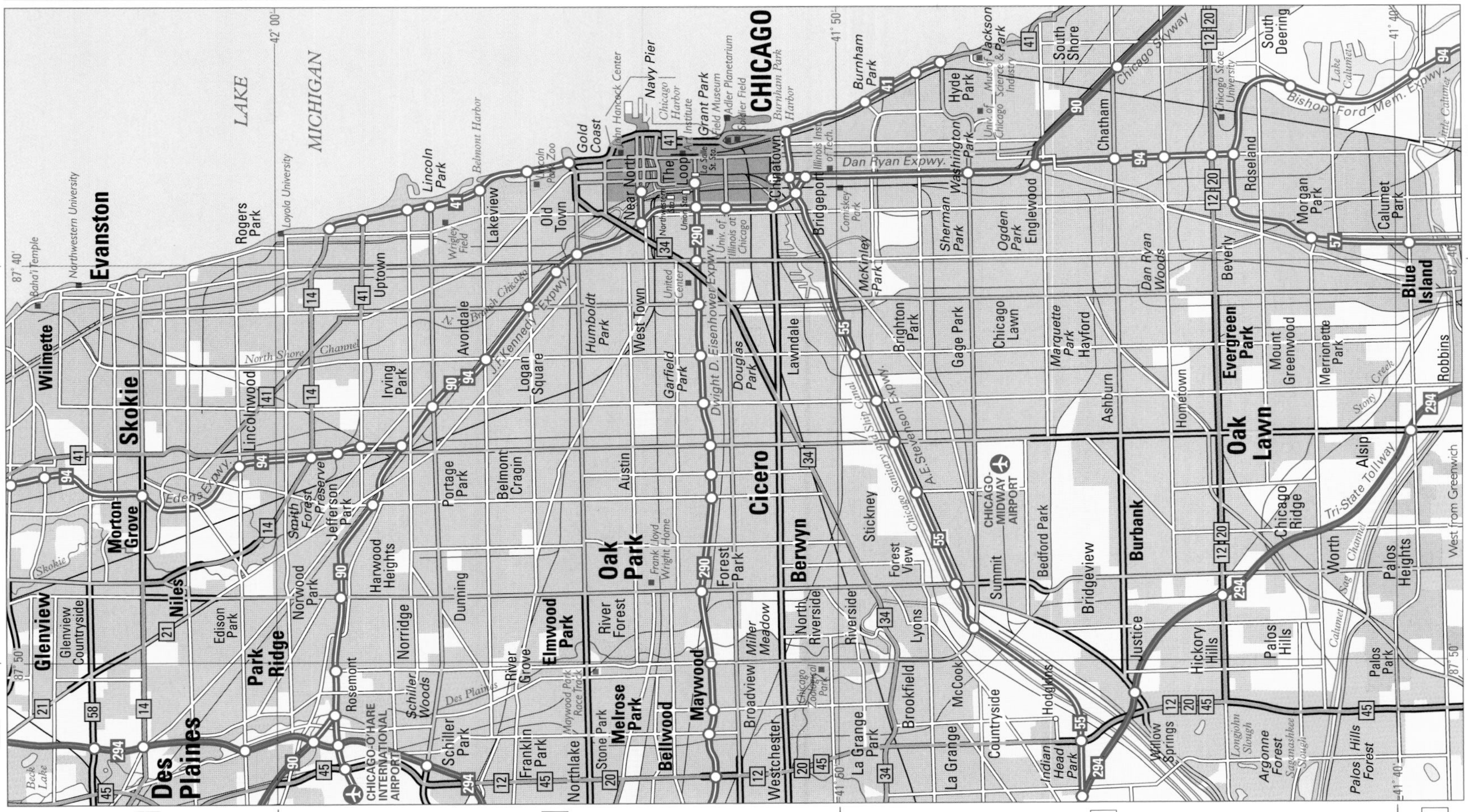

CHICAGO-O'HARE INTERNATIONAL AIRPORT

Westchester · La Grange Park · La Grange · Countryside · Western Springs · Indian Head Park · Hodgkins · McCook · Summit · Stickney · Forest View · Bedford Park · Bridgeview · Justice · Willow Springs · Hickory Hills · Palos Hills · Palos Park · Palos Heights · Worth · Chicago Ridge · Burbank · Oak Lawn · Evergreen Park · Mount Greenwood · Merrionette Park · Beverly · Morgan Park · Blue Island · Robbins · Alsip

CHICAGO MIDWAY AIRPORT

Brighton Park · Gage Park · Marquette Park · Hayford · Chicago Lawn · Ashburn · Hometown · McKinley Park · Bridgeport · Comiskey Park · Sherman Park · Ogden Park · Englewood · Chatham · Washington Park · Hyde Park · University of Chicago · Museum of Science & Industry · South Shore · Roseland · Calumet Park · South Deering · Lake Calumet · Little Calumet

Illinois Inst. of Tech. · Dan Ryan Expwy. · Dan Ryan Woods · Chicago Sanitary and Ship Canal · A.E. Stevenson Expwy. · J.F. Kennedy Expwy. · Dwight D. Eisenhower Expwy. · Edens Expwy. · North Shore Channel · Des Plaines R. · Tri-State Tollway · Chicago Skyway · Bishop Ford Mem. Expwy. · West from Greenwich

Central Chicago

km 0 1
miles 0 0.5

LAKE MICHIGAN

Outer Harbor · Navy Pier · Olive Park · Ohio St Beach · Lake Point Tower · Streeter Dr · Chicago Harbor · Chicago Yacht Club · Shedd Aquarium · Adler Planetarium · Merrill C. Meigs Field · Burnham Park · Burnham Park Harbor · McCormack Place East · McCormack Place West

Oak St Beach · Gold Coast · John Hancock Center · Water Tower Place · Northwestern Memorial Hosp-l · Northwestern Univ. · Tribune Tower · Wrigley Bldg. · Marshall Field's · Prudential Building · Art Institute of Chicago · Grant Park · Buckingham Fountain · Roosevelt Road Sta. · Field Museum of Nat. History · Soldier Field

Near North · River North · The Loop · Printer's Row · South Loop · Chinatown · Merchandise Mart · City Hall & County Bldg. · La Salle St. Sta. · Randolph St. Sta. · Van Buren Sta. · Northwestern Sta. · Union Sta. · Main Post Office · Opera House · Sears Tower

E Lake Shore Drive · N Lake Shore Drive · S Lake Shore Drive · South Lake Shore Drive East · South Lake Shore Drive West · N Wacker Dr · S Wacker Dr · Michigan Avenue · State Street · Wabash Ave · Congress Pkwy · Roosevelt Road · Cermak Road · Chicago River · South Branch · North Branch · E Solidarity Dr · E Columbus Drive · S Columbus Drive · Fairbanks Court · Canal Street · Clinton

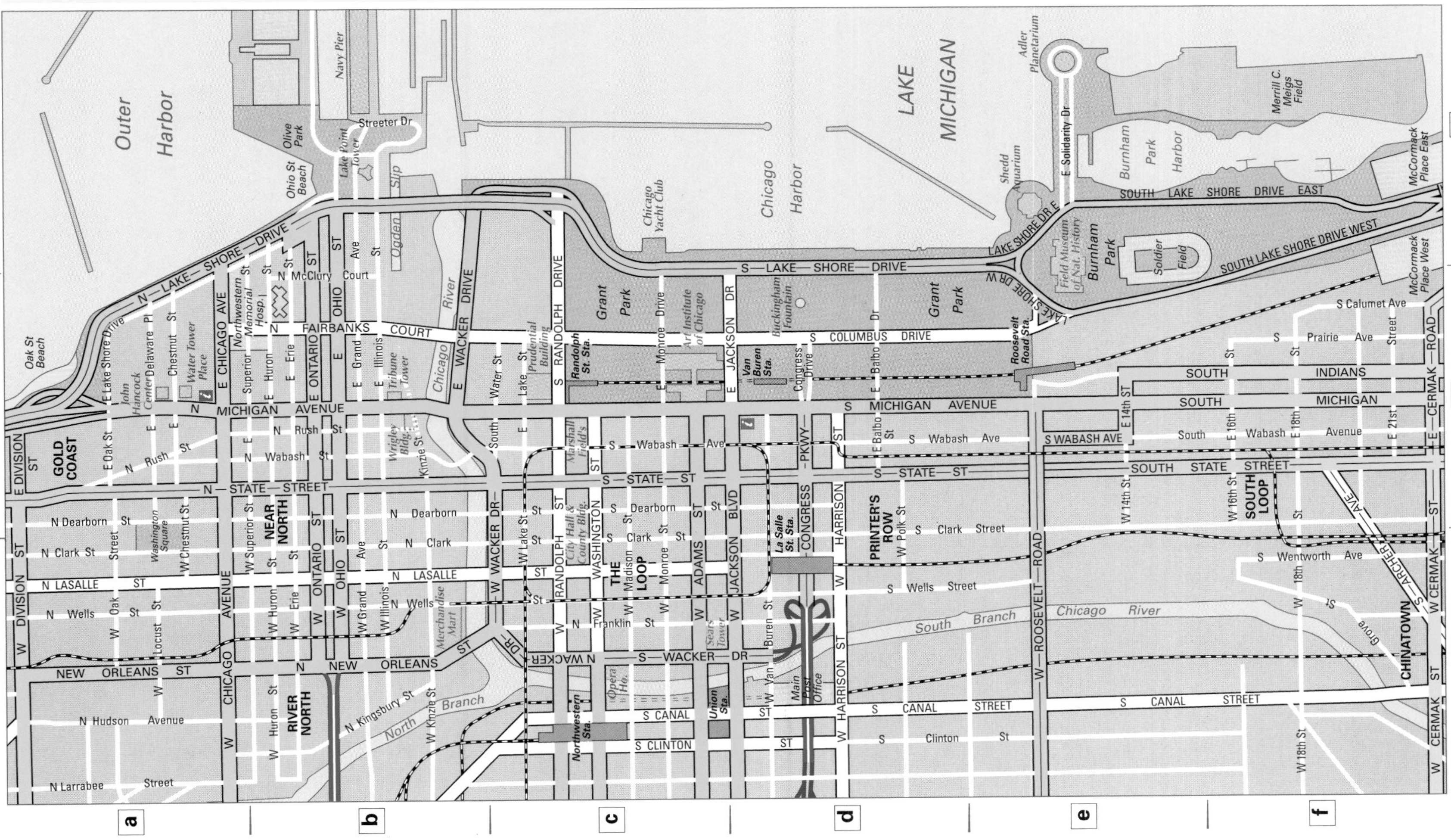

COPYRIGHT GEORGE PHILIP LTD.

Copenhagen

Central Copenhagen

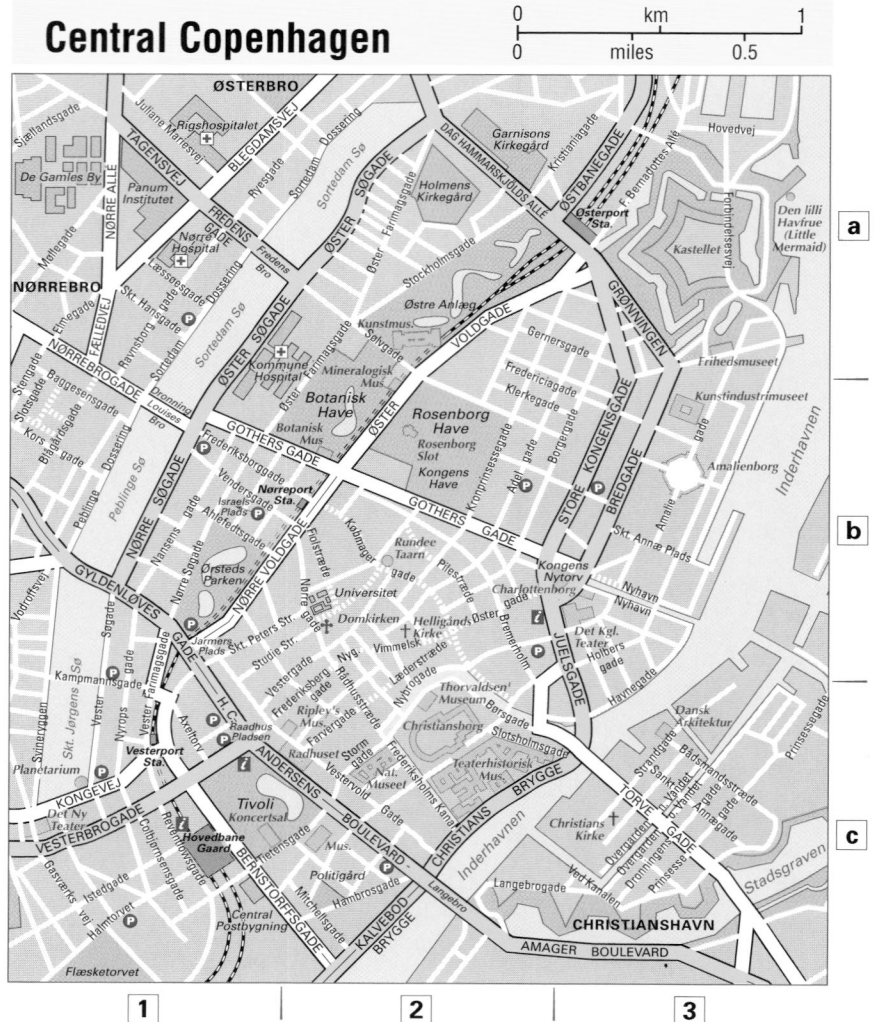

Delhi

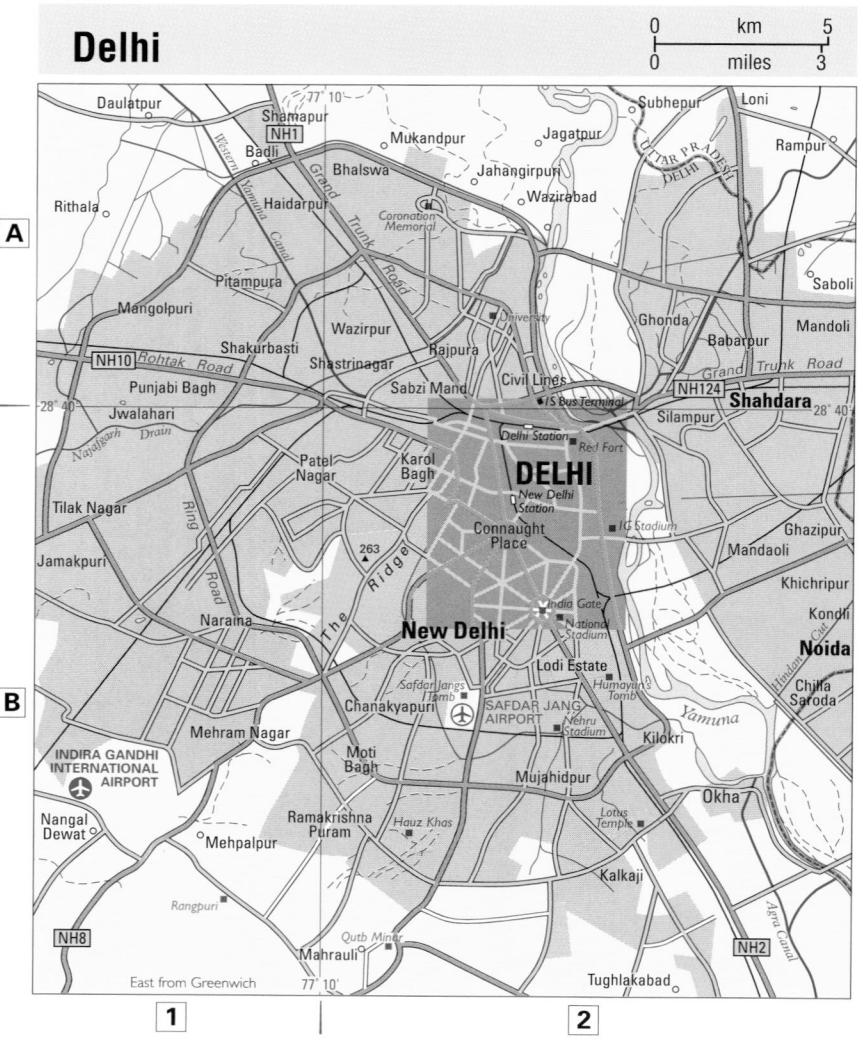

Central Delhi

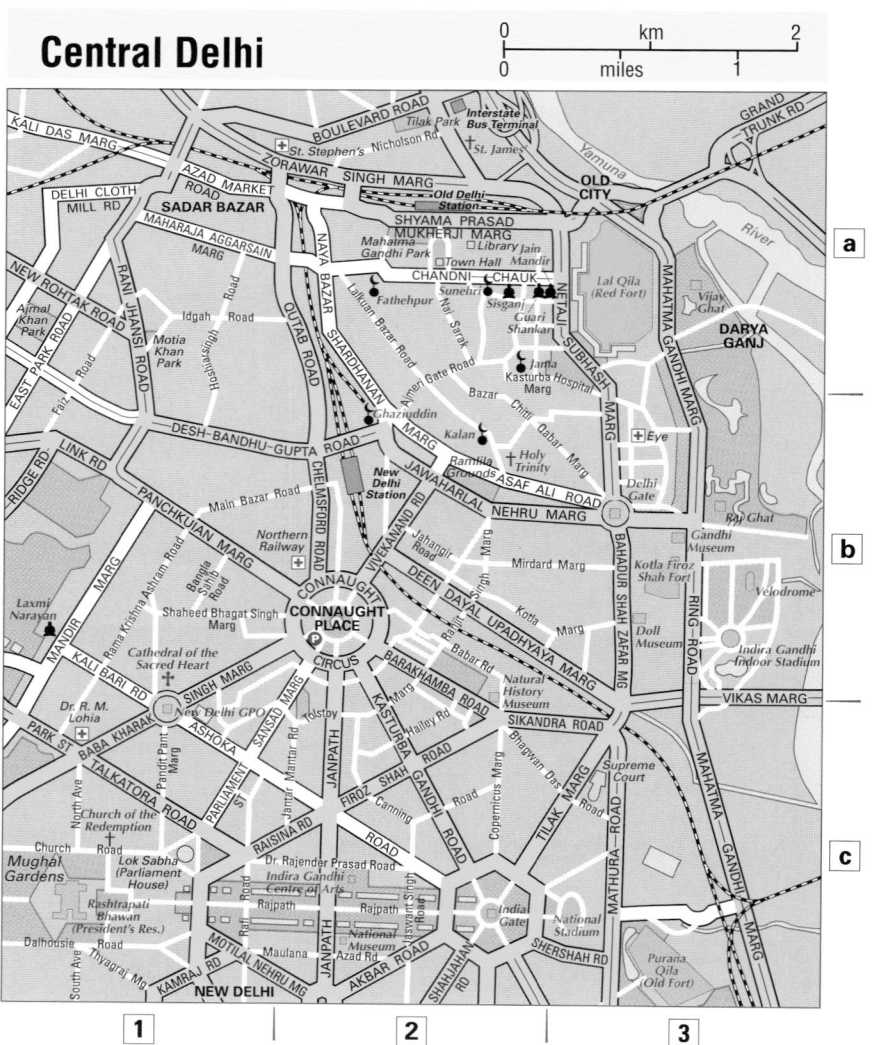

COPYRIGHT GEORGE PHILIP LTD.

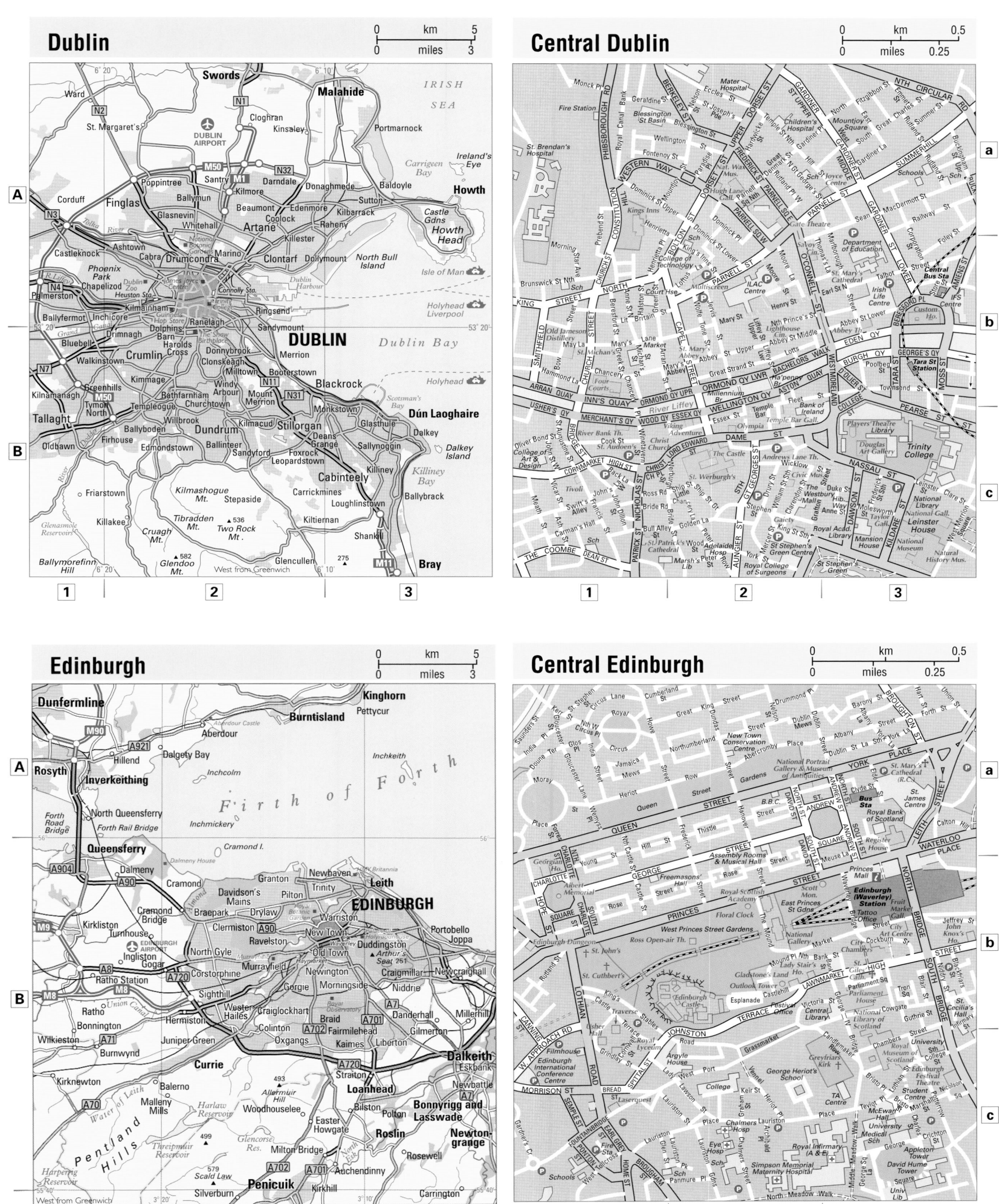
Dublin
0 km 5
0 miles 3
Swords
Malahide
IRISH SEA
Ward
St. Margaret's
Cloghran
DUBLIN AIRPORT
Kinsaley
Portmarnock
Ireland's Eye
Santry
Darndale
Donaghmede
Baldoyle
Howth
Poppintree
Corduff
Finglas
Ballymun
Kilmore
Beaumont
Edenmore
Sutton
Kilbarrack
Castle Gdns
Howth Head
Glasnevin
Coolock
Raheny
Whitehall
Artane
Killester
Castleknock
Ashtown
Cabra
Drumcondra
Marino
Clontarf
Dollymount
North Bull Island
Phoenix Park
Chapelizod
Isle of Man
Palmerston
Kilmainham
Ringsend
Holyhead Liverpool
Ballyfermot
Inchicore
Ranelagh
Sandymount
Drimnagh
Dolphins Barn
Harolds Cross
DUBLIN
Dublin Bay
Bluebell
Crumlin
Merrion
Walkinstown
Donnybrook
Clonskeagh
Milltown
Booterstown
Kilnamanagh
Kimmage
Blackrock
Greenhills
Rathfarnham
Windy Arbour
Mount Merrion
Holyhead
Tymon North
Templeogue
Churchtown
Monkstown
Dún Laoghaire
Tallaght
Willbrook
Kilmacud
Stillorgan
Glasthule
Ballyboden
Dundrum
Dalkey
Oldbawn
Firhouse
Deans Grange
Sallynoggin
Edmondstown
Ballinteer
Sandyford
Foxrock
Dalkey Island
Leopardstown
Cabinteely
Killiney
Killiney Bay
Friarstown
Kilmashogue Mt.
Stepaside
Carrickmines
Ballybrack
Loughlinstown
Killakee
Tibradden Mt.
536
Two Rock Mt.
Kiltiernan
Glenasmole Reservoirs
Cruagh Mt.
Shankill
Ballymorefinn Hill
582
Glendoo Mt.
West from Greenwich
Glencullen
275
Bray
1 2 3
A B

Central Dublin
0 km 0.5
0 miles 0.25
Trinity College
Central Bus Sta
Tara St Station
River Liffey
Dublin Castle
St. Patrick's Cathedral
1 2 3
a b c

Edinburgh
0 km 5
0 miles 3
Dunfermline
Kinghorn
Pettycur
Burntisland
Aberdour
Rosyth
Hillend
Dalgety Bay
Inchkeith
Inverkeithing
Inchcolm
Firth of Forth
North Queensferry
Forth Road Bridge
Forth Rail Bridge
Inchmickery
Queensferry
Cramond I.
Dalmeny
Newhaven
Cramond
Granton
Leith
Davidson's Mains
Trinity
Pilton
EDINBURGH
Kirkliston
Cramond Bridge
Braepark
Drylaw
Clermiston
Warriston
Portobello
Turnhouse
Ravelston
New Town
Joppa
EDINBURGH AIRPORT
Duddingston
Ingliston
North Gyle
Old Town
Arthur's Seat 251
Gogar
Murrayfield
Newington
Craigmillar
Newcraighall
Ratho Station
Corstorphine
Gorgie
Morningside
Niddrie
Sighthill
Ratho
Union Canal
Wester Hailes
Craiglockhart
Danderhall
Millerhill
Bonnington
Hermiston
Braid
Fairmilehead
Gilmerton
Wilkieston
Burnwynd
Colinton
Oxgangs
Kaimes
Liberton
Juniper Green
Dalkeith
Currie
Eskbank
Straiton
Kirknewton
Balerno
493
Allermuir Hill
Loanhead
Newbattle
Malleny Mills
Harlaw Reservoir
Woodhouselee
Bilston
Bonnyrigg and Lasswade
Polton
Easter Howgate
Roslin
Newtongrange
Pentland Hills
499
Threipmuir Reservoir
Glencorse Res.
Milton Bridge
Rosewell
579
Scald Law
Auchendinny
Harperrig Reservoir
Silverburn
Penicuik
Kirkhill
Carrington
West from Greenwich
1 2 3
A B

Central Edinburgh
0 km 0.5
0 miles 0.25
Edinburgh (Waverley) Station
Edinburgh Castle
Royal Mile
Princes Street
1 2 3
a b c

COPYRIGHT GEORGE PHILIP LTD.

Helsinki

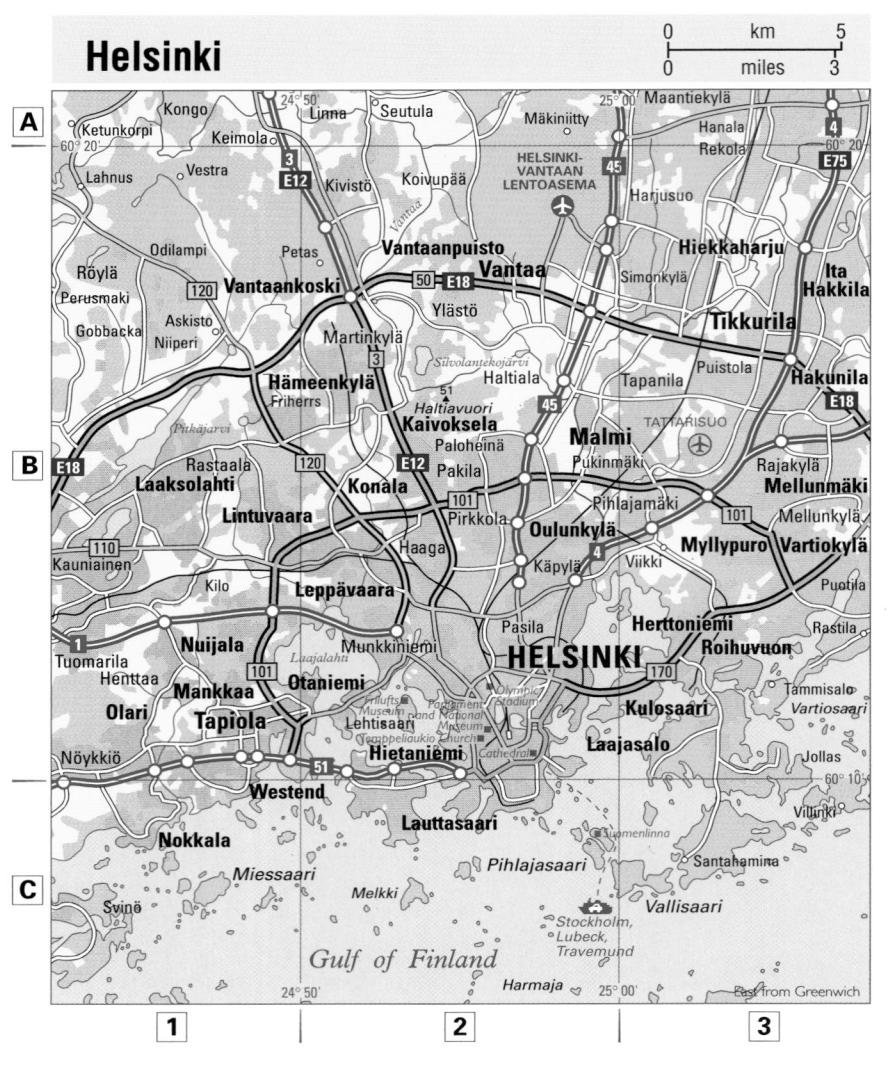

Istanbul

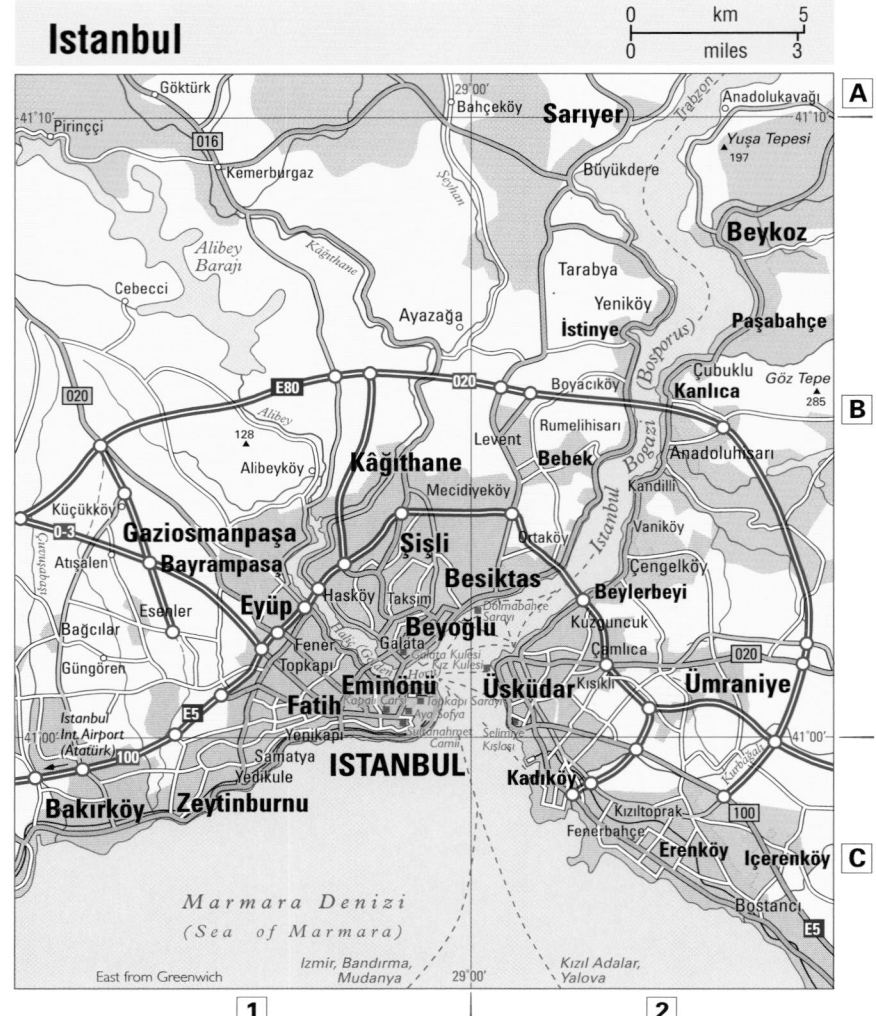

Hong Kong

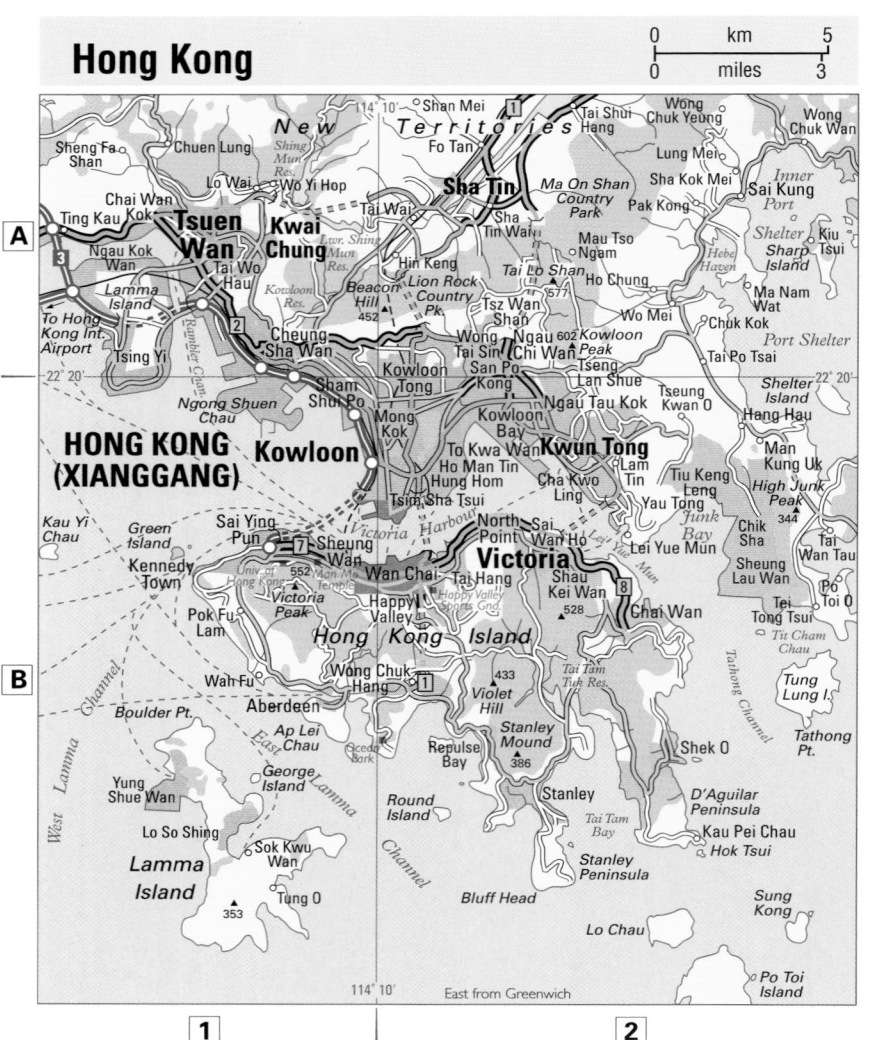

Central Hong Kong

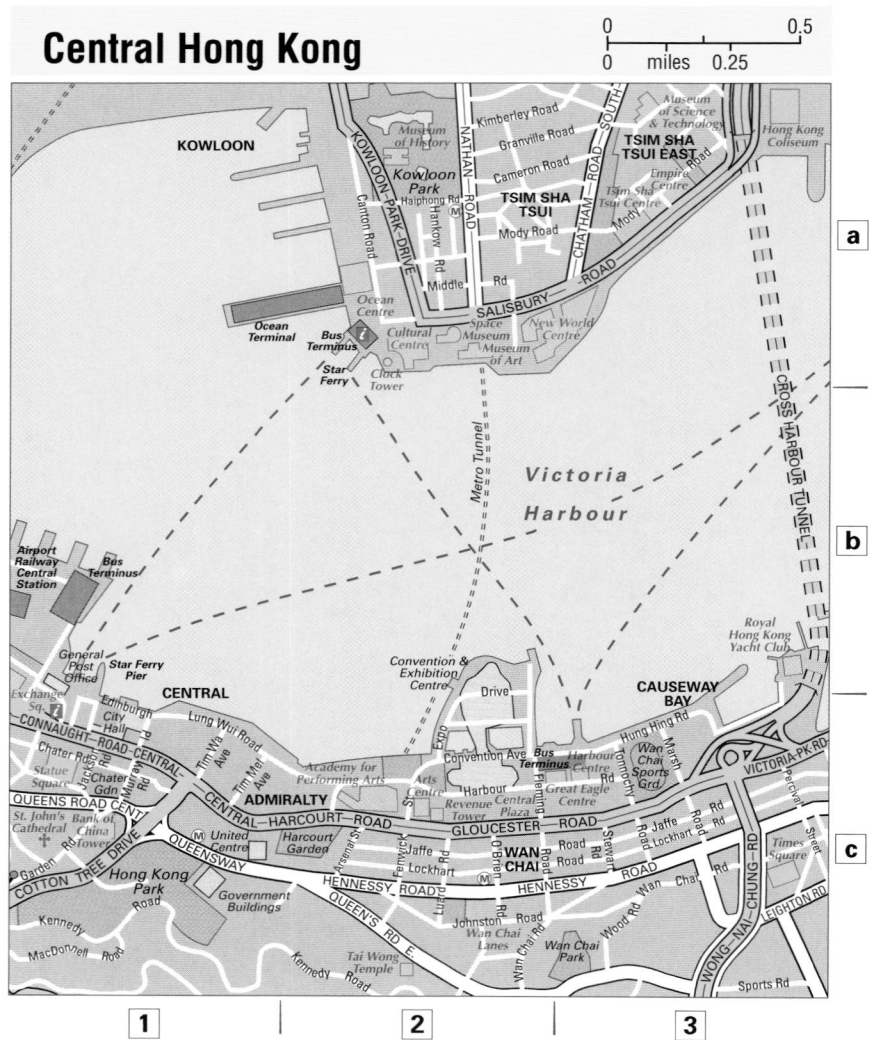

COPYRIGHT GEORGE PHILIP LTD.

Jerusalem

km 5 / miles 3

Deir Ibzi'e · Ein Arik · **Rām Allāh** · **El-Bira** · Deir Dibwan
Beit Ghur el-Fawqa · Pesagot · Burqa
455 · 60 · Ma'ale Mikhmas
Beitunya · 436 · ATAROT AIRPORT · Kafr 'Aqab · Mukhmas
443 · Giv'at Ze'ev · Qalandya · Judeira · Jaba · Geva Binyamin
Tira · Rafat
Beit I'nan · 832 · Ram · 60
Bidu · Beit Hanina · Hizma · Almon
Qatane · 815 · Har Adar · Beit Surik · Ramot · Shu'afat
Ma'ale Ha-Khamisha · Beit Nekofa · Beit Iksa
Abu Ghosh · 1 · Mevaseret Tsiyon · WEST BANK ISRAEL · Anata · 1
Ein Naquba · Ein Rafa · 821 · Motsa Ilit · Motsa · **JERUSALEM (Yerushalayim) (Al Quds)** · Eizariya
Giv'at Ye'arim · Tsova · Beit Zayit · National Hebrew University · Israel Museum · Mt of Olives · Ma'ale Adumim
Even Sapir · Ora · Aminadav · Old City · Railway Station · Abu Dis · Kedar
785
Bar Giyora · Mevo Beitar · Batir · Khirbet Jub e-Rum
Tsur Hadassa · Gilo
Wadi Fukin · Beitar Ilit · El-Khadr · **Bethlehem (Bayt Laḥm) (Beit Lekhem)** · Ubeidiya
Rachel's Tomb · Beit Jala · Beit Sahur · Basilica of Nativity
1949 Cease fire line · Daheisha · 60 · Artas

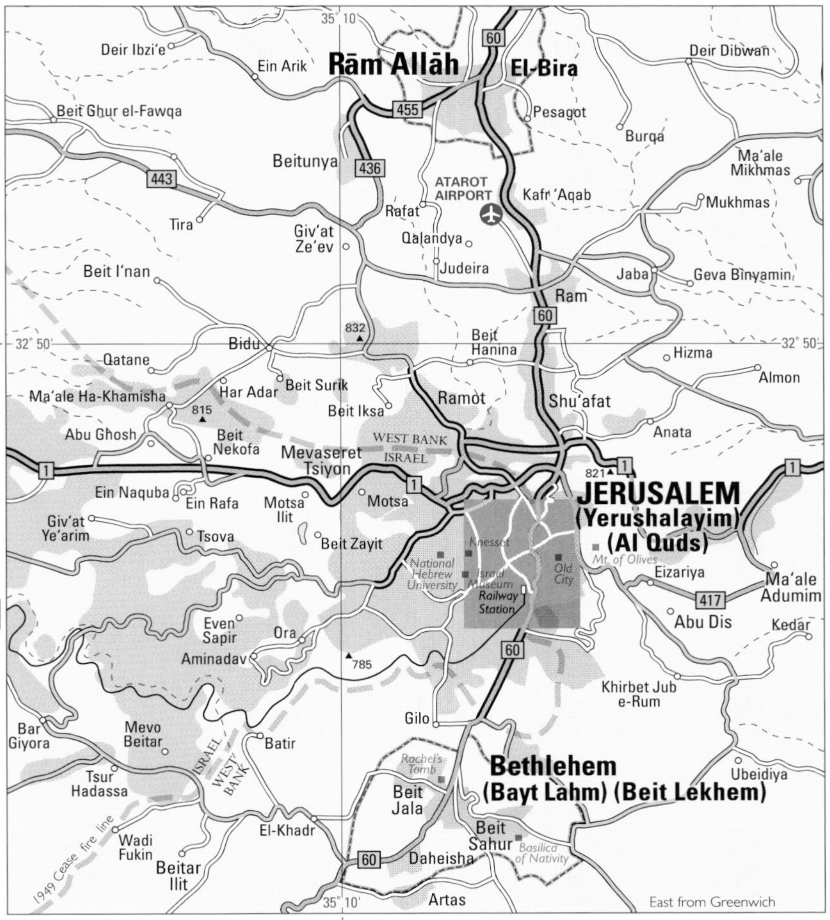

East from Greenwich

Central Jerusalem

km 1 / miles 0.5

YIRMIYAHU · BAR ILAN · Zayit Ra'anan · Shim'on Ha · DEREKI HA SHALOM · Tomb of the Kings · Shemi el Ben 'Adaya
Rehovot · SHEMU'EL HA NAVI · St George's Cathedral · Rockefeller Museum · Tomb of Virgin St Mary
Zefanya · NATHAN STRAUSS · St George's Salah'd A Din · Herod's Gate · St Stephen's Gate
Rashi · Yellin · **ME'A SHE' ARIM** · SULEIMAN · **MUSLIM QUARTER**
Ha Turim · Yafo · Ha Nevi'im · Damascus Gate · Via Dolorosa · Church of All Nations
Agripas · Yafo · Ben Yehuda · Holy Sepulchre · **OLD CITY** · **TEMPLE MOUNT** Dome of the Rock
Convention Hall · Betsal'el · Hillel · **CHRISTIAN QUARTER** · Western Wall · Al-Aqsa Mosque
Sacker Park · Independence Park · Jaffa Gate · David's Citadel · **ARMENIAN QUARTER** · **JEWISH QUARTER** · Dung Gate
President's Park · Knesset · Hekhal Shlomo · **YEMIN MOSHE** · David's Tomb · Mount Zion · **SILWAN**
Israel Museum · Monastery of the Cross · Museum of Islamic Art · Mishkenot Shaananim · President's Residence · Bloomfield Park · En Roge!
Abraham Granot · Bezalel Bank · Railway Sta. · Gikhon Na'omi · Peace Forest
EMEK REFA'IM
GONEN

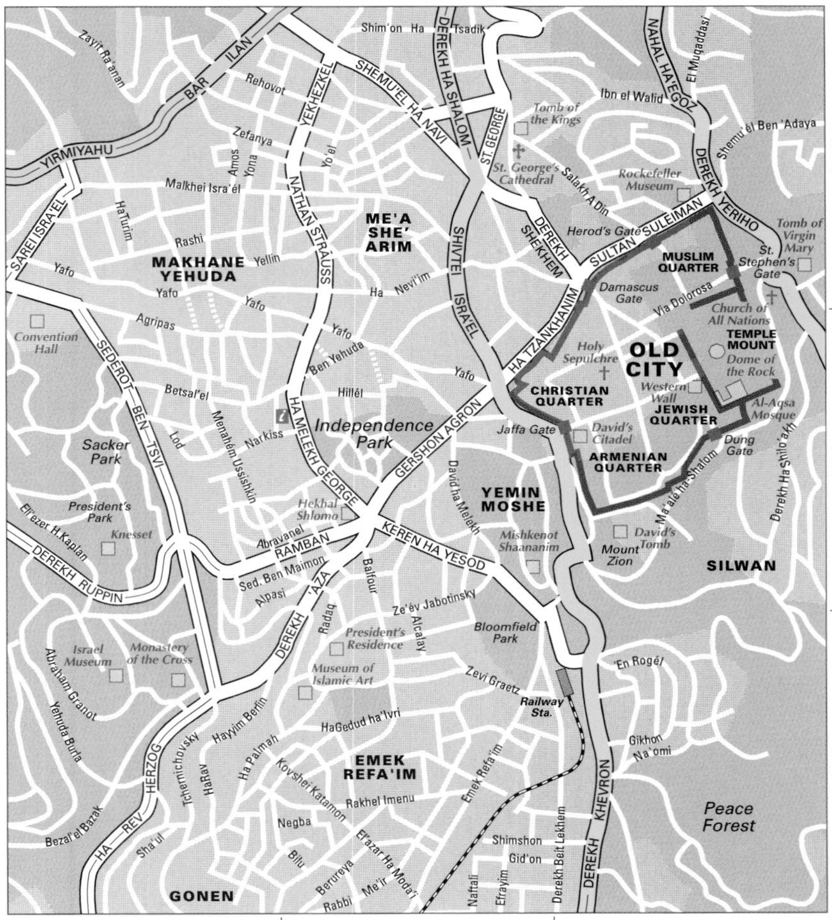

Jakarta

km 5 / miles 3

J A V A S E A

Sukarno-Hatta Int. Airport · Waduk Pluit · *Teluk Jakarta* · Koja Utara
Penjaringan · Sunda Kelapa Harbour · Taman Impian Jaya Ancol · Cilincing
Cengkareng · Ancol · Tanjung Priok · Koja
Kota · International Trade Centre · Sunter
Tambora · Taman Sari · Sawah Besar · **JAKARTA**
Grogol Petamburin · Gambir · Istiqlal Mosque · Kemayoran · Sunter
Tanjung Daren · National Monument/National Museum · Gambir Station · Cathedral · Kayu Putih
Kebon Jeruk · Orchid Palace · Slipi · Kampung I Bali · Welcome Monument · Senen · Cempaka Putih · Race Course
Parliament House · Tanah Abang · Menteng · Taman Ismail Marzuki · University · Pulo Gadung
Olympic Stadium · Setia Budi · Matraman · Rawamangun
Kebayoran Lama · Kebayoran Baru · Kuningan · Jatinegara
Psangrahan · Kemang · Tebet
Pondok Indah · Cipete · Mampang Prapatan · Kramat Jati · **HALIM PERDANAKUSUMA INTERNATIONAL AIRPORT**
Cilandak · Pasar Minggu

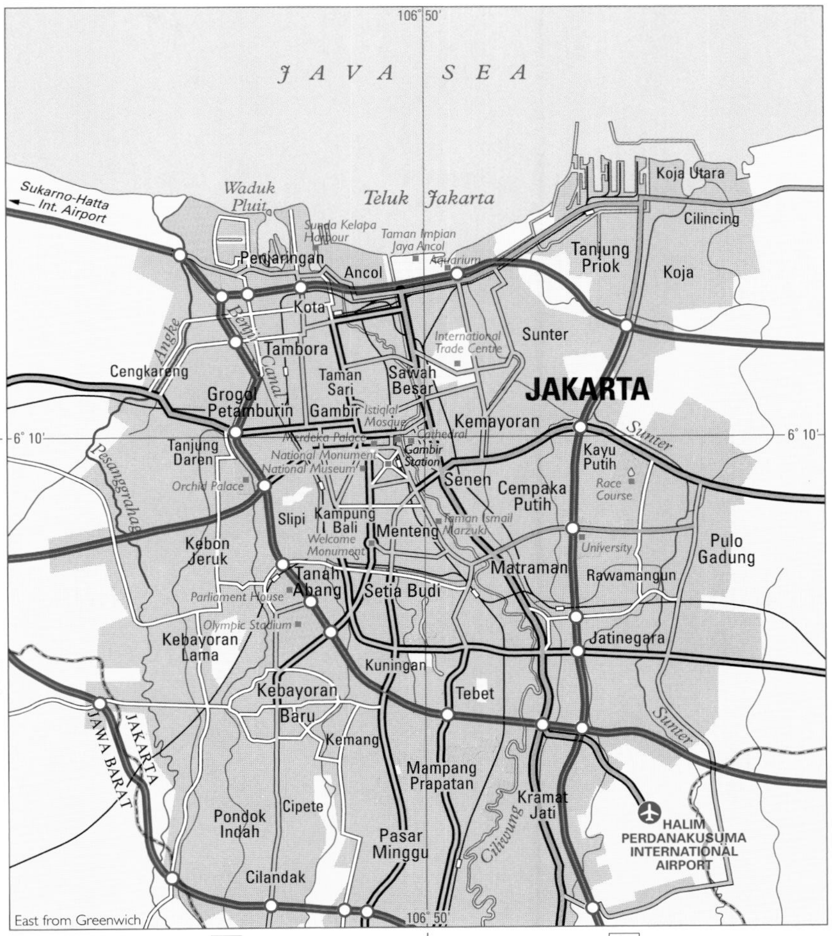

East from Greenwich

Johannesburg

km 5 / miles 3

Bryanston · N1 · R55 · Morningside · Kelvin · N3
Randburg · R27 · **Sandton** · Modderfontein · Linbropark
Randpark Ridge · Ferndale · Parkmore · Sandown · **Alexandra** · Lakeside
Weltevreden Park · Fontainebleau · Blairgowrie · Hyde Park · M1 · Lombardy East · R25
Windsor · Florence Bloom Bird Sanctuary · Craighall Park · Atholl · Bramley · **Edenvale**
Fairland · Linden · Parkhurst · Waverley · Highlands North · R25 · Dunvegan · Jan Smuts Airport
Quellerina · Northcliff · Parktown North · Parkwood · Norwood · Sydenham
N1 · Emmarentia Park · Parkview · Zoo · Houghton · Linksfield
West Park · The Wilds · Observatory · Bezuidenhout Park · R24 · Bedfordview
Florida · Newlands · Westdene · Westcliff · Parktown · Post Office Tower · 11 · N3
Bosmont · Auckland Park · Univ. of Witwatersrand · **JOHANNESBURG** · Kensington · Primrose
R24 · Industria · Crosby · Mayfair · Doornfontein · Malvern · R29
New Canada Dam · Riverlea · Selby · M2 · **Germiston** · Simmer and Jack Mines Victoria Lake
Noordgesig · New Canada · Crown Mine · Ophirton · Wemmer Pan · 31 · Rosherville Dam · RAND AIRPORT
Soweto · Soccer Stadium · Gold Reef City · M1 · Race Course · Regents Park · South Hills
Orlando East · Diepkloof · National Exhibition Centre · Turffontein · Rosettenville
Orlando Dam · Robertsham · Linmeyer · **Alberton**
M70 · Mondeor · 1818 · Randhart · Florentia
M27 · Meredale · Glenvista · N3
N1 · Klipriviersberg Nature Reserve · Kibler Park · Mulbarton · R26 · Meyersdal · Alrode

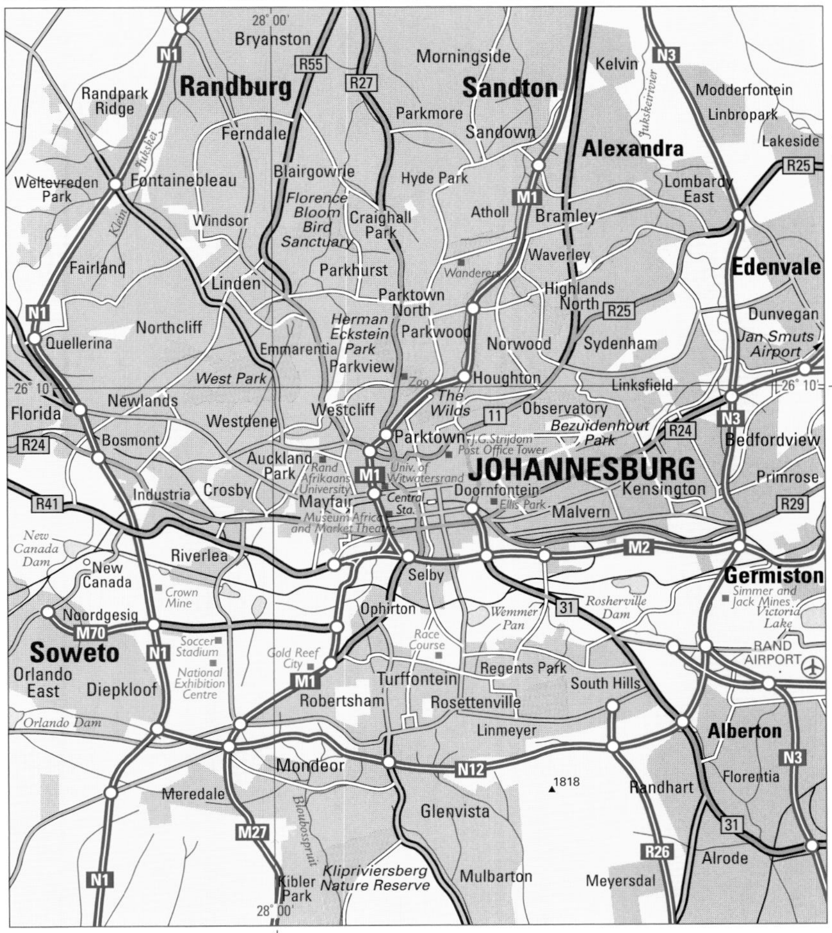

COPYRIGHT GEORGE PHILIP LTD.

Karachi

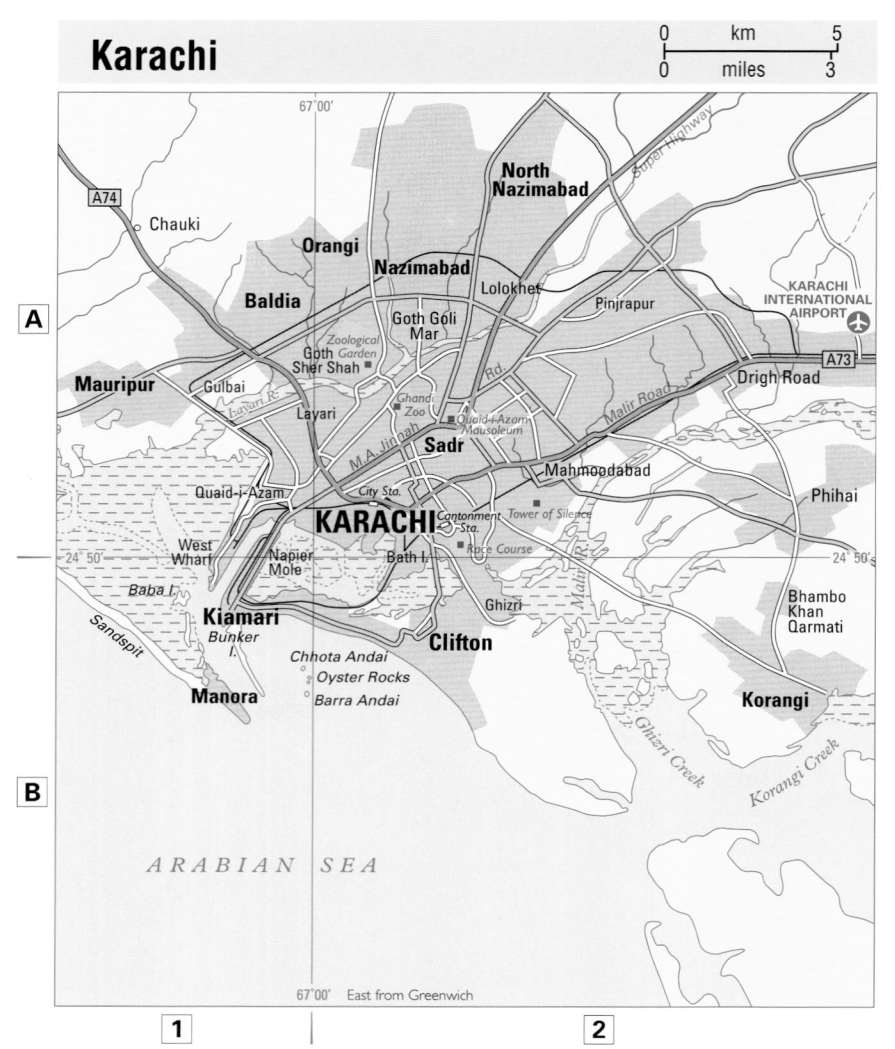

Lagos

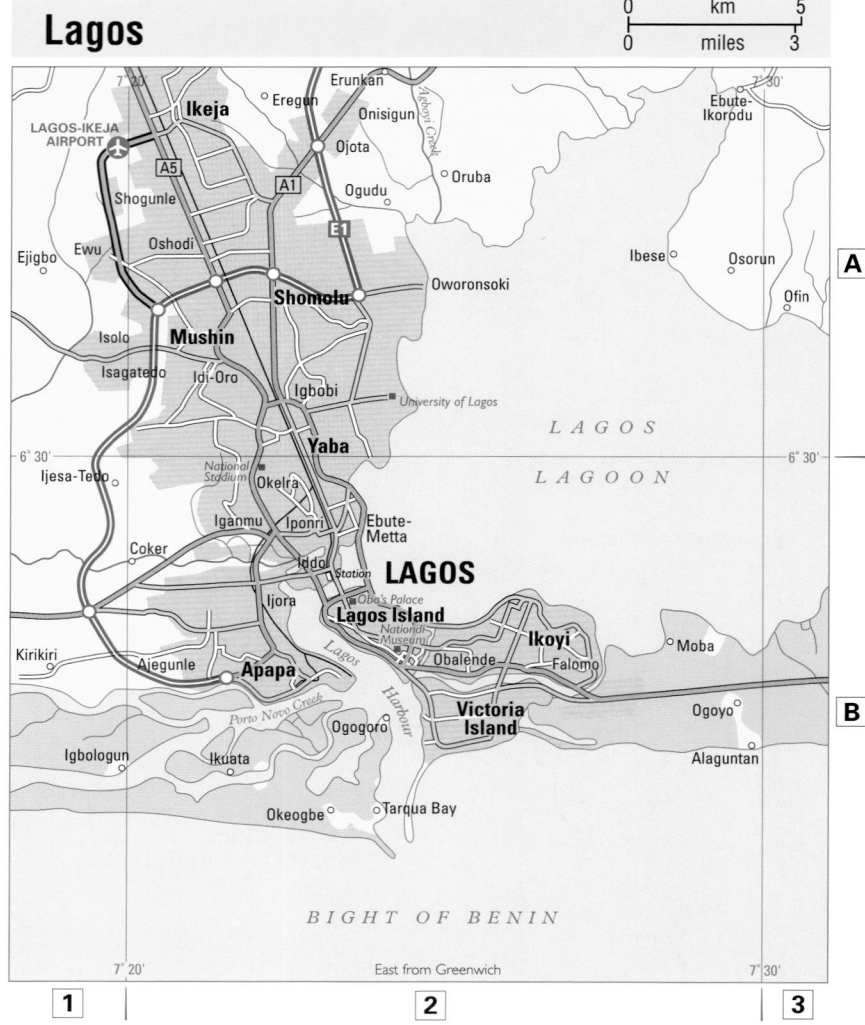

Lisbon

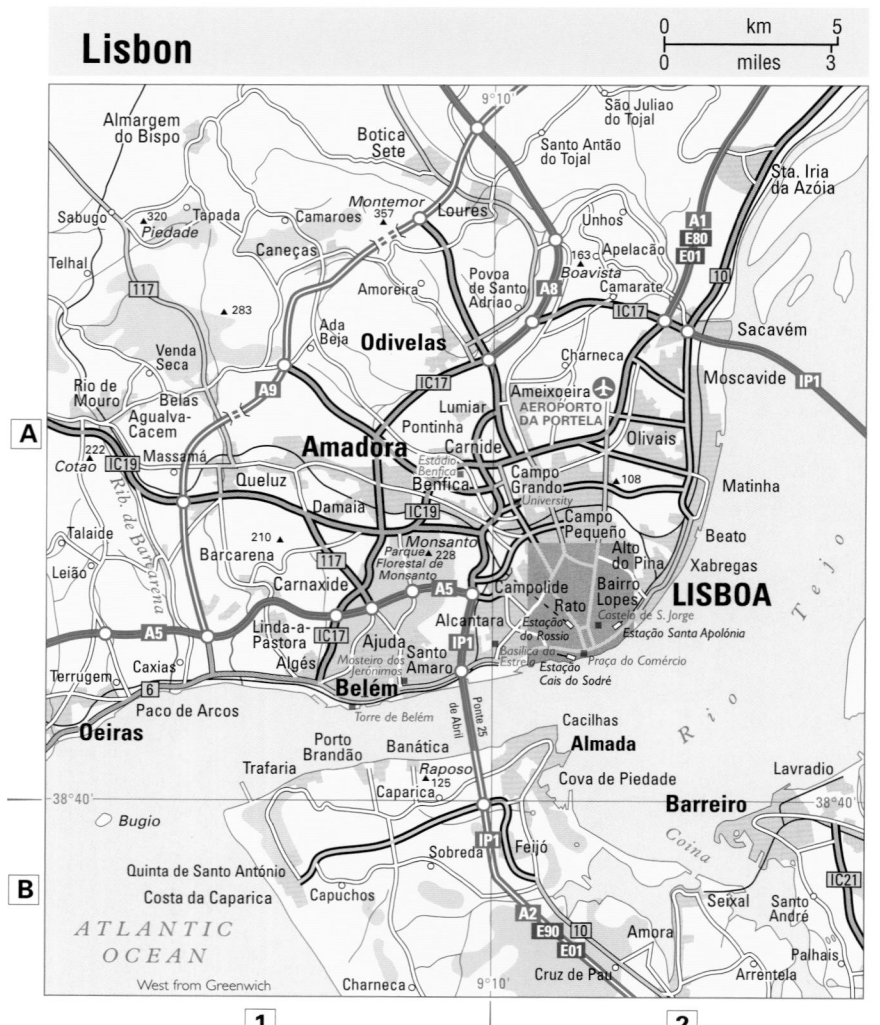

Central Lisbon

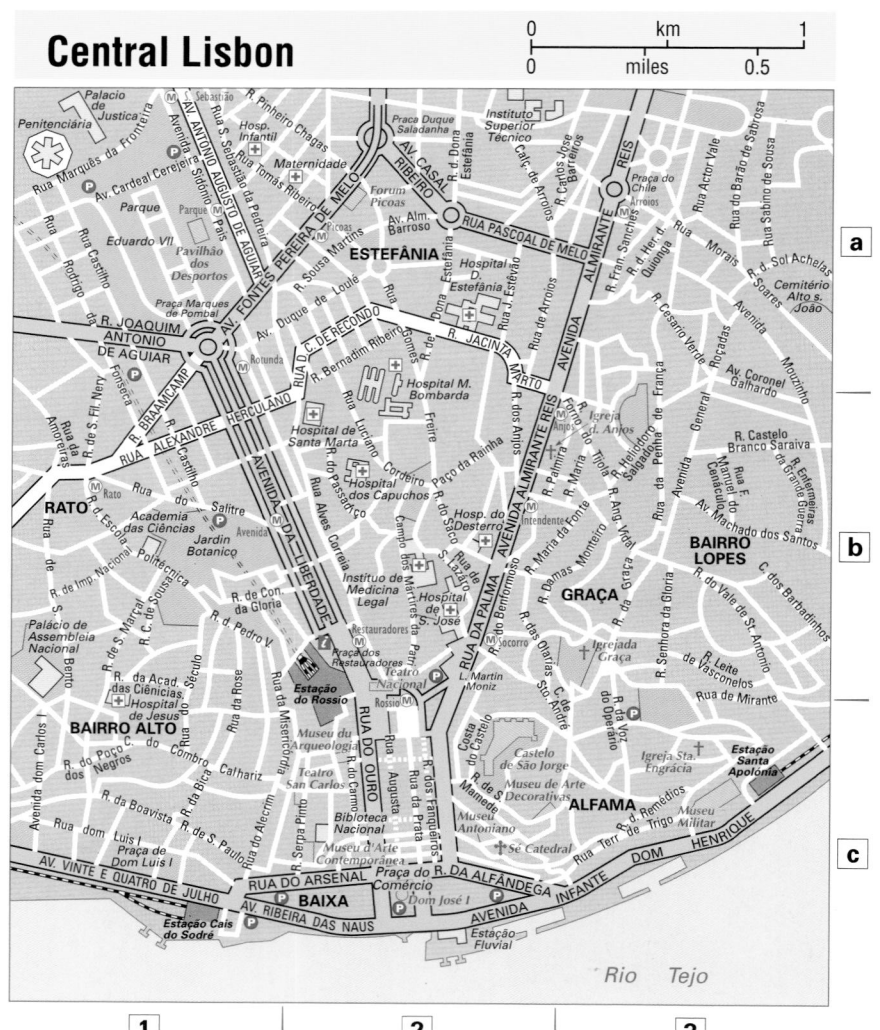

COPYRIGHT GEORGE PHILIP LTD.

London

km 0 — 5
miles 0 — 3

Northwood, Pinner Green, Ruislip Common, Eastcote, Ruislip, Rayners Lane, Ickenham, South Ruislip, Hillingdon, Cowley, Hayes End, Hayes, West Drayton, Sipson, Harlington, Cranford, HEATHROW AIRPORT, West Bedfont, Ashford, Feltham, Hanworth, Hampton, Sunbury-on-Thames, Shepperton, Walton on Thames, Weybridge, Esher

Hatch End, Harrow Weald, Pinner, Wealdstone, Harrow, Greenhill, Kenton, Northolt, Perivale, Greenford, Southall, Hanwell, Ealing, Acton, Gunnersbury, Turnham Green, Chiswick, Brentford, Isleworth, Hounslow, Twickenham, Whitton, East Bedfont, Teddington, Bushy Park, Hampton Wick, Hampton Court Palace, East Molesey, West Molesey, Thames Ditton, Long Ditton, Surbiton, Tolworth, Hook

Stanmore, Belmont, Queensbury, Colindale, Hendon, Wembley, Sudbury, Alperton, Kingsbury, Cricklewood, Willesden, Harlesden, Kensal Green, Kilburn, Park Royal

Mill Hill, Burnt Oak, Colney Hatch, Barnet, Finchley, Church End, East Finchley, Muswell Hill, Highgate, Hampstead Heath, Hampstead Garden Suburb, Golders Green, Child's Hill, Dollis Hill, Hampstead, Regent's Park, St John's Wood, Paddington, Notting Hill, Shepherd's Bush, Hammersmith, Kensington, Chelsea, Fulham, Putney, Barnes, Mortlake, Kew Gardens, Richmond, Richmond upon Thames, Roehampton, East Sheen, Mortlake

Wood Green, Hornsey, Crouch End, Stamford Hill, Finsbury Park, Stoke Newington, Highbury, Holloway, Tufnell Park, Kentish Town, Camden, Islington, Dalston, Clapton, Hackney, Homerton, Bethnal Green, Shoreditch, Finsbury, City, LONDON, Westminster, Southwark, Bermondsey, Rotherhithe, Deptford, Camberwell, Peckham, New Cross, Brockley, Nunhead, Vauxhall, Lambeth, Battersea, Clapham, Brixton, Herne Hill, Dulwich

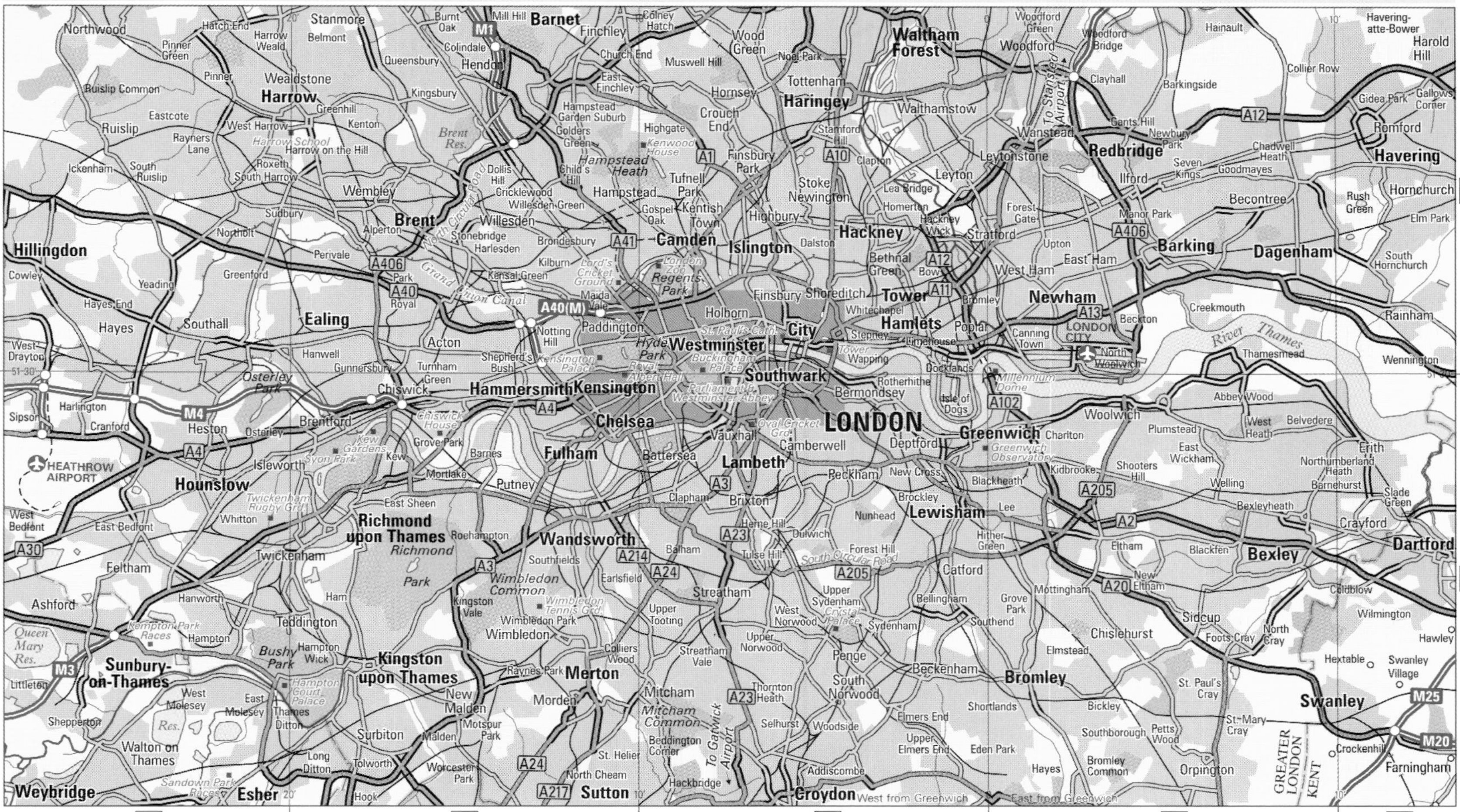

Waltham Forest, Woodford, Wanstead, Leyton, Leytonstone, Stratford, West Ham, East Ham, Upton, Manor Park, Canning Town, Poplar, Isle of Dogs, Greenwich, Charlton, Woolwich, Blackheath, Lewisham, Catford, Lee, Eltham, Mottingham

Haringey, Tottenham, Walthamstow, Hackney, Tower Hamlets, Wapping, Newham, Barking, Dagenham, Redbridge, Ilford, Goodmayes, Seven Kings, Becontree, Chadwell Heath

Romford, Gidea Park, Harold Hill, Havering, Hornchurch, Elm Park, Rainham, Wennington, Thamesmead, Abbey Wood, Belvedere, Erith, Northumberland Heath, Slade Green, Crayford, Dartford, Bexleyheath, Welling, Bexley, Sidcup, Blackfen, Chislehurst, Bromley, Beckenham, Penge, Sydenham, Forest Hill, Streatham, Wandsworth, Wimbledon, Merton, Morden, Mitcham, Sutton, Croydon, Kingston upon Thames, New Malden, Worcester Park, North Cheam, Carshalton, Wallington, Purley, Coulsdon, Orpington, Petts Wood, St Mary Cray, St Paul's Cray, Swanley, Farningham, Crockenhall, Hextable, Swanley Village, Wilmington

GREATER LONDON KENT

Rivers: River Thames, Grand Union Canal, Regent's Canal

Motorways/Roads: M1, M4, M3, M25, M20, A1, A10, A12, A13, A40(M), A41, A406, A2, A20, A205, A214, A23, A24, A3, A217, A102

Grid: A B along left and right edges; 1 2 3 4 5 along bottom

Central London

km 0 — 2
miles 0 — 1

KENSAL RISE, WEST KILBURN, MAIDA VALE, WESTBOURNE GREEN, ST JOHN'S WOOD, Queen's Park, Kilburn, Lord's Cricket Ground, REGENT'S PARK, London Zoo, Open Air Theatre, Queen Mary's Gardens, London Mosque, Madame Tussaud's, Marylebone, Planetarium, PADDINGTON, BAYSWATER, NOTTING HILL, Westbourne Park, Royal Oak, Notting Hill Gate, KENSINGTON GARDENS, HYDE PARK, Kensington Palace, Serpentine Gallery, Apsley House & Wellington Mus., MAYFAIR, HOLLAND PARK, Holland Park, KENSINGTON, Commonwealth Institute, Olympia, Olympia Exhibition Hall, KNIGHTSBRIDGE, Royal Albert Hall, Imperial Coll. of Science, Victoria & Albert Mus., Nat. History & Geological Mus., Brompton Oratory, BROMPTON, BELGRAVIA, SOUTH KENSINGTON, WEST KENSINGTON, Earl's Court Exhibition Hall, Hammersmith Cemetery, CHELSEA, Chelsea Royal Hosp., Nat. Army Mus., PIMLICO, Victoria Coach Sta., Victoria, Westminster Cath., Westminster Abbey, Tate Britain

BLOOMSBURY, British Museum, HOLBORN, SOHO, Oxford Circus, Piccadilly Circus, Leicester Sq., Covent Gdn., Transport Mus., ST JAMES'S, Royal Acad., St James's Palace, St James's Park, Green Park, Buckingham Palace, Queen's Gall., Trafalgar Sq., Charing Cross, National Gall., Banqueting House, Downing Street, Horse Guards, Cabinet War Rooms, Houses of Parliament, St Thomas's Hosp., Lambeth Palace, LAMBETH, Imperial War Mus., KENNINGTON, Oval Cricket Gd., The Oval, WALWORTH, KENNINGTON

Euston, St Pancras, King's Cross, King's Cross Thameslink, British Lib., CLERKENWELL, Farringdon, HOXTON, SHOREDITCH, Old Street, Wesley's Chapel, Barbican, Moorgate, Mus. of London, Liverpool St, Whitechapel Art Gall., CITY, St Paul's, Bank, Aldgate, Mansion House, Cannon St, Fenchurch St, Leadenhall, Monument, Tower of London, Tower Gateway (DLR), River Thames, SOUTHWARK, Tate Modern, Southwark Cath., London Bridge, Borough, HMS Belfast, London Dungeon, Guy's Hosp., The Design Museum, BERMONDSEY, NEWINGTON, Elephant & Castle, NEW KENT RD, Waterloo International, Waterloo East, BFI London IMAX, National, Royal Festival Hall, Qn. Elizabeth Hall, Hayward Gall.

Grid: a b c along left and right edges; 1 2 3 4 5 along bottom

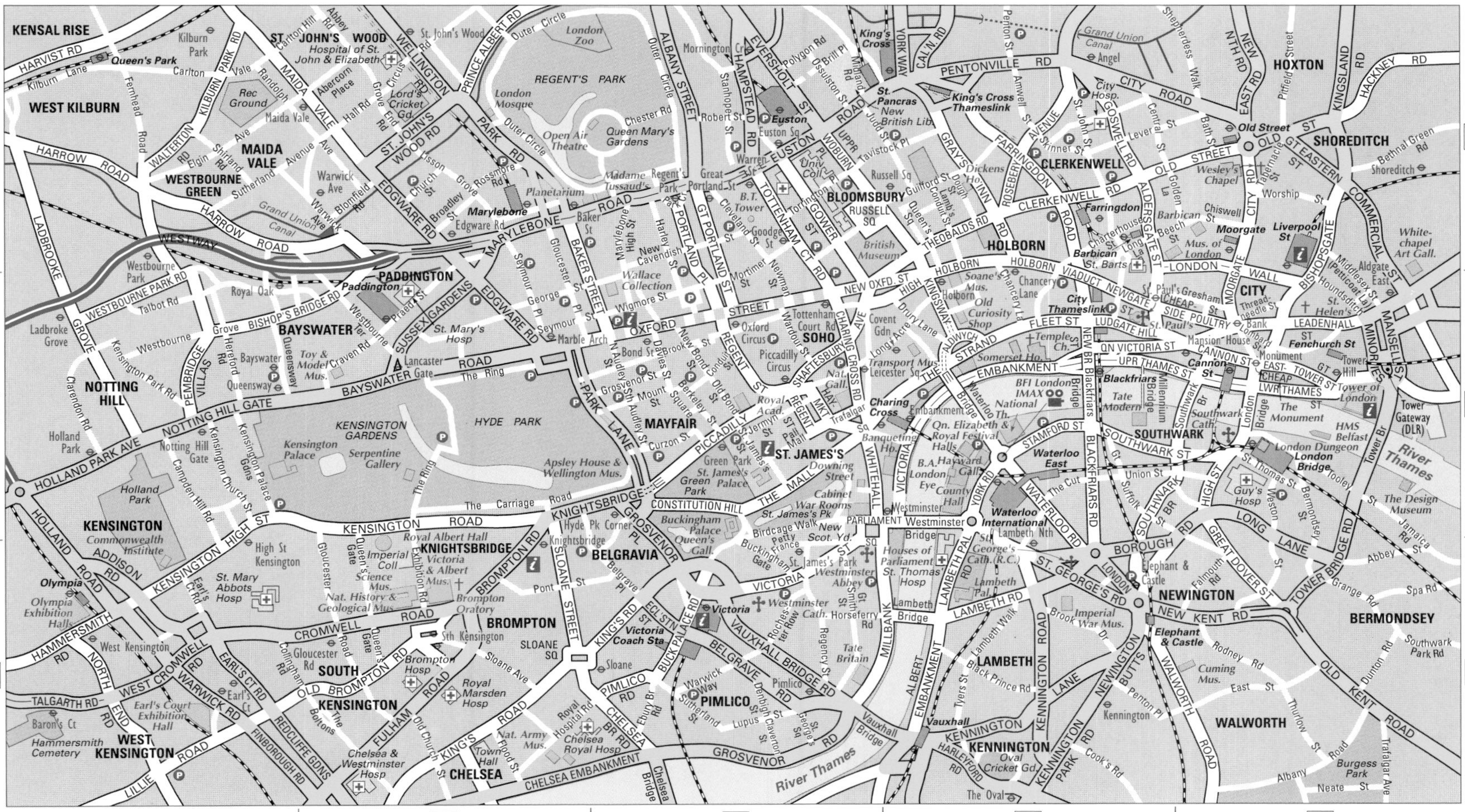

COPYRIGHT GEORGE PHILIP LTD.

Los Angeles

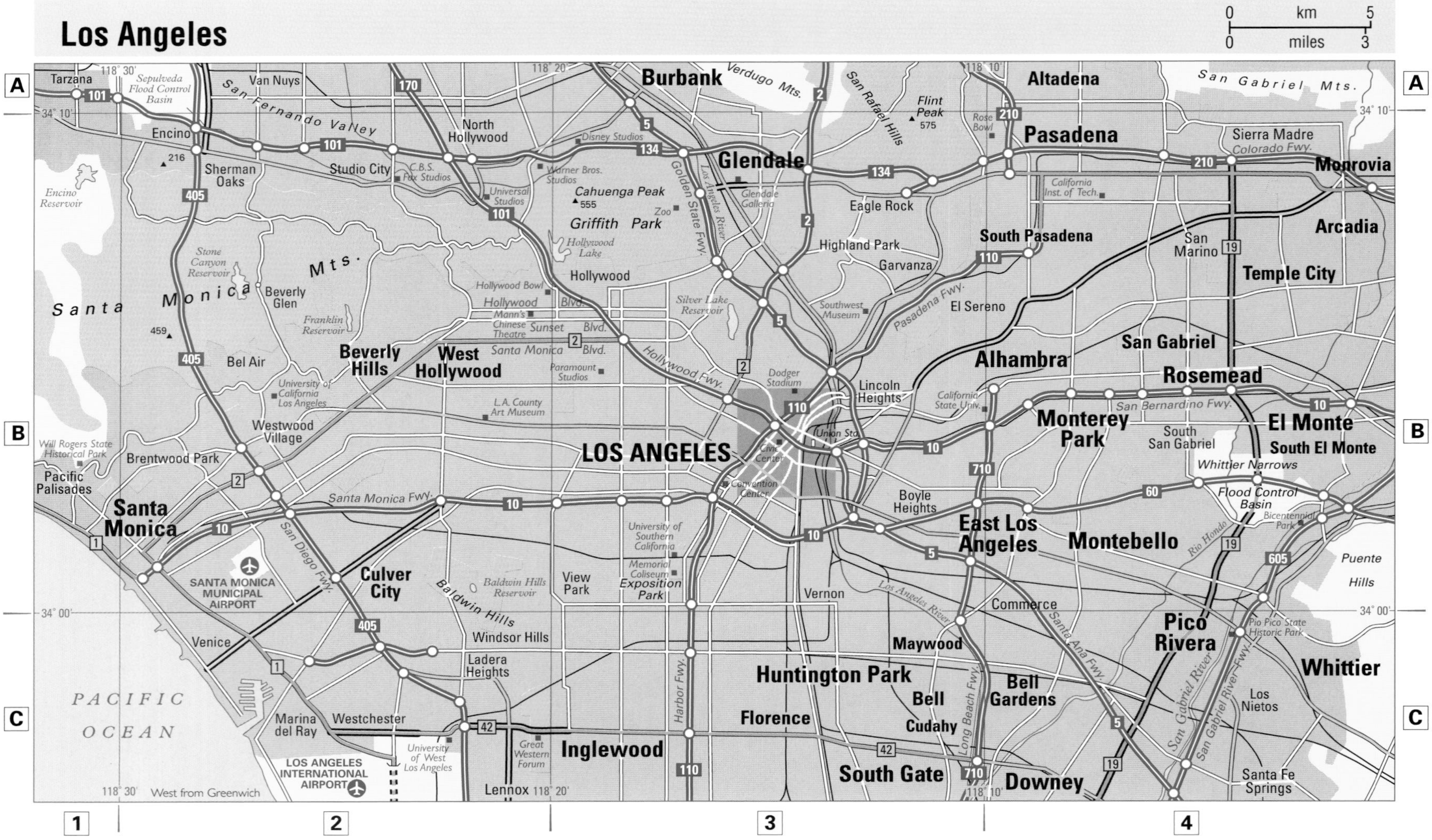

0 km 5
0 miles 3

Tarzana · 118° 30'
101
Sepulveda Flood Control Basin
Van Nuys
170
North Hollywood
Burbank
Verdugo Mts.
2
San Rafael Hills
Flint Peak 575
Altadena
210
San Gabriel Mts.
A

34° 10'
Encino
101
216
Sherman Oaks
405
Studio City
C.B.S.
Disney Studios
5
134
Warner Bros. Studios
Universal Studios
Glendale
Glendale Galleria
134
California Inst. of Tech
Pasadena
Sierra Madre Colorado Fwy.
210
Monrovia

Encino Reservoir
Stone Canyon Reservoir
459 ▲
Cahuenga Peak 555 ▲
Griffith Park
Hollywood Lake
Golden State Fwy.
L.A. River
2
Eagle Rock
Highland Park
Garvanza
South Pasadena
110
El Sereno
Southwest Museum
San Marino
19
Arcadia
Temple City

Santa Monica Mts.
Beverly Glen
Franklin Reservoir
Hollywood Bowl
Hollywood
Mann's Chinese Theatre
Sunset Blvd.
Hollywood Blvd.
Paramount Studios
Santa Monica Blvd.
2
Sunset Blvd.
Silver Lake Reservoir
5
Dodger Stadium
Lincoln Heights
California State Univ.
Alhambra
San Gabriel
Rosemead
10

405
Bel Air
University of California Los Angeles
Beverly Hills
West Hollywood
L.A. County Art Museum
110
LOS ANGELES
Union Sta.
Civic Center
Monterey Park
South San Gabriel
San Bernardino Fwy.
Whittier Narrows
El Monte
South El Monte
B

34° 10'
Westwood Village
Brentwood Park
2
Will Rogers State Historical Park
Pacific Palisades
Santa Monica Fwy.
10
Convention Center
University of Southern California
Memorial Coliseum Exposition Park
Boyle Heights
60
10
East Los Angeles
710
Montebello
Rio Hondo
Flood Control Basin
Bicentennial Park
19
605
Puente Hills

Santa Monica
10
1
San Diego Fwy.
SANTA MONICA MUNICIPAL AIRPORT
Culver City
Baldwin Hills Reservoir
Windsor Hills
View Park
405
Vernon
Commerce
Los Angeles River
Santa Ana Fwy.
Maywood
Pico Rivera
Pio Pico State Historic Park
Los Nietos
Whittier
34° 00'

Venice
1
Ladera Heights
Baldwin Hills
Huntington Park
Florence
Bell
Cudahy
Bell Gardens
Long Beach Fwy.
5
Santa Fe Springs
C

PACIFIC OCEAN
Marina del Rey
Westchester
42
University of West Los Angeles
Great Western Forum
Inglewood
110
42
Harbor Fwy.
South Gate
710
Downey
19

LOS ANGELES INTERNATIONAL AIRPORT
Lennox · 118° 20'
118° 10'

118° 30' West from Greenwich

1   2   3   4

Lima

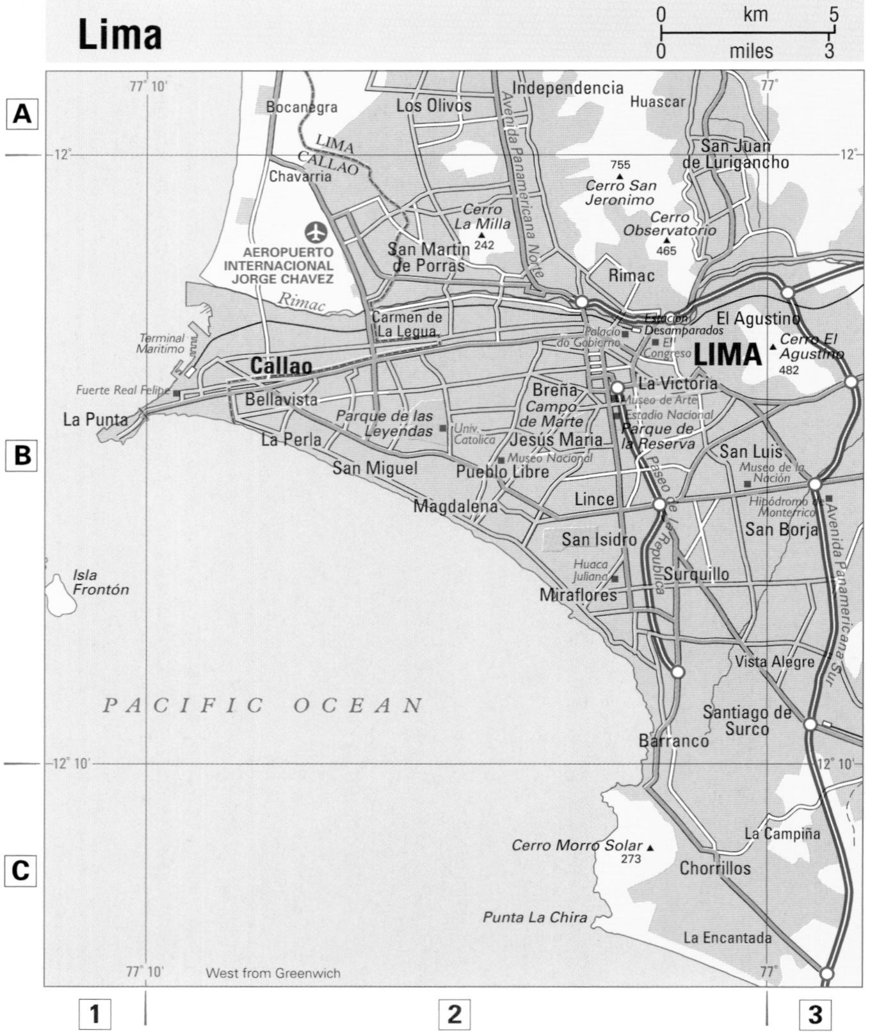

0 km 5
0 miles 3

Bocanegra
Los Olivos
Independencia
Huascar
77°
A

77° 10'
12°
LIMA CALLAO
Chavarria
AEROPUERTO INTERNACIONAL JORGE CHAVEZ
San Martin de Porras
755
Cerro San Jeronimo
Cerro La Milla 242
Cerro Observatorio 465
San Juan de Lurigancho
12°

Terminal Maritimo
Rimac
Carmen de La Legua
Rimac
El Agustino
Cerro El Agustino 482

Callao
Fuerte Real Felipe
Bellavista
La Perla
Breña
Campo de Marte
Jesús Maria
Univ. Catolica
Palacio de Gobierno
Estacion Desamparados
El Congreso
Museo de Arte
Estadio Nacional
LIMA
Museo de la Victoria
B

La Punta
San Miguel
Parque de las Leyendas
Pueblo Libre
Museo Nacional
San Luis

Magdalena
Lince
Parque de la Reserva
Paseo de la Republica
San Borja
San Isidro
Huaca Juliana
Hipodromo de Montefrico

Surquillo
Miraflores
Avenida Panamericana Sur

Isla Frontón
Vista Alegre

PACIFIC OCEAN
12° 10'
Santiago de Surco
C

Cerro Morro Solar 273
Chorrillos
Barranco
La Campiña

Punta La Chira
La Encantada

77° 10' West from Greenwich 77°

1   2   3

Central Los Angeles

0 km 1
0 miles 0.5

Echo Park
Elysian Park Ave
Dodger Stadium
Elysian Park
SUNSET BOULEVARD
ECHO PARK
GLENDALE BLVD
BROADWAY
SPRING STREET
a

CHINA TOWN
NORTH
MAIN STREET
ALAMEDA
Cardinal St

Temple
Street
Hollywood Freeway
SUNSET BOULEVARD
Terminal Annex Post Office
County Jail
Board of Education
Hall of Admin
CIVIC CENTER
County Courthouse
Law Lib
Hall of Justice
City Hall
U.S. Ct Ho
El Pueblo de Los Angeles Hist. Park
Union Sta.
Federal Bldg
SANTA ANA FREEWAY
MACY STREET
b

2ND STREET
1ST STREET
World Trade Center
Music Center
Miramar
Hall of Records
LITTLE TOKYO
Commercial
Los Angeles River

FIGUEROA
Wilshire Blvd
Arco Plaza
Wells Fargo Center
California Plaza
Museum of Contemporary Art
Central Library
Bradbury Bldg
Parker Center
Turner
ALAMEDA
1ST
SAN PEDRO
Santa Fe Ave
c

Pershing Square
BROADWAY
MAIN STREET
6TH
SPRING STREET
OLYMPIC BLVD
Greyhound Bus Depot
Factory Pl

1   2   3

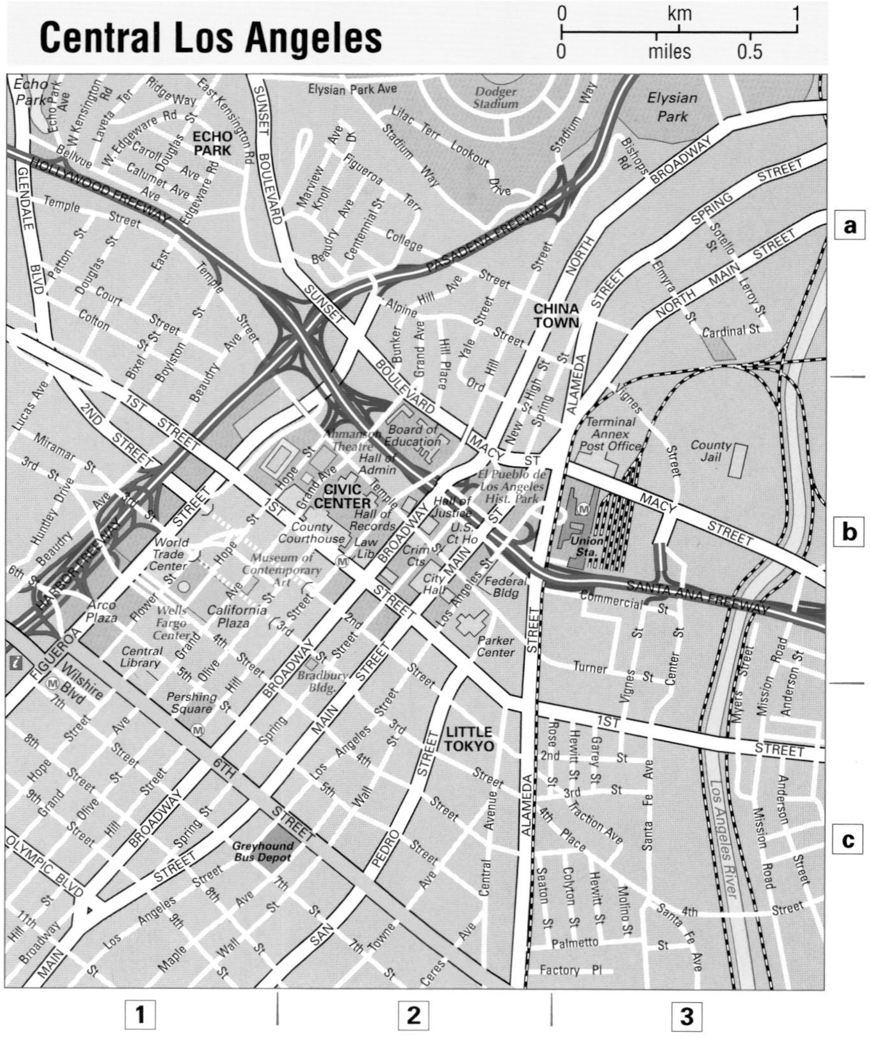

COPYRIGHT GEORGE PHILIP LTD.

Madrid

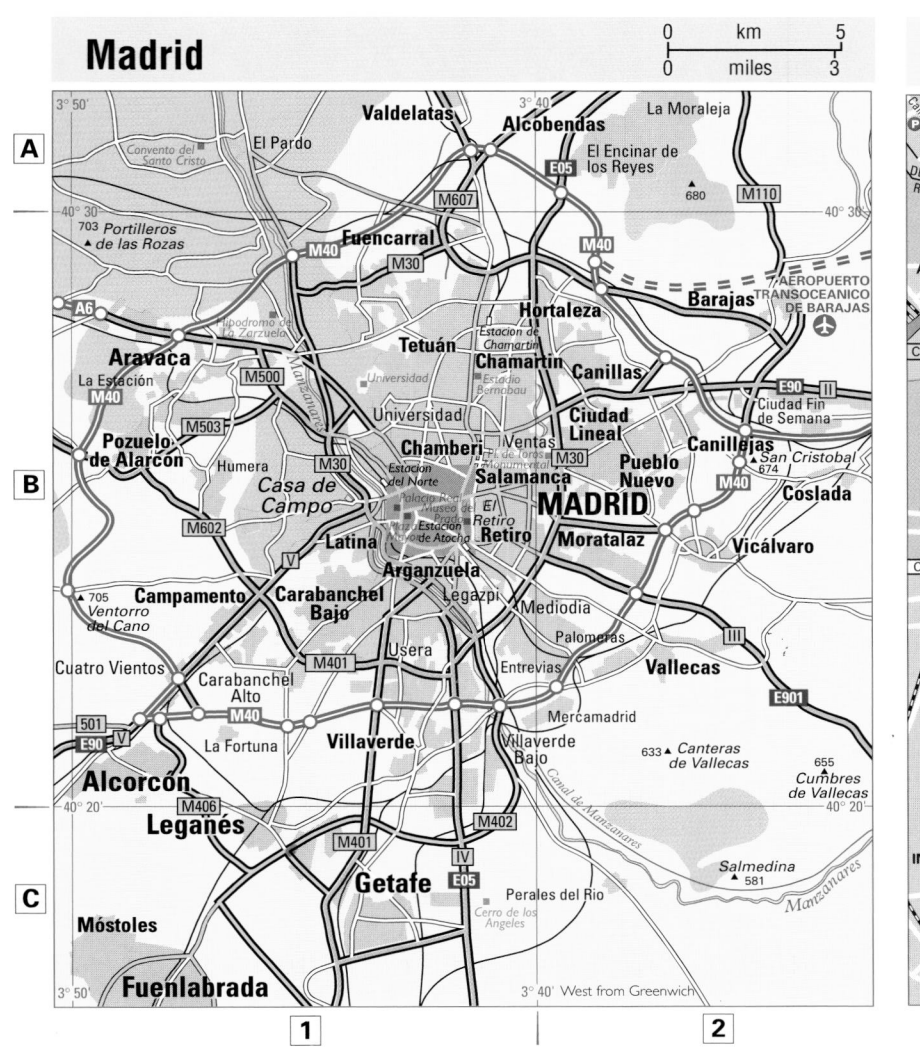

Central Madrid

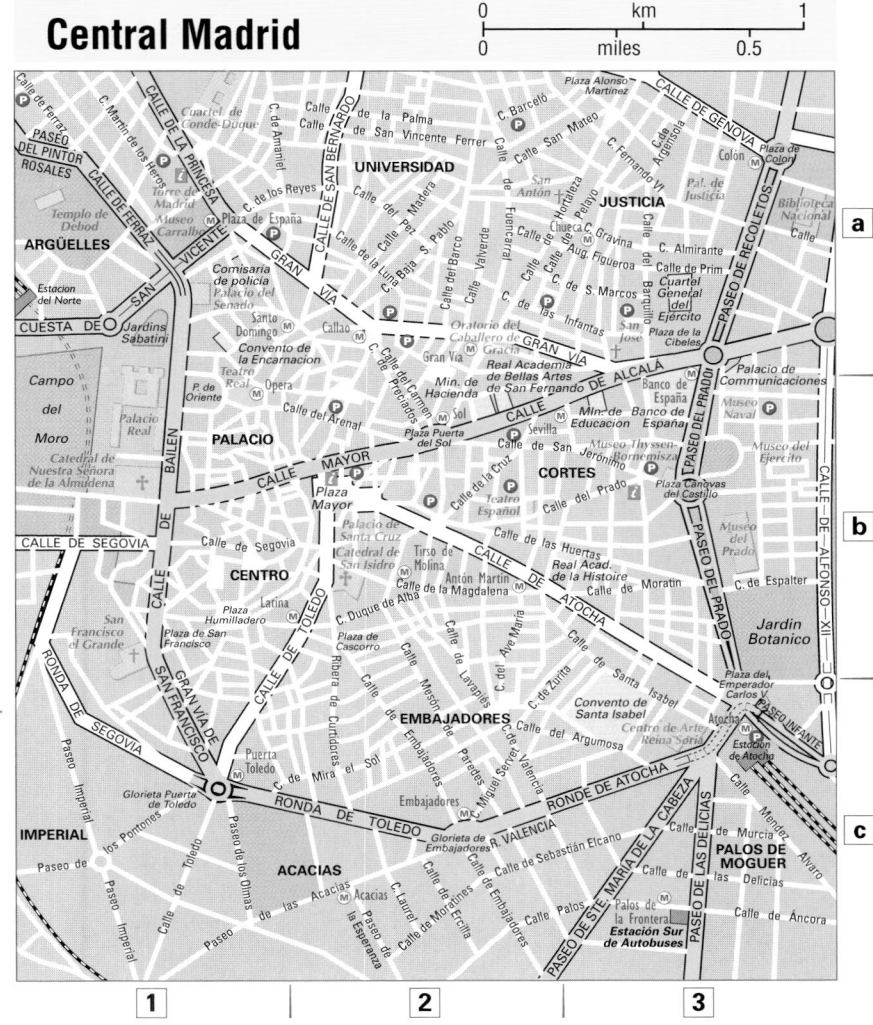

Manila

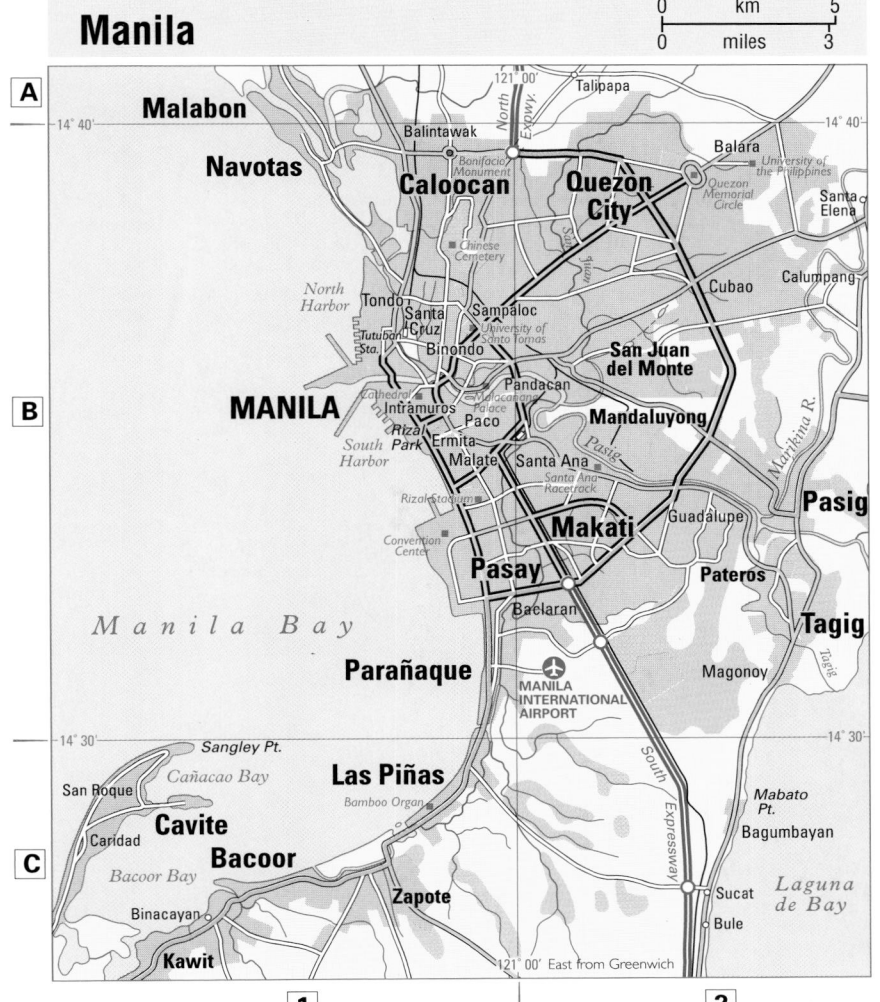

Melbourne

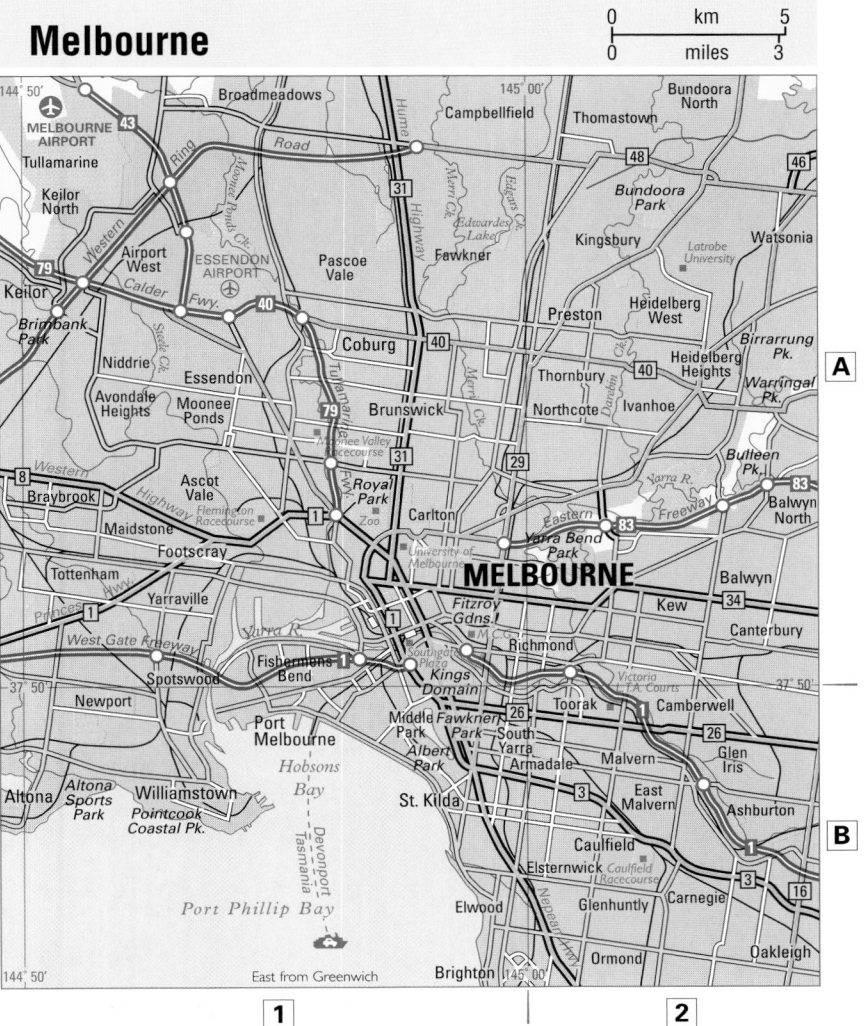

COPYRIGHT GEORGE PHILIP LTD.

Mexico City

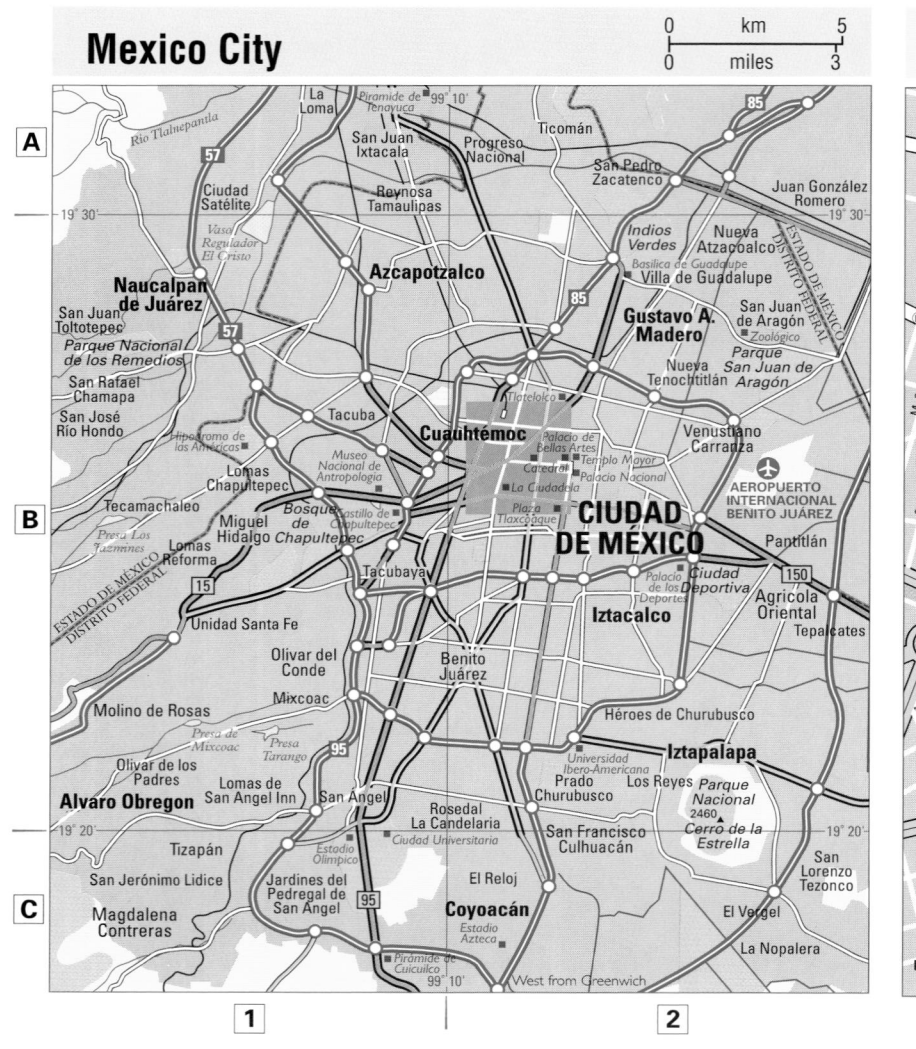

Central Mexico City

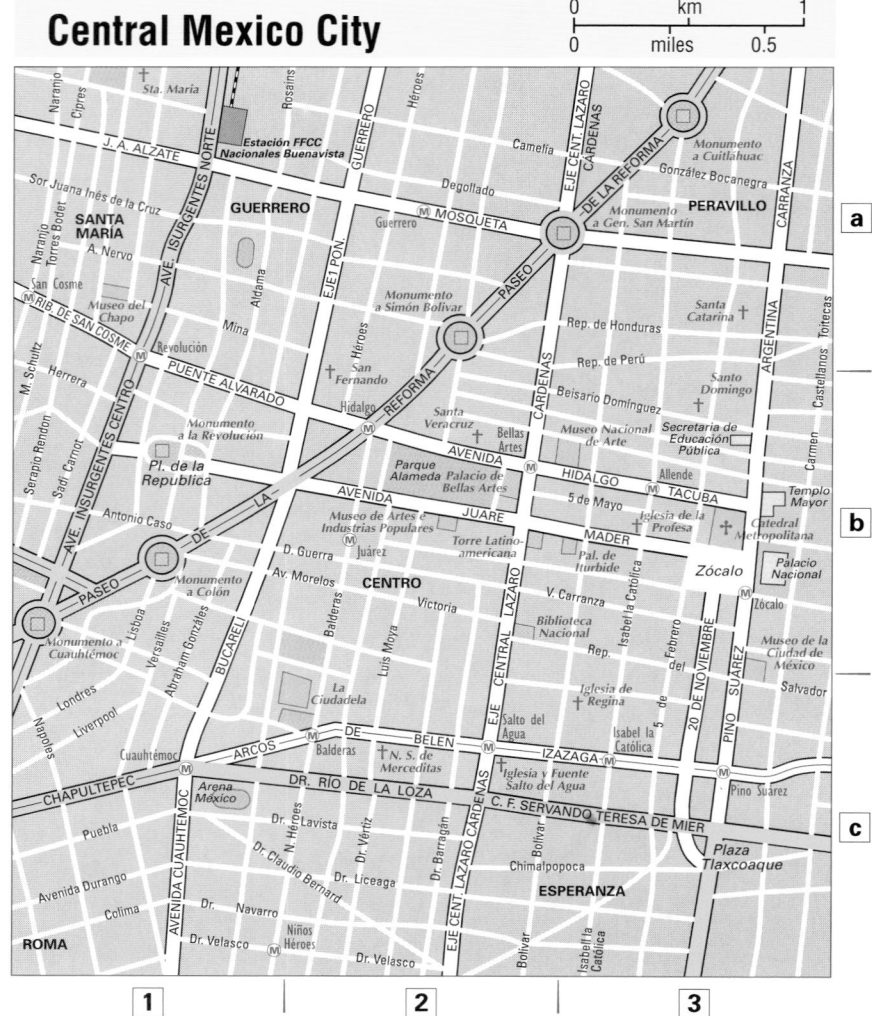

Miami

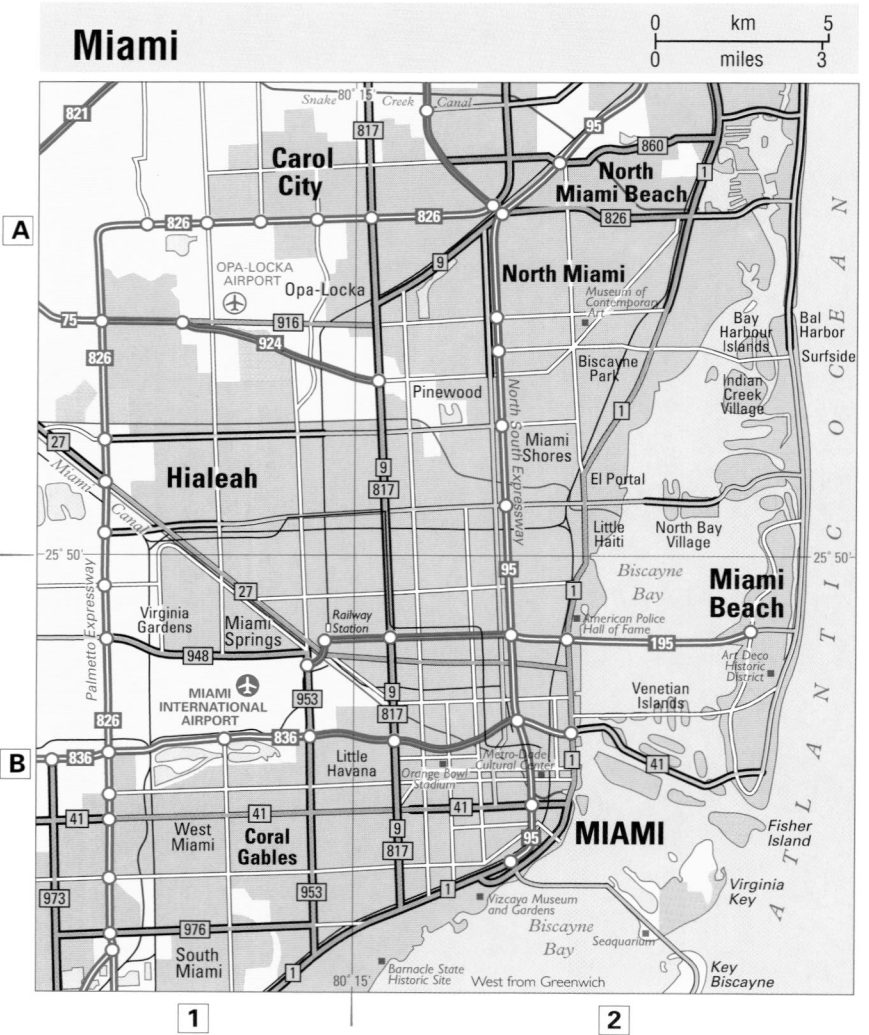

Milan

COPYRIGHT GEORGE PHILIP LTD.

Moscow

km 0 — 5
miles 0 — 3

Rows: A, B, C — Columns: 1, 2, 3, 4, 5, 6

Novonikolyskoye, Mitino, Putilkovo, Sheremetyevo Airport, Bratsevo, Degunino, Vladykino, Babushkin 157, Medvezhiy Ozyora, Medvezhiy Ozyora, 38

Chernyovo, Penyaging, Nikolskiy, Khimki-Khovrino, Dzerzhinskiy Park, Gorod Moskva, Almazova, Pekhra-Pokrovskoye

Krasnogorsk, Golyevo, Pavshino, Myakinino, Strogino, Petrovsko-Razumovskoye, Ostankino, Sokolniki Park, Bogorodskoye, Galyanovo, Vostochnyy 140, Gorenki, Balashikha, Novaya, M7

Tushino, M10, Nikolskiy, Timiryazev Park, Dzerzhinskiy Park, Izmaylovo, Pekhra-Yakovievskaya

Arkhangelskoye, Troitse-Lykovo, M9, Zakharkovo, Rublovo, Khorosovo, Frunze, Sverdlov, Leningrad Station, Yaroslavl Station, Kazan Station, Izmayloskiy Park, 150, Vishnyaki, Nikolyskoye, Saltykovka, Reutov

Razdory, Cherepkovo, Krylatskoye, MOSKVA, Krasno-Presnenskaya, Bolshoy Theatre, Red Square, St. Basil's Cath., Lenin Museum, Kremlin, Bauman Station, Kursk Station, Novogireyevo, Perovo, Kuskovo, Serebryanka, Kutsino, Zheleznodorozhnyy

Barvikha, Romashkovo, Kuntsevo, Fili-Mazilovo, Kiev Station, Tretyakov Art Gallery, Zhdanov, Kuznetsovo, Plyushchevo, Veshnyaki, Fenino, Temnikovo

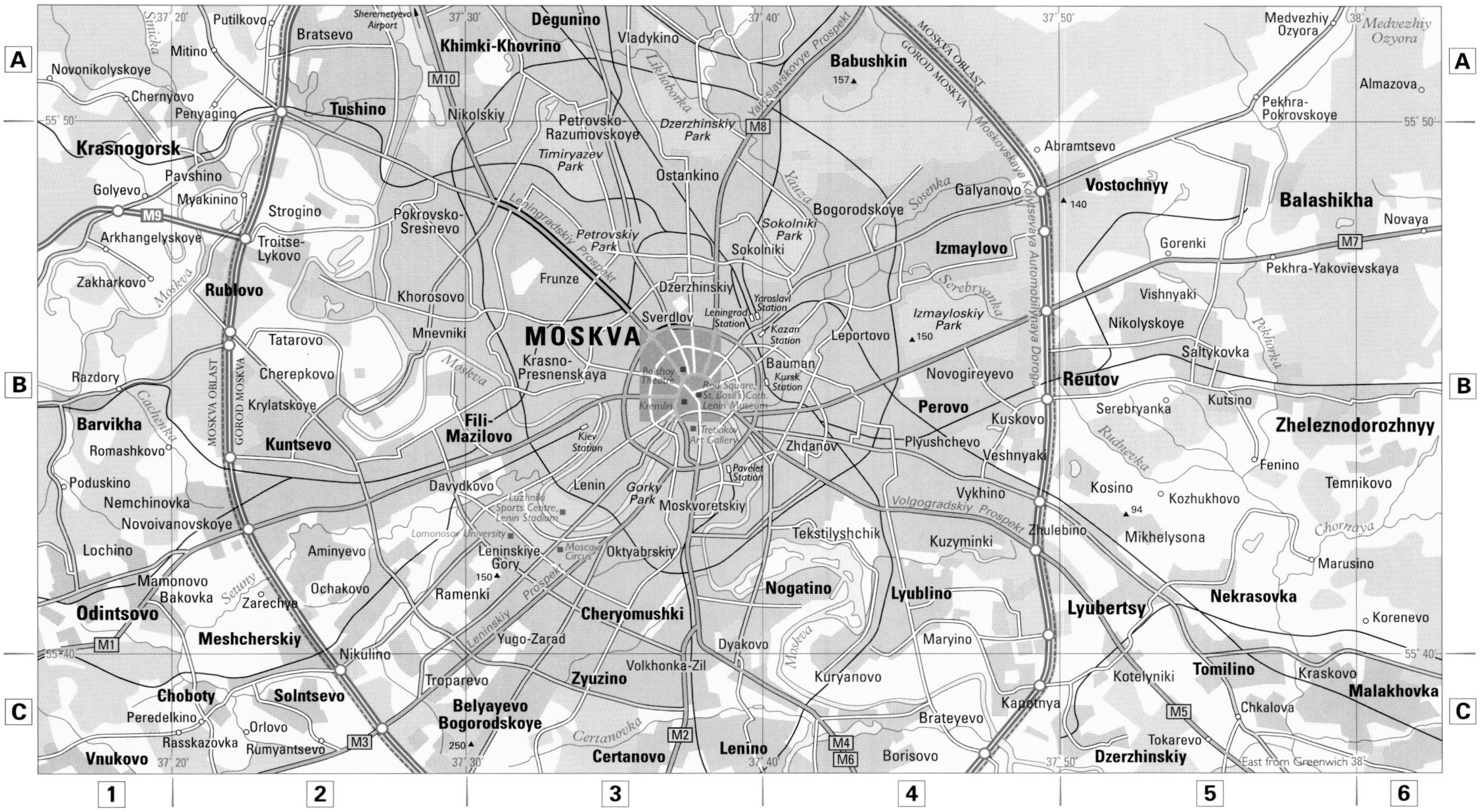

Poduskino, Nemchinovka, Davydkovo, Lenin, Gorky Park, Moskvoretskiy, Pavelet Station, Vykhino, Kosino, Kozhukhovo

Novoivanovskoye, Lochino, Luzhniki Sports Centre, Lenin Stadium, Lomonosov University, Leninskiye-Gory, Moscow Circus, Oktyabrskiy, Tekstilyshchik, Kuzyminki, 94, Mikhelysona, Chornaya, Marusino

Mamonovo, Bakovka, Zarechye, Aminyevo, Ochakovo, Ramenki, 150, Yugo-Zarad, Cheryomushki, Dyakovo, Maryino, Koptyevo

Odintsovo, Meshcherskiy, M1, Nikulino, Troparevo, Zyuzino, Volkhonka-Zil, Nogatino, Lyublino, Lyubertsy, Nekrasovka, Korenevo

Choboty, Solntsevo, Belyayevo Bogorodskoye, Kuryanovo, Kotelniki, Tomilino, Kraskovo, Malakhovka

Peredelkino, Rasskazovka, Orlovo, Rumyantsevo, M3, 250, Certanovo, Certanovka, M2, Lenino, Brateyevo, Borisovo, Kamptyna, Chkalova, Dzerzhinskiy, M5

Vnukovo, M4, M6, Tokarevo, East from Greenwich 38

Montréal

km 0 — 5
miles 0 — 3

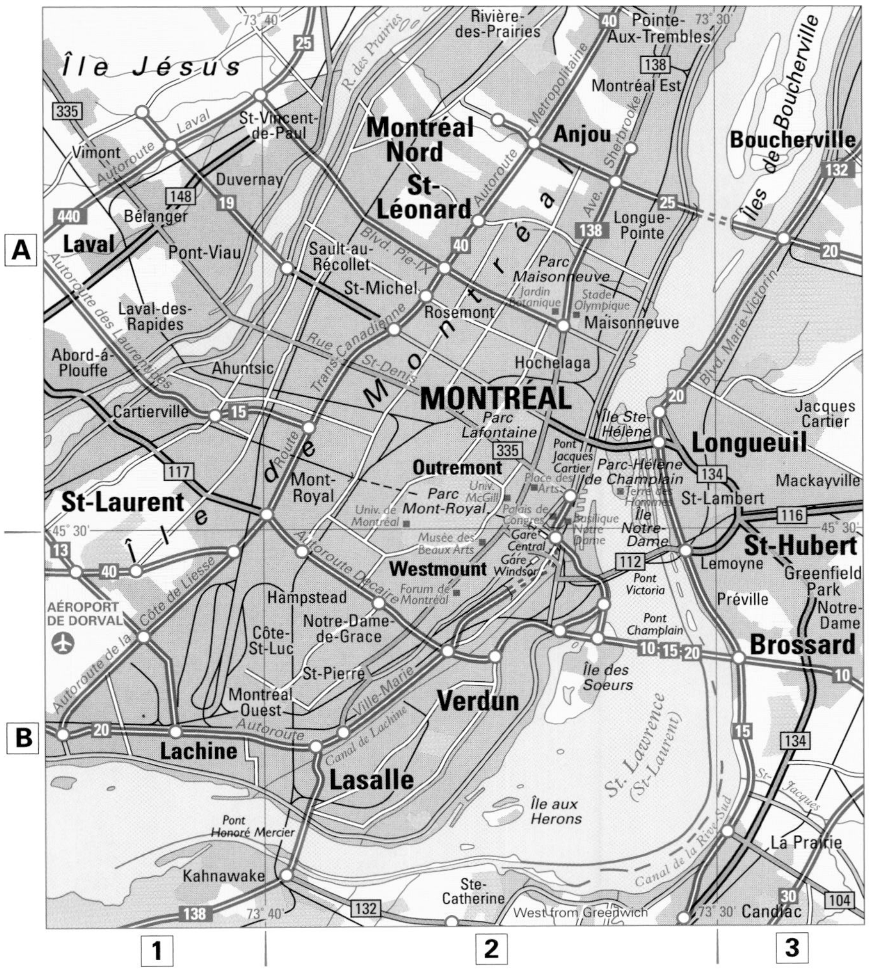

Île Jésus, Rivière-des-Prairies, Pointe-Aux-Trembles, Montréal Est, Boucherville

Vimont, St-Vincent-de-Paul, Montréal Nord, Anjou, Boucherville

Laval, Duvernay, Montréal Nord, St-Léonard, Laval, Bélanger, Pont-Viau, Sault-au-Récollet, St-Michel, Parc Maisonneuve, Jardin Botanique, Stade Olympique, Longue-Pointe, Îles de Boucherville

Laval-des-Rapides, Ahuntsic, Rosemont, Maisonneuve

Abord-à-Plouffe, Cartierville, Hochelaga

St-Laurent, Mont-Royal, MONTRÉAL, Parc Lafontaine, Île Ste Hélène, Jacques Cartier, Longueuil, Mackayville

Outremont, Parc Jean-Drapeau, Parc Hélène-de-Champlain, St-Lambert

Hampstead, Westmount, Forum de Montréal, Musée des Beaux Arts, Gare Centrale, Basilique Notre-Dame, Lemoyne, St-Hubert, Greenfield Park, Notre-Dame

Côte-St-Luc, Notre-Dame-de-Grace, Pont Victoria, Préville

AÉROPORT DE DORVAL, St-Pierre, Pont Champlain, Brossard

Verdun, Île des Soeurs, Montréal Ouest

Lachine, Lasalle, Île aux Herons, St-Lawrence (St-Laurent), La Prairie

Kahnawake, Pont Honoré Mercier, Ste-Catherine, West from Greenwich, Candiac

Central Moscow

km 0 — 1
miles 0 — 0.5

Rows: a, b, c — Columns: 1, 2, 3

Sad-Samotechnaya, Sad-Suharevskaya, Sad-Spasskaya, Sad-Triumfalnaya Ulitsa, Svetnoy Boulevard, Suharevskaya, Sergievskiy Per., Koshanskiy Per.

Mayakovskiy Ploshchad, Tchaikovsky Concert Hall, Old Moscow Circus, Rozhdestvenskiy Boulevard, Sretenka, Chistiy Prudy

Youth Theatre, Mayakovskaya, Sadovskich, Pushkinskaya, Petrovsky Boulevard, Trubnaya Pl., Turgenevskaya Pl., Convent of the Nativity of the Virgin, Turgenevskaya Per.

Museum of the Revolution, Tverskaya, Strastnoy Boulevard, Stoleshnikov, Petrovka, Petrovskiy Passage, Varsonofyevsky Per., Lubyanka

Pushkin Ploshchad, Chekovskaya, Kuznetsky Most, Detskiy Theatre, Novaya

Gorky Theatre, Bolshoi Theatre, Teatralnaya, Teatralniy Proj., Lubyanskaya, Komsomolsky Bld.

Mal Bronnaya Ulitsa, Gorky House Museum, Chekhov Theatre, Okhotny Ryad, Ploshchad Revolyutsii, Slavianski Bazar, Bolshoy Per. Devyatinskiy, Polytechnic Museum, Nogina

Gersena, Ulitsa Stanislavskovo, Ulitsa Nezhdanovoy, Central Post Office, Ermolovoy Theatre, Revolution Square, Lenin Museum, Lubyanskaya Ul.

Moscow Conservatoire, University, Central Exhibition Hall, Manezhnaya Ploshchad, Historical Museum, Gum Shopping Arcade, Kitai Gorod, Vladimirova Pereulok, Slavyanskaya Pl.

Arbatskaya Ploshchad, Vozdvizhenka U., Aleksandrovsky Sad, Arsenal, Red Square, Lenin Mausoleum, St. Basil's Cathedral, Ulitsa Varvarka, Central Concert Hall

Ulitsa Arbat, Arbatskaya, U. Znamenka, Okhotny Ryad, Manezhnaya, Alexander Garden, Council of Ministers, Ivan Square, Presidium of the Supreme Soviet, Kremlin

Marx-Engels Museum, Borovitskaya Ploshchad, Lenin State Library, Palace of Congress, Terem Palace, Kremlin Palace, Cathedral Square, Armoury Palace, Archangel Cathedral

Pushkin Fine Arts Museum, Gogolevsky Boulevard, Volkhonka Ulitsa, Kremlevskaya Naberezhnaya, Moskva, Moskvorets. Nab., Raushskaya Nab.

Ryleyev Ulitsa, Kropotkinskaya, Moscow Swimming Pool, Sofiyskaya Naberezhnaya, Bolotnaya Nab., Vodootvodny Kanal, Sadovnicheskaya Nab., Ovchinnikovskaya, Bolshoy Kamenniy Most, Kadashevskaya Nab., Ovchinnikovskaya Nab.

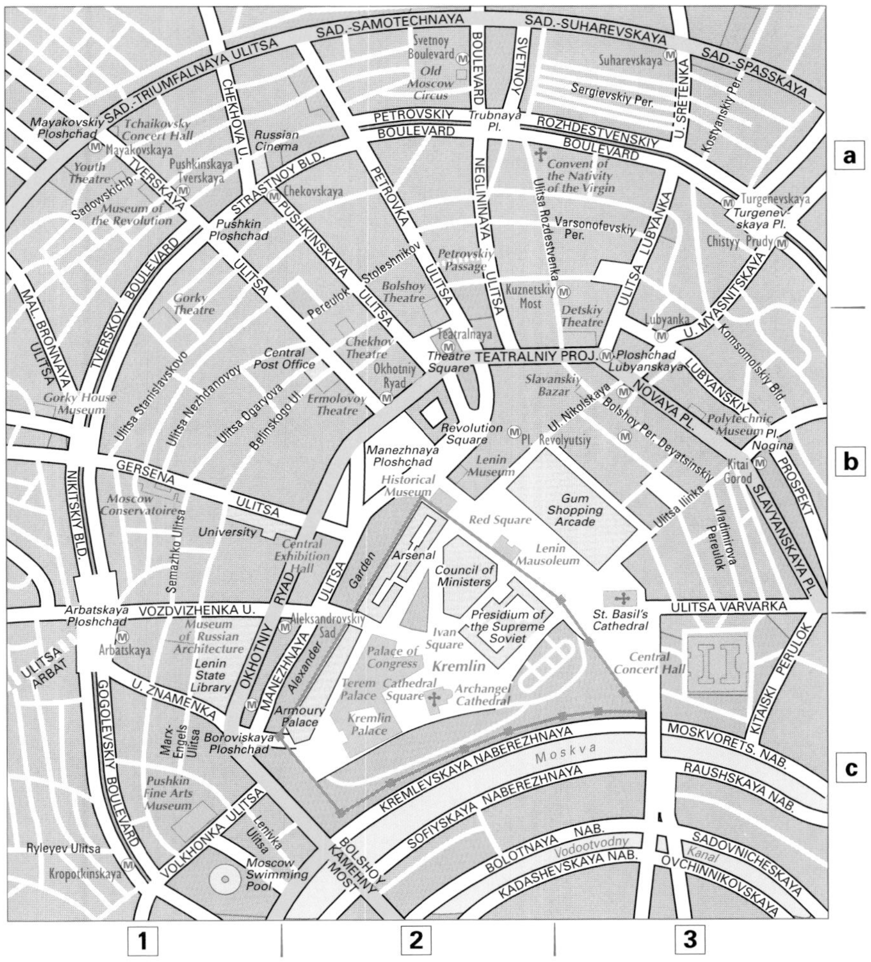

COPYRIGHT GEORGE PHILIP LTD.

Mumbai

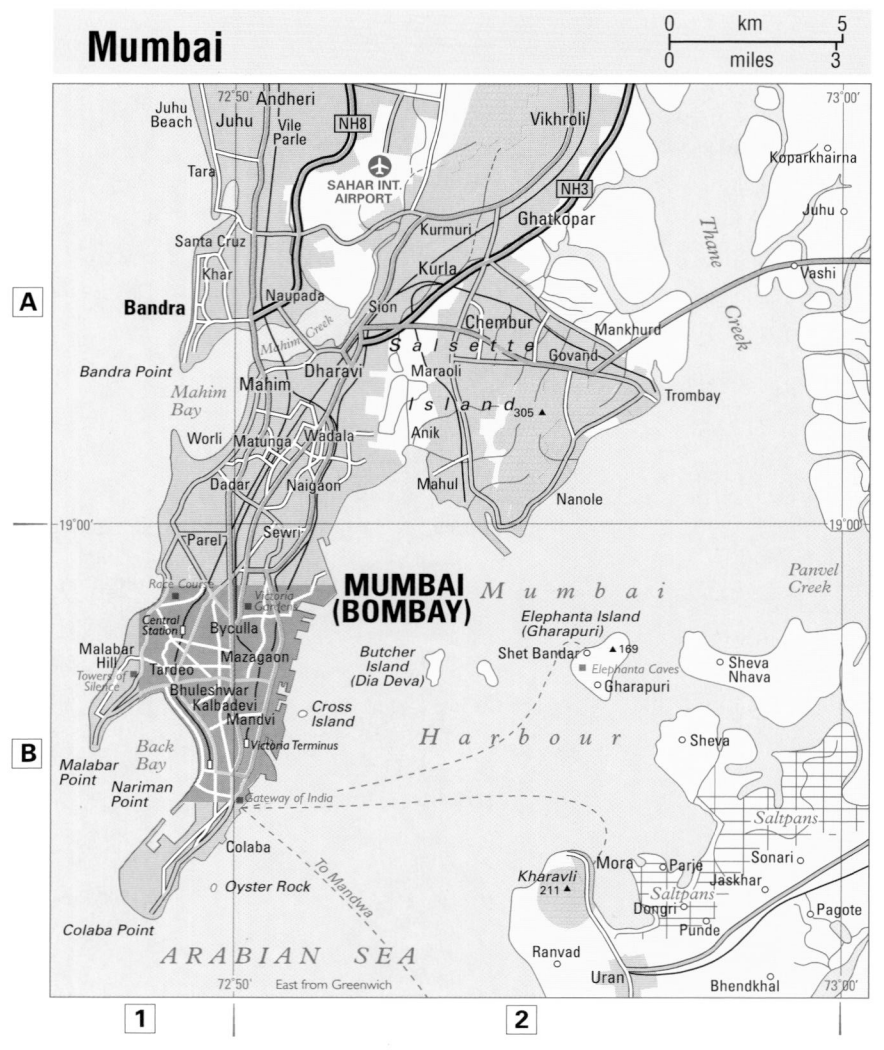

Central Mumbai

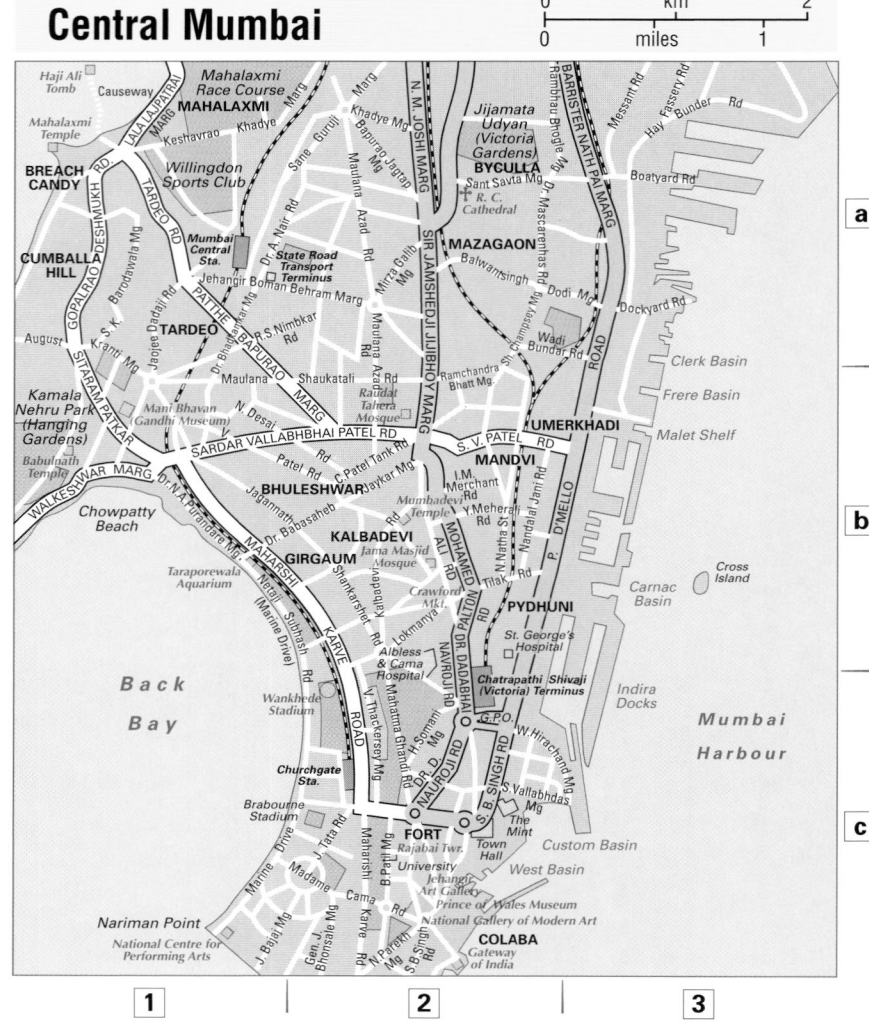

Munich

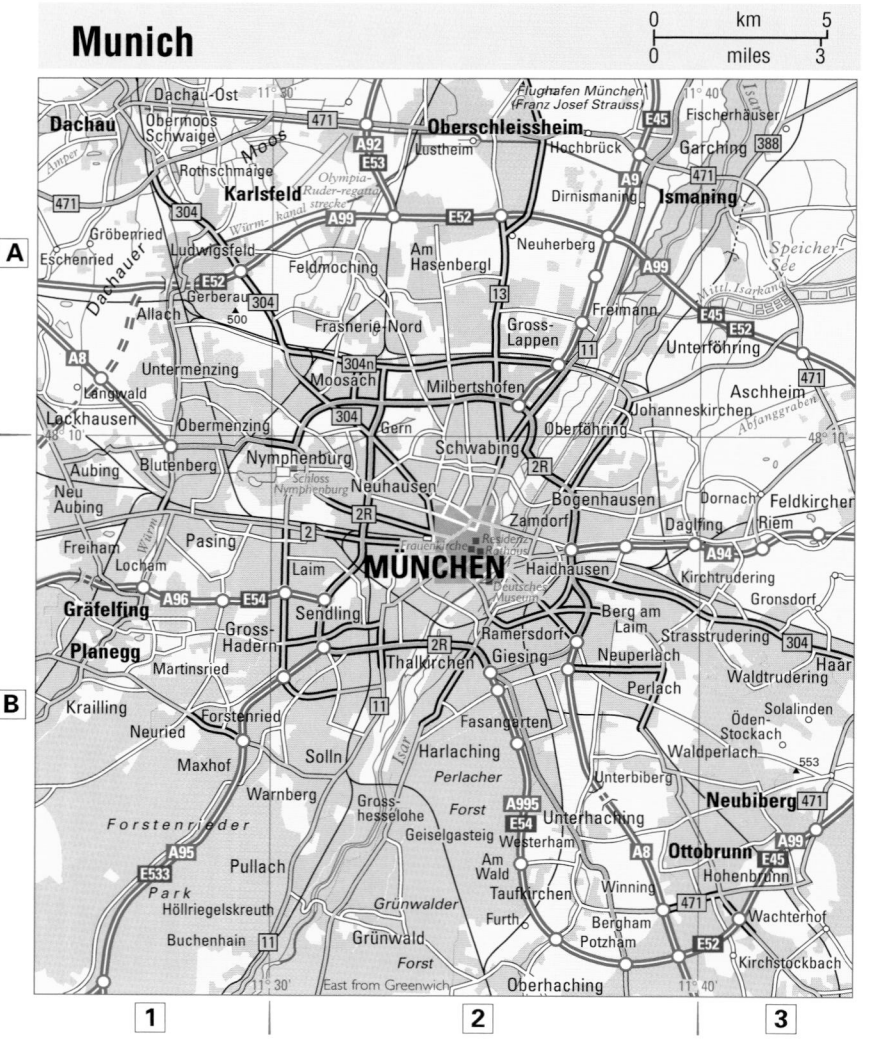

Central Munich

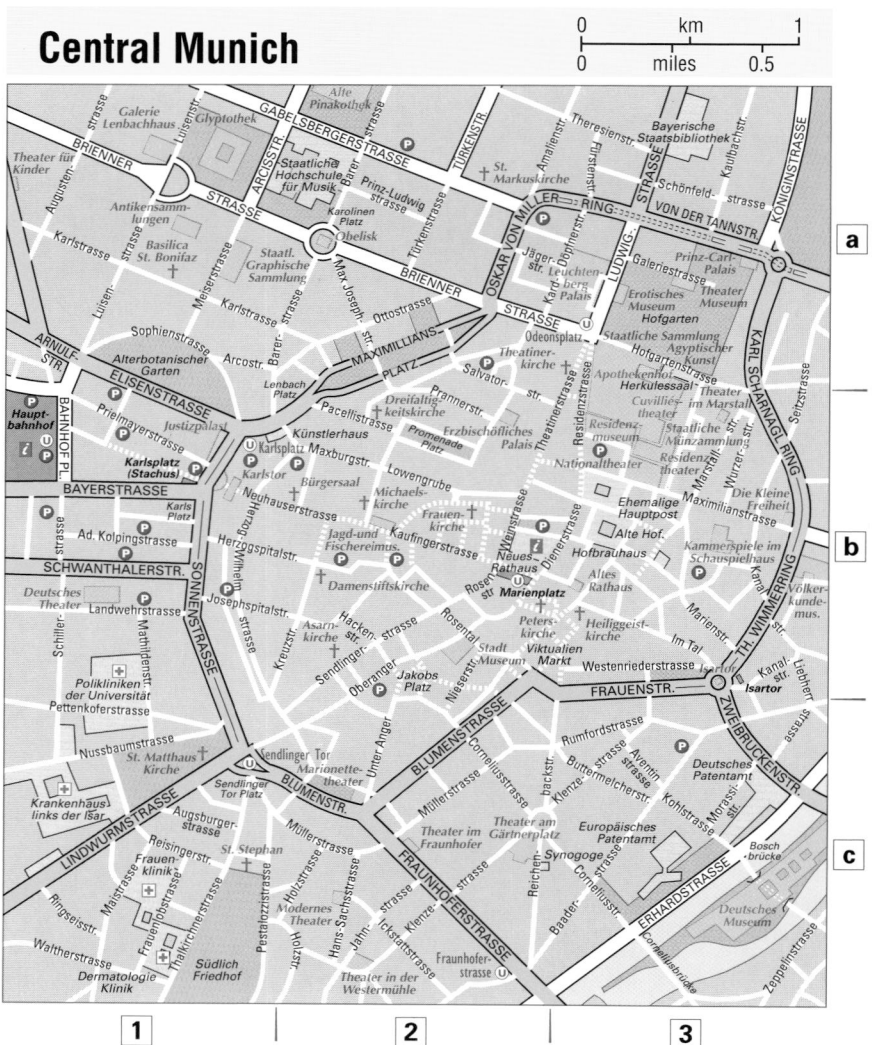

New York

0 — km — 5
0 — miles — 3

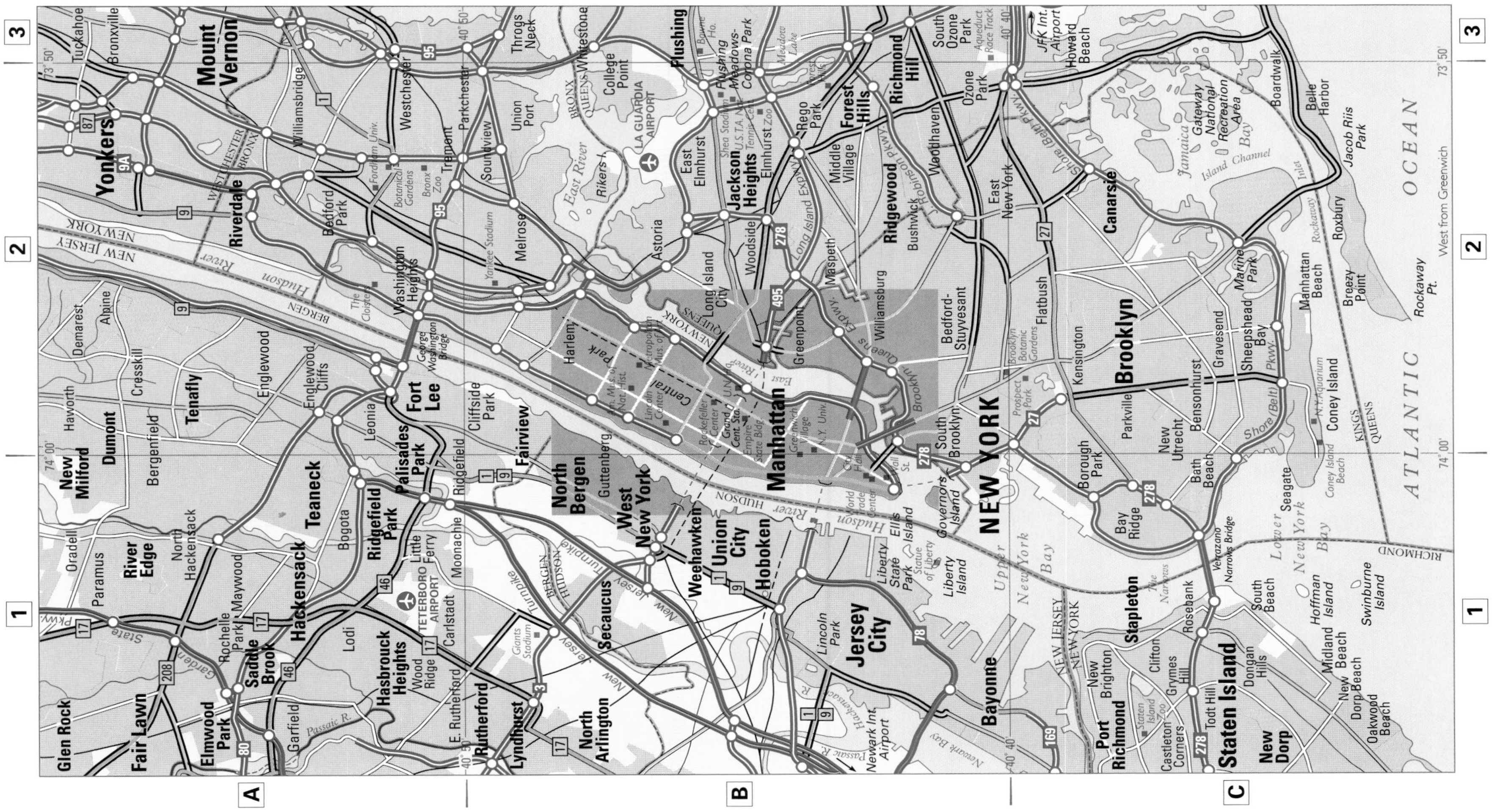

Tuckahoe · Bronxville · Mount Vernon · Yonkers · Williamsbridge · Westchester · Throgs Neck · Whitestone · College Point · Flushing · Flushing Meadows-Corona Park · South Ozone Park · JFK Int. Airport · Howard Beach · Boardwalk

Riverdale · Bedford Park · Fordham Univ. · BRONX · Bronx Zoo · Parkchester · Union Port · Trippent · LA GUARDIA AIRPORT · East River · Rikers I. · East Elmhurst · Jackson Heights · Woodside · Rego Park · Forest Hills · Richmond Hill · Ozone Park · Jamaica Bay · Gateway National Recreation Area · Belle Harbor

NEW YORK · NEW JERSEY · Alpine · Demarest · Cresskill · Englewood · Englewood Cliffs · Fort Lee · George Washington Bridge · Washington Heights · Yankee Stadium · Melrose · Astoria · Long Island City · Greenpoint · Maspeth · Ridgewood · Bushwick · East New York · Bedford-Stuyvesant · Williamsburg · Brooklyn · Canarsie · Marine Park · Manhattan Beach · Breezy Point · Rockaway Pt. · ATLANTIC OCEAN

New Milford · Dumont · Tenafly · Leonia · Cliffside Park · Fairview · North Bergen · Guttenberg · West New York · Harlem · Central Park · Manhattan · NEW YORK · Prospect Park · Flatbush · Kensington · Gravesend · Sheepshead Bay · Coney Island · KINGS

Haworth · Oradell · River Edge · North Hackensack · Teaneck · Ridgefield Park · Bogota · Palisades Park · Ridgefield · Moonachie · Weehawken · Union City · Hoboken · Hudson River · Ellis Island · Liberty Island · Governor's Island · Borough Park · New Utrecht · Bath Beach · Bay Ridge · Bensonhurst · Lower New York Bay

Paramus · Hackensack · Rochelle Park · Maywood · Lodi · Garfield · Hasbrouck Heights · Wood Ridge · Carlstadt · TETERBORO AIRPORT · Secaucus · Jersey City · Liberty State Park · Upper New York Bay · NEW YORK · NEW JERSEY · Stapleton · Clifton · Grymes Hill · Dongan Hills · Midland Beach · South Beach · Hoffman Island · Swinburne Island

Glen Rock · Fair Lawn · Elmwood Park · Saddle Brook · E. Rutherford · Lyndhurst · North Arlington · Passaic R. · North Bergen · Newark Int. Airport · Bayonne · Port Richmond · New Richmond · Castleton Corners · Todt Hill · Staten Island · New Dorp · Oakwood Beach

A · B · C
1 · 2 · 3

Central New York

0 — km — 2
0 — miles — 1

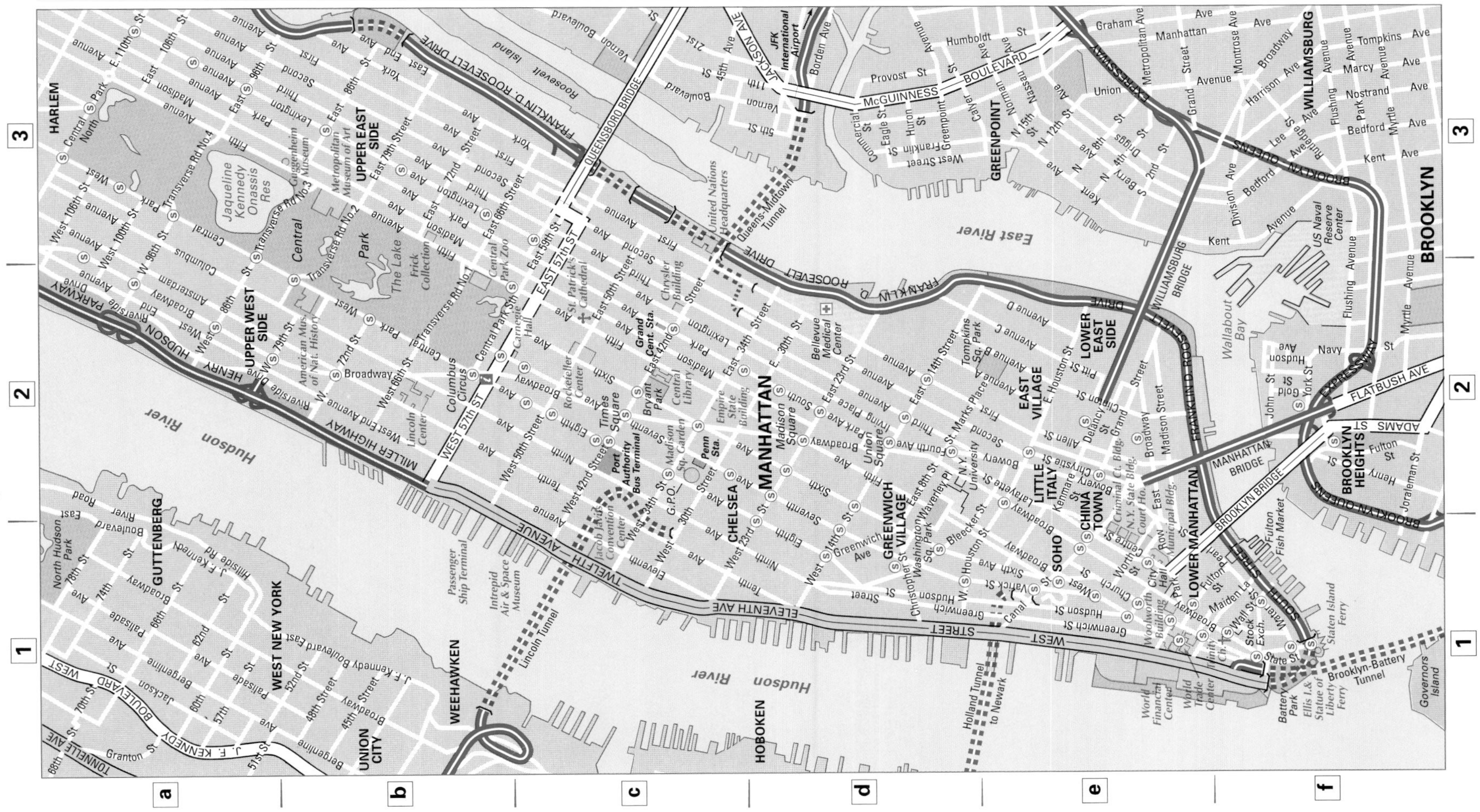

HARLEM · UPPER EAST SIDE · UPPER WEST SIDE · Central Park · Jacqueline Kennedy Onassis Res. · The Lake · Metropolitan Museum of Art · Guggenheim Museum · Frick Collection · Am. Mus. of Nat. History · Lincoln Center · Columbus Circle · Central Park Zoo · Roosevelt Island · QUEENSBORO BRIDGE · United Nations Headquarters · JFK International Airport · GREENPOINT · WILLIAMSBURG · BROOKLYN

HUDSON RIVER · Hudson River · Weehawken · Union City · Hoboken · GUTTENBERG · WEST NEW YORK · NORTH HUDSON · MILLER HIGHWAY · HENRY HUDSON PARKWAY · TWELFTH AVENUE · ELEVENTH AVENUE · WEST STREET · CHELSEA · MANHATTAN · Times Square · Port Authority Bus Terminal · Penn Sta. · G.P.O. · Madison Square · Empire State Building · Bryant Park · Rockefeller Center · St. Patrick's Cathedral · Chrysler Building · Grand Cent. Sta. · Central Library · Bellevue Medical Center · East Village · Lower East Side · Williamsburg Bridge · US Naval Reserve Center · Wallabout Bay

Intrepid Air & Space Museum · Jacob Javits Convention Center · Passenger Ship Terminal · Lincoln Tunnel · GREENWICH VILLAGE · N.Y. University · Union Square · Washington Sq. Park · SOHO · LITTLE ITALY · CHINA TOWN · Bowery · Tompkins Sq. Park · East River · FRANKLIN D. ROOSEVELT DRIVE · FRANKLIN D. ROOSEVELT DRIVE · Manhattan Bridge · BROOKLYN HEIGHTS · ADAMS · FLATBUSH AVE

Holland Tunnel to Newark · LOWER MANHATTAN · Woolworth Building · City Hall · Fulton Fish Market · Brooklyn Bridge · Brooklyn-Battery Tunnel · World Financial Center · World Trade Center · Battery Park · Ellis I. & Statue of Liberty Ferry · Staten Island Ferry · Stock Exch. · Wall St. · Governors Island

a · b · c · d · e · f
1 · 2 · 3

COPYRIGHT GEORGE PHILIP LTD.

Osaka

0 km 5
0 miles 3

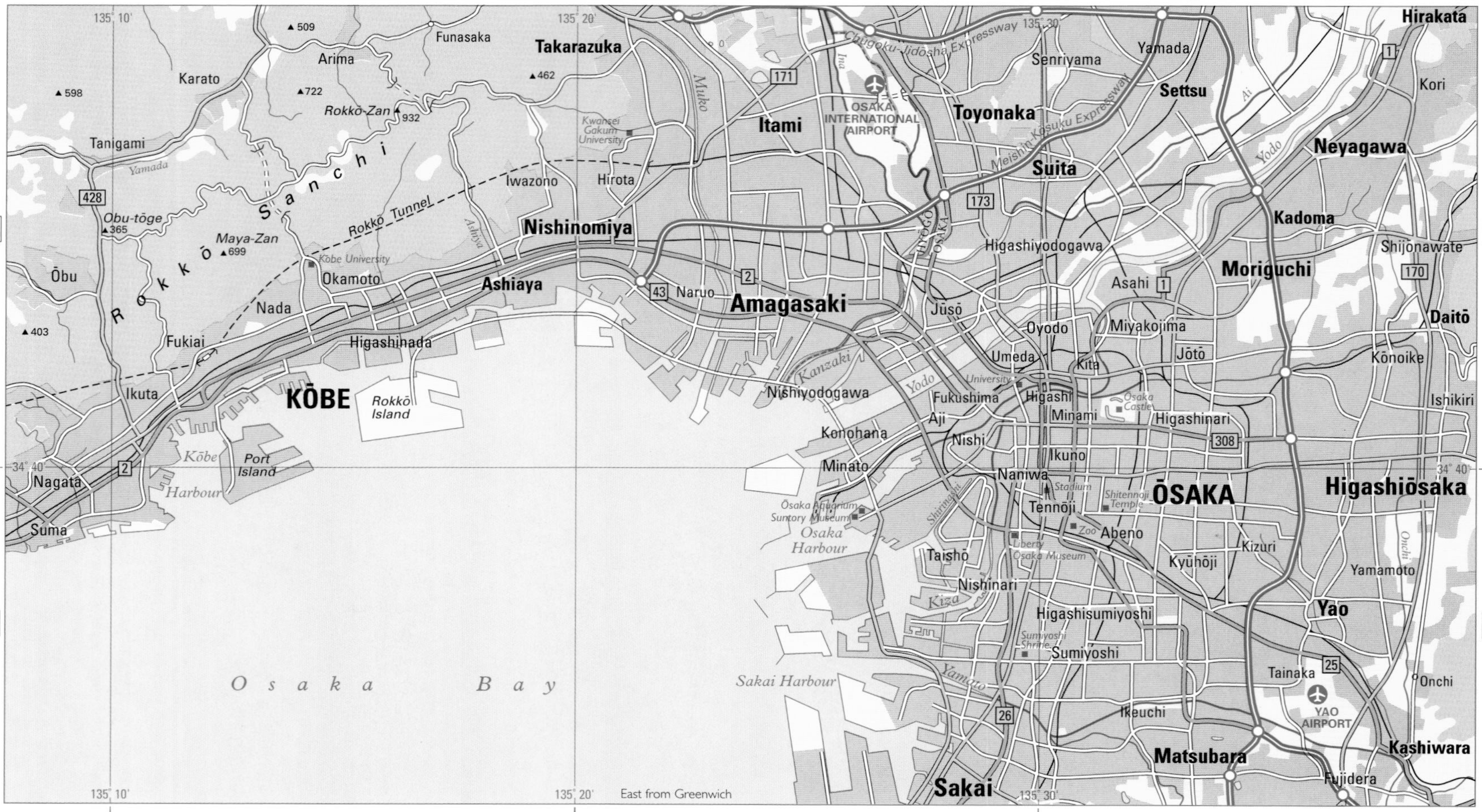

135° 10'
▲509 Funasaka
Karato Arima **Takarazuka** Yamada Senriyama Kori **Hirakata**
▲598 ▲722 Rokkō-Zan 932 ▲462 135° 30' Settsu
Tanigami _Yamada_ 171 **OSAKA** **Toyonaka** **Neyagawa**
428 Rokkō Tunnel Iwazono INTERNATIONAL
Obu-tōge ▲365 Maya-Zan Hirota 173 **Suita** AIRPORT **Kadoma**
A ▲699 Kōbe University **Nishinomiya** Higashiyodogawa **Moriguchi** **A**
Ōbu Okamoto 43 Naruo Asahi 1 Shijonawate
Nada **Ashiaya** **Amagasaki** Jūsō 2 Miyakojima Daitō
Fukiai Higashinada Jūsō Oyodo Jōtō 170
▲403 Nishiyodogawa Umeda Kita Ōsaka Kōnoike
Ikuta Konohana Fukushima Higashi Castle 308 Ishikiri
Suma **KŌBE** Rokkō Aji Nishi Minami Higashinari
Nagata Port Island Minato Naniwa Ikuno **ŌSAKA** **Higashiōsaka**
34° 40' 2 Kōbe Island Osaka Aquarium Stadium Shitennō Temple 34° 40'
Suma _Kōbe Harbour_ Suntory Museum Taishō Tennōji Zoo Abeno Kizuri Yamamoto
Osaka Harbour Nishinari Osaka Museum Kyūhōji
B _Sakai Harbour_ Higashisumiyoshi **Yao** **B**
Sumiyoshi Yamato Tainaka 25
_O s a k a   B a y_ Sumiyoshi Shrine Ōnchi
Sumiyoshi YAO
26 Ikeuchi AIRPORT **Kashiwara**
Matsubara Fujidera
135° 10' 135° 20' East from Greenwich **Sakai** 135° 30'

1 **2** **3** **4**

Oslo

0 km 5
0 miles 3

60°00' 10° 30' 10° 40' 10° 50' 60°00'
OSLO Tryvannshøgda Maridalen
AKERSHUS ▲531 _Maridalsvatn_
Bogstadvatn Holmenkollen Alnsjøen
Burudvatn ▲418 Kjelsås **Gorud**
Ila Røa Ris **OSLO** Rødtvet
Bærums 168 Ullevål 4 163
Verk Lijordet Sinsen
Bryn 168 ▲379 Haslum Skøyen **Ullern** Universitetet Alna E6
A E16 **Kolsås** 160 Stabekk Lysaker Vestbane Tøyen Bryn **A**
Tanum Stabekk 166 sta. Sentralst. Ryen
164 Høvik E18 Norsk Folke Akershus Oppsal
Slependen **Bærum** Museum Slott E6
Hvalstad Nesbru Snarøya Bygdøy Hovedøya E18 Bekkelaget Bøler
Nesøya FORNEBU Lindøya Lambertseter
Frederikshaven Ormøya Nordstrand Østmark-
Sandvika Forneby Helsingborg kapellet
København Oksval Ljabru
Nesøya Hirtshals, Kiel **Nesoddtangen** Malmøya
E18 Brønnøya Flaskebekk Skoklefall 155
Asker Hauketo
59° 50' 165 Holmenfjorden Klemetsrud
B 167 Vollen Nesodden 157 ▲215 Ingierstrand **B**
Blakstad Torvvik
Fjellstrand 156 Gjersjøen **Kolbotn**
Slemmestad Svestad Hasle Oppegård E6
Oppgård 152 Myrvoll
10° 30' Garder Blylaget 134 E18
Nærsnes 10° 40' East from Greenwich 10° 50' **Oppegård**

1 **2** **3** **4**

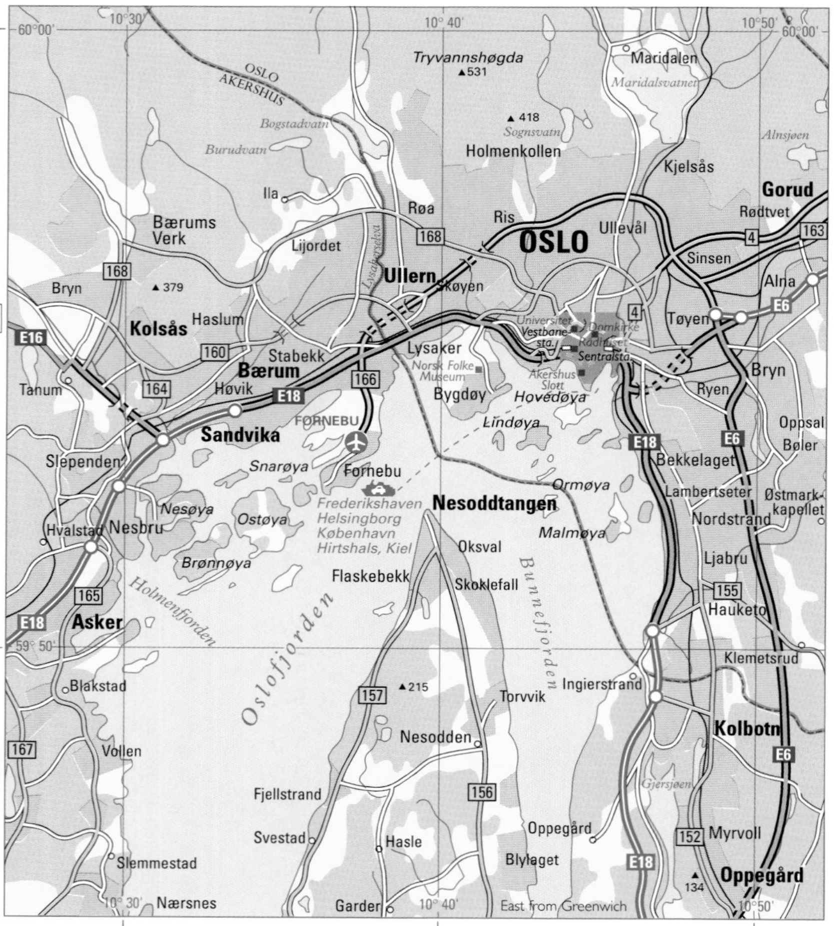

Central Oslo

0 km 0.5
0 miles 0.25

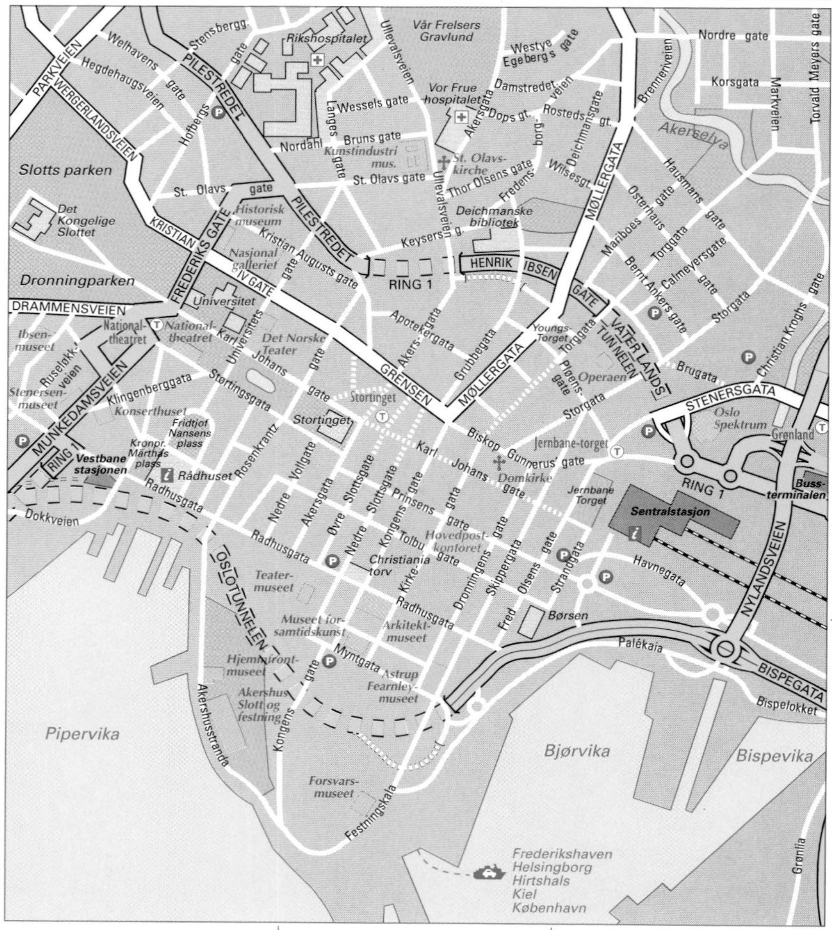

PARKVEIEN Wethavens Stensberg Riks-hospitalet Vår Frelsers Nordre gate
Wergelandsveien Hegdehaugsveien gate PILESTREDET Ullevålsveien Gravlund Westye Korsgata
Egebergs gate Martveien
Hofborg Lønnes Wessels gate Vor Frue Damstredet Brennerveien Torvald Meyers gate **a**
Slotts parken Nordahl hospitalet Rostedsgate Akerselva
Kunstindustri Bruns gate St. Olavs Deichmanske
mus. St. Olavs gate kirke Hauemann
Det St. Olavs gate Thor Olsens gate Deichmanske
Kongelige Historisk Universitetsgate bibliotek
Slottet museum Kristian Augusts gate
Dronningparken Nasjonal Keysers g Calmeyers gate Storgata
DRAMMENSVEIEN galleriet Apotekergata Youngs Bernt Ankers gate
b
Ibsen- National Universitet Akers Torget Christian Krohgs gate Brugata
museet museet Det Norske Grønlands-torget
Stenersen- National Teater Grubbegata Operaen STENERSGATA
museet theatret Stortorvet gate Biskop STENERSGATA
MUNKEDAMSVEIEN theatret Fridtjof Stortinget Gunnerus Oslo
RING Nansens Jernbane Spektrum
Vestbane plass Stortinget Gunnerus gate Torget RING 1 Buss-
stasjonen Rådhuset Karl Johans gate Domkirke **Sentralstasjon** terminalen
Hovedpost- Prinsens gate
Dokkveien kontoret Christiania Havnegata
Teater- torv Skippergata
museet Radhusgata Fred NYLANDSVEIEN
Piervika Museet for Myntgata Astrup Børsen BISPEGATA
samtidskunst Arkitekt- Fearnley
Hjemmefront- museet Palékaia Bispefolket
museet Akershus Palékaia
Slott og _Bjørvika_ _Bispevika_ **c**
festning OSLOTUNNELEN
Forsvars- Akershusstranda
museet Festningspl.
Frederikshaven
Helsingborg
Hirtshals
Kiel
København

1 **2** **3**

COPYRIGHT GEORGE PHILIP LTD.

Paris

km 0 — 5
miles 0 — 3

Carrières-sous-Poissy · Achères · Maisons-Laffitte · Forêt · **Argenteuil Sartrouville** · Gennevilliers · Villeneuve-la-Garenne · **St.-Denis** · Stains · Parc de la Courneuve · Le Blanc-Mesnil · **Aulnay-sous-Bois** · Sevran · Tremblay-en-France · Villeparisis

Poissy · Mesnil-le-Roi · St.-Germain-en-Laye · Houilles · Bois-Colombes · La Courneuve · Le Bourget · **Drancy** · Livry-Gargan · Vaujours · Coubron · Le Pin · Courtry · Villevaudé

Chambourcy · Aigremont · **Colombes** · **Asnières** · **Aubervilliers** · Bobigny · Les Pavillons-sous-Bois · Clichy-sous-Bois · Montfermeil · Montjay-la-Tour

St.-Germain-en-Laye · Le Vésinet · La Garenne-Colombes · Clichy · St.-Ouen · Pantin · Le Pré-St.-Gervais · Les Lilas · Bondy · Le Raincy · Gagny · Brou-sur-Chantereine

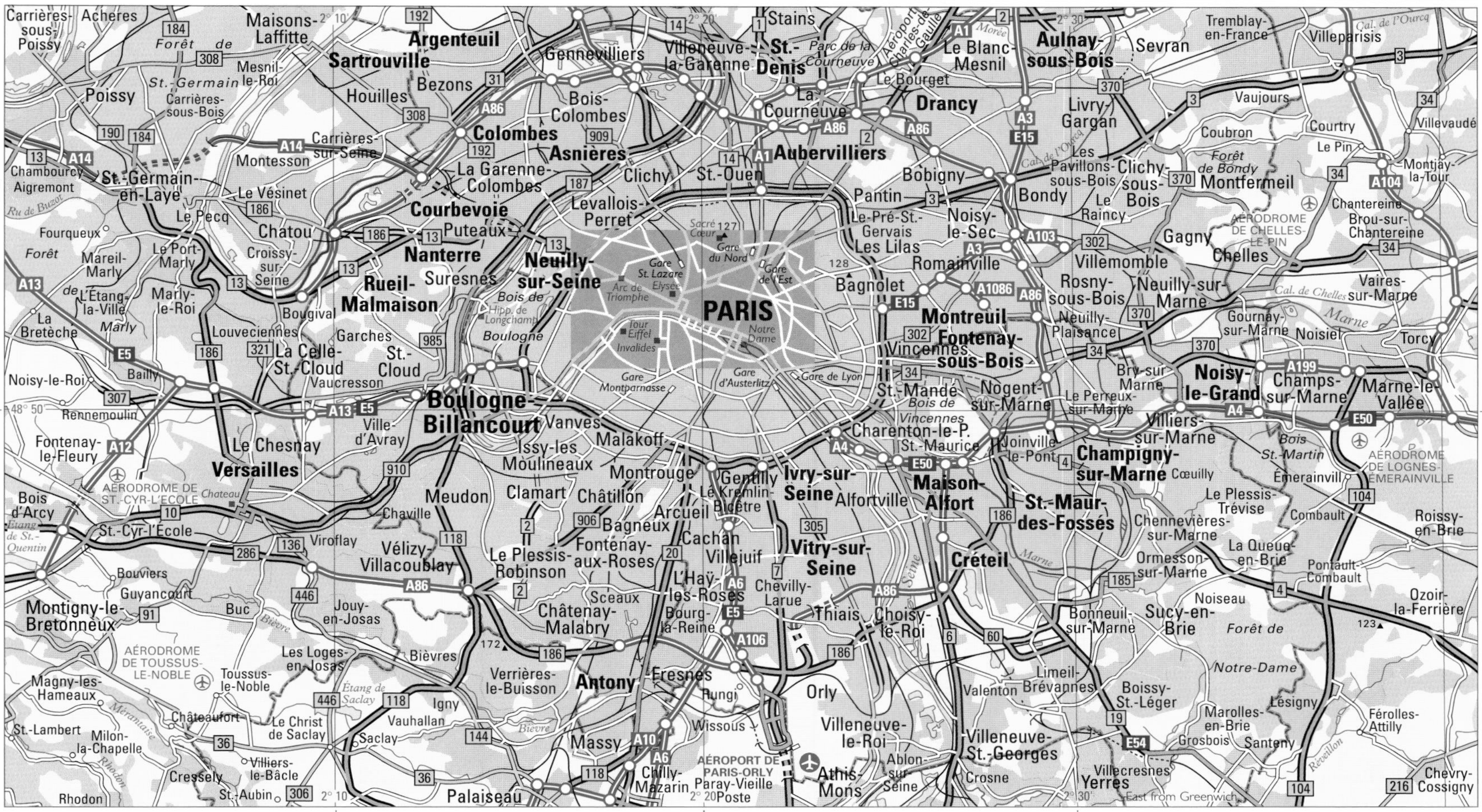

Le Pecq · **Courbevoie** · **Puteaux** · Levallois-Perret · Sacré Cœur · Romainville · Villemomble · **Chelles**

Chatou · Croissy-sur-Seine · **Nanterre** · **Neuilly-sur-Seine** · Gare St.-Lazare · Gare du Nord · Gare de l'Est · Bagnolet · **Montreuil** · Rosny-sous-Bois · **Neuilly-sur-Marne** · Gournay-sur-Marne · Noisiel · Torcy

Le Port-Marly · Suresnes · Arc de Triomphe · **PARIS** · Notre-Dame · **Fontenay-sous-Bois** · Vincennes · Neuilly-Plaisance

Marly-le-Roi · **Rueil-Malmaison** · Garches · Boulogne · Tour Eiffel · Invalides · Gare de Lyon · St.-Mandé · Nogent-sur-Marne · Le Perreux-sur-Marne · **Noisy-le-Grand** · **Champs-sur-Marne** · **Marne-la-Vallée**

La Bretèche · Louveciennes · Bougival · La Celle-St.-Cloud · St.-Cloud · Vaucresson · **Boulogne-Billancourt** · Charenton-le-P. · St.-Maurice · Joinville-le-Pont · Villiers-sur-Marne

Noisy-le-Roi · Bailly · **Le Chesnay** · Vanves · Malakoff · Gare Montparnasse · Gare d'Austerlitz · **Champigny-sur-Marne**

Rennemoulin · Ville-d'Avray · Issy-les-Moulineaux · Montrouge · Le Kremlin-Bicêtre · **Ivry-sur-Seine** · **Maisons-Alfort** · **St.-Maur-des-Fossés** · Chennevières-sur-Marne

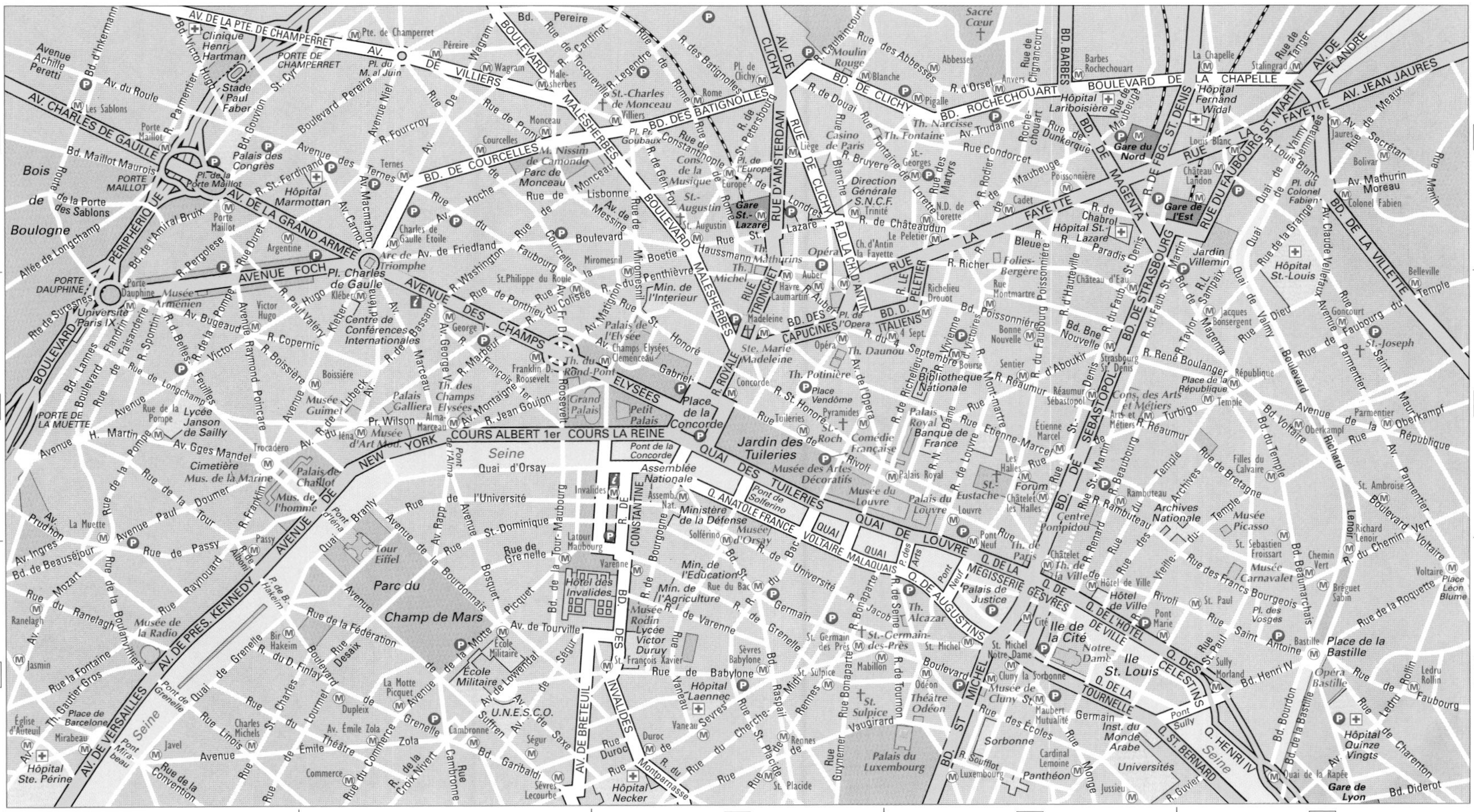

Fontenay-le-Fleury · **Versailles** · Meudon · Clamart · Châtillon · **Vitry-sur-Seine** · Alfortville · **Créteil** · Le Plessis-Trévise · Combault

Bois d'Arcy · St.-Cyr-l'École · Viroflay · Chaville · Bagneux · Arcueil · Cachan · Villejuif · Ormesson-sur-Marne · La Queue-en-Brie · Roissy-en-Brie

Montigny-le-Bretonneux · Bouviers · **Vélizy-Villacoublay** · Le Plessis-Robinson · Fontenay-aux-Roses · L'Haÿ-les-Roses · Chevilly-Larue · Choisy-le-Roi · Bonneuil-sur-Marne · Sucy-en-Brie · Ozoir-la-Ferrière

Guyancourt · Jouy-en-Josas · Sceaux · Bourg-la-Reine · Thiais · Noiseau · Forêt de Notre-Dame

Magny-les-Hameaux · Châteaufort · Milon-la-Chapelle · Les Loges-en-Josas · Bièvres · Verrières-le-Buisson · **Antony** · Fresnes · Rungis · Orly · Valenton · Boissy-St.-Léger · Marolles-en-Brie · Santeny · Férolles-Attilly

St.-Lambert · Toussus-le-Noble · Igny · Vauhallan · Wissous · Villeneuve-le-Roi · Limeil-Brévannes · Lésigny

Cresselly · Villiers-le-Bâcle · Saclay · Massy · Chilly-Mazarin · AÉROPORT DE PARIS-ORLY · Athis-Mons · Ablon-sur-Seine · Villeneuve-St.-Georges · Crosne · Villecresnes · Yerres · Chevry-Cossigny

Rhodon · St.-Aubin · Palaiseau · Paray-Vieille-Poste

Central Paris

km 0 — 1
miles 0 — 0.5

COPYRIGHT GEORGE PHILIP LTD.

Prague

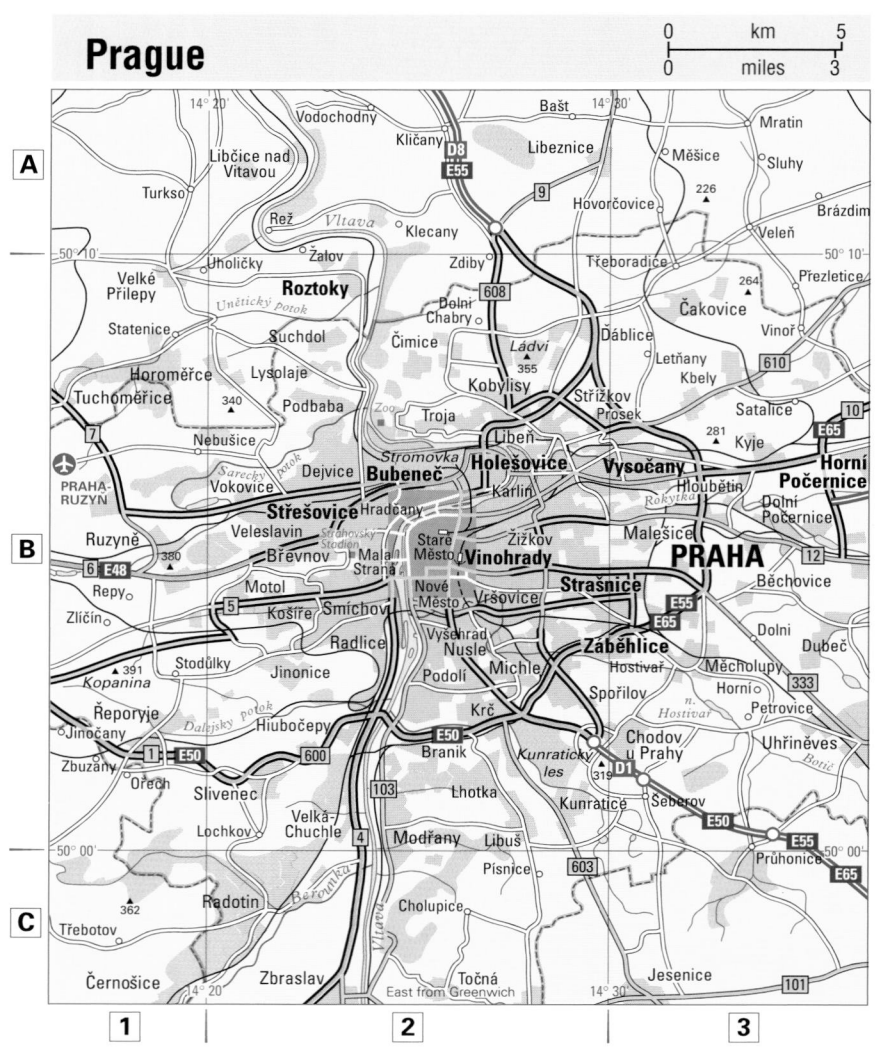

Central Prague

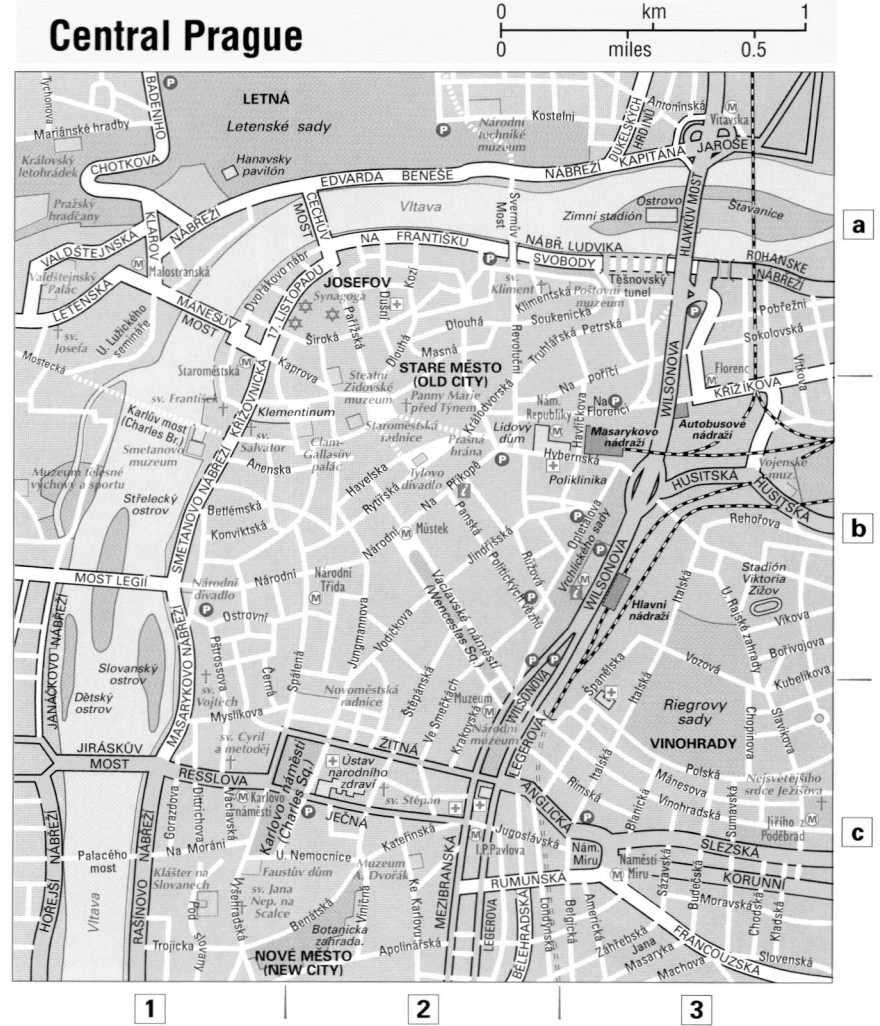

Rio de Janeiro

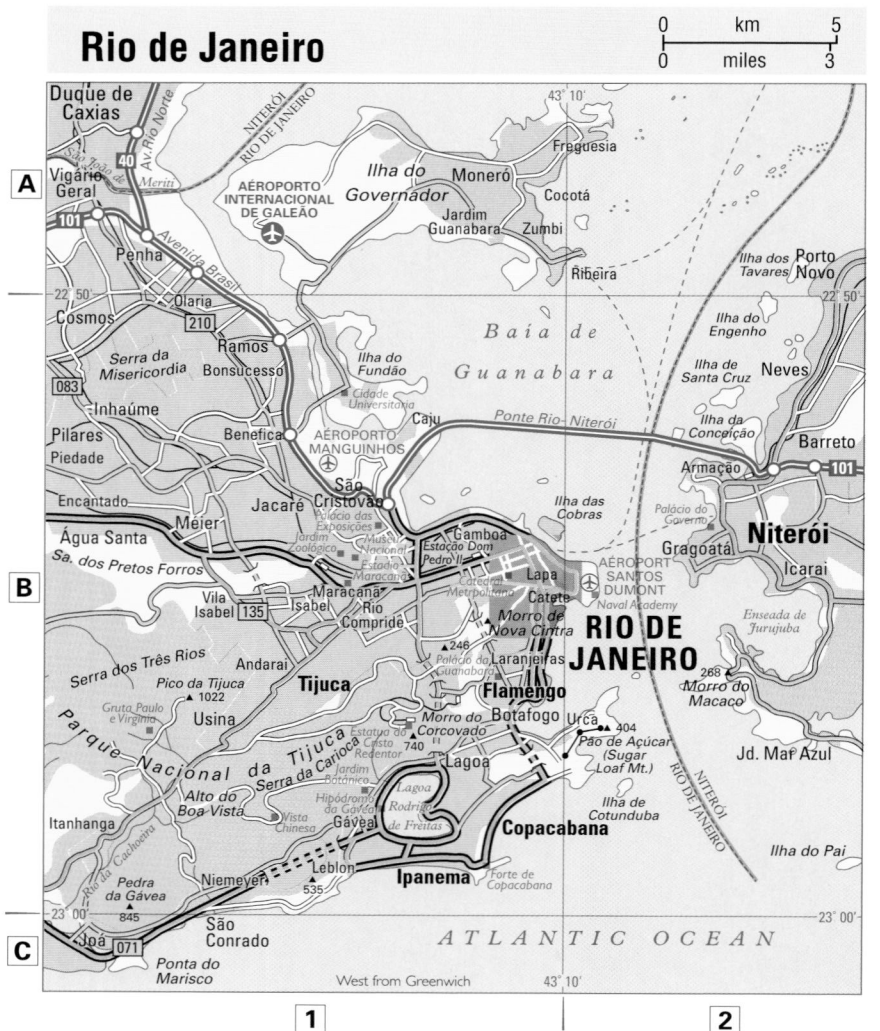

Central Rio de Janeiro

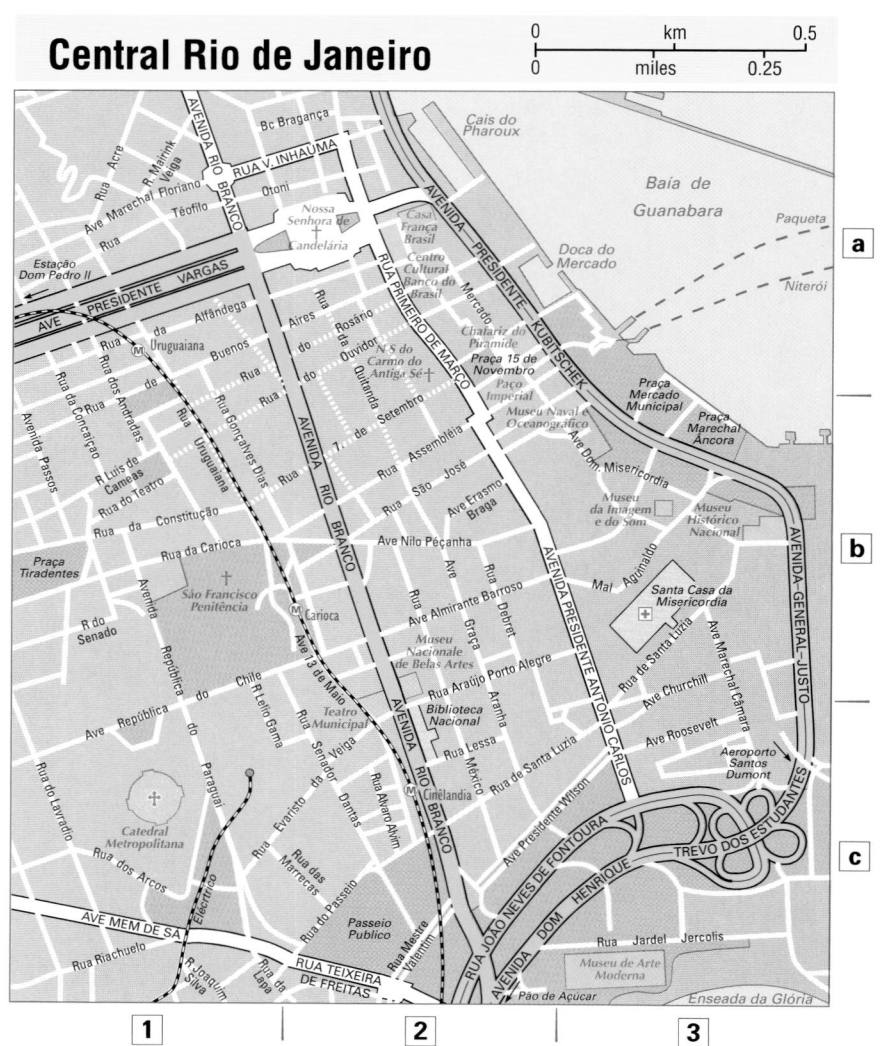

COPYRIGHT GEORGE PHILIP LTD.

Rome

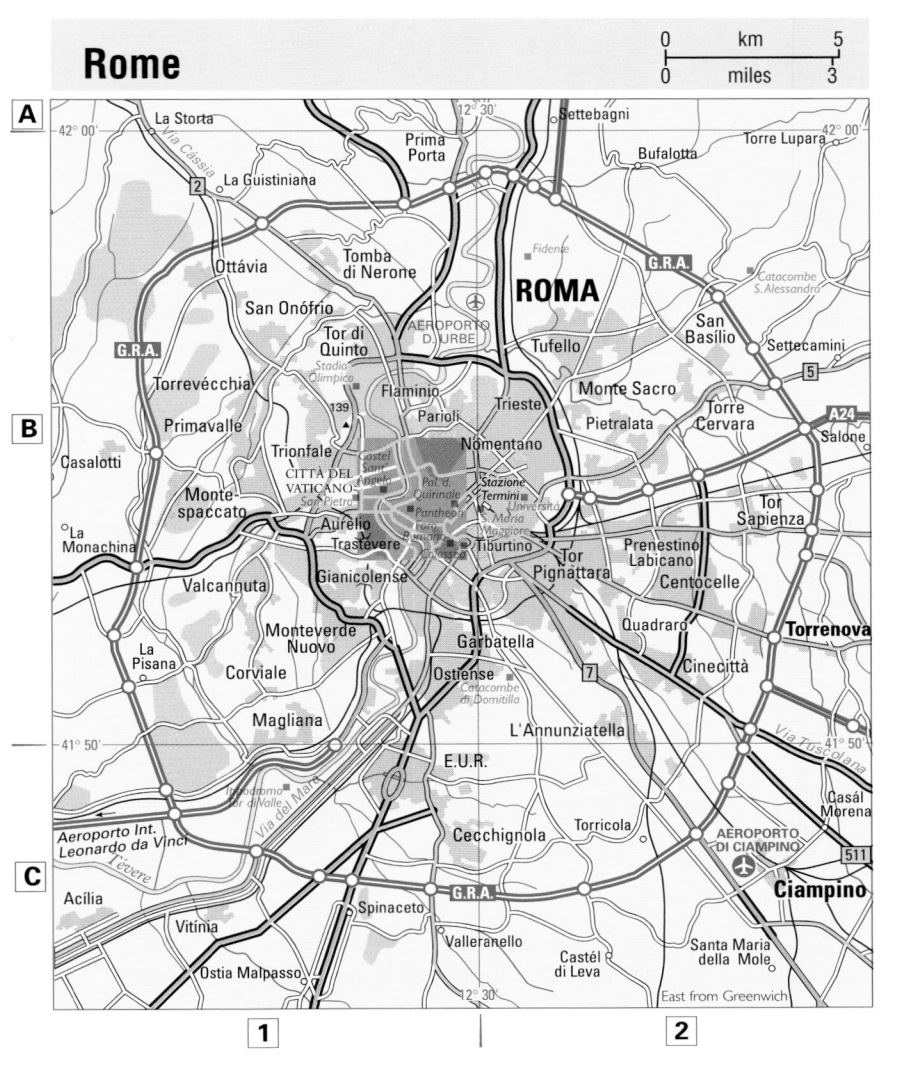

Central Rome

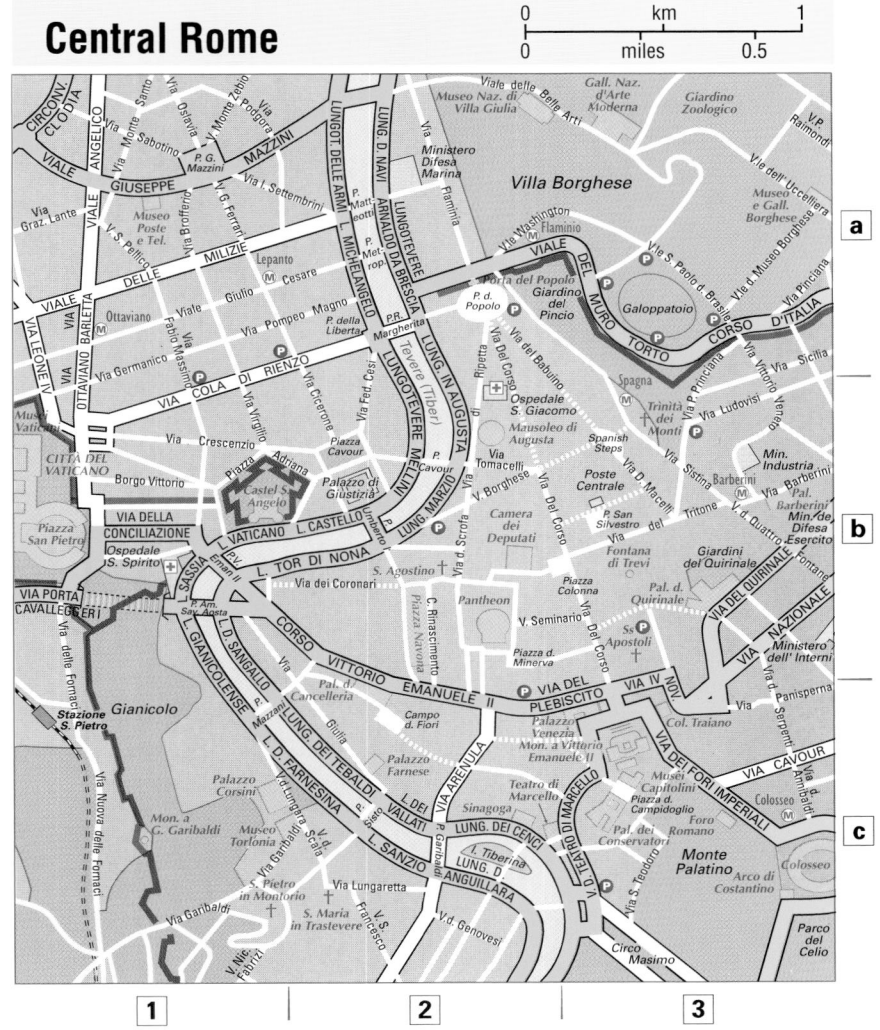

San Francisco

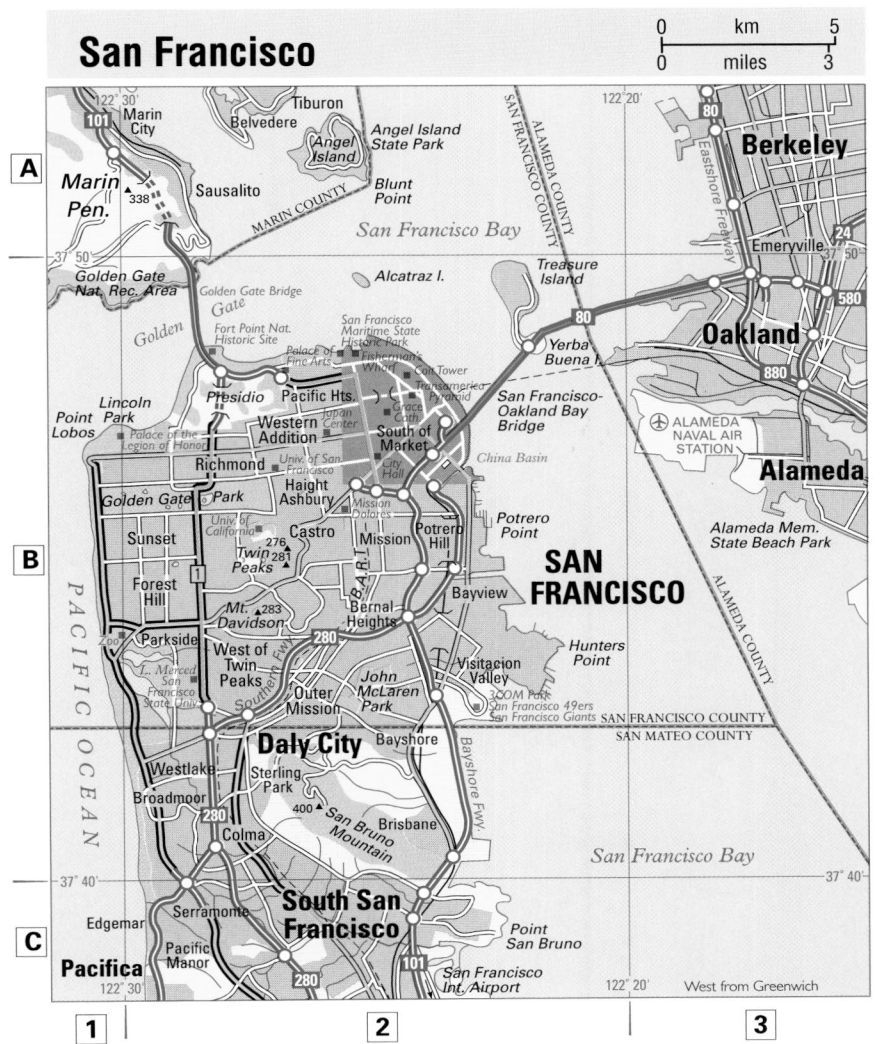

Central San Francisco

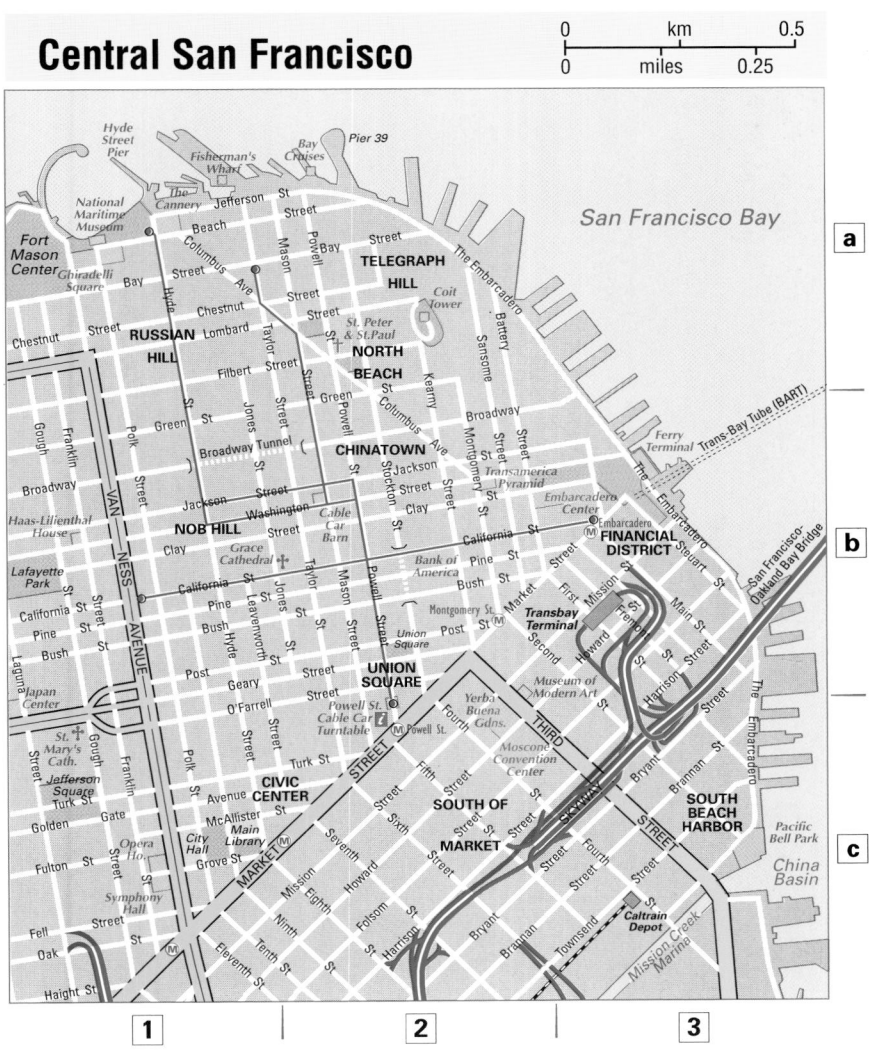

COPYRIGHT GEORGE PHILIP LTD.

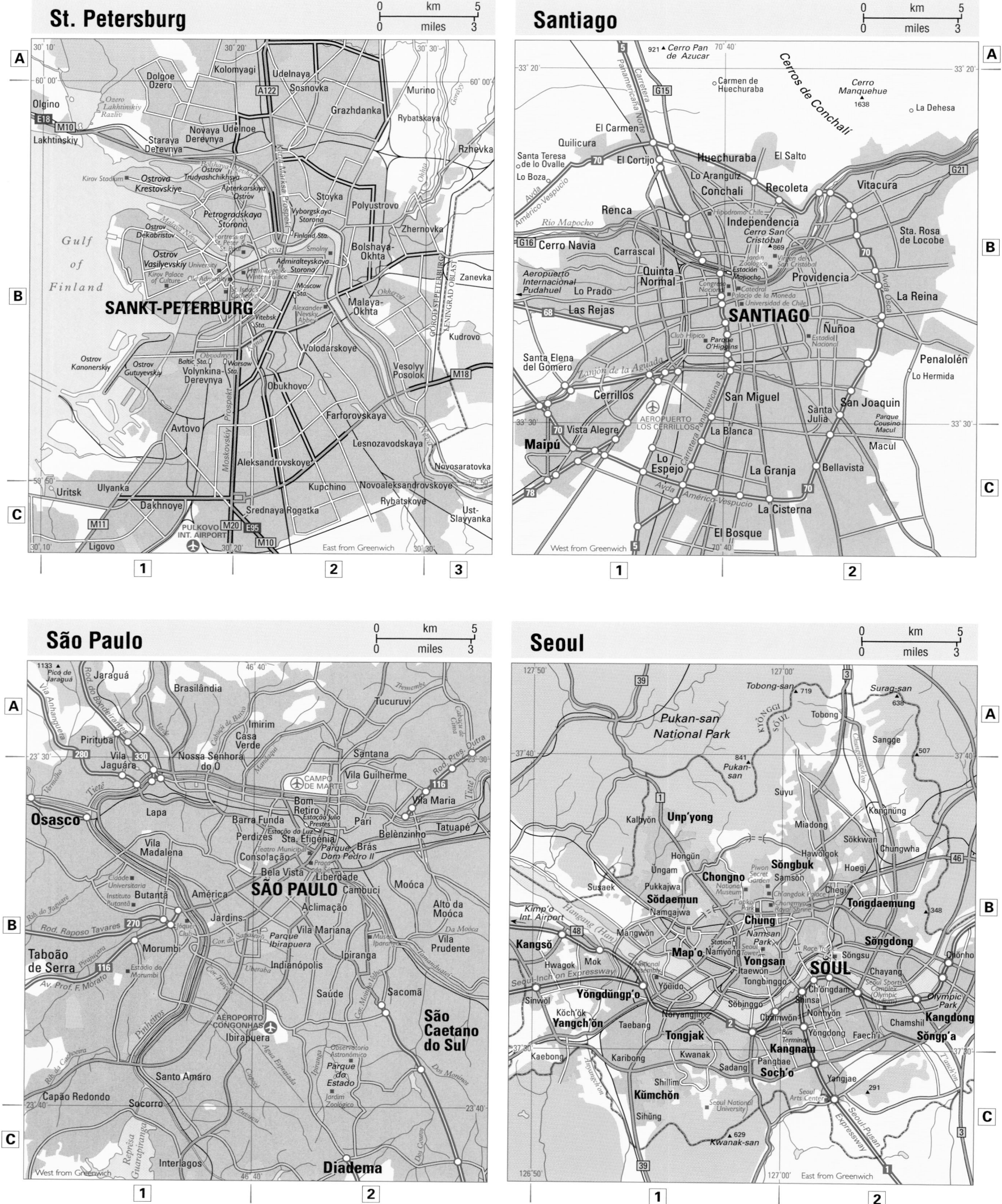
St. Petersburg
0 km 5
0 miles 3
SANKT-PETERBURG
Gulf of Finland
Kolomyagi
Udelnaya
Sosnovka
Dolgoe Ozero
Olgino
Lakhtinskiy
Murino
Grazhdanka
Rybatskaya
Novaya Derevnya
Udelnoe
Staraya Derevnya
Rzhevka
Ostrova Krestovskiye
Petrogradskaya Storona
Stoyka
Polyustrovo
Zhernovka
Bolshaya-Okhta
Zanevka
Malaya-Okhta
Kudrovo
Volodarskoye
Vesolyy Posolok
Volynkina-Derevnya
Obukhovo
Farforovskaya
Avtovo
Lesnozavodskaya
Aleksandrovskoye
Novosaratovka
Uritsk
Ulyanka
Kupchino
Novoaleksandrovskoye
Dakhnoye
Srednaya Rogatka
Rybatskoye
Ust-Slavyanka
Ligovo
PULKOVO INT. AIRPORT
East from Greenwich
Santiago
0 km 5
0 miles 3
SANTIAGO
Cerros de Conchalí
Cerro Pan de Azucar
Carmen de Huechuraba
Cerro Manquehue
La Dehesa
El Carmen
Quilicura
Huechuraba
El Salto
El Cortijo
Lo Aranguiz
Conchali
Recoleta
Vitacura
Renca
Independencia
Cerro San Cristóbal
Sta. Rosa de Locobe
Cerro Navia
Carrascal
Quinta Normal
Providencia
Aeropuerto Internacional Pudahuel
Lo Prado
La Reina
Las Rejas
Ñuñoa
Santa Elena del Gomero
Penalolén
Lo Hermida
Cerrillos
San Miguel
San Joaquin
Santa Julia
AEROPUERTO LOS CERRILLOS
Vista Alegre
La Blanca
Maipú
Macul
Lo Espejo
La Granja
Bellavista
La Cisterna
El Bosque
West from Greenwich
São Paulo
0 km 5
0 miles 3
SÃO PAULO
Jaraguá
Brasilândia
Tucuruvi
Imirim
Casa Verde
Pirituba
Vila Jaguará
Nossa Senhora do Ó
Santana
Vila Guilherme
CAMPO DE MARTE
Vila Maria
Osasco
Lapa
Bom Retiro
Barra Funda
Pari
Belènzinho
Tatuapé
Vila Madalena
Perdizes
Sta. Efigênia
Brás
Consolação
Bela Vista
Liberdade
Moóca
Butantã
América
Cambuci
Alto da Moóca
Jardins
Aclimação
Vila Mariana
Vila Prudente
Taboão de Serra
Morumbi
Parque Ibirapuera
Ipiranga
Indianópolis
Saúde
Sacomã
AEROPORTO CONGONHAS
Ibirapuera
São Caetano do Sul
Santo Amaro
Capão Redondo
Socorro
Interlagos
Diadema
West from Greenwich
Seoul
0 km 5
0 miles 3
SŎUL
Pukan-san National Park
Tobong-san
Surag-san
Tobong
Sangge
Pukan-san
Suyu
Kalhyŏn
Unp'yong
Kongnŭng
Miadong
Sŏkkwan
Hongŭn
Chungwha
Hawŏlgok
Ŭngam
Sŏngbuk
Hoegi
Chongno
Susaek
Pukkajwa
Sŏdaemun
Tongdaemung
Namgajwa
Chung
Kimp'o Int. Airport
Kangsŏ
Mangwŏn
Sŏngdong
Map'o
Namyŏng
Yongsan
Sŏngsu
Hwagok
Mok
Itaewon
Chayang
Ch'ŏnho
Yŏngdŭngp'o
Yŏido
Tongbinggo
Ch'ŏngdam
Olympic Park
Sinwŏl
Noryangjin
Sŏbinggo
Sinsa
Kangdong
Yangch'ŏn
Chamwŏn
Nonhyŏn
Chamshil
Taebang
Tongjak
Yŏngdong
Faech'i
Sŏngp'a
Kaebong
Karibong
Kwanak
Kangnam
Sadang
Pangbae
Soch'o
Shillim
Yangjae
Kŭmchŏn
Sihŭng
Kwanak-san
Seoul-Pusan Expressway
East from Greenwich

COPYRIGHT GEORGE PHILIP LTD.

Shanghai

0 — km — 5
0 — miles — 3

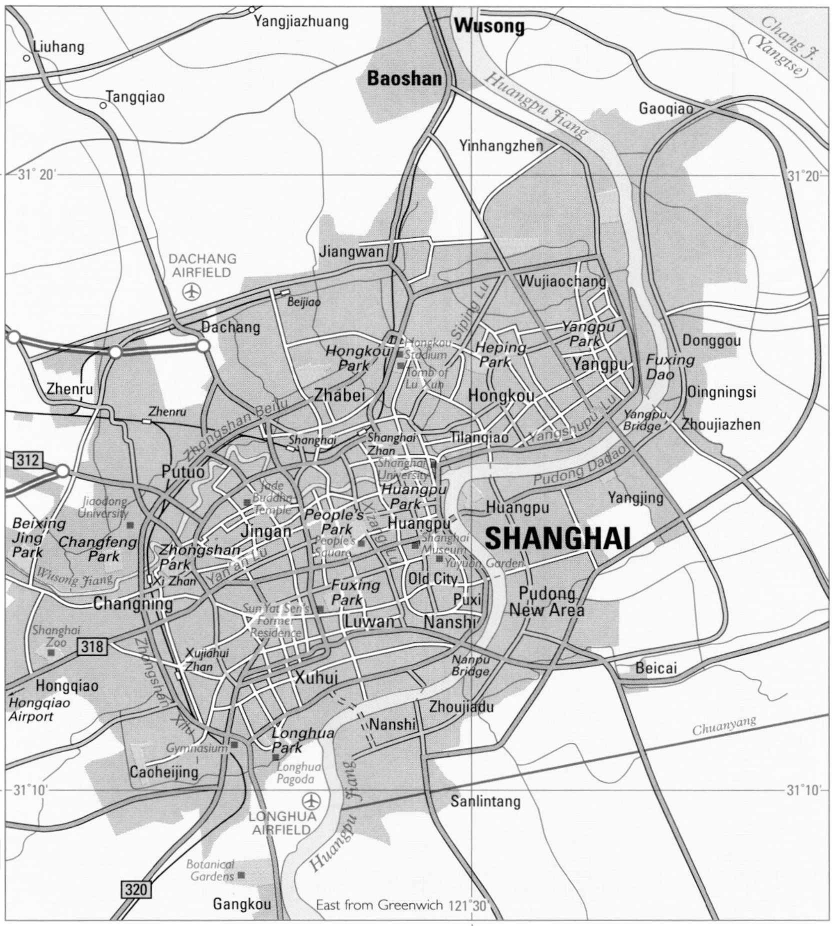

Liuhang
Yangjiazhuang
Wusong
Tangqiao
Baoshan
Gaoqiao
Yinhangzhen
Chang J. (Yangtse)
Huangpu Jiang
31°20'
31°20'
Jiangwan
DACHANG AIRFIELD
Beijiao
Wujiaochang
Dachang
Heping Park
Yangpu Park
Donggou
Zhenru
Hongkou Park
Tomb of Lu Xun
Yangpu
Fuxing Dao
Zhenru
Zhabei
Hongkou
Qingningsi
Hongkou Stadium
Zhoujiazhen
Shanghai Zhan
Tilangiao
Yangpu Bridge
Jade Buddha Temple
Putuo
Huangpu Park
Yangjing
Jiaodong University
Zhongshan Park
People's Park
Huangpu
Huangpu
Beixing Jing Park
Changfeng Park
Jingan
People's Square
Shanghai Museum
Yangjing
Changning
Fuxing Park
Old City
Puxi
Pudong New Area
Sun Yat Sen's former Residence
Luwan
Nanshi
Yuyuan Garden
Shanghai Zoo
Xujiahui Zhan
Xuhui
Nanpu Bridge
Beicai
Hongqiao
Hongqiao Airport
Zhoujiadu
Chuanyang
Longhua Park
Nanshi
31°10'
31°10'
Caoheijing
Gymnasium
Longhua Pagoda
Sanlintang
Botanical Gardens
LONGHUA AIRFIELD
Gangkou
East from Greenwich 121°30'

Central Singapore

0 — km — 1
0 — miles — 0.5

CARNHILL ROAD
Istana (President's Residence)
Kandang Kerbau Hospital
BUKIT TIMAH ROAD
Cuff Rd.
Upper Weld Rd.
CLEMENCEAU AVE
Central Park
Edinburgh
Sophia Road
MacKenzie
Serangoon Road
Short Street
Dunlop St.
Abdul Gafoor Mosque
JALAN BESAR
ROCHOR CANAL RD.
Bus Station
BIDEFORD RD.
ORCHARD ROAD
Thong Sia Bldg.
Emerald Hill Rd.
Cuppage Centre
Faber House
Centre-point
Cuppage Road
Orchard Plaza
Sri Temasek
Wilkie Road
Sophia Road
Sin Lim Square
MIDDLE ROAD
Blanco Court
Bencoolen Mosque
Waterloo Street
St. Joseph's Church
COLONIAL DISTRICT
ORCHARD
N2 Somerset
Handy Road
BENCOOLEN STREET
Raffles Hotel
ROAD
PENANG ROAD
Dhoby Ghaut
St. Andrews Rd.
Seah St.
KILLINEY
Lloyd Rd.
Chesed-El Synagogue
AVENUE
Singapore Art Museum
BRAS BASAH
Westin Plaza
RIVER VALLEY ROAD
OXLEY
Sacred Heart Church
BOULEVARD
Singapore Hist. Mus.
STAMFORD
Battle Box
VICTORIA STREET
War Memorial Park
Sri Thandayuthapani Temple
Fort Canning Park
Singapore Cric. Mus.
Hong San See Temple
TANK ROAD
Canning Rise
Asian Civ. Mus.
C2 City Hall
CITY CENTRE
Van Kleef Aquarium
St. Andrew's Cathedral
Singapore Philatelic Mus.
HILL STREET
City Hall
Esplanade Park
CLEMENCEAU
Clarke Quay
North Boat Quay
Supreme Court
Singapore Cricket Club
Singapore River
Boat Quay
Parliament Hse.
Victoria Concert Hall & Theatre
HAVELOCK ROAD
MERCHANT ROAD
Raffles Landing Site
Empress Pl. Museum
Melaka Mosque
N CANAL RD.
Merlion Park
Marina Bay
Swee Road
UPPER CROSS ROAD
PICKERING STREET
CHULIA ST.
CENTRAL EXPRESSWAY
Pearl's Hill City Park
Pearl's Hill Reservoir
Wak Hai Cheng Bio Temple
OUB Centre
Clifford Pier
SENTOSA
Chin
Outram Park
NEW BRIDGE
People's Park Complex
SOUTH BRIDGE
Jamae Mosque
CHINATOWN
Fuk Tak Ch'i Temple
Raffles Place
Oriental Theatre
Sri Mariamman Temple
RAFFLES QUAY

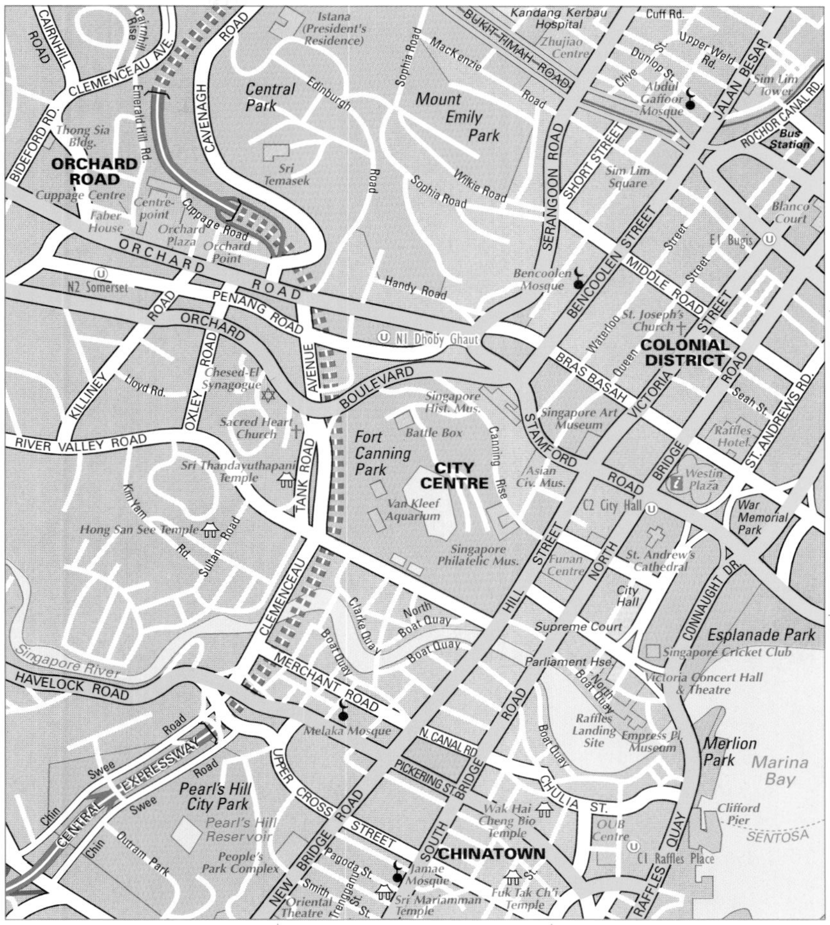

Singapore

0 — km — 10
0 — miles — 6

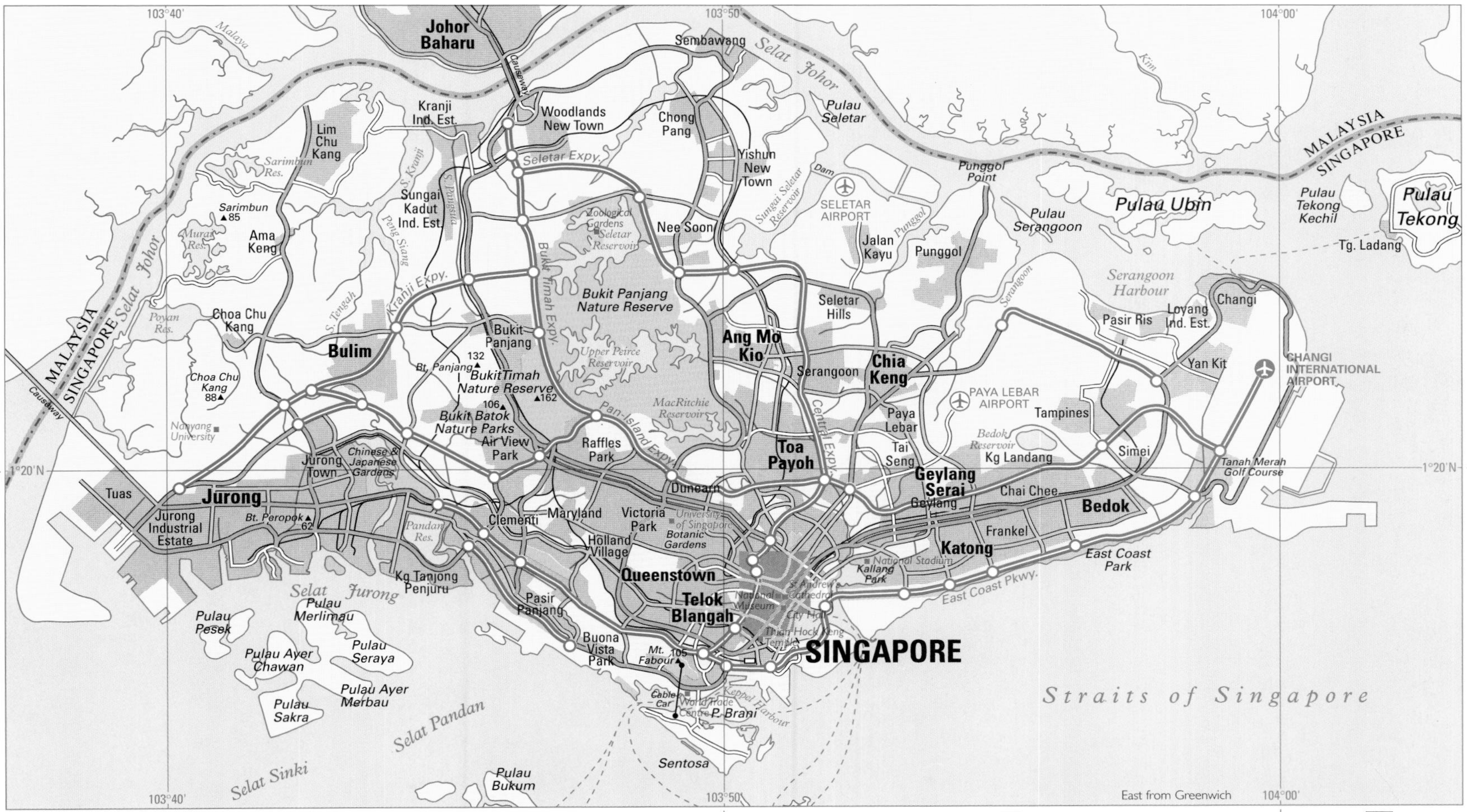

103°40'
103°50'
104°00'
Malaysia
Johor Baharu
Selat Johor
MALAYSIA SINGAPORE
Sembawang
Pulau Tekong
Kranji Ind. Est.
Woodlands New Town
Chong Pang
Pulau Seletar
Pulau Tekong Kechil
Lim Chu Kang
Sarimbun Res.
Seletar Expy.
Yishun New Town
Dam
Tg. Ladang
Sarimbun 85
Ama Keng
Sungei Kadut Ind. Est.
Zoological Gardens
Seletar Reservoir
Nee Soon
SELETAR AIRPORT
Punggol Point
Pulau Ubin
Murai Res.
Panjang Res.
Bukit Timah Expy.
Jalan Kayu
Pulau Serangoon
Pulau Tekong
Choa Chu Kang
Kranji Expy.
Bukit Panjang Nature Reserve
Punggol
Serangoon Harbour
Changi
Bulim
Bukit Panjang
Upper Peirce Reservoir
Ang Mo Kio
Seletar Hills
Pasir Ris
Loyang Ind. Est.
Choa Chu Kang 88▲
Bt. Panjang 132
Bukit Timah Nature Reserve
▲162
Chia Keng
Serangoon
Yan Kit
CHANGI INTERNATIONAL AIRPORT
Nanyang University
106 Bukit Batok Nature Parks
MacRitchie Reservoir
Paya Lebar
PAYA LEBAR AIRPORT
Air View Park
Raffles Park
Tai Seng
Bedok Reservoir
Kg Landang
Tampines
Tanah Merah Golf Course
Jurong Town
Chinese & Japanese Gardens
Pan-Island Expy.
Toa Payoh
Geylang Serai
Simei
1°20'N
Jürong
Bt. Peropok▲
Duncan
Geylang
Chai Chee
1°20'N
Tuas
Jurong Industrial Estate
Bt. Peropok▲ 62
Clementi
Maryland
Victoria Park
University of Singapore
Bedok
Pandan Res.
Holland Village
Botanic Gardens
Katong
Frankel
East Coast Park
Pulau Pesek
Pulau Merlimau
Pasir Panjang
Queenstown
Telok Blangah
Kallang Park
East Coast Pkwy.
Pulau Ayer Chawan
Buona Vista Park
Mt. Faber
National Stadium
Selat Jurong
Kg Tanjong Penjuru
Cable Car
World Trade Centre
P. Brani
SINGAPORE
Thian Hock Keng Temple
Pulau Ayer Merbau
B
Straits of Singapore
Pulau Seraya
Pulau Sakra
Selat Pandan
Sentosa
Pulau Bukum
Selat Sinki
East from Greenwich
104°00'

COPYRIGHT GEORGE PHILIP LTD.

Stockholm

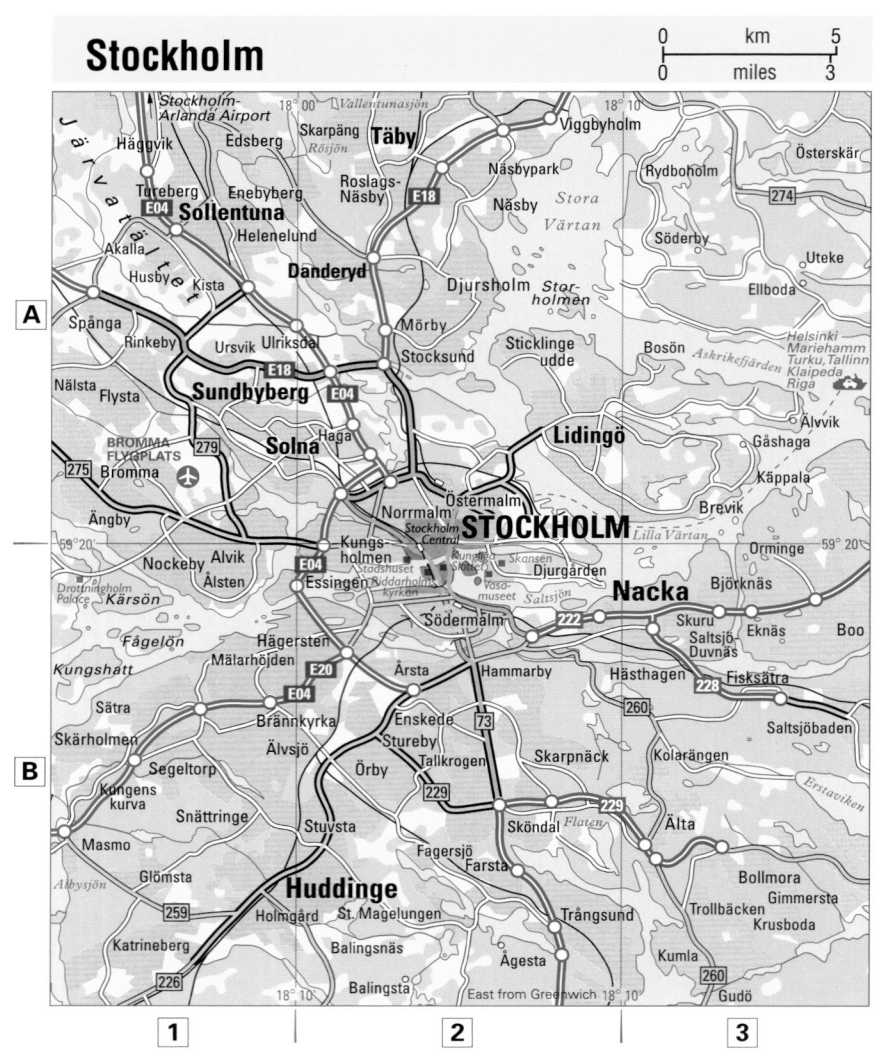

Central Stockholm

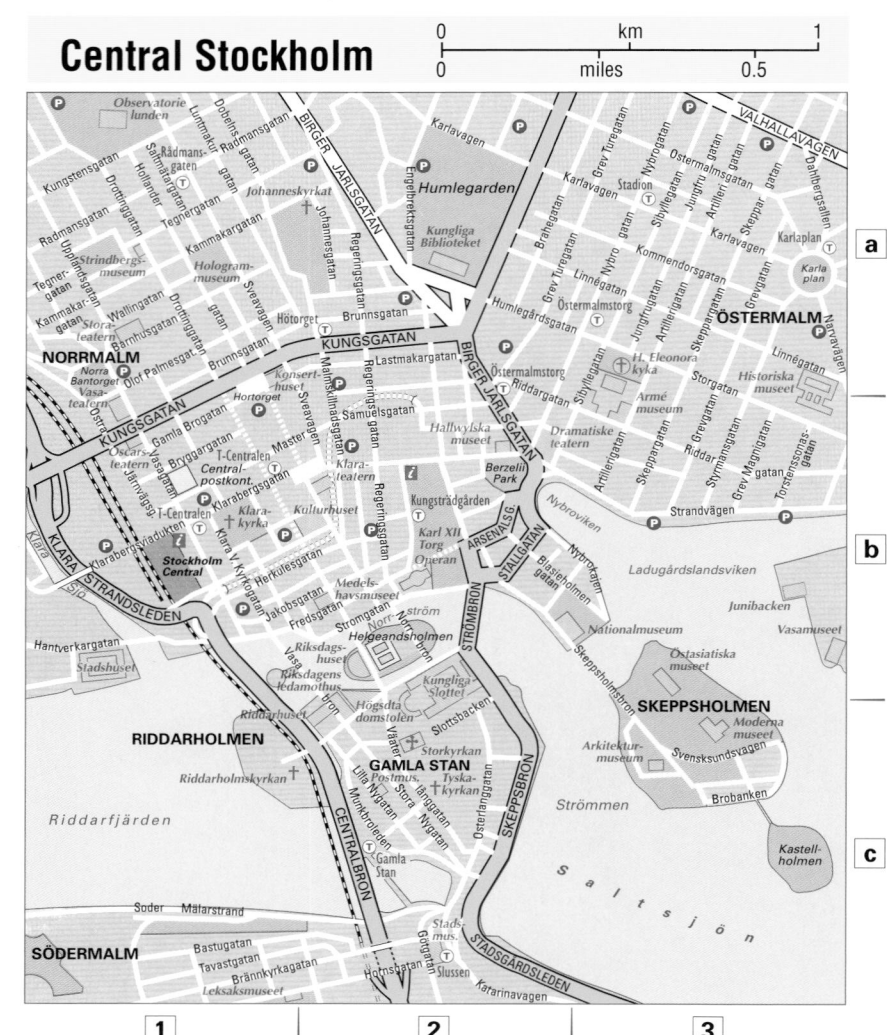

Sydney

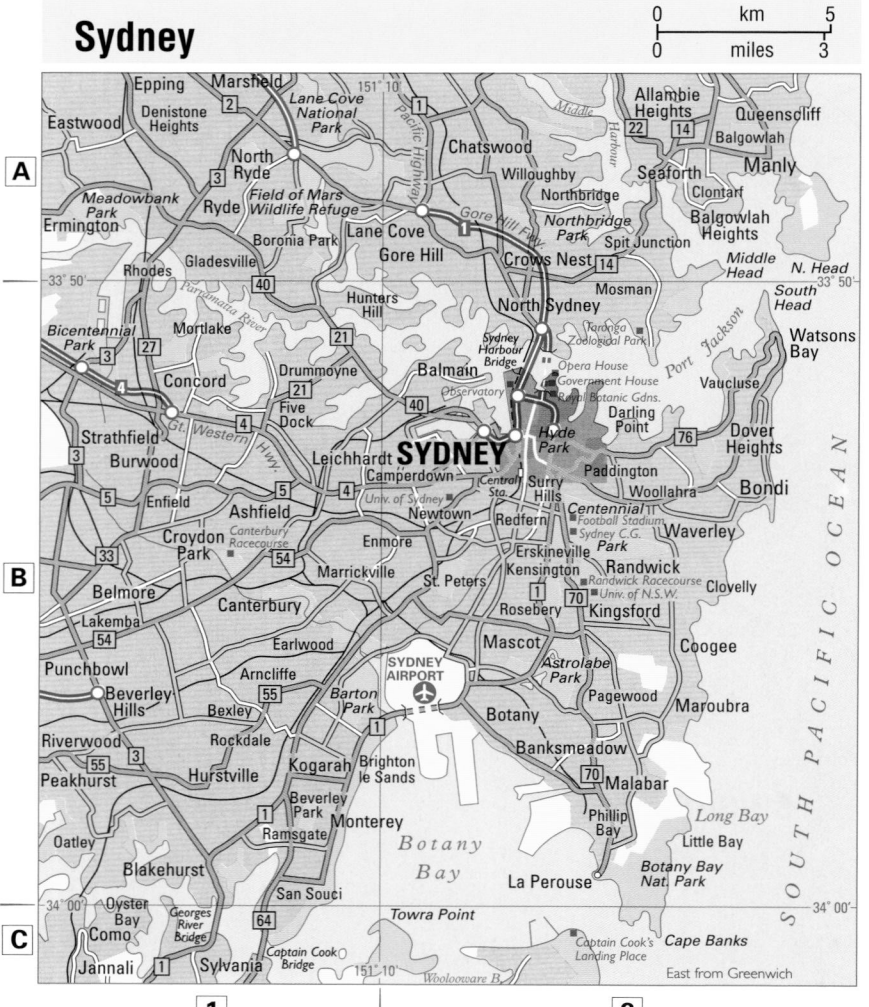

Central Sydney

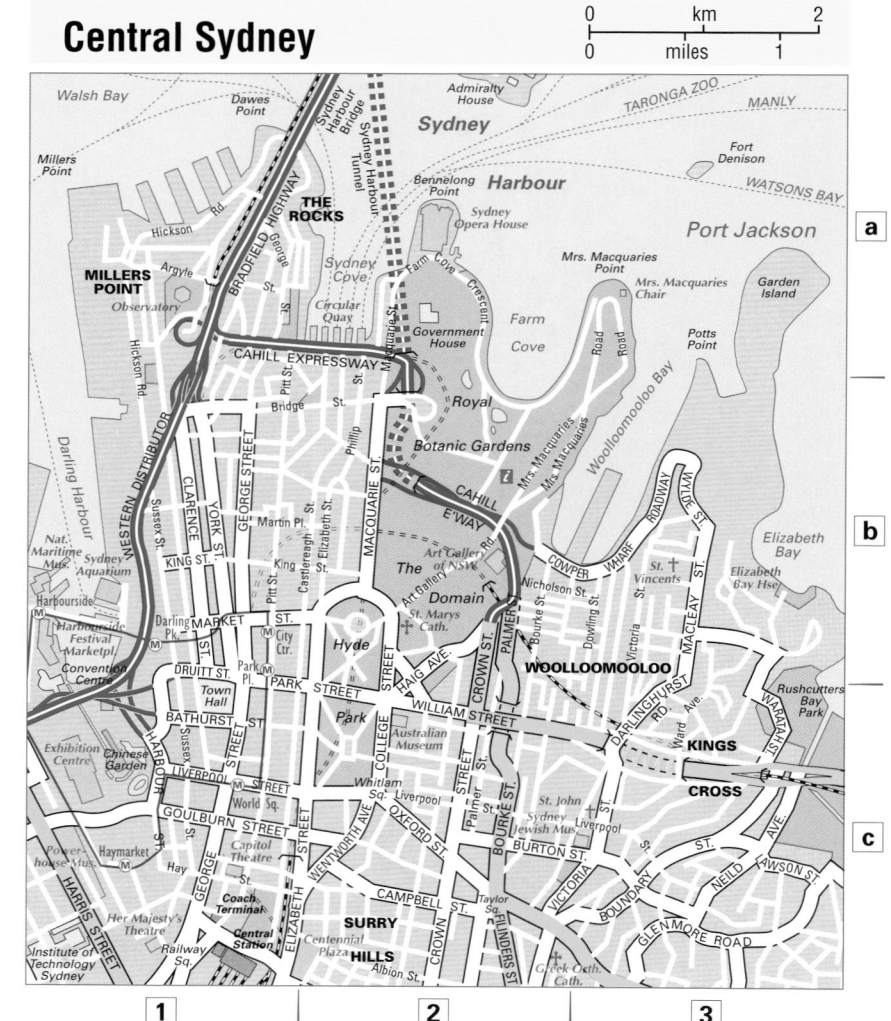

COPYRIGHT GEORGE PHILIP LTD.

Tokyo

0 km 5
0 miles 3

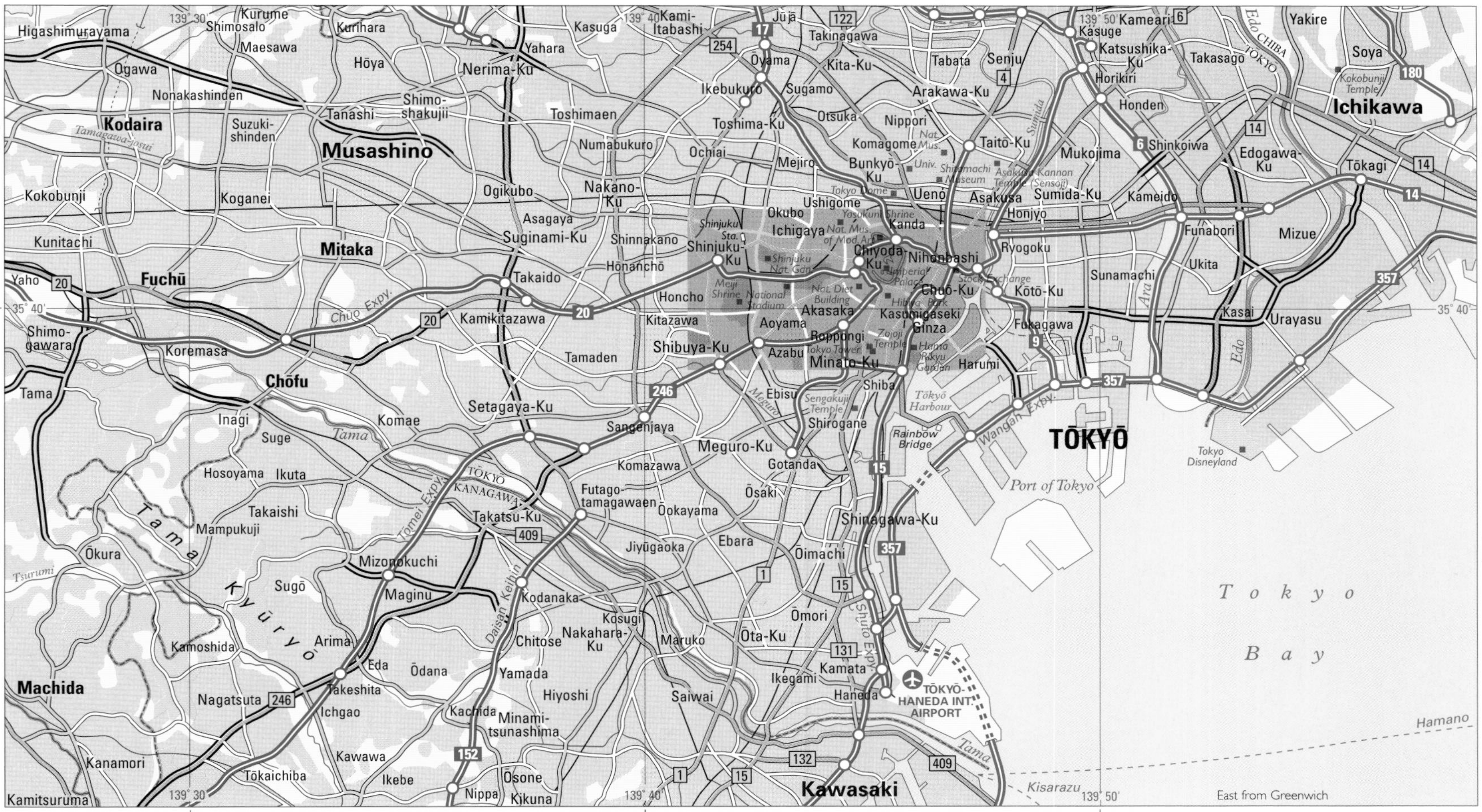

Higashimurayama · Shimosalo · Kurume · Kurihara · Kasuga · Yahara · Kami-Itabashi · Jūjō · Takinagawa · Kasuge · Katsushika-Ku · Takasago · Yakire · Soya · Kobunji Temple

Kodaira · Shimoshakuji · Nerima-Ku · Ōyama · Kita-Ku · Tabata · Senju · Horikiri · Takasago · Ichikawa

Musashino · Ogawa · Nonakashinden · Hōya · Tanashi · Shimo-shakuji · Toshimaen · Ikebukuro · Sugamo · Arakawa-Ku · Shinkoiwa · Edogawa-Ku · Tōkagi

Mitaka · Kokubunji · Koganei · Ogikubo · Asagaya · Nakano-Ku · Toshima-Ku · Otsuka · Nippori · Komagome · Mukojima · Funabori · Mizue

Fuchū · Kunitachi · Suginami-Ku · Shinnakano · Mejiro · Bunkyō-Ku · Ueno · Asakusa · Sumida-Ku · Honjyo · Kameido · Ukita · Kasai

Chōfu · Takaido · Honcho · Kamikitazawa · Shinjuku-Ku · Chiyoda-Ku · Nihonbashi · Chūō-Ku · Kōtō-Ku · Fukagawa · Urayasu

Shimogawara · Tama · Koremasa · Inagi · Suge · Komae · Setagaya-Ku · Sangenjaya · Shibuya-Ku · Azabu · Minato-Ku · Shiba · Harumi · TŌKYŌ · Tokyo Disneyland

Machida · Okura · Hosoyama · Ikuta · Takaishi · Mizonokuchi · Futago-tamagawaen · Meguro-Ku · Gotanda · Ōsaki · Shinagawa-Ku · Port of Tokyo

Kamitsuruma · Kanamori · Nagatsuta · Takeshita · Ōdana · Yamada · Jiyūgaoka · Ebara · Ōimachi · Ōmori · Tokyo Bay

Kawasaki · Kisarazu · Hamano · East from Greenwich

TŌKYŌ HANEDA INT'L AIRPORT

Central Tokyo

0 km 1
0 miles 0.5

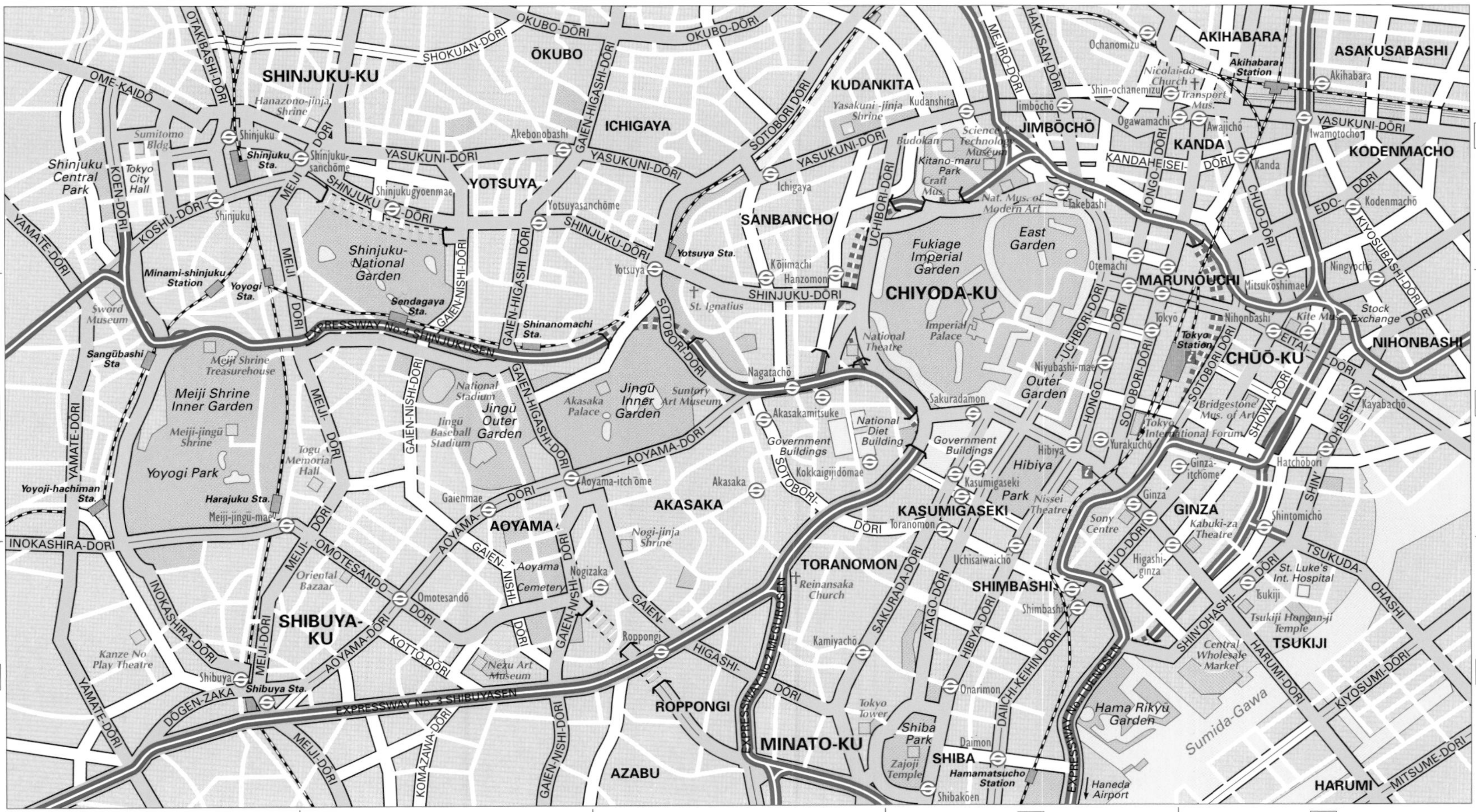

SHINJUKU-KU · ŌKUBO · KUDANKITA · AKIHABARA · ASAKUSABASHI · ICHIGAYA · JIMBOCHO · KANDA · KODENMACHO · YOTSUYA · SANBANCHO · CHIYODA-KU · MARUNŌUCHI · NIHONBASHI · Fukiage Imperial Garden · East Garden · Imperial Palace · CHŪŌ-KU · AOYAMA · AKASAKA · KASUMIGASEKI · GINZA · TSUKUDA · TORANOMON · SHIMBASHI · TSUKIJI · SHIBUYA-KU · ROPPONGI · MINATO-KU · SHIBA · HARUMI · AZABU

Meiji Shrine Inner Garden · Yoyogi Park · Shinjuku National Garden · Jingū Outer Garden · Jingū Inner Garden · Hama Rikyū Garden · Shiba Park

COPYRIGHT GEORGE PHILIP LTD.

Tehran

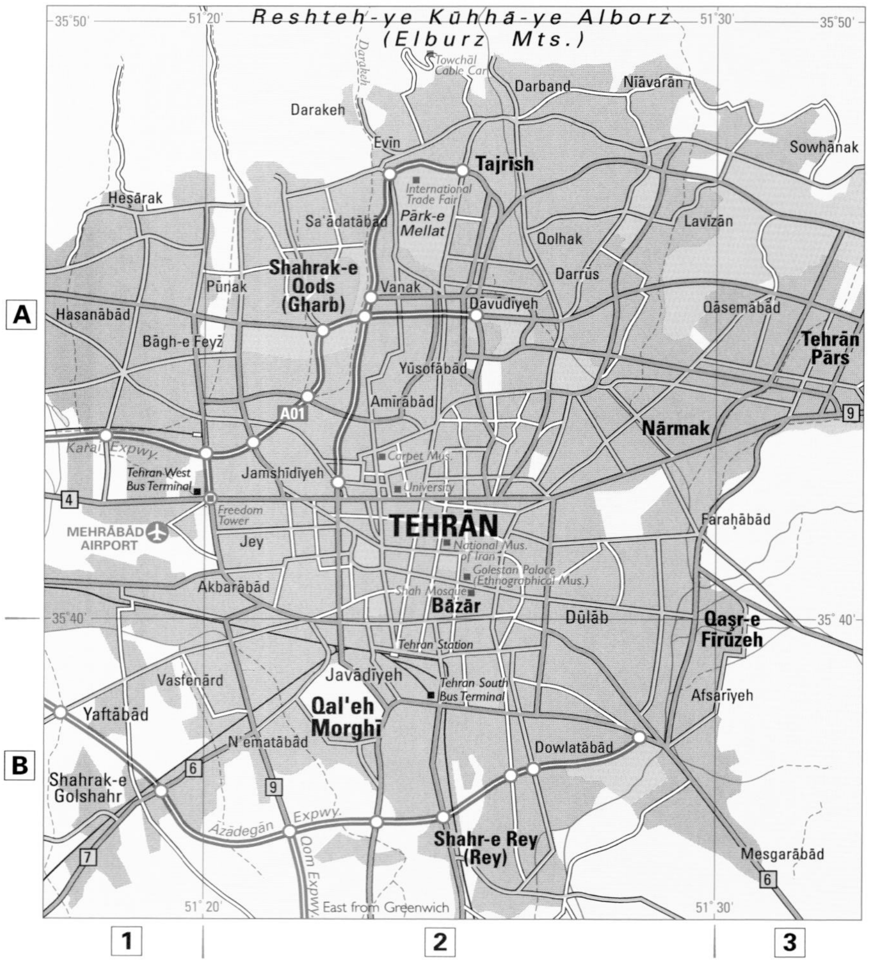

km 5 / miles 3

Reshteh-ye Kūhhā-ye Alborz (Elburz Mts.)

Darband
Darakeh
Niāvarān
Sowhānak
Evin
Tajrīsh
Sa'ādatābād
Pārk-e Mellat
International Trade Fair
Towchāl Cable Car
Hesārak
Lavīzān
Qolhak
Shahrak-e Qods (Gharb)
Vanak
Darrūs
Pūnak
Dāvūdīyeh
Qāsemābād
Bāgh-e Feyż
Hasanābād
Yūsofābād
Tehrān Pārs
Amīrābād
Nārmak
Kāraj Expwy.
Jamshīdīyeh
Carpet Mus.
University
Tehran West Bus Terminal
Freedom Tower
MEHRĀBĀD AIRPORT
Jey
National Mus. of Iran
Golestan Palace (Ethnographical Mus.)
TEHRĀN
Farahābād
Akbarābād
Shah Mosque
Bāzār
Dūlāb
Qasr-e Fīrūzeh
Tehran Station
Vasfenārd
Javādīyeh
Tehran South Bus Terminal
Afsarīyeh
Yaftābād
Qal'eh Morghī
N'ematābād
Dowlatābād
Shahrak-e Golshahr
Āzādegān
Shahr-e Rey (Rey)
Mesgarābād
Qom Expwy.
East from Greenwich

Tianjin

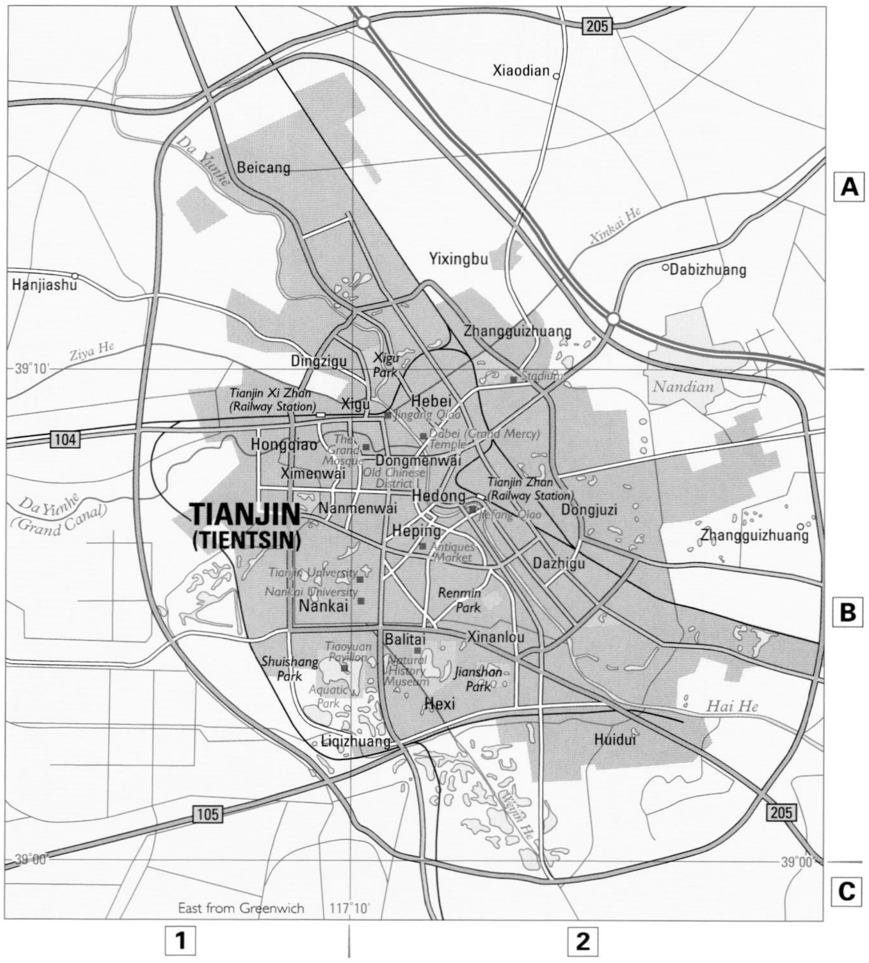

km 5 / miles 3

Xiaodian
Beicang
Da Yunhe
Xinkai He
Nandian
Hanjiashū
Yixingbu
Dabizhuang
Ziya He
Zhangguizhuang
Dingzigu
Xigu Park
Tianjin Xi Zhan (Railway Station)
Xigu
Hebei
Hongqiao
Dongmenwai
Tianjin Zhan (Railway Station)
Ximenwai
Old Chinese District
Hedong
Dongjuzi
TIANJIN (TIENTSIN)
Da Yunhe (Grand Canal)
Nanmenwai
Heping
Zhangguizhuang
Tianjin University
Nankai University
Nankai
Renmin Park
Dazhigu
Xinanlou
Shuishang Park
Balitai
Aquatic Park
Hexi
Hai He
Liqizhuang
Huidui
East from Greenwich

Toronto

km 5 / miles 3

Fairport
Markham
Thornhill
Brown
Concord
Metro Toronto Zoo
West Rouge
Rouge Hill
Woodbridge
Pine Grove
Edgeley
Newtonbrook
Agincourt
Malvern
Highland Creek
Port Union
Fisherville
Willowdale
York University
Northmount
North York
Woburn
West Hill
Humber Summit
Black Creek Pioneer Village
Lansing
York Mills
Bendale
Beaumonte Heights
Armour Heights
Scarborough
Thistletown
DOWNSVIEW AIRPORT
Don Mills
Wexford
Cliffside
Kipling Heights
Downsview
Lawrence Heights
Wilket Creek Park
Rexdale
Humberlea
Ontario Science Centre
Danforth
Malton
Woodbine Race Track
Weston
Leaside
Thorncliffe
Demonia Park
Forest Hill
East York
Birch Cliff
TORONTO INTERNATIONAL AIRPORT (LESTER B. PEARSON)
Humber Valley Village
York
Casa Loma
Riverdale Park
Kew Gardens
Hanlon
Lambton Mills
Mount Dennis
Swansea
University of Toronto
City Hall
Parliament Buildings
Etobicoke
Islington
Kingsway
High Park
CN Tower
SkyDome
Union Sta.
Gardiner Expwy.
Markland Wood
Humber Bay
Parkdale
Old Fort York
Exhibition Place
TORONTO CITY CENTRE AIRPORT
TORONTO
Burnhamthorpe
Summerville
Ontario Place
Island Park
Toronto Harbour
Mimico
Toronto Islands
Gibraltar Point
LAKE ONTARIO
Cooksville
Mississauga
Long Branch
New Toronto
Elizabeth Way
West from Greenwich

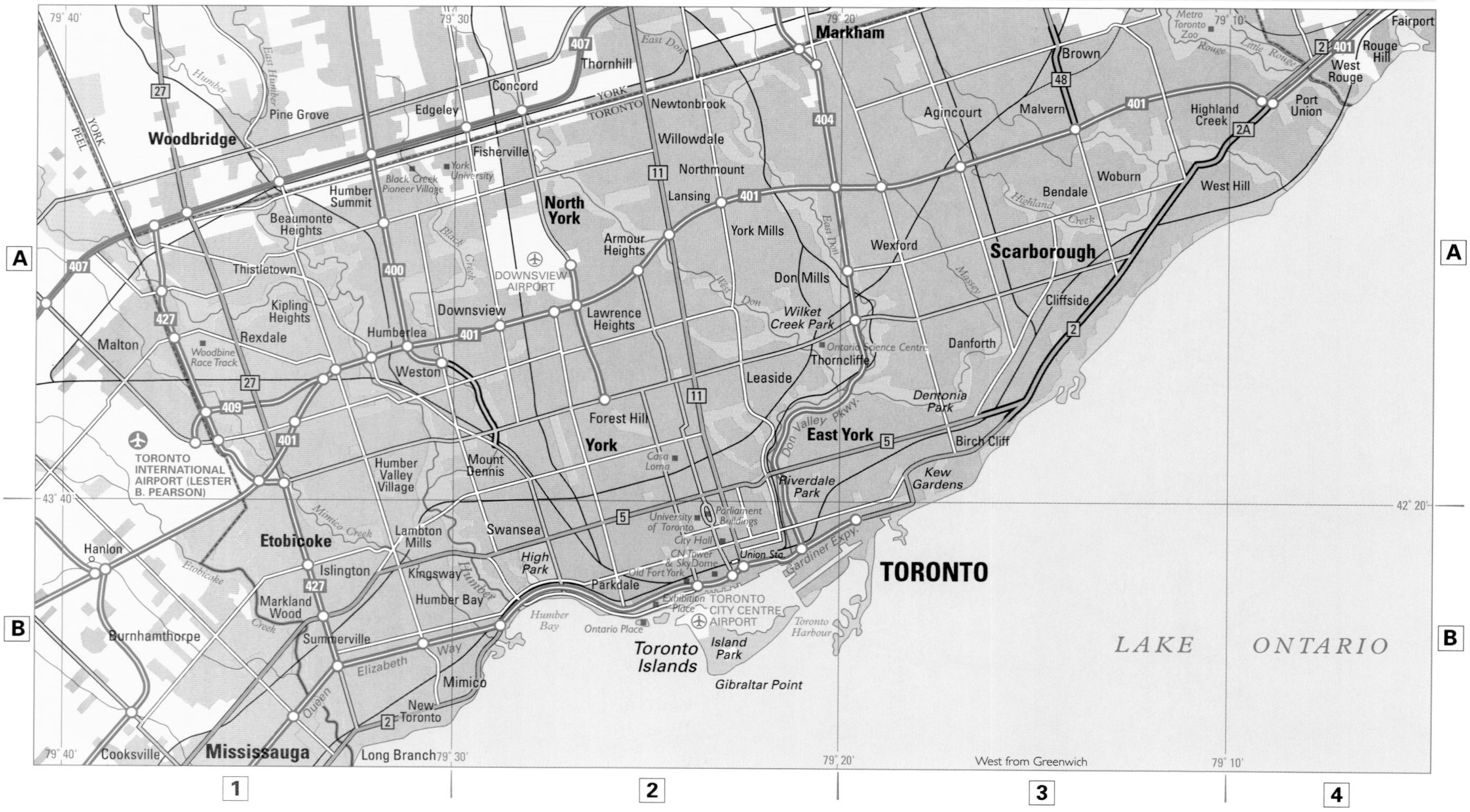

COPYRIGHT GEORGE PHILIP LTD.

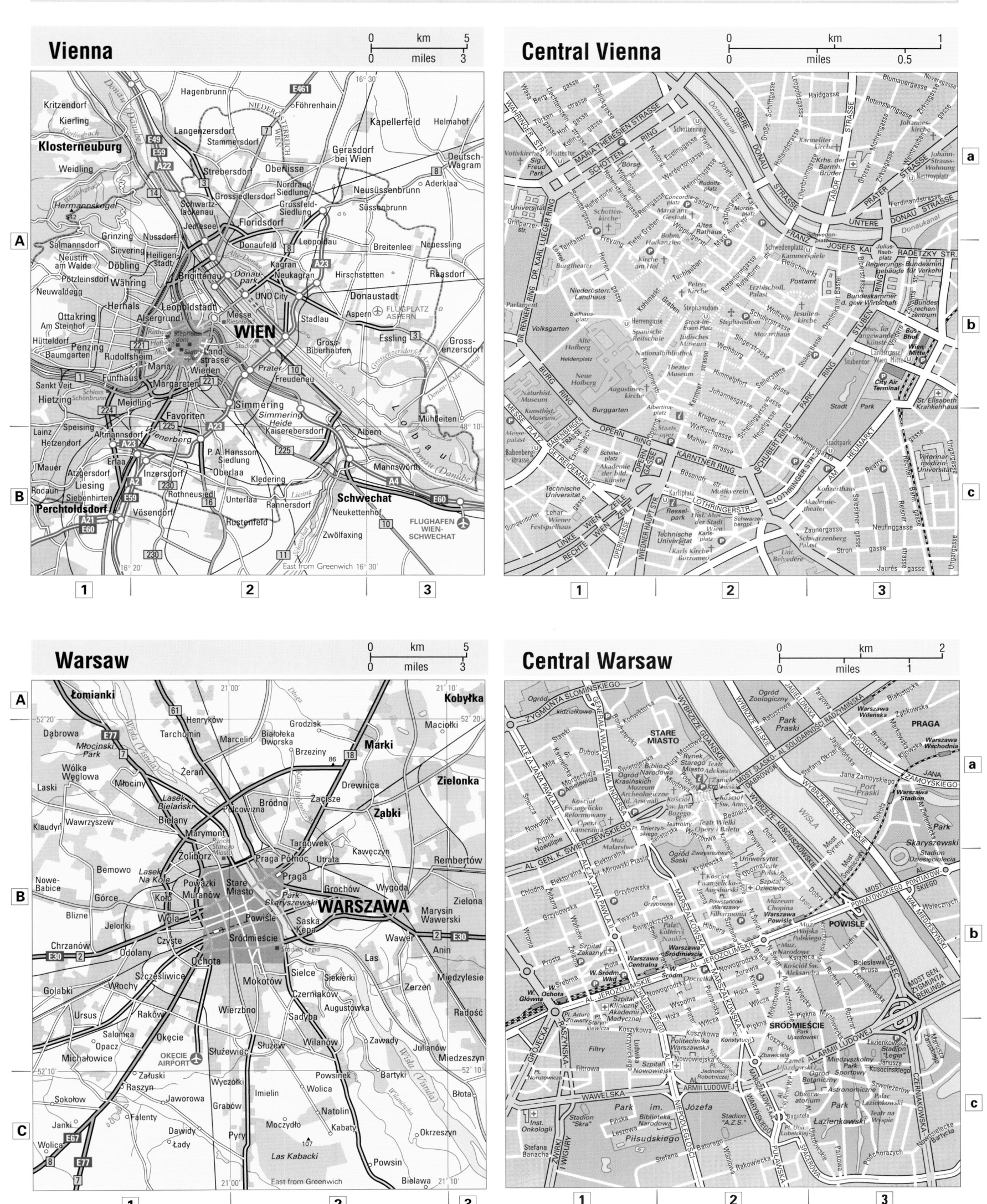

Vienna

km 5 / miles 3

Kritzendorf, Kierling, Kierlingbach, Klosterneuburg, Weidling, Hermannskogel, Grinzing, Nussdorf, Sievering, Heiligenstadt, Döbling, Währing, Sälmannsdorf, Neustift am Walde, Pötzleinsdorf, Neuwaldegg, Ottakring, Am Steinhof, Hütteldorf, Penzing, Baumgarten, Rudolfsheim, Sankt Veit, Hietzing, Schloss Schönbrunn, Lainz, Speising, Hetzendorf, Altmannsdorf, Mauer, Atzgersdorf, Liesing, Siebenhirten, Rodaun, Perchtoldsdorf, Vösendorf

Hagenbrunn, Föhrenhain, E461, NIEDERÖSTERREICH WIEN, Kapellerfeld, Helmahof, Langenzersdorf, Stammersdorf, Strebersdorf, Gerasdorf bei Wien, Deutsch-Wagram, E49, E59, A22, Schwartz-lackenau, Nordrand-Siedlung, Grossfeld-Siedlung, Neusüssenbrunn, Süssenbrunn, Jedlesee, Floridsdorf, Grossjedlersdorf, Aderklaa, Donaufeld, Leopoldau, Kagran, Neukagran, Breitenlee, Neuessling, Brigittenau, Leopoldstadt, Donau park, UNO City, Stadlau, Hirschstetten, Raasdorf, Donaustadt, Aspern, FLUGPLATZ ASPERN, Alsergrund, Messe, Riesenrad, WIEN, Land-strasse, Gross-Biberhaufen, Gross-enzersdorf, Maria, Wieden, Prater, Margareten, Freudenau, Essling, Funfhaus, Meidling, Favoriten, Simmering, Simmering Heide, Kaiserebersdorf, Albern, Mühlleiten, P.A. Hansson Siedlung, Oberlaa, Kledering, Erlaa, Inzersdorf, Rothneusiedl, Unterlaa, Rannersdorf, Schwechat, Neukettenhof, Rustenfeld, Zwölfaxing, FLUGHAFEN WIEN-SCHWECHAT, Mannswörth, Neusiedl, Lobau, Donau (Danube)

East from Greenwich 16° 30'

Central Vienna

km 1 / miles 0.5

Warsaw

km 5 / miles 3

Łomianki, Dąbrowa, Młocinski Park, Wólka Węglowa, Laski, Klaudyn, Nowe-Babice, Górce, Blizne, Jelonki, Chrzanów, Odolany, Golabki, Ursus, Szczęśliwice, Salomea, Opacz, Michałowice, Janki, Wolica, Sokołów, Raszyn, Falenty, Henryków, Tarchomin, Marcelin, Młociny, Wawrzyszew, Bemowo, Koło, Wola, Czyste, Ochota, Włochy, Raków, Okęcie, OKECIE AIRPORT, Dawidy, Łady, Grodzisk, Białołęka Dworska, Brzeziny, Żerań, Lasek Bielański, Bielany, Marymont, Żoliborz, Powązki, Muranów, Stare Miasto, Park Skaryszewski, Powiśle, Śródmieście, Mokotów, Sielce, Wierzbno, Sadyba, Służew, Służewiec, Wilanów, Pyry, Kabaty, Las Kabacki, Kobyłka, Maciołki, Marki, Zielonka, Drewnica, Ząbki, Bródno, Żacisze, Targówek, Kawęczyn, Praga Północ, Praga, Utrata, WARSZAWA, Grochów, Wygoda, Zielona, Marysin Wawerski, Saska Kępa, Wawer, Las, Miedzylesie, Zerzeń, Zawady, Julianów, Miedzeszyn, Powsinek, Bartyki, Błota, Wyczółki, Imielin, Wolica, Grabów, Natolin, Moczydło, Okrzeszyn, Powsin, Bielawa

East from Greenwich 21° 00' / 21° 10'

Central Warsaw

km 2 / miles 1

STARE MIASTO, PRAGA, Ogród Zoologiczny, Park Praski, Warszawa Wileńska, Warszawa Wschodnia, Port Praski, Warszawa Stadion, POWIŚLE, Skaryszewski, Stadion Dziesięciolecia, SRÓDMIEŚCIE, Warszawa Centralna, W. Śródm., Warszawa Śródmieście, Ochota, Pl. Artura Zawiszy, Filtry, Pole Mokotowskie, Stadion "Skra", Stadion "AZS", Pola Mokotowskie, Ogród Botaniczny, Łazienkowski Park, Stadion "Legia", Piłsudskiego

COPYRIGHT GEORGE PHILIP LTD.

Washington

| 0 | km | 5 |
| 0 | miles | 3 |

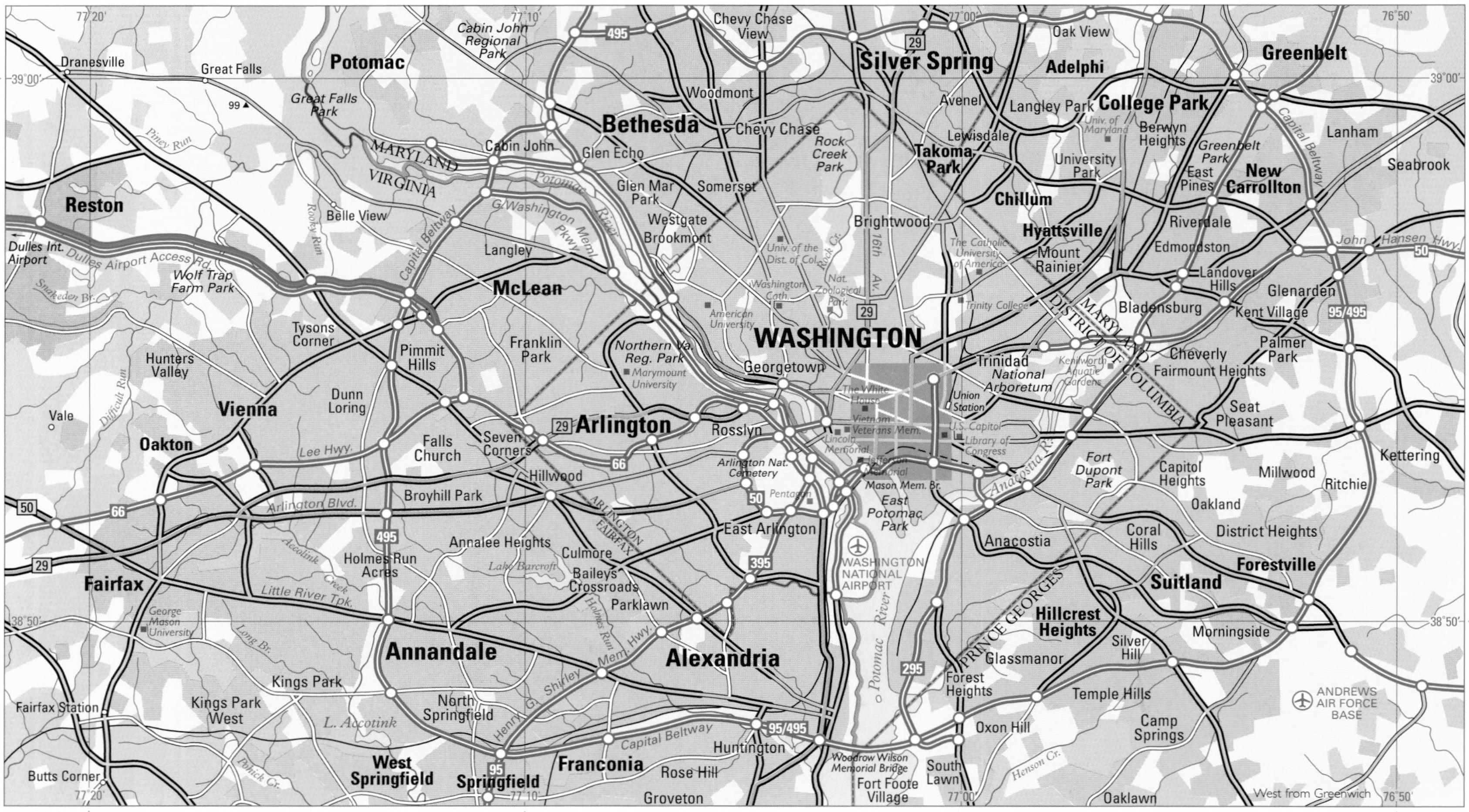

Dranesville
Great Falls
Potomac
Cabin John Regional Park
Chevy Chase View
Silver Spring
Adelphi
Oak View
Greenbelt

Woodmont
Avenel
Langley Park
College Park
Lanham

Great Falls Park
Chevy Chase
Lewisdale
Berwyn Heights
Greenbelt Park
Seabrook

Bethesda
Takoma Park
University Park
New Carrollton

Reston
MARYLAND
VIRGINIA
Cabin John
Glen Echo
Somerset
Westgate
Brookmont
Rock Creek Park
Brightwood
Chillum
Hyattsville
Riverdale
Edmonston

Belle View
Langley
Glen Mar Park
Mount Rainier
Landover Hills
Glenarden

Dulles Int. Airport
Wolf Trap Farm Park
McLean
Franklin Park
Northern Va. Reg. Park
American University
WASHINGTON
Georgetown
Trinidad
National Arboretum
Bladensburg
Kent Village
95/495

Hunters Valley
Tysons Corner
Pimmit Hills
Marymount University
Cheverly
Fairmount Heights
Palmer Park

Vale
Vienna
Dunn Loring
Arlington
Rosslyn
Union Station
Seat Pleasant

Oakton
Falls Church
Seven Corners
Hillwood
Arlington Nat. Cemetery
Pentagon
Fort Dupont Park
Capitol Heights
Kettering

Lee Hwy.
Broyhill Park
East Arlington
East Potomac Park
Anacostia
Oakland
Millwood
Ritchie

Fairfax
Annalee Heights
Holmes Run Acres
Baileys Crossroads
Culmore
Parklawn
WASHINGTON NATIONAL AIRPORT
Coral Hills
District Heights

George Mason University
Annandale
Alexandria
Hillcrest Heights
Suitland
Forestville

Fairfax Station
Kings Park West
Kings Park
North Springfield
Glassmanor
Silver Hill
Morningside
ANDREWS AIR FORCE BASE

Butts Corner
West Springfield
Springfield
Franconia
Rose Hill
Huntington
Oxon Hill
Temple Hills
Camp Springs

Groveton
Woodrow Wilson Memorial Bridge
Fort Foote Village
South Lawn
Oaklawn

West from Greenwich

Central Washington

| 0 | km | 1 |
| 0 | miles | 0.5 |

Logan Circle
Scott Circle
NORTH WEST
Mt. Vernon Sq.
Thomas Circle
Convention Center
Union Station

Farragut North
Franklin Square
Metro Center
Gallery Place

Farragut West
Lafayette Square
McPherson Sq.
Mt. Vernon Square

World Bank
The White House
National Place
Nat. Mus. of American Art
Judiciary Sq.
Union Station Plaza

Dept. of the Interior
Zero Milestone
National Theater
Fords Theater
Federal Triangle
Navy Mem.
Columbus Circle

The Ellipse
Nat. Museum of American History
Nat. Gallery of Art
CONSTITUTION AVE.
Supreme Court

Reflecting Pool
Washington Monument
Madison
The Mall
Jefferson
Smithsonian Inst.
National Gallery of Art
Hirshhorn
Nat. Air & Space Museum
U.S. Capitol
Library of Congress
Botanic Gardens

Tidal Basin
D.C. War Memorial
U.S. Holocaust Memorial Museum
Smithsonian
INDEPENDENCE AVE.
Grant Statue

Jefferson Memorial
Outlet Bridge
L'Enfant Plaza
Federal Center SW
Capitol South

SOUTH WEST
SOUTHWEST FREEWAY

Potomac R.
Francis Case Mem. Bridge
East Potomac Park
Washington Channel
Waterfront

Wellington

| 0 | km | 5 |
| 0 | miles | 3 |

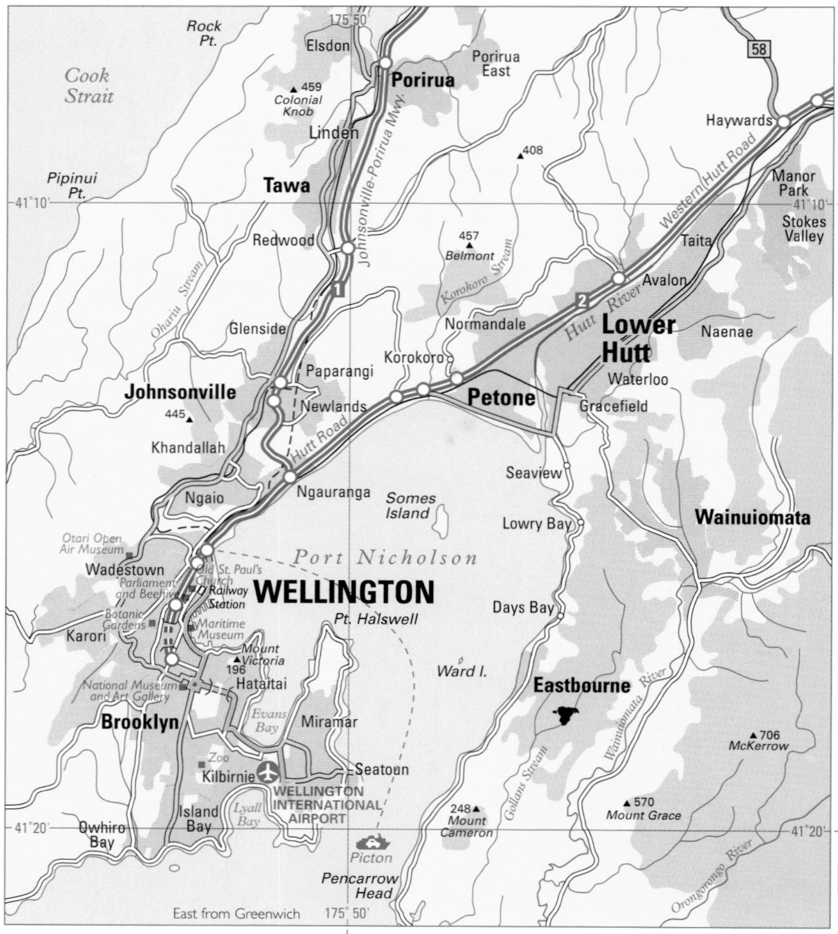

Cook Strait
Rock Pt.
Elsdon
Porirua East
58

459 Colonial Knob
Porirua
Haywards

Pipinui Pt.
Linden
408
Manor Park

Tawa
Taita
Stokes Valley

Redwood
457 Belmont
Avalon

Glenside
Normandale
Lower Hutt
Naenae

Johnsonville
Paparangi
Korokoro
Waterloo
Gracefield

445
Newlands
Khandallah
Ngauranga
Petone

Ngaio
Somes Island
Seaview

Otari Open Air Museum
Wadestown
Port Nicholson
Lowry Bay
Wainuiomata

Parliament
Old St. Paul's Church
Railway Station
WELLINGTON
Days Bay

Botanic Gardens
Maritime Museum
Pt. Halswell
Ward I.

Karori
National Museum and Art Gallery
196 Mount Victoria
Hataitai
Evans Bay
Eastbourne

Brooklyn
Zoo
Miramar

Kilbirnie
WELLINGTON INTERNATIONAL AIRPORT
Seatoun
248 Mount Cameron
570 Mount Grace
706 McKerrow

Owhiro Bay
Island Bay
Lyall Bay
Picton
Pencarrow Head

East from Greenwich

COPYRIGHT GEORGE PHILIP LTD

INDEX TO CITY MAPS

The index contains the names of all the principal places and features shown on the City Maps. Each name is followed by an additional entry in italics giving the name of the City Map within which it is located.

The number in bold type which follows each name refers to the number of the City Map page where that feature or place will be found.

The letter and figure which are immediately after the page number give the grid square on the map within which the feature or place is situated. The letter represents the latitude and the figure the longitude. Upper case letters refer to the City Maps, lower case letters to the Central Area Maps. The full geographic reference is provided in the border of the City Maps.

The location given is the centre of the city, suburb or feature and is not necessarily the name. Rivers, canals and roads are indexed to their name. Rivers carry the symbol → after their name.

An explanation of the alphabetical order rules and a list of the abbreviations used are to be found at the beginning of the World Map Index.

A

Aalām, *Baghdad* **3** B2
Aalsmeer, *Amsterdam* **2** B1
Abbey Wood, *London* **15** B4
Abcoude, *Amsterdam* **2** B2
Âbdin, *Cairo* **7** A2
Abeno, *Osaka* **22** B4
Aberdeen, *Hong Kong* **12** B2
Aberdour, *Edinburgh* **11** A2
Aberdour Castle, *Edinburgh* **11** A2
Abfanggraben →, *Munich* **20** A3
Ablon-sur-Seine, *Paris* **23** B3
Abord-à-Plouffe, *Montreal* **19** A1
Abramtsevo, *Moscow* **19** B4
Abu Dis, *Jerusalem* **13** B2
Abû en Numrus, *Cairo* **7** B2
Abu Ghosh, *Jerusalem* **13** B1
Acacias, *Madrid* **17** c2
Acassuso, *Buenos Aires* **7** A1
Accotink Cr. →, *Washington* **32** B2
Acheres, *Paris* **23** A1
Acília, *Rome* **25** C1
Aclimação, *São Paulo* **26** B2
Acton, *London* **15** A2
Açúcar, Pão de, *Rio de Janeiro* **24** B2
Ada Beja, *Lisbon* **14** A1
Adams Park, *Atlanta* **3** B2
Adams Shore, *Boston* **6** B4
Addiscombe, *London* **15** B3
Adelphi, *Washington* **32** A4
Aderklaa, *Vienna* **31** A3
Admiralteyskaya Storona, *St. Petersburg* **26** B2
Áffori, *Milan* **18** A2
Aflandshage, *Copenhagen* **10** B3
Afsarīyeh, *Tehran* **30** B2
Agboyi Cr. →, *Lagos* **14** A2
Ågerup, *Copenhagen* **10** A1
Ågesta, *Stockholm* **28** B2
Agincourt, *Toronto* **30** A3
Agora, Arhéa, *Athens* **2** c1
Agra Canal, *Delhi* **10** B2
Agricola Oriental, *Mexico City* **18** B2
Agua Espraiada →, *São Paulo* **26** B2
Agualva-Cacem, *Lisbon* **14** A1
Agustino, Cerro El, *Lima* **16** B2
Ahrensfelde, *Berlin* **5** A4
Ahuntsic, *Montreal* **19** A1
Ai →, *Osaka* **22** A4
Aigremont, *Paris* **23** A1
Air View Park, *Singapore* **27** A2
Airport West, *Melbourne* **17** A1
Aiyaleo, *Athens* **2** B2
Aiyáleos, Óros, *Athens* **2** B1
Ajegunle, *Lagos* **14** B2
Aji, *Osaka* **22** A3
Ajuda, *Lisbon* **14** A1
Akalla, *Stockholm* **28** A1
Akasaka, *Tokyo* **29** b3
Akbarābād, *Tehran* **30** A2
Akershus Slott, *Oslo* **22** A3
Akihabara, *Tokyo* **29** a5
Akrópolis, *Athens* **2** c2
Al 'Azamiyah, *Baghdad* **3** A2
Al Quds = Jerusalem, *Jerusalem* **13** B2
Alaguntan, *Lagos* **14** B2
Alameda, *San Francisco* **25** B3
Alameda, Parque, *Mexico City* **18** b2
Alameda Memorial State Beach Park, *San Francisco* **25** B3
Albern, *Vienna* **31** B2
Albert Park, *Melbourne* **17** B1
Alberton, *Johannesburg* **13** B2
Albertslund, *Copenhagen* **10** B2
Albysjön, *Stockholm* **28** B1
Alcantara, *Lisbon* **14** A1
Alcatraz I., *San Francisco* **25** B2
Alcobendas, *Madrid* **17** A2
Alcorcón, *Madrid* **17** B1
Aldershof, *Berlin* **5** B4
Aldo Bonzi, *Buenos Aires* **7** C1
Aleksandrovskoye, *St. Petersburg* **26** B2
Alexander Nevsky Abbey, *St. Petersburg* **26** B2
Alexander Soutzos Moussío, *Athens* **2** b3
Alexandra, *Johannesburg* **13** A2
Alexandra, *Singapore* **27** B2
Alexandria, *Washington* **32** C3
Alfama, *Lisbon* **14** c3
Alfortville, *Paris* **23** B3
Algés, *Lisbon* **14** A1
Alhambra, *Los Angeles* **16** B4
Alibey →, *Istanbul* **12** B1
Alibey Barajı, *Istanbul* **12** B1
Alibeyköy, *Istanbul* **12** B1
Alimos, *Athens* **2** B2
Alipur, *Calcutta* **8** B1
Allach, *Munich* **20** A1
Allambie Heights, *Sydney* **28** A2
Allard Pierson Museum, *Amsterdam* **2** b2
Allermuir Hill, *Edinburgh* **11** B2
Allerton, Pt., *Boston* **6** B4
Allston, *Boston* **6** A3
Almada, *Lisbon* **14** A2
Almagro, *Buenos Aires* **7** B2
Almargem do Bispo, *Lisbon* **14** A1
Almazovo, *Moscow* **19** A6
Almirante G. Brown, Parque, *Buenos Aires* **7** C2
Almon, *Jerusalem* **13** B2
Almond →, *Edinburgh* **11** B2
Alnabru, *Oslo* **22** A4
Alnsjøen, *Oslo* **22** A4
Alperton, *London* **15** A2
Alpine, *New York* **21** A2
Alrode, *Johannesburg* **13** B2
Alsemerg, *Brussels* **6** B1
Alsergrund, *Vienna* **31** A2
Alsip, *Chicago* **9** C2
Ålsten, *Stockholm* **28** B1
Älta, *Stockholm* **28** B3
Altadena, *Los Angeles* **16** A4
Alte-Donau →, *Vienna* **31** A2
Alte Hofburg, *Vienna* **31** b1
Alter Finkenkrug, *Berlin* **5** A1
Altes Rathaus, *Munich* **20** b3
Altglienicke, *Berlin* **5** B4
Altlandsberg, *Berlin* **5** A5
Altlandsberg Nord, *Berlin* **5** A5
Altmannsdorf, *Vienna* **31** B1
Alto da Moóca, *São Paulo* **26** B2
Alto do Pina, *Lisbon* **14** A2
Altona, *Melbourne* **17** B1
Alvaro Obregon, *Mexico City* **18** B1
Alvik, *Stockholm* **28** B1
Älvsjo, *Stockholm* **28** B2
Älvvik, *Stockholm* **28** A3
Am Hasenbergl, *Munich* **20** A2
Am Steinhof, *Vienna* **31** A1
Am Wald, *Munich* **20** B2
Ama Keng, *Singapore* **27** A2
Amadora, *Lisbon* **14** A1
Amagasaki, *Osaka* **22** A3
Amager, *Copenhagen* **10** B3
Amāl Qādisiya, *Baghdad* **3** B2
Amalienborg, *Copenhagen* **10** b3
Amata, *Milan* **18** A1
Ameixoeira, *Lisbon* **14** A2
América, *São Paulo* **26** B1
Amin, *Baghdad* **3** B2
Aminadov, *Jerusalem* **13** B1
Aminyevo, *Moscow* **19** B2
Amīrābād, *Tehran* **30** A2
Amora, *Lisbon* **14** B2
Amoreira, *Lisbon* **14** A1
Ampelokipi, *Athens* **2** B2
Amper →, *Munich* **20** A1
Amstel, *Amsterdam* **2** b2
Amstel →, *Amsterdam* **2** c2
Amstel-Drecht-Kanaal, *Amsterdam* **2** B2
Amstel Station, *Amsterdam* **2** c3
Amstelhof, *Amsterdam* **2** b2
Amstelveen, *Amsterdam* **2** B2
Amsterdam, *Amsterdam* **2** A2
Amsterdam-Rijnkanaal, *Amsterdam* **2** B3
Amsterdam Zoo, *Amsterdam* **2** b3
Amsterdam Zuidoost, *Amsterdam* **2** B2
Amsterdamse Bos, *Amsterdam* **2** B1
Anacostia, *Washington* **32** B4
Anadoluhisarı, *Istanbul* **12** B2
Anadolukavağı, *Istanbul* **12** A2
Anata, *Jerusalem* **13** B2
Ancol, *Jakarta* **13** A1
'Andalus, *Baghdad* **3** B1
Andarai, *Rio de Janeiro* **24** B1
Anderlecht, *Brussels* **6** A1
Anderson Park, *Atlanta* **3** B2
Andingmen, *Beijing* **4** B2
Andrews Air Force Base, *Washington* **32** C4
Ang Mo Kio, *Singapore* **27** A3
Ängby, *Stockholm* **28** A1
Angel I., *San Francisco* **25** A2
Angel Island State Park, *San Francisco* **25** A2
Angke, Kali →, *Jakarta* **13** A1
Angyalföld, *Budapest* **7** A2
Anik, *Mumbai* **20** A2
Anin, *Warsaw* **31** B2
Anjou, *Montreal* **19** A2
Annalee Heights, *Washington* **32** B2
Annandale, *Washington* **32** C2
Anne Frankhuis, *Amsterdam* **2** a1
Antony, *Paris* **23** B2
Anyangch'on, *Seoul* **26** C1
Aoyama, *Tokyo* **29** b2
Ap Lei Chau, *Hong Kong* **12** B1
Apapa, *Lagos* **14** B2
Apelacão, *Lisbon* **14** A2
Apterkarskiy Ostrov, *St. Petersburg* **26** B2
Ar Kazimiyah, *Baghdad* **3** B1
Ara →, *Tokyo* **29** A4
Arakawa-Ku, *Tokyo* **29** A3
Arany-hegyi-patak →, *Budapest* **7** A2
Aravaca, *Madrid* **17** B1
Arbataash, *Baghdad* **3** A1
Arc de Triomphe, *Paris* **23** a2
Arcadia, *Los Angeles* **16** B4
Arceuil, *Paris* **23** B2
Arco Plaza, *Los Angeles* **16** b1
Arese, *Milan* **18** A1
Arganzuela, *Madrid* **17** B1
Argenteuil, *Paris* **23** A2
Argonne Forest, *Chicago* **9** C1
Argüelles, *Madrid* **17** a1
Arima, *Osaka* **22** A2
Arima, *Tokyo* **29** B2
Ários Págos, *Athens* **2** c1
Arkhangelyskoye, *Moscow* **19** B1
Arlington, *Boston* **6** A2
Arlington, *Washington* **32** B3
Arlington Heights, *Boston* **6** A2
Arlington Nat. Cemetery, *Washington* **32** B3
Armação, *Rio de Janeiro* **24** B2
Armadale, *Melbourne* **17** B2
Armenian Quarter, *Jerusalem* **13** b3
Armour Heights, *Toronto* **30** A2
Arncliffe, *Sydney* **28** B1
Arnold Arboretum, *Boston* **6** B3
Árpádföld, *Budapest* **7** A3
Arrentela, *Lisbon* **14** B2
Årsta, *Stockholm* **28** B2
Art Institute, *Chicago* **9** c2
Artane, *Dublin* **11** A2
Artas, *Jerusalem* **13** B2
Arthur's Seat, *Edinburgh* **11** B3
Aryiróupolis, *Athens* **2** B2
Asagaya, *Tokyo* **29** A2
Asahi, *Osaka* **22** A4
Asakusa, *Tokyo* **29** A3
Asakusabashi, *Tokyo* **29** a5
Asati, *Calcutta* **8** C1
Aschheim, *Munich* **20** A3
Ascot Vale, *Melbourne* **17** A1
Ashburn, *Chicago* **9** C2
Ashburton, *Melbourne* **17** B2
Ashfield, *Sydney* **28** B1
Ashford, *London* **15** B1
Ashiya, *Osaka* **22** A2
Ashiya →, *Osaka* **22** A2
Ashtown, *Dublin* **11** A2
Askisto, *Helsinki* **12** B1
Askrikefjärden, *Stockholm* **28** A3
Asnières, *Paris* **23** A2
Aspern, *Vienna* **31** A2
Aspern, Flugplatz, *Vienna* **31** A3
Assago, *Milan* **18** B1
Assemblée Nationale, *Paris* **23** b3
Assendelft, *Amsterdam* **2** A1
Assiano, *Milan* **18** B1
Astoria, *New York* **21** B2
Astrolabe Park, *Sydney* **28** B2
Atarot Airport, *Jerusalem* **13** A2
Atghara, *Calcutta* **8** B2
Athens = Athínai, *Athens* **2** B2
Athínai, *Athens* **2** B2
Athinai-Ellinikón Airport, *Athens* **2** B2
Athis-Mons, *Paris* **23** B3
Athlone, *Cape Town* **8** A2
Atholl, *Johannesburg* **13** A2
Atīfīya, *Baghdad* **3** A2
Atişalen, *Istanbul* **12** B1
Atlanta, *Atlanta* **3** B2
Atlanta History Center, *Atlanta* **3** B2
Atomium, *Brussels* **6** A2
Attiki, *Athens* **2** A2
Atzgersdorf, *Vienna* **31** B1
Aubervilliers, *Paris* **23** A3
Aubing, *Munich* **20** B1
Auburndale, *Boston* **6** A2
Aucherdinny, *Edinburgh* **11** B2
Auckland Park, *Johannesburg* **13** B2
Auderghem, *Brussels* **6** B2
Augusta, Mausoleo di, *Rome* **25** b2
Augustówka, *Warsaw* **31** B2
Aulnay-sous-Bois, *Paris* **23** A3
Aurelio, *Rome* **25** B1
Ausîm, *Cairo* **7** A1
Austerlitz, Gare d', *Paris* **23** A3
Austin, *Chicago* **9** B2
Avalon, *Wellington* **32** B2
Avedøre, *Copenhagen* **10** B2
Avellaneda, *Buenos Aires* **7** C2
Avenel, *Washington* **32** B4
Avondale, *Chicago* **9** B2
Avondale Heights, *Melbourne* **17** A1
Avtovo, *St. Petersburg* **26** B1
Ayazağa, *Istanbul* **12** B1
Ayer Chawan, P., *Singapore* **27** B2
Ayer Merbau, P., *Singapore* **27** B2
Ayía Marina, *Athens* **2** C3
Ayía Paraskevi, *Athens* **2** A2
Áyios Dhimitrios, *Athens* **2** B2
Áyios Ioánnis Rendis, *Athens* **2** B1
Azabu, *Tokyo* **29** c3
Azcapotzalco, *Mexico City* **18** B1
Azteca, Estadia, *Mexico City* **18** C2
Azucar, Cerro Pan de, *Santiago* **26** A1

B

Baambrugge, *Amsterdam* **2** B2
Baba I., *Karachi* **14** B1
Babarpur, *Delhi* **10** A2
Babushkin, *Moscow* **19** A4
Back B., *Mumbai* **20** B1
Baclaran, *Manila* **17** B2
Bacoor, *Manila* **17** C1
Bacoor B., *Manila* **17** C1
Badalona, *Barcelona* **4** A2
Badhoevedorp, *Amsterdam* **2** A1
Badli, *Delhi* **10** A1
Bærum, *Oslo* **22** A2
Bağcılar, *Istanbul* **12** B1
Bággio, *Milan* **18** B1
Bāgh-e-Feyz, *Tehran* **30** A1
Baghdād, *Baghdad* **3** A2
Bagmari, *Calcutta* **8** B2
Bagneux, *Paris* **23** B2
Bagnolet, *Paris* **23** A3
Bagsværd, *Copenhagen* **10** A2
Bagsværd Sø, *Copenhagen* **10** A2
Baguiati, *Calcutta* **8** B2
Bagumbayan, *Manila* **17** C2
Bahçeköy, *Istanbul* **12** A1
Bahtîm, *Cairo* **7** A2
Baileys Crossroads, *Washington* **32** B3
Bailly, *Paris* **23** A1
Bairro Alto, *Lisbon* **14** c1
Bairro Lopes, *Lisbon* **14** b3
Baisha, *Canton* **8** B2
Baisha →, *Canton* **8** B2
Baixa, *Lisbon* **14** c2
Baiyun Airport, *Canton* **8** A2
Baiyun Hill Scenic Spot, *Canton* **8** B2
Bakırköy, *Istanbul* **12** C1
Bakovka, *Moscow* **19** B2
Bal Harbor, *Miami* **18** A2
Balara, *Manila* **17** B2
Balashikha, *Moscow* **19** B5
Baldia, *Karachi* **14** A1
Baldoyle, *Dublin* **11** A3
Baldwin Hills, *Los Angeles* **16** B2
Baldwin Hills Res., *Los Angeles* **16** B2
Balgowlah, *Sydney* **28** A2
Balgowlah Heights, *Sydney* **28** A2
Balham, *London* **15** B3
Bali, *Calcutta* **8** B1
Baliganja, *Calcutta* **8** B2
Balingsnäs, *Stockholm* **28** B2
Balingsta, *Stockholm* **28** B2
Balintawak, *Manila* **17** B1
Balitai, *Tianjin* **30** B2
Ballerup, *Copenhagen* **10** A2
Ballinteer, *Dublin* **11** B2
Ballyboden, *Dublin* **11** B2
Ballybrack, *Dublin* **11** B3
Ballyfermot, *Dublin* **11** A1
Ballymorefinn Hill, *Dublin* **11** B1
Ballymun, *Dublin* **11** A2
Balmain, *Sydney* **28** B2
Baluhati, *Calcutta* **8** B1
Balvanera, *Buenos Aires* **7** B2
Balwyn, *Melbourne* **17** A2
Balwyn North, *Melbourne* **17** A2
Banática, *Lisbon* **14** A1
Banco do Brasil, Centro Cultural, *Rio de Janeiro* **24** a2
Bandra, *Mumbai* **20** A1
Bandra Pt., *Mumbai* **20** A1
Bang Kapi, *Bangkok* **3** B2
Bang Kholaem, *Bangkok* **3** A2
Bang Na, *Bangkok* **3** B2
Bang Phlad, *Bangkok* **3** a1
Bangkhen, *Bangkok* **3** A2
Bangkok = Krung Thep, *Bangkok* **3** B2
Bangkok Noi, *Bangkok* **3** B1
Bangkok Yai, *Bangkok* **3** B1
Banglamphoo, *Bangkok* **3** b2
Banglo, *Calcutta* **8** B1
Bangrak, *Bangkok* **3** B2
Bangsu, *Bangkok* **3** B2
Bank, *London* **15** b5
Bank of America, *San Francisco* **25** b2
Bank of China Tower, *Hong Kong* **12** c1
Banks, C., *Sydney* **28** C2
Banksmeadow, *Sydney* **28** B2
Banstala, *Calcutta* **8** B2
Bantra, *Calcutta* **8** B1
Baoshan, *Shanghai* **27** A1
Bar Giyora, *Jerusalem* **13** B1
Barahanagar, *Calcutta* **8** B2
Barajas, *Madrid* **17** B2
Barajas, Aeropuerto Transoceanico de, *Madrid* **17** B2
Barakpur, *Calcutta* **8** A2
Barberini, Palazzo, *Rome* **25** b3
Barbican, *London* **15** a4
Barcarena, *Lisbon* **14** A1
Barcarena, Rib. de →, *Lisbon* **14** A1
Barcelona, *Barcelona* **4** A2
Barcelona-Prat, Aeropuerta de, *Barcelona* **4** B1
Barceloneta, *Barcelona* **4** A2
Barking, *London* **15** A4
Barkingside, *London* **15** A4
Barnes, *London* **15** B2
Barnet, *London* **15** A2
Barra Andai, *Karachi* **14** B2
Barra Funda, *São Paulo* **26** B2
Barracas, *Buenos Aires* **7** B2
Barranco, *Lima* **16** B2
Barreiro, *Lisbon* **14** B2
Barreto, *Rio de Janeiro* **24** B2
Bartala, *Calcutta* **8** B1
Barton Park, *Sydney* **28** B1
Bartyki, *Warsaw* **31** C2
Barvikha, *Moscow* **19** B1
Bastille, Place de la, *Paris* **23** c5
Basus, *Cairo* **7** A2
Batanagar, *Calcutta* **8** B1
Bath Beach, *New York* **21** C1
Bath I., *Karachi* **14** B2
Batir, *Jerusalem* **13** B1
Batok, Bukit, *Singapore* **27** A2
Battersea, *London* **15** B3
Battery Park, *New York* **21** f1
Bauman, *Moscow* **19** B4
Baumgarten, *Vienna* **31** A1
Bay Harbour Islands, *Miami* **18** A2
Bay Ridge, *New York* **21** C1
Bayonne, *New York* **21** B1
Bayshore, *San Francisco* **25** B3
Bayswater, *London* **15** b2
Bayt Lahm = Bethlehem, *Jerusalem* **13** B2
Bayview, *San Francisco* **25** B2
Bāzār, *Tehran* **30** A2
Beachmont, *Boston* **6** A4
Beacon Hill, *Hong Kong* **12** A2
Beato, *Lisbon* **14** A2
Beaumont, *Dublin* **11** A2
Beaumonte Heights, *Toronto* **30** A1
Bebek, *Istanbul* **12** B2
Běchovice, *Prague* **24** B3
Beck L., *Chicago* **9** A1
Beckenham, *London* **15** B3
Beckton, *London* **15** A4
Becontree, *London* **15** A4
Beddington Corner, *London* **15** B3
Bedford, *Boston* **6** A2
Bedford Park, *Chicago* **9** C2
Bedford Park, *New York* **21** A2
Bedford Stuyvesant, *New York* **21** B2
Bedford View, *Johannesburg* **13** B2
Bedok, *Singapore* **27** B3
Bedok, Res., *Singapore* **27** A3
Beersel, *Brussels* **6** B1
Behala, *Calcutta* **8** B1
Bei Hai, *Beijing* **4** B2
Beicai, *Shanghai* **27** B2
Beicang, *Tianjin* **30** A1
Beihai Park, *Beijing* **4** b2
Beijing, *Beijing* **4** B1
Beit Ghur el-Fawqa, *Jerusalem* **13** A1
Beit Hanina, *Jerusalem* **13** B2
Beit Iksa, *Jerusalem* **13** B2
Beit I'nan, *Jerusalem* **13** A1
Beit Jala, *Jerusalem* **13** B2
Beit Lekhem = Bethlehem, *Jerusalem* **13** B2
Beit Nekofa, *Jerusalem* **13** B1
Beit Sahur, *Jerusalem* **13** B2
Beit Surik, *Jerusalem* **13** B1
Beit Zayit, *Jerusalem* **13** B1
Beitaipingzhuan, *Beijing* **4** B1
Beitar Ilit, *Jerusalem* **13** B1
Beitsun, *Canton* **8** B2
Beitunya, *Jerusalem* **13** A2
Beixing Jing Park, *Shanghai* **27** B1
Békásmegyer, *Budapest* **7** A2
Bekkelaget, *Oslo* **22** A3
Bel Air, *Los Angeles* **16** B2
Bela Vista, *São Paulo* **26** B2
Bélanger, *Montreal* **19** A1
Belas, *Lisbon* **14** A1
Belas Artes, Museu Nacionale de, *Rio de Janeiro* **24** b2
Beleghata, *Calcutta* **8** B2
Belém, *Lisbon* **14** A1
Belém, Torre de, *Lisbon* **14** A1
Belènzinho, *São Paulo* **26** B2
Belgachiya, *Calcutta* **8** B2
Belgharia, *Calcutta* **8** B2
Belgrano, *Buenos Aires* **7** B2
Belgravia, *London* **15** c3
Bell, *Los Angeles* **16** C3
Bell Gardens, *Los Angeles* **16** C4
Bell Tower, *Beijing* **4** a2
Bellavista, *Lima* **16** B2
Bellavista, *Santiago* **26** C2
Belle Harbor, *New York* **21** C2
Belle View, *Washington* **32** B2
Bellevue, Schloss, *Berlin* **5** a2
Bellingham, *London* **15** B3
Bellwood, *Chicago* **9** B1
Belmont, *Boston* **6** A2
Belmont, *London* **15** A2
Belmont, *Wellington* **32** B2
Belmont Harbor, *Chicago* **9** B3
Belmore, *Sydney* **28** B1
Belur, *Calcutta* **8** B2
Belvedere, *Atlanta* **3** B3
Belvedere, *London* **15** B4
Belvedere, *San Francisco* **25** A2
Belyayevo Bogorodskoye, *Moscow* **19** C3
Bemowo, *Warsaw* **31** B1
Benaki, Moussío, *Athens* **2** b3
Bendale, *Toronto* **30** A3
Bendkhal, *Mumbai* **20** B2
Benefica, *Rio de Janeiro* **24** B1
Benfica, *Lisbon* **14** A1
Benito Juárez, *Mexico City* **18** B2
Benito Juárez, Aeropuerto Int., *Mexico City* **18** B2
Bensonhurst, *New York* **21** C2
Berchem-Sainte-Agathe, *Brussels* **6** A1
Berg am Laim, *Munich* **20** B2
Bergenfield, *New York* **21** A2
Bergham, *Munich* **20** B2
Bergvliet, *Cape Town* **8** B1
Beri, *Barcelona* **4** A1
Berkeley, *San Francisco* **25** A3
Berlin, *Berlin* **5** A3
Bermondsey, *London* **15** B3
Bernabeu, Estadio, *Madrid* **17** B1
Bernal Heights, *San Francisco* **25** B2
Berwyn, *Chicago* **9** B2
Berwyn Heights, *Washington* **32** B4
Besiktas, *Istanbul* **12** B2
Besós →, *Barcelona* **4** A2
Bethesda, *Washington* **32** B3
Bethlehem, *Jerusalem* **13** B2
Bethnal Green, *London* **15** A3
Betor, *Calcutta* **8** B1
Beurs, *Amsterdam* **2** b2
Beverley Hills, *Sydney* **28** B1
Beverley Park, *Sydney* **28** B1
Beverly, *Chicago* **9** C3
Beverly Glen, *Los Angeles* **16** B2
Beverly Hills, *Los Angeles* **16** B2
Bexley, *London* **15** B4
Bexley, *Sydney* **28** B1
Bexleyheath, *London* **15** B4
Beykoz, *Istanbul* **12** B2
Beylerbeyi, *Istanbul* **12** B2
Beyoğlu, *Istanbul* **12** B1
Bezons, *Paris* **23** A2
Bezuidenhout Park, *Johannesburg* **13** B2
Bhadrakali, *Calcutta* **8** A2
Bhalswa, *Delhi* **10** A2
Bhambo Khan Qarmati, *Karachi* **14** B2
Bhatsala, *Calcutta* **8** B1
Bhawanipur, *Calcutta* **8** B2
Bhuleshwar, *Mumbai* **20** b2
Białołeka Dworska, *Warsaw* **31** B2
Biblioteca Nacional, *Rio de Janeiro* **24** c2
Bicentennial Park, *Sydney* **28** B1
Bickley, *London* **15** B4
Bidu, *Jerusalem* **13** B1
Bielany, *Warsaw* **31** B1
Bielawa, *Warsaw* **31** C2
Biesdorf, *Berlin* **5** A4
Bièvre →, *Paris* **23** B1
Bièvres, *Paris* **23** B2
Bilston, *Edinburgh* **11** B2
Binacayan, *Manila* **17** C1
Binondo, *Manila* **17** B1
Birak el Kiyam, *Cairo* **7** A1
Birch Cliff, *Toronto* **30** A3
Birkenstein, *Berlin* **5** A5
Birkholz, *Berlin* **5** A4
Birkholzaue, *Berlin* **5** A4
Birrarrung Park, *Melbourne* **17** A2
Biscayne Bay, *Miami* **18** B2
Biscayne Park, *Miami* **18** A2
Bishop Lavis, *Cape Town* **8** A2
Bishopscourt, *Cape Town* **8** A1
Bispebjerg, *Copenhagen* **10** A3
Biwon Secret Garden, *Seoul* **26** B1
Björknas, *Stockholm* **28** B3
Black Cr. →, *Toronto* **30** A2
Blackfen, *London* **15** B4
Blackheath, *London* **15** B4
Blackrock, *Dublin* **11** B2
Bladensburg, *Washington* **32** B4
Blair Village, *Atlanta* **3** C2
Blairgowrie, *Johannesburg* **13** A2
Blakehurst, *Sydney* **28** B1
Blakstad, *Oslo* **22** B1
Blankenburg, *Berlin* **5** A3
Blankenfelde, *Berlin* **5** A3
Blizne, *Warsaw* **31** B1
Bloomsbury, *London* **15** a3
Błota, *Warsaw* **31** C3
Blue Island, *Chicago* **9** C2
Bluebell, *Dublin* **11** B1
Bluff Hd., *Hong Kong* **12** B2
Blumberg, *Berlin* **5** A4
Blunt Pt., *San Francisco* **25** A2
Blutenberg, *Munich* **20** B1
Blylaget, *Oslo* **22** B3
Bo-Kaap Museum, *Cape Town* **8** c2
Boa Vista, Alto do, *Rio de Janeiro* **24** B1
Boardwalk, *New York* **21** C3
Boavista, *Lisbon* **14** A2
Bobigny, *Paris* **23** A3
Bocanegra, *Lima* **16** A2
Boedo, *Buenos Aires* **7** B2
Bogenhausen, *Munich* **20** B2
Bogorodskoye, *Moscow* **19** B4
Bogota, *New York* **21** A1
Bogstadvatnet, *Oslo* **22** A2
Bohnsdorf, *Berlin* **5** B4
Bois-Colombes, *Paris* **23** A2
Bois-d'Arcy, *Paris* **23** B1
Boissy-St.-Léger, *Paris* **23** B4
Boldinasco, *Milan* **18** B1
Bøler, *Oslo* **22** A4
Bollate, *Milan* **18** A1
Bollebeek, *Brussels* **6** A1
Bollensdorf, *Berlin* **5** A5
Bollmora, *Stockholm* **28** B3
Bolshaya-Okhta, *St. Petersburg* **26** B2
Bolton, *Atlanta* **3** B2
Bom Retiro, *São Paulo* **26** B2
Bombay = Mumbai, *Mumbai* **20** B2
Bondi, *Sydney* **28** B2
Bondy, *Paris* **23** A3
Bondy, Forêt de, *Paris* **23** A4
Bonifacio Monument, *Manila* **17** B1
Bonneuil-sur-Marne, *Paris* **23** B4
Bonnington, *Edinburgh* **11** B1
Bonnyrig and Lasswade, *Edinburgh* **11** B3
Bonsucesso, *Rio de Janeiro* **24** B1
Bonteheuwel, *Cape Town* **8** A2
Boo, *Stockholm* **28** A3
Booterstown, *Dublin* **11** B2
Borisovo, *Moscow* **19** C4
Borle, *Mumbai* **20** A2
Boronia Park, *Sydney* **28** A1
Borough Park, *New York* **21** C2
Bosmont, *Johannesburg* **13** B1
Bosön, *Stockholm* **28** A3
Bosporus = Istanbul Boğazi, *Istanbul* **12** B2
Bostancı, *Istanbul* **12** C2
Boston Harbor, *Boston* **6** A4
Botafogo, *Rio de Janeiro* **24** B1
Botanisk Have, *Copenhagen* **10** b2
Botany, *Sydney* **28** B2
Botany B., *Sydney* **28** B2
Botany Bay Nat. Park, *Sydney* **28** B2
Botič →, *Prague* **24** B3
Botica Sete, *Lisbon* **14** A1
Boucherville, *Montreal* **19** A3
Boucherville, Îs. de, *Montreal* **19** A3
Bougival, *Paris* **23** A1
Boulder Pt., *Hong Kong* **12** B1
Boulogne, Bois de, *Paris* **23** A2
Boulogne-Billancourt, *Paris* **23** A2
Bourg-la-Reine, *Paris* **23** B2
Bouviers, *Paris* **23** B1
Bovenkerk, *Amsterdam* **2** B2
Bovenkerker Polder, *Amsterdam* **2** B2
Bovisa, *Milan* **18** A2
Bow, *London* **15** A3
Bowery, *New York* **21** e2
Boyacıköy, *Istanbul* **12** B2
Boyle Heights, *Los Angeles* **16** B3
Bradbury Building, *Los Angeles* **16** b2
Braepark, *Edinburgh* **11** B2
Braid, *Edinburgh* **11** B2
Bramley, *Johannesburg* **13** A2
Brandenburger Tor, *Berlin* **5** A3
Brani, P., *Singapore* **27** B3
Branik, *Prague* **24** B2
Brännkyrka, *Stockholm* **28** B2
Brás, *São Paulo* **26** B2
Brasilândia, *São Paulo* **26** A1
Brateyevo, *Moscow* **19** C4
Bratsevo, *Moscow* **19** A2
Bray, *Dublin* **11** B3
Braybrook, *Melbourne* **17** A1
Brázdim, *Prague* **24** A3
Breach Candy, *Mumbai* **20** a1
Breakheart Reservation, *Boston* **6** A3
Brede, *Copenhagen* **10** A3
Breeds Pond, *Boston* **6** A4
Breezy Point, *New York* **21** C2
Breitenlee, *Vienna* **31** A3
Breña, *Lima* **16** B2
Brent, *London* **15** A2
Brent Res., *London* **15** A2
Brentford, *London* **15** B2
Brentwood Park, *Los Angeles* **16** B2
Brera, *Milan* **18** B2
Bresso, *Milan* **18** A2
Brevik, *Stockholm* **28** A3
Břevnov, *Prague* **24** B2
Bridgeport, *Chicago* **9** B3
Bridgetown, *Cape Town* **8** A2
Bridgeview, *Chicago* **9** C2
Brighton, *Boston* **6** A3
Brighton, *Melbourne* **17** B1
Brighton le Sands, *Sydney* **28** B1
Brighton Park, *Chicago* **9** C2
Brightwood, *Washington* **32** B3
Brigittenau, *Vienna* **31** A2
Brimbank Park, *Melbourne* **17** A1
Brisbane, *San Francisco* **25** B2
British Museum, *London* **15** a3
Britz, *Berlin* **5** B3
Brixton, *London* **15** B3
Broad Sd., *Boston* **6** A4
Broadmeadows, *Melbourne* **17** A1
Broadmoor, *San Francisco* **25** B2
Broadview, *Chicago* **9** B1
Broadway, *New York* **21** e1
Brockley, *London* **15** B3
Bródno, *Warsaw* **31** B2
Bródnowski, Kanal, *Warsaw* **31** B2
Broek in Waterland, *Amsterdam* **2** A2
Bromley, *London* **15** B4
Bromley Common, *London* **15** B4
Bromma, *Stockholm* **28** A1
Bromma flygplats, *Stockholm* **28** A1
Brompton, *London* **15** c2
Brøndby Strand, *Copenhagen* **10** B2
Brøndbyøster, *Copenhagen* **10** B2
Brøndbyvester, *Copenhagen* **10** B2
Brondesbury, *London* **15** A2
Brønnøya, *Oslo* **22** A2
Brønshøj, *Copenhagen* **10** A2

Bronxville, *New York* 21 A3
Brookfield, *Chicago* 9 C1
Brookhaven, *Atlanta* 3 A2
Brookline, *Boston* 6 B3
Brooklyn, *Cape Town* 8 A1
Brooklyn, *New York* 21 C2
Brooklyn, *Wellington* 32 B1
Brooklyn Bridge, *New York* 21 f2
Brookmont, *Washington* 32 B3
Brossard, *Montreal* 19 B3
Brou-sur-Chantereine, *Paris* 23 A4
Brown, *Toronto* 30 A3
Broyhill Park, *Washington* 32 B2
Brughério, *Milan* 18 A2
Brunswick, *Melbourne* 17 A1
Brush Hill, *Boston* 6 B1
Brussegem, *Brussels* 6 A1
Brussel Nat. Luchthaven, *Brussels* 6 A2
Brussels = Bruxelles, *Brussels* 6 A2
Bruxelles, *Brussels* 6 A2
Bruzzano, *Milan* 18 A2
Bry-sur-Marne, *Paris* 23 A4
Bryanston, *Johannesburg* 13 A1
Bryn, *Oslo* 22 A1
Brzeziny, *Warsaw* 31 B2
Bubeneč, *Prague* 24 B2
Buc, *Paris* 23 B1
Buchenhain, *Munich* 20 B1
Buchholz, *Berlin* 5 A3
Buckhead, *Atlanta* 3 A2
Buckingham Palace, *London* 15 b3
Buckow, *Berlin* 5 B3
Buda, *Budapest* 7 A2
Budafok, *Budapest* 7 B2
Budaörs, *Budapest* 7 B1
Budapest, *Budapest* 7 B2
Budatétény, *Budapest* 7 B2
Budavaripalota, *Budapest* 7 b2
Buddinge, *Copenhagen* 10 A3
Budokan, *Tokyo* 29 a4
Buena Vista, *San Francisco* 25 B2
Buenos Aires, *Buenos Aires* 7 B2
Bufalotta, *Rome* 25 B2
Bugio, *Lisbon* 14 B1
Buiksloot, *Amsterdam* 2 A2
Buitenveldert, *Amsterdam* 2 B2
Buizingen, *Brussels* 6 B1
Bukit Panjang Nature Reserve, *Singapore* 27 A2
Bukit Timah Nature Reserve, *Singapore* 27 A2
Bukum, P., *Singapore* 27 B2
Būlāq, *Cairo* 7 A2
Bule, *Manila* 17 C2
Bulim, *Singapore* 27 A2
Bullen Park, *Melbourne* 17 A2
Bundoora North, *Melbourne* 17 A2
Bundoora Park, *Melbourne* 17 A2
Bunker I., *Karachi* 14 B1
Bunkyo-Ku, *Tokyo* 29 A3
Bunnefjorden, *Oslo* 22 A3
Buona Vista Park, *Singapore* 27 B2
Burbank, *Chicago* 9 C2
Burbank, *Los Angeles* 16 A3
Burlington, *Boston* 6 A2
Burnham Park, *Chicago* 9 c2
Burnham Park Harbor, *Chicago* 9 B3
Burnhamthorpe, *Toronto* 30 B1
Burnt Oak, *London* 15 A2
Burntisland, *Edinburgh* 11 A2
Burnwynd, *Edinburgh* 11 B1
Burqa, *Jerusalem* 13 A2
Burtus, *Cairo* 7 A1
Burudvatn, *Oslo* 22 A2
Burwood, *Sydney* 28 B1
Bushwick, *New York* 21 B2
Bushy Park, *London* 15 B1
Butantã, *São Paulo* 26 B1
Butcher I., *Mumbai* 20 B2
Butts Corner, *Washington* 32 C2
Büyükdere, *Istanbul* 12 B2
Byculla, *Mumbai* 20 B2
Bygdøy, *Oslo* 22 A3

C

C.N. Tower, *Toronto* 30 B2
Cabaçu de Cima →, *São Paulo* 26 A2
Caballito, *Buenos Aires* 7 B2
Cabin John, *Washington* 32 B2
Cabin John Regional Park, *Washington* 32 A2
Cabinteely, *Dublin* 11 B3
Cabra, *Dublin* 11 A2
Cabuçú de Baixo →, *São Paulo* 26 A1
Cachan, *Paris* 23 B2
Cachenka →, *Moscow* 19 B1
Cachoeira, Rib. da →, *São Paulo* 26 B1
Cacilhas, *Lisbon* 14 A2
Cahuenga Pk., *Los Angeles* 16 B3
Cairo = El Qâhira, *Cairo* 7 A2
Caju, *Rio de Janeiro* 24 B1
Čakovice, *Prague* 24 B3
Calcutta = Kolkata, *Calcutta* 8 B2
California Inst. of Tech., *Los Angeles* 16 B4
California Plaza, *Los Angeles* 16 b1
California State Univ., *Los Angeles* 16 B3
Callao, *Lima* 16 B2
Caloocan, *Manila* 17 B1
Calumet Park, *Chicago* 9 C3
Calumet Sag Channel →, *Chicago* 9 C2
Calumpang, *Manila* 17 B2
Calvairate, *Milan* 18 B2
Camarate, *Lisbon* 14 A2
Camaroes, *Lisbon* 14 A1
Camberwell, *London* 15 B3
Camberwell, *Melbourne* 17 B2
Cambridge, *Boston* 6 A3
Cambridge Res., *Boston* 6 A2
Cambuci, *São Paulo* 26 B2
Camden, *London* 15 A3
Cameron, Mt., *Wellington* 32 B2
Çamlıca, *Istanbul* 12 B2
Camp Springs, *Washington* 32 C4
Campamento, *Madrid* 17 B1
Campbellfield, *Melbourne* 17 A1
Camperdown, *Sydney* 28 B2
Campidoglio, *Rome* 25 c3
Campo, Casa de, *Madrid* 17 B1
Campo F.C. Barcelona, *Barcelona* 4 A1
Campo Grande, *Lisbon* 14 A2
Campo Pequeño, *Lisbon* 14 A2
Campolide, *Lisbon* 14 A2
Camps Bay, *Cape Town* 8 A1
C'an San Joan, *Barcelona* 4 A2
Cañacao B., *Manila* 17 C1
Canarsie, *New York* 21 C2
Cancelleria, Palazzo dei, *Rome* 25 c2
Candiac, *Montreal* 19 B3
Caneças, *Lisbon* 14 A1
Canillas, *Madrid* 17 B2
Canillejas, *Madrid* 17 B2
Canning Town, *London* 15 A4
Canteras de Vallecas, *Madrid* 17 B2
Canterbury, *Melbourne* 17 A2
Canterbury, *Sydney* 28 B1
Canton = Guangzhou, *Canton* 8 B2
Caoheijing, *Shanghai* 27 B1
Capão Redondo, *São Paulo* 26 B1
Caparica, *Lisbon* 14 A2
Caparica, Costa da, *Lisbon* 14 B1
Cape Flats, *Cape Town* 8 B2
Cape Town, *Cape Town* 8 A1
Capitol Heights, *Washington* 32 B4
Capitol Hill, *Washington* 32 B4
Capitolini, Musei, *Rome* 25 c3
Captain Cook Bridge, *Sydney* 28 C1
Captain Cook Landing Place Park, *Sydney* 28 C2
Capuchos, *Lisbon* 14 B1
Carabanchel Alto, *Madrid* 17 B1
Carabanchel Bajo, *Madrid* 17 B1
Carapachay, *Buenos Aires* 7 B1
Caraza, *Buenos Aires* 7 C2
Caridad, *Manila* 17 C1
Carioca, Sa. da, *Rio de Janeiro* 24 B1
Carlstadt, *New York* 21 A1
Carlton, *Melbourne* 17 A1
Carmen de Huechuraba, *Santiago* 26 B1
Carmen de la Legua, *Lima* 16 B2
Carnaxide, *Lisbon* 14 A1
Carnegie, *Melbourne* 17 B2
Carnegie Hall, *New York* 21 c2
Carnide, *Lisbon* 14 A1
Carol City, *Miami* 18 A1
Carrascal, *Santiago* 26 B1
Carrickmines, *Dublin* 11 B3
Carrières-sous-Bois, *Paris* 23 A1
Carrières-sous-Poissy, *Paris* 23 A1
Carrières-sur-Seine, *Paris* 23 A2
Carrigeen Bay, *Dublin* 11 A3
Cartierville, *Montreal* 19 A1
Casa Verde, *São Paulo* 26 A1
Casal Morena, *Rome* 25 C2
Casalotti, *Rome* 25 B1
Cascade Heights, *Atlanta* 3 B2
Castél di Leva, *Rome* 25 C2
Castel Sant'Angelo, *Rome* 25 B1
Castle, *Dublin* 11 c2
Castle, *Edinburgh* 11 b2
Castle of Good Hope, *Cape Town* 8 c3
Castleknock, *Dublin* 11 A1
Castleton Corners, *New York* 21 C1
Catedral Metropolitana, *Mexico City* 18 b3
Catedral Metropolitana, *Rio de Janeiro* 24 c1
Catete, *Rio de Janeiro* 24 B1
Catford, *London* 15 B3
Caulfield, *Melbourne* 17 B2
Causeway Bay, *Hong Kong* 12 c3
Cavite, *Manila* 17 C1
Caxias, *Lisbon* 14 A1
Cebecci, *Istanbul* 12 B1
Cecchignola, *Rome* 25 C2
Cecilienhof, Schloss, *Berlin* 5 B1
Cedar Grove, *Atlanta* 3 C3
Cempaka Putih, *Jakarta* 13 B2
Çengelköy, *Istanbul* 12 B2
Cengkareng, *Jakarta* 13 A1
Centennial Park, *Sydney* 28 B2
Center Hill, *Atlanta* 3 B2
Centocelle, *Rome* 25 B2
Centraal Station, *Amsterdam* 2 a2
Central Park, *New York* 21 B2
Cerillos, *Santiago* 26 B1
Cerro de la Estrella, *Mexico City* 18 B2
Cerro de los Angeles, *Madrid* 17 C1
Cerro Navia, *Santiago* 26 B1
Certanovka →, *Moscow* 19 C3
Certanovo, *Moscow* 19 C3
Cesano Boscone, *Milan* 18 B1
Cesate, *Milan* 18 A1
Cha Kwo Ling, *Hong Kong* 12 B2
Chacarrita, *Buenos Aires* 7 B2
Chadwell Heath, *London* 15 A4
Chai Chee, *Singapore* 27 B3
Chai Wan, *Hong Kong* 12 B2
Chai Wan Kok, *Hong Kong* 12 A1
Chaillot, Palais de, *Paris* 23 b2
Chakdaha, *Calcutta* 8 C1
Chamartin, *Madrid* 17 B1
Chamberi, *Madrid* 17 B1
Chambourcy, *Paris* 23 A1
Champ de Mars, Parc du, *Paris* 23 c2
Champigny-sur-Marne, *Paris* 23 B4
Champlain, Pont, *Montreal* 19 B2
Champs Elysées, Avenue des, *Paris* 23 b2
Champs-sur-Marne, *Paris* 23 A4
Chamrail, *Calcutta* 8 B1
Chamshil, *Seoul* 26 B2
Chamwŏn, *Seoul* 26 B2
Chanakyapuri, *Delhi* 10 B2
Chanditala, *Calcutta* 8 A1
Changfeng Park, *Shanghai* 27 B1
Changi, *Singapore* 27 A3
Changi Int. Airport, *Singapore* 27 A3
Changning, *Shanghai* 27 B1
Chantereine, *Paris* 23 A4
Chantian, *Canton* 8 A2
Chao Phraya →, *Bangkok* 3 B2
Chaoyang, *Beijing* 4 B2
Chaoyangmen, *Beijing* 4 B2
Chapelizod, *Dublin* 11 A1
Chapultepec, Bosque de, *Mexico City* 18 B1
Chapultepec, Castillo de, *Mexico City* 18 B1
Charenton-le-Pont, *Paris* 23 B3
Charing Cross, *London* 15 b4
Charleroi, Kanal de →, *Brussels* 6 B1
Charles Bridge, *Prague* 24 b1
Charles Square, *Prague* 24 c1
Charlestown, *Boston* 6 A3
Charlottenburg, *Berlin* 5 A2
Charlottenburg, Schloss, *Berlin* 5 A2
Charlottenlund, *Copenhagen* 10 A3
Charlton, *London* 15 B4
Charneca, *Lisbon* 14 A2
Charneca, *Lisbon* 14 B1
Châteaufort, *Paris* 23 B1
Châtenay-Malabry, *Paris* 23 B2
Chatham, *Chicago* 9 C3
Châtillon, *Paris* 23 B2
Chatou, *Paris* 23 A1
Chatpur, *Calcutta* 8 B2
Chatswood, *Sydney* 28 A2
Chatuchak, *Bangkok* 3 B2
Chatuchak Park, *Bangkok* 3 B2
Chauki, *Karachi* 14 A1
Chavarria, *Lima* 16 B2
Chaville, *Paris* 23 B2
Chayang, *Seoul* 26 B2
Chegi, *Seoul* 26 B2
Chelles, *Paris* 23 A4
Chelles, Canal de, *Paris* 23 A4
Chells-le-Pin, Aérodrome, *Paris* 23 A4
Chelsea, *Boston* 6 A3
Chelsea, *London* 15 B2
Chelsea, *New York* 21 c1
Chembur, *Mumbai* 20 A2
Chennevières-sur-Marne, *Paris* 23 B4
Cheops, *Cairo* 7 B1
Cherepkovo, *Moscow* 19 B2
Chernyovo, *Moscow* 19 A1
Cheryomushki, *Moscow* 19 B3
Chestnut Hill, *Boston* 6 B2
Cheung Sha Wan, *Hong Kong* 12 A1
Cheverly, *Washington* 32 B4
Chevilly-Larue, *Paris* 23 B3
Chevry-Cossigny, *Paris* 23 B4
Chevy Chase, *Washington* 32 B3
Chevy Chase View, *Washington* 32 A3
Chia Keng, *Singapore* 27 A3
Chiaravalle Milanese, *Milan* 18 B2
Chicago, *Chicago* 9 B3
Chicago Harbor, *Chicago* 9 B3
Chicago Lawn, *Chicago* 9 C2
Chicago-Midway Airport, *Chicago* 9 C2
Chicago-O'Hare Int. Airport, *Chicago* 9 B1
Chicago Ridge, *Chicago* 9 C2
Chicago Sanitary and Ship Canal, *Chicago* 9 C2
Chienzui, *Canton* 8 A3
Chik Sha, *Hong Kong* 12 B2
Child's Hill, *London* 15 A2
Chilla Saroda, *Delhi* 10 B2
Chillum, *Washington* 32 B4
Chilly-Mazarin, *Paris* 23 B2
Chinatown, *Los Angeles* 16 a3
Chinatown, *New York* 21 e2
Chinatown, *San Francisco* 25 b2
Chinatown, *Singapore* 27 c2
Chingupota, *Calcutta* 8 C1
Chislehurst, *London* 15 B4
Chiswick, *London* 15 B2
Chiswick House, *London* 15 B2
Chitose, *Tokyo* 29 B2
Chitralada Palace, *Bangkok* 3 B2
Chiyoda-Ku, *Tokyo* 29 b4
Chkalova, *Moscow* 19 C5
Choa Chu Kang, *Singapore* 27 A2
Choboty, *Moscow* 19 C2
Chodov u Prahy, *Prague* 24 B3
Chōfu, *Tokyo* 29 B2
Choisy-le-Roi, *Paris* 23 B3
Cholupice, *Prague* 24 C2
Chom Thong, *Bangkok* 3 B1
Chong Pang, *Singapore* 27 A2
Ch'ŏngdam, *Seoul* 26 B2
Chongmyo Royal Shrine, *Seoul* 26 B1
Chongno, *Seoul* 26 B1
Chongwen, *Beijing* 4 B2
Chŏnho, *Seoul* 26 B2
Chopin, Muzeum, *Warsaw* 31 b2
Chornaya →, *Moscow* 19 B6
Chorrillos, *Lima* 16 C2
Chowpatty Beach, *Mumbai* 20 b1
Christian Quarter, *Jerusalem* 13 b3
Christiansborg, *Copenhagen* 10 c2
Christianshavn, *Copenhagen* 10 A3
Chrysler Building, *New York* 21 c2
Chrzanów, *Warsaw* 31 B1
Chuen Lung, *Hong Kong* 12 A1
Chuk Kok, *Hong Kong* 12 A2
Chulalongkorn Univ., *Bangkok* 3 B2
Chung, *Seoul* 26 B1
Chunghwa, *Seoul* 26 B2
Chungnangch'on →, *Seoul* 26 B1
Chūō-Ku, *Tokyo* 29 b5
Church End, *London* 15 A2
Churchtown, *Dublin* 11 B2
Ciampino, *Rome* 25 C2
Ciampino, Aeroporto di, *Rome* 25 C2
Cicero, *Chicago* 9 B2
Cilandak, *Jakarta* 13 B1
Cilincing, *Jakarta* 13 A2
Ciliwung →, *Jakarta* 13 B2
Čimice, *Prague* 24 B2
Cinecittà, *Rome* 25 B2
Cinisello Bálsamo, *Milan* 18 A2
Cinkota, *Budapest* 7 A3
Cipete, *Jakarta* 13 B1
Citadella, *Budapest* 7 c2
Città degli Studi, *Milan* 18 B2
Città del Vaticano, *Rome* 25 B1
City, *London* 15 A3
City Hall, *New York* 21 e1
Ciudad Deportiva, *Mexico City* 18 B2
Ciudad Fin de Semana, *Madrid* 17 B2
Ciudad General Belgrano, *Buenos Aires* 7 C1
Ciudad Lineál, *Madrid* 17 B2
Ciudad Satélite, *Mexico City* 18 A1
Ciudad Universitaria, *Buenos Aires* 7 B2
Ciudad Universitaria, *Mexico City* 18 C1
Ciutadella, Parc de la, *Barcelona* 4 b3
Civic Center, *Los Angeles* 16 b2
Clamart, *Paris* 23 B2
Clapham, *London* 15 B3
Clapton, *London* 15 A3
Claremont, *Cape Town* 8 A1
Clayhall, *London* 15 A4
Clerkenwell, *London* 15 a4
Clermiston, *Edinburgh* 11 B1
Clichy, *Paris* 23 A2
Clichy-sous-Bois, *Paris* 23 A4
Cliffside, *Toronto* 30 A3
Cliffside Park, *New York* 21 B2
Clifton, *Boston* 6 A4
Clifton, *Karachi* 14 B2
Clifton, *New York* 21 C1
Cliftondale, *Boston* 6 A3
Cloghran, *Dublin* 11 A2
Clonskeagh, *Dublin* 11 B2
Clontarf, *Dublin* 11 A2
Clontarf, *Sydney* 28 A2
Clovelly, *Sydney* 28 B2
Cobras, I. das, *Rio de Janeiro* 24 B2
Coburg, *Melbourne* 17 A1
Cochituate, *Boston* 6 A1
Cochituate, L., *Boston* 6 B1
Cocotá, *Rio de Janeiro* 24 A1
Cœuilly, *Paris* 23 B4
Coina, *Lisbon* 14 B2
Coit Tower, *San Francisco* 25 a2
Coker, *Lagos* 14 B2
Colaba, *Mumbai* 20 B1
Colaba Pt., *Mumbai* 20 B1
Colegiales, *Buenos Aires* 7 B2
Colindale, *London* 15 A2
Colinton, *Edinburgh* 11 B2
College Park, *Atlanta* 3 C2
College Park, *Washington* 32 B4
College Point, *New York* 21 B2
Collégien, *Paris* 23 A4
Collier Row, *London* 15 A4
Colliers Wood, *London* 15 B2
Colma, *San Francisco* 25 B2
Colney Hatch, *London* 15 A3
Cologno Monzese, *Milan* 18 A2
Colombes, *Paris* 23 A2
Colón, Monumente, *Barcelona* 4 c3
Colon, Plaza de, *Madrid* 17 a3
Colonia Güell, *Barcelona* 4 A1
Colonial Knob, *Wellington* 32 A1
Colosseo, *Rome* 25 c3
Columbus Circus, *New York* 21 b2
Combault, *Paris* 23 B4
Comércio, Praça do, *Lisbon* 14 A2
Commerce, *Los Angeles* 16 B4
Como, *Sydney* 28 C1
Company's Gardens, *Cape Town* 8 c2
Conceição, I. da, *Rio de Janeiro* 24 B2
Concertgebouw, *Amsterdam* 2 c1
Conchali, *Santiago* 26 B2
Concord, *Boston* 6 A1
Concord, *Sydney* 28 B1
Concord, *Toronto* 30 A2
Concorde, Place de la, *Paris* 23 b3
Concorezzo, *Milan* 18 A2
Coney Island, *New York* 21 C2
Congonhas, Aéroporto, *São Paulo* 26 B2
Connaught Place, *Delhi* 10 B2
Conservatori, Palazzo dei, *Rome* 25 c3
Consolação, *São Paulo* 26 B2
Constantia, *Cape Town* 8 B1
Constitución, *Buenos Aires* 7 B2
Constitution, *Atlanta* 3 B2
Convention and Exhibition Centre, *Hong Kong* 12 b2
Coogee, *Sydney* 28 B2
Cook Str., *Wellington* 32 A1
Cooksville, *Toronto* 30 B1
Coolock, *Dublin* 11 A2
Copacabana, *Rio de Janeiro* 24 B1
Copenhagen = København, *Copenhagen* 10 A2
Coral Gables, *Miami* 18 B2
Coral Hills, *Washington* 32 B4
Corcovado, Morro do, *Rio de Janeiro* 24 B1
Corduff, *Dublin* 11 A1
Cormano, *Milan* 18 A2
Cornaredo, *Milan* 18 A1
Córsico, *Milan* 18 B1
Corsini, Palazzo, *Rome* 25 c1
Corviale, *Rome* 25 B1
Coslada, *Madrid* 17 B2
Cossigny, *Paris* 23 B4
Cossipore, *Calcutta* 8 B2
Costantino, Arco di, *Rome* 25 c3
Costorphine, *Edinburgh* 11 B2
Cotao, *Lisbon* 14 A1
Côte St.-Luc, *Montreal* 19 B2
Cotunduba, I. de, *Rio de Janeiro* 24 B2
Coubron, *Paris* 23 A4
Countryside, *Chicago* 9 C1
Courbevoie, *Paris* 23 A2
Courtry, *Paris* 23 A4
Covent Garden, *London* 15 b4
Cowgate, *Edinburgh* 11 b3
Cowley, *London* 15 A1
Coyoacán, *Mexico City* 18 B2
Cragin, *Chicago* 9 B2
Craighall Park, *Johannesburg* 13 A2
Craiglockhart, *Edinburgh* 11 B2
Craigmillar, *Edinburgh* 11 B3
Cramond, *Edinburgh* 11 B2
Cramond Bridge, *Edinburgh* 11 B1
Cramond I., *Edinburgh* 11 B1
Cranford, *London* 15 B1
Crawford, *Cape Town* 8 A2
Crayford, *London* 15 B5
Creekmouth, *London* 15 A4
Crescenzago, *Milan* 18 A2
Cressely, *Paris* 23 B1
Cresskill, *New York* 21 A2
Creteil, *Paris* 23 B3
Cricklewood, *London* 15 A2
Cristo Redentor, Estatua do, *Rio de Janeiro* 24 B1
Crockenhill, *London* 15 B4
Croissy-Beaubourg, *Paris* 23 B4
Croissy-sur-Seine, *Paris* 23 A1
Crosby, *Johannesburg* 13 B1
Crosne, *Paris* 23 B3
Cross I., *Mumbai* 20 B2
Crouch End, *London* 15 A3
Crown Mine, *Johannesburg* 13 B1
Crows Nest, *Sydney* 28 A2
Croydon, *London* 15 B3
Croydon Park, *Sydney* 28 B1
Cruagh Mt., *Dublin* 11 B2
Crumlin, *Dublin* 11 B2
Cruz de Pau, *Lisbon* 14 B2
Crystal Palace, *London* 15 B3
Csepel, *Budapest* 7 B2
Csepelsziget, *Budapest* 7 B2
Csillaghegy, *Budapest* 7 A2
Csillagtelep, *Budapest* 7 B2
Csömör, *Budapest* 7 A3
Csömöri-patak →, *Budapest* 7 A3
Cuatro Vientos, *Madrid* 17 B1
Cuauhtémoc, *Mexico City* 18 B2
Cubao, *Manila* 17 B2
Çubuklu, *Istanbul* 12 B2
Cudahy, *Los Angeles* 16 C3
Cuicuilco, Pirámido de, *Mexico City* 18 C1
Culver City, *Los Angeles* 16 B2
Cumballa Hill, *Mumbai* 20 a1
Cumbres de Vallecas, *Madrid* 17 B2
Cupecê, *São Paulo* 26 B1
Currie, *Edinburgh* 11 B2
Cusago, *Milan* 18 B1
Cusano Milanino, *Milan* 18 A2
Custom House, *Dublin* 11 b3
Çuvuşabaşi →, *Istanbul* 12 B1
Czerniaków, *Warsaw* 31 B2
Czyste, *Warsaw* 31 B1

D

D.F. Malan Airport, *Cape Town* 8 A2
Da Moóca →, *São Paulo* 26 B2
Da Yunhe →, *Tianjin* 30 A1
Dabizhuang, *Tianjin* 30 A2
Ďáblice, *Prague* 24 B2
Dąbrowa, *Warsaw* 31 B1
Dachang, *Shanghai* 27 B1
Dachang Airfield, *Shanghai* 27 B1
Dachau-Ost, *Munich* 20 A1
Dachauer Moos, *Munich* 20 A1
Dadar, *Mumbai* 20 A2
Dagenham, *London* 15 A4
Daglfing, *Munich* 20 B2
Daheisha, *Jerusalem* 13 B2
Dahlem, *Berlin* 5 B2
Dahlwitz-Hoppegarten, *Berlin* 5 A5
Dahongmen, *Beijing* 4 C2
Daitō, *Osaka* 22 A4
Dajiaoting, *Beijing* 4 B2
Dakhnoye, *St. Petersburg* 26 C1
Dalejsky potok →, *Prague* 24 B2
Dalgety Bay, *Edinburgh* 11 A1
Dalkeith, *Edinburgh* 11 B3
Dalkey, *Dublin* 11 B3
Dalkey Island, *Dublin* 11 B3
Dallgow, *Berlin* 5 A1
Dalmeny, *Edinburgh* 11 B1
Dalston, *London* 15 A3
Daly City, *San Francisco* 25 B2
Dam, *Amsterdam* 2 b2
Dam Rak, *Amsterdam* 2 a2
Damaia, *Lisbon* 14 A1
Dämeritzsee, *Berlin* 5 B5
Dan Ryan Woods, *Chicago* 9 C2
Danderhall, *Edinburgh* 11 B3
Danderyd, *Stockholm* 28 A2
Danforth, *Toronto* 30 A3
Darakeh, *Tehran* 30 A2
Darband, *Tehran* 30 A2
Darling Harbour, *Sydney* 28 b1
Darling Point, *Sydney* 28 B2
Darndale, *Dublin* 11 A2
Darrūs, *Tehran* 30 A2
Dartford, *London* 15 B5
Darya Ganj, *Delhi* 1 a3
Dashi, *Canton* 8 B2
Datansha, *Canton* 8 B2
Datun, *Beijing* 4 B2
Daulatpur, *Delhi* 10 A1
David's Citadel, *Jerusalem* 13 b3
David's Tomb, *Jerusalem* 13 b3
Davidson, Mt., *San Francisco* 25 B2
Davidson's Mains, *Edinburgh* 11 B2
Dāvūdiyeh, *Tehran* 30 A2
Davydkovo, *Moscow* 19 B2
Dawidy, *Warsaw* 31 C1
Days Bay, *Wellington* 32 B2
Dazhigu, *Tianjin* 30 B2
De Waag, *Amsterdam* 2 b2
Decatur, *Atlanta* 3 B3
Dedham, *Boston* 6 B2
Deer I., *Boston* 6 A4
Degunino, *Moscow* 19 A3
Deir Dibwan, *Jerusalem* 13 A2
Deir Ibzi'e, *Jerusalem* 13 A1
Dejvice, *Prague* 24 B2
Dekabristov, Ostrov, *St. Petersburg* 26 B1
Delhi, *Delhi* 10 B2
Delhi Gate, *Delhi* 1 b3
Demarest, *New York* 21 A2
Den Ilp, *Amsterdam* 2 A2
Denistone Heights, *Sydney* 28 A1
Dentonia Park, *Toronto* 30 A3
Deptford, *London* 15 B3
Deputati, Camera dei, *Rome* 25 b2
Des Plaines, *Chicago* 9 A1
Des Plaines →, *Chicago* 9 B1
Deshengmen, *Beijing* 4 B2
Deutsch-Wagram, *Vienna* 31 A3
Deutsche Oper, *Berlin* 5 A2
Deutscher Museum, *Munich* 20 B2
Devil's Peak, *Cape Town* 8 A1
Dhāfni, *Athens* 2 B2
Dhakuria, *Calcutta* 8 B2
Dhamarakia, *Athens* 2 B1
Dharavi, *Mumbai* 20 A2
Dhrapersón, *Athens* 2 B1
Diadema, *São Paulo* 26 C2
Diegen, *Brussels* 6 A2
Diemen, *Amsterdam* 2 A2
Diepkloof, *Johannesburg* 13 B1
Diepriviet, *Cape Town* 8 B1
Difficult Run →, *Washington* 32 B2
Dilbeek, *Brussels* 6 A1
Dinzigu, *Tianjin* 30 A1
Dirnismaning, *Munich* 20 A2
District Heights, *Washington* 32 B4
Ditan Park, *Beijing* 4 a2
Diyāla →, *Baghdad* 3 B3
Djursholm, *Stockholm* 28 A2
Döberitz, *Berlin* 5 A1
Döbling, *Vienna* 31 A2
Docklands, *London* 15 A3
Dodder, R. →, *Dublin* 11 B1
Dodger Stadium, *Los Angeles* 16 B3
Dolgoe Ozero, *St. Petersburg* 26 A1
Doll Museum, *Delhi* 1 b3
Dollis Hill, *London* 15 A2
Dollymount, *Dublin* 11 A3
Dolni, *Prague* 24 B3
Dolni Chabry, *Prague* 24 B2
Dolni Počernice, *Prague* 24 B3
Dolphins Barn, *Dublin* 11 B2
Dom Pedro II, Parque, *São Paulo* 26 B2
Domain, The, *Sydney* 28 b2
Dome of the Rock, *Jerusalem* 13 b3
Don Mills, *Toronto* 30 A2
Don Muang Int. Airport, *Bangkok* 3 A2
Donaghmede, *Dublin* 11 A3
Donau-Oder Kanal, *Vienna* 31 A3
Donaufeld, *Vienna* 31 A2
Donaupark, *Vienna* 31 A2
Donaustadt, *Vienna* 31 A2
Dongan Hills, *New York* 21 C1
Dongcheng, *Beijing* 4 B2
Dongguo, *Shanghai* 27 B2
Dongjiao, *Canton* 8 B2
Dongjuzi, *Tianjin* 30 B2
Dongmenwai, *Tianjin* 30 B2
Dongri, *Mumbai* 20 B2
Dongshanhu Park, *Canton* 8 B2
Dongzhimen, *Beijing* 4 B2
Donnybrook, *Dublin* 11 B2
Doornfontein, *Johannesburg* 13 B2
Dorchester, *Boston* 6 B3
Dorchester B., *Boston* 6 B3
Dornach, *Munich* 20 B3
Dorval, Aéroport de, *Montreal* 19 B1
Dos Couros →, *São Paulo* 26 C2
Dos Moninos →, *São Paulo* 26 C2
Douglas Park, *Chicago* 9 B2
Dover Heights, *Sydney* 28 B2
Dowlatābād, *Tehran* 30 B2
Downey, *Los Angeles* 16 C4
Downsview, *Toronto* 30 A1
Dragør, *Copenhagen* 10 B3
Drancy, *Paris* 23 A3
Dranesville, *Washington* 32 A1
Dreilinden, *Berlin* 5 B2
Drewnica, *Warsaw* 31 B2
Drigh Road, *Karachi* 14 A2
Drimnagh, *Dublin* 11 B2
Drogenbos, *Brussels* 6 B1
Druid Hills, *Atlanta* 3 B2
Drum Towwer, *Beijing* 4 a2
Drumcondra, *Dublin* 11 A2
Drummoyne, *Sydney* 28 B1
Drylaw, *Edinburgh* 11 B2
Dubeč, *Prague* 24 B3
Dublin, *Dublin* 11 A2
Dublin Airport, *Dublin* 11 A2
Dublin Bay, *Dublin* 11 B3
Dublin Harbour, *Dublin* 11 A2
Duddingston, *Edinburgh* 11 B3
Dugnano, *Milan* 18 A2
Dūlāb, *Tehran* 30 B2
Dulwich, *London* 15 B3
Dum Dum, *Calcutta* 8 B2
Dum Dum Int. Airport, *Calcutta* 8 B2
Dumont, *New York* 21 A2
Dūn Laoghaire, *Dublin* 11 B3
Duna →, *Budapest* 7 A2
Duncan Dock, *Cape Town* 8 a3
Dundrum, *Dublin* 11 B2
Dunearn, *Singapore* 27 B2
Dunfermline, *Edinburgh* 11 A1
Dunn Loring, *Washington* 32 B2
Dunning, *Chicago* 9 B2
Dunvegan, *Johannesburg* 13 A2
Duomo, *Milan* 18 B2
Duque de Caxias, *Rio de Janeiro* 24 A1
Dusit, *Bangkok* 3 B2
Dusit Zoo, *Bangkok* 3 a2
Duvernay, *Montreal* 19 A1
Dworp, *Brussels* 6 B1
Dyakovo, *Moscow* 19 B3
Dzerzhinskiy, *Moscow* 19 C5
Dzerzhinskiy, *Moscow* 19 B3
Dzerzhinskiy Park, *Moscow* 19 B3

E

Eagle Rock, *Los Angeles* 16 B3
Ealing, *London* 15 A2
Earl's Court, *London* 15 c1
Earlsfield, *London* 15 B2
Earlwood, *Sydney* 28 B1
East Acton, *London* 15 A1
East Arlington, *Boston* 6 A3
East Arlington, *Washington* 32 B3
East Bedfont, *London* 15 B1
East Boston, *Boston* 6 A3
East Don →, *Toronto* 30 A2
East Elmhurst, *New York* 21 B2
East Finchley, *London* 15 A2
East Ham, *London* 15 A4
East Humber →, *Toronto* 30 A1
East Lamma Channel, *Hong Kong* 12 B1
East Lexington, *Boston* 6 A2
East Los Angeles, *Los Angeles* 16 B3
East Molesey, *London* 15 B1
East New York, *New York* 21 B2
East Pines, *Washington* 32 B4
East Point, *Atlanta* 3 B2
East Potomac Park, *Washington* 32 B3
East Pt., *Boston* 6 A4
East River →, *New York* 21 B2
East Rutherford, *New York* 21 A1
East Sheen, *London* 15 B2
East Village, *New York* 21 e2
East Wickham, *London* 15 B4
East York, *Toronto* 30 A2
Eastbourne, *Wellington* 32 B2
Eastcote, *London* 15 A1
Easter Howgate, *Edinburgh* 11 B2
Eastwood, *Sydney* 28 A1
Ebara, *Tokyo* 29 B3
Ebisu, *Tokyo* 29 B3
Ebute-Ikorodu, *Lagos* 14 A2
Ebute-Metta, *Lagos* 14 B2
Echo Park, *Los Angeles* 16 a1
Eda, *Tokyo* 29 B2
Edendale, *Johannesburg* 13 A2
Edenmore, *Dublin* 11 A2
Edgars Cr. →, *Melbourne* 17 A1
Edgeley, *Toronto* 30 A1
Edgemar, *San Francisco* 25 C2
Edinburgh, *Edinburgh* 11 B2
Edison Park, *Chicago* 9 A2
Edmondston, *Washington* 32 B4
Edmondstown, *Dublin* 11 B2
Edo →, *Tokyo* 29 B4
Edogawa-Ku, *Tokyo* 29 A4
Edsberg, *Stockholm* 28 A1
Edwards L., *Melbourne* 17 A1
Eiche, *Berlin* 5 A4
Eiche Sud, *Berlin* 5 A4
Eiffel, Tour, *Paris* 23 A2
Ein Arik, *Jerusalem* 13 A1
Ein Naquba, *Jerusalem* 13 B1
Ein Rafa, *Jerusalem* 13 B1
Eizariya, *Jerusalem* 13 B2
Ejby, *Copenhagen* 10 A2
Ejigbo, *Lagos* 14 A1
Ekeberg, *Oslo* 22 A3
Eknäs, *Stockholm* 28 B3
El 'Abbasiya, *Cairo* 7 A2
El Agustino, *Lima* 16 B2
El Baragil, *Cairo* 7 A1
El Basātīn, *Cairo* 7 B2
El-Bira, *Jerusalem* 13 A2
El Bosque, *Santiago* 26 C2
El Carmen, *Santiago* 26 B1
El Cortijo, *Santiago* 26 B1
El Duqqi, *Cairo* 7 A2
El Encinar de los Reyes, *Madrid* 17 A2
El Ghurīya, *Cairo* 7 A2
El Gīza, *Cairo* 7 A2
El-Khadr, *Jerusalem* 13 B1
El Khalīfa, *Cairo* 7 A2
El Kôm el Ahmar, *Cairo* 7 A2
El Ma'ādi, *Cairo* 7 B2
El Matarīya, *Cairo* 7 A2
El Mohandessin, *Cairo* 7 A2
El Monte, *Los Angeles* 16 B4
El Mūskī, *Cairo* 7 A2
El Pardo, *Madrid* 17 A1
El Portal, *Miami* 18 A2
El Prat de Llobregat, *Barcelona* 4 B1
El Pueblo de L.A. Historic Park, *Los Angeles* 16 b2
El Qâhira, *Cairo* 7 A2
El Qubba, *Cairo* 7 A2
El Reloj, *Mexico City* 18 C2
El Retiro, *Madrid* 17 B1
El Salto, *Santiago* 26 B2
El Sereno, *Los Angeles* 16 B3
El Talibīya, *Cairo* 7 B2
El Vergel, *Mexico City* 18 C2
El Wāhli, *Cairo* 7 A2
El Zamālik, *Cairo* 7 A2
El Zeitūn, *Cairo* 7 A2
Elephanta Caves, *Mumbai* 20 B2
Elephanta I., *Mumbai* 20 B2
Ellboda, *Stockholm* 28 A3
Ellinikón, *Athens* 2 B2
Ellis I., *New York* 21 B1
Elm Park, *London* 15 A5
Elmers End, *London* 15 B3
Elmhurst, *New York* 21 B2
Elmstead, *London* 15 B4
Elmwood Park, *Chicago* 9 B2
Elmwood Park, *New York* 21 A1
Elsdon, *Wellington* 32 A1
Elsiesrivier, *Cape Town* 8 A2
Elsternwick, *Melbourne* 17 B2
Eltham, *London* 15 B4
Elwood, *Melbourne* 17 B1
Élysée, *Paris* 23 A2
Elysian Park, *Los Angeles* 16 a3
Embajadores, *Madrid* 17 c2
Embarcadero Center, *San Francisco* 25 b3
Emek Refa'im, *Jerusalem* 13 c2
Émerainville, *Paris* 23 B4
Emeryville, *San Francisco* 25 A3
Eminönü, *Istanbul* 12 B1
Emmarentia, *Johannesburg* 13 A2
Empire State Building, *New York* 21 c2
Encantado, *Rio de Janeiro* 24 B1
Encino, *Los Angeles* 16 B2
Encino Res., *Los Angeles* 16 B1
Enebyberg, *Stockholm* 28 A1
Enfield, *Sydney* 28 B1
Engenho, I. do, *Rio de Janeiro* 24 B2
Englewood, *Chicago* 9 C3
Englewood, *New York* 21 A2
Englewood Cliffs, *New York* 21 A2
Enmore, *Sydney* 28 B2
Enskede, *Stockholm* 28 B2
Entrevias, *Madrid* 17 B1
Epping, *Sydney* 28 A1
Erawan Shrine, *Bangkok* 3 c3
Eregun, *Lagos* 14 A2
Erenköy, *Istanbul* 12 C2
Erith, *London* 15 B5
Erlaa, *Vienna* 31 B1
Ermington, *Sydney* 28 A1
Ermita, *Manila* 17 B1
Ershatou, *Canton* 8 B2
Erskineville, *Sydney* 28 B2
Erunkan, *Lagos* 14 A2
Erzsébet-Telep, *Budapest* 7 B3
Eschenried, *Munich* 20 A1
Esenler, *Istanbul* 12 B1
Esher, *London* 15 B1
Eskbank, *Edinburgh* 11 B3
Esperanza, *Mexico City* 18 c3
Esplanade Park, *Singapore* 27 c3
Esplugas, *Barcelona* 4 A1
Esposizione Univ. di Roma (E.U.R.), *Rome* 25 C1
Essendon, *Melbourne* 17 A1
Essendon Airport, *Melbourne* 17 A1
Essingen, *Stockholm* 28 B1
Essling, *Vienna* 31 A3
Est, Gare de l', *Paris* 23 a5
Estadio Maracanã, *Rio de Janeiro* 24 B1
Estado, Parque do, *São Paulo* 26 B2
Estefânia, *Lisbon* 14 a2
Estrela, Basilica da, *Lisbon* 14 A2
Ethnikó Arheologiko Moussío, *Athens* 2 a2
Etobicoke, *Toronto* 30 B1
Etobicoke Cr. →, *Toronto* 30 B1
Etterbeek, *Brussels* 6 B2
Euston, *London* 15 a3
Evanston, *Chicago* 9 A2
Even Sapir, *Jerusalem* 13 B1
Evere, *Brussels* 6 A2
Everett, *Boston* 6 A3
Evergreen Park, *Chicago* 9 C2
Evīn, *Tehran* 30 A2
Évzonos, *Athens* 2 B2
Ewu, *Lagos* 14 A1
Exchange Square, *Hong Kong* 12 c1
Exposições, Palácio das, *Rio de Janeiro* 24 B1
Eyüp, *Istanbul* 12 B1

F

Fabour, Mt., *Singapore* 27 B2
Faechi, *Seoul* 26 B2
Fælledparken, *Copenhagen* 10 A3
Fågelön, *Stockholm* 28 B1
Fagersjö, *Stockholm* 28 B2
Fair Lawn, *New York* 21 A1
Fairfax, *Washington* 32 B2
Fairfax Station, *Washington* 32 C2
Fairhaven Bay, *Boston* 6 A1
Fairhaven Hill, *Boston* 6 A1
Fairland, *Johannesburg* 13 A1
Fairmilehead, *Edinburgh* 11 B2
Fairmount Heights, *Washington* 32 B4
Fairport, *Toronto* 30 A4
Fairview, *New York* 21 B1
Falenty, *Warsaw* 31 C1
Fálirou, Órmos, *Athens* 2 B2
Falkenburg, *Berlin* 5 A4
Falkenhagen, *Berlin* 5 A1
Falkensee, *Berlin* 5 A1
Falls Church, *Washington* 32 B2
Falomo, *Lagos* 14 B2
False Bay, *Cape Town* 8 B2
Fangcun, *Canton* 8 B2
Farahābād, *Tehran* 30 A2
Farforovskaya, *St. Petersburg* 26 B2
Farningham, *London* 15 B5
Farrar Pond, *Boston* 6 A1
Farsta, *Stockholm* 28 B2
Fasanerie-Nord, *Munich* 20 A2
Fasangarten, *Munich* 20 B2
Fasting Palace, *Beijing* 4 c2
Fatih, *Istanbul* 12 B1
Favoriten, *Vienna* 31 B2
Fawkner, *Melbourne* 17 A1

Kapellerfeld 35

Fawkner Park, *Melbourne* 17 B1
Feijó, *Lisbon* 14 B2
Feldkirchen, *Munich* 20 B3
Feldmoching, *Munich* 20 A2
Feltham, *London* 15 B1
Fener, *Istanbul* 12 B1
Fenerbahçe, *Istanbul* 12 C2
Fengtai, *Beijing* 4 C1
Fenino, *Moscow* 19 B5
Ferencváros, *Budapest* 7 B2
Ferihegyi Airport, *Budapest* 7 B3
Ferndale, *Johannesburg* 13 A2
Férolles-Attilly, *Paris* 23 B4
Fichtenau, *Berlin* 5 B5
Fields Corner, *Boston* 6 B3
Fiera Camp, *Milan* 18 B1
Fifth Avenue, *New York* 21 b3
Figino, *Milan* 18 B1
Fijir, *Baghdad* 3 A2
Filadhélfia, *Athens* 2 A2
Fili-Mazilovo, *Moscow* 19 B2
Filothei, *Athens* 2 A2
Finchley, *London* 15 A2
Finglas, *Dublin* 11 A2
Finsbury, *London* 15 A3
Finsbury Park, *London* 15 A3
Fiorito, *Buenos Aires* 7 C2
Firhouse, *Dublin* 11 B2
Fischerhäuser, *Munich* 20 A3
Fisher Island, *Miami* 18 B2
Fishermans Bend, *Melbourne* 17 A1
Fisherman's Wharf, *San Francisco* 25 a1
Fisherville, *Toronto* 30 A2
Fisksätra, *Stockholm* 28 B3
Fitzroy Gardens, *Melbourne* 17 A1
Five Dock, *Sydney* 28 B1
Fjellstrand, *Oslo* 22 B2
Flamengo, *Rio de Janeiro* 24 B1
Flaminio, *Rome* 25 B1
Flaskebekk, *Oslo* 22 A2
Flatbush, *New York* 21 C2
Flaten, *Stockholm* 28 B2
Flemington Racecourse, *Melbourne* 17 A1
Flint Pk., *Los Angeles* 16 B3
Florence, *Los Angeles* 16 C3
Florence Bloom Bird Sanctuary, *Johannesburg* 13 A2
Florentia, *Johannesburg* 13 B2
Flores, *Buenos Aires* 7 B2
Floresta, *Buenos Aires* 7 B2
Florida, *Buenos Aires* 7 B2
Florida, *Johannesburg* 13 B1
Floridsdorf, *Vienna* 31 A2
Flushing, *New York* 21 B3
Flushing Meadows Corona Park, *New York* 21 B2
Flysta, *Stockholm* 28 A1
Fo Tan, *Hong Kong* 12 A2
Föhrenhain, *Vienna* 31 A2
Fontainebleau, *Johannesburg* 13 A1
Fontenay-aux-Roses, *Paris* 23 B2
Fontenay-le-Fleury, *Paris* 23 B1
Fontenay-sous-Bois, *Paris* 23 A3
Foots Cray, *London* 15 B4
Footscray, *Melbourne* 17 A1
Foreshore, *Cape Town* 8 a3
Forest, *Brussels* 6 B1
Forest Gate, *London* 15 A4
Forest Heights, *Washington* 32 C3
Forest Hill, *London* 15 B3
Forest Hill, *Toronto* 30 A2
Forest Hills, *New York* 21 B2
Forest Park, *Chicago* 9 B2
Forest View, *Chicago* 9 C2
Forestville, *Washington* 32 B4
Fornebu, *Oslo* 22 A2
Fornebu Airport, *Oslo* 22 A2
Foro Romano, *Rome* 25 c3
Forstenried, *Munich* 20 B1
Forstenrieder Park, *Munich* 20 B1
Fort, *Mumbai* 20 c2
Fort Canning Park, *Singapore* 27 b2
Fort Dupont Park, *Washington* 32 B4
Fort Foote Village, *Washington* 32 C3
Fort Lee, *New York* 21 A2
Fort Mason Center, *San Francisco* 25 a1
Forth, Firth of, *Edinburgh* 11 A2
Forth Rail Bridge, *Edinburgh* 11 A1
Forth Road Bridge, *Edinburgh* 11 A1
Fót, *Budapest* 7 A3
Fourqueux, *Paris* 23 A1
Foxrock, *Dublin* 11 B2
Framingham, *Boston* 6 B1
Franconia, *Washington* 32 C3
Frankel, *Singapore* 27 B3
Franklin Park, *Boston* 6 B3
Franklin Park, *Chicago* 9 B1
Franklin Park, *Washington* 32 B3
Franklin Res., *Los Angeles* 16 B2
Frauenkirche, *Munich* 20 b2
Frederiksberg, *Copenhagen* 10 A3
Frederiksdal, *Copenhagen* 10 A2
Fredersdorf, *Berlin* 5 A5
Freguesia, *Rio de Janeiro* 24 A1
Freidrichshain, Volkspark, *Berlin* 5 A3
Freiham, *Munich* 20 B1
Freimann, *Munich* 20 A2
Fresh Pond, *Boston* 6 A3
Fresnes, *Paris* 23 B2
Freudenau, *Vienna* 31 A2
Friarstown, *Dublin* 11 B1
Frick Collection, *New York* 21 b3
Friedenau, *Berlin* 5 B3
Friedrichsfelde, *Berlin* 5 B4
Friedrichshagen, *Berlin* 5 B5
Friedrichshain, *Berlin* 5 A3
Friedrichslust, *Berlin* 5 A5
Friherrs, *Helsinki* 12 B1
Frontón, I., *Lima* 16 B1
Frunze, *Moscow* 19 B3
Fuchū, *Tokyo* 29 A1
Fuencarral, *Madrid* 17 B1
Fuenlabrada, *Madrid* 17 C1
Fujidera, *Osaka* 22 B4
Fukagawa, *Tokyo* 29 B3
Fukiage Imperial Garden, *Tokyo* 29 a4
Fukiai, *Osaka* 22 A2
Fukushima, *Osaka* 22 A3
Fulham, *London* 15 B2
Funabori, *Tokyo* 29 A4
Funasaka, *Osaka* 22 A2
Fundão, I. do, *Rio de Janeiro* 24 B1
Fünfhaus, *Vienna* 31 A2
Furesø, *Copenhagen* 10 A2
Furth, *Munich* 20 B2
Futago-tamagawaen, *Tokyo* 29 B2
Fuxing Dao, *Shanghai* 27 B2
Fuxing Park, *Shanghai* 27 B1
Fuxinglu, *Beijing* 4 B1

G

Gage Park, *Chicago* 9 C2
Gagny, *Paris* 23 A4
Galata, *Istanbul* 12 B1
Galátsion, *Athens* 2 A2
Galeão, Aéroporto Int. de, *Rio de Janeiro* 24 A1
Galyanovo, *Moscow* 19 B4
Gambir, *Jakarta* 13 A1
Gamboa, *Rio de Janeiro* 24 B1
Gambolóita, *Milan* 18 B2
Gamla Stan, *Stockholm* 28 c2
Gamlebyen, *Oslo* 22 A3
Gangtou, *Canton* 8 A1
Gangwei, *Canton* 8 B2
Ganjiakou, *Beijing* 4 B1
Ganshoren, *Brussels* 6 A1
Gants Hill, *London* 15 A4
Gaoqiao, *Shanghai* 27 A2
Garbagnate Milanese, *Milan* 18 A1
Garbatella, *Rome* 25 B2
Garches, *Paris* 23 A2
Garching, *Munich* 20 A3
Garden City, *Cairo* 7 A2
Garden Reach, *Calcutta* 8 B1
Garder, *Oslo* 22 B2
Garfield, *New York* 21 A1
Garfield Park, *Chicago* 9 B2
Gargareta, *Athens* 2 B2
Garvanza, *Los Angeles* 16 B3
Gåshaga, *Stockholm* 28 A3
Gateway National Recreation Area, *New York* 21 C2
Gateway of India, *Mumbai* 20 B2
Gatow, *Berlin* 5 B1
Gávea, *Rio de Janeiro* 24 B1
Gávea, Pedra da, *Rio de Janeiro* 24 B1
Gazdagrét, *Budapest* 7 B1
Gebel el Ahmar, *Cairo* 7 A2
Gebel el Muqattam, *Cairo* 7 A2
Gebel el Tura, *Cairo* 7 B2
Geiselgasteig, *Munich* 20 B2
General San Martín, *Buenos Aires* 7 B1
Gennevilliers, *Paris* 23 A2
Gentilly, *Paris* 23 B3
Gentofte, *Copenhagen* 10 A3
Genval, *Brussels* 6 B2
George I., *Hong Kong* 12 B1
Georges I., *Boston* 6 B4
Georges River Bridge, *Sydney* 28 C1
Georgetown, *Washington* 32 B3
Georgia Dome, *Atlanta* 3 B2
Gerasdorf bei Wien, *Vienna* 31 A2
Gerberau, *Munich* 20 A1
Gerli, *Buenos Aires* 7 C2
Germiston, *Johannesburg* 13 B2
Gern, *Munich* 20 B2
Gesîrat el Rauda, *Cairo* 7 A2
Getafe, *Madrid* 17 C1
Geva Binyamin, *Jerusalem* 13 A2
Geylang Serai, *Singapore* 27 B3
Gezîrat el Dhahab, *Cairo* 7 B2
Gharapuri, *Mumbai* 20 B2
Ghatkopar, *Mumbai* 20 A2
Ghazipur, *Delhi* 10 B2
Ghizri, *Karachi* 14 B2
Ghizri Cr. →, *Karachi* 14 B2
Ghonda, *Delhi* 10 A2
Ghusuri, *Calcutta* 8 B2
Gianicolense, *Rome* 25 B1
Gianicolo, *Rome* 25 c1
Gibraltar Pt., *Toronto* 30 B2
Gidea Park, *London* 15 A5
Giesing, *Munich* 20 B2
Gilmerton, *Edinburgh* 11 B3
Gilo, *Jerusalem* 13 B2
Gimmersta, *Stockholm* 28 B3
Ginza, *Tokyo* 29 b5
Girgaum, *Mumbai* 20 b2
Giv'at Ye'arim, *Jerusalem* 13 B1
Giv'at Ze'ev, *Jerusalem* 13 A2
Giza Pyramids = Pyramids, *Cairo* 7 B1
Gjersjøen, *Oslo* 22 B3
Gladesville, *Sydney* 28 B1
Gladsakse, *Copenhagen* 10 A2
Glasnevin, *Dublin* 11 A2
Glassmanor, *Washington* 32 C3
Glasthule, *Dublin* 11 B3
Glen Iris, *Melbourne* 17 B2
Glen Mar Park, *Washington* 32 B3
Glen Rock, *New York* 21 A1
Glenarden, *Washington* 32 B4
Glenasmole Reservoirs, *Dublin* 11 B1
Glencorse Res., *Edinburgh* 11 B2
Glencullen, *Dublin* 11 B2
Glendale, *Los Angeles* 16 B3
Glendoo Mt., *Dublin* 11 B2
Glenhuntly, *Melbourne* 17 B2
Glenside, *Wellington* 32 B1
Glenview, *Chicago* 9 A2
Glenview Countryside, *Chicago* 9 A2
Glenvista, *Johannesburg* 13 B2
Glifádha, *Athens* 2 B2
Glömsta, *Stockholm* 28 B1
Glostrup, *Copenhagen* 10 B2
Gogar, *Edinburgh* 11 B2
Göktürk, *Istanbul* 12 B1
Golabari, *Calcutta* 8 B2
Golabki, *Warsaw* 31 B1
Gold Coast, *Chicago* 9 a2
Golden Gate, *San Francisco* 25 B2
Golden Gate Bridge, *San Francisco* 25 B2
Golden Gate Park, *San Francisco* 25 B2
Golden Horn, *Istanbul* 12 B1
Golders Green, *London* 15 A2
Gollans Stream →, *Wellington* 32 B2
Golyevo, *Moscow* 19 B1
Goodman Hill, *Boston* 6 A1
Goodmayes, *London* 15 A4
Goodwood, *Cape Town* 8 A2
Gopalpur, *Calcutta* 8 B2
Górce, *Warsaw* 31 B1
Gore Hill, *Sydney* 28 A2
Gorelyy →, *St. Petersburg* 26 A3
Gorenki, *Moscow* 19 B5
Gorgie, *Edinburgh* 11 B2
Gorky Park, *Moscow* 19 B3
Gosen, *Berlin* 5 B5
Gosener kanal, *Berlin* 5 B5
Gospel Oak, *London* 15 A3
Gotanda, *Tokyo* 29 B3
Goth Goli Mar, *Karachi* 14 A2
Goth Sher Shah, *Karachi* 14 A1
Gournay-sur-Marne, *Paris* 23 A4
Governador, I. do, *Rio de Janeiro* 24 A1
Governor's I., *New York* 21 B1
Graben, *Vienna* 31 b2
Grabów, *Warsaw* 31 C1
Graça, *Lisbon* 14 b3
Grace, Mt., *Wellington* 32 B2
Grace Cathedral, *San Francisco* 25 b1
Gracefield, *Wellington* 32 B2
Gràcia, *Barcelona* 4 A2
Gräfelfing, *Munich* 20 B1
Gragoatá, *Rio de Janeiro* 24 B2
Grand Cemtral Station, *New York* 21 c2
Grand Union Canal, *London* 15 A2
Grande Place, *Brussels* 6 b2
Grant Park, *Atlanta* 3 B2
Grant Park, *Chicago* 9 c2
Granton, *Edinburgh* 11 B2
Grape I., *Boston* 6 B4
Grassy Park, *Cape Town* 8 B2
Gratosóglio, *Milan* 18 B2
Gratzwalde, *Berlin* 5 B5
Gravesend, *New York* 21 C2
Grazhdanka, *St. Petersburg* 26 B2
Great Falls, *Washington* 32 B2
Great Falls Park, *Washington* 32 B2
Great Hall of the People, *Beijing* 4 b2
Great Meadows National Wildlife Refuge, *Boston* 6 A1
Greco, *Milan* 18 A2
Green I., *Hong Kong* 12 B1
Green Point, *Cape Town* 8 A1
Greenbelt, *Washington* 32 A4
Greenbelt Park, *Washington* 32 B4
Greenfield Park, *Montreal* 19 B3
Greenford, *London* 15 A1
Greenhill, *London* 15 A2
Greenhills, *Dublin* 11 B1
Greenmarket Square, *Cape Town* 8 c2
Greenpoint, *New York* 21 B2
Greenwich, *London* 15 B3
Greenwich Observatory, *London* 15 B3
Greenwich Village, *New York* 21 B2
Greenwood, *Boston* 6 A3
Grefsen, *Oslo* 22 A3
Gresham Park, *Atlanta* 3 B2
Greve Strand, *Copenhagen* 10 B1
Greyfriars Kirk, *Edinburgh* 11 c2
Griebnitzsee, *Berlin* 5 B1
Griffen Park, *Los Angeles* 16 B3
Grimbergen, *Brussels* 6 A2
Grinzing, *Vienna* 31 A2
Gröbenried, *Munich* 20 A1
Grochów, *Warsaw* 31 B2
Grodzisk, *Warsaw* 31 B2
Groenendaal, *Brussels* 6 B2
Grogol Petamburin, *Jakarta* 13 A1
Gronsdorf, *Munich* 20 B3
Grorud, *Oslo* 22 A4
Gross Glienicke, *Berlin* 5 B1
Gross-Hadern, *Munich* 20 B1
Gross-Lappen, *Munich* 20 A2
Grosse Krampe, *Berlin* 5 B5
Grosse Müggelsee, *Berlin* 5 B4
Grossenzersdorf, *Vienna* 31 A3
Grossenzersdorfer Arm →, *Vienna* 31 A3
Grosser Biberhaufen, *Vienna* 31 A2
Grosser Wannsee, *Berlin* 5 B2
Grossfeld-Siedlung, *Vienna* 31 A2
Grosshesselohe, *Munich* 20 B2
Grossjedlersdorf, *Vienna* 31 A2
Grossziethen, *Berlin* 5 B3
Grove Hall, *Boston* 6 B3
Grove Park, *Atlanta* 3 B2
Grove Park, *London* 15 B4
Grove Park, *London* 15 B3
Groveton, *Washington* 32 C3
Grünau, *Berlin* 5 B4
Grunewald, *Berlin* 5 B2
Grünwald, *Munich* 20 B2
Grünwalder Forst, *Munich* 20 B2
Grymes Hill, *New York* 21 C1
Guadalupe, *Manila* 17 B2
Guadalupe, Basilica de, *Mexico City* 18 B2
Guanabara, B. de, *Rio de Janeiro* 24 B1
Guanabara, Jardim, *Rio de Janeiro* 24 A1
Guanabara, Palácio da, *Rio de Janeiro* 24 B1
Guang'anmen, *Beijing* 4 B1
Guangqumen, *Beijing* 4 B2
Guangzhou, *Canton* 8 B2
Guanshuo, *Canton* 8 B3
Gudö, *Stockholm* 28 B3
Güell, Parque de, *Barcelona* 4 A2
Guerrero, *Mexico City* 18 a1
Guggenheim Museum, *New York* 21 b3
Guinardó, *Barcelona* 4 A2
Gulbai, *Karachi* 14 A1
Güngören, *Istanbul* 12 B1
Gunnersbury, *London* 15 B2
Gustavo A. Madero, *Mexico City* 18 B2
Guttenberg, *New York* 21 B1
Gutuyevskiy, Ostrov, *St. Petersburg* 26 B1
Guyancourt, *Paris* 23 B1
Gyál, *Budapest* 7 B3
Gyáli-patak →, *Budapest* 7 B2

H

Haaga, *Helsinki* 12 B2
Haar, *Munich* 20 B3
Hackbridge, *London* 15 B3
Hackensack, *New York* 21 A1
Hackensack →, *New York* 21 A1
Hackney, *London* 15 A3
Hackney Wick, *London* 15 A3
Haga, *Stockholm* 28 A2
Hagenbrunn, *Vienna* 31 A2
Hägersten, *Stockholm* 28 B1
Häggvik, *Stockholm* 28 A1
Hai He →, *Tianjin* 30 B2
Haidian, *Beijing* 4 B1
Haidarpur, *Delhi* 10 A1
Haidhausen, *Munich* 20 B2
Haight-Ashbury, *San Francisco* 25 B2
Hainault, *London* 15 A4
Haizhu Guangchang, *Canton* 8 B2
Hakunila, *Helsinki* 12 B3
Halásztelek, *Budapest* 7 B1
Haliç = Golden Horn, *Istanbul* 12 B1
Halim Perdanakusuma International Airport, *Jakarta* 13 B2
Halle, *Brussels* 6 B1
Haltiala, *Helsinki* 12 B2
Haltiavuori, *Helsinki* 12 B2
Ham, *London* 15 B2
Hämeenkylä, *Helsinki* 12 B1
Hammarby, *Stockholm* 28 B2
Hamme, *Brussels* 6 A1
Hammersmith, *London* 15 B2
Hampstead, *London* 15 A2
Hampstead, *Montreal* 19 B2
Hampstead Garden Suburb, *London* 15 A2
Hampstead Heath, *London* 15 A2
Hampton, *London* 15 B1
Hampton Court Palace, *London* 15 B1
Hampton Wick, *London* 15 B2
Hamrā', *Baghdad* 3 B1
Hanala, *Helsinki* 12 B3
Haneda, *Tokyo* 29 B3
Hang Hau, *Hong Kong* 12 B2
Hanging Gardens, *Mumbai* 20 b1
Hanjiashu, *Tianjin* 30 A1
Hanlon, *Toronto* 30 B1
Hanwell, *London* 15 A1
Hanworth, *London* 15 B1
Haora, *Calcutta* 8 B1
Hapeville, *Atlanta* 3 C2
Happy Valley, *Hong Kong* 12 B2
Har Adar, *Jerusalem* 13 B1
Haren, *Brussels* 6 A2
Hareskovby, *Copenhagen* 10 A2
Haringey, *London* 15 A3
Harjusuo, *Helsinki* 12 B3
Harlaching, *Munich* 20 B2
Harlaw Res., *Edinburgh* 11 B2
Harlem, *New York* 21 B2
Harlesden, *London* 15 A2
Harlington, *London* 15 B1
Harmaja, *Helsinki* 12 C2
Harmashatar hegy, *Budapest* 7 A2
Harolds Cross, *Dublin* 11 B2
Háros, *Budapest* 7 B2
Harperrig Reservoir, *Edinburgh* 11 B1
Harrow, *London* 15 A1
Harrow on the Hill, *London* 15 A1
Harrow School, *London* 15 A1
Harrow Weald, *London* 15 A1
Hartsfield-Atlanta International Airport, *Atlanta* 3 C2
Harumi, *Tokyo* 29 c5
Harvard Univ., *Boston* 6 A3
Harwood Heights, *Chicago* 9 B2
Hasanābād, *Tehran* 30 A1
Hasbrouck Heights, *New York* 21 A1
Haselhorst, *Berlin* 5 A2
Hasköy, *Istanbul* 12 B1
Hasle, *Oslo* 22 B2
Haslum, *Oslo* 22 A2
Hästhagen, *Stockholm* 28 B2
Hataitai, *Wellington* 32 B1
Hatch End, *London* 15 A1
Hatiara, *Calcutta* 8 B2
Hauketo, *Oslo* 22 A3
Havel →, *Berlin* 5 A2
Havelkanal, *Berlin* 5 A2
Havering, *London* 15 A5
Havering-atte-Bower, *London* 15 A5
Hawŏlgok, *Seoul* 26 B2
Haworth, *New York* 21 A2
Hayes, *London* 15 B4
Hayes, *London* 15 A1
Hayes End, *London* 15 A1
Hayford, *Chicago* 9 C2
Haywards, *Wellington* 32 A2
Heard Pond, *Boston* 6 A1
Heathfield, *Cape Town* 8 B1
Heathrow Airport, *London* 15 B1
Hebe Haven, *Hong Kong* 12 A2
Hebei, *Tianjin* 30 B2
Hedong, *Canton* 8 B2
Hedong, *Tianjin* 30 B2
Heidelberg Heights, *Melbourne* 17 A2
Heidelberg West, *Melbourne* 17 A2
Heidemühle, *Berlin* 5 B5
Heideveld, *Cape Town* 8 A2
Heiligensee, *Berlin* 5 A2
Heiligenstadt, *Vienna* 31 A2
Heinersdorf, *Berlin* 5 A3
Heldenplatz, *Vienna* 31 b1
Hélène Champlain, Parc, *Montreal* 19 A2
Helenelund, *Stockholm* 28 A1
Heliopolis = Masr el Gedida, *Cairo* 7 A2
Hellersdorf, *Berlin* 5 A4
Hellerup, *Copenhagen* 10 A3
Helmahof, *Vienna* 31 A3
Helsingfors = Helsinki, *Helsinki* 12 B2
Helsinki, *Helsinki* 12 B2
Helsinki Airport, *Helsinki* 12 B2
Hendon, *London* 15 A2
Hengsha, *Canton* 8 B2
Hennigsdorf, *Berlin* 5 A2
Henryków, *Warsaw* 31 B1
Henson Cr. →, *Washington* 32 C4
Henttaa, *Helsinki* 12 B1
Heping, *Tianjin* 30 B2
Heping Park, *Shanghai* 27 B2
Hepingli, *Beijing* 4 B2
Herlev, *Copenhagen* 10 A2
Herman Eckstein Park, *Johannesburg* 13 A2
Hermannskogel, *Vienna* 31 A1
Hermiston, *Edinburgh* 11 B2
Hermitage and Winter Palace, *St. Petersburg* 26 B1
Hermsdorf, *Berlin* 5 A2
Hernals, *Vienna* 31 A2
Herne Hill, *London* 15 B3
Héroes de Churubusco, *Mexico City* 18 B2
Herons, Î. aux, *Montreal* 19 B2
Herstedøster, *Copenhagen* 10 A2
Herttoniemi, *Helsinki* 12 B3
Ḥeṣārak, *Tehran* 30 A1
Heston, *London* 15 B1
Hetzendorf, *Vienna* 31 B1
Hexi, *Tianjin* 30 B2
Hextable, *London* 15 B5
Hialeah, *Miami* 18 A1
Hickory Hills, *Chicago* 9 C2
Hiekkaharju, *Helsinki* 12 B3
Hietaniemi, *Helsinki* 12 B2
Hietzing, *Vienna* 31 A1
Higashi, *Osaka* 22 A4
Higashimurayama, *Tokyo* 29 A1
Higashinada, *Osaka* 22 A2
Higashinari, *Osaka* 22 A4
Higashiōsaka, *Osaka* 22 B4
Higashisumiyoshi, *Osaka* 22 B4
Higashiyodogawa, *Osaka* 22 A3
High Park, *Toronto* 30 B2
Highbury, *London* 15 A3
Highgate, *London* 15 A3
Highland Cr. →, *Toronto* 30 A3
Highland Creek, *Toronto* 30 A3
Highland Park, *Los Angeles* 16 B3
Highlands North, *Johannesburg* 13 A2
Hillcrest Heights, *Washington* 32 C4
Hillend, *Edinburgh* 11 A1
Hillingdon, *London* 15 A1
Hillwood, *Washington* 32 B3
Hilmīya, *Cairo* 7 A2
Hin Keng, *Hong Kong* 12 A2
Hingham, *Boston* 6 B4
Hingham B., *Boston* 6 B4
Hingham Harbor, *Boston* 6 B4
Hirakata, *Osaka* 22 A4
Hirota, *Osaka* 22 A3
Hirschstetten, *Vienna* 31 A2
Histórico Nacional, Museu, *Rio de Janeiro* 24 b3
Hither Green, *London* 15 B3
Hiyoshi, *Tokyo* 29 B2
Hizma, *Jerusalem* 13 B2
Hjortekær, *Copenhagen* 10 A3
Hjortespring, *Copenhagen* 10 A2
Hlubočepy, *Prague* 24 B2
Ho Chung, *Hong Kong* 12 A2
Ho Man Tin, *Hong Kong* 12 B2
Hoboken, *New York* 21 B1
Hobsons B., *Melbourne* 17 B1
Hochbrück, *Munich* 20 A2
Hochelaga, *Montreal* 19 A2
Hodgkins, *Chicago* 9 C1
Hoegi, *Seoul* 26 B2
Hoeilaart, *Brussels* 6 B2
Hofberg, *Vienna* 31 A2
Hoffman I., *New York* 21 C1
Hofgarten, *Munich* 20 a3
Högsdtadomstolen, *Stockholm* 28 c2
Hohenbrunn, *Munich* 20 B3
Hohenschönhausen, *Berlin* 5 A4
Holborn, *London* 15 a4
Holešovice, *Prague* 24 B2
Holland Village, *Singapore* 27 B2
Höllriegelskreuth, *Munich* 20 B1
Hollywood, *Los Angeles* 16 B3
Holmenkollen, *Oslo* 22 A3
Holmes Run Acres, *Washington* 32 B2
Holmgård, *Stockholm* 28 B1
Holysloot, *Amsterdam* 2 A3
Homerton, *London* 15 A3
Hometown, *Chicago* 9 C2
Hōnanchō, *Tokyo* 29 A2
Honcho, *Tokyo* 29 A3
Honden, *Tokyo* 29 A2
Hondo, Rio →, *Los Angeles* 16 B4
Hong Kong, *Hong Kong* 12 B1
Hong Kong, Univ. of, *Hong Kong* 12 B1
Hong Kong I., *Hong Kong* 12 B2
Hong Kong Park, *Hong Kong* 12 c1
Hongkou, *Shanghai* 27 B1
Hongkou Park, *Shanghai* 27 B1
Hongmiao, *Beijing* 4 B2
Hongqiao, *Shanghai* 27 B1
Hongqiao, *Tianjin* 30 B1
Hongqiao Airport, *Shanghai* 27 B1
Hongūn, *Seoul* 26 B1
Honjyo, *Tokyo* 29 A3
Honoré Mercier, Pont, *Montreal* 19 B1
Hönow, *Berlin* 5 A4
Hooghly = Hugli →, *Calcutta* 8 A2
Hook, *London* 15 B2
Horikiri, *Tokyo* 29 A4
Horn Pond, *Boston* 6 A2
Hornchurch, *London* 15 A5
Horni, *Prague* 24 B3
Horni Počernice, *Prague* 24 B3
Hornsey, *London* 15 A3
Horoměřice, *Prague* 24 B1
Hortaleza, *Madrid* 17 B2
Hosoyama, *Tokyo* 29 B2
Hostafrancs, *Barcelona* 4 A1
Hostivař, *Prague* 24 B3
Hôtel des Invalides, *Paris* 23 c2
Houbětin, *Prague* 24 B3
Houghs Neck, *Boston* 6 B4
Houghton, *Johannesburg* 13 B2
Houilles, *Paris* 23 A2
Hounslow, *London* 15 B1
Houses of Parliament, *London* 15 c3
Hout Bay, *Cape Town* 8 B1
Hove Å →, *Copenhagen* 10 A1
Hovedøya, *Oslo* 22 A3
Høvik, *Oslo* 22 A2
Hovorčovice, *Prague* 24 A3
Howard Beach, *New York* 21 C2
Howth, *Dublin* 11 A3
Howth Head, *Dublin* 11 A3
Hoxton, *London* 15 a5
Hōya, *Tokyo* 29 A2
Hradčany, *Prague* 24 B2
Huanghuagang Mausoleum of the 72 Martyrs, *Canton* 8 B2
Huangpu, *Shanghai* 27 B2
Huangpu Jiang →, *Shanghai* 27 B1
Huangpu Park, *Shanghai* 27 B1
Huangtugang, *Beijing* 4 C1
Huascar, *Lima* 16 A2
Huay Khwang, *Bangkok* 3 B2
Huddinge, *Stockholm* 28 B2
Hudson →, *New York* 21 A2
Huechuraba, *Santiago* 26 B1
Huertas de San Beltran, *Barcelona* 4 A1
Hugli →, *Calcutta* 8 A2
Huidui, *Tianjin* 30 B2
Huizingen, *Brussels* 6 B1
Hull, *Boston* 6 B4
Humber →, *Toronto* 30 A1
Humber B., *Toronto* 30 B2
Humber Bay, *Toronto* 30 B2
Humber Summit, *Toronto* 30 A1
Humber Valley Village, *Toronto* 30 A1
Humberlea, *Toronto* 30 A1
Humboldt Park, *Chicago* 9 B2
Humera, *Madrid* 17 B1
Hunaydī, *Baghdad* 3 B2
Hundige, *Copenhagen* 10 B1
Hundige Strand, *Copenhagen* 10 B2
Hung Hom, *Hong Kong* 12 B2
Hunters Hill, *Sydney* 28 B1
Hunters Pt., *San Francisco* 25 B2
Hunters Valley, *Washington* 32 B2
Huntington, *Washington* 32 C3
Huntington Park, *Los Angeles* 16 C3
Hurīya, *Baghdad* 3 A1
Hurstville, *Sydney* 28 B1
Husby, *Stockholm* 28 A1
Husum, *Copenhagen* 10 A2
Hutt R. →, *Wellington* 32 B2
Hütteldorf, *Vienna* 31 A1
Hűvösvölgy, *Budapest* 7 A2
Hvalstad, *Oslo* 22 A1
Hvalstrand, *Oslo* 22 A2
Hvidovre, *Copenhagen* 10 B2
Hwagok, *Seoul* 26 B1
Hyattsville, *Washington* 32 B4
Hyde Park, *Boston* 6 B3
Hyde Park, *Chicago* 9 C3
Hyde Park, *Johannesburg* 13 A2
Hyde Park, *London* 15 A2
Hyde Park, *Sydney* 28 B2

I

Ibese, *Lagos* 14 A2
Ibirapuera, *São Paulo* 26 B1
Ibirapuera, Parque, *São Paulo* 26 B2
Icarai, *Rio de Janeiro* 24 B2
Içerenköy, *Istanbul* 12 C2
Ichgao, *Tokyo* 29 B2
Ichigaya, *Tokyo* 29 a3
Ichikawa, *Tokyo* 29 A4
Ickenham, *London* 15 A1
Iddo, *Lagos* 14 B2
Idi-Oro, *Lagos* 14 B2
Iganmu, *Lagos* 14 B2
Igbobi, *Lagos* 14 B2
Igbologun, *Lagos* 14 B1
Igny, *Paris* 23 B2
IJ, Het →, *Amsterdam* 2 A2
IJ-meer, *Amsterdam* 2 A3
Ijesa-Tedo, *Lagos* 14 B1
Ijora, *Lagos* 14 B2
IJtunnel, *Amsterdam* 2 a3
Ikebe, *Tokyo* 29 B2
Ikebukuro, *Tokyo* 29 A3
Ikegami, *Tokyo* 29 B3
Ikeja, *Lagos* 14 A2
Ikeuchi, *Osaka* 22 B4
Ikoyi, *Lagos* 14 B2
Ikuata, *Lagos* 14 B2
Ikuno, *Osaka* 22 A4
Ikuta, *Osaka* 22 A2
Ikuta, *Tokyo* 29 B2
Ila, *Oslo* 22 A2
Ilford, *London* 15 A4
Ilioúpolis, *Athens* 2 B2
Ilpendam, *Amsterdam* 2 A2
Ilsós →, *Athens* 2 B2
Imagem e do Som, Museu da, *Rio de Janeiro* 24 b3
Imbâbah, *Cairo* 7 A2
Imielin, *Warsaw* 31 C2
Imirim, *São Paulo* 26 A2
Imittós, *Athens* 2 B2
Imittós, Óros, *Athens* 2 B2
Imperial Palace Museum, *Beijing* 4 b2
Inagi, *Tokyo* 29 B2
Inchcolm, *Edinburgh* 11 A2
Inchicore, *Dublin* 11 A1
Inchkeith, *Edinburgh* 11 A3
Inchmickery, *Edinburgh* 11 A2
Incirano, *Milan* 18 A1
Independencia, *Lima* 16 A2
Independencia, *Santiago* 26 B2
India Gate, *Delhi* 1 c2
Indian Creek Village, *Miami* 18 A2
Indian Head Park, *Chicago* 9 C1
Indianópolis, *São Paulo* 26 B2
Indios Verdes, *Mexico City* 18 B2
Indira Ghandi International Airport, *Delhi* 10 B1
Industria, *Johannesburg* 13 B1
Ingierstrand, *Oslo* 22 B3
Inglewood, *Los Angeles* 16 C3
Ingliston, *Edinburgh* 11 B1
Inhaúme, *Rio de Janeiro* 24 B1
Inner Port Shelter, *Hong Kong* 12 A2
Interlagos, *São Paulo* 26 C1
Intramuros, *Manila* 17 B1
Invalides, *Paris* 23 A2
Inverkeithing, *Edinburgh* 11 A1
Inzersdorf, *Vienna* 31 B2
Ipanema, *Rio de Janeiro* 24 B1
Ipiranga, *São Paulo* 26 B2
Ipiranga →, *São Paulo* 26 B2
Iponri, *Lagos* 14 B2
Ireland's Eye, *Dublin* 11 A3
Irving Park, *Chicago* 9 B2
Isabel, *Rio de Janeiro* 24 B1
Isagatedo, *Lagos* 14 A1
Isar →, *Munich* 20 A3
Ishbīliya, *Baghdad* 3 A2
Ishikiri, *Osaka* 22 A4
Ishøj Strand, *Copenhagen* 10 B2
Island Bay, *Wellington* 32 B1
Island Park, *Toronto* 30 B2
Isle of Dogs, *London* 15 B3
Islev, *Copenhagen* 10 A2
Isleworth, *London* 15 B2
Islington, *London* 15 A3
Islington, *Toronto* 30 B1
Ismaning, *Munich* 20 A3
Ismaylovsky Park, *Moscow* 19 B4
Isolo, *Lagos* 14 A1
Issy-les-Moulineaux, *Paris* 23 B2
Istanbul, *Istanbul* 12 C1
Istanbul Boğazi, *Istanbul* 12 B2
Istinye, *Istanbul* 12 B2
Itä Hakkila, *Helsinki* 12 B3
Itaewŏn, *Seoul* 26 B1
Itahanga, *Rio de Janeiro* 24 B1
Itami, *Osaka* 22 A3
Ivanhoe, *Melbourne* 17 A2
Ivry-sur-Seine, *Paris* 23 B3
Iwazono, *Osaka* 22 A2
Ixelles, *Brussels* 6 B2
Izmaylovo, *Moscow* 19 B4
Iztacalco, *Mexico City* 18 B2
Iztapalapa, *Mexico City* 18 B2

J

Jaba, *Jerusalem* 13 A2
Jababpur, *Calcutta* 8 C2
Jacaré, *Rio de Janeiro* 24 B1
Jackson Heights, *New York* 21 B2
Jackson Park, *Chicago* 9 C3
Jacques Cartier, *Montreal* 19 A3
Jacques Cartier, Pont, *Montreal* 19 A2
Jade Buddha Temple, *Shanghai* 27 B1
Jægersborg, *Copenhagen* 10 A3
Jægersborg Dyrehave, *Copenhagen* 10 A3
Jagadishpur, *Calcutta* 8 B1
Jagatpur, *Delhi* 10 A2
Jaguaré, Rib. do →, *São Paulo* 26 B1
Jahangirpur, *Delhi* 10 A2
Jakarta, *Jakarta* 13 A2
Jakarta, Teluk, *Jakarta* 13 A1
Jalan Kayu, *Singapore* 27 A3
Jamaica B., *New York* 21 C3
Jamaica Plain, *Boston* 6 B3
Jamakpuri, *Delhi* 10 B1
Jamshīdīyeh, *Tehran* 30 A2
Janki, *Warsaw* 31 C1
Jannali, *Sydney* 28 C1
Japan Center, *San Francisco* 25 c1
Jaraguá, *São Paulo* 26 A1
Jaraguá, Pico de, *São Paulo* 26 A1
Jardim Paulista, *São Paulo* 26 B1
Jardin Botanique, *Brussels* 6 a3
Järvatältet, *Stockholm* 28 A1
Jaskhar, *Mumbai* 20 B2
Jatinegara, *Jakarta* 13 B2
Javādīyeh, *Tehran* 30 B2
Jaworowa, *Warsaw* 31 C1
Jedlesee, *Vienna* 31 A2
Jefferson Memorial, *Washington* 32 c1
Jefferson Park, *Chicago* 9 B2
Jelonki, *Warsaw* 31 B1
Jerónimos, Mosteiro dos, *Lisbon* 14 A1
Jersey City, *New York* 21 B1
Jerusalem, *Jerusalem* 13 B2
Jésus, Î., *Montreal* 19 A1
Jesús María, *Lima* 16 B2
Jette, *Brussels* 6 A1
Jewish Quarter, *Jerusalem* 13 b3
Jey, *Tehran* 30 B2
Jianguomen, *Beijing* 4 B2
Jiangwan, *Shanghai* 27 B1
Jianshan Park, *Tianjin* 30 B2
Jihād, *Baghdad* 3 B1
Jim Thompson's House, *Bangkok* 3 b3
Jimbōchō, *Tokyo* 29 a4
Jingan, *Shanghai* 27 B1
Jingu Outer Garden, *Tokyo* 29 b2
Jinočany, *Prague* 24 B1
Jinonice, *Prague* 24 B2
Jiyūgaoka, *Tokyo* 29 B3
Jizā'ir, *Baghdad* 3 B2
Jizīra, *Baghdad* 3 B2
Johannesburg, *Johannesburg* 13 B2
Johanneskirchen, *Munich* 20 A2
Johannesstift, *Berlin* 5 A2
Johannisthal, *Berlin* 5 B4
John Hancock Center, *Chicago* 9 a2
John McLaren Park, *San Francisco* 25 B2
Johnsonville, *Wellington* 32 B1
Joinville-le-Pont, *Paris* 23 B3
Joli-Bois, *Brussels* 6 B2
Jollas, *Helsinki* 12 B3
Jonstrup, *Copenhagen* 10 A2
Joppa, *Edinburgh* 11 B3
Jorge Chavez, Aeropuerto Int., *Lima* 16 B2
Jorge Newbury, Aeroparque, *Buenos Aires* 7 B2
Józefa Piłsudskiego Park, *Warsaw* 31 B1
Jōtō, *Osaka* 22 A4
Jouy-en-Josas, *Paris* 23 B2
Juan Anchorena, *Buenos Aires* 7 A2
Juan González Romero, *Mexico City* 18 A2
Judeira, *Jerusalem* 13 A2
Juhu, *Mumbai* 20 A2
Jūjō, *Tokyo* 29 A3
Jukskeirivier →, *Johannesburg* 13 A2
Julianów, *Warsaw* 31 B2
Jungfernheide, Volkspark, *Berlin* 5 A2
Jungfernsee, *Berlin* 5 B1
Juniper Green, *Edinburgh* 11 B2
Junk B., *Hong Kong* 12 B2
Jurong, *Singapore* 27 B2
Jurong, Selat, *Singapore* 27 B2
Jurong Industrial Estate, *Singapore* 27 B1
Jurujuba, Enseada de, *Rio de Janeiro* 24 B2
Jūsō, *Osaka* 22 A3
Justice, *Chicago* 9 C2
Justicia, *Madrid* 17 a3
Jwalahari, *Delhi* 10 B1

K

Kabaty, *Warsaw* 31 C2
Kadıköy, *Istanbul* 12 C2
Kadoma, *Osaka* 22 A4
Kaebong, *Seoul* 26 C1
Kafr 'Aqab, *Jerusalem* 13 A2
Kâğıthane, *Istanbul* 12 B1
Kâğıthane →, *Istanbul* 12 B1
Kagran, *Vienna* 31 A2
Kahnawake, *Montreal* 19 B1
Kaimes, *Edinburgh* 11 B2
Kaisariani, *Athens* 2 B2
Kaiser Wilhelm Kirche, *Berlin* 5 b2
Kaiserebersdorf, *Vienna* 31 B2
Kaivoksela, *Helsinki* 12 B2
Kalamákion, *Athens* 2 B2
Kalbadevi, *Mumbai* 20 b2
Kalhyŏn, *Seoul* 26 B1
Kalipur, *Calcutta* 8 A1
Kalkaji, *Delhi* 10 B2
Kallithéa, *Athens* 2 B2
Kalveboderne, *Copenhagen* 10 B3
Kamarhati, *Calcutta* 8 A2
Kamata, *Tokyo* 29 B3
Kameari, *Tokyo* 29 A4
Kameido, *Tokyo* 29 A4
Kami-Itabashi, *Tokyo* 29 A3
Kamikitazawa, *Tokyo* 29 B2
Kamitsuruma, *Tokyo* 29 B1
Kamoshida, *Tokyo* 29 B2
Kampong Landang, *Singapore* 27 A3
Kampong Tanjong Penjuru, *Singapore* 27 B2
Kampung Bali, *Jakarta* 13 B1
Kanamori, *Tokyo* 29 B1
Kanda, *Tokyo* 29 a5
Kandilli, *Istanbul* 12 B2
Kangdong, *Seoul* 26 B2
Kangnam, *Seoul* 26 B1
Kangsŏ, *Seoul* 26 B1
Kankurgachi, *Calcutta* 8 B2
Kanlıca, *Istanbul* 12 B2
Kanonerskiy, Ostrov, *St. Petersburg* 26 B1
Kanzaki →, *Osaka* 22 A3
Kapellerfeld, *Vienna* 31 A2

Káposztásmegyer, *Budapest* 7 A2
Kapotnya, *Moscow* 19 C4
Käppala, *Stockholm* 28 A3
Käpylä, *Helsinki* 12 B2
Karachi, *Karachi* 14 A2
Karachi Int. Airport, *Karachi* 14 A2
Karato, *Osaka* 22 A2
Karibong, *Seoul* 26 C1
Karkh, *Baghdad* 3 A2
Karlin, *Prague* 24 B2
Karlsfeld, *Munich* 20 A1
Karlshorst, *Berlin* 5 B4
Karlsplatz, *Munich* 20 b1
Karntner Strasse, *Vienna* 31 b2
Karol Bagh, *Delhi* 10 B2
Karolinenhof, *Berlin* 5 B4
Karori, *Wellington* 32 B1
Karow, *Berlin* 5 A3
Karrādah, *Baghdad* 3 B2
Kärsön, *Stockholm* 28 B1
Kasai, *Tokyo* 29 B4
Kashiwara, *Osaka* 22 B4
Kastellet, *Copenhagen* 10 a3
Kastrup, *Copenhagen* 10 B3
Kastrup Lufthavn, *Copenhagen* 10 B3
Kasuga, *Tokyo* 29 A2
Kasuge, *Tokyo* 29 A3
Kasumigaseki, *Tokyo* 29 b4
Katong, *Singapore* 27 B3
Katrineberg, *Stockholm* 28 B1
Katsushika-Ku, *Tokyo* 29 A4
Kau Pei Chau, *Hong Kong* 12 B2
Kau Yi Chau, *Hong Kong* 12 B1
Kaulsdorf, *Berlin* 5 B4
Kauniainen, *Helsinki* 12 B1
Kawasaki, *Tokyo* 29 B3
Kawawa, *Tokyo* 29 B2
Kawęczyn, *Warsaw* 31 B2
Kayu Putih, *Jakarta* 13 B2
Kbely, *Prague* 24 B3
Kebayoran Baru, *Jakarta* 13 B1
Kebayoran Lama, *Jakarta* 13 B1
Kebon Jeruk, *Jakarta* 13 B1
Kedar, *Jerusalem* 13 B2
Keilor, *Melbourne* 17 A1
Keilor North, *Melbourne* 17 A1
Keimola, *Helsinki* 12 A1
Kelenföld, *Budapest* 7 B2
Kelvin, *Johannesburg* 13 A2
Kemang, *Jakarta* 13 B1
Kemayoran, *Jakarta* 13 B2
Kemerburgaz, *Istanbul* 12 B1
Kempton Park Races, *London* 15 B1
Kendall Green, *Boston* 6 A2
Kenilworth, *Cape Town* 8 A1
Kennedy Town, *Hong Kong* 12 B1
Kennington, *London* 15 c4
Kensal Green, *London* 15 A2
Kensal Rise, *London* 15 a1
Kensington, *Johannesburg* 13 B2
Kensington, *London* 15 B2
Kensington, *New York* 21 C2
Kensington, *Sydney* 28 B2
Kensington Palace, *London* 15 A2
Kent Village, *Washington* 32 B4
Kentish Town, *London* 15 A3
Kenton, *London* 15 A2
Kenwood House, *London* 15 A3
Kepa, *Warsaw* 31 B2
Keppel Harbour, *Singapore* 27 B2
Keramíkos, *Athens* 2 b1
Kettering, *Washington* 32 B5
Kew, *London* 15 B2
Kew, *Melbourne* 17 A2
Kew Gardens, *London* 15 B2
Kew Gardens, *Toronto* 30 B3
Key Biscayne, *Miami* 18 B2
Khaidhárion, *Athens* 2 A1
Khalándrion, *Athens* 2 A2
Khalīj, *Baghdad* 3 B2
Khandallah, *Wellington* 32 B1
Khansā', *Baghdad* 3 A2
Kharavli, *Mumbai* 20 B2
Khefren, *Cairo* 7 B1
Khichripur, *Delhi* 10 B2
Khidirpur, *Calcutta* 8 B1
Khimki-Khovrino, *Moscow* 19 A3
Khirbet Jub e-Rum, *Jerusalem* 13 B2
Khlong San, *Bangkok* 3 B2
Khlong Toey, *Bangkok* 3 B2
Kholargós, *Athens* 2 B2
Khorel, *Calcutta* 8 A1
Khorosovo, *Moscow* 19 B2
Kiamari, *Karachi* 14 B1
Kierling, *Vienna* 31 A1
Kierlingbach →, *Vienna* 31 A1
Kifisós →, *Athens* 2 B2
Kikuna, *Tokyo* 29 B2
Kilbarrack, *Dublin* 11 A3
Kilbirnie, *Wellington* 32 B1
Kilburn, *London* 15 A2
Killakee, *Dublin* 11 B2
Killester, *Dublin* 11 A2
Killiney, *Dublin* 11 B3
Killiney Bay, *Dublin* 11 B3
Kilmacud, *Dublin* 11 B2
Kilmainham, *Dublin* 11 A2
Kilmashogue Mt., *Dublin* 11 B2
Kilmore, *Dublin* 11 A2
Kilnamanagh, *Dublin* 11 B1
Kilo, *Helsinki* 12 B1
Kilokri, *Delhi* 10 B2
Kiltiernan, *Dublin* 11 B2
Kimmage, *Dublin* 11 B2
Kindi, *Baghdad* 3 B2
Kinghorn, *Edinburgh* 11 A2
King's Cross, *London* 15 a4
Kings Cross, *Sydney* 28 c3
Kings Domain, *Melbourne* 17 A1
Kings Park, *Washington* 32 C2
Kings Park West, *Washington* 32 C2
Kingsbury, *London* 15 A2
Kingsbury, *Melbourne* 17 A2
Kingsford, *Sydney* 28 B2
Kingston upon Thames, *London* 15 B2
Kingston Vale, *London* 15 B2
Kingsway, *Toronto* 30 B1
Kinsaley, *Dublin* 11 A2
Kipling Heights, *Toronto* 30 A1
Kipséli, *Athens* 2 B2
Kirchstockbach, *Munich* 20 B3
Kirchtrudering, *Munich* 20 B3
Kirikiri, *Lagos* 14 B1
Kirke Værløse, *Copenhagen* 10 A1
Kirkhill, *Edinburgh* 11 B2
Kirkliston, *Edinburgh* 11 B1
Kirknewton, *Edinburgh* 11 B1
Kirov Palace of Culture, *St. Petersburg* 26 B1
Kısıklı, *Istanbul* 12 B2
Kispest, *Budapest* 7 B2
Kista, *Stockholm* 28 A1
Kita, *Osaka* 22 A4
Kita-Ku, *Tokyo* 29 A3
Kitazawa, *Tokyo* 29 B3
Kiu Tsiu, *Hong Kong* 12 A2
Kivistö, *Helsinki* 12 B2
Kızıltoprak, *Istanbul* 12 C2
Kizu →, *Osaka* 22 B3
Kizuri, *Osaka* 22 B4
Kjelsås, *Oslo* 22 A3
Kladow, *Berlin* 5 B1
Klampenborg, *Copenhagen* 10 A3
Klaudyń, *Warsaw* 31 B1
Klecany, *Prague* 24 A2
Kledering, *Vienna* 31 B2
Klein Jukskei →, *Johannesburg* 13 A1
Kleinmachnow, *Berlin* 5 B2
Kleinschönebeck, *Berlin* 5 B5
Klemetsrud, *Oslo* 22 A4
Kličany, *Prague* 24 A2
Klipriviersberg Nature Reserve, *Johannesburg* 13 B2
Klosterneuburg, *Vienna* 31 A1
Knesset, *Jerusalem* 13 b1
Knightsbridge, *London* 15 c2
Köbánya, *Budapest* 7 B2
Kobbegem, *Brussels* 6 A1
Kōbe, *Osaka* 22 A2
Kōbe Harbour, *Osaka* 22 B2
København, *Copenhagen* 10 A2
Kobylisy, *Prague* 24 B2
Kobyłka, *Warsaw* 31 A3
Kŏch'ŏk, *Seoul* 26 B1
Kodaira, *Tokyo* 29 A1
Kodanaka, *Tokyo* 29 B2
Kodenmacho, *Tokyo* 29 a5
Koekelberg, *Brussels* 6 A1
Koganei, *Tokyo* 29 A2
Kogarah, *Sydney* 28 B1
Køge Bugt, *Copenhagen* 10 B2
Koivupää, *Helsinki* 12 B2
Koja, *Jakarta* 13 A2
Koja Utara, *Jakarta* 13 A2
Kokobunji, *Tokyo* 29 A1
Kokobunji-Temple, *Tokyo* 29 A4
Kolarängen, *Stockholm* 28 B3
Kolbotn, *Oslo* 22 B3
Kolkata, *Calcutta* 8 B2
Koło, *Warsaw* 31 B1
Kolokinthóu, *Athens* 2 B2
Kolomyagi, *St. Petersburg* 26 A1
Kolónos, *Athens* 2 B2
Kolsås, *Oslo* 22 A2
Komae, *Tokyo* 29 B2
Komagome, *Tokyo* 29 A3
Komazawa, *Tokyo* 29 B3
Kona, *Calcutta* 8 B1
Konala, *Helsinki* 12 B2
Kondli, *Delhi* 10 B2
Kongelige Slottet, *Oslo* 22 a1
Kongelunden, *Copenhagen* 10 B3
Kongens Lyngby, *Copenhagen* 10 A3
Kongnŭng, *Seoul* 26 B2
Kongo, *Helsinki* 12 A1
Koninklijk Paleis, *Amsterdam* 2 b2
Konnagar, *Calcutta* 8 A2
Konohana, *Osaka* 22 A3
Kōnoike, *Osaka* 22 A4
Konradshöhe, *Berlin* 5 A2
Kopanina, *Prague* 24 B1
Koparkhairna, *Mumbai* 20 A2
Köpenick, *Berlin* 5 B4
Korangi, *Karachi* 14 B2
Koremasa, *Tokyo* 29 B1
Korenevo, *Moscow* 19 B6
Kori, *Osaka* 22 A4
Koridhallós, *Athens* 2 B1
Korokoro, *Wellington* 32 B2
Korokoro Stream →, *Wellington* 32 B2
Kosino, *Moscow* 19 B5
Kosugi, *Tokyo* 29 B2
Kota, *Jakarta* 13 A1
Kotelyniki, *Moscow* 19 C5
Kōtō-Ku, *Tokyo* 29 A3
Kotrung, *Calcutta* 8 A2
Kouponia, *Athens* 2 B2
Kowloon, *Hong Kong* 12 B1
Kowloon Park, *Hong Kong* 12 a2
Kowloon Peak, *Hong Kong* 12 A2
Kowloon Res., *Hong Kong* 12 A1
Kowloon Tong, *Hong Kong* 12 A2
Kozhukhovo, *Moscow* 19 B5
Kraainem, *Brussels* 6 A2
Krailling, *Munich* 20 B1
Krampnitz, *Berlin* 5 B1
Krampnitzsee, *Berlin* 5 B1
Kranji, Sungei →, *Singapore* 27 A2
Kranji Industrial Estate, *Singapore* 27 A2
Kraskovo, *Moscow* 19 C5
Krasno-Presnenskaya, *Moscow* 19 B3
Krasnogorsk, *Moscow* 19 B1
Krč, *Prague* 24 B2
Krestovskiye, Ostrov, *St. Petersburg* 26 B1
Kreuzberg, *Berlin* 5 A3
Kritzendorf, *Vienna* 31 A1
Krumme Lanke, *Berlin* 5 B2
Krummensee, *Berlin* 5 A5
Krung Thep, *Bangkok* 3 B2
Krusboda, *Stockholm* 28 B3
Krylatskoye, *Moscow* 19 B2
Küçükköy, *Istanbul* 12 B1
Kudankita, *Tokyo* 29 a3
Kudrovo, *St. Petersburg* 26 B3
Kulosaari, *Helsinki* 12 B3
Kulturforum, *Berlin* 5 b3
Kultury i Nauki, Palac, *Warsaw* 31 b2
Kŭmch'ŏn, *Seoul* 26 C1
Kumla, *Stockholm* 28 B3
Kungens kurva, *Stockholm* 28 B1
Kungliga Slottet, *Stockholm* 28 b2
Kungshatt, *Stockholm* 28 B1
Kungsholmen, *Stockholm* 28 A2
Kuningan, *Jakarta* 13 B1
Kunitachi, *Tokyo* 29 A1
Kunming Hu, *Beijing* 4 B1
Kunratice, *Prague* 24 B2
Kunsthistorischesmuseum, *Vienna* 31 b1
Kuntsevo, *Moscow* 19 B2
Kupchino, *St. Petersburg* 26 B2
Kurbağalı →, *Istanbul* 12 C2
Kurihara, *Tokyo* 29 A2
Kurla, *Mumbai* 20 A2
Kurmuri, *Mumbai* 20 A2
Kurume, *Tokyo* 29 A2
Kuryanovo, *Moscow* 19 C4
Kuskovo, *Moscow* 19 B4
Kustia, *Calcutta* 8 B2
Kutsino, *Moscow* 19 B5
Kuzguncuk, *Istanbul* 12 B2
Kuzyminki, *Moscow* 19 B4
Kwai Chung, *Hong Kong* 12 A1
Kwanak, *Seoul* 26 C1
Kwanak-san, *Seoul* 26 C1
Kyje, *Prague* 24 B3
Kyūhōji, *Osaka* 22 B4

L

La Blanca, *Santiago* 26 C2
La Boca, *Buenos Aires* 7 B2
La Bretèche, *Paris* 23 A1
La Campiña, *Lima* 16 C2
La Celle-St.-Cloud, *Paris* 23 A1
La Ciudadela, *Mexico City* 18 c2
La Courneuve, *Paris* 23 A3
La Dehesa, *Santiago* 26 B2
La Encantada, *Lima* 16 C2
La Estación, *Madrid* 17 B1
La Floresta, *Barcelona* 4 A1
La Fortuna, *Madrid* 17 B1
La Fransa, *Barcelona* 4 A1
La Garenne-Colombes, *Paris* 23 A2
La Giustiniana, *Rome* 25 B1
La Grange, *Chicago* 9 C1
La Grange Park, *Chicago* 9 C1
La Granja, *Santiago* 26 C2
La Guardia Airport, *New York* 21 B2
La Hulpe, *Brussels* 6 B2
La Llacuna, *Barcelona* 4 A2
La Loma, *Mexico City* 18 A1
La Lucila, *Buenos Aires* 7 B2
La Maladrerie, *Paris* 23 A1
La Milla, Cerro, *Lima* 16 B2
La Monachina, *Rome* 25 B1
La Moraleja, *Madrid* 17 A2
La Nopalera, *Mexico City* 18 C2
La Paternal, *Buenos Aires* 7 B2
La Perla, *Lima* 16 B2
La Perouse, *Sydney* 28 B2
La Pineda, *Barcelona* 4 B1
La Pisana, *Rome* 25 B1
La Prairie, *Montreal* 19 B3
La Punta, *Lima* 16 B1
La Puntigala, *Barcelona* 4 A2
La Queue-en-Brie, *Paris* 23 B4
La Reina, *Santiago* 26 B2
La Ribera, *Barcelona* 4 A1
La Sagrera, *Barcelona* 4 A2
La Salada, *Buenos Aires* 7 C2
La Scala, *Milan* 18 B2
La Storta, *Rome* 25 A1
La Taxonera, *Barcelona* 4 A2
La Victoria, *Lima* 16 B2
Laajalahti, *Helsinki* 12 B1
Laajasalo, *Helsinki* 12 B3
Laaksolahti, *Helsinki* 12 B1
Lablâba, W. el →, *Cairo* 7 A2
Lac Cisterna, *Santiago* 26 C2
Lachine, *Montreal* 19 B1
Lad Phrao, *Bangkok* 3 B2
Ladera Heights, *Los Angeles* 16 C2
Ládví, *Prague* 24 B2
Łady, *Warsaw* 31 C1
Lafontaine, Parc, *Montreal* 19 A2
Lagoa, *Rio de Janeiro* 24 B1
Lagos, *Lagos* 14 B2
Lagos Harbour, *Lagos* 14 B2
Lagos-Ikeja Airport, *Lagos* 14 A1
Lagos Island, *Lagos* 14 B2
Lagos Lagoon, *Lagos* 14 B2
Laguna de B., *Manila* 17 C2
Laim, *Munich* 20 B2
Lainate, *Milan* 18 A1
Lainz, *Vienna* 31 B1
Lakemba, *Sydney* 28 B1
Lakeside, *Cape Town* 8 B1
Lakeside, *Johannesburg* 13 A2
Lakeview, *Chicago* 9 B3
Lakewood Park, *Atlanta* 3 B2
Lakhtinskiy, *St. Petersburg* 26 B1
Lakhtinskiy Razliv, Oz., *St. Petersburg* 26 B1
Lakshmanpur, *Calcutta* 8 B1
Lal Qila, *Delhi* 1 a3
Lam Tin, *Hong Kong* 12 B2
Lambert, *Oslo* 22 A3
Lambeth, *London* 15 B3
Lambrate, *Milan* 18 B2
Lambro, Parco, *Milan* 18 B2
Lambton Mills, *Toronto* 30 B1
Lamma I., *Hong Kong* 12 B1
Landover Hills, *Washington* 32 B4
Landsmeer, *Amsterdam* 2 A2
Landstrasse, *Vienna* 31 A2
Landwehr kanal, *Berlin* 5 B3
Lane Cove, *Sydney* 28 A1
Lane Cove National Park, *Sydney* 28 A1
Langa, *Cape Town* 8 A2
Langenzersdorf, *Vienna* 31 A2
Langer See, *Berlin* 5 B4
Langley, *Washington* 32 B2
Langley Park, *Washington* 32 B4
Langwald, *Munich* 20 A1
Lanham, *Washington* 32 B4
Lankwitz, *Berlin* 5 B3
L'Annunziatella, *Rome* 25 C2
Lansdowne, *Cape Town* 8 A2
Lansing, *Toronto* 30 A2
Lanús, *Buenos Aires* 7 C2
Lapa, *Rio de Janeiro* 24 B1
Laranjeiras, *Rio de Janeiro* 24 B1
Larísa Sta., *Athens* 2 a1
Las, *Warsaw* 31 B2
Las Corts, *Barcelona* 4 A1
Las Kabacki, *Warsaw* 31 C2
Las Pinas, *Manila* 17 C1
Las Rejas, *Santiago* 26 B1
Lasalle, *Montreal* 19 B2
Lasek Bielański, *Warsaw* 31 B1
Lasek Na Kole, *Warsaw* 31 B1
Laski, *Warsaw* 31 B1
Latina, *Madrid* 17 B1
Laurence G. Hanscom Field, *Boston* 6 A2
Lauttasaari, *Helsinki* 12 C2
Laval, *Montreal* 19 A1
Laval-des-Rapides, *Montreal* 19 A1
Lavīzān, *Tehran* 30 A2
Lavradio, *Lisbon* 14 A2
Lawndale, *Chicago* 9 B2
Lawrence Heights, *Toronto* 30 A2
Layari, *Karachi* 14 A2
Layari →, *Karachi* 14 A1
Lazare, Gare St., *Paris* 23 a3
Łazienkowski, Palac, *Warsaw* 31 c3
Łazienkowski Park, *Warsaw* 31 B2
Le Blanc-Mesnil, *Paris* 23 A3
Le Bourget, *Paris* 23 A3
Le Chenoi, *Brussels* 6 B2
Le Chesnay, *Paris* 23 B1
Le Christ de Saclay, *Paris* 23 B2
Le Kremlin-Bicêtre, *Paris* 23 B3
Le Mesnil-le-Roi, *Paris* 23 A1
Le Pecq, *Paris* 23 A1
Le Perreux, *Paris* 23 A3
Le Pin, *Paris* 23 A4
Le Plessis-Robinson, *Paris* 23 B2
Le Plessis-Trévise, *Paris* 23 B4
Le Port-Marly, *Paris* 23 A1
Le Pré-St.-Gervais, *Paris* 23 A3
Le Raincy, *Paris* 23 A4
Le Vésinet, *Paris* 23 A1
Lea Bridge, *London* 15 A3
Leaside, *Toronto* 30 A2
Leblon, *Rio de Janeiro* 24 B1
Lee, *London* 15 B4
Leganés, *Madrid* 17 C1
Legazpi, *Madrid* 17 B1
Lehtisaari, *Helsinki* 12 B2
Lei Yue Mun, *Hong Kong* 12 B2
Leião, *Lisbon* 14 A1
Leicester Square, *London* 15 b3
Leichhardt, *Sydney* 28 B1
Leith, *Edinburgh* 11 B3
Lemoyne, *Montreal* 19 B3
Lenin, *Moscow* 19 B3
Lenino, *Moscow* 19 C3
Leninskiye Gory, *Moscow* 19 B3
Lennox, *Los Angeles* 16 C2
Leonia, *New York* 21 A2
Leopardstown, *Dublin* 11 B2
Leopoldau, *Vienna* 31 A2
Leopoldstadt, *Vienna* 31 A2
Leportovo, *Moscow* 19 B4
Leppävaara, *Helsinki* 12 B1
Les Lilas, *Paris* 23 A3
Les Loges-en-Josas, *Paris* 23 B1
Les Pavillons-sous-Bois, *Paris* 23 A4
Lésigny, *Paris* 23 B4
Lesnozavodskaya, *St. Petersburg* 26 B2
L'Étang-la-Ville, *Paris* 23 A1
Letná, *Prague* 24 a1
Letňany, *Prague* 24 B3
Levallois-Perret, *Paris* 23 A2
Levent, *Istanbul* 12 B2
Lewisdale, *Washington* 32 B4
Lewisham, *London* 15 B3
Lexington, *Boston* 6 A2
Leyton, *London* 15 A3
Leytonstone, *London* 15 A4
L'Hay-les-Roses, *Paris* 23 B3
L'Hospitalet de Llobregat, *Barcelona* 4 A1
Lhotka, *Prague* 24 B2
Liangshui He →, *Beijing* 4 C2
Lianhua Chi, *Beijing* 4 B1
Lianhua He →, *Beijing* 4 B1
Libčice nad Vitavou, *Prague* 24 A2
Libeň, *Prague* 24 B2
Liberdade, *São Paulo* 26 B2
Liberdade, Ave da, *Lisbon* 14 b1
Liberton, *Edinburgh* 11 B3
Liberty I., *New York* 21 B1
Liberty State Park, *New York* 21 B1
Libeznice, *Prague* 24 A2
Library of Congress, *Washington* 32 c3
Libuš, *Prague* 24 B2
Lichiao, *Canton* 8 B2
Lichtenburg, *Berlin* 5 A4
Lichterfelde, *Berlin* 5 B2
Lidingö, *Stockholm* 28 A2
Lieshi Lingyuan, *Canton* 8 B2
Liesing, *Vienna* 31 B1
Liesing →, *Vienna* 31 B2
Liffey, R. →, *Dublin* 11 A1
Ligovo, *St. Petersburg* 26 C1
Lijordet, *Oslo* 22 A2
Likavitos, *Athens* 2 b3
Likhoborka →, *Moscow* 19 A3
Lilla Värtan, *Stockholm* 28 A3
Lille Værløse, *Copenhagen* 10 A2
Liluah, *Calcutta* 8 B1
Lim Chu Kang, *Singapore* 27 A2
Lima, *Lima* 16 B2
Limbiate, *Milan* 18 A1
Limehouse, *London* 15 A3
Limeil-Brévannes, *Paris* 23 B3
Linate, Aeroporto Internazionale di, *Milan* 18 B2
Linbropark, *Johannesburg* 13 A2
Lincoln, *Boston* 6 A2
Lincoln Center, *New York* 21 b2
Lincoln Heights, *Los Angeles* 16 B3
Lincoln Park, *Chicago* 9 B3
Lincoln Park, *New York* 21 B1
Lincoln Park, *San Francisco* 25 B1
Lincolnwood, *Chicago* 9 A2
Linda-a-Pastora, *Lisbon* 14 A1
Linden, *Johannesburg* 13 A2
Linden, *Wellington* 32 A1
Lindenberg, *Berlin* 5 A4
Lindøya, *Oslo* 22 A3
Liniers, *Buenos Aires* 7 B1
Linkebeek, *Brussels* 6 B2
Linksfield, *Johannesburg* 13 A2
Linmeyer, *Johannesburg* 13 B2
Linna, *Helsinki* 12 A2
Lintuvaara, *Helsinki* 12 B1
Lion Rock Country Park, *Hong Kong* 12 A2
Lioúmi, *Athens* 2 B2
Liqizhuang, *Tianjin* 30 B2
Lisboa, *Lisbon* 14 A2
Lisbon = Lisboa, *Lisbon* 14 A2
Lishui, *Canton* 8 A1
Little B., *Sydney* 28 B2
Little Calumet →, *Chicago* 9 D3
Little Ferry, *New York* 21 A1
Little Italy, *New York* 21 e2
Little Mermaid, *Copenhagen* 10 a3
Little Rouge →, *Toronto* 30 A4
Little Tokyo, *Los Angeles* 16 c2
Liuhang, *Shanghai* 27 A1
Liurong Temple, *Canton* 8 B2
Liuxi →, *Canton* 8 B2
Liverpool Street, *London* 15 a5
Livry-Gargan, *Paris* 23 A4
Ljan, *Oslo* 22 A3
Llano de Can Gineu, *Barcelona* 4 A2
Llobregat →, *Barcelona* 4 A1
Lo Aranguiz, *Santiago* 26 B2
Lo Boza, *Santiago* 26 B1
Lo Chau, *Hong Kong* 12 B2
Lo Espejo, *Santiago* 26 C1
Lo Hermida, *Santiago* 26 B2
Lo Prado, *Santiago* 26 B1
Lo So Shing, *Hong Kong* 12 B1
Lo Wai, *Hong Kong* 12 A1
Loanhead, *Edinburgh* 11 B3
Lobau, *Vienna* 31 A3
Lobos, Pt., *San Francisco* 25 B1
Locham, *Munich* 20 B1
Lochino, *Moscow* 19 B1
Lochkov, *Prague* 24 B2
Lockhausen, *Munich* 20 A1
Lodi, *New York* 21 A1
Lodi Estate, *Delhi* 10 B2
Logan Int. Airport, *Boston* 6 A4
Logan Square, *Chicago* 9 B2
Lognes-Émerainville, Aérodrome de, *Paris* 23 B4
Löhme, *Berlin* 5 A5
Lolokhet, *Karachi* 14 A2
Lomas Chapultepec, *Mexico City* 18 B1
Lomas de San Angel Inn, *Mexico City* 18 B1
Lomas de Zamora, *Buenos Aires* 7 C2
Lombardy East, *Johannesburg* 13 A2
Łomianki, *Warsaw* 31 A1
Lomus Reforma, *Mexico City* 18 B1
London, *London* 15 A3
London Bridge, *London* 15 b5
London City Airport, *London* 15 A4
London Zoo, *London* 15 A3
Long B., *Sydney* 28 B2
Long Branch, *Toronto* 30 B1
Long Brook →, *Washington* 32 C2
Long Ditton, *London* 15 B2
Long I., *Boston* 6 B4
Long Island City, *New York* 21 B2
Long Street, *Cape Town* 8 c2
Longchamp, Hippodrôme de, *Paris* 23 A2
Longhua Pagoda, *Shanghai* 27 B1
Longhua Park, *Shanghai* 27 B1
Longjohn Slough, *Chicago* 9 C1
Longtan Hu →, *Beijing* 4 B2
Longue-Pointe, *Montreal* 19 A2
Longueuil, *Montreal* 19 A3
Loni, *Delhi* 10 A2
Loop, The, *Chicago* 9 c1
Lord's Cricket Ground, *London* 15 A2
Loreto, *Milan* 18 B2
Los Angeles Int. Airport, *Los Angeles* 16 C2
Los Cerrillos, Aeropuerto, *Santiago* 26 B1
Los Nietos, *Los Angeles* 16 C4
Los Olivos, *Lima* 16 A2
Los Reyes, *Mexico City* 18 B2
Lot, *Brussels* 6 B1
Loughlinstown, *Dublin* 11 B3
Loures, *Lisbon* 14 A1
Louveciennes, *Paris* 23 A1
Louvre, Musée du, *Paris* 23 b4
Louvre, Palais du, *Paris* 23 b4
Lower East Side, *New York* 21 e2
Lower Hutt, *Wellington* 32 B2
Lower Manhattan, *New York* 21 e1
Lower New York B., *New York* 21 C1
Lower Shing Mun Res., *Hong Kong* 12 A1
Lowry Bay, *Wellington* 32 B2
Lu Xun Museum, *Beijing* 4 b1
Lübars, *Berlin* 5 A3
Ludwigsfeld, *Munich* 20 A1
Luhu, *Canton* 8 B2
Lumiar, *Lisbon* 14 A2
Lumphini Park, *Bangkok* 3 B2
Lundtofte, *Copenhagen* 10 A3
Lung Mei, *Hong Kong* 12 A2
Luojiang, *Canton* 8 B2
Lustheim, *Munich* 20 A2
Luwan, *Shanghai* 27 B1
Luxembourg, Palais du, *Paris* 23 c4
Luzhniki Sports Centre, *Moscow* 19 B3
Lyndhurst, *New York* 21 B1
Lynn, *Boston* 6 A4
Lynn Harbor, *Boston* 6 A4
Lynn Woods Res., *Boston* 6 A3
Lyon, Gare de, *Paris* 23 c5
Lyons, *Chicago* 9 C2
Lysaker, *Oslo* 22 A2
Lysakerselva →, *Oslo* 22 A2
Lysolaje, *Prague* 24 B2
Lyubertsy, *Moscow* 19 B5
Lyublino, *Moscow* 19 B4

M

Ma Nam Wat, *Hong Kong* 12 A2
Ma On Shan Country Park, *Hong Kong* 12 A2
Ma'ale Adumim, *Jerusalem* 13 B2
Ma'ale Ha Khamisha, *Jerusalem* 13 B1
Ma'ale Mikhmas, *Jerusalem* 13 A2
Maantiekylä, *Helsinki* 12 A3
Maarifa, *Baghdad* 3 B2
Mabato Pt., *Manila* 17 C2
Macaco, Morro do, *Rio de Janeiro* 24 B2
McCook, *Chicago* 9 C2
Machelen, *Brussels* 6 A2
Machida, *Tokyo* 29 B1
Maciołki, *Warsaw* 31 B2
Mackayville, *Montreal* 19 A3
McKerrow, *Wellington* 32 B2
McKinley Park, *Chicago* 9 C2
Mclean, *Washington* 32 B2
Macopocho, R. →, *Santiago* 26 B1
MacRitchie Res., *Singapore* 27 A2
Macul, *Santiago* 26 C2
Madame Tussaud's, *London* 15 a3
Madhudaha, *Calcutta* 8 B2
Madhyamgram, *Calcutta* 8 A2
Madīnah Al Mansūr, *Baghdad* 3 B2
Mâdinet Nasr, *Cairo* 7 A2
Madison Avenue, *New York* 21 c2
Madison Square, *New York* 21 d2
Madrid, *Madrid* 17 B1
Madrona, *Barcelona* 4 A1
Maesawa, *Tokyo* 29 A2
Magdalena, *Lima* 16 B2
Magdalena Contreras, *Mexico City* 18 C1
Maghreb, *Baghdad* 3 A2
Maginu, *Tokyo* 29 B2
Magliana, *Rome* 25 B1
Magny-les-Hameaux, *Paris* 23 B1
Magonoy, *Manila* 17 B2
Mahalaxmi, *Mumbai* 20 a1
Maheshtala, *Calcutta* 8 C1
Mahim, *Mumbai* 20 A2
Mahim B., *Mumbai* 20 A1
Mahlsdorf, *Berlin* 5 A4
Mahmoodabad, *Karachi* 14 A2
Mahrauli, *Delhi* 10 B1
Mahul, *Mumbai* 20 A2
Maida Vale, *London* 15 a1
Maidstone, *Melbourne* 17 A1
Maipú, *Santiago* 26 C1
Maisonneuve, Parc, *Montreal* 19 A2
Maisons-Alfort, *Paris* 23 B3
Maisons-Laffitte, *Paris* 23 A1
Maissoneuve, *Montreal* 19 A2
Maitland, *Cape Town* 8 A1
Makati, *Manila* 17 B2
Mäkiniitty, *Helsinki* 12 A2
Mala Straná, *Prague* 24 B2
Malabar, *Mumbai* 20 B1
Malabar, *Sydney* 28 B2
Malabar Hill, *Mumbai* 20 B1
Malabar Pt., *Mumbai* 20 B1
Malabon, *Manila* 17 B1
Malacañang Palace, *Manila* 17 B1
Malahide, *Dublin* 11 A3
Malakhovka, *Moscow* 19 C6
Malakoff, *Paris* 23 B2
Mälarhöjaen, *Stockholm* 28 B1
Malate, *Manila* 17 B1
Malay Quarter, *Cape Town* 8 c2
Malaya Neva, *St. Petersburg* 26 B1
Malaya-Okhta, *St. Petersburg* 26 B2
Malchow, *Berlin* 5 A3
Malden, *Boston* 6 A3
Malden, *London* 15 B2
Maleizen, *Brussels* 6 B3
Malešice, *Prague* 24 B3
Malir →, *Karachi* 14 B2
Mall, The, *Washington* 32 b2
Malleny Mills, *Edinburgh* 11 B2
Malmi, *Helsinki* 12 B2
Malmøya, *Oslo* 22 A3
Måløv, *Copenhagen* 10 A2
Malpasso, Ost., *Rome* 25 C1
Malton, *Toronto* 30 A1
Malvern, *Johannesburg* 13 B2
Malvern, *Melbourne* 17 B2
Malvern, *Toronto* 30 A3
Mamonovo, *Moscow* 19 B2
Mampang Prapatan, *Jakarta* 13 B1
Mampukuji, *Tokyo* 29 B2
Man Budrukh, *Mumbai* 20 A2
Man Khurd, *Mumbai* 20 A2
Mandaluyong, *Manila* 17 B2
Mandaoli, *Delhi* 10 B2
Mandaqui →, *São Paulo* 26 A2
Mandoli, *Delhi* 10 A2
Mandvi, *Mumbai* 20 B2
Manenberg, *Cape Town* 8 A2
Mang Kung Uk, *Hong Kong* 12 B2
Mangolpuri, *Delhi* 10 A1
Manguinhos, Aéroporto, *Rio de Janeiro* 24 B1
Mangwŏn, *Seoul* 26 B1
Manhattan, *New York* 21 B2
Manhattan Beach, *New York* 21 C2
Manila, *Manila* 17 B1
Manila B., *Manila* 17 B1
Manila Int. Airport, *Manila* 17 B2
Mankkaa, *Helsinki* 12 B1
Manly, *Sydney* 28 A2
Mannswörth, *Vienna* 31 B3
Manor Park, *London* 15 A4
Manor Park, *Wellington* 32 A2
Manora, *Karachi* 14 B1
Manquehue, Cerro, *Santiago* 26 B2
Manzanares, Canal de, *Madrid* 17 C2
Mao Mausoleum, *Beijing* 4 c2
Map'o, *Seoul* 26 B1
Maracanã, *Rio de Janeiro* 24 B1
Maraoli, *Mumbai* 20 A2
Marblehead, *Boston* 6 A4
Marcelin, *Warsaw* 31 B1
Mareil-Marly, *Paris* 23 A1
Margareten, *Vienna* 31 A2
Maria, *Vienna* 31 A2
Maridalen, *Oslo* 22 A3
Maridalsvatnet, *Oslo* 22 A3
Mariendorf, *Berlin* 5 B3
Marienfelde, *Berlin* 5 B3
Marienplatz, *Munich* 20 b2
Marikina →, *Manila* 17 B2
Marin City, *San Francisco* 25 A1
Marin Headlands State Park, *San Francisco* 25 A2
Marin Pen., *San Francisco* 25 A1
Marina del Rey, *Los Angeles* 16 C2
Marine Drive, *Mumbai* 20 b1
Marino, *Dublin* 11 A2
Maritim, Museu, *Barcelona* 4 c2
Markham, *Toronto* 30 A2
Marki, *Warsaw* 31 B2
Markland Wood, *Toronto* 30 B1
Marly, Forêt de, *Paris* 23 A1
Marly-le-Roi, *Paris* 23 A1
Marne →, *Paris* 23 B3
Marne-la-Vallée, *Paris* 23 A4
Marolles-en-Brie, *Paris* 23 B4
Maroubra, *Sydney* 28 B2
Marquette Park, *Chicago* 9 C2
Marrickville, *Sydney* 28 B1
Marsfield, *Sydney* 28 A1
Marshall Field's, *Chicago* 9 c2
Marte, Campo de, *São Paulo* 26 B2
Martesana, Navíglio della, *Milan* 18 A2
Martin Luther King National Historic Site, *Atlanta* 3 B2
Martinez, *Buenos Aires* 7 A1
Martinkylä, *Helsinki* 12 B2
Martinsried, *Munich* 20 B1
Maruko, *Tokyo* 29 B3
Marunouchi, *Tokyo* 29 b4
Marusino, *Moscow* 19 B5
Maryino, *Moscow* 19 B4
Maryland, *Singapore* 27 B2
Marylebone, *London* 15 A2
Marymont, *Warsaw* 31 B1
Marysin Wawerski, *Warsaw* 31 B2
Marzahn, *Berlin* 5 A4
Mascot, *Sydney* 28 B2
Masmo, *Stockholm* 28 B1
Maspeth, *New York* 21 B2
Masr el Gedida, *Cairo* 7 A2
Masr el Qadîma, *Cairo* 7 A2
Massachusetts B., *Boston* 6 A4
Massachusett's Inst. of Tech., *Boston* 6 A3
Massamá, *Lisbon* 14 A1
Massey →, *Toronto* 30 A3
Massy, *Paris* 23 B2
Matihutong, *Beijing* 4 B1
Matinha, *Lisbon* 14 A2
Matramam, *Jakarta* 13 B2
Matsubara, *Osaka* 22 B4
Mattapan, *Boston* 6 B3
Mátyásföld, *Budapest* 7 A3
Mátyástemplom, *Budapest* 7 b1
Mau Tso Ngam, *Hong Kong* 12 A2
Mauer, *Vienna* 31 B1
Mauripur, *Karachi* 14 A1
Maxhof, *Munich* 20 B1
Maya-Zan, *Osaka* 22 A2
Mayfair, *Johannesburg* 13 B2
Mayfair, *London* 15 b3
Mayor, Plaza, *Madrid* 17 b2
Maywood, *Chicago* 9 B1
Maywood, *Los Angeles* 16 C3
Maywood, *New York* 21 A1
Mazagaon, *Mumbai* 20 a2
Me'a She' Arim, *Jerusalem* 13 a2
Meadowbank Park, *Sydney* 28 A1
Měcholupy, *Prague* 24 B3
Měčice, *Prague* 24 A3
Mecidiyeköy, *Istanbul* 12 B2
Medford, *Boston* 6 A3
Mediodia, *Madrid* 17 B2
Medvezhiy Ozyora, *Moscow* 19 A5
Meguro →, *Tokyo* 29 B3
Meguro-Ku, *Tokyo* 29 B3
Mehpalpur, *Delhi* 10 B1
Mehrābād Airport, *Tehran* 30 A1
Mehram Nagar, *Delhi* 10 B1
Mehrow, *Berlin* 5 A4
Mei Lanfang, *Beijing* 4 a2
Meidling, *Vienna* 31 A2
Méier, *Rio de Janeiro* 24 B1
Meiji Shrine, *Tokyo* 29 b1
Meise, *Brussels* 6 A1
Mejiro, *Tokyo* 29 A3
Melbourne, *Melbourne* 17 A1
Melbourne Airport, *Melbourne* 17 A1
Melkki, *Helsinki* 12 C2
Mellunkylä, *Helsinki* 12 B3
Mellunmäki, *Helsinki* 12 B3
Melrose, *Boston* 6 A3
Melrose, *New York* 21 B2
Melrose Park, *Chicago* 9 B1
Melsbroek, *Brussels* 6 A2
Menteng, *Jakarta* 13 B1
Mérantaise →, *Paris* 23 B1
Mercamadrid, *Madrid* 17 B2
Merced, L., *San Francisco* 25 B2
Meredale, *Johannesburg* 13 B1
Merlimau, P., *Singapore* 27 B2
Merri Cr. →, *Melbourne* 17 A1
Merrion, *Dublin* 11 B2
Merrionette Park, *Chicago* 9 C2
Merton, *London* 15 B2
Mesgarābād, *Tehran* 30 B3
Meshcherskiy, *Moscow* 19 B2
Messe, *Vienna* 31 A2
Messe-palast, *Vienna* 31 c1
Metanópoli, *Milan* 18 B2
Metropolitan Museum of Art, *New York* 21 b3
Meudon, *Paris* 23 B2
Mevaseret Tsiyon, *Jerusalem* 13 B1
Mevo Beitar, *Jerusalem* 13 B1
México, Ciudad de, *Mexico City* 18 B1
Meyersdal, *Johannesburg* 13 B2
Mezzano, *Milan* 18 B2
Mezzate, *Milan* 18 B2
Miadong, *Seoul* 26 B2
Miami, *Miami* 18 B2
Miami Beach, *Miami* 18 B2
Miami Canal →, *Miami* 18 A1
Miami Int. Airport, *Miami* 18 B1
Miami Shores, *Miami* 18 A2
Miami Springs, *Miami* 18 B1
Miasto, *Warsaw* 31 B2
Michałowice, *Warsaw* 31 B1
Michigan Avenue, *Chicago* 9 b2
Michle, *Prague* 24 B2
Middle Harbour, *Sydney* 28 A2
Middle Hd., *Sydney* 28 A2
Middle Park, *Melbourne* 17 B1
Middle Village, *New York* 21 B2
Middlesex Fells Reservation, *Boston* 6 A3
Midi, Gare du, *Brussels* 6 c1
Midland Beach, *New York* 21 C1
Miedzeszyn, *Warsaw* 31 B3
Międzylesie, *Warsaw* 31 B3
Miessaari, *Helsinki* 12 C1
Miguel Hidalgo, *Mexico City* 18 B1
Mikhelysona, *Moscow* 19 B5
Milano, *Milan* 18 B1
Milano Due, *Milan* 18 B2
Milano San Felice, *Milan* 18 B2
Milbertshofen, *Munich* 20 A2
Mill Hill, *London* 15 A2
Millennium Dome, *London* 15 A4
Miller Meadow, *Chicago* 9 B2
Millerhill, *Edinburgh* 11 B3
Millers Point, *Sydney* 28 a1
Milltown, *Dublin* 11 B2
Millwood, *Washington* 32 B4
Milnerton, *Cape Town* 8 A1
Milon-la-Chapelle, *Paris* 23 B1
Milton, *Boston* 6 B3
Milton Bridge, *Edinburgh* 11 B2
Mimico, *Toronto* 30 B2
Minami, *Osaka* 22 A4
Minamitsunashima, *Tokyo* 29 B2
Minato, *Osaka* 22 B3
Minato-Ku, *Tokyo* 29 c3
Minshât el Bekkarî, *Cairo* 7 A1
Minute Man Nat. Hist. Park, *Boston* 6 A2
Miraflores, *Lima* 16 B2
Miramar, *Wellington* 32 B1
Misericordia, Sa. da, *Rio de Janeiro* 24 B1
Mission, *San Francisco* 25 B2
Mississauga, *Toronto* 30 B1
Mitaka, *Tokyo* 29 A2
Mitcham, *London* 15 B2
Mitcham Common, *London* 15 B3
Mitchell's Plain, *Cape Town* 8 B2
Mitino, *Moscow* 19 A2
Mitte, *Berlin* 5 A3
Mittel Isarkanal →, *Munich* 20 A3
Mixcoac, *Mexico City* 18 B1
Mixcoac, Presa de, *Mexico City* 18 B1
Miyakojima, *Osaka* 22 A4
Mizonokuchi, *Tokyo* 29 B2
Mizue, *Tokyo* 29 A4
Młocinski Park, *Warsaw* 31 B1
Młociny, *Warsaw* 31 B1
Mnevniki, *Moscow* 19 B2
Moba, *Lagos* 14 B2
Moczydło, *Warsaw* 31 C2
Modderfontein, *Johannesburg* 13 A2
Modřany, *Prague* 24 B2
Mogyoród, *Budapest* 7 A3
Moinho Velho, Cor. →, *São Paulo* 26 B2
Mok, *Seoul* 26 B1
Mokotów, *Warsaw* 31 B2
Molenbeek-Saint-Jean, *Brussels* 6 A1
Molino de Rosas, *Mexico City* 18 B1
Mollem, *Brussels* 6 A1
Mollins de Rey, *Barcelona* 4 A1
Mondeor, *Johannesburg* 13 B2
Moneda, Palacio de la, *Santiago* 26 B2
Moneró, *Rio de Janeiro* 24 A1
Mong Kok, *Hong Kong* 12 B2
Monkstown, *Dublin* 11 B3
Monnickendam, *Amsterdam* 2 A3
Monrovia, *Los Angeles* 16 B4
Monsanto, *Lisbon* 14 A1
Monsanto, Parque Florestal de, *Lisbon* 14 A1
Mont Royal, *Montreal* 19 A2
Mont-Royal, Parc, *Montreal* 19 A2
Montana de Montjuich, *Barcelona* 4 A1
Monte Chingolo, *Buenos Aires* 7 C2

Raffles Park 37

Monte Palatino, *Rome* 25 c3
Montebello, *Los Angeles* 16 B4
Montemor, *Lisbon* 14 A1
Monterey Park, *Los Angeles* 16 B4
Montespaccato, *Rome* 25 B1
Montesson, *Paris* 23 A1
Monteverde Nuovo, *Rome* 25 B1
Montfermeil, *Paris* 23 A4
Montigny-le-Bretonneux, *Paris* 23 B1
Montjay-la-Tour, *Paris* 23 A4
Montjuic, Parc de, *Barcelona* 4 c1
Montparnasse, Gare, *Paris* 23 A2
Montréal, *Montreal* 19 A2
Montréal, Î. de, *Montreal* 19 A2
Montréal, Univ. de, *Montreal* 19 B2
Montréal Est, *Montreal* 19 A2
Montréal Nord, *Montreal* 19 A2
Montréal Ouest, *Montreal* 19 B1
Montreuil, *Paris* 23 A3
Montrouge, *Paris* 23 B2
Montserrat, *Buenos Aires* 7 B2
Monza, *Milan* 18 A2
Monzoro, *Milan* 18 B1
Moóca, *São Paulo* 26 B2
Moonachie, *New York* 21 B1
Moonee Ponds, *Melbourne* 17 A1
Moonee Valley Racecourse, *Melbourne* 17 A1
Moosach, *Munich* 20 A2
Mora, *Mumbai* 20 B2
Moratalaz, *Madrid* 17 B2
Mörby, *Stockholm* 28 A2
Morden, *London* 15 B2
Morée →, *Paris* 23 A3
Morgan Park, *Chicago* 9 C3
Moriguchi, *Osaka* 22 A4
Morivione, *Milan* 18 B2
Morningside, *Edinburgh* 11 B2
Morningside, *Johannesburg* 13 A2
Morningside, *Washington* 32 C4
Morro Solar, Cerro, *Lima* 16 C2
Mortlake, *London* 15 B2
Mortlake, *Sydney* 28 B1
Morton Grove, *Chicago* 9 A2
Morumbi, *São Paulo* 26 B1
Moscavide, *Lisbon* 14 A2
Moscow = Moskva, *Moscow* 19 B3
Moskhaton, *Athens* 2 B2
Moskva, *Moscow* 19 B3
Moskva →, *Moscow* 19 B2
Moskvoretskiy, *Moscow* 19 B3
Mosman, *Sydney* 28 A2
Móstoles, *Madrid* 17 C1
Moti Bagh, *Delhi* 10 B2
Motol, *Prague* 24 B1
Motsa, *Jerusalem* 13 B2
Motsa Ilit, *Jerusalem* 13 B1
Motspur Park, *London* 15 B2
Mottingham, *London* 15 B4
Moulin Rouge, *Paris* 23 a3
Mount Dennis, *Toronto* 30 A2
Mount Greenwood, *Chicago* 9 C2
Mount Hood Memorial Park, *Boston* 6 A3
Mount Merrion, *Dublin* 11 B2
Mount Rainier, *Washington* 32 B4
Mount Vernon, *New York* 21 A3
Mount Vernon Square, *Washington* 32 a2
Mount Zion, *Jerusalem* 13 b3
Mozarthaus, *Vienna* 31 b2
Müggelberge, *Berlin* 5 B4
Müggelheim, *Berlin* 5 B5
Muggiò, *Milan* 18 A2
Mughal Gardens, *Delhi* 1 c1
Mühleiten, *Vienna* 31 A3
Mühlenfliess →, *Berlin* 5 A5
Muiden, *Amsterdam* 2 A3
Muiderpoort Station, *Amsterdam* 2 b3
Muizenberg, *Cape Town* 8 B1
Mujahidpur, *Delhi* 10 B2
Mukandpur, *Delhi* 10 A2
Mukhmas, *Jerusalem* 13 A2
Muko →, *Osaka* 22 A3
Mukojima, *Tokyo* 29 A3
Mulbarton, *Johannesburg* 13 B2
Mumbai, *Mumbai* 20 B2
Mumbai Harbour, *Mumbai* 20 B2
Münchehofe, *Berlin* 5 B5
München, *Munich* 20 B2
Munich = München, *Munich* 20 B2
Munkkiniemi, *Helsinki* 12 B2
Munro, *Buenos Aires* 7 B1
Murai Res., *Singapore* 27 A2
Muranów, *Warsaw* 31 B1
Murino, *St. Petersburg* 26 B2
Murrayfield, *Edinburgh* 11 B2
Musashino, *Tokyo* 29 A2
Museu Nacional, *Rio de Janeiro* 24 B1
Mushin, *Lagos* 14 A2
Musiektheater, *Amsterdam* 2 b2
Muslim Quarter, *Jerusalem* 13 a3
Musocco, *Milan* 18 B1
Mustansirīya, *Baghdad* 3 A2
Musturud, *Cairo* 7 A2
Muswell Hill, *London* 15 A3
Mutanabi, *Baghdad* 3 B2
Muthana, *Baghdad* 3 B2
Myakinino, *Moscow* 19 B2
Mykerinos, *Cairo* 7 B1
Myllypuro, *Helsinki* 12 B3

N

Nacka, *Stockholm* 28 B3
Nada, *Osaka* 22 A2
Naenae, *Wellington* 32 B2
Nærsnes, *Oslo* 22 B1
Nagata, *Osaka* 22 B1
Nagatsuta, *Tokyo* 29 B2
Nagytétény, *Budapest* 7 B1
Nahant, *Boston* 6 A4
Nahant B., *Boston* 6 A4
Nahant Harbor, *Boston* 6 A4
Nahr Dijlah →, *Baghdad* 3 B2
Najafgarh Drain →, *Delhi* 10 B1
Nakahara-Ku, *Tokyo* 29 B2
Nakano-Ku, *Tokyo* 29 A2
Namgajwa, *Seoul* 26 B1
Namsan Park, *Seoul* 26 B1
Namyŏng, *Seoul* 26 B1
Nanbiancun, *Canton* 8 B1
Nanchang He →, *Beijing* 4 B1
Nandang, *Canton* 8 B2
Nandian, *Tianjin* 30 A2
Nangal Dewat, *Delhi* 10 B1
Naniwa, *Osaka* 22 B3
Nankai, *Tianjin* 30 B1
Nanmenwai, *Tianjin* 30 B2
Nanole, *Mumbai* 20 A2
Nanpu Bridge, *Shanghai* 27 B2
Nanshi, *Shanghai* 27 B1
Nantasket Beach, *Boston* 6 B4
Nanterre, *Paris* 23 A2
Naoabad, *Calcutta* 8 C2
Napier Mole, *Karachi* 14 B1
Naraina, *Delhi* 10 B1
Nariman Point, *Mumbai* 20 c1
Nariman Pt., *Mumbai* 20 B1
Nārmak, *Tehran* 30 A2
Naruo, *Osaka* 22 A3
Näsby, *Stockholm* 28 A2
Näsbypark, *Stockholm* 28 A2
Nathan Road, *Hong Kong* 12 a2
Natick, *Boston* 6 B2
National Maritime Museum, *San Francisco* 25 a1
National Museum, *Bangkok* 3 b1
Nationalmuseum, *Stockholm* 28 b2
Natolin, *Warsaw* 31 C2
Naturhistorischesmuseum, *Vienna* 31 b1
Naucalpan de Juárez, *Mexico City* 18 B1
Naupada, *Mumbai* 20 A2
Navíglio di Pavia, *Milan* 18 B1
Navíglio Grande, *Milan* 18 B1
Navona, Piazza, *Rome* 25 b2
Navotas, *Manila* 17 B1
Navy Pier, *Chicago* 9 b3
Nazal Hikmat Beg, *Baghdad* 3 A2
Nazimabad, *Karachi* 14 A2
Nazlet el Simmân, *Cairo* 7 B1
Néa Alexandhria, *Athens* 2 B2
Néa Faliron, *Athens* 2 B1
Néa Ionía, *Athens* 2 A2
Néa Liósia, *Athens* 2 A2
Néa Smírni, *Athens* 2 B2
Neapolis, *Athens* 2 B2
Near North, *Chicago* 9 b2
Nebušice, *Prague* 24 B1
Nederhorst, *Amsterdam* 2 B3
Nedlitz, *Berlin* 5 B1
Nee Soon, *Singapore* 27 A2
Needham Heights, *Boston* 6 B2
Nekrasovka, *Moscow* 19 B5
N'ematābād, *Tehran* 30 B2
Nemchinovka, *Moscow* 19 B1
Nemzeti Muz, *Budapest* 7 c3
Neponsit, *New York* 21 C2
Nerima-Ku, *Tokyo* 29 A3
Nesodden, *Oslo* 22 B3
Nesoddtangen, *Oslo* 22 A3
Nesøya, *Oslo* 22 A2
Neu Aubing, *Munich* 20 B1
Neu Buch, *Berlin* 5 A4
Neu Buchhorst, *Berlin* 5 B5
Neu Fahrland, *Berlin* 5 B1
Neu Lindenberg, *Berlin* 5 A4
Neubiberg, *Munich* 20 B3
Neue Hofburg, *Vienna* 31 b1
Neuenhagen, *Berlin* 5 A4
Neuessling, *Vienna* 31 A3
Neuhausen, *Munich* 20 B2
Neuherberg, *Munich* 20 A2
Neuhönow, *Berlin* 5 A5
Neuilly-Plaisance, *Paris* 23 A4
Neuilly-sur-Marne, *Paris* 23 A4
Neuilly-sur-Seine, *Paris* 23 A2
Neukagran, *Vienna* 31 A2
Neukettenhof, *Vienna* 31 B2
Neukölln, *Berlin* 5 B3
Neuperlach, *Munich* 20 B2
Neuried, *Munich* 20 B1
Neustift am Walde, *Vienna* 31 A1
Neusüssenbrunn, *Vienna* 31 A2
Neuwaldegg, *Vienna* 31 A1
Neva →, *St. Petersburg* 26 B2
Neves, *Rio de Janeiro* 24 B2
New Baghdād, *Baghdad* 3 B2
New Barakpur, *Calcutta* 8 A2
New Brighton, *New York* 21 C1
New Canada, *Johannesburg* 13 B1
New Canada Dam, *Johannesburg* 13 B1
New Carrollton, *Washington* 32 B4
New Cross, *London* 15 B3
New Delhi, *Delhi* 10 B2
New Dorp, *New York* 21 C1
New Dorp Beach, *New York* 21 C1
New Malden, *London* 15 B2
New Milford, *New York* 21 A1
New Territories, *Hong Kong* 12 A1
New Toronto, *Toronto* 30 B1
New Town, *Edinburgh* 11 B2
New Utrecht, *New York* 21 C2
Newark B., *New York* 21 B1
Newbattle, *Edinburgh* 11 B3
Newbury Park, *London* 15 A4
Newcraighall, *Edinburgh* 11 B3
Newham, *London* 15 A4
Newhaven, *Edinburgh* 11 B2
Newington, *Edinburgh* 11 B2
Newington, *London* 15 c5
Newlands, *Johannesburg* 13 B1
Newlands, *Wellington* 32 B1
Newport, *Melbourne* 17 B1
Newton, *Boston* 6 B2
Newtonbrook, *Toronto* 30 A2
Newtongrange, *Edinburgh* 11 B3
Newtonville, *Boston* 6 A2
Newtown, *Sydney* 28 B2
Neyagawa, *Osaka* 22 A4
Ngaio, *Wellington* 32 B1
Ngau Chi Wan, *Hong Kong* 12 A2
Ngau Tau Kok, *Hong Kong* 12 B2
Ngauranga, *Wellington* 32 B1
Ngong Shuen Chau, *Hong Kong* 12 B1
Ngua Kok Wan, *Hong Kong* 12 A1
Nīāvarān, *Tehran* 30 A2
Nibra, *Calcutta* 8 B1
Nidāl, *Baghdad* 3 B2
Niddrie, *Edinburgh* 11 B3
Niddrie, *Melbourne* 17 A1
Nieder Neuendorf, *Berlin* 5 A2
Niederschöneweide, *Berlin* 5 B3
Niederschönhausen, *Berlin* 5 A3
Niemeyer, *Rio de Janeiro* 24 B1
Nieuw Zuid, *Amsterdam* 2 c2
Nieuwe Kerk, *Amsterdam* 2 b2
Nieuwendam, *Amsterdam* 2 A2
Nihonbashi, *Tokyo* 29 b5
Niipperi, *Helsinki* 12 B1
Níkaia, *Athens* 2 B1
Nikolassee, *Berlin* 5 B2
Nikolskiy, *Moscow* 19 B2
Nikolyskoye, *Moscow* 19 B5
Nikulino, *Moscow* 19 B2
Nil, Nahr en →, *Cairo* 7 B2
Nile = Nil, Nahr en →, *Cairo* 7 B2
Niles, *Chicago* 9 A2
Nimta, *Calcutta* 8 A2
Ningyuan, *Tianjin* 30 B2
Nippa, *Tokyo* 29 B2
Nippori, *Tokyo* 29 A3
Nishi, *Osaka* 22 A3
Nishinari, *Osaka* 22 B3
Nishiyodogawa, *Osaka* 22 A3
Niterói, *Rio de Janeiro* 24 B2
Nob Hill, *San Francisco* 25 b1
Nockeby, *Stockholm* 28 B1
Noel Park, *London* 15 A3
Nogatino, *Moscow* 19 B4
Nogent-sur-Marne, *Paris* 23 A3
Noida, *Delhi* 10 B2
Noiseau, *Paris* 23 B4
Noisiel, *Paris* 23 A4
Noisy-le-Grand, *Paris* 23 A4
Noisy-le-Roi, *Paris* 23 A1
Noisy-le-Sec, *Paris* 23 A3
Nokkala, *Helsinki* 12 C1
Nomentano, *Rome* 25 B2
Nonakashinden, *Tokyo* 29 A2
Nongminyundong Jiangxisuo, *Canton* 8 B2
Nonhyŏn, *Seoul* 26 B2
Nonthaburi, *Bangkok* 3 A1
Noon Gun, *Cape Town* 8 b1
Noorder Kerk, *Amsterdam* 2 a1
Noordgesig, *Johannesburg* 13 B1
Noordzeekanaal, *Amsterdam* 2 A1
Nord, Gare du, *Paris* 23 a4
Nordrand-Siedlung, *Vienna* 31 A2
Nordstrand, *Oslo* 22 A3
Normandale, *Wellington* 32 B2
Nørrebro, *Copenhagen* 10 a1
Norridge, *Chicago* 9 B2
Norrmalm, *Stockholm* 28 a1
North Arlington, *New York* 21 B1
North Bay Village, *Miami* 18 A2
North Bergen, *New York* 21 B1
North Branch Chicago River →, *Chicago* 9 B2
North Bull Island, *Dublin* 11 A3
North Cambridge, *Boston* 6 A3
North Cheam, *London* 15 B2
North Cohasset, *Boston* 6 B4
North Cray, *London* 15 B4
North Decatur, *Atlanta* 3 B3
North Druid Hills, *Atlanta* 3 B3
North Esk →, *Edinburgh* 11 B2
North Gyle, *Edinburgh* 11 B2
North Hackensack, *New York* 21 A1
North Harbor, *Manila* 17 B1
North Hd., *Sydney* 28 A2
North Hollywood, *Los Angeles* 16 B2
North Lexington, *Boston* 6 A2
North Miami, *Miami* 18 A2
North Miami Beach, *Miami* 18 A2
North Nazimabad, *Karachi* 14 A2
North Pt., *Hong Kong* 12 B2
North Queensferry, *Edinburgh* 11 A1
North Quincy, *Boston* 6 B3
North Res., *Boston* 6 A3
North Riverside, *Chicago* 9 B2
North Saugus, *Boston* 6 A3
North Shore Channel →, *Chicago* 9 B2
North Springfield, *Washington* 32 C2
North Sudbury, *Boston* 6 A1
North Sydney, *Sydney* 28 B2
North Woolwich, *London* 15 A4
North York, *Toronto* 30 A2
Northbridge, *Sydney* 28 A2
Northbridge Park, *Sydney* 28 A2
Northcliff, *Johannesburg* 13 A1
Northcote, *Melbourne* 17 A2
Northlake, *Chicago* 9 B1
Northmount, *Toronto* 30 A2
Northolt, *London* 15 A1
Northumberland Heath, *London* 15 B5
Northwood, *London* 15 A1
Norumbega Res., *Boston* 6 B2
Norwood, *Johannesburg* 13 A2
Norwood Park, *Chicago* 9 B2
Noryangjin, *Seoul* 26 B1
Nossa Senhora de Candelária, *Rio de Janeiro* 24 a2
Nossa Senhora do Ó, *São Paulo* 26 B1
Nossegem, *Brussels* 6 A3
Notre-Dame, *Montreal* 19 B3
Notre-Dame, *Paris* 23 c4
Notre-Dame, Bois, *Paris* 23 B4
Notre-Dame-de-Grace, *Montreal* 19 B2
Notting Hill, *London* 15 b1
Nova Milanese, *Milan* 18 A2
Novate Milanese, *Milan* 18 A1
Novaya Derevnya, *St. Petersburg* 26 A1
Nové Město, *Prague* 24 B2
Novoaleksandrovskoye, *St. Petersburg* 26 B2
Novogireyevo, *Moscow* 19 B4
Novoivanovskoye, *Moscow* 19 B1
Novonikolyskoye, *Moscow* 19 A1
Novosaratovka, *St. Petersburg* 26 B3
Nowe-Babice, *Warsaw* 31 B1
Nöykkiö, *Helsinki* 12 B1
Nueva Atzacoalco, *Mexico City* 18 B2
Nueva Pompeya, *Buenos Aires* 7 C2
Nueva Tenochtitlán, *Mexico City* 18 B2
Nuijala, *Helsinki* 12 B1
Numabukuro, *Tokyo* 29 A2
Nunez, *Buenos Aires* 7 B2
Nunhead, *London* 15 B3
Ñuñoa, *Santiago* 26 B2
Nusle, *Prague* 24 B2
Nussdorf, *Vienna* 31 A2
Nyanga, *Cape Town* 8 A2
Nymphenburg, *Munich* 20 B2
Nymphenburg, Schloss, *Munich* 20 B2

O

Oak Grove, *Atlanta* 3 A3
Oak Island, *Boston* 6 A4
Oak Lawn, *Chicago* 9 C2
Oak Park, *Chicago* 9 B2
Oak View, *Washington* 32 A4
Oakdale, *Atlanta* 3 A2
Oakland, *San Francisco* 25 B3
Oakland, *Washington* 32 B4
Oaklawn, *Washington* 32 C4
Oakleigh, *Melbourne* 17 B2
Oakton, *Washington* 32 B2
Oakwood Beach, *New York* 21 C1
Oatley, *Sydney* 28 B1
Obalende, *Lagos* 14 B2
Oba's Palace, *Lagos* 14 B2
Oberföhring, *Munich* 20 B2
Oberhaching, *Munich* 20 B2
Oberlaa, *Vienna* 31 B2
Oberlisse, *Vienna* 31 A2
Obermenzing, *Munich* 20 A1
Obermoos Schwaige, *Munich* 20 A1
Oberschleissheim, *Munich* 20 A2
Oberschöneweide, *Berlin* 5 B4
Observatory, *Johannesburg* 13 B2
Observatory, *Sydney* 28 a1
Ōbu, *Osaka* 22 A1
Obu-tōge, *Osaka* 22 A1
Óbuda, *Budapest* 7 A2
Obukhovo, *St. Petersburg* 26 B2
Obvodnyy Kanal, *St. Petersburg* 26 B1
Ocean Park, *Hong Kong* 12 B2
Ochakovo, *Moscow* 19 B2
Ochota, *Warsaw* 31 B1
O'Connell Street, *Dublin* 11 b2
Ōdana, *Tokyo* 29 B2
Öden-Stockach, *Munich* 20 B3
Odilampi, *Helsinki* 12 B1
Odintsovo, *Moscow* 19 B1
Odivelas, *Lisbon* 14 A1
Odolany, *Warsaw* 31 B1
Oeiras, *Lisbon* 14 A1
Ofin, *Lagos* 14 A3
Ogawa, *Tokyo* 29 A1
Ogden Park, *Chicago* 9 C2
Ogikubo, *Tokyo* 29 A2
Ogogoro, *Lagos* 14 B2
Ogoyo, *Lagos* 14 B2
Ogudu, *Lagos* 14 A2
Ohariu Stream →, *Wellington* 32 B1
O'Higgins, Parque, *Santiago* 26 B2
Ōimachi, *Tokyo* 29 B3
Ojota, *Lagos* 14 A2
Okamoto, *Osaka* 22 A2
Okęcie, *Warsaw* 31 B1
Okęcie Airport, *Warsaw* 31 B1
Okelra, *Lagos* 14 B2
Okeogbe, *Lagos* 14 B2
Okha, *Delhi* 10 B2
Okhta →, *St. Petersburg* 26 B2
Okkervil →, *St. Petersburg* 26 B2
Okrzeszyn, *Warsaw* 31 C2
Oksval, *Oslo* 22 A3
Oktyabrskiy, *Moscow* 19 B3
Ōkubo, *Tokyo* 29 a2
Ōkura, *Tokyo* 29 B1
Olari, *Helsinki* 12 B1
Olaria, *Rio de Janeiro* 24 B1
Old Admiralty, *St. Petersburg* 26 B1
Old City, *Delhi* 1 a3
Old City, *Jerusalem* 13 b3
Old City, *Shanghai* 27 B1
Old Fort = Purana Qila, *Delhi* 1 c3
Old Harbor, *Boston* 6 B3
Old Town, *Chicago* 9 B3
Old Town, *Edinburgh* 11 B2
Oldbawn, *Dublin* 11 B1
Olgino, *St. Petersburg* 26 A1
Olimpico, Estadio, *Mexico City* 18 C1
Olivais, *Lisbon* 14 A2
Olivar de los Padres, *Mexico City* 18 B1
Olivar del Conde, *Mexico City* 18 B1
Olivos, *Buenos Aires* 7 B2
Olona →, *Milan* 18 B1
Olympia, *London* 15 c1
Olympic Stadium, *Helsinki* 12 B2
Olympique, Stade, *Montreal* 19 A2
Omonias, Pl., *Athens* 2 b1
Ōmori, *Tokyo* 29 B3
Onchi, *Osaka* 22 B4
Onchi →, *Osaka* 22 B4
Onisigun, *Lagos* 14 A2
Ōokayama, *Tokyo* 29 B3
Oosterpark, *Amsterdam* 2 b3
Oostzaan, *Amsterdam* 2 A2
Opa-Locka, *Miami* 18 A1
Opa-Locka Airport, *Miami* 18 A1
Opacz, *Warsaw* 31 B1
Opera House, *Sydney* 28 a2
Ophirton, *Johannesburg* 13 B2
Oppegård, *Oslo* 22 B3
Oppem, *Brussels* 6 A1
Oppsal, *Oslo* 22 A4
Ora, *Jerusalem* 13 B1
Oradell, *New York* 21 A1
Orange Bowl Stadium, *Miami* 18 B2
Orangi, *Karachi* 14 A2
Orchard Road, *Singapore* 27 a1
Ordrup, *Copenhagen* 10 A3
Orech, *Prague* 24 B1
Øresund, *Copenhagen* 10 A3
Orient Heights, *Boston* 6 A4
Orlando Dam, *Johannesburg* 13 B1
Orlando East, *Johannesburg* 13 B1
Orlovo, *Moscow* 19 C2
Orly, *Paris* 23 B3
Ormesson-sur-Marne, *Paris* 23 B4
Ormond, *Melbourne* 17 B2
Ormøya, *Oslo* 22 A3
Orpington, *London* 15 B4
Orsay, Musée d', *Paris* 23 b3
Országház, *Budapest* 7 b2
Országos Levétár, *Budapest* 7 b1
Ortaköy, *Istanbul* 12 B2
Ortica, *Milan* 18 B2
Oruba, *Lagos* 14 A2
Orvostörteneti Múz., *Budapest* 7 c2
Ōsaka, *Osaka* 22 B4
Osaka B., *Osaka* 22 B2
Osaka Castle, *Osaka* 22 A4
Osaka Harbour, *Osaka* 22 B3
Osaka International Airport, *Osaka* 22 A3
Ōsaki, *Tokyo* 29 B3
Osasco, *São Paulo* 26 B1
Osdorf, *Berlin* 5 B3
Osdorp, *Amsterdam* 2 A1
Oshodi, *Lagos* 14 A2
Oslo, *Oslo* 22 A3
Oslofjorden, *Oslo* 22 B2
Ōsone, *Tokyo* 29 B2
Osorun, *Lagos* 14 A2
Ospiate, *Milan* 18 A1
Ostankino, *Moscow* 19 B3
Östasiatiskamuséet, *Stockholm* 28 b3
Österalm, *Stockholm* 28 a3
Østerbro, *Copenhagen* 10 a1
Osterley, *London* 15 B1
Osterley Park, *London* 15 B1
Östermalm, *Stockholm* 28 A2
Österskär, *Stockholm* 28 A3
Ostiense, *Rome* 25 B1
Østmarkkapellet, *Oslo* 22 A4
Ostøya, *Oslo* 22 A2
Østre Aker, *Oslo* 22 A3
Ōta-Ku, *Tokyo* 29 B3
Otaniemi, *Helsinki* 12 B1
Otari Open Air Museum, *Wellington* 32 B1
Otsuka, *Tokyo* 29 A3
Ottakring, *Vienna* 31 A1
Ottávia, *Rome* 25 B1
Ottery, *Cape Town* 8 B2
Ottobrunn, *Munich* 20 B3
Oud Zuid, *Amsterdam* 2 b1
Oude Kerk, *Amsterdam* 2 b2
Ouderkerk, *Amsterdam* 2 B2
Oulunkylä, *Helsinki* 12 B2
Ourcq, Canal de l', *Paris* 23 A3
Outer Mission, *San Francisco* 25 B2
Outremont, *Montreal* 19 A2
Overijse, *Brussels* 6 B3
Owhiro Bay, *Wellington* 32 C1
Oworonsoki, *Lagos* 14 A2
Oxford Street, *London* 15 b3
Oxgangs, *Edinburgh* 11 B2
Oxon Hill, *Washington* 32 C4
Oyodo, *Osaka* 22 A3
Oyster B., *Sydney* 28 C1
Oyster Rock, *Mumbai* 20 B1
Oyster Rocks, *Karachi* 14 B2
Ozoir-la-Ferrière, *Paris* 23 B4
Ozone Park, *New York* 21 B2

P

Pacific Heights, *San Francisco* 25 B2
Pacific Manor, *San Francisco* 25 C2
Pacific Palisades, *Los Angeles* 16 B1
Pacifica, *San Francisco* 25 C2
Paco, *Manila* 17 B1
Paco de Arcos, *Lisbon* 14 A1
Paco Imperial, *Rio de Janeiro* 24 a2
Paddington, *London* 15 b2
Paddington, *Sydney* 28 B2
Paderno, *Milan* 18 A1
Pagewood, *Sydney* 28 B2
Pagote, *Mumbai* 20 B2
Pai, I. do, *Rio de Janeiro* 24 B2
Pak Kong, *Hong Kong* 12 A2
Pakila, *Helsinki* 12 B2
Palacio de Bellas Artes, *Mexico City* 18 b2
Palacio de Communicaciones, *Madrid* 17 a3
Palacio Nacional, *Mexico City* 18 b3
Palacio Real, *Barcelona* 4 b3
Palacio Real, *Madrid* 17 b1
Palaión Fáliron, *Athens* 2 B2
Palais de Justice, *Brussels* 6 c2
Palais Royal, *Paris* 23 b4
Palais Royale, *Brussels* 6 b3
Palaiseau, *Paris* 23 B2
Palau Nacional Museu d'Art, *Barcelona* 4 c1
Palazzolo, *Milan* 18 A1
Palermo, *Buenos Aires* 7 B2
Palhais, *Lisbon* 14 B2
Palisades Park, *New York* 21 A1
Palmer Park, *Washington* 32 B4
Palmerston, *Dublin* 11 A1
Paloheinä, *Helsinki* 12 B2
Palomeras, *Madrid* 17 B2
Palos Heights, *Chicago* 9 D2
Palos Hills, *Chicago* 9 C2
Palos Hills Forest, *Chicago* 9 C1
Palos Park, *Chicago* 9 C1
Palpara, *Calcutta* 8 B2
Panchur, *Calcutta* 8 B1
Pandacan, *Manila* 17 B2
Pandan, Selat, *Singapore* 27 B2
Pandan Res., *Singapore* 27 B2
Panepistimio, *Athens* 2 b2
Pangbae, *Seoul* 26 C1
Pangrati, *Athens* 2 B2
Pangsua, Sungei →, *Singapore* 27 A2
Panihati, *Calcutta* 8 A2
Panjang, Bukit, *Singapore* 27 A2
Panje, *Mumbai* 20 B2
Panke →, *Berlin* 5 A3
Pankow, *Berlin* 5 A3
Panthéon, *Paris* 23 c4
Pantheon, *Rome* 25 b2
Pantin, *Paris* 23 A3
Pantitlán, *Mexico City* 18 B2
Panvel Cr. →, *Mumbai* 20 B2
Paparangi, *Wellington* 32 B1
Papiol, *Barcelona* 4 A1
Paramus, *New York* 21 A1
Paranaque, *Manila* 17 B1
Paray-Vieille-Poste, *Paris* 23 B3
Parco Regionale, *Milan* 18 A1
Parel, *Mumbai* 20 B1
Pari, *São Paulo* 26 B2
Parioli, *Rome* 25 B1
Paris, *Paris* 23 A3
Paris-Orly, Aéroport de, *Paris* 23 B3
Pārk-e Mellat, *Tehran* 30 A2
Park Ridge, *Chicago* 9 A1
Park Royal, *London* 15 A2
Parkchester, *New York* 21 B2
Parkdale, *Toronto* 30 B2
Parkhurst, *Johannesburg* 13 A2
Parklawn, *Washington* 32 B3
Parkmore, *Johannesburg* 13 A2
Parkside, *San Francisco* 25 B2
Parktown, *Johannesburg* 13 B2
Parktown North, *Johannesburg* 13 A2
Parkview, *Johannesburg* 13 A2
Parkville, *New York* 21 C2
Parkwood, *Cape Town* 8 B1
Parkwood, *Johannesburg* 13 A2
Parow, *Cape Town* 8 A2
Parque Chabuco, *Buenos Aires* 7 B2
Parque Patricios, *Buenos Aires* 7 B2
Parramatta →, *Sydney* 28 A1
Parthenon, *Athens* 2 c2
Paşabahçe, *Istanbul* 12 B2
Pasadena, *Los Angeles* 16 B4
Pasar Minggu, *Jakarta* 13 B1
Pasay, *Manila* 17 B1
Pascoe Vale, *Melbourne* 17 A1
Paseo de la Reforma, *Mexico City* 18 b2
Pasig, *Manila* 17 B2
Pasig →, *Manila* 17 B2
Pasila, *Helsinki* 12 B2
Pasing, *Munich* 20 B1
Pasir Panjang, *Singapore* 27 B2
Pasir Ris, *Singapore* 27 A3
Passaic →, *New York* 21 B1
Passirana, *Milan* 18 A1
Patel Nagar, *Delhi* 10 B1
Pateros, *Manila* 17 B2
Pathersville, *Atlanta* 3 B3
Pathumwan, *Bangkok* 3 B2
Patipukur, *Calcutta* 8 B2
Patisia, *Athens* 2 A2
Paulo E. Virginia, Gruta, *Rio de Janeiro* 24 B1
Paulshof, *Berlin* 5 A5
Pavshino, *Moscow* 19 B1
Paya Lebar, *Singapore* 27 A3
Peachtree →, *Atlanta* 3 B2
Peakhurst, *Sydney* 28 B1
Peania, *Athens* 2 B3
Peckham, *London* 15 B3
Peddocks I., *Boston* 6 B4
Pederstrup, *Copenhagen* 10 A2
Pedralbes, *Barcelona* 4 A1
Pedregal de San Angel, Jardines del, *Mexico City* 18 C1
Pekhorka →, *Moscow* 19 C6
Pekhra-Pokrovskoye, *Moscow* 19 A5
Pekhra-Yakovievskaya, *Moscow* 19 B5
Peking = Beijing, *Beijing* 4 B1
Pelcowizna, *Warsaw* 31 B2
Pelopónnisos Sta., *Athens* 2 a1
Penalolén, *Santiago* 26 B2
Pencarrow Hd., *Wellington* 32 C2
Peng Siang →, *Singapore* 27 A2
Penge, *London* 15 B3
Penha, *Rio de Janeiro* 24 A1
Penicuik, *Edinburgh* 11 B2
Penjaringan, *Jakarta* 13 A1
Penn Station, *New York* 21 c2
Pennsylvania Avenue, *Washington* 32 b1
Pentland Hills, *Edinburgh* 11 B1
Penyagino, *Moscow* 19 A2
Penzing, *Vienna* 31 A1
People's Park, *Shanghai* 27 B1
People's Square, *Shanghai* 27 B1
Perales del Rio, *Madrid* 17 C2
Peravillo, *Mexico City* 18 a3
Perchtoldsdorf, *Vienna* 31 B1
Perdizes, *São Paulo* 26 B2
Peredelkino, *Moscow* 19 C2
Pergamon Museum, *Berlin* 5 a4
Peristérion, *Athens* 2 A2
Perivale, *London* 15 A2
Perk, *Brussels* 6 A2
Perlach, *Munich* 20 B2
Perlacher Forst, *Munich* 20 B2
Pero, *Milan* 18 A1
Peropok, Bukit, *Singapore* 27 B2
Perovo, *Moscow* 19 B4
Pershing Square, *Los Angeles* 16 c1
Pertusella, *Milan* 18 A1
Pesagot, *Jerusalem* 13 A2
Pesanggrahag, Kali →, *Jakarta* 13 B1
Peschiera Borromeo, *Milan* 18 B2
Pesek, P., *Singapore* 27 B2
Pest, *Budapest* 7 B2
Pesterzsébet, *Budapest* 7 B2
Pesthidegkút, *Budapest* 7 A1
Pestimre, *Budapest* 7 B3
Pestlörinc, *Budapest* 7 B3
Pestújhely, *Budapest* 7 A2
Petas, *Helsinki* 12 B2
Petone, *Wellington* 32 B2
Petrogradskaya Storona, *St. Petersburg* 26 B2
Petroúpolis, *Athens* 2 A2
Petrovice, *Prague* 24 B3
Petrovskiy Park, *Moscow* 19 B3
Petrovsko-Razumovskoye, *Moscow* 19 B3
Pettycur, *Edinburgh* 11 A2
Peutie, *Brussels* 6 A2
Pfaueninsel, *Berlin* 5 B1
Phaya Thai, *Bangkok* 3 B2
Phihai, *Karachi* 14 A2
Phillip B., *Sydney* 28 B2
Phoenix Park, *Dublin* 11 A2
Phra Khanong, *Bangkok* 3 B2
Phra Pradaeng, *Bangkok* 3 C2
Phranakhon, *Bangkok* 3 B1
Picasso, Museu, *Barcelona* 4 c2
Piccadilly, *London* 15 b3
Pico Rivera, *Los Angeles* 16 C4
Piedade, *Lisbon* 14 A1
Piedade, *Rio de Janeiro* 24 B1
Piedade, Cova da, *Lisbon* 14 A2
Piedmont Park, *Atlanta* 3 B2
Pietralata, *Rome* 25 B2
Pihlajamäki, *Helsinki* 12 B2
Pihlajasaari, *Helsinki* 12 C2
Pilares, *Rio de Janeiro* 24 B1
Pilton, *Edinburgh* 11 B2
Pimlico, *London* 15 c3
Pimmit Hills, *Washington* 32 B2
Pine Grove, *Toronto* 30 A1
Pinewood, *Miami* 18 A2
Piney Run →, *Washington* 32 B2
Pinganli, *Beijing* 4 B2
Pingzhou, *Canton* 8 B2
Pinheiros →, *São Paulo* 26 B1
Pinjrapur, *Karachi* 14 A2
Pinner, *London* 15 A1
Pinner Green, *London* 15 A1
Pioltello, *Milan* 18 A2
Pipinui Pt., *Wellington* 32 A1
Piraévs, *Athens* 2 B1
Pirajuçara →, *São Paulo* 26 B1
Pirinççi, *Istanbul* 12 B1
Pirituba, *São Paulo* 26 A1
Pirkkola, *Helsinki* 12 B2
Písnice, *Prague* 24 C2
Pitampura, *Delhi* 10 A1
Pitkäjärvi, *Helsinki* 12 B1
Planegg, *Munich* 20 B1
Plumstead, *Cape Town* 8 B1
Plumstead, *London* 15 B4
Plyushchevo, *Moscow* 19 B4
Pníka, *Athens* 2 c1
Po Toi I., *Hong Kong* 12 B2
Po Toi O, *Hong Kong* 12 B2
Poasco, *Milan* 18 B2
Podbaba, *Prague* 24 B2
Podoli, *Prague* 24 B2
Poduskino, *Moscow* 19 B1
Pointe-Aux-Trembles, *Montreal* 19 A2
Poissy, *Paris* 23 A1
Pok Fu Lam, *Hong Kong* 12 B1
Pokrovsko-Sresnevo, *Moscow* 19 B2
Polton, *Edinburgh* 11 B3
Polyustrovo, *St. Petersburg* 26 B2
Pompidou, Centre, *Paris* 23 b4
Pomprap, *Bangkok* 3 B2
Pondok Indah, *Jakarta* 13 B1
Pont-Viau, *Montreal* 19 A1
Ponta do Marisco, *Rio de Janeiro* 24 C1
Pontault-Combault, *Paris* 23 B4
Pontinha, *Lisbon* 14 A1
Poplar, *London* 15 A3
Popolo, Porta del, *Rome* 25 a2
Poppintree, *Dublin* 11 A2
Porirua, *Wellington* 32 A2
Porirua East, *Wellington* 32 A2
Port I., *Osaka* 22 A2
Port Melbourne, *Melbourne* 17 B1
Port Nicholson, *Wellington* 32 B2
Port Philip Bay, *Melbourne* 17 B1
Port Richmond, *New York* 21 C1
Port Shelter, *Hong Kong* 12 A2
Port Union, *Toronto* 30 A4
Portage Park, *Chicago* 9 B2
Portal de la Pau, Pl., *Barcelona* 4 c2
Portela, Aeroporto da, *Lisbon* 14 A2
Portmarnock, *Dublin* 11 A3
Porto Brandão, *Lisbon* 14 A1
Porto Novo, *Rio de Janeiro* 24 A2
Porto Novo Cr. →, *Lagos* 14 B2
Portobello, *Edinburgh* 11 B3
Portrero, *San Francisco* 25 B3
Potomac, *Washington* 32 A2
Potomac →, *Washington* 32 B3
Potrero Pt., *San Francisco* 25 B2
Potsdam, *Berlin* 5 B1
Potsdamer Platz, *Berlin* 5 b3
Potzham, *Munich* 20 B2
Pötzleinsdorf, *Vienna* 31 A1
Povoa de Santo Adriao, *Lisbon* 14 A2
Powązki, *Warsaw* 31 B1
Powiśle, *Warsaw* 31 B2
Powsin, *Warsaw* 31 C2
Powsinek, *Warsaw* 31 C2
Poyan Res., *Singapore* 27 A2
Pozuelo de Alarcon, *Madrid* 17 B1
Prado, Museo del, *Madrid* 17 b3
Prado Churubusco, *Mexico City* 18 B2
Praga, *Warsaw* 31 B2
Prague = Praha, *Prague* 24 B2
Praha, *Prague* 24 B2
Praha-Ruzyně Airport, *Prague* 24 B1
Praires, R. des →, *Montreal* 19 A2
Prater, *Vienna* 31 A2
Precotto, *Milan* 18 A2
Prenestino Labicano, *Rome* 25 B2
Prenzlauerberg, *Berlin* 5 A3
Preston, *Melbourne* 17 A1
Pretos Forros, Sa. dos, *Rio de Janeiro* 24 B1
Préville, *Montreal* 19 B3
Přezletice, *Prague* 24 B3
Prima Porta, *Rome* 25 B1
Primavalle, *Rome* 25 B1
Primrose, *Johannesburg* 13 B2
Princes Street, *Edinburgh* 11 b2
Printer's Row, *Chicago* 9 d2
Progreso Nacional, *Mexico City* 18 A2
Prosek, *Prague* 24 B3
Prospect Hill Park, *Boston* 6 A2
Providencia, *Santiago* 26 B2
Prudential Building, *Chicago* 9 c2
Průhonice, *Prague* 24 C3
Psikhikón, *Athens* 2 A2
Pudong New Area, *Shanghai* 27 B2
Pueblo Libre, *Lima* 16 B2
Pueblo Nuevo, *Barcelona* 4 A2
Pueblo Nuevo, *Madrid* 17 B2
Puerta del Sol, Plaza, *Madrid* 17 b2
Puerto Madero, *Buenos Aires* 7 B2
Puerto Retiro, *Buenos Aires* 7 B2
Puhuangyu, *Beijing* 4 B2
Puistola, *Helsinki* 12 B3
Pukan-san, *Seoul* 26 B1
Pukinmäki, *Helsinki* 12 B2
Pukkajwa, *Seoul* 26 B1
Pulkovo Int. Airport, *St. Petersburg* 26 C1
Pullach, *Munich* 20 B1
Pulo Gadung, *Jakarta* 13 B2
Pūnak, *Tehran* 30 A2
Punchbowl, *Sydney* 28 B1
Punde, *Mumbai* 20 B2
Punggol, *Singapore* 27 A3
Punggol, Sungei →, *Singapore* 27 A3
Punggol Pt., *Singapore* 27 A3
Punjabi Bagh, *Delhi* 10 A1
Puotila, *Helsinki* 12 B3
Purana Qila, *Delhi* 1 c3
Puteaux, *Paris* 23 A2
Putilkovo, *Moscow* 19 A2
Putney, *London* 15 B2
Putuo, *Shanghai* 27 B1
Putxet, *Barcelona* 4 A1
Puxi, *Shanghai* 27 B1
Pydhuni, *Mumbai* 20 b2
Pyramids, *Cairo* 7 B1
Pyry, *Warsaw* 31 C1

Q

Qalandya, *Jerusalem* 13 A2
Qal'eh Morghī, *Tehran* 30 B2
Qanâ el Ismâ'ilîya, *Cairo* 7 A2
Qāsemābād, *Tehran* 30 A3
Qasr-e Firūzeh, *Tehran* 30 B3
Qatane, *Jerusalem* 13 B1
Qianmen, *Beijing* 4 B2
Qinghuayuan, *Beijing* 4 B1
Qingningsi, *Shanghai* 27 B2
Qolhak, *Tehran* 30 A2
Quadraro, *Rome* 25 B2
Quaid-i-Azam, *Karachi* 14 A1
Quartiere Zingone, *Milan* 18 B1
Quds, *Baghdad* 3 A2
Queen Mary Res., *London* 15 B1
Queen Street, *Edinburgh* 11 a1
Queensbury, *London* 15 A2
Queenscliffe, *Sydney* 28 A2
Queensferry, *Edinburgh* 11 B1
Queenstown, *Singapore* 27 B2
Quellerina, *Johannesburg* 13 A1
Queluz, *Lisbon* 14 A1
Quezon City, *Manila* 17 B2
Quezon Memorial Circle, *Manila* 17 B2
Quilicura, *Santiago* 26 B1
Quincy, *Boston* 6 B3
Quincy B., *Boston* 6 B4
Quinta Normal, *Santiago* 26 B1
Quinto de Stampi, *Milan* 18 B2
Quinto Romano, *Milan* 18 B1
Quirinale, *Rome* 25 B1
Quirinale, Palazzo dei, *Rome* 25 b3

R

Raasdorf, *Vienna* 31 A3
Rådhuset, *Oslo* 22 A3
Radlice, *Prague* 24 B2
Radość, *Warsaw* 31 B3
Radotin, *Prague* 24 C2
Rafat, *Jerusalem* 13 A2
Raffles Hotel, *Singapore* 27 b3
Raffles Park, *Singapore* 27 B2

38 Raheny

Raheny, Dublin 11 A3
Rahnsdorf, Berlin 5 B5
Rainham, London 15 A5
Raj Ghat, Delhi 1 b3
Rajakylä, Helsinki 12 B3
Rajpath, Delhi 1 c2
Rajpura, Delhi 10 A2
Rákos-patak ✈, Budapest 7 B3
Rákoshegy, Budapest 7 B3
Rákoskeresztúr, Budapest 7 B3
Rákoskert, Budapest 7 B3
Rákosliget, Budapest 7 B3
Rákospalota, Budapest 7 A2
Rákosszentmihály, Budapest 7 A2
Raków, Warsaw 31 B1
Ram, Jerusalem 13 A2
Rām Allāh, Jerusalem 13 A2
Ramadān, Baghdad 3 B2
Ramakrishna Puram, Delhi 10 B1
Ramanathpur, Calcutta 8 A1
Rambla, La, Barcelona 4 b2
Rambler Channel, Hong Kong 12 A1
Ramenki, Moscow 19 B2
Ramersdorf, Munich 20 B2
Ramos, Rio de Janeiro 24 B1
Ramos Mejia, Buenos Aires 7 B1
Ramot, Jerusalem 13 B2
Rampur, Delhi 10 A2
Ramsgate, Sydney 28 B1
Rand Afrikaans Univ., Johannesburg 13 B2
Rand Airport, Johannesburg 13 B2
Randburg, Johannesburg 13 A1
Randhart, Johannesburg 13 B2
Randpark Ridge, Johannesburg 13 A1
Randwick, Sydney 28 B2
Ranelagh, Dublin 11 A2
Rannersdorf, Vienna 31 B2
Ransbèche, Brussels 6 B2
Ransdorp, Amsterdam 2 A2
Ranvad, Mumbai 20 B2
Raposo, Lisbon 14 A1
Rashtrapati Bhawan, Delhi 1 c1
Rasskazovka, Moscow 19 C2
Rastaala, Helsinki 12 B1
Rastila, Helsinki 12 B3
Raszyn, Warsaw 31 C1
Ratcha Thewi, Bangkok 3 b3
Rathfarnham, Dublin 11 B2
Ratho, Edinburgh 11 B1
Ratho Station, Edinburgh 11 B1
Rato, Lisbon 14 A2
Ravelston, Edinburgh 11 B2
Rawamangun, Jakarta 13 B2
Rayners Lane, London 15 A1
Raynes Park, London 15 B2
Raypur, Calcutta 8 C2
Razdory, Moscow 19 B1
Real Felipe, Fuerte, Lima 16 B2
Recoleta, Buenos Aires 7 B2
Recoleta, Santiago 26 B2
Red Fort = Lal Qila, Delhi 1 a3
Redbridge, London 15 A4
Redfern, Sydney 28 B2
Redwood, Wellington 32 B1
Reeves Hill, Boston 6 A1
Refshaleøen, Copenhagen 10 A3
Regents Park, Johannesburg 13 B2
Regent's Park, London 15 a2
Rego Park, New York 21 B2
Reichstag, Berlin 5 a3
Reina Sofia, Centro de Arte, Madrid 17 c3
Reinickendorf, Berlin 5 A3
Rekola, Helsinki 12 B3
Rembertów, Warsaw 31 B2
Rembrandthuis, Amsterdam 2 b2
Rembrandtpark, Amsterdam 2 A2
Rembrandtsplein, Amsterdam 2 b2
Remedios, Parque Nacional de los, Mexico City 18 B1
Remedios de Escalada, Buenos Aires 7 C2
Rémola, Laguna del, Barcelona 4 B1
Renca, Santiago 26 B1
Renmin Park, Tianjin 30 B2
Rennemoulin, Paris 23 A1
Reporyje, Prague 24 B1
Republica, Plaza de la, Mexico City 18 b1
République, Place de la, Paris 23 b5
Repulse Bay, Hong Kong 12 B2
Repy, Prague 24 B1
Residenz, Munich 20 B2
Residenzmuseum, Munich 20 b3
Reston, Washington 32 B2
Retiro, Buenos Aires 7 B2
Retiro, Madrid 17 B1
Retreat, Cape Town 8 B1
Reutov, Moscow 19 B5
Réveillon ✈, Paris 23 B4
Revere, Boston 6 A3
Rexdale, Toronto 30 A1
Reynosa Tamaulipas, Mexico City 18 A1
Rho, Milan 18 A1
Rhodes, Sydney 28 A1
Rhodon, Paris 23 B1
Rhodon ✈, Paris 23 B1
Ribeira, Rio de Janeiro 24 A1
Ricarda, Laguna de la, Barcelona 4 B1
Richmond, Melbourne 17 A2
Richmond, San Francisco 25 B2
Richmond Hill, New York 21 B2
Richmond Park, London 15 B2
Richmond upon Thames, London 15 B2
Riddarholmen, Stockholm 28 c1
Riddarhuset, Stockholm 28 c2
Ridgefield, New York 21 B1
Ridgefield Park, New York 21 A1
Ridgewood, New York 21 B2
Riem, Munich 20 B3
Rijksmuseum, Amsterdam 2 b1
Rikers I., New York 21 B2
Riksdagensledamothus, Stockholm 28 b2
Riksdagshuset, Stockholm 28 b2
Rimac, Lima 16 B2
Ringsend, Dublin 11 A2
Rinkeby, Stockholm 28 A1
Rio Comprido, Rio de Janeiro 24 B1
Rio de Janeiro, Rio de Janeiro 24 B1
Rio de la Plata, Buenos Aires 7 B2
Rio de Mouro, Lisbon 14 A1
Ripollet, Barcelona 4 A1
Ris, Oslo 22 A3
Risby, Copenhagen 10 A1
Rishra, Calcutta 8 A2
Ritchie, Washington 32 B4
Rithala, Delhi 10 A1
Rive Sud, Canal de la, Montreal 19 B2
River Edge, New York 21 A1
River Forest, Chicago 9 B2
River Grove, Chicago 9 B1
Riverdale, New York 21 A2
Riverdale, Washington 32 B4
Riverdale Park, Toronto 30 A2
Riverlea, Johannesburg 13 B1
Riverside, Chicago 9 C2
Riverwood, Sydney 28 B1
Rivière-des-Praires, Montreal 19 A2
Rixensart, Brussels 6 B3
Riyad, Baghdad 3 B2
Rizal Park, Manila 17 B1
Rizal Stadium, Manila 17 B1
Røa, Oslo 22 A2
Robbins, Chicago 9 D2
Robertsham, Johannesburg 13 B2
Rochelle Park, New York 21 A1
Rock Cr. ✈, Washington 32 B3
Rock Creek Park, Washington 32 B3
Rock Pt., Wellington 32 A1
Rockaway Pt., New York 21 C2
Rockdale, Sydney 28 B1
Rockefeller Center, New York 21 c2
Rodaon, Vienna 31 B1
Rødovre, Copenhagen 10 A2
Rodrigo de Freitas, L., Rio de Janeiro 24 B1
Roehampton, London 15 B2
Rogers Park, Chicago 9 A2
Roihuvuori, Helsinki 12 B3
Roissy-en-Brie, Paris 23 B4
Rokin, Amsterdam 2 b2
Rokkō I., Osaka 22 A2
Rokkō Sanchi, Osaka 22 A2
Rokkō-Zan, Osaka 22 A2
Rokytka ✈, Prague 24 B3
Roma, Rome 25 B1
Római-Fürdö, Budapest 7 A2
Romainville, Paris 23 A3
Romano Banco, Milan 18 B1
Romashkovo, Moscow 19 B1
Rome = Roma, Rome 25 B1
Romford, London 15 A5
Rondebosch, Cape Town 8 A1
Roppongi, Tokyo 29 c3
Rose Hill, Washington 32 C3
Rosebank, New York 21 C1
Rosebery, Sydney 28 B2
Rosedal La Candelaria, Mexico City 18 B2
Roseland, Chicago 9 C3
Rosemead, Los Angeles 16 B4
Rosemont, Montreal 19 A2
Rosenborg Have, Copenhagen 10 A3
Rosenthal, Berlin 5 A3
Rosettenville, Johannesburg 13 B2
Rosewell, Edinburgh 11 B3
Rosherville Dam, Johannesburg 13 B2
Rösjön, Stockholm 28 A2
Roslags-Näsby, Stockholm 28 A2
Roslin, Edinburgh 11 B3
Roslindale, Boston 6 B3
Rosny-sous-Bois, Paris 23 A4
Rosslyn, Washington 32 B3
Rosyth, Edinburgh 11 A1
Rotherhithe, London 15 B3
Rothneusiedl, Vienna 31 B2
Rothschmaige, Munich 20 A1
Rouge Hill, Toronto 30 A4
Round I., Hong Kong 12 B2
Roxbury, Boston 6 B3
Roxeth, London 15 A1
Royal Botanic Garden, Edinburgh 11 B2
Royal Botanic Gardens, Sydney 28 b2
Royal Grand Palace, Bangkok 3 b1
Royal Observatory, Edinburgh 11 B2
Royal Park, Melbourne 17 A1
Royal Turf Club, Bangkok 3 b2
Röylä, Helsinki 12 B1
Rozas, Portilleros de las, Madrid 17 B1
Roztoky, Prague 24 B2
Rozzano, Milan 18 B1
Rubi ✈, Barcelona 4 A1
Rublovo, Moscow 19 B2
Rudnevka ✈, Moscow 19 B5
Rudolfsheim, Vienna 31 A2
Rudolfshöhe, Berlin 5 A5
Rudow, Berlin 5 B3
Rueil-Malmaison, Paris 23 A2
Ruisbroek, Brussels 6 B1
Ruislip, London 15 A1
Rumelihisarı, Istanbul 12 B2
Rumyantsevo, Moscow 19 C2
Rungis, Paris 23 B3
Rusāfa, Baghdad 3 A2
Rush Green, London 15 A5
Russa, Calcutta 8 C2
Russian Hill, San Francisco 25 a1
Rustenfeld, Vienna 31 B2
Rutherford, New York 21 B1
Ruzyně, Prague 24 B1
Rybatskaya, St. Petersburg 26 B2
Rydboholm, Stockholm 28 A3
Ryde, Sydney 28 A1
Rynek, Warsaw 31 a2
Ryogoku, Tokyo 29 A3
Rzhevka, St. Petersburg 26 B3

S

Sa'ādatābād, Tehran 30 A2
Saadūn, Baghdad 3 B2
Saavedra, Buenos Aires 7 B2
Saboli, Delhi 10 A2
Sabugo, Lisbon 14 A1
Sabzi Mand, Delhi 10 A2
Sacavém, Lisbon 14 A2
Saclay, Paris 23 B2
Saclay, Étang de, Paris 23 B1
Sacomã, São Paulo 26 B2
Sacré Cœur, Paris 23 a4
Sacrow, Berlin 5 B1
Sacrower See, Berlin 5 B1
Sadang, Seoul 26 C1
Sadar Bazar, Delhi 1 a1
Saddām City, Baghdad 3 A2
Saddle Brook, New York 21 A1
Sadr, Karachi 14 A2
Sadyba, Warsaw 31 B2
Saft el Laban, Cairo 7 A2
Saganashkee Slough, Chicago 9 C1
Sagene, Oslo 22 A3
Sagrada Familia, Templo de, Barcelona 4 A2
Sagrado Familia, Templo de, Barcelona 4 a2
Sahar Int. Airport, Mumbai 20 A2
Sai Kung, Hong Kong 12 A2
Sai Wan Ho, Hong Kong 12 B2
Sai Ying Pun, Hong Kong 12 B1
St.-Aubin, Paris 23 B1
St.-Cloud, Paris 23 A2
St.-Cyr-l'École, Paris 23 B1
St.-Cyr-l'École, Aérodrome de, Paris 23 B1
St.-Denis, Paris 23 A3
St.-Germain, Forêt de, Paris 23 A1
St.-Germain-en-Laye, Paris 23 A1
St. Giles Cathedral, Edinburgh 11 b2
St. Helier, London 15 B2
St.-Hubert, Montreal 19 B3
St. Hubert, Galerie, Brussels 6 b2
St. Isaac's Cathedral, St. Petersburg 26 B1
St. Jacques ✈, Montreal 19 B3
St. James's, London 15 b3
St. John's Cathedral, Hong Kong 12 c1
St. Kilda, Melbourne 17 B1
St. Lambert, Montreal 19 A3
St.-Lambert, Paris 23 B1
St.-Laurent, Montreal 19 A1
St. Lawrence ✈, Montreal 19 B2
St.-Lazare, Gare, Paris 23 A2
St. Leonard, Montreal 19 A2
St. Magelungen, Stockholm 28 B2
St.-Mandé, Paris 23 A3
St. Margaret's, Dublin 11 A2
St.-Martin, Bois, Paris 23 B4
St. Mary Cray, London 15 B4
St.-Maur-des-Fossés, Paris 23 B3
St.-Maurice, Paris 23 B3
St.-Michel, Montreal 19 A2
St. Nikolaus-Kirken, Prague 24 B2
St.-Ouen, Paris 23 A3
St. Patrick's Cathedral, Dublin 11 c1
St. Patrick's Cathedral, New York 21 c2
St. Paul's Cathedral, London 15 b4
St. Paul's Cray, London 15 B4
St. Peters, Sydney 28 B2
St. Petersburg = Sankt Peterburg, St. Petersburg 26 B1
St.-Pierre, Montreal 19 B2
St.-Quentin, Étang de, Paris 23 B1
St. Stephen's Green, Dublin 11 c3
St.-Vincent-de-Paul, Montreal 19 A2
Ste.-Catherine, Montreal 19 B2
Ste.-Hélène, Î., Montreal 19 A2
Saiwai, Tokyo 29 B3
Sakai, Osaka 22 B3
Sakai Harbour, Osaka 22 B3
Sakra, P., Singapore 27 B2
Salam, Baghdad 3 A2
Salamanca, Madrid 17 B1
Sällynoggin, Dublin 11 B3
Salmannsdorf, Vienna 31 A1
Salmedina, Madrid 17 C2
Salomea, Warsaw 31 B1
Salsette I., Mumbai 20 A2
Salt Lake City, Calcutta 8 B2
Salt River, Cape Town 8 A1
Salt Water L., Calcutta 8 B2
Saltsjö-Duvnäs, Stockholm 28 B3
Saltykovka, Moscow 19 B5
Samatya, Istanbul 12 C1
Sampaloc, Manila 17 B1
Samphan Thawong, Bangkok 3 B2
Samsön, Seoul 26 B2
San Andrés, Barcelona 4 A2
San Angel, Mexico City 18 B1
San Angelo, Castel, Rome 25 b1
San Basilio, Rome 25 B2
San Borja, Lima 16 B3
San Bóvio, Milan 18 B2
San Bruno, Pt., San Francisco 25 C2
San Bruno Mt., San Francisco 25 B2
San Cristobal, Buenos Aires 7 B2
San Cristobal, Madrid 17 B2
San Cristóbal, Cerro, Santiago 26 B2
San Cristoforo, Milan 18 B1
San Donato Milanese, Milan 18 B2
San Francisco, San Francisco 25 B2
San Francisco B., San Francisco 25 B3
San Francisco Culhuacán, Mexico City 18 C2
San Fruttuoso, Milan 18 A2
San Gabriel, Los Angeles 16 B4
San Giuliano Milanese, Milan 18 B2
San Isidro, Lima 16 B2
San Jerónimo Lídice, Mexico City 18 C1
San Joaquin, Santiago 26 B2
San José Rio Hondo, Mexico City 18 B1
San Juan ✈, Manila 17 B2
San Juan de Aragón, Mexico City 18 B2
San Juan de Aragón, Parque, Mexico City 18 B2
San Juan de Lurigancho, Lima 16 A2
San Juan del Monte, Manila 17 B2
San Juan Ixtacala, Mexico City 18 A1
San Juan Toltotepec, Mexico City 18 B1
San Just Desvern, Barcelona 4 A1
San Justo, Buenos Aires 7 C1
San Lorenzo Tezonco, Mexico City 18 C2
San Luis, Lima 16 B2
San Marino, Los Angeles 16 B4
San Martin, Barcelona 4 A2
San Martin de Porras, Lima 16 B2
San Miguel, Lima 16 B2
San Miguel, Santiago 26 B2
San Nicolas, Buenos Aires 7 B2
San Onofrio, Rome 25 B1
San Pedro Martir, Barcelona 4 A1
San Pedro Zacatenco, Mexico City 18 A2
San Pietro, Piazza, Rome 25 b1
San Po Kong, Hong Kong 12 A2
San Rafael Chamapa, Mexico City 18 B1
San Rafael Hills, Los Angeles 16 A3
San Roque, Manila 17 B2
San Siro, Milan 18 B1
San Souci, Sydney 28 B1
San Telmo, Buenos Aires 7 B2
San Vicenc dels Horts, Barcelona 4 A1
Sanbancho, Tokyo 29 a3
Sandown, Johannesburg 13 A2
Sandown Park Races, London 15 B1
Sandton, Johannesburg 13 A2
Sandvika, Oslo 22 A2
Sandy Pond, Boston 6 A2
Sandyford, Dublin 11 B2
Sandymount, Dublin 11 B2
Sangenjaya, Tokyo 29 B2
Sangge, Seoul 26 B2
Sangley Pt., Manila 17 C1
Sankrail, Calcutta 8 B1
Sankt Peterburg, St. Petersburg 26 B1
Sankt Veit, Vienna 31 A1
Sanlihe, Beijing 4 B1
Sanlintang, Shanghai 27 C1
Sans, Barcelona 4 A1
Sant Agusti, Barcelona 4 c2
Sant Ambrogio, Basilica di, Milan 18 B2
Sant Boi de Llobregat, Barcelona 4 A1
Sant Cugat, Barcelona 4 A1
Sant Feliu de Llobregat, Barcelona 4 A1
Sant Joan Despi, Barcelona 4 A1
Sant Maria del Mar, Barcelona 4 b3
Sant Pau del Camp, Barcelona 4 c2
Santa Ana, Manila 17 B2
Santa Coloma de Gramanet, Barcelona 4 A2
Santa Cruz, Manila 17 B1
Santa Cruz, Mumbai 20 A1
Santa Cruz, I. de, Rio de Janeiro 24 B2
Santa Cruz de Olorde, Barcelona 4 A1
Santa Efigênia, São Paulo 26 B2
Santa Elena, Manila 17 B2
Santa Elena del Gomero, Santiago 26 B1
Santa Eulalia, Barcelona 4 A2
Santa Fe Springs, Los Angeles 16 C4
Santa Iria da Azóia, Lisbon 14 A2
Santa Julia, Santiago 26 C2
Santa Maria, Mexico City 18 a1
Santa Monica, Los Angeles 16 B2
Santa Monica Mts., Los Angeles 16 B2
Santa Rosa De Locobe, Santiago 26 B2
Santa Teresa de la Ovalle, Santiago 26 B1
Santahamina, Helsinki 12 C3
Santana, São Paulo 26 A2
Santeny, Paris 23 B4
Santiago, Santiago 26 B2
Santiago de Surco, Lima 16 B2
Santo Amaro, Lisbon 14 A1
Santo Amaro, São Paulo 26 B1
Santo Andre, Lisbon 14 B2
Santo Antão do Tojal, Lisbon 14 A2
Santo António, Qta. de, Lisbon 14 B1
Santo Tomas, Univ. of, Manila 17 B1
Santos Dumont, Aéroport, Rio de Janeiro 24 B2
Santoshpur, Calcutta 8 B1
Santragachi, Calcutta 8 B1
Santry, Dublin 11 A2
Sanyuanli, Canton 8 B2
São Caetano do Sul, São Paulo 26 B2
São Conrado, Rio de Janeiro 24 C1
São Cristovão, Rio de Janeiro 24 B1
São Francisco Penitência, Rio de Janeiro 24 b1
São Jorge, Castelo de, Lisbon 14 A2
São Juliao do Tojal, Lisbon 14 A2
São Paulo, São Paulo 26 B2
Sapa, Calcutta 8 B1
Sapateiro, Cor. do ✈, São Paulo 26 B1
Sarandi, Buenos Aires 7 C2
Saraswati ✈, Calcutta 8 A1
Sarecky potok ✈, Prague 24 B2
Sarimbun, Singapore 27 A2
Sarimbun Res., Singapore 27 A2
Sarıyer, Istanbul 12 A2
Saronikós Kólpos, Athens 2 B1
Sarriá, Barcelona 4 A1
Sarsuna, Calcutta 8 C1
Sartrouville, Paris 23 A2
Sasad, Budapest 7 B2
Sashalom, Budapest 7 A3
Saska, Warsaw 31 B2
Satalice, Prague 24 B3
Satgachi, Calcutta 8 B2
Sathorn, Bangkok 3 B2
Satpukur, Calcutta 8 B2
Sätra, Stockholm 28 B1
Sattru Pha, Bangkok 3 b2
Saúde, São Paulo 26 B2
Saugus, Boston 6 A3
Saugus ✈, Boston 6 A3
Sault-au-Récollet, Montreal 19 A2
Sausalito, San Francisco 25 A2
Sawah Besar, Jakarta 13 A1
Saxonville, Boston 6 B1
Scald Law, Edinburgh 11 B2
Scarborough, Toronto 30 A3
Sceaux, Paris 23 B2
Schaerbeek, Brussels 6 A2
Scharfenberg, Berlin 5 A2
Scheepvartmuseum, Amsterdam 2 b3
Schiller Park, Chicago 9 B1
Schiller Woods, Chicago 9 B1
Schiphol, Luchthaven, Amsterdam 2 B1
Schlachtensee, Berlin 5 B2
Schlossgarten, Berlin 5 A2
Schmargendorf, Berlin 5 B2
Schönblick, Berlin 5 B5
Schönbrunn, Schloss, Vienna 31 A1
Schöneberg, Berlin 5 B3
Schöneiche, Berlin 5 B5
Schönwalde, Berlin 5 A1
Schotschekloof, Cape Town 8 b1
Schulzendorf, Berlin 5 A2
Schwabing, Munich 20 B2
Schwanebeck, Berlin 5 A4
Schwanenwerder, Berlin 5 B2
Schwarzlackenau, Vienna 31 A2
Schwechat, Vienna 31 B2
Scitrek Museum, Atlanta 3 B2
Scott Monument, Edinburgh 11 b2
Scottdale, Atlanta 3 B3
Sea Point, Cape Town 8 A1
Seabrook, Washington 32 B5
Seacliff, San Francisco 25 B2
Seaforth, Sydney 28 A2
Seagate, New York 21 C1
Sears Tower, Chicago 9 c1
Seat Pleasant, Washington 32 B4
Seaview, Wellington 32 B2
Seberov, Prague 24 B3
Secaucus, New York 21 B1
Seddinsee, Berlin 5 B5
Seeberg, Berlin 5 A5
Seeburg, Berlin 5 A1
Seefeld, Berlin 5 A5
Seegefeld, Berlin 5 A1
Seehof, Berlin 5 B2
Segeltorp, Stockholm 28 B1
Segrate, Milan 18 B2
Seguro, Milan 18 B1
Seine ✈, Paris 23 B3
Seixal, Lisbon 14 B2
Selby, Johannesburg 13 B2
Seletar, P., Singapore 27 A3
Seletar Hills, Singapore 27 A3
Seletar Res., Singapore 27 A2
Selhurst, London 15 B3
Sembawang, Singapore 27 A2
Senago, Milan 18 A1
Sendinger Tor Platz, Munich 20 c1
Sendling, Munich 20 B2
Senju, Tokyo 29 A3
Sennyama, Osaka 22 A4
Sentosa, P., Singapore 27 B2
Seoul = Sŏul, Seoul 26 B2
Seoul National Univ., Seoul 26 C1
Seoul Tower, Seoul 26 B1
Sepolia, Athens 2 A2
Sepulveda Flood Control Basin, Los Angeles 16 A2
Serangoon, Singapore 27 A3
Serangoon, P., Singapore 27 A3
Serangoon, Sungei ✈, Singapore 27 A3
Serangoon Harbour, Singapore 27 A3
Seraya, P., Singapore 27 B2
Serebryanka, Moscow 19 B5
Serebryanka ✈, Moscow 19 B4
Serramonte, San Francisco 25 C2
Sesto San Giovanni, Milan 18 A2
Sesto Ulteriano, Milan 18 B2
Setagaya-Ku, Tokyo 29 B2
Seter, Oslo 22 A3
Setia Budi, Jakarta 13 B1
Settebagni, Rome 25 A2
Settecamini, Rome 25 B2
Séttimo Milanese, Milan 18 B1
Settsu, Osaka 22 A4
Setuny ✈, Moscow 19 B2
Seutula, Helsinki 12 A2
Seven Corners, Washington 32 B3
Seven Kings, London 15 A4
Sévesco ✈, Milan 18 A1
Sevran, Paris 23 A4
Sewri, Mumbai 20 B2
Sforzesso, Castello, Milan 18 B2
Sha Kok Mei, Hong Kong 12 A2
Sha Tin, Hong Kong 12 A2
Sha Tin Wai, Hong Kong 12 A2
Shabrâmant, Cairo 7 B2
Shahdara, Delhi 10 A2
Shahe, Canton 8 B2
Shahr-e Rey, Tehran 30 B2
Shahrak-e Golshahr, Tehran 30 B1
Shahrak-e Qods, Tehran 30 A2
Shaikh Aomar, Baghdad 3 A2
Shakurbasti, Delhi 10 A1
Shalkiya, Calcutta 8 B2
Sham Shui Po, Hong Kong 12 A1
Shamapur, Delhi 10 A1
Shamian, Canton 8 B2
Shan Mei, Hong Kong 12 A2
Shanghai, Shanghai 27 B2
Shankill, Dublin 11 B3
Sharp I., Hong Kong 12 A2
Shastrinagar, Delhi 10 A2
Shau Kei Wan, Hong Kong 12 B2
Shawocun, Beijing 4 B1
Shayuan, Canton 8 B2
Sheepshead Bay, New York 21 C2
Shek O, Hong Kong 12 B2
Shelter I., Hong Kong 12 B2
Sheng Fa Shan, Hong Kong 12 A1
Shepherds Bush, London 15 A2
Shepperton, London 15 B1
Sherman Oaks, Los Angeles 16 B2
Sherman Park, Chicago 9 C2
Shet Bandar, Mumbai 20 B2
Sheung Lau Wan, Hong Kong 12 B2
Sheung Wan, Hong Kong 12 B1
Sheva, Mumbai 20 B2
Sheva Nhava, Mumbai 20 B2
Shiba, Tokyo 29 c4
Shibpur, Calcutta 8 B1
Shibuya-Ku, Tokyo 29 c1
Shijōnawate, Osaka 22 A4
Shillim, Seoul 26 C1
Shimogawara, Tokyo 29 B1
Shimosalo, Tokyo 29 A2
Shimoshakujii, Tokyo 29 A2
Shinagawa-Ku, Tokyo 29 B3
Shing Mun Res., Hong Kong 12 A1
Shinjuku-Ku, Tokyo 29 a1
Shinjuku National Garden, Tokyo 29 a2
Shinkoiwa, Tokyo 29 A4
Shinnakano, Tokyo 29 A3
Shinsa, Seoul 26 B2
Shipai, Canton 8 B3
Shirinashi ✈, Osaka 22 A3
Shirogane, Tokyo 29 B3
Shiweitang, Canton 8 B2
Shogunle, Lagos 14 A2
Shomolu, Lagos 14 B2
Shooters Hill, London 15 B4
Shoreditch, London 15 a5
Shortlands, London 15 B4
Shu' afat, Jerusalem 13 B2
Shubrā, Cairo 7 A2
Shubrā el Kheima, Cairo 7 A2
Shuikuo, Canton 8 A2
Shuishang Park, Tianjin 30 B1
Sidcup, London 15 B4
Siebenhirten, Vienna 31 B1
Siedlung, Berlin 5 A1
Siekierki, Warsaw 31 B2
Sielce, Warsaw 31 B2
Siemensstadt, Berlin 5 A2
Sierra Madre, Los Angeles 16 B4
Sievering, Vienna 31 A2
Sighthill, Edinburgh 11 B2
Signal Hill, Cape Town 8 A1
Sihŭng, Seoul 26 C1
Sikátorpuszta, Budapest 7 A3
Silampur, Delhi 10 B2
Silver Hill, Boston 6 A2
Silver Hill, Washington 32 C4
Silver Spring, Washington 32 A3
Silvermine Nature Reserve, Cape Town 8 B1
Silvolantekojärvi, Helsinki 12 B2
Simei, Singapore 27 B3
Simla, Calcutta 8 B2
Simmering, Vienna 31 A2
Simmering Heide, Vienna 31 A2
Simonkylä, Helsinki 12 B3
Simpang, Singapore 27 B3
Singapore, Singapore 27 B2
Singapore, Univ. of, Singapore 27 B2
Sinicka ✈, Moscow 19 A1
Sinki, Selat, Singapore 27 B2
Sint-Genesius-Rode, Brussels 6 B2
Sinwŏl, Seoul 26 B1
Sion, Mumbai 20 A2
Sipson, London 15 B1
Siqeil, Cairo 7 A1
Şişli, Istanbul 12 B1
Skansen, Stockholm 28 B2
Skärholmen, Stockholm 28 B2
Skarpäng, Stockholm 28 A2
Skarpnäck, Stockholm 28 B2
Skaryszewski Park, Warsaw 31 B2
Skeppsholmen, Stockholm 28 c3
Skokie, Chicago 9 A2
Skokie ✈, Chicago 9 A2
Skoklefall, Oslo 22 A3
Sköndal, Stockholm 28 B2
Skovlunde, Copenhagen 10 A2
Skovshoved, Copenhagen 10 A3
Skuru, Stockholm 28 B3
Skyland, Atlanta 3 A3
Slade Green, London 15 B5
Slemmestad, Oslo 22 B1
Slependen, Oslo 22 A2
Slipi, Jakarta 13 B1
Slivenec, Prague 24 B2
Sloten, Amsterdam 2 A1
Sloterpark, Amsterdam 2 A1
Sluhy, Prague 24 A3
Służew, Warsaw 31 B2
Służewiec, Warsaw 31 B2
Smíchov, Prague 24 B2
Smith Forest Preserve, Chicago 9 B2
Smithsonian Institute, Washington 32 b2
Smolny, St. Petersburg 26 B2
Snake Creek Canal ✈, Miami 18 A2
Snarøya, Oslo 22 A2
Snättringe, Stockholm 28 B1
Sŏbinggo, Seoul 26 B1
Søborg, Copenhagen 10 A2
Sobreda, Lisbon 14 B1
Soch'o, Seoul 26 C1
Södaemun, Seoul 26 B1
Söderby, Stockholm 28 A3
Södermalm, Stockholm 28 B2
Sodpur, Calcutta 8 A2
Soeurs, Î. des, Montreal 19 B2
Sognsvatn, Oslo 22 A3
Soho, London 15 b3
Soho, New York 21 e1
Soignes, Forêt de, Brussels 6 B2
Sok Kwu Wan, Hong Kong 12 B1
Sŏkkwan, Seoul 26 B2
Sokolniki, Moscow 19 B4
Sokolniki Park, Moscow 19 B4
Sokołów, Warsaw 31 C1
Solalinden, Munich 20 B3
Soldier Field, Chicago 9 e3
Sollentuna, Stockholm 28 A1
Solln, Munich 20 B2
Solna, Stockholm 28 A1
Solntsevo, Moscow 19 C2
Somerset, Washington 32 B3
Somerville, Boston 6 A3
Somes I., Wellington 32 B2
Sonari, Mumbai 20 B2
Sønderso, Copenhagen 10 A2
Sŏngbuk, Seoul 26 B2
Sŏngdong, Seoul 26 B2
Sŏngp'a, Seoul 26 B2
Sŏngsu, Seoul 26 B2
Soong Qingling, Former Res. of, Beijing 4 a2
Soroksár, Budapest 7 B2
Soroksari Duna ✈, Budapest 7 B2
Sosenka ✈, Moscow 19 B4
Sosnovka, St. Petersburg 26 B2
Sŏul, Seoul 26 B2
Soundview, New York 21 B2
South Beach, New York 21 C1
South Beach Harbor, San Francisco 25 c3
South Bend Park, Atlanta 3 B2
South Boston, Boston 6 A3
South Brooklyn, New York 21 B2
South Decatur, Atlanta 3 B3
South Deering, Chicago 9 C3
South El Monte, Los Angeles 16 B4
South Gate, Los Angeles 16 C3
South Harbor, Manila 17 B1
South Harrow, London 15 A1
South Hd., Sydney 28 B2
South Hills, Johannesburg 13 B2
South Hornchurch, London 15 A5
South Kensington, London 15 c2
South Lawn, Washington 32 C3
South Lincoln, Boston 6 A2
South Miami, Miami 18 B1
South Norwood, London 15 B3
South of Market, San Francisco 25 B2
South Ozone Park, New York 21 B3
South Pasadena, Los Angeles 16 B4
South Res., Boston 6 A3
South Ruislip, London 15 A1
South San Francisco, San Francisco 25 C2
South San Gabriel, Los Angeles 16 B4
South Shore, Chicago 9 C3
South Sudbury, Boston 6 A1
Southall, London 15 A1
Southborough, London 15 B4
Southend, London 15 B3
Southfields, London 15 B2
Southwark, London 15 B3
Søvang, Copenhagen 10 B3
Soweto, Johannesburg 13 B1
Sowhānak, Tehran 30 A3
Soya, Tokyo 29 A4
Spandau, Berlin 5 A1
Spånga, Stockholm 28 A1
Spanische Reitschule, Vienna 31 b1
Spectacle I., Boston 6 A4
Speicher-See, Munich 20 A3
Speising, Vienna 31 B1
Sphinx, Cairo 7 B1
Spinaceto, Rome 25 C1
Spit Junction, Sydney 28 A2
Spořilov, Prague 24 B3
Spot Pond, Boston 6 A3
Spotswood, Melbourne 17 B1
Spree ✈, Berlin 5 A2
Spring Pond, Boston 6 A4
Springeberg, Berlin 5 B5
Springfield, Washington 32 C2
Squantum, Boston 6 B3
Srednaya Rogatka, St. Petersburg 26 C2
Śródmieście, Warsaw 31 B2
Saint-Gilles, Brussels 6 B2
Saint-Josse-Ten-Noode, Brussels 6 A2
Saint-Pieters-Leeuw, Brussels 6 B1
Saint-Stevens-Woluwe, Brussels 6 A2
Staaken, Berlin 5 A1
Stabekk, Oslo 22 A2
Stadhion, Athens 2 c3
Stadhuis, Amsterdam 2 b2
Stadlau, Vienna 31 A2
Stadshuset, Stockholm 28 b1
Stains, Paris 23 A3
Stamford Hill, London 15 A3
Stammersdorf, Vienna 31 A2
Stanley, Hong Kong 12 B2
Stanley Mound, Hong Kong 12 B2
Stanley Pen., Hong Kong 12 B2
Stanmore, London 15 A2
Stapleton, New York 21 C1
Star Ferry, Hong Kong 12 a2
Staraya Derevnya, St. Petersburg 26 B1
Stare, Warsaw 31 B2
Staré Město, Prague 24 B2
Starego Miasto, Warsaw 31 a2
Staten Island Zoo, New York 21 C1
Statenice, Prague 24 B1
Statue Square, Hong Kong 12 c1
Stedelijk Museum, Amsterdam 2 c1
Steele Creek, Melbourne 17 A1
Steenokkerzeel, Brussels 6 A2
Steglitz, Berlin 5 B2
Stepaside, Dublin 11 B2
Stephansdom, Vienna 31 b2
Stepney, London 15 A3
Sterling Park, San Francisco 25 B2
Sticklinge udde, Stockholm 28 A2
Stickney, Chicago 9 C2
Stillorgan, Dublin 11 B2
Stockholm, Stockholm 28 B2
Stocksund, Stockholm 28 A2
Stodůlky, Prague 24 B1
Stoke Newington, London 15 A3
Stokes Valley, Wellington 32 B2
Stone Canyon Res., Los Angeles 16 B2
Stone Park, Chicago 9 B1
Stonebridge, London 15 A2
Stoneham, Boston 6 A3
Stony Brook Res., Boston 6 B3
Stora Värtan, Stockholm 28 A2
Store Hareskov, Copenhagen 10 A2
Store Magleby, Copenhagen 10 B3
Storholmen, Stockholm 28 A2
Stoyka, St. Petersburg 26 B2
Straiton, Edinburgh 11 B3
Strand, London 15 b4
Strandfontein, Cape Town 8 B2
Strašnice, Prague 24 B2
Strasstrudering, Munich 20 B3
Stratford, London 15 A4
Strathfield, Sydney 28 B1
Streatham, London 15 B3
Streatham Vale, London 15 B3
Strebersdorf, Vienna 31 A2
Střešovice, Prague 24 B2
Strížkov, Prague 24 B2
Strogino, Moscow 19 B2
Strombeek-Bever, Brussels 6 A2
Stromovka, Prague 24 B2
Studio City, Los Angeles 16 B2
Stureby, Stockholm 28 B2
Stuvsta, Stockholm 28 B2
Subhepur, Delhi 10 A2
Sucat, Manila 17 C2
Suchdol, Prague 24 B2
Sucy-en-Brie, Paris 23 B4
Sudbury, Boston 6 A1
Sugamo, Tokyo 29 A3
Sugar Loaf Mt. = Açúcar, Pão de, Rio de Janeiro 24 B2
Suge, Tokyo 29 B2
Suginami-Ku, Tokyo 29 A2
Sugō, Tokyo 29 B2
Suita, Osaka 22 A4
Suitland, Washington 32 B4
Sukchar, Calcutta 8 A2
Suma, Osaka 22 B1
Sumida ✈, Tokyo 29 A3
Sumida-Ku, Tokyo 29 A3
Sumiyoshi, Osaka 22 B4
Summerville, Toronto 30 B1
Summit, Chicago 9 C2
Sunamachi, Tokyo 29 A4
Sunbury-on-Thames, London 15 B1
Sundbyberg, Stockholm 28 A1
Sundbyerne, Copenhagen 10 B3
Sung Kong, Hong Kong 12 B2
Sungei Kadut Industrial Estate, Singapore 27 A2
Sungei Selatar Res., Singapore 27 A3
Sunter, Jakarta 13 A2
Sunter, Kali ✈, Jakarta 13 B2
Suomenlinna, Helsinki 12 C2
Supreme Court, Washington 32 b3
Sura, Calcutta 8 B2
Surag-san, Seoul 26 A2
Surbiton, London 15 B2
Suresnes, Paris 23 A2
Surfside, Miami 18 A2
Surquillo, Lima 16 B2
Surrey Hills, Sydney 28 B2
Susaek, Seoul 26 B1
Süssenbrunn, Vienna 31 A2
Sutton, Dublin 11 A3
Sutton, London 15 B2
Suyu, Seoul 26 B2
Suzukishinden, Tokyo 29 A2
Svanemøllen, Copenhagen 10 A3
Sverdlov, Moscow 19 B3
Svestad, Oslo 22 B2
Svinö, Helsinki 12 C1
Swampscott, Boston 6 A4
Swanley, London 15 B5
Swansea, Toronto 30 B2
Swinburne I., New York 21 C1
Swords, Dublin 11 A2
Sydenham, Johannesburg 13 A2
Sydney, Sydney 28 B2
Sydney, Univ. of, Sydney 28 B2
Sydney Airport, Sydney 28 B2
Sydney Harbour Bridge, Sydney 28 B2
Sydstranden, Copenhagen 10 B3
Sylvania, Sydney 28 C1
Syntagma, Pl., Athens 2 b3
Syon Park, London 15 B2
Szczęśliwice, Warsaw 31 B1
Széchnenyi-hegy, Budapest 7 B1
Szent Istvánbaz, Budapest 7 b2
Széphalom, Budapest 7 A1

T

Tabata, Tokyo 29 A3
Tablada, Buenos Aires 7 C1
Table Bay, Cape Town 8 A1
Table Mountain, Cape Town 8 A1
Taboão da Serra, São Paulo 26 B1
Täby, Stockholm 28 A2

Zyuzino 39

Tacuba, *Mexico City* 18 B1
Tacubaya, *Mexico City* 18 B1
Taebang, *Seoul* 26 B1
Tagig, *Manila* 17 B2
Tagig →, *Manila* 17 B2
Tai Hang, *Hong Kong* 12 B2
Tai Lo Shan, *Hong Kong* 12 A2
Tai Po Tsai, *Hong Kong* 12 A2
Tai Seng, *Singapore* 27 A3
Tai Shui Hang, *Hong Kong* 12 A2
Tai Tam B., *Hong Kong* 12 B2
Tai Tam Tuk Res., *Hong Kong* 12 B2
Tai Wai, *Hong Kong* 12 A1
Tai Wan Tau, *Hong Kong* 12 B2
Tai Wo Hau, *Hong Kong* 12 A1
Tainaka, *Osaka* 22 B4
Taishō, *Osaka* 22 B3
Taita, *Wellington* 32 B2
Tajrīsh, *Tehran* 30 A2
Takaido, *Tokyo* 29 A2
Takaishi, *Tokyo* 29 B2
Takarazuka, *Osaka* 22 A2
Takasago, *Tokyo* 29 A4
Takatsu-Ku, *Tokyo* 29 B2
Takeshita, *Tokyo* 29 B2
Takinegawa, *Tokyo* 29 A3
Takoma Park, *Washington* 32 B3
Taksim, *Istanbul* 12 B1
Talaide, *Lisbon* 14 A1
Taliganga, *Calcutta* 8 B2
Talipapa, *Manila* 17 A2
Tallaght, *Dublin* 11 B1
Tallkrogen, *Stockholm* 28 B2
Tama, *Tokyo* 29 B1
Tama →, *Tokyo* 29 B2
Tama Kyūryō, *Tokyo* 29 B2
Tamaden, *Tokyo* 29 B2
Tamagawa-josui →, *Tokyo* 29 A1
Taman Sari, *Jakarta* 13 A1
Tamanduateí →, *São Paulo* 26 B2
Tamboerskloof, *Cape Town* 8 A1
Tambora, *Jakarta* 13 A1
Tammisalo, *Helsinki* 12 B3
Tammūh, *Cairo* 7 B2
Tampines, *Singapore* 27 A3
Tanah Abang, *Jakarta* 13 B1
Tanigami, *Osaka* 22 A2
Tanjung Duren, *Jakarta* 13 B1
Tanjung Priok, *Jakarta* 13 A2
Tanum, *Oslo* 22 A1
Taoranting Park, *Beijing* 4 c2
Tapada, *Lisbon* 14 A1
Tapanila, *Helsinki* 12 B3
Tapiales, *Buenos Aires* 7 C1
Tapiola, *Helsinki* 12 B1
Tapsia, *Calcutta* 8 B2
Tara, *Mumbai* 20 A1
Tarabya, *Istanbul* 12 B2
Tarango, Presa, *Mexico City* 18 B1
Tårbæk, *Copenhagen* 10 A3
Tarchomin, *Warsaw* 31 B1
Tardeo, *Mumbai* 20 B1
Targówek, *Warsaw* 31 B2
Tårnby, *Copenhagen* 10 B3
Tarqua Bay, *Lagos* 14 B2
Tåstrup, *Copenhagen* 10 B1
Tatarovo, *Moscow* 19 B2
Tathong Channel, *Hong Kong* 12 B2
Tathong Pt., *Hong Kong* 12 B2
Tatuapé, *São Paulo* 26 B2
Taufkirchen, *Munich* 20 B2
Tavares, I. dos, *Rio de Janeiro* 24 A2
Távros, *Athens* 2 B2
Tawa, *Wellington* 32 A1
Teaneck, *New York* 21 A1
Teatro Municipal, *Rio de Janeiro* 24 c2
Tebet, *Jakarta* 13 B2
Tecamachaleo, *Mexico City* 18 B1
Teddington, *London* 15 B1
Tegel, *Berlin* 5 A2
Tegel, Flughafen, *Berlin* 5 A2
Tegeler See, *Berlin* 5 A2
Tegelort, *Berlin* 5 A2
Tehrān, *Tehran* 30 A2
Tehrān Pārs, *Tehran* 30 A3
Tei Tong Tsui, *Hong Kong* 12 B2
Tejo, Rio →, *Lisbon* 14 A2
Tekstilyshchik, *Moscow* 19 B4
Telegraph hill, *San Francisco* 25 a2
Telhal, *Lisbon* 14 A1
Telok Blangah, *Singapore* 27 B2
Teltow, *Berlin* 5 B2
Teltow kanal, *Berlin* 5 B3
Temnikovo, *Moscow* 19 B6
Tempelhof, *Berlin* 5 B3
Tempelhof, Flughafen, *Berlin* 5 B3
Temple City, *Los Angeles* 16 B4
Temple Hills Park, *Washington* 32 C4
Temple Mount, *Jerusalem* 13 b3
Templeogue, *Dublin* 11 B2
Templo Mayor, *Mexico City* 18 b3
Tenafly, *New York* 21 A2
Tenayuca, Pirámide de, *Mexico City* 18 A1
Tengah →, *Singapore* 27 A2
Tennoji, *Osaka* 22 B4
Tepalcates, *Mexico City* 18 B2
Terrazzano, *Milan* 18 A1
Terrugem, *Lisbon* 14 A1
Tervuren, *Brussels* 6 B3
Tervuren, Park van, *Brussels* 6 B3
Tetuán, *Madrid* 17 B1
Teufelsberg, *Berlin* 5 B2
Tévere →, *Rome* 25 B1
Thalkirchen, *Munich* 20 B2
Thames →, *London* 15 B3
Thames Ditton, *London* 15 B1
Thamesmead, *London* 15 A4
Thana Cr. →, *Mumbai* 20 A2
The Loop, *Chicago* 9 B3
The Ridge, *Delhi* 10 B2
The Wilds, *Johannesburg* 13 B2
Theater Carré, *Amsterdam* 2 b2
Théatro Dionissou, *Athens* 2 c2
Thiais, *Paris* 23 B3
Thissío, *Athens* 2 c1
Thistletown, *Toronto* 30 A1
Thomastown, *Melbourne* 17 A2
Thompson I., *Boston* 6 B4
Thon Buri, *Bangkok* 3 B1
Thornbury, *Melbourne* 17 A2
Thorncliffe, *Toronto* 30 A2
Thornhill, *Toronto* 30 A2
Thornton, *Cape Town* 8 A2
Thornton Heath, *London* 15 B3
Threipmuir Res., *Edinburgh* 11 B2
Throgs Neck, *New York* 21 B3
Thyssen Bornemisza, Museo, *Madrid* 17 b3
Tian'anmen Square, *Beijing* 4 B2
Tiancun, *Beijing* 4 B1
Tianjin, *Tianjin* 30 B1
Tiantan Park, *Beijing* 4 c2
Tibidabo, *Barcelona* 4 A1
Tibradden Mt., *Dublin* 11 B2
Tiburon, *San Francisco* 25 A2
Tiburtino, *Rome* 25 B2
Ticomán, *Mexico City* 18 A2
Tiefersee, *Berlin* 5 B1
Tiejiangyin, *Beijing* 4 C2
Tientsin = Tianjin, *Tianjin* 30 B1
Tiergarten, *Berlin* 5 A3
Tietê →, *São Paulo* 26 B2
Tigerhof, *Cape Town* 8 A2
Tigris = Nahr Dijlah →, *Baghdad* 3 B2
Tijuca, *Rio de Janeiro* 24 B1
Tijuca, Parque Nacional da, *Rio de Janeiro* 24 B1
Tijuca, Pico da, *Rio de Janeiro* 24 B1
Tikkurila, *Helsinki* 12 B3
Tilak Nagar, *Delhi* 10 B1
Tilanqiao, *Shanghai* 27 B1
Timah, Bukit, *Singapore* 27 A2
Times Square, *New York* 21 c2
Timiryazev Park, *Moscow* 19 B3
Ting Kau, *Hong Kong* 12 A1
Tira, *Jerusalem* 13 A1
Tirsa, *Cairo* 7 B2
Tishrīyaa, *Baghdad* 3 B2
Tiu Keng Leng, *Hong Kong* 12 B2
Tivoli, *Copenhagen* 10 a3
Tizapán, *Mexico City* 18 C1
Tlalnepantla →, *Mexico City* 18 A1
To Kwai Wan, *Hong Kong* 12 B2
Toa Payoh, *Singapore* 27 A3
Tobong, *Seoul* 26 B2
Tobong-san, *Seoul* 26 A2
Točná, *Prague* 24 C2
Toco Hills, *Atlanta* 3 A2
Todt Hill, *New York* 21 C1
Tōkagi, *Tokyo* 29 A4
Tokai Plantation, *Cape Town* 8 B1
Tōkaichiba, *Tokyo* 29 B2
Tokarevo, *Moscow* 19 C5
Tōkyō, *Tokyo* 29 B3
Tokyo B., *Tokyo* 29 B4
Tokyo-Haneda Int. Airport, *Tokyo* 29 B3
Tokyo Harbour, *Tokyo* 29 B3
Tolka R. →, *Dublin* 11 A1
Tolworth, *London* 15 B2
Tomb of Lu Xun, *Shanghai* 27 B1
Tomb of the Kings, *Jerusalem* 13 a2
Tomba di Nerone, *Rome* 25 B1
Tomilino, *Moscow* 19 C5
Tondo, *Manila* 17 B1
Tongbinggo, *Seoul* 26 B1
Tongjak, *Seoul* 26 B1
Tongmaemung, *Seoul* 26 B2
Tongqiao, *Shanghai* 27 A1
Toorak, *Melbourne* 17 B2
Topkapı, *Istanbul* 12 B1
Tor di Quinto, *Rome* 25 B1
Tor Pignattara, *Rome* 25 B2
Tor Sapienza, *Rome* 25 B2
Toranomon, *Tokyo* 29 c3
Torcy, *Paris* 23 A4
Toronto, *Toronto* 30 B3
Toronto, Univ. of, *Toronto* 30 B2
Toronto Harbour, *Toronto* 30 B2
Toronto I., *Toronto* 30 B2
Toronto Int. Airport, *Toronto* 30 A1
Toros Las Arenas, Pl. de, *Barcelona* 4 c1
Toros Monumental, Templo de, *Barcelona* 4 a3
Torre Latino-americana, *Mexico City* 18 b2
Torre Lupara, *Rome* 25 B2
Torre Nova, *Rome* 25 B2
Torrellas →, *Barcelona* 4 A1
Torrevécchia, *Rome* 25 B1
Toshima-Ku, *Tokyo* 29 A3
Toshimaen, *Tokyo* 29 A2
Tottenham, *London* 15 A3
Tottenham, *Melbourne* 17 A1
Tour Eiffel, *Paris* 23 c2
Toussus-le-Noble, *Paris* 23 B1
Toussus-le-Noble, Aérodrome de, *Paris* 23 B1
Tower Bridge, *London* 15 b5
Tower Hamlets, *London* 15 A3
Tower of London, *London* 15 b5
Towra Pt., *Sydney* 28 C2
Tøyen, *Oslo* 22 A3
Toyonaka, *Osaka* 22 A3
Trafalgar Square, *London* 15 b3
Trafaria, *Lisbon* 14 A1
Traição, Cor. →, *São Paulo* 26 B2
Tranegilde, *Copenhagen* 10 B2
Trångsund, *Stockholm* 28 B2
Transamerica Pyramid, *San Francisco* 25 b2
Transbay Terminal, *San Francisco* 25 b3
Trappenfelde, *Berlin* 5 A4
Trastévere, *Rome* 25 B1
Treasure I., *San Francisco* 25 B2
Třeboradice, *Prague* 24 B3
Třebotov, *Prague* 24 C1
Tremblay-en-France, *Paris* 23 A4
Tremembe →, *São Paulo* 26 A2
Tremont, *New York* 21 A2
Trenno, *Milan* 18 B1
Treptow, *Berlin* 5 B3
Trés Rios, Sa. dos, *Rio de Janeiro* 24 B1
Trevi, Fontana di, *Rome* 25 b3
Trezzano sul Navíglio, *Milan* 18 B1
Tribune Tower, *Chicago* 9 b2
Trieste, *Rome* 25 B2
Trinidad, *Washington* 32 B4
Trinity, *Edinburgh* 11 B2
Trinity College, *Dublin* 11 c3
Trionfale, *Rome* 25 B1
Triulzo, *Milan* 18 B2
Trocadero, *Paris* 23 b1
Troitse-Lykovo, *Moscow* 19 B2
Troja, *Prague* 24 B2
Trollbäcken, *Stockholm* 28 B3
Trombay, *Mumbai* 20 A2
Troparevo, *Moscow* 19 C2
Tropenmuseum, *Amsterdam* 2 b3
Trudyashchikhsya, Ostrov, *St. Petersburg* 26 B1
Tryvasshøgda, *Oslo* 22 A3
Tseng Lan Shue, *Hong Kong* 12 A2
Tsim Sha Tsui, *Hong Kong* 12 a2
Tsing Yi, *Hong Kong* 12 A1
Tsova, *Jerusalem* 13 B1
Tsuen Wan, *Hong Kong* 12 A1
Tsukiji, *Tokyo* 29 c5
Tsur Hadassa, *Jerusalem* 13 B1
Tsurumi →, *Tokyo* 29 B3
Tsz Wan Shan, *Hong Kong* 12 A2
Tuas, *Singapore* 27 B1
Tuchoměřice, *Prague* 24 B1
Tuckahoe, *New York* 21 A3
Tucuruvi, *São Paulo* 26 A2
Tufello, *Rome* 25 B2
Tufnell Park, *London* 15 A3
Tughlakabad, *Delhi* 10 B2
Tuileries, Jardin des, *Paris* 23 b3
Tuindorp Oostzaan, *Amsterdam* 2 A2
Tullamarine, *Melbourne* 17 A1
Tulse Hill, *London* 15 B3
Tung Lung I., *Hong Kong* 12 B2
Tung O, *Hong Kong* 12 B1
Tunis, *Baghdad* 3 A2
Tuomarila, *Helsinki* 12 B1
Tureberg, *Stockholm* 28 A1
Turffontein, *Johannesburg* 13 B2
Turkso, *Prague* 24 A1
Turnham Green, *London* 15 B2
Turnhouse, *Edinburgh* 11 B1
Tuscolana, Via, *Rome* 25 B2
Tushino, *Moscow* 19 A2
Twelve Apostles, *Cape Town* 8 A1
Twickenham, *London* 15 B1
Twickenham Rugby Ground, *London* 15 B1
Twin Peaks, *San Francisco* 25 B2
Two Rock Mt., *Dublin* 11 B2
Tymon North, *Dublin* 11 B1
Tysons Corner, *Washington* 32 B2

U

U.S. Capitol, *Washington* 32 b3
Ubeidiya, *Jerusalem* 13 B2
Uberaba →, *São Paulo* 26 B2
Ubin, P., *Singapore* 27 A3
Uccle, *Brussels* 6 B2
Udelnaya, *St. Petersburg* 26 A2
Udelnoe, *St. Petersburg* 26 B1
Udding, *Munich* 20 A1
Ueno, *Tokyo* 29 A3
Úholičky, *Prague* 24 B1
Uhříněves, *Prague* 24 B3
Uithoorn, *Amsterdam* 2 B1
Újpalota, *Budapest* 7 A2
Újpest, *Budapest* 7 A2
Ukita, *Tokyo* 29 A4
Ullerup, *Copenhagen* 10 B3
Ullevål, *Oslo* 22 A3
Ulriksdal, *Stockholm* 28 A1
Ulyanka, *St. Petersburg* 26 B1
Um Al-Khanazir Island, *Baghdad* 3 B2
Umeda, *Osaka* 22 A3
Umerkhadi, *Mumbai* 20 b2
Ümraniye, *Istanbul* 12 B2
Underground Atlanta, *Atlanta* 3 B2
Uněticky potok →, *Prague* 24 B2
Ŭngam, *Seoul* 26 B1
Unhos, *Lisbon* 14 A2
Unidad Santa Fe, *Mexico City* 18 B1
Union City, *New York* 21 B1
Union Port, *New York* 21 B2
Union Square, *New York* 21 d2
Union Square, *San Francisco* 25 b2
Union Station, *Washington* 32 b3
United Nations H.Q., *New York* 21 c3
Universidad, *Madrid* 17 B1
Universidad de Chile, *Santiago* 26 B2
University Park, *Washington* 32 B4
Unp'yong, *Seoul* 26 B1
Unter den Linden, *Berlin* 5 a4
Unterbiberg, *Munich* 20 B2
Unterföhring, *Munich* 20 A3
Unterhaching, *Munich* 20 B2
Unterlaa, *Vienna* 31 B2
Untermenzing, *Munich* 20 A1
Upper East Side, *New York* 21 b3
Upper Elmers End, *London* 15 B3
Upper New York B., *New York* 21 C1
Upper Norwood, *London* 15 B3
Upper Peirce Res., *Singapore* 27 A2
Upper Sydenham, *London* 15 B3
Upper Tooting, *London* 15 B3
Upper West Side, *New York* 21 a2
Upton, *London* 15 A4
Uptown, *Chicago* 9 B2
Uran, *Mumbai* 20 B2
Urayasu, *Tokyo* 29 B4
Urbe, Aeroporto d', *Rome* 25 B2
Urca, *Rio de Janeiro* 24 B2
Uritsk, *St. Petersburg* 26 C1
Üröm, *Budapest* 7 A2
Ursus, *Warsaw* 31 B1
Ursvik, *Stockholm* 28 A1
Usera, *Madrid* 17 B1
Ushigome, *Tokyo* 29 A3
Usina, *Rio de Janeiro* 24 B1
Üsküdar, *Istanbul* 12 B2
Ust-Slavyanka, *St. Petersburg* 26 C3
Uteke, *Stockholm* 28 A3
Utrata, *Warsaw* 31 B2
Uttarpara, *Calcutta* 8 B1
Utterslev Mose, *Copenhagen* 10 A2

V

Vadaul, *Mumbai* 20 A2
Vaires-sur-Marne, *Paris* 23 A4
Valby, *Copenhagen* 10 B2
Valcannuta, *Rome* 25 B1
Valdelatas, *Madrid* 17 A1
Vale, *Washington* 32 B1
Valenton, *Paris* 23 B3
Valera, *Milan* 18 A1
Vallcarca, *Barcelona* 4 A1
Valldoreix, *Barcelona* 4 A1
Vallecas, *Madrid* 17 B2
Vallensbæk, *Copenhagen* 10 B2
Vallensbæk Strand, *Copenhagen* 10 B2
Vallentunasjön, *Stockholm* 28 A2
Valleranello, *Rome* 25 C1
Vallisaari, *Helsinki* 12 C3
Vallvidrera, *Barcelona* 4 A1
Valvidrera →, *Barcelona* 4 A1
Van Goghmuseum, *Amsterdam* 2 c1
Vanak, *Tehran* 30 A2
Vangede, *Copenhagen* 10 A3
Vaniköy, *Istanbul* 12 B2
Vanløse, *Copenhagen* 10 A2
Vantaa, *Helsinki* 12 B2
Vantaa →, *Helsinki* 12 B2
Vantaankoski, *Helsinki* 12 B2
Vantaanpuisto, *Helsinki* 12 B2
Vanves, *Paris* 23 B2
Varedo, *Milan* 18 A1
Varkiza, *Athens* 2 C2
Varszínház, *Budapest* 7 b2
Vartiokylä, *Helsinki* 12 B3
Vartiosaari, *Helsinki* 12 B3
Vasamuseet, *Stockholm* 28 b3
Vasco, *Cape Town* 8 A2
Vasfanārd, *Tehran* 30 B2
Vashi, *Mumbai* 20 A2
Vasilyevskiy, Ostrov, *St. Petersburg* 26 B1
Vaso Regulador El Cristo, *Mexico City* 18 B1
Vaucluse, *Sydney* 28 B2
Vaucresson, *Paris* 23 A1
Vauhallan, *Paris* 23 B2
Vaujours, *Paris* 23 A4
Vauxhall, *London* 15 c4
Vecsés, *Budapest* 7 B3
Veleň, *Prague* 24 A3
Veleslavin, *Prague* 24 B2
Vélizy-Villacoublay, *Paris* 23 B2
Velka-Chuchle, *Prague* 24 B2
Velké Přilepy, *Prague* 24 B1
Venda Seca, *Lisbon* 14 A1
Venetian Islands, *Miami* 18 B2
Venezia, Palazzo, *Rome* 25 c2
Venice, *Los Angeles* 16 C2
Ventas, *Madrid* 17 B1
Ventorro del Cano, *Madrid* 17 B1
Venustiano Carranza, *Mexico City* 18 B2
Verde →, *São Paulo* 26 A1
Verdi, *Athens* 2 A2
Verdun, *Montreal* 19 B2
Vérhalom, *Budapest* 7 A2
Vermelho →, *São Paulo* 26 B1
Vernon, *Los Angeles* 16 B3
Verrières-le-Buisson, *Paris* 23 B2
Versailles, *Buenos Aires* 7 B1
Versailles, *Paris* 23 B1
Veshnyaki, *Moscow* 19 B4
Vesolyy Posolok, *St. Petersburg* 26 B2
Vestra, *Helsinki* 12 B1
Vestskoven, *Copenhagen* 10 A2
Vicálvaro, *Madrid* 17 B2
Vicente Lopez, *Buenos Aires* 7 B2
Victoria, *Hong Kong* 12 B2
Victoria, *London* 15 c3
Victoria, Mt., *Wellington* 32 B1
Victoria, Pont, *Montreal* 19 B2
Victoria and Albert Waterfront, *Cape Town* 8 a1
Victoria Gardens, *Mumbai* 20 B2
Victoria Harbour, *Hong Kong* 12 B2
Victoria Island, *Lagos* 14 B2
Victoria L., *Johannesburg* 13 B2
Victoria Lawn Tennis Courts, *Melbourne* 17 B2
Victoria Park, *Singapore* 27 B2
Victoria Peak, *Hong Kong* 12 B1
Victoria Wharf, *Cape Town* 8 a2
Vienna = Wien, *Vienna* 31 A2
Vienna, *Washington* 32 B2
View Park, *Los Angeles* 16 B3
Vigário Geral, *Rio de Janeiro* 24 A1
Vigentino, *Milan* 18 B2
Viggbyholm, *Stockholm* 28 A2
Vighignolo, *Milan* 18 B1
Viikki, *Helsinki* 12 B3
Vikhroli, *Mumbai* 20 A2
Vila Guilherme, *São Paulo* 26 B2
Vila Isabel, *Rio de Janeiro* 24 B1
Vila Jaguára, *São Paulo* 26 B1
Vila Madalena, *São Paulo* 26 B1
Vila Maria, *São Paulo* 26 B2
Vila Mariana, *São Paulo* 26 B2
Vila Prudente, *São Paulo* 26 B2
Viladecans, *Barcelona* 4 B1
Vile Parle, *Mumbai* 20 A2
Villa Adelina, *Buenos Aires* 7 B1
Villa Ballester, *Buenos Aires* 7 B1
Villa Barilari, *Buenos Aires* 7 C2
Villa Borghese, *Rome* 25 a3
Villa Bosch, *Buenos Aires* 7 B1
Villa C. Colon, *Buenos Aires* 7 C2
Villa Ciudadela, *Buenos Aires* 7 B1
Villa de Guadalupe, *Mexico City* 18 B2
Villa Devoto, *Buenos Aires* 7 B1
Villa Diamante, *Buenos Aires* 7 C2
Villa Dominico, *Buenos Aires* 7 C3
Villa Lugano, *Buenos Aires* 7 C2
Villa Lynch, *Buenos Aires* 7 B1
Villa Madero, *Buenos Aires* 7 C1
Villa Sáenz Pena, *Buenos Aires* 7 B1
Villa Urquiza, *Buenos Aires* 7 B2
Villaverde, *Madrid* 17 B1
Villaverde Bajo, *Madrid* 17 B1
Ville-d'Avray, *Paris* 23 B2
Villecresnes, *Paris* 23 B4
Villejuif, *Paris* 23 B3
Villemomble, *Paris* 23 A4
Villeneuve-la-Garenne, *Paris* 23 A2
Villeneuve-le-Roi, *Paris* 23 B3
Villeneuve-St.-Georges, *Paris* 23 B3
Villeparisis, *Paris* 23 A4
Villevaudé, *Paris* 23 A4
Villiers-le-Bâcle, *Paris* 23 B1
Villiers-sur-Marne, *Paris* 23 B4
Villinki, *Helsinki* 12 C3
Villoresi, Canale, *Milan* 18 A1
Vilvoorde, *Brussels* 6 A2
Vimodrone, *Milan* 18 A2
Vimont, *Montreal* 19 A1
Vinanmek Palace, *Bangkok* 3 a2
Vincennes, *Paris* 23 A3
Vincennes, Bois de, *Paris* 23 B3
Vinings, *Atlanta* 3 A2
Vinohrady, *Prague* 24 c3
Vinoř, *Prague* 24 B3
Violet Hill, *Hong Kong* 12 B2
Virányos, *Budapest* 7 A1
Virgen del San Cristóbal, *Santiago* 26 B2
Virginia Gardens, *Miami* 18 B1
Virginia Key, *Miami* 18 B2
Viroflay, *Paris* 23 B2
Víron, *Athens* 2 B2
Virum, *Copenhagen* 10 A2
Vishnyaki, *Moscow* 19 B5
Visitacion Valley, *San Francisco* 25 B2
Vista Alegre, *Lima* 16 B3
Vista Alegre, *Santiago* 26 C1
Vista Grove, *Atlanta* 3 A3
Vitacura, *Santiago* 26 B2
Vitinia, *Rome* 25 C1
Vitry-sur-Seine, *Paris* 23 B3
Vizandinó, Moussío, *Athens* 2 b3
Vladykino, *Moscow* 19 A3
Vlezenbeek, *Brussels* 6 B1
Vltava →, *Prague* 24 A2
Vnukovo, *Moscow* 19 C1
Vokovice, *Prague* 24 B2
Volgelsdorf, *Berlin* 5 B5
Volkhonka-Zil, *Moscow* 19 C3
Vollen, *Oslo* 22 B1
Volodarskoye, *St. Petersburg* 26 B2
Volynkina-Derevnya, *St. Petersburg* 26 B1
Vondelpark, *Amsterdam* 2 A2
Vösendorf, *Vienna* 31 B2
Vostochnyy, *Moscow* 19 B5
Voula, *Athens* 2 C2
Vouliagmeni, *Athens* 2 C2
Vredehoek, *Cape Town* 8 A1
Vršovice, *Prague* 24 B2
Vyborgskaya Storona, *St. Petersburg* 26 B2
Vykhino, *Moscow* 19 B4
Vyšehrad, *Prague* 24 B2

W

Wachterhof, *Munich* 20 B3
Wadala, *Mumbai* 20 A2
Wadestown, *Wellington* 32 B1
Wadi Fukin, *Jerusalem* 13 B1
Wah Fu, *Hong Kong* 12 B1
Wahda, *Baghdad* 3 B2
Währing, *Vienna* 31 A2
Waidmannslust, *Berlin* 5 A3
Wainuiomata, *Wellington* 32 B2
Wainuiomata R. →, *Wellington* 32 B2
Wakefield, *Boston* 6 A3
Waldesruh, *Berlin* 5 B4
Waldperlach, *Munich* 20 B3
Waldtrudering, *Munich* 20 B3
Walkinstown, *Dublin* 11 B1
Wall Street, *New York* 21 f1
Waltham, *Boston* 6 A2
Waltham Forest, *London* 15 A3
Walthamstow, *London* 15 A3
Walton on Thames, *London* 15 B1
Wambeek, *Brussels* 6 A3
Wan Chai, *Hong Kong* 12 B2
Wan Chai Lanes, *Hong Kong* 12 c2
Wandsworth, *London* 15 B2
Wankhede Stadium, *Mumbai* 20 c2
Wannsee, *Berlin* 5 B1
Wansdorf, *Berlin* 5 A1
Wanstead, *London* 15 A4
Wapping, *London* 15 A3
Ward, *Dublin* 11 A1
Ward I., *Wellington* 32 B2
Warnberg, *Munich* 20 B2
Warrāq el 'Arab, *Cairo* 7 A2
Warrâq el Hadr, *Cairo* 7 A2
Warringen Park, *Melbourne* 17 A2
Warriston, *Edinburgh* 11 B2
Warsaw = Warszawa, *Warsaw* 31 B2
Warszawa, *Warsaw* 31 B2
Wartenberg, *Berlin* 5 A4
Washington, *Washington* 32 B3
Washington Heights, *New York* 21 A2
Washington Monument, *Washington* 32 b1
Washington Nat. Airport, *Washington* 32 B3
Washington Park, *Chicago* 9 C3
Wat Arun, *Bangkok* 3 b1
Wat Pho, *Bangkok* 3 b1
Wat Phra Keo, *Bangkok* 3 b1
Wat Traimit, *Bangkok* 3 c2
Water of Leith, *Edinburgh* 11 B1
Water Tower Place, *Chicago* 9 a2
Watergraafsmeer, *Amsterdam* 2 A2
Waterland, *Amsterdam* 2 A2
Waterloo, *Brussels* 6 B2
Waterloo, *Wellington* 32 B2
Waterloo International, *London* 15 b4
Watermael-Boitsfort, *Brussels* 6 B2
Watertown, *Boston* 6 A2
Watsonia, *Melbourne* 17 A2
Waverley, *Boston* 6 A2
Waverley, *Johannesburg* 13 A2
Waverley, *Sydney* 28 B2
Waverley Station, *Edinburgh* 11 b3
Wawer, *Warsaw* 31 B2
Wawrzyszew, *Warsaw* 31 B1
Wayland, *Boston* 6 A1
Wazirabad, *Delhi* 10 A2
Waziriya, *Baghdad* 3 A2
Wazirpur, *Delhi* 10 A2
Wealdstone, *London* 15 A1
Wedding, *Berlin* 5 A3
Weehawken, *New York* 21 B1
Weesp, *Amsterdam* 2 B3
Weidling, *Vienna* 31 A1
Weidlingbach, *Vienna* 31 A1
Weigongcun, *Beijing* 4 B1
Weijin He →, *Tianjin* 30 B2
Weissensee, *Berlin* 5 A3
Wellesley, *Boston* 6 B2
Wellesley Falls, *Boston* 6 B2
Wellesley Hills, *Boston* 6 B2
Welling, *London* 15 B4
Wellington, *Boston* 6 A3
Wellington, *Wellington* 32 B1
Wells Fargo Center, *Los Angeles* 16 b1
Weltevreden Park, *Johannesburg* 13 A1
Wembley, *London* 15 A2
Wemmel, *Brussels* 6 A1
Wemmer Pan, *Johannesburg* 13 B2
Wenceslas Square, *Prague* 24 b2
Wendenschloss, *Berlin* 5 B4
Wenhuagong, *Tianjin* 30 B2
Wennington, *London* 15 A5
Werneuchen, *Berlin* 5 A5
West Bedford, *Boston* 6 A2
West Concord, *Boston* 6 A1
West Don →, *Toronto* 30 A2
West Drayton, *London* 15 A1
West Ham, *London* 15 A4
West Harrow, *London* 15 A1
West Heath, *London* 15 B4
West Hill, *Toronto* 30 A3
West Hollywood, *Los Angeles* 16 B2
West Kensington, *London* 15 c1
West Kilburn, *London* 15 a1
West Lamma Channel, *Hong Kong* 12 B1
West Lynn, *Boston* 6 A4
West Medford, *Boston* 6 A3
West Miami, *Miami* 18 B1
West Molesey, *London* 15 B1
West New York, *New York* 21 B1
West of Twin Peaks, *San Francisco* 25 B2
West Park, *Johannesburg* 13 A1
West Rouge, *Toronto* 30 A4
West Roxbury, *Boston* 6 B3
West Springfield, *Washington* 32 C2
West Town, *Chicago* 9 B2
West Wharf, *Karachi* 14 B1
Westbourne Green, *London* 15 a1
Westchester, *Chicago* 9 B1
Westchester, *Los Angeles* 16 C2
Westchester, *New York* 21 A2
Westcliff, *Johannesburg* 13 B2
Westdene, *Johannesburg* 13 B1
Westend, *Helsinki* 12 C1
Wester Hailes, *Edinburgh* 11 B2
Westerham, *Munich* 20 B2
Western Addition, *San Francisco* 25 B2
Western Wall, *Jerusalem* 13 b3
Westgate, *Washington* 32 B3
Westlake, *Cape Town* 8 B1
Westlake, *San Francisco* 25 B2
Westminster, *London* 15 A3
Westmount, *Montreal* 19 B2
Weston, *Boston* 6 A2
Weston, *Toronto* 30 A1
Weston Res., *Boston* 6 A2
Westwood Village, *Los Angeles* 16 B2
Westzaan, *Amsterdam* 2 A1
Wetton, *Cape Town* 8 B2
Wexford, *Toronto* 30 A3
Weybridge, *London* 15 B1
Wezembeek-Oppem, *Brussels* 6 A2
White House, The, *Washington* 32 b1
Whitechapel, *London* 15 A3
Whitehall, *Dublin* 11 A2
Whitehall, *London* 15 b3
Whittier, *Los Angeles* 16 C4
Whitton, *London* 15 B1
Wieden, *Vienna* 31 A2
Wien, *Vienna* 31 A2
Wien-Schwechat, Flughafen, *Vienna* 31 B3
Wienerberg, *Vienna* 31 B2
Wierzbno, *Warsaw* 31 B2
Wijde Wormer, *Amsterdam* 2 A2
Wilanów, *Warsaw* 31 B2
Wilanówka →, *Warsaw* 31 C2
Wilhelmshagen, *Berlin* 5 B5
Wilket Creek Park, *Toronto* 30 A2
Wilkieston, *Edinburgh* 11 B1
Willbrook, *Dublin* 11 B2
Willesden, *London* 15 A2
Willesden Green, *London* 15 A2
Williamsbridge, *New York* 21 A2
Williamsburg, *New York* 21 B2
Williamstown, *Melbourne* 17 B1
Willoughby, *Sydney* 28 A2
Willow Springs, *Chicago* 9 C1
Willowdale, *Toronto* 30 A2
Wilmersdorf, *Berlin* 5 c1
Wilmette, *Chicago* 9 A2
Wilmington, *London* 15 B5
Wilshire Boulevard, *Los Angeles* 16 c1
Wimbledon, *London* 15 B2
Wimbledon Common, *London* 15 B2
Wimbledon Park, *London* 15 B2
Wimbledon Tennis Ground, *London* 15 B2
Winchester, *Boston* 6 A3
Windermere, *Cape Town* 8 A2
Windsor, *Johannesburg* 13 A1
Windsor Hills, *Los Angeles* 16 C2
Windy Arbour, *Dublin* 11 B2
Winning, *Munich* 20 B2
Winthrop, *Boston* 6 A4
Wissous, *Paris* 23 B2
Wittenau, *Berlin* 5 A2
Witwatersrand, Univ. of, *Johannesburg* 13 B2
Włochy, *Warsaw* 31 B1
Wo Mei, *Hong Kong* 12 A2
Wo Yi Hop, *Hong Kong* 12 A1
Woburn, *Boston* 6 A3
Woburn, *Toronto* 30 A3
Woduk Pluit, *Jakarta* 13 A1
Wola, *Warsaw* 31 B1
Wolf Trap Farm Park, *Washington* 32 B2
Wolica, *Warsaw* 31 C2
Wolica, *Warsaw* 31 C1
Wólka Węglowa, *Warsaw* 31 B1
Wollaston, *Boston* 6 B3
Woltersdorf, *Berlin* 5 B5
Woluwe-Saint-Lambert, *Brussels* 6 A2
Woluwe-Saint-Pierre, *Brussels* 6 A2
Wong Chuk Hang, *Hong Kong* 12 B2
Wong Chuk Wan, *Hong Kong* 12 A2
Wong Chuk Yeung, *Hong Kong* 12 A2
Wong Tai Sin, *Hong Kong* 12 A2
Wood Green, *London* 15 A3
Wood Ridge, *New York* 21 A1
Woodbridge, *Toronto* 30 A1
Woodford, *London* 15 A4
Woodford Bridge, *London* 15 A4
Woodford Green, *London* 15 A4
Woodhaven, *New York* 21 B2
Woodhouselee, *Edinburgh* 11 B2
Woodlands New Town, *Singapore* 27 A2
Woodmont, *Washington* 32 B3
Woodside, *London* 15 B3
Woodside, *New York* 21 B2
Woodstock, *Cape Town* 8 A1
Woollahra, *Sydney* 28 B2
Woolloomooloo, *Sydney* 28 b2
Woolooware B., *Sydney* 28 C1
Woolwich, *London* 15 B4
Woolworth Building, *New York* 21 e1
World Trade Center, *New York* 21 B1
Worli, *Mumbai* 20 A1
Worth, *Chicago* 9 C2
Wren's Nest, *Atlanta* 3 B2
Wrigley Building, *Chicago* 9 b2
Wuhlgarten, *Berlin* 5 A4
Wujiaochang, *Shanghai* 27 B2
Würm →, *Munich* 20 B1
Würm-kanal, *Munich* 20 A1
Wusong, *Shanghai* 27 A1
Wyczółki, *Warsaw* 31 C1
Wygoda, *Warsaw* 31 B2
Wynberg, *Cape Town* 8 B1

X

Xabregas, *Lisbon* 14 A2
Xianggang = Hong Kong, *Hong Kong* 12 B1
Xiaodian, *Tianjin* 30 A2
Xiaogang Park, *Canton* 8 B2
Xiaoping, *Canton* 8 A2
Xiasha chong, *Canton* 8 B1
Xichang, *Canton* 8 B2
Xicheng, *Beijing* 4 B1
Xidan, *Beijing* 4 B2
Xigu Park, *Tianjin* 30 A2
Xigucun, *Tianjin* 30 A1
Ximenwai, *Tianjin* 30 B1
Xinanlou, *Tianjin* 30 B2
Xinkai He →, *Tianjin* 30 A2
Xizhimen, *Beijing* 4 B1
Xu Beihong Mem. Hall, *Beijing* 4 a1
Xuanwu, *Beijing* 4 B1
Xuhui, *Shanghai* 27 B1

Y

Yaba, *Lagos* 14 A2
Yaftābād, *Tehran* 30 B1
Yahara, *Tokyo* 29 A2
Yaho, *Tokyo* 29 A1
Yakire, *Tokyo* 29 A4
Yamada, *Osaka* 22 A4
Yamada, *Tokyo* 29 B2
Yamamoto, *Osaka* 22 B4
Yamato →, *Osaka* 22 B3
Yamuna →, *Delhi* 10 B2
Yan Kit, *Singapore* 27 A3
Yanbu, *Canton* 8 B1
Yangch'ŏn, *Seoul* 26 B1
Yanghuayuan, *Beijing* 4 C1
Yangjae, *Seoul* 26 C2
Yangjiazhuang, *Shanghai* 27 A1
Yangpu, *Shanghai* 27 B2
Yangpu Park, *Shanghai* 27 B2
Yao, *Osaka* 22 B4
Yao Airport, *Osaka* 22 A4
Yarmūk, *Baghdad* 3 B1
Yarra →, *Melbourne* 17 A1
Yarra Bend Park, *Melbourne* 17 A2
Yarraville, *Melbourne* 17 A1
Yau Tong, *Hong Kong* 12 B2
Yauza →, *Moscow* 19 A4
Yeading, *London* 15 A1
Yedikule, *Istanbul* 12 C1
Yemin Moshe, *Jerusalem* 13 b2
Yenikapı, *Istanbul* 12 B1
Yeniköy, *Istanbul* 12 B2
Yerba Buena Gardens, *San Francisco* 25 c2
Yerba Buena I., *San Francisco* 25 B2
Yerres, *Paris* 23 B4
Yerushalayim = Jerusalem, *Jerusalem* 13 B2
Yiheyuan, *Beijing* 4 A1
Yinhangzhen, *Shanghai* 27 A2
Yishun New Town, *Singapore* 27 A3
Yixingbu, *Tianjin* 30 A2
Ylästö, *Helsinki* 12 B2
Yodo →, *Osaka* 22 A4
Yongdingman, *Beijing* 4 B2
Yŏngdong, *Seoul* 26 B2
Yŏngdŭngp'o, *Seoul* 26 B1
Yongfucun, *Canton* 8 B2
Yongjing, *Shanghai* 27 B2
Yongsan, *Seoul* 26 B1
Yonkers, *New York* 21 A2
York, *Toronto* 30 A2
York Mills, *Toronto* 30 A2
Yotsuya, *Tokyo* 29 a2
You'anmen, *Beijing* 4 B2
Yŏŭido, *Seoul* 26 B1
Youndsfield, *Cape Town* 8 B1
Yuanxiatian, *Canton* 8 A2
Yugo-Zarad, *Moscow* 19 B3
Yung Shue Wan, *Hong Kong* 12 B1
Yūsofābād, *Tehran* 30 A2
Yuyuantan Park, *Beijing* 4 b2

Z

Zaandam, *Amsterdam* 2 A1
Zaandijk, *Amsterdam* 2 A1
Zaanstad, *Amsterdam* 2 A1
Zāběhlice, *Prague* 24 B2
Ząbki, *Warsaw* 31 B2
Zacisze, *Warsaw* 31 B2
Zahrā, *Baghdad* 3 A1
Zakharkovo, *Moscow* 19 B1
Žalov, *Prague* 24 A2
Załuski, *Warsaw* 31 C1
Zamdorf, *Munich* 20 B2
Zamek Królewski, *Warsaw* 31 a2
Zamek Ujazdowski, *Warsaw* 31 c3
Zanevka, *St. Petersburg* 26 B3
Zapote, *Manila* 17 C1
Záppeio, *Athens* 2 c2
Zarechye, *Moscow* 19 B2
Zaventem, *Brussels* 6 A2
Zawady, *Warsaw* 31 B2
Zāwiyet Abû Musallam, *Cairo* 7 B1
Zawrā' Park, *Baghdad* 3 B2
Zbraslav, *Prague* 24 C2
Zbuzany, *Prague* 24 B1
Zdiby, *Prague* 24 B2
Zeekoevlei, *Cape Town* 8 B2
Zehlendorf, *Berlin* 5 B2
Zenne →, *Brussels* 6 B1
Zerań, *Warsaw* 31 B2
Zerzeń, *Warsaw* 31 B2
Zeytinburnu, *Istanbul* 12 C1
Zhabei, *Shanghai* 27 B1
Zhangguizhuang, *Tianjin* 30 B2
Zhdanov, *Moscow* 19 B4
Zheleznodorozhnyy, *Moscow* 19 B6
Zhenru, *Shanghai* 27 B1
Zhernovka, *St. Petersburg* 26 B2
Zhicun, *Canton* 8 B2
Zhongshan Park, *Beijing* 4 b2
Zhongshan Park, *Shanghai* 27 B1
Zhoucun, *Canton* 8 A2
Zhoujiadu, *Shanghai* 27 B1
Zhoujiazhen, *Shanghai* 27 B2
Zhu Jiang →, *Canton* 8 B3
Zhulebino, *Moscow* 19 B5
Zhushadi, *Canton* 8 A3
Zielona, *Warsaw* 31 B3
Zielonka, *Warsaw* 31 B3
Ziya He →, *Tianjin* 30 A1
Žižkov, *Prague* 24 B2
Zličín, *Prague* 24 B1
Zócalo, *Mexico City* 18 b3
Zografos, *Athens* 2 B2
Zoliborz, *Warsaw* 31 B1
Zonnenbloem, *Cape Town* 8 A1
Zoo, *Beijing* 4 a1
Zugliget, *Budapest* 7 B1
Zugló, *Budapest* 7 A2
Zuiderwoude, *Amsterdam* 2 A3
Zumbi, *Rio de Janeiro* 24 A1
Zunderdorp, *Amsterdam* 2 A2
Zuvuvu →, *São Paulo* 26 C1
Zwanenburg, *Amsterdam* 2 A1
Zwölfaxing, *Vienna* 31 B2
Zyuzino, *Moscow* 19 C3

CITY GAZETTEER

The entries below provide information on places of interest in cities throughout the world that have particularly large numbers of visitors, whether in a business or tourist capacity. The map page reference at the start of an entry indicates that one or more relevant maps are included in the City Maps section.

Accra, Ghana

Accra is not the most beautiful city in West Africa, but its people are considered to be among the friendliest and best educated. It has several lively markets and a National Museum with displays of West African art and artefacts. Near the city are some beautiful sandy beaches, although visitors should be alert to the powerful undertow. Further along the coast are forts and castles that once served as slave-trading centres, including St George's Castle at Elmina, the oldest European structure in sub-Saharan Africa.

Agra, India

Agra is visited primarily for its architectural wonders, especially the 17th-century Taj Mahal. This magical building, a symbol of Mughal emperor Shah Jahan's love for his favourite wife, Mumtaz Mahal, captures the imagination even when crowded with tourists in the heat of the day. Agra's 16th-century Red Fort contains elaborately decorated royal apartments and gardens that give a vivid impression of life at the Mughal court. Just 40 km (25 miles) away is the Mughal 'ghost city' of Fatehpur Sikri which was abandoned almost immediately after it had been built in the 1570s.

Taj Mahal, Agra

Amsterdam, The Netherlands   *Map page 2*

In the centre of Amsterdam is a network of canals, crossed by around a thousand bridges and edged with tree-lined streets of 17th- and 18th-century gabled houses. Canal cruises are an excellent way to get to know the city, and visitors can also hire bicycles – a major form of transport in Amsterdam. Among the museums are the Rijksmuseum, with its famous art collection, the Van Gogh Museum, and the Stedelijk Museum, housing modern art. The heart of the city is Dam Square, with the royal palace and Anne Frank's house (now a museum) close by. Rembrandt's house can also be visited in an area full of bars, nightclubs and restaurants.

Athens, Greece   *Map page 2*

Athens is a curious mixture of ancient and modern, where ugly concrete tower blocks rub shoulders with Classical monuments. Dominating the centre of the city are the ruins on the Acropolis, dating from the 5th century BC and crowned by the magnificent Parthenon. Other interesting ruins include the Temple of Olympian Zeus, the largest temple in Greece. The National Archaeological Museum houses gold artefacts from Mycenae and spectacular Minoan frescoes.

Nestling beneath the Acropolis is the engaging Pláka quarter, with its small Byzantine churches and bustling tavernas. For most visitors the centre of Athens is Sindagma Square, with its large hotels, banks and open-air cafés. Ferries to the islands depart from the port of Piraeus, 10 km (6 miles) from the square.

Atlanta, Georgia, USA   *Map page 3*

Beneath the glittering high-rise buildings of Atlanta's modern financial centre lies 'Underground Atlanta' – the revitalized old centre, complete with cobbled, gas-lit streets and packed with shops and restaurants. The piazza above it is filled with street entertainers and flanked by the Coca-Cola Museum. Atlanta is most famously associated with Martin Luther King, and an area of the city is devoted to his memory and to the history of the civil rights movement. The Centennial Olympic Park, with its Fountain of Rings, is an entertaining outdoor venue, and the adjacent CNN Center provides an interesting studio tour.

Auckland, New Zealand

The heart of Auckland is the magnificent Waitemata Harbour, where sailing is a popular pastime. The city is not renowned for its nightlife, but it is pleasant to walk its streets, perhaps following the 13 km (8-mile) Coast-to-Coast Walkway from the Ferry Building to Manukau Harbour. On the route, in an area of parkland known as The Domain, is the Auckland Museum, with a unique collection of Maori and Pacific Island artefacts. Beyond is the inner suburb of Parnell, with its colonial buildings, east of which is Underwater World, a particularly impressive aquarium. There are several city beaches, and surfing beaches beyond the Waitakere Ranges.

Baghdad, Iraq   *Map page 3*

Baghdad is a city where modern shops and restaurants rub shoulders with bazaars. Buildings dating from as early as the 13th century include the Abbasid Palace and an Islamic Law School (the Mustansiriyah), both now museums. The National Museum contains artefacts from ancient civilizations, including Mesopotomia and Babylonia. At the time of writing, Baghdad is effectively closed to Western visitors.

Bangkok, Thailand   *Map page 3*

With its choking traffic, Bangkok can be both a daunting and an exhilarating city for short-stay visitors. Something of the old Siam can be uncovered by using the river-bus service to visit the Royal Grand Palace and the ornate Temple of the Emerald Buddha (Wat Phra Keo). Other Buddhist temples include the Temple of the Dawn (Wat Arun), whose 82 m (266 ft) high gilded stupa is best seen from the Chao Phraya River. At Jim Thompson's House there is an extraordinary private museum of Thai domestic architecture. The network of canals, with their floating markets, is well worth exploring, as are the shops for silk and other textiles, clothes, jewellery and handicrafts. Night-time entertainment includes traditional dancing and Thai boxing.

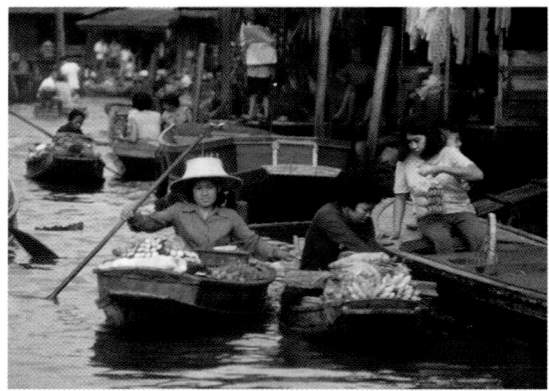
Floating market, Bangkok

Barcelona, Spain   *Map page 4*

The capital of Catalonia and Spain's second city, Barcelona is a major port with a fashionable, cosmopolitan cultural life. Particularly enjoyable is strolling along the Ramblas, a broad avenue which bisects central Barcelona, and has a vibrant street life. At the southern end is the renovated harbour area, with shops, restaurants and tapas bars. The district of greatest historic interest is the Barri Gòtic, where medieval houses cluster around the great Gothic cathedral, La Seu. Barcelona has over 50 museums and galleries, including world-class museums dedicated to the works of Picasso and Miró, but it is the buildings of Antonio Gaudí that are most often associated with the city. His incomplete Sagrada Família Cathedral has become a symbol for Barcelona, and is perhaps the most fantastic of all his eccentric creations.

Beijing, China   *Map page 4*

Despite Beijing's daunting scale, extreme climate and heavy traffic, its sights are well worth visiting. They include the massive Tiananmen Square, the Mao Mausoleum, the Great Hall of the People, the Imperial Palace (Forbidden City), the buildings of the Summer Palace along the shore of Kunming Lake, and the 15th-century Temple of Heaven. Beijing has many interesting parks, including Beihai Park with its historic buildings and exquisite Jade Island. However, perhaps the most famous attraction of all is the Great Wall, which can be visited at Badaling, just 70 km (40 miles) north-west of the city, on a trip that also takes in the Ming tombs in the Shisan Ling Valley.

Berlin, Germany   *Map page 5*

After decades of being divided into West and East Berlin, the city is once again the capital of a united Germany. From the modern dome on the renovated Reichstag building there are fine views of the new buildings rising in the former no-man's-land between the two sectors, whose distinct character can still be felt. The city's youthful 'alternative' scene also continues to thrive, as does its famous nightlife in and around, for example, Savignyplatz in the west and the Scheunenviertel in the east. To the east of the Brandenburg Gate is an area of grand old squares and streets containing Berlin's main museums, including the Pergamon, with its collection of Ancient, Oriental and Islamic art. To the west is the landscaped Tiergarten, the famous zoo, with its exotic pastiche architecture, and the wealthy, modern heart of former West Berlin.

Boston, Massachusetts, USA
Map page 6

The oldest areas of Boston have a European feel, their street plan based on meandering farm tracks. The Beacon Hill district contains splendid 19th-century brick houses and narrow alleyways, and the Massachusetts State House. A 'Freedom Trail', marked by a line of red bricks, takes the visitor past 17th- and 18th-century buildings, some of which are associated with the American Revolution. There are also guided tours of the USA's oldest surviving battleship – the USS *Constitution*, built in 1797 – moored in Boston Harbour. Across the Charles River lies Cambridge, with Harvard University and Square. Boston is a relatively unthreatening city for visitors, with a lively intellectual and artistic life, and a 'necklace' of city parks and tree-lined streets within a compact central area.

Brisbane, Queensland, Australia

The relaxed atmosphere and compactness of its centre make Brisbane a pleasant place to stroll around. Its historic precinct, next to the Botanic Gardens, contains some fine 19th-century buildings, among them the Treasury. South of the River Brisbane is the State Art Gallery and the Cultural Centre, which includes two theatres and a superb concert hall. Day trips are possible to the beaches of the Gold and Sunshine Coasts.

Brussels, Belgium
Map page 6

The centre of government for the European Union, Brussels is renowned for its excellent restaurants and shops, with everything from flea markets to the designer boutiques in the Galéries St Hubert. The imposing Hôtel de Ville, the gilded 17th-century houses and the Maison du Roi make the Grand-Place one of the world's most beautiful central squares. To the east lies the Gothic cathedral, the Palais Royale and the Royal Art Museums, containing both ancient and modern art. The city is full of fine examples of Art Nouveau architecture, including the museum dedicated to the founder of the movement, Victor Horta. A popular tourist site is the irreverent 17th-century statue, Manneken Pis.

Budapest, Hungary
Map page 7

The Danube and Parliament building, Budapest

Formerly two cities, Buda and Pest, on opposite sides of the Danube, the capital of Hungary is a fascinating destination. The Castle Hill district of Buda includes the cobbled streets and medieval houses of the Old Town, and the Royal Palace (Budavári palota), containing the national art gallery and museum. The Fishermen's Bastion gives sweeping views over the city. A network of grand 19th-century boulevards forms the centre of the larger, more cosmopolitan Pest, with its imposing Parliament building (Orzágház).

There are many elegant spa baths (gyógyfürdo) dotted around the city, and extensive Roman remains, including an amphitheatre, at Óbuda and Rómaifürdo. Famous for its cafés, Budapest has excellent restaurants and offers a huge range of entertainment, including opera, jazz and discos.

Buenos Aires, Argentina
Map page 7

The centre of Buenos Aires is laid out on a grand scale, with wide boulevards, imposing 19th-century buildings, modern tower blocks, and spacious plazas. Around this area, however, are the more intimate districts (*barrios*), each with its distinctive character. San Telmo is the artists' quarter, while La Boca, with its brightly painted houses, is the city's port district. The most fashionable district, Recoleta, houses the National Museum of Art, but is best known for the ornate tombs of its cemetery.

La Boca, Buenos Aires

Cairo, Egypt
Map page 7

The largest city in Africa, Cairo is full of hooting taxis and bustling crowds. Modern buildings have risen next to the minarets of the old mosques, while a maze of markets provide potential bargains. The Pyramids of Giza are visible from the upper storeys of buildings all over the city. Famous worldwide for its unrivalled collection of antiquities, the Egyptian Museum houses the treasures of the Pharaoh Tutankhamun, and more than 100,000 other relics and antiquities from all periods of ancient Egyptian history. Experiences not to be missed include the *Son et Lumière* that takes place daily by the Sphinx at Giza, and drifting on the Nile in a *felucca* while watching the sun sink below the Cairo skyline.

Calcutta (Kolkata), India
Map page 8

The capital of West Bengal, Calcutta (Kolkata) is regarded by many as the cultural and intellectual centre of India. It also has a reputation for extreme poverty and squalor. One of the great colonial cities of Asia, its main historic sites date from the days of the British Raj and include the white marble Victoria Memorial, the neo-Gothic St Paul's Cathedral, and the Indian Museum, with sculptures from all over India. These buildings are all in the vicinity of the Maidan, one of the largest city parks in the world, where hundreds of different interests – among them yoga, cricket and riding – are regularly pursued, and live entertainment is provided.

Canton (Guangzhou), China
Map page 8

An economic success but a planning disaster, Guangzhou holds more attraction for the business traveller than for those seeking historic sites.

There are, however, numerous decaying French and British colonial buildings on Shamian Island, which provides a haven of peace from the bustle of Guangzhou's streets. A climb to the top of the 11th-century Temple of Six Banyan Trees provides a fine view. Another way of seeing the city is to take a cruise on the Pearl River.

Cape Town, South Africa
Map page 8

South Africa's oldest city, Cape Town has several buildings of historic interest, including the Castle of Good Hope, the Old Town House, the Tuynhuis and the Parliament building. Artefacts from all over Africa are sold at the Saturday market in Greenmarket Square. The city lies below the spectacular Table Mountain, accessible by cable car. There are numerous good beaches, such as those at Clifton and Camps Bay on the cold Atlantic Ocean, and at Muizenberg and Fishoek on the warmer Indian Ocean. The old docks have been developed as the Victoria and Albert Waterfront, which boasts a range of restaurants. Boat trips run from here to the infamous Robben Island, where Nelson Mandela was imprisoned.

Cartagena, Colombia

Several impressive 16th-century forts overlook the channel leading to the bay of Cartagena, evidence of the city's origins as an imperial Spanish stronghold. Huge 17th- and 18th-century walls surround narrow streets, palaces, churches, monasteries and plazas. The Palace of the Inquisition is a fine example of colonial architecture, with its magnificent Baroque gateway.

Chicago, Illinois, USA
Map page 9

Built on the shore of Lake Michigan, Chicago played a key role in the economic development of the USA, serving as a railhead for the cattle trade of the Midwest. Its skyline includes skyscrapers dating from the 1890s, buildings in the International Style of the 1950s, and particularly fine examples of more recent architecture. The Sears Tower provides fantastic views of four states from its Space Deck. A closer view can be had on a boat trip up the Chicago River or from 'The Loop', an elevated railway that lends its name to the area it encircles. There are several important museums, including the vast Museum of Science and Industry and the Art Institute of Chicago. For outdoor pursuits, there is the extensive Grant Park, bordering the lake. The city is renowned for its rich musical life and, as well as a world-class symphony orchestra, there is a multitude of clubs offering blues, jazz, rock and folk music.

Skyline with Sears Tower, Chicago

Cologne, Germany

Despite the almost total destruction of central Cologne during World War II, many historic buildings have been restored to their former glory, including the massive and beautiful twin-towered Gothic cathedral (Dom). Among the museums and art galleries are the Roman-Germanic Museum and the Imhoff-Stollwek Museum of Chocolate. The city's unique beer, *kslsch*, can be sampled in the numerous beer halls. Short boat trips on the Rhine provide views of the impressive riverfront, while longer boat excursions go to, for example, Königswinter and Linz.

Copenhagen, Denmark   *Map page 10*

Scandinavia's largest and liveliest city, Copenhagen has excellent art collections, royal palaces, churches and other historic buildings as well as entertainment late into the night. Punctuated by parks, lakes, fountains and squares, the city is easily explored on foot or bicycle. The old harbour of Nyhavn, with its tall, brightly painted buildings, is packed with pavement cafés and bars, while the Latin Quarter is good for restaurants. From the top of the Round Tower (Rundee Taarn), Europe's oldest functioning observatory, there are magnificent views over the city. The famous Tivoli Gardens is a delightfully varied amusement park dating from 1843. A bridge now links Copenhagen to the attractive Swedish city of Malmö.

Delhi, India   *Map page 10*

Red Fort, Delhi

The capital of India, Delhi is a city with two centres: New Delhi, which was established by the British in 1911, and Old Delhi, whose present layout dates from the 17th century. The streets of the old town, and in particular Chandni Chauk, are famously frenetic. The massive walls of the Red Fort and the Lahore Gate enclose a host of palace buildings, although many have been stripped of their fine decoration. India's largest mosque, the Jama Masjid, is also in the old town. The new city, with its broad avenues and imposing marble buildings, contains some older sites, including the 16th-century tomb of Humayun and the 12th-century Qutb Minar tower.

Dublin, Ireland   *Map page 11*

Built on the River Iffey, Ireland's capital contains elegant 18th-century buildings, two Norman cathedrals, a castle, and some fine museums, three of them in Leinster House. One of the oldest books in the world, the 9th-century illuminated Book of Kells, is housed in Trinity College library, while the Writers' Museum pays homage to local literary figures such as W. B. Yeats, James Joyce and Oscar Wilde. Dublin has a relaxed, friendly atmosphere, and plenty of pubs and restaurants. In summer, outdoor events are often held in Phoenix Park. The famous Easter Uprising of 1916 is commemorated at Kilmainham Jail, where many heroes of Irish independence were once incarcerated.

Edinburgh, Scotland   *Map page 11*

Set on a dramatic rock that soars 76 m (250 ft) from the valley floor, the Old Town of Edinburgh is a collection of historic buildings, towering tenements and narrow passages huddling beneath a romantic castle. The Royal Mile, lined with 16th- and 17th-century buildings, leads from the castle to the royal residence of Holyrood. The Royal Museum lies to its south, as does the lively Grassmarket district with its bars and restaurants. The small but elegant National Gallery sits in Princes Street Gardens to the north. Beyond lie graceful Georgian squares, terraces and crescents of the New Town. Scotland's capital has a rich cultural life, including the world-famous International and Fringe festivals.

Esfahan, Iran

On the four sides of the vast central square of Esfahan, with its formal lawns and pool, are the delicately tiled façades of public buildings. These include the opulent Royal Mosque and the magnificent entrance to the bazaar, whose crowded streets twist and turn towards the steps of the Great Mosque, a complex of buildings spanning a 700-year period. Among other historic sites are the shrine of Imamzadeh Ahmad and several royal palaces. Esfahan's high altitude keeps it relatively cool, making it pleasant to stroll through the streets and parks, and sample the many teahouses.

Fès, Morocco

The old part of Fès – Fès el-Bali – is one of the largest living medieval cities in the world. A fascinating labyrinth of some 94,000 streets and lanes, its covered bazaars are crammed with every conceivable sort of craft workshop, restaurants and market stalls, as well as extensive dye pits and tanneries. On the edge of the old town, the Museum of Moroccan Arts houses a splendid collection of artefacts, including colourful tribal carpets and the city's famous blue pottery.

Florence, Italy

The pedestrianized streets in the beautiful centre of Florence enable visitors to wander about freely, visiting such well-known Renaissance sites as the cathedral, with its red-roofed dome, and the spacious Piazza della Signoria, dominated by the crenellated Palazzo Vecchio. Between the piazza and the River Arno is the Uffizi Gallery, containing famous works by Botticelli and Titian among many others. The 14th-century Ponte Vecchio bridge, lined on both sides with jewellery and gift shops, provides a route to the imposing Pitti Palace. The city's churches range in style from the exquisite San Miniato, through the austere Santo Croce to the classically inspired San Lorenzo. Of the many religious frescoes, those by Fra Angelico in the monastery of San Marco, and by Masaccio in the church of Santa Maria del Carmine, stand out. The Bargello has a fine collection of sculpture, while the Accademia houses Michelangelo's *David*.

Cathedral with Brunelleshci's dome, Florence

Geneva, Switzerland

Geneva enjoys one of the world's most dramatic locations, straddling the Rhône where it leaves Lake Geneva, and overlooked by the Alps on one side and the Jura mountains on the other. A cosmopolitan, French-speaking city, it is a world centre for banking and commerce as well as for international organizations, such as the Red Cross. South of the river, the oldest part has excellent museums, galleries and historic buildings, including St Peter's Cathedral, where John Calvin preached. Geneva lives up to its reputation for efficiency, cleanliness and safety, but all this comes at a price: restaurants, clubs and other entertainments are smart and expensive.

Hamburg, Germany

Germany's largest port (there are daily harbour tours from March to November), Hamburg combines its busy commercial life with a graceful, old-world charm. Situated on the River Elbe and criss-crossed by a network of canals, at its heart is the Alster lake, where boating is a popular pastime in the summer. The city has many extensive parks, stylish shopping arcades, elegant boulevards, museums and art galleries, among them the Kunsthalle with a fine collection of art spanning several centuries. There are numerous inviting café-bars and all-night entertainment, most notably in the St Pauli Quarter, where The Beatles famously performed in the 1960s.

Hanoi, Vietnam

Built on the Red River, around several large lakes, Hanoi has both peaceful tree-lined avenues and parks, and a bustling old city where almost anything can be purchased, including silk, lacquerware, puppets and jewellery. Bikes are the main form of transport. The city's many religious buildings include the One-Pillar Pagoda and the 11th-century Temple of Literature. Ho Chi Minh's mausoleum provides a memorable experience, with visitors being escorted to view the embalmed body. A day trip can be made to the Perfume Pagoda – actually a complex of pagodas and Buddhist shrines carved out of limestone cliffs. A cruise from Haiphong around the limestone islands of Halong Bay is also recommended.

Havana, Cuba

Ironically for a country that is proud of its independence from imperialism, one of the main attractions of Cuba's capital is its colonial past. The vast open space of Plaza de la Revolución and the post-colonial buildings of the Vedado district are worth seeing, but it is the boulevards and squares of Old Havana that are most fascinating.

The palaces surrounding the Plaza de Armas, the Baroque cathedral and the elegant thoroughfare 'The Paseo' are all fine examples of colonial architecture. There are few cars on the streets, but many bicycles. There are also many nightclubs, where salsa is the predominant dance style.

Capitol building and Grand Theatre, Havana

Helsinki, Finland   Map page 12

Helsinki is almost surrounded by water and is full of the sounds and scents of the sea. Among its architectural gems are the 19th-century Neo-classical buildings of Senate Square – which also contains the blue-domed Lutheran Cathedral – and the rock-hewn church of Temppeliauko (1969) where many concerts are held. Although its combination of attractive buildings, good restaurants and excellent art galleries and museums make it a year-round tourist destination, Helsinki really comes to life in summer, with open-air cafés, concerts, and boat trips to the ruined fortress on nearby Suomenlinna Island.

Hong Kong, China   Map page 12

Most visitors to Hong Kong take the short ferry ride from Kowloon across the harbour, with its spectacular view of the high-rise buildings on the waterfront of Hong Kong Island. A visit to the Man Mo temple, with its ornate interior, provides a complete contrast. A funicular goes to the top of Victoria Peak where there are shady paths through lush vegetation. The Tsim Sha Tsui area of Kowloon contains a group of modern exhibition buildings, including the Space Museum and the Hong Kong Museum of History, as well as air-conditioned shopping malls. A ferry goes to the islands of Lamma, where there are relatively uncrowded beaches, country walks and seafood restaurants. A hydrofoil goes to Macau.

Istanbul, Turkey   Map page 12

Formerly known as Constantinople, Istanbul has an imperial history dating back to the time of the Roman Empire. Its stategic position straddling the Bosporus Strait makes it both a European and an Asian city. Among the churches built in the 6th century by Emperor Constantine is the domed Hagia Sophia (Aya Sofya), which was converted into a mosque in 1453 and is now a museum. The 17th-century Blue Mosque (Sultanahmet Camii) is a masterpiece of Ottoman architecture, while the Topkapi Palace, with its imperial treasury stuffed with gold and jewels, is on every itinerary. In old Istanbul is the labyrinthine Kapali Carsi (the world's largest covered bazaar) where more than 4,000 shops and stalls sell carpets, jewellery, ceramics, brass and leatherware. A fascinating mixture of both the ancient and modern, Istanbul also has a renowned cuisine.

Jaipur, India

Known as the 'Pink City' because of the salmon-coloured wash applied to many of its buildings, Jaipur is the capital of the colourful state of Rajasthan. It is divided into areas dedicated to specialist activities, such as elephant-handling or the sale of textiles, silver or gems. Within the walled town are the Palace of Winds (Hawa Mahal), with its delicately screened windows, the City Palace – now a museum – and Jai Singh's extraordinary Observatory, with its huge angular stone instruments. Nearby is the hill town and Rajput palace complex of Amber.

Jakarta, Indonesia   Map page 13

Jakarta's glinting high-rise office blocks contrast sharply with the cobbled square at the heart of what was 18th-century Batavia (now known as Kota). Much can be discovered of this colonial period at the dock of Sunda Kelapa, where many magnificent schooners are moored and a maritime museum has been created in an old warehouse. The National Museum has excellent displays on Indonesia's ethnic groups. There is a theme park at Taman Impian Jaya Ancol, and Balinese dancing and traditional music at Taman Ismail Marzuki. Jakarta also offers a fine range of restaurants.

Jerusalem, Israel   Map page 13

The focus of most visits to Jerusalem is the Old City with its different quarters. The heart of the Christian quarter is the Church of the Holy Sepulchre, the site of Christ's crucifixion. This is reached along the Via Dolorosa, much of which passes through the Muslim quarter, with its impressive Mamluk architecture. The Western (Wailing) Wall is in the Jewish quarter, which also contains the multi-layered Temple Mount Excavations. The Armenian quarter, the centre of the Armenian Church, contains the impressive Citadel. Towering over all these is the golden Dome of the Rock, a sacred Muslim site in the Temple Mount compound.

Dome of the Rock, Jerusalem

Johannesburg, South Africa   Map page 13

The richest city in Africa, Johannesburg is also a lively centre of South African culture. Museum-Africa has collections relating to the history and art of all sections of the community, while the nearby Market Theatre Complex, which contains four theatres, is an attractive place in which to eat and drink, and listen to music. Visitors, however, should be aware of the high crime rate in the downtown area, and enjoy instead the restaurants and gardens of northern suburbs such as Rosebank and Melville. Outside the city is Soweto, the vast black township which has a lively music and theatre scene but is best visited on a guided tour.

Kairouan, Tunisia

An important centre for the Muslim faith, Tunisia's holy city has over 130 mosques, including the 9th-century Great Mosque, which once doubled as a fortress. A special permit is required to visit the holy sites. Kairouan's maze of buildings and narrow, winding streets is enclosed by ancient city walls, and it is a fascinating place in which to stroll. Artisans carry out the traditional trades of weaving and carpentry, and carpet sellers try to attract visitors to their stalls in the souk (bazaar).

Karachi, Pakistan   Map page 14

Developed as a city by the British from the 1840s, Karachi is a business rather than a tourist centre. It does, however, have many colourful bazaars in Saddar, the central district, which specialize in such products as jewellery, cloth, dried fruit and bottles. It also has a fascinating coastline which can be viewed on a traditional lateen-sailed boat trip from the harbour. Clifton Beach, with its camel rides and fairground, is well equipped for families, while other, rather less commercialized beaches are a short drive away.

Katmandu, Nepal

Street scene, Katmandu

Katmandu is a popular holiday destination – an intriguing mixture of modern buildings and narrow, traffic-clogged streets with intricately carved temples and shrines. Many of these ancient buildings are grouped around Durbar Square, including the Jaganath Temple, with its erotic carvings. The Old Royal Palace houses an interesting museum. Jochne, better known as 'Freak Street', is a focal point for many visitors, with its fascinating shops, cheap hotels and restaurants. Outside the city are three huge temples: the Hindu Pashupatinath complex, with its riverside ghats, and the Buddhist stupas of Boudhanath and Swayambunath.

Kraków, Poland

Having come through World War II virtually unscathed, and with not a high-rise building in sight, Kraków's densely packed old centre is full of historic churches and picturesque streets and squares. The central market square, which is reputed to be the largest medieval town square in Europe, contains a number of interesting buildings, among them the largely 16th-century Cloth Hall. The square is also the focus of the city's vigorous cultural life. There are several jazz and cabaret clubs in the Old Town, as well as numerous attractive cafés, bars and restaurants. To the south are the castle and cathedral of Wawel, behind which lies Kazimierz, the gradually reviving Jewish district.

Kuala Lumpur, Malaysia

A city that has sprung up since the 1860s, Kuala Lumpur is short on historic sites but has plenty to offer the visitor. Its colonial, 19th-century heart is Merdeka Square. Nearby is the most spectacular of the city's mosques, Masjid Jamek. Chinatown and Little India provide much of interest, and Malaysian craftwork and antiques can be bought at the Art Deco Central Market. The 'Golden Triangle' business area includes the Petronas Tower, the world's tallest building. The Lake Gardens contain a Bird Park, Orchid Garden and Butterfly Park. A half-hour drive outside the city are the Batu Caves, used as Hindu temples. Day trips can be made to the historic city of Malacca and the Genting Highlands Casino Complex.

Kyoto, Japan

Japan's capital for over 1,000 years, Kyoto has numerous Buddhist temples, Shinto shrines, palaces and gardens. Despite extensive modern development, there are still traditional wooden houses and craft shops in the back streets. A city that is particularly spectacular when clad in either cherry blossom or autumnal colours, its main sights include the 1,001 gilded statues of Buddha lined up in the Hall of the Thirty-Three Bays, the view from the temple of Kiyomizu-dera, and the intriguing gardens of Ginkaku-ji. Other famous gardens include the lake-garden of Kinkaku-ji, and the 500-year-old garden of Ryoan-ji. The city of Nara, 35 km (22 miles) south, contains the huge bronze Buddha of Todai-ji, and other fine examples of early Japanese art and architecture.

Temple of Kiyomizu-dera, Kyoto

Lagos, Nigeria   Map page 14

Although no longer the capital of Nigeria, Lagos is by far the largest city in West Africa. At its heart lies Lagos Island, a business centre whose skyline is spiked by skyscrapers. The National Museum provides a fascinating insight into the country's cultural heritage and includes works of art dating back 2,800 years, including beautiful Benin bronzes. The city's main attraction, however, is modern African music, and many of the country's best-known singers have nightclubs here.

Lahore, Pakistan

Lahore is renowned for its Mughal architecture. The most attractive of its many mosques is that of Wazir Kahn, covered in intricate glazed mosaic tiles, but the largest is the Badshahi Mosque. The massive walls of Lahore Fort surround a compound of elegant buildings. Away from the centre is Jahangir's tomb and the Shalimar Garden, with its geometrically arranged terraces, ponds, fountains and, in February and March, its spectacular flowers.

Las Vegas, Nevada, USA

A city whose population grew from 30 to half a million in just 90 years, Las Vegas is continually reinventing itself, with the casinos on The Strip providing ever bigger and better spectacles. The most famous is Caesar's Palace, with staff dressed as centurions and Cleopatra lookalikes. New York, New York entices with its replica skyscrapers and a Statue of Liberty. Treasure Island has a mock sea battle, Mirage an erupting volcano and Circus Circus live fire-eaters. Food and lodging are cheap, particularly midweek, with the real profits being made on the gambling tables and slot machines. Las Vegas is popular for outrageous weddings, with services being conducted in the most unlikely places – in a 'drive-through' chapel, the nearby Grand Canyon, or even in mid-air.

The Strip, Las Vegas

Lima, Peru   Map page 16

A once-beautiful city, Lima has suffered badly at the hands of modern developers. It is worth visiting primarily for its fine museums, which provide background information about Peru's Inca sites. It is also a useful base from which to explore the surrounding countryside, including the beautiful beaches to the south, over which towers the temple complex of Pachacamac.

Lisbon, Portugal   Map page 14

There are many hills to climb and much to see in Portugal's capital. Stretching north from the Rio Tejo, the Baixa district – rebuilt after the devastating earthquake of 1755 – contains many of the city's museums and theatres. The old Moorish area, the Alfama, survived the earthquake and its warren of narrow streets, stairways and squares leads up to the hilltop Castle of St George, with magnificent views. On the edge of the city the Belém area contains fine examples of 16th-century architecture, including the marvellous Jerônimos Monastery and the famous white Belém Tower. At night the haunting traditional *fado* music is played in bars in, for example, the Bairro Alto district. Day trips can be made to the hill town of Sintra or to the beaches on the Estoril coast.

London, England   Map page 15

Europe's largest city, London is a lively, cosmopolitan metropolis, offering a huge range of attractions to the visitor. From the grand squares of Knightsbridge and Belgravia to the business district of the City, central London is made up of a mosaic of areas, each with its own distinctive atmosphere and architectural style. Historic buildings include the Tower of London (containing the Crown Jewels), St Paul's Cathedral, Westminster Abbey, the Houses of Parliament and Buckingham Palace. Among the many art galleries are the new Tate Modern, housed in a converted power station on the South Bank of the River Thames, and The National Gallery, overlooking Trafalgar Square. The British Museum contains a monumental collection of Egyptian, Greek and Roman artefacts. Soho, Piccadilly and Covent Garden form the heart of the theatre district, with numerous restaurants, clubs and bars. Day excursions can be made to Hampton Court Palace, Windsor Castle, Canterbury Cathedral, the Royal Pavilion in Brighton, and the historic university towns of Oxford and Cambridge.

Los Angeles, California, USA   Map page 16

Among the skyscrapers in Los Angeles' downtown area are some notable public buildings, including the Museum of Contemporary Art. To the southwest is Exposition Park, home to three museums, including the interactive California Space Center. Most visitors, however, flock to Hollywood in search of film stars, although the big names have long since left for more salubrious neighbourhoods, such as Beverly Hills and elegant Bel Air. Other attractions include the Warner Bros. Studio Tour, and the thrilling rides at Universal Studios. On the coast, the long sandy beach linking Santa Monica and Venice is a magnet for Los Angeles' more colourful characters.

Luxembourg City, Luxembourg

The picturesque old walled city of Luxembourg perches above the Pétrusse and Alzette valleys, overlooked by the ruins of its ancient fortress with a labyrinth of defensive tunnels and underground chambers (the casemates), which is a UNESCO World Heritage Site. Running between the Citadelle du St Esprit, which provides spectacular views, and the Grand Ducal Palace is the elegant Chemin de la Corniche, one of Europe's most beautiful pedestrian promenades.

Madrid, Spain   Map page 17

Spain's capital is a huge metropolis with a remarkable collection of museums and art galleries, beautiful parks and a famously vibrant nightlife centred on Plaza de Santa Ana. The city is made up of a number of districts (*barrios*), each with its own distinct character. The area of most interest to visitors is around the 17th-century Plaza Mayor, with the elaborately decorated Royal Palace, the Opera House (Teatro Real) and the famous Prado Museum all within easy reach. The city has a vivacious character and a buzzing street life. Tapas bars are everywhere, and shoppers can explore the busy Gran Via or the atmospheric Rastro flea market centred on Plaza de Cascorro. Excursions can be made to the austere monastery of El Escorial and to the historic towns of Toledo, Segovia, Avila and Aranjuez.

Plaza Mayor, Madrid

Manila, Philippines   *Map page 17*

Many people visit Manila purely for its bars and nightlife, and the city provides plenty to choose from in the business district of Makati and the streets behind Roxes Boulevard. The walled area known as Intramuros contains the most significant historic sites, including Fort Santiago and the imposing Romanesque cathedral. Rizal Park, projecting out into Manila Bay, contains a lagoon, a spectacular fountain, a replica of Beijing's Summer Palace, a Japanese Garden and planetarium. Manila's Chinatown (on the border of Santa Cruz and Binondo) is the place to go for silk, porcelain and Chinese dumplings.

Marrakech, Morocco

Famous for its lively street life, Marrakech is also known for the pink colour that dominates the city from the earth walls around the old town centre to the flat-roofed houses. Every evening in Djemaa El Fna, the old town's central square, acrobats, snake charmers and storytellers perform. Nearby is the labyrinthine souk (bazaar), with its hundreds of small shops selling jewellery, carpets, metalware and leather. There are several beautiful gardens, and the Museum of Arts contains a magnificent display of carpets. Just an hour's drive away are the spectacular High Atlas mountains.

The souk, Marrakech

Melbourne, Victoria, Australia   *Map page 17*

Central Melbourne, on the north bank of the River Yarra, is a striking blend of past and present. Ornate 19th-century buildings sit alongside towering skyscrapers, as in Collins Street where the 1980s Rialto Towers provide splendid views from an Observation Deck. Elsewhere, the Old Melbourne Gaol is a major historic attraction and there are many fine parks and gardens, including the outstanding Botanic Gardens. The city's multi-ethnic nature is apparent in the popular Queen Victoria Market and in the huge variety of restaurants. Outside the centre several inner suburbs, each with a distinct character, can be explored by tram. Places of interest nearby include the Yarra Valley with its wineries and wildlife sanctuaries, and Phillip Island with its penguins.

Mexico City, Mexico   *Map page 18*

It is worth braving the traffic and pollution of Mexico City to see the impressive architecture of the buildings surrounding the main square (Zócalo), including the National Palace, with its murals by Diego Rivera. Nearby are the fascinating excavations of an Aztec temple (Templo Mayor). Bosque de Chapultepec, with its boating lakes, gardens and zoo, provides some relief from the hectic street life. It is also home to the outstanding

Museo de Antropologia, whose indoor and outdoor exhibition spaces house the world's greatest collection of Mexican art and artefacts. Just 48 km (30 miles) away from the centre are the splendid ruins of the ancient city of Teotihuacán.

Miami, Florida, USA   *Map page 18*

Miami is spread out along the fragmented coastline of Biscayne Bay. The Spanish language predominates and the downtown area, with its modern tower blocks, is greatly enlivened by the Latin American street life. Little Havana and Little Haiti are two areas worth visiting for their strong culture. The city's most elegant neighbourhood is Coral Gables, built as a 'model suburb' in the 1920s. Miami Beach, on an island linked to the mainland by causeways, has many fine examples of Art Deco buildings and miles of sandy beaches, hotels and bars.

Milan, Italy   *Map page 18*

Famous as a world centre for design and fashion, and for its grand opera house, La Scala, Milan has many historic buildings alongside its modern skyscrapers. The enormous Gothic cathedral dominates the main square, Piazza del Duomo, and the nearby convent of Santa Maria delle Grazie houses Leonardo da Vinci's fresco *The Last Supper*. Italy's most beautiful shopping arcade, the Galleria Vittorio Emanuele II, runs between the cathedral and La Scala. The Castello Sforzesco, a striking red-brick castle which was once the seat of the Dukes of Milan, houses the excellent municipal art collections. Excursions can be made to the old university town of Pavia and to the lake resorts such as Varenna and Bellagio on Lake Como, and Stresa on Lake Maggiore.

Montréal, Québec, Canada   *Map page 19*

Situated on the St Lawrence River, Montréal is Canada's second-largest city. The multi-ethnic nature of its population, of whom around 60% are French-speaking, is evident in the diversity of its cuisine and cultural festivals. The Parisian-style old city has numerous 17th-, 18th- and 19th-century buildings, among them the Neo-gothic Basilique Notre-Dame. By the river a public space has been created out of the old shipyards, complete with exhibitions and amusements. Boat trips can be taken up and down the St Lawrence, including one through the Lachine Rapids. The collection in the Art Museum is wide-ranging and includes a display of Inuit art. There are also particularly interesting Botanic Gardens.

Moscow, Russia   *Map page 19*

Moscow radiates outwards from the Kremlin in a series of rings, of which the innermost is of greatest interest to visitors and is small enough to be explored on foot. Among the buildings enclosed by the thick red-brick walls of the Kremlin are three imposing palaces and the Archangel Cathedral. Outside is Red Square, with the exotic, multi-coloured domes of St Basil's Cathedral, the Lenin Mausoleum, the Historical Museum and the magnificent 19th-century state department store, GUM, facing each other across the famous cobbled parade ground. There are also numerous literary museums and art galleries. The palatial metro system with its glittering chandeliers and fabulous marble architecture should not be missed.

St Basil's Cathedral, Moscow

Mumbai (Bombay), India   *Map page 20*

Home to India's thriving film industry, Mumbai also has the largest slum area of any city in Asia. The influence of the British colonial heritage is apparent in the Victorian Gothic buildings of the Fort district, the triumphal Gateway of India arch, and the red double-decker buses. The frenetic streets and bazaars are, however, pure India. Malabar Hill, with its Hanging Gardens, provides some relief from the crowds, as do the Mahatma Gandhi Museum and an impressive new National Gallery of Modern Art. Most visitors take a boat trip across the large harbour to Elephanta Island, to see the Hindu temples hewn out of the rock.

Munich, Germany   *Map page 20*

Munich is a cosmopolitan city, close to the Bavarian Alps, with many beautiful buildings and a wide variety of theatres, museums, galleries and restaurants. In the centre of the old town is the Marienplatz with its famous old town hall (Rathaus), and several historic churches. Many visitors shop in the glamorous Maximilianstrasse and spend an evening at the opera or drink in one of the city's many historic beer cellars, such as the famous Hofbräuhaus. Another attraction is the beer festival in October. Just outside the city is the Baroque palace of Nymphenburg.

Nairobi, Kenya

East Africa's most modern city has broad streets lined with jacaranda trees. The compact city centre can be walked in 20 minutes, but visitors should be aware that street robberies are a growing problem. The National Museum details the history of Kenyan tribal groups. Close to the city is the Bomas of Kenya, where traditional dances and songs are performed, and the Nairobi National Park where zebras, giraffes, lions, leopards and rhinos are among the animals that can be seen, particularly from July to September.

New Orleans, Louisiana, USA

Its fantastic mix of cultures – French, Spanish, Native American, African and Caribbean – makes New Orleans one of America's most stimulating cities. It is famous as the 'cradle of jazz', and trad jazz is still played in Preservation Hall. The best way to see the elegant architecture of the French Quarter is on foot, starting in Jackson Square – a park that is surrounded by some of the city's most important public buildings, including the Louisiana State Museum. Many visitors go to New Orleans simply to enjoy its restaurants, including the Creole and Cajun cuisines, both variations on the French. Popular times to visit are during the Mardi Gras carnival in February or March, and the annual Jazz Festival in April or May.

New York, NY, USA
Map page 21

Manhattan and the Statue of Liberty, New York

New York is the ultimate destination for those who love cities, with most of its main attractions on Manhattan Island. Its famous skyline includes the 1930s Empire State Building and the twin towers of the World Trade Center. There are dozens of art galleries, including the Metropolitan Museum of Art and the Guggenheim Museum of predominantly 20th-century art. The ferry to Staten Island provides panoramic views of Manhattan, while the Circle Line runs ferries across the magnificent natural harbour to the Statue of Liberty and Ellis Island. Districts to be toured on foot include Greenwich Village, with its cafés, SoHo, renowned for its art galleries and boutiques, and Little Italy. Some visitors are drawn to the city by stores such as Macy's or Bloomingdales, others by the vibrancy of its nightlife. Providing a haven from the big-city traffic is Central Park, where there is often live entertainment.

Osaka, Japan
Map page 22

The Japanese city most welcoming to foreign visitors, Osaka is enjoyed mainly for its lively nightlife and varied cuisine. It has some fine historic sites, such as the castle and the red-painted Sumiyoshi Shinto shrine to the gods of the sea. Its museums include the Liberty Osaka Museum of Human Rights and the Suntory Museum of 20th-century graphic art. The spectacular Osaka Aquarium is another attraction.

Oslo, Norway
Map page 22

The oldest of Scandinavia's capitals, Oslo is an attractive city situated at the head of Oslofjord. The impressive medieval Akershus castle contains grand staterooms, dungeons and the Norwegian Resistance Museum. The Munch Museum has over 5,000 drawings and paintings by Edvard Munch, while in the beautiful Vigeland Park, sculptures by Gustav Vigeland are on permanent display. Across the harbour is the BygdØy peninsula with good beaches, an open-air folk museum and maritime museums containing Viking ships as well as Thor Heyerdahl's raft, *Kon-Tiki*.

Panama City, Panama

Bristling with skyscrapers and fronted by palm-fringed beaches, Panama is a thriving modern city. In the Casco Viejo district, grand Spanish colonial buildings overlook the Bay of Panama from the tip of a fortified peninsula. The old sea wall provides excellent views across the bay and there are restaurants in its restored colonial dungeons. Other attractions include the 17th-century Presidential Palace, the cathedral and the Panama Canal. The 16th-century ruins of Old Panama (Panamá Viejo) lie 6.5 km (4 miles) to the east.

Paris, France
Map page 23

Famously beautiful in springtime, Paris is fascinating at any time of year. Packed with historic buildings, world-famous art collections, fine restaurants and street cafés, it is one of the world's most elegant cities. Compact enough to explore on foot, the centre is made up of a number of distinct areas or *quartiers*, each with its own character. On a hill crowned by the basilica of Sacré-Coeur is Montmartre, with its village-like atmosphere, street artists, nearby flea markets and a splendid view over the city. The Notre Dame Cathedral and Sainte Chapelle are on the peaceful Île de la Cité, an island in the River Seine. The Picasso Museum is set among the beautiful old houses and courtyards of the Marais. The colourful Pompidou Centre looms above the galleries and cafés of the Beaubourg. The Louvre occupies a vast stretch of the Right Bank of the Seine, and there is a magnificent unbroken view through the Tuileries gardens and along the Champs Elysées to the Arc de Triomphe. Attractions on the Left Bank include the Musée d'Orsay – containing a huge collection of Impressionist art – and the Eiffel Tower. Excursions can be made to the royal palaces of Versailles and Fontainebleu, Monet's house at Giverney, and the beautiful cathedral at Chartres.

The Seine and Notre Dame, Paris

Perth, Western Australia, Australia

Situated on a sweep of the Swan River, Perth has lots of sunshine and an easy-going atmosphere. Its centre is relatively compact and dominated by skyscrapers, among which are scattered some Victorian buildings, such as the ornate Government House and the Old Flour Mill. A few miles to the west lie excellent sandy beaches and opportunities for surfing, while cruise companies offer dolphin- and whale-watching trips. The port of Fremantle, just 20 km (12 miles) away, is worth visiting, as is Rottnest Island.

Prague, Czech Republic
Map page 24

With a centre full of beautiful buildings covering 900 years of architecture it is easy to see why Prague, on the River Vitava, is one of Europe's top tourist attractions. Prague Castle (Prazsky Hrad), encompassing the 10th-century Church of St George and the Gothic St Vitus' Cathedral, is the focus of most visits to the city. Other architectural treasures include Baroque and Rococo palaces and the Neoclassical National Theatre (Náordní divadlo). The Old Jewish Quarter (Josefov) contains the Jewish Cemetery and several synagogues, including the Old-New Synagogue (Staranová). Prague's rich cultural life centres especially on its music – it is home to two fine orchestras. It is also arguably the beer-drinking capital of the world, and has several famous beer halls as well as numerous pubs and bars.

Quito, Ecuador

At a height of 2,850 m (9,350 ft), Quito escapes the oppressive temperature and pollution of many Latin American cities. The historic centre, with its whitewashed buildings and red roofs, is a UNESCO heritage site and includes a 16th-century monastery and cathedral, as well as a number of museums. There is also a fascinating vivarium, with displays of many of Ecuador's reptiles, both living and dead.

Reykjavik, Iceland

The world's northernmost capital, Reykjavik is a small modern city with colourful buildings, fashionable shops and a lively nightlife. The Arni Magnússon Institute houses a famous collection of Icelandic saga manuscripts, while the National Museum in the Old Town displays relics from the earliest days of settlement. The modern church of Hallgrímskirkja is built in the shape of a lava mountain and offers excellent views over the city from its 75 m (246 ft) high tower.

Riga, Latvia

A bustling industrial city, Riga also has a waterfront castle, a medieval centre and a lively cultural life. Places to visit include the cavernous Dome Cathedral, the Riga Motor Museum, an open-air ethnographical museum and St Peter's Church – with a view over Old Riga from the spire, which is reached by a lift. To the west, a string of resort towns known collectively as Jurmala stretches for 20 km (12 miles) along the coast, with peaceful beaches and good restaurants.

Rio de Janeiro, Brazil
Map page 24

With a spectacular location at the entrance to a bay, Rio has two famous landmarks that provide breathtaking views: Corcovado Mountain, topped by a huge statue of Christ, and Sugar Loaf Mountain. There are many museums, including the National Historical and the wide-ranging National. The city is best known, however, for its lively beaches, including Copacabana, and the more up-market Ipanema. At night, the bars, clubs and discos of Rio resound to jazz and rock. There are samba shows primarily for tourists as well as more authentic dancehalls. A particularly popular time to visit is during the spectacular Mardi Gras Carnaval, in February or March.

View from Sugar Loaf Mountain, Rio de Janeiro

Rome, Italy
Map page 25

The historic capital of the Roman Empire, of Latin Christendom and now of Italy, Rome is exceptionally rich in treasures from many eras. Ancient buildings include the Colosseum, the Arch of Constantine, Trajan's Column, the Roman Forum

and the Pantheon. Among the early Christian sites are the famous catacombs and the basilicas of Santa Maria Maggiore and San Giovanni in Laterano (near the Colosseum). Michelangelo's Piazza del Campidoglio – bordered by three palaces – is a fine example of Renaissance town planning, but Rome is known more for its Baroque buildings and squares, and landmarks such as the Trevi Fountain and the Spanish Steps. In the centre of Rome, the Vatican City is the world's smallest independent state, containing St Peter's Square, St Peter's Basilica, the Sistine Chapel and ten museums. Increased pedestrianization of the centre has made it easier to enjoy the exuberant street life for which the city is famous.

St Petersburg, Russia   *Map page 26*

Situated in the Neva River delta, St Petersburg is a city of canals, bridges and elegant architecture. Founded in 1703 by Peter the Great, its oldest landmark is the massive Peter-Paul Fortress, with the slender spire of the Cathedral of St Peter and St Paul rising above it. At the heart of the city is Palace Square, dominated by the pastel-coloured façade of the Winter Palace. The palace is part of the Hermitage Museum, which contains one of the world's greatest collections of European art. Along the Nevsky Prospekt are the former homes of many famous Russians as well as several palaces, department stores, theatres, restaurants, churches and the richly decorated Kazan Cathedral. Day trips can be taken to several summer palaces, among them Pushkin and Petrodvorets.

San Francisco, California, USA   *Map page 25*

One of the USA's most spectacular cities, San Francisco's trademarks are its elegant suspension bridges (Golden Gate and Oakland Bay Bridge) and the street cars that service the steep streets. It is also famous as America's gay capital, the main focus of the gay community being the Castro district. The city has a thriving Chinatown, and its North Beach area (between Russian and Telegraph hills) has long been associated with alternative culture. The northern waterfront includes the famous and crowded Fisherman's Wharf development, with its numerous restaurants. The Golden Gate Park is home to several specialist gardens, art galleries and museums. A boat takes visitors to Alcatraz, the notorious island prison.

Santiago, Chile   *Map page 26*

Santiago is a sprawling city set on a wide plain at the foot of the Andes. However, its central area is relatively compact, and its tree-lined streets and landscaped parks are pleasant to explore on foot, with diversions to the Museum of Pre-Colombian Art in the Real Casa de Aduana and the Santiago Museum, close to the cathedral. A funicular goes to the peak of San Cristóbal and the Pablo Neruda Museum. Day trips can be made to the beaches of Valparaiso and the ski resort of Valle Nevado.

São Paulo, Brazil   *Map page 26*

Although much of São Paulo is modern, the area around the central square (Praça da Sé) contains several interesting old buildings, such as the whitewashed Palácio do Colégio, (a 19th-century replica of Baroque buildings), the Igreja de Santo Antônio and the Solar da Marquesa de Santos. The city has plenty of nightlife and a varied cuisine,

some of its best bars and restaurants being in the suburb known as the Jardins. The nearby Parque do Ibirapuera is a centre for sporting activities and home to several of the city's museums, as well as providing a haven of peace in its 'reading woods'.

Seattle, Washington, USA

The sparkling skyscrapers of downtown Seattle, including the trademark 'flying saucer' of the Space Needle, rise from the shores of Elliott Bay against the spectacular backdrop of the snowy peak of Mount Rainier. A recent surge in the city's prosperity (Seattle is home to the Microsoft Corporation) has led to much new building and the restoration of the historic centre. The city is a centre for contemporary arts and music, the embodiment of which is the high-tech Experience Music Project building. It also contains the headquarters of the Boeing Corporation, whose out-of-town Museum of Flight is a popular attraction.

Seoul, South Korea   *Map page 26*

Secret Garden of palace of Ch'angdok , Seoul

Selected as the site of the ruling dynasty's capital in 1394, Seoul today consists of a series of linked districts, each with its own centre. The National Assembly and financial institutions are on the small island of Youido. Spread around the old centre is a series of royal palaces, the best preserved of which is Ch'angdok, with its Secret Garden of wooded hills and ponds. T'apkol Park is a good place to meet the locals, while Namsan Park is home to the Botanic Gardens, and also to Seoul Tower, which provides a fine view of the city.

Shanghai, China   *Map page 27*

Rapidly regaining its status as a major trading and commercial centre, Shanghai's colonial past is clearly visible in the massive 1920s Neoclassical buildings of its waterfront trading area, famous as 'The Bund'. The maze of narrow streets in the Old City and the crowded bazaar of Yuyuan Park provide a complete contrast. Chinese culture is celebrated in the impressive collection of paintings, ceramics, calligraphy, and sculpture in the new Shanghai Museum. Just 80 km (50 miles) away are the famous city gardens of Suzhou, some of which are over 1,000 years old.

Singapore City, Singapore   *Map page 27*

Singapore is a popular 'stopover' city because it is relatively compact, has an efficient infrastructure and its shopping malls are a source of bargains. Amid the high-rise developments are colonial, Chinese, Malay and Indian enclaves that have retained their character, and some fine historic buildings, such as Coleman's Parliament building, the Buddhist Temple of Heavenly Happiness (Thian Hock Keng Temple) and the colourful Sri

Mariamman Hindu Temple. On the riverside are the restored old shops of Boat and Clarke Quays, both of which are relatively lively nightspots. To the south a cable car and causeway go to the island of Sentosa, which has beaches and attractions such as the impressive Underwater World, while to the north is the well-designed zoo, which features a night safari park. To the west attractions include the Jurong Bird Park and Tang Dynasty City.

Stockholm, Sweden   *Map page 28*

Built on 14 islands, between Lake Mälaren and the Baltic Sea, Stockholm is a beautiful city with numerous parks. It has an essentially modern feel, with many fine 20th-century buildings, although there is still a medieval Old Town (Gamla Stan), with narrow streets and a 15th-century cathedral (Storkyrkan). A ferry goes to Drottningholm – the royal family's island castle, complete with lakeside gardens and an 18th-century theatre. The island of Djurgarden is home to an open-air museum of Swedish vernacular architecture (Skansen) and the cathedral-like building that covers the Vasa – a beautifully restored 17th-century warship.

Sydney, NSW, Australia   *Map page 28*

Australia's oldest and largest city is built around a beautiful harbour that is both a major port and recreational area. Best known for its sail-shaped opera house and striking steel-arched harbour bridge, Sydney also has excellent beaches such as Manly, which can be reached by ferry, and the famous Bondi. In the centre, ferries and harbour cruises set out from Circular Quay, near which is The Rocks, with a restored historic quarter. Another area of waterside redevelopment is Darling Harbour, not far from which is the bustling Sydney Fish Market. Away from the harbour, inner suburbs worth visiting include Glebe, Newtown and Paddington, each with a distinct character and attractive 19th-century terraced houses. With an exciting mix of Asian and European cultures, the city offers a cosmopolitan choice of restaurants, theatres and music. The many museums and art galleries include the Australian Museum, which has a gallery devoted to Aboriginal history. A day trip can be made by train to the spectacular Blue Mountains only 80 km (50 miles) away.

Opera House, Sydney

Tehran, Iran   *Map page 30*

Most visitors to Tehran concentrate on its excellent museums. The National Museum and the Golestan Palace Museum house many ancient objects, including those taken from famous sites such as Persepolis. The Museum of Glass and Ceramics is well designed and organized, and the Reza Abbasis Museum displays Islamic art. For those willing to brave the heat and noise, Iran has an extensive bazaar.

Tianjin, China
Map page 30

The centre of Tianjin, for decades an important trading port, is a mixture of international architectural styles – British, French, German and Japanese – from the late 19th century. The Ancient Culture Street, a major draw for visitors, is an attempt to re-create the feel of ancient China. For a more authentic experience of Chinese culture, it is worth going to the Antiques Market and taking a walk through the Hai River Park.

Tokyo, Japan
Map page 29

Visitors to Tokyo, faced with a vast urban sprawl, normally work outwards from the Imperial Palace and the surrounding gardens, which contain the remains of Edo Castle. Immediately to the east is the downtown area, with a wide choice of restaurants and shops and some fine examples of modern architecture, including the Tokyo International Forum, with a 60 m (200 ft) high glass atrium. To the west is the Meijii Shrine, set in attractive gardens. The city centre has many art galleries, exhibiting both Japanese and European art. However, many of the largest museums, including the Tokyo National Museum, are further north, in Ueno. The adjacent Asakusa district reveals a more tranquil world of wooden houses, temples and shrines, including the magnificent temple of Senso-ji.

Toronto, Ontario, Canada
Map page 30

Standing on the shore of Lake Ontario, Toronto is Canada's leading commercial city. In its centre is the tallest free-standing structure in the world: the CN Tower. Glass-fronted lifts transport visitors to the Space Deck, 442 m (1,400 ft high), from where it is possible to see as far as Niagara Falls. The city's museums include the Royal Ontario Museum and the Gallery of Inuit Art. Along the waterfront an area of old warehouses has been developed as the Harbourfront Park, with hotels, theatres, shops and restaurants. Toronto's large immigrant population has helped create a vibrant city culture, with a thriving music scene.

Vancouver, British Columbia, Canada

Built around a natural harbour, Vancouver is a major port and city of inlets and green spaces, set against a mountain backdrop. The downtown area contains a cluster of sparkling, glass-fronted skyscrapers. Vancouver has a thriving Chinatown and a dynamic artistic and musical scene that encompasses classical, jazz and rock music. Of the many museums, the Museum of Anthropology is the finest. Stanley Park – a peninsula containing a large area of semi-wilderness – has three of Vancouver's many city beaches and the Vancouver Aquarium. Nearby is Vancouver Island, with its rainforest and glacial mountain peaks.

Varanasi, India

Built on the banks of the sacred River Ganges, Varanasi is famous for the flights of stone steps (ghats), lining 5 km (3 miles) of the river banks, where Hindu pilgrims bathe in the waters and cremate their dead. The old town consists of a maze of narrow alleyways at the heart of which is the Golden Temple, dedicated to the god Shiva. The city is also sacred for Buddhists, and at nearby Sarnath there is a collection of restored temples.

Venice, Italy

Distant view of Church of Santa Maria delle Salute, Venice

Built on a collection of islands and criss-crossed by 177 canals, Venice is a city like no other, where boats are the only means of transport. A journey by gondola or vaporetto along the Grand Canal passes many grand palaces, including the Gothic Ca' d'Oro and Ca' Foscari, the Renaissance Palazzo Grimani and the Baroque Rezzonico. The familiar landmark of the Rialto Bridge presides over the busiest shopping area in Venice. Around St Mark's Square is the stunning 11th-century Byzantine Basilica, the Pala d'Oro, and the Doge's Palace. A lift to the top of the towering Campanile provides exceptional views over the city and the lagoon, across which lies the Lido, with beaches and hotels. The Accademia contains the world's most comprehensive collection of Venetian art, including paintings by Titian, while the Peggy Guggenheim collection is one of the most important of 20th-century art outside the USA.

Vienna, Austria
Map page 31

Formerly the capital of the Habsburg and Austro-Hungarian empires, today's Vienna preserves an atmosphere of historic grandeur. A city of cafés, beer cellars, parks and elegant boulevards, it has a centre, the Innere Stadt, that is sufficiently compact to be explored on foot. It contains numerous Baroque churches and palaces, the magnificent Gothic St Stephen's Cathedral, and the Hofburg – the Habsburgs' imperial palace, which is now home to the famous Spanish Riding School. Among the city's many museums are the Kunsthistorisches (Art History Museum), with an unrivalled collection of paintings by Peter Breugel the Elder, and the fine 18th-century Belvedere palace complex which features paintings by Klimt and Schiele among others. Outside the centre is Schönbrunn, the Habsburgs' impressive summer palace, and the Prater (in Leopoldstadt), a vast park featuring Vienna's giant ferris wheel. To the north the hills of Kahlenberg and Leopoldsberg provide magnificent views over the city.

Warsaw, Poland
Map page 31

The old centre of Warsaw, on the left bank of the River Vistula, was reduced to rubble during World War II, but it has been meticulously rebuilt and is now a UNESCO World Heritage site. All the buildings appear to date from the 18th century or earlier. They include St John's Cathedral and the Renaissance and Baroque merchants' houses surrounding the Old Market Square (Rynek Starego Miasta). There is also the excellent Historical Museum of Warsaw, many lively cafés and some fine restaurants. Outside the Old Town is the beautiful Lazienki park and palace complex and, 6 km (4 miles) further south, the restored Baroque Wilanów park and palace.

Washington DC, USA
Map page 32

The main public buildings of Washington DC are grouped on and around the National Mall – a broad swathe of parkland containing the Washington Monument, the Lincoln and Jefferson memorials, and the V-shaped polished black stone wall incised with thousands of names, which commemorates the Americans who fell in Vietnam. On the north side of the Mall is the White House, and over-looking all from the eastern end is the Capitol building, with its 55 m (180 ft) high rotunda. Home to the House of Representatives and the Senate, it is open to visitors. The National Gallery of Art and the National Air and Space Museum are two of the many museums. Central Washington DC can be dangerous at night. Georgetown is more relaxed, with its restaurants, bars and handsome streets. Within easy reach of the city are Chesapeake Bay and several Civil War battle sites.

Wellington, New Zealand
Map page 32

Overlooked by Mount Victoria, Wellington is the political and commercial capital of New Zealand. Wooden Victorian houses climb the steep hills surrounding the magnificent harbour of Port Nicholson, and a cable car provides a spectacular view of the city. Among the historic buildings in the centre are the Old Government Buildings, while the city's museums include the recently opened Museum of New Zealand (Te Papa). A lively, cosmopolitan city, Wellington has an exciting cultural scene, as evidenced in February and March by the annual Fringe Festival and the biennial International Festival of the Arts.

View over the harbour, Wellington

Xi'ian, China

As well as being a base from which to visit the famous Army of Terracotta Warriors, Xi'an possesses its own historic sites. These include the impressive city walls that all but surround the old town, and the 64 m (200 ft) high Big Goose Pagoda. Xi'an also has a strong Islamic culture and its Great Mosque is the largest in China. The Shaanxi Provincial Museum presents a fascinating history of the Silk Road.

Yangon (Rangoon), Burma (Myanmar)

The main focus of any visit to Yangon will be the magnificent Shwedagon stupa. The stupa is 90 m (290 ft) high and shaped like a bell. Completely covered in gold, it is surrounded by a host of smaller gilded stupas, statues, temples and pavilions. Of the many other Buddhist sites around the city, the huge reclining Buddha at Chauk-htatgyi Paya is the most impressive. Two large lakes provide areas of recreation, and the many tree-lined streets and areas of near-jungle give some parts an almost rural feel.

WORLD MAPS

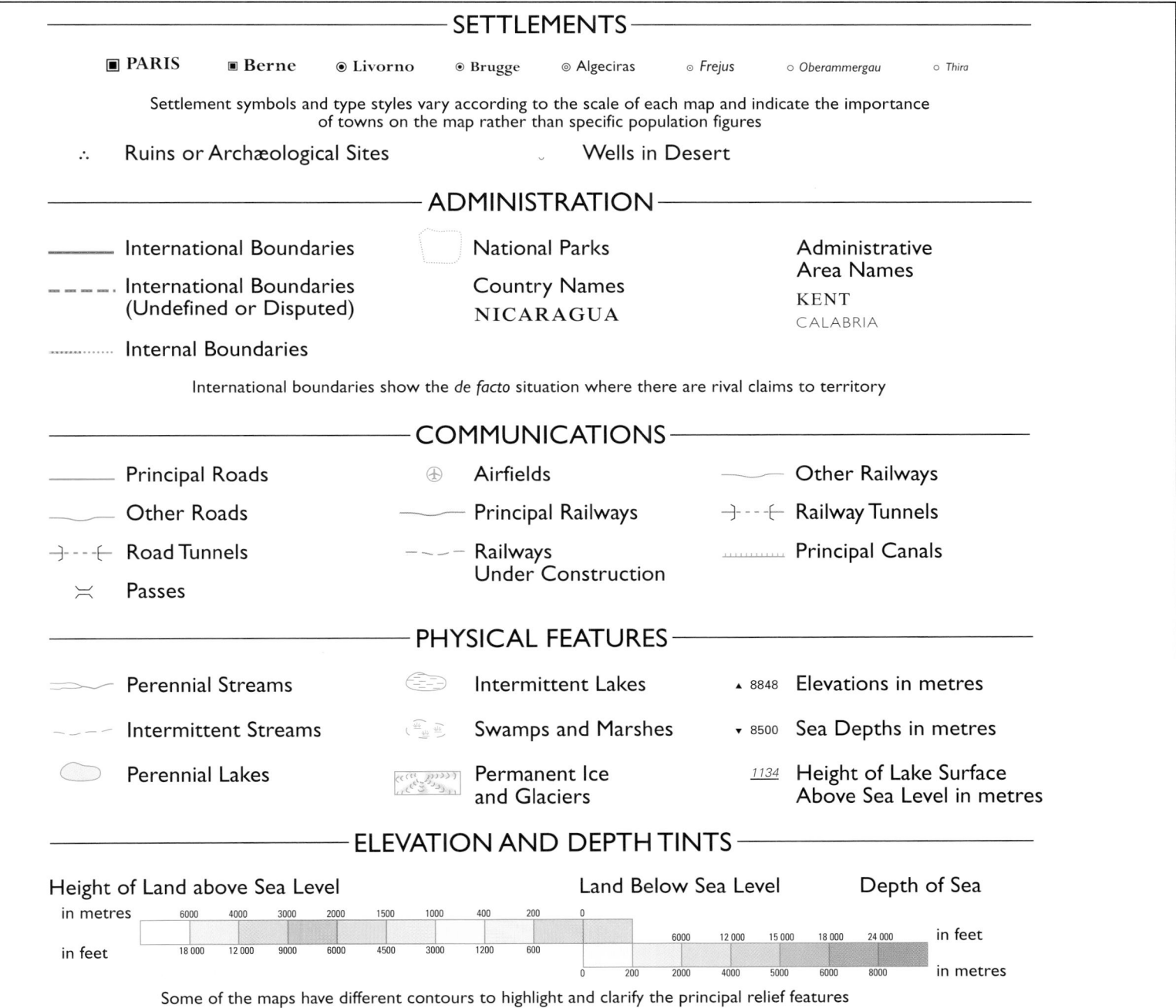

SETTLEMENTS

◼ PARIS   ◾ Berne   ◉ Livorno   ⊙ Brugge   ◎ Algeciras   ∘ Frejus   ○ Oberammergau   ○ Thira

Settlement symbols and type styles vary according to the scale of each map and indicate the importance
of towns on the map rather than specific population figures

∴   Ruins or Archæological Sites   ◡   Wells in Desert

ADMINISTRATION

──────── International Boundaries

─ ─ ─ ─ International Boundaries
(Undefined or Disputed)

············· Internal Boundaries

National Parks

Country Names
NICARAGUA

Administrative
Area Names

KENT
CALABRIA

International boundaries show the *de facto* situation where there are rival claims to territory

COMMUNICATIONS

──────── Principal Roads

──────── Other Roads

─⊣···⊢── Road Tunnels

⋈   Passes

⊕   Airfields

──────── Principal Railways

─ ⌒ ─ Railways
Under Construction

──────── Other Railways

─⊣···⊢── Railway Tunnels

············· Principal Canals

PHYSICAL FEATURES

⌇   Perennial Streams

─ ─ ─ Intermittent Streams

◯   Perennial Lakes

Intermittent Lakes

Swamps and Marshes

Permanent Ice
and Glaciers

▲ 8848   Elevations in metres

▼ 8500   Sea Depths in metres

1134   Height of Lake Surface
Above Sea Level in metres

ELEVATION AND DEPTH TINTS

Height of Land above Sea Level   Land Below Sea Level   Depth of Sea

in metres	6000	4000	3000	2000	1500	1000	400	200	0						
										6000	12 000	15 000	18 000	24 000	in feet
in feet	18 000	12 000	9000	6000	4500	3000	1200	600							
									0	200	2000	4000	5000	6000	8000	in metres

Some of the maps have different contours to highlight and clarify the principal relief features

1
2
3
4
5
6
7
8
9
A
B
C
D
E
F
G
H
180
160
140
120
100
80
60
40
20
Beaufort Sea
Parry Is.
Queen Elizabeth Is.
Ellesmere I.
Banks I.
Devon I.
GREENLAND
(Denmark)
Baffin Bay
Victoria I.
Bering Strait
St. Lawrence I.
Yukon
Fairbanks
ALASKA
(U.S.A.)
Anchorage
Great Bear L.
Yellowknife
Great Slave L.
Baffin I.
Davis Str.
Nuuk
Denmark Str.
ICELAND
Reykjavik
Norwegian Sea
Arctic Circle
G. of Alaska
Kodiak I.
Hudson Bay
Churchill
Faroe Is.
(Den.)
Aleutian Is. (U.S.A.)
Queen Charlotte Is.
Nelson
Edmonton
Calgary
CANADA
Schefferville
UNITED KINGDOM
Glasgow
Dublin
IRELAND
LONDON
Vancouver
Vancouver I.
L. Winnipeg
Winnipeg
Seattle
Portland
Missouri
UNITED STATES OF AMERICA
L. Superior
Québec
Newfoundland
St. John's
Ottawa
Montréal
Minneapolis
L. Michigan
L. Huron
Toronto
Halifax
Milwaukee
Detroit
Boston
FRANCE
Bordeaux
Salt Lake City
CHICAGO
Cleveland
Pittsburgh
NEW YORK
PHILADELPHIA
Baltimore
Washington D.C.
SAN FRANCISCO
Sacramento
Denver
Kansas City
St. Louis
Cincinnati
Madrid
SPAIN
PORTUGAL
Lisbon
International Date Line
Colorado
LOS ANGELES
Phoenix
Memphis
Atlanta
NORTH ATLANTIC OCEAN
Azores
(Port.)
San Diego
Dallas
El Paso
Mississippi
Tangier
Rabat
Casablanca
Midway Is.
Ciudad Juárez
Rio Grande
Houston
New Orleans
Jacksonville
Bermuda
(U.K.)
Madeira
(Port.)
Marrakesh
MOROCCO
Guadalupe I.
(Mexico)
Hawaiian Is.
(U.S.A.)
Monterrey
Gulf of Mexico
Canary Is.
(Sp.)
El Aaiun
Tropic of Cancer
G. of California
Miami
BAHAMAS
WESTERN SAHARA
MEXICO
Honolulu
Oahu
Hawaii
León
Havana
CUBA
Turks & Caicos Is.
(U.K.)
Guadalajara
MÉXICO
Revilla Gigedo Is.
(Mexico)
Cayman Is. (U.K.)
HAITI
DOMINICAN REP.
Port-au-Prince
Santo Domingo
JAMAICA
Kingston
PUERTO RICO
Virgin Is. (U.S.A.) & (U.K.)
ANTIGUA & BARBUDA
ST. KITTS & NEVIS
Nouakchott
MAURITANIA
Puebla
Belmopan
BELIZE
GUATEMALA
Guatemala
HONDURAS
Tegucigalpa
San Salvador
EL SALVADOR
NICARAGUA
Managua
Caribbean Sea
GUADELOUPE (Fr.)
DOMINICA
MARTINIQUE (Fr.)
ST. LUCIA
ST. VINCENT & THE GRENADINES
BARBADOS
GRENADA
TRINIDAD & TOBAGO
NETH. ANTILLES
Timbuktu
MALI
CAPE VERDE IS.
Dakar
SENEGAL
GAMBIA
GUINEA-BISSAU
Bissau
GUINEA
Bamako
BURKINA FASO
Ouagadougou
Barranquilla
Caracas
Clipperton I.
(Fr.)
San José
COSTA RICA
Panamá
PANAMA
Conakry
Freetown
SIERRA LEONE
IVORY COAST
GHANA
Yamoussoukro
Monrovia
LIBERIA
Abidjan
Accra
PACIFIC OCEAN
Palmyra Is.
(U.S.A.)
Orinoco
VENEZUELA
Georgetown
GUYANA
Paramaribo
SURINAM
Cayenne
FRENCH GUIANA
Medellín
Coco I.
(C. Rica)
Malpelo
(Colombia)
Cali
BOGOTÁ
COLOMBIA
Kiritimati
Howland I. (U.S.A.)
Baker I. (U.S.A.)
Jarvis I.
(U.S.A.)
Equator
Negro
Gulf of Guinea
São Paulo
(Brazil)
Galápagos
(Ecuador)
Quito
ECUADOR
Guayaquil
Japurá
Manaus
Amazon
Belém
Iquitos
Fortaleza
Fernando de Noronha
(Brazil)
Abariringa
KIRIBATI
Malden I.
Phoenix Is.
Starbuck I.
Xingu
Natal
Recife
Tokelau Is.
(N.Z.)
Penrhyn Is.
Marquesas Is.
Ucayali
Marañón
Madeira
Tocantins
BRAZIL
Ascension I.
(U.K.)
São Francisco
Wallis & Futuna
(Fr.)
WESTERN SAMOA
Manihiki
Flint I.
FRENCH POLYNESIA
PERU
LIMA
Callao
Salvador
AMERICAN SAMOA
FIJI
TONGA
Niue
(N.Z.)
Cook Is.
(N.Z.)
Society Is.
Tahiti
Tuamotu Is.
Arequipa
L. Titicaca
La Paz
BOLIVIA
Sucre
Brasília
St. Helena
(U.K.)
Belo Horizonte
SOUTH ATLANTIC OCEAN
Trindade
(Brazil)
Tubuai Is.
Tropic of Capricorn
Antofagasta
PARAGUAY
SÃO PAULO
RIO DE JANEIRO
Asunción
Santos
Curitiba
Pitcairn I.
(U.K.)
Ducie I.
Rapa
Easter I.
(Chile)
Sala-y-Gómez
(Chile)
San Felix
(Chile)
San Ambrosio
(Chile)
Tucumán
CHILE
Paraná
Uruguay
Pôrto Alegre
Córdoba
Paraná
Rio Grande
Kermadec Is. (N.Z.)
Valparaíso
Rosario
URUGUAY
Juan Fernández
(Chile)
SANTIAGO
BUENOS AIRES
Montevideo
Talcahuano
ARGENTINA
Tristan da Cunha
(U.K.)
Bahía Blanca
Gough I.
(U.K.)
Chiloé I.
Chatham Is.
(N.Z.)
Falkland Is.
(U.K.)
Punta Arenas
Tierra del Fuego
Scotia Sea
South Georgia
(U.K.)
C. Horn
South Sandwich Is.
(U.K.)
Drake Passage
South Orkney Is.
South Shetland Is.
Antarctic Circle
Bellingshausen Sea
Weddell Sea
Amundsen Sea
Antar
West from Greenwich

Projection: *Hammer Equal Area*

ARCTIC OCEAN

Svalbard (Nor.)

Barents Sea

Novaya Zemlya

Kara Sea

Severnaya Zemlya

Laptev Sea

East Siberian Sea

New Siberian Is.

Wrangel I.

Arctic Circle

A

Murmansk

Norilsk

Salekhard

Verkhoyansk

Lena

Yakutsk

Magadan

Okhotsk

Bering Sea

B

NORWAY SWEDEN FINLAND

Oslo Stockholm Helsinki EST.

Arkhangelsk

Perm

Yekaterinburg

Tomsk Krasnoyarsk

Irkutsk L. Baikal Ulan Ude

Petropavlovsk-Kamchatskiy

International Date Line

RUSSIA

DENMARK LATVIA LITH.

Copenhagen ST.PETERSBURG

Hamburg, NETH. POLAND BELARUS

Amsterdam Berlin

BELG. GERMANY CZECH Warsaw Kiev

PARIS LUX. Vienna REP. SLOVAK

Volga

MOSCOW Kazan

Samara

Chelyabinsk Omsk Novosibirsk

Astana Barnaul

Komsomolsk

Sakhalin

Kuril Is.

Khabarovsk

Sapporo

C

AUSTRIA HUNG.

Milan SLOV. CROATIA Budapest

Lyons SWITZ.

Barcelona ITALY ROMANIA

Rome Belgrade Bucharest

Marseilles Naples B-H. YUG.

Sardinia MAC. BULGARIA Black

Algiers Tunis GREECE Sofia Sea

Tunis MALTA ISTANBUL

Mediterranean Athens Ankara TURKEY

Sea CYPRUS İzmir

Saratov

Volgograd

Astrakhan

Aral Sea

KAZAKSTAN

L. Balkhash

Almaty

Bishkek

ULAN BATOR MONGOLIA

Ürümqi

Changchun

Harbin

Vladivostok

SHENYANG

BEIJING TIANJIN

NORTH KOREA Pyongyang

SEOUL JAPAN

TŌKYŌ

PACIFIC

OCEAN

GEORGIA Tbilisi Baku

ARM. AZER.

Yerevan

UZBEKISTAN KYRGYZSTAN

Samarkand Tashkent

TURKMENISTAN TAJIKISTAN

Ashkhabad Dushanbe

CHINA

Lanzhou Taiyuan

Dalian

SOUTH KOREA

Ōsaka

Kitakyushu

Qaraghandy

Tabriz Mashhad

TEHRĀN

SYRIA Damascus Baghdād Esfahan

Beirut LEB. Kābul

Jerusalem ISR. Amman IRAQ IRAN AFGHANISTAN

JORDAN Shīrāz Islamabad

Xi'an Nanjing

Hwang ho

SHANGHAI

East China Sea

Bonin Is. (Japan)

Marcus I. (Japan)

Tropic of Cancer

C

LIBYA EGYPT CAIRO

Alexandria

KUWAIT

Riyadh QATAR Abu Dhabi

BAHRAIN U.A.E.

SAUDI ARABIA OMAN Muscat

Mecca

The Gulf

PAKISTAN

Lahore TIBET

Lhasa

NEPAL Katmandu BHU.

DELHI New Delhi JAMMU & KASHMIR

Kanpur

Ahmadabad INDIA

Chengdu Wuhan

CHONGQING

Kunming Fuzhou

GUANGZHOU

HONG KONG

Hainan

Taipei TAIWAN

Ryukyus

Volcano Is. (Japan)

Wake I. (U.S.A.)

NIGER CHAD SUDAN

Omdurmân Khartoum

Niamey Ndjamena

L. Chad

Asmara San'ā YEMEN

ERITREA

Red Sea

Nile

Arabian

Sea

Nagpur CALCUTTA (Kolkata)

DACCA BANGLA-DESH

BURMA MYANMAR

Rangoon

Hanoi

South China Sea

D

NIGERIA Kano

TOGO Abuja

Ibadan CAMEROON

Lagos Douala

EQUATORIAL GUINEA GABON

Yaoundé Bangui

CENTRAL AFRICAN REP.

Addis Ababa

DJIBOUTI

SOMALI REP.

ETHIOPIA

MUMBAI (Bombay)

Hyderabad

Bay of Bengal

Andaman Is. (India)

BANGKOK

THAILAND CAMBODIA

VIET-NAM

MANILA

PHILIPPINES

NORTHERN MARIANAS (U.S.A.)

GUAM (U.S.A.)

MARSHALL IS.

Hyderabad

Bangalore CHENNAI (Madras)

Lakshadweep Is. (India)

SRI LANKA

Vientiane

Phnom Penh

Ho Chi Minh City

Yap

PALAU

Truk

Caroline Is.

Pohnpei

FEDERATED STATES OF MICRONESIA

Colombo

Nicobar Is. (India)

MALDIVES

Equator

Medan MALAYSIA

Kuala Lumpur SABAH

PEN. MALAYSIA BRUNEI

SINGAPORE SARAWAK

Borneo

Gilbert Is.

NAURU KIRIBATI

INDIAN

OCEAN

SEYCHELLES

Amirante Is.

Diego Garcia

Chagos Arch. (U.K.)

Palembang

Banjarmasin

INDONESIA Ujung Pandang

JAKARTA

Bandung Surabaya

Java

IRIAN JAYA

PAPUA NEW GUINEA

Port Moresby

New Ireland

New Britain

SOLOMON IS.

Santa Cruz I.

E

SÃO TOMÉ & PRÍNCIPE

CABINDA (Angola)

CONGO (DEM.REP. OF THE)

Brazzaville Kinshasa

Luanda

ANGOLA

Benguela

Kisangani Kampala UGANDA

Kananga RWANDA Kigali KENYA

BURUNDI Bujumbura Nairobi

Zaïre L. Victoria

Mombasa

TANZANIA Zanzibar

Dodoma Dar es Salaam

L. Tanganyika

Aldabra Is.

Agalega Is. (Fr.)

Cargados Carajos

Mogadishu

L. Turkana

MALDIVES

Cocos Is. (Austral.)

Christmas I. (Austral.)

Timor

EAST TIMOR

Arafura Sea

C. York

Darwin

TUVALU

VANUATU

FIJI

Suva

F

Lubumbashi

ZAMBIA

Lusaka Lilongwe

MALAWI

ZIMBABWE MOZAMBIQUE

Harare

Bulawayo

NAMIBIA

BOTSWANA

Windhoek Gaborone

Pretoria

Johannesburg

SOUTH LESOTHO SWAZILAND

AFRICA Maputo

Cape Town Durban

C. of Good Hope Port Elizabeth

L. Malawi

Malawi

Mozambique Channel

MADAGASCAR

Antananarivo

COMOROS Mayotte (Fr.)

RÉUNION (Fr.) MAURITIUS

Rodriguez

Tropic of Capricorn

Amsterdam I. (Fr.)

St.Paul (Fr.)

Port Hedland

Geraldton

Perth Kalgoorlie-Boulder

Fremantle

AUSTRALIA

Alice Springs

Cairns

Townsville

Rockhampton

Brisbane

Lord Howe I. (Austral.)

Norfolk I. (Austral.)

NEW CALEDONIA (Fr.)

Great Australian Bight

Adelaide Darling

Melbourne

Canberra

Sydney

Newcastle

Tasman

Auckland

North I.

NEW ZEALAND

Wellington

F

Prince Edward Is. (S.Africa)

Crozet Is. (Fr.)

Kerguelen (Fr.)

McDonald Is. (Austral.) Heard I. (Austral.)

Bouvet I. (Nor.)

SOUTHERN OCEAN

Tasmania

Hobart

Christchurch

South I.

Stewart I. Dunedin

Bounty Is. (N.Z.) Antipodes Is. (N.Z.)

Macquarie Is. (Austral.)

Campbell I. (N.Z.) Auckland Is. (N.Z.)

G

Antarctic Circle

An ta rc ti ca

East from Greenwich

Ross Sea

H

Hanoi ◉ Capital Cities

COPYRIGHT GEORGE PHILIP LTD.

100 0   200   400   600   800 1000 1200 1400 km
100 0   200   400   600   800 1000 miles

18   **17**   180   **16**   160   **15**

JAPAN

PACIFIC OCEAN

Aleutian Islands (U.S.A.)
Near Is. (U.S.A.)
▼ 7822
Komandorskiye Ostrova
Kurilskiye Ostrova (Russia)
La Perouse Str.
Hokkaidō

Bering Sea

Dutch Harbor
Mys Lopatka
Petropavlovsk-Kamchatskiy
Gora Klyuchevskaya 4850

Sakhalin (Russia)
Sakhalinskiy Zaliv
Vanino

Unimak I.

Pribilof Is. (U.S.A.)
▼ 42
Ostrov Karaginskiy
Mys Olyutorski

Poluostrov Kamchatka

Sea of Okhotsk

Nikolayevsk
Ulbanskiy Zaliv
Udskaya Guba

Amur
Khabarovsk

Kodiak I.
Bristol Bay
St. Matthew (U.S.A.)

Penzhino
Penzhinskaya G.
Gizhiginskaya Guba
Tauiskaya Guba

Nunivak
St. Lawrence I. (U.S.A.)
Mys Navarin

Anadyrskiy Zaliv

Anadyr

S

Kolymskoye Nagorye

Okhotsk

G. of Alaska
Seward
Prince William Sd.
Anchorage
Cordova
Nome
Norton Sd.
Bering Str.

Mys Dezhneva
Chukotskoye Nagorye

Omolon
Kolyma
Nizhne Kolymsk
Srednekolymsk

Stanovoy Khrebet

Mt. St. Elias 5489
Mt. McKinley 6194
Fairbanks
Pt. of Wales
C. Prince of Wales
Kotzebue Sd.
Pt. Hope
C. Lisburne

Proliv Longa

Indigirka
Zashiversk

Verkhoyansk
Kolyma
Kazachye

Yakutsk
Aldan
Lena
Olekma

Skagway
Mt. Logan 6050
Whitehorse

ALASKA (U.S.A.)
Yukon
Koyukuk
Kobuk

Chukchi Sea
Ostrov Vrangelya (Russia)
Chaunskaya G.

Russkoye Ustie

Verkhoyansk
Yana

Vilyuy
Zhigansk

Rocky Mountains
Dawson
Fort Yukon

Prudhoe Bay
Pt. Barrow
C. Halkett
Harrison Bay
Pt. Barrow

b

Lyakhovskiye Ostrova
Lena
Bulun

A S I

Dawson Creek
Fort Simpson
Peace
Liard
Fort McPherson
Herschel I.

Beaufort Sea

ARCTIC

Novosibirskiye Ostrova

Kotelnyy
Tiksi

Lena
Olenek

Lena

Fort Vermilion
Athabasca
Yellowknife
Great Slave Lake

Mackenzie
Fort Good Hope
Tulita
Great Bear Lake

Mackenzie Bay
C. Bathurst
▲ 3767

O. Bennetta (Russia)

Laptev Sea

Anabar
Nordvik

Nizhnyaya Tunguska

NORTH

Coppermine
Kugluktuk

C. Kellett
C. Prince Alfred

Canada Basin

Mendeleyev Ridge

80
3327

Ostrova Petra

Poluostrov Taymyr

Pyasina

Khatanga
Kheta

Gory Putorana

AMERICA

Athabasca Lake

Dolphin & Union Str.
Banks I.
Prince Patrick I.

3546

3849

Severnaya Zemlya

Ozero Taymyr

Norilsk

Coronation G.
Wollaston Pen.
Prince Albert Pen.
Victoria Island
Melville I.

4007
Alpha Cordillera

Lomonosov Ridge
4100

O. Oktyabrskoy Revolyutsii

Pyasina

A

Chesterfield
Boothia Pen.
King William I.
M'Clintock Chan.
Viscount Melville Sd.
Parry Is.
Borden I.
3700

Makarov Basin

NORTH POLE
4484

Fram Basin

Nansen Cordillera

Igarka
Dudinka
Golchikha

Yenisey

Hudson Bay

Back
Prince of Wales I.
Bathurst I.
North Magnetic Pole 1990
Elef Ringnes I.
Sverdrup Is.
Axel Heiberg I.

2104
4418

Nansen Basin

O. Uedineniya
O. Ushakova

O. Vise

Taz

Roes Welcome Sd.
Somerset I.
Prince Regent Inlet
Gulf of Boothia
Barrow Str.
Lancaster Sd.
Jones Sound
Devon I.
Eureka
Nansen Sd.
2104

3741

Zemlya Frantsa Iosifa (Russia)
O. Graham Bell
Z. Vilcheka

O. Belyy

Urengoy

Southampton I.
Coats I.
Melville Pen.
Hecla Str.
Bylot I.
Ellesmere I. (Canada)
Alert
C. Columbia
Lincoln Sea

Z. Aleksandry (Russia)
Zemlya Georga

Kara Sea

Poluostrov Yamal
Novyy Port
Nadym

Mansel I.
Foxe Basin
Prince Charles I.
Smith Sund
Kane Basin
Robeson Chan.
Knud Rasmussen Land

Peary Land
C. Morris Jesup

McKinley Sea

Novaya

Novaya Zemlya

Baydaratskaya Guba

Ob
Vorkuta
Salekhard

Berezovo

Baffin Bay

2399
Uummannaq
K. York
Sermersuaq
Kong Frederik VIII.s Land
Independence Fjord

A

Nordkapp

Nordaustlandet

Kolguyev
O. Kolguyev

1894
Narodnaya

Ural'skie

Tobolsk

C. Wolstenholme
Nettilling L.
Iqaluit
C. Dyer
Upernavik
Qaanaaq

Kong Frederik VI.s Land
Kong Christian X.s Land

2571
Vestspitsbergen
Svalbard (Norway)
Longyearbyen
Edgeøya

Barents Sea

Mys Kanin Nos

Pechora

Surgut

YEKATERINBURG

BAFFIN I.

Foxe Chan.

Davis Str.
Qeqertarsuaq
Uummannaq
Qeqertarsuaq

GREENLAND (Denmark)
KALAALLIT NUNAAT

Greenland Sea

Bjørnøya

Mezen
Onega
Sev. Dvina

Murmansk
Kolskiy Poluostrov
Arkhangelsk
Beloye More

Narodnaya
Berezovo

PERM

Labrador
Hamilton Inlet
Resolution I.
C. Chidley

Nuuk
Paamiut

Mt. Forel
Kong Christian IX.s Land
Kong Frederik VI.s Kyst

Nordkapp
Hammerfest
Vardø

Varangerfjorden

Onezhskoye Ozero

RUSSIA

UFA

Qaqortoq
Alluitsup Paa
Kap Farvel (Nunap Isua)

Ammassalik
3360
Kong Oscar Fjord
Kong Franz Joseph Fd.
Ittoqqortoormiit
Kap Brewster

Jan Mayen (Norway)

B

Nordkapp
Tromsø
Lofoten

Ladozhskoye Ozero
Volga

SAMARA

Iceland Plateau
Horn
Breiðafjörður
Fontur

3800
▼

Iceland

Trondheim

S
W
E
D
E
N

N
O
R
W
A
Y

FINLAND

Helsinki
ST. PETERBURG

Chudskoye Ozero

MOSKVA

Saratov

4755
▼

ICELAND
Reykjavik
Öræfajökull 2119

Norwegian Sea

C

Arctic Circle

Bergen

Oslo

Gulf of Bothnia

Tornio

STOCKHOLM
Tallinn
EST.
Rīga

VOLGOGRAD

Mid-Atlantic Ridge

Føroyar (Den.)

Shetland Is. (U.K.)

North Sea

Skagerrak

KØBENHAVN
DENMARK

Baltic Sea

Gulf of Finland

LAT.
LITH.
Vilnius
Kaliningrad

BELARUS

KYYIV

ROSTOV

ATLANTIC OCEAN

Rockall (U.K.)
Hebrides (U.K.)

SCOTLAND
Edinburgh

Orkney Is. (U.K.)

HAMBURG
NETH.
BERLIN
GERMANY
Elbe
Wisła

UKRAINE

ODESA

UNITED KINGDOM
Belfast
Dublin
IRELAND
C. Clear

ENGLAND
LONDON

AMSTERDAM
POLAND
PRAHA

Black Sea

6   20   **7**   West from Greenwich   0   East from Greenwich   **8**   20   **9**

Legend:

— — — Maximum extent of sea ice

▨ Summer extent of sea ice

▢ Ice caps and permanent ice shelf

ft   m
12 000   4000
6000   2000
4500   1500
3000   1000
1200   400
600   200
0   0
500   1500
1000   3000
2000   6000
3000   9000
4000   12 000
5000   15 000
m   ft

Projection : Zenithal Equidistant

CARTOGRAPHY BY PHILIP'S

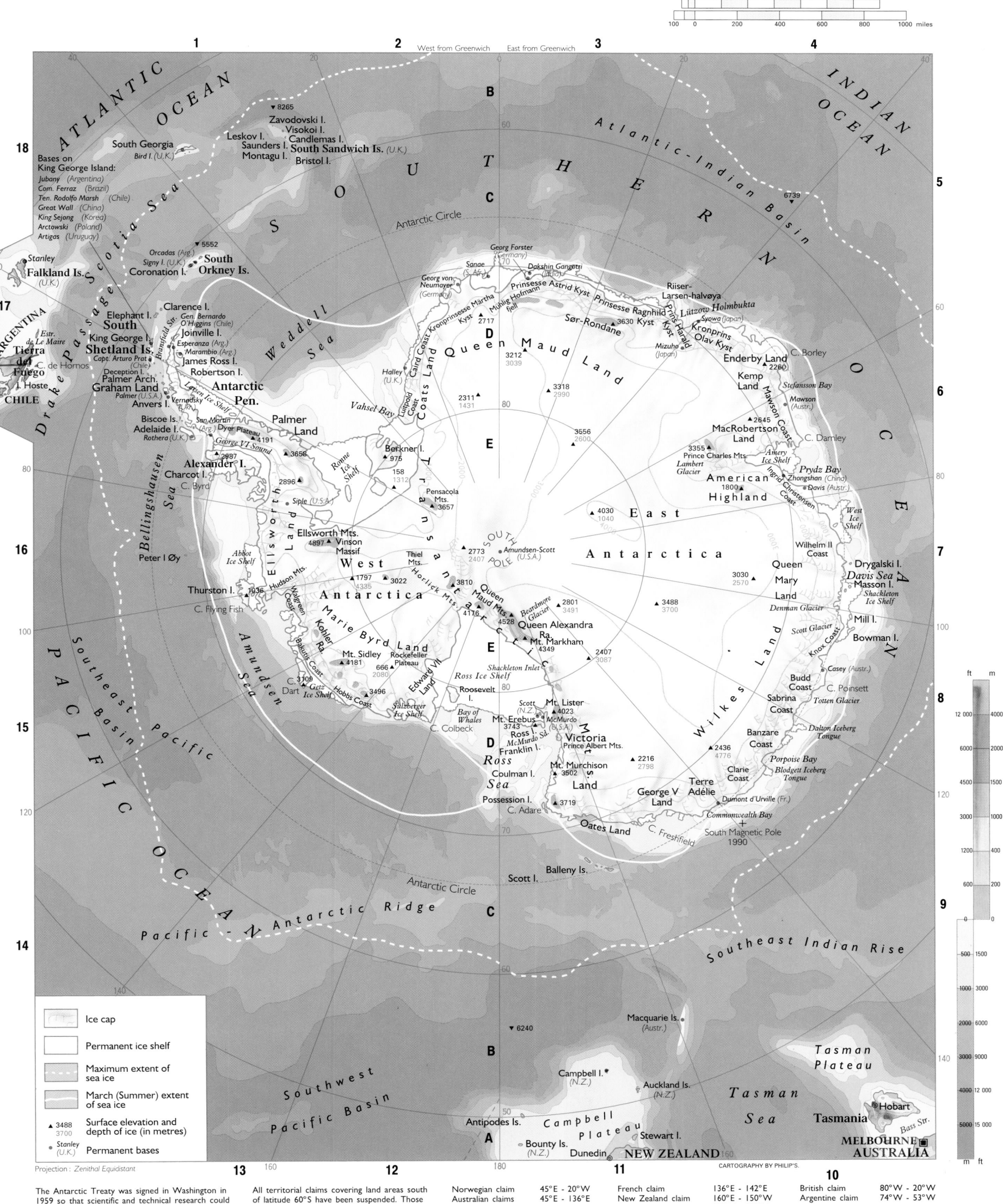

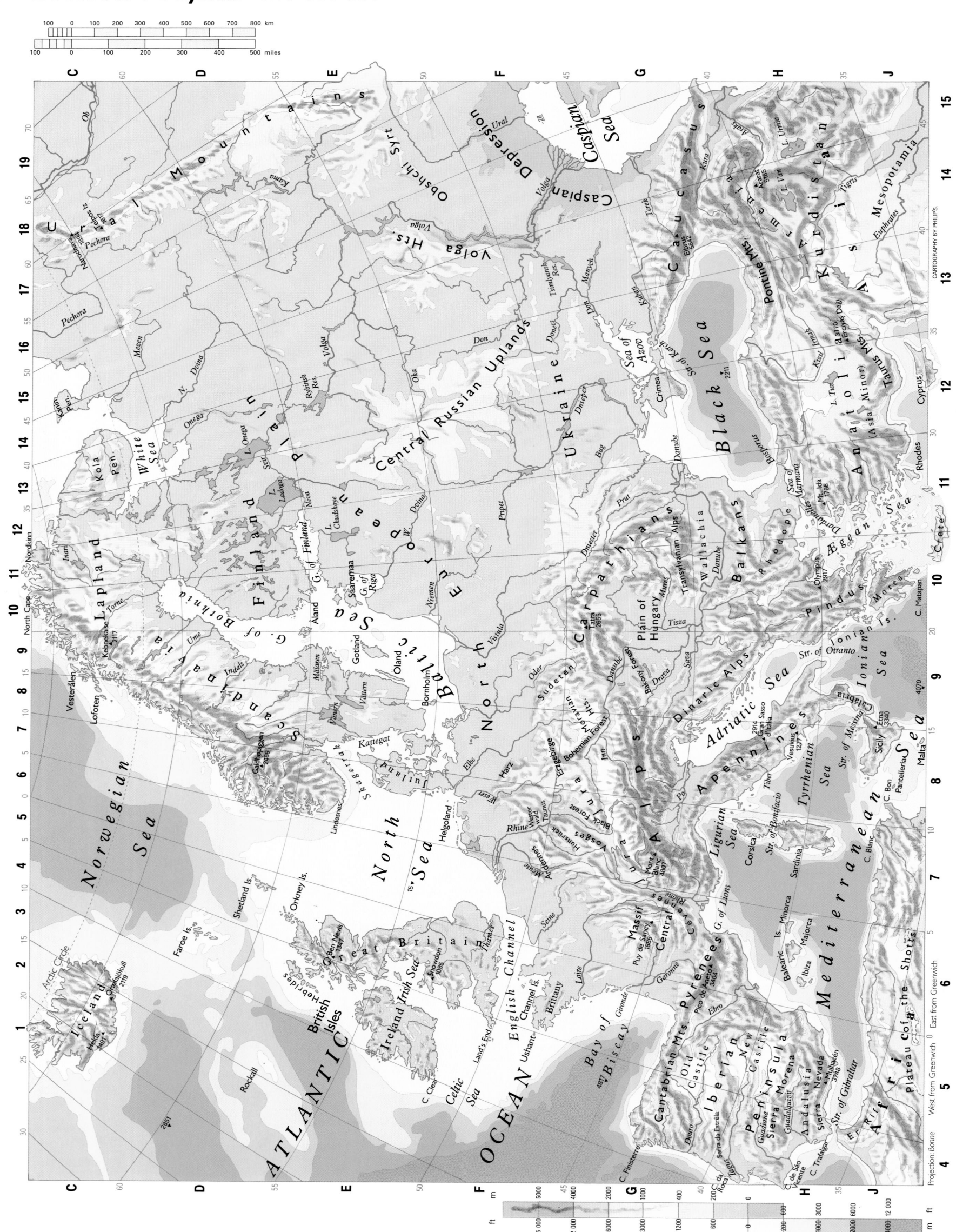
Norwegian Sea
North Sea
Baltic Sea
ATLANTIC OCEAN
Bay of Biscay
Mediterranean Sea
Black Sea
Caspian Sea
Adriatic Sea
Tyrrhenian Sea
Ionian Sea
Ægean Sea
Ural Mountains
North European Plain
Central Russian Uplands
Scandinavia
Finland
Lapland
Iceland
British Isles
Great Britain
Ireland
Alps
Carpathians
Pyrenees
Apennines
Caucasus
Balkans
Iberian Peninsula
Anatolia (Asia Minor)
Africa
CARTOGRAPHY BY PHILIPS
Projection: Bonne
West from Greenwich
East from Greenwich

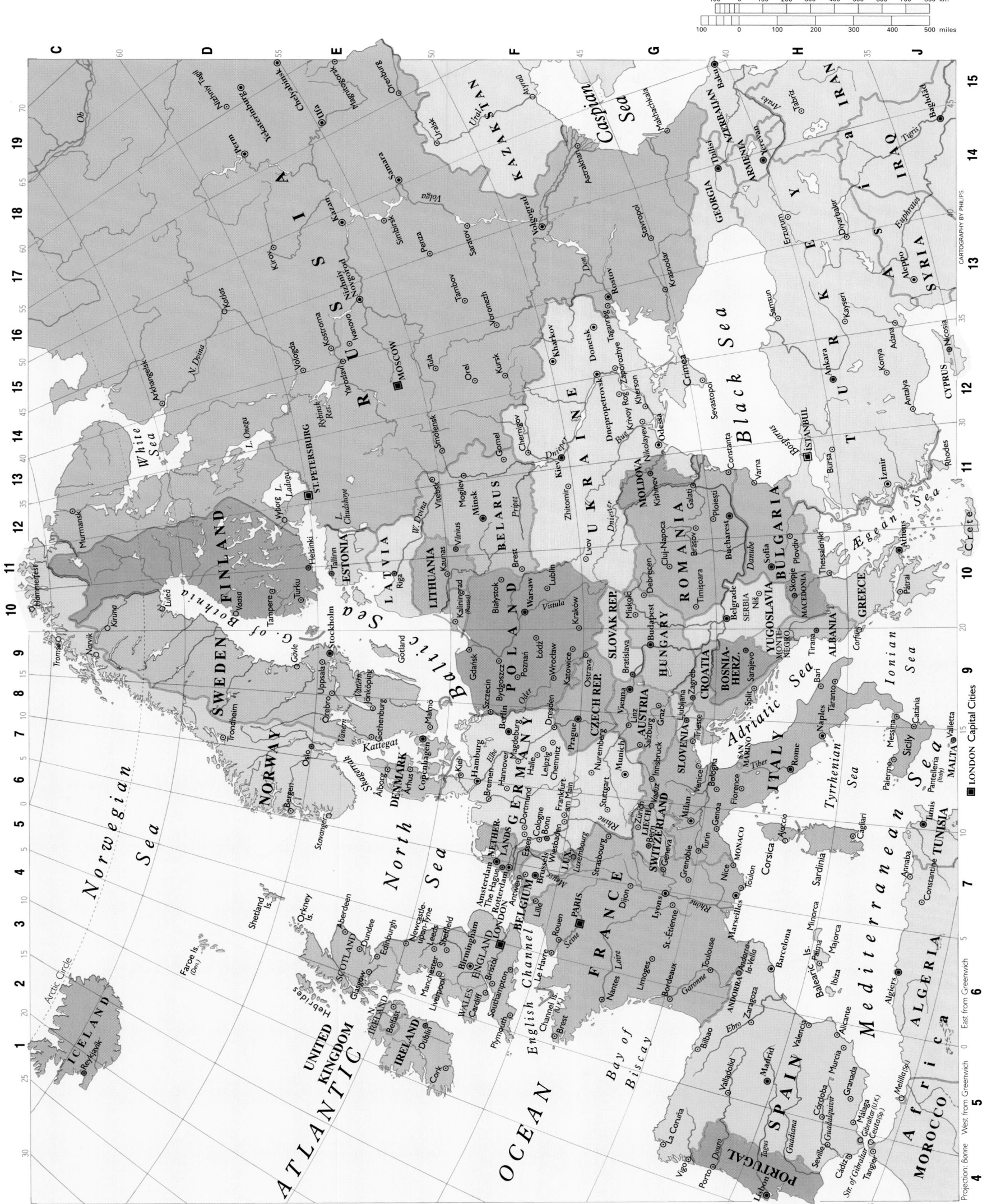

CARTOGRAPHY BY PHILIP'S

Projection: Bonne

■ LONDON Capital Cities

SCANDINAVIA 1:4 400 000

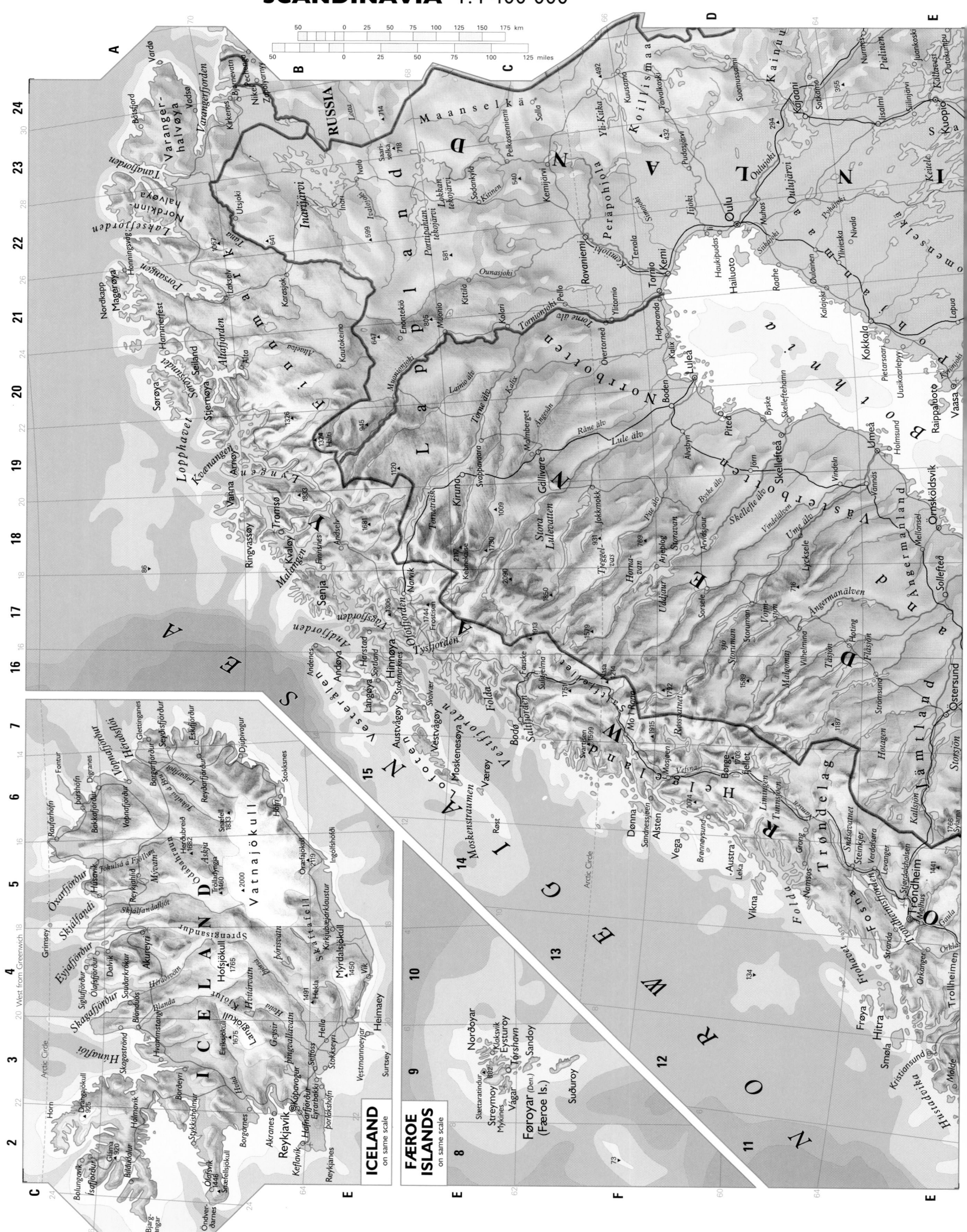

50   0   25   50   75   100 125 150 175 km
50   0   25   50   75   100   125 miles

A B C D E

RUSSIA

Vardø
Vadsø
Varangerfjorden
Båtsfjord
Kirkenes
Nikel
Zapolyarnyy
Vranger-halvøya
Nordkinn halvøya
Laksefjorden
Tanafjorden

Lotta

Maanselkä

Koillismaa

Salla
Saariselkä
Pelkosenniemi

Ivalo
Inari
Utsjoki

Sodankylä
Kittilä
Kemijärvi

Rovaniemi
Kemijoki
Kemi
Tornio
Haparanda
Kalix
Luleå
Boden
Piteå
Skellefteå
Umeå

Oulu
Muhos

Kuopio
Kajaani
Iisalmi

FINLAND

LAPPLAND

Nordkapp
Magerøya
Hammerfest
Honningsvåg
Nordkapp
Sørøya
Seiland
Altafjorden
Alta
Kautokeino
Enontekiö

Karasjok

Tromsø
Narvik
Bodø
Mo i Rana
Mosjøen

Lofoten
Vesterålen
Moskenstraumen
Værøy
Røst

NORGE

NORWAY

Trondheim
Trøndelag
Østersund
Jämtland

ICELAND
on same scale

FÆROE
ISLANDS
on same scale

ICELAND

Vatnajökull
Reykjavík
Akureyri

Reykjanes

Arctic Circle

FÆROE ISLANDS
Føroyar
(Faeroe Is.)
(Den.)
Tórshavn
Eysturoy
Streymoy
Vágar
Sandoy
Suðuroy
Norðoyar

Arctic Circle

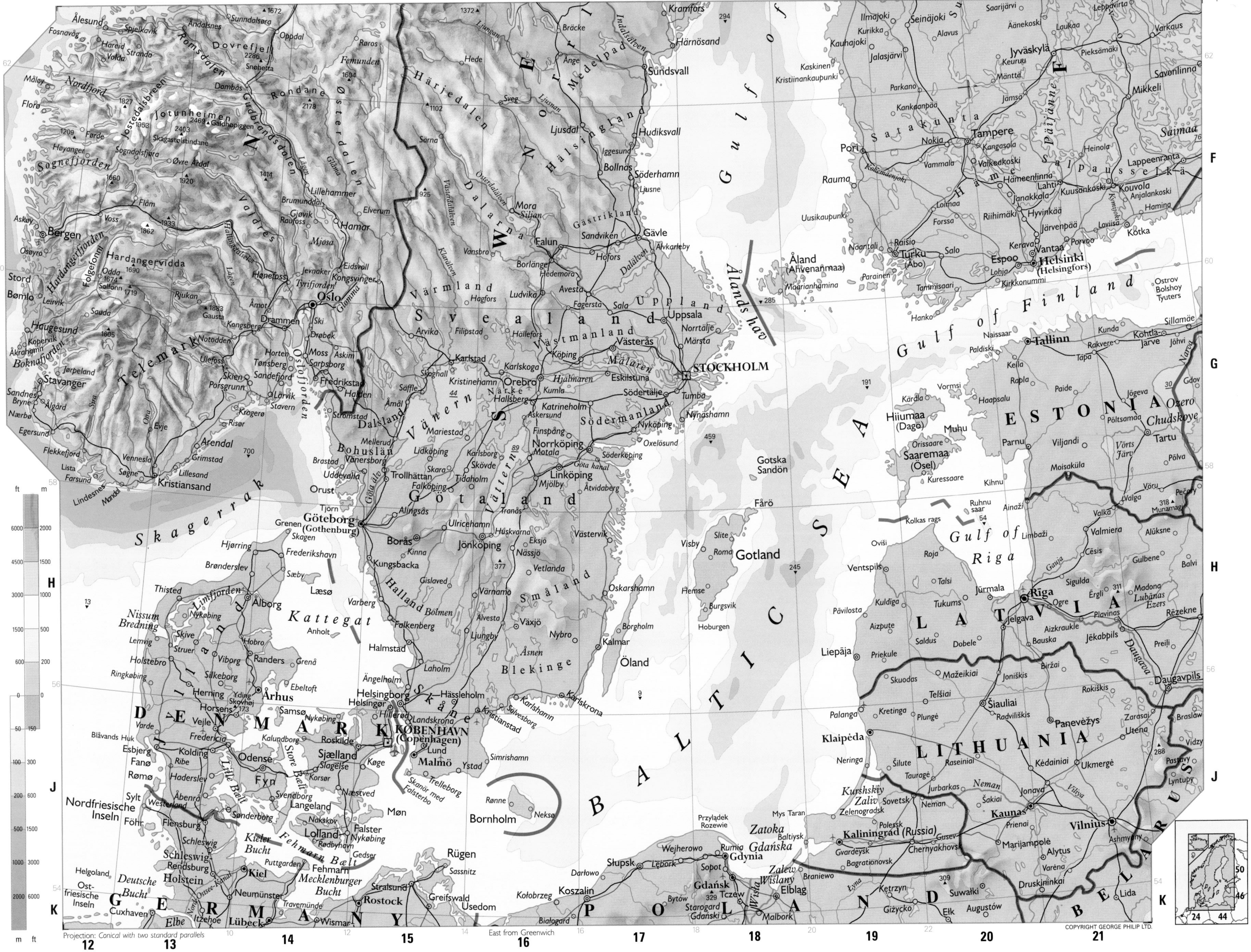

COPYRIGHT GEORGE PHILIP LTD.

FINLAND

Saimaa

Varkaus · Savonlinna · Mikkeli · Lappeenranta · Kotka · Kouvola · Lahti · Helsinki (Helsingfors) · Espoo · Tampere · Turku (Åbo) · Pori · Rauma · Uusikaupunki

Gulf of Finland

Åland (Ahvenanmaa)

Ålands hav

Gulf of Bothnia

ESTONIA

Tallinn · Narva · Tartu · Pärnu · Viljandi · Haapsalu · Paldiski · Hiiumaa (Dagö) · Saaremaa (Ösel) · Kuressaare

Lake Peipus / Ozero Chudskoye

LATVIA

Riga · Jūrmala · Jelgava · Ventspils · Liepāja · Daugavpils · Rēzekne · Valmiera · Cēsis · Sigulda · Talsi · Tukums · Saldus

Gulf of Riga

Daugava

LITHUANIA

Vilnius · Kaunas · Šiauliai · Panevėžys · Klaipėda · Marijampolė · Utena · Telšiai · Plungė

Kaliningrad (Russia)

Chernyakhovsk · Gusev · Sovetsk

BALTIC SEA

Gotland · Visby · Fårö · Öland · Kalmar · Bornholm · Rønne

SWEDEN

STOCKHOLM · Uppsala · Västerås · Eskilstuna · Örebro · Norrköping · Linköping · Jönköping · Göteborg (Gothenburg) · Borås · Gävle · Sundsvall · Härnösand · Falun · Karlstad · Halmstad · Helsingborg · Malmö · Lund · Kristianstad · Karlskrona · Kalmar · Växjö

Vänern · Vättern · Mälaren

Uppland · Södermanland · Östergötland · Småland · Västergötland · Bohuslän · Halland · Skåne · Blekinge · Dalarna · Värmland · Hälsingland · Härjedalen · Medelpad · Ångermanland

NORWAY

Oslo · Bergen · Stavanger · Kristiansand · Hamar · Lillehammer · Drammen · Tønsberg · Skien · Porsgrunn · Arendal · Ålesund

Oslofjorden · Sognefjord · Hardangerfjord · Hardangervidda · Jotunheimen · Dovrefjell · Rondane · Gudbrandsdalen · Østerdalen · Telemark · Valdres

Skagerrak · Kattegat

DENMARK

KØBENHAVN (Copenhagen) · Århus · Ålborg · Odense · Esbjerg · Randers · Kolding · Horsens · Vejle · Roskilde · Helsingør · Hillerød · Slagelse · Næstved

Sjælland · Fyn · Lolland · Falster · Møn · Bornholm · Langeland

Lille Bælt · Store Bælt · Fehmarn Bælt

Jylland (Jutland)

GERMANY

Kiel · Lübeck · Rostock · Flensburg · Schleswig · Neumünster · Wismar · Greifswald · Stralsund · Heide · Husum · Cuxhaven

Rügen · Usedom · Fehmarn · Helgoland

Nordfriesische Inseln · Ostfriesische Inseln

Deutsche Bucht · Mecklenburger Bucht · Kieler Bucht

Elbe · Weser

POLAND

Gdańsk · Gdynia · Sopot · Szczecin · Koszalin · Słupsk · Kołobrzeg · Malbork · Elbląg · Tczew · Starogard Gdański · Bytów

Zalew Wiślany · Zatoka Gdańska · Wisła

BELARUS

Lida · Ashmyany

RUSSIA

m ft — 6000 4500 3000 1500 1000 600 300 150 0 — 2000 1500 1000 500 200 100 50 0

Major labels

Countries / Regions: AUST-AGDER, GERMANY, POLAND, DENMARK, SVERIGE (Sweden)

Seas / Waters: BALTIC SEA, Kattegat, Skagerrak, Kalmar sund, Hanöbukten, Store Bælt, Øresund, Fehmarn Belt, Langelandsbælt

Swedish Län: GÖTEBORGS OCH BOHUS LÄN, ÄLVSBORGS LÄN, SKARABORGS LÄN, ÖSTERGÖTLANDS LÄN, JÖNKÖPINGS LÄN, HALLANDS LÄN, KRONOBERGS LÄN, KALMAR LÄN, BLEKINGE LÄN, SKÅNE, GOTLANDS LÄN

Danish Amt: NORDJYLLANDS AMT, VIBORG AMT, ÅRHUS AMT, RINGKØBING AMT, VEJLE AMT, RIBE AMT, SØNDERJYLLANDS AMT, FYNS AMT, VESTSJÆLLANDS AMT, STORSTRØMS AMT, FREDERIKSBORG AMT, ROSKILDE AMT, KØBENHAVNS AMT, BORNHOLMS AMT

Major cities: Göteborg, Norrköping, Linköping, Jönköping, Borås, Halmstad, Helsingborg, Malmö, Kalmar, Karlskrona, Kristianstad, Landskrona, Visby, KØBENHAVN, Helsingør, Roskilde, Odense, Århus, Ålborg, Randers, Viborg, Herning, Esbjerg, Kolding, Vejle, Fredericia, Horsens, Silkeborg, Frederikshavn, Skagen, Flensburg, Rønne, Bornholm

Islands: Gotland (Sweden), Öland (Sweden), Læsø (Denmark), Anholt (Denmark), Samsø, Fyn, Sjælland, Lolland, Falster, Møn, Ærø, Als, Langeland, Bornholm (Denmark), Fehmarn, Sylt, Rømø, Fanø, Hiddensee

Grid references: F, G, H, J, K (left/right margins); 2–11 (bottom); letters and numbers along edges

Projection : Lambert's Conformal Conic

East from Greenwich

COPYRIGHT GEORGE PHILIP LTD.

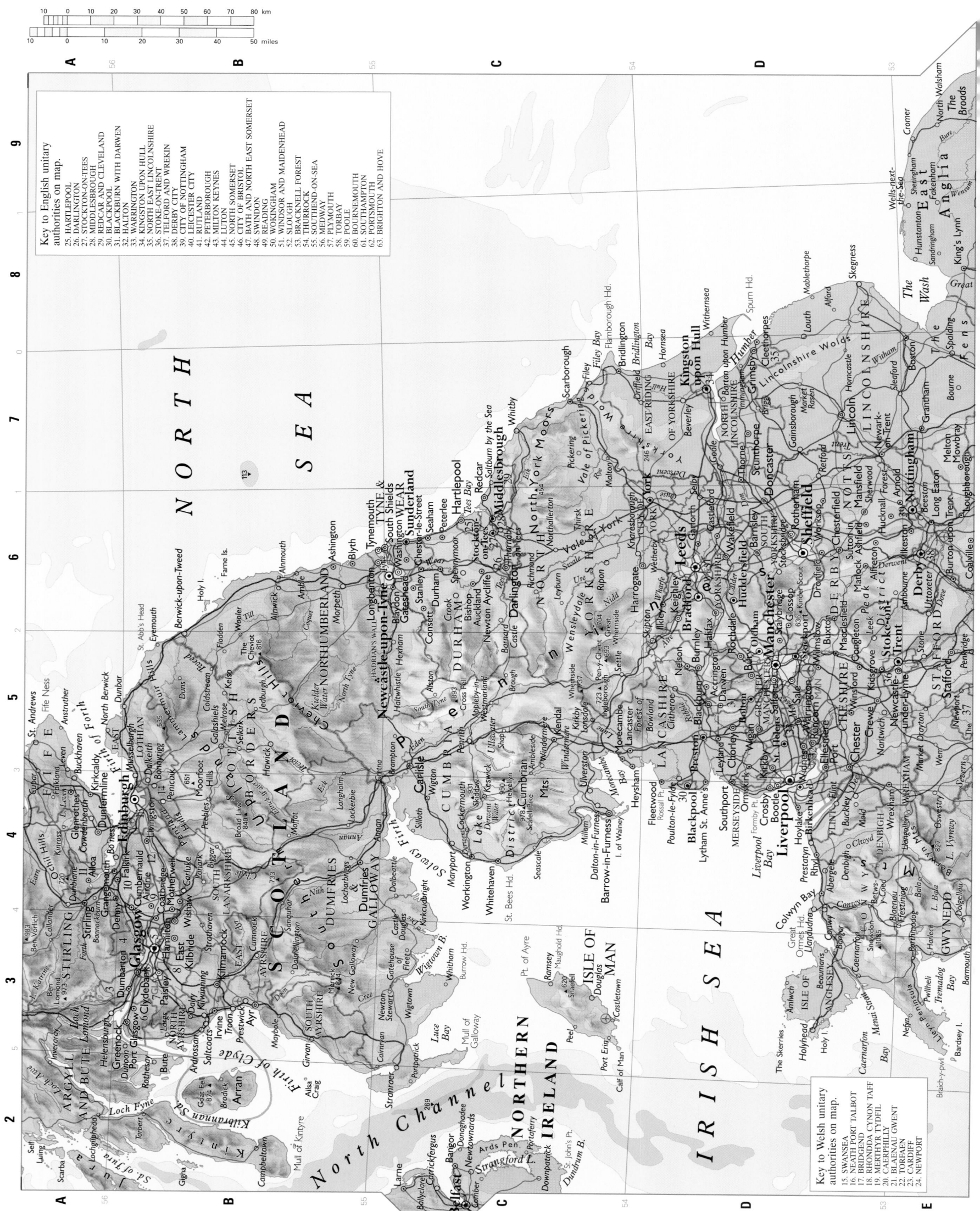

Key to English unitary
authorities on map.

25. HARTLEPOOL
26. DARLINGTON
27. STOCKTON-ON-TEES
28. MIDDLESBROUGH
29. REDCAR AND CLEVELAND
30. BLACKPOOL
31. BLACKBURN WITH DARWEN
32. HALTON
33. WARRINGTON
34. KINGSTON UPON HULL
35. NORTH EAST LINCOLNSHIRE
36. STOKE-ON-TRENT
37. TELFORD AND WREKIN
38. DERBY CITY
39. CITY OF NOTTINGHAM
40. LEICESTER CITY
41. RUTLAND
42. PETERBOROUGH
43. MILTON KEYNES
44. LUTON
45. NORTH SOMERSET
46. CITY OF BRISTOL
47. BATH AND NORTH EAST SOMERSET
48. SWINDON
49. READING
50. WOKINGHAM
51. WINDSOR AND MAIDENHEAD
52. SLOUGH
53. BRACKNELL FOREST
54. THURROCK
55. SOUTHEND-ON-SEA
56. MEDWAY
57. PLYMOUTH
58. TORBAY
59. POOLE
60. BOURNEMOUTH
61. SOUTHAMPTON
62. PORTSMOUTH
63. BRIGHTON AND HOVE

Key to Welsh unitary
authorities on map.

15. SWANSEA
16. NEATH PORT TALBOT
17. BRIDGEND
18. RHONDDA CYNON TAFF
19. MERTHYR TYDFIL
20. CAERPHILLY
21. BLAENAU GWENT
22. TORFAEN
23. CARDIFF
24. NEWPORT

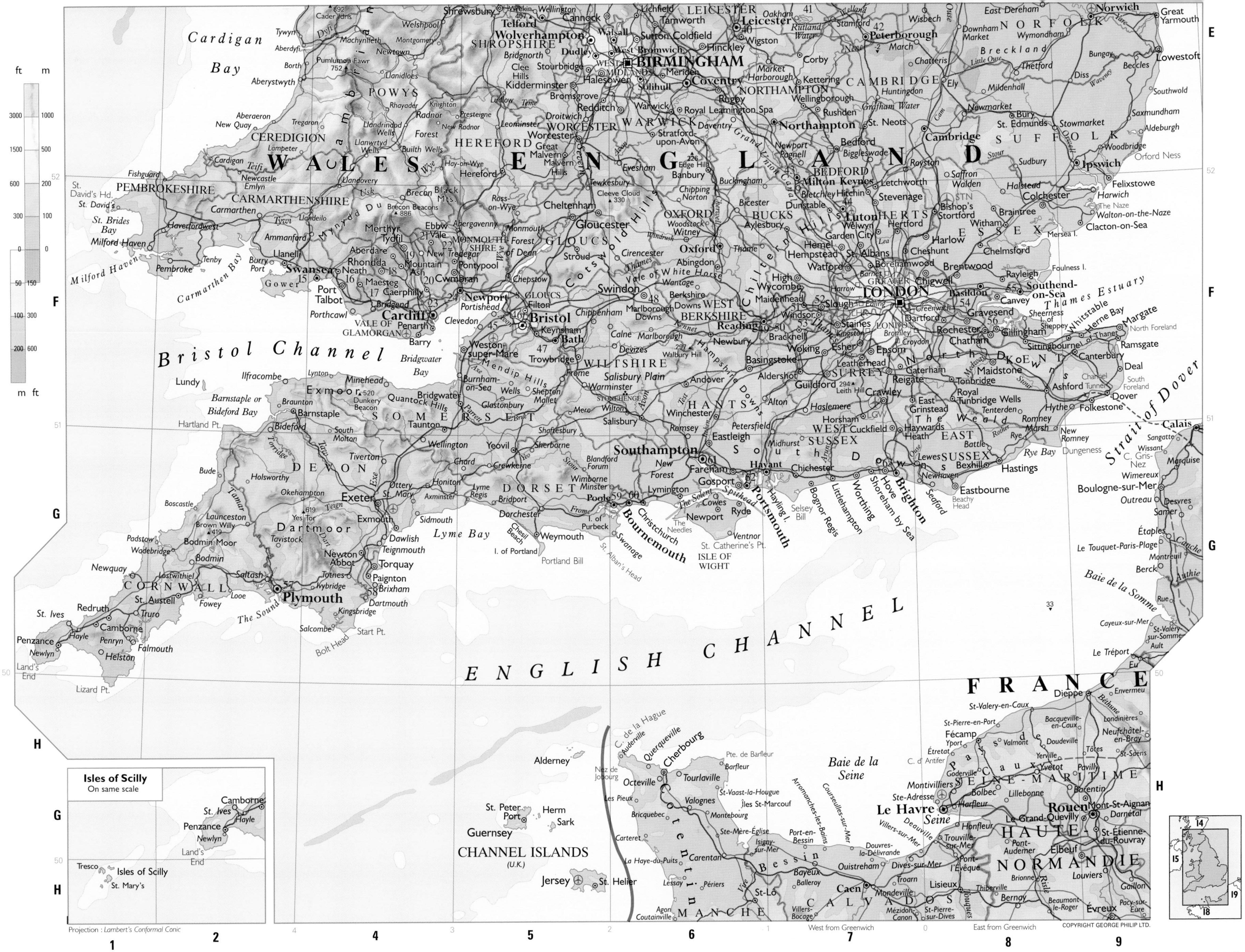

ENGLAND

WALES

FRANCE

NORMANDIE

SEINE-MARITIME

HAUTE

CALVADOS

ENGLISH CHANNEL

Bristol Channel

Cardigan Bay

Strait of Dover

Thames Estuary

Baie de la Somme

Baie de la Seine

LONDON

Birmingham

Bristol

Cardiff

Swansea

Plymouth

Exeter

Bournemouth

Southampton

Portsmouth

Brighton

Leicester

Wolverhampton

Newport

Le Havre

Rouen

Caen

Cherbourg

Dieppe

Calais

Boulogne-sur-Mer

CHANNEL ISLANDS (U.K.)

Jersey — St. Helier

Guernsey — St. Peter Port

Alderney

Sark

Herm

Isles of Scilly
On same scale

St. Mary's
Tresco
Isles of Scilly

Land's End

Lizard Pt.

Penzance

Newlyn

St. Ives

Camborne

Truro

Falmouth

Redruth

Newquay

CORNWALL

DEVON

DORSET

SOMERSET

WILTSHIRE

HAMPSHIRE

SUSSEX

SURREY

KENT

ESSEX

SUFFOLK

NORFOLK

CAMBRIDGE

BEDFORD

BUCKS

OXFORD

BERKSHIRE

GLOUCS

WORCESTER

WARWICK

SHROPSHIRE

HEREFORD

POWYS

CEREDIGION

PEMBROKESHIRE

CARMARTHENSHIRE

GLAMORGAN

VALE OF GLAMORGAN

LEICESTER

NORTHAMPTON

HERTS

WEST SUSSEX

EAST SUSSEX

Projection : Lambert's Conformal Conic

COPYRIGHT GEORGE PHILIP LTD.

East from Greenwich

West from Greenwich

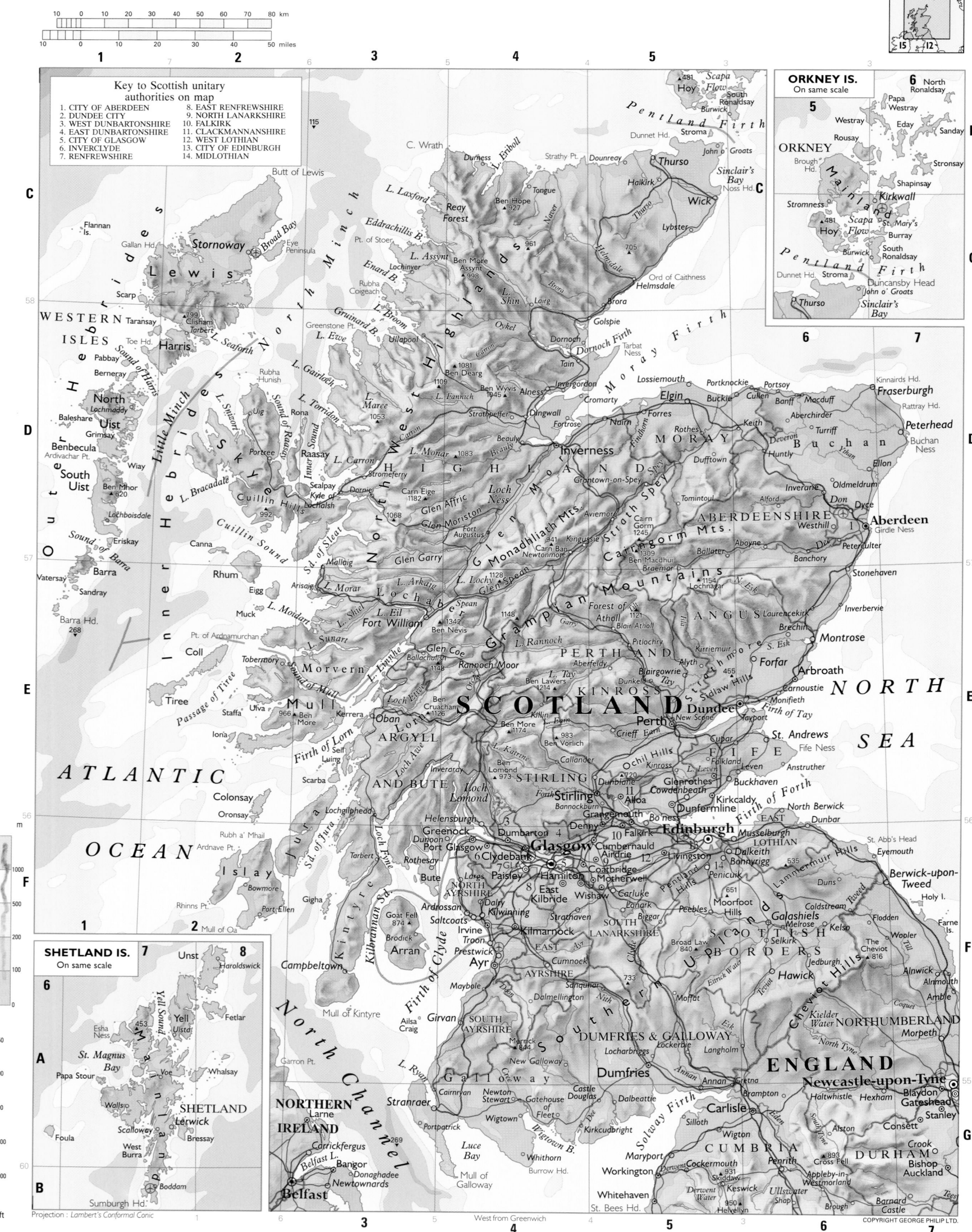

Key to Scottish unitary authorities on map
1. CITY OF ABERDEEN
2. DUNDEE CITY
3. WEST DUNBARTONSHIRE
4. EAST DUNBARTONSHIRE
5. CITY OF GLASGOW
6. INVERCLYDE
7. RENFREWSHIRE
8. EAST RENFREWSHIRE
9. NORTH LANARKSHIRE
10. FALKIRK
11. CLACKMANNANSHIRE
12. WEST LOTHIAN
13. CITY OF EDINBURGH
14. MIDLOTHIAN

ORKNEY IS.
On same scale
ORKNEY

SHETLAND IS.
On same scale
SHETLAND

SCOTLAND

NORTH SEA

ATLANTIC OCEAN

ENGLAND

NORTHERN IRELAND

North Channel

Projection : Lambert's Conformal Conic

COPYRIGHT GEORGE PHILIP LTD.

West from Greenwich

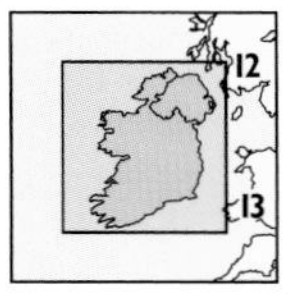

10 0 10 20 30 40 50 60 70 80 km
10 0 10 20 30 40 50 miles

ATLANTIC OCEAN

NORTH CHANNEL

Kintyre
Campbeltown
Mull of Oa
Mull of Kintyre
Arran
Brodick
Firth of Clyde
Ailsa Craig
Cairnryan
Stranraer
Portpatrick

Malin Hd.
Tory I.
Sheep Haven
Lough Swilly
Malin Pen.
Carndonagh
Moville
Giants Causeway
Rathlin I.
Fair Hd.
Ballycastle
Garron Pt.
554 Trostan

Inishowen Pen.
Buncrana
Portstewart
Portrush
Limavady
Ballymoney
269

Bloody Foreland
Inishfree B.
Gweedore
Errigal 752
The Rosses
Rathmelton
Aran I.
L. Foyle
Coleraine
LONDONDERRY
Londonderry
ANTRIM
Ballymena
Larne
Cairnryan

Crohy Hd.
683
Letterkenny
DONEGAL
Lifford
Strabane
Sawel Mt. 683
Sperrin Mts.
Magherafelt
Randalstown Ballyclare
Carrickfergus
Gweebarra B.
Dawros Hd.
Glenties
Sion Mills
Newtownstewart
Moneymore
Cookstown
Lough Neagh
Antrim
Belfast L.
Bangor
Loughros More B.
Lavagh More 676
Castlederg
TYRONE
Omagh
Coalisland
Dungannon
Belfast
Newtownabbey
Donaghadee
Newtownards
Rossan Pt.
Killybegs
Donegal
Finn
Derg
Ulster
Dromore
Irvinestown
Craigavon
Portadown
Lurgan
Lisburn
Comber
Ards Pen.
Strangford L.
St. John's Pt.
Donegal Bay
Ballyshannon
Bundoran
Erne
Lower L. Erne
Enniskillen
FERMANAGH
Monaghan
Armagh
ARMAGH
Middletown
Keady
Banbridge
Tandragee
Ballynahinch
Portaferry
Ballyquintin Pt.
Broad Haven
Erris Hd.
Downpatrick Hd.
Killala B.
Upper L. Erne
Clones
Belturbet
MONAGHAN
577
Castleblaney
Cootehill
Newry
Slieve Gullion
Mourne Mts.
852 Slieve Donard
Newcastle
DOWN
Dundrum
Dundrum B.
St. John's Pt.
Mullet Pen.
Belmullet
Inishkea North
Inishkea South
Blacksod Bay
Killala
Ballina
Dromore West
544 Slieve Gamph
Colooney
L. Allen
LEITRIM
Leitrim
Cavan
L. Gowna
CAVAN
Carrickmacross
Kingscourt
Louth
Ardee
Dundalk
Greenore
Carlingford L.
Dundalk Bay
Clogher Hd.
Achill Hd.
Achill I.
Corraun Pen.
L. Conn
806 Nephin
Newport
Castlebar
Swinford
Charlestown
Boyle
Carrick-on-Shannon
Annalee
L. Sheelin
Oldcastle
Ceanannus Mor (Kells)
Blackwater
Dunleer
MEATH
Drogheda
Clare I.
Clew Bay
Westport
MAYO
Knock
Ballyhaunis
Ballaghaderreen
ROSCOMMON
Castlerea
L. Arrow
Granard
LONGFORD
Castlepollard
Balbriggan
Inishturk
Croagh Patrick 765
Mweelrea 819
Killary Harbour
Inishbofin
Inishshark
Connacht
Connemara
Ballinrobe
Claremorris
Glennamaddy
Roscommon
Longford
An Uaimh (Navan)
Boyne
Rush
Lambay I.
Slyne Hd.
Clifden
Oughterard
Lough Mask
Tuam
IRELAND
Inny
Athboy
Trim
Swords
Malahide
Howth Hd.
Lough Corrib
Lough Ree
Mullingar
WESTMEATH
Leinster
Maynooth
DUBLIN
Bertraghboy B.
Kilkieran B.
GALWAY
Athenry
Athlone
Moate
Royal Canal
Dublin
Dun Laoghaire
Slyne Hd.
Galway
Galway Bay
Ballinasloe
Suck
Clara
Edenderry
KILDARE
Clondalkin
Bray
Greystones
Aran Is.
Inishmore
Inishmaan
Inisheer
Black Hd.
368
Slieve Aughty
Portumna
Loughrea
Shannon
Birr
OFFALY
Tullamore
Daingean
Bog of Allen
Kildare
Naas
Clane
Droichead Nua
Kippure 754
WICKLOW
123
Ennistimon
Hags Hd.
Liscannor Bay
Gort
Lough Derg
Roscrea
Slieve Bloom 529 Arderin
Mountmellick
Portarlington
Port Laoise
Monasterevin
Athy
Poulaphouca Res.
Wicklow Mts.
Lugnaquilla 926
Wicklow
Wicklow Hd.
Mal Bay
Mutton I.
Tulla
Ennis
CLARE
Killaloe
Nenagh
LAOIS
Durrow
Mountrath
Carlow
Tullow
Rathdrum
Avoca
Arklow
Mizen Hd.
Kilkee
Loop Hd.
Kilrush
Sixmilebridge
Shannon Airport
694 Keeper Hill
Templemore
Thurles
CARLOW
Muine Bheag
Shillelagh
Gorey
Mouth of the Shannon
Foynes
Limerick
TIPPERARY
Kilkenny
KILKENNY
Callan
796 Mt. Leinster
Bunclody
Enniscorthy
Kerry Hd.
Rathkeale
Golden Vale
LIMERICK
Tipperary
Cashel
Cahore Pt.
Smerwick Harbour
Brandon B.
Tralee B.
953
Brandon Mt.
Dingle
Slieve Mish 853
Maine
Tralee
Newcastle West
Kilfinnane
Galtymore 920 Galty Mts.
Caher
Slievenamon 722
Clonmel
Carrick-on-Suir
Nore
Barrow
Suir
New Ross
WEXFORD
Enniscorthy
Wexford Harbour
Rosslare
Great Blasket I.
Dunmore Hd.
Dingle
Dingle Bay
KERRY
Newmarket
Kanturk
Buttevant
Mitchelstown
Fermoy
Knockmealdown Mts. 795
Comeragh Mts. 792
WATERFORD
Lismore
Waterford
Tramore
Tramore B.
Waterford Harbour
Hook Hd.
Saltee Is.
Carnsore Pt.
Inishvickillane
Valencia I.
Puffin I.
Great Skellig
Killorglin
Laune
Killarney
Carrauntoohill 1041
L. Leane
Macroom
Boggeragh Mts. 646
Mallow
Blackwater
Dungarvan
Dungarvan Harbour
St. David's Hd.
St. David's
St. Brides Bay
Ballinskelligs B.
Cahirciveen
Kenmare
Macgillycuddy's Reeks
Kenmare River
Caha Mts. 686
Glengarriff
Dunmanway
Bandon
CORK
Cork
Blarney
Lee
Passage West
Cobh
Midleton
Youghal
Youghal B.
115
Dursey I.
Castletown Bearhaven
Bear I.
Bantry Bay
Bantry
Clonakilty
Kinsale
Crosshaven
Cork Harbour
Old Head of Kinsale
Crow Hd.
Scariff I.
Dunmanus B.
Skull
Long I.
Baltimore
Sherkin I.
Clear I.
C. Clear
Galley Hd.
Clonakilty B.

CELTIC SEA

IRISH SEA

St. George's Channel

COPYRIGHT GEORGE PHILIP LTD.

Projection: Lambert's Conformal Conic

West from Greenwich

ft m
1500 500
600 200
300 100
0 0
150
100 300
200 600
500 1500
1000 3000
2000 6000
m ft

Projection: Conical with two standard parallels

ATLANTIC OCEAN

NORWAY
Bergen
Askøy
Osøyro
Stord
Bømlo
Leirvik
Haugesund
Kopervik
Åkrahamn
Boknafjorden
Stavanger
Sandnes
Bryne
Nærbø

Shetland Is.
Yell
Unst
Fetlar
Mainland
Lerwick
Foula
Fair Isle

Orkney Is.
Westray
Sanday
Stronsay
Mainland
Hoy
Kirkwall
South Ronaldsay

C. Wrath
Pentland Firth
Thurso
Wick

Lewis
Stornoway
Outer Hebrides
Harris
St. Kilda
North Uist
Benbecula
South Uist
Barra

North Minch
Ullapool
Lairg
Helmsdale
Golspie
Tain
Invergordon
Dingwall
L. Ness
Inverness
Nairn
Elgin
Buckie
Banff
Fraserburgh
Huntly
Peterhead
Inverurie
Aberdeen

North West Highlands
Portree
Skye
Mallaig
Rhum
Eigg
Fort William
Ben Nevis 1342
Aviemore
Spey
Dee
Ballater
Stonehaven

SCOTLAND
GRAMPIAN MTS.
Coll
Tiree
Tobermory
Mull
Oban
Colonsay
L. Lomond
973
Perth
Dundee
St. Andrews
Stirling
Glenrothes
Kirkcaldy
Dunfermline
Dunbar
Forfar
Montrose
Arbroath

Jura
Islay
Greenock
Paisley
Glasgow
Edinburgh
East Kilbride
Hamilton
Berwick-upon-Tweed
Campbeltown
Arran
Kilmarnock
Ayr
SOUTHERN UPLANDS
Galashiels
Jedburgh
Hawick
Cheviot Hills
Alnwick

Malin Hd.
North Channel
Girvan
Dumfries
Annan
Hexham
Newcastle-upon-Tyne
South Shields
Firth of Clyde
Kirkcudbright
Carlisle
Gateshead
Durham
Sunderland
Hartlepool
Redcar
Workington
Cumbrian Mts.
Darlington
Middlesbrough
Stockton-on-Tees

NORTH SEA

Buncrana
Aran I.
Coleraine
Ballymena
Larne
Letterkenny
Londonderry
Bangor
Lifford
NORTHERN IRELAND
Belfast
Donegal
ULSTER
Lough Neagh
Omagh
Portadown
Lurgan
Bundoran
Lower L. Erne
Enniskillen
Armagh
Newry
Sligo
Leitrim
Cavan
Castleblaney
Clones

UNITED KINGDOM

Whitehaven
Barrow-in-Furness
I. of Man
Douglas
Lancaster
Harrogate
York
Scarborough
Bridlington
Beverley
Kingston upon Hull

IRISH SEA

Achill I.
Ballina
Castlebar
L. Conn
Westport
Lough Mask
Roscommon
Longford
Boyne
Drogheda
Dundalk
Ceanannus Mor
Lough Corrib
Athlone
Lough Ree
Mullingar
Connemara
Galway B.
Galway
Ballinasloe
Tullamore
L. Derg
Dublin
Dun Laoghaire
Bray
Holyhead
Anglesey
Blackpool
Preston
Blackburn
Burnley
Keighley
Bradford
Leeds
Halifax
Huddersfield
Barnsley
Doncaster
Scunthorpe
Grimsby
Bolton
Manchester
Oldham
Rotherham
Sheffield
Stockport
Warrington
Liverpool
Chester
Crewe
Chesterfield
Mansfield
Lincoln
Louth
Skegness

IRELAND
Aran Is.
Ennis
Lough Derg
Nenagh
Thurles
Kilrush
Limerick
Carlow
Kilkenny
MUNSTER
Tipperary
Carrick-on-Suir
Clonmel
Kilkenny
Wexford
Rosslare
Wicklow Mts.
Arklow
LEINSTER
Port Laoise
Athy
Liffey

Shannon
Listowel
Tralee
Dingle
Killarney
Mallow
Carrantoohill 1041
Macgillycuddy's Reeks
Valencia
Bantry
Kinsale
Cork
Bandon
Cóbh
Youghal
Dungarvan
Waterford
Blackwater

Snowdon 1085
Cambrian Mts.
Colwyn Bay
Bangor
Pwllheli
Wrexham
Stoke on Trent
Derby
Nottingham
Stafford
Shrewsbury
Telford
Trent
Grantham
King's Lynn
Norwich
Great Yarmouth
Lowestoft
Cromer

ENGLAND
Cardigan Bay
Aberystwyth
Welshpool
WALES
Wolverhampton
BIRMINGHAM
Leicester
Nuneaton
Coventry
Rugby
Corby
Peterborough
Thetford
Ely
Bury St. Edmunds
Ipswich
Felixstowe
Harwich
Colchester
Chelmsford

Carmarthen
Brecon
Merthyr Tydfil
Neath
Llanelli
Swansea
Port Talbot
Rhondda
Cwmbran
Newport
Cardiff
Barry
Redditch
Worcester
Hereford
Cheltenham
Gloucester
Royal Leamington Spa
Northampton
Bedford
Milton Keynes
Cambridge
Stevenage
Luton
Harlow
Southend-on-Sea
Bristol Channel
Bristol
Bath
Swindon
Newbury
Reading
Slough
Watford
Basildon
LONDON
Chatham
Margate
Canterbury
Dover
Reigate
Maidstone
Folkestone

St. George's Channel
Fishguard
Haverfordwest
Milford Haven
Pembroke
High Wycombe
Hemel Hempstead
Oxford
Cotswold Hills

Weston-super-Mare
Barnstaple
Exmoor
Taunton
Salisbury
Basingstoke
Guildford
Winchester
Crawley
Ashford
Hastings
Eastbourne
Str. of Dover
Bude
Newquay
Truro
St. Austell
Dartmoor
Exeter
Yeovil
Bournemouth
Poole
Southampton
Fareham
Portsmouth
Brighton
Worthing
Havant
Isle of Wight
Newport
Weymouth
Exmouth

Land's End
Penzance
Falmouth
Plymouth
Torbay
Isles of Scilly

CELTIC SEA

ENGLISH CHANNEL

FRANCE
C. de la Hague
Pte. de Barfleur
Alderney
Guernsey
St. Peter Port
Sark
Channel Is. (U.K.)
St. Helier
Jersey
Cotentin
Cherbourg
Valognes
Bayeux
Trouville-sur-Mer
Caen
Lisieux
Seine
Elbeuf
Bolbec
Rouen
Le Havre
Fécamp
Pays de Caux
Dieppe
Le Tréport
Abbeville
St-Quentin
Amiens
PICARDIE
Cambrai
Valenciennes

NETHERLANDS
's-Gravenhage (Den Haag)
ROTTERDAM
Dordrecht
Texel
Den Helder
Alkmaar
Haarlem
Hoek van Holland

BELGIUM
BRUSSEL (Bruxelles)
Antwerpen
Brugge
Gent
Mechelen
Oostende
Zeebrugge
Vlissingen
Dunkerque
Calais
Boulogne-sur-Mer
Le Touquet-Paris-Plage
Gris Nez
St-Omer
Béthune
Bruay-la-Buissière
Lens
Lille
Roubaix
Tourcoing
Tournai
Villeneuve-d'Ascq

West from Greenwich
East from Greenwich
COPYRIGHT GEORGE PHILIP LTD.

10 0 10 20 30 40 50 60 70 80 90 km
10 0 10 20 30 40 50 60 miles

NORTH SEA

UNITED KINGDOM

NETHERLANDS

BELGIUM

GERMANY

FRANCE

LUXEMBOURG

Waddeneilanden

Ostfriesische Inseln

FRIESLAND

GRONINGEN

DRENTHE

OVERIJSSEL

GELDERLAND

HOLLAND

ZUID-HOLLAND

NOORD-BRABANT

ZEELAND

LIMBURG

NORDRHEIN-WESTFALEN

RHEINLAND-PFALZ

SAARLAND

PAS-DE-CALAIS

NORD

PICARDIE

SOMME

OISE

AISNE

ARDENNES

SEINE-ET-MARNE

LORRAINE

MOSELLE

MEUSE

MARNE

Amsterdam · Haarlem · 's-Gravenhage (Den Haag) · Rotterdam · Utrecht · Leiden · Groningen · Leeuwarden · Assen · Zwolle · Arnhem · Nijmegen · Eindhoven · Tilburg · Breda · Dordrecht · Enschede · Apeldoorn · Amersfoort

Antwerpen · Brussel (Bruxelles) · Gent (Gand) · Brugge · Oostende · Namur · Charleroi · Liège · Mons · Hasselt · Leuven · Mechelen

Luxembourg

Köln · Düsseldorf · Dortmund · Essen · Duisburg · Bonn · Münster · Oldenburg · Bremerhaven · Wilhelmshaven · Osnabrück · Wiesbaden · Mainz · Kaiserslautern · Saarbrücken · Trier · Koblenz

Lille · Calais · Dunkerque · Boulogne-sur-Mer · Amiens · Reims · Nancy · Strasbourg · Paris · Metz · Charleville-Mézières · Châlons-en-Champagne · Valenciennes · Douai · Arras · St-Quentin · Compiègne · Beauvais

Projection : Lambert's Conformal Conic

East from Greenwich

COPYRIGHT GEORGE PHILIP LTD.

Underlined towns give their name to the administrative area in which they stand.

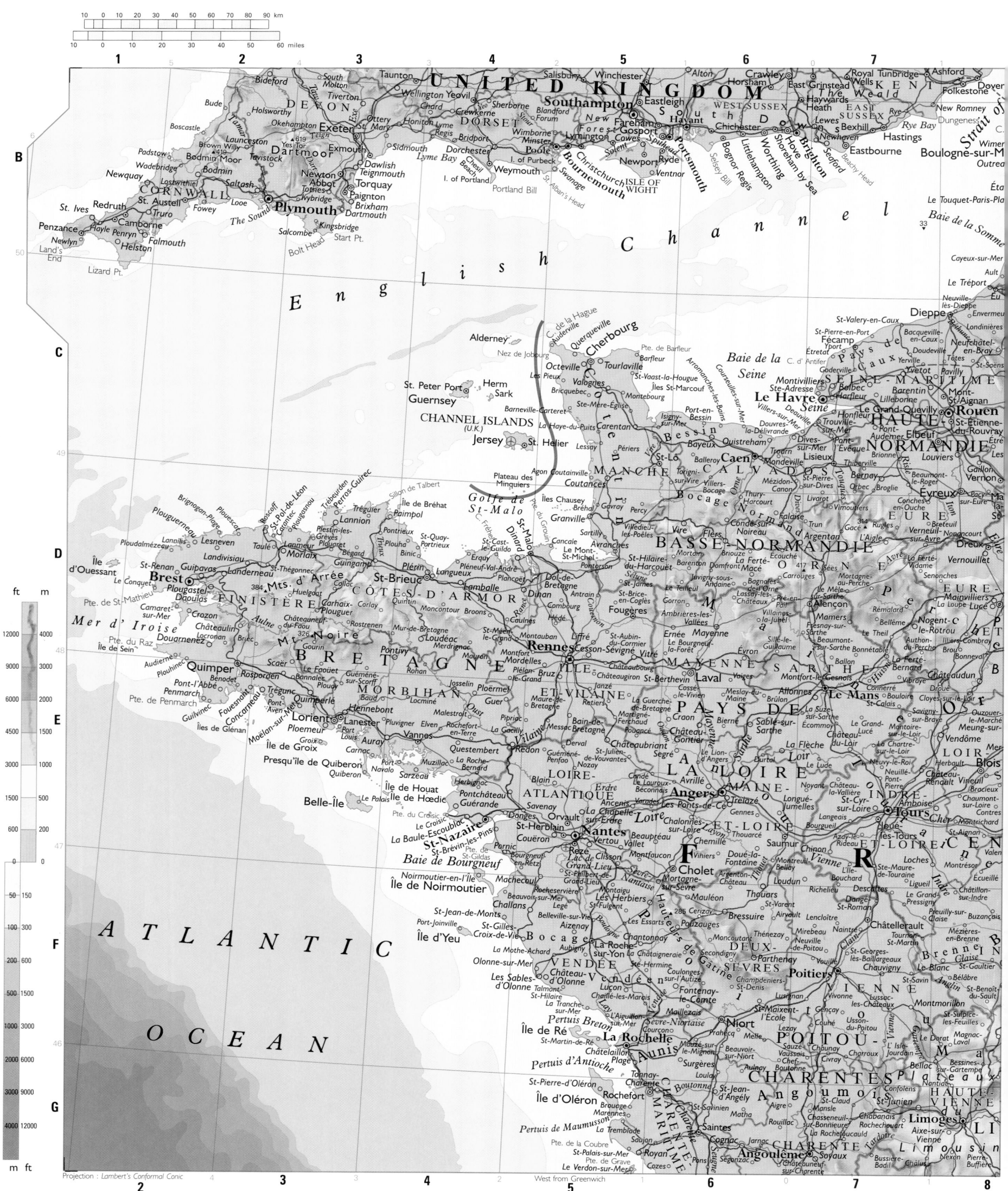

Projection : Lambert's Conformal Conic

DÉPARTEMENTS IN THE PARIS AREA
1. Ville de Paris   3. Val-de-Marne
2. Seine-St-Denis   4. Hauts-de-Seine

Underlined towns give their name to the
administrative area in which they stand.

COPYRIGHT GEORGE PHILIP LTD.

East from Greenwich

Projection : Lambert's Conformal Conic   West from Greenwich   East from Greenwich

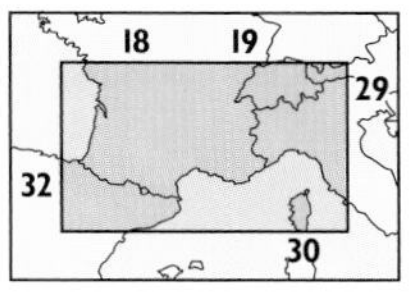

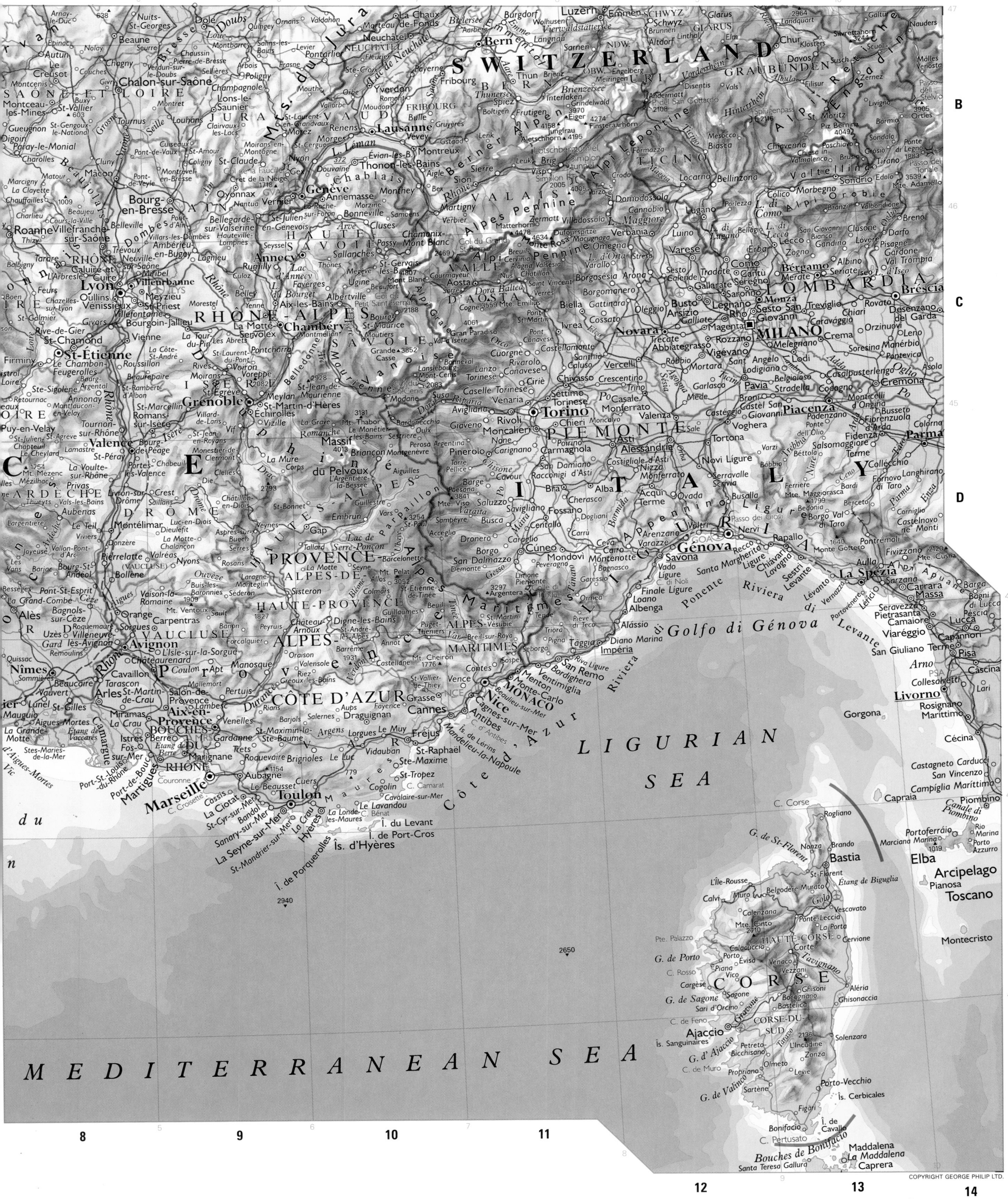

SWITZERLAND

ITALY

FRANCE

LIGURIAN SEA

MEDITERRANEAN SEA

Golfe de Gênova

Côte d'Azur

SAÔNE-ET-LOIRE · JURA · VAUD · BERN · GRAUBÜNDEN · TICINO · LOMBARDIA · AIN · HAUTE-SAVOIE · VALAIS · VALLE D'AOSTA · RHÔNE-ALPES · SAVOIE · PIEMONTE · ISÈRE · DRÔME · HAUTES-ALPES · LIGURIA · ARDÈCHE · PROVENCE · ALPES-DE-HAUTE-PROVENCE · ALPES-MARITIMES · VAUCLUSE · BOUCHES-DU-RHÔNE · CÔTE D'AZUR · HAUTE-CORSE · CORSE · CORSE-DU-SUD · TOSCANO

Lyon · Genève · Lausanne · Bern · Neuchâtel · Fribourg · Annecy · Chambéry · Grenoble · St-Étienne · Valence · Torino · Milano · Bergamo · Brescia · Novara · Pavia · Piacenza · Parma · Cuneo · Savona · Génova · La Spezia · Carrara · Massa · Lucca · Pisa · Livorno · Nice · Monaco · Menton · Cannes · Antibes · San Remo · Imperia · Marseille · Toulon · Avignon · Nîmes · Arles · Aix-en-Provence · Bastia · Ajaccio · Porto-Vecchio · Bonifacio

Elba · Arcipelago Toscano · Pianosa · Montecristo · Capraia · Gorgona · Corse · Îles d'Hyères · Île du Levant · Île de Port-Cros · Île de Porquerolles

COPYRIGHT GEORGE PHILIP LTD.

MIDDLE EUROPE 1:4 400 000

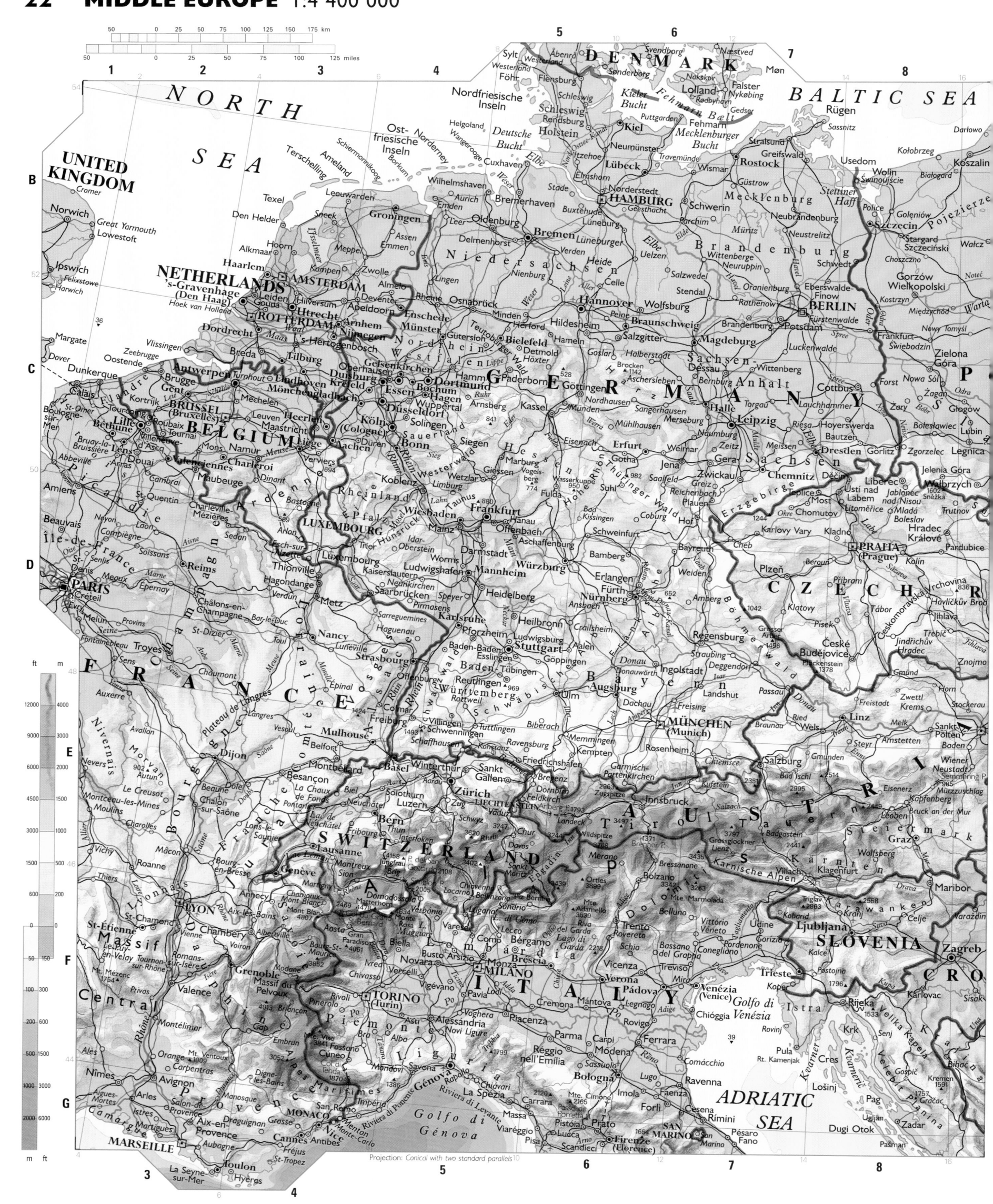

km
miles
NORTH SEA
BALTIC SEA
ADRIATIC SEA
Golfo di Venézia
Golfo di Génova
UNITED KINGDOM
NETHERLANDS
BELGIUM
LUXEMBOURG
FRANCE
GERMANY
DENMARK
POLAND
CZECH REPUBLIC
AUSTRIA
SWITZERLAND
LIECHTENSTEIN
ITALY
SLOVENIA
CROATIA
MONACO
SAN MARINO
AMSTERDAM
'S-Gravenhage (Den Haag)
ROTTERDAM
BRUSSEL (Bruxelles)
PARIS
BERLIN
HAMBURG
MÜNCHEN (Munich)
PRAHA (Prague)
MILANO
TORINO (Turin)
LYON
MARSEILLE
Ljubljana
Zagreb
Frankfurt
Stuttgart
Zürich
Genève
Bern
Venézia (Venice)
Génova
Firenze (Florence)
Köln (Cologne)
Niedersachsen
Brandenburg
Sachsen-Anhalt
Sachsen
Hessen
Bayern
Baden-Württemberg
Nordrhein-Westfalen
Rheinland-Pfalz
Mecklenburg
Tirol
Steiermark
Kärnten
Lombardia
Piemonte
Liguria
Provence
Massif Central
Alsace
Lorraine
Champagne
Bourgogne
Franche-Comté
Picardie
Île-de-France
Dauphiné
Savoie
Ardennes
Schwarzwald
Erzgebirge
Böhmerwald
Alpes Maritimes
Dolomiti
Hohe Tauern
Karawanken
Projection: Conical with two standard parallels
ft
m

9 10 11 12 13 14 15 16

18 20 22 24 26 28 30

Zatoka Gdańska
Baltiysk
Polessk
Kaliningrad (Russia)
Prienai
Vilnius
Vileyka
Maladzyechna
Barysaw
Krupki
Shklow
Mstsislaw
Słupsk
Wejherowo
Rumia
Gdynia
Gvardeysk
Gusev
Chernyakhovsk
Marijampolė
LITHUANIA
Ashmyany
Smarhon
342
Zhodzina
Dnyapro
Lębork
Sopot
Zalew Wiślany
Braniewo
Bagrationovsk
Varėna
Valozhyn
MINSK
Mahilyow
S
Krychaw
Gdańsk
Tczew
Elbląg
Łyna
309
Druskininkai
Cherven
Cherykaw
Slawharad
Bytów
329
Kętrzyn
Giżycko
Suwałki
Lida
346
B E L A R U S
Bykhaw
Pomorskie
Malbork
Pojezierze Mazurskie
Augustów
Dzyarzhynsk
Hrodzyanka
Drut
Dnyapro
Starogard Gdański
Kwidzyn
Olsztyn
Ełk
Hrodna
323
Navahrudak
Sozh
Szczecinek
Chojnice
Iława
Ostróda
Nyoman
Dzyatlava
Stowbtsy
Nyasvizh
Asipovichy
Babruysk
Rahachow
Świecie
Wisła
Grudziądz
Szczytno
Sokółka
Masty
Baranavichy
Slutsk
Zhlobin
Wałcz
Chełmno
Brodnica
Działdowo
Narew
Łomża
Białystok
Vawkavysk
Slonim
Klyetsk
Byarezina
Bydgoszcz
Mława
Ostrołęka
Lyakhavichy
Hantsavichy
Salihorsk
Glusk
Ptsich
Aktsyabrski
Homyel
Piła
Toruń
Rypin
Wkra
Ostrów Mazowiecka
Hajnówka
Svislach
Ivatsevichy
Svyetlahorsk
Rechytsa
Dobrush
Inowrocław
Ciechanów
Bielsk Podlaski
Pruzhany
Bereza
Tsyelyakhany
Vasilevichi
Kalinkavichy
Wisła
Włocławek
Bug
Pułtusk
Sokołów Podlaski
Yaselda
Luninyets
Pyetrikaw
Loyew
Gniezno
Płock
Legionowo
Kobryn
Dragichyn
Ivanava
Pripyats
Pripet
Mazyr
Khoyniki
Poznań
Września
Vistula
Kutno
WARSZAWA (Warsaw)
Mińsk Mazowiecki
Biała Podlaska
Zhabinka
Brest
Pinsk
Horyn
Davyd Haradok
Yelsk
Koło
Łęczyca
Pruszków
Otwock
Siedlce
Malaryta
Stolin
Ubort
Śrem
Konin
Łowicz
Żyrardów
Międzyrzec Podlaski
P r i p e t   M a r s h e s
Kościan
Prosna
Turek
Skierniewice
N
Łuków
D
Kamin-Kashyrskyy
316
Ovruch
Chornobyl
Leszno
O
L
A
Zduńska Wola
Łódź
Grójec
Pilica
Wieprz
Dubrovytsya
Uzh
Prypyat
Oster
Krotoszyn
Kalisz
Pabianice
Włodawa
Olevsk
C
Ostrów Wielkopolski
Sieradz
Tomaszów Mazowiecki
Radom
Puławy
Belokorovichi
Kyyivske Vdskh.
Desna
Warta
Piotrków Trybunalski
Lublin
Chełm
Lyuboml
Kovel
Staryy Chartoryisk
Korosten
Dymer
Oleśnica
Wieluń
Końskie
Skarżysko-Kamienna
Świdnik
Sluch
Irpin
Radomsko
Starachowice
Kraśnik
Novovolynsk
Rozhyshche
Kivertsi
Kostopil
Novohrad-Volynskyy
Malyn
Teterev
Wrocław
Kluczbork
Kielce
612
Volodymyr-Volynskyy
Oleksandriya
Korets
Radomyshl
KYYIV (Kiev)
Oława
Częstochowa
Ostrowiec-Świętokrzyski
Sandomierz
Zamość
Lutsk
Rivne
Zdolbuniv
Zhytomyr
Korostyshev
Vasylkiv
Świdnica
Opole
Myszków
Stalowa Wola
Sokal
Horokhiv
Dubno
341
Ostroh
Slavuta
Pershotravensk
Fastiv
Dzierżoniów
Tarnowskie Góry
Jędrzejów
Pińczów
Tarnobrzeg
Rava-Ruska
Chervonohrad
Berestechko
Kremenets
Shepetivka
Polonne
Berdychiv
Bila Tserkva
Kłodzko
Nysa
Zabrze
Bytom
Sosnowiec
Zawiercie
Wisła
Mielec
San
Radekhiv
Izyaslav
Kozyatyn
Skvyra
Tarashcha
Gliwice
Chorzów
Katowice
Nesterov
Kamyanka-Buzka
Brody
U K R A I N E
Racibórz
Tychy
Oświęcim
Kraków
Tarnów
Rzeszów
Dębica
Jarosław
Yavoriv
Starokonstyantyniv
Khmelnik
Tetiyev
1425
1492
Opava
Karviná
Bochnia
Przemyśl
Mostyska
Lviv (Lvov)
Zolochiv
Zbarazh
Ternopil
Khmelnytskyy
Lipovets
Zhashkiv
Šumperk
Ostrava
Havířov
Bielsko-Biała
Jasło
Krosno
Horodok
Skalat
Podilska Vysochyna
Vinnytsya
D
Olomouc
Frýdek-Místek
Český Těšín
Cieszyn
C a r p a t h i a n s
Nowy Sącz
Sanok
Sambir
Khodoriv
Berezhany
Hrymayliv
Horodok
384
Zhmerynka
E
R.
Prostějov
1324
Přerov
Zywiec
1725
Západné Beskydy
Nowy Targ
Východné Beskydy
Dukelský Průsmyk
502
Drohobych
Rogatyn
Terebovlya
Kopychyntsi
Bar
327
Haysyn
Vyškov
Zlín
Povážská Bystrica
Žilina
Zakopane
Tatry
2655
Poprad
Bardejov
1157
1248
Boryslav
Truskavets
Stryy
Kalush
Dnister
Buchach
Chortkiv
Skala-Podilska
Tulchyn
270
Uman
Brno
Bielé Karpaty
Martin
Ružomberok
Prešov
Humenné
Skole
Bolekhiv
Ivano-Frankivsk
Horodenka
Zalishchyky
Kamyanets-Podilskyy
Vapnyarka
Buh
Hayvoron
Trenčín
Nízke Tatry
2043
Banská Bystrica
S L O V A K R E P.
Michalovce
Nadvirna
Kolomyya
Khotyn
Mohyliv-Podilskyy
Bershad
Hodonín
768
Prievidza
1458
Košice
Uzhhorod
Volovets
Pechenizhyn
Yaremcha
Snyatyn
Novoselytsya
Lipcani
Ocnița
Balta
Malé Karpaty
Morava
Váh
Topoľčany
Slovenské Rudohorie
Zvolen
Sátoraljaújhely
Chop
Mukacheve
1881
Yasinya
Chernivtsi
Hlyboka
Edineț
Yampil
Drochia
Soroca
Ananyiv
Trnava
Nitra
Lučenec
Berehove
Khust
Rakhiv
Storozhynets
Florești
Kotovsk
Levice
Ózd
Sajó
Hernád
Bodrog
Vynohradiv
Tyachiv
Rădăuți
Dorohoi
Siret
Bălți
Râbnița
WIEN (Vienna)
Bratislava
Nové Zámky
Hron
Salgótarján
Miskolc
Nyíregyháza
Satu Mare
Sighetu Marmației
1565
Suceava
Botoșani
Fălești
Dubăsari Vdkhr.
Bruck an der Leitha
Dunaj
Eger
Carei
Baia Mare
Borșa
2303
Pietrosul
Fălticeni
Cornești
Dubăsari
Neusiedler See
Komárno
Gyöngyös
Vác
Mezőkövesd
Hajdúböszörmény
Someș
Pașcani
M O L D O V A
Orhei
Mosonmagyaróvár
Esztergom
Dunakeszi
Hatvan
Debrecen
Ungheni
Chișinău
Tiraspol
E
Sopron
Rába
Győr
Tatabánya
Jászberény
Vatra-Dornei
Iași
Rozdilna
Pápa
Érd
BUDAPEST
Tisza
Karcag
2102
Pietrosul
1864
Bistrița
Roman
418
Tighina
Szombathely
709
Székesfehérvár
Cegléd
Zalău
Dej
Bistrița
Huși
Cimișlia
Dnister
H U N G A R Y
Bakony
Ajka
Veszprém
Szolnok
Mezőtúr
Oradea
Reghin
Mureș
Piatra Neamț
Vaslui
Leova
Basarabeasca
Nistru
Bilhorod-Dnistrovskyy
Balaton
Dunaújváros
Nagykőrös
Kecskemét
Cluj-Napoca
Târgu Mureș
1777
Bacău
Prut
Comrat
Zalaegerszeg
Siófok
Kiskunfélegyháza
Körös
Salonta
Békéscsaba
1836
Turda
Odorheiu Secuiesc
Miercurea Ciuc
Siret
Bârlad
Artsyz
Csongrád
Szentes
Crișul Negru
Munții Bihor
1848
Onești
Ciadâr-Lunga
46
Nagykanizsa
Kalocsa
Kiskőrös
Gyula
Orosháza
Abrud
Aiud
Târnăveni
Sighișoara
Sfântu Gheorghe
Bârlad
Tatarbunary
Kaposvár
Duna
Kiskunhalas
Hódmezővásárhely
Makó
Crișul Alb
Arad
T r a n s i l v a n i a
Mediaș
1783
Tecuci
Cahul
Ozero Sasyk
Szekszárd
Szeged
Brad
Alba-Iulia
Focșani
Vulcanești
Bolhrad
Kiliya
Vylkove
681
Baja
Sânnicolau Mare
Mureș
Deva
Sibiu
Olt
Făgăraș
Brașov
Izmayil
Reni
Koprivnica
Pécs
Subotica
Simeria
R O M A N I A
Săcele
Râmnicu Sărat
Galați
Sulina
Drava
Mohács
Senta
Kikinda
Lugoj
1380
Carpații Meridionali
P. Turnu Roșu
2543
Moldoveanu
2507
Vf. Omul
Brăila
F
Bjelovar
Virovitica
Sombor
Timișoara
Hunedoara
Dunărea (Danube)
Buzău
Tulcea
ATIA
Bečej
Tisa
Caransebeș
Vf. Peleaga 2509
Petroșani
Câmpulung
Câmpina
Buzău
Babadag
Osijek
Vukovar
Vojvodina
Vulcan
2518 Parângul Mare
Curtea de Argeș
Lacul Razelm
984
Novska
Novi Sad
Zrenjanin
Vršac
Reșița
Porta Orientalis
Râmnicu Vâlcea
Târgoviște
Ploiești
Dobrogea
Slavonski Brod
Vinkovci
Petrovaradin
Târgu-Jiu
Ialomița
Slobozia
Bosanska Gradiška
Sava
Sremska Mitrovica
Pančevo
Bela Crkva
Jiu
Pitești
Dâmbovița
Fetești
978
Bosna
Brčko
Zemun
1226
Portile de Fier
Drăgășani
Argeș
BUCUREȘTI (Bucharest)
Medgidia
Năvodari
Banja Luka
Doboj
Bijeljina
Šabac
BEOGRAD (Belgrade)
Smederevo
Orșova
Drobeta-Turnu-Severin
W a l l a c h i a
Călărași
Constanța
Sana
Tuzla
Drina
Dunav
Požarevac
Slatina
Olt
Oltenița
44
BOSNIA-
YUGOSLAVIA
Negotin
Craiova
Roșiori-de-Vede
Silistra
Mangalia
Vrbas
1943
Travnik
Žepče
Zenica
Valjevo
1366
Bor
Vedea
Alexandria
Tutrakan
HERZEGOVINA
Han Pijesak
Srebrenica
Kragujevac
Jagodina
Zaječar
Băilești
Caracal
Turnu Măgurele
Giurgiu
Ruse
Dobrich
Balchik
G
1913
2006
2112
Užice
Čačak
Kraljevo
Vidin
Corabia
Zimnicea
Razgrad
Nos Kaliakra
Treglav
Cincar
Sarajevo
Višegrad
Morava
Timok
Lom
Oryakhovo
B U L G A R I A
Varna
18
East from Greenwich
20
22
24
26

9 10 11 12 13 14 15

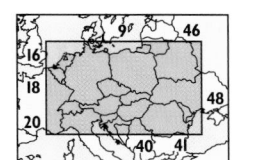

COPYRIGHT GEORGE PHILIP LTD.

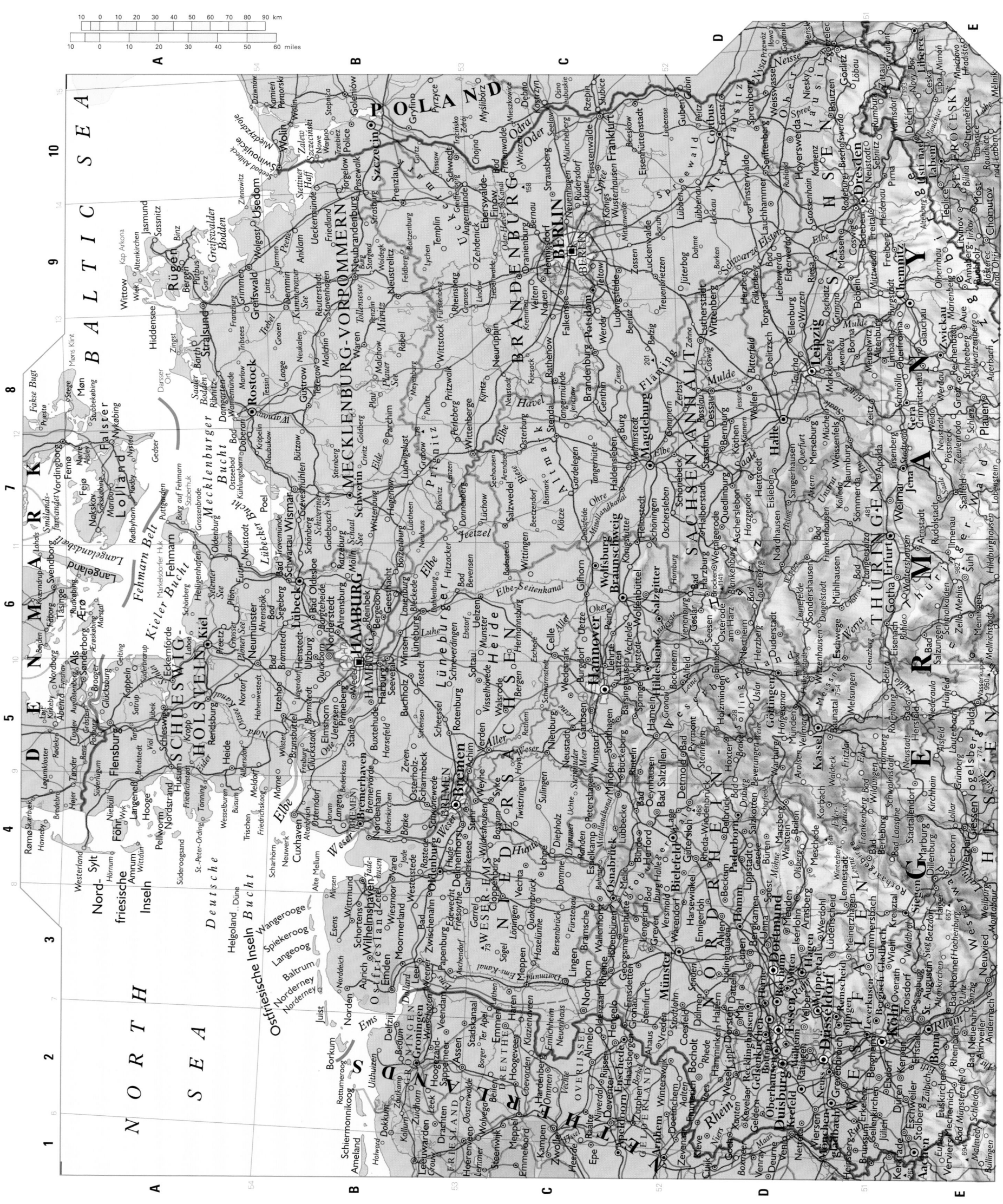
10 0 10 20 30 40 50 60 70 80 90 km
10 0 10 20 30 40 50 60 miles
NORTH SEA
BALTIC SEA
DENMARK
POLAND
GERMANY
NETHERLANDS
SCHLESWIG-HOLSTEIN
MECKLENBURG-VORPOMMERN
BRANDENBURG
NIEDERSACHSEN
SACHSEN-ANHALT
NORDRHEIN-WESTFALEN
THÜRINGEN
SACHSEN
HESSEN
BERLIN
HAMBURG
Bremen
Hannover
Kiel
Lübeck
Rostock
Magdeburg
Leipzig
Dresden
Dortmund
Düsseldorf
Köln
Bonn
Münster
Kassel
Erfurt
Chemnitz
Halle
Szczecin
Ostfriesische Inseln
Nordfriesische Inseln
Deutsche Bucht
Mecklenburger Bucht
Kieler Bucht
Fehmarn Belt

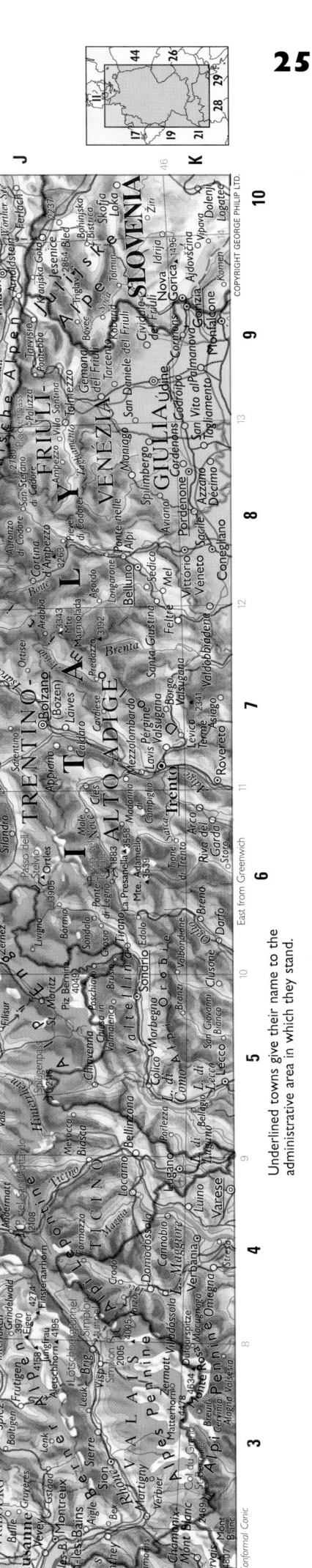

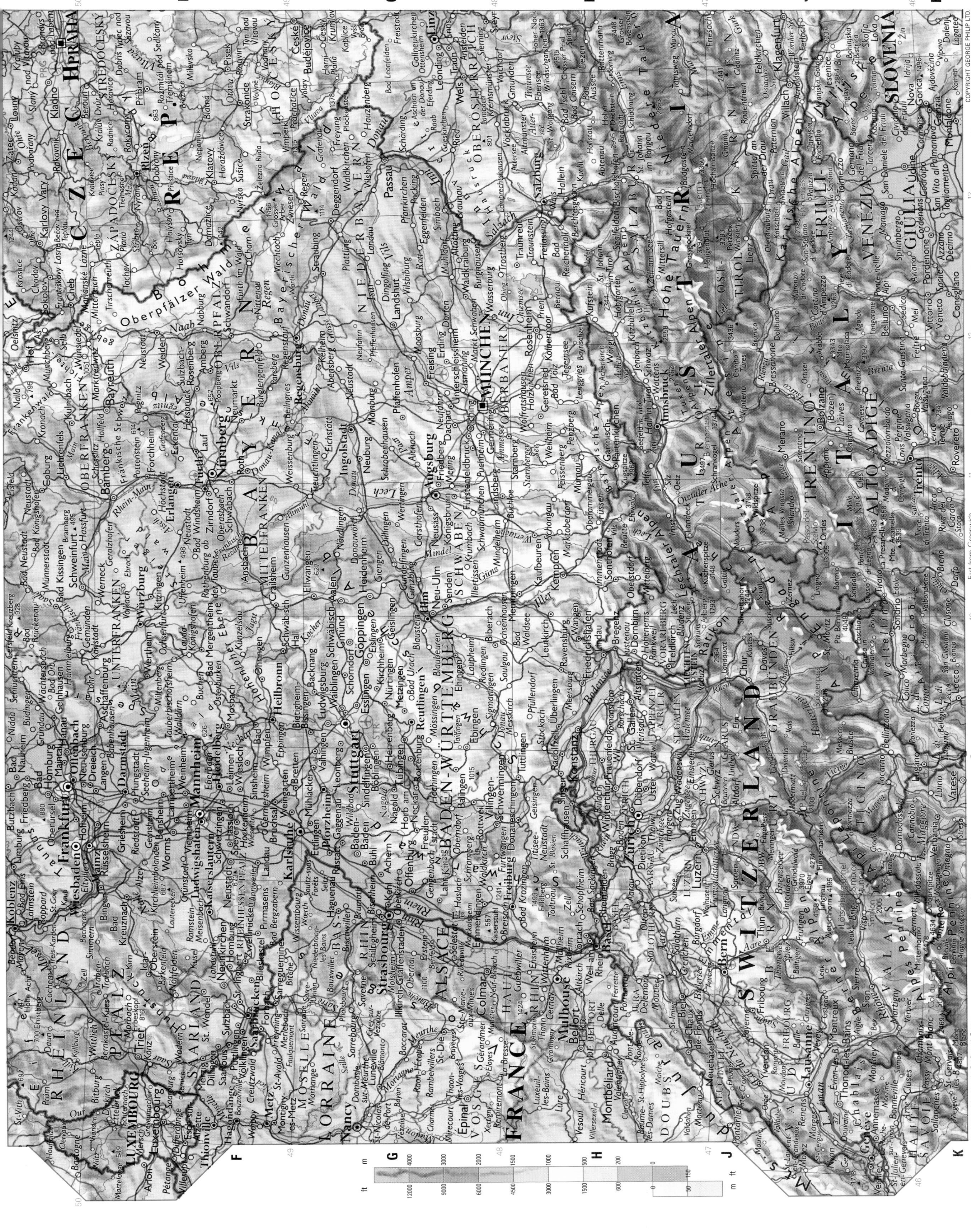

Underlined towns give their name to the administrative area in which they stand.

Projection: Lambert's Conformal Conic

East from Greenwich

COPYRIGHT GEORGE PHILIP LTD.

km
miles
Projection : Lambert's Conformal Conic
ft
m
GERMANY
AUSTRIA
CZECH REP.
ITALY
SLOVENIA
SWITZERLAND
THÜRINGEN
BAYERN
OBERFRANKEN
UNTERFRANKEN
MITTELFRANKEN
OBERPFALZ
NIEDERBAYERN
OBERBAYERN
SCHWABEN
ZÁPADOČESKÝ
STŘEDOČESKÝ
SEVEROČESKÝ
JIHOČESKÝ
VÝCHODOČESKÝ
OBERÖSTERREICH
NIEDERÖSTERREICH
SALZBURG
STEIERMARK
KÄRNTEN
TIROL
OST-TIROL
VORARLBERG
TRENTINO-ALTO ADIGE
FRIULI-VENÉZIA GIULIA
VÉNETO
LOMBARDIA
LIECHTENSTEIN
PRAHA
MÜNCHEN
Dresden
Chemnitz
Nürnberg
Stuttgart
Augsburg
Regensburg
Würzburg
Erfurt
Plzeň
České Budějovice
Linz
Salzburg
Innsbruck
Graz
Klagenfurt
Ljubljana
Maribor
Zagreb
Trieste
Venézia
Bolzano
Trento
Vicenza
Brescia
Bergamo
Udine
Sankt Pölten
Golfo di Venézia
Bodensee
Donau
Inn
Hohe Tauern
Niedere Tauern
Zillertaler Alpen
Karnische Alpen
Bayerischer Wald
Böhmerwald
Erzgebirge
Thüringer Wald

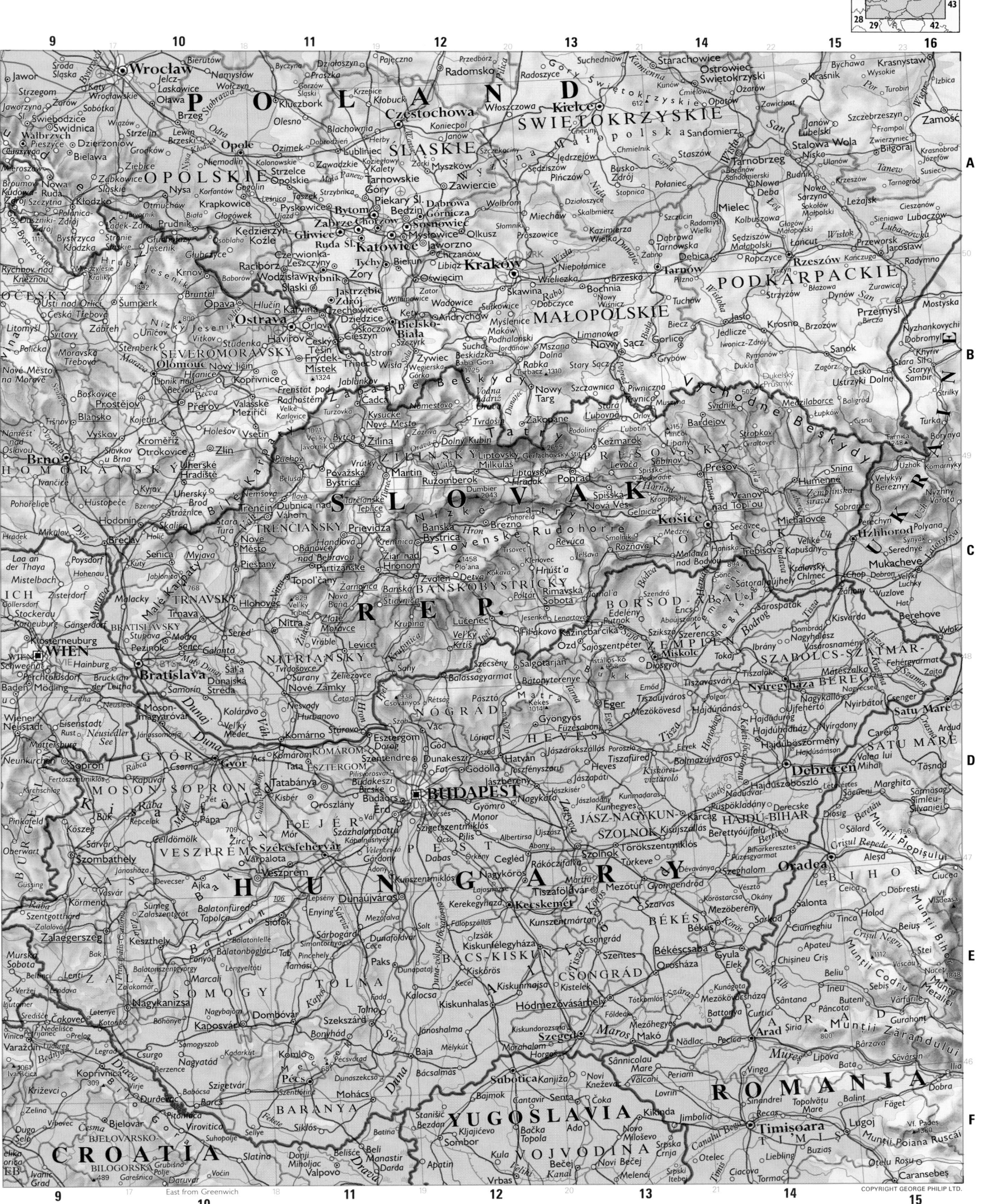

Underlined towns give their name to the
administrative area in which they stand.

Underlined towns give their name to the
administrative area in which they stand.

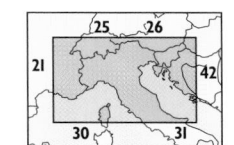

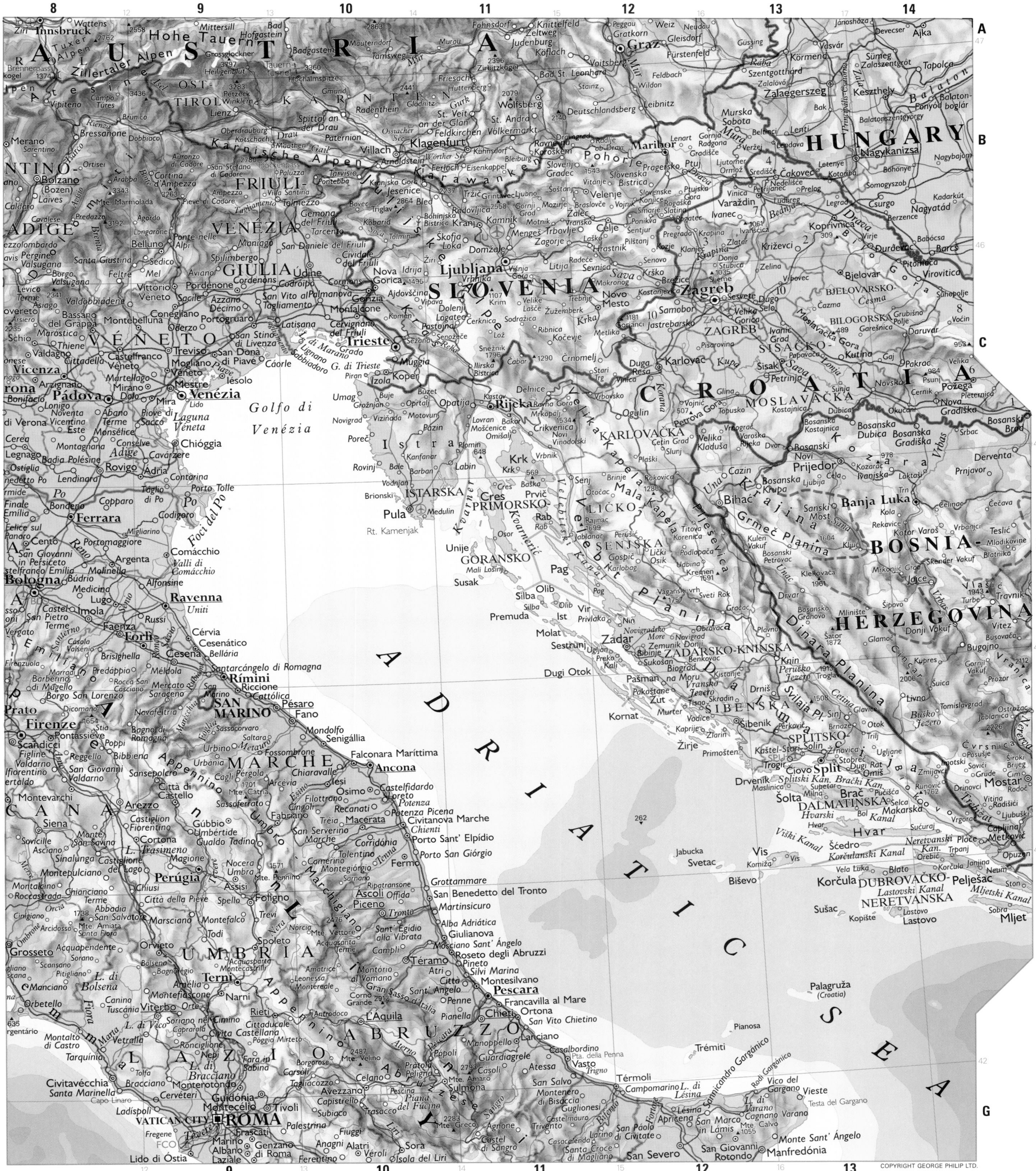

Administrative divisions in Croatia:

1. Brodsko-Posavska	4. Medimurska	8. Virovitičko-Podravska
2. Koprivničko-Križevačka	6. Požeško-Slavonska	10. Zagrebačka
3. Krapinsko-Zagorska	7. Varaždinska	

Inter-entity boundaries as agreed
at the 1995 Dayton Peace Agreement.

COPYRIGHT GEORGE PHILIP LTD.

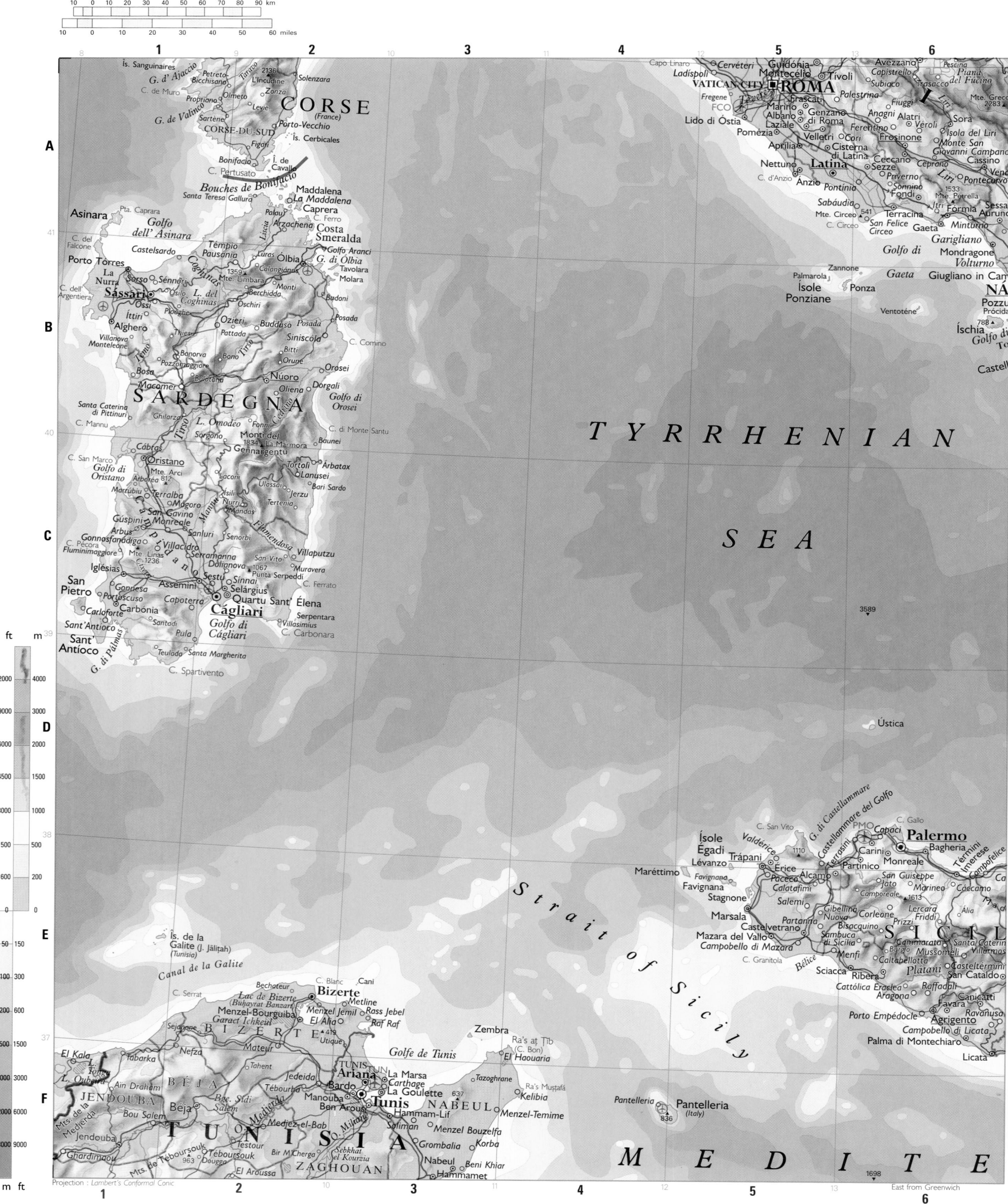

ft m

10 0 10 20 30 40 50 60 70 80 90 km
10 0 10 20 30 40 50 60 miles

CORSE
(France)

CORSE-DU-SUD

Bouches de Bonifacio

SARDEGNA

TYRRHENIAN

SEA

Strait of Sicily

SICIL

Palermo

TUNISIA

ZAGHOUAN

MEDITE

Projection : Lambert's Conformal Conic

East from Greenwich

ADRIATIC

SEA

IONIAN

SEA

RRANEAN SEA

Underlined towns give their name to the
administrative area in which they stand.

10 0 10 20 30 40 50 60 70 80 90 km
10 0 10 20 30 40 50 60 miles
FRANCE
SPAIN
ANDORRA
ARAGÓN
CATALUÑA
NAVARRA
LA RIOJA
CASTILLA Y LEÓN
PAÍS VASCO
MIDI-PYRÉNÉES
ROUSSILLON
LANGUEDOC-
Golfe de Gascogne
Costa Brava
Costa Dorada
Costa del Azahar
BALEARES
BARCELONA
Zaragoza
Toulouse
MADRID
Bilbao
Pamplona
Vitoria-Gasteiz
Donostia-San Sebastián
Tarragona
Lleida (Lérida)
Perpignan
Castelló de la Plana
Palma de Mallorca
MENORCA
MALLORCA

MEDITERRANEAN SEA

BALEARIC SEA

Golfo de Valencia

ISLAS BALEARES

Palma · Manacor · Cabrera
EIVISSA (IBIZA) · Formentera

VALENCIA · Torrent · Sueca · Gandía · Denia · Calpe · Benidorm
Alicante · Elche · Santa Pola · Torrevieja
MURCIA · Cartagena · Mar Menor · Lorca · Águilas
ALBACETE · CASTILLA–LA MANCHA · CIUDAD REAL
Granada · Sierra Nevada · Almería · G. de Almería · C. de Gata
Guadix · Motril · Adra · Costa del Sol

Melilla (Sp.) · Nador · Alborán (Sp.) · Islas Chafarinas (Sp.)

ALGER (Algiers) · Blida · Médéa · TIPASA · Cherchell · AÏN DEFLA · MÉDÉA
Ech Cheliff · El Marsa · Ténès · RELIZANE · MOSTAGANEM · Mostaganem
ORAN (Ouahran) · Arzew · Golfe d'Arzew · Sidi-bel-Abbès · MASCARA · Mascara
TIARET · Tiaret · TISSEMSILT · DJELFA · TÉMOUCHENT

Projection: Lambert's Conformal Conic
COPYRIGHT GEORGE PHILIP LTD.

m ft scale bar

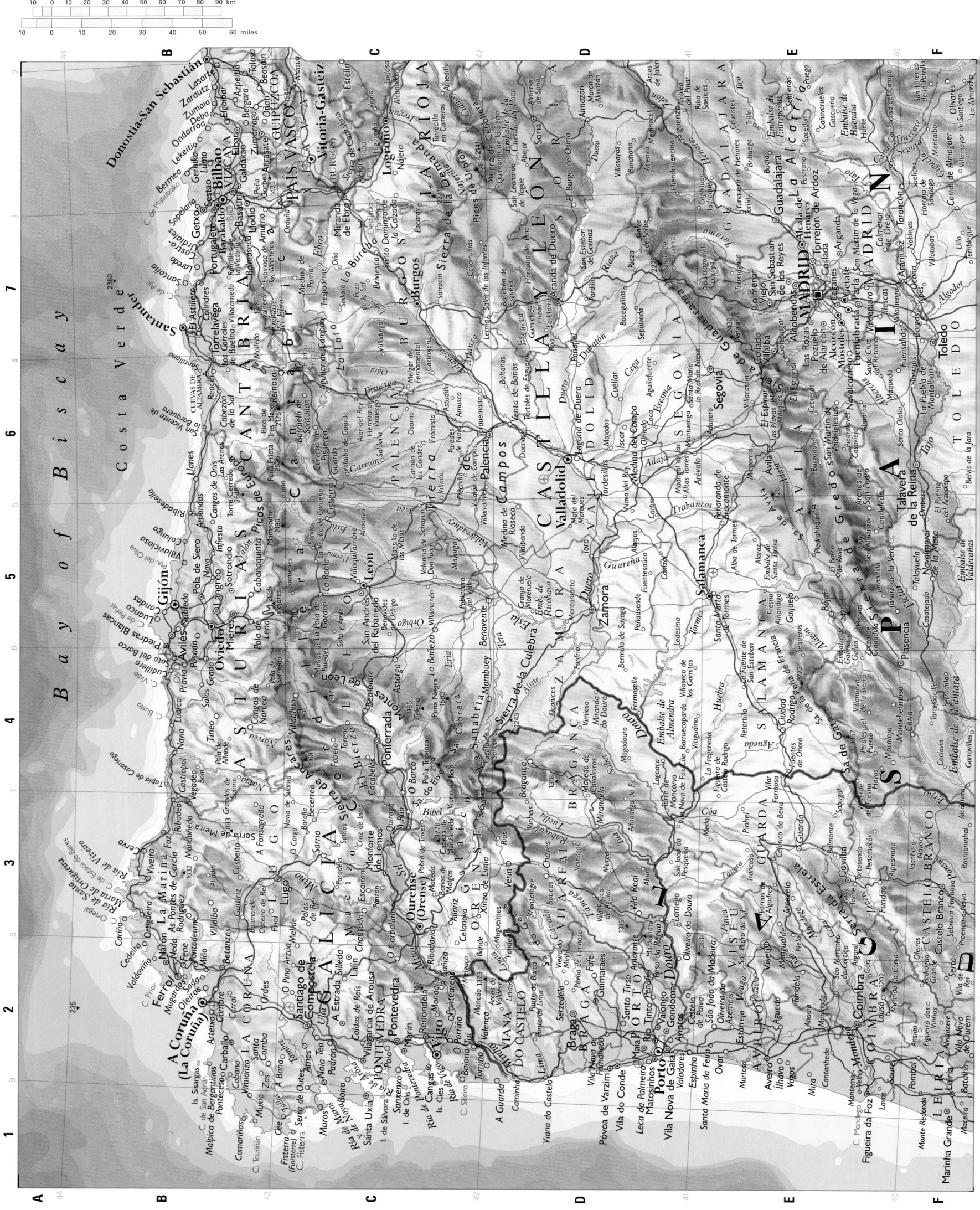
10 0 10 20 30 40 50 60 70 80 90 km
10 0 10 20 30 40 50 60 miles
Bay of Biscay
Costa Verde
Donostia-San Sebastián
Bilbao
Santander
Vitoria-Gasteiz
PAÍS VASCO
LA RIOJA
Logroño
Burgos
CANTABRIA
ASTURIAS
Oviedo
Gijón
Avilés
León
Palencia
Valladolid
CASTILLA Y LEÓN
Zamora
Salamanca
Segovia
Ávila
MADRID
Guadalajara
Toledo
Talavera de la Reina
Plasencia
GALICIA
A Coruña (La Coruña)
Ferrol
Lugo
Santiago de Compostela
Pontevedra
Vigo
Ourense (Orense)
Ponferrada
Bragança
Braga
Porto
Vila Nova de Gaia
Aveiro
Coimbra
Viseu
Guarda
Castelo Branco
Leiria
Figueira da Foz
Picos de Europa
Sierra de Gredos
Serra da Estrela
Sierra de Guadarrama
Douro
Duero
Tajo
Miño
SPAIN

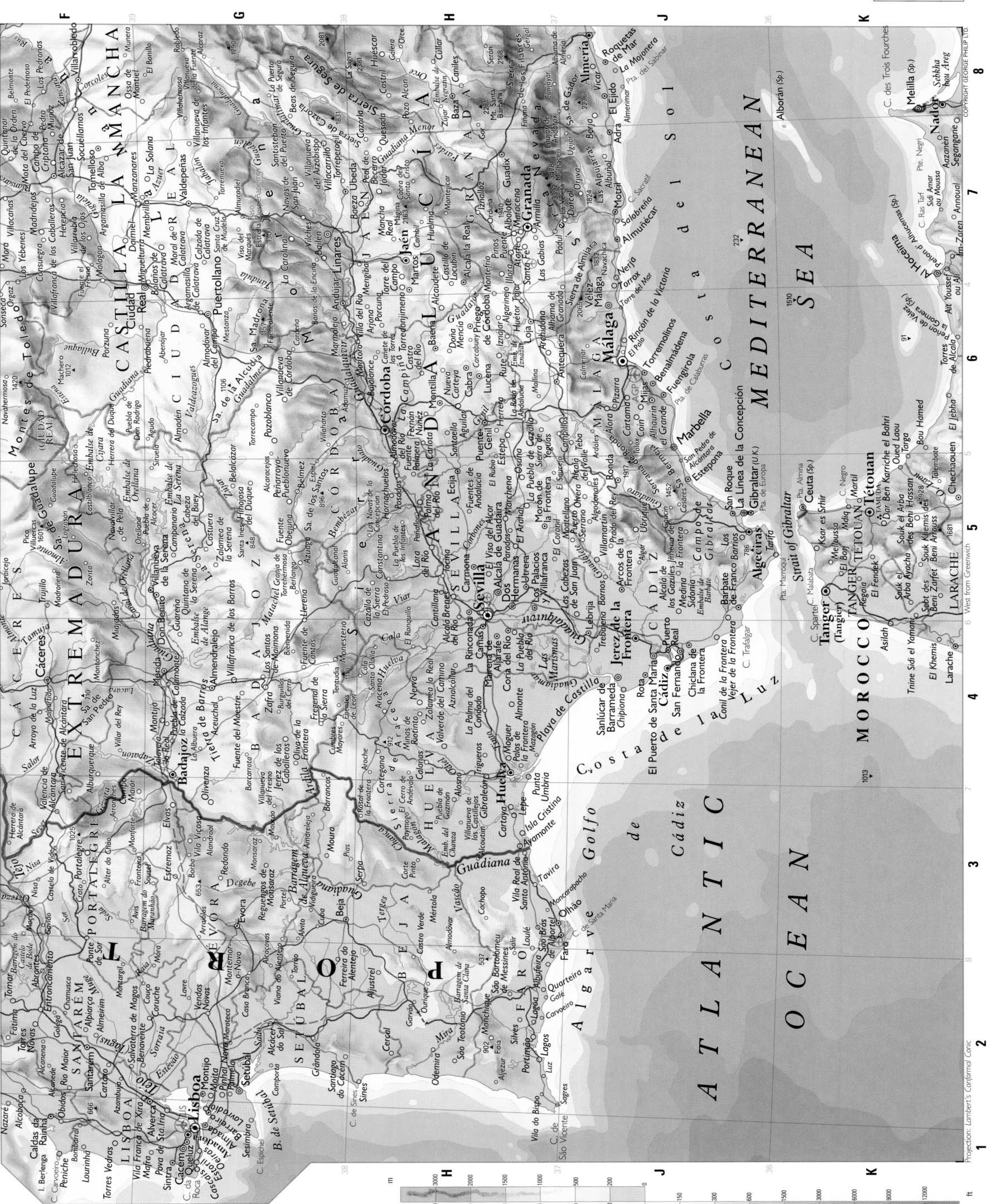

COPYRIGHT GEORGE PHILIP LTD.

Projection: Lambert's Conformal Conic

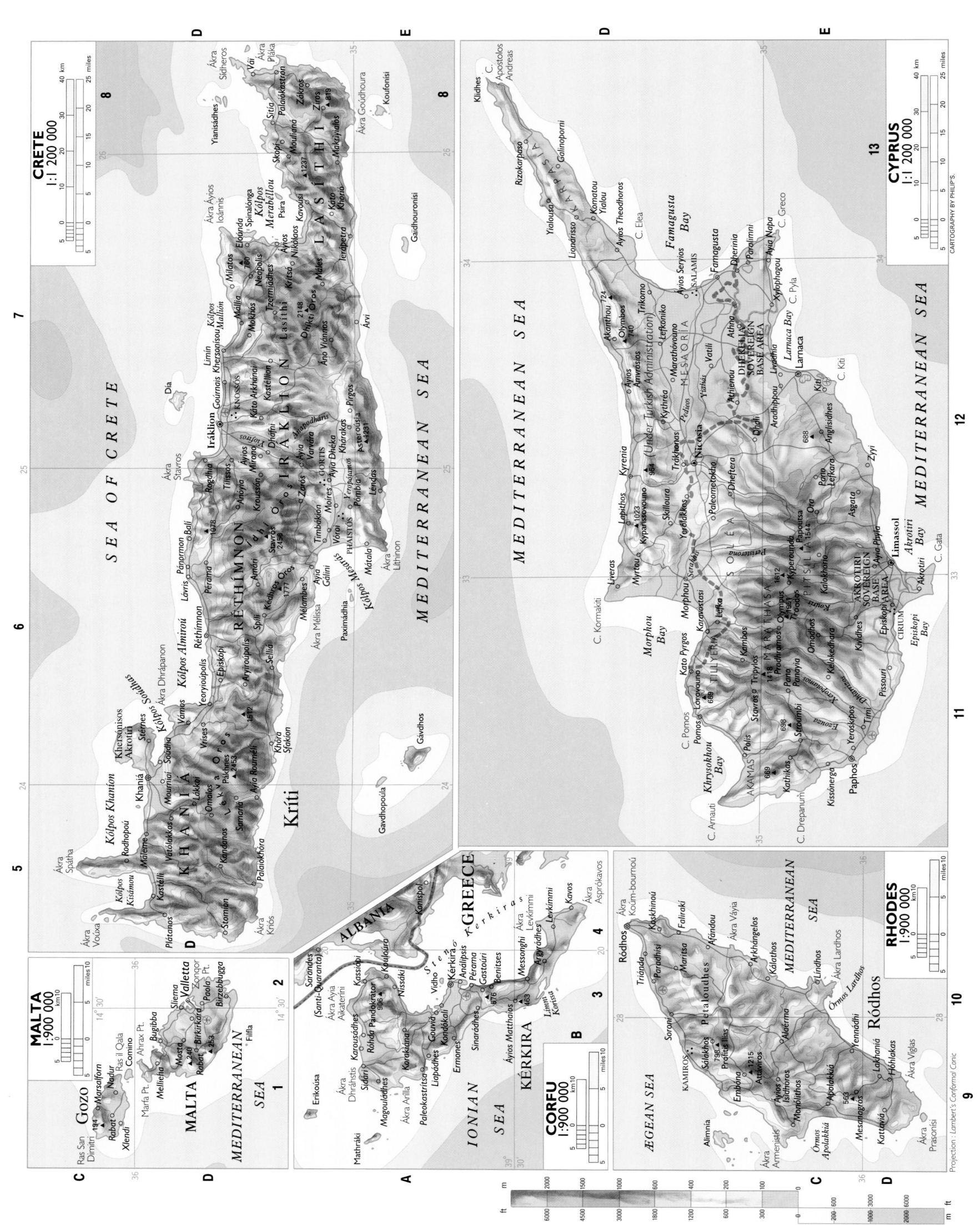

CRETE
1:1 200 000

MALTA
1:900 000

CORFU
1:900 000

RHODES
1:900 000

CYPRUS
1:1 200 000

CARTOGRAPHY BY PHILIP'S

Projection: Lambert's Conformal Conic

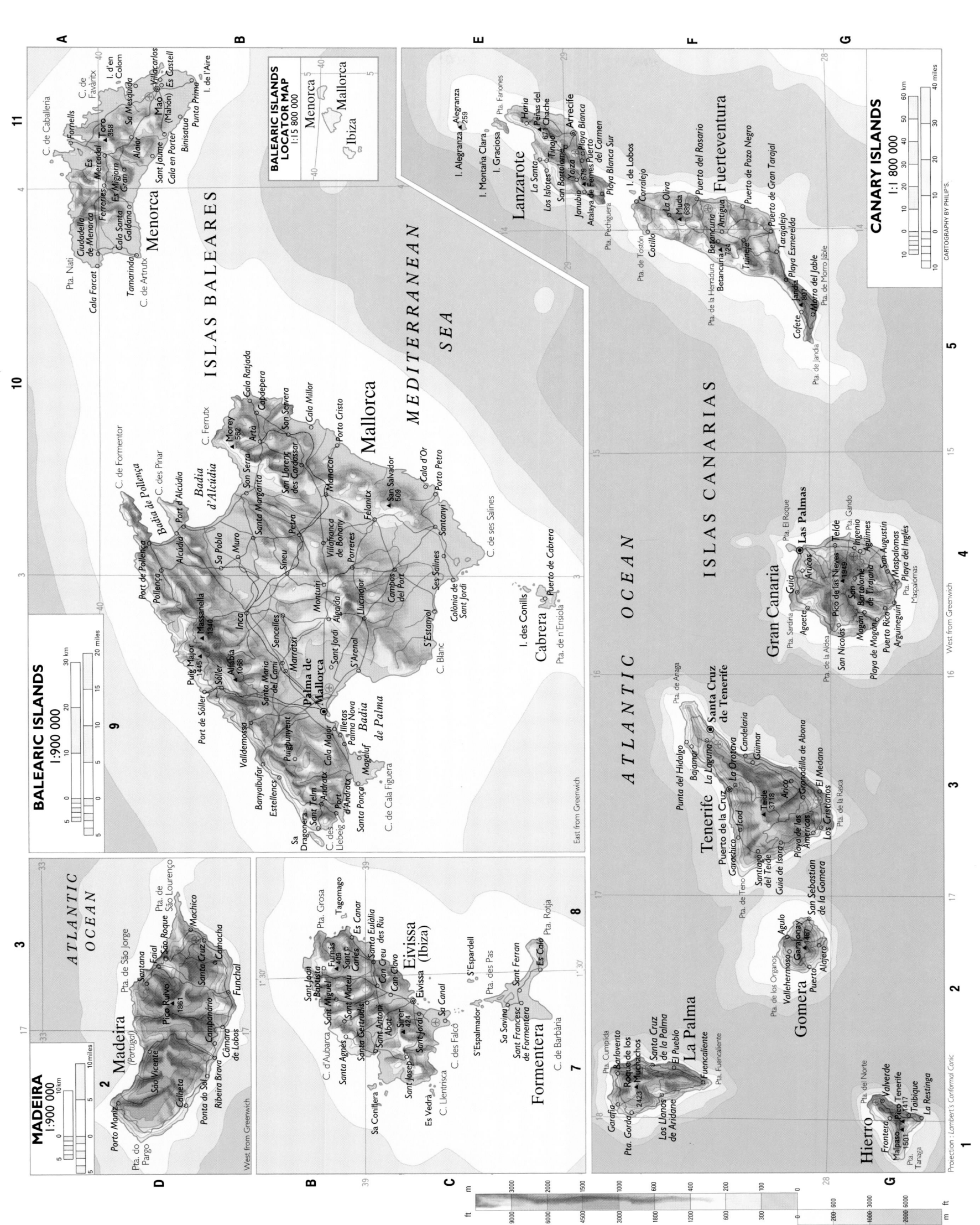

THE BALEARICS, THE CANARIES AND MADEIRA

ISLAS BALEARES

Menorca

C. de Caballeria
Fornells
Es Mercadal
▲Toro 358
Villacarlos
Es Castell
Maó (Mahón)
Punta Prima
I. de l'Aire
Cala en Porter
Binisafua
Sant Jaume
Alaior
Sa Mesquida
I. d'en Colom
C. de Favàritx
Cala Santa Galdana
Es Migjorn Gran
Ferreries
Ciudadella de Menorca
Cala Santa
Tamarinda
C. de Artrutx
Pta. Nati
Cala Forcat

BALEARIC ISLANDS LOCATOR MAP 1:15 800 000

Menorca
Mallorca
Ibiza

MEDITERRANEAN SEA

ISLAS BALEARES

Mallorca

C. de Formentor
Pollença
Port de Pollença
Port de Sóller
Badia de Pollença
C. des Pinar
Port d'Alcúdia
Alcúdia
Badia d'Alcúdia
Cala Ratjada
Capdepera
Cala Millor
San Severa
Artà
Morey 562▲
C. Ferrutx
Son Serra
Santa Margarita
Sa Pobla
Muro
Inca
Sineu
Petra
Manacor
Porto Cristo
Cala d'Or
Porto Petro
C. Blanc
Puig Major ▲1445
Massanella ▲1340
Sóller
Alfàbia ▲1068
Santa Maria del Camí
Sencelles
Marratxí
Valldemossa
Banyalbufar
Estellencs
Puigpunyent
Palma de Mallorca
S'Arenal
Illetas
Palma Nova
Magaluf
Badia de Palma
Cala Major
S'Estanyol
Sant Jordi
Algaida
Montuïri
Villafranca de Bonany
Porreres
Llucmajor
Campos del Port
Ses Salines
Santanyí
Felanitx
San Salvador 509▲
S. Llorenç des Cardassar
C. des Salines
Sant Telm
Andratx
Port d'Andratx
Sa Dragonera
C. des Llebeig
Santa Ponça
C. de Cala Figuera
Colònia de Sant Jordi
Puerto de Cabrera

Cabrera
I. des Conills
Pta. de n'Ensiola
C. de ses Salines

ATLANTIC OCEAN

MADEIRA 1:900 000

Madeira (Portugal)

Pta. de São Lourenço
Ponta de São Jorge
São Roque
Machico
Santana
Faial
Santa Cruz
Caniço
Caniçal
Funchal
Câmara de Lobos
Pico Ruivo ▲1861
São Vicente
Porto Moniz
Pta. do Pargo
Seixal
Ribeira Brava
Ponta do Sol
Calheta
Campanário

ATLANTIC OCEAN

Eivissa (Ibiza)

Pta. Grosa
Tagomago
Pta. de sa Creu
Portinatx
Santa Eulalia des Riu
Sant Carles
Es Canar
Sant Vicent
Sant Joan Baptista
Furnas 409
Sant Miguel
Sant Mateu
C. d'Aubarca
Santa Gertrudis
Santa Agnès
Sant Antoni Abat
Sant Josep
Sa Talaia 424
Eivissa
Sant Jordi
Can Clavo
Can Negre
Es Vedrà
C. Llentrisca
C. des Falcó

Formentera

S'Espardell
Pta. des Pas
Es Caló
Pta. Rotja
Sant Ferran
Sant Francesc de Formentera
Sa Savina
Sa Canal
C. de Barbària
S'Espalmador
Sa Conillera

East from Greenwich
West from Greenwich

CANARY ISLANDS 1:1 800 000
CARTOGRAPHY BY PHILIP'S.

ISLAS CANARIAS

ATLANTIC OCEAN

Lanzarote
I. Alegranza
Alegranza 289
I. Montaña Clara
I. Graciosa
La Santa
Haria
Peñas del Chache 671
Teguise
Arrecife
Los Islotes
San Bartolomé
Yaiza
Playa Blanca
Puerto del Carmen
Janubio 679
Atalaya de Femés
I. de Lobos
Playa Blanca Sur
Corralejo
Pta. de Tostón
Cotillo
La Oliva
Muda 689
Puerto del Rosario
Tindaya
Fuerteventura
Puerto de Gran Tarajal
Puerto del Pozo Negro
Betancuria ▲724
Antigua
Tuineje
Tarajalejo
Jandía
Playa Esmerelda
Pta. de la Herradura
Cofete
Morro del Jable
Pta. de Morro Jable
Pta. de Jandía
Pta. Pechiguera

Gran Canaria
Las Palmas
Pta. El Roque
Arucas
Guía
Gáldar
Agaete
Telde
Pico de las Nieves ▲1949
Ingenio
Agüimes
San Mateo
San Nicolás
San Bartolomé de Tirajana
Mogán
Playa de Mogán
Puerto Rico
Arguineguín
Maspalomas
Playa del Inglés
Pta. Maspalomas
Pta. de la Aldea

Tenerife
Punta del Hidalgo
Pta. de Anaga
Santa Cruz de Tenerife
La Laguna
Bajamar
La Orotova
Puerto de la Cruz
Candelaria
Icod
Garachico
Teide ▲3718
Güimar
Arico
Granadilla de Abona
El Médano
Pta. de Teno
Buenavista
Playa de las Américas
Los Cristianos
Guía de Isora
Pta. de la Rasca

Gomera
Pta. de los Órganos
Agulo
Vallehermoso
Garajonay ▲1487
Hermigua
San Sebastián de la Gomera
Puerto
Alojera
Alajeró

La Palma
Pta. Cumplida
Barlovento
Roque de los Muchachos ▲2423
Garafia
Santa Cruz de la Palma
El Pueblo
Los Llanos de Aridane
Pta. Gorda
Tazacorte
Fuencaliente
Pta. Fuencaliente

Hierro
Valverde
Frontera
Pico Tenerife 1501
▲1417
Malpaso
Taibique
La Restinga
Pta. del Norte
Pta. Tenaga

ISLAS CANARIAS

West from Greenwich

Projection : Lambert's Conformal Conic

m / ft elevation scale

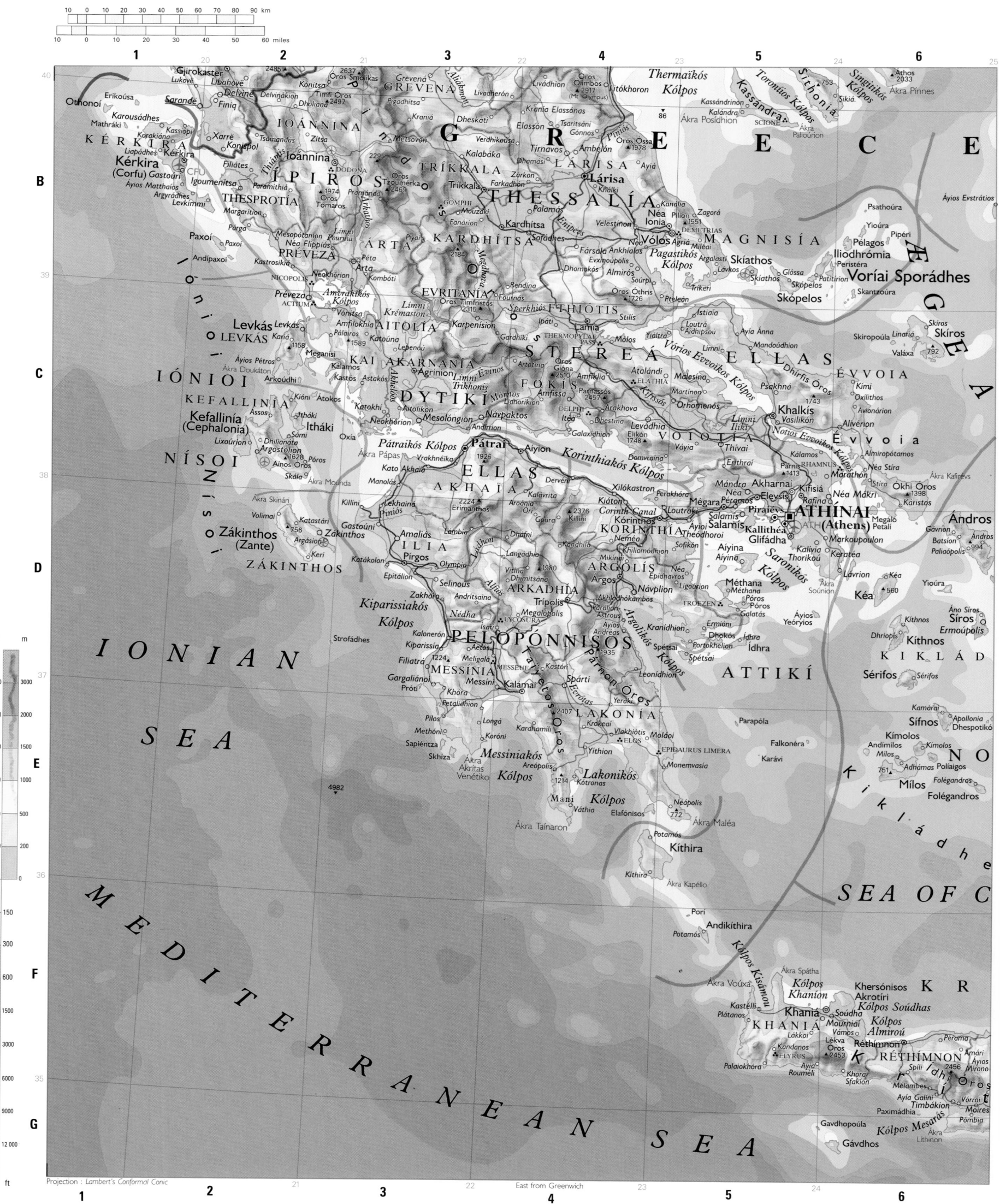

ft   m
9000   3000
6000   2000
4500   1500
3000   1000
1500   500
600   200
0   0
50   150
100   300
200   600
500   1500
1000   3000
2000   6000
3000   9000
4000   12 000
m   ft

Projection : Lambert's Conformal Conic

East from Greenwich

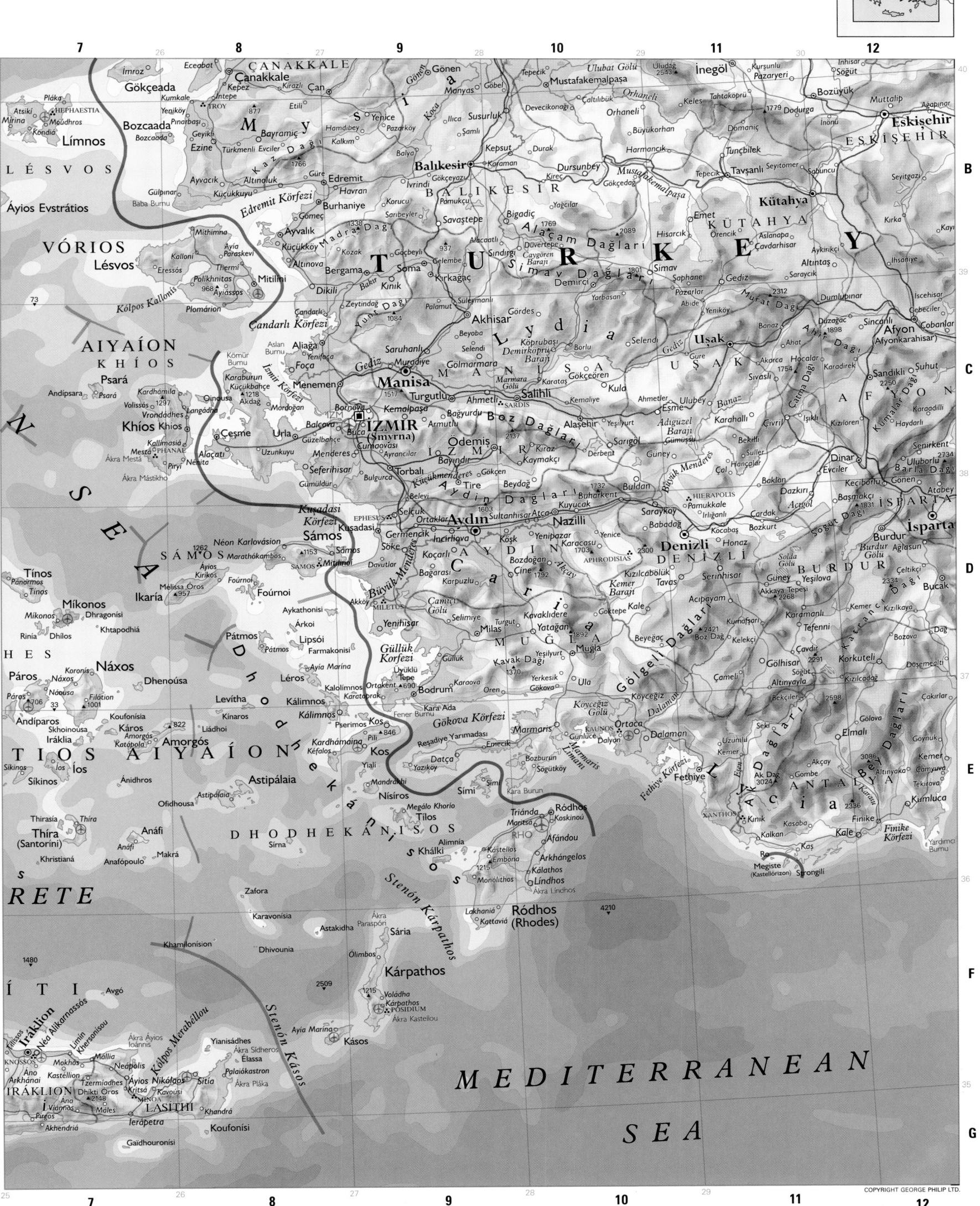
7
8
9
10
11
12
B
C
D
E
F
G
Çanakkale
ÇANAKKALE
Gökçeada
İmroz
Eceabat
Kepez
Intepe
TROY
Kumkale
Bozcaada
Ezine
Bayramiç
Çan
Gönen
Manyas
Mustafakemalpaşa
Ulubat Gölü
Uludağ 2543
İnegöl
Pazaryeri
Söğüt
Bozüyük
Eskişehir
ESKİŞEHİR
Límnos
Mírina
Moúdhros
HEPHAESTIA
LÉSVOS
Áyios Evstrátios
Edremit
Edremit Körfezi
Havran
Burhaniye
Ayvacık
Altınoluk
Küçükkuyu
Kaz Dağı
1766
Balıkesir
BALIKESİR
Susurluk
Kepsut
Dursunbey
Bigadiç
Savaştepe
Sındırgı
Simav
Simav Dağları
Alaçam Dağları
Kütahya
KÜTAHYA
Tavşanlı
Tunçbilek
Emet
Gediz
Murat Dağı
2312
Demirci
VÓRIOS
Lésvos
Mitilíni
Mithimna
Kalloní
Kólpos Kallonís
Plomárion
Ayvalık
Küçükköy
Altınova
Dikili
Bergama
Soma
Kınık
Kırkağaç
Madra Dağı
Çandarlı Körfezi
Çandarlı
Zeytindağ
Akhisar
Gördes
Selendi
Uşak
UŞAK
Banaz
Afyon
(Afyonkarahisar)
Sandıklı
Şuhut
AFYON
Dumlupınar
Sincanlı
Çobanlar
AIYAÍON
KHÍOS
Psará
Andípsara
Khíos
Oinoúsa
Çeşme
Urla
Alaçatı
Aliağa
Foça
Menemen
Manisa
MANISA
Turgutlu
Salihli
Gediz
Demirköprü Barajı
Kula
Eşme
Karahallı
Sivaslı
Çivril
İzmir
(Smyrna)
İZMİR
İzmir Körfezi
Bornova
Buca
Kemalpaşa
Ödemiş
Bayındır
Torbalı
Tire
Boz Dağları
Küçükmenderes
Seferihisar
Menderes
Alaşehir
Sarıgöl
Buldan
Büyük Menderes
HIERAPOLIS
Pamukkale
Dinar
Evciler
Keçiborlu
Gönen
Barla Dağı
Uluborlu
Senirkent
Isparta
ISPARTA
Atabey
Aydın Dağları
Aydın
AYDIN
Nazilli
Sultanhisar
Atça
Kuşadası
Kuşadası Körfezi
Selçuk
EPHESUS
Germencik
İncirliova
Söke
Koçarlı
Çine
Karacasu
APHRODISIAS
Denizli
DENİZLİ
Honaz
Sarayköy
Tavas
Serinhisar
Acıpayam
Burdur
Burdur Gölü
BURDUR
Ağlasun
Yeşilova
Bucak
Sámos
SÁMOS
Karlovásion
Ikaría
Foúrnoi
MILETUS
Akköy
Bafa Gölü
Yenihisar
Milas
Yatağan
Muğla
MUĞLA
Kavaklıdere
Beyağaç
Gölgeli Dağları
Boz Dağ
2421
Tefenni
Gölhisar
Çavdır
Altınyayla
Korkuteli
Döşemealtı
Tínos
Míkonos
Dhílos
Rínia
Náxos
Páros
Andíparos
Dhenoúsa
Pátmos
Lipsói
Arkoi
Léros
Farmakonisi
Güllük Körfezi
Bodrum
Kálimnos
Kos
Gökova Körfezi
Marmaris
Köyceğiz
Köyceğiz Gölü
KAUNOS
Dalyan
Ortaca
Dalaman
Fethiye
Fethiye Körfezi
Elmalı
Bey Dağları
Ak Dağ
3024
Lycia
ANTALYA
Kemer
Kumluca
Finike
Finike Körfezi
Kale
Kaş
Kalkan
XANTHOS
Megiste
(Kastellórizon)
Strongilí
Amorgós
Astipálaia
Nísiros
Tílos
Sími
Khálki
Ródhos
RHODOS
Lindhos
Arkhángelos
Kámiros
Ródhos
(Rhodes)
DHODHEKÁNISOS
Dhodhekánisos
Íos
Síkinos
Thíra
(Santoríni)
Anáfi
Iráklia
Schinoússa
Koufonísia
Kéros
Ánidhros
Kárpathos
Sária
Kásos
Stenón Kárpathos
Stenón Kásos
Astakidha
Karavonísia
Zafora
Dhivounia
Khamilonísion
MEDITERRANEAN
SEA
CRETE
Iráklion
IRÁKLION
KNOSSOS
Mália
Áyios Nikólaos
Sitía
LASITHI
Ierápetra
Koufonísi
Gaidhouronísi
Kólpos Merabéllou
TURKEY
Mysia
Lydia
Caria
AIYAÍON
SEA
4210
2509
1480
COPYRIGHT GEORGE PHILIP LTD.

East from Greenwich

------ Inter-entity boundaries as agreed
at the 1995 Dayton Peace Agreement.

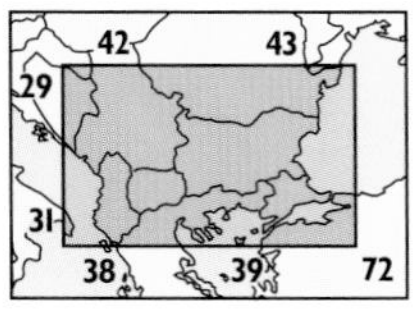

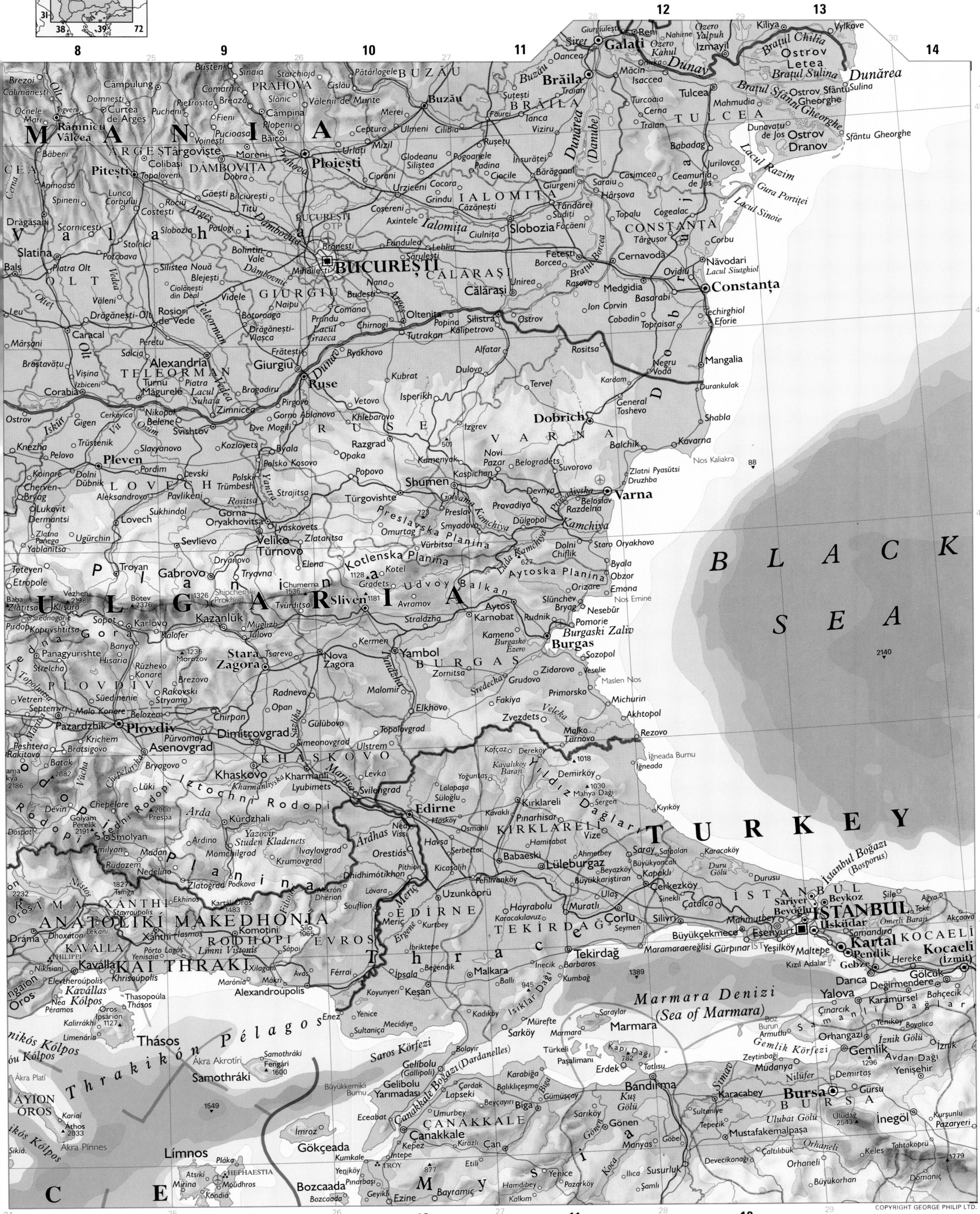

Underlined towns give their name to the administrative area in which they stand.

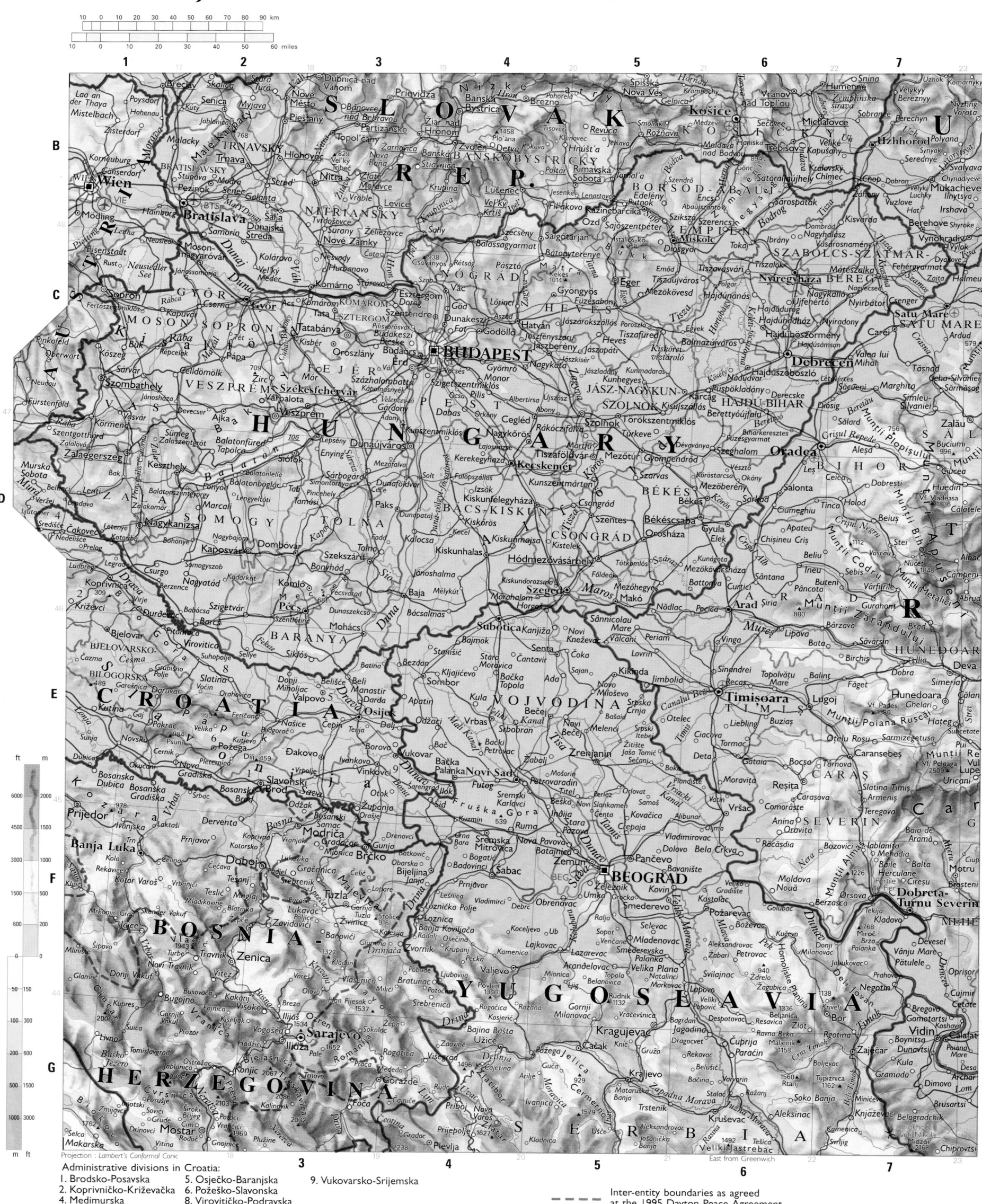

Administrative divisions in Croatia:
1. Brodsko-Posavska
2. Koprivničko-Križevačka
4. Medimurska
5. Osječko-Baranjska
6. Požeško-Slavonska
8. Virovitičko-Podravska
9. Vukovarsko-Srijemska

Projection : Lambert's Conformal Conic

East from Greenwich

Inter-entity boundaries as agreed
at the 1995 Dayton Peace Agreement.

Underlined towns give their name to the administrative area in which they stand.

COPYRIGHT GEORGE PHILIP LTD.

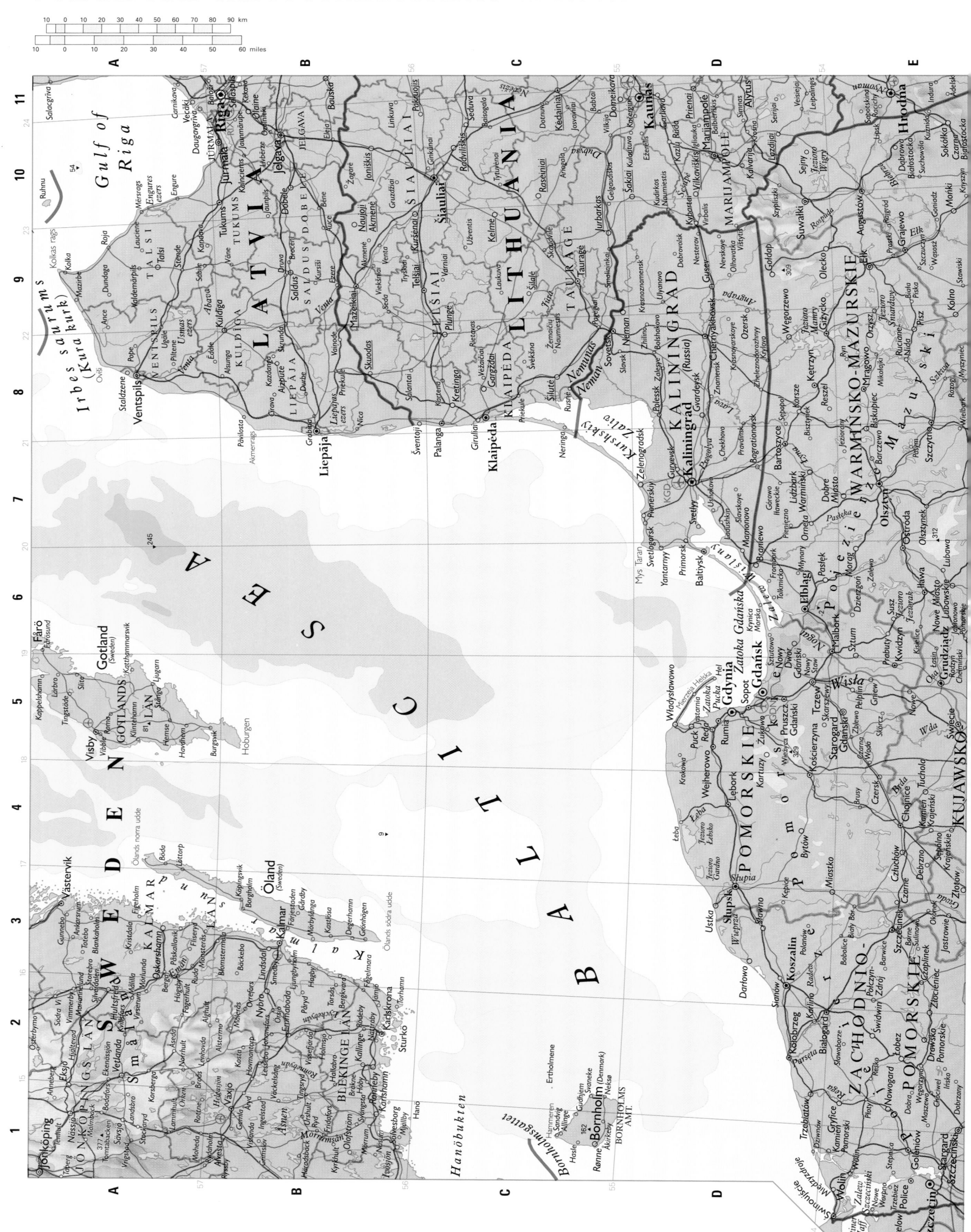

10 0 10 20 30 40 50 60 70 80 90 km
10 0 10 20 30 40 50 60 miles
A
B
C
D
E
1
2
3
4
5
6
7
8
9
10
11
BALTIC SEA
SWEDEN
LATVIA
LITHUANIA
KALININGRAD (Russia)
Gulf of Riga
Irbes šaurums (Kura kurk)
Kurshskiy Zaliv
Zatoka Gdańska
Zalew Wiślany
Hanöbukten
Bornholmsgattet
Kalmar sund
Gotland (Sweden)
Öland (Sweden)
Bornholm (Denmark)
POMORSKIE
WARMIŃSKO-MAZURSKIE
ZACHODNIO-POMORSKIE
KUJAWSKO-
Riga
Kaunas
Šiauliai
Klaipėda
Liepāja
Ventspils
Kaliningrad
Gdańsk
Gdynia
Szczecin
Elbląg
Olsztyn
Koszalin
Słupsk
Kalmar
Karlskrona
Visby
Jönköping
Hrodna
Jelgava
Jūrmala
Marijampolė
Suwałki

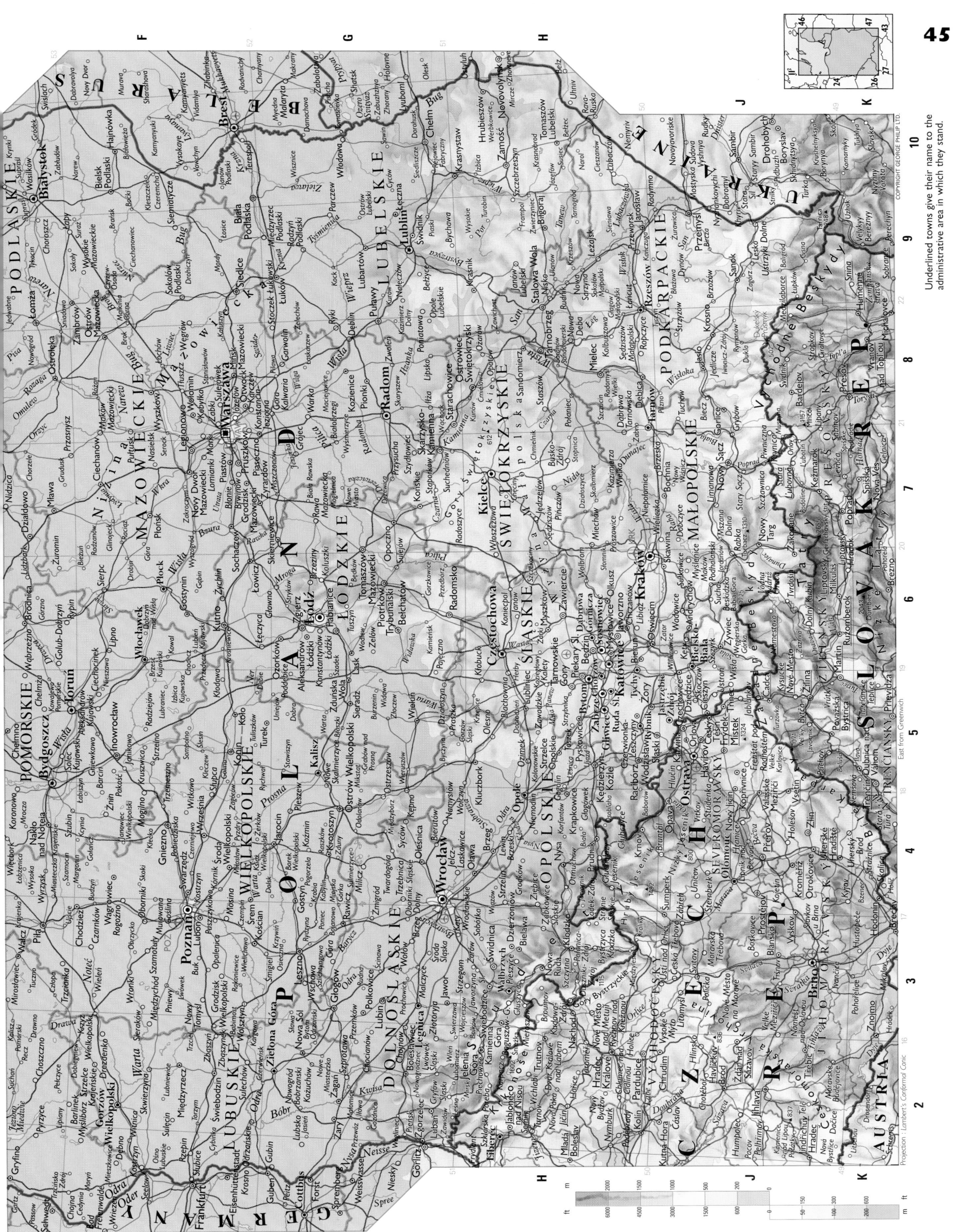

Underlined towns give their name to the
administrative area in which they stand.

East from Greenwich

Projection : Lambert's Conformal Conic

COPYRIGHT GEORGE PHILIP LTD.

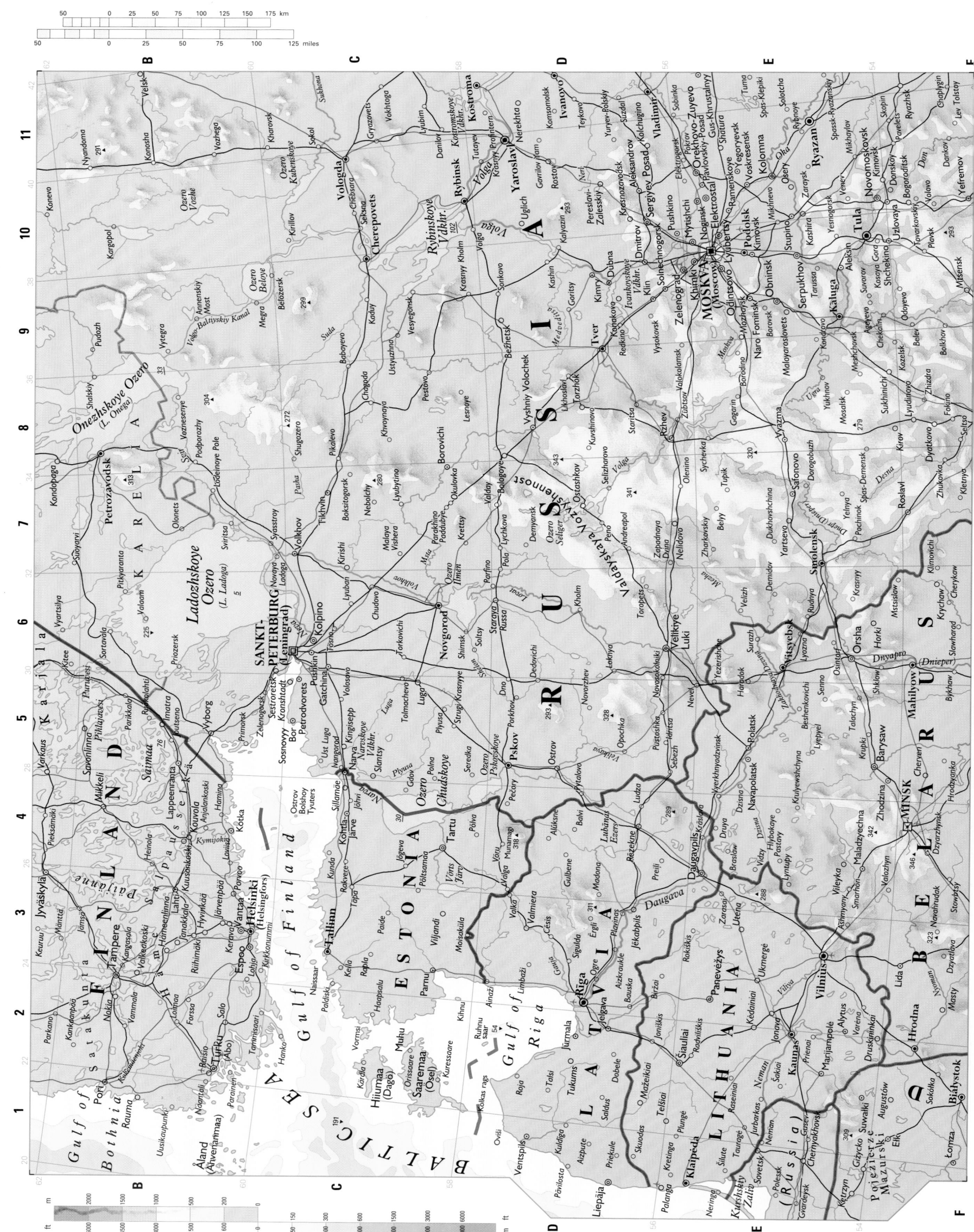

0 25 50 75 100 125 150 175 km
0 25 50 75 100 125 miles
FINLAND
ESTONIA
LATVIA
LITHUANIA
BELARUS
RUSSIA
(Russia)
KARELIA
Gulf of Finland
Gulf of Bothnia
Gulf of Riga
BALTIC SEA
Ladozhskoye Ozero (L. Ladoga)
Onezhskoye Ozero (L. Onega)
Ozero Chudskoye
Valdayskaya Vozvyshennost
Rybinskoye Vdkhr.
SANKT-PETERBURG (Leningrad)
MOSKVA (Moscow)
MINSK
Helsinki (Helsingfors)
Tallinn
Riga
Vilnius
Kaunas
Tartu
Pskov
Novgorod
Tver
Smolensk
Vitsyebsk
Daugavpils
Klaipėda
Liepāja
Tampere
Turku (Åbo)
Yaroslavl
Vologda
Kostroma
Tula
Kaluga
Ryazan
Hrodna
Białystok
Mahilyow
Orsha
Daugava
Volga
Dnyapro (Dnieper)
Neman

m 2000 1500 1000 500 200 0
ft 6000 4500 3000 1500 600 0
0 50 150 300 600 1500 3000 6000 ft
0 50 100 200 500 1000 2000 m

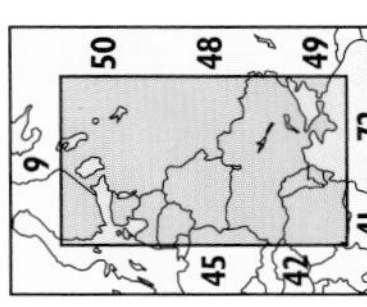

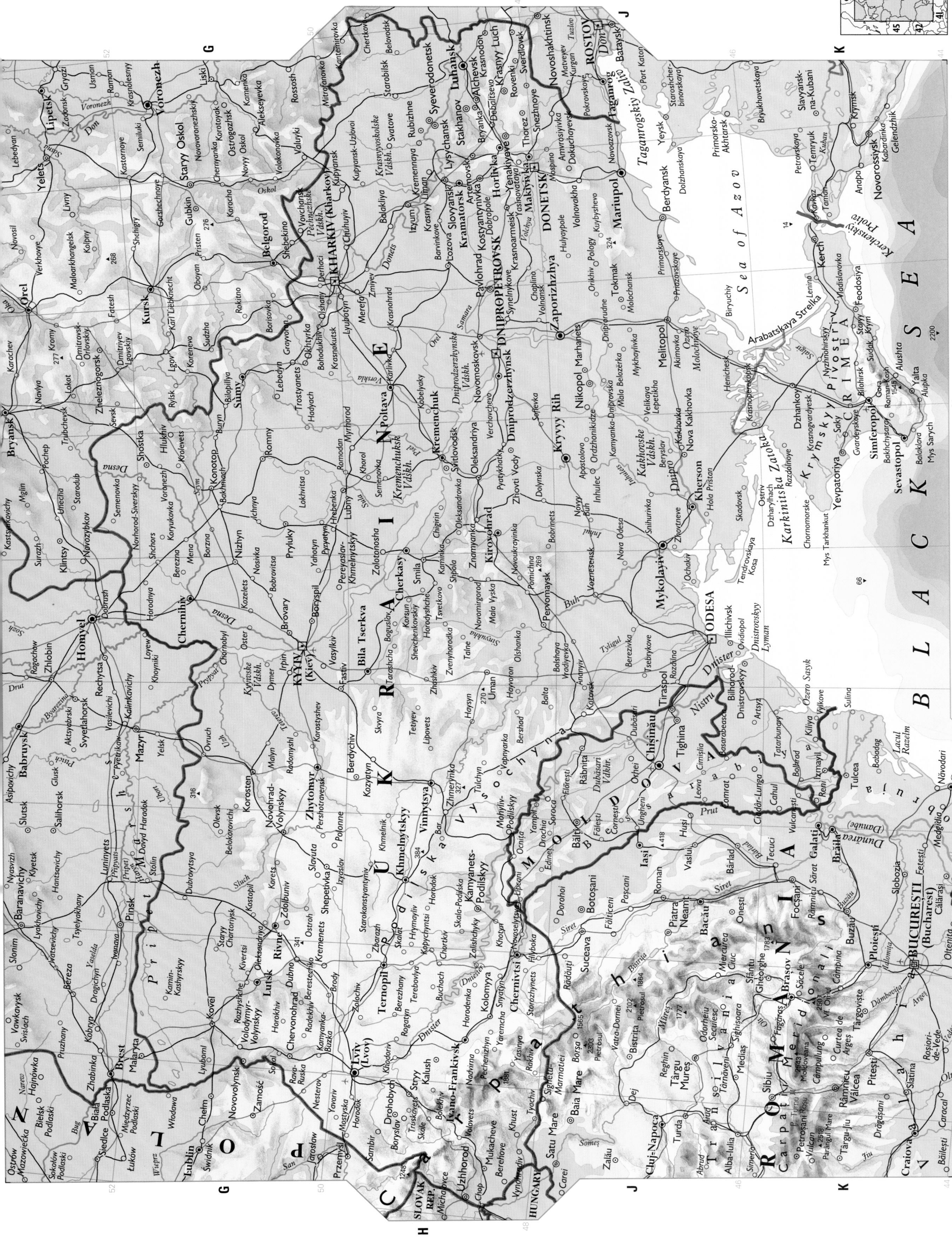

50 48 49
45 42 41 72

Map of Ukraine and surrounding region

Lipetsk Yelets Lebedyan Zadonsk Gryazi Usman Raman
Orel Livny Voronezh
Bryansk Kursk
Belgorod
KHARKIV (Kharkov)
Sumy
Poltava
Luhansk
ROSTOV Don Bataysk
Taganrog

DONETSK
Makiyivka
Mariupol
Berdyansk

Sea of Azov

Kerch
CRIMEA
Simferopol
Sevastopol Yalta Alushta
Feodosiya
Novorossiysk Anapa

B L A C K   S E A

DNIPROPETROVSK
Dniprodzerzhynsk
Zaporizhzhya
Melitopol
Kryvyy Rih
Kirovohrad
Kremenchuk
Svitlovodsk
Cherkasy
Bila Tserkva
KYIV (Kiev)
Chernihiv
Homel
Babruysk
Mazyr
Pinsk
Brest

Zhytomyr
Vinnytsya
Khmelnytskyy
Ternopil
Rivne
Lutsk
Lviv (Lvov)
Ivano-Frankivsk
Chernivtsi
Uzhhorod

Mykolayiv
ODESA
Kherson

Chisinău
Tighina
MOLDOVA
Tiraspol

ROMANIA
BUCUREȘTI (Bucharest)
Ploiești
Brașov
Sibiu
Cluj-Napoca
Galați
Brăila
Iași
Constanța

BULGARIA
Ruse
Dobrich

HUNGARY
SLOVAK REP.
POLAND
Lublin

CARPATHIANS

Dniester (Dunărea / Danube)

CARTOGRAPHY BY PHILIP'S.

East from Greenwich

Projection: Conical with two standard parallels

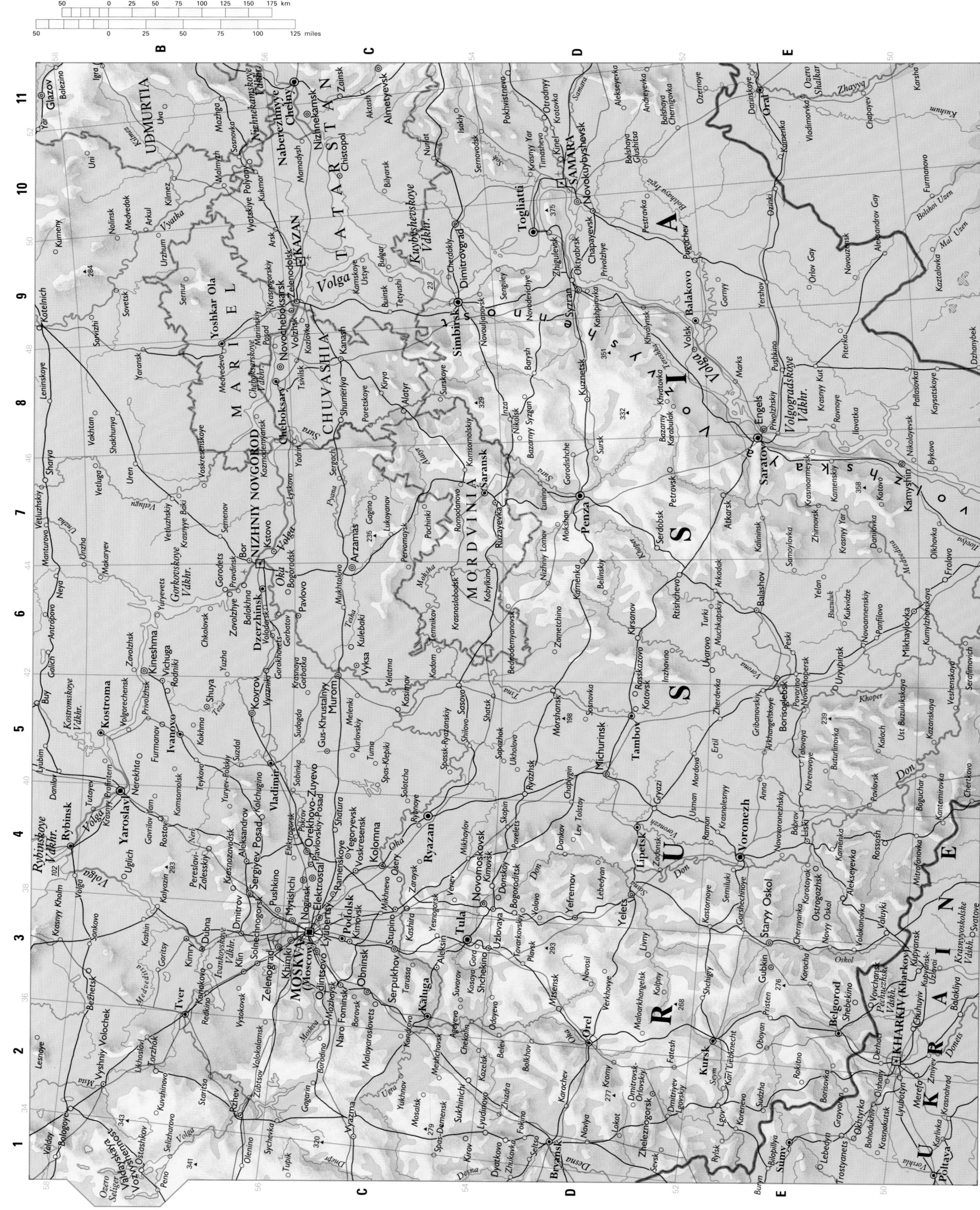
50 0 25 50 75 100 125 150 175 km
50 0 25 50 75 100 125 miles
UDMURTIA
TATARSTAN
MARI EL
CHUVASHIA
MORDVINIA
RUSSIA
UKRAINE
MOSKVA (Moscow)
NIZHNIY NOVGOROD
KAZAN
SAMARA
KHARKIV (Kharkov)
Yaroslavl
Kostroma
Ivanovo
Vladimir
Tver
Ryazan
Tula
Kaluga
Orel
Kursk
Belgorod
Voronezh
Lipetsk
Tambov
Penza
Saransk
Simbirsk
Togliatti
Saratov
Engels
Cheboksary
Yoshkar Ola
Naberezhnyye Chelny
Bryansk
Volga
Oka
Don
Rybinskoye Vdkhr.
Gorkovskoye Vdkhr.
Kuybyshevskoye Vdkhr.
Volgogradskoye Vdkhr.

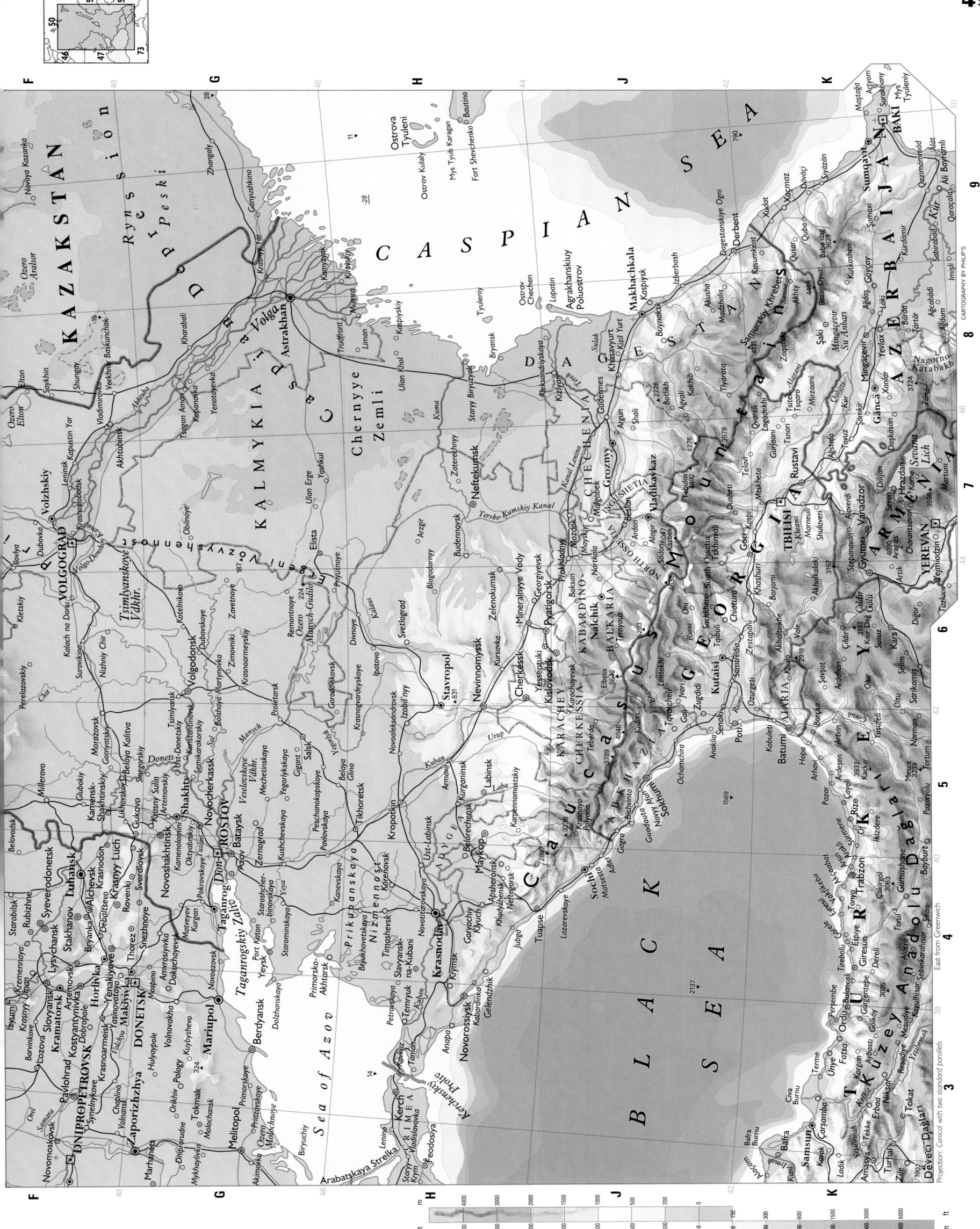
KAZAKSTAN
CASPIAN SEA
BLACK SEA
Sea of Azov
Taganrogskiy Zaliv
Caspian Depression
Ryn Peski
KALMYKIA
Chernyye Zemli
Ergeni Vozvyshennost
Prikubanskaya Nizmennost
DAGESTAN
CHECHENIA
INGUSHETIA
NORTH OSSETIA
KABARDINO-BALKARIA
KARACHEY-CHERKESSIA
ADYGEA
ABKHAZIA
South Ossetia
AJARIA
GEORGIA
ARMENIA
AZERBAIJAN
TURKEY
CRIMEA
Caucasus Mountains
Samurskiy Khrebet
Kuzey Anadolu Dağları
Nagorno-Karabakh
Ostrova Tyuleni
Agrakhanskiy Poluostrov
Kerchenskiy Proliv
Arabatskaya Strelka
Tsimlyanskoye Vdkhr.
Veselovskoye Vdkhr.
Mingäçevir Su Anbarı
Sevana Lich
Çıldır Gölü
Ozero Elton
Ozero Aralsor
Ozero Manych-Gudilo
VOLGOGRAD
Volzhskiy
Astrakhan
ROSTOV
Novocherkassk
Shakhty
Taganrog
DONETSK
DNIPROPETROVSK
Zaporizhzhya
Luhansk
Mariupol
Melitopol
Berdyansk
Krasnodar
Stavropol
Novorossiysk
Maykop
Sochi
Tuapse
Sokhumi
Batumi
Kutaisi
TBILISI
Rustavi
YEREVAN
Gyumri
Vanadzor
BAKI
Sumqayıt
Gäncä
Makhachkala
Derbent
Groznyy
Vladikavkaz
Nalchik
Pyatigorsk
Elista
Kerch
Feodosiya
Trabzon
Samsun
Rize
Kars
Elbrus 5642
Kazbek 5047
F G H J K
3 4 5 6 7 8 9
Projection: Conical with two standard parallels
East from Greenwich
CARTOGRAPHY BY PHILIP'S.

RUSSIA
1 Adygea
2 Karachey-Cherkessia
3 Kabardino-Balkaria
4 North Ossetia
5 Ingushetia
6 Chechenia
7 Dagestan
8 Mordvinia
9 Chuvashia
10 Mari El
11 Tatarstan
12 Udmurtia
13 Khakassia
AZERBAIJAN
14 Naxçivan
GEORGIA   UKRAINE
15 Ajaria   17 Crimea
16 Abkhazia

Projection: Conical Orthomorphic with two standard parallels

East from Greenwich

A
B
C
D
E
F
8
9
10
11
12
13
14
15
16
17
18
19
Mys Dezhneva (East C.)
Uelen
Chukchi Sea
St. Lawrence I. (U.S.A.)
Provideniya
Anadyrskiy Zaliv
Beringovskiy
Egvekinot
Vankarem
Chukotskoye Nagorye
Pevek
Ostrov Vrangelya
East Siberian Sea
Ostrov Gennyetty
Ostrov Zhannetty
Ostrova Delonga
Ostrov Zhokhova
Ostrov Bennetta
Novosibirskiye Ostrova
Ostrov Faddeyevskiy
Ostrov Novaya Sibir
Ostrov Belkovskiy
Ostrov Kotelnyy
Ostrov Stolbovoy
Ostrov Malyy Lyakhovskiy
Ostrov Bolshoy Lyakhovskiy
Lyakhovskiye Ostrova
Proliv Dmitriya Lapteva
Laptev Sea
OCEAN
Ostrov Shmidta
Mys Arkticheskiy
Ostrov Komsomolets
Ostrov Oktyabrskoy Revolyutsii
Ostrov Pioner
Ostrov Bolshevik
Severnaya Zemlya
Proliv Vilkitskogo
Mys Chelyuskin
Poluostrov Taymyr
Gory Byrranga
Oz. Taymyr
Ostrov Bolshoy Begichev
Nordvik
Ostrova Medvezhi
Ostrov Ayon
Ambarchik
Cherskiy
Ust Chaun
Bilibino
Anadyr
Bolshoy Anyuy
Oloy
Yeropol
Markovo
Penzhino
Koryakskoye Nagorye
Khatyrka
Bering Sea
Korf
Tilichiki
Kamenskoye
Omolon
Nizhne Kolymsk
Srednekolymsk
Chokurdakh
Indigirka
Mys Buorkhaya
Tiksi
Kazachye
Ust Kuyga
Deputatskiy
Druzhina
Ust Olenek
Tit-Ary
Bulun
Kyusyur
Saskylakh
Novorybnoye
Khatanga
Volochanka
Kheta
Zhilinda
Olenek
Verkhoyansk
Batagai
Verkhoyanskiy Khrebet
Khrebet Cherskogo
Khonuu
Zyryanka
Kolyma
Pobeda 3147
Gora Chen
Ust-Nera
Taskan
Omsukchan
Orotukan
Evensk
Kolymskoye Nagorye
Gizhiga
Paren
Penzhinskaya Guba
Gizhiginskaya Guba
Zaliv Shelikhova
Palana
Sredinnyy Khrebet
Ossora
Ostrov Karaginskiy
Ust-Kamchatsk
Komandorskiye Ostrova
Nikolskoye
Uka
Gora Klyuchevskaya
Poluostrov Kamchatka
Tigil
Ust Khayryuzovo
Petropavlovsk-Kamchatskiy
Kirovskiy
Ust-Bolsheretsk
Severo-Kurilsk
Ostrov Paramushir
Ostrov Onekotan
Kurilskiye Ostrova
Ostrov Simushir
Ostrov Urup
Ostrov Iturup
Kurilsk
Ostrov Kunashir
Dudinka
Norilsk
Gory Putorana
Yessey
Kystatyam
Zhigansk
Arctic Circle
Susuman
Yagodnoye
Atka
Palatka
Magadan
Ust-Omchug
Oymyakon
Khandyga
Okhotskiy Perevoz
Arka
Okhotsk
Ulya
Sangar
Lena
Batamay
Borogontsy
Ytyk Kyuyel
Vilyuysk
Verkhnevilyuysk
Namtsy
Yakutsk
Mayya
Amga
Ust Maya
Nyurba
Pokrovsk
Suntar
Mirnyy
Chernyshevskiy
Sinsk
Ust-Mil
Aim
Maya
Nelkan
Khrebet Dzhugdzur
Chagda
Uchur
Ayan
Sea of Okhotsk
Ostrov Bolshoy Shantar
Sakhalinskiy Zaliv
Okha
Sakhalin
Turukhansk
Noginsk
Nizhnyaya Tunguska
Tura
Yukta
Vilyuy
Yerbogachen
Olekminsk
Tommot
Aldan
Lensk
Kuyumba
Mutoray
Vanavara
Podkamennaya Tunguska
Yartsevo
Severo-Yeniseyskiy
Vitim
Yenyuka
Olekma
Neryungri
Chumikan
Tugur
Nikolayevsk-na-Amur
Aleksandrovsk-Sakhalinskiy
Gora Lopatina
Poronaysk
Uglegorsk
Kezhma
Korshunovo
Mama
Bodaybo
Chara
Nagornyy
Stanovoy Khrebet
Uda
Amgun
Amur
Khrebet Sikhote Alin
Yeniseysk
Strelka
Boguchany
Ust-Ilimsk
Kirensk
Makarovo
Karalon
Ust-Nyukzha
Tynda
Zeya
Selemdzha
Vanino
Yuzhno-Sakhalinsk
Kondratyevo
Chuna
Zheleznogorsk-Ilimskiy
Ust-Kut
Magistralnyy
Kalakan
Skovorodino
Dzhalinda
Ushumun
Norsk
Bureya
Komsomolsk
Amursk
Kholmsk
Korsakov
Wakkanai
Achinsk
Kansk
Ilanskiy
Tayshet
Bratsk
Krasnoyarsk
Bagdarin
Mogocha
Yablonovyy Khrebet
Gulian
Shimanovsk
Svobodnyy
Belogorsk
Chegdomyn
Zavitinsk
Raychikhinsk
Obluchye
Birobidzhan
Smidovich
Khabarovsk
Artemovsk
Nizhneudinsk
Tulun
Zima
Vostochnyy Sayan
Chernogorsk
Minusinsk
Abakan
Barguzin
Vitim
Bukachacha
Sretensk
Shilka
Nerchinsk
Argun
Da Hinggan Ling
Blagoveshchensk
Poyarkovo
Vyazemskiy
Bikin
Amgu
Terney
Rumoi
Abashiri
Kushiro
Obihiro
SAPPORO
Hokkaidō
Otaru
Hakodate
Cheremkhovo
Usolye Sibirskoye
Angarsk
Irkutsk
Ulan Ude
Chita
Aginskoye
Munku-Sardyk
Ozero Baykal
Buryatiya
Zapadnyy Sayan
Turan
Toora-Khem
Kyzyl
Chadan
TUVA
Slyudyanka
Hövsgöl Nuur
Petrovsk-Zabaykalskiy
Khilok
Olovyannaya
Borzya
Zabaykalsk
Hailar
Nenjiang
QIQIHAR
Hegang
Jiamusi
Songhua Jiang
Dalnerechensk
Lesozavodsk
Spassk Dalniy
Dalnegorsk
Olga
Tannu Ola
Samagaltay
Uvs Nuur
Erzin
Hatgal
Gusinoozersk
Kyakhta
Zakamensk
Darhan
Khapcheranga
Manzhouli
Hulun Nur
HARBIN
Ussuriysk
Artem
Vladivostok
Nakhodka
Khanka
Aomori
Hachinohe
Har Us Nuur
Hyargas Nuur
Hangayn Nuruu
Hentiyn Nuruu
Onon
Choybalsan
Tamsagbulag
Ang'angxi
Nen Jiang
Dongbei
Mudanjiang
Kraskino
Akita
Döröö Nuur
Uliastay
Hovd
Ulaanbaatar
Lun
Tsetserleg
Öndörhaan
Tao'an
JILIN
Yanji
Chŏngjin
Sea of Japan
Honshū
CHANGCHUN
Siping
MONGOLIA
Altay
FUSHUN
Tonghua
Linxi
Niigata
Xilinhot
Chifeng
SHENYANG
ANSHAN
NORTH KOREA
Saynshand
Gobi
CHINA
Dandong
Wŏnsan
Kanazawa
Fuji-San
Erenhot
Yingkou
P'YŎNGYANG
Nampo
Kansŏng
JAPAN
Dalandzadgad
Chengde
SŎUL
Seoul
DALIAN
INCH'ŎN
SOUTH KOREA
TAEJŎN
TAEGU
PUSAN
ŌSAKA
Hami
Gaxun Nur
Baotou
Hohhot
Zhangjiakou
BEIJING
COPYRIGHT GEORGE PHILIP LTD.

ASIA : Physical 1:44 400 000

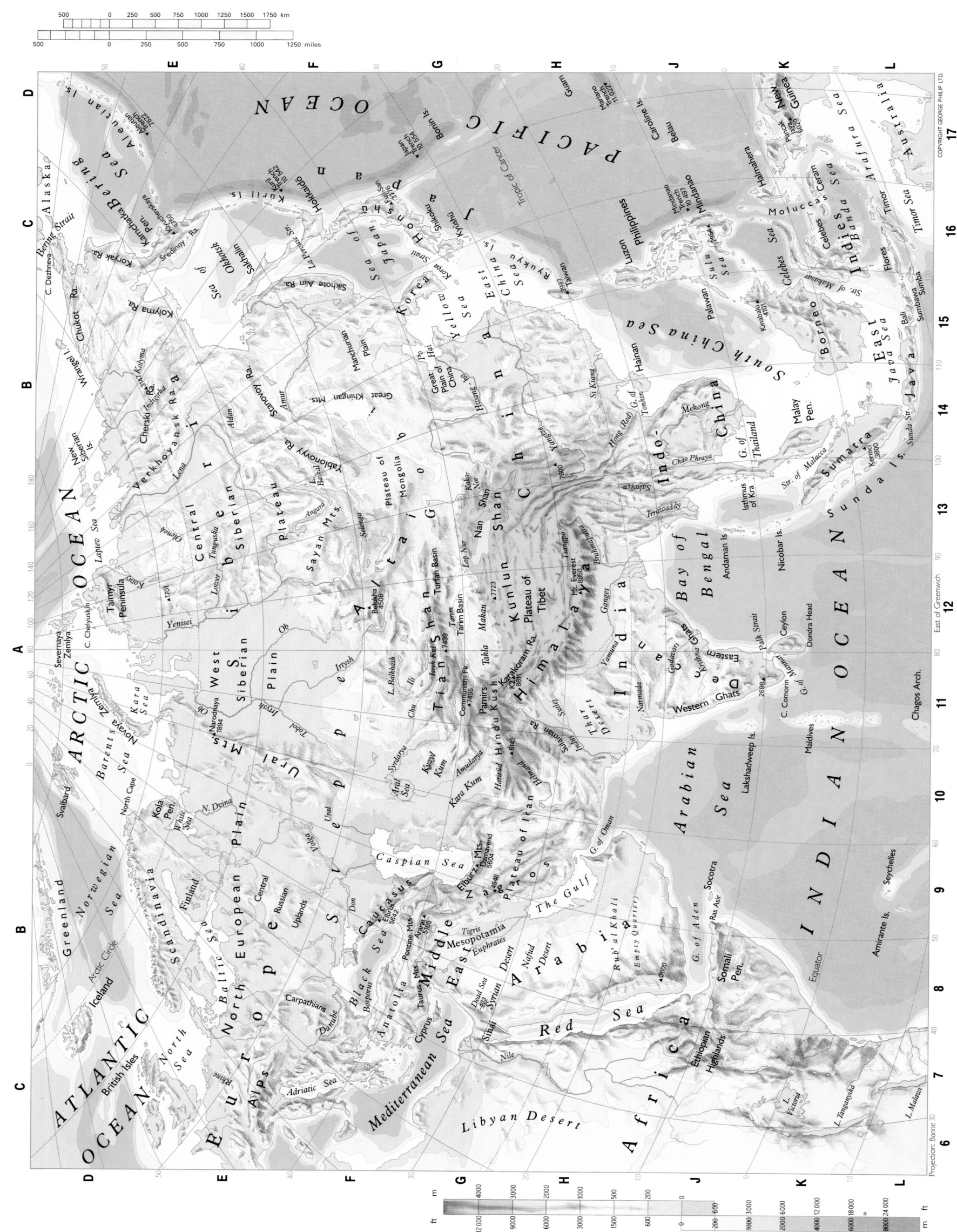
500 0 250 500 750 1000 1250 1500 1750 km
500 0 250 500 750 1000 1250 miles
ARCTIC OCEAN
PACIFIC OCEAN
INDIAN OCEAN
ATLANTIC OCEAN
Siberia
Europe
Steppe
China
Gobi
Altai
Japan
India
Arabia
Africa
Indo-China
East Indies
Greenland
Svalbard
Iceland
British Isles
Norwegian Sea
North Sea
Barents Sea
Kara Sea
Laptev Sea
Baltic Sea
Black Sea
Caspian Sea
Mediterranean Sea
Red Sea
Arabian Sea
Bay of Bengal
South China Sea
East China Sea
Yellow Sea
Sea of Japan
Sea of Okhotsk
Bering Sea
Scandinavia
Finland
North European Plain
Central Russian Uplands
Ural Mts.
West Siberian Plain
Central Siberian Plateau
Verkhoyansk Ra.
Cherski Ra.
Kolyma Ra.
Stanovoy Ra.
Yablonovyy Ra.
Sayan Mts.
Plateau of Mongolia
Great Khingan Mts.
Manchurian Plain
Caucasus
Anatolia
Middle East
Mesopotamia
Syrian Desert
Nafud Desert
Rub' al Khali (Empty Quarter)
Plateau of Iran
Elburz Mts.
Zagros
Tian Shan
Turfan Basin
Tarim Basin
Takla Makan
Pamirs
Hindu Kush
Karakoram Ra.
Kunlun
Plateau of Tibet
Himalaya
Mt. Everest 8850
Thar Desert
Deccan
Western Ghats
Eastern Ghats
Ethiopian Highlands
Somali Pen.
Libyan Desert
Philippines
Borneo
Sumatra
Java
Celebes
New Guinea
Australia
Tropic of Cancer
Arctic Circle
Equator
Projection: Bonne
East of Greenwich
COPYRIGHT GEORGE PHILIP LTD.
ft m
12 000 4000
9000 3000
6000 2000
3000 1000
1500 500
600 200
0 0
200 600
1000 3000
2000 6000
4000 12 000
6000 18 000
8000 24 000
m ft

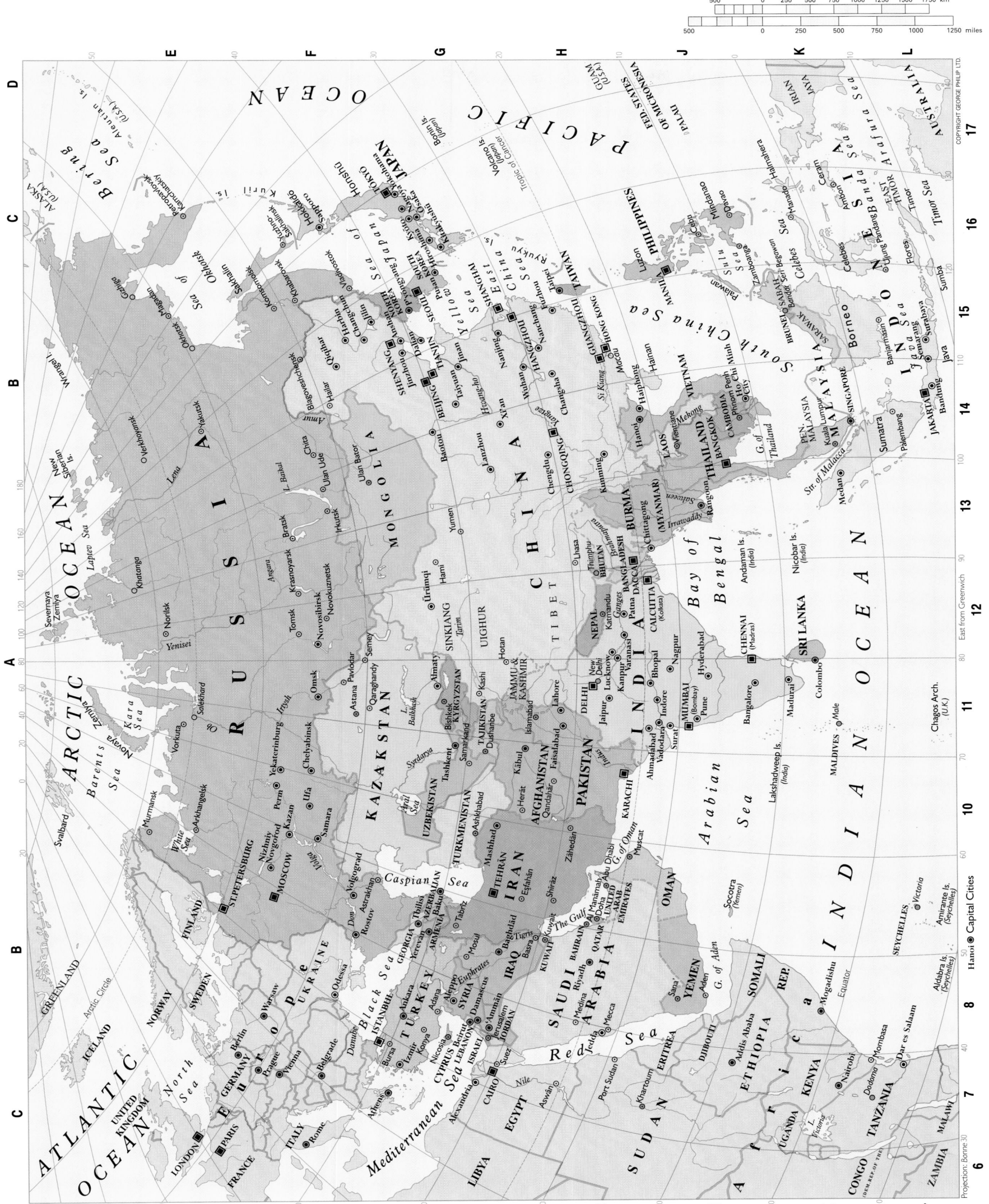

COPYRIGHT GEORGE PHILIP LTD.

Projection: Bonne

Hanoi ⊙ Capital Cities

JAPAN 1:4 400 000

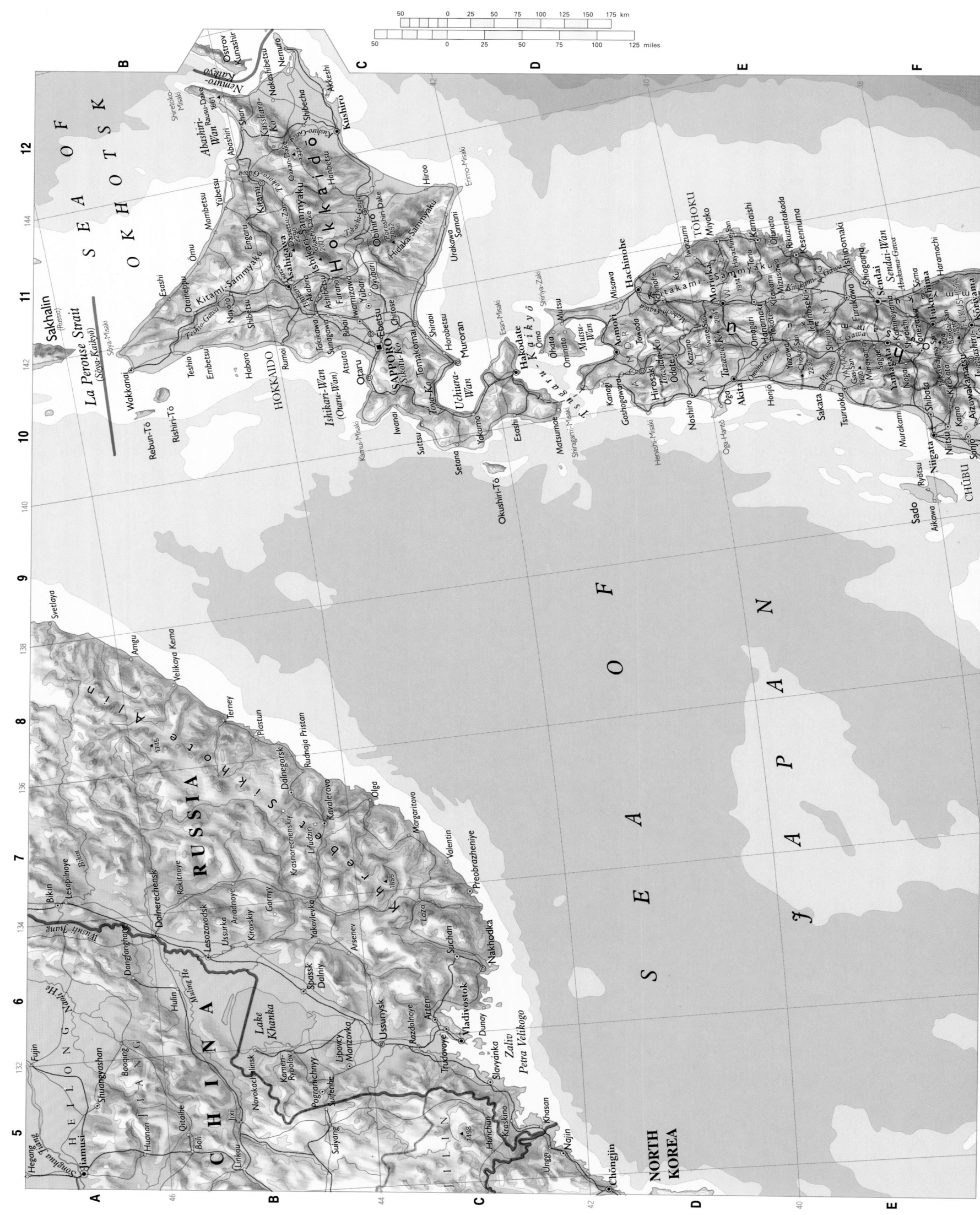

SEA OF OKHOTSK

Sakhalin
(Rossiya)

La Perouse Strait
(Sōya-Kaikyō)

Ostrov
Kunashir

Nemuro-
Kaikyō

HOKKAIDŌ

HOKKAIDO

SAPPORO

RUSSIA

CHINA

Lake
Khanka

Vladivostok

NORTH
KOREA

SEA OF JAPAN

TŌHOKU

HONSHU

Hakodate

Tsugaru-kaikyō

Aomori

Akita

Sendai

Sendai-Wan

CHŪBU

Sado

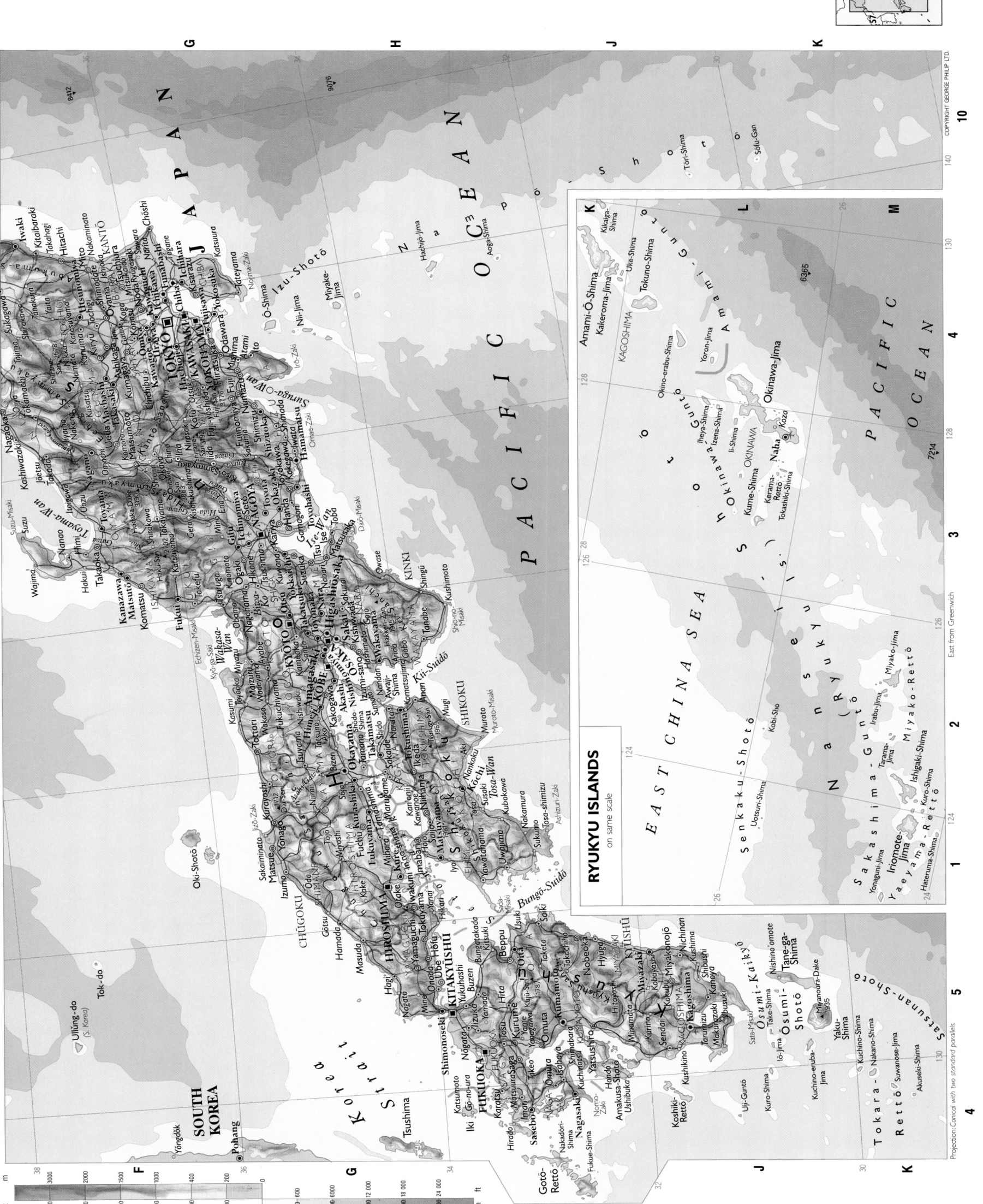

RYUKYU ISLANDS
on same scale

COPYRIGHT GEORGE PHILIP LTD.

Projection: Conical with two standard parallels

East from Greenwich

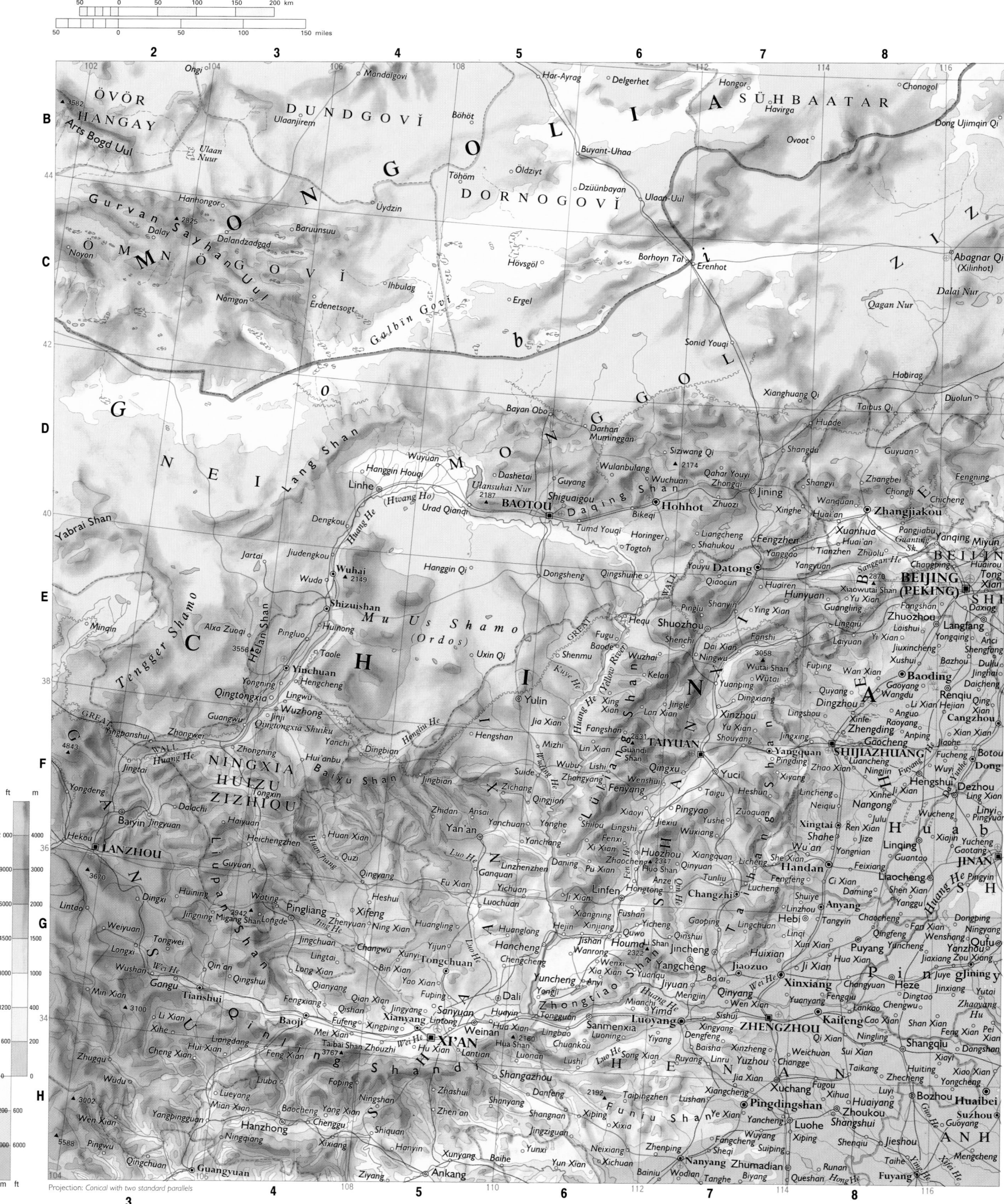

50   0   50   100   150   200 km
50   0   50   100   150 miles

Projection: Conical with two standard parallels

ft   m
12 000   4000
9000   3000
6000   2000
4500   1500
3000   1000
1200   400
600   200
0   0
200   600
2000   6000
m   ft

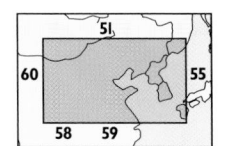

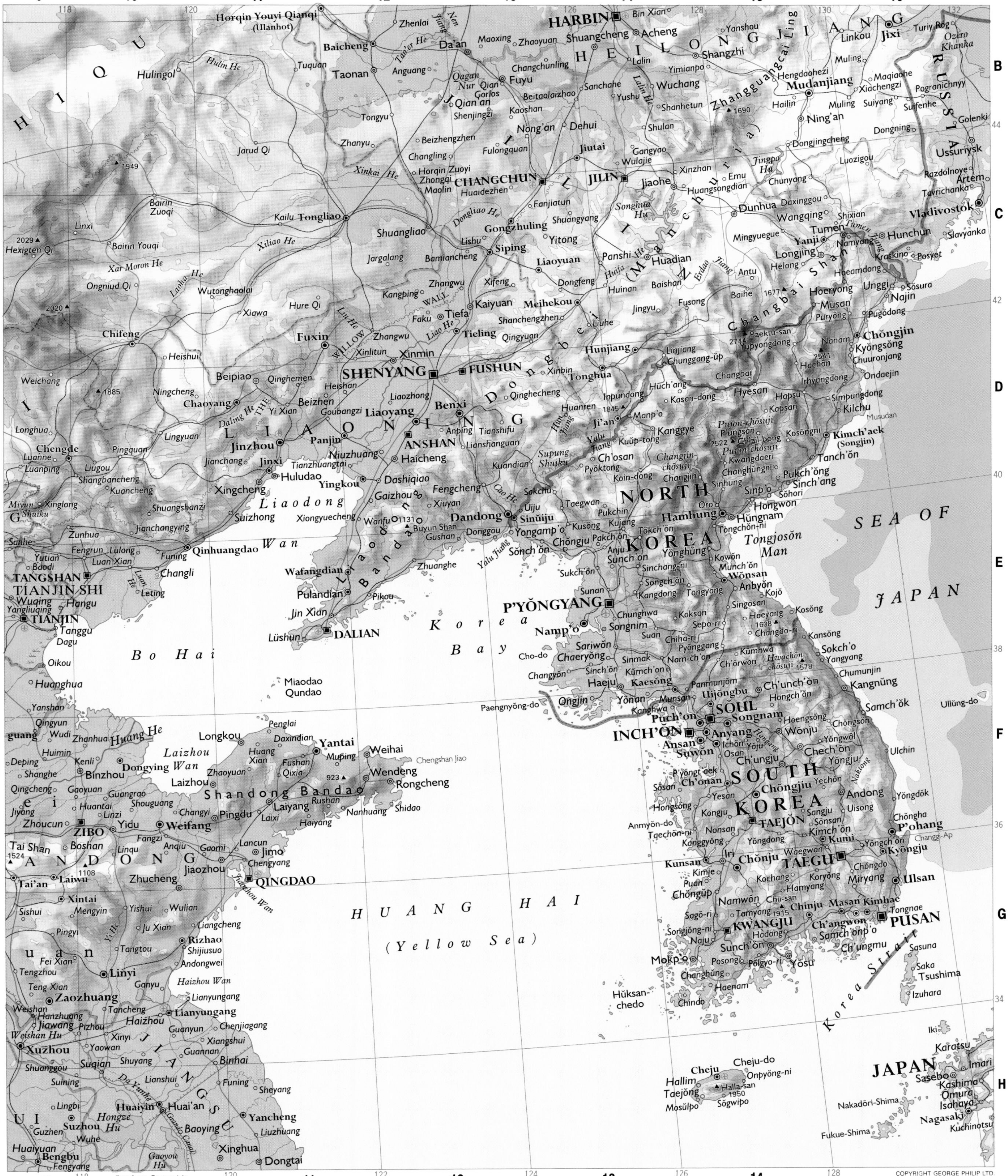

East from Greenwich

COPYRIGHT GEORGE PHILIP LTD.

Horqin Youyi Qianqi (Ulanhot) · Zhenlai · Da'an · HARBIN · Bin Xian · Acheng · Yanshou · Linkou · Jixi · Turiy Rog · Ozero Khanka

Baicheng · Maoxing · Zhaoyuan · Shuangcheng · Changchunling · Shangzhi · Muling · RUSSIA

Hulingol · Hulin He · Tuquan · Anguang · Fuyu · Lalin · Yimianpo · Hengdaohezi · Maqiaohe · Muling · Pogranichnyy · Golenki

Qagan Nur Qian Gorlos · Beitaolaizhao · Sanchahe · Wuchang · Shanhetun · Hailin · Mudanjiang · Xiachengzi · Suiyang · Suifenhe

Tongyu · Shenjingzi · Kaoshan · Yushu · Shulan · Ning'an · Dongjingcheng · Dongning · Ussuriysk

Jarud Qi · Beizhengzhen · Nong'an · Dehui · Gangyao · Wulajie · Xinzhan · Emu · Jingpo Hu · Luozigou · Razdolnoye · Artem

Zhanyu · Changling · Fulongquan · Jiutai · Jiaohe · Dunhua · Daxinggou · Wangqing · Shixian · Tavrichanka

Bairin Zuoqi · Kailu · Tongliao · Shuangliao · Lishu · Gongzhuling · Shuangyang · Panshi · Huadian · Chunyang · Mingyuegue · Tumen · Hunchun · Vladivostok · Slavyanka

Linxi · Bairin Youqi · Xar Moron He · Jargalang · Bamiancheng · Siping · Yitong · Liaoyuan · Dongfeng · Huinan · Baishan · Baihe · Longjing · Helong · Hoeamdong · Kraskino · Posyet

Hexigten Qi · Chifeng · Liaohe · Wutonghaolai · Xiawa · Hure Qi · Zhangwu · Xifeng · Qingyuan · Jingyu · Fusong · Changbai Shan · Paektu-san · Hoeryong · Musan · Puryong · Unggi · Najin

Ongniud Qi · Kangping · Faku · Tiefa · Shanchengzhen · Liuhe · Tonghua · Linjiang · Chunggang-ŭp · Changbai · Yupyongdong · Hyesan · Musan · Puryong · Pugŏdong

Weichang · Beipiao · Fuxin · Xinlitun · Xinmin · Kaiyuan · Meihekou · Hunjiang · Huch'ang · Irhyangdong · Ondaejin · Chŏngjin · Kyŏngsŏng

Chaoyang · Ningcheng · SHENYANG · FUSHUN · Liaozhong · Qinghecheng · Huanren · Ipundong · Pungsan · Kasan-dong · Hyesan · Hapsu · Kilchu · Chuuronjang

Longhua · Chengde · Lingyuan · Beizhen · Heishan · Goubangzi · Liaoyang · Benxi · Tianshifu · Huanren · Ji'an · Manp'o · Kanggye · Puon-chosuji · Chiail-bong · Kosŏng-ni · Kimch'aek (Songch'ŏn)

Luanne · Pingquan · Jinzhou · Jinxi · Panjin · ANSHAN · Haicheng · Anping · Kuandian · Ch'osan · Pyŏktong · Changjin-chosuji · Changjin · Kwangdaeri · Changhŭngni · Tanch'ŏn

Liugou · Shangbancheng · Xingcheng · Huludao · Tianzhuangtai · Niuzhuang · Fengcheng · Xiuyan · Sakchu · Koin-dong · Pukch'ŏng · Sinch'ang · Sŏhori

Miyun · Xinglong · Kuancheng · Suizhong · Yingkou · Dashiqiao · Gaizhou · Cao He · Uiju · Taegwan · Pukch'in · Sinp'o

Shuiku · Zunhua · Jianchangying · Shuangshanzi · Xiongyuecheng · Wanfu · Buyun Shan · Gushan · Dandong · Dongguo · Sinŭiju · Yongamp'o · Kusŏng · Kujang · Sinhŭng · Hŭngnam · Oro · Hongwon

Sanhe · Fengrun · Lulong · Qinhuangdao · Liaodong Wan · Zhuanghe · Pikou · Sŏnch'ŏn · Chŏngju · Pakch'ŏn · Anju · Yŏngwŏn · Tŏkch'ŏn · HAMHUNG · Tongch'ŏn-ni · Tongjosŏn Man

Yutian · Bodi · Changli · Leting · Pulandian · Changjŏn · Anak · Sukch'ŏn · Sunan · Sinchang-ni · Yangdŏk · Kowŏn · Munch'ŏn · SEA OF JAPAN

TANGSHAN · TIANJIN SHI · Funing · Luan Xian · Jin Xian · DALIAN · Lüshun · Kangdong · Yangdŏk · Songch'ŏn · WŎNSAN · Anbyŏn

Wuqing · Hangu · Tanggu · P'YŎNGYANG · Namp'o · Chunghwa · Kojŏ · Hoeyang · Kosŏng

Yangliuqing · TIANJIN · Dagu · Oikou · Bo Hai · Korea Bay · Cho-do · Chaeryŏng · Sariwŏn · Suan · Sinmak · Songnim · P'yŏnggang · Ch'ŏrwŏn · Sokch'o · Yangyang

Huanghua · Miaodao Qundao · Changyŏn · Sinch'ŏn · Kŭmch'ŏn · Kŭmhwa · Hwach'ŏn · Hwach'ŏn-chosuji

Yanshan · Huimin · Paengnyŏng-do · Ongjin · Haeju · Kaesŏng · Munsan · Ch'unch'ŏn · Kangnŭng

Qingyun · Wudi · Zhanhua · Longkou · Penglai · Yantai · Weihai · Ongjin · Yŏnan · Kanghwa · Uijŏngbu · SŎUL · Hongch'ŏn · Samch'ŏk

Deping · Kenli · Dongying · Laizhou Wan · Daxindian · Fushan · Muping · Chengshan Jiao · Puch'ŏn · Songnam · Hoengsŏng · Chŏngsŏn

Shanghe · Binzhou · Huang Xian · Zhaoyuan · Qixia · Wendeng · INCH'ŎN · Anyang · Wŏnju · Yŏngwŏl

Qingcheng · Gaoyuan · Guangrao · Shouguang · Laizhou · Wenden · Rongcheng · Ansan · Ich'ŏn · Yŏju · Ch'ungju · Chech'ŏn · Yŏngju · Ulchin

Jiyang · Huantai · Linzi · Changyi · Pingdu · Laixi · Laiyang · Rushan · Nanhuang · Shidao · Suwŏn · Osan · Ch'ungju

Zhoucun · ZIBO · Yidu · Weifang · Haiyang · SOUTH KOREA · P'yŏngt'aek · Ch'ŏnan · Sŏsan · Chŏngju · Yech'ŏn · Andong · Yŏngdŏk

Tai Shan · Boshan · Linqu · Anqiu · Gaomi · Lancun · Jimo · Sosan · Yesan · Hongsŏng · Kongju · Sangju · Uisong · Chŏngha

Tai'an · Laiwu · Jiaozhou · Chengyang · Anmyŏn-do · Taechŏn-ni · Nonsan · Sŏnsan · Kimch'ŏn · Kumi · P'OHANG

Xintai · Yishui · Wulian · Zhucheng · QINGDAO · Kunsan · Iri · Chŏnju · Waegwan · TAEGU · Yŏngch'ŏn · Kyŏngju

Sishui · Mengyin · Ju Xian · Liangcheng · Kunsan · Kimje · Kagang · Koryŏng · Chŏngdo · Ilsan

Pingyi · Yi He · Tangtou · Rizhao · Shijiusuo · Andongwei · Puan · Chŏngŭp · Namwŏn · Chii-san · Hamyang · Chinju · Miryang · Ulsan

Linyi · Ganyu · Haizhou Wan · HUANG HAI (Yellow Sea) · Sagŏ-ri · Masan · Kimhae · Tongnae · Sasuna

Zaozhuang · Tancheng · Haizhou · Lianyungang · KWANGJU · Hadong · Sunch'ŏn · Ch'angwŏn · PUSAN · Saka · Tsushima

Weishan Hu · Hanzhuang · Pizhou · Guanyun · Chenjiagang · Mokp'o · Posong · Pŏlgyo-ri · Yŏsu · Ch'ungmu · Izuhara

Jiawang · Xinyi · Guannan · Xiangshui · Changhŭng · Haenam · Korea Strait · Iki

Xuzhou · Yaowan · Binhai · Hüksan-chedo · Chindo · Karatsu

Shuangsou · Suqian · Shuyang · Funing · Sheyang · JAPAN · Sasebo · Imari

Suining · Lianshui · Cheju · Cheju-do · P'yŏngyŏn-ni · Nakadōri-Shima · Kashima · Omura · Isahaya

Lingbi · Hongze Hu · Huaiyin · Huai'an · Baoying · Yancheng · Hallim · Halla-san · Taejŏng · Sŏgwipo · Fukue-Shima · Nagasaki · Kuchinotsu

Suzhou · Guzhen · Wuhe · Xinghua · Liuzhuang · Mosŭlpo

Huaiyuan · Bengbu · Fengyang · Gaoyou Hu · Dongtai

SOUTHERN CHINA 1:5 300 000

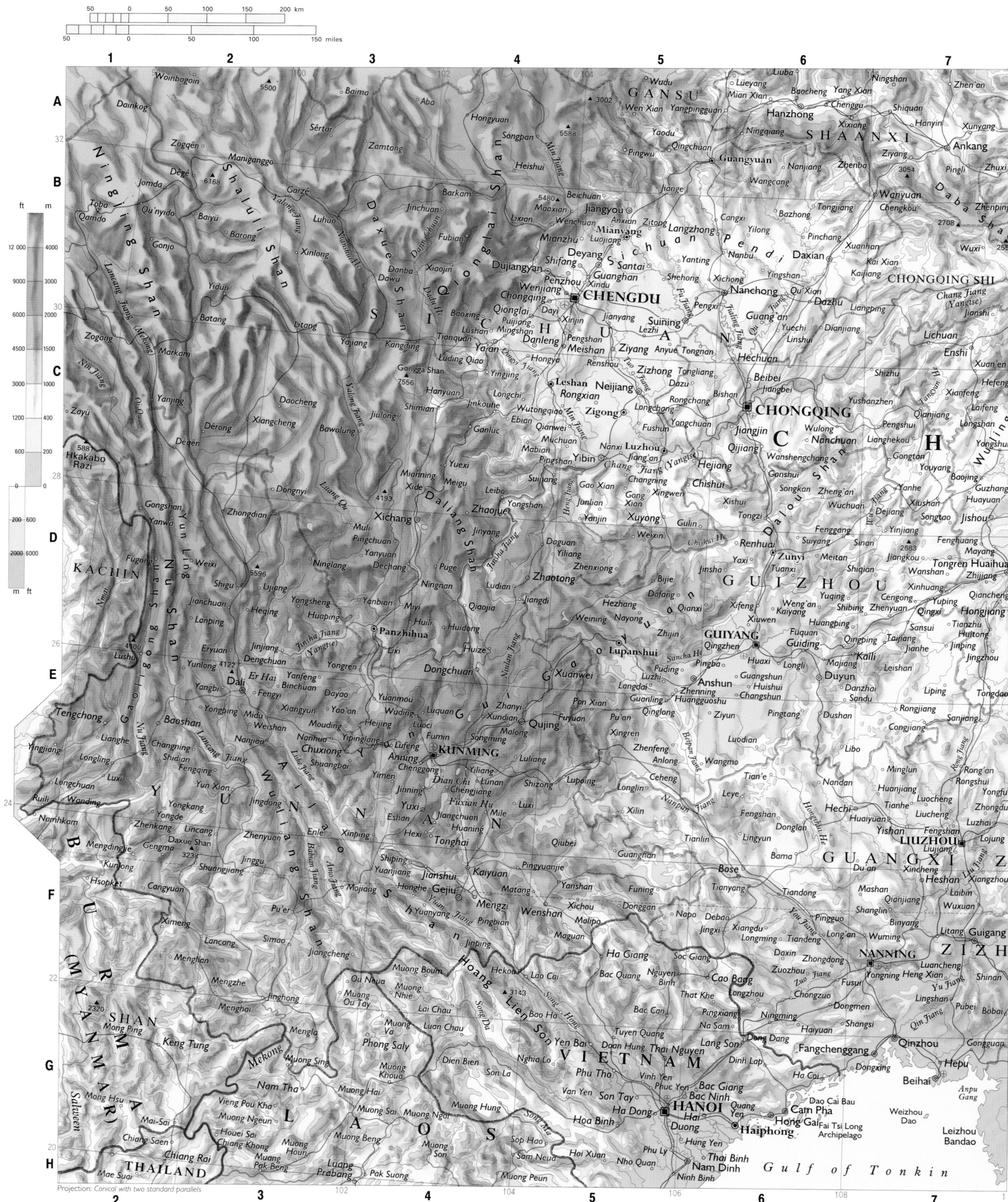
SICHUAN
CHENGDU
CHONGQING
KUNMING
GUIYANG
NANNING
HANOI
YUNNAN
GUIZHOU
GUANGXI
VIETNAM
LAOS
THAILAND
BURMA (MYANMAR)
SHAANXI
GANSU
CHONGQING SHI
Sichuan Pendi
Gulf of Tonkin
Projection: Conical with two standard parallels

8 9 10 11 12 13 14

A B C D E F G H

HENAN

JIANGSU

ANHUI

HUBEI

HUNAN

JIANGXI

ZHEJIANG

FUJIAN

GUANGDONG

HUANGZU

TAIWAN

NANJING

SHANGHAI

SHANGHAI SHI

WUHAN

HANGZHOU

NANCHANG

CHANGSHA

GUANGZHOU

HONG KONG (XIANGGANG)

T'AIPEI

KAOHSIUNG

Taiwan Strait

Luzon Strait

Tropic of Cancer

SOUTH CHINA SEA

East from Greenwich

8 9 10 11 12 13

COPYRIGHT GEORGE PHILIP LTD.

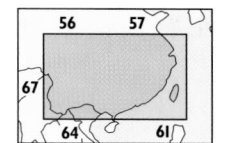

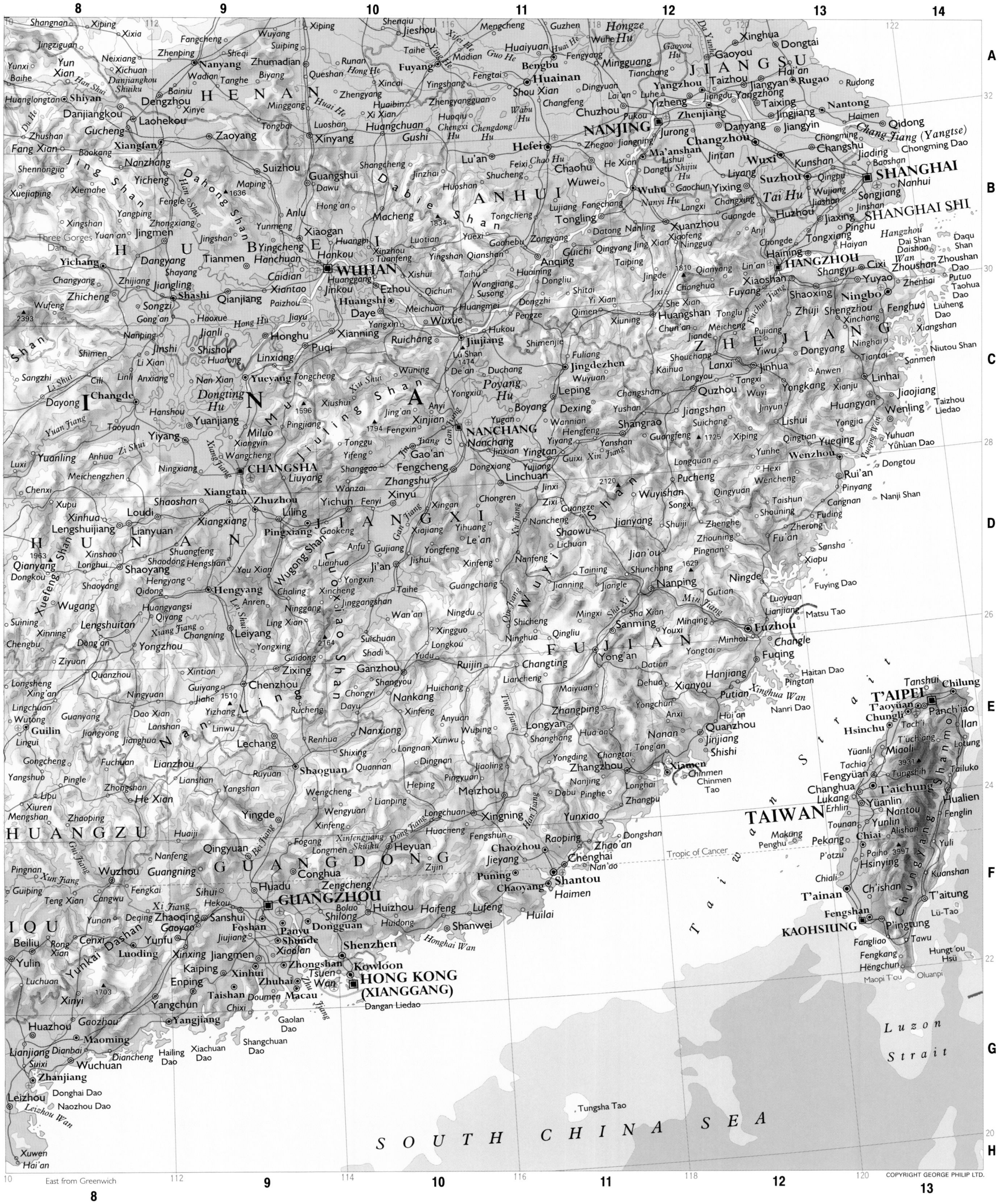

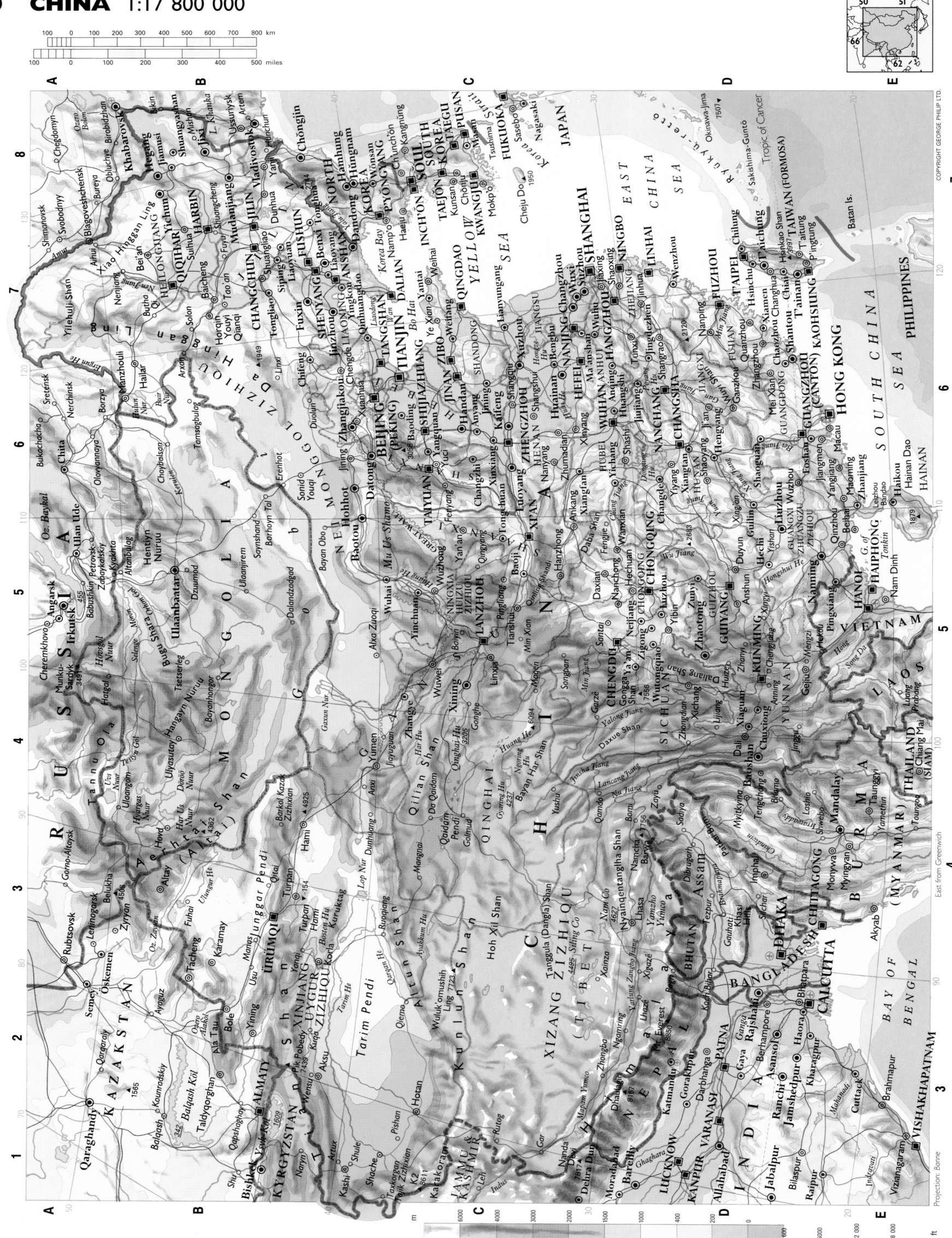
100 0 100 200 300 400 500 600 700 800 km
100 0 100 200 300 400 500 miles
RUSSIA
KAZAKSTAN
KYRGYZSTAN
MONGOLIA
CHINA
NEI MONGGOL ZIZHIQU
XINJIANG UYGUR ZIZHIQU
XIZANG ZIZHIQU (TIBET)
QINGHAI
SICHUAN
YUNNAN
JAMMU & KASHMIR
NEPAL
BHUTAN
BANGLADESH
INDIA
BURMA (MYANMAR)
THAILAND (SIAM)
LAOS
VIETNAM
PHILIPPINES
TAIWAN (FORMOSA)
NORTH KOREA
SOUTH KOREA
JAPAN
EAST CHINA SEA
SOUTH CHINA SEA
YELLOW SEA
BAY OF BENGAL
Tarim Pendi
Junggar Pendi
Kunlun Shan
Tian Shan
Qilian Shan
Altun Shan
Hoh Xil Shan
Gobi
Himalaya
BEIJING (PEKING)
SHANGHAI
TIANJIN
CHONGQING
CHENGDU
WUHAN
GUANGZHOU (CANTON)
HONG KONG
LANZHOU
ÜRÜMQI
HARBIN
SHENYANG
XI'AN
KUNMING
Lhasa
Ulaanbaatar
CALCUTTA
DHAKA
HANOI
Tropic of Cancer
Projection: Bonne
East from Greenwich
COPYRIGHT GEORGE PHILIP LTD.
m 6000 4000 3000 2000 1500 1000 400 200 0 200 2000 4000 6000
ft 18 000 12 000 9000 6000 4500 3000 1200 600 0 600 6000 12 000 18 000

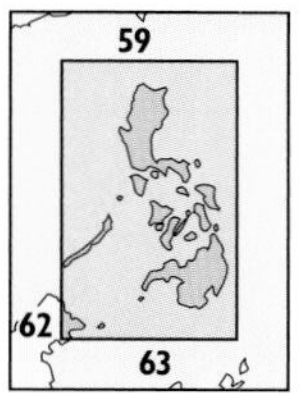

50 0 100 150 200 250 300 km
50 0 50 100 150 200 miles

A Itbayat I.
Batanes Is.
Batan I.

Balintang Channel

B Calayan I. Babuyan I.
Dalupiri I. Babuyan Camiguin I.
Islands
Mayraira Pt. Fuga I.
Babuyan Channel
Claveria Santa Ana
Bacarra Bangui Aparri Gonzaga
San Nicolas Laoag Kabugao Gattaran
C Batac 2360
Cabugao Tuao Mt. Cresta
Banued Tuguegarao 1685
Vigan Santa Lubuagan
Maria
Candon Roxas Santiago
Tagudin Bontoc
Balaoan San Mateo Ilagan
San Fernando Mt. Pulog Cordon Casiguran
2928 Solano
Baguio Bayombong
D Bolinao Rosario Mt. Anacauo C. San Ildefonso
Alaminos Dagupan 1852
Lingayen Baler Bay
San Carlos Bayambang San Manuel
Santa Cruz Moncada San Jose **Luzon**
Camiling Cuyapo Baler
Masinloc Victoria La
Iba Tarlac Paz Cabanatuan
2037 Concepcion Gapan Dingalan
1780 Angeles
San Antonio Mt. Pinatubo San Fernando Polillo Is.
Olongapo Orani Malabon Patnanongan I.
Bataan Caloocan Jomalig I.
Cavite **Quezon City**
MANILA Lamon Bay
Dasmariñas Pasay Santa Cruz Paracale
Nasugbu Tagatay San Pablo Atimonan Labo
Balayan Lipa Lucban Daet
Lemery Batangas Lucena Calauag Viga Catanduanes
Lobo Lopez Calabanga San Andres
Lubang Tayabas Bay Catanauan Naga Virac
Is. Boac Nabua Iriga
C. Calavite Marin- 2421 Tabaco
Mamburao duque Ligao Mayon Vol. Rapu Rapu I.
Mindoro Victoria Burias I. Legazpi Sorsogon
Sablayan Mt. Baco Pinamalayan *SIBUYAN* Donsol Gubat
2487 Ticao I. Magallanes
Bongabong Tablas I. Romblon Bulan San Bernardino Str.
Roxas Odiongan Sibuyan I. Irosin Allen
San Jose Aroroy Masbate
Busuanga I. Ilin I. *SEA* Mandaon Milagros
Semirara Is. Masbate Placer
Culion I. Calamian Pandan Kalibo Roxas *VISAYAN* Catbalogan
Group Dao Pilar *SEA* Bilinan I.
Linapacan Str. Tibiao 2117 Ajuy Sara Calubian
Linapacan I. **Panay** Passi Carigara
Taytay Cuyo Is. Bugasong Pototan Palompon
Cuyo Cuyo West Pass San Jose **Iloilo** Silay Cadiz Ormoc **Leyte**
Cuyo East Pass Jordan Victorias Tuburan Dulag
Palawan Guimaras 2450 San Carlos Danao Camotes Is.
Dumaran I. La Mandaue Sogod
1593 Hinigaran Carlota **Cebu**
Irahuan Honda Bay Binalbagan Guihulngan Maasin
Puerto Princesa Himamaylan Carcar Panaon I.
Kabankalan Argao Bohol I.
Cagayan Is. Sipalay Bais Oslob Tagbilaran
Mt. Mantalingajan Hinoba-an Tanjay **BOHOL**
G 2085 **Negros** Dumaguete Siquijor I. Camiguin I.
Bayawan Zamboanguita
Siaton Talisayan
C. Buliluyan *SULU* Dipolog Dapitan
Bugsuk I. *SEA* Alubijid
Balabac I. Manukan Oroquieta
Sindangan Ozamiz
Balabac Strait Labason
Balambangan Kabasalan Pagadian
Banggi Siocon Tubod
H Kudat Cagayan Sulu I. Margosatubig
Langkon Sibuca
Jembongan Datu Piang
Tenghilan Koto Belud Suba Talan Turtle Is. Kalamansig
Kota G. Kinabulu Sandakan Pangutaran Lebak
Kinabalu 4101 Group
Papar **SABAH** Jolo
Keningau Group Jolo
MALAYSIA Parang Talipao
Melalap Silam Tapul Pata I. Kiamba
J **Borneo** Kuamat Group
Banjaran Brassey Tg. Labian Siasi I.
Tawi-tawi Tapul
Group Group
Sibutu
Group

SOUTH
CHINA
SEA

PACIFIC
OCEAN

PHILIPPINES

Pandan

Lagonoy Gulf

TABLAS STRAIT

Samar
Borongan
Basey General MacArthur
Rita Guiuan
Santa Homonhon I.
Taft
Paranas
Mondragon Laoang
Catarman Gamay
Arteche
Oras
Calbayog

Leyte Gulf
Abuyog
Baybay Surigao Str.
Bato San Juan Dinagat I.
Camotes Dinagat
Sea Siargao I.
Placer 10 497
Surigao Bucas Grande I.
Mainit Carrascal
2012 Lanuza
Cabadbaran Tandag
Talisayan Nasipit Tago
Balingasag **Butuan** Bayugan Marihatag
Esperanza Lianga
Cagayan de Oro Talacogon Hinatuan
Iligan Malaybalay Bislig
2938
Marawi City Bunawan
L. Lanao Cateel
M i n d a n a o Baganga
2815 Panabo
Malabang Midsayap **Tagum** Pantukan
Illana Parang Manay
Bay Cotabato Mt. Apo Davao
Talayan Pikit 2954 **Davao**
Datu Piang Digos *Davao*
Kalamansig *Gulf* San Isidro
2083 Koronadal Malita
Palimbang **General**
Santos
Sarangani Bay C. San Agustin
Tinaca Pt.
Sarangani Is.

CELEBES
SEA

Mindanao Trench

Mindoro Strait
Verde I. Pass

INDONESIA Kep. Talaud

ft m
9000 3000
6000 2000
4500 1500
3000 1000
1200 400
600
0
200 600
4000 12 000
8000 24 000
m ft

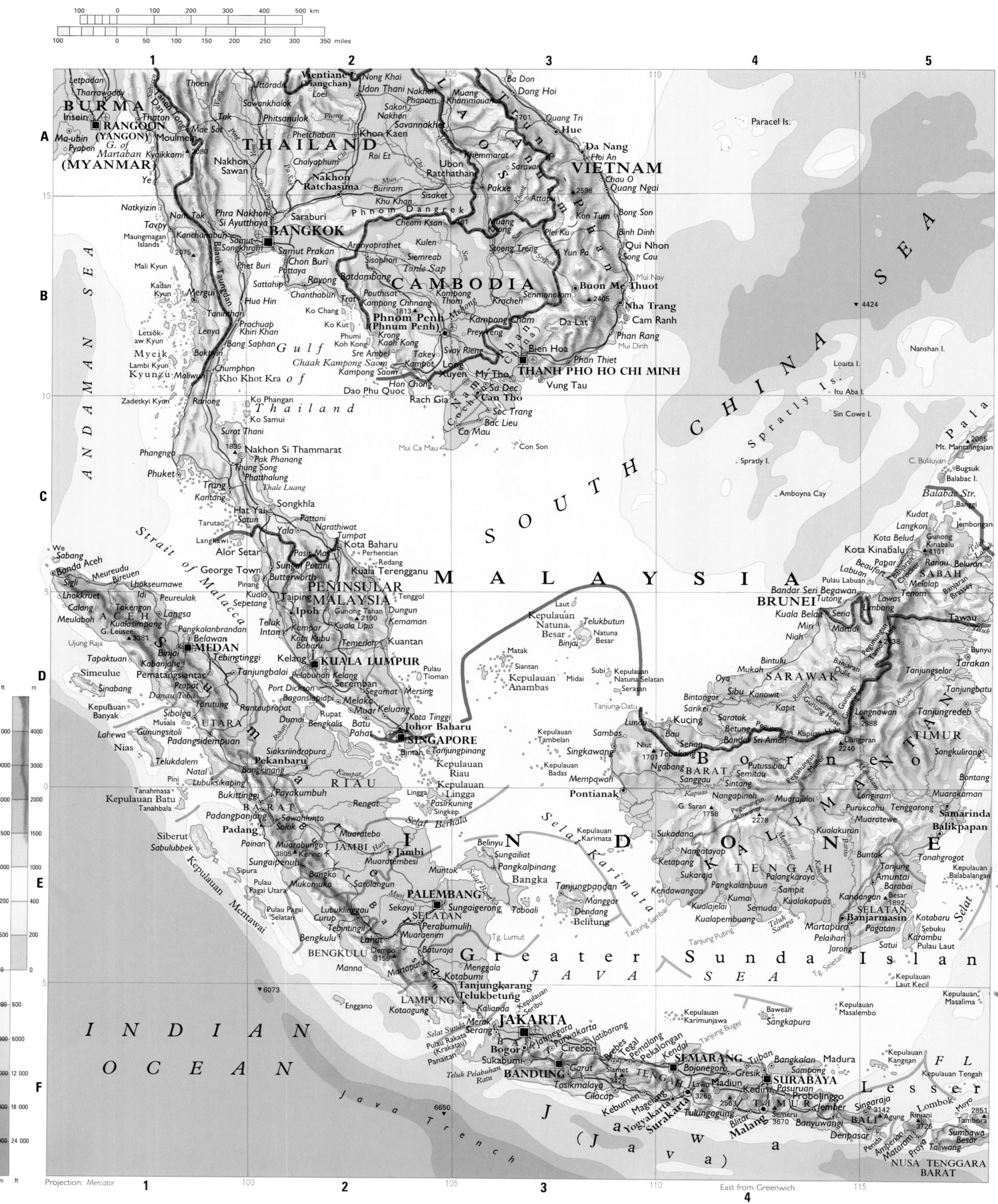
100 0 100 200 300 400 500 km
100 0 50 100 150 200 250 300 350 miles
BURMA (MYANMAR)
RANGOON (YANGON)
G. of Martaban
THAILAND
BANGKOK
LAOS
VIETNAM
CAMBODIA
Phnom Penh (Phnum Penh)
THANH PHO HO CHI MINH
Gulf of Thailand
ANDAMAN SEA
SOUTH CHINA SEA
Paracel Is.
Spratly Is.
MALAYSIA
PENINSULAR MALAYSIA
KUALA LUMPUR
SINGAPORE
Strait of Malacca
BRUNEI
SARAWAK
SABAH
Borneo
KALIMANTAN
Sumatera
MEDAN
Padang
PALEMBANG
JAKARTA
BANDUNG
SEMARANG
SURABAYA
JAVA SEA
Greater Sunda Islands
Jawa (Java)
INDIAN OCEAN
Java Trench
Selat Karimata
Kepulauan Riau
Bangka
Belitung
Lesser
Projection: Mercator
East from Greenwich

65
92
94

JAVA AND MADURA

1 : 6 700 000

50 0 50 100 150 200 250 300 km

50 0 50 100 150 200 miles

PACIFIC OCEAN

CELEBES SEA

SULU SEA

BANDA SEA

ARAFURA SEA

MOLUCCA SEA

FEDERATED STATES OF MICRONESIA

PALAU

PHILIPPINES

IRIAN JAYA

PAPUA NEW GUINEA

TIMOR TIMUR (EAST TIMOR)

Equator

COPYRIGHT GEORGE PHILIP LTD.

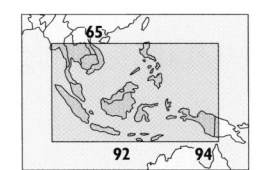

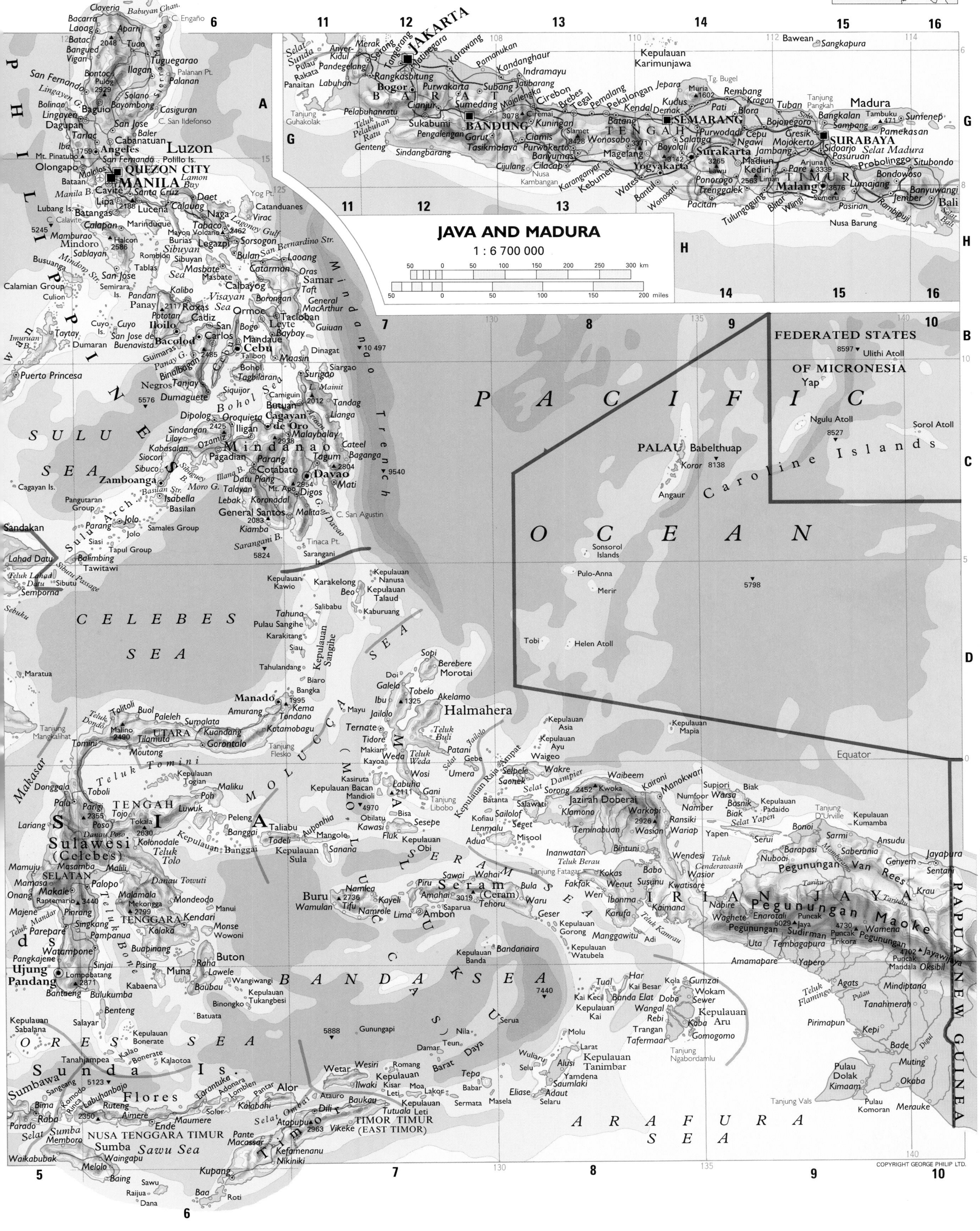

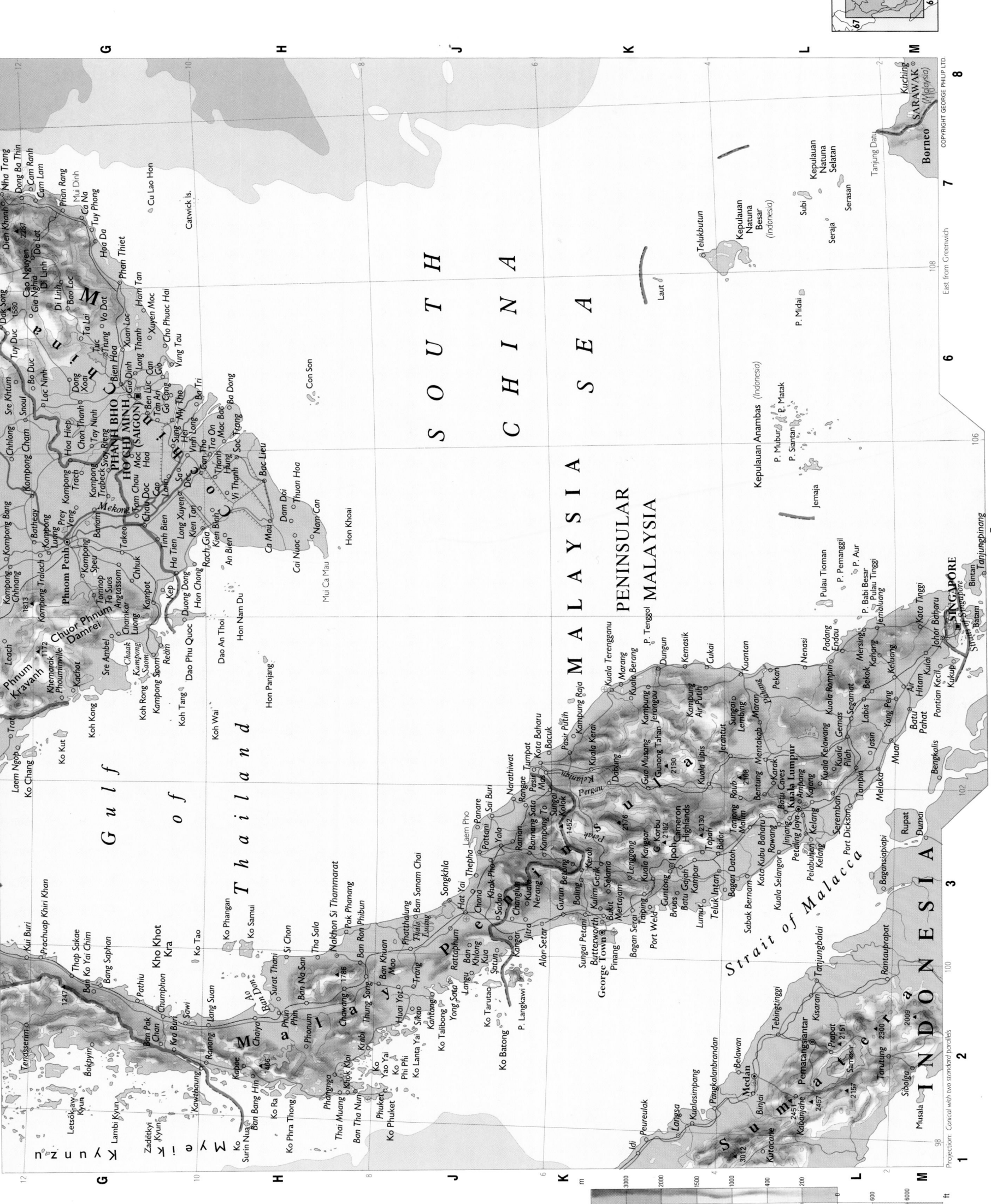

SOUTH

CHINA

SEA

MALAYSIA

PENINSULAR
MALAYSIA

Kepulauan Anambas *(Indonesia)*

Kepulauan
Natuna
Besar
(Indonesia)

SARAWAK
(Malaysia)

Borneo

Kuching

Tanjung Datu

East from Greenwich

COPYRIGHT GEORGE PHILIP LTD.

G   H   J   K   L   M

Nha Trang
Dong Ba Thin
Cam Ranh
Cam Lam
Phan Rang
Mui Dinh
Da Lat
Ca Na
Tuy Phong
Hoa Da
Phan Thiet
Phan Tan
Ham Tan

Dien Khanh
2287

Cu Lao Hon
Catwick Is.

Dak Song
1580
Cao Nguyen
Gia Nghia
Di Linh
Bao Loc
Ta Lai
Vo Dat

Sre Khtum
Loc Ninh
Ba Duc
Dong Xoai
Xuyen Moc
Xuan Loc
Cho Phuoc Hai
Vung Tau

Snoul
Chhlong
Kompong Cham
Hoa Hiep
Chon Thanh
Tay Ninh
Bien Hoa
Gio Dinh
Gia Dinh
Luc Can
Ben

Con Son

Kompong Bang
Batheay
Kompong
Luong
Prey
Veng
Kompong
Trach
Svay Rieng
Go Dau
Tan An
Go Cong
Ben Tri
Ba Dong

PHANH BHO
HO CHI MINH
(SAIGON)

Kompong Chhnang
Phnom Penh
Kompong Speu
Takeo
Tominop
Angtassom
Ta Suos
Kompot
Tan Chau
Moc Hoa
My Tho
Tra On
Soc Trang

Kompong Tralach
1813
Mekong
Banam
Trabeck
Chau Doc
Vinh Long
Hung

Kompong
Phuominville
Khemarak
1172
Chuor Phnum
Damrei
Chhuk
Kompong
Suom
Kampot
Kep
Ha Tien
Prey
Kien Tan
Long Xuyen
Deo
Can Tho
Thanh
Sa
Vi Thanh
Bac Lieu

Phnum
Kravanh
Leach
Phnum
Kcompong
Saom
Redri
Hon Chong
Rach Gia
Kien Binh
Thuan Hoa

Trat
Laem Ngop
Ko Chang
Sre Ambel
Kampong
Suam
Koh Rong
Koh Tang
Koh Wai
Duong Dong
Dao Phu Quoc
Hon Nam Du
Ca Mau
Dam Doi
Nam Can

Ko Kut
Koh Kong
Koh Tang
Koh Wai
Dao An Thoi
Hon Panjang
Cai Nuoc
Hon Khoai

Gulf

of

Thailand

Mui Ca Mau

Kui Buri
Prachuap Khiri Khan
Thap Sakae
Ban Ko Yai Chim
Bang Saphan
1247

Tenasserim
Kui Buri
Ban Pak
Chan
Chumphon
Pathiu
Lang Suan
Kra Buri
Sawi

Bokbyin
Ko Phangan
Ko Samui

Letsok-aw
Kyun
Zadetkyi
Kyun
Lambi Kyun

Kawthaung
Ranong
Kapoe
1465
Surin Nua

Ko Ra
Ban Bang Hin
Phangnga
Thai Muang
Phuket
Ko Phuket
Ko Yao Yai
Ko Phi Phi
Ko Lanta Yai

M
y
e
i
k
Archipelago

Ban Na San
Surat Thani
1786
Ban Ron Phibun
Phunphin
Chaiya

Si Chon
Tha Sala
Nakhon Si Thammarat
Pak Phanang

P
h
u
k
e
t

Kho Khot
Kra

Ko Tao

Ban Don
Ban Na San

Thai Ban Sanam Chai

Ban Khuan
Mao
Trang
Huai Yot
Sikao
Kantang

Phatthalung
Songkhla

Ko Lanta Yai
Yong Satta
Ko Tarutao
P. Langkawi
Ko Batong

Thale Luang

Pattani
Yala
Narathiwat
Tumpat
Kota Baharu
Pasir Putih

Peninsular

Ban Sanam Chai
Hat Yai
Sadao

Khlong
Satun
Kangar
Alor Setar

Chana
Khok Pho
Laem Pho

Rangae
Sungai
Kolok
Sungai Padi

Kampung Raja
Kuala Terengganu
Kuala Berang

Marang
Dungun
Kemasik
Cukai

MALAYSIA

Kulim
Butterworth
George Town
Pinang
Bagan Serai
Port Weld

Jitra
Sungai Petani

Grik
Baling
Gurun

Kroh
Selama
Kuala Kangsar
Taiping

Keroh
Pergau
1452
Banang Sata
Kampong To
Betong

Kota Baharu
Baculk

Kuala Kerai
Gunong Tahan
2190

Bacuk

Jerangau

Kuala
Kerau

Ipoh
Batu Gajah
Kampar
Tapah
Teluk Intan

Kuala Lumpur
Petaling Jaya
Port Kelang
Kelang

Gua Musang
Korbu
2176
Cameron
Highlands
2182
2130
Raub
Bentung
Batu Caves
Ampang
Kajang

Jerantut
Temerloh
Mentakab
Karak

Kuala Lipis
2608

Kuantan
Pekan

Padang
Endau
Pulau Tinggi

Seremban
Tampin
Melaka

Kuala Pilah
Bidor
Tapah

Jinjang
Rawang
Kajang

Jasin
Muar

Bahau
Labis
Yong Peng
Batu
Pahat
Bengkalis

Gemas
Segamat
Bekok
Kluang
Keluang

Kuala Rompin
Nenasi

Mersing
P. Babi Besar
Pulau Tinggi
Jemaluang

Air
Hitam
Pontian Kecil
Kukup

Kulai
Johor Baharu
SINGAPORE
Singapore

Kota Tinggi
Bintan
Tanjungpinang

Batu
Pahat

Rupat
Dumai

Bagansiapiapi

Strait of Malacca

Tanjungbalai
Rantauprapat

Kualasimpang
Langsa
Tebingtinggi
2008

di
Peureulak

Pangkalanbrandan
Belawan
Medan
Binjai

Pematangsiantar
2457
Prapat
2151
Samosir
2157

Kutacane
Kabanjahe
2451

INDONESIA

Musala
Sibolga
3012
2300

S
u
m
a
t
e
r
a

Projection: Conical with two standard parallels

ft   m
9000
6000
4500
3000
1500
1200
600
400
200
0
m   ft

P. Tenggol
P. Mubur
P. Matak
P. Siantan
Jemaja
Laut
P. Midai
Subi
Seraja
Serasan

Pulau Toman
P. Pemanggil
P. Aur
Telukbutun

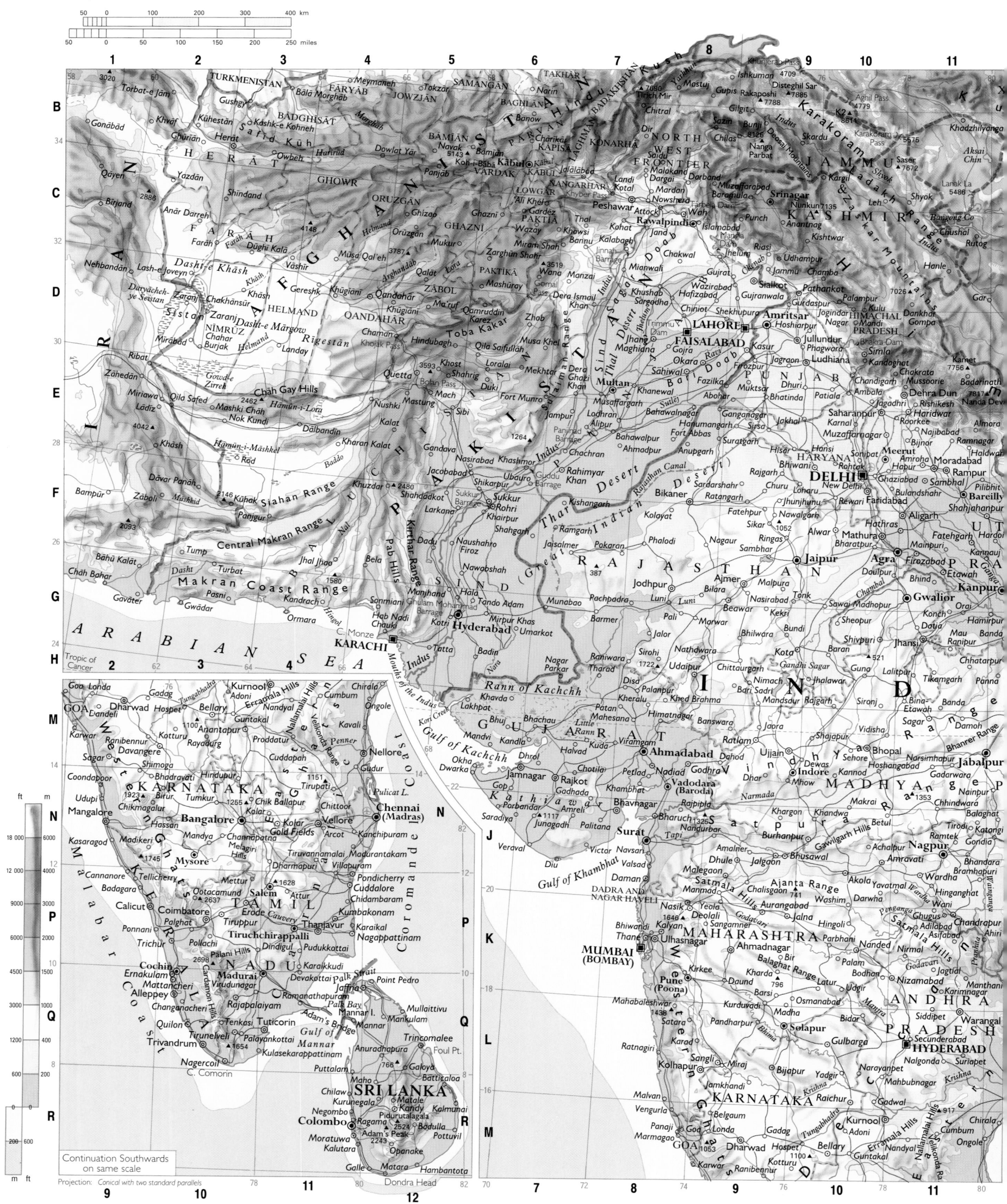

50 0   100   200   300   400 km

50 0   50   100   150   200   250 miles

Continuation Southwards
on same scale

Projection: Conical with two standard parallels

CHINA
XIZANG (TIBET)
QINGHAI
SICHUAN
YUNNAN
NEPAL
SIKKIM
BHUTAN
ARUNACHAL PRADESH
ASSAM
MEGHALAYA
NAGALAND
MANIPUR
MIZORAM
TRIPURA
BANGLADESH
East Bengal
DHAKA
WEST BENGAL
BIHAR
ORISSA
BURMA (MYANMAR)
KACHIN
SAGAING
CHIN
MAGWE
ARAKAN
SHAN
KAYAH
PEGU
IRRAWADDY
TENASSERIM
THAILAND
Huh Xil Shan
Bayan Har Shan
Tanggula (Dangla) Shan
Nganglong Kangri
Gangdisê Shan
Nyainqentanglha Shan
Siwalik Range
Arakan Yoma
Pegu Yoma
Kawthule
Tanen Tong Dan
BAY OF BENGAL
INDIAN OCEAN
G. of Martaban
Mouths of the Ganges
Mouths of the Irrawaddy
Preparis North Channel
Preparis South Channel
Arakan Coast
Northern Circars
Brahmaputra
Yarlung Zangbo Jiang
Ganga
Irrawaddy
Chindwin
Salween
Mekong
Nu Jiang
Lancang Jiang
Jinsha Jiang
Lhasa
Xigazê
Gyangzê
Nagqu
Qamdo
Yushu
Kathmandu
Mt. Everest 8850
Kanchenjunga 8598
Dhaulagiri 8172
Xixabangma Feng 8013
Thimphu
Gangtok
Darjiling
Shillong
Cherrapunji
Gauhati
Imphal
Kohima
Lucknow
Varanasi
Allahabad
Patna
Gaya
Dhanbad
Ranchi
Jamshedpur
Durgapur
CALCUTTA
Haora
Khulna
Chittagong
Cox's Bazar
Cuttack
Bhubaneshwar
Puri
Berhampur
Vishakhapatnam
Vizianagaram
Rajahmundry
Kakinada
Vijayawada
Machilipatnam
Raipur
Sittwe (Akyab)
Ramree I.
Cheduba I.
Mandalay
Myitkyina
Bhamo
Lashio
Taunggyi
Meiktila
Prome
Bassein
RANGOON
Moulmein
Martaban
Amherst
Ye
Tavoy
Moscos Is.
Coco Channel
Paripait Kyun (Burma)
Koko Kyunzu (Burma)
Chiang Mai
Lampang
Tak
Hkakabo Razi 5881
East from Greenwich
B C D E F G H J K L M
12 13 14 15 16 17 18 19 20 21 22

COPYRIGHT GEORGE PHILIP LTD.

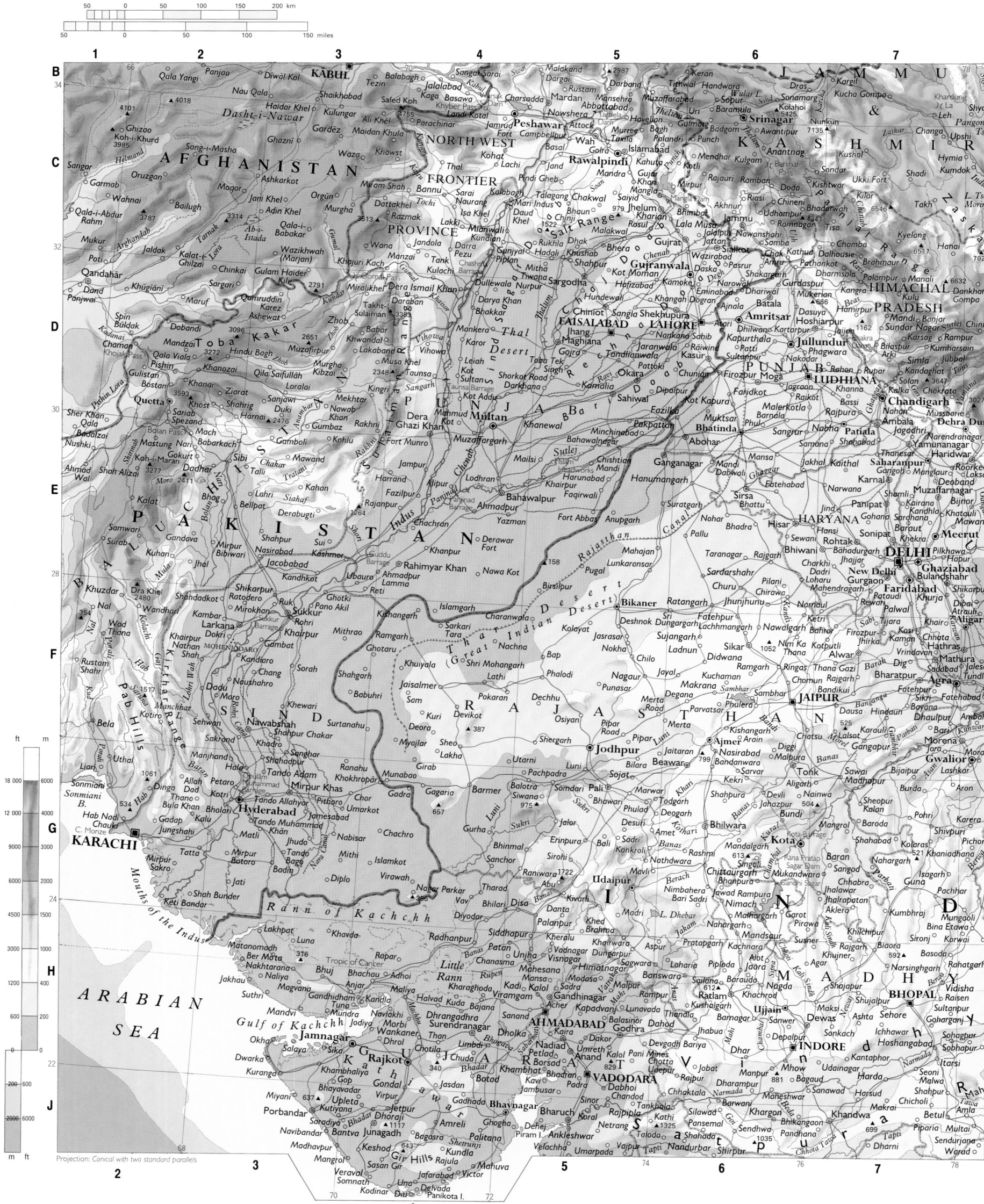
AFGHANISTAN
PAKISTAN
BALUCHISTAN
NORTH WEST FRONTIER PROVINCE
PUNJAB
SIND
RAJASTHAN
GUJARAT
MADHYA PRADESH
HARYANA
HIMACHAL PRADESH
JAMMU & KASHMIR
INDIA
ARABIAN SEA
KARACHI
KABUL
DELHI
New Delhi
JAIPUR
AHMADABAD
INDORE
BHOPAL
LAHORE
FAISALABAD
LUDHIANA
Multan
Hyderabad
Rawalpindi
Islamabad
Peshawar
Quetta
Srinagar
Amritsar
Jodhpur
Udaipur
Rajkot
Jamnagar
Vadodara
Bhavnagar
Chandigarh
Agra
Gwalior
Kota
Ajmer
Bikaner
Sukkur
Thar Desert (Great Indian Desert)
Rann of Kachchh
Gulf of Kachchh
Mouths of the Indus
Salt Range
Thal Desert
Kirthar Range
Pab Hills
Toba Kakar
Dasht-i-Nawar
Projection: Conical with two standard parallels
Tropic of Cancer

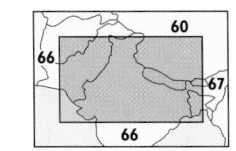

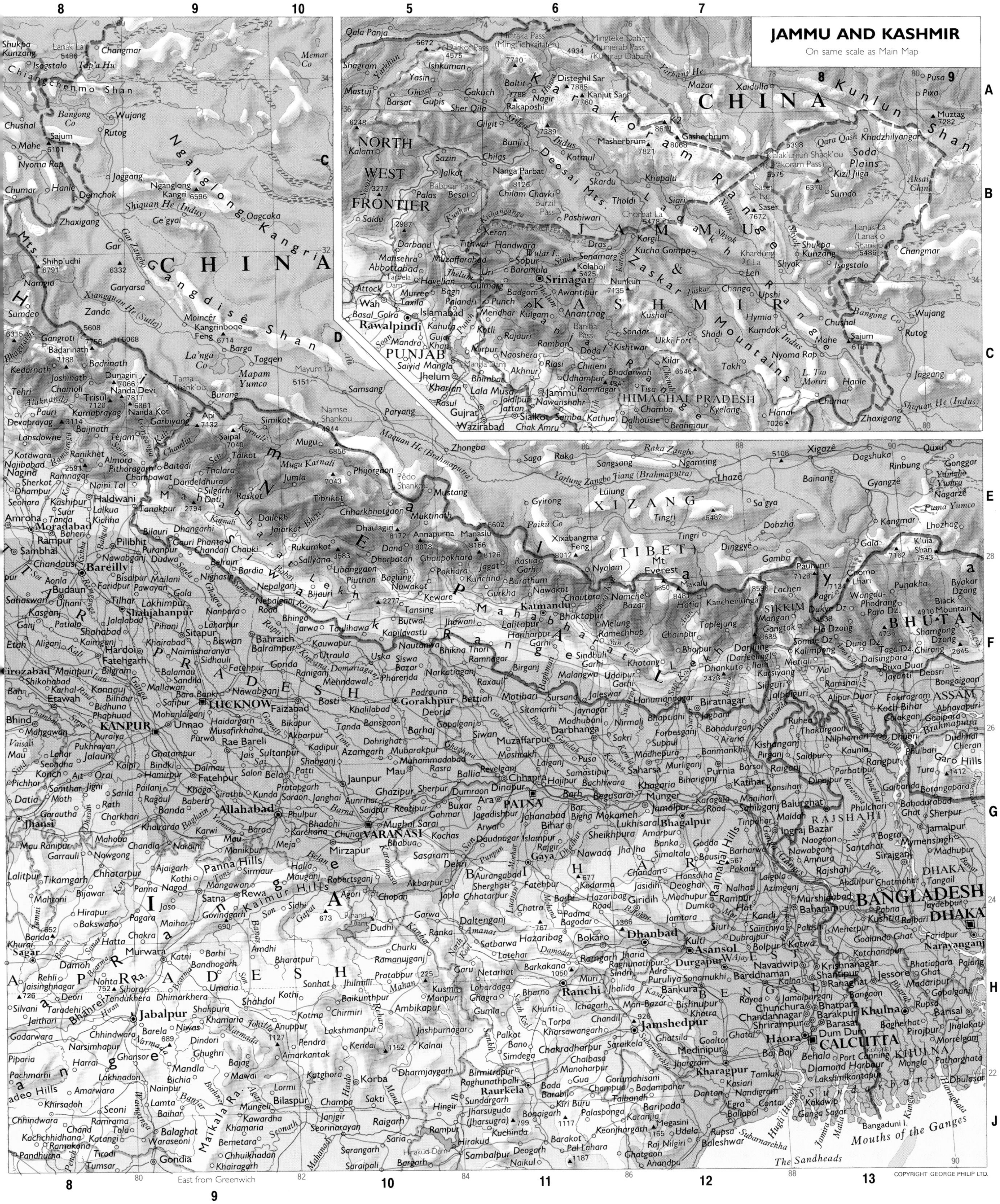

JAMMU AND KASHMIR
On same scale as Main Map

COPYRIGHT GEORGE PHILIP LTD.

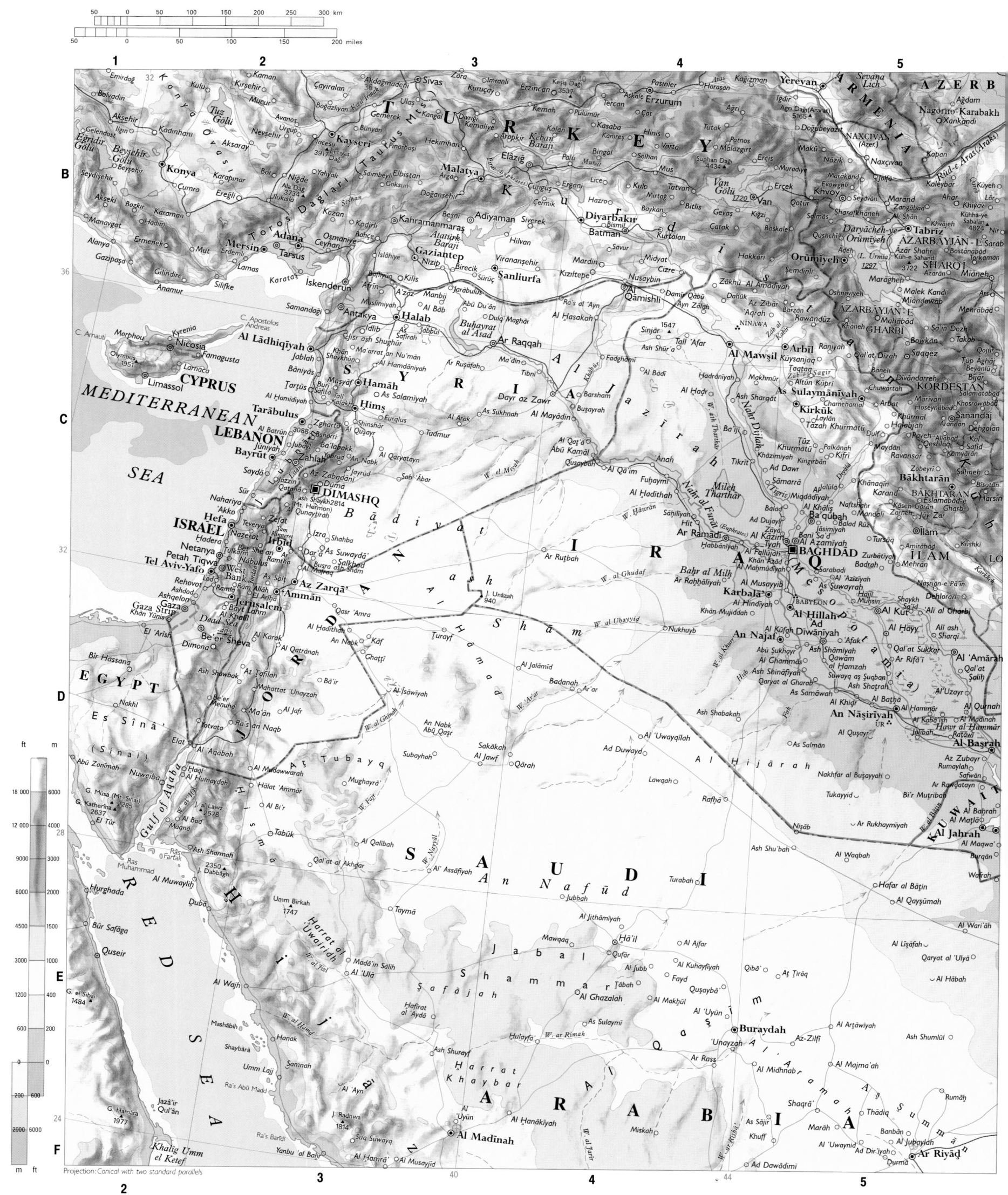

50 0 50 100 150 200 250 300 km
50 0 50 100 150 200 miles

MEDITERRANEAN SEA

RED SEA

EGYPT

ISRAEL

LEBANON

CYPRUS

JORDAN

SAUDI ARABIA

SYRIA

TURKEY

IRAQ

ARMENIA

AZERB

KUWAIT

Projection: Conical with two standard parallels

49
50
72
66
80
74

6 7 8 9 10

B C D E F

TURKMENISTAN

Kara Kum

CASPIAN SEA

IRAN

AFGHANISTAN

PAKISTAN

THE GULF

Gulf of Oman

QATAR

BAHRAIN

UNITED ARAB EMIRATES

OMAN

East from Greenwich

6 7 8 9

COPYRIGHT GEORGE PHILIP LTD.

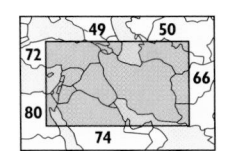

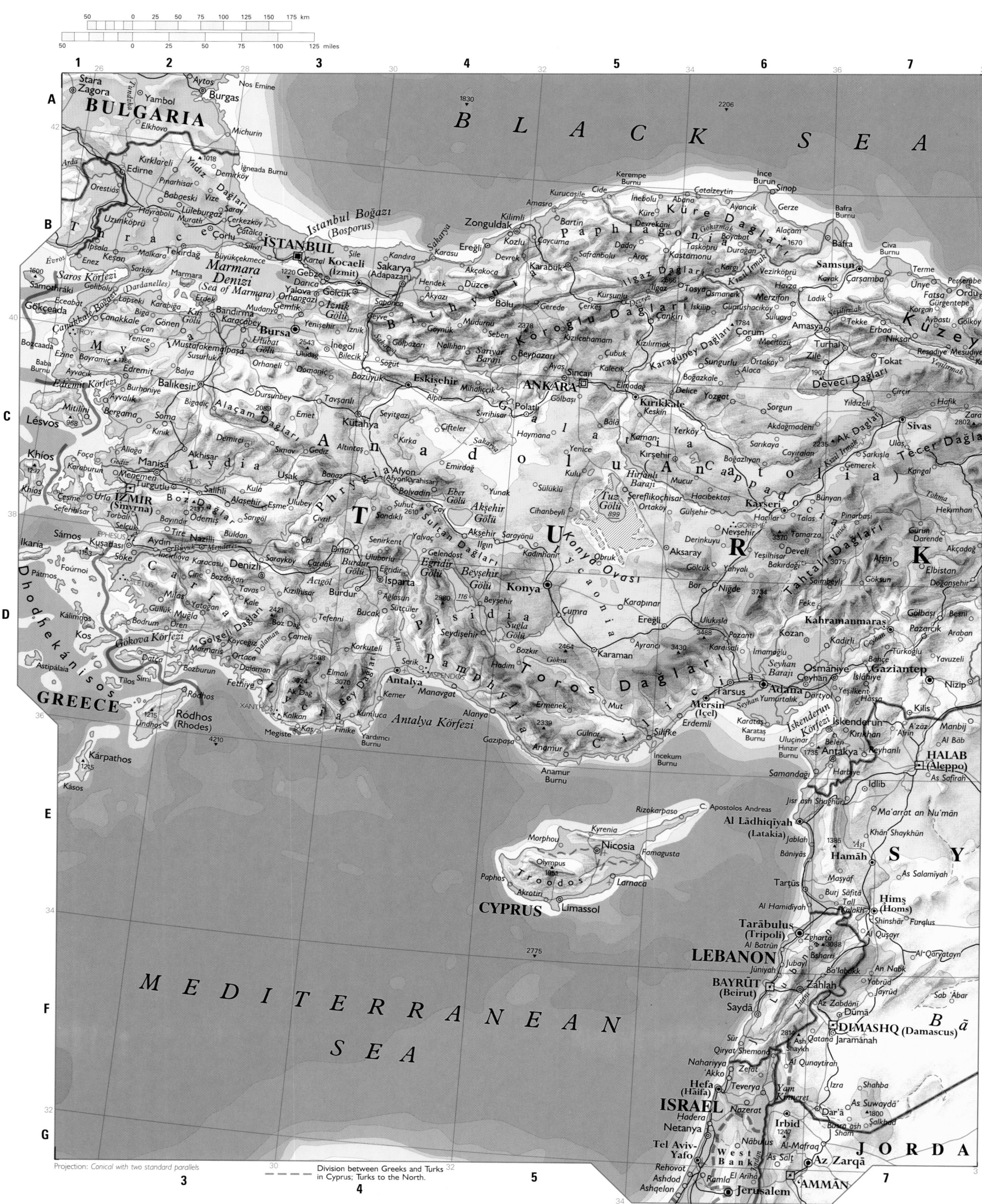

Projection: Conical with two standard parallels

Division between Greeks and Turks in Cyprus; Turks to the North.

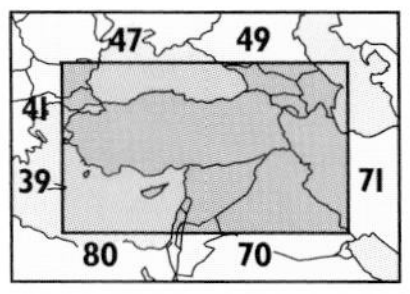

CASPIAN SEA

RUSSIA

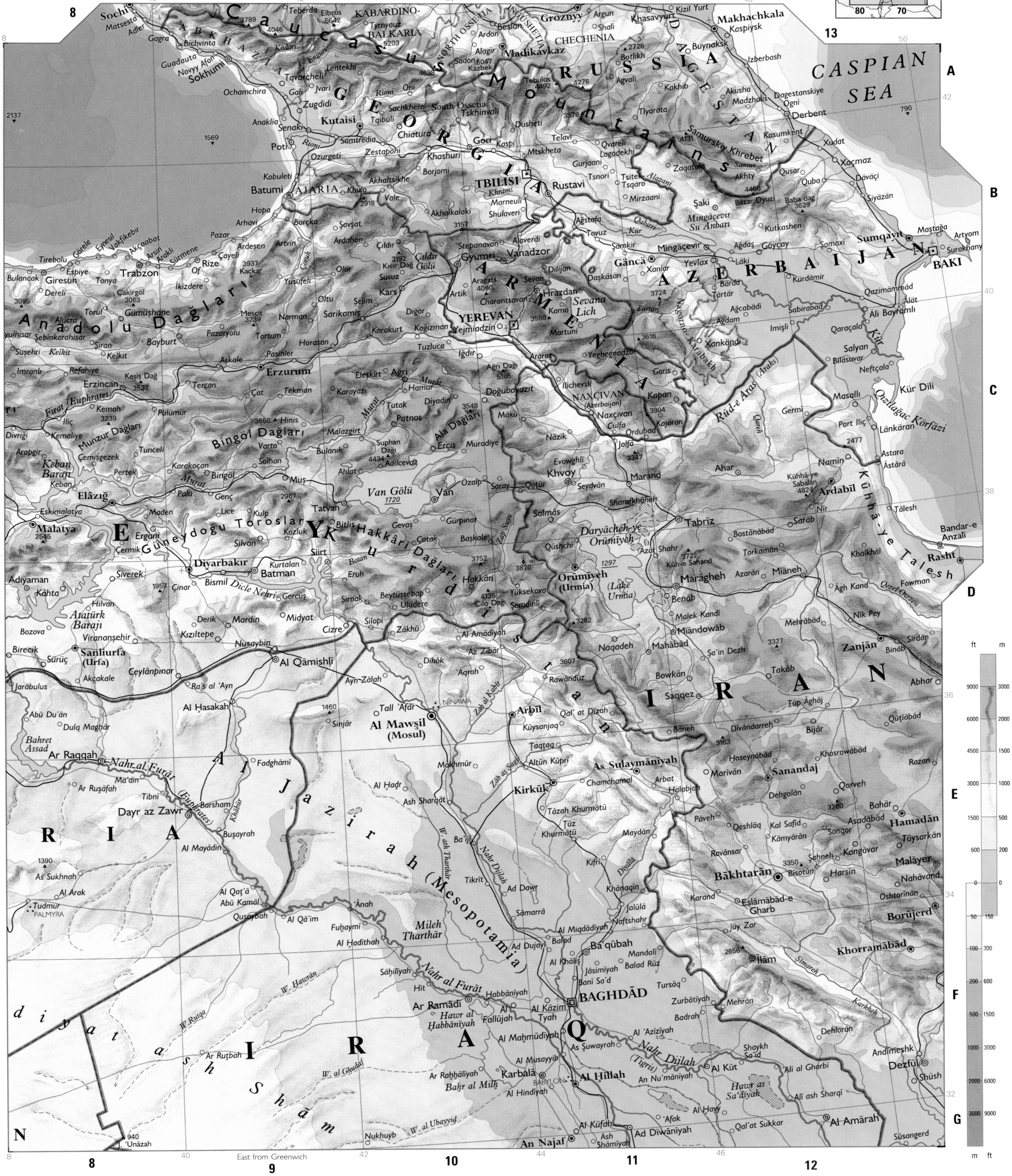

GEORGIA

Caucasus Mountains

ARMENIA

AZERBAIJAN

TBILISI

YEREVAN

BAKI

TURKEY

IRAN

IRAQ

SYRIA

BAGHDAD

Mesopotamia

Al Jazirah (Mesopotamia)

Van Gölü

Daryācheh-ye Orūmīyeh (Lake Urmia)

Anadolu Dağları

Güneydoğu Toroslar

Hakkâri Dağları

Kurdistan

Sochi • Matsesta • Adler • Gagra • Bichvinta • Guadauta • Novyy Afon • Sokhumi • Ochamchira • Gali • Zugdidi • Anaklia • Senaki • Poti • Kobuleti • Batumi • Kutaisi

Elbrus 5642 • KABARDINO-BALKARIA • Teberda • Tyrnyauz 4046 • 5203 • NORTH OSSETIA • Beslan • INGUSHETIA • Groznyy • Argun • Khasavyurt • Kizil Yurt • Makhachkala • Kaspiysk • Izberbash

Vladikavkaz • Kazbek 5047 • CHECHENIA • Shali • Buynaksk • 2726 • Botlikh • DAGESTAN • Derbent

TBILISI • Rustavi • Marneuli • Gyumri • Vanadzor • Sevan • Sevana Lich • Gäncä • Mingäçevir • Yevlax • Şamaxi • Sumqayıt • BAKI • Surakhany

Erzurum • Erzincan • Elâzığ • Diyarbakır • Batman • Malatya • Şanlıurfa (Urfa) • Mardin • Nusaybin • Al Qāmishlī • Al Ḥasakah • Ar Raqqah • Dayr az Zawr • Tabrīz • Orūmīyeh (Urmīa) • Marāgheh • Mīāneh • Zanjān • Ardabīl • Rasht • Bandar-e Anzalī

Al Mawşil (Mosul) • Arbīl • Kirkūk • As Sulaymānīyah • Sanandaj • Hamadān • Bākhtarān • Khorramābād • Borūjerd

BAGHDAD • Ar Ramādī • Al Fallūjah • Karbalā' • Al Ḥillah • An Najaf • BABYLON • Al Kūt • Al ʿAmārah • Dezfūl

East from Greenwich

PALMYRA • Tudmur

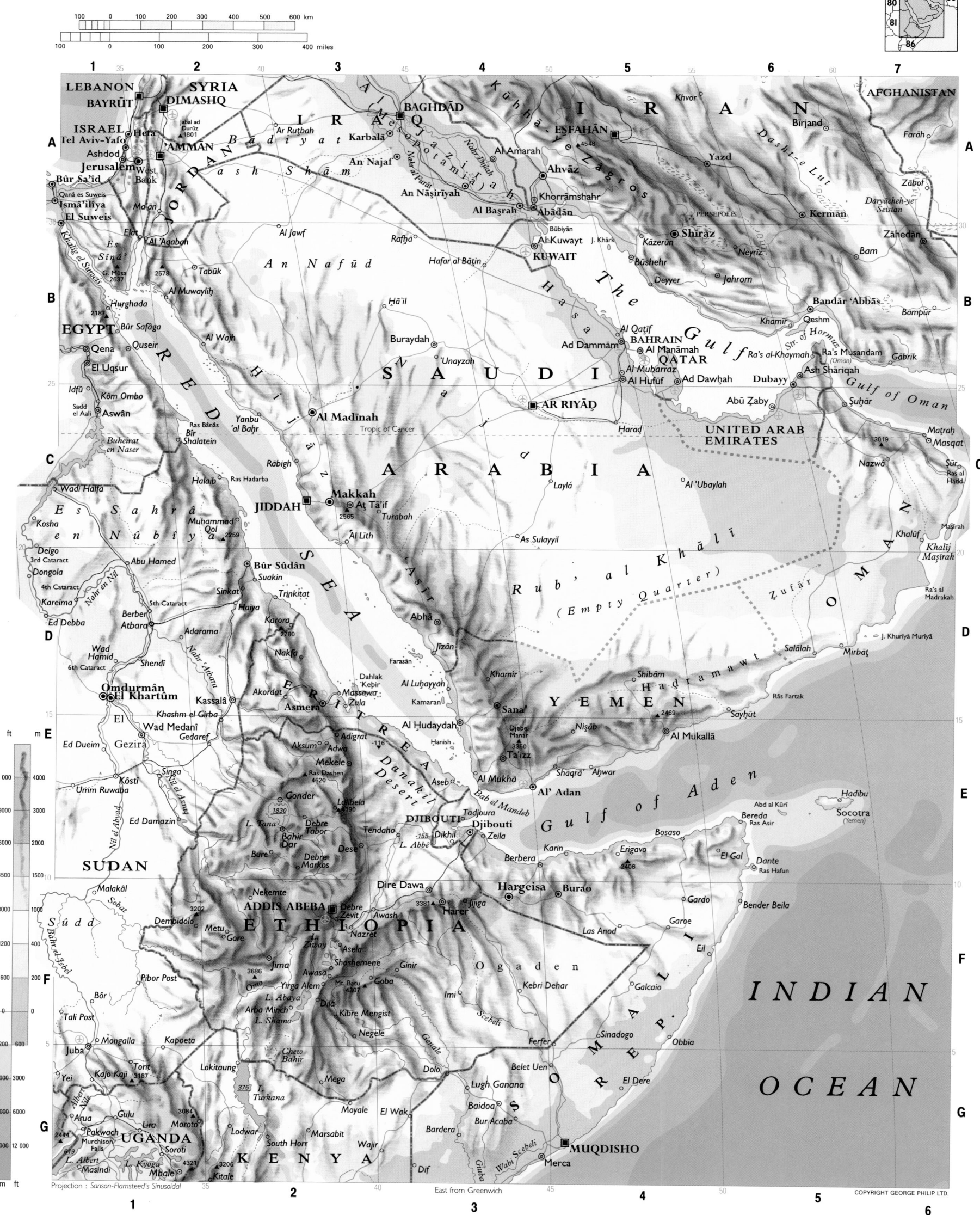

100 0 100 200 300 400 500 600 km
100 0 100 200 300 400 miles

LEBANON SYRIA
BAYRŪT DIMASHQ
ISRAEL 'AMMĀN Jabal ad Durūz 1801
Tel Aviv-Yafo Hefa
Ashdod Jerusalem West Bank
Būr Sa'īd Qanā es Suweis Ma'ān
Ismā'iliya
El Suweis Elat Al 'Aqabah
Khalīg el Suweis Es Sina' G. Mūsa 2637
2578 Tabūk
Hurghada Al Muwayliḥ
Būr Safāga
EGYPT Qena Quseir Al Wajh
Idfū Ras Bānās
Kōm Ombo Bīr Yanbu 'al Baḥr
Aswān Shalatein
Sadd el Aali Muhammad Qol 2259
Buheirat en Naser Halaib Ras Hadarba
Wadi Halfa Rābigh
Kosha Halā'ib
Delgo 3rd Cataract
Dongola 4th Cataract Makkah
Nahr en Nīl Abu Hamed JIDDAH Aţ Ţā'if 2565
Kareima 5th Cataract Ās Līth Turabah
Ed Debba Berber Atbara
Wad Hamid Adarama Sinkat Trinkitat
6th Cataract Shendī Haiya
Khashm el Girba Karora 2780
Nahr 'Atbara Nakfa Jīzān
El Omdurmān Kassalâ Akordat Farasān
El Khartūm Adigrat Dahlak Kebir
Wad Medanî Asmera Massawa Al Luḥayyah
Gedaref Zula Kamaran
SUDAN Aksum Adwa Al Ḥudaydah
Ed Dueim El Obeid Mekele Ḥanīsh
Umm Ruwaba Gezira Ras Dashen 4620 Ta'izz
Kôsti Singa Lalibela 4190 Al Mukhā
Gonder 1830 Bab el Mandeb
Debre Tabor Djibouti Zeila
Ed Damazin Bahir Dar Aseb
Bure DJIBOUTI
Malakāl Dese Tadjoura
ADDIS ABEBA Debre Dikhil L. Abbé
Nekemte Zevit Awash
Dembidola 3202 Nazret 3381
ETHIOPIA Harer Jijiga
Metu Gore Asela Dire Dawa
Jima Shashemene HARGEISA Burao
3686 Ginir
Pibor Post L. Ziway Goba
Bōr Yirga Alem Mt. Batu 4307
Arba Minch Dilo Kebri Dehar
L. Abaya Kibre Mengist Imi
L. Shamo Negele
Mongalla Chew Genale Galcaio
Juba Kapoeta Bahir Dolo
Yei Kajo Kaji 3187 Mega El Wak
Lokitaung Moyale Bur Acaba
375 L. Turkana Bardera
Arua Gulu Lira 3084 Lodwar Wajir
2444 Pakwach Moroto South Horr Marsabit Dif
819 Murchison Falls Soroti Kitale MUQDISHO
L. Albert Masindi UGANDA Mbale 4321 3206 KENYA Merca
L. Kyoga

IRAQ
BAGHDĀD Ar Ruţbah
Karbalā Nahr Dijlah
An Najaf Al Amarah
An Nāşirīyah Nahr al Furāt
Kūhhā-ye Zagros
ESFAHĀN 4548
Ahvāz
IRAN Yazd
Khorramshahr
Al Başrah Ābādān Kermān
Al Kuwayt Bīrjand
KUWAIT J. Khārk Zābol
Būbiyān Farāh
Kāzerūn Daryācheh-ye Seistan
Būshehr Shīrāz AFGHANISTAN
Hafar al Bāţin Deyyer Jahrom Neyrīz
Rafḥā Bam
Al Jawf Zāhedān
An Nafūd
Ḥā'il Bandar 'Abbās
Khamīr Qeshm Bampur
Burayda Al Qaţīf Ras al-Khaymah Ra's Musandam (Oman) Gābrik
'Unayzah Ad Dammān BAHRAIN Str. of Hormuz
SAUDI Al Manāmah QATAR Dubayy Ash Shāriqah
Al Mubarraz Ra's al Hadd Şuḥār
Al Hufūf Ad Dawḥah Abū Ẓaby Gulf of Oman
AR RIYĀḌ UNITED ARAB EMIRATES 3019 Maţraḥ Masqaţ
Tropic of Cancer Ḥaraḍ Nazwā Şūr Ras al Hadd
ARABIA OMAN
Layla Al 'Ubaylah Khalūf
As Sulayyil Khalīj Maşīrah
Rub' al Khālī Maşīrah
(Empty Quarter) Zufār
Khamir Shibām Salālah Mirbāţ
Sana' Nişāb Ra's al Madrakah
Djebel Manar 3350 2469 J. Khuriyā Mūriyā
YEMEN Al Mukallā
Shaqrā Aḥwar Sayḥūt Rās Fartak
Al' Adan Hadibu Socotra (Yemen)
Gulf of Aden Abd al Kūrī Bereda Ras Asir
Bosaso Dante
Karin Erigavo 2406 Ras Hafun
Berbera El Gal
Gardo Bender Beila
Las Anod Garoe
Ogaden Eil
Ferfer Obbia
Scebeli Sinadogo
Belet Uen El Dere
Lugh Ganana
SOMALI REP.
Baidoa
Juba
Wabi Scebeli

INDIAN OCEAN

ft m
12 000 4000
9000 3000
6000 2000
4500 1500
3000 1000
1200 400
600 200
0 0
200 600
1000 3000
2000 6000
4000 12 000
m ft

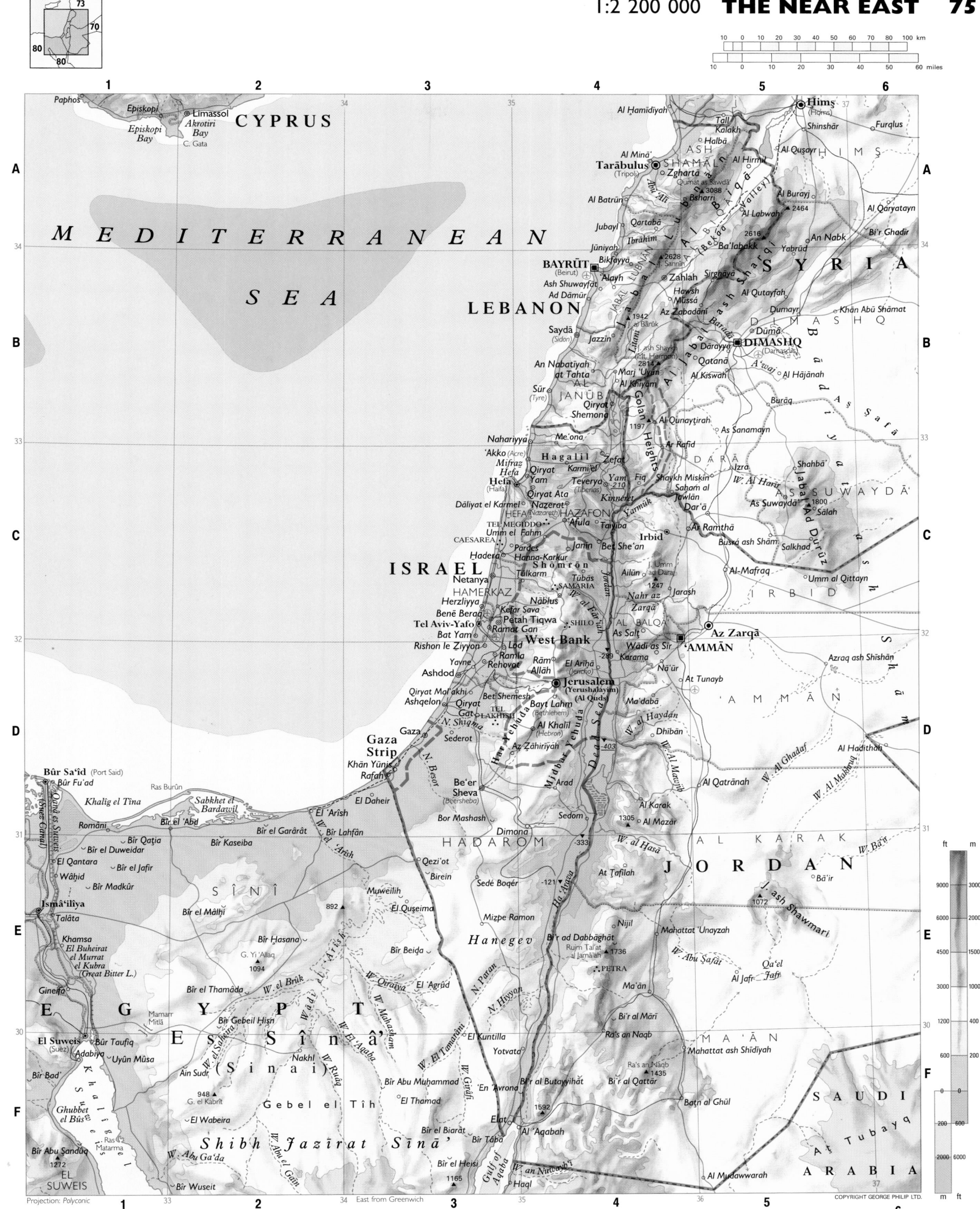

73
70
80
80

10 0 10 20 30 40 50 60 70 80 100 km
10 0 10 20 30 40 50 60 miles

1 **2** **3** **4** **5** **6**

CYPRUS

Paphos
Episkopi
Akrotiri
Bay
Episkopi
Bay
Limassol
C. Gata

Al Hamidiyah
Tall
Kalakh
Shinshār
Furqlus

● Hims
(Homs)
37

A Halbā ASH
Tarābulus ◉ SHAMĀL Al Hirmil
(Tripoli) Zgharta Al Quṣayr Al Qaryatayn **A**
Al Batrūn Qumat as Sawdā' ▲3088 Al Burayj
Qartaba Bsharri Al Labwah ▲2464
Jubayl Ibrāhīm 2616 An Nabk Bi'r Ghadir
Jūniyah Bikfayyā Ba'labakk Yabrūd

M E D I T E R R A N E A N
34 ▲2628 34
Sannin
BAYRŪT Sirghāyā **S Y R I A**
(Beirut) Alayh Zahlah
Ash Shuwayfāt Hawsh Al Qutayfah
S E A Ad Dāmūr Mūssá Khān Abū Shāmat
Az Zabadānī Dumayr DIMASHQ
1942 al Bārūk Darayyā ◉ **DIMASHQ**
LEBANON Saydā ▲2814 ◉ (Damascus)
B (Sidon) Ash Shaykh Al Khiyām Qaṭanā A'waj Al Hājānah **B**
Jazzin (Mt. Hermon) Marj 'Uyūn Al Kiswah
An Nabaṭīyah Burāq
at Tahta AL Al Quṇayṭirah As Sanamayn
Sūr JANŪB 1197 As Safā
(Tyre) Qiryat Ar Rafid DARĀ
33 Naharīyya Me'ona Shemona Golan Izra Shahbā' As SUWAYDĀ 33
'Akko (Acre) Zefat Heights W. Al Harīr ▲1800
Mifraz Karmi'el Shaykh Miskin Jabal Ad Durūz
Hefa Qiryat Teverya Fiq Sāḥam al Salkhad Ad
Hefa Yam (Tiberias) Kinneret Jawlān As Suwaydā ● Sālah
(Haifa) Qiryat Ata Yam ▲210 Yarmūk Dar'ā
Dāliyat el Karmel Nazerat Al Ramthā
C TEL MEGIDDO Afula Tayiba Irbid ● Umm al Qittayn **C**
CAESAREA Umm el Fahm HAZAFON Busrā ash Shām
Hadera Pardes Janin Bet She'an Ailūn Umm al-Mafraq
Hanna-Karkur Tulkarm ad Daraj Umm al Qittayn
ISRAEL Shōmrōn SAMARIA Jordan 1247 Jarash **I R B I D**
Netanya Tūbās Nahr az Jarash
HAMERKAZ Nāblus Zarqā'
Herzliyya Kefar Sava
Benē Beraq Petah Tiqwa SHILO AL BALQĀ Az Zarqā
32 Tel Aviv-Yafo Ramat Gan West Bank As Salt ◉ **AMMĀN** **32**
Bat Yam Rām Karama Wādi as Sīr
Rishon le Ziyyon Allāh ▲289 Na'ūr Azraq ash Shīshān
Yavne Ramla At Tunayb
Rehovot El Arīḥā 'A M M Ā N
Ashdod (Jericho)
Qiryat Mol'akhi Jerusalem Ma'dabā
Bet Shemesh ◉ (Yerushalayim)
Ashqelon Qiryat (Al Quds)
Gat TEL Bayt Lahm W. al Haydān Dhībān
D Gaza LAKHISH (Bethlehem) Al Hadithah **D**
Strip N. Shiqma Sederot Al Khalīl W. al Mawjib
Khān Yūnis Az Zāhirīyah (Hebron) Al Qatrānah
Rafah Be'er ▲-403 Al Karak
Bûr Sa'îd (Port Said) Sheva Arad W. Al Mawjib
Bûr Fu'ad (Beersheba) Sedom A L K A R A K
Ras Burûn Bor Mashash 1305 ● Al Mazār
31 Khalîg el Tîna Dimona W. al Hasā ▲ 31
Români Bîr el 'Abd El Daheir ▲-333 J O R D A N W. Bā'ir
Bîr Qatia **H A D A R O M** At Ṭafilah Bā'ir
Qanâ es Suweis El 'Arîsh Bā'ir
El Qantara Bîr el Garârât Bîr Lahfân -121 Bā'ir
Wâhid Bîr el Duweidar Qezi'ot Sedé Boqér 1072 J. ash Shawmari
Bîr Madkûr Bîr Kaseiba Birein
E Ismâ'ilîya S Î N Î Muweilih Mizpe Ramon Nijil Mahattat 'Unayzah **E**
Talâta 892▲ El Quşeima Bi'r ad Dabbāghāt
Khamsa Bîr el Mâlḥî Rujm Tal'at Qa'el
El Buheirat Bîr Hasana H a n e g e v al Jamā'ah ▲1736 W. Abū Safāi Jafr
el Murrat G. Yi 'Allaq El 'Agrûd N. Paran W. Abū Safāi Al Jafr
el Kubra 1094 El Qudeirat PETRA
(Great Bitter L.) Bîr Beida Ma'ān
F Gineifa Bîr el Thamâda W. el Brûk N. Hiyyon Bi'r al Mārī M A 'Ā N **F**
El Suweis Bûr Taufîq Bîr Gebeil Hisn W. el Saharâ El 'Agrûd Ra's an Naqb
(Suez) Adabiya Bîr Bad' Nakhl W. el Tamarâni El Kuntilla Mahaṭṭat ash Shīdīyah
Uyûn Mûsa W. Ruda Yotvata S A U D I
Bîr Bad' Âin Sudr W. el 'Aqaba Ra's an Nāqb ▲1435
Ghubbet 948▲ Bîr Abu Muhammad En 'Avrona Bi'r al Qattār
el Bûs G. el Kabrît Bîr al Butayyihāt Batn al Ghūl **A R A B I A**
1272 Ras Gebel el Tîh El Thamad 1592▲
EL Matarma Elat
SUWEIS Shibh Jazîrat Sînâ' Bîr Tâba Al 'Aqabah Al Mudawwarah
Bîr el Biarât At Tubayq
Bîr Abu Sandûq W. Abu Ga'da W. an Nuwaybi'
1165▲
Haql
37

Projection: Polyconic **1** 33 **2** 34 East from Greenwich **3** 35 **4** 36 **5** **6**
COPYRIGHT GEORGE PHILIP LTD.

━ ━ ━ 1974 Cease Fire Lines

ft m
9000 3000
6000 2000
4500 1500
3000 1000
1200 400
600 200
0 0
200 600
2000 6000
m ft

AFRICA : Physical 1:37 300 000

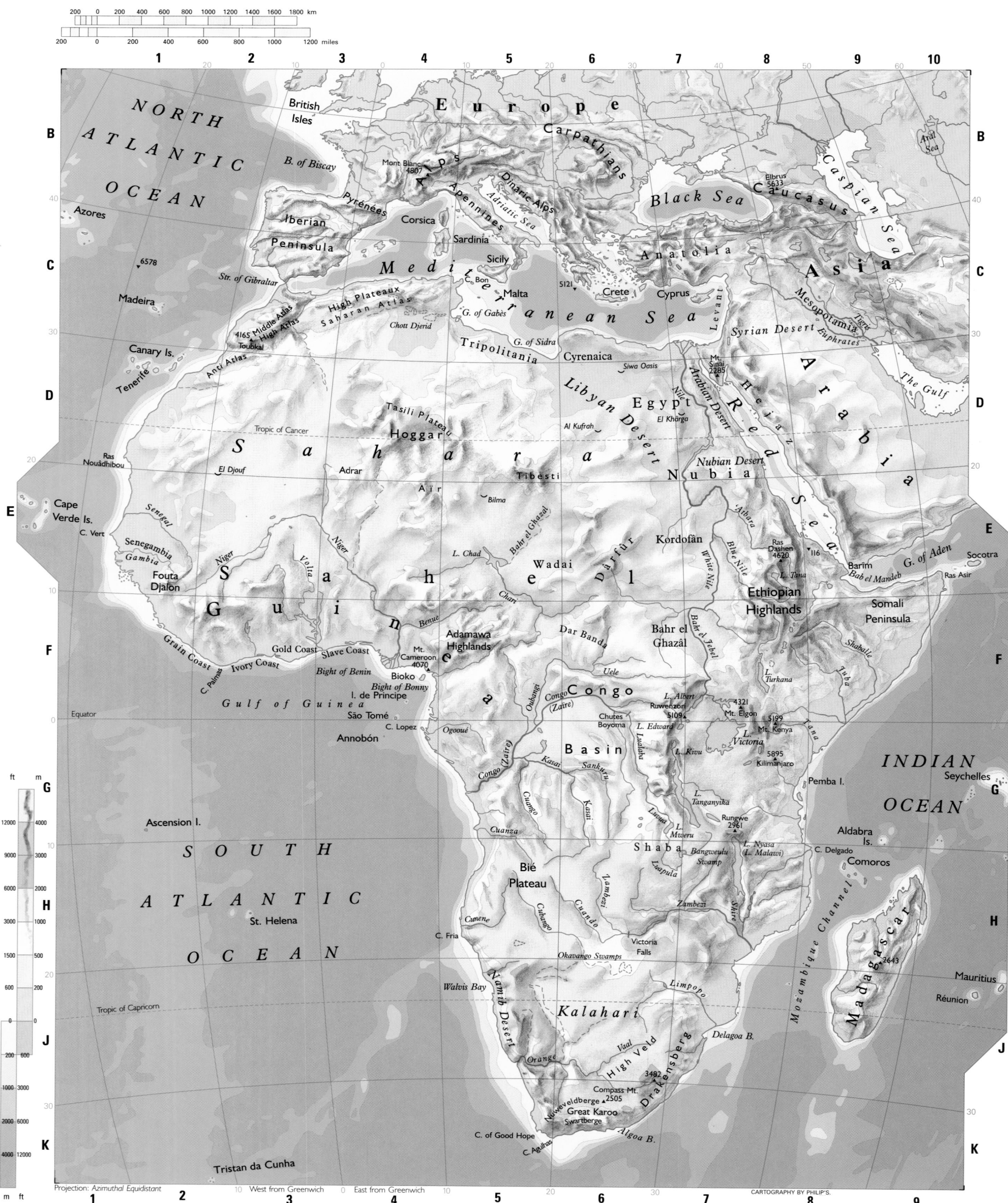

NORTH ATLANTIC OCEAN
British Isles
Europe
Carpathians
B. of Biscay
Mont Blanc 4807
Alps
Dinaric Alps
Apennines
Adriatic Sea
Black Sea
Elbrus 5633
Caucasus
Caspian Sea
Aral Sea
Azores
Pyrénées
Iberian Peninsula
Corsica
Sardinia
Sicily
Anatolia
Asia
6578
Madeira
Str. of Gibraltar
Mediterranean Sea
C. Bon
Malta
5121
Crete
Cyprus
Mesopotamia
Tigris
High Plateaux
Saharan Atlas
Middle Atlas
High Atlas
4165
Toubkal
G. of Gabès
Chott Djerid
Levant
Syrian Desert
Euphrates
Canary Is.
G. of Sidra
Tripolitania
Cyrenaica
Siwa Oasis
Mt. Sinai 2285
Arabia
The Gulf
Anti Atlas
Tenerife
Libyan Desert
Nile
Egypt
El Kharga
Arabian Desert
Hejaz
Red Sea
Tropic of Cancer
Tasili Plateau
Hoggar
Al Kufrah
Ras Nouâdhibou
Sahara
El Djouf
Adrar
Tibesti
Nubian Desert
Nubia
Aïr
Bilma
Cape Verde Is.
C. Vert
Senegal
Senegambia
Gambia
Niger
Volta
L. Chad
Bahr el Ghazal
Wadai
Dârfûr
Kordofân
White Nile
Blue Nile
'Atbara
Ras Dashen 4620
116
Barim
G. of Aden
Socotra
Bab el Mandeb
Ras Asir
L. Tana
Fouta Djalon
Sahel
Ethiopian Highlands
Somali Peninsula
Chari
Guinea
Benue
Dar Banda
Bahr el Ghazâl
Bahr el Jebel
Shaballe
Juba
Grain Coast
Gold Coast
Slave Coast
Mt. Cameroon 4070
Adamawa Highlands
Ivory Coast
C. Palmas
Bight of Benin
Bioko
Bight of Bonny
Uele
L. Turkana
I. de Principe
Oubangi
Congo (Zaïre)
Congo
L. Albert
Ruwenzori 5109
4321
Mt. Elgon
5199
Mt. Kenya
Tana
Gulf of Guinea
Equator
São Tomé
C. Lopez
Ogooué
Chutes Boyoma
L. Edward
L. Victoria
Annobón
Basin
Lualaba
L. Kivu
5895
Kilimanjaro
INDIAN OCEAN
Seychelles
Kasai
Sankuru
Pemba I.
Cuango
Kasai
L. Tanganyika
Ascension I.
Lwowa
L. Mweru
Rungwe 2961
Cuanza
Aldabra Is.
SOUTH ATLANTIC OCEAN
Shaba
Bangweulu Swamp
L. Nyasa (L. Malawi)
C. Delgado
Comoros
Bié Plateau
Luapula
Zambezi
Mozambique Channel
Cunene
Cubango
Cuando
Shire
Madagascar
St. Helena
C. Fria
Victoria Falls
Okavango Swamps
2643
Namib Desert
Walvis Bay
Limpopo
Mauritius
Réunion
Tropic of Capricorn
Kalahari
Delagoa B.
Vaal
High Veld
Orange
Drakensberg
3482
Compass Mt. 2505
Nuweveldberge
Great Karoo
Swartberge
C. of Good Hope
C. Agulhas
Algoa B.
Tristan da Cunha
Projection: Azimuthal Equidistant
West from Greenwich
East from Greenwich
CARTOGRAPHY BY PHILIP'S.
km
miles
ft
m

200 0 200 400 600 800 1000 1200 1400 1600 1800 km
200 0 200 400 600 800 1000 1200 miles

NORTH ATLANTIC OCEAN

UNITED KINGDOM
LONDON

NETH. GERMANY POLAND Warsaw RUSSIA KAZAKSTAN

BELG. Kiev Volgograd

PARIS Prague CZECH REP. UKRAINE

FRANCE SWITZ. AUSTRIA SLOVAK REP. HUNGARY Odessa Black Sea Aral Sea

Vienna CROATIA BOS.- ROMANIA GEORGIA Caspian Sea

HERZ. YUG. BULGARIA Ankara ARM. AZER. Baku TURKMEN.

B. of Biscay ITALY MAC. Rome ALB. GREECE TURKEY Mosul TEHRĀN

Corsica Sardinia Athens CYPRUS SYRIA Tigris Eşfahān

PORTUGAL SPAIN Madrid Sicily Crete LEB. Aleppo Damascus Baghdād Euphrates IRAN

Lisbon MALTA Tel Aviv Jerusalem Basra

Madeira Rabat Tétouan Tunis ISRAEL Syrian Desert KUWAIT

(Port.) Casablanca Fès Mediterranean Sea Alexandria Port Said JORDAN The Gulf

Canary Is. Marrakesh MOROCCO Algiers Annaba Constantine Tripoli Misrātah CAIRO Suez BAHRAIN

(Sp.) TUNISIA Benghazi El Faiyûm SAUDI Riyadh QATAR

El Aaiún ALGERIA Chott Djerid EGYPT Asyût ARABIA Medina

Dakhla In Salah LIBYA Al Jawf Aswân Mecca YEMEN

Fdérik Tropic of Cancer Marzûq Wadi Halfa Jedda

Ras Nouâdhibou S a h a r a Port Sudan Medewa Socotra

CAPE VERDE IS. MAURITANIA Tombouctou NIGER CHAD Atbara ERITREA G. of Aden (Yemen)

Praia Nouakchott Agadès SUDAN Omdurmân Khartoum Asmera Berbera Ras Asir

St-Louis Senegal Niamey L. Chad Abéché El Fâsher Wâd Medani DJIBOUTI

C. Vert MALI BURKINA Kano Ndjamena El Obeid Blue Nile Djibouti SOMALI REP.

Dakar SENEGAL Bamako FASO Ouagadougou Maiduguri Chari White Nile L. Tana

GAMBIA Banjul Bobo- NIGERIA Abuja Wau Addis Ababa Harer

GUINEA Bissau GUINEA Dioulasso BENIN Ibadan Enugu Benue CENTRAL Bahr el Jebel ETHIOPIA Shabelle

BISSAU Conakry SIERRA IVORY GHANA TOGO Lagos AFRICAN REP. Malakâl

Freetown LEONE COAST Bouaké Lomé Port CAMEROON Bangui L. Turkana Mogadishu

Monrovia Yamoussoukro Kumasi Accra Harcourt Douala UGANDA Jubba

LIBERIA Abidjan Sekondi- Bight of Benin EQUATORIAL Yaoundé Ôbangi Kisangani L. Albert Kampala KENYA

Takoradi Gulf of Guinea GUINEA Congo Mbandaka L. Edward Kisumu Kismayu

Equator SÃO TOMÉ & PRINCIPE Libreville (Zaïre) RWANDA Kigali L. Victoria Nairobi INDIAN

C. López GABON CONGO CONGO RWANDA Kivu BURUNDI Mombasa OCEAN

Annobón Brazzaville (DEM. REP. OF THE) Bujumbura SEYCHELLES

Pointe-Noire Kasai TANZANIA Zanzibar

CABINDA Matadi Kinshasa Kananga Dodoma Dar es Salaam Aldabra

(Angola) Congo L. Tanganyika Is.

Luanda Cuango L. Mweru

ASCENSION I. Cubango ANGOLA Likasi L. Malawi C. Delgado COMOROS Antsiranana

(U.K.) Lobito Lubumbashi Moroni Mayotte

Huambo Ndola Lilongwe MALAWI Moçambique (Fr.)

SOUTH Namibe Cunene ZAMBIA Lusaka Zambezi Blantyre MOZAMBIQUE Mahajanga

ATLANTIC St. Helena C. Fria Livingstone Harare Beira MADAGASCAR Toamasina

(U.K.) Bulawayo MAURITIUS

OCEAN NAMIBIA BOTSWANA ZIMBABWE Limpopo Fianarantsoa Antananarivo

Windhoek Gaborone Moçambique Channel Réunion Port Louis

Johannesburg Pretoria Maputo (Fr.)

Kimberley Vaal Mbabane SWAZ.

Maseru LESOTHO Durban

Cape Town SOUTH AFRICA East London

C. of Good Hope Port Elizabeth

C. Agulhas

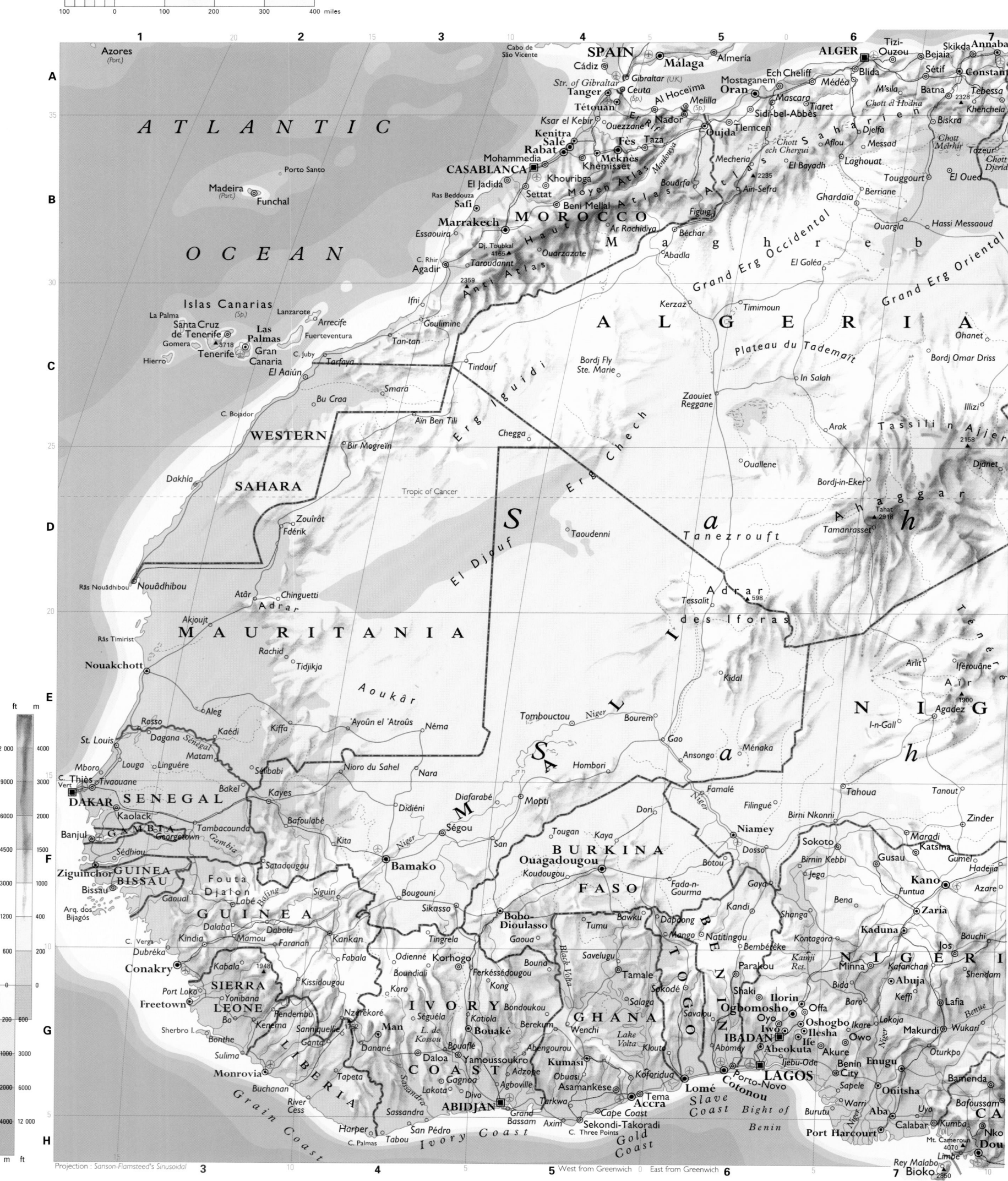

100   0   100   200   300   400   500   600 km
100   0   100   200   300   400 miles

1 | 20 | **2** | 15 | **3** | 10 | **4** | 5 | **5** | **6** | 0 | **7**

A

Azores
(Port.)

SPAIN
Cabo de
São Vicente
Cádiz • Málaga Almería ALGER Tizi- Skikda • Annaba
Ouzou
Str. of Gibraltar Gibraltar (U.K.) Mostaganem Ech Cheliff Médéa • Blida Bejaia Sétif
Tanger • Ceuta Oran Mascara M'sila Chott el Hodna 2328 Constan-
Tétouan Al Hoceïma Sidi-bel-Abbès Tiaret Djelfa Batna Tebessa
Melilla (Sp.) Oujda Tlemcen Aflou Messad Biskra Khenchela

35 Kenitra Fès Taza Chott ech Chergui El Bayadh Laghouat Chott
Salé Meknès Mecheria Touggourt Melrhir Tozeur
Rabat Khémisset Moulouya   Aïn-Sefra Ghardaïa Berriane El Oued Chott
Mohammedia Khouribga 2235 Bouârfa Djerid
CASABLANCA El Jadida Settat Figuig Béchar Ouargla Hassi Messaoud
B Ras Beddouza Beni Mellal Ar Rachidiya Abadla El Goléa
Safi Marrakech **MOROCCO** M Ouarzazate a g h r e b
Essaouira Dj. Toubkal Grand Erg Occidental
4165 Haut Atlas Kerzaz Grand Erg Oriental
C. Rhir Taroudannt Timimoun Ohanet
30 Agadir 2359 Anti Atlas **A L G E R I A**
Ifni Goulimine Plateau du Tademaït
Islas Canarias Tan-tan Zaouiet Bordj Omar Driss
La Palma (Sp.) Lanzarote Reggane In Salah
Santa Cruz Arrecife Arak
Gomera 3718 de Tenerife Fuerteventura C. Juby Tarfaya Tindouf Illizi
Hierro Tenerife Gran El Aaiún 2158
C Canaria Smara Erg Chech Tassili n'Ajjer
Bu Craa Chegga S Djanet
C. Bojador Aïn Ben Tili Ouallene Bordj-in-Eker
WESTERN Bir Mogreïn a Ahaggar Tahat
Dakhla Tropic of Cancer h 2918 Tamanrasset
SAHARA **S** a Taoudenni Tanezrouft
D Zouîrat El Djouf Adrar 598
Fdérik des Iforas Tessalit
Rås Nouâdhibou Nouâdhibou Atâr Chinguetti Adrar Ténéré
20 Rachid Kidal Arlit Iférouâne
MAURITANIA Tidjikja Aïr
Rås Timiris 1900
Nouakchott Aoukâr **N I G** Agadez
E Aleg Tombouctou Niger Bourem I-n-Gall
St. Louis Rosso Kaédi Kiffa 'Ayoûn el 'Atroûs Néma Gao **e** **r**
Dagana Sénégal Matam Ansongo Ménaka Tahoua Tanout
Mboro Louga Linguère Nioro du Sahel Nara Hombori **S** a h
15 C. Vert Tivaouane Sélibabi Famalé Birni Nkonni Zinder
DAKAR Thiès Bakel Kayes Didiéni Mopti Niger Filingué Margai
SENEGAL Diafarabé Dori **Niamey** Dosso Sokoto Katsina
Kaolack Tambacounda Gambia Ségou Tougan Kaya Birnin Kebbi Gusau
F Banjul Georgetown Kita San **BURKINA** Botou Jega Gumel Hadejia
GAMBIA Satadougou Bamako **Ouagadougou** Gaya **KANO**
Sédhiou Bafoulabé Koudougou Shanga Funtua Azare
Ziguinchor **GUINEA** Fouta Siguiri **FASO** Fada-N-Gourma Kandi Kontagora **Zaria**
BISSAU Djalon Labé Boling Bougouni Sikasso Bawku Dapaong Bena Kaduna Bauchi
Bissau Gaoual Bobo- Gaoua Tumu Mango Natitingou Bembéréke Minna Jos Shendam
Arq. dos C. Verga Dalaba Mamou Dioulasso Tingrela Savelugu Abuja Kafanchan
Bijagós Kindia **GUINEA** Faranah Fabala Odienné Korhogo Bouna Tamale Parakou Gaya **N I G E R I**
G Conakry Kabala 1948 Kissidougou Koro Ferkéssédougou Kong Sokodé Baro Bida Lafia
Dubréka Kankan Boundiali Kainji Benue
Port Loko **SIERRA** Kenema Nzérékoré Koidu Katiola Salaga Res. Minna
Freetown **LEONE** Hendembu **IVORY** Séguéla Bouaké Wenchi Lake Ilorin Offa Oshogbo Owo Makurdi Wukari
Bonthe Bo Sanniquellie Man L. de Berekum Volta **IBADAN** Iwo Ilesha Benin Enugu
Sherbro I. Ganta Kossou **GHANA** Abengourou **GHANA** Abomey Ife City Oturkpo
COAST Danané Bouaflé **Kumasi** Koforidua **LAGOS** Ijebu-Ode
H Monrovia Tapeta Daloa Yamoussoukro Adzope Obuasi Porto-Novo Onitsha Bamenda
LIBERIA Grand Gagnoa Asamankese Lomé Cotonou Sapele
Buchanan Divo Aboisso Tarkwa **Accra** Slave Warri **CA**
River Bassam Tema Coast Port Harcourt Uyo Calabar Kumba
Cess Sassandra Lakota Cape Coast Bight of Nko
Harper San Pédro Tabou **Ivory Coast** Sekondi-Takoradi Benin Mt. Cameroun Dou
C. Palmas C. Three Points 4070
Gold Rey Malabo 2850
Coast **7** Bioko

Projection : Sanson-Flamsteed's Sinusoïdal
3 | 10 | **4** | 5 | West from Greenwich | 0 | East from Greenwich | **6** | 10 | **7**

ft m
12 000 4000
9 000 3000
6 000 2000
4500 1500
3000 1000
1200 400
600 200
0 0
200 600
1000 3000
2000 6000
4000 12 000
m ft

A T L A N T I C

O C E A N

Madeira
(Port.)
Porto Santo
Funchal

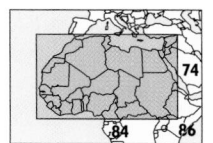

MEDITERRANEAN SEA

GREECE · Iráklion · Kríti · Ródhos · CYPRUS · Nicosia · **TURKEY** · Antalya · **ADANA** · Antakya · **HALAB** · Al Lādhiqiyah · **SYRIA** · Tarābulus · Hims · **LEBANON** · **BAYRŪT** · **DIMASHQ** · **IRAQ** · Ar Rutbah · Jabal ad Durūz · **AMMĀN** · Bādiyat · ash Shām

Bizerte · Ariana · Béja · **TUNIS** · CARTHAGE · Nabeul · Sousse · Mahdia · Kairouan · Sicilia · **MALTA** · Valletta · Sfax · Golfe de Gabès · Île de Djerba · Gabès · Zarzis · Gafsa · Médenine · Tataouine · Dehibat

Zuwārah · **Tarābulus** · Al Khums · Misrātah · Az Zāwiyah · Gharyān · 968 · Surt · Khalīj Surt · Banghāzī · Al Marj · Darnah · Zāwiyat al Baydā · Suluq · Tubruq · Bardīyah · Salūm · **EL ISKANDARĪYA** · Marsá Matrûh · El Alamein

Mizdah · Daraj · Ghudāmis · Hūn · T r i p o l i t a n i a · C y r e n a i c a · Ajdābiyah · Awjilah · Al Jaghbūb · −133 · Munkhafed el Qattâra · Sīwa

L I B Y A · I d e h a n A w b ā r ī · Brach · Awbārī · Sabhah · Zillah · 1200 · S a h r â ' L î b î y a · Qasr Farâfra · El Wâhât el-Dakhla · Mût · El Khârga · El Wâhât el-Khârga

F e z z a n · Ghat · Marzūq · Wāw al Kabīr · Al Qatrūn · S a h r â ' R e b i a n a · Al Jawf · Al Kufrah

S a h a r a · Toummo · Madama · Chirfa · Bardai · Pic Toussidé 3265 · Aozou · 3150 Tarso Emissi · T i b e s t i · Zouar · Emi Koussi 3415 · Ma'tan as Sarra · 1082 · J. Uweinat 1893 · El Wâhât el Selîma · ABU SIMBEL · Wâdi Halfa

EGYPT · Misr · El Mahalla el Kubra · Damanhûr · Dumyât · Bûr Sa'id · Tanta · El Mansûra · Zagazig · Isma'iliya · **EL QAHIRA** · **EL GÎZA** · El Suweis · Helwân · El Faiyûm · Beni Suef · El Minyâ · Maghâgha · Mallawi · Manfalût · Asyût · 2187 · Sohâg · Tahta · Girga · THEBES · KARNAK · Qena · El Uqsur · Idfû · Kom Ombo · Sadd el Aali · Aswân

Jerusalem · West Bank · ISRAEL · Tel Aviv-Yafo · Hefa · Ashdod · Ma'ân · Elat · Al 'Aqabah · Es Sinâ' · G. Mûsa 2637 · 2578 · Tabûk · Khalîg el Suweis · Hurghada · Bûr Safâga · Quseir · Al Muwaylih · **SAUDI ARABIA** · Al Wajh · H i j a z · Yanbu' al Bahr · Rābigh · Al Jawf

RED SEA · Buheirat en Naser · Bîr Shalatein · Ras Bânâs · Halaib · Ras Hadarba

E s S a h r â Esh Sharqiya · E s S a h r â e n N û b î y a · Muhammad Qol 2259 · Kosha · Delgo · 3rd Cataract · Abu Hamed · Dongola · Kareima · 4th Cataract · 5th Cataract · **Bûr Sûdân** · Suakin · Sinkat · Trinkitât · Haiya · Karora 2780 · Nakfa · **ERITREA** · Akordat

SUDAN · Ed Debba · Nahr en Nîl · Berber · Atbara · Adarama · Kassalâ · Wad Hamid · 6th Cataract · Shendî · Nahr Atbara · Omdurmân · **El Khartûm** · Khashm el Girba · Gedaref · El Gezira · Wad Medanî · Bir 'Atrun · Malha · 1954 · Kutum · El Fâsher · Sodiri · Umm Keddada · El Wuz · El Obeid · Kôstî · Singa · **ETHIOPIA** · Gonder 1830 · L. Tana · Bahir Dar · Debre Markos · Nekemte · Metu · Gore · Jima · 3686 · L. Abaya · Arba Minch · L. Shamo · Chew Bahir · L. Turkana · 3202 · Dembidolo

Al Junaynah · Zalingei · Djebel Mara 3088 · Nyâlâ · D a r f û r · En Nahud · Abu Zabad · Er Rahad · Umm Ruwaba · Ed Damazin · K o r d o f â n · 1325 · Kâdugli · Nil el Azraq

CHAD · Boultoum · Nguigmi · Bosso · Zigey · Mao · Lac Tchad · Moussoro · Ati · Bahr el Ghazal · Massakory · Massaguet · **Ndjamena** · Kousseri · Bokoro · Mongo · Abéché · Oum Hadjer · Goz Beïda · Abou-Deïa · Am-Timan · Birao · Songa

NIGER · E r d i · Faya-Largeau · Fada · E n n e d i · 1310 · Z a g a o u a · Oum Chalouba · Erg du Djourab · Dépression du Mourdi · B o r k o u · Ouanianga Sérir · Bilma · Fachi · Grand Erg du Bilma

Gashua · Nguru · Geidam · **Maiduguri** · Potiskum · Duku · Gombe · Bajoga · Kumo · Biu · Mubi · Bama · **CAMEROON** · Numan · Yola · Garoua · Guider · Maroua · Bongor · Laï · Pala · Kourna · Moundou · Doba · Sarh · Massenya · Chari · Logone · Baïbokoum · Bétaré Oya · Ngaoundéré · Bossangoa · Massif de l'Adamaoua · Foumban · Yoko · Nanga-Eboko · **Yaoundé** · Banyo · Gashaka · ngsamba ala

1226 · Sa'id Bundas · Raga · B a h r e l G h a z â l · Jur · S û d d · Malakâl · Sobat · Gogrîal · Wâw · Tonj · Rumbêk · Bôr · Toïnya · Bahr el Jebel · Pibor Post · Amâdi · Juba · Kapoeta · Lokitaung · Torit 3187 · Kajo Kaji · Yei · Faradje · Dungu · El Istiwa'iya · Mongalla · Yâmbiô · Obo · Bakouma · Ippy · Bambari · Bangassou · Mobaye · Mobayi · Bomu · Bondo · Ango · Uele

CENTRAL AFRICAN REPUBLIC · Kaga Bandoro · Yalinga · Bouar · Bozoum · Paoua · Bouca · Sibut · Carnot · Bossembélé · **Bangui** · Berbérati · Mbaïki · Zongo · Bosobolo · Libenge · Oubangui

Batouri · Bertoua · Abong-Mbang

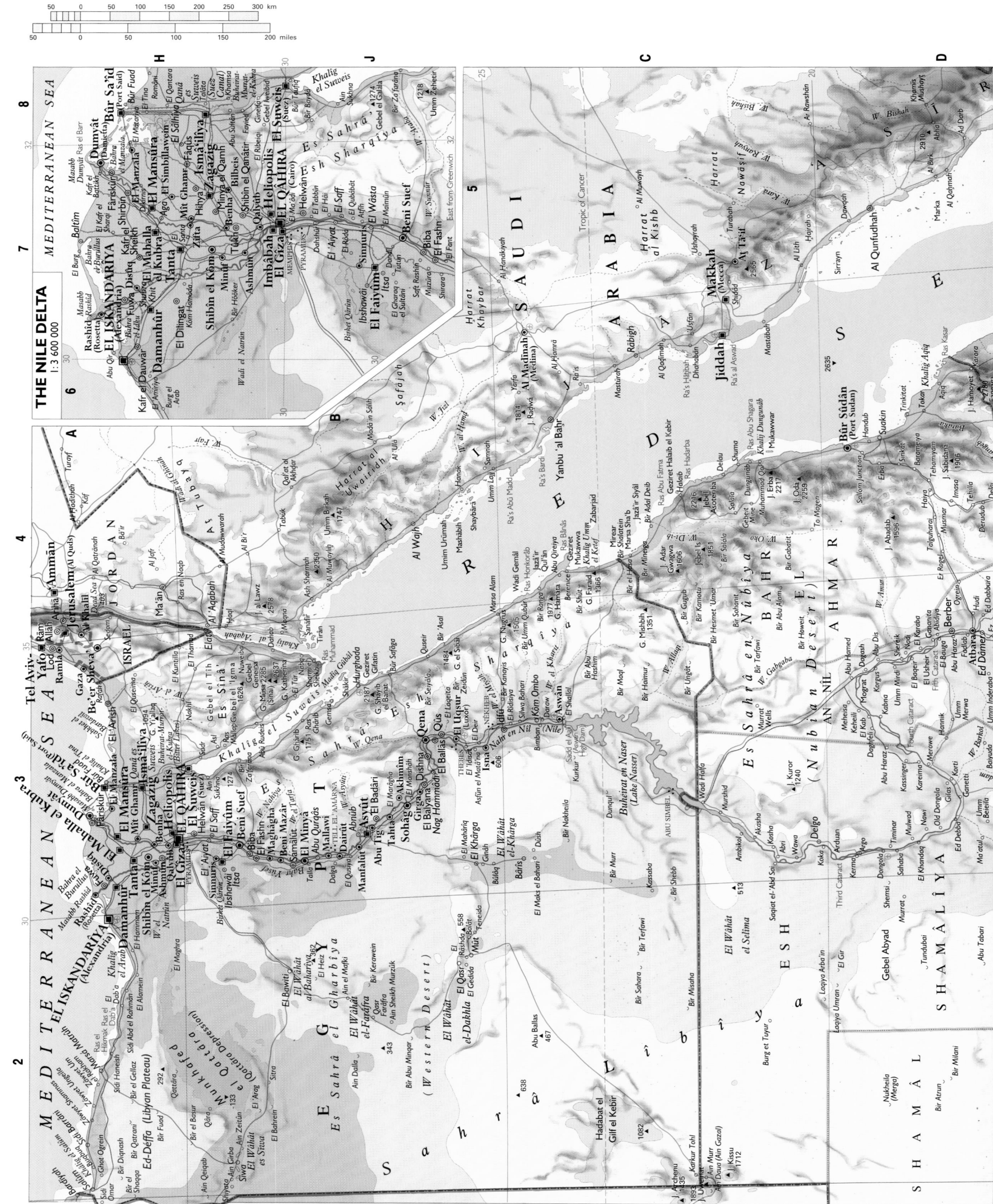

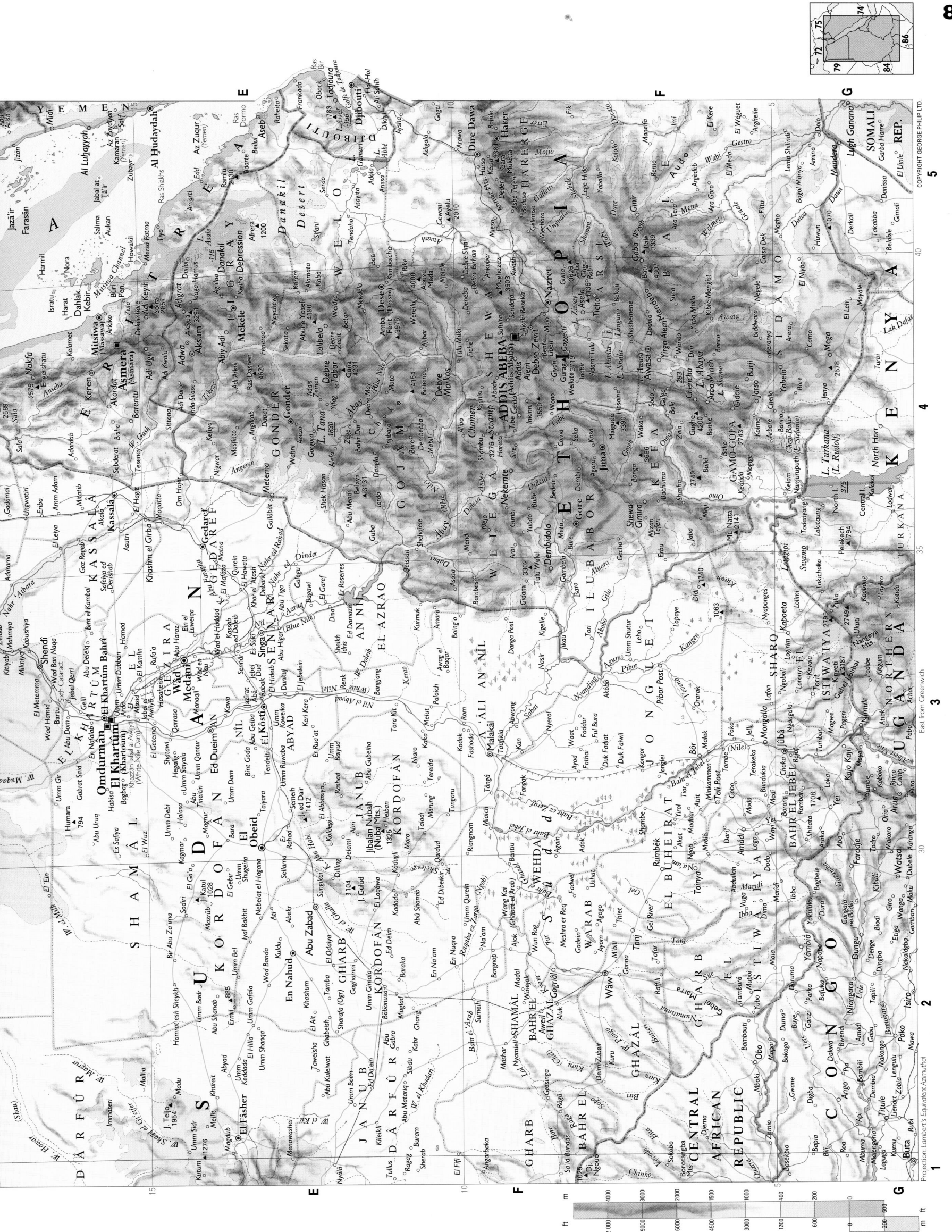

SUDAN
ETHIOPIA
ERITREA
KENYA
UGANDA
CONGO
CENTRAL AFRICAN REPUBLIC
SOMALI REP.
DJIBOUTI
YEMEN
DÂRFÛR
SHAMÂL
KORDOFÂN
EL KHARTÛM
KASSALÂ
GEZIRA
GEDAREF
SENNAR
NÎL ABYAD
AN NÎL EL AZRAQ
JANUB KORDOFÂN
GHARB KORDOFÂN
JANUB DÂRFÛR
A'ÂLI AN NÎL
WEHDA
WARAB
JONGLEI
EL BUHEIRAT
BAHR EL JEBEL
SHARQ EL ISTIWA'IYA
GHARB EL ISTIWA'IYA
GHARB BAHR EL GHAZÂL
SHAMÂL BAHR EL GHAZÂL
TIGRAY
GONDER
GOJAM
WELO
SHEWA
WELEGA
ILUBABOR
KEFA
GAMO-GOFA
SIDAMO
BALE
ARSI
HARERGE
Dankil Desert
Danakil Depression
Sudd
Omdurmân
El Khartûm (Khartoum)
El Khartûm Bahrî
Wad Medani
Kassalâ
Gedaref
El Obeid
Kôstî
Malakâl
Wâw
Jûbâ
El Fâsher
En Nahud
Abu Zabad
Asmera (Asmara)
Mitsiwa (Massawa)
Keren
Aksum
Mekele
Gonder
Dese (Dessye)
ADDIS ABEBA (Addis Ababa)
Nazret
Dire Dawa
Harer
Jima
Gore
Nekemte
Awasa
Djibouti
Al Hudaydah
L. Tana
L. Turkana (L. Rudolf)
L. Abaya
Blue Nile
White Nile
Nahr 'Atbara
Projection: Lambert's Equivalent Azimuthal
East from Greenwich
COPYRIGHT GEORGE PHILIP LTD.

Projection : Lambert's Equivalent Azimuthal

West from Greenwich

4 5 6 7

A B C D E

Erg i-n Sâkâne
Timeiaouine 598
I-n-Ouzzal
Tassili Tin-Rerhoh
I-n-Oudad
Admer
A L G E R I A
Touaret
Massif de Terazit
Ténéré
Tessalit
In Akhmed
Mabrouk
Monts Timétrine
Tin Ethisane
Adrar des Iforas
Aguelhok
In Koufi
Estouk
Vallée du Tilemsi
853
Kidal
Ti-n-Zaouatène
In-Guezzam
O. Tin-Barraouene
Assamakka
Arlit
Ourârene
Zourika
1800
I-n-Tadreft
Aïr
Iférouane
Ti-n-Amzi
Sidaouet
Talak (Azbine)
Timia
Monts Bagzane 1900
Arbre du Ténéré
Aouderas
G a o
Tabankort
Oudeika
Almoustarat
In Tebezas
Iracher Zeggerene
Anou Mellene
Teguidda i-n-Tessoum
Agadez
Agadez (Agadès)
Bamba
Kerchoual
Bourem
Gourma-Rharous
Tondibi
Tin Gornai
Gao
Iménas
Teletaye
Vallée de l'Azaouak
Ilatane
I-n-Gall
Doro
In Tallak
Tirdout
Gargouna
Ouassouas
Ménaka
Tillia
N I G E R
Abalemma
Gossi
Ansongo
In Delimane
Akzar
Tchin Tabaraden
Tilemses
Fafa
Andéranboukane
Tahoua
Bagam
Aderbissinat
Hombori
1155
Tessit
Ouatagouna
Labbézenga
Azaouak
Abalak
509
Tahoua
Tamaské
Keita
Tanout
Sabonkafi
Tasker
Boultoum
Oursi
Markoye
Yatakala
Ayorou
Bani Bangou
Abala
Dallol Bosso
Dallol Maouri
Talcho
Illéla
Badéguichéri
Bouza
Dakoro
Gangara
Gamou
Manga
Nguigmi
Gorom Gorom
Tillabéri
Tondi Kiwindi
Bankilaré
Djibo
Aribinda
Kokoro
Tillabéri
Ouallam
Filingué
Dabnou
Madaoua
Mir
Gouré
Ouidi
Dori
Téra
Dargol
Gothèye
Karma
Tabla
Bonkoukou
Matankari
Bayzo
Malbaza
Doguéraoua
Birni Nkonni
Mayahi
Tessaoua
Aguié
Tibiri
Zinder
Mirria
Guidiguir
Guidimouni
Goudoumaria
Kalmalo
Dogondoutchi
Loga
Yéni
Kiessé
Tangaza
SOKOTO
Rima
Goronyo
Maradi
Dankama
Gazaoua
Matameye
Kantché
Karguéri
Alkamari
Adebour
Kabi
Bouroum
Barsalogho
Dani
Sebba
Bossé Bangou
Niamey
Koré Mayroua
Dosso
Binji
Gwadabawa
Rabah
Isa
Shinkafe
Jibiya
Daura
Magaria
Matsena
Mallaoua
Kumaganum
Maïne-Soroa
Zari
Kongoussi
Tougouri
Kaya
Pissila
Boussouma
Soulougou
Say
Birni Ngaouré
Sokoto
Bodinga
Gandi
Moriki
Katsina
Mashi
Baure
Maigatari
Nguru
Gashua
Geidam
Bogandé
Bilanga
Gayéri
Bohongou
Botou
Kirtachi
Lido
Argungu
Denge
Talata Mafara
Faru
Kaura Namoda
Runka
Kazaure
Babura
Gorgoram
Gwio Kura
Dapchi
Gubio
Boussé
Ziniaré
Ouagadougou
Kantchari
Matiakoali
Gulma
Gwandu
Jega
Maru
Bunsuru
Yashi
Gwarzo
JIGAWA
Gagarawa
Hadejia
Katagum
Gorgoram
Kombissiri
Zorgo
Koupéla
Fada-n-Gourma
Diapaga
Birnin Kebbi
Bunza
Gummi
Zamfara
Anka
Gusau
Jikamshi
Dawaki
KANO
Ringim
Keffin Hausa
Gamawa
Lantewa
Bornu Yassa
Titiwa
Sapone
Diapangou
Ougarou
Kamba
Maiyema
ZAMFARA
Sauri
Malumfashi
Kano
Gaya
Jamaari
Madara
Lajere
YOBE
Potiskum
Dankalwa
Tenkodogo
Garango
Sapouy
Manga
Bané
Ouargaye
Arly
Guéné
Dakingari
Fokku
Mahuta
Dan-Gulbi
Ka
Funtua
Bakori
Garko
Dangora
Azare
Dambatu
Dapchi
Zoumra
Nebbou
Pô
Bittou
Pama
Pendjari
Banikoara
Alibori
Kandi
Angara-Débou
Kende
Koko
Dabai
Zuru
853
Danja
Birnin Kudu
Disina
633
Zadawa
Daura
Goniri
Masba
Zabré
Paga
Zebila
Bawku
Navrongo
Zuarungu
Garu
Dapaong
KEBBI
Giro
Duku
Sakaba
Bena
Zaria
Ikara
Ningi
Fagam
Foggo
Sade
Fika
Gabarin
Nafada
Yajua
Dumboa
Bolgatanga
Nalerigu
Bogou
Tanguiéta
Mékrou
Kérou
Ségbana
Yelwa
Rijau
Kotonkoro
Mariga
Birnin Gwari
KADUNA
Soba
Dutsan Wai
Burra
Darazo
Kafin Madaki
Duku
Bajoga
Chibuk
Meringa
Valembele
Gambaga
Gogonou
Bérouboay
Kainji Res.
Babana
Bin Yauri
Kusheriki
Kushaka
Rigacikun
Kauru
BAUCHI
GOMBE
Biu
Shaffa
Yagaba
Walewale
Mango
635
Natitingou
Sinendé
Dunkassa
510
450
Kontagora
Kaduna
Kajuru
Lere
Lame
Bauchi
Kafareti
Hinna
Gombe
Wuyo
Shani
Garkida
Gombi
Janga
Boukombé
Bembéréke
Auna
Kainji Dam
NIGER
Tegina
Gwagwada
Bununu Dass
Yamrat
Gwaram
Deba Habe
Gaanda
Yan
Daboya
Savelugu
Karaga
Gushiago
Kanté
Guessou-Sud
Djougou
Nikki
Yashikera
Wawa
Mashegu
Zungeru
Minna
Kachia
Kafanchan
Jos
Bukuru
1780
Plateau
Bununu
Kasa
Pindiga
Kumo
Tula
867
Zummo
Nyankpala
Tamale
Yendi
Kabou
Lama Kara
Ndali
Saya
New Bussa
Kaiama
Eban
Bokani
Wushishi
Kafin
Kagarko
Panyam
Boi
1585
Dawaki
Kaltungo
Dadiya
Numan
NORTHERN
Zan
Zabzugu
Bafilo
850
Bassar
Bétérou
Parakou
Gwasero
Mokwa
Bida
Gawu
Bokkos
Pankshin
Amper
Dengi
Kpabia
Sokodé
Bassila
Tchaourou
Gwanara
Okuta
Kishi
Jebba
Bode Sadu
Lapai
Zuba
Abuja
Wamba
PLATEAU
Wase
Lau
Yola
Bimbila
Wulehe
Kambolé
Kilibo
Ilesha
Igbeti
Lafiagi
Badeggi
Agaie
Gwi
Keffi
Kwolla
Shendam
Jalingo
Mayo Faran
GHANA
Salaga
Ayengré
Kpandae
Agofie
Blitta
Pira
Aklampa
Shaki
Igboho
545
OYO
Ilorin
Pategi
Isanlu
Baro
FED. CAP. TERR.
Nasarawa
NASSARAWA
Assaikio
Mutum Biyu
ADAMAWA
Kintampo
Kedjebi
Akaba
Kpessi
Savalou
Ogbomosho
Offa
Osi
Makutu
Toto
Doma
Lafia
Azara
Gassol
Gandole
Shebshi Mts.
Vogel Pk.
2042
Ganye
Atebubu
Prang
Kete Krachi
Ahamansu
Tchetti
Agouna
Dassa
Iseyin
Oyo
Ilobu
Ila
Ikurun
Oshogbo
Irele
KOGI
NIGERIA
Koton-Karifi
Lokoja
Loko
Ibi
TARABA
Bakundi
Kam
Kogin Baba
Toungo
Kontcha
Mts. Gan Goriama
BRONG-AHAFO
Atakpamé
Anié
Savè
Ede
Fiditi
Ilora
Iwo
OSUN
731
Ado-Ekiti
Kabba
Okene
Abocho
Riti
Wukari
Taraba
Ejura
Sene
Mampong
Lake Volta
Afram
Hohoe
Abomey
Kétou
Meko
Igbo-Ora
IBADAN
Ife
Ilesha
EKITI
Ikare
Ikerre-Ekiti
Egume
Boju
Igbor
Makurdi
Gboko
Takum
Donga
Baissa
Gashaka
Gotel Mts.
Kloutou
Notsé
Zagnanado
Pobé
OGUN
Abeokuta
Ikire
Akure
Ondo
Owo
Auchi
Idah
Ete
Otukpa
Oturkpo
BENUE
Ihugh
Katsina Ala
Bissaula
Mayo Darlé
Galim
ASHANTI
Kpalimé
986
Kouvé
Allada
Sakété
Ilaro
Shagamu
Ijebu-Igbo
Ijebu-Ode
ONDO
Ifon
Ubiaja
Enugu Ezike
Nsukka
Opi
Obudu
Katsina Ala
Gembu
Banyo
Mts. Atsoum
Konongo
Nkawkaw
788
Agbélouvé
Tsévié
Athiémé
Adjohon
Ado
Ikeja
Epe
Mushin
LAGOS
Okitipupa
Gbekebo
Siluko
EDO
Ogwashi-Uku
Enugu
Nike
Eha Amufu
Ogoja
Nkambe
M'boukou Res.
Tibati
Bekwai
Obuasi
EASTERN
Akosombo Dam
Ho
Yogan
Lomé
Aného
Grand Popo
Ouidah
Cotonou
Porto-Novo
Badagri
Lagos
Benin City
ANAMBRA
Asaba
Udi
EBONYI
Amagunze
Abakaliki
2000
Wum
Mme
Kumbo
Bafut
Bamkin
Kade
Oda
Tafo
Koforidua
Asamankese
Sogakofe
Denu
Keta
Keta Lagoon
Sapele
Onitsha
Awka
Mberubu
Afikpo
CROSS RIVER
Ikom
Bali
Bamenda
Ngambé
Foso
Nyakrom
Nsawam
Ada
Volta
Prampram
Benin
Escravos
Warri
Usoro
Obiaruku
Kwale
Ihiala
Okija
Orodo
Okigwi
Obubra
Ugep
Mamfé
2679
Foumban
Zengbe
CENTRAL
Valley
Swedru
Apam
ACCRA
Tema
Forcados
DELTA
Burutu
Ughelli
Oguta
Owerri
IMO
Umuahia
ABIA
1060
Fontem
Dschang
Foumbot
Bafoussam
Yoko
1500
Dunkwa
Saltpond
Winneba
Senya Beraku
Ramos
Amassama
Yenagoa
Ahoada
Omoko
Elele
Ovoro
Ikot Ekpene
Arochukwu
Oban
Mts. Manengouba
Bangangté
Elmina
Cape Coast
Slave Coast
Bight of Benin
Ogwe
Aba
Uyo
Calabar
2300
Bafang
Mankim
Sekondi-Takoradi
Pennington
BAYELSA
Buguma
Degema
Abonnema
Port Harcourt
Okrika
Bori
Eket
Oron
AKWA-IBOM
Ikang
Kumba
Nkongsamba
Bafia
Nanga Eboko
Sanaga
Mbam
Gold Coast
Niger Delta
Bonny
RIVERS
Imo
Opobo
Cross
Rio-del-Rey
M'bonge
Mont Cameroun 4070
Ndikiniméki
Yabassi
Nguila
Ntui
Guéle Mendouka
Brass
Bonny
Buea
Tiko
Mbanga
DOUALA
Ngambé
Obala
Bikoué
Limbe
Yaoundé
Nyong
Rey Malabo
Pico Santa Isabel
Bioko
Butuku-Luba
Basilé
2850
Ri-Aba
Cameroun
Édéa
Eséka
Otélé
Akonolinga
Mésamena
Makak
Oloma
Mbalmayo
Bengbis
Lolodorf
CAMEROON
GULF OF GUINEA
EQUATORIAL GUINEA
Bight of Bonny
Pta. de Santiago
Kribi
Bipindi
Ebolowa
Sangmélima
Massif de l'Adamaoua

N.E. NIGERIA
on same scale as general map

NIGER
Bosso
Lac Tchad
Yobe
Gashagar
CHAD
Zari
Kukawa
Mongonu
Dabilda
Makari
Gubio
Marte
BORNO
Ngala
Titiwa
Dikwa
Kala
Maiduguri
Masba
Konduga
Bama
Yajua
Dumboa
Gwoza
Mora
Chibuk
Madagali
Mokolo
Maroua
Uba
Michika
Garkida
Mubi
Yedseram
Gombi
Kaélé
Guider
Song
Zummo
Binder
Malabu
Léré
Ribado
Garoua
Gurin
ADAMAWA
CAMEROON
Poli

East from Greenwich
0 5 10 15 20

COPYRIGHT, GEORGE PHILIP LTD.

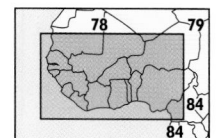

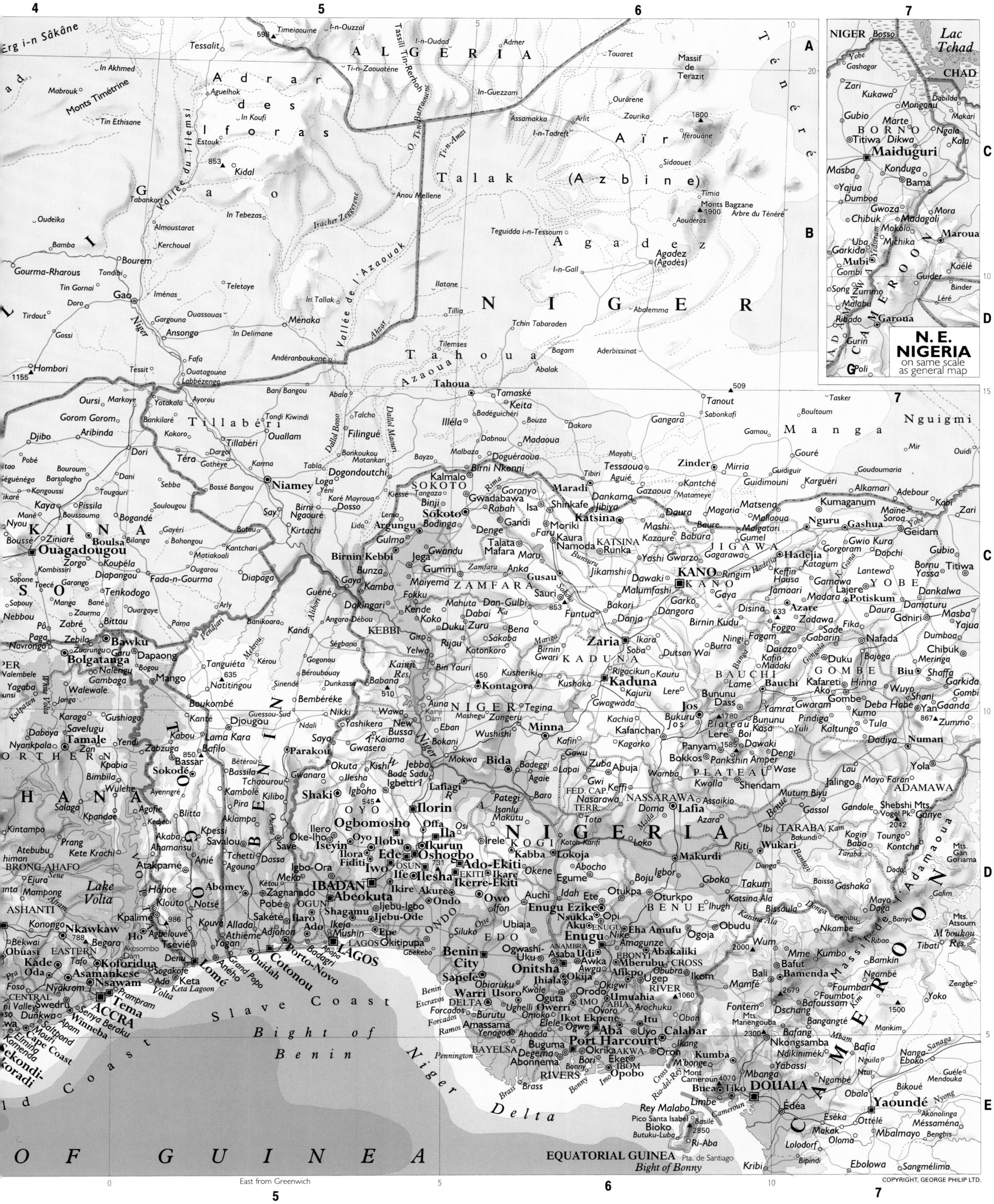

CENTRAL AND SOUTHERN AFRICA 1:13 300 000

100 0 100 200 300 400 500 600 km
100 0 100 200 300 400 miles
SUDAN
ETHIOPIA
ERITREA
KENYA
UGANDA
TANZANIA
RWANDA
BURUNDI
CHAD
NIGERIA
NIGER
CAMEROON
CENTRAL AFRICAN REPUBLIC
CONGO (DEM. REP. OF THE)
CONGO
GABON
EQUATORIAL GUINEA
Omdurmân
El Khartûm
ADDIS ABEBA
Asmera
NAIROBI
Kampala
Kigali
Bujumbura
DAR ES SALAAM
Mombasa
Ndjamena
Bangui
Yaoundé
Douala
Libreville
Brazzaville
KINSHASA
LUANDA
Kisangani
Lake Victoria
L. Turkana
L. Tanganyika
Congo Basin
Massif de l'Adamaoua
Lac Tchad
Danakil Desert
Sudd
Bahr el Ghazal
Lualaba
Kano
Juba
Mbandaka
Kananga
Mbuji-Mayi
Lubumbashi
Kolwezi
Pointe-Noire
Cabinda

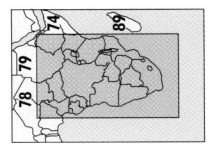

MADAGASCAR
On same scale as
General Map

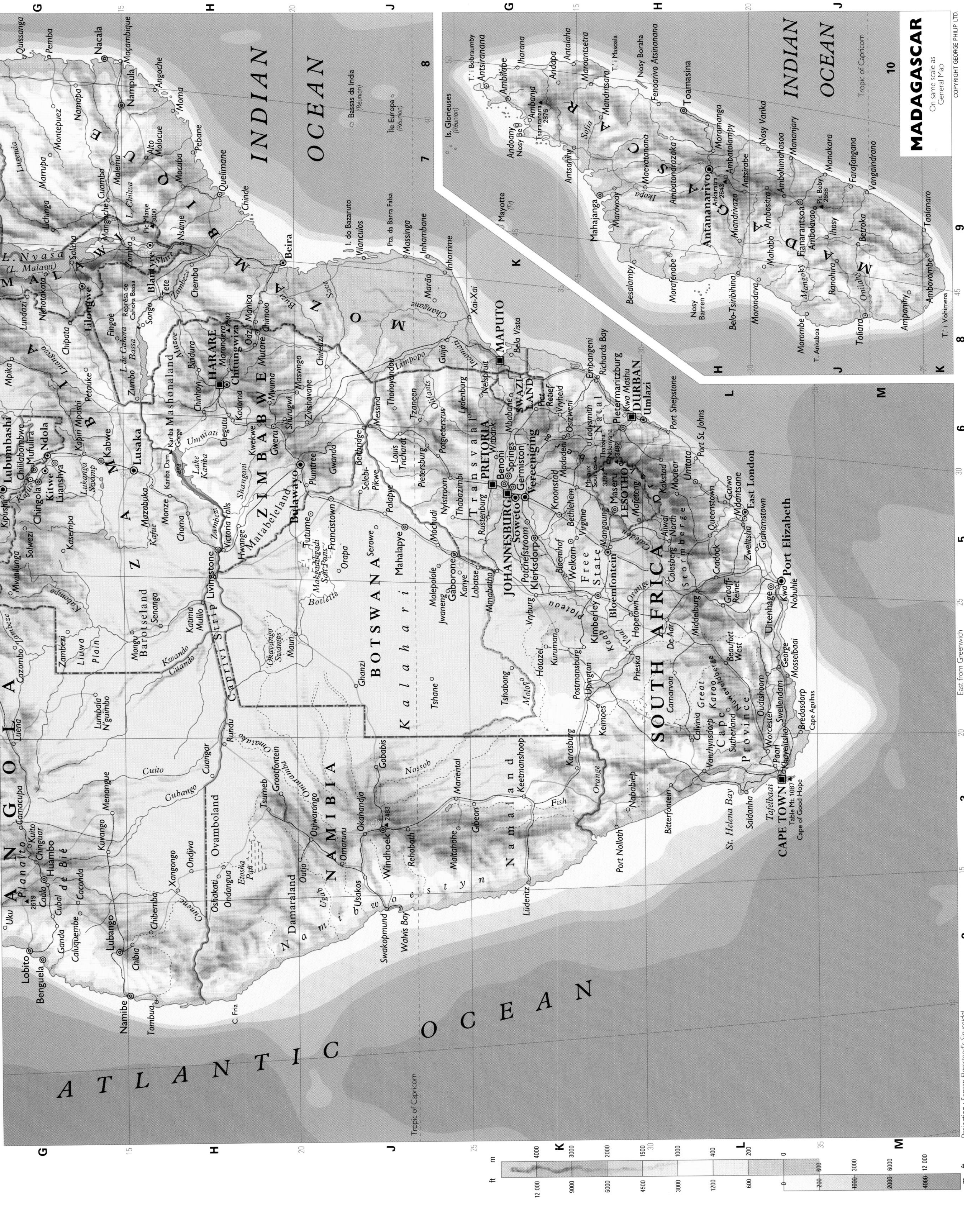

COPYRIGHT GEORGE PHILIP LTD.

INDIAN OCEAN

ATLANTIC OCEAN

Projection : Sanson-Flamsteed's Sinusoidal

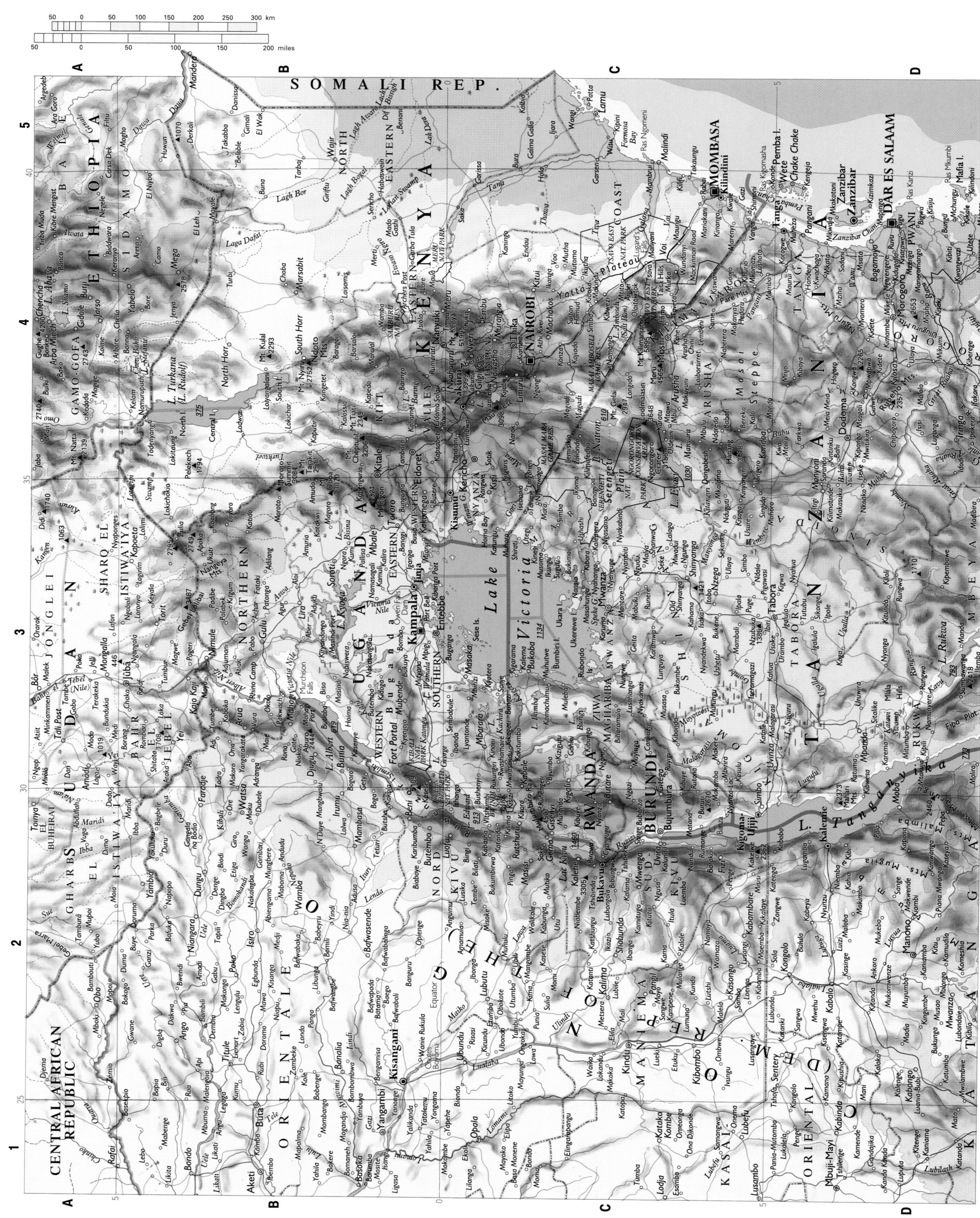
50 0 50 100 150 200 250 300 km
50 0 50 100 150 200 miles
CENTRAL AFRICAN REPUBLIC
SUDAN
ETHIOPIA
SOMALI REP.
KENYA
UGANDA
TANZANIA
RWANDA
BURUNDI
DEM. REP. OF THE CONGO
NAIROBI
MOMBASA
DAR ES SALAAM
Zanzibar
Kampala
Kisangani
Lake Victoria
L. Turkana (L. Rudolf)
L. Tanganyika
L. Albert
L. Kyoga
L. Rukwa

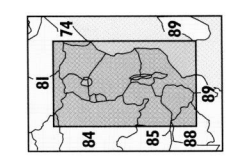

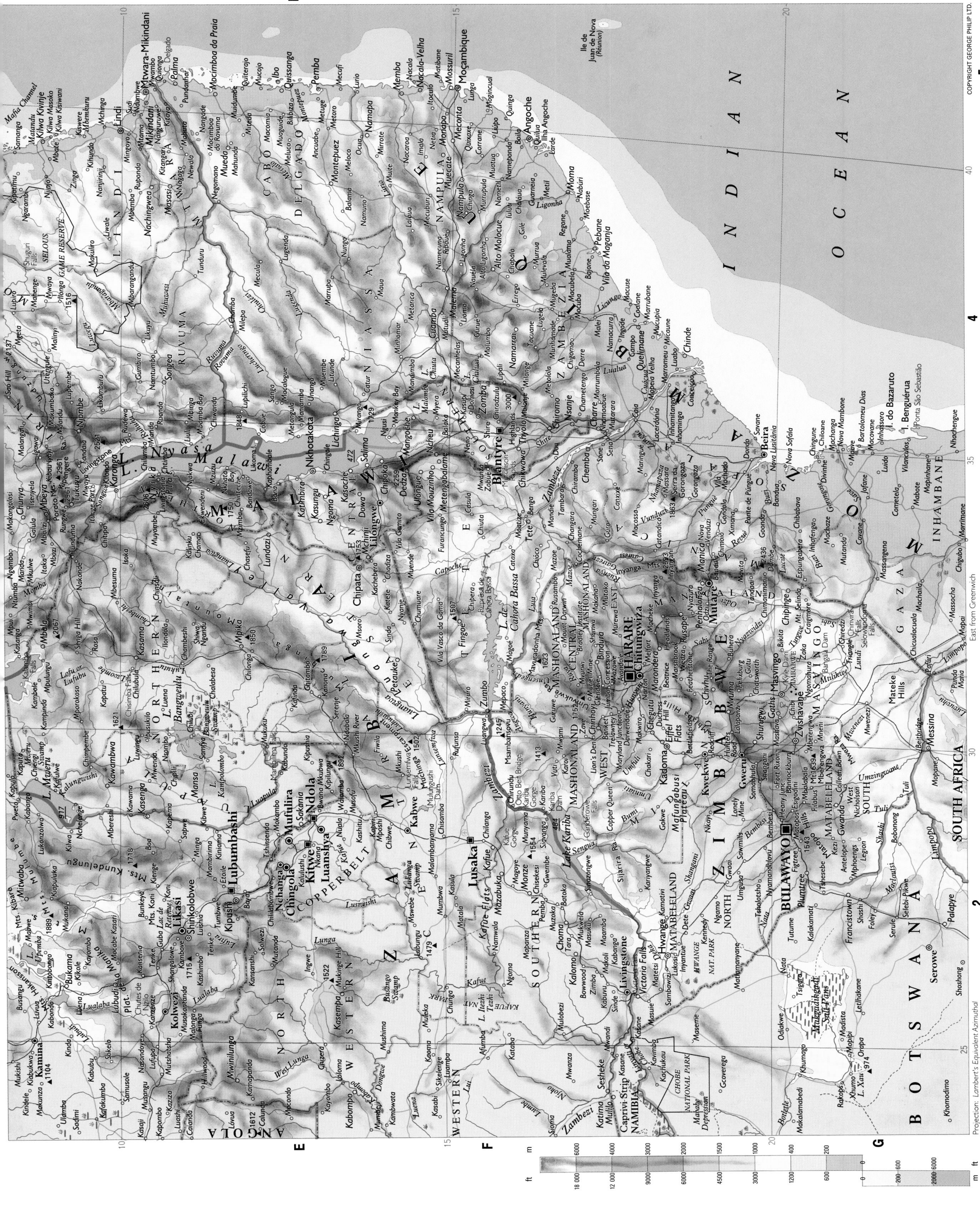

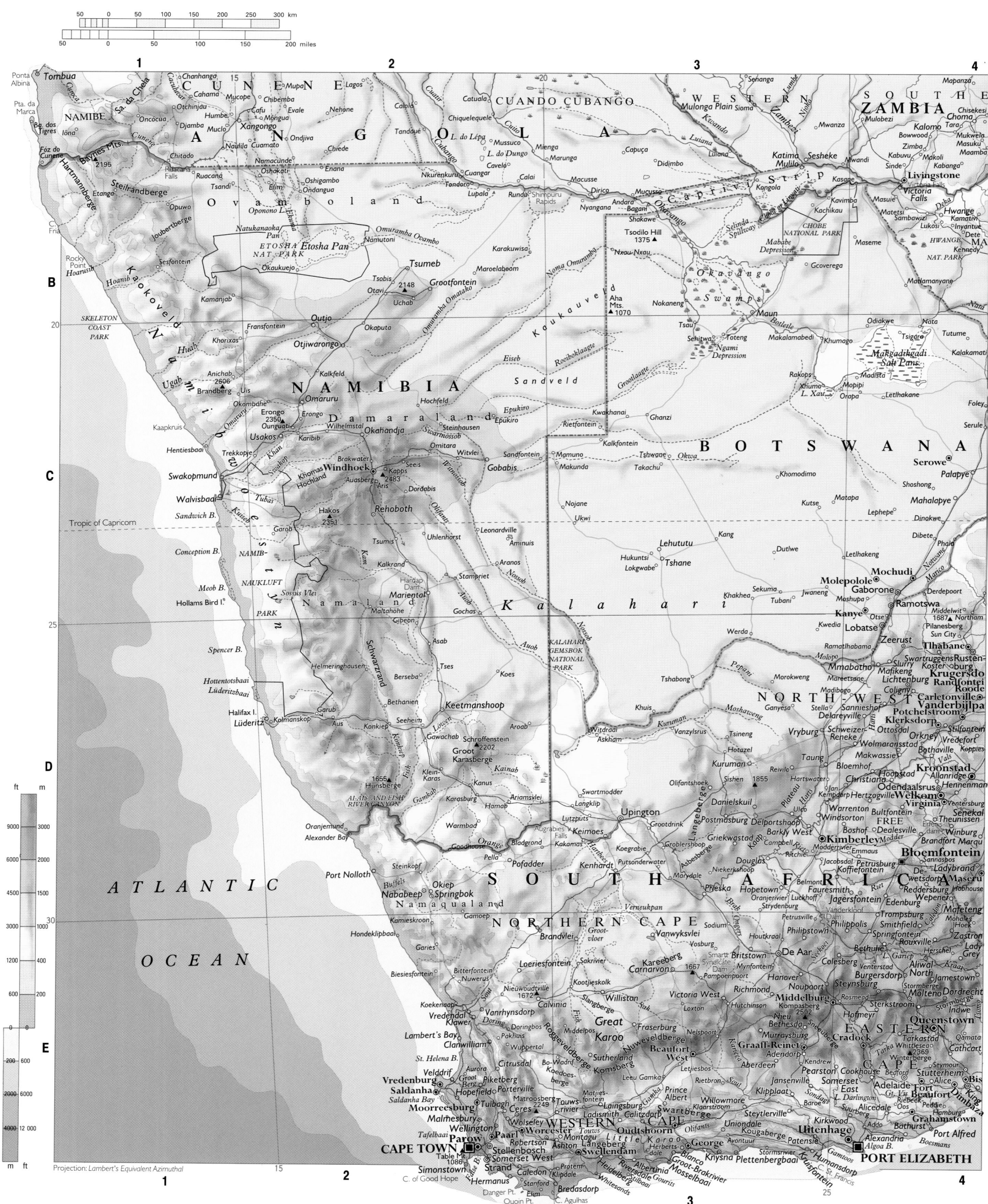
50 0 50 100 150 200 250 300 km
50 0 50 100 150 200 miles
ANGOLA
CUNENE
NAMIBE
CUANDO CUBANGO
ZAMBIA
SOUTHERN
WESTERN
NAMIBIA
BOTSWANA
SOUTH AFRICA
NORTH-WEST
FREE
NORTHERN CAPE
WESTERN CAPE
EASTERN CAPE
ATLANTIC OCEAN
Ovamboland
Damaraland
Namaland
Namaqualand
Kaokoveld
Namib Desert
Kalahari
Sandveld
Kaukauveld
Caprivi Strip
Okavango Swamps
Makgadikgadi Salt Pans
Ngami Depression
Etosha Pan
ETOSHA NAT. PARK
SKELETON COAST PARK
NAMIB-NAUKLUFT PARK
KALAHARI GEMSBOK NATIONAL PARK
CHOBE NATIONAL PARK
HWANGE NAT. PARK
Great Karoo
Tropic of Capricorn
Windhoek
Swakopmund
Walvisbaai
Lüderitz
Keetmanshoop
Rehoboth
Okahandja
Otjiwarongo
Tsumeb
Grootfontein
Outjo
Gobabis
Mariental
Maun
Serowe
Mochudi
Molepolole
Gaborone
Ramotswa
Kanye
Lobatse
Livingstone
Victoria Falls
Upington
Kimberley
Bloemfontein
Welkom
Kroonstad
Vryburg
De Aar
Beaufort West
Graaff-Reinet
Queenstown
Grahamstown
Uitenhage
PORT ELIZABETH
CAPE TOWN
Parow
Paarl
Stellenbosch
Worcester
Oudtshoorn
George
Mosselbaai
Saldanha
Vredenburg
Springbok
Port Nolloth
Alexander Bay
C. of Good Hope
C. Agulhas
Projection: Lambert's Equivalent Azimuthal

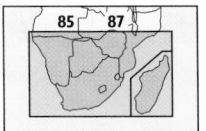

MADAGASCAR

On same scale as General Map

COPYRIGHT GEORGE PHILIP LTD.

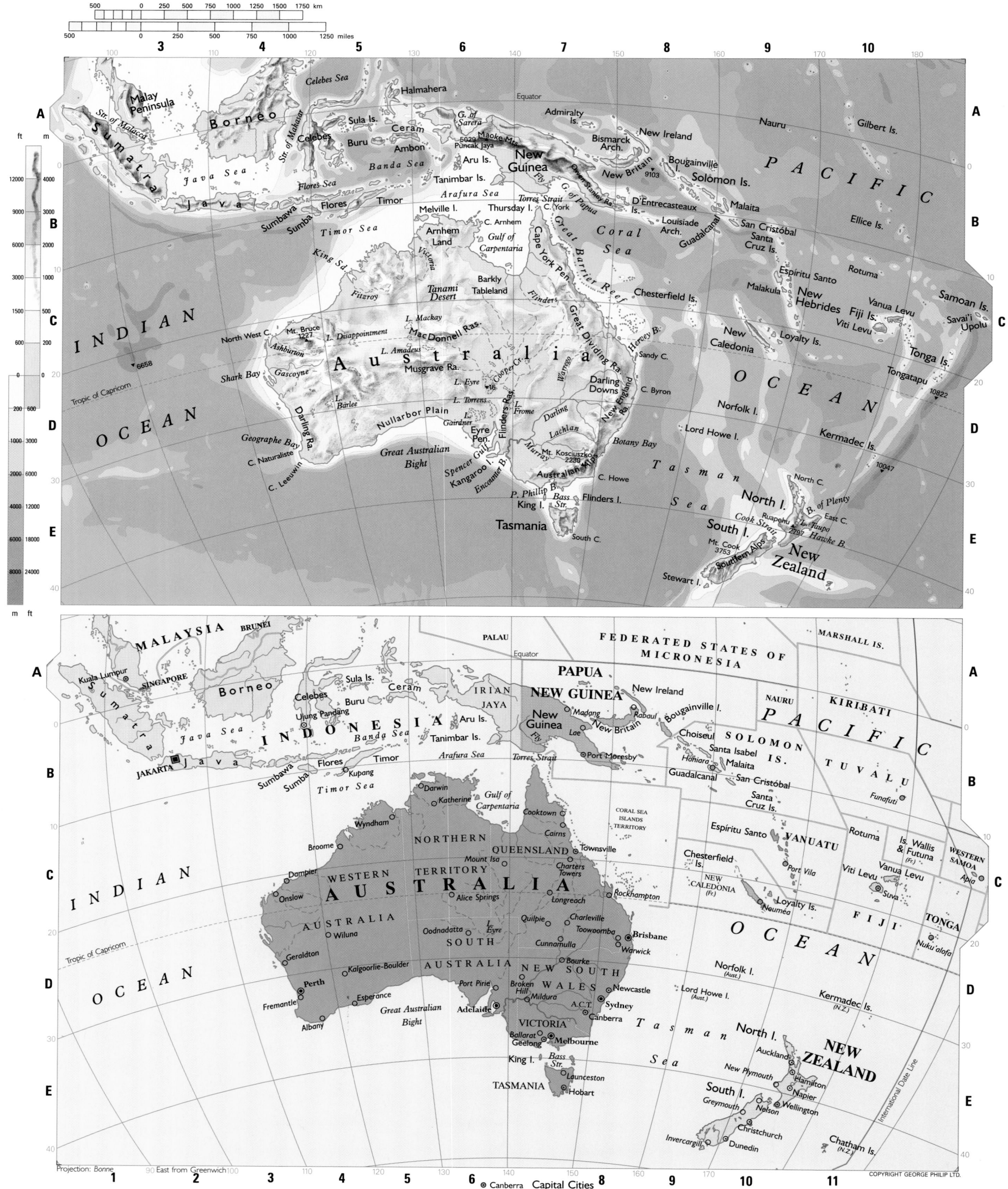

500 0 250 500 750 1000 1250 1500 1750 km
500 0 250 500 750 1000 1250 miles
ft m
12000 4000
9000 3000
6000 2000
3000 1000
1500 500
600 200
0 0
200 600
1000 3000
2000 6000
4000 12000
6000 18000
8000 24000
m ft
Equator
Malay Peninsula
Str. of Malacca
Sumatra
Borneo
Celebes Sea
Str. of Makasar
Celebes
Sula Is.
Halmahera
Buru
Ceram
Ambon
Banda Sea
Java Sea
Java
Flores Sea
Sumbawa
Sumba
Flores
Timor
Timor Sea
G. of Sarera
5029 Puncak Jaya
Maoke Mts.
New Guinea
Aru Is.
Tanimbar Is.
Arafura Sea
Fly
Torres Strait
Thursday I.
C. York
Admiralty Is.
Bismarck Arch.
New Ireland
New Britain
9103
Bougainville I.
Solomon Is.
Owen Stanley Ra.
G. of Papua
D'Entrecasteaux Is.
Louisiade Arch.
Malaita
Guadalcanal
San Cristóbal
Santa Cruz Is.
Nauru
Gilbert Is.
PACIFIC
Ellice Is.
Melville I.
C. Arnhem
Arnhem Land
Gulf of Carpentaria
Victoria
Cape York Pen.
Great Barrier Reef
Coral Sea
King Sd.
Fitzroy
Tanami Desert
Barkly Tableland
Flinders
Great Dividing Ra.
Chesterfield Is.
Espíritu Santo
Malakula
New Hebrides
Rotuma
Fiji Is.
Vanua Levu
Viti Levu
Samoan Is.
Savai'i
Upolu
INDIAN
OCEAN
6658
North West C.
Mt. Bruce 1227
L. Disappointment
L. Mackay
MacDonnell Ras.
L. Amadeus
Ashburton
Australia
Musgrave Ra.
Cooper Cr.
Warrego
Hervey B.
Sandy C.
New Caledonia
Loyalty Is.
Tonga Is.
Tongatapu
10822
Shark Bay
Gascoyne
Tropic of Capricorn
L. Eyre
-16
L. Torrens
L. Barlee
Darling Downs
C. Byron
New England Ra.
Nullarbor Plain
L. Gairdner
Eyre Pen.
Flinders Ra.
L. Frome
Darling
Lachlan
Norfolk I.
Lord Howe I.
Kermadec Is.
Geographe Bay
Darling Ra.
C. Naturaliste
C. Leeuwin
Great Australian Bight
Spencer Gulf
Kangaroo I.
Encounter B.
Murray
Mt. Kosciuszko 2230
Australian Alps
Botany Bay
C. Howe
Tasman Sea
10047
North C.
North I.
B. of Plenty
East C.
Ruapehu 2797
L. Taupo
Hawke B.
Cook Strait
P. Phillip B.
King I.
Bass Str.
Flinders I.
Tasmania
South C.
South I.
Mt. Cook 3753
Southern Alps
New Zealand
Stewart I.
MALAYSIA
BRUNEI
PALAU
FEDERATED STATES OF MICRONESIA
MARSHALL IS.
Kuala Lumpur
SINGAPORE
Ujung Pandang
IRIAN JAYA
PAPUA NEW GUINEA
Madang
Lae
Rabaul
Port Moresby
INDONESIA
JAKARTA
Kupang
Choiseul
Santa Isabel
SOLOMON IS.
Honiara
NAURU
KIRIBATI
TUVALU
Funafuti
Darwin
Katherine
Wyndham
Cooktown
Cairns
Townsville
CORAL SEA ISLANDS TERRITORY
Broome
NORTHERN TERRITORY
QUEENSLAND
Mount Isa
Charters Towers
VANUATU
Port Vila
Is. Wallis & Futuna (Fr.)
WESTERN SAMOA
Apia
Dampier
WESTERN AUSTRALIA
Onslow
Alice Springs
Longreach
Rockhampton
NEW CALEDONIA (Fr.)
Nouméa
Suva
FIJI
TONGA
Nuku'alofa
Wiluna
Oodnadatta
Quilpie
Charleville
Toowoomba
Brisbane
Warwick
Cunnamulla
SOUTH AUSTRALIA
Geraldton
Kalgoorlie-Boulder
Bourke
NEW SOUTH WALES
Perth
Fremantle
Port Pirie
Broken Hill
Mildura
Newcastle
Sydney
A.C.T.
Canberra
Esperance
Albany
Adelaide
VICTORIA
Ballarat
Geelong
Melbourne
Norfolk I. (Aust.)
Lord Howe I. (Aust.)
Kermadec Is. (N.Z.)
Launceston
Hobart
TASMANIA
Auckland
NEW ZEALAND
New Plymouth
Hamilton
Napier
Wellington
Greymouth
Nelson
Christchurch
Invercargill
Dunedin
Chatham Is. (N.Z.)
International Date Line
Projection: Bonne
East from Greenwich
Canberra Capital Cities

COPYRIGHT GEORGE PHILIP LTD.

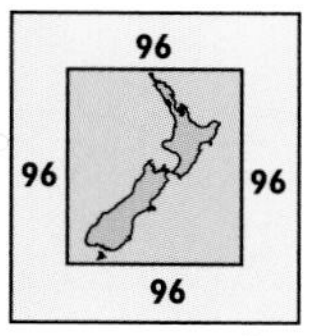

96
96 96 96
96

50 0 50 100 150 200 km
50 0 50 100 150 miles

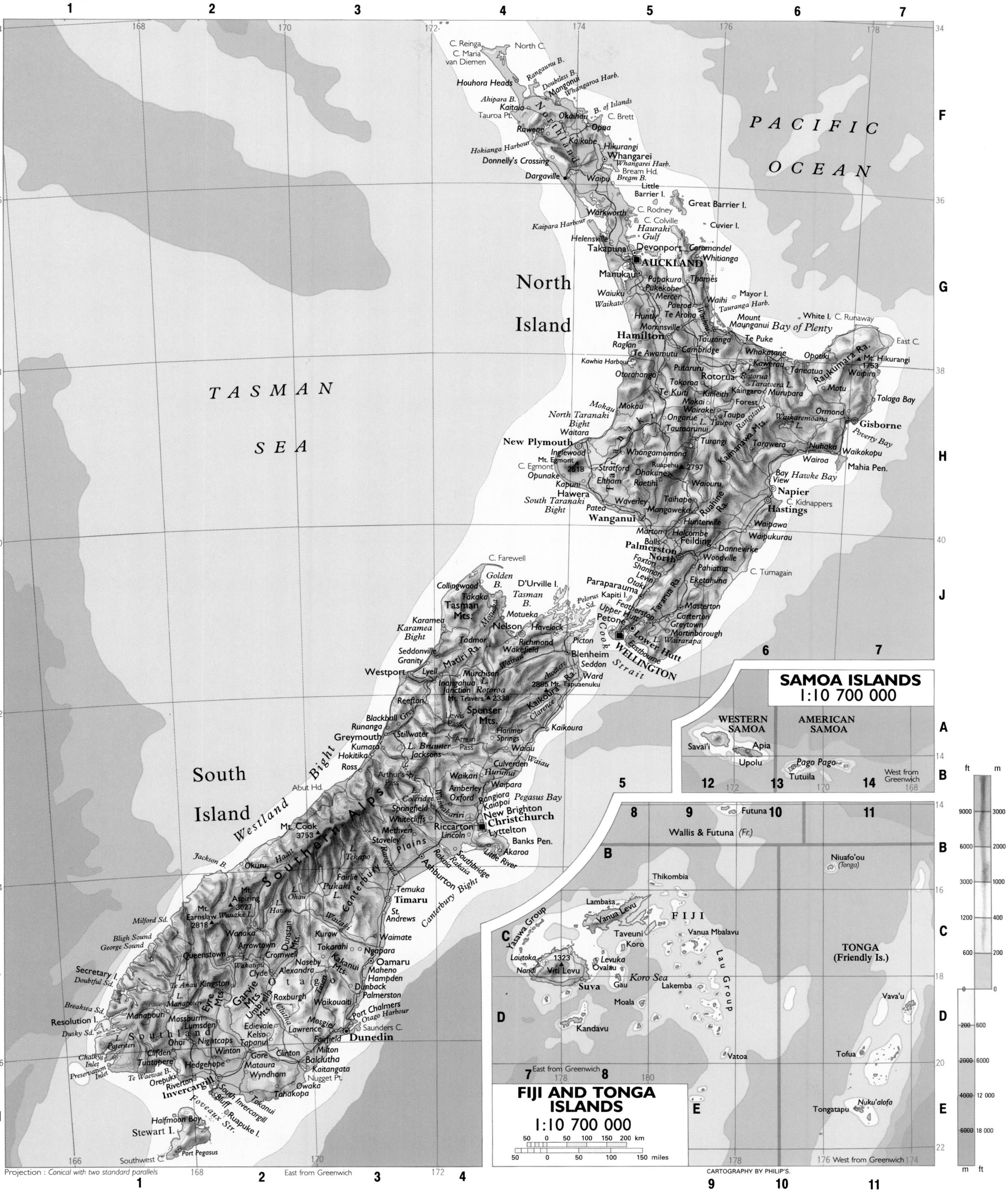

PACIFIC

OCEAN

C. Reinga
C. Maria
van Diemen
North C.
Rangaunu B.
Houhora Heads
Doubless B.
Mangonui
Whangaroa Harb.
Ahipara B.
Kaitaia
Okaihau
B. of Islands
Tauroa Pt.
C. Brett
Rawene
Kaikohe
Hikurangi
Hokianga Harbour
Whangarei
Donnelly's Crossing
Whangarei Harb.
Bream Hd.
Dargaville
Waipu
Bream B.
Little
Barrier I.
Great Barrier I.

North
Kaipara Harbour
Helensville
Warkworth
C. Rodney
C. Colville
Cuvier I.

Island
Takapuna
Devonport
Coromandel
Whitianga
Manukau
■ AUCKLAND
Papakura
Thames
Waiuku
Pukekohe
Mercer
Waihi
Mayor I.
Waikato
Paeroa
Tauranga Harb.
Huntly
Te Aroha
Mount
Maunganui
Bay of Plenty
White I. C. Runaway
Raglan
Morrinsville
Hamilton
Cambridge
Tauranga
Te Puke
Whakatane
Opotiki
East C.
Te Awamutu
Kawhia Harbour
Putaruru
Kowerau
Taneatua
Raukumara Ra.
Otorohanga
Tokoroa
Rotorua
Rotorua L.
Taratawera L.
Murupara
Waipiro
Mt. Hikurangi 1753
Mokau
Te Kuiti
Kaingaroa
Motu
Mokau
Mokai
Waikite
Forest
Tolaga Bay
North Taranaki
Bight
Ongarue
Taupo L.
Ormond
Waitara
Taumarunui
Taupo
Rangitaiki
Waikaremoana L.
Gisborne
New Plymouth
Whangamomona
Turangi
Kaimanawa Mts.
Targwera
Nuhaka
Poverty Bay
Inglewood
Mt. Egmont
Ruapehu 2797
Waikokopu
C. Egmont 2518
Stratford
Ohakune
Waiouru
Bay Hawke Bay
Mahia Pen.
Opunake
Eltham
Raetihi
View
Kapuni
Hawera
Waverley
Mangaweka
Taihape
Napier
South Taranaki
Patea
Mangaweka
Hunterville
Hastings
Bight
Wanganui
Marton
Halcombe
Waipawa
C. Kidnappers
Bulls
Feilding
Waipukurau
Foxton
Palmerston
Dannevirke
Shannon
North
Woodville
Levin
Pahiatua
Otaki
Eketahuna
C. Turnagain

TASMAN

SEA

C. Farewell
Collingwood
Golden
B.
D'Urville I.
Paraparauma
Takaka
Tasman
B.
Kapiti I.
Masterton
Tasman
Pelorus Sd.
Upper
Carterton
Mts.
Motueka
Featherston
Greytown
Karamea
Nelson
Petone
Martinborough
Karamea
Havelock
Picton
Lower Hutt
Wairarapa
Bight
Tadmor
Richmond
■ **WELLINGTON**
Wakefield
Cook
Westport
Lyell
Murchison
Blenheim
Strait
Inangahua
Wairau
Seddon
Junction Rotoroa
Ward
Mt. Travers ▲2338
2885 Mt. Tapuaenuku
Reefton
Lewis
Spenser
Clarence
Kaikoura
Blackball
Grey
Pass
Mts.
Runanga
Stillwater
Amuri
Hanmer
Kaikoura
Greymouth
Pass
Springs
Kumara
L. Brunner
Waiau
Hokitika
Jacksons
Culverden
Ross
Arthur's
Waikari
Hurunui
Pass
Amberley
Waipara

South
Abut Hd.
rangiora
Pegasus Bay
Oxford
Kaiapoi
Island
Coleridge
New Brighton
Springfield
Riccarton
Christchurch
Westland
Whitecliffs
Lincoln
Lyttelton
Bight
Mt. Cook
Methven
Banks Pen.
3753
Staveley
Akaroa
Southern Alps
Tekapo
Southbridge
Little River
Rakaia
Jackson B.
Okuru
Haast
Pukaki
Rakaia
Fairlie
Ashburton
Mt.
L.
Canterbury
Bight
Milford Sd.
Aspiring
Ohau
3027
L.
Temuka
Bligh Sound
Earnslaw
Wanaka L.
St.
Timaru
George Sound
2818
Wanaka
Plains
Andrews
Arrowtown
Tekapo
Secretary I.
Queenstown
Cromwell
Kurow
Waimate
Doubtful Sd.
Wakatipu
Clyde
Tokarahi
Ngapara
Te Anau Kingston
Naseby
Oamaru
Breaksea Sd.
L.
Alexandra
Maheno
Resolution I.
Manapouri
Garvie
Roxburgh
Hampden
Dusky Sd.
Eyre
Mts.
Dunback
Mossburn
Umbrella
Palmerston
Lumsden
Kelso
Port Chalmers
Preservation Inlet
Ohai
Nightcaps
Edievale
Lawrence
Otago Harbour
Chalky
Clifden
Winton
Tapanui
Fairfield
Saunders C.
Inlet
Tuatapere
Mataura
Milton
Dunedin
Te Waewae B.
Orepuki
Hedgehope
Clinton
Kaitangata
Riverton
Wyndham
Owaka
Southland
Tokanui
Gore
Nugget Pt.
Invercargill
South Invercargill
Tahakopa
Bluff Ruapuke I.
Foveaux Str.

Halfmoon Bay
Stewart I.
Southwest C.
Port Pegasus

SAMOA ISLANDS
1:10 700 000

WESTERN
SAMOA
AMERICAN
SAMOA
Savai'i
Apia
Upolu
Pago Pago
West from
Tutuila
Greenwich

Wallis & Futuna (Fr.)
Futuna

Niuafo'ou
(Tonga)

Thikombia
Lambasa
Vanua Levu
Yasawa Group
Taveuni
Vanua Mbalavu
Koro
FIJI
Lautoka
1323
Levuka
Lau Group
TONGA
Nandi
Viti Levu
Ovalau
(Friendly Is.)
Gau
Vava'u
Suva
Koro Sea
Lakemba
Moala
Tofua
Kandavu
Vatoa
Tongatapu
Nuku'alofa

FIJI AND TONGA
ISLANDS
1:10 700 000

50 0 50 100 150 200 km
50 0 50 100 150 miles

ft   m
9000   3000
6000   2000
3000   1000
1200   400
600   200
0   0
200   600
2000   6000
4000   12000
6000   18000
m   ft

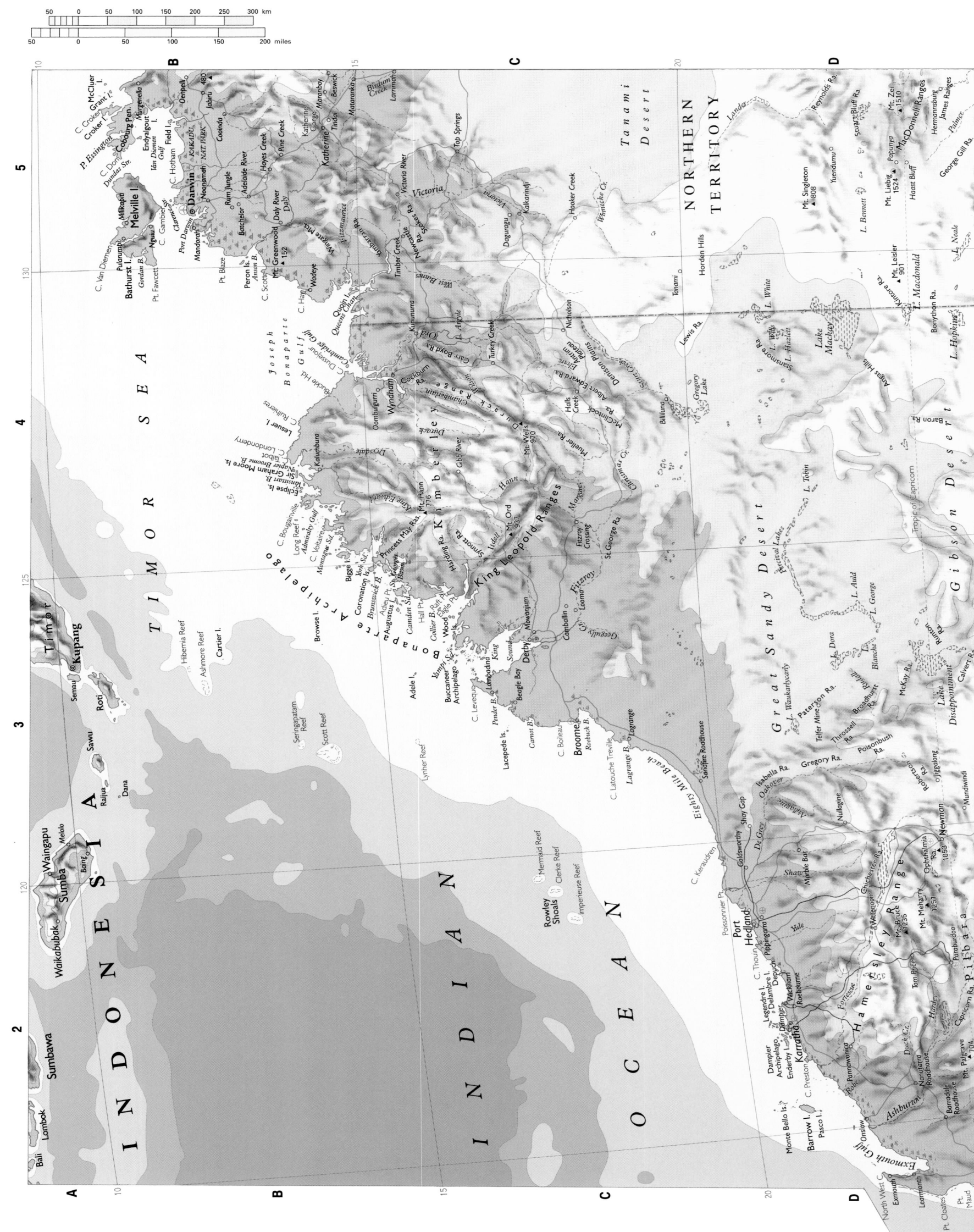
50 0 50 100 150 200 250 300 km
50 0 50 100 150 200 miles
INDONESIA
TIMOR SEA
INDIAN OCEAN
NORTHERN TERRITORY
Tanami Desert
Great Sandy Desert
Gibson Desert
Bali
Lombok
Sumbawa
Waikabubak
Sumba
Waingapu
Melolo
Baing
Raijua
Dana
Sawu
Roti
Semau
Kupang
Timor
Hibernia Reef
Ashmore Reef
Cartier I.
Seringapatam Reef
Scott Reef
Browse I.
Adele I.
Lynher Reef
Rowley Shoals
Mermaid Reef
Clerke Reef
Imperieuse Reef
Bonaparte Archipelago
Buccaneer Archipelago
Lacepede Is.
King Sound
Derby
Broome
Roebuck B.
Lagrange
Eighty Mile Beach
Sandfire Roadhouse
Port Hedland
Goldsworthy
Shay Gap
Dampier Archipelago
Karratha
Roebourne
Barrow I.
Monte Bello Is.
Onslow
Exmouth Gulf
Exmouth
Hamersley Range
Pilbara
Mt. Bruce 1235
Mt. Meharry 1251
Tom Price
Paraburdoo
Newman
Marble Bar
Nullagine
Telfer Mine
Lake Disappointment
Tropic of Capricorn
Kimberley
King Leopold Ranges
Mt. Hann 776
Mt. Ord 937
Mt. Wells 970
Fitzroy Crossing
Halls Creek
Kalumburu
Wyndham
Kununurra
Joseph Bonaparte Gulf
Cambridge Gulf
Gregory Lake
Billiluna
Lake Mackay
L. Hopkins
L. Macdonald
Darwin
Melville I.
Bathurst I.
Katherine
Timber Creek
Victoria River
Kalkarindji
Hooker Creek
Tanami
Mt. Singleton 808
Mt. Liebig 1524
Mt. Zeil 1510
MacDonnell Ranges

WESTERN AUSTRALIA

SOUTH AUSTRALIA

Great Victoria Desert

Nullarbor Plain

Hampton Tableland

Great Australian Bight

INDIAN OCEAN

SOUTHERN OCEAN

Archipelago of the Recherche

PERTH
Fremantle
Kwinana
Rockingham
Mandurah
Bunbury
Australind
Busselton
Albany
Geraldton
Carnarvon
Kalgoorlie-Boulder
Coolgardie
Norseman
Esperance
Northam
Merredin
Narrogin
Katanning
Collie
Kalbarri
Meekatharra
Wiluna
Leonora
Laverton
Southern Cross
Hopetoun
Ravensthorpe
Eucla
Forrest
Cook
Ooldea
Nullarbor
Madura
Cocklebiddy
Balladonia
Rawlinna
Zanthus
Naretha

Mt. Augustus 1105
Mt. Essendon 906
Ayers Rock 868
Mt. Olga 1069
Mt. Woodroffe 1440
Musgrave Ranges
Petermann Ranges
Everard Ranges
Mt. Ragged 585
Stirling Ra. 1073
Bluff Knoll

L. Moore
L. Barlee
L. Ballard
L. Carey
L. Lefroy
L. Cowan
L. Dundas
L. Carnegie
L. Wells
L. Amadeus

Shark Bay
Hamelin Pool
Dirk Hartog I.
Bernier I.
Dorre I.
Houtman Abrolhos
Rottnest I.
C. Leeuwin
Pt. D'Entrecasteaux
Geographe B.

1 2 3 4 5
E F G
115 120 125 130
30 35

East from Greenwich

Projection: Bonne

COPYRIGHT GEORGE PHILIP LTD.

ft m
3000 1000
1200 400
600 200
0 0
200 600
2000 6000
4000 12 000
m ft

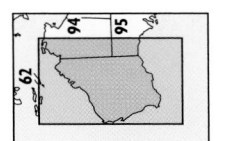

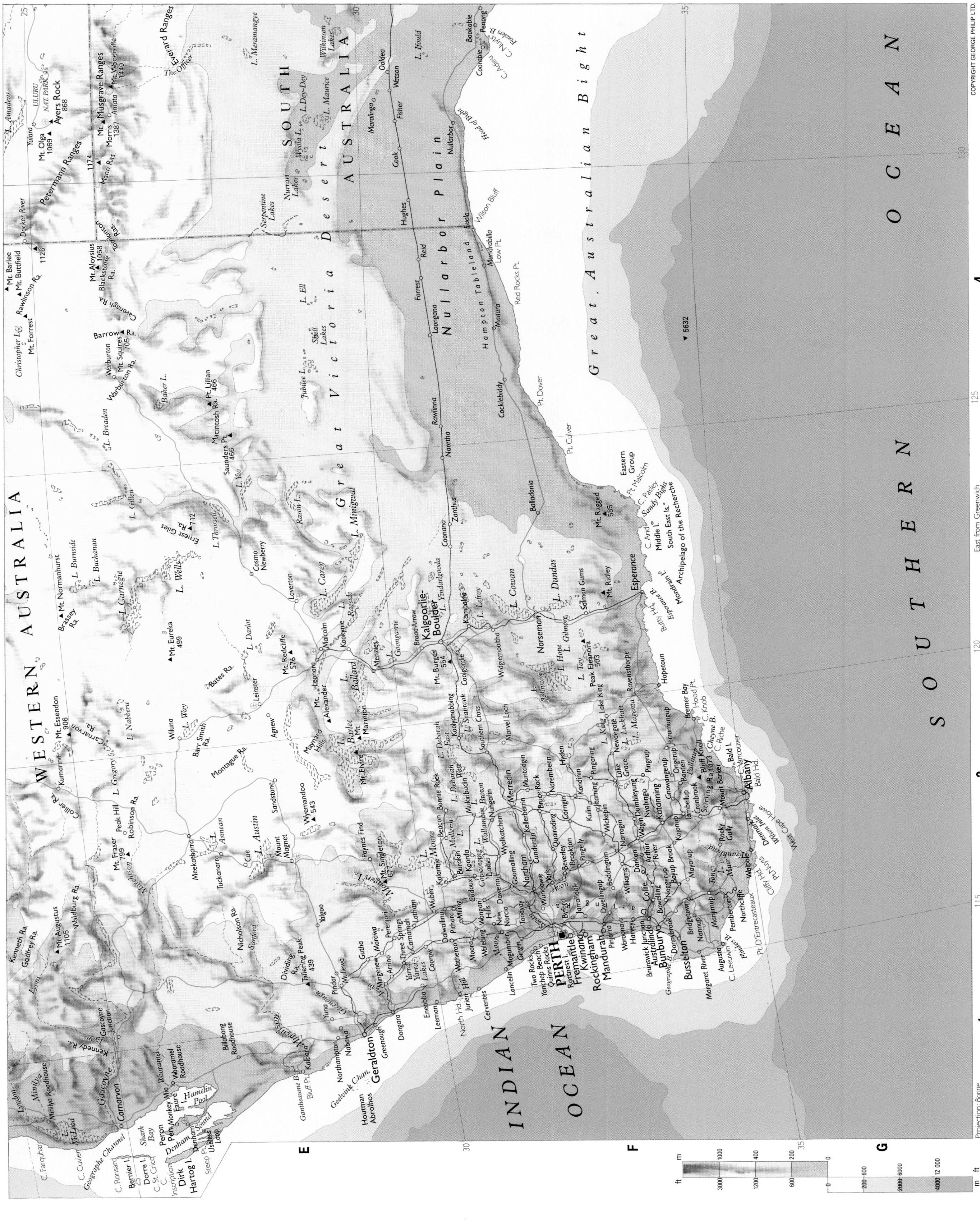

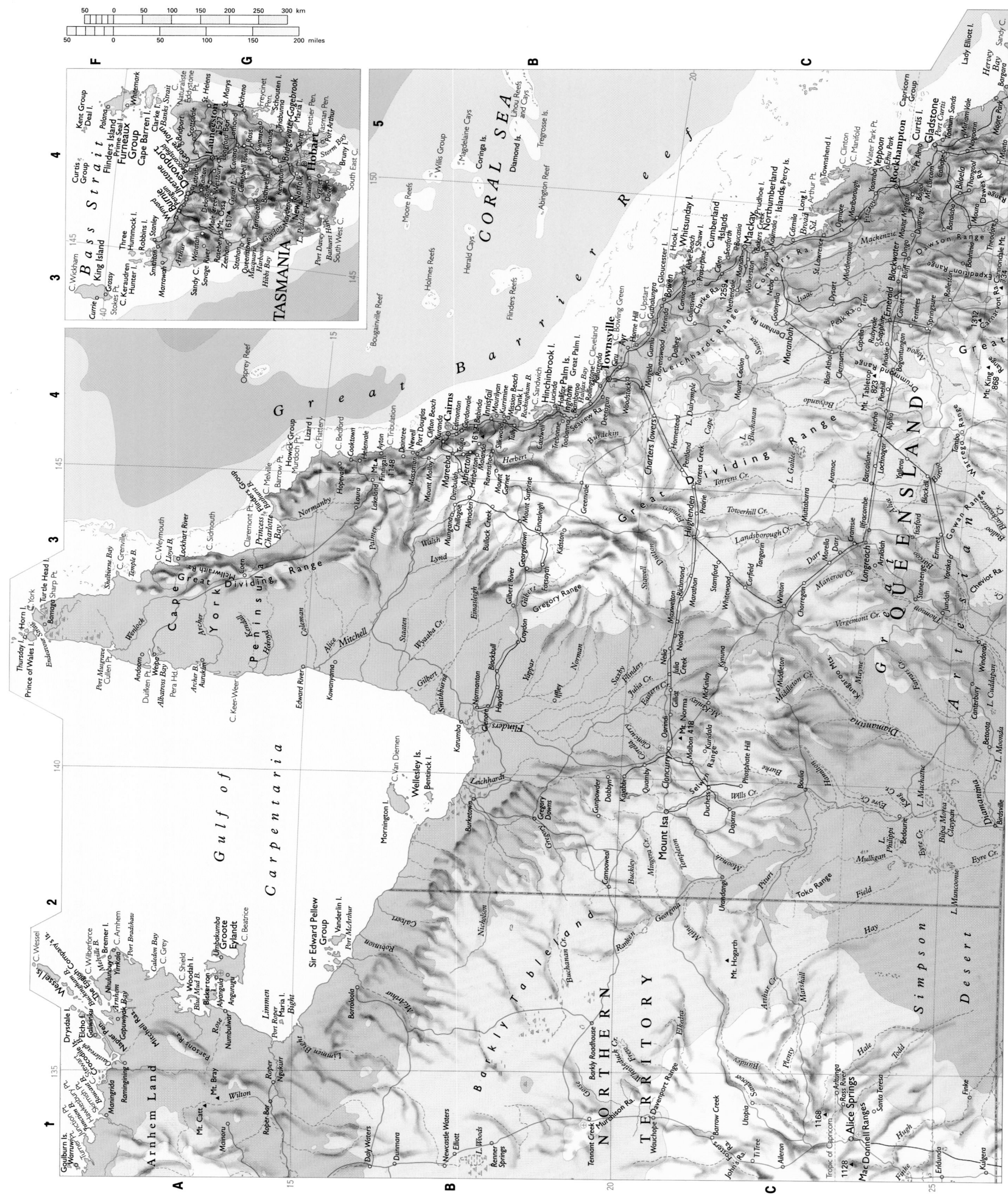

50 0 50 100 150 200 250 300 km
50 0 50 100 150 200 miles
TASMANIA
Bass Strait
King Island
Flinders Island
Furneaux Group
Cape Barren I.
Launceston
Devonport
Burnie
Hobart
Great Barrier Reef
CORAL SEA
Gulf of Carpentaria
Cape York Peninsula
Great Dividing Range
QUEENSLAND
NORTHERN TERRITORY
Great Artesian Basin
Simpson Desert
Barkly Tableland
Arnhem Land
Groote Eylandt
Wellesley Is.
Mornington I.
Sir Edward Pellew Group
Cairns
Townsville
Mackay
Rockhampton
Gladstone
Mount Isa
Cloncurry
Longreach
Charters Towers
Alice Springs
Tennant Creek
Mac Donnell Ranges
Tropic of Capricorn
Birdsville
Boulia
Hughenden
Emerald
Bowen
Whitsunday I.
Hinchinbrook I.
Normanton
Burketown
Borroloola
Roper Bar
Ngukurr
Newcastle Waters

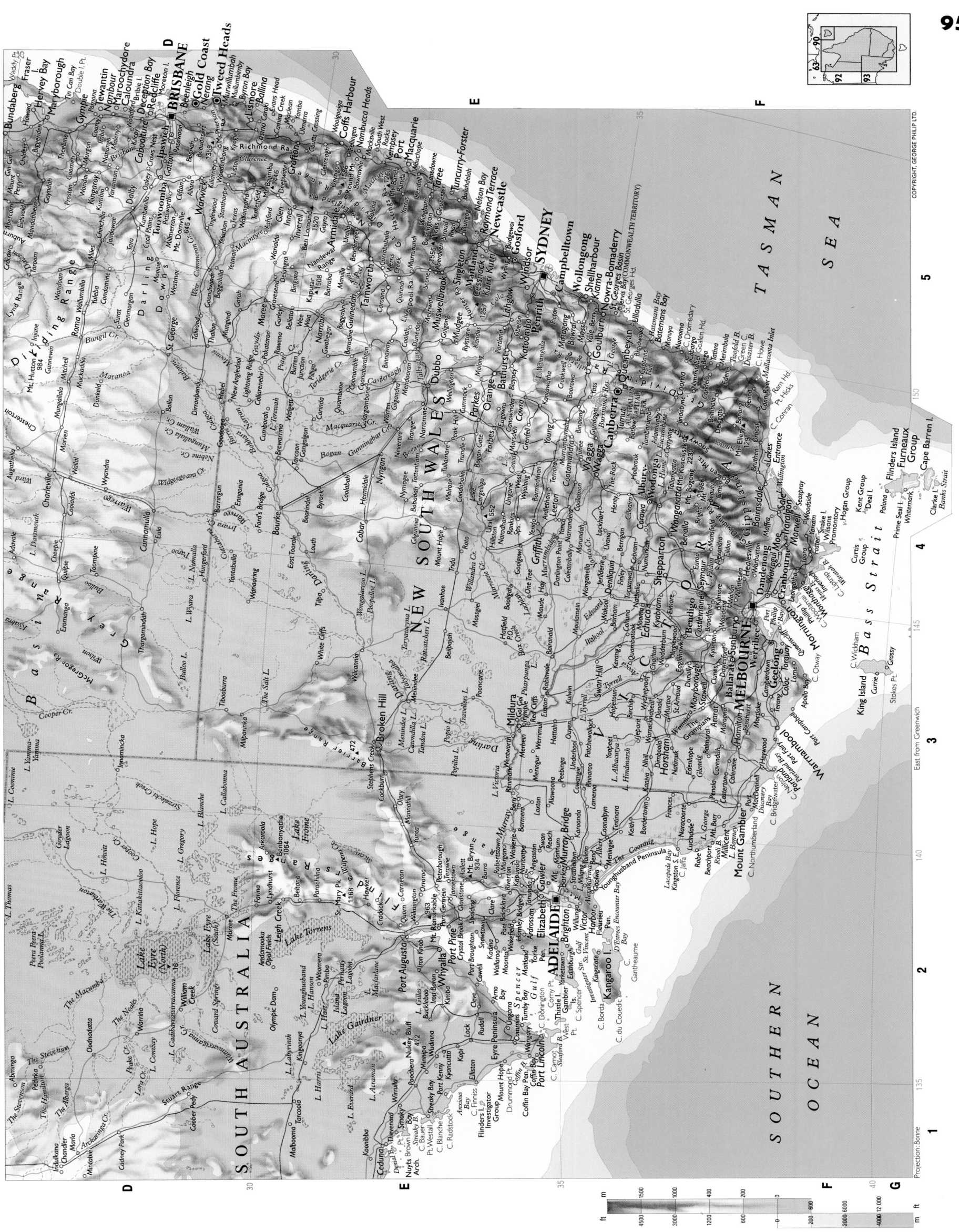

SOUTH AUSTRALIA
NEW SOUTH WALES
VICTORIA
TASMAN SEA
SOUTHERN OCEAN
Bass Strait
BRISBANE
SYDNEY
MELBOURNE
ADELAIDE
Canberra
AUSTRALIAN CAPITAL TERR.
(COMMONWEALTH TERRITORY)
Gold Coast
Tweed Heads
Newcastle
Wollongong
Geelong
Ballarat
Bendigo
Broken Hill
Mildura
Port Augusta
Port Pirie
Whyalla
Port Lincoln
Mount Gambier
Warrnambool
Dubbo
Orange
Bathurst
Wagga Wagga
Albury-Wodonga
Tamworth
Armidale
Toowoomba
Ipswich
Coffs Harbour
Port Macquarie
Lake Eyre (North)
Lake Eyre (South)
Lake Torrens
Lake Frome
Lake Gairdner
Flinders Ranges
Great Dividing Range
Grey Range
Darling Downs
Kangaroo I.
King Island
Flinders Island
Furneaux Group
Cape Barren I.
Spencer Gulf
East from Greenwich
Projection: Bonne
COPYRIGHT, GEORGE PHILIP LTD.

7 8 9 10

6

1 2 3 4 5

B

MOSKVA
Volga
Yekaterinburg
R U S S I A
Tomsk
Oб
Lena
Sea of Okhotsk
Okhotsk
Poluostrov Kamchatka
Komandorskiye Ostrova (Russia)
Near Is. (U.S.A.)
Bering Sea
Andreanof Is. (U.S.A.)

Novosibirsk
Astana (Aqmola)
Semey
Irkutsk
Oz. Baykal
Chita
Blagoveshchensk
Amur
Sakhalin
Petropavlovsk-Kamchatskiy
7822
Aleutian
Aleutian Trench

50
KAZAKSTAN
Aral Sea
Balqash Köl
Altai
MONGOLIA
Ulaanbaatar
Khabarovsk
La Perouse Str.
Kurilskiye Ostrova (Russia)
10,542
Kuril Trench

C
Almaty
Ürümqi
Changchun
Harbin
Sapporo
Vladivostok
Hakodate
Sea of Japan

40
Toshkent
KYRGYZSTAN
SHENYANG
NORTH KOREA
Emperor Seamount Chain

TAJIKISTAN
BEIJING
TIANJIN
Taiyuan
DALIAN
SŌUL
SOUTH KOREA
Nagoya
Fuji-San 3776
TOKYO
Sendai

D
AFGHANISTAN
Kabul
Srinagar
Kunlun Shan
CHINA
Lanzhou
Xi'an
Qingdao
Kyoto
Osaka
Yokohama
JAPAN
Japan Trench
10,554

PAKISTAN
Lahore
DELHI
XIZANG
Himalaya
Lhasa
CHONGQING
Nanjing
Wuhan
Yellow Sea
Kitakyushū
Shikoku
Kyūshū

30
Kanpur
8850 Mt. Everest
NEPAL
Chang Jiang
HANGZHOU
SHANGHAI
East China Sea
Ogasawara Gunto (Japan)
Midway Is. (U.S.A.)

Ganga
Brahmaputra
Changsha
Minami-Tori-Shima (Japan)
Lisianski I. (U.S.A.)

E
BANGLADESH
Kunming
Fuzhou
Taipei
Ryūkyū-retto (Japan)
Kazan-Rettō (Japan)

CALCUTTA
DHAKA
GUANGZHOU
TAIWAN

20
INDIA
BURMA
Mandalay
HONG KONG
Macau
South Honshu Ridge
Wake I. (U.S.A.)
Necker Ridge

Hyderabad
LAOS
Hanoi
NORTHERN MARIANAS (U.S.A.)
Marcus
P A

F
Bay of Bengal
Rangoon
THAILAND
Hainan
C. Engano
Luzon
Paracel Is.
MANILA
Saipan
MARSHALL IS.

CHENNAI (Madras)
BANGKOK
CAMBODIA
Mindoro
PHILIPPINES
GUAM (U.S.A.)
11,022
Enewetak Atoll
Bikini Atoll

Andaman Is. (India)
Phnom Penh
G. of Thailand
Palawan
Samar
10,497
Mariana Trench
Yap
Caroline Is.
M i c r o

10
SRI LANKA
Nicobar Is. (India)
Phanh Bho Ho Chi Minh
South China Sea
Sulu Sea
Mindanao
Truk
Dalap-Uliga-Darrit

Colombo
MALAYSIA
4101
BRUNEI
SABAH
Mindanao Trench
Koror
PALAU
FEDERATED STATES OF MICRONESIA
Pohnpei
Palikir
Jaluit I.

G
Kuala Lumpur
PEN. MALAYSIA
SARAWAK
Celebes Sea
M e l
n e s i a
O

0
SINGAPORE
Borneo
Sulawesi
Halmahera
PAPUA NEW GUINEA
NAURU
Tarawa
Gilbert Is.
Banaba
Howland I. (U.S.A.)
Baker I. (U.S.A.)

H
Sumatera
INDONESIA
Palembang
Java Sea
Ujung Pandang
Buru
Seram
Admiralty Is.
New Ireland
Bismarck Arch.
New Britain
Rabaul
Bougainville
Butaritari
Phoenix Is.
Abariringa
Enderbury

JAKARTA
Jawa
Surabaya
Flores Sea
Banda Sea
7440
Punçak Jaya 5029
IRIAN JAYA
New Guinea
Lae
SOLOMON IS.
Fongafale
TUVALU
K I R

10
Selat Sunda
Sunda Islands
Bali
Sumbawa
Sumba
Flores
Timor
Arafura Sea
Torres Strait
C. York
Port Moresby
Honiara
Guadalcanal
Santa Cruz I.
9165
Tokelau Is. (N.Z.)

Cocos Is. (Austral.)
Christmas I. (Austral.)
Java Trench
C. Arnhem
Gulf of Carpentaria
Louisiade Arch.
Rotuma
Is. Wallis & Futuna (Fr.)
WESTERN SAMOA

INDIAN
Darwin
Coral Sea
VANUATU
Espiritu Santo
Is. Chesterfield
Apia
Vanua Levu

20
OCEAN
Broome
Cairns
Townsville
Port Vila
Viti Levu
FIJI
Suva

North West C.
Mount Isa
7570
NEW CALEDONIA (Fr.)
Noumea
Is. Loyauté
Nuku'alofa
TONGA

AUSTRALIA
Alice Springs
Rockhampton
Great Dividing Ra.
10,822
Tonga Trench

30
Geraldton
L. Eyre
Brisbane
Norfolk I. (Austral.)
Kermadec Is. (N.Z.)

Perth
Darling
Lord Howe I. (Austral.)
Kermadec Trench
10,047

L
Nouvelle Amsterdam (Fr.)
I. St. Paul (Fr.)
Great Australian Bight
Sydney
Canberra
Tasman Sea
NEW ZEALAND

Albany
Adelaide
Murray
Mt. Kosciuszko 2237
Auckland

40
Mid-Indian Ridge
Bass Str.
Melbourne
Cook Strait
Wellington

M
Is. Crozet (Fr.)
Tasmania
Hobart
Aoraki Mt. Cook 3753
Christchurch
Chatham Is. (N.Z.)

Kerguelen (Fr.)
Dunedin
Bounty Is. (N.Z.)

50
Invercargill
Antipodes Is. (N.Z.)

N
Heard I. (Austral.)
Auckland Is. (N.Z.)
Campbell I. (N.Z.)
Macquarie I. (Austral.)

ft m
12 000 4000
9000 3000
6000 2000
3000 1000
1500 500
600 200
0 0
200 600
1000 3000
2000 6000
4000 12 000
6000 18 000
8000 24 000
m ft

Projection: Mollweide's Homolographic
East from Greenwich

1 2 3 4 5 6 7 8 9 10

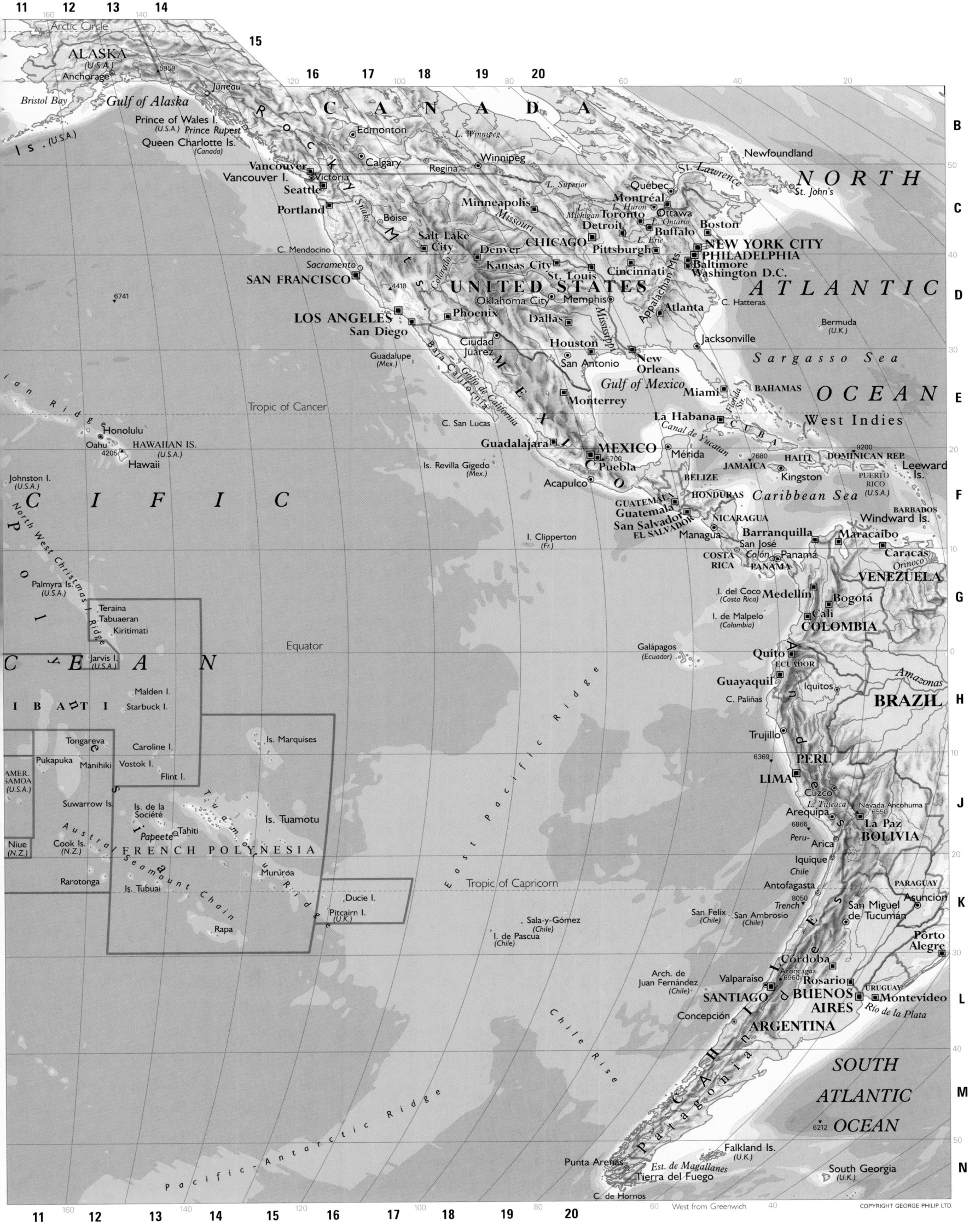

Arctic Circle
ALASKA
(U.S.A.)
Anchorage
Juneau
Bristol Bay
Gulf of Alaska
Prince of Wales I.
(U.S.A.) Prince Rupert
Queen Charlotte Is.
(Canada)
Is. (U.S.A.)

CANADA

NORTH

Edmonton
Calgary
Regina
Winnipeg
L. Winnipeg
Newfoundland

Vancouver
Vancouver I.
Victoria
Seattle
Portland

St. Lawrence
Québec
Montréal
Ottawa
Boston
St. John's

Boise
Minneapolis
L. Superior
L. Michigan
L. Huron
Toronto
Detroit
L. Ontario
Buffalo
L. Erie

Salt Lake
City
Denver
CHICAGO
Pittsburgh
NEW YORK CITY
PHILADELPHIA
Baltimore
Washington D.C.

C. Mendocino
Sacramento
SAN FRANCISCO
Kansas City
UNITED STATES
St. Louis
Cincinnati

ATLANTIC

6741
Oklahoma City
Memphis
Appalachian Mts.
Atlanta
C. Hatteras

4418
LOS ANGELES
San Diego
Phoenix
Dallas
Houston
Jacksonville

Bermuda
(U.K.)

Ciudad
Juárez
San Antonio
New
Orleans
Guadalupe
(Mex.)
Monterrey
Gulf of Mexico
Miami
BAHAMAS
Sargasso Sea

OCEAN

Tropic of Cancer
C. San Lucas
Gulfo de California
La Habana
West Indies
CUBA

Honolulu
Oahu
HAWAIIAN IS.
4205
Hawaii
(U.S.A.)
Hawaii

Guadalajara
MEXICO
Puebla
Mérida
Canal de Yucatán
7680
9200
HAITI
DOMINICAN REP.
Leeward
Is.
JAMAICA
Kingston
PUERTO
RICO
(U.S.A.)

Is. Revilla Gigedo
(Mex.)
Acapulco
BELIZE
GUATEMALA
HONDURAS
Caribbean Sea
BARBADOS
Windward Is.
Guatemala
San Salvador
EL SALVADOR
NICARAGUA
Managua
Barranquilla
Maracaibo
I. Clipperton
(Fr.)
San José
Colón
Panamá
Caracas
VENEZUELA
COSTA
RICA
PANAMA
Orinoco

Johnston I.
(U.S.A.)
PACIFIC

North West Christmas Ridge

Palmyra Is.
(U.S.A.)
I. del Coco
(Costa Rica)
Medellín
Bogotá
I. de Malpelo
(Colombia)
Cali
COLOMBIA

Teraina
Tabuaeran
Kiritimati

OCEAN
Equator
Galápagos
(Ecuador)
Quito
ECUADOR

Jarvis I.
(U.S.A.)
Guayaquil
Iquitos
Amazonas

Malden I.
Starbuck I.
C. Paliñas
BRAZIL

IBA OTI
Tongareva
Caroline I.
Trujillo

AMER.
SAMOA
(U.S.A.)
Pukapuka
Manihiki
Vostok I.
Flint I.
6369
PERU

Suwarrow Is.
Is. Marquises
LIMA
Cuzco

Niue
(N.Z.)
Is. de la
Société
Is. Tuamotu
Arequipa
L. Titicaca
Nevada Ancohuma
6550

Cook Is.
(N.Z.)
Papeete
Tahiti
FRENCH POLYNESIA
6866
Peru
Arica
La Paz
BOLIVIA

Rarotonga
Is. Tubuai
Mururoa
Iquique
Chile

Tropic of Capricorn
PARAGUAY
Antofagasta
Asunción

Ducie I.
8050
Trench
San Felix
(Chile)
San Ambrosio
(Chile)
San Miguel
de Tucumán

Pitcairn I.
(U.K.)
Rapa
Pôrto
Alegre

Sala-y-Gómez
(Chile)
Córdoba
I. de Pascua
(Chile)
Aconcagua
6960
Rosario
URUGUAY

Arch. de
Juan Fernández
(Chile)
Valparaíso
SANTIAGO
BUENOS
AIRES
Montevideo
Río de la Plata

Concepción
ARGENTINA

SOUTH

Chile Rise

ATLANTIC

East Pacific Ridge

OCEAN
6212

Pacific-Antarctic Ridge

Punta Arenas
Falkland Is.
(U.K.)
South Georgia
(U.K.)
Est. de Magallanes
Tierra del Fuego
C. de Hornos
West from Greenwich
COPYRIGHT GEORGE PHILIP LTD.

B C D E F G H J K L M N

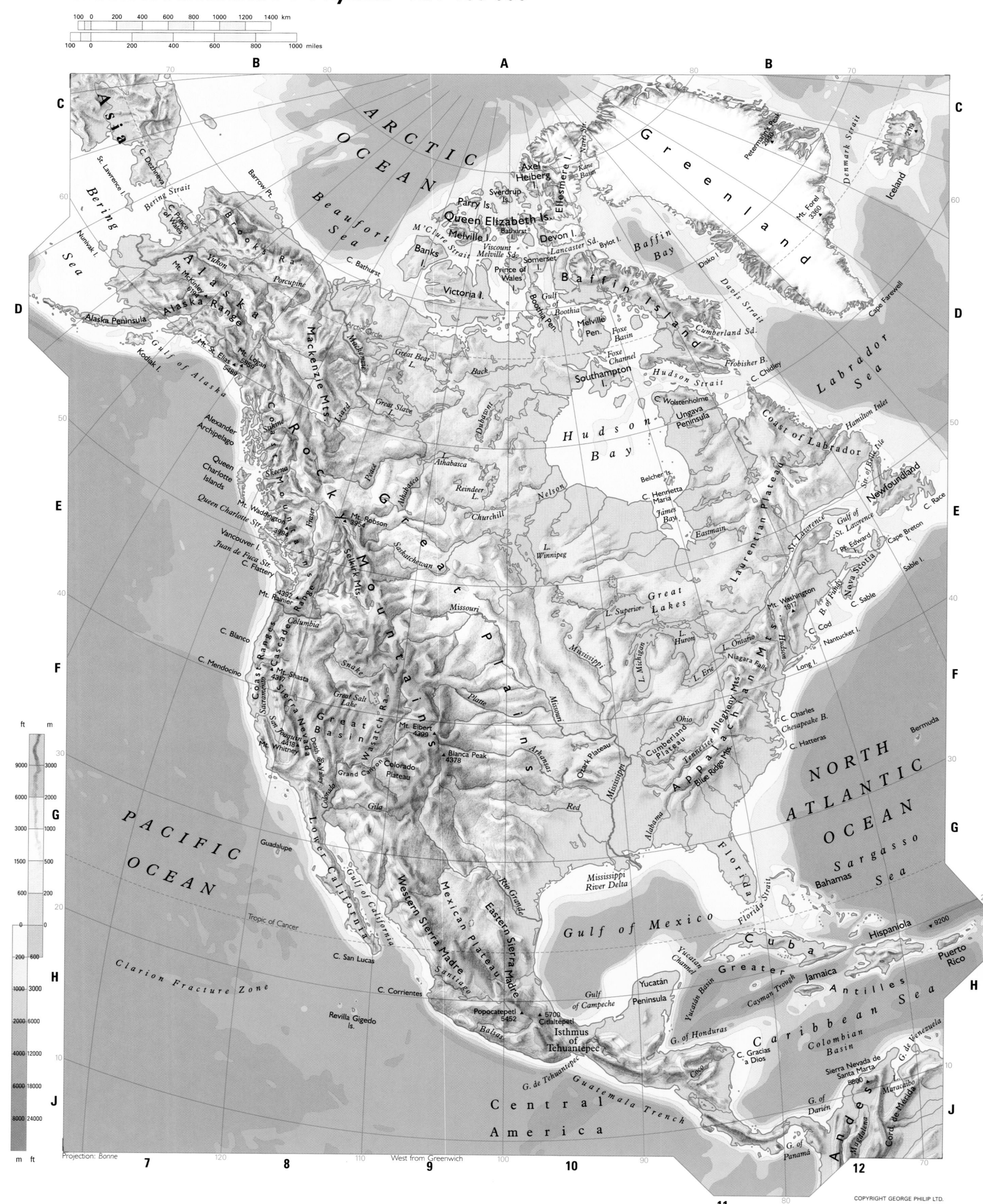

COPYRIGHT GEORGE PHILIP LTD.

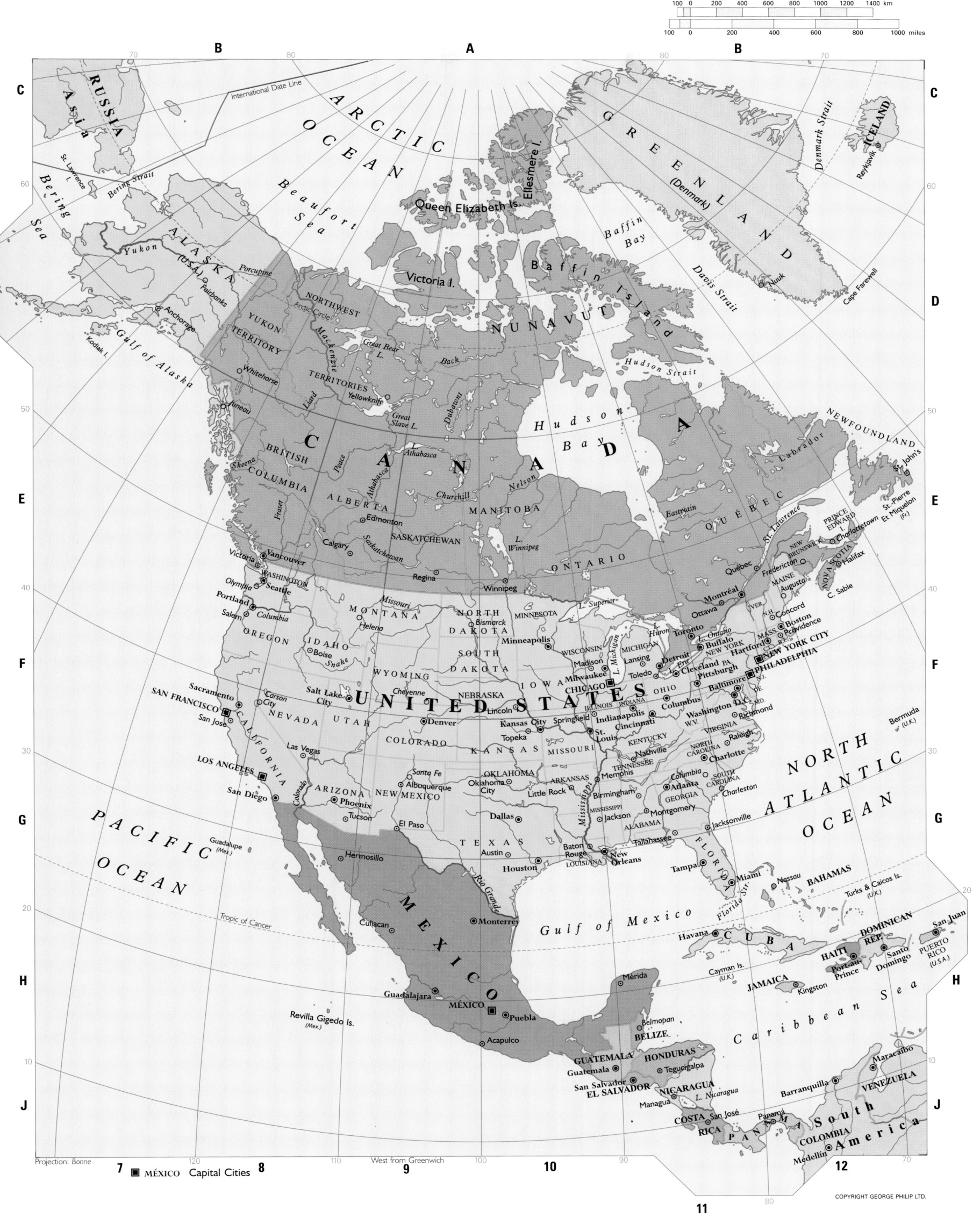

100 0 200 400 600 800 1000 1200 1400 km
100 0 200 400 600 800 1000 miles

RUSSIA

Asia

St. Lawrence I.

Bering Strait

Bering Sea

International Date Line

ARCTIC OCEAN

Beaufort Sea

Queen Elizabeth Is.

Ellesmere I.

GREENLAND (Denmark)

Denmark Strait

ICELAND

Reykjavik

Baffin Bay

Victoria I.

ALASKA (U.S.A.)

Yukon

Porcupine

Fairbanks

Anchorage

Kodiak I.

Gulf of Alaska

Juneau

Whitehorse

YUKON TERRITORY

NORTHWEST

Arctic Circle

Mackenzie

Great Bear L.

Back

NUNAVUT

Baffin Island

Davis Strait

Nuuk

Cape Farewell

TERRITORIES

Yellowknife

Liard

Great Slave L.

Duhawnt

Hudson Strait

NEWFOUNDLAND

CANADA

Peace

Athabasca

Athabasca L.

Churchill

Nelson

Hudson Bay

Eastmain

Labrador

St. John's

Skeena

BRITISH COLUMBIA

ALBERTA

Fraser

Edmonton

Calgary

SASKATCHEWAN

Saskatchewan

Regina

MANITOBA

L. Winnipeg

ONTARIO

QUÉBEC

St. Lawrence

PRINCE EDWARD I.

Charlottetown

St-Pierre Et Miquelon (Fr.)

Victoria

Vancouver

WASHINGTON

Olympia

Seattle

Portland

Salem

Columbia

OREGON

MONTANA

Missouri

Helena

IDAHO

Boise

Snake

WYOMING

Winnipeg

NORTH DAKOTA

Bismarck

SOUTH DAKOTA

MINNESOTA

Minneapolis

Madison

WISCONSIN

L. Superior

L. Michigan

MICHIGAN

Lansing

Milwaukee

CHICAGO

Ottawa

Montréal

Québec

Fredericton

NEW BRUNSWICK

MAINE

Augusta

N.H.

Concord

VER.

MASS.

Boston

Hartford

Providence

R.I.

NOVA SCOTIA

Halifax

C. Sable

L. Huron

Toronto

L. Ontario

Buffalo

Detroit

Cleveland

Erie

Pittsburgh

PA

NEW YORK

NEW YORK CITY

PHILADELPHIA

Baltimore

Washington D.C.

DE.

MD.

Richmond

VIRGINIA

Raleigh

Sacramento

SAN FRANCISCO

San José

CALIFORNIA

Carson City

NEVADA

UTAH

Salt Lake City

Las Vegas

Cheyenne

NEBRASKA

Denver

COLORADO

Lincoln

Kansas City

Topeka

KANSAS

IOWA

ILLINOIS

Springfield

St. Louis

MISSOURI

INDIANA

Indianapolis

OHIO

Columbus

Cincinnati

KENTUCKY

Nashville

W.V.

TENNESSEE

NORTH CAROLINA

Charlotte

Columbia

SOUTH CAROLINA

Charleston

Bermuda (U.K.)

NORTH ATLANTIC OCEAN

LOS ANGELES

San Diego

ARIZONA

Phoenix

Tucson

Colorado

Santa Fe

NEW MEXICO

Albuquerque

El Paso

OKLAHOMA

Oklahoma City

ARKANSAS

Little Rock

Memphis

Birmingham

MISSISSIPPI

Jackson

ALABAMA

Montgomery

GEORGIA

Atlanta

Jacksonville

FLORIDA

PACIFIC OCEAN

Guadalupe (Mex.)

Dallas

TEXAS

Austin

Houston

Baton Rouge

LOUISIANA

New Orleans

Tallahassee

Tampa

Miami

Nassau

BAHAMAS

Turks & Caicos Is. (U.K.)

San Juan

DOMINICAN REP.

PUERTO RICO (U.S.A.)

Tropic of Cancer

Hermosillo

Culiacan

Monterrey

Rio Grande

MEXICO

Gulf of Mexico

Havana

CUBA

Cayman Is. (U.K.)

HAITI

Port-au-Prince

Santo Domingo

JAMAICA

Kingston

Florida Str.

Revilla Gigedo Is. (Mex.)

Guadalajara

MÉXICO

Puebla

Acapulco

Mérida

Belmopan

BELIZE

GUATEMALA

Guatemala

San Salvador

EL SALVADOR

HONDURAS

Tegucigalpa

NICARAGUA

L. Nicaragua

Managua

Caribbean Sea

Maracaibo

Barranquilla

VENEZUELA

COSTA RICA

San José

PANAMA

COLOMBIA

Medellín

South America

Projection: Bonne

7 ■ MÉXICO Capital Cities 8

120 110 West from Greenwich 100 9 10 90 80 11 70 12

COPYRIGHT GEORGE PHILIP LTD.

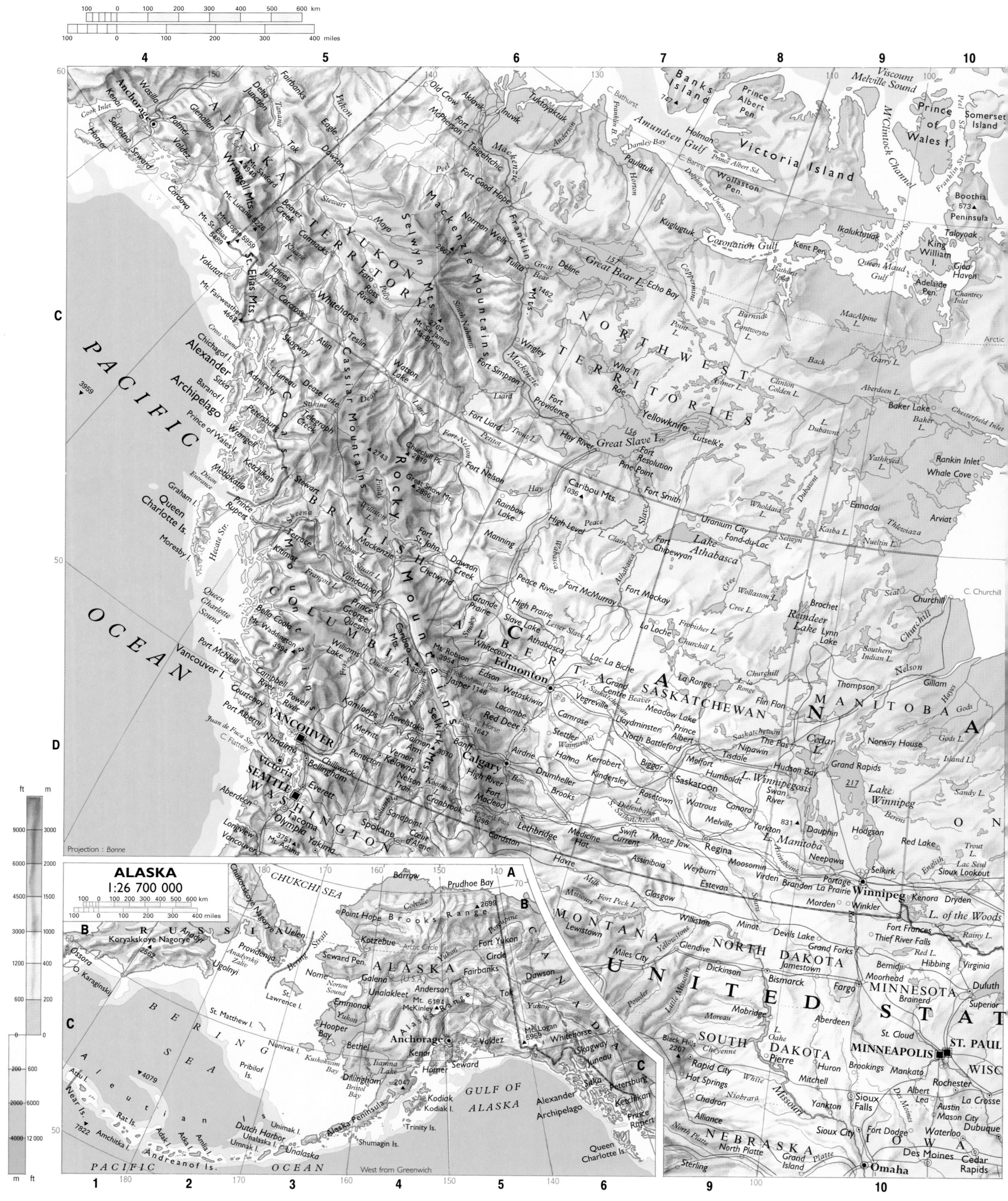

100 0 100 200 300 400 500 600 km
100 0 100 200 300 400 miles
PACIFIC OCEAN
ALASKA
YUKON TERRITORY
NORTHWEST TERRITORIES
BRITISH COLUMBIA
ALBERTA
SASKATCHEWAN
MANITOBA
WASHINGTON
MONTANA
NORTH DAKOTA
SOUTH DAKOTA
NEBRASKA
IOWA
MINNESOTA
UNITED STATES
Rocky Mountains
Mackenzie Mountains
Cassiar Mountains
Coast Mts.
Selwyn Mts.
Wrangell Mts.
St. Elias Mts.
Victoria Island
Banks Island
Great Bear L.
Great Slave L.
Lake Athabasca
Lake Winnipeg
Anchorage
Whitehorse
Yellowknife
Edmonton
Calgary
VANCOUVER
SEATTLE
Victoria
Saskatoon
Regina
Winnipeg
MINNEAPOLIS
ST. PAUL
Omaha
Projection : Bonne
ALASKA
1:26 700 000
100 0 100 200 300 400 500 600 km
100 0 100 200 300 400 miles
CHUKCHI SEA
BERING SEA
GULF OF ALASKA
Brooks Range
Alaska Range
Aleutian Is.
West from Greenwich
ft m
9000 3000
6000 2000
4500 1500
3000 1000
1200 400
600 200
0 0
200 600
2000 6000
4000 12 000
m ft

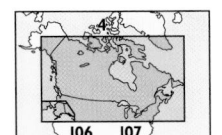
B

11 12 13 14 15 16

Devon I.
Lancaster Sound
Arctic Bay
Brodeur
Peninsula
Borden Pen.
Bylot I.
Eclipse Sd.
Pond Inlet
C. Adair
Clyde River
C. Raper
Baffin Bay
Nuvanik
Uummannaq
Ilulissat
Qeqertarsuaq
Qasigiannguit
Sisimiut

G R E E N L A N D
(KALAALLIT NUNAAT)
(Denmark)

Ammassalik

Kangerlussuaq
Maniitsoq
Nuuk
Kong Frederik VI's Kyst
Arsuk
Paamiut
Qaqortoq
Nanortalik
Qeqertarsuatsiaat
Uummannarsuaq

A T L A N T I C

60

C

Gulf of
Boothia
Fury and Hecla Str.
Igloolik
Simpson Pen.
Melville Peninsula
Committee B.
Pelly Bay
Sanirajak
Prince Charles I.
Air Force I.
Foxe Basin
C. Dorchester
Amadjuak L.
Foxe Pen.
Cape Dorset
Meta Incognita
Kimmirut
Iqaluit
Hall Peninsula
Frobisher Bay
Resolution I.

Cumberland Peninsula
Pangnirtung
C. Dyer
Qikiqtarjuaq

Davis Strait

Labrador Sea

50

Circle Rae Isthmus Repulse Bay
N U N A V U T
Iglurjuaq
C. Tatnam
Roes Welcome Sd.
Southampton I.
Coats I.
Mansel I.
Nottingham I.
Salisbury I.
Hudson Strait
Ivujivik
Salluit
Quaqtaq
Akpatok I.
C. Chidley

H u d s o n

B a y

Sleeper Is.
King George Is.
Baker's Dozen Is.
Belcher Is.
Ottawa Is.

Kangiqsujuaq
Kangirsuk
Ungava Bay
Kangiqsualujjuaq
Hebron
Nain
Hopedale
C. Harrison
Rigolet
Cartwright
Port Hope Simpson
Belle Isle
St. Anthony

Puvirnituq
Péninsule d'Ungava
Inukjuak
Kuujjuaq

N E W F O U N D L A N D

L a b r a d o r

Smallwood Res.
North West River
Happy Valley-Goose Bay
Churchill Falls

Q U É B E C

James Bay
Chisasibi
La Grande
Schefferville
Labrador City
Fermont
Gagnon
Sept-Îles
Natashquan
St-Augustin
Deer Lake
Corner Brook
Gander
Bonavista
St. John's
Carbonear
Placentia
C. Race

O C E A N

Wemindji
Eastmain
Waskaganish
Mistassini
Chibougamau
Baie Comeau
Matane
Gaspé
Î. d'Anticosti
Gulf of St. Lawrence
Cabot Str.
Channel-Port aux Basques
Stephenville

40

O N T A R I O
Moosonee
Fort Albany
Hearst
Cochrane
Timmins
Kapuskasing
Val-d'Or
Rouyn-Noranda
La Tuque
Chicoutimi
Jonquière
Rimouski
Rivière-du-Loup
Edmundston
Campbellton
Bathurst
Miramichi
N E W B R U N S W I C K
Moncton
PR. EDWARD I.
Charlottetown
Summerside
Sydney
Cape Breton I.
N O V A S C O T I A

Thunder Bay
Lake Superior
Sault Ste. Marie
Sudbury
North Bay
Ottawa
MONTRÉAL
Québec
Trois-Rivières
Sherbrooke
M A I N E
Fredericton
Saint John
Amherst
Truro
Halifax
Dartmouth
Yarmouth

TORONTO
Hamilton
Kitchener
London
BUFFALO
NEW YORK
VERMONT
NEW HAMPSHIRE
Montpelier
Concord
Manchester
MASS.
BOSTON
Providence
HARTFORD
CONN.
NEW YORK

CHICAGO DETROIT
CLEVELAND
MILWAUKEE
WISCONSIN
MICHIGAN
ILLINOIS INDIANA OHIO PENNSYLVANIA

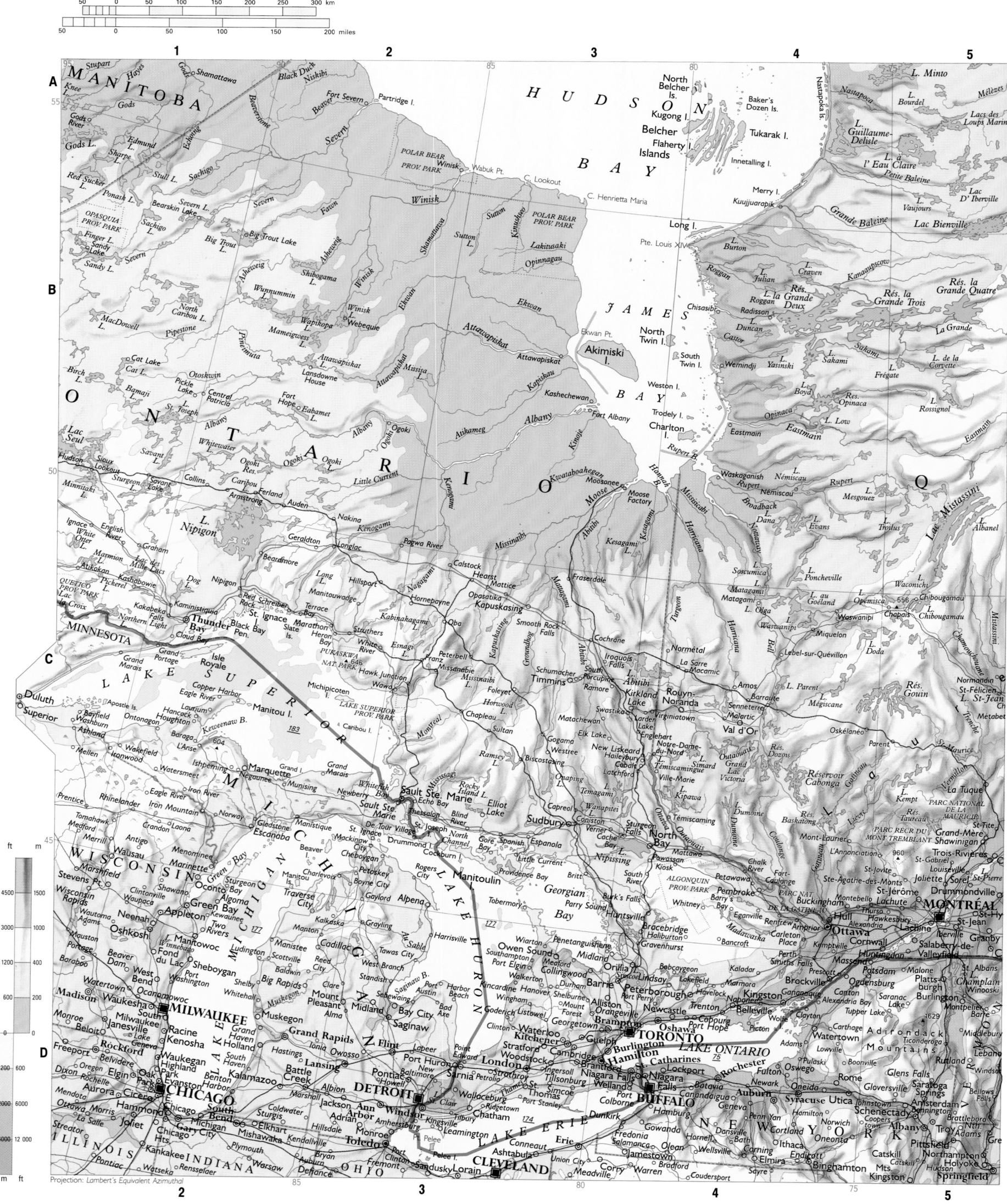
50 0 50 100 150 200 250 300 km
50 0 50 100 150 200 miles
1 2 3 4 5
A B C D
MANITOBA
ONTARIO
HUDSON BAY
JAMES BAY
MINNESOTA
WISCONSIN
MICHIGAN
ILLINOIS
INDIANA
OHIO
NEW YORK
LAKE SUPERIOR
LAKE MICHIGAN
LAKE HURON
LAKE ONTARIO
LAKE ERIE
Georgian Bay
Belcher Islands
Akimiski I.
L. Nipigon
Lac Mistassini
Réservoir Cabonga
POLAR BEAR PROV. PARK
OPASQUIA PROV. PARK
QUETICO PROV. PARK
PUKASKWA NAT. PARK
LAKE SUPERIOR PROV. PARK
ALGONQUIN PROV. PARK
Thunder Bay
Sault Ste. Marie
Sudbury
Timmins
North Bay
Moosonee
Kapuskasing
Rouyn-Noranda
Val d'Or
MONTRÉAL
Ottawa
Hull
Kingston
TORONTO
Hamilton
London
Windsor
DETROIT
CLEVELAND
BUFFALO
Rochester
Syracuse
MILWAUKEE
CHICAGO
Duluth
Marquette
Green Bay
Grand Rapids
Lansing
Toledo
Erie
Albany
Trois-Rivières
Joliette
ft m
4500 1500
3000 1000
1200 400
600 200
0 0
200 600
2000 6000
4000 12 000
m ft
Projection: Lambert's Equivalent Azimuthal

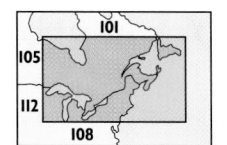

6 7 8 9

LABRADOR SEA

A

Nain
South Aulatsivik I.
Voisey B.
Paul I.
Davis Inlet
Tunungayualok I.
Kogaluk
Nunaksaluk I.
Hopedale
Kanairiktok B.
Makkovik
Adlavik Is.
Aillik
C. Harrison
Holton
Indian Harbour
Groswater
B.
Sandwich B.
Cartwright
Table B.
Black Tickle
Island of Ponds

NEWFOUNDLAND

Smallwood Reservoir
Schefferville
Menihek
Esker
Churchill Falls
Churchill
Ossokmanuan L.
North West River
Goose
Happy Valley-Goose Bay
Melville
Mealy Mts.
Charlottetown
Alexis
Square Islands
Williams harbour
Port Hope
Simpson
Battle Harbour
Lodge Bay
Red
Bay
Belle Isle
L'Anse au Loup
Forteau
Blanc-Sablon
St. Anthony
L'Anse aux Meadows
Groais I.
Hare B.

Labrador

Twin Falls
Winokapau L.
Minipi L.
Little Mecatina
Natashquan
Burnt L.
St-Augustin
Rivière St-Paul
St-Paul
Str. of Belle Isle
Roddickton
Englee
Bell I.

QUÉBEC

Gagnon
Labrador City
Fermont
Wabush
Ashuanipi L.
St-Augustin
Port au Choix
Hawke's Bay
Daniel's Harbour
Jackson's Arm
Springdale
Baie Verte
Notre Dame B.
Fogo I.
Twillingate
Musgrave Harbour
C. Freels

Newfoundland

GROS MORNE NAT. PARK
Rocky Harbour
Norris Point
Trout River
Deer Lake
South Brook
Botwood
Bishop's Falls
Glenwood
Gander
Gambo
Glovertown
TERRA NOVA NAT PARK
Bonavista
C. Bonavista
Catalina
Trinity B.

Sept-Îles
Moisie
Port-Cartier
Mingan
Havre-St-Pierre
Natashquan
Sheldrake
Romaine
Keggaska
L. Musquaro

Î. d'Anticosti
Dét. de Jacques-Cartier
Pte. de l'Ouest
Port-Menier
Pte. Heath

GULF OF ST. LAWRENCE

Corner Brook
Pasadena
B. of Islands
Buchans
Grand Falls
Windsor
Badger
Red Indian L.
L. Meelpaeg Res.
Gander

Î. Brion
Grande-Entrée
Cap-aux-Meules
Îs. de la Madeleine (Québec)
Havre-Aubert
St. Paul I.
Cape North

Port au Port
Petit Jardin
Stephenville
St. George's
St. George's B.
St. David's
South Branch
Great Codroy
St. Andrew's
Channel-Port aux Basques
Isle aux Morts

Granite L.
St. Alban's
Burgeo
François
Rose Blanche

St-Pierre
Fortune
Grand Bank
Burin
Marystown
Belleoram
Fortune B.
Terrenceville
Clarenville
Trinity
Heart's Content
Carbonear
Old Perlican
Conception B.
Wabana
Harbour Grace
Bay Roberts
St. John's
Mt. Pearl
Torbay
Holyrood
Whitless Bay
Argentia
Placentia
Placentia B.
St. Bride's
Avalon Peninsula
Ferryland
Trepassey
St. Mary's B.
C. Pine
C. St. Mary's
C. Race

ST-PIERRE ET MIQUELON (France)
Miquelon
Langlade

NEW BRUNSWICK

Matane
Mont-Joli
Rimouski
Amqui
Causapscal
Pén. de Gaspé
Chic-Chocs
Gaspé
Percé
Grande-Rivière
Chandler
Bonaventure
New Richmond
Paspébiac
Miscou I.
Shippegan
Tracadie-Sheila
Caraquet
Bathurst
Dalhousie
Campbellton
Chaleur Bay
Miramichi
Newcastle
Rogersville
Richibucto
Buctouche
Shediac
Moncton
Sackville
Amherst

PRINCE EDWARD ISLAND
North Cape
Tignish
Alberton
Summerside
Kensington
Borden
Charlottetown
Souris
East Pt.
Georgetown
Montague
Cape Tormentine
Murray Hr.

NOVA SCOTIA

Pleasant Bay
CAPE BRETON HIGHLANDS NAT. PARK
Chéticamp
Ingonish
St. Ann's B.
Sydney Mines
New Waterford
Glace Bay
Louisbourg
Cape Breton Island
Inverness
N. Sydney
Sydney
Port Hood
Port Hawkesbury
Antigonish
Mulgrave
Canso
Chedabucto B.
Î. Madame

Pictou
New Glasgow
Stellarton
Truro
Parrsboro
Springhill
Minas Basin
Windsor
Kentville
Middleton
Annapolis Royal
Digby
Sherbrooke
Sheet Harbour
Musquodoboit Harbour
Dartmouth
Halifax
Mahone Bay
Lunenburg
Bridgewater
Liverpool
Milton
KEJIMKUJIK NAT. PARK
Weymouth
L. Rossignol
Shelburne
Lockeport
Clark's Harbour
C. Sable
Yarmouth
Wedgeport

MAINE

Jackman
Moosehead L.
Millinocket
Patten
Lincoln
Greenville
Bingham
Skowhegan
Waterville
Belfast
Bangor
Brewer
Old Town
Ellsworth
Bar Harbor
Mount Desert I.
Machias
Eastport
Calais
St. Stephen
Saint John
Bay of Fundy
St. George
Rothesay
Sussex
Fredericton
Oromocto
Woodstock
Houlton
Presque Isle
Caribou
Van Buren
Edmundston
Grand Falls
Plaster Rock
Perth-Andover

NEW HAMPSHIRE
Berlin
Norway
Augusta
Auburn
Lewiston
Brunswick
Bath
Portland
Saco
Biddeford
Sanford
Rochester
Dover
Concord
Portsmouth
Manchester
Nashua
Keene
Laconia

MASS.
Haverhill
Lawrence
Lowell
Lynn
Newton
BOSTON
Quincy
Brockton
Woonsocket
Worcester

UNITED STATES

ATLANTIC OCEAN

Sable I. (Nova Scotia)

QUÉBEC
Québec
Lévis
Charny
Montmagny
Beaupré
Î. d'Orléans
Donnaconna
La Pérade
Cap-de-la-Madeleine
Trois-Pistoles
Rivière-du-Loup
Cabano
Dégelis
St-Pascal
La Pocatière
St-Jean-Port-Joli
Montmagny
Ste-Marie
St-Georges
Beauceville
Plessisville
Victoriaville
Thetford Mines
Asbestos
East Angus
Sherbrooke
Magog
Coaticook
Newport
Island Pond
St. Johnsbury
Hanover
Roberval
Alma
Chicoutimi
Jonquière
La Baie
Saguenay
St-Siméon
Tadoussac
Les Escoumins
La Malbaie
Baie-St-Paul
Baie-Comeau
Godbout
Betsiamites
Forestville
Chute-aux-Outardes
Baie-Trinité

D

C

B

55

50

45

COPYRIGHT GEORGE PHILIP LTD.

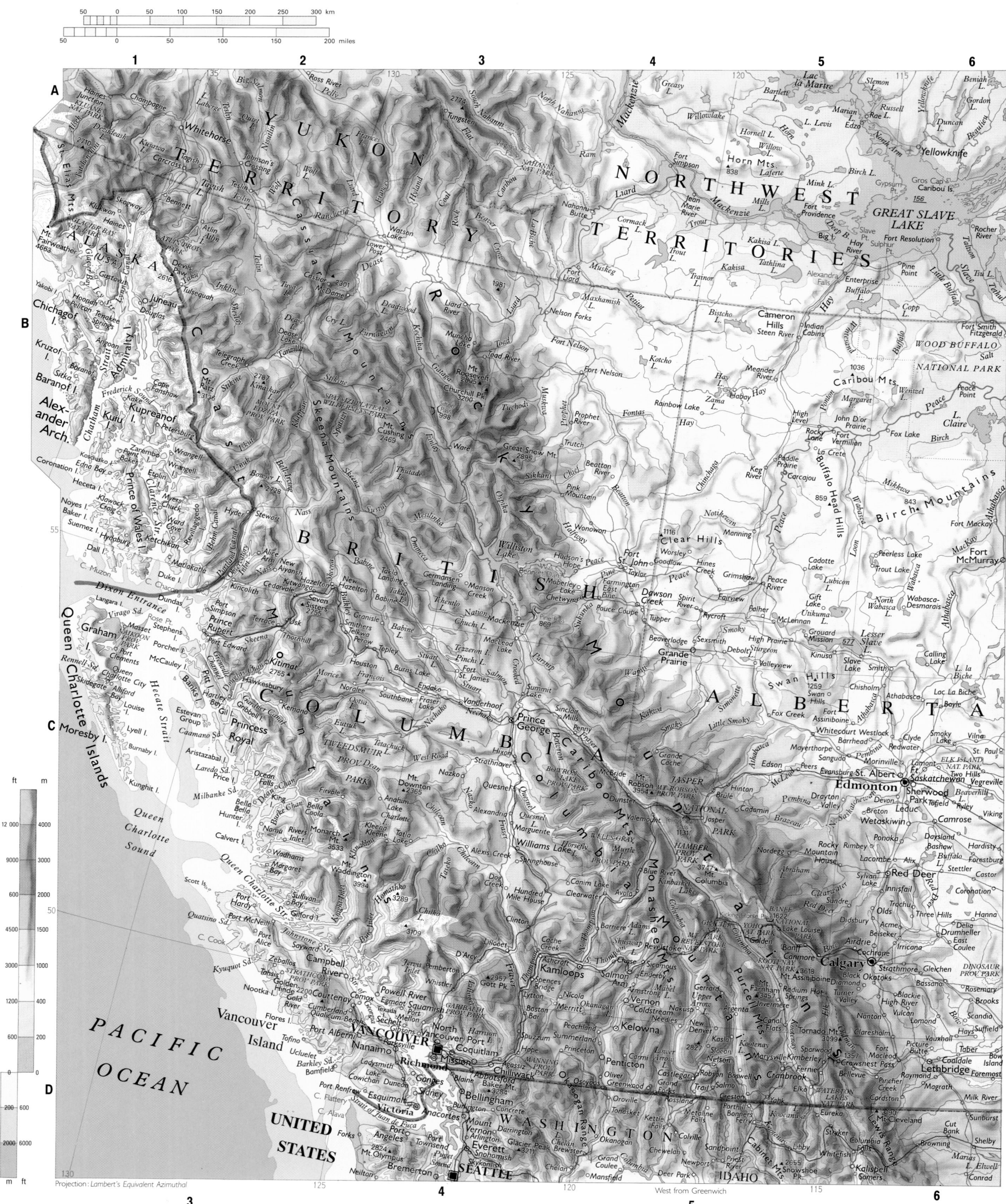
YUKON TERRITORY
NORTHWEST TERRITORIES
BRITISH COLUMBIA
ALBERTA
ALASKA (U.S.A.)
WASHINGTON
IDAHO
UNITED STATES
PACIFIC OCEAN
GREAT SLAVE LAKE
Whitehorse
Yellowknife
Juneau
Prince Rupert
Prince George
Edmonton
Calgary
Kamloops
Kelowna
VANCOUVER
Victoria
Vancouver Island
Queen Charlotte Islands
SEATTLE
Lethbridge
Red Deer
Projection: Lambert's Equivalent Azimuthal
West from Greenwich

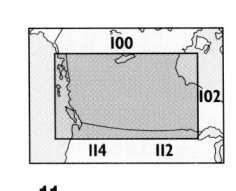

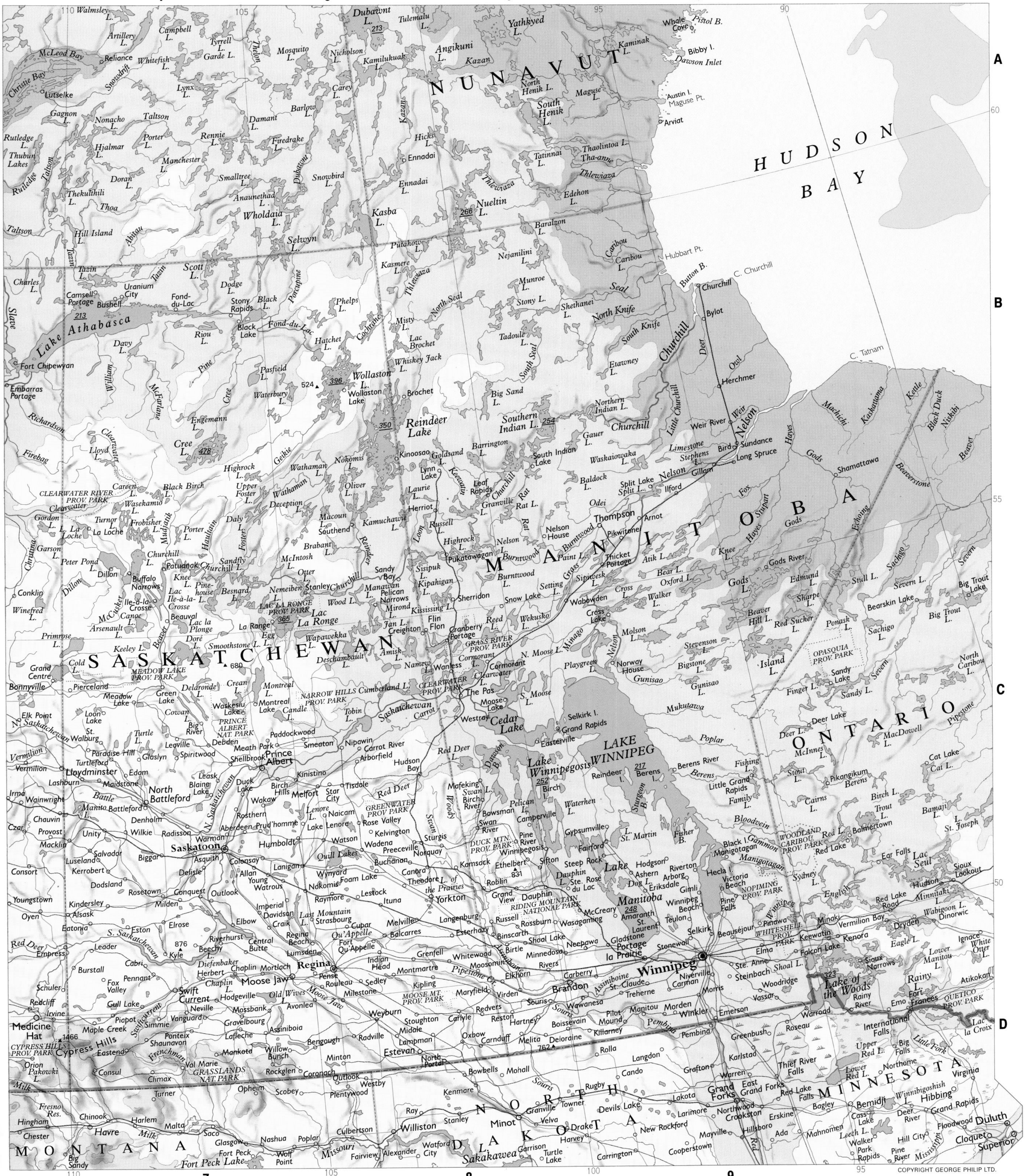

NUNAVUT

HUDSON BAY

SASKATCHEWAN

MANITOBA

ONTARIO

MONTANA

NORTH DAKOTA

MINNESOTA

Lake Athabasca

Reindeer Lake

LAKE WINNIPEG

Lake Winnipegosis

Cree L.

Wollaston Lake

Lac La Ronge

Cedar Lake

Lake of the Woods

Cypress Hills

Missouri

Saskatchewan

Churchill

Nelson

Saskatoon · Regina · Moose Jaw · Prince Albert · North Battlefield · Lloydminster · Medicine Hat · Swift Current

Winnipeg · Brandon · Thompson · Churchill · Dauphin · Portage la Prairie · Selkirk

Duluth · Grand Forks · Minot · Williston

COPYRIGHT GEORGE PHILIP LTD.

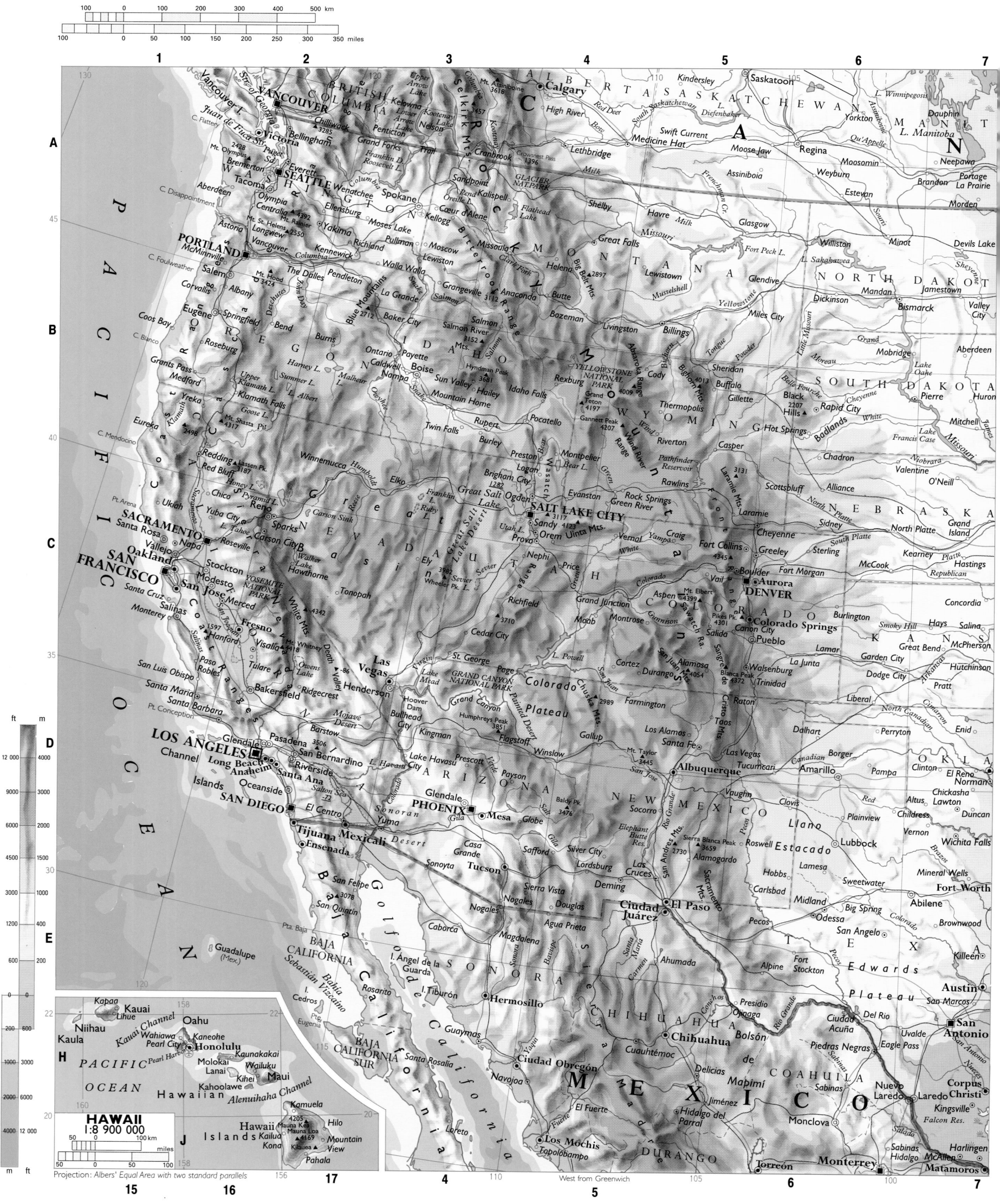

Projection: Albers' Equal Area with two standard parallels

HAWAII 1:8 900 000

8 9 10 11 12 13

Lake Winnipeg
Berens
Trout L.
L. St. Joseph
Albany
O N T A R I O
C A N A D A
Q U É B E C
Moosonee
Moose
Nottaway
Chibougamau
L. Chibougamau
L. au Goéland
Matagami
L. Matagami
Baie-Comeau
St. Lawrence
Matane
Rimouski
Rivière-du-Loup
Edmundston
NEW BRUNSWICK
L. Seul
English
Sioux Lookout
Nakina
Kenogami
Missinaibi
Abitibi
Bell
Rés. Gouin
L. St-Jean
Alma
Chicoutimi
Jonquière
Roberval
St-Maurice
La Tuque
Winnipeg
Kenora
Lake of the Woods
Dryden
Lake Nipigon
Geraldton
Hearst
Cochrane
Amos
L. Abitibi
Rouyn-Noranda
L. Kempt
Québec
Fort Kent
Caribou
Presque Isle
Houlton
Millinocket
Saint John
Calais
Nipigon
Marathon
Timmins
Kirkland Lake
L. Témiscamingue
Rés. Cabonga
Rés. Baskatong
Shawinigan
Trois-Rivières
Joliette
Drummondville
Moosehead L.
Rainy L.
Fort Frances
International Falls
Thunder Bay
I. Royale
L. St. Ignace
Wawa
Michipicoten I.
Grafton
Thief River Falls
Red Lake
Ely
Lake Superior
183
Grand Forks
Bemidji
Hibbing
Virginia
Two Harbors
Houghton
Keweenaw Bay
Whitefish Bay
Sault Ste. Marie
Sudbury
North Bay
Ottawa
Mont-Laurier
MONTRÉAL
Sherbrooke
M A I N E
Bangor
Belfast
Waterville
Penobscot Bay
Moorhead
Fargo
M I N N E S O T A
Leech L.
Duluth
Superior
Apostle Is.
Marquette
Ishpeming
Sault Ste. Marie
North Channel
L. Nipissing
Manitoulin I.
Pembroke
Hull
Cornwall
L. Champlain
Granby
Farmington
Augusta
Lewiston
Brunswick
Fergus Falls
Brainerd
Mille Lacs L.
Ashland
Ironwood
Iron Mountain
Manistique
Escanaba
Parry Sound
Georgian Bay
Huntsville
Ogdensburg
Plattsburgh
Burlington
VERMONT
Berlin
White Mts.
1917
NEW HAMPSHIRE
Portland
St. Cloud
Rice Lake
Rhinelander
Menominee
Petoskey
Alpena
Lake Huron
177
Orillia
Peterborough
Kingston
Adirondack Mts.
1629
Montpelier
Rutland
Concord
Manchester
Big Stone Lake
Willmar
Coon Rapids
Merrill
Wausau
Traverse City
Saginaw Bay
Owen Sound
Barrie
Oshawa
Picton
Watertown
Glens Falls
Nashua
Lawrence
Lowell
Watertown
MINNEAPOLIS
ST. PAUL
Eau Claire
Stevens Point
Manistee
Cadillac
TORONTO
Lake Ontario
75
Oswego
Utica
Troy
MASS.
BOSTON
C. Cod
Red Wing
Green Bay
Appleton
Ludington
Bay City
Kitchener
Niagara Falls
Rochester
Syracuse
Schenectady
Albany
Worcester
Brookings
Minnesota
Owatonna
Winona
W I S C O N S I N
Oshkosh
Manitowoc
Midland
Saginaw
London
Hamilton
BUFFALO
N E W   Y O R K
Ithaca
Catskill Mts.
1281
Springfield
Providence
R.I.
Fall River
New Bedford
Nantucket I.
Martha's Vineyard
Mankato
Rochester
Austin
La Crosse
Sheboygan
Lake Michigan
Muskegon
Flint
Port Huron
Madison
Worthington
Albert Lea
Mason City
Portage
Grand Rapids
Lansing
DETROIT
Lake Erie
174
Erie
Jamestown
Bradford
Elmira
Binghamton
Poughkeepsie
CONN.
HARTFORD
New Haven
Sioux Falls
Des Moines
Spencer
Cedar
Charles City
Madison
MILWAUKEE
Battle Creek
Ann Arbor
Windsor
L. St. Clair
Ashtabula
Warren
Scranton
Wilkes-Barre
Bridgeport
Yonkers
Long I.
Paterson
NEW YORK
Yankton
Sioux City
Cherokee
Fort Dodge
Waterloo
Cedar Rapids
Janesville
Racine
Kenosha
Dubuque
Elgin
Kalamazoo
Jackson
Toledo
CLEVELAND
Oil City
Williamsport
P E N N S Y L V A N I A
Newark
Jersey City
Allentown
I O W A
Rockford
Clinton
CHICAGO
Elkhart
Sandusky
Akron
Youngstown
Altoona
Reading
NEW JERSEY
Trenton
PHILADELPHIA
Norfolk
Columbus
Ames
Iowa City
Davenport
Aurora
Joliet
Gary
Kankakee
South Bend
Fort Wayne
Findlay
Mansfield
Canton
Johnstown
Harrisburg
Lancaster
Atlantic City
Omaha
Lincoln
Council Bluffs
Ottumwa
Galesburg
Rock Island
Midwest
Marion
Lima
Marion
O H I O
PITTSBURGH
Wheeling
Wilmington
BALTIMORE
Dover
Red Oak
Creston
Burlington
Peoria
Bloomington
Lafayette
Kokomo
Muncie
COLUMBUS
Zanesville
Cumberland
Frederick
Annapolis
MARYLAND
DEL.
C. May
Delaware B.
Beatrice
Maryville
Kirksville
Champaign
Danville
INDIANAPOLIS
Richmond
Dayton
Springfield
Morgantown
Clarksburg
WASHINGTON D.C.
Elkins
Potomac
Salisbury
Illinois
Springfield
Decatur
I L L I N O I S
I N D I A N A
CINCINNATI
Parkersburg
Portsmouth
W E S T   V I R G I N I A
1482
Harrisonburg
St. Joseph
Chillicothe
Quincy
Hannibal
Mattoon
Effingham
Terre Haute
Bloomington
Columbus
Maysville
Huntington
Charleston
Charlottesville
Chesapeake Bay
Manhattan
Leavenworth
Kansas
KANSAS CITY
Columbia
ST. LOUIS
Alton
East St. Louis
Vincennes
Wabash
Louisville
Frankfort
Lexington
James
Richmond
C. Charles
Newport News
Virginia Beach
Topeka
Lawrence
Jefferson City
Sedalia
M I S S O U R I
Mount Vernon
Evansville
Owensboro
Danville
Richmond
Big Sandy
Beckley
Kanawha
Lynchburg
Petersburg
Norfolk
Emporia
L. of the Ozarks
Rolla
Carbondale
Henderson
Marion
K E N T U C K Y
Hazard
Bluefield
Roanoke
Danville
Roanoke
Elizabeth City
Albemarle Sd.
Newton
Wichita
Fort Scott
Nevada
Lebanon
Cape Girardeau
Green
Bowling Green
Cumberland
Somerset
Radford
Pulaski
Kingsport
Greensboro
Durham
Rocky Mount
Greenville
Pamlico Sd.
C. Hatteras
Parsons
Pittsburg
Springfield
Ozark Plateau
Poplar Bluff
Paducah
Hopkinsville
Clarksville
Middlesboro
Johnson City
Winston-Salem
Raleigh
Goldsboro
Arkansas City
Bartlesville
Joplin
510
West Plains
Mayfield
Nashville
Oak Ridge
Knoxville
2037
Hickory
N O R T H   C A R O L I N A
New Bern
Ponca City
Tulsa
Fayetteville
Boston Mts.
781
Paragould
Blytheville
Dyersburg
Murfreesboro
Asheville
CHARLOTTE
Fayetteville
Jacksonville
Onslow Bay
Stillwater
Muskogee
Jonesboro
Jackson
T E N N E S S E E
Columbia
Athens
Spartanburg
Greenville
Rock Hill
Cape Fear
Wilmington
Oklahoma City
Shawnee
Russellville
Newport
Conway
Memphis
Chattanooga
Anderson
Florence
Columbia
C. Fear
Fort Smith
McAlester
A R K A N S A S
Little Rock
Stuttgart
Corinth
Florence
Huntsville
Gainesville
Rome
Sumter
Myrtle Beach
Long Bay
Canadian
Ouachita Mts.
811
Hot Springs
Arkansas
Tupelo
Decatur
Gadsden
Anniston
Roswell
ATLANTA
Athens
SOUTH CAROLINA
Georgetown
Ardmore
Clarksdale
Oxford
Augusta
Orangeburg
C. Romain
Durant
Pine Bluff
Cleveland
Greenwood
Columbus
Birmingham
Charleston
Paris
Hope
Camden
Greenville
Tuscaloosa
La Grange
Macon
Savannah
Sherman
Texarkana
El Dorado
M I S S I S S I P P I
Yazoo City
A L A B A M A
Auburn
G E O R G I A
Statesboro
Denton
Ouachita
Demopolis
Columbus
Dublin
Altamaha
DALLAS
Arlington
Marshall
Shreveport
Monroe
Meridian
Selma
Montgomery
Cordele
Douglas
Longview
Tyler
Vicksburg
Jackson
Troy
Albany
Waycross
Brunswick
Corsicana
Palestine
Toledo Bend Res.
Sabine
Natchez
Tombigbee
Greenville
Alabama
Chattahoochee
Flint
Tifton
Valdosta
Waco
Nacogdoches
Red
Natchitoches
Mississippi
Laurel
Hattiesburg
McComb
Andalusia
Dothan
Thomasville
Lake City
St. Johns
Jacksonville
Lufkin
Alexandria
Trinity
Huntsville
De Ridder
L O U I S I A N A
Bogalusa
Mobile
Tallahassee
St. Augustine
Temple
Bryan
Brazos
Lake Charles
Baton Rouge
Biloxi
Gulfport
L. Pontchartrain
Pensacola
Panama City
C. San Blas
Apalachicola
F L O R I D A
L. George
Daytona Beach
Beaumont
Lafayette
New Iberia
NEW ORLEANS
Apalachee B.
Gainesville
Ocala
Deltona
C. Canaveral
HOUSTON
Pasadena
Port Arthur
Houma
Breton Sd.
Orlando
Melbourne
Palm Bay
Indian River
Marsh I.
Atchafalaya B.
Morgan City
Mississippi River Delta
Galveston
TAMPA
Lakeland
Fort Pierce
Victoria
Freeport
Clearwater
St. Petersburg
Tampa B.
Sarasota
West Palm Beach
Grand Bahama I.
Little Abaco I.
Port Lavaca
Great Abaco I.
Freeport
N.E. Providence Channel
Matagorda I.
L. Okeechobee
Aransas Pass
Charlotte Harbor
Cape Coral
Fort Myers
Fort Lauderdale
N.W. Providence Channel
BAHAMAS
Eleuthera I.
The Everglades
MIAMI
Naples
Nassau
New Providence I.
Cat I.
Padre I.
G U L F   O F   M E X I C O
Laguna Madre
C. Sable
Florida Bay
Florida Keys
Straits of Florida
Exuma Sound
Brownsville
Rio Grande
Key West
Andros I.
Great Exuma I.
Long I.
A T L A N T I C   O C E A N

A B C D E F

45 40 35 30 25

95 90 85 80 75

8 9 10 11 12

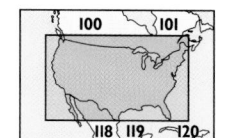

COPYRIGHT GEORGE PHILIP LTD.

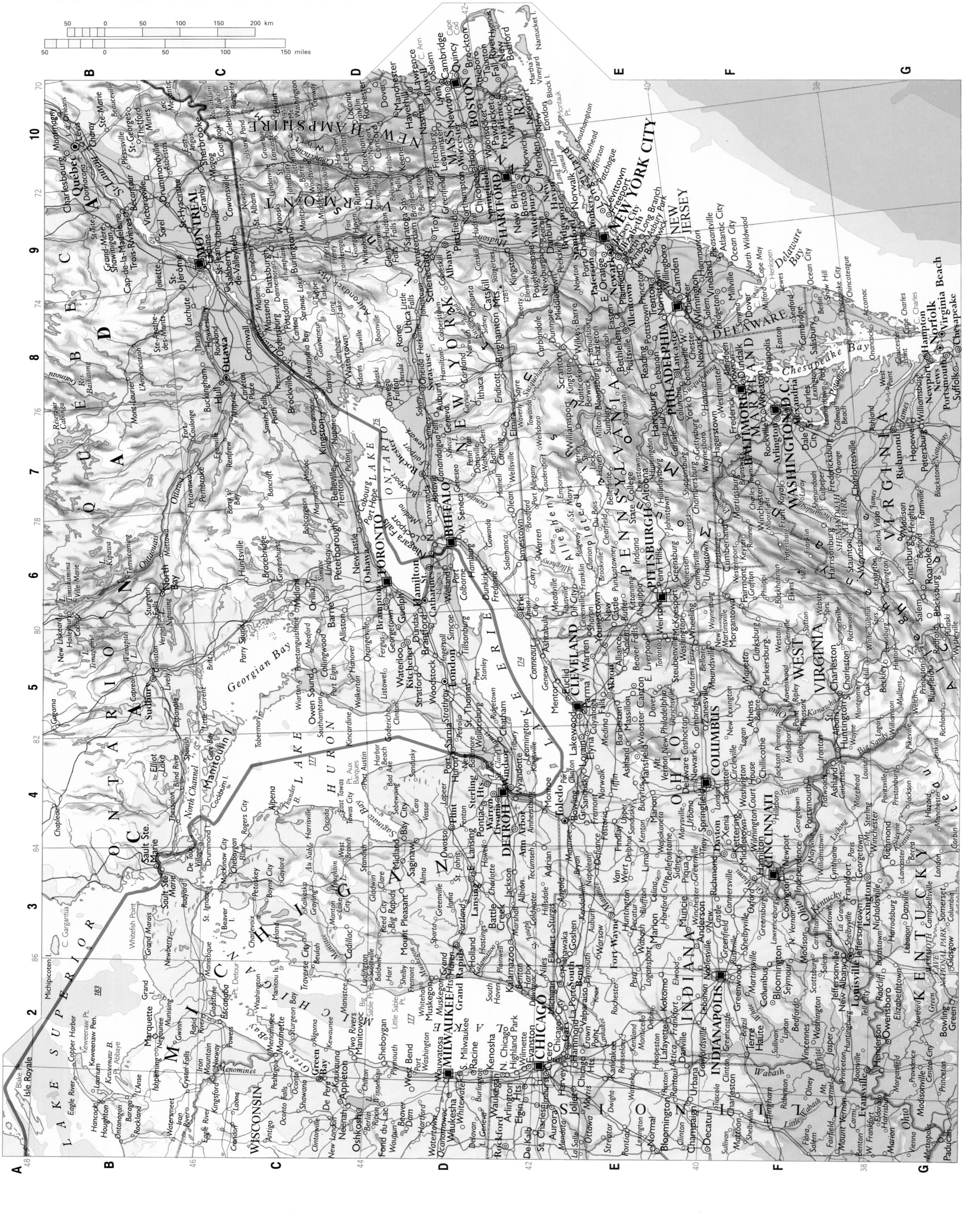

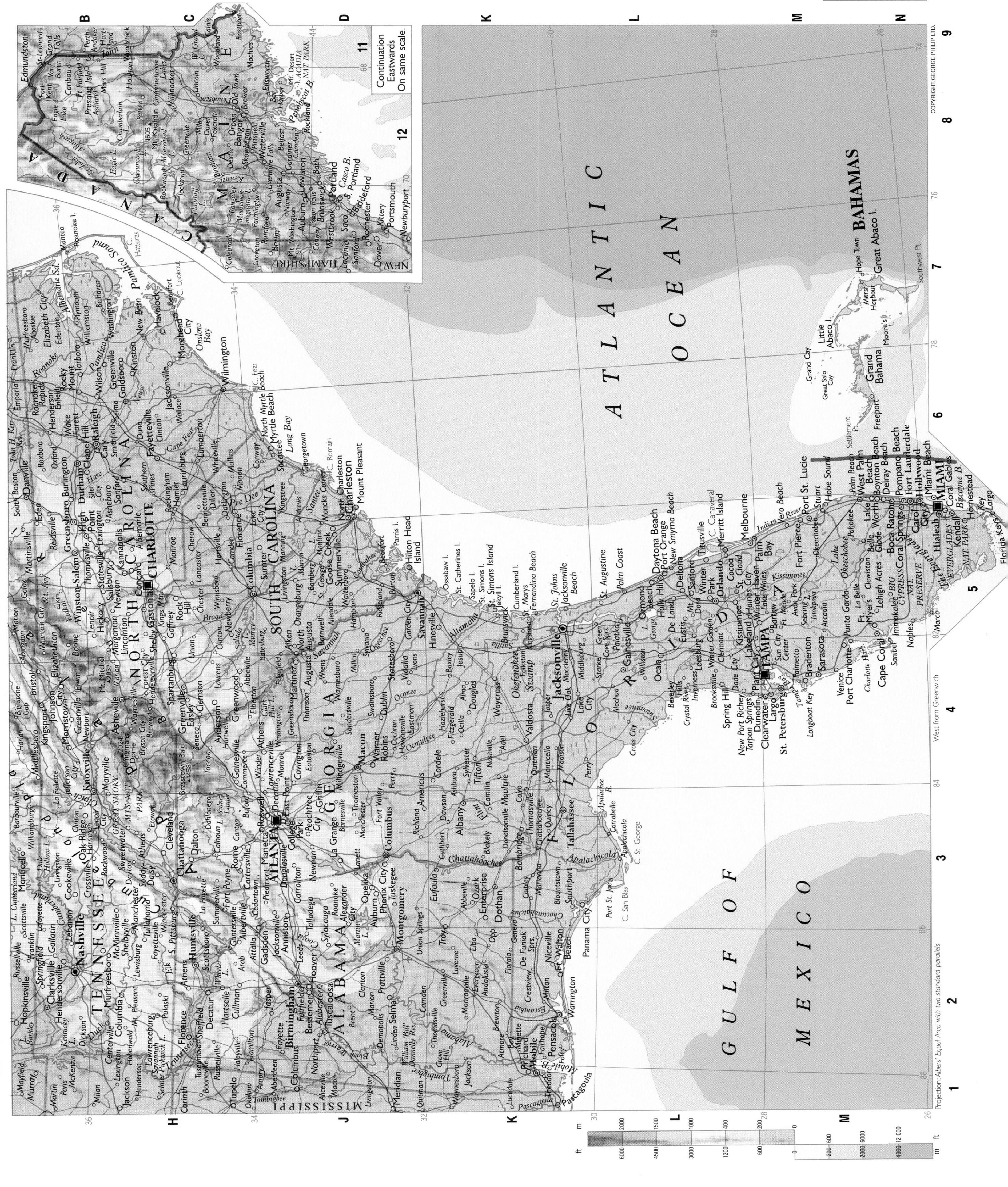

ATLANTIC OCEAN

GULF OF MEXICO

BAHAMAS

CANADA

MAINE

NEW HAMPSHIRE

TENNESSEE
NORTH CAROLINA
SOUTH CAROLINA
GEORGIA
ALABAMA
MISSISSIPPI
FLORIDA

Nashville · Charlotte · Atlanta · Tampa · MIAMI · Jacksonville · Birmingham · Montgomery · Columbia · Raleigh · Wilmington · Savannah · Tallahassee · Orlando · St. Petersburg

Continuation
Eastwards
On same scale.

Projection: Albers' Equal Area with two standard parallels

West from Greenwich

COPYRIGHT GEORGE PHILIP LTD.

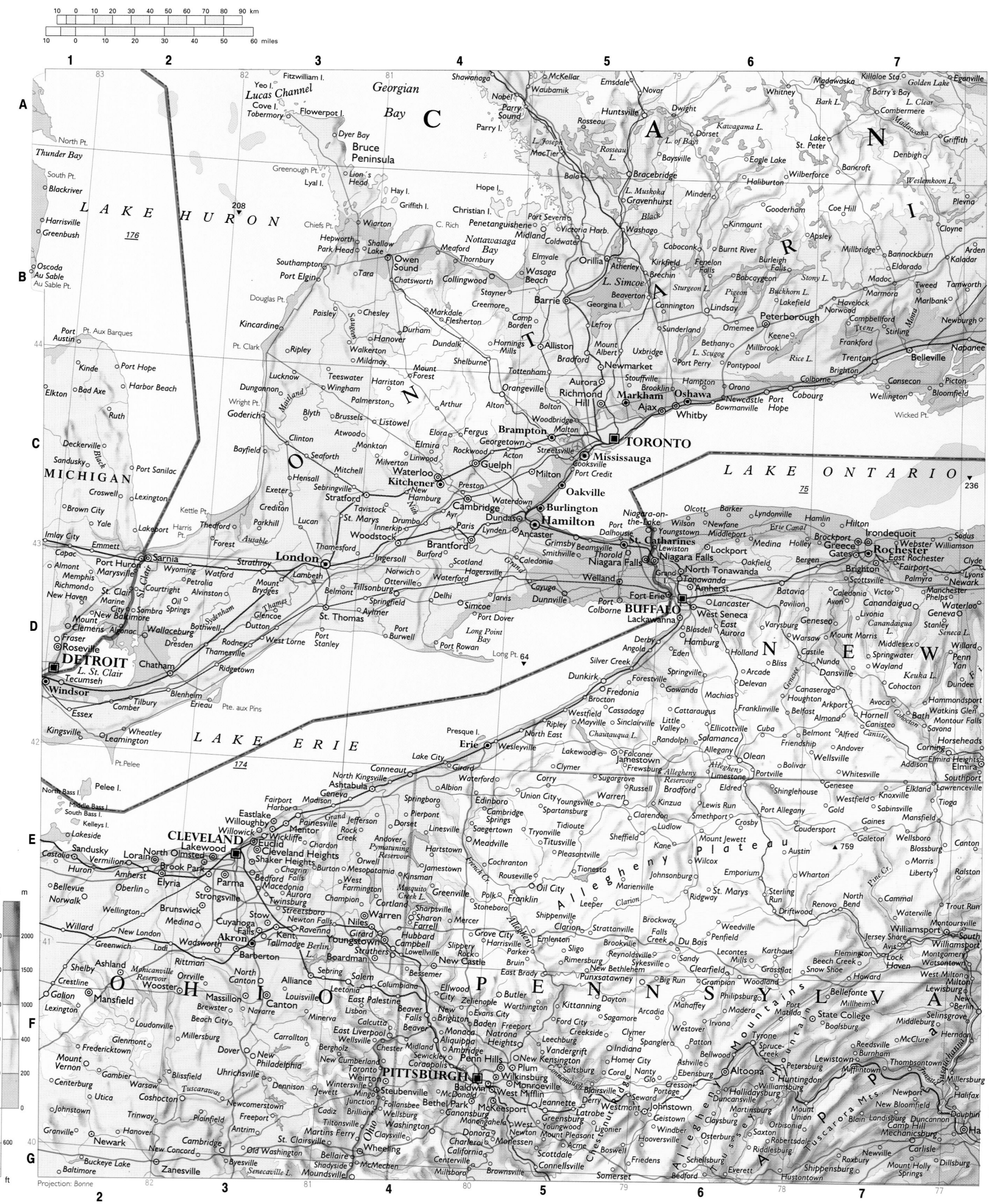

LAKE HURON
LAKE ERIE
LAKE ONTARIO
Georgian Bay
Bruce Peninsula
MICHIGAN
ONTARIO
NEW YORK
OHIO
PENNSYLVANIA
Allegheny Plateau
Allegheny Mountains
TORONTO
Mississauga
Hamilton
London
Kitchener
BUFFALO
CLEVELAND
PITTSBURGH
DETROIT
Windsor
Rochester
Erie
Akron
Youngstown
Projection: Bonne

102
108
108

8 9 10 11 12 13 14

A B C D E F G

CANADA
ONTARIO
QUÉBEC
MONTREAL
Ottawa
Hull
Sherbrooke
L. Champlain
Adirondack Mountains
Green Mountains
White Mountains
Catskill Mts.
Kittatinny Mts.
Blue Mountains
VERMONT
NEW HAMPSHIRE
MAINE
NEW YORK
MASSACHUSETTS
CONNECTICUT
RHODE ISLAND
NEW JERSEY
PENNSYLVANIA
BOSTON
HARTFORD
Providence
Albany
Syracuse
Utica
Binghamton
PHILADELPHIA
NEW YORK
Long Island
Long Island Sound
Block Island Sound
Martha's Vineyard
ATLANTIC OCEAN

West from Greenwich 76 74 73 72 71

COPYRIGHT GEORGE PHILIP LTD.

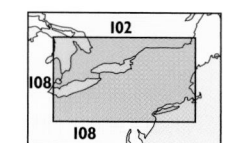

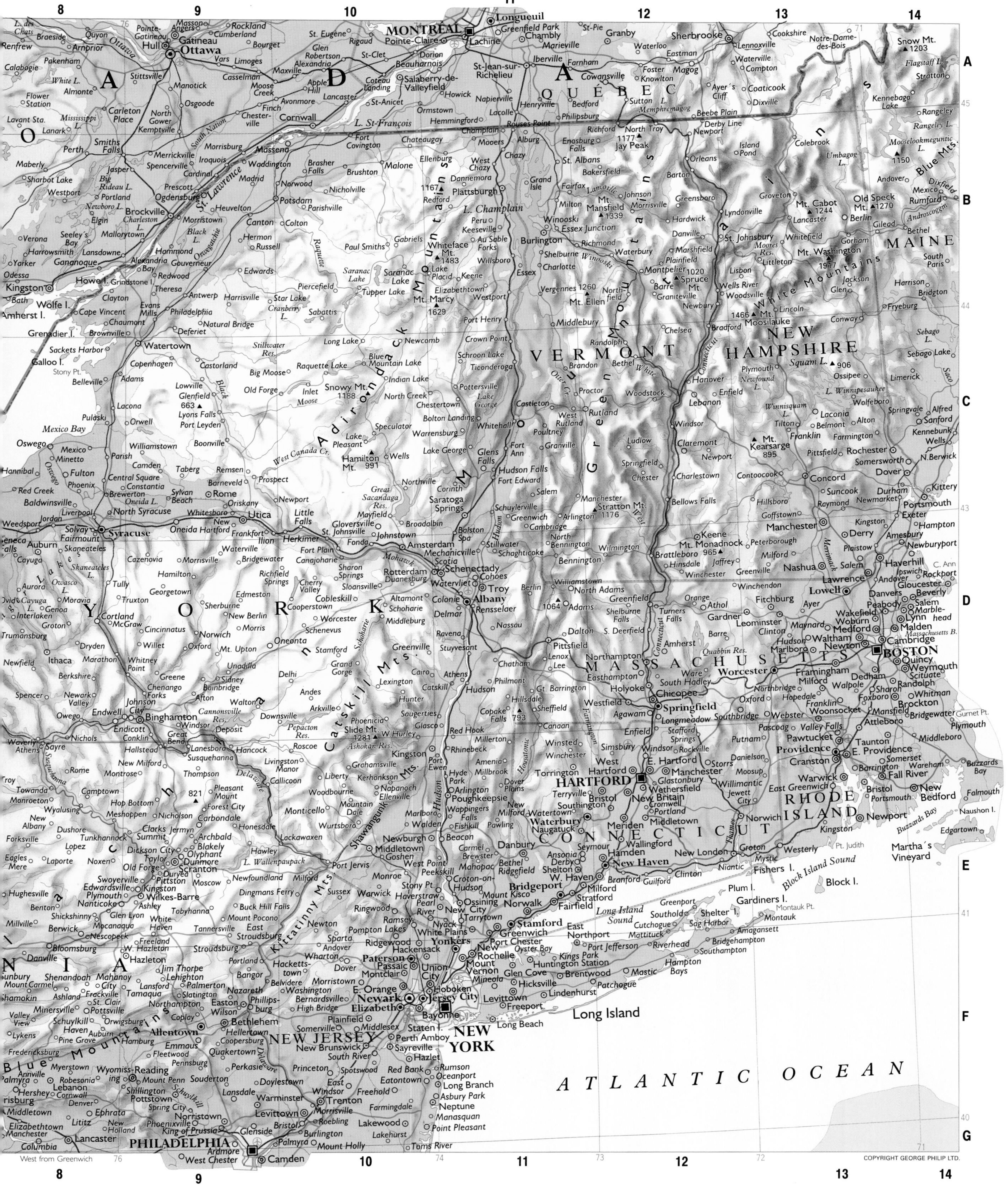

MIDDLE UNITED STATES 1:5 300 000

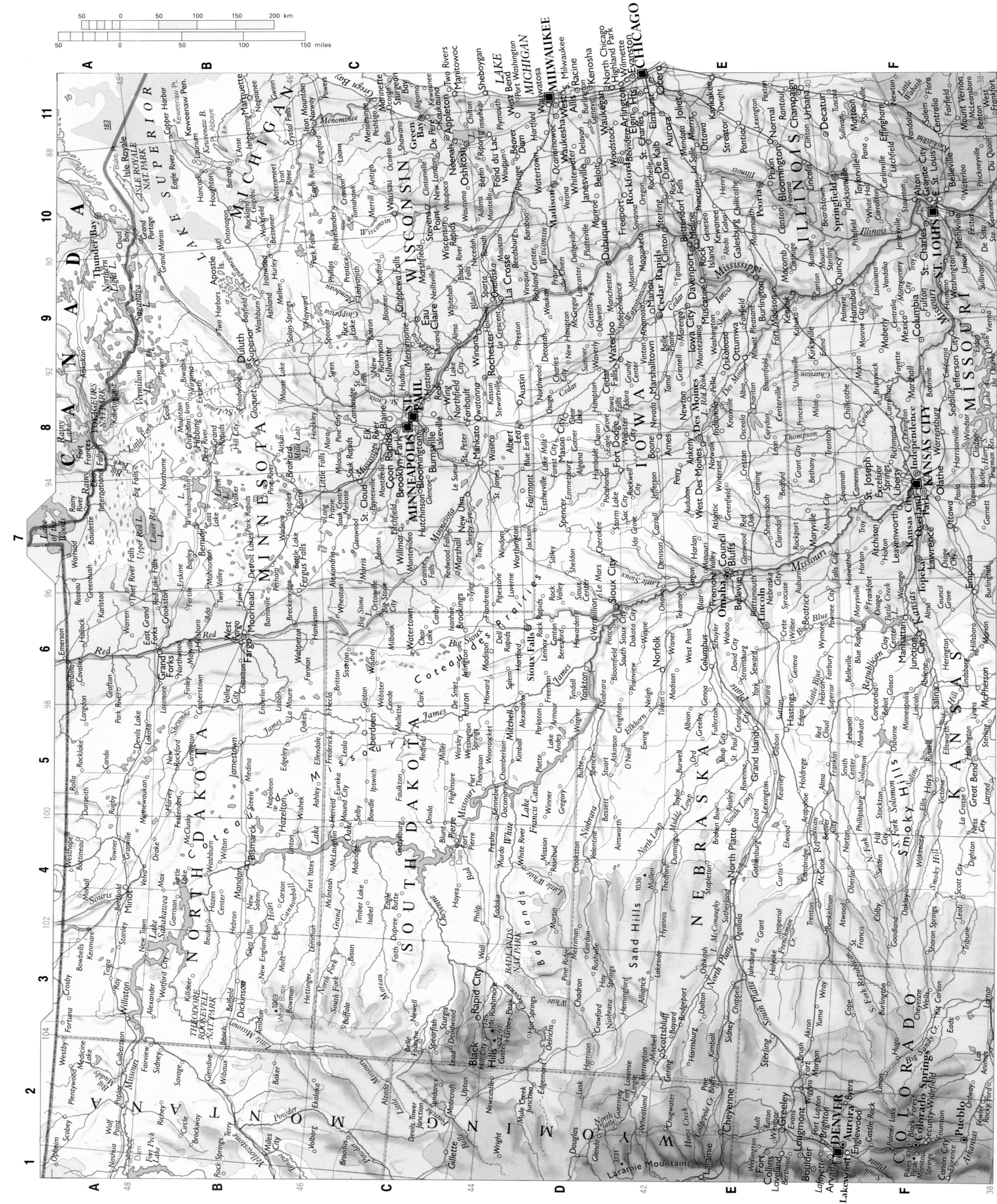
50 0 50 100 150 200 km
50 0 50 100 150 miles
CANADA
NORTH DAKOTA
SOUTH DAKOTA
NEBRASKA
KANSAS
MINNESOTA
IOWA
WISCONSIN
ILLINOIS
MISSOURI
MONTANA
WYOMING
COLORADO
MICHIGAN
LAKE SUPERIOR
LAKE MICHIGAN
MINNEAPOLIS
ST. PAUL
MILWAUKEE
CHICAGO
KANSAS CITY
ST. LOUIS
DENVER

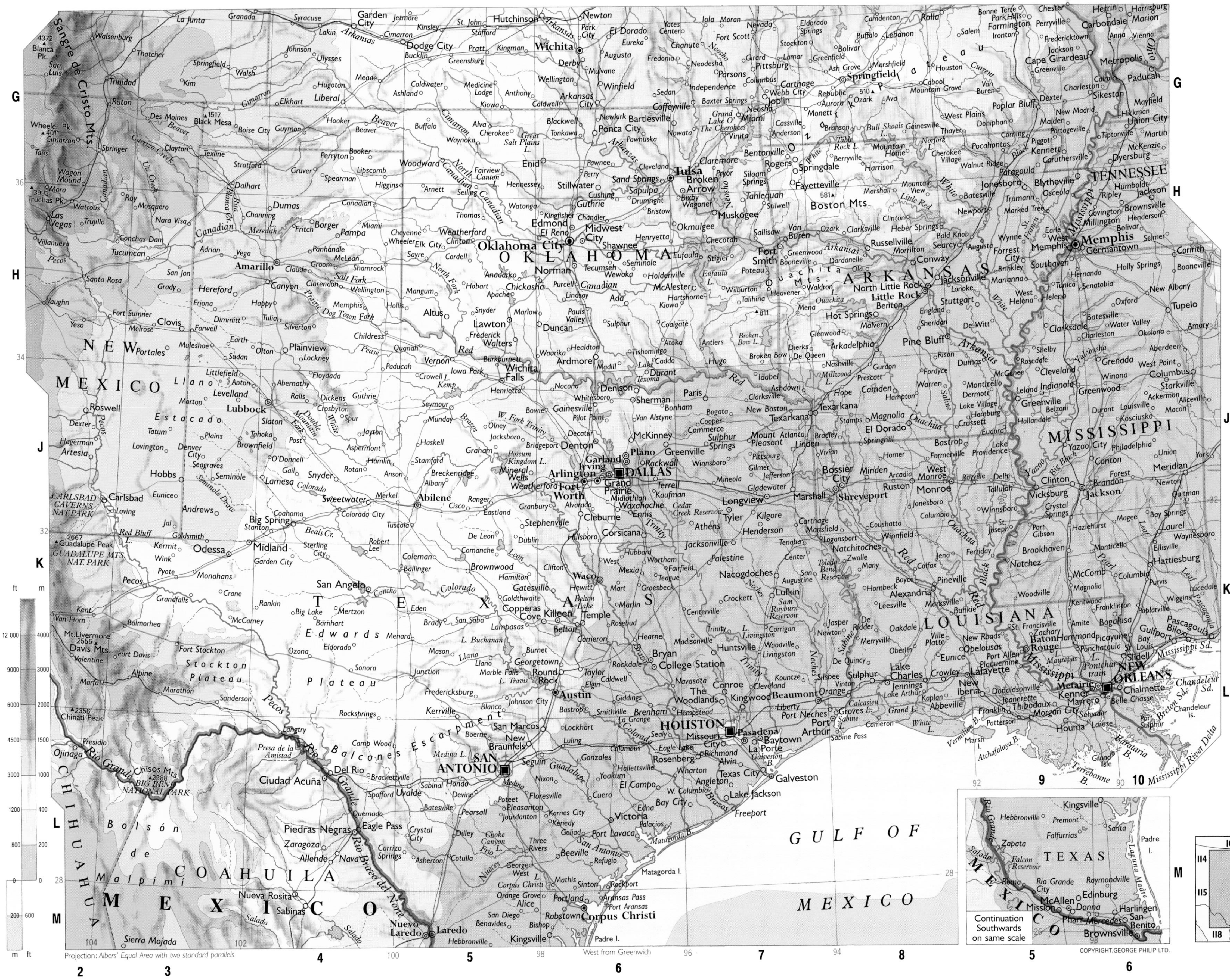

COPYRIGHT GEORGE PHILIP LTD.

Projection: Albers' Equal Area with two standard parallels

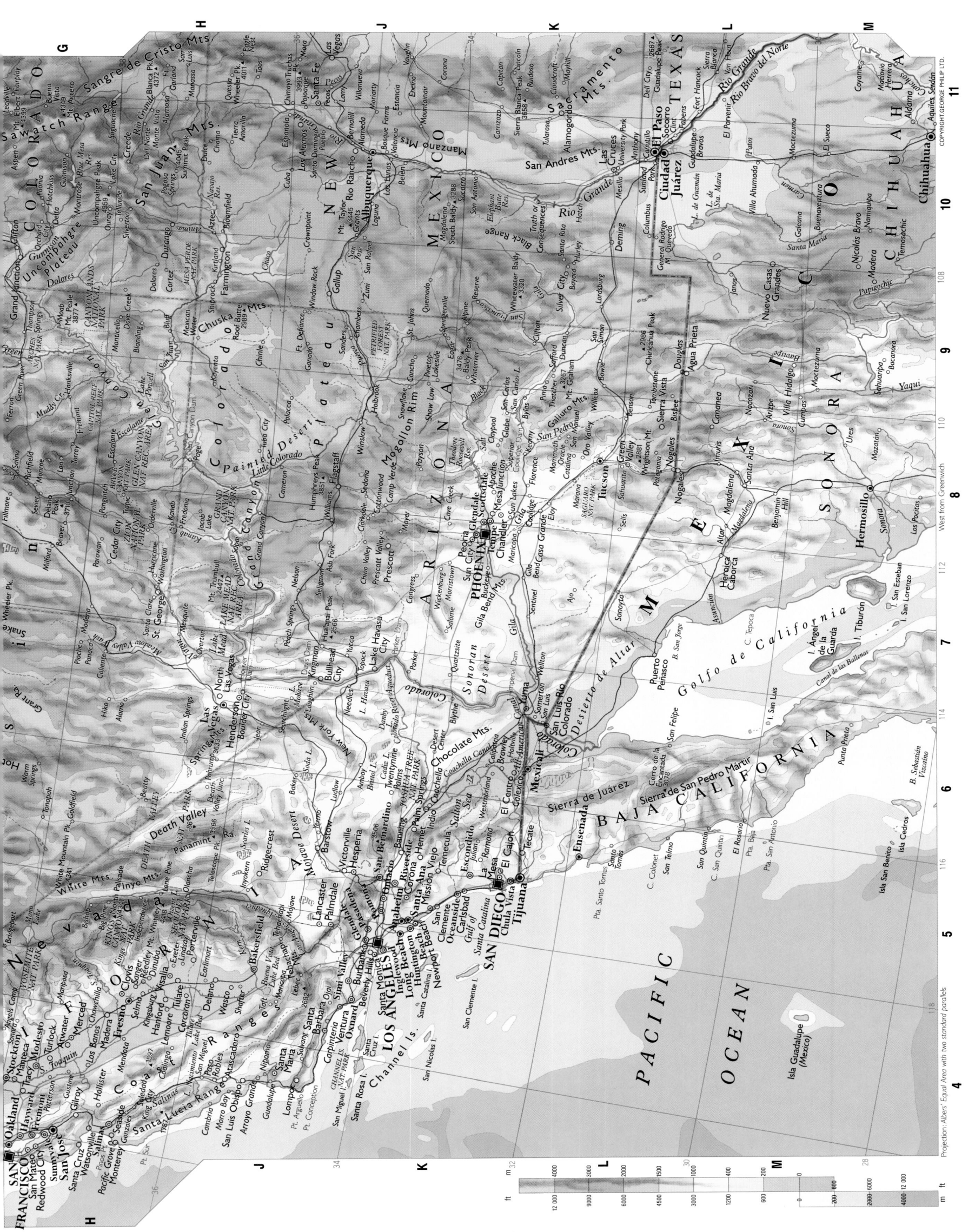
PACIFIC OCEAN
COLORADO
NEW MEXICO
ARIZONA
TEXAS
SONORA
CHIHUAHUA
MEXICO
BAJA CALIFORNIA
Golfo de California
Colorado Plateau
Sawatch Range
Sangre de Cristo Mts.
San Juan Mts.
Sacramento Mts.
Mojave Desert
Sonoran Desert
Painted Desert
Desierto de Altar
Death Valley
Grand Canyon
Mogollon Rim
Chocolate Mts.
Channel Is.
Salton Sea
SAN FRANCISCO
Oakland
San Jose
Fresno
Bakersfield
LOS ANGELES
SAN DIEGO
Tijuana
Mexicali
Ensenada
Las Vegas
PHOENIX
Tucson
Flagstaff
Albuquerque
Santa Fe
El Paso
Ciudad Juárez
Chihuahua
Hermosillo
Nogales
Yuma
Isla Guadalupe (Mexico)
I. Tiburón
I. Ángel de la Guarda
West from Greenwich
Projection: Albers' Equal Area with two standard parallels
COPYRIGHT GEORGE PHILIP LTD.
ft
m
12 000
9000
6000
4500
3000
1200
600
0
4000
3000
2000
1500
1000
400
200
0
200
600
2000
6000
4000
12 000
m
ft

WESTERN WASHINGTON REGION
On same scale

PACIFIC OCEAN

COPYRIGHT GEORGE PHILIP LTD.

West from Greenwich

Scale

10 0 10 20 30 40 50 60 70 80 90 km

10 0 10 20 30 40 50 60 miles

NEVADA

ARIZONA

C A L I F O R N I A

M E X I C O

BAJA CALIFORNIA

P A C I F I C   O C E A N

Channel Islands

M O J A V E   D E S E R T

S O N O R A N   D E S E R T

Death Valley

Amargosa Range

Panamint Ra.

San Bernardino Mts.

San Gabriel Mts.

Tehachapi Mts.

San Rafael Mts.

Santa Ynez Mts.

Temblor Range

Chocolate Mts.

Providence Mts.

Sonoran Desert

Santa Barbara Channel

San Pedro Channel

Santa Monica Mts.

Lake Mead

Colorado River

Salton Sea

Imperial Valley

Coachella Canal

Coachella Valley

DEATH VALLEY NATIONAL MONUMENT

JOSHUA TREE NATIONAL PARK

MOJAVE NATIONAL PRESERVE

LAKE MEAD NATIONAL RECREATION AREA

CHANNEL ISLANDS NATIONAL PARK

SANTA MONICA MTS. NAT. REC. AREA

Major cities and places

Las Vegas
North Las Vegas
Henderson
Boulder City
Kingman
Bullhead City
Lake Havasu City
Needles
Parker
Blythe
Yuma
Mexicali
Calexico
El Centro
Brawley
San Diego
Tijuana
Chula Vista
National City
Coronado
La Mesa
El Cajon
Escondido
Oceanside
Carlsbad
Encinitas
San Clemente
San Juan Capistrano
Mission Viejo
Laguna Beach
Irvine
Newport Beach
Santa Ana
Costa Mesa
Huntington Beach
Long Beach
Garden Grove
Anaheim
Fullerton
Orange
Riverside
San Bernardino
Redlands
Moreno Valley
Hemet
Palm Springs
Palm Desert
Indio
Banning
Fontana
Ontario
Pomona
Rancho Cucamonga
Claremont
Chino
Corona
Norco
Lake Elsinore
Temecula
Perris
Sun City
Fallbrook
Vista
San Marcos
Poway
Santee
Lakeside
LOS ANGELES
Burbank
Glendale
Pasadena
Alhambra
Monterey Park
Whittier
Downey
Norwalk
Compton
Inglewood
Torrance
Redondo Beach
Palos Verdes Estates
Pt. Palos Verdes
Santa Monica
Malibu
Beverly Hills
West Covina
El Monte
Baldwin Park
Azusa
Covina
Diamond Bar
Santa Clarita
Newhall
San Fernando
Simi Valley
Thousand Oaks
Moorpark
Camarillo
Oxnard
Ventura
Port Hueneme
El Rio
Fillmore
Santa Paula
Ojai
Carpinteria
Montecito
Santa Barbara
Goleta
Isla Vista
Los Olivos
Solvang
Santa Ynez
Lompoc
Santa Maria
Guadalupe
Pismo Beach
Grover City
Arroyo Grande
Nipomo
Oceano
San Luis Obispo
Bakersfield
Delano
McFarland
Wasco
Shafter
Oildale
Lamont
Arvin
Tehachapi
Mojave
California City
Boron
Edwards
Lancaster
Palmdale
Rosamond
Victorville
Hesperia
Apple Valley
Adelanto
Barstow
Yermo
Daggett
Newberry Springs
Ludlow
Amboy
Essex
Twentynine Palms
Joshua Tree
Yucca Valley
Morongo Valley
Desert Hot Springs
Cathedral City
Ridgecrest
Trona
Johannesburg
Randsburg
Searchlight
Nipton
Baker
Shoshone
Tecopa
Death Valley Junction
Furnace Creek
Stovepipe Wells
Scotty's Castle
Beatty
Amargosa Valley
Pahrump
Mt. Charleston
Indian Springs
Mercury
Overton
Logandale
Moapa
Laughlin
Topock
Chloride
Oatman
Quartzsite
Ehrenberg
Ripley
Palo Verde
Vidal
Rice
Cadiz
Bristol L.
Danby L.
Soda Lake
Silver Lake
Rogers L.

Elevations (selected)

Jumbo Pk. 1357
Mt. Tipton 2179
Mt. Charleston 3633
Potosi Mt. 2581
McCullough Mt. 2142
Kingston Pk. 2232
Telescope Pk. 3366
Olancha Pk. 3695
Argus Pk. 2030
Coso Pk. 2457
San Gorgonio Mt. 3505
San Jacinto 3293
Toro Pk. 2657
Mt. San Antonio 3068
Signal Pk. 1487
Avawatz Mts. 1816
Cima 1412
1315

114 115 116 117 118 119

Elevation scale

ft	m
12 000	4000
9000	3000
6000	2000
4500	1500
3000	1000
1200	400
600	200
0	0

m	ft
200	600
2000	6000

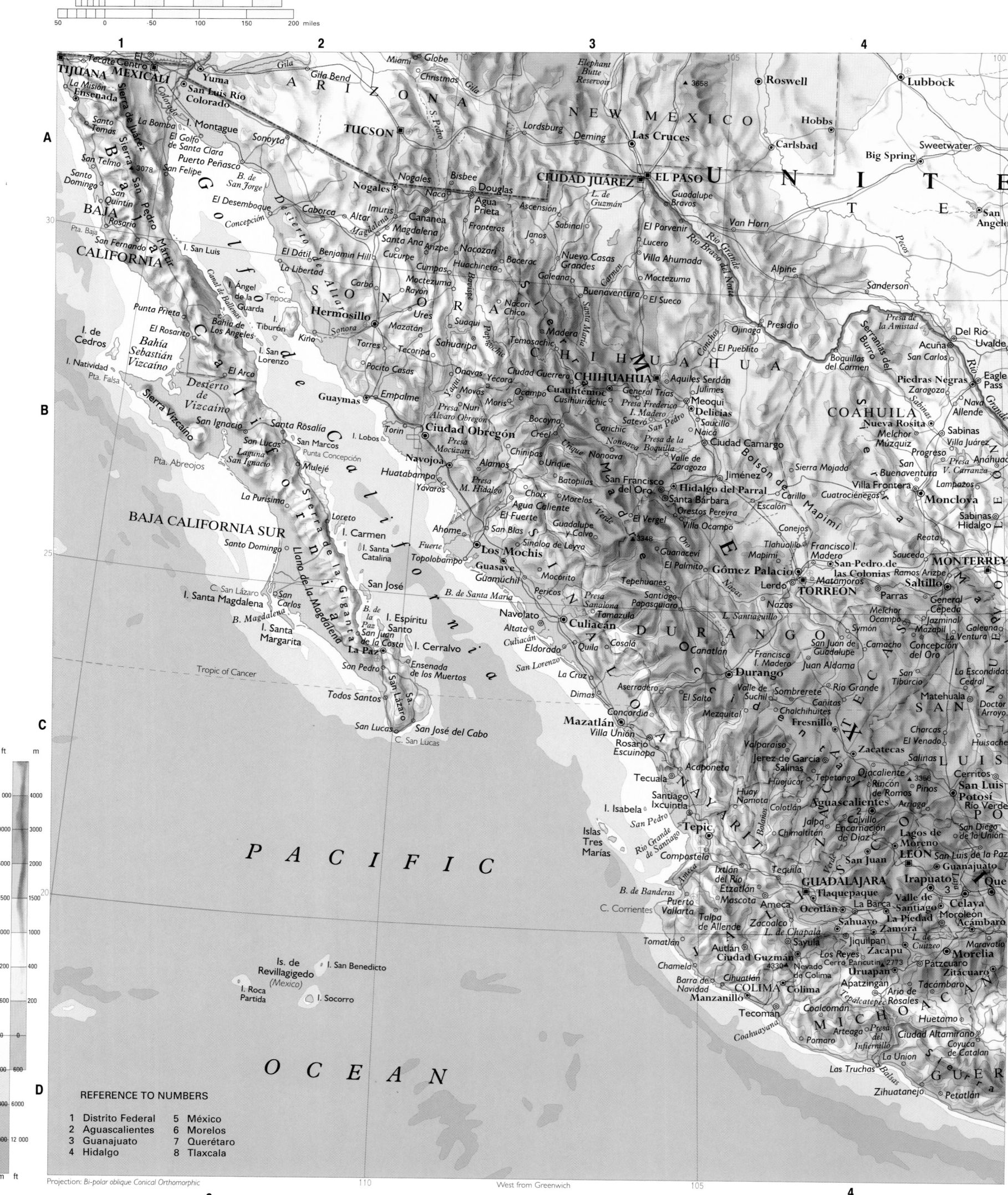

50 0 50 100 150 200 250 300 km
50 0 -50 100 150 200 miles

1   **2**   **3**   **4**

Tecate Centro   El
TIJUANA   **MEXICALI**
La Misión   Yuma
Ensenada   San Luis Río Colorado

Miami   Globe
Christmas
Gila
Elephant Butte Reservoir
▲3658   Roswell   Lubbock

Santo Tomás
La Bomba
Sierra de Juárez
El Golfo de Santa Clara
Puerto Peñasco
San Telmo   ▲3078   San Felipe
Santo Domingo
San Quintín
Rosario

A R I Z O N A
TUCSON
S. Pedro
Lordsburg
Deming
NEW MEXICO
Las Cruces
CIUDAD JUÁREZ   EL PASO
Hobbs
Carlsbad
Big Spring
Sweetwater

Sonoyta
Nogales
Nogales
Naco   Bisbee   Douglas
Agua Prieta
Ascensión
L. de Guzmán
Guadalupe Bravos
Van Horn
San Angelo

A

BAJA
Santo Domingo
Pta. Baja
San Fernando
Pta. Prieta

B. de San Jorge
El Desemboque
Concepción
Caborca
Altar
Imuris
Magdalena
Santa Ana Arizpe
Cucurpe
Cumpas
Nacozari
Moctezuma
Rayón
Huachineta
Bacerac
Nuevo Casas Grandes
Janos
Galeana
Sabinal
El Porvenir
Lucero   Villa Ahumada
Moctezuma
Carmen
Alpine
Sanderson

30

CALIFORNIA
San Luis
El Dátil
Benjamin Hill
La Libertad

C.
Tepoca

G O L F O

S O N O R A
Hermosillo
Ures
Mazatán
Sonora
Torres
Tecoripa
Pocito Casas
Empalme
Guaymas

Arizpe
Nacozari
Moctezuma
Rayón
Carbó
Moctezuma
Madera
Temosachic
Nácori Chico
El Sueco
Buenaventura
Ojinaga
Presidio
Presa de la Amistad
Serranías del Burro
Del Río
Uvalde
Acuña
San Carlos

B

I. de Cedros
I. Natividad
Pta. Falsa

Punta Prieta
El Rosarito
Bahía Sebastián Vizcaíno
Sierra Vizcaíno
Desierto de Vizcaíno

I. Ángel de la Guarda
Bahía de Los Angeles
El Arco
I. Tiburón
Kino
I. San Lorenzo

Guaymas
Suaqui
Sahuaripa
Onavas
Yécora
Ciudad Guerrero
Ocampo

C H I H U A H U A
CHIHUAHUA
Aquiles Serdán
Julimes
General Trías
Cuauhtémoc
Cusihuiriáchic
Meoqui
Delicias
Saucillo
Naica
Ciudad Camargo

COAHUILA
Boquillas del Carmen
Piedras Negras
Zaragoza
Nava
Allende
Sabinas
Villa Juárez
Múzquiz
Melchor
Progreso
San Buenaventura
Villa Frontera
Cuatrociénegas
Monclova
Sabinas Hidalgo

San Rosalía
Santa Rosalía
San Ignacio
Mulegé
Punta Concepción
I. Lobos
Torín
Ciudad Obregón
Navojoa
Álamos
Creel
Carichic
Chínipas
Uruique
Batopilas
San Francisco del Oro
Hidalgo del Parral
Santa Bárbara
Orestos Pereyra
Escalón
Conejos
Sierra Mojada
Villa Frontera
Carillo
Cuatrociénegas
Bolsón de Mapimí
Reata
Sauceda
MONTERREY
Saltillo

Huatabampo
Yávaros
Presa M. Hidalgo
Choix
El Fuerte
Agua Caliente
Morelos
Guadalupe y Calvo
El Vergel
▲3348
Villa Ocampo
Guanaceví
El Palmito
Mapimí
Tlahualilo
Francisco I. Madero
Mapimí
San Pedro de las Colonias
Ramos Arizpe
Parras
General Cepeda

25

BAJA CALIFORNIA SUR
La Purísima
Loreto
I. Carmen
I. Santa Catalina
Santo Domingo
C. San Lázaro
I. Santa Magdalena
San Carlos
B. Magdalena
I. Santa Margarita

Llano de la Magdalena
Sierra de la Giganta
B. de la Paz
San Juan de la Costa
La Paz
San Pedro
Espíritu Santo
I. Cerralvo
Ensenada de los Muertos

Topolobampo
Los Mochis
Guasave
Guamúchil
Navolato
Culiacán
Culiacán
Eldorado
Quila
Cosalá

Navolato
Altata
B. de Santa María
Pericos
Presa Sanalona
Santiago Papasquiaro
Nazas
L. Santiaguillo
Canatlán
Francisco I. Madero
Juan Aldama
Símbolo
Camacho
Concepción del Oro

D U R A N G O
Durango
Valle de Suchil
Sombrerete
Río Grande
San Tiburcio
La Ventura
Galeana
Matehuala
Cedral
La Escondida

S A N

C

Tropic of Cancer

San Lucas
San José del Cabo
C. San Lucas

Concordia
Mazatlán
Villa Unión
Rosario
Escuinapa
Tecuala
Acaponeta

Dimas
Aserradero
El Salto
Mezquital
Chalchihuites
Fresnillo
Valparaíso
Zacatecas
Jerez de García
Salinas
Huejúcar
Tepetongo
Ojocaliente
Rincón de Romos
▲3356   Pinos
Cerritos
San Luis Potosí
Río Verde
Charcas
El Venado
Salinas
Huisache
Doctor Arroyo

1
Santiago Ixcuintla
I. Isabela
Islas Tres Marías
San Pedro
Huay Namota
Colotlán
Jalpa
Calvillo
Aguascalientes
Encarnación de Díaz
Lagos de Moreno
San Luis de la Paz
San Diego de la Unión

PACIFIC

Is. de Revillagigedo (México)
I. San Benedicto
I. Roca Partida
I. Socorro

Tepic
Ixtlán del Río
Etzatlán
Mascota
Puerto Vallarta
C. Corrientes
B. de Banderas
Talpa de Allende
Tomatlán
Chamela

Compostela
Ameca
Tequila
Zacoalco
Autlán
Ciudad Guzmán
▲4330   Nevado de Colima
Cerro Paricutín ▲2773
Uruapan

San Juan
GUADALAJARA
Tlaquepaque
La Barca
Ocotlán
Santiago
Sahuayo
Jiquilpan
Los Reyes
Zacapu
Cihuatlán
Apatzingán
Ario de Rosales
Coalcomán

LEÓN
Guanajuato
Irapuato
Celaya
Moroleón
Acámbaro
L. de Cuitzeo
Pátzcuaro
Morelia
Zitácuaro
Tácambaro

20

O C E A N

Barra de Navidad
Manzanillo
COLIMA
Colima
Tecomán

Coahuayana
Pomaro
Artega
Presa del Infiernillo
La Unión
Coyuca de Catalán
Las Truchas
Zihuatanejo
Petatlán

M I C H O A C A N
Huetamo
Ciudad Altamirano
G U E R

D

REFERENCE TO NUMBERS

1   Distrito Federal   5   México
2   Aguascalientes   6   Morelos
3   Guanajuato   7   Querétaro
4   Hidalgo   8   Tlaxcala

Projection: Bi-polar oblique Conical Orthomorphic

West from Greenwich

2   110   **3**   105   **4**

ft m
12 000   4000
9000   3000
6000   2000
4500   1500
3000   1000
1200   400
600   200
0   0
200   600
2000   6000
4000   12 000
m ft

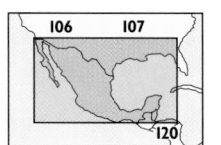

5   6   7   8

Wichita Falls
Denison Sherman
Denton Greenville Paris Red Hope Camden
Possum Kingdom Res. Texarkana El Dorado Greenville
FORT WORTH DALLAS Marshall ARKANSAS MISSISSIPPI Tuscaloosa Opelika
Abilene Ranger Cleburne Longview Tyler Monroe Vicksburg Jackson Meridian Selma Montgomery Columbus McRae
Brownwood Hillsboro Corsicana Shreveport Tallulah Natchez Laurel Hattiesburg Troy Americus Cordele A
Waco Palestine Nacogdoches Alexandria McComb Bogalusa Flomaton Dothan Albany Tifton GEORGIA Waycross
Temple Lufkin Sam Rayburn Reservoir Baton Biloxi MOBILE Pensacola Jim Woodruff Res. Chattahoochee Tallahassee Valdosta
Huntsville Bryan Sabine Rouge Hammond Gulfport Panama City FLORIDA Lake City 30
Austin Navasota Lake Charles Lafayette NEW ORLEANS C. San Blas Apalachee Bay Suwannee
HOUSTON Beaumont Port Arthur Terrebonne Bay Mississippi River Delta Breton Sd. B
SAN ANTONIO Rosenberg Galveston Atchafalaya Bay Clearwater
Dilley Victoria
Alice Corpus Christi GULF OF
Laredo Kingsville
Nuevo Laredo Zapata
Camargo Laguna Madre
McAllen Harlingen Brownsville MEXICO 25
Reynosa Matamoros
Valle Hermoso Santa Teresa Laguna Madre
Linares San Fernando C
Villagrán Tropic of Cancer La Esperanza
Hidalgo Santander Jiménez CUBA
Zaragoza La Pesca Guane
Ciudad Victoria Soto la Marina La Fé
Ciudad Mante I. Desterrada C. San Antonio C. Corrientes
Altamira I. Pérez (Mexico) Canal de Yucatán
Ciudad Madero Pta. Yalkubul Río Lagartos C. Catoche
Tampico Progreso Dzilam de Bravo El Cuyo Cancún
Pánuco Motul Temax Tizimín Puerto Juárez
Ozuluama Mérida Izamal Espita Puerto Morelos
TOSÍ Tempoal CHICHEN ITZA Valladolid Isla 20
Tamazunchale YUCATÁN Sotuta Cozumel Cozumel
Tuxpan Maxcanú Ticul Peto
Poza Rica Papantla Tenabo Tekax Vigía Chico B. de la Ascensión
Huauchinango Bolonchenticul QUINTANA
Pachuca Tulancingo Campeche Hopelchén Felipe Carrillo ROO B. del Espíritu Santo
El Oro Teziutlán Jalapa Champotón Puerto Banco Chinchorro
MÉXICO Apizaco Enríquez Chenkán Bacalar B. de
Toluca Amecameca Veracruz Ciudad del Chetumal Chetumal
Puebla Coatepec Carmen L. de Matamoros Ambergris Cay
Cuernavaca Orizaba Córdoba Términos Corozal
Taxco Tehuacán Alvarado Frontera CAMPECHE Orange Walk Turneffe Is.
Iguala Chiautla Tlacotalpan Paraíso Palizada Concepción Belize City BELIZE
RERO Acatlán San Andrés Coatzacoalcos TABASCO Balancán Belmopan Dangriga
Chilapa Huajuapan Tuxtla Comalcalco Villahermosa Uaxactún San Ignacio Golfo de Honduras
Chilpancingo de León Minatitlán Cárdenas Macuspana Tenosique Benque Viejo Is. de la Bahía
Acapulco Oaxaca Istmo de Jesús Carranza Teapa Simojovel Flores Maya Mts. Roatán Puerto Castilla
OAXACA Tehuantepec Raudales de Ocosingo L. Petén Itzá Monkey River Trujillo
Ocotlán Netzahualcoyotl Copainalá Chiapa de La Libertad San Luis Punta Gorda Puerto Tela
CHIAPAS Tuxtla Corzo San Cristóbal de San Antonio Livingston Barrios San Pedro Sula HONDURAS
Juchitán Gutiérrez las Casas La Independencia El Progreso E 15
Tehuantepec Arriaga Tonalá Comitán GUATEMALA Cobán Santa Rosa de Copán Tegucigalpa
Salina Cruz La Concordia Cuchumatanes Zacapa Comayagua
Golfo de Puerto Arista Motozintla Huehuetenango GUATEMALA La Esperanza Juticalpa Catacamas
Pijijiapan San Marcos Totonicapán Jalapa Chiquimula La Paz
Tehuantepec Tapachula Coatepeque GUATEMALA

COPYRIGHT GEORGE PHILIP LTD.

5   6   7

GULF OF MEXICO

U.S.A.
Fort Myers
Naples
C. Romano
Everglades
The
C. Sable
MIAMI
Hialeah
Dry Tortugas (U.S.A.)
Key West
Florida Keys
Straits of Florida
L. Okeechobee
West Palm Beach
Boca Raton
Fort Lauderdale
West End
Freeport
Hope Town
Little Abaco I.
Grand Bahama
Northwest Providence Channel
Great Abaco I.
BAH
Dunmore Town
Eleuthera
Nassau
New Providence
Adelaide
Andros Town
New Portsmouth (Rock Sound)
Exuma Sound
Bimini Is.
Berry Is.
Nicolls Town
Governor's Harbour
Great Exuma I.
Jumentos Cays
Northeast Providence Channel

LA HABANA (Havana)
MARIANAO
Guanabacoa
Guanajay
Bahía Honda
La Esperanza
Los Palacios
San Antonio de los Baños
Güines
Matanzas
Cárdenas
Jovellanos
Colón
Sagua la Grande
Caibarién
Morón
Cayo Romano
Duncan Town
Santa Cruz del Norte
Canal Nicholás
Cay Sal Bank
Santaren Channel
Canal Viejo de Bahama
Great Bahama Bank
Pinar del Río
Guane
San Luis
La Fé
I. de la Juventud
Nueva Gerona
Cienfuegos
Santa Clara
Placetas
Trinidad
Arch. de los Canarreos
Jagüey Grande
CUBA
Ciego de Avila
Júcaro
Sancti Spíritus
Tunas de Zaza
Florida
Camagüey
Santa Cruz del Sur
Arch. de Jardines de la Reina
Golfo de Guacanayabo
Manzanillo
Bayamo
Victoria de las Tunas
Puerto Manatí
Puerto Padre
Gibara
HOLGUÍN
Palma Soriano
Sierra Maestra
2000
C. Cruz
SANTIAGO DE CUBA
Nuevitas

Cayman Islands (U.K.)
Georgetown
Grand Cayman
Cayman Brac
Little Cayman
7680

Montego Bay
Lucea
Negril
Falmouth
St. Ann's Bay
Port Maria
Annotto Bay
Port Antonio
South Negril Pt.
Savanna-la-Mar
Cambridge
Black River
Mandeville
May Pen
JAMAICA
KINGSTON
Spanish Town
Port Morant
Morant
Morant Cays (Jamaica)
Pedro Cays (Jamaica)
Bajo Nuevo (Colombia)

GREATER

Punta Yalkubul
C. Catoche
Río Lagartos
El Cuyo
Cancún
Puerto Juárez
El Diaz
Puerto Morelos
Cozumel
Isla Cozumel
Progreso
Dzilam de Bravo
Motul
Temax
Tizimín
Espita
Valladolid
MÉRIDA
DZIBILCHALTÚN
Izamal
Maxcanú
Sotuta
CHICHÉN ITZÁ
MAYAPÁN
Ticul
Tekax
Peto
Vigia Chico
B. de la Ascensión
YUCATÁN
Campeche
Champotón
Chankán
Hopelchen
Bolonchenticul
UXMAL
Calkini
Tenabo
San José Carpizo
Felipe Carrillo Puerto
B. del Espíritu Santo
Pedro Antonio Santos
QUINTANA ROO
Banco Chinchorro
Ciudad del Carmen
I. de Términos
Palizada
Pital
Balancán
Matamoros
Concepción
Escárcega
MEXICO
CAMPECHE
Bacalar
Chetumal
Corozal
B. de Chetumal
Orange Walk
Hondo
Ambergris Cay

I. Desterrada
I. Pérez (Mexico)
Canal de Yucatán
C. San Antonio
Corrientes
C. San Antonio

PALENQUE
Ocosingo
La Independencia
Comitán
Sierra de los Cuchumatanes
3993
Cuilco
San Marcos
Ayutla
Tenosique
Uaxactún
USUMACINTA
TIKAL
L. Petén Itzá
La Libertad
Flores
Sebol
Cobán
Livingston
Punta Gorda
GUATEMALA
Huehuetenango
Totonicapán
QUETZALTENANGO
Quetzaltenango
Retalhuleu
Mazatenango
Escuintla
San José
Ahuachapán
Sonsonate
Acajutla
Nueva San Salvador
SAN SALVADOR
EL SALVADOR
Usulután
San Miguel
La Unión
G. de Fonseca
Puerto Morazán
Chinandega
Corinto
León
La Paz Centro
San Ignacio
Benque Viejo
Belize City
Belmopan
Middlesex
BELIZE
Turneffe Is.
Dangriga
Maya Mts.
Golfo de Honduras
Monkey River
San Antonio
Is. de la Bahía
Roatán
Puerto Cortés
Puerto Barrios
Tela
La Ceiba
Trujillo
Balfate
Savá
Olanchito
Yoro
SAN PEDRO SULA
El Progreso
Santa Bárbara
Santa Rosa de Copán
L. de Yojoa
El Jaral
Comayagua
HONDURAS
Juticalpa
Catacamas
Iriona
C. Camarón
Punta Patuca
Brus Laguna
Laguna Caratasca
Mosquitia
C. Falso
C. Gracias a Dios
Puerto Castilla
Sierra de las Minas
Gualán
Zacapa
Chiquimula
Jalapa
Antigua
GUATEMALA
Amatitlán
Cojutepeque
Zacatecoluca
Chalatenango
Santa Ana
Suchitoto
Coatepeque
Sololá
UTATLÁN
Jalpa
La Esperanza
La Paz
Yuscarán
Danlí
Ocotal
Somoto
Esteli
Tegucigalpa
Nacaome
Choluteca
El Sauce
Matagalpa
Muy Muy
San Pedro del Norte
Río Grande
Coco (Segovia)
Puerto Cabo Gracias á Dios
Kisalaya
Puerto Cabezas
Cayos Miskitos (Nicaragua)
Pta. Gorda
Bonanza
Siuna
Cord. Isabelia
Prinzapolca
Bluefields
El Bluff
Tungla
San Pedro del Norte

PACIFIC OCEAN

San Juan del Sur
B. de Salinas
C. Santa Elena
G. de Papagayo
Pta. Velas
C. Blanco
Liberia
Santa Cruz
Nicoya
Carmona
Pen. de Nicoya
G. de Nicoya
Puntarenas
Esparta
Puerto Quepos
B. de Coronado
Pen. de Osa
Pta. Burica
NICARAGUA
MANAGUA
Masaya
Granada
Diriamba
Jinotepe
Boaco
Juigalpa
L. de Managua
Rivas
I. de Ometepe
Lago de Nicaragua
San Carlos
La Cruz
Los Chiles
San Juan
B. de San Juan del Norte
San Juan del Norte
Santo Domingo
Rama
Cord. de Yolaina
Pta. Mico
Punta de Perlas
Is. del Maíz (Nicaragua, U.S.A.)
Cayos de Albuquerque (Colombia)
I. de San Andrés (Colombia)
I. de Providencia (Colombia)
Cayos Roncador (U.S.A. & Colombia)
Swan Islands (U.S.A. & Honduras)

COSTA RICA
Cord. de Guanacaste
Alajuela
SAN JOSÉ
Cartago
Cord. Central
Guápiles
Siquirres
Limón
Cord. de Talamanca
3837
Chirripó Grande
Buenos Aires
San Vito
Golfito
G. Dulce
Pta. Mona
Bribri
Bocas del Toro
Pandora
Almirante
Volcán Barú
3374
Boquete
La Concepción
David
Remedios
Santiago
Soná
G. de Chiriquí
I. de Coiba
I. de Cebaco
Pta. Mala
Pen. de Azuero
Chitré
Las Tablas
Pocrí
Tonosí
I. Jicarón
Punta Mariato
Serranía de Tabasara
L. de Chiriquí
G. de los Mosquitos
Portobelo
Nombre de Dios
Colón
Panama Canal
L. Gatún
Balboa
PANAMA
La Chorrera
Chepo
Penonomé
Río Hato
Aguadulce
Chimán
Arch. de las Perlas
San Miguel
I. del Rey
Golfo de Panamá
La Palma
Yaviza
El Real
Garachiné
Serranía del Darién
Golfo del Darién
G. de Urabá
G. de Morrosquillo
I. de San Bernardo
Lorica
Cereté
Montería
CÓR
Monte
CARTAGE
CARIB

Projection: Conical with two standard parallels

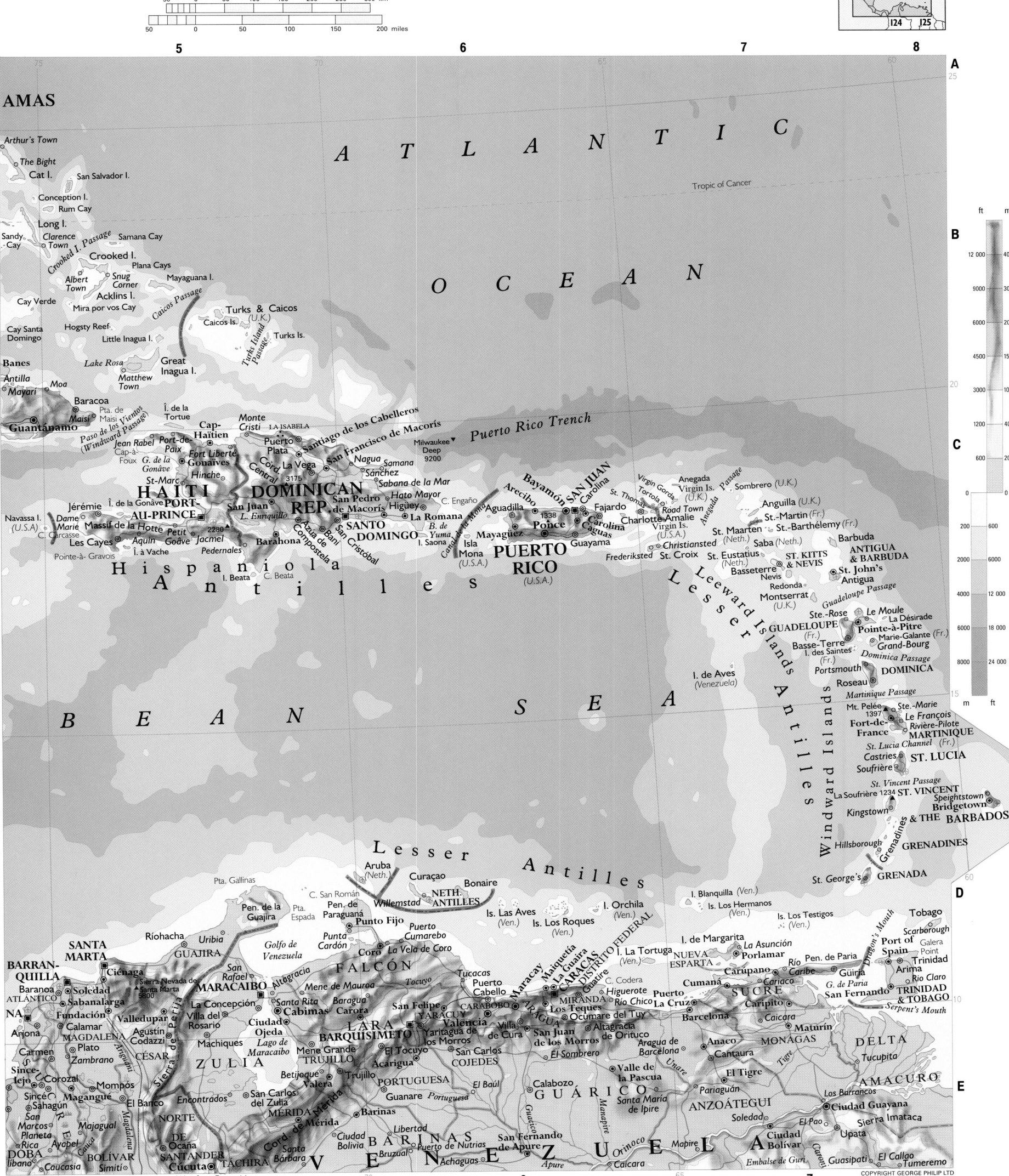

50 0 50 100 150 200 250 300 km

50 0 50 100 150 200 miles

AMAS

A T L A N T I C

Arthur's Town

The Bight
Cat I.

San Salvador I.

Conception I.

Rum Cay

Long I.

Sandy
Cay   Clarence
        Town   Samana Cay

Crooked I.
            Plana Cays

Albert
Town   Snug
        Corner   Mayaguana I.

Acklins I.

Cay Verde   Mira por vos Cay

Cay Santa
Domingo   Hogsty Reef   Little Inagua I.

Banes

Antilla
Moa
Mayari

Baracoa

Maisi

Guantanamo

Tropic of Cancer

O C E A N

Turks & Caicos
(U.K.)

Caicos Is.

Turks Island Passage

Turks Is.

Lake Rosa

Great
Inagua I.

Matthew
Town

Î. de la
Tortue   Monte
Cristi   LA ISABELA

Cap-
Haïtien

Pta. de
Maisi

Jean Rabel   Port-de-
Paix   Puerto
Plata   Santiago de los Cabelleros

Puerto Rico Trench

San Francisco de Macoris

Milwaukee
Deep
9200

Nagua   Samana

Fort Liberté   La Vega

Cord.   Sánchez

G. de la
Gonâve   Gonaïves   Central   3175

Sabana de la Mar

Cap-à-
Foux   Hinche   DOMINICAN
REP   San Pedro
de Macoris   Higüey

Jérémie   Î. de la Gonâve   PORT-
AU-PRINCE   San Juan   Hato Mayor

St-Marc   HAITI   L. Enriquillo   La Romana   C. Engaño

Dame
Marie   Massif de la Hotte   2280   Azua de   San Cristóbal   Isla
Mona
(U.S.A.)

Navassa I.
(U.S.A.)   Petit   Jacmel   Compostela   B. de
Yuma

C. Carcasse   Les Cayes   Aquin   Goâve   Barahona   SANTO
DOMINGO   I. Saona

Pointe-à- Gravois   Î. à Vache   Pedernales

Hispaniola   C. Beata   I. Beata

A n t i l l e s

Bayamón   SAN JUAN

Arecibo   Carolina

Aguadilla   1338   Fajardo

Mayagüez   Ponce   Caguas   Guayama

PUERTO
RICO
(U.S.A.)

Virgin Gorda
Virgin Is.
(U.K.)   Anegada

Tortola   Road Town

St. Thomas   Virgin Is.
(U.S.A.)   Charlotte Amalie

Christiansted   St. Croix

Frederiksted

Anegada Passage

Sombrero (U.K.)

Anguilla (U.K.)

St.-Martin (Fr.)
St. Maarten (Neth.)   St.-Barthélemy (Fr.)

Saba (Neth.)   Barbuda

St. Eustatius
(Neth.)   ANTIGUA
& BARBUDA

ST. KITTS
& NEVIS   St. John's

Basseterre   Antigua

Nevis   Redonda   Guadeloupe Passage

Montserrat
(U.K.)   Ste.-Rose   Le Moule
La Désirade

GUADELOUPE   Pointe-à-Pitre
(Fr.)   Marie-Galante (Fr.)

Basse-Terre   Grand-Bourg
(Fr.)   I. des Saintes

I. de Aves
(Venezuela)   Dominica Passage

Portsmouth   DOMINICA

Roseau

Martinique Passage

B E A N   S E A

Lesser   Antilles

Aruba
(Neth.)   Curaçao   Bonaire

Pta. Gallinas   C. San Román   NETH.
ANTILLES

Pen. de
la   Pta.
Espada   Pen. de
Paraguaná   Willemstad

Guajira   Punto Fijo

Mt. Pelée
1397   Ste.-Marie
Le François

Fort-de-
France   Rivière-Pilote
MARTINIQUE

St. Lucia Channel
(Fr.)

Castries   ST. LUCIA

Soufrière

St. Vincent Passage

La Soufrière 1234   ST. VINCENT
Speightstown

Kingstown   Bridgetown
Grenadines   & THE BARBADOS

Hillsborough   GRENADINES

St. George's   GRENADA

I. Blanquilla (Ven.)

I. Los Hermanos
(Ven.)

I. Los Testigos
(Ven.)

Tobago
Scarborough

Port of
Spain

Galera
Point

I. Orchila
(Ven.)   I. de Margarita   NUEVA
ESPARTA   La Asunción   Trinidad

Is. Las Aves
(Ven.)   Is. Los Roques
(Ven.)   I. La Tortuga
(Ven.)   Porlamar   Arima
Río Claro

RÍohacha   Uribia   Golfo de
Venezuela   Punta   Maiquetía   La Guaira   Cumaná   Carúpano   Güiria   San Fernando

SANTA
MARTA   GUAJIRA   Cardón   Coro   La Vela de Coro   Maracay   CARACAS   Pen. de Paria   Caribe   TRINIDAD
& TOBAGO

BARRAN-
QUILLA   Ciénaga   FALCÓN   Tucacas   DISTRITO FEDERAL   Cariaco   SUCRE

Baranoa   Sierra Nevada de   San   Puerto   MIRANDA   Río Chico   Barcelona   Caripito

ATLÁNTICO   Soledad   Santa Marta
5800   Rafael   Altagracia   Mene de Mauroa   Cabello   Los Teques   Puerto
La Cruz   Maturín

NA   Sabanalarga   Villa del   Mene Grande   CARABOBO   Ocumare del Tuy   Anaco

Fundación   La Concepción   Rosario   MARACAIBO   Baragua   Carora   San Felipe   YARACUY   Villa   Altagracia   DELTA

Arjona   Calamar   Agustín   Cabimas   LARA   de Cura   San Juan   de Orituco   Cantaura   Tucupita

MAGDALENA   Codazzi   Ciudad   Yaritagua de   BARQUISIMETO   San Carlos   de Barcelona   MONAGAS   AMACURO

Plato   Ojeda   Lago de   los Morros   Aragua de

Carmen   Zambrano   CÉSAR   Machiques   Maracaibo   Mene Grande   El Tocuyo   COJEDES   Valle de
la Pascua   El Tigre

Since-   Mompós   ZULIA   San Carlos   Acarigua   PORTUGUESA   El Baúl   GUÁRICO   ANZOÁTEGUI   Ciudad Guayana

lejo   Magangué   El Banco   del Zulia   Trujillo   Guanare   Portuguesa   Santa María
de Ipire   Soledad   Sierra Imataca

Since   Majagual   Betijoque   Valera   El Pao

San   El Barco   NORTE   MÉRIDA   Barinas   Libertad   Calabozo   Pariaguán   Upata

Marcos   Planeta   DE   Mérida   Barinas   San Fernando   Ciudad

DOBA   Rica   Ayapel   OCAÑA   SANTANDER   Ciudad   BARINAS   Puerto de Nutrias   de Apure   El Callao

libano   Caucasia   BOLÍVAR   Cúcuta   Santa   Bolivia   Bruzual   Mapire   Guasipati

Simití   TÁCHIRA   Bárbara   **V E N E Z U E L A**   Orinoco   Ciudad   Tumeremo
Bolívar

West from Greenwich   Achaguas   Apure   Caicara   Embalse de Guri

COPYRIGHT GEORGE PHILIP LTD

ft   m
12 000   4000
9000   3000
6000   2000
4500   1500
3000   1000
1200   400
600   200
0   0
200   600
2000   6000
4000   12 000
6000   18 000
8000   24 000
m   ft

100 0 200 400 600 800 1000 1200 1400 km

100 0 200 400 600 800 1000 miles

1　　　　2　　　　3　　　　4　　　　5　　　　6　　　　7

Tropic of Cancer

A

Yucatan Channel

Cuba

Greater Antilles

Turks & Caicos Is.

Gulf of Campeche

Yucatán Peninsula

Hispaniola

9200

Puerto Rico

B

Isthmus of Tehuantepec

G. de Honduras

Jamaica

Coco

C. Gracias a Dios

Lesser Antilles

Guadeloupe
Dominica
Martinique
St. Lucia
Barbados
St. Vincent
Grenada
Tobago

NORTH

ATLANTIC

OCEAN

Guatemala Trench

L. Nicaragua

Caribbean Sea

I. Margarita

Trinidad

Panama Canal

Gulf of Panamá

C. de la Aguja

Sierra Nevada de Santa Marta

5800

L. Maracaibo

C. de Manita

Orinoco

Meta

Llanos

Guiana Highlands

Mt. Roraima 2810

C. Orange

C

Gulf of Darién

Cordillera Occidental
Cordillera Central
Cord. Oriental
Magdalena

Guaviare

Sierra Pacaraima

Caroní
Caura
Essequibo
Serra Tumucumaque

C. de San Francisco

Caquetá

Negro

Branco

Equator

Cotopaxi 5897

Chimborazo 6267

Putumayo

Japurá

Amazon

Marajó I.

D

Galapagos Is.

G. of Guayaquil

Pta. Pariñas

Pta. Negra

Napo

Marañón

Ucuali

Amazon

Juruá

Purus

Madeira

Roosevelt

Aripuanã

Tapajós

Teles Pires

Xingu

Araguaia

Tocantins

Parnaíba

C. de São Roque

Plat. of Borborema

Huascaran 6769

Madre de Dios

Mamoré

Guaporé

Arinos

São Francisco

10

Chincha Alta

L. Titicaca

Nevada Ancohuma 6550

Plateau of Mato Grosso

Brazilian Highlands

E

PACIFIC

Bolivian Plateau

L. de Poopó

Paraguay

Serra da Mantiqueira 2890

C. Frio

20

Tropic of Capricorn

San Félix

San Ambrosio

Atacama Desert

8050

Cerro Ojos del Salado 6863

Salinas Grandes

Gran Chaco

Pilcomayo

Paraná

Salado

Entre Ríos

Iguaçu Falls

Uruguay

Serra do Mar

F

OCEAN

Arch. de Juan Fernández

Mt. Aconcagua 6980

Sierra de Córdoba

L. Mar Chiquita

Paraná

L. dos Patos

Andes

G

Pampas

Río de la Plata

SOUTH

ATLANTIC

Colorado

Negro

Bahía Blanca

Patagonia

Chubut

G. San Matías

Valdés Peninsula

Argentine Basin

OCEAN

40

Chile Rise

Chiloé I.

Chonos Archipelago

Mte. San Valentin 4058

Gulf of San Jorge

6212

H

Taitao Peninsula

Gulf of Penas

Wellington I.

Madre de Dios I.

Magellan's Str.

West Falkland

Falkland Is.

East Falkland

South Georgia

Santa Inés I.

Canal Cockburn

Canal Beagle

Tierra del Fuego

Staten I.

C. Horn

West from Greenwich

ft　m

12000　4000

9000　3000

6000　2000

3000　1000

1500　500

600　200

200　600

0　0

0　0

200　600

1000　3000

2000　6000

4000　12000

6000　18000

8000　24000

m　ft

Projection: Lambert's Azimuthal Equal Area

CARTOGRAPHY BY PHILIP'S.

100 0 200 400 600 800 1000 1200 1400 km
100 0 200 400 600 800 1000 miles

NORTH

ATLANTIC

OCEAN

Havana
CUBA
BAHAMAS
Turks & Caicos Is.
(U.K.)

HAITI
DOMINICAN
REP.
Virgin Is.
(U.K.)
San Juan
ANTIGUA &
BARBUDA
JAMAICA
Kingston
Port-au-
Prince
PUERTO
RICO
(U.S.A.)
ST. KITTS
& NEVIS
GUADELOUPE
(Fr.)
Basse-Terre

MEXICO
BELIZE
Caribbean Sea
DOMINICA
Fort-de-France
MARTINIQUE
(Fr.)

GUATEMALA
HONDURAS
Castries
ST. LUCIA

Guatemala
Tegucigalpa
ST. VINCENT
BARBADOS
Bridgetown

San Salvador
NICARAGUA
Kingstown
GRENADA
St. George's

EL SALVADOR
Managua
Aruba
Curaçao
Port of
Spain
TRINIDAD &
TOBAGO

COSTA
San José
C. de
la Aguja

RICA
Panamá
Barranquilla
Maracaibo
Caracas

PANAMA
Cartagena
Valencia

G. of
Darién
Barquisimeto
Orinoco

Gulf of Panama
Cúcuta
San Cristóbal
Ciudad Guayana

Medellín
Bucaramanga
VENEZUELA
Georgetown
Paramaribo

Cali
Bogotá
GUYANA
Cayenne
C. Orange

SURINAM
FRENCH
GUIANA

COLOMBIA
RORAIMA
Branco

Essequibo
AMAPÁ

Galapagos Is.
(Ecuador)
Quito
Equator

ECUADOR
Napo
Japurá
Amazon
Marajó
I.
Belém

Guayaquil
Putumayo
Santarém
São Luís

G. of Guayaquil
Iquitos
Manaus
Fortaleza

Marañón
AMAZONAS
Amazon
PARÁ
C. de
São Roque

Chiclayo
Juruá
Madeira
MARANHÃO
Teresina
CEARÁ
RIO G.
DO NORTE
Natal

Trujillo
Ucayali
Purus
Tapajós
Xingu
Tocantins
PARAÍBA
Campina Grande

Chimbote
ACRE
Pôrto Velho
PIAUÍ
PERNAMBUCO
Recife

PERU
RONDÔNIA
B R A Z I L
ALAGOAS
Maceió

Callao
LIMA
Cuzco
Madre de Dios
MATO GROSSO
TOCANTINS
SERGIPE
Aracaju

Mamoré
BAHÍA
Salvador

L.
Titicaca
BOLIVIA
GOIÁS
DIS. FED.
Brasília
São Francisco

Arequipa
La Paz
Cochabamba
Cuiabá

PACIFIC
Santa Cruz
Goiânia
MINAS GERAIS

Sucre
MATO GROSSO
DO SUL
Paraguay
Belo
Horizonte
ESPÍRITO
SANTO

Iquique
Ribeirão
Prêto
Vitória

Paraná
SÃO PAULO
Juiz
de Fora

PARAGUAY
Campos

Tropic of Capricorn
Antofagasta
Pilcomayo
Asunción
PARANÁ
SÃO
PAULO
Campinas
R. DE J.
Niterói
RIO DE
JANEIRO

San Félix
(Chile)
San Ambrosio
(Chile)
Salta
Curitiba

San Miguel
de Tucumán
SANTA CATARINA

OCEAN
Resistencia
Corrientes
Uruguay
RIO GRANDE
DO SUL

Salado
Pôrto Alegre

Córdoba
Santa Fe
Paraná
Pelotas

Arch. de Juan Fernández
(Chile)
Viña del Mar
Valparaíso
San Juan
Mendoza
Rosario
URUGUAY

SANTIAGO
BUENOS AIRES
Montevideo
SOUTH

Talca
La Plata
Río de la Plata

Concepción
CHILE
Bahía
Blanca
Mar del Plata
ATLANTIC

Colorado

Valdivia
ARGENTINA
Negro

Puerto Montt
Viedma
OCEAN

Chubut

Comodoro Rivadavia
Gulf of San Jorge

Gulf of Penas

West Falkland
FALKLAND IS.
(U.K.)
Stanley
East Falkland

Magellan's Str.
South Georgia
(U.K.)

Punta Arenas
Tierra del Fuego
C. Horn

■ LIMA Capital Cities
West from Greenwich
CARTOGRAPHY BY PHILIP'S.

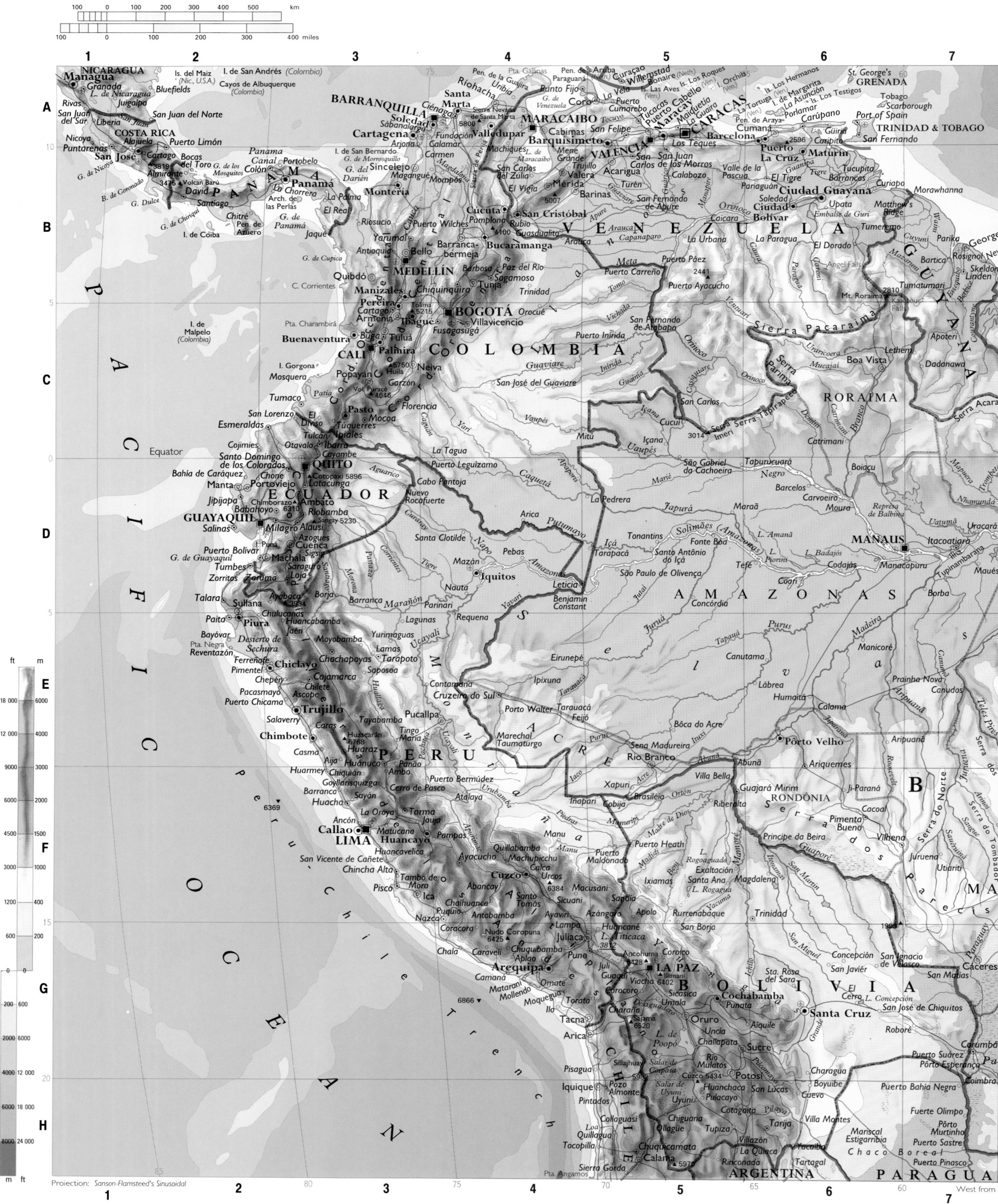

100 0 100 200 300 400 500 km
100 0 100 200 300 400 miles
NICARAGUA
Managua
Granada
L. de Nicaragua
COSTA RICA
San José
Puerto Limón
Bluefields
San Juan del Norte
I. de San Andrés (Colombia)
Panama Canal
Colón
Panamá
P A N A M A
David
G. de Panamá
I. de Coiba
BARRANQUILLA
Cartagena
Santa Marta
Riohacha
MARACAIBO
Valledupar
Barquisimeto
VALENCIA
CARACAS
Barcelona
Cumaná
Maturín
Ciudad Bolívar
Ciudad Guayana
Port of Spain
TRINIDAD & TOBAGO
St. George's
GRENADA
Aruba
Curaçao
Willemstad
Bonaire
V E N E Z U E L A
San Cristóbal
Mérida
Cúcuta
Bucaramanga
Montería
MEDELLÍN
Manizales
Pereira
Armenia
Ibagué
BOGOTÁ
Villavicencio
Tunja
CALI
Palmira
Buenaventura
Quibdó
Popayán
Pasto
Neiva
C O L O M B I A
Puerto Carreño
Puerto Ayacucho
Puerto Inírida
Angel Falls
Mt. Roraima
Sierra Pacaraima
G U Y A N A
Georgetown
Linden
Lethem
Boa Vista
RORAIMA
Equator
QUITO
Ibarra
Esmeraldas
Santo Domingo de los Colorados
Portoviejo
Manta
Ambato
Riobamba
Cotopaxi 5896
Chimborazo 6310
E C U A D O R
GUAYAQUIL
Machala
Cuenca
Loja
Tumbes
Talara
Sullana
Piura
Chiclayo
Cajamarca
Trujillo
Chimbote
Huascarán 6768
Huánuco
Cerro de Pasco
Pucallpa
Iquitos
Leticia
Callao
LIMA
Huancayo
Ayacucho
Pisco
Ica
Nazca
Cuzco
Arequipa
Tacna
Arica
P E R U
P A C I F I C O C E A N
Peru-Chile Trench
L. Titicaca
Puno
Juliaca
LA PAZ
Oruro
Cochabamba
Sucre
Potosí
Santa Cruz
Trinidad
B O L I V I A
Calama
Antofagasta
Iquique
C H I L E
ARGENTINA
P A R A G U A Y
Manaus
A M A Z O N A S
Amazonas
Solimões
Japurá
Rio Negro
Madeira
Purus
Juruá
Porto Velho
Rio Branco
RONDÔNIA
ACRE
Cruzeiro do Sul
Tefé
Coari
São Gabriel da Cachoeira
Barcelos
Humaitá
Ariquemes
Vilhena
Guajará Mirim
Cobija
Riberalta
Corumbá
Puerto Suárez
Chaco Boreal

Projection: Sanson-Flamsteed's Sinusoidal

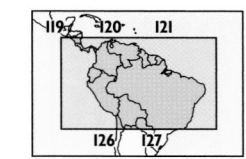

8   9   10   11   12   13

A

A T L A N T I C

B

O C E A N

C

town
Amsterdam
Nieuw Nickerie
Totness   Paramaribo
Kwakoegron   Albina   Nieuw Amsterdam
   Moengo
   St-Laurent
Prof. Van   Iracoubo
Blommesteinmeer   Sinnamary
    Kourou
    Kaw   Cayenne
  Approuague
SURINAM   ▲1230   St-Georges
Julianatop   Oiapoque   C. Orange
Tapanahoni
**FRENCH
GUIANA**

Camopi

C. Orange

São Paulo
(Braz.)

Serra Tumucumaque
Amapá
AMAPÁ
Meriruma   Serra do
   Navio
Macapá   I. de Maracá

Equator

D

Faro   Óbidos   Monte   Mazagão   I. Caviana   I. Mexiana
   Alegre   Almeirim   Chaves   C. Maguarinho
Aleixquer   Prainha   I. Grande   Afuá   Soure   Curuçá Salinópolis
   de Gurupá   Breves   I. de   Bragança
Santarém   Gurupá   Gurupá   Vigia   Viseu
Belterra   Pôrto de Móz   Marajó   **BELÉM**   Castanhal   Gururupu
Aveiro   Almeirim   Currralinho   Abaetetuba   Turiaçu
Juruti   Brasília Legal   Cametá   Alcântara   **São Luís**   Barreirinhas
Parintins   Itaituba   Baião   Pinheiro   Tutóia   Luís Correia
Amazonas   Amazon   Santa Inês   Rosário   Parnaíba   Camocim

Equator

5

D

P A R A
Altamira   Tucuruí   Viana   Itapecuru-   Granja   Itapipoca
   Bacabal   Mirim   Piracuruca   Caucaia
Represa de   Açailândia   Coroatá   Brejo   Piripiri   Sobral   **FORTALEZA**
Tucuruí   Pedreiras   Codó   Campo   Ipu   Maranguape
   Caxias   Maior   Oiticica   Quixadá   Cascavel
Serra dos Carajás   Marabá   **MARANHÃO**   Crateús   Baturité   Aracati
São João do   **Imperatriz**   Barra   **Teresina**   **C E A R Á**   Russas   Areia Branca
Araguaia   Carajás   do Corda   Senador Pompeu   Mossoró   Macau
Carajás   Grajaú   Colinas   **RIO GRANDE**   Ceará Mirim
Tocantinópolis   Pôrto Franco   Amarante   Valença   Iguatu   Caraúbas   **DO NORTE**   C. de São Roque
Conceição do   Estreito   do Piauí   Caicó   Currais   **Natal**
Araguaia   Carolina   Floriano   Oeiras   Cedro   Sousa   Novos   Canguaretama
   Riachão   Picos   Cajàzeiras   Patos   Alagoa   Mamanguape
Araguacema   Loreto   Nova Iorque   Crato   **PARAÍBA**   Grande   Cabedelo
Serra do Cachimbo   Uruçuí   **P I A U Í**   Juàzeiro   **Campina**   **João Pessoa**
   Chapada do Araripe   do Norte   **Grande**   **Olinda**
Ouricuri   Salgueiro   Caruaru   **RECIFE**

E

R   Serra Formosa   Pedro Afonso   São João   Paulistana   Pesqueira   **Jaboatão**
   do Piauí   **PERNAMBUCO**   Garanhuns   Vitória de Santo Antão
Apiacás   **A**   Palmas   Santa   Caracol   Petrolina   Petrolândia   Palmares
   Filomena   Sa. Dois Irmãos   Palmeira   Rio Largo
Santa Isabel   **Z**   Novo Remanso   Nova Casa   São Francisco   dos   Arapiraca
do Morro   Nova   Juàzeiro   Índios   **Maceió**
   Represa de   Paulo Afonso   **ALAGOAS**
   I   Sobradinho   Senhor do   Própria   Penedo
Serra do Roncador   Parnaguá   Bonfim   **SERGIPE**   6059▾   10
   Capela
TOCANTINS   Barra   Jacobina   Queimadas   **Aracaju**
   Xique-Xique   Mundo   Serrinha   **São Cristóvão**
Gurupi   Pôrto Nacional   Novo   Estância
   Taguatinga   **B**   **A**   **H**   **Í**   **A**
Peixe   Paranã   Barreiras   Ibotirama   **Feira de**
   Campos Belos   **Santana**   Alagoinhas

F

Serra Formosa   São Domingos   Santa Maria   Bom Jesus   Itaberaba   Cachoeira   **Santo Amaro**
Diamantino   da Vitória   da Lapa   Serra do Sincorá   Castro   Valença   **SALVADOR**
Planalto do   Uruaçu   Posse   Carinhanha   Alves   Nazaré
Cuiabá   **Mato Grosso**   Niquelândia   Caetité   Brumado   Jequié
Santo Antonio   1678▲   Carinhanha   Ubaitaba
Barra do Garças   Aruanã   Condeúba   Vitória da   Itabuna
Rondonópolis   Formosa   Januária   Monte Azul   Conquista   Ilhéus

G

DIST.   Taguatinga   FED   São Francisco   Janaúba   Pedra Azul   Canavieiras
Anápolis   **BRASÍLIA**   Salinas   Belmonte
Goiás   Luziânia   Montes   Araçuaí   Jequitinhonha   Pôrto Seguro
Goiânia   Vianópolis   Claros   Itamaraju
G O I Á S   Alto Araguaia   Paracatu   Pirapora   Teófilo Otoni   Prado   Caravelas
Morrinhos   Ipameri   Nanuque   Mucuri
MATO GROSSO   Rio Verde   Catalão   Patos de   Diamantina   Governador   Conceição da Barra
Jataí   Itumbiara   Minas   Valadares   São Mateus
DO SUL   Quirinópolis   Araguari   Corinto   Ipatinga   Nova   Linhares
Coxim   Paranaíba   **M I N A S**   **G E R A I S**   Itabira   Veneza   Colatina
   Uberlândia   Patrocínio   Sête Lagoas   Caratinga

H

Campo   Miranda   Santa Fé do Sul   Uberaba   Ibiá   Araxá   **BELO HORIZONTE**   Ponte Nova   **Cariacica**
Grande   Água Clara   Frutal   Prata   Curvelo   Sabará   2890   **Vitória**
Aquidauana   São José do   Barretos   Igarapava   Divinópolis   Nova   Ouro   **Vila Velha**
   Rio Prêto   Ribas   Andradina   Franca   Passos   Lima   Prêto   Cachoeiro de Itapemirim
   do Rio   Três Lagoas   Conselheiro   Ubá   Trindade
   Pardo   Araçatuba   **Ribeirão Prêto**   Lafaiete   (Braz.)
Dourados   Panorama   Penápolis   Guaxupé   São João   Barbacena   Itaperuna
Bela   Presidente Epitácio   Catanduva   Araraquara   Poços de   del Rei   **Campos**
Vista   Presidente   Marília   São Carlos   Caldas   São   **Juiz de Fora**
Pedro Juan   Prudente   Jaú   Limeira   Moji-Mirim   Lourenço   Três Rios
Caballero   Assis   **Bauru**   Piracicaba   Nova Friburgo
   Botucatu   **Campinas**   2787▲   **Petrópolis**
   SÃO PAULO   Volta   RIO DE   Cabo Frio
Y   Redonda   JANEIRO   Niterói
Greenwich   55   **RIO DE JANEIRO**

COPYRIGHT GEORGE PHILIP LTD.

8   9   10   11   12   13

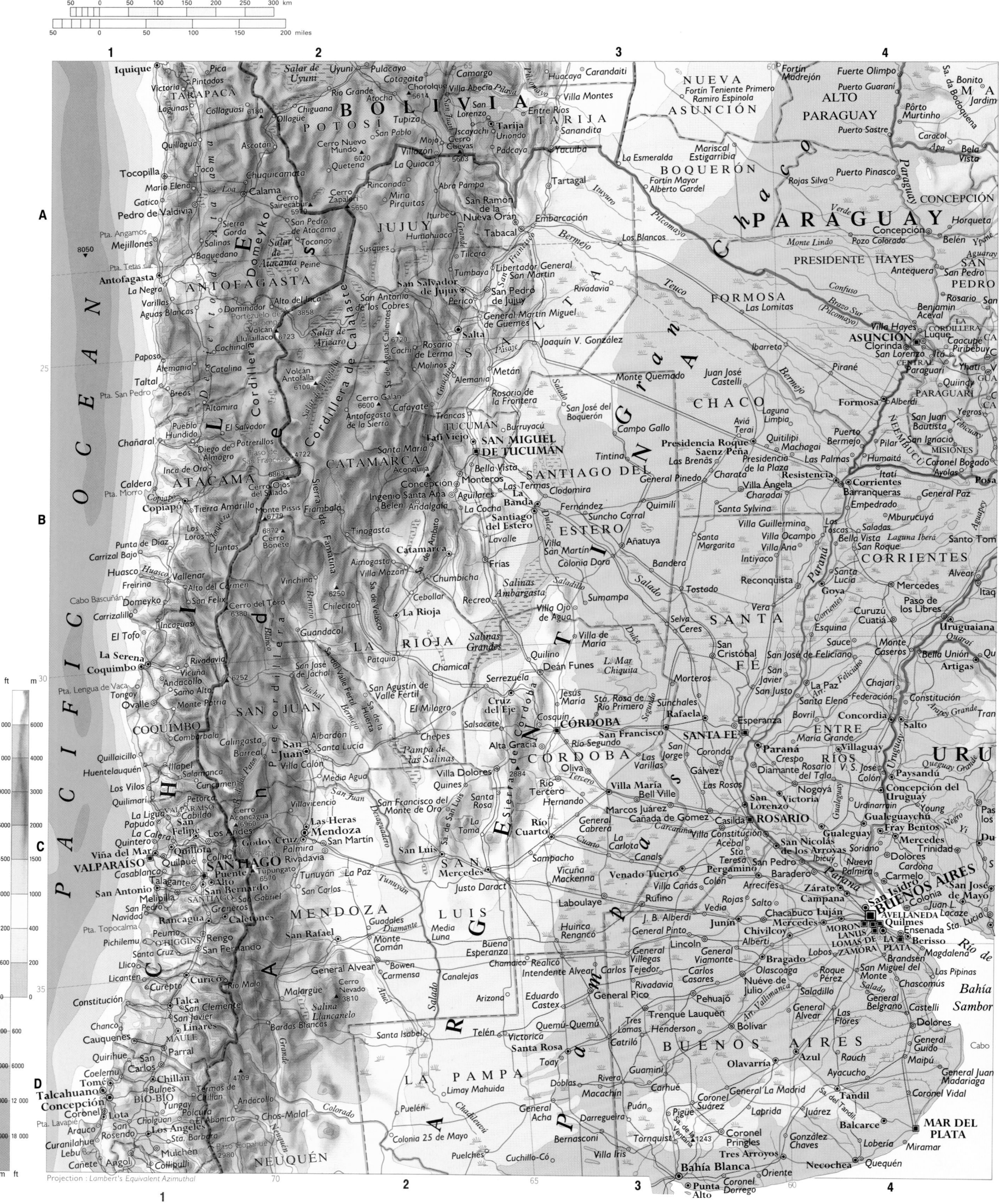
50 0 50 100 150 200 250 300 km
50 0 50 100 150 200 miles
1
2
3
4
A
B
C
D
PACIFIC OCEAN
BOLIVIA
PARAGUAY
ARGENTINA
CHILE
URU
Andes
Cordillera Domeyko
Cordillera de Calalaste
Gran Chaco
Pampas
TARAPACÁ
ANTOFAGASTA
ATACAMA
COQUIMBO
VALPARAÍSO
SANTIAGO
O'HIGGINS
MAULE
BIO-BIO
POTOSÍ
TARIJA
JUJUY
SALTA
TUCUMÁN
CATAMARCA
LA RIOJA
SAN JUAN
MENDOZA
SAN LUIS
CÓRDOBA
SANTIAGO DEL ESTERO
CHACO
FORMOSA
SANTA FÉ
ENTRE RÍOS
CORRIENTES
MISIONES
BUENOS AIRES
LA PAMPA
NEUQUÉN
NUEVA ASUNCIÓN
BOQUERÓN
ALTO PARAGUAY
PRESIDENTE HAYES
CONCEPCIÓN
SAN PEDRO
CORDILLERA
CENTRAL
PARAGUARÍ
ÑEEMBUCÚ
Iquique
Pica
Pintados
Victoria
Lagunas
Collaguasi
Quillagua
Tocopilla
María Elena
Gatico
Pedro de Valdivia
Calama
Chuquicamata
Mejillones
Pta. Angamos
Pta. Tetas
Antofagasta
La Negra
Baquedano
San Pedro de Atacama
Toconao
Salar de Atacama
Peine
Paposo
Taltal
Pta. San Pedro
Chañaral
Diego de Almagro
El Salvador
Potrerillos
Caldera
Pta. Morro
Copiapó
Tierra Amarilla
Vallenar
Huasco
Freirina
Domeyko
Carrizal Bajo
Carrizalillo
Cabo Bascuñán
El Tofo
La Serena
Coquimbo
Vicuña
Andacollo
Ovalle
Monte Patria
Pta. Lengua de Vaca
Tongoy
Combarbalá
Illapel
Salamanca
Quillaicillo
Huentelauquén
Los Vilos
Quilimarí
La Ligua
Papudo
San Felipe
Los Andes
La Calera
Quintero
Viña del Mar
VALPARAÍSO
Quilpue
Casablanca
Talagante
SANTIAGO
Puente Alto
San Bernardo
San Antonio
Melipilla
San Pedro
Navidad
Pta. Topocalma
Rancagua
Rengo
San Fernando
Pichilemu
Peumo
Curicó
Llico
Licantén
Curepto
Constitución
Talca
San Clemente
San Javier
Linares
Chanco
Cauquenes
Parral
Quirihue
San Carlos
Coelemu
Tomé
Chillán
Bulnes
Talcahuano
Concepción
Coronel
Lota
Pta. Lavapié
Arauco
Los Angeles
Curanilahue
Lebu
Cañete
Angol
Mulchén
Collipulli
Salar de Uyuni
Uyuni
Pulacayo
Cotagaita
Camargo
Huacaya
Carandaití
Villa Montes
Entre Ríos
Tarija
Uriondo
Padcaya
Yacuiba
Tupiza
Villazón
La Quiaca
Abra Pampa
Humahuaca
Tilcara
San Salvador de Jujuy
Perico
San Pedro de Jujuy
Libertador General San Martín
Tartagal
Embarcación
San Ramón de la Nueva Orán
Tabacal
Salta
General Martín Miguel de Güemes
Joaquín V. González
Metán
Rosario de la Frontera
Cafayate
San Miguel de Tucumán
Tafí Viejo
Monteros
Concepción
Aguilares
Santiago del Estero
La Banda
Frías
Catamarca
Andalgalá
Belén
Tinogasta
Fiambalá
Chilecito
La Rioja
Chamical
Patquia
Chepes
San Juan
San José de Jáchal
Villa Colón
Mendoza
Godoy Cruz
San Martín
Tunuyán
San Rafael
General Alvear
Malargüe
Bardas Blancas
Cerro Aconcagua
6960
Tupungato
6570
Volcán Llullaillaco
6723
Ojos del Salado
6863
Monte Pissis
6779
Cerro Bonete
6872
Cerro del Toro
6380
Volcán Antofalla
6100
Cerro Galán
6600
San Luis
Mercedes
Justo Daract
Villa Dolores
Río Cuarto
Río Tercero
Córdoba
Cruz del Eje
Deán Funes
Jesús María
Alta Gracia
Villa María
Bell Ville
San Francisco
Rafaela
Santa Fé
Esperanza
Paraná
Rosario
Venado Tuerto
Rufino
Laboulaye
Junín
Pergamino
San Nicolás de los Arroyos
Zárate
Campana
Luján
Mercedes
Chivilcoy
San Isidro
BUENOS AIRES
AVELLANEDA
Quilmes
LA PLATA
Ensenada
Berisso
Magdalena
Chascomús
Dolores
Azul
Tandil
Olavarría
Bolívar
Trenque Lauquen
Pehuajó
General Pico
Santa Rosa
General Acha
Victorica
Bahía Blanca
Punta Alto
Coronel Dorrego
Tres Arroyos
Necochea
Quequén
Miramar
MAR DEL PLATA
Balcarce
Lobería
Maipú
General Madariaga
Coronel Vidal
Cabo San Antonio
Bahía Samborombón
Río de la Plata
Colonia
San José de Mayo
Juan L. Lacaze
Carmelo
Nueva Palmira
Dolores
Mercedes
Fray Bentos
Paysandú
Salto
Artigas
Bella Unión
Concordia
Concepción del Uruguay
Gualeguaychú
Gualeguay
Victoria
Villaguay
Colón
Federación
Chajarí
La Paz
Corrientes
Resistencia
Barranqueras
Goya
Esquina
Mercedes
Curuzú Cuatiá
Paso de los Libres
Uruguaiana
Formosa
Clorinda
ASUNCIÓN
Villa Hayes
San Lorenzo
Pilar
Presidencia Roque Sáenz Peña
Charata
Villa Ángela
Reconquista
Tostado
Añatuya
Monte Quemado
Concepción
Horqueta
Belén
Antequera
Puerto Casado
Puerto Pinasco
Fuerte Olimpo
Bahía Negra
Mariscal Estigarribia
Fortín Teniente Primero Ramiro Espinola
Fortín Madrejón
Río Colorado
Río Negro
Río Salado
Río Bermejo
Río Pilcomayo
Río Paraná
Río Uruguay
Río Paraguay
Laguna Iberá
Salinas Grandes
Salinas Ambargasta
Mar Chiquita
Sierra de Córdoba
Sierras de San Luis
Sierra de la Ventana
1243
Projection : Lambert's Equivalent Azimuthal
70
65
60

BELO
HORIZONTE
Nova Lima
Itabirito
Congonhas
Conselheiro
Lafaiete
Oliveira
Ouro
Prêto
Ponte Nova
Pico da
Bandeira
2890
Vitória
Itaquari
Vila
Velha
Guarapari

Vitória

5

Três Lagoas
Andradina
Mirassol
Olímpia
São José
do Rio Prêto
Passos
Batatais
São Sebastião
do Paraíso
Oliveira
Campo Belo
São João
del Rei
Carangola
Muriaé
Alegre
Castelo
Cachoeiro
de Itapemirim

6

Xavantina
Mirandópolis
Panorama
Araçatuba
Catanduva
Bebedouro
Ribeirão
Prêto
Guaxupé
Pontas
Lavras
Barbacena
Cataguases
Itaperuna

Sidrolândia
Nioaque
Guia Lopes
da Laguna
Maracaju

TO GROSSO

Presidente
Epitácio
Adamantina
Santo
Anastácio
Penápolis
Lins
Jaboticabal
Mococa
Casa
Branca
Alfenas
Varginha
Três
Corações
Santos
Dumont
Leopoldina
RIO DE JANEIRO
Cabo de
São Tomé
Guarus

DO SUL

Dourados
Rio
Brilhante
Nova
Andradina
do Sul
Martinópolis
Presidente
Prudente
Araraquara
São
Carlos
São João
da Boa Vista
Pinhal
Poços de
Caldas
Ubá
Juiz de Fora
Além Paraíba
CAMPOS

Ponta Pora
Dourados
Ivinhema
Rancharia
Marília
Garça
Bariri
Jaú
Rio Claro
Limeira
Americana
Mogi-Mirim
Ouro Fino
Pouso
Alegre
São
Lourenço
Mansa
Três
Rios
Paraíba do Sul
Nova Friburgo
Macaé

Pedro Juan Caballero
Naviraí
Paranavaí
Nova
Esperança
Apucarana
Joaquim
Távora
Ourinhos
Avaré
Botucatu
Piracicaba
CAMPINAS
Guaratinguetá
Cruzeiro
Volta
Redonda
Barra do Piraí
Petrópolis
DUQUE DE CAXIAS
SÃO GONÇALO

Amambaí
Amambai
Maringá
Cianorte
Mandaguari
Londrina
Cornélio
Procópio
Jacarèzinho
Jundiaí
São José dos C.
NOVA IGUAÇU
NITERÓI
RIO DE JANEIRO

BRAZIL

PARANÁ

Umuarama
Cruzeiro
do Oeste
Goio-Erê
Campo
Mourão
Ibaiti
Itapetininga
SÃO PAULO
Moji das Cruzes
SANTO ANDRÉ
São Bernardo
do Campo
São Vicente
SANTOS
Guarujá
Ilha de São Sebastião
Pta. de Boi

Tropic of Capricorn

Guaíra
Toledo
Ubiratã
Cândido de Abreu
Pitanga
Itararé
Apiaí
Juquiá
Registro
Itanhaém

Cascavel
Sa. das Araras
Prudentópolis
Ponta
Grossa
Palmeira
CURITIBA
Ilha Comprida
Ilha do Cardoso

Foz do Iguaçu
Guarapuava
Irati
Antonina
Paranaguá
Matinhos
Guaratuba

Medianeira
Ciudad del Este
Francisco
Beltrão
Laranjeiras
do Sul
Lapa
São Mateus
do Sul
Rio Negro
Mafra
Joinville
São Francisco do Sul

PARANÁ

Bernardo
de Irigoyen
Pato Branco
União da
Vitória
Pôrto União
Itajaí

Eldorado
Clevelândia
Palmas
Caçador
SANTA
CATARINA
Blumenau
Santa Cecília
Brusque

MISIONES

San
Pedro
São Miguel
do Oeste
Xanxerê
Chapecó
Joaçaba
Rio do Sul
São José
Ilha de Santa Catarina
Florianópolis

Uruguai
Monteagudo
Frederico
Westphalen
Erechim
Campos
Novos
Curitibanos

San Javier
Santa Rosa
Palmeira
das Missões
Passo
Fundo
Lajes

Obera
Leandro N. Alem
São Luís
Gonzaga
Ijuí
Caràzinho
Pelotas
Lagoa
Vermelha
São
Joaquim

Apóstoles
Santo Angelo
Cruz Alta
Coxilha Grande
Vacaria
Tubarão
Laguna
Cabo Santa Marta Grande

São Borja
Sa. do Espinilho
Guaporé
Bento Gonçalves
Criciúma
Araranguá

RIO GRANDE

Santiago
Santa Maria
Caxias do Sul
Torres

Santa Cruz
do Sul
Montenegro
Nôvo Hamburgo
Taquara

DO SUL

Alegrete
Rosário do Sul
Cachoeira do Sul
Canoas
São
Leopoldo
Osorio

Santana do
Livramento
São
Gabriel
Caçapava
do Sul
Sa.
Encantadas
PÔRTO ALEGRE
Viamão

Rivera
Dom Pedro
Camaquã
Tapes

Bagé
Sa. do Canguçu
Mostardas

GUAY

Tacuarembó
Pinheiro
Machado
Pelotas
Canguçu
Lagoa dos Patos
São Lourenço
do Sul
Rio
Grande

Melo
Jaguarão
São José do Norte
Rio Grande

Fraile
Muerto
Río
Branco

San Gregorio
Cerro
Chato
Vergara
Lagoa
Mirim

Sarandi del Yi
Santa Vitória do Palmar
Chuy

José Batlle
y Ordóñez
Lascano
Santa Vitória do Palmar

Florida
Aigua
Castillos

Tala
Minas
Rocha

Canelones
Las Piedras
San Carlos

MONTEVIDEO
Maldonado

la Plata

ombón

San Antonio

A T L A N T I C

O C E A N

5304

A

B

C

D

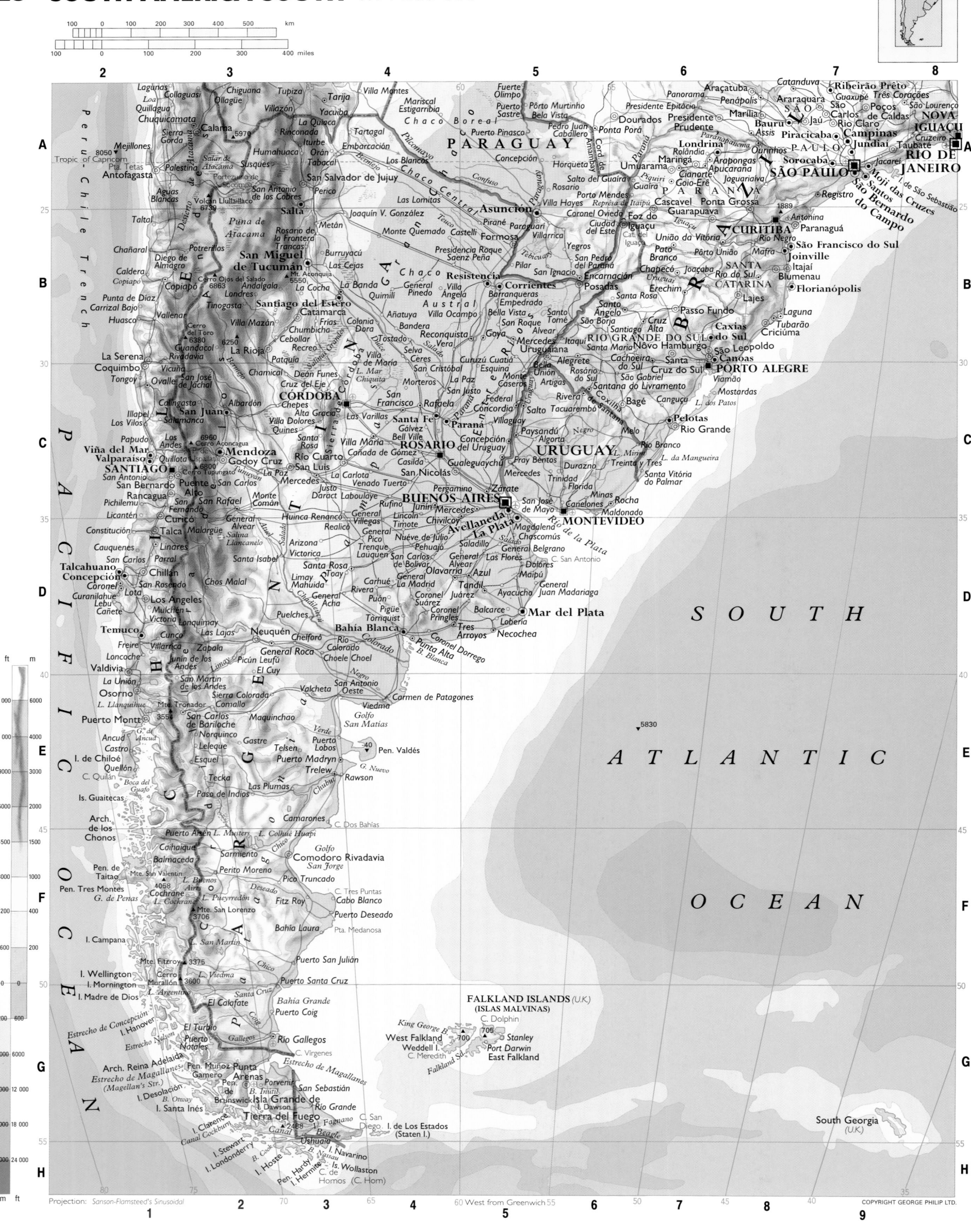

COPYRIGHT GEORGE PHILIP LTD.

Projection: Sanson-Flamsteed's Sinusoidal

INDEX

The index contains the names of all the principal places and features shown on the World Maps. Each name is followed by an additional entry in italics giving the country or region within which it is located. The alphabetical order of names composed of two or more words is governed primarily by the first word and then by the second. This is an example of the rule:

Mīr Kūh, *Iran*	**71**	**E8**
Mīr Shahdād, *Iran*	**71**	**E8**
Mira, *Italy*	**29**	**C9**
Mira por vos Cay, *Bahamas* . .	**121**	**B5**
Miraj, *India*	**66**	**L9**

Physical features composed of a proper name (Erie) and a description (Lake) are positioned alphabetically by the proper name. The description is positioned after the proper name and is usually abbreviated:

Erie, L., *N. Amer.* **110** **D4**

Where a description forms part of a settlement or administrative name however, it is always written in full and put in its true alphabetic position:

Mount Morris, *U.S.A.* **110** **D7**

Names beginning with M' and Mc are indexed as if they were spelled Mac. Names beginning St. are alphabetised under Saint, but Sankt, Sint, Sant', Santa and San are all spelt in full and are alphabetised accordingly. If the same place name occurs two or more times in the index and all are in the same country, each is followed by the name of the administrative subdivision in which it is located. The names are placed in the alphabetical order of the subdivisions. For example:

Jackson, *Ky., U.S.A.*	**108**	**G4**
Jackson, *Mich., U.S.A.*	**108**	**D3**
Jackson, *Minn., U.S.A.*	**112**	**D7**

The number in bold type which follows each name in the index refers to the number of the map page where that feature or place will be found. This is usually the largest scale at which the place or feature appears.

The letter and figure which are in bold type immediately after the page number give the grid square on the map page, within which the feature is situated. The letter represents the latitude and the figure the longitude.

In some cases the feature itself may fall within the specified square, while the name is outside. This is usually the case only with features which are larger than a grid square.

Rivers are indexed to their mouths or confluences, and carry the symbol → after their names. A solid square ■ follows the name of a country, while an open square □ refers to a first order administrative area.

ABBREVIATIONS USED IN THE INDEX

A.C.T. – Australian Capital Territory
Afghan. – Afghanistan
Ala. – Alabama
Alta. – Alberta
Amer. – America(n)
Arch. – Archipelago
Ariz. – Arizona
Ark. – Arkansas
Atl. Oc. – Atlantic Ocean
B. – Baie, Bahía, Bay, Bucht, Bugt
B.C. – British Columbia
Bangla. – Bangladesh
Barr. – Barrage
Bos.-H. – Bosnia-Herzegovina
C. – Cabo, Cap, Cape, Coast
C.A.R. – Central African Republic
C. Prov. – Cape Province
Calif. – California
Cent. – Central
Chan. – Channel
Colo. – Colorado
Conn. – Connecticut
Cord. – Cordillera
Cr. – Creek
Czech. – Czech Republic
D.C. – District of Columbia
Del. – Delaware
Dep. – Dependency
Des. – Desert
Dist. – District
Dj. – Djebel
Domin. – Dominica
Dom. Rep. – Dominican Republic
E. – East

E. Salv. – El Salvador
Eq. Guin. – Equatorial Guinea
Fla. – Florida
Falk. Is. – Falkland Is.
G. – Golfe, Golfo, Gulf, Guba, Gebel
Ga. – Georgia
Gt. – Great, Greater
Guinea-Biss. – Guinea-Bissau
H.K. – Hong Kong
H.P. – Himachal Pradesh
Hants. – Hampshire
Harb. – Harbor, Harbour
Hd. – Head
Hts. – Heights
I.(s). – Île, Ilha, Insel, Isla, Island, Isle
Ill. – Illinois
Ind. – Indiana
Ind. Oc. – Indian Ocean
Ivory C. – Ivory Coast
J. – Jabal, Jebel, Jazira
Junc. – Junction
K. – Kap, Kapp
Kans. – Kansas
Kep. – Kepulauan
Ky. – Kentucky
L. – Lac, Lacul, Lago, Lagoa, Lake, Limni, Loch, Lough
La. – Louisiana
Liech. – Liechtenstein
Lux. – Luxembourg
Mad. P. – Madhya Pradesh
Madag. – Madagascar
Man. – Manitoba
Mass. – Massachusetts

Md. – Maryland
Me. – Maine
Medit. S. – Mediterranean Sea
Mich. – Michigan
Minn. – Minnesota
Miss. – Mississippi
Mo. – Missouri
Mont. – Montana
Mozam. – Mozambique
Mt.(e) – Mont, Monte, Monti, Montaña, Mountain
N. – Nord, Norte, North, Northern, Nouveau
N.B. – New Brunswick
N.C. – North Carolina
N. Cal. – New Caledonia
N. Dak. – North Dakota
N.H. – New Hampshire
N.I. – North Island
N.J. – New Jersey
N. Mex. – New Mexico
N.S. – Nova Scotia
N.S.W. – New South Wales
N.W.T. – North West Territory
N.Y. – New York
N.Z. – New Zealand
Nebr. – Nebraska
Neths. – Netherlands
Nev. – Nevada
Nfld. – Newfoundland
Nic. – Nicaragua
O. – Oued, Ouadi
Occ. – Occidentale
Okla. – Oklahoma
Ont. – Ontario
Or. – Orientale

Oreg. – Oregon
Os. – Ostrov
Oz. – Ozero
P. – Pass, Passo, Pasul, Pulau
P.E.I. – Prince Edward Island
Pa. – Pennsylvania
Pac. Oc. – Pacific Ocean
Papua N.G. – Papua New Guinea
Pass. – Passage
Pen. – Peninsula, Péninsule
Pk. – Park, Peak
Plat. – Plateau
Prov. – Province, Provincial
Pt. – Point
Pta. – Ponta, Punta
Pte. – Pointe
Qué. – Québec
Queens. – Queensland
R. – Rio, River
R.I. – Rhode Island
Ra.(s). – Range(s)
Raj. – Rajasthan
Reg. – Region
Rep. – Republic
Res. – Reserve, Reservoir
S. – San, South, Sea
Si. Arabia – Saudi Arabia
S.C. – South Carolina
S. Dak. – South Dakota
S.I. – South Island
S. Leone – Sierra Leone
Sa. – Serra, Sierra
Sask. – Saskatchewan
Scot. – Scotland
Sd. – Sound

Sev. – Severnaya
Sib. – Siberia
Sprs. – Springs
St. – Saint
Sta. – Santa, Station
Ste. – Sainte
Sto. – Santo
Str. – Strait, Stretto
Switz. – Switzerland
Tas. – Tasmania
Tenn. – Tennessee
Tex. – Texas
Tg. – Tanjung
Trin. & Tob. – Trinidad & Tobago
U.A.E. – United Arab Emirates
U.K. – United Kingdom
U.S.A. – United States of America
Ut. P. – Uttar Pradesh
Va. – Virginia
Vdkhr. – Vodokhranilishche
Vf. – Vîrful
Vic. – Victoria
Vol. – Volcano
Vt. – Vermont
W. – Wadi, West
W. Va. – West Virginia
Wash. – Washington
Wis. – Wisconsin
Wlkp. – Wielkopolski
Wyo. – Wyoming
Yorks. – Yorkshire
Yug. – Yugoslavia

A

A Baña, *Spain* 34 C2
A Cañiza, *Spain* 34 C2
A Coruña, *Spain* 34 B2
A Estrada, *Spain* 34 C2
A Fonsagrada, *Spain* 34 B3
A Guarda, *Spain* 34 D2
A Gudiña, *Spain* 34 C3
A Rúa, *Spain* 34 C3
Aachen, *Germany* 24 E2
Aalborg = Ålborg, *Denmark* 11 G3
Aalen, *Germany* 25 G6
A'âli an Nîl □, *Sudan* 81 F3
Aalst, *Belgium* 17 D4
Aalten, *Neths.* 17 C6
Aalter, *Belgium* 17 C3
Äänekoski, *Finland* 9 E21
Aarau, *Switz.* 25 H4
Aarberg, *Switz.* 25 H3
Aare →, *Switz.* 25 H4
Aargau □, *Switz.* 25 H4
Aarhus = Århus, *Denmark* 11 H4
Aarschot, *Belgium* 17 D4
Aba, *China* 58 A3
Aba, *Dem. Rep. of the Congo* 86 B3
Aba, *Nigeria* 83 D6
Âbâ, Jazîrat, *Sudan* 81 E3
Abadab, J., *Sudan* 80 D4
Ābādān, *Iran* 71 D6
Abade, *Ethiopia* 81 F4
Ābādeh, *Iran* 71 D7
Abadin, *Spain* 34 B3
Abadla, *Algeria* 78 B5
Abaetetuba, *Brazil* 125 D9
Abagnar Qi, *China* 56 C9
Abai, *Paraguay* 127 B4
Abak, *Nigeria* 83 E6
Abakaliki, *Nigeria* 83 D6
Abakan, *Russia* 51 D10
Abala, *Niger* 83 C5
Abalak, *Niger* 83 B6
Abalemma, *Niger* 83 B6
Abana, *Turkey* 72 B6
Abancay, *Peru* 124 F4
Abano Terme, *Italy* 29 C8
Abarán, *Spain* 33 G3
Abariringa, *Kiribati* 96 H10
Abarqū, *Iran* 71 D7
Abashiri, *Japan* 54 C12
Abashiri-Wan, *Japan* 54 C12
Abaújszántó, *Hungary* 42 B6
Abava →, *Latvia* 44 A8
Ābay = Nîl el Azraq →, *Sudan* 81 D3
Abay, *Kazakstan* 50 E8
Abaya, L., *Ethiopia* 81 F4
Abaza, *Russia* 50 D10
Abbadia San Salvatore, *Italy* 29 F8
'Abbāsābād, *Iran* 71 C8
Abbay = Nîl el Azraq →, *Sudan* 81 D3
Abbaye, Pt., *U.S.A.* 108 B1
Abbé, L., *Ethiopia* 81 E5
Abbeville, *France* 19 B8
Abbeville, *Ala., U.S.A.* 109 K3
Abbeville, *La., U.S.A.* 113 L8
Abbeville, *S.C., U.S.A.* 109 H4
Abbiategrasso, *Italy* 28 C5
Abbot Ice Shelf, *Antarctica* 5 D16
Abbottabad, *Pakistan* 68 B5
Abd al Kūrī, *Ind. Oc.* 74 E5
Ābdar, *Iran* 71 D7
'Abdolābād, *Iran* 71 C8
Abdulpur, *Bangla.* 69 G13
Abéché, *Chad* 79 F10
Abejar, *Spain* 32 D2
Abekr, *Sudan* 81 E2
Abengourou, *Ivory C.* 82 D4
Abenójar, *Spain* 35 G6
Åbenrå, *Denmark* 11 J3
Abensberg, *Germany* 25 G7
Abeokuta, *Nigeria* 83 D5
Aber, *Uganda* 86 B3
Aberaeron, *U.K.* 13 E3
Aberayron = Aberaeron, *U.K.* 13 E3
Aberchirder, *U.K.* 14 D6
Abercorn = Mbala, *Zambia* 87 D3
Abercorn, *Australia* 95 D5
Aberdare, *U.K.* 13 F4
Aberdare Ra., *Kenya* 86 C4
Aberdeen, *Australia* 95 E5
Aberdeen, *Canada* 105 C7
Aberdeen, *S. Africa* 88 E3
Aberdeen, *U.K.* 14 D6
Aberdeen, *Ala., U.S.A.* 109 J1
Aberdeen, *Idaho, U.S.A.* 114 E7
Aberdeen, *Md., U.S.A.* 108 F7
Aberdeen, *S. Dak., U.S.A.* 112 C5
Aberdeen, *Wash., U.S.A.* 116 D3
Aberdeen, City of □, *U.K.* 14 D6
Aberdeenshire □, *U.K.* 14 D6
Aberdovey = Aberdyfi, *U.K.* 13 E3
Aberdyfi, *U.K.* 13 E3
Aberfeldy, *U.K.* 14 E5
Abergavenny, *U.K.* 13 F4
Abergele, *U.K.* 12 D4
Abernathy, *U.S.A.* 113 J4
Abert, L., *U.S.A.* 114 E3
Aberystwyth, *U.K.* 13 E3
Abhā, *Si. Arabia* 74 D3
Abhar, *Iran* 71 B6
Abhayapuri, *India* 69 F14
Abia □, *Nigeria* 83 D6
Abide, *Turkey* 39 C11
Abidiya, *Sudan* 80 D3
Abidjan, *Ivory C.* 82 D4
Abilene, *Kans., U.S.A.* 112 F6
Abilene, *Tex., U.S.A.* 113 J5
Abingdon, *U.K.* 13 F6
Abingdon, *U.S.A.* 109 G5
Abington Reef, *Australia* 94 B4
Abitau →, *Canada* 105 B7
Abitibi →, *Canada* 102 B3
Abitibi, L., *Canada* 102 C4
Abiy Adi, *Ethiopia* 81 E4
Abkhaz Republic = Abkhazia □, *Georgia* 49 J5
Abkhazia □, *Georgia* 49 J5
Abminga, *Australia* 95 D1
Abnûb, *Egypt* 80 B3
Åbo = Turku, *Finland* 9 F20
Abocho, *Nigeria* 83 D6
Abohar, *India* 68 D6
Aboisso, *Ivory C.* 82 D4
Abomey, *Benin* 83 D5
Abong-Mbang, *Cameroon* 84 D2
Abonnema, *Nigeria* 83 E6
Abony, *Hungary* 42 C5
Aboso, *Ghana* 82 D4
Abou-Deïa, *Chad* 79 F9
Aboyne, *U.K.* 14 D6
Abra Pampa, *Argentina* 126 A2
Abraham L., *Canada* 104 C5
Abrantes, *Portugal* 35 F2
Abreojos, Pta., *Mexico* 118 B2
Abri, *Esh Shamâliya, Sudan* 80 C3
Abri, *Janub Kordofân, Sudan* 81 E3
Abrud, *Romania* 42 D8
Abruzzo □, *Italy* 29 F10
Absaroka Range, *U.S.A.* 114 D9
Abtenau, *Austria* 26 D6
Abu, *India* 68 G5
Abū al Abyad, *U.A.E.* 71 E7
Abū al Khaşīb, *Iraq* 71 D6
Abū 'Alī, *Si. Arabia* 71 E6
Abū 'Alī →, *Lebanon* 75 A4
Abu Ballas, *Egypt* 80 C2
Abu Deleiq, *Sudan* 81 D3
Abu Dhabi = Abū Z̧āby, *U.A.E.* 71 E7
Abu Dis, *Sudan* 80 D3
Abu Dom, *Sudan* 81 D3
Abū Du'ān, *Syria* 70 B3
Abu el Gairi, W. →, *Egypt* 75 F2
Abu Fatma, Ras, *Sudan* 80 C4
Abu Gabra, *Sudan* 81 E2
Abu Ga'da, W. →, *Egypt* 75 F1
Abu Gelba, *Sudan* 81 E3
Abu Gubeiha, *Sudan* 81 E3
Abu Habl, Khawr →, *Sudan* 81 E3
Abū Ḩadrīyah, *Si. Arabia* 71 E6
Abu Hamed, *Sudan* 80 D3
Abu Haraz, *An Nîl el Azraq, Sudan* 80 D3
Abu Haraz, *El Gezira, Sudan* 81 E3
Abu Haraz, *Esh Shamâliya, Sudan* 80 D3
Abu Higar, *Sudan* 81 E3
Abū Kamāl, *Syria* 70 C4
Abu Kuleiwat, *Sudan* 81 E2
Abū Madd, Ra's, *Si. Arabia* 70 E3
Abu Matariq, *Sudan* 81 E2
Abu Mendi, *Ethiopia* 81 E4
Abū Mūsā, *U.A.E.* 71 E7
Abu Qir, *Egypt* 80 H7
Abu Qireiya, *Egypt* 80 C4
Abu Qurqâs, *Egypt* 80 B3
Abu Şafāt, W. →, *Jordan* 75 E5
Abu Shagara, Ras, *Sudan* 80 C4
Abu Shanab, *Sudan* 81 E2
Abu Simbel, *Egypt* 80 C3
Abū Şukhayr, *Iraq* 70 D5
Abu Sultân, *Egypt* 80 H8
Abu Tabari, *Sudan* 80 D2
Abu Tig, *Egypt* 80 B3
Abu Tiga, *Sudan* 81 E3
Abu Tineitin, *Sudan* 81 E3
Abu Uruq, *Sudan* 81 D3
Abu Zabad, *Sudan* 81 E2
Abū Z̧āby, *U.A.E.* 71 E7
Abū Zeydābād, *Iran* 71 C6
Abuja, *Nigeria* 83 D6
Abukuma-Gawa →, *Japan* 54 E10
Abukuma-Sammyaku, *Japan* 54 F10
Abunã, *Brazil* 124 E5
Abunã →, *Brazil* 124 E5
Abune Yosef, *Ethiopia* 81 E4
Aburo, *Dem. Rep. of the Congo* 86 B3
Abut Hd., *N.Z.* 91 K3
Abuye Meda, *Ethiopia* 81 E4
Abwong, *Sudan* 81 F3
Åby, *Sweden* 11 F10
Aby, Lagune, *Ivory C.* 82 D4
Abyad, *Sudan* 81 E2
Åbybro, *Denmark* 11 G3
Acadia National Park, *U.S.A.* 109 C11
Açailândia, *Brazil* 125 D9
Acajutla, *El Salv.* 120 D2
Acámbaro, *Mexico* 118 D4
Acanthus, *Greece* 40 F7
Acaponeta, *Mexico* 118 C3
Acapulco, *Mexico* 119 D5
Acarai, Serra, *Brazil* 124 C7
Acarigua, *Venezuela* 124 B5
Acatlán, *Mexico* 119 D5
Acayucan, *Mexico* 119 D6
Accéglio, *Italy* 28 D4
Accomac, *U.S.A.* 108 G8
Accous, *France* 20 E3
Accra, *Ghana* 83 D4
Accrington, *U.K.* 12 D5
Acebal, *Argentina* 126 C3
Aceh □, *Indonesia* 62 D1
Acerra, *Italy* 31 B7
Aceuchal, *Spain* 35 G4
Achalpur, *India* 66 J10
Acheng, *China* 57 B14
Achenkirch, *Austria* 26 D4
Achensee, *Austria* 26 D4
Acher, *India* 68 H5
Achern, *Germany* 25 G4
Achill Hd., *Ireland* 15 C1
Achill I., *Ireland* 15 C1
Achim, *Germany* 24 B5
Achinsk, *Russia* 51 D10
Acıgöl, *Turkey* 39 D11
Acıpayam, *Turkey* 39 D11
Acireale, *Italy* 31 E8
Ackerman, *U.S.A.* 113 J10
Acklins I., *Bahamas* 121 B5
Acme, *Canada* 104 C6
Acme, *U.S.A.* 110 F5
Aconcagua, Cerro, *Argentina* 126 C2
Aconquija, Mt., *Argentina* 126 B2
Açores, Is. dos = Azores, *Atl. Oc.* 78 A1
Acornhoek, *S. Africa* 89 C5
Acquapendente, *Italy* 29 F8
Acquasanta Terme, *Italy* 29 F10
Acquasparta, *Italy* 29 F9
Acquaviva delle Fonti, *Italy* 31 B9
Ácqui Terme, *Italy* 28 D5
Acraman, L., *Australia* 95 E2
Acre = 'Akko, *Israel* 75 C4
Acre □, *Brazil* 124 E4
Acre →, *Brazil* 124 E5
Acri, *Italy* 31 C9
Acs, *Hungary* 42 C3
Actium, *Greece* 38 C2
Acton, *Canada* 110 C4
Acuña, *Mexico* 118 B4
Ad Dammām, *Si. Arabia* 71 E6
Ad Dāmūr, *Lebanon* 75 B4
Ad Dawādimī, *Si. Arabia* 70 E5
Ad Dawḩah, *Qatar* 71 E6
Ad Dawr, *Iraq* 70 C4
Ad Dir'īyah, *Si. Arabia* 70 E5
Ad Dīwānīyah, *Iraq* 70 D5
Ad Dujayl, *Iraq* 70 C5
Ad Duwayd, *Si. Arabia* 70 D4
Ada, *Ghana* 83 D5
Ada, *Serbia, Yug.* 42 E5
Ada, *Minn., U.S.A.* 112 B6
Ada, *Okla., U.S.A.* 113 H6
Adabiya, *Egypt* 75 F1
Adair, C., *Canada* 101 A12
Adaja →, *Spain* 34 D6
Adak I., *U.S.A.* 100 C2
Adamaoua, Massif de l', *Cameroon* 83 D7
Adamawa □, *Nigeria* 83 D7
Adamawa Highlands = Adamaoua, Massif de l', *Cameroon* 83 D7
Adamello, Mte., *Italy* 28 B7
Adami Tulu, *Ethiopia* 81 F4
Adaminaby, *Australia* 95 F4
Adams, *Mass., U.S.A.* 111 D11
Adams, *N.Y., U.S.A.* 111 C8
Adams, *Wis., U.S.A.* 112 D10
Adam's Bridge, *Sri Lanka* 66 Q11
Adams L., *Canada* 104 C5
Adams Mt., *U.S.A.* 116 D5
Adam's Peak, *Sri Lanka* 66 R12
Adamuz, *Spain* 35 G6
Adana, *Turkey* 70 B2
Adanero, *Spain* 34 E6
Adapazarı = Sakarya, *Turkey* 72 B4
Adar Gwagwa, J., *Sudan* 80 C4
Adarama, *Sudan* 81 D3
Adare, C., *Antarctica* 5 D11
Adarte, *Eritrea* 81 E5
Adaut, *Indonesia* 63 F8
Adavale, *Australia* 95 D3
Adda →, *Italy* 28 C6
Addis Ababa = Addis Abeba, *Ethiopia* 81 F4
Addis Abeba, *Ethiopia* 81 F4
Addis Alem, *Ethiopia* 81 F4
Addis Zemen, *Ethiopia* 81 E4
Addison, *U.S.A.* 110 D7
Addo, *S. Africa* 88 E4
Adebour, *Niger* 83 C7
Ādeh, *Iran* 70 B5
Adel, *U.S.A.* 109 K4
Adelaide, *Australia* 95 E2
Adelaide, *Bahamas* 120 A4
Adelaide, *S. Africa* 88 E4
Adelaide I., *Antarctica* 5 C17
Adelaide Pen., *Canada* 100 B10
Adelaide River, *Australia* 92 B5
Adelanto, *U.S.A.* 117 L9
Adele I., *Australia* 92 C3
Adélie, Terre, *Antarctica* 5 C10
Adélie Land = Adélie, Terre, *Antarctica* 5 C10
Ademuz, *Spain* 32 E3
Aden = Al 'Adan, *Yemen* 74 E4
Aden, G. of, *Asia* 74 E4
Adendorp, *S. Africa* 88 E3
Aderbissinat, *Niger* 83 B6
Adh Dhayd, *U.A.E.* 71 E7
Adhoi, *India* 68 H4
Adi, *Indonesia* 63 E8
Adi Arkai, *Ethiopia* 81 E4
Adi Daro, *Ethiopia* 81 E4
Adi Keyih, *Eritrea* 81 E4
Adi Kwala, *Eritrea* 81 E4
Adi Ugri, *Eritrea* 81 E4
Adieu, C., *Australia* 93 F5
Adieu Pt., *Australia* 92 C3
Adigala, *Ethiopia* 81 E5
Adige →, *Italy* 29 C9
Adigrat, *Ethiopia* 81 E4
Adıgüzel Barajı, *Turkey* 39 C11
Adilabad, *India* 66 K11
Adilcevaz, *Turkey* 73 C10
Adin Khel, *Afghan.* 66 C6
Adirondack Mts., *U.S.A.* 111 C10
Adıyaman, *Turkey* 73 D8
Adjohon, *Benin* 83 D5
Adjud, *Romania* 43 D12
Adjumani, *Uganda* 86 B3
Adlavik Is., *Canada* 103 A8
Adler, *Russia* 49 J4
Admer, *Algeria* 83 A6
Admiralty G., *Australia* 92 B4
Admiralty I., *U.S.A.* 104 B2
Admiralty Is., *Papua N. G.* 96 H6
Ado, *Nigeria* 83 D5
Ado-Ekiti, *Nigeria* 83 D6
Adok, *Sudan* 81 F3
Adola, *Ethiopia* 81 E5
Adonara, *Indonesia* 63 F6
Adoni, *India* 66 M10
Adony, *Hungary* 42 C3
Adour →, *France* 20 E2
Adra, *India* 69 H12
Adra, *Spain* 35 J7
Adrano, *Italy* 31 E7
Adrar, *Mauritania* 78 D3
Adrar des Iforas, *Algeria* 76 D4
Ádria, *Italy* 29 C9
Adrian, *Mich., U.S.A.* 108 E3
Adrian, *Tex., U.S.A.* 113 H3
Adriatic Sea, *Medit. S.* 6 G9
Adua, *Indonesia* 63 E7
Adwa, *Ethiopia* 81 E4
Adygea □, *Russia* 49 H5
Adzhar Republic = Ajaria □, *Georgia* 49 K6
Adzopé, *Ivory C.* 82 D4
Ægean Sea, *Medit. S.* 39 C7
Aerhtai Shan, *Mongolia* 60 B4
Ærø, *Denmark* 11 K4
Ærøskøbing, *Denmark* 11 K4
Aëtós, *Greece* 38 D3
'Afak, *Iraq* 70 C5
Afándou, *Greece* 36 C10
Afghanistan ■, *Asia* 66 C4
Afikpo, *Nigeria* 83 D6
Aflou, *Algeria* 78 B6
Afragóla, *Italy* 31 B7
Afram →, *Ghana* 83 D4
Afrera, *Ethiopia* 81 E5
Africa 76 E6
'Afrīn, *Syria* 70 B3
Afşin, *Turkey* 72 C7
Afton, *N.Y., U.S.A.* 111 D9
Afton, *Wyo., U.S.A.* 114 E8
Afuá, *Brazil* 125 D8
'Afula, *Israel* 75 C4
Afyon, *Turkey* 39 C12
Afyon □, *Turkey* 39 C12
Afyonkarahisar = Afyon, *Turkey* 39 C12
Aga, *Egypt* 80 H7
Agadès = Agadez, *Niger* 83 B6
Agadez, *Niger* 83 B6
Agadir, *Morocco* 78 B4
Agaete, *Canary Is.* 37 F4
Agaie, *Nigeria* 83 D6
Again, *Sudan* 81 F2
Ağapınar, *Turkey* 39 B12
Agar, *India* 68 H7
Agaro, *Ethiopia* 81 F4
Agartala, *India* 67 H17
Agăş, *Romania* 43 D11
Agassiz, *Canada* 104 D4
Agats, *Indonesia* 63 F9
Agawam, *U.S.A.* 111 D12
Agbélouvé, *Togo* 83 D5
Agboville, *Ivory C.* 82 D4
Ağcabädi, *Azerbaijan* 49 K8
Ağdam, *Azerbaijan* 49 L8
Ağdaş, *Azerbaijan* 49 K8
Agde, *France* 20 E7
Agde, C. d', *France* 20 E7
Agdzhabedi = Ağcabädi, *Azerbaijan* 49 K8
Agen, *France* 20 D4
Agerbæk, *Denmark* 11 J2
Agersø, *Denmark* 11 J5
Ageyevo, *Russia* 46 E9
Āgh Kand, *Iran* 71 B6
Aghireşu, *Romania* 43 D8
Aginskoye, *Russia* 51 D12
Ağlasun, *Turkey* 39 D12
Agly →, *France* 20 F7
Agnew, *Australia* 93 E3
Agnibilékrou, *Ivory C.* 82 D4
Agnita, *Romania* 43 E9
Agnone, *Italy* 29 G11
Agofie, *Ghana* 83 D5
Agogna →, *Italy* 28 C5
Agogo, *Sudan* 81 F2
Agön, *Sweden* 10 C11
Agon Coutainville, *France* 18 C5
Ágordo, *Italy* 29 B9
Agori, *India* 69 G10
Agouna, *Benin* 83 D5
Agout →, *France* 20 E5
Agra, *India* 68 F7
Agrakhanskiy Poluostrov, *Russia* 49 J8
Agramunt, *Spain* 32 D6
Agreda, *Spain* 32 D3
Ağri, *Turkey* 73 C10
Agri →, *Italy* 31 B9
Ağrı Dağı, *Turkey* 70 B5
Agriá, *Greece* 38 B5
Agrigento, *Italy* 30 E6
Agrínion, *Greece* 38 C3
Agrópoli, *Italy* 31 B7
Ağstafa, *Azerbaijan* 49 K7
Agua Caliente, *Baja Calif., Mexico* 117 N10
Agua Caliente, *Sinaloa, Mexico* 118 B3
Agua Caliente Springs, *U.S.A.* 117 N10
Água Clara, *Brazil* 125 H8
Agua Hechicero, *Mexico* 117 N10
Agua Prieta, *Mexico* 118 A3
Aguadilla, *Puerto Rico* 121 C6
Aguadulce, *Panama* 120 E3
Aguanga, *U.S.A.* 117 M10
Aguanish, *Canada* 103 B7
Aguanus →, *Canada* 103 B7
Aguapey →, *Argentina* 126 B4
Aguaray Guazú →, *Paraguay* 126 A4
Aguarico →, *Ecuador* 124 D3
Aguas →, *Spain* 32 D4
Aguas Blancas, *Chile* 126 A2
Aguas Calientes, Sierra de, *Argentina* 126 B2
Aguascalientes, *Mexico* 118 C4
Aguascalientes □, *Mexico* 118 C4
Agudo, *Spain* 35 G6
Águeda, *Portugal* 34 E2
Agueda →, *Spain* 34 D4
Aguelhok, *Mali* 83 B5
Aguié, *Niger* 83 C6
Aguilafuente, *Spain* 34 D6
Aguilar, *Spain* 35 H6
Aguilar de Campóo, *Spain* 34 C6
Aguilares, *Argentina* 126 B2
Aguilas, *Spain* 33 H3
Agüimes, *Canary Is.* 37 G4
Aguja, C. de la, *Colombia* 122 B3
Agulaa, *Ethiopia* 81 E4
Agulhas, C., *S. Africa* 88 E3
Agulo, *Canary Is.* 37 F2
Agung, *Indonesia* 62 F5
Agur, *Uganda* 86 B3
Agusan →, *Phil.* 61 G6
Ağva, *Turkey* 41 E13
Agvali, *Russia* 49 J8
Aha Mts., *Botswana* 88 B3
Ahaggar, *Algeria* 78 D7
Ahamansu, *Ghana* 83 D5
Ahar, *Iran* 70 B5
Ahat, *Turkey* 39 C11
Ahaus, *Germany* 24 C2
Ahipara B., *N.Z.* 91 F4
Ahir Dağı, *Turkey* 39 C12
Ahiri, *India* 66 K12
Ahlat, *Turkey* 73 C10
Ahlen, *Germany* 24 D3
Ahmad Wal, *Pakistan* 68 E1
Ahmadabad, *India* 68 H5
Aḩmadābād, *Khorāsān, Iran* 71 C9
Aḩmadābād, *Khorāsān, Iran* 71 C8
Aḩmadī, *Iran* 71 E8
Ahmadnagar, *India* 66 K9
Ahmadpur, *Pakistan* 68 E4
Ahmadpur Lamma, *Pakistan* 68 E4
Ahmar, *Ethiopia* 81 F5
Ahmedabad = Ahmadabad, *India* 68 H5
Ahmednagar = Ahmadnagar, *India* 66 K9
Ahmetbey, *Turkey* 41 E11
Ahmetler, *Turkey* 39 C11
Ahmetli, *Turkey* 39 C9
Ahoada, *Nigeria* 83 D6
Ahome, *Mexico* 118 B3
Ahoskie, *U.S.A.* 109 G7
Ahr →, *Germany* 24 E3
Ahram, *Iran* 71 D6
Ahrax Pt., *Malta* 36 D1
Ahrensbök, *Germany* 24 A6
Ahrensburg, *Germany* 24 B6
Āhū, *Iran* 71 C6
Ahuachapán, *El Salv.* 120 D2
Ahun, *France* 19 F9
Åhus, *Sweden* 11 J8
Ahvāz, *Iran* 71 D6
Ahvenanmaa = Åland, *Finland* 9 F19
Aḩwar, *Yemen* 74 E4
Ahzar →, *Mali* 83 B5
Ai →, *India* 69 F14
Ai-Ais, *Namibia* 88 D2
Aichach, *Germany* 25 G7
Aichi □, *Japan* 55 G8
Aigle, *Switz.* 25 J2
Aignay-le-Duc, *France* 19 E11
Aigoual, Mt., *France* 20 D7
Aigre, *France* 20 C4
Aigua, *Uruguay* 127 C5
Aigueperse, *France* 19 F10
Aigues →, *France* 21 D8
Aigues-Mortes, *France* 21 E8
Aigues-Mortes, G. d', *France* 21 E8
Aiguilles, *France* 21 D10
Aiguillon, *France* 20 D4
Aigurande, *France* 19 F8
Aihui, *China* 60 A7
Aija, *Peru* 124 E3
Aikawa, *Japan* 54 E9
Aiken, *U.S.A.* 109 J5
Ailao Shan, *China* 58 F3
Aileron, *Australia* 94 C1
Aillant-sur-Tholon, *France* 19 E10
Aillik, *Canada* 103 A8
Ailsa Craig, *U.K.* 14 F3
'Ailūn, *Jordan* 75 C4
Aim, *Russia* 51 D14
Aimere, *Indonesia* 63 F6
Aimogasta, *Argentina* 126 B2
Ain □, *France* 19 F12
Ain →, *France* 21 C9
Aïn Ben Tili, *Mauritania* 78 C4

Ain Dalla, *Egypt* 80 B2
Ain el Mafki, *Egypt* 80 B2
Ain Girba, *Egypt* 80 B2
Ain Murr, *Sudan* 80 C2
Ain Qeiqab, *Egypt* 80 B1
Aïn-Sefra, *Algeria* 78 B5
Ain Sheikh Murzûk, *Egypt* 80 B2
Ain Sudr, *Egypt* 75 F2
Ain Sukhna, *Egypt* 80 J8
Ain Zeitûn, *Egypt* 80 B2
Ainaži, *Latvia* 9 H21
Aínos Óros, *Greece* 38 C2
Ainsworth, *U.S.A.* 112 D5
Aiquile, *Bolivia* 124 G5
Aïr, *Niger* 83 B6
Air Force I., *Canada* 101 B12
Air Hitam, *Malaysia* 65 M4
Airaines, *France* 19 C8
Airdrie, *Canada* 104 C6
Airdrie, *U.K.* 14 F5
Aire →, *France* 19 C11
Aire →, *U.K.* 12 D7
Aire, I. de l', *Spain* 37 B11
Aire-sur-la-Lys, *France* 19 B9
Aire-sur-l'Adour, *France* 20 E3
Airlie Beach, *Australia* 94 C4
Airvault, *France* 18 F6
Aisch →, *Germany* 25 F6
Aisne □, *France* 19 C10
Aisne →, *France* 19 C9
Ait, *India* 69 G8
Aitana, Sierra de, *Spain* 33 G4
Aitkin, *U.S.A.* 112 B8
Aitolía Kai Akarnanía □, *Greece* 38 C3
Aitolikón, *Greece* 38 C3
Aiud, *Romania* 43 D8
Aix-en-Provence, *France* 21 E9
Aix-la-Chapelle = Aachen, *Germany* 24 E2
Aix-les-Bains, *France* 21 C9
Aixe-sur-Vienne, *France* 20 C5
Áíyina, *Greece* 38 D5
Aiyínion, *Greece* 40 F6
Aíyion, *Greece* 38 C4
Aizawl, *India* 67 H18
Aizenay, *France* 18 F5
Aizkraukle, *Latvia* 9 H21
Aizpute, *Latvia* 9 H19
Aizuwakamatsu, *Japan* 54 F9
Ajaccio, *France* 21 G12
Ajaccio, G. d', *France* 21 G12
Ajaigarh, *India* 69 G9
Ajalpan, *Mexico* 119 D5
Ajanta Ra., *India* 66 J9
Ajari Rep. = Ajaria □, *Georgia* 49 K6
Ajaria □, *Georgia* 49 K6
Ajax, *Canada* 110 C5
Ajdâbiyah, *Libya* 79 B10
Ajdovščina, *Slovenia* 29 C10
Ajibar, *Ethiopia* 81 E4
Ajka, *Hungary* 42 C2
'Ajmān, *U.A.E.* 71 E7
Ajmer, *India* 68 F6
Ajnala, *India* 68 D6
Ajo, *U.S.A.* 115 K7
Ajo, C. de, *Spain* 34 B7
Ajok, *Sudan* 81 F2
Ajuy, *Phil.* 61 F5
Ak Dağ, *Turkey* 39 E11
Ak Dağları, *Muğla, Turkey* 39 E11
Ak Dağları, *Sivas, Turkey* 72 C7
Akaba, *Togo* 83 D5
Akabira, *Japan* 54 C11
Akaki Beseka, *Ethiopia* 81 F4
Akala, *Sudan* 81 D4
Akamas □, *Cyprus* 36 D11
Akanthou, *Cyprus* 36 D12
Akarca, *Turkey* 39 C11
Akaroa, *N.Z.* 91 K4
Akasha, *Sudan* 80 C3
Akashi, *Japan* 55 G7
Akbarpur, *Bihar, India* 69 G10
Akbarpur, *Ut. P., India* 69 F10
Akçaabat, *Turkey* 73 B8
Akçadağ, *Turkey* 72 C7
Akçakale, *Turkey* 73 D8
Akçakoca, *Turkey* 72 B4
Akçaova, *Turkey* 41 E13
Akçay, *Turkey* 39 E11
Akçay →, *Turkey* 39 D10
Akdağ, *Turkey* 39 C8
Akdağmadeni, *Turkey* 72 C6
Akelamo, *Indonesia* 63 D7
Åkers styckebruk, *Sweden* 10 E11
Åkersberga, *Sweden* 10 E12
Aketi, *Dem. Rep. of the Congo* 84 D4
Akhaïa □, *Greece* 38 C3
Akhalkalaki, *Georgia* 49 K6
Akhaltsikhe, *Georgia* 49 K6
Akharnaí, *Greece* 38 C5
Akhelóös →, *Greece* 38 C3
Akhendria, *Greece* 39 G7
Akhisar, *Turkey* 39 C9
Akhladhókambos, *Greece* 38 D4
Akhmîm, *Egypt* 80 B3
Akhnur, *India* 69 C6
Akhtopol, *Bulgaria* 41 D11
Akhtuba →, *Russia* 49 G8
Akhtubinsk, *Russia* 49 F8
Akhty, *Russia* 49 K8
Akhtyrka = Okhtyrka, *Ukraine* 47 G8
Aki, *Japan* 55 H6
Akimiski I., *Canada* 102 B3
Akimovka, *Ukraine* 47 J8
Åkirkeby, *Denmark* 11 J8
Akita, *Japan* 54 E10
Akita □, *Japan* 54 E10
Akjoujt, *Mauritania* 82 B2
Akka, *Mali* 82 B4
Akkaya Tepesi, *Turkey* 39 D11
Akkeshi, *Japan* 54 C12
'Akko, *Israel* 75 C4
Akköy, *Turkey* 39 D9
Aklampa, *Benin* 83 D5
Aklavik, *Canada* 100 B6
Aklera, *India* 68 G7
Akmenė, *Lithuania* 44 B9
Akmenrags, *Latvia* 44 B8
Akmolinsk = Astana, *Kazakstan* 50 D8
Akmonte = Almonte, *Spain* 35 H4
Akō, *Japan* 55 G7
Ako, *Nigeria* 83 C7
Akôbô, *Sudan* 81 F3
Akobo →, *Ethiopia* 81 F3
Akola, *India* 66 J10
Akonolinga, *Cameroon* 83 E7
Akor, *Mali* 82 C3
Akordat, *Eritrea* 81 D4
Akosombo Dam, *Ghana* 83 D5
Akot, *Sudan* 81 F3
Akoupé, *Ivory C.* 82 D4
Akpatok I., *Canada* 101 B13
Åkrahamn, *Norway* 9 G11
Akranes, *Iceland* 8 D2
Akreïjit, *Mauritania* 82 B3
Akrítas Venétiko, Ákra, *Greece* 38 E3
Akron, *Colo., U.S.A.* 112 E3
Akron, *Ohio, U.S.A.* 110 E3
Akrotiri, *Cyprus* 36 E11
Akrotíri, Ákra, *Greece* 41 F9
Akrotiri Bay, *Cyprus* 36 E12
Aksai Chin, *India* 69 B8
Aksaray, *Turkey* 70 B2
Aksay, *Kazakstan* 50 D6
Akşehir, *Turkey* 70 B1
Akşehir Gölü, *Turkey* 72 C4
Akstafa = Ağstafa, *Azerbaijan* 49 K7
Aksu, *China* 60 B3
Aksu →, *Turkey* 72 D4
Aksum, *Ethiopia* 81 E4
Aktash, *Russia* 48 C11
Aktogay, *Kazakstan* 50 E8
Aktsyabrski, *Belarus* 47 F5
Aktyubinsk = Aqtöbe, *Kazakstan* 50 D6
Aku, *Nigeria* 83 D6
Akure, *Nigeria* 83 D6
Akureyri, *Iceland* 8 D4
Akuseki-Shima, *Japan* 55 K4
Akusha, *Russia* 49 J8
Akwa-Ibom □, *Nigeria* 83 E6
Akyab = Sittwe, *Burma* 67 J18
Akyazı, *Turkey* 72 B4
Al 'Adan, *Yemen* 74 E4
Al Aḥsā = Hasa □, *Si. Arabia* 71 E6
Al Ajfar, *Si. Arabia* 70 E4
Al Amādīyah, *Iraq* 70 B4
Al 'Amārah, *Iraq* 70 D5
Al 'Aqabah, *Jordan* 75 F4
Al Arak, *Syria* 70 C3
Al 'Aramah, *Si. Arabia* 70 E5
Al Arṭāwīyah, *Si. Arabia* 70 E5
Al 'Āṣimah = 'Ammān □, *Jordan* 75 D5
Al 'Assāfīyah, *Si. Arabia* 70 D3
Al 'Ayn, *Oman* 71 E7
Al 'Ayn, *Si. Arabia* 70 E3
Al 'Azamīyah, *Iraq* 70 C5
Al 'Azīzīyah, *Iraq* 70 C5
Al Bāb, *Syria* 70 B3
Al Bad', *Si. Arabia* 70 D2
Al Bādī, *Iraq* 70 C4
Al Baḥrah, *Kuwait* 70 D5
Al Baḥral Mayyit = Dead Sea, *Asia* 75 D4
Al Balqā' □, *Jordan* 75 C4
Al Bārūk, J., *Lebanon* 75 B4
Al Baṣrah, *Iraq* 70 D5
Al Baṭḥā, *Iraq* 70 D5
Al Batrūn, *Lebanon* 75 A4
Al Bayḍā, *Libya* 79 B10
Al Biqā, *Lebanon* 75 A5
Al Bi'r, *Si. Arabia* 70 D3
Al Burayj, *Syria* 75 A5
Al Faḍilī, *Si. Arabia* 71 E6
Al Fallūjah, *Iraq* 70 C4
Al Fāw, *Iraq* 71 D6
Al Fujayrah, *U.A.E.* 71 E8
Al Ghadaf, W. →, *Jordan* 75 D5
Al Ghammās, *Iraq* 70 D5
Al Ghazālah, *Si. Arabia* 70 E4
Al Hābah, *Si. Arabia* 70 E5
Al Ḥadīthah, *Iraq* 70 C4
Al Ḥadīthah, *Si. Arabia* 75 D6
Al Ḥaḍr, *Iraq* 70 C4
Al Ḥājānah, *Syria* 75 B5
Al Hajar al Gharbi, *Oman* 71 E8
Al Hāmad, *Si. Arabia* 70 D3
Al Hamdānīyah, *Syria* 70 C3
Al Ḥamīdīyah, *Syria* 75 A4
Al Ḥammār, *Iraq* 70 D5
Al Ḥamrā', *Si. Arabia* 70 E3
Al Ḥanākīyah, *Si. Arabia* 70 E4
Al Ḥarīr, W. →, *Syria* 75 C4
Al Ḥasā, W. →, *Jordan* 75 D4
Al Ḥasakah, *Syria* 70 B4
Al Haydān, W. →, *Jordan* 75 D4
Al Ḥayy, *Iraq* 70 C5
Al Ḥijarah, *Asia* 70 D4
Al Ḥillah, *Iraq* 70 C5
Al Hindīyah, *Iraq* 70 C5
Al Hirmil, *Lebanon* 75 A5
Al Hoceïma, *Morocco* 78 A5
Al Ḥudaydah, *Yemen* 74 E3
Al Hufūf, *Si. Arabia* 71 E6
Al Ḥumayḍah, *Si. Arabia* 70 D2
Al Ḥunayy, *Si. Arabia* 71 E6
Al Īsāwīyah, *Si. Arabia* 70 D3
Al Jafr, *Jordan* 75 E5
Al Jāfūrah, *Si. Arabia* 71 E7
Al Jaghbūb, *Libya* 79 C10
Al Jahrah, *Kuwait* 70 D5
Al Jalāmīd, *Si. Arabia* 70 D3
Al Jamalīyah, *Qatar* 71 E6
Al Janūb □, *Lebanon* 75 B4
Al Jawf, *Libya* 79 D10
Al Jawf, *Si. Arabia* 70 D3
Al Jazirah, *Iraq* 70 C5
Al Jithāmīyah, *Si. Arabia* 70 E4
Al Jubayl, *Si. Arabia* 71 E6
Al Jubaylah, *Si. Arabia* 70 E5
Al Jubb, *Si. Arabia* 70 E4
Al Junaynah, *Sudan* 79 F10
Al Kabā'ish, *Iraq* 70 D5
Al Karak, *Jordan* 75 D4
Al Karak □, *Jordan* 75 E5
Al Kāẓim Tyah, *Iraq* 70 C5
Al Khābūra, *Oman* 71 F8
Al Khafji, *Si. Arabia* 71 E6
Al Khalīl, *West Bank* 75 D4
Al Khāliṣ, *Iraq* 70 C5
Al Kharsānīyah, *Si. Arabia* 71 E6
Al Khaṣab, *Oman* 71 E8
Al Khawr, *Qatar* 71 E6
Al Khiḍr, *Iraq* 70 D5
Al Khiyām, *Lebanon* 75 B4
Al Khums, *Libya* 79 B8
Al Kiswah, *Syria* 75 B5
Al Kūfah, *Iraq* 70 C5
Al Kufrah, *Libya* 79 D10
Al Kuhayfīyah, *Si. Arabia* 70 E4
Al Kūt, *Iraq* 70 C5
Al Kuwayt, *Kuwait* 70 D5
Al Labwah, *Lebanon* 75 A5
Al Lādhiqīyah, *Syria* 70 C2
Al Līth, *Si. Arabia* 74 C3
Al Liwā', *Oman* 71 E8
Al Luḥayyah, *Yemen* 74 D3
Al Madīnah, *Iraq* 70 D5
Al Madīnah, *Si. Arabia* 70 E3
Al Mafraq, *Jordan* 75 C5
Al Maḥmūdīyah, *Iraq* 70 C5
Al Majma'ah, *Si. Arabia* 70 E5
Al Makhruq, W. →, *Jordan* 75 D6
Al Makḥūl, *Si. Arabia* 70 E4
Al Manāmah, *Bahrain* 71 E6
Al Maqwa', *Kuwait* 70 D5
Al Marj, *Libya* 79 B10
Al Maṭlā, *Kuwait* 70 D5
Al Mawjib, W. →, *Jordan* 75 D4
Al Mawṣil, *Iraq* 70 B4
Al Mayādin, *Syria* 70 C4
Al Mazār, *Jordan* 75 D4
Al Midhnab, *Si. Arabia* 70 E5
Al Minā', *Lebanon* 75 A4
Al Miqdādīyah, *Iraq* 70 C5
Al Mubarraz, *Si. Arabia* 71 E6
Al Mudawwarah, *Jordan* 75 F5
Al Mughayrā', *U.A.E.* 71 E7
Al Muḥarraq, *Bahrain* 71 E6
Al Mukallā, *Yemen* 74 E4
Al Mukhā, *Yemen* 74 E3
Al Musayjīd, *Si. Arabia* 70 E3
Al Musayyib, *Iraq* 70 C5
Al Muwayh, *Si. Arabia* 80 C5
Al Muwayliḥ, *Si. Arabia* 70 E2
Al Owuho = Otukpa, *Nigeria* 83 D6
Al Qā'im, *Iraq* 70 C4
Al Qalībah, *Si. Arabia* 70 D3
Al Qāmishlī, *Syria* 70 B4
Al Qaryatayn, *Syria* 75 A6
Al Qaṣīm, *Si. Arabia* 70 E4
Al Qaṭ'ā, *Syria* 70 C4
Al Qaṭīf, *Si. Arabia* 71 E6
Al Qatrānah, *Jordan* 75 D5
Al Qaṭrūn, *Libya* 79 D9
Al Qayṣūmah, *Si. Arabia* 70 D5
Al Quds = Jerusalem, *Israel* 75 D4
Al Qunayṭirah, *Syria* 75 C4
Al Qunfudhah, *Si. Arabia* 80 D5
Al Qurnah, *Iraq* 70 D5
Al Quṣayr, *Iraq* 70 D5
Al Quṣayr, *Syria* 75 A5
Al Qutayfah, *Syria* 75 B5
Al 'Ubaylah, *Si. Arabia* 74 C5
Al 'Uḍaylīyah, *Si. Arabia* 71 E6
Al 'Ulā, *Si. Arabia* 70 E3
Al 'Uqayr, *Si. Arabia* 71 E6
Al 'Uthmānīyah, *Si. Arabia* 71 E6
Al 'Uwaynid, *Si. Arabia* 70 E5
Al 'Uwayqīlah, *Si. Arabia* 70 D4
Al 'Uyūn, *Ḥijāz, Si. Arabia* 70 E3
Al 'Uyūn, *Najd, Si. Arabia* 70 E4
Al 'Uzayr, *Iraq* 70 D5
Al Wajh, *Si. Arabia* 70 E3
Al Wakrah, *Qatar* 71 E6
Al Wannān, *Si. Arabia* 71 E6
Al Waqbah, *Si. Arabia* 70 D5
Al Wari'āh, *Si. Arabia* 70 E5
Al Wusayl, *Qatar* 71 E6
Ala, *Italy* 28 C8
Ala Dağ, *Turkey* 70 B2
Ala Dağları, *Turkey* 73 C10
Alabama □, *U.S.A.* 109 J2
Alabama →, *U.S.A.* 109 K2
Alabaster, *U.S.A.* 109 J2
Alaca, *Turkey* 72 B6
Alacaatlı, *Turkey* 39 B10
Alaçam, *Turkey* 72 B6
Alaçam Dağları, *Turkey* 39 B10
Alaçatı, *Turkey* 39 C8
Alachua, *U.S.A.* 109 L4
Alaejos, *Spain* 34 D5
Alaérma, *Greece* 36 C9
Alagir, *Russia* 49 J7
Alagna Valsésia, *Italy* 28 C4
Alagoa Grande, *Brazil* 125 E11
Alagoas □, *Brazil* 125 E11
Alagoinhas, *Brazil* 125 F11
Alagón, *Spain* 32 D3
Alagón →, *Spain* 34 F4
Alaior, *Spain* 37 B11
Alajero, *Canary Is.* 37 F2
Alajuela, *Costa Rica* 120 D3
Alakamisy, *Madag.* 89 C8
Alaknanda →, *India* 69 D8
Alamarvdasht, *Iran* 71 E7
Alamata, *Ethiopia* 81 E4
Alameda, *Calif., U.S.A.* 116 H4
Alameda, *N. Mex., U.S.A.* 115 J10
Alaminos, *Phil.* 61 C3
Alamo, *U.S.A.* 117 J11
Alamo Crossing, *U.S.A.* 117 L13
Alamogordo, *U.S.A.* 115 K11
Alamos, *Mexico* 118 B3
Alamosa, *U.S.A.* 115 H11
Åland, *Finland* 9 F19
Alandroal, *Portugal* 35 G3
Ålands hav, *Sweden* 9 F18
Alandur, *India* 66 N12
Alange, Presa de, *Spain* 35 G4
Alania = North Ossetia □, *Russia* 49 J7
Alanís, *Spain* 35 G5
Alanya, *Turkey* 70 B1
Alaotra, Farihin', *Madag.* 89 B8
Alapayevsk, *Russia* 50 D7
Alar del Rey, *Spain* 34 C6
Alaraz, *Spain* 34 E5
Alarcón, Embalse de, *Spain* 32 F2
Alarobia-Vohiposa, *Madag.* 89 C8
Alaşehir, *Turkey* 39 C10
Alaska □, *U.S.A.* 100 B5
Alaska, G. of, *Pac. Oc.* 100 C5
Alaska Peninsula, *U.S.A.* 100 C4
Alaska Range, *U.S.A.* 100 B4
Alássio, *Italy* 28 E5
Älät, *Azerbaijan* 49 L9
Alatri, *Italy* 29 G10
Alatyr, *Russia* 48 C8
Alatyr →, *Russia* 48 C8
Alausi, *Ecuador* 124 D3
Álava □, *Spain* 32 C2
Alava, C., *U.S.A.* 114 B1
Alaverdi, *Armenia* 49 K7
Alavus, *Finland* 9 E20
Alawoona, *Australia* 95 E3
'Alayh, *Lebanon* 75 B4
Alazani →, *Azerbaijan* 49 K8
Alba, *Italy* 28 D5
Alba □, *Romania* 43 D8
Alba Adriática, *Italy* 29 F10
Alba de Tormes, *Spain* 34 E5
Alba-Iulia, *Romania* 43 D8
Albac, *Romania* 42 D7
Albacete, *Spain* 33 F3
Albacete □, *Spain* 33 G3
Albacutya, L., *Australia* 95 F3
Ålbæk, *Denmark* 11 G4
Ålbæk Bugt, *Denmark* 11 G4
Albaida, *Spain* 33 G4
Albalate de las Nogueras, *Spain* 32 E2
Albalate del Arzobispo, *Spain* 32 D4
Alban, *France* 20 E6
Albanel, L., *Canada* 102 B5
Albania ■, *Europe* 40 E4
Albano Laziale, *Italy* 29 G9
Albany, *Australia* 93 G2
Albany, *Ga., U.S.A.* 109 K3
Albany, *N.Y., U.S.A.* 111 D11
Albany, *Oreg., U.S.A.* 114 D2
Albany, *Tex., U.S.A.* 113 J5
Albany →, *Canada* 102 B3
Albardón, *Argentina* 126 C2
Albarracín, *Spain* 32 E3
Albarracín, Sierra de, *Spain* 32 E3
Albatera, *Spain* 33 G4
Albatross B., *Australia* 94 A3
Albegna →, *Italy* 29 F8
Albemarle, *U.S.A.* 109 H5
Albemarle Sd., *U.S.A.* 109 H7
Albenga, *Italy* 28 D5
Alberche →, *Spain* 34 F6
Alberdi, *Paraguay* 126 B4
Alberes, Mts., *France* 20 F6
Ålberga, *Sweden* 11 F10
Albersdorf, *Germany* 24 A5
Albert, *France* 19 C9
Albert, L., *Australia* 95 F2
Albert Edward Ra., *Australia* 92 C4
Albert L., *Africa* 86 B3
Albert Lea, *U.S.A.* 112 D8
Albert Nile →, *Uganda* 86 B3
Albert Town, *Bahamas* 121 B5
Alberta □, *Canada* 104 C6
Alberti, *Argentina* 126 D3
Albertinia, *S. Africa* 88 E3
Albertirsa, *Hungary* 42 C4
Alberton, *Canada* 103 C7
Albertville = Kalemie, *Dem. Rep. of the Congo* 86 D2
Albertville, *France* 21 C10
Albertville, *U.S.A.* 109 H2
Albi, *France* 20 E6
Albia, *U.S.A.* 112 E8
Albina, *Surinam* 125 B8
Albina, Ponta, *Angola* 88 B1
Albino, *Italy* 28 C6
Albion, *Mich., U.S.A.* 108 D3
Albion, *Nebr., U.S.A.* 112 E6
Albion, *Pa., U.S.A.* 110 E4
Albocácer, *Spain* 32 E5
Albolote, *Spain* 35 H7
Alborán, *Medit. S.* 35 K7
Alborea, *Spain* 33 F3
Ålborg, *Denmark* 11 G3
Ålborg Bugt, *Denmark* 11 H4
Alborz, Reshteh-ye Kūhhā-ye, *Iran* 71 C7
Albox, *Spain* 33 H2
Albufeira, *Portugal* 35 H2
Albula →, *Switz.* 25 J5
Albuñol, *Spain* 35 J7
Albuquerque, *U.S.A.* 115 J10
Albuquerque, Cayos de, *Caribbean* 120 D3
Alburg, *U.S.A.* 111 B11
Alburno, Mte., *Italy* 31 B8
Alburquerque, *Spain* 35 F4
Albury-Wodonga, *Australia* 95 F4
Alcácer do Sal, *Portugal* 35 G2
Alcáçovas, *Portugal* 35 G2
Alcalá de Chivert, *Spain* 32 E5
Alcalá de Guadaira, *Spain* 35 H5
Alcalá de Henares, *Spain* 34 E7
Alcalá de los Gazules, *Spain* 35 J5
Alcalá del Júcar, *Spain* 33 F3
Alcalá del Río, *Spain* 35 H5
Alcalá del Valle, *Spain* 35 J5
Alcalá la Real, *Spain* 35 H7
Álcamo, *Italy* 30 E5
Alcanadre, *Spain* 32 C2
Alcanadre →, *Spain* 32 D4
Alcanar, *Spain* 32 E5
Alcanede, *Portugal* 35 F2
Alcanena, *Portugal* 35 F2
Alcañices, *Spain* 34 D4
Alcañiz, *Spain* 32 D4
Alcântara, *Brazil* 125 D10
Alcántara, *Spain* 34 F4
Alcántara, Embalse de, *Spain* 34 F4
Alcantarilla, *Spain* 33 H3
Alcaracejos, *Spain* 35 G6
Alcaraz, *Spain* 33 G2
Alcaraz, Sierra de, *Spain* 33 G2
Alcaudete, *Spain* 35 H6
Alcázar de San Juan, *Spain* 35 F7
Alchevsk, *Ukraine* 47 H10
Alcira = Alzira, *Spain* 33 F4
Alcobaça, *Portugal* 35 F2
Alcobendas, *Spain* 34 E7
Alcolea del Pinar, *Spain* 32 D2
Alcora, *Spain* 32 E4
Alcorcón, *Spain* 34 E7
Alcoutim, *Portugal* 35 H3
Alcova, *U.S.A.* 114 E10
Alcoy, *Spain* 33 G4
Alcubierre, Sierra de, *Spain* 32 D4
Alcublas, *Spain* 32 F4
Alcúdia, *Spain* 37 B10
Alcúdia, B. d', *Spain* 37 B10
Alcudia, Sierra de la, *Spain* 35 G6
Aldabra Is., *Seychelles* 77 G8
Aldama, *Mexico* 119 C5
Aldan, *Russia* 51 D13
Aldan →, *Russia* 51 C13
Aldea, Pta. de la, *Canary Is.* 37 G4
Aldeburgh, *U.K.* 13 E9
Alder Pk., *U.S.A.* 116 K5
Alderney, *U.K.* 13 H5
Aldershot, *U.K.* 13 F7
Åled, *Sweden* 11 H6
Aledo, *U.S.A.* 112 E9
Alefa, *Ethiopia* 81 E4
Aleg, *Mauritania* 82 B2
Alegranza, *Canary Is.* 37 E6
Alegranza, I., *Canary Is.* 37 E6
Alegre, *Brazil* 127 A7
Alegrete, *Brazil* 127 B4
Aleisk, *Russia* 50 D9
Aleksandriya = Oleksandriya, *Kirovohrad, Ukraine* 47 H7
Aleksandriya = Oleksandriya, *Rivne, Ukraine* 47 G4
Aleksandriyskaya, *Russia* 49 J8
Aleksandrov, *Russia* 46 D10
Aleksandrov Gay, *Russia* 48 E9
Aleksandrovac, *Serbia, Yug.* 40 C5
Aleksandrovac, *Serbia, Yug.* 40 B5
Aleksandrovka = Oleksandrovka, *Ukraine* 47 H7
Aleksandrovo, *Bulgaria* 41 C8
Aleksandrovsk-Sakhalinskiy, *Russia* 51 D15
Aleksandrów Kujawski, *Poland* 45 F5
Aleksandrów Łódźki, *Poland* 45 G6
Alekseyevka, *Samara, Russia* 48 D10
Alekseyevka, *Voronezh, Russia* 47 G10
Aleksin, *Russia* 46 E9
Aleksinac, *Serbia, Yug.* 40 C5
Além Paraíba, *Brazil* 127 A7
Alemania, *Argentina* 126 B2
Alemania, *Chile* 126 B2
Alençon, *France* 18 D7
Alenquer, *Brazil* 125 D8
Alenuihaha Channel, *U.S.A.* 106 H17
Alépé, *Ivory C.* 82 D4
Aleppo = Ḥalab, *Syria* 70 B3
Aléria, *France* 21 F13
Alès, *France* 21 D8
Aleşd, *Romania* 42 C7
Alessándria, *Italy* 28 D5
Ålestrup, *Denmark* 11 H3
Ålesund, *Norway* 9 E12
Alet-les-Bains, *France* 20 F6
Aletschhorn, *Switz.* 25 J4
Aleutian Is., *Pac. Oc.* 100 C2
Aleutian Trench, *Pac. Oc.* 96 C10

Alexander, *U.S.A.* 112 B3
Alexander, Mt., *Australia* 93 E3
Alexander Arch., *U.S.A.* 100 C6
Alexander Bay, *S. Africa* 88 D2
Alexander City, *U.S.A.* 109 J3
Alexander I., *Antarctica* 5 C17
Alexandra, *Australia* 95 F4
Alexandra, *N.Z.* 91 L2
Alexandra Falls, *Canada* 104 A5
Alexandria = El Iskandarîya, *Egypt* 80 H7
Alexandria, *B.C., Canada* 104 C4
Alexandria, *Ont., Canada* 102 C5
Alexandria, *Romania* 43 G10
Alexandria, *S. Africa* 88 E4
Alexandria, *U.K.* 14 F4
Alexandria, *La., U.S.A.* 113 K8
Alexandria, *Minn., U.S.A.* 112 C7
Alexandria, *S. Dak., U.S.A.* 112 D6
Alexandria, *Va., U.S.A.* 108 F7
Alexandria Bay, *U.S.A.* 111 B9
Alexandrina, L., *Australia* 95 F2
Alexandroúpolis, *Greece* 41 F9
Alexis →, *Canada* 103 B8
Alexis Creek, *Canada* 104 C4
Alfabia, *Spain* 37 B9
Alfambra, *Spain* 32 E3
Alfândega da Fé, *Portugal* 34 D4
Alfaro, *Spain* 32 C3
Alfatar, *Bulgaria* 41 C11
Alfaz del Pi, *Spain* 33 G4
Alfeld, *Germany* 24 D5
Alfenas, *Brazil* 127 A6
Alfiós →, *Greece* 38 D3
Alföld, *Hungary* 42 D5
Alfonsine, *Italy* 29 D9
Alford, *Aberds., U.K.* 14 D6
Alford, *Lincs., U.K.* 12 D8
Alfred, *Maine, U.S.A.* 111 C14
Alfred, *N.Y., U.S.A.* 110 D7
Alfreton, *U.K.* 12 D6
Alfta, *Sweden* 10 C10
Alga, *Kazakstan* 50 E6
Algaida, *Spain* 37 B9
Algar, *Spain* 35 J5
Ålgård, *Norway* 9 G11
Algarinejo, *Spain* 35 H6
Algarve, *Portugal* 35 J2
Algeciras, *Spain* 35 J5
Algemesí, *Spain* 33 F4
Alger, *Algeria* 78 A6
Algeria ■, *Africa* 78 C6
Alghero, *Italy* 30 B1
Älghult, *Sweden* 11 G9
Algiers = Alger, *Algeria* 78 A6
Algoa B., *S. Africa* 88 E4
Algodonales, *Spain* 35 J5
Algodor →, *Spain* 34 F7
Algoma, *U.S.A.* 108 C2
Algona, *U.S.A.* 112 D7
Algonac, *U.S.A.* 110 D2
Algonquin Prov. Park, *Canada* 102 C4
Algorta, *Uruguay* 128 C5
Alhama de Almería, *Spain* 35 J8
Alhama de Aragón, *Spain* 32 D3
Alhama de Granada, *Spain* 35 H7
Alhama de Murcia, *Spain* 33 H3
Alhambra, *U.S.A.* 117 L8
Alhaurín el Grande, *Spain* 35 J6
Alhucemas = Al Hoceïma, *Morocco* 78 A5
'Alī al Gharbī, *Iraq* 70 C5
'Alī ash Sharqī, *Iraq* 70 C5
Äli Bayramlı, *Azerbaijan* 49 L9
'Alī Khēl, *Afghan.* 68 C3
Ali Sahīh, *Djibouti* 81 E5
Alī Shāh, *Iran* 70 B5
Ália, *Italy* 30 E6
'Alīābād, *Khorāsān, Iran* 71 C8
'Alīābād, *Kordestān, Iran* 70 C5
'Alīābād, *Yazd, Iran* 71 D7
Aliaga, *Spain* 32 E4
Aliağa, *Turkey* 39 C8
Aliákmon →, *Greece* 40 F6
Alibo, *Ethiopia* 81 F4
Alibori →, *Benin* 83 C5
Alibunar, *Serbia, Yug.* 42 E5
Alicante, *Spain* 33 G4
Alicante □, *Spain* 33 G4
Alice, *S. Africa* 88 E4
Alice, *U.S.A.* 113 M5
Alice →, *Queens., Australia* 94 C3
Alice →, *Queens., Australia* 94 B3
Alice, Punta, *Italy* 31 C10
Alice Arm, *Canada* 104 B3
Alice Springs, *Australia* 94 C1
Alicedale, *S. Africa* 88 E4
Aliceville, *U.S.A.* 109 J1
Alicudi, *Italy* 31 D7
Aliganj, *India* 69 F8
Aligarh, *Raj., India* 68 G7
Aligarh, *Ut. P., India* 68 F8
Alīgūdarz, *Iran* 71 C6
Alijó, *Portugal* 34 D3
Alimnía, *Greece* 36 C9
Alingsås, *Sweden* 11 G6
Alipur, *Pakistan* 68 E4
Alipur Duar, *India* 67 F16
Aliquippa, *U.S.A.* 110 F4
Alishan, *Taiwan* 59 F13
Aliste →, *Spain* 34 D5
Alitus = Alytus, *Lithuania* 9 J21
Alivérion, *Greece* 38 C6
Aliwal North, *S. Africa* 88 E4
Alix, *Canada* 104 C6
Aljezur, *Portugal* 35 H2
Aljustrel, *Portugal* 35 H2
Alkamari, *Niger* 83 C7
Alkmaar, *Neths.* 17 B4
All American Canal, *U.S.A.* 115 K6
Allada, *Benin* 83 D5
Allagash →, *U.S.A.* 109 B11
Allah Dad, *Pakistan* 68 G2
Allahabad, *India* 69 G9
Allan, *Canada* 105 C7
Allanche, *France* 20 C6
Allanmyo, *Burma* 67 K19
Allanridge, *S. Africa* 88 D4
Allaqi, Wadi →, *Egypt* 80 C3
Allariz, *Spain* 34 C3
Allassac, *France* 20 C5
Ålleberg, *Sweden* 11 F7
Allegany, *U.S.A.* 110 D6
Allegheny →, *U.S.A.* 110 F5
Allegheny Mts., *U.S.A.* 108 G6
Allegheny Reservoir, *U.S.A.* 110 E6
Allègre, *France* 20 C7
Allen, Bog of, *Ireland* 15 C5
Allen, L., *Ireland* 15 B3
Allendale, *U.S.A.* 109 J5
Allende, *Mexico* 118 B4
Allentown, *U.S.A.* 111 F9
Allentsteig, *Austria* 26 C8
Alleppey, *India* 66 Q10
Allepuz, *Spain* 32 E4
Aller →, *Germany* 24 C5
Alliance, *Nebr., U.S.A.* 112 D3
Alliance, *Ohio, U.S.A.* 110 F3
Allier □, *France* 19 F9
Allier →, *France* 19 F10
Alliford Bay, *Canada* 104 C2
Allinge, *Denmark* 11 J8
Alliston, *Canada* 102 D4
Alloa, *U.K.* 14 E5
Allones, *France* 18 D8
Allora, *Australia* 95 D5
Allos, *France* 21 D10
Alluitsup Paa, *Greenland* 4 C5
Alma, *Canada* 103 C5
Alma, *Ga., U.S.A.* 109 K4
Alma, *Kans., U.S.A.* 112 F6
Alma, *Mich., U.S.A.* 108 D3
Alma, *Nebr., U.S.A.* 112 E5
Alma Ata = Almaty, *Kazakstan* 50 E8
Almacelles, *Spain* 32 D5
Almada, *Portugal* 35 G1
Almaden, *Australia* 94 B3
Almadén, *Spain* 35 G6
Almanor, L., *U.S.A.* 114 F3
Almansa, *Spain* 33 G3
Almanza, *Spain* 34 C5
Almanzor, Pico, *Spain* 34 E5
Almanzora →, *Spain* 33 H3
Almaş, Munţii, *Romania* 42 F7
Almassora, *Spain* 32 F4
Almaty, *Kazakstan* 50 E8
Almazán, *Spain* 32 D2
Almeirim, *Brazil* 125 D8
Almeirim, *Portugal* 35 F2
Almelo, *Neths.* 17 B6
Almenar de Soria, *Spain* 32 D2
Almenara, *Spain* 32 F4
Almenara, Sierra de la, *Spain* 33 H3
Almendra, Embalse de, *Spain* 34 D4
Almendralejo, *Spain* 35 G4
Almere-Stad, *Neths.* 17 B5
Almería, *Spain* 35 J8
Almería □, *Spain* 33 H2
Almería, G. de, *Spain* 33 J2
Almetyevsk, *Russia* 48 C11
Älmhult, *Sweden* 11 H8
Almirante, *Panama* 120 E3
Almiropótamos, *Greece* 38 C6
Almirós, *Greece* 38 B4
Almiroú, Kólpos, *Greece* 36 D6
Almodôvar, *Portugal* 35 H2
Almodóvar del Campo, *Spain* 35 G6
Almodóvar del Río, *Spain* 35 H5
Almond, *U.S.A.* 110 D7
Almont, *U.S.A.* 110 D1
Almonte, *Canada* 111 A8
Almonte, *Spain* 35 H4
Almora, *India* 69 E8
Almoradí, *Spain* 33 G4
Almorox, *Spain* 34 E6
Almoustarat, *Mali* 83 B5
Älmsta, *Sweden* 10 E12
Almudévar, *Spain* 32 C4
Almuñécar, *Spain* 35 J7
Almunge, *Sweden* 10 E12
Almuradiel, *Spain* 35 G7
Alness, *U.K.* 14 D4
Alnmouth, *U.K.* 12 B6
Alnwick, *U.K.* 12 B6
Aloi, *Uganda* 86 B3
Alon, *Burma* 67 H19
Alor, *Indonesia* 63 F6
Alor Setar, *Malaysia* 65 J3
Álora, *Spain* 35 J6
Alosno, *Spain* 35 H3
Alot, *India* 68 H6
Aloysius, Mt., *Australia* 93 E4
Alpaugh, *U.S.A.* 116 K7
Alpedrinha, *Portugal* 34 E3
Alpena, *U.S.A.* 108 C4
Alpes-de-Haute-Provence □, *France* 21 D10
Alpes-Maritimes □, *France* 21 E11
Alpha, *Australia* 94 C4
Alphen aan den Rijn, *Neths.* 17 B4
Alpiarça, *Portugal* 35 F2
Alpine, *Ariz., U.S.A.* 115 K9
Alpine, *Calif., U.S.A.* 117 N10
Alpine, *Tex., U.S.A.* 113 K3
Alps, *Europe* 6 F7
Alpu, *Turkey* 72 C4
Alqueta, Barragem do, *Portugal* 35 G3
Alrø, *Denmark* 11 J4
Als, *Denmark* 11 K3
Alsace, *France* 19 D14
Alsask, *Canada* 105 C7
Alsasua, *Spain* 32 C2
Alsek →, *U.S.A.* 104 B1
Alsfeld, *Germany* 24 E5
Alsten, *Norway* 8 D15
Alstermo, *Sweden* 11 H9
Alston, *U.K.* 12 C5
Alta, *Norway* 8 B20
Alta, Sierra, *Spain* 32 E3
Alta Gracia, *Argentina* 126 C3
Alta Sierra, *U.S.A.* 117 K8
Altaelva →, *Norway* 8 B20
Altafjorden, *Norway* 8 A20
Altai = Aerhtai Shan, *Mongolia* 60 B4
Altamaha →, *U.S.A.* 109 K5
Altamira, *Brazil* 125 D8
Altamira, *Chile* 126 B2
Altamira, *Mexico* 119 C5
Altamira, Cuevas de, *Spain* 34 B6
Altamont, *U.S.A.* 111 D10
Altamura, *Italy* 31 B9
Altanbulag, *Mongolia* 60 A5
Altar, *Mexico* 118 A2
Altar, Desierto de, *Mexico* 118 B2
Altata, *Mexico* 118 C3
Altavista, *U.S.A.* 108 G6
Altay, *China* 60 B3
Altdorf, *Switz.* 25 J4
Alte Mellum, *Germany* 24 B4
Altea, *Spain* 33 G4
Altenberg, *Germany* 24 E9
Altenbruch, *Germany* 24 B4
Altenburg, *Germany* 24 E8
Altenkirchen, *Mecklenburg-Vorpommern, Germany* 24 A9
Altenkirchen, *Rhld-Pfz., Germany* 24 E3
Altenmarkt, *Austria* 26 D7
Alter do Chão, *Portugal* 35 F3
Altınoluk, *Turkey* 39 B8
Altınova, *Turkey* 39 B8
Altıntaş, *Turkey* 39 B12
Altınyaka, *Turkey* 39 E12
Altınyayla, *Turkey* 39 D11
Altiplano = Bolivian Plateau, *S. Amer.* 122 E4
Altkirch, *France* 19 E14
Altmark, *Germany* 24 C7
Altmühl →, *Germany* 25 G7
Altmunster, *Austria* 26 D6
Alto Adige = Trentino-Alto Adige □, *Italy* 29 B8
Alto Araguaia, *Brazil* 125 G8
Alto Cuchumatanes = Cuchumatanes, Sierra de los, *Guatemala* 120 C1
Alto del Carmen, *Chile* 126 B1
Alto del Inca, *Chile* 126 A2
Alto Ligonha, *Mozam.* 87 F4
Alto Molocue, *Mozam.* 87 F4
Alto Paraguay □, *Paraguay* 126 A4
Alto Paraná □, *Paraguay* 127 B5
Alton, *Canada* 110 C4
Alton, *U.K.* 13 F7
Alton, *Ill., U.S.A.* 112 F9
Alton, *N.H., U.S.A.* 111 C13
Altoona, *U.S.A.* 110 F6
Altötting, *Germany* 25 G8
Altstätten, *Switz.* 25 H5
Altūn Kūprī, *Iraq* 70 C5
Altun Shan, *China* 60 C3
Alturas, *U.S.A.* 114 F3
Altus, *U.S.A.* 113 H5
Alubijid, *Phil.* 61 G6
Alucra, *Turkey* 73 B8
Aluk, *Sudan* 81 F2
Alūksne, *Latvia* 9 H22
Alunda, *Sweden* 10 D12
Alunite, *U.S.A.* 117 K12
Aluoro →, *Ethiopia* 81 F3
Alupka, *Ukraine* 47 K8
Alushta, *Ukraine* 47 K8
Alusi, *Indonesia* 63 F8
Alustante, *Spain* 32 E3
Alva, *U.S.A.* 113 G5
Alvaiázere, *Portugal* 34 F2
Alvängen, *Sweden* 11 G6
Alvarado, *Mexico* 119 D5
Alvarado, *U.S.A.* 113 J6
Alvaro Obregón, Presa, *Mexico* 118 B3
Älvdalen, *Sweden* 10 C8
Alvear, *Argentina* 126 B4
Alverca, *Portugal* 35 G1
Alvesta, *Sweden* 11 H8
Alvin, *U.S.A.* 113 L7
Alvinston, *Canada* 110 D3
Alvito, *Portugal* 35 G3
Älvkarleby, *Sweden* 10 D11
Alvord Desert, *U.S.A.* 114 E4
Älvros, *Sweden* 10 B8
Älvsborgs län □, *Sweden* 11 F6
Älvsbyn, *Sweden* 8 D19
Alwar, *India* 68 F7
Alxa Zuoqi, *China* 56 E3
Alyangula, *Australia* 94 A2
Alyata = Älät, *Azerbaijan* 49 L9
Alyth, *U.K.* 14 E5
Alytus, *Lithuania* 9 J21
Alzada, *U.S.A.* 112 C2
Alzey, *Germany* 25 F4
Alzira, *Spain* 33 F4
Am-Timan, *Chad* 79 F10
Amadeus, L., *Australia* 93 D5
Amadi, *Dem. Rep. of the Congo* 86 B2
Amâdi, *Sudan* 81 F3
Amadjuak L., *Canada* 101 B12
Amadora, *Portugal* 35 G1
Amagansett, *U.S.A.* 111 F12
Amagasaki, *Japan* 55 G7
Amager, *Denmark* 11 J6
Amagunze, *Nigeria* 83 D6
Amahai, *Indonesia* 63 E7
Amakusa-Shotō, *Japan* 55 H5
Åmål, *Sweden* 10 E6
Amalfi, *Italy* 31 B7
Amaliás, *Greece* 38 D3
Amalner, *India* 66 J9
Amamapare, *Indonesia* 63 E9
Amambaí, *Brazil* 127 A4
Amambaí →, *Brazil* 127 A5
Amambay □, *Paraguay* 127 A4
Amambay, Cordillera de, *S. Amer.* 127 A4
Amami-Guntō, *Japan* 55 L4
Amami-Ō-Shima, *Japan* 55 L4
Amaná, L., *Brazil* 124 D6
Amanat →, *India* 69 G11
Amanda Park, *U.S.A.* 116 C3
Amangeldy, *Kazakstan* 50 D7
Amantea, *Italy* 31 C9
Amapá, *Brazil* 125 C8
Amapá □, *Brazil* 125 C8
Amara, *Sudan* 81 E3
Amarante, *Brazil* 125 E10
Amarante, *Portugal* 34 D2
Amaranth, *Canada* 105 C9
Amareleja, *Portugal* 35 G3
Amargosa →, *U.S.A.* 117 J10
Amargosa Range, *U.S.A.* 117 J10
Amári, *Greece* 36 D6
Amarillo, *U.S.A.* 113 H4
Amarkantak, *India* 69 H9
Amârna, Tell el', *Sudan* 80 B3
Amaro, Mte., *Italy* 29 F11
Amarpur, *India* 69 G12
Amarti, *Eritrea* 81 E5
Amarwara, *India* 69 H8
Amasra, *Turkey* 72 B5
Amassama, *Nigeria* 83 D6
Amasya, *Turkey* 72 B6
Amata, *Australia* 93 E5
Amatikulu, *S. Africa* 89 D5
Amatitlán, *Guatemala* 120 D1
Amatrice, *Italy* 29 F10
Amay, *Belgium* 17 D5
Amazon = Amazonas →, *S. Amer.* 122 D5
Amazonas □, *Brazil* 124 E6
Amazonas →, *S. Amer.* 122 D5
Amba Ferit, *Ethiopia* 81 E4
Ambah, *India* 68 F8
Ambahakily, *Madag.* 89 C7
Ambahita, *Madag.* 89 C8
Ambala, *India* 68 D7
Ambalavao, *Madag.* 89 C8
Ambanja, *Madag.* 89 A8
Ambararata, *Madag.* 89 B8
Ambarchik, *Russia* 51 C17
Ambarijeby, *Madag.* 89 A8
Ambaro, Helodranon', *Madag.* 89 A8
Ambato, *Ecuador* 124 D3
Ambato, *Madag.* 89 A8
Ambato, Sierra de, *Argentina* 126 B2
Ambato Boeny, *Madag.* 89 B8
Ambatofinandrahana, *Madag.* 89 C8
Ambatolampy, *Madag.* 89 B8
Ambatomainty, *Madag.* 89 B8
Ambatomanoina, *Madag.* 89 B8
Ambatondrazaka, *Madag.* 89 B8
Ambatosoratra, *Madag.* 89 B8
Ambelón, *Greece* 38 B4
Ambenja, *Madag.* 89 B8
Amberg, *Germany* 25 F7
Ambergris Cay, *Belize* 119 D7
Ambérieu-en-Bugey, *France* 21 C9
Amberley, *N.Z.* 91 K4
Ambert, *France* 20 C7
Ambidédi, *Mali* 82 C2
Ambikapur, *India* 69 H10
Ambikol, *Sudan* 80 C3
Ambilobé, *Madag.* 89 A8
Ambinanindrano, *Madag.* 89 C8
Ambinanitelo, *Madag.* 89 B8
Ambinda, *Madag.* 89 B8
Amble, *U.K.* 12 B6
Ambleside, *U.K.* 12 C5
Ambo, *Peru* 124 F3
Amboahangy, *Madag.* 89 C8
Ambodifototra, *Madag.* 89 B8
Ambodilazana, *Madag.* 89 B8
Ambodiriana, *Madag.* 89 B8
Ambohidratrimo, *Madag.* 89 B8
Ambohidray, *Madag.* 89 B8
Ambohimahamasina, *Madag.* 89 C8
Ambohimahasoa, *Madag.* 89 C8
Ambohimanga, *Madag.* 89 C8
Ambohimitombo, *Madag.* 89 C8
Ambohitra, *Madag.* 89 A8
Amboise, *France* 18 E8
Ambon, *Indonesia* 63 E7
Ambondro, *Madag.* 89 D8
Amboseli, L., *Kenya* 86 C4
Ambositra, *Madag.* 89 C8
Ambovombe, *Madag.* 89 D8
Amboy, *U.S.A.* 117 L11
Amboyna Cay, *S. China Sea* 62 C4
Ambridge, *U.S.A.* 110 F4
Ambriz, *Angola* 84 F2
Amchitka I., *U.S.A.* 100 C1
Amderma, *Russia* 50 C7
Amdhi, *India* 69 H9
Ameca, *Mexico* 118 C4
Ameca →, *Mexico* 118 C3
Amecameca, *Mexico* 119 D5
Ameland, *Neths.* 17 A5
Amélia, *Italy* 29 F9
Amendolara, *Italy* 31 C9
Amenia, *U.S.A.* 111 E11
American Falls, *U.S.A.* 114 E7
American Falls Reservoir, *U.S.A.* 114 E7
American Fork, *U.S.A.* 114 F8
American Highland, *Antarctica* 5 D6
American Samoa ■, *Pac. Oc.* 91 B13
Americana, *Brazil* 127 A6
Americus, *U.S.A.* 109 K3
Amersfoort, *Neths.* 17 B5
Amersfoort, *S. Africa* 89 D4
Amery Ice Shelf, *Antarctica* 5 C6
Ames, *Spain* 34 C2
Ames, *U.S.A.* 112 E8
Amesbury, *U.S.A.* 111 D14
Amet, *India* 68 G5
Amfíklia, *Greece* 38 C4
Amfilokhía, *Greece* 38 C3
Amfípolis, *Greece* 40 F7
Ámfissa, *Greece* 38 C4
Amga, *Russia* 51 C14
Amga →, *Russia* 51 C14
Amgu, *Russia* 51 E14
Amgun →, *Russia* 51 D14
Amherst, *Burma* 67 L20
Amherst, *Canada* 103 C7
Amherst, *Mass., U.S.A.* 111 D12
Amherst, *N.Y., U.S.A.* 110 D6
Amherst, *Ohio, U.S.A.* 110 E2
Amherst I., *Canada* 111 B8
Amherstburg, *Canada* 102 D3
Amiata, Mte., *Italy* 29 F8
Amidon, *U.S.A.* 112 B3
Amiens, *France* 19 C9
Amindaion, *Greece* 40 F5
Åminne, *Sweden* 11 G7
Amino, *Ethiopia* 81 G5
Aminuis, *Namibia* 88 C2
Amīrābād, *Iran* 70 C5
Amirante Is., *Seychelles* 52 K9
Amisk L., *Canada* 105 C8
Amistad, Presa de la, *Mexico* 118 B4
Amite, *U.S.A.* 113 K9
Amla, *India* 68 J8
Amlia I., *U.S.A.* 100 C2
Amlwch, *U.K.* 12 D3
Amm Adam, *Sudan* 81 D4
'Ammān, *Jordan* 75 D4
'Ammān □, *Jordan* 75 D5
Ammanford, *U.K.* 13 F4
Ammassalik = Tasiilaq, *Greenland* 4 C6
Ammerån →, *Sweden* 10 A10
Ammersee, *Germany* 25 G7
Ammon, *U.S.A.* 114 E8
Amnat Charoen, *Thailand* 64 E5
Amnura, *Bangla.* 69 G13
Amo Jiang →, *China* 58 F3
Āmol, *Iran* 71 B7
Amorgós, *Greece* 39 E7
Amory, *U.S.A.* 109 J1
Amos, *Canada* 102 C4
Åmot, *Norway* 9 G13
Åmotfors, *Sweden* 10 E6
Amoy = Xiamen, *China* 59 E12
Ampanavoana, *Madag.* 89 B9
Ampang, *Malaysia* 65 L3
Ampangalana, Lakandranon', *Madag.* 89 C8
Ampanihy, *Madag.* 89 C7
Amparafaravola, *Madag.* 89 B8
Ampasinambo, *Madag.* 89 C8
Ampasindava, Helodranon', *Madag.* 89 A8
Ampasindava, Saikanosy, *Madag.* 89 A8
Ampenan, *Indonesia* 62 F5
Amper, *Nigeria* 83 D6
Amper →, *Germany* 25 G7
Ampezzo, *Italy* 29 B9
Ampitsikinana, *Réunion* 89 A8
Ampombiantambo, *Madag.* 89 A8
Amposta, *Spain* 32 E5
Ampotaka, *Madag.* 89 D7
Ampoza, *Madag.* 89 C7
Amqui, *Canada* 103 C6
Amravati, *India* 66 J10
Amreli, *India* 68 J4
Amritsar, *India* 68 D6
Amroha, *India* 69 E8
Amrum, *Germany* 24 A4
Amsterdam, *Neths.* 17 B4
Amsterdam, *U.S.A.* 111 D10
Amsterdam, I. = Nouvelle-Amsterdam, I., *Ind. Oc.* 3 F13
Amstetten, *Austria* 26 C7
Amudarya →, *Uzbekistan* 50 E6
Amundsen Gulf, *Canada* 100 A7
Amundsen Sea, *Antarctica* 5 D15
Amungen, *Sweden* 10 C9
Amuntai, *Indonesia* 62 E5
Amur →, *Russia* 51 D15
Amur, W. →, *Sudan* 80 D3
Amurang, *Indonesia* 63 D6
Amuri Pass, *N.Z.* 91 K4
Amurrio, *Spain* 32 B1
Amursk, *Russia* 51 D14
Amusco, *Spain* 34 C6
Amvrakikós Kólpos, *Greece* 38 C2
Amvrosiyivka, *Ukraine* 47 J10
Amyderya = Amudarya →, *Uzbekistan* 50 E6

An Bien, *Vietnam* 65 H5
An Hoa, *Vietnam* 64 E7
An Nabatīyah at Tahta, *Lebanon* 75 B4
An Nabk, *Si. Arabia* 70 D3
An Nabk, *Syria* 75 A5
An Nabk Abū Qaşr, *Si. Arabia* 70 D3
An Nafūd, *Si. Arabia* 70 D4
An Najaf, *Iraq* 70 C5
An Nāşirīyah, *Iraq* 70 D5
An Nhon, *Vietnam* 64 F7
An Nîl □, *Sudan* 80 D3
An Nîl el Abyad □, *Sudan* 81 E3
An Nîl el Azraq □, *Sudan* 81 E3
An Nu'ayrīyah, *Si. Arabia* 71 E6
An Nu'mānīyah, *Iraq* 73 F11
An Nuwayb'ī, W. →, *Si. Arabia* 75 F3
An Thoi, Dao, *Vietnam* 65 H4
An Uaimh, *Ireland* 15 C5
Anabar →, *Russia* 51 B12
'Anabtā, *West Bank* 75 C4
Anaconda, *U.S.A.* 114 C7
Anacortes, *U.S.A.* 116 B4
Anacuao, Mt., *Phil.* 61 C4
Anadarko, *U.S.A.* 113 H5
Anadia, *Portugal* 34 E2
Anadolu, *Turkey* 72 C5
Anadyr, *Russia* 51 C18
Anadyr →, *Russia* 51 C18
Anadyrskiy Zaliv, *Russia* 51 C19
Anáfi, *Greece* 39 E7
Anafópoulo, *Greece* 39 E7
Anaga, Pta. de, *Canary Is.* 37 F3
Anagni, *Italy* 29 G10
'Ānah, *Iraq* 70 C4
Anaheim, *U.S.A.* 117 M9
Anahim Lake, *Canada* 104 C3
Anáhuac, *Mexico* 118 B4
Anakapalle, *India* 67 L13
Anakie, *Australia* 94 C4
Anaklia, *Georgia* 49 J5
Analalava, *Madag.* 89 A8
Analavoka, *Madag.* 89 C8
Análipsis, *Greece* 36 A3
Anambar →, *Pakistan* 68 D3
Anambas, Kepulauan, *Indonesia* 65 L6
Anambas Is. = Anambas, Kepulauan, *Indonesia* 65 L6
Anambra □, *Nigeria* 83 D6
Anamosa, *U.S.A.* 112 D9
Anamur, *Turkey* 70 B2
Anamur Burnu, *Turkey* 72 D5
Anan, *Japan* 55 H7
Anand, *India* 68 H5
Anánes, *Greece* 38 E6
Anantnag, *India* 69 C6
Ananyiv, *Ukraine* 47 J5
Anapa, *Russia* 47 K9
Anapodháris →, *Greece* 36 E7
Anápolis, *Brazil* 125 G9
Anapu →, *Brazil* 125 D8
Anār, *Iran* 71 D7
Anārak, *Iran* 71 C7
Anarisfjällen, *Sweden* 10 A7
Anas →, *India* 68 H5
Anatolia = Anadolu, *Turkey* 72 C5
Anatsogno, *Madag.* 89 C7
Añatuya, *Argentina* 126 B3
Anaunethad L., *Canada* 105 A8
Anbyŏn, *N. Korea* 57 E14
Ancares, Sierra de, *Spain* 34 C4
Ancaster, *Canada* 110 C5
Ancenis, *France* 18 E5
Anchor Bay, *U.S.A.* 116 G3
Anchorage, *U.S.A.* 100 B5
Anci, *China* 56 E9
Ancohuma, Nevada, *Bolivia* 122 E4
Ancón, *Peru* 124 F3
Ancona, *Italy* 29 E10
Ancud, *Chile* 128 E2
Ancud, G. de, *Chile* 128 E2
Ancy-le-Franc, *France* 19 E11
Andacollo, *Argentina* 126 D1
Andacollo, *Chile* 126 C1
Andaingo, *Madag.* 89 B8
Andalgalá, *Argentina* 126 B2
Åndalsnes, *Norway* 9 E12
Andalucía □, *Spain* 35 H6
Andalusia = Andalucía □, *Spain* 35 H6
Andalusia, *U.S.A.* 109 K2
Andaman Is., *Ind. Oc.* 52 H13
Andaman Sea, *Ind. Oc.* 62 B1
Andamooka Opal Fields, *Australia* 95 E2
Andapa, *Madag.* 89 A8
Andara, *Namibia* 88 B3
Andelot-Blancheville, *France* 19 D12
Andenes, *Norway* 8 B17
Andenne, *Belgium* 17 D5
Andéranboukane, *Mali* 83 B5
Andermatt, *Switz.* 25 J4
Andernach, *Germany* 24 E3
Andernos-les-Bains, *France* 20 D2
Anderslöv, *Sweden* 11 J7
Anderson, *Alaska, U.S.A.* 100 B5
Anderson, *Calif., U.S.A.* 114 F2
Anderson, *Ind., U.S.A.* 108 E3
Anderson, *Mo., U.S.A.* 113 G7
Anderson, *S.C., U.S.A.* 109 H4
Anderson →, *Canada* 100 B7
Anderstorp, *Sweden* 11 G7
Andes, *U.S.A.* 111 D10
Andes, Cord. de los, *S. Amer.* 122 F4
Andfjorden, *Norway* 8 B17
Andhra Pradesh □, *India* 66 L11
Andijon, *Uzbekistan* 50 E8
Andikíthira, *Greece* 38 F5
Andilamena, *Madag.* 89 B8
Andīmeshk, *Iran* 71 C6
Andímilos, *Greece* 38 E6
Andíparos, *Greece* 39 D7
Andípaxoi, *Greece* 38 B2
Andípsara, *Greece* 39 C7
Andírrion, *Greece* 38 C3
Andizhan = Andijon, *Uzbekistan* 50 E8
Andoain, *Spain* 32 B2
Andoany, *Madag.* 89 A8
Andong, *S. Korea* 57 F15
Andongwei, *China* 57 G10
Andoom, *Australia* 94 A3
Andorra, *Spain* 32 E4
Andorra ■, *Europe* 20 F5
Andorra La Vella, *Andorra* 20 F5
Andover, *U.K.* 13 F6
Andover, *Maine, U.S.A.* 111 B14
Andover, *Mass., U.S.A.* 111 D13
Andover, *N.J., U.S.A.* 111 F10
Andover, *N.Y., U.S.A.* 110 D7
Andover, *Ohio, U.S.A.* 110 E4
Andøya, *Norway* 8 B16
Andradina, *Brazil* 125 H8
Andrahary, Mt., *Madag.* 89 A8
Andramasina, *Madag.* 89 B8
Andranopasy, *Madag.* 89 C7
Andranovory, *Madag.* 89 C7
Andratx, *Spain* 37 B9
Andreanof Is., *U.S.A.* 100 C2
Andreapol, *Russia* 46 D7
Andrews, *S.C., U.S.A.* 109 J6
Andrews, *Tex., U.S.A.* 113 J3
Andreyevka, *Russia* 48 D10
Ándria, *Italy* 31 A9
Andriamena, *Madag.* 89 B8
Andriandampy, *Madag.* 89 C8
Andriba, *Madag.* 89 B8
Andrijevica, *Montenegro, Yug.* 40 D3
Andrítsaina, *Greece* 38 D3
Androka, *Madag.* 89 C7
Andropov = Rybinsk, *Russia* 46 C10
Ándros, *Greece* 38 D6
Andros I., *Bahamas* 120 B4
Andros Town, *Bahamas* 120 B4
Androscoggin →, *U.S.A.* 111 C14
Andrychów, *Poland* 45 J6
Andselv, *Norway* 8 B18
Andújar, *Spain* 35 G6
Andulo, *Angola* 84 G3
Aneby, *Sweden* 11 G8
Anegada I., *Virgin Is.* 121 C7
Anegada Passage, *W. Indies* 121 C7
Anécho, *Togo* 83 D5
Anenni-Noi, *Moldova* 43 D14
Aneto, Pico de, *Spain* 32 C5
Anfu, *China* 59 D10
Ang Thong, *Thailand* 64 E3
Angamos, Punta, *Chile* 126 A1
Angara →, *Russia* 51 D10
Angara-Débou, *Benin* 83 C5
Angarab, *Ethiopia* 81 E4
Angarbaka, *Sudan* 81 F1
Angarsk, *Russia* 51 D11
Angas Hills, *Australia* 92 D4
Angaston, *Australia* 95 E2
Angaur I., *Pac. Oc.* 63 C8
Ånge, *Sweden* 10 B9
Ángel, Salto = Angel Falls, *Venezuela* 124 B6
Ángel de la Guarda, I., *Mexico* 118 B2
Angel Falls, *Venezuela* 124 B6
Angeles, *Phil.* 61 D4
Ängelholm, *Sweden* 11 H6
Angels Camp, *U.S.A.* 116 G6
Ängelsberg, *Sweden* 10 E10
Anger →, *Ethiopia* 81 F4
Angereb →, *Ethiopia* 81 E4
Ångermanälven →, *Sweden* 10 B11
Ångermanland, *Sweden* 8 E18
Angermünde, *Germany* 24 B9
Angers, *Canada* 111 A9
Angers, *France* 18 E6
Angerville, *France* 19 D9
Ångesån →, *Sweden* 8 C20
Angikuni L., *Canada* 105 A9
Angkor, *Cambodia* 64 F4
Anglès, *Spain* 32 D7
Anglesey, Isle of □, *U.K.* 12 D3
Anglet, *France* 20 E2
Angleton, *U.S.A.* 113 L7
Anglin →, *France* 20 B4
Anglisidhes, *Cyprus* 36 E12
Anglure, *France* 19 D10
Angmagssalik = Tasiilaq, *Greenland* 4 C6
Ango, *Dem. Rep. of the Congo* 86 B2
Angoche, *Mozam.* 87 F4
Angoche, I., *Mozam.* 87 F4
Angol, *Chile* 126 D1
Angola, *Ind., U.S.A.* 108 E3
Angola, *N.Y., U.S.A.* 110 D5
Angola ■, *Africa* 85 G3
Angoulême, *France* 20 C4
Angoumois, *France* 20 C4
Angra dos Reis, *Brazil* 127 A7
Angren, *Uzbekistan* 50 E8
Angtassom, *Cambodia* 65 G5
Angu, *Dem. Rep. of the Congo* 86 B1
Anguang, *China* 57 B12
Anguilla ■, *W. Indies* 121 C7
Anguo, *China* 56 E8
Angurugu, *Australia* 94 A2
Angus □, *U.K.* 14 E6
Angwa →, *Zimbabwe* 89 B5
Anhanduí →, *Brazil* 127 A5
Anholt, *Denmark* 11 H5
Anhua, *China* 59 C8
Anhui □, *China* 59 B11
Anhwei = Anhui □, *China* 59 B11
Anichab, *Namibia* 88 C1
Ánidhros, *Greece* 39 E7
Anié, *Togo* 83 D5
Animas →, *U.S.A.* 115 H9
Anina, *Romania* 42 E6
Aninoasa, *Romania* 43 F9
Anivorano, *Madag.* 89 B8
Anjalankoski, *Finland* 9 F22
Anjar, *India* 68 H4
Anji, *China* 59 B12
Anjidiv I., *India* 66 M9
Anjou, *France* 18 E6
Anjozorobe, *Madag.* 89 B8
Anju, *N. Korea* 57 E13
Anka, *Nigeria* 83 C6
Ankaboa, Tanjona, *Madag.* 89 C7
Ankang, *China* 56 H5
Ankara, *Turkey* 72 C5
Ankaramena, *Madag.* 89 C8
Ankaratra, *Madag.* 85 H9
Ankarsrum, *Sweden* 11 G10
Ankasakasa, *Madag.* 89 B7
Ankavandra, *Madag.* 89 B8
Ankazoabo, *Madag.* 89 C7
Ankazobe, *Madag.* 89 B8
Ankeny, *U.S.A.* 112 E8
Ankilimalinika, *Madag.* 89 C7
Ankilizato, *Madag.* 89 C8
Ankisabe, *Madag.* 89 B8
Anklam, *Germany* 24 B9
Ankober, *Ethiopia* 81 F4
Ankoro, *Dem. Rep. of the Congo* 86 D2
Ankororoka, *Madag.* 89 D8
Anlong, *China* 58 E5
Anlu, *China* 59 B9
Anmyŏn-do, *S. Korea* 57 F14
Ånn, *Sweden* 10 A6
Ann, C., *U.S.A.* 111 D14
Ann Arbor, *U.S.A.* 108 D4
Anna, *Russia* 48 E5
Anna, *U.S.A.* 113 G10
Annaba, *Algeria* 78 A7
Annaberg-Buchholz, *Germany* 24 E9
Annalee →, *Ireland* 15 B4
Annam, *Vietnam* 64 E7
Annamitique, Chaîne, *Asia* 64 D6
Annan, *U.K.* 14 G5
Annan →, *U.K.* 14 G5
Annapolis, *U.S.A.* 108 F7
Annapolis Royal, *Canada* 103 D6
Annapurna, *Nepal* 69 E10
Annean, L., *Australia* 93 E2
Anneberg, *Sweden* 11 G8
Annecy, *France* 21 C10
Annecy, Lac d', *France* 21 C10
Annemasse, *France* 19 F13
Annenskiy Most, *Russia* 46 B9
Anning, *China* 58 E4
Anniston, *U.S.A.* 109 J3
Annobón, *Atl. Oc.* 77 G4
Annonay, *France* 21 C8
Annot, *France* 21 E10
Annotto Bay, *Jamaica* 120 C4
Ånnsjön, *Sweden* 10 A6
Annville, *U.S.A.* 111 F8
Annweiler, *Germany* 25 F3
Áno Arkhánai, *Greece* 39 F7
Áno Porróia, *Greece* 40 E7
Áno Síros, *Greece* 38 D6
Áno Viánnos, *Greece* 36 D7
Anorotsangana, *Madag.* 89 A8
Anosibe, *Madag.* 89 B8
Anou Mellene, *Mali* 83 B5
Anoumaba, *Ivory C.* 82 D4
Anóyia, *Greece* 36 D6
Anping, *Hebei, China* 56 E8
Anping, *Liaoning, China* 57 D12
Anpu Gang, *China* 58 G7
Anqing, *China* 59 B11
Anqiu, *China* 57 F10
Anren, *China* 59 D9
Ansager, *Denmark* 11 J2
Ansai, *China* 56 F5
Ansbach, *Germany* 25 F6
Anseba →, *Eritrea* 81 D4
Ansfelden, *Austria* 26 C7
Anshan, *China* 57 D12
Anshun, *China* 58 D5
Ansião, *Portugal* 34 F2
Ansley, *U.S.A.* 112 E5
Ansó, *Spain* 32 C4
Ansoain, *Spain* 32 C3
Anson, *U.S.A.* 113 J5
Anson B., *Australia* 92 B5
Ansongo, *Mali* 83 B5
Ansonia, *U.S.A.* 111 E11
Anstruther, *U.K.* 14 E6
Ansudu, *Indonesia* 63 E9
Antabamba, *Peru* 124 F4
Antakya, *Turkey* 70 B3
Antalaha, *Madag.* 89 A9
Antalya, *Turkey* 72 D4
Antalya □, *Turkey* 39 E12
Antalya Körfezi, *Turkey* 72 D4
Antambohobe, *Madag.* 89 C8
Antanambao-Manampotsy, *Madag.* 89 B8
Antanambe, *Madag.* 89 B8
Antananarivo, *Madag.* 89 B8
Antananarivo □, *Madag.* 89 B8
Antanifotsy, *Madag.* 89 B8
Antanimbaribe, *Madag.* 89 C7
Antanimora, *Madag.* 89 C8
Antarctic Pen., *Antarctica* 5 C18
Antarctica 5 E3
Antelope, *Zimbabwe* 87 G2
Antequera, *Paraguay* 126 A4
Antequera, *Spain* 35 H6
Antero, Mt., *U.S.A.* 115 G10
Antevamena, *Madag.* 89 C7
Anthemoús, *Greece* 40 F7
Anthony, *Kans., U.S.A.* 113 G5
Anthony, *N. Mex., U.S.A.* 115 K10
Anti Atlas, *Morocco* 78 C4
Anti-Lebanon = Ash Sharqi, Al Jabal, *Lebanon* 75 B5
Antibes, *France* 21 E11
Antibes, C. d', *France* 21 E11
Anticosti, Î. d', *Canada* 103 C7
Antifer, C. d', *France* 18 C7
Antigo, *U.S.A.* 112 C10
Antigonish, *Canada* 103 C7
Antigua, *Canary Is.* 37 F5
Antigua, *W. Indies* 121 C7
Antigua & Barbuda ■, *W. Indies* 121 C7
Antigua Guatemala, *Guatemala* 120 D1
Antilla, *Cuba* 120 B4
Antilles = West Indies, *Cent. Amer.* 121 D7
Antioch, *U.S.A.* 116 G5
Antioche, Pertuis d', *France* 20 B2
Antioquia, *Colombia* 124 B3
Antipodes Is., *Pac. Oc.* 96 M9
Antlers, *U.S.A.* 113 H7
Antoetra, *Madag.* 89 C8
Antofagasta, *Chile* 126 A1
Antofagasta □, *Chile* 126 A2
Antofagasta de la Sierra, *Argentina* 126 B2
Antofalla, *Argentina* 126 B2
Antofalla, Salar de, *Argentina* 126 B2
Anton, *U.S.A.* 113 J3
Antongila, Helodrano, *Madag.* 89 B8
Antonibé, *Madag.* 89 B8
Antonibé, Presqu'île d', *Madag.* 89 A8
Antonina, *Brazil* 127 B6
Antrain, *France* 18 D5
Antrim, *U.K.* 15 B5
Antrim, *U.S.A.* 110 F3
Antrim □, *U.K.* 15 B5
Antrim, Mts. of, *U.K.* 15 A5
Antrim Plateau, *Australia* 92 C4
Antrodoco, *Italy* 29 F10
Antropovo, *Russia* 48 A6
Antsakabary, *Madag.* 89 B8
Antsalova, *Madag.* 89 B7
Antsenavolo, *Madag.* 89 C8
Antsiafabositra, *Madag.* 89 B8
Antsirabe, *Antananarivo, Madag.* 89 B8
Antsirabe, *Antsiranana, Madag.* 89 A8
Antsirabe, *Mahajanga, Madag.* 89 B8
Antsiranana, *Madag.* 89 A8
Antsiranana □, *Madag.* 89 A8
Antsohihy, *Madag.* 89 A8
Antsohimbondrona Seranana, *Madag.* 89 A8
Antu, *China* 57 C15
Antwerp = Antwerpen, *Belgium* 17 C4
Antwerp, *U.S.A.* 111 B9
Antwerpen, *Belgium* 17 C4
Antwerpen □, *Belgium* 17 C4
Anupgarh, *India* 68 E5
Anuppur, *India* 69 H9
Anuradhapura, *Sri Lanka* 66 Q12
Anveh, *Iran* 71 E7
Anvers = Antwerpen, *Belgium* 17 C4
Anvers I., *Antarctica* 5 C17
Anwen, *China* 59 C13
Anxi, *Fujian, China* 59 E12
Anxi, *Gansu, China* 60 B4
Anxian, *China* 58 B5
Anxiang, *China* 59 C9
Anxious B., *Australia* 95 E1
Anyama, *Ivory C.* 82 D4
Anyang, *China* 56 F8
Anyer-Kidul, *Indonesia* 63 G11
Anyi, *Jiangxi, China* 59 C10
Anyi, *Shanxi, China* 56 G6
Anyuan, *China* 59 E10
Anyue, *China* 58 B5
Anza, *U.S.A.* 117 M10
Anze, *China* 56 F7
Anzhero-Sudzhensk, *Russia* 50 D9
Ánzio, *Italy* 30 A5
Aoga-Shima, *Japan* 55 H9
Aoiz, *Spain* 32 C3
Aomen = Macau, *Asia* 59 F9
Aomori, *Japan* 54 D10
Aomori □, *Japan* 54 D10
Aonla, *India* 69 E8
Aosta, *Italy* 28 C4
Aoudéras, *Niger* 83 B6
Aoukâr, *Mauritania* 82 B3
Aozou, *Chad* 79 D9
Apa →, *S. Amer.* 126 A4
Apache, *U.S.A.* 113 H5
Apache Junction, *U.S.A.* 115 K8
Apalachee B., *U.S.A.* 109 L4
Apalachicola, *U.S.A.* 109 L3
Apalachicola →, *U.S.A.* 109 L3
Apam, *Ghana* 83 D4
Apapa, *Nigeria* 83 D5
Apaporis →, *Colombia* 124 D5
Aparri, *Phil.* 61 B4
Apateu, *Romania* 42 D6
Apatin, *Serbia, Yug.* 42 E4
Apatity, *Russia* 50 C4
Apatzingán, *Mexico* 118 D4
Apeldoorn, *Neths.* 17 B5
Apen, *Germany* 24 B3
Apennines = Appennini, *Italy* 28 E7
Aphrodisias, *Turkey* 39 D10
Apia, *W. Samoa* 91 A13
Apiacás, Serra dos, *Brazil* 124 E7
Apies →, *S. Africa* 89 D4
Apizaco, *Mexico* 119 D5
Aplao, *Peru* 124 G4
Apo, Mt., *Phil.* 63 C7
Apolakkiá, *Greece* 36 C9
Apolakkiá, Órmos, *Greece* 36 C9
Apolda, *Germany* 24 D7
Apollo Bay, *Australia* 95 F3
Apollonia, *Greece* 38 E6
Apolo, *Bolivia* 124 F5
Aporé →, *Brazil* 125 G8
Apostle Is., *U.S.A.* 112 B9
Apóstoles, *Argentina* 127 B4
Apostolos Andreas, C., *Cyprus* 36 D13
Apostolovo, *Ukraine* 47 J7
Apoteri, *Guyana* 124 C7
Appalachian Mts., *U.S.A.* 108 G6
Äppelbo, *Sweden* 10 D8
Appennini, *Italy* 28 E7
Appennino Ligure, *Italy* 28 D6
Appenzell-Ausser Rhoden □, *Switz.* 25 H5
Appenzell-Inner Rhoden □, *Switz.* 25 H5
Appiano, *Italy* 29 B8
Apple Hill, *Canada* 111 A10
Apple Valley, *U.S.A.* 117 L9
Appleby-in-Westmorland, *U.K.* 12 C5
Appleton, *U.S.A.* 108 C1
Approuague →, *Fr. Guiana* 125 C8
Apricena, *Italy* 29 G12
Aprília, *Italy* 30 A5
Apsheronsk, *Russia* 49 H4
Apsley, *Canada* 110 B6
Apt, *France* 21 E9
Apuane, Alpi, *Italy* 28 D7
Apucarana, *Brazil* 127 A5
Apulia = Púglia □, *Italy* 31 A9
Apure →, *Venezuela* 124 B5
Apurimac →, *Peru* 124 F4
Apuseni, Munţii, *Romania* 42 D7
Āqā Jarī, *Iran* 71 D6
Aqaba = Al 'Aqabah, *Jordan* 75 F4
Aqaba, G. of, *Red Sea* 70 D2
'Aqabah, Khalīj al = Aqaba, G. of, *Red Sea* 70 D2
'Aqdā, *Iran* 71 C7
Aqîq, *Sudan* 80 D4
Aqîq, Khalîg, *Sudan* 80 D4
Aqmola = Astana, *Kazakstan* 50 D8
Aqrah, *Iraq* 70 B4
Aqtaū, *Kazakstan* 50 E6
Aqtöbe, *Kazakstan* 50 D6
Aquidauana, *Brazil* 125 H7
Aquiles Serdán, *Mexico* 118 B3
Aquin, *Haiti* 121 C5
Aquitaine □, *France* 20 D3
Ar Rachidiya, *Morocco* 78 B5
Ar Rafīd, *Syria* 75 C4
Ar Raḩḩālīyah, *Iraq* 70 C4
Ar Ramādī, *Iraq* 70 C4
Ar Ramthā, *Jordan* 75 C5
Ar Raqqah, *Syria* 70 C3
Ar Rass, *Si. Arabia* 70 E4
Ar Rawshān, *Si. Arabia* 80 C5
Ar Rifā'ī, *Iraq* 70 D5
Ar Riyāḍ, *Si. Arabia* 70 E5
Ar Ru'ays, *Qatar* 71 E6
Ar Rukhaymīyah, *Iraq* 70 D5
Ar Ruqayyidah, *Si. Arabia* 71 E6
Ar Ruşāfah, *Syria* 70 C3
Ar Ruţbah, *Iraq* 70 C4
Ara, *India* 69 G11
Ara Goro, *Ethiopia* 81 F5
Ara Tera, *Ethiopia* 81 F5
Arab, *U.S.A.* 109 H2
'Arab, Bahr el →, *Sudan* 81 F2
Arab, Khalîg el, *Egypt* 80 A2
'Araba, W. →, *Egypt* 80 J8
'Arabābād, *Iran* 71 C8
Araban, *Turkey* 72 D7
Arabatskaya Strelka, *Ukraine* 47 K8
Arabba, *Italy* 29 B8
Arabia, *Asia* 52 G8
Arabian Desert = Es Sahrâ' Esh Sharqîya, *Egypt* 80 B3
Arabian Gulf = Gulf, The, *Asia* 71 E6
Arabian Sea, *Ind. Oc.* 52 H10
Araç, *Turkey* 72 B5
Aracaju, *Brazil* 125 F11
Aracati, *Brazil* 125 D11
Araçatuba, *Brazil* 127 A5
Aracena, *Spain* 35 H4
Aracena, Sierra de, *Spain* 35 H4
Aračinovo, *Macedonia* 40 D5
Araçuaí, *Brazil* 125 G10
'Arad, *Israel* 75 D4
Arad, *Romania* 42 D6
Arad □, *Romania* 42 D6
Arādān, *Iran* 71 C7
Aradhippou, *Cyprus* 36 E12
Arafura Sea, *E. Indies* 52 K17
Aragats, *Armenia* 49 K7
Aragón □, *Spain* 32 D4
Aragón →, *Spain* 32 C3
Aragona, *Italy* 30 E6

Araguacema, *Brazil* 125 E9
Araguaia →, *Brazil* 122 D6
Araguaína, *Brazil* 125 E9
Araguari, *Brazil* 125 G9
Araguari →, *Brazil* 125 C9
Arain, *India* 68 F6
Arak, *Algeria* 78 C6
Arāk, *Iran* 71 C6
Araka, *Sudan* 81 G3
Arakan Coast, *Burma* 67 K19
Arakan Yoma, *Burma* 67 K19
Arákhova, *Greece* 38 C4
Arakli, *Turkey* 73 B8
Araks = Aras, Rūd-e →, *Azerbaijan* 49 K9
Aral, *Kazakstan* 50 E7
Aral Sea, *Asia* 50 E7
Aral Tengizi = Aral Sea, *Asia* 50 E7
Aralsk = Aral, *Kazakstan* 50 E7
Aralskoye More = Aral Sea, *Asia* 50 E7
Aralsor, Ozero, *Kazakstan* 49 F9
Aramac, *Australia* 94 C4
Aran I., *Ireland* 15 A3
Aran Is., *Ireland* 15 C2
Aranda de Duero, *Spain* 34 D7
Arandān, *Iran* 70 C5
Aranđelovac, *Serbia, Yug.* 40 B4
Aranjuez, *Spain* 34 E7
Aranos, *Namibia* 88 C2
Aransas Pass, *U.S.A.* 113 M6
Aranyaprathet, *Thailand* 64 F4
Araouane, *Mali* 82 B4
Arapahoe, *U.S.A.* 112 E5
Arapey Grande →, *Uruguay* 126 C4
Arapgir, *Turkey* 70 B3
Arapiraca, *Brazil* 125 E11
Arapongas, *Brazil* 127 A5
Ar'ar, *Si. Arabia* 70 D4
Araranguá, *Brazil* 127 B6
Araraquara, *Brazil* 125 H9
Ararás, Serra das, *Brazil* 127 B5
Ararat, *Armenia* 73 C11
Ararat, *Australia* 95 F3
Ararat, Mt. = Ağrı Dağı, *Turkey* 70 B5
Araria, *India* 69 F12
Araripe, Chapada do, *Brazil* 125 E11
Araruama, L. de, *Brazil* 127 A7
Aras, Rūd-e →, *Azerbaijan* 49 K9
Aratāne, *Mauritania* 82 B3
Arauca, *Colombia* 124 B4
Arauca →, *Venezuela* 124 B5
Arauco, *Chile* 126 D1
Arawa, *Ethiopia* 81 F5
Araxá, *Brazil* 125 G9
Araya, Pen. de, *Venezuela* 124 A6
Arba Gugu, *Ethiopia* 81 F5
Arba Minch, *Ethiopia* 81 F4
Arbat, *Iraq* 70 C5
Árbatax, *Italy* 30 C2
Arbi, *Ethiopia* 81 F4
Arbīl, *Iraq* 70 B5
Arboga, *Sweden* 10 E9
Arbois, *France* 19 F12
Arbore, *Ethiopia* 81 F4
Arboréa, *Italy* 30 C1
Arborfield, *Canada* 105 C8
Arborg, *Canada* 105 C9
Arbre du Ténéré, *Niger* 83 B7
Arbroath, *U.K.* 14 E6
Arbuckle, *U.S.A.* 116 F4
Arbus, *Italy* 30 C1
Arc →, *France* 21 C10
Arc-lès-Gray, *France* 19 E12
Arcachon, *France* 20 D2
Arcachon, Bassin d', *France* 20 D2
Arcade, *Calif., U.S.A.* 117 L8
Arcade, *N.Y., U.S.A.* 110 D6
Arcadia, *Fla., U.S.A.* 109 M5
Arcadia, *La., U.S.A.* 113 J8
Arcadia, *Pa., U.S.A.* 110 F6
Arcata, *U.S.A.* 114 F1
Arcévia, *Italy* 29 E9
Archangel = Arkhangelsk, *Russia* 50 C5
Archar, *Bulgaria* 40 C6
Archbald, *U.S.A.* 111 E9
Archena, *Spain* 33 G3
Archer →, *Australia* 94 A3
Archer B., *Australia* 94 A3
Archers Post, *Kenya* 86 B4
Arches National Park, *U.S.A.* 115 G9
Archidona, *Spain* 35 H6
Arci, Mte., *Italy* 30 C1
Arcidosso, *Italy* 29 F8
Arcis-sur-Aube, *France* 19 D11
Arckaringa Cr. →, *Australia* 95 D2
Arco, *Italy* 28 C7
Arco, *U.S.A.* 114 E7
Arcos = Arcos de Jalón, *Spain* 32 D2
Arcos de Jalón, *Spain* 32 D2
Arcos de la Frontera, *Spain* 35 J5
Arcos de Valdevez, *Portugal* 34 D2
Arcot, *India* 66 N11
Arcozelo, *Portugal* 34 E3
Arctic Bay, *Canada* 101 A11
Arctic Ocean, *Arctic* 4 B18
Arctic Red River = Tsiigehtchic, *Canada* 100 B6
Arda →, *Bulgaria* 41 E10
Arda →, *Italy* 28 C7
Ardabīl, *Iran* 71 B6
Ardahan, *Turkey* 73 B10
Ardakān = Sepīdān, *Iran* 71 D7
Ardakān, *Iran* 71 C7
Ardala, *Sweden* 11 F7
Ardales, *Spain* 35 J6
Ardèche □, *France* 21 D8
Ardèche →, *France* 21 D8
Ardee, *Ireland* 15 C5
Arden, *Canada* 110 B8
Arden, *Denmark* 11 H3
Arden, *Calif., U.S.A.* 116 G5
Arden, *Nev., U.S.A.* 117 J11
Ardenne, *Belgium* 6 F7
Ardennes = Ardenne, *Belgium* 6 F7
Ardennes □, *France* 19 C11
Ardentes, *France* 19 F8
Arderin, *Ireland* 15 C4
Ardeşen, *Turkey* 73 B9
Ardestān, *Iran* 71 C7
Árdhas →, *Greece* 41 E10
Ardhéa, *Greece* 40 F6
Ardila →, *Portugal* 35 G3
Ardino, *Bulgaria* 41 E9
Ardivachar Pt., *U.K.* 14 D1
Ardlethan, *Australia* 95 E4
Ardmore, *Okla., U.S.A.* 113 H6
Ardmore, *Pa., U.S.A.* 111 G9
Ardnamurchan, Pt. of, *U.K.* 14 E2
Ardnave Pt., *U.K.* 14 F2
Ardon, *Russia* 49 J7
Ardore, *Italy* 31 D9
Ardres, *France* 19 B8
Ardrossan, *Australia* 95 E2
Ardrossan, *U.K.* 14 F4
Ards Pen., *U.K.* 15 B6
Arduan, *Sudan* 80 D3
Ardud, *Romania* 42 C7
Åre, *Sweden* 10 A7
Arecibo, *Puerto Rico* 121 C6
Areia Branca, *Brazil* 125 E11
Arena, Pt., *U.S.A.* 116 G3
Arenal, *Honduras* 120 C2
Arenas = Las Arenas, *Spain* 34 B6
Arenas de San Pedro, *Spain* 34 E5
Arendal, *Norway* 9 G13
Arendsee, *Germany* 24 C7
Arenys de Mar, *Spain* 32 D7
Arenzano, *Italy* 28 D5
Areópolis, *Greece* 38 E4
Arequipa, *Peru* 124 G4
Arero, *Ethiopia* 81 G4
Arès, *France* 20 D2
Arévalo, *Spain* 34 D6
Arezzo, *Italy* 29 E8
Arga, *Turkey* 70 B3
Arga →, *Spain* 32 C3
Argalastí, *Greece* 38 B5
Argamasilla de Alba, *Spain* 35 F7
Argamasilla de Calatrava, *Spain* 35 G6
Arganda, *Spain* 34 E7
Arganil, *Portugal* 34 E2
Argedeb, *Ethiopia* 81 F5
Argelès-Gazost, *France* 20 E3
Argelès-sur-Mer, *France* 20 F7
Argens →, *France* 21 E10
Argent-sur-Sauldre, *France* 19 E9
Argenta, *Canada* 104 C5
Argenta, *Italy* 29 D8
Argentan, *France* 18 D6
Argentário, Mte., *Italy* 29 F8
Argentat, *France* 20 C5
Argentera, *Italy* 28 D4
Argenteuil, *France* 19 D9
Argentia, *Canada* 103 C9
Argentiera, C. dell', *Italy* 30 B1
Argentina ■, *S. Amer.* 128 D3
Argentina Is., *Antarctica* 5 C17
Argentino, L., *Argentina* 128 G2
Argenton-Château, *France* 18 F6
Argenton-sur-Creuse, *France* 19 F8
Argeş □, *Romania* 43 F9
Argeş →, *Romania* 43 F11
Arghandab →, *Afghan.* 68 D1
Argheile, *Ethiopia* 81 F5
Argo, *Sudan* 80 D3
Argolikós Kólpos, *Greece* 38 D4
Argolís □, *Greece* 38 D4
Argonne, *France* 19 C12
Árgos, *Greece* 38 D4
Árgos Orestikón, *Greece* 40 F5
Argostólion, *Greece* 38 C2
Arguedas, *Spain* 32 C3
Arguello, Pt., *U.S.A.* 117 L6
Arguineguín, *Canary Is.* 37 G4
Argun, *Russia* 49 J7
Argun →, *Russia* 51 D13
Argungu, *Nigeria* 83 C5
Argus Pk., *U.S.A.* 117 K9
Argyle, L., *Australia* 92 C4
Argyll & Bute □, *U.K.* 14 E3
Arhavi, *Turkey* 73 B9
Århus, *Denmark* 11 H4
Århus Amtskommune □, *Denmark* 11 H4
Ariadnoye, *Russia* 54 B7
Ariamsvlei, *Namibia* 88 D2
Ariana, *Tunisia* 79 A7
Ariano Irpino, *Italy* 31 A8
Aribinda, *Burkina Faso* 83 C4
Arica, *Chile* 124 G4
Arica, *Colombia* 124 D4
Arico, *Canary Is.* 37 F3
Arid, C., *Australia* 93 F3
Arida, *Japan* 55 G7
Ariège □, *France* 20 F5
Ariège →, *France* 20 E5
Arieş →, *Romania* 43 D8
Arīhā, *Israel* 80 A4
Arilje, *Serbia, Yug.* 40 C4
Arílla, Ákra, *Greece* 36 A3
Arima, *Trin. & Tob.* 121 D7
Arinos →, *Brazil* 122 E5
Ario de Rosales, *Mexico* 118 D4
Ariogala, *Lithuania* 44 C10
Aripuanã, *Brazil* 124 E6
Aripuanã →, *Brazil* 122 D4
Ariquemes, *Brazil* 124 E6
Arisaig, *U.K.* 14 E3
Arîsh, W. el →, *Egypt* 80 A3
Arissa, *Ethiopia* 81 E5
Aristazabal I., *Canada* 104 C3
Arivonimamo, *Madag.* 89 B8
Ariza, *Spain* 32 D2
Arizaro, Salar de, *Argentina* 126 A2
Arizona, *Argentina* 126 D2
Arizona □, *U.S.A.* 115 J8
Arizpe, *Mexico* 118 A2
Årjäng, *Sweden* 10 E6
Arjeplog, *Sweden* 8 D18
Arjona, *Colombia* 124 A3
Arjona, *Spain* 35 H6
Arjuna, *Indonesia* 63 G15
Arka, *Russia* 51 C15
Arkadak, *Russia* 48 E6
Arkadelphia, *U.S.A.* 113 H8
Arkadhía □, *Greece* 38 D4
Arkaig, L., *U.K.* 14 E3
Arkalyk = Arqalyk, *Kazakstan* 50 D7
Arkansas □, *U.S.A.* 113 H8
Arkansas →, *U.S.A.* 113 J9
Arkansas City, *U.S.A.* 113 G6
Arkaroola, *Australia* 95 E2
Árkathos →, *Greece* 38 B3
Arkhángelos, *Greece* 36 C10
Arkhangelsk, *Russia* 50 C5
Arkhangelskoye, *Russia* 48 E5
Arki, *India* 68 D7
Arkiko, *Eritrea* 81 D4
Arklow, *Ireland* 15 D5
Árkoi, *Greece* 39 D8
Arkona, Kap, *Germany* 24 A9
Arkösund, *Sweden* 11 F10
Arkoúdhi, *Greece* 38 C2
Arkport, *U.S.A.* 110 D7
Arkticheskiy, Mys, *Russia* 51 A10
Arkul, *Russia* 48 B10
Arkville, *U.S.A.* 111 D10
Ärla, *Sweden* 10 E10
Arlanza →, *Spain* 34 C6
Arlanzón →, *Spain* 34 C6
Arlbergpass, *Austria* 26 D3
Arles, *France* 21 E8
Arlington, *S. Africa* 89 D4
Arlington, *N.Y., U.S.A.* 111 E11
Arlington, *Oreg., U.S.A.* 114 D3
Arlington, *S. Dak., U.S.A.* 112 C6
Arlington, *Tex., U.S.A.* 113 J6
Arlington, *Va., U.S.A.* 108 F7
Arlington, *Vt., U.S.A.* 111 C11
Arlington, *Wash., U.S.A.* 116 B4
Arlington Heights, *U.S.A.* 108 D2
Arlit, *Niger* 78 E7
Arlon, *Belgium* 17 E5
Arltunga, *Australia* 94 C1
Arly, *Burkina Faso* 83 C5
Armagh, *U.K.* 15 B5
Armagh □, *U.K.* 15 B5
Armagnac, *France* 20 E4
Armançon →, *France* 19 E10
Armavir, *Russia* 49 H5
Armenia, *Colombia* 124 C3
Armenia ■, *Asia* 49 K7
Armeniş, *Romania* 42 E7
Armenistís, Ákra, *Greece* 36 C9
Armentières, *France* 19 B9
Armidale, *Australia* 95 E5
Armilla, *Spain* 35 H7
Armour, *U.S.A.* 112 D5
Armstrong, *B.C., Canada* 104 C5
Armstrong, *Ont., Canada* 102 B2
Armutlu, *Bursa, Turkey* 41 F12
Armutlu, *İzmir, Turkey* 39 C9
Arnaía, *Greece* 40 F7
Arnarfjörður, *Iceland* 8 D2
Arnaud →, *Canada* 101 B12
Arnauti, C., *Cyprus* 36 D11
Arnay-le-Duc, *France* 19 E11
Arnedillo, *Spain* 32 C2
Arnedo, *Spain* 32 C2
Arnett, *U.S.A.* 113 G5
Arnhem, *Neths.* 17 C5
Arnhem, C., *Australia* 94 A2
Arnhem B., *Australia* 94 A2
Arnhem Land, *Australia* 94 A1
Árnissa, *Greece* 40 F5
Arno →, *Italy* 28 E7
Arno Bay, *Australia* 95 E2
Arnold, *U.K.* 12 D6
Arnold, *U.S.A.* 116 G6
Arnoldstein, *Austria* 26 E6
Arnon →, *France* 19 E9
Arnot, *Canada* 105 B9
Arnøy, *Norway* 8 A19
Arnprior, *Canada* 102 C4
Arnsberg, *Germany* 24 D4
Arnstadt, *Germany* 24 E6
Aroab, *Namibia* 88 D2
Aroánia Óri, *Greece* 38 D4
Aroche, *Spain* 35 H4
Arochuku, *Nigeria* 83 D6
Arolsen, *Germany* 24 D5
Aron, *India* 68 G6
Aron →, *France* 19 F10
Arona, *Italy* 28 C5
Aroroy, *Phil.* 61 E5
Arosa, Ría de, *Spain* 34 C2
Arpajon, *France* 19 D9
Arpajon-sur-Cère, *France* 20 D6
Arpaşu de Jos, *Romania* 43 E9
Arqalyk, *Kazakstan* 50 D7
Arrah = Ara, *India* 69 G11
Arrah, *Ivory C.* 82 D4
Arraiolos, *Portugal* 35 G3
Arran, *U.K.* 14 F3
Arras, *France* 19 B9
Arrasate, *Spain* 32 B2
Arrats →, *France* 20 D4
Arreau, *France* 20 F4
Arrecife, *Canary Is.* 37 F6
Arrecifes, *Argentina* 126 C3
Arrée, Mts. d', *France* 18 D3
Arresø, *Denmark* 11 J6
Arriaga, *Chiapas, Mexico* 119 D6
Arriaga, *San Luis Potosí, Mexico* 118 C4
Arrilalah, *Australia* 94 C3
Arrino, *Australia* 93 E2
Arriondas, *Spain* 34 B5
Arromanches-les-Bains, *France* 18 C6
Arronches, *Portugal* 35 F3
Arros →, *France* 20 E3
Arrow, L., *Ireland* 15 B3
Arrowhead, L., *U.S.A.* 117 L9
Arrowtown, *N.Z.* 91 L2
Arroyo de la Luz, *Spain* 35 F4
Arroyo Grande, *U.S.A.* 117 K6
Års, *Denmark* 11 H3
Ars, *Iran* 70 B5
Ars-sur-Moselle, *France* 19 C13
Arsenault L., *Canada* 105 B7
Arsenev, *Russia* 54 B6
Arsi □, *Ethiopia* 81 F4
Arsiero, *Italy* 29 C8
Arsin, *Turkey* 73 B8
Arsk, *Russia* 48 B9
Årsunda, *Sweden* 10 D10
Árta, *Greece* 38 B3
Artà, *Spain* 37 B10
Árta □, *Greece* 38 B3
Arteaga, *Mexico* 118 D4
Arteche, *Phil.* 61 E6
Arteijo = Arteixo, *Spain* 34 B2
Arteixo, *Spain* 34 B2
Artem = Artyom, *Azerbaijan* 49 K10
Artem, *Russia* 54 C6
Artemovsk, *Russia* 51 D10
Artemovsk, *Ukraine* 47 H9
Artemovskiy, *Russia* 49 G5
Artenay, *France* 19 D8
Artern, *Germany* 24 D7
Artesa de Segre, *Spain* 32 D6
Artesia = Mosomane, *Botswana* 88 C4
Artesia, *U.S.A.* 113 J2
Arthington, *Liberia* 82 D2
Arthur, *Canada* 110 C4
Arthur →, *Australia* 94 G3
Arthur Cr. →, *Australia* 94 C2
Arthur Pt., *Australia* 94 C5
Arthur River, *Australia* 93 F2
Arthur's Pass, *N.Z.* 91 K3
Arthur's Town, *Bahamas* 121 B4
Artigas, *Uruguay* 126 C4
Artik, *Armenia* 49 K6
Artillery L., *Canada* 105 A7
Artois, *France* 19 B9
Artotína, *Greece* 38 C4
Artrutx, C. de, *Spain* 37 B10
Artsyz, *Ukraine* 47 J5
Artvin, *Turkey* 73 B9
Artyom, *Azerbaijan* 49 K10
Aru, Kepulauan, *Indonesia* 63 F8
Aru Is. = Aru, Kepulauan, *Indonesia* 63 F8
Arua, *Uganda* 86 B3
Aruanã, *Brazil* 125 F8
Aruba ■, *W. Indies* 121 D6
Arucas, *Canary Is.* 37 F4
Arudy, *France* 20 E3
Arun →, *Nepal* 69 F12
Arun →, *U.K.* 13 G7
Arunachal Pradesh □, *India* 67 F19
Arusha, *Tanzania* 86 C4
Arusha □, *Tanzania* 86 C4
Arusha Chini, *Tanzania* 86 C4
Aruwimi →, *Dem. Rep. of the Congo* 86 B1
Arvada, *Colo., U.S.A.* 112 F2
Arvada, *Wyo., U.S.A.* 114 D10
Arve →, *France* 19 F13
Árvi, *Greece* 36 E7
Arviat, *Canada* 105 A10
Arvidsjaur, *Sweden* 8 D18
Arvika, *Sweden* 10 E6
Arvin, *U.S.A.* 117 K8
Arwal, *India* 69 G11
Arxan, *China* 60 B6
Åryd, *Sweden* 11 H8
Aryirádhes, *Greece* 36 B3
Aryiroúpolis, *Greece* 36 D6
Arys, *Kazakstan* 50 E7
Arzachena, *Italy* 30 A2
Arzamas, *Russia* 48 C6
Arzgir, *Russia* 49 H7
Arzignano, *Italy* 29 C8
Arzúa, *Spain* 34 C2
Aš, *Czech Rep.* 26 A5
Ås, *Sweden* 10 A8
As Pontes de García Rodríquez, *Spain* 34 B3
Aş Şadr, *U.A.E.* 71 E7
Aş Şafā, *Syria* 75 B6
As Saffānīyah, *Si. Arabia* 71 E6
As Safīrah, *Syria* 70 B3
Aş Şahm, *Oman* 71 E8
As Sājir, *Si. Arabia* 70 E5
As Salamīyah, *Syria* 70 C3
As Salmān, *Iraq* 70 D5
As Salṭ, *Jordan* 75 C4
As Sal'w'a, *Qatar* 71 E6
As Samāwah, *Iraq* 70 D5
As Sanamayn, *Syria* 75 B5
As Sohar = Şuḩār, *Oman* 71 E8
As Sukhnah, *Syria* 70 C3
As Sulaymānīyah, *Iraq* 70 C5
As Sulaymī, *Si. Arabia* 70 E4
As Sulayyil, *Si. Arabia* 74 C4
As Summān, *Si. Arabia* 70 E5
As Suwaydā', *Syria* 75 C5
As Suwaydā' □, *Syria* 75 C5
As Suwayq, *Oman* 71 F8
As Şuwayrah, *Iraq* 70 C5
Åsa, *Sweden* 11 G6
Asab, *Namibia* 88 D2
Asaba, *Nigeria* 83 D6
Asad, Buḩayrat al, *Syria* 70 C3
Asadābād, *Iran* 73 E13
Asafo, *Ghana* 82 D4
Asahi-Gawa →, *Japan* 55 G6
Asahigawa, *Japan* 54 C11
Asale, L., *Ethiopia* 81 E5
Asamankese, *Ghana* 83 D4
Asan →, *India* 69 F8
Asansol, *India* 69 H12
Åsarna, *Sweden* 10 B8
Asayita, *Ethiopia* 81 E5
Asbe Teferi, *Ethiopia* 81 F5
Asbesberge, *S. Africa* 88 D3
Asbestos, *Canada* 103 C5
Asbury Park, *U.S.A.* 111 F10
Ascea, *Italy* 31 B8
Ascensión, *Mexico* 118 A3
Ascensión, B. de la, *Mexico* 119 D7
Ascension I., *Atl. Oc.* 77 G2
Aschach an der Donau, *Austria* 26 C7
Aschaffenburg, *Germany* 25 F5
Aschendorf, *Germany* 24 B3
Aschersleben, *Germany* 24 D7
Asciano, *Italy* 29 E8
Áscoli Piceno, *Italy* 29 F10
Áscoli Satriano, *Italy* 31 A8
Ascope, *Peru* 124 E3
Ascotán, *Chile* 126 A2
Aseb, *Eritrea* 81 E5
Åseda, *Sweden* 11 G9
Asela, *Ethiopia* 81 F4
Åsen, *Sweden* 10 C7
Asenovgrad, *Bulgaria* 41 D8
Aserradero, *Mexico* 118 C3
Asfeld, *France* 19 C11
Asfûn el Matâ'na, *Egypt* 80 B3
Asgata, *Cyprus* 36 E12
Ash Fork, *U.S.A.* 115 J7
Ash Grove, *U.S.A.* 113 G8
Ash Shabakah, *Iraq* 70 D4
Ash Shamāl □, *Lebanon* 75 A5
Ash Shāmīyah, *Iraq* 70 D5
Ash Shāriqah, *U.A.E.* 71 E7
Ash Sharmah, *Si. Arabia* 70 D2
Ash Sharqāt, *Iraq* 70 C4
Ash Sharqi, Al Jabal, *Lebanon* 75 B5
Ash Shaṭrah, *Iraq* 70 D5
Ash Shawbak, *Jordan* 70 D2
Ash Shawmari, J., *Jordan* 75 E5
Ash Shināfīyah, *Iraq* 70 D5
Ash Shu'bah, *Si. Arabia* 70 D5
Ash Shumlūl, *Si. Arabia* 70 E5
Ash Shūr'a, *Iraq* 70 C4
Ash Shurayf, *Si. Arabia* 70 E3
Ash Shuwayfāt, *Lebanon* 75 B4
Ashanti □, *Ghana* 83 D4
Ashau, *Vietnam* 64 D6
Ashbourne, *U.K.* 12 D6
Ashburn, *U.S.A.* 109 K4
Ashburton, *N.Z.* 91 K3
Ashburton →, *Australia* 92 D1
Ashcroft, *Canada* 104 C4
Ashdod, *Israel* 75 D3
Ashdown, *U.S.A.* 113 J7
Asheboro, *U.S.A.* 109 H6
Ashern, *Canada* 105 C9
Asherton, *U.S.A.* 113 L5
Asheville, *U.S.A.* 109 H4
Ashewat, *Pakistan* 68 D3
Asheweig →, *Canada* 102 B2
Ashford, *Australia* 95 D5
Ashford, *U.K.* 13 F8
Ashgabat, *Turkmenistan* 50 F6
Ashibetsu, *Japan* 54 C11
Ashikaga, *Japan* 55 F9
Ashington, *U.K.* 12 B6
Ashizuri-Zaki, *Japan* 55 H6
Ashkarkot, *Afghan.* 68 C2
Ashkhabad = Ashgabat, *Turkmenistan* 50 F6
Āshkhāneh, *Iran* 71 B8
Ashland, *Kans., U.S.A.* 113 G5
Ashland, *Ky., U.S.A.* 108 F4
Ashland, *Mont., U.S.A.* 114 D10
Ashland, *Ohio, U.S.A.* 110 F2
Ashland, *Oreg., U.S.A.* 114 E2
Ashland, *Pa., U.S.A.* 111 F8
Ashland, *Va., U.S.A.* 108 G7
Ashland, *Wis., U.S.A.* 112 B9
Ashley, *N. Dak., U.S.A.* 112 B5
Ashley, *Pa., U.S.A.* 111 E9
Ashmore Reef, *Australia* 92 B3
Ashmûn, *Egypt* 80 H7
Ashmyany, *Belarus* 9 J21
Ashokan Reservoir, *U.S.A.* 111 E10
Ashqelon, *Israel* 75 D3
Ashta, *India* 68 H7
Ashtabula, *U.S.A.* 110 E4
Ashton, *S. Africa* 88 E3
Ashton, *U.S.A.* 114 D8
Ashuanipi, L., *Canada* 103 B6
Ashville, *U.S.A.* 110 F6
'Āṣī →, *Asia* 72 D6
Asia 52 E11
Asia, Kepulauan, *Indonesia* 63 D8
Āsīā Bak, *Iran* 71 C6
Asiago, *Italy* 29 C8

Asifabad, India 66 K11
Asinara, Italy 30 A1
Asinara, G. dell', Italy 30 A1
Asino, Russia 50 D9
Asipovichy, Belarus 46 F5
'Asīr □, Si. Arabia 74 D3
Asir, Ras, Somali Rep. 74 E5
Aşkale, Turkey 73 C9
Askersund, Sweden 11 F8
Askham, S. Africa 88 D3
Askim, Norway 9 G14
Askja, Iceland 8 D5
Askøy, Norway 9 F11
Asl, Egypt 80 B3
Aslan Burnu, Turkey 39 C8
Aslanapa, Turkey 39 B11
Asmara = Asmera, Eritrea 81 D4
Asmera, Eritrea 81 D4
Asnæs, Denmark 11 J4
Åsnen, Sweden 11 H8
Ásola, Italy 28 C7
Asosa, Ethiopia 81 E3
Asoteriba, Jebel, Sudan 80 C4
Aspe, Spain 33 G4
Aspen, U.S.A. 115 G10
Aspendos, Turkey 72 D4
Aspermont, U.S.A. 113 J4
Aspet, France 20 E4
Aspiring, Mt., N.Z. 91 L2
Aspres-sur-Buëch, France 21 D9
Asprókavos, Ákra, Greece 36 B4
Aspromonte, Italy 31 D9
Aspur, India 68 H6
Asquith, Canada 105 C7
Assâba, Massif de l', Mauritania 82 B2
Assaikio, Nigeria 83 D6
Assal, L., Djibouti 81 E5
Assam □, India 67 G18
Assamakka, Niger 83 B6
Asse, Belgium 17 D4
Assémini, Italy 30 C1
Assen, Neths. 17 A6
Assens, Denmark 11 J3
Assini, Ivory C. 82 D4
Assiniboia, Canada 105 D7
Assiniboine →, Canada 105 D9
Assiniboine, Mt., Canada 104 C5
Assis, Brazil 127 A5
Assisi, Italy 29 E9
Ássos, Greece 38 C2
Assynt, L., U.K. 14 C3
Astaffort, France 20 D4
Astakidha, Greece 39 F8
Astakós, Greece 38 C3
Astana, Kazakstan 50 D8
Āstāneh, Iran 71 B6
Astara, Azerbaijan 71 B6
Āstārā, Iran 73 C13
Asteroúsia, Greece 36 E7
Asti, Italy 28 D5
Astipálaia, Greece 39 E8
Astorga, Spain 34 C4
Astoria, U.S.A. 116 D3
Åstorp, Sweden 11 H6
Astrakhan, Russia 49 G9
Astudillo, Spain 34 C6
Asturias □, Spain 34 B5
Asunción, Paraguay 126 B4
Asunción Nochixtlán, Mexico 119 D5
Åsunden, Sweden 11 F9
Asutri, Sudan 81 D4
Aswa →, Uganda 86 B3
Aswad, Ra's al, Si. Arabia 80 C4
Aswân, Egypt 80 C3
Aswân High Dam = Sadd el Aali, Egypt 80 C3
Asyût, Egypt 80 B3
Asyûti, Wadi →, Egypt 80 B3
Aszód, Hungary 42 C4
At Ţafilah, Jordan 75 E4
Aţ Tā'if, Si. Arabia 74 C3
Aţ Ţirāq, Si. Arabia 70 E5
Aţ Tubayq, Si. Arabia 70 D3
Atabey, Turkey 39 D12
Atacama □, Chile 126 B2
Atacama, Desierto de, Chile 126 A2
Atacama, Salar de, Chile 126 A2
Atakpamé, Togo 83 D5
Atalándi, Greece 38 C4
Atalaya, Peru 124 F4
Atalaya de Femes, Canary Is. 37 F6
Atami, Japan 55 G9
Atapupu, Indonesia 63 F6
Atâr, Mauritania 78 D3
Atarfe, Spain 35 H7
Atari, Pakistan 68 D6
Atascadero, U.S.A. 116 K6
Atasu, Kazakstan 50 E8
Atatürk Barajı, Turkey 73 D8
Atauro, Indonesia 63 F7
Atbara, Sudan 80 D3
'Atbara →, Sudan 80 D3
Atbasar, Kazakstan 50 D7
Atça, Turkey 39 D10
Atchafalaya B., U.S.A. 113 L9
Atchison, U.S.A. 112 F7
Atebubu, Ghana 83 D4
Ateca, Spain 32 D3
Aterno →, Italy 29 F10
Āteshān, Iran 71 C7
Atesine, Alpi, Italy 29 B8
Atessa, Italy 29 F11
Atfîh, Egypt 80 J7
Ath, Belgium 17 D3
Athabasca, Canada 104 C6
Athabasca →, Canada 105 B6
Athabasca, L., Canada 105 B7
Athboy, Ireland 15 C5
Athenry, Ireland 15 C3
Athens = Athínai, Greece 38 D5
Athens, Ala., U.S.A. 109 H2
Athens, Ga., U.S.A. 109 J4
Athens, N.Y., U.S.A. 111 D11
Athens, Ohio, U.S.A. 108 F4
Athens, Pa., U.S.A. 111 E8
Athens, Tenn., U.S.A. 109 H3
Athens, Tex., U.S.A. 113 J7
Atherley, Canada 110 B5
Atherton, Australia 94 B4
Athiéme, Benin 83 D5
Athienou, Cyprus 36 D12
Athínai, Greece 38 D5
Athlone, Ireland 15 C4
Athna, Cyprus 36 D12
Athol, U.S.A. 111 D12
Atholl, Forest of, U.K. 14 E5
Atholville, Canada 103 C6
Áthos, Greece 41 F8
Athy, Ireland 15 C5
Ati, Chad 79 F9
Ati, Sudan 81 E2
Atiak, Uganda 86 B3
Atienza, Spain 32 D2
Atiit, Sudan 81 F3
Atik L., Canada 105 B9
Atikameg →, Canada 102 B3
Atikokan, Canada 102 C1
Atikonak L., Canada 103 B7
Atimonan, Phil. 61 E4
Atka, Russia 51 C16
Atka I., U.S.A. 100 C2
Atkarsk, Russia 48 E7
Atkinson, U.S.A. 112 D5
Atlanta, Ga., U.S.A. 109 J3
Atlanta, Tex., U.S.A. 113 J7
Atlantic, U.S.A. 112 E7
Atlantic City, U.S.A. 108 F8
Atlantic Ocean 2 E9
Atlas Mts. = Haut Atlas, Morocco 78 B4
Atlin, Canada 104 B2
Atlin, L., Canada 104 B2
Atlin Prov. Park, Canada 104 B2
Atmore, U.S.A. 109 K2
Atoka, U.S.A. 113 H6
Atokos, Greece 38 C2
Atolia, U.S.A. 117 K9
Atrai →, Bangla. 69 G13
Atrak = Atrek →, Turkmenistan 71 B8
Ätran, Sweden 11 G6
Ätran →, Sweden 11 H6
Atrauli, India 68 E8
Atrek →, Turkmenistan 71 B8
Atri, Italy 29 F10
Atsikí, Greece 39 B7
Atsoum, Mts., Cameroon 83 D7
Atsuta, Japan 54 C10
Attalla, U.S.A. 109 H2
Attapu, Laos 64 E6
Attáviros, Greece 36 C9
Attawapiskat, Canada 102 B3
Attawapiskat →, Canada 102 B3
Attawapiskat L., Canada 102 B2
Attersee, Austria 26 D6
Attica, Ind., U.S.A. 108 E2
Attica, Ohio, U.S.A. 110 E2
Attichy, France 19 C10
Attigny, France 19 C11
Attikamagen L., Canada 103 B6
Attikí □, Greece 38 D5
Attleboro, U.S.A. 111 E13
Attock, Pakistan 68 C5
Attopeu = Attapu, Laos 64 E6
Attu I., U.S.A. 100 C1
Attur, India 66 P11
Atuel →, Argentina 126 D2
Åtvidaberg, Sweden 11 F10
Atwater, U.S.A. 116 H6
Atwood, Canada 110 C3
Atwood, U.S.A. 112 F4
Atyraū, Kazakstan 50 E6
Au Sable, U.S.A. 110 B1
Au Sable →, U.S.A. 108 C4
Au Sable Forks, U.S.A. 111 B11
Au Sable Pt., U.S.A. 110 B1
Aubagne, France 21 E9
Aubarca, C. d', Spain 37 B7
Aube □, France 19 D11
Aube →, France 19 D10
Aubenas, France 21 D8
Aubenton, France 19 C11
Auberry, U.S.A. 116 H7
Aubigny-sur-Nère, France 19 E9
Aubin, France 20 D6
Aubrac, Mts. d', France 20 D7
Auburn, Ala., U.S.A. 109 J3
Auburn, Calif., U.S.A. 116 G5
Auburn, Ind., U.S.A. 108 E3
Auburn, Maine, U.S.A. 109 C10
Auburn, N.Y., U.S.A. 111 D8
Auburn, Nebr., U.S.A. 112 E7
Auburn, Pa., U.S.A. 111 F8
Auburn, Wash., U.S.A. 116 C4
Auburn Ra., Australia 95 D5
Aubusson, France 20 C6
Auce, Latvia 44 B9
Auch, France 20 E4
Auchi, Nigeria 83 D6
Auckland, N.Z. 91 G5
Auckland Is., Pac. Oc. 96 N8
Aude □, France 20 E6
Aude →, France 20 E7
Auden, Canada 102 B2
Auderville, France 18 C5
Audierne, France 18 D2
Audincourt, France 19 E13
Audo, Ethiopia 81 F5
Audubon, U.S.A. 112 E7
Aue, Germany 24 E8
Auerbach, Germany 24 E8
Augathella, Australia 95 D4
Aughnacloy, U.K. 15 B5
Augrabies Falls, S. Africa 88 D3
Augsburg, Germany 25 G6
Augusta, Australia 93 F2
Augusta, Italy 31 E8
Augusta, Ark., U.S.A. 113 H9
Augusta, Ga., U.S.A. 109 J5
Augusta, Kans., U.S.A. 113 G6
Augusta, Maine, U.S.A. 101 D13
Augusta, Mont., U.S.A. 114 C7
Augustenborg, Denmark 11 K3
Augustów, Poland 44 E9
Augustus, Mt., Australia 93 D2
Augustus I., Australia 92 C3
Aukan, Eritrea 81 D5
Aukum, U.S.A. 116 G6
Auld, L., Australia 92 D3
Aulla, Italy 28 D6
Aulnay, France 20 B3
Aulne →, France 18 D2
Aulnoye-Aymeries, France 19 B10
Ault, France 18 B8
Ault, U.S.A. 112 E2
Aulus-les-Bains, France 20 F5
Aumale, France 19 C8
Aumont-Aubrac, France 20 D7
Auna, Nigeria 83 C5
Auning, Denmark 11 H4
Aunis, France 20 B3
Auponhia, Indonesia 63 E7
Aups, France 21 E10
Aur, Pulau, Malaysia 65 L5
Auraiya, India 69 F8
Aurangabad, Bihar, India 69 G11
Aurangabad, Maharashtra, India 66 K9
Auray, France 18 E4
Aurich, Germany 24 B3
Aurillac, France 20 D6
Auronzo di Cadore, Italy 29 B9
Aurora, Canada 110 C5
Aurora, S. Africa 88 E2
Aurora, Colo., U.S.A. 112 F2
Aurora, Ill., U.S.A. 108 E1
Aurora, Mo., U.S.A. 113 G8
Aurora, N.Y., U.S.A. 111 D8
Aurora, Nebr., U.S.A. 112 E6
Aurora, Ohio, U.S.A. 110 E3
Aurukun, Australia 94 A3
Aus, Namibia 88 D2
Ausable →, Canada 110 C3
Auschwitz = Oświęcim, Poland 45 H6
Austerlitz = Slavkov u Brna, Czech Rep. 27 B9
Austin, Minn., U.S.A. 112 D8
Austin, Nev., U.S.A. 114 G5
Austin, Pa., U.S.A. 110 E6
Austin, Tex., U.S.A. 113 K6
Austin, L., Australia 93 E2
Austin I., Canada 105 A10
Austra, Norway 8 D14
Austral Is. = Tubuai Is., Pac. Oc. 97 K13
Austral Seamount Chain, Pac. Oc. 97 K13
Australia ■, Oceania 96 K5
Australian Capital Territory □, Australia 95 F4
Australind, Australia 93 F2
Austria ■, Europe 26 E7
Austvågøy, Norway 8 B16
Auterive, France 20 E5
Authie →, France 19 B8
Authon-du-Perche, France 18 D7
Autlán, Mexico 118 D4
Autun, France 19 F11
Auvergne, France 20 C7
Auvergne, Mts. d', France 20 C6
Auvézère →, France 20 C4
Auxerre, France 19 E10
Auxi-le-Château, France 19 B9
Auxonne, France 19 E12
Auzances, France 19 F9
Ava, U.S.A. 113 G8
Avallon, France 19 E10
Avalon, U.S.A. 117 M8
Avalon Pen., Canada 103 C9
Avanos, Turkey 70 B2
Avaré, Brazil 127 A6
Ávas, Greece 41 F9
Avawatz Mts., U.S.A. 117 K10
Avdan Dağı, Turkey 41 F13
Aveiro, Brazil 125 D7
Aveiro, Portugal 34 E2
Aveiro □, Portugal 34 E2
Āvej, Iran 71 C6
Avellaneda, Argentina 126 C4
Avellino, Italy 31 B7
Avenal, U.S.A. 116 K6
Aversa, Italy 31 B7
Avery, U.S.A. 114 C6
Aves, Is. las, Venezuela 121 D6
Avesnes-sur-Helpe, France 19 B10
Avesta, Sweden 10 D10
Aveyron □, France 20 D6
Aveyron →, France 20 D5
Avezzano, Italy 29 F10
Avgó, Greece 39 F7
Aviá Terai, Argentina 126 B3
Aviano, Italy 29 B9
Aviemore, U.K. 14 D5
Avigliana, Italy 28 C4
Avigliano, Italy 31 B8
Avignon, France 21 E8
Ávila, Spain 34 E6
Ávila □, Spain 34 E6
Ávila, Sierra de, Spain 34 E5
Avila Beach, U.S.A. 117 K6
Avilés, Spain 34 B5
Avintes, Portugal 34 D2
Avionárion, Greece 38 C6
Avis, Portugal 35 F3
Avis, U.S.A. 110 E7
Avísio →, Italy 28 B8
Aviz = Avis, Portugal 35 F3
Avize, France 19 D11
Avlum, Denmark 11 H2
Avoca, U.S.A. 110 D7
Avoca →, Australia 95 F3
Avoca →, Ireland 15 D5
Avola, Canada 104 C5
Avola, Italy 31 F8
Avon, U.S.A. 110 D7
Avon →, Australia 93 F2
Avon →, Bristol, U.K. 13 F5
Avon →, Dorset, U.K. 13 G6
Avon →, Warks., U.K. 13 E5
Avon Park, U.S.A. 109 M5
Avondale, Zimbabwe 87 F3
Avonlea, Canada 105 D8
Avonmore, Canada 111 A10
Avramov, Bulgaria 41 D10
Avranches, France 18 D5
Avre →, France 18 D8
Avrig, Romania 43 E9
Avrillé, France 18 E6
Avtovac, Bos.-H. 40 C2
Awag el Baqar, Sudan 81 E3
A'waj →, Syria 75 B5
Awaji-Shima, Japan 55 G7
'Awālī, Bahrain 71 E6
Awantipur, India 69 C6
Awasa, Ethiopia 81 F4
Awasa, L., Ethiopia 81 F4
Awash, Ethiopia 81 F5
Awash →, Ethiopia 81 E5
Awaso, Ghana 82 D4
Awatere →, N.Z. 91 J5
Awbārī, Libya 79 C8
Awe, L., U.K. 14 E3
Aweil, Sudan 81 F2
Awgu, Nigeria 83 D6
Awjilah, Libya 79 C10
Awka, Nigeria 83 D6
Ax-les-Thermes, France 20 F5
Axat, France 20 F6
Axe →, U.K. 13 F5
Axel Heiberg I., Canada 4 B3
Axim, Ghana 82 E4
Axintele, Romania 43 F11
Axiós →, Greece 40 F6
Axminster, U.K. 13 G4
Axvall, Sweden 11 F7
Ay, France 19 C11
Ayabaca, Peru 124 D3
Ayabe, Japan 55 G7
Ayacucho, Argentina 126 D4
Ayacucho, Peru 124 F4
Ayaguz, Kazakstan 50 E9
Ayamé, Ivory C. 82 D4
Ayamonte, Spain 35 H3
Ayan, Russia 51 D14
Ayancık, Turkey 72 B6
Ayas, Turkey 72 B5
Ayaviri, Peru 124 F4
Aybastı, Turkey 72 B7
Aydın, Turkey 72 D2
Aydin □, Turkey 39 D9
Aydin Dağları, Turkey 39 D10
Ayelu, Ethiopia 81 E5
Ayenngré, Togo 83 D5
Ayer, U.S.A. 111 D13
Ayerbe, Spain 32 C4
Ayer's Cliff, Canada 111 A12
Ayers Rock, Australia 93 E5
Ayiá, Greece 38 B4
Ayia Aikateríni, Ákra, Greece 36 A3
Ayía Ánna, Greece 38 C5
Ayia Dhéka, Greece 36 D6
Ayia Gálini, Greece 36 D6
Ayía Marína, Kásos, Greece 39 F8
Ayía Marína, Léros, Greece 39 D8
Ayia Napa, Cyprus 36 E13
Ayía Paraskeví, Greece 39 B8
Ayia Phyla, Cyprus 36 E12
Ayía Rouméli, Greece 38 F5
Ayía Varvára, Greece 36 D7
Ayiássos, Greece 39 B8
Áyioi Theódhoroi, Greece 38 D5
Áyion Óros □, Greece 41 F8
Áyios Amvrósios, Cyprus 36 D12
Áyios Andréas, Greece 38 D4
Áyios Evstrátios, Greece 38 B6
Áyios Ioánnis, Ákra, Greece 36 D7
Áyios Isidhoros, Greece 36 C9
Áyios Kiríkos, Greece 39 D8
Áyios Matthaíos, Greece 36 B3
Áyios Mírono, Greece 39 F7
Áyios Nikólaos, Greece 36 D7
Áyios Pétros, Greece 38 C2
Áyios Seryios, Cyprus 36 D12
Ayios Theodhoros, Cyprus 36 D13
Áyios Yeóryios, Greece 38 D5
Aykathonisi, Greece 39 D8
Aykirikçi, Turkey 39 B12
Aylesbury, U.K. 13 F7
Aylmer, Canada 110 D4
Aylmer, L., Canada 100 B8
'Ayn, Wādī al, Oman 71 F7
Ayn Dār, Si. Arabia 71 E7
Ayn Zālah, Iraq 70 B4
Ayna, Spain 33 G2
Ayod, Sudan 81 F3
Ayolas, Paraguay 126 B4
Ayom, Sudan 81 F2
Ayon, Ostrov, Russia 51 C17
Ayora, Spain 33 F3
Ayorou, Niger 83 C5
'Ayoûn el 'Atroûs, Mauritania 82 B3
Ayr, Australia 94 B4
Ayr, Canada 110 C4
Ayr, U.K. 14 F4
Ayr →, U.K. 14 F4
Ayrancı, Turkey 72 D5
Ayrancılar, Turkey 39 C9
Ayre, Pt. of, U.K. 12 C3
Aysha, Ethiopia 81 E5
Ayton, Australia 94 B4
Aytos, Bulgaria 41 D11
Aytoska Planina, Bulgaria 41 D11
Ayu, Kepulauan, Indonesia 63 D8
Ayutla, Guatemala 120 D1
Ayutla, Mexico 119 D5
Ayvacık, Turkey 72 C2
Ayvalık, Turkey 39 B8
Az Zabadānī, Syria 75 B5
Az Ẓāhirīyah, West Bank 75 D3
Az Ẓahrān, Si. Arabia 71 E6
Az Zarqā, Jordan 75 C5
Az Zarqā', U.A.E. 71 E7
Az Zāwiyah, Libya 79 B8
Az Zībār, Iraq 70 B5
Az Zilfī, Si. Arabia 70 E5
Az Zubayr, Iraq 70 D5
Az Zuqur, Yemen 81 E5
Azambuja, Portugal 35 F2
Azamgarh, India 69 F10
Azangaro, Peru 124 F4
Azaoua, Niger 83 B5
Azaouad, Mali 82 B4
Azaouak, Vallée de l', Mali 83 B5
Āzār Shahr, Iran 70 B5
Azara, Nigeria 83 D6
Azarān, Iran 70 B5
Azärbayjan = Azerbaijan ■, Asia 49 K9
Āzarbāyjān-e Gharbī □, Iran 70 B5
Āzarbāyjān-e Sharqī □, Iran 70 B5
Azare, Nigeria 83 C7
Azay-le-Rideau, France 18 E7
A'zāz, Syria 70 B3
Azbine = Aïr, Niger 83 B6
Azerbaijan ■, Asia 49 K9
Azerbaijchan = Azerbaijan ■, Asia 49 K9
Azezo, Ethiopia 81 E4
Azimganj, India 69 G13
Aznalcóllar, Spain 35 H4
Azogues, Ecuador 124 D3
Azores, Atl. Oc. 78 A1
Azov, Russia 47 J10
Azov, Sea of, Europe 47 J9
Azovskoye More = Azov, Sea of, Europe 47 J9
Azpeitia, Spain 32 B2
Azraq ash Shīshān, Jordan 75 D5
Aztec, U.S.A. 115 H10
Azúa de Compostela, Dom. Rep. 121 C5
Azuaga, Spain 35 G5
Azuara, Spain 32 D4
Azuer →, Spain 35 F7
Azuero, Pen. de, Panama 120 E3
Azuga, Romania 43 E10
Azul, Argentina 126 D4
Azusa, U.S.A. 117 L9
Azzano Décimo, Italy 29 C9

B

Ba Don, Vietnam 64 D6
Ba Dong, Vietnam 65 H6
Ba Ngoi = Cam Lam, Vietnam 65 G7
Ba Tri, Vietnam 65 G6
Ba Xian = Bazhou, China 56 E9
Baa, Indonesia 63 F6
Baamonde, Spain 34 B3
Baarle-Nassau, Belgium 17 C4
Bab el Mandeb, Red Sea 74 E3
Baba, Bulgaria 40 D7
Baba Burnu, Turkey 39 B8
Baba dag, Azerbaijan 49 K9
Bābā Kalū, Iran 71 D6
Babadag, Romania 43 F13
Babadağ, Turkey 39 D10
Babadayhan, Turkmenistan 50 F7
Babaeski, Turkey 41 E11
Babahoyo, Ecuador 124 D3
Babai = Sarju →, India 69 F9
Babana, Nigeria 83 C5
Babanusa, Sudan 81 E2
Babar, Indonesia 63 F7
Babar, Pakistan 68 D3
Babarkach, Pakistan 68 E3
Babayevo, Russia 46 C8
Babb, U.S.A. 114 B7
Babelthuap, Pac. Oc. 63 C8
Babenhausen, Germany 25 F4
Băbeni, Romania 43 F9
Baberu, India 69 G9
Babi Besar, Pulau, Malaysia 65 L4
Babia Gora, Europe 45 J6
Babian Jiang →, China 58 F3
Babile, Ethiopia 81 F5
Babimost, Poland 45 F2
Babinda, Australia 94 B4
Babine, Canada 104 B3
Babine →, Canada 104 B3
Babine L., Canada 104 C3
Babo, Indonesia 63 E8
Babócsa, Hungary 42 D2
Bābol, Iran 71 B7
Bābol Sar, Iran 71 B7
Baborów, Poland 45 H5

Babruysk, Belarus 47 F5
Babuhri, India 68 F3
Babuna, Macedonia 40 E5
Babura, Nigeria 83 C6
Babusar Pass, Pakistan 69 B5
Babušnica, Serbia, Yug. 40 C6
Babuyan Chan., Phil. 61 B4
Babylon, Iraq 70 C5
Bač, Serbia, Yug. 42 E4
Bâc →, Moldova 43 D14
Bac Can, Vietnam 58 F5
Bac Giang, Vietnam 58 G6
Bac Lieu, Vietnam 65 H5
Bac Ninh, Vietnam 58 G6
Bac Phan, Vietnam 64 B5
Bac Quang, Vietnam 58 F5
Bacabal, Brazil 125 D10
Bacalar, Mexico 119 D7
Bacan, Kepulauan, Indonesia 63 E7
Bacarra, Phil. 61 B4
Bacău, Romania 43 D11
Bacău □, Romania 43 D11
Baccarat, France 19 D13
Bacerac, Mexico 118 A3
Băceşti, Romania 43 D12
Bach Long Vi, Dao, Vietnam 64 B6
Bacharach, Germany 25 E3
Bachelina, Russia 50 D7
Bachhwara, India 69 G11
Bachuma, Ethiopia 81 F4
Bačina, Serbia, Yug. 40 C5
Back →, Canada 100 B9
Bačka Palanka, Serbia, Yug. 42 E4
Bačka Topola, Serbia, Yug. 42 E4
Bäckebo, Sweden 11 H10
Bäckefors, Sweden 11 F6
Bäckhammar, Sweden 10 E8
Bački Petrovac, Serbia, Yug. 42 E4
Backnang, Germany 25 G5
Baco, Mt., Phil. 61 E4
Bacolod, Phil. 61 F5
Bacqueville-en-Caux, France 18 C8
Bács-Kiskun □, Hungary 42 D4
Bácsalmás, Hungary 42 D4
Bacuag = Placer, Phil. 61 G6
Bacuk, Malaysia 65 J4
Bād, Iran 71 C7
Bad →, U.S.A. 112 C4
Bad Aussee, Austria 26 D6
Bad Axe, U.S.A. 110 C2
Bad Bergzabern, Germany 25 F3
Bad Berleburg, Germany 24 D4
Bad Bevensen, Germany 24 B6
Bad Bramstedt, Germany 24 B5
Bad Brückenau, Germany 25 E5
Bad Doberan, Germany 24 A7
Bad Driburg, Germany 24 D5
Bad Ems, Germany 25 E3
Bad Frankenhausen, Germany 24 D7
Bad Freienwalde, Germany 24 C10
Bad Goisern, Austria 26 D6
Bad Harzburg, Germany 24 D6
Bad Hersfeld, Germany 24 E5
Bad Hofgastein, Austria 26 D6
Bad Homburg, Germany 25 E4
Bad Honnef, Germany 24 E3
Bad Iburg, Germany 24 C4
Bad Ischl, Austria 26 D6
Bad Kissingen, Germany 25 E6
Bad Königshofen, Germany 25 E6
Bad Kreuznach, Germany 25 F3
Bad Krozingen, Germany 25 H3
Bad Laasphe, Germany 24 E4
Bad Lands, U.S.A. 112 D3
Bad Langensalza, Germany 24 D6
Bad Lauterberg, Germany 24 D6
Bad Leonfelden, Austria 26 C7
Bad Liebenwerda, Germany 24 D9
Bad Mergentheim, Germany 25 F5
Bad Münstereifel, Germany 24 E2
Bad Nauheim, Germany 25 E4
Bad Neuenahr-Ahrweiler, Germany 24 E3
Bad Neustadt, Germany 25 E6
Bad Oeynhausen, Germany 24 C4
Bad Oldesloe, Germany 24 B6
Bad Orb, Germany 25 E5
Bad Pyrmont, Germany 24 D5
Bad Reichenhall, Germany 25 H8
Bad Säckingen, Germany 25 H3
Bad Salzuflen, Germany 24 C4
Bad Salzungen, Germany 24 E6
Bad Schwartau, Germany 24 B6
Bad Segeberg, Germany 24 B6
Bad St. Leonhard, Austria 26 E7
Bad Tölz, Germany 25 H7
Bad Urach, Germany 25 G5
Bad Vöslau, Austria 27 D9
Bad Waldsee, Germany 25 H5
Bad Wildungen, Germany 24 D5
Bad Wimpfen, Germany 25 F5
Bad Windsheim, Germany 25 F6
Bad Zwischenahn, Germany 24 B4
Bada Barabil, India 69 H11
Badagara, India 66 P9
Badagri, Nigeria 83 D5
Badajós, L., Brazil 124 D6
Badajoz, Spain 35 G4
Badajoz □, Spain 35 G4
Badalona, Spain 32 D7
Badalzai, Afghan. 68 E1
Badampahar, India 67 H15
Badanah, Si. Arabia 70 D4
Badarinath, India 69 D8
Badas, Kepulauan, Indonesia 62 D3
Baddo →, Pakistan 66 F4
Bade, Indonesia 63 F9
Badeggi, Nigeria 83 D6
Badéguichéri, Niger 83 C6
Baden, Austria 27 C9
Baden, Switz. 25 H4
Baden, U.S.A. 110 F4
Baden-Baden, Germany 25 G4
Baden-Württemberg □, Germany 25 G4
Badgastein, Austria 26 D6
Badger, Canada 103 C8
Badger, U.S.A. 116 J7
Bādghīsāt □, Afghan. 66 B3
Badgom, India 69 B6
Badia Polésine, Italy 29 C8
Badin, Pakistan 68 G3
Badlands National Park, U.S.A. 112 D3
Badogo, Mali 82 C3
Badoumbé, Mali 82 C2
Badrah, Iraq 70 C5
Badrinath, India 69 D8
Badulla, Sri Lanka 66 R12
Baena, Spain 35 H6
Baeza, Spain 35 H7
Bafang, Cameroon 83 D7
Bafatá, Guinea-Biss. 82 C2
Baffin B., Canada 4 B4
Baffin I., Canada 101 B12
Bafia, Cameroon 83 E7
Bafilo, Togo 83 D5
Bafing →, Mali 82 C2
Bafliyūn, Syria 70 B3
Bafoulabé, Mali 82 C2
Bafoussam, Cameroon 83 D7
Bāfq, Iran 71 D7
Bafra, Turkey 72 B6
Bafra Burnu, Turkey 72 B7
Bāft, Iran 71 D8
Bafut, Cameroon 83 D7
Bafwasende, Dem. Rep. of the Congo 86 B2
Bagam, Niger 83 B6
Bagamoyo, Tanzania 86 D4
Bagan Datoh, Malaysia 65 L3
Bagan Serai, Malaysia 65 K3
Baganga, Phil. 61 H7
Bagani, Namibia 88 B3
Bagansiapiapi, Indonesia 62 D2
Bagasra, India 68 J4
Bagaud, India 68 H6
Bagawi, Sudan 81 E3
Bagbag, Sudan 81 D3
Bagdad, U.S.A. 117 L11
Bagdarin, Russia 51 D12
Bagé, Brazil 127 C5
Bagenalstown = Muine Bheag, Ireland 15 D5
Baggs, U.S.A. 114 F10
Bagh, Pakistan 69 C5
Baghain →, India 69 G9
Baghdād, Iraq 70 C5
Bagheria, Italy 30 D6
Baghlān, Afghan. 66 A6
Bagley, U.S.A. 112 B7
Bagnara Cálabra, Italy 31 D8
Bagnasco, Italy 28 D5
Bagnères-de-Bigorre, France 20 E4
Bagnères-de-Luchon, France 20 F4
Bagni di Lucca, Italy 28 D7
Bagno di Romagna, Italy 29 E8
Bagnoles-de-l'Orne, France 18 D6
Bagnols-sur-Cèze, France 21 D8
Bagnorégio, Italy 29 F9
Bago = Pegu, Burma 67 L20
Bagodar, India 69 G11
Bagrationovsk, Russia 9 J19
Bagrdan, Serbia, Yug. 40 B5
Baguio, Phil. 61 C4
Bağyurdu, Turkey 39 C9
Bagzane, Monts, Niger 83 B6
Bah, India 69 F8
Bahabón de Esgueva, Spain 34 D7
Bahadurganj, India 69 F12
Bahadurgarh, India 68 E7
Bahama, Canal Viejo de, W. Indies 120 B4
Bahamas ■, N. Amer. 121 B5
Bahār, Iran 73 E13
Baharampur, India 69 G13
Baharîya, El Wâhât al, Egypt 80 B2
Bahawalnagar, Pakistan 68 E5
Bahawalpur, Pakistan 68 E4
Bahçe, Turkey 72 D7
Bahçecik, Turkey 41 F13
Baheri, India 69 E8
Bahgul →, India 69 F8
Bahi, Tanzania 86 D4
Bahi Swamp, Tanzania 86 D4
Bahía = Salvador, Brazil 125 F11
Bahía □, Brazil 125 F10
Bahía, Is. de la, Honduras 120 C2
Bahía Blanca, Argentina 126 D3
Bahía de Caráquez, Ecuador 124 D2
Bahía Honda, Cuba 120 B3
Bahía Laura, Argentina 128 F3
Bahía Negra, Paraguay 124 H7
Bahir Dar, Ethiopia 81 E4
Bahmanzād, Iran 71 D6
Bahr el Ahmar □, Sudan 80 D4
Bahr el Ghazâl □, Sudan 81 F2
Bahr el Jabal □, Sudan 81 G3
Bahr Yûsef →, Egypt 80 B3
Bahraich, India 69 F9
Bahrain ■, Asia 71 E6
Bahror, India 68 F7
Bāhū Kalāt, Iran 71 E9
Bai, Mali 82 C4
Bai Bung, Mui = Ca Mau, Mui, Vietnam 65 H5
Bai Duc, Vietnam 64 C5
Bai Thuong, Vietnam 64 C5
Baia de Aramă, Romania 42 E7
Baia Mare, Romania 43 C8
Baia-Sprie, Romania 43 C8
Baião, Brazil 125 D9
Baïbokoum, Chad 79 G9
Baicheng, China 57 B12
Băicoi, Romania 43 E10
Baidoa, Somali Rep. 74 G3
Baie Comeau, Canada 103 C6
Baie-St-Paul, Canada 103 C5
Baie Trinité, Canada 103 C6
Baie Verte, Canada 103 C8
Baignes-Ste-Radegonde, France 20 C3
Baigneux-les-Juifs, France 19 E11
Baihar, India 69 H9
Baihe, China 56 H6
Ba'ījī, Iraq 70 C4
Baijnath, India 69 E8
Baikal, L. = Baykal, Oz., Russia 51 D11
Baikunthpur, India 69 H10
Baile Atha Cliath = Dublin, Ireland 15 C5
Băile Govora, Romania 43 E9
Băile Herculane, Romania 42 F7
Băile Olăneşti, Romania 43 E9
Băile Tuşnad, Romania 43 D10
Bailén, Spain 35 G7
Băileşti, Romania 43 F8
Baima, China 58 A3
Bain-de-Bretagne, France 18 E5
Bainbridge, Ga., U.S.A. 109 K3
Bainbridge, N.Y., U.S.A. 111 D9
Baing, Indonesia 63 F6
Bainiu, China 56 H7
Baiona, Spain 34 C2
Bā'ir, Jordan 75 E5
Bairin Youqi, China 57 C10
Bairin Zuoqi, China 57 C10
Bairnsdale, Australia 95 F4
Bais, Phil. 61 G5
Baisha, China 56 G7
Baissa, Nigeria 83 D7
Baitadi, Nepal 69 E9
Baiyin, China 56 F3
Baiyü, China 58 B2
Baiyu Shan, China 56 F4
Baiyuda, Sudan 80 D3
Baj Baj, India 69 H13
Baja, Hungary 42 D3
Baja, Pta., Mexico 118 B1
Baja California, Mexico 118 A1
Baja California □, Mexico 118 B2
Baja California Sur □, Mexico 118 B2
Bajag, India 69 H9
Bajamar, Canary Is. 37 F3
Bajana, India 68 H4
Bājgīrān, Iran 71 B8
Bajimba, Mt., Australia 95 D5
Bajina Bašta, Serbia, Yug. 40 C3
Bajmok, Serbia, Yug. 42 E4
Bajo Nuevo, Caribbean 120 C4
Bajoga, Nigeria 83 C7
Bajool, Australia 94 C5
Bak, Hungary 42 D1
Bakar, Croatia 29 C11
Bakel, Senegal 82 C2
Baker, Calif., U.S.A. 117 K10
Baker, Mont., U.S.A. 112 B2
Baker, L., Canada 100 B10
Baker City, U.S.A. 114 D5
Baker I., Pac. Oc. 96 G10
Baker I., U.S.A. 104 B2
Baker L., Australia 93 E4
Baker Lake, Canada 100 B10
Baker Mt., U.S.A. 114 B3
Bakers Creek, Australia 94 C4
Baker's Dozen Is., Canada 102 A4
Bakersfield, Calif., U.S.A. 117 K8
Bakersfield, Vt., U.S.A. 111 B12
Bakhchysaray, Ukraine 47 K7
Bakhmach, Ukraine 47 G7
Bākhtarān, Iran 70 C5
Bākhtarān □, Iran 70 C5
Bakı, Azerbaijan 49 K9
Bakır →, Turkey 39 C9
Bakırdaği, Turkey 72 C6
Bakkafjörður, Iceland 8 C6
Baklan, Turkey 39 C11
Bako, Ethiopia 81 F4
Bako, Ivory C. 82 D3
Bakony, Hungary 42 C2
Bakony Forest = Bakony, Hungary 42 C2
Bakori, Nigeria 83 C6
Bakouma, C.A.R. 84 C4
Baksan, Russia 49 J6
Bakswaho, India 69 G8
Baku = Bakı, Azerbaijan 49 K9
Bakundi, Nigeria 83 D7
Bakutis Coast, Antarctica 5 D15
Baky = Bakı, Azerbaijan 49 K9
Bala, Canada 110 A5
Bala, Senegal 82 C2
Bâlâ, Turkey 72 C5
Bala, U.K. 12 E4
Bala, L., U.K. 12 E4
Balabac I., Phil. 62 C5
Balabac Str., E. Indies 62 C5
Balabagh, Afghan. 68 B4
Ba'labakk, Lebanon 75 B5
Balabalangan, Kepulauan, Indonesia 62 E5
Bălăciţa, Romania 43 F8
Balad, Iraq 70 C5
Balad Rūz, Iraq 70 C5
Bālādeh, Fārs, Iran 71 D6
Bālādeh, Māzandaran, Iran 71 B6
Balaghat, India 66 J12
Balaghat Ra., India 66 K10
Balaguer, Spain 32 D5
Balakhna, Russia 48 B6
Balaklava, Ukraine 47 K7
Balakliya, Ukraine 47 H9
Balakovo, Russia 48 D8
Balamau, India 69 F9
Bălan, Romania 43 D10
Balancán, Mexico 119 D6
Balashov, Russia 48 E6
Balasinor, India 68 H5
Balasore = Baleshwar, India 67 J15
Balassagyarmat, Hungary 42 B4
Balât, Egypt 80 B2
Balaton, Hungary 42 D2
Balatonboglár, Hungary 42 D2
Balatonfüred, Hungary 42 D2
Balatonszentgyörgy, Hungary 42 D2
Balayan, Phil. 61 E4
Balazote, Spain 33 G2
Balbieriškis, Lithuania 44 D10
Balbigny, France 21 C8
Balbina, Représa de, Brazil 124 D7
Balboa, Panama 120 E4
Balbriggan, Ireland 15 C5
Balcarce, Argentina 126 D4
Balcarres, Canada 105 C8
Bălceşti, Romania 43 F8
Balchik, Bulgaria 41 C12
Balclutha, N.Z. 91 M2
Balcones Escarpment, U.S.A. 113 L5
Balçova, Turkey 39 C9
Bald Hd., Australia 93 G2
Bald I., Australia 93 F2
Bald Knob, U.S.A. 113 H9
Baldock L., Canada 105 B9
Baldwin, Mich., U.S.A. 108 D3
Baldwin, Pa., U.S.A. 110 F5
Baldwinsville, U.S.A. 111 C8
Baldy Mt., U.S.A. 114 B9
Baldy Peak, U.S.A. 115 K9
Bale, Croatia 29 C10
Bale, Ethiopia 81 F5
Bale □, Ethiopia 81 F5
Baleares, Is., Spain 37 B10
Balearic Is. = Baleares, Is., Spain 37 B10
Baleine = Whale →, Canada 103 A6
Băleni, Romania 43 E12
Baler, Phil. 61 D4
Baler Bay, Phil. 61 D4
Baleshare, U.K. 14 D1
Baleshwar, India 67 J15
Balezino, Russia 48 B11
Balfate, Honduras 120 C2
Bali, Cameroon 83 D7
Balí, Greece 36 D6
Bali, India 68 G5
Bali □, Indonesia 62 F5
Bali, Selat, Indonesia 63 H16
Balia, S. Leone 82 D2
Baliapal, India 69 J12
Baligród, Poland 45 J9
Balıkeşir, Turkey 39 B9
Balıkeşir □, Turkey 39 B9
Balıklıçeşme, Turkey 41 F11
Balikpapan, Indonesia 62 E5
Balimbing, Phil. 63 C5
Baling, Malaysia 65 K3
Balingen, Germany 25 G4
Balinţ, Romania 42 E6
Balintang Channel, Phil. 61 B4
Balipara, India 67 F18
Balkan Mts. = Stara Planina, Bulgaria 40 C7
Balkhash = Balqash, Kazakstan 50 E8
Balkhash, Ozero = Balqash Köl, Kazakstan 50 E8
Balla, Bangla. 67 G17
Ballachulish, U.K. 14 E3
Balladonia, Australia 93 F3
Ballaghaderreen, Ireland 15 C3
Ballarat, Australia 95 F3
Ballard, L., Australia 93 E3
Ballater, U.K. 14 D5
Ballé, Mali 82 B3
Ballenas, Canal de, Mexico 118 B2
Balleny Is., Antarctica 5 C11
Balleroy, France 18 C6
Ballerup, Denmark 11 J6
Ballı, Turkey 41 F11
Ballia, India 69 G11
Ballina, Australia 95 D5
Ballina, Ireland 15 B2
Ballinasloe, Ireland 15 C3
Ballinger, U.S.A. 113 K5
Ballinrobe, Ireland 15 C2
Ballinskelligs B., Ireland 15 E1
Ballon, France 18 D7
Ballsh, Albania 40 F3
Ballston Spa, U.S.A. 111 D11
Ballycastle, U.K. 15 A5
Ballyclare, U.K. 15 B5
Ballyhaunis, Ireland 15 C3
Ballymena, U.K. 15 B5
Ballymoney, U.K. 15 A5
Ballymote, Ireland 15 B3
Ballynahinch, U.K. 15 B6
Ballyquintin Pt., U.K. 15 B6
Ballyshannon, Ireland 15 B3
Balmaceda, Chile 128 F2
Balmaseda, Spain 32 B1
Balmazújváros, Hungary 42 C6
Balmertown, Canada 105 C10
Balmoral, Australia 95 F3
Balmorhea, U.S.A. 113 K3
Balonne →, Australia 95 D4
Balotra, India 68 G5
Balqash, Kazakstan 50 E8
Balqash Köl, Kazakstan 50 E8
Balrampur, India 69 F10
Balranald, Australia 95 E3
Balş, Romania 43 F9
Balsas, Mexico 119 D5
Balsas →, Brazil 125 E9
Balsas →, Mexico 118 D4
Bålsta, Sweden 10 E11
Balston Spa, U.S.A. 111 D11
Balta, Romania 42 F7
Balta, Ukraine 47 H5
Baltanás, Spain 34 D6
Bălţi, Moldova 43 C12
Baltic Sea, Europe 9 H18
Baltîm, Egypt 80 H7
Baltimore, Ireland 15 E2
Baltimore, Md., U.S.A. 108 F7
Baltimore, Ohio, U.S.A. 110 G2
Baltit, Pakistan 69 A6
Baltiysk, Russia 9 J18
Baltrum, Germany 24 B3
Baluchistan □, Pakistan 66 F4
Balurghat, India 69 G13
Balvi, Latvia 9 H22
Balya, Turkey 39 B9
Bam, Iran 71 D8
Bama, China 58 E6
Bama, Nigeria 83 C7
Bamaga, Australia 94 A3
Bamaji L., Canada 102 B1
Bamako, Mali 82 C3
Bamba, Mali 83 B4
Bambara Maoundé, Mali 82 B4
Bambari, C.A.R. 84 C4
Bambaroo, Australia 94 B4
Bambaya, Guinea 82 D2
Bamberg, Germany 25 F6
Bamberg, U.S.A. 109 J5
Bambesi, Ethiopia 81 F3
Bambey, Senegal 82 C1
Bambey, Senegal 82 C1
Bambili, Dem. Rep. of the Congo 86 B2
Bamboi, Ghana 82 D4
Bamenda, Cameroon 83 D7
Bamfield, Canada 104 D3
Bāmīān □, Afghan. 66 B5
Bamiancheng, China 57 C13
Bamkin, Cameroon 83 D7
Bampūr, Iran 71 E9
Ban, Burkina Faso 82 C4
Ban Ban, Laos 64 C4
Ban Bang Hin, Thailand 65 H2
Ban Chiang Klang, Thailand 64 C3
Ban Chik, Laos 64 D4
Ban Choho, Thailand 64 E4
Ban Dan Lan Hoi, Thailand 64 D2
Ban Don = Surat Thani, Thailand 65 H2
Ban Don, Vietnam 64 F6
Ban Don, Ao →, Thailand 65 H2
Ban Dong, Thailand 64 C3
Ban Hong, Thailand 64 C2
Ban Kaeng, Thailand 64 D3
Ban Kantang, Thailand 65 J2
Ban Keun, Laos 64 C4
Ban Khai, Thailand 64 F3
Ban Kheun, Laos 64 B3
Ban Khlong Kua, Thailand 65 J3
Ban Khuan Mao, Thailand 65 J2
Ban Ko Yai Chim, Thailand 65 G2
Ban Kok, Thailand 64 D4
Ban Laem, Thailand 64 F2
Ban Lao Ngam, Laos 64 E6
Ban Le Kathe, Thailand 64 E2
Ban Mae Chedi, Thailand 64 C2
Ban Mae Laeng, Thailand 64 B2
Ban Mae Sariang, Thailand 64 C1
Ban Mê Thuôt = Buon Ma Thuot, Vietnam 64 F7
Ban Mi, Thailand 64 E3
Ban Muong Mo, Laos 64 C4
Ban Na Mo, Laos 64 D5
Ban Na San, Thailand 65 H2
Ban Na Tong, Laos 64 B3
Ban Nam Bac, Laos 64 B4
Ban Nam Ma, Laos 64 A3
Ban Ngang, Laos 64 E6
Ban Nong Bok, Laos 64 D5
Ban Nong Boua, Laos 64 E6
Ban Nong Pling, Thailand 64 E3
Ban Pak Chan, Thailand 65 G2
Ban Phai, Thailand 64 D4
Ban Pong, Thailand 64 F2
Ban Ron Phibun, Thailand 65 H2
Ban Sanam Chai, Thailand 65 J3
Ban Sangkha, Thailand 64 E4
Ban Tak, Thailand 64 D2
Ban Tako, Thailand 64 E4
Ban Tha Dua, Thailand 64 D2
Ban Tha Li, Thailand 64 D3
Ban Tha Nun, Thailand 65 H2
Ban Thahine, Laos 64 E5
Ban Xien Kok, Laos 64 B3
Ban Yen Nhan, Vietnam 64 B6
Banaba, Kiribati 96 H8
Banalia, Dem. Rep. of the Congo 86 B2
Banam, Cambodia 65 G5
Banamba, Mali 82 C3
Banana Is., S. Leone 82 D2
Bananal, I. do, Brazil 125 F8
Banaras = Varanasi, India 69 G10
Banas →, Gujarat, India 68 H4
Banas →, Mad. P., India 69 G9
Bânâs, Ras, Egypt 80 C4
Banaz, Turkey 39 C11
Banaz →, Turkey 39 C11
Banbān, Si. Arabia 70 E5
Banbridge, U.K. 15 B5
Banbury, U.K. 13 E6
Banchory, U.K. 14 D6
Banco, Ethiopia 81 F4

Batie

Bancroft, *Canada* 102 C4
Band, *Romania* 43 D9
Band Bonī, *Iran* 71 E8
Band Qīr, *Iran* 71 D6
Banda, *Mad. P., India* 69 G8
Banda, *Ut. P., India* 69 G9
Banda, Kepulauan, *Indonesia* 63 E7
Banda Aceh, *Indonesia* 62 C1
Banda Banda, Mt., *Australia* 95 E5
Banda Elat, *Indonesia* 63 F8
Banda Is. = Banda, Kepulauan, *Indonesia* 63 E7
Banda Sea, *Indonesia* 63 F7
Bandai-San, *Japan* 54 F10
Bandama →, *Ivory C.* 82 D3
Bandama Blanc →, *Ivory C.* 82 D3
Bandama Rouge →, *Ivory C.* 82 D4
Bandān, *Iran* 71 D9
Bandanaira, *Indonesia* 63 E7
Bandanwara, *India* 68 F6
Bandar = Machilipatnam, *India* 67 L12
Bandār 'Abbās, *Iran* 71 E8
Bandar-e Anzalī, *Iran* 71 B6
Bandar-e Bushehr = Būshehr, *Iran* 71 D6
Bandar-e Chārak, *Iran* 71 E7
Bandar-e Deylam, *Iran* 71 D6
Bandar-e Khomeynı, *Iran* 71 D6
Bandar-e Lengeh, *Iran* 71 E7
Bandar-e Maqām, *Iran* 71 E7
Bandar-e Ma'shur, *Iran* 71 D6
Bandar-e Nakhīlū, *Iran* 71 E7
Bandar-e Rīg, *Iran* 71 D6
Bandar-e Torkeman, *Iran* 71 B7
Bandar Maharani = Muar, *Malaysia* 65 L4
Bandar Penggaram = Batu Pahat, *Malaysia* 65 M4
Bandar Seri Begawan, *Brunei* 62 C4
Bandar Sri Aman, *Malaysia* 62 D4
Bandawe, *Malawi* 87 E3
Bande, *Spain* 34 C3
Bandeira, Pico da, *Brazil* 127 A7
Bandera, *Argentina* 126 B3
Banderas, B. de, *Mexico* 118 C3
Bandhogarh, *India* 69 H9
Bandi →, *India* 68 F6
Bandiagara, *Mali* 82 C4
Bandikui, *India* 68 F7
Bandırma, *Turkey* 41 F11
Bandol, *France* 21 E9
Bandon, *Ireland* 15 E3
Bandon →, *Ireland* 15 E3
Bandula, *Mozam.* 87 F3
Bandundu, *Dem. Rep. of the Congo* 84 E3
Bandung, *Indonesia* 63 G12
Bané, *Burkina Faso* 83 C4
Băneasa, *Romania* 43 E12
Bāneh, *Iran* 70 C5
Bañeres, *Spain* 33 G4
Banes, *Cuba* 121 B4
Banff, *Canada* 104 C5
Banff, *U.K.* 14 D6
Banff Nat. Park, *Canada* 104 C5
Banfora, *Burkina Faso* 82 C4
Bang Fai →, *Laos* 64 D5
Bang Hieng →, *Laos* 64 D5
Bang Krathum, *Thailand* 64 D3
Bang Lamung, *Thailand* 64 F3
Bang Mun Nak, *Thailand* 64 D3
Bang Pa In, *Thailand* 64 E3
Bang Rakam, *Thailand* 64 D3
Bang Saphan, *Thailand* 65 G2
Bangaduni I., *India* 69 J13
Bangala Dam, *Zimbabwe* 87 G3
Bangalore, *India* 66 N10
Banganga →, *India* 68 F6
Bangangté, *Cameroon* 83 D7
Bangaon, *India* 69 H13
Bangassou, *C.A.R.* 84 D4
Banggai, *Indonesia* 63 E6
Banggai, Kepulauan, *Indonesia* 63 E6
Banggai Arch. = Banggai, Kepulauan, *Indonesia* 63 E6
Banggi, *Malaysia* 62 C5
Banghāzī, *Libya* 79 B10
Bangjang, *Sudan* 81 E3
Bangka, *Sulawesi, Indonesia* 63 D7
Bangka, *Sumatera, Indonesia* 62 E3
Bangka, Selat, *Indonesia* 62 E3
Bangkalan, *Indonesia* 63 G15
Bangkinang, *Indonesia* 62 D2
Bangko, *Indonesia* 62 E2
Bangkok, *Thailand* 64 F3
Bangladesh ■, *Asia* 67 H17
Bangolo, *Ivory C.* 82 D3
Bangong Co, *India* 69 B8
Bangor, *Down, U.K.* 15 B6
Bangor, *Gwynedd, U.K.* 12 D3
Bangor, *Maine, U.S.A.* 101 D13
Bangor, *Pa., U.S.A.* 111 F9
Bangued, *Phil.* 61 C4
Bangui, *C.A.R.* 84 D3
Bangui, *Phil.* 61 B4
Banguru, *Dem. Rep. of the Congo* 86 B2
Bangweulu, L., *Zambia* 87 E3
Bangweulu Swamp, *Zambia* 87 E3
Bani, *Dom. Rep.* 121 C5
Bani →, *Mali* 82 C4
Bani Bangou, *Niger* 83 B5
Banī Sa'd, *Iraq* 70 C5
Bania, *Ivory C.* 82 D4
Banihal Pass, *India* 69 C6
Banikoara, *Benin* 83 C5
Bāniyās, *Syria* 70 C3
Banja Luka, *Bos.-H.* 42 F2
Banjar, *India* 68 D7
Banjar →, *India* 69 H9
Banjarmasin, *Indonesia* 62 E4
Banjul, *Gambia* 82 C1
Banka, *India* 69 G12
Bankas, *Mali* 82 C4
Bankeryd, *Sweden* 11 G8
Banket, *Zimbabwe* 87 F3
Bankilaré, *Niger* 83 C5
Bankipore, *India* 67 G14
Banks I., *B.C., Canada* 104 C3
Banks I., *N.W.T., Canada* 100 A7
Banks Pen., *N.Z.* 91 K4
Banks Str., *Australia* 94 G4
Bankura, *India* 69 H12
Bankya, *Bulgaria* 40 D7
Banmankhi, *India* 69 G12
Bann →, *Arm., U.K.* 15 B5
Bann →, *L'derry., U.K.* 15 A5
Bannalec, *France* 18 E3
Bannang Sata, *Thailand* 65 J3
Banning, *U.S.A.* 117 M10
Banningville = Bandundu, *Dem. Rep. of the Congo* 84 E3
Banno, *Ethiopia* 81 G4
Bannockburn, *Canada* 110 B7
Bannockburn, *U.K.* 14 E5
Bannockburn, *Zimbabwe* 87 G2
Bannu, *Pakistan* 66 C7
Bano, *India* 69 H11
Bañolas = Banyoles, *Spain* 32 C7
Banon, *France* 21 D9
Baños de la Encina, *Spain* 35 G7
Baños de Molgas, *Spain* 34 C3
Bánovce nad Bebravou, *Slovak Rep.* 27 C11
Banovići, *Bos.-H.* 42 F3
Bansgaon, *India* 69 F10
Banská Bystrica, *Slovak Rep.* 27 C12
Banská Štiavnica, *Slovak Rep.* 27 C11
Bansko, *Bulgaria* 40 E7
Banskobystrický □, *Slovak Rep.* 27 C12
Banswara, *India* 68 H6
Bantaeng, *Indonesia* 63 F5
Bantaji, *Nigeria* 83 D7
Bantayan, *Phil.* 61 F5
Bantry, *Ireland* 15 E2
Bantry B., *Ireland* 15 E2
Bantul, *Indonesia* 63 G14
Bantva, *India* 68 J4
Banu, *Afghan.* 66 B6
Banya, *Bulgaria* 41 D8
Banyak, Kepulauan, *Indonesia* 62 D1
Banyalbufar, *Spain* 37 B9
Banyo, *Cameroon* 83 D7
Banyoles, *Spain* 32 C7
Banyuls-sur-Mer, *France* 20 F7
Banyumas, *Indonesia* 63 G13
Banyuwangi, *Indonesia* 63 H16
Banzare Coast, *Antarctica* 5 C9
Banzyville = Mobayi, *Dem. Rep. of the Congo* 84 D4
Bao Ha, *Vietnam* 58 F5
Bao Lac, *Vietnam* 64 A5
Bao Loc, *Vietnam* 65 G6
Bao'an = Shenzhen, *China* 59 F10
Baocheng, *China* 56 H4
Baode, *China* 56 E6
Baodi, *China* 57 E9
Baoding, *China* 56 E8
Baoji, *China* 56 G4
Baojing, *China* 58 C7
Baokang, *China* 59 B8
Baoshan, *Shanghai, China* 59 B13
Baoshan, *Yunnan, China* 58 E2
Baotou, *China* 56 D6
Baoxing, *China* 58 B4
Baoying, *China* 57 H10
Bap, *India* 68 F5
Bapatla, *India* 67 M12
Bapaume, *France* 19 B9
Bāqerābād, *Iran* 71 C6
Ba'qūbah, *Iraq* 70 C5
Baquedano, *Chile* 126 A2
Bar, *Montenegro, Yug.* 40 D3
Bar, *Ukraine* 47 H4
Bar Bigha, *India* 69 G11
Bar Harbor, *U.S.A.* 109 C11
Bar-le-Duc, *France* 19 D12
Bar-sur-Aube, *France* 19 D11
Bar-sur-Seine, *France* 19 D11
Bara, *India* 69 G9
Bâra, *Romania* 43 C12
Bara Banki, *India* 69 F9
Barabai, *Indonesia* 62 E5
Baraboo, *U.S.A.* 112 D10
Baracoa, *Cuba* 121 B5
Baradā →, *Syria* 75 B5
Baradero, *Argentina* 126 C4
Baradine, *Australia* 95 E4
Baraga, *U.S.A.* 112 B10
Bărăganul, *Romania* 43 F12
Barah →, *India* 68 F6
Barahona, *Dom. Rep.* 121 C5
Barahona, *Spain* 32 D2
Barail Range, *India* 67 G18
Baraka, *Sudan* 81 E2
Baraka →, *Sudan* 80 D4
Barakaldo, *Spain* 32 B2
Barakar →, *India* 69 G12
Barakhola, *India* 67 G18
Barakot, *India* 69 J11
Barakpur, *India* 69 H13
Baralaba, *Australia* 94 C4
Baralla, *Spain* 34 C3
Baralzon L., *Canada* 105 B9
Barameiya, *Sudan* 80 D4
Baramula, *India* 69 B6
Baran, *India* 68 G7
Baran →, *Pakistan* 68 G3
Barañain, *Spain* 32 C3
Baranavichy, *Belarus* 47 F4
Barani, *Burkina Faso* 82 C4
Baranof, *U.S.A.* 104 B2
Baranof I., *U.S.A.* 100 C6
Baranów Sandomierski, *Poland* 45 H8
Baranya □, *Hungary* 42 E3
Baraolt, *Romania* 43 D10
Barapasi, *Indonesia* 63 E9
Barasat, *India* 69 H13
Barat Daya, Kepulauan, *Indonesia* 63 F7
Barataria B., *U.S.A.* 113 L10
Barauda, *India* 68 H6
Baraut, *India* 68 E7
Barbacena, *Brazil* 127 A7
Barbados ■, *W. Indies* 121 D8
Barban, *Croatia* 29 C11
Barbària, C. de, *Spain* 37 C7
Barbaros, *Turkey* 41 F11
Barbastro, *Spain* 32 C5
Barbate = Barbate de Franco, *Spain* 35 J5
Barbate de Franco, *Spain* 35 J5
Barberino di Mugello, *Italy* 29 E8
Barberton, *S. Africa* 89 D5
Barberton, *U.S.A.* 110 E3
Barbezieux-St-Hilaire, *France* 20 C3
Barbosa, *Colombia* 124 B4
Barbourville, *U.S.A.* 109 G4
Barbuda, *W. Indies* 121 C7
Bârca, *Romania* 43 G8
Barcaldine, *Australia* 94 C4
Barcarrota, *Spain* 35 G4
Barcellona Pozzo di Gotto, *Italy* 31 D8
Barcelona, *Spain* 32 D7
Barcelona, *Venezuela* 124 A6
Barcelona □, *Spain* 32 D7
Barcelonette, *France* 21 D10
Barcelos, *Brazil* 124 D6
Barcin, *Poland* 45 F4
Barclayville, *Liberia* 82 E3
Barcoo →, *Australia* 94 D3
Barcs, *Hungary* 42 E2
Barczewo, *Poland* 44 E7
Bärdä, *Azerbaijan* 49 K8
Bardaï, *Chad* 79 D9
Bardas Blancas, *Argentina* 126 D2
Barddhaman, *India* 69 H12
Bardejov, *Slovak Rep.* 27 B14
Bardera, *Somali Rep.* 74 G3
Bardi, *Italy* 28 D6
Bardīyah, *Libya* 79 B10
Bardolino, *Italy* 28 C7
Bardonécchia, *Italy* 28 C3
Bardsey I., *U.K.* 12 E3
Bardstown, *U.S.A.* 108 G3
Bareilly, *India* 69 E8
Barela, *India* 69 H9
Barentin, *France* 18 C7
Barenton, *France* 18 D6
Barents Sea, *Arctic* 4 B9
Barentu, *Eritrea* 81 D4
Barfleur, *France* 18 C5
Barfleur, Pte. de, *France* 18 C5
Barga, *Italy* 28 D7
Bargara, *Australia* 94 C5
Bargas, *Spain* 34 F6
Bârgăului Bistrița, *Romania* 43 C9
Barge, *Italy* 28 D4
Bargnop, *Sudan* 81 F2
Bargteheide, *Germany* 24 B6
Barguzin, *Russia* 51 D11
Barh, *India* 69 G11
Barhaj, *India* 69 F10
Barham, *Australia* 95 F3
Barharwa, *India* 69 G12
Barhi, *India* 69 G11
Bari, *India* 68 F7
Bari, *Italy* 31 A9
Bari Doab, *Pakistan* 68 D5
Bari Sadri, *India* 68 G6
Bari Sardo, *Italy* 30 C2
Barīdī, Ra's, *Si. Arabia* 70 E3
Barīm, *Yemen* 76 E8
Barinas, *Venezuela* 124 B4
Baring, C., *Canada* 100 B8
Baringo, *Kenya* 86 B4
Baringo, L., *Kenya* 86 B4
Bârîs, *Egypt* 80 C3
Barisal, *Bangla.* 67 H17
Barisan, Bukit, *Indonesia* 62 E2
Barito →, *Indonesia* 62 E4
Barjac, *France* 21 D8
Barjols, *France* 21 E10
Bark L., *Canada* 110 A7
Barka = Baraka →, *Sudan* 80 D4
Barkakana, *India* 69 H11
Barkam, *China* 58 B4
Barker, *U.S.A.* 110 C6
Barkley, L., *U.S.A.* 109 G2
Barkley Sound, *Canada* 104 D3
Barkly East, *S. Africa* 88 E4
Barkly Roadhouse, *Australia* 94 B2
Barkly Tableland, *Australia* 94 B2
Barkly West, *S. Africa* 88 D3
Barkol, Wadi →, *Sudan* 80 D3
Barla Dağı, *Turkey* 39 C12
Bârlad, *Romania* 43 D12
Bârlad →, *Romania* 43 E12
Barlee, L., *Australia* 93 E2
Barlee, Mt., *Australia* 93 D4
Barletta, *Italy* 31 A9
Barlinek, *Poland* 45 F2
Barlovento, *Canary Is.* 37 F2
Barlow L., *Canada* 105 A8
Barmedman, *Australia* 95 E4
Barmer, *India* 68 G4
Barmera, *Australia* 95 E3
Barmouth, *U.K.* 12 E3
Barmstedt, *Germany* 24 B5
Barna →, *India* 69 G10
Barnagar, *India* 68 H6
Barnala, *India* 68 D6
Barnard Castle, *U.K.* 12 C6
Barnaul, *Russia* 50 D9
Barnesville, *U.S.A.* 109 J3
Barnet, *U.K.* 13 F7
Barneveld, *Neths.* 17 B5
Barneveld, *U.S.A.* 111 C9
Barneville-Cartevert, *France* 18 C5
Barnhart, *U.S.A.* 113 K4
Barnsley, *U.K.* 12 D6
Barnstaple, *U.K.* 13 F3
Barnstaple Bay = Bideford Bay, *U.K.* 13 F3
Barnsville, *U.S.A.* 112 B6
Barnwell, *U.S.A.* 109 J5
Baro, *Nigeria* 83 D6
Baro →, *Ethiopia* 81 F3
Baroda = Vadodara, *India* 68 H5
Baroda, *India* 68 G7
Baroe, *S. Africa* 88 E3
Baron Ra., *Australia* 92 D4
Barong, *China* 58 B2
Barotseland, *Zambia* 85 H4
Barouéli, *Mali* 82 C3
Barpeta, *India* 67 F17
Barques, Pt. Aux, *U.S.A.* 110 B2
Barquísimeto, *Venezuela* 124 A5
Barr, Ras el, *Egypt* 80 H7
Barr Smith Range, *Australia* 93 E3
Barra, *Brazil* 125 F10
Barra, *U.K.* 14 E1
Barra, Sd. of, *U.K.* 14 D1
Barra de Navidad, *Mexico* 118 D4
Barra do Corda, *Brazil* 125 E9
Barra do Piraí, *Brazil* 127 A7
Barra Falsa, Pta. da, *Mozam.* 89 C6
Barra Hd., *U.K.* 14 E1
Barra Mansa, *Brazil* 127 A7
Barraba, *Australia* 95 E5
Barrackpur = Barakpur, *India* 69 H13
Barradale Roadhouse, *Australia* 92 D1
Barrafranca, *Italy* 31 E7
Barraigh = Barra, *U.K.* 14 E1
Barranca, *Lima, Peru* 124 F3
Barranca, *Loreto, Peru* 124 D3
Barrancabermeja, *Colombia* 124 B4
Barrancas, *Venezuela* 124 B6
Barrancos, *Portugal* 35 G4
Barranqueras, *Argentina* 126 B4
Barranquilla, *Colombia* 124 A4
Barraute, *Canada* 102 C4
Barre, *Mass., U.S.A.* 111 D12
Barre, *Vt., U.S.A.* 111 B12
Barreal, *Argentina* 126 C2
Barreiras, *Brazil* 125 F10
Barreirinhas, *Brazil* 125 D10
Barreiro, *Portugal* 35 G1
Barrême, *France* 21 E10
Barren, Nosy, *Madag.* 89 B7
Barretos, *Brazil* 125 H9
Barrhead, *Canada* 104 C6
Barrie, *Canada* 102 D4
Barrier Ra., *Australia* 95 E3
Barrière, *Canada* 104 C4
Barrington, *U.S.A.* 111 E13
Barrington L., *Canada* 105 B8
Barrington Tops, *Australia* 95 E5
Barringun, *Australia* 95 D4
Barro do Garças, *Brazil* 125 G8
Barron, *U.S.A.* 112 C9
Barrow, *U.S.A.* 100 A4
Barrow →, *Ireland* 15 D5
Barrow Creek, *Australia* 94 C1
Barrow I., *Australia* 92 D2
Barrow-in-Furness, *U.K.* 12 C4
Barrow Pt., *Australia* 94 A3
Barrow Pt., *U.S.A.* 98 B4
Barrow Ra., *Australia* 93 E4
Barrow Str., *Canada* 4 B3
Barruecopardo, *Spain* 34 D4
Barruelo de Santullán, *Spain* 34 C6
Barry, *U.K.* 13 F4
Barry's Bay, *Canada* 102 C4
Barsalogho, *Burkina Faso* 83 C4
Barsat, *Pakistan* 69 A5
Barsham, *Syria* 70 C4
Barsi, *India* 66 K9
Barsinghausen, *Germany* 24 C5
Barsoi, *India* 67 G15
Barstow, *U.S.A.* 117 L9
Barth, *Germany* 24 A8
Barthélemy, Col, *Vietnam* 64 C5
Bartica, *Guyana* 124 B7
Bartin, *Turkey* 72 B5
Bartlesville, *U.S.A.* 113 G7
Bartlett, *U.S.A.* 116 J8
Bartlett, L., *Canada* 104 A5
Bartolomeu Dias, *Mozam.* 87 G4
Barton, *U.S.A.* 111 B12
Barton upon Humber, *U.K.* 12 D7
Bartoszyce, *Poland* 44 D7
Bartow, *U.S.A.* 109 M5
Barú, Volcan, *Panama* 120 E3
Barumba, *Dem. Rep. of the Congo* 86 B1
Baruth, *Germany* 24 C9
Baruunsuu, *Mongolia* 56 C3
Barvinkove, *Ukraine* 47 H9
Barwani, *India* 68 H6
Barwice, *Poland* 44 E3
Barycz →, *Poland* 45 G3
Barysaw, *Belarus* 46 E5
Barysh, *Russia* 48 D8
Barzān, *Iraq* 70 B5
Bârzava, *Romania* 42 D6
Bas-Rhin □, *France* 19 D14
Bašaid, *Serbia, Yug.* 42 E5
Bāsa'idū, *Iran* 71 E7
Basal, *Pakistan* 68 C5
Basankusa, *Dem. Rep. of the Congo* 84 D3
Basarabeasca, *Moldova* 43 D13
Basarabi, *Romania* 43 F13
Basauri, *Spain* 32 B2
Basawa, *Afghan.* 68 B4
Bascuñán, C., *Chile* 126 B1
Basel, *Switz.* 25 H3
Basel-Landschaft □, *Switz.* 25 H3
Basento →, *Italy* 31 B9
Bashākerd, Kūhhā-ye, *Iran* 71 E8
Bashaw, *Canada* 104 C6
Bāshī, *Iran* 71 D6
Bashkir Republic = Bashkortostan □, *Russia* 50 D6
Bashkortostan □, *Russia* 50 D6
Basibasy, *Madag.* 89 C7
Basilan I., *Phil.* 61 H5
Basilan Str., *Phil.* 61 H5
Basildon, *U.K.* 13 F8
Basilé, *Eq. Guin.* 83 E6
Basilicata □, *Italy* 31 B9
Basim = Washim, *India* 66 J10
Basin, *U.S.A.* 114 D9
Basingstoke, *U.K.* 13 F6
Baška, *Croatia* 29 D11
Başkale, *Turkey* 73 C10
Baskatong, Rés., *Canada* 102 C4
Basle = Basel, *Switz.* 25 H3
Başmakçı, *Turkey* 39 D12
Basoda, *India* 68 H7
Basoka, *Dem. Rep. of the Congo* 86 B1
Basque, Pays, *France* 20 E2
Basque Provinces = País Vasco □, *Spain* 32 C2
Basra = Al Başrah, *Iraq* 70 D5
Bass Str., *Australia* 94 F4
Bassano, *Canada* 104 C6
Bassano del Grappa, *Italy* 29 C8
Bassar, *Togo* 83 D5
Bassas da India, *Ind. Oc.* 85 J7
Basse-Normandie □, *France* 18 D6
Basse Santa-Su, *Gambia* 82 C2
Basse-Terre, *Guadeloupe* 121 C7
Bassein, *Burma* 67 L19
Basseterre, *St. Kitts & Nevis* 121 C7
Bassett, *U.S.A.* 112 D5
Bassi, *India* 68 D7
Bassigny, *France* 19 E12
Bassikounou, *Mauritania* 82 B3
Bassila, *Benin* 83 D5
Bassum, *Germany* 24 C4
Båstad, *Sweden* 11 H6
Bastak, *Iran* 71 E7
Baştām, *Iran* 71 B7
Bastar, *India* 67 K12
Bastelica, *France* 21 F13
Basti, *India* 69 F10
Bastia, *France* 21 F13
Bastogne, *Belgium* 17 D5
Bastrop, *La., U.S.A.* 113 J9
Bastrop, *Tex., U.S.A.* 113 K6
Bat Yam, *Israel* 75 C3
Bata, *Eq. Guin.* 84 D1
Bata, *Romania* 42 D7
Bataan □, *Phil.* 61 D4
Batabanó, *Cuba* 120 B3
Batabanó, G. de, *Cuba* 120 B3
Batac, *Phil.* 61 B4
Batagai, *Russia* 51 C14
Batajnica, *Serbia, Yug.* 40 B4
Batak, *Bulgaria* 41 E8
Batala, *India* 68 D6
Batalha, *Portugal* 34 F2
Batama, *Dem. Rep. of the Congo* 86 B2
Batamay, *Russia* 51 C13
Batang, *China* 58 B2
Batang, *Indonesia* 63 G13
Batangas, *Phil.* 61 E4
Batanta, *Indonesia* 63 E8
Batatais, *Brazil* 127 A6
Batavia, *U.S.A.* 110 D6
Bataysk, *Russia* 47 J10
Batchelor, *Australia* 92 B5
Batdambang, *Cambodia* 64 F4
Bateman's B., *Australia* 95 F5
Batemans Bay, *Australia* 95 F5
Bates Ra., *Australia* 93 E3
Batesburg, *U.S.A.* 109 J5
Batesville, *Ark., U.S.A.* 113 H9
Batesville, *Miss., U.S.A.* 113 H10
Batesville, *Tex., U.S.A.* 113 L5
Bath, *Canada* 111 B8
Bath, *U.K.* 13 F5
Bath, *Maine, U.S.A.* 109 D11
Bath, *N.Y., U.S.A.* 110 D7
Bath & North East Somerset □, *U.K.* 13 F5
Batheay, *Cambodia* 65 G5
Bathurst = Banjul, *Gambia* 82 C1
Bathurst, *Australia* 95 E4
Bathurst, *Canada* 103 C6
Bathurst, *S. Africa* 88 E4
Bathurst, C., *Canada* 100 A7
Bathurst B., *Australia* 94 A3
Bathurst Harb., *Australia* 94 G4
Bathurst I., *Australia* 92 B5
Bathurst I., *Canada* 4 B2
Bathurst Inlet, *Canada* 100 B9
Bati, *Ethiopia* 81 E5
Batie, *Burkina Faso* 82 D4

Batlow, Australia 95 F4
Batman, Turkey 70 B4
Baṭn al Ghūl, Jordan 75 F4
Batna, Algeria 78 A7
Batobato = San Isidro, Phil. 61 H7
Batočina, Serbia, Yug. 40 B5
Batoka, Zambia 87 F2
Baton Rouge, U.S.A. 113 K9
Batong, Ko, Thailand 65 J2
Bátonyterenye, Hungary 42 C4
Batopilas, Mexico 118 B3
Batouri, Cameroon 84 D2
Båtsfjord, Norway 8 A23
Battambang = Batdambang, Cambodia 64 F4
Batticaloa, Sri Lanka 66 R12
Battipáglia, Italy 31 B7
Battle, U.K. 13 G8
Battle →, Canada 105 C7
Battle Creek, U.S.A. 108 D3
Battle Ground, U.S.A. 116 E4
Battle Harbour, Canada 103 B8
Battle Lake, U.S.A. 112 B7
Battle Mountain, U.S.A. 114 F5
Battlefields, Zimbabwe 87 F2
Battleford, Canada 105 C7
Battonya, Hungary 42 D6
Batu, Ethiopia 81 F4
Batu, Kepulauan, Indonesia 62 E1
Batu Caves, Malaysia 65 L3
Batu Gajah, Malaysia 65 K3
Batu Is. = Batu, Kepulauan, Indonesia 62 E1
Batu Pahat, Malaysia 65 M4
Batuata, Indonesia 63 F6
Batumi, Georgia 49 K5
Baturaja, Indonesia 62 E2
Baturité, Brazil 125 D11
Bau, Malaysia 62 D4
Baubau, Indonesia 63 F6
Bauchi, Nigeria 83 C6
Bauchi □, Nigeria 83 C7
Baud, France 18 E3
Baudette, U.S.A. 112 A7
Bauer, C., Australia 95 E1
Bauhinia, Australia 94 C4
Baukau, Indonesia 63 F7
Bauld, C., Canada 101 C14
Baume-les-Dames, France . 19 E13
Baunatal, Germany 24 D5
Baunei, Italy 30 B2
Baure, Nigeria 83 C6
Bauru, Brazil 127 A6
Bausi, India 69 G12
Bauska, Latvia 9 H21
Bautino, Kazakstan 49 H10
Bautzen, Germany 24 D10
Bauya, S. Leone 82 D2
Bavānāt, Iran 71 D7
Bavanište, Serbia, Yug. 42 F5
Bavaria = Bayern □, Germany 25 G7
Båven, Sweden 10 E10
Bavispe →, Mexico 118 B3
Bawdwin, Burma 67 H20
Bawean, Indonesia 62 F4
Bawku, Ghana 83 C4
Bawlake, Burma 67 K20
Bawolung, China 58 C3
Baxley, U.S.A. 109 K4
Baxoi, China 58 B1
Baxter, U.S.A. 112 B7
Baxter Springs, U.S.A. 113 G7
Bay, L. de, Phil. 61 D4
Bay City, Mich., U.S.A. 108 D4
Bay City, Tex., U.S.A. 113 L7
Bay Minette, U.S.A. 109 K2
Bay Roberts, Canada 103 C9
Bay St. Louis, U.S.A. 113 K10
Bay Springs, U.S.A. 113 K10
Bay View, N.Z. 91 H6
Baya, Dem. Rep. of the Congo . 87 E2
Bayamo, Cuba 120 B4
Bayamón, Puerto Rico 121 C6
Bayan Har Shan, China 60 C4
Bayan Hot = Alxa Zuoqi, China 56 E3
Bayan Obo, China 56 D5
Bayan-Ovoo = Erdenetsogt, Mongolia 56 C4
Bayana, India 68 F7
Bayanaūyl, Kazakstan 50 D8
Bayandalay, Mongolia 56 C2
Bayanhongor, Mongolia 60 B5
Bayard, N. Mex., U.S.A. .. 115 K9
Bayard, Nebr., U.S.A. 112 E3
Bayawan, Phil. 61 G5
Baybay, Phil. 61 F6
Bayburt, Turkey 73 B9
Bayelsa □, Nigeria 83 E6
Bayerische Alpen, Germany 25 H7
Bayerischer Wald, Germany 25 G8
Bayern □, Germany 25 G7
Bayeux, France 18 C6
Bayfield, Canada 110 C3
Bayfield, U.S.A. 112 B9
Bayındır, Turkey 39 C9
Baykal, Oz., Russia 51 D11
Baykan, Turkey 70 B4
Baykonur = Bayqongyr, Kazakstan 50 E7
Baynes Mts., Namibia 88 B1
Bayombong, Phil. 61 C4
Bayon, France 19 D13
Bayona = Baiona, Spain ... 34 C2
Bayonne, France 20 E2
Bayonne, U.S.A. 111 F10
Bayovar, Peru 124 E2
Bayqongyr, Kazakstan 50 E7

Bayram-Ali = Bayramaly, Turkmenistan 50 F7
Bayramaly, Turkmenistan .. 50 F7
Bayramiç, Turkey 39 B8
Bayreuth, Germany 25 F7
Bayrischzell, Germany 25 H8
Bayrūt, Lebanon 75 B4
Bays, L. of, Canada 110 A5
Baysville, Canada 110 A5
Bayt Laḥm, West Bank 75 D4
Baytown, U.S.A. 113 L7
Bayzo, Niger 83 C5
Baza, Spain 35 H8
Bazar Dyuzi, Russia 49 K8
Bazardüzü = Bazar Dyuzi, Russia 49 K8
Bazarny Karabulak, Russia . 48 D8
Bazarnyy Syzgan, Russia .. 48 D8
Bazaruto, I. do, Mozam. .. 89 C6
Bazas, France 20 D3
Bazhong, China 58 B6
Bazhou, China 56 E9
Bazmān, Kūh-e, Iran 71 D9
Beach, U.S.A. 112 B3
Beach City, U.S.A. 110 F3
Beachport, Australia 95 F3
Beachy Hd., U.K. 13 G8
Beacon, Australia 93 F2
Beacon, U.S.A. 111 E11
Beaconsfield, Australia 94 G4
Beagle, Canal, S. Amer. .. 122 J4
Beagle Bay, Australia 92 C3
Bealanana, Madag. 89 A8
Beals Cr. →, U.S.A. 113 J4
Beamsville, Canada 110 C5
Bear →, Calif., U.S.A. ... 116 G5
Bear →, Utah, U.S.A. 106 B4
Béar, C., France 20 F7
Bear I., Ireland 15 E2
Bear L., Canada 105 B9
Bear L., U.S.A. 114 F4
Beardmore, Canada 102 C2
Beardmore Glacier, Antarctica 5 E11
Beardstown, U.S.A. 112 F9
Bearma →, India 69 G8
Béarn, France 20 E3
Bearpaw Mts., U.S.A. 114 B9
Bearskin Lake, Canada 102 B1
Beas →, India 68 D6
Beas de Segura, Spain 35 G8
Beasain, Spain 32 B2
Beata, C., Dom. Rep. 121 C5
Beata, I., Dom. Rep. 121 C5
Beatrice, U.S.A. 112 E6
Beatrice, Zimbabwe 87 F3
Beatrice, C., Australia 94 A2
Beatton →, Canada 104 B4
Beatton River, Canada 104 B4
Beatty, U.S.A. 116 J10
Beaucaire, France 21 E8
Beauce, Plaine de la, France 19 D8
Beauceville, Canada 103 C5
Beaudesert, Australia 95 D5
Beaufort, France 21 C10
Beaufort, Malaysia 62 C5
Beaufort, N.C., U.S.A. 109 H7
Beaufort, S.C., U.S.A. 109 J5
Beaufort Sea, Arctic 4 B1
Beaufort West, S. Africa .. 88 E3
Beaugency, France 19 E8
Beauharnois, Canada 111 A11
Beaujeu, France 19 F11
Beaujolais, France 19 F11
Beaulieu →, Canada 104 A6
Beaulieu-sur-Dordogne, France 20 D5
Beaulieu-sur-Mer, France . 21 E11
Beauly, U.K. 14 D4
Beauly →, U.K. 14 D4
Beaumaris, U.K. 12 D3
Beaumont, Belgium 17 D4
Beaumont, France 20 D4
Beaumont, U.S.A. 113 K7
Beaumont-de-Lomagne, France 20 E5
Beaumont-le-Roger, France 18 C7
Beaumont-sur-Sarthe, France 18 D7
Beaune, France 19 E11
Beaune-la-Rolande, France . 19 C9
Beaupré, Canada 103 C5
Beaupréau, France 18 E6
Beauraing, Belgium 17 D4
Beaurepaire, France 21 C9
Beauséjour, Canada 105 C9
Beauvais, France 19 C9
Beauval, Canada 105 B7
Beauvoir-sur-Mer, France . 18 F4
Beauvoir-sur-Niort, France . 20 B3
Beaver, Okla., U.S.A. 113 G4
Beaver, Pa., U.S.A. 110 F4
Beaver, Utah, U.S.A. 115 G7
Beaver →, B.C., Canada .. 104 B4
Beaver →, Ont., Canada .. 102 A2
Beaver →, Sask., Canada . 105 B7
Beaver →, U.S.A. 113 G5
Beaver City, U.S.A. 112 E5
Beaver Creek, Canada 100 B5
Beaver Dam, U.S.A. 112 D10
Beaver Falls, U.S.A. 110 F4
Beaver Hill L., Canada 105 C10
Beaver I., U.S.A. 108 C3
Beaverhill L., Canada 104 C6
Beaverlodge, Canada 104 B5
Beaverstone →, Canada .. 102 B2
Beaverton, Canada 110 B5
Beaverton, U.S.A. 116 E4
Beawar, India 68 F6
Bebedouro, Brazil 127 A6
Beboa, Madag. 89 B7
Bebra, Germany 24 E5

Beccles, U.K. 13 E9
Bečej, Serbia, Yug. 42 E5
Beceni, Romania 43 E11
Becerreá, Spain 34 C3
Béchar, Algeria 78 B5
Bechyně, Czech Rep. 26 B7
Beckley, U.S.A. 108 G5
Beckum, Germany 24 D4
Beclean, Romania 43 C9
Bečov nad Teplou, Czech Rep. 26 A5
Bečva →, Czech Rep. 27 B10
Bédar, Spain 33 H3
Bédarieux, France 20 E7
Beddouza, Ras, Morocco .. 78 B4
Bedele, Ethiopia 81 F4
Bederkesa, Germany 24 B4
Bedeso, Ethiopia 81 F5
Bedford, Canada 111 A12
Bedford, S. Africa 88 E4
Bedford, U.K. 13 E7
Bedford, Ind., U.S.A. 108 F2
Bedford, Iowa, U.S.A. 112 E7
Bedford, Ohio, U.S.A. 110 E3
Bedford, Pa., U.S.A. 110 F6
Bedford, Va., U.S.A. 108 G6
Bedford, C., Australia 94 B4
Bedfordshire □, U.K. 13 E7
Będków, Poland 45 G6
Bednja →, Croatia 29 B13
Bednodemyanovsk, Russia . 48 D6
Bedónia, Italy 28 D6
Bedourie, Australia 94 C2
Bedum, Neths. 17 A6
Będzin, Poland 45 H6
Beebe Plain, Canada 111 A12
Beech Creek, U.S.A. 110 E7
Beelitz, Germany 24 C8
Beenleigh, Australia 95 D5
Be'er Menuha, Israel 70 D2
Be'er Sheva, Israel 75 D3
Beersheba = Be'er Sheva, Israel 75 D3
Beeskow, Germany 24 C10
Beestekraal, S. Africa 89 D4
Beeston, U.K. 12 E6
Beetzendorf, Germany 24 C7
Beeville, U.S.A. 113 L6
Befale, Dem. Rep. of the Congo . 84 D4
Befandriana, Mahajanga, Madag. 89 B8
Befandriana, Toliara, Madag. 89 C7
Befasy, Madag. 89 C7
Béfotaka, Antsiranana, Madag. 89 A8
Befotaka, Fianarantsoa, Madag. 89 C8
Bega, Australia 95 F4
Bega, Canalul, Romania .. 42 E5
Bégard, France 18 D3
Beğendik, Turkey 41 F10
Begoro, Ghana 83 D4
Begusarai, India 69 G12
Behābād, Iran 71 C8
Behala, India 69 H13
Behara, Madag. 89 C8
Behbehān, Iran 71 D6
Behm Canal, U.S.A. 104 B2
Behshahr, Iran 71 B7
Bei Jiang →, China 59 F9
Bei'an, China 60 B7
Beibei, China 58 C6
Beichuan, China 58 B5
Beihai, China 58 G7
Beijing, China 56 E9
Beijing □, China 56 E9
Beilen, Neths. 17 B6
Beiliu, China 59 F8
Beilngries, Germany 25 F7
Beilpajah, Australia 95 E3
Beilul, Eritrea 81 E5
Beinn na Faoghla = Benbecula, U.K. 14 D1
Beipan Jiang →, China 58 E5
Beipiao, China 57 D11
Beira, Mozam. 87 F3
Beirut = Bayrūt, Lebanon . 75 B4
Beiseker, Canada 104 C6
Beitaolaizhao, China 57 B13
Beitbridge, Zimbabwe 87 G3
Beiuş, Romania 42 D7
Beizhen = Binzhou, China . 57 F10
Beizhen, China 57 D11
Beizhengzhen, China 57 B12
Beja, Portugal 35 G3
Béja, Tunisia 79 A7
Beja □, Portugal 35 H3
Béjar, Spain 34 E5
Bejestān, Iran 71 C8
Bekçiler, Turkey 39 E11
Békés, Hungary 42 D6
Békés □, Hungary 42 D6
Békéscsaba, Hungary 42 D6
Bekilli, Turkey 39 C11
Bekily, Madag. 89 C8
Bekisopa, Madag. 89 C8
Bekitro, Madag. 89 C8
Bekodoka, Madag. 89 B8
Bekoji, Ethiopia 81 F4
Bekok, Malaysia 65 L4
Bekopaka, Madag. 89 B7
Bekwai, Ghana 83 D4
Bela, India 69 G10
Bela, Pakistan 68 F2
Bela Crkva, Serbia, Yug. . 42 F6
Bela Palanka, Serbia, Yug. 40 C6
Bela Vista, Brazil 126 A4
Bela Vista, Mozam. 89 D5

Bélâbre, France 20 B5
Belalcázar, Spain 35 G5
Belan →, India 69 G9
Belanovica, Serbia, Yug. .. 40 B4
Belarus ■, Europe 46 F4
Belau = Palau ■, Pac. Oc. 52 J17
Belavenona, Madag. 89 C8
Belawan, Indonesia 62 D1
Belaya, Ethiopia 81 E4
Belaya Glina, Russia 49 G5
Belaya Kalitva, Russia 49 F5
Belaya Tserkov = Bila Tserkva, Ukraine 47 H6
Belcești, Romania 43 C12
Bełchatów, Poland 45 G6
Belcher Is., Canada 102 A3
Belchite, Spain 32 D4
Belden, U.S.A. 116 E5
Belém, Brazil 125 D9
Belén, Argentina 126 B2
Belén, Paraguay 126 A4
Belen, U.S.A. 115 J10
Belene, Bulgaria 41 C9
Beleni, Turkey 72 D7
Bélesta, France 20 F5
Belet Uen, Somali Rep. ... 74 G4
Belev, Russia 46 F9
Belevi, Turkey 39 C9
Belfair, U.S.A. 116 C4
Belfast, S. Africa 89 D5
Belfast, U.K. 15 B6
Belfast, Maine, U.S.A. 109 C11
Belfast, N.Y., U.S.A. 110 D6
Belfast L., U.K. 15 B6
Belfield, U.S.A. 112 B3
Belfort, France 19 E13
Belfort, Territoire de □, France 19 E13
Belfry, U.S.A. 114 D9
Belgaum, India 66 M9
Belgioioso, Italy 28 C6
Belgium ■, Europe 17 D4
Belgodère, France 21 F13
Belgorod, Russia 47 G9
Belgorod-Dnestrovskiy = Bilhorod-Dnistrovskyy, Ukraine 47 J6
Belgrade = Beograd, Serbia, Yug. 40 B4
Belgrade, U.S.A. 114 D8
Belhaven, U.S.A. 109 H7
Beli Drim →, Europe 40 D4
Beli Manastir, Croatia 42 E3
Beli Timok →, Serbia, Yug. 40 C6
Bélice →, Italy 30 E5
Belinskiy, Russia 48 D6
Belinyu, Indonesia 62 E3
Beliton Is. = Belitung, Indonesia 62 E3
Belitung, Indonesia 62 E3
Beliu, Romania 42 D6
Belize ■, Cent. Amer. 119 D7
Belize City, Belize 119 D7
Beljakovci, Macedonia 40 D5
Beljanica, Serbia, Yug. ... 40 B5
Belkovskiy, Ostrov, Russia . 51 B14
Bell →, Canada 102 C4
Bell I., Canada 103 B8
Bell-Irving →, Canada 104 B3
Bell Peninsula, Canada 101 B11
Bell Ville, Argentina 126 C3
Bella, Italy 31 B8
Bella Bella, Canada 104 C3
Bella Coola, Canada 104 C3
Bella Unión, Uruguay 126 C4
Bella Vista, Corrientes, Argentina 126 B4
Bella Vista, Tucuman, Argentina 126 B2
Bellac, France 20 B5
Bellágio, Italy 28 C6
Bellaire, U.S.A. 110 F4
Bellária, Italy 29 D9
Bellary, India 66 M10
Bellata, Australia 95 D4
Belle-Chasse, U.S.A. 113 L10
Belle Fourche, U.S.A. 112 C3
Belle Fourche →, U.S.A. . 112 C3
Belle Glade, U.S.A. 109 M5
Belle-Île, France 18 E3
Belle Isle, Canada 103 B8
Belle Isle, Str. of, Canada . 103 B8
Belle Plaine, U.S.A. 112 E8
Belle Yella, Liberia 82 D3
Belledonne, France 21 C10
Bellefontaine, U.S.A. 108 E4
Bellefonte, U.S.A. 110 F7
Bellegarde, France 19 E9
Bellegarde-en-Marche, France 20 C6
Bellegarde-sur-Valserine, France 19 F12
Bellême, France 18 D7
Belleoram, Canada 103 C8
Belleville, Canada 102 D4
Belleville, France 19 F11
Belleville, Ill., U.S.A. 112 F10
Belleville, Kans., U.S.A. .. 112 F6
Belleville, N.Y., U.S.A. ... 111 C8
Belleville-sur-Vie, France . 18 F5
Bellevue, Canada 104 D6
Bellevue, Idaho, U.S.A. .. 114 E6
Bellevue, Nebr., U.S.A. .. 112 E7
Bellevue, Ohio, U.S.A. ... 110 E2
Bellevue, Wash., U.S.A. .. 116 C4
Belley, France 21 C9
Bellin = Kangirsuk, Canada 101 B13
Bellinge, Denmark 11 J4
Bellingen, Australia 95 E5
Bellingham, U.S.A. 100 D7

Bellingshausen Sea, Antarctica 5 C17
Bellinzona, Switz. 25 J5
Bello, Colombia 124 B3
Bellows Falls, U.S.A. 111 C12
Bellpat, Pakistan 68 E3
Bellpuig d'Urgell, Spain ... 32 D6
Belluno, Italy 29 B9
Bellwood, U.S.A. 110 F6
Bélmez, Spain 35 G5
Belmont, Canada 110 D3
Belmont, S. Africa 88 D3
Belmont, U.S.A. 110 D6
Belmonte, Brazil 125 G11
Belmonte, Portugal 34 E3
Belmonte, Spain 33 F2
Belmopan, Belize 119 D7
Belmullet, Ireland 15 B2
Belo Horizonte, Brazil 125 G10
Belo-sur-Mer, Madag. 89 C7
Belo-Tsiribihina, Madag. .. 89 B7
Belogorsk = Bilohirsk, Ukraine 47 K8
Belogorsk, Russia 51 D13
Belogradchik, Bulgaria 40 C6
Belogradets, Bulgaria 41 C11
Beloha, Madag. 89 D8
Beloit, Kans., U.S.A. 112 F5
Beloit, Wis., U.S.A. 112 D10
Belokorovichi, Ukraine 47 G5
Belomorsk, Russia 50 C4
Belonia, India 67 H17
Belopolye = Bilopillya, Ukraine 47 G8
Belorechensk, Russia 49 H4
Belorussia = Belarus ■, Europe 46 F4
Beloslav, Bulgaria 41 C11
Belovo, Bulgaria 41 D8
Belovo, Russia 50 D9
Belovodsk, Ukraine 47 H10
Beloye, Ozero, Russia 46 B9
Beloye More, Russia 50 C4
Belozem, Bulgaria 41 D9
Belozersk, Russia 46 B9
Belpasso, Italy 31 E7
Belpre, U.S.A. 108 F5
Belrain, India 69 E9
Belt, U.S.A. 114 C8
Beltana, Australia 95 E2
Belterra, Brazil 125 D8
Beltinci, Slovenia 29 B13
Belton, U.S.A. 113 K6
Beltsy = Bălți, Moldova .. 43 C12
Belturbet, Ireland 15 B4
Belukha, Russia 50 E9
Beluran, Malaysia 62 C5
Beluša, Slovak Rep. 27 B11
Belušić, Serbia, Yug. 40 C5
Belvedere Maríttimo, Italy . 31 C8
Belvès, France 20 D5
Belvidere, Ill., U.S.A. 112 D10
Belvidere, N.J., U.S.A. ... 111 F9
Belvis de la Jara, Spain ... 34 F6
Belyando →, Australia 94 C4
Belyy, Russia 46 E7
Belyy, Ostrov, Russia 50 B8
Belyy Yar, Russia 50 D9
Bełżec, Poland 45 H10
Belzig, Germany 24 C8
Belzoni, U.S.A. 113 J9
Bełżyce, Poland 45 G9
Bemaraha, Lembalemban' i, Madag. 89 B7
Bemarivo, Madag. 89 C7
Bemarivo →, Antsiranana, Madag. 89 A9
Bemarivo →, Mahajanga, Madag. 89 B8
Bemavo, Madag. 89 C8
Bembéréke, Benin 83 C5
Bembesi, Zimbabwe 87 G2
Bembesi →, Zimbabwe ... 87 F2
Bembézar →, Spain 35 H5
Bembibre, Spain 34 C4
Bemetara, India 69 J9
Bemidji, U.S.A. 112 B7
Bemolanga, Madag. 89 B8
Ben, Iran 71 C6
Ben Cruachan, U.K. 14 E3
Ben Dearg, U.K. 14 D4
Ben Hope, U.K. 14 C4
Ben Lawers, U.K. 14 E4
Ben Lomond, Vietnam ... 65 G6
Ben Lomond, N.S.W., Australia 95 E5
Ben Lomond, Tas., Australia 95 G4
Ben Lomond, U.K. 14 E4
Ben Luc, Vietnam 65 G6
Ben Macdhui, U.K. 14 D5
Ben Mhor, Arg. & Bute, U.K. 14 E2
Ben More, Stirl., U.K. 14 E4
Ben More Assynt, U.K. ... 14 C4
Ben Nevis, U.K. 14 E3
Ben Quang, Vietnam 64 D6
Ben Vorlich, U.K. 14 E4
Ben Wyvis, U.K. 14 D4
Bena, Nigeria 83 C6
Benāb, Iran 73 D12
Benalla, Australia 95 F4
Benalmádena, Spain 35 J6
Benares = Varanasi, India . 69 G10
Bénat, C., France 21 E10
Benavente, Portugal 35 G2
Benavente, Spain 34 C5
Benavides de Órbigo, Spain 34 C5
Benavides, U.S.A. 113 M5
Benbecula, U.K. 14 D1
Benbonyathe, Australia ... 95 E2

Bend, U.S.A. 114 D3
Bendemeer, Australia 95 E5
Bender Beila, Somali Rep. .. 74 F5
Bendery = Tighina, Moldova 43 D14
Bendigo, Australia 95 F3
Bendorf, Germany 24 E3
Benē Beraq, Israel 75 C3
Bénéna, Mali 82 C4
Benenitra, Madag. 89 C8
Benešov, Czech Rep. 26 B7
Benevento, Italy 31 A7
Benfeld, France 19 D14
Benga, Mozam. 87 F3
Bengal, Bay of, Ind. Oc. ... 67 M17
Bengbis, Cameroon 83 E7
Bengbu, China 57 H9
Benghazi = Banghāzī, Libya 79 B10
Bengkalis, Indonesia 62 D2
Bengkulu, Indonesia 62 E2
Bengkulu □, Indonesia 62 E2
Bengough, Canada 105 D7
Bengtsfors, Sweden 10 E6
Benguela, Angola 85 G2
Benguérua, I., Mozam. 89 C6
Benha, Egypt 80 H7
Beni,
  Dem. Rep. of the Congo . 86 B2
Beni →, Bolivia 124 F5
Beni Mazâr, Egypt 80 B3
Beni Mellal, Morocco 78 B4
Beni Suef, Egypt 80 J7
Beniah L., Canada 104 A6
Benicarló, Spain 32 E5
Benicàssim, Spain 32 E5
Benicia, U.S.A. 116 G4
Benidorm, Spain 33 G4
Benin ■, Africa 83 D5
Benin →, Nigeria 83 D6
Benin, Bight of, W. Afr. ... 83 E5
Benin City, Nigeria 83 D6
Benisa, Spain 33 G5
Benitses, Greece 36 A3
Benjamin Aceval, Paraguay 126 A4
Benjamin Constant, Brazil . 124 D4
Benjamin Hill, Mexico 118 A2
Benkelman, U.S.A. 112 E4
Benkovac, Croatia 29 D12
Bennett, Canada 104 B2
Bennett, L., Australia 92 D5
Bennetta, Ostrov, Russia .. 51 B15
Bennettsville, U.S.A. 109 H6
Bennichchâb, Mauritania .. 82 B1
Bennington, N.H., U.S.A. . 111 D11
Bennington, Vt., U.S.A. ... 111 D11
Bénodet, France 18 E2
Benoni, S. Africa 89 D4
Benque Viejo, Belize 119 D7
Bensheim, Germany 25 F4
Benson, Ariz., U.S.A. 115 L8
Benson, Minn., U.S.A. 112 C7
Bent, Iran 71 E8
Benteng, Indonesia 63 F6
Bentinck I., Australia 94 B2
Bentiu, Sudan 81 F2
Bento Gonçalves, Brazil ... 127 B5
Benton, Ark., U.S.A. 113 H8
Benton, Calif., U.S.A. 116 H8
Benton, Ill., U.S.A. 112 G10
Benton, Pa., U.S.A. 111 E8
Benton Harbor, U.S.A. 108 D2
Bentonville, U.S.A. 113 G7
Bentu Liben, Ethiopia 81 F4
Bentung, Malaysia 65 L3
Benue □, Nigeria 83 D6
Benue →, Nigeria 83 D6
Benxi, China 57 D12
Beo, Indonesia 63 D7
Beograd, Serbia, Yug. 40 B4
Beoumi, Ivory C. 82 D3
Bepan Jiang →, China 58 E6
Beppu, Japan 55 H5
Beqaa Valley = Al Biqâ,
  Lebanon 75 A5
Ber Mota, India 68 H3
Berach →, India 68 G6
Beraketa, Madag. 89 C7
Berane, Montenegro, Yug. . 40 D3
Berati, Albania 40 F3
Berau, Teluk, Indonesia ... 63 E8
Beravina, Madag. 89 B8
Berber, Sudan 80 D3
Berbera, Somali Rep. 74 E4
Berbérati, C.A.R. 84 D3
Berbice →, Guyana 124 B7
Berceto, Italy 28 D6
Berchidda, Italy 30 B2
Berchtesgaden, Germany .. 25 H8
Berck, France 19 B8
Berdichev = Berdychiv,
  Ukraine 47 H5
Berdsk, Russia 50 D9
Berdyansk, Ukraine 47 J9
Berdychiv, Ukraine 47 H5
Berea, U.S.A. 108 G3
Berebere, Indonesia 63 D7
Bereda, Somali Rep. 74 E5
Berehove, Ukraine 47 H2
Berekum, Ghana 82 D4
Berenice, Egypt 80 C4
Berens →, Canada 105 C9
Berens I., Canada 105 C9
Berens River, Canada 105 C9
Beresford, U.S.A. 112 D6
Berestechko, Ukraine 47 G3
Berești, Romania 43 D12
Beretău →, Romania 42 C6
Berettyó →, Hungary 42 D6
Berettyóújfalu, Hungary .. 42 D6
Berevo, Mahajanga, Madag. 89 B7
Berevo, Toliara, Madag. ... 89 B7
Bereza, Belarus 47 F3

Berezhany, Ukraine 47 H3
Berezina = Byarezina →,
  Belarus 47 F6
Berezivka, Ukraine 47 J6
Berezna, Ukraine 47 G6
Berezniki, Russia 50 C5
Berezniki, Russia 50 D6
Berezovo, Russia 50 C7
Berga, Spain 32 C6
Berga, Sweden 11 G10
Bergama, Turkey 39 B9
Bérgamo, Italy 28 C6
Bergara, Spain 32 B2
Bergby, Sweden 10 D11
Bergedorf, Germany 24 B6
Bergeforsen, Sweden 10 B11
Bergen,
  Mecklenburg-Vorpommern,
  Germany 24 A9
Bergen, Niedersachsen,
  Germany 24 C5
Bergen, Neths. 17 B4
Bergen, Norway 9 F11
Bergen, U.S.A. 110 C7
Bergen op Zoom, Neths. .. 17 C4
Bergerac, France 20 D4
Bergheim, Germany 24 E2
Bergholz, U.S.A. 110 F4
Bergisch Gladbach, Germany 17 D7
Bergkamen, Germany 24 D3
Bergkvara, Sweden 11 H10
Bergshamra, Sweden 10 E12
Bergsjö, Sweden 10 C11
Bergues, France 19 B9
Bergviken, Sweden 10 C10
Bergville, S. Africa 89 D4
Berhala, Selat, Indonesia .. 62 E2
Berhampore = Baharampur,
  India 69 G13
Berhampur = Brahmapur,
  India 67 K14
Berheci →, Romania 43 E12
Bering Sea, Pac. Oc. 100 C1
Bering Strait, Pac. Oc. 100 B3
Beringovskiy, Russia 51 C18
Berisso, Argentina 126 C4
Berja, Spain 35 J8
Berkeley, U.S.A. 116 H4
Berkner I., Antarctica 5 D18
Berkovitsa, Bulgaria 40 C7
Berkshire, U.S.A. 111 D8
Berkshire Downs, U.K. ... 13 F6
Berlanga, Spain 35 G5
Berlenga, I., Portugal 35 F1
Berlin, Germany 24 C9
Berlin, Md., U.S.A. 108 F8
Berlin, N.H., U.S.A. 111 B13
Berlin, N.Y., U.S.A. 111 D11
Berlin, Wis., U.S.A. 108 D1
Berlin □, Germany 24 C9
Berlin L., U.S.A. 110 E4
Bermeja, Sierra, Spain 35 J5
Bermejo →, Formosa,
  Argentina 126 B4
Bermejo →, San Juan,
  Argentina 126 C2
Bermen, L., Canada 103 B6
Bermeo, Spain 32 B2
Bermillo de Sayago, Spain . 34 D4
Bermuda ■, Atl. Oc. 98 F13
Bern, Switz. 25 J3
Bern □, Switz. 25 J3
Bernalda, Italy 31 B9
Bernalillo, U.S.A. 115 J10
Bernardo de Irigoyen,
  Argentina 127 B5
Bernardo O'Higgins □, Chile 126 C1
Bernardsville, U.S.A. 111 F10
Bernasconi, Argentina 126 D3
Bernau, Bayern, Germany . 25 H8
Bernau, Brandenburg,
  Germany 24 C9
Bernay, France 18 C7
Bernburg, Germany 24 D7
Berndorf, Austria 26 D9
Berne = Bern, Switz. 25 J3
Berne = Bern □, Switz. ... 25 J3
Berner Alpen, Switz. 25 J3
Berneray, U.K. 14 D1
Bernier I., Australia 93 D1
Bernina, Piz, Switz. 25 J5
Bernkastel-Kues, Germany . 25 F3
Beroroha, Madag. 89 C8
Bérouбouay, Benin 83 C5
Beroun, Czech Rep. 26 B7
Berounka →, Czech Rep. . 26 B7
Berovo, Macedonia 40 E6
Berre, Étang de, France ... 21 E9
Berre-l'Étang, France 21 E9
Berri, Australia 95 E3
Berriane, Algeria 78 B6
Berrigan, Australia 95 F4
Berry, Australia 95 E5
Berry, France 19 F8
Berry Is., Bahamas 120 A4
Berryessa L., U.S.A. 116 G4
Berryville, U.S.A. 113 G8
Berseba, Namibia 88 D2
Bersenbrück, Germany ... 24 C3
Bershad, Ukraine 47 H5
Berthold, U.S.A. 112 A4
Berthoud, U.S.A. 112 E2
Bertincourt, France 19 B9
Bertoua, Cameroon 84 D2
Bertraghboy B., Ireland ... 15 C2
Berwick, U.S.A. 111 E8
Berwick-upon-Tweed, U.K. 12 B6
Berwyn Mts., U.K. 12 E4
Beryslav, Ukraine 47 J7
Berzasca, Romania 42 F6
Berzence, Hungary 42 D2

Besal, Pakistan 69 B5
Besalampy, Madag. 89 B7
Besançon, France 19 E13
Besar, Indonesia 62 E5
Beshenkovichi, Belarus ... 46 E5
Beška, Serbia, Yug. 42 E5
Beslan, Russia 49 J7
Besna Kobila, Serbia, Yug. . 40 D6
Besnard L., Canada 105 B7
Besni, Turkey 70 B3
Besor, N. →, Egypt 75 D3
Bessarabiya, Moldova 47 J5
Bessarabka = Basarabeasca,
  Moldova 43 D13
Bessèges, France 21 D8
Bessemer, Ala., U.S.A. ... 109 J2
Bessemer, Mich., U.S.A. .. 112 B9
Bessemer, Pa., U.S.A. 110 F4
Bessin, France 18 C6
Bessines-sur-Gartempe,
  France 20 B5
Beswick, Australia 92 B5
Bet She'an, Israel 75 C4
Bet Shemesh, Israel 75 D4
Betafo, Madag. 89 B8
Betancuria, Canary Is. 37 F5
Betanzos, Spain 34 B2
Bétaré Oya, Cameroon ... 84 C2
Betatao, Madag. 89 B8
Bétera, Spain 33 F4
Bétérou, Benin 83 D5
Bethal, S. Africa 89 D4
Bethanien, Namibia 88 D2
Bethany, Canada 110 B6
Bethany, U.S.A. 112 E7
Bethel, Alaska, U.S.A. ... 100 B3
Bethel, Conn., U.S.A. 111 E11
Bethel, Maine, U.S.A. ... 111 B14
Bethel, Vt., U.S.A. 111 C12
Bethel Park, U.S.A. 110 F4
Béthenville, France 19 C11
Bethlehem = Bayt Lahm,
  West Bank 75 D4
Bethlehem, S. Africa 89 D4
Bethlehem, U.S.A. 111 F9
Bethulie, S. Africa 88 E4
Béthune, France 19 B9
Béthune →, France 18 C8
Betioky, Madag. 89 C7
Betong, Thailand 65 K3
Betoota, Australia 94 D3
Betor, Ethiopia 81 E4
Betroka, Madag. 89 C8
Betsiamites, Canada 103 C6
Betsiamites →, Canada ... 103 C6
Betsiboka →, Madag. 89 B8
Bettendorf, U.S.A. 112 E9
Bettiah, India 69 F11
Bettna, Sweden 11 F10
Béttola, Italy 28 D6
Betul, India 66 J10
Betung, Malaysia 62 D4
Betws-y-Coed, U.K. 12 D4
Betxi, Spain 32 F4
Betzdorf, Germany 24 E3
Beuil, France 21 D10
Beulah, Mich., U.S.A. 108 C2
Beulah, N. Dak., U.S.A. .. 112 B4
Beuvron →, France 18 E8
Beveren, Belgium 17 C4
Beverley, Australia 93 F2
Beverley, U.K. 12 D7
Beverley Hills, U.S.A. 109 L4
Beverly, U.S.A. 111 D14
Beverly Hills, U.S.A. 117 L8
Beverungen, Germany ... 24 D5
Bevoalavo, Madag. 89 D7
Bewas →, India 69 H8
Bex, Switz. 25 J3
Bexhill, U.K. 13 G8
Bey Dağları, Turkey 39 E12
Beyānlū, Iran 70 C5
Beyazköy, Turkey 41 E11
Beyçayırı, Turkey 41 F10
Beydağ, Turkey 39 C10
Beyeğaç, Turkey 39 D10
Beyin, Ghana 82 D4
Beykoz, Turkey 41 E13
Beyla, Guinea 82 D3
Beynat, France 20 C5
Beyneu, Kazakhstan 50 E6
Beyoba, Turkey 39 C9
Beyoğlu, Turkey 41 E12
Beypazarı, Turkey 72 B4
Beyşehir, Turkey 72 D4
Beyşehir Gölü, Turkey ... 70 B1
Beytüşşebap, Turkey 73 D10
Bezdan, Serbia, Yug. 42 E3
Bezhetsk, Russia 46 D9
Béziers, France 20 E7
Bezwada = Vijayawada,
  India 67 L12
Bhabua, India 69 G10
Bhachau, India 66 H7
Bhadar →, Gujarat, India . 68 H5
Bhadar →, Gujarat, India . 68 J3
Bhadarwah, India 69 C6
Bhadohi, India 69 G10
Bhadra, India 68 E6
Bhadrakh, India 67 J15
Bhadran, India 68 H5
Bhadravati, India 66 N9
Bhag, Pakistan 68 E2
Bhagalpur, India 69 G12
Bhagirathi →, Ut. P., India 69 D8
Bhagirathi →, W. Bengal,
  India 69 H13
Bhakkar, Pakistan 68 D4
Bhakra Dam, India 68 D7
Bhamo, Burma 67 G20
Bhandara, India 66 J11

Bhanpura, India 68 G6
Bhanrer Ra., India 69 H8
Bhaptiahi, India 69 F12
Bharat = India ■, Asia ... 66 K11
Bharatpur, Mad. P., India . 69 H9
Bharatpur, Raj., India 68 F7
Bharno, India 69 H11
Bhatinda, India 68 D6
Bhatpara, India 69 H13
Bhattu, India 68 E6
Bhaun, Pakistan 68 C5
Bhaunagar = Bhavnagar,
  India 66 J8
Bhavnagar, India 66 J8
Bhawanipatna, India 67 K12
Bhawari, India 68 G5
Bhayavadar, India 68 J4
Bhera, Pakistan 68 C5
Bhikangaon, India 68 J6
Bhilsa = Vidisha, India ... 68 H7
Bhilwara, India 68 G6
Bhima →, India 66 L10
Bhimavaram, India 67 L12
Bhimbar, Pakistan 69 C6
Bhind, India 69 F8
Bhinga, India 69 F9
Bhinmal, India 68 G5
Bhiwandi, India 66 K8
Bhiwani, India 68 E7
Bhogava →, India 68 H5
Bhola, Bangla. 67 H17
Bholari, Pakistan 68 G3
Bhopal, India 68 H7
Bhubaneshwar, India ... 67 J14
Bhuj, India 68 H3
Bhusaval, India 66 J9
Bhutan ■, Asia 67 F17
Biafra, B. of = Bonny, Bight
  of, Africa 83 E6
Biak, Indonesia 63 E9
Biała, Poland 45 H4
Biała →, Poland 45 H7
Biała Piska, Poland 44 E9
Biała Podlaska, Poland .. 45 F10
Biała Rawska, Poland ... 45 G7
Białobrzegi, Poland 45 G7
Białogard, Poland 44 D2
Białowieża, Poland 45 F10
Biały Bór, Poland 44 E3
Białystok, Poland 45 E10
Biancavilla, Italy 31 E7
Bianco, Italy 31 D9
Biankouma, Ivory C. 82 D3
Biaora, India 68 H7
Bīārjmand, Iran 71 B7
Biaro, Indonesia 63 D7
Biarritz, France 20 E2
Biasca, Switz. 25 J4
Biba, Egypt 80 J7
Bibai, Japan 54 C10
Bibbiena, Italy 29 E8
Bibby I., Canada 105 A10
Bibel →, Spain 34 C3
Biberach, Germany 25 G5
Bibiani, Ghana 82 D4
Bibungwa,
  Dem. Rep. of the Congo . 86 C2
Bic, Canada 103 C6
Bicaj, Albania 40 E4
Bicaz, Romania 43 D11
Bicazu Ardelean, Romania 43 D10
Bíccari, Italy 31 A8
Bicester, U.K. 13 F6
Bichena, Ethiopia 81 E4
Bicheno, Australia 94 G4
Bichia, India 69 H9
Bichvinta, Georgia 49 J5
Bickerton I., Australia .. 94 A2
Bicske, Hungary 42 C3
Bida, Nigeria 83 D6
Bidar, India 66 L10
Biddeford, U.S.A. 109 D10
Biddwara, Ethiopia 81 F4
Bideford, U.K. 13 F3
Bideford Bay, U.K. 13 F3
Bidhuna, India 69 F8
Bidor, Malaysia 65 K3
Bie, Sweden 10 E10
Bié, Planalto de, Angola . 85 G3
Bieber, U.S.A. 114 F3
Biebrza →, Poland 45 E9
Biecz, Poland 45 J8
Biel, Switz. 25 H3
Bielawa, Poland 45 H3
Bielefeld, Germany 24 C4
Bielersee, Switz. 25 H3
Biella, Italy 28 C5
Bielsk Podlaski, Poland . 45 F10
Bielsko-Biała, Poland ... 45 J6
Bien Hoa, Vietnam 65 G6
Bienne = Biel, Switz. ... 25 H3
Bienvenida, Spain 35 G4
Bienville, L., Canada ... 102 A5
Bierné, France 18 E6
Bierun, Poland 45 H6
Bierutów, Poland 45 G4
Biescas, Spain 32 C4
Biese →, Germany 24 C7
Biesiesfontein, S. Africa . 88 E2
Bietigheim-Bissingen,
  Germany 25 G5
Bieżuń, Poland 45 F6
Biferno →, Italy 29 G12
Big →, Canada 103 B8
Big B., Canada 105 A8
Big Bear City, U.S.A. .. 117 L10
Big Bear Lake, U.S.A. . 117 L10
Big Belt Mts., U.S.A. .. 114 C8
Big Bend, Swaziland .. 89 D5
Big Bend National Park,
  U.S.A. 113 L3

Big Black →, U.S.A. ... 113 K9
Big Blue →, U.S.A. 112 F6
Big Creek, U.S.A. 116 H7
Big Cypress National
  Preserve, U.S.A. 109 M5
Big Cypress Swamp, U.S.A. 109 M5
Big Falls, U.S.A. 112 A8
Big Fork →, U.S.A. ... 112 A8
Big Horn Mts. = Bighorn
  Mts., U.S.A. 114 D10
Big I., Canada 104 A5
Big Lake, U.S.A. 113 K4
Big Moose, U.S.A. 111 C10
Big Muddy Cr. →, U.S.A. 112 A2
Big Pine, U.S.A. 116 H8
Big Piney, U.S.A. 114 E8
Big Rapids, U.S.A. 108 D3
Big Rideau L., Canada . 111 B8
Big River, Canada 105 C7
Big Run, U.S.A. 110 F6
Big Sable Pt., U.S.A. .. 108 C2
Big Salmon →, Canada . 104 A2
Big Sand L., Canada ... 105 B9
Big Sandy, U.S.A. 114 B8
Big Sandy →, U.S.A. .. 108 F4
Big Sandy Cr. →, U.S.A. 112 F3
Big Sioux →, U.S.A. .. 112 D6
Big Spring, U.S.A. 113 J4
Big Stone City, U.S.A. . 112 C6
Big Stone Gap, U.S.A. . 109 G4
Big Stone L., U.S.A. ... 112 C6
Big Sur, U.S.A. 116 J5
Big Timber, U.S.A. ... 114 D9
Big Trout L., Canada .. 102 B2
Big Trout Lake, Canada . 102 B2
Biğa, Turkey 41 F11
Biga →, Turkey 41 F11
Bigadiç, Turkey 39 B10
Biganos, France 20 D3
Biggar, Canada 105 C7
Biggar, U.K. 14 F5
Bigge I., Australia 92 B4
Biggenden, Australia .. 95 D5
Biggleswade, U.K. 13 E7
Biggs, U.S.A. 116 F5
Bighorn, U.S.A. 114 C10
Bighorn →, U.S.A. ... 114 C10
Bighorn L., U.S.A. 114 D9
Bighorn Mts., U.S.A. . 114 D10
Bignona, Senegal 82 C1
Bigorre, France 20 E4
Bigstone L., Canada .. 105 C9
Biguglia, Étang de, France 21 F13
Bigwa, Tanzania 86 D4
Bihać, Bos.-H. 29 D12
Bihar, India 69 G11
Bihar □, India 69 G12
Biharamulo, Tanzania . 86 C3
Bihariganj, India 69 G12
Biharkeresztes, Hungary . 42 C6
Bihor □, Romania 42 D7
Bihor, Munții, Romania . 42 D7
Bijagós, Arquipélago dos,
  Guinea-Biss. 82 C1
Bijaipur, India 68 F7
Bijapur, Karnataka, India . 66 L9
Bijapur, Mad. P., India . 67 K12
Bījār, Iran 70 C5
Bijawar, India 69 G8
Bijeljina, Bos.-H. 42 F4
Bijelo Polje,
  Montenegro, Yug. ... 40 C3
Bijie, China 58 D5
Bijnor, India 68 E8
Bikaner, India 68 E5
Bikapur, India 69 F10
Bikeqi, China 56 D6
Bikfayyā, Lebanon ... 75 B4
Bikin, Russia 51 E14
Bikin →, Russia 54 A7
Bikini Atoll, Marshall Is. . 96 F8
Bikita, Zimbabwe 89 C5
Bikoué, Cameroon ... 83 E7
Bila Tserkva, Ukraine . 47 H6
Bilanga, Burkina Faso . 83 C4
Bilara, India 68 F5
Bilaspur, Mad. P., India 69 H10
Bilaspur, Punjab, India . 68 D7
Biläsuvar, Azerbaijan .. 73 C13
Bilauk Taungdan, Thailand 64 F2
Bilbao, Spain 32 B2
Bilbeis, Egypt 80 H7
Bilbo = Bilbao, Spain . 32 B2
Bilbor, Romania 43 C10
Bilciurești, Romania . 43 F10
Bíldudalur, Iceland .. 8 D2
Bílé Karpaty, Europe . 27 B11
Bileća, Bos.-H. 40 D2
Bilecik, Turkey 72 B4
Biłgoraj, Poland 45 H9
Bilgram, India 69 F9
Bilhaur, India 69 F9
Bilhorod-Dnistrovskyy,
  Ukraine 47 J6
Bilibino, Russia 51 C17
Biliboza, Mozam. ... 87 E5
Bilishti, Albania 40 F5
Billabalong Roadhouse,
  Australia 93 E2
Billdal, Sweden 11 G5
Billiluna, Australia .. 92 C4
Billings, U.S.A. 114 D9
Billiton Is. = Belitung,
  Indonesia 62 E3
Billsta, Sweden 10 A13
Billund, Denmark ... 11 J3
Bilma, Niger 79 E8
Bilo Gora, Croatia .. 42 E2
Biloela, Australia ... 94 C5
Bilohirsk, Ukraine .. 47 K8
Bilopillya, Ukraine .. 47 G8

Biloxi, *U.S.A.* 113 K10
Bilpa Morea Claypan, *Australia* 94 D3
Biltine, *Chad* 79 F10
Bilyarsk, *Russia* 48 C10
Bima, *Indonesia* 63 F5
Bimban, *Egypt* 80 C3
Bimbila, *Ghana* 83 D5
Bimini Is., *Bahamas* 120 A4
Bin Xian, *Heilongjiang, China* 57 B14
Bin Xian, *Shaanxi, China* 56 G5
Bin Yauri, *Nigeria* 83 C5
Bina-Etawah, *India* 68 G8
Bināb, *Iran* 71 B6
Binalbagan, *Phil.* 61 F5
Binalong, *Australia* 95 E4
Bīnālūd, Kūh-e, *Iran* 71 B8
Binatang = Bintangor, *Malaysia* 62 D4
Binche, *Belgium* 17 D4
Binchuan, *China* 58 E3
Binder, *Chad* 83 D7
Bindki, *India* 69 F9
Bindslev, *Denmark* 11 G4
Bindura, *Zimbabwe* 87 F3
Binefar, *Spain* 32 D5
Bingara, *Australia* 95 D5
Bingen, *Germany* 25 F3
Bingerville, *Ivory C.* 82 D4
Bingham, *U.S.A.* 109 C11
Binghamton, *U.S.A.* 111 D9
Bingöl, *Turkey* 70 B4
Bingöl Dağları, *Turkey* 73 C9
Bingsjö, *Sweden* 10 C9
Binh Dinh = An Nhon, *Vietnam* 64 F7
Binh Khe, *Vietnam* 64 F7
Binh Son, *Vietnam* 64 E7
Binhai, *China* 57 G10
Binic, *France* 18 D4
Binisatua, *Spain* 37 B11
Binjai, *Indonesia* 62 D3
Binji, *Nigeria* 83 C5
Binnaway, *Australia* 95 E4
Binongko, *Indonesia* 63 F6
Binscarth, *Canada* 105 C8
Bint Goda, *Sudan* 81 E3
Bintan, *Indonesia* 62 D2
Bintangor, *Malaysia* 62 D4
Bintulu, *Malaysia* 62 D4
Bintuni, *Indonesia* 63 E8
Binyang, *China* 58 F7
Binz, *Germany* 24 A9
Binzert = Bizerte, *Tunisia* 79 A7
Binzhou, *China* 57 F10
Bío Bío □, *Chile* 126 D1
Biograd na Moru, *Croatia* 29 E12
Bioko, *Eq. Guin.* 83 E6
Biokovo, *Croatia* 29 E14
Bipindi, *Cameroon* 83 E7
Bir, *India* 66 K9
Bir, Ras, *Djibouti* 81 E5
Bîr Abu Hashim, *Egypt* 80 C3
Bîr Abu Minqar, *Egypt* 80 B2
Bîr Abu Muḥammad, *Egypt* 75 F3
Bi'r ad Dabbāghāt, *Jordan* 75 E4
Bîr Adal Deib, *Sudan* 80 C4
Bi'r al Butayyihāt, *Jordan* 75 F4
Bi'r al Mārī, *Jordan* 75 E4
Bi'r al Qattār, *Jordan* 75 F4
Bîr 'Asal, *Egypt* 80 B3
Bîr Atrun, *Sudan* 80 D2
Bîr Beiḍa, *Egypt* 75 E3
Bîr Diqnash, *Egypt* 80 A2
Bîr el 'Abd, *Egypt* 75 D2
Bîr el Basur, *Egypt* 80 B2
Bîr el Biarât, *Egypt* 75 F3
Bîr el Duweidar, *Egypt* 75 E1
Bîr el Garârât, *Egypt* 75 D2
Bîr el Gellaz, *Egypt* 80 A2
Bîr el Heisi, *Egypt* 75 F3
Bîr el Jafir, *Egypt* 75 E1
Bîr el Mâlḥi, *Egypt* 75 E2
Bîr el Shaqqa, *Egypt* 80 A2
Bîr el Thamâda, *Egypt* 75 E2
Bîr Fuad, *Egypt* 80 A2
Bîr Gebeil Ḥiṣn, *Egypt* 75 E2
Bi'r Ghadīr, *Syria* 75 A6
Bîr Haimur, *Egypt* 80 C3
Bîr Ḥasana, *Egypt* 75 E2
Bîr Hôôker, *Egypt* 80 H7
Bîr Kanayis, *Egypt* 80 C3
Bîr Kaseiba, *Egypt* 75 E2
Bîr Kerawein, *Egypt* 80 B2
Bîr Lahfân, *Egypt* 75 E2
Bîr Madkûr, *Egypt* 75 E1
Bîr Maql, *Egypt* 80 C3
Bîr Mîneiga, *Sudan* 80 C4
Bîr Misaha, *Egypt* 80 C2
Bir Mogreïn, *Mauritania* 78 C3
Bîr Murr, *Egypt* 80 C3
Bi'r Muṭribah, *Kuwait* 70 D5
Bîr Nakheila, *Egypt* 80 C3
Bîr Qaṭia, *Egypt* 75 E1
Bîr Qatrani, *Egypt* 80 A2
Bîr Ranga, *Egypt* 80 C4
Bîr Sahara, *Egypt* 80 C2
Bîr Seiyâla, *Egypt* 80 B3
Bîr Shalatein, *Egypt* 80 C4
Bîr Shebb, *Egypt* 80 C2
Bîr Shût, *Egypt* 80 C4
Bîr Terfawi, *Egypt* 80 C2
Bîr Umm Qubûr, *Egypt* 80 C3
Bîr Ungât, *Egypt* 80 C3
Bîr Za'farâna, *Egypt* 80 J8
Bîr Zeidûn, *Egypt* 80 B3
Biramféro, *Guinea* 82 C3
Biratnagar, *Nepal* 69 F12
Birawa, *Dem. Rep. of the Congo* 86 C2
Birch →, *Canada* 104 B6
Birch Hills, *Canada* 105 C7
Birch I., *Canada* 105 C9
Birch L., *N.W.T., Canada* 104 A5
Birch L., *Ont., Canada* 102 B1
Birch Mts., *Canada* 104 B6
Birch River, *Canada* 105 C8
Birchip, *Australia* 95 F3
Birchiş, *Romania* 42 E7
Bird, *Canada* 105 B10
Bird I. = Las Aves, Is., *W. Indies* 121 C7
Birdsville, *Australia* 94 D2
Birdum Cr., *Australia* 92 C5
Birecik, *Turkey* 70 B3
Birein, *Israel* 75 E3
Bireuen, *Indonesia* 62 C1
Biri →, *Sudan* 81 F2
Birifo, *Gambia* 82 C2
Birigui, *Brazil* 127 A5
Birjand, *Iran* 71 C8
Birkenfeld, *Germany* 25 F3
Birkenhead, *U.K.* 12 D4
Birkerød, *Denmark* 11 J6
Birket Qârûn, *Egypt* 80 J7
Birkfeld, *Austria* 26 D8
Bîrlad = Bârlad, *Romania* 43 D12
Birmingham, *U.K.* 13 E6
Birmingham, *U.S.A.* 109 J2
Birmitrapur, *India* 67 H14
Birni Ngaouré, *Niger* 83 C5
Birni Nkonni, *Niger* 83 C6
Birnin Gwari, *Nigeria* 83 C6
Birnin Kebbi, *Nigeria* 83 C5
Birnin Kudu, *Nigeria* 83 C6
Birobidzhan, *Russia* 51 E14
Birr, *Ireland* 15 C4
Birrie →, *Australia* 95 D4
Birsilpur, *India* 68 E5
Birsk, *Russia* 50 D6
Birštonas, *Lithuania* 44 D11
Birtle, *Canada* 105 C8
Birur, *India* 66 N9
Biryuchiy, *Ukraine* 47 J8
Biržai, *Lithuania* 9 H21
Birżebbugga, *Malta* 36 D2
Bisa, *Indonesia* 63 E7
Bisáccia, *Italy* 31 A8
Bisacquino, *Italy* 30 E6
Bisalpur, *India* 69 E8
Bisbee, *U.S.A.* 115 L9
Biscarosse, *France* 20 D2
Biscarrosse et de Parentis, Étang de, *France* 20 D2
Biscay, B. of, *Atl. Oc.* 6 F5
Biscayne B., *U.S.A.* 109 N5
Biscéglie, *Italy* 31 A9
Bischheim, *France* 19 D14
Bischofshofen, *Austria* 26 D6
Bischofswerda, *Germany* 24 D10
Bischwiller, *France* 19 D14
Biscoe Bay, *Antarctica* 5 D13
Biscoe Is., *Antarctica* 5 C17
Biscostasing, *Canada* 102 C3
Biševo, *Croatia* 29 F13
Bisha, *Eritrea* 81 D4
Bishah, W. →, *Si. Arabia* 80 C5
Bishan, *China* 58 C6
Bishkek, *Kyrgyzstan* 50 E8
Bishnupur, *India* 69 H12
Bisho, *S. Africa* 89 E4
Bishop, *Calif., U.S.A.* 116 H8
Bishop, *Tex., U.S.A.* 113 M6
Bishop Auckland, *U.K.* 12 C6
Bishop's Falls, *Canada* 103 C8
Bishop's Stortford, *U.K.* 13 F8
Bisignano, *Italy* 31 C9
Bisina, L., *Uganda* 86 B3
Biskra, *Algeria* 78 B7
Biskupiec, *Poland* 44 E7
Bismarck, *U.S.A.* 112 B4
Bismarck Arch., *Papua N. G.* 96 H7
Bismark, *Germany* 24 C7
Bismil, *Turkey* 73 D9
Biso, *Uganda* 86 B3
Bison, *U.S.A.* 112 C3
Bīsotūn, *Iran* 70 C5
Bispgården, *Sweden* 10 A10
Bissagos = Bijagós, Arquipélago dos, *Guinea-Biss.* 82 C1
Bissau, *Guinea-Biss.* 82 C1
Bissaula, *Nigeria* 83 D7
Bissikrima, *Guinea* 82 C2
Bissorã, *Guinea-Biss.* 82 C1
Bistcho L., *Canada* 104 B5
Bistreţ, *Romania* 43 G8
Bistrica = Ilirska-Bistrica, *Slovenia* 29 C11
Bistriţa, *Romania* 43 C9
Bistriţa →, *Romania* 43 D11
Bistriţa Năsăud □, *Romania* 43 C9
Bistriţei, Munţii, *Romania* 43 C10
Biswan, *India* 69 F9
Bisztynek, *Poland* 44 D7
Bitburg, *Germany* 25 F2
Bitche, *France* 19 C14
Bithynia, *Turkey* 72 B4
Bitlis, *Turkey* 70 B4
Bitola, *Macedonia* 40 E5
Bitolj = Bitola, *Macedonia* 40 E5
Bitonto, *Italy* 31 A9
Bitter Creek, *U.S.A.* 114 F9
Bitter L. = Buheirat-Murrat-el-Kubra, *Egypt* 80 H8
Bitterfeld, *Germany* 24 D8
Bitterfontein, *S. Africa* 88 E2
Bitterroot →, *U.S.A.* 114 C6
Bitterroot Range, *U.S.A.* 114 D6
Bitterwater, *U.S.A.* 116 J6
Bitti, *Italy* 30 B2
Bittou, *Burkina Faso* 83 C4
Biu, *Nigeria* 83 C7
Bivolari, *Romania* 43 C12
Bivolu, Vf., *Romania* 43 C10
Biwa-Ko, *Japan* 55 G8
Biwabik, *U.S.A.* 112 B8
Bixad, *Romania* 43 C8
Bixby, *U.S.A.* 113 H7
Biyang, *China* 56 H7
Biysk, *Russia* 50 D9
Bizana, *S. Africa* 89 E4
Bizen, *Japan* 55 G7
Bizerte, *Tunisia* 79 A7
Bjargtangar, *Iceland* 8 D1
Bjärnum, *Sweden* 11 H7
Bjästa, *Sweden* 10 A12
Bjelasica, *Montenegro, Yug.* 40 D3
Bjelašnica, *Bos.-H.* 42 G3
Bjelovar, *Croatia* 29 C13
Bjerringbro, *Denmark* 11 H3
Björbo, *Sweden* 10 D8
Björklinge, *Sweden* 10 D11
Björneborg, *Sweden* 10 E8
Bjørnevatn, *Norway* 8 B23
Bjørnøya, *Arctic* 4 B8
Bjursås, *Sweden* 10 D9
Bjuv, *Sweden* 11 H6
Bla, *Mali* 82 C3
Blace, *Serbia, Yug.* 40 C5
Blachownia, *Poland* 45 H5
Black = Da →, *Vietnam* 58 G5
Black →, *Canada* 110 B5
Black →, *Ariz., U.S.A.* 115 K8
Black →, *Ark., U.S.A.* 113 H9
Black →, *Mich., U.S.A.* 110 D2
Black →, *N.Y., U.S.A.* 111 C8
Black →, *Wis., U.S.A.* 112 D9
Black Bay Pen., *Canada* 102 C2
Black Birch L., *Canada* 105 B7
Black Diamond, *Canada* 104 C6
Black Duck →, *Canada* 102 A2
Black Forest = Schwarzwald, *Germany* 25 G4
Black Forest, *U.S.A.* 112 F2
Black Hd., *Ireland* 15 C2
Black Hills, *U.S.A.* 112 D3
Black I., *Canada* 105 C9
Black L., *Canada* 105 B7
Black L., *Mich., U.S.A.* 108 C3
Black L., *N.Y., U.S.A.* 111 B9
Black Lake, *Canada* 105 B7
Black Mesa, *U.S.A.* 113 G3
Black Mt. = Mynydd Du, *U.K.* 13 F4
Black Mts., *U.K.* 13 F4
Black Range, *U.S.A.* 115 K10
Black River, *Jamaica* 120 C4
Black River Falls, *U.S.A.* 112 C9
Black Sea, *Eurasia* 6 G12
Black Tickle, *Canada* 103 B8
Black Volta →, *Africa* 82 D4
Black Warrior →, *U.S.A.* 109 J2
Blackall, *Australia* 94 C4
Blackball, *N.Z.* 91 K3
Blackbull, *Australia* 94 B3
Blackburn, *U.K.* 12 D5
Blackburn with Darwen □, *U.K.* 12 D5
Blackfoot, *U.S.A.* 114 E7
Blackfoot →, *U.S.A.* 114 C7
Blackfoot River Reservoir, *U.S.A.* 114 E8
Blackie, *Canada* 104 C6
Blackpool, *U.K.* 12 D4
Blackpool □, *U.K.* 12 D4
Blackriver, *U.S.A.* 110 B1
Blacks Harbour, *Canada* 103 C6
Blacksburg, *U.S.A.* 108 G5
Blacksod B., *Ireland* 15 B1
Blackstone, *U.S.A.* 108 G7
Blackstone Ra., *Australia* 93 E4
Blackwater, *Australia* 94 C4
Blackwater →, *Meath, Ireland* 15 C4
Blackwater →, *Waterford, Ireland* 15 D4
Blackwater →, *U.K.* 15 B5
Blackwell, *U.S.A.* 113 G6
Blackwells Corner, *U.S.A.* 117 K7
Blaenau Ffestiniog, *U.K.* 12 E4
Blaenau Gwent □, *U.K.* 13 F4
Blagaj, *Bos.-H.* 40 C1
Blagnac, *France* 20 E5
Blagodarnoye = Blagodarnyy, *Russia* 49 H6
Blagodarnyy, *Russia* 49 H6
Blagoevgrad, *Bulgaria* 40 D7
Blagoveshchensk, *Russia* 51 D13
Blain, *France* 18 E5
Blain, *U.S.A.* 110 F7
Blaine, *Minn., U.S.A.* 112 C8
Blaine, *Wash., U.S.A.* 116 B4
Blaine Lake, *Canada* 105 C7
Blair, *U.S.A.* 112 E6
Blair Athol, *Australia* 94 C4
Blair Atholl, *U.K.* 14 E5
Blairgowrie, *U.K.* 14 E5
Blairsden, *U.S.A.* 116 F6
Blairsville, *U.S.A.* 110 F5
Blaj, *Romania* 43 D8
Blake Pt., *U.S.A.* 112 A10
Blakely, *Ga., U.S.A.* 109 K3
Blakely, *Pa., U.S.A.* 111 E9
Blâmont, *France* 19 D13
Blanc, C., *Spain* 37 B9
Blanc, Mont, *Alps* 21 C10
Blanc-Sablon, *Canada* 103 B8
Blanca, B., *Argentina* 122 G4
Blanca Peak, *U.S.A.* 115 H11
Blanche, C., *Australia* 95 E1
Blanche, L., *S. Austral., Australia* 95 D2
Blanche, L., *W. Austral., Australia* 92 D3
Blanco, *S. Africa* 88 E3
Blanco, *U.S.A.* 113 K5
Blanco →, *Argentina* 126 C2
Blanco, C., *Costa Rica* 120 E2
Blanco, C., *U.S.A.* 114 E1
Blanda →, *Iceland* 8 D3
Blandford Forum, *U.K.* 13 G5
Blanding, *U.S.A.* 115 H9
Blanes, *Spain* 32 D7
Blangy-sur-Bresle, *France* 19 C8
Blanice →, *Czech Rep.* 26 B7
Blankaholm, *Sweden* 11 G10
Blankenberge, *Belgium* 17 C3
Blankenburg, *Germany* 24 D6
Blanquefort, *France* 20 D3
Blanquilla, I., *Venezuela* 121 D7
Blanquillo, *Uruguay* 127 C4
Blansko, *Czech Rep.* 27 B9
Blantyre, *Malawi* 87 F4
Blarney, *Ireland* 15 E3
Blasdell, *U.S.A.* 110 D6
Błaszki, *Poland* 45 G5
Blatná, *Czech Rep.* 26 B6
Blato, *Croatia* 29 F13
Blaubeuren, *Germany* 25 G5
Blaustein, *Germany* 25 G5
Blåvands Huk, *Denmark* 11 J2
Blaydon, *U.K.* 12 C6
Blaye, *France* 20 C3
Blaye-les-Mines, *France* 20 D6
Blayney, *Australia* 95 E4
Blaze, Pt., *Australia* 92 B5
Błażowa, *Poland* 45 J9
Bleckede, *Germany* 24 B6
Bled, *Slovenia* 29 B11
Bleiburg, *Austria* 26 E7
Blejeşti, *Romania* 43 F10
Blekinge, *Sweden* 9 H16
Blekinge län □, *Sweden* 11 H9
Blenheim, *Canada* 110 D3
Blenheim, *N.Z.* 91 J4
Bléone →, *France* 21 D10
Blérancourt, *France* 19 C10
Bletchley, *U.K.* 13 F7
Blida, *Algeria* 78 A6
Blidö, *Sweden* 10 E12
Blidsberg, *Sweden* 11 G7
Blieskastel, *Germany* 25 F3
Bligh Sound, *N.Z.* 91 L1
Blind River, *Canada* 102 C3
Blinishti, *Albania* 40 E3
Bliss, *Idaho, U.S.A.* 114 E6
Bliss, *N.Y., U.S.A.* 110 D6
Blissfield, *U.S.A.* 110 F3
Blitar, *Indonesia* 63 H15
Blitta, *Togo* 83 D5
Block I., *U.S.A.* 111 E13
Block Island Sd., *U.S.A.* 111 E13
Blodgett Iceberg Tongue, *Antarctica* 5 C9
Bloemfontein, *S. Africa* 88 D4
Bloemhof, *S. Africa* 88 D4
Blois, *France* 18 E8
Blomskog, *Sweden* 10 E6
Blomstermåla, *Sweden* 11 H10
Blönduós, *Iceland* 8 D3
Błonie, *Poland* 45 F7
Bloodvein →, *Canada* 105 C9
Bloody Foreland, *Ireland* 15 A3
Bloomer, *U.S.A.* 112 C9
Bloomfield, *Canada* 110 C7
Bloomfield, *Iowa, U.S.A.* 112 E8
Bloomfield, *N. Mex., U.S.A.* 115 H10
Bloomfield, *Nebr., U.S.A.* 112 D6
Bloomington, *Ill., U.S.A.* 112 E10
Bloomington, *Ind., U.S.A.* 108 F2
Bloomington, *Minn., U.S.A.* 112 C8
Bloomsburg, *U.S.A.* 111 F8
Blora, *Indonesia* 63 G14
Blossburg, *U.S.A.* 110 E7
Blouberg, *S. Africa* 89 C4
Blountstown, *U.S.A.* 109 K3
Bludenz, *Austria* 26 D2
Blue Earth, *U.S.A.* 112 D8
Blue Mesa Reservoir, *U.S.A.* 115 G10
Blue Mountain Lake, *U.S.A.* 111 C10
Blue Mts., *Maine, U.S.A.* 111 B14
Blue Mts., *Oreg., U.S.A.* 114 D4
Blue Mts., *Pa., U.S.A.* 111 F8
Blue Mud B., *Australia* 94 A2
Blue Nile = Nîl el Azraq →, *Sudan* 81 D3
Blue Rapids, *U.S.A.* 112 F6
Blue Ridge Mts., *U.S.A.* 109 G5
Blue River, *Canada* 104 C5
Bluefield, *U.S.A.* 108 G5
Bluefields, *Nic.* 120 D3
Bluff, *Australia* 94 C4
Bluff, *N.Z.* 91 M2
Bluff, *U.S.A.* 115 H9
Bluff Knoll, *Australia* 93 F2
Bluff Pt., *Australia* 93 E1
Bluffton, *U.S.A.* 108 E3
Blumenau, *Brazil* 127 B6
Blunt, *U.S.A.* 112 C5
Bly, *U.S.A.* 114 E3
Blyth, *Canada* 110 C3
Blyth, *U.K.* 12 B6
Blythe, *U.S.A.* 117 M12
Blytheville, *U.S.A.* 113 H10
Bo, *S. Leone* 82 D2
Bo Duc, *Vietnam* 65 G6
Bo Hai, *China* 57 E10
Bo Xian = Bozhou, *China* 56 H8
Boa Vista, *Brazil* 124 C6
Boac, *Phil.* 61 E4
Boaco, *Nic.* 120 D2
Bo'ai, *China* 56 G7
Boal, *Spain* 34 B4
Boalsburg, *U.S.A.* 110 F7
Boane, *Mozam.* 89 D5
Boardman, *U.S.A.* 110 E4
Bobadah, *Australia* 95 E4
Bobai, *China* 58 F7
Bobbili, *India* 67 K13
Bóbbio, *Italy* 28 D6
Bobcaygeon, *Canada* 102 D4
Böblingen, *Germany* 25 G5
Bobo-Dioulasso, *Burkina Faso* 82 C4
Bobolice, *Poland* 44 E3
Boboshevo, *Bulgaria* 40 D7
Bobov Dol, *Bulgaria* 40 D6
Bóbr →, *Poland* 45 F2
Bobraomby, Tanjon' i, *Madag.* 89 A8
Bobrinets, *Ukraine* 47 H7
Bobrov, *Russia* 48 E5
Bobrovitsa, *Ukraine* 47 G6
Bobruysk = Babruysk, *Belarus* 47 F5
Boby, Pic, *Madag.* 85 J9
Bôca do Acre, *Brazil* 124 E5
Boca Raton, *U.S.A.* 109 M5
Bocanda, *Ivory C.* 82 D4
Bocas del Toro, *Panama* 120 E3
Boceguillas, *Spain* 34 D7
Bochnia, *Poland* 45 J7
Bocholt, *Germany* 24 D2
Bochum, *Germany* 24 D3
Bockenem, *Germany* 24 C6
Boćki, *Poland* 45 F10
Bocognano, *France* 21 F13
Bocoyna, *Mexico* 118 B3
Bocşa, *Romania* 42 E6
Böda, *Kalmar, Sweden* 11 G11
Boda, *Kopparberg, Sweden* 10 C9
Boda, *Västernorrland, Sweden* 10 B10
Bodafors, *Sweden* 11 G8
Bodaybo, *Russia* 51 D12
Boddam, *U.K.* 14 B7
Boddington, *Australia* 93 F2
Bode Sadu, *Nigeria* 83 D5
Bodega Bay, *U.S.A.* 116 G3
Boden, *Sweden* 8 D19
Bodensee, *Europe* 25 H5
Bodenteich, *Germany* 24 C6
Bodhan, *India* 66 K10
Bodinga, *Nigeria* 83 C6
Bodmin, *U.K.* 13 G3
Bodmin Moor, *U.K.* 13 G3
Bodø, *Norway* 8 C16
Bodrog →, *Hungary* 42 B6
Bodrum, *Turkey* 39 D9
Bódva →, *Hungary* 42 B5
Boën, *France* 21 C8
Boende, *Dem. Rep. of the Congo* 84 E4
Boerne, *U.S.A.* 113 L5
Boesmans →, *S. Africa* 88 E4
Boffa, *Guinea* 82 C2
Bogalusa, *U.S.A.* 113 K10
Bogan →, *Australia* 95 D4
Bogan Gate, *Australia* 95 E4
Bogandé, *Burkina Faso* 83 C4
Bogantungan, *Australia* 94 C4
Bogata, *U.S.A.* 113 J7
Bogatić, *Serbia, Yug.* 40 B3
Boğazkale, *Turkey* 72 B6
Boğazlıyan, *Turkey* 72 C6
Bogen, *Sweden* 10 D6
Bogense, *Denmark* 11 J4
Bogetići, *Montenegro, Yug.* 40 D2
Boggabilla, *Australia* 95 D5
Boggabri, *Australia* 95 E5
Boggeragh Mts., *Ireland* 15 D3
Boglan = Solhan, *Turkey* 70 B4
Bognor Regis, *U.K.* 13 G7
Bogo, *Phil.* 61 F6
Bogodukhov = Bohodukhiv, *Ukraine* 47 G8
Bogol Manya, *Ethiopia* 81 G5
Bogong, Mt., *Australia* 95 F4
Bogor, *Indonesia* 63 G12
Bogoroditsk, *Russia* 46 F10
Bogorodsk, *Russia* 48 B6
Bogoso, *Ghana* 82 D4
Bogotá, *Colombia* 124 C4
Bogotol, *Russia* 50 D9
Bogou, *Togo* 83 C5
Bogra, *Bangla.* 67 G16
Boguchany, *Russia* 51 D10
Boguchar, *Russia* 48 F5
Bogué, *Mauritania* 82 B2
Boguslav, *Ukraine* 47 H6
Boguszów-Gorce, *Poland* 45 H3
Bohain-en-Vermandois, *France* 19 C10
Bohemian Forest = Böhmerwald, *Germany* 25 F9
Bohinjska Bistrica, *Slovenia* 29 B11
Böhmerwald, *Germany* 25 F9
Bohmte, *Germany* 24 C4
Bohodukhiv, *Ukraine* 47 G8
Bohol □, *Phil.* 61 G6
Bohol Sea, *Phil.* 63 C6
Bohongou, *Burkina Faso* 83 C5
Böhönye, *Hungary* 42 D2
Bohuslän, *Sweden* 11 F5
Boi, *Nigeria* 83 D6
Boi, Pta. de, *Brazil* 127 A6
Boiaçu, *Brazil* 124 D6
Boileau, C., *Australia* 92 C3
Boing'o, *Sudan* 81 F3
Boiro, *Spain* 34 C2
Boise, *U.S.A.* 114 E5
Boise City, *U.S.A.* 113 G3

Boissevain, *Canada* 105 D8
Bóite →, *Italy* 29 B9
Boitzenburg, *Germany* 24 B9
Boizenburg, *Germany* 24 B6
Bojador C., *W. Sahara* 78 C3
Bojana →, *Albania* 40 E3
Bojano, *Italy* 31 A7
Bojanowo, *Poland* 45 G3
Bøjden, *Denmark* 11 J4
Bojnūrd, *Iran* 71 B8
Bojonegoro, *Indonesia* 63 G14
Boju, *Nigeria* 83 D6
Boka, *Serbia, Yug.* 42 E5
Boka Kotorska, *Montenegro, Yug.* 40 D2
Bokala, *Ivory C.* 82 D4
Bokani, *Nigeria* 83 D6
Bokaro, *India* 69 H11
Boké, *Guinea* 82 C2
Bokhara →, *Australia* 95 D4
Bokkos, *Nigeria* 83 D6
Boknafjorden, *Norway* 9 G11
Bokoro, *Chad* 79 F9
Bokpyin, *Burma* 65 G2
Boksitogorsk, *Russia* 46 C7
Bol, *Croatia* 29 E13
Bolama, *Guinea-Biss.* 82 C1
Bolan →, *Pakistan* 68 E2
Bolan Pass, *Pakistan* 66 E5
Bolaños →, *Mexico* 118 C4
Bolaños de Calatrava, *Spain* 35 G7
Bolayır, *Turkey* 41 F10
Bolbec, *France* 18 C7
Boldājī, *Iran* 71 D6
Boldeşti-Scăeni, *Romania* 43 E11
Bole, *China* 60 B3
Bole, *Ethiopia* 81 F4
Bole, *Ghana* 82 D4
Bolekhiv, *Ukraine* 47 H2
Bolesławiec, *Poland* 45 G2
Bolgatanga, *Ghana* 83 C4
Bolgrad = Bolhrad, *Ukraine* 47 K5
Bolhrad, *Ukraine* 47 K5
Bolinao, *Phil.* 61 C3
Bolintin-Vale, *Romania* 43 F10
Bolívar, *Argentina* 126 D3
Bolivar, *Mo., U.S.A.* 113 G8
Bolivar, *N.Y., U.S.A.* 110 D6
Bolivar, *Tenn., U.S.A.* 113 H10
Bolivia ■, *S. Amer.* 124 G6
Bolivian Plateau, *S. Amer.* 122 E4
Boljevac, *Serbia, Yug.* 40 C5
Bolkhov, *Russia* 46 F9
Bolków, *Poland* 45 H3
Bollebygd, *Sweden* 11 G6
Bollène, *France* 21 D8
Bollnäs, *Sweden* 10 C10
Bollon, *Australia* 95 D4
Bollstabruk, *Sweden* 10 B11
Bolmen, *Sweden* 11 H7
Bolobo, *Dem. Rep. of the Congo* 84 E3
Bologna, *Italy* 29 D8
Bologoye, *Russia* 46 D8
Bolonchenticul, *Mexico* 119 D7
Bolótana, *Italy* 30 B1
Boloven, Cao Nguyen, *Laos* 64 E6
Bolpur, *India* 69 H12
Bolsena, *Italy* 29 F8
Bolsena, L. di, *Italy* 29 F8
Bolshaya Chernigovka, *Russia* 48 D10
Bolshaya Glushitsa, *Russia* 48 D10
Bolshaya Martynovka, *Russia* 49 G5
Bolshaya Vradiyevka, *Ukraine* 47 J6
Bolshevik, Ostrov, *Russia* 51 B11
Bolshoi Kavkas = Caucasus Mountains, *Eurasia* 49 J7
Bolshoy Anyuy →, *Russia* 51 C17
Bolshoy Begichev, Ostrov, *Russia* 51 B12
Bolshoy Lyakhovskiy, Ostrov, *Russia* 51 B15
Bolshoy Tokmak = Tokmak, *Ukraine* 47 J8
Bolshoy Tyuters, Ostrov, *Russia* 9 G22
Bolsward, *Neths.* 17 A5
Bolt Head, *U.K.* 13 G4
Boltaña, *Spain* 32 C5
Boltigen, *Switz.* 25 J3
Bolton, *Canada* 110 C5
Bolton, *U.K.* 12 D5
Bolton Landing, *U.S.A.* 111 C11
Bolu, *Turkey* 72 B4
Bolungavík, *Iceland* 8 C2
Boluo, *China* 59 F10
Bolvadin, *Turkey* 70 B1
Bolzano, *Italy* 29 B8
Bom Jesus da Lapa, *Brazil* 125 F10
Boma, *Dem. Rep. of the Congo* 84 F2
Bombala, *Australia* 95 F4
Bombarral, *Portugal* 35 F1
Bombay = Mumbai, *India* 66 K8
Bomboma, *Dem. Rep. of the Congo* 84 D3
Bombombwa, *Dem. Rep. of the Congo* 86 B2
Bomi Hills, *Liberia* 82 D2
Bomili, *Dem. Rep. of the Congo* 86 B2
Bømlo, *Norway* 9 G11
Bomokandi →, *Dem. Rep. of the Congo* 86 B2
Bomu →, *C.A.R.* 84 D4
Bon, C., *Tunisia* 76 C5
Bon Sar Pa, *Vietnam* 64 F6
Bonaigarh, *India* 69 J11
Bonaire, *Neth. Ant.* 121 D6
Bonang, *Australia* 95 F4
Bonanza, *Nic.* 120 D3
Bonaparte Arch., *Australia* 92 B3
Boñar, *Spain* 34 C5
Bonaventure, *Canada* 103 C6
Bonavista, *Canada* 103 C9
Bonavista, C., *Canada* 103 C9
Bonavista B., *Canada* 103 C9
Bondeno, *Italy* 29 D8
Bondo, *Dem. Rep. of the Congo* 86 B1
Bondoukou, *Ivory C.* 82 D4
Bondowoso, *Indonesia* 63 G15
Bone, Teluk, *Indonesia* 63 E6
Bonerate, *Indonesia* 63 F6
Bonerate, Kepulauan, *Indonesia* 63 F6
Bo'ness, *U.K.* 14 E5
Bonete, Cerro, *Argentina* 126 B2
Bong Son = Hoai Nhon, *Vietnam* 64 E7
Bonga, *Ethiopia* 81 F4
Bongabong, *Phil.* 61 E4
Bongor, *Chad* 79 F9
Bongouanou, *Ivory C.* 82 D4
Bonham, *U.S.A.* 113 J6
Boni, *Mali* 82 B4
Bonifacio, *France* 21 G13
Bonifacio, Bouches de, *Medit. S.* 30 A2
Bonin Is. = Ogasawara Gunto, *Pac. Oc.* 52 G18
Bonke, *Ethiopia* 81 F4
Bonkoukou, *Niger* 83 C5
Bonn, *Germany* 24 E3
Bonnat, *France* 19 F8
Bonne Terre, *U.S.A.* 113 G9
Bonners Ferry, *U.S.A.* 114 B5
Bonnétable, *France* 18 D7
Bonneval, *Eure-et-Loir, France* 18 D8
Bonneval, *Savoie, France* 21 C11
Bonneville, *France* 19 F13
Bonney, L., *Australia* 95 F3
Bonnie Rock, *Australia* 93 F2
Bonny, *Nigeria* 83 E6
Bonny →, *Nigeria* 83 E6
Bonny, Bight of, *Africa* 83 E6
Bonny-sur-Loire, *France* 19 E9
Bonnyrigg, *U.K.* 14 F5
Bonnyville, *Canada* 105 C6
Bono, *Italy* 30 B2
Bonoi, *Indonesia* 63 E9
Bonorva, *Italy* 30 B1
Bonsall, *U.S.A.* 117 M9
Bontang, *Indonesia* 62 D5
Bonthe, *S. Leone* 82 D2
Bontoc, *Phil.* 61 C4
Bonyeri, *Ghana* 82 D4
Bonyhád, *Hungary* 42 D3
Bonython Ra., *Australia* 92 D4
Bookabie, *Australia* 93 F5
Booker, *U.S.A.* 113 G4
Boola, *Guinea* 82 D3
Booligal, *Australia* 95 E3
Boonah, *Australia* 95 D5
Boone, *Iowa, U.S.A.* 112 D8
Boone, *N.C., U.S.A.* 109 G5
Booneville, *Ark., U.S.A.* 113 H8
Booneville, *Miss., U.S.A.* 109 H1
Boonville, *Calif., U.S.A.* 116 F3
Boonville, *Ind., U.S.A.* 108 F2
Boonville, *Mo., U.S.A.* 112 F8
Boonville, *N.Y., U.S.A.* 111 C9
Boorindal, *Australia* 95 E4
Boorowa, *Australia* 95 E4
Boothia, Gulf of, *Canada* 101 A11
Boothia Pen., *Canada* 100 A10
Bootle, *U.K.* 12 D4
Booué, *Gabon* 84 E2
Boppard, *Germany* 25 E3
Boquete, *Panama* 120 E3
Boquilla, Presa de la, *Mexico* 118 B3
Boquillas del Carmen, *Mexico* 118 B4
Bor, *Czech Rep.* 26 B5
Bor, *Russia* 48 B7
Bor, *Serbia, Yug.* 40 B6
Bôr, *Sudan* 81 F3
Bor, *Sweden* 11 G8
Bor, *Turkey* 72 D6
Bor Mashash, *Israel* 75 D3
Borah Peak, *U.S.A.* 114 D7
Borang, *Sudan* 81 G3
Borås, *Sweden* 11 G6
Borāzjān, *Iran* 71 D6
Borba, *Brazil* 124 D7
Borba, *Portugal* 35 G3
Borborema, Planalto da, *Brazil* 122 D7
Borcea, *Romania* 43 F12
Borçka, *Turkey* 73 B9
Bord Khūn-e Now, *Iran* 71 D6
Borda, C., *Australia* 95 F2
Bordeaux, *France* 20 D3
Borden, *Australia* 93 F2
Borden, *Canada* 103 C7
Borden I., *Canada* 4 B2
Borden Pen., *Canada* 101 A11
Borders = Scottish Borders □, *U.K.* 14 F6
Bordertown, *Australia* 95 F3
Borðeyri, *Iceland* 8 D3
Bordighera, *Italy* 28 E4
Bordj Fly Ste. Marie, *Algeria* 78 C5
Bordj-in-Eker, *Algeria* 78 D7
Bordj Omar Driss, *Algeria* 78 C7
Bore, *Ethiopia* 81 G4
Borehamwood, *U.K.* 13 F7
Borek Wielkopolski, *Poland* 45 G4
Borensberg, *Sweden* 11 F9
Borgå = Porvoo, *Finland* 9 F21
Borgarfjörður, *Iceland* 8 D7
Borgarnes, *Iceland* 8 D3
Børgefjellet, *Norway* 8 D15
Borger, *Neths.* 17 B6
Borger, *U.S.A.* 113 H4
Borgholm, *Sweden* 11 H10
Bórgia, *Italy* 31 D9
Borgo San Dalmazzo, *Italy* 28 D4
Borgo San Lorenzo, *Italy* 29 E8
Borgo Val di Taro, *Italy* 28 D6
Borgo Valsugana, *Italy* 29 B8
Borgomanero, *Italy* 28 C5
Borgorose, *Italy* 29 F10
Borgosésia, *Italy* 28 C5
Borhoyn Tal, *Mongolia* 56 C6
Bori, *Nigeria* 83 E6
Borikhane, *Laos* 64 C4
Borisoglebsk, *Russia* 48 E6
Borisov = Barysaw, *Belarus* 46 E5
Borisovka, *Russia* 47 G9
Borja, *Peru* 124 D3
Borja, *Spain* 32 D3
Borjas Blancas = Les Borges Blanques, *Spain* 32 D5
Borjomi, *Georgia* 49 K6
Borken, *Germany* 24 D9
Børkop, *Denmark* 11 J3
Borkou, *Chad* 79 E9
Borkum, *Germany* 24 B2
Borlänge, *Sweden* 10 D9
Borley, C., *Antarctica* 5 C5
Borlu, *Turkey* 39 C10
Bormida →, *Italy* 28 D5
Bórmio, *Italy* 28 B7
Borna, *Germany* 24 D8
Borne Sulinowo, *Poland* 44 E3
Borneo, *E. Indies* 62 D5
Bornholm, *Denmark* 11 J8
Bornholms Amtskommune □, *Denmark* 11 J8
Bornholmsgattet, *Europe* 11 J8
Borno □, *Nigeria* 83 C7
Bornos, *Spain* 35 J5
Bornova, *Turkey* 39 C9
Bornu Yassa, *Nigeria* 83 C7
Boro →, *Sudan* 81 F2
Borodino, *Russia* 46 E8
Borogontsy, *Russia* 51 C14
Boromo, *Burkina Faso* 82 C4
Boron, *U.S.A.* 117 L9
Borongan, *Phil.* 61 F6
Borotangba Mts., *C.A.R.* 81 F2
Borotou, *Ivory C.* 82 D3
Borovan, *Bulgaria* 40 C7
Borovichi, *Russia* 46 C7
Borovsk, *Russia* 46 E9
Borrby, *Sweden* 11 J8
Borrego Springs, *U.S.A.* 117 M10
Borriol, *Spain* 32 E4
Borroloola, *Australia* 94 B2
Borşa, *Cluj, Romania* 43 D8
Borşa, *Maramureş, Romania* 43 C9
Borsad, *India* 68 H5
Borsec, *Romania* 43 D10
Borsod-Abaúj-Zemplén □, *Hungary* 42 B6
Bort-les-Orgues, *France* 20 C6
Borth, *U.K.* 13 E3
Börtnan, *Sweden* 10 B7
Borūjerd, *Iran* 71 C6
Boryslav, *Ukraine* 47 H2
Boryspil, *Ukraine* 47 G6
Borzhomi = Borjomi, *Georgia* 49 K6
Borzna, *Ukraine* 47 G7
Borzya, *Russia* 51 D12
Bosa, *Italy* 30 B1
Bosanska Dubica, *Bos.-H.* 29 C13
Bosanska Gradiška, *Bos.-H.* 42 E2
Bosanska Kostajnica, *Bos.-H.* 29 C13
Bosanska Krupa, *Bos.-H.* 29 D13
Bosanski Brod, *Bos.-H.* 42 E2
Bosanski Novi, *Bos.-H.* 29 C13
Bosanski Petrovac, *Bos.-H.* 29 D13
Bosanski Šamac, *Bos.-H.* 42 E3
Bosansko Grahovo, *Bos.-H.* 29 D13
Bosaso, *Somali Rep.* 74 E4
Boscastle, *U.K.* 13 G3
Bose, *China* 58 F6
Boshan, *China* 57 F9
Boshof, *S. Africa* 88 D4
Boshrūyeh, *Iran* 71 C8
Bosilegrad, *Serbia, Yug.* 40 D6
Boskovice, *Czech Rep.* 27 B9
Bosna →, *Bos.-H.* 42 E3
Bosna i Hercegovina = Bosnia-Herzegovina ■, *Europe* 42 G2
Bosnia-Herzegovina ■, *Europe* 42 G2
Bosnik, *Indonesia* 63 E9
Bosobolo, *Dem. Rep. of the Congo* 84 D3
Bosporus = İstanbul Boğazı, *Turkey* 41 E13
Bosque Farms, *U.S.A.* 115 J10
Bossangoa, *C.A.R.* 84 C3
Bossé Bangou, *Niger* 83 C5
Bossier City, *U.S.A.* 113 J8
Bosso, *Niger* 83 C7
Bosso, Dallol →, *Niger* 83 C5
Bostan, *Pakistan* 68 D2
Bostānābād, *Iran* 70 B5
Bosten Hu, *China* 60 B3
Boston, *U.K.* 12 E7
Boston, *U.S.A.* 111 D13
Boston Bar, *Canada* 104 D4
Boston Mts., *U.S.A.* 113 H8
Bosut →, *Croatia* 42 E3
Boswell, *Canada* 104 D5
Boswell, *U.S.A.* 110 F5
Botad, *India* 68 H4
Botan →, *Turkey* 73 D10
Botene, *Laos* 64 D3
Botev, *Bulgaria* 41 D8
Botevgrad, *Bulgaria* 40 D7
Bothaville, *S. Africa* 88 D4
Bothnia, G. of, *Europe* 8 E19
Bothwell, *Australia* 94 G4
Bothwell, *Canada* 110 D3
Boticas, *Portugal* 34 D3
Botletle →, *Botswana* 88 C3
Botlikh, *Russia* 49 J8
Botna →, *Moldova* 43 D14
Botoroaga, *Romania* 43 F10
Botoşani, *Romania* 43 C11
Botoşani □, *Romania* 43 C11
Botou, *Burkina Faso* 83 C5
Botricello, *Italy* 31 D9
Botro, *Ivory C.* 82 D3
Botswana ■, *Africa* 88 C3
Bottineau, *U.S.A.* 112 A4
Bottnaryd, *Sweden* 11 G7
Bottrop, *Germany* 17 C6
Botucatu, *Brazil* 127 A6
Botwood, *Canada* 103 C8
Bou Djébéha, *Mali* 82 B4
Bou Rjeïmât, *Mauritania* 82 B1
Bouaflé, *Ivory C.* 82 D3
Bouaké, *Ivory C.* 82 D3
Bouar, *C.A.R.* 84 C3
Bouârfa, *Morocco* 78 B5
Boucaut B., *Australia* 94 A1
Bouches-du-Rhône □, *France* 21 E9
Bougainville, C., *Australia* 92 B4
Bougainville I., *Papua N. G.* 96 H7
Bougainville Reef, *Australia* 94 B4
Bougie = Bejaia, *Algeria* 78 A7
Bougouni, *Mali* 82 C3
Bouillon, *Belgium* 17 E5
Boukombé, *Benin* 83 C5
Boulal, *Mali* 82 B3
Boulazac, *France* 20 C4
Boulder, *Colo., U.S.A.* 112 E2
Boulder, *Mont., U.S.A.* 114 C7
Boulder City, *U.S.A.* 117 K12
Boulder Creek, *U.S.A.* 116 H4
Boulder Dam = Hoover Dam, *U.S.A.* 117 K12
Bouli, *Mauritania* 82 B2
Boulia, *Australia* 94 C2
Bouligny, *France* 19 C12
Boulogne →, *France* 18 E5
Boulogne-sur-Gesse, *France* 20 E4
Boulogne-sur-Mer, *France* 19 B8
Bouloire, *France* 18 E7
Boulouli, *Mali* 82 B3
Boulsa, *Burkina Faso* 83 C4
Boultoum, *Niger* 83 C7
Boûmdeïd, *Mauritania* 82 B2
Boun Neua, *Laos* 64 B3
Boun Tai, *Laos* 64 B3
Bouna, *Ivory C.* 82 D4
Boundary Peak, *U.S.A.* 116 H8
Boundiali, *Ivory C.* 82 D3
Bountiful, *U.S.A.* 114 F8
Bounty Is., *Pac. Oc.* 96 M9
Boura, *Mali* 82 C4
Bourbon-Lancy, *France* 19 F10
Bourbon-l'Archambault, *France* 19 F10
Bourbonnais, *France* 19 F10
Bourbonne-les-Bains, *France* 19 E12
Bourbourg, *France* 19 B9
Bourdel L., *Canada* 102 A5
Bourem, *Mali* 83 B4
Bourg, *France* 20 C3
Bourg-Argental, *France* 21 C8
Bourg-de-Péage, *France* 21 C9
Bourg-en-Bresse, *France* 19 F12
Bourg-Lastic, *France* 20 C6
Bourg-Madame, *France* 20 F5
Bourg-St-Andéol, *France* 21 D8
Bourg-St-Maurice, *France* 21 C10
Bourganeuf, *France* 20 C5
Bourges, *France* 19 E9
Bourget, *Canada* 111 A9
Bourget, Lac du, *France* 21 C9
Bourgneuf, B. de, *France* 18 E4
Bourgneuf-en-Retz, *France* 18 E5
Bourgogne, *France* 19 F11
Bourgoin-Jallieu, *France* 21 C9
Bourgueil, *France* 18 E7
Bourke, *Australia* 95 E4
Bourne, *U.K.* 12 E7
Bournemouth, *U.K.* 13 G6
Bournemouth □, *U.K.* 13 G6
Bouroum, *Burkina Faso* 83 C4
Bouse, *U.S.A.* 117 M13
Boussac, *France* 19 F9
Boussé, *Burkina Faso* 83 C4
Boussouma, *Burkina Faso* 83 C4
Boutilimit, *Mauritania* 82 B2
Boutonne →, *France* 20 C3
Bouvet I. = Bouvetøya, *Antarctica* 3 G10
Bouvetøya, *Antarctica* 3 G10
Bouxwiller, *France* 19 D14
Bouza, *Niger* 83 C6
Bouzonville, *France* 19 C13
Bova Marina, *Italy* 31 E8
Bovalino Marina, *Italy* 31 D9
Bovec, *Slovenia* 29 B10
Bovill, *U.S.A.* 114 C5
Bovino, *Italy* 31 A8
Bovril, *Argentina* 126 C4
Bow →, *Canada* 104 C6
Bow Island, *Canada* 104 D6
Bowbells, *U.S.A.* 112 A3
Bowdle, *U.S.A.* 112 C5
Bowelling, *Australia* 93 F2
Bowen, *Argentina* 126 D2
Bowen, *Australia* 94 C4
Bowen Mts., *Australia* 95 F4
Bowie, *Ariz., U.S.A.* 115 K9
Bowie, *Tex., U.S.A.* 113 J6
Bowkān, *Iran* 70 B5
Bowland, Forest of, *U.K.* 12 D5
Bowling Green, *Ky., U.S.A.* 108 G2
Bowling Green, *Ohio, U.S.A.* 108 E4
Bowling Green, C., *Australia* 94 B4
Bowman, *U.S.A.* 112 B3
Bowman I., *Antarctica* 5 C8
Bowmanville, *Canada* 110 C6
Bowmore, *U.K.* 14 F2
Bowral, *Australia* 95 E5
Bowraville, *Australia* 95 E5
Bowron →, *Canada* 104 C4
Bowron Lake Prov. Park, *Canada* 104 C4
Bowser L., *Canada* 104 B3
Bowsman, *Canada* 105 C8
Bowwood, *Zambia* 87 F2
Box Cr. →, *Australia* 95 E3
Boxholm, *Sweden* 11 F9
Boxmeer, *Neths.* 17 C5
Boxtel, *Neths.* 17 C5
Boyabat, *Turkey* 72 B6
Boyalıca, *Turkey* 41 F13
Boyang, *China* 59 C11
Boyce, *U.S.A.* 113 K8
Boyd L., *Canada* 102 B4
Boyle, *Canada* 104 C6
Boyle, *Ireland* 15 C3
Boyne →, *Ireland* 15 C5
Boyne City, *U.S.A.* 108 C3
Boynitsa, *Bulgaria* 40 C6
Boynton Beach, *U.S.A.* 109 M5
Boyolali, *Indonesia* 63 G14
Boyoma, Chutes, *Dem. Rep. of the Congo* 86 B2
Boysen Reservoir, *U.S.A.* 114 E9
Boyuibe, *Bolivia* 124 G6
Boyup Brook, *Australia* 93 F2
Boz Burun, *Turkey* 41 F12
Boz Dağ, *Turkey* 39 D11
Boz Dağları, *Turkey* 39 C10
Bozburun, *Turkey* 39 E10
Bozcaada, *Turkey* 72 C2
Bozdoğan, *Turkey* 39 D10
Bozeman, *U.S.A.* 114 D8
Bozen = Bolzano, *Italy* 29 B8
Boževac, *Serbia, Yug.* 40 B5
Bozhou, *China* 56 H8
Bozkır, *Turkey* 72 D5
Bozkurt, *Turkey* 39 D11
Bozouls, *France* 20 D6
Bozoum, *C.A.R.* 84 C3
Bozova, *Antalya, Turkey* 39 D12
Bozova, *Sanliurfa, Turkey* 73 D8
Bozovici, *Romania* 42 F7
Bozüyük, *Turkey* 39 B12
Bra, *Italy* 28 D4
Braås, *Sweden* 11 G9
Brabant □, *Belgium* 17 D4
Brabant L., *Canada* 105 B8
Brabrand, *Denmark* 11 H4
Brač, *Croatia* 29 E13
Bracadale, L., *U.K.* 14 D2
Bracciano, *Italy* 29 F9
Bracciano, L. di, *Italy* 29 F9
Bracebridge, *Canada* 102 C4
Brach, *Libya* 79 C8
Bracieux, *France* 18 E8
Bräcke, *Sweden* 10 B9
Brackettville, *U.S.A.* 113 L4
Bračkì Kanal, *Croatia* 29 E13
Bracknell, *U.K.* 13 F7
Bracknell Forest □, *U.K.* 13 F7
Brad, *Romania* 42 D7
Brădano →, *Italy* 31 B9
Bradenton, *U.S.A.* 109 M4
Bradford, *Canada* 110 B5
Bradford, *U.K.* 12 D6
Bradford, *Pa., U.S.A.* 110 E6
Bradford, *Vt., U.S.A.* 111 C12
Bradley, *Ark., U.S.A.* 113 J8
Bradley, *Calif., U.S.A.* 116 K6
Bradley Institute, *Zimbabwe* 87 F3
Brady, *U.S.A.* 113 K5
Brædstrup, *Denmark* 11 J3
Braemar, *U.K.* 14 D5
Braeside, *Canada* 111 A8
Braga, *Portugal* 34 D2
Braga □, *Portugal* 34 D2
Bragadiru, *Romania* 43 G10
Bragado, *Argentina* 126 D3
Bragança, *Brazil* 125 D9
Bragança, *Portugal* 34 D4
Bragança □, *Portugal* 34 D4
Bragança Paulista, *Brazil* 127 A6
Brahmanbaria, *Bangla.* 67 H17
Brahmani →, *India* 67 J15
Brahmapur, *India* 67 K14
Brahmaputra →, *India* 69 H13
Braich-y-pwll, *U.K.* 12 E3
Braidwood, *Australia* 95 F4
Brăila, *Romania* 43 E12
Brăila □, *Romania* 43 E12
Brainerd, *U.S.A.* 112 B7
Braintree, *U.K.* 13 F8
Braintree, *U.S.A.* 111 D14
Brak →, *S. Africa* 88 D3
Brake, *Germany* 24 B4
Brakel, *Germany* 24 D5

Bräkne-Hoby, *Sweden* 11 H9
Brakwater, *Namibia* 88 C2
Brålanda, *Sweden* 11 F6
Bramberg, *Germany* 25 E6
Bramdrupdam, *Denmark* 11 J3
Bramming, *Denmark* 11 J2
Brämön, *Sweden* 10 B11
Brampton, *Canada* 102 D4
Brampton, *U.K.* 12 C5
Bramsche, *Germany* 24 C3
Branco →, *Brazil* 122 D4
Brandberg, *Namibia* 88 B2
Brande, *Denmark* 11 J3
Brandenburg = Neubrandenburg, *Germany* 24 B9
Brandenburg, *Germany* 24 C8
Brandenburg □, *Germany* 24 C9
Brandfort, *S. Africa* 88 D4
Brando, *France* 21 F13
Brandon, *Canada* 105 D9
Brandon, *U.S.A.* 111 C11
Brandon B., *Ireland* 15 D1
Brandon Mt., *Ireland* 15 D1
Brandsen, *Argentina* 126 D4
Brandvlei, *S. Africa* 88 E3
Brandýs nad Labem, *Czech Rep.* 26 A7
Brănești, *Romania* 43 F11
Branford, *U.S.A.* 111 E12
Braniewo, *Poland* 44 D6
Bransfield Str., *Antarctica* 5 C18
Brańsk, *Poland* 45 F9
Branson, *U.S.A.* 113 G8
Brantford, *Canada* 102 D3
Brantôme, *France* 20 C4
Branzi, *Italy* 28 B6
Bras d'Or L., *Canada* 103 C7
Brasher Falls, *U.S.A.* 111 B10
Brasil, Planalto, *Brazil* 122 E6
Brasiléia, *Brazil* 124 F5
Brasília, *Brazil* 125 G9
Brasília Legal, *Brazil* 125 D7
Braslaw, *Belarus* 9 J22
Braslovče, *Slovenia* 29 B12
Brașov, *Romania* 43 E10
Brașov □, *Romania* 43 E10
Brass, *Nigeria* 83 E6
Brass →, *Nigeria* 83 E6
Brassac-les-Mines, *France* 20 C7
Brasschaat, *Belgium* 17 C4
Brassey, Banjaran, *Malaysia* 62 D5
Brassey Ra., *Australia* 93 E3
Brasstown Bald, *U.S.A.* 109 H4
Brastad, *Sweden* 11 F5
Brastavățu, *Romania* 43 G9
Bratan = Morozov, *Bulgaria* 41 D9
Brateș, *Romania* 43 E11
Bratislava, *Slovak Rep.* 27 C10
Bratislavský □, *Slovak Rep.* 27 C10
Bratsigovo, *Bulgaria* 41 D8
Bratsk, *Russia* 51 D11
Brattleboro, *U.S.A.* 111 D12
Bratunac, *Bos.-H.* 42 F4
Braunau, *Austria* 26 C6
Braunschweig, *Germany* 24 C6
Braunton, *U.K.* 13 F3
Bravicea, *Moldova* 43 C13
Bråviken, *Sweden* 11 F10
Bravo del Norte, Rio = Grande, Rio →, *U.S.A.* 113 N6
Brawley, *U.S.A.* 117 N11
Bray, *Ireland* 15 C5
Bray, Mt., *Australia* 94 A1
Bray-sur-Seine, *France* 19 D10
Brazeau →, *Canada* 104 C5
Brazil, *U.S.A.* 108 F2
Brazil ■, *S. Amer.* 125 F9
Brazilian Highlands = Brasil, Planalto, *Brazil* 122 E6
Brazo Sur →, *S. Amer.* 126 B4
Brazos →, *U.S.A.* 113 L7
Brazzaville, *Congo* 84 E3
Brčko, *Bos.-H.* 42 F3
Brda →, *Poland* 45 E5
Brdy, *Czech Rep.* 26 B6
Breaden, L., *Australia* 93 E4
Breaksea Sd., *N.Z.* 91 L1
Bream B., *N.Z.* 91 F5
Bream Hd., *N.Z.* 91 F5
Breas, *Chile* 126 B1
Breaza, *Romania* 43 E10
Brebes, *Indonesia* 63 G13
Brechin, *Canada* 110 B5
Brechin, *U.K.* 14 E6
Brecht, *Belgium* 17 C4
Breckenridge, *Colo., U.S.A.* 114 G10
Breckenridge, *Minn., U.S.A.* 112 B6
Breckenridge, *Tex., U.S.A.* 113 J5
Breckland, *U.K.* 13 E8
Břeclav, *Czech Rep.* 27 C9
Brecon, *U.K.* 13 F4
Brecon Beacons, *U.K.* 13 F4
Breda, *Neths.* 17 C4
Bredaryd, *Sweden* 11 G7
Bredasdorp, *S. Africa* 88 E3
Bredebro, *Denmark* 11 J2
Bredstedt, *Germany* 24 A4
Bree, *Belgium* 17 C5
Bregalnica →, *Macedonia* 40 E6
Bregenz, *Austria* 26 D2
Bregovo, *Bulgaria* 40 B6
Bréhal, *France* 18 D5
Bréhat, Î. de, *France* 18 D4
Breiðafjörður, *Iceland* 8 D2
Breil-sur-Roya, *France* 21 E11
Breisach, *Germany* 25 G3
Brejo, *Brazil* 125 D10
Bremen, *Germany* 24 B4
Bremen □, *Germany* 24 B4
Bremer Bay, *Australia* 93 F2
Bremer I., *Australia* 94 A2
Bremerhaven, *Germany* 24 B4
Bremerton, *U.S.A.* 116 C4
Bremervörde, *Germany* 24 B5
Brenes, *Spain* 35 H5
Brenham, *U.S.A.* 113 K6
Brenne, *France* 20 B5
Brennerpass, *Austria* 26 D4
Breno, *Italy* 28 C7
Brent, *U.S.A.* 109 J2
Brenta →, *Italy* 29 C9
Brentwood, *U.K.* 13 F8
Brentwood, *Calif., U.S.A.* 116 H5
Brentwood, *N.Y., U.S.A.* 111 F11
Bréscia, *Italy* 28 C7
Breskens, *Neths.* 17 C3
Breslau = Wrocław, *Poland* 45 G4
Bresle →, *France* 18 B8
Bressanone, *Italy* 29 B8
Bressay, *U.K.* 14 A7
Bresse, *France* 19 F12
Bressuire, *France* 18 F6
Brest, *Belarus* 47 F2
Brest, *France* 18 D2
Brest-Litovsk = Brest, *Belarus* 47 F2
Bretagne, *France* 18 D3
Bretçu, *Romania* 43 D11
Bretenoux, *France* 20 D5
Breteuil, *Eure, France* 18 D7
Breteuil, *Oise, France* 19 C9
Breton, *Canada* 104 C6
Breton, Pertuis, *France* 20 B2
Breton Sd., *U.S.A.* 113 L10
Brett, C., *N.Z.* 91 F5
Bretten, *Germany* 25 F4
Breuil-Cervínia, *Italy* 28 C4
Brevard, *U.S.A.* 109 H4
Breves, *Brazil* 125 D8
Brewarrina, *Australia* 95 E4
Brewer, *U.S.A.* 109 C11
Brewer, Mt., *U.S.A.* 116 J8
Brewerville, *Liberia* 82 D2
Brewster, *N.Y., U.S.A.* 111 E11
Brewster, *Ohio, U.S.A.* 110 F3
Brewster, *Wash., U.S.A.* 114 B4
Brewster, Kap = Kangikajik, *Greenland* 4 B6
Brewton, *U.S.A.* 109 K2
Breyten, *S. Africa* 89 D5
Breza, *Bos.-H.* 42 F3
Brezhnev = Naberezhnyye Chelny, *Russia* 48 C11
Brežice, *Slovenia* 29 C12
Březnice, *Czech Rep.* 26 B6
Breznik, *Bulgaria* 40 D6
Brezno, *Slovak Rep.* 27 C12
Brezoi, *Romania* 43 E9
Brezovica, *Kosovo, Yug.* 40 D5
Brezovo, *Bulgaria* 41 D9
Briançon, *France* 21 D10
Briare, *France* 19 E9
Briático, *Italy* 31 D9
Bribie I., *Australia* 95 D5
Bribri, *Costa Rica* 120 E3
Briceni, *Moldova* 43 B12
Bricquebec, *France* 18 C5
Bridgehampton, *U.S.A.* 111 F12
Bridgend, *U.K.* 13 F4
Bridgend □, *U.K.* 13 F4
Bridgeport, *Calif., U.S.A.* 116 G7
Bridgeport, *Conn., U.S.A.* 111 E11
Bridgeport, *Nebr., U.S.A.* 112 E3
Bridgeport, *Tex., U.S.A.* 113 J6
Bridger, *U.S.A.* 114 D9
Bridgeton, *U.S.A.* 108 F8
Bridgetown, *Australia* 93 F2
Bridgetown, *Barbados* 121 D8
Bridgetown, *Canada* 103 D6
Bridgewater, *Canada* 103 D7
Bridgewater, *Mass., U.S.A.* 111 E14
Bridgewater, *N.Y., U.S.A.* 111 D9
Bridgewater, C., *Australia* 95 F3
Bridgewater-Gagebrook, *Australia* 94 G4
Bridgnorth, *U.K.* 13 E5
Bridgton, *U.S.A.* 111 B14
Bridgwater, *U.K.* 13 F5
Bridgwater B., *U.K.* 13 F4
Bridlington, *U.K.* 12 C7
Bridlington B., *U.K.* 12 C7
Bridport, *Australia* 94 G4
Bridport, *U.K.* 13 G5
Briec, *France* 18 D2
Brienne-le-Château, *France* 19 D11
Brienon-sur-Armançon, *France* 19 E10
Brienz, *Switz.* 25 J4
Brienzersee, *Switz.* 25 J3
Brig, *Switz.* 25 J3
Brigg, *U.K.* 12 D7
Brigham City, *U.S.A.* 114 F7
Bright, *Australia* 95 F4
Brighton, *Australia* 95 F2
Brighton, *Canada* 110 B7
Brighton, *U.K.* 13 G7
Brighton, *Colo., U.S.A.* 112 F2
Brighton, *N.Y., U.S.A.* 110 C7
Brignogan-Plage, *France* 18 D2
Brignoles, *France* 21 E10
Brihuega, *Spain* 32 E2
Brikama, *Gambia* 82 C1
Brilliant, *U.S.A.* 110 F4
Brilon, *Germany* 24 D4
Bríndisi, *Italy* 31 B10
Brinje, *Croatia* 29 D12
Brinkley, *U.S.A.* 113 H9
Brinnon, *U.S.A.* 116 C4
Brion, I., *Canada* 103 C7
Brionne, *France* 18 C7
Brionski, *Croatia* 29 D10
Brioude, *France* 20 C7
Briouze, *France* 18 D6
Brisbane, *Australia* 95 D5
Brisbane →, *Australia* 95 D5
Brisighella, *Italy* 29 D8
Bristol, *U.K.* 13 F5
Bristol, *Conn., U.S.A.* 111 E12
Bristol, *Pa., U.S.A.* 111 F10
Bristol, *R.I., U.S.A.* 111 E13
Bristol, *Tenn., U.S.A.* 109 G4
Bristol, City of □, *U.K.* 13 F5
Bristol B., *U.S.A.* 100 C4
Bristol Channel, *U.K.* 13 F3
Bristol I., *Antarctica* 5 B1
Bristol L., *U.S.A.* 115 J5
Bristow, *U.S.A.* 113 H6
Britain = Great Britain, *Europe* 6 E5
British Columbia □, *Canada* 104 C3
British Indian Ocean Terr. = Chagos Arch., *Ind. Oc.* 52 K11
British Isles, *Europe* 6 E5
Brits, *S. Africa* 89 D4
Britstown, *S. Africa* 88 E3
Britt, *Canada* 102 C3
Brittany = Bretagne, *France* 18 D3
Britton, *U.S.A.* 112 C6
Brive-la-Gaillarde, *France* 20 C5
Briviesca, *Spain* 34 C7
Brixen = Bressanone, *Italy* 29 B8
Brixham, *U.K.* 13 G4
Brnaze, *Croatia* 29 E13
Brno, *Czech Rep.* 27 B9
Broad →, *U.S.A.* 109 J5
Broad Arrow, *Australia* 93 F3
Broad B., *U.K.* 14 C2
Broad Haven, *Ireland* 15 B2
Broad Law, *U.K.* 14 F5
Broad Sd., *Australia* 94 C4
Broadalbin, *U.S.A.* 111 C10
Broadback →, *Canada* 102 B4
Broadford, *Australia* 95 F4
Broadhurst Ra., *Australia* 92 D3
Broads, The, *U.K.* 12 E9
Broadus, *U.S.A.* 112 C2
Broager, *Denmark* 11 K3
Broby, *Sweden* 11 H8
Broceni, *Latvia* 44 B9
Brochet, *Canada* 105 B8
Brochet, L., *Canada* 105 B8
Brocken, *Germany* 24 D6
Brockport, *U.S.A.* 110 C7
Brockton, *U.S.A.* 111 D13
Brockville, *Canada* 102 D4
Brockway, *Mont., U.S.A.* 112 B2
Brockway, *Pa., U.S.A.* 110 E6
Brocton, *U.S.A.* 110 D5
Brod, *Macedonia* 40 E5
Brodarevo, *Serbia, Yug.* 40 C3
Brodeur Pen., *Canada* 101 A11
Brodhead, Mt., *U.S.A.* 110 E7
Brodick, *U.K.* 14 F3
Brodnica, *Poland* 45 E6
Brody, *Ukraine* 47 G3
Brogan, *U.S.A.* 114 D5
Broglie, *France* 18 C7
Brok, *Poland* 45 F8
Broken Arrow, *U.S.A.* 113 G7
Broken Bow, *Nebr., U.S.A.* 112 E5
Broken Bow, *Okla., U.S.A.* 113 H7
Broken Bow Lake, *U.S.A.* 113 H7
Broken Hill = Kabwe, *Zambia* 87 E2
Broken Hill, *Australia* 95 E3
Brokind, *Sweden* 11 F9
Bromley, *U.K.* 13 F8
Bromölla, *Sweden* 11 H8
Bromsgrove, *U.K.* 13 E5
Brønderslev, *Denmark* 11 G3
Brong-Ahafo □, *Ghana* 82 D4
Broni, *Italy* 28 C6
Bronkhorstspruit, *S. Africa* 89 D4
Brønnøysund, *Norway* 8 D15
Bronte, *Italy* 31 E7
Brook Park, *U.S.A.* 110 E4
Brookhaven, *U.S.A.* 113 K9
Brookings, *Oreg., U.S.A.* 114 E1
Brookings, *S. Dak., U.S.A.* 112 C6
Brooklin, *Canada* 110 C6
Brooklyn Park, *U.S.A.* 112 C8
Brooks, *Canada* 104 C6
Brooks Range, *U.S.A.* 100 B5
Brooksville, *U.S.A.* 109 L4
Brookton, *Australia* 93 F2
Brookville, *U.S.A.* 110 E5
Broom, L., *U.K.* 14 D3
Broome, *Australia* 92 C3
Broons, *France* 18 D4
Brora, *U.K.* 14 C5
Brora →, *U.K.* 14 C5
Brørup, *Denmark* 11 J2
Brösarp, *Sweden* 11 J8
Brosna →, *Ireland* 15 C4
Broșteni, *Mehedinți, Romania* 42 F7
Broșteni, *Suceava, Romania* 43 C10
Brothers, *U.S.A.* 114 E3
Brou, *France* 18 D8
Brouage, *France* 20 C2
Brough, *U.K.* 12 C5
Brough Hd., *U.K.* 14 B5
Broughton Island = Qikiqtarjuaq, *Canada* 101 B13
Broumov, *Czech Rep.* 27 A9
Brovary, *Ukraine* 47 G6
Brovst, *Denmark* 11 G3
Brown, L., *Australia* 93 F2
Brown, Pt., *Australia* 95 E1
Brown City, *U.S.A.* 110 C2
Brown Willy, *U.K.* 13 G3
Brownfield, *U.S.A.* 113 J3
Browning, *U.S.A.* 114 B7
Brownsville, *Oreg., U.S.A.* 114 D2
Brownsville, *Pa., U.S.A.* 110 F5
Brownsville, *Tenn., U.S.A.* 113 H10
Brownsville, *Tex., U.S.A.* 113 N6
Brownville, *U.S.A.* 111 C9
Brownwood, *U.S.A.* 113 K5
Browse I., *Australia* 92 B3
Bruas, *Malaysia* 65 K3
Bruay-la-Buissière, *France* 19 B9
Bruce, Mt., *Australia* 92 D2
Bruce Pen., *Canada* 110 B3
Bruce Rock, *Australia* 93 F2
Bruche →, *France* 19 D14
Bruchsal, *Germany* 25 F4
Bruck an der Leitha, *Austria* 27 C9
Bruck an der Mur, *Austria* 26 D8
Brue →, *U.K.* 13 F5
Bruges = Brugge, *Belgium* 17 C3
Brugg, *Switz.* 25 H4
Brugge, *Belgium* 17 C3
Bruin, *U.S.A.* 110 E5
Brûlé, *Canada* 104 C5
Brûlon, *France* 18 E6
Brumado, *Brazil* 125 F10
Brumath, *France* 19 D14
Brumunddal, *Norway* 9 F14
Bruneau, *U.S.A.* 114 E6
Bruneau →, *U.S.A.* 114 E6
Bruneck = Brunico, *Italy* 29 B8
Brunei = Bandar Seri Begawan, *Brunei* 62 C4
Brunei ■, *Asia* 62 D4
Brunflo, *Sweden* 10 A8
Brunico, *Italy* 29 B8
Brunna, *Sweden* 10 E11
Brunnen, *Switz.* 25 J4
Brunner, L., *N.Z.* 91 K3
Brunsbüttel, *Germany* 24 B5
Brunssum, *Neths.* 17 D5
Brunswick = Braunschweig, *Germany* 24 C6
Brunswick, *Ga., U.S.A.* 109 K5
Brunswick, *Maine, U.S.A.* 109 D11
Brunswick, *Md., U.S.A.* 108 F7
Brunswick, *Mo., U.S.A.* 112 F8
Brunswick, *Ohio, U.S.A.* 110 E3
Brunswick, Pen. de, *Chile* 128 G2
Brunswick B., *Australia* 92 C3
Brunswick Junction, *Australia* 93 F2
Bruntál, *Czech Rep.* 27 B10
Bruny I., *Australia* 94 G4
Brus Laguna, *Honduras* 120 C3
Brusartsi, *Bulgaria* 40 C7
Brush, *U.S.A.* 112 E3
Brushton, *U.S.A.* 111 B10
Brusio, *Switz.* 25 J6
Brusque, *Brazil* 127 B6
Brussel, *Belgium* 17 D4
Brussels = Brussel, *Belgium* 17 D4
Brussels, *Canada* 110 C3
Brusy, *Poland* 44 E4
Bruthen, *Australia* 95 F4
Bruxelles = Brussel, *Belgium* 17 D4
Bruyères, *France* 19 D13
Bruz, *France* 18 D5
Brwinów, *Poland* 45 F7
Bryagovo, *Bulgaria* 41 E9
Bryan, *Ohio, U.S.A.* 108 E3
Bryan, *Tex., U.S.A.* 113 K6
Bryan, Mt., *Australia* 95 E2
Bryanka, *Ukraine* 47 H10
Bryansk, *Bryansk, Russia* 47 F8
Bryansk, *Dagestan, Russia* 49 H8
Bryanskoye = Bryansk, *Russia* 49 H8
Bryce Canyon National Park, *U.S.A.* 115 H7
Bryne, *Norway* 9 G11
Bryson City, *U.S.A.* 109 H4
Bryukhovetskaya, *Russia* 47 K10
Brza Palanka, *Serbia, Yug.* 40 B6
Brzeg, *Poland* 45 H4
Brzeg Dolny, *Poland* 45 G3
Brześć Kujawski, *Poland* 45 F5
Brzesko, *Poland* 45 J7
Brzeziny, *Poland* 45 G6
Brzozów, *Poland* 45 J9
Bsharri, *Lebanon* 75 A5
Bū Baqarah, *U.A.E.* 71 E8
Bu Craa, *W. Sahara* 78 C3
Bū Ḥasā, *U.A.E.* 71 F7
Bua, *Sweden* 11 G6
Bua Yai, *Thailand* 64 E4
Buapinang, *Indonesia* 63 E6
Buba, *Guinea-Biss.* 82 C2
Bubanza, *Burundi* 86 C2
Bubaque, *Guinea-Biss.* 82 C1
Bube, *Ethiopia* 81 F4
Būbiyān, *Kuwait* 71 D6
Buca, *Turkey* 39 C9
Bucak, *Turkey* 39 D12
Bucaramanga, *Colombia* 124 B4
Bucas Grande I., *Phil.* 61 G6
Bucasia, *Australia* 94 C4
Buccaneer Arch., *Australia* 92 C3
Buccino, *Italy* 31 B8
Bucecea, *Romania* 43 C11
Buchach, *Ukraine* 47 H3
Buchan, *U.K.* 14 D6
Buchan Ness, *U.K.* 14 D7
Buchanan, *Canada* 105 C8
Buchanan, *Liberia* 82 D2
Buchanan, L., *Queens., Australia* 94 C4
Buchanan, L., *W. Austral., Australia* 93 E3
Buchanan, L., *U.S.A.* 113 K5
Buchanan Cr. →, *Australia* 94 B2
Buchans, *Canada* 103 C8
Bucharest = București, *Romania* 43 F11
Buchen, *Germany* 25 F5
Buchholz, *Germany* 24 B5
Buchloe, *Germany* 25 G6
Buchon, Pt., *U.S.A.* 116 K6
Buciumi, *Romania* 42 C8
Buck Hill Falls, *U.S.A.* 111 E9
Bückeburg, *Germany* 24 C5
Buckeye, *U.S.A.* 115 K7
Buckeye Lake, *U.S.A.* 110 G2
Buckhannon, *U.S.A.* 108 F5
Buckhaven, *U.K.* 14 E5
Buckhorn L., *Canada* 110 B6
Buckie, *U.K.* 14 D6
Buckingham, *Canada* 102 C4
Buckingham, *U.K.* 13 F7
Buckingham B., *Australia* 94 A2
Buckinghamshire □, *U.K.* 13 F7
Buckle Hd., *Australia* 92 B4
Buckleboo, *Australia* 95 E2
Buckley, *U.K.* 12 D4
Buckley →, *Australia* 94 C2
Bucklin, *U.S.A.* 113 G5
Bucks L., *U.S.A.* 116 F5
Bucquoy, *France* 19 B9
Buctouche, *Canada* 103 C7
București, *Romania* 43 F11
Bucyrus, *U.S.A.* 108 E4
Budacu, Vf., *Romania* 43 C10
Budalin, *Burma* 67 H19
Budaörs, *Hungary* 42 C3
Budapest, *Hungary* 42 C4
Budapest □, *Hungary* 42 C4
Budaun, *India* 69 E8
Budd Coast, *Antarctica* 5 C8
Buddusò, *Italy* 30 B2
Bude, *U.K.* 13 G3
Budennovsk, *Russia* 49 H7
Budești, *Romania* 43 F11
Budge Budge = Baj Baj, *India* 69 H13
Budgewoi, *Australia* 95 E5
Budia, *Spain* 32 E2
Büdingen, *Germany* 25 E5
Budjala, *Dem. Rep. of the Congo* 84 D3
Budoni, *Italy* 30 B2
Búdrio, *Italy* 29 D8
Budva, *Montenegro, Yug.* 40 D2
Budzyń, *Poland* 45 F3
Buea, *Cameroon* 83 E6
Buellton, *U.S.A.* 117 L6
Buena Esperanza, *Argentina* 126 C2
Buena Park, *U.S.A.* 117 M9
Buena Vista, *Colo., U.S.A.* 115 G10
Buena Vista, *Va., U.S.A.* 108 G6
Buena Vista Lake Bed, *U.S.A.* 117 K7
Buenaventura, *Colombia* 124 C3
Buenaventura, *Mexico* 118 B3
Buendía, Embalse de, *Spain* 32 E2
Buenos Aires, *Argentina* 126 C4
Buenos Aires, *Costa Rica* 120 E3
Buenos Aires □, *Argentina* 126 D4
Buenos Aires, L., *Chile* 128 F2
Buffalo, *Mo., U.S.A.* 113 G8
Buffalo, *N.Y., U.S.A.* 110 D6
Buffalo, *Okla., U.S.A.* 113 G5
Buffalo, *S. Dak., U.S.A.* 112 C3
Buffalo, *Wyo., U.S.A.* 114 D10
Buffalo →, *Canada* 104 A5
Buffalo →, *S. Africa* 89 D5
Buffalo Head Hills, *Canada* 104 B5
Buffalo L., *Alta., Canada* 104 C6
Buffalo L., *N.W.T., Canada* 104 A5
Buffalo Narrows, *Canada* 105 B7
Buffels →, *S. Africa* 88 D2
Buford, *U.S.A.* 109 H4
Bug = Buh →, *Ukraine* 47 J6
Bug →, *Poland* 45 F8
Buga, *Colombia* 124 C3
Buganda, *Uganda* 86 C3
Buganga, *Uganda* 86 C3
Bugasong, *Phil.* 61 F5
Bugeat, *France* 20 C5
Bugel, Tanjung, *Indonesia* 63 G14
Bugibba, *Malta* 36 D1
Bugojno, *Bos.-H.* 42 F2
Bugsuk, *Phil.* 62 C5
Buguma, *Nigeria* 83 E6
Bugun Shara, *Mongolia* 60 B5
Buguruslan, *Russia* 50 D6
Buh →, *Ukraine* 47 J6
Buharkent, *Turkey* 39 D10
Buheirat-Murrat-el-Kubra, *Egypt* 80 H8
Buhera, *Zimbabwe* 89 B5
Bühl, *Germany* 25 G4
Buhl, *U.S.A.* 114 E6
Buhuși, *Romania* 43 D11
Builth Wells, *U.K.* 13 E4
Buinsk, *Russia* 48 C9
Buir Nur, *Mongolia* 60 B6
Buis-les-Baronnies, *France* 21 D9
Buitrago = Buitrago del Lozoya, *Spain* 34 E7
Buitrago del Lozoya, *Spain* 34 E7
Bujalance, *Spain* 35 H6
Bujanovac, *Serbia, Yug.* 40 D5
Bujaraloz, *Spain* 32 D4
Buje, *Croatia* 29 C10
Bujumbura, *Burundi* 86 C2
Bük, *Hungary* 42 C1
Buk, *Poland* 45 F3
Bukachacha, *Russia* 51 D12
Bukama, *Dem. Rep. of the Congo* 87 D2

Calhoun

Bukavu, *Dem. Rep. of the Congo* 86 C2
Bukene, *Tanzania* 86 C3
Bukhara = Bukhoro, *Uzbekistan* 50 F7
Bukhoro, *Uzbekistan* 50 F7
Bukima, *Tanzania* 86 C3
Bukit Mertajam, *Malaysia* 65 K3
Bukittinggi, *Indonesia* 62 E2
Bükk, *Hungary* 42 B5
Bukoba, *Tanzania* 86 C3
Bukuru, *Nigeria* 83 D6
Bukuya, *Uganda* 86 B3
Būl, Kuh-e, *Iran* 71 D7
Bula, *Guinea-Biss.* 82 C1
Bula, *Indonesia* 63 E8
Bülach, *Switz.* 25 H4
Bulahdelah, *Australia* 95 E5
Bulan, *Phil.* 61 E5
Bulancak, *Turkey* 73 B8
Bulandshahr, *India* 68 E7
Bulanık, *Turkey* 73 C10
Bûlâq, *Egypt* 80 B3
Bulawayo, *Zimbabwe* 87 G2
Buldan, *Turkey* 39 C10
Bulgar, *Russia* 48 C9
Bulgaria ■, *Europe* 41 D9
Bulgheria, Monte, *Italy* 31 B8
Bulgurca, *Turkey* 39 C9
Buli, Teluk, *Indonesia* 63 D7
Buliluyan, C., *Phil.* 61 G2
Bulki, *Ethiopia* 81 F4
Bulkley —►, *Canada* 104 B3
Bull Shoals L., *U.S.A.* 113 G8
Bullaque —►, *Spain* 35 G6
Bullas, *Spain* 33 G3
Bulle, *Switz.* 25 J3
Bullhead City, *U.S.A.* 117 K12
Büllingen, *Belgium* 17 D6
Bullock Creek, *Australia* 94 B3
Bulloo —►, *Australia* 95 D3
Bulloo L., *Australia* 95 D3
Bulls, *N.Z.* 91 J5
Bully-les-Mines, *France* 19 B9
Bulnes, *Chile* 126 D1
Bulqiza, *Albania* 40 E4
Bulsar = Valsad, *India* 66 J8
Bultfontein, *S. Africa* 88 D4
Bulukumba, *Indonesia* 63 F6
Bulun, *Russia* 51 B13
Bumba, *Dem. Rep. of the Congo* 84 D4
Bumbeşti-Jiu, *Romania* 43 E8
Bumbiri I., *Tanzania* 86 C3
Bumbuna, *S. Leone* 82 D2
Bumhpa Bum, *Burma* 67 F20
Bumi —►, *Zimbabwe* 87 F2
Buna, *Kenya* 86 B4
Bunawan, *Phil.* 61 G6
Bunazi, *Tanzania* 86 C3
Bunbury, *Australia* 93 F2
Bunclody, *Ireland* 15 D5
Buncrana, *Ireland* 15 A4
Bundaberg, *Australia* 95 C5
Bünde, *Germany* 24 C4
Bundey —►, *Australia* 94 C2
Bundi, *India* 68 G6
Bundoran, *Ireland* 15 B3
Bundukia, *Sudan* 81 F3
Bung Kan, *Thailand* 64 C4
Bunga —►, *Nigeria* 83 C6
Bungatakada, *Japan* 55 H5
Bungay, *U.K.* 13 E9
Bungil Cr. —►, *Australia* 95 D4
Bungo-Suidō, *Japan* 55 H6
Bungoma, *Kenya* 86 B3
Bungu, *Tanzania* 86 D4
Bunia, *Dem. Rep. of the Congo* 86 B3
Bunji, *Pakistan* 69 B6
Bunkie, *U.S.A.* 113 K8
Buñol, *Spain* 33 F4
Bunsuru, *Nigeria* 83 C5
Buntok, *Indonesia* 62 E4
Bununu Dass, *Nigeria* 83 C6
Bununu Kasa, *Nigeria* 83 D6
Bünyan, *Turkey* 72 C6
Bunyu, *Indonesia* 62 D5
Bunza, *Nigeria* 83 C5
Buol, *Indonesia* 63 D6
Buon Brieng, *Vietnam* 64 F7
Buon Ma Thuot, *Vietnam* 64 F7
Buong Long, *Cambodia* 64 F6
Buorkhaya, Mys, *Russia* 51 B14
Buqayq, *Si. Arabia* 71 E6
Buqbuq, *Egypt* 80 A2
Bur Acaba, *Somali Rep.* 74 G3
Bûr Fuad, *Egypt* 80 H8
Bûr Safâga, *Egypt* 70 E2
Bûr Sa'îd, *Egypt* 80 H8
Bûr Sûdân, *Sudan* 80 D4
Bûr Taufiq, *Egypt* 80 J8
Bura, *Kenya* 86 C4
Burakin, *Australia* 93 F2
Buram, *Sudan* 81 E2
Burao, *Somali Rep.* 74 F4
Burāq, *Syria* 75 B5
Buraydah, *Si. Arabia* 70 E5
Burbank, *U.S.A.* 117 L8
Burda, *India* 68 G6
Burdekin —►, *Australia* 94 B4
Burdur, *Turkey* 39 D12
Burdur □, *Turkey* 39 D12
Burdur Gölü, *Turkey* 39 D12
Burdwan = Barddhaman, *India* 69 H12
Bure, *Gojam, Ethiopia* 81 E4
Bure, *Ilubabor, Ethiopia* 81 F4
Bure —►, *U.K.* 12 E9
Büren, *Germany* 24 D4
Bureya —►, *Russia* 51 E13
Burford, *Canada* 110 C4
Burg, *Germany* 24 C7
Burg auf Fehmarn, *Germany* 24 A7
Burg el Arab, *Egypt* 80 H6
Burg et Tuyur, *Sudan* 80 C2
Burg Stargard, *Germany* 24 B9
Burgas, *Bulgaria* 41 D11
Burgas □, *Bulgaria* 41 D10
Burgaski Zaliv, *Bulgaria* 41 D11
Burgdorf, *Germany* 24 C6
Burgdorf, *Switz.* 25 H3
Burgenland □, *Austria* 27 D9
Burgeo, *Canada* 103 C8
Burgersdorp, *S. Africa* 88 E4
Burges, Mt., *Australia* 93 F3
Burghausen, *Germany* 25 G8
Búrgio, *Italy* 30 E6
Burglengenfeld, *Germany* 25 F8
Burgohondo, *Spain* 34 E6
Burgos, *Spain* 34 C7
Burgos □, *Spain* 34 C7
Burgstädt, *Germany* 24 E8
Burgsvik, *Sweden* 11 G12
Burguillos del Cerro, *Spain* 35 G4
Burgundy = Bourgogne, *France* 19 F11
Burhaniye, *Turkey* 39 B8
Burhanpur, *India* 66 J10
Burhi Gandak —►, *India* 69 G12
Burhner —►, *India* 69 H9
Buri Pen., *Eritrea* 81 D4
Burias I., *Phil.* 61 E5
Burica, Pta., *Costa Rica* 120 E3
Burien, *U.S.A.* 116 C4
Burigi, L., *Tanzania* 86 C3
Burin, *Canada* 103 C8
Buriram, *Thailand* 64 E4
Burj Sāfitā, *Syria* 70 C3
Burji, *Ethiopia* 81 F4
Burkburnett, *U.S.A.* 113 H5
Burke —►, *Australia* 94 C2
Burke Chan., *Canada* 104 C3
Burketown, *Australia* 94 B2
Burkina Faso ■, *Africa* 82 C4
Burk's Falls, *Canada* 102 C4
Burlada, *Spain* 32 C3
Burleigh Falls, *Canada* 110 B6
Burley, *U.S.A.* 114 E7
Burlingame, *U.S.A.* 116 H4
Burlington, *Canada* 102 D4
Burlington, *Colo., U.S.A.* 112 F3
Burlington, *Iowa, U.S.A.* 112 E9
Burlington, *Kans., U.S.A.* 112 F7
Burlington, *N.C., U.S.A.* 109 G6
Burlington, *N.J., U.S.A.* 111 F10
Burlington, *Vt., U.S.A.* 111 B11
Burlington, *Wash., U.S.A.* 116 B4
Burlington, *Wis., U.S.A.* 108 D1
Burlyu-Tyube, *Kazakstan* 50 E8
Burma ■, *Asia* 67 J20
Burnaby I., *Canada* 104 C2
Burnet, *U.S.A.* 113 K5
Burney, *U.S.A.* 114 F3
Burnham, *U.S.A.* 110 F7
Burnham-on-Sea, *U.K.* 13 F5
Burnie, *Australia* 94 G4
Burnley, *U.K.* 12 D5
Burns, *U.S.A.* 114 E4
Burns Lake, *Canada* 104 C3
Burnside —►, *Canada* 100 B9
Burnside, L., *Australia* 93 E3
Burnsville, *U.S.A.* 112 C8
Burnt L., *Canada* 103 B7
Burnt River, *Canada* 110 B6
Burntwood —►, *Canada* 105 B9
Burntwood L., *Canada* 105 B8
Burqān, *Kuwait* 70 D5
Burra, *Australia* 95 E2
Burra, *Nigeria* 83 C6
Burray, *U.K.* 14 C6
Burreli, *Albania* 40 E4
Burren Junction, *Australia* 95 E4
Burriana, *Spain* 32 F4
Burrinjuck Res., *Australia* 95 F4
Burro, Serranías del, *Mexico* 118 B4
Burrow Hd., *U.K.* 14 G4
Burruyacú, *Argentina* 126 B3
Burry Port, *U.K.* 13 F3
Bursa, *Turkey* 41 F13
Burseryd, *Sweden* 11 G7
Burstall, *Canada* 105 C7
Burton, *Ohio, U.S.A.* 110 E3
Burton, *S.C., U.S.A.* 109 J5
Burton, L., *Canada* 102 B4
Burton upon Trent, *U.K.* 12 E6
Buru, *Indonesia* 63 E7
Burullus, Bahra el, *Egypt* 80 H7
Burûn, Râs, *Egypt* 75 D2
Burundi ■, *Africa* 86 C3
Bururi, *Burundi* 86 C2
Burutu, *Nigeria* 83 D6
Burwell, *U.S.A.* 112 E5
Burwick, *U.K.* 14 C5
Bury, *U.K.* 12 D5
Bury St. Edmunds, *U.K.* 13 E8
Buryatia □, *Russia* 51 D11
Buryn, *Ukraine* 47 G7
Burzenin, *Poland* 45 G5
Busalla, *Italy* 28 D5
Busango Swamp, *Zambia* 87 E2
Buşayrah, *Syria* 70 C4
Busca, *Italy* 28 D4
Bushati, *Albania* 40 E3
Büshehr, *Iran* 71 D6
Büshehr □, *Iran* 71 D6
Bushell, *Canada* 105 B7
Bushenyi, *Uganda* 86 C3
Bushire = Büshehr, *Iran* 71 D6
Busie, *Ghana* 82 C4
Businga, *Dem. Rep. of the Congo* 84 D4
Busko-Zdrój, *Poland* 45 H7
Busovača, *Bos.-H.* 42 F2
Buşra ash Shām, *Syria* 75 C5
Busselton, *Australia* 93 F2
Busseri —►, *Sudan* 81 F2
Busseto, *Italy* 28 D7
Bussière-Badil, *France* 20 C4
Bussolengo, *Italy* 28 C7
Bussum, *Neths.* 17 B5
Buşteni, *Romania* 43 E10
Busto, C., *Spain* 34 B4
Busto Arsízio, *Italy* 28 C5
Busu-Djanoa, *Dem. Rep. of the Congo* 84 D4
Busuanga I., *Phil.* 61 E3
Büsum, *Germany* 24 A4
Buta, *Dem. Rep. of the Congo* 86 B1
Butare, *Rwanda* 86 C2
Butaritari, *Kiribati* 96 G9
Bute, *U.K.* 14 F3
Bute Inlet, *Canada* 104 C4
Butemba, *Uganda* 86 B3
Butembo, *Dem. Rep. of the Congo* 86 B2
Buteni, *Romania* 42 D7
Butera, *Italy* 31 E7
Butha Qi, *China* 60 B7
Butiaba, *Uganda* 86 B3
Butler, *Mo., U.S.A.* 112 F7
Butler, *Pa., U.S.A.* 110 F5
Buton, *Indonesia* 63 E6
Butte, *Mont., U.S.A.* 114 C7
Butte, *Nebr., U.S.A.* 112 D5
Butte Creek —►, *U.S.A.* 116 F5
Butterworth = Gcuwa, *S. Africa* 89 E4
Butterworth, *Malaysia* 65 K3
Buttevant, *Ireland* 15 D3
Buttfield, Mt., *Australia* 93 D4
Button B., *Canada* 105 B10
Buttonwillow, *U.S.A.* 117 K7
Butty Hd., *Australia* 93 F3
Butuan, *Phil.* 61 G6
Butuku-Luba, *Eq. Guin.* 83 E6
Butung = Buton, *Indonesia* 63 E6
Buturlinovka, *Russia* 48 E5
Butzbach, *Germany* 25 E4
Bützow, *Germany* 24 B7
Buxa Duar, *India* 69 F13
Buxar, *India* 69 G10
Buxtehude, *Germany* 24 B5
Buxton, *U.K.* 12 D6
Buxy, *France* 19 F11
Buy, *Russia* 48 A5
Buynaksk, *Russia* 49 J8
Buyo, *Ivory C.* 82 D3
Buyo, L. de, *Ivory C.* 82 D3
Büyük Menderes —►, *Turkey* 39 D9
Büyükçekmece, *Turkey* 41 E12
Büyükkariştiran, *Turkey* 41 E11
Büyükkemikli Burnu, *Turkey* 41 F10
Büyükorhan, *Turkey* 39 B10
Büyükyoncalı, *Turkey* 41 E11
Buzançais, *France* 18 F8
Buzău, *Romania* 43 E11
Buzău □, *Romania* 43 E11
Buzău —►, *Romania* 43 E12
Buzău, Pasul, *Romania* 43 E11
Buzen, *Japan* 55 H5
Buzet, *Croatia* 29 C10
Buzi —►, *Mozam.* 87 F3
Buziaş, *Romania* 42 E6
Buzuluk, *Russia* 50 D6
Buzuluk —►, *Russia* 48 E6
Buzzards B., *U.S.A.* 111 E14
Buzzards Bay, *U.S.A.* 111 E14
Bwana Mkubwe, *Dem. Rep. of the Congo* 87 E2
Byala, *Ruse, Bulgaria* 41 C9
Byala, *Varna, Bulgaria* 41 D11
Byala Slatina, *Bulgaria* 40 C7
Byarezina —►, *Belarus* 47 F6
Bychawa, *Poland* 45 G9
Byczyna, *Poland* 45 G5
Bydgoszcz, *Poland* 45 E5
Byelarus = Belarus ■, *Europe* 46 F4
Byelorussia = Belarus ■, *Europe* 46 F4
Byers, *U.S.A.* 112 F2
Byesville, *U.S.A.* 110 G3
Byford, *Australia* 93 F2
Bykhaw, *Belarus* 46 F6
Bykhov = Bykhaw, *Belarus* 46 F6
Bykovo, *Russia* 48 F7
Bylas, *U.S.A.* 115 K8
Bylot, *Canada* 105 B10
Bylot I., *Canada* 101 A12
Byrd, C., *Antarctica* 5 C17
Byrock, *Australia* 95 E4
Byron Bay, *Australia* 95 D5
Byrranga, Gory, *Russia* 51 B11
Byrranga Mts. = Byrranga, Gory, *Russia* 51 B11
Byrum, *Denmark* 11 G5
Byske, *Sweden* 8 D19
Byske älv —►, *Sweden* 8 D19
Bystrzyca —►, *Dolnośląskie, Poland* 45 G3
Bystrzyca —►, *Lubelskie, Poland* 45 G9
Bystrzyca Kłodzka, *Poland* 45 H3
Bytča, *Slovak Rep.* 27 B11
Bytom, *Poland* 45 H5
Bytom Odrzański, *Poland* 45 G2
Bytów, *Poland* 44 D4
Byumba, *Rwanda* 86 C3
Bzenec, *Czech Rep.* 27 C10
Bzura —►, *Poland* 45 F7

C

Ca —►, *Vietnam* 64 C5
Ca Mau, *Vietnam* 65 H5
Ca Mau, Mui, *Vietnam* 65 H5
Ca Na, *Vietnam* 65 G7
Caacupé, *Paraguay* 126 B4
Caála, *Angola* 85 G3
Caamano Sd., *Canada* 104 C3
Caazapá, *Paraguay* 126 B4
Caazapá □, *Paraguay* 127 B4
Cabadbaran, *Phil.* 61 G6
Cabalian = San Juan, *Phil.* 61 F6
Cabana, *Spain* 34 B2
Cabañaquinta, *Spain* 34 B5
Cabanatuan, *Phil.* 61 D4
Cabanes, *Spain* 32 E5
Cabano, *Canada* 103 C6
Čabar, *Croatia* 29 C11
Cabazon, *U.S.A.* 117 M10
Cabedelo, *Brazil* 125 E12
Cabeza del Buey, *Spain* 35 G5
Cabezón de la Sal, *Spain* 34 B6
Cabildo, *Chile* 126 C1
Cabimas, *Venezuela* 124 A4
Cabinda, *Angola* 84 F2
Cabinda □, *Angola* 84 F2
Cabinet Mts., *U.S.A.* 114 C6
Cabo Blanco, *Argentina* 128 F3
Cabo Frio, *Brazil* 127 A7
Cabo Pantoja, *Peru* 124 D3
Cabonga, Réservoir, *Canada* 102 C4
Cabool, *U.S.A.* 113 G8
Caboolture, *Australia* 95 D5
Cabora Bassa Dam = Cahora Bassa, Reprêsa de, *Mozam.* 87 F3
Caborca, *Mexico* 118 A2
Cabot, Mt., *U.S.A.* 111 B13
Cabot Hd., *Canada* 110 A3
Cabot Str., *Canada* 103 C8
Cabra, *Spain* 35 H6
Cabra del Santo Cristo, *Spain* 35 H7
Cábras, *Italy* 30 C1
Cabrera, *Spain* 37 B9
Cabrera, Sierra, *Spain* 34 C4
Cabri, *Canada* 105 C7
Cabriel —►, *Spain* 33 F3
Cabugao, *Phil.* 61 C4
Cacabelos, *Spain* 34 C4
Caçador, *Brazil* 127 B5
Čačak, *Serbia, Yug.* 40 C4
Caçapava do Sul, *Brazil* 127 C5
Cáccamo, *Italy* 30 E6
Cacém, *Portugal* 35 G1
Cáceres, *Brazil* 124 G7
Cáceres, *Spain* 35 F4
Cáceres □, *Spain* 34 F5
Cache Bay, *Canada* 102 C4
Cache Cr. —►, *U.S.A.* 116 G5
Cache Creek, *Canada* 104 C4
Cacheu, *Guinea-Biss.* 82 C1
Cachi, *Argentina* 126 B2
Cachimbo, Serra do, *Brazil* 125 E7
Cachinal de la Sierra, *Chile* 126 A2
Cachoeira, *Brazil* 125 F11
Cachoeira de Itapemirim, *Brazil* 127 A7
Cachoeira do Sul, *Brazil* 127 C5
Cachopo, *Portugal* 35 H3
Cacine, *Guinea-Biss.* 82 C1
Cacoal, *Brazil* 124 F6
Cacólo, *Angola* 84 G3
Caconda, *Angola* 85 G3
Čadca, *Slovak Rep.* 27 B11
Caddo, *U.S.A.* 113 H6
Cader Idris, *U.K.* 13 E4
Cadereyta, *Mexico* 118 B5
Cadí, Sierra del, *Spain* 32 C6
Cadibarrawirracanna, L., *Australia* 95 D2
Cadillac, *France* 20 D3
Cadillac, *U.S.A.* 108 C3
Cadiz, *Phil.* 61 F5
Cádiz, *Spain* 35 J4
Cadiz, *Calif., U.S.A.* 117 L11
Cadiz, *Ohio, U.S.A.* 110 F4
Cádiz □, *Spain* 35 J5
Cádiz, G. de, *Spain* 35 J3
Cadiz L., *U.S.A.* 115 J6
Cadney Park, *Australia* 95 D1
Cadomin, *Canada* 104 C5
Cadotte Lake, *Canada* 104 B5
Cadours, *France* 20 E5
Cadoux, *Australia* 93 F2
Caen, *France* 18 C6
Caernarfon, *U.K.* 12 D3
Caernarfon B., *U.K.* 12 D3
Caernarvon = Caernarfon, *U.K.* 12 D3
Caerphilly, *U.K.* 13 F4
Caerphilly □, *U.K.* 13 F4
Caesarea, *Israel* 75 C3
Caetité, *Brazil* 125 F10
Cafayate, *Argentina* 126 B2
Cafu, *Angola* 88 B2
Cagayan —►, *Phil.* 61 B4
Cagayan de Oro, *Phil.* 61 G6
Cagayan Is., *Phil.* 61 G4
Cagayan Sulu I., *Phil.* 61 H3
Cagli, *Italy* 29 E9
Cágliari, *Italy* 30 C2
Cágliari, G. di, *Italy* 30 C2
Cagnano Varano, *Italy* 29 G12
Cagnes-sur-Mer, *France* 21 E11
Caguán —►, *Colombia* 124 D4
Caguas, *Puerto Rico* 121 C6
Caha Mts., *Ireland* 15 E2
Cahama, *Angola* 88 B1
Caher, *Ireland* 15 D4
Caherciveen, *Ireland* 15 E1
Cahora Bassa, Reprêsa de, *Mozam.* 87 F3
Cahore Pt., *Ireland* 15 D5
Cahors, *France* 20 D5
Cahul, *Moldova* 43 E13
Cai Bau, Dao, *Vietnam* 58 G6
Cai Nuoc, *Vietnam* 65 H5
Caia, *Mozam.* 87 F4
Caianda, *Angola* 87 E1
Caibarién, *Cuba* 120 B4
Caibiran, *Phil.* 61 F6
Caicara, *Venezuela* 124 B5
Caicó, *Brazil* 125 E11
Caicos Is., *W. Indies* 121 B5
Caicos Passage, *W. Indies* 121 B5
Caidian, *China* 59 B10
Căinari, *Moldova* 43 D14
Caird Coast, *Antarctica* 5 D1
Cairn Gorm, *U.K.* 14 D5
Cairngorm Mts., *U.K.* 14 D5
Cairnryan, *U.K.* 14 G3
Cairns, *Australia* 94 B4
Cairns L., *Canada* 105 C10
Cairo = El Qâhira, *Egypt* 80 H7
Cairo, *Ga., U.S.A.* 109 K3
Cairo, *Ill., U.S.A.* 113 G10
Cairo, *N.Y., U.S.A.* 111 D11
Cairo Montenotte, *Italy* 28 D5
Caithness, Ord of, *U.K.* 14 C5
Cajamarca, *Peru* 124 E3
Cajarc, *France* 20 D5
Cajàzeiras, *Brazil* 125 E11
Čajetina, *Serbia, Yug.* 40 C3
Çakirgol, *Turkey* 73 B8
Çakırlar, *Turkey* 39 E12
Čakovec, *Croatia* 29 B13
Çal, *Turkey* 39 C11
Cala, *Spain* 35 H4
Cala —►, *Spain* 35 H4
Cala Cadolar, Punta de = Rotja, Pta., *Spain* 33 G6
Cala d'Or, *Spain* 37 B10
Cala en Porter, *Spain* 37 B11
Cala Figuera, C. de, *Spain* 37 B9
Cala Forcat, *Spain* 37 B10
Cala Major, *Spain* 37 B9
Cala Mezquida = Sa Mesquida, *Spain* 37 B11
Cala Millor, *Spain* 37 B10
Cala Ratjada, *Spain* 37 B10
Cala Santa Galdana, *Spain* 37 B10
Calabanga, *Phil.* 61 E5
Calabar, *Nigeria* 83 E6
Calabogie, *Canada* 111 A8
Calabozo, *Venezuela* 124 B5
Calábria □, *Italy* 31 C9
Calaburras, Pta. de, *Spain* 35 J6
Calaceite, *Spain* 32 D5
Calacuccia, *France* 21 F13
Calafat, *Romania* 42 G7
Calafate, *Argentina* 128 G2
Calafell, *Spain* 32 D6
Calahorra, *Spain* 32 C3
Calais, *France* 19 B8
Calais, *U.S.A.* 109 C12
Calalaste, Cord. de, *Argentina* 126 B2
Calama, *Brazil* 124 E6
Calama, *Chile* 126 A2
Calamar, *Colombia* 124 A4
Calamian Group, *Phil.* 61 F3
Calamocha, *Spain* 32 E3
Calamonte, *Spain* 35 G4
Călan, *Romania* 42 E7
Calañas, *Spain* 35 H4
Calanda, *Spain* 32 E4
Calang, *Indonesia* 62 D1
Calangiánus, *Italy* 30 B2
Calapan, *Phil.* 61 E4
Călărasi, *Moldova* 43 C13
Călăraşi, *Romania* 43 F12
Călăraşi □, *Romania* 43 F12
Calasparra, *Spain* 33 G3
Calatafimi, *Italy* 30 E5
Calatayud, *Spain* 32 D3
Călăţele, *Romania* 42 D8
Calato = Kálathos, *Greece* 39 E10
Calauag, *Phil.* 61 E5
Calavà, C., *Italy* 31 D7
Calavite, C., *Phil.* 61 E4
Calayan, *Phil.* 61 B4
Calbayog, *Phil.* 61 E6
Calca, *Peru* 124 F4
Calcasieu L., *U.S.A.* 113 L8
Calcutta, *India* 69 H13
Calcutta, *U.S.A.* 110 F4
Caldaro, *Italy* 29 B8
Caldas da Rainha, *Portugal* 35 F1
Caldas de Reis, *Spain* 34 C2
Calder —►, *U.K.* 12 D6
Caldera, *Chile* 126 B1
Caldwell, *Idaho, U.S.A.* 114 E5
Caldwell, *Kans., U.S.A.* 113 G6
Caldwell, *Tex., U.S.A.* 113 K6
Caledon, *S. Africa* 88 E2
Caledon —►, *S. Africa* 88 E4
Caledon B., *Australia* 94 A2
Caledonia, *Canada* 110 C5
Caledonia, *U.S.A.* 110 D7
Calella, *Spain* 32 D7
Calemba, *Angola* 88 B2
Calen, *Australia* 94 C4
Calenzana, *France* 21 F12
Caletones, *Chile* 126 C1
Calexico, *U.S.A.* 117 N11
Calf of Man, *U.K.* 12 C3
Calgary, *Canada* 104 C6
Calheta, *Madeira* 37 D2
Calhoun, *U.S.A.* 109 H3

Cali, *Colombia* 124 **C3**
Calicut, *India* 66 **P9**
Caliente, *U.S.A.* 115 **H6**
California, *Mo., U.S.A.* 112 **F8**
California, *Pa., U.S.A.* 110 **F5**
California □, *U.S.A.* 116 **H7**
California, Baja, *Mexico* 118 **A1**
California, Baja, T.N. = Baja California □, *Mexico* 118 **B2**
California, Baja, T.S. = Baja California Sur □, *Mexico* 118 **B2**
California, G. de, *Mexico* 118 **B2**
California City, *U.S.A.* 117 **K9**
California Hot Springs, *U.S.A.* 117 **K8**
Călimăneşti, *Romania* 43 **E9**
Călimani, Munţii, *Romania* 43 **C10**
Calingasta, *Argentina* 126 **C2**
Calipatria, *U.S.A.* 117 **M11**
Calistoga, *U.S.A.* 116 **G4**
Calitri, *Italy* 31 **B8**
Calitzdorp, *S. Africa* 88 **E3**
Callabonna, L., *Australia* 95 **D3**
Callac, *France* 18 **D3**
Callan, *Ireland* 15 **D4**
Callander, *U.K.* 14 **E4**
Callao, *Peru* 124 **F3**
Calles, *Mexico* 119 **C5**
Callicoon, *U.S.A.* 111 **E9**
Calling Lake, *Canada* 104 **B6**
Calliope, *Australia* 94 **C5**
Callosa de Ensarriá, *Spain* 33 **G4**
Callosa de Segura, *Spain* 33 **G4**
Calne, *U.K.* 13 **F6**
Calola, *Angola* 88 **B2**
Calolbon = San Andres, *Phil.* 61 **E6**
Calonge, *Spain* 32 **D8**
Caloocan, *Phil.* 61 **D4**
Calore →, *Italy* 31 **A7**
Caloundra, *Australia* 95 **D5**
Calpe, *Spain* 33 **G5**
Calpella, *U.S.A.* 116 **F3**
Calpine, *U.S.A.* 116 **F6**
Calstock, *Canada* 102 **C3**
Caltabellotta, *Italy* 30 **E6**
Caltagirone, *Italy* 31 **E7**
Caltanissetta, *Italy* 31 **E7**
Çaltılıbük, *Turkey* 41 **G12**
Caluire-et-Cuire, *France* 19 **G11**
Calulo, *Angola* 84 **G2**
Caluso, *Italy* 28 **C4**
Calvados □, *France* 18 **C6**
Calvert →, *Australia* 94 **B2**
Calvert I., *Canada* 104 **C3**
Calvert Ra., *Australia* 92 **D3**
Calvi, *France* 21 **F12**
Calviá, *Spain* 33 **F7**
Calvillo, *Mexico* 118 **C4**
Calvinia, *S. Africa* 88 **E2**
Calvo = Calvo, Mte., *Italy* 29 **G12**
Calvo, Mte., *Italy* 29 **G12**
Calwa, *U.S.A.* 116 **J7**
Calzada Almuradiel = Almuradiel, *Spain* 35 **G7**
Calzada de Calatrava, *Spain* 35 **G7**
Cam →, *U.K.* 13 **E8**
Cam Lam, *Vietnam* 65 **G7**
Cam Pha, *Vietnam* 58 **G6**
Cam Ranh, *Vietnam* 65 **G7**
Cam Xuyen, *Vietnam* 64 **C6**
Camabatela, *Angola* 84 **F3**
Camacha, *Madeira* 37 **D3**
Camacho, *Mexico* 118 **C4**
Camacupa, *Angola* 85 **G3**
Camagüey, *Cuba* 120 **B4**
Camaiore, *Italy* 28 **E7**
Camaná, *Peru* 124 **G4**
Camanche Reservoir, *U.S.A.* 116 **G6**
Camaquã, *Brazil* 127 **C5**
Camaquã →, *Brazil* 127 **C5**
Câmara de Lobos, *Madeira* 37 **D3**
Camarat, C., *France* 21 **E10**
Camarès, *France* 20 **E6**
Camaret-sur-Mer, *France* 18 **D2**
Camargo, *Mexico* 119 **B5**
Camargue, *France* 21 **E8**
Camarillo, *U.S.A.* 117 **L7**
Camariñas, *Spain* 34 **B1**
Camarón, C., *Honduras* 120 **C2**
Camarones, *Argentina* 128 **E3**
Camas, *Spain* 35 **H4**
Camas, *U.S.A.* 116 **E4**
Camas Valley, *U.S.A.* 114 **E2**
Camballin, *Australia* 92 **C3**
Cambará, *Brazil* 127 **A5**
Cambay = Khambhat, *India* 68 **H5**
Cambay, G. of = Khambhat, G. of, *India* 66 **J8**
Cambil, *Spain* 35 **H7**
Cambo-les-Bains, *France* 20 **E2**
Cambodia ■, *Asia* 64 **F5**
Camborne, *U.K.* 13 **G2**
Cambrai, *France* 19 **B10**
Cambre, *Spain* 34 **B2**
Cambria, *U.S.A.* 116 **K5**
Cambrian Mts., *U.K.* 13 **E4**
Cambridge, *Canada* 102 **D3**
Cambridge, *Jamaica* 120 **C4**
Cambridge, *N.Z.* 91 **G5**
Cambridge, *U.K.* 13 **E8**
Cambridge, *Mass., U.S.A.* 111 **D13**
Cambridge, *Minn., U.S.A.* 112 **C8**
Cambridge, *N.Y., U.S.A.* 111 **C11**
Cambridge, *Nebr., U.S.A.* 112 **E4**
Cambridge, *Ohio, U.S.A.* 110 **F3**
Cambridge Bay = Ikaluktutiak, *Canada* 100 **B9**
Cambridge G., *Australia* 92 **B4**
Cambridge Springs, *U.S.A.* 110 **E4**
Cambridgeshire □, *U.K.* 13 **E7**
Cambrils, *Spain* 32 **D6**
Cambuci, *Brazil* 127 **A7**
Cambundi-Catembo, *Angola* 84 **G3**
Camden, *Ala., U.S.A.* 109 **K2**
Camden, *Ark., U.S.A.* 113 **J8**
Camden, *Maine, U.S.A.* 109 **C11**
Camden, *N.J., U.S.A.* 111 **G9**
Camden, *N.Y., U.S.A.* 111 **C9**
Camden, *S.C., U.S.A.* 109 **H5**
Camden Sd., *Australia* 92 **C3**
Camdenton, *U.S.A.* 113 **F8**
Çameli, *Turkey* 39 **D11**
Camenca, *Moldova* 43 **B13**
Camerino, *Italy* 29 **E10**
Cameron, *Ariz., U.S.A.* 115 **J8**
Cameron, *La., U.S.A.* 113 **L8**
Cameron, *Mo., U.S.A.* 112 **F7**
Cameron, *Tex., U.S.A.* 113 **K6**
Cameron Highlands, *Malaysia* 65 **K3**
Cameron Hills, *Canada* 104 **B5**
Cameroon ■, *Africa* 84 **C2**
Camerota, *Italy* 31 **B8**
Cameroun →, *Cameroon* 83 **E6**
Cameroun, Mt., *Cameroon* 83 **E6**
Cametá, *Brazil* 125 **D9**
Çamiçi Gölü, *Turkey* 39 **D9**
Camiguin □, *Phil.* 61 **G6**
Camiguin I., *Phil.* 61 **B4**
Camiling, *Phil.* 61 **D4**
Camilla, *U.S.A.* 109 **K3**
Caminha, *Portugal* 34 **D2**
Camino, *U.S.A.* 116 **G6**
Camira Creek, *Australia* 95 **D5**
Cammal, *U.S.A.* 110 **E7**
Cammarata, *Italy* 30 **E6**
Camocim, *Brazil* 125 **D10**
Camooweal, *Australia* 94 **B2**
Camopi, *Fr. Guiana* 125 **C8**
Camotes Is., *Phil.* 61 **F6**
Camotes Sea, *Phil.* 61 **F6**
Camp Borden, *Canada* 110 **B5**
Camp Hill, *U.S.A.* 110 **F8**
Camp Nelson, *U.S.A.* 117 **J8**
Camp Pendleton, *U.S.A.* 117 **M9**
Camp Verde, *U.S.A.* 115 **J8**
Camp Wood, *U.S.A.* 113 **L5**
Campagna, *Italy* 31 **B8**
Campana, *Argentina* 126 **C4**
Campana, I., *Chile* 128 **F1**
Campanário, *Madeira* 37 **D2**
Campanario, *Spain* 35 **G5**
Campánia □, *Italy* 31 **B7**
Campbell, *S. Africa* 88 **D3**
Campbell, *Calif., U.S.A.* 116 **H5**
Campbell, *Ohio, U.S.A.* 110 **E4**
Campbell I., *Pac. Oc.* 96 **N8**
Campbell L., *Canada* 105 **A7**
Campbell River, *Canada* 104 **C3**
Campbell Town, *Australia* 94 **G4**
Campbellford, *Canada* 110 **B7**
Campbellpur, *Pakistan* 68 **C5**
Campbellsville, *U.S.A.* 108 **G3**
Campbellton, *Canada* 103 **C6**
Campbelltown, *Australia* 95 **E5**
Campbeltown, *U.K.* 14 **F3**
Campeche, *Mexico* 119 **D6**
Campeche □, *Mexico* 119 **D6**
Campeche, Golfo de, *Mexico* 119 **D6**
Campello, *Spain* 33 **G4**
Câmpeni, *Romania* 42 **D8**
Camperdown, *Australia* 95 **F3**
Camperville, *Canada* 105 **C8**
Campi Salentina, *Italy* 31 **B11**
Câmpia Turzii, *Romania* 43 **D8**
Campidano, *Italy* 30 **C1**
Campíglia Maríttima, *Italy* 28 **E7**
Campillo de Altobuey, *Spain* 33 **F3**
Campillos, *Spain* 35 **H6**
Câmpina, *Romania* 43 **E10**
Campina Grande, *Brazil* 125 **E11**
Campinas, *Brazil* 127 **A6**
Campli, *Italy* 29 **F10**
Campo, *Spain* 32 **C5**
Campo de Criptana, *Spain* 35 **F7**
Campo de Gibraltar, *Spain* 35 **J5**
Campo Grande, *Brazil* 125 **H8**
Campo Maíor, *Brazil* 125 **D10**
Campo Maior, *Portugal* 35 **F3**
Campo Mourão, *Brazil* 127 **A5**
Campo Túres, *Italy* 29 **B8**
Campobasso, *Italy* 31 **A7**
Campobello di Licata, *Italy* 30 **E6**
Campobello di Mazara, *Italy* 30 **E5**
Campofelice di Roccella, *Italy* 30 **E6**
Campomarino, *Italy* 29 **G12**
Camporeale, *Italy* 30 **E6**
Camporrobles, *Spain* 32 **F3**
Campos, *Brazil* 127 **A7**
Campos Belos, *Brazil* 125 **F9**
Campos del Puerto, *Spain* 37 **B10**
Campos Novos, *Brazil* 127 **B5**
Camprodón, *Spain* 32 **C7**
Camptonville, *U.S.A.* 116 **F5**
Camptown, *U.S.A.* 111 **E8**
Câmpulung, *Argeş, Romania* 43 **E10**
Câmpulung, *Suceava, Romania* 43 **C10**
Câmpuri, *Romania* 43 **D11**
Camrose, *Canada* 104 **C6**
Camsell Portage, *Canada* 105 **B7**
Çamyuva, *Turkey* 39 **E12**
Çan, *Turkey* 41 **F11**
Can Clavo, *Spain* 37 **C7**
Can Creu, *Spain* 37 **C7**
Can Gio, *Vietnam* 65 **G6**
Can Tho, *Vietnam* 65 **G5**
Canaan, *U.S.A.* 111 **D11**
Canada ■, *N. Amer.* 100 **C10**
Cañada de Gómez, *Argentina* 126 **C3**
Canadian, *U.S.A.* 113 **H4**
Canadian →, *U.S.A.* 113 **H7**
Canajoharie, *U.S.A.* 111 **D10**
Çanakkale, *Turkey* 41 **F10**
Çanakkale □, *Turkey* 41 **F10**
Çanakkale Boğazı, *Turkey* 41 **F10**
Canal Flats, *Canada* 104 **C5**
Canalejas, *Argentina* 126 **D2**
Canals, *Argentina* 126 **C3**
Canals, *Spain* 33 **G4**
Canandaigua, *U.S.A.* 110 **D7**
Canandaigua L., *U.S.A.* 110 **D7**
Cananea, *Mexico* 118 **A2**
Canarias, Is., *Atl. Oc.* 37 **F4**
Canarreos, Arch. de los, *Cuba* 120 **B3**
Canary Is. = Canarias, Is., *Atl. Oc.* 37 **F4**
Canaseraga, *U.S.A.* 110 **D7**
Canatlán, *Mexico* 118 **C4**
Canaveral, C., *U.S.A.* 109 **L5**
Cañaveruelas, *Spain* 32 **E2**
Canavieiras, *Brazil* 125 **G11**
Canberra, *Australia* 95 **F4**
Canby, *Calif., U.S.A.* 114 **F3**
Canby, *Minn., U.S.A.* 112 **C6**
Canby, *Oreg., U.S.A.* 116 **E4**
Cancale, *France* 18 **D5**
Canche →, *France* 19 **B8**
Cancún, *Mexico* 119 **C7**
Candanchu, *Spain* 32 **C4**
Çandarlı, *Turkey* 39 **C8**
Çandarlı Körfezi, *Turkey* 39 **C8**
Candas, *Spain* 34 **B5**
Candé, *France* 18 **E5**
Candela, *Italy* 31 **A8**
Candelaria, *Argentina* 127 **B4**
Candelaria, *Canary Is.* 37 **F3**
Candeleda, *Spain* 34 **E5**
Candelo, *Australia* 95 **F4**
Candia = Iráklion, *Greece* 36 **D7**
Candia, Sea of = Crete, Sea of, *Greece* 39 **E7**
Candle L., *Canada* 105 **C7**
Candlemas I., *Antarctica* 5 **B1**
Cando, *U.S.A.* 112 **A5**
Candon, *Phil.* 61 **C4**
Canea = Khaniá, *Greece* 36 **D6**
Canelli, *Italy* 28 **D5**
Canelones, *Uruguay* 127 **C4**
Canet-Plage, *France* 20 **F7**
Cañete, *Chile* 126 **D1**
Cañete, *Peru* 124 **F3**
Cañete, *Spain* 32 **E3**
Cañete de las Torres, *Spain* 35 **H6**
Cangas, *Spain* 34 **C2**
Cangas de Narcea, *Spain* 34 **B4**
Cangas de Onís, *Spain* 34 **B5**
Cangnan, *China* 59 **D13**
Canguaretama, *Brazil* 125 **E11**
Canguçu, *Brazil* 127 **C5**
Canguçu, Serra do, *Brazil* 127 **C5**
Cangwu, *China* 59 **F8**
Cangxi, *China* 58 **B5**
Cangyuan, *China* 58 **F2**
Cangzhou, *China* 56 **E9**
Caniapiscau →, *Canada* 103 **A6**
Caniapiscau Rés. de, *Canada* 103 **B6**
Canicattì, *Italy* 30 **E6**
Canicattini Bagni, *Italy* 31 **E8**
Caniles, *Spain* 35 **H8**
Canim Lake, *Canada* 104 **C4**
Canindeyu □, *Paraguay* 127 **A5**
Canino, *Italy* 29 **F8**
Canisteo, *U.S.A.* 110 **D7**
Canisteo →, *U.S.A.* 110 **D7**
Cañitas, *Mexico* 118 **C4**
Cañizal, *Spain* 34 **D5**
Canjáyar, *Spain* 35 **H8**
Çankırı, *Turkey* 72 **B5**
Cankuzo, *Burundi* 86 **C3**
Canmore, *Canada* 104 **C5**
Cann River, *Australia* 95 **F4**
Canna, *U.K.* 14 **D2**
Cannanore, *India* 66 **P9**
Cannes, *France* 21 **E11**
Canning Town = Port Canning, *India* 69 **H13**
Cannington, *Canada* 110 **B5**
Cannóbio, *Italy* 28 **B5**
Cannock, *U.K.* 13 **E5**
Cannon Ball →, *U.S.A.* 112 **B4**
Cannondale Mt., *Australia* 94 **D4**
Cannonsville Reservoir, *U.S.A.* 111 **D9**
Cannonvale, *Australia* 94 **C4**
Canoas, *Brazil* 127 **B5**
Canoe L., *Canada* 105 **B7**
Canon City, *U.S.A.* 112 **F2**
Canora, *Canada* 105 **C8**
Canosa di Púglia, *Italy* 31 **A9**
Canowindra, *Australia* 95 **E4**
Canso, *Canada* 103 **C7**
Cantabria □, *Spain* 34 **B7**
Cantabria, Sierra de, *Spain* 32 **C2**
Cantabrian Mts. = Cantábrica, Cordillera, *Spain* 34 **C5**
Cantábrica, Cordillera, *Spain* 34 **C5**
Cantal □, *France* 20 **C6**
Cantal, Plomb du, *France* 20 **C6**
Cantanhede, *Portugal* 34 **E2**
Cantavieja, *Spain* 32 **E4**
Čantavir, *Serbia, Yug.* 42 **E4**
Cantemir, *Moldova* 43 **D13**
Canterbury, *Australia* 94 **D3**
Canterbury, *U.K.* 13 **F9**
Canterbury □, *N.Z.* 91 **K3**
Canterbury Bight, *N.Z.* 91 **L3**
Canterbury Plains, *N.Z.* 91 **K3**
Cantil, *U.S.A.* 117 **K9**
Cantillana, *Spain* 35 **H5**
Canton = Guangzhou, *China* 59 **F9**
Canton, *Ga., U.S.A.* 109 **H3**
Canton, *Ill., U.S.A.* 112 **E9**
Canton, *Miss., U.S.A.* 113 **J9**
Canton, *Mo., U.S.A.* 112 **E9**
Canton, *N.Y., U.S.A.* 111 **B9**
Canton, *Ohio, U.S.A.* 110 **F3**
Canton, *Pa., U.S.A.* 110 **E8**
Canton, *S. Dak., U.S.A.* 112 **D6**
Canton L., *U.S.A.* 113 **G5**
Cantù, *Italy* 28 **C6**
Canudos, *Brazil* 124 **E7**
Canumã →, *Brazil* 124 **D7**
Canutama, *Brazil* 124 **E6**
Canutillo, *U.S.A.* 115 **L10**
Canvey, *U.K.* 13 **F8**
Canyon, *U.S.A.* 113 **H4**
Canyonlands National Park, *U.S.A.* 115 **G9**
Canyonville, *U.S.A.* 114 **E2**
Cao Bang, *Vietnam* 58 **F6**
Cao He →, *China* 57 **D13**
Cao Lanh, *Vietnam* 65 **G5**
Cao Xian, *China* 56 **G8**
Cáorle, *Italy* 29 **C9**
Cap-aux-Meules, *Canada* 103 **C7**
Cap-Chat, *Canada* 103 **C6**
Cap-de-la-Madeleine, *Canada* 102 **C5**
Cap-Haïtien, *Haiti* 121 **C5**
Capac, *U.S.A.* 110 **C2**
Capáccio, *Italy* 31 **B8**
Capaci, *Italy* 30 **D6**
Capanaparo →, *Venezuela* 124 **B5**
Capánnori, *Italy* 28 **E7**
Capbreton, *France* 20 **E2**
Capdenac, *France* 20 **D6**
Capdepera, *Spain* 32 **F8**
Cape →, *Australia* 94 **C4**
Cape Barren I., *Australia* 94 **G4**
Cape Breton Highlands Nat. Park, *Canada* 103 **C7**
Cape Breton I., *Canada* 103 **C7**
Cape Charles, *U.S.A.* 108 **G8**
Cape Coast, *Ghana* 83 **D4**
Cape Coral, *U.S.A.* 109 **M5**
Cape Dorset, *Canada* 101 **B12**
Cape Fear →, *U.S.A.* 109 **H6**
Cape Girardeau, *U.S.A.* 113 **G10**
Cape May, *U.S.A.* 108 **F8**
Cape May Point, *U.S.A.* 108 **F8**
Cape Province, *S. Africa* 85 **L3**
Cape Tormentine, *Canada* 103 **C7**
Cape Town, *S. Africa* 88 **E2**
Cape Verde Is. ■, *Atl. Oc.* 77 **E1**
Cape Vincent, *U.S.A.* 111 **B8**
Cape York Peninsula, *Australia* 94 **A3**
Capela, *Brazil* 125 **F11**
Capella, *Australia* 94 **C4**
Capendu, *France* 20 **E6**
Capestang, *France* 20 **E7**
Capim →, *Brazil* 125 **D9**
Capistrello, *Italy* 29 **G10**
Capitan, *U.S.A.* 115 **K11**
Capitol Reef National Park, *U.S.A.* 115 **G8**
Capitola, *U.S.A.* 116 **J5**
Capizzi, *Italy* 31 **E7**
Capoche →, *Mozam.* 87 **F3**
Capoterra, *Italy* 30 **C1**
Cappadocia, *Turkey* 72 **C6**
Capraia, *Italy* 28 **E6**
Caprara, Pta., *Italy* 30 **A1**
Caprarola, *Italy* 29 **F9**
Capreol, *Canada* 102 **C3**
Caprera, *Italy* 30 **A2**
Capri, *Italy* 31 **B7**
Capricorn Group, *Australia* 94 **C5**
Capricorn Ra., *Australia* 92 **D2**
Caprino Veronese, *Italy* 28 **C7**
Caprivi Strip, *Namibia* 88 **B3**
Captain's Flat, *Australia* 95 **F4**
Captieux, *France* 20 **D3**
Caquetá →, *Colombia* 122 **D4**
Caracal, *Romania* 43 **F9**
Caracas, *Venezuela* 124 **A5**
Caracol, *Mato Grosso do Sul, Brazil* 126 **A4**
Caracol, *Piauí, Brazil* 125 **E10**
Caráglio, *Italy* 28 **D4**
Carajas, *Brazil* 125 **E8**
Carajás, Serra dos, *Brazil* 125 **E8**
Carangola, *Brazil* 127 **A7**
Caransebeş, *Romania* 42 **E7**
Carantec, *France* 18 **D3**
Caraquet, *Canada* 103 **C6**
Caras, *Peru* 124 **E3**
Caraş Severin □, *Romania* 42 **E7**
Caraşova, *Romania* 42 **E6**
Caratasca, L., *Honduras* 120 **C3**
Caratinga, *Brazil* 125 **G10**
Caraúbas, *Brazil* 125 **E11**
Caravaca = Caravaca de la Cruz, *Spain* 33 **G3**
Caravaca de la Cruz, *Spain* 33 **G3**
Caravággio, *Italy* 28 **C6**
Caravela, *Guinea-Biss.* 82 **C1**
Caravelas, *Brazil* 125 **G11**
Caraveli, *Peru* 124 **G4**
Caràzinho, *Brazil* 127 **B5**
Carballino = O Carballiño, *Spain* 34 **C2**
Carballo, *Spain* 34 **B2**
Carberry, *Canada* 105 **D9**
Carbó, *Mexico* 118 **B2**
Carbonara, C., *Italy* 30 **C2**
Carbondale, *Colo., U.S.A.* 114 **G10**
Carbondale, *Ill., U.S.A.* 113 **G10**
Carbondale, *Pa., U.S.A.* 111 **E9**
Carbonear, *Canada* 103 **C9**
Carboneras, *Spain* 33 **J3**
Carboneras de Guadazaón, *Spain* 32 **F3**
Carbónia, *Italy* 30 **C1**
Carcabuey, *Spain* 35 **H6**
Carcagente = Carcaixent, *Spain* 33 **F4**
Carcaixent, *Spain* 33 **F4**
Carcajou, *Canada* 104 **B5**
Carcar, *Phil.* 61 **F5**
Carcarana →, *Argentina* 126 **C3**
Carcasse, C., *Haiti* 121 **C5**
Carcassonne, *France* 20 **E6**
Carcross, *Canada* 104 **A2**
Çardak, *Çanakkale, Turkey* 41 **F10**
Çardak, *Denizli, Turkey* 39 **D11**
Cardamon Hills, *India* 66 **Q10**
Cardeña, *Spain* 35 **G6**
Cárdenas, *Cuba* 120 **B3**
Cárdenas, *San Luis Potosí, Mexico* 119 **C5**
Cárdenas, *Tabasco, Mexico* 119 **D6**
Cardenete, *Spain* 32 **F3**
Cardiff, *U.K.* 13 **F4**
Cardiff □, *U.K.* 13 **F4**
Cardiff-by-the-Sea, *U.S.A.* 117 **M9**
Cardigan, *U.K.* 13 **E3**
Cardigan B., *U.K.* 13 **E3**
Cardinal, *Canada* 111 **B9**
Cardona, *Spain* 32 **D6**
Cardona, *Uruguay* 126 **C4**
Cardoner →, *Spain* 32 **D6**
Cardoso, Ilha do, *Brazil* 127 **B5**
Cardston, *Canada* 104 **D6**
Cardwell, *Australia* 94 **B4**
Careen L., *Canada* 105 **B7**
Carei, *Romania* 42 **C7**
Careme = Ciremai, *Indonesia* 63 **G13**
Carentan, *France* 18 **C5**
Carey, *U.S.A.* 114 **E7**
Carey, L., *Australia* 93 **E3**
Carey L., *Canada* 105 **A8**
Careysburg, *Liberia* 82 **D2**
Cargèse, *France* 21 **F12**
Carhaix-Plouguer, *France* 18 **D3**
Carhué, *Argentina* 126 **D3**
Caria, *Turkey* 39 **D10**
Cariacica, *Brazil* 125 **H10**
Cariati, *Italy* 31 **C9**
Caribbean Sea, *W. Indies* 121 **D5**
Cariboo Mts., *Canada* 104 **C4**
Caribou, *U.S.A.* 109 **B12**
Caribou →, *Man., Canada* 105 **B10**
Caribou →, *N.W.T., Canada* 104 **A3**
Caribou I., *Canada* 102 **C2**
Caribou Is., *Canada* 104 **A6**
Caribou L., *Man., Canada* 105 **B9**
Caribou L., *Ont., Canada* 102 **B2**
Caribou Mts., *Canada* 104 **B5**
Carichic, *Mexico* 118 **B3**
Carigara, *Phil.* 61 **F6**
Carignan, *France* 19 **C12**
Carignano, *Italy* 28 **D4**
Carillo, *Mexico* 118 **B4**
Carinda, *Australia* 95 **E4**
Cariñena, *Spain* 32 **D3**
Carinhanha, *Brazil* 125 **F10**
Carinhanha →, *Brazil* 125 **F10**
Carini, *Italy* 30 **D6**
Cariño, *Spain* 34 **B3**
Carínola, *Italy* 30 **A6**
Carinthia = Kärnten □, *Austria* 26 **E6**
Caripito, *Venezuela* 124 **A6**
Carlbrod = Dimitrovgrad, *Serbia, Yug.* 40 **C6**
Carlet, *Spain* 33 **F4**
Carleton, Mt., *Canada* 103 **C6**
Carleton Place, *Canada* 102 **C4**
Carletonville, *S. Africa* 88 **D4**
Cârlibaba, *Romania* 43 **C10**
Carlin, *U.S.A.* 114 **F5**
Carlingford L., *U.K.* 15 **B5**
Carlinville, *U.S.A.* 112 **F10**
Carlisle, *U.K.* 12 **C5**
Carlisle, *U.S.A.* 110 **F7**
Carlit, Pic, *France* 20 **F5**
Carloforte, *Italy* 30 **C1**
Carlos Casares, *Argentina* 126 **D3**
Carlos Tejedor, *Argentina* 126 **D3**
Carlow, *Ireland* 15 **D5**
Carlow □, *Ireland* 15 **D5**
Carlsbad, *Calif., U.S.A.* 117 **M9**
Carlsbad, *N. Mex., U.S.A.* 113 **J2**
Carlsbad Caverns National Park, *U.S.A.* 113 **J2**
Carluke, *U.K.* 14 **F5**
Carlyle, *Canada* 105 **D8**
Carmacks, *Canada* 100 **B6**
Carmagnola, *Italy* 28 **D4**
Carman, *Canada* 105 **D9**
Carmarthen, *U.K.* 13 **F3**
Carmarthen B., *U.K.* 13 **F3**
Carmarthenshire □, *U.K.* 13 **F3**
Carmaux, *France* 20 **D6**
Carmel, *U.S.A.* 111 **E11**
Carmel-by-the-Sea, *U.S.A.* 116 **J5**
Carmel Valley, *U.S.A.* 116 **J5**
Carmelo, *Uruguay* 126 **C4**
Carmen, *Colombia* 124 **B3**
Carmen, *Paraguay* 127 **B4**
Carmen →, *Mexico* 118 **A3**
Carmen, I., *Mexico* 118 **B2**
Carmen de Patagones, *Argentina* 128 **E4**
Cármenes, *Spain* 34 **C5**
Carmensa, *Argentina* 126 **D2**

Carmi, *Canada* 104 D5
Carmi, *U.S.A.* 108 F1
Carmichael, *U.S.A.* 116 G5
Carmila, *Australia* 94 C4
Carmona, *Costa Rica* 120 E2
Carmona, *Spain* 35 H5
Carn Ban, *U.K.* 14 D4
Carn Eige, *U.K.* 14 D3
Carnamah, *Australia* 93 E2
Carnarvon, *Australia* 93 D1
Carnarvon, *S. Africa* 88 E3
Carnarvon Ra., *Queens., Australia* 94 D4
Carnarvon Ra., *W. Austral., Australia* 93 E3
Carnation, *U.S.A.* 116 C5
Carndonagh, *Ireland* 15 A4
Carnduff, *Canada* 105 D8
Carnegie, *U.S.A.* 110 F4
Carnegie, L., *Australia* 93 E3
Carnic Alps = Karnische Alpen, *Europe* 26 E6
Carniche Alpi = Karnische Alpen, *Europe* 26 E6
Carnot, *C.A.R.* 84 D3
Carnot, C., *Australia* 95 E2
Carnot B., *Australia* 92 C3
Carnoustie, *U.K.* 14 E6
Carnsore Pt., *Ireland* 15 D5
Caro, *U.S.A.* 108 D4
Carol City, *U.S.A.* 109 N5
Carolina, *Brazil* 125 E9
Carolina, *Puerto Rico* 121 C6
Carolina, *S. Africa* 89 D5
Caroline I., *Kiribati* 97 H12
Caroline Is., *Micronesia* 52 J17
Caroni →, *Venezuela* 124 B6
Caroníe = Nébrodi, Monti, *Italy* 31 E7
Caroona, *Australia* 95 E5
Carpathians, *Europe* 6 F10
Carpații Meridionali, *Romania* 43 E9
Carpentaria, G. of, *Australia* 94 A2
Carpentras, *France* 21 D9
Carpi, *Italy* 28 D7
Cărpineni, *Moldova* 43 D13
Carpinteria, *U.S.A.* 117 L7
Carpio, *Spain* 34 D5
Carr Boyd Ra., *Australia* 92 C4
Carrabelle, *U.S.A.* 109 L3
Carral, *Spain* 34 B2
Carranza, Presa V., *Mexico* 118 B4
Carrara, *Italy* 28 D7
Carrascal, *Phil.* 61 G6
Carrascosa del Campo, *Spain* 32 E2
Carrauntoohill, *Ireland* 15 D2
Carrick-on-Shannon, *Ireland* 15 C3
Carrick-on-Suir, *Ireland* 15 D4
Carrickfergus, *U.K.* 15 B6
Carrickmacross, *Ireland* 15 C5
Carrieton, *Australia* 95 E2
Carrington, *U.S.A.* 112 B5
Carrión →, *Spain* 34 D6
Carrión de los Condes, *Spain* 34 C6
Carrizal Bajo, *Chile* 126 B1
Carrizalillo, *Chile* 126 B1
Carrizo Cr. →, *U.S.A.* 113 G3
Carrizo Springs, *U.S.A.* 113 L5
Carrizozo, *U.S.A.* 115 K11
Carroll, *U.S.A.* 112 D7
Carrollton, *Ga., U.S.A.* 109 J3
Carrollton, *Ill., U.S.A.* 112 F9
Carrollton, *Ky., U.S.A.* 108 F3
Carrollton, *Mo., U.S.A.* 112 F8
Carrollton, *Ohio, U.S.A.* 110 F3
Carron →, *U.K.* 14 D4
Carron, L., *U.K.* 14 D3
Carrot →, *Canada* 105 C8
Carrot River, *Canada* 105 C8
Carrouges, *France* 18 D6
Carrù, *Italy* 28 D4
Carruthers, *Canada* 105 C7
Carsa Dek, *Ethiopia* 81 F4
Çarşamba, *Turkey* 72 B7
Carsóli, *Italy* 29 F10
Carson, *Calif., U.S.A.* 117 M8
Carson, *N. Dak., U.S.A.* 112 B4
Carson →, *U.S.A.* 116 F8
Carson City, *U.S.A.* 116 F7
Carson Sink, *U.S.A.* 114 G4
Cartagena, *Colombia* 124 A3
Cartagena, *Spain* 33 H4
Cartago, *Colombia* 124 C3
Cartago, *Costa Rica* 120 E3
Cártama, *Spain* 35 J6
Cartaxo, *Portugal* 35 F2
Cartaya, *Spain* 35 H3
Cartersville, *U.S.A.* 109 H3
Carterton, *N.Z.* 91 J5
Carthage, *Tunisia* 30 F3
Carthage, *Ill., U.S.A.* 112 E9
Carthage, *Mo., U.S.A.* 113 G7
Carthage, *N.Y., U.S.A.* 108 D8
Carthage, *Tex., U.S.A.* 113 J7
Cartier I., *Australia* 92 B3
Cartwright, *Canada* 103 B8
Caruaru, *Brazil* 125 E11
Carúpano, *Venezuela* 124 A6
Caruthersville, *U.S.A.* 113 G10
Carvin, *France* 19 B9
Carvoeiro, *Brazil* 124 D6
Carvoeiro, C., *Portugal* 35 F1
Cary, *U.S.A.* 109 H6
Casa Branca, *Portugal* 35 G2
Casa Grande, *U.S.A.* 115 K8
Casablanca, *Chile* 126 C1
Casablanca, *Morocco* 78 B4
Casacalenda, *Italy* 29 G11
Casalbordino, *Italy* 29 F11
Casale Monferrato, *Italy* 28 C5
Casalmaggiore, *Italy* 28 D7
Casalpusterlengo, *Italy* 28 C6
Casamance →, *Senegal* 82 C1
Casarano, *Italy* 31 B11
Casares, *Spain* 35 J5
Casas Ibáñez, *Spain* 33 F3
Casasimarro, *Spain* 33 F2
Casatejada, *Spain* 34 F5
Casavieja, *Spain* 34 E6
Cascade, *Idaho, U.S.A.* 114 D5
Cascade, *Mont., U.S.A.* 114 C8
Cascade Locks, *U.S.A.* 116 E5
Cascade Ra., *U.S.A.* 116 D5
Cascade Reservoir, *U.S.A.* 114 D5
Cascais, *Portugal* 35 G1
Cascavel, *Brazil* 127 A5
Cáscina, *Italy* 28 E7
Casco B., *U.S.A.* 109 D10
Caselle Torinese, *Italy* 28 C4
Caserta, *Italy* 31 A7
Cashel, *Ireland* 15 D4
Casiguran, *Phil.* 61 C5
Casilda, *Argentina* 126 C3
Casimcea, *Romania* 43 F13
Casino, *Australia* 95 D5
Casiquiare →, *Venezuela* 124 C5
Čáslav, *Czech Rep.* 26 B8
Casma, *Peru* 124 E3
Casmalia, *U.S.A.* 117 L6
Cásola Valsénio, *Italy* 29 D8
Cásoli, *Italy* 29 F11
Caspe, *Spain* 32 D4
Casper, *U.S.A.* 114 E10
Caspian Depression, *Eurasia* 49 G9
Caspian Sea, *Eurasia* 50 E6
Cass Lake, *U.S.A.* 112 B7
Cassà de la Selva, *Spain* 32 D7
Cassadaga, *U.S.A.* 110 D5
Cassano allo Iónio, *Italy* 31 C9
Casse, Grande, *France* 21 C10
Cassel, *France* 19 B9
Casselman, *Canada* 111 A9
Casselton, *U.S.A.* 112 B6
Cassiar, *Canada* 104 B3
Cassiar Mts., *Canada* 104 B2
Cassino, *Italy* 30 A6
Cassis, *France* 21 E9
Cassville, *U.S.A.* 113 G8
Castagneto Carducci, *Italy* 28 E7
Castaic, *U.S.A.* 117 L8
Castalia, *U.S.A.* 110 E2
Castanhal, *Brazil* 125 D9
Castéggio, *Italy* 28 C6
Castejón de Monegros, *Spain* 32 D4
Castèl di Sangro, *Italy* 29 G11
Castèl San Giovanni, *Italy* 28 C6
Castèl San Pietro Terme, *Italy* 29 D8
Castelbuono, *Italy* 31 E7
Castelfidardo, *Italy* 29 E10
Castelfiorentino, *Italy* 28 E7
Castelfranco Emília, *Italy* 28 D8
Castelfranco Véneto, *Italy* 29 C8
Casteljaloux, *France* 20 D4
Castellabate, *Italy* 31 B7
Castellammare, G. di, *Italy* 30 D5
Castellammare del Golfo, *Italy* 30 D5
Castellammare di Stábia, *Italy* 31 B7
Castellamonte, *Italy* 28 C4
Castellane, *France* 21 E10
Castellaneta, *Italy* 31 B9
Castelli, *Argentina* 126 D4
Castelló de la Plana, *Spain* 32 F4
Castellón de la Plana □, *Spain* 32 E4
Castellote, *Spain* 32 E4
Castelmáuro, *Italy* 29 G11
Castelnau-de-Médoc, *France* 20 C3
Castelnau-Magnoac, *France* 20 E4
Castelnaudary, *France* 20 E5
Castelnovo ne' Monti, *Italy* 28 D7
Castelnuovo di Val di Cécina, *Italy* 28 E7
Castelo, *Brazil* 127 A7
Castelo Branco, *Portugal* 34 F3
Castelo Branco □, *Portugal* 34 F3
Castelo de Paiva, *Portugal* 34 D2
Castelo de Vide, *Portugal* 35 F3
Castelsardo, *Italy* 30 B1
Castelsarrasin, *France* 20 D5
Casteltérmini, *Italy* 30 E6
Castelvetrano, *Italy* 30 E5
Casterton, *Australia* 95 F3
Castets, *France* 20 E2
Castiglion Fiorentino, *Italy* 29 E8
Castiglione del Lago, *Italy* 29 E9
Castiglione della Pescáia, *Italy* 28 F7
Castiglione delle Stiviere, *Italy* 28 C7
Castilblanco, *Spain* 35 F5
Castile, *U.S.A.* 110 D6
Castilla, Playa de, *Spain* 35 J4
Castilla-La Mancha □, *Spain* 6 H5
Castilla y Leon □, *Spain* 34 D6
Castillo de Locubín, *Spain* 35 H7
Castillon-en-Couserans, *France* 20 F5
Castillonès, *France* 20 D4
Castillos, *Uruguay* 127 C5
Castle Dale, *U.S.A.* 114 G8
Castle Douglas, *U.K.* 14 G5
Castle Rock, *Colo., U.S.A.* 112 F2
Castle Rock, *Wash., U.S.A.* 116 D4
Castlebar, *Ireland* 15 C2
Castleblaney, *Ireland* 15 B5
Castlederg, *U.K.* 15 B4
Castleford, *U.K.* 12 D6
Castlegar, *Canada* 104 D5
Castlemaine, *Australia* 95 F3
Castlepollard, *Ireland* 15 C4
Castlerea, *Ireland* 15 C3
Castlereagh →, *Australia* 95 E4
Castlereagh B., *Australia* 94 A2
Castleton, *U.S.A.* 111 C11
Castletown, *U.K.* 12 C3
Castletown Bearhaven, *Ireland* 15 E2
Castor, *Canada* 104 C6
Castor →, *Canada* 102 B4
Castorland, *U.S.A.* 111 C9
Castres, *France* 20 E6
Castricum, *Neths.* 17 B4
Castries, *St. Lucia* 121 D7
Castril, *Spain* 35 H8
Castro, *Brazil* 127 A6
Castro, *Chile* 128 E2
Castro Alves, *Brazil* 125 F11
Castro del Río, *Spain* 35 H6
Castro-Urdiales, *Spain* 34 B7
Castro Verde, *Portugal* 35 H2
Castrojeriz, *Spain* 34 C6
Castropol, *Spain* 34 B4
Castroreale, *Italy* 31 D8
Castrovillari, *Italy* 31 C9
Castroville, *U.S.A.* 116 J5
Castuera, *Spain* 35 G5
Çat, *Turkey* 73 C9
Cat Ba, Dao, *Vietnam* 64 B6
Cat I., *Bahamas* 121 B4
Cat L., *Canada* 102 B1
Cat Lake, *Canada* 102 B1
Čata, *Slovak Rep.* 27 D11
Catacamas, *Honduras* 120 D2
Cataguases, *Brazil* 127 A7
Çatak, *Turkey* 73 C10
Catalão, *Brazil* 125 G9
Çatalca, *Turkey* 41 E12
Catalina, *Canada* 103 C9
Catalina, *Chile* 126 B2
Catalina, *U.S.A.* 115 K8
Catalonia = Cataluña □, *Spain* 32 D6
Cataluña □, *Spain* 32 D6
Çatalzeytin, *Turkey* 72 B6
Catamarca, *Argentina* 126 B2
Catamarca □, *Argentina* 126 B2
Catanauan, *Phil.* 61 E5
Catanduanes □, *Phil.* 61 E6
Catanduva, *Brazil* 127 A6
Catánia, *Italy* 31 E8
Catánia, G. di, *Italy* 31 E8
Catanzaro, *Italy* 31 D9
Catarman, *Phil.* 61 E6
Catbalogan, *Phil.* 61 F6
Cateel, *Phil.* 61 H7
Catembe, *Mozam.* 89 D5
Caterham, *U.K.* 13 F7
Cathcart, *S. Africa* 88 E4
Cathlamet, *U.S.A.* 116 D3
Catio, *Guinea-Biss.* 82 C1
Catlettsburg, *U.S.A.* 108 F4
Çatma Dağı, *Turkey* 39 C11
Catoche, C., *Mexico* 119 C7
Cátria, Mte., *Italy* 29 E9
Catriló, *Argentina* 126 D3
Catrimani, *Brazil* 124 C6
Catrimani →, *Brazil* 124 C6
Catskill, *U.S.A.* 111 D11
Catskill Mts., *U.S.A.* 111 D10
Catt, Mt., *Australia* 94 A1
Cattaraugus, *U.S.A.* 110 D6
Cattólica, *Italy* 29 E9
Cattólica Eraclea, *Italy* 30 E6
Catuala, *Angola* 88 B2
Catuane, *Mozam.* 89 D5
Catur, *Mozam.* 87 E4
Catwick Is., *Vietnam* 65 G7
Cauca →, *Colombia* 124 B4
Caucaia, *Brazil* 125 D11
Caucasus Mountains, *Eurasia* 49 J7
Caudete, *Spain* 33 G3
Caudry, *France* 19 B10
Caulnes, *France* 18 D4
Caulónia, *Italy* 31 D9
Caungula, *Angola* 84 F3
Cauquenes, *Chile* 126 D1
Caura →, *Venezuela* 124 B6
Cauresi →, *Mozam.* 87 F3
Căușani, *Moldova* 43 D14
Causapscal, *Canada* 103 C6
Caussade, *France* 20 D5
Causse-Méjean, *France* 20 D7
Cauterets, *France* 20 F3
Cauvery →, *India* 66 P11
Caux, Pays de, *France* 18 C7
Cava de' Tirreni, *Italy* 31 B7
Cávado →, *Portugal* 34 D2
Cavaillon, *France* 21 E9
Cavalaire-sur-Mer, *France* 21 E10
Cavalese, *Italy* 29 B8
Cavalier, *U.S.A.* 112 A6
Cavalla = Cavally →, *Africa* 82 E3
Cavalleria, C. de, *Spain* 37 A11
Cavallo, I. de, *France* 21 G13
Cavally →, *Africa* 82 E3
Cavan, *Ireland* 15 B4
Cavan □, *Ireland* 15 C4
Cavárzere, *Italy* 29 C9
Çavdarhisar, *Turkey* 39 B11
Çavdır, *Turkey* 39 D11
Cave Creek, *U.S.A.* 115 K7
Cavenagh Ra., *Australia* 93 E4
Cavendish, *Australia* 95 F3
Caviana, I., *Brazil* 125 C8
Cavite, *Phil.* 61 D4
Cavnic, *Romania* 43 C8
Cavour, *Italy* 28 D4
Cavtat, *Croatia* 40 D2
Cawndilla L., *Australia* 95 E3
Cawnpore = Kanpur, *India* 69 F9
Caxias, *Brazil* 125 D10
Caxias do Sul, *Brazil* 127 B5
Çay, *Turkey* 72 C4
Cay Sal Bank, *Bahamas* 120 B4
Cayambe, *Ecuador* 124 C3
Çaycuma, *Turkey* 72 B5
Çayeli, *Turkey* 73 B9
Cayenne, *Fr. Guiana* 125 B8
Caygören Barajı, *Turkey* 39 B10
Cayiralan, *Turkey* 72 C6
Caylus, *France* 20 D5
Cayman Brac, *Cayman Is.* 120 C4
Cayman Is. ■, *W. Indies* 120 C3
Cayo Romano, *Cuba* 120 B4
Cayres, *France* 20 D7
Cayuga, *Canada* 110 D5
Cayuga, *U.S.A.* 111 D8
Cayuga L., *U.S.A.* 111 D8
Cazalla de la Sierra, *Spain* 35 H5
Căzănești, *Romania* 43 F12
Cazaubon, *France* 20 E3
Cazaux et de Sanguinet, Étang de, *France* 20 D2
Cazenovia, *U.S.A.* 111 D9
Cazères, *France* 20 E5
Cazin, *Bos.-H.* 29 D12
Čazma, *Croatia* 29 C13
Cazombo, *Angola* 85 G4
Cazorla, *Spain* 35 H7
Cazorla, Sierra de, *Spain* 35 G8
Cea →, *Spain* 34 C5
Ceamurlia de Jos, *Romania* 43 F13
Ceanannus Mor, *Ireland* 15 C5
Ceará = Fortaleza, *Brazil* 125 D11
Ceará □, *Brazil* 125 E11
Ceará Mirim, *Brazil* 125 E11
Ceauru, L., *Romania* 43 F8
Cebaco, I. de, *Panama* 120 E3
Cebollar, *Argentina* 126 B2
Cebollera, Sierra de, *Spain* 32 D2
Cebreros, *Spain* 34 E6
Cebu, *Phil.* 61 F5
Čečava, *Bos.-H.* 42 F2
Ceccano, *Italy* 30 A6
Cece, *Hungary* 42 D3
Cechi, *Ivory C.* 82 D4
Cecil Plains, *Australia* 95 D5
Cécina, *Italy* 28 E7
Cécina →, *Italy* 28 E7
Ceclavín, *Spain* 34 F4
Cedar →, *U.S.A.* 112 E9
Cedar City, *U.S.A.* 115 H7
Cedar Creek Reservoir, *U.S.A.* 113 J6
Cedar Falls, *Iowa, U.S.A.* 112 D8
Cedar Falls, *Wash., U.S.A.* 116 C5
Cedar L., *Canada* 105 C9
Cedar Rapids, *U.S.A.* 112 E9
Cedartown, *U.S.A.* 109 H3
Cedarvale, *Canada* 104 B3
Cedarville, *S. Africa* 89 E4
Cedeira, *Spain* 34 B2
Cedral, *Mexico* 118 C4
Cedrino →, *Italy* 30 B2
Cedro, *Brazil* 125 E11
Cedros, I. de, *Mexico* 118 B1
Ceduna, *Australia* 95 E1
Cedynia, *Poland* 45 F1
Cée, *Spain* 34 C1
Cefalù, *Italy* 31 D7
Cega →, *Spain* 34 D6
Cegléd, *Hungary* 42 C4
Céglie Messápico, *Italy* 31 B10
Cehegín, *Spain* 33 G3
Ceheng, *China* 58 E5
Cehu-Silvaniei, *Romania* 43 C8
Ceica, *Romania* 42 D7
Ceira →, *Portugal* 34 E2
Čelákovice, *Czech Rep.* 26 A7
Celano, *Italy* 29 F10
Celanova, *Spain* 34 C3
Celaya, *Mexico* 118 C4
Celebes Sea, *Indonesia* 63 D6
Čelić, *Bos.-H.* 42 F3
Celina, *U.S.A.* 108 E3
Celinac, *Bos.-H.* 42 F2
Celje, *Slovenia* 29 B12
Celldömölk, *Hungary* 42 C2
Celle, *Germany* 24 C6
Celorico da Beira, *Portugal* 34 E3
Çeltikçi, *Turkey* 39 D12
Çemişgezek, *Turkey* 73 C8
Cenderwasih, Teluk, *Indonesia* 63 E9
Cengong, *China* 58 D7
Ceno →, *Italy* 28 D7
Centallo, *Italy* 28 D4
Centelles, *Spain* 32 D7
Center, *N. Dak., U.S.A.* 112 B4
Center, *Tex., U.S.A.* 113 K7
Centerburg, *U.S.A.* 110 F2
Centerville, *Calif., U.S.A.* 116 J7
Centerville, *Iowa, U.S.A.* 112 E8
Centerville, *Pa., U.S.A.* 110 F5
Centerville, *Tenn., U.S.A.* 109 H2
Centerville, *Tex., U.S.A.* 113 K7
Cento, *Italy* 29 D8
Central □, *Ghana* 83 D4
Central □, *Kenya* 86 C4
Central □, *Malawi* 87 E3
Central □, *Zambia* 87 E2
Central, Cordillera, *Colombia* 122 C3
Central, Cordillera, *Costa Rica* 120 D3
Central, Cordillera, *Dom. Rep.* 121 C5
Central, Cordillera, *Phil.* 61 C4
Central African Rep. ■, *Africa* 84 C4
Central America, *America* 98 H11
Central Butte, *Canada* 105 C7
Central City, *Colo., U.S.A.* 114 G11
Central City, *Ky., U.S.A.* 108 G2
Central City, *Nebr., U.S.A.* 112 E6
Central I., *Kenya* 86 B4
Central Makran Range, *Pakistan* 66 F4
Central Patricia, *Canada* 102 B1
Central Point, *U.S.A.* 114 E2
Central Russian Uplands, *Europe* 6 E13
Central Siberian Plateau, *Russia* 52 C14
Central Square, *U.S.A.* 111 C8
Centralia, *Ill., U.S.A.* 112 F10
Centralia, *Mo., U.S.A.* 112 F8
Centralia, *Wash., U.S.A.* 116 D4
Cenxi, *China* 59 F8
Čeotina →, *Bos.-H.* 40 C2
Cephalonia = Kefallinía, *Greece* 38 C2
Čepin, *Croatia* 42 E3
Ceprano, *Italy* 30 A6
Ceptura, *Romania* 43 E11
Cepu, *Indonesia* 63 G14
Ceram = Seram, *Indonesia* 63 E7
Ceram Sea = Seram Sea, *Indonesia* 63 E7
Cerbère, *France* 20 F7
Cerbicales, Is., *France* 21 G13
Cercal, *Portugal* 35 H2
Cerdaña, *Spain* 32 C6
Cère →, *France* 20 D5
Cerea, *Italy* 29 C8
Ceredigion □, *U.K.* 13 E3
Ceres, *Argentina* 126 B3
Ceres, *S. Africa* 88 E2
Ceres, *U.S.A.* 116 H6
Céret, *France* 20 F6
Cergy, *France* 19 C9
Cerignola, *Italy* 31 A8
Cerigo = Kíthira, *Greece* 38 E5
Cérilly, *France* 19 F9
Cerisiers, *France* 19 D10
Cerizay, *France* 18 F6
Çerkeş, *Turkey* 72 B5
Çerkezköy, *Turkey* 41 E12
Cerknica, *Slovenia* 29 C11
Cerkovica, *Bulgaria* 41 C8
Cermerno, *Serbia, Yug.* 40 C4
Çermik, *Turkey* 73 C8
Cerna, *Romania* 43 E13
Cerna →, *Romania* 43 F8
Cernavodă, *Romania* 43 F13
Cernay, *France* 19 E14
Cernik, *Croatia* 42 E2
Cerralvo, I., *Mexico* 118 C3
Cërrik, *Albania* 40 E3
Cerritos, *Mexico* 118 C4
Cerro Chato, *Uruguay* 127 C4
Certaldo, *Italy* 28 E8
Cervaro →, *Italy* 31 A8
Cervati, Monte, *Italy* 31 B8
Cerventes, *Australia* 93 F2
Cervera, *Spain* 32 D6
Cervera de Pisuerga, *Spain* 34 C6
Cervera del Río Alhama, *Spain* 32 C3
Cervéteri, *Italy* 29 F9
Cérvia, *Italy* 29 D9
Cervignano del Friuli, *Italy* 29 C10
Cervinara, *Italy* 31 A7
Cervione, *France* 21 F13
Cervo, *Spain* 34 B3
Cesarò, *Italy* 31 E7
Cesena, *Italy* 29 D9
Cesenático, *Italy* 29 D9
Cēsis, *Latvia* 9 H21
Česká Lípa, *Czech Rep.* 26 A7
Česká Třebová, *Czech Rep.* 27 B9
České Budějovice, *Czech Rep.* 26 C7
České Velenice, *Czech Rep.* 26 C7
Českomoravská Vrchovina, *Czech Rep.* 26 B8
Český Brod, *Czech Rep.* 26 A7
Český Krumlov, *Czech Rep.* 26 C7
Český Těšín, *Czech Rep.* 27 B11
Česma →, *Croatia* 29 C13
Çeşme, *Turkey* 39 C8
Cessnock, *Australia* 95 E5
Cesson-Sévigné, *France* 18 D5
Cestas, *France* 20 D3
Cestos →, *Liberia* 82 D3
Cetate, *Romania* 42 F8
Cetin Grad, *Croatia* 29 C12
Cetina →, *Croatia* 29 E13
Cetinje, *Montenegro, Yug.* 40 D2
Cetraro, *Italy* 31 C8
Ceuta, *N. Afr.* 78 A4
Ceva, *Italy* 28 D5
Cévennes, *France* 20 D7
Ceyhan, *Turkey* 70 B2
Ceyhan →, *Turkey* 72 D6
Ceylânpınar, *Turkey* 73 D9
Ceylon = Sri Lanka ■, *Asia* 66 R12
Cèze →, *France* 21 D8
Cha-am, *Thailand* 64 F2
Cha Pa, *Vietnam* 64 A4
Chabanais, *France* 20 C4
Chabeuil, *France* 21 D9
Chablais, *France* 19 F13
Chablis, *France* 19 E10
Chacabuco, *Argentina* 126 C3
Chachapoyas, *Peru* 124 E3
Chachoengsao, *Thailand* 64 F3
Chachran, *Pakistan* 66 E7
Chachro, *Pakistan* 68 G4
Chaco □, *Argentina* 126 B3
Chaco □, *Paraguay* 126 B4

Chaco →, *U.S.A.* 115 H9
Chaco Austral, *S. Amer.* 128 B4
Chaco Boreal, *S. Amer.* 128 H6
Chaco Central, *S. Amer.* 128 A4
Chacon, C., *U.S.A.* 104 C2
Chad ■, *Africa* 79 E9
Chad, L. = Tchad, L., *Chad* 79 F8
Chadan, *Russia* 51 D10
Chadileuvú →, *Argentina* 126 D2
Chadiza, *Zambia* 87 E3
Chadron, *U.S.A.* 112 D3
Chadyr-Lunga = Ciadâr-Lunga, *Moldova* 43 D13
Chae Hom, *Thailand* 64 C2
Chaem →, *Thailand* 64 C2
Chaeryŏng, *N. Korea* 57 E13
Chagai Hills, *Afghan.* 66 E3
Chagda, *Russia* 51 D14
Chagny, *France* 19 F11
Chagoda, *Russia* 46 C8
Chagos Arch., *Ind. Oc.* 52 K11
Chagrin Falls, *U.S.A.* 110 E3
Chāh Ākhvor, *Iran* 71 C8
Chāh Bahār, *Iran* 71 E9
Chāh-e Kavīr, *Iran* 71 C8
Chahar Burjak, *Afghan.* 66 D3
Chahār Mahāll va Bakhtīarī □, *Iran* 71 C6
Chaibasa, *India* 67 H14
Chaillé-les-Marais, *France* 20 B2
Chainat, *Thailand* 64 E3
Chaiya, *Thailand* 65 H2
Chaj Doab, *Pakistan* 68 C5
Chajari, *Argentina* 126 C4
Chak Amru, *Pakistan* 68 C6
Chaka, *Sudan* 81 G3
Chakar →, *Pakistan* 68 E3
Chakari, *Zimbabwe* 89 B4
Chake Chake, *Tanzania* 86 D4
Chakhānsūr, *Afghan.* 66 D3
Chakonipau, L., *Canada* 103 A6
Chakradharpur, *India* 69 H11
Chakrata, *India* 68 D7
Chakwal, *Pakistan* 68 C5
Chala, *Peru* 124 G4
Chalais, *France* 20 C4
Chalchihuites, *Mexico* 118 C4
Chalcis = Khalkís, *Greece* 38 C5
Châlette-sur-Loing, *France* 19 D9
Chaleur B., *Canada* 103 C6
Chalfant, *U.S.A.* 116 H8
Chalhuanca, *Peru* 124 F4
Chalindrey, *France* 19 E12
Chaling, *China* 59 D9
Chalisgaon, *India* 66 J9
Chalk River, *Canada* 102 C4
Chalky Inlet, *N.Z.* 91 M1
Challans, *France* 18 F5
Challapata, *Bolivia* 124 G5
Challis, *U.S.A.* 114 D6
Chalmette, *U.S.A.* 113 L10
Chalon-sur-Saône, *France* 19 F11
Chalonnes-sur-Loire, *France* 18 E6
Châlons-en-Champagne, *France* 19 D11
Châlus, *France* 20 C4
Chalyaphum, *Thailand* 64 E4
Cham, *Germany* 25 F8
Cham, Cu Lao, *Vietnam* 64 E7
Chama, *U.S.A.* 115 H10
Chamaicó, *Argentina* 126 D3
Chaman, *Pakistan* 66 D5
Chamba, *India* 68 C7
Chamba, *Tanzania* 87 E4
Chambal →, *India* 69 F8
Chamberlain, *U.S.A.* 112 D5
Chamberlain →, *Australia* 92 C4
Chamberlain L., *U.S.A.* 109 B11
Chambers, *U.S.A.* 115 J9
Chambersburg, *U.S.A.* 108 F7
Chambéry, *France* 21 C9
Chambeshi →, *Zambia* 84 G6
Chambly, *Canada* 111 A11
Chambord, *Canada* 103 C5
Chamboulive, *France* 20 C5
Chamchamal, *Iraq* 70 C5
Chamela, *Mexico* 118 D3
Chamical, *Argentina* 126 C2
Chamkar Luong, *Cambodia* 65 G4
Chamoli, *India* 69 D8
Chamonix-Mont Blanc, *France* 21 C10
Chamouchouane →, *Canada* 102 C5
Champa, *India* 69 H10
Champagne, *Canada* 104 A1
Champagne, *France* 19 D11
Champagnole, *France* 19 F12
Champaign, *U.S.A.* 108 E1
Champassak, *Laos* 64 E5
Champaubert, *France* 19 D10
Champawat, *India* 69 E9
Champdeniers-St-Denis, *France* 20 B3
Champdoré, L., *Canada* 103 A6
Champeix, *France* 20 C7
Champion, *U.S.A.* 110 E4
Champlain, *U.S.A.* 111 B11
Champlain, L., *U.S.A.* 111 B11
Champlitte, *France* 19 E12
Champotón, *Mexico* 119 D6
Champua, *India* 69 H11
Chamusca, *Portugal* 35 F2
Chana, *Thailand* 65 J3
Chañaral, *Chile* 126 B1
Chanārān, *Iran* 71 B8
Chanasma, *India* 68 H5
Chanco, *Chile* 126 D1
Chand, *India* 69 J8
Chandan, *India* 69 G12
Chandan Chauki, *India* 69 E9
Chandannagar, *India* 69 H13
Chandausi, *India* 69 E8
Chandeleur Is., *U.S.A.* 113 L10
Chandeleur Sd., *U.S.A.* 113 L10
Chandigarh, *India* 68 D7
Chandil, *India* 69 H12
Chandler, *Australia* 95 D1
Chandler, *Canada* 103 C7
Chandler, *Ariz., U.S.A.* 115 K8
Chandler, *Okla., U.S.A.* 113 H6
Chandod, *India* 68 J5
Chandpur, *Bangla.* 67 H17
Chandrapur, *India* 66 K11
Chānf, *Iran* 71 E9
Chang, *Pakistan* 68 F3
Chang, Ko, *Thailand* 65 F4
Ch'ang Chiang = Chang Jiang →, *China* 59 B13
Chang Jiang →, *China* 59 B13
Changa, *India* 69 C7
Changanacheri, *India* 66 Q10
Changane →, *Mozam.* 89 C5
Changbai, *China* 57 D15
Changbai Shan, *China* 57 C15
Changchiak'ou = Zhangjiakou, *China* 56 D8
Ch'angchou = Changzhou, *China* 59 B12
Changchun, *China* 57 C13
Changchunling, *China* 57 B13
Changde, *China* 59 C8
Changdo-ri, *N. Korea* 57 E14
Changfeng, *China* 59 A11
Changhai = Shanghai, *China* 59 B13
Changhua, *China* 59 B12
Changhua, *Taiwan* 59 E13
Changhŭng, *S. Korea* 57 G14
Changhŭngni, *N. Korea* 57 D15
Changjiang, *China* 64 C7
Changjin, *N. Korea* 57 D14
Changjin-chŏsuji, *N. Korea* 57 D14
Changle, *China* 59 E12
Changli, *China* 57 E10
Changling, *China* 57 B12
Changlun, *Malaysia* 65 J3
Changning, *Hunan, China* 59 D9
Changning, *Sichuan, China* 58 C5
Changning, *Yunnan, China* 58 E2
Changping, *China* 56 D9
Changsha, *China* 59 C9
Changshan, *China* 59 C12
Changshu, *China* 59 B13
Changshun, *China* 58 D6
Changtai, *China* 59 E11
Changting, *China* 59 E11
Changwu, *China* 56 G4
Changxing, *China* 59 B12
Changyang, *China* 59 B8
Changyi, *China* 57 F10
Changyŏn, *N. Korea* 57 E13
Changyuan, *China* 56 G8
Changzhi, *China* 56 F7
Changzhou, *China* 59 B12
Chanhanga, *Angola* 88 B1
Chanlar = Xanlar, *Azerbaijan* 49 K8
Channapatna, *India* 66 N10
Channel Is., *U.K.* 13 H5
Channel Is., *U.S.A.* 117 M7
Channel Islands National Park, *U.S.A.* 117 M8
Channel-Port aux Basques, *Canada* 103 C8
Channel Tunnel, *Europe* 13 F9
Channing, *U.S.A.* 113 H3
Chantada, *Spain* 34 C3
Chanthaburi, *Thailand* 64 F4
Chantilly, *France* 19 C9
Chantonnay, *France* 18 F5
Chantrey Inlet, *Canada* 100 B10
Chanute, *U.S.A.* 113 G7
Chanza →, *Spain* 35 H3
Chao Hu, *China* 59 B11
Chao Phraya →, *Thailand* 64 F3
Chao Phraya Lowlands, *Thailand* 64 E3
Chaocheng, *China* 56 F8
Chaohu, *China* 59 B11
Chaoyang, *Guangdong, China* 59 F11
Chaoyang, *Liaoning, China* 57 D11
Chaozhou, *China* 59 F11
Chapais, *Canada* 102 C5
Chapala, *Mozam.* 87 F4
Chapala, L. de, *Mexico* 118 C4
Chapayev, *Kazakstan* 48 E10
Chapayevsk, *Russia* 48 D9
Chapecó, *Brazil* 127 B5
Chapel Hill, *U.S.A.* 109 H6
Chapleau, *Canada* 102 C3
Chaplin, *Canada* 105 C7
Chaplin L., *Canada* 105 C7
Chaplino, *Ukraine* 47 H9
Chaplygin, *Russia* 46 F11
Chappell, *U.S.A.* 112 E3
Chapra = Chhapra, *India* 69 G11
Chara, *Russia* 51 D12
Charadai, *Argentina* 126 B4
Charagua, *Bolivia* 124 G6
Charambirá, Punta, *Colombia* 124 C3
Charaña, *Bolivia* 124 G5
Charantsavan, *Armenia* 49 K7
Charanwala, *India* 68 F5
Charata, *Argentina* 126 B3
Charcas, *Mexico* 118 C4
Chard, *U.K.* 13 G5
Chardon, *U.S.A.* 110 E3
Chardzhou = Chärjew, *Turkmenistan* 50 F7
Charente □, *France* 20 C4
Charente →, *France* 20 C2
Charente-Maritime □, *France* 20 C3
Charenton-du-Cher, *France* 19 F9
Chari →, *Chad* 79 F8
Chārīkār, *Afghan.* 66 B6
Chariton →, *U.S.A.* 112 F8
Chärjew, *Turkmenistan* 50 F7
Charkhari, *India* 69 G8
Charkhi Dadri, *India* 68 E7
Charleroi, *Belgium* 17 D4
Charleroi, *U.S.A.* 110 F5
Charles, C., *U.S.A.* 108 G8
Charles City, *U.S.A.* 112 D8
Charles L., *Canada* 105 B6
Charles Town, *U.S.A.* 108 F7
Charleston, *Ill., U.S.A.* 108 F1
Charleston, *Miss., U.S.A.* 113 H9
Charleston, *Mo., U.S.A.* 113 G10
Charleston, *S.C., U.S.A.* 109 J6
Charleston, *W. Va., U.S.A.* 108 F5
Charleston L., *Canada* 111 B9
Charleston Peak, *U.S.A.* 117 J11
Charlestown, *Ireland* 15 C3
Charlestown, *S. Africa* 89 D4
Charlestown, *Ind., U.S.A.* 108 F3
Charlestown, *N.H., U.S.A.* 111 C12
Charleville = Rath Luirc, *Ireland* 15 D3
Charleville, *Australia* 95 D4
Charleville-Mézières, *France* 19 C11
Charlevoix, *U.S.A.* 108 C3
Charlieu, *France* 19 F11
Charlotte, *Mich., U.S.A.* 108 D3
Charlotte, *N.C., U.S.A.* 109 H5
Charlotte, *Vt., U.S.A.* 111 B11
Charlotte Amalie, *Virgin Is.* 121 C7
Charlotte Harbor, *U.S.A.* 109 M4
Charlotte L., *Canada* 104 C3
Charlottenberg, *Sweden* 10 E6
Charlottesville, *U.S.A.* 108 F6
Charlottetown, *Nfld., Canada* 103 B8
Charlottetown, *P.E.I., Canada* 103 C7
Charlton, *Australia* 95 F3
Charlton, *U.S.A.* 112 E8
Charlton I., *Canada* 102 B4
Charmes, *France* 19 D13
Charny, *Canada* 103 C5
Charolles, *France* 19 F11
Chârost, *France* 19 F9
Charre, *Mozam.* 87 F4
Charroux, *France* 20 B4
Charsadda, *Pakistan* 68 B4
Charters Towers, *Australia* 94 C4
Chartres, *France* 18 D8
Chascomús, *Argentina* 126 D4
Chasefu, *Zambia* 87 E3
Chashma Barrage, *Pakistan* 68 C4
Chasseneuil-sur-Bonnieure, *France* 20 C4
Chât, *Iran* 71 B7
Chatal Balkan = Udvoy Balkan, *Bulgaria* 41 D10
Château-Arnoux, *France* 21 D10
Château-Chinon, *France* 19 E10
Château-d'Olonne, *France* 20 B2
Château-du-Loir, *France* 18 E7
Château-Gontier, *France* 18 E6
Château-la-Vallière, *France* 18 E7
Château-Landon, *France* 19 D9
Château-Renault, *France* 18 E7
Château-Salins, *France* 19 D13
Château-Thierry, *France* 19 C10
Châteaubourg, *France* 18 D5
Châteaubriant, *France* 18 E5
Châteaudun, *France* 18 D8
Châteauguay, *U.S.A.* 111 B10
Châteaugiron, *France* 18 D5
Châteauguay, L., *Canada* 103 A5
Châteaulin, *France* 18 D2
Châteaumeillant, *France* 19 F9
Châteauneuf-du-Faou, *France* 18 D3
Châteauneuf-sur-Charente, *France* 20 C3
Châteauneuf-sur-Cher, *France* 19 F9
Châteauneuf-sur-Loire, *France* 19 E9
Châteaurenard, *Bouches-du-Rhône, France* 21 E8
Châteaurenard, *Loiret, France* 19 E9
Châteauroux, *France* 19 F8
Châteauvillain, *France* 19 D11
Châtelaillon-Plage, *France* 20 B2
Châtelguyon, *France* 20 C7
Châtellerault, *France* 18 F7
Châtelus-Malvaleix, *France* 19 F9
Chatham = Miramichi, *Canada* 103 C6
Chatham, *Canada* 102 D3
Chatham, *U.K.* 13 F8
Chatham, *U.S.A.* 111 D11
Chatham Is., *Pac. Oc.* 96 M10
Châtillon, *Italy* 28 C4
Châtillon-Coligny, *France* 19 E9
Châtillon-en-Diois, *France* 21 D9
Châtillon-sur-Indre, *France* 18 F8
Châtillon-sur-Loire, *France* 19 E9
Châtillon-sur-Seine, *France* 19 E11
Chatmohar, *Bangla.* 69 G13
Chatra, *India* 69 G11
Chatrapur, *India* 67 K14
Chats, L. des, *Canada* 111 A8
Chatsu, *India* 68 F6
Chatsworth, *Canada* 110 B4
Chatsworth, *Zimbabwe* 87 F3
Chattahoochee, *U.S.A.* 109 K3
Chattahoochee →, *U.S.A.* 109 K3
Chattanooga, *U.S.A.* 109 H3
Chatteris, *U.K.* 13 E8
Chaturat, *Thailand* 64 E3
Chau Doc, *Vietnam* 65 G5
Chaudes-Aigues, *France* 20 D7
Chauffailles, *France* 19 F11
Chauk, *Burma* 67 J19
Chaukan La, *Burma* 67 F20
Chaumont, *France* 19 D12
Chaumont, *U.S.A.* 111 B8
Chaumont-en-Vexin, *France* 19 C8
Chaumont-sur-Loire, *France* 18 E8
Chaunay, *France* 20 B4
Chauny, *France* 19 C10
Chausey, Îs., *France* 18 D5
Chaussin, *France* 19 F12
Chautauqua L., *U.S.A.* 110 D5
Chauvigny, *France* 18 F7
Chauvin, *Canada* 105 C6
Chavanges, *France* 19 D11
Chaves, *Brazil* 125 D9
Chaves, *Portugal* 34 D3
Chawang, *Thailand* 65 H2
Chazelles-sur-Lyon, *France* 21 C8
Chazy, *U.S.A.* 111 B11
Cheb, *Czech Rep.* 26 A5
Cheboksarskoye Vdkhr., *Russia* 48 B8
Cheboksary, *Russia* 48 B8
Cheboygan, *U.S.A.* 108 C3
Chebsara, *Russia* 46 C10
Chech, Erg, *Africa* 78 D5
Chechen, Ostrov, *Russia* 49 H8
Chechenia □, *Russia* 49 J7
Checheno-Ingush Republic = Chechenia □, *Russia* 49 J7
Chechnya = Chechenia □, *Russia* 49 J7
Chech'ŏn, *S. Korea* 57 F15
Chęciny, *Poland* 45 H7
Checotah, *U.S.A.* 113 H7
Chedabucto B., *Canada* 103 C7
Cheduba I., *Burma* 67 K18
Cheepie, *Australia* 95 D4
Chef-Boutonne, *France* 20 B3
Chegdomyn, *Russia* 51 D14
Chegga, *Mauritania* 78 C4
Chegutu, *Zimbabwe* 87 F3
Chehalis, *U.S.A.* 116 D4
Chehalis →, *U.S.A.* 116 D3
Cheiron, Mt., *France* 21 E10
Cheju do, *S. Korea* 57 H14
Chekalin, *Russia* 46 E9
Chekiang = Zhejiang □, *China* 59 C13
Chel = Kuru, Bahr el →, *Sudan* 81 F2
Chela, Sa. da, *Angola* 88 B1
Chelan, *U.S.A.* 114 C4
Chelan, L., *U.S.A.* 114 B3
Cheleken, *Turkmenistan* 50 F6
Cheleken Yarymadasy, *Turkmenistan* 71 B7
Chelforó, *Argentina* 128 D3
Chelkar = Shalqar, *Kazakstan* 50 E6
Chelkar Tengiz, Solonchak, *Kazakstan* 50 E7
Chella, *Ethiopia* 81 F4
Chelles, *France* 19 D9
Chełm, *Poland* 45 G10
Chełmno, *Poland* 45 E5
Chelmsford, *U.K.* 13 F8
Chełmża, *Poland* 45 E5
Chelsea, *U.S.A.* 111 C12
Cheltenham, *U.K.* 13 F5
Chelva, *Spain* 32 F4
Chelyabinsk, *Russia* 50 D7
Chelyuskin, C., *Russia* 52 B14
Chemainus, *Canada* 116 B3
Chemba, *Mozam.* 85 H6
Chembar = Belinskiy, *Russia* 48 D6
Chemillé, *France* 18 E6
Chemnitz, *Germany* 24 E8
Chemult, *U.S.A.* 114 E3
Chen, Gora, *Russia* 51 C15
Chenab →, *Pakistan* 68 D4
Chenango Forks, *U.S.A.* 111 D9
Chencha, *Ethiopia* 81 F4
Chenchiang = Zhenjiang, *China* 59 A12
Cheney, *U.S.A.* 114 C5
Cheng Xian, *China* 56 H3
Chengbu, *China* 59 D8
Chengcheng, *China* 56 G5
Chengchou = Zhengzhou, *China* 56 G7
Chengde, *China* 57 D9
Chengdong Hu, *China* 59 A11
Chengdu, *China* 58 B5
Chenggong, *China* 58 E4
Chenggu, *China* 56 H4
Chenghai, *China* 59 F11
Chengjiang, *China* 58 E4
Chengkou, *China* 58 B7
Ch'engmai, *China* 64 C7
Ch'engtu = Chengdu, *China* 58 B5
Chengwu, *China* 56 G8
Chengxi Hu, *China* 59 A11
Chengyang, *China* 57 F11
Chenjiagang, *China* 57 G10
Chenkán, *Mexico* 119 D6
Chennai, *India* 66 N12
Chenôve, *France* 19 E12
Chenxi, *China* 59 C8
Chenzhou, *China* 59 E9
Cheo Reo, *Vietnam* 62 B3
Cheom Ksan, *Cambodia* 64 E5
Chepelare, *Bulgaria* 41 E8
Chepén, *Peru* 124 E3
Chepes, *Argentina* 126 C2
Chepo, *Panama* 120 E4
Chepstow, *U.K.* 13 F5
Cheptulil, Mt., *Kenya* 86 B4
Chequamegon B., *U.S.A.* 112 B9
Cher □, *France* 19 E9
Cher →, *France* 18 E7
Chéradi, *Italy* 31 B10
Cherasco, *Italy* 28 D4
Cheraw, *U.S.A.* 109 H6
Cherbourg, *France* 18 C5
Cherdakly, *Russia* 48 C9
Cherdyn, *Russia* 50 C6
Cheremkhovo, *Russia* 51 D11
Cherepanovo, *Russia* 50 D9
Cherepovets, *Russia* 46 C9
Chergui, Chott ech, *Algeria* 78 B6
Cherikov = Cherykaw, *Belarus* 46 F6
Cherkasy, *Ukraine* 47 H7
Cherkessk, *Russia* 49 H6
Cherlak, *Russia* 50 D8
Chernaya, *Russia* 51 B9
Cherni, *Bulgaria* 40 D7
Chernigov = Chernihiv, *Ukraine* 47 G6
Chernihiv, *Ukraine* 47 G6
Chernivtsi, *Ukraine* 47 H3
Chernobyl = Chornobyl, *Ukraine* 47 G6
Chernogorsk, *Russia* 51 D10
Chernomorskoye = Chornomorske, *Ukraine* 47 K7
Chernovtsy = Chernivtsi, *Ukraine* 47 H3
Chernyakhovsk, *Russia* 9 J19
Chernyanka, *Russia* 47 G9
Chernysheyskiy, *Russia* 51 C12
Chernyye Zemli, *Russia* 49 H8
Cherokee, *Iowa, U.S.A.* 112 D7
Cherokee, *Okla., U.S.A.* 113 G5
Cherokee Village, *U.S.A.* 113 G9
Cherokees, Grand Lake O' The, *U.S.A.* 113 G7
Cherrapunji, *India* 67 G17
Cherry Valley, *Calif., U.S.A.* 117 M10
Cherry Valley, *N.Y., U.S.A.* 111 D10
Cherskiy, *Russia* 51 C17
Cherskogo Khrebet, *Russia* 51 C15
Chertkovo, *Russia* 47 H11
Cherven, *Belarus* 46 F5
Cherven-Bryag, *Bulgaria* 41 C8
Chervonohrad, *Ukraine* 47 G3
Cherwell →, *U.K.* 13 F6
Cherykaw, *Belarus* 46 F6
Chesapeake, *U.S.A.* 108 G7
Chesapeake B., *U.S.A.* 108 G7
Cheshire □, *U.K.* 12 D5
Cheshskaya Guba, *Russia* 50 C5
Cheshunt, *U.K.* 13 F7
Chesil Beach, *U.K.* 13 G5
Chesley, *Canada* 110 B3
Cheste, *Spain* 33 F4
Chester, *U.K.* 12 D5
Chester, *Calif., U.S.A.* 114 F3
Chester, *Ill., U.S.A.* 113 G10
Chester, *Mont., U.S.A.* 114 B8
Chester, *Pa., U.S.A.* 108 F8
Chester, *S.C., U.S.A.* 109 H5
Chester, *Vt., U.S.A.* 111 C12
Chester, *W. Va., U.S.A.* 110 F4
Chester-le-Street, *U.K.* 12 C6
Chesterfield, *U.K.* 12 D6
Chesterfield, Is., *N. Cal.* 96 J7
Chesterfield Inlet, *Canada* 100 B10
Chesterton Ra., *Australia* 95 D4
Chestertown, *U.S.A.* 111 C11
Chesterville, *Canada* 111 A9
Chestnut Ridge, *U.S.A.* 110 F5
Chesuncook L., *U.S.A.* 109 C11
Chéticamp, *Canada* 103 C7
Chetrosu, *Moldova* 43 B12
Chetumal, *Mexico* 119 D7
Chetumal, B. de, *Mexico* 119 D7
Chetwynd, *Canada* 104 B4
Chevanceaux, *France* 20 C3
Cheviot, The, *U.K.* 12 B5
Cheviot Hills, *U.K.* 12 B5
Cheviot Ra., *Australia* 94 D3
Chew Bahir, *Ethiopia* 81 G4
Chewelah, *U.S.A.* 114 B5
Cheyenne, *Okla., U.S.A.* 113 H5
Cheyenne, *Wyo., U.S.A.* 112 E2
Cheyenne →, *U.S.A.* 112 C4
Cheyenne Wells, *U.S.A.* 112 F3
Cheyne B., *Australia* 93 F2
Chhabra, *India* 68 G7
Chhaktala, *India* 68 H6
Chhapra, *India* 69 G11
Chhata, *India* 68 F7
Chhatarpur, *Bihar, India* 69 G11
Chhatarpur, *Mad. P., India* 69 G8
Chhep, *Cambodia* 64 F5
Chhindwara, *Mad. P., India* 69 H8
Chhindwara, *Mad. P., India* 69 H8
Chhlong, *Cambodia* 65 F5
Chhota Tawa →, *India* 68 H7
Chhoti Kali Sindh →, *India* 68 G6
Chhuikhadan, *India* 69 J9
Chhuk, *Cambodia* 65 G5
Chi →, *Thailand* 64 E5
Chiai, *Taiwan* 59 F13
Chiali, *Taiwan* 59 F13
Chiamboni, *Somali Rep.* 84 E8
Chiamussu = Jiamusi, *China* 60 B8
Chianciano Terme, *Italy* 29 E8
Chiang Dao, *Thailand* 64 C2
Chiang Kham, *Thailand* 64 C3
Chiang Khan, *Thailand* 64 D3
Chiang Khong, *Thailand* 58 G3
Chiang Mai, *Thailand* 64 C2
Chiang Rai, *Thailand* 58 H2

Chiang Saen, *Thailand* 58 G3
Chiapa →, *Mexico* 119 D6
Chiapa de Corzo, *Mexico* 119 D6
Chiapas □, *Mexico* 119 D6
Chiaramonte Gulfi, *Italy* 31 E7
Chiaravalle, *Italy* 29 E10
Chiaravalle Centrale, *Italy* 31 D9
Chiari, *Italy* 28 C6
Chiatura, *Georgia* 49 J6
Chiautla, *Mexico* 119 D5
Chiávari, *Italy* 28 D6
Chiavenna, *Italy* 28 B6
Chiba, *Japan* 55 G10
Chiba □, *Japan* 55 G10
Chibabava, *Mozam.* 89 C5
Chibemba, *Cunene, Angola* 85 H2
Chibemba, *Huila, Angola* 88 B2
Chibi, *Zimbabwe* 89 C5
Chibia, *Angola* 85 H2
Chibougamau, *Canada* 102 C5
Chibougamau, L., *Canada* 102 C5
Chibuk, *Nigeria* 83 C7
Chibuto, *Mozam.* 89 C5
Chic-Chocs, Mts., *Canada* 103 C6
Chicacole = Srikakulam, *India* 67 K13
Chicago, *U.S.A.* 108 E2
Chicago Heights, *U.S.A.* 108 E2
Chichagof I., *U.S.A.* 100 C6
Chichén-Itzá, *Mexico* 119 C7
Chicheng, *China* 56 D8
Chichester, *U.K.* 13 G7
Chichester Ra., *Australia* 92 D2
Chichibu, *Japan* 55 F9
Ch'ich'ihaerh = Qiqihar, *China* 51 E13
Chicholi, *India* 68 H8
Chickasha, *U.S.A.* 113 H6
Chiclana de la Frontera, *Spain* 35 J4
Chiclayo, *Peru* 124 E3
Chico, *U.S.A.* 116 F5
Chico →, *Chubut, Argentina* 128 E3
Chico →, *Santa Cruz, Argentina* 128 G3
Chicomo, *Mozam.* 89 C5
Chicontepec, *Mexico* 119 C5
Chicopee, *U.S.A.* 111 D12
Chicoutimi, *Canada* 103 C5
Chicualacuala, *Mozam.* 89 C5
Chidambaram, *India* 66 P11
Chidenguele, *Mozam.* 89 C5
Chidley, C., *Canada* 101 B13
Chiducuane, *Mozam.* 89 C5
Chiede, *Angola* 88 B2
Chiefs Pt., *Canada* 110 B3
Chiem Hoa, *Vietnam* 64 A5
Chiemsee, *Germany* 25 H8
Chiengi, *Zambia* 87 D2
Chiengmai = Chiang Mai, *Thailand* 64 C2
Chienti →, *Italy* 29 E10
Chieri, *Italy* 28 C4
Chiers →, *France* 19 C11
Chiesa in Valmalenco, *Italy* 28 B6
Chiese →, *Italy* 28 C7
Chieti, *Italy* 29 F11
Chifeng, *China* 57 C10
Chigirin, *Ukraine* 47 H7
Chignecto B., *Canada* 103 C7
Chiguana, *Bolivia* 126 A2
Chigwell, *U.K.* 13 F8
Chiha-ri, *N. Korea* 57 E14
Chihli, G. of = Bo Hai, *China* 57 E10
Chihuahua, *Mexico* 118 B3
Chihuahua □, *Mexico* 118 B3
Chiili, *Kazakstan* 50 E7
Chik Bollapur, *India* 66 N10
Chikmagalur, *India* 66 N9
Chikwawa, *Malawi* 87 F3
Chilac, *Mexico* 119 D5
Chilam Chavki, *Pakistan* 69 B6
Chilanga, *Zambia* 87 F2
Chilapa, *Mexico* 119 D5
Chilas, *Pakistan* 69 B6
Chilaw, *Sri Lanka* 66 R11
Chilcotin →, *Canada* 104 C4
Childers, *Australia* 95 D5
Childress, *U.S.A.* 113 H4
Chile ■, *S. Amer.* 128 D2
Chile Rise, *Pac. Oc.* 97 L18
Chilecito, *Argentina* 126 B2
Chilete, *Peru* 124 E3
Chilia, Braţul →, *Romania* 43 E14
Chililabombwe, *Zambia* 87 E2
Chilin = Jilin, *China* 57 C14
Chilka L., *India* 67 K14
Chilko →, *Canada* 104 C4
Chilko L., *Canada* 104 C4
Chillagoe, *Australia* 94 B3
Chillán, *Chile* 126 D1
Chillicothe, *Ill., U.S.A.* 112 E10
Chillicothe, *Mo., U.S.A.* 112 F8
Chillicothe, *Ohio, U.S.A.* 108 F4
Chilliwack, *Canada* 104 D4
Chilo, *India* 68 F5
Chiloane, I., *Mozam.* 89 C5
Chiloé, I. de, *Chile* 122 H3
Chilpancingo, *Mexico* 119 D5
Chiltern Hills, *U.K.* 13 F7
Chilton, *U.S.A.* 108 C1
Chilubi, *Zambia* 87 E2
Chilubula, *Zambia* 87 E3
Chilumba, *Malawi* 87 E3
Chilung, *Taiwan* 59 E13
Chilwa, L., *Malawi* 87 F4
Chimaltitán, *Mexico* 118 C4
Chimán, *Panama* 120 E4
Chimanimani, *Zimbabwe* 89 B5
Chimay, *Belgium* 17 D4
Chimayo, *U.S.A.* 115 H11
Chimbay, *Uzbekistan* 50 E6
Chimborazo, *Ecuador* 122 D3
Chimbote, *Peru* 124 E3
Chimkent = Shymkent, *Kazakstan* 50 E7
Chimoio, *Mozam.* 87 F3
Chimpembe, *Zambia* 87 D2
Chin □, *Burma* 67 J18
Chin Ling Shan = Qinling Shandi, *China* 56 H5
China, *Mexico* 119 B5
China ■, *Asia* 60 D6
China Lake, *U.S.A.* 117 K9
Chinan = Jinan, *China* 56 F9
Chinandega, *Nic.* 120 D2
Chinati Peak, *U.S.A.* 113 L2
Chincha Alta, *Peru* 122 E3
Chinchaga →, *Canada* 104 B5
Chinchilla, *Australia* 95 D5
Chinchilla de Monte Aragón, *Spain* 33 G3
Chinchorro, Banco, *Mexico* 119 D7
Chinchou = Jinzhou, *China* 57 D11
Chincoteague, *U.S.A.* 108 G8
Chinde, *Mozam.* 87 F4
Chindo, *S. Korea* 57 G14
Chindwin →, *Burma* 67 J19
Chineni, *India* 69 C6
Chinga, *Mozam.* 87 F4
Chingola, *Zambia* 87 E2
Chingole, *Malawi* 87 E3
Ch'ingtao = Qingdao, *China* 57 F11
Chinguetti, *Mauritania* 78 D3
Chingune, *Mozam.* 89 C5
Chinhae, *S. Korea* 57 G15
Chinhanguanine, *Mozam.* 89 D5
Chinhoyi, *Zimbabwe* 87 F3
Chini, *India* 68 D8
Chiniot, *Pakistan* 68 D5
Chínipas, *Mexico* 118 B3
Chinji, *Pakistan* 68 C5
Chinju, *S. Korea* 57 G15
Chinle, *U.S.A.* 115 H9
Chinmen, *Taiwan* 59 E13
Chinmen Tao, *Taiwan* 59 E12
Chinnampo = Namp'o, *N. Korea* 57 E13
Chino, *Japan* 55 G9
Chino, *U.S.A.* 117 L9
Chino Valley, *U.S.A.* 115 J7
Chinon, *France* 18 E7
Chinook, *U.S.A.* 114 B9
Chinsali, *Zambia* 87 E3
Chióggia, *Italy* 29 C9
Chíos = Khíos, *Greece* 39 C8
Chipata, *Zambia* 87 E3
Chiperceni, *Moldova* 43 C13
Chipinge, *Zimbabwe* 87 G3
Chipiona, *Spain* 35 J4
Chipley, *U.S.A.* 109 K3
Chipman, *Canada* 103 C6
Chipoka, *Malawi* 87 E3
Chippenham, *U.K.* 13 F5
Chippewa →, *U.S.A.* 112 C8
Chippewa Falls, *U.S.A.* 112 C9
Chipping Norton, *U.K.* 13 F6
Chiprovtsi, *Bulgaria* 40 C6
Chiputneticook Lakes, *U.S.A.* 109 C11
Chiquián, *Peru* 124 F3
Chiquimula, *Guatemala* 120 D2
Chiquinquira, *Colombia* 124 B4
Chir →, *Russia* 49 F6
Chirala, *India* 66 M12
Chiramba, *Mozam.* 87 F3
Chirawa, *India* 68 E6
Chirchiq, *Uzbekistan* 50 E7
Chiredzi, *Zimbabwe* 89 C5
Chirfa, *Niger* 79 D8
Chiricahua Peak, *U.S.A.* 115 L9
Chiriquí, G. de, *Panama* 120 E3
Chiriquí, L. de, *Panama* 120 E3
Chirivira Falls, *Zimbabwe* 87 G3
Chirmiri, *India* 67 H13
Chirnogi, *Romania* 43 F11
Chirpan, *Bulgaria* 41 D9
Chirripó Grande, Cerro, *Costa Rica* 120 E3
Chirundu, *Zimbabwe* 89 B4
Chisamba, *Zambia* 87 E2
Chisapani Garhi, *Nepal* 67 F14
Chisasibi, *Canada* 102 B4
Ch'ishan, *Taiwan* 59 F13
Chisholm, *Canada* 104 C6
Chisholm, *U.S.A.* 112 B8
Chishtian Mandi, *Pakistan* 68 E5
Chishui, *China* 58 C5
Chishui He →, *China* 58 C5
Chisimaio, *Somali Rep.* 77 G8
Chisimba Falls, *Zambia* 87 E3
Chişinău, *Moldova* 43 C13
Chişineu Criş, *Romania* 42 D6
Chisone →, *Italy* 28 D4
Chisos Mts., *U.S.A.* 113 L3
Chistopol, *Russia* 48 C10
Chita, *Russia* 51 D12
Chitipa, *Malawi* 87 D3
Chitose, *Japan* 54 C10
Chitral, *Pakistan* 66 B7
Chitré, *Panama* 120 E3
Chittagong, *Bangla.* 67 H17
Chittagong □, *Bangla.* 67 G17
Chittaurgarh, *India* 68 G6
Chittoor, *India* 66 N11
Chitungwiza, *Zimbabwe* 87 F3
Chiusi, *Italy* 29 E8
Chiva, *Spain* 33 F4
Chivasso, *Italy* 28 C4
Chivhu, *Zimbabwe* 87 F3
Chivilcoy, *Argentina* 126 C4
Chiwanda, *Tanzania* 87 E3
Chixi, *China* 59 G9
Chizera, *Zambia* 87 E2
Chkalov = Orenburg, *Russia* 50 D6
Chkolovsk, *Russia* 48 B6
Chloride, *U.S.A.* 117 K12
Chlumec nad Cidlinou, *Czech Rep.* 26 A8
Chmielnik, *Poland* 45 H7
Cho Bo, *Vietnam* 58 G5
Cho-do, *N. Korea* 57 E13
Cho Phuoc Hai, *Vietnam* 65 G6
Choba, *Kenya* 86 B4
Chobe National Park, *Botswana* 88 B4
Choch'iwŏn, *S. Korea* 57 F14
Chocianów, *Poland* 45 G2
Chociwel, *Poland* 44 E2
Chocolate Mts., *U.S.A.* 117 M11
Choctawatchee →, *U.S.A.* 109 K3
Chodecz, *Poland* 45 F6
Chodov, *Czech Rep.* 26 A5
Chodziez, *Poland* 45 F3
Choele Choel, *Argentina* 128 D3
Choix, *Mexico* 118 B3
Chojna, *Poland* 45 F1
Chojnice, *Poland* 44 E4
Chojnów, *Poland* 45 G2
Chōkai-San, *Japan* 54 E10
Choke, *Ethiopia* 81 E4
Choke Canyon L., *U.S.A.* 113 L5
Chokurdakh, *Russia* 51 B15
Cholame, *U.S.A.* 116 K6
Cholet, *France* 18 E6
Cholguan, *Chile* 126 D1
Choluteca, *Honduras* 120 D2
Choluteca →, *Honduras* 120 D2
Chom Bung, *Thailand* 64 F2
Chom Thong, *Thailand* 64 C2
Choma, *Zambia* 87 F2
Chomen Swamp, *Ethiopia* 81 F4
Chomun, *India* 68 F6
Chomutov, *Czech Rep.* 26 A6
Chon Buri, *Thailand* 64 F3
Chon Thanh, *Vietnam* 65 G6
Ch'onan, *S. Korea* 57 F14
Chone, *Ecuador* 124 D3
Chong Kai, *Cambodia* 64 F4
Chong Mek, *Thailand* 64 E5
Chongde, *China* 59 B13
Chŏngdo, *S. Korea* 57 G15
Chŏngha, *S. Korea* 57 F15
Chŏngjin, *N. Korea* 57 D15
Chŏngjiu, *S. Korea* 57 F14
Chŏngju, *N. Korea* 57 E13
Chongli, *China* 56 D8
Chongming, *China* 59 B13
Chongming Dao, *China* 59 B13
Chongqing, *Chongqing, China* 58 C6
Chongqing, *Sichuan, China* 58 B4
Chongqing □, *China* 60 C5
Chongqing Shi □, *China* 58 C6
Chongren, *China* 59 D11
Chonguene, *Mozam.* 89 C5
Chŏngŭp, *S. Korea* 57 G14
Chongyi, *China* 59 E10
Chongzuo, *China* 58 F6
Chŏnju, *S. Korea* 57 G14
Chonos, Arch. de los, *Chile* 122 H3
Chop, *Ukraine* 47 H2
Chopim →, *Brazil* 127 B5
Chor, *Pakistan* 68 G3
Chorbat La, *India* 69 B7
Chorley, *U.K.* 12 D5
Chornobyl, *Ukraine* 47 G6
Chornomorske, *Ukraine* 47 K7
Chorolque, Cerro, *Bolivia* 126 A2
Choroszcz, *Poland* 45 E9
Chorregon, *Australia* 94 C3
Chortkiv, *Ukraine* 47 H3
Ch'ŏrwon, *S. Korea* 57 E14
Chorzele, *Poland* 45 E7
Chorzów, *Poland* 45 H5
Chos-Malal, *Argentina* 126 D1
Ch'osan, *N. Korea* 57 D13
Choszczno, *Poland* 45 E2
Choteau, *U.S.A.* 114 C7
Chotěboř, *Czech Rep.* 26 B8
Chotila, *India* 68 H4
Chotta Udepur, *India* 68 H6
Chowchilla, *U.S.A.* 116 H6
Choybalsan, *Mongolia* 60 B6
Christchurch, *N.Z.* 91 K4
Christchurch, *U.K.* 13 G6
Christian I., *Canada* 110 B4
Christiana, *S. Africa* 88 D4
Christiansfeld, *Denmark* 11 J3
Christiansted, *Virgin Is.* 121 C7
Christie B., *Canada* 105 A6
Christina →, *Canada* 105 B6
Christmas Cr. →, *Australia* 92 C4
Christmas I. = Kiritimati, *Kiribati* 97 G12
Christmas I., *Ind. Oc.* 96 J2
Christopher L., *Australia* 93 D4
Chrudim, *Czech Rep.* 26 B8
Chrzanów, *Poland* 45 H6
Chtimba, *Malawi* 87 E3
Chu = Shu, *Kazakstan* 50 E8
Chu = Shu →, *Kazakstan* 52 E10
Chu →, *Vietnam* 64 C5
Chu Lai, *Vietnam* 64 E7
Ch'uanchou = Quanzhou, *China* 59 E12
Chuankou, *China* 56 G6
Chubbuck, *U.S.A.* 114 E7
Chūbu □, *Japan* 55 F8
Chubut →, *Argentina* 122 H4
Chuchi L., *Canada* 104 B4
Chuda, *India* 68 H4
Chudovo, *Russia* 46 C6
Chudskoye, Ozero, *Russia* 9 G22
Chūgoku □, *Japan* 55 G6
Chūgoku-Sanchi, *Japan* 55 G6
Chuguyev = Chuhuyiv, *Ukraine* 47 H9
Chugwater, *U.S.A.* 112 E2
Chuhuyiv, *Ukraine* 47 H9
Chukchi Sea, *Russia* 51 C19
Chukotskoye Nagorye, *Russia* 51 C18
Chula Vista, *U.S.A.* 117 N9
Chulucanas, *Peru* 124 E2
Chulym →, *Russia* 50 D9
Chum Phae, *Thailand* 64 D4
Chum Saeng, *Thailand* 64 E3
Chumar, *India* 69 C8
Chumbicha, *Argentina* 126 B2
Chumerna, *Bulgaria* 41 D9
Chumikan, *Russia* 51 D14
Chumphon, *Thailand* 65 G2
Chumuare, *Mozam.* 87 E3
Chumunjin, *S. Korea* 57 F15
Chuna →, *Russia* 51 D10
Chun'an, *China* 59 C12
Ch'unch'ŏn, *S. Korea* 57 F14
Chunchura, *India* 69 H13
Chunga, *Zambia* 87 F2
Chunggang-ŭp, *N. Korea* 57 D14
Chunghwa, *N. Korea* 57 E13
Ch'ungju, *S. Korea* 57 F14
Chungking = Chongqing, *China* 58 C6
Chungli, *Taiwan* 59 E13
Ch'ungmu, *S. Korea* 57 G15
Chungt'iaoshan = Zhongtiao Shan, *China* 56 G6
Chungyang Shanmo, *Taiwan* 59 F13
Chunian, *Pakistan* 68 D6
Chunya, *Tanzania* 87 D3
Chunyang, *China* 57 C15
Chuquibamba, *Peru* 124 G4
Chuquicamata, *Chile* 126 A2
Chur, *Switz.* 25 J5
Churachandpur, *India* 67 G18
Churchill, *Canada* 105 B10
Churchill →, *Man., Canada* 105 B10
Churchill →, *Nfld., Canada* 103 B7
Churchill, C., *Canada* 105 B10
Churchill Falls, *Canada* 103 B7
Churchill L., *Canada* 105 B7
Churchill Pk., *Canada* 104 B3
Churki, *India* 69 H10
Churu, *India* 68 E6
Churún Merú = Angel Falls, *Venezuela* 124 B6
Chushal, *India* 69 C8
Chuska Mts., *U.S.A.* 115 H9
Chusovoy, *Russia* 50 D6
Chute-aux-Outardes, *Canada* 103 C6
Chuuronjang, *N. Korea* 57 D15
Chuvash Republic = Chuvashia □, *Russia* 48 C8
Chuvashia □, *Russia* 48 C8
Chuwārtah, *Iraq* 70 C5
Chuxiong, *China* 58 E3
Chuy, *Uruguay* 127 C5
Chuzhou, *China* 59 A12
Ci Xian, *China* 56 F8
Ciacova, *Romania* 42 E6
Ciadâr-Lunga, *Moldova* 43 D13
Ciamis, *Indonesia* 63 G13
Cianjur, *Indonesia* 63 G12
Cianorte, *Brazil* 127 A5
Cibola, *U.S.A.* 117 M12
Cicero, *U.S.A.* 108 E2
Cidacos →, *Spain* 32 C3
Cide, *Turkey* 72 B5
Ciechanów, *Poland* 45 F7
Ciechanowiec, *Poland* 45 F9
Ciechocinek, *Poland* 45 F5
Ciego de Avila, *Cuba* 120 B4
Ciénaga, *Colombia* 124 A4
Cienfuegos, *Cuba* 120 B3
Cierp, *France* 20 F4
Cíes, Is., *Spain* 34 C2
Cieszanów, *Poland* 45 H10
Cieszyn, *Poland* 45 J5
Cieza, *Spain* 33 G3
Çifteler, *Turkey* 72 C4
Cifuentes, *Spain* 32 E2
Cihanbeyli, *Turkey* 72 C5
Cihuatlán, *Mexico* 118 D4
Cijara, Embalse de, *Spain* 35 F6
Cijulang, *Indonesia* 63 G13
Cilacap, *Indonesia* 63 G13
Çıldır, *Turkey* 73 B10
Çıldır Gölü, *Turkey* 73 B10
Cili, *China* 59 C8
Cilibia, *Romania* 43 E12
Cilicia, *Turkey* 72 D5
Cill Chainnigh = Kilkenny, *Ireland* 15 D4
Cilo Dağı, *Turkey* 73 D10
Cima, *U.S.A.* 117 K11
Cimarron, *Kans., U.S.A.* 113 G4
Cimarron, *N. Mex., U.S.A.* 113 G2
Cimarron →, *U.S.A.* 113 G6
Cimişlia, *Moldova* 43 D13
Cimone, Mte., *Italy* 28 D7
Çinar, *Turkey* 73 D9
Çınarcık, *Turkey* 41 F13
Cinca →, *Spain* 32 D5
Cincar, *Bos.-H.* 42 G2
Cincinnati, *U.S.A.* 108 F3
Cincinnatus, *U.S.A.* 111 D9
Çine, *Turkey* 39 D10
Ciney, *Belgium* 17 D5
Cíngoli, *Italy* 29 E10
Cinigiano, *Italy* 29 F8
Cinto, Mte., *France* 21 F12
Cintruénigo, *Spain* 32 C3
Ciocile, *Romania* 43 F12
Ciolănești din Deal, *Romania* 43 F10
Ciorani, *Romania* 43 F11
Čiovo, *Croatia* 29 E13
Circeo, Mte., *Italy* 30 A6
Çirçir, *Turkey* 72 C7
Circle, *Alaska, U.S.A.* 100 B5
Circle, *Mont., U.S.A.* 112 B2
Circleville, *U.S.A.* 108 F4
Cirebon, *Indonesia* 63 G13
Ciremai, *Indonesia* 63 G13
Cirencester, *U.K.* 13 F6
Cireşu, *Romania* 42 F7
Cirey-sur-Vezouze, *France* 19 D13
Ciriè, *Italy* 28 C4
Cirium, *Cyprus* 36 E11
Cirò, *Italy* 31 C10
Cirò Marina, *Italy* 31 C10
Ciron →, *France* 20 D3
Cisco, *U.S.A.* 113 J5
Cislău, *Romania* 43 E11
Cisna, *Poland* 45 J9
Cisnădie, *Romania* 43 E9
Cisterna di Latina, *Italy* 30 A5
Cisternino, *Italy* 31 B10
Cistierna, *Spain* 34 C5
Citeli-Ckaro = Tsiteli-Tsqaro, *Georgia* 49 K8
Citlaltépetl, *Mexico* 119 D5
Citrus Heights, *U.S.A.* 116 G5
Citrusdal, *S. Africa* 88 E2
Città della Pieve, *Italy* 29 F9
Città di Castello, *Italy* 29 E9
Città Sant' Angelo, *Italy* 29 F11
Cittadella, *Italy* 29 C8
Cittaducale, *Italy* 29 F9
Cittanova, *Italy* 31 D9
Ciuc, Munţii, *Romania* 43 D11
Ciucaş, Vf., *Romania* 43 E10
Ciucea, *Romania* 42 D7
Ciuciulea, *Moldova* 43 C12
Ciuciuleni, *Moldova* 43 C13
Ciudad Altamirano, *Mexico* 118 D4
Ciudad Bolívar, *Venezuela* 124 B6
Ciudad Camargo, *Mexico* 118 B3
Ciudad de Valles, *Mexico* 119 C5
Ciudad del Carmen, *Mexico* 119 D6
Ciudad del Este, *Paraguay* 127 B5
Ciudad Delicias = Delicias, *Mexico* 118 B3
Ciudad Guayana, *Venezuela* 124 B6
Ciudad Guerrero, *Mexico* 118 B3
Ciudad Guzmán, *Mexico* 118 D4
Ciudad Juárez, *Mexico* 118 A3
Ciudad Madero, *Mexico* 119 C5
Ciudad Mante, *Mexico* 119 C5
Ciudad Obregón, *Mexico* 118 B3
Ciudad Real, *Spain* 35 G7
Ciudad Real □, *Spain* 35 G7
Ciudad Rodrigo, *Spain* 34 E4
Ciudad Trujillo = Santo Domingo, *Dom. Rep.* 121 C6
Ciudad Victoria, *Mexico* 119 C5
Ciudadela, *Spain* 37 B10
Ciulniţa, *Romania* 43 F12
Ciumeghiu, *Romania* 42 D6
Ciuperceni, *Romania* 42 F8
Civa Burnu, *Turkey* 72 B7
Cividale del Friuli, *Italy* 29 B10
Cívita Castellana, *Italy* 29 F9
Civitanova Marche, *Italy* 29 E10
Civitavécchia, *Italy* 29 F8
Civray, *France* 20 B4
Çivril, *Turkey* 39 C11
Cixerri →, *Italy* 30 C1
Cixi, *China* 59 B13
Cizre, *Turkey* 70 B4
Cizur Mayor, *Spain* 32 C3
Clackmannanshire □, *U.K.* 14 E5
Clacton-on-Sea, *U.K.* 13 F9
Clain →, *France* 18 F7
Claire, L., *Canada* 104 B6
Clairton, *U.S.A.* 110 F5
Clairvaux-les-Lacs, *France* 19 F12
Claise →, *France* 20 B5
Clallam Bay, *U.S.A.* 116 B2
Clamecy, *France* 19 E10
Clanton, *U.S.A.* 109 J2
Clanwilliam, *S. Africa* 88 E2
Clara, *Ireland* 15 C4
Claraville, *U.S.A.* 117 K8
Clare, *Australia* 95 E2
Clare, *U.S.A.* 108 D3
Clare □, *Ireland* 15 D3
Clare →, *Ireland* 15 C2
Clare I., *Ireland* 15 C1
Claremont, *Calif., U.S.A.* 117 L9
Claremont, *N.H., U.S.A.* 111 C12
Claremont Pt., *Australia* 94 A3
Claremore, *U.S.A.* 113 G7
Claremorris, *Ireland* 15 C3
Clarence →, *Australia* 95 D5
Clarence →, *N.Z.* 91 K4
Clarence, I., *Chile* 128 G2
Clarence I., *Antarctica* 5 C18
Clarence Str., *Australia* 92 B5
Clarence Town, *Bahamas* 121 B5
Clarendon, *Pa., U.S.A.* 110 E5
Clarendon, *Tex., U.S.A.* 113 H4
Clarenville, *Canada* 103 C9
Claresholm, *Canada* 104 D6
Clarie Coast, *Antarctica* 5 C9
Clarinda, *U.S.A.* 112 E7
Clarion, *Iowa, U.S.A.* 112 D8
Clarion, *Pa., U.S.A.* 110 E5
Clarion →, *U.S.A.* 110 E5
Clark, *U.S.A.* 112 C6
Clark, Pt., *Canada* 110 B3
Clark Fork, *U.S.A.* 114 B5
Clark Fork →, *U.S.A.* 114 B5

Clark Hill L., *U.S.A.* 109 J4
Clarkdale, *U.S.A.* 115 J7
Clarke City, *Canada* 103 B6
Clarke I., *Australia* 94 G4
Clarke Ra., *Australia* 94 C4
Clark's Fork →, *U.S.A.* 114 D9
Clark's Harbour, *Canada* .. 103 D6
Clarks Summit, *U.S.A.* 111 E9
Clarksburg, *U.S.A.* 108 F5
Clarksdale, *U.S.A.* 113 H9
Clarksville, *Ark., U.S.A.* 113 H8
Clarksville, *Tenn., U.S.A.* 109 G2
Clarksville, *Tex., U.S.A.* 113 J7
Clatskanie, *U.S.A.* 116 D3
Claude, *U.S.A.* 113 H4
Claveria, *Phil.* 61 B4
Clay □, *Romania* 43 D8
Clay, *U.S.A.* 116 G5
Clay Center, *U.S.A.* 112 F6
Claypool, *U.S.A.* 115 K8
Claysburg, *U.S.A.* 110 F6
Claysville, *U.S.A.* 110 F4
Clayton, *N. Mex., U.S.A.* 113 G3
Clayton, *N.Y., U.S.A.* 111 B8
Clear, C., *Ireland* 15 E2
Clear, L., *Canada* 110 A7
Clear Hills, *Canada* 104 B5
Clear I., *Ireland* 15 E2
Clear, L., *U.S.A.* 116 F4
Clear Lake, *Iowa, U.S.A.* 112 D8
Clear Lake, *S. Dak., U.S.A.* 112 C6
Clear Lake Reservoir,
    U.S.A. 114 F3
Clearfield, *Pa., U.S.A.* 110 E6
Clearfield, *Utah, U.S.A.* 114 F8
Clearlake, *U.S.A.* 114 G2
Clearlake Highlands, *U.S.A.* 116 G4
Clearwater, *Canada* 104 C4
Clearwater, *U.S.A.* 109 M4
Clearwater →, *Alta.,*
    Canada 104 C6
Clearwater →, *Alta.,*
    Canada 105 B6
Clearwater L., *Canada* 105 C9
Clearwater Mts., *Canada* 114 C6
Clearwater Prov. Park,
    Canada 105 C8
Clearwater River Prov. Park,
    Canada 105 B7
Cleburne, *U.S.A.* 113 J6
Clee Hills, *U.K.* 13 E5
Cleethorpes, *U.K.* 12 D7
Cleeve Cloud, *U.K.* 13 F6
Clelles, *France* 21 D9
Clemson, *U.S.A.* 109 H4
Clerke Reef, *Australia* 92 C2
Clermont, *Australia* 94 C4
Clermont, *France* 19 C9
Clermont, *U.S.A.* 109 L5
Clermont-en-Argonne,
    France 19 C12
Clermont-Ferrand, *France* .. 20 C7
Clermont-l'Hérault, *France* . 20 E7
Clerval, *France* 19 E13
Clervaux, *Lux.* 17 D6
Cles, *Italy* 28 B8
Cleve, *Australia* 95 E2
Clevedon, *U.K.* 13 F5
Cleveland, *Miss., U.S.A.* 113 J9
Cleveland, *Ohio, U.S.A.* 110 E3
Cleveland, *Okla., U.S.A.* 113 G6
Cleveland, *Tenn., U.S.A.* 109 H3
Cleveland, *Tex., U.S.A.* 113 K7
Cleveland, C., *Australia* 94 B4
Cleveland, Mt., *U.S.A.* 114 B7
Cleveland Heights, *U.S.A.* . 110 E3
Clevelândia, *Brazil* 127 B5
Clew B., *Ireland* 15 C2
Clewiston, *U.S.A.* 109 M5
Clifden, *Ireland* 15 C1
Clifden, *N.Z.* 91 M1
Cliffdell, *U.S.A.* 116 D5
Cliffy Hd., *Australia* 93 G2
Clifton, *Australia* 95 D5
Clifton, *Ariz., U.S.A.* 115 K9
Clifton, *Colo., U.S.A.* 115 G9
Clifton, *Tex., U.S.A.* 113 K6
Clifton Beach, *Australia* 94 B4
Climax, *Canada* 105 D7
Clinch →, *U.S.A.* 109 H3
Clingmans Dome, *U.S.A.* 109 H4
Clint, *U.S.A.* 115 L10
Clinton, *B.C., Canada* 104 C4
Clinton, *Ont., Canada* 102 D3
Clinton, *N.Z.* 91 M2
Clinton, *Ark., U.S.A.* 113 H8
Clinton, *Conn., U.S.A.* 111 E12
Clinton, *Ill., U.S.A.* 112 E10
Clinton, *Ind., U.S.A.* 108 F2
Clinton, *Iowa, U.S.A.* 112 E9
Clinton, *Mass., U.S.A.* 111 D13
Clinton, *Miss., U.S.A.* 113 J9
Clinton, *Mo., U.S.A.* 112 F8
Clinton, *N.C., U.S.A.* 109 H6
Clinton, *Okla., U.S.A.* 113 H5
Clinton, *S.C., U.S.A.* 109 H5
Clinton, *Tenn., U.S.A.* 109 G3
Clinton, *Wash., U.S.A.* 116 C4
Clinton C., *Australia* 94 C5
Clinton Colden L., *Canada* . 100 B9
Clintonville, *U.S.A.* 112 C10
Clipperton, I., *Pac. Oc.* 97 F17
Clisham, *U.K.* 14 D2
Clisson, *France* 18 E5
Clitheroe, *U.K.* 12 D5
Clo-oose, *Canada* 116 B2
Cloates, Pt., *Australia* 92 D1
Clocolan, *S. Africa* 89 D4
Clodomira, *Argentina* 126 B3
Clogher Hd., *Ireland* 15 C5
Clonakilty, *Ireland* 15 E3
Clonakilty B., *Ireland* 15 E3

Cloncurry, *Australia* 94 C3
Cloncurry →, *Australia* 94 B3
Clondalkin, *Ireland* 15 C5
Clones, *Ireland* 15 B4
Clonmel, *Ireland* 15 D4
Cloppenburg, *Germany* 24 C4
Cloquet, *U.S.A.* 112 B8
Clorinda, *Argentina* 126 B4
Cloud Bay, *Canada* 102 C2
Cloud Peak, *U.S.A.* 114 D10
Cloudcroft, *U.S.A.* 115 K11
Cloverdale, *U.S.A.* 116 G4
Clovis, *Calif., U.S.A.* 116 J7
Clovis, *N. Mex., U.S.A.* 113 H3
Cloyes-sur-le-Loir, *France* .. 18 E8
Cloyne, *Canada* 110 B7
Cluj □, *Romania* 43 D8
Cluj-Napoca, *Romania* 43 D8
Clunes, *Australia* 95 F3
Cluny, *France* 19 F11
Cluses, *France* 19 F13
Clusone, *Italy* 28 C6
Clutha →, *N.Z.* 91 M2
Clwyd →, *U.K.* 12 D4
Clyde, *Canada* 104 C6
Clyde, *N.Z.* 91 L2
Clyde, *U.S.A.* 110 C8
Clyde →, *U.K.* 14 F4
Clyde, Firth of, *U.K.* 14 F3
Clyde River, *Canada* 101 A13
Clydebank, *U.K.* 14 F4
Clymer, *N.Y., U.S.A.* 110 D5
Clymer, *Pa., U.S.A.* 110 D5
Ćmielów, *Poland* 45 H8
Côa →, *Portugal* 34 D3
Coachella, *U.S.A.* 117 M10
Coachella Canal, *U.S.A.* 117 N12
Coahoma, *U.S.A.* 113 J4
Coahuayana →, *Mexico* 118 D4
Coahuila □, *Mexico* 118 B4
Coal →, *Canada* 104 B3
Coalane, *Mozam.* 87 F4
Coalcomán, *Mexico* 118 D4
Coaldale, *Canada* 104 D6
Coalgate, *U.S.A.* 113 H6
Coalinga, *U.S.A.* 116 J6
Coalisland, *U.K.* 15 B5
Coalville, *U.K.* 12 E6
Coalville, *U.S.A.* 114 F8
Coari, *Brazil* 124 D6
Coast □, *Kenya* 86 C4
Coast Mts., *Canada* 104 C3
Coast Ranges, *U.S.A.* 116 G4
Coatbridge, *U.K.* 14 F4
Coatepec, *Mexico* 119 D5
Coatepeque, *Guatemala* 120 D1
Coatesville, *U.S.A.* 108 F8
Coaticook, *Canada* 103 C5
Coats I., *Canada* 101 B11
Coats Land, *Antarctica* 5 D1
Coatzacoalcos, *Mexico* 119 D6
Cobadin, *Romania* 43 F13
Cobalt, *Canada* 102 C4
Cobán, *Guatemala* 120 C1
Çobanlar, *Turkey* 39 C12
Cobar, *Australia* 95 E4
Cobargo, *Australia* 95 F4
Cóbh, *Ireland* 15 E3
Cobija, *Bolivia* 124 F5
Cobleskill, *U.S.A.* 111 D10
Coboconk, *Canada* 110 B6
Cobourg, *Canada* 102 D4
Cobourg Pen., *Australia* 92 B5
Cobram, *Australia* 95 F4
Cóbué, *Mozam.* 87 E3
Coburg, *Germany* 25 E6
Coca, *Spain* 34 D6
Cocanada = Kakinada, *India* 67 L13
Cocentaina, *Spain* 33 G4
Cochabamba, *Bolivia* 124 G5
Cochem, *Germany* 25 E3
Cochemane, *Mozam.* 87 F3
Cochin, *India* 66 Q10
Cochin China, *Vietnam* 65 G6
Cochran, *U.S.A.* 109 J4
Cochrane, *Alta., Canada* 104 C6
Cochrane, *Ont., Canada* 102 C3
Cochrane, *Chile* 128 F2
Cochrane →, *Canada* 105 B8
Cochrane, L., *Chile* 128 F2
Cochranton, *U.S.A.* 110 E4
Cockburn, *Australia* 95 E3
Cockburn, Canal, *Chile* 122 J3
Cockburn I., *Canada* 102 C3
Cockburn Ra., *Australia* 92 C4
Cockermouth, *U.K.* 12 C4
Cocklebiddy, *Australia* 93 F4
Coco →, *Cent. Amer.* 120 D3
Coco, I. del, *Pac. Oc.* 97 G19
Cocoa, *U.S.A.* 109 L5
Cocobeach, *Gabon* 84 D1
Cocora, *Romania* 43 F12
Cocos Is., *Ind. Oc.* 96 J1
Cod, C., *U.S.A.* 108 D10
Codajás, *Brazil* 124 D6
Codigoro, *Italy* 29 D9
Codlea, *Romania* 43 E10
Codó, *Brazil* 125 D10
Codogno, *Italy* 28 C6
Codróipo, *Italy* 29 C10
Codru, Munţii, *Romania* 42 D7
Cody, *U.S.A.* 114 D9
Coe Hill, *Canada* 110 B7
Coelemu, *Chile* 126 D1
Coen, *Australia* 94 A3
Coesfeld, *Germany* 24 D3
Cœur d'Alene, *U.S.A.* 114 C5
Cœur d'Alene L., *U.S.A.* 114 C5
Coevorden, *Neths.* 17 B6
Cofete, *Canary Is.* 37 F5
Coffeyville, *U.S.A.* 113 G7

Coffin B., *Australia* 95 E2
Coffin Bay, *Australia* 95 E2
Coffin Bay Peninsula,
    Australia 95 E2
Coffs Harbour, *Australia* 95 E5
Cofrentes, *Spain* 33 F3
Cogalnic →, *Moldova* 43 E14
Cogealac, *Romania* 43 F13
Coghinas →, *Italy* 30 B1
Coghinas, L. del, *Italy* 30 B2
Cognac, *France* 20 C3
Cogne, *Italy* 28 C4
Cogolin, *France* 21 E10
Cogolludo, *Spain* 32 E1
Cohocton, *U.S.A.* 110 D7
Cohocton →, *U.S.A.* 110 D7
Cohoes, *U.S.A.* 111 D11
Cohuna, *Australia* 95 F3
Coiba, I., *Panama* 120 E3
Coig →, *Argentina* 128 G3
Coigeach, Rubha, *U.K.* 14 C3
Coihaique, *Chile* 128 F2
Coimbatore, *India* 66 P10
Coimbra, *Brazil* 124 G7
Coimbra, *Portugal* 34 E2
Coimbra □, *Portugal* 34 E2
Coín, *Spain* 35 J6
Coipasa, Salar de, *Bolivia* .. 124 G5
Cojimies, *Ecuador* 124 C3
Cojocna, *Romania* 43 D8
Cojutepequé, *El Salv.* 120 D2
Coka, *Serbia, Yug.* 42 E5
Cokeville, *U.S.A.* 114 E8
Colac, *Australia* 95 F3
Colatina, *Brazil* 125 G10
Colbeck, C., *Antarctica* 5 D13
Colborne, *Canada* 110 C7
Colby, *U.S.A.* 112 F4
Colchester, *U.K.* 13 F8
Cold L., *Canada* 105 C7
Coldstream, *Canada* 104 C5
Coldstream, *U.K.* 14 F6
Coldwater, *Canada* 110 B5
Coldwater, *Kans., U.S.A.* 113 G5
Coldwater, *Mich., U.S.A.* 108 E3
Coleambally, *Australia* 95 E4
Colebrook, *U.S.A.* 111 B13
Coleman, *U.S.A.* 113 K5
Coleman →, *Australia* 94 B3
Colenso, *S. Africa* 89 D4
Coleraine, *Australia* 95 F3
Coleraine, *U.K.* 15 A5
Coleridge, L., *N.Z.* 91 K3
Colesberg, *S. Africa* 88 E4
Coleville, *U.S.A.* 116 G7
Colfax, *Calif., U.S.A.* 116 F6
Colfax, *La., U.S.A.* 113 K8
Colfax, *Wash., U.S.A.* 114 C5
Colhué Huapi, L., *Argentina* 128 F3
Colibaşi, *Moldova* 43 E13
Colibaşi, *Romania* 43 F9
Cólico, *Italy* 28 B6
Coligny, *France* 19 F12
Coligny, *S. Africa* 89 D4
Colima, *Mexico* 118 D4
Colima □, *Mexico* 118 D4
Colima, Nevado de, *Mexico* 118 D4
Colina, *Chile* 126 C1
Colina do Norte,
    Guinea-Biss. 82 C2
Colinas, *Brazil* 125 E10
Colindres, *Spain* 34 B7
Coll, *U.K.* 14 E2
Collaguasi, *Chile* 126 A2
Collarada, Peña, *Spain* 32 C4
Collarenebri, *Australia* 95 D4
Colle di Val d'Elsa, *Italy* 28 E8
Collécchio, *Italy* 28 D7
Colleen Bawn, *Zimbabwe* 87 G2
College Park, *U.S.A.* 109 J3
College Station, *U.S.A.* 113 K6
Collesalvetti, *Italy* 28 E7
Collie, *Australia* 93 F2
Collier B., *Australia* 92 C3
Collier Ra., *Australia* 93 D2
Collina, Passo di, *Italy* 28 D7
Collingwood, *Canada* 102 D3
Collingwood, *N.Z.* 91 J4
Collins, *Canada* 102 B2
Collinsville, *Australia* 94 C4
Collipulli, *Chile* 126 D1
Collooney, *Ireland* 15 B3
Colmar, *France* 19 D14
Colmars, *France* 21 D10
Colmenar, *Spain* 35 J6
Colmenar de Oreja, *Spain* .. 34 E7
Colmenar Viejo, *Spain* 34 E7
Colo →, *Australia* 95 E5
Cologne = Köln, *Germany* .. 24 E2
Colom, I. d'en, *Spain* 37 B11
Coloma, *U.S.A.* 116 G6
Colomb-Béchar = Béchar,
    Algeria 78 B4
Colombey-les-Belles, *France* 19 D12
Colombey-les-Deux-Églises,
    France 19 D11
Colombia ■, *S. Amer.* 124 C4
Colombian Basin, *S. Amer.* 98 H12
Colombo, *Sri Lanka* 66 R11
Colomiers, *France* 20 E5
Colón, *Buenos Aires,*
    Argentina 126 C3
Colón, *Entre Ríos, Argentina* 126 C4
Colón, *Cuba* 120 B3
Colón, *Panama* 120 E4
Colonia de Sant Jordi, *Spain* 37 B9
Colonia del Sacramento,
    Uruguay 126 C4
Colonia Dora, *Argentina* 126 B3
Colonial Beach, *U.S.A.* 108 F7
Colonie, *U.S.A.* 111 D11

Colonna, C., *Italy* 31 C10
Colonsay, *Canada* 105 C7
Colonsay, *U.K.* 14 E2
Colorado □, *U.S.A.* 115 G10
Colorado →, *Argentina* 128 D4
Colorado →, *N. Amer.* 115 L6
Colorado →, *U.S.A.* 113 L7
Colorado City, *U.S.A.* 113 J4
Colorado Plateau, *U.S.A.* 115 H8
Colorado River Aqueduct,
    U.S.A. 117 L12
Colorado Springs, *U.S.A.* 112 F2
Colorno, *Italy* 28 D7
Colotlán, *Mexico* 118 C4
Colstrip, *U.S.A.* 114 D10
Colton, *U.S.A.* 111 B10
Columbia, *Ky., U.S.A.* 108 G3
Columbia, *La., U.S.A.* 113 J8
Columbia, *Miss., U.S.A.* 113 K10
Columbia, *Mo., U.S.A.* 112 F8
Columbia, *Pa., U.S.A.* 111 F8
Columbia, *S.C., U.S.A.* 109 J5
Columbia, *Tenn., U.S.A.* 109 H2
Columbia →, *N. Amer.* 116 D2
Columbia, C., *Canada* 4 A4
Columbia, District of □,
    U.S.A. 108 F7
Columbia, Mt., *Canada* 104 C5
Columbia Basin, *U.S.A.* 114 C4
Columbia Falls, *U.S.A.* 114 B6
Columbia Mts., *Canada* 104 C5
Columbia Plateau, *U.S.A.* 114 D5
Columbiana, *U.S.A.* 110 F4
Columbretes, Is., *Spain* 32 F5
Columbus, *Ga., U.S.A.* 109 J3
Columbus, *Ind., U.S.A.* 108 F3
Columbus, *Kans., U.S.A.* 113 G7
Columbus, *Miss., U.S.A.* 109 J1
Columbus, *Mont., U.S.A.* .. 114 D9
Columbus, *N. Mex., U.S.A.* 115 L10
Columbus, *Nebr., U.S.A.* 112 E6
Columbus, *Ohio, U.S.A.* 108 F4
Columbus, *Tex., U.S.A.* 113 L6
Colunga, *Spain* 34 B5
Colusa, *U.S.A.* 116 F4
Colville, *U.S.A.* 114 B5
Colville →, *U.S.A.* 100 A4
Colville, C., *N.Z.* 91 G5
Colwood, *Canada* 116 B3
Colwyn Bay, *U.K.* 12 D4
Coma, *Ethiopia* 81 F4
Comácchio, *Italy* 29 D9
Comalcalco, *Mexico* 119 D6
Comallo, *Argentina* 128 E2
Comana, *Romania* 43 F11
Comanche, *U.S.A.* 113 K5
Comăneşti, *Romania* 43 D11
Comarnic, *Romania* 43 E10
Comayagua, *Honduras* 120 D2
Combahee →, *U.S.A.* 109 J5
Combarbalá, *Chile* 126 C1
Combeaufontaine, *France* .. 19 E12
Comber, *Canada* 110 D2
Comber, *U.K.* 15 B6
Combermere, *Canada* 110 A7
Comblain-au-Pont, *Belgium* 17 D5
Combourg, *France* 18 D5
Combrailles, *France* 19 F9
Combronde, *France* 20 C7
Comeragh Mts., *Ireland* 15 D4
Comet, *Australia* 94 C4
Comilla, *Bangla.* 67 H17
Comino, *Malta* 36 C1
Comino, C., *Italy* 30 B2
Cómiso, *Italy* 31 F7
Comitán, *Mexico* 119 D6
Commentry, *France* 19 F9
Commerce, *Ga., U.S.A.* 109 H4
Commerce, *Tex., U.S.A.* 113 J7
Commercy, *France* 19 D12
Committee B., *Canada* 101 B11
Commonwealth B.,
    Antarctica 5 C10
Commoron Cr. →, *Australia* 95 D5
Communism Pk. =
    Kommunizma, Pik,
    Tajikistan 50 F8
Como, *Italy* 28 C6
Como, Lago di, *Italy* 28 B6
Comodoro Rivadavia,
    Argentina 128 F3
Comorâşte, *Romania* 42 E6
Comorin, C., *India* 66 Q10
Comoro Is. = Comoros ■,
    Ind. Oc. 77 H8
Comoros ■, *Ind. Oc.* 77 H8
Comox, *Canada* 104 D4
Compiègne, *France* 19 C9
Comporta, *Portugal* 35 G2
Compostela, *Mexico* 118 C4
Comprida, I., *Brazil* 127 A6
Compton, *Canada* 111 A13
Compton, *U.S.A.* 117 M8
Comrat, *Moldova* 43 D13
Con Cuong, *Vietnam* 64 C5
Con Son, *Vietnam* 65 H6
Conakry, *Guinea* 82 D2
Conara, *Australia* 94 G4
Concarneau, *France* 18 E3
Conceição, *Mozam.* 87 F4
Conceição da Barra, *Brazil* . 125 G11
Conceição do Araguaia,
    Brazil 125 E9
Concepción, *Argentina* 126 B2
Concepción, *Bolivia* 124 G6
Concepción, *Chile* 126 D1
Concepción, *Mexico* 119 D6
Concepción, *Paraguay* 126 A4
Concepción □, *Chile* 126 D1
Concepción →, *Mexico* 118 A2
Concepción, Est. de, *Chile* . 128 G2

Concepción, L., *Bolivia* 124 G6
Concepción, Punta, *Mexico* 118 B2
Concepción del Oro, *Mexico* 118 C4
Concepción del Uruguay,
    Argentina 126 C4
Conception, Pt., *U.S.A.* 117 L6
Conception B., *Canada* 103 C9
Conception B., *Namibia* 88 C1
Conception I., *Bahamas* 121 B4
Concession, *Zimbabwe* 87 F3
Conchas Dam, *U.S.A.* 113 H2
Conches-en-Ouche, *France* . 18 D7
Concho, *U.S.A.* 115 J9
Concho →, *U.S.A.* 113 K5
Conchos →, *Chihuahua,*
    Mexico 118 B4
Conchos →, *Tamaulipas,*
    Mexico 119 B5
Concord, *Calif., U.S.A.* 116 H4
Concord, *N.C., U.S.A.* 109 H5
Concord, *N.H., U.S.A.* 111 C13
Concordia, *Argentina* 126 C4
Concórdia, *Brazil* 124 D5
Concordia, *Mexico* 118 C3
Concordia, *U.S.A.* 112 F6
Concrete, *U.S.A.* 114 B3
Condamine, *Australia* 95 D5
Condat, *France* 20 C6
Conde, *U.S.A.* 112 C5
Condé-sur-Noireau, *France* . 18 D6
Condeúba, *Brazil* 125 F10
Condobolin, *Australia* 95 E4
Condom, *France* 20 E4
Condon, *U.S.A.* 114 D3
Conegliano, *Italy* 29 C9
Conejera, I. = Conills, I.
    des, *Spain* 37 B9
Conejos, *Mexico* 118 B4
Confolens, *France* 20 B4
Confuso →, *Paraguay* 126 B4
Congaz, *Moldova* 43 D13
Conghua, *China* 59 F9
Congjiang, *China* 58 E7
Congleton, *U.K.* 12 D5
Congo (Kinshasa) = Congo,
    Dem. Rep. of the ■,
    Africa 84 E4
Congo ■, *Africa* 84 E3
Congo →, *Africa* 84 F2
Congo, Dem. Rep. of the ■,
    Africa 84 E4
Congo Basin, *Africa* 84 E4
Congonhas, *Brazil* 127 A7
Congress, *U.S.A.* 115 J7
Conil = Conil de la
    Frontera, *Spain* 35 J4
Conil de la Frontera, *Spain* . 35 J4
Conills, I. des, *Spain* 37 B9
Coniston, *Canada* 102 C3
Conjeeveram =
    Kanchipuram, *India* 66 N11
Conklin, *Canada* 105 B6
Conklin, *U.S.A.* 111 D9
Conn, L., *Ireland* 15 B2
Connacht □, *Ireland* 15 C2
Conneaut, *U.S.A.* 110 E4
Connecticut □, *U.S.A.* 111 E12
Connecticut →, *U.S.A.* 111 E12
Connell, *U.S.A.* 114 C4
Connellsville, *U.S.A.* 110 F5
Connemara, *Ireland* 15 C2
Connemaugh →, *U.S.A.* 110 F5
Connerré, *France* 18 D7
Connersville, *U.S.A.* 108 F3
Connors Ra., *Australia* 94 C4
Conques, *France* 20 D6
Conquest, *Canada* 105 C7
Conrad, *U.S.A.* 114 B8
Conran, C., *Australia* 95 F4
Conroe, *U.S.A.* 113 K7
Consecon, *Canada* 110 C7
Conselheiro Lafaiete, *Brazil* 127 A7
Conselve, *Italy* 29 C9
Consett, *U.K.* 12 C6
Consort, *Canada* 105 C7
Constance = Konstanz,
    Germany 25 H5
Constance, L. = Bodensee,
    Europe 25 H5
Constanţa, *Romania* 43 F13
Constanţa □, *Romania* 43 F13
Constantia, *U.S.A.* 111 C8
Constantina, *Spain* 35 H5
Constantine, *Algeria* 78 A7
Constitución, *Chile* 126 D1
Constitución, *Uruguay* 126 C4
Consuegra, *Spain* 35 F7
Consul, *Canada* 105 D7
Contact, *U.S.A.* 114 F6
Contai, *India* 69 J12
Contamana, *Peru* 124 E4
Contarina, *Italy* 29 C9
Contas →, *Brazil* 125 F11
Contes, *France* 21 E11
Contoocook, *U.S.A.* 111 C13
Contra Costa, *Mozam.* 89 D5
Contres, *France* 18 E8
Contrexéville, *France* 19 D12
Contwoyto L., *Canada* 100 B8
Conversano, *Italy* 31 A10
Conway = Conwy, *U.K.* 12 D4
Conway = Conwy →, *U.K.* .. 12 D4
Conway, *Ark., U.S.A.* 113 H8
Conway, *N.H., U.S.A.* 111 C13
Conway, *S.C., U.S.A.* 109 J6
Conway, L., *Australia* 95 D2
Conwy □, *U.K.* 12 D4
Conwy →, *U.K.* 12 D4
Coober Pedy, *Australia* 95 D1

Cuillin Sd.

Cooch Behar = Koch Bihar, *India* 67 F16
Cooinda, *Australia* 92 B5
Cook, *Australia* 93 F5
Cook, *U.S.A.* 112 B8
Cook, B., *Chile* 128 H3
Cook, C., *Canada* 104 C3
Cook, Mt., *N.Z.* 91 K3
Cook Inlet, *U.S.A.* 100 C4
Cook Is., *Pac. Oc.* 97 J12
Cook Strait, *N.Z.* 91 J5
Cookeville, *U.S.A.* 109 G3
Cookhouse, *S. Africa* 88 E4
Cookshire, *Canada* 111 A13
Cookstown, *U.K.* 15 B5
Cooksville, *Canada* 110 C5
Cooktown, *Australia* 94 B4
Coolabah, *Australia* 95 E4
Cooladdi, *Australia* 95 D4
Coolah, *Australia* 95 E4
Coolamon, *Australia* 95 E4
Coolgardie, *Australia* 93 F3
Coolidge, *U.S.A.* 115 K8
Coolidge Dam, *U.S.A.* 115 K8
Cooma, *Australia* 95 F4
Coon Rapids, *U.S.A.* 112 C8
Coonabarabran, *Australia* 95 E4
Coonalpyn, *Australia* 95 F2
Coonamble, *Australia* 95 E4
Coonana, *Australia* 93 F3
Coondapoor, *India* 66 N9
Cooninie, L., *Australia* 95 D2
Cooper, *U.S.A.* 113 J7
Cooper Cr. →, *Australia* 95 D2
Cooperstown, *N. Dak., U.S.A.* 112 B5
Cooperstown, *N.Y., U.S.A.* 111 D10
Coorabie, *Australia* 93 F5
Coorow, *Australia* 93 E2
Cooroy, *Australia* 95 D5
Coos Bay, *U.S.A.* 114 E1
Coosa →, *U.S.A.* 109 J2
Cootamundra, *Australia* 95 E4
Cootehill, *Ireland* 15 B4
Copahue Paso, *Argentina* 126 D1
Copainalá, *Mexico* 119 D6
Copake Falls, *U.S.A.* 111 D11
Copalnic Mănăştur, *Romania* 43 C8
Copán, *Honduras* 120 D2
Cope, *U.S.A.* 112 F3
Cope, C., *Spain* 33 H3
Copenhagen = København, *Denmark* 11 J6
Copenhagen, *U.S.A.* 111 C9
Copertino, *Italy* 31 B11
Copiapó, *Chile* 126 B1
Copiapó →, *Chile* 126 B1
Coplay, *U.S.A.* 111 F9
Copp L., *Canada* 104 A6
Copparo, *Italy* 29 D8
Coppename →, *Surinam* 125 B7
Copper Harbor, *U.S.A.* 108 B2
Copper Queen, *Zimbabwe* 87 F2
Copperas Cove, *U.S.A.* 113 K6
Copperbelt □, *Zambia* 87 E2
Coppermine = Kugluktuk, *Canada* 100 B8
Coppermine →, *Canada* 100 B8
Copperopolis, *U.S.A.* 116 H6
Copşa Mică, *Romania* 43 D9
Coquet →, *U.K.* 12 B6
Coquilhatville = Mbandaka, *Dem. Rep. of the Congo* 84 D3
Coquille, *U.S.A.* 114 E1
Coquimbo, *Chile* 126 C1
Coquimbo □, *Chile* 126 C1
Corabia, *Romania* 43 G9
Coracora, *Peru* 124 G4
Coraki, *Australia* 95 D5
Coral, *U.S.A.* 110 F5
Coral Gables, *U.S.A.* 109 N5
Coral Harbour = Salliq, *Canada* 101 B11
Coral Sea, *Pac. Oc.* 96 J7
Coral Springs, *U.S.A.* 109 M5
Coraopolis, *U.S.A.* 110 F4
Corato, *Italy* 31 A9
Corbeil-Essonnes, *France* 19 D9
Corbie, *France* 19 C9
Corbières, *France* 20 F6
Corbigny, *France* 19 E10
Corbin, *U.S.A.* 108 G3
Corbones →, *Spain* 35 H5
Corbu, *Romania* 43 F13
Corby, *U.K.* 13 E7
Corcaigh = Cork, *Ireland* 15 E3
Corcoran, *U.S.A.* 116 J7
Cordele, *U.S.A.* 109 K4
Cordell, *U.S.A.* 113 H5
Cordenòns, *Italy* 29 C9
Cordes, *France* 20 D5
Córdoba, *Argentina* 126 C3
Córdoba, *Mexico* 119 D5
Córdoba, *Spain* 35 H6
Córdoba □, *Argentina* 126 C3
Córdoba □, *Spain* 35 G6
Córdoba, Sierra de, *Argentina* 126 C3
Cordon, *Phil.* 61 C4
Cordova, *U.S.A.* 100 B5
Corella, *Spain* 32 C3
Corella →, *Australia* 94 B3
Corfield, *Australia* 94 C3
Corfu = Kérkira, *Greece* 36 A3
Corfu, Str. of, *Greece* 36 A4
Corgo = O Corgo, *Spain* 34 C3
Cori, *Italy* 30 A5
Coria, *Spain* 34 F4
Coria del Río, *Spain* 35 H4
Corigliano Cálabro, *Italy* 31 C9
Coringa Is., *Australia* 94 B4
Corinth = Kórinthos, *Greece* 38 D4
Corinth, *Miss., U.S.A.* 109 H1
Corinth, *N.Y., U.S.A.* 111 C11
Corinth, *N.Y., U.S.A.* 111 C11
Corinth, G. of = Korinthiakós Kólpos, *Greece* 38 C4
Corinth Canal, *Greece* 38 D4
Corinto, *Brazil* 125 G10
Corinto, *Nic.* 120 D2
Cork, *Ireland* 15 E3
Cork □, *Ireland* 15 E3
Cork Harbour, *Ireland* 15 E3
Corlay, *France* 18 D3
Corleone, *Italy* 30 E6
Corleto Perticara, *Italy* 31 B9
Çorlu, *Turkey* 41 E11
Cormack L., *Canada* 104 A4
Cormòns, *Italy* 29 C10
Cormorant, *Canada* 105 C8
Cormorant L., *Canada* 105 C8
Corn Is. = Maiz, Is. del, *Nic.* 120 D3
Cornélio Procópio, *Brazil* 127 A5
Corner Brook, *Canada* 103 C8
Corneşti, *Moldova* 43 C13
Corníglio, *Italy* 28 D7
Corning, *Ark., U.S.A.* 113 G9
Corning, *Calif., U.S.A.* 114 G2
Corning, *Iowa, U.S.A.* 112 E7
Corning, *N.Y., U.S.A.* 110 D7
Corno Grande, *Italy* 29 F10
Cornwall, *Canada* 102 C5
Cornwall, *U.S.A.* 111 F8
Cornwall □, *U.K.* 13 G3
Corny Pt., *Australia* 95 E2
Coro, *Venezuela* 124 A5
Coroatá, *Brazil* 125 D10
Corocoro, *Bolivia* 124 G5
Coroico, *Bolivia* 124 G5
Coromandel, *N.Z.* 91 G5
Coromandel Coast, *India* 66 N12
Corona, *Calif., U.S.A.* 117 M9
Corona, *N. Mex., U.S.A.* 115 J11
Coronach, *Canada* 105 D7
Coronado, *U.S.A.* 117 N9
Coronado, B. de, *Costa Rica* 120 E3
Coronados, Is. los, *U.S.A.* 117 N9
Coronation, *Canada* 104 C6
Coronation Gulf, *Canada* 100 B8
Coronation I., *Antarctica* 5 C18
Coronation Is., *Australia* 92 B3
Coronda, *Argentina* 126 C3
Coronel, *Chile* 126 D1
Coronel Bogado, *Paraguay* 126 B4
Coronel Dorrego, *Argentina* 126 D3
Coronel Oviedo, *Paraguay* 126 B4
Coronel Pringles, *Argentina* 126 D3
Coronel Suárez, *Argentina* 126 D3
Coronel Vidal, *Argentina* 126 D4
Coropuna, Nevado, *Peru* 124 G4
Çorovoda, *Albania* 40 F4
Corowa, *Australia* 95 F4
Corozal, *Belize* 119 D7
Corps, *France* 21 D9
Corpus, *Argentina* 127 B4
Corpus Christi, *U.S.A.* 113 M6
Corpus Christi, L., *U.S.A.* 113 L6
Corral de Almaguer, *Spain* 34 F7
Corralejo, *Canary Is.* 37 F6
Corraun Pen., *Ireland* 15 C2
Corréggio, *Italy* 28 D7
Correntes, C. das, *Mozam.* 89 C6
Corrèze □, *France* 20 C5
Corrèze →, *France* 20 C5
Corrib, L., *Ireland* 15 C2
Corridónia, *Italy* 29 E10
Corrientes, *Argentina* 126 B4
Corrientes □, *Argentina* 126 B4
Corrientes →, *Argentina* 126 C4
Corrientes →, *Peru* 124 D4
Corrientes, C., *Colombia* 124 B3
Corrientes, C., *Cuba* 120 B3
Corrientes, C., *Mexico* 118 C3
Corrigan, *U.S.A.* 113 K7
Corrigin, *Australia* 93 F2
Corry, *U.S.A.* 110 E5
Corryong, *Australia* 95 F4
Corse, *France* 21 G13
Corse, C., *France* 21 E13
Corse-du-Sud □, *France* 21 G13
Corsica = Corse, *France* 21 G13
Corsicana, *U.S.A.* 113 J6
Corte, *France* 21 F13
Corte Pinto, *Portugal* 35 H3
Cortegana, *Spain* 35 H4
Cortez, *U.S.A.* 115 H9
Cortina d'Ampezzo, *Italy* 29 B9
Cortland, *N.Y., U.S.A.* 111 D8
Cortland, *Ohio, U.S.A.* 110 E4
Cortona, *Italy* 29 E8
Corubal →, *Guinea-Biss.* 82 C2
Coruche, *Portugal* 35 G2
Çoruh →, *Turkey* 49 K5
Çorum, *Turkey* 72 B6
Corumbá, *Brazil* 124 G7
Corund, *Romania* 43 D10
Corunna = A Coruña, *Spain* 34 B2
Corvallis, *U.S.A.* 114 D2
Corvette, L. de la, *Canada* 102 B5
Corydon, *U.S.A.* 112 E8
Cosalá, *Mexico* 118 C3
Cosamaloapan, *Mexico* 119 D5
Cosenza, *Italy* 31 C9
Coşereni, *Romania* 43 F11
Coshocton, *U.S.A.* 110 F3
Cosmo Newberry, *Australia* 93 E3
Cosne-Cours-sur-Loire, *France* 19 E9
Coso Junction, *U.S.A.* 117 J9
Coso Pk., *U.S.A.* 117 J9
Cospeito, *Spain* 34 B3
Cosquín, *Argentina* 126 C3
Cossato, *Italy* 28 C5
Cossé-le-Vivien, *France* 18 E6
Cosson →, *France* 18 E8
Costa Blanca, *Spain* 33 G4
Costa Brava, *Spain* 32 D8
Costa del Sol, *Spain* 35 J6
Costa Dorada, *Spain* 32 D6
Costa Mesa, *U.S.A.* 117 M9
Costa Rica ■, *Cent. Amer.* 120 E3
Costa Smeralda, *Italy* 30 A2
Costeşti, *Romania* 43 F9
Costigliole d'Asti, *Italy* 28 D5
Cosumnes →, *U.S.A.* 116 G5
Coswig, *Sachsen, Germany* 24 D9
Coswig, *Sachsen-Anhalt, Germany* 24 D8
Cotabato, *Phil.* 61 H6
Cotagaita, *Bolivia* 126 A2
Côte d'Azur, *France* 21 E11
Côte-d'Ivoire = Ivory Coast ■, *Africa* 82 D4
Côte d'Or, *France* 19 E11
Côte-d'Or □, *France* 19 E11
Coteau des Prairies, *U.S.A.* 112 C6
Coteau du Missouri, *U.S.A.* 112 B4
Coteau Landing, *Canada* 111 A10
Cotentin, *France* 18 C5
Côtes-d'Armor □, *France* 18 D4
Côtes de Meuse, *France* 19 C12
Côtes-du-Nord = Côtes-d'Armor □, *France* 18 D4
Cotiella, *Spain* 32 C5
Cotillo, *Canary Is.* 37 F5
Cotiujeni, *Moldova* 43 C13
Cotonou, *Benin* 83 D5
Cotopaxi, *Ecuador* 122 D3
Cotronei, *Italy* 31 C9
Cotswold Hills, *U.K.* 13 F5
Cottage Grove, *U.S.A.* 114 E2
Cottbus, *Germany* 24 D10
Cottonwood, *U.S.A.* 115 J7
Cotulla, *U.S.A.* 113 L5
Coubre, Pte. de la, *France* 20 C2
Couches, *France* 19 F11
Couço, *Portugal* 35 G2
Coudersport, *U.S.A.* 110 E6
Couedic, C. du, *Australia* 95 F2
Couëron, *France* 18 E5
Couesnon →, *France* 18 D5
Couhé, *France* 20 B4
Coulanges-sur-Yonne, *France* 19 E10
Coulee City, *U.S.A.* 114 C4
Coulman I., *Antarctica* 5 D11
Coulommiers, *France* 19 D10
Coulon →, *France* 21 E9
Coulonge →, *Canada* 102 C4
Coulonges-sur-l'Autize, *France* 20 B3
Coulounieix-Chamiers, *France* 20 C4
Coulterville, *U.S.A.* 116 H6
Council, *U.S.A.* 114 D5
Council Bluffs, *U.S.A.* 112 E7
Council Grove, *U.S.A.* 112 F6
Coupeville, *U.S.A.* 116 B4
Courantyne →, *S. Amer.* 122 C5
Courcelles, *Belgium* 17 D4
Courçon, *France* 20 B3
Courmayeur, *Italy* 28 C3
Couronne, C., *France* 21 E9
Cours-la-Ville, *France* 19 F11
Coursan, *France* 20 E7
Courseulles-sur-Mer, *France* 18 C6
Courtenay, *Canada* 104 D4
Courtenay, *France* 19 D10
Courtland, *U.S.A.* 116 G5
Courtrai = Kortrijk, *Belgium* 17 D3
Courtright, *Canada* 110 D2
Coushatta, *U.S.A.* 113 J8
Coutances, *France* 18 C5
Coutras, *France* 20 C3
Coutts Crossing, *Australia* 95 D5
Couvin, *Belgium* 17 D4
Covarrubias, *Spain* 34 C7
Covasna, *Romania* 43 E11
Covasna □, *Romania* 43 E10
Cove I., *Canada* 110 A3
Coventry, *U.K.* 13 E6
Covilhã, *Portugal* 34 E3
Covington, *Ga., U.S.A.* 109 J4
Covington, *Ky., U.S.A.* 108 F3
Covington, *Okla., U.S.A.* 113 G6
Covington, *Tenn., U.S.A.* 113 H10
Covington, *Va., U.S.A.* 108 G5
Cowal, L., *Australia* 95 E4
Cowan, L., *Australia* 93 F3
Cowan L., *Canada* 105 C7
Cowangie, *Australia* 95 F3
Cowansville, *Canada* 102 C5
Coward Springs, *Australia* 95 D2
Cowcowing Lakes, *Australia* 93 F2
Cowdenbeath, *U.K.* 14 E5
Cowell, *Australia* 95 E2
Cowes, *U.K.* 13 G6
Cowichan L., *Canada* 116 B2
Cowlitz →, *U.S.A.* 116 D4
Cowra, *Australia* 95 E4
Cox, *Spain* 33 G4
Coxilha Grande, *Brazil* 127 B5
Coxim, *Brazil* 125 G8
Cox's Bazar, *Bangla.* 67 J17
Coyote Wells, *U.S.A.* 117 N11
Coyuca de Benítez, *Mexico* 119 D4
Coyuca de Catalan, *Mexico* 118 D4
Cozad, *U.S.A.* 112 E5
Cozes, *France* 20 C3
Cozumel, *Mexico* 119 C7
Cozumel, Isla, *Mexico* 119 C7
Cracow = Kraków, *Poland* 45 H6
Cracow, *Australia* 95 D5
Cradock, *Australia* 95 E2
Cradock, *S. Africa* 88 E4
Craig, *U.S.A.* 114 F10
Craigavon, *U.K.* 15 B5
Craigmore, *Zimbabwe* 87 G3
Craik, *Canada* 105 C7
Crailsheim, *Germany* 25 F6
Craiova, *Romania* 43 F8
Cramsie, *Australia* 94 C3
Cranberry L., *U.S.A.* 111 B10
Cranberry Portage, *Canada* 105 C8
Cranbrook, *Australia* 93 F2
Cranbrook, *Canada* 104 D5
Crandon, *U.S.A.* 112 C10
Crane, *Oreg., U.S.A.* 114 E4
Crane, *Tex., U.S.A.* 113 K3
Cranston, *U.S.A.* 111 E13
Craon, *France* 18 E6
Craonne, *France* 19 C10
Craponne-sur-Arzon, *France* 20 C7
Crasna, *Romania* 43 D12
Crasna →, *Romania* 42 C7
Crasnei, Munţii, *Romania* 43 C8
Crater L., *U.S.A.* 114 E2
Crater Lake National Park, *U.S.A.* 114 E2
Crateús, *Brazil* 125 E10
Crati →, *Italy* 31 C9
Crato, *Brazil* 125 E11
Crato, *Portugal* 35 F3
Craven, L., *Canada* 102 B4
Crawford, *U.S.A.* 112 D3
Crawfordsville, *U.S.A.* 108 E2
Crawley, *U.K.* 13 F7
Crazy Mts., *U.S.A.* 114 C8
Crean L., *Canada* 105 C7
Crécy-en-Ponthieu, *France* 19 B8
Crediton, *Canada* 110 C3
Cree →, *Canada* 105 B7
Cree →, *U.K.* 14 G4
Cree L., *Canada* 105 B7
Creede, *U.S.A.* 115 H10
Creekside, *U.S.A.* 110 F5
Creel, *Mexico* 118 B3
Creemore, *Canada* 110 B4
Creighton, *Canada* 105 C8
Creighton, *U.S.A.* 112 D6
Creil, *France* 19 C9
Crema, *Italy* 28 C6
Cremona, *Italy* 28 C7
Crepaja, *Serbia, Yug.* 42 E5
Crépy, *France* 19 C10
Crépy-en-Valois, *France* 19 C9
Cres, *Croatia* 29 D11
Crescent City, *U.S.A.* 114 F1
Crescentino, *Italy* 28 C5
Crespo, *Argentina* 126 C3
Cresson, *U.S.A.* 110 F6
Crest, *France* 21 D9
Cresta, Mt., *Phil.* 61 C5
Crestline, *Calif., U.S.A.* 117 L9
Crestline, *Ohio, U.S.A.* 110 F2
Creston, *Canada* 104 D5
Creston, *Calif., U.S.A.* 116 K6
Creston, *Iowa, U.S.A.* 112 E7
Crestview, *Calif., U.S.A.* 116 H8
Crestview, *Fla., U.S.A.* 109 K2
Crêt de la Neige, *France* 19 F12
Crete = Kríti, *Greece* 36 D7
Crete, *U.S.A.* 112 E6
Crete, Sea of, *Greece* 39 E7
Créteil, *France* 19 D9
Creus, C. de, *Spain* 32 C8
Creuse □, *France* 19 F9
Creuse →, *France* 20 B4
Creutzwald, *France* 19 C13
Creuzburg, *Germany* 24 D6
Crèvecœur-le-Grand, *France* 19 C9
Crevillente, *Spain* 33 G4
Crewe, *U.K.* 12 D5
Crewkerne, *U.K.* 13 G5
Criciúma, *Brazil* 127 B6
Cricova, *Moldova* 43 C13
Crieff, *U.K.* 14 E5
Crikvenica, *Croatia* 29 C11
Crimea □, *Ukraine* 47 K8
Crimean Pen. = Krymskyy Pivostriv, *Ukraine* 47 K8
Crimmitschau, *Germany* 24 E8
Cristuru Secuiesc, *Romania* 43 D10
Crişul Alb →, *Romania* 42 D6
Crişul Negru →, *Romania* 42 D6
Crişul Repede →, *Romania* 42 D5
Criuleni, *Moldova* 43 C14
Crivitz, *Germany* 24 B7
Crna →, *Macedonia* 40 E5
Crna Gora = Montenegro □, *Yugoslavia* 40 D3
Crna Gora, *Macedonia* 40 D5
Crna Reka = Crna →, *Macedonia* 40 E5
Crna Trava, *Serbia, Yug.* 40 D6
Crni Drim →, *Macedonia* 40 E4
Crni Timok →, *Serbia, Yug.* 40 C6
Crnoljeva Planina, *Kosovo, Yug.* 40 D5
Črnomelj, *Slovenia* 29 C12
Croagh Patrick, *Ireland* 15 C2
Croatia ■, *Europe* 29 C13
Crocker, Banjaran, *Malaysia* 62 C5
Crockett, *U.S.A.* 113 K7
Crocodile = Krokodil →, *Mozam.* 89 D5
Crocodile Is., *Australia* 94 A1
Crocq, *France* 20 C6
Crodo, *Italy* 28 B5
Crohy Hd., *Ireland* 15 B3
Croisette, C., *France* 21 E9
Croisic, Pte. du, *France* 18 E4
Croix, L. La, *Canada* 102 C1
Croker, C., *Australia* 92 B5
Croker, C., *Canada* 110 B4
Croker I., *Australia* 92 B5
Cromarty, *U.K.* 14 D4
Cromer, *U.K.* 12 E9
Cromwell, *N.Z.* 91 L2
Cromwell, *U.S.A.* 111 E12
Cronat, *France* 19 F10
Crook, *U.K.* 12 C6
Crooked →, *Canada* 104 C4
Crooked →, *U.S.A.* 114 D3
Crooked I., *Bahamas* 121 B5
Crooked Island Passage, *Bahamas* 121 B5
Crookston, *Minn., U.S.A.* 112 B6
Crookston, *Nebr., U.S.A.* 112 D4
Crookwell, *Australia* 95 E4
Crosby, *U.K.* 12 D4
Crosby, *N. Dak., U.S.A.* 112 A3
Crosby, *Pa., U.S.A.* 110 E6
Crosbyton, *U.S.A.* 113 J4
Crosía, *Italy* 31 C9
Cross →, *Nigeria* 83 E6
Cross City, *U.S.A.* 109 L4
Cross Fell, *U.K.* 12 C5
Cross L., *Canada* 105 C9
Cross Lake, *Canada* 105 C9
Cross River □, *Nigeria* 83 D6
Cross Sound, *U.S.A.* 100 C6
Crossett, *U.S.A.* 113 J9
Crosshaven, *Ireland* 15 E3
Crossville, *U.S.A.* 109 G3
Croswell, *U.S.A.* 110 C2
Croton-on-Hudson, *U.S.A.* 111 E11
Crotone, *Italy* 31 C10
Crow →, *Canada* 104 B4
Crow Agency, *U.S.A.* 114 D10
Crow Hd., *Ireland* 15 E1
Crowell, *U.S.A.* 113 J5
Crowley, *U.S.A.* 113 K8
Crowley, L., *U.S.A.* 116 H8
Crown Point, *Ind., U.S.A.* 108 E2
Crown Point, *N.Y., U.S.A.* 111 C11
Crownpoint, *U.S.A.* 115 J9
Crows Landing, *U.S.A.* 116 H5
Crows Nest, *Australia* 95 D5
Crowsnest Pass, *Canada* 104 D6
Croydon, *Australia* 94 B3
Croydon, *U.K.* 13 F7
Crozet, Is., *Ind. Oc.* 3 G12
Crozon, *France* 18 D2
Cruz, C., *Cuba* 120 C4
Cruz Alta, *Brazil* 127 B5
Cruz de Incio, *Spain* 34 C3
Cruz del Eje, *Argentina* 126 C3
Cruzeiro, *Brazil* 127 A7
Cruzeiro do Oeste, *Brazil* 127 A5
Cruzeiro do Sul, *Brazil* 124 E4
Cry L., *Canada* 104 B3
Crystal Bay, *U.S.A.* 116 F7
Crystal Brook, *Australia* 95 E2
Crystal City, *U.S.A.* 113 L5
Crystal Falls, *U.S.A.* 108 B1
Crystal River, *U.S.A.* 109 L4
Crystal Springs, *U.S.A.* 113 K9
Csenger, *Hungary* 42 C7
Csongrád, *Hungary* 42 D5
Csongrád □, *Hungary* 42 D5
Csorna, *Hungary* 42 C2
Csurgo, *Hungary* 42 D2
Cu Lao Hon, *Vietnam* 65 G7
Cua Rao, *Vietnam* 64 C5
Cuácua →, *Mozam.* 87 F4
Cuamato, *Angola* 88 B2
Cuamba, *Mozam.* 87 E4
Cuando →, *Angola* 85 H4
Cuando Cubango □, *Angola* 88 B3
Cuangar, *Angola* 88 B2
Cuanza →, *Angola* 76 G5
Cuarto →, *Argentina* 126 C3
Cuatrociénegas, *Mexico* 118 B4
Cuauhtémoc, *Mexico* 118 B3
Cuba, *Portugal* 35 G3
Cuba, *N. Mex., U.S.A.* 115 J10
Cuba, *N.Y., U.S.A.* 110 D6
Cuba ■, *W. Indies* 120 B4
Cubango →, *Africa* 88 B3
Çubuk, *Turkey* 72 B5
Cuchumatanes, Sierra de los, *Guatemala* 120 C1
Cuckfield, *U.K.* 13 F7
Cucuí, *Brazil* 124 C5
Cucurpe, *Mexico* 118 A2
Cúcuta, *Colombia* 124 B4
Cudalbi, *Romania* 43 E12
Cuddalore, *India* 66 P11
Cuddapah, *India* 66 M11
Cuddapan, L., *Australia* 94 D3
Cudillero, *Spain* 34 B4
Cue, *Australia* 93 E2
Cuéllar, *Spain* 34 D6
Cuenca, *Ecuador* 124 D3
Cuenca, *Spain* 32 E2
Cuenca □, *Spain* 32 F3
Cuenca, Serranía de, *Spain* 32 F3
Cuerdo del Pozo, Embalse de la, *Spain* 32 D2
Cuernavaca, *Mexico* 119 D5
Cuero, *U.S.A.* 113 L6
Cuers, *France* 21 E10
Cuevas del Almanzora, *Spain* 33 H3
Cuevo, *Bolivia* 124 H6
Cugir, *Romania* 43 E8
Cugnaux, *France* 20 E5
Cuhai-Bakony →, *Hungary* 42 C2
Cuiabá, *Brazil* 125 G7
Cuiabá →, *Brazil* 125 G7
Cuijk, *Neths.* 17 C5
Cuilco, *Guatemala* 120 C1
Cuillin Hills, *U.K.* 14 D2
Cuillin Sd., *U.K.* 14 D2

Cuiseaux, *France* 19 F12
Cuito →, *Angola* 88 B3
Cuitzeo, L. de, *Mexico* 118 D4
Cujmir, *Romania* 42 F7
Cukai, *Malaysia* 65 K4
Culbertson, *U.S.A.* 112 A2
Culcairn, *Australia* 95 F4
Culebra, Sierra de la, *Spain* 34 D4
Culfa, *Azerbaijan* 73 C11
Culgoa →, *Australia* 95 D4
Culiacán, *Mexico* 118 C3
Culiacán →, *Mexico* 118 C3
Culion, *Phil.* 61 F4
Cúllar, *Spain* 35 H8
Cullarin Ra., *Australia* 95 E4
Cullen, *U.K.* 14 D6
Cullen Pt., *Australia* 94 A3
Cullera, *Spain* 33 F4
Cullman, *U.S.A.* 109 H2
Culoz, *France* 21 C9
Culpeper, *U.S.A.* 108 F7
Culuene →, *Brazil* 125 F8
Culver, Pt., *Australia* 93 F3
Culverden, *N.Z.* 91 K4
Cumaná, *Venezuela* 124 A6
Cumaovası, *Turkey* 39 C9
Cumberland, *B.C., Canada* 104 D4
Cumberland, *Ont., Canada* 111 A9
Cumberland, *U.S.A.* 108 F6
Cumberland →, *U.S.A.* 109 G2
Cumberland, L., *U.S.A.* 109 G3
Cumberland I., *U.S.A.* 109 K5
Cumberland Is., *Australia* 94 C4
Cumberland L., *Canada* 105 C8
Cumberland Pen., *Canada* 101 B13
Cumberland Plateau, *U.S.A.* 109 H3
Cumberland Sd., *Canada* 101 B13
Cumbernauld, *U.K.* 14 F5
Cumborah, *Australia* 95 D4
Cumbres Mayores, *Spain* 35 G4
Cumbria □, *U.K.* 12 C5
Cumbrian Mts., *U.K.* 12 C5
Cumbum, *India* 66 M11
Cuminá →, *Brazil* 125 D7
Cummings Mt., *U.S.A.* 117 K8
Cummins, *Australia* 95 E2
Cumnock, *Australia* 95 E4
Cumnock, *U.K.* 14 F4
Cumpas, *Mexico* 118 B3
Cumplida, Pta., *Canary Is.* 37 F2
Çumra, *Turkey* 72 D5
Cunco, *Chile* 128 D2
Cuncumén, *Chile* 126 C1
Cunderdin, *Australia* 93 F2
Cunene →, *Angola* 88 B1
Cúneo, *Italy* 28 D4
Çüngüş, *Turkey* 70 B3
Cunillera, I. = Sa Conillera, *Spain* 37 C7
Cunlhat, *France* 20 C7
Cunnamulla, *Australia* 95 D4
Cuorgnè, *Italy* 28 C4
Cupar, *Canada* 105 C8
Cupar, *U.K.* 14 E5
Cupcini, *Moldova* 43 B12
Cupica, G. de, *Colombia* 124 B3
Ćuprija, *Serbia, Yug.* 40 C5
Curaçao, *Neth. Ant.* 121 D6
Curanilahue, *Chile* 126 D1
Curaray →, *Peru* 124 D4
Cure →, *France* 19 E10
Curepto, *Chile* 126 D1
Curiapo, *Venezuela* 124 B6
Curicó, *Chile* 126 C1
Curinga, *Italy* 31 D9
Curitiba, *Brazil* 127 B6
Curitibanos, *Brazil* 127 B5
Currabubula, *Australia* 95 E5
Currais Novos, *Brazil* 125 E11
Curralinho, *Brazil* 125 D9
Currant, *U.S.A.* 114 G6
Current →, *U.S.A.* 113 G9
Currie, *Australia* 94 F3
Currie, *U.S.A.* 114 F6
Curtea de Argeş, *Romania* 43 E9
Curtici, *Romania* 42 D6
Curtis, *U.S.A.* 112 E4
Curtis Group, *Australia* 94 F4
Curtis I., *Australia* 94 C5
Curuápanema →, *Brazil* 125 D7
Curuçá, *Brazil* 125 D9
Curuguaty, *Paraguay* 127 A4
Curup, *Indonesia* 62 E2
Cururupu, *Brazil* 125 D10
Curuzú Cuatiá, *Argentina* 126 B4
Curvelo, *Brazil* 125 G10
Cushing, *U.S.A.* 113 H6
Cushing, Mt., *Canada* 104 B3
Cusihuiriáchic, *Mexico* 118 B3
Cusna, Mte., *Italy* 28 D7
Cusset, *France* 19 F10
Custer, *U.S.A.* 112 D3
Cut Bank, *U.S.A.* 114 B7
Cutchogue, *U.S.A.* 111 E12
Cuthbert, *U.S.A.* 109 K3
Cutler, *U.S.A.* 116 J7
Cutro, *Italy* 31 C9
Cuttaburra →, *Australia* 95 D3
Cuttack, *India* 67 J14
Cuvier, C., *Australia* 93 D1
Cuvier I., *N.Z.* 91 G5
Cuxhaven, *Germany* 24 B4
Cuyahoga Falls, *U.S.A.* 110 E3
Cuyapo, *Phil.* 61 D4
Cuyo, *Phil.* 61 F4
Cuyo East Pass, *Phil.* 61 F4
Cuyo West Pass, *Phil.* 61 F4
Cuyuni →, *Guyana* 124 B7
Cuzco, *Bolivia* 124 H5
Cuzco, *Peru* 124 F4
Čvrsnica, *Bos.-H.* 42 G2
Cwmbran, *U.K.* 13 F4
Cyangugu, *Rwanda* 86 C2
Cybinka, *Poland* 45 F1
Cyclades = Kikládhes, *Greece* 38 E6
Cygnet, *Australia* 94 G4
Cynthiana, *U.S.A.* 108 F3
Cypress Hills, *Canada* 105 D7
Cypress Hills Prov. Park, *Canada* 105 D7
Cyprus ■, *Asia* 36 E12
Cyrenaica, *Libya* 79 C10
Czaplinek, *Poland* 44 E3
Czar, *Canada* 105 C6
Czarna →, *Łódzkie, Poland* 45 G6
Czarna →, *Świętokrzyskie, Poland* 45 H8
Czarna Białostocka, *Poland* 45 E10
Czarna Woda, *Poland* 44 E5
Czarne, *Poland* 44 E3
Czarnków, *Poland* 45 F3
Czech Rep. ■, *Europe* 26 B8
Czechowice-Dziedzice, *Poland* 45 J5
Czempiń, *Poland* 45 F3
Czeremcha, *Poland* 45 F10
Czerniejewo, *Poland* 45 F4
Czersk, *Poland* 44 E4
Czerwieńsk, *Poland* 45 F2
Czerwionka-Leszczyny, *Poland* 45 H5
Częstochowa, *Poland* 45 H6
Człopa, *Poland* 45 E3
Człuchów, *Poland* 44 E4
Czyżew-Osada, *Poland* 45 F9

D

Da →, *Vietnam* 58 G5
Da Hinggan Ling, *China* 60 B7
Da Lat, *Vietnam* 65 G7
Da Nang, *Vietnam* 64 D7
Da Qaidam, *China* 60 C4
Da Yunhe →, *China* 57 G11
Da'an, *China* 57 B13
Dab'a, Ras el, *Egypt* 80 H6
Daba Shan, *China* 58 B7
Dabai, *Nigeria* 83 C6
Dabakala, *Ivory C.* 82 D4
Dabas, *Hungary* 42 C4
Dabat, *Ethiopia* 81 E4
Dabbagh, Jabal, *Si. Arabia* 70 E2
Dabhoi, *India* 68 H5
Dąbie, *Poland* 45 F5
Dabie Shan, *China* 59 B10
Dabilda, *Cameroon* 83 C7
Dabnou, *Niger* 83 C6
Dabo = Pasirkuning, *Indonesia* 62 E2
Dabola, *Guinea* 82 C2
Dabou, *Ivory C.* 82 D4
Daboya, *Ghana* 83 D4
Dąbrowa Białostocka, *Poland* 44 E10
Dąbrowa Górnicza, *Poland* 45 H6
Dąbrowa Tarnowska, *Poland* 45 H7
Dabu, *China* 59 E11
Dabung, *Malaysia* 65 K4
Dabus →, *Ethiopia* 81 E4
Dacato →, *Ethiopia* 81 F5
Dacca = Dhaka, *Bangla.* 69 H14
Dacca = Dhaka □, *Bangla.* 69 G14
Dachau, *Germany* 25 G7
Dachstein, Hoher, *Austria* 26 D6
Dačice, *Czech Rep.* 26 B8
Dadanawa, *Guyana* 124 C7
Daday, *Turkey* 72 B5
Dade City, *U.S.A.* 109 L4
Dadhar, *Pakistan* 68 E2
Dadiya, *Nigeria* 83 D7
Dadra & Nagar Haveli □, *India* 66 J8
Dadri = Charkhi Dadri, *India* 68 E7
Dadu, *Pakistan* 68 F2
Dadu He →, *China* 58 C4
Daet, *Phil.* 61 D5
Dafang, *China* 58 D5
Dağ, *Turkey* 39 D12
Dagana, *Senegal* 82 B1
Dagash, *Sudan* 80 D3
Dagestan □, *Russia* 49 J8
Dagestanskiye Ogni, *Russia* 49 J9
Daggett, *U.S.A.* 117 L10
Daghestan Republic = Dagestan □, *Russia* 49 J8
Daghfeli, *Sudan* 80 D3
Dağlıq Qarabağ = Nagorno-Karabakh, *Azerbaijan* 70 B5
Dagö = Hiiumaa, *Estonia* 9 G20
Dagu, *China* 57 E9
Daguan, *China* 58 D4
Dagupan, *Phil.* 61 C4
Daguragu, *Australia* 92 C5
Dahab, *Egypt* 80 B3
Dahlak Kebir, *Eritrea* 81 D5
Dahlenburg, *Germany* 24 B6
Dahlonega, *U.S.A.* 109 H4
Dahme, *Germany* 24 D9
Dahod, *India* 68 H6
Dahomey = Benin ■, *Africa* 83 D5
Dahong Shan, *China* 59 B9
Dahra, *Senegal* 82 B1
Dahshûr, *Egypt* 80 J7
Dahūk, *Iraq* 70 B3
Dai Hao, *Vietnam* 64 C6
Dai-Sen, *Japan* 55 G6
Dai Shan, *China* 59 B14
Dai Xian, *China* 56 E7
Daicheng, *China* 56 E9
Daimiel, *Spain* 35 F7
Daingean, *Ireland* 15 C4
Dainkog, *China* 58 A1
Daintree, *Australia* 94 B4
Daiō-Misaki, *Japan* 55 G8
Dair, J. ed, *Sudan* 81 E3
Dairût, *Egypt* 80 B3
Daisetsu-Zan, *Japan* 54 C11
Dajarra, *Australia* 94 C2
Dajin Chuan →, *China* 58 B3
Dak Dam, *Cambodia* 64 F6
Dak Nhe, *Vietnam* 64 E6
Dak Pek, *Vietnam* 64 E6
Dak Song, *Vietnam* 65 F6
Dak Sui, *Vietnam* 64 E6
Dakar, *Senegal* 82 C1
Dakhla, *W. Sahara* 78 D2
Dakhla, El Wâhât el-, *Egypt* 80 B2
Dakingari, *Nigeria* 83 C5
Dakor, *India* 68 H5
Dakoro, *Niger* 83 C6
Dakota City, *U.S.A.* 112 D6
Đakovica, *Kosovo, Yug.* 40 D4
Đakovo, *Croatia* 42 E3
Dalaba, *Guinea* 82 C2
Dalachi, *China* 56 F3
Dalai Nur, *China* 56 C9
Dālakī, *Iran* 71 D6
Dalälven, *Sweden* 10 D10
Dalaman, *Turkey* 39 E10
Dalaman →, *Turkey* 39 E10
Dalandzadgad, *Mongolia* 56 C3
Dalap-Uliga-Darrit, *Marshall Is.* 96 G9
Dalarna, *Sweden* 10 D8
Dālbandīn, *Pakistan* 66 E4
Dalbeattie, *U.K.* 14 G5
Dalbeg, *Australia* 94 C4
Dalbosjön, *Sweden* 11 F6
Dalby, *Australia* 95 D5
Dalby, *Sweden* 11 J7
Dale City, *U.S.A.* 108 F7
Dale Hollow L., *U.S.A.* 109 G3
Dalga, *Egypt* 80 B3
Dalgān, *Iran* 71 E8
Dalhart, *U.S.A.* 113 G3
Dalhousie, *Canada* 103 C6
Dalhousie, *India* 68 C6
Dali, *Shaanxi, China* 56 G5
Dali, *Yunnan, China* 58 E3
Dalian, *China* 57 E11
Daliang Shan, *China* 58 D4
Daling He →, *China* 57 D11
Dāliyat el Karmel, *Israel* 75 C4
Dalj, *Croatia* 42 E3
Dalkeith, *U.K.* 14 F5
Dallas, *Oreg., U.S.A.* 114 D2
Dallas, *Tex., U.S.A.* 113 J6
Dallol, *Ethiopia* 81 E5
Dalmā, *U.A.E.* 71 E7
Dalmacija, *Croatia* 29 E13
Dalmas, L., *Canada* 103 B5
Dalmatia = Dalmacija, *Croatia* 29 E13
Dalmau, *India* 69 F9
Dalmellington, *U.K.* 14 F4
Dalnegorsk, *Russia* 51 E14
Dalnerechensk, *Russia* 51 E14
Daloa, *Ivory C.* 82 D3
Dalou Shan, *China* 58 C6
Dalry, *U.K.* 14 F4
Dalrymple, L., *Australia* 94 C4
Dals Långed, *Sweden* 11 F6
Dalsjöfors, *Sweden* 11 G7
Dalsland, *Sweden* 11 F6
Daltenganj, *India* 69 H11
Dalton, *Ga., U.S.A.* 109 H3
Dalton, *Mass., U.S.A.* 111 D11
Dalton, *Nebr., U.S.A.* 112 E3
Dalton Iceberg Tongue, *Antarctica* 5 C9
Dalton-in-Furness, *U.K.* 12 C4
Dalupiri I., *Phil.* 61 B4
Dalvík, *Iceland* 8 D4
Dalwallinu, *Australia* 93 F2
Daly →, *Australia* 92 B5
Daly City, *U.S.A.* 116 H4
Daly L., *Canada* 105 B7
Daly River, *Australia* 92 B5
Daly Waters, *Australia* 94 B1
Dalyan, *Turkey* 39 E10
Dam Doi, *Vietnam* 65 H5
Dam Ha, *Vietnam* 64 B6
Daman, *India* 66 J8
Dāmaneh, *Iran* 71 C6
Damanhûr, *Egypt* 80 H7
Damant L., *Canada* 105 A7
Damanzhuang, *China* 56 E9
Damar, *Indonesia* 63 F7
Damaraland, *Namibia* 88 C2
Damascus = Dimashq, *Syria* 75 B5
Damaturu, *Nigeria* 83 C7
Damāvand, *Iran* 71 C7
Damāvand, Qolleh-ye, *Iran* 71 C7
Damba, *Angola* 84 F3
Dâmboviţa □, *Romania* 43 F10
Dâmboviţa →, *Romania* 43 F11
Dâmbovnic →, *Romania* 43 F10
Dame Marie, *Haiti* 121 C5
Dāmghān, *Iran* 71 B7
Dămienesti, *Romania* 43 D11
Damietta = Dumyât, *Egypt* 80 H7
Daming, *China* 56 F8
Damīr Qābū, *Syria* 70 B4
Dammam = Ad Dammām, *Si. Arabia* 71 E6
Dammarie-les-Lys, *France* 19 D9
Dammartin-en-Goële, *France* 19 C9
Damme, *Germany* 24 C4
Damodar →, *India* 69 H12
Damoh, *India* 69 H8
Dampier, *Australia* 92 D2
Dampier, Selat, *Indonesia* 63 E8
Dampier Arch., *Australia* 92 D2
Damrei, Chuor Phnum, *Cambodia* 65 G4
Damvillers, *France* 19 C12
Dan-Gulbi, *Nigeria* 83 C6
Dan Xian, *China* 64 C7
Dana, *Indonesia* 63 F6
Dana, L., *Canada* 102 B4
Dana, Mt., *U.S.A.* 116 H7
Danakil Depression, *Ethiopia* 81 E5
Danakil Desert, *Ethiopia* 81 E5
Danané, *Ivory C.* 82 D3
Danao, *Phil.* 61 F6
Danau Poso, *Indonesia* 63 E6
Danba, *China* 58 B3
Danbury, *U.S.A.* 111 E11
Danby L., *U.S.A.* 115 J6
Dand, *Afghan.* 68 D1
Dandeldhura, *Nepal* 69 E9
Dandeli, *India* 66 M9
Dandenong, *Australia* 95 F4
Dandīl, *Egypt* 80 J7
Dandong, *China* 57 D13
Danfeng, *China* 56 H6
Dangan Liedao, *China* 59 F10
Dangé-St-Roman, *France* 20 B4
Dângeni, *Romania* 43 C11
Danger Is. = Pukapuka, *Cook Is.* 97 J11
Danger Pt., *S. Africa* 88 E2
Dangla, *Ethiopia* 81 E4
Dangla Shan = Tanggula Shan, *China* 60 C4
Dangora, *Nigeria* 83 C6
Dangouadougou, *Burkina Faso* 82 D4
Dangrek, Phnom, *Thailand* 64 E5
Dangriga, *Belize* 119 D7
Dangshan, *China* 56 G9
Dangtu, *China* 59 B12
Dangyang, *China* 59 B8
Dani, *Burkina Faso* 83 C4
Daniel, *U.S.A.* 114 E8
Daniel's Harbour, *Canada* 103 B8
Danielskuil, *S. Africa* 88 D3
Danielson, *U.S.A.* 111 E13
Danilov, *Russia* 46 C11
Danilovgrad, *Montenegro, Yug.* 40 D3
Danilovka, *Russia* 48 E7
Daning, *China* 56 F6
Danissa, *Kenya* 86 B5
Danja, *Nigeria* 83 C6
Danjiangkou, *China* 59 A8
Danjiangkou Shuiku, *China* 59 A8
Ðank, *Oman* 71 F8
Dankalwa, *Nigeria* 83 C7
Dankama, *Nigeria* 83 C6
Dankhar Gompa, *India* 66 C11
Dankov, *Russia* 46 F10
Danleng, *China* 58 B4
Danlí, *Honduras* 120 D2
Dannemora, *U.S.A.* 111 B11
Dannenberg, *Germany* 24 B7
Dannevirke, *N.Z.* 91 J6
Dannhauser, *S. Africa* 89 D5
Dansville, *U.S.A.* 110 D7
Danta, *India* 68 G5
Dantan, *India* 69 J12
Dante, *Somali Rep.* 74 E5
Danube = Dunărea →, *Europe* 43 E14
Danvers, *U.S.A.* 111 D14
Danville, *Ill., U.S.A.* 108 E2
Danville, *Ky., U.S.A.* 108 G3
Danville, *Pa., U.S.A.* 111 F8
Danville, *Va., U.S.A.* 109 G6
Danville, *Vt., U.S.A.* 111 B12
Danyang, *China* 59 B12
Danzhai, *China* 58 D6
Danzig = Gdańsk, *Poland* 44 D5
Dão →, *Portugal* 34 E2
Dao Xian, *China* 59 E8
Daocheng, *China* 58 C3
Daoukro, *Ivory C.* 82 D4
Dapaong, *Togo* 83 C5
Dapchi, *Nigeria* 83 C7
Dapitan, *Phil.* 61 G5
Daqing Shan, *China* 56 D6
Daqu Shan, *China* 59 B14
Dar Banda, *Africa* 76 F6
Dar el Beida = Casablanca, *Morocco* 78 B4
Dar es Salaam, *Tanzania* 86 D4
Dar Mazār, *Iran* 71 D8
Dar'ā, *Syria* 75 C5
Dar'ā □, *Syria* 75 C5
Dārāb, *Iran* 71 D7
Daraban, *Pakistan* 68 D4
Darabani, *Romania* 43 B11
Daraina, *Madag.* 89 A8
Daraj, *Libya* 79 B8
Dārān, *Iran* 71 C6
Daravica, *Kosovo, Yug.* 40 D4
Daraw, *Egypt* 80 C3
Dārayyā, *Syria* 75 B5
Darazo, *Nigeria* 83 C7
Darband, *Pakistan* 68 B5
Darband, Kūh-e, *Iran* 71 D8
Darbhanga, *India* 69 F11
D'Arcy, *Canada* 104 C4
Darda, *Croatia* 42 E3
Dardanelle, *Ark., U.S.A.* 113 H8
Dardanelle, *Calif., U.S.A.* 116 G7
Dardanelles = Çanakkale Boğazı, *Turkey* 41 F10
Dare →, *Ethiopia* 81 F5
Darende, *Turkey* 72 C7
Dārestān, *Iran* 71 D8
Darfo, *Italy* 28 C7
Dârfûr, *Sudan* 79 F10
Dargai, *Pakistan* 68 B4
Dargan Ata, *Uzbekistan* 50 E7
Dargaville, *N.Z.* 91 F4
Dargol, *Niger* 83 C5
Darhan Muminggan Lianheqi, *China* 56 D6
Dari, *Sudan* 81 F3
Darıca, *Turkey* 72 B3
Darién, G. del, *Colombia* 122 C3
Dariganga = Ovoot, *Mongolia* 56 B7
Darinskoye, *Kazakstan* 48 E10
Darjeeling = Darjiling, *India* 69 F13
Darjiling, *India* 69 F13
Darkan, *Australia* 93 F2
Darkhana, *Pakistan* 68 D5
Darkhazīneh, *Iran* 71 D6
Darkot Pass, *Pakistan* 69 A5
Darling →, *Australia* 95 E3
Darling Downs, *Australia* 95 D5
Darling Ra., *Australia* 93 F2
Darlington, *U.K.* 12 C6
Darlington, *U.S.A.* 109 H6
Darlington □, *U.K.* 12 C6
Darlington, L., *S. Africa* 88 E4
Darlington Point, *Australia* 95 E4
Darlot, L., *Australia* 93 E3
Darłowo, *Poland* 44 D3
Dărmănești, *Bacău, Romania* 43 D11
Dărmănești, *Suceava, Romania* 43 C11
Darmstadt, *Germany* 25 F4
Darnah, *Libya* 79 B10
Darnall, *S. Africa* 89 D5
Darney, *France* 19 D13
Darnley, C., *Antarctica* 5 C6
Darnley B., *Canada* 100 B7
Daroca, *Spain* 32 D3
Darou-Mousti, *Senegal* 82 B1
Darr →, *Australia* 94 C3
Darra Pezu, *Pakistan* 68 C4
Darrequeira, *Argentina* 126 D3
Darrington, *U.S.A.* 114 B3
Darsser Ort, *Germany* 24 A8
Dart →, *U.K.* 13 G4
Dart, C., *Antarctica* 5 D14
Dartford, *U.K.* 13 F8
Dartmoor, *U.K.* 13 G4
Dartmouth, *Canada* 103 D7
Dartmouth, *U.K.* 13 G4
Dartmouth, L., *Australia* 95 D4
Dartuch, C. = Artrutx, C. de, *Spain* 37 B10
Daruvar, *Croatia* 42 E2
Darvaza, *Turkmenistan* 50 E6
Darvel, Teluk = Lahad Datu, Teluk, *Malaysia* 63 D5
Darwen, *U.K.* 12 D5
Darwendale, *Zimbabwe* 89 B5
Darwha, *India* 66 J10
Darwin, *Australia* 92 B5
Darwin, *U.S.A.* 117 J9
Darya Khan, *Pakistan* 68 D4
Daryoi Amu = Amudarya →, *Uzbekistan* 50 E6
Dās, *U.A.E.* 71 E7
Dashen, Ras, *Ethiopia* 81 E4
Dashetai, *China* 56 D5
Dashhowuz, *Turkmenistan* 50 E6
Dashkesan = Daşkäsän, *Azerbaijan* 49 K7
Dashköpri, *Turkmenistan* 71 B9
Dasht, *Iran* 71 B8
Dasht →, *Pakistan* 66 G2
Daska, *Pakistan* 68 C6
Daşkäsän, *Azerbaijan* 49 K7
Dassa, *Benin* 83 D5
Dasuya, *India* 68 D6
Datça, *Turkey* 39 E9
Datia, *India* 69 G8
Datian, *China* 59 E11
Datong, *Anhui, China* 59 B11
Datong, *Shanxi, China* 56 D7
Dattakhel, *Pakistan* 68 C3
Datteln, *Germany* 24 D3
Datu, Tanjung, *Indonesia* 62 D3
Datu Piang, *Phil.* 61 H6
Daud Khel, *Pakistan* 68 C4
Daudnagar, *India* 69 G11
Daugava →, *Latvia* 9 H21
Daugavpils, *Latvia* 9 J22
Daulpur, *India* 68 F7
Daun, *Germany* 25 E2
Dauphin, *Canada* 105 C8
Dauphin, *U.S.A.* 110 F8
Dauphin L., *Canada* 105 C9
Dauphiné, *France* 21 C9
Daura, *Borno, Nigeria* 83 C7
Daura, *Katsina, Nigeria* 83 C6
Dausa, *India* 68 F7
Däväçi, *Azerbaijan* 49 K9
Davangere, *India* 66 M9
Davao, *Phil.* 61 H6
Davao G., *Phil.* 61 H6
Dāvar Panāh, *Iran* 71 E9
Davenport, *Calif., U.S.A.* 116 H4
Davenport, *Iowa, U.S.A.* 112 E9
Davenport, *Wash., U.S.A.* 114 C4
Davenport Ra., *Australia* 94 C1
Daventry, *U.K.* 13 E6
David, *Panama* 120 E3
David City, *U.S.A.* 112 E6
David Gorodok = Davyd Haradok, *Belarus* 47 F4
Davidson, *Canada* 105 C7
Davis, *U.S.A.* 116 G5
Davis Dam, *U.S.A.* 117 K12

Davis Inlet, *Canada* 103 A7
Davis Mts., *U.S.A.* 113 K2
Davis Sea, *Antarctica* 5 C7
Davis Str., *N. Amer.* 101 B14
Davo →, *Ivory C.* 82 D3
Davos, *Switz.* 25 J5
Davutlar, *Turkey* 39 D9
Davy L., *Canada* 105 B7
Davyd Haradok, *Belarus* 47 F4
Dawa →, *Ethiopia* 81 G5
Dawaki, *Bauchi, Nigeria* 83 D6
Dawaki, *Kano, Nigeria* 83 C6
Dawei, *Burma* 64 E2
Dawes Ra., *Australia* 94 C5
Dawlish, *U.K.* 13 G4
Dawros Hd., *Ireland* 15 B3
Dawson, *Canada* 100 B6
Dawson, *U.S.A.* 109 K3
Dawson, I., *Chile* 128 G2
Dawson B., *Canada* 105 C8
Dawson Creek, *Canada* 104 B4
Dawson Inlet, *Canada* 105 A10
Dawson Ra., *Australia* 94 C4
Dawu, *Hubei, China* 59 B9
Dawu, *Sichuan, China* 58 B3
Dax, *France* 20 E2
Daxian, *China* 58 B6
Daxin, *China* 58 F6
Daxindian, *China* 57 F11
Daxinggou, *China* 57 C15
Daxue Shan, *Sichuan, China* 58 B3
Daxue Shan, *Yunnan, China* 58 F2
Dayao, *China* 58 E3
Daye, *China* 59 B10
Dayet en Naharat, *Mali* 82 B4
Dayi, *China* 58 B4
Daylesford, *Australia* 95 F3
Dayong, *China* 59 C8
Dayr az Zawr, *Syria* 70 C4
Daysland, *Canada* 104 C6
Dayton, *Nev., U.S.A.* 116 F7
Dayton, *Ohio, U.S.A.* 108 F3
Dayton, *Pa., U.S.A.* 110 F5
Dayton, *Tenn., U.S.A.* 109 H3
Dayton, *Wash., U.S.A.* 114 C4
Dayton, *Wyo., U.S.A.* 114 D10
Daytona Beach, *U.S.A.* 109 L5
Dayu, *China* 59 E10
Dayville, *U.S.A.* 114 D4
Dazhu, *China* 58 B6
Dazkırı, *Turkey* 39 D11
Dazu, *China* 58 C5
De Aar, *S. Africa* 88 E3
De Funiak Springs, *U.S.A.* 109 K2
De Grey →, *Australia* 92 D2
De Haan, *Belgium* 17 C3
De Kalb, *U.S.A.* 112 E10
De Land, *U.S.A.* 109 L5
De Leon, *U.S.A.* 113 J5
De Panne, *Belgium* 17 C2
De Pere, *U.S.A.* 108 C1
De Queen, *U.S.A.* 113 H7
De Quincy, *U.S.A.* 113 K8
De Ridder, *U.S.A.* 113 K8
De Smet, *U.S.A.* 112 C6
De Soto, *U.S.A.* 112 F9
De Tour Village, *U.S.A.* 108 C4
De Witt, *U.S.A.* 113 H9
Dead Sea, *Asia* 75 D4
Deadwood, *U.S.A.* 112 C3
Deadwood L., *Canada* 104 B3
Deal, *U.K.* 13 F9
Deal I., *Australia* 94 F4
Dealesville, *S. Africa* 88 D4
De'an, *China* 59 C10
Dean →, *Canada* 104 C3
Dean, Forest of, *U.K.* 13 F5
Dean Chan., *Canada* 104 C3
Deán Funes, *Argentina* 126 C3
Dease →, *Canada* 104 B3
Dease L., *Canada* 104 B2
Dease Lake, *Canada* 104 B2
Death Valley, *U.S.A.* 117 J10
Death Valley Junction, *U.S.A.* 117 J10
Death Valley National Park, *U.S.A.* 117 J10
Deauville, *France* 18 C7
Deba, *Spain* 32 B2
Deba Habe, *Nigeria* 83 C7
Debaltsevo, *Ukraine* 47 H10
Debao, *China* 58 F6
Debar, *Macedonia* 40 E4
Debden, *Canada* 105 C7
Dębica, *Poland* 45 H8
Dęblin, *Poland* 45 G8
Dębno, *Poland* 45 F1
Débo, L., *Mali* 82 B4
Debolt, *Canada* 104 B5
Deborah East, L., *Australia* 93 F2
Deborah West, L., *Australia* 93 F2
Debrc, *Serbia, Yug.* 40 B3
Debre Birhan, *Ethiopia* 81 F4
Debre Markos, *Ethiopia* 81 E4
Debre May, *Ethiopia* 81 E4
Debre Sina, *Ethiopia* 81 F4
Debre Tabor, *Ethiopia* 81 E4
Debre Zevit, *Ethiopia* 81 F4
Debre Zeyit, *Ethiopia* 81 E4
Debrecen, *Hungary* 42 C6
Debrzno, *Poland* 44 E4
Dečani, *Kosovo, Yug.* 40 D4
Decatur, *Ala., U.S.A.* 109 H2
Decatur, *Ga., U.S.A.* 109 J3
Decatur, *Ill., U.S.A.* 112 F10
Decatur, *Ind., U.S.A.* 108 E3
Decatur, *Tex., U.S.A.* 113 J6
Decazeville, *France* 20 D6
Deccan, *India* 66 L11
Deception Bay, *Australia* 95 D5
Deception L., *Canada* 105 B8
Dechang, *China* 58 D4
Dechhu, *India* 68 F5
Děčín, *Czech Rep.* 26 A7
Decize, *France* 19 F10
Deckerville, *U.S.A.* 110 C2
Decollatura, *Italy* 31 C9
Decorah, *U.S.A.* 112 D9
Deda, *Romania* 43 D9
Dedéagach = Alexandroúpolis, *Greece* 41 F9
Deder, *Ethiopia* 81 F5
Dedham, *U.S.A.* 111 D13
Dédougou, *Burkina Faso* 82 C4
Dedovichi, *Russia* 46 D5
Dedza, *Malawi* 87 E3
Dee →, *Aberds., U.K.* 14 D6
Dee →, *Dumf. & Gall., U.K.* 14 G4
Dee →, *Wales, U.K.* 12 D4
Deep B., *Canada* 104 A5
Deepwater, *Australia* 95 D5
Deer →, *Canada* 105 B10
Deer L., *Canada* 105 C10
Deer Lake, *Nfld., Canada* 103 C8
Deer Lake, *Ont., Canada* 105 C10
Deer Lodge, *U.S.A.* 114 C7
Deer Park, *U.S.A.* 114 C5
Deer River, *U.S.A.* 112 B8
Deeragun, *Australia* 94 B4
Deerdepoort, *S. Africa* 88 C4
Deferiet, *U.S.A.* 111 B9
Defiance, *U.S.A.* 108 E3
Degana, *India* 68 F6
Dêgê, *China* 58 B2
Degebe →, *Portugal* 35 G3
Degeberga, *Sweden* 11 J8
Dégelis, *Canada* 103 C6
Degema, *Nigeria* 83 E6
Degerfors, *Sweden* 10 E8
Degerhamn, *Sweden* 11 H10
Deggendorf, *Germany* 25 G8
Degh →, *Pakistan* 68 D5
Değirmendere, *Turkey* 41 F13
Deh Bīd, *Iran* 71 D7
Deh-e Shīr, *Iran* 71 D7
Dehaj, *Iran* 71 D7
Dehak, *Iran* 71 E9
Dehdez, *Iran* 71 D6
Dehej, *India* 68 J5
Dehestān, *Iran* 71 D7
Dehgolān, *Iran* 70 C5
Dehi Titan, *Afghan.* 66 C3
Dehibat, *Tunisia* 79 B8
Dehlorān, *Iran* 70 C5
Dehnow-e Kūhestān, *Iran* 71 E8
Dehra Dun, *India* 68 D8
Dehri, *India* 69 G11
Dehua, *China* 59 E12
Dehui, *China* 57 B13
Deim Zubeir, *Sudan* 81 F2
Deinze, *Belgium* 17 D3
Dej, *Romania* 43 C8
Deje, *Sweden* 10 E7
Dejiang, *China* 58 C7
Deka →, *S. Africa* 88 B4
Dekemhare, *Eritrea* 81 D4
Dekese, *Dem. Rep. of the Congo* 84 E4
Del Mar, *U.S.A.* 117 N9
Del Norte, *U.S.A.* 115 H10
Del Rio, *U.S.A.* 113 L4
Delai, *Sudan* 80 D4
Delambre I., *Australia* 92 D2
Delami, *Sudan* 81 E3
Delano, *U.S.A.* 117 K7
Delano Peak, *U.S.A.* 115 G7
Delareyville, *S. Africa* 88 D4
Delaronde L., *Canada* 105 C7
Delavan, *U.S.A.* 112 D10
Delaware, *U.S.A.* 108 E4
Delaware □, *U.S.A.* 108 F8
Delaware →, *U.S.A.* 111 G9
Delaware B., *U.S.A.* 108 F8
Delay →, *Canada* 103 A5
Delbrück, *Germany* 24 D4
Delčevo, *Macedonia* 40 E6
Delegate, *Australia* 95 F4
Delémont, *Switz.* 25 H3
Delevan, *U.S.A.* 110 D6
Delft, *Neths.* 17 B4
Delfzijl, *Neths.* 17 A6
Delgado, C., *Mozam.* 87 E5
Delgerhet, *Mongolia* 56 B6
Delgo, *Sudan* 80 C3
Delhi, *Canada* 110 D4
Delhi, *India* 68 E7
Delhi, *La., U.S.A.* 113 J9
Delhi, *N.Y., U.S.A.* 111 D10
Deli Jovan, *Serbia, Yug.* 40 B6
Delia, *Canada* 104 C6
Delice, *Turkey* 72 C6
Delicias, *Mexico* 118 B3
Delījān, *Iran* 71 C6
Déline, *Canada* 100 B7
Delisle, *Canada* 105 C7
Delitzsch, *Germany* 24 D8
Dell City, *U.S.A.* 115 L11
Dell Rapids, *U.S.A.* 112 D6
Delle, *France* 19 E14
Delmar, *U.S.A.* 111 D11
Delmenhorst, *Germany* 24 B4
Delnice, *Croatia* 29 C11
Delong, Ostrova, *Russia* 51 B15
Deloraine, *Australia* 94 G4
Deloraine, *Canada* 105 D8
Delphi, *Greece* 38 C4
Delphi, *U.S.A.* 108 E2
Delphos, *U.S.A.* 108 E3
Delportshoop, *S. Africa* 88 D3
Delray Beach, *U.S.A.* 109 M5
Delsbo, *Sweden* 10 C10
Delta, *Colo., U.S.A.* 115 G9
Delta, *Utah, U.S.A.* 114 G7
Delta □, *Nigeria* 83 D6
Delta Junction, *U.S.A.* 100 B5
Deltona, *U.S.A.* 109 L5
Delungra, *Australia* 95 D5
Delvada, *India* 68 J4
Delvinákion, *Greece* 38 B2
Delvinë, *Albania* 40 G4
Demak, *Indonesia* 63 G14
Demanda, Sierra de la, *Spain* 32 C2
Demavand = Damāvand, *Iran* 71 C7
Dembecha, *Ethiopia* 81 E4
Dembi, *Ethiopia* 81 F4
Dembia, *Dem. Rep. of the Congo* 86 B2
Dembidolo, *Ethiopia* 81 F3
Demchok, *India* 69 C8
Demer →, *Belgium* 17 D4
Demetrias, *Greece* 38 B5
Demidov, *Russia* 46 E6
Deming, *N. Mex., U.S.A.* 115 K10
Deming, *Wash., U.S.A.* 116 B4
Demini →, *Brazil* 124 D6
Demirci, *Turkey* 39 B10
Demirköprü Barajı, *Turkey* 39 C10
Demirköy, *Turkey* 41 E11
Demmin, *Germany* 24 B9
Demonte, *Italy* 28 D4
Demopolis, *U.S.A.* 109 J2
Dempo, *Indonesia* 62 E2
Demyansk, *Russia* 46 D7
Den Burg, *Neths.* 17 A4
Den Chai, *Thailand* 64 D3
Den Haag = 's-Gravenhage, *Neths.* 17 B4
Den Helder, *Neths.* 17 B4
Den Oever, *Neths.* 17 B5
Denain, *France* 19 B10
Denair, *U.S.A.* 116 H6
Denau, *Uzbekistan* 50 F7
Denbigh, *Canada* 110 A7
Denbigh, *U.K.* 12 D4
Denbighshire □, *U.K.* 12 D4
Dendang, *Indonesia* 62 E3
Dendermonde, *Belgium* 17 C4
Deneba, *Ethiopia* 81 F4
Dengchuan, *China* 58 E3
Denge, *Nigeria* 83 C6
Dengfeng, *China* 56 G7
Dengi, *Nigeria* 83 D6
Dengkou, *China* 56 D4
Dengzhou, *China* 59 A9
Denham, *Australia* 93 E1
Denham Ra., *Australia* 94 C4
Denham Sd., *Australia* 93 E1
Denholm, *Canada* 105 C7
Denia, *Spain* 33 G5
Denial B., *Australia* 95 E1
Deniliquin, *Australia* 95 F3
Denison, *Iowa, U.S.A.* 112 E7
Denison, *Tex., U.S.A.* 113 J6
Denison Plains, *Australia* 92 C4
Denizli, *Turkey* 39 D11
Denizli □, *Turkey* 39 D11
Denman Glacier, *Antarctica* 5 C7
Denmark, *Australia* 93 F2
Denmark ■, *Europe* 11 J3
Denmark Str., *Atl. Oc.* 4 C6
Dennison, *U.S.A.* 110 F3
Denny, *U.K.* 14 E5
Denpasar, *Indonesia* 62 F5
Denton, *Mont., U.S.A.* 114 C9
Denton, *Tex., U.S.A.* 113 J6
D'Entrecasteaux, Pt., *Australia* 93 F2
Denu, *Ghana* 83 D5
Denver, *Colo., U.S.A.* 112 F2
Denver, *Pa., U.S.A.* 111 F8
Denver City, *U.S.A.* 113 J3
Deoband, *India* 68 E7
Deogarh, *India* 68 G5
Deoghar, *India* 69 G12
Deolali, *India* 66 K8
Deoli = Devli, *India* 68 G6
Déols, *France* 19 F8
Deora, *India* 68 F4
Deori, *India* 69 H8
Deoria, *India* 69 F10
Deosai Mts., *Pakistan* 69 B6
Deosri, *India* 69 F14
Depalpur, *India* 68 H6
Deping, *China* 57 F9
Deposit, *U.S.A.* 111 D9
Depuch I., *Australia* 92 D2
Deputatskiy, *Russia* 51 C14
Dêqên, *China* 58 C2
Deqing, *China* 59 F8
Dera Ghazi Khan, *Pakistan* 68 D4
Dera Ismail Khan, *Pakistan* 68 D4
Derabugti, *Pakistan* 68 E3
Derawar Fort, *Pakistan* 68 E4
Derbent, *Russia* 49 J9
Derbent, *Turkey* 39 C10
Derby, *Australia* 92 C3
Derby, *U.K.* 12 E6
Derby, *Conn., U.S.A.* 111 E11
Derby, *Kans., U.S.A.* 113 G6
Derby, *N.Y., U.S.A.* 110 D6
Derby City □, *U.K.* 12 E6
Derby Line, *U.S.A.* 111 B12
Derbyshire □, *U.K.* 12 D6
Derecske, *Hungary* 42 C6
Dereköy, *Turkey* 41 E11
Dereli, *Turkey* 73 B8
Derg →, *U.K.* 15 B4
Derg, L., *Ireland* 15 D3
Dergachi = Derhaci, *Ukraine* 47 G9
Dergaon, *India* 67 F19
Derhaci, *Ukraine* 47 G9
Derik, *Turkey* 73 D9
Derinkuyu, *Turkey* 72 C6
Dermantsi, *Bulgaria* 41 C8
Dermott, *U.S.A.* 113 J9
Dêrong, *China* 58 C2
Derry = Londonderry, *U.K.* 15 B4
Derry = Londonderry □, *U.K.* 15 B4
Derry, *N.H., U.S.A.* 111 D13
Derry, *Pa., U.S.A.* 110 F5
Derryveagh Mts., *Ireland* 15 B3
Derudub, *Sudan* 80 D4
Derval, *France* 18 E5
Dervéni, *Greece* 38 C4
Derventa, *Bos.-H.* 42 F2
Derwent →, *Cumb., U.K.* 12 C4
Derwent →, *Derby, U.K.* 12 E6
Derwent →, *N. Yorks., U.K.* 12 D7
Derwent Water, *U.K.* 12 C4
Des Moines, *Iowa, U.S.A.* 112 E8
Des Moines, *N. Mex., U.S.A.* 113 G3
Des Moines →, *U.S.A.* 112 E9
Desa, *Romania* 42 G8
Desaguadero →, *Argentina* 126 C2
Desaguadero →, *Bolivia* 124 G5
Descanso, Pta., *Mexico* 117 N9
Descartes, *France* 20 B4
Deschaillons, *Canada* 103 C5
Deschambault L., *Canada* 105 C8
Deschutes →, *U.S.A.* 114 D3
Dese, *Ethiopia* 81 E4
Deseado →, *Argentina* 128 F3
Desenzano del Garda, *Italy* 28 C7
Desert Center, *U.S.A.* 117 M11
Desert Hot Springs, *U.S.A.* 117 M10
Deshnok, *India* 68 F5
Desna →, *Ukraine* 47 G6
Desnătui →, *Romania* 43 G8
Desolación, I., *Chile* 128 G2
Despeñaperros, Paso, *Spain* 35 G7
Despotovac, *Serbia, Yug.* 40 B5
Dessau, *Germany* 24 D8
Dessye = Dese, *Ethiopia* 81 E4
D'Estrees B., *Australia* 95 F2
Desuri, *India* 68 G5
Desvres, *France* 19 B8
Det Udom, *Thailand* 64 E5
Deta, *Romania* 42 E6
Dete, *S. Africa* 88 B4
Dete, *Zimbabwe* 87 F2
Đetinja →, *Serbia, Yug.* 40 C4
Detmold, *Germany* 24 D4
Detour, Pt., *U.S.A.* 108 C2
Detroit, *U.S.A.* 110 D1
Detroit Lakes, *U.S.A.* 112 B7
Detva, *Slovak Rep.* 27 C12
Deurne, *Neths.* 17 C5
Deutsche Bucht, *Germany* 24 A4
Deutschlandsberg, *Austria* 26 E8
Deux-Sèvres □, *France* 18 F6
Deva, *Romania* 42 E7
Devakottai, *India* 66 Q11
Devaprayag, *India* 69 D8
Dévaványa, *Hungary* 42 C5
Deveci Dağları, *Turkey* 72 B7
Devecikonağı, *Turkey* 41 G12
Devecser, *Hungary* 42 C2
Develi, *Turkey* 72 C6
Deventer, *Neths.* 17 B6
Deveron →, *U.K.* 14 D6
Devesel, *Romania* 42 F7
Devgadh Bariya, *India* 68 H5
Devikot, *India* 68 F4
Devils Den, *U.S.A.* 116 K7
Devils Lake, *U.S.A.* 112 A5
Devils Paw, *Canada* 104 B2
Devils Tower Junction, *U.S.A.* 112 C2
Devin, *Bulgaria* 41 E8
Devine, *U.S.A.* 113 L5
Devizes, *U.K.* 13 F6
Devli, *India* 68 G6
Devnya, *Bulgaria* 41 C11
Devolii →, *Albania* 40 F4
Devon, *Canada* 104 C6
Devon □, *U.K.* 13 G4
Devon I., *Canada* 4 B3
Devonport, *Australia* 94 G4
Devonport, *N.Z.* 91 G5
Devrek, *Turkey* 72 B4
Devrekâni, *Turkey* 72 B5
Devrez →, *Turkey* 72 B6
Dewas, *India* 68 H7
Dewetsdorp, *S. Africa* 88 D4
Dexing, *China* 59 C11
Dexter, *Maine, U.S.A.* 109 C11
Dexter, *Mo., U.S.A.* 113 G10
Dexter, *N. Mex., U.S.A.* 113 J2
Dey-Dey, L., *Australia* 93 E5
Deyang, *China* 58 B5
Deyhūk, *Iran* 71 C8
Deyyer, *Iran* 71 E6
Dezadeash L., *Canada* 104 A1
Dezfūl, *Iran* 71 C6
Dezhneva, Mys, *Russia* 51 C19
Dezhou, *China* 56 F9
Dhadhar →, *India* 69 G11
Dháfni, *Kríti, Greece* 36 D7
Dháfni, *Pelóponnisos, Greece* 38 D4
Dhahabān, *Si. Arabia* 80 C4
Dhahiriya = Aẓ Ẓāhirīyah, *West Bank* 75 D3
Dhahran = Aẓ Ẓahrān, *Si. Arabia* 71 E6
Dhak, *Pakistan* 68 C5
Dhaka, *Bangla.* 69 H14
Dhaka □, *Bangla.* 69 G14
Dhali, *Cyprus* 36 D12
Dhamási, *Greece* 38 B4
Dhampur, *India* 69 E8
Dhamtari, *India* 67 J12
Dhanbad, *India* 69 H12
Dhangarhi, *Nepal* 67 E12
Dhankuta, *Nepal* 69 F12
Dhar, *India* 68 H6
Dharampur, *India* 68 H6
Dharamsala = Dharmsala, *India* 68 C7
Dhariwal, *India* 68 D6
Dharla →, *Bangla.* 69 G13
Dharmapuri, *India* 66 N11
Dharmjaygarh, *India* 69 H10
Dharmsala, *India* 68 C7
Dharni, *India* 68 J7
Dhasan →, *India* 69 G8
Dhaulagiri, *Nepal* 69 E10
Dhebar, L., *India* 68 G6
Dheftera, *Cyprus* 36 D12
Dhenkanal, *India* 67 J14
Dhenoúsa, *Greece* 39 D7
Dherinia, *Cyprus* 36 D12
Dheskáti, *Greece* 40 G5
Dhespotikó, *Greece* 38 E6
Dhestina, *Greece* 38 C4
Dhiarrizos →, *Cyprus* 36 E11
Dhībān, *Jordan* 75 D4
Dhidhimótikhon, *Greece* 41 E10
Dhíkti Óros, *Greece* 36 D7
Dhilianáta, *Greece* 38 C2
Dhílos, *Greece* 39 D7
Dhilwan, *India* 68 D6
Dhimarkhera, *India* 69 H9
Dhimitsána, *Greece* 38 D4
Dhírfis = Dhírfis Óros, *Greece* 38 C5
Dhírfis Óros, *Greece* 38 C5
Dhodhekánisos, *Greece* 39 E8
Dhodhekánisos □, *Greece* 39 E8
Dhokós, *Greece* 38 D5
Dholiana, *Greece* 38 B2
Dholka, *India* 68 H5
Dhomokós, *Greece* 38 B4
Dhoraji, *India* 68 J4
Dhoxáton, *Greece* 41 E8
Dhragonísi, *Greece* 39 D7
Dhráhstis, Ákra, *Greece* 36 A3
Dhrangadhra, *India* 68 H4
Dhrápanon, Ákra, *Greece* 36 D6
Dhriopís, *Greece* 38 D6
Dhrol, *India* 68 H4
Dhuburi, *India* 67 F16
Dhule, *India* 66 J9
Di-ib, W. →, *Sudan* 80 C4
Di Linh, *Vietnam* 65 G7
Di Linh, Cao Nguyen, *Vietnam* 65 G7
Día, *Greece* 36 D7
Diabakania, *Guinea* 82 C2
Diablo, Mt., *U.S.A.* 116 H5
Diablo Range, *U.S.A.* 116 J5
Diafarabé, *Mali* 82 C4
Diala, *Mali* 82 C3
Dialakoro, *Mali* 82 C3
Dialakoto, *Senegal* 82 C2
Diallassagou, *Mali* 82 C4
Diamante, *Argentina* 126 C3
Diamante, *Italy* 31 C8
Diamante →, *Argentina* 126 C2
Diamantina, *Brazil* 125 G10
Diamantina →, *Australia* 95 D2
Diamantino, *Brazil* 125 F7
Diamond Bar, *U.S.A.* 117 L9
Diamond Harbour, *India* 69 H13
Diamond Is., *Australia* 94 B5
Diamond Mts., *U.S.A.* 114 G6
Diamond Springs, *U.S.A.* 116 G6
Dian Chi, *China* 58 E4
Dianalund, *Denmark* 11 J5
Dianbai, *China* 59 G8
Diancheng, *China* 59 G8
Dianjiang, *China* 58 B6
Diano Marina, *Italy* 28 E5
Dianra, *Ivory C.* 82 D3
Diapaga, *Burkina Faso* 83 C5
Diapangou, *Burkina Faso* 83 C5
Diariguila, *Guinea* 82 C2
Dībā, *Oman* 71 E8
Dibai, *India* 68 E8
Dibaya-Lubue, *Dem. Rep. of the Congo* 84 E3
Dibete, *Botswana* 88 C4
Dibrugarh, *India* 67 F19
Dickens, *U.S.A.* 113 J4
Dickinson, *U.S.A.* 112 B3
Dickson = Dikson, *Russia* 50 B9
Dickson, *U.S.A.* 109 G2
Dickson City, *U.S.A.* 111 E9
Dicle Nehri →, *Turkey* 73 D9
Dicomano, *Italy* 29 E8
Didesa, W. →, *Ethiopia* 81 E4
Didi, *Sudan* 81 F3
Didiéni, *Mali* 82 C3
Didsbury, *Canada* 104 C6
Didwana, *India* 68 F6
Die, *France* 21 D9
Diébougou, *Burkina Faso* 82 C4
Diecke, *Guinea* 82 D3
Diefenbaker, L., *Canada* 105 C7
Diego de Almagro, *Chile* 126 B1
Diego Garcia, *Ind. Oc.* 3 E13
Diekirch, *Lux.* 17 E6
Diéma, *Mali* 82 C3
Diembéring, *Senegal* 82 C1
Dien Ban, *Vietnam* 64 E7
Dien Bien, *Vietnam* 58 G4
Dien Khanh, *Vietnam* 65 F7
Diepholz, *Germany* 24 C4
Dieppe, *France* 18 C8
Dierks, *U.S.A.* 113 H8
Diest, *Belgium* 17 D5

Dietikon

Dietikon, *Switz.* 25 H4
Dieulefit, *France* 21 D9
Dieuze, *France* 19 D13
Dif, *Somali Rep.* 74 G3
Differdange, *Lux.* 17 E5
Dig, *India* 68 F7
Digba, *Dem. Rep. of the Congo* 86 B2
Digby, *Canada* 103 D6
Diggi, *India* 68 F6
Dighinala, *Bangla.* 67 H18
Dighton, *U.S.A.* 112 F4
Digna, *Mali* 82 C3
Digne-les-Bains, *France* 21 D10
Digoin, *France* 19 F11
Digor, *Turkey* 73 B10
Digos, *Phil.* 61 H6
Digranes, *Iceland* 8 C6
Digul →, *Indonesia* 63 F9
Dihang →, *India* 67 F19
Dijlah, Nahr →, *Asia* 70 D5
Dijon, *France* 19 E12
Dikhil, *Djibouti* 81 E5
Dikili, *Turkey* 39 B8
Dikirnis, *Egypt* 80 H7
Dikkil = Dikhil, *Djibouti* 81 E5
Dikodougou, *Ivory C.* 82 D3
Diksmuide, *Belgium* 17 C2
Dikson, *Russia* 50 B9
Dikwa, *Nigeria* 83 C7
Dila, *Ethiopia* 81 F4
Dili, *Indonesia* 63 F7
Dilijan, *Armenia* 49 K7
Dilizhan = Dilijan, *Armenia* 49 K7
Dilj, *Croatia* 42 E3
Dillenburg, *Germany* 24 E4
Dilley, *U.S.A.* 113 L5
Dilling, *Sudan* 81 E2
Dillingen, *Bayern, Germany* 25 G6
Dillingen, *Saarland, Germany* 25 F2
Dillingham, *U.S.A.* 100 C4
Dillon, *Canada* 105 B7
Dillon, *Mont., U.S.A.* 114 D7
Dillon, *S.C., U.S.A.* 109 H6
Dillon →, *Canada* 105 B7
Dillsburg, *U.S.A.* 110 F7
Dilly, *Mali* 82 C3
Dilolo, *Dem. Rep. of the Congo* 84 G4
Dimas, *Mexico* 118 C3
Dimashq, *Syria* 75 B5
Dimashq □, *Syria* 75 B5
Dimbaza, *S. Africa* 89 E4
Dimbokro, *Ivory C.* 82 D4
Dimboola, *Australia* 95 F3
Dîmbovița = Dâmbovița →, *Romania* 43 F11
Dimbulah, *Australia* 94 B4
Dimitrovgrad, *Bulgaria* 41 D9
Dimitrovgrad, *Russia* 48 C9
Dimitrovgrad, *Serbia, Yug.* 40 C6
Dimitrovo = Pernik, *Bulgaria* 40 D7
Dimmitt, *U.S.A.* 113 H3
Dimo, *Sudan* 81 F2
Dimona, *Israel* 75 D4
Dimovo, *Bulgaria* 40 C6
Dinagat, *Phil.* 61 F6
Dinajpur, *Bangla.* 67 G16
Dinan, *France* 18 D4
Dīnān Āb, *Iran* 71 C8
Dinant, *Belgium* 17 D4
Dinapur, *India* 69 G11
Dinar, *Turkey* 39 C12
Dīnār, Kūh-e, *Iran* 71 D6
Dinara Planina, *Croatia* 29 D13
Dinard, *France* 18 D4
Dinaric Alps = Dinara Planina, *Croatia* 29 D13
Dindanko, *Mali* 82 C3
Dinder, Nahr ed →, *Sudan* 81 E3
Dindigul, *India* 66 P11
Dindori, *India* 69 H9
Ding Xian = Dingzhou, *China* 56 E8
Dinga, *Pakistan* 68 G2
Dingalan, *Phil.* 61 D4
Dingbian, *China* 56 F4
Dingelstädt, *Germany* 24 D6
Dingle, *Ireland* 15 D1
Dingle, *Sweden* 11 F5
Dingle B., *Ireland* 15 D1
Dingmans Ferry, *U.S.A.* 111 E10
Dingnan, *China* 59 E10
Dingo, *Australia* 94 C4
Dingolfing, *Germany* 25 G8
Dingtao, *China* 56 G8
Dinguira, *Mali* 82 C2
Dinguiraye, *Guinea* 82 C2
Dingwall, *U.K.* 14 D4
Dingxi, *China* 56 G3
Dingxiang, *China* 56 E7
Dingyuan, *China* 59 A11
Dingzhou, *China* 56 E8
Dinh, Mui, *Vietnam* 65 G7
Dinh Lap, *Vietnam* 58 G6
Dinokwe, *Botswana* 88 C4
Dinorwic, *Canada* 105 D10
Dinosaur National Monument, *U.S.A.* 114 F9
Dinosaur Prov. Park, *Canada* 104 C6
Dinuba, *U.S.A.* 116 J7
Diö, *Sweden* 11 H8
Dioïla, *Mali* 82 C3
Dioka, *Mali* 82 C2
Diongoï, *Mali* 82 C3
Diósgyör, *Hungary* 42 B5
Diosig, *Romania* 42 C7
Diougani, *Mali* 82 C4
Diouloulou, *Senegal* 82 C1
Dioura, *Mali* 82 C3
Diourbel, *Senegal* 82 C1
Dipalpur, *Pakistan* 68 D5
Diplo, *Pakistan* 68 G3
Dipolog, *Phil.* 61 G5
Dir, *Pakistan* 66 B7
Diré, *Mali* 82 B4
Dire Dawa, *Ethiopia* 81 F5
Diriamba, *Nic.* 120 D2
Dirk Hartog I., *Australia* 93 E1
Dirranbandi, *Australia* 95 D4
Disa, *India* 68 G5
Disa, *Sudan* 81 E3
Disappointment, C., *U.S.A.* 114 C2
Disappointment, L., *Australia* 92 D3
Disaster B., *Australia* 95 F4
Discovery B., *Australia* 95 F3
Disentis Muster, *Switz.* 25 J4
Dishna, *Egypt* 80 B3
Disina, *Nigeria* 83 C6
Disko = Qeqertarsuaq, *Greenland* 4 C5
Disko Bugt, *Greenland* 4 C5
Disna = Dzisna →, *Belarus* 46 E5
Diss, *U.K.* 13 E9
Disteghil Sar, *Pakistan* 69 A6
Distrito Federal □, *Brazil* 125 G9
Distrito Federal □, *Mexico* 119 D5
Disûq, *Egypt* 80 H7
Diu, *India* 68 J4
Dīvāndarreh, *Iran* 70 C5
Dives →, *France* 18 C6
Dives-sur-Mer, *France* 18 C6
Divichi = Däväçi, *Azerbaijan* 49 K9
Divide, *U.S.A.* 114 D7
Dividing Ra., *Australia* 93 E2
Divinópolis, *Brazil* 125 H10
Divjake, *Albania* 40 F3
Divnoye, *Russia* 49 H6
Divo, *Ivory C.* 82 D3
Divriği, *Turkey* 73 C8
Dīwāl Kol, *Afghan.* 68 B2
Dixie Mt., *U.S.A.* 116 F6
Dixon, *Calif., U.S.A.* 116 G5
Dixon, *Ill., U.S.A.* 112 E10
Dixon Entrance, *U.S.A.* 100 C6
Dixville, *Canada* 111 A13
Diyadin, *Turkey* 73 C10
Diyālā →, *Iraq* 70 C5
Diyarbakır, *Turkey* 70 B4
Diyodar, *India* 68 G4
Djakarta = Jakarta, *Indonesia* 63 G12
Djamba, *Angola* 88 B1
Djambala, *Congo* 84 E2
Djanet, *Algeria* 78 D7
Djawa = Jawa, *Indonesia* 63 G14
Djelfa, *Algeria* 78 B6
Djema, *C.A.R.* 86 A2
Djenné, *Mali* 82 C4
Djerba, I. de, *Tunisia* 79 B8
Djerid, Chott, *Tunisia* 78 B7
Djibo, *Burkina Faso* 83 C4
Djibouti, *Djibouti* 81 E5
Djibouti ■, *Africa* 81 E5
Djolu, *Dem. Rep. of the Congo* 84 D4
Djougou, *Benin* 83 D5
Djoum, *Cameroon* 84 D2
Djourab, Erg du, *Chad* 79 E9
Djugu, *Dem. Rep. of the Congo* 86 B3
Djúpivogur, *Iceland* 8 D6
Djurås, *Sweden* 10 D9
Djursland, *Denmark* 11 H4
Dmitriya Lapteva, Proliv, *Russia* 51 B15
Dmitriyev Lgovskiy, *Russia* 47 F8
Dmitrov, *Russia* 46 D9
Dmitrovsk-Orlovskiy, *Russia* 47 F8
Dnepr → = Dnipro →, *Ukraine* 47 J7
Dneprodzerzhinsk = Dniprodzerzhynsk, *Ukraine* 47 H8
Dneprodzerzhinskoye Vdkhr. = Dniprodzerzhynske Vdskh., *Ukraine* 47 H8
Dnepropetrovsk = Dnipropetrovsk, *Ukraine* 47 H8
Dneprorudnoye = Dniprorudne, *Ukraine* 47 J8
Dnestr → = Dnister →, *Europe* 47 J6
Dnestrovski = Belgorod, *Russia* 47 G9
Dnieper = Dnipro →, *Ukraine* 47 J7
Dniester = Dnister →, *Europe* 47 J6
Dnipro →, *Ukraine* 47 J7
Dniprodzerzhynsk, *Ukraine* 47 H8
Dniprodzerzhynske Vdskh., *Ukraine* 47 H8
Dnipropetrovsk, *Ukraine* 47 H8
Dniprorudne, *Ukraine* 47 J8
Dnister →, *Europe* 47 J6
Dnistrovskyy Lyman, *Ukraine* 47 J6
Dno, *Russia* 46 D5
Dnyapro = Dnipro →, *Ukraine* 47 J7
Doaktown, *Canada* 103 C6
Doan Hung, *Vietnam* 58 G5
Doany, *Madag.* 89 A8
Doba, *Chad* 79 G9
Dobandi, *Pakistan* 68 D2
Dobbiaco, *Italy* 29 B9
Dobbyn, *Australia* 94 B3
Dobczyce, *Poland* 45 J7
Dobele, *Latvia* 9 H20
Dobele □, *Latvia* 44 B10
Döbeln, *Germany* 24 D9
Doberai, Jazirah, *Indonesia* 63 E8
Dobiegniew, *Poland* 45 F2
Doblas, *Argentina* 126 D3
Dobo, *Indonesia* 63 F8
Doboj, *Bos.-H.* 42 F3
Dobra, *Wielkopolskie, Poland* 45 G5
Dobra, *Zachodnio-Pomorskie, Poland* 44 E2
Dobra, *Dîmbovita, Romania* 43 F10
Dobra, *Hunedoara, Romania* 42 E7
Dobre Miasto, *Poland* 44 E7
Dobreşti, *Romania* 42 D7
Dobreta-Turnu Severin, *Romania* 42 F7
Dobrich, *Bulgaria* 41 C11
Dobrinishta, *Bulgaria* 40 E7
Dobříš, *Czech Rep.* 26 B7
Dobrodzień, *Poland* 45 H5
Dobropole, *Ukraine* 47 H9
Dobruja, *Europe* 43 F13
Dobrush, *Belarus* 47 F6
Dobrzany, *Poland* 44 E2
Dobrzyń nad Wisłą, *Poland* 45 F6
Doc, Mui, *Vietnam* 64 D6
Docker River, *Australia* 93 D4
Docksta, *Sweden* 10 A12
Doctor Arroyo, *Mexico* 118 C4
Doda, *India* 69 C6
Doda, L., *Canada* 102 C4
Dodecanese = Dhodhekánisos, *Greece* 39 E8
Dodge City, *U.S.A.* 113 G5
Dodge L., *Canada* 105 B7
Dodgeville, *U.S.A.* 112 D9
Dodo, *Cameroon* 83 D7
Dodo, *Sudan* 81 F2
Dodola, *Ethiopia* 81 F4
Dodoma, *Tanzania* 86 D4
Dodoma □, *Tanzania* 86 D4
Dodona, *Greece* 38 B2
Dodsland, *Canada* 105 C7
Dodson, *U.S.A.* 114 B9
Dodurga, *Turkey* 39 B11
Doesburg, *Neths.* 17 B6
Doetinchem, *Neths.* 17 C6
Dog Creek, *Canada* 104 C4
Dog L., *Man., Canada* 105 C9
Dog L., *Ont., Canada* 102 C2
Doğanşehir, *Turkey* 72 C7
Dogi, *Afghan.* 66 C3
Dogliani, *Italy* 28 D4
Dogondoutchi, *Niger* 83 C5
Dogran, *Pakistan* 68 D5
Doğubayazıt, *Turkey* 70 B5
Doguéraoua, *Niger* 83 C6
Doha = Ad Dawḩah, *Qatar* 71 E6
Dohazari, *Bangla.* 67 H18
Dohrighat, *India* 69 F10
Doi, *Indonesia* 63 D7
Doi Luang, *Thailand* 64 C3
Doi Saket, *Thailand* 64 C2
Dois Irmãos, Sa., *Brazil* 125 E10
Dojransko Jezero, *Macedonia* 40 E6
Dokkum, *Neths.* 17 A5
Dokri, *Pakistan* 68 F3
Dokuchayevsk, *Ukraine* 47 J9
Dol-de-Bretagne, *France* 18 D5
Dolac, *Kosovo, Yug.* 40 D4
Dolak, Pulau, *Indonesia* 63 F9
Dolbeau, *Canada* 103 C5
Dole, *France* 19 E12
Doleib, Wadi →, *Sudan* 81 E3
Dolenji Logatec, *Slovenia* 29 C11
Dolgellau, *U.K.* 12 E4
Dolgelley = Dolgellau, *U.K.* 12 E4
Dolhasca, *Romania* 43 C11
Dolianova, *Italy* 30 C2
Dolinskaya = Dolynska, *Ukraine* 47 H7
Dolj □, *Romania* 43 F8
Dollard, *Neths.* 17 A7
Dolna Banya, *Bulgaria* 40 D7
Dolni Chiflik, *Bulgaria* 41 D11
Dolni Dŭbnik, *Bulgaria* 41 C8
Dolnośląskie □, *Poland* 45 G3
Dolný Kubín, *Slovak Rep.* 27 B12
Dolo, *Ethiopia* 81 G5
Dolo, *Italy* 29 C9
Dolomites = Dolomiti, *Italy* 29 B8
Dolomiti, *Italy* 29 B8
Dolores, *Argentina* 126 D4
Dolores, *Uruguay* 126 C4
Dolores, *U.S.A.* 115 H9
Dolores →, *U.S.A.* 115 G9
Dolovo, *Serbia, Yug.* 42 F5
Dolphin, C., *Falk. Is.* 128 G5
Dolphin and Union Str., *Canada* 100 B8
Dolsk, *Poland* 45 G4
Dolynska, *Ukraine* 47 H7
Dolzhanskaya, *Russia* 47 J9
Dom Pedrito, *Brazil* 127 C5
Doma, *Nigeria* 83 D6
Domaniç, *Turkey* 39 B11
Domariaganj →, *India* 69 F10
Domasi, *Malawi* 87 F4
Domažlice, *Czech Rep.* 26 B5
Dombarovskiy, *Russia* 50 D6
Dombås, *Norway* 9 E13
Dombasle-sur-Meurthe, *France* 19 D13
Dombes, *France* 21 C9
Dombóvár, *Hungary* 42 D3
Dombrád, *Hungary* 42 B6
Domel I. = Letsôk-aw Kyun, *Burma* 65 G2
Domérat, *France* 19 F9
Domeyko, *Chile* 126 B1
Domeyko, Cordillera, *Chile* 126 A2
Domfront, *France* 18 D6
Dominador, *Chile* 126 A2
Dominica ■, *W. Indies* 121 C7
Dominica Passage, *W. Indies* 121 C7
Dominican Rep. ■, *W. Indies* 121 C5
Dömitz, *Germany* 24 B7
Domme, *France* 20 D5
Domneşti, *Romania* 43 E9
Domodóssola, *Italy* 28 B5
Dompaire, *France* 19 D13
Dompierre-sur-Besbre, *France* 19 F10
Dompim, *Ghana* 82 D4
Domrémy-la-Pucelle, *France* 19 D12
Domville, Mt., *Australia* 95 D5
Domvraína, *Greece* 38 C4
Domžale, *Slovenia* 29 B11
Don →, *Russia* 47 J10
Don →, *Aberds., U.K.* 14 D6
Don →, *S. Yorks., U.K.* 12 D7
Don, C., *Australia* 92 B5
Don Benito, *Spain* 35 G5
Dona Ana = Nhamaabué, *Mozam.* 87 F4
Doña Mencía, *Spain* 35 H6
Donaghadee, *U.K.* 15 B6
Donald, *Australia* 95 F3
Donaldsonville, *U.S.A.* 113 K9
Donalsonville, *U.S.A.* 109 K3
Donau = Dunărea →, *Europe* 43 E14
Donau →, *Austria* 17 D3
Donaueschingen, *Germany* 25 H4
Donauwörth, *Germany* 25 G6
Doncaster, *U.K.* 12 D6
Dondo, *Mozam.* 87 F3
Dondo, Teluk, *Indonesia* 63 D6
Dondra Head, *Sri Lanka* 66 S12
Donduşeni, *Moldova* 43 B12
Donegal, *Ireland* 15 B3
Donegal □, *Ireland* 15 B4
Donegal B., *Ireland* 15 B3
Donets →, *Russia* 49 G5
Donetsk, *Ukraine* 47 J9
Dong Ba Thin, *Vietnam* 65 F7
Dong Dang, *Vietnam* 58 G6
Dong Giam, *Vietnam* 64 C5
Dong Ha, *Vietnam* 64 D6
Dong Hene, *Laos* 64 D5
Dong Hoi, *Vietnam* 64 D6
Dong Jiang →, *China* 59 F10
Dong Khe, *Vietnam* 64 A6
Dong Ujimqin Qi, *China* 56 B9
Dong Van, *Vietnam* 64 A5
Dong Xoai, *Vietnam* 65 G6
Donga, *Nigeria* 83 D7
Donga →, *Nigeria* 83 D7
Dong'an, *China* 59 D8
Dongara, *Australia* 93 E1
Dongbei, *China* 57 D13
Dongchuan, *China* 58 D4
Donges, *France* 18 E4
Dongfang, *China* 64 C7
Dongfeng, *China* 57 C13
Donggala, *Indonesia* 63 E5
Donggan, *China* 58 F5
Donggou, *China* 57 E13
Dongguan, *China* 59 F9
Dongguang, *China* 56 F9
Donghai Dao, *China* 59 G8
Dongjingcheng, *China* 57 B15
Dongkou, *China* 59 D8
Donglan, *China* 58 E6
Dongliu, *China* 59 B11
Dongmen, *China* 58 F6
Dongning, *China* 57 B16
Dongnyi, *China* 58 C3
Dongola, *Sudan* 80 D3
Dongping, *China* 56 G9
Dongshan, *China* 59 F11
Dongsheng, *China* 56 E6
Dongtai, *China* 57 H11
Dongting Hu, *China* 59 C9
Dongtou, *China* 59 D13
Dongxiang, *China* 59 C11
Dongxing, *China* 58 G7
Dongyang, *China* 59 C13
Dongzhi, *China* 59 B11
Donington, C., *Australia* 95 E2
Doniphan, *U.S.A.* 113 G9
Donja Stubica, *Croatia* 29 C12
Donji Dušnik, *Serbia, Yug.* 40 C6
Donji Miholjac, *Croatia* 42 E3
Donji Milanovac, *Serbia, Yug.* 40 B6
Donji Vakuf, *Bos.-H.* 42 F2
Dønna, *Norway* 8 C15
Donna, *U.S.A.* 113 M5
Donnaconna, *Canada* 103 C5
Donnelly's Crossing, *N.Z.* 91 F4
Donnybrook, *Australia* 93 F2
Donnybrook, *S. Africa* 89 D4
Donora, *U.S.A.* 110 F5
Donostia = Donostia-San Sebastián, *Spain* 32 B3
Donostia-San Sebastián, *Spain* 32 B3
Donskoy, *Russia* 46 F10
Donsol, *Phil.* 61 E5
Donzère, *France* 21 D8
Donzy, *France* 19 E10
Doon →, *U.K.* 14 F4
Dora, L., *Australia* 92 D3
Dora Báltea →, *Italy* 28 C5
Dora Ripária →, *Italy* 28 C4
Doran L., *Canada* 105 A7
Dorchester, *U.K.* 13 G5
Dorchester, C., *Canada* 101 B12
Dordabis, *Namibia* 88 C2
Dordogne □, *France* 20 C4
Dordogne →, *France* 20 C3
Dordrecht, *Neths.* 17 C4
Dordrecht, *S. Africa* 88 E4
Dore →, *France* 20 C7
Dore, Mts., *France* 20 C6
Doré L., *Canada* 105 C7
Doré Lake, *Canada* 105 C7
Dorfen, *Germany* 25 G8
Dorgali, *Italy* 30 B2
Dori, *Burkina Faso* 83 C4
Doring →, *S. Africa* 88 E2
Doringbos, *S. Africa* 88 E2
Dorion, *Canada* 111 A10
Dormaa-Ahenkro, *Ghana* 82 D4
Dormans, *France* 19 C10
Dormo, Ras, *Eritrea* 81 E5
Dornbirn, *Austria* 26 D2
Dornes, *France* 19 F10
Dorneşti, *Romania* 43 C11
Dornie, *U.K.* 14 D3
Dornoch, *U.K.* 14 D4
Dornoch Firth, *U.K.* 14 D4
Dornogovĭ □, *Mongolia* 56 C6
Doro, *Mali* 83 B4
Dorog, *Hungary* 42 C3
Dorogobuzh, *Russia* 46 E7
Dorohoi, *Romania* 43 C11
Döröö Nuur, *Mongolia* 60 B4
Dorr, *Iran* 71 C6
Dorre I., *Australia* 93 E1
Dorrigo, *Australia* 95 E5
Dorris, *U.S.A.* 114 F3
Dorset, *Canada* 110 A6
Dorset, *U.S.A.* 110 E4
Dorset □, *U.K.* 13 G5
Dorsten, *Germany* 24 D2
Dortmund, *Germany* 24 D3
Dortmund-Ems-Kanal →, *Germany* 24 D3
Dörtyol, *Turkey* 72 D7
Dorum, *Germany* 24 B4
Doruma, *Dem. Rep. of the Congo* 86 B2
Dorūneh, *Iran* 71 C8
Dos Bahías, C., *Argentina* 128 E3
Dos Hermanas, *Spain* 35 H5
Dos Palos, *U.S.A.* 116 J6
Döşemealtı, *Turkey* 39 D12
Dosso, *Niger* 83 C5
Dothan, *U.S.A.* 109 K3
Doty, *U.S.A.* 116 D3
Douai, *France* 19 B10
Douako, *Guinea* 82 D2
Douala, *Cameroon* 83 E6
Douarnenez, *France* 18 D2
Doubabougou, *Mali* 82 C3
Double Island Pt., *Australia* 95 D5
Double Mountain Fork →, *U.S.A.* 113 J4
Doubrava →, *Czech Rep.* 26 A8
Doubs □, *France* 19 E13
Doubs →, *France* 19 F12
Doubtful Sd., *N.Z.* 91 L1
Doubtless B., *N.Z.* 91 F4
Doudeville, *France* 18 C7
Doué-la-Fontaine, *France* 18 E6
Douentza, *Mali* 82 C4
Douglas, *S. Africa* 88 D3
Douglas, *U.K.* 12 C3
Douglas, *Ariz., U.S.A.* 115 L9
Douglas, *Ga., U.S.A.* 109 K4
Douglas, *Wyo., U.S.A.* 112 D2
Douglas Chan., *Canada* 104 C3
Douglas Pt., *Canada* 110 B3
Douglasville, *U.S.A.* 109 J3
Doukáton, Ákra, *Greece* 38 C2
Doulevant-le-Château, *France* 19 D11
Doullens, *France* 19 B9
Doumen, *China* 59 F9
Douna, *Mali* 82 C3
Douna, *Mali* 83 C4
Dounreay, *U.K.* 14 C5
Dourada, Serra, *Brazil* 125 F9
Dourados, *Brazil* 127 A5
Dourados →, *Brazil* 127 A5
Dourados, Serra dos, *Brazil* 127 A5
Dourdan, *France* 19 D9
Douro →, *Europe* 34 D2
Douvaine, *France* 19 F13
Douvres-la-Délivrande, *France* 18 C6
Douze →, *France* 20 E3
Dove →, *U.K.* 12 E6
Dove Creek, *U.S.A.* 115 H9
Dover, *Australia* 94 G4
Dover, *U.K.* 13 F9
Dover, *Del., U.S.A.* 108 F8
Dover, *N.H., U.S.A.* 111 C14
Dover, *N.J., U.S.A.* 111 F10
Dover, *Ohio, U.S.A.* 110 F3
Dover, Pt., *Australia* 93 F4
Dover, Str. of, *Europe* 13 G9
Dover-Foxcroft, *U.S.A.* 109 C11
Dover Plains, *U.S.A.* 111 E11
Dovey = Dyfi →, *U.K.* 13 E3
Dovrefjell, *Norway* 9 E13
Dow Rūd, *Iran* 71 C6
Dowa, *Malawi* 87 E3
Dowagiac, *U.S.A.* 108 E2
Dowerin, *Australia* 93 F2
Dowgha'i, *Iran* 71 B8
Dowlatābād, *Iran* 71 D8
Down □, *U.K.* 15 B5
Downey, *Calif., U.S.A.* 117 M8
Downey, *Idaho, U.S.A.* 114 E7

Eauze

Downham Market, *U.K.* 13 E8
Downieville, *U.S.A.* 116 F6
Downpatrick, *U.K.* 15 B6
Downpatrick Hd., *Ireland* 15 B2
Downsville, *U.S.A.* 111 D10
Downton, Mt., *Canada* 104 C4
Dowsārī, *Iran* 71 D8
Doyle, *U.S.A.* 116 E6
Doylestown, *U.S.A.* 111 F9
Dozois, Rés., *Canada* 102 C4
Dra Khel, *Pakistan* 68 F2
Drac →, *France* 21 C9
Dračevo, *Macedonia* 40 E5
Drachten, *Neths.* 17 A6
Drăgăneşti, *Moldova* 43 C13
Drăgăneşti-Olt, *Romania* 43 F9
Drăgăneşti-Vlaşca, *Romania* 43 F10
Dragaš, *Kosovo, Yug.* 40 D4
Drăgăşani, *Romania* 43 F9
Dragichyn, *Belarus* 47 F3
Dragocvet, *Serbia, Yug.* 40 C5
Dragovishtitsa, *Bulgaria* 40 D6
Draguignan, *France* 21 E10
Drain, *U.S.A.* 114 E2
Drake, *U.S.A.* 112 B4
Drake Passage, *S. Ocean* 5 B17
Drakensberg, *S. Africa* 89 D4
Dráma, *Greece* 41 E8
Dráma □, *Greece* 41 E8
Drammen, *Norway* 9 G14
Drangajökull, *Iceland* 8 C2
Dranov, Ostrov, *Romania* 43 F14
Dras, *India* 69 B6
Drau = Drava →, *Croatia* 42 E3
Drava →, *Croatia* 42 E3
Dravograd, *Slovenia* 29 B12
Drawa →, *Poland* 45 F2
Drawno, *Poland* 45 E2
Drawsko Pomorskie, *Poland* 44 E2
Drayton Valley, *Canada* 104 C6
Dreieich, *Germany* 25 E4
Dren, *Kosovo, Yug.* 40 C4
Drenthe □, *Neths.* 17 B6
Drepanum, C., *Cyprus* 36 E11
Dresden, *Canada* 110 D2
Dresden, *Germany* 24 D9
Dreux, *France* 18 D8
Drezdenko, *Poland* 45 F2
Driffield, *U.K.* 12 C7
Driftwood, *U.S.A.* 110 E6
Driggs, *U.S.A.* 114 E8
Drin i Zi →, *Albania* 40 E4
Drina →, *Bos.-H.* 40 B3
Drincea →, *Romania* 42 F7
Drini →, *Albania* 40 D3
Drinjača →, *Bos.-H.* 42 F4
Drissa = Vyerkhnyadzvinsk, *Belarus* 46 E4
Drniš, *Croatia* 29 E13
Drøbak, *Norway* 9 G14
Drobin, *Poland* 45 F6
Drochia, *Moldova* 43 B12
Drogheda, *Ireland* 15 C5
Drogichin = Dragichyn, *Belarus* 47 F3
Drogobych = Drohobych, *Ukraine* 47 H2
Drohiczyn, *Poland* 45 F9
Drohobych, *Ukraine* 47 H2
Droichead Atha = Drogheda, *Ireland* 15 C5
Droichead Nua, *Ireland* 15 C5
Droitwich, *U.K.* 13 E5
Drôme □, *France* 21 D9
Drôme →, *France* 21 D8
Dromedary, C., *Australia* 95 F5
Dromore, *U.K.* 15 B4
Dromore West, *Ireland* 15 B3
Dronero, *Italy* 28 D4
Dronfield, *U.K.* 12 D6
Dronne →, *France* 20 C3
Dronninglund, *Denmark* 11 G4
Dronten, *Neths.* 17 B5
Dropt →, *France* 20 D3
Drosendorf, *Austria* 26 C8
Droué, *France* 18 D8
Drumbo, *Canada* 110 C4
Drumheller, *Canada* 104 C6
Drummond, *U.S.A.* 114 C7
Drummond I., *U.S.A.* 108 C4
Drummond Pt., *Australia* 95 E2
Drummond Ra., *Australia* 94 C4
Drummondville, *Canada* 102 C5
Drumright, *U.S.A.* 113 H6
Druskininkai, *Lithuania* 9 J20
Drut →, *Belarus* 47 F6
Druya, *Belarus* 46 E4
Druzhba, *Bulgaria* 41 C12
Druzhina, *Russia* 51 C15
Drvar, *Bos.-H.* 29 D13
Drvenik, *Croatia* 29 E13
Drwęca →, *Poland* 45 E5
Dry Tortugas, *U.S.A.* 120 B3
Dryanovo, *Bulgaria* 41 D9
Dryden, *Canada* 105 D10
Dryden, *U.S.A.* 111 D8
Drygalski I., *Antarctica* 5 C7
Drysdale →, *Australia* 92 B4
Drysdale I., *Australia* 94 A2
Drzewica, *Poland* 45 G7
Drzewiczka →, *Poland* 45 G7
Dschang, *Cameroon* 83 D7
Du Bois, *U.S.A.* 110 E6
Du Gué →, *Canada* 102 A5
Du He, *China* 59 A8
Du Quoin, *U.S.A.* 112 G10
Du'an, *China* 58 F7
Duanesburg, *U.S.A.* 111 D10
Duaringa, *Australia* 94 C4
Ḍubā, *Si. Arabia* 70 E2
Dubai = Dubayy, *U.A.E.* 71 E7
Dubăsari, *Moldova* 43 C14
Dubăsari Vdkhr., *Moldova* 43 C13
Dubawnt →, *Canada* 105 A8
Dubawnt, L., *Canada* 105 A8
Dubayy, *U.A.E.* 71 E7
Dubbo, *Australia* 95 E4
Dubele, *Dem. Rep. of the Congo* 86 B2
Dübendorf, *Switz.* 25 H4
Dubica, *Croatia* 29 C13
Dublin, *Ireland* 15 C5
Dublin, *Ga., U.S.A.* 109 J4
Dublin, *Tex., U.S.A.* 113 J5
Dublin □, *Ireland* 15 C5
Dubna, *Russia* 46 D9
Dubnica nad Váhom, *Slovak Rep.* 27 C11
Dubno, *Ukraine* 47 G3
Dubois, *U.S.A.* 114 D7
Dubossary = Dubăsari, *Moldova* 43 C14
Dubossary Vdkhr. = Dubăsari Vdkhr., *Moldova* 43 C13
Dubovka, *Russia* 49 F7
Dubovskoye, *Russia* 49 G6
Dubrajpur, *India* 69 H12
Dubréka, *Guinea* 82 D2
Dubrovitsa = Dubrovytsya, *Ukraine* 47 G4
Dubrovnik, *Croatia* 40 D2
Dubrovytsya, *Ukraine* 47 G4
Dubuque, *U.S.A.* 112 D9
Dubysa →, *Lithuania* 44 C10
Duchang, *China* 59 C11
Duchesne, *U.S.A.* 114 F8
Duchess, *Australia* 94 C2
Ducie I., *Pac. Oc.* 97 K15
Duck →, *U.S.A.* 109 G2
Duck Cr. →, *Australia* 92 D2
Duck Lake, *Canada* 105 C7
Duck Mountain Prov. Park, *Canada* 105 C8
Duckwall, Mt., *U.S.A.* 116 H6
Duderstadt, *Germany* 24 D6
Dudhi, *India* 67 G13
Dudinka, *Russia* 51 C9
Dudley, *U.K.* 13 E5
Dudwa, *India* 69 E9
Duékoué, *Ivory C.* 82 D3
Dueñas, *Spain* 34 D6
Duero = Douro →, *Europe* 34 D2
Dufftown, *U.K.* 14 D5
Dufourspitz, *Switz.* 25 K3
Dugi Otok, *Croatia* 29 D11
Dugo Selo, *Croatia* 29 C13
Duifken Pt., *Australia* 94 A3
Duisburg, *Germany* 24 D2
Duiwelskloof, *S. Africa* 89 C5
Dujiangyan, *China* 58 B4
Duk Fadiat, *Sudan* 81 F3
Duk Faiwil, *Sudan* 81 F3
Dukati, *Albania* 40 F3
Dūkdamīn, *Iran* 71 C8
Dukelský Průsmyk, *Slovak Rep.* 27 B14
Dukhān, *Qatar* 71 E6
Dukhovshchina, *Russia* 46 E7
Duki, *Pakistan* 66 D6
Dukla, *Poland* 45 J8
Duku, *Bauchi, Nigeria* 83 C7
Duku, *Sokoto, Nigeria* 83 C5
Dulag, *Phil.* 61 F6
Dulce, *U.S.A.* 115 H10
Dulce →, *Argentina* 126 C3
Dulce, G., *Costa Rica* 120 E3
Dulf, *Iraq* 70 C5
Dŭlgopol, *Bulgaria* 41 C11
Dulit, Banjaran, *Malaysia* 62 D4
Duliu, *China* 56 E9
Dullewala, *Pakistan* 68 D4
Dullstroom, *S. Africa* 89 D5
Dülmen, *Germany* 24 D3
Dulovo, *Bulgaria* 41 C11
Dulq Maghār, *Syria* 70 B3
Duluth, *U.S.A.* 112 B8
Dum Dum, *India* 69 H13
Dum Duma, *India* 67 F19
Dūmā, *Syria* 75 B5
Dumaguete, *Phil.* 61 G5
Dumai, *Indonesia* 62 D2
Dumaran, *Phil.* 61 F3
Dumas, *Ark., U.S.A.* 113 J9
Dumas, *Tex., U.S.A.* 113 H4
Ḍumayr, *Syria* 75 B5
Dumbarton, *U.K.* 14 F4
Ďumbier, *Slovak Rep.* 27 C12
Dumbleyung, *Australia* 93 F2
Dumboa, *Nigeria* 83 C7
Dumbrăveni, *Romania* 43 D9
Dumfries, *U.K.* 14 F5
Dumfries & Galloway □, *U.K.* 14 F5
Dumitreşti, *Romania* 43 E11
Dumka, *India* 69 G12
Dumlupınar, *Turkey* 39 C12
Dümmer, *Germany* 24 C4
Dumoine →, *Canada* 102 C4
Dumoine, L., *Canada* 102 C4
Dumraon, *India* 69 G11
Dumyât, *Egypt* 80 H7
Dumyât, Masabb, *Egypt* 80 H7
Dún Dealgan = Dundalk, *Ireland* 15 B5
Dun Laoghaire, *Ireland* 15 C5
Dun-le-Palestel, *France* 19 F8
Dun-sur-Auron, *France* 19 F9
Dun-sur-Meuse, *France* 19 C12
Duna = Dunărea →, *Europe* 43 E14
Duna →, *Hungary* 42 E3
Duna-völgyi-főcsatorna, *Hungary* 42 D4
Dunaföldvár, *Hungary* 42 D3
Dunagiri, *India* 69 D8
Dunaj = Dunărea →, *Europe* 43 E14
Dunaj →, *Slovak Rep.* 27 D11
Dunajec →, *Poland* 45 H7
Dunajská Streda, *Slovak Rep.* 27 C10
Dunakeszi, *Hungary* 42 C4
Dunapataj, *Hungary* 42 D4
Dunărea →, *Europe* 43 E14
Dunaszekcső, *Hungary* 42 D3
Dunaújváros, *Hungary* 42 D3
Dunav = Dunărea →, *Europe* 43 E14
Dunavaţu de Jos, *Romania* 43 F14
Dunavtsi, *Bulgaria* 40 C6
Dunay, *Russia* 54 C6
Dunback, *N.Z.* 91 L3
Dunbar, *U.K.* 14 E6
Dunblane, *U.K.* 14 E5
Duncan, *Canada* 104 D4
Duncan, *Ariz., U.S.A.* 115 K9
Duncan, *Okla., U.S.A.* 113 H6
Duncan, L., *Canada* 102 B4
Duncan L., *Canada* 104 A6
Duncan Town, *Bahamas* 120 B4
Duncannon, *U.S.A.* 110 F7
Duncansby Head, *U.K.* 14 C5
Duncansville, *U.S.A.* 110 F6
Dundaga, *Latvia* 44 A9
Dundalk, *Canada* 110 B4
Dundalk, *Ireland* 15 B5
Dundalk, *U.S.A.* 108 F7
Dundalk Bay, *Ireland* 15 C5
Dundas, *Canada* 110 C5
Dundas, L., *Australia* 93 F3
Dundas I., *Canada* 104 C2
Dundas Str., *Australia* 92 B5
Dundee, *S. Africa* 89 D5
Dundee, *U.K.* 14 E6
Dundee, *U.S.A.* 110 D8
Dundee City □, *U.K.* 14 E6
Dundgovĭ □, *Mongolia* 56 B4
Dundrum, *U.K.* 15 B6
Dundrum B., *U.K.* 15 B6
Dunedin, *N.Z.* 91 L3
Dunedin, *U.S.A.* 109 L4
Dunedoo, *Australia* 95 E4
Dunfermline, *U.K.* 14 E5
Dungannon, *Canada* 110 C3
Dungannon, *U.K.* 15 B5
Dungarpur, *India* 68 H5
Dungarvan, *Ireland* 15 D4
Dungarvan Harbour, *Ireland* 15 D4
Dungeness, *U.K.* 13 G8
Dungo, L. do, *Angola* 88 B2
Dungog, *Australia* 95 E5
Dungu, *Dem. Rep. of the Congo* 86 B2
Dungun, *Malaysia* 65 K4
Dungunâb, *Sudan* 80 C4
Dungunâb, Khalij, *Sudan* 80 C4
Dunhua, *China* 57 C15
Dunhuang, *China* 60 B4
Dunk I., *Australia* 94 B4
Dunkassa, *Benin* 83 C5
Dunkeld, *Australia* 95 E4
Dunkeld, *U.K.* 14 E5
Dunkerque, *France* 19 A9
Dunkery Beacon, *U.K.* 13 F4
Dunkirk = Dunkerque, *France* 19 A9
Dunkirk, *U.S.A.* 110 D5
Dunkuj, *Sudan* 81 E3
Dunkwa, *Central, Ghana* 82 D4
Dunkwa, *Central, Ghana* 83 D4
Dúnleary = Dun Laoghaire, *Ireland* 15 C5
Dunleer, *Ireland* 15 C5
Dunmanus B., *Ireland* 15 E2
Dunmanway, *Ireland* 15 E2
Dunmara, *Australia* 94 B1
Dunmore, *U.S.A.* 111 E9
Dunmore Hd., *Ireland* 15 D1
Dunmore Town, *Bahamas* 120 A4
Dunn, *U.S.A.* 109 H6
Dunnet Hd., *U.K.* 14 C5
Dunning, *U.S.A.* 112 E4
Dunnville, *Canada* 110 D5
Dunolly, *Australia* 95 F3
Dunoon, *U.K.* 14 F4
Dunphy, *U.S.A.* 114 F5
Dunqul, *Egypt* 80 C3
Duns, *U.K.* 14 F6
Dunseith, *U.S.A.* 112 A4
Dunsmuir, *U.S.A.* 114 F2
Dunstable, *U.K.* 13 F7
Dunstan Mts., *N.Z.* 91 L2
Dunster, *Canada* 104 C5
Dunvegan L., *Canada* 105 A7
Duolun, *China* 56 C9
Duong Dong, *Vietnam* 65 G4
Dupree, *U.S.A.* 112 C4
Dupuyer, *U.S.A.* 114 B7
Duque de Caxias, *Brazil* 127 A7
Durack →, *Australia* 92 C4
Durack Ra., *Australia* 92 C4
Durağan, *Turkey* 72 B6
Durak, *Turkey* 39 B10
Đurakovac, *Kosovo, Yug.* 40 D4
Durance →, *France* 21 E8
Durand, *U.S.A.* 112 C9
Durango, *Mexico* 118 C4
Durango, *U.S.A.* 115 H10
Durango □, *Mexico* 118 C4
Durankulak, *Bulgaria* 41 C12
Durant, *Miss., U.S.A.* 113 J10
Durant, *Okla., U.S.A.* 113 J6
Duratón →, *Spain* 34 D6
Durazno, *Uruguay* 126 C4
Durazzo = Durrësi, *Albania* 40 E3
Durban, *France* 20 F6
Durban, *S. Africa* 89 D5
Durbuy, *Belgium* 17 D5
Dúrcal, *Spain* 35 J7
Đurđevac, *Croatia* 42 D2
Düren, *Germany* 24 E2
Durg, *India* 67 J12
Durgapur, *India* 69 H12
Durham, *Canada* 102 D3
Durham, *U.K.* 12 C6
Durham, *Calif., U.S.A.* 116 F5
Durham, *N.C., U.S.A.* 109 H6
Durham, *N.H., U.S.A.* 111 C14
Durham □, *U.K.* 12 C6
Durleşti, *Moldova* 43 C13
Ḍurmā, *Si. Arabia* 70 E5
Durmitor, *Montenegro, Yug.* 40 C2
Durness, *U.K.* 14 C4
Durrësi, *Albania* 40 E3
Durrow, *Ireland* 15 D4
Dursey I., *Ireland* 15 E1
Dursunbey, *Turkey* 39 B10
Durtal, *France* 18 E6
Duru, *Dem. Rep. of the Congo* 86 B2
Duru Gölü, *Turkey* 41 E12
Durusu, *Turkey* 41 E12
Durūz, Jabal ad, *Jordan* 75 C5
D'Urville, Tanjung, *Indonesia* 63 E9
D'Urville I., *N.Z.* 91 J4
Duryea, *U.S.A.* 111 E9
Dûsh, *Egypt* 80 C3
Dushak, *Turkmenistan* 50 F7
Dushan, *China* 58 E6
Dushanbe, *Tajikistan* 50 F7
Dusheti, *Georgia* 49 J7
Dushore, *U.S.A.* 111 E8
Dusky Sd., *N.Z.* 91 L1
Dussejour, C., *Australia* 92 B4
Düsseldorf, *Germany* 24 D2
Duszniki-Zdrój, *Poland* 45 H3
Dutch Harbor, *U.S.A.* 100 C3
Dutlwe, *Botswana* 88 C3
Dutsan Wai, *Nigeria* 83 C6
Dutton, *Canada* 110 D3
Dutton →, *Australia* 94 C3
Duved, *Sweden* 10 A6
Düvertepe, *Turkey* 39 B10
Duwayhin, Khawr, *U.A.E.* 71 E6
Duyun, *China* 58 D6
Düzağac, *Turkey* 39 C12
Düzce, *Turkey* 72 B4
Duzdab = Zāhedān, *Iran* 71 D9
Dve Mogili, *Bulgaria* 41 C9
Dvina, Severnaya →, *Russia* 50 C5
Dvinsk = Daugavpils, *Latvia* 9 J22
Dvor, *Croatia* 29 C13
Dvůr Králové nad Labem, *Czech Rep.* 26 A8
Dwarka, *India* 68 H3
Dwellingup, *Australia* 93 F2
Dwight, *Canada* 110 A5
Dwight, *U.S.A.* 108 E1
Dyatkovo, *Russia* 46 F8
Dyatlovo = Dzyatlava, *Belarus* 46 F3
Dyce, *U.K.* 14 D6
Dyer, C., *Canada* 101 B13
Dyer Bay, *Canada* 110 A3
Dyer Plateau, *Antarctica* 5 D17
Dyersburg, *U.S.A.* 113 G10
Dyfi →, *U.K.* 13 E3
Dyje →, *Czech Rep.* 27 C9
Dymer, *Ukraine* 47 G6
Dynów, *Poland* 45 J9
Dysart, *Australia* 94 C4
Dzamin Üüd = Borhoyn Tal, *Mongolia* 56 C6
Dzerzhinsk, *Russia* 48 B6
Dzhalinda, *Russia* 51 D13
Dzhambul = Zhambyl, *Kazakstan* 50 E8
Dzhankoy, *Ukraine* 47 K8
Dzhanybek, *Kazakstan* 48 F8
Dzharylhach, Ostriv, *Ukraine* 47 J7
Dzhezkazgan = Zhezqazghan, *Kazakstan* 50 E7
Dzhizak = Jizzakh, *Uzbekistan* 50 E7
Dzhugdzur, Khrebet, *Russia* 51 D14
Dzhvari = Jvari, *Georgia* 49 J6
Działdowo, *Poland* 45 E7
Działoszyce, *Poland* 45 H7
Działoszyn, *Poland* 45 G5
Dzibilchaltun, *Mexico* 119 C7
Dzierzgoń, *Poland* 44 E6
Dzierżoniów, *Poland* 45 H3
Dzilam de Bravo, *Mexico* 119 C7
Dzisna, *Belarus* 46 E5
Dzisna →, *Belarus* 46 E5
Dziwnów, *Poland* 44 D1
Dzungaria = Junggar Pendi, *China* 60 B3
Dzuumod, *Mongolia* 60 B5
Dzyarzhynsk, *Belarus* 46 F4
Dzyatlava, *Belarus* 46 F3

E

Eabamet L., *Canada* 102 B2
Eads, *U.S.A.* 112 F3
Eagar, *U.S.A.* 115 J9
Eagle, *Alaska, U.S.A.* 100 B5
Eagle, *Colo., U.S.A.* 114 G10
Eagle →, *Canada* 103 B8
Eagle Butte, *U.S.A.* 112 C4
Eagle Grove, *U.S.A.* 112 D8
Eagle L., *Canada* 105 D10
Eagle L., *Calif., U.S.A.* 114 F3
Eagle L., *Maine, U.S.A.* 109 B11
Eagle Lake, *Canada* 110 A6
Eagle Lake, *Maine, U.S.A.* 109 B11
Eagle Lake, *Tex., U.S.A.* 113 L6
Eagle Mountain, *U.S.A.* 117 M11
Eagle Nest, *U.S.A.* 115 H11
Eagle Pass, *U.S.A.* 113 L4
Eagle Pk., *U.S.A.* 116 G7
Eagle Pt., *Australia* 92 C3
Eagle River, *Mich., U.S.A.* 108 B1
Eagle River, *Wis., U.S.A.* 112 C10
Eaglehawk, *Australia* 95 F3
Eagles Mere, *U.S.A.* 111 E8
Ealing, *U.K.* 13 F7
Ear Falls, *Canada* 105 C10
Earle, *U.S.A.* 113 H9
Earlimart, *U.S.A.* 117 K7
Earn →, *U.K.* 14 E5
Earn, L., *U.K.* 14 E4
Earnslaw, Mt., *N.Z.* 91 L2
Earth, *U.S.A.* 113 H3
Easley, *U.S.A.* 109 H4
East Anglia, *U.K.* 12 E9
East Angus, *Canada* 103 C5
East Aurora, *U.S.A.* 110 D6
East Ayrshire □, *U.K.* 14 F4
East Bengal, *Bangla.* 67 H17
East Beskids = Vychodné Beskydy, *Europe* 27 B15
East Brady, *U.S.A.* 110 F5
East C., *N.Z.* 91 G7
East Chicago, *U.S.A.* 108 E2
East China Sea, *Asia* 60 C7
East Coulee, *Canada* 104 C6
East Dereham, *U.K.* 13 E8
East Dunbartonshire □, *U.K.* 14 F4
East Falkland, *Falk. Is.* 122 J5
East Grand Forks, *U.S.A.* 112 B6
East Greenwich, *U.S.A.* 111 E13
East Grinstead, *U.K.* 13 F8
East Hartford, *U.S.A.* 111 E12
East Helena, *U.S.A.* 114 C8
East Indies, *Asia* 52 K15
East Kilbride, *U.K.* 14 F4
East Lansing, *U.S.A.* 108 D3
East Liverpool, *U.S.A.* 110 F4
East London, *S. Africa* 89 E4
East Lothian □, *U.K.* 14 F6
East Main = Eastmain, *Canada* 102 B4
East Northport, *U.S.A.* 111 F11
East Orange, *U.S.A.* 111 F10
East Pacific Ridge, *Pac. Oc.* 97 J17
East Palestine, *U.S.A.* 110 F4
East Pine, *Canada* 104 B4
East Point, *U.S.A.* 109 J3
East Providence, *U.S.A.* 111 E13
East Pt., *Canada* 103 C7
East Renfrewshire □, *U.K.* 14 F4
East Retford = Retford, *U.K.* 12 D7
East Riding of Yorkshire □, *U.K.* 12 D7
East Rochester, *U.S.A.* 110 C7
East St. Louis, *U.S.A.* 112 F9
East Schelde = Oosterschelde →, *Neths.* 17 C4
East Siberian Sea, *Russia* 51 B17
East Stroudsburg, *U.S.A.* 111 E9
East Sussex □, *U.K.* 13 G8
East Tawas, *U.S.A.* 108 C4
East Timor = Timor Timur □, *Indonesia* 63 F7
East Toorale, *Australia* 95 E4
East Walker →, *U.S.A.* 116 G7
East Windsor, *U.S.A.* 111 F10
Eastbourne, *N.Z.* 91 J5
Eastbourne, *U.K.* 13 G8
Eastend, *Canada* 105 D7
Easter I. = Pascua, I. de, *Pac. Oc.* 97 K17
Eastern □, *Ghana* 83 D4
Eastern □, *Kenya* 86 C4
Eastern □, *Uganda* 86 B3
Eastern Cape □, *S. Africa* 88 E4
Eastern Cr. →, *Australia* 94 C3
Eastern Ghats, *India* 66 N11
Eastern Group = Lau Group, *Fiji* 91 C9
Eastern Group, *Australia* 93 F3
Eastern Province □, *S. Leone* 82 D2
Eastern Transvaal = Mpumalanga □, *S. Africa* 89 B5
Easterville, *Canada* 105 C9
Easthampton, *U.S.A.* 111 D12
Eastlake, *U.S.A.* 110 E3
Eastland, *U.S.A.* 113 J5
Eastleigh, *U.K.* 13 G6
Eastmain, *Canada* 102 B4
Eastmain →, *Canada* 102 B4
Eastman, *Canada* 111 A12
Eastman, *U.S.A.* 109 J4
Easton, *Md., U.S.A.* 108 F7
Easton, *Pa., U.S.A.* 111 F9
Easton, *Wash., U.S.A.* 116 C5
Eastpointe, *U.S.A.* 110 D2
Eastport, *U.S.A.* 109 C12
Eastsound, *U.S.A.* 116 B4
Eaton, *U.S.A.* 112 E2
Eatonia, *Canada* 105 C7
Eatonton, *U.S.A.* 109 J4
Eatontown, *U.S.A.* 111 F10
Eatonville, *U.S.A.* 116 D4
Eau Claire, *U.S.A.* 112 C9
Eau Claire, L. à l', *Canada* 102 A5
Eauze, *France* 20 E4

Eban, *Nigeria* 83 D5
Ebbw Vale, *U.K.* 13 F4
Ebeltoft, *Denmark* 11 H4
Ebeltoft Vig, *Denmark* .. 11 H4
Ebensburg, *U.S.A.* 110 F6
Ebensee, *Austria* 26 D6
Eber Gölü, *Turkey* 72 C4
Eberbach, *Germany* 25 F4
Ebersalde-Finow, *Germany* 24 C9
Ebetsu, *Japan* 54 C10
Ebian, *China* 58 C4
Ebingen, *Germany* 25 G5
Éboli, *Italy* 31 B8
Ebolowa, *Cameroon* 83 E7
Ebonyi □, *Nigeria* 83 D6
Ebrach, *Germany* 25 F6
Ébrié, Lagune, *Ivory C.* .. 82 D4
Ebro →, *Spain* 32 E5
Ebro, Embalse del, *Spain* . 34 C7
Ebstorf, *Germany* 24 B6
Eceabat, *Turkey* 41 F10
Ech Cheliff, *Algeria* 78 A6
Echigo-Sammyaku, *Japan* . 55 F9
Échirolles, *France* 21 C9
Echizen-Misaki, *Japan* ... 55 G7
Echmiadzin = Yejmiadzin,
  Armenia 49 K7
Echo Bay, *N.W.T., Canada* 100 B8
Echo Bay, *Ont., Canada* .. 102 C3
Echoing →, *Canada* 102 B1
Echternach, *Lux.* 17 E6
Echuca, *Australia* 95 F3
Ecija, *Spain* 35 H5
Eckental, *Germany* 25 F7
Eckernförde, *Germany* 24 A5
Eclipse Is., *Australia* 92 B4
Eclipse Sd., *Canada* 101 A11
Écommoy, *France* 18 E7
Écouché, *France* 18 D6
Ecuador ■, *S. Amer.* 124 D3
Écueillé, *France* 18 E8
Ed, *Sweden* 11 F5
Ed Dabbura, *Sudan* 80 D3
Ed Da'ein, *Sudan* 81 E2
Ed Damazin, *Sudan* 79 F12
Ed Dâmer, *Sudan* 80 D3
Ed Debba, *Sudan* 80 D3
Ed-Déffa, *Egypt* 80 A2
Ed Deim, *Sudan* 81 E2
Ed Dueim, *Sudan* 81 E3
Edam, *Canada* 105 C7
Edam, *Neths.* 17 B5
Edane, *Sweden* 10 E6
Eday, *U.K.* 14 B6
Edd, *Eritrea* 81 E5
Eddrachillis B., *U.K.* 14 C3
Eddystone Pt., *Australia* .. 94 G4
Ede, *Neths.* 17 B5
Ede, *Nigeria* 83 D5
Edéa, *Cameroon* 83 E7
Edebäck, *Sweden* 10 D7
Edehon L., *Canada* 105 A9
Edelény, *Hungary* 42 E6
Eden, *Australia* 95 F4
Eden, *N.C., U.S.A.* 109 G6
Eden, *N.Y., U.S.A.* 110 D6
Eden, *Tex., U.S.A.* 113 K5
Eden →, *U.K.* 12 C4
Edenburg, *S. Africa* 88 D4
Edendale, *S. Africa* 89 D5
Edenderry, *Ireland* 15 C4
Edenhope, *Australia* 95 F3
Edenton, *U.S.A.* 109 G7
Edenville, *S. Africa* 89 D4
Eder →, *Germany* 24 D5
Eder-Stausee, *Germany* ... 24 D4
Edgar, *U.S.A.* 112 E6
Edgartown, *U.S.A.* 111 E14
Edge Hill, *U.K.* 13 E6
Edgefield, *U.S.A.* 109 J5
Edgeley, *U.S.A.* 112 B5
Edgemont, *U.S.A.* 112 D3
Edgeøya, *Svalbard* 4 B9
Édhessa, *Greece* 40 F6
Edievale, *N.Z.* 91 L2
Edina, *Liberia* 82 D2
Edina, *U.S.A.* 112 E8
Edinboro, *U.S.A.* 110 E4
Edinburg, *U.S.A.* 113 M5
Edinburgh, *U.K.* 14 F5
Edinburgh, City of □, *U.K.* 14 F5
Edineţ, *Moldova* 43 B12
Edirne, *Turkey* 41 E10
Edirne □, *Turkey* 41 E10
Edison, *U.S.A.* 116 B4
Edithburgh, *Australia* 95 F2
Edmeston, *U.S.A.* 111 D9
Edmond, *U.S.A.* 113 H6
Edmonds, *U.S.A.* 116 C4
Edmonton, *Australia* 94 B4
Edmonton, *Canada* 104 C6
Edmund L., *Canada* 102 B1
Edmundston, *Canada* 103 C6
Edna, *U.S.A.* 113 L6
Edo □, *Nigeria* 83 D6
Edolo, *Italy* 28 B7
Edremit, *Turkey* 39 B9
Edremit Körfezi, *Turkey* .. 39 B8
Edsbro, *Sweden* 10 E12
Edsbyn, *Sweden* 10 C9
Edson, *Canada* 104 C5
Eduardo Castex, *Argentina* 126 D3
Edward →, *Australia* 95 F3
Edward, L., *Africa* 86 C2
Edward River, *Australia* .. 94 A3
Edward VII Land, *Antarctica* 5 E13
Edwards, *Calif., U.S.A.* .. 117 L9
Edwards, *N.Y., U.S.A.* .. 111 B9
Edwards Air Force Base,
  U.S.A. 117 L9

Edwards Plateau, *U.S.A.* .. 113 K4
Edwardsville, *U.S.A.* 111 E9
Edzo, *Canada* 104 A5
Eeklo, *Belgium* 17 C3
Eferding, *Austria* 26 C7
Effingham, *U.S.A.* 108 F1
Eforie, *Romania* 43 F13
Ega →, *Spain* 32 C3
Égadi, Ísole, *Italy* 30 E5
Egan Range, *U.S.A.* 114 G6
Eganville, *Canada* 102 C4
Eger = Cheb, *Czech Rep.* . 26 A5
Eger, *Hungary* 42 C5
Eger →, *Hungary* 42 C5
Egersund, *Norway* 9 G12
Egg L., *Canada* 105 B7
Eggenburg, *Austria* 26 C8
Eggenfelden, *Germany* 25 G8
Éghezée, *Belgium* 17 D4
Égletons, *France* 20 C6
Egmont, *Canada* 104 D4
Egmont, C., *N.Z.* 91 H4
Egmont, Mt., *N.Z.* 91 H5
Egra, *India* 69 J12
Eğridir, *Turkey* 72 D4
Eğridir Gölü, *Turkey* 70 B1
Egtved, *Denmark* 11 J3
Egume, *Nigeria* 83 D6
Éguzon-Chantôme, *France* . 19 F8
Egvekinot, *Russia* 51 C19
Egyek, *Hungary* 42 C5
Egypt ■, *Africa* 80 B3
Eha Amufu, *Nigeria* 83 D6
Ehime □, *Japan* 55 H6
Ehingen, *Germany* 25 G5
Ehrenberg, *U.S.A.* 117 M12
Ehrwald, *Austria* 26 D3
Eibar, *Spain* 32 B2
Eichstätt, *Germany* 25 G7
Eider →, *Germany* 24 A4
Eidsvold, *Australia* 95 D5
Eidsvoll, *Norway* 9 F14
Eifel, *Germany* 25 E2
Eiffel Flats, *Zimbabwe* ... 87 F3
Eiger, *Switz.* 28 B5
Eigg, *U.K.* 14 E2
Eighty Mile Beach, *Australia* 92 C3
Eil, *Somali Rep.* 74 F4
Eil, L., *U.K.* 14 E3
Eildon, *Australia* 95 F4
Eildon, L., *Australia* 95 F4
Eilenburg, *Germany* 24 D8
Ein el Luweiqa, *Sudan* ... 81 E3
Einasleigh, *Australia* 94 B3
Einasleigh →, *Australia* .. 94 B3
Einbeck, *Germany* 24 D5
Eindhoven, *Neths.* 17 C5
Einsiedeln, *Switz.* 25 H4
Eire = Ireland ■, *Europe* . 15 C4
Eiríksjökull, *Iceland* 8 D3
Eirunepé, *Brazil* 124 E5
Eiseb →, *Namibia* 88 C2
Eisenach, *Germany* 24 E6
Eisenberg, *Germany* 24 E7
Eisenerz, *Austria* 26 D7
Eisenhüttenstadt, *Germany* . 24 C10
Eisenkappel, *Austria* 26 E7
Eisenstadt, *Austria* 27 D9
Eisfeld, *Germany* 25 E6
Eisleben, *Germany* 24 D7
Eislingen, *Germany* 25 G5
Eivissa, *Spain* 37 C7
Eixe, Serra do, *Spain* ... 34 C4
Ejea de los Caballeros, *Spain* 32 C3
Ejeda, *Madag.* 89 C7
Ejura, *Ghana* 83 D4
Ejutla, *Mexico* 119 D5
Ekalaka, *U.S.A.* 112 C2
Ekenässjön, *Sweden* 11 G9
Ekerö, *Sweden* 10 E11
Eket, *Nigeria* 83 E6
Eketahuna, *N.Z.* 91 J5
Ekhínos, *Greece* 41 E9
Ekibastuz, *Kazakstan* 50 D8
Ekiti □, *Nigeria* 83 D6
Ekoli,
  Dem. Rep. of the Congo . 86 C1
Ekoln, *Sweden* 10 E11
Ekshärad, *Sweden* 10 D7
Eksjö, *Sweden* 11 G8
Ekuma →, *Namibia* 88 B2
Ekwan →, *Canada* 102 B3
Ekwan Pt., *Canada* 102 B3
El Aaiún, *W. Sahara* 78 C3
El Abanico, *Chile* 126 D1
El Abbasia, *Sudan* 81 E3
El 'Agrûd, *Egypt* 75 E3
El Ait, *Sudan* 81 E2
El 'Aiyat, *Egypt* 80 J7
El Alamein, *Egypt* 80 A2
El 'Aqaba, W. →, *Egypt* . 75 E2
El 'Arag, *Egypt* 80 B2
El Arahal, *Spain* 35 H5
El Arîha, *West Bank* 75 D4
El 'Arîsh, *Egypt* 75 D2
El 'Arîsh, W. →, *Egypt* .. 75 D2
El Asnam = Ech Cheliff,
  Algeria 78 A6
El Astillero, *Spain* 34 B7
El Badâri, *Egypt* 80 B3
El Bahrein, *Egypt* 80 B2
El Ballâs, *Egypt* 80 B3
El Balyana, *Egypt* 80 B3
El Baqeir, *Sudan* 80 D3
El Barco de Ávila, *Spain* . 34 E5
El Barco de Valdeorras = O
  Barco, *Spain* 34 C4
El Bauga, *Sudan* 80 D3
El Bawiti, *Egypt* 80 B2
El Bayadh, *Algeria* 78 B6
El Bierzo, *Spain* 34 C4

El Bluff, *Nic.* 120 D3
El Bonillo, *Spain* 33 G2
El Brûk, W. →, *Egypt* ... 75 E2
El Buheirat □, *Sudan* 81 F3
El Burgo de Osma, *Spain* . 32 D1
El Cajon, *U.S.A.* 117 N10
El Campo, *U.S.A.* 113 L6
El Centro, *U.S.A.* 117 N11
El Cerro, *Bolivia* 124 G6
El Cerro de Andévalo, *Spain* 35 H4
El Compadre, *Mexico* 117 N10
El Coronil, *Spain* 35 H5
El Cuy, *Argentina* 128 D3
El Cuyo, *Mexico* 119 C7
El Dab'a, *Egypt* 80 H6
El Daheir, *Egypt* 75 D3
El Dátil, *Mexico* 118 B2
El Deir, *Egypt* 80 B3
El Dere, *Somali Rep.* 74 G4
El Descanso, *Mexico* 117 N10
El Desemboque, *Mexico* .. 118 A2
El Dilingat, *Egypt* 80 H7
El Diviso, *Colombia* 124 C3
El Djouf, *Mauritania* 78 D4
El Dorado, *Ark., U.S.A.* . 113 J8
El Dorado, *Kans., U.S.A.* 113 G6
El Dorado, *Venezuela* 124 B6
El 'Ein, *Sudan* 81 D2
El Ejido, *Spain* 35 J8
El Escorial, *Spain* 34 E6
El Espinar, *Spain* 34 D6
El Faiyûm, *Egypt* 80 J7
El Fâsher, *Sudan* 81 E2
El Fashn, *Egypt* 80 J7
El Ferrol = Ferrol, *Spain* . 34 B2
El Fifi, *Sudan* 81 E2
El Fuerte, *Mexico* 118 B3
El Ga'a, *Sudan* 81 E2
El Gal, *Somali Rep.* 74 E5
El Garef, *Sudan* 81 E3
El Gebir, *Sudan* 81 E2
El Gedida, *Egypt* 80 B2
El Geneina = Al Junaynah,
  Sudan 79 F10
El Geteina, *Sudan* 81 E3
El Gezira □, *Sudan* 81 E3
El Gîr, *Sudan* 80 D2
El Gîza, *Egypt* 80 J7
El Goléa, *Algeria* 78 B6
El Grau, *Spain* 33 G4
El Hagiz, *Sudan* 81 D4
El Hâi, *Egypt* 80 J7
El Hammam, *Egypt* 80 A2
El Hawata, *Sudan* 81 E3
El Heiz, *Egypt* 80 B2
El Hideib, *Sudan* 81 E3
El Hilla, *Sudan* 81 E2
El 'Idisât, *Egypt* 80 B3
El Iskandarîya, *Egypt* 80 H7
El Istiwa'iya, *Sudan* 79 G11
El Jadida, *Morocco* 78 B4
El Jardal, *Honduras* 120 D2
El Jebelein, *Sudan* 81 E3
El Kab, *Sudan* 80 D3
El Kabrît, G., *Egypt* 75 E1
El Kafr el Sharqi, *Egypt* .. 80 H7
El Kamlin, *Sudan* 81 D3
El Karaba, *Sudan* 80 D3
El Kere, *Ethiopia* 81 F5
El Khandaq, *Sudan* 80 D3
El Khârga, *Egypt* 80 B3
El Khartûm, *Sudan* 81 D3
El Khartûm □, *Sudan* ... 81 D3
El Khartûm Bahrî, *Sudan* . 81 D3
El Kuntilla, *Egypt* 75 E3
El Laqâwa, *Sudan* 81 E2
El Laqeita, *Egypt* 80 B3
El Leh, *Ethiopia* 81 G4
El Leiya, *Sudan* 81 D4
El Maestrazgo, *Spain* 32 E4
El Mafâza, *Sudan* 81 E3
El Maghra, *Egypt* 80 A2
El Mahalla el Kubra, *Egypt* 80 H7
El Mahârîq, *Egypt* 80 B3
El Maîmûn, *Egypt* 80 J7
El Maks el Bahari, *Egypt* . 80 C3
El Manshâh, *Egypt* 80 B3
El Mansûra, *Egypt* 80 H7
El Manzala, *Egypt* 80 H7
El Marâgha, *Egypt* 80 B3
El Masid, *Sudan* 81 D3
El Masnou, *Spain* 32 D7
El Matariya, *Egypt* 80 H8
El Meda, *Ethiopia* 81 F5
El Medano, *Canary Is.* ... 37 F3
El Metemma, *Sudan* 81 D3
El Milagro, *Argentina* ... 126 C2
El Minyâ, *Egypt* 80 B3
El Monte, *U.S.A.* 117 L8
El Montseny, *Spain* 32 D7
El Mreyye, *Mauritania* ... 82 B3
El Niybo, *Ethiopia* 81 G4
El Obeid, *Sudan* 81 E3
El Odaiya, *Sudan* 81 E2
El Oro, *Mexico* 119 D4
El Oued, *Algeria* 78 B7
El Palmito, Presa, *Mexico* . 118 B3
El Paso, *U.S.A.* 115 L10
El Paso Robles, *U.S.A.* .. 116 K6
El Pedernoso, *Spain* 33 F2
El Pedroso, *Spain* 35 H5
El Pobo de Dueñas, *Spain* . 32 E3
El Portal, *U.S.A.* 116 H7
El Porvenir, *Mexico* 118 A3
El Prat de Llobregat, *Spain* 32 D7
El Progreso, *Honduras* ... 120 C2
El Pueblito, *Mexico* 118 B3
El Pueblo, *Canary Is.* 37 F2
El Puente del Arzobispo,
  Spain 34 F5

El Puerto de Santa María,
  Spain 35 J4
El Qâhira, *Egypt* 80 H7
El Qantara, *Egypt* 75 E1
El Qasr, *Egypt* 80 B2
El Qubâbât, *Egypt* 80 J7
El Quseima, *Egypt* 75 E3
El Qusîya, *Egypt* 80 B3
El Râshda, *Egypt* 80 B2
El Real, *Panama* 124 B3
El Reno, *U.S.A.* 113 H6
El Rîdisiya, *Egypt* 80 C3
El Rio, *U.S.A.* 117 L7
El Ronquillo, *Spain* 35 H4
El Roque, Pta., *Canary Is.* . 37 F4
El Rosarito, *Mexico* 118 B2
El Rubio, *Spain* 35 H5
El Saff, *Egypt* 80 J7
El Saheira, W. →, *Egypt* . 75 E2
El Salto, *Mexico* 118 C3
El Salvador ■, *Cent. Amer.* 120 D2
El Sauce, *Nic.* 120 D2
El Saucejo, *Spain* 35 H5
El Shallal, *Egypt* 80 C3
El Simbillawein, *Egypt* ... 80 H7
El Sueco, *Mexico* 118 B3
El Suweis, *Egypt* 80 J8
El Tabbîn, *Egypt* 80 J7
El Tamarâni, W. →, *Egypt* 75 E3
El Thamad, *Egypt* 75 F3
El Tigre, *Venezuela* 124 B6
El Tîh, Gebal, *Egypt* 75 F2
El Tîna, *Egypt* 80 H8
El Tîna, Khalîg, *Egypt* ... 75 D1
El Tofo, *Chile* 126 B1
El Tránsito, *Chile* 126 B1
El Tûr, *Egypt* 70 D2
El Turbio, *Argentina* 128 G2
El Uqsur, *Egypt* 80 B3
El Venado, *Mexico* 118 C4
El Vendrell, *Spain* 32 D6
El Vergel, *Mexico* 118 B3
El Vigía, *Venezuela* 124 B4
El Viso del Alcor, *Spain* .. 35 H5
El Wabeira, *Egypt* 75 F2
El Wak, *Kenya* 86 B5
El Waqf, *Egypt* 80 B3
El Weguet, *Ethiopia* 81 F5
El Wuz, *Sudan* 81 D3
Elafónisos, *Greece* 38 E4
Élancourt, *France* 19 D8
Élassa, *Greece* 39 F8
Elassón, *Greece* 38 B4
Elat, *Israel* 75 F3
Eláthia, *Greece* 38 C4
Elâzığ, *Turkey* 70 B3
Elba, *Italy* 28 F7
Elba, *U.S.A.* 109 K2
Elbasani, *Albania* 40 E4
Elbe, *U.S.A.* 116 D4
Elbe →, *Europe* 24 B4
Elbe-Seitenkanal, *Germany* 24 C6
Elbert, Mt., *U.S.A.* 115 G10
Elberton, *U.S.A.* 109 H4
Elbeuf, *France* 18 C8
Elbidtan, *Turkey* 70 B3
Elbing = Elblag, *Poland* .. 44 D6
Elbistan, *Turkey* 72 C7
Elblag, *Poland* 44 D6
Elbow, *Canada* 105 C7
Elbrus, *Asia* 49 J6
Elburz Mts. = Alborz,
  Reshteh-ye Kûhhâ-ye, *Iran* 71 C7
Elche, *Spain* 33 G4
Elche de la Sierra, *Spain* . 33 G2
Elcho I., *Australia* 94 A2
Elda, *Spain* 33 G4
Elde →, *Germany* 24 B7
Eldon, *Mo., U.S.A.* 112 F8
Eldon, *Wash., U.S.A.* ... 116 C3
Eldora, *U.S.A.* 112 D8
Eldorado, *Argentina* 127 B5
Eldorado, *Canada* 110 B7
Eldorado, *Mexico* 118 C3
Eldorado, *Ill., U.S.A.* ... 108 G1
Eldorado, *Tex., U.S.A.* .. 113 K4
Eldorado Springs, *U.S.A.* . 113 G8
Eldoret, *Kenya* 86 B4
Eldred, *U.S.A.* 110 E6
Elea, C., *Cyprus* 36 D13
Eleanora, Pk., *Australia* .. 93 F3
Elefantes →, *Mozam.* 89 C5
Elektrogorsk, *Russia* 46 E10
Elektrostal, *Russia* 46 E10
Elele, *Nigeria* 83 D6
Elena, *Bulgaria* 41 D9
Elephant Butte Reservoir,
  U.S.A. 115 K10
Elephant I., *Antarctica* ... 5 C18
Eleshnitsa, *Bulgaria* 40 E7
Eleşkirt, *Turkey* 73 C10
Eleuthera, *Bahamas* 120 B4
Elevsís, *Greece* 38 C5
Elevtheroúpolis, *Greece* .. 41 F8
Elgin, *Canada* 111 B8
Elgin, *U.K.* 14 D5
Elgin, *Ill., U.S.A.* 108 D1
Elgin, *N. Dak., U.S.A.* .. 112 B4
Elgin, *Oreg., U.S.A.* 114 D5
Elgin, *Tex., U.S.A.* 113 K6
Elgoibar, *Spain* 32 B2
Elgon, Mt., *Africa* 86 B3
Eliase, *Indonesia* 63 F8
Elikón, *Greece* 38 C4
Elim, *Namibia* 88 B2
Elim, *S. Africa* 88 E2
Elin Pelin, *Bulgaria* 40 D7
Elisabethville =
  Lubumbashi,
  Dem. Rep. of the Congo . 87 E2
Elista, *Russia* 49 G7

Elizabeth, *Australia* 95 E2
Elizabeth, *N.J., U.S.A.* .. 111 F10
Elizabeth, *Pa., U.S.A.* ... 111 F10
Elizabeth City, *U.S.A.* ... 109 G7
Elizabethton, *U.S.A.* 109 G4
Elizabethtown, *Ky., U.S.A.* 108 G3
Elizabethtown, *N.Y., U.S.A.* 111 B11
Elizabethtown, *Pa., U.S.A.* 111 F8
Elizondo, *Spain* 32 B3
Ełk, *Poland* 44 E9
Elk →, *Canada* 104 C5
Elk →, *Poland* 44 E9
Elk →, *U.S.A.* 109 H2
Elk City, *U.S.A.* 113 H5
Elk Creek, *U.S.A.* 116 F4
Elk Grove, *U.S.A.* 116 G5
Elk Island Nat. Park,
  Canada 104 C6
Elk Lake, *Canada* 102 C3
Elk Point, *Canada* 105 C6
Elk River, *Idaho, U.S.A.* . 114 C5
Elk River, *Minn., U.S.A.* . 112 C8
Elkedra →, *Australia* 94 C2
Elkhart, *Ind., U.S.A.* ... 108 E3
Elkhart, *Kans., U.S.A.* .. 113 G4
Elkhorn, *Canada* 105 D8
Elkhorn →, *U.S.A.* 112 E6
Elkhovo, *Bulgaria* 41 D10
Elkin, *U.S.A.* 109 G5
Elkins, *U.S.A.* 108 F6
Elkland, *U.S.A.* 110 E7
Elko, *Canada* 104 D5
Elko, *U.S.A.* 114 F6
Elkton, *U.S.A.* 110 C1
Ell, L., *Australia* 93 E4
Ellef Ringnes I., *Canada* .. 4 B2
Ellen, Mt., *U.S.A.* 111 B12
Ellenburg, *U.S.A.* 111 B11
Ellendale, *U.S.A.* 112 B5
Ellensburg, *U.S.A.* 114 C3
Ellenville, *U.S.A.* 111 E10
Ellery, Mt., *Australia* 95 F4
Ellesmere, L., *N.Z.* 91 M4
Ellesmere I., *Canada* 4 B4
Ellesmere Port, *U.K.* 12 D5
Ellice Is. = Tuvalu ■,
  Pac. Oc. 96 H9
Ellicottville, *U.S.A.* 110 D6
Elliot, *Australia* 94 B1
Elliot, *S. Africa* 89 E4
Elliot Lake, *Canada* 102 C3
Elliotdale = Xhora, *S. Africa* 89 E4
Ellis, *U.S.A.* 112 F5
Elliston, *Australia* 95 E1
Ellisville, *U.S.A.* 113 K10
Ellon, *U.K.* 14 D6
Ellore = Eluru, *India* 67 L12
Ellsworth, *Kans., U.S.A.* . 112 F5
Ellsworth, *Maine, U.S.A.* . 109 C11
Ellsworth Land, *Antarctica* . 5 D16
Ellsworth Mts., *Antarctica* . 5 D16
Ellwangen, *Germany* 25 G6
Ellwood City, *U.S.A.* 110 F4
Elm, *Switz.* 25 C8
Elma, *Canada* 105 D9
Elma, *U.S.A.* 116 D3
Elmadağ, *Turkey* 72 C5
Elmalı, *Turkey* 39 E11
Elmhurst, *U.S.A.* 108 E2
Elmina, *Ghana* 83 D4
Elmira, *Canada* 110 C4
Elmira, *U.S.A.* 110 D8
Elmira Heights, *U.S.A.* .. 110 D8
Elmore, *Australia* 95 F3
Elmore, *U.S.A.* 117 M11
Elmshorn, *Germany* 24 B5
Elmvale, *Canada* 110 B5
Elne, *France* 20 F6
Elora, *Canada* 110 C4
Elos, *Greece* 38 E4
Eloúnda, *Greece* 36 D7
Eloy, *U.S.A.* 115 K8
Éloyes, *France* 19 D13
Elrose, *Canada* 105 C7
Elsdorf, *Germany* 24 E2
Elsie, *U.S.A.* 116 E3
Elsinore = Helsingør,
  Denmark 11 H6
Elster →, *Germany* 24 D7
Elsterwerda, *Germany* ... 24 D9
Eltham, *N.Z.* 91 H5
Elton, *Russia* 49 F8
Elton, Ozero, *Russia* 49 F8
Eltville, *Germany* 25 E4
Eluru, *India* 67 L12
Elvas, *Portugal* 35 G3
Elven, *France* 18 E4
Elverum, *Norway* 9 F14
Elvire →, *Australia* 92 C4
Elvire, Mt., *Australia* 93 E2
Elvo →, *Italy* 28 C5
Elwell, L., *U.S.A.* 114 B8
Elwood, *Ind., U.S.A.* 108 E3
Elwood, *Nebr., U.S.A.* ... 112 E5
Elx = Elche, *Spain* 33 G4
Ely, *U.K.* 13 E8
Ely, *Minn., U.S.A.* 112 B8
Ely, *Nev., U.S.A.* 114 G6
Elyria, *U.S.A.* 110 E2
Elyrus, *Greece* 38 F5
Elz →, *Germany* 25 G3
Emådalen, *Sweden* 10 C8
Emāmrūd, *Iran* 71 B7
Emån →, *Sweden* 11 G10
Emba, *Kazakstan* 50 E6
Emba →, *Kazakstan* 50 E6
Embarcación, *Argentina* .. 126 A3
Embarras Portage, *Canada* . 105 B6
Embetsu, *Japan* 54 B10
Embi = Emba, *Kazakstan* . 50 E6

Embi = Emba →, *Kazakstan* 50 E6
Embóna, *Greece* 36 C9
Embrun, *France* 21 D10
Embu, *Kenya* 86 C4
Emden, *Germany* 24 B3
Emecik, *Turkey* 39 E9
Emerald, *Australia* 94 C4
Emerson, *Canada* 105 D9
Emet, *Turkey* 39 B11
Emi Koussi, *Chad* 79 E9
Emília-Romagna □, *Italy* 28 D8
Emilius, Mte., *Italy* 28 C4
Eminabad, *Pakistan* 68 C6
Emine, Nos, *Bulgaria* 41 D11
Emirdağ, *Turkey* 72 C4
Emlenton, *U.S.A.* 110 E5
Emlichheim, *Germany* 24 C2
Emmaboda, *Sweden* 11 H9
Emmaus, *S. Africa* 88 D4
Emmaus, *U.S.A.* 111 F9
Emme →, *Switz.* 25 H3
Emmeloord, *Neths.* 17 B5
Emmen, *Neths.* 17 B6
Emmen, *Switz.* 25 H4
Emmendingen, *Germany* 25 G3
Emmental, *Switz.* 25 J3
Emmerich, *Germany* 24 D2
Emmet, *Australia* 94 C3
Emmetsburg, *U.S.A.* 112 D7
Emmett, *Idaho, U.S.A.* 114 E5
Emmett, *Mich., U.S.A.* 110 D2
Emmonak, *U.S.A.* 100 B3
Emo, *Canada* 105 D10
Emőd, *Hungary* 42 C5
Emona, *Bulgaria* 41 D11
Empalme, *Mexico* 118 B2
Empangeni, *S. Africa* 89 D5
Empedrado, *Argentina* 126 B4
Emperor Seamount Chain, *Pac. Oc.* 96 D9
Empoli, *Italy* 28 E7
Emporia, *Kans., U.S.A.* 112 F6
Emporia, *Va., U.S.A.* 109 G7
Emporium, *U.S.A.* 110 E6
Empress, *Canada* 105 C7
Empty Quarter = Rub' al Khālī, *Si. Arabia* 74 D4
Ems →, *Germany* 24 B3
Emsdale, *Canada* 110 A5
Emsdetten, *Germany* 24 C3
Emu, *China* 57 C15
Emu Park, *Australia* 94 C5
'En 'Avrona, *Israel* 75 F4
En Nahud, *Sudan* 81 E2
En Nofalab, *Sudan* 81 D3
Ena, *Japan* 55 G8
Enana, *Namibia* 88 B2
Enånger, *Sweden* 10 C11
Enaratoli, *Indonesia* 63 E9
Enard B., *U.K.* 14 C3
Enare = Inarijärvi, *Finland* 8 B22
Encampment, *U.S.A.* 114 F10
Encantadas, Serra, *Brazil* 127 C5
Encarnación, *Paraguay* 127 B4
Encarnación de Diaz, *Mexico* 118 C4
Enchi, *Ghana* 82 D4
Encinitas, *U.S.A.* 117 M9
Encino, *U.S.A.* 115 J11
Encounter B., *Australia* 95 F2
Encs, *Hungary* 42 B6
Endako, *Canada* 104 C3
Ende, *Indonesia* 63 F6
Endeavour Str., *Australia* 94 A3
Endelave, *Denmark* 11 J4
Enderbury I., *Kiribati* 96 H10
Enderby, *Canada* 104 C5
Enderby I., *Australia* 92 D2
Enderby Land, *Antarctica* 5 C5
Enderlin, *U.S.A.* 112 B6
Endicott, *U.S.A.* 111 D8
Endwell, *U.S.A.* 111 D8
Endyalgout I., *Australia* 92 B5
Eneabba, *Australia* 93 E2
Enewetak Atoll, *Marshall Is.* 96 F8
Enez, *Turkey* 41 F10
Enfield, *Canada* 103 D7
Enfield, *Conn., U.S.A.* 111 E12
Enfield, *N.H., U.S.A.* 111 C12
Engadin, *Switz.* 25 J6
Engaño, C., *Dom. Rep.* 121 C6
Engaño, C., *Phil.* 63 A6
Engaru, *Japan* 54 B11
Engcobo, *S. Africa* 89 E4
Engelberg, *Switz.* 25 J4
Engels, *Russia* 48 E8
Engemann L., *Canada* 105 B7
Engershatu, *Eritrea* 81 D4
Enggano, *Indonesia* 62 F2
England, *U.S.A.* 113 H9
England □, *U.K.* 12 D7
Englee, *Canada* 103 B8
Englehart, *Canada* 102 C4
Englewood, *U.S.A.* 112 F2
English →, *Canada* 105 C10
English Bazar = Ingraj Bazar, *India* 69 G13
English Channel, *Europe* 13 G6
English River, *Canada* 102 C1
Engures ezers, *Latvia* 44 A10
Enguri →, *Georgia* 49 J5
Enid, *U.S.A.* 113 G6
Enipévs →, *Greece* 38 B4
Enkhuizen, *Neths.* 17 B5
Enköping, *Sweden* 10 E11
Enle, *China* 58 F3
Enna, *Italy* 31 E7
Ennadai, *Canada* 105 A8
Ennadai L., *Canada* 105 A8
Ennedi, *Chad* 79 E10
Enngonia, *Australia* 95 D4
Ennigerloh, *Germany* 24 D4
Ennis, *Ireland* 15 D3
Ennis, *Mont., U.S.A.* 114 D8
Ennis, *Tex., U.S.A.* 113 J6
Enniscorthy, *Ireland* 15 D5
Enniskillen, *U.K.* 15 B4
Ennistimon, *Ireland* 15 D2
Enns, *Austria* 26 C7
Enns →, *Austria* 26 C7
Enontekiö, *Finland* 8 B20
Enosburg Falls, *U.S.A.* 111 B12
Enping, *China* 59 F9
Enriquillo, L., *Dom. Rep.* 121 C5
Enschede, *Neths.* 17 B6
Ensenada, *Argentina* 126 C4
Ensenada, *Mexico* 118 A1
Ensenada de los Muertos, *Mexico* 118 C2
Enshi, *China* 58 B7
Ensiola, Pta. de n', *Spain* 37 B9
Ensisheim, *France* 19 E14
Entebbe, *Uganda* 86 B3
Enterprise, *Canada* 104 A5
Enterprise, *Ala., U.S.A.* 109 K3
Enterprise, *Oreg., U.S.A.* 114 D5
Entraygues-sur-Truyère, *France* 20 D6
Entre Ríos, *Bolivia* 126 A3
Entre Ríos □, *Argentina* 126 C4
Entrepeñas, Embalse de, *Spain* 32 E2
Entroncamento, *Portugal* 35 F2
Enugu, *Nigeria* 83 D6
Enugu □, *Nigeria* 83 D6
Enugu Ezike, *Nigeria* 83 D6
Enumclaw, *U.S.A.* 116 C5
Envermeu, *France* 18 C8
Enviken, *Sweden* 10 D9
Enying, *Hungary* 42 D3
Enza →, *Italy* 28 D7
Eólie, Ís., *Italy* 31 D7
Epanomí, *Greece* 40 F6
Epe, *Neths.* 17 B5
Epe, *Nigeria* 83 D5
Épernay, *France* 19 C10
Épernon, *France* 19 D8
Ephesus, *Turkey* 39 D9
Ephraim, *U.S.A.* 114 G8
Ephrata, *Pa., U.S.A.* 111 F8
Ephrata, *Wash., U.S.A.* 114 C4
Epidaurus Limera, *Greece* 38 E5
Épila, *Spain* 32 D3
Épinac, *France* 19 F11
Épinal, *France* 19 D13
Episkopi, *Cyprus* 36 E11
Episkopí, *Greece* 36 D6
Episkopi Bay, *Cyprus* 36 E11
Epitálion, *Greece* 38 D3
Eppan = Appiano, *Italy* 29 B8
Eppingen, *Germany* 25 F4
Epsom, *U.K.* 13 F7
Epukiro, *Namibia* 88 C2
Equatorial Guinea ■, *Africa* 84 D1
Er Hai, *China* 58 E3
Er Rahad, *Sudan* 81 E3
Er Rif, *Morocco* 78 A5
Er Rogel, *Sudan* 80 D4
Er Roseires, *Sudan* 81 E3
Er Rua'at, *Sudan* 81 E3
Eraclea, *Italy* 29 C9
Erāwadī Myit = Irrawaddy →, *Burma* 67 M19
Erba, *Italy* 28 C6
Erba, *Sudan* 80 D4
Erba, J., *Sudan* 80 C4
Erbaa, *Turkey* 72 B7
Erbeskopf, *Germany* 25 F3
Erbil = Arbīl, *Iraq* 70 B5
Erbu, *Ethiopia* 81 E3
Erçek, *Turkey* 70 B4
Erçiş, *Turkey* 73 C10
Erciyaş Dağı, *Turkey* 70 B2
Érd, *Hungary* 42 C3
Erdao Jiang →, *China* 57 C14
Erdek, *Turkey* 41 F11
Erdemli, *Turkey* 72 D6
Erdene = Ulaan-Uul, *Mongolia* 56 B6
Erdenetsogt, *Mongolia* 56 C4
Erding, *Germany* 25 G7
Erdre →, *France* 18 E5
Erebus, Mt., *Antarctica* 5 D11
Erechim, *Brazil* 127 B5
Ereğli, *Konya, Turkey* 70 B2
Ereğli, *Zonguldak, Turkey* 72 B4
Erei, Monti, *Italy* 31 E7
Erenhot, *China* 56 C7
Eresma →, *Spain* 34 D6
Eressós, *Greece* 39 B7
Erewadi Myitwanya, *Burma* 67 M19
Erfenisdam, *S. Africa* 88 D4
Erfstadt, *Germany* 24 E2
Erft →, *Germany* 24 D2
Erfurt, *Germany* 24 E7
Erg Iguidi, *Africa* 78 C4
Ergani, *Turkey* 70 B3
Ergel, *Mongolia* 56 C5
Ergene →, *Turkey* 41 E10
Ergeni Vozvyshennost, *Russia* 49 G7
Ērgli, *Latvia* 9 H21
Erhlin, *Taiwan* 59 F13
Eria →, *Spain* 34 C5
Eriba, *Sudan* 81 D4
Eriboll, L., *U.K.* 14 C4
Érice, *Italy* 30 D5
Erie, *U.S.A.* 110 D4
Erie, L., *N. Amer.* 110 D4
Erie Canal, *U.S.A.* 110 C7
Erieau, *Canada* 110 D3
Erigavo, *Somali Rep.* 74 E4
Erikoúsa, *Greece* 36 A3
Eriksdale, *Canada* 105 C9
Erímanthos, *Greece* 38 D3
Erimo-misaki, *Japan* 54 D11
Erinpura, *India* 68 G5
Eriskay, *U.K.* 14 D1
Erithraí, *Greece* 38 C5
Eritrea ■, *Africa* 81 E4
Erjas →, *Portugal* 34 F3
Erkelenz, *Germany* 24 D2
Erkner, *Germany* 24 C9
Erlangen, *Germany* 25 F6
Erldunda, *Australia* 94 D1
Ermelo, *Neths.* 17 B5
Ermelo, *S. Africa* 89 D4
Ermenek, *Turkey* 70 B2
Ermil, *Sudan* 81 E2
Ermióni, *Greece* 38 D5
Ermones, *Greece* 36 A3
Ermoúpolis = Síros, *Greece* 38 D6
Ernakulam = Cochin, *India* 66 Q10
Erne →, *Ireland* 15 B3
Erne, Lower L., *U.K.* 15 B4
Erne, Upper L., *U.K.* 15 B4
Ernée, *France* 18 D6
Ernest Giles Ra., *Australia* 93 E3
Ernstberg, *Germany* 25 E2
Erode, *India* 66 P10
Eromanga, *Australia* 95 D3
Erongo, *Namibia* 88 C2
Erquy, *France* 18 D4
Erramala Hills, *India* 66 M11
Errer →, *Ethiopia* 81 F5
Errigal, *Ireland* 15 A3
Erris Hd., *Ireland* 15 B1
Erseka, *Albania* 40 F4
Erskine, *U.S.A.* 112 B7
Erstein, *France* 19 D14
Ertholmene, *Denmark* 11 J9
Ertil, *Russia* 48 E5
Ertis = Irtysh →, *Russia* 50 C7
Eruh, *Turkey* 73 D10
Eruwa, *Nigeria* 83 D5
Ervy-le-Châtel, *France* 19 D10
Erwin, *U.S.A.* 109 G4
Eryuan, *China* 58 D2
Erzgebirge, *Germany* 24 E8
Erzin, *Russia* 51 D10
Erzincan, *Turkey* 70 B3
Erzurum, *Turkey* 70 B4
Es Caló, *Spain* 37 C8
Es Canar, *Spain* 37 B8
Es Mercadal, *Spain* 37 B11
Es Migjorn Gran, *Spain* 37 B11
Es Safiya, *Sudan* 81 D3
Es Sahrâ' Esh Sharqîya, *Egypt* 80 B3
Es Sînâ', *Egypt* 75 F3
Es Sûkî, *Sudan* 81 E3
Es Vedrà, *Spain* 37 C7
Esambo, *Dem. Rep. of the Congo* 86 C1
Esan-Misaki, *Japan* 54 D10
Esashi, *Hokkaidō, Japan* 54 B11
Esashi, *Hokkaidō, Japan* 54 D10
Esbjerg, *Denmark* 11 J2
Escalante, *U.S.A.* 115 H8
Escalante →, *U.S.A.* 115 H8
Escalón, *Mexico* 118 B4
Escambia →, *U.S.A.* 109 K2
Escanaba, *U.S.A.* 108 C2
Esch-sur-Alzette, *Lux.* 17 E6
Eschede, *Germany* 24 C6
Eschwege, *Germany* 24 D6
Eschweiler, *Germany* 24 E2
Escondido, *U.S.A.* 117 M9
Escravos →, *Nigeria* 83 D6
Escuinapa, *Mexico* 118 C3
Escuintla, *Guatemala* 120 D1
Eséka, *Cameroon* 83 E7
Eşen →, *Turkey* 39 E11
Esenguly, *Turkmenistan* 50 F6
Esens, *Germany* 24 B3
Esenyurt, *Turkey* 41 E12
Esera →, *Spain* 32 C5
Eşfahān, *Iran* 71 C6
Eşfahān □, *Iran* 71 C6
Esfarāyen, *Iran* 71 B8
Esfideh, *Iran* 71 C8
Esgueva →, *Spain* 34 D6
Esh Sham = Dimashq, *Syria* 75 B5
Esh Shamâlîya □, *Sudan* 80 D2
Esha Ness, *U.K.* 14 A7
Eshan, *China* 58 E4
Esher, *U.K.* 13 F7
Eshowe, *S. Africa* 89 D5
Esiama, *Ghana* 82 E4
Esigodini, *Zimbabwe* 89 C4
Esil = Ishim →, *Russia* 50 D8
Esino →, *Italy* 29 E10
Esira, *Madag.* 89 C8
Esk →, *Cumb., U.K.* 14 G5
Esk →, *N. Yorks., U.K.* 12 C7
Eskān, *Iran* 71 E9
Esker, *Canada* 103 B6
Eskifjörður, *Iceland* 8 D7
Eskilsäter, *Sweden* 11 F7
Eskilstuna, *Sweden* 10 E10
Eskimalatya, *Turkey* 73 C8
Eskimo Pt., *Canada* 100 B10
Eskişehir, *Turkey* 39 B12
Eskişehir □, *Turkey* 39 B12
Esla →, *Spain* 34 D4
Eslāmābād-e Gharb, *Iran* 70 C5
Eslāmshahr, *Iran* 71 C6
Eslöv, *Sweden* 11 J7
Eşme, *Turkey* 39 C10
Esmeraldas, *Ecuador* 124 C3
Esnagi L., *Canada* 102 C3
Espalion, *France* 20 D6
Espanola, *Canada* 102 C3
Espanola, *U.S.A.* 115 H10
Esparreguera, *Spain* 32 D6
Esparta, *Costa Rica* 120 E3
Espelkamp, *Germany* 24 C4
Esperance, *Australia* 93 F3
Esperance B., *Australia* 93 F3
Esperanza, *Argentina* 126 C3
Esperanza, *Phil.* 61 G6
Espéraza, *France* 20 F6
Espichel, C., *Portugal* 35 G1
Espiel, *Spain* 35 G5
Espigão, Serra do, *Brazil* 127 B5
Espinazo, Sierra del = Espinhaço, Serra do, *Brazil* 125 G10
Espinhaço, Serra do, *Brazil* 125 G10
Espinho, *Portugal* 34 D2
Espinilho, Serra do, *Brazil* 127 B5
Espinosa de los Monteros, *Spain* 34 B7
Espírito Santo □, *Brazil* 125 H10
Espíritu Santo, *Vanuatu* 96 J8
Espíritu Santo, B. del, *Mexico* 119 D7
Espíritu Santo, I., *Mexico* 118 C2
Espita, *Mexico* 119 C7
Espiye, *Turkey* 73 B8
Espluga de Francolí, *Spain* 32 D6
Espoo, *Finland* 9 F21
Espuña, Sierra de, *Spain* 33 H3
Espungabera, *Mozam.* 89 C5
Esquel, *Argentina* 128 E2
Esquimalt, *Canada* 104 D4
Esquina, *Argentina* 126 C4
Essaouira, *Morocco* 78 B4
Essebie, *Dem. Rep. of the Congo* 86 B3
Essen, *Belgium* 17 C4
Essen, *Germany* 24 D3
Essendon, Mt., *Australia* 93 E3
Essequibo →, *Guyana* 122 C5
Essex, *Canada* 110 D2
Essex, *Calif., U.S.A.* 117 L11
Essex, *N.Y., U.S.A.* 111 B11
Essex □, *U.K.* 13 F8
Essex Junction, *U.S.A.* 111 B11
Esslingen, *Germany* 25 G5
Essonne □, *France* 19 D9
Estaca de Bares, C. de, *Spain* 34 B3
Estadilla, *Spain* 32 C5
Estados, I. de Los, *Argentina* 122 J4
Estagel, *France* 20 F6
Eşţahbānāt, *Iran* 71 D7
Estância, *Brazil* 125 F11
Estancia, *U.S.A.* 115 J10
Estārm, *Iran* 71 D8
Estarreja, *Portugal* 34 E2
Estats, Pic d', *Spain* 32 C6
Estcourt, *S. Africa* 89 D4
Este, *Italy* 29 C8
Estelí, *Nic.* 120 D2
Estella, *Spain* 32 C2
Estellencs, *Spain* 37 B9
Estena →, *Spain* 35 F6
Estepa, *Spain* 35 H6
Estepona, *Spain* 35 J5
Esterhazy, *Canada* 105 C8
Esternay, *France* 19 D10
Esterri d'Aneu, *Spain* 32 C6
Estevan, *Canada* 105 D8
Estevan Group, *Canada* 104 C3
Estherville, *U.S.A.* 112 D7
Estissac, *France* 19 D10
Eston, *Canada* 105 C7
Estonia ■, *Europe* 9 G21
Estoril, *Portugal* 35 G1
Estouk, *Mali* 83 B5
Estreito, *Brazil* 125 E9
Estrela, Serra da, *Portugal* 34 E3
Estrella, *Spain* 35 G7
Estremoz, *Portugal* 35 G3
Estrondo, Serra do, *Brazil* 125 E9
Esztergom, *Hungary* 42 C3
Et Tîdra, *Mauritania* 82 B1
Etah, *India* 69 F8
Étain, *France* 19 C12
Étampes, *France* 19 D9
Etanga, *Namibia* 88 B1
Étaples, *France* 19 B8
Etawah, *India* 69 F8
Etawney L., *Canada* 105 B9
Ete, *Nigeria* 83 D6
Ethel, *U.S.A.* 116 D4
Ethelbert, *Canada* 105 C8
Ethiopia ■, *Africa* 74 F3
Ethiopian Highlands, *Ethiopia* 52 J7
Etili, *Turkey* 41 G10
Etive, L., *U.K.* 14 E3
Etna, *Italy* 31 E7
Etoile, *Dem. Rep. of the Congo* 87 E2
Etosha Nat. Park, *Namibia* 88 B2
Etosha Pan, *Namibia* 88 B2
Etowah, *U.S.A.* 109 H3
Étréchy, *France* 19 D9
Étrépagny, *France* 19 C8
Étretat, *France* 18 C7
Etropole, *Bulgaria* 41 D8
Ettelbruck, *Lux.* 17 E6
Ettlingen, *Germany* 25 G4
Ettrick Water →, *U.K.* 14 F6
Etuku, *Dem. Rep. of the Congo* 86 C2
Etulia, *Moldova* 43 E13
Etzatlán, *Mexico* 118 C4
Etzná, *Mexico* 119 D6
Eu, *France* 18 B8
Euboea = Évvoia, *Greece* 38 C6
Eucla, *Australia* 93 F4
Euclid, *U.S.A.* 110 E3
Eucumbene, L., *Australia* 95 F4
Eudora, *U.S.A.* 113 J9
Eufaula, *Ala., U.S.A.* 109 K3
Eufaula, *Okla., U.S.A.* 113 H7
Eufaula L., *U.S.A.* 113 H7
Eugene, *U.S.A.* 114 E2
Eugowra, *Australia* 95 E4
Eulo, *Australia* 95 D4
Eunice, *La., U.S.A.* 113 K8
Eunice, *N. Mex., U.S.A.* 113 J3
Eupen, *Belgium* 17 D6
Euphrates = Furāt, Nahr al →, *Asia* 70 D5
Eure □, *France* 18 C8
Eure →, *France* 18 C8
Eure-et-Loir □, *France* 18 D8
Eureka, *Canada* 4 B3
Eureka, *Calif., U.S.A.* 114 F1
Eureka, *Kans., U.S.A.* 113 G6
Eureka, *Mont., U.S.A.* 114 B6
Eureka, *Nev., U.S.A.* 114 G5
Eureka, *S. Dak., U.S.A.* 112 C5
Eureka, Mt., *Australia* 93 E3
Euroa, *Australia* 95 F4
Europa, Île, *Ind. Oc.* 85 J8
Europa, Picos de, *Spain* 34 B6
Europa, Pta. de, *Gib.* 35 J5
Europe 6 E10
Europoort, *Neths.* 17 C4
Euskirchen, *Germany* 24 E2
Eustis, *U.S.A.* 109 L5
Euston, *Australia* 95 E3
Eutin, *Germany* 24 A6
Eutsuk L., *Canada* 104 C3
Evale, *Angola* 88 B2
Evans, *U.S.A.* 112 E2
Evans, L., *Canada* 102 B4
Evans City, *U.S.A.* 110 F4
Evans Head, *Australia* 95 D5
Evans Mills, *U.S.A.* 111 B9
Evansburg, *Canada* 104 C5
Evanston, *Ill., U.S.A.* 108 E2
Evanston, *Wyo., U.S.A.* 114 F8
Evansville, *U.S.A.* 108 G2
Évaux-les-Bains, *France* 19 F9
Evaz, *Iran* 71 E7
Evciler, *Afyon, Turkey* 39 C11
Evciler, *Çanakkale, Turkey* 39 B8
Eveleth, *U.S.A.* 112 B8
Evensk, *Russia* 51 C16
Everard, L., *Australia* 95 E2
Everard Ranges, *Australia* 93 E5
Everest, Mt., *Nepal* 69 E12
Everett, *Pa., U.S.A.* 110 F6
Everett, *Wash., U.S.A.* 116 C4
Everglades, The, *U.S.A.* 109 N5
Everglades National Park, *U.S.A.* 109 N5
Evergreen, *Ala., U.S.A.* 109 K2
Evergreen, *Mont., U.S.A.* 114 B6
Everöd, *Sweden* 11 J8
Evertsberg, *Sweden* 10 C7
Evesham, *U.K.* 13 E6
Évian-les-Bains, *France* 19 F13
Évinos →, *Greece* 38 C3
Évisa, *France* 21 F12
Evje, *Norway* 9 G12
Évora, *Portugal* 35 G3
Évora □, *Portugal* 35 G3
Evowghlī, *Iran* 70 B5
Évreux, *France* 18 C8
Evritanía □, *Greece* 38 B3
Évron, *France* 18 D6
Évros □, *Greece* 41 E10
Évros →, *Bulgaria* 72 B2
Evrótas →, *Greece* 38 E4
Évry, *France* 19 D9
Évvoia, *Greece* 38 C6
Évvoia □, *Greece* 38 C5
Evxinoúpolis, *Greece* 38 B4
Ewe, L., *U.K.* 14 D3
Ewing, *U.S.A.* 112 D5
Ewo, *Congo* 84 E2
Exaltación, *Bolivia* 124 F5
Excelsior Springs, *U.S.A.* 112 F7
Excideuil, *France* 20 C5
Exe →, *U.K.* 13 G4
Exeter, *Canada* 110 C3
Exeter, *U.K.* 13 G4
Exeter, *Calif., U.S.A.* 116 J7
Exeter, *N.H., U.S.A.* 111 D14
Exmoor, *U.K.* 13 F4
Exmouth, *Australia* 92 D1
Exmouth, *U.K.* 13 G4
Exmouth G., *Australia* 92 D1
Expedition Ra., *Australia* 94 C4
Extremadura □, *Spain* 35 F4
Exuma Sound, *Bahamas* 120 B4
Eyasi, L., *Tanzania* 86 C4
Eye Pen., *U.K.* 14 C2
Eyemouth, *U.K.* 14 F6
Eygurande, *France* 19 G9
Eyjafjörður, *Iceland* 8 C4
Eymet, *France* 20 D4
Eymoutiers, *France* 20 C5
Eynesil, *Turkey* 73 B8
Eyre (North), L., *Australia* 95 D2
Eyre (South), L., *Australia* 95 D2
Eyre Mts., *N.Z.* 91 L2
Eyre Pen., *Australia* 95 E2
Eysturoy, *Færoe Is.* 8 E9
Eyvānkī, *Iran* 71 C6
Ez Zeidab, *Sudan* 80 D3
Ezcaray, *Spain* 32 C1
Ežerėlis, *Lithuania* 44 D10
Ezhou, *China* 59 B10
Ezine, *Turkey* 39 B8
Ezouza →, *Cyprus* 36 E11

F

F.Y.R.O.M. = Macedonia ■, Europe 40 E5
Fabala, Guinea 82 D3
Fabens, U.S.A. 115 L10
Fabero, Spain 34 C4
Fåborg, Denmark 11 J4
Fabriano, Italy 29 E9
Făcăeni, Romania 43 F12
Fachi, Niger 79 E8
Fada, Chad 79 E10
Fada-n-Gourma, Burkina Faso 83 C5
Fadd, Hungary 42 D3
Faddeyevskiy, Ostrov, Russia 51 B15
Faddor, Sudan 81 F3
Fadghāmī, Syria 70 C4
Fadlab, Sudan 80 D3
Faenza, Italy 29 D8
Færoe Is. = Føroyar, Atl. Oc. 8 F9
Fafa, Mali 83 B5
Fafe, Portugal 34 D2
Fagam, Nigeria 83 C7
Făgăras, Romania 43 E9
Făgăras, Munţii, Romania 43 E9
Fågelmara, Sweden 11 H9
Fagerhult, Sweden 11 G9
Fagersta, Sweden 10 D9
Făget, Romania 42 E7
Făget, Munţii, Romania 43 C8
Fagnano, L., Argentina 128 G3
Fagnières, France 19 D11
Faguibine, L., Mali 82 B4
Fahlīān, Iran 71 D6
Fahraj, Kermān, Iran 71 D8
Fahraj, Yazd, Iran 71 D7
Fai Tsi Long Archipelago, Vietnam 58 G6
Faial, Madeira 37 D3
Fair Haven, U.S.A. 108 D9
Fair Hd., U.K. 15 A5
Fair Oaks, U.S.A. 116 G5
Fairbanks, U.S.A. 100 B5
Fairbury, U.S.A. 112 E6
Fairfax, U.S.A. 111 B11
Fairfield, Ala., U.S.A. 109 J2
Fairfield, Calif., U.S.A. 116 G4
Fairfield, Conn., U.S.A. 111 E11
Fairfield, Idaho, U.S.A. 114 E6
Fairfield, Ill., U.S.A. 108 F1
Fairfield, Iowa, U.S.A. 112 E9
Fairfield, Tex., U.S.A. 113 K7
Fairford, Canada 105 C9
Fairhope, U.S.A. 109 K2
Fairlie, N.Z. 91 L3
Fairmead, U.S.A. 116 H6
Fairmont, Minn., U.S.A. 112 D7
Fairmont, W. Va., U.S.A. 108 F5
Fairmount, Calif., U.S.A. 117 L8
Fairmount, N.Y., U.S.A. 111 C8
Fairplay, U.S.A. 115 G11
Fairport, U.S.A. 110 C7
Fairport Harbor, U.S.A. 110 E3
Fairview, Canada 104 B5
Fairview, Mont., U.S.A. 112 B2
Fairview, Okla., U.S.A. 113 G5
Fairweather, Mt., U.S.A. 104 B1
Faisalabad, Pakistan 68 D5
Faith, U.S.A. 112 C3
Faizabad, India 69 F10
Fajardo, Puerto Rico 121 C6
Fajr, W. →, Si. Arabia 70 D3
Fakenham, U.K. 12 E8
Fåker, Sweden 10 A8
Fakfak, Indonesia 63 E8
Fakiya, Bulgaria 41 D11
Fakobli, Ivory C. 82 D3
Fakse, Denmark 11 J6
Fakse Bugt, Denmark 11 J6
Fakse Ladeplads, Denmark 11 J6
Faku, China 57 C12
Falaba, S. Leone 82 D2
Falaise, France 18 D6
Falaise, Mui, Vietnam 64 C5
Falakrón Óros, Greece 40 E7
Falam, Burma 67 H18
Falces, Spain 32 C3
Fălciu, Romania 43 D13
Falcó, C. des, Spain 37 C7
Falcón, Presa, Mexico 119 B5
Falcon Lake, Canada 105 D9
Falcon Reservoir, U.S.A. 113 M5
Falconara Marittima, Italy 29 E10
Falcone, C. del, Italy 30 B1
Falconer, U.S.A. 110 D5
Faléa, Mali 82 C2
Falémé →, Senegal 82 C2
Falerum, Sweden 11 F10
Faleshty = Făleşti, Moldova 43 C12
Făleşti, Moldova 43 C12
Falfurrias, U.S.A. 113 M5
Falher, Canada 104 B5
Falirakí, Greece 36 C10
Falkenberg, Germany 24 D9
Falkenberg, Sweden 11 H6
Falkensee, Germany 24 C9
Falkirk, U.K. 14 F5
Falkirk □, U.K. 14 F5
Falkland, U.K. 14 E5
Falkland Is. □, Atl. Oc. 128 G5
Falkland Sd., Falk. Is. 128 G5
Falkonéra, Greece 38 E5
Falköping, Sweden 11 F7
Fall River, U.S.A. 111 E13
Fallbrook, U.S.A. 117 M9
Fallon, U.S.A. 114 G4
Falls City, U.S.A. 112 E7
Falls Creek, U.S.A. 110 E6
Falmouth, Jamaica 120 C4
Falmouth, U.K. 13 G2
Falmouth, U.S.A. 111 E14
Falsa, Pta., Mexico 118 B1
False B., S. Africa 88 E2
Falso, C., Honduras 120 C3
Falster, Denmark 11 K5
Falsterbo, Sweden 9 J15
Fălticeni, Romania 43 C11
Falun, Sweden 10 D9
Famagusta, Cyprus 36 D12
Famagusta Bay, Cyprus 36 D13
Famalé, Niger 78 F6
Famatina, Sierra de, Argentina 126 B2
Family L., Canada 105 C9
Famoso, U.S.A. 117 K7
Fan Xian, China 56 G8
Fana, Mali 82 C3
Fanad Hd., Ireland 15 A4
Fanárion, Greece 38 B3
Fandriana, Madag. 89 C8
Fang, Thailand 58 H2
Fang Xian, China 59 A8
Fangaga, Sudan 80 D4
Fangak, Sudan 81 F3
Fangchang, China 59 B12
Fangcheng, China 56 H7
Fangchenggang, China 58 G7
Fangliao, Taiwan 59 F13
Fangshan, China 56 E6
Fangzi, China 57 F10
Fani i Madh →, Albania 40 E4
Fanjakana, Madag. 89 C8
Fanjiatun, China 57 C13
Fannich, L., U.K. 14 D4
Fannūj, Iran 71 E8
Fanø, Denmark 11 J2
Fano, Italy 29 E10
Fanshi, China 56 E7
Fao = Al Fāw, Iraq 71 D6
Faqirwali, Pakistan 68 E5
Fâqûs, Egypt 80 H7
Fara in Sabina, Italy 29 F9
Faradje, Dem. Rep. of the Congo 86 B2
Farafangana, Madag. 89 C8
Farâfra, El Wâhât el-, Egypt 80 B2
Farāh, Afghan. 66 C3
Farāh □, Afghan. 66 C3
Farahalana, Madag. 89 A9
Faraid, Gebel, Egypt 80 C4
Farako, Ivory C. 82 D4
Faramana, Burkina Faso 82 C4
Faranah, Guinea 82 C2
Farasān, Jazā'ir, Si. Arabia 74 D3
Farasan Is. = Farasān, Jazā'ir, Si. Arabia 74 D3
Faratsiho, Madag. 89 B8
Fardes →, Spain 35 H7
Fareham, U.K. 13 G6
Farewell, C., N.Z. 91 J4
Farewell C. = Nunap Isua, Greenland 4 D5
Färgelanda, Sweden 11 F5
Farghona, Uzbekistan 50 E8
Fargo, U.S.A. 112 B6
Fār'iah, W. al →, West Bank 75 C4
Faribault, U.S.A. 112 C8
Faridabad, India 68 E6
Faridkot, India 68 D6
Faridpur, Bangla. 69 H13
Faridpur, India 69 E8
Färila, Sweden 10 C9
Farim, Guinea-Biss. 82 C1
Farīmān, Iran 71 C8
Farina, Australia 95 E2
Fariones, Pta., Canary Is. 37 E6
Fâriskûr, Egypt 80 H7
Färjestaden, Sweden 11 H10
Farkadhón, Greece 38 B4
Farmakonisi, Greece 39 D9
Farmerville, U.S.A. 113 J8
Farmingdale, U.S.A. 111 F10
Farmington, Canada 104 B4
Farmington, Calif., U.S.A. 116 H6
Farmington, Maine, U.S.A. 109 C10
Farmington, Mo., U.S.A. 113 G9
Farmington, N.H., U.S.A. 111 C13
Farmington, N. Mex., U.S.A. 115 H9
Farmington, Utah, U.S.A. 114 F8
Farmington →, U.S.A. 111 E12
Farmville, U.S.A. 108 G6
Färnäs, Sweden 10 D8
Farne Is., U.K. 12 B6
Farnham, Canada 111 A12
Farnham, Mt., Canada 104 C5
Faro, Brazil 125 D7
Faro, Canada 100 B6
Faro, Portugal 35 H3
Fårö, Sweden 9 H18
Faro □, Portugal 35 H2
Fårösund, Sweden 11 G13
Farquhar, C., Australia 93 D1
Farrars Cr. →, Australia 94 D3
Farrāshband, Iran 71 D7
Farrell, U.S.A. 110 E4
Farrokhī, Iran 71 C8
Farruch, C. = Ferrutx, C., Spain 37 B10
Farrukhabad-cum-Fatehgarh, India 66 F11
Fārs □, Iran 71 D7
Fársala, Greece 38 B4
Farsø, Denmark 11 H3
Farson, U.S.A. 114 E9
Farsund, Norway 9 G12
Fartak, Râs, Si. Arabia 70 D2
Fartak, Ra's, Yemen 74 D5
Fârţăneşti, Romania 43 E12
Fartura, Serra da, Brazil 127 B5
Faru, Nigeria 83 C6
Fārūj, Iran 71 B8
Fårup, Denmark 11 H3
Farvel, Kap = Nunap Isua, Greenland 4 D5
Farwell, U.S.A. 113 H3
Fasā, Iran 71 D7
Fasano, Italy 31 B10
Fashoda, Sudan 81 F3
Fassa, Mali 82 C3
Fastiv, Ukraine 47 G5
Fastov = Fastiv, Ukraine 47 G5
Fatagar, Tanjung, Indonesia 63 E8
Fatehabad, Haryana, India 68 E6
Fatehabad, Ut. P., India 68 F8
Fatehgarh, India 69 F8
Fatehpur, Bihar, India 69 G11
Fatehpur, Raj., India 68 F6
Fatehpur, Ut. P., India 69 G9
Fatehpur, Ut. P., India 69 F9
Fatehpur Sikri, India 68 F6
Fatesh, Russia 47 F8
Fathai, Sudan 81 F3
Fatick, Senegal 82 C1
Fatima, Canada 103 C7
Fátima, Portugal 35 F2
Fatoya, Guinea 82 C3
Fatsa, Turkey 72 B7
Faucille, Col de la, France 19 F13
Faulkton, U.S.A. 112 C5
Faulquemont, France 19 C13
Faure I., Australia 93 E1
Făurei, Romania 43 E12
Fauresmith, S. Africa 88 D4
Fauske, Norway 8 C16
Favara, Italy 30 E6
Faváritx, C. de, Spain 37 B11
Faverges, France 21 C10
Favignana, Italy 30 E5
Favignana, I., Italy 30 E5
Fawcett, Pt., Australia 92 B5
Fawn →, Canada 102 A2
Fawnskin, U.S.A. 117 L10
Faxaflói, Iceland 8 D2
Faxälven →, Sweden 10 A10
Faya-Largeau, Chad 79 E9
Fayd, Si. Arabia 70 E4
Fayence, France 21 E10
Fayette, Ala., U.S.A. 109 J2
Fayette, Mo., U.S.A. 112 F8
Fayetteville, Ark., U.S.A. 113 G7
Fayetteville, N.C., U.S.A. 109 H6
Fayetteville, Tenn., U.S.A. 109 H2
Fayied, Egypt 80 H8
Fayón, Spain 32 D5
Fazilka, India 68 D6
Fazilpur, Pakistan 68 E4
Fdérik, Mauritania 78 D3
Feale →, Ireland 15 D2
Fear, C., U.S.A. 109 J7
Feather →, U.S.A. 114 G3
Feather Falls, U.S.A. 116 F5
Featherston, N.Z. 91 J5
Featherstone, Zimbabwe 87 F3
Fécamp, France 18 C7
Fedala = Mohammedia, Morocco 78 B4
Federación, Argentina 126 C4
Féderal, Argentina 128 C5
Federal Capital Terr. □, Nigeria 83 D6
Federal Way, U.S.A. 116 C4
Fedeshkūh, Iran 71 D7
Fehérgyarmat, Hungary 42 C7
Fehmarn, Germany 24 A7
Fehmarn Bælt, Europe 11 K5
Fehmarn Belt = Fehmarn Bælt, Europe 11 K5
Fei Xian, China 57 G9
Feijó, Brazil 124 E4
Feilding, N.Z. 91 J5
Feira de Santana, Brazil 125 F11
Feixi, China 59 B11
Feixiang, China 56 F8
Fejér □, Hungary 42 C3
Fejø, Denmark 11 K5
Feke, Turkey 72 D6
Fekete →, Hungary 42 E3
Felanitx, Spain 37 B10
Feldbach, Austria 26 E8
Feldberg, Baden-W., Germany 25 H3
Feldberg, Mecklenburg-Vorpommern, Germany 24 B9
Feldkirch, Austria 26 D2
Feldkirchen, Austria 26 E7
Felipe Carrillo Puerto, Mexico 119 D7
Felixburg, Zimbabwe 89 B5
Felixstowe, U.K. 13 F9
Felletin, France 20 C6
Fellingsbro, Sweden 10 E9
Felton, U.S.A. 116 H4
Feltre, Italy 29 B8
Femer Bælt = Fehmarn Bælt, Europe 11 K5
Femø, Denmark 11 K5
Femunden, Norway 9 E14
Fen He →, China 56 G6
Fene, Spain 34 B2
Fenelon Falls, Canada 110 B6
Fener Burnu, Turkey 39 E9
Feneroa, Ethiopia 81 E4
Feng Xian, Jiangsu, China 56 G9
Feng Xian, Shaanxi, China 56 H4
Fengári, Greece 41 F9
Fengcheng, Jiangxi, China 59 C10
Fengcheng, Liaoning, China 57 D13
Fengfeng, China 56 F8
Fenggang, China 58 D6
Fenghua, China 59 C13
Fenghuang, China 58 D7
Fengkai, China 59 F8
Fengkang, Taiwan 59 F13
Fengle, China 59 B9
Fenglin, Taiwan 59 F13
Fengning, China 56 D9
Fengqing, China 58 E2
Fengqiu, China 56 G8
Fengrun, China 57 E10
Fengshan, Guangxi Zhuangzu, China 58 E7
Fengshan, Guangxi Zhuangzu, China 58 E6
Fengshan, Taiwan 59 F13
Fengshun, China 59 F11
Fengtai, Anhui, China 59 A11
Fengtai, Beijing, China 56 E9
Fengxian, China 59 B13
Fengxiang, China 56 G4
Fengxin, China 59 C10
Fengyang, China 57 H9
Fengyi, China 58 E3
Fengyüan, Taiwan 59 E13
Fengzhen, China 56 D7
Feno, C. de, France 21 G12
Fenoarivo, Fianarantsoa, Madag. 89 C8
Fenoarivo, Fianarantsoa, Madag. 89 C8
Fenoarivo Afovoany, Madag. 89 B8
Fenoarivo Atsinanana, Madag. 89 B8
Fens, The, U.K. 12 E7
Fensmark, Denmark 11 J5
Fenton, U.S.A. 108 D4
Fenxi, China 56 F6
Fenyang, China 56 F6
Fenyi, China 59 D10
Feodosiya, Ukraine 47 K8
Ferdows, Iran 71 C8
Fère-Champenoise, France 19 D10
Fère-en-Tardenois, France 19 C10
Ferentino, Italy 29 G10
Ferfer, Somali Rep. 74 F4
Fergana = Farghona, Uzbekistan 50 E8
Fergus, Canada 110 C4
Fergus Falls, U.S.A. 112 B6
Feričanci, Croatia 42 E2
Ferkéssédougou, Ivory C. 82 D3
Ferlach, Austria 26 E7
Ferland, Canada 102 B2
Ferlo, Vallée du, Senegal 82 B2
Fermanagh □, U.K. 15 B4
Fermo, Italy 29 E10
Fermont, Canada 103 B6
Fermoselle, Spain 34 D4
Fermoy, Ireland 15 D3
Fernán Nuñéz, Spain 35 H6
Fernández, Argentina 126 B3
Fernandina Beach, U.S.A. 109 K5
Fernando de Noronha, Brazil 125 D12
Fernando Póo = Bioko, Eq. Guin. 83 E6
Ferndale, U.S.A. 116 B4
Fernie, Canada 104 D5
Fernlees, Australia 94 C4
Fernley, U.S.A. 114 G4
Ferozepore = Firozpur, India 68 D6
Férrai, Greece 41 F10
Ferrandina, Italy 31 B9
Ferrara, Italy 29 D8
Ferrato, C., Italy 30 C2
Ferreira do Alentejo, Portugal 35 G2
Ferreñafe, Peru 124 E3
Ferrerías, Spain 37 B11
Ferret, C., France 20 D2
Ferrette, France 19 E14
Ferriday, U.S.A. 113 K9
Ferriere, Italy 28 D6
Ferrières, France 19 D9
Ferro, Capo, Italy 30 A2
Ferrol, Spain 34 B2
Ferron, U.S.A. 115 G8
Ferrutx, C., Spain 37 B10
Ferryland, Canada 103 C9
Fertile, U.S.A. 112 B6
Fertőszentmiklós, Hungary 42 C1
Fès, Morocco 78 B5
Fessenden, U.S.A. 112 B5
Festus, U.S.A. 112 F9
Feté Bowé, Senegal 82 C2
Feteşti, Romania 43 F12
Fethiye, Turkey 39 E11
Fethiye Körfezi, Turkey 39 E10
Fetlar, U.K. 14 A8
Feuilles →, Canada 101 C12
Feurs, France 21 C8
Fez = Fès, Morocco 78 B5
Fezzan, Libya 79 C8
Fiambalá, Argentina 126 B2
Fianarantsoa, Madag. 89 C8
Fianarantsoa □, Madag. 89 B8
Fiche, Ethiopia 81 F4
Fichtelgebirge, Germany 25 E7
Ficksburg, S. Africa 89 D4
Fidenza, Italy 28 D7
Fiditi, Nigeria 83 D5
Field →, Australia 94 C2
Field I., Australia 92 B5
Fieni, Romania 43 E10
Fieri, Albania 40 F3
Fierzë, Albania 40 D4
Fife □, U.K. 14 E5
Fife Ness, U.K. 14 E6
Fifth Cataract, Sudan 80 D3
Figari, France 21 G13
Figeac, France 20 D6
Figeholm, Sweden 11 G10
Figline Valdarno, Italy 29 E8
Figtree, Zimbabwe 87 G2
Figueira Castelo Rodrigo, Portugal 34 E4
Figueira da Foz, Portugal 34 E2
Figueiró dos Vinhos, Portugal 34 F2
Figueres, Spain 32 C7
Figuig, Morocco 78 B5
Fihaonana, Madag. 89 B8
Fiherenana, Madag. 89 B8
Fiherenana →, Madag. 89 C7
Fiji ■, Pac. Oc. 91 C8
Fik, Ethiopia 81 F5
Fika, Nigeria 83 C7
Filabres, Sierra de los, Spain 35 H8
Filabusi, Zimbabwe 89 C4
Filadélfia, Italy 31 D9
Fil'akovo, Slovak Rep. 27 C12
Filey, U.K. 12 C7
Filey B., U.K. 12 C7
Filfla, Malta 36 D1
Filiaşi, Romania 43 F8
Filiátes, Greece 38 B2
Filiatrá, Greece 38 D3
Filicudi, Italy 31 D7
Filingué, Niger 83 C5
Filiourí →, Greece 41 E9
Filipstad, Sweden 10 E8
Filisur, Switz. 25 J5
Fillmore, Calif., U.S.A. 117 L8
Fillmore, Utah, U.S.A. 115 G7
Filótion, Greece 39 D7
Filottrano, Italy 29 E10
Filtu, Ethiopia 81 F5
Finale Emília, Italy 29 D8
Finale Lígure, Italy 28 D5
Fiñana, Spain 35 H8
Finch, Canada 111 A9
Findhorn →, U.K. 14 D5
Findlay, U.S.A. 108 E4
Finger L., Canada 102 B1
Finger Lakes, U.S.A. 111 D8
Fíngoè, Mozam. 87 E3
Finike, Turkey 39 E12
Finike Körfezi, Turkey 39 E12
Finiq, Albania 40 G4
Finistère □, France 18 D3
Finisterre = Fisterra, Spain 34 C1
Finisterre, C. = Fisterra, C., Spain 34 C1
Finke, Australia 94 D1
Finland ■, Europe 8 E22
Finland, G. of, Europe 9 G21
Finlay →, Canada 104 B3
Finley, Australia 95 F4
Finley, U.S.A. 112 B6
Finn →, Ireland 15 B4
Finneródja, Sweden 11 F8
Finnigan, Mt., Australia 94 B4
Finniss, C., Australia 95 E1
Finnmark, Norway 8 B20
Finnsnes, Norway 8 B18
Finspång, Sweden 11 F9
Finsteraarhorn, Switz. 25 J4
Finsterwalde, Germany 24 D9
Fiora →, Italy 29 F8
Fiorenzuola d'Arda, Italy 28 D6
Fīq, Syria 75 C4
Firat = Furāt, Nahr al →, Asia 70 D5
Firebag →, Canada 105 B6
Firebaugh, U.S.A. 116 J6
Firedrake L., Canada 105 A8
Firenze, Italy 29 E8
Firenzuola, Italy 29 D8
Firk →, Iraq 70 D5
Firmi, France 20 D6
Firminy, France 21 C8
Firozabad, India 69 F8
Firozpur, India 68 D6
Firozpur-Jhirka, India 68 F7
Fīrūzābād, Iran 71 D7
Fīrūzkūh, Iran 71 C7
Firvale, Canada 104 C3
Fish →, Namibia 88 D2
Fish →, S. Africa 88 E3
Fish River Canyon, Namibia 88 D2
Fisher, Australia 93 F5
Fisher B., Canada 105 C9
Fishers I., U.S.A. 111 E13
Fishguard, U.K. 13 E3
Fishing L., Canada 105 C9
Fishkill, U.S.A. 111 E11
Fismes, France 19 C10
Fisterra, Spain 34 C1
Fisterra, C., Spain 34 C1
Fitchburg, U.S.A. 111 D13
Fitz Roy, Argentina 128 F3
Fitzgerald, Canada 104 B6
Fitzgerald, U.S.A. 109 K4
Fitzmaurice →, Australia 92 B5
Fitzroy →, Queens., Australia 94 C5
Fitzroy →, W. Austral., Australia 92 C3
Fitzroy, Mte., Argentina 128 F2
Fitzroy Crossing, Australia 92 C4
Fitzwilliam I., Canada 110 A3
Fiuggi, Italy 29 G10
Fiume = Rijeka, Croatia 29 C11
Five Points, U.S.A. 116 J6
Fivizzano, Italy 28 D7
Fizi, Dem. Rep. of the Congo 86 C2
Fjällbacka, Sweden 11 F5
Fjärdhundra, Sweden 10 E10
Fjellerup, Denmark 11 H4
Fjerritslev, Denmark 11 G3

Fritch

Fjugesta, *Sweden* 10 E8
Flagstaff, *U.S.A.* 115 J8
Flagstaff L., *U.S.A.* 109 C10
Flaherty I., *Canada* 102 A4
Flåm, *Norway* 9 F12
Flambeau →, *U.S.A.* 112 C9
Flamborough Hd., *U.K.* 12 C7
Fläming, *Germany* 24 C8
Flaming Gorge Reservoir, *U.S.A.* 114 F9
Flamingo, Teluk, *Indonesia* 63 F9
Flanders = Flandre, *Europe* 19 B9
Flandre, *Europe* 19 B9
Flandre Occidentale = West-Vlaanderen □, *Belgium* 17 D2
Flandre Orientale = Oost-Vlaanderen □, *Belgium* 17 C3
Flandreau, *U.S.A.* 112 C6
Flanigan, *U.S.A.* 116 E7
Flannan Is., *U.K.* 14 C1
Flåsjön, *Sweden* 8 D16
Flat →, *Canada* 104 A3
Flathead L., *U.S.A.* 114 C7
Flattery, C., *Australia* 94 A4
Flattery, C., *U.S.A.* 116 B2
Flatwoods, *U.S.A.* 108 F4
Fleetwood, *U.K.* 12 D4
Fleetwood, *U.S.A.* 111 F9
Flekkefjord, *Norway* 9 G12
Flemington, *U.S.A.* 110 E7
Flen, *Sweden* 10 E10
Flensburg, *Germany* 24 A5
Flers, *France* 18 D6
Flesherton, *Canada* 110 B4
Flesko, Tanjung, *Indonesia* 63 D6
Fleurance, *France* 20 E4
Fleurier, *Switz.* 25 J2
Fleurieu Pen., *Australia* 95 F2
Flevoland □, *Neths.* 17 B5
Flin Flon, *Canada* 105 C8
Flinders →, *Australia* 94 B3
Flinders B., *Australia* 93 F2
Flinders Group, *Australia* 94 A3
Flinders I., *S. Austral., Australia* 95 E1
Flinders I., *Tas., Australia* 94 G4
Flinders Ranges, *Australia* 95 E2
Flinders Reefs, *Australia* 94 B4
Flint, *U.K.* 12 D4
Flint, *U.S.A.* 108 D4
Flint →, *U.S.A.* 109 K3
Flint I., *Kiribati* 97 J12
Flintshire □, *U.K.* 12 D4
Fliseryd, *Sweden* 11 G10
Flix, *Spain* 32 D5
Flixecourt, *France* 19 B9
Floby, *Sweden* 11 F7
Floda, *Sweden* 11 G6
Flodden, *U.K.* 12 B5
Flogny-la-Chapelle, *France* 19 E10
Floodwood, *U.S.A.* 112 B8
Flora, *U.S.A.* 108 F1
Florac, *France* 20 D7
Florala, *U.S.A.* 109 K2
Florence = Firenze, *Italy* 29 E8
Florence, *Ala., U.S.A.* 109 H2
Florence, *Ariz., U.S.A.* 115 K8
Florence, *Colo., U.S.A.* 112 F2
Florence, *Oreg., U.S.A.* 114 E1
Florence, *S.C., U.S.A.* 109 H6
Florence, L., *Australia* 95 D2
Florencia, *Colombia* 124
Florennes, *Belgium* 17 D4
Florensac, *France* 20 E7
Florenville, *Belgium* 17 E5
Flores, *Guatemala* 120 C2
Flores, *Indonesia* 63 F6
Flores I., *Canada* 104 D3
Flores Sea, *Indonesia* 63 F6
Floreşti, *Moldova* 43 C13
Floresville, *U.S.A.* 113 L5
Floriano, *Brazil* 125 E10
Florianópolis, *Brazil* 127 B6
Florida, *Cuba* 120 B4
Florida, *Uruguay* 127 C4
Florida □, *U.S.A.* 109 L5
Florida, Straits of, *U.S.A.* 120 B4
Florida B., *U.S.A.* 120 B3
Florida Keys, *U.S.A.* 109 N5
Florídia, *Italy* 31 E8
Flórina, *Greece* 40 F5
Flórina □, *Greece* 40 F5
Florø, *Norway* 9 F11
Flower Station, *Canada* 111 A8
Flowerpot I., *Canada* 110 A3
Floydada, *U.S.A.* 113 J4
Fluk, *Indonesia* 63 E7
Flúmen →, *Spain* 32 D4
Flumendosa →, *Italy* 30 C2
Fluminimaggiore, *Italy* 30 C1
Flushing = Vlissingen, *Neths.* 17 C3
Fluviá →, *Spain* 32 C8
Flying Fish, C., *Antarctica* 5 D15
Foam Lake, *Canada* 105 C8
Foča, *Bos.-H.* 40 C2
Foça, *Turkey* 39 C8
Focşani, *Romania* 43 E12
Fodécontéa, *Guinea* 82 C2
Fogang, *China* 59 F9
Fóggia, *Italy* 31 A8
Foggo, *Nigeria* 83 C6
Foglia →, *Italy* 29 E9
Fogo, *Canada* 103 C9
Fogo I., *Canada* 103 C9
Fohnsdorf, *Austria* 26 D7
Föhr, *Germany* 24 A4
Foia, *Portugal* 35 H2
Foix, *France* 20 E5
Fojnica, *Bos.-H.* 42 G2
Fokino, *Russia* 46 F8
Fokís □, *Greece* 38 C4
Fokku, *Nigeria* 83 C5
Folda, *Nord-Trøndelag, Norway* 8 D14
Folda, *Nordland, Norway* 8 C16
Földeák, *Hungary* 42 D5
Folégandros, *Greece* 38 E6
Foley, *Botswana* 88 C4
Foley, *U.S.A.* 109 K2
Foleyet, *Canada* 102 C3
Folgefonni, *Norway* 9 F12
Foligno, *Italy* 29 F9
Folkestone, *U.K.* 13 F9
Folkston, *U.S.A.* 109 K5
Follansbee, *U.S.A.* 110 F4
Follónica, *Italy* 28 F7
Follónica, G. di, *Italy* 28 F7
Folsom L., *U.S.A.* 116 G5
Folteşti, *Romania* 43 E13
Fond-du-Lac, *Canada* 105 B7
Fond du Lac, *U.S.A.* 112 D10
Fond-du-Lac →, *Canada* 105 B7
Fonda, *U.S.A.* 111 D10
Fondi, *Italy* 30 A6
Fonfría, *Spain* 34 D4
Fongafale, *Tuvalu* 96 H9
Fonni, *Italy* 30 B2
Fonsagrada = A Fonsagrada, *Spain* 34 B3
Fonseca, G. de, *Cent. Amer.* 120 D2
Font-Romeu, *France* 20 F5
Fontaine-Française, *France* 19 E12
Fontainebleau, *France* 19 D9
Fontana, *U.S.A.* 117 L9
Fontas →, *Canada* 104 B4
Fonte Boa, *Brazil* 124 D5
Fontem, *Cameroon* 83 D6
Fontenay-le-Comte, *France* 20 B3
Fontenelle Reservoir, *U.S.A.* 114 E8
Fontur, *Iceland* 8 C6
Fonyód, *Hungary* 42 D2
Foochow = Fuzhou, *China* 59 D12
Foping, *China* 56 H5
Forbach, *France* 19 C13
Forbes, *Australia* 95 E4
Forbesganj, *India* 69 F12
Forcados, *Nigeria* 83 D6
Forcados →, *Nigeria* 83 D6
Forcalquier, *France* 21 E9
Forchheim, *Germany* 25 F7
Ford City, *Calif., U.S.A.* 117 K7
Ford City, *Pa., U.S.A.* 110 F5
Førde, *Norway* 9 F11
Ford's Bridge, *Australia* 95 D4
Fordyce, *U.S.A.* 113 J8
Forécariah, *Guinea* 82 D2
Forel, Mt., *Greenland* 4 C6
Foremost, *Canada* 104 D6
Forest, *Canada* 110 C3
Forest, *U.S.A.* 113 J10
Forest City, *Iowa, U.S.A.* 112 D8
Forest City, *N.C., U.S.A.* 109 H5
Forest City, *Pa., U.S.A.* 111 E9
Forest Grove, *U.S.A.* 116 E3
Forestburg, *Canada* 104 C6
Foresthill, *U.S.A.* 116 F6
Forestier Pen., *Australia* 94 G4
Forestville, *Canada* 103 C6
Forestville, *Calif., U.S.A.* 116 G4
Forestville, *N.Y., U.S.A.* 110 D5
Forez, Mts. du, *France* 20 C7
Forfar, *U.K.* 14 E6
Forks, *U.S.A.* 116 C2
Forksville, *U.S.A.* 111 E8
Forlì, *Italy* 29 D9
Forman, *U.S.A.* 112 B6
Formazza, *Italy* 28 B5
Formby Pt., *U.K.* 12 D4
Formentera, *Spain* 37 C7
Formentor, C. de, *Spain* 37 B10
Former Yugoslav Republic of Macedonia = Macedonia ■, *Europe* 40 E5
Fórmia, *Italy* 30 A6
Formígine, *Italy* 28 D7
Formosa = Taiwan ■, *Asia* 59 F13
Formosa, *Argentina* 126 B4
Formosa, *Brazil* 125 G9
Formosa □, *Argentina* 126 B4
Formosa, Serra, *Brazil* 125 F8
Formosa Bay, *Kenya* 86 C5
Formosa Strait = Taiwan Strait, *Asia* 59 E12
Fornells, *Spain* 37 A11
Fornos de Algodres, *Portugal* 34 E3
Fornovo di Taro, *Italy* 28 D7
Føroyar, *Atl. Oc.* 8 F9
Forres, *U.K.* 14 D5
Forrest, *Australia* 93 F4
Forrest, Mt., *Australia* 93 D4
Forrest City, *U.S.A.* 113 H9
Fors, *Sweden* 10 D10
Forsayth, *Australia* 94 B3
Forshaga, *Sweden* 10 E7
Förslöv, *Sweden* 11 H6
Forsmo, *Sweden* 10 A11
Forssa, *Finland* 9 F20
Forst, *Germany* 24 D10
Forsvik, *Sweden* 11 F8
Forsyth, *U.S.A.* 114 C10
Fort Abbas, *Pakistan* 68 E5
Fort Albany, *Canada* 102 B3
Fort Ann, *U.S.A.* 111 C11
Fort Assiniboine, *Canada* 104 C6
Fort Augustus, *U.K.* 14 D4
Fort Beaufort, *S. Africa* 88 E4
Fort Benton, *U.S.A.* 114 C8
Fort Bragg, *U.S.A.* 114 G2
Fort Bridger, *U.S.A.* 114 F8
Fort Chipewyan, *Canada* 105 B6
Fort Collins, *U.S.A.* 112 E2
Fort-Coulonge, *Canada* 102 C4
Fort Covington, *U.S.A.* 111 B10
Fort Davis, *U.S.A.* 113 K3
Fort-de-France, *Martinique* 121 D7
Fort Defiance, *U.S.A.* 115 J9
Fort Dodge, *U.S.A.* 112 D7
Fort Edward, *U.S.A.* 111 C11
Fort Erie, *Canada* 110 D6
Fort Fairfield, *U.S.A.* 109 B12
Fort Frances, *Canada* 105 D10
Fort Garland, *U.S.A.* 115 H11
Fort George = Chisasibi, *Canada* 102 B4
Fort Good-Hope, *Canada* 100 B7
Fort Hancock, *U.S.A.* 115 L11
Fort Hertz = Putao, *Burma* 67 F20
Fort Hope, *Canada* 102 B2
Fort Irwin, *U.S.A.* 117 K10
Fort Jameson = Chipata, *Zambia* 87 E3
Fort Kent, *U.S.A.* 109 B11
Fort Klamath, *U.S.A.* 114 E3
Fort-Lamy = Ndjamena, *Chad* 79 F8
Fort Laramie, *U.S.A.* 112 D2
Fort Lauderdale, *U.S.A.* 109 M5
Fort Liard, *Canada* 104 A4
Fort Liberté, *Haiti* 121 C5
Fort Lupton, *U.S.A.* 112 E2
Fort Mackay, *Canada* 104 B6
Fort Macleod, *Canada* 104 D6
Fort McMurray, *Canada* 104 B6
Fort McPherson, *Canada* 100 B6
Fort Madison, *U.S.A.* 112 E9
Fort Meade, *U.S.A.* 109 M5
Fort Morgan, *U.S.A.* 112 E3
Fort Munro, *Pakistan* 68 E3
Fort Myers, *U.S.A.* 109 M5
Fort Nelson, *Canada* 104 B4
Fort Nelson →, *Canada* 104 B4
Fort Norman = Tulita, *Canada* 100 B7
Fort Payne, *U.S.A.* 109 H3
Fort Peck, *U.S.A.* 114 B10
Fort Peck Dam, *U.S.A.* 114 C10
Fort Peck L., *U.S.A.* 114 C10
Fort Pierce, *U.S.A.* 109 M5
Fort Pierre, *U.S.A.* 112 C4
Fort Plain, *U.S.A.* 111 D10
Fort Portal, *Uganda* 86 B3
Fort Providence, *Canada* 104 A5
Fort Qu'Appelle, *Canada* 105 C8
Fort Resolution, *Canada* 104 A6
Fort Rixon, *Zimbabwe* 87 G2
Fort Rosebery = Mansa, *Zambia* 87 E2
Fort Ross, *U.S.A.* 116 G3
Fort Rupert = Waskaganish, *Canada* 102 B4
Fort St. James, *Canada* 104 C4
Fort St. John, *Canada* 104 B4
Fort Sandeman = Zhob, *Pakistan* 68 D3
Fort Saskatchewan, *Canada* 104 C6
Fort Scott, *U.S.A.* 113 G7
Fort Severn, *Canada* 102 A2
Fort Shevchenko, *Kazakstan* 49 H10
Fort Simpson, *Canada* 104 A4
Fort Smith, *Canada* 104 B6
Fort Smith, *U.S.A.* 113 H7
Fort Stockton, *U.S.A.* 113 K3
Fort Sumner, *U.S.A.* 113 H2
Fort Thompson, *U.S.A.* 112 C5
Fort Trinquet = Bir Mogreïn, *Mauritania* 78 C3
Fort Valley, *U.S.A.* 109 J4
Fort Vermilion, *Canada* 104 B5
Fort Walton Beach, *U.S.A.* 109 K2
Fort Wayne, *U.S.A.* 108 E3
Fort William, *U.K.* 14 E3
Fort Worth, *U.S.A.* 113 J6
Fort Yates, *U.S.A.* 112 B4
Fort Yukon, *U.S.A.* 100 B5
Fortaleza, *Brazil* 125 D11
Forteau, *Canada* 103 B8
Fortescue →, *Australia* 92 D2
Forth →, *U.K.* 14 E5
Forth, Firth of, *U.K.* 14 E6
Fortore →, *Italy* 29 G12
Fortrose, *U.K.* 14 D4
Fortuna, *Spain* 33 G3
Fortuna, *Calif., U.S.A.* 114 F1
Fortuna, *N. Dak., U.S.A.* 112 A3
Fortune, *Canada* 103 C8
Fortune B., *Canada* 103 C8
Forūr, *Iran* 71 E7
Fos-sur-Mer, *France* 21 E8
Foshan, *China* 59 F9
Fosna, *Norway* 8 E14
Fosnavåg, *Norway* 9 E11
Foso, *Ghana* 83 D4
Fossano, *Italy* 28 D4
Fossil, *U.S.A.* 114 D3
Fossombrone, *Italy* 29 E9
Foster, *Australia* 95 F4
Foster, *Canada* 111 A12
Foster →, *Canada* 105 B7
Fosters Ra., *Australia* 94 C1
Fostoria, *U.S.A.* 108 E4
Fotadrevo, *Madag.* 89 C8
Fouesnant, *France* 18 E2
Fougères, *France* 18 D5
Foul Pt., *Sri Lanka* 66 Q12
Foula, *U.K.* 14 A6
Foulalaba, *Mali* 82 C3
Foulness I., *U.K.* 13 F8
Foulpointe, *Madag.* 89 B8
Foulweather, C., *U.S.A.* 106 B2
Foumban, *Cameroon* 83 D7
Foumbot, *Cameroon* 83 D7
Foundiougne, *Senegal* 82 C1
Fountain, *U.S.A.* 112 F2
Fountain Springs, *U.S.A.* 117 K8
Fourchambault, *France* 19 E10
Fouriesburg, *S. Africa* 88 D4
Fourmies, *France* 19 B11
Fournás, *Greece* 38 B3
Foúrnoi, *Greece* 39 D8
Fours, *France* 19 F10
Fourth Cataract, *Sudan* 80 D3
Fouta Djalon, *Guinea* 82 C2
Foux, Cap-à-, *Haiti* 121 C5
Foveaux Str., *N.Z.* 91 M2
Fowey, *U.K.* 13 G3
Fowler, *Calif., U.S.A.* 116 J7
Fowler, *Colo., U.S.A.* 112 F3
Fowlers B., *Australia* 93 F5
Fowman, *Iran* 71 B6
Fox →, *Canada* 105 B10
Fox Creek, *Canada* 104 C5
Fox Lake, *Canada* 104 B6
Fox Valley, *Canada* 105 C7
Foxboro, *U.S.A.* 111 D13
Foxe Basin, *Canada* 101 B12
Foxe Chan., *Canada* 101 B11
Foxe Pen., *Canada* 101 B12
Foxen, *Sweden* 10 E5
Foxton, *N.Z.* 91 J5
Foyle, Lough, *U.K.* 15 A4
Foynes, *Ireland* 15 D2
Foz, *Spain* 34 B3
Fóz do Cunene, *Angola* 88 B1
Foz do Iguaçu, *Brazil* 127 B5
Frackville, *U.S.A.* 111 F8
Fraga, *Spain* 32 D5
Fraile Muerto, *Uruguay* 127 C5
Framingham, *U.S.A.* 111 D13
Frampol, *Poland* 45 H9
Franca, *Brazil* 125 H9
Francavilla al Mare, *Italy* 29 F11
Francavilla Fontana, *Italy* 31 B10
France ■, *Europe* 7 F6
Frances, *Australia* 95 F3
Frances →, *Canada* 104 A3
Frances L., *Canada* 104 A3
Franceville, *Gabon* 84 E2
Franche-Comté, *France* 19 F12
Francis Case, L., *U.S.A.* 112 D5
Francisco Beltrão, *Brazil* 127 B5
Francisco I. Madero, *Coahuila, Mexico* 118 B4
Francisco I. Madero, *Durango, Mexico* 118 C4
Francistown, *Botswana* 89 C4
Francofonte, *Italy* 31 E7
François, *Canada* 103 C8
François L., *Canada* 104 C3
Francker, *Neths.* 17 A5
Frankado, *Djibouti* 81 E5
Frankenberg, *Germany* 24 D4
Frankenwald, *Germany* 25 E7
Frankford, *Canada* 110 B7
Frankfort, *S. Africa* 89 D4
Frankfort, *Ind., U.S.A.* 108 E2
Frankfort, *Kans., U.S.A.* 112 F6
Frankfort, *Ky., U.S.A.* 108 F3
Frankfort, *N.Y., U.S.A.* 111 C9
Frankfurt, *Brandenburg, Germany* 24 C10
Frankfurt, *Hessen, Germany* 25 E4
Fränkische Alb, *Germany* 25 F7
Fränkische Rezat →, *Germany* 25 F7
Fränkische Saale →, *Germany* 25 E5
Fränkische Schweiz, *Germany* 25 F7
Frankland →, *Australia* 93 G2
Franklin, *Ky., U.S.A.* 109 G2
Franklin, *La., U.S.A.* 113 L9
Franklin, *Mass., U.S.A.* 111 D13
Franklin, *N.H., U.S.A.* 111 C13
Franklin, *Nebr., U.S.A.* 112 E5
Franklin, *Pa., U.S.A.* 110 E5
Franklin, *Va., U.S.A.* 109 G7
Franklin, *W. Va., U.S.A.* 108 F6
Franklin B., *Canada* 100 B7
Franklin D. Roosevelt L., *U.S.A.* 114 B4
Franklin I., *Antarctica* 5 D11
Franklin L., *U.S.A.* 114 F6
Franklin Mts., *Canada* 100 B7
Franklin Str., *Canada* 100 A10
Franklinton, *U.S.A.* 113 K9
Franklinville, *U.S.A.* 110 D6
Franks Pk., *U.S.A.* 114 E9
Frankston, *Australia* 95 F4
Frånö, *Sweden* 10 B11
Fransfontein, *Namibia* 88 C2
Fränsta, *Sweden* 10 B10
Frantsa Iosifa, Zemlya, *Russia* 50 A6
Franz, *Canada* 102 C3
Franz Josef Land = Frantsa Iosifa, Zemlya, *Russia* 50 A6
Franzburg, *Germany* 24 A8
Frascati, *Italy* 29 G9
Fraser, *U.S.A.* 110 D2
Fraser →, *B.C., Canada* 104 D4
Fraser →, *Nfld., Canada* 103 A7
Fraser, Mt., *Australia* 93 E2
Fraser I., *Australia* 95 D5
Fraser Lake, *Canada* 104 C4
Fraserburg, *S. Africa* 88 E3
Fraserburgh, *U.K.* 14 D6
Fraserdale, *Canada* 102 C3
Frashëri, *Albania* 40 F4
Frasne, *France* 19 F13
Frăteşti, *Romania* 43 G10
Frauenfeld, *Switz.* 25 H4
Fray Bentos, *Uruguay* 126 C4
Frechilla, *Spain* 34 C6
Fredericia, *Denmark* 11 J3
Frederick, *Md., U.S.A.* 108 F7
Frederick, *Okla., U.S.A.* 113 H5
Frederick, *S. Dak., U.S.A.* 112 C5
Fredericksburg, *Pa., U.S.A.* 111 F8
Fredericksburg, *Tex., U.S.A.* 113 K5
Fredericksburg, *Va., U.S.A.* 108 F7
Fredericktown, *Mo., U.S.A.* 113 G9
Fredericktown, *Ohio, U.S.A.* 110 F2
Frederico I. Madero, Presa, *Mexico* 118 B3
Frederico Westphalen, *Brazil* 127 B5
Fredericton, *Canada* 103 C6
Fredericton Junction, *Canada* 103 C6
Frederiksborg Amtskommune □, *Denmark* 11 J6
Frederikshåb = Paamiut, *Greenland* 4 C5
Frederikshavn, *Denmark* 11 G4
Frederikssund, *Denmark* 11 J6
Frederiksted, *Virgin Is.* 121 C7
Frederiksværk, *Denmark* 11 J6
Fredonia, *Ariz., U.S.A.* 115 H7
Fredonia, *Kans., U.S.A.* 113 G7
Fredonia, *N.Y., U.S.A.* 110 D5
Fredriksberg, *Sweden* 10 D8
Fredrikstad, *Norway* 9 G14
Free State □, *S. Africa* 88 D4
Freehold, *U.S.A.* 111 F10
Freel Peak, *U.S.A.* 116 G7
Freeland, *U.S.A.* 111 E9
Freels, C., *Canada* 103 C9
Freeman, *Calif., U.S.A.* 117 K9
Freeman, *S. Dak., U.S.A.* 112 D6
Freeport, *Bahamas* 120 A4
Freeport, *Ill., U.S.A.* 112 D10
Freeport, *N.Y., U.S.A.* 111 F11
Freeport, *Ohio, U.S.A.* 110 F3
Freeport, *Pa., U.S.A.* 110 F5
Freeport, *Tex., U.S.A.* 113 L7
Freetown, *S. Leone* 82 D2
Frégate, L., *Canada* 102 B5
Fregenal de la Sierra, *Spain* 35 G4
Fregene, *Italy* 29 G9
Fréhel, C., *France* 18 D4
Freiberg, *Germany* 24 E9
Freibourg = Fribourg, *Switz.* 25 J3
Freiburg, *Baden-W., Germany* 25 H3
Freiburg, *Niedersachsen, Germany* 24 B5
Freilassing, *Germany* 25 H8
Freire, *Chile* 128 D2
Freirina, *Chile* 126 B1
Freising, *Germany* 25 G7
Freistadt, *Austria* 26 C7
Freital, *Germany* 24 D9
Fréjus, *France* 21 E10
Fremantle, *Australia* 93 F2
Fremont, *Calif., U.S.A.* 116 H4
Fremont, *Mich., U.S.A.* 108 D3
Fremont, *Nebr., U.S.A.* 112 E6
Fremont, *Ohio, U.S.A.* 108 E4
Fremont →, *U.S.A.* 115 G8
French Camp, *U.S.A.* 116 H5
French Creek →, *U.S.A.* 110 E5
French Guiana ■, *S. Amer.* 125 C8
French Pass, *N.Z.* 91 J4
French Polynesia ■, *Pac. Oc.* 97 K13
Frenchman Cr. →, *N. Amer.* 114 B10
Frenchman Cr. →, *U.S.A.* 112 E4
Frenštát pod Radhoštěm, *Czech Rep.* 27 B11
Fresco, *Ivory C.* 82 D3
Fresco →, *Brazil* 125 E8
Freshfield, C., *Antarctica* 5 C10
Fresnay-sur-Sarthe, *France* 18 D7
Fresnillo, *Mexico* 118 C4
Fresno, *U.S.A.* 116 J7
Fresno Alhandiga, *Spain* 34 E5
Fresno Reservoir, *U.S.A.* 114 B9
Freudenstadt, *Germany* 25 G4
Frévent, *France* 19 B9
Frew →, *Australia* 94 C2
Frewsburg, *U.S.A.* 110 D5
Freycinet Pen., *Australia* 94 G4
Freyming-Merlebach, *France* 19 C13
Freyung, *Germany* 25 G9
Fria, *Guinea* 82 C2
Fria, C., *Namibia* 88 B1
Friant, *U.S.A.* 116 J7
Frías, *Argentina* 126 B2
Fribourg, *Switz.* 25 J3
Fribourg □, *Switz.* 25 J3
Fridafors, *Sweden* 11 H8
Friday Harbor, *U.S.A.* 116 B3
Friedberg, *Bayern, Germany* 25 G6
Friedberg, *Hessen, Germany* 25 E4
Friedens, *U.S.A.* 110 F6
Friedland, *Germany* 24 B9
Friedrichshafen, *Germany* 25 H5
Friedrichskoog, *Germany* 24 A4
Friedrichstadt, *Germany* 24 A5
Friendly Is. = Tonga ■, *Pac. Oc.* 91 D11
Friendship, *U.S.A.* 110 D6
Friesach, *Austria* 26 E7
Friesack, *Germany* 24 C8
Friesland □, *Neths.* 17 A5
Friesoythe, *Germany* 24 B3
Friggesund, *Sweden* 10 C10
Frillesås, *Sweden* 11 G6
Frinnaryd, *Sweden* 11 G8
Frio →, *U.S.A.* 113 L5
Frio, C., *Brazil* 122 F6
Friol, *Spain* 34 B3
Friona, *U.S.A.* 113 H3
Fristad, *Sweden* 11 G6
Fritch, *U.S.A.* 113 H4

Fritsla, *Sweden* 11 G6
Fritzlar, *Germany* 24 D5
Friuli-Venézia Giulia □, *Italy* 29 B9
Frobisher B., *Canada* 101 B13
Frobisher Bay = Iqaluit, *Canada* 101 B13
Frobisher L., *Canada* 105 B7
Frohavet, *Norway* 8 E13
Frohnleiten, *Austria* 26 D8
Frolovo, *Russia* 48 F6
Frombork, *Poland* 44 D6
Frome, *U.K.* 13 F5
Frome →, *U.K.* 13 G5
Frome, L., *Australia* 95 E2
Frómista, *Spain* 34 C6
Front Range, *U.S.A.* 106 C5
Front Royal, *U.S.A.* 108 F6
Fronteira, *Portugal* 35 F3
Frontera, *Canary Is.* 37 G2
Frontera, *Mexico* 119 D6
Fronteras, *Mexico* 118 A3
Frontignan, *France* 20 E7
Frosinone, *Italy* 30 A6
Frostburg, *U.S.A.* 108 F6
Frostisen, *Norway* 8 B17
Frouard, *France* 19 D13
Frövi, *Sweden* 10 E9
Frøya, *Norway* 8 E13
Frumoasa, *Romania* 43 D10
Frunze = Bishkek, *Kyrgyzstan* 50 E8
Fruška Gora, *Serbia, Yug.* 42 E4
Frutal, *Brazil* 125 H9
Frutigen, *Switz.* 25 J3
Frýdek-Místek, *Czech Rep.* 27 B11
Frýdlant, *Czech Rep.* 26 A8
Fryeburg, *U.S.A.* 111 B14
Fryvaldov = Jeseník, *Czech Rep.* 27 A10
Fthiótis □, *Greece* 38 C4
Fu Jiang →, *China* 58 C6
Fu Xian = Wafangdian, *China* 57 E11
Fu Xian, *China* 56 G5
Fu'an, *China* 59 D12
Fubian, *China* 58 B4
Fucécchio, *Italy* 28 E7
Fucheng, *China* 56 F9
Fuchou = Fuzhou, *China* 59 D12
Fuchū, *Japan* 55 G6
Fuchuan, *China* 59 E8
Fuchun Jiang →, *China* 59 B13
Fúcino, Piana del, *Italy* 29 F10
Fuding, *China* 59 D13
Fuencaliente, *Canary Is.* 37 F2
Fuencaliente, *Spain* 35 G6
Fuencaliente, Pta., *Canary Is.* 37 F2
Fuengirola, *Spain* 35 J6
Fuenlabrada, *Spain* 34 E7
Fuensalida, *Spain* 34 E6
Fuente-Alamo, *Spain* 33 G3
Fuente-Álamo de Murcia, *Spain* 33 H3
Fuente de Cantos, *Spain* 35 G4
Fuente del Maestre, *Spain* 35 G4
Fuente el Fresno, *Spain* 35 F7
Fuente Obejuna, *Spain* 35 G5
Fuente Palmera, *Spain* 35 H5
Fuentes de Andalucía, *Spain* 35 H5
Fuentes de Ebro, *Spain* 32 D4
Fuentes de León, *Spain* 35 G4
Fuentes de Oñoro, *Spain* 34 E4
Fuentesaúco, *Spain* 34 D5
Fuerte →, *Mexico* 118 B3
Fuerte Olimpo, *Paraguay* 126 A4
Fuerteventura, *Canary Is.* 37 F6
Fufeng, *China* 56 G5
Fuga I., *Phil.* 61 B4
Fugong, *China* 58 D2
Fugou, *China* 56 G8
Fugu, *China* 56 E6
Fuhai, *China* 60 B3
Fuḩaymī, *Iraq* 70 C4
Fuji, *Japan* 55 G9
Fuji-San, *Japan* 55 G9
Fuji-yoshida, *Japan* 55 G9
Fujian □, *China* 59 E12
Fujinomiya, *Japan* 55 G9
Fujisawa, *Japan* 55 G9
Fujiyama, Mt. = Fuji-San, *Japan* 55 G9
Fukien = Fujian □, *China* 59 E12
Fukuchiyama, *Japan* 55 G7
Fukue-Shima, *Japan* 55 H4
Fukui, *Japan* 55 F8
Fukui □, *Japan* 55 G8
Fukuoka, *Japan* 55 H5
Fukuoka □, *Japan* 55 H5
Fukushima, *Japan* 54 F10
Fukushima □, *Japan* 54 F10
Fukuyama, *Japan* 55 G6
Fulacunda, *Guinea-Biss.* 82 C1
Fulda, *Germany* 24 E5
Fulda →, *Germany* 24 D5
Fulford Harbour, *Canada* 116 B3
Fuliang, *China* 59 C11
Fullerton, *Calif., U.S.A.* 117 M9
Fullerton, *Nebr., U.S.A.* 112 E6
Fulongquan, *China* 57 B13
Fülöpszállás, *Hungary* 42 D4
Fulton, *Mo., U.S.A.* 112 F9
Fulton, *N.Y., U.S.A.* 111 C8
Fuluälven →, *Sweden* 10 C7
Fulufjället, *Sweden* 10 C6
Fumay, *France* 19 C11
Fumel, *France* 20 D4
Fumin, *China* 58 E4
Funabashi, *Japan* 55 G10
Funäsdalen, *Sweden* 10 B6
Funchal, *Madeira* 37 D3
Fundación, *Colombia* 124 A4
Fundão, *Portugal* 34 E3
Fundu Moldovei, *Romania* 43 C10
Fundulea, *Romania* 43 F11
Fundy, B. of, *Canada* 103 D6
Funhalouro, *Mozam.* 89 C5
Funing, *Hebei, China* 57 E10
Funing, *Jiangsu, China* 57 H10
Funing, *Yunnan, China* 58 F5
Funiu Shan, *China* 56 H7
Funsi, *Ghana* 82 C4
Funtua, *Nigeria* 83 C6
Fuping, *Hebei, China* 56 E8
Fuping, *Shaanxi, China* 56 G5
Fuqing, *China* 59 E12
Fuquan, *China* 58 D6
Furano, *Japan* 54 C11
Furāt, Nahr al →, *Asia* 70 D5
Fūrg, *Iran* 71 D7
Furmanov, *Russia* 48 B5
Furmanovo, *Kazakstan* 48 F9
Furnás, *Spain* 37 B8
Furnas, Represa de, *Brazil* 127 A6
Furneaux Group, *Australia* 94 G4
Furqlus, *Syria* 75 A6
Fürstenau, *Germany* 24 C3
Fürstenberg, *Germany* 24 B9
Fürstenfeld, *Austria* 26 D9
Fürstenfeldbruck, *Germany* 25 G7
Fürstenwalde, *Germany* 24 C10
Fürth, *Germany* 25 F6
Furth im Wald, *Germany* 25 F8
Furtwangen, *Germany* 25 G4
Furudal, *Sweden* 10 C9
Furukawa, *Japan* 54 E10
Furulund, *Sweden* 11 J7
Fury and Hecla Str., *Canada* 101 B11
Fusagasuga, *Colombia* 124 C4
Fuscaldo, *Italy* 31 C9
Fushan, *Shandong, China* 57 F11
Fushan, *Shanxi, China* 56 G6
Fushë Arrëzi, *Albania* 40 D4
Fushë-Krujë, *Albania* 40 E3
Fushun, *Liaoning, China* 57 D12
Fushun, *Sichuan, China* 58 C5
Fusong, *China* 57 C14
Füssen, *Germany* 25 H6
Fusui, *China* 58 F6
Futog, *Yugoslavia* 42 E4
Futuna, *Wall. & F. Is.* 91 B8
Fuwa, *Egypt* 80 H7
Fuxian Hu, *China* 58 E4
Fuxin, *China* 57 C11
Fuyang, *Anhui, China* 56 H8
Fuyang, *Zhejiang, China* 59 B12
Fuyang He →, *China* 56 E9
Fuying Dao, *China* 59 D13
Fuyu, *China* 57 B13
Fuyuan, *China* 58 E5
Füzesgyarmat, *Hungary* 42 C6
Fuzhou, *China* 59 D12
Fylde, *U.K.* 12 D5
Fyn, *Denmark* 11 J4
Fyne, L., *U.K.* 14 F3
Fyns Amtskommune □, *Denmark* 11 J4
Fynshav, *Denmark* 11 K3

G

Ga, *Ghana* 82 D4
Gaanda, *Nigeria* 83 C7
Gabarin, *Nigeria* 83 C7
Gabas →, *France* 20 E3
Gabela, *Angola* 84 G2
Gabès, *Tunisia* 79 B8
Gabès, G. de, *Tunisia* 79 B8
Gabgaba, W. →, *Egypt* 80 C3
Gąbin, *Poland* 45 F6
Gabon ■, *Africa* 84 E2
Gaborone, *Botswana* 88 C4
Gabriels, *U.S.A.* 111 B10
Gābrīk, *Iran* 71 E8
Gabrovo, *Bulgaria* 41 D9
Gacé, *France* 18 D7
Gāch Sār, *Iran* 71 B6
Gachsārān, *Iran* 71 D6
Gacko, *Bos.-H.* 40 C2
Gadag, *India* 66 M9
Gadamai, *Sudan* 81 D4
Gadap, *Pakistan* 68 G2
Gadarwara, *India* 69 H8
Gadebusch, *Germany* 24 B7
Gadein, *Sudan* 81 F2
Gadhada, *India* 68 J4
Gádor, Sierra de, *Spain* 35 J8
Gadra, *Pakistan* 68 G4
Gadsden, *U.S.A.* 109 H3
Gadwal, *India* 66 L10
Gadyach = Hadyach, *Ukraine* 47 G8
Găeşti, *Romania* 43 F10
Gaeta, *Italy* 30 A6
Gaeta, G. di, *Italy* 30 A6
Gaffney, *U.S.A.* 109 H5
Gafsa, *Tunisia* 78 B7
Gagarawa, *Nigeria* 83 C6
Gagaria, *India* 68 G4
Gagarin, *Russia* 46 E8
Gaggenau, *Germany* 25 G4
Gaghamni, *Sudan* 81 E2
Gagino, *Russia* 48 C7
Gagliano del Capo, *Italy* 31 C11
Gagnef, *Sweden* 10 D9
Gagnoa, *Ivory C.* 82 D3
Gagnon, *Canada* 103 B6
Gagnon, L., *Canada* 105 A6
Gagra, *Georgia* 49 J5
Gahini, *Rwanda* 86 C3
Gahmar, *India* 69 G10
Gai Xian = Gaizhou, *China* 57 D12
Gaïdhouronísi, *Greece* 36 E7
Gail, *U.S.A.* 113 J4
Gail →, *Austria* 26 E6
Gaillac, *France* 20 E5
Gaillimh = Galway, *Ireland* 15 C2
Gaillon, *France* 18 C8
Gaines, *U.S.A.* 110 E7
Gainesville, *Fla., U.S.A.* 109 L4
Gainesville, *Ga., U.S.A.* 109 H4
Gainesville, *Mo., U.S.A.* 113 G8
Gainesville, *Tex., U.S.A.* 113 J6
Gainsborough, *U.K.* 12 D7
Gairdner, L., *Australia* 95 E2
Gairloch, L., *U.K.* 14 D3
Gaizhou, *China* 57 D12
Gaj, *Croatia* 42 E2
Gaj →, *Pakistan* 68 F2
Gakuch, *Pakistan* 69 A5
Galala, Gebel el, *Egypt* 80 J8
Galán, Cerro, *Argentina* 126 B2
Galana →, *Kenya* 86 C5
Galanta, *Slovak Rep.* 27 C10
Galapagar, *Spain* 34 E7
Galápagos, *Pac. Oc.* 122 D1
Galashiels, *U.K.* 14 F6
Galatás, *Greece* 38 D5
Galaţi, *Romania* 43 E13
Galaţi □, *Romania* 43 E12
Galatia, *Turkey* 72 C5
Galatina, *Italy* 31 B11
Galátone, *Italy* 31 B11
Galax, *U.S.A.* 109 G5
Galaxídhion, *Greece* 38 C4
Galcaio, *Somali Rep.* 74 F4
Galdhøpiggen, *Norway* 9 F12
Galeana, *Chihuahua, Mexico* 118 A3
Galeana, *Nuevo León, Mexico* 118 A3
Galegu, *Sudan* 81 E4
Galela, *Indonesia* 63 D7
Galena, *U.S.A.* 100 B4
Galera, *Spain* 33 H2
Galera Point, *Trin. & Tob.* 121 D7
Galesburg, *U.S.A.* 112 E9
Galeton, *U.S.A.* 110 E7
Galga, *Ethiopia* 81 F4
Gali, *Georgia* 49 J5
Galicea Mare, *Romania* 43 F8
Galich, *Russia* 48 A6
Galiche, *Bulgaria* 40 C7
Galicia □, *Spain* 34 C3
Galilee = Hagalil, *Israel* 75 C4
Galilee, L., *Australia* 94 C4
Galilee, Sea of = Yam Kinneret, *Israel* 75 C4
Galim, *Cameroon* 83 D7
Galinoporni, *Cyprus* 36 D13
Galion, *U.S.A.* 110 F2
Galiuro Mts., *U.S.A.* 115 K8
Galiwinku, *Australia* 94 A2
Gallabat, *Sudan* 81 E4
Gallan Hd., *U.K.* 14 C1
Gallarate, *Italy* 28 C5
Gallatin, *U.S.A.* 109 G2
Galle, *Sri Lanka* 66 R12
Gállego →, *Spain* 32 D4
Gallegos →, *Argentina* 128 G3
Galletti →, *Ethiopia* 81 F5
Galley Hd., *Ireland* 15 E3
Galliate, *Italy* 28 C5
Gallinas, Pta., *Colombia* 124 A4
Gallipoli = Gelibolu, *Turkey* 41 F10
Gallípoli, *Italy* 31 B10
Gallipolis, *U.S.A.* 108 F4
Gällivare, *Sweden* 8 C19
Gallneukirchen, *Austria* 26 C7
Gällö, *Sweden* 10 B9
Gallo, C., *Italy* 30 D6
Gallocanta, L. de, *Spain* 32 E3
Galloo I., *U.S.A.* 111 C8
Galloway, *U.K.* 14 F4
Galloway, Mull of, *U.K.* 14 G4
Gallup, *U.S.A.* 115 J9
Gallur, *Spain* 32 D3
Galoya, *Sri Lanka* 66 Q12
Galt, *U.S.A.* 116 G5
Galten, *Denmark* 11 H3
Galtür, *Austria* 26 E3
Galty Mts., *Ireland* 15 D3
Galtymore, *Ireland* 15 D3
Galva, *U.S.A.* 112 E9
Galve de Sorbe, *Spain* 32 D1
Galveston, *U.S.A.* 113 L7
Galveston B., *U.S.A.* 113 L7
Gálvez, *Argentina* 126 C3
Galway, *Ireland* 15 C2
Galway □, *Ireland* 15 C2
Galway B., *Ireland* 15 C2
Gam →, *Vietnam* 64 B5
Gamagori, *Japan* 55 G8
Gamari, L., *Ethiopia* 81 E5
Gamawa, *Nigeria* 83 C7
Gamay, *Phil.* 61 E6
Gambaga, *Ghana* 83 C4
Gambat, *Pakistan* 68 F3
Gambela, *Ethiopia* 81 F3
Gambhir →, *India* 68 F6
Gambia ■, *W. Afr.* 82 C1
Gambia →, *W. Afr.* 82 C1
Gambier, *U.S.A.* 110 F2
Gambier, C., *Australia* 92 B5
Gambier Is., *Australia* 95 F2
Gambo, *Canada* 103 C9
Gamboli, *Pakistan* 68 E3
Gamboma, *Congo* 84 E3
Gamka →, *S. Africa* 88 E3
Gamkab →, *Namibia* 88 D2
Gamla Uppsala, *Sweden* 10 E11
Gamlakarleby = Kokkola, *Finland* 8 E20
Gamleby, *Sweden* 11 G10
Gammon →, *Canada* 105 C9
Gamo-Gofa □, *Ethiopia* 81 F4
Gamou, *Niger* 83 C6
Gamtoos →, *S. Africa* 88 E4
Gan, *France* 20 E3
Gan Goriama, Mts., *Cameroon* 83 D7
Gan Jiang →, *China* 59 C11
Ganado, *U.S.A.* 115 J9
Gananita, *Sudan* 80 D3
Gananoque, *Canada* 102 D4
Ganāveh, *Iran* 71 D6
Gäncä, *Azerbaijan* 49 K8
Gancheng, *China* 64 C7
Gand = Gent, *Belgium* 17 C3
Ganda, *Angola* 85 G2
Gandajika, *Dem. Rep. of the Congo* 84 F4
Gandak →, *India* 69 G11
Gandava, *Pakistan* 68 E2
Gander, *Canada* 103 C9
Gander L., *Canada* 103 C9
Ganderkesee, *Germany* 24 B4
Ganderowe Falls, *Zimbabwe* 87 F2
Gandesa, *Spain* 32 D5
Gandhi Sagar, *India* 68 G6
Gandhinagar, *India* 68 H5
Gandi, *Nigeria* 83 C6
Gandía, *Spain* 33 G4
Gandino, *Italy* 28 C6
Gando, Pta., *Canary Is.* 37 G4
Gandole, *Nigeria* 83 D7
Gâneb, *Mauritania* 82 B2
Ganedidalem = Gani, *Indonesia* 63 E7
Ganetti, *Sudan* 80 D3
Ganga →, *India* 69 H14
Ganga Sagar, *India* 69 J13
Gangafani, *Mali* 82 C4
Gangan →, *India* 69 E8
Ganganagar, *India* 68 E5
Gangapur, *India* 68 F7
Gangara, *Niger* 83 C6
Gangaw, *Burma* 67 H19
Gangdisê Shan, *China* 67 D12
Ganges = Ganga →, *India* 69 H14
Ganges, *Canada* 104 D4
Ganges, *France* 20 E7
Ganges, Mouths of the, *India* 69 J14
Gånghester, *Sweden* 11 G7
Gangi, *Italy* 31 E7
Gângiova, *Romania* 43 G8
Gangoh, *India* 68 E7
Gangroti, *India* 69 D8
Gangtok, *India* 67 F16
Gangu, *China* 56 G3
Gangyao, *China* 57 B14
Gani, *Indonesia* 63 E7
Ganj, *India* 69 F8
Ganluc, *China* 58 C4
Gannat, *France* 19 F10
Gannett Peak, *U.S.A.* 114 E9
Ganquan, *China* 56 F5
Gänserdorf, *Austria* 27 C9
Ganshui, *China* 58 C6
Gansu □, *China* 56 G3
Ganta, *Liberia* 82 D3
Gantheaume, C., *Australia* 95 F2
Gantheaume B., *Australia* 93 E1
Gantsevichi = Hantsavichy, *Belarus* 47 F4
Ganye, *Nigeria* 83 D7
Ganyem = Genyem, *Indonesia* 63 E10
Ganyu, *China* 57 G10
Ganyushkino, *Kazakstan* 49 G9
Ganzhou, *China* 59 E10
Gao, *Mali* 83 B4
Gao, *Mali* 83 B5
Gao Xian, *China* 58 C5
Gao'an, *China* 59 C10
Gaochun, *China* 59 B12
Gaohe, *China* 59 F9
Gaohebu, *China* 59 B11
Gaokeng, *China* 59 D9
Gaolan Dao, *China* 59 G9
Gaoligong Shan, *China* 58 E2
Gaomi, *China* 57 F10
Gaoming, *China* 59 F9
Gaoping, *China* 56 G7
Gaotang, *China* 56 F9
Gaoua, *Burkina Faso* 82 C4
Gaoual, *Guinea* 82 C2
Gaoxiong = Kaohsiung, *Taiwan* 59 F13
Gaoyang, *China* 56 E8
Gaoyao, *China* 59 F9
Gaoyou, *China* 59 A12
Gaoyou Hu, *China* 57 H10
Gaoyuan, *China* 57 F9
Gaozhou, *China* 59 G8
Gap, *France* 21 D10
Gapan, *Phil.* 61 D4
Gapat →, *India* 69 G10
Gapuwiyak, *Australia* 94 A2
Gar, *China* 60 C2
Garabogazköl Aylagy, *Turkmenistan* 50 E6
Garachico, *Canary Is.* 37 F3
Garachiné, *Panama* 120 E4
Garafia, *Canary Is.* 37 F2
Garah, *Australia* 95 D4
Garajonay, *Canary Is.* 37 F2
Garango, *Burkina Faso* 83 C4
Garanhuns, *Brazil* 125 E11
Garautha, *India* 69 G8
Garawe, *Liberia* 82 E3
Garba Tula, *Kenya* 86 B4
Garberville, *U.S.A.* 114 F2
Garbiyang, *India* 69 D9
Garbsen, *Germany* 24 C5
Gard □, *France* 21 D8
Gard →, *France* 21 E8
Garda, L. di, *Italy* 28 C7
Gardanne, *France* 21 E9
Gårdby, *Sweden* 11 H10
Garde L., *Canada* 105 A7
Gardelegen, *Germany* 24 C7
Garden City, *Ga., U.S.A.* 109 J5
Garden City, *Kans., U.S.A.* 113 G4
Garden City, *Tex., U.S.A.* 113 K4
Garden Grove, *U.S.A.* 117 M9
Gardēz, *Afghan.* 68 C3
Gardhíki, *Greece* 38 C3
Gardiner, *Maine, U.S.A.* 109 C11
Gardiner, *Mont., U.S.A.* 114 D8
Gardiners I., *U.S.A.* 111 E12
Gardner, *U.S.A.* 111 D13
Gardner Canal, *Canada* 104 C3
Gardnerville, *U.S.A.* 116 G7
Gardno, Jezioro, *Poland* 44 D4
Gardo, *Somali Rep.* 74 F4
Gardone Val Trómpia, *Italy* 28 C7
Gárdony, *Hungary* 42 C3
Garešnica, *Croatia* 29 C13
Garéssio, *Italy* 28 D5
Garey, *U.S.A.* 117 L6
Garfield, *U.S.A.* 114 C5
Garforth, *U.K.* 12 D6
Gargaliánoi, *Greece* 38 D3
Gargan, Mt., *France* 20 C5
Gargouna, *Mali* 83 B5
Gargždai, *Lithuania* 44 C8
Garibaldi Prov. Park, *Canada* 104 D4
Gariep, L., *S. Africa* 88 E4
Garies, *S. Africa* 88 E2
Garigliano →, *Italy* 30 A6
Garissa, *Kenya* 86 C4
Garkida, *Nigeria* 83 C7
Garko, *Nigeria* 83 C6
Garland, *Tex., U.S.A.* 113 J6
Garland, *Utah, U.S.A.* 114 F7
Garlasco, *Italy* 28 C5
Garliava, *Lithuania* 44 D10
Garlin, *France* 20 E3
Garm, *Tajikistan* 50 F8
Garmāb, *Iran* 71 C8
Garmisch-Partenkirchen, *Germany* 25 H7
Garmsār, *Iran* 71 C7
Garner, *U.S.A.* 112 D8
Garnett, *U.S.A.* 112 F7
Garo Hills, *India* 69 G14
Garoe, *Somali Rep.* 74 F4
Garonne →, *France* 20 C3
Garonne, Canal Latéral à la, *France* 20 D4
Garot, *India* 68 G6
Garoua, *Cameroon* 83 D7
Garpenberg, *Sweden* 10 D10
Garphyttan, *Sweden* 10 E8
Garrauli, *India* 69 G8
Garrel, *Germany* 24 C4
Garrigue = Garrigues, *France* 20 E7
Garrigues, *France* 20 E7
Garrison, *Mont., U.S.A.* 114 C7
Garrison, *N. Dak., U.S.A.* 112 B4
Garrison Res. = Sakakawea, L., *U.S.A.* 112 B4
Garron Pt., *U.K.* 15 A6
Garrovillas, *Spain* 35 F4
Garrucha, *Spain* 33 H3
Garry →, *U.K.* 14 E5
Garry, L., *Canada* 100 B9
Garsen, *Kenya* 86 C5
Gärsnäs, *Sweden* 11 J8
Garson L., *Canada* 105 B6
Gartempe →, *France* 20 B4
Gartz, *Germany* 24 B10
Garu, *Ghana* 83 C4
Garu, *India* 69 H11
Garub, *Namibia* 88 D2
Garut, *Indonesia* 63 G12
Garvão, *Portugal* 35 H2
Garvie Mts., *N.Z.* 91 L2
Garwa = Garoua, *Cameroon* 83 D7
Garwa, *India* 69 G10
Garwolin, *Poland* 45 G8
Gary, *U.S.A.* 108 E2
Garz, *Germany* 24 A9
Garzê, *China* 58 B3
Garzón, *Colombia* 124 C3
Gas-San, *Japan* 54 E10
Gasan Kuli = Esenguly, *Turkmenistan* 50 F6
Gascogne, *France* 20 E4
Gascogne, G. de, *Europe* 20 E2
Gascony = Gascogne, *France* 20 E4
Gascoyne →, *Australia* 93 D1
Gascoyne Junction, *Australia* 93 E2
Gascueña, *Spain* 32 E2
Gash, Wadi →, *Ethiopia* 81 D4
Gashagar, *Nigeria* 83 C7
Gashaka, *Nigeria* 83 D7
Gasherbrum, *Pakistan* 69 B7
Gashua, *Nigeria* 83 C7
Gaspé, *Canada* 103 C7
Gaspé, C. de, *Canada* 103 C7
Gaspé, Pén. de, *Canada* 103 C6
Gaspésie, Parc de Conservation de la, *Canada* 103 C6
Gassan, *Burkina Faso* 82 C4
Gassol, *Nigeria* 83 D7
Gasteiz = Vitoria-Gasteiz, *Spain* 32 C2
Gastonia, *U.S.A.* 109 H5

Gastoúni, *Greece* 38 D3
Gastoúri, *Greece* 38 B1
Gastre, *Argentina* 128 E3
Gästrikland, *Sweden* 10 D10
Gata, C., *Cyprus* 36 E12
Gata, C. de, *Spain* 33 J2
Gata, Sierra de, *Spain* 34 E4
Gataga →, *Canada* 104 B3
Gătaia, *Romania* 42 E6
Gatchina, *Russia* 46 C6
Gatehouse of Fleet, *U.K.* 14 G4
Gates, *U.S.A.* 110 C7
Gateshead, *U.K.* 12 C6
Gatesville, *U.S.A.* 113 K6
Gaths, *Zimbabwe* 87 G3
Gatico, *Chile* 126 A1
Gâtinais, *France* 19 D9
Gâtine, Hauteurs de, *France* 20 B3
Gatineau, *Canada* 111 A9
Gatineau →, *Canada* 102 C4
Gatineau, Parc Nat. de la, *Canada* 102 C4
Gattaran, *Phil.* 61 B4
Gattinara, *Italy* 28 C5
Gatton, *Australia* 95 D5
Gatun, L., *Panama* 120 E4
Gatyana, *S. Africa* 89 E4
Gau, *Fiji* 91 D8
Gaucín, *Spain* 35 J5
Gauer L., *Canada* 105 B9
Gauhati, *India* 67 F17
Gauja →, *Latvia* 9 H21
Gaula →, *Norway* 8 E14
Gauri Phanta, *India* 69 E9
Gausta, *Norway* 9 G13
Gauteng □, *S. Africa* 89 D4
Gāv Koshī, *Iran* 71 D8
Gāvakān, *Iran* 71 D7
Gavarnie, *France* 20 F3
Gavāter, *Iran* 71 E9
Gāvbandī, *Iran* 71 E7
Gavdhopoúla, *Greece* 36 E6
Gávdhos, *Greece* 36 E6
Gavi, *Italy* 28 D5
Gavião, *Portugal* 35 F3
Gaviota, *U.S.A.* 117 L6
Gāvkhūnī, Bāţlāq-e, *Iran* 71 C7
Gävle, *Sweden* 10 D11
Gävleborgs län □, *Sweden* 10 C10
Gävlebukten, *Sweden* 10 D11
Gavorrano, *Italy* 28 F7
Gavray, *France* 18 D5
Gavrilov Yam, *Russia* 46 D10
Gávrion, *Greece* 38 D6
Gawachab, *Namibia* 88 D2
Gawilgarh Hills, *India* 66 J10
Gawler, *Australia* 95 E2
Gawu, *Nigeria* 83 D6
Gaxun Nur, *China* 60 B5
Gaya, *India* 69 G11
Gaya, *Niger* 83 C5
Gaya, *Nigeria* 83 C6
Gayéri, *Burkina Faso* 83 C5
Gaylord, *U.S.A.* 108 C3
Gayndah, *Australia* 95 D5
Gaysin = Haysyn, *Ukraine* 47 H5
Gayvoron = Hayvoron, *Ukraine* 47 H5
Gaza, *Gaza Strip* 75 D3
Gaza □, *Mozam.* 89 C5
Gaza Strip □, *Asia* 75 D3
Gazanjyk, *Turkmenistan* 71 B7
Gazaoua, *Niger* 83 C6
Gāzbor, *Iran* 71 D8
Gazi, *Dem. Rep. of the Congo* 86 B1
Gaziantep, *Turkey* 70 B3
Gazipaşa, *Turkey* 72 D5
Gbarnga, *Liberia* 82 D3
Gbekebo, *Nigeria* 83 D5
Gboko, *Nigeria* 83 D6
Gbongan, *Nigeria* 83 D5
Gcoverega, *Botswana* 88 B3
Gcuwa, *S. Africa* 89 E4
Gdańsk, *Poland* 44 D5
Gdańska, Zatoka, *Poland* 44 D6
Gdov, *Russia* 9 G22
Gdynia, *Poland* 44 D5
Geba →, *Guinea-Biss.* 82 C1
Gebe, *Indonesia* 63 D7
Gebeciler, *Turkey* 39 C12
Gebeit Mine, *Sudan* 80 C4
Gebel Abyad, *Sudan* 80 D2
Gebel Iweibid, *Egypt* 80 H8
Gebze, *Turkey* 41 F13
Gecha, *Ethiopia* 81 F4
Gedaref, *Sudan* 81 E4
Gedaref □, *Sudan* 81 E4
Gediz, *Turkey* 39 B11
Gediz →, *Turkey* 39 C8
Gedo, *Ethiopia* 81 F4
Gèdre, *France* 20 F4
Gedser, *Denmark* 11 K5
Geegully Cr. →, *Australia* 92 C3
Geel, *Belgium* 17 C4
Geelong, *Australia* 95 F3
Geelvink B. = Cenderwasih, Teluk, *Indonesia* 63 E9
Geelvink Chan., *Australia* 93 E1
Geesthacht, *Germany* 24 B6
Geidam, *Nigeria* 83 C7
Geikie →, *Canada* 105 B8
Geilenkirchen, *Germany* 24 E2
Geili, *Sudan* 81 D3
Geisingen, *Germany* 25 H4
Geislingen, *Germany* 25 G5
Geistown, *U.S.A.* 110 F6
Geita, *Tanzania* 86 C3
Gejiu, *China* 58 F4
Gel →, *Sudan* 81 F2
Gel, Meydān-e, *Iran* 71 D7
Gel River, *Sudan* 81 F2
Gela, *Italy* 31 E7
Gela, G. di, *Italy* 31 F7
Gelahun, *Liberia* 82 D2
Gelderland □, *Neths.* 17 B6
Geldern, *Germany* 24 D2
Geldrop, *Neths.* 17 C5
Geleen, *Neths.* 17 D5
Gelehun, *S. Leone* 82 D2
Gelembe, *Turkey* 39 B9
Gelemso, *Ethiopia* 81 F5
Gelendost, *Turkey* 72 C4
Gelendzhik, *Russia* 47 K10
Gelibolu, *Turkey* 41 F10
Gelibolu Yarımadası, *Turkey* 41 F10
Gelidonya Burnu, *Turkey* 72 D4
Gelnhausen, *Germany* 25 E5
Gelnica, *Slovak Rep.* 27 C13
Gelsenkirchen, *Germany* 24 D3
Gelting, *Germany* 24 A5
Gemas, *Malaysia* 65 L4
Gembloux, *Belgium* 17 D4
Gembu, *Nigeria* 83 D7
Gemena, *Dem. Rep. of the Congo* 84 D3
Gemerek, *Turkey* 70 B3
Gemla, *Sweden* 11 H8
Gemlik, *Turkey* 41 F13
Gemlik Körfezi, *Turkey* 41 F12
Gemona del Friuli, *Italy* 29 B10
Gemsa, *Egypt* 80 B3
Gemünden, *Germany* 25 E5
Genale →, *Ethiopia* 81 F4
Genç, *Turkey* 73 C9
Gençay, *France* 20 B4
Geneina, Gebel, *Egypt* 80 B3
General Acha, *Argentina* 126 D3
General Alvear, *Buenos Aires, Argentina* 126 D4
General Alvear, *Mendoza, Argentina* 126 D2
General Artigas, *Paraguay* 126 B4
General Belgrano, *Argentina* 126 D4
General Cabrera, *Argentina* 126 C3
General Cepeda, *Mexico* 118 B4
General Guido, *Argentina* 126 D4
General Juan Madariaga, *Argentina* 126 D4
General La Madrid, *Argentina* 126 D3
General MacArthur, *Phil.* 61 F6
General Martin Miguel de Güemes, *Argentina* 126 A3
General Paz, *Argentina* 126 B4
General Pico, *Argentina* 126 D3
General Pinedo, *Argentina* 126 B3
General Pinto, *Argentina* 126 C3
General Roca, *Argentina* 128 D3
General Santos, *Phil.* 61 H6
General Toshevo, *Bulgaria* 41 C12
General Trevino, *Mexico* 119 B5
General Trías, *Mexico* 118 B3
General Viamonte, *Argentina* 126 D3
General Villegas, *Argentina* 126 D3
Genesee, *Idaho, U.S.A.* 114 C5
Genesee, *Pa., U.S.A.* 110 E7
Genesee →, *U.S.A.* 110 C7
Geneseo, *Ill., U.S.A.* 112 E9
Geneseo, *N.Y., U.S.A.* 110 D7
Geneva = Genève, *Switz.* 25 J2
Geneva, *Ala., U.S.A.* 109 K3
Geneva, *N.Y., U.S.A.* 110 D8
Geneva, *Nebr., U.S.A.* 112 E6
Geneva, *Ohio, U.S.A.* 110 E4
Geneva, L. = Léman, L., *Europe* 19 F13
Geneva, L., *U.S.A.* 108 D1
Genève, *Switz.* 25 J2
Gengenbach, *Germany* 25 G4
Gengma, *China* 58 F2
Genichesk = Henichesk, *Ukraine* 47 J8
Genil →, *Spain* 35 H5
Genk, *Belgium* 17 D5
Genlis, *France* 19 E12
Gennargentu, Mti. del, *Italy* 30 B2
Gennes, *France* 18 E6
Genoa = Génova, *Italy* 28 D5
Genoa, *Australia* 95 F4
Genoa, *N.Y., U.S.A.* 111 D8
Genoa, *Nebr., U.S.A.* 112 E6
Genoa, *Nev., U.S.A.* 116 F7
Génova, *Italy* 28 D5
Génova, G. di, *Italy* 28 E6
Genriyetty, Ostrov, *Russia* 51 B16
Gent, *Belgium* 17 C3
Genteng, *Indonesia* 63 G12
Genthin, *Germany* 24 C8
Genyem, *Indonesia* 63 E10
Genzano di Lucánia, *Italy* 31 B9
Genzano di Roma, *Italy* 29 G9
Geoagiu, *Romania* 43 E8
Geographe B., *Australia* 93 F2
Geographe Chan., *Australia* 93 D1
Geokchay = Göyçay, *Azerbaijan* 49 K8
Georga, Zemlya, *Russia* 50 A5
George, *S. Africa* 88 E3
George →, *Canada* 103 A6
George, L., *N.S.W., Australia* 95 F4
George, L., *S. Austral., Australia* 95 F3
George, L., *W. Austral., Australia* 92 D3
George, L., *Uganda* 86 B3
George, L., *Fla., U.S.A.* 109 L5
George, L., *N.Y., U.S.A.* 111 C11
George Gill Ra., *Australia* 92 D5
George River = Kangiqsualujjuaq, *Canada* 101 C13
George Sound, *N.Z.* 91 L1
George Town, *Australia* 94 G4
George Town, *Bahamas* 120 B4
George Town, *Malaysia* 65 K3
George V Land, *Antarctica* 5 C10
George VI Sound, *Antarctica* 5 D17
George West, *U.S.A.* 113 L5
Georgetown, *Australia* 94 B3
Georgetown, *Ont., Canada* 102 D4
Georgetown, *P.E.I., Canada* 103 C7
Georgetown, *Cayman Is.* 120 C3
Georgetown, *Gambia* 82 C2
Georgetown, *Guyana* 124 B7
Georgetown, *Calif., U.S.A.* 116 G6
Georgetown, *Colo., U.S.A.* 114 G11
Georgetown, *Ky., U.S.A.* 108 F3
Georgetown, *N.Y., U.S.A.* 111 D9
Georgetown, *Ohio, U.S.A.* 108 F4
Georgetown, *S.C., U.S.A.* 109 J6
Georgetown, *Tex., U.S.A.* 113 K6
Georgia □, *U.S.A.* 109 K5
Georgia ■, *Asia* 49 J6
Georgia, Str. of, *Canada* 104 D4
Georgian B., *Canada* 102 C3
Georgina →, *Australia* 94 C2
Georgina I., *Canada* 110 B5
Georgiu-Dezh = Liski, *Russia* 47 G10
Georgiyevsk, *Russia* 49 H6
Georgsmarienhütte, *Germany* 24 C4
Gera, *Germany* 24 E8
Geraardsbergen, *Belgium* 17 D3
Geral, Serra, *Brazil* 127 B6
Geral de Goiás, Serra, *Brazil* 125 F9
Geraldine, *U.S.A.* 114 C8
Geraldton, *Australia* 93 E1
Geraldton, *Canada* 102 C2
Gérardmer, *France* 19 D13
Gercüş, *Turkey* 73 D9
Gerede, *Turkey* 72 B5
Gerês, Sierra do, *Portugal* 34 D3
Gereshk, *Afghan.* 66 D4
Geretsried, *Germany* 25 H7
Gérgal, *Spain* 33 H2
Gerik, *Malaysia* 65 K3
Gering, *U.S.A.* 112 E3
Gerlach, *U.S.A.* 114 F4
Gerlachovský štit, *Slovak Rep.* 27 B13
German Planina, *Macedonia* 40 D6
Germansen Landing, *Canada* 104 B4
Germantown, *U.S.A.* 113 M10
Germany ■, *Europe* 24 E6
Germencik, *Turkey* 39 D9
Germering, *Germany* 25 G7
Germersheim, *Germany* 25 F4
Germī, *Iran* 71 B6
Germiston, *S. Africa* 89 D4
Gernika-Lumo, *Spain* 32 B2
Gernsheim, *Germany* 25 F4
Gero, *Japan* 55 G8
Gerolzhofen, *Germany* 25 F6
Gerona = Girona, *Spain* 32 D7
Gerrard, *Canada* 104 C5
Gers □, *France* 20 E4
Gers →, *France* 20 D4
Gersfeld, *Germany* 24 E5
Gersthofen, *Germany* 25 G6
Gerzat, *France* 20 C7
Gerze, *Turkey* 72 B6
Geseke, *Germany* 24 D4
Geser, *Indonesia* 63 E8
Gesso →, *Italy* 28 D4
Gestro, Wabi →, *Ethiopia* 81 G5
Getafe, *Spain* 34 E7
Getinge, *Sweden* 11 H6
Gettysburg, *Pa., U.S.A.* 108 F7
Gettysburg, *S. Dak., U.S.A.* 112 C5
Getxo, *Spain* 32 B2
Getz Ice Shelf, *Antarctica* 5 D14
Gevaş, *Turkey* 73 C10
Gévaudan, *France* 20 D7
Gevgelija, *Macedonia* 40 E6
Gévora →, *Spain* 35 G4
Gewani, *Ethiopia* 81 E5
Gex, *France* 19 F13
Geyikli, *Turkey* 39 B8
Geyser, *U.S.A.* 114 C8
Geyserville, *U.S.A.* 116 G4
Geyve, *Turkey* 72 B4
Ghâbat el Arab = Wang Kai, *Sudan* 81 F2
Ghabeish, *Sudan* 81 E2
Ghaggar →, *India* 68 E6
Ghaghara →, *India* 69 G11
Ghaghat →, *Bangla.* 69 G13
Ghagra, *India* 69 H11
Ghagra →, *India* 69 F9
Ghalla, Wadi el →, *Sudan* 81 E2
Ghana ■, *W. Afr.* 83 D4
Ghansor, *India* 69 H9
Ghanzi, *Botswana* 88 C3
Gharb el Istiwa'iya □, *Sudan* 81 G3
Gharb Kordofân, *Sudan* 81 E2
Gharbîya, Es Sahrâ el, *Egypt* 80 B2
Ghardaïa, *Algeria* 78 B6
Ghârib, G., *Egypt* 80 B3
Gharig, *Sudan* 81 E2
Gharyān, *Libya* 79 B8
Ghat, *Libya* 79 D8
Ghatal, *India* 69 H12
Ghatampur, *India* 69 F9
Ghatsila, *India* 69 H12
Ghaţţī, *Si. Arabia* 70 D3
Ghawdex = Gozo, *Malta* 36 C1
Ghazal, Bahr el →, *Chad* 79 F9
Ghazâl, Bahr el →, *Sudan* 81 F3
Ghaziabad, *India* 68 E7
Ghazipur, *India* 69 G10
Ghaznī, *Afghan.* 68 C3
Ghaznī □, *Afghan.* 66 C6
Ghedi, *Italy* 28 C7
Ghelari, *Romania* 42 E7
Ghent = Gent, *Belgium* 17 C3
Gheorghe Gheorghiu-Dej = Oneşti, *Romania* 43 D11
Gheorgheni, *Romania* 43 D10
Gherla, *Romania* 43 C8
Ghidigeni, *Romania* 43 D12
Ghilarza, *Italy* 30 B1
Ghimeş-Făget, *Romania* 43 D11
Ghīnah, Wādī al, *Si. Arabia* 70 D3
Ghīnah, Wādī al →, *Si. Arabia* 80 B4
Ghisonaccia, *France* 21 F13
Ghisoni, *France* 21 F13
Ghizao, *Afghan.* 68 C1
Ghizar →, *Pakistan* 69 A5
Ghot Ogrein, *Egypt* 80 A2
Ghotaru, *India* 68 F4
Ghotki, *Pakistan* 68 E3
Ghowr □, *Afghan.* 66 C4
Ghudaf, W. al →, *Iraq* 70 C4
Ghudāmis, *Libya* 79 B7
Ghughri, *India* 69 H9
Ghugus, *India* 66 K11
Ghulam Mohammad Barrage, *Pakistan* 68 G3
Ghūrīān, *Afghan.* 66 B2
Gia Dinh, *Vietnam* 65 G6
Gia Lai = Plei Ku, *Vietnam* 64 F7
Gia Nghia, *Vietnam* 65 G6
Gia Ngoc, *Vietnam* 64 E7
Gia Vuc, *Vietnam* 64 E7
Giannutri, *Italy* 28 F8
Giant Forest, *U.S.A.* 116 J8
Giant Mts. = Krkonoše, *Czech Rep.* 26 A8
Giants Causeway, *U.K.* 15 A5
Giarabub = Al Jaghbūb, *Libya* 79 C10
Giarre, *Italy* 31 E8
Giaveno, *Italy* 28 C4
Gibara, *Cuba* 120 B4
Gibb River, *Australia* 92 C4
Gibbon, *U.S.A.* 112 E5
Gibe →, *Ethiopia* 81 F4
Gibellina Nuova, *Italy* 30 E5
Gibeon, *Namibia* 88 D2
Gibraleón, *Spain* 35 H4
Gibraltar ■, *Europe* 35 J5
Gibraltar, Str. of, *Medit. S.* 35 K5
Gibson Desert, *Australia* 92 D4
Gibsons, *Canada* 104 D4
Gibsonville, *U.S.A.* 116 F6
Giddings, *U.S.A.* 113 K6
Gidole, *Ethiopia* 81 F4
Gien, *France* 19 E9
Giengen, *Germany* 25 G6
Giessen, *Germany* 24 E4
Gīfān, *Iran* 71 B8
Gifatin, Geziret, *Egypt* 80 B3
Gifhorn, *Germany* 24 C6
Gift Lake, *Canada* 104 B5
Gifu, *Japan* 55 G8
Gifu □, *Japan* 55 G8
Gigant, *Russia* 49 G5
Giganta, Sa. de la, *Mexico* 118 B2
Gigen, *Bulgaria* 41 C8
Gigha, *U.K.* 14 F3
Giglio, *Italy* 28 F7
Gignac, *France* 20 E7
Gigüela →, *Spain* 35 F7
Gijón, *Spain* 34 B5
Gil I., *Canada* 104 C3
Gila →, *U.S.A.* 115 K6
Gila Bend, *U.S.A.* 115 K7
Gila Bend Mts., *U.S.A.* 115 K7
Gīlān □, *Iran* 71 B6
Gilău, *Romania* 43 D8
Gilbert →, *Australia* 94 B3
Gilbert Is., *Kiribati* 96 G9
Gilbert River, *Australia* 94 B3
Gilead, *U.S.A.* 111 B14
Gilf el Kebîr, Hadabat el, *Egypt* 80 C2
Gilford I., *Canada* 104 C3
Gilgandra, *Australia* 95 E4
Gilgil, *Kenya* 86 C4
Gilgit, *India* 69 B6
Gilgit →, *Pakistan* 69 B6
Gilgunnia, *Australia* 95 E4
Giljeva Planina, *Serbia, Yug.* 40 C3
Gillam, *Canada* 105 B10
Gilleleje, *Denmark* 11 H6
Gillen, L., *Australia* 93 E3
Gilles, L., *Australia* 95 E2
Gillette, *U.S.A.* 112 C2
Gilliat, *Australia* 94 C3
Gillingham, *U.K.* 13 F8
Gilmer, *U.S.A.* 113 J7
Gilmore, L., *Australia* 93 F3
Gilo →, *Ethiopia* 81 F3
Gilort →, *Romania* 43 F8
Gilroy, *U.S.A.* 116 H5
Gimbi, *Ethiopia* 81 F4
Gimli, *Canada* 105 C9
Gimo, *Sweden* 10 D12
Gimone →, *France* 20 E5
Gimont, *France* 20 E4
Gin Gin, *Australia* 95 D5
Ginâh, *Egypt* 80 B3
Gineifa, *Egypt* 80 H8
Gingin, *Australia* 93 F2
Gingindlovu, *S. Africa* 89 D5
Ginir, *Ethiopia* 81 F5
Ginosa, *Italy* 31 B9
Ginzo de Limia = Xinzo de Limia, *Spain* 34 C3
Gióia, G. di, *Italy* 31 D8
Gióia del Colle, *Italy* 31 B9
Gióia Táuro, *Italy* 31 D8
Gioiosa Iónica, *Italy* 31 D9
Gioiosa Marea, *Italy* 31 D7
Gióna, Óros, *Greece* 38 C4
Giovi, Passo dei, *Italy* 28 D5
Giovinazzo, *Italy* 31 A9
Gippsland, *Australia* 95 F4
Gir Hills, *India* 68 J4
Girab, *India* 68 F4
Girâfi, W. →, *Egypt* 75 F3
Giraltovce, *Slovak Rep.* 27 B14
Girard, *Kans., U.S.A.* 113 G7
Girard, *Ohio, U.S.A.* 110 E4
Girard, *Pa., U.S.A.* 110 D4
Girard, *Pa., U.S.A.* 110 E4
Girdle Ness, *U.K.* 14 D6
Giresun, *Turkey* 73 B8
Girga, *Egypt* 80 B3
Giri →, *India* 68 D7
Giridih, *India* 69 G12
Girifalco, *Italy* 31 D9
Girne = Kyrenia, *Cyprus* 36 D12
Giro, *Nigeria* 83 C5
Giromagny, *France* 19 E13
Girona, *Spain* 32 D7
Girona □, *Spain* 32 C7
Gironde □, *France* 20 D3
Gironde →, *France* 20 C2
Gironella, *Spain* 32 C6
Giru, *Australia* 94 B4
Girvan, *U.K.* 14 F4
Gisborne, *N.Z.* 91 H7
Gisenyi, *Rwanda* 86 C2
Gislaved, *Sweden* 11 G7
Gisors, *France* 19 C8
Gitega, *Burundi* 86 C2
Giuba →, *Somali Rep.* 74 G3
Giugliano in Campania, *Italy* 31 B7
Giulianova, *Italy* 29 F10
Giurgeni, *Romania* 43 F12
Giurgiu, *Romania* 43 G10
Giurgiu □, *Romania* 43 F10
Giurgiuleşti, *Moldova* 43 E13
Give, *Denmark* 11 J3
Givet, *France* 19 B11
Givors, *France* 21 C8
Givry, *France* 19 F11
Giyon, *Ethiopia* 81 F4
Giza = El Gîza, *Egypt* 80 J7
Gizhiga, *Russia* 51 C17
Gizhiginskaya Guba, *Russia* 51 C16
Giżycko, *Poland* 44 D8
Gizzeria, *Italy* 31 D9
Gjalicës e Lumës, Mal, *Albania* 40 D4
Gjegjani, *Albania* 40 E4
Gjirokastra, *Albania* 40 F4
Gjoa Haven, *Canada* 100 B10
Gjøvik, *Norway* 9 F14
Gjuhës, Kep i, *Albania* 40 F3
Glace Bay, *Canada* 103 C8
Glacier Bay National Park and Preserve, *U.S.A.* 104 B1
Glacier National Park, *Canada* 104 C5
Glacier National Park, *U.S.A.* 114 B7
Glacier Peak, *U.S.A.* 114 B3
Gladewater, *U.S.A.* 113 J7
Gladstone, *Queens., Australia* 94 C5
Gladstone, *S. Austral., Australia* 95 E2
Gladstone, *Canada* 105 C9
Gladstone, *U.S.A.* 108 C2
Gladwin, *U.S.A.* 108 D3
Glafsfjorden, *Sweden* 10 E6
Głagów Małapolski, *Poland* 45 H8
Glåma = Glomma →, *Norway* 9 G14
Gláma, *Iceland* 8 D2
Glamis, *U.S.A.* 117 N11
Glamoč, *Bos.-H.* 29 D13
Glamsbjerg, *Denmark* 11 J4
Glarus, *Switz.* 25 H5
Glarus □, *Switz.* 25 J5
Glasco, *Kans., U.S.A.* 112 F6
Glasco, *N.Y., U.S.A.* 111 D11
Glasgow, *U.K.* 14 F4
Glasgow, *Ky., U.S.A.* 108 G3
Glasgow, *Mont., U.S.A.* 114 B10
Glasgow, City of □, *U.K.* 14 F4
Glaslyn, *Canada* 105 C7
Glastonbury, *U.K.* 13 F5
Glastonbury, *U.S.A.* 111 E12
Glauchau, *Germany* 24 E8
Glava, *Sweden* 10 E6
Glavice, *Croatia* 29 E13
Glazov, *Russia* 48 A11
Gleichen, *Canada* 104 C6
Gleisdorf, *Austria* 26 D8
Gleiwitz = Gliwice, *Poland* 45 H5
Glen, *U.S.A.* 111 B13
Glen Affric, *U.K.* 14 D3
Glen Canyon, *U.S.A.* 115 H8
Glen Canyon Dam, *U.S.A.* 115 H8
Glen Canyon National Recreation Area, *U.S.A.* 115 H8
Glen Coe, *U.K.* 14 E3
Glen Cove, *U.S.A.* 111 F11
Glen Garry, *U.K.* 14 D3
Glen Innes, *Australia* 95 D5
Glen Lyon, *U.S.A.* 111 E8
Glen Mor, *U.K.* 14 D4
Glen Moriston, *U.K.* 14 D4
Glen Robertson, *Canada* 111 A10
Glen Spean, *U.K.* 14 E4
Glen Ullin, *U.S.A.* 112 B4
Glénan, Îs. de, *France* 18 E3

Glencoe, *Canada* 110 D3
Glencoe, *S. Africa* 89 D5
Glencoe, *U.S.A.* 112 C7
Glendale, *Ariz., U.S.A.* 115 K7
Glendale, *Calif., U.S.A.* 117 L8
Glendale, *Zimbabwe* 87 F3
Glendive, *U.S.A.* 112 B2
Glendo, *U.S.A.* 112 D2
Glenelg →, *Australia* 95 F3
Glenfield, *U.S.A.* 111 C9
Glengarriff, *Ireland* 15 E2
Glenmont, *U.S.A.* 110 F2
Glenmorgan, *Australia* 95 D4
Glenn, *U.S.A.* 116 F4
Glennallen, *U.S.A.* 100 B5
Glennamaddy, *Ireland* 15 C3
Glenns Ferry, *U.S.A.* 114 E6
Glenore, *Australia* 94 B3
Glenreagh, *Australia* 95 E5
Glenrock, *U.S.A.* 114 E11
Glenrothes, *U.K.* 14 E5
Glens Falls, *U.S.A.* 111 C11
Glenside, *U.S.A.* 111 F9
Glenties, *Ireland* 15 B3
Glenville, *U.S.A.* 108 F5
Glenwood, *Canada* 103 C9
Glenwood, *Ark., U.S.A.* 113 H8
Glenwood, *Hawaii, U.S.A.* 106 J17
Glenwood, *Iowa, U.S.A.* 112 E7
Glenwood, *Minn., U.S.A.* 112 C7
Glenwood, *Wash., U.S.A.* 116 D5
Glenwood Springs, *U.S.A.* 114 G10
Glettinganes, *Iceland* 8 D7
Glifádha, *Greece* 38 D5
Glimåkra, *Sweden* 11 H8
Glina, *Croatia* 29 C13
Glinojeck, *Poland* 45 F7
Gliwice, *Poland* 45 H5
Globe, *U.S.A.* 115 K8
Glodeanu Siliştea, *Romania* 43 F11
Glodeni, *Moldova* 43 C12
Glödnitz, *Austria* 26 E7
Gloggnitz, *Austria* 26 D8
Głogów, *Poland* 45 G3
Głogówek, *Poland* 45 H4
Glomma →, *Norway* 9 G14
Glorieuses, Is., *Ind. Oc.* 89 A8
Glóssa, *Greece* 38 B5
Glossop, *U.K.* 12 D6
Gloucester, *Australia* 95 E5
Gloucester, *U.K.* 13 F5
Gloucester, *U.S.A.* 111 D14
Gloucester I., *Australia* 94 C4
Gloucester Point, *U.S.A.* 108 G7
Gloucestershire □, *U.K.* 13 F5
Gloversville, *U.S.A.* 111 C10
Glovertown, *Canada* 103 C9
Głowno, *Poland* 45 G6
Głubczyce, *Poland* 45 H4
Glubokiy, *Russia* 49 F5
Glubokoye = Hlybokaye, *Belarus* 46 E4
Głuchołazy, *Poland* 45 H4
Glücksburg, *Germany* 24 A5
Glückstadt, *Germany* 24 B5
Glukhov = Hlukhiv, *Ukraine* 47 G7
Glusk, *Belarus* 47 F5
Głuszyca, *Poland* 45 H3
Glyngøre, *Denmark* 11 H2
Gmünd, *Kärnten, Austria* 26 E6
Gmünd, *Niederösterreich, Austria* 26 C8
Gmunden, *Austria* 26 D6
Gnarp, *Sweden* 10 B11
Gnesta, *Sweden* 10 E11
Gniew, *Poland* 44 E5
Gniewkowo, *Poland* 45 F5
Gniezno, *Poland* 45 F4
Gnjilane, *Kosovo, Yug.* 40 D5
Gnoien, *Germany* 24 B8
Gnosjö, *Sweden* 11 G7
Gnowangerup, *Australia* 93 F2
Go Cong, *Vietnam* 65 G6
Gō-no-ura, *Japan* 55 H4
Goa, *India* 66 M8
Goa □, *India* 66 M8
Goalen Hd., *Australia* 95 F5
Goalpara, *India* 67 F17
Goaltor, *India* 69 H12
Goalundo Ghat, *Bangla.* 69 H13
Goaso, *Ghana* 82 D4
Goat Fell, *U.K.* 14 F3
Goba, *Ethiopia* 81 F4
Goba, *Mozam.* 89 D5
Gobabis, *Namibia* 88 C2
Göbel, *Turkey* 41 F12
Gobi, *Asia* 56 C6
Gobō, *Japan* 55 H7
Gobo, *Sudan* 81 F3
Göçbeyli, *Turkey* 39 B9
Goch, *Germany* 24 D2
Gochas, *Namibia* 88 C2
Godavari →, *India* 67 L13
Godavari Pt., *India* 67 L13
Godbout, *Canada* 103 C6
Godda, *India* 69 G12
Godech, *Bulgaria* 40 C7
Goderich, *Canada* 102 D3
Goderville, *France* 18 C7
Godfrey Ra., *Australia* 93 D2
Godhavn = Qeqertarsuaq, *Greenland* 4 C5
Godhra, *India* 68 H5
Gödöllő, *Hungary* 42 C4
Godoy Cruz, *Argentina* 126 C2
Gods →, *Canada* 102 A1
Gods L., *Canada* 102 B1
Gods River, *Canada* 105 C10
Godthåb = Nuuk, *Greenland* 101 B14
Godwin Austen = K2, *Pakistan* 69 B7
Goeie Hoop, Kaap die = Good Hope, C. of, *S. Africa* 88 E2
Goéland, L. au, *Canada* 102 C4
Goeree, *Neths.* 17 C3
Goes, *Neths.* 17 C3
Goffstown, *U.S.A.* 111 C13
Gogama, *Canada* 102 C3
Gogebic, L., *U.S.A.* 112 B10
Goggetti, *Ethiopia* 81 F4
Gogolin, *Poland* 45 H5
Gogonou, *Benin* 83 C5
Gogra = Ghaghara →, *India* 69 G11
Gogriâl, *Sudan* 81 F2
Gogti, *Ethiopia* 81 E5
Gohana, *India* 68 E7
Goharganj, *India* 68 H7
Goi →, *India* 68 H6
Goiânia, *Brazil* 125 G9
Goiás, *Brazil* 125 G8
Goiás □, *Brazil* 125 F9
Goio-Ere, *Brazil* 127 A5
Góis, *Portugal* 34 E2
Gojam □, *Ethiopia* 81 E4
Gojeb, Wabi →, *Ethiopia* 81 F4
Gojō, *Japan* 55 G7
Gojra, *Pakistan* 68 D5
Gökçeada, *Turkey* 41 F9
Gökçedağ, *Turkey* 39 B10
Gökçen, *Turkey* 39 C9
Gökçeören, *Turkey* 39 C10
Gökçeyazı, *Turkey* 39 B9
Gökırmak →, *Turkey* 72 B6
Gökova, *Turkey* 39 D10
Gökova Körfezi, *Turkey* 39 E9
Göksu →, *Turkey* 72 D6
Göksun, *Turkey* 72 C7
Gokteik, *Burma* 67 H20
Göktepe, *Turkey* 39 D10
Gokurt, *Pakistan* 68 E2
Gokwe, *Zimbabwe* 89 B4
Gol Gol, *Australia* 95 E3
Gola, *India* 69 E9
Golakganj, *India* 69 F13
Golan Heights = Hagolan, *Syria* 75 C4
Gołańcz, *Poland* 45 F4
Golāshkerd, *Iran* 71 E8
Golaya Pristen = Hola Pristan, *Ukraine* 47 J7
Gölbaşı, *Adiyaman, Turkey* 72 D7
Gölbaşı, *Ankara, Turkey* 72 C5
Golchikha, *Russia* 4 B12
Golconda, *U.S.A.* 114 F5
Gölcük, *Kocaeli, Turkey* 41 F13
Gölcük, *Niğde, Turkey* 72 C6
Gold, *U.S.A.* 110 E7
Gold Beach, *U.S.A.* 114 E1
Gold Coast, *W. Afr.* 83 E4
Gold Hill, *U.S.A.* 114 E2
Gold River, *Canada* 104 D3
Goldap, *Poland* 44 D9
Goldberg, *Germany* 24 B8
Golden, *Canada* 104 C5
Golden B., *N.Z.* 91 J4
Golden Gate, *U.S.A.* 114 H2
Golden Hinde, *Canada* 104 D3
Golden Lake, *Canada* 110 A7
Golden Vale, *Ireland* 15 D3
Goldendale, *U.S.A.* 114 D3
Goldfield, *U.S.A.* 115 H5
Goldsand L., *Canada* 105 B8
Goldsboro, *U.S.A.* 109 H7
Goldsmith, *U.S.A.* 113 K3
Goldsworthy, *Australia* 92 D2
Goldthwaite, *U.S.A.* 113 K5
Golegã, *Portugal* 35 F2
Goleniów, *Poland* 44 E1
Golestānak, *Iran* 71 D7
Goleta, *U.S.A.* 117 L7
Golfito, *Costa Rica* 120 E3
Golfo Aranci, *Italy* 30 B2
Gölgeli Dağları, *Turkey* 39 D10
Gölhisar, *Turkey* 39 D11
Goliad, *U.S.A.* 113 L6
Golija, *Montenegro, Yug.* 40 C2
Golija, *Serbia, Yug.* 40 C4
Golina, *Poland* 45 F5
Gölköy, *Turkey* 72 B7
Göllersdorf, *Austria* 26 C9
Gölmarmara, *Turkey* 39 C9
Golo →, *France* 21 F13
Gölova, *Turkey* 39 E12
Golpāyegān, *Iran* 71 C6
Gölpazarı, *Turkey* 72 B4
Golra, *Pakistan* 68 C5
Golspie, *U.K.* 14 D5
Golub-Dobrzyń, *Poland* 45 E6
Golubac, *Serbia, Yug.* 40 B5
Golyam Perelik, *Bulgaria* 41 E8
Golyama Kamchiya →, *Bulgaria* 41 C11
Goma, *Dem. Rep. of the Congo* 86 C2
Gomal Pass, *Pakistan* 68 D3
Gomati →, *India* 69 G10
Gombari, *Dem. Rep. of the Congo* 86 B2
Gombe, *Nigeria* 83 C7
Gombe, *Turkey* 39 E11
Gombe □, *Nigeria* 83 C7
Gombe →, *Tanzania* 86 C3
Gombi, *Nigeria* 83 C7
Gomel = Homyel, *Belarus* 47 F6
Gomera, *Canary Is.* 37 F2
Gómez Palacio, *Mexico* 118 B4
Gomīshān, *Iran* 71 B7
Gommern, *Germany* 24 C7
Gomogomo, *Indonesia* 63 F8
Gomoh, *India* 67 H15
Gomotartsi, *Bulgaria* 40 B6
Gompa = Ganta, *Liberia* 82 D3
Gomphi, *Greece* 38 B3
Gonābād, *Iran* 71 C8
Gonaïves, *Haiti* 121 C5
Gonâve, G. de la, *Haiti* 121 C5
Gonâve, I. de la, *Haiti* 121 C5
Gonbad-e Kāvūs, *Iran* 71 B7
Gönc, *Hungary* 42 B6
Gonda, *India* 69 F9
Gondal, *India* 68 J4
Gonder, *Ethiopia* 81 E4
Gonder □, *Ethiopia* 81 E4
Gondia, *India* 66 J12
Gondola, *Mozam.* 87 F3
Gondomar, *Portugal* 34 D2
Gondrecourt-le-Château, *France* 19 D12
Gönen, *Balıkesir, Turkey* 41 F11
Gönen, *Isparta, Turkey* 39 D12
Gönen →, *Turkey* 41 F11
Gong Xian, *China* 58 C5
Gong'an, *China* 59 B9
Gongcheng, *China* 59 E8
Gongga Shan, *China* 58 C3
Gongguan, *China* 58 G7
Gonghe, *China* 60 C5
Gongola →, *Nigeria* 83 D7
Gongolgon, *Australia* 95 E4
Gongshan, *China* 58 D2
Gongtan, *China* 58 C7
Gongzhuling, *China* 57 C13
Goniadz, *Poland* 44 E9
Goniri, *Nigeria* 83 C7
Gonjo, *China* 58 B2
Gonnesa, *Italy* 30 C1
Gónnos, *Greece* 38 B4
Gonnosfanádiga, *Italy* 30 C1
Gonzaga, *Phil.* 61 B5
Gonzales, *Calif., U.S.A.* 116 J5
Gonzales, *Tex., U.S.A.* 113 L6
González Chaves, *Argentina* 126 D3
Good Hope, C. of, *S. Africa* 88 E2
Gooderham, *Canada* 110 B6
Goodhouse, *S. Africa* 88 D2
Gooding, *U.S.A.* 114 E6
Goodland, *U.S.A.* 112 F4
Goodlow, *Canada* 104 B4
Goodooga, *Australia* 95 D4
Goodsprings, *U.S.A.* 117 K11
Goole, *U.K.* 12 D7
Goolgowi, *Australia* 95 E4
Goolwa, *Australia* 95 F2
Goomalling, *Australia* 93 F2
Goomeri, *Australia* 95 D5
Goonda, *Mozam.* 87 F3
Goondiwindi, *Australia* 95 D5
Goongarrie, L., *Australia* 93 F3
Goonyella, *Australia* 94 C4
Goose →, *Canada* 103 B7
Goose Creek, *U.S.A.* 109 J5
Goose L., *U.S.A.* 114 F3
Gop, *India* 66 H6
Gopalganj, *India* 69 F11
Göppingen, *Germany* 25 G5
Gor, *Spain* 35 H8
Góra, *Dolnośląskie, Poland* 45 G3
Góra, *Mazowieckie, Poland* 45 F7
Góra Kalwaria, *Poland* 45 G8
Gorakhpur, *India* 69 F10
Goražde, *Bos.-H.* 42 G3
Gorbatov, *Russia* 48 B6
Gorbea, Peña, *Spain* 32 B2
Gorda, *U.S.A.* 116 K5
Gorda, Pta., *Canary Is.* 37 F2
Gorda, Pta., *Nic.* 120 D3
Gordan B., *Australia* 92 B5
Gördes, *Turkey* 39 C10
Gordon, *U.S.A.* 112 D3
Gordon →, *Australia* 94 G4
Gordon L., *Alta., Canada* 105 B6
Gordon L., *N.W.T., Canada* 104 A6
Gordonvale, *Australia* 94 B4
Gore, *Ethiopia* 81 F4
Gore, *N.Z.* 91 M2
Gore Bay, *Canada* 102 C3
Görele, *Turkey* 73 B8
Goreme, *Turkey* 72 C6
Gorey, *Ireland* 15 D5
Gorg, *Iran* 71 D8
Gorgān, *Iran* 71 B7
Gorgona, *Italy* 28 E6
Gorgona, I., *Colombia* 124 C3
Gorgora, *Ethiopia* 81 E4
Gorgoram, *Nigeria* 83 C7
Gorham, *U.S.A.* 111 B13
Gori, *Georgia* 49 J7
Goriganga →, *India* 69 E9
Gorinchem, *Neths.* 17 C4
Goris, *Armenia* 73 C12
Goritsy, *Russia* 46 D9
Gorízia, *Italy* 29 C10
Gorj □, *Romania* 43 E8
Gorki = Horki, *Belarus* 46 E6
Gorki = Nizhniy Novgorod, *Russia* 48 B7
Gorkiy = Nizhniy Novgorod, *Russia* 48 B7
Gorkovskoye Vdkhr., *Russia* 48 B6
Gorlice, *Poland* 45 J8
Görlitz, *Germany* 24 D10
Gorlovka = Horlivka, *Ukraine* 47 H10
Gorman, *U.S.A.* 117 L8
Gorna Dzhumayo = Blagoevgrad, *Bulgaria* 40 D7
Gorna Oryakhovitsa, *Bulgaria* 41 C9
Gornja Radgona, *Slovenia* 29 B13
Gornja Tuzla, *Bos.-H.* 42 F3
Gornji Grad, *Slovenia* 29 B11
Gornji Milanovac, *Serbia, Yug.* 40 B4
Gornji Vakuf, *Bos.-H.* 42 G2
Gorno Ablanovo, *Bulgaria* 41 C9
Gorno-Altay □, *Russia* 50 D9
Gorno-Altaysk, *Russia* 50 D9
Gornyatskiy, *Russia* 49 F5
Gornyy, *Saratov, Russia* 48 E9
Gornyy, *Sib., Russia* 54 B6
Gorodenka = Horodenka, *Ukraine* 47 H3
Gorodets, *Russia* 48 B6
Gorodishche = Horodyshche, *Ukraine* 47 H6
Gorodishche, *Russia* 48 D7
Gorodnya = Horodnya, *Ukraine* 47 G6
Gorodok = Haradok, *Belarus* 46 E6
Gorodok = Horodok, *Ukraine* 47 H2
Gorodovikovsk, *Russia* 49 G5
Gorokhov = Horokhiv, *Ukraine* 47 G3
Gorokhovets, *Russia* 48 B6
Gorom Gorom, *Burkina Faso* 83 C4
Goromonzi, *Zimbabwe* 87 F3
Gorong, Kepulauan, *Indonesia* 63 E8
Gorongose →, *Mozam.* 89 C5
Gorongoza, *Mozam.* 87 F3
Gorongoza, Sa. da, *Mozam.* 87 F3
Gorontalo, *Indonesia* 63 D6
Goronyo, *Nigeria* 83 C6
Górowo Iławeckie, *Poland* 44 D7
Gorron, *France* 18 D6
Gorshechnoye, *Russia* 47 G10
Gort, *Ireland* 15 C3
Gortis, *Greece* 36 D6
Góry Bystrzyckie, *Poland* 45 H3
Goryachiy Klyuch, *Russia* 49 H4
Gorzkowice, *Poland* 45 G6
Górzno, *Poland* 45 E6
Gorzów Śląski, *Poland* 45 G5
Gorzów Wielkopolski, *Poland* 45 F2
Gosford, *Australia* 95 E5
Goshen, *Calif., U.S.A.* 116 J7
Goshen, *Ind., U.S.A.* 108 E3
Goshen, *N.Y., U.S.A.* 111 E10
Goshogawara, *Japan* 54 D10
Goslar, *Germany* 24 D6
Gospič, *Croatia* 29 D12
Gosport, *U.K.* 13 G6
Gossas, *Senegal* 82 C1
Gosse →, *Australia* 94 B1
Gossi, *Mali* 83 B4
Gossinga, *Sudan* 81 F2
Gostivar, *Macedonia* 40 E4
Gostyń, *Poland* 45 G4
Gostynin, *Poland* 45 F6
Göta älv →, *Sweden* 11 G5
Göta kanal, *Sweden* 11 F9
Götaland, *Sweden* 11 G8
Göteborg, *Sweden* 11 G5
Göteborgs och Bohus län □, *Sweden* 11 F5
Götene, *Sweden* 11 F7
Goteşti, *Moldova* 43 D13
Gotha, *Germany* 24 E6
Gothenburg = Göteborg, *Sweden* 11 G5
Gothenburg, *U.S.A.* 112 E4
Gothèye, *Niger* 83 C5
Gotland, *Sweden* 11 G12
Gotlands län □, *Sweden* 11 G12
Gotō-Rettō, *Japan* 55 H4
Gotse Delchev, *Bulgaria* 40 E7
Gotska Sandön, *Sweden* 9 G18
Gōtsu, *Japan* 55 G6
Gott Pk., *Canada* 104 C4
Góttero, Monte, *Italy* 28 D6
Göttingen, *Germany* 24 D5
Gottwald = Zmiyev, *Ukraine* 47 H9
Gottwaldov = Zlín, *Czech Rep.* 27 B10
Goubangzi, *China* 57 D11
Gouda, *Neths.* 17 B4
Goúdhoura, Ákra, *Greece* 36 E8
Goudiry, *Senegal* 82 C2
Goudoumaria, *Niger* 83 C7
Gouéké, *Guinea* 82 D3
Gough I., *Atl. Oc.* 2 G9
Gouin, Rés., *Canada* 102 C5
Gouitafla, *Ivory C.* 82 D3
Goulburn, *Australia* 95 E4
Goulburn Is., *Australia* 94 A1
Goulia, *Ivory C.* 82 C3
Goulimine, *Morocco* 78 C3
Goumbou, *Mali* 82 B3
Gouménissa, *Greece* 40 F6
Goundam, *Mali* 82 B4
Goúra, *Greece* 38 D4
Gourbassi, *Mali* 82 C2
Gourdon, *France* 20 D5
Gouré, *Niger* 83 C7
Gourin, *France* 18 D3
Gourits →, *S. Africa* 88 E3
Gourma-Rharous, *Mali* 83 B4
Goúrnais, *Greece* 36 D7
Gournay-en-Bray, *France* 19 C8
Goursi, *Burkina Faso* 82 C4
Gouverneur, *U.S.A.* 111 B9
Gouviá, *Greece* 36 A3
Gouzon, *France* 19 F9
Governador Valadares, *Brazil* 125 G10
Governor's Harbour, *Bahamas* 120 A4
Govindgarh, *India* 69 G9
Gowan Ra., *Australia* 94 D4
Gowanda, *U.S.A.* 110 D6
Gowd-e Zirreh, *Afghan.* 66 E3
Gower, *U.K.* 13 F3
Gowna, L., *Ireland* 15 C4
Goya, *Argentina* 126 B4
Göyçay, *Azerbaijan* 49 K8
Goyder Lagoon, *Australia* 95 D2
Goyllarisquisga, *Peru* 124 F3
Göynük, *Antalya, Turkey* 39 E12
Göynük, *Bolu, Turkey* 72 B4
Goz Beïda, *Chad* 79 F10
Goz Regeb, *Sudan* 81 D4
Gozdnica, *Poland* 45 G2
Gozo, *Malta* 36 C1
Graaff-Reinet, *S. Africa* 88 E3
Grabo, *Ivory C.* 82 D3
Grabow, *Germany* 24 B7
Grabów nad Prosną, *Poland* 45 G5
Gračac, *Croatia* 29 D12
Gračanica, *Bos.-H.* 42 F3
Graçay, *France* 19 E8
Gracias a Dios, C., *Honduras* 120 D3
Graciosa, I., *Canary Is.* 37 E6
Grad Sofiya □, *Bulgaria* 40 D7
Gradac, *Montenegro, Yug.* 40 C3
Gradačac, *Bos.-H.* 42 F3
Gradeška Planina, *Macedonia* 40 E6
Gradets, *Bulgaria* 41 D10
Gradišče, *Slovenia* 29 B12
Grădiştea de Munte, *Romania* 43 E8
Grado, *Italy* 29 C10
Grado, *Spain* 34 B4
Grady, *U.S.A.* 113 H3
Graeca, Lacul, *Romania* 43 F11
Grafenau, *Germany* 25 G9
Gräfenberg, *Germany* 25 F7
Grafham Water, *U.K.* 13 E7
Grafton, *Australia* 95 D5
Grafton, *N. Dak., U.S.A.* 112 A6
Grafton, *W. Va., U.S.A.* 108 F5
Graham, *Canada* 102 C1
Graham, *U.S.A.* 113 J5
Graham, Mt., *U.S.A.* 115 K9
Graham Bell, Ostrov = Greem-Bell, Ostrov, *Russia* 50 A7
Graham I., *B.C., Canada* 104 C2
Graham I., *N.W.T., Canada* 100 C6
Graham Land, *Antarctica* 5 C17
Grahamstown, *S. Africa* 88 E4
Grahamsville, *U.S.A.* 111 E10
Grahovo, *Montenegro, Yug.* 40 D2
Graie, Alpi, *Europe* 21 C11
Grain Coast, *W. Afr.* 82 E3
Grajaú, *Brazil* 125 E9
Grajaú →, *Brazil* 125 D10
Grajewo, *Poland* 44 E9
Gramada, *Bulgaria* 40 C6
Gramat, *France* 20 D5
Grammichele, *Italy* 31 E7
Grámmos, Óros, *Greece* 40 F4
Grampian, *U.S.A.* 110 F6
Grampian Highlands = Grampian Mts., *U.K.* 14 E5
Grampian Mts., *U.K.* 14 E5
Grampians, The, *Australia* 95 F3
Gramsh, *Albania* 40 F4
Gran Canaria, *Canary Is.* 37 G4
Gran Chaco, *S. Amer.* 126 B3
Gran Paradiso, *Italy* 28 C4
Gran Sasso d'Itália, *Italy* 29 F10
Granada, *Nic.* 120 D2
Granada, *Spain* 35 H7
Granada, *U.S.A.* 113 F3
Granada □, *Spain* 35 H7
Granadilla de Abona, *Canary Is.* 37 F3
Granard, *Ireland* 15 C4
Granbury, *U.S.A.* 113 J6
Granby, *Canada* 102 C5
Granby, *U.S.A.* 114 F11
Grand →, *Canada* 110 D5
Grand →, *Mo., U.S.A.* 112 F8
Grand →, *S. Dak., U.S.A.* 112 C4
Grand Bahama, *Bahamas* 120 A4
Grand Bank, *Canada* 103 C8
Grand Bassam, *Ivory C.* 82 D4
Grand Béréby, *Ivory C.* 82 E3
Grand-Bourg, *Guadeloupe* 121 C7
Grand Canal = Yun Ho →, *China* 57 E9
Grand Canyon, *U.S.A.* 115 H7
Grand Canyon National Park, *U.S.A.* 115 H7
Grand Cayman, *Cayman Is.* 120 C3
Grand Centre, *Canada* 105 C6
Grand Cess, *Liberia* 82 E3
Grand Coulee, *U.S.A.* 114 C4
Grand Coulee Dam, *U.S.A.* 114 C4
Grand Erg du Bilma, *Niger* 79 E8
Grand Erg Occidental, *Algeria* 78 B6
Grand Erg Oriental, *Algeria* 78 B7
Grand Falls, *Canada* 103 C6
Grand Falls-Windsor, *Canada* 103 C8
Grand Forks, *Canada* 104 D5
Grand Forks, *U.S.A.* 112 B6
Grand Gorge, *U.S.A.* 111 D10
Grand Haven, *U.S.A.* 108 D2
Grand I., *Mich., U.S.A.* 108 B2
Grand I., *N.Y., U.S.A.* 110 D6
Grand Island, *U.S.A.* 112 E5
Grand Isle, *La., U.S.A.* 113 L9
Grand Isle, *Vt., U.S.A.* 111 B11
Grand Junction, *U.S.A.* 115 G9
Grand L., *N.B., Canada* 103 C6

Grand L., Nfld., Canada 103 C8
Grand L., Nfld., Canada 103 B7
Grand L., U.S.A. 113 L8
Grand Lahou, Ivory C. 82 D3
Grand Lake, U.S.A. 114 F11
Grand-Lieu, L. de, France 18 E5
Grand Manan I., Canada 103 D6
Grand Marais, Canada 112 B9
Grand Marais, U.S.A. 108 B3
Grand-Mère, Canada 102 C5
Grand Popo, Benin 83 D5
Grand Portage, U.S.A. 112 B10
Grand Prairie, U.S.A. 113 J6
Grand Rapids, Canada 105 C9
Grand Rapids, Mich., U.S.A. 108 D2
Grand Rapids, Minn., U.S.A. 112 B8
Grand St-Bernard, Col du, Europe 25 K3
Grand Teton, U.S.A. 114 E8
Grand Teton National Park, U.S.A. 114 D8
Grand Union Canal, U.K. 13 E7
Grand View, Canada 105 C8
Grandas de Salime, Spain 34 B4
Grande →, Jujuy, Argentina 126 A2
Grande →, Mendoza, Argentina 126 D2
Grande →, Bolivia 124 G6
Grande →, Bahia, Brazil 125 F10
Grande →, Minas Gerais, Brazil 125 H8
Grande, B., Argentina 128 G3
Grande, Rio →, U.S.A. 113 N6
Grande Baleine, R. de la →, Canada 102 A4
Grande Cache, Canada 104 C5
Grande-Entrée, Canada 103 C7
Grande Prairie, Canada 104 B5
Grande-Rivière, Canada 103 C7
Grande-Vallée, Canada 103 C6
Grandfalls, U.S.A. 113 K3
Grândola, Portugal 35 G2
Grandpré, France 19 C11
Grandview, U.S.A. 114 C4
Grandvilliers, France 19 C8
Graneros, Chile 126 C1
Grangemouth, U.K. 14 E5
Granger, U.S.A. 114 F9
Grängesberg, Sweden 10 D9
Grangeville, U.S.A. 114 D5
Granisle, Canada 104 C3
Granite City, U.S.A. 112 F9
Granite Falls, U.S.A. 112 C7
Granite L., Canada 103 C8
Granite Mt., U.S.A. 117 M10
Granite Pk., U.S.A. 114 D9
Graniteville, U.S.A. 111 B12
Granitola, C., Italy 30 E5
Granity, N.Z. 91 J3
Granja, Brazil 125 D10
Granja de Moreruela, Spain 34 D5
Granja de Torrehermosa, Spain 35 G5
Gränna, Sweden 11 F8
Granollers, Spain 32 D7
Gransee, Germany 24 B9
Grant, U.S.A. 112 E4
Grant, Mt., U.S.A. 114 G4
Grant City, U.S.A. 112 E7
Grant I., Australia 92 B5
Grant Range, U.S.A. 115 G6
Grantham, U.K. 12 E7
Grantown-on-Spey, U.K. 14 D5
Grants, U.S.A. 115 J10
Grants Pass, U.S.A. 114 E2
Grantsville, U.S.A. 114 F7
Granville, France 18 D5
Granville, N. Dak., U.S.A. 112 A4
Granville, N.Y., U.S.A. 111 C11
Granville, Ohio, U.S.A. 110 F2
Granville L., Canada 105 B8
Graskop, S. Africa 89 C5
Gräsö, Sweden 10 D12
Grass →, Canada 105 B9
Grass Range, U.S.A. 114 C9
Grass River Prov. Park, Canada 105 C8
Grass Valley, Calif., U.S.A. 116 F6
Grass Valley, Oreg., U.S.A. 114 D3
Grassano, Italy 31 B9
Grasse, France 21 E10
Grassflat, U.S.A. 110 F6
Grasslands Nat. Park, Canada 105 D7
Grassy, Australia 94 G3
Gråsten, Denmark 11 K3
Grästorp, Sweden 11 F6
Gratkorn, Austria 26 D8
Graubünden □, Switz. 25 J5
Graulhet, France 20 E5
Graus, Spain 32 C5
Grave, Pte. de, France 20 C2
Gravelbourg, Canada 105 D7
Gravelines, France 19 A9
's-Gravenhage, Neths. 17 B4
Gravenhurst, Canada 102 D4
Gravesend, Australia 95 D5
Gravesend, U.K. 13 F8
Gravina in Púglia, Italy 31 B9
Gravois, Pointe-à-, Haiti 121 C5
Gravone →, France 21 G12
Gray, France 19 E12
Grayling, U.S.A. 108 C3
Grays Harbor, U.S.A. 114 C1
Grays L., U.S.A. 114 E8
Grays River, U.S.A. 116 D3
Grayvoron, Russia 47 G8
Graz, Austria 26 D8
Grdelica, Serbia, Yug. 40 D6
Greasy L., Canada 104 A4
Great Abaco I., Bahamas 120 A4
Great Artesian Basin, Australia 94 C3
Great Australian Bight, Australia 93 F5
Great Bahama Bank, Bahamas 120 B4
Great Barrier I., N.Z. 91 G5
Great Barrier Reef, Australia 94 B4
Great Barrington, U.S.A. 111 D11
Great Basin, U.S.A. 114 G5
Great Basin Nat. Park, U.S.A. 114 G6
Great Bear →, Canada 100 B7
Great Bear L., Canada 100 B7
Great Belt = Store Bælt, Denmark 11 J4
Great Bend, Kans., U.S.A. 112 F5
Great Bend, Pa., U.S.A. 111 E9
Great Blasket I., Ireland 15 D1
Great Britain, Europe 6 E5
Great Codroy, Canada 103 C8
Great Dividing Ra., Australia 94 C4
Great Driffield = Driffield, U.K. 12 C7
Great Exuma I., Bahamas 120 B4
Great Falls, U.S.A. 114 C8
Great Fish = Groot Vis →, S. Africa 88 E4
Great Guana Cay, Bahamas 120 B4
Great Inagua I., Bahamas 121 B5
Great Indian Desert = Thar Desert, India 68 F5
Great Karoo, S. Africa 88 E3
Great Lake, Australia 94 G4
Great Lakes, N. Amer. 98 E11
Great Malvern, U.K. 13 E5
Great Miami →, U.S.A. 108 F3
Great Ormes Head, U.K. 12 D4
Great Ouse →, U.K. 12 E8
Great Palm I., Australia 94 B4
Great Plains, N. Amer. 106 A6
Great Ruaha →, Tanzania 86 D4
Great Sacandaga Res., U.S.A. 111 C10
Great Saint Bernard Pass = Grand St-Bernard, Col du, Europe 25 K3
Great Salt L., U.S.A. 114 F7
Great Salt Lake Desert, U.S.A. 114 F7
Great Salt Plains L., U.S.A. 113 G5
Great Sandy Desert, Australia 92 D3
Great Sangi = Sangihe, Pulau, Indonesia 63 D7
Great Scarcies →, S. Leone 82 D2
Great Skellig, Ireland 15 E1
Great Slave L., Canada 104 A5
Great Smoky Mts. Nat. Park, U.S.A. 109 H4
Great Snow Mt., Canada 104 B4
Great Stour = Stour →, U.K. 13 F9
Great Victoria Desert, Australia 93 E4
Great Wall, China 56 E5
Great Whernside, U.K. 12 C6
Great Yarmouth, U.K. 13 E9
Greater Antilles, W. Indies 121 C5
Greater London □, U.K. 13 F7
Greater Manchester □, U.K. 12 D5
Greater Sunda Is., Indonesia 62 F4
Grebbestad, Sweden 11 F5
Grebenka = Hrebenka, Ukraine 47 G7
Greco, C., Cyprus 36 E13
Greco, Mte., Italy 29 G10
Gredos, Sierra de, Spain 34 E6
Greece, U.S.A. 110 C7
Greece ■, Europe 38 B3
Greeley, Colo., U.S.A. 112 E2
Greeley, Nebr., U.S.A. 112 E5
Greem-Bell, Ostrov, Russia 50 A7
Green, U.S.A. 114 E2
Green →, Ky., U.S.A. 108 G2
Green →, Utah, U.S.A. 115 G9
Green B., U.S.A. 108 C2
Green Bay, U.S.A. 108 C2
Green C., Australia 95 F5
Green Cove Springs, U.S.A. 109 L5
Green Lake, Canada 105 C7
Green Mts., U.S.A. 111 C12
Green River, Utah, U.S.A. 115 G8
Green River, Wyo., U.S.A. 114 F9
Green Valley, U.S.A. 115 L8
Greenbank, U.S.A. 116 B4
Greenbush, Mich., U.S.A. 110 B1
Greenbush, Minn., U.S.A. 112 A6
Greencastle, U.S.A. 108 F2
Greene, U.S.A. 111 D9
Greenfield, Calif., U.S.A. 116 J5
Greenfield, Calif., U.S.A. 117 K8
Greenfield, Ind., U.S.A. 108 F3
Greenfield, Iowa, U.S.A. 112 E7
Greenfield, Mass., U.S.A. 111 D12
Greenfield, Mo., U.S.A. 113 G8
Greenfield Park, Canada 111 A11
Greenland ■, N. Amer. 4 C5
Greenland Sea, Arctic 4 B7
Greenock, U.K. 14 F4
Greenore, Ireland 15 B5
Greenore Pt., Ireland 15 D5
Greenough, Australia 93 E1
Greenough →, Australia 93 E1
Greenough Pt., Canada 110 B3
Greenport, U.S.A. 111 E12
Greensboro, Ga., U.S.A. 109 J4
Greensboro, N.C., U.S.A. 109 G6
Greensboro, Vt., U.S.A. 111 B12
Greensburg, Ind., U.S.A. 108 F3
Greensburg, Kans., U.S.A. 113 G5
Greensburg, Pa., U.S.A. 110 F5
Greenstone Pt., U.K. 14 D3
Greenvale, Australia 94 B4
Greenville, Liberia 82 D3
Greenville, Ala., U.S.A. 109 K2
Greenville, Calif., U.S.A. 116 E6
Greenville, Maine, U.S.A. 109 C11
Greenville, Mich., U.S.A. 108 D3
Greenville, Miss., U.S.A. 113 J9
Greenville, Mo., U.S.A. 113 G9
Greenville, N.C., U.S.A. 109 H7
Greenville, N.H., U.S.A. 111 D13
Greenville, N.Y., U.S.A. 111 D10
Greenville, Ohio, U.S.A. 108 E3
Greenville, Pa., U.S.A. 110 E4
Greenville, S.C., U.S.A. 109 H4
Greenville, Tenn., U.S.A. 109 G4
Greenville, Tex., U.S.A. 113 J6
Greenwater Lake Prov. Park, Canada 105 C8
Greenwich, U.K. 13 F8
Greenwich, Conn., U.S.A. 111 E11
Greenwich, N.Y., U.S.A. 111 C11
Greenwich, Ohio, U.S.A. 110 E2
Greenwood, Canada 104 D5
Greenwood, Ark., U.S.A. 113 H7
Greenwood, Ind., U.S.A. 108 F2
Greenwood, Miss., U.S.A. 113 J9
Greenwood, S.C., U.S.A. 109 H4
Greenwood, Mt., Australia 92 B5
Gregbe, Ivory C. 82 D3
Gregory, U.S.A. 112 D5
Gregory →, Australia 94 B2
Gregory, L., S. Austral., Australia 95 D2
Gregory, L., W. Austral., Australia 93 E2
Gregory Downs, Australia 94 B2
Gregory L., Australia 92 D4
Gregory Ra., Queens., Australia 94 B3
Gregory Ra., W. Austral., Australia 92 D3
Greiffenberg, Germany 24 B9
Greifswald, Germany 24 A9
Greifswalder Bodden, Germany 24 A9
Grein, Austria 26 C7
Greiz, Germany 24 E8
Gremikha, Russia 50 C4
Grenå, Denmark 11 H4
Grenada, U.S.A. 113 J10
Grenada ■, W. Indies 121 D7
Grenade, France 20 E5
Grenadier I., U.S.A. 111 B8
Grenadines, W. Indies 121 D7
Grenchen, Switz. 25 H3
Grenen, Denmark 11 G4
Grenfell, Australia 95 E4
Grenfell, Canada 105 C8
Grenoble, France 21 C9
Grenville, C., Australia 94 A3
Grenville Chan., Canada 104 C3
Gréoux-les-Bains, France 21 E9
Gresham, U.S.A. 116 E4
Gresik, Indonesia 63 G15
Gretna, U.K. 14 F5
Greven, Germany 24 C3
Grevená, Greece 40 F5
Grevená □, Greece 40 F5
Grevenbroich, Germany 24 D2
Grevenmacher, Lux. 17 E6
Grevesmühlen, Germany 24 B7
Grevestrand, Denmark 11 J6
Grey →, Canada 103 C8
Grey →, N.Z. 91 K3
Grey, C., Australia 94 A2
Grey Ra., Australia 95 D3
Greybull, U.S.A. 114 D9
Greymouth, N.Z. 91 K3
Greystones, Ireland 15 C5
Greytown, N.Z. 91 J5
Greytown, S. Africa 89 D5
Gribanovskiy, Russia 48 E5
Gribbell I., Canada 104 C3
Gribës, Mal i, Albania 40 F3
Gridley, U.S.A. 116 F5
Griekwastad, S. Africa 88 D3
Griesheim, Germany 25 F4
Grieskirchen, Austria 26 C6
Griffin, U.S.A. 109 J3
Griffith, Australia 95 E4
Griffith, Canada 110 A7
Griffith I., Canada 110 B4
Grignols, France 20 D3
Grigoriopol, Moldova 43 C14
Grimaylov = Hrymayliv, Ukraine 47 H4
Grimes, U.S.A. 116 F5
Grimma, Germany 24 D8
Grimmen, Germany 24 A9
Grimsay, U.K. 14 D1
Grimsby, Canada 110 C5
Grimsby, U.K. 12 D7
Grímsey, Iceland 8 C5
Grimshaw, Canada 104 B5
Grimslöv, Sweden 11 H8
Grimstad, Norway 9 G13
Grindelwald, Switz. 25 J4
Grindsted, Denmark 11 J2
Grindstone I., Canada 111 B8
Grindu, Romania 43 F11
Grinnell, U.S.A. 112 E8
Grintavec, Slovenia 29 B11
Gris-Nez, C., France 19 B8
Grisolles, France 20 E5
Grisons = Graubünden □, Switz. 25 J5
Grisslehamn, Sweden 10 D12
Grmeč Planina, Bos.-H. 29 D13
Groais I., Canada 103 B8
Grobiņa, Latvia 44 B8
Groblersdal, S. Africa 89 D4
Grobming, Austria 26 D6
Grocka, Serbia, Yug. 40 B4
Gródek, Poland 45 E10
Grodków, Poland 45 H4
Grodno = Hrodna, Belarus 46 F2
Grodzisk Mazowiecki, Poland 45 F7
Grodzisk Wielkopolski, Poland 45 F3
Grodzyanka = Hrodzyanka, Belarus 46 F5
Groesbeck, U.S.A. 113 K6
Groix, France 18 E3
Groix, Î. de, France 18 E3
Grójec, Poland 45 G7
Gronau, Niedersachsen, Germany 24 C5
Gronau, Nordrhein-Westfalen, Germany 24 C3
Grong, Norway 8 D15
Grönhögen, Sweden 11 H10
Groningen, Neths. 17 A6
Groningen □, Neths. 17 A6
Groom, U.S.A. 113 H4
Groot →, S. Africa 88 E3
Groot Berg →, S. Africa 88 E2
Groot-Brakrivier, S. Africa 88 E3
Groot Karasberge, Namibia 88 D2
Groot-Kei →, S. Africa 89 E4
Groot Vis →, S. Africa 88 E4
Grootdrink, S. Africa 88 D3
Groote Eylandt, Australia 94 A2
Grootfontein, Namibia 88 B2
Grootlaagte →, Africa 88 C3
Grootvloer →, S. Africa 88 E3
Gros C., Canada 104 A6
Gros Morne Nat. Park, Canada 103 C8
Grósio, Italy 28 B7
Grosne →, France 19 F11
Grossa, Pta., Spain 37 B8
Grossenbrode, Germany 24 A7
Grossenhain, Germany 24 D9
Grosser Arber, Germany 25 F9
Grosser Plöner See, Germany 24 A6
Grosseto, Italy 29 F8
Grossgerungs, Austria 26 C7
Grossglockner, Austria 26 D5
Groswater B., Canada 103 B8
Groton, Conn., U.S.A. 111 E12
Groton, N.Y., U.S.A. 111 D8
Groton, S. Dak., U.S.A. 112 C5
Grottáglie, Italy 31 B10
Grottaminarda, Italy 31 A8
Grottammare, Italy 29 F10
Grouard Mission, Canada 104 B5
Grouin, Pte. du, France 18 D5
Groundhog →, Canada 102 C3
Grouw, Neths. 17 A5
Grove City, U.S.A. 110 E4
Grove Hill, U.S.A. 109 K2
Groveland, U.S.A. 116 H6
Grover City, U.S.A. 117 K6
Groves, U.S.A. 113 L8
Groveton, U.S.A. 111 B13
Grožnjan, Croatia 29 C10
Groznyy, Russia 49 J7
Grubišno Polje, Croatia 42 E2
Grudovo, Bulgaria 41 D11
Grudusk, Poland 45 E7
Grudziądz, Poland 44 E5
Gruinard B., U.K. 14 D3
Gruissan, France 20 E7
Grumo Áppula, Italy 31 A9
Grums, Sweden 10 E7
Grünberg, Germany 24 E4
Gründau, Germany 25 E5
Grundy Center, U.S.A. 112 D8
Grünstadt, Germany 25 F4
Gruvberget, Sweden 10 C10
Gruver, U.S.A. 113 G4
Gruyères, Switz. 25 J3
Gruža, Serbia, Yug. 40 C4
Gryazi, Russia 47 F10
Gryazovets, Russia 46 C11
Grybów, Poland 45 J7
Grycksbo, Sweden 10 D9
Gryfice, Poland 44 E2
Gryfino, Poland 45 E1
Gryfów Śląski, Poland 45 G2
Grythyttan, Sweden 10 E8
Gstaad, Switz. 25 J3
Gua, India 67 H14
Gua Musang, Malaysia 65 K3
Guacanayabo, G. de, Cuba 120 B4
Guachípas →, Argentina 126 B2
Guadajoz →, Spain 35 H6
Guadalajara, Mexico 118 C4
Guadalajara, Spain 32 E1
Guadalajara □, Spain 32 E2
Guadalcanal, Solomon Is. 96 H8
Guadalcanal, Spain 35 G5
Guadalén →, Spain 35 G7
Guadales, Argentina 126 C2
Guadalete →, Spain 35 J4
Guadalimar →, Spain 35 G7
Guadalmena →, Spain 35 G8
Guadalmez →, Spain 35 G5
Guadalope →, Spain 32 D4
Guadalquivir →, Spain 35 J4
Guadalupe = Guadeloupe ■, W. Indies 121 C7
Guadalupe, Mexico 117 N10
Guadalupe, Spain 35 F5
Guadalupe, U.S.A. 117 L6
Guadalupe →, Mexico 117 N10
Guadalupe →, U.S.A. 113 L6
Guadalupe, Sierra de, Spain 35 F5
Guadalupe Bravos, Mexico 118 A3
Guadalupe I., Pac. Oc. 98 G8
Guadalupe Mts. Nat. Park, U.S.A. 113 K2
Guadalupe Peak, U.S.A. 113 K2
Guadalupe y Calvo, Mexico 118 B3
Guadarrama, Sierra de, Spain 34 E7
Guadauta, Georgia 49 J5
Guadeloupe ■, W. Indies 121 C7
Guadeloupe Passage, W. Indies 121 C7
Guadiamar →, Spain 35 J4
Guadiana →, Portugal 35 H3
Guadiana Menor →, Spain 35 H7
Guadiaro →, Spain 35 J5
Guadiato →, Spain 35 H5
Guadiela →, Spain 32 E2
Guadix, Spain 35 H7
Guafo, Boca del, Chile 128 E2
Guainía →, Colombia 124 C5
Guaíra, Brazil 127 A5
Guaíra □, Paraguay 126 B4
Guaitecas, Is., Chile 128 E2
Guajará-Mirim, Brazil 124 F5
Guajira, Pen. de la, Colombia 124 A4
Gualán, Guatemala 120 C2
Gualdo Tadino, Italy 29 E9
Gualeguay, Argentina 126 C4
Gualeguaychú, Argentina 126 C4
Gualequay →, Argentina 126 C4
Guam ■, Pac. Oc. 96 F6
Guaminí, Argentina 126 D3
Guamúchil, Mexico 118 B3
Guanabacoa, Cuba 120 B3
Guanacaste, Cordillera del, Costa Rica 120 D2
Guanaceví, Mexico 118 B3
Guanahani = San Salvador I., Bahamas 121 B5
Guanajay, Cuba 120 B3
Guanajuato, Mexico 118 C4
Guanajuato □, Mexico 118 C4
Guandacol, Argentina 126 B2
Guane, Cuba 120 B3
Guang'an, China 58 B6
Guangchang, China 59 D11
Guangde, China 59 B12
Guangdong □, China 59 F9
Guangfeng, China 59 C12
Guanghan, China 58 B5
Guangling, China 56 E8
Guangnan, China 58 E5
Guangning, China 59 F9
Guangrao, China 57 F10
Guangshui, China 59 B9
Guangshun, China 58 D6
Guangwu, China 56 F3
Guangxi Zhuangzu Zizhiqu □, China 58 F7
Guangyuan, China 58 A5
Guangze, China 59 D11
Guangzhou, China 59 F9
Guanipa →, Venezuela 124 B6
Guanling, China 58 E5
Guannan, China 57 G10
Guantánamo, Cuba 121 B4
Guantao, China 56 F8
Guanyang, China 59 E8
Guanyun, China 57 G10
Guápiles, Costa Rica 120 D3
Guaporé, Brazil 127 B5
Guaporé →, Brazil 122 E4
Guaqui, Bolivia 124 G5
Guara, Sierra de, Spain 32 C4
Guarapari, Brazil 127 A7
Guarapuava, Brazil 127 B5
Guaratinguetá, Brazil 127 A6
Guaratuba, Brazil 127 B6
Guarda, Portugal 34 E3
Guarda □, Portugal 34 E3
Guardafui, C. = Asir, Ras, Somali Rep. 74 E5
Guardamar del Segura, Spain 33 G4
Guardavalle, Italy 31 D9
Guárdia Sanframondi, Italy 31 A7
Guardiagrele, Italy 29 F11
Guardo, Spain 34 C6
Guareña, Spain 35 G4
Guareña →, Spain 34 D5
Guárico □, Venezuela 124 B5
Guarujá, Brazil 127 A6
Guarus, Brazil 127 A7
Guasave, Mexico 118 B3
Guasdualito, Venezuela 124 B4
Guastalla, Italy 28 D7
Guatemala, Guatemala 120 D1
Guatemala ■, Cent. Amer. 120 C1
Guaviare →, Colombia 122 C4
Guaxupé, Brazil 127 A6
Guayama, Puerto Rico 121 C6
Guayaquil, Ecuador 124 D3
Guayaquil, G. de, Ecuador 122 D2
Guaymas, Mexico 118 B2
Guazhou, China 59 A12
Guba, Dem. Rep. of the Congo 87 E2
Guba, Ethiopia 81 E4
Gûbâl, Madîq, Egypt 80 B3
Gubat, Phil. 61 E6
Gúbbio, Italy 29 E9
Guben, Germany 24 D10
Gubin, Poland 45 G1
Gubio, Nigeria 83 C7
Gubkin, Russia 47 G9
Guča, Serbia, Yug. 40 C4

Gucheng, *China* 59 A8
Gudata = Guadauta, *Georgia* 49 J5
Gudbrandsdalen, *Norway* 9 F14
Guddu Barrage, *Pakistan* 66 E6
Gudenå →, *Denmark* 11 H4
Gudermes, *Russia* 49 J8
Gudhjem, *Denmark* 11 J8
Gudivada, *India* 67 L12
Gudur, *India* 66 M11
Guebwiller, *France* 19 E14
Guecho = Getxo, *Spain* 32 B2
Guékédou, *Guinea* 82 D2
Guéle Mendouka, *Cameroon* 83 E7
Guelph, *Canada* 102 D3
Guéméné-Penfao, *France* 18 E5
Guéméné-sur-Scorff, *France* 18 D3
Guéné, *Benin* 83 C5
Guer, *France* 18 E4
Guérande, *France* 18 E4
Guéret, *France* 19 F8
Guérigny, *France* 19 E10
Guerneville, *U.S.A.* 116 G4
Guernica = Gernika-Lumo, *Spain* 32 B2
Guernsey, *U.K.* 13 H5
Guernsey, *U.S.A.* 112 D2
Guerrero □, *Mexico* 119 D5
Guessou-Sud, *Benin* 83 C5
Gueugnon, *France* 19 F11
Guéyo, *Ivory C.* 82 D3
Gughe, *Ethiopia* 81 F4
Gügher, *Iran* 71 D8
Guglionesi, *Italy* 29 G11
Guhakolak, Tanjung, *Indonesia* 63 G11
Gui Jiang →, *China* 59 F8
Guia, *Canary Is.* 37 F4
Guia de Isora, *Canary Is.* 37 F3
Guia Lopes da Laguna, *Brazil* 127 A4
Guiana, *S. Amer.* 122 C4
Guibéroua, *Ivory C.* 82 D3
Guichi, *China* 59 B11
Guider, *Cameroon* 83 D7
Guidiguir, *Niger* 83 C6
Guidimouni, *Niger* 83 C6
Guiding, *China* 58 D6
Guidong, *China* 59 D9
Guidónia-Montecélio, *Italy* 29 F9
Guiers, L. de, *Senegal* 82 B1
Guigang, *China* 58 F7
Guiglo, *Ivory C.* 82 D3
Guihulñgan, *Phil.* 61 F5
Guijá, *Mozam.* 89 C5
Guijuelo, *Spain* 34 E5
Guildford, *U.K.* 13 F7
Guilford, *U.S.A.* 111 E12
Guilin, *China* 59 E8
Guillaume-Delisle L., *Canada* 102 A4
Guillaumes, *France* 21 D10
Guillestre, *France* 21 D10
Guilvinec, *France* 18 E2
Güimar, *Canary Is.* 37 F3
Guimarães, *Portugal* 34 D2
Guimaras □, *Phil.* 61 F5
Guinda, *U.S.A.* 116 G4
Guinea, *Africa* 76 F4
Guinea ■, *W. Afr.* 82 C2
Guinea, Gulf of, *Atl. Oc.* 83 E5
Guinea-Bissau ■, *Africa* 82 C2
Güines, *Cuba* 120 B3
Guingamp, *France* 18 D3
Guinguinéo, *Senegal* 82 C1
Guipavas, *France* 18 D2
Guiping, *China* 59 F8
Guipúzcoa □, *Spain* 32 B2
Guir, *Mali* 82 B4
Guirel, *Mauritania* 82 B3
Güiria, *Venezuela* 124 A6
Guiscard, *France* 19 C10
Guise, *France* 19 C10
Guitiriz, *Spain* 34 B3
Guitri, *Ivory C.* 82 D3
Guiuan, *Phil.* 61 F6
Guixi, *China* 59 C11
Guiyang, *Guizhou, China* 58 D6
Guiyang, *Hunan, China* 59 E9
Guizhou □, *China* 58 D6
Gujan-Mestras, *France* 20 D2
Gujar Khan, *Pakistan* 68 C5
Gujarat □, *India* 68 H4
Gujiang, *China* 59 D10
Gujranwala, *Pakistan* 68 C6
Gujrat, *Pakistan* 68 C6
Gukovo, *Russia* 49 F5
Gulargambone, *Australia* 95 E4
Gulbarga, *India* 66 L10
Gulbene, *Latvia* 9 H22
Gulf, The, *Asia* 71 E6
Gulfport, *U.S.A.* 113 K10
Gulgong, *Australia* 95 E4
Gulin, *China* 58 C5
Gulistan, *Pakistan* 68 D2
Gull Lake, *Canada* 105 C7
Gullbrandstorp, *Sweden* 11 H6
Gullspång, *Sweden* 11 F8
Güllük, *Turkey* 39 D9
Güllük Korfezi, *Turkey* 39 D9
Gulma, *Nigeria* 83 C5
Gulmarg, *India* 69 B6
Gülnar, *Turkey* 72 D5
Gülpınar, *Turkey* 39 B8
Gülşehir, *Turkey* 72 C6
Gulshad, *Kazakstan* 50 E8
Gulu, *Uganda* 86 B3
Gŭlŭbovo, *Bulgaria* 41 D9
Gulud, J., *Sudan* 81 E2
Gulwe, *Tanzania* 86 D4
Gulyaypole = Hulyaypole, *Ukraine* 47 J9
Gumal →, *Pakistan* 68 D4
Gumbaz, *Pakistan* 68 D3
Gumel, *Nigeria* 83 C6
Gumiel de Hizán, *Spain* 34 D7
Gumla, *India* 69 H11
Gumlu, *Australia* 94 B4
Gumma □, *Japan* 55 F9
Gummersbach, *Germany* 24 D3
Gummi, *Nigeria* 83 C6
Gümüldür, *Turkey* 39 C9
Gümüşçay, *Turkey* 41 F11
Gümüşhacıköy, *Turkey* 72 B6
Gümüşhane, *Turkey* 73 B8
Gümüşsu, *Turkey* 39 C11
Gumzai, *Indonesia* 63 F8
Guna, *Ethiopia* 81 F4
Guna, *India* 68 G7
Gundelfingen, *Germany* 25 G6
Güney, *Burdur, Turkey* 39 D11
Güney, *Denizli, Turkey* 39 C11
Güneydoğu Toroslar, *Turkey* 73 C9
Gunisao →, *Canada* 105 C9
Gunisao L., *Canada* 105 C9
Gunjyal, *Pakistan* 68 C4
Günlüce, *Turkey* 39 E10
Gunnarskog, *Sweden* 10 E6
Gunnbjørn Fjeld, *Greenland* 4 C6
Gunnebo, *Sweden* 11 G10
Gunnedah, *Australia* 95 E5
Gunnewin, *Australia* 95 D4
Gunningbar Cr. →, *Australia* 95 E4
Gunnison, *Colo., U.S.A.* 115 G10
Gunnison, *Utah, U.S.A.* 114 G8
Gunnison →, *U.S.A.* 115 G9
Gunpowder, *Australia* 94 B2
Guntakal, *India* 66 M10
Guntersville, *U.S.A.* 109 H2
Guntong, *Malaysia* 65 K3
Guntur, *India* 67 L12
Gunungapi, *Indonesia* 63 F7
Gunungsitoli, *Indonesia* 62 D1
Günz →, *Germany* 25 G6
Gunza, *Angola* 84 G2
Günzburg, *Germany* 25 G6
Gunzenhausen, *Germany* 25 F6
Guo He →, *China* 57 H9
Guoyang, *China* 56 H9
Gupis, *Pakistan* 69 A5
Gura Humorului, *Romania* 43 C10
Gura-Teghii, *Romania* 43 E11
Gurag, *Ethiopia* 81 F4
Gurahonţ, *Romania* 42 D7
Gurdaspur, *India* 68 C6
Gurdon, *U.S.A.* 113 J8
Güre, *Balıkesir, Turkey* 39 B8
Güre, *Uşak, Turkey* 39 C11
Gurgaon, *India* 68 E7
Gürgentepe, *Turkey* 72 B7
Gurghiu, Munţii, *Romania* 43 D10
Gurgueia →, *Brazil* 125 E10
Gurha, *India* 68 G4
Guri, Embalse de, *Venezuela* 124 B6
Gurin, *Nigeria* 83 D7
Gurjaani, *Georgia* 49 K7
Gurk →, *Austria* 26 E7
Gurkha, *Nepal* 69 E11
Gurley, *Australia* 95 D4
Gurnet Point, *U.S.A.* 111 D14
Gürpınar, *İst., Turkey* 41 F12
Gürpınar, *Van, Turkey* 73 C10
Gürsu, *Turkey* 41 F13
Gurué, *Mozam.* 87 F4
Gurun, *Malaysia* 65 K3
Gürün, *Turkey* 72 C7
Gurupá, *Brazil* 125 D8
Gurupá, I. Grande de, *Brazil* 125 D8
Gurupi, *Brazil* 125 F9
Gurupi →, *Brazil* 125 D9
Guruwe, *Zimbabwe* 89 B5
Guryev = Atyraū, *Kazakstan* 50 E6
Gus-Khrustalnyy, *Russia* 48 C5
Gusau, *Nigeria* 83 C6
Gusev, *Russia* 9 J20
Gushan, *China* 57 E12
Gushgy, *Turkmenistan* 50 F7
Gushi, *China* 59 A10
Gushiago, *Ghana* 83 D4
Gusinje, *Montenegro, Yug.* 40 D3
Gusinoozersk, *Russia* 51 D11
Gúspini, *Italy* 30 C1
Güssing, *Austria* 27 D9
Gustavsberg, *Sweden* 10 E12
Gustavus, *U.S.A.* 104 B1
Gustine, *U.S.A.* 116 H6
Güstrow, *Germany* 24 B8
Gusum, *Sweden* 11 F10
Guta = Kolárovo, *Slovak Rep.* 27 D10
Gütersloh, *Germany* 24 D4
Gutha, *Australia* 93 E2
Guthalungra, *Australia* 94 B4
Guthrie, *Okla., U.S.A.* 113 H6
Guthrie, *Tex., U.S.A.* 113 J4
Gutian, *China* 59 D12
Guttenberg, *U.S.A.* 112 D9
Gutu, *Zimbabwe* 89 B5
Guyana ■, *S. Amer.* 124 C7
Guyane française = French Guiana ■, *S. Amer.* 125 C8
Guyang, *China* 56 D6
Guyenne, *France* 20 D4
Guymon, *U.S.A.* 113 G4
Guyra, *Australia* 95 E5
Guyuan, *Hebei, China* 56 D8
Guyuan, *Ningxia Huizu, China* 56 G4
Güzelbahçe, *Turkey* 39 C8
Guzhang, *China* 58 C7
Guzhen, *China* 57 H9
Guzmán, L. de, *Mexico* 118 A3
Gvardeysk, *Russia* 9 J19
Gvardeyskoye, *Ukraine* 47 K8
Gwa, *Burma* 67 L19
Gwaai, *Zimbabwe* 87 F2
Gwabegar, *Australia* 95 E4
Gwadabawa, *Nigeria* 83 C6
Gwādar, *Pakistan* 66 G3
Gwagwada, *Nigeria* 83 C6
Gwalior, *India* 68 F8
Gwanara, *Nigeria* 83 D5
Gwanda, *Zimbabwe* 87 G2
Gwandu, *Nigeria* 83 C5
Gwane, *Dem. Rep. of the Congo* 86 B2
Gwaram, *Nigeria* 83 C7
Gwarzo, *Nigeria* 83 C6
Gwasero, *Nigeria* 83 D5
Gwda →, *Poland* 45 E3
Gweebarra B., *Ireland* 15 B3
Gweedore, *Ireland* 15 A3
Gweru, *Zimbabwe* 87 F2
Gwi, *Nigeria* 83 D6
Gwinn, *U.S.A.* 108 B2
Gwio Kura, *Nigeria* 83 C7
Gwoza, *Nigeria* 83 C7
Gwydir →, *Australia* 95 D4
Gwynedd □, *U.K.* 12 E3
Gyandzha = Gäncä, *Azerbaijan* 49 K8
Gyaring Hu, *China* 60 C4
Gydanskiy Poluostrov, *Russia* 50 C8
Gympie, *Australia* 95 D5
Gyomaendrőd, *Hungary* 42 D5
Gyöngyös, *Hungary* 42 C4
Győr, *Hungary* 42 C2
Győr-Moson-Sopron □, *Hungary* 42 C2
Gypsum Pt., *Canada* 104 A6
Gypsumville, *Canada* 105 C9
Gyueshevo, *Bulgaria* 40 D6
Gyula, *Hungary* 42 D6
Gyumri, *Armenia* 49 K6
Gyzylarbat, *Turkmenistan* 50 F6
Gyzyletrek, *Turkmenistan* 71 B7
Gzhatsk = Gagarin, *Russia* 46 E8

H

Ha 'Arava →, *Israel* 75 E4
Ha Coi, *Vietnam* 58 G6
Ha Dong, *Vietnam* 58 G5
Ha Giang, *Vietnam* 58 F5
Ha Tien, *Vietnam* 65 G5
Ha Tinh, *Vietnam* 64 C5
Ha Trung, *Vietnam* 64 C5
Haaksbergen, *Neths.* 17 B6
Haapsalu, *Estonia* 9 G20
Haarlem, *Neths.* 17 B4
Haast →, *N.Z.* 91 K2
Haast Bluff, *Australia* 92 D5
Hab →, *Pakistan* 68 G3
Hab Nadi Chauki, *Pakistan* 68 G2
Habaswein, *Kenya* 86 B4
Habay, *Canada* 104 B5
Ḩabbānīyah, *Iraq* 70 C4
Ḩabbānīyah, Hawr al, *Iraq* 73 F10
Habo, *Sweden* 11 G8
Haboro, *Japan* 54 B10
Ḩabshān, *U.A.E.* 71 F7
Hachenburg, *Germany* 24 E3
Hachijō-Jima, *Japan* 55 H9
Hachinohe, *Japan* 54 D10
Hachiōji, *Japan* 55 G9
Hachŏn, *N. Korea* 57 D15
Hacıbektaş, *Turkey* 72 C6
Hacılar, *Turkey* 72 C6
Hackås, *Sweden* 10 B8
Hackensack, *U.S.A.* 111 F10
Hackettstown, *U.S.A.* 111 F10
Hadali, *Pakistan* 68 C5
Hadarba, Ras, *Sudan* 80 C4
Hadarom □, *Israel* 75 E4
Hadd, Ra's al, *Oman* 74 C6
Hadejia, *Nigeria* 83 C7
Hadejia →, *Nigeria* 83 C7
Hadera, *Israel* 75 C3
Hadera, N. →, *Israel* 75 C3
Haderslev, *Denmark* 11 J3
Hadhramaut = Ḩaḑramawt, *Yemen* 74 D4
Hadibu, *Yemen* 74 E5
Hadım, *Turkey* 72 D5
Hadong, *S. Korea* 57 G14
Ḩaḑramawt, *Yemen* 74 D4
Ḩadrānīyah, *Iraq* 70 C4
Hadrian's Wall, *U.K.* 12 B5
Hadsten, *Denmark* 11 H4
Hadsund, *Denmark* 11 H4
Hadyach, *Ukraine* 47 G8
Haeju, *N. Korea* 57 E13
Haenam, *S. Korea* 57 G14
Haenertsburg, *S. Africa* 89 C4
Haerhpin = Harbin, *China* 57 B14
Hafar al Bāţin, *Si. Arabia* 70 D5
Hafik, *Turkey* 72 C7
Ḩafīrat al 'Aydā, *Si. Arabia* 70 E3
Ḩafit, *Oman* 71 F7
Ḩafit, Jabal, *Oman* 71 E7
Hafizabad, *Pakistan* 68 C5
Haflong, *India* 67 G18
Hafnarfjörður, *Iceland* 8 D3
Haft Gel, *Iran* 71 D6
Hafun, Ras, *Somali Rep.* 74 E5
Hagalil, *Israel* 75 C4
Hagby, *Sweden* 11 H10
Hagen, *Germany* 24 D3
Hagenow, *Germany* 24 B7
Hagerman, *U.S.A.* 113 J2
Hagerstown, *U.S.A.* 108 F7
Hagersville, *Canada* 110 D4
Hagetmau, *France* 20 E3
Hagfors, *Sweden* 10 D7
Hagi, *Japan* 55 G5
Hagolan, *Syria* 75 C4
Hagondange, *France* 19 C13
Hags Hd., *Ireland* 15 D2
Hague, C. de la, *France* 18 C5
Hague, The = 's-Gravenhage, *Neths.* 17 B4
Haguenau, *France* 19 D14
Hai Duong, *Vietnam* 58 G6
Hai'an, *Guangdong, China* 59 G8
Hai'an, *Jiangsu, China* 59 A13
Haicheng, *Fujian, China* 59 E11
Haicheng, *Liaoning, China* 57 D12
Haidar Khel, *Afghan.* 68 C3
Haidargarh, *India* 69 F9
Haifa = Hefa, *Israel* 75 C4
Haifeng, *China* 59 F10
Haiger, *Germany* 24 E4
Haikou, *China* 60 D6
Ḩā'il, *Si. Arabia* 70 E4
Hailar, *China* 60 B6
Hailey, *U.S.A.* 114 E6
Haileybury, *Canada* 102 C4
Hailin, *China* 57 B15
Hailing Dao, *China* 59 G8
Hailong, *China* 57 C13
Hailuoto, *Finland* 8 D21
Haimen, *Guangdong, China* 59 F11
Haimen, *Jiangsu, China* 59 B13
Hainan □, *China* 60 E5
Hainaut □, *Belgium* 17 D4
Hainburg, *Austria* 27 C9
Haines, *Alaska, U.S.A.* 104 B1
Haines, *Oreg., U.S.A.* 114 D5
Haines City, *U.S.A.* 109 L5
Haines Junction, *Canada* 104 A1
Hainfeld, *Austria* 26 C8
Haining, *China* 59 B13
Haiphong, *Vietnam* 58 G6
Haitan Dao, *China* 59 E12
Haiti ■, *W. Indies* 121 C5
Haiya, *Sudan* 80 D4
Haiyan, *China* 59 B13
Haiyang, *China* 57 F11
Haiyuan, *Guangxi Zhuangzu, China* 58 F6
Haiyuan, *Ningxia Huizu, China* 56 F3
Haizhou, *China* 57 G10
Haizhou Wan, *China* 57 G10
Hajdú-Bihar □, *Hungary* 42 C6
Hajdúböszörmény, *Hungary* 42 C6
Hajdúdurog, *Hungary* 42 C6
Hajdúhadház, *Hungary* 42 C6
Hajdúnánás, *Hungary* 42 C6
Hajdúsámson, *Hungary* 42 C6
Hajdúszoboszló, *Hungary* 42 C6
Hajipur, *India* 69 G11
Ḩājjī Muḩsin, *Iraq* 70 C5
Ḩājjīābād, *Iran* 71 D7
Ḩājjīābād-e Zarrīn, *Iran* 71 C7
Hajnówka, *Poland* 45 F10
Hakansson, Mts., *Dem. Rep. of the Congo* 87 D2
Hakkâri, *Turkey* 70 B4
Hakkâri Dağları, *Turkey* 73 C10
Hakken-Zan, *Japan* 55 G7
Hakodate, *Japan* 54 D10
Hakos, *Namibia* 88 C2
Håksberg, *Sweden* 10 D9
Haku-San, *Japan* 55 F8
Hakui, *Japan* 55 F8
Hala, *Pakistan* 66 G6
Ḩalab, *Syria* 70 B3
Ḩalabjah, *Iraq* 70 C5
Halaib, *Sudan* 80 C4
Halasa, *Sudan* 81 E3
Hālat 'Ammār, *Si. Arabia* 70 D3
Halbā, *Lebanon* 75 A5
Halberstadt, *Germany* 24 D7
Halcombe, *N.Z.* 91 J5
Halcon, *Phil.* 63 B6
Halden, *Norway* 9 G14
Haldensleben, *Germany* 24 C7
Haldia, *India* 67 H16
Haldwani, *India* 69 E8
Hale →, *Australia* 94 C2
Haleakala Crater, *U.S.A.* 106 H16
Halesowen, *U.K.* 13 E5
Haleyville, *U.S.A.* 109 H2
Half Assini, *Ghana* 82 D4
Halfway →, *Canada* 104 B4
Halia, *India* 69 G10
Haliburton, *Canada* 102 C4
Halifax, *Australia* 94 B4
Halifax, *Canada* 103 D7
Halifax, *U.K.* 12 D6
Halifax, *U.S.A.* 110 F8
Halifax B., *Australia* 94 B4
Halifax I., *Namibia* 88 D2
Halīl →, *Iran* 71 E8
Halkirk, *U.K.* 14 C5
Hall Beach = Sanirajak, *Canada* 101 B11
Hall in Tirol, *Austria* 26 D4
Hall Pen., *Canada* 101 B13
Hall Pt., *Australia* 92 C3
Hallabro, *Sweden* 11 H9
Halland, *Sweden* 9 H15
Hallands län □, *Sweden* 11 H6
Hallands Väderö, *Sweden* 11 H6
Hallandsås, *Sweden* 11 H7
Hällbybrunn, *Sweden* 10 E10
Halle, *Belgium* 17 D4
Halle, *Nordrhein-Westfalen, Germany* 24 C4
Halle, *Sachsen-Anhalt, Germany* 24 D7
Hällefors, *Sweden* 10 E8
Hälleforsnäs, *Sweden* 10 E10
Hallein, *Austria* 26 D6
Hällekis, *Sweden* 11 F7
Hallen, *Sweden* 10 A8
Hallett, *Australia* 95 E2
Hallettsville, *U.S.A.* 113 L6
Hallim, *S. Korea* 57 H14
Hallingdalselvi →, *Norway* 9 F13
Hallock, *U.S.A.* 112 A6
Halls Creek, *Australia* 92 C4
Hallsberg, *Sweden* 10 E9
Hallstahammar, *Sweden* 10 E10
Hallstatt, *Austria* 26 D6
Hallstavik, *Sweden* 10 D12
Hallstead, *U.S.A.* 111 E9
Halmahera, *Indonesia* 63 D7
Halmeu, *Romania* 42 C8
Halmstad, *Sweden* 11 H6
Hals, *Denmark* 11 H4
Hälsingborg = Helsingborg, *Sweden* 11 H6
Hälsingland, *Sweden* 10 C10
Halstead, *U.K.* 13 F8
Haltern, *Germany* 24 D3
Halti, *Finland* 8 B19
Halton □, *U.K.* 12 D5
Haltwhistle, *U.K.* 12 C5
Halul, *Qatar* 71 E7
Halvad, *India* 68 H4
Ḩalvān, *Iran* 71 C8
Ham, *France* 19 C10
Ham Tan, *Vietnam* 65 G6
Ham Yen, *Vietnam* 64 A5
Hamab, *Namibia* 88 D2
Hamad, *Sudan* 81 D3
Hamada, *Japan* 55 G6
Hamadān, *Iran* 71 C6
Hamadān □, *Iran* 71 C6
Ḩamāh, *Syria* 70 C3
Hamamatsu, *Japan* 55 G8
Hamar, *Norway* 9 F14
Hamâta, Gebel, *Egypt* 70 E2
Hambantota, *Sri Lanka* 66 R12
Hamber Prov. Park, *Canada* 104 C5
Hamburg, *Germany* 24 B5
Hamburg, *Ark., U.S.A.* 113 J9
Hamburg, *N.Y., U.S.A.* 110 D6
Hamburg, *Pa., U.S.A.* 111 F9
Hamburg □, *Germany* 24 B5
Ḩamḑ, W. al →, *Si. Arabia* 70 E3
Hamden, *U.S.A.* 111 E12
Hamdibey, *Turkey* 39 B9
Häme, *Finland* 9 F20
Hämeenlinna, *Finland* 9 F21
Hamélé, *Ghana* 82 C4
Hamelin Pool, *Australia* 93 E1
Hameln, *Germany* 24 C5
Hamerkaz □, *Israel* 75 C3
Hamersley Ra., *Australia* 92 D2
Hamhung, *N. Korea* 57 E14
Hami, *China* 60 B4
Hamilton, *Australia* 95 F3
Hamilton, *Canada* 102 D4
Hamilton, *N.Z.* 91 G5
Hamilton, *U.K.* 14 F4
Hamilton, *Ala., U.S.A.* 109 H1
Hamilton, *Mont., U.S.A.* 114 C6
Hamilton, *N.Y., U.S.A.* 111 D9
Hamilton, *Ohio, U.S.A.* 108 F3
Hamilton, *Tex., U.S.A.* 113 K5
Hamilton →, *Australia* 94 C2
Hamilton City, *U.S.A.* 116 F4
Hamilton Inlet, *Canada* 103 B8
Hamilton Mt., *U.S.A.* 111 C10
Hamina, *Finland* 9 F22
Hamirpur, *H.P., India* 68 D7
Hamirpur, *Ut. P., India* 69 G9
Hamitabat, *Turkey* 41 E11
Hamlet, *U.S.A.* 109 H6
Hamley Bridge, *Australia* 95 E2
Hamlin = Hameln, *Germany* 24 C5
Hamlin, *N.Y., U.S.A.* 110 C7
Hamlin, *Tex., U.S.A.* 113 J4
Hamm, *Germany* 24 D3
Ḩammār, Hawr al, *Iraq* 70 D5
Hammarstrand, *Sweden* 10 A10
Hammelburg, *Germany* 25 E5
Hammeren, *Denmark* 11 J8
Hammerfest, *Norway* 8 A20
Hammerum, *Denmark* 11 H3
Hamminkeln, *Germany* 24 D2
Hammond, *Ind., U.S.A.* 108 E2
Hammond, *La., U.S.A.* 113 K9
Hammond, *N.Y., U.S.A.* 111 B9
Hammondsport, *U.S.A.* 110 D7
Hammonton, *U.S.A.* 108 F8
Hamneda, *Sweden* 11 H7
Hamoyet, Jebel, *Sudan* 80 D4
Hampden, *N.Z.* 91 L3
Hampshire □, *U.K.* 13 F6
Hampshire Downs, *U.K.* 13 F6
Hampton, *N.B., Canada* 103 C6
Hampton, *Ont., Canada* 110 C6
Hampton, *Ark., U.S.A.* 113 J8
Hampton, *Iowa, U.S.A.* 112 D8
Hampton, *N.H., U.S.A.* 111 D14
Hampton, *S.C., U.S.A.* 109 J5
Hampton, *Va., U.S.A.* 108 G7
Hampton Bays, *U.S.A.* 111 F12
Hampton Tableland, *Australia* 93 F4
Hamra, *Sweden* 10 C8
Hamrat esh Sheykh, *Sudan* 81 E2
Hamur, *Turkey* 73 C10
Hamyang, *S. Korea* 57 G14
Han Jiang →, *China* 59 F11

Han Shui, China 58 A7
Han Shui →, China 59 B10
Hana, U.S.A. 106 H17
Hanak, Si. Arabia 70 E3
Hanamaki, Japan 54 E10
Hanang, Tanzania 86 C4
Hanau, Germany 25 E4
Hanbogd = Ihbulag,
    Mongolia 56 C4
Hançalar, Turkey 39 C11
Hâncești, Moldova 43 D13
Hancheng, China 56 G6
Hanchuan, China 59 B9
Hancock, Mich., U.S.A. .. 112 B10
Hancock, N.Y., U.S.A. ... 111 E9
Handa, Japan 55 G8
Handan, China 56 F8
Handeni, Tanzania 86 D4
Handlová, Slovak Rep. ... 27 C11
Handub, Sudan 80 D4
Handwara, India 69 B6
Hanegev, Israel 75 E4
Hanford, U.S.A. 116 J7
Hang Chat, Thailand 64 C2
Hang Dong, Thailand ... 64 C2
Hangang →, S. Korea ... 57 F14
Hangayn Nuruu, Mongolia 60 B4
Hangchou = Hangzhou,
    China 59 B13
Hanggin Houqi, China ... 56 D4
Hanggin Qi, China 56 E5
Hangu, China 57 E9
Hangzhou, China 59 B13
Hangzhou Wan, China ... 59 B13
Hanhongor, Mongolia ... 56 C3
Ḥanīdh, Si. Arabia 71 E6
Ḥanīsh, Yemen 74 E3
Haniska, Slovak Rep. 27 C14
Hanjiang, China 59 E12
Hankinson, U.S.A. 112 B6
Hanko, Finland 9 G20
Hankou, China 59 B10
Hanksville, U.S.A. 115 G8
Hanle, India 69 C8
Hanmer Springs, N.Z. ... 91 K4
Hann →, Australia 92 C4
Hann, Mt., Australia ... 92 C4
Hanna, Canada 104 C6
Hanna, U.S.A. 114 F10
Hannah B., Canada 102 B4
Hannibal, Mo., U.S.A. .. 112 F9
Hannibal, N.Y., U.S.A. . 111 C8
Hannik, Sudan 80 D3
Hannover, Germany 24 C5
Hanö, Sweden 11 H8
Hanöbukten, Sweden ... 11 J8
Hanoi, Vietnam 58 G5
Hanover = Hannover,
    Germany 24 C5
Hanover, Canada 102 D3
Hanover, S. Africa 88 E3
Hanover, N.H., U.S.A. . 111 C12
Hanover, Ohio, U.S.A. . 110 F2
Hanover, Pa., U.S.A. .. 108 F7
Hanover, I., Chile 128 G2
Hansdiha, India 69 G12
Hanshou, China 59 C8
Hansi, India 68 E6
Hanson, L., Australia .. 95 E2
Hanstholm, Denmark ... 11 G2
Hantsavichy, Belarus ... 47 F4
Hanumangarh, India ... 68 E6
Hanyin, China 58 A7
Hanyuan, China 58 C4
Hanzhong, China 56 H4
Hanzhuang, China 57 G9
Haora, India 69 H13
Haoxue, China 59 B9
Haparanda, Sweden ... 8 D21
Happy, U.S.A. 113 H4
Happy Camp, U.S.A. ... 114 F2
Happy Valley-Goose Bay,
    Canada 103 B7
Hapsu, N. Korea 57 D15
Hapur, India 68 E7
Haql, Si. Arabia 75 D3
Har, Indonesia 63 F8
Har-Ayrag, Mongolia .. 56 B5
Har Hu, China 60 C4
Har Us Nuur, Mongolia . 60 B4
Har Yehuda, Israel 75 D3
Ḥaraḍ, Si. Arabia 74 C4
Haradok, Belarus 46 E6
Häradsbäck, Sweden ... 11 H8
Haranomachi, Japan ... 54 F10
Harare, Zimbabwe 87 F3
Harat, Eritrea 81 D4
Harbin, China 57 B14
Harbiye, Turkey 72 D7
Harbo, Sweden 10 D11
Harboør, Denmark 11 H2
Harbor Beach, U.S.A. .. 110 C2
Harbour Breton, Canada . 103 C8
Harbour Deep, Canada .. 103 B8
Harburg, Germany 24 B5
Hårby, Denmark 11 J4
Harda, India 68 H7
Hardangerfjorden, Norway 9 F12
Hardangervidda, Norway . 9 F12
Hardap Dam, Namibia ... 88 C2
Hardenberg, Neths. 17 B6
Harderwijk, Neths. 17 B5
Hardey →, Australia ... 92 D2
Hardin, U.S.A. 114 D10
Harding, S. Africa 89 E4
Harding Ra., Australia .. 92 C3
Hardisty, Canada 104 C6
Hardoi, India 69 F9
Hardwar = Haridwar, India 68 E8
Hardwick, U.S.A. 111 B12
Hardy, Pen., Chile 128 H3

Hare B., Canada 103 B8
Hareid, Norway 9 E12
Haren, Germany 24 C3
Harer, Ethiopia 81 F5
Harerge □, Ethiopia 81 F5
Hareto, Ethiopia 81 F4
Harfleur, France 18 C7
Hargeisa, Somali Rep. ... 74 F3
Harghita □, Romania ... 43 D10
Harghita, Munții, Romania . 43 D10
Hargshamn, Sweden ... 10 D12
Hari →, Indonesia 62 E2
Haria, Canary Is. 37 E6
Haridwar, India 68 E8
Harim, Jabal al, Oman .. 71 E8
Haringhata →, Bangla. .. 67 J16
Harīrūd →, Asia 66 A2
Härjedalen, Sweden 10 B7
Harlan, Iowa, U.S.A. ... 112 E7
Harlan, Ky., U.S.A. 109 G4
Hârlău, Romania 43 C11
Harlech, U.K. 12 E3
Harlem, U.S.A. 114 B9
Hårlev, Denmark 11 J6
Harlingen, Neths. 17 A5
Harlingen, U.S.A. 113 M6
Harlow, U.K. 13 F8
Harlowton, U.S.A. 114 C9
Harmancık, Turkey 39 B11
Harmånger, Sweden ... 10 C11
Harmil, Eritrea 81 D5
Harnai, Pakistan 68 D2
Harney Basin, U.S.A. .. 114 E4
Harney L., U.S.A. 114 E4
Harney Peak, U.S.A. ... 112 D3
Härnön, Sweden 10 B12
Härnösand, Sweden ... 10 B11
Haro, Spain 32 C2
Haroldswick, U.K. 14 A8
Harp L., Canada 103 A7
Harper, Liberia 82 E3
Harplinge, Sweden 11 H6
Harr, Mauritania 82 B2
Harrai, India 69 H8
Harrand, Pakistan 68 E4
Ḥarrat Khaybar, Si. Arabia 80 B5
Ḥarrat Nawāşīf, Si. Arabia 80 C5
Harricana →, Canada .. 102 B4
Harriman, U.S.A. 109 H3
Harrington Harbour, Canada 103 B8
Harris, U.K. 14 D2
Harris, Sd. of, U.K. ... 14 D1
Harris L., Australia ... 95 E2
Harris Pt., Canada 110 C2
Harrisburg, Ill., U.S.A. . 113 G10
Harrisburg, Nebr., U.S.A. . 112 E3
Harrisburg, Pa., U.S.A. . 110 F8
Harrismith, S. Africa .. 89 D4
Harrison, Ark., U.S.A. . 113 G8
Harrison, Maine, U.S.A. . 111 B14
Harrison, Nebr., U.S.A. . 112 D3
Harrison, C., Canada ... 103 B8
Harrison L., Canada ... 104 D4
Harrisonburg, U.S.A. .. 108 F6
Harrisonville, U.S.A. .. 112 F7
Harriston, Canada 110 C4
Harrisville, Mich., U.S.A. . 110 B1
Harrisville, N.Y., U.S.A. . 111 B9
Harrisville, Pa., U.S.A. . 110 E5
Harrodsburg, U.S.A. ... 108 G3
Harrogate, U.K. 12 C6
Harrow, U.K. 13 F7
Harrowsmith, Canada .. 111 B8
Harry S. Truman Reservoir,
    U.S.A. 112 F7
Harsefeld, Germany ... 24 B5
Harsewinkel, Germany .. 24 D4
Harsīn, Iran 70 C5
Harsprånget, Sweden .. 8 C18
Harstad, Norway 8 B17
Harsud, India 68 H7
Hart, U.S.A. 108 D2
Hart, L., Australia 95 E2
Hartbees →, S. Africa . 88 D3
Hartberg, Austria 26 D8
Hartford, Conn., U.S.A. . 111 E12
Hartford, Ky., U.S.A. .. 108 G2
Hartford, S. Dak., U.S.A. . 112 D6
Hartford, Wis., U.S.A. .. 112 D10
Hartford City, U.S.A. .. 108 E3
Hartland, Canada 103 C6
Hartland Pt., U.K. 13 F3
Hartlepool, U.K. 12 C6
Hartlepool □, U.K. 12 C6
Hartley Bay, Canada ... 104 C3
Hartmannberge, Namibia . 88 B1
Hartney, Canada 105 D8
Hârtop, Moldova 43 D13
Harts →, S. Africa 88 D3
Hartselle, U.S.A. 109 H2
Hartshorne, U.S.A. 113 H7
Hartstown, U.S.A. 110 E4
Hartsville, U.S.A. 109 H5
Hartswater, S. Africa .. 88 D3
Hartwell, U.S.A. 109 H4
Harunabad, Pakistan .. 68 E5
Harvand, Iran 71 D7
Harvey, Australia 93 F2
Harvey, Ill., U.S.A. ... 108 E2
Harvey, N. Dak., U.S.A. . 112 B5
Harwich, U.K. 13 F9
Haryana □, India 68 E7
Haryn →, Belarus 47 F4
Harz, Germany 24 D6
Harzgerode, Germany .. 24 D7
Hasa □, Si. Arabia 71 E6
Hasaheisa, Sudan 81 E3
Hasanābād, Iran 71 C7
Hasdo →, India 69 J10
Haselünne, Germany .. 24 C3
Hashimoto, Japan 55 G7

Hashtjerd, Iran 71 C6
Haskell, U.S.A. 113 J5
Hasköy, Turkey 41 E10
Haslach, Germany 25 G4
Hasle, Denmark 11 J8
Haslemere, U.K. 13 F7
Haslev, Denmark 11 J5
Hasparren, France 20 E2
Hassa, Turkey 72 D7
Hassela, Sweden 10 B10
Hasselt, Belgium 17 D5
Hassfurt, Germany 25 E6
Hassi Messaoud, Algeria . 78 B7
Hässleholm, Sweden .. 11 H7
Hassloch, Germany ... 25 F4
Hästholmen, Sweden .. 11 F8
Hastings, N.Z. 91 H6
Hastings, U.K. 13 G8
Hastings, Mich., U.S.A. . 108 D3
Hastings, Minn., U.S.A. . 112 C8
Hastings, Nebr., U.S.A. . 112 E5
Hastings Ra., Australia . 95 E5
Hästveda, Sweden 11 H7
Hat Yai, Thailand 65 J3
Hatanbulag = Ergel,
    Mongolia 56 C5
Hatay = Antalya, Turkey .. 72 D4
Hatch, U.S.A. 115 K10
Hatchet L., Canada ... 105 B8
Hațeg, Romania 42 E7
Hateruma-Shima, Japan . 55 M1
Hatfield P.O., Australia . 95 E3
Hatgal, Mongolia 60 A5
Hathras, India 68 F8
Hatia, Bangla. 67 H17
Hato Mayor, Dom. Rep. . 121 C6
Hatta, India 69 G8
Hattah, Australia 95 E3
Hatteras, C., U.S.A. ... 109 H8
Hattiesburg, U.S.A. ... 113 K10
Hatvan, Hungary 42 C4
Hau Bon = Cheo Reo,
    Vietnam 62 B3
Hau Duc, Vietnam 64 E7
Haugesund, Norway ... 9 G11
Haukipudas, Finland .. 8 D21
Haultain →, Canada .. 105 B7
Hauraki G., N.Z. 91 G5
Hausruck, Austria 26 C6
Haut Atlas, Morocco .. 78 B4
Haut-Rhin □, France .. 19 E14
Haut-Zaïre = Orientale □,
    Dem. Rep. of the Congo . 86 B2
Haute-Corse □, France . 21 F13
Haute-Garonne □, France . 20 E5
Haute-Loire □, France .. 20 C7
Haute-Marne □, France . 19 D12
Haute-Normandie □, France 18 C7
Haute-Saône □, France . 19 E13
Haute-Savoie □, France . 21 C10
Haute-Vienne □, France . 20 C5
Hautes-Alpes □, France . 21 D10
Hautes Fagnes = Hohe
    Venn, Belgium 17 D6
Hautes-Pyrénées □, France . 20 F4
Hauteville-Lompnès, France 21 C9
Hautmont, France 19 B10
Hauts-de-Seine □, France . 19 D9
Hauts Plateaux, Algeria . 76 C4
Hauzenberg, Germany . 25 G9
Havana = La Habana, Cuba 120 B3
Havana, U.S.A. 112 E9
Havant, U.K. 13 G7
Havârna, Romania 43 B11
Havasu, L., U.S.A. 117 L12
Havdhem, Sweden 11 G12
Havel →, Germany ... 24 C8
Havelian, Pakistan ... 68 B5
Havelock, Canada 102 D4
Havelock, N.Z. 91 J4
Havelock, U.S.A. 109 H7
Haverfordwest, U.K. .. 13 F3
Haverhill, U.S.A. 111 D13
Haverstraw, U.S.A. ... 111 E11
Håverud, Sweden 11 F6
Havığa, Mongolia 56 B7
Havířov, Czech. 27 B11
Havlíčkův Brod, Czech Rep. . 26 B8
Havneby, Denmark ... 11 J2
Havran, Turkey 39 B9
Havre, U.S.A. 114 B9
Havre-Aubert, Canada . 103 C7
Havre-St.-Pierre, Canada . 103 B7
Havsa, Turkey 41 E10
Havza, Turkey 72 B6
Hawaii □, U.S.A. 106 H16
Hawaii I., Pac. Oc. ... 106 J17
Hawaiian Is., Pac. Oc. . 106 H17
Hawaiian Ridge, Pac. Oc. . 97 E11
Hawarden, U.S.A. 112 D6
Hawea, L., N.Z. 91 L2
Hawera, N.Z. 91 H5
Hawick, U.K. 14 F6
Hawk Junction, Canada . 102 C3
Hawke, B., N.Z. 91 H6
Hawker, Australia 95 E2
Hawkesbury, Canada .. 102 C5
Hawkesbury I., Canada . 104 C3
Hawkesbury Pt., Australia 94 A1
Hawkinsville, U.S.A. .. 109 J4
Hawley, Minn., U.S.A. . 112 B6
Hawley, Pa., U.S.A. ... 111 E9
Ḥawrān, W. →, Iraq .. 70 C4
Hawsh Mūssá, Lebanon . 75 B4
Hawthorne, U.S.A. ... 114 G4
Hay, Australia 95 E3
Hay →, Australia 94 C2
Hay →, Canada 104 A5
Hay, C., Australia 92 B4

Hay I., Canada 110 B4
Hay L., Canada 104 B5
Hay-on-Wye, U.K. 13 E4
Hay River, Canada 104 A5
Hay Springs, U.S.A. ... 112 D3
Haya = Tehoru, Indonesia . 63 E7
Hayachine-San, Japan .. 54 E10
Hayange, France 19 C13
Haydarlı, Turkey 39 C12
Hayden, U.S.A. 114 F10
Haydon, Australia 94 B3
Hayes, U.S.A. 112 C4
Hayes →, Canada 102 A1
Hayes Creek, Australia . 92 B5
Hayle, U.K. 13 G2
Hayling I., U.K. 13 G7
Haymana, Turkey 72 C5
Hayrabolu, Turkey 41 E11
Hays, Canada 104 C6
Hays, U.S.A. 112 F5
Haysyn, Ukraine 47 H5
Hayvoron, Ukraine ... 47 H5
Hayward, Calif., U.S.A. . 116 H4
Hayward, Wis., U.S.A. . 112 B9
Haywards Heath, U.K. . 13 G7
Hazafon □, Israel 75 C4
Hazārān, Kūh-e, Iran .. 71 D8
Hazard, U.S.A. 108 G4
Hazaribag, India 69 H11
Hazaribag Road, India . 69 G11
Hazebrouck, France ... 19 B9
Hazelton, Canada 104 B3
Hazelton, U.S.A. 112 B4
Hazen, U.S.A. 112 B4
Hazlehurst, Ga., U.S.A. . 109 K4
Hazlehurst, Miss., U.S.A. . 113 K9
Hazlet, U.S.A. 111 F10
Hazleton, U.S.A. 111 F9
Hazlett, L., Australia .. 92 D4
Hazro, Turkey 70 B4
He Xian, Anhui, China .. 59 B12
He Xian,
    Guangxi Zhuangzu, China 59 E8
Head of Bight, Australia . 93 F5
Headlands, Zimbabwe .. 87 F3
Healdsburg, U.S.A. 116 G4
Healdton, U.S.A. 113 H6
Healesville, Australia .. 95 F4
Heany Junction, Zimbabwe 89 C4
Heard I., Ind. Oc. 3 G13
Hearne, U.S.A. 113 K6
Hearst, Canada 102 C3
Heart →, U.S.A. 112 B4
Heart's Content, Canada . 103 C9
Heath Pt., Canada 103 C7
Heavener, U.S.A. 113 H7
Hebbronville, U.S.A. .. 113 M5
Hebei □, China 56 E9
Hebel, Australia 95 D4
Heber, U.S.A. 117 N11
Heber City, U.S.A. 114 F8
Heber Springs, U.S.A. . 113 H9
Hebert, Canada 105 C7
Hebgen L., U.S.A. 114 D8
Hebi, China 56 G8
Hebrides, U.K. 6 D4
Hebron = Al Khalīl,
    West Bank 75 D4
Hebron, Canada 101 C13
Hebron, N. Dak., U.S.A. . 112 B3
Hebron, Nebr., U.S.A. . 112 E6
Heby, Sweden 10 E10
Hecate Str., Canada ... 104 C2
Heceta I., U.S.A. 104 B2
Hechi, China 58 E7
Hechingen, Germany .. 25 G4
Hechuan, China 58 B6
Hecla, U.S.A. 112 C5
Hecla I., Canada 105 C9
Hédé, France 18 D5
Hede, Sweden 10 B7
Hedemora, Sweden ... 10 D9
Hedensted, Denmark .. 11 J3
Hedesunda, Sweden .. 10 D10
Heerde, Neths. 17 B6
Heerenveen, Neths. ... 17 B5
Heerhugowaard, Neths. . 17 B4
Heerlen, Neths. 17 D5
Ḥefa, Israel 75 C4
Ḥefa □, Israel 75 C4
Hefei, China 59 B11
Hefeng, China 59 C8
Hegalig, Sudan 81 E3
Hegang, China 60 B8
Heiban, Sudan 81 E3
Heichengzhen, China .. 56 F4
Heide, Germany 24 A5
Heidelberg, Germany .. 25 F4
Heidelberg, S. Africa .. 88 E3
Heidenau, Germany ... 24 E9
Heidenheim, Germany . 25 G6
Heijing, China 58 E3
Heilbad Heiligenstadt,
    Germany 24 D6
Heilbron, S. Africa ... 89 D4
Heilbronn, Germany .. 25 F5
Heiligenblut, Austria .. 26 D5
Heiligenhafen, Germany 24 A6
Heilongjiang □, China . 60 B7
Heilunkiang =
    Heilongjiang □, China . 60 B7
Heimaey, Iceland 8 E3
Heinola, Finland 9 F22
Heinsberg, Germany .. 24 D2
Heinze Is., Burma 67 M20
Heishan, China 57 D12
Heishui, Liaoning, China . 57 C10
Heishui, Sichuan, China . 58 A4
Hejaz = Hijāz □, Si. Arabia 70 E3
Hejian, China 56 E9
Hejiang, China 58 C5

Hejin, China 56 G6
Hekımhan, Turkey 70 B3
Hekla, Iceland 8 E4
Hekou, Guangdong, China 59 F9
Hekou, Yunnan, China . 58 F4
Hel, Poland 44 D5
Helagsfjället, Sweden . 10 B6
Helan Shan, China ... 56 E3
Helechosa, Spain 35 F6
Helen Atoll, Pac. Oc. . 63 D8
Helena, Ark., U.S.A. .. 113 H9
Helena, Mont., U.S.A. . 114 C7
Helendale, U.S.A. 117 L9
Helensburgh, U.K. ... 14 E4
Helensville, N.Z. 91 G5
Helenvale, Australia .. 94 B4
Helgasjön, Sweden ... 11 H8
Helgeland, Norway ... 8 C15
Helgoland, Germany .. 24 A3
Heligoland = Helgoland,
    Germany 24 A3
Heligoland B. = Deutsche
    Bucht, Germany 24 A4
Heliopolis, Egypt 80 H7
Hella, Iceland 8 E3
Hellertown, U.S.A. ... 111 F9
Hellespont = Çanakkale
    Boğazı, Turkey 41 F10
Hellevoetsluis, Neths. . 17 C4
Hellín, Spain 33 G3
Helmand □, Afghan. .. 66 D4
Helmand →, Afghan. . 66 D2
Helme →, Germany .. 24 D7
Helmeringhausen, Namibia . 88 D2
Helmond, Neths. 17 C5
Helmsdale, U.K. 14 C5
Helmsdale →, U.K. .. 14 C5
Helmstedt, Germany .. 24 C7
Helong, China 57 C15
Helper, U.S.A. 114 G8
Helsingborg, Sweden . 11 H6
Helsinge, Denmark ... 11 H6
Helsingfors = Helsinki,
    Finland 9 F21
Helsingør, Denmark .. 11 H6
Helsinki, Finland 9 F21
Helska, Mierzeja, Poland . 44 D5
Helston, U.K. 13 G2
Helvellyn, U.K. 12 C4
Helwân, Egypt 80 J7
Hemel Hempstead, U.K. . 13 F7
Hemet, U.S.A. 117 M10
Hemingford, U.S.A. .. 112 D3
Hemmingford, Canada . 111 A11
Hempstead, U.S.A. ... 113 K6
Hemse, Sweden 11 G12
Hemsön, Sweden 10 B12
Henán, Sweden 11 F5
Henan □, China 56 H8
Henares →, Spain ... 34 E7
Henashi-Misaki, Japan . 54 D9
Hendaye, France 20 E2
Hendek, Turkey 72 B4
Henderson, Argentina . 126 D3
Henderson, Ky., U.S.A. . 108 G2
Henderson, N.C., U.S.A. . 109 G6
Henderson, Nev., U.S.A. . 117 J12
Henderson, Tenn., U.S.A. . 109 H1
Henderson, Tex., U.S.A. . 113 J7
Hendersonville, N.C.,
    U.S.A. 109 H4
Hendersonville, Tenn.,
    U.S.A. 109 G2
Hendījān, Iran 71 D6
Hendorābī, Iran 71 E7
Heng Jiang, China ... 58 C5
Heng Xian, China 58 F7
Hengcheng, China 56 E4
Héngchun, Taiwan ... 59 F13
Hengdaohezi, China .. 57 B15
Hengelo, Neths. 17 B6
Hengfeng, China 59 C10
Hengshan, Hunan, China . 59 D9
Hengshan, Shaanxi, China 56 F5
Hengshui, China 56 F8
Hengyang, Hunan, China . 59 D9
Hengyang, Hunan, China . 59 D9
Henichesk, Ukraine .. 47 J8
Hénin-Beaumont, France . 19 B9
Henlopen, C., U.S.A. . 108 F8
Hennan, Sweden 10 B9
Hennebont, France ... 18 E3
Hennenman, S. Africa . 88 D4
Hennessey, U.S.A. ... 113 G6
Hennigsdorf, Germany . 24 C9
Henrietta, U.S.A. 113 J5
Henrietta, Ostrov =
    Genriyetty, Ostrov, Russia 51 B16
Henrietta Maria, C., Canada 102 A3
Henry, U.S.A. 112 E10
Henryetta, U.S.A. 113 H7
Henryville, Canada ... 111 A11
Hensall, Canada 110 C3
Henstedt-Ulzburg, Germany 24 B6
Hentiesbaai, Namibia . 88 C1
Hentiyn Nuruu, Mongolia . 60 B5
Henty, Australia 95 F4
Henzada, Burma 67 L19
Hephaestia, Greece ... 39 B7
Heping, China 59 E10
Heppner, U.S.A. 114 D4
Hepu, China 58 G7
Hepworth, Canada ... 110 B3
Heqing, China 58 D3
Hequ, China 56 E6
Heràðsflói, Iceland ... 8 D6
Heráðsvötn →, Iceland . 8 D4
Herald Cays, Australia . 94 B4
Herāt, Afghan. 66 B3
Herāt □, Afghan. 66 B3
Hérault □, France ... 20 E7

Hérault →, *France* 20 E7
Herbault, *France* 18 E8
Herbert →, *Australia* 94 B4
Herberton, *Australia* 94 B4
Herbertsdale, *S. Africa* 88 E3
Herbignac, *France* 18 E4
Herborn, *Germany* 24 E4
Herby, *Poland* 45 H5
Herceg-Novi, *Montenegro, Yug.* 40 D2
Herchmer, *Canada* 105 B10
Herðubreið, *Iceland* 8 D5
Hereford, *U.K.* 13 E5
Hereford, *U.S.A.* 113 H3
Herefordshire □, *U.K.* 13 E5
Hereke, *Turkey* 41 F13
Herencia, *Spain* 35 F7
Herentals, *Belgium* 17 C4
Herford, *Germany* 24 C4
Héricourt, *France* 19 E13
Herington, *U.S.A.* 112 F6
Herisau, *Switz.* 25 H5
Hérisson, *France* 19 F9
Herkimer, *U.S.A.* 111 D10
Herlong, *U.S.A.* 116 E6
Herm, *U.K.* 13 H5
Hermann, *U.S.A.* 112 F9
Hermannsburg, *Australia* 92 D5
Hermannsburg, *Germany* 24 C6
Hermanus, *S. Africa* 88 E2
Herment, *France* 20 C6
Hermidale, *Australia* 95 E4
Hermiston, *U.S.A.* 114 D4
Hermitage, *N.Z.* 91 K3
Hermite, I., *Chile* 128 H3
Hermon, *U.S.A.* 111 B9
Hermon, Mt. = Shaykh, J. ash, *Lebanon* 75 B4
Hermosillo, *Mexico* 118 B2
Hernád →, *Hungary* 42 C6
Hernandarias, *Paraguay* 127 B5
Hernandez, *U.S.A.* 116 J6
Hernando, *Argentina* 126 C3
Hernando, *U.S.A.* 113 H10
Hernani, *Spain* 32 B3
Herndon, *U.S.A.* 110 F8
Herne, *Germany* 17 C7
Herne Bay, *U.K.* 13 F9
Herning, *Denmark* 11 H2
Heroica = Caborca, *Mexico* 118 A2
Heroica Nogales = Nogales, *Mexico* 118 A2
Heron Bay, *Canada* 102 C2
Herradura, Pta. de la, *Canary Is.* 37 F5
Herreid, *U.S.A.* 112 C4
Herrenberg, *Germany* 25 G4
Herrera, *Spain* 35 H6
Herrera de Alcántara, *Spain* 35 F3
Herrera de Pisuerga, *Spain* 34 C6
Herrera del Duque, *Spain* 35 F5
Herrestad, *Sweden* 11 F5
Herrin, *U.S.A.* 113 G10
Herriot, *Canada* 105 B8
Herrljunga, *Sweden* 11 F7
Hersbruck, *Germany* 25 F7
Hershey, *U.S.A.* 111 F8
Hersonissos, *Greece* 36 D7
Herstal, *Belgium* 17 D5
Hertford, *U.K.* 13 F7
Hertfordshire □, *U.K.* 13 F7
's-Hertogenbosch, *Neths.* 17 C5
Hertzogville, *S. Africa* 88 D4
Hervás, *Spain* 34 E5
Hervey B., *Australia* 94 C5
Herzberg, *Brandenburg, Germany* 24 D9
Herzberg, *Niedersachsen, Germany* 24 D6
Herzliyya, *Israel* 75 C3
Herzogenburg, *Austria* 26 C8
Ḥeşār, *Fārs, Iran* 71 D6
Ḥeşār, *Markazī, Iran* 71 C6
Hesdin, *France* 19 B9
Heshan, *China* 58 F7
Heshui, *China* 56 G5
Heshun, *China* 56 F7
Hesperia, *U.S.A.* 117 L9
Hesse = Hessen □, *Germany* 24 E4
Hessen □, *Germany* 24 E4
Hestra, *Sweden* 11 G7
Hetch Hetchy Aqueduct, *U.S.A.* 116 H5
Hettinger, *U.S.A.* 112 C3
Hettstedt, *Germany* 24 D7
Heuvelton, *U.S.A.* 111 B9
Heves, *Hungary* 42 C5
Heves □, *Hungary* 42 C5
Hewitt, *U.S.A.* 113 K6
Hexham, *U.K.* 12 C5
Hexi, *Yunnan, China* 58 E4
Hexi, *Zhejiang, China* 59 D12
Hexigten Qi, *China* 57 C9
Ḥeydarābād, *Iran* 71 D7
Heysham, *U.K.* 12 C5
Heyuan, *China* 59 F10
Heywood, *Australia* 95 F3
Heze, *China* 56 G8
Hezhang, *China* 58 D5
Hi Vista, *U.S.A.* 117 L9
Hialeah, *U.S.A.* 109 N5
Hiawatha, *U.S.A.* 112 F7
Hibbing, *U.S.A.* 112 B8
Hibbs B., *Australia* 94 G4
Hibernia Reef, *Australia* 92 B3
Hickman, *U.S.A.* 113 G10
Hickory, *U.S.A.* 109 H5
Hicks, Pt., *Australia* 95 F4
Hicks L., *Canada* 105 A9
Hicksville, *U.S.A.* 111 F11
Hida, *Romania* 43 C8
Hida-Gawa →, *Japan* 55 G8
Hida-Sammyaku, *Japan* 55 F8
Hidaka-Sammyaku, *Japan* 54 C11
Hidalgo, *Mexico* 119 C5
Hidalgo □, *Mexico* 119 C5
Hidalgo, Presa M., *Mexico* 118 B3
Hidalgo, Pta. del, *Canary Is.* 37 F3
Hidalgo del Parral, *Mexico* 118 B3
Hiddensee, *Germany* 24 A9
Hieflau, *Austria* 26 D7
Hiendelaencina, *Spain* 32 D2
Hierro, *Canary Is.* 37 G1
Higashiajima-San, *Japan* 54 F10
Higashiōsaka, *Japan* 55 G7
Higgins, *U.S.A.* 113 G4
Higgins Corner, *U.S.A.* 116 F5
High Atlas = Haut Atlas, *Morocco* 78 B4
High Bridge, *U.S.A.* 111 F10
High Level, *Canada* 104 B5
High Point, *U.S.A.* 109 H6
High Prairie, *Canada* 104 B5
High River, *Canada* 104 C6
High Tatra = Tatry, *Slovak Rep.* 27 B13
High Veld, *Africa* 76 J6
High Wycombe, *U.K.* 13 F7
Highland □, *U.K.* 14 D4
Highland Park, *U.S.A.* 108 D2
Highmore, *U.S.A.* 112 C5
Highrock L., *Man., Canada* 105 B8
Highrock L., *Sask., Canada* 105 B7
Higüey, *Dom. Rep.* 121 C6
Hihya, *Egypt* 80 H7
Hiiumaa, *Estonia* 9 G20
Híjar, *Spain* 32 D4
Ḥijāz □, *Si. Arabia* 70 E3
Hijo = Tagum, *Phil.* 61 H6
Hikari, *Japan* 55 H5
Hikmak, Ras el, *Egypt* 80 A2
Hiko, *U.S.A.* 116 H11
Hikone, *Japan* 55 G8
Hikurangi, *N.Z.* 91 F5
Hikurangi, Mt., *N.Z.* 91 H6
Hildburghausen, *Germany* 24 E6
Hildesheim, *Germany* 24 C5
Hill →, *Australia* 93 F2
Hill City, *Idaho, U.S.A.* 114 E6
Hill City, *Kans., U.S.A.* 112 F5
Hill City, *S. Dak., U.S.A.* 112 D3
Hill Island L., *Canada* 105 A7
Hillared, *Sweden* 11 G7
Hillcrest Center, *U.S.A.* 117 K8
Hillegom, *Neths.* 17 B4
Hillerød, *Denmark* 11 J6
Hillerstorp, *Sweden* 11 G7
Hillsboro, *Kans., U.S.A.* 112 F6
Hillsboro, *N. Dak., U.S.A.* 112 B6
Hillsboro, *N.H., U.S.A.* 111 C13
Hillsboro, *Ohio, U.S.A.* 108 F4
Hillsboro, *Oreg., U.S.A.* 116 E4
Hillsboro, *Tex., U.S.A.* 113 J6
Hillsborough, *Grenada* 121 D7
Hillsdale, *Mich., U.S.A.* 108 E3
Hillsdale, *N.Y., U.S.A.* 111 D11
Hillsport, *Canada* 102 C2
Hillston, *Australia* 95 E4
Hilo, *U.S.A.* 106 J17
Hilton, *U.S.A.* 110 C7
Hilton Head Island, *U.S.A.* 109 J5
Hilvan, *Turkey* 73 D8
Hilversum, *Neths.* 17 B5
Himachal Pradesh □, *India* 68 D7
Himalaya, *Asia* 69 E11
Himamaylan, *Phil.* 61 F5
Himara, *Albania* 40 F3
Himatnagar, *India* 66 H8
Himeji, *Japan* 55 G7
Himi, *Japan* 55 F8
Himmerland, *Denmark* 11 H3
Ḥimş, *Syria* 75 A5
Ḥimş □, *Syria* 75 A6
Hinche, *Haiti* 121 C5
Hinchinbrook I., *Australia* 94 B4
Hinckley, *U.K.* 13 E6
Hinckley, *U.S.A.* 112 B8
Hindaun, *India* 68 F7
Hindmarsh, L., *Australia* 95 F3
Hindsholm, *Denmark* 11 J4
Hindu Bagh, *Pakistan* 68 D2
Hindu Kush, *Asia* 66 B7
Hindubagh, *Pakistan* 66 D5
Hindupur, *India* 66 N10
Hines Creek, *Canada* 104 B5
Hinesville, *U.S.A.* 109 K5
Hinganghat, *India* 66 J11
Hingham, *U.S.A.* 114 B8
Hingir, *India* 69 J10
Hingoli, *India* 66 K10
Hinigaran, *Phil.* 61 F5
Hinis, *Turkey* 73 C9
Hinna = Imi, *Ethiopia* 81 F5
Hinna, *Nigeria* 83 C7
Hinnerup, *Denmark* 11 H4
Hinnøya, *Norway* 8 B16
Hinojosa del Duque, *Spain* 35 G5
Hinsdale, *U.S.A.* 111 D12
Hinterrhein →, *Switz.* 25 J5
Hinton, *Canada* 104 C5
Hinton, *U.S.A.* 108 G5
Hınzır Burnu, *Turkey* 72 D6
Hirado, *Japan* 55 H4
Hirakud Dam, *India* 67 J13
Hiran →, *India* 69 H8
Hirapur, *India* 69 G8
Hiratsuka, *Japan* 55 G9
Hirfanlı Baraji, *Turkey* 72 C5
Hiroo, *Japan* 54 C11
Hirosaki, *Japan* 54 D10
Hiroshima, *Japan* 55 G6
Hiroshima □, *Japan* 55 G6
Hirson, *France* 19 C11
Hirtshals, *Denmark* 11 G3
Hisar, *India* 68 E6
Hisarcık, *Turkey* 39 B11
Hisaria, *Bulgaria* 41 D8
Hisb →, *Iraq* 70 D5
Ḥismá, *Si. Arabia* 70 D3
Hispaniola, *W. Indies* 121 C5
Hīt, *Iraq* 70 C4
Hita, *Japan* 55 H5
Hitachi, *Japan* 55 F10
Hitchin, *U.K.* 13 F7
Hitoyoshi, *Japan* 55 H5
Hitra, *Norway* 8 E13
Hitzacker, *Germany* 24 B7
Hixon, *Canada* 104 C4
Ḥiyyon, N. →, *Israel* 75 E4
Hjalmar L., *Canada* 105 A7
Hjälmaren, *Sweden* 10 E9
Hjältevad, *Sweden* 11 G9
Hjo, *Sweden* 11 F8
Hjørring, *Denmark* 11 G3
Hjortkvarn, *Sweden* 11 F9
Hlinsko, *Czech Rep.* 26 B8
Hlobane, *S. Africa* 89 D5
Hlohovec, *Slovak Rep.* 27 C10
Hlučín, *Czech Rep.* 27 B11
Hluhluwe, *S. Africa* 89 D5
Hlukhiv, *Ukraine* 47 G7
Hlyboka, *Ukraine* 47 H3
Hlybokaye, *Belarus* 46 E4
Hnúšt'a, *Slovak Rep.* 27 C12
Ho, *Ghana* 83 D5
Ho Chi Minh City = Phanh Bho Ho Chi Minh, *Vietnam* 65 G6
Ho Thuong, *Vietnam* 64 C5
Hoa Binh, *Vietnam* 58 G5
Hoa Da, *Vietnam* 65 G7
Hoa Hiep, *Vietnam* 65 G5
Hoai Nhon, *Vietnam* 64 E7
Hoang Lien Son, *Vietnam* 58 F4
Hoanib →, *Namibia* 88 B2
Hoare B., *Canada* 101 B13
Hoarusib →, *Namibia* 88 B2
Hobart, *Australia* 94 G4
Hobart, *U.S.A.* 113 H5
Hobbs, *U.S.A.* 113 J3
Hobbs Coast, *Antarctica* 5 D14
Hobe Sound, *U.S.A.* 109 M5
Hoboken, *U.S.A.* 111 F10
Hobro, *Denmark* 11 H3
Hoburgen, *Sweden* 11 H12
Hocalar, *Turkey* 39 C11
Hochfeld, *Namibia* 88 C2
Hochschwab, *Austria* 26 D8
Höchstadt, *Germany* 25 F6
Hockenheim, *Germany* 25 F4
Hodaka-Dake, *Japan* 55 F8
Hodgeville, *Canada* 105 C7
Hodgson, *Canada* 105 C9
Hódmezővásárhely, *Hungary* 42 D5
Hodna, Chott el, *Algeria* 78 A6
Hodonín, *Czech Rep.* 27 C10
Hoeamdong, *N. Korea* 57 C16
Hœdic, Î. de, *France* 18 E4
Hoek van Holland, *Neths.* 17 C4
Hoengsŏng, *S. Korea* 57 F14
Hoeryong, *N. Korea* 57 C15
Hoeyang, *N. Korea* 57 E14
Hof, *Germany* 25 E7
Hofgeismar, *Germany* 24 D5
Hofheim, *Germany* 25 E4
Hofmeyr, *S. Africa* 88 E4
Höfn, *Iceland* 8 D6
Hofors, *Sweden* 10 D10
Hofsjökull, *Iceland* 8 D4
Hōfu, *Japan* 55 G5
Hogan Group, *Australia* 95 F4
Höganäs, *Sweden* 11 H6
Hogarth, Mt., *Australia* 94 C2
Hoggar = Ahaggar, *Algeria* 78 D7
Högsäter, *Sweden* 11 F6
Högsby, *Sweden* 11 G10
Högsjö, *Sweden* 10 E9
Hogsty Reef, *Bahamas* 121 B5
Hoh →, *U.S.A.* 116 C2
Hohe Acht, *Germany* 25 E3
Hohe Tauern, *Austria* 26 D5
Hohe Venn, *Belgium* 17 D6
Hohenau, *Austria* 27 C9
Hohenems, *Austria* 26 D2
Hohenloher Ebene, *Germany* 25 F5
Hohenwald, *U.S.A.* 109 H2
Hohenwestedt, *Germany* 24 A5
Hoher Rhön = Rhön, *Germany* 24 E5
Hohhot, *China* 56 D6
Hóhlakas, *Greece* 36 D9
Hohoe, *Ghana* 83 D5
Hoi An, *Vietnam* 64 E7
Hoi Xuan, *Vietnam* 58 G5
Hoisington, *U.S.A.* 112 F5
Højer, *Denmark* 11 K2
Hōjō, *Japan* 55 H6
Hok, *Sweden* 11 G8
Hökensås, *Sweden* 11 G8
Hökerum, *Sweden* 11 G7
Hokianga Harbour, *N.Z.* 91 F4
Hokitika, *N.Z.* 91 K3
Hokkaidō □, *Japan* 54 C11
Hol-Hol, *Djibouti* 81 E5
Hola Pristan, *Ukraine* 47 J7
Holbæk, *Denmark* 11 J5
Holbrook, *Australia* 95 F4
Holbrook, *U.S.A.* 115 J8
Holden, *U.S.A.* 114 G7
Holdenville, *U.S.A.* 113 H6
Holdrege, *U.S.A.* 112 E5
Holešov, *Czech Rep.* 27 B10
Holguín, *Cuba* 120 B4
Holíč, *Slovak Rep.* 27 C10
Holice, *Czech Rep.* 26 A8
Höljes, *Sweden* 10 D6
Hollabrunn, *Austria* 26 C9
Hollams Bird I., *Namibia* 88 C1
Holland, *Mich., U.S.A.* 108 D2
Holland, *N.Y., U.S.A.* 110 D6
Hollandale, *U.S.A.* 113 J9
Hollandia = Jayapura, *Indonesia* 63 E10
Holley, *U.S.A.* 110 C6
Hollfeld, *Germany* 25 F7
Hollidaysburg, *U.S.A.* 110 F6
Hollis, *U.S.A.* 113 H5
Hollister, *Calif., U.S.A.* 116 J5
Hollister, *Idaho, U.S.A.* 114 E6
Höllviken, *Sweden* 11 J6
Holly Hill, *U.S.A.* 109 L5
Holly Springs, *U.S.A.* 113 H10
Hollywood, *Calif., U.S.A.* 106 D3
Hollywood, *Fla., U.S.A.* 109 N5
Holman, *Canada* 100 A8
Hólmavík, *Iceland* 8 D3
Holmen, *U.S.A.* 112 D9
Holmes Reefs, *Australia* 94 B4
Holmsjö, *Sweden* 11 H9
Holmsjön, *Västernorrland, Sweden* 10 B10
Holmsjön, *Västernorrland, Sweden* 10 B9
Holmsland Klit, *Denmark* 11 J2
Holmsund, *Sweden* 8 E19
Holod, *Romania* 42 D7
Holroyd →, *Australia* 94 A3
Holstebro, *Denmark* 11 H2
Holsworthy, *U.K.* 13 G3
Holton, *Canada* 103 B8
Holton, *U.S.A.* 112 F7
Holtville, *U.S.A.* 117 N11
Holwerd, *Neths.* 17 A5
Holy I., *Angl., U.K.* 12 D3
Holy I., *Northumb., U.K.* 12 B6
Holyhead, *U.K.* 12 D3
Holyoke, *Colo., U.S.A.* 112 E3
Holyoke, *Mass., U.S.A.* 111 D12
Holyrood, *Canada* 103 C9
Holzkirchen, *Germany* 25 H7
Holzminden, *Germany* 24 D5
Homa Bay, *Kenya* 86 C3
Homalin, *Burma* 67 G19
Homand, *Iran* 71 C8
Homathko →, *Canada* 104 C4
Homberg, *Germany* 24 D5
Hombori, *Mali* 83 B4
Homburg, *Germany* 25 F3
Home B., *Canada* 101 B13
Home Hill, *Australia* 94 B4
Homedale, *U.S.A.* 114 E5
Homer, *Alaska, U.S.A.* 100 C4
Homer, *La., U.S.A.* 113 J8
Homer City, *U.S.A.* 110 F5
Homestead, *Australia* 94 C4
Homestead, *U.S.A.* 109 N5
Homewood, *U.S.A.* 116 F6
Homoine, *Mozam.* 89 C6
Homoljske Planina, *Serbia, Yug.* 40 B5
Homorod, *Romania* 43 D10
Homs = Ḥimş, *Syria* 75 A5
Homyel, *Belarus* 47 F6
Hon Chong, *Vietnam* 65 G5
Hon Me, *Vietnam* 64 C5
Honan = Henan □, *China* 56 H8
Honaz, *Turkey* 39 D11
Honbetsu, *Japan* 54 C11
Honcut, *U.S.A.* 116 F5
Honda Bay, *Phil.* 61 G3
Hondarribia, *Spain* 32 B3
Hondeklipbaai, *S. Africa* 88 E2
Hondo, *Japan* 55 H5
Hondo, *U.S.A.* 113 L5
Hondo →, *Belize* 119 D7
Honduras ■, *Cent. Amer.* 120 D2
Honduras, G. de, *Caribbean* 120 C2
Hønefoss, *Norway* 9 F14
Honesdale, *U.S.A.* 111 E9
Honey L., *U.S.A.* 116 E6
Honfleur, *France* 18 C7
Høng, *Denmark* 11 J5
Hong →, *Vietnam* 58 F5
Hong Gai, *Vietnam* 58 G6
Hong He →, *China* 56 H8
Hong Hu, *China* 59 C9
Hong Kong □, *China* 59 F10
Hong'an, *China* 59 B10
Hongch'ŏn, *S. Korea* 57 F14
Honghai Wan, *China* 59 F10
Honghe, *China* 58 F4
Honghu, *China* 59 C9
Hongjiang, *China* 58 D7
Hongliu He →, *China* 56 F5
Hongor, *Mongolia* 56 B7
Hongsa, *Laos* 64 C3
Hongshui He →, *China* 58 F7
Hongsŏng, *S. Korea* 57 F14
Hongtong, *China* 56 F6
Honguedo, Détroit d', *Canada* 103 C7
Hongwon, *N. Korea* 57 E14
Hongya, *China* 58 C4
Hongyuan, *China* 58 A4
Hongze Hu, *China* 57 H10
Honiara, *Solomon Is.* 96 H7
Honiton, *U.K.* 13 G4
Honjō, *Japan* 54 E10
Honkorâb, Ras, *Egypt* 80 C4
Honningsvåg, *Norway* 8 A21
Hönö, *Sweden* 11 G5
Honolulu, *U.S.A.* 106 H16
Honshū, *Japan* 55 G9
Hontoria del Pinar, *Spain* 32 D1
Hood, Mt., *U.S.A.* 114 D3
Hood, Pt., *Australia* 93 F2
Hood River, *U.S.A.* 114 D3
Hoodsport, *U.S.A.* 116 C3
Hooge, *Germany* 24 A4
Hoogeveen, *Neths.* 17 B6
Hoogezand-Sappemeer, *Neths.* 17 A6
Hooghly = Hugli →, *India* 69 J13
Hooghly-Chinsura = Chunchura, *India* 69 H13
Hook Hd., *Ireland* 15 D5
Hook I., *Australia* 94 C4
Hook of Holland = Hoek van Holland, *Neths.* 17 C4
Hooker, *U.S.A.* 113 G4
Hooker Creek, *Australia* 92 C5
Hoonah, *U.S.A.* 104 B1
Hooper Bay, *U.S.A.* 100 B3
Hoopeston, *U.S.A.* 108 E2
Hoopstad, *S. Africa* 88 D4
Höör, *Sweden* 11 J7
Hoorn, *Neths.* 17 B5
Hoover, *U.S.A.* 109 J2
Hoover Dam, *U.S.A.* 117 K12
Hooversville, *U.S.A.* 110 F6
Hop Bottom, *U.S.A.* 111 E9
Hopa, *Turkey* 73 B9
Hope, *Canada* 104 D4
Hope, *Ariz., U.S.A.* 117 M13
Hope, *Ark., U.S.A.* 113 J8
Hope, L., *S. Austral., Australia* 95 D2
Hope, L., *W. Austral., Australia* 93 F3
Hope I., *Canada* 110 B4
Hope Town, *Bahamas* 120 A4
Hopedale, *Canada* 103 A7
Hopedale, *U.S.A.* 111 D13
Hopefield, *S. Africa* 88 E2
Hopei = Hebei □, *China* 56 E9
Hopelchén, *Mexico* 119 D7
Hopetoun, *Vic., Australia* 95 F3
Hopetoun, *W. Austral., Australia* 93 F3
Hopetown, *S. Africa* 88 D3
Hopevale, *Australia* 94 B4
Hopewell, *U.S.A.* 108 G7
Hopfgarten, *Austria* 26 D5
Hopkins, L., *Australia* 92 D4
Hopkinsville, *U.S.A.* 109 G2
Hopland, *U.S.A.* 116 G3
Hoquiam, *U.S.A.* 116 D3
Horasan, *Turkey* 73 B10
Horažďovice, *Czech Rep.* 26 B6
Horb, *Germany* 25 G4
Hörby, *Sweden* 11 J7
Horcajo de Santiago, *Spain* 32 F1
Horden Hills, *Australia* 92 D5
Horezu, *Romania* 43 E8
Horgen, *Switz.* 25 H4
Horgoš, *Serbia, Yug.* 42 D4
Hořice, *Czech Rep.* 26 A8
Horinger, *China* 56 D6
Horki, *Belarus* 46 E6
Horlick Mts., *Antarctica* 5 E15
Horlivka, *Ukraine* 47 H10
Hormak, *Iran* 71 D9
Hormoz, *Iran* 71 E7
Hormoz, Jaz.-ye, *Iran* 71 E8
Hormozgān □, *Iran* 71 E8
Hormuz, Kūh-e, *Iran* 71 E7
Hormuz, Str. of, *The Gulf* 71 E8
Horn, *Austria* 26 C8
Horn, *Iceland* 8 C2
Horn, *Sweden* 11 G9
Horn →, *Canada* 104 A5
Horn, Cape = Hornos, C. de, *Chile* 122 J4
Horn Head, *Ireland* 15 A3
Horn I., *Australia* 94 A3
Horn Mts., *Canada* 104 A5
Hornachuelos, *Spain* 35 H5
Hornavan, *Sweden* 8 C17
Hornbeck, *U.S.A.* 113 K8
Hornbrook, *U.S.A.* 114 F2
Hornburg, *Germany* 24 C6
Horncastle, *U.K.* 12 D7
Horndal, *Sweden* 10 D10
Hornell, *U.S.A.* 110 D7
Hornell L., *Canada* 104 A5
Hornepayne, *Canada* 102 C3
Horní Planá, *Czech Rep.* 26 C7
Hornings Mills, *Canada* 110 B4
Hornitos, *U.S.A.* 116 H6
Hornos, C. de, *Chile* 122 J4
Hornoy-le-Bourg, *France* 19 C8
Hornsea, *U.K.* 12 D7
Hornslandet, *Sweden* 10 C11
Hörnum, *Germany* 24 A4
Horobetsu, *Japan* 54 C10
Horodenka, *Ukraine* 47 H3
Horodnya, *Ukraine* 47 G6
Horodok, *Khmelnytskyy, Ukraine* 47 H4
Horodok, *Lviv, Ukraine* 47 H2
Horodyshche, *Ukraine* 47 H6
Horokhiv, *Ukraine* 47 G3
Horovice, *Czech Rep.* 26 B6
Horqin Youyi Qianqi, *China* 57 A12
Horqueta, *Paraguay* 126 A4
Horred, *Sweden* 11 G6
Horse Creek, *U.S.A.* 112 E3
Horse Is., *Canada* 103 B8
Horsefly L., *Canada* 104 C4
Horseheads, *U.S.A.* 110 D8
Horsens, *Denmark* 11 J3
Horsham, *Australia* 95 F3
Horsham, *U.K.* 13 F7
Horšovský Týn, *Czech Rep.* 26 B5
Horten, *Norway* 9 G14

Hortobágy →, *Hungary* 42 C6
Horton, *U.S.A.* 112 F7
Horton →, *Canada* 100 B7
Horwood L., *Canada* 102 C3
Hosaina, *Ethiopia* 81 F4
Hose, Gunung-Gunung, *Malaysia* 62 D4
Ḩoseynābād, *Khuzestān, Iran* 71 C6
Ḩoseynābād, *Kordestān, Iran* 70 C5
Hoshangabad, *India* 68 H7
Hoshiarpur, *India* 68 D6
Hospet, *India* 66 M10
Hoste, I., *Chile* 128 H3
Hostens, *France* 20 D3
Hot, *Thailand* 64 C2
Hot Creek Range, *U.S.A.* 114 G6
Hot Springs, *Ark., U.S.A.* 113 H8
Hot Springs, *S. Dak., U.S.A.* 112 D3
Hotagen, *Sweden* 8 E16
Hotan, *China* 60 C2
Hotazel, *S. Africa* 88 D3
Hotchkiss, *U.S.A.* 115 G10
Hotham, C., *Australia* 92 B5
Hoting, *Sweden* 8 D17
Hotolishti, *Albania* 40 E4
Hotte, Massif de la, *Haiti* 121 C5
Hottentotsbaai, *Namibia* 88 D1
Houat, Î. de, *France* 18 E4
Houdan, *France* 19 D8
Houei Sai, *Laos* 58 G3
Houeillès, *France* 20 D4
Houffalize, *Belgium* 17 D5
Houghton, *Mich., U.S.A.* 112 B10
Houghton, *N.Y., U.S.A.* 110 D6
Houghton L., *U.S.A.* 108 C3
Houhora Heads, *N.Z.* 91 F4
Houlton, *U.S.A.* 109 B12
Houma, *U.S.A.* 113 L9
Houndé, *Burkina Faso* 82 C4
Hourtin, *France* 20 C2
Hourtin-Carcans, Étang d', *France* 20 C2
Housatonic →, *U.S.A.* 111 E11
Houston, *Canada* 104 C3
Houston, *Mo., U.S.A.* 113 G9
Houston, *Tex., U.S.A.* 113 L7
Hout →, *S. Africa* 89 C4
Houtkraal, *S. Africa* 88 E3
Houtman Abrolhos, *Australia* 93 E1
Hovd, *Mongolia* 60 B4
Hove, *U.K.* 13 G7
Hoveyzeh, *Iran* 71 D6
Hovmantorp, *Sweden* 11 H9
Hövsgöl, *Mongolia* 56 C5
Hövsgöl Nuur, *Mongolia* 60 A5
Hovsta, *Sweden* 10 E9
Howakil, *Eritrea* 81 D5
Howar, Wadi →, *Sudan* 81 D2
Howard, *Australia* 95 D5
Howard, *Pa., U.S.A.* 110 F7
Howard, *S. Dak., U.S.A.* 112 C6
Howe, *U.S.A.* 114 E7
Howe, C., *Australia* 95 F5
Howe I., *Canada* 111 B8
Howell, *U.S.A.* 108 D4
Howick, *Canada* 111 A11
Howick, *S. Africa* 89 D5
Howick Group, *Australia* 94 A4
Howitt, L., *Australia* 95 D2
Howland I., *Pac. Oc.* 96 G10
Howrah = Haora, *India* 69 H13
Howth Hd., *Ireland* 15 C5
Höxter, *Germany* 24 D5
Hoy, *U.K.* 14 C5
Hoya, *Germany* 24 C5
Høyanger, *Norway* 9 F12
Hoyerswerda, *Germany* 24 D10
Hoylake, *U.K.* 12 D4
Hoyos, *Spain* 34 E4
Hpa-an = Pa-an, *Burma* 67 L20
Hpungan Pass, *Burma* 67 F20
Hradec Králové, *Czech Rep.* 26 A8
Hrádek, *Czech Rep.* 27 C9
Hranice, *Czech Rep.* 27 B10
Hrazdan, *Armenia* 49 K7
Hrebenka, *Ukraine* 47 G7
Hrodna, *Belarus* 46 F2
Hrodzyanka, *Belarus* 46 F5
Hron →, *Slovak Rep.* 27 D11
Hrubieszów, *Poland* 45 H10
Hrubý Jeseník, *Czech Rep.* 27 A10
Hrvatska = Croatia ■, *Europe* 29 C13
Hrymayliv, *Ukraine* 47 H4
Hsenwi, *Burma* 67 H20
Hsiamen = Xiamen, *China* 59 E12
Hsian = Xi'an, *China* 56 G5
Hsinchu, *Taiwan* 59 E13
Hsinhailien = Lianyungang, *China* 57 G10
Hsinying, *Taiwan* 59 F13
Hsopket, *Burma* 58 F2
Hsüchou = Xuzhou, *China* 57 G9
Hu Xian, *China* 56 G5
Hua Hin, *Thailand* 64 F2
Hua Xian, *Henan, China* 56 G8
Hua Xian, *Shaanxi, China* 56 G5
Hua'an, *China* 59 E11
Huab →, *Namibia* 88 B2
Huacheng, *China* 59 E10
Huachinera, *Mexico* 118 A3
Huacho, *Peru* 124 F3
Huade, *China* 56 D7
Huadian, *China* 57 C14
Huadu, *China* 59 F9
Huai He →, *China* 59 A12
Huai Yot, *Thailand* 65 J2
Huai'an, *Hebei, China* 56 D8
Huai'an, *Jiangsu, China* 57 H10
Huaibei, *China* 56 G9
Huaibin, *China* 59 A10
Huaide = Gongzhuling, *China* 57 C13
Huaidezhen, *China* 57 C13
Huaihua, *China* 58 D7
Huaiji, *China* 59 F9
Huainan, *China* 59 A11
Huaining, *China* 59 B11
Huairen, *China* 56 E7
Huairou, *China* 56 D9
Huaiyang, *China* 56 H8
Huaiyin, *China* 57 H10
Huaiyuan, *Anhui, China* 57 H9
Huaiyuan, *Guangxi Zhuangzu, China* 58 E7
Huajianzi, *China* 57 D13
Huajuapan de Leon, *Mexico* 119 D5
Hualapai Peak, *U.S.A.* 115 J7
Hualien, *Taiwan* 59 E13
Huallaga →, *Peru* 124 E3
Huambo, *Angola* 85 G3
Huan Jiang →, *China* 56 G5
Huan Xian, *China* 56 F4
Huancabamba, *Peru* 124 E3
Huancane, *Peru* 124 G5
Huancavelica, *Peru* 124 F3
Huancayo, *Peru* 124 F3
Huanchaca, *Bolivia* 124 H5
Huang Hai = Yellow Sea, *China* 57 G12
Huang He →, *China* 57 F10
Huang Xian, *China* 57 F11
Huangchuan, *China* 59 A10
Huanggang, *China* 59 B10
Huangguoshu, *China* 58 E5
Huangling, *China* 56 G5
Huanglong, *China* 56 G5
Huanglongtan, *China* 59 A8
Huangmei, *China* 59 B10
Huangpi, *China* 59 B10
Huangping, *China* 58 D6
Huangshan, *China* 59 C12
Huangshi, *China* 59 B10
Huangsongdian, *China* 57 C14
Huangyan, *China* 59 C13
Huangyangsi, *China* 59 D8
Huaning, *China* 58 E4
Huanjiang, *China* 58 E7
Huantai, *China* 57 F9
Huánuco, *Peru* 124 E3
Huaping, *China* 58 D3
Huaraz, *Peru* 124 E3
Huarmey, *Peru* 124 F3
Huarong, *China* 59 C9
Huascarán, *Peru* 122 D3
Huasco, *Chile* 126 B1
Huasco →, *Chile* 126 B1
Huasna, *U.S.A.* 117 K6
Huatabampo, *Mexico* 118 B3
Huauchinango, *Mexico* 119 C5
Huautla de Jiménez, *Mexico* 119 D5
Huaxi, *China* 58 D6
Huay Namota, *Mexico* 118 C4
Huayin, *China* 56 G6
Huayuan, *China* 58 C7
Huayun, *China* 58 B6
Huazhou, *China* 59 G8
Hubbard, *Ohio, U.S.A.* 110 E4
Hubbard, *Tex., U.S.A.* 113 K6
Hubbart Pt., *Canada* 105 B10
Hubei □, *China* 59 B9
Hubli, *India* 66 M9
Huch'ang, *N. Korea* 57 D14
Hucknall, *U.K.* 12 D6
Huddersfield, *U.K.* 12 D6
Hude, *Germany* 24 B4
Hudi, *Sudan* 80 D3
Hudiksvall, *Sweden* 10 C11
Hudson, *Canada* 102 B1
Hudson, *Mass., U.S.A.* 111 D13
Hudson, *N.Y., U.S.A.* 111 D11
Hudson, *Wis., U.S.A.* 112 C8
Hudson, *Wyo., U.S.A.* 114 E9
Hudson →, *U.S.A.* 111 F10
Hudson Bay, *N.W.T., Canada* 101 C11
Hudson Bay, *Sask., Canada* 105 C8
Hudson Falls, *U.S.A.* 111 C11
Hudson Mts., *Antarctica* 5 D16
Hudson Str., *Canada* 101 B13
Hudson's Hope, *Canada* 104 B4
Hue, *Vietnam* 64 D6
Huebra →, *Spain* 34 D4
Huedin, *Romania* 42 D8
Huehuetenango, *Guatemala* 120 C1
Huejúcar, *Mexico* 118 C4
Huélamo, *Spain* 32 E3
Huelgoat, *France* 18 D3
Huelma, *Spain* 35 H7
Huelva, *Spain* 35 H4
Huelva □, *Spain* 35 H4
Huelva →, *Spain* 35 H5
Huentelauquén, *Chile* 126 C1
Huércal-Overa, *Spain* 33 H3
Huerta, Sa. de la, *Argentina* 126 C2
Huertas, C. de las, *Spain* 33 G4
Huerva →, *Spain* 32 D4
Huesca, *Spain* 32 C4
Huesca □, *Spain* 32 C5
Huéscar, *Spain* 33 H2
Huetamo, *Mexico* 118 D4
Huete, *Spain* 32 E2
Hugh →, *Australia* 94 D1
Hughenden, *Australia* 94 C3
Hughes, *Australia* 93 F4
Hughesville, *U.S.A.* 111 E8
Hugli →, *India* 69 J13
Hugo, *Colo., U.S.A.* 112 F3
Hugo, *Okla., U.S.A.* 113 H7
Hugoton, *U.S.A.* 113 G4
Hui Xian = Huixian, *China* 56 G7
Hui Xian, *China* 56 H4
Hui'an, *China* 59 E12
Hui'anbu, *China* 56 F4
Huichang, *China* 59 E10
Huichapán, *Mexico* 119 C5
Huidong, *Guangdong, China* 59 F10
Huidong, *Sichuan, China* 58 D4
Huifa He →, *China* 57 C14
Huila, Nevado del, *Colombia* 124 C3
Huilai, *China* 59 F11
Huili, *China* 58 D4
Huimin, *China* 57 F9
Huinan, *China* 57 C14
Huinca Renancó, *Argentina* 126 C3
Huining, *China* 56 G3
Huinong, *China* 56 E4
Huisache, *Mexico* 118 C4
Huishui, *China* 58 D6
Huisne →, *France* 18 E7
Huiting, *China* 56 G9
Huitong, *China* 58 D7
Huixian, *China* 56 G7
Huixtla, *Mexico* 119 D6
Huize, *China* 58 D4
Huizhou, *China* 59 F10
Hukawng Valley, *Burma* 67 F20
Hukou, *China* 59 C11
Hukuntsi, *Botswana* 88 C3
Ḩulayfā', *Si. Arabia* 70 E4
Huld = Ulaanjirem, *Mongolia* 56 B3
Hulin He →, *China* 57 B12
Hull = Kingston upon Hull, *U.K.* 12 D7
Hull, *Canada* 102 C4
Hull →, *U.K.* 12 D7
Hulst, *Neths.* 17 C4
Hultsfred, *Sweden* 11 G9
Hulun Nur, *China* 60 B6
Hulyaypole, *Ukraine* 47 J9
Humahuaca, *Argentina* 126 A2
Humaitá, *Brazil* 124 E6
Humaitá, *Paraguay* 126 B4
Humansdorp, *S. Africa* 88 E3
Humara, J., *Sudan* 81 D3
Humbe, *Angola* 88 B1
Humber →, *U.K.* 12 D7
Humboldt, *Canada* 105 C7
Humboldt, *Iowa, U.S.A.* 112 D7
Humboldt, *Tenn., U.S.A.* 113 H10
Humboldt →, *U.S.A.* 114 F4
Humboldt Gletscher, *Greenland* 4 B4
Hume, *U.S.A.* 116 J8
Hume, L., *Australia* 95 F4
Humenné, *Slovak Rep.* 27 C14
Hummelsta, *Sweden* 10 E10
Humphreys, Mt., *U.S.A.* 116 H8
Humphreys Peak, *U.S.A.* 115 J8
Humpolec, *Czech Rep.* 26 B8
Humptulips, *U.S.A.* 116 C3
Hūn, *Libya* 79 C9
Hun Jiang →, *China* 57 D13
Húnaflói, *Iceland* 8 D3
Hunan □, *China* 59 D9
Hunchun, *China* 57 C16
Hundested, *Denmark* 11 J5
Hundewali, *Pakistan* 68 D5
Hundred Mile House, *Canada* 104 C4
Hunedoara, *Romania* 42 E7
Hunedoara □, *Romania* 42 E7
Hünfeld, *Germany* 24 E5
Hung Yen, *Vietnam* 58 G6
Hungary ■, *Europe* 27 D12
Hungary, Plain of, *Europe* 6 F10
Hungerford, *Australia* 95 D3
Hŭngnam, *N. Korea* 57 E14
Hungt'ou Hsü, *Taiwan* 59 F13
Huni Valley, *Ghana* 82 D4
Hunneberg, *Sweden* 11 F6
Hunnebostrand, *Sweden* 11 F5
Hunsberge, *Namibia* 88 D2
Hunsrück, *Germany* 25 F3
Hunstanton, *U.K.* 12 E8
Hunte →, *Germany* 24 B4
Hunter, *U.S.A.* 111 D10
Hunter I., *Australia* 94 G3
Hunter I., *Canada* 104 C3
Hunter Ra., *Australia* 95 E5
Hunters Road, *Zimbabwe* 87 F2
Hunterville, *N.Z.* 91 H5
Huntingburg, *U.S.A.* 108 F2
Huntingdon, *Canada* 102 C5
Huntingdon, *U.K.* 13 E7
Huntingdon, *U.S.A.* 110 F6
Huntington, *Ind., U.S.A.* 108 E3
Huntington, *Oreg., U.S.A.* 114 D5
Huntington, *Utah, U.S.A.* 114 G8
Huntington, *W. Va., U.S.A.* 108 F4
Huntington Beach, *U.S.A.* 117 M9
Huntington Station, *U.S.A.* 111 F11
Huntly, *N.Z.* 91 G5
Huntly, *U.K.* 14 D6
Huntsville, *Canada* 102 C4
Huntsville, *Ala., U.S.A.* 109 H2
Huntsville, *Tex., U.S.A.* 113 K7
Hunyani →, *Zimbabwe* 87 F3
Hunyuan, *China* 56 E7
Hunza →, *India* 69 B6
Huo Xian = Huozhou, *China* 56 F6
Huong Hoa, *Vietnam* 64 D6
Huong Khe, *Vietnam* 64 C5
Huonville, *Australia* 94 G4
Huoqiu, *China* 59 A11
Huoshan, *Anhui, China* 59 A12
Huoshan, *Anhui, China* 59 B11
Huoshao Dao = Lü-Tao, *Taiwan* 59 F13
Huozhou, *China* 56 F6
Hupeh = Hubei □, *China* 59 B9
Ḩūr, *Iran* 71 D8
Hurbanovo, *Slovak Rep.* 27 D11
Hurd, C., *Canada* 110 A3
Hure Qi, *China* 57 C11
Hurezani, *Romania* 43 F8
Hurghada, *Egypt* 80 B3
Hurley, *N. Mex., U.S.A.* 115 K9
Hurley, *Wis., U.S.A.* 112 B9
Huron, *Calif., U.S.A.* 116 J6
Huron, *Ohio, U.S.A.* 110 E2
Huron, *S. Dak., U.S.A.* 112 C5
Huron, L., *U.S.A.* 110 B2
Hurricane, *U.S.A.* 115 H7
Hurso, *Ethiopia* 81 F5
Hurunui →, *N.Z.* 91 K4
Hurup, *Denmark* 11 H2
Húsavík, *Iceland* 8 C5
Huşi, *Romania* 43 D13
Huskvarna, *Sweden* 11 G8
Hustadvika, *Norway* 8 E12
Hustontown, *U.S.A.* 110 F6
Hustopeče, *Czech Rep.* 27 C9
Husum, *Germany* 24 A5
Husum, *Sweden* 10 A13
Hutchinson, *Kans., U.S.A.* 113 F6
Hutchinson, *Minn., U.S.A.* 112 C7
Hutte Sauvage, L. de la, *Canada* 103 A7
Hüttenberg, *Austria* 26 E7
Hutton, Mt., *Australia* 95 D4
Huwun, *Ethiopia* 81 G5
Huy, *Belgium* 17 D5
Huzhou, *China* 59 B13
Hvalpsund, *Denmark* 11 H3
Hvammstangi, *Iceland* 8 D3
Hvar, *Croatia* 29 E13
Hvarski Kanal, *Croatia* 29 E13
Hvítá →, *Iceland* 8 D3
Hwachŏn-chŏsuji, *S. Korea* 57 E14
Hwang Ho = Huang He →, *China* 57 F10
Hwange, *Zimbabwe* 87 F2
Hwange Nat. Park, *Zimbabwe* 88 B4
Hyannis, *Mass., U.S.A.* 108 E10
Hyannis, *Nebr., U.S.A.* 112 E4
Hyargas Nuur, *Mongolia* 60 B4
Hybo, *Sweden* 10 C10
Hydaburg, *U.S.A.* 104 B2
Hyde Park, *U.S.A.* 111 E11
Hyden, *Australia* 93 F2
Hyder, *U.S.A.* 104 B2
Hyderabad, *India* 66 L11
Hyderabad, *Pakistan* 68 G3
Hyères, *France* 21 E10
Hyères, Îs. d', *France* 21 F10
Hyesan, *N. Korea* 57 D15
Hyland →, *Canada* 104 B3
Hyltebruk, *Sweden* 11 H7
Hymia, *India* 69 C8
Hyndman Peak, *U.S.A.* 114 E6
Hyōgo □, *Japan* 55 G7
Hyrum, *U.S.A.* 114 F8
Hysham, *U.S.A.* 114 C10
Hythe, *U.K.* 13 F9
Hyūga, *Japan* 55 H5
Hyvinge = Hyvinkää, *Finland* 9 F21
Hyvinkää, *Finland* 9 F21

I

I-n-Gall, *Niger* 83 B6
I-n-Oudad, *Algeria* 83 A5
I-n-Ouzzal, *Algeria* 83 A5
I-n-Tadreft, *Niger* 83 B6
Iablaniţa, *Romania* 42 F7
Iaco →, *Brazil* 124 E5
Iacobeni, *Romania* 43 C10
Iakora, *Madag.* 89 C8
Ialomiţa □, *Romania* 43 F12
Ialomiţa →, *Romania* 43 F12
Ialoveni, *Moldova* 43 D13
Ialpug →, *Moldova* 43 E13
Ianca, *Romania* 43 E12
Iara, *Romania* 43 D8
Iarda, *Ethiopia* 81 E4
Iargara, *Moldova* 43 D13
Iaşi, *Romania* 43 C12
Iaşi □, *Romania* 43 C12
Íasmos, *Greece* 41 E9
Ib →, *India* 69 J10
Iba, *Phil.* 61 D3
Ibadan, *Nigeria* 83 D5
Ibagué, *Colombia* 124 C3
Iballja, *Albania* 40 D4
Ibăneşti, *Botoşani, Romania* 43 B11
Ibăneşti, *Mureş, Romania* 43 D9
Ibar →, *Serbia, Yug.* 40 C4
Ibaraki □, *Japan* 55 F10
Ibarra, *Ecuador* 124 C3
Ibba, *Sudan* 81 G2
Ibba, Bahr el →, *Sudan* 81 F2
Ibbenbüren, *Germany* 24 C3
Ibembo, *Dem. Rep. of the Congo* 86 B1
Ibera, L., *Argentina* 126 B4
Iberian Peninsula, *Europe* 6 H5
Iberville, *Canada* 102 C5
Iberville, Lac d', *Canada* 102 A5
Ibi, *Nigeria* 83 D6
Ibi, *Spain* 33 G4
Ibiá, *Brazil* 125 G9
Ibicuí →, *Brazil* 127 B4
Ibicuy, *Argentina* 126 C4
Ibioapaba, Sa. da, *Brazil* 125 D10
Ibiza = Eivissa, *Spain* 37 C7
Íblei, Monti, *Italy* 31 E7
Ibo, *Mozam.* 87 E5
Ibonma, *Indonesia* 63 E8
Ibotirama, *Brazil* 125 F10
Ibrāhīm →, *Lebanon* 75 A4
'Ibrī, *Oman* 71 F8
İbriktepe, *Turkey* 41 E10
Ibshawâi, *Egypt* 80 J7
Ibu, *Indonesia* 63 D7
Ibusuki, *Japan* 55 J5
Ica, *Peru* 124 F3
Iça →, *Brazil* 124 D5
Içana, *Brazil* 124 C5
Içana →, *Brazil* 124 C5
Içel = Mersin, *Turkey* 70 B2
Iceland ■, *Europe* 8 D4
Ich'ang = Yichang, *China* 59 B8
Ichchapuram, *India* 67 K14
Ichhawar, *India* 68 H7
Ichihara, *Japan* 55 G10
Ichikawa, *Japan* 55 G9
Ichilo →, *Bolivia* 124 G6
Ichinohe, *Japan* 54 D10
Ichinomiya, *Japan* 55 G8
Ichinoseki, *Japan* 54 E10
Ichnya, *Ukraine* 47 G7
Ichŏn, *S. Korea* 57 F14
Icod, *Canary Is.* 37 F3
Ida Grove, *U.S.A.* 112 D7
Idabel, *U.S.A.* 113 J7
Idaga Hamus, *Ethiopia* 81 E4
Idah, *Nigeria* 83 D6
Idaho □, *U.S.A.* 114 D7
Idaho City, *U.S.A.* 114 E6
Idaho Falls, *U.S.A.* 114 E7
Idanha-a-Nova, *Portugal* 34 F3
Idar-Oberstein, *Germany* 25 F3
Idfû, *Egypt* 80 C3
Ídhi Óros, *Greece* 36 D6
Ídhra, *Greece* 38 D5
Idi, *Indonesia* 62 C1
Idiofa, *Dem. Rep. of the Congo* 84 E3
Idkerberget, *Sweden* 10 D9
Idku, Bahra el, *Egypt* 80 H7
Idlib, *Syria* 70 C3
Idre, *Sweden* 10 C6
Idria, *U.S.A.* 116 J6
Idrija, *Slovenia* 29 C11
Idritsa, *Russia* 46 D5
Idutywa, *S. Africa* 89 E4
Ieper, *Belgium* 17 D2
Ierápetra, *Greece* 36 E7
Ierissós, *Greece* 40 F7
Ierissóu Kólpos, *Greece* 40 F7
Iernut, *Romania* 43 D9
Iesi, *Italy* 29 E10
Iésolo, *Italy* 29 C9
Ifach, Peñón de, *Spain* 33 G5
Ifakara, *Tanzania* 84 F7
'Ifāl, W. al →, *Si. Arabia* 70 D2
Ifanadiana, *Madag.* 89 C8
Ife, *Nigeria* 83 D5
Iférouâne, *Niger* 83 B6
Iffley, *Australia* 94 B3
Ifni, *Morocco* 78 C3
Ifon, *Nigeria* 83 D6
Iforas, Adrar des, *Mali* 83 B5
Ifould, L., *Australia* 93 F5
Iganga, *Uganda* 86 B3
Igarapava, *Brazil* 125 H9
Igarka, *Russia* 50 C9
Igatimi, *Paraguay* 127 A4
Igbetti, *Nigeria* 83 D5
Igbo-Ora, *Nigeria* 83 D5
Igboho, *Nigeria* 83 D5
Igbor, *Nigeria* 83 D6
Iğdır, *Turkey* 73 C11
Igelfors, *Sweden* 11 F9
Iggesund, *Sweden* 10 C11
Iglésias, *Italy* 30 C1
Igloolik, *Canada* 101 B11
Igluligaarjuk, *Canada* 101 B10
'Igma, Gebel el, *Egypt* 80 B3
Ignace, *Canada* 102 C1
İğneada, *Turkey* 41 E11
İğneada Burnu, *Turkey* 41 E12
Igoumenítsa, *Greece* 38 B2
Igra, *Russia* 48 B11
Iguaçu →, *Brazil* 127 B5
Iguaçu, Cat. del, *Brazil* 127 B5
Iguaçu Falls = Iguaçu, Cat. del, *Brazil* 127 B5
Iguala, *Mexico* 119 D5
Igualada, *Spain* 32 D6
Iguassu = Iguaçu →, *Brazil* 127 B5
Iguatu, *Brazil* 125 E11
Iharana, *Madag.* 89 A9
Ihbulag, *Mongolia* 56 C4
Iheya-Shima, *Japan* 55 L3
Ihiala, *Nigeria* 83 D6
Ihosy, *Madag.* 89 C8
Ihotry, Farihy, *Madag.* 89 C7
Ihugh, *Nigeria* 83 D6
Ii, *Finland* 8 D21
Ii-Shima, *Japan* 55 L3
Iida, *Japan* 55 G8
Iijoki →, *Finland* 8 D21
Iisalmi, *Finland* 8 E22
Iiyama, *Japan* 55 F9
Iizuka, *Japan* 55 H5
Ijebu-Igbo, *Nigeria* 83 D5
Ijebu-Ode, *Nigeria* 83 D5
IJmuiden, *Neths.* 17 B4
IJssel →, *Neths.* 17 B5
IJsselmeer, *Neths.* 17 B5
Ijuí, *Brazil* 127 B5
Ijuí →, *Brazil* 127 B4
Ikalamavony, *Madag.* 89 C8
Ikale, *Nigeria* 83 D6
Ikaluktutiak, *Canada* 100 B9

Ikang, *Nigeria* 83 E6
Ikara, *Nigeria* 83 C6
Ikare, *Nigeria* 83 D6
Ikaría, *Greece* 39 D8
Ikast, *Denmark* 11 H3
Ikeda, *Japan* 55 G6
Ikeja, *Nigeria* 83 D5
Ikela, *Dem. Rep. of the Congo* 84 E4
Ikerre-Ekiti, *Nigeria* 83 D6
Ikhtiman, *Bulgaria* 40 D7
Iki, *Japan* 55 H4
Ikimba L., *Tanzania* 86 C3
Ikire, *Nigeria* 83 D5
İkizdere, *Turkey* 73 B9
Ikom, *Nigeria* 83 D6
Ikongo, *Madag.* 89 C8
Ikopa →, *Madag.* 89 B8
Ikot Ekpene, *Nigeria* 83 D6
Ikungu, *Tanzania* 86 C3
Ikurun, *Nigeria* 83 D5
Ila, *Nigeria* 83 D5
Ilagan, *Phil.* 61 C4
Ilaka, *Madag.* 89 B8
Īlām, *Iran* 70 C5
Ilam, *Nepal* 69 F12
Ilam □, *Iran* 70 C5
Ilan, *Taiwan* 59 E13
Ilanskiy, *Russia* 51 D10
Ilaro, *Nigeria* 83 D5
Ilatane, *Niger* 83 B5
Iława, *Poland* 44 E6
Ile-à-la-Crosse, *Canada* 105 B7
Ile-à-la-Crosse, Lac, *Canada* 105 B7
Île-de-France □, *France* 19 D9
Ileanda, *Romania* 43 C8
Ilebo, *Dem. Rep. of the Congo* 84 E4
Ilek, *Russia* 50 D6
Ilero, *Nigeria* 83 D5
Ilesha, *Kwara, Nigeria* 83 D5
Ilesha, *Oyo, Nigeria* 83 D5
Ilford, *Canada* 105 B9
Ilfracombe, *Australia* 94 C3
Ilfracombe, *U.K.* 13 F3
Ilgaz, *Turkey* 72 B5
Ilgaz Dağları, *Turkey* 72 B5
Ilgın, *Turkey* 72 C4
Ílhavo, *Portugal* 34 E2
Ilhéus, *Brazil* 125 F11
Ili →, *Kazakstan* 50 E8
Ilia, *Romania* 42 E7
Ilia □, *Greece* 38 D3
Iliamna L., *U.S.A.* 100 C4
Iliç, *Turkey* 73 C8
Ilıca, *Turkey* 39 B9
Ilichevsk, *Azerbaijan* 73 C11
Iligan, *Phil.* 61 G6
Iligan Bay, *Phil.* 61 G6
Ilíki, L., *Greece* 38 C5
Ilin I., *Phil.* 61 E4
Iliodhrómia, *Greece* 38 B5
Ilion, *U.S.A.* 111 D9
Ilirska-Bistrica, *Slovenia* 29 C11
Ilkeston, *U.K.* 12 E6
Ilkley, *U.K.* 12 D6
Illampu = Ancohuma, Nevada, *Bolivia* 122 E4
Illana B., *Phil.* 61 H5
Illapel, *Chile* 126 C1
Ille-et-Vilaine □, *France* 18 D5
Ille-sur-Têt, *France* 20 F6
Illéla, *Niger* 83 C6
Iller →, *Germany* 25 G5
Illertissen, *Germany* 25 G6
Illescas, *Spain* 34 E7
Illetas, *Spain* 37 B9
Illichivsk, *Ukraine* 47 J6
Illiers-Combray, *France* 18 D8
Illimani, Nevado, *Bolivia* 124 G5
Illinois □, *U.S.A.* 112 E10
Illinois →, *U.S.A.* 107 C8
Illium = Troy, *Turkey* 39 B8
Illizi, *Algeria* 78 C7
Illkirch-Graffenstaden, *France* 19 D14
Illoqqortoormiit, *Greenland* 4 B6
Íllora, *Spain* 35 H7
Ilm →, *Germany* 24 D7
Ilmajoki, *Finland* 9 E20
Ilmen, Ozero, *Russia* 46 C6
Ilmenau, *Germany* 24 E6
Ilo, *Peru* 124 G4
Ilobu, *Nigeria* 83 D5
Iloilo, *Phil.* 61 F5
Ilora, *Nigeria* 83 D5
Ilorin, *Nigeria* 83 D5
Ilovatka, *Russia* 48 E7
Ilovlya, *Russia* 49 F7
Ilovlya →, *Russia* 49 F7
Iłowa, *Poland* 45 G2
Ilubabor □, *Ethiopia* 81 F4
Ilva Mică, *Romania* 43 C9
Ilwaco, *U.S.A.* 116 D2
Ilwaki, *Indonesia* 63 F7
Ilyichevsk = Illichivsk, *Ukraine* 47 J6
Iłża, *Poland* 45 G8
Iłżanka →, *Poland* 45 G8
Imabari, *Japan* 55 G6
Imaloto →, *Madag.* 89 C8
İmamoğlu, *Turkey* 72 D6
Imandra, Ozero, *Russia* 50 C4
Imanombo, *Madag.* 89 C8
Imari, *Japan* 55 H4
Imasa, *Sudan* 80 D4
Imathía □, *Greece* 40 F6
Imatra, *Finland* 46 B5
Imbil, *Australia* 95 D5
Iménas, *Mali* 83 B5
imeni 26 Bakinskikh Komissarov = Neftçala, *Azerbaijan* 71 B6
imeni 26 Bakinskikh Komissarov, *Turkmenistan* 71 B7
Imeri, Serra, *Brazil* 124 C5
Imerimandroso, *Madag.* 89 B8
Imi, *Ethiopia* 81 F5
Imishly = İmişli, *Azerbaijan* 49 L9
İmişli, *Azerbaijan* 49 L9
Imlay, *U.S.A.* 114 F4
Imlay City, *U.S.A.* 110 D1
Immaseri, *Sudan* 81 D2
Immenstadt, *Germany* 25 H6
Immingham, *U.K.* 12 D7
Immokalee, *U.S.A.* 109 M5
Imo □, *Nigeria* 83 D6
Imo →, *Nigeria* 83 E6
Ímola, *Italy* 29 D8
Imotski, *Croatia* 29 E14
Imperatriz, *Brazil* 125 E9
Impéria, *Italy* 28 E5
Imperial, *Canada* 105 C7
Imperial, *Calif., U.S.A.* 117 N11
Imperial, *Nebr., U.S.A.* 112 E4
Imperial Beach, *U.S.A.* 117 N9
Imperial Dam, *U.S.A.* 117 N12
Imperial Reservoir, *U.S.A.* 117 N12
Imperial Valley, *U.S.A.* 117 N11
Imperieuse Reef, *Australia* 92 C2
Impfondo, *Congo* 84 D3
Imphal, *India* 67 G18
Imphy, *France* 19 F10
İmranlı, *Turkey* 73 C8
İmroz = Gökçeada, *Turkey* 41 F9
İmroz, *Turkey* 41 F9
Imst, *Austria* 26 D3
Imuris, *Mexico* 118 A2
Imuruan B., *Phil.* 63 B5
In Akhmed, *Mali* 83 B4
In-Aleï, *Mali* 82 B4
In Delimane, *Mali* 83 B5
In-Guezzam, *Niger* 83 B6
In Koufi, *Mali* 83 B5
In Salah, *Algeria* 78 C6
In Tallak, *Mali* 83 B5
In Tebezas, *Mali* 83 B5
Ina, *Japan* 55 G8
Inangahua Junction, *N.Z.* 91 J3
Inanwatan, *Indonesia* 63 E8
Iñapari, *Peru* 124 F5
Inari, *Finland* 8 B22
Inarijärvi, *Finland* 8 B22
Inawashiro-Ko, *Japan* 54 F10
Inca, *Spain* 37 B9
Inca de Oro, *Chile* 126 B2
Incaguasi, *Chile* 126 B1
İnce Burun, *Turkey* 72 A6
İncekum Burnu, *Turkey* 72 D5
İncesu, *Turkey* 70 B2
Inch'ŏn, *S. Korea* 57 F14
Incio = Cruz de Incio, *Spain* 34 C3
İncirliova, *Turkey* 39 D9
Incline Village, *U.S.A.* 114 G4
Incomáti →, *Mozam.* 89 D5
Inda Silase, *Ethiopia* 81 E4
Indal, *Sweden* 10 B11
Indalsälven →, *Sweden* 10 B11
Indaw, *Burma* 67 G20
Indbir, *Ethiopia* 81 F4
Independence, *Calif., U.S.A.* 116 J8
Independence, *Iowa, U.S.A.* 112 D9
Independence, *Kans., U.S.A.* 113 G7
Independence, *Ky., U.S.A.* 108 F3
Independence, *Mo., U.S.A.* 112 F7
Independence Fjord, *Greenland* 4 A6
Independence Mts., *U.S.A.* 114 F5
Independenţa, *Romania* 43 E12
Index, *U.S.A.* 116 C5
India ■, *Asia* 66 K11
Indian →, *U.S.A.* 109 M5
Indian Cabins, *Canada* 104 B5
Indian Harbour, *Canada* 103 B8
Indian Head, *Canada* 105 C8
Indian Lake, *U.S.A.* 111 C10
Indian Ocean 52 K11
Indian Springs, *U.S.A.* 117 J11
Indiana, *U.S.A.* 110 F5
Indiana □, *U.S.A.* 108 F3
Indianapolis, *U.S.A.* 108 F2
Indianola, *Iowa, U.S.A.* 112 E8
Indianola, *Miss., U.S.A.* 113 J9
Indigirka →, *Russia* 51 B15
Inđija, *Serbia, Yug.* 42 E5
Indio, *U.S.A.* 117 M10
Indo-China, *Asia* 52 H14
Indonesia ■, *Asia* 62 F5
Indore, *India* 68 H6
Indramayu, *Indonesia* 63 G13
Indravati →, *India* 67 K12
Indre □, *France* 19 F8
Indre →, *France* 18 E7
Indre-et-Loire □, *France* 18 E7
Indulkana, *Australia* 95 D1
Indus →, *Pakistan* 68 G2
Indus, Mouth of the, *Pakistan* 68 H3
İnebolu, *Turkey* 72 B5
İnecik, *Turkey* 41 F11
İnegöl, *Turkey* 41 F13
Ineu, *Romania* 42 D6
Infantes = Villanueva de los Infantes, *Spain* 35 G7
Infiernillo, Presa del, *Mexico* 118 D4
Infiesto, *Spain* 34 B5
Ingelstad, *Sweden* 11 H8
Ingenio, *Canary Is.* 37 G4
Ingenio Santa Ana, *Argentina* 126 B2
Ingersoll, *Canada* 102 D3
Ingham, *Australia* 94 B4
Ingleborough, *U.K.* 12 C5
Inglewood, *Queens., Australia* 95 D5
Inglewood, *Vic., Australia* 95 F3
Inglewood, *N.Z.* 91 H5
Inglewood, *U.S.A.* 117 M8
Ingólfshöfði, *Iceland* 8 E5
Ingolstadt, *Germany* 25 G7
Ingomar, *U.S.A.* 114 C10
Ingonish, *Canada* 103 C7
Ingore, *Guinea-Biss.* 82 C1
Ingraj Bazar, *India* 69 G13
Ingrid Christensen Coast, *Antarctica* 5 C6
Ingul → = Inhul →, *Ukraine* 47 J7
Ingulec = Inhulec, *Ukraine* 47 J7
Ingulets → = Inhulets →, *Ukraine* 47 J7
Inguri → = Enguri →, *Georgia* 49 J5
Ingushetia □, *Russia* 49 J7
Ingwavuma, *S. Africa* 89 D5
Inhaca, *Mozam.* 89 D5
Inhafenga, *Mozam.* 89 C5
Inhambane, *Mozam.* 89 C6
Inhambane □, *Mozam.* 89 C5
Inhaminga, *Mozam.* 87 F4
Inharrime, *Mozam.* 89 C6
Inharrime →, *Mozam.* 89 C6
Inhisar, *Turkey* 39 A12
Inhul →, *Ukraine* 47 J7
Inhulec, *Ukraine* 47 J7
Inhulets →, *Ukraine* 47 J7
Iniesta, *Spain* 33 F3
Ining = Yining, *China* 50 E9
Inírida →, *Colombia* 124 C5
Inishbofin, *Ireland* 15 C1
Inisheer, *Ireland* 15 C2
Inishfree B., *Ireland* 15 A3
Inishkea North, *Ireland* 15 B1
Inishkea South, *Ireland* 15 B1
Inishmaan, *Ireland* 15 C2
Inishmore, *Ireland* 15 C2
Inishowen Pen., *Ireland* 15 A4
Inishshark, *Ireland* 15 C1
Inishturk, *Ireland* 15 C1
Inishvickillane, *Ireland* 15 D1
Injibara, *Ethiopia* 81 E4
Injune, *Australia* 95 D4
Inklin →, *Canada* 104 B2
Inle L., *Burma* 67 J20
Inlet, *U.S.A.* 111 C10
Inn →, *Austria* 26 C6
Innamincka, *Australia* 95 D3
Inner Hebrides, *U.K.* 14 E2
Inner Mongolia = Nei Mongol Zizhiqu □, *China* 56 D7
Inner Sound, *U.K.* 14 D3
Innerkip, *Canada* 110 C4
Innetalling I., *Canada* 102 A4
Innisfail, *Australia* 94 B4
Innisfail, *Canada* 104 C6
In'no-shima, *Japan* 55 G6
Innsbruck, *Austria* 26 D4
Innviertel, *Austria* 26 C6
Inny →, *Ireland* 15 C4
Inongo, *Dem. Rep. of the Congo* 84 E3
İnönü, *Turkey* 39 B12
Inoucdjouac = Inukjuak, *Canada* 101 C12
Inowrocław, *Poland* 45 F5
Inpundong, *N. Korea* 57 D14
Inscription, C., *Australia* 93 E1
Insein, *Burma* 67 L20
Insjön, *Sweden* 10 D9
Ińsko, *Poland* 44 E2
Însurăţei, *Romania* 43 F12
Inta, *Russia* 50 C6
Intendente Alvear, *Argentina* 126 D3
Intepe, *Turkey* 39 A8
Interlaken, *Switz.* 25 J3
Interlaken, *U.S.A.* 111 D8
International Falls, *U.S.A.* 112 A8
Intiyaco, *Argentina* 126 B3
Întorsura Buzăului, *Romania* 43 E11
Inukjuak, *Canada* 101 C12
Inútil, B., *Chile* 128 G2
Inuvik, *Canada* 100 B6
Inveraray, *U.K.* 14 E3
Inverbervie, *U.K.* 14 E6
Invercargill, *N.Z.* 91 M2
Inverclyde □, *U.K.* 14 F4
Inverell, *Australia* 95 D5
Invergordon, *U.K.* 14 D4
Inverloch, *Australia* 95 F4
Invermere, *Canada* 104 C5
Inverness, *Canada* 103 C7
Inverness, *U.K.* 14 D4
Inverness, *U.S.A.* 109 L4
Inverurie, *U.K.* 14 D6
Investigator Group, *Australia* 95 E1
Investigator Str., *Australia* 95 F2
Inya, *Russia* 50 D9
Inyanga, *Zimbabwe* 87 F3
Inyangani, *Zimbabwe* 87 F3
Inyantue, *Zimbabwe* 88 B4
Inyo Mts., *U.S.A.* 116 J9
Inyokern, *U.S.A.* 117 K9
Inza, *Russia* 48 D8
Inzhavino, *Russia* 48 D6
Iō-Jima, *Japan* 55 J5
Ioánnina, *Greece* 38 B2
Ioánnina □, *Greece* 38 B2
Iola, *U.S.A.* 113 G7
Ion Corvin, *Romania* 43 F12
Iona, *U.K.* 14 E2
Ione, *U.S.A.* 116 G6
Ionia, *U.S.A.* 108 D3
Ionian Is. = Iónioi Nísoi, *Greece* 38 C2
Ionian Sea, *Medit. S.* 6 H9
Iónioi Nísoi, *Greece* 38 C2
Iónioi Nísoi □, *Greece* 38 C2
Íos, *Greece* 39 E7
Iowa □, *U.S.A.* 112 D8
Iowa →, *U.S.A.* 112 E9
Iowa City, *U.S.A.* 112 E9
Iowa Falls, *U.S.A.* 112 D8
Iowa Park, *U.S.A.* 113 J5
Ipala, *Tanzania* 86 C3
Ipameri, *Brazil* 125 G9
Ipáti, *Greece* 38 C4
Ipatinga, *Brazil* 125 G10
Ipatovo, *Russia* 49 H6
Ipel' →, *Europe* 27 D11
Ipiales, *Colombia* 124 C3
Ipin = Yibin, *China* 58 C5
Ípiros □, *Greece* 38 B2
Ipixuna, *Brazil* 124 E4
Ipoh, *Malaysia* 65 K3
Ippy, *C.A.R.* 84 C4
Ipsala, *Turkey* 41 F10
Ipsárion, Óros, *Greece* 41 F8
Ipswich, *Australia* 95 D5
Ipswich, *U.K.* 13 E9
Ipswich, *Mass., U.S.A.* 111 D14
Ipswich, *S. Dak., U.S.A.* 112 C5
Ipu, *Brazil* 125 D10
Iqaluit, *Canada* 101 B13
Iquique, *Chile* 124 H4
Iquitos, *Peru* 124 D4
Irabu-Jima, *Japan* 55 M2
Iracoubo, *Fr. Guiana* 125 B8
Īrafshān, *Iran* 71 E9
Irahuan, *Phil.* 61 G3
Iráklia, *Kikládhes, Greece* 39 E7
Iráklia, *Sérrai, Greece* 40 E7
Iráklion, *Greece* 36 D7
Iráklion □, *Greece* 36 D7
Irala, *Paraguay* 127 B5
Iran ■, *Asia* 71 C7
Iran, Gunung-Gunung, *Malaysia* 62 D4
Iran, Plateau of, *Asia* 52 F9
Iran Ra. = Iran, Gunung-Gunung, *Malaysia* 62 D4
Īrānshahr, *Iran* 71 E9
Irapuato, *Mexico* 118 C4
Iraq ■, *Asia* 70 C5
Irati, *Brazil* 127 B5
Irbes saurums, *Latvia* 44 A9
Irbid, *Jordan* 75 C4
Irbid □, *Jordan* 75 C5
Iregua →, *Spain* 32 C7
Ireland ■, *Europe* 15 C4
Irele, *Nigeria* 83 D6
Irgiz, Bolshaya →, *Russia* 48 D9
Irhyangdong, *N. Korea* 57 D15
Iri, *S. Korea* 57 G14
Irian Jaya □, *Indonesia* 63 E9
Irié, *Guinea* 82 D3
Iriga, *Phil.* 61 E5
Iringa, *Tanzania* 86 D4
Iringa □, *Tanzania* 86 D4
Iriomote-Jima, *Japan* 55 M1
Iriona, *Honduras* 120 C2
Iriri →, *Brazil* 125 D8
Irish Republic ■, *Europe* 15 C3
Irish Sea, *U.K.* 12 D3
Irkutsk, *Russia* 51 D11
Irlıganlı, *Turkey* 39 D11
Irma, *Canada* 105 C6
Irō-Zaki, *Japan* 55 G9
Iroise, Mer d', *France* 18 D2
Iron Baron, *Australia* 95 E2
Iron Gate = Portile de Fier, *Europe* 42 F7
Iron Knob, *Australia* 95 E2
Iron Mountain, *U.S.A.* 108 C1
Iron River, *U.S.A.* 112 B10
Irondequoit, *U.S.A.* 110 C7
Ironton, *Mo., U.S.A.* 113 G9
Ironton, *Ohio, U.S.A.* 108 F4
Ironwood, *U.S.A.* 112 B9
Iroquois, *Canada* 111 B9
Iroquois Falls, *Canada* 102 C3
Irosin, *Phil.* 61 E6
Irpin, *Ukraine* 47 G6
Irrara Cr. →, *Australia* 95 D4
Irrawaddy □, *Burma* 67 L19
Irrawaddy →, *Burma* 67 M19
Irricana, *Canada* 104 C6
Irsina, *Italy* 31 B9
Irtysh →, *Russia* 50 C7
Irumu, *Dem. Rep. of the Congo* 86 B2
Irún, *Spain* 32 B3
Irunea = Pamplona, *Spain* 32 C3
Irurzun, *Spain* 32 C3
Irvine, *Canada* 105 D6
Irvine, *U.K.* 14 F4
Irvine, *Calif., U.S.A.* 117 M9
Irvine, *Ky., U.S.A.* 108 G4
Irvinestown, *U.K.* 15 B4
Irving, *U.S.A.* 113 J6
Irvona, *U.S.A.* 110 F6
Irwin →, *Australia* 93 E1
Irymple, *Australia* 95 E3
Is, Jebel, *Sudan* 80 C4
Is-sur-Tille, *France* 19 E12
Isa, *Nigeria* 83 C6
Isa Khel, *Pakistan* 68 C4
Isaac →, *Australia* 94 C4
Isabel, *U.S.A.* 112 C4
Isabela, *Phil.* 61 H5
Isabela, I., *Mexico* 118 C3
Isabelia, Cord., *Nic.* 120 D2
Isabella Ra., *Australia* 92 D3
Isaccea, *Romania* 43 E13
Ísafjarðardjúp, *Iceland* 8 C2
Ísafjörður, *Iceland* 8 C2
Isagarh, *India* 68 G7
Isahaya, *Japan* 55 H5
Isaka, *Tanzania* 86 C3
Isakly, *Russia* 48 C10
Işalniţa, *Romania* 43 F8
Isan →, *India* 69 F9
Isana = Içana →, *Brazil* 124 C5
Isanlu Makutu, *Nigeria* 83 D6
Isar →, *Germany* 25 G8
Isarco →, *Italy* 29 B8
Ísari, *Greece* 38 D3
Íscar, *Spain* 34 D6
Iscehisar, *Turkey* 39 C12
Íschia, *Italy* 30 B6
Isdell →, *Australia* 92 C3
Ise, *Japan* 55 G8
Ise-Wan, *Japan* 55 G8
Isefjord, *Denmark* 11 J5
Isel →, *Austria* 26 E5
Iseo, *Italy* 28 C7
Iseo, L. d', *Italy* 28 C7
Iseramagazi, *Tanzania* 86 C3
Isère □, *France* 21 C9
Isère →, *France* 21 D8
Iserlohn, *Germany* 24 D3
Isérnia, *Italy* 31 A7
Iseyin, *Nigeria* 83 D5
Isfahan = Eşfahān, *Iran* 71 C6
Ishigaki-Shima, *Japan* 55 M2
Ishikari-Gawa →, *Japan* 54 C10
Ishikari-Sammyaku, *Japan* 54 C11
Ishikari-Wan, *Japan* 54 C10
Ishikawa □, *Japan* 55 F8
Ishim, *Russia* 50 D7
Ishim →, *Russia* 50 D8
Ishinomaki, *Japan* 54 E10
Ishioka, *Japan* 55 F10
Ishkuman, *Pakistan* 69 A5
Ishmi, *Albania* 40 E3
Ishpeming, *U.S.A.* 108 B2
Isigny-sur-Mer, *France* 18 C5
Isıklar Dağı, *Turkey* 41 F11
Işıklı, *Turkey* 39 C11
Isil Kul, *Russia* 50 D8
Ísili, *Italy* 30 C2
Isiolo, *Kenya* 86 B4
Isiro, *Dem. Rep. of the Congo* 86 B2
Isisford, *Australia* 94 C3
Iskenderun, *Turkey* 70 B3
Iskenderun Körfezi, *Turkey* 72 D6
Iskilip, *Turkey* 72 B6
Iskŭr →, *Bulgaria* 41 C8
Iskŭr, Yazovir, *Bulgaria* 40 D7
Iskut →, *Canada* 104 B2
Isla →, *U.K.* 14 E5
Isla Cristina, *Spain* 35 H3
Isla Vista, *U.S.A.* 117 L7
Islâhiye, *Turkey* 72 D7
Islam Headworks, *Pakistan* 68 E5
Islamabad, *Pakistan* 68 C5
Islamgarh, *Pakistan* 68 F4
Islamkot, *Pakistan* 68 G4
Islampur, *India* 69 G11
Island L., *Canada* 105 C10
Island Lagoon, *Australia* 95 E2
Island Pond, *U.S.A.* 111 B13
Islands, B. of, *Canada* 103 C8
Islay, *U.K.* 14 F2
Isle →, *France* 20 D3
Isle aux Morts, *Canada* 103 C8
Isle of Wight □, *U.K.* 13 G6
Isle Royale, *U.S.A.* 112 B10
Isle Royale National Park, *U.S.A.* 112 B10
Isleton, *U.S.A.* 116 G5
Ismail = Izmayil, *Ukraine* 47 K5
Ismâ'ilîya, *Egypt* 80 H8
Ismaning, *Germany* 25 G7
Isna, *Egypt* 80 B3
Isoanala, *Madag.* 89 C8
Isogstalo, *India* 69 B8
Ísola del Liri, *Italy* 29 G10
Ísola della Scala, *Italy* 28 C7
Ísola di Capo Rizzuto, *Italy* 31 D10
Isparta, *Turkey* 39 D12
Isperikh, *Bulgaria* 41 C10
Íspica, *Italy* 31 F7
Israel ■, *Asia* 75 D3
Isratu, *Eritrea* 81 D4
Issia, *Ivory C.* 82 D3
Issoire, *France* 20 C7
Issoudun, *France* 19 F8
Issyk-Kul, Ozero = Ysyk-Köl, Ozero, *Kyrgyzstan* 50 E8
Ist, *Croatia* 29 D11
Istállós-kő, *Hungary* 42 B5
İstanbul, *Turkey* 41 E12
İstanbul □, *Turkey* 41 E12
İstanbul Boğazı, *Turkey* 41 E13
Istiaía, *Greece* 38 C5
Istok, *Kosovo, Yug.* 40 D4
Istokpoga, L., *U.S.A.* 109 M5
Istra, *Croatia* 29 C10
Istres, *France* 21 E8
Istria = Istra, *Croatia* 29 C10
Itá, *Paraguay* 126 B4
Itaberaba, *Brazil* 125 F10
Itabira, *Brazil* 125 G10
Itabirito, *Brazil* 127 A7
Itabuna, *Brazil* 125 F11
Itacaunas →, *Brazil* 125 E9
Itacoatiara, *Brazil* 124 D7
Itaipú, Represa de, *Brazil* 127 B5
Itaituba, *Brazil* 125 D7
Itajaí, *Brazil* 127 B6
Itajubá, *Brazil* 127 A6

Itaka, *Tanzania* 87 D3
Italy ■, *Europe* 7 G8
Itamaraju, *Brazil* 125 G11
Itampolo, *Madag.* 89 C7
Itandrano, *Madag.* 89 C8
Itapecuru-Mirim, *Brazil* 125 D10
Itaperuna, *Brazil* 127 A7
Itapetininga, *Brazil* 127 A6
Itapeva, *Brazil* 127 A6
Itapicuru →, *Bahia, Brazil* 125 F11
Itapicuru →, *Maranhão, Brazil* 125 D10
Itapipoca, *Brazil* 125 D11
Itapuá □, *Paraguay* 127 B4
Itaquari, *Brazil* 127 A7
Itaquí, *Brazil* 126 B4
Itararé, *Brazil* 127 A6
Itarsi, *India* 68 H7
Itatí, *Argentina* 126 B4
Itbayat, *Phil.* 61 A4
Itchen →, *U.K.* 13 G6
Itéa, *Greece* 38 C4
Itezhi Tezhi, L., *Zambia* 87 F2
Ithaca = Itháki, *Greece* 38 C2
Ithaca, *U.S.A.* 111 D8
Itháki, *Greece* 38 C2
Itiquira →, *Brazil* 125 G7
Ito, *Japan* 55 G9
Ito Aba I., *S. China Sea* 62 B4
Itoigawa, *Japan* 55 F8
Iton →, *France* 18 C8
Itonamas →, *Bolivia* 124 F6
Itri, *Italy* 30 A6
Itsa, *Egypt* 80 J7
Íttiri, *Italy* 30 B1
Itu, *Brazil* 127 A6
Itu, *Nigeria* 83 D6
Ituiutaba, *Brazil* 125 G9
Itumbiara, *Brazil* 125 G9
Ituna, *Canada* 105 C8
Itunge Port, *Tanzania* 87 D3
Iturbe, *Argentina* 126 A2
Ituri →, *Dem. Rep. of the Congo* 86 B2
Iturup, Ostrov, *Russia* 51 E15
Ituxi →, *Brazil* 124 E6
Ituyuro →, *Argentina* 126 A3
Itzehoe, *Germany* 24 B5
Ivahona, *Madag.* 89 C8
Ivaí →, *Brazil* 127 A5
Ivalo, *Finland* 8 B22
Ivalojoki →, *Finland* 8 B22
Ivanava, *Belarus* 47 F3
Ivančice, *Czech Rep.* 27 B9
Ivănești, *Romania* 43 D12
Ivangorod, *Russia* 46 C5
Ivanhoe, *Australia* 95 E3
Ivanhoe, *Calif., U.S.A.* 116 J7
Ivanhoe, *Minn., U.S.A.* 112 C6
Ivanić Grad, *Croatia* 29 C13
Ivanjica, *Serbia, Yug.* 40 C4
Ivanjska, *Bos.-H.* 42 F2
Ivankoyskoye Vdkhr., *Russia* 46 D9
Ivano-Frankivsk, *Ukraine* 47 H3
Ivano-Frankovsk = Ivano-Frankivsk, *Ukraine* 47 H3
Ivanovo = Ivanava, *Belarus* 47 F3
Ivanovo, *Russia* 46 D11
Ivanšćica, *Croatia* 29 B13
Ivato, *Madag.* 89 C8
Ivatsevichy, *Belarus* 47 F3
Ivaylovgrad, *Bulgaria* 41 E10
Ivinheima →, *Brazil* 127 A5
Ivinhema, *Brazil* 127 A5
Ivohibe, *Madag.* 89 C8
Ivory Coast, *W. Afr.* 82 E4
Ivory Coast ■, *Africa* 82 D4
Ivösjön, *Sweden* 11 H8
Ivrea, *Italy* 28 C4
İvrindi, *Turkey* 39 B9
Ivujivik, *Canada* 101 B12
Ivybridge, *U.K.* 13 G4
Iwaizumi, *Japan* 54 E10
Iwaki, *Japan* 55 F10
Iwakuni, *Japan* 55 G6
Iwamizawa, *Japan* 54 C10
Iwanai, *Japan* 54 C10
Iwata, *Japan* 55 G8
Iwate □, *Japan* 54 E10
Iwate-San, *Japan* 54 E10
Iwo, *Nigeria* 83 D5
Iwonicz-Zdrój, *Poland* 45 J8
Ixiamas, *Bolivia* 124 F5
Ixopo, *S. Africa* 89 E5
Ixtepec, *Mexico* 119 D5
Ixtlán del Río, *Mexico* 118 C4
Iyal Bakhit, *Sudan* 81 E2
Iyo, *Japan* 55 H6
Izabal, L. de, *Guatemala* 120 C2
Izamal, *Mexico* 119 C7
Izberbash, *Russia* 49 J8
Izbica, *Poland* 45 H10
Izbica Kujawska, *Poland* 45 F5
Izbiceni, *Romania* 43 G9
Izena-Shima, *Japan* 55 L3
Izgrev, *Bulgaria* 41 C10
Izhevsk, *Russia* 50 D6
Izmayil, *Ukraine* 47 K5
İzmir, *Turkey* 39 C9
İzmir □, *Turkey* 39 C9
İzmir Körfezi, *Turkey* 39 C8
İzmit = Kocaeli, *Turkey* 41 F13
Iznájar, *Spain* 35 H6
Iznalloz, *Spain* 35 H7
İznik, *Turkey* 72 B3
İznik Gölü, *Turkey* 41 F13
Izobil'nyy, *Russia* 49 H5
Izola, *Slovenia* 29 C10
Izra, *Syria* 75 C5
Iztochni Rodopi, *Bulgaria* 41 E9
Izu-Shotō, *Japan* 55 G10
Izúcar de Matamoros, *Mexico* 119 D5
Izumi-sano, *Japan* 55 G7
Izumo, *Japan* 55 G6
Izyaslav, *Ukraine* 47 G4
Izyum, *Ukraine* 47 H9

J

Jaba, *Ethiopia* 81 F4
Jabal al Awliyā, *Sudan* 81 D3
Jabal at Tā'ir, *Eritrea* 81 D5
Jabalón →, *Spain* 35 G6
Jabalpur, *India* 69 H8
Jabbūl, *Syria* 70 B3
Jabiru, *Australia* 92 B5
Jablah, *Syria* 70 C3
Jablanac, *Croatia* 29 D11
Jablanica, *Bos.-H.* 42 G2
Jablonec nad Nisou, *Czech Rep.* 26 A8
Jablonica, *Slovak Rep.* 27 C10
Jabłonowo Pomorskie, *Poland* 44 E6
Jablunkov, *Czech Rep.* 27 B11
Jaboatão, *Brazil* 125 E11
Jaboticabal, *Brazil* 127 A6
Jabukovac, *Serbia, Yug.* 40 B6
Jaca, *Spain* 32 C4
Jacareí, *Brazil* 127 A6
Jacarèzinho, *Brazil* 127 A6
Jackman, *U.S.A.* 109 C10
Jacksboro, *U.S.A.* 113 J5
Jackson, *Ala., U.S.A.* 109 K2
Jackson, *Calif., U.S.A.* 116 G6
Jackson, *Ky., U.S.A.* 108 G4
Jackson, *Mich., U.S.A.* 108 D3
Jackson, *Minn., U.S.A.* 112 D7
Jackson, *Miss., U.S.A.* 113 J9
Jackson, *Mo., U.S.A.* 113 G10
Jackson, *N.H., U.S.A.* 111 B13
Jackson, *Ohio, U.S.A.* 108 F4
Jackson, *Tenn., U.S.A.* 109 H1
Jackson, *Wyo., U.S.A.* 114 E8
Jackson B., *N.Z.* 91 K2
Jackson L., *U.S.A.* 114 E8
Jacksons, *N.Z.* 91 K3
Jackson's Arm, *Canada* 103 C8
Jacksonville, *Ala., U.S.A.* 109 J3
Jacksonville, *Ark., U.S.A.* 113 H8
Jacksonville, *Calif., U.S.A.* 116 H6
Jacksonville, *Fla., U.S.A.* 109 K5
Jacksonville, *Ill., U.S.A.* 112 F9
Jacksonville, *N.C., U.S.A.* 109 H7
Jacksonville, *Tex., U.S.A.* 113 K7
Jacksonville Beach, *U.S.A.* 109 K5
Jacmel, *Haiti* 121 C5
Jacob Lake, *U.S.A.* 115 H7
Jacobabad, *Pakistan* 68 E3
Jacobina, *Brazil* 125 F10
Jacques Cartier, Dét. de, *Canada* 103 C7
Jacques-Cartier, Mt., *Canada* 103 C6
Jacques Cartier, Parc Prov., *Canada* 103 C5
Jacqueville, *Ivory C.* 82 D4
Jacuí →, *Brazil* 127 C5
Jacumba, *U.S.A.* 117 N10
Jacundá →, *Brazil* 125 D8
Jade, *Germany* 24 B4
Jadebusen, *Germany* 24 B4
Jadotville = Likasi, *Dem. Rep. of the Congo* 87 E2
Jadovnik, *Serbia, Yug.* 40 C3
Jadraque, *Spain* 32 E2
Jaén, *Peru* 124 E3
Jaén, *Spain* 35 H7
Jaén □, *Spain* 35 H7
Jafarabad, *India* 68 J4
Jaffa = Tel Aviv-Yafo, *Israel* 75 C3
Jaffa, C., *Australia* 95 F2
Jaffna, *Sri Lanka* 66 Q12
Jaffrey, *U.S.A.* 111 D12
Jagadhri, *India* 68 D7
Jagadishpur, *India* 69 G11
Jagdalpur, *India* 67 K13
Jagersfontein, *S. Africa* 88 D4
Jaghīn →, *Iran* 71 E8
Jagodina, *Serbia, Yug.* 40 B5
Jagraon, *India* 66 D9
Jagst →, *Germany* 25 F5
Jagtial, *India* 66 K11
Jaguariaíva, *Brazil* 127 A6
Jaguaribe →, *Brazil* 125 D11
Jagüey Grande, *Cuba* 120 B3
Jahanabad, *India* 69 G11
Jahazpur, *India* 68 G6
Jahrom, *Iran* 71 D7
Jaijon, *India* 68 D7
Jailolo, *Indonesia* 63 D7
Jailolo, Selat, *Indonesia* 63 D7
Jaipur, *India* 68 F6
Jais, *India* 69 F9
Jaisalmer, *India* 68 F4
Jaisinghnagar, *India* 69 H8
Jaitaran, *India* 68 F5
Jaithari, *India* 69 H8
Jājarm, *Iran* 71 B8
Jajce, *Bos.-H.* 42 F2
Jakam →, *India* 68 H6
Jakarta, *Indonesia* 63 G12
Jakhal, *India* 68 E6
Jakhau, *India* 68 H3
Jakobstad = Pietarsaari, *Finland* 8 E20
Jakupica, *Macedonia* 40 E5
Jal, *U.S.A.* 113 J3
Jalalabad, *Afghan.* 68 B4
Jalalabad, *India* 69 F8
Jalalpur Jattan, *Pakistan* 68 C6
Jalama, *U.S.A.* 117 L6
Jalapa, *Guatemala* 120 D2
Jalapa Enríquez, *Mexico* 119 D5
Jalasjärvi, *Finland* 9 E20
Jalaun, *India* 69 F8
Jaldhaka →, *Bangla.* 69 F13
Jalesar, *India* 68 F8
Jaleswar, *Nepal* 69 F11
Jalgaon, *Maharashtra, India* 66 J10
Jalgaon, *Maharashtra, India* 66 J9
Jalībah, *Iraq* 70 D5
Jalingo, *Nigeria* 83 D7
Jalisco □, *Mexico* 118 D4
Jalkot, *Pakistan* 69 B5
Jallas →, *Spain* 34 C1
Jalna, *India* 66 K9
Jalón →, *Spain* 32 D3
Jalor, *India* 68 G5
Jalpa, *Mexico* 118 C4
Jalpaiguri, *India* 67 F16
Jaluit I., *Marshall Is.* 96 G8
Jalūlā, *Iraq* 70 C5
Jamaari, *Nigeria* 83 C6
Jamaica ■, *W. Indies* 120 C4
Jamalpur, *Bangla.* 67 G16
Jamalpur, *India* 69 G12
Jamalpurganj, *India* 69 H13
Jamanxim →, *Brazil* 125 D7
Jambi, *Indonesia* 62 E2
Jambi □, *Indonesia* 62 E2
Jambusar, *India* 68 H5
James →, *S. Dak., U.S.A.* 112 D6
James →, *Va., U.S.A.* 108 G7
James B., *Canada* 102 B3
James Ranges, *Australia* 92 D5
James Ross I., *Antarctica* 5 C18
Jamesabad, *Pakistan* 68 G3
Jamestown, *Australia* 95 E2
Jamestown, *S. Africa* 88 E4
Jamestown, *N. Dak., U.S.A.* 112 B5
Jamestown, *N.Y., U.S.A.* 110 D5
Jamestown, *Pa., U.S.A.* 110 E4
Jamīlābād, *Iran* 71 C6
Jamiltepec, *Mexico* 119 D5
Jamira →, *India* 69 J13
Jämjö, *Sweden* 11 H9
Jamkhandi, *India* 66 L9
Jammerbugt, *Denmark* 11 G3
Jammu, *India* 68 C6
Jammu & Kashmir □, *India* 69 B7
Jamnagar, *India* 68 H4
Jamni →, *India* 69 G8
Jampur, *Pakistan* 68 E4
Jamrud, *Pakistan* 68 C4
Jämsä, *Finland* 9 F21
Jamshedpur, *India* 69 H12
Jamtara, *India* 69 H12
Jämtland, *Sweden* 8 E15
Jämtlands län □, *Sweden* 10 B7
Jan L., *Canada* 105 C8
Jan Mayen, *Arctic* 4 B7
Janakkala, *Finland* 9 F21
Janaúba, *Brazil* 125 G10
Jand, *Pakistan* 68 C5
Jandaq, *Iran* 71 C7
Jandia, *Canary Is.* 37 F5
Jandia, Pta. de, *Canary Is.* 37 F5
Jandola, *Pakistan* 68 C4
Jandowae, *Australia* 95 D5
Jándula →, *Spain* 35 G6
Janesville, *U.S.A.* 112 D10
Janga, *Ghana* 83 C4
Jangamo, *Mozam.* 89 C6
Janghai, *India* 69 G10
Janikowo, *Poland* 45 F5
Janīn, *West Bank* 75 C4
Janinà = Ioánnina □, *Greece* 38 B2
Janja, *Bos.-H.* 42 F4
Janjevo, *Kosovo, Yug.* 40 D5
Janjgir, *India* 69 J10
Janjina, *Croatia* 29 F14
Janjina, *Madag.* 89 C8
Janos, *Mexico* 118 A3
Jánoshalma, *Hungary* 42 D4
Jánosháza, *Hungary* 42 C2
Jánossomorja, *Hungary* 42 C2
Janów, *Poland* 45 H6
Janów Lubelski, *Poland* 45 H9
Janów Podlaski, *Poland* 45 F10
Janowiec Wielkopolski, *Poland* 45 F4
Januária, *Brazil* 125 G10
Janub Dârfûr □, *Sudan* 81 E2
Janub Kordofân □, *Sudan* 81 E3
Janubio, *Canary Is.* 37 F6
Janville, *France* 19 D8
Janzé, *France* 18 E5
Jaora, *India* 68 H6
Japan ■, *Asia* 55 G8
Japan, Sea of, *Asia* 54 E7
Japan Trench, *Pac. Oc.* 52 F18
Japen = Yapen, *Indonesia* 63 E9
Japla, *India* 69 G11
Japurá →, *Brazil* 122 D4
Jaquarão, *Brazil* 127 C5
Jaqué, *Panama* 120 E4
Jarābulus, *Syria* 70 B3
Jaraicejo, *Spain* 35 F5
Jaraíz de la Vera, *Spain* 34 E5
Jarama →, *Spain* 34 E7
Jaramānah, *Syria* 72 F7
Jarandilla, *Spain* 34 E5
Jaranwala, *Pakistan* 68 D5
Jarash, *Jordan* 75 C4
Järbo, *Sweden* 10 D10
Jardim, *Brazil* 126 A4
Jardín →, *Spain* 33 G2
Jardines de la Reina, Arch. de los, *Cuba* 120 B4
Jargalang, *China* 57 C12
Jargalant = Hovd, *Mongolia* 60 B4
Jari →, *Brazil* 125 D8
Jarīr, W. al →, *Si. Arabia* 70 E4
Järlåsa, *Sweden* 10 E11
Jarmen, *Germany* 24 B9
Järna, *Kopparberg, Sweden* 10 D8
Järna, *Stockholm, Sweden* 10 E11
Jarnac, *France* 20 C3
Jarny, *France* 19 C12
Jarocin, *Poland* 45 G4
Jaroměř, *Czech Rep.* 26 A8
Jarosław, *Poland* 45 H9
Järpås, *Sweden* 11 F6
Järpen, *Sweden* 10 A7
Jarrahdale, *Australia* 93 F2
Jarrahi →, *Iran* 71 D6
Jarres, Plaine des, *Laos* 64 C4
Jarso, *Ethiopia* 81 F4
Jartai, *China* 56 E3
Jarud Qi, *China* 57 B11
Järvenpää, *Finland* 9 F21
Jarvis, *Canada* 110 D4
Jarvis I., *Pac. Oc.* 97 H12
Jarvorník, *Czech Rep.* 27 A10
Järvsö, *Sweden* 10 C10
Jarwa, *India* 69 F10
Jaša Tomić, *Serbia, Yug.* 42 E5
Jasdan, *India* 68 H4
Jashpurnagar, *India* 69 H11
Jasidih, *India* 69 G12
Jasień, *Poland* 45 G2
Jāsimīyah, *Iraq* 70 C5
Jasin, *Malaysia* 65 L4
Jāsk, *Iran* 71 E8
Jasło, *Poland* 45 J8
Jasmund, *Germany* 24 A9
Jaso, *India* 69 G9
Jasper, *Alta., Canada* 104 C5
Jasper, *Ont., Canada* 111 B9
Jasper, *Ala., U.S.A.* 109 J2
Jasper, *Fla., U.S.A.* 109 K4
Jasper, *Ind., U.S.A.* 108 F2
Jasper, *Tex., U.S.A.* 113 K8
Jasper Nat. Park, *Canada* 104 C5
Jasrasar, *India* 68 F5
Jastarnia, *Poland* 44 D5
Jastrebarsko, *Croatia* 29 C12
Jastrowie, *Poland* 44 E3
Jastrzębie Zdrój, *Poland* 45 J5
Jász-Nagykun-Szolnok □, *Hungary* 42 C5
Jászapáti, *Hungary* 42 C5
Jászárokszállás, *Hungary* 42 C4
Jászberény, *Hungary* 42 C4
Jászkisér, *Hungary* 42 C5
Jászladány, *Hungary* 42 C5
Jataí, *Brazil* 125 G8
Jati, *Pakistan* 68 G3
Jatibarang, *Indonesia* 63 G13
Jatinegara, *Indonesia* 63 G12
Játiva = Xátiva, *Spain* 33 G4
Jättendal, *Sweden* 10 C11
Jaú, *Brazil* 127 A6
Jauja, *Peru* 124 F3
Jaunpur, *India* 69 G10
Java = Jawa, *Indonesia* 63 G14
Java Barat □, *Indonesia* 63 G12
Java Sea, *Indonesia* 62 E3
Java Tengah □, *Indonesia* 63 G14
Java Timur □, *Indonesia* 63 G15
Java Trench, *Ind. Oc.* 62 F3
Javalambre, Sa. de, *Spain* 32 E4
Jávea, *Spain* 33 G5
Javhlant = Uliastay, *Mongolia* 60 B4
Jawa, *Indonesia* 63 G14
Jawad, *India* 68 G6
Jawor, *Poland* 45 G3
Jaworzno, *Poland* 45 H6
Jaworzyna Śląska, *Poland* 45 H3
Jay Peak, *U.S.A.* 111 B12
Jaya, Puncak, *Indonesia* 63 E9
Jayanti, *India* 67 F16
Jayapura, *Indonesia* 63 E10
Jayawijaya, Pegunungan, *Indonesia* 63 E9
Jaynagar, *India* 67 F15
Jayrūd, *Syria* 70 C3
Jayton, *U.S.A.* 113 J4
Jāz Mūrīān, Hāmūn-e, *Iran* 71 E8
Jazīreh-ye Shīf, *Iran* 71 D6
Jazminal, *Mexico* 118 C4
Jazzīn, *Lebanon* 75 B4
Jean, *U.S.A.* 117 K11
Jean Marie River, *Canada* 104 A4
Jean Rabel, *Haiti* 121 C5
Jeanerette, *U.S.A.* 113 L9
Jeanette, Ostrov = Zhannetty, Ostrov, *Russia* 51 B16
Jeannette, *U.S.A.* 110 F5
Jebāl Bārez, Kūh-e, *Iran* 71 D8
Jebba, *Nigeria* 83 D5
Jebel, Bahr el →, *Sudan* 81 F3
Jebel Dud, *Sudan* 81 E3
Jebel Qerri, *Sudan* 81 D3
Jedburgh, *U.K.* 14 F6
Jedda = Jiddah, *Si. Arabia* 74 C2
Jeddore L., *Canada* 103 C8
Jedlicze, *Poland* 45 J8
Jędrzejów, *Poland* 45 H7
Jedwabne, *Poland* 45 E9
Jeetzel →, *Germany* 24 B7
Jefferson, *Iowa, U.S.A.* 112 D7
Jefferson, *Ohio, U.S.A.* 110 E4
Jefferson, *Tex., U.S.A.* 113 J7
Jefferson, Mt., *Nev., U.S.A.* 114 G5
Jefferson, Mt., *Oreg., U.S.A.* 114 D3
Jefferson City, *Mo., U.S.A.* 112 F8
Jefferson City, *Tenn., U.S.A.* 109 G4
Jeffersontown, *U.S.A.* 108 F3
Jeffersonville, *U.S.A.* 108 F3
Jeffrey City, *U.S.A.* 114 E10
Jega, *Nigeria* 83 C5
Jēkabpils, *Latvia* 9 H21
Jekyll I., *U.S.A.* 109 K5
Jelcz-Laskowice, *Poland* 45 G4
Jelenia Góra, *Poland* 45 H2
Jelgava, *Latvia* 9 H20
Jelgava □, *Latvia* 44 B10
Jelica, *Serbia, Yug.* 40 C4
Jelli, *Sudan* 81 F3
Jelšava, *Slovak Rep.* 27 C13
Jemaja, *Indonesia* 65 L5
Jemaluang, *Malaysia* 65 L4
Jember, *Indonesia* 63 H15
Jembongan, *Malaysia* 62 C5
Jena, *Germany* 24 E7
Jena, *U.S.A.* 113 K8
Jenbach, *Austria* 26 D4
Jenkins, *U.S.A.* 108 G4
Jenner, *U.S.A.* 116 G3
Jennings, *U.S.A.* 113 K8
Jepara, *Indonesia* 63 G14
Jeparit, *Australia* 95 F3
Jequié, *Brazil* 125 F10
Jequitinhonha, *Brazil* 125 G10
Jequitinhonha →, *Brazil* 125 G11
Jerantut, *Malaysia* 65 L4
Jérémie, *Haiti* 121 C5
Jerez, Punta, *Mexico* 119 C5
Jerez de García Salinas, *Mexico* 118 C4
Jerez de la Frontera, *Spain* 35 J4
Jerez de los Caballeros, *Spain* 35 G4
Jericho = El Arīḥā, *West Bank* 75 D4
Jericho, *Australia* 94 C4
Jerichow, *Germany* 24 C8
Jerilderie, *Australia* 95 F4
Jermyn, *U.S.A.* 111 E9
Jerome, *U.S.A.* 114 E6
Jerramungup, *Australia* 93 F2
Jersey, *U.K.* 13 H5
Jersey City, *U.S.A.* 111 F10
Jersey Shore, *U.S.A.* 110 E7
Jerseyville, *U.S.A.* 112 F9
Jerusalem, *Israel* 75 D4
Jervis B., *Australia* 95 F5
Jervis Inlet, *Canada* 104 C4
Jerzu, *Italy* 30 C2
Jesenice, *Slovenia* 29 B11
Jeseník, *Czech Rep.* 27 A10
Jesenké, *Slovak Rep.* 27 C13
Jesselton = Kota Kinabalu, *Malaysia* 62 C5
Jessnitz, *Germany* 24 D8
Jessore, *Bangla.* 67 H16
Jesup, *U.S.A.* 109 K5
Jesús Carranza, *Mexico* 119 D5
Jesús María, *Argentina* 126 C3
Jetmore, *U.S.A.* 113 F5
Jetpur, *India* 68 J4
Jeumont, *France* 19 B11
Jevnaker, *Norway* 9 F14
Jewett, *U.S.A.* 110 F3
Jewett City, *U.S.A.* 111 E13
Jeyḥūnābād, *Iran* 71 C6
Jeypore, *India* 67 K13
Jeziorak, Jezioro, *Poland* 44 E6
Jeziorany, *Poland* 44 E7
Jeziorka →, *Poland* 45 F8
Jha Jha, *India* 69 G12
Jhabua, *India* 68 H6
Jhajjar, *India* 68 E7
Jhal, *Pakistan* 68 E2
Jhal Jhao, *Pakistan* 66 F4
Jhalawar, *India* 68 G7
Jhalida, *India* 69 H11
Jhalrapatan, *India* 68 G7
Jhang Maghiana, *Pakistan* 68 D5
Jhansi, *India* 69 G8
Jhargram, *India* 69 H12
Jharia, *India* 69 H12
Jharsuguda, *India* 67 J14
Jhelum, *Pakistan* 68 C5
Jhelum →, *Pakistan* 68 D5
Jhilmilli, *India* 69 H10
Jhudo, *Pakistan* 68 G3
Jhunjhunu, *India* 68 E6
Ji-Paraná, *Brazil* 124 F6
Ji Xian, *Hebei, China* 56 F8
Ji Xian, *Henan, China* 56 G8
Ji Xian, *Shanxi, China* 56 F6
Jia Xian, *Henan, China* 56 H7
Jia Xian, *Shaanxi, China* 56 E6
Jiading, *China* 59 B13
Jiahe, *China* 59 E9
Jialing Jiang →, *China* 58 C6
Jiamusi, *China* 60 B8
Ji'an, *Jiangxi, China* 59 D10
Ji'an, *Jilin, China* 57 D14
Jianchang, *China* 57 D11
Jianchangying, *China* 57 D10
Jianchuan, *China* 58 D2
Jiande, *China* 59 C12
Jiang'an, *China* 58 C5
Jiangbei, *China* 58 C6
Jiangcheng, *China* 58 F3
Jiangchuan, *China* 58 E4
Jiangdi, *China* 58 D4
Jiangdu, *China* 59 A12
Jiange, *China* 58 A5
Jianghua, *China* 59 E8
Jiangjin, *China* 58 C6
Jiangkou, *China* 58 D7
Jiangle, *China* 59 D11
Jiangling, *China* 59 B9

Jiangmen, *China* 59 F9
Jiangning, *China* 59 B12
Jiangshan, *China* 59 C12
Jiangsu □, *China* 57 H11
Jiangxi □, *China* 59 D11
Jiangyan, *China* 59 A13
Jiangyin, *China* 59 B13
Jiangyong, *China* 59 E8
Jiangyou, *China* 58 B5
Jianhe, *China* 58 D7
Jianli, *China* 59 C9
Jianning, *China* 59 D11
Jian'ou, *China* 59 D12
Jianshi, *China* 58 B7
Jianshui, *China* 58 F4
Jianyang, *Fujian, China* 59 D12
Jianyang, *Sichuan, China* 58 B5
Jiao Xian = Jiaozhou, *China* 57 F11
Jiaohe, *Hebei, China* 56 E9
Jiaohe, *Jilin, China* 57 C14
Jiaojiang, *China* 59 C13
Jiaoling, *China* 59 E11
Jiaozhou, *China* 57 F11
Jiaozhou Wan, *China* 57 F11
Jiaozuo, *China* 56 G7
Jiashan, *China* 59 B13
Jiawang, *China* 57 G9
Jiaxiang, *China* 56 G9
Jiaxing, *China* 59 B13
Jiayi = Chiai, *Taiwan* 59 F13
Jiayu, *China* 59 C9
Jibiya, *Nigeria* 83 C6
Jibou, *Romania* 43 C8
Jibuti = Djibouti ■, *Africa* 81 E5
Jicarón, I., *Panama* 120 E3
Jičín, *Czech Rep.* 26 A8
Jiddah, *Si. Arabia* 74 C2
Jido, *India* 67 E19
Jieshou, *China* 56 H8
Jiexiu, *China* 56 F6
Jieyang, *China* 59 F11
Jigawa □, *Nigeria* 83 C6
Jiggalong, *Australia* 92 D3
Jigni, *India* 69 G8
Jihlava, *Czech Rep.* 26 B8
Jihlava →, *Czech Rep.* 27 C9
Jihočeský □, *Czech Rep.* 26 B7
Jihomoravský □, *Czech Rep.* 27 B9
Jijiga, *Ethiopia* 74 F3
Jikamshi, *Nigeria* 83 C6
Jikau, *Sudan* 81 F3
Jilin, *China* 57 C14
Jilin □, *China* 57 C14
Jiloca →, *Spain* 32 D3
Jilong = Chilung, *Taiwan* 59 E13
Jim Thorpe, *U.S.A.* 111 F9
Jima, *Ethiopia* 81 F4
Jimbolia, *Romania* 42 E5
Jimena de la Frontera, *Spain* 35 J5
Jiménez, *Mexico* 118 B4
Jimo, *China* 57 F11
Jin Jiang →, *China* 59 C10
Jin Xian = Jinzhou, *China* 56 E8
Jin Xian, *China* 57 E11
Jinan, *China* 56 F9
Jincheng, *China* 56 G7
Jinchuan, *China* 58 B4
Jind, *India* 68 E7
Jindabyne, *Australia* 95 F4
Jindřichův Hradec, *Czech Rep.* 26 B8
Jing He →, *China* 56 G5
Jing Shan, *China* 59 B8
Jing Xian, *China* 59 B12
Jing'an, *China* 59 C10
Jingbian, *China* 56 F5
Jingchuan, *China* 56 G4
Jingde, *China* 59 B12
Jingdezhen, *China* 59 C11
Jingdong, *China* 58 E3
Jinggangshan, *China* 59 D10
Jinggu, *China* 58 F3
Jinghai, *China* 56 E9
Jinghong, *China* 58 G3
Jingjiang, *China* 59 A13
Jingle, *China* 56 E6
Jingmen, *China* 59 B9
Jingning, *China* 56 G3
Jingpo Hu, *China* 57 C15
Jingshan, *China* 59 B9
Jingtai, *China* 56 F3
Jingxi, *China* 58 F6
Jingxing, *China* 56 E8
Jingyang, *China* 56 G5
Jingyu, *China* 57 C14
Jingyuan, *China* 56 F3
Jingzhou, *China* 58 D7
Jingziguan, *China* 56 H6
Jinhua, *China* 59 C12
Jining, *Nei Mongol Zizhiqu, China* 56 D7
Jining, *Shandong, China* 56 G9
Jinja, *Uganda* 86 B3
Jinjang, *Malaysia* 65 L3
Jinji, *China* 56 F4
Jinjiang, *Fujian, China* 59 E12
Jinjiang, *Yunnan, China* 58 D3
Jinjie, *China* 58 F6
Jinjini, *Ghana* 82 D4
Jinkou, *China* 59 B10
Jinkouhe, *China* 58 C4
Jinmen Dao, *China* 59 E12
Jinnah Barrage, *Pakistan* 66 C7
Jinning, *China* 58 E4
Jinotega, *Nic.* 120 D2
Jinotepe, *Nic.* 120 D2
Jinping, *Guizhou, China* 58 D7
Jinping, *Yunnan, China* 58 F4
Jinsha, *China* 58 D6
Jinsha Jiang →, *China* 58 C5
Jinshan, *China* 59 B13
Jinshi, *China* 59 C8
Jintan, *China* 59 B12
Jinxi, *Jiangxi, China* 59 D11
Jinxi, *Liaoning, China* 57 D11
Jinxian, *China* 59 C11
Jinxiang, *China* 56 G9
Jinyang, *China* 58 D4
Jinyun, *China* 59 C13
Jinzhai, *China* 59 B10
Jinzhou, *Hebei, China* 56 E8
Jinzhou, *Liaoning, China* 57 D11
Jiparaná →, *Brazil* 124 E6
Jipijapa, *Ecuador* 124 D2
Jiquilpan, *Mexico* 118 D4
Jishan, *China* 56 G6
Jishou, *China* 58 C7
Jishui, *China* 59 D10
Jisr ash Shughūr, *Syria* 70 C3
Jitarning, *Australia* 93 F2
Jitra, *Malaysia* 65 J3
Jiu →, *Romania* 43 G8
Jiudengkou, *China* 56 E4
Jiujiang, *Guangdong, China* 59 F9
Jiujiang, *Jiangxi, China* 59 C10
Jiuling Shan, *China* 59 C10
Jiulong, *China* 58 C3
Jiutai, *China* 57 B13
Jiuxiangcheng, *China* 56 H8
Jiuxincheng, *China* 56 E8
Jiuyuhang, *China* 59 B12
Jixi, *Anhui, China* 59 B12
Jixi, *Heilongjiang, China* 57 B16
Jiyang, *China* 57 F9
Jiyuan, *China* 56 G7
Jīzān, *Si. Arabia* 74 D3
Jize, *China* 56 F8
Jizera →, *Czech Rep.* 26 A7
Jizl, W. →, *Si. Arabia* 80 B4
Jizl, Wādī al, *Si. Arabia* 70 E3
Jizō-Zaki, *Japan* 55 G6
Jizzakh, *Uzbekistan* 50 E7
Joaçaba, *Brazil* 127 B5
Joal Fadiout, *Senegal* 82 C1
João Pessoa, *Brazil* 125 E12
Joaquín V. González, *Argentina* 126 B3
Jobat, *India* 68 H6
Jobourg, Nez de, *France* 18 C5
Jódar, *Spain* 35 H7
Jodhpur, *India* 68 F5
Jodiya, *India* 68 H4
Jōetsu, *Japan* 55 F9
Jœuf, *France* 19 C12
Jofane, *Mozam.* 89 C5
Jogbani, *India* 69 F12
Jõgeva, *Estonia* 9 G22
Jogjakarta = Yogyakarta, *Indonesia* 63 G14
Johannesburg, *S. Africa* 89 D4
Johannesburg, *U.S.A.* 117 K9
Johansfors, *Sweden* 11 H9
Johilla →, *India* 69 H9
John Day, *U.S.A.* 114 D4
John Day →, *U.S.A.* 114 D3
John D'Or Prairie, *Canada* 104 B5
John H. Kerr Reservoir, *U.S.A.* 109 G6
John o' Groats, *U.K.* 14 C5
Johnnie, *U.S.A.* 117 J10
John's Ra., *Australia* 94 C1
Johnson, *Kans., U.S.A.* 113 G4
Johnson, *Vt., U.S.A.* 111 B12
Johnson City, *N.Y., U.S.A.* 111 D9
Johnson City, *Tenn., U.S.A.* 109 G4
Johnson City, *Tex., U.S.A.* 113 K5
Johnsonburg, *U.S.A.* 110 E6
Johnsondale, *U.S.A.* 117 K8
Johnson's Crossing, *Canada* 104 A2
Johnston, L., *Australia* 93 F3
Johnston Falls = Mambilima Falls, *Zambia* 87 E2
Johnston I., *Pac. Oc.* 97 F11
Johnstone Str., *Canada* 104 C3
Johnstown, *N.Y., U.S.A.* 111 C10
Johnstown, *Ohio, U.S.A.* 110 F2
Johnstown, *Pa., U.S.A.* 110 F6
Johor Baharu, *Malaysia* 65 M4
Jõhvi, *Estonia* 9 G22
Joigny, *France* 19 E10
Joinville, *Brazil* 127 B6
Joinville, *France* 19 D12
Joinville I., *Antarctica* 5 C18
Jojutla, *Mexico* 119 D5
Jokkmokk, *Sweden* 8 C18
Jökulsá á Bru →, *Iceland* 8 D6
Jökulsá á Fjöllum →, *Iceland* 8 C5
Jolfā, *Āzarbājān-e Sharqī, Iran* 70 B5
Jolfā, *Eşfahan, Iran* 71 C6
Joliet, *U.S.A.* 108 E1
Joliette, *Canada* 102 C5
Jolo, *Phil.* 61 J4
Jolon, *U.S.A.* 116 K5
Jomalig I., *Phil.* 61 D5
Jombang, *Indonesia* 63 G15
Jomda, *China* 58 B2
Jonava, *Lithuania* 9 J21
Jones Sound, *Canada* 4 B3
Jonesboro, *Ark., U.S.A.* 113 H9
Jonesboro, *La., U.S.A.* 113 J8
Jong →, *S. Leone* 82 D2
Jonglei, *Sudan* 81 F3
Jonglei □, *Sudan* 81 F3
Joniškis, *Lithuania* 9 H20
Jönköping, *Sweden* 11 G8
Jönköpings län □, *Sweden* 11 G8
Jonquière, *Canada* 103 C5
Jonsered, *Sweden* 11 G6
Jonzac, *France* 20 C3
Joplin, *U.S.A.* 113 G7
Jora, *India* 68 F6
Jordan, *Mont., U.S.A.* 114 C10
Jordan, *N.Y., U.S.A.* 111 C8
Jordan ■, *Asia* 75 E5
Jordan →, *Asia* 75 D4
Jordan Valley, *U.S.A.* 114 E5
Jordanów, *Poland* 45 J6
Jorhat, *India* 67 F19
Jörn, *Sweden* 8 D19
Jorong, *Indonesia* 62 E4
Jørpeland, *Norway* 9 G11
Jorquera →, *Chile* 126 B2
Jos, *Nigeria* 83 D6
Jos Plateau, *Nigeria* 83 D6
Jošanička Banja, *Serbia, Yug.* 40 C4
José Batlle y Ordóñez, *Uruguay* 127 C4
Joseni, *Romania* 43 D10
Joseph, L., *Nfld., Canada* 103 B6
Joseph, L., *Ont., Canada* 110 A5
Joseph Bonaparte G., *Australia* 92 B4
Joshinath, *India* 69 D8
Joshua Tree, *U.S.A.* 117 L10
Joshua Tree National Park, *U.S.A.* 117 M10
Josselin, *France* 18 E4
Jostedalsbreen, *Norway* 9 F12
Jotunheimen, *Norway* 9 F13
Joubertberge, *Namibia* 88 B1
Joué-lès-Tours, *France* 18 E7
Jourdanton, *U.S.A.* 113 L5
Joutseno, *Finland* 46 B5
Jovellanos, *Cuba* 120 B3
Joyeuse, *France* 21 D8
Józefów, *Lubelskie, Poland* 45 H10
Józefów, *Mazowieckie, Poland* 45 F8
Ju Xian, *China* 57 F10
Juan Aldama, *Mexico* 118 C4
Juan Bautista Alberdi, *Argentina* 126 C3
Juan de Fuca Str., *Canada* 116 B3
Juan de Nova, *Ind. Oc.* 89 B7
Juan Fernández, Arch. de, *Pac. Oc.* 122 G2
Juan José Castelli, *Argentina* 126 B3
Juan L. Lacaze, *Uruguay* 126 C4
Juankoski, *Finland* 8 E23
Juárez, *Argentina* 126 D4
Juárez, *Mexico* 117 N11
Juárez, Sierra de, *Mexico* 118 A1
Juàzeiro, *Brazil* 125 E10
Juàzeiro do Norte, *Brazil* 125 E11
Juba, *Sudan* 81 G3
Jubayl, *Lebanon* 75 A4
Jubbah, *Si. Arabia* 70 D4
Jubbal, *India* 68 D7
Jubbulpore = Jabalpur, *India* 69 H8
Jübek, *Germany* 24 A5
Jubga, *Russia* 49 H4
Jubilee L., *Australia* 93 E4
Juby, C., *Morocco* 78 C3
Júcar = Xúquer →, *Spain* 33 F4
Júcaro, *Cuba* 120 B4
Juchitán, *Mexico* 119 D5
Judaea = Har Yehuda, *Israel* 75 D3
Judenburg, *Austria* 26 D7
Judith →, *U.S.A.* 114 C9
Judith, Pt., *U.S.A.* 111 E13
Judith Gap, *U.S.A.* 114 C9
Juelsminde, *Denmark* 11 J4
Jugoslavia = Yugoslavia ■, *Europe* 40 C4
Juigalpa, *Nic.* 120 D2
Juillac, *France* 20 C5
Juist, *Germany* 24 B2
Juiz de Fora, *Brazil* 127 A7
Jujuy □, *Argentina* 126 A2
Julesburg, *U.S.A.* 112 E3
Juli, *Peru* 124 G5
Julia Cr. →, *Australia* 94 C3
Julia Creek, *Australia* 94 C3
Juliaca, *Peru* 124 G4
Julian, *U.S.A.* 117 M10
Julian Alps = Julijske Alpe, *Slovenia* 29 B11
Julian L., *Canada* 102 B4
Julianatop, *Surinam* 125 C7
Julianehåb = Qaqortoq, *Greenland* 4 C5
Jülich, *Germany* 24 E2
Julijske Alpe, *Slovenia* 29 B11
Julimes, *Mexico* 118 B3
Jullundur, *India* 68 D6
Julu, *China* 56 F8
Jumbo, *Zimbabwe* 87 F3
Jumbo Pk., *U.S.A.* 117 J12
Jumentos Cays, *Bahamas* 120 B4
Jumilla, *Spain* 33 G3
Jumla, *Nepal* 69 E10
Jumna = Yamuna →, *India* 69 G9
Junagadh, *India* 68 J4
Junction, *Tex., U.S.A.* 113 K5
Junction, *Utah, U.S.A.* 115 G7
Junction B., *Australia* 94 A1
Junction City, *Kans., U.S.A.* 112 F6
Junction City, *Oreg., U.S.A.* 114 D2
Junction Pt., *Australia* 94 A1
Jundah, *Australia* 94 C3
Jundiaí, *Brazil* 127 A6
Juneau, *U.S.A.* 104 B2
Junee, *Australia* 95 E4
Jungfrau, *Switz.* 25 J3
Junggar Pendi, *China* 60 B3
Jungshahi, *Pakistan* 68 G2
Juniata →, *U.S.A.* 110 F7
Junín, *Argentina* 126 C3
Junín de los Andes, *Argentina* 128 D2
Jūniyah, *Lebanon* 75 B4
Junlian, *China* 58 C5
Juntas, *Chile* 126 B2
Juntura, *U.S.A.* 114 E4
Jur, Nahr el →, *Sudan* 81 F2
Jura = Jura, Mts. du, *Europe* 19 F13
Jura = Schwäbische Alb, *Germany* 25 G5
Jura, *U.K.* 14 F3
Jura □, *France* 19 F12
Jura □, *Switz.* 25 H3
Jūra →, *Lithuania* 44 C9
Jura, Mts. du, *Europe* 19 F13
Jura, Sd. of, *U.K.* 14 F3
Jurbarkas, *Lithuania* 9 J20
Jurien, *Australia* 93 F2
Jurilovca, *Romania* 43 F13
Jūrmala, *Latvia* 9 H20
Jurong, *China* 59 B12
Juruá →, *Brazil* 122 D4
Juruena, *Brazil* 124 F7
Juruena →, *Brazil* 124 E7
Juruti, *Brazil* 125 D7
Jussey, *France* 19 E12
Justo Daract, *Argentina* 126 C2
Jutaí →, *Brazil* 124 D5
Jüterbog, *Germany* 24 D9
Juticalpa, *Honduras* 120 D2
Jutland = Jylland, *Denmark* 11 H3
Juventud, I. de la, *Cuba* 120 B3
Juvigny-sous-Andaine, *France* 18 D6
Juwain, *Afghan.* 66 D2
Jūy Zar, *Iran* 70 C5
Juye, *China* 56 G9
Juzennecourt, *France* 19 D11
Jvari, *Georgia* 49 J6
Jwaneng, *Botswana* 85 J4
Jyderup, *Denmark* 11 J5
Jylland, *Denmark* 11 H3
Jyväskylä, *Finland* 9 E21

K

K2, *Pakistan* 69 B7
Ka →, *Nigeria* 83 C5
Kaap Plateau, *S. Africa* 88 D3
Kaapkruis, *Namibia* 88 C1
Kaapstad = Cape Town, *S. Africa* 88 E2
Kaba, *Guinea* 82 C2
Kabaena, *Indonesia* 63 F6
Kabala, *S. Leone* 82 D2
Kabale, *Uganda* 86 C3
Kabalo, *Dem. Rep. of the Congo* 86 D2
Kabambare, *Dem. Rep. of the Congo* 86 C2
Kabango, *Dem. Rep. of the Congo* 87 D2
Kabanjahe, *Indonesia* 62 D1
Kabankalan, *Phil.* 61 G5
Kabara, *Mali* 82 B4
Kabardinka, *Russia* 47 K10
Kabardino-Balkar Republic = Kabardino-Balkaria □, *Russia* 49 J6
Kabardino-Balkaria □, *Russia* 49 J6
Kabarega Falls = Murchison Falls, *Uganda* 86 B3
Kabasalan, *Phil.* 61 H5
Kabba, *Nigeria* 83 D6
Kabetogama, *U.S.A.* 112 A8
Kabi, *Niger* 83 C7
Kabin Buri, *Thailand* 64 F3
Kabinakagami L., *Canada* 102 C3
Kabinda, *Dem. Rep. of the Congo* 84 F4
Kabna, *Sudan* 80 D3
Kabompo, *Zambia* 87 E1
Kabompo →, *Zambia* 85 G4
Kabondo, *Dem. Rep. of the Congo* 87 D2
Kabongo, *Dem. Rep. of the Congo* 86 D2
Kabot, *Guinea* 82 C2
Kabou, *Togo* 83 D5
Kabr, *Sudan* 81 E2
Kabūd Gonbad, *Iran* 71 B8
Kabugao, *Phil.* 61 B4
Kābul, *Afghan.* 68 B3
Kābul □, *Afghan.* 66 B6
Kabul →, *Pakistan* 68 C5
Kabunga, *Dem. Rep. of the Congo* 86 C2
Kaburuang, *Indonesia* 63 D7
Kabushiya, *Sudan* 81 D3
Kabwe, *Zambia* 87 E2
Kačanik, *Kosovo, Yug.* 40 D5
Kačerginė, *Lithuania* 44 D10
Kachchh, Gulf of, *India* 68 H3
Kachchh, Rann of, *India* 68 H4
Kachchhidhana, *India* 69 J8
Kachebera, *Zambia* 87 E3
Kachia, *Nigeria* 83 D6
Kachikau, *Botswana* 88 B3
Kachin □, *Burma* 58 D1
Kachira, L., *Uganda* 86 C3
Kachiry, *Kazakstan* 50 D8
Kachisi, *Ethiopia* 81 F4
Kachnara, *India* 68 H6
Kachot, *Cambodia* 65 G4
Kaçkar, *Turkey* 73 B9
Kadan, *Czech Rep.* 26 A6
Kadan Kyun, *Burma* 64 F2
Kadanai →, *Afghan.* 68 D1
Kadarkút, *Hungary* 42 D2
Kade, *Ghana* 83 D4
Kadi, *India* 68 H5
Kadina, *Australia* 95 E2
Kadınhanı, *Turkey* 72 C5
Kadiolo, *Mali* 82 C3
Kadipur, *India* 69 F10
Kadirli, *Turkey* 70 B3
Kadiyevka = Stakhanov, *Ukraine* 47 H10
Kadodo, *Sudan* 81 E2
Kadoka, *U.S.A.* 112 D4
Kadom, *Russia* 48 C6
Kadoma, *Zimbabwe* 87 F2
Kâdugli, *Sudan* 81 E2
Kaduna, *Nigeria* 83 C6
Kaduna □, *Nigeria* 83 C6
Kaduy, *Russia* 46 C9
Kaédi, *Mauritania* 82 B2
Kaélé, *Cameroon* 83 C7
Kaeng Khoï, *Thailand* 64 E3
Kaesŏng, *N. Korea* 57 F14
Kāf, *Si. Arabia* 70 D3
Kafan = Kapan, *Armenia* 70 B5
Kafanchan, *Nigeria* 83 D6
Kafareti, *Nigeria* 83 C7
Kaffrine, *Senegal* 82 C1
Kafin, *Nigeria* 83 D6
Kafin Madaki, *Nigeria* 83 C6
Kafinda, *Zambia* 87 E3
Kafirévs, Ákra, *Greece* 38 C6
Kafr el Battikh, *Egypt* 80 H7
Kafr el Dauwâr, *Egypt* 80 H7
Kafr el Sheikh, *Egypt* 80 H7
Kafue, *Zambia* 87 F2
Kafue →, *Zambia* 85 H5
Kafue Flats, *Zambia* 87 F2
Kafue Nat. Park, *Zambia* 87 F2
Kafulwe, *Zambia* 87 D2
Kaga, *Afghan.* 68 B4
Kaga Bandoro, *C.A.R.* 84 C3
Kagan, *Uzbekistan* 50 F7
Kagarko, *Nigeria* 83 D6
Kagawa □, *Japan* 55 G7
Kagera □, *Tanzania* 86 C3
Kagera →, *Uganda* 86 C3
Kağızman, *Turkey* 70 B4
Kagmar, *Sudan* 81 E3
Kagoshima, *Japan* 55 J5
Kagoshima □, *Japan* 55 J5
Kagul = Cahul, *Moldova* 43 E13
Kahak, *Iran* 71 B6
Kahama, *Tanzania* 86 C3
Kahan, *Pakistan* 68 E3
Kahang, *Malaysia* 65 L4
Kahayan →, *Indonesia* 62 E4
Kahe, *Tanzania* 86 C4
Kahnūj, *Iran* 71 E8
Kahoka, *U.S.A.* 112 E9
Kahoolawe, *U.S.A.* 106 H16
Kahramanmaraş, *Turkey* 70 B3
Kâhta, *Turkey* 73 D8
Kahuta, *Pakistan* 68 C5
Kai, Kepulauan, *Indonesia* 63 F8
Kai Besar, *Indonesia* 63 F8
Kai Is. = Kai, Kepulauan, *Indonesia* 63 F8
Kai Kecil, *Indonesia* 63 F8
Kai Xian, *China* 58 B7
Kaiama, *Nigeria* 83 D5
Kaiapoi, *N.Z.* 91 K4
Kaieteur Falls, *Guyana* 124 B7
Kaifeng, *China* 56 G8
Kaihua, *China* 59 C12
Kaijiang, *China* 58 B6
Kaikohe, *N.Z.* 91 F4
Kaikoura, *N.Z.* 91 K4
Kaikoura Ra., *N.Z.* 91 J4
Kailahun, *S. Leone* 82 D2
Kaili, *China* 58 D6
Kailu, *China* 57 C11
Kailua Kona, *U.S.A.* 106 J17
Kaimana, *Indonesia* 63 E8
Kaimanawa Mts., *N.Z.* 91 H5
Kaimganj, *India* 69 F8
Kaimur Hills, *India* 69 G10
Kainab →, *Namibia* 88 D2
Kaingaroa Forest, *N.Z.* 91 H6
Kainji Dam, *Nigeria* 83 D5
Kainji Res., *Nigeria* 83 C5
Kainuu, *Finland* 8 D23
Kaipara Harbour, *N.Z.* 91 G5
Kaiping, *China* 59 F9
Kaipokok B., *Canada* 103 B8
Kaira, *India* 68 H5
Kairana, *India* 68 E7
Kaironi, *Indonesia* 63 E8
Kairouan, *Tunisia* 79 A8
Kaiserslautern, *Germany* 25 F3
Kaiserstuhl, *Germany* 25 G3
Kaitaia, *N.Z.* 91 F4
Kaitangata, *N.Z.* 91 M2
Kaithal, *India* 68 E7
Kaitu →, *Pakistan* 68 C4
Kaiwi Channel, *U.S.A.* 106 H16
Kaiyang, *China* 58 D6
Kaiyuan, *Liaoning, China* 57 C13
Kaiyuan, *Yunnan, China* 58 F4
Kajaani, *Finland* 8 D22
Kajabbi, *Australia* 94 C3
Kajana = Kajaani, *Finland* 8 D22
Kajang, *Malaysia* 65 L3
Kajaran, *Armenia* 73 C12
Kajiado, *Kenya* 86 C4
Kajo Kaji, *Sudan* 81 G3
Kajuru, *Nigeria* 83 C6
Kaka, *Sudan* 81 E3
Kakabeka Falls, *Canada* 102 C2
Kakadu Nat. Park, *Australia* 92 B5
Kakamas, *S. Africa* 88 D3
Kakamega, *Kenya* 86 B3

Kakanj, *Bos.-H.* 42 F3
Kakanui Mts., *N.Z.* 91 L3
Kakata, *Liberia* 82 D2
Kakdwip, *India* 69 J13
Kake, *Japan* 55 G6
Kake, *U.S.A.* 104 B2
Kakegawa, *Japan* 55 G9
Kakeroma-Jima, *Japan* 55 K4
Kakhib, *Russia* 49 J8
Kakhovka, *Ukraine* 47 J7
Kakhovske Vdskh., *Ukraine* 47 J7
Kakinada, *India* 67 L13
Kakisa →, *Canada* 104 A5
Kakisa L., *Canada* 104 A5
Kakogawa, *Japan* 55 G7
Kakwa →, *Canada* 104 C5
Kāl Gūsheh, *Iran* 71 D8
Kal Safīd, *Iran* 70 C5
Kala, *Nigeria* 83 C7
Kalaallit Nunaat = Greenland ■, *N. Amer.* 4 C5
Kalabagh, *Pakistan* 68 C4
Kalabahi, *Indonesia* 63 F6
Kalabáka, *Greece* 38 B3
Kalabana, *Mali* 82 C3
Kalach, *Russia* 48 E5
Kalach na Donu, *Russia* 49 F6
Kaladan →, *Burma* 67 J18
Kaladar, *Canada* 102 D4
Kalahari, *Africa* 88 C3
Kalahari Gemsbok Nat. Park, *S. Africa* 88 D3
Kalajoki, *Finland* 8 D20
Kālak, *Iran* 71 E8
Kalakamati, *Botswana* 89 C4
Kalakan, *Russia* 51 D12
K'alak'unlun Shank'ou = Karakoram Pass, *Pakistan* 69 B7
Kalam, *Pakistan* 69 B5
Kalama, *Dem. Rep. of the Congo* 86 C2
Kalama, *U.S.A.* 116 E4
Kalámai, *Greece* 38 D4
Kalamariá, *Greece* 40 F6
Kalamata = Kalámai, *Greece* 38 D4
Kalamazoo, *U.S.A.* 108 D3
Kalamazoo →, *U.S.A.* 108 D2
Kalambo Falls, *Tanzania* 87 D3
Kálamos, *Attikí, Greece* 38 C5
Kálamos, *Iónioi Nísoi, Greece* 38 C2
Kalan, *Turkey* 70 B3
Kalankalan, *Guinea* 82 C3
Kalannie, *Australia* 93 F2
Kalāntarī, *Iran* 71 C7
Kalao, *Indonesia* 63 F6
Kalaotoa, *Indonesia* 63 F6
Kälarne, *Sweden* 10 B10
Kalasin, *Thailand* 64 D4
Kalat, *Pakistan* 66 E5
Kalāteh, *Iran* 71 B7
Kalāteh-ye Ganj, *Iran* 71 E8
Kálathos, *Greece* 39 E10
Kalaus →, *Russia* 49 H7
Kalávrita, *Greece* 38 C4
Kalbarri, *Australia* 93 E1
Kale, *Antalya, Turkey* 39 E12
Kale, *Denizli, Turkey* 39 D10
Kalecik, *Turkey* 72 B5
Kalegauk Kyun, *Burma* 67 M20
Kalehe, *Dem. Rep. of the Congo* 86 C2
Kalema, *Tanzania* 86 C3
Kalemie, *Dem. Rep. of the Congo* 86 D2
Kalety, *Poland* 45 H5
Kalewa, *Burma* 67 H19
Kaleybar, *Iran* 70 B5
Kalgan = Zhangjiakou, *China* 56 D8
Kalgoorlie-Boulder, *Australia* 93 F3
Kali →, *India* 69 F8
Kali Sindh →, *India* 68 G6
Kaliakra, Nos, *Bulgaria* 41 C12
Kalianda, *Indonesia* 62 F3
Kalibo, *Phil.* 61 F5
Kalima, *Dem. Rep. of the Congo* 86 C2
Kalimantan □, *Indonesia* 62 E4
Kalimantan Barat □, *Indonesia* 62 E4
Kalimantan Selatan □, *Indonesia* 62 E5
Kalimantan Tengah □, *Indonesia* 62 E4
Kalimantan Timur □, *Indonesia* 62 D5
Kálimnos, *Greece* 39 D8
Kalimpong, *India* 69 F13
Kalinin = Tver, *Russia* 46 D8
Kaliningrad, *Russia* 9 J19
Kalininsk, *Russia* 48 E7
Kalinkavichy, *Belarus* 47 F5
Kalinkovichi = Kalinkavichy, *Belarus* 47 F5
Kalinovik, *Bos.-H.* 40 C2
Kalipetrovo, *Bulgaria* 41 B11
Kaliro, *Uganda* 86 B3
Kalirrákhi, *Greece* 41 F8
Kalispell, *U.S.A.* 114 B6
Kalisz, *Poland* 45 G5
Kalisz Pomorski, *Poland* 45 E2
Kaliua, *Tanzania* 86 D3
Kalívia Thorikoú, *Greece* 38 D5
Kalix, *Sweden* 8 D20
Kalix →, *Sweden* 8 D20
Kalka, *India* 68 D7
Kalkan, *Turkey* 39 E11
Kalkarindji, *Australia* 92 C5
Kalkaska, *U.S.A.* 108 C3
Kalkfeld, *Namibia* 88 C2
Kalkfontein, *Botswana* 88 C3
Kalkım, *Turkey* 39 B9
Kalkrand, *Namibia* 88 C2
Kållandsö, *Sweden* 11 F7
Kallavesi, *Finland* 8 E22
Källby, *Sweden* 11 F7
Kållered, *Sweden* 11 G6
Kallimasiá, *Greece* 39 C8
Kallinge, *Sweden* 11 H9
Kallithéa, *Greece* 38 D5
Kallmeti, *Albania* 40 E3
Kalloní, *Greece* 39 B8
Kallonís, Kólpos, *Greece* 39 B8
Kallsjön, *Sweden* 8 E15
Kalmalo, *Nigeria* 83 C6
Kalmar, *Sweden* 11 H10
Kalmar län □, *Sweden* 11 G10
Kalmar sund, *Sweden* 11 H10
Kalmyk Republic = Kalmykia □, *Russia* 49 G8
Kalmykia □, *Russia* 49 G8
Kalmykovo, *Kazakstan* 50 E6
Kalna, *India* 69 H13
Kalnai, *India* 69 H10
Kalocsa, *Hungary* 42 D4
Kalofer, *Bulgaria* 41 D8
Kalokhorio, *Cyprus* 36 E12
Kaloko, *Dem. Rep. of the Congo* 86 D2
Kalol, *Gujarat, India* 68 H5
Kalol, *Gujarat, India* 68 H5
Kalolímnos, *Greece* 39 D9
Kalomo, *Zambia* 87 F2
Kalonerón, *Greece* 38 D3
Kalpi, *India* 69 F8
Kaltern = Caldaro, *Italy* 29 B8
Kaltungo, *Nigeria* 83 D7
Kalu, *Pakistan* 68 G2
Kaluga, *Russia* 46 E9
Kalulushi, *Zambia* 87 E2
Kalundborg, *Denmark* 11 J5
Kalush, *Ukraine* 47 H3
Kałuszyn, *Poland* 45 F8
Kalutara, *Sri Lanka* 66 R12
Kalvarija, *Lithuania* 44 D10
Kalyazin, *Russia* 46 D9
Kam →, *Nigeria* 83 D7
Kama, *Dem. Rep. of the Congo* 86 C2
Kama →, *Russia* 6 D16
Kamachumu, *Tanzania* 86 C3
Kamaishi, *Japan* 54 E10
Kamalia, *Pakistan* 68 D5
Kaman, *India* 68 F6
Kaman, *Turkey* 72 C5
Kamanjab, *Namibia* 88 B2
Kamapanda, *Zambia* 87 E1
Kamaran, *Yemen* 74 D3
Kamativi, *Zimbabwe* 88 B4
Kamba, *Nigeria* 83 C5
Kambalda, *Australia* 93 F3
Kambar, *Pakistan* 68 F3
Kambia, *S. Leone* 82 D2
Kambolé, *Togo* 83 D5
Kambolé, *Zambia* 87 D3
Kambos, *Cyprus* 36 D11
Kambove, *Dem. Rep. of the Congo* 87 E2
Kamchatka, Poluostrov, *Russia* 51 D16
Kamchatka Pen. = Kamchatka, Poluostrov, *Russia* 51 D16
Kamchiya →, *Bulgaria* 41 C11
Kamen, *Russia* 50 D9
Kamen-Rybolov, *Russia* 54 B6
Kamenica, *Serbia, Yug.* 40 C6
Kamenica, *Serbia, Yug.* 40 B3
Kamenice nad Lipou, *Czech Rep.* 26 B8
Kamenjak, Rt., *Croatia* 29 D10
Kamenka = Kaminka, *Ukraine* 47 H7
Kamenka, *Kazakstan* 48 E10
Kamenka, *Penza, Russia* 48 D6
Kamenka, *Voronezh, Russia* 47 G10
Kamenka Bugskaya = Kamyanka-Buzka, *Ukraine* 47 G3
Kamenka Dneprovskaya = Kamyanka-Dniprovska, *Ukraine* 47 J8
Kamennomostskiy, *Russia* 49 H5
Kameno, *Bulgaria* 41 D11
Kamenolomini, *Russia* 49 G5
Kamensk-Shakhtinskiy, *Russia* 49 F5
Kamensk Uralskiy, *Russia* 50 D7
Kamenskiy, *Russia* 48 E7
Kamenskoye, *Russia* 51 C17
Kamenyak, *Bulgaria* 41 C10
Kamenz, *Germany* 24 D10
Kameoka, *Japan* 55 G7
Kami, *Albania* 40 D4
Kamiah, *U.S.A.* 114 C5
Kamień Krajeński, *Poland* 44 E4
Kamień Pomorski, *Poland* 44 E1
Kamienna →, *Poland* 45 G8
Kamienna Góra, *Poland* 45 H3
Kamieńsk, *Poland* 45 G6
Kamieskroon, *S. Africa* 88 E2
Kamilukuak, L., *Canada* 105 A8
Kamin-Kashyrskyy, *Ukraine* 47 G3
Kamina, *Dem. Rep. of the Congo* 87 D2
Kaminak L., *Canada* 105 A10
Kaministiquia, *Canada* 102 C1
Kaminka, *Ukraine* 47 H7
Kaminoyama, *Japan* 54 E10
Kamiros, *Greece* 36 C9
Kamituga, *Dem. Rep. of the Congo* 86 C2
Kamla →, *India* 69 G12
Kamloops, *Canada* 104 C4
Kamnik, *Slovenia* 29 B11
Kamo, *Armenia* 49 K7
Kamo, *Japan* 54 F9
Kamoke, *Pakistan* 68 C6
Kamp →, *Austria* 26 C8
Kampala, *Uganda* 86 B3
Kampang Chhnang, *Cambodia* 65 F5
Kampar, *Malaysia* 65 K3
Kampar →, *Indonesia* 62 D2
Kampen, *Neths.* 17 B5
Kampene, *Dem. Rep. of the Congo* 84 E5
Kamphaeng Phet, *Thailand* 64 D2
Kampolombo, L., *Zambia* 87 E2
Kampong Saom, *Cambodia* 65 G4
Kampong Saom, Chaak, *Cambodia* 65 G4
Kampong To, *Thailand* 65 J3
Kampot, *Cambodia* 65 G5
Kampti, *Burkina Faso* 82 C4
Kampuchea = Cambodia ■, *Asia* 64 F5
Kampung Air Putih, *Malaysia* 65 K4
Kampung Jerangau, *Malaysia* 65 K4
Kampung Raja, *Malaysia* 65 K4
Kampungbaru = Tolitoli, *Indonesia* 63 D6
Kamrau, Teluk, *Indonesia* 63 E8
Kamsack, *Canada* 105 C8
Kamsai, *Guinea* 82 C2
Kamskoye Ustye, *Russia* 48 C9
Kamuchawie L., *Canada* 105 B8
Kamuela, *U.S.A.* 106 H17
Kamui-Misaki, *Japan* 54 C10
Kamyanets-Podilskyy, *Ukraine* 47 H4
Kamyanka-Buzka, *Ukraine* 47 G3
Kamyanka-Dniprovska, *Ukraine* 47 J8
Kāmyārān, *Iran* 70 C5
Kamyshin, *Russia* 48 E7
Kamyzyak, *Russia* 49 G9
Kan, *Sudan* 81 F3
Kanaaupscow, *Canada* 102 B4
Kanaaupscow →, *Canada* 101 C12
Kanab, *U.S.A.* 115 H7
Kanab →, *U.S.A.* 115 H7
Kanagi, *Japan* 54 D10
Kanairiktok →, *Canada* 103 A7
Kanália, *Greece* 38 B4
Kananga, *Dem. Rep. of the Congo* 84 F4
Kanash, *Russia* 48 C8
Kanaskat, *U.S.A.* 116 C5
Kanastraíon, Ákra = Palioúrion, Ákra, *Greece* 40 G7
Kanawha →, *U.S.A.* 108 F4
Kanazawa, *Japan* 55 F8
Kanchanaburi, *Thailand* 64 E2
Kanchenjunga, *Nepal* 69 F13
Kanchipuram, *India* 66 N11
Kańczuga, *Poland* 45 J9
Kandaghat, *India* 68 D7
Kandahar = Qandahār, *Afghan.* 66 D4
Kandalaksha, *Russia* 50 C4
Kandalu, *Afghan.* 66 E3
Kandangan, *Indonesia* 62 E5
Kandanghaur, *Indonesia* 63 G13
Kandanos, *Greece* 36 D5
Kandava, *Latvia* 44 A9
Kandhíla, *Greece* 38 D4
Kandhkot, *Pakistan* 68 E3
Kandhla, *India* 68 E7
Kandi, *Benin* 83 C5
Kandi, *India* 69 H13
Kandiaro, *Pakistan* 68 F3
Kandıra, *Turkey* 72 B4
Kandla, *India* 68 H4
Kandos, *Australia* 95 E4
Kandreho, *Madag.* 89 B8
Kandy, *Sri Lanka* 66 R12
Kane, *U.S.A.* 110 E6
Kane Basin, *Greenland* 4 B4
Kanel, *Senegal* 82 B2
Kaneohe, *U.S.A.* 106 H16
Kanevskaya, *Russia* 49 G4
Kanfanar, *Croatia* 29 C10
Kang, *Botswana* 88 C3
Kangaba, *Mali* 82 C3
Kangal, *Turkey* 72 C7
Kangān, *Fārs, Iran* 71 E7
Kangān, *Hormozgān, Iran* 71 E8
Kangar, *Malaysia* 65 J3
Kangaré, *Mali* 82 C3
Kangaroo I., *Australia* 95 F2
Kangaroo Mts., *Australia* 94 C3
Kangasala, *Finland* 9 F21
Kangāvar, *Iran* 71 C6
Kangding, *China* 58 B3
Kangdong, *N. Korea* 57 E14
Kangean, Kepulauan, *Indonesia* 62 F5
Kangean Is. = Kangean, Kepulauan, *Indonesia* 62 F5
Kangen →, *Sudan* 81 F3
Kanggye, *N. Korea* 57 D14
Kanggyŏng, *S. Korea* 57 F14
Kanghwa, *S. Korea* 57 F14
Kangikajik, *Greenland* 4 B6
Kangiqsualujjuaq, *Canada* 101 C13
Kangiqsujuaq, *Canada* 101 B12
Kangirsuk, *Canada* 101 B13
Kangnŭng, *S. Korea* 57 F15
Kangping, *China* 57 C12
Kangra, *India* 68 C7
Kangto, *India* 67 F18
Kanhar →, *India* 69 G10
Kani, *Ivory C.* 82 D3
Kaniama, *Dem. Rep. of the Congo* 86 D1
Kaniapiskau = Caniapiscau →, *Canada* 103 A6
Kaniapiskau, Res. = Caniapiscau Rés. de, *Canada* 103 B6
Kanin, Poluostrov, *Russia* 50 C5
Kanin Nos, Mys, *Russia* 50 C5
Kanin Pen. = Kanin, Poluostrov, *Russia* 50 C5
Kanina, *Albania* 40 F3
Kaniva, *Australia* 95 F3
Kanjiža, *Serbia, Yug.* 42 D5
Kanjut Sar, *Pakistan* 69 A6
Kankaanpää, *Finland* 9 F20
Kankakee, *U.S.A.* 108 E2
Kankakee →, *U.S.A.* 108 E1
Kankan, *Guinea* 82 C3
Kankendy = Xankändi, *Azerbaijan* 70 B5
Kanker, *India* 67 J12
Kankossa, *Mauritania* 82 B2
Kankroli, *India* 68 G5
Kannapolis, *U.S.A.* 109 H5
Kannauj, *India* 69 F8
Kannod, *India* 66 H10
Kano, *Nigeria* 83 C6
Kano □, *Nigeria* 83 C6
Kan'onji, *Japan* 55 G6
Kanoroba, *Ivory C.* 82 D3
Kanowit, *Malaysia* 62 D4
Kanoya, *Japan* 55 J5
Kanpetlet, *Burma* 67 J18
Kanpur, *India* 69 F9
Kansas □, *U.S.A.* 112 F6
Kansas →, *U.S.A.* 112 F7
Kansas City, *Kans., U.S.A.* 112 F7
Kansas City, *Mo., U.S.A.* 112 F7
Kansenia, *Dem. Rep. of the Congo* 87 E2
Kansk, *Russia* 51 D10
Kansŏng, *S. Korea* 57 E15
Kansu = Gansu □, *China* 56 G3
Kantaphor, *India* 68 H7
Kantchari, *Burkina Faso* 83 C5
Kantché, *Niger* 83 C6
Kanté, *Togo* 83 D5
Kantemirovka, *Russia* 47 H10
Kantharalak, *Thailand* 64 E5
Kantli →, *India* 68 E6
Kantō □, *Japan* 55 F9
Kantō-Sanchi, *Japan* 55 G9
Kanturk, *Ireland* 15 D3
Kanuma, *Japan* 55 F9
Kanus, *Namibia* 88 D2
Kanye, *Botswana* 88 C4
Kanzenze, *Dem. Rep. of the Congo* 87 E2
Kanzi, Ras, *Tanzania* 86 D4
Kaohsiung, *Taiwan* 59 F13
Kaokoveld, *Namibia* 88 B1
Kaolack, *Senegal* 82 C1
Kaoshan, *China* 57 B13
Kapaa, *U.S.A.* 106 G15
Kapadvanj, *India* 68 H5
Kapaklı, *Turkey* 41 E11
Kapan, *Armenia* 70 B5
Kapanga, *Dem. Rep. of the Congo* 84 F4
Kapchagai = Qapshaghay, *Kazakstan* 50 E8
Kapela = Velika Kapela, *Croatia* 29 C12
Kapéllo, Ákra, *Greece* 38 E5
Kapema, *Dem. Rep. of the Congo* 87 E2
Kapfenberg, *Austria* 26 D8
Kapı Dağı, *Turkey* 41 F11
Kapiri Mposhi, *Zambia* 87 E2
Kapiskau →, *Canada* 102 B3
Kapit, *Malaysia* 62 D4
Kapiti I., *N.Z.* 91 J5
Kaplan, *U.S.A.* 113 K8
Kaplice, *Czech Rep.* 26 C7
Kapoe, *Thailand* 65 H2
Kapoeta, *Sudan* 81 G3
Kápolnásnyék, *Hungary* 42 C3
Kapos →, *Hungary* 42 D3
Kaposvár, *Hungary* 42 D2
Kapowsin, *U.S.A.* 116 D4
Kappeln, *Germany* 24 A5
Kappelshamn, *Sweden* 11 G12
Kapps, *Namibia* 88 C2
Kaprije, *Croatia* 29 E12
Kapsan, *N. Korea* 57 D15
Kapsukas = Marijampolė, *Lithuania* 9 J20
Kapuas →, *Indonesia* 62 E3
Kapuas Hulu, Pegunungan, *Malaysia* 62 D4
Kapuas Hulu Ra. = Kapuas Hulu, Pegunungan, *Malaysia* 62 D4
Kapulo, *Dem. Rep. of the Congo* 87 D2
Kapunda, *Australia* 95 E2
Kapuni, *N.Z.* 91 H5
Kapurthala, *India* 68 D6
Kapuskasing, *Canada* 102 C3
Kapuskasing →, *Canada* 102 C3
Kapustin Yar, *Russia* 49 F7
Kaputar, *Australia* 95 E5
Kaputir, *Kenya* 86 B4
Kapuvár, *Hungary* 42 C2
Kara, *Russia* 50 C7
Karā, W. →, *Si. Arabia* 80 C5
Kara Ada, *Turkey* 39 E9
Kara Bogaz Gol, Zaliv = Garabogazköl Aylagy, *Turkmenistan* 50 E6
Kara Burun, *Turkey* 39 E9
Kara Kalpak Republic = Karakalpakstan □, *Uzbekistan* 50 E6
Kara Kum, *Turkmenistan* 50 F6
Kara Sea, *Russia* 50 B7
Karaadilli, *Turkey* 39 C12
Karabiğa, *Turkey* 41 F11
Karabük, *Turkey* 72 B5
Karaburun, *Turkey* 39 C8
Karaburuni, *Albania* 40 F3
Karabutak = Qarabutaq, *Kazakstan* 50 E7
Karacabey, *Turkey* 41 F12
Karacakılavuz, *Turkey* 41 E11
Karacaköy, *Turkey* 41 E12
Karacasu, *Turkey* 39 D10
Karachala = Qaraçala, *Azerbaijan* 49 L9
Karachayevsk, *Russia* 49 J5
Karachev, *Russia* 47 F8
Karachey-Cherkessia □, *Russia* 49 J5
Karachi, *Pakistan* 68 G2
Karad, *India* 66 L9
Karadirek, *Turkey* 39 C12
Karaga, *Ghana* 83 D4
Karaganda = Qaraghandy, *Kazakstan* 50 E8
Karagayly, *Kazakstan* 50 E8
Karaginskiy, Ostrov, *Russia* 51 D17
Karagola Road, *India* 69 G12
Karagüney Dağları, *Turkey* 72 B6
Karahallı, *Turkey* 39 C11
Karaikal, *India* 66 P11
Karaikkudi, *India* 66 P11
Karaisali, *Turkey* 72 D6
Karaj, *Iran* 71 C6
Karak, *Malaysia* 65 L4
Karakalpakstan □, *Uzbekistan* 50 E6
Karakelong, *Indonesia* 63 D7
Karakitang, *Indonesia* 63 D7
Karaklis = Vanadzor, *Armenia* 49 K7
Karakoçan, *Turkey* 73 C9
Karakoram Pass, *Pakistan* 69 B7
Karakoram Ra., *Pakistan* 69 B7
Karakurt, *Turkey* 73 B10
Karakuwisa, *Namibia* 88 B2
Karalon, *Russia* 51 D12
Karama, *Jordan* 75 D4
Karaman, *Balıkesir, Turkey* 39 B9
Karaman, *Konya, Turkey* 70 B2
Karamanlı, *Turkey* 39 D11
Karamay, *China* 60 B3
Karambu, *Indonesia* 62 E5
Karamea Bight, *N.Z.* 91 J3
Karamnasa →, *India* 69 G10
Karamürsel, *Turkey* 41 F13
Karand, *Iran* 70 C5
Karangana, *Mali* 82 C3
Karanganyar, *Indonesia* 63 G13
Karanjia, *India* 69 J11
Karankasso, *Burkina Faso* 82 C4
Karaova, *Turkey* 39 D9
Karapınar, *Turkey* 72 D5
Karasburg, *Namibia* 88 D2
Karasino, *Russia* 50 C9
Karasjok, *Norway* 8 B21
Karasu, *Turkey* 72 B4
Karasu →, *Turkey* 39 E12
Karasuk, *Russia* 50 D8
Karasuyama, *Japan* 55 F10
Karataş, *Adana, Turkey* 72 D6
Karataş, *Manisa, Turkey* 39 C10
Karataş Burnu, *Turkey* 72 D6
Karatau = Qarataū, *Kazakstan* 50 E8
Karatau, Khrebet, *Kazakstan* 50 E7
Karatoprak, *Turkey* 39 D9
Karatsu, *Japan* 55 H5
Karaul, *Russia* 50 B9
Karauli, *India* 68 F7
Karavastasë, L. e, *Albania* 40 F3
Karávi, *Greece* 38 E5
Karavostasi, *Cyprus* 36 D11
Karawang, *Indonesia* 63 G12
Karawanken, *Europe* 26 E7
Karayazı, *Turkey* 73 C10
Karazhal, *Kazakstan* 50 E8
Karbalā', *Iraq* 70 C5
Kårböle, *Sweden* 10 C9
Karcag, *Hungary* 42 C5
Karcha →, *Pakistan* 69 B7
Karchana, *India* 69 G9
Karczew, *Poland* 45 F8
Kardam, *Bulgaria* 41 C12
Kardeljovo = Ploče, *Croatia* 29 E14
Kardhámila, *Greece* 39 C8
Kardhamíli, *Greece* 38 E4
Kardhítsa, *Greece* 38 B3
Kardhítsa □, *Greece* 38 B3
Kärdla, *Estonia* 9 G20
Kareeberge, *S. Africa* 88 E3
Kareha →, *India* 69 G12
Kareima, *Sudan* 80 D3
Karelia □, *Russia* 50 C4
Karelian Republic = Karelia □, *Russia* 50 C4
Karera, *India* 68 G8
Karevāndar, *Iran* 71 E9
Kargasok, *Russia* 50 D9
Kargat, *Russia* 50 D9
Kargı, *Turkey* 72 B6
Kargil, *India* 69 B7
Kargopol, *Russia* 46 B10
Kargowa, *Poland* 45 F2

Karguéri

Karguéri, *Niger* 83 C7
Karhal, *India* 69 F8
Kariá, *Greece* 38 C2
Kariaí, *Greece* 41 F8
Karīān, *Iran* 71 E8
Karianga, *Madag.* 89 C8
Kariba, *Zimbabwe* 87 F2
Kariba, L., *Zimbabwe* 87 F2
Kariba Dam, *Zimbabwe* 87 F2
Kariba Gorge, *Zambia* 87 F2
Karibib, *Namibia* 88 C2
Karimata, Kepulauan, *Indonesia* 62 E3
Karimata, Selat, *Indonesia* 62 E3
Karimata Is. = Karimata, Kepulauan, *Indonesia* 62 E3
Karimnagar, *India* 66 K11
Karimunjawa, Kepulauan, *Indonesia* 62 F4
Karin, *Somali Rep.* 74 E4
Káristos, *Greece* 38 C6
Karīt, *Iran* 71 C8
Kariya, *Japan* 55 G8
Kariyangwe, *Zimbabwe* 89 B4
Karjala, *Finland* 46 A5
Karkaralinsk = Qarqaraly, *Kazakstan* 50 E8
Karkheh →, *Iran* 70 D5
Karkinitska Zatoka, *Ukraine* 47 K7
Karkinitskiy Zaliv = Karkinitska Zatoka, *Ukraine* 47 K7
Karkur Tohl, *Egypt* 80 C2
Karl Liebknecht, *Russia* 47 G8
Karl-Marx-Stadt = Chemnitz, *Germany* 24 E8
Karlholmsbruk, *Sweden* 10 D11
Karlino, *Poland* 44 D2
Karlivka, *Ukraine* 47 H8
Karlobag, *Croatia* 29 D12
Karlovac, *Croatia* 29 C12
Karlovka = Karlivka, *Ukraine* 47 H8
Karlovo, *Bulgaria* 41 D8
Karlovy Vary, *Czech Rep.* 26 A5
Karlsbad = Karlovy Vary, *Czech Rep.* 26 A5
Karlsborg, *Sweden* 11 F8
Karlshamn, *Sweden* 11 H8
Karlskoga, *Sweden* 10 E8
Karlskrona, *Sweden* 11 H9
Karlsruhe, *Germany* 25 F4
Karlstad, *Sweden* 10 E7
Karlstad, *U.S.A.* 112 A6
Karlstadt, *Germany* 25 F5
Karma, *Niger* 83 C5
Karmėlava, *Lithuania* 44 D11
Karmi'el, *Israel* 75 C4
Karnak, *Egypt* 79 C12
Karnal, *India* 68 E7
Karnali →, *Nepal* 69 E9
Karnaphuli Res., *Bangla.* 67 H18
Karnaprayag, *India* 69 D8
Karnataka □, *India* 66 N10
Karnes City, *U.S.A.* 113 L6
Karnische Alpen, *Europe* 26 E6
Karnobat, *Bulgaria* 41 D10
Kärnten □, *Austria* 26 E6
Karo, *Mali* 82 C4
Karoi, *Zimbabwe* 87 F2
Karonga, *Malawi* 87 D3
Karoonda, *Australia* 95 F2
Karor, *Pakistan* 68 D4
Karora, *Sudan* 80 D4
Káros, *Greece* 39 E7
Karounga, *Mali* 82 B3
Karousádhes, *Greece* 38 B1
Karpacz, *Poland* 45 H2
Karpasia □, *Cyprus* 36 D13
Kárpathos, *Greece* 39 F9
Kárpathos, Stenón, *Greece* 39 F9
Karpenísion, *Greece* 38 C3
Karpuz Burnu = Apostolos Andreas, C., *Cyprus* 36 D13
Karpuzlu, *Turkey* 39 D9
Karratha, *Australia* 92 D2
Kars, *Turkey* 73 B10
Karsakpay, *Kazakstan* 50 E7
Karsha, *Kazakstan* 48 F10
Karshi = Qarshi, *Uzbekistan* 50 F7
Karsiyang, *India* 69 F13
Karsog, *India* 68 D7
Karst = Kras, *Croatia* 29 C10
Kartal, *Turkey* 41 F13
Kartál Óros, *Greece* 41 E9
Kartaly, *Russia* 50 D7
Kartapur, *India* 68 D6
Karthaus, *U.S.A.* 110 E6
Kartuzy, *Poland* 44 D5
Karufa, *Indonesia* 63 E8
Karumba, *Australia* 94 B3
Karumo, *Tanzania* 86 C3
Karumwa, *Tanzania* 86 C3
Kārūn →, *Iran* 71 D6
Karungu, *Kenya* 86 C3
Karup, *Denmark* 11 H3
Karviná, *Czech Rep.* 27 B11
Karwan →, *India* 68 F8
Karwar, *India* 66 M9
Karwi, *India* 69 G9
Kaş, *Turkey* 39 E11
Kasaba, *Turkey* 39 E11
Kasache, *Malawi* 87 E3
Kasai →, *Dem. Rep. of the Congo* 84 E3
Kasaï-Oriental □, *Dem. Rep. of the Congo* 86 D1
Kasaji, *Dem. Rep. of the Congo* 87 E1
Kasama, *Zambia* 87 E3
Kasan-dong, *N. Korea* 57 D14
Kasane, *Namibia* 88 B3
Kasanga, *Tanzania* 87 D3
Kasar, Ras, *Sudan* 80 D4
Kasaragod, *India* 66 N9
Kasba L., *Canada* 105 A8
Kāseh Garān, *Iran* 70 C5
Kasempa, *Zambia* 87 E2
Kasenga, *Dem. Rep. of the Congo* 87 E2
Kasese, *Uganda* 86 B3
Kasewa, *Zambia* 87 E2
Kasganj, *India* 69 F8
Kashabowie, *Canada* 102 C1
Kashaf, *Iran* 71 C9
Kāshān, *Iran* 71 C6
Kashechewan, *Canada* 102 B3
Kashi, *China* 60 C2
Kashimbo, *Dem. Rep. of the Congo* 87 E2
Kashin, *Russia* 46 D9
Kashipur, *India* 69 E8
Kashira, *Russia* 46 E10
Kashiwazaki, *Japan* 55 F9
Kashk-e Kohneh, *Afghan.* 66 B3
Kashkū'īyeh, *Iran* 71 D7
Kāshmar, *Iran* 71 C8
Kashmir, *Asia* 69 C7
Kashmor, *Pakistan* 68 E3
Kashpirovka, *Russia* 48 D9
Kashun Noerh = Gaxun Nur, *China* 60 B5
Kasiari, *India* 69 H12
Kasimov, *Russia* 48 C5
Kasinge, *Dem. Rep. of the Congo* 86 D2
Kasiruta, *Indonesia* 63 E7
Kaskaskia →, *U.S.A.* 112 G10
Kaskattama →, *Canada* 105 B10
Kaskinen, *Finland* 9 E19
Kaslo, *Canada* 104 D5
Kasmere L., *Canada* 105 B8
Kasongo, *Dem. Rep. of the Congo* 86 C2
Kasongo Lunda, *Dem. Rep. of the Congo* 84 F3
Kásos, *Greece* 39 F8
Kásos, Stenón, *Greece* 39 F8
Kaspi, *Georgia* 49 K7
Kaspichan, *Bulgaria* 41 C11
Kaspiysk, *Russia* 49 J8
Kaspiyskiy, *Russia* 49 H8
Kassab ed Doleib, *Sudan* 81 E3
Kassaba, *Egypt* 80 C2
Kassalâ, *Sudan* 81 D4
Kassalâ □, *Sudan* 81 D4
Kassándra, *Greece* 40 F7
Kassándrinon, *Greece* 40 F7
Kassel, *Germany* 24 D5
Kassinger, *Sudan* 80 D3
Kassiópi, *Greece* 36 A3
Kasson, *U.S.A.* 112 C8
Kastamonu, *Turkey* 72 B5
Kastav, *Croatia* 29 C11
Kastélli, *Greece* 36 D5
Kastéllion, *Greece* 36 D7
Kastellórizon = Megiste, *Greece* 39 E11
Kástellos, *Greece* 39 E9
Kastellou, Ákra, *Greece* 39 F9
Kasterlee, *Belgium* 17 C4
Kastlösa, *Sweden* 11 H10
Kastóri, *Greece* 38 D4
Kastoría, *Greece* 40 F5
Kastoría □, *Greece* 40 F5
Kastorías, Límni, *Greece* 40 F5
Kastornoye, *Russia* 47 G10
Kastós, *Greece* 38 C2
Kastrosikiá, *Greece* 38 B2
Kastsyukovichy, *Belarus* 46 F7
Kasulu, *Tanzania* 86 C3
Kasumi, *Japan* 55 G7
Kasumkent, *Russia* 49 K9
Kasungu, *Malawi* 87 E3
Kasur, *Pakistan* 68 D6
Kataba, *Zambia* 87 F2
Katagum, *Nigeria* 83 C7
Katahdin, Mt., *U.S.A.* 109 C11
Katako Kombe, *Dem. Rep. of the Congo* 86 C1
Katákolon, *Greece* 38 D3
Katale, *Tanzania* 86 C3
Katanda, *Katanga, Dem. Rep. of the Congo* 86 D1
Katanda, *Nord-Kivu, Dem. Rep. of the Congo* 86 C2
Katanga □, *Dem. Rep. of the Congo* 86 D2
Katangi, *India* 66 J11
Katanning, *Australia* 93 F2
Katastári, *Greece* 38 D2
Katavi Swamp, *Tanzania* 86 D3
Kateríni, *Greece* 40 F6
Katghora, *India* 69 H10
Katherîna, Gebel, *Egypt* 70 D2
Katherine, *Australia* 92 B5
Katherine Gorge, *Australia* 92 B5
Kathi, *India* 68 J6
Kathiawar, *India* 68 H4
Kathikas, *Cyprus* 36 E11
Kathua, *India* 68 C6
Kati, *Mali* 82 C3
Katihar, *India* 69 G12
Katima Mulilo, *Zambia* 88 B3
Katimbira, *Malawi* 87 E3
Katingan = Mendawai →, *Indonesia* 62 E4
Katiola, *Ivory C.* 82 D3
Katlanovo, *Macedonia* 40 E5
Katmandu, *Nepal* 69 F11
Katni, *India* 69 H9
Kato Akhaïa, *Greece* 38 C3
Káto Arkhánai, *Greece* 36 D7
Káto Khorió, *Greece* 36 D7
Kato Pyrgos, *Cyprus* 36 D11
Káto Stavros, *Greece* 40 F7
Katokhí, *Greece* 38 C3
Katompe, *Dem. Rep. of the Congo* 86 D2
Katonga →, *Uganda* 86 B3
Katoomba, *Australia* 95 E5
Katoúna, *Greece* 38 C3
Katowice, *Poland* 45 H6
Katrancı Dağı, *Turkey* 39 D12
Katrine, L., *U.K.* 14 E4
Katrineholm, *Sweden* 11 E10
Katsepe, *Madag.* 89 B8
Katsina, *Nigeria* 83 C6
Katsina □, *Nigeria* 83 C6
Katsina Ala, *Nigeria* 83 D6
Katsina Ala →, *Nigeria* 83 D6
Katsumoto, *Japan* 55 H4
Katsuura, *Japan* 55 G10
Katsuyama, *Japan* 55 F8
Kattaviá, *Greece* 36 D9
Kattegat, *Denmark* 11 H5
Katthammarsvik, *Sweden* 11 G12
Katul, J., *Sudan* 81 E2
Katumba, *Dem. Rep. of the Congo* 86 D2
Katungu, *Kenya* 86 C5
Katwa, *India* 69 H13
Katwijk, *Neths.* 17 B4
Kąty Wrocławskie, *Poland* 45 G3
Kauai, *U.S.A.* 106 H15
Kauai Channel, *U.S.A.* 106 H15
Kaub, *Germany* 25 E3
Kaufbeuren, *Germany* 25 H6
Kaufman, *U.S.A.* 113 J6
Kauhajoki, *Finland* 9 E20
Kaukauna, *U.S.A.* 108 C1
Kaukauveld, *Namibia* 88 C3
Kaunakakai, *U.S.A.* 106 H16
Kaunas, *Lithuania* 9 J20
Kaunia, *Bangla.* 69 G13
Kaunos, *Turkey* 39 E10
Kaura Namoda, *Nigeria* 83 C6
Kauru, *Nigeria* 83 C6
Kautokeino, *Norway* 8 B20
Kauwapur, *India* 69 F10
Kavacha, *Russia* 51 C17
Kavadarci, *Macedonia* 40 E6
Kavaja, *Albania* 40 E3
Kavak, *Turkey* 72 B7
Kavak Dağı, *Turkey* 39 D10
Kavaklı, *Turkey* 41 E11
Kavaklıdere, *Turkey* 39 D10
Kavalerovo, *Russia* 54 B7
Kavali, *India* 66 M12
Kavála, *Greece* 41 F8
Kavála □, *Greece* 41 E8
Kavála Kólpos, *Greece* 41 F8
Kavār, *Iran* 71 D7
Kavarna, *Bulgaria* 41 C12
Kavi, *India* 68 H5
Kavimba, *Botswana* 88 B3
Kavīr, Dasht-e, *Iran* 71 C7
Kavkaz, *Russia* 47 K9
Kävlinge, *Sweden* 11 J7
Kavos, *Greece* 36 B4
Kavoúsi, *Greece* 39 F7
Kaw, *Fr. Guiana* 125 C8
Kawa, *Sudan* 81 E3
Kawagama L., *Canada* 110 A6
Kawagoe, *Japan* 55 G9
Kawaguchi, *Japan* 55 G9
Kawaihae, *U.S.A.* 106 H17
Kawambwa, *Zambia* 87 D2
Kawanoe, *Japan* 55 G6
Kawardha, *India* 69 J9
Kawasaki, *Japan* 55 G9
Kawasi, *Indonesia* 63 E7
Kawerau, *N.Z.* 91 H6
Kawhia Harbour, *N.Z.* 91 H5
Kawio, Kepulauan, *Indonesia* 63 D7
Kawnro, *Burma* 67 H21
Kawthaung, *Burma* 65 H2
Kawthoolei = Kawthule □, *Burma* 67 L20
Kawthule □, *Burma* 67 L20
Kaxholmen, *Sweden* 11 G8
Kaya, *Burkina Faso* 83 C4
Kayah □, *Burma* 67 K20
Kayalıköy Barajı, *Turkey* 41 E11
Kayan →, *Indonesia* 62 D5
Kaycee, *U.S.A.* 114 E10
Kayeli, *Indonesia* 63 E7
Kayenta, *U.S.A.* 115 H8
Kayes, *Mali* 82 C2
Kayı, *Turkey* 39 B12
Kayima, *S. Leone* 82 D2
Kayin = Kawthule □, *Burma* 67 L20
Kaymakçı, *Turkey* 39 C10
Kayoa, *Indonesia* 63 D7
Kayomba, *Zambia* 87 E1
Kaysatskoye, *Russia* 48 F8
Kayseri, *Turkey* 70 B2
Kaysville, *U.S.A.* 114 F8
Kaz Dağı, *Turkey* 39 B8
Kazachye, *Russia* 51 B14
Kazakstan ■, *Asia* 50 E7
Kazan, *Russia* 48 C9
Kazan →, *Canada* 105 A9
Kazan-Rettō, *Pac. Oc.* 96 E6
Kazanlŭk, *Bulgaria* 41 D9
Kazanskaya, *Russia* 48 F5
Kazatin = Kozyatyn, *Ukraine* 47 H5
Kazaure, *Nigeria* 83 C6
Kazbek, *Russia* 49 J7
Kāzerūn, *Iran* 71 D6
Kazi Magomed = Qazimämmäd, *Azerbaijan* 49 K9
Kazimierz Dolny, *Poland* 45 G8
Kazimierza Wielka, *Poland* 45 H7
Kazincbarcika, *Hungary* 42 B5
Kazlų Rūda, *Lithuania* 44 D10
Kaztalovka, *Kazakstan* 48 F9
Kazuno, *Japan* 54 D10
Kazym →, *Russia* 50 C7
Kcynia, *Poland* 45 F4
Ké-Macina, *Mali* 82 C3
Kéa, *Greece* 38 D6
Keady, *U.K.* 15 B5
Kearney, *U.S.A.* 112 E5
Kearny, *U.S.A.* 115 K8
Kearsarge, Mt., *U.S.A.* 111 C13
Keban, *Turkey* 73 C8
Keban Baraji, *Turkey* 70 B3
Kebbi □, *Nigeria* 83 C5
Kébi, *Ivory C.* 82 D3
Kebnekaise, *Sweden* 8 C18
Kebri Dehar, *Ethiopia* 74 F3
Kebumen, *Indonesia* 63 G13
Kecel, *Hungary* 42 D4
Kechika →, *Canada* 104 B3
Keçiborlu, *Turkey* 39 D12
Kecskemét, *Hungary* 42 D4
Kedada, *Ethiopia* 81 F4
Kėdainiai, *Lithuania* 9 J21
Kedarnath, *India* 69 D8
Kedgwick, *Canada* 103 C6
Kédhros Óros, *Greece* 36 D6
Kediri, *Indonesia* 63 G15
Kedjebi, *Ghana* 83 D5
Kédougou, *Senegal* 82 C2
Kędzierzyn-Koźle, *Poland* 45 H5
Keeler, *U.S.A.* 116 J9
Keeley L., *Canada* 105 C7
Keeling Is. = Cocos Is., *Ind. Oc.* 96 J1
Keelung = Chilung, *Taiwan* 59 E13
Keene, *Canada* 110 B6
Keene, *Calif., U.S.A.* 117 K8
Keene, *N.H., U.S.A.* 111 D12
Keene, *N.Y., U.S.A.* 111 B11
Keeper Hill, *Ireland* 15 D3
Keer-Weer, C., *Australia* 94 A3
Keeseville, *U.S.A.* 111 B11
Keetmanshoop, *Namibia* 88 D2
Keewatin, *Canada* 105 D10
Keewatin →, *Canada* 105 B8
Kefa □, *Ethiopia* 81 F4
Kefallinía, *Greece* 38 C2
Kefallinía □, *Greece* 38 C2
Kéfalos, *Greece* 39 E8
Kefamenanu, *Indonesia* 63 F6
Kefar Sava, *Israel* 75 C3
Keffi, *Nigeria* 83 D6
Keffin Hausa, *Nigeria* 83 C6
Keflavík, *Iceland* 8 D2
Keftya, *Ethiopia* 81 E4
Keg River, *Canada* 104 B5
Kegaska, *Canada* 103 B7
Keheili, *Sudan* 80 D3
Kehl, *Germany* 25 G3
Keighley, *U.K.* 12 D6
Keila, *Estonia* 9 G21
Keimoes, *S. Africa* 88 D3
Keita, *Niger* 83 C6
Keitele, *Finland* 8 E22
Keith, *Australia* 95 F3
Keith, *U.K.* 14 D6
Keizer, *U.S.A.* 114 D2
Kejimkujik Nat. Park, *Canada* 103 D6
Kejser Franz Joseph Fd., *Greenland* 4 B6
Kekri, *India* 68 G6
Kelam, *Ethiopia* 81 G4
Kelamet, *Eritrea* 81 D4
Kelan, *China* 56 E6
Kelang, *Malaysia* 65 L3
Kelantan →, *Malaysia* 65 J4
Këlcyra, *Albania* 40 F4
Kelekçi, *Turkey* 39 D11
Keles, *Turkey* 41 G13
Keleti-főcsatorna, *Hungary* 42 C6
Kelheim, *Germany* 25 G7
Kelkit, *Turkey* 73 B8
Kelkit →, *Turkey* 72 B7
Kellerberrin, *Australia* 93 F2
Kellett, C., *Canada* 4 B1
Kelleys I., *U.S.A.* 110 E2
Kellogg, *U.S.A.* 114 C5
Kells = Ceanannus Mor, *Ireland* 15 C5
Kelmė, *Lithuania* 44 C9
Kelokedhara, *Cyprus* 36 E11
Kelowna, *Canada* 104 D5
Kelseyville, *U.S.A.* 116 G4
Kelso, *N.Z.* 91 L2
Kelso, *U.K.* 14 F6
Kelso, *U.S.A.* 116 D4
Keluang, *Malaysia* 65 L4
Kelvington, *Canada* 105 C8
Kem, *Russia* 50 C4
Kema, *Indonesia* 63 D7
Kemah, *Turkey* 70 B3
Kemaliye, *Erzincan, Turkey* 73 C8
Kemaliye, *Manisa, Turkey* 39 C10
Kemalpaşa, *Turkey* 39 C9
Kemaman, *Malaysia* 62 D2
Kemano, *Canada* 104 C3
Kemasik, *Malaysia* 65 K4
Kembolcha, *Ethiopia* 81 E4
Kemer, *Antalya, Turkey* 39 E12
Kemer, *Burdur, Turkey* 39 D12
Kemer, *Muğla, Turkey* 39 E11
Kemer Barajı, *Turkey* 39 D10
Kemerovo, *Russia* 50 D9
Kemi, *Finland* 8 D21
Kemi älv = Kemijoki →, *Finland* 8 D21
Kemijärvi, *Finland* 8 C22
Kemijoki →, *Finland* 8 D21
Kemmerer, *U.S.A.* 114 F8
Kemmuna = Comino, *Malta* 36 C1
Kemp, L., *U.S.A.* 113 J5
Kemp Land, *Antarctica* 5 C5
Kempsey, *Australia* 95 E5
Kempt, L., *Canada* 102 C5
Kempten, *Germany* 25 H6
Kempton, *Australia* 94 G4
Kemptville, *Canada* 102 D4
Ken →, *India* 69 G9
Kenai, *U.S.A.* 100 B4
Kendai, *India* 69 H10
Kendal, *Indonesia* 63 G14
Kendal, *U.K.* 12 C5
Kendall, *Australia* 95 E5
Kendall, *U.S.A.* 109 N5
Kendall →, *Australia* 94 A3
Kendallville, *U.S.A.* 108 E3
Kendari, *Indonesia* 63 E6
Kendawangan, *Indonesia* 62 E4
Kende, *Nigeria* 83 C5
Kendrapara, *India* 67 J15
Këndrevicës, Maja e, *Albania* 40 F3
Kendrew, *S. Africa* 88 E3
Kene Thao, *Laos* 64 D3
Kenedy, *U.S.A.* 113 L6
Kenema, *S. Leone* 82 D2
Keng Kok, *Laos* 64 D5
Keng Tawng, *Burma* 67 J21
Keng Tung, *Burma* 58 G2
Kengeja, *Tanzania* 86 D4
Kenhardt, *S. Africa* 88 D3
Kéniéba, *Mali* 82 C2
Kenitra, *Morocco* 78 B4
Kenli, *China* 57 F10
Kenmare, *Ireland* 15 E2
Kenmare, *U.S.A.* 112 A3
Kenmare River, *Ireland* 15 E2
Kennebago Lake, *U.S.A.* 111 A14
Kennebec, *U.S.A.* 112 D5
Kennebec →, *U.S.A.* 109 D11
Kennebunk, *U.S.A.* 111 C14
Kennedy, *Zimbabwe* 88 B4
Kennedy Ra., *Australia* 93 D2
Kennedy Taungdeik, *Burma* 67 H18
Kenner, *U.S.A.* 113 L9
Kennet →, *U.K.* 13 F7
Kenneth Ra., *Australia* 93 D2
Kennett, *U.S.A.* 113 G9
Kennewick, *U.S.A.* 114 C4
Kenogami →, *Canada* 102 B3
Kenora, *Canada* 105 D10
Kenosha, *U.S.A.* 108 D2
Kensington, *Canada* 103 C7
Kent, *Ohio, U.S.A.* 110 E3
Kent, *Tex., U.S.A.* 113 K2
Kent, *Wash., U.S.A.* 116 C4
Kent □, *U.K.* 13 F8
Kent Group, *Australia* 94 F4
Kent Pen., *Canada* 100 B9
Kentau, *Kazakstan* 50 E7
Kentland, *U.S.A.* 108 E2
Kenton, *U.S.A.* 108 E4
Kentucky □, *U.S.A.* 108 G3
Kentucky →, *U.S.A.* 108 F3
Kentucky L., *U.S.A.* 109 G2
Kentville, *Canada* 103 C7
Kentwood, *U.S.A.* 113 K9
Kenya ■, *Africa* 86 B4
Kenya, Mt., *Kenya* 86 C4
Keo Neua, Deo, *Vietnam* 64 C5
Keokuk, *U.S.A.* 112 E9
Keonjhargarh, *India* 69 J11
Kep, *Cambodia* 65 G5
Kep, *Vietnam* 64 B6
Kepez, *Turkey* 41 F10
Kepi, *Indonesia* 63 F9
Kępice, *Poland* 44 D3
Kępno, *Poland* 45 G4
Kepsut, *Turkey* 39 B10
Kerala □, *India* 66 P10
Kerama-Rettō, *Japan* 55 L3
Keran, *Pakistan* 69 B5
Kerang, *Australia* 95 F3
Keranyo, *Ethiopia* 81 F4
Kerao →, *Sudan* 81 E3
Keratéa, *Greece* 38 D5
Keraudren, C., *Australia* 92 C2
Kerava, *Finland* 9 F21
Kerch, *Ukraine* 47 K9
Kerchenskiy Proliv, *Black Sea* 47 K9
Kerchoual, *Mali* 83 B5
Kerempe Burnu, *Turkey* 72 A5
Keren, *Eritrea* 81 D4
Kerewan, *Gambia* 82 C1
Kerguelen, *Ind. Oc.* 3 G13
Keri, *Greece* 38 D2
Keri Kera, *Sudan* 81 E3
Kericho, *Kenya* 86 C4
Kerinci, *Indonesia* 62 E2
Kerki, *Turkmenistan* 50 F7
Kerkinitis, Límni, *Greece* 40 E7
Kérkira, *Greece* 36 A3
Kérkira □, *Greece* 38 B1
Kerkrade, *Neths.* 17 D6
Kerma, *Sudan* 80 D3
Kermadec Is., *Pac. Oc.* 96 L10
Kermadec Trench, *Pac. Oc.* 96 L10
Kermān, *Iran* 71 D8
Kerman, *U.S.A.* 116 J6
Kermān □, *Iran* 71 D8
Kermān, Bīābān-e, *Iran* 71 D8
Kermānshāh = Bākhtarān, *Iran* 70 C5
Kermen, *Bulgaria* 41 D10

Kermit, U.S.A. 113 K3
Kern →, U.S.A. 117 K7
Kernhof, Austria 26 D8
Kernville, U.S.A. 117 K8
Keroh, Malaysia 65 K3
Kérou, Benin 83 C5
Kérouane, Guinea 82 D3
Kerpen, Germany 24 E2
Kerrera, U.K. 14 E3
Kerrobert, Canada 105 C7
Kerrville, U.S.A. 113 K5
Kerry □, Ireland 15 D2
Kerry Hd., Ireland 15 D2
Kersa, Ethiopia 81 F5
Kerulen →, Asia 60 B6
Kerzaz, Algeria 78 C5
Kesagami →, Canada 102 B4
Kesagami L., Canada 102 B3
Keşan, Turkey 41 F10
Kesennuma, Japan 54 E10
Keshit, Iran 71 D8
Keşiş Dağ, Turkey 73 C8
Keskin, Turkey 72 C5
Kestell, S. Africa 89 D4
Kestenga, Russia 50 C4
Keswick, U.K. 12 C4
Keszthely, Hungary 42 D2
Ket →, Russia 50 D9
Keta, Ghana 83 D5
Keta Lagoon, Ghana 83 D5
Ketapang, Indonesia 62 E4
Ketchikan, U.S.A. 104 B2
Ketchum, U.S.A. 114 E6
Kete Krachi, Ghana 83 D4
Ketef, Khalîg Umm el, Egypt 70 F2
Keti Bandar, Pakistan 68 G2
Kétou, Benin 83 D5
Ketri, India 68 E6
Kętrzyn, Poland 44 D8
Kettering, U.K. 13 E7
Kettering, U.S.A. 108 F3
Kettle →, Canada 105 B11
Kettle Falls, U.S.A. 114 B4
Kettle Pt., Canada 110 C2
Kettleman City, U.S.A. 116 J7
Kęty, Poland 45 J6
Keuka L., U.S.A. 110 D7
Keuruu, Finland 9 E21
Kevelaer, Germany 24 D2
Kewanee, U.S.A. 112 E10
Kewaunee, U.S.A. 108 C2
Keweenaw B., U.S.A. 108 B1
Keweenaw Pen., U.S.A. 108 B2
Keweenaw Pt., U.S.A. 108 B2
Key Largo, U.S.A. 109 N5
Key West, U.S.A. 107 F10
Keyala, Sudan 81 G3
Keynsham, U.K. 13 F5
Keyser, U.S.A. 108 F6
Kezhma, Russia 51 D11
Kezi, Zimbabwe 89 C4
Kežmarok, Slovak Rep. 27 B13
Khabarovsk, Russia 51 E14
Khabr, Iran 71 D8
Khābūr →, Syria 70 C4
Khachmas = Xaçmaz, Azerbaijan 49 K9
Khachrod, India 68 H6
Khadari, W. el →, Sudan 81 E2
Khadro, Pakistan 68 F3
Khadyzhensk, Russia 49 H4
Khadzhilyangar, India 69 B8
Khaga, India 69 G9
Khagaria, India 69 G12
Khaipur, Pakistan 68 E5
Khair, India 68 F7
Khairabad, India 69 F9
Khairagarh, India 69 J9
Khairpur, Pakistan 68 F3
Khairpur Nathan Shah, Pakistan 68 F2
Khairwara, India 68 H5
Khaisor →, Pakistan 68 D3
Khajuri Kach, Pakistan 68 C3
Khakassia □, Russia 50 D9
Khakhea, Botswana 88 C3
Khalafābād, Iran 71 D6
Khalilabad, India 69 F10
Khalīlī, Iran 71 E7
Khalkhāl, Iran 71 B6
Khálki, Dhodhekánisos, Greece 39 E9
Khálki, Thessalía, Greece 38 B4
Khalkidhikí □, Greece 40 F7
Khalkís, Greece 38 C5
Khalmer-Sede = Tazovskiy, Russia 50 C8
Khalmer Yu, Russia 50 C7
Khalūf, Oman 74 C6
Kham Keut, Laos 64 C5
Khamaria, India 69 H9
Khambhaliya, India 68 H3
Khambhat, India 68 H5
Khambhat, G. of, India 66 J8
Khamilonísion, Greece 39 F8
Khamīr, Iran 71 E7
Khamir, Yemen 74 D3
Khamsa, Egypt 75 E1
Khan →, Namibia 88 C2
Khān Abū Shāmat, Syria 75 B5
Khān Azād, Iraq 70 C5
Khān Mujiddah, Iraq 70 C4
Khān Shaykhūn, Syria 70 C3
Khān Yūnis, Gaza Strip 75 D3
Khanai, Pakistan 68 D2
Khānaqīn, Iraq 70 C5
Khānbāghī, Iran 71 B7
Khandrá, Greece 39 F8
Khandwa, India 66 J10
Khandyga, Russia 51 C14
Khāneh, Iran 70 B5
Khanewal, Pakistan 68 D4
Khangah Dogran, Pakistan 68 D5
Khanh Duong, Vietnam 64 F7
Khaniá, Greece 36 D6
Khaniá □, Greece 36 D6
Khaniadhana, India 68 G8
Khaníon, Kólpos, Greece 36 D5
Khanka, L., Asia 51 E14
Khankendy = Xankändi, Azerbaijan 70 B5
Khanna, India 68 D7
Khanozai, Pakistan 68 D2
Khanpur, Pakistan 68 E4
Khanty-Mansiysk, Russia 50 C7
Khapalu, Pakistan 69 B7
Khapcheranga, Russia 51 E12
Kharabali, Russia 49 G8
Kharaghoda, India 68 H4
Kharagpur, India 69 H12
Khárakas, Greece 36 D7
Kharan Kalat, Pakistan 66 E4
Kharānaq, Iran 71 C7
Kharda, India 66 K9
Khardung La, India 69 B7
Khârga, El Wâhât-el, Egypt 80 B3
Khargon, India 66 J9
Khari →, India 68 G6
Kharian, Pakistan 68 C5
Kharit, Wadi el →, Egypt 80 C3
Khārk, Jazīreh-ye, Iran 71 D6
Kharkiv, Ukraine 47 H9
Kharkov = Kharkiv, Ukraine 47 H9
Kharmanli, Bulgaria 41 E9
Kharovsk, Russia 46 C11
Kharsawangarh, India 69 H11
Kharta, Turkey 72 B3
Khartoum = El Khartûm, Sudan 81 D3
Khasan, Russia 54 C5
Khasavyurt, Russia 49 J8
Khāsh, Iran 66 E2
Khashm el Girba, Sudan 81 E4
Khashum, Sudan 81 E2
Khashuri, Georgia 49 J6
Khaskovo, Bulgaria 41 E9
Khaskovo □, Bulgaria 41 E9
Khatanga, Russia 51 B11
Khatanga →, Russia 51 B11
Khatauli, India 68 E7
Khatra, India 69 H12
Khātūnābād, Iran 71 D7
Khatyrka, Russia 51 C18
Khavda, India 68 H3
Khaybar, Harrat, Si. Arabia 70 E4
Khayelitsha, S. Africa 85 L3
Khāzimiyah, Iraq 70 C4
Khazzān Jabal al Awliyā, Sudan 81 D3
Khe Bo, Vietnam 64 C5
Khe Long, Vietnam 64 B5
Khed Brahma, India 66 G8
Khekra, India 68 E7
Khemarak Phouminville, Cambodia 65 G4
Khemisset, Morocco 78 B4
Khemmarat, Thailand 64 D5
Khenāmān, Iran 71 D8
Khenchela, Algeria 78 A7
Khersān →, Iran 71 D6
Khérson, Greece 40 E6
Kherson, Ukraine 47 J7
Khersónisos Akrotíri, Greece 36 D6
Kheta →, Russia 51 B11
Khewari, Pakistan 68 F3
Khilchipur, India 68 G7
Khiliomódhion, Greece 38 D4
Khilok, Russia 51 D12
Khimki, Russia 46 E9
Khíos, Greece 39 C8
Khíos □, Greece 39 C8
Khirsadoh, India 69 H8
Khiuma = Hiiumaa, Estonia 9 G20
Khiva, Uzbekistan 50 E7
Khīyāv, Iran 70 B5
Khlebarovo, Bulgaria 41 C10
Khlong Khlung, Thailand 64 D2
Khmelnik, Ukraine 47 H4
Khmelnitskiy = Khmelnytskyy, Ukraine 47 H4
Khmelnytskyy, Ukraine 47 H4
Khmer Rep. = Cambodia ■, Asia 64 F5
Khoai, Hon, Vietnam 65 H5
Khodoriv, Ukraine 47 H3
Khodzent = Khudzhand, Tajikistan 50 E7
Khojak Pass, Afghan. 68 D2
Khok Kloi, Thailand 65 H2
Khok Pho, Thailand 65 J3
Kholm, Russia 46 D6
Kholmsk, Russia 51 E15
Khomas Hochland, Namibia 88 C2
Khombole, Senegal 82 C1
Khomeyn, Iran 71 C6
Khomeynī Shahr, Iran 71 C6
Khomodino, Botswana 88 C3
Khon Kaen, Thailand 64 D4
Khong →, Cambodia 64 F5
Khong Sedone, Laos 64 E5
Khonuu, Russia 51 C15
Khoper →, Russia 48 F6
Khor el 'Atash, Sudan 81 E3
Khóra, Greece 38 D3
Khóra Sfakíon, Greece 36 D6
Khorāsān □, Iran 71 C8
Khorat = Nakhon Ratchasima, Thailand 64 E4
Khorat, Cao Nguyen, Thailand 64 E4
Khorixas, Namibia 88 C1
Khorol, Ukraine 47 H7
Khorramābād, Khorāsān, Iran 71 C8
Khorramābād, Lorestān, Iran 71 C6
Khorrāmshahr, Iran 71 D6
Khorugh, Tajikistan 50 F8
Khosravī, Iran 71 D6
Khosrowābād, Khuzestān, Iran 71 D6
Khosrowābād, Kordestān, Iran 70 C5
Khost, Pakistan 68 D2
Khosūyeh, Iran 71 D7
Khotyn, Ukraine 47 H4
Khouribga, Morocco 78 B4
Khowai, Bangla. 67 G17
Khowst, Afghan. 68 C3
Khoyniki, Belarus 47 G5
Khrami →, Georgia 49 K7
Khrenovoye, Russia 48 E5
Khrisoúpolis, Greece 41 F8
Khristianá, Greece 39 E7
Khrysokhou B., Cyprus 36 D11
Khtapodhiá, Greece 39 D7
Khu Khan, Thailand 64 E5
Khudzhand, Tajikistan 50 E7
Khuff, Si. Arabia 70 E5
Khūgīānī, Afghan. 68 D1
Khuis, Botswana 88 D3
Khuiyala, India 68 F4
Khujner, India 68 H7
Khulna, Bangla. 67 H16
Khulna □, Bangla. 67 H16
Khulo, Georgia 49 K6
Khumago, Botswana 88 C3
Khūnsorkh, Iran 71 E8
Khunti, India 69 H11
Khūr, Iran 71 C8
Khurai, India 68 G8
Khurayş, Si. Arabia 71 E6
Khureit, Sudan 81 E2
Khurīyā Murīyā, Jazā 'ir, Oman 74 D6
Khurja, India 68 E7
Khūrmāl, Iraq 70 C5
Khurr, Wādī al, Iraq 70 C4
Khūsf, Iran 71 C8
Khush, Afghan. 66 C3
Khushab, Pakistan 68 C5
Khust, Ukraine 47 H2
Khuzdar, Pakistan 68 F2
Khūzestān □, Iran 71 D6
Khvāf, Iran 71 C9
Khvājeh, Iran 70 B5
Khvalynsk, Russia 48 D9
Khvānsār, Iran 71 D7
Khvatovka, Russia 48 D8
Khvor, Iran 71 C7
Khvorgū, Iran 71 E8
Khvormūj, Iran 71 D6
Khvoy, Iran 70 B5
Khvoynaya, Russia 46 C8
Khyber Pass, Afghan. 68 B4
Kiabukwa, Dem. Rep. of the Congo 87 D1
Kiama, Australia 95 E5
Kiamba, Phil. 61 H6
Kiambi, Dem. Rep. of the Congo 86 D2
Kiambu, Kenya 86 C4
Kiangara, Madag. 89 B8
Kiangsi = Jiangxi □, China 59 D11
Kiangsu = Jiangsu □, China 57 H11
Kiáton, Greece 38 C4
Kibæk, Denmark 11 H2
Kibanga Port, Uganda 86 B3
Kibara, Tanzania 86 C3
Kibare, Mts., Dem. Rep. of the Congo 86 D2
Kibombo, Dem. Rep. of the Congo 86 C2
Kibondo, Tanzania 86 C3
Kibre Mengist, Ethiopia 81 F4
Kibumbu, Burundi 86 C2
Kibungo, Rwanda 86 C3
Kibuye, Burundi 86 C2
Kibuye, Rwanda 86 C2
Kibwesa, Tanzania 86 D2
Kibwezi, Kenya 86 C4
Kicasalih, Turkey 41 E10
Kičevo, Macedonia 40 E4
Kichha, India 69 E8
Kichha →, India 69 E8
Kicking Horse Pass, Canada 104 C5
Kidal, Mali 83 B5
Kidderminster, U.K. 13 E5
Kidete, Tanzania 86 D4
Kidira, Senegal 82 C2
Kidnappers, C., N.Z. 91 H6
Kidsgrove, U.K. 12 D5
Kidston, Australia 94 B3
Kidugallo, Tanzania 86 D4
Kiel, Germany 24 A6
Kiel Canal = Nord-Ostsee-Kanal, Germany 24 A5
Kielce, Poland 45 H7
Kielder Water, U.K. 12 B5
Kieler Bucht, Germany 24 A6
Kiembara, Burkina Faso 82 C4
Kien Binh, Vietnam 65 H5
Kien Tan, Vietnam 65 G5
Kienge, Dem. Rep. of the Congo 87 E2
Kiessé, Niger 83 C5
Kiev = Kyyiv, Ukraine 47 G6
Kifaya, Guinea 82 C2
Kiffa, Mauritania 82 B2
Kifisiá, Greece 38 C5
Kifissós →, Greece 38 C5
Kifrī, Iraq 70 C5
Kigali, Rwanda 86 C3
Kigarama, Tanzania 86 C3
Kigelle, Sudan 81 F3
Kigoma □, Tanzania 86 D3
Kigoma-Ujiji, Tanzania 86 C2
Kigomasha, Ras, Tanzania 86 C4
Kığzı, Turkey 70 B4
Kihei, U.S.A. 106 H16
Kihnu, Estonia 9 G21
Kii-Sanchi, Japan 55 G8
Kii-Suidō, Japan 55 H7
Kikaiga-Shima, Japan 55 K4
Kikinda, Serbia, Yug. 42 E5
Kikládhes, Greece 38 E6
Kikládhes □, Greece 38 D6
Kikwit, Dem. Rep. of the Congo 84 E3
Kil, Sweden 10 E7
Kilafors, Sweden 10 C10
Kilar, India 68 C7
Kilauea, U.S.A. 106 J14
Kilauea Crater, U.S.A. 106 J17
Kilbrannan Sd., U.K. 14 F3
Kilchu, N. Korea 57 D15
Kilcoy, Australia 95 D5
Kildare, Ireland 15 C5
Kildare □, Ireland 15 C5
Kileikli, Sudan 81 E2
Kilfinnane, Ireland 15 D3
Kilgore, U.S.A. 113 J7
Kilibo, Benin 83 D5
Kilifi, Kenya 86 C4
Kilimanjaro, Tanzania 86 C4
Kilimanjaro □, Tanzania 86 C4
Kilimli, Turkey 72 B4
Kilindini, Kenya 86 C4
Kilis, Turkey 70 B3
Kiliya, Ukraine 47 K5
Kilkee, Ireland 15 D2
Kilkeel, U.K. 15 B5
Kilkenny, Ireland 15 D4
Kilkenny □, Ireland 15 D4
Kilkieran B., Ireland 15 C2
Kilkís, Greece 40 F6
Kilkís □, Greece 40 E6
Killala, Ireland 15 B2
Killala B., Ireland 15 B2
Killaloe, Ireland 15 D3
Killaloe Sta., Canada 110 A7
Killarney, Australia 95 D5
Killarney, Canada 105 D9
Killarney, Ireland 15 D2
Killary Harbour, Ireland 15 C2
Killdeer, U.S.A. 112 B3
Killeberg, Sweden 11 H8
Killeen, U.S.A. 113 K6
Killin, U.K. 14 E4
Killíni, Ilía, Greece 38 D3
Killíni, Korinthía, Greece 38 D4
Killorglin, Ireland 15 D2
Killybegs, Ireland 15 B3
Kilmarnock, U.K. 14 F4
Kilmez, Russia 48 B10
Kilmez →, Russia 48 B10
Kilmore, Australia 95 F3
Kilondo, Tanzania 87 D3
Kilosa, Tanzania 86 D4
Kilrush, Ireland 15 D2
Kilwa Kisiwani, Tanzania 87 D4
Kilwa Kivinje, Tanzania 87 D4
Kilwa Masoko, Tanzania 87 D4
Kilwinning, U.K. 14 F4
Kim, U.S.A. 113 G3
Kim →, Cameroon 83 D7
Kimaam, Indonesia 63 F9
Kimamba, Tanzania 86 D4
Kimba, Australia 95 E2
Kimball, Nebr., U.S.A. 112 E3
Kimball, S. Dak., U.S.A. 112 D5
Kimberley, Australia 92 C4
Kimberley, Canada 104 D5
Kimberley, S. Africa 88 D3
Kimberly, U.S.A. 114 E6
Kimch'aek, N. Korea 57 D15
Kimch'ŏn, S. Korea 57 F15
Kími, Greece 38 C6
Kimje, S. Korea 57 G14
Kimmirut, Canada 101 B13
Kímolos, Greece 38 E6
Kimovsk, Moskva, Russia 46 E9
Kimovsk, Tula, Russia 46 E10
Kimparana, Mali 82 C4
Kimpese, Dem. Rep. of the Congo 84 F2
Kimry, Russia 46 D9
Kimstad, Sweden 11 F9
Kinabalu, Gunong, Malaysia 62 C5
Kínaros, Greece 39 E8
Kinaskan L., Canada 104 B2
Kinbasket L., Canada 104 C5
Kincardine, Canada 102 D3
Kincolith, Canada 104 B3
Kinda, Dem. Rep. of the Congo 87 D2
Kindberg, Austria 26 D8
Kinde, U.S.A. 110 C2
Kinder Scout, U.K. 12 D6
Kindersley, Canada 105 C7
Kindia, Guinea 82 D2
Kindu, Dem. Rep. of the Congo 86 C2
Kinel, Russia 48 D10
Kineshma, Russia 48 B6
Kinesi, Tanzania 86 C3
King, L., Australia 93 F2
King, Mt., Australia 94 D4
King City, U.S.A. 116 J5
King Cr. →, Australia 94 C2
King Edward →, Australia 92 B4
King Frederick VI Land = Kong Frederik VI Kyst, Greenland 4 C5
King George B., Falk. Is. 128 G4
King George I., Antarctica 5 C18
King George Is., Canada 101 C11
King I. = Kadan Kyun, Burma 64 F2
King I., Australia 94 F3
King I., Canada 104 C3
King Leopold Ranges, Australia 92 C4
King of Prussia, U.S.A. 111 F9
King Sd., Australia 92 C3
King William I., Canada 100 B10
King William's Town, S. Africa 88 E4
Kingaroy, Australia 95 D5
Kingfisher, U.S.A. 113 H6
Kingirbān, Iraq 70 C5
Kingisepp = Kuressaare, Estonia 9 G20
Kingisepp, Russia 46 C5
Kingman, Ariz., U.S.A. 117 K12
Kingman, Kans., U.S.A. 113 G5
Kingoonya, Australia 95 E2
Kingri, Pakistan 68 D3
Kings →, U.S.A. 116 J7
Kings Canyon National Park, U.S.A. 116 J8
King's Lynn, U.K. 12 E8
Kings Mountain, U.S.A. 109 H5
Kings Park, U.S.A. 111 F11
King's Peak, U.S.A. 114 F8
Kingsbridge, U.K. 13 G4
Kingsburg, U.S.A. 116 J7
Kingscote, Australia 95 F2
Kingscourt, Ireland 15 C5
Kingsford, U.S.A. 108 C1
Kingsland, U.S.A. 109 K5
Kingsley, U.S.A. 112 D7
Kingsport, U.S.A. 109 G4
Kingston, Canada 102 D4
Kingston, Jamaica 120 C4
Kingston, N.Z. 91 L2
Kingston, N.H., U.S.A. 111 D13
Kingston, N.Y., U.S.A. 111 E11
Kingston, Pa., U.S.A. 111 E9
Kingston, R.I., U.S.A. 111 E13
Kingston Pk., U.S.A. 117 K11
Kingston South East, Australia 95 F2
Kingston upon Hull, U.K. 12 D7
Kingston upon Hull □, U.K. 12 D7
Kingston-upon-Thames, U.K. 13 F7
Kingstown, St. Vincent 121 D7
Kingstree, U.S.A. 109 J6
Kingsville, Canada 102 D3
Kingsville, U.S.A. 113 M6
Kingussie, U.K. 14 D4
Kingwood, U.S.A. 113 K7
Kınık, Antalya, Turkey 39 E11
Kınık, İzmir, Turkey 39 B9
Kinistino, Canada 105 C7
Kinkala, Congo 84 E2
Kinki □, Japan 55 H8
Kinleith, N.Z. 91 H5
Kinmount, Canada 110 B6
Kinna, Sweden 11 G6
Kinnairds Hd., U.K. 14 D6
Kinnared, Sweden 11 G7
Kinnarodden, Norway 6 A11
Kinnarp, Sweden 11 F7
Kinneviken, Sweden 11 F7
Kino, Mexico 118 B2
Kinoje →, Canada 102 B3
Kinomoto, Japan 55 G8
Kinoni, Uganda 86 C3
Kinoosao, Canada 105 B8
Kinross, U.K. 14 E5
Kinsale, Ireland 15 E3
Kinsale, Old Hd. of, Ireland 15 E3
Kinsha = Chang Jiang →, China 59 B13
Kinshasa, Dem. Rep. of the Congo 84 E3
Kinsley, U.S.A. 113 G5
Kinsman, U.S.A. 110 E4
Kinston, U.S.A. 109 H7
Kintampo, Ghana 83 D4
Kintore Ra., Australia 92 D4
Kintyre, U.K. 14 F3
Kintyre, Mull of, U.K. 14 F3
Kinushseo →, Canada 102 A3
Kinuso, Canada 104 B5
Kinyangiri, Tanzania 86 C3
Kinyeti, Sudan 81 G3
Kinzig →, Germany 25 G3
Kinzua, U.S.A. 110 E6
Kinzua Dam, U.S.A. 110 E6
Kióni, Greece 38 C2
Kiosk, Canada 102 C4
Kiowa, Kans., U.S.A. 113 G5
Kiowa, Okla., U.S.A. 113 H7
Kipahigan L., Canada 105 B8
Kipanga, Tanzania 86 D4
Kiparissía, Greece 38 D3
Kiparissiakós Kólpos, Greece 38 D3
Kipawa, L., Canada 102 C4
Kipembawe, Tanzania 86 D3
Kipengere Ra., Tanzania 87 D3
Kipili, Tanzania 86 D3
Kipini, Kenya 86 C5
Kipling, Canada 105 C8
Kippure, Ireland 15 C5
Kipushi, Dem. Rep. of the Congo 87 E2
Kirane, Mali 82 B2
Kiranomena, Madag. 89 B8
Kiraz, Turkey 39 C10
Kirazlı, Turkey 41 F10
Kirchhain, Germany 24 E4
Kirchheim, Germany 25 G5
Kirchheimbolanden, Germany 25 F3

Kirchschlag, *Austria* 27 D9
Kireç, *Turkey* 39 B10
Kirensk, *Russia* 51 D11
Kirghizia = Kyrgyzstan ■, *Asia* 50 E8
Kirghizstan = Kyrgyzstan ■, *Asia* 50 E8
Kiribati ■, *Pac. Oc.* 96 H10
Kırıkhan, *Turkey* 72 D7
Kırıkkale, *Turkey* 72 C5
Kirillov, *Russia* 46 C10
Kirin = Jilin, *China* 57 C14
Kirishi, *Russia* 46 C7
Kiritimati, *Kiribati* 97 G12
Kırka, *Turkey* 39 B12
Kirkağaç, *Turkey* 39 B9
Kirkby, *U.K.* 12 D5
Kirkby Lonsdale, *U.K.* 12 C5
Kirkcaldy, *U.K.* 14 E5
Kirkcudbright, *U.K.* 14 G4
Kirkee, *India* 66 K8
Kirkenes, *Norway* 8 B23
Kirkfield, *Canada* 110 B6
Kirkjubæjarklaustur, *Iceland* 8 E4
Kirkkonummi, *Finland* 9 F21
Kirkland Lake, *Canada* 102 C3
Kırklareli, *Turkey* 41 E11
Kırklareli □, *Turkey* 41 E11
Kirksville, *U.S.A.* 112 E8
Kirkūk, *Iraq* 70 C5
Kirkwall, *U.K.* 14 C6
Kirkwood, *S. Africa* 88 E4
Kirn, *Germany* 25 F3
Kirov, *Kaluga, Russia* 46 E8
Kirov, *Kirov, Russia* 50 D5
Kirovabad = Gäncä, *Azerbaijan* 49 K8
Kirovakan = Vanadzor, *Armenia* 49 K7
Kirovograd = Kirovohrad, *Ukraine* 47 H7
Kirovohrad, *Ukraine* 47 H7
Kirovsk = Babadayhan, *Turkmenistan* 50 F7
Kirovskiy, *Astrakhan, Russia* 49 H9
Kirovskiy, *Kamchatka, Russia* 51 D16
Kirovskiy, *Primorsk, Russia* 54 B6
Kirriemuir, *U.K.* 14 E5
Kirsanov, *Russia* 48 D6
Kırşehir, *Turkey* 70 B2
Kirtachi, *Niger* 83 C5
Kirthar Range, *Pakistan* 68 F2
Kirtland, *U.S.A.* 115 H9
Kiruna, *Sweden* 8 C19
Kirundu, *Dem. Rep. of the Congo* 86 C2
Kirya, *Russia* 48 C8
Kiryū, *Japan* 55 F9
Kisa, *Sweden* 11 G9
Kisaga, *Tanzania* 86 C3
Kisalaya, *Nic.* 120 D3
Kisalföld, *Hungary* 42 C2
Kisámou, Kólpos, *Greece* 36 D5
Kisanga, *Dem. Rep. of the Congo* 86 B2
Kisangani, *Dem. Rep. of the Congo* 86 B2
Kisar, *Indonesia* 63 F7
Kisarawe, *Tanzania* 86 D4
Kisarazu, *Japan* 55 G9
Kisbér, *Hungary* 42 C3
Kishanganga →, *Pakistan* 69 B5
Kishanganj, *India* 69 F13
Kishangarh, *Raj., India* 68 F6
Kishangarh, *Raj., India* 68 F4
Kishi, *Nigeria* 83 D5
Kishinev = Chişinău, *Moldova* 43 C13
Kishiwada, *Japan* 55 G7
Kishtwar, *India* 69 C6
Kisielice, *Poland* 44 E6
Kisii, *Kenya* 86 C3
Kisiju, *Tanzania* 86 D4
Kisir, *Turkey* 73 B10
Kisizi, *Uganda* 86 C2
Kiskomárom = Zalakomár, *Hungary* 42 D2
Kiskőrei-víztároló, *Hungary* 42 C5
Kiskőrös, *Hungary* 42 D4
Kiskundorozsma, *Hungary* 42 D5
Kiskunfélegyháza, *Hungary* 42 D4
Kiskunhalas, *Hungary* 42 D4
Kiskunmajsa, *Hungary* 42 D4
Kislovodsk, *Russia* 49 J6
Kismayu = Chisimaio, *Somali Rep.* 77 G8
Kiso-Gawa →, *Japan* 55 G8
Kiso-Sammyaku, *Japan* 55 G8
Kisofukushima, *Japan* 55 G8
Kisoro, *Uganda* 86 C2
Kissidougou, *Guinea* 82 D2
Kissimmee, *U.S.A.* 109 L5
Kissimmee →, *U.S.A.* 109 M5
Kississing L., *Canada* 105 B8
Kissónerga, *Cyprus* 36 E11
Kissu, J., *Sudan* 80 C2
Kistanje, *Croatia* 29 E12
Kisújszállás, *Hungary* 42 C5
Kisumu, *Kenya* 86 C3
Kisvárda, *Hungary* 42 B7
Kiswani, *Tanzania* 86 C4
Kiswere, *Tanzania* 87 D4
Kit Carson, *U.S.A.* 112 F3
Kita, *Mali* 82 C3
Kitaibaraki, *Japan* 55 F10
Kitakami, *Japan* 54 E10
Kitakami-Gawa →, *Japan* 54 E10
Kitakami-Sammyaku, *Japan* 54 E10
Kitakata, *Japan* 54 F9
Kitakyūshū, *Japan* 55 H5
Kitale, *Kenya* 86 B4
Kitami, *Japan* 54 C11
Kitami-Sammyaku, *Japan* 54 B11
Kitangiri, L., *Tanzania* 86 C3
Kitaya, *Tanzania* 87 E5
Kitchener, *Canada* 102 D3
Kitee, *Finland* 46 A6
Kitega = Gitega, *Burundi* 86 C2
Kitengo, *Dem. Rep. of the Congo* 86 D1
Kitgum, *Uganda* 86 B3
Kíthira, *Greece* 38 E5
Kíthnos, *Greece* 38 D6
Kiti, *Cyprus* 36 E12
Kiti, C., *Cyprus* 36 E12
Kitimat, *Canada* 104 C3
Kitinen →, *Finland* 8 C22
Kitiyab, *Sudan* 81 D3
Kítros, *Greece* 40 F6
Kitsuki, *Japan* 55 H5
Kittakittaooloo, L., *Australia* 95 D2
Kittanning, *U.S.A.* 110 F5
Kittatinny Mts., *U.S.A.* 111 F10
Kittery, *U.S.A.* 109 D10
Kittilä, *Finland* 8 C21
Kitui, *Kenya* 86 C4
Kitwanga, *Canada* 104 B3
Kitwe, *Zambia* 87 E2
Kitzbühel, *Austria* 26 D5
Kitzbühler Alpen, *Austria* 26 D5
Kitzingen, *Germany* 25 F6
Kivarli, *India* 68 G5
Kivertsi, *Ukraine* 47 G3
Kividhes, *Cyprus* 36 E11
Kivik, *Sweden* 11 J8
Kivotós, *Greece* 40 F5
Kivu, L., *Dem. Rep. of the Congo* 86 C2
Kiyev = Kyyiv, *Ukraine* 47 G6
Kiyevskoye Vdkhr. = Kyyivske Vdskh., *Ukraine* 47 G6
Kıyıköy, *Turkey* 41 E12
Kiziguru, *Rwanda* 86 C3
Kızıl Adalar, *Turkey* 41 F13
Kızıl Irmak →, *Turkey* 72 B6
Kizil Jilga, *India* 69 B8
Kizil Yurt, *Russia* 49 J8
Kızılcabölük, *Turkey* 39 D11
Kızılcadağ, *Turkey* 39 D11
Kızılcahamam, *Turkey* 72 B5
Kızılhisar, *Turkey* 72 D3
Kızılırmak, *Turkey* 72 B5
Kızılkaya, *Turkey* 39 D12
Kızılören, *Turkey* 39 C12
Kızıltepe, *Turkey* 70 B4
Kizimkazi, *Tanzania* 86 D4
Kizlyar, *Russia* 49 J8
Kizyl-Arvat = Gyzylarbat, *Turkmenistan* 50 F6
Kjellerup, *Denmark* 11 H3
Kjölur, *Iceland* 8 D4
Kladanj, *Bos.-H.* 42 F3
Kladnica, *Serbia, Yug.* 40 C4
Kladno, *Czech Rep.* 26 A7
Kladovo, *Serbia, Yug.* 40 B6
Klaeng, *Thailand* 64 F3
Klagenfurt, *Austria* 26 E7
Klaipėda, *Lithuania* 9 J19
Klaipėda □, *Lithuania* 44 C8
Klaksvík, *Færoe Is.* 8 E9
Klamath →, *U.S.A.* 114 F1
Klamath Falls, *U.S.A.* 114 E3
Klamath Mts., *U.S.A.* 114 F2
Klamono, *Indonesia* 63 E8
Klanjec, *Croatia* 29 B12
Klappan →, *Canada* 104 B3
Klarälven →, *Sweden* 10 E7
Klässbol, *Sweden* 10 E6
Klatovy, *Czech Rep.* 26 B6
Klawer, *S. Africa* 88 E2
Klazienaveen, *Neths.* 17 B6
Klé, *Mali* 82 C3
Klecko, *Poland* 45 F4
Kleczew, *Poland* 45 F5
Kleena Kleene, *Canada* 104 C4
Klein-Karas, *Namibia* 88 D2
Klekovača, *Bos.-H.* 29 D13
Klenoec, *Macedonia* 40 E4
Klenovec, *Slovak Rep.* 27 C12
Klerksdorp, *S. Africa* 88 D4
Kleszczele, *Poland* 45 F10
Kletnya, *Russia* 46 F7
Kletsk = Klyetsk, *Belarus* 47 F4
Kletskiy, *Russia* 49 F6
Kleve, *Germany* 24 D2
Klickitat, *U.S.A.* 114 D3
Klickitat →, *U.S.A.* 116 E5
Klidhes, *Cyprus* 36 D13
Klimovichi, *Belarus* 46 F6
Klin, *Russia* 46 D9
Klina, *Kosovo, Yug.* 40 D4
Klinaklini →, *Canada* 104 C3
Klintehamn, *Sweden* 11 G12
Klintsy, *Russia* 47 F7
Klip →, *S. Africa* 89 D4
Klipdale, *S. Africa* 88 E2
Klippan, *Sweden* 11 H7
Klipplaat, *S. Africa* 88 E3
Klisura, *Bulgaria* 41 D8
Kljajićevo, *Serbia, Yug.* 42 E4
Ključ, *Bos.-H.* 29 D13
Kłobuck, *Poland* 45 H5
Klockestrand, *Sweden* 10 B11
Kłodawa, *Poland* 45 F5
Kłodzko, *Poland* 45 H3
Klosi, *Albania* 40 E4
Klosterneuburg, *Austria* 27 C9
Klosters, *Switz.* 25 J5
Klötze, *Germany* 24 C7
Klouto, *Togo* 83 D5
Kluane L., *Canada* 100 B6
Kluane Nat. Park, *Canada* 104 A1
Kluczbork, *Poland* 45 H5
Klukwan, *U.S.A.* 104 B1
Klyetsk, *Belarus* 47 F4
Klyuchevskaya, Gora, *Russia* 51 D17
Knäred, *Sweden* 11 H7
Knaresborough, *U.K.* 12 C6
Knee L., *Man., Canada* 102 A1
Knee L., *Sask., Canada* 105 B7
Knezha, *Bulgaria* 41 C8
Knić, *Serbia, Yug.* 40 C4
Knight Inlet, *Canada* 104 C3
Knighton, *U.K.* 13 E4
Knights Ferry, *U.S.A.* 116 H6
Knights Landing, *U.S.A.* 116 G5
Knin, *Croatia* 29 D13
Knislinge, *Sweden* 11 H8
Knittelfeld, *Austria* 26 D7
Knivsta, *Sweden* 10 E11
Knjaževac, *Serbia, Yug.* 40 C6
Knob, C., *Australia* 93 F2
Knock, *Ireland* 15 C3
Knockmealdown Mts., *Ireland* 15 D4
Knokke-Heist, *Belgium* 17 C3
Knossós, *Greece* 36 D7
Knowlton, *Canada* 111 A12
Knox, *U.S.A.* 108 E2
Knox Coast, *Antarctica* 5 C8
Knoxville, *Iowa, U.S.A.* 112 E8
Knoxville, *Pa., U.S.A.* 110 E7
Knoxville, *Tenn., U.S.A.* 109 H4
Knysna, *S. Africa* 88 E3
Knyszyn, *Poland* 44 E9
Ko Kha, *Thailand* 64 C2
Koartac = Quaqtaq, *Canada* 101 B13
Koba, *Indonesia* 63 F8
Kobarid, *Slovenia* 29 B10
Kobayashi, *Japan* 55 J5
Kobdo = Hovd, *Mongolia* 60 B4
Kōbe, *Japan* 55 G7
Kobelyaky, *Ukraine* 47 H8
København, *Denmark* 11 J6
Københavns Amtskommune □, *Denmark* 11 J6
Kobenni, *Mauritania* 82 B3
Kōbi-Sho, *Japan* 55 M1
Koblenz, *Germany* 25 E3
Kobo, *Ethiopia* 81 E4
Kobryn, *Belarus* 47 F3
Kobuleti, *Georgia* 49 K5
Kobylin, *Poland* 45 G4
Kobyłka, *Poland* 45 F8
Kobylkino, *Russia* 48 C6
Koca →, *Turkey* 41 F11
Kocabaş, *Turkey* 39 D11
Kocaeli, *Turkey* 41 F13
Kocaeli □, *Turkey* 41 F13
Kočane, *Serbia, Yug.* 40 C5
Kočani, *Macedonia* 40 E6
Koçarlı, *Turkey* 39 D9
Koceljevo, *Serbia, Yug.* 40 B3
Kočevje, *Slovenia* 29 C11
Koch Bihar, *India* 67 F16
Kochang, *S. Korea* 57 G14
Kochas, *India* 69 G10
Kocher →, *Germany* 25 F5
Kōchi, *Japan* 55 H6
Kōchi □, *Japan* 55 H6
Kochiu = Gejiu, *China* 58 F4
Kock, *Poland* 45 G9
Kodarma, *India* 69 G11
Kode, *Sweden* 11 G5
Kodiak, *U.S.A.* 100 C4
Kodiak I., *U.S.A.* 100 C4
Kodinar, *India* 68 J4
Kodok, *Sudan* 81 F3
Kodori →, *Georgia* 49 J5
Koedoesberge, *S. Africa* 88 E3
Koes, *Namibia* 88 D2
Kofçaz, *Turkey* 41 E11
Koffiefontein, *S. Africa* 88 D4
Kofiau, *Indonesia* 63 E7
Köflach, *Austria* 26 D8
Koforidua, *Ghana* 83 D4
Kōfu, *Japan* 55 G9
Koga, *Japan* 55 F9
Kogaluk →, *Canada* 103 A7
Køge, *Denmark* 11 J6
Køge Bugt, *Denmark* 11 J6
Kogi □, *Nigeria* 83 D6
Kogin Baba, *Nigeria* 83 D7
Koh-i-Bābā, *Afghan.* 66 B5
Koh-i-Khurd, *Afghan.* 68 C1
Koh-i-Maran, *Pakistan* 68 E2
Kohat, *Pakistan* 68 C4
Kohima, *India* 67 G19
Kohkīlūyeh va Būyer Aḥmadi □, *Iran* 71 D6
Kohler Ra., *Antarctica* 5 D15
Kohlu, *Pakistan* 68 E3
Kohtla-Järve, *Estonia* 9 G22
Koillismaa, *Finland* 8 D23
Koin-dong, *N. Korea* 57 D14
Koinare, *Bulgaria* 41 C8
Koindu, *S. Leone* 82 D2
Kojetín, *Czech Rep.* 27 B10
Kojō, *N. Korea* 57 E14
Kojonup, *Australia* 93 F2
Kojūr, *Iran* 71 B6
Koka, *Sudan* 80 C3
Kokand = Qūqon, *Uzbekistan* 50 E8
Kokas, *Indonesia* 63 E8
Kokava, *Slovak Rep.* 27 C12
Kokchetav = Kökshetaū, *Kazakstan* 50 D7
Kokemäenjoki →, *Finland* 9 F19
Kokhma, *Russia* 48 B5
Koki, *Senegal* 82 B1
Kokkola, *Finland* 8 E20
Koko, *Nigeria* 83 C5
Koko Kyunzu, *Burma* 67 M18
Kokolopozo, *Ivory C.* 82 D3
Kokomo, *U.S.A.* 108 E2
Kokoro, *Niger* 83 C5
Koksan, *N. Korea* 57 E14
Kökshetaū, *Kazakstan* 50 D7
Koksoak →, *Canada* 101 C13
Kokstad, *S. Africa* 89 E4
Kokubu, *Japan* 55 J5
Kola, *Indonesia* 63 F8
Kola Pen. = Kolskiy Poluostrov, *Russia* 50 C4
Kolachi →, *Pakistan* 68 F2
Kolahoi, *India* 69 B6
Kolahun, *Liberia* 82 D2
Kolaka, *Indonesia* 63 E6
Kolar, *India* 66 N11
Kolar Gold Fields, *India* 66 N11
Kolaras, *India* 68 G6
Kolari, *Finland* 8 C20
Kolárovo, *Slovak Rep.* 27 D10
Kolašin, *Montenegro, Yug.* 40 D3
Kolayat, *India* 66 F8
Kolbäck, *Sweden* 10 E10
Kolbäcksån →, *Sweden* 10 E10
Kolbermoor, *Germany* 25 H8
Kolbuszowa, *Poland* 45 H8
Kolchugino = Leninsk-Kuznetskiy, *Russia* 50 D9
Kolchugino, *Russia* 46 D10
Kolda, *Senegal* 82 C2
Koldegi, *Sudan* 81 E3
Kolding, *Denmark* 11 J3
Kolepom = Dolak, Pulau, *Indonesia* 63 F9
Kolguyev, Ostrov, *Russia* 50 C5
Kolhapur, *India* 66 L9
Kolia, *Ivory C.* 82 D3
Kolín, *Czech Rep.* 26 A8
Kolind, *Denmark* 11 H4
Kolkas rags, *Latvia* 9 H20
Kölleda, *Germany* 24 D7
Kollum, *Neths.* 17 A6
Kolmanskop, *Namibia* 88 D2
Köln, *Germany* 24 E2
Kolno, *Poland* 44 E8
Koło, *Poland* 45 F5
Kołobrzeg, *Poland* 44 D2
Kolokani, *Mali* 82 C3
Koloko, *Burkina Faso* 82 C3
Kololo, *Ethiopia* 81 F5
Kolomna, *Russia* 46 E10
Kolomyya, *Ukraine* 47 H3
Kolondiéba, *Mali* 82 C3
Kolonodale, *Indonesia* 63 E6
Kolonowskie, *Poland* 45 H5
Kolosib, *India* 67 G18
Kolpashevo, *Russia* 50 D9
Kolpino, *Russia* 46 C6
Kolpny, *Russia* 47 F9
Kolskiy Poluostrov, *Russia* 50 C4
Kolsva, *Sweden* 10 E9
Kolubara →, *Serbia, Yug.* 40 B4
Koluszki, *Poland* 45 G6
Kolwezi, *Dem. Rep. of the Congo* 87 E2
Kolyma →, *Russia* 51 C17
Kolymskoye Nagorye, *Russia* 51 C16
Kôm Hamâda, *Egypt* 80 H7
Kôm Ombo, *Egypt* 80 C3
Komadugu Gana →, *Nigeria* 83 C7
Komandorskiye Is. = Komandorskiye Ostrova, *Russia* 51 D17
Komandorskiye Ostrova, *Russia* 51 D17
Komárno, *Slovak Rep.* 27 D11
Komárom, *Hungary* 42 C3
Komárom-Esztergom □, *Hungary* 42 C3
Komatipoort, *S. Africa* 89 D5
Komatou Yialou, *Cyprus* 36 D13
Komatsu, *Japan* 55 F8
Komatsujima, *Japan* 55 H7
Kombissiri, *Burkina Faso* 83 C4
Kombori, *Burkina Faso* 82 C4
Kombóti, *Greece* 38 B3
Komen, *Slovenia* 29 C10
Komenda, *Ghana* 83 D4
Komi □, *Russia* 50 C6
Komiža, *Croatia* 29 E13
Komló, *Hungary* 42 D3
Kommunarsk = Alchevsk, *Ukraine* 47 H10
Kommunizma, Pik, *Tajikistan* 50 F8
Komodo, *Indonesia* 63 F5
Komoé →, *Ivory C.* 82 D4
Komoran, Pulau, *Indonesia* 63 F9
Komoro, *Japan* 55 F9
Komotini, *Greece* 41 E9
Komovi, *Montenegro, Yug.* 40 D3
Kompasberg, *S. Africa* 88 E3
Kompong Bang, *Cambodia* 65 F5
Kompong Cham, *Cambodia* 65 F5
Kompong Chhnang = Kampang Chhnang, *Cambodia* 65 F5
Kompong Chikreng, *Cambodia* 64 F5
Kompong Kleang, *Cambodia* 64 F5
Kompong Luong, *Cambodia* 65 G5
Kompong Pranak, *Cambodia* 64 F5
Kompong Som = Kampong Saom, *Cambodia* 65 G4
Kompong Som, Chhung = Kampong Saom, Chaak, *Cambodia* 65 G4
Kompong Speu, *Cambodia* 65 G5
Kompong Sralao, *Cambodia* 64 E5
Kompong Thom, *Cambodia* 64 F5
Kompong Trabeck, *Cambodia* 64 F5
Kompong Trabeck, *Cambodia* 65 G5
Kompong Trach, *Cambodia* 65 G5
Kompong Tralach, *Cambodia* 65 G5
Komrat = Comrat, *Moldova* 43 D13
Komsberg, *S. Africa* 88 E3
Komsomolets, Ostrov, *Russia* 51 A10
Komsomolsk, *Amur, Russia* 51 D14
Komsomolsk, *Ivanovo, Russia* 46 D11
Komsomolskiy, *Russia* 48 C7
Kömür Burnu, *Turkey* 39 C8
Kon Tum, *Vietnam* 64 E7
Kon Tum, Plateau du, *Vietnam* 64 E7
Kona, *Mali* 82 C4
Konakovo, *Russia* 46 D9
Konarhā □, *Afghan.* 66 B7
Konārī, *Iran* 71 D6
Konch, *India* 69 G8
Konde, *Tanzania* 86 C4
Kondiá, *Greece* 39 B7
Kondinin, *Australia* 93 F2
Kondoa, *Tanzania* 86 C4
Kondókali, *Greece* 36 A3
Kondopaga, *Russia* 46 A8
Kondratyevo, *Russia* 51 D10
Kondrovo, *Russia* 46 E8
Konduga, *Nigeria* 83 C7
Köneürgench, *Turkmenistan* 50 E6
Konevo, *Russia* 46 A10
Kong = Khong →, *Cambodia* 64 F5
Kong, *Ivory C.* 82 D4
Kong, Koh, *Cambodia* 65 G4
Kong Christian IX Land, *Greenland* 4 C6
Kong Christian X Land, *Greenland* 4 B6
Kong Frederik IX Land, *Greenland* 4 C5
Kong Frederik VI Kyst, *Greenland* 4 C5
Kong Frederik VIII Land, *Greenland* 4 B6
Kong Oscar Fjord, *Greenland* 4 B6
Kongeå →, *Denmark* 11 J2
Kongerslev, *Denmark* 11 H4
Kongju, *S. Korea* 57 F14
Konglu, *Burma* 67 F20
Kongola, *Namibia* 88 B3
Kongolo, *Kasai-Or., Dem. Rep. of the Congo* 86 D1
Kongolo, *Katanga, Dem. Rep. of the Congo* 86 D2
Kongor, *Sudan* 81 F3
Kongoussi, *Burkina Faso* 83 C4
Kongsberg, *Norway* 9 G13
Kongsvinger, *Norway* 9 F15
Kongwa, *Tanzania* 86 D4
Koni, *Dem. Rep. of the Congo* 87 E2
Koni, Mts., *Dem. Rep. of the Congo* 87 E2
Koniakari, *Mali* 82 C2
Koniecpol, *Poland* 45 H6
Königs Wusterhausen, *Germany* 24 C9
Königsberg = Kaliningrad, *Russia* 9 J19
Königsbrunn, *Germany* 25 G6
Königslutter, *Germany* 24 C6
Konin, *Poland* 45 F5
Konispoli, *Albania* 40 G4
Kónitsa, *Greece* 38 A2
Konjic, *Bos.-H.* 42 G2
Konkiep, *Namibia* 88 D2
Konkouré →, *Guinea* 82 D2
Könnern, *Germany* 24 D7
Kono, *S. Leone* 82 D2
Konongo, *Ghana* 83 D4
Konosha, *Russia* 46 B11
Kōnosu, *Japan* 55 F9
Konotop, *Ukraine* 47 G7
Konsankoro, *Guinea* 82 D3
Końskie, *Poland* 45 G7
Konstancin-Jeziorna, *Poland* 45 F8
Konstantinovka = Kostyantynivka, *Ukraine* 47 H9
Konstantinovsk, *Russia* 49 G5
Konstantynów Łódźki, *Poland* 45 G6
Konstanz, *Germany* 25 H5
Kont, *Iran* 71 E9
Kontagora, *Nigeria* 83 C6
Kontcha, *Cameroon* 83 D7
Konya, *Turkey* 70 B2
Konya Ovası, *Turkey* 72 C5
Konz, *Germany* 25 F2
Konza, *Kenya* 86 C4
Koocanusa, L., *Canada* 114 B6
Kookynie, *Australia* 93 E3
Koolyanobbing, *Australia* 93 F2
Koonibba, *Australia* 95 E1
Koorawatha, *Australia* 95 E4
Koorda, *Australia* 93 F2
Kooskia, *U.S.A.* 114 C6
Kootenay →, *U.S.A.* 104 D5
Kootenay L., *Canada* 104 D5
Kootenay Nat. Park, *Canada* 104 C5
Kootjieskolk, *S. Africa* 88 E3
Kopanovka, *Russia* 49 G8
Kopaonik, *Yugoslavia* 40 C4
Kópavogur, *Iceland* 8 D3
Koper, *Slovenia* 29 C10
Kopervik, *Norway* 9 G11

Kopet Dagh, *Asia* 71 B8
Kopi, *Australia* 95 E2
Köping, *Sweden* 10 E10
Köpingsvik, *Sweden* 11 H10
Kopište, *Croatia* 29 F13
Kopliku, *Albania* 40 D3
Köpmanholmen, *Sweden* 10 A12
Kopparberg, *Sweden* 10 E9
Kopparbergs län □, *Sweden* 10 C8
Koppeh Dāgh = Kopet Dagh, *Asia* 71 B8
Koppies, *S. Africa* 89 D4
Koppom, *Sweden* 10 E6
Koprivlen, *Bulgaria* 40 E7
Koprivnica, *Croatia* 29 B13
Kopřivnice, *Czech Rep.* 27 B11
Koprivshtitsa, *Bulgaria* 41 D8
Köprübaşı, *Turkey* 39 C10
Kopychyntsi, *Ukraine* 47 H3
Korab, *Macedonia* 40 E4
Korakiána, *Greece* 36 A3
Koral, *India* 68 J5
Korarou, L., *Mali* 82 B4
Korba, *India* 69 H10
Korbach, *Germany* 24 D4
Korbu, G., *Malaysia* 65 K3
Korça, *Albania* 40 F4
Korce = Korça, *Albania* 40 F4
Korčula, *Croatia* 29 F13
Korčulanski Kanal, *Croatia* 29 E13
Kord Kūy, *Iran* 71 B7
Kord Sheykh, *Iran* 71 D7
Kordestān □, *Iran* 70 C5
Kordofân, *Sudan* 79 F11
Koré Mayroua, *Niger* 83 C5
Korea, North ■, *Asia* 57 E14
Korea, South ■, *Asia* 57 G15
Korea Bay, *Korea* 57 E13
Korea Strait, *Asia* 57 H15
Korem, *Ethiopia* 81 E4
Korenevo, *Russia* 47 G8
Korenovsk, *Russia* 49 H4
Korets, *Ukraine* 47 G4
Korfantów, *Poland* 45 H4
Korgan, *Turkey* 72 B7
Korgus, *Sudan* 80 D3
Korhogo, *Ivory C.* 82 D3
Koribundu, *S. Leone* 82 D2
Korienzé, *Mali* 82 B4
Korinthía □, *Greece* 38 D4
Korinthiakós Kólpos, *Greece* 38 C4
Kórinthos, *Greece* 38 D4
Korioumé, *Mali* 82 B4
Korissa, Límni, *Greece* 36 B3
Kōriyama, *Japan* 54 F10
Korkuteli, *Turkey* 39 D12
Kormakiti, C., *Cyprus* 36 D11
Körmend, *Hungary* 42 C1
Kornat, *Croatia* 29 E12
Korneshty = Corneşti, *Moldova* 43 C13
Korneuburg, *Austria* 27 C9
Kórnik, *Poland* 45 F4
Koro, *Fiji* 91 C8
Koro, *Ivory C.* 82 D3
Koro, *Mali* 82 C4
Koro Sea, *Fiji* 91 C9
Korocha, *Russia* 47 G9
Köroğlu Dağları, *Turkey* 72 B5
Korogwe, *Tanzania* 86 D4
Koronadal, *Phil.* 61 H6
Koróni, *Greece* 38 E3
Korónia, Limni, *Greece* 40 F7
Koronís, *Greece* 39 D7
Koronowo, *Poland* 45 E4
Koror, *Palau* 63 C8
Körös →, *Hungary* 42 D5
Köröstarcsa, *Hungary* 42 D6
Korosten, *Ukraine* 47 G5
Korostyshev, *Ukraine* 47 G5
Korotoyak, *Russia* 47 G10
Korraraika, Helodranon' i, *Madag.* 89 B7
Korsakov, *Russia* 51 E15
Korsberga, *Sweden* 11 G9
Korshunovo, *Russia* 51 D12
Korsør, *Denmark* 11 J5
Korsun Shevchenkovskiy, *Ukraine* 47 H6
Korsze, *Poland* 44 D8
Korti, *Sudan* 80 D3
Kortrijk, *Belgium* 17 D3
Korucu, *Turkey* 39 B9
Korwai, *India* 68 G8
Koryakskoye Nagorye, *Russia* 51 C18
Koryŏng, *S. Korea* 57 G15
Koryukovka, *Ukraine* 47 G7
Kos, *Greece* 39 E9
Kosa, *Ethiopia* 81 F4
Kosaya Gora, *Russia* 46 E9
Kościan, *Poland* 45 F3
Kościerzyna, *Poland* 44 D4
Kosciusko, *U.S.A.* 113 J10
Kosciuszko, Mt., *Australia* 95 F4
Kösély →, *Hungary* 42 C6
Kosha, *Sudan* 80 C3
Koshava, *Bulgaria* 40 B7
K'oshih = Kashi, *China* 60 C2
Koshiki-Rettō, *Japan* 55 J4
Kosi, *India* 68 F7
Kosi →, *India* 69 E8
Košice, *Slovak Rep.* 27 C14
Košický □, *Slovak Rep.* 27 C14
Kosjerić, *Serbia, Yug.* 40 B3
Köşk, *Turkey* 39 D10
Koskhinoú, *Greece* 36 C10
Koslan, *Russia* 50 C5
Kosŏng, *N. Korea* 57 E15
Kosovo □, *Yugoslavia* 40 D4
Kosovo Polje, *Kosovo, Yug.* 40 D5
Kosovska Kamenica, *Kosovo, Yug.* 40 D5
Kosovska Mitrovica, *Kosovo, Yug.* 40 D4
Kossou, L. de, *Ivory C.* 82 D3
Kosta, *Sweden* 11 H9
Kostajnica, *Croatia* 29 C13
Kostanjevica, *Slovenia* 29 C12
Kostenets, *Bulgaria* 40 D7
Koster, *S. Africa* 88 D4
Kôstî, *Sudan* 81 E3
Kostinbrod, *Bulgaria* 40 D7
Kostolac, *Serbia, Yug.* 40 B5
Kostopil, *Ukraine* 47 G4
Kostroma, *Russia* 46 D11
Kostromskoye Vdkhr., *Russia* 46 D11
Kostrzyn, *Lubuskie, Poland* 45 F1
Kostrzyn, *Wielkopolskie, Poland* 45 F4
Kostyantynivka, *Ukraine* 47 H9
Kostyukovichi = Kastsyukovichy, *Belarus* 46 F7
Koszalin, *Poland* 44 D3
Kőszeg, *Hungary* 42 C1
Kot Addu, *Pakistan* 68 D4
Kot Kapura, *India* 68 D6
Kot Moman, *Pakistan* 68 C5
Kot Sultan, *Pakistan* 68 D4
Kota, *India* 68 G6
Kota Baharu, *Malaysia* 65 J4
Kota Barrage, *India* 68 G6
Kota Belud, *Malaysia* 62 C5
Kota Kinabalu, *Malaysia* 62 C5
Kota Kubu Baharu, *Malaysia* 65 L3
Kota Tinggi, *Malaysia* 65 M4
Kotaagung, *Indonesia* 62 F2
Kotabaru, *Indonesia* 62 E5
Kotabumi, *Indonesia* 62 E2
Kotamobagu, *Indonesia* 63 D6
Kotcho L., *Canada* 104 B4
Kotdwara, *India* 69 E8
Kotel, *Bulgaria* 41 D10
Kotelnich, *Russia* 48 A9
Kotelnikovo, *Russia* 49 G6
Kotelnyy, Ostrov, *Russia* 51 B14
Kothari →, *India* 68 G6
Köthen, *Germany* 24 D7
Kothi, *Mad. P., India* 69 H10
Kothi, *Mad. P., India* 69 G9
Kotiro, *Pakistan* 68 F2
Kotka, *Finland* 9 F22
Kotlas, *Russia* 50 C5
Kotlenska Planina, *Bulgaria* 41 D10
Kotli, *Pakistan* 68 C5
Kotma, *India* 69 H9
Kotmul, *Pakistan* 69 B6
Koton-Karifi, *Nigeria* 83 D6
Kotonkoro, *Nigeria* 83 C6
Kotor, *Montenegro, Yug.* 40 D2
Kotor Varoš, *Bos.-H.* 42 F2
Kotoriba, *Croatia* 29 B13
Kotovo, *Russia* 48 E7
Kotovsk, *Russia* 48 D5
Kotovsk, *Ukraine* 47 J5
Kotputli, *India* 68 F7
Kotri, *Pakistan* 68 G3
Kótronas, *Greece* 38 E4
Kötschach-Mauthen, *Austria* 26 E6
Kottayam, *India* 66 Q10
Kotturu, *India* 66 M10
Kotuy →, *Russia* 51 B11
Kotzebue, *U.S.A.* 100 B3
Koudougou, *Burkina Faso* 82 C4
Koufonísi, *Greece* 36 E8
Koufonísia, *Greece* 39 E7
Kougaberge, *S. Africa* 88 E3
Kouibli, *Ivory C.* 82 D3
Kouilou →, *Congo* 84 E2
Koula Moutou, *Gabon* 84 E2
Koulen = Kulen, *Cambodia* 64 F5
Koulikoro, *Mali* 82 C3
Kouloúra, *Greece* 36 A3
Koúm-bournoú, Ákra, *Greece* 36 C10
Koumala, *Australia* 94 C4
Koumankou, *Mali* 82 C3
Koumbia, *Burkina Faso* 82 C4
Koumbia, *Guinea* 82 C2
Koumboum, *Guinea* 82 C2
Koumpenntoum, *Senegal* 82 C2
Koumra, *Chad* 79 G9
Koun-Fao, *Ivory C.* 82 D4
Koundara, *Guinea* 82 C2
Koundian, *Guinea* 82 C3
Koungheul, *Senegal* 82 C2
Kounradskiy, *Kazakstan* 50 E8
Kountze, *U.S.A.* 113 K7
Koupéla, *Burkina Faso* 83 C4
Kourémalé, *Mali* 82 C3
Kouris →, *Cyprus* 36 E11
Kourou, *Fr. Guiana* 125 B8
Kourouba, *Mali* 82 C2
Kouroukoto, *Mali* 82 C2
Kourouma, *Burkina Faso* 82 C4
Kourouninkoto, *Mali* 82 C3
Kouroussa, *Guinea* 82 C3
Koussanar, *Senegal* 82 C2
Koussané, *Mali* 82 C2
Koussane, *Senegal* 82 C2
Kousseri, *Cameroon* 79 F8
Koutiala, *Mali* 82 C3
Kouto, *Ivory C.* 82 D3
Kouvé, *Togo* 83 D5
Kouvola, *Finland* 9 F22
Kovačica, *Serbia, Yug.* 42 E5
Kovel, *Ukraine* 47 G3
Kovin, *Serbia, Yug.* 42 F5
Kovrov, *Russia* 48 B5
Kowal, *Poland* 45 F6
Kowalewo Pomorskie, *Poland* 45 E5
Kowanyama, *Australia* 94 B3
Kowloon, *H.K.* 59 F10
Kowŏn, *N. Korea* 57 E14
Köyceğiz, *Turkey* 39 E10
Köyceğız Gölü, *Turkey* 39 E10
Koyulhisar, *Turkey* 72 B7
Koyunyeri, *Turkey* 41 F10
Koza, *Japan* 55 L3
Kozak, *Turkey* 39 B9
Kozan, *Turkey* 70 B2
Kozáni, *Greece* 40 F5
Kozáni □, *Greece* 40 F5
Kozara, *Bos.-H.* 29 D14
Kozarac, *Bos.-H.* 29 D13
Kozelets, *Ukraine* 47 G6
Kozelsk, *Russia* 46 E8
Kozhikode = Calicut, *India* 66 P9
Koziegłowy, *Poland* 45 H6
Kozienice, *Poland* 45 G8
Kozje, *Slovenia* 29 B12
Kozloduy, *Bulgaria* 40 C7
Kozlovets, *Bulgaria* 41 C9
Kozlovka, *Russia* 48 C9
Kozlu, *Turkey* 72 B4
Kozluk, *Turkey* 73 C9
Koźmin, *Poland* 45 G4
Kozmodemyansk, *Russia* 48 B8
Kożuchów, *Poland* 45 G2
Kozyatyn, *Ukraine* 47 H5
Kpabia, *Ghana* 83 D4
Kpalimé, *Togo* 83 D5
Kpandae, *Ghana* 83 D4
Kpessi, *Togo* 83 D5
Kra, Isthmus of = Kra, Kho Khot, *Thailand* 65 G2
Kra, Kho Khot, *Thailand* 65 G2
Kra Buri, *Thailand* 65 G2
Kraai →, *S. Africa* 88 E4
Krabi, *Thailand* 65 H2
Kracheh, *Cambodia* 64 F6
Kragan, *Indonesia* 63 G14
Kragerø, *Norway* 9 G13
Kragujevac, *Serbia, Yug.* 40 B4
Krajenka, *Poland* 45 E3
Krajina, *Bos.-H.* 29 D13
Krakatau = Rakata, Pulau, *Indonesia* 62 F3
Krakatoa = Rakata, Pulau, *Indonesia* 62 F3
Krakor, *Cambodia* 64 F5
Kraków, *Poland* 45 H6
Kralanh, *Cambodia* 64 F4
Králíky, *Czech Rep.* 27 A9
Kraljevo, *Serbia, Yug.* 40 C4
Královský Chlmec, *Slovak Rep.* 27 C14
Kralupy nad Vltavou, *Czech Rep.* 26 A7
Kramatorsk, *Ukraine* 47 H9
Kramfors, *Sweden* 10 B11
Kraniá, *Greece* 40 G5
Kranía Elassónas, *Greece* 38 B4
Kranídhion, *Greece* 38 D5
Kranj, *Slovenia* 29 B11
Kranjska Gora, *Slovenia* 29 B10
Krankskop, *S. Africa* 89 D5
Krapina, *Croatia* 29 B12
Krapina →, *Croatia* 29 C12
Krapkowice, *Poland* 45 H4
Kras, *Croatia* 29 C10
Kraskino, *Russia* 51 E14
Krāslava, *Latvia* 46 E4
Kraslice, *Czech Rep.* 26 A5
Krasnaya Gorbatka, *Russia* 48 C5
Krasnaya Polyana, *Russia* 49 J5
Kraśnik, *Poland* 45 H9
Krasnoarmeisk, *Ukraine* 47 H9
Krasnoarmeysk, *Russia* 48 E7
Krasnoarmeyskiy, *Russia* 49 G6
Krasnobrod, *Poland* 45 H10
Krasnodar, *Russia* 49 H4
Krasnodon, *Ukraine* 47 H10
Krasnogorskiy, *Russia* 48 B9
Krasnograd = Krasnohrad, *Ukraine* 47 H8
Krasnogvardeyskoye, *Russia* 49 H5
Krasnogvardyesk, *Ukraine* 47 K8
Krasnohrad, *Ukraine* 47 H8
Krasnokutsk, *Ukraine* 47 G8
Krasnolesnyy, *Russia* 47 G10
Krasnoperekopsk, *Ukraine* 47 J7
Krasnorechenskiy, *Russia* 54 B7
Krasnoselkup, *Russia* 50 C9
Krasnoslobodsk, *Mordvinia, Russia* 48 C6
Krasnoslobodsk, *Volgograd, Russia* 49 F7
Krasnoturinsk, *Russia* 50 D7
Krasnovodsk = Türkmenbashi, *Turkmenistan* 50 E6
Krasnoyarsk, *Russia* 51 D10
Krasnoye = Krasnyy, *Russia* 46 E6
Krasnozavodsk, *Russia* 46 D10
Krasny Sulin, *Russia* 47 J11
Krasnystaw, *Poland* 45 H10
Krasnyy, *Russia* 46 E6
Krasnyy Kholm, *Russia* 46 C9
Krasnyy Kut, *Russia* 48 E8
Krasnyy Liman, *Ukraine* 47 H9
Krasnyy Luch, *Ukraine* 47 H10
Krasnyy Profintern, *Russia* 46 D11
Krasnyy Yar, *Astrakhan, Russia* 49 G9
Krasnyy Yar, *Samara, Russia* 48 D10
Krasnyy Yar, *Volgograd, Russia* 48 E7
Krasnyye Baki, *Russia* 48 B7
Krasnyyoskolske Vdskh., *Ukraine* 47 H9
Kraszna →, *Hungary* 42 B7
Kratie = Kracheh, *Cambodia* 64 F6
Kratovo, *Macedonia* 40 D6
Krau, *Indonesia* 63 E10
Kravanh, Chuor Phnum, *Cambodia* 65 G4
Krefeld, *Germany* 24 D2
Krémaston, Límni, *Greece* 38 C3
Kremen, *Croatia* 29 D12
Kremenchug = Kremenchuk, *Ukraine* 47 H7
Kremenchuk, *Ukraine* 47 H7
Kremenchuksk Vdskh., *Ukraine* 47 H7
Kremenets, *Ukraine* 47 G3
Kremennaya, *Ukraine* 47 H10
Kremges = Svitlovodsk, *Ukraine* 47 H7
Kremmen, *Germany* 24 C9
Kremmling, *U.S.A.* 114 F10
Kremnica, *Slovak Rep.* 27 C11
Krems, *Austria* 26 C8
Kremsmünster, *Austria* 26 C7
Kretinga, *Lithuania* 9 J19
Krettsy, *Russia* 46 C7
Kreuzberg, *Germany* 25 E5
Kreuztal, *Germany* 24 E4
Kría Vrísi, *Greece* 40 F6
Kribi, *Cameroon* 83 E6
Krichem, *Bulgaria* 41 D8
Krichev = Krychaw, *Belarus* 46 F6
Krim, *Slovenia* 29 C11
Kriós, Ákra, *Greece* 36 D5
Krishna →, *India* 67 M12
Krishnanagar, *India* 69 H13
Kristdala, *Sweden* 11 G10
Kristiansand, *Norway* 9 G13
Kristianstad, *Sweden* 11 H8
Kristiansund, *Norway* 8 E12
Kristiinankaupunki, *Finland* 9 E19
Kristinehamn, *Sweden* 10 E8
Kristinestad = Kristiinankaupunki, *Finland* 9 E19
Kríti, *Greece* 36 D7
Kritsá, *Greece* 36 D7
Kriva →, *Macedonia* 40 D5
Kriva Palanka, *Macedonia* 40 D6
Krivaja →, *Bos.-H.* 42 F3
Krivelj, *Serbia, Yug.* 40 B6
Krivoy Rog = Kryvyy Rih, *Ukraine* 47 J7
Križevci, *Croatia* 29 B13
Krk, *Croatia* 29 C11
Krka →, *Slovenia* 29 C12
Krkonoše, *Czech Rep.* 26 A8
Krnov, *Czech Rep.* 27 A10
Krobia, *Poland* 45 G3
Krokeaí, *Greece* 38 E4
Krokek, *Sweden* 11 F10
Krokodil →, *Mozam.* 89 D5
Krokom, *Sweden* 10 A8
Krokowa, *Poland* 44 D5
Krolevets, *Ukraine* 47 G7
Kroměříž, *Czech Rep.* 27 B10
Krompachy, *Slovak Rep.* 27 C13
Kromy, *Russia* 47 F8
Kronach, *Germany* 25 E7
Krong Kaoh Kong, *Cambodia* 62 B2
Kronobergs län □, *Sweden* 11 H8
Kronprins Olav Kyst, *Antarctica* 5 C5
Kronshtadt, *Russia* 46 C5
Kroonstad, *S. Africa* 88 D4
Kröpelin, *Germany* 24 A7
Kropotkin, *Russia* 49 H5
Kropp, *Germany* 24 A5
Krosna, *Lithuania* 44 D10
Krośniewice, *Poland* 45 F6
Krosno, *Poland* 45 J8
Krosno Odrzańskie, *Poland* 45 F2
Krotoszyn, *Poland* 45 G4
Krotovka, *Russia* 48 D10
Kroussón, *Greece* 36 D6
Krraba, *Albania* 40 E3
Krško, *Slovenia* 29 C12
Krstača, *Serbia, Yug.* 40 D4
Kruger Nat. Park, *S. Africa* 89 C5
Krugersdorp, *S. Africa* 89 D4
Kruisfontein, *S. Africa* 88 E3
Kruja, *Albania* 40 E3
Krulevshchina = Krulyewshchyna, *Belarus* 46 E4
Krulyewshchyna, *Belarus* 46 E4
Kruma, *Albania* 40 D4
Krumbach, *Germany* 25 G6
Krumovgrad, *Bulgaria* 41 E9
Krung Thep = Bangkok, *Thailand* 64 F3
Krupanj, *Serbia, Yug.* 40 B3
Krupina, *Slovak Rep.* 27 C12
Krupinica →, *Slovak Rep.* 27 C11
Krupki, *Belarus* 46 E5
Kruševac, *Serbia, Yug.* 40 C5
Kruševo, *Macedonia* 40 E5
Kruszwica, *Poland* 45 F5
Krychaw, *Belarus* 46 F6
Krymsk, *Russia* 47 K10
Krymskiy Poluostrov = Krymskyy Pivostriv, *Ukraine* 47 K8
Krymskyy Pivostriv, *Ukraine* 47 K8
Krynica, *Poland* 45 J7
Krynica Morska, *Poland* 44 D6
Krynki, *Poland* 45 E10
Kryvyy Rih, *Ukraine* 47 J7
Krzepice, *Poland* 45 H5
Krzeszów, *Poland* 45 H9
Krzna →, *Poland* 45 F10
Krzywiń, *Poland* 45 G3
Krzyż Wielkopolski, *Poland* 45 F2
Ksar el Kebir, *Morocco* 78 B4
Ksar es Souk = Ar Rachidiya, *Morocco* 78 B5
Książ Wielkopolski, *Poland* 45 F4
Kstovo, *Russia* 48 B7
Ku, W. el →, *Sudan* 81 E2
Kuala Belait, *Malaysia* 62 D4
Kuala Berang, *Malaysia* 65 K4
Kuala Dungun = Dungun, *Malaysia* 65 K4
Kuala Kangsar, *Malaysia* 65 K3
Kuala Kelawang, *Malaysia* 65 L4
Kuala Kerai, *Malaysia* 65 K4
Kuala Lipis, *Malaysia* 65 K4
Kuala Lumpur, *Malaysia* 65 L3
Kuala Nerang, *Malaysia* 65 J3
Kuala Pilah, *Malaysia* 65 L4
Kuala Rompin, *Malaysia* 65 L4
Kuala Selangor, *Malaysia* 65 L3
Kuala Sepetang, *Malaysia* 65 K3
Kuala Terengganu, *Malaysia* 65 K4
Kualajelai, *Indonesia* 62 E4
Kualakapuas, *Indonesia* 62 E4
Kualakurun, *Indonesia* 62 E4
Kualapembuang, *Indonesia* 62 E4
Kualasimpang, *Indonesia* 62 D1
Kuancheng, *China* 57 D10
Kuandang, *Indonesia* 63 D6
Kuandian, *China* 57 D13
Kuangchou = Guangzhou, *China* 59 F9
Kuanshan, *Taiwan* 59 F13
Kuantan, *Malaysia* 65 L4
Kuba = Quba, *Azerbaijan* 49 K9
Kuban →, *Russia* 47 K9
Kubenskoye, Ozero, *Russia* 46 C10
Kubokawa, *Japan* 55 H6
Kubrat, *Bulgaria* 41 C10
Kučevo, *Serbia, Yug.* 40 B5
Kucha Gompa, *India* 69 B7
Kuchaman, *India* 68 F6
Kuchenspitze, *Austria* 26 D3
Kuchinda, *India* 69 J11
Kuching, *Malaysia* 62 D4
Kuchino-eruba-Jima, *Japan* 55 J5
Kuchino-Shima, *Japan* 55 K4
Kuchinotsu, *Japan* 55 H5
Kuchl, *Austria* 26 D6
Kucing = Kuching, *Malaysia* 62 D4
Kuçovë, *Albania* 40 F3
Küçükbahçe, *Turkey* 39 C8
Küçükköy, *Turkey* 39 B8
Küçükkuyu, *Turkey* 39 B8
Küçükmenderes →, *Turkey* 39 D9
Kud →, *Pakistan* 68 F2
Kuda, *India* 66 H7
Kudat, *Malaysia* 62 C5
Kudirkos Naumiestis, *Lithuania* 44 D9
Kudowa-Zdrój, *Poland* 45 H3
Kudus, *Indonesia* 63 G14
Kudymkar, *Russia* 50 D6
Kueiyang = Guiyang, *China* 58 D6
Kufra Oasis = Al Kufrah, *Libya* 79 D10
Kufstein, *Austria* 26 D5
Kugluktuk, *Canada* 100 B8
Kugong I., *Canada* 102 A4
Kūhak, *Iran* 66 F3
Kuhan, *Pakistan* 68 E2
Kūhbonān, *Iran* 71 D8
Kūhestak, *Iran* 71 E8
Kuhin, *Iran* 71 B6
Kūhīrī, *Iran* 71 E9
Kuhnsdorf, *Austria* 26 E7
Kūhpāyeh, *Eşfahan, Iran* 71 C7
Kūhpāyeh, *Kermān, Iran* 71 D8
Kührān, Kūh-e, *Iran* 71 E8
Kui Buri, *Thailand* 65 F2
Kuiseb →, *Namibia* 88 B2
Kuito, *Angola* 85 G3
Kuiu I., *U.S.A.* 104 B2
Kujang, *N. Korea* 57 E14
Kujawsko-Pomorskie □, *Poland* 44 E5
Kuji, *Japan* 54 D10
Kujū-San, *Japan* 55 H5
Kukavica, *Serbia, Yug.* 40 D5
Kukawa, *Nigeria* 83 C7
Kukësi, *Albania* 40 D4
Kukmor, *Russia* 48 B10
Kukup, *Malaysia* 65 M4
Kukvidze, *Russia* 48 E6
Kula, *Bulgaria* 40 C6
Kula, *Serbia, Yug.* 42 E4
Kula, *Turkey* 39 C10
Kulachi, *Pakistan* 68 D4
Kulai, *Malaysia* 65 M4
Kulal, Mt., *Kenya* 86 B4
Kulaly, Ostrov, *Kazakstan* 49 H10
Kulasekarappattinam, *India* 66 Q11
Kulautuva, *Lithuania* 44 D10
Kuldīga, *Latvia* 9 H19
Kuldīga □, *Latvia* 44 B8
Kuldja = Yining, *China* 50 E9
Kuldu, *Sudan* 81 E2
Kulebaki, *Russia* 48 C6
Kulen, *Cambodia* 64 F5
Kulen Vakuf, *Bos.-H.* 29 D13
Kulgam, *India* 69 C6
Kulgera, *Australia* 94 D1
Kulim, *Malaysia* 65 K3
Kulin, *Australia* 93 F2
Kullen, *Sweden* 11 H6
Kulmbach, *Germany* 25 E7
Kŭlob, *Tajikistan* 50 F7
Kulp, *Turkey* 73 C9
Kulpawn →, *Ghana* 83 D4

Kulsary, *Kazakstan* 50 E6
Kulti, *India* 69 H12
Kulu, *India* 68 D7
Kulu, *Turkey* 72 C5
Kulumbura, *Australia* 92 B4
Kulunda, *Russia* 50 D8
Kulungar, *Afghan.* 68 C3
Külvand, *Iran* 71 D7
Kulwin, *Australia* 95 F3
Kulyab = Kŭlob, *Tajikistan* 50 F7
Kuma →, *Russia* 49 H8
Kumafşarı, *Turkey* 39 D11
Kumaganum, *Nigeria* 83 C7
Kumagaya, *Japan* 55 F9
Kumai, *Indonesia* 62 E4
Kumalar Dağı, *Turkey* 39 C12
Kumamba, Kepulauan, *Indonesia* 63 E9
Kumamoto, *Japan* 55 H5
Kumamoto □, *Japan* 55 H5
Kumanovo, *Macedonia* 40 D5
Kumara, *N.Z.* 91 K3
Kumarina, *Australia* 93 D2
Kumasi, *Ghana* 82 D4
Kumayri = Gyumri, *Armenia* 49 K6
Kumba, *Cameroon* 83 E6
Kumbağ, *Turkey* 41 F11
Kumbakonam, *India* 66 P11
Kumbarilla, *Australia* 95 D5
Kumbhraj, *India* 68 G7
Kumbia, *Australia* 95 D5
Kumbo, *Cameroon* 83 D7
Kŭmch'ŏn, *N. Korea* 57 E14
Kumdok, *India* 69 C8
Kume-Shima, *Japan* 55 L3
Kumeny, *Russia* 48 A9
Kumharsain, *India* 68 D7
Kŭmhwa, *S. Korea* 57 E14
Kumi, *Uganda* 86 B3
Kumkale, *Turkey* 41 G10
Kumla, *Sweden* 10 E9
Kumluca, *Turkey* 39 E12
Kummerower See, *Germany* 24 B8
Kumo, *Nigeria* 83 C7
Kumon Bum, *Burma* 67 F20
Kumylzhenskaya, *Russia* 48 F6
Kunágota, *Hungary* 42 D6
Kunashir, Ostrov, *Russia* 51 E15
Kunda, *Estonia* 9 G22
Kunda, *India* 69 G9
Kundar →, *Pakistan* 68 D3
Kundian, *Pakistan* 68 C4
Kundla, *India* 68 J4
Kunga →, *Bangla.* 69 J13
Kungälv, *Sweden* 11 G5
Kunghit I., *Canada* 104 C2
Kungrad = Qŭnghirot, *Uzbekistan* 50 E6
Kungsängen, *Sweden* 10 E11
Kungsbacka, *Sweden* 11 G6
Kungsgården, *Sweden* 10 D10
Kungshamn, *Sweden* 11 F5
Kungsör, *Sweden* 10 E10
Kungur, *Russia* 50 D6
Kunhar →, *Pakistan* 69 B5
Kunhegyes, *Hungary* 42 C5
Kuningan, *Indonesia* 63 G13
Kunlong, *Burma* 58 F2
Kunlun Shan, *Asia* 60 C3
Kunmadaras, *Hungary* 42 C5
Kunming, *China* 58 E4
Kunów, *Poland* 45 H8
Kunsan, *S. Korea* 57 G14
Kunshan, *China* 59 B13
Kunszentmárton, *Hungary* 42 D5
Kunszentmiklós, *Hungary* 42 C4
Kuntaur, *Senegal* 82 C2
Kununurra, *Australia* 92 C4
Kunwari →, *India* 69 F8
Kunya-Urgench = Köneürgench, *Turkmenistan* 50 E6
Künzelsau, *Germany* 25 F5
Kuopio, *Finland* 8 E22
Kupa →, *Croatia* 29 C13
Kupang, *Indonesia* 63 F6
Kupreanof I., *U.S.A.* 104 B2
Kupres, *Bos.-H.* 42 G2
Kupyansk, *Ukraine* 47 H9
Kupyansk-Uzlovoi, *Ukraine* 47 H9
Kuqa, *China* 60 B3
Kür →, *Azerbaijan* 73 C13
Kür Dili, *Azerbaijan* 71 B6
Kura = Kür →, *Azerbaijan* 73 C13
Kuranda, *Australia* 94 B4
Kuranga, *India* 68 H3
Kurashiki, *Japan* 55 G6
Kurayoshi, *Japan* 55 G6
Kürdämir, *Azerbaijan* 49 K9
Kurdistan, *Asia* 73 D10
Kŭrdzhali, *Bulgaria* 41 E9
Kure, *Japan* 55 G6
Küre, *Turkey* 72 B5
Küre Dağları, *Turkey* 72 B6
Kuressaare, *Estonia* 9 G20
Kurgan, *Russia* 50 D7
Kurganinsk, *Russia* 49 H5
Kurgannaya = Kurganinsk, *Russia* 49 H5
Kuri, *India* 68 F4
Kuria Maria Is. = Khurīyā Murīyā, Jazā 'ir, *Oman* 74 D6
Kuridala, *Australia* 94 C3
Kurigram, *Bangla.* 67 G16
Kurikka, *Finland* 9 E20
Kuril Is. = Kurilskiye Ostrova, *Russia* 51 E15
Kuril Trench, *Pac. Oc.* 52 E19
Kurilsk, *Russia* 51 E15
Kurilskiye Ostrova, *Russia* 51 E15
Kurino, *Japan* 55 J5
Kurinskaya Kosa = Kür Dili, *Azerbaijan* 71 B6
Kurkur, *Egypt* 80 C3
Kurlovskiy, *Russia* 48 C5
Kurmuk, *Sudan* 81 E3
Kurnool, *India* 66 M11
Kuro-Shima, *Kagoshima, Japan* 55 J4
Kuro-Shima, *Okinawa, Japan* 55 M2
Kuror, J., *Sudan* 80 C3
Kurow, *N.Z.* 91 L3
Kurów, *Poland* 45 G9
Kurram →, *Pakistan* 68 C4
Kurri Kurri, *Australia* 95 E5
Kurrimine, *Australia* 94 B4
Kursavka, *Russia* 49 H6
Kuršėnai, *Lithuania* 44 B9
Kurshskiy Zaliv, *Russia* 9 J19
Kursk, *Russia* 47 G9
Kuršumlija, *Serbia, Yug.* 40 C5
Kuršumlijska Banja, *Serbia, Yug.* 40 C5
Kurşunlu, *Bursa, Turkey* 41 F13
Kurşunlu, *Çankırı, Turkey* 72 B5
Kurtalan, *Turkey* 73 D9
Kurtbey, *Turkey* 41 E10
Kuru, *Sudan* 81 F2
Kuru, Bahr el →, *Sudan* 81 F2
Kurucaşile, *Turkey* 72 B5
Kuruçay, *Turkey* 70 B3
Kuruktag, *China* 60 B3
Kuruman, *S. Africa* 88 D3
Kuruman →, *S. Africa* 88 D3
Kurume, *Japan* 55 H5
Kurun →, *Sudan* 81 F3
Kurunegala, *Sri Lanka* 66 R12
Kurya, *Russia* 50 C6
Kus Gölü, *Turkey* 41 F11
Kuşadası, *Turkey* 72 D2
Kuşadası Körfezi, *Turkey* 39 D8
Kusatsu, *Japan* 55 F9
Kusawa L., *Canada* 104 A1
Kusel, *Germany* 25 F3
Kushaka, *Nigeria* 83 C6
Kushalgarh, *India* 68 H6
Kushchevskaya, *Russia* 49 G4
Kusheriki, *Nigeria* 83 C6
Kushikino, *Japan* 55 J5
Kushima, *Japan* 55 J5
Kushimoto, *Japan* 55 H7
Kushiro, *Japan* 54 C12
Kushiro-Gawa →, *Japan* 54 C12
Kūshk, *Iran* 71 D8
Kushka = Gushgy, *Turkmenistan* 50 F7
Kūshkī, *Iran* 70 C5
Kushol, *India* 69 C7
Kushtia, *Bangla.* 67 H16
Kushum →, *Kazakstan* 48 F10
Kuskokwim B., *U.S.A.* 100 C3
Kusmi, *India* 69 H10
Kussharo-Ko, *Japan* 54 C12
Kustanay = Qostanay, *Kazakstan* 50 D7
Kut, Ko, *Thailand* 65 G4
Kütahya, *Turkey* 39 B12
Kütahya □, *Turkey* 39 B11
Kutaisi, *Georgia* 49 J6
Kutaraja = Banda Aceh, *Indonesia* 62 C1
Kutch, Gulf of = Kachchh, Gulf of, *India* 68 H3
Kutch, Rann of = Kachchh, Rann of, *India* 68 H4
Kutina, *Croatia* 29 C13
Kutiyana, *India* 68 J4
Kutjevo, *Croatia* 42 E2
Kutkashen, *Azerbaijan* 49 K8
Kutná Hora, *Czech Rep.* 26 B8
Kutno, *Poland* 45 F6
Kutse, *Botswana* 88 C3
Kutu, *Dem. Rep. of the Congo* 84 E3
Kutum, *Sudan* 81 E1
Kúty, *Slovak Rep.* 27 C10
Kuujjuaq, *Canada* 101 C13
Kuujjuarapik, *Canada* 102 A4
Kuŭp-tong, *N. Korea* 57 D14
Kuusamo, *Finland* 8 D23
Kuusankoski, *Finland* 9 F22
Kuvshinovo, *Russia* 46 D8
Kuwait = Al Kuwayt, *Kuwait* 70 D5
Kuwait ■, *Asia* 70 D5
Kuwana, *Japan* 55 G8
Kuwana →, *India* 69 F10
Kuybyshev = Samara, *Russia* 48 D10
Kuybyshev, *Russia* 50 D8
Kuybyshevo, *Ukraine* 47 J9
Kuybyshevskoye Vdkhr., *Russia* 48 C9
Kuye He →, *China* 56 E6
Kūyeh, *Iran* 70 B5
Kūysanjaq, *Iraq* 70 B5
Kuyucak, *Turkey* 39 D10
Kuyumba, *Russia* 51 C10
Kuzey Anadolu Dağları, *Turkey* 72 B7
Kuzmin, *Serbia, Yug.* 42 E4
Kuznetsk, *Russia* 48 D8
Kuzomen, *Russia* 50 C4
Kvænangen, *Norway* 8 A19
Kværndrup, *Denmark* 11 J4
Kvaløy, *Norway* 8 B18
Kvänum, *Sweden* 11 F7
Kvareli = Qvareli, *Georgia* 49 K7
Kvarner, *Croatia* 29 D11
Kvarnerič, *Croatia* 29 D11
Kvicksund, *Sweden* 10 E10
Kvillsfors, *Sweden* 11 G9
Kvismare kanal, *Sweden* 10 E9
Kvissleby, *Sweden* 10 B11
Kwa-Nobuhle, *S. Africa* 85 L5
Kwabhaca, *S. Africa* 89 E4
Kwakhanai, *Botswana* 88 C3
Kwakoegron, *Surinam* 125 B7
Kwale, *Kenya* 86 C4
Kwale, *Nigeria* 83 D6
KwaMashu, *S. Africa* 89 D5
Kwando →, *Africa* 88 B3
Kwangdaeri, *N. Korea* 57 D14
Kwangju, *S. Korea* 57 G14
Kwango →, *Dem. Rep. of the Congo* 77 G5
Kwangsi-Chuang = Guangxi Zhuangzu Zizhiqu □, *China* 58 F7
Kwangtung = Guangdong □, *China* 59 F9
Kwara □, *Nigeria* 83 D6
Kwataboahegan →, *Canada* 102 B3
Kwatisore, *Indonesia* 63 E8
KwaZulu Natal □, *S. Africa* 89 D5
Kweichow = Guizhou □, *China* 58 D6
Kwekwe, *Zimbabwe* 87 F2
Kwidzyn, *Poland* 44 E5
Kwiha, *Ethiopia* 81 E4
Kwinana New Town, *Australia* 93 F2
Kwisa →, *Poland* 45 G2
Kwoka, *Indonesia* 63 E8
Kwolla, *Nigeria* 83 D6
Kyabra Cr. →, *Australia* 95 D3
Kyabram, *Australia* 95 F4
Kyaikto, *Burma* 64 D1
Kyakhta, *Russia* 51 D11
Kyancutta, *Australia* 95 E2
Kyangin, *Burma* 67 K19
Kyaukpadaung, *Burma* 67 J19
Kyaukpyu, *Burma* 67 K18
Kyaukse, *Burma* 67 J20
Kybartai, *Lithuania* 44 D9
Kyburz, *U.S.A.* 116 G6
Kyelang, *India* 68 C7
Kyenjojo, *Uganda* 86 B3
Kyjov, *Czech Rep.* 27 B10
Kyle, *Canada* 105 C7
Kyle Dam, *Zimbabwe* 87 G3
Kyle of Lochalsh, *U.K.* 14 D3
Kyll →, *Germany* 25 F2
Kyllburg, *Germany* 25 E2
Kymijoki →, *Finland* 9 F22
Kyneton, *Australia* 95 F3
Kynuna, *Australia* 94 C3
Kyō-ga-Saki, *Japan* 55 G7
Kyoga, L., *Uganda* 86 B3
Kyogle, *Australia* 95 D5
Kyom →, *Sudan* 81 F2
Kyongju, *S. Korea* 57 G15
Kyongpyaw, *Burma* 67 L19
Kyŏngsŏng, *N. Korea* 57 D15
Kyōto, *Japan* 55 G7
Kyōto □, *Japan* 55 G7
Kyparissovouno, *Cyprus* 36 D12
Kyperounda, *Cyprus* 36 E11
Kyrenia, *Cyprus* 36 D12
Kyrgyzstan ■, *Asia* 50 E8
Kyritz, *Germany* 24 C8
Kyrkhult, *Sweden* 11 H8
Kyrönjoki →, *Finland* 8 E19
Kystatyam, *Russia* 51 C13
Kysucké Nové Mesto, *Slovak Rep.* 27 B11
Kythréa, *Cyprus* 36 D12
Kyunhla, *Burma* 67 H19
Kyuquot Sound, *Canada* 104 D3
Kyurdamir = Kürdämir, *Azerbaijan* 49 K9
Kyūshū, *Japan* 55 H5
Kyūshū □, *Japan* 55 H5
Kyūshū-Sanchi, *Japan* 55 H5
Kyustendil, *Bulgaria* 40 D6
Kyusyur, *Russia* 51 B13
Kyyiv, *Ukraine* 47 G6
Kyyivske Vdskh., *Ukraine* 47 G6
Kyzyl, *Russia* 51 D10
Kyzyl Kum, *Uzbekistan* 50 E7
Kyzyl-Kyya, *Kyrgyzstan* 50 E8
Kyzyl-Orda = Qyzylorda, *Kazakstan* 50 E7

L

La Albuera, *Spain* 35 G4
La Alcarria, *Spain* 32 E2
La Almarcha, *Spain* 32 F2
La Almunia de Doña Godina, *Spain* 32 D3
La Asunción, *Venezuela* 124 A6
La Baie, *Canada* 103 C5
La Banda, *Argentina* 126 B3
La Bañeza, *Spain* 34 C5
La Barca, *Mexico* 118 C4
La Barge, *U.S.A.* 114 E8
La Bastide-Puylaurent, *France* 20 D7
La Baule-Escoubiac, *France* 18 E4
La Belle, *U.S.A.* 109 M5
La Biche →, *Canada* 104 B4
La Biche, L., *Canada* 104 C6
La Bisbal d'Empordà, *Spain* 32 D8
La Bomba, *Mexico* 118 A1
La Bresse, *France* 19 D13
La Bureba, *Spain* 34 C7
La Calera, *Chile* 126 C1
La Campiña, *Spain* 35 H6
La Canal = Sa Canal, *Spain* 37 C7
La Cañiza = A Cañiza, *Spain* 34 C2
La Canourgue, *France* 20 D7
La Capelle, *France* 19 C10
La Carlota, *Argentina* 126 C3
La Carlota, *Phil.* 61 F5
La Carlota, *Spain* 35 H6
La Carolina, *Spain* 35 G7
La Cavalerie, *France* 20 D7
La Ceiba, *Honduras* 120 C2
La Chaise-Dieu, *France* 20 C7
La Chapelle d'Angillon, *France* 19 E9
La Chapelle-St-Luc, *France* 19 D11
La Chapelle-sur-Erdre, *France* 18 E5
La Charité-sur-Loire, *France* 19 E10
La Chartre-sur-le-Loir, *France* 18 E7
La Châtaigneraie, *France* 20 B3
La Châtre, *France* 19 F9
La Chaux-de-Fonds, *Switz.* 25 H2
La Chorrera, *Panama* 120 E4
La Ciotat, *France* 21 E9
La Clayette, *France* 19 F11
La Cocha, *Argentina* 126 B2
La Concepción = Ri-Aba, *Eq. Guin.* 83 E6
La Concepción, *Panama* 120 E3
La Concordia, *Mexico* 119 D6
La Coruña = A Coruña, *Spain* 34 B2
La Coruña □, *Spain* 34 B2
La Côte-St-André, *France* 21 C9
La Courtine-le-Trucq, *France* 20 C6
La Crau, *Bouches-du-Rhône, France* 21 E8
La Crau, *Var, France* 21 E10
La Crescent, *U.S.A.* 112 D9
La Crete, *Canada* 104 B5
La Crosse, *Kans., U.S.A.* 112 F5
La Crosse, *Wis., U.S.A.* 112 D9
La Cruz, *Costa Rica* 120 D2
La Cruz, *Mexico* 118 C3
La Désirade, *Guadeloupe* 121 C7
La Escondida, *Mexico* 118 C5
La Esmeralda, *Paraguay* 126 A3
La Esperanza, *Cuba* 120 B3
La Esperanza, *Honduras* 120 D2
La Estrada = A Estrada, *Spain* 34 C2
La Faouët, *France* 18 D3
La Fayette, *U.S.A.* 109 H3
La Fé, *Cuba* 120 B3
La Fère, *France* 19 C10
La Ferté-Bernard, *France* 18 D7
La Ferté-Gaucher, *France* 19 D10
La Ferté-Macé, *France* 18 D6
La Ferté-St-Aubin, *France* 19 E8
La Ferté-sous-Jouarre, *France* 19 D10
La Ferté-Vidame, *France* 18 D7
La Flèche, *France* 18 E6
La Follette, *U.S.A.* 109 G3
La Fregeneda, *Spain* 34 E4
La Fuente de San Esteban, *Spain* 34 E4
La Gacilly, *France* 18 E4
La Gineta, *Spain* 33 F2
La Grand-Combe, *France* 21 D8
La Grande, *U.S.A.* 114 D4
La Grande →, *Canada* 102 B5
La Grande Deux, Rés., *Canada* 102 B4
La Grande-Motte, *France* 21 E8
La Grande Quatre, Rés., *Canada* 102 B5
La Grande Trois, Rés., *Canada* 102 B4
La Grange, *Calif., U.S.A.* 116 H6
La Grange, *Ga., U.S.A.* 109 J3
La Grange, *Ky., U.S.A.* 108 F3
La Grange, *Tex., U.S.A.* 113 L6
La Grave, *France* 21 C10
La Guaira, *Venezuela* 124 A5
La Guardia = A Guarda, *Spain* 34 D2
La Gudiña = A Gudiña, *Spain* 34 C3
La Guerche-de-Bretagne, *France* 18 E5
La Guerche-sur-l'Aubois, *France* 19 F9
La Habana, *Cuba* 120 B3
La Haye-du-Puits, *France* 18 C5
La Horra, *Spain* 34 D7
La Independencia, *Mexico* 119 D6
La Isabela, *Dom. Rep.* 121 C5
La Jonquera, *Spain* 32 C7
La Junta, *U.S.A.* 113 F3
La Laguna, *Canary Is.* 37 F3
La Libertad, *Guatemala* 120 C1
La Libertad, *Mexico* 118 B2
La Ligua, *Chile* 126 C1
La Línea de la Concepción, *Spain* 35 J5
La Loche, *Canada* 105 B7
La Londe-les-Maures, *France* 21 E10
La Lora, *Spain* 34 C7
La Loupe, *France* 18 D8
La Louvière, *Belgium* 17 D4
La Machine, *France* 19 F10
La Maddalena, *Italy* 30 A2
La Malbaie, *Canada* 103 C5
La Mancha, *Spain* 33 F2
La Mariña, *Spain* 34 B3
La Martre, L., *Canada* 104 A5
La Mesa, *U.S.A.* 117 N9
La Misión, *Mexico* 118 A1
La Mothe-Achard, *France* 18 F5
La Motte, *France* 21 D10
La Motte-Chalançon, *France* 21 D9
La Motte-Servolex, *France* 21 C9
La Moure, *U.S.A.* 112 B5
La Muela, *Spain* 32 D3
La Mure, *France* 21 D9
La Negra, *Chile* 126 A1
La Oliva, *Canary Is.* 37 F6
La Orotava, *Canary Is.* 37 F3
La Oroya, *Peru* 124
La Pacaudière, *France* 19 F10
La Palma, *Canary Is.* 37 F2
La Palma, *Panama* 120 E4
La Palma del Condado, *Spain* 35 H4
La Paloma, *Chile* 126 C1
La Pampa □, *Argentina* 126 D2
La Paragua, *Venezuela* 124 B6
La Paz, *Entre Ríos, Argentina* 126 C4
La Paz, *San Luis, Argentina* 126 C2
La Paz, *Bolivia* 124 G5
La Paz, *Honduras* 120 D2
La Paz, *Mexico* 118 C2
La Paz, *Phil.* 61 D4
La Paz Centro, *Nic.* 120 D2
La Pedrera, *Colombia* 124 D5
La Pérade, *Canada* 103 C5
La Perouse Str., *Asia* 54 B11
La Pesca, *Mexico* 119 C5
La Piedad, *Mexico* 118 C4
La Pine, *U.S.A.* 114 E3
La Plata, *Argentina* 126 D4
La Pobla de Lillet, *Spain* 32 C6
La Pocatière, *Canada* 103 C5
La Pola de Gordón, *Spain* 34 C5
La Porta, *France* 21 F13
La Porte, *Ind., U.S.A.* 108 E2
La Porte, *Tex., U.S.A.* 113 L7
La Presanella, *Italy* 28 B7
La Puebla = Sa Pobla, *Spain* 32 F8
La Puebla de Cazalla, *Spain* 35 H5
La Puebla de los Infantes, *Spain* 35 H5
La Puebla de Montalbán, *Spain* 34 F6
La Puebla del Río, *Spain* 35 H4
La Puerta de Segura, *Spain* 35 G8
La Purísima, *Mexico* 118 B2
La Push, *U.S.A.* 116 C2
La Quiaca, *Argentina* 126 A2
La Réole, *France* 20 D3
La Restinga, *Canary Is.* 37 G2
La Rioja, *Argentina* 126 B2
La Rioja □, *Argentina* 126 B2
La Rioja □, *Spain* 32 C2
La Robla, *Spain* 34 C5
La Roche-Bernard, *France* 18 E4
La Roche-Canillac, *France* 20 C5
La Roche-en-Ardenne, *Belgium* 17 D5
La Roche-sur-Foron, *France* 19 F13
La Roche-sur-Yon, *France* 18 F5
La Rochefoucauld, *France* 20 C4
La Rochelle, *France* 20 B2
La Roda, *Spain* 33 F2
La Roda de Andalucía, *Spain* 35 H6
La Romana, *Dom. Rep.* 121 C6
La Ronge, *Canada* 105 B7
La Rumorosa, *Mexico* 117 N10
La Sabina = Sa Savina, *Spain* 37 C7
La Sagra, *Spain* 33 H2
La Salle, *U.S.A.* 112 E10
La Sanabria, *Spain* 34 C4
La Santa, *Canary Is.* 37 E6
La Sarre, *Canada* 102 C4
La Scie, *Canada* 103 C8
La Selva, *Spain* 32 C7
La Selva Beach, *U.S.A.* 116 J5
La Selva del Camp, *Spain* 32 D6
La Serena, *Chile* 126 B1
La Serena, *Spain* 35 G5
La Seu d'Urgell, *Spain* 32 C6
La Seyne-sur-Mer, *France* 21 E9
La Sila, *Italy* 31 C9
La Solana, *Spain* 35 G7
La Soufrière, *St. Vincent* 121 D7
La Souterraine, *France* 19 F8
La Spézia, *Italy* 28 D6
La Suze-sur-Sarthe, *France* 18 E7
La Tagua, *Colombia* 124 C4
La Teste, *France* 20 D2
La Tortuga, *Venezuela* 121 D6
La Tour-du-Pin, *France* 21 C9
La Tranche-sur-Mer, *France* 18 F5
La Tremblade, *France* 20 C2
La Tuque, *Canada* 102 C5
La Unión, *Chile* 128 E2
La Unión, *El Salv.* 120 D2
La Unión, *Mexico* 118 D4
La Unión, *Spain* 33 H4
La Urbana, *Venezuela* 124 B5
La Vall d'Uixó, *Spain* 32 F4
La Vecilla de Curveño, *Spain* 34 C5
La Vega, *Dom. Rep.* 121 C5
La Vela de Coro, *Venezuela* 124 A5
La Veleta, *Spain* 35 H7
La Venta, *Mexico* 119 D6
La Ventura, *Mexico* 118 C4
La Voulte-sur-Rhône, *France* 21 D8
Laa an der Thaya, *Austria* 27 C9
Laaber, Grosse →, *Germany* 25 G8
Laage, *Germany* 24 B8
Laatzen, *Germany* 24 C5
Laba →, *Russia* 49 H4
Labason, *Phil.* 61 G5
Labastide-Murat, *France* 20 D5
Labastide-Rouairoux, *France* 20 E6
Labbézenga, *Mali* 83 B5

Labe = Elbe →, *Europe* 24 B4
Labé, *Guinea* 82 C2
Laberge, L., *Canada* 104 A1
Labin, *Croatia* 29 C11
Labinsk, *Russia* 49 H5
Labis, *Malaysia* 65 L4
Łabiszyn, *Poland* 45 F4
Labo, *Phil.* 61 D5
Laboe, *Germany* 24 A6
Laborec →, *Slovak Rep.* 27 C14
Labouheyre, *France* 20 D3
Laboulaye, *Argentina* 126 C3
Labrador, *Canada* 103 B7
Labrador City, *Canada* 103 B6
Labrador Sea, *Atl. Oc.* 101 C14
Lábrea, *Brazil* 124 E6
Labrède, *France* 20 D3
Labruguière, *France* 20 E6
Labuan, *Malaysia* 62 C5
Labuan, Pulau, *Malaysia* 62 C5
Labuha, *Indonesia* 63 E7
Labuhan, *Indonesia* 63 G11
Labuhanbajo, *Indonesia* 63 F6
Labuk, Telok, *Malaysia* 62 C5
Labyrinth, L., *Australia* 95 E2
Labytnangi, *Russia* 50 C7
Laç, *Albania* 40 E3
Lac Bouchette, *Canada* 103 C5
Lac Édouard, *Canada* 102 C5
Lac La Biche, *Canada* 104 C6
Lac la Martre = Wha Ti, *Canada* 100 B8
Lac La Ronge Prov. Park, *Canada* 105 B7
Lac-Mégantic, *Canada* 103 C5
Lac Seul, Res., *Canada* 102 B1
Lac Thien, *Vietnam* 64 F7
Lacanau, *France* 20 D2
Lacanau, Étang de, *France* 20 D2
Lacantúm →, *Mexico* 119 D6
Lacara →, *Spain* 35 G4
Lacaune, *France* 20 E6
Lacaune, Mts. de, *France* 20 E6
Laccadive Is. = Lakshadweep Is., *Ind. Oc.* 52 H11
Lacepede B., *Australia* 95 F2
Lacepede Is., *Australia* 92 C3
Lacerdónia, *Mozam.* 87 F4
Lacey, *U.S.A.* 116 C4
Lachhmangarh, *India* 68 F6
Lachi, *Pakistan* 68 C4
Lachine, *Canada* 102 C5
Lachlan →, *Australia* 95 E3
Lachute, *Canada* 102 C5
Lackawanna, *U.S.A.* 110 D6
Lackawaxen, *U.S.A.* 111 E10
Lacolle, *Canada* 111 A11
Lacombe, *Canada* 104 C6
Lacona, *U.S.A.* 111 C8
Láconi, *Italy* 30 C2
Laconia, *U.S.A.* 111 C13
Lacq, *France* 20 E3
Ladakh Ra., *India* 69 C8
Lądek-Zdrój, *Poland* 45 H3
Ládhon →, *Greece* 38 D3
Ladik, *Turkey* 72 B6
Ladismith, *S. Africa* 88 E3
Ladíspoli, *Italy* 29 G9
Lādīz, *Iran* 71 D9
Ladnun, *India* 68 F6
Ladoga, L. = Ladozhskoye Ozero, *Russia* 46 B6
Ladozhskoye Ozero, *Russia* 46 B6
Lady Elliott I., *Australia* 94 C5
Lady Grey, *S. Africa* 88 E4
Ladybrand, *S. Africa* 88 D4
Ladysmith, *Canada* 104 D4
Ladysmith, *S. Africa* 89 D4
Ladysmith, *U.S.A.* 112 C9
Lae, *Papua N. G.* 96 H6
Laem Ngop, *Thailand* 65 F4
Laem Pho, *Thailand* 65 J3
Læsø, *Denmark* 11 G5
Læsø Rende, *Denmark* 11 G4
Lafayette, *Colo., U.S.A.* 112 F2
Lafayette, *Ind., U.S.A.* 108 E2
Lafayette, *La., U.S.A.* 113 K9
Lafayette, *Tenn., U.S.A.* 109 G2
Laferte →, *Canada* 104 A5
Lafia, *Nigeria* 83 D6
Lafiagi, *Nigeria* 83 D6
Lafleche, *Canada* 105 D7
Lafon, *Sudan* 81 F3
Lagan, *Sweden* 11 H7
Lagan →, *Sweden* 11 H6
Lagan →, *U.K.* 15 B6
Lagarfljót →, *Iceland* 8 D6
Lage, *Germany* 24 D4
Lågen →, *Oppland, Norway* 9 F14
Lågen →, *Vestfold, Norway* 9 G14
Lägerdorf, *Germany* 24 B5
Laghouat, *Algeria* 78 B6
Lagnieu, *France* 21 C9
Lagny-sur-Marne, *France* 19 D9
Lago, *Italy* 31 C9
Lagôa, *Portugal* 35 H2
Lagoa Vermelha, *Brazil* 127 B5
Lagoaça, *Portugal* 34 D4
Lagodekhi, *Georgia* 49 K8
Lagónegro, *Italy* 31 B8
Lagonoy G., *Phil.* 61 E5
Lagos, *Nigeria* 83 D5
Lagos, *Portugal* 35 H2
Lagos □, *Nigeria* 83 D5
Lagos de Moreno, *Mexico* 118 C4
Lagrange, *Australia* 92 C3
Lagrange B., *Australia* 92 C3
Laguardia, *Spain* 32 C2
Laguépie, *France* 20 D5
Laguna, *Brazil* 127 B6
Laguna, *U.S.A.* 115 J10
Laguna Beach, *U.S.A.* 117 M9
Laguna de Duera, *Spain* 34 D6
Laguna Limpia, *Argentina* 126 B4
Laguna Madre, *U.S.A.* 119 B5
Lagunas, *Chile* 126 A2
Lagunas, *Peru* 124 E3
Lahad Datu, *Malaysia* 63 C5
Lahad Datu, Teluk, *Malaysia* 63 D5
Lahan Sai, *Thailand* 64 E4
Lahanam, *Laos* 64 D5
Lahar, *India* 69 F8
Laharpur, *India* 69 F9
Lahat, *Indonesia* 62 E2
Lahewa, *Indonesia* 62 D1
Lāhījān, *Iran* 71 B6
Lahn →, *Germany* 25 E3
Lahnstein, *Germany* 25 E3
Laholm, *Sweden* 11 H7
Laholmsbukten, *Sweden* 11 H6
Lahore, *Pakistan* 68 D6
Lahr, *Germany* 25 G3
Lahri, *Pakistan* 68 E3
Lahti, *Finland* 9 F21
Lahtis = Lahti, *Finland* 9 F21
Laï, *Chad* 79 G9
Lai Chau, *Vietnam* 58 F4
Lai'an, *China* 59 A12
Laibin, *China* 58 F7
Laifeng, *China* 58 C7
L'Aigle, *France* 18 D7
Laignes, *France* 19 E11
L'Aiguillon-sur-Mer, *France* 20 B2
Laila = Laylá, *Si. Arabia* 74 C4
Laingsburg, *S. Africa* 88 E3
Lainio älv →, *Sweden* 8 C20
Lairg, *U.K.* 14 C4
Laishui, *China* 56 E8
Laissac, *France* 20 D6
Láives, *Italy* 29 B8
Laiwu, *China* 57 F9
Laixi, *China* 57 F11
Laiyang, *China* 57 F11
Laiyuan, *China* 56 E8
Laizhou, *China* 57 F10
Laizhou Wan, *China* 57 F10
Laja →, *Mexico* 118 C4
Lajere, *Nigeria* 83 C7
Lajes, *Brazil* 127 B5
Lajkovac, *Serbia, Yug.* 40 B4
Lajosmizse, *Hungary* 42 C4
Lak Sao, *Laos* 64 C5
Lakaband, *Pakistan* 68 D3
Lakamané, *Mali* 82 C3
Lake Alpine, *U.S.A.* 116 G7
Lake Andes, *U.S.A.* 112 D5
Lake Arthur, *U.S.A.* 113 K8
Lake Cargelligo, *Australia* 95 E4
Lake Charles, *U.S.A.* 113 K8
Lake City, *Colo., U.S.A.* 115 G10
Lake City, *Fla., U.S.A.* 109 K4
Lake City, *Mich., U.S.A.* 108 C3
Lake City, *Minn., U.S.A.* 112 C8
Lake City, *Pa., U.S.A.* 110 D4
Lake City, *S.C., U.S.A.* 109 J6
Lake Cowichan, *Canada* 104 D4
Lake District, *U.K.* 12 C4
Lake Elsinore, *U.S.A.* 117 M9
Lake George, *U.S.A.* 111 C11
Lake Grace, *Australia* 93 F2
Lake Harbour = Kimmirut, *Canada* 101 B13
Lake Havasu City, *U.S.A.* 117 L12
Lake Hughes, *U.S.A.* 117 L8
Lake Isabella, *U.S.A.* 117 K8
Lake Jackson, *U.S.A.* 113 L7
Lake Junction, *U.S.A.* 114 D8
Lake King, *Australia* 93 F2
Lake Lenore, *Canada* 105 C8
Lake Louise, *Canada* 104 C5
Lake Mead National Recreation Area, *U.S.A.* 117 K12
Lake Mills, *U.S.A.* 112 D8
Lake Placid, *U.S.A.* 111 B11
Lake Pleasant, *U.S.A.* 111 C10
Lake Providence, *U.S.A.* 113 J9
Lake St. Peter, *Canada* 110 A6
Lake Superior Prov. Park, *Canada* 102 C3
Lake Village, *U.S.A.* 113 J9
Lake Wales, *U.S.A.* 109 M5
Lake Worth, *U.S.A.* 109 M5
Lakefield, *Canada* 102 D4
Lakehurst, *U.S.A.* 111 F10
Lakeland, *Australia* 94 B3
Lakeland, *U.S.A.* 109 M5
Lakemba, *Fiji* 91 D9
Lakeport, *Calif., U.S.A.* 116 F4
Lakeport, *Mich., U.S.A.* 110 C2
Lakes Entrance, *Australia* 95 F4
Lakeside, *Ariz., U.S.A.* 115 J9
Lakeside, *Calif., U.S.A.* 117 N10
Lakeside, *Nebr., U.S.A.* 112 D3
Lakeside, *Ohio, U.S.A.* 110 E2
Lakeview, *U.S.A.* 114 E3
Lakeville, *U.S.A.* 112 C8
Lakewood, *Colo., U.S.A.* 112 F2
Lakewood, *N.J., U.S.A.* 111 F10
Lakewood, *N.Y., U.S.A.* 110 D5
Lakewood, *Ohio, U.S.A.* 110 E3
Lakewood, *Wash., U.S.A.* 116 C4
Lakha, *India* 68 F4
Lakhaniá, *Greece* 36 D9
Lakhimpur, *India* 69 F9
Lakhnadon, *India* 69 H8
Lakhonpheng, *Laos* 64 E5
Lakhpat, *India* 68 H3
Läki, *Azerbaijan* 49 K8
Lakin, *U.S.A.* 113 G4
Lakitusaki →, *Canada* 102 B3
Lakki, *Pakistan* 68 C4
Lákkoi, *Greece* 36 D5
Lakonía □, *Greece* 38 E4
Lakonikós Kólpos, *Greece* 38 E4
Lakor, *Indonesia* 63 F7
Lakota, *Ivory C.* 82 D3
Lakota, *U.S.A.* 112 A5
Laksar, *India* 68 E8
Laksefjorden, *Norway* 8 A22
Lakselv, *Norway* 8 A21
Lakshadweep Is., *Ind. Oc.* 52 H11
Lakshmanpur, *India* 69 H10
Lakshmikantapur, *India* 69 H13
Lala Ghat, *India* 67 G18
Lala Musa, *Pakistan* 68 C5
Lalago, *Tanzania* 86 C3
Lalapanzi, *Zimbabwe* 87 F3
Lalapaşa, *Turkey* 41 E10
Lalbenque, *France* 20 D5
L'Albufera, *Spain* 33 F4
Lalganj, *India* 69 G11
Lalgola, *India* 69 G13
Lālī, *Iran* 71 C6
Lalibela, *Ethiopia* 81 E4
Lalin, *China* 57 B14
Lalín, *Spain* 34 C2
Lalin He →, *China* 57 B13
Lalinde, *France* 20 D4
Lalitapur = Patan, *Nepal* 67 F14
Lalitpur, *India* 69 G8
Lalkua, *India* 69 E8
Lalsot, *India* 68 F7
Lam, *Vietnam* 64 B6
Lam Pao Res., *Thailand* 64 D4
Lama Kara, *Togo* 83 D5
Lamaing, *Burma* 67 M20
Lamar, *Colo., U.S.A.* 112 F3
Lamar, *Mo., U.S.A.* 113 G7
Lamas, *Peru* 124 E3
Lamastre, *France* 21 D8
Lambach, *Austria* 26 C6
Lamballe, *France* 18 D4
Lambaréné, *Gabon* 84 E2
Lambasa, *Fiji* 91 C8
Lambay I., *Ireland* 15 C5
Lambert Glacier, *Antarctica* 5 D6
Lambert's Bay, *S. Africa* 88 E2
Lambesc, *France* 21 E9
Lambeth, *Canada* 110 D3
Lambi Kyun, *Burma* 65 G2
Lámbia, *Greece* 38 D3
Lambomakondro, *Madag.* 89 C7
Lambro →, *Italy* 28 C6
Lame, *Nigeria* 83 C6
Lame Deer, *U.S.A.* 114 D10
Lamego, *Portugal* 34 D3
Lamèque, *Canada* 103 C7
Lameroo, *Australia* 95 F3
Lamesa, *U.S.A.* 113 J4
Lamía, *Greece* 38 C4
Lamitan, *Phil.* 61 H5
Lammermuir Hills, *U.K.* 14 F6
Lammhult, *Sweden* 11 G8
Lamoille →, *U.S.A.* 111 B11
Lamon B., *Phil.* 61 D5
Lamont, *Canada* 104 C6
Lamont, *Calif., U.S.A.* 117 K8
Lamont, *Wyo., U.S.A.* 114 E10
Lamotte-Beuvron, *France* 19 E9
Lampa, *Peru* 124 G4
Lampang, *Thailand* 64 C2
Lampasas, *U.S.A.* 113 K5
Lampazos de Naranjo, *Mexico* 118 B4
Lampertheim, *Germany* 25 F4
Lampeter, *U.K.* 13 E3
Lampman, *Canada* 105 D8
Lamprechtshausen, *Austria* 26 D5
Lampung □, *Indonesia* 62 F2
Lamta, *India* 69 H9
Lamu, *Kenya* 86 C5
Lamy, *U.S.A.* 115 J11
Lan Xian, *China* 56 E6
Lan Yu = Hungt'ou Hsü, *Taiwan* 59 F13
Lanai, *U.S.A.* 106 H16
Lanak La, *India* 69 B8
Lanak'o Shank'ou = Lanak La, *India* 69 B8
Lanao, L., *Phil.* 61 H6
Lanark, *Canada* 111 A8
Lanark, *U.K.* 14 F5
Lancang, *China* 58 F2
Lancang Jiang →, *China* 58 G3
Lancashire □, *U.K.* 12 D5
Lancaster, *Canada* 111 A10
Lancaster, *U.K.* 12 C5
Lancaster, *Calif., U.S.A.* 117 L8
Lancaster, *Ky., U.S.A.* 108 G3
Lancaster, *N.H., U.S.A.* 111 B13
Lancaster, *N.Y., U.S.A.* 110 D6
Lancaster, *Ohio, U.S.A.* 108 F4
Lancaster, *Pa., U.S.A.* 111 F8
Lancaster, *S.C., U.S.A.* 109 H5
Lancaster, *Wis., U.S.A.* 112 D9
Lancaster Sd., *Canada* 101 A11
Lancelin, *Australia* 93 F2
Lanchow = Lanzhou, *China* 56 F2
Lanciano, *Italy* 29 F11
Lancun, *China* 57 F11
Łańcut, *Poland* 45 H9
Landau, *Bayern, Germany* 25 G8
Landau, *Rhld-Pfz., Germany* 25 F4
Landeck, *Austria* 26 D3
Lander, *U.S.A.* 114 E9
Lander →, *Australia* 92 D5
Landerneau, *France* 18 D2
Landeryd, *Sweden* 11 G7
Landes, *France* 20 D2
Landes □, *France* 20 E3
Landete, *Spain* 32 F3
Landi Kotal, *Pakistan* 68 B4
Landisburg, *U.S.A.* 110 F7
Landivisiau, *France* 18 D2
Landquart, *Switz.* 25 J5
Landrecies, *France* 19 B10
Land's End, *U.K.* 13 G2
Landsberg, *Germany* 25 G6
Landsborough Cr. →, *Australia* 94 C3
Landsbro, *Sweden* 11 G8
Landshut, *Germany* 25 G8
Landskrona, *Sweden* 11 J6
Landstuhl, *Germany* 25 F3
Landvetter, *Sweden* 11 G6
Lanesboro, *U.S.A.* 111 E9
Lanester, *France* 18 E3
Lanett, *U.S.A.* 109 J3
Lang Qua, *Vietnam* 64 A5
Lang Shan, *China* 56 D4
Lang Son, *Vietnam* 58 G6
Lang Suan, *Thailand* 65 H2
Langå, *Denmark* 11 H3
La'nga Co, *China* 67 D12
Lángadhás, *Greece* 40 F7
Langádhia, *Greece* 38 D4
Långan →, *Sweden* 10 A8
Langano, L., *Ethiopia* 81 F4
Langar, *Iran* 71 C9
Langara I., *Canada* 104 C2
Långås, *Sweden* 11 H6
Langdai, *China* 58 D5
Langdon, *U.S.A.* 112 A5
Långe Jan = Ölands södra udde, *Sweden* 11 H10
Langeac, *France* 20 C7
Langeais, *France* 18 E7
Langeb Baraka →, *Sudan* 80 D4
Langeberg, *S. Africa* 88 E3
Langeberge, *S. Africa* 88 D3
Langeland, *Denmark* 11 K4
Langelands Bælt, *Denmark* 11 K4
Langen, *Hessen, Germany* 25 F4
Langen, *Niedersachsen, Germany* 24 B4
Langenburg, *Canada* 105 C8
Langeneß, *Germany* 24 A4
Langenlois, *Austria* 26 C8
Langeoog, *Germany* 24 B3
Langeskov, *Denmark* 11 J4
Länghem, *Sweden* 11 G7
Langhirano, *Italy* 28 D7
Langholm, *U.K.* 14 F5
Langjökull, *Iceland* 8 D3
Langkawi, Pulau, *Malaysia* 65 J2
Langklip, *S. Africa* 88 D3
Langkon, *Malaysia* 62 C5
Langlade, *St- P. & M.* 103 C8
Langley, *Canada* 116 A4
Langnau, *Switz.* 25 J3
Langogne, *France* 20 D7
Langon, *France* 20 D3
Langøya, *Norway* 8 B16
Langreo, *Spain* 34 B5
Langres, *France* 19 E12
Langres, Plateau de, *France* 19 E12
Langsa, *Indonesia* 62 D1
Långsele, *Sweden* 10 A11
Långshyttan, *Sweden* 10 D10
Langtry, *U.S.A.* 113 L4
Langu, *Thailand* 65 J2
Languedoc, *France* 20 E7
Languedoc-Roussillon □, *France* 20 E6
Langxi, *China* 59 B12
Langxiangzhen, *China* 56 E9
Langzhong, *China* 58 B5
Lanigan, *Canada* 105 C7
Lankao, *China* 56 G8
Länkäran, *Azerbaijan* 71 B6
Lanmeur, *France* 18 D3
Lannemezan, *France* 20 E4
Lannilis, *France* 18 D2
Lannion, *France* 18 D3
L'Annonciation, *Canada* 102 C5
Lanouaille, *France* 20 C5
Lanping, *China* 58 D2
Lansdale, *U.S.A.* 111 F9
Lansdowne, *Australia* 95 E5
Lansdowne, *Canada* 111 B8
Lansdowne, *India* 69 E8
Lansdowne House, *Canada* 102 B2
L'Anse, *Mich., U.S.A.* 108 B1
L'Anse, *Mich., U.S.A.* 112 B10
L'Anse au Loup, *Canada* 103 B8
L'Anse aux Meadows, *Canada* 103 B8
Lansford, *U.S.A.* 111 F9
Lanshan, *China* 59 E9
Lansing, *U.S.A.* 108 D3
Lanslebourg-Mont-Cenis, *France* 21 C10
Lanta Yai, Ko, *Thailand* 65 J2
Lantewa, *Nigeria* 83 C7
Lantian, *China* 56 G5
Lanus, *Argentina* 126 C4
Lanusei, *Italy* 30 C2
Lanuza, *Phil.* 61 G7
Lanxi, *China* 59 C12
Lanzarote, *Canary Is.* 37 F6
Lanzhou, *China* 56 F2
Lanzo Torinese, *Italy* 28 C4
Lao →, *Italy* 31 C8
Lao Bao, *Laos* 64 D6
Lao Cai, *Vietnam* 58 F4
Laoag, *Phil.* 61 B4
Laoang, *Phil.* 61 E6
Laoha He →, *China* 57 C11
Laohekou, *China* 59 A8
Laois □, *Ireland* 15 D4
Laon, *France* 19 C10
Laona, *U.S.A.* 108 C1
Laos ■, *Asia* 64 D5
Lapa, *Brazil* 127 B6
Lapai, *Nigeria* 83 D6
Lapalisse, *France* 19 F10
Lapeer, *U.S.A.* 108 D4
Lapeyrade, *France* 20 D3
Lapithos, *Cyprus* 36 D12
Lapland = Lappland, *Europe* 8 B21
Laporte, *U.S.A.* 111 E8
Lapovo, *Serbia, Yug.* 40 B5
Lappeenranta, *Finland* 9 F23
Lappland, *Europe* 8 B21
Laprida, *Argentina* 126 D3
Lapseki, *Turkey* 41 F10
Laptev Sea, *Russia* 51 B13
Lapua, *Finland* 8 E20
Lăpuş →, *Romania* 43 C8
Lapuş, Munţii, *Romania* 43 C8
Lăpuşna, *Moldova* 43 D13
Łapy, *Poland* 45 F9
Laqiya Arba'in, *Sudan* 80 C2
Laqiya Umran, *Sudan* 80 D2
L'Aquila, *Italy* 29 F10
Lār, *Āzarbājān-e Sharqī, Iran* 70 B5
Lār, *Fārs, Iran* 71 E7
Larabanga, *Ghana* 82 D4
Laragne-Montéglin, *France* 21 D9
Laramie, *U.S.A.* 112 E2
Laramie →, *U.S.A.* 114 F11
Laramie Mts., *U.S.A.* 112 E2
Laranjeiras do Sul, *Brazil* 127 B5
Larantuka, *Indonesia* 63 F6
Larat, *Indonesia* 63 F8
L'Arbresle, *France* 21 C8
Lärbro, *Sweden* 11 G12
Larde, *Mozam.* 87 F4
Larder Lake, *Canada* 102 C4
Lardhos, Ákra = Líndhos, Ákra, *Greece* 36 C10
Lardhos, Órmos, *Greece* 36 C10
Laredo, *Spain* 34 B7
Laredo, *U.S.A.* 113 M5
Laredo Sd., *Canada* 104 C3
Largentière, *France* 21 D8
L'Argentière-la-Bessée, *France* 21 D10
Largo, *U.S.A.* 109 M4
Largs, *U.K.* 14 F4
Lari, *Italy* 28 E7
Lariang, *Indonesia* 63 E5
Larimore, *U.S.A.* 112 B6
Lārīn, *Iran* 71 C7
Larino, *Italy* 29 G11
Lárisa, *Greece* 38 B4
Lárisa □, *Greece* 38 B4
Larkana, *Pakistan* 68 F3
Larnaca, *Cyprus* 36 E12
Larnaca Bay, *Cyprus* 36 E12
Larne, *U.K.* 15 B6
Larned, *U.S.A.* 112 F5
Laroquebrou, *France* 20 D6
Larose, *U.S.A.* 113 L9
Larrimah, *Australia* 92 C5
Larsen Ice Shelf, *Antarctica* 5 C17
Laruns, *France* 20 F3
Larvik, *Norway* 9 G14
Larzac, Causse du, *France* 20 E7
Las Alpujarras, *Spain* 33 J1
Las Animas, *U.S.A.* 112 F3
Las Anod, *Somali Rep.* 74 F4
Las Arenas, *Spain* 34 B6
Las Aves, Is., *W. Indies* 121 C7
Las Brenãs, *Argentina* 126 B3
Las Cabezas de San Juan, *Spain* 35 J5
Las Cejas, *Argentina* 128 B4
Las Chimeneas, *Mexico* 117 N10
Las Cruces, *U.S.A.* 115 K10
Las Flores, *Argentina* 126 D4
Las Heras, *Argentina* 126 C2
Las Lajas, *Argentina* 128 D2
Las Lomitas, *Argentina* 126 A3
Las Marismas, *Spain* 35 H4
Las Minas, *Spain* 33 G3
Las Navas de la Concepción, *Spain* 35 H5
Las Navas del Marqués, *Spain* 34 E6
Las Palmas, *Argentina* 126 B4
Las Palmas, *Canary Is.* 37 F4
Las Palmas →, *Mexico* 117 N10
Las Pedroñas, *Spain* 33 F2
Las Piedras, *Uruguay* 127 C4
Las Pipinas, *Argentina* 126 D4
Las Plumas, *Argentina* 128 E3
Las Rosas, *Argentina* 126 C3
Las Rozas, *Spain* 34 E7
Las Tablas, *Panama* 120 E3
Las Termas, *Argentina* 126 B3
Las Toscas, *Argentina* 126 B4
Las Truchas, *Mexico* 118 D4
Las Varillas, *Argentina* 126 C3
Las Vegas, *N. Mex., U.S.A.* 115 J11
Las Vegas, *Nev., U.S.A.* 117 J11
Lasarte, *Spain* 32 B2
Lascano, *Uruguay* 127 C5
Lashburn, *Canada* 105 C7
Lashio, *Burma* 67 H20
Lashkar, *India* 68 F8
Łasin, *Poland* 44 E6
Lasíthi, *Greece* 36 D7
Lasíthi □, *Greece* 36 D7
Lāsjerd, *Iran* 71 C7
Lask, *Poland* 45 G6
Łaskarzew, *Poland* 45 G8
Laško, *Slovenia* 29 B12
Lassay-les-Châteaux, *France* 18 D6
Lassen Pk., *U.S.A.* 114 F3
Lassen Volcanic National Park, *U.S.A.* 114 F3
Last Mountain L., *Canada* 105 C7
Lastchance Cr. →, *U.S.A.* 116 E5

Lastoursville, *Gabon* 84 E2
Lastovo, *Croatia* 29 F13
Lastovski Kanal, *Croatia* ... 29 F14
Lat Yao, *Thailand* 64 E2
Latacunga, *Ecuador* 124 D3
Latakia = Al Lādhiqīyah,
 Syria 70 C2
Latchford, *Canada* 102 C4
Latehar, *India* 69 H11
Laterza, *Italy* 31 B9
Latham, *Australia* 93 E2
Lathen, *Germany* 24 C3
Lathi, *India* 68 F4
Lathrop Wells, *U.S.A.* 117 J10
Latiano, *Italy* 31 B10
Latina, *Italy* 30 A5
Latisana, *Italy* 29 C10
Latium = Lazio □, *Italy* ... 29 F9
Laton, *U.S.A.* 116 J7
Latorytsya →, *Slovak Rep.* . 27 C14
Latouche Treville, C.,
 Australia 92 C3
Latrobe, *Australia* 94 G4
Latrobe, *U.S.A.* 110 F5
Latrónico, *Italy* 31 B9
Latvia ■, *Europe* 9 H20
Lau, *Nigeria* 83 D7
Lau Group, *Fiji* 91 C9
Lauchhammer, *Germany* ... 24 D9
Lauda-Königshofen,
 Germany 25 F5
Lauenburg, *Germany* 24 B6
Lauf, *Germany* 25 F7
Laughlin, *U.S.A.* 115 J6
Laujar de Andarax, *Spain* .. 33 H2
Laukaa, *Finland* 9 E21
Launceston, *Australia* 94 G4
Launceston, *U.K.* 13 G3
Laune →, *Ireland* 15 D2
Launglon Bok, *Burma* 64 F1
Laupheim, *Germany* 25 G5
Laura, *Australia* 94 B3
Laureana di Borrello, *Italy* . 31 D9
Laurel, *Miss., U.S.A.* 113 K10
Laurel, *Mont., U.S.A.* 114 D9
Laurencekirk, *U.K.* 14 E6
Laurens, *U.S.A.* 109 H4
Laurentian Plateau, *Canada* 103 B6
Lauria, *Italy* 31 B8
Laurie L., *Canada* 105 B8
Laurinburg, *U.S.A.* 109 H6
Laurium, *U.S.A.* 108 B1
Lausanne, *Switz.* 25 J2
Laut, *Indonesia* 65 K6
Laut, Pulau, *Indonesia* ... 62 E5
Laut Kecil, Kepulauan,
 Indonesia 62 E5
Lauterbach, *Germany* 24 E5
Lauterecken, *Germany* 25 F3
Lautoka, *Fiji* 91 C7
Lauzès, *France* 20 D5
Lavagh More, *Ireland* 15 B3
Lavagna, *Italy* 28 D6
Laval, *France* 18 D6
Lavalle, *Argentina* 126 B2
Lavant Station, *Canada* ... 111 A8
Lāvar Meydān, *Iran* 71 D7
Lávara, *Greece* 41 E10
Lavardac, *France* 20 D4
Lavaur, *France* 20 E5
Lavelanet, *France* 20 F5
Lavello, *Italy* 31 A8
Laverton, *Australia* 93 E3
Lavìs, *Italy* 28 B8
Lávkos, *Greece* 38 B5
Lavos, *Portugal* 34 E2
Lavradio, *Portugal* 35 G1
Lavras, *Brazil* 127 A7
Lavre, *Portugal* 35 G2
Lávrion, *Greece* 38 D6
Lávris, *Greece* 36 D6
Lavumisa, *Swaziland* 89 D5
Lawas, *Malaysia* 62 D5
Lawele, *Indonesia* 63 F6
Lawng Pit, *Burma* 67 G20
Lawqah, *Si. Arabia* 70 D4
Lawra, *Ghana* 82 C4
Lawrence, *N.Z.* 91 L2
Lawrence, *Kans., U.S.A.* ... 112 F7
Lawrence, *Mass., U.S.A.* ... 111 D13
Lawrenceburg, *Ind., U.S.A.* 108 F3
Lawrenceburg, *Tenn.,
 U.S.A.* 109 H2
Lawrenceville, *Ga., U.S.A.* 109 J4
Lawrenceville, *Pa., U.S.A.* . 110 E7
Laws, *U.S.A.* 116 H8
Lawton, *U.S.A.* 113 H5
Lawu, *Indonesia* 63 G14
Lawz, J. al, *Si. Arabia* ... 80 B4
Laxå, *Sweden* 11 F8
Laxford, L., *U.K.* 14 C3
Laxou, *France* 19 D13
Lay →, *France* 20 B2
Laylá, *Si. Arabia* 74 C4
Laylān, *Iraq* 70 C5
Layon →, *France* 18 E6
Layton, *U.S.A.* 114 F7
Laytonville, *U.S.A.* 114 G2
Lazarevac, *Serbia, Yug.* ... 40 B4
Lazarevskoye, *Russia* 49 J4
Lazarivo, *Madag.* 89 C8
Lazdijai, *Lithuania* 44 D10
Lazio □, *Italy* 29 F9
Lazo, *Moldova* 43 C13
Lazo, *Russia* 54 C6
Le Beausset, *France* 21 E9
Le Blanc, *France* 20 B5
Le Bleymard, *France* 20 D7
Le Bourgneuf-la-Fôret,
 France 18 D6
Le Bugue, *France* 20 D4

Le Canourgue = La
 Canourgue, *France* 20 D7
Le Cateau Cambrésis, *France* 19 B10
Le Caylar, *France* 20 E7
Le Chambon-Feugerolles,
 France 21 C8
Le Châtelet, *France* 19 F9
Le Chesne, *France* 19 C11
Le Cheylard, *France* 21 D8
Le Conquet, *France* 18 D2
Le Creusot, *France* 19 F11
Le Croisic, *France* 18 E4
Le Donjon, *France* 19 F10
Le Dorat, *France* 20 B5
Le François, *Martinique* .. 121 D7
Le Grand-Lucé, *France* 18 E7
Le Grand-Pressigny, *France* 18 F7
Le Grand-Quevilly, *France* . 18 C8
Le Havre, *France* 18 C7
Le Lavandou, *France* 21 E10
Le Lion-d'Angers, *France* .. 18 E6
Le Louroux-Béconnais,
 France 18 E6
Le Luc, *France* 21 E10
Le Lude, *France* 18 E7
Le Mans, *France* 18 D7
Le Mars, *U.S.A.* 112 D6
Le Mayet-de-Montagne,
 France 19 F10
Le Mêle-sur-Sarthe, *France* . 18 D7
Le Monastier-sur-Gazeille,
 France 20 D7
Le Monêtier-les-Bains,
 France 21 D10
Le Mont-Dore, *France* 20 C6
Le Mont-St-Michel, *France* . 18 D5
Le Moule, *Guadeloupe* 121 C7
Le Muy, *France* 21 E10
Le Palais, *France* 18 E3
Le Perthus, *France* 20 F6
Le Puy-en-Velay, *France* ... 20 C7
Le Sueur, *U.S.A.* 112 C8
Le Teil, *France* 21 D8
Le Teilleul, *France* 18 D6
Le Theil, *France* 18 D7
Le Thillot, *France* 19 E13
Le Thuy, *Vietnam* 64 D6
Le Touquet-Paris-Plage,
 France 19 B8
Le Tréport, *France* 18 B8
Le Val-d'Ajol, *France* 19 E13
Le Verdon-sur-Mer, *France* 20 C2
Le Vigan, *France* 20 E7
Lea →, *U.K.* 13 F8
Leach, *Cambodia* 65 F4
Lead, *U.S.A.* 112 C3
Leader, *Canada* 105 C7
Leadville, *U.S.A.* 115 G10
Leaf →, *U.S.A.* 113 K10
Leaf Rapids, *Canada* 105 B9
Leamington, *Canada* 102 D3
Leamington, *U.S.A.* 114 G7
Leamington Spa = Royal
 Leamington Spa, *U.K.* ... 13 E6
Le'an, *China* 59 D10
Leandro Norte Alem,
 Argentina 127 B4
Leane, L., *Ireland* 15 D2
Learmonth, *Australia* 92 D1
Leask, *Canada* 105 C7
Leatherhead, *U.K.* 13 F7
Leavenworth, *Kans., U.S.A.* 112 F7
Leavenworth, *Wash., U.S.A.* 114 C3
Łeba, *Poland* 44 D4
Łeba →, *Poland* 44 D4
Lebach, *Germany* 25 F2
Lebak, *Phil.* 61 H6
Lebam, *U.S.A.* 116 D3
Lebane, *Serbia, Yug.* 40 D5
Lebanon, *Ind., U.S.A.* 108 E2
Lebanon, *Kans., U.S.A.* ... 112 F5
Lebanon, *Ky., U.S.A.* 108 G3
Lebanon, *Mo., U.S.A.* 113 G8
Lebanon, *N.H., U.S.A.* 111 C12
Lebanon, *Oreg., U.S.A.* ... 114 D2
Lebanon, *Pa., U.S.A.* 111 F8
Lebanon, *Tenn., U.S.A.* ... 109 G2
Lebanon ■, *Asia* 75 B5
Lebec, *U.S.A.* 117 L8
Lebedyan, *Russia* 47 F11
Lebedyn, *Ukraine* 47 G8
Lebel-sur-Quévillon, *Canada* 102 C4
Lebomboberge, *S. Africa* .. 89 C5
Lębork, *Poland* 44 D4
Lebrija, *Spain* 35 J4
Łebsko, Jezioro, *Poland* ... 44 D4
Lebu, *Chile* 126 D1
Leca da Palmeira, *Portugal* . 34 D2
Lecce, *Italy* 31 B11
Lecco, *Italy* 28 C6
Lecco, L. di, *Italy* 28 C6
Lécera, *Spain* 32 D4
Lech, *Austria* 26 D3
Lech →, *Germany* 25 G6
Lechang, *China* 59 E9
Lechtaler Alpen, *Austria* .. 26 D3
Lecontes Mills, *U.S.A.* 110 E6
Lectoure, *France* 20 E4
Łęczna, *Poland* 45 G9
Łęczyca, *Poland* 45 F6
Ledesma, *Spain* 34 D5
Ledong, *China* 64 C7
Leduc, *Canada* 104 C6
Lee, *U.S.A.* 111 D11
Lee →, *Ireland* 15 E3
Lee Vining, *U.S.A.* 116 H7
Leech L., *U.S.A.* 112 B7
Leechburg, *U.S.A.* 110 F5
Leeds, *U.K.* 12 D6
Leeds, *U.S.A.* 109 J2
Leek, *Neths.* 17 A6

Leek, *U.K.* 12 D5
Leeman, *Australia* 93 E1
Leeper, *U.S.A.* 110 E5
Leer, *Germany* 24 B3
Leesburg, *U.S.A.* 109 L5
Leesville, *U.S.A.* 113 K8
Leeton, *Australia* 95 E4
Leetonia, *Australia* 110 F4
Leeu Gamka, *S. Africa* 88 E3
Leeuwarden, *Neths.* 17 A5
Leeuwin, C., *Australia* 93 F2
Leeward Is., *Atl. Oc.* 121 C7
Lefka, *Cyprus* 36 D11
Lefkoniko, *Cyprus* 36 D12
Lefroy, *Canada* 110 B5
Lefroy, L., *Australia* 93 F3
Łęg →, *Poland* 45 H8
Leganés, *Spain* 34 E7
Legazpi, *Phil.* 61 E5
Lège, *France* 20 D2
Lege Hida, *Ethiopia* 81 F5
Legendre I., *Australia* 92 D2
Leghorn = Livorno, *Italy* .. 28 E7
Legionowo, *Poland* 45 F7
Legnago, *Italy* 29 C8
Legnano, *Italy* 28 C5
Legnica, *Poland* 45 G3
Legrad, *Croatia* 29 B13
Leh, *India* 69 B7
Lehigh Acres, *U.S.A.* 109 M5
Lehighton, *U.S.A.* 111 F9
Lehliu, *Romania* 43 F11
Leho, *Sudan* 81 F3
Lehrte, *Germany* 24 C5
Lehututu, *Botswana* 88 C3
Lei Shui →, *China* 59 D9
Leiah, *Pakistan* 68 D4
Leibnitz, *Austria* 26 E8
Leibo, *China* 58 C4
Leicester, *U.K.* 13 E6
Leicester City □, *U.K.* ... 13 E6
Leicestershire □, *U.K.* ... 13 E6
Leichhardt →, *Australia* .. 94 B2
Leichhardt Ra., *Australia* . 94 C4
Leiden, *Neths.* 17 B4
Leie →, *Belgium* 17 C3
Leifers = Láives, *Italy* ... 29 B8
Leigh Creek, *Australia* 95 E2
Leimen, *Germany* 25 F4
Leine →, *Germany* 24 C5
Leinefelde, *Germany* 24 D6
Leinster, *Australia* 93 E3
Leinster □, *Ireland* 15 C4
Leinster, Mt., *Ireland* ... 15 D5
Leipalingis, *Lithuania* ... 44 D10
Leipzig, *Germany* 24 D8
Leiria, *Portugal* 34 F2
Leiria □, *Portugal* 34 F2
Leirvik, *Norway* 9 G11
Leishan, *China* 58 D7
Leisler, Mt., *Australia* ... 92 D4
Leith, *U.K.* 14 F5
Leith Hill, *U.K.* 13 F7
Leitha →, *Europe* 27 D10
Leitrim, *Ireland* 15 B3
Leitrim □, *Ireland* 15 B4
Leitza, *Spain* 32 B3
Leiyang, *China* 59 D9
Leizhou, *China* 59 G8
Leizhou Bandao, *China* 58 G7
Leizhou Wan, *China* 59 G8
Lek →, *Neths.* 17 C4
Leka, *Norway* 8 D14
Lekáni, *Greece* 41 E8
Lekbibaj, *Albania* 40 D3
Lekeitio, *Spain* 32 B2
Lekhainá, *Greece* 38 D3
Lekoui, *Burkina Faso* 82 C4
Leksand, *Sweden* 10 D9
Lékva Óros, *Greece* 36 D6
Leland, *Mich., U.S.A.* 108 C3
Leland, *Miss., U.S.A.* 113 J9
Leláng, *Sweden* 10 E6
Leleque, *Argentina* 128 E2
Lelystad, *Neths.* 17 B5
Lem, *Denmark* 11 H2
Lema, *Nigeria* 83 C5
Lema Shilindi, *Ethiopia* ... 81 G5
Léman, L., *Europe* 19 F13
Lemera,
 Dem. Rep. of the Congo . 86 C2
Lemery, *Phil.* 61 E4
Lemhi Ra., *U.S.A.* 114 D7
Lemmer, *Neths.* 17 B5
Lemmon, *U.S.A.* 112 C3
Lemon Grove, *U.S.A.* 117 N9
Lemoore, *U.S.A.* 116 J7
Lempdes, *France* 20 C7
Lemvig, *Denmark* 11 H2
Lena →, *Russia* 51 B13
Lenart, *Slovenia* 29 B12
Lenartovce, *Slovak Rep.* .. 27 C13
Lencloître, *France* 18 F7
Léndas, *Greece* 36 E6
Lendava, *Slovenia* 29 B13
Lendeh, *Iran* 71 D6
Lendinara, *Italy* 29 C8
Lengerich, *Germany* 24 C3
Lenggong, *Malaysia* 65 K3
Lenggries, *Germany* 25 H7
Lengshuijiang, *China* 59 D8
Lengshuitan, *China* 59 D8
Lengua de Vaca, Pta., *Chile* 126 C1
Lengyeltóti, *Hungary* 42 D2
Lenhovda, *Sweden* 11 G9
Lenina, Kanal →, *Russia* .. 49 J7
Leninabad = Khudzhand,
 Tajikistan 50 E7
Leninakan = Gyumri,
 Armenia 49 K6

Leningrad = Sankt-
 Peterburg, *Russia* 46 C6
Lenino, *Ukraine* 47 K8
Leninogorsk, *Kazakstan* ... 50 D9
Leninsk, *Russia* 49 F7
Leninsk-Kuznetskiy, *Russia* 50 D9
Leninskoye, *Russia* 48 A8
Lenk, *Switz.* 25 J3
Lenkoran = Länkäran,
 Azerbaijan 49 B6
Lenmalu, *Indonesia* 63 E8
Lenne →, *Germany* 24 D3
Lennestadt, *Germany* 24 D4
Lennox, *U.S.A.* 112 D6
Lennoxville, *Canada* 111 A13
Leno, *Italy* 28 C7
Lenoir, *U.S.A.* 109 H5
Lenoir City, *U.S.A.* 109 H3
Lenore L., *Canada* 105 C8
Lenox, *U.S.A.* 111 D11
Lens, *France* 19 B9
Lensahn, *Germany* 24 A6
Lensk, *Russia* 51 C12
Lentekhi, *Georgia* 49 J6
Lenti, *Hungary* 42 D1
Lentini, *Italy* 31 E8
Lenwood, *U.S.A.* 117 L9
Lenya, *Burma* 62 B1
Lenzen, *Germany* 24 B7
Léo, *Burkina Faso* 82 C4
Leoben, *Austria* 26 D8
Leodhas = Lewis, *U.K.* 14 C2
Leola, *U.S.A.* 112 C5
Leominster, *U.K.* 13 E5
Leominster, *U.S.A.* 111 D13
León, *France* 20 E2
León, *Mexico* 118 C4
León, *Nic.* 120 D2
León, *Spain* 34 C5
León, *U.S.A.* 112 E8
León □, *Spain* 34 C5
León →, *U.S.A.* 113 K6
León, Montes de, *Spain* ... 34 C4
Leonardtown, *U.S.A.* 108 F7
Leonardville, *Namibia* 88 C2
Leonberg, *Germany* 25 G5
Leonding, *Austria* 26 C7
Leonessa, *Italy* 29 F9
Leonforte, *Italy* 31 E7
Leongatha, *Australia* 95 F4
Leonídhion, *Greece* 38 D4
Leonora, *Australia* 93 E3
Léopold II, Lac = Mai-
 Ndombe, L.,
 Dem. Rep. of the Congo . 84 E3
Leopoldina, *Brazil* 127 A7
Leopoldsburg, *Belgium* ... 17 C5
Léopoldville = Kinshasa,
 Dem. Rep. of the Congo . 84 E3
Leoti, *U.S.A.* 112 F4
Leova, *Moldova* 43 D13
Leoville, *Canada* 105 C7
Lepe, *Spain* 35 H3
Lepel = Lyepyel, *Belarus* .. 46 E5
Lepenoú, *Greece* 38 C3
Leping, *China* 59 C11
Lépo, L. do, *Angola* 88 B2
Lepontine, Alpi, *Italy* ... 28 B5
Leppävirta, *Finland* 9 E22
Lepsény, *Hungary* 42 D3
Lequeitio = Lekeitio, *Spain* 32 B2
Lercara Friddi, *Italy* 30 E6
Lerdo, *Mexico* 118 B4
Léré, *Chad* 83 D7
Léré, *Mali* 82 B4
Lere, *Bauchi, Nigeria* 83 D6
Lere, *Kaduna, Nigeria* 83 C6
Leribe, *Lesotho* 89 D4
Lérici, *Italy* 28 D6
Lérida = Lleida, *Spain* ... 32 D5
Lérins, Îs. de, *France* ... 21 E11
Lerma, *Spain* 34 C7
Léros, *Greece* 39 D8
Lérouville, *France* 19 D12
Lerum, *Sweden* 11 G6
Lerwick, *U.K.* 14 A7
Leş, *Romania* 42 D6
Les Abrets, *France* 21 C9
Les Andelys, *France* 18 C8
Les Borges Blanques, *Spain* 32 D5
Les Cayes, *Haiti* 121 C5
Les Essarts, *France* 18 F5
Les Herbiers, *France* 18 F5
Les Minquiers, Plateau des,
 Chan. Is. 18 D4
Les Pieux, *France* 18 C5
Les Ponts-de-Cé, *France* .. 18 E6
Les Riceys, *France* 19 E11
Les Sables-d'Olonne, *France* 20 B2
Les Vans, *France* 21 D8
Lesbos = Lésvos, *Greece* .. 39 B8
L'Escala, *Spain* 32 C8
Lésina, *Italy* 29 G12
Lésina, L. di, *Italy* 29 G12
Lesjöfors, *Sweden* 10 E8
Lesko, *Poland* 45 J9
Leskov I., *Antarctica* 5 B1
Leskovac, *Serbia, Yug.* ... 40 C5
Leskoviku, *Albania* 40 F4
Leśna, *Poland* 45 G2
Lesneven, *France* 18 D2
Lešnica, *Serbia, Yug.* 40 B3
Lesnoye, *Russia* 46 C8
Lesopilnoye, *Russia* 54 A7
Lesotho ■, *Africa* 89 D4
Lesozavodsk, *Russia* 51 E14
Lesparre-Médoc, *France* ... 20 C3
Lessay, *France* 18 C5
Lesse →, *Belgium* 17 D4

Lessebo, *Sweden* 11 H9
Lesser Antilles, *W. Indies* . 121 D7
Lesser Slave L., *Canada* .. 104 B5
Lesser Sunda Is., *Indonesia* 63 F6
Lessines, *Belgium* 17 D3
Lester, *U.S.A.* 116 C5
Lestock, *Canada* 105 C8
Lesuer I., *Australia* 92 B4
Lésvos, *Greece* 39 B8
Leszno, *Poland* 45 G3
Letaba, *S. Africa* 89 C5
Letälven, *Sweden* 10 E8
Létavértes, *Hungary* 42 C6
Letchworth, *U.K.* 13 F7
Letea, Ostrov, *Romania* ... 43 E14
Lethbridge, *Canada* 104 D6
Lethem, *Guyana* 124 C7
Leti, Kepulauan, *Indonesia* 63 F7
Leti Is. = Leti, Kepulauan,
 Indonesia 63 F7
Letiahau →, *Botswana* 88 C3
Leticia, *Colombia* 124 D5
Leting, *China* 57 E10
Letjiesbos, *S. Africa* 88 E3
Letlhakane, *Botswana* 88 C4
Letlhakeng, *Botswana* 88 C3
Letong, *Indonesia* 62 D3
Letpadan, *Burma* 67 L19
Letpan, *Burma* 67 K19
Letsôk-aw Kyun, *Burma* ... 65 G2
Letterkenny, *Ireland* 15 B4
Leu, *Romania* 43 F9
Leucadia, *U.S.A.* 117 M9
Leucate, *France* 20 F7
Leucate, Étang de, *France* . 20 F7
Leuk, *Switz.* 25 J3
Leuşeni, *Moldova* 43 D13
Leuser, G., *Indonesia* 62 D1
Leutkirch, *Germany* 25 H6
Leuven, *Belgium* 17 D4
Leuze-en-Hainaut, *Belgium* 17 D3
Lev Tolstoy, *Russia* 46 F10
Levádhia, *Greece* 38 C4
Levanger, *Norway* 8 E14
Levani, *Albania* 40 F3
Levant, Î. du, *France* 21 E10
Lévanto, *Italy* 28 D6
Lévanzo, *Italy* 30 D5
Levelland, *U.S.A.* 113 J3
Leven, *U.K.* 14 E6
Leven, L., *U.K.* 14 E5
Leven, Toraka, *Madag.* 89 A8
Leveque C., *Australia* 92 C3
Leverano, *Italy* 31 B10
Leverkusen, *Germany* 24 D3
Levice, *Slovak Rep.* 27 C11
Lévico Terme, *Italy* 29 C8
Levie, *France* 21 F13
Levier, *France* 19 F13
Levin, *N.Z.* 91 J5
Lévis, *Canada* 103 C5
Levis, L., *Canada* 104 A5
Levítha, *Greece* 39 D8
Levittown, *N.Y., U.S.A.* .. 111 F11
Levittown, *Pa., U.S.A.* ... 111 F10
Levka, *Bulgaria* 41 E10
Levkás, *Greece* 38 C2
Levkás □, *Greece* 38 C2
Levkímmi, *Greece* 36 B4
Levkímmi, Ákra, *Greece* ... 36 B4
Levkôsia = Nicosia, *Cyprus* 36 D12
Levoča, *Slovak Rep.* 27 B13
Levroux, *France* 19 F8
Levski, *Bulgaria* 41 C9
Levskigrad = Karlovo,
 Bulgaria 41 D8
Lewes, *U.K.* 13 G8
Lewes, *U.S.A.* 108 F8
Lewin Brzeski, *Poland* 45 H4
Lewis, *U.K.* 14 C2
Lewis →, *U.S.A.* 116 E4
Lewis, Butt of, *U.K.* 14 C2
Lewis Ra., *Australia* 92 D4
Lewis Range, *U.S.A.* 114 C7
Lewis Run, *U.S.A.* 110 E6
Lewisburg, *Pa., U.S.A.* ... 110 F8
Lewisburg, *Tenn., U.S.A.* . 109 H2
Lewisburg, *W. Va., U.S.A.* 108 G5
Lewisporte, *Canada* 103 C8
Lewiston, *Idaho, U.S.A.* .. 114 C5
Lewiston, *Maine, U.S.A.* .. 109 C11
Lewiston, *N.Y., U.S.A.* ... 110 C5
Lewistown, *Mont., U.S.A.* . 114 C9
Lewistown, *Pa., U.S.A.* ... 110 F7
Lexington, *Ill., U.S.A.* ... 112 E10
Lexington, *Ky., U.S.A.* ... 108 F3
Lexington, *Mich., U.S.A.* . 110 C2
Lexington, *Mo., U.S.A.* ... 112 F8
Lexington, *N.C., U.S.A.* .. 109 H5
Lexington, *N.Y., U.S.A.* .. 111 D10
Lexington, *Nebr., U.S.A.* . 112 E5
Lexington, *Ohio, U.S.A.* .. 110 F2
Lexington, *Tenn., U.S.A.* . 109 H1
Lexington, *Va., U.S.A.* ... 108 G6
Lexington Park, *U.S.A.* ... 108 F7
Leyburn, *U.K.* 12 C6
Leye, *China* 58 E6
Leyland, *U.K.* 12 D5
Leyre →, *France* 20 D2
Leyte □, *Phil.* 61 F6
Leyte Gulf, *Phil.* 61 F6
Leżajsk, *Poland* 45 H9
Lezay, *France* 20 B3
Lezha, *Albania* 40 E3
Lezhi, *China* 58 B5
Lézignan-Corbières, *France* 20 E6
Lezoux, *France* 20 C7
Lgov, *Russia* 47 G8
Lhasa, *China* 60 D4
Lhazê, *China* 60 D3
Lhokkruet, *Indonesia* 62 D1

Lhokseumawe, *Indonesia* 62 C1
L'Hospitalet de Llobregat, *Spain* 32 D7
Lhuntsi Dzong, *India* 67 F17
Li, *Thailand* 64 D2
Li Shui →, *China* 59 C9
Li Xian, *Gansu, China* 56 G3
Li Xian, *Hebei, China* 56 E8
Li Xian, *Hunan, China* 59 C8
Liádhoi, *Greece* 39 E8
Liancheng, *China* 59 E11
Lianga, *Phil.* 61 G7
Liangcheng, *Nei Mongol Zizhiqu, China* 56 D7
Liangcheng, *Shandong, China* 57 G10
Liangdang, *China* 56 H4
Lianghe, *China* 58 E2
Lianghekou, *China* 58 C7
Liangping, *China* 58 B6
Liangpran, *Indonesia* 62 D4
Lianhua, *China* 59 D9
Lianjiang, *Fujian, China* 59 D12
Lianjiang, *Guangdong, China* 59 G8
Lianping, *China* 59 E10
Lianshan, *China* 59 E9
Lianshanguan, *China* 57 D12
Lianshui, *China* 57 H10
Lianyuan, *China* 59 D8
Lianyungang, *China* 57 G10
Lianzhou, *China* 59 E9
Liao He →, *China* 57 D11
Liaocheng, *China* 56 F8
Liaodong Bandao, *China* 57 E12
Liaodong Wan, *China* 57 D11
Liaoning □, *China* 57 D12
Liaoyang, *China* 57 D12
Liaoyuan, *China* 57 C13
Liaozhong, *China* 57 D12
Liapádhes, *Greece* 38 B1
Liard →, *Canada* 104 A4
Liard River, *Canada* 104 B3
Liari, *Pakistan* 68 G2
Libau = Liepāja, *Latvia* 9 H19
Libby, *U.S.A.* 114 B6
Libenge, *Dem. Rep. of the Congo* 84 D3
Liberal, *U.S.A.* 113 G4
Liberec, *Czech Rep.* 26 A8
Liberia, *Costa Rica* 120 D2
Liberia ■, *W. Afr.* 82 D3
Liberty, *Mo., U.S.A.* 112 F7
Liberty, *N.Y., U.S.A.* 111 E10
Liberty, *Pa., U.S.A.* 110 E7
Liberty, *Tex., U.S.A.* 113 K7
Libiąż, *Poland* 45 H6
Lîbîya, Sahrâ', *Africa* 79 C10
Libo, *China* 58 E6
Libobo, Tanjung, *Indonesia* 63 E7
Libode, *S. Africa* 89 E4
Libohava, *Albania* 40 F4
Libourne, *France* 20 D3
Libramont, *Belgium* 17 E5
Librazhdi, *Albania* 40 E4
Libreville, *Gabon* 84 D1
Libya ■, *N. Afr.* 79 C9
Libyan Desert = Lîbîya, Sahrâ', *Africa* 79 C10
Libyan Plateau = Ed-Déffa, *Egypt* 80 A2
Licantén, *Chile* 126 D1
Licata, *Italy* 30 E6
Lice, *Turkey* 73 C9
Licheng, *China* 56 F7
Lichfield, *U.K.* 13 E6
Lichinga, *Mozam.* 87 E4
Lichtenburg, *S. Africa* 88 D4
Lichtenfels, *Germany* 25 E7
Lichuan, *Hubei, China* 58 B7
Lichuan, *Jiangxi, China* 59 D11
Licking →, *U.S.A.* 108 F3
Licosa, Punta, *Italy* 31 B7
Lida, *Belarus* 9 K21
Liden, *Sweden* 10 B10
Lidhoríkion, *Greece* 38 C4
Lidhult, *Sweden* 11 H7
Lidköping, *Sweden* 11 F7
Lido, *Italy* 29 C9
Lido, *Niger* 83 C5
Lido di Roma = Óstia, Lido di, *Italy* 29 G9
Lidzbark, *Poland* 45 E6
Lidzbark Warmiński, *Poland* 44 D7
Liebenwalde, *Germany* 24 C9
Lieberose, *Germany* 24 D10
Liebig, Mt., *Australia* 92 D5
Liebling, *Romania* 42 E6
Liechtenstein ■, *Europe* 25 H5
Liège, *Belgium* 17 D5
Liège □, *Belgium* 17 D5
Liegnitz = Legnica, *Poland* 45 G3
Lienart, *Dem. Rep. of the Congo* 86 B2
Lienyünchiangshih = Lianyungang, *China* 57 G10
Lienz, *Austria* 26 E5
Liepāja, *Latvia* 9 H19
Liepāja □, *Latvia* 44 B8
Liepājas ezers, *Latvia* 44 B8
Lier, *Belgium* 17 C4
Liernais, *France* 19 E11
Lieşti, *Romania* 43 E12
Liévin, *France* 19 B9
Lièvre →, *Canada* 102 C4
Liezen, *Austria* 26 D7
Liffey →, *Ireland* 15 C5
Lifford, *Ireland* 15 B4
Liffré, *France* 18 D5
Lifudzin, *Russia* 54 B7
Ligao, *Phil.* 61 E5
Lightning Ridge, *Australia* 95 D4
Lignano Sabbiadoro, *Italy* 29 C10
Ligny-en-Barrois, *France* 19 D12
Ligonier, *U.S.A.* 110 F5
Ligoúrion, *Greece* 38 D5
Ligueil, *France* 18 E7
Liguria □, *Italy* 28 D5
Ligurian Sea, *Medit. S.* 6 G7
Lihou Reefs and Cays, *Australia* 94 B5
Lihue, *U.S.A.* 106 H15
Lijiang, *China* 58 D3
Likasi, *Dem. Rep. of the Congo* 87 E2
Likenäs, *Sweden* 10 D8
Likhoslavl, *Russia* 46 D8
Likhovskoy, *Russia* 47 H11
Likoma I., *Malawi* 87 E3
Likumburu, *Tanzania* 87 D4
L'Île-Bouchard, *France* 18 E7
L'Île-Rousse, *France* 21 F12
Liling, *China* 59 D9
Lilla Edet, *Sweden* 11 F6
Lille, *France* 19 B10
Lille Bælt, *Denmark* 11 J3
Lillebonne, *France* 18 C7
Lillehammer, *Norway* 9 F14
Lillesand, *Norway* 9 G13
Lillhärdal, *Sweden* 10 C8
Lillian Pt., *Australia* 93 E4
Lillo, *Spain* 34 F7
Lillooet, *Canada* 104 C4
Lillooet →, *Canada* 104 D4
Lilongwe, *Malawi* 87 E3
Liloy, *Phil.* 63 C6
Lim →, *Bos.-H.* 40 C3
Lima, *Indonesia* 63 E7
Lima, *Peru* 124 F3
Lima, *Mont., U.S.A.* 114 D7
Lima, *Ohio, U.S.A.* 108 E3
Lima →, *Portugal* 34 D2
Liman, *Indonesia* 63 G14
Liman, *Russia* 49 H8
Limanowa, *Poland* 45 J7
Limassol, *Cyprus* 36 E12
Limavady, *U.K.* 15 A5
Limay →, *Argentina* 128 D3
Limay Mahuida, *Argentina* 126 D2
Limbach-Oberfrohna, *Germany* 24 E8
Limbang, *Brunei* 62 D5
Limbara, Mte., *Italy* 30 B2
Limbaži, *Latvia* 9 H21
Limbdi, *India* 68 H4
Limbe, *Cameroon* 83 E6
Limburg, *Germany* 25 E4
Limburg □, *Belgium* 17 C5
Limburg □, *Neths.* 17 C5
Limedsforsen, *Sweden* 10 D7
Limeira, *Brazil* 127 A6
Limenária, *Greece* 41 F8
Limerick, *Ireland* 15 D3
Limerick, *U.S.A.* 111 C14
Limerick □, *Ireland* 15 D3
Limestone, *U.S.A.* 110 D6
Limestone →, *Canada* 105 B10
Limfjorden, *Denmark* 11 H3
Limia = Lima →, *Portugal* 34 D2
Limín Khersonísou, *Greece* 39 F7
Limingen, *Norway* 8 D15
Limmared, *Sweden* 11 G7
Limmen Bight, *Australia* 94 A2
Limmen Bight →, *Australia* 94 B2
Límni, *Greece* 38 C5
Límnos, *Greece* 39 B7
Limoges, *Canada* 111 A9
Limoges, *France* 20 C5
Limón, *Costa Rica* 120 E3
Limon, *U.S.A.* 112 F3
Limone Piemonte, *Italy* 28 D4
Limousin, *France* 20 C5
Limousin, Plateaux du, *France* 20 C5
Limoux, *France* 20 E6
Limpopo →, *Africa* 89 D5
Limuru, *Kenya* 86 C4
Lin Xian, *China* 56 F6
Lin'an, *China* 59 B12
Linapacan I., *Phil.* 61 F3
Linapacan Str., *Phil.* 61 F3
Linares, *Chile* 126 D1
Linares, *Mexico* 119 C5
Linares, *Spain* 35 G7
Linaro, Capo, *Italy* 29 F8
Línas Mte., *Italy* 30 C1
Lincang, *China* 58 F3
Lincheng, *China* 56 F8
Linchuan, *China* 59 D11
Lincoln, *Argentina* 126 C3
Lincoln, *N.Z.* 91 K4
Lincoln, *U.K.* 12 D7
Lincoln, *Calif., U.S.A.* 116 G5
Lincoln, *Ill., U.S.A.* 112 E10
Lincoln, *Kans., U.S.A.* 112 F5
Lincoln, *Maine, U.S.A.* 109 C11
Lincoln, *N.H., U.S.A.* 111 B13
Lincoln, *N. Mex., U.S.A.* 115 K11
Lincoln, *Nebr., U.S.A.* 112 E6
Lincoln City, *U.S.A.* 114 D1
Lincoln Hav = Lincoln Sea, *Arctic* 4 A5
Lincoln Sea, *Arctic* 4 A5
Lincolnshire □, *U.K.* 12 D7
Lincolnshire Wolds, *U.K.* 12 D7
Lincolnton, *U.S.A.* 109 H5
L'Incudine, *France* 21 G13
Lind, *U.S.A.* 114 C4
Linda, *U.S.A.* 116 F5
Lindau, *Germany* 25 H5
Linden, *Guyana* 124 B7
Linden, *Ala., U.S.A.* 109 J2
Linden, *Calif., U.S.A.* 116 G5
Linden, *Tex., U.S.A.* 113 J7
Lindenhurst, *U.S.A.* 111 F11
Lindesberg, *Sweden* 10 E9
Lindesnes, *Norway* 9 H12
Líndhos, *Greece* 36 C10
Líndhos, Ákra, *Greece* 36 C10
Lindi, *Tanzania* 87 D4
Lindi □, *Tanzania* 87 D4
Lindi →, *Dem. Rep. of the Congo* 86 B2
Lindö, *Sweden* 11 F10
Lindome, *Sweden* 11 G6
Lindoso, *Portugal* 34 D2
Lindow, *Germany* 24 C8
Lindsay, *Canada* 102 D4
Lindsay, *Calif., U.S.A.* 116 J7
Lindsay, *Okla., U.S.A.* 113 H6
Lindsborg, *U.S.A.* 112 F6
Lindsdal, *Sweden* 11 H10
Linesville, *U.S.A.* 110 E4
Linfen, *China* 56 F6
Ling Xian, *Hunan, China* 59 D9
Ling Xian, *Shandong, China* 56 F9
Lingao, *China* 64 C7
Lingayen, *Phil.* 63 A6
Lingayen G., *Phil.* 61 C4
Lingbi, *China* 57 H9
Lingbo, *Sweden* 10 C10
Lingchuan, *Guangxi Zhuangzu, China* 59 E8
Lingchuan, *Shanxi, China* 56 G7
Lingen, *Germany* 24 C3
Lingga, *Indonesia* 62 E2
Lingga, Kepulauan, *Indonesia* 62 E2
Lingga Arch. = Lingga, Kepulauan, *Indonesia* 62 E2
Linghem, *Sweden* 11 F9
Lingle, *U.S.A.* 112 D2
Lingqiu, *China* 56 E8
Lingshan, *China* 58 F7
Lingshi, *China* 56 F6
Lingshou, *China* 56 E8
Lingshui, *China* 64 C8
Lingtai, *China* 56 G4
Linguère, *Senegal* 82 B1
Lingui, *China* 59 E8
Lingwu, *China* 56 E4
Lingyuan, *China* 57 D10
Lingyun, *China* 58 E6
Linhai, *China* 59 C13
Linhares, *Brazil* 125 G10
Linhe, *China* 56 D4
Linjiang, *China* 57 D14
Linköping, *Sweden* 11 F9
Linkou, *China* 57 B16
Linli, *China* 59 C8
Linnhe, L., *U.K.* 14 E3
Linqi, *China* 56 G7
Linqing, *China* 56 F8
Linqu, *China* 57 F10
Linru, *China* 56 G7
Lins, *Brazil* 127 A6
Linshui, *China* 58 B6
Linta →, *Madag.* 89 D7
Linth →, *Switz.* 25 H5
Linthal, *Switz.* 25 J5
Linton, *Ind., U.S.A.* 108 F2
Linton, *N. Dak., U.S.A.* 112 B4
Lintong, *China* 56 G5
Linwood, *Canada* 110 C4
Linwu, *China* 59 E9
Linxi, *China* 57 C10
Linxia, *China* 60 C5
Linxiang, *China* 59 C9
Linyanti →, *Africa* 88 B4
Linyi, *China* 57 G10
Linz, *Austria* 26 C7
Linz, *Germany* 24 E3
Linzhenzhen, *China* 56 F5
Linzi, *China* 57 F10
Lion, G. du, *France* 20 E7
Lionárisso, *Cyprus* 36 D13
Lioni, *Italy* 31 B8
Lions, G. of = Lion, G. du, *France* 20 E7
Lion's Den, *Zimbabwe* 87 F3
Lion's Head, *Canada* 110 B3
Liozno = Lyozna, *Belarus* 46 E6
Lipa, *Phil.* 61 E4
Lipali, *Mozam.* 87 F4
Lipany, *Slovak Rep.* 27 B13
Lípari, *Italy* 31 D7
Lípari, I., *Italy* 31 D7
Lípari, Is. = Eólie, Ís., *Italy* 31 D7
Lipcani, *Moldova* 43 B11
Lipetsk, *Russia* 47 F10
Lipiany, *Poland* 45 E1
Liping, *China* 58 D7
Lipkany = Lipcani, *Moldova* 43 B11
Lipljan, *Kosovo, Yug.* 40 D5
Lipník nad Bečvou, *Czech Rep.* 27 B10
Lipno, *Poland* 45 F6
Lipova, *Romania* 42 D6
Lipovcy Manzovka, *Russia* 54 B6
Lipovets, *Ukraine* 47 H5
Lippe →, *Germany* 24 D2
Lippstadt, *Germany* 24 D4
Lipscomb, *U.S.A.* 113 G4
Lipsk, *Poland* 44 E10
Lipsko, *Poland* 45 G8
Lipsói, *Greece* 39 D8
Liptovský Hrádok, *Slovak Rep.* 27 B12
Liptovský Milkuláš, *Slovak Rep.* 27 B12
Liptrap C., *Australia* 95 F4
Lipu, *China* 59 E8
Lira, *Uganda* 86 B3
Liri →, *Italy* 30 A6
Liria = Llíria, *Spain* 33 F4
Lisala, *Dem. Rep. of the Congo* 84 D4
Lisboa, *Portugal* 35 G1
Lisboa □, *Portugal* 35 F1
Lisbon = Lisboa, *Portugal* 35 G1
Lisbon, *N. Dak., U.S.A.* 112 B6
Lisbon, *N.H., U.S.A.* 111 B13
Lisbon, *Ohio, U.S.A.* 110 F4
Lisbon Falls, *U.S.A.* 109 D10
Lisburn, *U.K.* 15 B5
Liscannor B., *Ireland* 15 D2
Liscia →, *Italy* 30 A2
Lishe Jiang →, *China* 58 E3
Lishi, *China* 56 F6
Lishu, *China* 57 C13
Lishui, *Jiangsu, China* 59 B12
Lishui, *Zhejiang, China* 59 C12
Lisianski I., *Pac. Oc.* 96 E10
Lisichansk = Lysychansk, *Ukraine* 47 H10
Lisieux, *France* 18 C7
Liski, *Russia* 47 G10
L'Isle-Jourdain, *Gers, France* 20 E5
L'Isle-Jourdain, *Vienne, France* 20 B4
L'Isle-sur-la-Sorgue, *France* 21 E9
Lisle-sur-Tarn, *France* 20 E5
Lismore, *Australia* 95 D5
Lismore, *Ireland* 15 D4
Lista, *Norway* 9 G12
Lister, Mt., *Antarctica* 5 D11
Liston, *Australia* 95 D5
Listowel, *Canada* 102 D3
Listowel, *Ireland* 15 D2
Lit, *Sweden* 10 A8
Lit-et-Mixe, *France* 20 D2
Litang, *Guangxi Zhuangzu, China* 58 F7
Litang, *Sichuan, China* 58 B3
Litang Qu →, *China* 58 C3
Litani →, *Lebanon* 75 B4
Litchfield, *Calif., U.S.A.* 116 E6
Litchfield, *Conn., U.S.A.* 111 E11
Litchfield, *Ill., U.S.A.* 112 F10
Litchfield, *Minn., U.S.A.* 112 C7
Liteni, *Romania* 43 C11
Lithgow, *Australia* 95 E5
Líthinon, Ákra, *Greece* 36 E6
Lithuania ■, *Europe* 9 J20
Litija, *Slovenia* 29 B11
Lititz, *U.S.A.* 111 F8
Litókhoron, *Greece* 40 F6
Litoměřice, *Czech Rep.* 26 A7
Litomyšl, *Czech Rep.* 27 B9
Litschau, *Austria* 26 C8
Little Abaco I., *Bahamas* 120 A4
Little Barrier I., *N.Z.* 91 G5
Little Belt Mts., *U.S.A.* 114 C8
Little Blue →, *U.S.A.* 112 F6
Little Buffalo →, *Canada* 104 A6
Little Cayman, I., *Cayman Is.* 120 C3
Little Churchill →, *Canada* 105 B9
Little Colorado →, *U.S.A.* 115 H8
Little Current, *Canada* 102 C3
Little Current →, *Canada* 102 B3
Little Falls, *Minn., U.S.A.* 112 C7
Little Falls, *N.Y., U.S.A.* 111 C10
Little Fork →, *U.S.A.* 112 A8
Little Grand Rapids, *Canada* 105 C9
Little Humboldt →, *U.S.A.* 114 F5
Little Inagua I., *Bahamas* 121 B5
Little Karoo, *S. Africa* 88 E3
Little Lake, *U.S.A.* 117 K9
Little Laut Is. = Laut Kecil, Kepulauan, *Indonesia* 62 E5
Little-Mecatina = Petit-Mécatina →, *Canada* 103 B8
Little Minch, *U.K.* 14 D2
Little Missouri →, *U.S.A.* 112 B3
Little Ouse →, *U.K.* 13 E9
Little Rann, *India* 68 H4
Little Red →, *U.S.A.* 113 H9
Little River, *N.Z.* 91 K4
Little Rock, *U.S.A.* 113 H8
Little Ruaha →, *Tanzania* 86 D4
Little Sable Pt., *U.S.A.* 108 D2
Little Scarcies →, *S. Leone* 82 D2
Little Sioux →, *U.S.A.* 112 E6
Little Smoky →, *Canada* 104 C5
Little Snake →, *U.S.A.* 114 F9
Little Valley, *U.S.A.* 110 D6
Little Wabash →, *U.S.A.* 108 G1
Little White →, *U.S.A.* 112 D4
Littlefield, *U.S.A.* 113 J3
Littlehampton, *U.K.* 13 G7
Littleton, *U.S.A.* 111 B13
Litvinov, *Czech Rep.* 26 A6
Liu He →, *China* 57 D11
Liu Jiang →, *China* 58 F7
Liuba, *China* 56 H4
Liucheng, *China* 58 E7
Liugou, *China* 57 D10
Liuhe, *China* 57 C13
Liuheng Dao, *China* 59 C14
Liujiang, *China* 58 E7
Liukang Tenggaja = Sabalana, Kepulauan, *Indonesia* 63 F5
Liuli, *Tanzania* 87 E3
Liuwa Plain, *Zambia* 85 G4
Liuyang, *China* 59 C9
Liuzhou, *China* 58 E7
Liuzhuang, *China* 57 H11
Livada, *Romania* 42 C8
Livadherón, *Greece* 40 F5
Livadhia, *Cyprus* 36 E12
Liváđhion, *Greece* 38 A4
Livarot, *France* 18 D7
Live Oak, *Calif., U.S.A.* 116 F5
Live Oak, *Fla., U.S.A.* 109 K4
Liveras, *Cyprus* 36 D11
Livermore, *U.S.A.* 116 H5
Livermore, Mt., *U.S.A.* 113 K2
Livermore Falls, *U.S.A.* 109 C11
Liverpool, *Canada* 103 D7
Liverpool, *U.K.* 12 D4
Liverpool, *U.S.A.* 111 C8
Liverpool Bay, *U.K.* 12 D4
Liverpool Plains, *Australia* 95 E5
Liverpool Ra., *Australia* 95 E5
Livigno, *Italy* 28 B7
Livingston, *Guatemala* 120 C2
Livingston, *U.K.* 14 F5
Livingston, *Ala., U.S.A.* 109 J1
Livingston, *Calif., U.S.A.* 116 H6
Livingston, *Mont., U.S.A.* 114 D8
Livingston, *S.C., U.S.A.* 109 J5
Livingston, *Tenn., U.S.A.* 109 G3
Livingston, *Tex., U.S.A.* 113 K7
Livingston, L., *U.S.A.* 113 K7
Livingston Manor, *U.S.A.* 111 E10
Livingstone, *Zambia* 87 F2
Livingstone Mts., *Tanzania* 87 D3
Livingstonia, *Malawi* 87 E3
Livno, *Bos.-H.* 42 G2
Livny, *Russia* 47 F9
Livonia, *Mich., U.S.A.* 108 D4
Livonia, *N.Y., U.S.A.* 110 D7
Livorno, *Italy* 28 E7
Livramento, *Brazil* 127 C4
Livron-sur-Drôme, *France* 21 D8
Liwale, *Tanzania* 87 D4
Liwiec →, *Poland* 45 F8
Lixi, *China* 58 D3
Lixian, *China* 58 B4
Lixoúrion, *Greece* 38 C2
Liyang, *China* 59 B12
Lizard I., *Australia* 94 A4
Lizard Pt., *U.K.* 13 H2
Lizzano, *Italy* 31 B10
Ljig, *Serbia, Yug.* 40 B4
Ljubija, *Bos.-H.* 29 D13
Ljubinje, *Bos.-H.* 40 D2
Ljubljana, *Slovenia* 29 B11
Ljubno, *Slovenia* 29 B11
Ljubovija, *Serbia, Yug.* 40 B3
Ljugarn, *Sweden* 11 G12
Ljung, *Sweden* 11 G7
Ljungan →, *Sweden* 10 B11
Ljungaverk, *Sweden* 10 B10
Ljungby, *Sweden* 9 H15
Ljungbyholm, *Sweden* 11 H10
Ljungdalen, *Sweden* 10 B6
Ljungsbro, *Sweden* 11 F9
Ljungskile, *Sweden* 11 F5
Ljusdal, *Sweden* 10 C10
Ljusfallshammar, *Sweden* 11 F9
Ljusnan →, *Sweden* 10 C11
Ljusne, *Sweden* 10 C11
Ljutomer, *Slovenia* 29 B13
Llagostera, *Spain* 32 D7
Llancanelo, Salina, *Argentina* 126 D2
Llandeilo, *U.K.* 13 F4
Llandovery, *U.K.* 13 F4
Llandrindod Wells, *U.K.* 13 E4
Llandudno, *U.K.* 12 D4
Llanelli, *U.K.* 13 F3
Llanes, *Spain* 34 B6
Llangollen, *U.K.* 12 E4
Llanidloes, *U.K.* 13 E4
Llano, *U.S.A.* 113 K5
Llano →, *U.S.A.* 113 K5
Llano Estacado, *U.S.A.* 113 J3
Llanos, *S. Amer.* 122 C3
Llanquihue, L., *Chile* 128 E1
Llanwrtyd Wells, *U.K.* 13 E4
Llebeig, C. des, *Spain* 37 B9
Lleida, *Spain* 32 D5
Lleida □, *Spain* 32 C6
Llentrisca, C., *Spain* 37 C7
Llera, *Mexico* 119 C5
Llerena, *Spain* 35 G5
Lleyn Peninsula, *U.K.* 12 E3
Llico, *Chile* 126 C1
Lliria, *Spain* 33 F4
Llobregat →, *Spain* 32 D7
Llodio, *Spain* 32 B2
Lloret de Mar, *Spain* 32 D7
Lloyd B., *Australia* 94 A3
Lloyd L., *Canada* 105 B7
Lloydminster, *Canada* 105 C7
Llucena del Cid, *Spain* 32 E4
Llucmajor, *Spain* 37 B9
Llullaillaco, Volcán, *S. Amer.* 126 A2
Lo →, *Vietnam* 64 B5
Loa, *U.S.A.* 115 G8
Loa →, *Chile* 126 A1
Loaita I., *S. China Sea* 62 B4
Loange →, *Dem. Rep. of the Congo* 84 E4
Loano, *Italy* 28 D5
Lobatse, *Botswana* 88 D4
Löbau, *Germany* 24 D10
Lobenstein, *Germany* 24 E7
Lobería, *Argentina* 126 D4
Löberöd, *Sweden* 11 J7
Łobez, *Poland* 44 E2
Lobito, *Angola* 85 G2
Lobo →, *Ivory C.* 82 D3
Lobos, *Argentina* 126 D4
Lobos, I., *Mexico* 118 B2
Lobos, I. de, *Canary Is.* 37 F6
Łobżenica, *Poland* 45 E4
Loc Binh, *Vietnam* 64 B6
Loc Ninh, *Vietnam* 65 G6
Locarno, *Switz.* 25 J4
Loch Baghasdail = Lochboisdale, *U.K.* 14 D1

Loch Garman

Loch Garman = Wexford, *Ireland* 15 D5
Loch Nam Madadh = Lochmaddy, *U.K.* 14 D1
Lochaber, *U.K.* 14 E3
Locharbriggs, *U.K.* 14 F5
Lochboisdale, *U.K.* 14 D1
Loche, L. La, *Canada* 105 B7
Lochem, *Neths.* 17 B6
Loches, *France* 18 E7
Lochgilphead, *U.K.* 14 E3
Lochinver, *U.K.* 14 C3
Lochmaddy, *U.K.* 14 D1
Lochnagar, *Australia* 94 C4
Lochnagar, *U.K.* 14 E5
Łochów, *Poland* 45 F8
Lochy, L., *U.K.* 14 E4
Lock, *Australia* 95 E2
Lock Haven, *U.S.A.* 110 E7
Lockeford, *U.S.A.* 116 G5
Lockeport, *Canada* 103 D6
Lockerbie, *U.K.* 14 F5
Lockhart, *Australia* 95 F4
Lockhart, *U.S.A.* 113 L6
Lockhart, L., *Australia* 93 F2
Lockhart River, *Australia* 94 A3
Lockney, *U.S.A.* 113 H4
Lockport, *U.S.A.* 110 C6
Locminé, *France* 18 E4
Locri, *Italy* 31 D9
Locronan, *France* 18 D2
Lod, *Israel* 75 D3
Lodeinoye Pole, *Russia* 46 B7
Lodève, *France* 20 E7
Lodge Bay, *Canada* 103 B8
Lodge Grass, *U.S.A.* 114 D10
Lodgepole Cr. →, *U.S.A.* 112 E2
Lodhran, *Pakistan* 68 E4
Lodi, *Italy* 28 C6
Lodi, *Calif., U.S.A.* 116 G5
Lodi, *Ohio, U.S.A.* 110 E3
Lodja, *Dem. Rep. of the Congo* 86 C1
Lodosa, *Spain* 32 C2
Lödöse, *Sweden* 11 F6
Lodwar, *Kenya* 86 B4
Łódź, *Poland* 45 G6
Łódzkie □, *Poland* 45 G6
Loei, *Thailand* 64 D3
Loengo, *Dem. Rep. of the Congo* 86 C2
Loeriesfontein, *S. Africa* 88 E2
Lofa →, *Liberia* 83 D2
Lofer, *Austria* 26 D5
Lofoten, *Norway* 8 B15
Lofsdalen, *Sweden* 10 B7
Lofsen →, *Sweden* 10 B7
Loftahammar, *Sweden* 11 G10
Loga, *Niger* 83 C5
Logan, *Iowa, U.S.A.* 112 E7
Logan, *Ohio, U.S.A.* 108 F4
Logan, *Utah, U.S.A.* 114 F8
Logan, *W. Va., U.S.A.* 108 G5
Logan, Mt., *Canada* 100 B5
Logandale, *U.S.A.* 117 J12
Logansport, *Ind., U.S.A.* 108 E2
Logansport, *La., U.S.A.* 113 K8
Logirim, *Sudan* 81 G3
Logo, *Sudan* 81 F3
Logone →, *Chad* 79 F9
Logroño, *Spain* 32 C2
Logrosán, *Spain* 35 F5
Løgstør, *Denmark* 11 H3
Løgumkloster, *Denmark* 11 J2
Lohals, *Denmark* 11 J4
Lohardaga, *India* 69 H11
Loharia, *India* 68 H6
Loharu, *India* 68 E6
Lohja, *Finland* 9 F21
Löhne, *Germany* 24 C4
Lohr, *Germany* 25 F5
Lohri Wah →, *Pakistan* 68 F2
Loi-kaw, *Burma* 67 K20
Loimaa, *Finland* 9 F20
Loir →, *France* 18 E6
Loir-et-Cher □, *France* 18 E8
Loire □, *France* 21 C8
Loire →, *France* 18 E4
Loire-Atlantique □, *France* 18 E5
Loiret □, *France* 19 E9
Loitz, *Germany* 24 B9
Loja, *Ecuador* 124 D3
Loja, *Spain* 35 H6
Loji = Kawasi, *Indonesia* 63 E7
Løjt Kirkeby, *Denmark* 11 J3
Lojung, *China* 58 E7
Loka, *Sudan* 81 G3
Lokandu, *Dem. Rep. of the Congo* 86 C2
Lokeren, *Belgium* 17 C3
Lokgwabe, *Botswana* 88 C3
Lokhvitsa, *Ukraine* 47 G7
Lokichokio, *Kenya* 86 B3
Lokitaung, *Kenya* 86 B4
Lokkan tekojärvi, *Finland* 8 C22
Løkken, *Denmark* 11 G3
Loknya, *Russia* 46 D6
Loko, *Nigeria* 83 D6
Lokoja, *Nigeria* 83 D6
Lokot, *Russia* 47 F8
Lol →, *Sudan* 81 F2
Lola, *Guinea* 82 D3
Lola, Mt., *U.S.A.* 116 F6
Lolibai, Gebel, *Sudan* 81 G3
Lolimi, *Sudan* 81 G3
Loliondo, *Tanzania* 86 C4
Lolland, *Denmark* 11 K5
Lollar, *Germany* 24 E4
Lolo, *U.S.A.* 114 C6
Lolodorf, *Cameroon* 83 E7
Lom, *Bulgaria* 40 C7
Lom →, *Bulgaria* 40 C7
Lom Kao, *Thailand* 64 D3
Lom Sak, *Thailand* 64 D3
Loma, *U.S.A.* 114 C8
Loma Linda, *U.S.A.* 117 L9
Lomami →, *Dem. Rep. of the Congo* 86 B1
Lomas de Zamóra, *Argentina* 126 C4
Lombadina, *Australia* 92 C3
Lombárdia □, *Italy* 28 C6
Lombardy = Lombárdia □, *Italy* 28 C6
Lombez, *France* 20 E4
Lomblen, *Indonesia* 63 F6
Lombok, *Indonesia* 62 F5
Lomé, *Togo* 83 D5
Lomela, *Dem. Rep. of the Congo* 84 E4
Lomela →, *Dem. Rep. of the Congo* 84 E4
Lomianki, *Poland* 45 F7
Lomma, *Sweden* 11 J7
Lommel, *Belgium* 17 C5
Lomond, *Canada* 104 C6
Lomond, L., *U.K.* 14 E4
Lomphat, *Cambodia* 64 F6
Lompobatang, *Indonesia* 63 F5
Lompoc, *U.S.A.* 117 L6
Łomża, *Poland* 45 E9
Loncoche, *Chile* 128 D2
Londa, *India* 66 M9
Londiani, *Kenya* 86 C4
Londinières, *France* 18 C8
London, *Canada* 102 D3
London, *U.K.* 13 F7
London, *Ky., U.S.A.* 108 G3
London, *Ohio, U.S.A.* 108 F4
London, Greater □, *U.K.* 13 F7
Londonderry, *U.K.* 15 B4
Londonderry □, *U.K.* 15 B4
Londonderry, C., *Australia* 92 B4
Londonderry, I., *Chile* 128 H2
Londres, *Argentina* 128 B3
Londrina, *Brazil* 127 A5
Lone Pine, *U.S.A.* 116 J8
Lonely Mine, *Zimbabwe* 89 B4
Long B., *U.S.A.* 109 J6
Long Beach, *Calif., U.S.A.* 117 M8
Long Beach, *N.Y., U.S.A.* 111 F11
Long Beach, *Wash., U.S.A.* 116 D2
Long Branch, *U.S.A.* 111 F11
Long Creek, *U.S.A.* 114 D4
Long Eaton, *U.K.* 12 E6
Long I., *Australia* 94 C4
Long I., *Bahamas* 121 B4
Long I., *Canada* 102 B4
Long I., *Ireland* 15 E2
Long I., *U.S.A.* 111 F11
Long Island Sd., *U.S.A.* 111 E12
Long L., *Canada* 102 C2
Long Lake, *U.S.A.* 111 C10
Long Point B., *Canada* 110 D4
Long Prairie →, *U.S.A.* 112 C7
Long Pt., *Canada* 110 D4
Long Range Mts., *Canada* 103 C8
Long Reef, *Australia* 92 B4
Long Spruce, *Canada* 105 B10
Long Str. = Longa, Proliv, *Russia* 4 C16
Long Thanh, *Vietnam* 65 G6
Long Xian, *China* 56 G4
Long Xuyen, *Vietnam* 65 G5
Longá, *Greece* 38 E3
Longa, Proliv, *Russia* 4 C16
Long'an, *China* 58 F6
Longarone, *Italy* 29 B9
Longbenton, *U.K.* 12 B6
Longboat Key, *U.S.A.* 109 M4
Longchang, *China* 58 C5
Longchi, *China* 58 C4
Longchuan, *Guangdong, China* 59 E10
Longchuan, *Yunnan, China* 58 E1
Longde, *China* 56 G4
Longeau, *France* 19 E12
Longford, *Australia* 94 G4
Longford, *Ireland* 15 C4
Longford □, *Ireland* 15 C4
Longguan, *China* 56 D8
Longhai, *China* 59 E11
Longhua, *China* 57 D9
Longhui, *China* 59 D8
Longido, *Tanzania* 86 C4
Longiram, *Indonesia* 62 E5
Longkou, *Jiangxi, China* 59 D10
Longkou, *Shandong, China* 57 F11
Longlac, *Canada* 102 C2
Longli, *China* 58 D6
Longlin, *China* 58 E5
Longling, *China* 58 E2
Longmeadow, *U.S.A.* 111 D12
Longmen, *China* 59 F10
Longming, *China* 58 F6
Longmont, *U.S.A.* 112 E2
Longnan, *China* 59 E10
Longnawan, *Indonesia* 62 D4
Longobucco, *Italy* 31 C9
Longquan, *China* 59 C12
Longreach, *Australia* 94 C3
Longshan, *China* 58 C7
Longsheng, *China* 59 E8
Longué-Jumelles, *France* 18 E6
Longueau, *France* 19 C9
Longueuil, *Canada* 111 A11
Longuyon, *France* 19 C12
Longvic, *France* 19 E12
Longview, *Tex., U.S.A.* 113 J7
Longview, *Wash., U.S.A.* 116 D4
Longwy, *France* 19 C12
Longxi, *China* 56 G3
Longyan, *China* 59 E11
Longyou, *China* 59 C12
Longzhou, *China* 58 F6
Lonigo, *Italy* 29 C8
Löningen, *Germany* 24 C3
Lonja →, *Croatia* 29 C13
Lonoke, *U.S.A.* 113 H9
Lonquimay, *Chile* 128 D2
Lons-le-Saunier, *France* 19 F12
Lönsboda, *Sweden* 11 H8
Looe, *U.K.* 13 G3
Lookout, C., *Canada* 102 A3
Lookout, C., *U.S.A.* 109 H7
Loolmalasin, *Tanzania* 86 C4
Loon →, *Alta., Canada* 104 B5
Loon →, *Man., Canada* 105 B8
Loon Lake, *Canada* 105 C7
Loongana, *Australia* 93 F4
Loop Hd., *Ireland* 15 D2
Lop Buri, *Thailand* 64 E3
Lop Nor = Lop Nur, *China* 60 B4
Lop Nur, *China* 60 B4
Lopare, *Bos.-H.* 42 F3
Lopatin, *Russia* 49 J8
Lopatina, Gora, *Russia* 51 D15
Lopaye, *Sudan* 81 F3
Lopez, *Phil.* 61 E5
Lopez, *U.S.A.* 111 E8
Lopez, C., *Gabon* 84 E1
Lopphavet, *Norway* 8 A19
Lora →, *Afghan.* 66 D4
Lora, Hamun-i-, *Pakistan* 66 E4
Lora Cr. →, *Australia* 95 D2
Lora del Río, *Spain* 35 H5
Lorain, *U.S.A.* 110 E2
Loralai, *Pakistan* 68 D3
Lorca, *Spain* 33 H3
Lord Howe I., *Pac. Oc.* 96 L7
Lord Howe Ridge, *Pac. Oc.* 96 L8
Lordsburg, *U.S.A.* 115 K9
Lorestan □, *Iran* 71 C6
Loreto, *Brazil* 125 E9
Loreto, *Italy* 29 E10
Loreto, *Mexico* 118 B2
Lorgues, *France* 21 E10
Lorhosso, *Burkina Faso* 82 C4
Lorient, *France* 18 E3
Lőrinci, *Hungary* 42 C4
Lormi, *India* 69 H9
Lorn, *U.K.* 14 E3
Lorn, Firth of, *U.K.* 14 E3
Lorne, *Australia* 95 F3
Loronyo, *Sudan* 81 G3
Lorovouno, *Cyprus* 36 D11
Lörrach, *Germany* 25 H3
Lorraine □, *France* 19 D13
Los, *Sweden* 10 C9
Los, Îles de, *Guinea* 82 D2
Los Alamos, *Calif., U.S.A.* 117 L6
Los Alamos, *N. Mex., U.S.A.* 115 J10
Los Altos, *U.S.A.* 116 H4
Los Andes, *Chile* 126 C1
Los Angeles, *Chile* 126 D1
Los Angeles, *U.S.A.* 117 M8
Los Angeles, Bahia de, *Mexico* 118 B2
Los Angeles Aqueduct, *U.S.A.* 117 K9
Los Banos, *U.S.A.* 116 H6
Los Barrios, *Spain* 35 J5
Los Blancos, *Argentina* 126 A3
Los Chiles, *Costa Rica* 120 D3
Los Corrales de Buelna, *Spain* 34 B6
Los Cristianos, *Canary Is.* 37 F3
Los Gallardos, *Spain* 33 H3
Los Gatos, *U.S.A.* 116 H5
Los Hermanos Is., *Venezuela* 121 D7
Los Islotes, *Canary Is.* 37 E6
Los Llanos de Aridane, *Canary Is.* 37 F2
Los Loros, *Chile* 126 B1
Los Lunas, *U.S.A.* 115 J10
Los Mochis, *Mexico* 118 B3
Los Monegros, *Spain* 32 D4
Los Nietos, *Spain* 33 H4
Los Olivos, *U.S.A.* 117 L6
Los Palacios, *Cuba* 120 B3
Los Palacios y Villafranca, *Spain* 35 H5
Los Reyes, *Mexico* 118 D4
Los Roques Is., *Venezuela* 121 D6
Los Santos de Maimona, *Spain* 35 G4
Los Teques, *Venezuela* 124 A5
Los Testigos, Is., *Venezuela* 124 A6
Los Vilos, *Chile* 126 C1
Los Yébenes, *Spain* 35 F7
Łosice, *Poland* 45 F9
Loskop Dam, *S. Africa* 89 D4
Løsning, *Denmark* 11 J3
Lossiemouth, *U.K.* 14 D5
Lostwithiel, *U.K.* 13 G3
Lot □, *France* 20 D5
Lot →, *France* 20 D4
Lot-et-Garonne □, *France* 20 D4
Lota, *Chile* 126 D1
Lotagipi Swamp, *Sudan* 81 G3
Loṭfābād, *Iran* 71 B8
Lothair, *S. Africa* 89 D5
Lotorp, *Sweden* 11 F9
Lötschbergtunnel, *Switz.* 25 J3
Löttorp, *Sweden* 11 G11
Lotung, *Taiwan* 59 E13
Loubomo, *Congo* 84 E2
Loudéac, *France* 18 D4
Loudi, *China* 59 D8
Loudonville, *U.S.A.* 110 F2
Loudun, *France* 18 E7
Loue →, *France* 19 E12
Louga, *Senegal* 82 B1
Loughborough, *U.K.* 12 E6
Loughrea, *Ireland* 15 C3
Loughros More B., *Ireland* 15 B3
Louhans, *France* 19 F12
Louis Trichardt, *S. Africa* 89 C4
Louis XIV, Pte., *Canada* 102 B4
Louisa, *U.S.A.* 108 F4
Louisbourg, *Canada* 103 C8
Louise I., *Canada* 104 C2
Louiseville, *Canada* 102 C5
Louisiade Arch., *Papua N. G.* 96 J7
Louisiana, *U.S.A.* 112 F9
Louisiana □, *U.S.A.* 113 K9
Louisville, *Ky., U.S.A.* 108 F3
Louisville, *Miss., U.S.A.* 113 J10
Louisville, *Ohio, U.S.A.* 110 F3
Loulay, *France* 20 B3
Loulé, *Portugal* 35 H3
Louny, *Czech Rep.* 26 A6
Loup City, *U.S.A.* 112 E5
Loups Marins, Lacs des, *Canada* 102 A5
Lourdes, *France* 20 E3
Lourenço-Marques = Maputo, *Mozam.* 89 D5
Lourinhã, *Portugal* 35 F1
Lousã, *Portugal* 34 E2
Louta, *Burkina Faso* 82 C4
Louth, *Australia* 95 E4
Louth, *Ireland* 15 C5
Louth, *U.K.* 12 D7
Louth □, *Ireland* 15 C5
Loutrá Aidhipsoú, *Greece* 38 C5
Loutráki, *Greece* 38 D4
Louvain = Leuven, *Belgium* 17 D4
Louviers, *France* 18 C8
Louwsburg, *S. Africa* 89 D5
Lovat →, *Russia* 46 C6
Lovćen, *Montenegro, Yug.* 40 D2
Lovech, *Bulgaria* 41 C8
Lovech □, *Bulgaria* 41 C8
Loveland, *U.S.A.* 112 E2
Lovell, *U.S.A.* 114 D9
Lovelock, *U.S.A.* 114 F4
Lóvere, *Italy* 28 C7
Lövestad, *Sweden* 11 J7
Loviisa, *Finland* 9 F22
Loving, *U.S.A.* 113 J2
Lovington, *U.S.A.* 113 J3
Lovisa = Loviisa, *Finland* 9 F22
Lovosice, *Czech Rep.* 26 A7
Lovran, *Croatia* 29 C11
Lovrin, *Romania* 42 E5
Lövstabruk, *Sweden* 10 D11
Lövstabukten, *Sweden* 10 D11
Low, L., *Canada* 102 B4
Low Pt., *Australia* 93 F4
Low Tatra = Nízké Tatry, *Slovak Rep.* 27 C12
Lowa, *Dem. Rep. of the Congo* 86 C2
Lowa →, *Dem. Rep. of the Congo* 86 C2
Lowell, *U.S.A.* 111 D13
Lowellville, *U.S.A.* 110 E4
Löwen →, *Namibia* 88 D2
Lower Alkali L., *U.S.A.* 114 F3
Lower Arrow L., *Canada* 104 D5
Lower Austria = Niederösterreich □, *Austria* 26 C8
Lower California = Baja California, *Mexico* 118 A1
Lower Hutt, *N.Z.* 91 J5
Lower Lake, *U.S.A.* 116 G4
Lower Manitou L., *Canada* 105 D10
Lower Post, *Canada* 104 B3
Lower Red L., *U.S.A.* 112 B7
Lower Saxony = Niedersachsen □, *Germany* 24 C4
Lower Tunguska = Tunguska, Nizhnyaya →, *Russia* 51 C9
Lowestoft, *U.K.* 13 E9
Łowicz, *Poland* 45 F6
Lowville, *U.S.A.* 111 C9
Loxton, *Australia* 95 E3
Loxton, *S. Africa* 88 E3
Loyalton, *U.S.A.* 116 F6
Loyalty Is. = Loyauté, Is., *N. Cal.* 96 K8
Loyang = Luoyang, *China* 56 G7
Loyauté, Is., *N. Cal.* 96 K8
Loyev = Loyew, *Belarus* 47 G6
Loyew, *Belarus* 47 G6
Loyoro, *Uganda* 86 B3
Lož, *Slovenia* 29 C11
Lozère □, *France* 20 D7
Loznica, *Serbia, Yug.* 40 B3
Lozova, *Ukraine* 47 H9
Lü Shan, *China* 59 C11
Lü-Tao, *Taiwan* 59 F13
Luachimo, *Angola* 84 F4
Luajan →, *India* 69 G11
Lualaba →, *Dem. Rep. of the Congo* 86 B2
Luampa, *Zambia* 87 F1
Lu'an, *China* 59 B11
Luan Chau, *Vietnam* 58 G4
Luan He →, *China* 57 E10
Luan Xian, *China* 57 E10
Luancheng, *Guangxi Zhuangzu, China* 58 F7
Luancheng, *Hebei, China* 56 F8
Luanco, *Spain* 34 B5
Luanda, *Angola* 84 F2
Luang, Thale, *Thailand* 65 J3
Luang Prabang, *Laos* 58 H4
Luangwa, *Zambia* 87 F3
Luangwa →, *Zambia* 87 E3
Luangwa Valley, *Zambia* 87 E3
Luanne, *China* 57 D9
Luanping, *China* 57 D9
Luanshya, *Zambia* 87 E2
Luapula □, *Zambia* 87 E2
Luapula →, *Africa* 87 D2
Luarca, *Spain* 34 B4
Luashi, *Dem. Rep. of the Congo* 87 E1
Luau, *Angola* 84 G4
Lubaczów, *Poland* 45 H10
Lubań, *Poland* 45 G2
Lubana, Ozero = Lubānas Ezers, *Latvia* 9 H22
Lubānas Ezers, *Latvia* 9 H22
Lubang, *Phil.* 61 E4
Lubang Is., *Phil.* 63 B6
Lubartów, *Poland* 45 G9
Lubawa, *Poland* 44 E6
Lübbecke, *Germany* 24 C4
Lübben, *Germany* 24 D9
Lübbenau, *Germany* 24 D9
Lubbock, *U.S.A.* 113 J4
Lübeck, *Germany* 24 B6
Lübecker Bucht, *Germany* 24 A6
Lubefu, *Dem. Rep. of the Congo* 86 C1
Lubefu →, *Dem. Rep. of the Congo* 86 C1
Lubelskie □, *Poland* 45 G9
Lubero = Luofu, *Dem. Rep. of the Congo* 86 C2
Lubersac, *France* 20 C5
Lubicon L., *Canada* 104 B5
Lubień Kujawski, *Poland* 45 F6
Lubilash →, *Dem. Rep. of the Congo* 84 F4
Lubin, *Poland* 45 G3
Lublin, *Poland* 45 G9
Lubliniec, *Poland* 45 H5
Lubnān, Jabal, *Lebanon* 75 B4
Lubniewice, *Poland* 45 F2
Lubny, *Ukraine* 47 G7
Lubomierz, *Poland* 45 G2
Luboń, *Poland* 45 F3
Lubongola, *Dem. Rep. of the Congo* 86 C2
L'ubotín, *Slovak Rep.* 27 B13
Lubraniec, *Poland* 45 F5
Lubsko, *Poland* 45 G1
Lübtheen, *Germany* 24 B7
Lubuagan, *Phil.* 61 C4
Lubudi, *Dem. Rep. of the Congo* 84 F5
Lubudi →, *Dem. Rep. of the Congo* 87 D2
Lubuklinggau, *Indonesia* 62 E2
Lubuksikaping, *Indonesia* 62 D2
Lubumbashi, *Dem. Rep. of the Congo* 87 E2
Lubunda, *Dem. Rep. of the Congo* 86 D2
Lubungu, *Zambia* 87 E2
Lubuskie □, *Poland* 45 F2
Lubutu, *Dem. Rep. of the Congo* 86 C2
Luc An Chau, *Vietnam* 64 A5
Luc-en-Diois, *France* 21 D9
Lucan, *Canada* 110 C3
Lucania, Mt., *Canada* 100 B5
Lucas Channel, *Canada* 110 A3
Lucban, *Phil.* 61 D4
Lucca, *Italy* 28 E7
Lucé, *France* 18 D8
Luce Bay, *U.K.* 14 G4
Lucea, *Jamaica* 120 C4
Lucedale, *U.S.A.* 109 K1
Lucena, *Phil.* 61 E4
Lucena, *Spain* 35 H6
Lučenec, *Slovak Rep.* 27 C12
Lucera, *Italy* 31 A8
Lucerne = Luzern, *Switz.* 25 H4
Lucerne, *U.S.A.* 116 F4
Lucerne Valley, *U.S.A.* 117 L10
Lucero, *Mexico* 118 A3
Luchena →, *Spain* 33 H3
Lucheng, *China* 56 F7
Lucheringo →, *Mozam.* 87 E4
Lüchow, *Germany* 24 C7
Luchuan, *China* 59 F8
Lucia, *U.S.A.* 116 J5
Lucinda, *Australia* 94 B4
Lucindale, *Australia* 95 F3
Luckau, *Germany* 24 D9
Luckenwalde, *Germany* 24 C9
Luckhoff, *S. Africa* 88 D3
Lucknow, *Canada* 110 C3
Lucknow, *India* 69 F9
Luçon, *France* 20 B2
Lüda = Dalian, *China* 57 E11
Luda Kamchiya →, *Bulgaria* 41 C11
Ludbreg, *Croatia* 29 B13
Lüdenscheid, *Germany* 24 D3
Lüderitz, *Namibia* 88 D2
Lüderitzbaai, *Namibia* 88 D2
Ludhiana, *India* 68 D6
Ludian, *China* 58 D4
Luding Qiao, *China* 58 C4
Lüdinghausen, *Germany* 24 D3
Ludington, *U.S.A.* 108 D2
Ludlow, *U.K.* 13 E5
Ludlow, *Calif., U.S.A.* 117 L10
Ludlow, *Pa., U.S.A.* 110 E6
Ludlow, *Vt., U.S.A.* 111 C12
Ludus, *Romania* 43 D9
Ludvika, *Sweden* 10 D9
Ludwigsburg, *Germany* 25 G5
Ludwigsfelde, *Germany* 24 C9
Ludwigshafen, *Germany* 25 F4
Ludwigslust, *Germany* 24 B7

Ludza, *Latvia* 46 D4
Lueki, *Dem. Rep. of the Congo* 86 C2
Luena, *Dem. Rep. of the Congo* 87 D2
Luena, *Zambia* 87 E3
Lüeyang, *China* 56 H4
Lufeng, *Guangdong, China* 59 F10
Lufeng, *Yunnan, China* 58 E4
Lufira →, *Dem. Rep. of the Congo* 87 D2
Lufkin, *U.S.A.* 113 K7
Lufupa, *Dem. Rep. of the Congo* 87 E1
Luga, *Russia* 46 C5
Luga →, *Russia* 46 C5
Lugano, *Switz.* 25 J4
Lugano, L. di, *Switz.* 28 C6
Lugansk = Luhansk, *Ukraine* 47 H10
Lugard's Falls, *Kenya* 86 C4
Lugela, *Mozam.* 87 F4
Lugenda →, *Mozam.* 87 E4
Lugh Ganana, *Somali Rep.* 74 G3
Lugnaquilla, *Ireland* 15 D5
Lugo, *Italy* 29 D8
Lugo, *Spain* 34 B3
Lugo □, *Spain* 34 C3
Lugoj, *Romania* 42 E6
Lugovoy, *Kazakstan* 50 E8
Luhansk, *Ukraine* 47 H10
Luhe, *China* 59 A12
Luhe →, *Germany* 24 B6
Luhuo, *China* 58 B3
Luiana, *Angola* 88 B3
Luimneach = Limerick, *Ireland* 15 D3
Luing, *U.K.* 14 E3
Luino, *Italy* 28 C5
Luís Correia, *Brazil* 125 D10
Luitpold Coast, *Antarctica* 5 D1
Luiza, *Dem. Rep. of the Congo* 84 F4
Luizi, *Dem. Rep. of the Congo* 86 D2
Luján, *Argentina* 126 C4
Lujiang, *China* 59 B11
Lukang, *Taiwan* 59 E13
Lukanga Swamp, *Zambia* 87 E2
Lukavac, *Bos.-H.* 42 F3
Lukenie →, *Dem. Rep. of the Congo* 84 E3
Lukhisaral, *India* 69 G12
Lŭki, *Bulgaria* 41 E8
Lukolela, *Dem. Rep. of the Congo* 86 D1
Lukosi, *Zimbabwe* 87 F2
Lukovë, *Albania* 40 G3
Lukovit, *Bulgaria* 41 C8
Łuków, *Poland* 45 G9
Lukoyanov, *Russia* 48 C7
Lule älv →, *Sweden* 8 D19
Luleå, *Sweden* 8 D20
Lüleburgaz, *Turkey* 41 E11
Luliang, *China* 58 E4
Luling, *U.S.A.* 113 L6
Lulong, *China* 57 E10
Lulonga →, *Dem. Rep. of the Congo* 84 D3
Lulua →, *Dem. Rep. of the Congo* 84 E4
Luluabourg = Kananga, *Dem. Rep. of the Congo* 84 F4
Lumajang, *Indonesia* 63 H15
Lumbala N'guimbo, *Angola* 85 G4
Lumberton, *U.S.A.* 109 H6
Lumbwa, *Kenya* 86 C4
Lumsden, *Canada* 105 C8
Lumsden, *N.Z.* 91 L2
Lumut, *Malaysia* 65 K3
Lumut, Tanjung, *Indonesia* 62 E3
Luna, *India* 68 H3
Lunan, *China* 58 E4
Lunavada, *India* 68 H5
Lunca, *Romania* 43 C10
Lunca Corbului, *Romania* 43 F9
Lund, *Sweden* 11 J7
Lundazi, *Zambia* 87 E3
Lunderskov, *Denmark* 11 J3
Lundi →, *Zimbabwe* 87 G3
Lundu, *Malaysia* 62 D3
Lundy, *U.K.* 13 F3
Lune →, *U.K.* 12 C5
Lüneburg, *Germany* 24 B6
Lüneburg Heath = Lüneburger Heide, *Germany* 24 B6
Lüneburger Heide, *Germany* 24 B6
Lunel, *France* 21 E8
Lünen, *Germany* 24 D3
Lunenburg, *Canada* 103 D7
Lunéville, *France* 19 D13
Lunga →, *Zambia* 87 E2
Lungi Airport, *S. Leone* 82 D2
Lunglei, *India* 67 H18
Luni, *India* 68 G5
Luni →, *India* 68 G4
Luninets = Luninyets, *Belarus* 47 F4
Luning, *U.S.A.* 114 G4
Lunino, *Russia* 48 D7
Luninyets, *Belarus* 47 F4
Lunkaransar, *India* 68 E5
Lunsemfwa →, *Zambia* 87 E3
Lunsemfwa Falls, *Zambia* 87 E2
Luo He →, *China* 56 G6
Luocheng, *China* 58 E7
Luochuan, *China* 56 G5
Luoci, *China* 58 E4
Luodian, *China* 58 E6
Luoding, *China* 59 F8
Luofu, *Dem. Rep. of the Congo* 86 C2
Luohe, *China* 56 H8
Luojiang, *China* 58 B5
Luonan, *China* 56 G6
Luoning, *China* 56 G6
Luoshan, *China* 59 A10
Luotian, *China* 59 B10
Luoxiao Shan, *China* 59 D10
Luoyang, *China* 56 G7
Luoyuan, *China* 59 D12
Luozigou, *China* 57 C16
Lupanshui, *China* 58 D5
Lupeni, *Romania* 43 E8
Lupilichi, *Mozam.* 87 E4
Łupków, *Poland* 45 J9
Lupoing, *China* 58 E5
Luquan, *China* 58 E4
Luque, *Paraguay* 126 B4
Lúras, *Italy* 30 B2
Luray, *U.S.A.* 108 F6
Lure, *France* 19 E13
Lurgan, *U.K.* 15 B5
Lusaka, *Zambia* 87 F2
Lusambo, *Dem. Rep. of the Congo* 86 C1
Lusangaye, *Dem. Rep. of the Congo* 86 C2
Luseland, *Canada* 105 C7
Lushan, *Henan, China* 56 H7
Lushan, *Sichuan, China* 58 B4
Lushi, *China* 56 G6
Lushnja, *Albania* 40 F3
Lushoto, *Tanzania* 86 C4
Lushui, *China* 58 E2
Lüshun, *China* 57 E11
Lusignan, *France* 20 B4
Lusigny-sur-Barse, *France* 19 D11
Lusk, *U.S.A.* 112 D2
Lussac-les-Châteaux, *France* 20 B4
Lustenau, *Austria* 26 D2
Lūt, Dasht-e, *Iran* 71 D8
Luta = Dalian, *China* 57 E11
Lutherstadt Wittenberg, *Germany* 24 D8
Luton, *U.K.* 13 F7
Luton □, *U.K.* 13 F7
Lutselke, *Canada* 105 A6
Lutsk, *Ukraine* 47 G3
Lützow Holmbukta, *Antarctica* 5 C4
Lutzputs, *S. Africa* 88 D3
Luverne, *Ala., U.S.A.* 109 K2
Luverne, *Minn., U.S.A.* 112 D6
Luvua, *Dem. Rep. of the Congo* 87 D2
Luvua →, *Dem. Rep. of the Congo* 86 D2
Luvuvhu →, *S. Africa* 89 C5
Luwegu →, *Tanzania* 87 D4
Luwuk, *Indonesia* 63 E6
Luxembourg, *Lux.* 17 E6
Luxembourg □, *Belgium* 17 E5
Luxembourg ■, *Europe* 7 F7
Luxeuil-les-Bains, *France* 19 E13
Luxi, *Hunan, China* 59 C8
Luxi, *Yunnan, China* 58 E4
Luxi, *Yunnan, China* 58 E2
Luxor = El Uqsur, *Egypt* 80 B3
Luy-de-Béarn →, *France* 20 E3
Luy-de-France →, *France* 20 E3
Luyi, *China* 56 H8
Luz-St-Sauveur, *France* 20 F4
Luzern, *Switz.* 25 H4
Luzern □, *Switz.* 25 H3
Luzhai, *China* 58 E7
Luzhi, *China* 58 D5
Luzhou, *China* 58 C5
Luziânia, *Brazil* 125 G9
Lužnice →, *Czech Rep.* 26 B7
Luzon, *Phil.* 61 D4
Luzy, *France* 19 F10
Luzzi, *Italy* 31 C9
Lviv, *Ukraine* 47 H3
Lvov = Lviv, *Ukraine* 47 H3
Lwówek, *Poland* 45 F3
Lwówek Śląski, *Poland* 45 G2
Lyakhavichy, *Belarus* 47 F4
Lyakhovskiye, Ostrova, *Russia* 51 B15
Lyaki = Läki, *Azerbaijan* 49 K8
Lyal I., *Canada* 110 B3
Lyallpur = Faisalabad, *Pakistan* 68 D5
Lyaskovets, *Bulgaria* 41 C9
Lybster, *U.K.* 14 C5
Lycaonia, *Turkey* 72 D5
Lychen, *Germany* 24 B9
Lychkova, *Russia* 46 D7
Lycia, *Turkey* 39 E11
Lyckebyån →, *Sweden* 11 H9
Lycksele, *Sweden* 8 D18
Lycosura, *Greece* 38 D4
Lydda = Lod, *Israel* 75 D3
Lydenburg, *S. Africa* 89 D5
Lydia, *Turkey* 39 C10
Łydynia →, *Poland* 45 F7
Lyell, *N.Z.* 91 J4
Lyell I., *Canada* 104 C2
Lyepyel, *Belarus* 46 E5
Lygnern, *Sweden* 11 G6
Lykens, *U.S.A.* 111 F8
Lyman, *U.S.A.* 114 F8
Lyme B., *U.K.* 13 G4
Lyme Regis, *U.K.* 13 G5
Lymington, *U.K.* 13 G6
Łyna →, *Poland* 9 J19
Lynchburg, *U.S.A.* 108 G6
Lynd →, *Australia* 94 B3
Lynd Ra., *Australia* 95 D4
Lynden, *Canada* 110 C4
Lynden, *U.S.A.* 116 B4
Lyndhurst, *Australia* 95 E2
Lyndon →, *Australia* 93 D1
Lyndonville, *N.Y., U.S.A.* 110 C6
Lyndonville, *Vt., U.S.A.* 111 B12
Lyngen, *Norway* 8 B19
Lynher Reef, *Australia* 92 C3
Lynn, *U.S.A.* 111 D14
Lynn Lake, *Canada* 105 B8
Lynnwood, *U.S.A.* 116 C4
Lynton, *U.K.* 13 F4
Lyntupy, *Belarus* 9 J22
Lynx L., *Canada* 105 A7
Lyon, *France* 21 C8
Lyonnais, *France* 21 C8
Lyons = Lyon, *France* 21 C8
Lyons, *Ga., U.S.A.* 109 J4
Lyons, *Kans., U.S.A.* 112 F5
Lyons, *N.Y., U.S.A.* 110 C8
Lyons →, *Australia* 93 E2
Lyons Falls, *U.S.A.* 111 C9
Lyozna, *Belarus* 46 E6
Lys = Leie →, *Belgium* 17 C3
Lysá nad Labem, *Czech Rep.* 26 A7
Lysekil, *Sweden* 11 F5
Lyskovo, *Russia* 48 B7
Lystrup, *Denmark* 11 H4
Lysvik, *Sweden* 10 D7
Lysychansk, *Ukraine* 47 H10
Lytham St. Anne's, *U.K.* 12 D4
Lyttelton, *N.Z.* 91 K4
Lytton, *Canada* 104 C4
Lyuban, *Russia* 46 C6
Lyubertsy, *Russia* 46 E9
Lyubim, *Russia* 46 C11
Lyubimets, *Bulgaria* 41 E10
Lyuboml, *Ukraine* 47 G3
Lyubotyn, *Ukraine* 47 H8
Lyubytino, *Russia* 46 C7
Lyudinovo, *Russia* 46 F8

M

M.R. Gomez, Presa, *Mexico* 119 B5
Ma →, *Vietnam* 58 H5
Ma'adaba, *Jordan* 75 E4
Maamba, *Zambia* 88 B4
Ma'ān, *Jordan* 75 E4
Ma'ān □, *Jordan* 75 F5
Maanselkä, *Finland* 8 C23
Ma'anshan, *China* 59 B12
Maarianhamina, *Finland* 9 F18
Ma'arrat an Nu'mān, *Syria* 70 C3
Maas →, *Neths.* 17 C4
Maaseik, *Belgium* 17 C5
Maasin, *Phil.* 63 B6
Maastricht, *Neths.* 17 D5
Maave, *Mozam.* 89 C5
Mababe Depression, *Botswana* 88 B3
Mabalane, *Mozam.* 89 C5
Mabel L., *Canada* 104 C5
Mabenge, *Dem. Rep. of the Congo* 86 B1
Maberly, *Canada* 111 B8
Mabian, *China* 58 C4
Mabil, *Ethiopia* 81 E4
Mablethorpe, *U.K.* 12 D8
Mably, *France* 19 F11
Maboma, *Dem. Rep. of the Congo* 86 B2
Mabonto, *S. Leone* 82 D2
Mabrouk, *Mali* 83 B4
Mac Bac, *Vietnam* 65 H6
Macachín, *Argentina* 126 D3
Macaé, *Brazil* 127 A7
Macael, *Spain* 33 H2
McAlester, *U.S.A.* 113 H7
McAllen, *U.S.A.* 113 M5
MacAlpine L., *Canada* 100 B9
Macamic, *Canada* 102 C4
Macao = Macau, *Asia* 59 F9
Macão, *Portugal* 35 F3
Macapá, *Brazil* 125 C8
McArthur →, *Australia* 94 B2
McArthur, Port, *Australia* 94 B2
Macau, *Brazil* 125 E11
Macau, *Asia* 59 F9
McBride, *Canada* 104 C4
McCall, *U.S.A.* 114 D5
McCamey, *U.S.A.* 113 K3
McCammon, *U.S.A.* 114 E7
McCauley I., *Canada* 104 C2
McCleary, *U.S.A.* 116 C3
Macclenny, *U.S.A.* 109 K4
Macclesfield, *U.K.* 12 D5
M'Clintock Chan., *Canada* 100 A9
McClintock Ra., *Australia* 92 C4
McCloud, *U.S.A.* 114 F2
McCluer I., *Australia* 92 B5
McClure, *U.S.A.* 110 F7
McClure, L., *U.S.A.* 116 H6
M'Clure Str., *Canada* 4 B2
McClusky, *U.S.A.* 112 B4
McComb, *U.S.A.* 113 K9
McConaughy, L., *U.S.A.* 112 E4
McCook, *U.S.A.* 112 E4
McCreary, *Canada* 105 C9
McCullough Mt., *U.S.A.* 117 K11
McCusker →, *Canada* 105 B7
McDame, *Canada* 104 B3
McDermitt, *U.S.A.* 114 F5
McDonald, *U.S.A.* 110 F4
Macdonald, L., *Australia* 92 D4
McDonald Is., *Ind. Oc.* 3 G13
MacDonnell Ranges, *Australia* 92 D5
MacDowell L., *Canada* 102 B1
Macduff, *U.K.* 14 D6
Maceda, *Spain* 34 C3
Macedonia, *U.S.A.* 110 E3
Macedonia ■, *Europe* 40 E5
Maceió, *Brazil* 125 E11
Maceira, *Portugal* 34 F2
Macenta, *Guinea* 82 D3
Macerata, *Italy* 29 E10
McFarland, *U.S.A.* 117 K7
McFarlane →, *Canada* 105 B7
Macfarlane, L., *Australia* 95 E2
McGehee, *U.S.A.* 113 J9
McGill, *U.S.A.* 114 G6
Macgillycuddy's Reeks, *Ireland* 15 E2
McGraw, *U.S.A.* 111 D8
McGregor, *U.S.A.* 112 D9
McGregor Ra., *Australia* 95 D3
Mach, *Pakistan* 66 E5
Māch Kowr, *Iran* 71 E9
Machado = Jiparaná →, *Brazil* 124 E6
Machagai, *Argentina* 126 B3
Machakos, *Kenya* 86 C4
Machala, *Ecuador* 124 D3
Machanga, *Mozam.* 89 C6
Machattie, L., *Australia* 94 C2
Machault, *France* 19 C11
Machava, *Mozam.* 89 D5
Machece, *Mozam.* 87 F4
Machecoul, *France* 18 F5
Macheke, *Zimbabwe* 89 B5
Macheng, *China* 59 B10
Machero, *Spain* 35 F6
Machhu →, *India* 68 H4
Machias, *Maine, U.S.A.* 109 C12
Machias, *N.Y., U.S.A.* 110 D6
Machichi →, *Canada* 105 B10
Machico, *Madeira* 37 D3
Machilipatnam, *India* 67 L12
Machiques, *Venezuela* 124 A4
Machupicchu, *Peru* 124 F4
Machynlleth, *U.K.* 13 E4
Macia, *Mozam.* 89 D5
Maciejowice, *Poland* 45 G8
McIlwraith Ra., *Australia* 94 A3
Măcin, *Romania* 43 E13
Macina, *Mali* 82 C4
McInnes L., *Canada* 105 C10
McIntosh, *U.S.A.* 112 C4
McIntosh L., *Canada* 105 B8
Macintosh Ra., *Australia* 93 E4
Macintyre →, *Australia* 95 D5
Macizo Galaico, *Spain* 34 C3
Mackay, *Australia* 94 C4
Mackay, *U.S.A.* 114 E7
MacKay →, *Canada* 104 B6
Mackay, L., *Australia* 92 D4
McKay Ra., *Australia* 92 D3
McKeesport, *U.S.A.* 110 F5
McKellar, *Canada* 110 A5
McKenna, *U.S.A.* 116 D4
Mackenzie, *Canada* 104 B4
McKenzie, *U.S.A.* 109 G1
Mackenzie →, *Australia* 94 C4
Mackenzie →, *Canada* 100 B6
McKenzie →, *U.S.A.* 114 D2
Mackenzie Bay, *Canada* 4 B1
Mackenzie City = Linden, *Guyana* 124 B7
Mackenzie Mts., *Canada* 100 B6
Mackinaw City, *U.S.A.* 108 C3
McKinlay, *Australia* 94 C3
McKinlay →, *Australia* 94 C3
McKinley, Mt., *U.S.A.* 100 B4
McKinley Sea, *Arctic* 4 A7
McKinney, *U.S.A.* 113 J6
Mackinnon Road, *Kenya* 86 C4
McKittrick, *U.S.A.* 117 K7
Macklin, *Canada* 105 C7
Macksville, *Australia* 95 E5
McLaughlin, *U.S.A.* 112 C4
Maclean, *Australia* 95 D5
McLean, *U.S.A.* 113 H4
McLeansboro, *U.S.A.* 112 F10
Maclear, *S. Africa* 89 E4
Macleay →, *Australia* 95 E5
McLennan, *Canada* 104 B5
McLeod →, *Canada* 104 C5
MacLeod, B., *Canada* 105 A7
McLeod, L., *Australia* 93 D1
MacLeod Lake, *Canada* 104 C4
McLoughlin, Mt., *U.S.A.* 114 E2
McMechen, *U.S.A.* 110 G4
McMinnville, *Oreg., U.S.A.* 114 D2
McMinnville, *Tenn., U.S.A.* 109 H3
McMurdo Sd., *Antarctica* 5 D11
McMurray = Fort McMurray, *Canada* 104 B6
McMurray, *U.S.A.* 116 B4
Macodoene, *Mozam.* 89 C6
Macomb, *U.S.A.* 112 E9
Macomer, *Italy* 30 B1
Mâcon, *France* 19 F11
Macon, *Ga., U.S.A.* 109 J4
Macon, *Miss., U.S.A.* 109 J1
Macon, *Mo., U.S.A.* 112 F8
Macossa, *Mozam.* 87 F3
Macoun L., *Canada* 105 B8
Macovane, *Mozam.* 89 C6
McPherson, *U.S.A.* 112 F6
McPherson Pk., *U.S.A.* 117 L7
McPherson Ra., *Australia* 95 D5
Macquarie →, *Australia* 95 E4
Macquarie Harbour, *Australia* 94 G4
Macquarie Is., *Pac. Oc.* 96 N7
MacRobertson Land, *Antarctica* 5 D6
Macroom, *Ireland* 15 E3
MacTier, *Canada* 110 A5
Macubela, *Mozam.* 87 F4
Macugnaga, *Italy* 28 C4
Macuiza, *Mozam.* 87 F3
Macusani, *Peru* 124 F4
Macuse, *Mozam.* 87 F4
Macuspana, *Mexico* 119 D6
Macusse, *Angola* 88 B3
Mada →, *Nigeria* 83 D6
Madadeni, *S. Africa* 89 D5
Madagali, *Nigeria* 83 C7
Madagascar ■, *Africa* 89 C8
Madā'in Sālih, *Si. Arabia* 70 E3
Madama, *Niger* 79 D8
Madame I., *Canada* 103 C7
Madan, *Bulgaria* 41 E8
Madaoua, *Niger* 83 C6
Madara, *Nigeria* 83 C7
Madaripur, *Bangla.* 67 H17
Madauk, *Burma* 67 L20
Madawaska, *Canada* 110 A7
Madawaska →, *Canada* 102 C4
Madaya, *Burma* 67 H20
Madbar, *Sudan* 81 F3
Maddalena, *Italy* 30 A2
Maddaloni, *Italy* 31 A7
Madeira, *Atl. Oc.* 37 D3
Madeira →, *Brazil* 122 D5
Madeleine, Îs. de la, *Canada* 103 C7
Maden, *Turkey* 73 C8
Madera, *Mexico* 118 B3
Madera, *Calif., U.S.A.* 116 J6
Madera, *Pa., U.S.A.* 110 F6
Madha, *India* 66 L9
Madhavpur, *India* 68 J3
Madhepura, *India* 69 F12
Madhubani, *India* 69 F12
Madhupur, *India* 69 G12
Madhya Pradesh □, *India* 68 J8
Madian, *China* 59 A11
Madidi →, *Bolivia* 124 F5
Madikeri, *India* 66 N9
Madill, *U.S.A.* 113 H6
Madimba, *Dem. Rep. of the Congo* 84 E3
Ma'din, *Syria* 70 C3
Madina, *Mali* 82 C3
Madinani, *Ivory C.* 82 D3
Madingou, *Congo* 84 E2
Madirovalo, *Madag.* 89 B8
Madison, *Calif., U.S.A.* 116 G5
Madison, *Fla., U.S.A.* 109 K4
Madison, *Ind., U.S.A.* 108 F3
Madison, *Nebr., U.S.A.* 112 E6
Madison, *Ohio, U.S.A.* 110 E3
Madison, *S. Dak., U.S.A.* 112 D6
Madison, *Wis., U.S.A.* 112 D10
Madison →, *U.S.A.* 114 D8
Madison Heights, *U.S.A.* 108 G6
Madisonville, *Ky., U.S.A.* 108 G2
Madisonville, *Tex., U.S.A.* 113 K7
Madista, *Botswana* 88 C4
Madiun, *Indonesia* 63 G14
Madoc, *Canada* 110 B7
Madol, *Sudan* 81 F2
Madon →, *France* 19 D13
Madona, *Latvia* 9 H22
Madonie, *Italy* 30 E6
Madonna di Campíglio, *Italy* 28 B7
Madra Dağı, *Turkey* 39 B9
Madrakah, Ra's al, *Oman* 74 D6
Madras = Chennai, *India* 66 N12
Madras = Tamil Nadu □, *India* 66 P10
Madras, *U.S.A.* 114 D3
Madre, L., *Mexico* 119 C5
Madre, Laguna, *U.S.A.* 113 M6
Madre, Sierra, *Phil.* 61 C5
Madre de Dios →, *Bolivia* 122 E4
Madre de Dios, I., *Chile* 122 J3
Madre del Sur, Sierra, *Mexico* 119 D5
Madre Occidental, Sierra, *Mexico* 118 B3
Madre Oriental, Sierra, *Mexico* 118 C5
Madri, *India* 68 G5
Madrid, *Spain* 34 E7
Madrid, *U.S.A.* 111 B9
Madrid □, *Spain* 34 E7
Madridejos, *Spain* 35 F7
Madrigal de las Altas Torres, *Spain* 34 D6
Madrona, Sierra, *Spain* 35 G6
Madroñera, *Spain* 35 F5
Madu, *Sudan* 81 E2
Madura, *Australia* 93 F4
Madura, *Indonesia* 63 G15
Madura, Selat, *Indonesia* 63 G15
Madurai, *India* 66 Q11
Madurantakam, *India* 66 N11
Madzhalis, *Russia* 49 J8
Mae Chan, *Thailand* 64 B2
Mae Hong Son, *Thailand* 64 C2
Mae Khlong →, *Thailand* 64 F3
Mae Phrik, *Thailand* 64 D2
Mae Ramat, *Thailand* 64 D2
Mae Rim, *Thailand* 64 C2
Mae Sot, *Thailand* 64 D2
Mae Suai, *Thailand* 58 H2
Mae Tha, *Thailand* 64 C2
Maebashi, *Japan* 55 F9
Maella, *Spain* 32 D5
Maesteg, *U.K.* 13 F4
Maestra, Sierra, *Cuba* 120 B4
Maevatanana, *Madag.* 89 B8
Mafeking = Mafikeng, *S. Africa* 88 D4
Mafeking, *Canada* 105 C8
Maféré, *Ivory C.* 82 D4
Mafeteng, *Lesotho* 88 D4
Maffra, *Australia* 95 F4

Mafia I., *Tanzania* 86 D4
Mafikeng, *S. Africa* 88 D4
Mafra, *Brazil* 127 B6
Mafra, *Portugal* 35 G1
Mafungabusi Plateau,
Zimbabwe 87 F2
Magadan, *Russia* 51 D16
Magadi, *Kenya* 86 C4
Magadi, L., *Kenya* 86 C4
Magaliesburg, *S. Africa* 89 D4
Magallanes, Estrecho de,
Chile 122 J3
Magaluf, *Spain* 33 F7
Magangué, *Colombia* 124 B4
Magaria, *Niger* 83 C6
Magburaka, *S. Leone* 82 D2
Magdalen Is. = Madeleine,
Îs. de la, *Canada* 103 C7
Magdalena, *Argentina* 126 D4
Magdalena, *Bolivia* 124 F6
Magdalena, *Mexico* 118 A2
Magdalena, *U.S.A.* 115 J10
Magdalena →, *Colombia* 122 B3
Magdalena →, *Mexico* 118 A2
Magdalena, B., *Mexico* 118 C2
Magdalena, Llano de la,
Mexico 118 C2
Magdeburg, *Germany* 24 C7
Magdelaine Cays, *Australia* 94 B5
Magdub, *Sudan* 81 E2
Magee, *U.S.A.* 113 K10
Magelang, *Indonesia* 63 G14
Magellan's Str. =
Magallanes, Estrecho de,
Chile 122 J3
Magenta, *Italy* 28 C5
Magenta, L., *Australia* 93 F2
Magerøya, *Norway* 8 A21
Maggia →, *Switz.* 25 J4
Maggiorasca, Mte., *Italy* 28 D6
Maggiore, Lago, *Italy* 28 C5
Maghâgha, *Egypt* 80 B3
Maghama, *Mauritania* 82 B2
Magherafelt, *U.K.* 15 B5
Maghreb, *N. Afr.* 78 B5
Magione, *Italy* 29 E9
Magistralnyy, *Russia* 51 D11
Maglaj, *Bos.-H.* 42 F3
Magliano in Toscana, *Italy* 29 F8
Máglie, *Italy* 31 B11
Magnac-Laval, *France* 20 B5
Magnetic Pole (North) =
North Magnetic Pole,
Canada 4 B2
Magnetic Pole (South) =
South Magnetic Pole,
Antarctica 5 C9
Magnisía □, *Greece* 38 B5
Magnitogorsk, *Russia* 50 D6
Magnolia, *Ark., U.S.A.* 113 J8
Magnolia, *Miss., U.S.A.* 113 K9
Magny-en-Vexin, *France* 19 C8
Magog, *Canada* 103 C5
Magoro, *Uganda* 86 B3
Magosa = Famagusta,
Cyprus 36 D12
Magouládhes, *Greece* 36 A3
Magoye, *Zambia* 87 F2
Magozal, *Mexico* 119 C5
Magpie, L., *Canada* 103 B7
Magrath, *Canada* 104 D6
Magre →, *Spain* 33 F4
Magrur, *Sudan* 81 E3
Magrur, Wadi →, *Sudan* 81 D2
Magta Lahjar, *Mauritania* 82 B2
Maguan, *China* 58 F5
Maguarinho, C., *Brazil* 125 D9
Magude, *Mozam.* 89 D5
Mağusa = Famagusta,
Cyprus 36 D12
Maguse L., *Canada* 105 A9
Maguse Pt., *Canada* 105 A10
Magvana, *India* 68 H3
Magwe, *Burma* 67 J19
Magwe, *Sudan* 81 G3
Maha Sarakham, *Thailand* 64 D4
Mahābād, *Iran* 70 B5
Mahabharat Lekh, *Nepal* 69 E10
Mahabo, *Madag.* 89 C7
Mahadeo Hills, *India* 69 H8
Mahaffey, *U.S.A.* 110 F6
Mahagi,
Dem. Rep. of the Congo 86 B3
Mahajamba →, *Madag.* 89 B8
Mahajamba, Helodranon' i,
Madag. 89 B8
Mahajan, *India* 68 E5
Mahajanga, *Madag.* 89 B8
Mahajanga □, *Madag.* 89 B8
Mahajilo →, *Madag.* 89 B8
Mahakam →, *Indonesia* 62 E5
Mahalapye, *Botswana* 88 C4
Maḩallāt, *Iran* 71 C6
Māhān, *Iran* 71 D8
Mahan →, *India* 69 H10
Mahanadi →, *India* 67 J15
Mahananda →, *India* 69 G12
Mahanoro, *Madag.* 89 B8
Mahanoy City, *U.S.A.* 111 F8
Maharashtra □, *India* 66 J9
Mahari Mts., *Tanzania* 86 D3
Mahasham, W. →, *Egypt* 75 E3
Mahasoa, *Madag.* 89 C8
Mahasolo, *Madag.* 89 B8
Mahattat ash Shīdīyah,
Jordan 75 F4
Mahattat 'Unayzah, *Jordan* 75 E4
Mahavavy →, *Madag.* 89 B8
Mahaxay, *Laos* 64 D5
Mahbubnagar, *India* 66 L10
Maḩḑah, *Oman* 71 E7
Mahdia, *Tunisia* 79 A8
Mahe, *India* 69 C8
Mahendragarh, *India* 68 E7
Mahenge, *Tanzania* 87 D4
Maheno, *N.Z.* 91 L3
Mahesana, *India* 68 H5
Maheshwar, *India* 68 H6
Mahgawan, *India* 69 F8
Mahi →, *India* 68 H5
Mahia Pen., *N.Z.* 91 H6
Mahilyow, *Belarus* 46 F6
Mahmiya, *Sudan* 81 D3
Mahmud Kot, *Pakistan* 68 D4
Mahmudia, *Romania* 43 E14
Mahmudiye, *Turkey* 39 B12
Mahmutbey, *Turkey* 41 E12
Mahnomen, *U.S.A.* 112 B7
Mahoba, *India* 69 G8
Mahón = Maó, *Spain* 37 B11
Mahone Bay, *Canada* 103 D7
Mahopac, *U.S.A.* 111 E11
Mahuta, *Nigeria* 83 C5
Mahuva, *India* 68 J4
Mahya Daği, *Turkey* 41 E11
Mai-Ndombe, L.,
Dem. Rep. of the Congo 84 E3
Mai-Sai, *Thailand* 58 G2
Maia, *Portugal* 34 D2
Maia, *Spain* 32 B3
Maials, *Spain* 32 D5
Maîche, *France* 19 E13
Maicurú →, *Brazil* 125 D8
Máida, *Italy* 31 D9
Maidan Khula, *Afghan.* 68 C3
Maidenhead, *U.K.* 13 F7
Maidstone, *Canada* 105 C7
Maidstone, *U.K.* 13 F8
Maiduguri, *Nigeria* 83 C7
Măieruş, *Romania* 43 E10
Maigatari, *Nigeria* 83 C6
Maignelay Montigny, *France* 19 C9
Maigo, *Phil.* 61 G5
Maigudo, *Ethiopia* 81 F4
Maihar, *India* 69 G9
Maijdi, *Bangla.* 67 H17
Maikala Ra., *India* 67 J12
Mailani, *India* 69 E9
Maillezais, *France* 20 B3
Mailsi, *Pakistan* 68 E5
Main →, *Germany* 25 F4
Main →, *U.K.* 15 B5
Mainburg, *Germany* 25 G7
Maine, *France* 18 D6
Maine □, *U.S.A.* 109 C11
Maine →, *Ireland* 15 D2
Maine-et-Loire □, *France* 18 E6
Maïne-Soroa, *Niger* 83 C7
Maingkwan, *Burma* 67 F20
Mainit, L., *Phil.* 61 G6
Mainland, *Orkney, U.K.* 14 C5
Mainland, *Shet., U.K.* 14 A7
Mainoru, *Australia* 94 A1
Mainpuri, *India* 69 F8
Maintal, *Germany* 25 E4
Maintenon, *France* 19 D8
Maintirano, *Madag.* 89 B7
Mainz, *Germany* 25 E4
Maipú, *Argentina* 126 D4
Maiquetía, *Venezuela* 124 A5
Máira →, *Italy* 28 D4
Mairabari, *India* 67 F18
Maisí, *Cuba* 121 B5
Maisí, Pta. de, *Cuba* 121 B5
Maitland, *N.S.W., Australia* 95 E5
Maitland, *S. Austral.,*
Australia 95 E2
Maitland →, *Canada* 110 C3
Maiyema, *Nigeria* 83 C5
Maiyuan, *China* 59 E11
Maiz, Is. del, *Nic.* 120 D3
Maizuru, *Japan* 55 G7
Majalengka, *Indonesia* 63 G13
Majene, *Indonesia* 63 E5
Majevica, *Bos.-H.* 42 F3
Maji, *Ethiopia* 81 F4
Majiang, *China* 58 D6
Majorca = Mallorca, *Spain* 37 B10
Maka, *Senegal* 82 C2
Makaha, *Zimbabwe* 89 B5
Makak, *Cameroon* 83 E7
Makalamabedi, *Botswana* 88 C3
Makale, *Indonesia* 63 E5
Makamba, *Burundi* 86 C2
Makari, *Cameroon* 83 C7
Makarikari = Makgadikgadi
Salt Pans, *Botswana* 88 C4
Makarovo, *Russia* 51 D11
Makarska, *Croatia* 29 E14
Makaryev, *Russia* 48 B6
Makasar = Ujung Pandang,
Indonesia 63 F5
Makasar, Selat, *Indonesia* 63 E5
Makasar, Str. of = Makasar,
Selat, *Indonesia* 63 E5
Makat, *Kazakstan* 50 E6
Makedonija = Macedonia ■,
Europe 40 E5
Makena, *U.S.A.* 106 H16
Makeni, *S. Leone* 82 D2
Makeyevka = Makiyivka,
Ukraine 47 H9
Makgadikgadi Salt Pans,
Botswana 88 C4
Makhachkala, *Russia* 49 J8
Makharadze = Ozurgeti,
Georgia 49 K5
Makhmūr, *Iraq* 70 C4
Makian, *Indonesia* 63 D7
Makindu, *Kenya* 86 C4
Makinsk, *Kazakstan* 50 D8
Makiyivka, *Ukraine* 47 H9
Makkah, *Si. Arabia* 74 C2
Makkovik, *Canada* 103 A8
Makó, *Hungary* 42 D5
Mako, *Senegal* 82 C2
Makokou, *Gabon* 84 D2
Makongo,
Dem. Rep. of the Congo 86 B2
Makoro,
Dem. Rep. of the Congo 86 B2
Maków Mazowiecki, *Poland* 45 F8
Maków Podhalański, *Poland* 45 J6
Makrá, *Greece* 39 E7
Makrai, *India* 66 H10
Makran Coast Range,
Pakistan 66 G4
Makrana, *India* 68 F6
Mákri, *Greece* 41 F9
Makriyialos, *Greece* 36 D7
Mākū, *Iran* 70 B5
Makunda, *Botswana* 88 C3
Makung, *Taiwan* 59 F12
Makurazaki, *Japan* 55 J5
Makurdi, *Nigeria* 83 D6
Makūyeh, *Iran* 71 D7
Makwassie, *S. Africa* 88 D4
Makwiro, *Zimbabwe* 89 B5
Mâl, *Mauritania* 82 B2
Mal B., *Ireland* 15 D2
Mala, Pta., *Panama* 120 E3
Mala Belozërka, *Ukraine* 47 J8
Mala Kapela, *Croatia* 29 D12
Mała Panew →, *Poland* 45 H4
Mala Vyska, *Ukraine* 47 H6
Malabang, *Phil.* 61 H6
Malabar Coast, *India* 66 P9
Malabo = Rey Malabo,
Eq. Guin. 83 E6
Malabon, *Phil.* 61 D4
Malabu, *Nigeria* 83 D7
Malacca, Str. of, *Indonesia* 65 L3
Malacky, *Slovak Rep.* 27 C10
Malad City, *U.S.A.* 114 E7
Maladeta, *Spain* 32 C5
Maladzyechna, *Belarus* 46 E4
Málaga, *Spain* 35 J6
Málaga □, *Spain* 35 J6
Malagarasi, *Tanzania* 86 D3
Malagarasi →, *Tanzania* 86 D2
Malagasy Rep. =
Madagascar ■, *Africa* 89 C8
Malagón, *Spain* 35 F7
Malagón →, *Spain* 35 H3
Malahide, *Ireland* 15 C5
Malaimbandy, *Madag.* 89 C8
Malakâl, *Sudan* 81 F3
Malakand, *Pakistan* 68 B4
Malakwal, *Pakistan* 68 C5
Malamala, *Indonesia* 63 E6
Malanda, *Australia* 94 B4
Malang, *Indonesia* 63 G15
Malangen, *Norway* 8 B18
Malanje, *Angola* 84 F3
Mälaren, *Sweden* 10 E11
Malargüe, *Argentina* 126 D2
Malartic, *Canada* 102 C4
Malaryta, *Belarus* 47 G3
Malatya, *Turkey* 70 B3
Malawi ■, *Africa* 87 E3
Malawi, L. = Nyasa, L.,
Africa 87 E3
Malay Pen., *Asia* 65 J3
Malaya Belozërka = Mala
Belozërka, *Ukraine* 47 J8
Malaya Vishera, *Russia* 46 C7
Malaya Viska = Mala Vyska,
Ukraine 47 H6
Malaybalay, *Phil.* 61 G6
Malāyer, *Iran* 71 C6
Malaysia ■, *Asia* 65 K4
Malazgirt, *Turkey* 70 B4
Malbaza, *Niger* 83 C6
Malbon, *Australia* 94 C3
Malbooma, *Australia* 95 E1
Malbork, *Poland* 44 D6
Malcésine, *Italy* 28 C7
Malchin, *Germany* 24 B8
Malchow, *Germany* 24 B8
Malcolm, *Australia* 93 E3
Malcolm, Pt., *Australia* 93 F3
Malczyce, *Poland* 45 G3
Maldah, *India* 69 G13
Maldegem, *Belgium* 17 C3
Malden, *Mass., U.S.A.* 111 D13
Malden, *Mo., U.S.A.* 113 G10
Malden I., *Kiribati* 97 H12
Maldives ■, *Ind. Oc.* 52 J11
Maldonado, *Uruguay* 127 C5
Maldonado, Punta, *Mexico* 119 D5
Malè, *Italy* 28 B7
Malé, *Maldives* 53 J11
Malé Karpaty, *Slovak Rep.* 27 C10
Maléa, Ákra, *Greece* 38 E5
Malegaon, *India* 66 J9
Malei, *Mozam.* 87 F4
Malek, *Sudan* 81 F3
Malek Kandī, *Iran* 70 B5
Malela,
Dem. Rep. of the Congo 86 C2
Malema, *Mozam.* 87 E4
Máleme, *Greece* 36 D5
Maleny, *Australia* 95 D5
Målerås, *Sweden* 11 H9
Malerkotla, *India* 68 D6
Máles, *Greece* 36 D7
Malesherbes, *France* 19 D9
Maleshevska Planina, *Europe* 40 E7
Malesína, *Greece* 38 C5
Malestroit, *France* 18 E4
Malfa, *Italy* 31 D7
Malgobek, *Russia* 49 J7
Malgomaj, *Sweden* 8 D17
Malgrat = Malgrat de Mar,
Spain 32 D7
Malgrat de Mar, *Spain* 32 D7
Malha, *Sudan* 81 D2
Malhargarh, *India* 68 G6
Malheur →, *U.S.A.* 114 D5
Malheur L., *U.S.A.* 114 E4
Mali, *Guinea* 82 C2
Mali ■, *Africa* 82 B4
Mali →, *Burma* 67 G20
Mali Kanal, *Serbia, Yug.* 42 E4
Mali Kyun, *Burma* 64 F2
Malibu, *U.S.A.* 117 L8
Maliku, *Indonesia* 63 E6
Malili, *Indonesia* 63 E6
Målilla, *Sweden* 11 G9
Malimba, Mts.,
Dem. Rep. of the Congo 86 D2
Malin Hd., *Ireland* 15 A4
Malin Pen., *Ireland* 15 A4
Malindi, *Kenya* 86 C5
Malines = Mechelen,
Belgium 17 C4
Malino, *Indonesia* 63 D6
Malinyi, *Tanzania* 87 D4
Malipo, *China* 58 F5
Maliqi, *Albania* 40 F4
Malita, *Phil.* 63 C7
Maliwun, *Burma* 62 B1
Maliya, *India* 68 H4
Maljenik, *Serbia, Yug.* 40 C5
Malkara, *Turkey* 41 F10
Małkinia Górna, *Poland* 45 F9
Malko Tŭrnovo, *Bulgaria* 41 E11
Mallacoota Inlet, *Australia* 95 F4
Mallaig, *U.K.* 14 D3
Mallaoua, *Niger* 83 C6
Mallawan, *India* 69 F9
Mallawi, *Egypt* 80 B3
Mallemort, *France* 21 E9
Málles Venosta, *Italy* 28 B7
Mállia, *Greece* 36 D7
Mallión, Kólpos, *Greece* 36 D7
Mallorca, *Spain* 37 B10
Mallorytown, *Canada* 111 B9
Mallow, *Ireland* 15 D3
Malmbäck, *Sweden* 11 G8
Malmberget, *Sweden* 8 C19
Malmédy, *Belgium* 17 D6
Malmesbury, *S. Africa* 88 E2
Malmköping, *Sweden* 10 E10
Malmö, *Sweden* 11 J6
Malmslätt, *Sweden* 11 F9
Malmyzh, *Russia* 48 B10
Malnaş, *Romania* 43 D10
Malo Konare, *Bulgaria* 41 D8
Maloarkhangelsk, *Russia* 47 F9
Malolos, *Phil.* 63 B6
Malombe L., *Malawi* 87 E4
Małomice, *Poland* 45 G2
Malomir, *Bulgaria* 41 D10
Malone, *U.S.A.* 111 B10
Malong, *China* 58 E4
Małopolskie □, *Poland* 45 J7
Malorad, *Bulgaria* 40 C7
Måløy, *Norway* 9 F11
Maloyaroslovets, *Russia* 46 E9
Malpartida, *Spain* 35 F4
Malpaso, *Canary Is.* 37 G1
Malpelo, I. de, *Colombia* 124 C2
Malpica de Bergantiños,
Spain 34 B2
Malpur, *India* 68 H5
Malpura, *India* 68 F6
Mals = Málles Venosta, *Italy* 28 B7
Malta, *Idaho, U.S.A.* 114 E7
Malta, *Mont., U.S.A.* 114 B10
Malta ■, *Europe* 36 D2
Maltahöhe, *Namibia* 88 C2
Maltepe, *Turkey* 41 F13
Malton, *Canada* 110 C5
Malton, *U.K.* 12 C7
Maluku, *Indonesia* 63 E7
Maluku □, *Indonesia* 63 E7
Maluku Sea = Molucca Sea,
Indonesia 63 E6
Malumfashi, *Nigeria* 83 C6
Malung, *Sweden* 10 D7
Malungsfors, *Sweden* 10 D7
Maluwe, *Ghana* 82 D4
Malvan, *India* 66 L8
Malvern, *U.S.A.* 113 H8
Malvern Hills, *U.K.* 13 E5
Malvinas, Is. = Falkland
Is. □, *Atl. Oc.* 128 G5
Malý Dunaj →, *Slovak Rep.* 27 D11
Malya, *Tanzania* 86 C3
Malyn, *Ukraine* 47 G5
Malyy Lyakhovskiy, Ostrov,
Russia 51 B15
Mama, *Russia* 51 D12
Mamadysh, *Russia* 48 C10
Mamanguape, *Brazil* 125 E11
Mamarr Mitlā, *Egypt* 75 E1
Mamasa, *Indonesia* 63 E5
Mambasa,
Dem. Rep. of the Congo 86 B2
Mamberamo →, *Indonesia* 63 E9
Mambilima Falls, *Zambia* 87 E2
Mambirima,
Dem. Rep. of the Congo 87 E2
Mambo, *Tanzania* 86 C4
Mambrui, *Kenya* 86 C5
Mamburao, *Phil.* 61 E4
Mameigwess L., *Canada* 102 B2
Mamers, *France* 18 D7
Mamfé, *Cameroon* 83 D6
Mammoth, *U.S.A.* 115 K8
Mammoth Cave National
Park, *U.S.A.* 108 G3
Mamoré →, *Bolivia* 122 E4
Mamou, *Guinea* 82 C2
Mampatá, *Guinea-Biss.* 82 C2
Mampikony, *Madag.* 89 B8
Mampong, *Ghana* 83 D4
Mamry, Jezioro, *Poland* 44 D8
Mamuju, *Indonesia* 63 E5
Mamuno, *Botswana* 88 C3
Mamuras, *Albania* 40 E3
Man, *Ivory C.* 82 D3
Man, I. of, *U.K.* 12 C3
Man-Bazar, *India* 69 H12
Man Na, *Burma* 67 H20
Mana →, *Fr. Guiana* 125 B8
Manaar, G. of = Mannar,
G. of, *Asia* 66 Q11
Manacapuru, *Brazil* 124 D6
Manacor, *Spain* 37 B10
Manado, *Indonesia* 63 D6
Managua, *Nic.* 120 D2
Managua, L. de, *Nic.* 120 D2
Manakara, *Madag.* 89 C8
Manali, *India* 68 C7
Manama = Al Manāmah,
Bahrain 71 E6
Manambao →, *Madag.* 89 B7
Manambato, *Madag.* 89 A8
Manambolo →, *Madag.* 89 B7
Manambolosy, *Madag.* 89 B8
Mananara, *Madag.* 89 B8
Mananara →, *Madag.* 89 C8
Mananjary, *Madag.* 89 C8
Manankoro, *Mali* 82 C3
Manantenina, *Madag.* 89 C8
Manaos = Manaus, *Brazil* 124 D7
Manapire →, *Venezuela* 124 B5
Manapouri, *N.Z.* 91 L1
Manapouri, L., *N.Z.* 91 L1
Manaqil, *Sudan* 81 E3
Manār, Jabal, *Yemen* 74 E3
Manaravolo, *Madag.* 89 C8
Manas, *China* 60 B3
Manas →, *India* 67 F17
Manaslu, *Nepal* 69 E11
Manasquan, *U.S.A.* 111 F10
Manassa, *U.S.A.* 115 H11
Manaung, *Burma* 67 K18
Manaus, *Brazil* 124 D7
Manavgat, *Turkey* 72 D4
Manawan L., *Canada* 105 B8
Manay, *Phil.* 61 H7
Manbij, *Syria* 70 B3
Mancha Real, *Spain* 35 H7
Manche □, *France* 18 C5
Manchegorsk, *Russia* 50 C4
Manchester, *U.K.* 12 D5
Manchester, *Calif., U.S.A.* 116 G3
Manchester, *Conn., U.S.A.* 111 E12
Manchester, *Ga., U.S.A.* 109 J3
Manchester, *Iowa, U.S.A.* 112 D9
Manchester, *Ky., U.S.A.* 108 G4
Manchester, *N.H., U.S.A.* 111 D13
Manchester, *N.Y., U.S.A.* 110 D7
Manchester, *Pa., U.S.A.* 111 F8
Manchester, *Tenn., U.S.A.* 109 H2
Manchester, *Vt., U.S.A.* 111 C11
Manchester L., *Canada* 105 A7
Manchhar L., *Pakistan* 68 F2
Manchuria = Dongbei,
China 57 D13
Manchurian Plain, *China* 52 E16
Manciano, *Italy* 29 F8
Mancifa, *Ethiopia* 81 F5
Mand →, *India* 69 J10
Mand →, *Iran* 71 D7
Manda, *Chunya, Tanzania* 86 D3
Manda, *Ludewe, Tanzania* 87 E3
Mandabé, *Madag.* 89 C7
Mandaguari, *Brazil* 127 A5
Mandah = Töhöm, *Mongolia* 56 B5
Mandal, *Norway* 9 G12
Mandala, Puncak, *Indonesia* 63 E10
Mandalay, *Burma* 67 J20
Mandale = Mandalay,
Burma 67 J20
Mandalgarh, *India* 68 G6
Mandalgovi, *Mongolia* 56 B4
Mandalī, *Iraq* 70 C5
Mandan, *U.S.A.* 112 B4
Mandaon, *Phil.* 61 E5
Mandar, Teluk, *Indonesia* 63 E5
Mándas, *Italy* 30 C2
Mandaue, *Phil.* 61 F5
Mandelieu-la-Napoule,
France 21 E10
Mandera, *Kenya* 86 B5
Mandi, *India* 68 D7
Mandi Dabwali, *India* 68 E6
Mandiana, *Guinea* 82 C3
Mandimba, *Mozam.* 87 E4
Mandioli, *Indonesia* 63 E7
Mandla, *India* 69 H9
Mandø, *Denmark* 11 J2
Mandorah, *Australia* 92 B5
Mandoto, *Madag.* 89 B8
Mandoúdhion, *Greece* 38 C5
Mándra, *Greece* 38 C5
Mandra, *Pakistan* 68 C5
Mandrákhi, *Greece* 39 E9
Mandrare →, *Madag.* 89 D8
Mandritsara, *Madag.* 89 B8
Mandronarivo, *Madag.* 89 C8
Mandsaur, *India* 68 G6
Mandurah, *Australia* 93 F2
Mandúria, *Italy* 31 B10
Mandvi, *India* 68 H3
Mandya, *India* 66 N10
Mandzai, *Pakistan* 68 D2
Mané, *Burkina Faso* 83 C4
Maneh, *Iran* 71 B8
Manengouba, Mts.,
Cameroon 83 E6

Manera, *Madag.* 89 C7
Manérbio, *Italy* 28 C7
Maneroo Cr. →, *Australia* 94 C3
Manfalût, *Egypt* 80 B3
Manfredónia, *Italy* 29 G12
Manfredónia, G. di, *Italy* 29 G13
Manga, *Burkina Faso* 83 C4
Manga, *Niger* 83 C7
Mangabeiras, Chapada das, *Brazil* 125 F9
Mangalia, *Romania* 43 G13
Mangalore, *India* 66 N9
Mangan, *India* 69 F13
Mangaung, *S. Africa* 85 K5
Mangawan, *India* 69 G9
Mangaweka, *N.Z.* 91 H5
Manggar, *Indonesia* 62 E3
Manggawitu, *Indonesia* 63 E8
Mangindrano, *Madag.* 89 A8
Mangkalihat, Tanjung, *Indonesia* 63 D5
Mangla, *Pakistan* 68 C5
Mangla Dam, *Pakistan* 69 C5
Manglaur, *India* 68 E7
Mangnai, *China* 60 C4
Mango, *Togo* 83 C5
Mangoche, *Malawi* 87 E4
Mangoky →, *Madag.* 89 C7
Mangole, *Indonesia* 63 E6
Mangombe, *Dem. Rep. of the Congo* 86 C2
Mangonui, *N.Z.* 91 F4
Mangoro →, *Madag.* 89 B8
Mangrol, *Mad. P., India* 68 J4
Mangrol, *Raj., India* 68 G6
Mangualde, *Portugal* 34 E3
Mangueira, L. da, *Brazil* 127 C5
Mangum, *U.S.A.* 113 H5
Mangyshlak Poluostrov, *Kazakstan* 50 E6
Manhattan, *U.S.A.* 112 F6
Manhiça, *Mozam.* 89 D5
Mania →, *Madag.* 89 B8
Maniago, *Italy* 29 B9
Manica, *Mozam.* 89 B5
Manica □, *Mozam.* 89 B5
Manicaland □, *Zimbabwe* 87 F3
Manicoré, *Brazil* 124 E6
Manicouagan →, *Canada* 103 C6
Manicouagan, Rés., *Canada* 103 B6
Maniema □, *Dem. Rep. of the Congo* 86 C2
Manīfah, *Si. Arabia* 71 E6
Manifold, C., *Australia* 94 C5
Maniganggo, *China* 58 B2
Manigotagan, *Canada* 105 C9
Manigotagan →, *Canada* 105 C9
Manihari, *India* 69 G12
Manihiki, *Cook Is.* 97 J11
Manika, Plateau de la, *Dem. Rep. of the Congo* 87 E2
Manikpur, *India* 69 G9
Manila, *Phil.* 61 D4
Manila, *U.S.A.* 114 F9
Manila B., *Phil.* 61 D4
Manilla, *Australia* 95 E5
Manimpé, *Mali* 82 C3
Maningrida, *Australia* 94 A1
Maninian, *Ivory C.* 82 C3
Manipur □, *India* 67 G19
Manipur →, *Burma* 67 H19
Manisa, *Turkey* 39 C9
Manisa □, *Turkey* 39 C9
Manistee, *U.S.A.* 108 C2
Manistee →, *U.S.A.* 108 C2
Manistique, *U.S.A.* 108 C2
Manito L., *Canada* 105 C7
Manitoba □, *Canada* 105 B9
Manitoba, L., *Canada* 105 C9
Manitou, *Canada* 105 D9
Manitou, L., *Canada* 103 B6
Manitou Is., *U.S.A.* 108 C3
Manitou Springs, *U.S.A.* 112 F2
Manitoulin I., *Canada* 102 C3
Manitouwadge, *Canada* 102 C2
Manitowoc, *U.S.A.* 108 C2
Manizales, *Colombia* 124 B3
Manja, *Madag.* 89 C7
Manjacaze, *Mozam.* 89 C5
Manjakandriana, *Madag.* 89 B8
Manjhand, *Pakistan* 68 G3
Manjil, *Iran* 71 B6
Manjimup, *Australia* 93 F2
Manjra →, *India* 66 K10
Mankato, *Kans., U.S.A.* 112 F5
Mankato, *Minn., U.S.A.* 112 C8
Mankayane, *Swaziland* 89 D5
Mankera, *Pakistan* 68 D4
Mankim, *Cameroon* 83 D7
Mankono, *Ivory C.* 82 D3
Mankota, *Canada* 105 D7
Manlay = Üydzin, *Mongolia* 56 B4
Manlleu, *Spain* 32 C7
Manmad, *India* 66 J9
Mann Ranges, *Australia* 93 E5
Manna, *Indonesia* 62 E2
Mannahill, *Australia* 95 E3
Mannar, *Sri Lanka* 66 Q11
Mannar, G. of, *Asia* 66 Q11
Mannar I., *Sri Lanka* 66 Q11
Mannheim, *Germany* 25 F4
Manning, *Canada* 104 B5
Manning, *Oreg., U.S.A.* 116 E3
Manning, *S.C., U.S.A.* 109 J5
Manning Prov. Park, *Canada* 104 D4
Mannu →, *Italy* 30 C2
Mannu, C., *Italy* 30 B1
Mannum, *Australia* 95 E2
Mano, *S. Leone* 82 D2
Mano →, *Liberia* 82 D2
Mano River, *Liberia* 82 D2
Manoharpur, *India* 69 H11
Manokwari, *Indonesia* 63 E8
Manolás, *Greece* 38 C3
Manombo, *Madag.* 89 C7
Manono, *Dem. Rep. of the Congo* 86 D2
Manoppello, *Italy* 29 F11
Manosque, *France* 21 E9
Manotick, *Canada* 111 A9
Manouane →, *Canada* 103 C5
Manouane, L., *Canada* 103 B5
Manp'o, *N. Korea* 57 D14
Manpojin = Manp'o, *N. Korea* 57 D14
Manpur, *Mad. P., India* 68 H6
Manpur, *Mad. P., India* 69 H10
Manresa, *Spain* 32 D6
Mansa, *Gujarat, India* 68 H5
Mansa, *Punjab, India* 68 E6
Mansa, *Zambia* 87 E2
Månsåsen, *Sweden* 10 A8
Mansehra, *Pakistan* 68 B5
Mansel I., *Canada* 101 B11
Mansfield, *Australia* 95 F4
Mansfield, *U.K.* 12 D6
Mansfield, *La., U.S.A.* 113 J8
Mansfield, *Mass., U.S.A.* 111 D13
Mansfield, *Ohio, U.S.A.* 110 F2
Mansfield, *Pa., U.S.A.* 110 E7
Mansfield, Mt., *U.S.A.* 111 B12
Mansilla de las Mulas, *Spain* 34 C5
Mansle, *France* 20 C4
Mansoa, *Guinea-Biss.* 82 C1
Manson Creek, *Canada* 104 B4
Manta, *Ecuador* 124 D2
Mantalingajan, Mt., *Phil.* 61 G2
Mantare, *Tanzania* 86 C3
Manteca, *U.S.A.* 116 H5
Manteo, *U.S.A.* 109 H8
Mantes-la-Jolie, *France* 19 D8
Manthani, *India* 66 K11
Manti, *U.S.A.* 114 G8
Mantiqueira, Serra da, *Brazil* 127 A7
Manton, *U.S.A.* 108 C3
Mantorp, *Sweden* 11 F9
Mántova, *Italy* 28 C7
Mänttä, *Finland* 9 E21
Mantua = Mántova, *Italy* 28 C7
Manturovo, *Russia* 48 A7
Manu, *Peru* 124 F4
Manu →, *Peru* 124 F4
Manua Is., *Amer. Samoa* 91 B14
Manuel Alves →, *Brazil* 125 F9
Manui, *Indonesia* 63 E6
Manuripi →, *Bolivia* 124 F5
Many, *U.S.A.* 113 K8
Manyara, L., *Tanzania* 86 C4
Manyas, *Turkey* 41 F11
Manych →, *Russia* 49 G5
Manych-Gudilo, Ozero, *Russia* 49 G6
Manyonga →, *Tanzania* 86 C3
Manyoni, *Tanzania* 86 D3
Manzai, *Pakistan* 68 C4
Manzala, Bahra el, *Egypt* 80 H7
Manzanares, *Spain* 35 F7
Manzaneda, *Spain* 34 C3
Manzanillo, *Cuba* 120 B4
Manzanillo, *Mexico* 118 D4
Manzanillo, Pta., *Panama* 120 E4
Manzano Mts., *U.S.A.* 115 J10
Manzarīyeh, *Iran* 71 C6
Manzhouli, *China* 60 B6
Manzini, *Swaziland* 89 D5
Mao, *Chad* 79 F9
Maó, *Spain* 37 B11
Maoke, Pegunungan, *Indonesia* 63 E9
Maolin, *China* 57 C12
Maoming, *China* 59 G8
Maopi T'ou, *China* 59 G13
Maouri, Dallol →, *Niger* 83 C5
Maoxian, *China* 58 B4
Maoxing, *China* 57 B13
Mapam Yumco, *China* 60 C3
Mapastepec, *Mexico* 119 D6
Mapia, Kepulauan, *Indonesia* 63 D8
Mapimí, *Mexico* 118 B4
Mapimí, Bolsón de, *Mexico* 118 B4
Maping, *China* 59 B9
Mapinga, *Tanzania* 86 D4
Mapinhane, *Mozam.* 89 C6
Maple Creek, *Canada* 105 D7
Maple Valley, *U.S.A.* 116 C4
Mapleton, *U.S.A.* 114 D2
Mapuera →, *Brazil* 124 D7
Mapulanguene, *Mozam.* 89 C5
Maputo, *Mozam.* 89 D5
Maputo □, *Mozam.* 89 D5
Maputo, B. de, *Mozam.* 89 D5
Maqiaohe, *China* 57 B16
Maqnā, *Si. Arabia* 70 D2
Maqueda, *Spain* 34 E6
Maquela do Zombo, *Angola* 84 F3
Maquinchao, *Argentina* 128 E3
Maquoketa, *U.S.A.* 112 D9
Mar, Serra do, *Brazil* 127 B6
Mar Chiquita, L., *Argentina* 126 C3
Mar del Plata, *Argentina* 126 D4
Mar Menor, *Spain* 33 H4
Mara, *Tanzania* 86 C3
Mara □, *Tanzania* 86 C3
Maraã, *Brazil* 124 D5
Marabá, *Brazil* 125 E9
Maracá, I. de, *Brazil* 125 C8
Maracaibo, *Venezuela* 124 A4
Maracaibo, L. de, *Venezuela* 122 C3
Maracaju, *Brazil* 127 A4
Maracay, *Venezuela* 124 A5
Maracena, *Spain* 35 H7
Maradi, *Niger* 83 C6
Marāgheh, *Iran* 70 B5
Marāh, *Si. Arabia* 70 E5
Marajó, I. de, *Brazil* 122 D6
Marākand, *Iran* 70 B5
Maralal, *Kenya* 86 B4
Maralinga, *Australia* 93 F5
Maramaraereğlisi, *Turkey* 41 F11
Marampa, *S. Leone* 82 D2
Maramureş □, *Romania* 43 C9
Maran, *Malaysia* 65 L4
Marana, *U.S.A.* 115 K8
Maranboy, *Australia* 92 B5
Maranchón, *Spain* 32 D2
Marand, *Iran* 70 B5
Marang, *Malaysia* 65 K4
Maranguape, *Brazil* 125 D11
Maranhão = São Luís, *Brazil* 125 D10
Maranhão □, *Brazil* 125 E9
Marano, L. di, *Italy* 29 C10
Maranoa →, *Australia* 95 D4
Marañón →, *Peru* 122 D3
Marão, *Mozam.* 89 C5
Maraş = Kahramanmaraş, *Turkey* 70 B3
Mărăşeşti, *Romania* 43 E12
Maratea, *Italy* 31 C8
Marateca, *Portugal* 35 G2
Marathasa □, *Cyprus* 36 E11
Marathókambos, *Greece* 39 D8
Marathon, *Australia* 94 C3
Marathon, *Canada* 102 C2
Marathón, *Greece* 38 C5
Marathon, *N.Y., U.S.A.* 111 D8
Marathon, *N.Y., U.S.A.* 111 D8
Marathon, *Tex., U.S.A.* 113 K3
Marathóvouno, *Cyprus* 36 D12
Maratua, *Indonesia* 63 D5
Maravatío, *Mexico* 118 D4
Marawi City, *Phil.* 61 G6
Marāwih, *U.A.E.* 71 E7
Marbella, *Spain* 35 J6
Marble Bar, *Australia* 92 D2
Marble Falls, *U.S.A.* 113 K5
Marblehead, *U.S.A.* 111 D14
Marburg, *Germany* 24 E4
Marcal →, *Hungary* 42 C2
Marcali, *Hungary* 42 D2
Marcaria, *Italy* 28 C7
Mărcăuţi, *Moldova* 43 B12
March, *U.K.* 13 E8
Marche, *France* 20 B5
Marche □, *Italy* 29 E10
Marche-en-Famenne, *Belgium* 17 D5
Marchena, *Spain* 35 H5
Marches = Marche □, *Italy* 29 E10
Marciana Marina, *Italy* 28 F7
Marcianise, *Italy* 31 A7
Marcigny, *France* 19 F11
Marcillat-en-Combraille, *France* 19 F9
Marck, *France* 19 B8
Marckolsheim, *France* 19 D14
Marco, *U.S.A.* 109 N5
Marcos Juárez, *Argentina* 126 C3
Mărculeşti, *Moldova* 43 C13
Marcus I. = Minami-Tori-Shima, *Pac. Oc.* 96 E7
Marcus Necker Ridge, *Pac. Oc.* 96 F9
Marcy, Mt., *U.S.A.* 111 B11
Mardan, *Pakistan* 68 B5
Mardin, *Turkey* 70 B4
Mårdsjön, *Sweden* 10 A9
Marécchia →, *Italy* 29 D9
Maree, L., *U.K.* 14 D3
Mareeba, *Australia* 94 B4
Mareetsane, *S. Africa* 88 D4
Maremma, *Italy* 29 F8
Maréna, *Mali* 82 C2
Maréna, *Mali* 82 C3
Marengo, *U.S.A.* 112 E8
Marennes, *France* 20 C2
Marenyi, *Kenya* 86 C4
Marerano, *Madag.* 89 C7
Maréttimo, *Italy* 30 E5
Mareuil, *France* 20 C4
Marfa, *U.S.A.* 113 K2
Marfa Pt., *Malta* 36 D1
Marganets = Marhanets, *Ukraine* 47 J8
Margaret →, *Australia* 92 C4
Margaret Bay, *Canada* 104 C3
Margaret L., *Canada* 104 B5
Margaret River, *Australia* 93 F2
Margarita, I. de, *Venezuela* 122 B4
Margarítion, *Greece* 38 B2
Margaritovo, *Russia* 54 C7
Margate, *S. Africa* 89 E5
Margate, *U.K.* 13 F9
Margeride, Mts. de la, *France* 20 D7
Margherita di Savóia, *Italy* 31 A9
Marghita, *Romania* 42 C7
Margonin, *Poland* 45 F4
Margosatubig, *Phil.* 61 H5
Mārgow, Dasht-e, *Afghan.* 66 D3
Marguerite, *Canada* 104 C4
Marhanets, *Ukraine* 47 J8
Mari El □, *Russia* 48 B8
Mari Indus, *Pakistan* 68 C4
Mari Republic = Mari El □, *Russia* 48 B8
María, Sa. de, *Spain* 33 H2
María Elena, *Chile* 126 A2
María Grande, *Argentina* 126 C4
Maria I., *N. Terr., Australia* 94 A2
Maria I., *Tas., Australia* 94 G4
Maria van Diemen, C., *N.Z.* 91 F4
Mariager, *Denmark* 11 H3
Mariager Fjord, *Denmark* 11 H4
Mariakani, *Kenya* 86 C4
Marian, *Australia* 94 C4
Marian L., *Canada* 104 A5
Mariana Trench, *Pac. Oc.* 52 H18
Marianao, *Cuba* 120 B3
Marianna, *Ark., U.S.A.* 113 H9
Marianna, *Fla., U.S.A.* 109 K3
Mariannelund, *Sweden* 11 G9
Mariánské Lázně, *Czech Rep.* 26 B5
Marias →, *U.S.A.* 114 C8
Mariato, Punta, *Panama* 120 E3
Mariazell, *Austria* 26 D8
Maribo, *Denmark* 11 K5
Maribor, *Slovenia* 29 B12
Marico →, *Africa* 88 C4
Maricopa, *Ariz., U.S.A.* 115 K7
Maricopa, *Calif., U.S.A.* 117 K7
Marīdī, *Sudan* 81 G2
Maridi, Wadi →, *Sudan* 81 F2
Marié →, *Brazil* 124 D5
Marie Byrd Land, *Antarctica* 5 D14
Marie-Galante, *Guadeloupe* 121 C7
Mariecourt = Kangiqsujuaq, *Canada* 101 B12
Mariefred, *Sweden* 10 E11
Marieholm, *Sweden* 11 J7
Mariembourg, *Belgium* 17 D4
Marienbad = Mariánské Lázně, *Czech Rep.* 26 B5
Marienberg, *Germany* 24 E9
Mariental, *Namibia* 88 C2
Marienville, *U.S.A.* 110 E5
Mariestad, *Sweden* 11 F7
Marietta, *Ga., U.S.A.* 109 J3
Marietta, *Ohio, U.S.A.* 108 F5
Marieville, *Canada* 111 A11
Mariga →, *Nigeria* 83 C6
Marignane, *France* 21 E9
Marihatag, *Phil.* 61 G7
Mariinsk, *Russia* 50 D9
Mariinskiy Posad, *Russia* 48 B8
Marijampolė, *Lithuania* 9 J20
Marijampolės □, *Lithuania* 44 D10
Marília, *Brazil* 127 A6
Marín, *Spain* 34 C2
Marina, *U.S.A.* 116 J5
Marinduque, *Phil.* 63 B6
Marine City, *U.S.A.* 110 D2
Marineo, *Italy* 30 E6
Marinette, *U.S.A.* 108 C2
Maringá, *Brazil* 127 A5
Marinha Grande, *Portugal* 34 F2
Marino, *Italy* 29 G9
Marion, *Ala., U.S.A.* 109 J2
Marion, *Ill., U.S.A.* 113 G10
Marion, *Ind., U.S.A.* 108 E3
Marion, *Iowa, U.S.A.* 112 D9
Marion, *Kans., U.S.A.* 112 F6
Marion, *N.C., U.S.A.* 109 H5
Marion, *Ohio, U.S.A.* 108 E4
Marion, *S.C., U.S.A.* 109 H6
Marion, *Va., U.S.A.* 109 G5
Marion, L., *U.S.A.* 109 J5
Mariposa, *U.S.A.* 116 H7
Mariscal Estigarribia, *Paraguay* 126 A3
Maritime Alps = Maritimes, Alpes, *Europe* 21 D11
Maritimes, Alpes, *Europe* 21 D11
Maritsa = Évros →, *Bulgaria* 72 B2
Maritsá, *Greece* 36 C10
Mariupol, *Ukraine* 47 J9
Marīvān, *Iran* 70 C5
Marj 'Uyūn, *Lebanon* 75 B4
Marka, *Si. Arabia* 80 D5
Markam, *China* 58 C2
Markaryd, *Sweden* 11 H7
Markazī □, *Iran* 71 C6
Markdale, *Canada* 110 B4
Marked Tree, *U.S.A.* 113 H9
Markelsdorfer Huk, *Germany* 24 A7
Market Drayton, *U.K.* 12 E5
Market Harborough, *U.K.* 13 E7
Market Rasen, *U.K.* 12 D7
Markham, *Canada* 110 C5
Markham, Mt., *Antarctica* 5 E11
Marki, *Poland* 45 F8
Markkleeberg, *Germany* 24 D8
Markleeville, *U.S.A.* 116 G7
Markoupoulon, *Greece* 38 D5
Markovac, *Serbia, Yug.* 40 B5
Markovo, *Russia* 51 C17
Markoye, *Burkina Faso* 83 C5
Marks, *Russia* 48 E8
Marksville, *U.S.A.* 113 K8
Markt Schwaben, *Germany* 25 G7
Marktoberdorf, *Germany* 25 H6
Marktredwitz, *Germany* 25 E8
Marl, *Germany* 24 D3
Marla, *Australia* 95 D1
Marlbank, *Canada* 110 B7
Marlboro, *Mass., U.S.A.* 111 D13
Marlboro, *N.Y., U.S.A.* 111 E11
Marlborough, *Australia* 94 C4
Marlborough, *U.K.* 13 F6
Marlborough Downs, *U.K.* 13 F6
Marle, *France* 19 C10
Marlin, *U.S.A.* 113 K6
Marlow, *Germany* 24 A8
Marlow, *U.S.A.* 113 H6
Marmagao, *India* 66 M8
Marmande, *France* 20 D4
Marmara, *Turkey* 41 F11
Marmara, Sea of = Marmara Denizi, *Turkey* 41 F12
Marmara Denizi, *Turkey* 41 F12
Marmara Gölü, *Turkey* 39 C10
Marmaris, *Turkey* 39 E10
Marmaris Limanı, *Turkey* 39 E10
Marmion, Mt., *Australia* 93 E2
Marmion L., *Canada* 102 C1
Marmolada, Mte., *Italy* 29 B8
Marmolejo, *Spain* 35 G6
Marmora, *Canada* 102 D4
Mármora, La, *Italy* 30 C2
Marnay, *France* 19 E12
Marne, *Germany* 24 B5
Marne □, *France* 19 D11
Marne →, *France* 19 D9
Marneuli, *Georgia* 49 K7
Maroala, *Madag.* 89 B8
Maroantsetra, *Madag.* 89 B8
Maroelaboom, *Namibia* 88 B2
Marofandilia, *Madag.* 89 C7
Marolambo, *Madag.* 89 C8
Maromandia, *Madag.* 89 A8
Marondera, *Zimbabwe* 87 F3
Maroni →, *Fr. Guiana* 125 B8
Marónia, *Greece* 41 F9
Maronne →, *France* 20 C5
Maroochydore, *Australia* 95 D5
Maroona, *Australia* 95 F3
Maros →, *Hungary* 42 D5
Marosakoa, *Madag.* 89 B8
Maroseranana, *Madag.* 89 B8
Maróstica, *Italy* 29 C8
Marotandrano, *Madag.* 89 B8
Marotaolano, *Madag.* 89 A8
Maroua, *Cameroon* 83 C7
Marovato, *Madag.* 89 B8
Marovoay, *Madag.* 89 B8
Marquard, *S. Africa* 88 D4
Marquesas Is. = Marquises, Is., *Pac. Oc.* 97 H14
Marquette, *U.S.A.* 108 B2
Marquise, *France* 19 B8
Marquises, Is., *Pac. Oc.* 97 H14
Marra, Djebel, *Sudan* 79 F10
Marra, Gebel, *Sudan* 81 F2
Marracuene, *Mozam.* 89 D5
Marradi, *Italy* 29 D8
Marrakech, *Morocco* 78 B4
Marratxi, *Spain* 32 F7
Marrawah, *Australia* 94 G3
Marree, *Australia* 95 D2
Marrero, *U.S.A.* 113 L9
Marrimane, *Mozam.* 89 C5
Marromeu, *Mozam.* 89 B6
Marroquí, Punta, *Spain* 35 K5
Marrowie Cr. →, *Australia* 95 E4
Marrubane, *Mozam.* 87 F4
Marrùbiu, *Italy* 30 C1
Marrupa, *Mozam.* 87 E4
Mars Hill, *U.S.A.* 109 B12
Marsa Alam, *Egypt* 80 B3
Marsá Matrûh, *Egypt* 80 A2
Marsa Sha'b, *Sudan* 80 C4
Marsabit, *Kenya* 86 B4
Marsala, *Italy* 30 E5
Marsalforn, *Malta* 36 C1
Mârşani, *Romania* 43 F9
Marsberg, *Germany* 24 D4
Marsciano, *Italy* 29 F9
Marsden, *Australia* 95 E4
Marseillan, *France* 20 E7
Marseille, *France* 21 E9
Marseilles = Marseille, *France* 21 E9
Marsh I., *U.S.A.* 113 L9
Marshall, *Liberia* 82 D2
Marshall, *Ark., U.S.A.* 113 H8
Marshall, *Mich., U.S.A.* 108 D3
Marshall, *Minn., U.S.A.* 112 C7
Marshall, *Mo., U.S.A.* 112 F8
Marshall, *Tex., U.S.A.* 113 J7
Marshall →, *Australia* 94 C2
Marshall Is. ■, *Pac. Oc.* 96 G9
Marshalltown, *U.S.A.* 112 D8
Marshbrook, *Zimbabwe* 89 B5
Marshfield, *Mo., U.S.A.* 113 G8
Marshfield, *Vt., U.S.A.* 111 B12
Marshfield, *Wis., U.S.A.* 112 C9
Marshūn, *Iran* 71 B6
Mársico Nuovo, *Italy* 31 B8
Märsta, *Sweden* 10 E11
Marstal, *Denmark* 11 K4
Marstrand, *Sweden* 11 G5
Mart, *U.S.A.* 113 K6
Marta →, *Italy* 29 F8
Martaban, *Burma* 67 L20
Martaban, G. of, *Burma* 67 L20
Martano, *Italy* 31 B11
Martapura, *Kalimantan, Indonesia* 62 E4
Martapura, *Sumatera, Indonesia* 62 E2
Marte, *Nigeria* 83 C7
Martel, *France* 20 D5
Martelange, *Belgium* 17 E5
Martellago, *Italy* 29 C9
Martés, Sierra, *Spain* 33 F4
Martfű, *Hungary* 42 C5
Martha's Vineyard, *U.S.A.* 111 E14
Martigné-Ferchaud, *France* 18 E5
Martigny, *Switz.* 25 J3
Martigues, *France* 21 E9
Martin, *Slovak Rep.* 27 B11
Martin, *S. Dak., U.S.A.* 112 D4
Martin, *Tenn., U.S.A.* 113 G10
Martín →, *Spain* 32 D4
Martin L., *U.S.A.* 109 J3
Martina Franca, *Italy* 31 B10
Martinborough, *N.Z.* 91 J5
Martinez, *Calif., U.S.A.* 116 G4
Martinez, *Ga., U.S.A.* 109 J4
Martinique ■, *W. Indies* 121 D7
Martinique Passage, *W. Indies* 121 C7
Martínon, *Greece* 38 C5

Martinópolis, Brazil 127 A5
Martins Ferry, U.S.A. 110 F4
Martinsberg, Austria 26 C8
Martinsburg, Pa., U.S.A. 110 F6
Martinsburg, W. Va., U.S.A. 108 F7
Martinsicuro, Italy 29 F10
Martinsville, Ind., U.S.A. 108 F2
Martinsville, Va., U.S.A. 109 G6
Marton, N.Z. 91 J5
Martorell, Spain 32 D6
Martos, Spain 35 H7
Martuni, Armenia 49 K7
Maru, Nigeria 83 C6
Marudi, Malaysia 62 D4
Ma'ruf, Afghan. 66 D5
Marugame, Japan 55 G6
Marunga, Angola 88 B3
Marungu, Mts., Dem. Rep. of the Congo 86 D3
Marv Dasht, Iran 71 D7
Marvast, Iran 71 D7
Marvejols, France 20 D7
Marvel Loch, Australia 93 F2
Marwar, India 68 G5
Mary, Turkmenistan 50 F7
Maryborough = Port Laoise, Ireland 15 C4
Maryborough, Queens., Australia 95 D5
Maryborough, Vic., Australia 95 F3
Maryfield, Canada 105 D8
Maryland □, U.S.A. 108 F7
Maryland Junction, Zimbabwe 87 F3
Maryport, U.K. 12 C4
Mary's Harbour, Canada 103 B8
Marystown, Canada 103 C8
Marysville, Canada 104 D5
Marysville, Calif., U.S.A. 116 F5
Marysville, Kans., U.S.A. 112 F6
Marysville, Mich., U.S.A. 110 D2
Marysville, Ohio, U.S.A. 108 E4
Marysville, Wash., U.S.A. 116 B4
Maryville, Mo., U.S.A. 112 E7
Maryville, Tenn., U.S.A. 109 H4
Marzūq, Libya 79 C8
Masahunga, Tanzania 86 C3
Masai Steppe, Tanzania 86 C4
Masaka, Uganda 86 C3
Masalembo, Kepulauan, Indonesia 62 F4
Masalima, Kepulauan, Indonesia 62 F5
Masallı, Azerbaijan 73 C13
Masamba, Indonesia 63 E6
Masan, S. Korea 57 G15
Masandam, Ra's, Oman 71 E8
Masasi, Tanzania 87 E4
Masaya, Nic. 120 D2
Masba, Nigeria 83 C7
Masbate, Phil. 61 E5
Máscali, Italy 31 E8
Mascara, Algeria 78 A6
Mascota, Mexico 118 C4
Masela, Indonesia 63 F7
Maseru, Lesotho 88 D4
Mashaba, Zimbabwe 87 G3
Mashābih, Si. Arabia 70 E3
Mashan, China 58 F7
Mashar, Sudan 81 F2
Mashegu, Nigeria 83 D6
Masherbrum, Pakistan 69 B7
Mashhad, Iran 71 B8
Mashi, Nigeria 83 C6
Mashīz, Iran 71 D8
Mashkel, Hamun-i, Pakistan 66 E3
Mashki Chāh, Pakistan 66 E3
Mashonaland, Zimbabwe 85 H6
Mashonaland Central □, Zimbabwe 89 B5
Mashonaland East □, Zimbabwe 89 B5
Mashonaland West □, Zimbabwe 89 B4
Mashrakh, India 69 F11
Mashtaga = Maştağa, Azerbaijan 49 K10
Masindi, Uganda 86 B3
Masindi Port, Uganda 86 B3
Maşīrah, Oman 74 C6
Maşīrah, Khalīj, Oman 74 C6
Masisi, Dem. Rep. of the Congo 86 C2
Masjed Soleyman, Iran 71 D6
Mask, L., Ireland 15 C2
Maskin, Oman 71 F8
Maslen Nos, Bulgaria 41 D11
Maslinica, Croatia 29 E13
Masnou = El Masnou, Spain 32 D7
Masoala, Tanjon' i, Madag. 89 B9
Masoarivo, Madag. 89 B7
Masohi = Amahai, Indonesia 63 E7
Masomeloka, Madag. 89 C8
Mason, Nev., U.S.A. 116 G7
Mason, Tex., U.S.A. 113 K5
Mason City, U.S.A. 112 D8
Maspalomas, Canary Is. 37 G4
Maspalomas, Pta., Canary Is. 37 G4
Masqat, Oman 74 C6
Massa, Italy 28 D7
Massa Maríttima, Italy 28 E7
Massachusetts □, U.S.A. 111 D13
Massachusetts B., U.S.A. 111 D14
Massafra, Italy 31 B10
Massakory, Chad 79 F9
Massanella, Spain 37 B9
Massangena, Mozam. 89 C5
Massango, Angola 84 F3
Massat, France 20 F5
Massawa = Mitsiwa, Eritrea 81 D4
Massena, U.S.A. 111 B10
Massénya, Chad 79 F9
Masset, Canada 104 C2
Masseube, France 20 E4
Massiac, France 20 C7
Massif Central, France 20 D7
Massigui, Mali 82 C3
Massillon, U.S.A. 110 F3
Massinga, Mozam. 89 C6
Massingir, Mozam. 89 C5
Mässlingen, Sweden 10 B6
Masson, Canada 111 A9
Masson I., Antarctica 5 C7
Maştağa, Azerbaijan 49 K10
Mastanli = Momchilgrad, Bulgaria 41 E9
Masterton, N.Z. 91 J5
Mastic, U.S.A. 111 F12
Mástikho, Ákra, Greece 39 C8
Mastuj, Pakistan 69 A5
Mastung, Pakistan 66 E5
Mastūrah, Si. Arabia 80 C4
Masty, Belarus 46 F3
Masuda, Japan 55 G5
Masvingo, Zimbabwe 87 G3
Masvingo □, Zimbabwe 87 G3
Maşyāf, Syria 70 C3
Maszewo, Poland 44 E2
Matabeleland, Zimbabwe 85 H5
Matabeleland North □, Zimbabwe 87 F2
Matabeleland South □, Zimbabwe 87 G2
Matachel →, Spain 35 G4
Matachewan, Canada 102 C3
Matadi, Dem. Rep. of the Congo 84 F2
Matagalpa, Nic. 120 D2
Matagami, Canada 102 C4
Matagami, L., Canada 102 C4
Matagorda B., U.S.A. 113 L6
Matagorda I., U.S.A. 113 L6
Matak, Indonesia 65 L6
Mátala, Greece 36 E6
Matam, Senegal 82 B2
Matameye, Niger 83 C6
Matamoros, Campeche, Mexico 119 D6
Matamoros, Coahuila, Mexico 118 B4
Matamoros, Tamaulipas, Mexico 119 B5
Ma'ţan as Sarra, Libya 79 D10
Matandu →, Tanzania 87 D3
Matane, Canada 103 C6
Matang, China 58 F5
Matankari, Niger 83 C5
Matanomadh, India 68 H3
Matanzas, Cuba 120 B3
Matapa, Botswana 88 C3
Matapan, C. = Taínaron, Ákra, Greece 38 E4
Matapédia, Canada 103 C6
Matara, Sri Lanka 66 S12
Mataram, Indonesia 62 F5
Matarani, Peru 124 G4
Mataranka, Australia 92 B5
Matarma, Râs, Egypt 75 E1
Mataró, Spain 32 D7
Matarraña →, Spain 32 D5
Mataruška Banja, Serbia, Yug. 40 C4
Matatiele, S. Africa 89 E4
Mataura, N.Z. 91 M2
Matehuala, Mexico 118 C4
Mateke Hills, Zimbabwe 87 G3
Matera, Italy 31 B9
Matese, Monti del, Italy 31 A7
Mátészalka, Hungary 42 C7
Matetsi, Zimbabwe 87 F2
Matfors, Sweden 10 B11
Matha, France 20 C3
Mathis, U.S.A. 113 L6
Mathráki, Greece 36 A3
Mathura, India 68 F7
Mati, Phil. 61 H7
Mati →, Albania 40 E3
Matiakoali, Burkina Faso 83 C5
Matiali, India 69 F13
Matías Romero, Mexico 119 D5
Matibane, Mozam. 87 E5
Matima, Botswana 88 C3
Matiri Ra., N.Z. 91 J4
Matjiesfontein, S. Africa 88 E3
Matla →, India 69 J13
Matlamanyane, Botswana 88 B4
Matli, Pakistan 68 G3
Matlock, U.K. 12 D6
Matna, Sudan 81 E4
Mato Grosso □, Brazil 125 F8
Mato Grosso, Planalto do, Brazil 122 E5
Mato Grosso do Sul □, Brazil 125 G8
Matochkin Shar, Russia 50 B6
Matopo Hills, Zimbabwe 87 G2
Matopos, Zimbabwe 87 G2
Matosinhos, Portugal 34 D2
Matour, France 19 F11
Maţraḩ, Oman 74 C6
Matroosberg, S. Africa 88 E2
Matsena, Nigeria 83 C7
Matsesta, Russia 49 J4
Matsu Tao, Taiwan 59 E13
Matsue, Japan 55 G6
Matsumae, Japan 54 D10
Matsumoto, Japan 55 F9
Matsusaka, Japan 55 G8
Matsutō, Japan 55 F8
Matsuura, Japan 55 H4
Matsuyama, Japan 55 H6
Mattagami →, Canada 102 B3
Mattancheri, India 66 Q10
Mattawa, Canada 102 C4
Matterhorn, Switz. 25 K3
Mattersburg, Austria 27 D9
Matthew Town, Bahamas 121 B5
Matthew's Ridge, Guyana 124 B6
Mattice, Canada 102 C3
Mattituck, U.S.A. 111 F12
Mattoon, U.S.A. 108 F1
Matuba, Mozam. 89 C5
Matucana, Peru 124 F3
Matūn = Khowst, Afghan. 68 C3
Maturín, Venezuela 124 B6
Matveyev Kurgan, Russia 47 J10
Matxitxako, C., Spain 32 B2
Mau, Mad. P., India 69 F8
Mau, Ut. P., India 69 G10
Mau, Ut. P., India 69 G9
Mau Escarpment, Kenya 86 C4
Mau Ranipur, India 69 G8
Maubeuge, France 19 B10
Maubourguet, France 20 E4
Maud, Pt., Australia 92 D1
Maude, Australia 95 E3
Maudin Sun, Burma 67 M19
Maués, Brazil 124 D7
Mauganj, India 67 G12
Maughold Hd., U.K. 12 C3
Mauguio, France 20 E7
Maui, U.S.A. 106 H16
Maulamyaing = Moulmein, Burma 67 L20
Maule □, Chile 126 D1
Mauléon-Licharre, France 20 E3
Maumee, U.S.A. 108 E4
Maumee →, U.S.A. 108 E4
Maumere, Indonesia 63 F6
Maumusson, Pertuis de, France 20 C2
Maun, Botswana 88 C3
Mauna Kea, U.S.A. 106 J17
Mauna Loa, U.S.A. 106 J17
Maungmagan Is., Burma 64 E1
Maungmagan Kyunzu, Burma 67 N20
Maupin, U.S.A. 114 D3
Maure-de-Bretagne, France 18 E5
Maurepas, L., U.S.A. 113 K9
Maures, France 21 E10
Mauriac, France 20 C6
Maurice, L., Australia 93 E5
Mauricie, Parc Nat. de la, Canada 102 C5
Maurienne, France 21 C10
Mauritania ■, Africa 78 E3
Mauritius ■, Ind. Oc. 77 J9
Mauron, France 18 D4
Maurs, France 20 D6
Mauston, U.S.A. 112 D9
Mauterndorf, Austria 26 D6
Mauthen, Austria 26 E6
Mauvezin, France 20 E4
Mauzé-sur-le-Mignon, France 20 B3
Mavli, India 68 G5
Mavrova, Albania 40 F3
Mavuradonha Mts., Zimbabwe 87 F3
Mawa, Dem. Rep. of the Congo 86 B2
Mawai, India 69 H9
Mawana, India 68 E7
Mawand, Pakistan 68 E3
Mawk Mai, Burma 67 J20
Mawlaik, Burma 67 H19
Mawlamyine = Moulmein, Burma 67 L20
Mawqaq, Si. Arabia 70 E4
Mawson Coast, Antarctica 5 C6
Max, U.S.A. 112 B4
Maxcanú, Mexico 119 C6
Maxesibeni, S. Africa 89 E4
Maxhamish L., Canada 104 B4
Maxixe, Mozam. 89 C6
Maxville, Canada 111 A10
Maxwell, U.S.A. 116 F4
Maxwelton, Australia 94 C3
May, C., U.S.A. 108 F8
May Pen, Jamaica 120 C4
Maya →, Russia 51 D14
Maya Mts., Belize 119 D7
Mayaguana, Bahamas 121 B5
Mayagüez, Puerto Rico 121 C6
Mayahi, Niger 83 C6
Mayals = Maials, Spain 32 D5
Mayāmey, Iran 71 B7
Mayang, China 58 D7
Mayanup, Australia 93 F2
Mayapan, Mexico 119 C7
Mayarí, Cuba 121 B4
Maybell, U.S.A. 114 F9
Maybole, U.K. 14 F4
Maychew, Ethiopia 81 E4
Maydān, Iraq 70 C5
Maydena, Australia 94 G4
Mayen, Germany 25 E3
Mayenne, France 18 D6
Mayenne □, France 18 D6
Mayenne →, France 18 E6
Mayer, U.S.A. 115 J7
Mayerthorpe, Canada 104 C5
Mayfield, Ky., U.S.A. 109 G1
Mayfield, N.Y., U.S.A. 111 C10
Mayhill, U.S.A. 115 K11
Maykop, Russia 49 H5
Maymyo, Burma 64 A1
Maynard, Mass., U.S.A. 111 D13
Maynard, Wash., U.S.A. 116 C4
Maynard Hills, Australia 93 E2
Mayne →, Australia 94 C3
Maynooth, Ireland 15 C5
Mayo, Canada 100 B6
Mayo □, Ireland 15 C2
Mayo Daga, Nigeria 83 D7
Mayo Faran, Nigeria 83 D7
Mayon Volcano, Phil. 61 E5
Mayor I., N.Z. 91 G6
Mayorga, Spain 34 C5
Mayotte, Ind. Oc. 85 G9
Mayraira Pt., Phil. 61 B4
Mayskiy, Russia 49 J7
Maysville, U.S.A. 108 F4
Mayu, Indonesia 63 D7
Mayville, N. Dak., U.S.A. 112 B6
Mayville, N.Y., U.S.A. 110 D5
Mayya, Russia 51 C14
Mazabuka, Zambia 87 F2
Mazagán = El Jadida, Morocco 78 B4
Mazagão, Brazil 125 D8
Mazamet, France 20 E6
Mazán, Peru 124 D4
Māzandarān □, Iran 71 B7
Mazapil, Mexico 118 C4
Mazara del Vallo, Italy 30 E5
Mazarrón, Spain 33 H3
Mazarrón, G. de, Spain 33 H3
Mazaruni →, Guyana 124 B7
Mazatán, Mexico 118 B2
Mazatenango, Guatemala 120 D1
Mazatlán, Mexico 118 C3
Mažeikiai, Lithuania 9 H20
Māzhān, Iran 71 C8
Mazīnān, Iran 71 B8
Mazoe, Mozam. 87 F3
Mazoe →, Mozam. 87 F3
Mazowe, Zimbabwe 87 F3
Mazowieckie □, Poland 45 F8
Mazrûb, Sudan 81 E2
Mazu Dao, China 59 D12
Mazurian Lakes = Mazurski, Pojezierze, Poland 44 E7
Mazurski, Pojezierze, Poland 44 E7
Mazyr, Belarus 47 F5
Mbaba, Senegal 82 C1
Mbabane, Swaziland 89 D5
Mbagne, Mauritania 82 B2
M'bahiakro, Ivory C. 82 D4
Mbaïki, C.A.R. 84 D3
Mbala, Zambia 87 D3
Mbalabala, Zimbabwe 89 C4
Mbale, Uganda 86 B3
Mbalmayo, Cameroon 83 E7
Mbam →, Cameroon 83 E7
Mbamba Bay, Tanzania 87 E3
Mbandaka, Dem. Rep. of the Congo 84 D3
Mbanga, Cameroon 83 E6
Mbanza Congo, Angola 84 F2
Mbanza Ngungu, Dem. Rep. of the Congo 84 F2
Mbarara, Uganda 86 C3
Mbashe →, S. Africa 89 E4
Mbatto, Ivory C. 82 D4
Mbenkuru →, Tanzania 87 D4
Mberengwa, Zimbabwe 87 G2
Mberengwa, Mt., Zimbabwe 87 G2
Mberubu, Nigeria 83 D6
Mbesuma, Zambia 87 E3
Mbeya, Tanzania 87 D3
Mbeya □, Tanzania 86 D3
M'bili, Sudan 81 F2
Mbinga, Tanzania 87 E4
Mbini □, Eq. Guin. 84 D2
Mboki, C.A.R. 81 F2
M'bonge, Cameroon 83 E6
Mboro, Senegal 82 B1
M'boukou Res., Cameroon 83 D7
Mboune, Senegal 82 C2
Mbour, Senegal 82 C1
Mbout, Mauritania 82 B2
Mbuji-Mayi, Dem. Rep. of the Congo 86 D1
Mbulu, Tanzania 86 C4
Mburucuyá, Argentina 126 B4
Mchinja, Tanzania 87 D4
Mchinji, Malawi 87 E3
Mdantsane, S. Africa 85 L5
Mead, L., U.S.A. 117 J12
Meade, U.S.A. 113 G4
Meadow Lake, Canada 105 C7
Meadow Lake Prov. Park, Canada 105 C7
Meadow Valley Wash →, U.S.A. 117 J12
Meadville, U.S.A. 110 E4
Meaford, Canada 102 D3
Mealhada, Portugal 34 E2
Mealy Mts., Canada 103 B8
Meander River, Canada 104 B5
Meares, C., U.S.A. 114 D2
Mearim →, Brazil 125 D10
Meath □, Ireland 15 C5
Meath Park, Canada 105 C7
Meaulne, France 19 F9
Meaux, France 19 D9
Mebechi-Gawa →, Japan 54 D10
Mecanhelas, Mozam. 87 F4
Mecca = Makkah, Si. Arabia 74 C2
Mecca, U.S.A. 117 M10
Mechanicsburg, U.S.A. 110 F8
Mechanicville, U.S.A. 111 D11
Mechara, Ethiopia 81 F5
Mechelen, Belgium 17 C4
Mecheria, Algeria 78 B5
Mechernich, Germany 24 E2
Mechetinskaya, Russia 49 G5
Mecidiye, Turkey 41 F10
Mecitözü, Turkey 72 B6
Mecklenburg-Vorpommern □, Germany 24 B8
Mecklenburger Bucht, Germany 24 A7
Meconta, Mozam. 87 E4
Mecsek, Hungary 42 D3
Meda, Portugal 34 E3
Medan, Indonesia 62 D1
Medanosa, Pta., Argentina 128 F3
Mede, Italy 28 C5
Médéa, Algeria 78 A6
Mededa, Bos.-H. 42 G4
Medellín, Colombia 124 B3
Medelpad, Sweden 10 B10
Medemblik, Neths. 17 B5
Mederdra, Mauritania 82 B1
Medford, Mass., U.S.A. 111 D13
Medford, Oreg., U.S.A. 114 E2
Medford, Wis., U.S.A. 112 C9
Medgidia, Romania 43 F13
Medi, Sudan 81 F3
Media Agua, Argentina 126 C2
Media Luna, Argentina 126 C2
Medianeira, Brazil 127 B5
Mediaş, Romania 43 D9
Medicina, Italy 29 D8
Medicine Bow, U.S.A. 114 F10
Medicine Bow Pk., U.S.A. 114 F10
Medicine Bow Ra., U.S.A. 114 F10
Medicine Hat, Canada 105 D6
Medicine Lake, U.S.A. 112 A2
Medicine Lodge, U.S.A. 113 G5
Medina = Al Madīnah, Si. Arabia 70 E3
Medina, N. Dak., U.S.A. 112 B5
Medina, N.Y., U.S.A. 110 C6
Medina, Ohio, U.S.A. 110 E3
Medina →, U.S.A. 113 L5
Medina de Pomar, Spain 34 C7
Medina de Ríoseco, Spain 34 D5
Medina del Campo, Spain 34 D6
Medina L., U.S.A. 113 L5
Medina Sidonia, Spain 35 J5
Medinaceli, Spain 32 D2
Medinipur, India 69 H12
Mediterranean Sea, Europe 6 H7
Médoc, France 20 C3
Medulin, Croatia 29 D10
Medveđa, Serbia, Yug. 40 D5
Medvedevo, Russia 48 B8
Medveditsa →, Tver, Russia 46 D9
Medveditsa →, Volgograd, Russia 48 F6
Medvedok, Russia 48 B10
Medvezhi, Ostrava, Russia 51 B17
Medvezhyegorsk, Russia 50 C4
Medway →, U.K. 13 F8
Medway Towns □, U.K. 13 F8
Medzev, Slovak Rep. 27 C13
Medzilaborce, Slovak Rep. 27 B14
Medžitlija, Macedonia 40 F5
Meekatharra, Australia 93 E2
Meeker, U.S.A. 114 F10
Meelpaeg Res., Canada 103 C8
Meersburg, Germany 25 H5
Meerut, India 68 E7
Meeteetse, U.S.A. 114 D9
Mega, Ethiopia 81 G4
Megálo Khorío, Greece 39 E9
Megálo Petalí, Greece 38 D6
Megalópolis, Greece 38 D4
Meganísi, Greece 38 C2
Mégara, Greece 38 D5
Megasini, India 69 J12
Megdhova →, Greece 38 B3
Megève, France 21 C10
Meghalaya □, India 67 G17
Meghezez, Ethiopia 81 F4
Mégiscane, L., Canada 102 C4
Megiste, Greece 39 E11
Megra, Russia 46 B9
Mehadia, Romania 42 F7
Meharry, Mt., Australia 92 D2
Mehedeby, Sweden 10 D11
Mehedinţi □, Romania 42 F7
Meheisa, Sudan 80 D3
Mehlville, U.S.A. 112 F9
Mehndawal, India 69 F10
Mehr Jān, Iran 71 C7
Mehrābād, Iran 70 B5
Mehrān, Iran 70 C5
Mehrīz, Iran 71 D7
Mehun-sur-Yèvre, France 19 E9
Mei Jiang →, China 59 E11
Mei Xian, China 56 G4
Meicheng, China 59 C12
Meichengzhen, China 59 C8
Meichuan, China 59 B10
Meigu, China 58 C4
Meiktila, Burma 67 J19
Meinerzhagen, Germany 24 D3
Meiningen, Germany 24 E6
Meira, Serra de, Spain 34 B3
Meiringen, Switz. 25 J4
Meishan, China 58 B4
Meissen, Germany 24 D9
Meissner, Germany 24 D5
Meitan, China 58 D6
Meizhou, China 59 E11
Meja, India 69 G10
Mejillones, Chile 126 A1
Mekdela, Ethiopia 81 E4
Mekele, Ethiopia 81 E4
Mekhtar, Pakistan 66 D6
Meknès, Morocco 78 B4
Meko, Nigeria 83 D5
Mekong →, Asia 65 H6
Mekongga, Indonesia 63 E6
Mekrou →, Benin 83 C5
Mekvari = Kür →, Azerbaijan 73 C13
Mel, Italy 29 B9
Melagiri Hills, India 66 N10
Melaka, Malaysia 65 L4
Melalap, Malaysia 62 C5

Mélambes, *Greece* 36 D6
Melanesia, *Pac. Oc.* 96 H7
Melbourne, *Australia* 95 F4
Melbourne, *U.S.A.* 109 L5
Melchor Múzquiz, *Mexico* 118 B4
Melchor Ocampo, *Mexico* 118 C4
Méldola, *Italy* 29 D9
Meldorf, *Germany* 24 A5
Melegnano, *Italy* 28 C6
Melenci, *Serbia, Yug.* 42 E5
Melenki, *Russia* 48 C5
Mélèzes →, *Qué., Canada* 101 C12
Mélèzes →, *Qué., Canada* 102 A5
Melfi, *Italy* 31 B8
Melfort, *Canada* 105 C8
Melfort, *Zimbabwe* 87 F3
Melgaço, *Portugal* 34 C2
Melgar de Fernamental, *Spain* 34 C6
Melhus, *Norway* 8 E14
Melide, *Spain* 34 C2
Meligalá, *Greece* 38 D3
Melilla, *N. Afr.* 78 A5
Melilli, *Italy* 31 E8
Melipilla, *Chile* 126 C1
Mélissa, Ákra, *Greece* 36 D6
Mélissa Óros, *Greece* 39 D8
Melita, *Canada* 105 D8
Mélito di Porto Salvo, *Italy* 31 E8
Melitopol, *Ukraine* 47 J8
Melk, *Austria* 26 C8
Mellan Fryken, *Sweden* 10 E7
Mellansel, *Sweden* 8 E18
Mellbystrand, *Sweden* 11 H6
Melle, *France* 20 B3
Melle, *Germany* 24 C4
Mellen, *U.S.A.* 112 B9
Mellerud, *Sweden* 11 F6
Mellette, *U.S.A.* 112 C5
Mellid = Melide, *Spain* 34 C2
Mellieha, *Malta* 36 D1
Mellit, *Sudan* 81 E2
Mellrichstadt, *Germany* 24 E6
Melnik, *Bulgaria* 40 E7
Mělník, *Czech Rep.* 26 A7
Melo, *Uruguay* 127 C5
Melolo, *Indonesia* 63 F6
Melouprey, *Cambodia* 64 F5
Melrose, *Australia* 95 E4
Melrose, *U.K.* 14 F6
Melrose, *Minn., U.S.A.* 112 C7
Melrose, *N. Mex., U.S.A.* 113 H3
Melstone, *U.S.A.* 114 C10
Melsungen, *Germany* 24 D5
Melton Mowbray, *U.K.* 12 E7
Melun, *France* 19 D9
Melut, *Sudan* 81 E3
Melville, *Canada* 105 C8
Melville, C., *Australia* 94 A3
Melville, L., *Canada* 103 B8
Melville B., *Australia* 94 A2
Melville I., *Australia* 92 B5
Melville I., *Canada* 4 B2
Melville Pen., *Canada* 101 B11
Mélykút, *Hungary* 42 D4
Memaliaj, *Albania* 40 F3
Memba, *Mozam.* 87 E5
Memboro, *Indonesia* 63 F5
Membrilla, *Spain* 35 G7
Memel = Klaipėda, *Lithuania* 9 J19
Memel, *S. Africa* 89 D4
Memmingen, *Germany* 25 H6
Mempawah, *Indonesia* 62 D3
Memphis, *Egypt* 80 J7
Memphis, *Mich., U.S.A.* 110 D2
Memphis, *Tenn., U.S.A.* 113 H10
Memphis, *Tex., U.S.A.* 113 H4
Memphremagog, L., *U.S.A.* 111 B12
Mena, *Ukraine* 47 G7
Mena, *U.S.A.* 113 H7
Mena →, *Ethiopia* 81 F5
Menai Strait, *U.K.* 12 D3
Ménaka, *Mali* 83 B5
Menan = Chao Phraya →, *Thailand* 64 F3
Menarandra →, *Madag.* 89 D7
Menard, *U.S.A.* 113 K5
Menawashei, *Sudan* 81 E1
Mendawai →, *Indonesia* 62 E4
Mende, *France* 20 D7
Mendebo, *Ethiopia* 81 F4
Menden, *Germany* 24 D3
Menderes, *Turkey* 39 C9
Mendez, *Mexico* 119 B5
Mendhar, *India* 69 C6
Mendi, *Ethiopia* 81 F4
Mendip Hills, *U.K.* 13 F5
Mendocino, *U.S.A.* 114 G2
Mendocino, C., *U.S.A.* 114 F1
Mendooran, *Australia* 95 E4
Mendota, *Calif., U.S.A.* 116 J6
Mendota, *Ill., U.S.A.* 112 E10
Mendoza, *Argentina* 126 C2
Mendoza □, *Argentina* 126 C2
Mene Grande, *Venezuela* 124 B4
Menemen, *Turkey* 39 C9
Menen, *Belgium* 17 D3
Menfi, *Italy* 30 E5
Mengdingjie, *China* 58 F2
Mengeš, *Slovenia* 29 B11
Menggala, *Indonesia* 62 E3
Menghai, *China* 58 G3
Mengíbar, *Spain* 35 H7
Mengjin, *China* 56 G7
Mengla, *China* 58 G3
Menglian, *China* 58 F2
Mengshan, *China* 59 E8
Mengyin, *China* 57 G9
Mengzhe, *China* 58 F3
Mengzi, *China* 58 F4
Menihek, *Canada* 103 B6
Menihek L., *Canada* 103 B6
Menin = Menen, *Belgium* 17 D3
Menindee, *Australia* 95 E3
Menindee L., *Australia* 95 E3
Meningie, *Australia* 95 F2
Menlo Park, *U.S.A.* 116 H4
Menominee, *U.S.A.* 108 C2
Menominee →, *U.S.A.* 108 C2
Menomonie, *U.S.A.* 112 C9
Menongue, *Angola* 85 G3
Menorca, *Spain* 37 B11
Mentakab, *Malaysia* 65 L4
Mentawai, Kepulauan, *Indonesia* 62 E1
Menton, *France* 21 E11
Mentor, *U.S.A.* 110 E3
Menzies, *Australia* 93 E3
Meob B., *Namibia* 88 B2
Me'ona, *Israel* 75 B4
Meoqui, *Mexico* 118 B3
Mepaco, *Mozam.* 87 F3
Meppel, *Neths.* 17 B6
Meppen, *Germany* 24 C3
Mequinenza, *Spain* 32 D5
Mequinenza, Embalse de, *Spain* 32 D5
Mer, *France* 18 E8
Merabéllou, Kólpos, *Greece* 36 D7
Merak, *Indonesia* 63 F12
Meramangye, L., *Australia* 93 E5
Meran = Merano, *Italy* 29 B8
Merano, *Italy* 29 B8
Merate, *Italy* 28 C6
Merauke, *Indonesia* 63 F10
Merbein, *Australia* 95 E3
Merca, *Somali Rep.* 74 G3
Mercato Saraceno, *Italy* 29 E9
Merced, *U.S.A.* 116 H6
Merced →, *U.S.A.* 116 H6
Merced Pk., *U.S.A.* 116 H7
Mercedes, *Buenos Aires, Argentina* 126 C4
Mercedes, *Corrientes, Argentina* 126 B4
Mercedes, *San Luis, Argentina* 126 C2
Mercedes, *Uruguay* 126 C4
Mercedes, *U.S.A.* 113 M6
Merceditas, *Chile* 126 B1
Mercer, *N.Z.* 91 G5
Mercer, *U.S.A.* 110 E4
Mercer Island, *U.S.A.* 116 C4
Mercury, *U.S.A.* 117 J11
Mercy C., *Canada* 101 B13
Merdrignac, *France* 18 D4
Mere, *U.K.* 13 F5
Meredith, C., *Falk. Is.* 128 G4
Meredith, L., *U.S.A.* 113 H4
Merefa, *Ukraine* 47 H9
Merei, *Romania* 43 E11
Merga = Nukheila, *Sudan* 80 D2
Mergui, *Burma* 64 F2
Mergui Arch. = Myeik Kyunzu, *Burma* 65 G1
Meriç, *Turkey* 41 E10
Meriç →, *Turkey* 41 F10
Mérida, *Mexico* 119 C7
Mérida, *Spain* 35 G4
Mérida, *Venezuela* 124 B4
Mérida, Cord. de, *Venezuela* 122 C3
Meriden, *U.K.* 13 E6
Meriden, *U.S.A.* 111 E12
Meridian, *Calif., U.S.A.* 116 F5
Meridian, *Idaho, U.S.A.* 114 E5
Meridian, *Miss., U.S.A.* 109 J1
Mérignac, *France* 20 D3
Merimbula, *Australia* 95 F4
Mérinaghène, *Senegal* 82 B1
Merinda, *Australia* 94 C4
Mering, *Germany* 25 G6
Meringa, *Nigeria* 83 C7
Meringur, *Australia* 95 E3
Merir, *Pac. Oc.* 63 D8
Merirumã, *Brazil* 125 C8
Merkel, *U.S.A.* 113 J5
Mermaid Reef, *Australia* 92 C2
Merowe, *Sudan* 80 D3
Merredin, *Australia* 93 F2
Merrick, *U.K.* 14 F4
Merrickville, *Canada* 111 B9
Merrill, *Oreg., U.S.A.* 114 E3
Merrill, *Wis., U.S.A.* 112 C10
Merrimack →, *U.S.A.* 111 D14
Merriman, *U.S.A.* 112 D4
Merritt, *Canada* 104 C4
Merritt Island, *U.S.A.* 109 L5
Merriwa, *Australia* 95 E5
Merry I., *Canada* 102 A4
Merryville, *U.S.A.* 113 K8
Mersa Fatma, *Eritrea* 81 E5
Mersch, *Lux.* 17 E6
Merse →, *Italy* 29 E8
Mersea I., *U.K.* 13 F8
Merseburg, *Germany* 24 D7
Mersey →, *U.K.* 12 D4
Merseyside □, *U.K.* 12 D4
Mersin, *Turkey* 70 B2
Mersing, *Malaysia* 65 L4
Merta, *India* 68 F6
Merta Road, *India* 68 F5
Merthyr Tydfil, *U.K.* 13 F4
Merthyr Tydfil □, *U.K.* 13 F4
Mértola, *Portugal* 35 H3
Mertzon, *U.S.A.* 113 K4
Méru, *France* 19 C9
Meru, *Kenya* 86 B4
Meru, *Tanzania* 86 C4
Merville, *France* 19 B9
Méry-sur-Seine, *France* 19 D10
Merzifon, *Turkey* 72 B6
Merzig, *Germany* 25 F2
Mesa, *U.S.A.* 115 K8
Mesa Verde National Park, *U.S.A.* 115 H9
Mesagne, *Italy* 31 B10
Mesanagrós, *Greece* 36 C9
Mesaoría □, *Cyprus* 36 D12
Mesarás, Kólpos, *Greece* 36 D6
Meschede, *Germany* 24 D4
Mescit, *Turkey* 73 B9
Mesfinto, *Ethiopia* 81 E4
Mesgouez, L., *Canada* 102 B5
Meshchovsk, *Russia* 46 E8
Meshed = Mashhad, *Iran* 71 B8
Meshoppen, *U.S.A.* 111 E8
Meshra er Req, *Sudan* 81 F2
Mesilinka →, *Canada* 104 B4
Mesilla, *U.S.A.* 115 K10
Meslay-du-Maine, *France* 18 E6
Mesocco, *Switz.* 25 J5
Mesolóngion, *Greece* 38 C3
Mesopotamia = Al Jazirah, *Iraq* 70 C5
Mesopotamia, *U.S.A.* 110 E4
Mesopótamon, *Greece* 38 B2
Mesoraca, *Italy* 31 C9
Mésou Volímais = Volímai, *Greece* 38 D2
Mesquite, *U.S.A.* 115 H6
Messac, *France* 18 E5
Messad, *Algeria* 78 B6
Messalo →, *Mozam.* 87 E4
Méssaména, *Cameroon* 83 E7
Messeue, *Greece* 38 D3
Messina, *Italy* 31 D8
Messina, *S. Africa* 89 C5
Messina, Str. di, *Italy* 31 D8
Messíni, *Greece* 38 D4
Messinía □, *Greece* 38 D3
Messiniakós Kólpos, *Greece* 38 E4
Messkirch, *Germany* 25 H5
Messonghi, *Greece* 36 B3
Mesta →, *Bulgaria* 40 E7
Mestá, Ákra, *Greece* 39 C7
Mestanza, *Spain* 35 G6
Mestre, *Italy* 29 C9
Mesudiye, *Turkey* 72 B7
Meta →, *S. Amer.* 122 C4
Meta Incognita Peninsula, *Canada* 101 B13
Metabetchouan, *Canada* 103 C5
Metairie, *U.S.A.* 113 L9
Metalici, Munţii, *Romania* 42 D7
Metaline Falls, *U.S.A.* 114 B5
Metallifere, Colline, *Italy* 28 E8
Metán, *Argentina* 126 B3
Metangula, *Mozam.* 87 E3
Metauro →, *Italy* 29 E10
Metema, *Ethiopia* 81 E4
Metengobalame, *Mozam.* 87 E3
Méthana, *Greece* 38 D5
Methóni, *Greece* 38 E3
Methven, *N.Z.* 91 K3
Metil, *Mozam.* 87 F4
Metkovets, *Bulgaria* 40 C7
Metković, *Croatia* 29 E14
Metlakatla, *U.S.A.* 100 C6
Metlika, *Slovenia* 29 C12
Metropolis, *U.S.A.* 113 G10
Métsovon, *Greece* 38 B3
Mettur Dam, *India* 66 P10
Metu, *Ethiopia* 81 F4
Metz, *France* 19 C13
Metzingen, *Germany* 25 G5
Meulaboh, *Indonesia* 62 D1
Meung-sur-Loire, *France* 19 E8
Meureudu, *Indonesia* 62 C1
Meurthe →, *France* 19 D13
Meurthe-et-Moselle □, *France* 19 D13
Meuse □, *France* 19 C12
Meuse →, *Europe* 17 D5
Meuselwitz, *Germany* 24 D8
Mexia, *U.S.A.* 113 K6
Mexiana, I., *Brazil* 125 D9
Mexicali, *Mexico* 117 N11
Mexican Plateau, *Mexico* 98 G9
Mexican Water, *U.S.A.* 115 H9
México, *Mexico* 119 D5
Mexico, *Maine, U.S.A.* 111 B14
Mexico, *Mo., U.S.A.* 112 F9
Mexico, *N.Y., U.S.A.* 111 C8
México □, *Mexico* 119 D5
Mexico ■, *Cent. Amer.* 118 C4
Mexico, G. of, *Cent. Amer.* 119 C7
Mexico B., *U.S.A.* 111 C8
Meydān-e Naftūn, *Iran* 71 D6
Meydani, Ra's-e, *Iran* 71 E8
Meyenburg, *Germany* 24 B8
Meymac, *France* 20 C6
Meymaneh, *Afghan.* 66 B4
Meyrueis, *France* 20 D7
Meyssac, *France* 20 C5
Meyzieu, *France* 21 C8
Mezdra, *Bulgaria* 40 C7
Mèze, *France* 20 E7
Mezen, *Russia* 50 C5
Mezen →, *Russia* 50 C5
Mézenc, Mt., *France* 21 D8
Mezeş, Munţii, *Romania* 42 C8
Mezha →, *Russia* 46 E6
Mezhdurechenskiy, *Russia* 50 D7
Mézidon-Canon, *France* 18 C6
Mézières-en-Brenne, *France* 20 B5
Mézilhac, *France* 21 D8
Mézin, *France* 20 D4
Mezőberény, *Hungary* 42 D6
Mezőfalva, *Hungary* 42 D3
Mezőhegyes, *Hungary* 42 D5
Mezőkövácsháza, *Hungary* 42 D5
Mezőkövesd, *Hungary* 42 C5
Mézos, *France* 20 D2
Mezőtúr, *Hungary* 42 C5
Mezquital, *Mexico* 118 C4
Mezzolombardo, *Italy* 28 B8
Mfolozi →, *S. Africa* 89 D5
Mgeta, *Tanzania* 87 D4
Mglin, *Russia* 47 F7
Mhlaba Hills, *Zimbabwe* 87 F3
Mhow, *India* 68 H6
Miahuatlán, *Mexico* 119 D5
Miajadas, *Spain* 35 F5
Miami, *Fla., U.S.A.* 109 N5
Miami, *Okla., U.S.A.* 113 G7
Miami, *Tex., U.S.A.* 113 H4
Miami Beach, *U.S.A.* 109 N5
Mian Xian, *China* 56 H4
Mianchi, *China* 56 G6
Mīāndarreh, *Iran* 71 C7
Mīāndowāb, *Iran* 70 B5
Miandrivazo, *Madag.* 89 B8
Mīāneh, *Iran* 70 B5
Mianning, *China* 58 C4
Mianwali, *Pakistan* 68 C4
Mianyang, *China* 58 B5
Mianzhu, *China* 58 B5
Miaoli, *Taiwan* 59 E13
Miarinarivo, *Antanarivo, Madag.* 89 B8
Miarinarivo, *Toamasina, Madag.* 89 B8
Miariravaratra, *Madag.* 89 C8
Miass, *Russia* 50 D7
Miasteczko Krajeńskie, *Poland* 45 E4
Miastko, *Poland* 44 E3
Mica, *S. Africa* 89 C5
Micăsasa, *Romania* 43 D9
Michalovce, *Slovak Rep.* 27 C14
Michigan □, *U.S.A.* 108 C3
Michigan, L., *U.S.A.* 108 D2
Michigan City, *U.S.A.* 108 E2
Michika, *Nigeria* 83 C7
Michipicoten I., *Canada* 102 C2
Michoacan □, *Mexico* 118 D4
Michurin, *Bulgaria* 41 D11
Michurinsk, *Russia* 48 D5
Mico, Pta., *Nic.* 120 D3
Micronesia, *Pac. Oc.* 96 G7
Micronesia, Federated States of ■, *Pac. Oc.* 96 G7
Midai, *Indonesia* 65 L6
Midale, *Canada* 105 D8
Middelburg, *Neths.* 17 C3
Middelburg, *Eastern Cape, S. Africa* 88 E4
Middelburg, *Mpumalanga, S. Africa* 89 D4
Middelfart, *Denmark* 11 J3
Middelpos, *S. Africa* 88 E3
Middelwit, *S. Africa* 88 C4
Middle Alkali L., *U.S.A.* 114 F3
Middle Bass I., *U.S.A.* 110 E2
Middle East, *Asia* 52 F7
Middle Fork Feather →, *U.S.A.* 116 F5
Middle I., *Australia* 93 F3
Middle Loup →, *U.S.A.* 112 E5
Middle Sackville, *Canada* 103 D7
Middleboro, *U.S.A.* 111 E14
Middleburg, *Fla., U.S.A.* 109 K5
Middleburg, *N.Y., U.S.A.* 111 D10
Middleburg, *Pa., U.S.A.* 110 F7
Middlebury, *U.S.A.* 111 B11
Middlemount, *Australia* 94 C4
Middleport, *N.Y., U.S.A.* 110 C6
Middleport, *Ohio, U.S.A.* 108 F4
Middlesboro, *U.S.A.* 109 G4
Middlesbrough, *U.K.* 12 C6
Middlesbrough □, *U.K.* 12 C6
Middlesex, *Belize* 120 C2
Middlesex, *N.J., U.S.A.* 111 F10
Middlesex, *N.Y., U.S.A.* 110 D7
Middleton, *Australia* 94 C3
Middleton, *Canada* 103 D6
Middleton Cr. →, *Australia* 94 C3
Middletown, *U.K.* 15 B5
Middletown, *Calif., U.S.A.* 116 G4
Middletown, *Conn., U.S.A.* 111 E12
Middletown, *N.Y., U.S.A.* 111 E10
Middletown, *Ohio, U.S.A.* 108 F3
Middletown, *Pa., U.S.A.* 111 F8
Midhurst, *U.K.* 13 G7
Mīdī, *Yemen* 81 D5
Midi, Canal du →, *France* 20 E5
Midi d'Ossau, Pic du, *France* 20 F3
Midi-Pyrénées □, *France* 20 E5
Midland, *Canada* 102 D4
Midland, *Calif., U.S.A.* 117 M12
Midland, *Mich., U.S.A.* 108 D3
Midland, *Pa., U.S.A.* 110 F4
Midland, *Tex., U.S.A.* 113 K3
Midlands □, *Zimbabwe* 87 F2
Midleton, *Ireland* 15 E3
Midlothian, *U.S.A.* 113 J6
Midlothian □, *U.K.* 14 F5
Midongy, Tangorombohitr' i, *Madag.* 89 C8
Midongy Atsimo, *Madag.* 89 C8
Midou →, *France* 20 E3
Midouze →, *France* 20 E3
Midsayap, *Phil.* 61 H6
Midu, *China* 58 E3
Midway Is., *Pac. Oc.* 96 E10
Midway Wells, *U.S.A.* 117 N11
Midwest, *U.S.A.* 107 B9
Midwest, *Wyo., U.S.A.* 114 E10
Midwest City, *U.S.A.* 113 H6
Midyat, *Turkey* 70 B4
Midžor, *Bulgaria* 40 C6
Mie □, *Japan* 55 G8
Miechów, *Poland* 45 H7
Miedwie, Jezioro, *Poland* 45 E1
Międzybórz, *Poland* 45 G4
Międzychód, *Poland* 45 F2
Międzylesie, *Poland* 45 H3
Międzyrzec Podlaski, *Poland* 45 G9
Międzyrzecz, *Poland* 45 F2
Międzyzdroje, *Poland* 44 E1
Miejska Górka, *Poland* 45 G3
Miélan, *France* 20 E4
Mielec, *Poland* 45 H8
Mienga, *Angola* 88 B2
Miercurea-Ciuc, *Romania* 43 D10
Miercurea Sibiului, *Romania* 43 E8
Mieres, *Spain* 34 B5
Mieroszów, *Poland* 45 H3
Mieso, *Ethiopia* 81 F5
Mieszkowice, *Poland* 45 F1
Mifflintown, *U.S.A.* 110 F7
Mifraz Hefa, *Israel* 75 C4
Migennes, *France* 19 E10
Migliarino, *Italy* 29 D8
Miguel Alemán, Presa, *Mexico* 119 D5
Miguelturra, *Spain* 35 G7
Mihăileni, *Romania* 43 C11
Mihăileşti, *Romania* 43 F10
Mihailovca, *Moldova* 43 D13
Mihalgazi, *Turkey* 39 A12
Mihaliççık, *Turkey* 72 C4
Mihara, *Japan* 55 G6
Miheşu de Cîmpie, *Romania* 43 D9
Mijas, *Spain* 35 J6
Mikese, *Tanzania* 86 D4
Mikha-Tskhakaya = Senaki, *Georgia* 49 J6
Mikhailovka = Mykhaylivka, *Ukraine* 47 J8
Mikhaylov, *Russia* 46 E10
Mikhaylovgrad = Montana, *Bulgaria* 40 C7
Mikhaylovka, *Russia* 48 E6
Mikhnevo, *Russia* 46 E9
Mikínai, *Greece* 38 D4
Mikkeli, *Finland* 9 F22
Mikkwa →, *Canada* 104 B6
Mikniya, *Sudan* 81 D3
Mikołajki, *Poland* 44 E8
Míkonos, *Greece* 39 D7
Mikrí Préspa, Límni, *Greece* 40 F5
Mikrón Dhérion, *Greece* 41 E10
Mikstat, *Poland* 45 G4
Mikulov, *Czech Rep.* 27 C9
Mikumi, *Tanzania* 86 D4
Milaca, *U.S.A.* 112 C8
Milagro, *Ecuador* 124 D3
Milagros, *Phil.* 61 E5
Milan = Milano, *Italy* 28 C6
Milan, *Mo., U.S.A.* 112 E8
Milan, *Tenn., U.S.A.* 109 H1
Milang, *Australia* 95 F2
Milange, *Mozam.* 87 F4
Milano, *Italy* 28 C6
Milanoa, *Madag.* 89 A8
Milâs, *Turkey* 39 D9
Mílatos, *Greece* 36 D7
Milazzo, *Italy* 31 D8
Milbank, *U.S.A.* 112 C6
Milbanke Sd., *Canada* 104 C3
Milden, *Canada* 105 C7
Mildenhall, *U.K.* 13 E8
Mildmay, *Canada* 110 B3
Mildura, *Australia* 95 E3
Mile, *China* 58 E4
Miléai, *Greece* 38 B5
Miles, *Australia* 95 D5
Miles City, *U.S.A.* 112 B2
Mileşti, *Moldova* 43 C13
Milestone, *Canada* 105 D8
Mileto, *Italy* 31 D9
Miletto, Mte., *Italy* 31 A7
Miletus, *Turkey* 39 D9
Milevsko, *Czech Rep.* 26 B7
Milford, *Calif., U.S.A.* 116 E6
Milford, *Conn., U.S.A.* 111 E11
Milford, *Del., U.S.A.* 108 F8
Milford, *Mass., U.S.A.* 111 D13
Milford, *N.H., U.S.A.* 111 D13
Milford, *Pa., U.S.A.* 111 E10
Milford, *Utah, U.S.A.* 115 G7
Milford Haven, *U.K.* 13 F2
Milford Sd., *N.Z.* 91 L1
Milh, Bahr al, *Iraq* 70 C4
Milicz, *Poland* 45 G4
Milikapiti, *Australia* 92 B5
Miling, *Australia* 93 F2
Militello in Val di Catánia, *Italy* 31 E7
Milk →, *U.S.A.* 114 B10
Milk, Wadi el →, *Sudan* 80 D3
Milk River, *Canada* 104 D6
Mill I., *Antarctica* 5 C8
Mill Valley, *U.S.A.* 116 H4
Millárs →, *Spain* 32 F4
Millau, *France* 20 D7
Millbridge, *Canada* 110 B7
Millbrook, *Canada* 110 B6
Millbrook, *U.S.A.* 111 E11
Mille Lacs, L. des, *Canada* 102 C1
Mille Lacs L., *U.S.A.* 112 B8
Milledgeville, *U.S.A.* 109 J4
Millen, *U.S.A.* 109 J5
Miller, *U.S.A.* 112 C5
Millerovo, *Russia* 49 F5
Millersburg, *Ohio, U.S.A.* 110 F3
Millersburg, *Pa., U.S.A.* 110 F8
Millerton, *U.S.A.* 111 E11
Millerton L., *U.S.A.* 116 J7
Millevaches, Plateau de, *France* 20 C6
Millheim, *U.S.A.* 110 F7
Millicent, *Australia* 95 F3

Millington, *U.S.A.* 113 H10
Millinocket, *U.S.A.* 109 C11
Millmerran, *Australia* 95 D5
Millom, *U.K.* 12 C4
Mills L., *Canada* 104 A5
Millsboro, *U.S.A.* 110 G5
Milltown Malbay, *Ireland* 15 D2
Millville, *N.J., U.S.A.* 108 F8
Millville, *Pa., U.S.A.* 111 E8
Millwood L., *U.S.A.* 113 J8
Milna, *Croatia* 29 E13
Milne →, *Australia* 94 C2
Milo, *U.S.A.* 109 C11
Mílos, *Greece* 38 E6
Miłosław, *Poland* 45 F4
Milot, *Albania* 40 E3
Milparinka, *Australia* 95 D3
Miltenberg, *Germany* 25 F5
Milton, *N.S., Canada* 103 D7
Milton, *Ont., Canada* 110 C5
Milton, *N.Z.* 91 M2
Milton, *Calif., U.S.A.* 116 G6
Milton, *Fla., U.S.A.* 109 K2
Milton, *Pa., U.S.A.* 110 F8
Milton, *Vt., U.S.A.* 111 B11
Milton-Freewater, *U.S.A.* 114 D4
Milton Keynes, *U.K.* 13 E7
Milton Keynes □, *U.K.* 13 E7
Miluo, *China* 59 C9
Milverton, *Canada* 110 C4
Milwaukee, *U.S.A.* 108 D2
Milwaukee Deep, *Atl. Oc.* 121 C6
Milwaukie, *U.S.A.* 116 E4
Mim, *Ghana* 82 D4
Mimizan, *France* 20 D2
Mimoň, *Czech Rep.* 26 A7
Min Jiang →, *Fujian, China* 59 E12
Min Jiang →, *Sichuan, China* 58 C5
Min Xian, *China* 56 G3
Mina Pirquitas, *Argentina* 126 A2
Mīnā Su'ud, *Si. Arabia* 71 D6
Mīnā'al Aḥmadī, *Kuwait* 71 D6
Minago →, *Canada* 105 C9
Minaki, *Canada* 105 D10
Minamata, *Japan* 55 H5
Minami-Tori-Shima, *Pac. Oc.* 96 E7
Minas, *Uruguay* 127 C4
Minas, Sierra de las, *Guatemala* 120 C2
Minas Basin, *Canada* 103 C7
Minas de Rio Tinto = Minas de Riotinto, *Spain* 35 H4
Minas de Riotinto, *Spain* 35 H4
Minas Gerais □, *Brazil* 125 G9
Minatitlán, *Mexico* 119 D6
Minbu, *Burma* 67 J19
Minchinabad, *Pakistan* 68 D5
Mincio →, *Italy* 28 C7
Minčol, *Slovak Rep.* 27 B13
Mindanao, *Phil.* 61 H6
Mindanao Sea = Bohol Sea, *Phil.* 63 C6
Mindanao Trench, *Pac. Oc.* 61 F7
Mindel →, *Germany* 25 G6
Mindelheim, *Germany* 25 G6
Minden, *Canada* 110 B6
Minden, *Germany* 24 C4
Minden, *La., U.S.A.* 113 J8
Minden, *Nev., U.S.A.* 116 G7
Mindiptana, *Indonesia* 63 F10
Mindoro, *Phil.* 61 E4
Mindoro Str., *Phil.* 61 E4
Mine, *Japan* 55 G5
Minehead, *U.K.* 13 F4
Mineola, *N.Y., U.S.A.* 111 F11
Mineola, *Tex., U.S.A.* 113 J7
Mineral King, *U.S.A.* 116 J8
Mineral Wells, *U.S.A.* 113 J5
Mineralnyye Vody, *Russia* 49 H6
Minersville, *U.S.A.* 111 F8
Minerva, *U.S.A.* 110 F3
Minervino Murge, *Italy* 31 A9
Minetto, *U.S.A.* 111 C8
Mingäçevir, *Azerbaijan* 49 K8
Mingäçevir Su Anbarı, *Azerbaijan* 49 K8
Mingan, *Canada* 103 B7
Mingechaur = Mingäçevir, *Azerbaijan* 49 K8
Mingechaurskoye Vdkhr. = Mingäçevir Su Anbarı, *Azerbaijan* 49 K8
Mingela, *Australia* 94 B4
Mingenew, *Australia* 93 E2
Mingera Cr. →, *Australia* 94 C2
Minggang, *China* 59 A10
Mingguang, *China* 59 A11
Mingin, *Burma* 67 H19
Mingir, *Moldova* 43 D13
Minglanilla, *Spain* 33 F3
Minglun, *China* 58 E7
Mingo Junction, *U.S.A.* 110 F4
Mingorria, *Spain* 34 E6
Mingshan, *China* 58 B4
Mingxi, *China* 59 D11
Mingyuegue, *China* 57 C15
Minho = Miño →, *Spain* 34 D2
Minhou, *China* 59 E12
Miničevo, *Serbia, Yug.* 42 G7
Minidoka, *U.S.A.* 114 E7
Minigwal, L., *Australia* 93 E3
Minilya →, *Australia* 93 D1
Minilya Roadhouse, *Australia* 93 D1
Minipi L., *Canada* 103 B7
Mink L., *Canada* 104 A5
Minkammen, *Sudan* 81 F3
Minna, *Nigeria* 83 D6
Minneapolis, *Kans., U.S.A.* 112 F6
Minneapolis, *Minn., U.S.A.* 112 C8
Minnedosa, *Canada* 105 C9
Minnesota □, *U.S.A.* 112 B8
Minnesota →, *U.S.A.* 112 C8
Minnewaukan, *U.S.A.* 112 A5
Minnipa, *Australia* 95 E2
Minnitaki L., *Canada* 102 C1
Mino, *Japan* 55 G8
Miño, *Spain* 34 B2
Miño →, *Spain* 34 D2
Minoa, *Greece* 39 F7
Minorca = Menorca, *Spain* 37 B11
Minot, *U.S.A.* 112 A4
Minqin, *China* 56 E2
Minqing, *China* 59 D12
Minsen, *Germany* 24 B3
Minsk, *Belarus* 46 F4
Mińsk Mazowiecki, *Poland* 45 F8
Mintabie, *Australia* 95 D1
Mintaka Pass, *Pakistan* 69 A6
Minteke Daban = Mintaka Pass, *Pakistan* 69 A6
Minto, *Canada* 103 C6
Minto, L., *Canada* 102 A5
Minton, *Canada* 105 D8
Minturn, *U.S.A.* 114 G10
Minturno, *Italy* 30 A6
Minûf, *Egypt* 80 H7
Minusinsk, *Russia* 51 D10
Minutang, *India* 67 E20
Minya el Qamh, *Egypt* 80 H7
Mionica, *Bos.-H.* 42 F3
Mionica, *Serbia, Yug.* 40 B4
Miquelon, *Canada* 102 C4
Miquelon, *St- P. & M.* 103 C8
Mir, *Niger* 83 C7
Mīr Kūh, *Iran* 71 E8
Mīr Shahdād, *Iran* 71 E8
Mira, *Italy* 29 C9
Mira, *Portugal* 34 E2
Mira →, *Portugal* 35 H2
Mira por vos Cay, *Bahamas* 121 B5
Mirabella Eclano, *Italy* 31 A7
Miraj, *India* 66 L9
Miram Shah, *Pakistan* 68 C4
Miramar, *Argentina* 126 D4
Miramar, *Mozam.* 89 C6
Miramas, *France* 21 E8
Mirambeau, *France* 20 C3
Miramichi, *Canada* 103 C6
Miramichi B., *Canada* 103 C7
Miramont-de-Guyenne, *France* 20 D4
Miranda, *Brazil* 125 H7
Miranda →, *Brazil* 124 G7
Miranda de Ebro, *Spain* 32 C2
Miranda do Corvo, *Portugal* 34 E2
Miranda do Douro, *Portugal* 34 D4
Mirande, *France* 20 E4
Mirandela, *Portugal* 34 D3
Mirándola, *Italy* 28 D8
Mirandópolis, *Brazil* 127 A5
Mirango, *Malawi* 87 E3
Mirano, *Italy* 29 C9
Miras, *Albania* 40 F4
Mirassol, *Brazil* 127 A6
Mirbāţ, *Oman* 74 D5
Mirear, *Egypt* 80 C4
Mirebeau, *Côte-d'Or, France* 19 E12
Mirebeau, *Vienne, France* 18 F7
Mirecourt, *France* 19 D13
Mirgorod = Myrhorod, *Ukraine* 47 H7
Miri, *Malaysia* 62 D4
Miriam Vale, *Australia* 94 C5
Miribel, *France* 19 G11
Mirim, L., *S. Amer.* 127 C5
Mirnyy, *Russia* 51 C12
Miroč, *Serbia, Yug.* 40 B6
Mirokhan, *Pakistan* 68 F3
Mirond L., *Canada* 105 B8
Mirosławiec, *Poland* 44 E3
Mirpur, *Pakistan* 69 C5
Mirpur Batoro, *Pakistan* 68 G3
Mirpur Bibiwari, *Pakistan* 68 E2
Mirpur Khas, *Pakistan* 68 G3
Mirpur Sakro, *Pakistan* 68 G2
Mirria, *Niger* 83 C6
Mirsk, *Poland* 45 H2
Mirtağ, *Turkey* 70 B4
Miryang, *S. Korea* 57 G15
Mirzaani, *Georgia* 49 K8
Mirzapur, *India* 69 G10
Mirzapur-cum-Vindhyachal = Mirzapur, *India* 69 G10
Misantla, *Mexico* 119 D5
Misawa, *Japan* 54 D10
Miscou I., *Canada* 103 C7
Mish'āb, Ra's al, *Si. Arabia* 71 D6
Mishan, *China* 60 B8
Mishawaka, *U.S.A.* 108 E2
Mishbih, Gebel, *Egypt* 80 C3
Mishima, *Japan* 55 G9
Misión, *Mexico* 117 N10
Misiones □, *Argentina* 127 B5
Misiones □, *Paraguay* 126 B4
Miskah, *Si. Arabia* 70 E4
Miskitos, Cayos, *Nic.* 120 D3
Miskolc, *Hungary* 42 B5
Misoke, *Dem. Rep. of the Congo* 86 C2
Misool, *Indonesia* 63 E8
Misrātah, *Libya* 79 B9
Missanabie, *Canada* 102 C3
Missinaibi →, *Canada* 102 B3
Missinaibi L., *Canada* 102 C3
Mission, *Canada* 104 D4
Mission, *S. Dak., U.S.A.* 112 D4
Mission, *Tex., U.S.A.* 113 M5
Mission Beach, *Australia* 94 B4
Mission Viejo, *U.S.A.* 117 M9
Missirah, *Senegal* 82 C1
Missisa L., *Canada* 102 B2
Missisicabi →, *Canada* 102 B4
Mississagi →, *Canada* 102 C3
Mississauga, *Canada* 110 C5
Mississippi □, *U.S.A.* 113 J10
Mississippi →, *U.S.A.* 113 L10
Mississippi L., *Canada* 111 A8
Mississippi River Delta, *U.S.A.* 113 L9
Mississippi Sd., *U.S.A.* 113 K10
Missoula, *U.S.A.* 114 C7
Missouri □, *U.S.A.* 112 F8
Missouri →, *U.S.A.* 112 F9
Missouri City, *U.S.A.* 113 L7
Missouri Valley, *U.S.A.* 112 E7
Mist, *U.S.A.* 116 E3
Mistassibi →, *Canada* 103 B5
Mistassini, *Canada* 103 C5
Mistassini →, *Canada* 103 C5
Mistassini, L., *Canada* 102 B5
Mistastin L., *Canada* 103 A7
Mistelbach, *Austria* 27 C9
Misterbianco, *Italy* 31 E8
Mistinibi, L., *Canada* 103 A7
Mistretta, *Italy* 31 E7
Misty L., *Canada* 105 B8
Misurata = Misrātah, *Libya* 79 B9
Mît Ghamr, *Egypt* 80 H7
Mitatib, *Sudan* 81 D4
Mitchell, *Australia* 95 D4
Mitchell, *Canada* 110 C3
Mitchell, *Nebr., U.S.A.* 112 E3
Mitchell, *Oreg., U.S.A.* 114 D3
Mitchell, *S. Dak., U.S.A.* 112 D6
Mitchell →, *Australia* 94 B3
Mitchell, Mt., *U.S.A.* 109 H4
Mitchell Ranges, *Australia* 94 A2
Mitchelstown, *Ireland* 15 D3
Mitha Tiwana, *Pakistan* 68 C5
Mithi, *Pakistan* 68 G3
Míthimna, *Greece* 39 B8
Mithrao, *Pakistan* 68 F3
Mitilíni, *Greece* 39 B8
Mitilinoí, *Greece* 39 D8
Mito, *Japan* 55 F10
Mitrofanovka, *Russia* 47 H10
Mitrovica = Kosovska Mitrovica, *Kosovo, Yug.* 40 D4
Mitsinjo, *Madag.* 89 B8
Mitsiwa, *Eritrea* 81 D4
Mitsiwa Channel, *Eritrea* 81 D5
Mitsukaidō, *Japan* 55 F9
Mittagong, *Australia* 95 E5
Mittelberg, *Austria* 26 D3
Mittelfranken □, *Germany* 25 F6
Mittellandkanal →, *Germany* 24 C4
Mittenwalde, *Germany* 24 C9
Mittersill, *Austria* 26 D5
Mitterteich, *Germany* 25 F8
Mittweida, *Germany* 24 E8
Mitú, *Colombia* 124 C4
Mitumba, *Tanzania* 86 D3
Mitumba, Mts., *Dem. Rep. of the Congo* 86 D2
Mitwaba, *Dem. Rep. of the Congo* 87 D2
Mityana, *Uganda* 86 B3
Mixteco →, *Mexico* 119 D5
Miyagi □, *Japan* 54 E10
Miyâh, W. el →, *Egypt* 80 C3
Miyāh, W. el →, *Syria* 70 C3
Miyake-Jima, *Japan* 55 G9
Miyako, *Japan* 54 E10
Miyako-Jima, *Japan* 55 M2
Miyako-Rettō, *Japan* 55 M2
Miyakonojō, *Japan* 55 J5
Miyani, *India* 68 J3
Miyanoura-Dake, *Japan* 55 J5
Miyazaki, *Japan* 55 J5
Miyazaki □, *Japan* 55 H5
Miyazu, *Japan* 55 G7
Miyet, Bahr el = Dead Sea, *Asia* 75 D4
Miyi, *China* 58 D4
Miyoshi, *Japan* 55 G6
Miyun, *China* 56 D9
Miyun Shuiku, *China* 57 D9
Mizan Teferi, *Ethiopia* 81 F4
Mizdah, *Libya* 79 B8
Mizen Hd., *Cork, Ireland* 15 E2
Mizen Hd., *Wick., Ireland* 15 D5
Mizhi, *China* 56 F6
Mizil, *Romania* 43 F11
Mizoram □, *India* 67 H18
Mizpe Ramon, *Israel* 75 E3
Mizusawa, *Japan* 54 E10
Mjällby, *Sweden* 11 H8
Mjöbäck, *Sweden* 11 G6
Mjölby, *Sweden* 11 F9
Mjörn, *Sweden* 11 G6
Mjøsa, *Norway* 9 F14
Mkata, *Tanzania* 86 D4
Mkokotoni, *Tanzania* 86 D4
Mkomazi, *Tanzania* 86 C4
Mkomazi →, *S. Africa* 89 E5
Mkulwe, *Tanzania* 87 D3
Mkumbi, Ras, *Tanzania* 86 D4
Mkushi, *Zambia* 87 E2
Mkushi River, *Zambia* 87 E2
Mkuze, *S. Africa* 89 D5
Mladá Boleslav, *Czech Rep.* 26 A7
Mladenovac, *Serbia, Yug.* 40 B4
Mlala Hills, *Tanzania* 86 D3
Mlange = Mulanje, *Malawi* 87 F4
Mlanje, Pic, *Malawi* 85 H7
Mlava →, *Serbia, Yug.* 40 B5
Mława, *Poland* 45 E7
Mlinište, *Bos.-H.* 29 D13
Mljet, *Croatia* 29 F14
Mljetski Kanal, *Croatia* 29 F14
Młynary, *Poland* 44 D6
Mmabatho, *S. Africa* 88 D4
Mme, *Cameroon* 83 D7
Mnichovo Hradiště, *Czech Rep.* 26 A7
Mo i Rana, *Norway* 8 C16
Moa, *Cuba* 121 B4
Moa, *Indonesia* 63 F7
Moa →, *S. Leone* 82 D2
Moab, *U.S.A.* 115 G9
Moala, *Fiji* 91 D8
Moama, *Australia* 95 F3
Moamba, *Mozam.* 89 D5
Moapa, *U.S.A.* 117 J12
Moate, *Ireland* 15 C4
Moba, *Dem. Rep. of the Congo* 86 D2
Mobārakābād, *Iran* 71 D7
Mobaye, *C.A.R.* 84 D4
Mobayi, *Dem. Rep. of the Congo* 84 D4
Moberley Lake, *Canada* 104 B4
Moberly, *U.S.A.* 112 F8
Mobile, *U.S.A.* 109 K1
Mobile B., *U.S.A.* 109 K2
Mobridge, *U.S.A.* 112 C4
Mobutu Sese Seko, L. = Albert L., *Africa* 86 B3
Moc Chau, *Vietnam* 64 B5
Moc Hoa, *Vietnam* 65 G5
Mocabe Kasari, *Dem. Rep. of the Congo* 87 D2
Moçambique, *Mozam.* 87 F5
Moçâmedes = Namibe, *Angola* 85 H2
Mocanaqua, *U.S.A.* 111 E8
Mochudi, *Botswana* 88 C4
Mocimboa da Praia, *Mozam.* 87 E5
Mociu, *Romania* 43 D9
Möckeln, *Sweden* 11 H8
Mockfjärd, *Sweden* 10 D8
Moclips, *U.S.A.* 116 C2
Mocoa, *Colombia* 124 C3
Mococa, *Brazil* 127 A6
Mocorito, *Mexico* 118 B3
Moctezuma, *Mexico* 118 B3
Moctezuma →, *Mexico* 119 C5
Mocuba, *Mozam.* 87 F4
Mocúzari, Presa, *Mexico* 118 B3
Modane, *France* 21 C10
Modasa, *India* 68 H5
Modder →, *S. Africa* 88 D3
Modderrivier, *S. Africa* 88 D3
Módena, *Italy* 28 D7
Modena, *U.S.A.* 115 H7
Modesto, *U.S.A.* 116 H6
Módica, *Italy* 31 F7
Mödling, *Austria* 27 C9
Modo, *Sudan* 81 F3
Modra, *Slovak Rep.* 27 C10
Modriča, *Bos.-H.* 42 F3
Moe, *Australia* 95 F4
Moebase, *Mozam.* 87 F4
Moëlan-sur-Mer, *France* 18 E3
Moengo, *Surinam* 125 B8
Moffat, *U.K.* 14 F5
Moga, *India* 68 D6
Mogadishu = Muqdisho, *Somali Rep.* 74 G4
Mogador = Essaouira, *Morocco* 78 B4
Mogadouro, *Portugal* 34 D4
Mogalakwena →, *S. Africa* 89 C4
Mogami-Gawa →, *Japan* 54 E10
Mogán, *Canary Is.* 37 G4
Mogaung, *Burma* 67 G20
Mogente = Moixent, *Spain* 33 G4
Mogho, *Ethiopia* 81 G5
Mogi das Cruzes, *Brazil* 127 A6
Mogi-Guaçu →, *Brazil* 127 A6
Mogi-Mirim, *Brazil* 127 A6
Mogielnica, *Poland* 45 G7
Mogige, *Ethiopia* 81 F4
Mogilev = Mahilyow, *Belarus* 46 F6
Mogilev-Podolskiy = Mohyliv-Podilskyy, *Ukraine* 47 H4
Mogilno, *Poland* 45 F4
Mogincual, *Mozam.* 87 F5
Mogliano Véneto, *Italy* 29 C9
Mogocha, *Russia* 51 D12
Mogok, *Burma* 67 H20
Mogollon Rim, *U.S.A.* 115 J8
Mógoro, *Italy* 30 C1
Mograt, *Sudan* 80 D3
Moguer, *Spain* 35 H4
Mogumber, *Australia* 93 F2
Mohács, *Hungary* 42 E3
Mohales Hoek, *Lesotho* 88 E4
Mohall, *U.S.A.* 112 A4
Moḥammadābād, *Iran* 71 B8
Mohammedia, *Morocco* 78 B4
Mohana →, *India* 69 G11
Mohanlalganj, *India* 69 F9
Mohave, L., *U.S.A.* 117 K12
Mohawk →, *U.S.A.* 111 D11
Moheda, *Sweden* 11 G8
Mohenjodaro, *Pakistan* 68 F3
Mohicanville Reservoir, *U.S.A.* 110 F3
Möhne →, *Germany* 24 D3
Mohoro, *Tanzania* 86 D4
Mohyliv-Podilskyy, *Ukraine* 47 H4
Moia, *Sudan* 81 F2
Moidart, L., *U.K.* 14 E3
Moinești, *Romania* 43 D11
Moira →, *Canada* 110 B7
Moirans, *France* 21 C9
Moirans-en-Montagne, *France* 19 F12
Moíres, *Greece* 36 D6
Moisaküla, *Estonia* 9 G21
Moisie, *Canada* 103 B6
Moisie →, *Canada* 103 B6
Moissac, *France* 20 D5
Moita, *Portugal* 35 G2
Moixent, *Spain* 33 G4
Möja, *Sweden* 10 E12
Mojácar, *Spain* 33 H3
Mojados, *Spain* 34 D6
Mojave, *U.S.A.* 117 K8
Mojave Desert, *U.S.A.* 117 L10
Mojiang, *China* 58 F3
Mojo →, *Ethiopia* 81 F5
Mojkovac, *Montenegro, Yug.* 40 D3
Mojo, *Bolivia* 126 A2
Mojo, *Ethiopia* 81 F4
Mojokerto, *Indonesia* 63 G15
Mokai, *N.Z.* 91 H5
Mokambo, *Dem. Rep. of the Congo* 87 E2
Mokameh, *India* 69 G11
Mokelumne →, *U.S.A.* 116 G5
Mokelumne Hill, *U.S.A.* 116 G6
Mokhós, *Greece* 36 D7
Mokhotlong, *Lesotho* 89 D4
Möklinta, *Sweden* 10 D10
Mokokchung, *India* 67 F19
Mokolo, *Cameroon* 83 C7
Mokolo →, *S. Africa* 89 C4
Mokp'o, *S. Korea* 57 G14
Mokra Gora, *Yugoslavia* 40 D4
Mokronog, *Slovenia* 29 C12
Moksha →, *Russia* 48 C6
Mokshan, *Russia* 48 D7
Mokwa, *Nigeria* 83 D6
Mol, *Belgium* 17 C5
Mola di Bari, *Italy* 31 A10
Molale, *Ethiopia* 81 E4
Moláoi, *Greece* 38 E4
Molara, *Italy* 30 B2
Molat, *Croatia* 29 D11
Molchanovo, *Russia* 50 D9
Mold, *U.K.* 12 D4
Moldava nad Bodvou, *Slovak Rep.* 27 C14
Moldavia = Moldova ■, *Europe* 43 C13
Moldavia, *Romania* 43 D12
Molde, *Norway* 8 E12
Moldova ■, *Europe* 43 C13
Moldova Nouă, *Romania* 42 F6
Moldoveana, Vf., *Romania* 43 E9
Moldoviţa, *Romania* 43 C10
Mole →, *U.K.* 13 F7
Mole Creek, *Australia* 94 G4
Molepolole, *Botswana* 88 C4
Molfetta, *Italy* 31 A9
Molina de Aragón, *Spain* 32 E3
Molina de Segura, *Spain* 33 G3
Moline, *U.S.A.* 112 E9
Molinella, *Italy* 29 D8
Molinos, *Argentina* 126 B2
Moliro, *Dem. Rep. of the Congo* 86 D3
Moliterno, *Italy* 31 B8
Molkom, *Sweden* 10 E7
Mölle, *Sweden* 11 H6
Molledo, *Spain* 34 B6
Mollendo, *Peru* 124 G4
Mollerin, L., *Australia* 93 F2
Mollerussa, *Spain* 32 D5
Mollina, *Spain* 35 H6
Mölln, *Germany* 24 B6
Mölltorp, *Sweden* 11 F8
Mölnlycke, *Sweden* 11 G6
Molochansk, *Ukraine* 47 J8
Molochnoye, Ozero, *Ukraine* 47 J8
Molodechno = Maladzyechna, *Belarus* 46 E4
Molokai, *U.S.A.* 106 H16
Molong, *Australia* 95 E4
Molopo →, *Africa* 88 D3
Mólos, *Greece* 38 C4
Molotov = Perm, *Russia* 50 D6
Molsheim, *France* 19 D14
Molson L., *Canada* 105 C9
Molteno, *S. Africa* 88 E4
Molu, *Indonesia* 63 F8
Molucca Sea, *Indonesia* 63 E6
Moluccas = Maluku, *Indonesia* 63 E7
Moma, *Dem. Rep. of the Congo* 86 C1
Moma, *Mozam.* 87 F4
Mombasa, *Kenya* 86 C4
Mombetsu, *Japan* 54 B11
Mombuey, *Spain* 34 C4
Momchilgrad, *Bulgaria* 41 E9
Momi, *Dem. Rep. of the Congo* 86 C2
Mompós, *Colombia* 124 B4
Møn, *Denmark* 11 K6
Mon →, *Burma* 67 J19
Mona, Canal de la, *W. Indies* 121 C6
Mona, Isla, *Puerto Rico* 121 C6
Mona, Pta., *Costa Rica* 120 E3
Monaca, *U.S.A.* 110 F4
Monaco ■, *Europe* 21 E11
Monadhliath Mts., *U.K.* 14 D4
Monadnock, Mt., *U.S.A.* 111 D12
Monaghan, *Ireland* 15 B5
Monaghan □, *Ireland* 15 B5
Monahans, *U.S.A.* 113 K3
Monapo, *Mozam.* 87 E5
Monar, L., *U.K.* 14 D3
Monarch Mt., *Canada* 104 C3
Monashee Mts., *Canada* 104 C5
Monasterevin, *Ireland* 15 C4

Monastir = Bitola, Macedonia 40 E5
Moncada, Phil. 61 D4
Moncalieri, Italy 28 D4
Moncalvo, Italy 28 C5
Monção, Portugal 34 C2
Moncarapacho, Portugal 35 H3
Moncayo, Sierra del, Spain 32 D3
Mönchengladbach, Germany 24 D2
Monchique, Portugal 35 H2
Moncks Corner, U.S.A. 109 J5
Monclova, Mexico 118 B4
Moncontour, France 18 D4
Moncton, Canada 103 C7
Mondariz, Spain 34 C2
Mondego →, Portugal 34 E2
Mondego, C., Portugal 34 E2
Mondeodo, Indonesia 63 E6
Mondeville, France 18 C6
Mondolfo, Italy 29 E10
Mondoñedo, Spain 34 B3
Mondovì, Italy 28 D4
Mondragon, Phil. 61 E6
Mondragone, Italy 30 A6
Mondrain I., Australia 93 F3
Monemvasía, Greece 38 E5
Monessen, U.S.A. 110 F5
Monesterio, Spain 35 G4
Monestier-de-Clermont, France 21 D9
Monett, U.S.A. 113 G8
Moneymore, U.K. 15 B5
Monfalcone, Italy 29 C10
Monflanquin, France 20 D4
Monforte, Portugal 35 F3
Monforte de Lemos, Spain 34 C3
Mong Hsu, Burma 58 G2
Mong Kung, Burma 67 J20
Mong Nai, Burma 67 J20
Mong Pawk, Burma 67 H21
Mong Ping, Burma 58 G2
Mong Ton, Burma 67 J21
Mong Wa, Burma 67 J22
Mong Yai, Burma 67 H21
Mongalla, Sudan 81 F3
Mongers, L., Australia 93 E2
Monghyr = Munger, India 69 G12
Mongibello = Etna, Italy 31 E7
Mongo, Chad 79 F9
Mongo →, S. Leone 82 D2
Mongolia ■, Asia 51 E10
Mongonu, Nigeria 83 C7
Mongu, Zambia 85 H4
Mônguâ, Angola 88 B2
Monifieth, U.K. 14 E6
Monistrol-sur-Loire, France 21 C8
Monkey Bay, Malawi 87 E4
Monkey Mia, Australia 93 E1
Monkey River, Belize 119 D7
Mońki, Poland 44 E9
Monkoto, Dem. Rep. of the Congo 84 E4
Monkton, Canada 110 C3
Monmouth, U.K. 13 F5
Monmouth, Ill., U.S.A. 112 E9
Monmouth, Oreg., U.S.A. 114 D2
Monmouthshire □, U.K. 13 F5
Mono L., U.S.A. 116 H7
Monolith, U.S.A. 117 K8
Monólithos, Greece 36 C9
Monongahela, U.S.A. 110 F5
Monópoli, Italy 31 B10
Monor, Hungary 42 C4
Monóvar, Spain 33 G4
Monreal del Campo, Spain 32 E3
Monreale, Italy 30 D6
Monroe, Ga., U.S.A. 109 J4
Monroe, La., U.S.A. 113 J8
Monroe, Mich., U.S.A. 108 E4
Monroe, N.C., U.S.A. 109 H5
Monroe, N.Y., U.S.A. 111 E10
Monroe, Utah, U.S.A. 115 G7
Monroe, Wash., U.S.A. 116 C5
Monroe, Wis., U.S.A. 112 D10
Monroe City, U.S.A. 112 F9
Monroeton, U.S.A. 111 E8
Monroeville, Ala., U.S.A. 109 K2
Monroeville, Pa., U.S.A. 110 F5
Monrovia, Liberia 82 D2
Mons, Belgium 17 D3
Møns Klint, Denmark 11 K6
Monsaraz, Portugal 35 G3
Monse, Indonesia 63 E6
Monségur, France 20 D4
Monsélice, Italy 29 C8
Mönsterås, Sweden 11 G10
Mont Cenis, Col du, France 21 C10
Mont-de-Marsan, France 20 E3
Mont-Joli, Canada 103 C6
Mont-Laurier, Canada 102 C4
Mont-Louis, Canada 103 C6
Mont-roig del Camp, Spain 32 D5
Mont-St-Michel, Le = Le Mont-St-Michel, France 18 D5
Mont Tremblant, Parc Recr. du, Canada 102 C5
Montabaur, Germany 24 E3
Montagnac, France 20 E7
Montagnana, Italy 29 C8
Montagu, S. Africa 88 E3
Montagu I., Antarctica 5 B1
Montague, Canada 103 C7
Montague, I., Mexico 118 A2
Montague Ra., Australia 93 E2
Montague Sd., Australia 92 B4
Montaigu, France 18 F5
Montalbán, Spain 32 E4
Montalbano Iónico, Italy 31 B9
Montalbo, Spain 32 F2
Montalcino, Italy 29 E8
Montalegre, Portugal 34 D3
Montalto, Italy 31 D8
Montalto di Castro, Italy 29 F8
Montalto Uffugo, Italy 31 C9
Montalvo, U.S.A. 117 L7
Montamarta, Spain 34 D5
Montana, Bulgaria 40 C7
Montaña, Peru 124 E4
Montana □, Bulgaria 40 C7
Montana □, U.S.A. 114 C9
Montaña Clara, I., Canary Is. 37 E6
Montánchez, Spain 35 F4
Montargil, Portugal 35 F2
Montargis, France 19 E9
Montauban, France 20 D5
Montauk, U.S.A. 111 E13
Montauk Pt., U.S.A. 111 E13
Montbard, France 19 E11
Montbarrey, France 19 E12
Montbéliard, France 19 E13
Montblanc, Spain 32 D6
Montbrison, France 21 C8
Montcalm, Pic de, France 20 F5
Montceau-les-Mines, France 19 F11
Montcenis, France 21 B8
Montclair, U.S.A. 111 F10
Montcornet, France 19 C11
Montcuq, France 20 D5
Montdidier, France 19 C9
Monte Albán, Mexico 119 D5
Monte Alegre, Brazil 125 D8
Monte Azul, Brazil 125 G10
Monte Bello Is., Australia 92 D2
Monte-Carlo, Monaco 21 E11
Monte Caseros, Argentina 126 C4
Monte Comán, Argentina 126 C2
Monte Cristi, Dom. Rep. 121 C5
Monte Lindo →, Paraguay 126 A4
Monte Patria, Chile 126 C1
Monte Quemado, Argentina 126 B3
Monte Redondo, Portugal 34 F2
Monte Rio, U.S.A. 116 G4
Monte San Giovanni Campano, Italy 30 A6
Monte San Savino, Italy 29 E8
Monte Sant' Ángelo, Italy 29 G12
Monte Santu, C. di, Italy 30 B2
Monte Vista, U.S.A. 115 H10
Monteagudo, Argentina 127 B5
Montealegre del Castillo, Spain 33 G3
Montebello, Canada 102 C5
Montebello Iónico, Italy 31 E8
Montebelluna, Italy 29 C9
Montebourg, France 18 C5
Montecastrilli, Italy 29 F9
Montecatini Terme, Italy 28 E7
Montecito, U.S.A. 117 L7
Montecristo, Italy 28 F7
Montefalco, Italy 29 F9
Montefiascone, Italy 29 F9
Montefrío, Spain 35 H7
Montegiórgio, Italy 29 E10
Montego Bay, Jamaica 120 C4
Montehermoso, Spain 34 E4
Montejicar, Spain 35 H7
Montélimar, France 21 D8
Montella, Italy 31 B8
Montellano, Spain 35 J5
Montello, U.S.A. 112 D10
Montemor-o-Novo, Portugal 35 G2
Montemor-o-Velho, Portugal 34 E2
Montemorelos, Mexico 119 B5
Montendre, France 20 C3
Montenegro, Brazil 127 B5
Montenegro □, Yugoslavia 40 D3
Montenero di Bisáccia, Italy 29 G11
Montepuez, Mozam. 87 E4
Montepuez →, Mozam. 87 E5
Montepulciano, Italy 29 E8
Montereale, Italy 29 F10
Montereau-Faut-Yonne, France 19 D9
Monterey, U.S.A. 116 J5
Monterey B., U.S.A. 116 J5
Montería, Colombia 124 B3
Monteros, Argentina 126 B2
Monterotondo, Italy 29 F9
Monterrey, Mexico 118 B4
Montes Claros, Brazil 125 G10
Montesano, U.S.A. 116 D3
Montesano sulla Marcellana, Italy 31 B8
Montesárchio, Italy 31 A7
Montescaglioso, Italy 31 B9
Montesilvano, Italy 29 F11
Montevarchi, Italy 29 E8
Montevideo, Uruguay 127 C4
Montevideo, U.S.A. 112 C7
Montezuma, U.S.A. 112 E8
Montfaucon, France 18 E5
Montfaucon-d'Argonne, France 19 C12
Montfaucon-en-Velay, France 21 C8
Montfort, France 18 D5
Montfort-le-Gesnois, France 18 D7
Montgenèvre, France 21 D10
Montgomery = Sahiwal, Pakistan 68 D5
Montgomery, U.K. 13 E4
Montgomery, Ala., U.S.A. 109 J2
Montgomery, Pa., U.S.A. 110 E8
Montgomery, W. Va., U.S.A. 108 F5
Montgomery City, U.S.A. 112 F9
Montguyon, France 20 C3
Monthermé, France 19 C11
Monthey, Switz. 25 J2
Monthois, France 19 C11
Monti, Italy 30 B2
Monticelli d'Ongina, Italy 28 C6
Monticello, Ark., U.S.A. 113 J9
Monticello, Fla., U.S.A. 109 K4
Monticello, Ind., U.S.A. 108 E2
Monticello, Iowa, U.S.A. 112 D9
Monticello, Ky., U.S.A. 109 G3
Monticello, Minn., U.S.A. 112 C8
Monticello, Miss., U.S.A. 113 K9
Monticello, N.Y., U.S.A. 111 E10
Monticello, Utah, U.S.A. 115 H9
Montichiari, Italy 28 C7
Montier-en-Der, France 19 D11
Montignac, France 20 C5
Montigny-les-Metz, France 19 C13
Montigny-sur-Aube, France 19 E11
Montijo, Portugal 35 G2
Montijo, Spain 35 G4
Montilla, Spain 35 H6
Montivilliers, France 18 C7
Montluçon, France 19 F9
Montmagny, Canada 103 C5
Montmarault, France 19 F9
Montmartre, Canada 105 C8
Montmédy, France 19 C12
Montmélian, France 21 C10
Montmirail, France 19 D10
Montmoreau-St-Cybard, France 20 C4
Montmorillon, France 20 B4
Montmort-Lucy, France 19 D10
Monto, Australia 94 C5
Montoire-sur-le-Loir, France 18 E7
Montório al Vomano, Italy 29 F10
Montoro, Spain 35 G6
Montour Falls, U.S.A. 110 D8
Montoursville, U.S.A. 110 E8
Montpelier, Idaho, U.S.A. 114 E8
Montpelier, Vt., U.S.A. 111 B12
Montpellier, France 20 E7
Montpezat-de-Quercy, France 20 D5
Montpon-Ménestérol, France 20 D4
Montréal, Canada 102 C5
Montréal, Aude, France 20 E6
Montréal, Gers, France 20 E4
Montreal →, Canada 102 C3
Montreal L., Canada 105 C7
Montreal Lake, Canada 105 C7
Montredon-Labessonnié, France 20 E6
Montrésor, France 18 E8
Montret, France 19 F12
Montreuil, Pas-de-Calais, France 19 B8
Montreuil, Seine-St-Denis, France 19 D9
Montreuil-Bellay, France 18 E6
Montreux, Switz. 25 J2
Montrevel-en-Bresse, France 19 F12
Montrichard, France 18 E8
Montrose, U.K. 14 E6
Montrose, Colo., U.S.A. 115 G10
Montrose, Pa., U.S.A. 111 E9
Monts, Pte. des, Canada 103 C6
Montsalvy, France 20 D6
Montsant, Serra de, Spain 32 D6
Montsauche-les-Settons, France 19 E11
Montsec, Serra del, Spain 32 C5
Montserrat, Spain 32 D6
Montserrat ■, W. Indies 121 C7
Montuenga, Spain 34 D6
Montuiri, Spain 37 B9
Monywa, Burma 67 H19
Monza, Italy 28 C6
Monze, Zambia 87 F2
Monze, C., Pakistan 68 G2
Monzón, Spain 32 D5
Mooers, U.S.A. 111 B11
Mooi →, S. Africa 89 D5
Mooi River, S. Africa 89 D4
Moonah →, Australia 94 C2
Moonda, L., Australia 94 D3
Moonie, Australia 95 D5
Moonie →, Australia 95 D4
Moonta, Australia 95 E2
Moora, Australia 93 F2
Moorcroft, U.S.A. 112 C2
Moore →, Australia 93 F2
Moore, L., Australia 93 E2
Moore Park, Australia 94 C5
Moore Reefs, Australia 94 B4
Moorefield, U.S.A. 108 F6
Moores Res., U.S.A. 111 B13
Moorfoot Hills, U.K. 14 F5
Moorhead, U.S.A. 112 B6
Moormerland, Germany 24 B3
Moorpark, U.S.A. 117 L8
Moorreesburg, S. Africa 88 E2
Moosburg, Germany 25 G7
Moose →, Canada 102 B3
Moose →, U.S.A. 111 C9
Moose Creek, Canada 111 A10
Moose Factory, Canada 102 B3
Moose Jaw, Canada 105 C7
Moose Jaw →, Canada 105 C7
Moose Lake, Canada 105 C8
Moose Lake, U.S.A. 112 B8
Moose Mountain Prov. Park, Canada 105 D8
Moosehead L., U.S.A. 109 C11
Mooselookmeguntic L., U.S.A. 109 C10
Moosilauke, Mt., U.S.A. 111 B13
Moosomin, Canada 105 C8
Moosonee, Canada 102 B3
Moosup, U.S.A. 111 E13
Mopane, S. Africa 89 C4
Mopeia Velha, Mozam. 87 F4
Mopipi, Botswana 88 C3
Mopoi, C.A.R. 86 A2
Mopti, Mali 82 C4
Moqatta, Sudan 81 E4
Moqor, Afghan. 68 C2
Moquegua, Peru 124 G4
Mór, Hungary 42 C3
Mora, Cameroon 83 C7
Móra, Portugal 35 G2
Mora, Spain 35 F7
Mora, Sweden 10 C8
Mora, Minn., U.S.A. 112 C8
Mora, N. Mex., U.S.A. 115 J11
Mora →, U.S.A. 113 H2
Mora de Ebro = Mòra d'Ebre, Spain 32 D5
Mora de Rubielos, Spain 32 E4
Mòra d'Ebre, Spain 32 D5
Mòra la Nova, Spain 32 D5
Morača →, Montenegro, Yug. 40 D3
Moradabad, India 69 E8
Morafenobe, Madag. 89 B7
Morąg, Poland 44 E6
Moral de Calatrava, Spain 35 G7
Moraleja, Spain 34 E4
Moramanga, Madag. 89 B8
Moran, Kans., U.S.A. 113 G7
Moran, Wyo., U.S.A. 114 E8
Moranbah, Australia 94 C4
Morano Cálabro, Italy 31 C9
Morant Cays, Jamaica 120 C4
Morant Pt., Jamaica 120 C4
Morar, India 68 F8
Morar, L., U.K. 14 E3
Moratalla, Spain 33 G3
Moratuwa, Sri Lanka 66 R11
Morava →, Slovak Rep. 27 C9
Moravia, U.S.A. 111 D8
Moravian Hts. = Českomoravská Vrchovina, Czech Rep. 26 B8
Moravica →, Serbia, Yug. 40 C4
Moraviţa, Romania 42 E6
Moravská Třebová, Czech Rep. 27 B9
Moravské Budějovice, Czech Rep. 26 B8
Morawa, Australia 93 E2
Morawhanna, Guyana 124 B7
Moray □, U.K. 14 D5
Moray Firth, U.K. 14 D5
Morbach, Germany 25 F3
Morbegno, Italy 28 B6
Morbi, India 68 H4
Morbihan □, France 18 E4
Mörbylånga, Sweden 11 H10
Morcenx, France 20 D3
Morcone, Italy 31 A7
Mordelles, France 18 D5
Morden, Canada 105 D9
Mordoğan, Turkey 39 C8
Mordovian Republic = Mordvinia □, Russia 48 C7
Mordovo, Russia 48 D5
Mordvinia □, Russia 48 C7
Mordy, Poland 45 F9
Morea, Greece 6 H10
Moreau →, U.S.A. 112 C4
Morecambe, U.K. 12 C5
Morecambe B., U.K. 12 C5
Moree, Australia 95 D4
Morehead, U.S.A. 108 F4
Morehead City, U.S.A. 109 H7
Morel →, India 68 F7
Morelia, Mexico 118 D4
Morella, Australia 94 C3
Morella, Spain 32 E4
Morelos, Mexico 118 B3
Morelos □, Mexico 119 D5
Morena, India 68 F8
Morena, Sierra, Spain 35 G7
Moreni, Romania 43 F10
Moreno Valley, U.S.A. 117 M10
Moresby I., Canada 104 C2
Morestel, France 21 C9
Moreton I., Australia 95 D5
Moreuil, France 19 C9
Morey, Spain 37 B10
Morez, France 19 F13
Morgan, U.S.A. 114 F8
Morgan City, U.S.A. 113 L9
Morgan Hill, U.S.A. 116 H5
Morganfield, U.S.A. 108 G2
Morganton, U.S.A. 109 H5
Morgantown, U.S.A. 108 F6
Morgenzon, S. Africa 89 D4
Morges, Switz. 25 J2
Morghak, Iran 71 D8
Morgongåva, Sweden 10 E10
Morhange, France 19 D13
Morhar →, India 69 G11
Mori, Italy 28 C7
Moriarty, U.S.A. 115 J10
Moribaya, Guinea 82 D3
Morice L., Canada 104 C3
Moriki, Nigeria 83 C6
Morinville, Canada 104 C6
Morioka, Japan 54 E10
Moris, Mexico 118 B3
Morlaàs, France 20 E3
Morlaix, France 18 D3
Mörlunda, Sweden 11 G9
Mormanno, Italy 31 C8
Mormant, France 19 D9
Mornington, Australia 95 F4
Mornington, I., Chile 128 F1
Mornington I., Australia 94 B2
Mórnos →, Greece 38 C3
Moro, Pakistan 68 F2
Moro, Sudan 81 E3
Moro →, Pakistan 68 E2
Moro G., Phil. 61 H5
Morocco ■, N. Afr. 78 B4
Morogoro, Tanzania 86 D4
Morogoro □, Tanzania 86 D4
Moroleón, Mexico 118 C4
Morombe, Madag. 89 C7
Moron, Argentina 126 C4
Morón, Cuba 120 B4
Morón de Almazán, Spain 32 D2
Morón de la Frontera, Spain 35 H5
Morona →, Peru 124 D3
Morondava, Madag. 89 C7
Morondo, Ivory C. 82 D3
Morongo Valley, U.S.A. 117 L10
Moroni, Comoros Is. 77 H8
Moroni, U.S.A. 114 G8
Moronou, Ivory C. 82 D4
Morotai, Indonesia 63 D7
Moroto, Uganda 86 B3
Moroto Summit, Kenya 86 B3
Morozov, Bulgaria 41 D9
Morozovsk, Russia 49 F5
Morpeth, U.K. 12 B6
Morphou, Cyprus 36 D11
Morphou Bay, Cyprus 36 D11
Morrilton, U.S.A. 113 H8
Morrinhos, Brazil 125 G9
Morrinsville, N.Z. 91 G5
Morris, Canada 105 D9
Morris, Ill., U.S.A. 112 E10
Morris, Minn., U.S.A. 112 C7
Morris, N.Y., U.S.A. 111 D9
Morris, Pa., U.S.A. 110 E7
Morris, Mt., Australia 93 E5
Morrisburg, Canada 111 B9
Morristown, Ariz., U.S.A. 115 K7
Morristown, N.J., U.S.A. 111 F10
Morristown, N.Y., U.S.A. 111 B9
Morristown, Tenn., U.S.A. 109 G4
Morrisville, N.Y., U.S.A. 111 D9
Morrisville, Pa., U.S.A. 111 F10
Morrisville, Vt., U.S.A. 111 B12
Morro, Pta., Chile 126 B1
Morro Bay, U.S.A. 116 K6
Morro del Jable, Canary Is. 37 F5
Morro Jable, Pta. de, Canary Is. 37 F5
Morrosquillo, G. de, Colombia 120 E4
Mörrum, Sweden 11 H8
Morrumbene, Mozam. 89 C6
Mörrumsån →, Sweden 11 H8
Mors, Denmark 11 H2
Morshansk, Russia 48 D5
Mörsil, Sweden 10 A7
Mortagne →, France 19 D13
Mortagne-au-Perche, France 18 D7
Mortagne-sur-Gironde, France 20 C3
Mortagne-sur-Sèvre, France 18 F6
Mortain, France 18 D6
Mortara, Italy 28 C5
Morteau, France 19 E13
Morteros, Argentina 126 C3
Mortlach, Canada 105 C7
Mortlake, Australia 95 F3
Morton, Tex., U.S.A. 113 J3
Morton, Wash., U.S.A. 116 D4
Morundah, Australia 95 E4
Moruya, Australia 95 F5
Morvan, France 19 E11
Morven, Australia 95 D4
Morvern, U.K. 14 E3
Morwell, Australia 95 F4
Moryń, Poland 45 F1
Morzine, France 19 F13
Mosalsk, Russia 46 E8
Mosbach, Germany 25 F5
Moščenice, Croatia 29 C11
Mosciano Sant' Ángelo, Italy 29 F10
Moscos Is. = Maungmagan Is., Burma 64 E1
Moscow = Moskva, Russia 46 E9
Moscow, Idaho, U.S.A. 114 C5
Moscow, Pa., U.S.A. 111 E9
Mosel →, Europe 19 B14
Moselle = Mosel →, Europe 19 B14
Moselle □, France 19 D13
Moses Lake, U.S.A. 114 C4
Mosgiel, N.Z. 91 L3
Moshaweng →, S. Africa 88 D3
Moshi, Tanzania 86 C4
Moshupa, Botswana 88 C4
Mosina, Poland 45 F3
Mosjøen, Norway 8 D15
Moskenesøya, Norway 8 C15
Moskenstraumen, Norway 8 C15
Moskva, Russia 46 E9
Moskva →, Russia 46 E10
Moslavačka Gora, Croatia 29 C13
Mosomane, Botswana 88 C4
Moson-magyaróvár, Hungary 42 C2
Mošorin, Serbia, Yug. 42 E5
Mospino, Ukraine 47 J9
Mosquera, Colombia 124 C3
Mosquero, U.S.A. 113 H3
Mosqueruela, Spain 32 E4
Mosquitia, Honduras 120 C3
Mosquito Coast = Mosquitia, Honduras 120 C3
Mosquito Creek L., U.S.A. 110 E4
Mosquito L., Canada 105 A8
Mosquitos, G. de los, Panama 120 E3
Moss, Norway 9 G14
Moss Vale, Australia 95 E5
Mossbank, Canada 105 D7
Mossburn, N.Z. 91 L2
Mosselbaai, S. Africa 88 E3

Mossendjo, *Congo* 84 E2
Mossgiel, *Australia* 95 E3
Mössingen, *Germany* 25 G5
Mossman, *Australia* 94 B4
Mossoró, *Brazil* 125 E11
Mossuril, *Mozam.* 87 E5
Most, *Czech Rep.* 26 A6
Mosta, *Malta* 36 D1
Moşţafáābād, *Iran* 71 C7
Mostaganem, *Algeria* 78 A6
Mostar, *Bos.-H.* 42 G2
Mostardas, *Brazil* 127 C5
Mostiska = Mostyska, *Ukraine* 47 H2
Móstoles, *Spain* 34 E7
Mosty = Masty, *Belarus* 46 F3
Mostyska, *Ukraine* 47 H2
Mosul = Al Mawşil, *Iraq* 70 B4
Mosŭlpo, *S. Korea* 57 H14
Mota, *Ethiopia* 81 E4
Mota del Cuervo, *Spain* 33 F2
Mota del Marqués, *Spain* 34 D5
Motagua →, *Guatemala* 120 C2
Motala, *Sweden* 11 F9
Motaze, *Mozam.* 89 C5
Moţca, *Romania* 43 C11
Moth, *India* 69 G8
Motherwell, *U.K.* 14 F5
Motihari, *India* 69 F11
Motilla del Palancar, *Spain* 33 F3
Motnik, *Slovenia* 29 B11
Motovun, *Croatia* 29 C10
Motozintla de Mendoza, *Mexico* 119 D6
Motril, *Spain* 35 J7
Motru, *Romania* 42 F7
Motru →, *Romania* 43 F8
Mott, *U.S.A.* 112 B3
Móttola, *Italy* 31 B10
Motueka, *N.Z.* 91 J4
Motueka →, *N.Z.* 91 J4
Motul, *Mexico* 119 C7
Mouchalagane →, *Canada* 103 B6
Moúdhros, *Greece* 39 B7
Mouding, *China* 58 E3
Moudjeria, *Mauritania* 82 B2
Moudon, *Switz.* 25 J2
Mouila, *Gabon* 84 E2
Moulamein, *Australia* 95 F3
Moulianá, *Greece* 36 D7
Moulins, *France* 19 F10
Moulmein, *Burma* 67 L20
Moulouya, O. →, *Morocco* 78 B5
Moultrie, *U.S.A.* 109 K4
Moultrie, L., *U.S.A.* 109 J5
Mound City, *Mo., U.S.A.* 112 E7
Mound City, *S. Dak., U.S.A.* 112 C4
Moúnda, Ákra, *Greece* 38 C2
Moundou, *Chad* 79 G9
Moundsville, *U.S.A.* 110 G4
Moung, *Cambodia* 64 F4
Mount Airy, *U.S.A.* 109 G5
Mount Albert, *Canada* 110 B5
Mount Barker, *S. Austral., Australia* 95 F2
Mount Barker, *W. Austral., Australia* 93 F2
Mount Beauty, *Australia* 95 F4
Mount Brydges, *Canada* 110 D3
Mount Burr, *Australia* 95 F3
Mount Carmel, *Ill., U.S.A.* 108 F2
Mount Carmel, *Pa., U.S.A.* 111 F8
Mount Charleston, *U.S.A.* 117 J11
Mount Clemens, *U.S.A.* 110 D2
Mount Coolon, *Australia* 94 C4
Mount Darwin, *Zimbabwe* 87 F3
Mount Desert I., *U.S.A.* 109 C11
Mount Dora, *U.S.A.* 109 L5
Mount Edziza Prov. Park, *Canada* 104 B2
Mount Fletcher, *S. Africa* 89 E4
Mount Forest, *Canada* 102 D3
Mount Gambier, *Australia* 95 F3
Mount Garnet, *Australia* 94 B4
Mount Holly, *U.S.A.* 111 G10
Mount Holly Springs, *U.S.A.* 110 F7
Mount Hope, *N.S.W., Australia* 95 E4
Mount Hope, *S. Austral., Australia* 95 E2
Mount Isa, *Australia* 94 C2
Mount Jewett, *U.S.A.* 110 E6
Mount Kisco, *U.S.A.* 111 E11
Mount Laguna, *U.S.A.* 117 N10
Mount Larcom, *Australia* 94 C5
Mount Lofty Ra., *Australia* 95 E2
Mount Magnet, *Australia* 93 E2
Mount Maunganui, *N.Z.* 91 G6
Mount Molloy, *Australia* 94 B4
Mount Morgan, *Australia* 94 C5
Mount Morris, *U.S.A.* 110 D7
Mount Pearl, *Canada* 103 C9
Mount Penn, *U.S.A.* 111 F9
Mount Perry, *Australia* 95 D5
Mount Pleasant, *Iowa, U.S.A.* 112 E9
Mount Pleasant, *Mich., U.S.A.* 108 D3
Mount Pleasant, *Pa., U.S.A.* 110 F5
Mount Pleasant, *S.C., U.S.A.* 109 J6
Mount Pleasant, *Tenn., U.S.A.* 109 H2
Mount Pleasant, *Tex., U.S.A.* 113 J7
Mount Pleasant, *Utah, U.S.A.* 114 G8
Mount Pocono, *U.S.A.* 111 E9
Mount Rainier Nat. Park, *U.S.A.* 116 D5
Mount Revelstoke Nat. Park, *Canada* 104 C5
Mount Robson Prov. Park, *Canada* 104 C5
Mount Selinda, *Zimbabwe* 89 C5
Mount Shasta, *U.S.A.* 114 F2
Mount Signal, *U.S.A.* 117 N11
Mount Sterling, *Ill., U.S.A.* 112 F9
Mount Sterling, *Ky., U.S.A.* 108 F4
Mount Surprise, *Australia* 94 B3
Mount Union, *U.S.A.* 110 F7
Mount Upton, *U.S.A.* 111 D9
Mount Vernon, *Ill., U.S.A.* 108 F1
Mount Vernon, *Ind., U.S.A.* 112 F10
Mount Vernon, *N.Y., U.S.A.* 111 F11
Mount Vernon, *Ohio, U.S.A.* 110 F2
Mount Vernon, *Wash., U.S.A.* 116 B4
Mountain Ash, *U.K.* 13 F4
Mountain Center, *U.S.A.* 117 M10
Mountain City, *Nev., U.S.A.* 114 F6
Mountain City, *Tenn., U.S.A.* 109 G5
Mountain Dale, *U.S.A.* 111 E10
Mountain Grove, *U.S.A.* 113 G8
Mountain Home, *Ark., U.S.A.* 113 G8
Mountain Home, *Idaho, U.S.A.* 114 E6
Mountain Iron, *U.S.A.* 112 B8
Mountain Pass, *U.S.A.* 117 K11
Mountain View, *Ark., U.S.A.* 113 H8
Mountain View, *Calif., U.S.A.* 116 H4
Mountain View, *Hawaii, U.S.A.* 106 J17
Mountainair, *U.S.A.* 115 J10
Mountlake Terrace, *U.S.A.* 116 C4
Mountmellick, *Ireland* 15 C4
Mountrath, *Ireland* 15 D4
Moura, *Australia* 94 C4
Moura, *Brazil* 124 D6
Moura, *Portugal* 35 G3
Mourão, *Portugal* 35 G3
Mourdi, Dépression du, *Chad* 79 E10
Mourdiah, *Mali* 82 C3
Mourenx-Ville-Nouvelle, *France* 20 E3
Mouri, *Ghana* 83 D4
Mourilyan, *Australia* 94 B4
Mourmelon-le-Grand, *France* 19 C11
Mourne →, *U.K.* 15 B4
Mourne Mts., *U.K.* 15 B5
Mourniaí, *Greece* 36 D6
Mournies = Mourniaí, *Greece* 36 D6
Mouscron, *Belgium* 17 D3
Moussoro, *Chad* 79 F9
Mouthe, *France* 19 F13
Moutier, *Switz.* 25 H3
Moûtiers, *France* 21 C10
Moutohara, *N.Z.* 91 H6
Moutong, *Indonesia* 63 D6
Mouy, *France* 19 C9
Mouzáki, *Greece* 38 B3
Mouzon, *France* 19 C12
Movas, *Mexico* 118 B3
Moville, *Ireland* 15 A4
Mowandjum, *Australia* 92 C3
Moy →, *Ireland* 15 B2
Moyale, *Kenya* 81 G4
Moyamba, *S. Leone* 82 D2
Moyen Atlas, *Morocco* 78 B4
Moyne, L. le, *Canada* 103 A6
Moyo, *Indonesia* 62 F5
Moyobamba, *Peru* 124 E3
Moyyero →, *Russia* 51 C11
Moyynty, *Kazakstan* 50 E8
Mozambique = Moçambique, *Mozam.* 87 F5
Mozambique ■, *Africa* 87 F4
Mozambique Chan., *Africa* 89 B7
Mozdok, *Russia* 49 J7
Mozdūrān, *Iran* 71 B9
Mozhaysk, *Russia* 46 E9
Mozhga, *Russia* 48 B11
Mozhnābād, *Iran* 71 C9
Mozirje, *Slovenia* 29 B11
Mozyr = Mazyr, *Belarus* 47 F5
Mpanda, *Tanzania* 86 D3
Mpésoba, *Mali* 82 C3
Mphoengs, *Zimbabwe* 89 C4
Mpika, *Zambia* 87 E3
Mpulungu, *Zambia* 87 D3
Mpumalanga, *S. Africa* 89 D5
Mpumalanga □, *S. Africa* 89 B5
Mpwapwa, *Tanzania* 86 D4
Mqanduli, *S. Africa* 89 E4
Mqinvartsveri = Kazbek, *Russia* 49 J7
Mrągowo, *Poland* 44 E8
Mramor, *Serbia, Yug.* 40 C5
Mrkonjić Grad, *Bos.-H.* 42 F2
Mrkopalj, *Croatia* 29 C11
Mrocza, *Poland* 45 E4
Msambansovu, *Zimbabwe* 87 F3
M'sila →, *Algeria* 78 A6
Msoro, *Zambia* 87 E3
Msta →, *Russia* 46 C6
Mstislavl = Mstsislaw, *Belarus* 46 E6
Mstsislaw, *Belarus* 46 E6
Mszana Dolna, *Poland* 45 J7
Mszczonów, *Poland* 45 G7
Mtama, *Tanzania* 87 E4
Mtamvuna →, *S. Africa* 89 E5
Mtilikwe →, *Zimbabwe* 87 G3
Mtsensk, *Russia* 46 F9
Mtskheta, *Georgia* 49 K7
Mtubatuba, *S. Africa* 89 D5
Mtwalume, *S. Africa* 89 E5
Mtwara-Mikindani, *Tanzania* 87 E5
Mu Gia, Deo, *Vietnam* 64 D5
Mu Us Shamo, *China* 56 E5
Muang Chiang Rai = Chiang Rai, *Thailand* 58 H2
Muang Khong, *Laos* 64 E5
Muang Lamphun, *Thailand* 64 C2
Muang Pak Beng, *Laos* 58 H3
Muar, *Malaysia* 65 L4
Muarabungo, *Indonesia* 62 E2
Muaraenim, *Indonesia* 62 E2
Muarajuloi, *Indonesia* 62 E4
Muarakaman, *Indonesia* 62 E5
Muaratebo, *Indonesia* 62 E2
Muaratembesi, *Indonesia* 62 E2
Muaratewe, *Indonesia* 62 E4
Mubarakpur, *India* 69 F10
Mubarraz = Al Mubarraz, *Si. Arabia* 71 E6
Mubende, *Uganda* 86 B3
Mubi, *Nigeria* 83 C7
Mubur, Pulau, *Indonesia* 65 L6
Mucajaí →, *Brazil* 124 C6
Muchachos, Roque de los, *Canary Is.* 37 F2
Mücheln, *Germany* 24 D7
Muchinga Mts., *Zambia* 87 E3
Muchkapskiy, *Russia* 48 E6
Muchuan, *China* 58 C5
Muck, *U.K.* 14 E2
Muckadilla, *Australia* 95 D4
Mucur, *Turkey* 72 C6
Mucuri, *Brazil* 125 G11
Mucusso, *Angola* 88 B3
Muda, *Canary Is.* 37 F6
Mudanjiang, *China* 57 B15
Mudanya, *Turkey* 41 F12
Muddy Cr. →, *U.S.A.* 115 H8
Mudgee, *Australia* 95 E4
Mudjatik →, *Canada* 105 B7
Mudurnu, *Turkey* 72 B4
Muecate, *Mozam.* 87 E4
Mueda, *Mozam.* 87 E4
Mueller Ra., *Australia* 92 C4
Muende, *Mozam.* 87 E3
Muerto, Mar, *Mexico* 119 D6
Mufu Shan, *China* 59 C10
Mufulira, *Zambia* 87 E2
Mufumbiro Range, *Africa* 86 C2
Mugardos, *Spain* 34 B2
Muge →, *Portugal* 35 F2
Múggia, *Italy* 29 C10
Mughal Sarai, *India* 69 G10
Mughayrā', *Si. Arabia* 70 D3
Mugi, *Japan* 55 H7
Mugia = Muxía, *Spain* 34 B1
Mugila, Mts., *Dem. Rep. of the Congo* 86 D2
Muğla, *Turkey* 39 D10
Muğla □, *Turkey* 39 D10
Muglad, *Sudan* 81 E2
Müglizh, *Bulgaria* 41 D9
Mugu, *Nepal* 69 E10
Muhammad, Ras, *Egypt* 70 E2
Muhammad Qol, *Sudan* 80 C4
Muhammadabad, *India* 69 F10
Muhesi →, *Tanzania* 86 D4
Mühlacker, *Germany* 25 G4
Mühldorf, *Germany* 25 G8
Mühlhausen, *Germany* 24 D6
Mühlig Hofmann fjell, *Antarctica* 5 D3
Mühlviertel, *Austria* 26 C7
Muhos, *Finland* 8 D22
Muhu, *Estonia* 9 G20
Muhutwe, *Tanzania* 86 C3
Muine Bheag, *Ireland* 15 D5
Muir, L., *Australia* 93 F2
Mukacheve, *Ukraine* 47 H2
Mukachevo = Mukacheve, *Ukraine* 47 H2
Mukah, *Malaysia* 62 D4
Mukandwara, *India* 68 G6
Mukawwa, Geziret, *Egypt* 80 C4
Mukawwar, *Sudan* 80 C4
Mukdahan, *Thailand* 64 D5
Mukden = Shenyang, *China* 57 D12
Mukerian, *India* 68 D6
Mukhtolovo, *Russia* 48 C6
Mukhtuya = Lensk, *Russia* 51 C12
Mukinbudin, *Australia* 93 F2
Mukishi, *Dem. Rep. of the Congo* 87 D1
Mukomuko, *Indonesia* 62 E2
Mukomwenze, *Dem. Rep. of the Congo* 86 D2
Muktsar, *India* 68 D6
Mukur = Moqor, *Afghan.* 68 C2
Mukutawa →, *Canada* 105 C9
Mukwela, *Zambia* 87 F2
Mula, *Spain* 33 G3
Mula →, *Pakistan* 68 F2
Mulange, *Dem. Rep. of the Congo* 86 C2
Mulanje, *Malawi* 87 F4
Mulchén, *Chile* 126 D1
Mulde →, *Germany* 24 D8
Mule Creek Junction, *U.S.A.* 112 D2
Muleba, *Tanzania* 86 C3
Mulejé, *Mexico* 118 B2
Muleshoe, *U.S.A.* 113 H3
Muletta, Gara, *Ethiopia* 81 F5
Mulgrave, *Canada* 103 C7
Mulhacén, *Spain* 35 H7
Mülheim, *Germany* 24 D2
Mulhouse, *France* 19 E14
Muli, *China* 58 D3
Muling, *China* 57 B16
Mull, *U.K.* 14 E3
Mull, Sound of, *U.K.* 14 E3
Mullaittivu, *Sri Lanka* 66 Q12
Mullen, *U.S.A.* 112 D4
Mullens, *U.S.A.* 108 G5
Muller, Pegunungan, *Indonesia* 62 D4
Mullet Pen., *Ireland* 15 B1
Mullewa, *Australia* 93 E2
Müllheim, *Germany* 25 H3
Mulligan →, *Australia* 94 D2
Mullingar, *Ireland* 15 C4
Mullins, *U.S.A.* 109 H6
Mullsjö, *Sweden* 11 G7
Mullumbimby, *Australia* 95 D5
Mulobezi, *Zambia* 87 F2
Mulroy B., *Ireland* 15 A4
Multan, *Pakistan* 68 D4
Mulumbe, Mts., *Dem. Rep. of the Congo* 87 D2
Mulungushi Dam, *Zambia* 87 E2
Mulvane, *U.S.A.* 113 G6
Mulwad, *Sudan* 80 D3
Mumbai, *India* 66 K8
Mumbwa, *Zambia* 87 F2
Mumra, *Russia* 49 H8
Mun →, *Thailand* 64 E5
Muna, *Indonesia* 63 F6
Munabao, *India* 68 G4
Munamagi, *Estonia* 9 H22
Münchberg, *Germany* 25 E7
Müncheberg, *Germany* 24 C10
München, *Germany* 25 G7
Munchen-Gladbach = Mönchengladbach, *Germany* 24 D2
Muncho Lake, *Canada* 104 B3
Munch'ŏn, *N. Korea* 57 E14
Muncie, *U.S.A.* 108 E3
Muncoonie, L., *Australia* 94 D2
Mundabbera, *Australia* 95 D5
Munday, *U.S.A.* 113 J5
Münden, *Germany* 24 D5
Mundiwindi, *Australia* 92 D3
Mundo →, *Spain* 33 G2
Mundo Novo, *Brazil* 125 F10
Mundra, *India* 68 H3
Mundrabilla, *Australia* 93 F4
Munera, *Spain* 33 F2
Mungallala, *Australia* 95 D4
Mungallala Cr. →, *Australia* 95 D4
Mungana, *Australia* 94 B3
Mungaoli, *India* 68 G8
Mungari, *Mozam.* 87 F3
Mungbere, *Dem. Rep. of the Congo* 86 B2
Mungeli, *India* 69 H9
Munger, *India* 69 G12
Munich = München, *Germany* 25 G7
Munising, *U.S.A.* 108 B2
Munka-Ljungby, *Sweden* 11 H6
Munkebo, *Denmark* 11 J4
Munkedal, *Sweden* 11 F5
Munkfors, *Sweden* 10 E7
Munku-Sardyk, *Russia* 51 D11
Münnerstadt, *Germany* 25 E6
Muñoz Gamero, Pen., *Chile* 128 G2
Munroe L., *Canada* 105 B9
Munsan, *S. Korea* 57 F14
Munster, *France* 19 D14
Munster, *Niedersachsen, Germany* 24 C6
Münster, *Nordrhein-Westfalen, Germany* 24 D3
Munster □, *Ireland* 15 D3
Muntadgin, *Australia* 93 F2
Muntele Mare, Vf., *Romania* 43 D8
Muntok, *Indonesia* 62 E3
Munyama, *Zambia* 87 F2
Munzur Dağları, *Turkey* 73 C8
Muong Beng, *Laos* 58 G3
Muong Boum, *Vietnam* 58 F4
Muong Et, *Laos* 64 B5
Muong Hai, *Laos* 58 G3
Muong Hiem, *Laos* 64 B4
Muong Houn, *Laos* 58 G3
Muong Hung, *Vietnam* 58 G4
Muong Kau, *Laos* 64 E5
Muong Khao, *Laos* 64 C4
Muong Khoua, *Laos* 58 G4
Muong Liep, *Laos* 64 C3
Muong May, *Laos* 64 E6
Muong Ngeun, *Laos* 58 G3
Muong Ngoi, *Laos* 58 G4
Muong Nhie, *Vietnam* 58 F4
Muong Nong, *Laos* 64 D6
Muong Ou Tay, *Laos* 58 F3
Muong Oua, *Laos* 64 C3
Muong Peun, *Laos* 58 G4
Muong Phalane, *Laos* 64 D5
Muong Phieng, *Laos* 64 C3
Muong Phine, *Laos* 64 D6
Muong Sai, *Laos* 58 G3
Muong Saiapoun, *Laos* 64 C3
Muong Sen, *Vietnam* 64 C5
Muong Sing, *Laos* 58 G3
Muong Son, *Laos* 58 G4
Muong Soui, *Laos* 64 C4
Muong Va, *Laos* 58 G4
Muong Xia, *Vietnam* 64 B5
Muonio, *Finland* 8 C20
Muonionjoki →, *Finland* 8 C20
Muping, *China* 57 F11
Mupoi, *Sudan* 81 F2
Muqaddam, Wadi →, *Sudan* 80 D3
Muqdisho, *Somali Rep.* 74 G4
Mur →, *Austria* 27 E9
Mur-de-Bretagne, *France* 18 D4
Muradiye, *Manisa, Turkey* 39 C9
Muradiye, *Van, Turkey* 73 C10
Murakami, *Japan* 54 E9
Murallón, Cerro, *Chile* 128 F2
Muranda, *Rwanda* 86 C2
Murang'a, *Kenya* 86 C4
Murashi, *Russia* 50 D5
Murat, *France* 20 C6
Murat →, *Turkey* 73 C9
Murat Dağı, *Turkey* 39 C11
Muratlı, *Turkey* 41 E11
Murato, *France* 21 F13
Murau, *Austria* 26 D7
Muravera, *Italy* 30 C2
Murayama, *Japan* 54 E10
Murban, *U.A.E.* 71 F7
Murça, *Portugal* 34 D3
Murchison →, *Australia* 93 E1
Murchison, Mt., *Antarctica* 5 D11
Murchison Falls, *Uganda* 86 B3
Murchison Ra., *Australia* 94 C1
Murchison Rapids, *Malawi* 87 F3
Murcia, *Spain* 33 G3
Murcia □, *Spain* 33 H3
Murdo, *U.S.A.* 112 D4
Murdoch Pt., *Australia* 94 A3
Mürefte, *Turkey* 41 F11
Mureş □, *Romania* 43 D9
Mureş →, *Romania* 42 D5
Mureşul = Mureş →, *Romania* 42 D5
Muret, *France* 20 E5
Murewa, *Zimbabwe* 89 B5
Murfreesboro, *N.C., U.S.A.* 109 G7
Murfreesboro, *Tenn., U.S.A.* 109 H2
Murgab = Murghob, *Tajikistan* 50 F8
Murgab →, *Turkmenistan* 71 B9
Murgenella, *Australia* 92 B5
Murgeni, *Romania* 43 D13
Murgha Kibzai, *Pakistan* 68 D3
Murghob, *Tajikistan* 50 F8
Murgon, *Australia* 95 D5
Muri, *India* 69 H11
Muria, *Indonesia* 63 G14
Muriaé, *Brazil* 127 A7
Murias de Paredes, *Spain* 34 C4
Muriel Mine, *Zimbabwe* 87 F3
Müritz, *Germany* 24 B8
Murka, *Kenya* 86 C4
Murliganj, *India* 69 G12
Murmansk, *Russia* 50 C4
Murnau, *Germany* 25 H7
Muro, *France* 21 F12
Muro, *Spain* 37 B10
Muro, C. de, *France* 21 G12
Muro de Alcoy, *Spain* 33 G4
Muro Lucano, *Italy* 31 B8
Murom, *Russia* 48 C6
Muroran, *Japan* 54 C10
Muros, *Spain* 34 C1
Muros y de Noya, Ría de, *Spain* 34 C1
Muroto, *Japan* 55 H7
Muroto-Misaki, *Japan* 55 H7
Murowana Goślina, *Poland* 45 F3
Murphy, *U.S.A.* 114 E5
Murphys, *U.S.A.* 116 G6
Murrat, *Sudan* 80 D2
Murrat Wells, *Sudan* 80 C3
Murray, *Ky., U.S.A.* 109 G1
Murray, *Utah, U.S.A.* 114 F8
Murray →, *Australia* 95 F2
Murray, L., *U.S.A.* 109 H5
Murray Bridge, *Australia* 95 F2
Murray Harbour, *Canada* 103 C7
Murraysburg, *S. Africa* 88 E3
Murree, *Pakistan* 68 C5
Murrieta, *U.S.A.* 117 M9
Murro di Porco, Capo, *Italy* 31 F8
Murrumbidgee →, *Australia* 95 E3
Murrumburrah, *Australia* 95 E4
Murrurundi, *Australia* 95 E5
Murshid, *Sudan* 80 C3
Murshidabad, *India* 69 G13
Murska Sobota, *Slovenia* 29 B13
Murtle L., *Canada* 104 C5
Murtoa, *Australia* 95 F3
Murtosa, *Portugal* 34 E2
Murungu, *Tanzania* 86 C3
Mururoa, *Pac. Oc.* 97 K14
Murwara, *India* 69 H9
Murwillumbah, *Australia* 95 D5
Mürz →, *Austria* 26 D8
Mürzzuschlag, *Austria* 26 D8
Muş, *Turkey* 70 B4
Mûsa, Gebel, *Egypt* 70 D2
Musa Khel, *Pakistan* 68 D3
Mūsá Qal'eh, *Afghan.* 66 C4
Musaffargarh, *Pakistan* 66 D7
Musafirkhana, *India* 69 F9
Musala, *Bulgaria* 40 D7
Musala, *Indonesia* 62 D1
Musan, *N. Korea* 57 C15
Musangu, *Dem. Rep. of the Congo* 87 E1
Musasa, *Tanzania* 86 C3
Musay'īd, *Qatar* 71 E6
Muscat = Masqat, *Oman* 74 C6
Muscat & Oman = Oman ■, *Asia* 74 C6
Muscatine, *U.S.A.* 112 E9
Musgrave Harbour, *Canada* 103 C9
Musgrave Ranges, *Australia* 93 E5
Mushie, *Dem. Rep. of the Congo* 84 E3
Mushin, *Nigeria* 83 D5

Natalinci

Musi →, *Indonesia* 62 E2
Muskeg →, *Canada* 104 A4
Muskegon, *U.S.A.* 108 D2
Muskegon →, *U.S.A.* 108 D2
Muskegon Heights, *U.S.A.* 108 D2
Muskogee, *U.S.A.* 113 H7
Muskoka, L., *Canada* 110 B5
Muskwa →, *Canada* 104 B4
Muslīmiyah, *Syria* 70 B3
Musmar, *Sudan* 80 D4
Musofu, *Zambia* 87 E2
Musoma, *Tanzania* 86 C3
Musquaro, L., *Canada* 103 B7
Musquodoboit Harbour, *Canada* 103 D7
Musselburgh, *U.K.* 14 F5
Musselshell →, *U.S.A.* 114 C10
Mussidan, *France* 20 C4
Mussomeli, *Italy* 30 E6
Mussoorie, *India* 68 D8
Mussuco, *Angola* 88 B2
Mustafakemalpaşa, *Turkey* 41 F12
Mustang, *Nepal* 69 E10
Musters, L., *Argentina* 128 F3
Musudan, *N. Korea* 57 D15
Muswellbrook, *Australia* 95 E5
Muszyna, *Poland* 45 J7
Mût, *Egypt* 80 B2
Mut, *Turkey* 70 B2
Mutanda, *Mozam.* 89 C5
Mutanda, *Zambia* 87 E2
Mutare, *Zimbabwe* 87 F3
Muting, *Indonesia* 63 F10
Mutoko, *Zimbabwe* 89 B5
Mutoray, *Russia* 51 C11
Mutshatsha, *Dem. Rep. of the Congo* 87 E1
Mutsu, *Japan* 54 D10
Mutsu-Wan, *Japan* 54 D10
Muttaburra, *Australia* 94 C3
Muttalip, *Turkey* 39 B12
Mutton I., *Ireland* 15 D2
Mutuáli, *Mozam.* 87 E4
Mutum Biyu, *Nigeria* 83 D7
Muweilih, *Egypt* 75 E3
Muxía, *Spain* 34 B1
Muy Muy, *Nic.* 120 D2
Muyinga, *Burundi* 86 C3
Muynak, *Uzbekistan* 50 E6
Muzaffarabad, *Pakistan* 69 B5
Muzaffargarh, *Pakistan* 68 D4
Muzaffarnagar, *India* 68 E7
Muzaffarpur, *India* 69 F11
Muzafirpur, *Pakistan* 68 D3
Muzhi, *Russia* 50 C7
Muzillac, *France* 18 E4
Muzūra, *Egypt* 80 J7
Mvôlô, *Sudan* 81 F2
Mvuma, *Zimbabwe* 87 F3
Mvurwi, *Zimbabwe* 87 F3
Mwadui, *Tanzania* 86 C3
Mwambo, *Tanzania* 87 E5
Mwandi, *Zambia* 87 F1
Mwanza, *Dem. Rep. of the Congo* 86 D2
Mwanza, *Tanzania* 86 C3
Mwanza, *Zambia* 87 F1
Mwanza □, *Tanzania* 86 C3
Mwaya, *Tanzania* 87 D3
Mweelrea, *Ireland* 15 C2
Mweka, *Dem. Rep. of the Congo* 84 E4
Mwenezi, *Zimbabwe* 87 G3
Mwenezi →, *Mozam.* 87 G3
Mwenga, *Dem. Rep. of the Congo* 86 C2
Mweru, L., *Zambia* 87 D2
Mweza Range, *Zimbabwe* 87 G3
Mwilambwe, *Dem. Rep. of the Congo* 86 D2
Mwimbi, *Tanzania* 87 D3
Mwinilunga, *Zambia* 87 E1
My Tho, *Vietnam* 65 G6
Myajlar, *India* 68 F4
Myanaung, *Burma* 67 K19
Myanmar = Burma ■, *Asia* 67 J20
Myaungmya, *Burma* 67 L19
Myeik Kyunzu, *Burma* 65 G1
Myers Chuck, *U.S.A.* 104 B2
Myerstown, *U.S.A.* 111 F8
Myingyan, *Burma* 67 J19
Myitkyina, *Burma* 67 G20
Myjava, *Slovak Rep.* 27 C10
Mykhaylivka, *Ukraine* 47 J8
Mykines, *Færoe Is.* 8 E9
Mykolayiv, *Ukraine* 47 J7
Mymensingh, *Bangla.* 67 G17
Mynydd Du, *U.K.* 13 F4
Mýrdalsjökull, *Iceland* 8 E4
Myrhorod, *Ukraine* 47 H7
Myrtle Beach, *U.S.A.* 109 J6
Myrtle Creek, *U.S.A.* 114 E2
Myrtle Point, *U.S.A.* 114 E1
Myrtou, *Cyprus* 36 D12
Mysia, *Turkey* 41 G11
Myślenice, *Poland* 45 J6
Myślibórz, *Poland* 45 F1
Mysłowice, *Poland* 45 H6
Mysore = Karnataka □, *India* 66 N10
Mysore, *India* 66 N10
Mystic, *U.S.A.* 111 E13
Myszków, *Poland* 45 H6
Myszyniec, *Poland* 44 E8
Mytishchi, *Russia* 46 E9
Mývatn, *Iceland* 8 D5
Mže →, *Czech Rep.* 26 B6
Mzimba, *Malawi* 87 E3
Mzimkulu →, *S. Africa* 89 E5
Mzimvubu →, *S. Africa* 89 E4
Mzuzu, *Malawi* 87 E3

N

Na Hearadh = Harris, *U.K.* 14 D2
Na Noi, *Thailand* 64 C3
Na Phao, *Laos* 64 D5
Na Sam, *Vietnam* 58 F6
Na San, *Vietnam* 64 B5
Naab →, *Germany* 25 F8
Na'am, *Sudan* 81 F2
Na'am →, *Sudan* 81 F2
Naantali, *Finland* 9 F19
Naas, *Ireland* 15 C5
Nababeep, *S. Africa* 88 D2
Nabadwip = Navadwip, *India* 69 H13
Nabari, *Japan* 55 G8
Nabawa, *Australia* 93 E1
Nabberu, L., *Australia* 93 E3
Nabburg, *Germany* 25 F8
Naberezhnyye Chelny, *Russia* 48 C11
Nabeul, *Tunisia* 79 A8
Nabha, *India* 68 D7
Nabīd, *Iran* 71 D8
Nabire, *Indonesia* 63 E9
Nabisar, *Pakistan* 68 G3
Nabisipi →, *Canada* 103 B7
Nabiswera, *Uganda* 86 B3
Nablus = Nābulus, *West Bank* 75 C4
Naboomspruit, *S. Africa* 89 C4
Nabou, *Burkina Faso* 82 C4
Nabua, *Phil.* 61 E5
Nābulus, *West Bank* 75 C4
Nacala, *Mozam.* 87 E5
Nacala-Velha, *Mozam.* 87 E5
Nacaome, *Honduras* 120 D2
Nacaroa, *Mozam.* 87 E4
Naches, *U.S.A.* 114 C3
Naches →, *U.S.A.* 116 D6
Nachicapau, L., *Canada* 103 A6
Nachingwea, *Tanzania* 87 E4
Nachna, *India* 68 F4
Náchod, *Czech Rep.* 26 A9
Nacimiento L., *U.S.A.* 116 K6
Naco, *Mexico* 118 A3
Nacogdoches, *U.S.A.* 113 K7
Nácori Chico, *Mexico* 118 B3
Nacozari, *Mexico* 118 A3
Nadi, *Sudan* 80 D3
Nadiad, *India* 68 H5
Nădlac, *Romania* 42 D5
Nador, *Morocco* 78 B5
Nadur, *Malta* 36 C1
Nadūshan, *Iran* 71 C7
Nadvirna, *Ukraine* 47 H3
Nadvoitsy, *Russia* 50 C4
Nadvornaya = Nadvirna, *Ukraine* 47 H3
Nadym, *Russia* 50 C8
Nadym →, *Russia* 50 C8
Nærbø, *Norway* 9 G11
Næstved, *Denmark* 11 J5
Nafada, *Nigeria* 83 C7
Naft-e Safīd, *Iran* 71 D6
Naftshahr, *Iran* 70 C5
Nafud Desert = An Nafūd, *Si. Arabia* 70 D4
Nag Hammâdi, *Egypt* 80 B3
Naga, *Phil.* 61 E5
Nagahama, *Japan* 55 G8
Nagai, *Japan* 54 E10
Nagaland □, *India* 67 G19
Nagano, *Japan* 55 F9
Nagano □, *Japan* 55 F9
Nagaoka, *Japan* 55 F9
Nagappattinam, *India* 66 P11
Nagar →, *Bangla.* 69 G13
Nagar Parkar, *Pakistan* 68 G4
Nagasaki, *Japan* 55 H4
Nagasaki □, *Japan* 55 H4
Nagato, *Japan* 55 G5
Nagaur, *India* 68 F5
Nagda, *India* 68 H6
Nagercoil, *India* 66 Q10
Nagina, *India* 69 E8
Nagīneh, *Iran* 71 C8
Nagir, *Pakistan* 69 A6
Naglarby, *Sweden* 10 D9
Nagod, *India* 69 G9
Nagold, *Germany* 25 G4
Nagold →, *Germany* 25 G4
Nagoorin, *Australia* 94 C5
Nagorno-Karabakh, *Azerbaijan* 70 B5
Nagornyy, *Russia* 51 D13
Nagoya, *Japan* 55 G8
Nagpur, *India* 66 J11
Nagua, *Dom. Rep.* 121 C6
Nagyatád, *Hungary* 42 D2
Nagyecsed, *Hungary* 42 C7
Nagykálló, *Hungary* 42 C6
Nagykanizsa, *Hungary* 42 D2
Nagykáta, *Hungary* 42 C4
Nagykőrös, *Hungary* 42 C4
Naha, *Japan* 55 L3
Nahan, *India* 68 D7
Nahanni Butte, *Canada* 104 A4
Nahanni Nat. Park, *Canada* 104 A4
Nahargarh, *Mad. P., India* 68 G6
Nahargarh, *Raj., India* 68 G7
Nahariyya, *Israel* 70 C2
Nahāvand, *Iran* 71 C6
Nahe →, *Germany* 25 F3
Nahîya, W. →, *Egypt* 80 B3
Naicá, *Mexico* 118 B3
Naicam, *Canada* 105 C8
Naikoon Prov. Park, *Canada* 104 C2
Naila, *Germany* 25 E7
Naimisharanya, *India* 69 F9
Nain, *Canada* 103 A7
Nā'īn, *Iran* 71 C7
Naini Tal, *India* 69 E8
Nainpur, *India* 66 H12
Naintré, *France* 18 F7
Nainwa, *India* 68 G6
Naipu, *Romania* 43 F10
Nairn, *U.K.* 14 D5
Nairobi, *Kenya* 86 C4
Naissaar, *Estonia* 9 G21
Naita, Mt., *Ethiopia* 81 F4
Naivasha, *Kenya* 86 C4
Naivasha, L., *Kenya* 86 C4
Najac, *France* 20 D5
Najafābād, *Iran* 71 C6
Najd, *Si. Arabia* 74 B3
Nájera, *Spain* 32 C2
Najerilla →, *Spain* 32 C2
Najibabad, *India* 68 E8
Najin, *N. Korea* 57 C16
Najmah, *Si. Arabia* 71 E6
Naju, *S. Korea* 57 G14
Nakadōri-Shima, *Japan* 55 H4
Nakalagba, *Dem. Rep. of the Congo* 86 B2
Nakaminato, *Japan* 55 F10
Nakamura, *Japan* 55 H6
Nakano, *Japan* 55 F9
Nakano-Shima, *Japan* 55 K4
Nakashibetsu, *Japan* 54 C12
Nakfa, *Eritrea* 81 D4
Nakhfar al Buşayyah, *Iraq* 70 D5
Nakhichevan = Naxçıvan, *Azerbaijan* 70 B5
Nakhichevan Republic = Naxçıvan □, *Azerbaijan* 50 F5
Nakhl, *Egypt* 75 F2
Nakhl-e Taqī, *Iran* 71 E7
Nakhodka, *Russia* 51 E14
Nakhon Nayok, *Thailand* 64 E3
Nakhon Pathom, *Thailand* 64 F3
Nakhon Phanom, *Thailand* 64 D5
Nakhon Ratchasima, *Thailand* 64 E4
Nakhon Sawan, *Thailand* 64 E3
Nakhon Si Thammarat, *Thailand* 65 H3
Nakhon Thai, *Thailand* 64 D3
Nakhtarana, *India* 68 H3
Nakina, *Canada* 102 B2
Nakło nad Noteią, *Poland* 45 E4
Nako, *Burkina Faso* 82 C4
Nakodar, *India* 68 D6
Nakskov, *Denmark* 11 K5
Naktong →, *S. Korea* 57 G15
Nakuru, *Kenya* 86 C4
Nakuru, L., *Kenya* 86 C4
Nakusp, *Canada* 104 C5
Nal, *Pakistan* 68 F2
Nal →, *Pakistan* 68 G1
Nalázi, *Mozam.* 89 C5
Nalchik, *Russia* 49 J6
Nałęczów, *Poland* 45 G9
Nalerigu, *Ghana* 83 C4
Nalgonda, *India* 66 L11
Nalhati, *India* 69 G12
Naliya, *India* 68 H3
Nallamalai Hills, *India* 66 M11
Nallıhan, *Turkey* 72 B4
Nalón →, *Spain* 34 B4
Nālūt, *Libya* 79 B8
Nam Can, *Vietnam* 65 H5
Nam-ch'on, *N. Korea* 57 E14
Nam Co, *China* 60 C4
Nam Dinh, *Vietnam* 58 G6
Nam Du, Hon, *Vietnam* 65 H5
Nam Ngum Dam, *Laos* 64 C4
Nam-Phan = Cochin China, *Vietnam* 65 G6
Nam Phong, *Thailand* 64 D4
Nam Tha, *Laos* 58 G3
Nam Tok, *Thailand* 64 E2
Namacunde, *Angola* 88 B2
Namacurra, *Mozam.* 89 B6
Namak, Daryācheh-ye, *Iran* 71 C7
Namak, Kavir-e, *Iran* 71 C8
Namakzār, Daryācheh-ye, *Iran* 71 C9
Namaland, *Namibia* 88 C2
Namangan, *Uzbekistan* 50 E8
Namapa, *Mozam.* 87 E4
Namaqualand, *S. Africa* 88 E2
Namasagali, *Uganda* 86 B3
Namber, *Indonesia* 63 E8
Nambour, *Australia* 95 D5
Nambucca Heads, *Australia* 95 E5
Namche Bazar, *Nepal* 69 F12
Namchonjŏm = Nam-ch'on, *N. Korea* 57 E14
Namecunda, *Mozam.* 87 E4
Nameponda, *Mozam.* 87 F4
Náměšť nad Oslavou, *Czech Rep.* 27 B9
Námestovo, *Slovak Rep.* 27 B12
Nametil, *Mozam.* 87 F4
Namew L., *Canada* 105 C8
Namgia, *India* 69 D8
Namhkam, *Burma* 58 E1
Namib Desert = Namibwoestyn, *Namibia* 88 C2
Namibe, *Angola* 85 H2
Namibe □, *Angola* 88 B1
Namibia ■, *Africa* 88 C2
Namibwoestyn, *Namibia* 88 C2
Namīn, *Iran* 73 C13
Namlea, *Indonesia* 63 E7
Namoi →, *Australia* 95 E4
Nampa, *U.S.A.* 114 E5
Nampala, *Mali* 82 B3
Namp'o, *N. Korea* 57 E13
Nampō-Shotō, *Japan* 55 J10
Nampula, *Mozam.* 87 F4
Namrole, *Indonesia* 63 E7
Namse Shankou, *China* 67 E13
Namsen →, *Norway* 8 D14
Namsos, *Norway* 8 D14
Namtsy, *Russia* 51 C13
Namtu, *Burma* 67 H20
Namtumbo, *Tanzania* 87 E4
Namu, *Canada* 104 C3
Namur, *Belgium* 17 D4
Namur □, *Belgium* 17 D4
Namutoni, *Namibia* 88 B2
Namwala, *Zambia* 87 F2
Namwŏn, *S. Korea* 57 G14
Namysłów, *Poland* 45 G4
Nan, *Thailand* 64 C3
Nan →, *Thailand* 64 E3
Nan-ch'ang = Nanchang, *China* 59 C10
Nan Ling, *China* 59 E8
Nan Xian, *China* 59 C9
Nana, *Romania* 43 F11
Nana Kru, *Liberia* 82 E3
Nanaimo, *Canada* 104 D4
Nanam, *N. Korea* 57 D15
Nanan, *China* 59 E12
Nanango, *Australia* 95 D5
Nan'ao, *China* 59 F11
Nanao, *Japan* 55 F8
Nanbu, *China* 58 B6
Nanchang, *Jiangxi, China* 59 C10
Nanchang, *Kiangsi, China* 59 C10
Nancheng, *China* 59 D11
Nanching = Nanjing, *China* 59 A12
Nanchong, *China* 58 B6
Nanchuan, *China* 58 C6
Nancy, *France* 19 D13
Nanda Devi, *India* 69 D8
Nanda Kot, *India* 69 D9
Nandan, *China* 58 E6
Nandan, *Japan* 55 G7
Nanded, *India* 66 K10
Nandewar Ra., *Australia* 95 E5
Nandi, *Fiji* 91 C7
Nandigram, *India* 69 H12
Nandurbar, *India* 66 J9
Nandyal, *India* 66 M11
Nanfeng, *Guangdong, China* 59 F8
Nanfeng, *Jiangxi, China* 59 D11
Nanga-Eboko, *Cameroon* 83 E7
Nanga Parbat, *Pakistan* 69 B6
Nangade, *Mozam.* 87 E4
Nangapinoh, *Indonesia* 62 E4
Nangarhār □, *Afghan.* 66 B7
Nangatayap, *Indonesia* 62 E4
Nangeya Mts., *Uganda* 86 B3
Nangis, *France* 19 D10
Nangong, *China* 56 F8
Nanhua, *China* 58 E3
Nanhuang, *China* 57 F11
Nanhui, *China* 59 B13
Nanjeko, *Zambia* 87 F1
Nanji Shan, *China* 59 D13
Nanjian, *China* 58 E3
Nanjiang, *China* 58 A6
Nanjing, *Fujian, China* 59 E11
Nanjing, *Jiangsu, China* 59 A12
Nanjirinji, *Tanzania* 87 D4
Nankana Sahib, *Pakistan* 68 D5
Nankang, *China* 59 E10
Nanking = Nanjing, *China* 59 A12
Nankoku, *Japan* 55 H6
Nanling, *China* 59 B12
Nanning, *China* 58 F7
Nannup, *Australia* 93 F2
Nanpan Jiang →, *China* 58 E6
Nanpara, *India* 69 F9
Nanpi, *China* 56 E9
Nanping, *Fujian, China* 59 D12
Nanping, *Henan, China* 59 C9
Nanri Dao, *China* 59 E12
Nanripe, *Mozam.* 87 E4
Nansei-Shotō = Ryūkyū-rettō, *Japan* 55 M3
Nansen Sd., *Canada* 4 A3
Nanshan I., *S. China Sea* 62 B5
Nansio, *Tanzania* 86 C3
Nant, *France* 20 D7
Nanterre, *France* 19 D9
Nantes, *France* 18 E5
Nantiat, *France* 20 B5
Nanticoke, *U.S.A.* 111 E8
Nanton, *Canada* 104 C6
Nantong, *China* 59 A13
Nantou, *Taiwan* 59 F13
Nantua, *France* 19 F12
Nantucket I., *U.S.A.* 108 E10
Nantwich, *U.K.* 12 D5
Nanty Glo, *U.S.A.* 110 F6
Nanuque, *Brazil* 125 G10
Nanusa, Kepulauan, *Indonesia* 63 D7
Nanutarra Roadhouse, *Australia* 92 D2
Nanxi, *China* 58 C5
Nanxiong, *China* 59 E10
Nanyang, *China* 56 H7
Nanyi Hu, *China* 59 B12
Nanyuan, *China* 56 E9
Nanyuki, *Kenya* 86 B4
Nanzhang, *China* 59 B8
Nao, C. de la, *Spain* 33 G5
Naococane, L., *Canada* 103 B5
Náousa, *Imathía, Greece* 40 F6
Náousa, *Kikládhes, Greece* 39 D7
Naozhou Dao, *China* 59 G8
Napa, *U.S.A.* 116 G4
Napa →, *U.S.A.* 116 G4
Napanee, *Canada* 102 D4
Napanoch, *U.S.A.* 111 E10
Nape, *Laos* 64 C5
Nape Pass = Keo Neua, Deo, *Vietnam* 64 C5
Napier, *N.Z.* 91 H6
Napier Broome B., *Australia* 92 B4
Napier Pen., *Australia* 94 A2
Napierville, *Canada* 111 A11
Naples = Nápoli, *Italy* 31 B7
Naples, *U.S.A.* 109 M5
Napo, *China* 58 F5
Napo →, *Peru* 122 D3
Napoleon, *N. Dak., U.S.A.* 112 B5
Napoleon, *Ohio, U.S.A.* 108 E3
Nápoli, *Italy* 31 B7
Nápoli, G. di, *Italy* 31 B7
Napopo, *Dem. Rep. of the Congo* 86 B2
Naqâda, *Egypt* 80 B3
Naqadeh, *Iran* 73 D11
Naqb, Ra's an, *Jordan* 75 F4
Naqqāsh, *Iran* 71 C6
Nara, *Japan* 55 G7
Nara, *Mali* 82 B3
Nara □, *Japan* 55 G8
Nara Canal, *Pakistan* 68 G3
Nara Visa, *U.S.A.* 113 H3
Naracoorte, *Australia* 95 F3
Naradhan, *Australia* 95 E4
Naraini, *India* 69 G9
Narasapur, *India* 67 L12
Narathiwat, *Thailand* 65 J3
Narayanganj, *Bangla.* 67 H17
Narayanpet, *India* 66 L10
Narbonne, *France* 20 E7
Narcea →, *Spain* 34 B4
Nardīn, *Iran* 71 B7
Nardò, *Italy* 31 B11
Narembeen, *Australia* 93 F2
Narendranagar, *India* 68 D8
Nares Str., *Arctic* 98 A13
Naretha, *Australia* 93 F3
Narew →, *Poland* 45 F7
Nari →, *Pakistan* 68 F2
Narin, *Afghan.* 66 A6
Narindra, Helodranon' i, *Madag.* 89 A8
Narita, *Japan* 55 G10
Närke, *Sweden* 10 E8
Narmada →, *India* 68 J5
Narman, *Turkey* 73 B9
Narmland, *Sweden* 9 F15
Narnaul, *India* 68 E7
Narni, *Italy* 29 F9
Naro, *Ghana* 82 C4
Naro Fominsk, *Russia* 46 E9
Narodnaya, *Russia* 6 B17
Narok, *Kenya* 86 C4
Narón, *Spain* 34 B2
Narooma, *Australia* 95 F5
Narowal, *Pakistan* 68 C6
Narrabri, *Australia* 95 E4
Narran →, *Australia* 95 D4
Narrandera, *Australia* 95 E4
Narrogin, *Australia* 93 F2
Narromine, *Australia* 95 E4
Narrow Hills Prov. Park, *Canada* 105 C8
Narsimhapur, *India* 69 H8
Narsinghgarh, *India* 68 H7
Nartes, L. e, *Albania* 40 F3
Nartkala, *Russia* 49 J6
Naruto, *Japan* 55 G7
Narva, *Estonia* 46 C5
Narva →, *Russia* 9 G22
Narvik, *Norway* 8 B17
Narvskoye Vdkhr., *Russia* 46 C5
Narwana, *India* 68 E7
Naryan-Mar, *Russia* 50 C6
Narym, *Russia* 50 D9
Naryn, *Kyrgyzstan* 50 E8
Nasa, *Norway* 8 C16
Nasarawa, *Nigeria* 83 D6
Năsăud, *Romania* 43 C9
Naseby, *N.Z.* 91 L3
Naselle, *U.S.A.* 116 D3
Naser, Buheirat en, *Egypt* 80 C3
Nashua, *Mont., U.S.A.* 114 B10
Nashua, *N.H., U.S.A.* 111 D13
Nashville, *Ark., U.S.A.* 113 J8
Nashville, *Ga., U.S.A.* 109 K4
Nashville, *Tenn., U.S.A.* 109 G2
Našice, *Croatia* 42 E3
Nasielsk, *Poland* 45 F7
Nasik, *India* 66 K8
Nasipit, *Phil.* 61 G6
Nasir, *Sudan* 81 F3
Nasirabad, *India* 68 F6
Nasirabad, *Pakistan* 68 E3
Naskaupi →, *Canada* 103 B7
Naso, *Italy* 31 D7
Naşrābād, *Iran* 71 C6
Naşriān-e Pā'īn, *Iran* 70 C5
Nass →, *Canada* 104 C3
Nassarawa □, *Nigeria* 83 D6
Nassau, *Bahamas* 120 A4
Nassau, *U.S.A.* 111 D11
Nassau, B., *Chile* 128 H3
Nasser, L. = Naser, Buheirat en, *Egypt* 80 C3
Nasser City = Kôm Ombo, *Egypt* 80 C3
Nassian, *Ivory C.* 82 D4
Nässjö, *Sweden* 11 G8
Nastapoka →, *Canada* 102 A4
Nastapoka, Is., *Canada* 102 A4
Nasugbu, *Phil.* 61 D4
Näsum, *Sweden* 11 H8
Näsviken, *Sweden* 10 C10
Nata, *Botswana* 88 C4
Nata →, *Botswana* 88 C4
Natal, *Brazil* 125 E11
Natal, *Indonesia* 62 D1
Natal, *S. Africa* 85 K6
Natalinci, *Serbia, Yug.* 42 F5

Naṭanz, *Iran* 71 C6
Natashquan, *Canada* 103 B7
Natashquan →, *Canada* 103 B7
Natchez, *U.S.A.* 113 K9
Natchitoches, *U.S.A.* 113 K8
Nathalia, *Australia* 95 F4
Nathdwara, *India* 68 G5
Nati, Pta., *Spain* 37 A10
Natimuk, *Australia* 95 F3
Nation →, *Canada* 104 B4
National City, *U.S.A.* 117 N9
Natitingou, *Benin* 83 C5
Natividad, I., *Mexico* 118 B1
Natkyizin, *Burma* 64 E1
Natron, L., *Tanzania* 86 C4
Natrona Heights, *U.S.A.* 110 F5
Natrûn, W. el →, *Egypt* 80 H7
Nättraby, *Sweden* 11 H9
Natukanaoka Pan, *Namibia* 88 B2
Natuna Besar, Kepulauan, *Indonesia* 65 L7
Natuna Is. = Natuna Besar, Kepulauan, *Indonesia* 65 L7
Natuna Selatan, Kepulauan, *Indonesia* 65 L7
Natural Bridge, *U.S.A.* 111 B9
Naturaliste, C., *Australia* 94 G4
Nau Qala, *Afghan.* 68 B3
Naucelle, *France* 20 D6
Nauders, *Austria* 26 E3
Nauen, *Germany* 24 C8
Naugatuck, *U.S.A.* 111 E11
Naujoji Akmenė, *Lithuania* 44 B9
Naumburg, *Germany* 24 D7
Nā'ūr at Tunayb, *Jordan* 75 D4
Nauru ■, *Pac. Oc.* 96 H8
Naushahra = Nowshera, *Pakistan* 66 C8
Naushahro, *Pakistan* 68 F3
Naushon I., *U.S.A.* 111 E14
Nauta, *Peru* 124 D4
Nautanwa, *India* 67 F13
Nautla, *Mexico* 119 C5
Nava, *Mexico* 118 B4
Nava, *Spain* 34 B5
Nava del Rey, *Spain* 34 D5
Navadwip, *India* 69 H13
Navahermosa, *Spain* 35 F6
Navahrudak, *Belarus* 46 F3
Navajo Reservoir, *U.S.A.* 115 H10
Navalcarnero, *Spain* 34 E6
Navalmoral de la Mata, *Spain* 34 F5
Navalvillar de Pela, *Spain* 35 F5
Navan = An Uaimh, *Ireland* 15 C5
Navapolatsk, *Belarus* 46 E5
Navarino, I., *Chile* 128 H3
Navarra □, *Spain* 32 C3
Navarre, *U.S.A.* 110 F3
Navarro →, *U.S.A.* 116 F3
Navas de San Juan, *Spain* 35 G7
Navasota, *U.S.A.* 113 K6
Navassa I., *W. Indies* 121 C5
Nävekvarn, *Sweden* 11 F10
Naver →, *U.K.* 14 C4
Navia, *Spain* 34 B4
Navia →, *Spain* 34 B4
Navia de Suarna, *Spain* 34 C3
Navibandar, *India* 68 J3
Navidad, *Chile* 126 C1
Naviraí, *Brazil* 127 A5
Navlakhi, *India* 68 H4
Navlya, *Russia* 47 F8
Năvodari, *Romania* 43 F13
Navoi = Nawoiy, *Uzbekistan* 50 E7
Navojoa, *Mexico* 118 B3
Navolato, *Mexico* 118 C3
Návpaktos, *Greece* 38 C3
Návplion, *Greece* 38 D4
Navrongo, *Ghana* 83 C4
Navsari, *India* 66 J8
Nawa Kot, *Pakistan* 68 E4
Nawab Khan, *Pakistan* 68 D3
Nawabganj, *Ut. P., India* 69 F9
Nawabganj, *Ut. P., India* 69 E8
Nawabshah, *Pakistan* 68 F3
Nawada, *India* 69 G11
Nawakot, *Nepal* 69 F11
Nawalgarh, *India* 68 F6
Nawanshahr, *India* 69 C6
Nawar, Dasht-i-, *Afghan.* 68 C3
Nawi, *Sudan* 80 D3
Nawoiy, *Uzbekistan* 50 E7
Naxçıvan, *Azerbaijan* 70 B5
Naxçıvan □, *Azerbaijan* 50 F5
Náxos, *Greece* 39 D7
Nay, *France* 20 E3
Nay, Mui, *Vietnam* 62 B3
Nāy Band, *Būshehr, Iran* 71 E7
Nāy Band, *Khorāsān, Iran* 71 C8
Nayakhan, *Russia* 51 C16
Nayarit □, *Mexico* 118 C4
Nayé, *Senegal* 82 C2
Nayong, *China* 58 D5
Nayoro, *Japan* 54 B11
Nayyāl, W. →, *Si. Arabia* 70 D3
Nazaré, *Brazil* 125 F11
Nazaré, *Portugal* 35 F1
Nazareth = Nazerat, *Israel* 75 C4
Nazareth, *U.S.A.* 111 F9
Nazas, *Mexico* 118 B4
Nazas →, *Mexico* 118 B4
Nazca, *Peru* 124 F4
Naze, The, *U.K.* 13 F9
Nazerat, *Israel* 75 C4
Nāzīk, *Iran* 70 B5
Nazilli, *Turkey* 39 D10
Nazir Hat, *Bangla.* 67 H17
Nazko, *Canada* 104 C4
Nazko →, *Canada* 104 C4
Nazret, *Ethiopia* 81 F4
Nazwá, *Oman* 74 C6
Nchanga, *Zambia* 87 E2
Ncheu, *Malawi* 87 E3
Ndala, *Tanzania* 86 C3
Ndalatando, *Angola* 84 F2
Ndali, *Benin* 83 D5
Ndareda, *Tanzania* 86 C4
Ndélé, *C.A.R.* 84 C4
Ndikiniméki, *Cameroon* 83 E7
N'Dioum, *Senegal* 82 B2
Ndjamena, *Chad* 79 F8
Ndola, *Zambia* 87 E2
Ndoto Mts., *Kenya* 86 B4
Nduguti, *Tanzania* 86 C3
Néa Alikarnassós, *Greece* 39 F7
Néa Ankhíalos, *Greece* 38 B4
Néa Epídhavros, *Greece* 38 D5
Néa Flippiás, *Greece* 38 B2
Néa Ionia, *Greece* 38 B4
Néa Kallikrátia, *Greece* 40 F7
Néa Mákri, *Greece* 38 C5
Néa Moudhaniá, *Greece* 40 F7
Néa Péramos, *Attikí, Greece* 38 C5
Néa Péramos, *Kavála, Greece* 41 F8
Néa Víssi, *Greece* 41 E10
Néa Zíkhna, *Greece* 40 E7
Neagh, Lough, *U.K.* 15 B5
Neah Bay, *U.S.A.* 116 B2
Neale, L., *Australia* 92 D5
Neamţ □, *Romania* 43 C11
Neápolis, *Kozáni, Greece* 40 F5
Neápolis, *Kríti, Greece* 36 D7
Neápolis, *Lakonía, Greece* 38 E5
Near Is., *U.S.A.* 100 C1
Neath, *U.K.* 13 F4
Neath Port Talbot □, *U.K.* 13 F4
Nebbou, *Burkina Faso* 83 C4
Nebelat el Hagana, *Sudan* 81 E2
Nebine Cr. →, *Australia* 95 D4
Nebitdag, *Turkmenistan* 50 F6
Nebo, *Australia* 94 C4
Nebolchy, *Russia* 46 C7
Nebraska □, *U.S.A.* 112 E5
Nebraska City, *U.S.A.* 112 E7
Nébrodi, Monti, *Italy* 31 E7
Necedah, *U.S.A.* 112 C9
Nechako →, *Canada* 104 C4
Neches →, *U.S.A.* 113 L8
Neckar →, *Germany* 25 F4
Necochea, *Argentina* 126 D4
Neda, *Spain* 34 B2
Nedelino, *Bulgaria* 41 E9
Nedelišće, *Croatia* 29 B13
Nédha →, *Greece* 38 D3
Needles, *Canada* 104 D5
Needles, *U.S.A.* 117 L12
Needles, The, *U.K.* 13 G6
Ñeembucú □, *Paraguay* 126 B4
Neemuch = Nimach, *India* 68 G6
Neenah, *U.S.A.* 108 C1
Neepawa, *Canada* 105 C9
Neftçala, *Azerbaijan* 71 B6
Neftegorsk, *Russia* 49 H4
Neftekumsk, *Russia* 49 H7
Nefyn, *U.K.* 12 E3
Négala, *Mali* 82 C3
Negapatam = Nagappattinam, *India* 66 P11
Negaunee, *U.S.A.* 108 B2
Negele, *Ethiopia* 81 F4
Negev Desert = Hanegev, *Israel* 75 E4
Negoiul, Vf., *Romania* 43 E9
Negombo, *Sri Lanka* 66 R11
Negotin, *Serbia, Yug.* 40 B6
Negotino, *Macedonia* 40 E6
Negra, Peña, *Spain* 34 C4
Negra, Pta., *Peru* 122 D2
Negrais, C. = Maudin Sun, *Burma* 67 M19
Negreşti, *Romania* 43 D12
Negreşti-Oaş, *Romania* 43 C8
Negril, *Jamaica* 120 C4
Negro →, *Argentina* 122 H4
Negro →, *Brazil* 122 D4
Negro →, *Uruguay* 127 C4
Negros, *Phil.* 61 G5
Negru Vodă, *Romania* 43 G13
Neguac, *Canada* 103 C6
Nehalem →, *U.S.A.* 116 E3
Nehāvand, *Iran* 71 C6
Nehbandān, *Iran* 71 D9
Nehoiu, *Romania* 43 E11
Nei Mongol Zizhiqu □, *China* 56 D7
Neijiang, *China* 58 C5
Neillsville, *U.S.A.* 112 C9
Neilton, *U.S.A.* 114 C2
Neiqiu, *China* 56 F8
Neiva, *Colombia* 124 C3
Neixiang, *China* 56 H6
Nejanilini L., *Canada* 105 B9
Nejd = Najd, *Si. Arabia* 74 B3
Nejo, *Ethiopia* 81 F4
Nekā, *Iran* 71 B7
Nekemte, *Ethiopia* 81 F4
Nêkheb, *Egypt* 80 B3
Neksø, *Denmark* 11 J9
Nelas, *Portugal* 34 E3
Nelia, *Australia* 94 C3
Nelidovo, *Russia* 46 D7
Neligh, *U.S.A.* 112 D5
Nelkan, *Russia* 51 D14
Nellore, *India* 66 M11
Nelson, *Canada* 104 D5
Nelson, *N.Z.* 91 J4
Nelson, *U.K.* 12 D5
Nelson, *Ariz., U.S.A.* 115 J7
Nelson, *Nev., U.S.A.* 117 K12
Nelson →, *Canada* 105 C9
Nelson, C., *Australia* 95 F3
Nelson, Estrecho, *Chile* 128 G2
Nelson Bay, *Australia* 95 E5
Nelson Forks, *Canada* 104 B4
Nelson House, *Canada* 105 B9
Nelson L., *Canada* 105 B8
Nelspoort, *S. Africa* 88 E3
Nelspruit, *S. Africa* 89 D5
Néma, *Mauritania* 82 B3
Neman, *Russia* 9 J20
Neman →, *Lithuania* 9 J20
Neméa, *Greece* 38 D4
Nemeiben L., *Canada* 105 B7
Nemërçkë, Mal, *Albania* 40 F4
Nemira, Vf., *Romania* 43 D11
Némiscau, *Canada* 102 B4
Némiscau, L., *Canada* 102 B4
Nemours, *France* 19 D9
Nemšová, *Slovak Rep.* 27 C11
Nemunas = Neman →, *Lithuania* 9 J20
Nemuro, *Japan* 54 C12
Nemuro-Kaikyō, *Japan* 54 C12
Nen Jiang →, *China* 57 B13
Nenagh, *Ireland* 15 D3
Nenasi, *Malaysia* 65 L4
Nene →, *U.K.* 13 E8
Nénita, *Greece* 39 C8
Nenjiang, *China* 60 B7
Neno, *Malawi* 87 F3
Neodesha, *U.S.A.* 113 G7
Neokhórion, *Aitolía kai Akarnanía, Greece* 38 C3
Neokhórion, *Árta, Greece* 38 B2
Néon Karlovásion, *Greece* 39 D8
Néon Petrítsi, *Greece* 40 E7
Neosho, *U.S.A.* 113 G7
Neosho →, *U.S.A.* 113 H7
Nepal ■, *Asia* 69 F11
Nepalganj, *Nepal* 69 E9
Nepalganj Road, *India* 69 E9
Nephi, *U.S.A.* 114 G8
Nephin, *Ireland* 15 B2
Nepi, *Italy* 29 F9
Nepomuk, *Czech Rep.* 26 B6
Neptune, *U.S.A.* 111 F10
Nera →, *Italy* 29 F9
Nera →, *Romania* 42 F6
Nérac, *France* 20 D4
Nerang, *Australia* 95 D5
Neratovice, *Czech Rep.* 26 A7
Nerchinsk, *Russia* 51 D12
Nereju, *Romania* 43 E11
Nerekhta, *Russia* 46 D11
Néret, L., *Canada* 103 B5
Neretvanski Kanal, *Croatia* 29 E14
Neringa, *Lithuania* 9 J19
Nerja, *Spain* 35 J7
Nerl →, *Russia* 46 D11
Nerpio, *Spain* 33 G2
Nerva, *Spain* 35 H4
Nervi, *Italy* 28 D6
Neryungri, *Russia* 51 D13
Nescopeck, *U.S.A.* 111 E8
Nesebŭr, *Bulgaria* 41 D11
Ness, L., *U.K.* 14 D4
Ness City, *U.S.A.* 112 F5
Nesterov, *Poland* 47 G2
Nestórion, *Greece* 40 F5
Néstos →, *Greece* 41 E8
Nesvady, *Slovak Rep.* 27 D11
Nesvizh = Nyasvizh, *Belarus* 47 F4
Netanya, *Israel* 75 C3
Netarhat, *India* 69 H11
Nete →, *Belgium* 17 C4
Netherdale, *Australia* 94 C4
Netherlands ■, *Europe* 17 C5
Netherlands Antilles ■, *W. Indies* 124 A5
Neto →, *Italy* 31 C10
Netrang, *India* 68 J5
Nettancourt, *France* 19 D11
Nettetal, *Germany* 24 D2
Nettilling L., *Canada* 101 B12
Nettuno, *Italy* 30 A5
Netzahualcoyotl, Presa, *Mexico* 119 D6
Neu-Isenburg, *Germany* 25 E4
Neu-Ulm, *Germany* 25 G6
Neubrandenburg, *Germany* 24 B9
Neubukow, *Germany* 24 A7
Neuburg, *Germany* 25 G7
Neuchâtel, *Switz.* 25 J2
Neuchâtel □, *Switz.* 25 J2
Neuchâtel, Lac de, *Switz.* 25 J2
Neudau, *Austria* 26 D9
Neuenhagen, *Germany* 24 C9
Neuenhaus, *Germany* 24 C2
Neuf-Brisach, *France* 19 D14
Neufahrn, *Bayern, Germany* 25 G8
Neufahrn, *Bayern, Germany* 25 G7
Neufchâteau, *Belgium* 17 E5
Neufchâteau, *France* 19 D12
Neufchâtel-en-Bray, *France* 18 C8
Neufchâtel-sur-Aisne, *France* 19 C11
Neuhaus, *Germany* 24 B6
Neuillé-Pont-Pierre, *France* 18 E7
Neuilly-St-Front, *France* 19 C10
Neukalen, *Germany* 24 B8
Neumarkt, *Germany* 25 F7
Neumünster, *Germany* 24 A5
Neung-sur-Beuvron, *France* 19 E8
Neunkirchen, *Austria* 26 D9
Neunkirchen, *Germany* 25 F3
Neuquén, *Argentina* 128 D3
Neuquén □, *Argentina* 126 D2
Neuruppin, *Germany* 24 C8
Neusäss, *Germany* 25 G6
Neuse →, *U.S.A.* 109 H7
Neusiedl, *Austria* 27 D9
Neusiedler See, *Austria* 27 D9
Neuss, *Germany* 24 D2
Neussargues-Moissac, *France* 20 C7
Neustadt, *Bayern, Germany* 25 F8
Neustadt, *Bayern, Germany* 25 G7
Neustadt, *Bayern, Germany* 25 F6
Neustadt, *Bayern, Germany* 25 E7
Neustadt, *Brandenburg, Germany* 24 C8
Neustadt, *Hessen, Germany* 24 E5
Neustadt, *Niedersachsen, Germany* 24 C5
Neustadt, *Rhld-Pfz., Germany* 25 F4
Neustadt, *Sachsen, Germany* 24 D10
Neustadt, *Schleswig-Holstein, Germany* 24 A6
Neustadt, *Thüringen, Germany* 24 E7
Neustrelitz, *Germany* 24 B9
Neuvic, *France* 20 C6
Neuville-sur-Saône, *France* 21 C8
Neuvy-le-Roi, *France* 18 E7
Neuvy-St-Sépulchre, *France* 19 F8
Neuvy-sur-Barangeon, *France* 19 E9
Neuwerk, *Germany* 24 B4
Neuwied, *Germany* 24 E3
Neva →, *Russia* 46 C6
Nevada, *Iowa, U.S.A.* 112 D8
Nevada, *Mo., U.S.A.* 113 G7
Nevada □, *U.S.A.* 114 G5
Nevada, Sierra, *Spain* 35 H7
Nevada, Sierra, *U.S.A.* 114 G3
Nevada City, *U.S.A.* 116 F6
Nevado, Cerro, *Argentina* 126 D2
Nevel, *Russia* 46 D5
Nevers, *France* 19 F10
Nevertire, *Australia* 95 E4
Nevesinje, *Bos.-H.* 40 C2
Neville, *Canada* 105 D7
Nevinnomyssk, *Russia* 49 H6
Nevis, *W. Indies* 121 C7
Nevrokop = Gotse Delchev, *Bulgaria* 40 E7
Nevşehir, *Turkey* 70 B2
New →, *U.S.A.* 108 F5
New Aiyansh, *Canada* 104 B3
New Albany, *Ind., U.S.A.* 108 F3
New Albany, *Miss., U.S.A.* 113 H10
New Albany, *Pa., U.S.A.* 111 E8
New Amsterdam, *Guyana* 124 B7
New Angledool, *Australia* 95 D4
New Baltimore, *U.S.A.* 110 D2
New Bedford, *U.S.A.* 111 E14
New Berlin, *N.Y., U.S.A.* 111 D9
New Berlin, *Pa., U.S.A.* 110 F8
New Bern, *U.S.A.* 109 H7
New Bethlehem, *U.S.A.* 110 F5
New Bloomfield, *U.S.A.* 110 F7
New Boston, *U.S.A.* 113 J7
New Braunfels, *U.S.A.* 113 L5
New Brighton, *N.Z.* 91 K4
New Brighton, *U.S.A.* 110 F4
New Britain, *Papua N. G.* 96 H7
New Britain, *U.S.A.* 111 E12
New Brunswick, *U.S.A.* 111 F10
New Brunswick □, *Canada* 103 C6
New Bussa, *Nigeria* 83 D5
New Caledonia ■, *Pac. Oc.* 96 K8
New Castile = Castilla-La Mancha □, *Spain* 6 H5
New Castle, *Ind., U.S.A.* 108 F3
New Castle, *Pa., U.S.A.* 110 F4
New City, *U.S.A.* 111 E11
New Concord, *U.S.A.* 110 G3
New Cumberland, *U.S.A.* 110 F4
New Cuyama, *U.S.A.* 117 L7
New Delhi, *India* 68 E7
New Denver, *Canada* 104 D5
New Don Pedro Reservoir, *U.S.A.* 116 H6
New England, *U.S.A.* 112 B3
New England Ra., *Australia* 95 E5
New Forest, *U.K.* 13 G6
New Galloway, *U.K.* 14 F4
New Glasgow, *Canada* 103 C7
New Guinea, *Oceania* 52 K17
New Hamburg, *Canada* 110 C4
New Hampshire □, *U.S.A.* 111 C13
New Hampton, *U.S.A.* 112 D8
New Hanover, *S. Africa* 89 D5
New Hartford, *U.S.A.* 111 C9
New Haven, *Conn., U.S.A.* 111 E12
New Haven, *Mich., U.S.A.* 110 D2
New Hazelton, *Canada* 104 B3
New Hebrides = Vanuatu ■, *Pac. Oc.* 96 J8
New Holland, *U.S.A.* 111 F8
New Iberia, *U.S.A.* 113 K9
New Ireland, *Papua N. G.* 96 H7
New Jersey □, *U.S.A.* 108 E8
New Kensington, *U.S.A.* 110 F5
New Lexington, *U.S.A.* 108 F4
New Liskeard, *Canada* 102 C4
New London, *Conn., U.S.A.* 111 E12
New London, *Ohio, U.S.A.* 110 E2
New London, *Wis., U.S.A.* 112 C10
New Madrid, *U.S.A.* 113 G10
New Martinsville, *U.S.A.* 108 F5
New Meadows, *U.S.A.* 114 D5
New Melones L., *U.S.A.* 116 H6
New Mexico □, *U.S.A.* 115 J10
New Milford, *Conn., U.S.A.* 111 E11
New Milford, *Pa., U.S.A.* 111 E9
New Norcia, *Australia* 93 F2
New Norfolk, *Australia* 94 G4
New Orleans, *U.S.A.* 113 L9
New Philadelphia, *U.S.A.* 110 F3
New Plymouth, *N.Z.* 91 H5
New Plymouth, *U.S.A.* 114 E5
New Port Richey, *U.S.A.* 109 L4
New Providence, *Bahamas* 120 A4
New Quay, *U.K.* 13 E3
New Radnor, *U.K.* 13 E4
New Richmond, *Canada* 103 C6
New Richmond, *U.S.A.* 112 C8
New Roads, *U.S.A.* 113 K9
New Rochelle, *U.S.A.* 111 F11
New Rockford, *U.S.A.* 112 B5
New Romney, *U.K.* 13 G8
New Ross, *Ireland* 15 D5
New Salem, *U.S.A.* 112 B4
New Scone, *U.K.* 14 E5
New Siberian I. = Novaya Sibir, Ostrov, *Russia* 51 B16
New Siberian Is. = Novosibirskiye Ostrova, *Russia* 51 B15
New Smyrna Beach, *U.S.A.* 109 L5
New South Wales □, *Australia* 95 E4
New Town, *U.S.A.* 112 B3
New Tredegar, *U.K.* 13 F4
New Ulm, *U.S.A.* 112 C7
New Waterford, *Canada* 103 C7
New Westminster, *Canada* 116 A4
New York, *U.S.A.* 111 F11
New York □, *U.S.A.* 111 D9
New York Mts., *U.S.A.* 115 J6
New Zealand ■, *Oceania* 91 J6
Newaj →, *India* 68 G7
Newala, *Tanzania* 87 E4
Newark, *Del., U.S.A.* 108 F8
Newark, *N.J., U.S.A.* 111 F10
Newark, *N.Y., U.S.A.* 110 C7
Newark, *Ohio, U.S.A.* 110 F2
Newark-on-Trent, *U.K.* 12 D7
Newark Valley, *U.S.A.* 111 D8
Newberg, *U.S.A.* 114 D2
Newberry, *Mich., U.S.A.* 108 B3
Newberry, *S.C., U.S.A.* 109 H5
Newberry Springs, *U.S.A.* 117 L10
Newboro L., *Canada* 111 B8
Newbridge = Droichead Nua, *Ireland* 15 C5
Newburgh, *Canada* 110 B8
Newburgh, *U.S.A.* 111 E10
Newbury, *U.K.* 13 F6
Newbury, *N.H., U.S.A.* 111 B12
Newbury, *Vt., U.S.A.* 111 B12
Newburyport, *U.S.A.* 109 D10
Newcastle, *Australia* 95 E5
Newcastle, *N.B., Canada* 103 C6
Newcastle, *Ont., Canada* 102 D4
Newcastle, *S. Africa* 89 D4
Newcastle, *U.K.* 15 B6
Newcastle, *Calif., U.S.A.* 116 G5
Newcastle, *Wyo., U.S.A.* 112 D2
Newcastle Emlyn, *U.K.* 13 E3
Newcastle Ra., *Australia* 92 C5
Newcastle-under-Lyme, *U.K.* 12 D5
Newcastle-upon-Tyne, *U.K.* 12 C6
Newcastle Waters, *Australia* 94 B1
Newcastle West, *Ireland* 15 D2
Newcomb, *U.S.A.* 111 C10
Newcomerstown, *U.S.A.* 110 F3
Newdegate, *Australia* 93 F2
Newell, *Australia* 94 B4
Newell, *U.S.A.* 112 C3
Newfane, *U.S.A.* 110 C6
Newfield, *U.S.A.* 111 D8
Newfound L., *U.S.A.* 111 C13
Newfoundland, *N. Amer.* 98 E14
Newfoundland, *U.S.A.* 111 E9
Newfoundland □, *Canada* 103 B8
Newhall, *U.S.A.* 117 L8
Newhaven, *U.K.* 13 G8
Newkirk, *U.S.A.* 113 G6
Newlyn, *U.K.* 13 G2
Newman, *Australia* 92 D2
Newman, *U.S.A.* 116 H5
Newmarket, *Canada* 110 B5
Newmarket, *Ireland* 15 D2
Newmarket, *U.K.* 13 E8
Newmarket, *N.H., U.S.A.* 111 C14
Newmarket, *N.H., U.S.A.* 111 C14
Newnan, *U.S.A.* 109 J3
Newport, *Ireland* 15 C2
Newport, *I. of W., U.K.* 13 G6
Newport, *Newp., U.K.* 13 F5
Newport, *Ark., U.S.A.* 113 H9
Newport, *Ky., U.S.A.* 108 F3
Newport, *N.H., U.S.A.* 111 C12
Newport, *N.Y., U.S.A.* 111 C9
Newport, *Oreg., U.S.A.* 114 D1
Newport, *Pa., U.S.A.* 110 F7
Newport, *R.I., U.S.A.* 111 E13
Newport, *Tenn., U.S.A.* 109 H4
Newport, *Vt., U.S.A.* 111 B12
Newport, *Wash., U.S.A.* 114 B5
Newport □, *U.K.* 13 F4
Newport Beach, *U.S.A.* 117 M9
Newport News, *U.S.A.* 108 G7
Newport Pagnell, *U.K.* 13 E7
Newquay, *U.K.* 13 G2
Newry, *U.K.* 15 B5
Newton, *Ill., U.S.A.* 112 F10
Newton, *Iowa, U.S.A.* 112 E8
Newton, *Kans., U.S.A.* 113 F6
Newton, *Mass., U.S.A.* 111 D13
Newton, *Miss., U.S.A.* 113 J10
Newton, *N.C., U.S.A.* 109 H5
Newton, *N.J., U.S.A.* 111 E10
Newton, *Tex., U.S.A.* 113 K8
Newton Abbot, *U.K.* 13 G4
Newton Aycliffe, *U.K.* 12 C6
Newton Falls, *U.S.A.* 110 E4
Newton Stewart, *U.K.* 14 G4
Newtonmore, *U.K.* 14 D4
Newtown, *U.K.* 13 E4
Newtownabbey, *U.K.* 15 B6

Newtownards, *U.K.* 15 B6
Newtownbarry = Bunclody, *Ireland* 15 D5
Newtownstewart, *U.K.* 15 B4
Newville, *U.S.A.* 110 F7
Nexon, *France* 20 C5
Neya, *Russia* 48 A6
Neyrīz, *Iran* 71 D7
Neyshābūr, *Iran* 71 B8
Nezhin = Nizhyn, *Ukraine* 47 G6
Nezperce, *U.S.A.* 114 C5
Ngabang, *Indonesia* 62 D3
Ngabordamlu, Tanjung, *Indonesia* 63 F8
N'Gage, *Angola* 84 F3
Ngala, *Nigeria* 83 C7
Ngambé, *Cameroon* 83 D7
Ngambé, *Cameroon* 83 D7
Ngami Depression, *Botswana* 88 C3
Ngamo, *Zimbabwe* 87 F2
Ngangala, *Sudan* 81 G3
Nganglong Kangri, *China* 67 C12
Ngao, *Thailand* 64 C2
Ngaoundéré, *Cameroon* 84 C2
Ngapara, *N.Z.* 91 L3
Ngara, *Tanzania* 86 C3
Ngawi, *Indonesia* 63 G14
Nghia Lo, *Vietnam* 58 G5
Ngoboli, *Sudan* 81 G3
Ngoma, *Malawi* 87 E3
Ngomahura, *Zimbabwe* 87 G3
Ngomba, *Tanzania* 87 D3
Ngop, *Sudan* 81 F3
Ngoring Hu, *China* 60 C4
Ngorkou, *Mali* 82 B4
Ngorongoro, *Tanzania* 86 C4
Ngozi, *Burundi* 86 C2
Ngudu, *Tanzania* 86 C3
Nguigmi, *Niger* 79 F8
Nguila, *Cameroon* 83 E7
Nguiu, *Australia* 92 B5
Ngukurr, *Australia* 94 A1
Ngulu Atoll, *Pac. Oc.* 63 C9
Ngunga, *Tanzania* 86 C3
Nguru, *Nigeria* 83 C7
Nguru Mts., *Tanzania* 86 D4
Nguyen Binh, *Vietnam* 58 F5
Nha Trang, *Vietnam* 65 F7
Nhacoongo, *Mozam.* 89 C6
Nhamaabué, *Mozam.* 87 F4
Nhamundá →, *Brazil* 125 D7
Nhangulaze, L., *Mozam.* 89 C5
Nhill, *Australia* 95 F3
Nho Quan, *Vietnam* 58 G5
Nhulunbuy, *Australia* 94 A2
Nia-nia, *Dem. Rep. of the Congo* 86 B2
Niafounké, *Mali* 82 B4
Niagara Falls, *Canada* 102 D4
Niagara Falls, *U.S.A.* 110 C6
Niagara-on-the-Lake, *Canada* 110 C5
Niah, *Malaysia* 62 D4
Niamey, *Niger* 83 C5
Niandan-Koro, *Guinea* 82 C3
Nianforando, *Guinea* 82 D2
Niangara, *Dem. Rep. of the Congo* 86 B2
Niangbo, *Ivory C.* 82 D3
Niangoloko, *Burkina Faso* 82 C4
Niantic, *U.S.A.* 111 E12
Niaro, *Sudan* 81 E3
Nias, *Indonesia* 62 D1
Niassa □, *Mozam.* 87 E4
Nibāk, *Si. Arabia* 71 E7
Nibe, *Denmark* 11 H3
Nicaragua ■, *Cent. Amer.* 120 D2
Nicaragua, L. de, *Nic.* 120 D2
Nicastro, *Italy* 31 D9
Nice, *France* 21 E11
Niceville, *U.S.A.* 109 K2
Nichicun, L., *Canada* 103 B5
Nichinan, *Japan* 55 J5
Nicholás, Canal, *W. Indies* 120 B3
Nicholasville, *U.S.A.* 108 G3
Nichols, *U.S.A.* 111 D8
Nicholson, *Australia* 92 C4
Nicholson, *U.S.A.* 111 E9
Nicholson →, *Australia* 94 B2
Nicholson L., *Canada* 105 A8
Nicholson Ra., *Australia* 93 E2
Nicholville, *U.S.A.* 111 B10
Nicobar Is., *Ind. Oc.* 52 J13
Nicola, *Canada* 104 C4
Nicolls Town, *Bahamas* 120 A4
Nicopolis, *Greece* 38 B2
Nicosia, *Cyprus* 36 D12
Nicosia, *Italy* 31 E7
Nicótera, *Italy* 31 D8
Nicoya, *Costa Rica* 120 D2
Nicoya, G. de, *Costa Rica* 120 E3
Nicoya, Pen. de, *Costa Rica* 120 E2
Nidd →, *U.K.* 12 D6
Nidda, *Germany* 25 E5
Nidda →, *Germany* 25 E4
Nidwalden □, *Switz.* 25 J4
Nidzica, *Poland* 45 E7
Niebüll, *Germany* 24 A4
Nied →, *Germany* 19 C13
Niederaula, *Germany* 24 E5
Niederbayern □, *Germany* 25 G8
Niederbronn-les-Bains, *France* 19 D14
Niedere Tauern, *Austria* 26 D7
Niederlausitz, *Germany* 24 D9
Niederösterreich □, *Austria* 26 C8
Niedersachsen □, *Germany* 24 C4
Niekerkshoop, *S. Africa* 88 D3
Niellé, *Ivory C.* 82 C3
Niemba, *Dem. Rep. of the Congo* 86 D2
Niemen = Neman →, *Lithuania* 9 J20
Niemodlin, *Poland* 45 H4
Nienburg, *Germany* 24 C5
Niepołomice, *Poland* 45 H7
Niers →, *Germany* 24 D1
Niesky, *Germany* 24 D10
Nieszawa, *Poland* 45 F5
Nieu Bethesda, *S. Africa* 88 E3
Nieuw Amsterdam, *Surinam* 125 B7
Nieuw Nickerie, *Surinam* 125 B7
Nieuwoudtville, *S. Africa* 88 E2
Nieuwpoort, *Belgium* 17 C2
Nieves, Pico de las, *Canary Is.* 37 G4
Nièvre □, *France* 19 E10
Niga, *Mali* 82 C3
Niğde, *Turkey* 70 B2
Nigel, *S. Africa* 89 D4
Niger □, *Nigeria* 83 D6
Niger ■, *W. Afr.* 83 B7
Niger →, *W. Afr.* 83 D6
Niger Delta, *Africa* 83 E6
Nigeria ■, *W. Afr.* 83 D6
Nighasin, *India* 69 E9
Nightcaps, *N.Z.* 91 L2
Nigríta, *Greece* 40 F7
Nii-Jima, *Japan* 55 G9
Niigata, *Japan* 54 F9
Niigata □, *Japan* 55 F9
Niihama, *Japan* 55 H6
Niihau, *U.S.A.* 106 H14
Niimi, *Japan* 55 G6
Niitsu, *Japan* 54 F9
Níjar, *Spain* 33 J2
Nijil, *Jordan* 75 E4
Nijkerk, *Neths.* 17 B5
Nijmegen, *Neths.* 17 C5
Nijverdal, *Neths.* 17 B6
Nīk Pey, *Iran* 71 B6
Nike, *Nigeria* 83 D6
Nikiniki, *Indonesia* 63 F6
Nikísiani, *Greece* 41 F8
Nikítas, *Greece* 40 F7
Nikki, *Benin* 83 D5
Nikkō, *Japan* 55 F9
Nikolayev = Mykolayiv, *Ukraine* 47 J7
Nikolayevsk, *Russia* 48 E7
Nikolayevsk-na-Amur, *Russia* 51 D15
Nikolsk, *Russia* 48 D8
Nikolskoye, *Russia* 51 D17
Nikopol, *Bulgaria* 41 C8
Nikopol, *Ukraine* 47 J8
Niksar, *Turkey* 72 B7
Nīkshahr, *Iran* 71 E9
Nikšić, *Montenegro, Yug.* 40 D2
Nîl, Nahr en →, *Africa* 80 H7
Nîl el Abyad →, *Sudan* 81 D3
Nîl el Azraq →, *Sudan* 81 D3
Nila, *Indonesia* 63 F7
Niland, *U.S.A.* 117 M11
Nile = Nîl, Nahr en →, *Africa* 80 H7
Niles, *Mich., U.S.A.* 108 E2
Niles, *Ohio, U.S.A.* 110 E4
Nilüfer →, *Turkey* 41 F12
Nim Ka Thana, *India* 68 F6
Nimach, *India* 68 G6
Nimbahera, *India* 68 G6
Nîmes, *France* 21 E8
Nimfaíon, Ákra = Pínnes, Ákra, *Greece* 41 F8
Nimmitabel, *Australia* 95 F4
Nimule, *Sudan* 81 G3
Nin, *Croatia* 29 D12
Nīnawá, *Iraq* 70 B4
Nindigully, *Australia* 95 D4
Nineveh = Nīnawá, *Iraq* 70 B4
Ning Xian, *China* 56 G4
Ning'an, *China* 57 B15
Ningbo, *China* 59 C13
Ningcheng, *China* 57 D10
Ningde, *China* 59 D12
Ningdu, *China* 59 D10
Ninggang, *China* 59 D9
Ningguo, *China* 59 B12
Ninghai, *China* 59 C13
Ninghua, *China* 59 D11
Ningi, *Nigeria* 83 C6
Ningjin, *China* 56 F8
Ningjing Shan, *China* 58 C2
Ninglang, *China* 58 D3
Ningling, *China* 56 G8
Ningming, *China* 58 F6
Ningnan, *China* 58 D4
Ningpo = Ningbo, *China* 59 C13
Ningqiang, *China* 56 H4
Ningshan, *China* 56 H5
Ningsia Hui A.R. = Ningxia Huizu Zizhiqu □, *China* 56 F4
Ningwu, *China* 56 E7
Ningxia Huizu Zizhiqu □, *China* 56 F4
Ningxiang, *China* 59 C9
Ningyang, *China* 56 G9
Ningyuan, *China* 59 E8
Ninh Binh, *Vietnam* 58 G5
Ninh Giang, *Vietnam* 64 B6
Ninh Hoa, *Vietnam* 64 F7
Ninh Ma, *Vietnam* 64 F7
Ninove, *Belgium* 17 D4
Nioaque, *Brazil* 127 A4
Niobrara, *U.S.A.* 112 D6
Niobrara →, *U.S.A.* 112 D6
Niono, *Mali* 82 C3
Nionsamoridougou, *Guinea* 82 D3
Nioro du Rip, *Senegal* 82 C1
Nioro du Sahel, *Mali* 82 B3
Niort, *France* 20 B3
Nipawin, *Canada* 105 C8
Nipfjället, *Sweden* 10 C6
Nipigon, *Canada* 102 C2
Nipigon, L., *Canada* 102 C2
Nipishish L., *Canada* 103 B7
Nipissing, L., *Canada* 102 C4
Nipomo, *U.S.A.* 117 K6
Nipton, *U.S.A.* 117 K11
Niquelândia, *Brazil* 125 F9
Nīr, *Iran* 70 B5
Nirasaki, *Japan* 55 G9
Nirmal, *India* 66 K11
Nirmali, *India* 69 F12
Niš, *Serbia, Yug.* 40 C5
Nisa, *Portugal* 35 F3
Nişāb, *Si. Arabia* 70 D5
Nişāb, *Yemen* 74 E4
Nišava →, *Serbia, Yug.* 40 C5
Niscemi, *Italy* 31 E7
Nishinomiya, *Japan* 55 G7
Nishino'omote, *Japan* 55 J5
Nishiwaki, *Japan* 55 G7
Nísíros, *Greece* 39 E9
Niška Banja, *Serbia, Yug.* 40 C6
Niskibi →, *Canada* 102 A2
Nisko, *Poland* 45 H9
Nisporeni, *Moldova* 43 C13
Nisqually →, *U.S.A.* 116 C4
Nissáki, *Greece* 36 A3
Nissan →, *Sweden* 11 H6
Nissum Bredning, *Denmark* 11 H2
Nissum Fjord, *Denmark* 11 H2
Nistru = Dnister →, *Europe* 47 J6
Nisutlin →, *Canada* 104 A2
Nitchequon, *Canada* 103 B5
Niterói, *Brazil* 127 A7
Nith →, *Canada* 110 C4
Nith →, *U.K.* 14 F5
Nitra, *Slovak Rep.* 27 C11
Nitra →, *Slovak Rep.* 27 D11
Nitriansky □, *Slovak Rep.* 27 C11
Nittenau, *Germany* 25 F8
Niuafo'ou, *Tonga* 91 B11
Niue, *Cook Is.* 97 J11
Niulan Jiang →, *China* 58 D4
Niut, *Indonesia* 62 D4
Niutou Shan, *China* 59 C13
Niuzhuang, *China* 57 D12
Nivala, *Finland* 8 E21
Nivelles, *Belgium* 17 D4
Nivernais, *France* 19 E10
Niwas, *India* 69 H9
Nixon, *U.S.A.* 113 L6
Nizamabad, *India* 66 K11
Nizamghat, *India* 67 E19
Nizhne Kolymsk, *Russia* 51 C17
Nizhnegorskiy = Nyzhnohirskyy, *Ukraine* 47 K8
Nizhnekamsk, *Russia* 48 C10
Nizhneudinsk, *Russia* 51 D10
Nizhnevartovsk, *Russia* 50 C8
Nizhniy Chir, *Russia* 49 F6
Nizhniy Lomov, *Russia* 48 D6
Nizhniy Novgorod, *Russia* 48 B7
Nizhniy Tagil, *Russia* 50 D6
Nizhyn, *Ukraine* 47 G6
Nizina Mazowiecka, *Poland* 45 F8
Nizip, *Turkey* 70 B3
Nízké Tatry, *Slovak Rep.* 27 C12
Nízký Jeseník, *Czech Rep.* 27 B10
Nizza Monferrato, *Italy* 28 D5
Njakwa, *Malawi* 87 E3
Njanji, *Zambia* 87 E3
Njegoš, *Montenegro, Yug.* 40 D2
Njinjo, *Tanzania* 87 D4
Njombe, *Tanzania* 87 D3
Njombe →, *Tanzania* 86 D4
Njurundabommen, *Sweden* 10 B11
Nkambe, *Cameroon* 83 D7
Nkana, *Zambia* 87 E2
Nkandla, *S. Africa* 89 D5
Nkawkaw, *Ghana* 83 D4
Nkayi, *Zimbabwe* 87 F2
Nkhotakota, *Malawi* 87 E3
Nkongsamba, *Cameroon* 83 E6
Nkurenkuru, *Namibia* 88 B2
Nkwanta, *Ghana* 82 D4
Nmai →, *Burma* 58 F2
Noakhali = Maijdi, *Bangla.* 67 H17
Nobel, *Canada* 110 A4
Nobeoka, *Japan* 55 H5
Noblejas, *Spain* 34 F7
Noblesville, *U.S.A.* 108 E3
Noce →, *Italy* 28 B8
Nocera Inferiore, *Italy* 31 B7
Nocera Umbra, *Italy* 29 E9
Noci, *Italy* 31 B10
Nocona, *U.S.A.* 113 J6
Nocrich, *Romania* 43 E9
Noda, *Japan* 55 G9
Nogales, *Mexico* 118 A2
Nogales, *U.S.A.* 115 L8
Nogaro, *France* 20 E3
Nogat →, *Poland* 44 D6
Nōgata, *Japan* 55 H5
Nogent, *France* 19 D12
Nogent-le-Rotrou, *France* 18 D7
Nogent-sur-Seine, *France* 19 D10
Noggerup, *Australia* 93 F2
Noginsk, *Moskva, Russia* 46 E10
Noginsk, *Tunguska, Russia* 51 C10
Nogoa →, *Australia* 94 C4
Nogoyá, *Argentina* 126 C4
Nógrád □, *Hungary* 42 C4
Noguera Pallaresa →, *Spain* 32 D5
Noguera Ribagorzana →, *Spain* 32 D5
Nohar, *India* 68 E6
Nohfelden, *Germany* 25 F3
Nohta, *India* 69 H8
Noia, *Spain* 34 C2
Noire, Montagne, *France* 20 E6
Noire, Mt., *France* 18 D3
Noirétable, *France* 20 C7
Noirmoutier, Î. de, *France* 18 F4
Noirmoutier-en-l'Île, *France* 18 F4
Nojane, *Botswana* 88 C3
Nojima-Zaki, *Japan* 55 G9
Nok Kundi, *Pakistan* 66 E3
Nokaneng, *Botswana* 88 B3
Nokia, *Finland* 9 F20
Nokomis, *Canada* 105 C8
Nokomis L., *Canada* 105 B8
Nol, *Sweden* 11 G6
Nola, *C.A.R.* 84 D3
Nola, *Italy* 31 B7
Nolay, *France* 19 F11
Noli, C. di, *Italy* 28 D5
Nolinsk, *Russia* 48 B9
Noma Omuramba →, *Namibia* 88 B3
Nombre de Dios, *Panama* 120 E4
Nome, *U.S.A.* 100 B3
Nomo-Zaki, *Japan* 55 H4
Nonacho L., *Canada* 105 A7
Nonancourt, *France* 18 D8
Nonda, *Australia* 94 C3
None, *Italy* 28 D4
Nong Chang, *Thailand* 64 E2
Nong Het, *Laos* 64 C4
Nong Khai, *Thailand* 64 D4
Nong'an, *China* 57 B13
Nongoma, *S. Africa* 89 D5
Nonoava, *Mexico* 118 B3
Nonoava →, *Mexico* 118 B3
Nonthaburi, *Thailand* 64 F3
Nontron, *France* 20 C4
Nonza, *France* 21 F13
Noonamah, *Australia* 92 B5
Noord Brabant □, *Neths.* 17 C5
Noord Holland □, *Neths.* 17 B4
Noordbeveland, *Neths.* 17 C3
Noordoostpolder, *Neths.* 17 B5
Noordwijk, *Neths.* 17 B4
Nootka I., *Canada* 104 D3
Nopiming Prov. Park, *Canada* 105 C9
Nora, *Eritrea* 81 D5
Nora, *Sweden* 10 E9
Noralee, *Canada* 104 C3
Noranda = Rouyn-Noranda, *Canada* 102 C4
Norberg, *Sweden* 10 D9
Nórcia, *Italy* 29 F10
Norco, *U.S.A.* 117 M9
Nord □, *France* 19 B10
Nord-Kivu □, *Dem. Rep. of the Congo* 86 C2
Nord-Ostsee-Kanal, *Germany* 24 A5
Nord-Pas-de-Calais □, *France* 19 B9
Nordaustlandet, *Svalbard* 4 B9
Nordborg, *Denmark* 11 J3
Nordby, *Denmark* 11 J2
Norddeich, *Germany* 24 B3
Nordegg, *Canada* 104 C5
Norden, *Germany* 24 B3
Nordenham, *Germany* 24 B4
Norderney, *Germany* 24 B3
Norderstedt, *Germany* 24 B6
Nordfjord, *Norway* 9 F11
Nordfriesische Inseln, *Germany* 24 A4
Nordhausen, *Germany* 24 D6
Nordhorn, *Germany* 24 C3
Norðoyar, *Færoe Is.* 8 E9
Nordingrå, *Sweden* 10 B12
Nordjyllands Amtskommune □, *Denmark* 11 G4
Nordkapp, *Norway* 8 A21
Nordkapp, *Svalbard* 4 A9
Nordkinn = Kinnarodden, *Norway* 6 A11
Nordkinn-halvøya, *Norway* 8 A22
Nördlingen, *Germany* 25 G6
Nordrhein-Westfalen □, *Germany* 24 D3
Nordstrand, *Germany* 24 A4
Nordvik, *Russia* 51 B12
Nore →, *Ireland* 15 D4
Norfolk, *Nebr., U.S.A.* 112 D6
Norfolk, *Va., U.S.A.* 108 G7
Norfolk □, *U.K.* 13 E8
Norfolk I., *Pac. Oc.* 96 K8
Norfork L., *U.S.A.* 113 G8
Norilsk, *Russia* 51 C9
Norma, Mt., *Australia* 94 C3
Normal, *U.S.A.* 112 E10
Norman, *U.S.A.* 113 H6
Norman →, *Australia* 94 B3
Norman Wells, *Canada* 100 B7
Normanby →, *Australia* 94 A3
Normandin, *Canada* 102 C5
Normanhurst, Mt., *Australia* 93 E3
Normanton, *Australia* 94 B3
Normétal, *Canada* 102 C4
Norquay, *Canada* 105 C8
Norquinco, *Argentina* 128 E2
Norra Dellen, *Sweden* 10 C10
Norra Ulvön, *Sweden* 10 A12
Norrahammar, *Sweden* 11 G8
Norrbotten □, *Sweden* 8 C19
Nørre Åby, *Denmark* 11 J3
Nørre Alslev, *Denmark* 11 K5
Nørresundby, *Denmark* 11 G3
Norrhult, *Sweden* 11 G9
Norris Point, *Canada* 103 C8
Norristown, *U.S.A.* 111 F9
Norrköping, *Sweden* 11 F10
Norrland, *Sweden* 9 E16
Norrsundet, *Sweden* 10 D11
Norrtälje, *Sweden* 10 E12
Norseman, *Australia* 93 F3
Norsk, *Russia* 51 D14
Norte, Pta. del, *Canary Is.* 37 G2
Norte, Serra do, *Brazil* 124
North, C., *Canada* 103 C7
North Adams, *U.S.A.* 111 D11
North Arm, *Canada* 104 A5
North Augusta, *U.S.A.* 109 J5
North Ayrshire □, *U.K.* 14 F4
North Bass I., *U.S.A.* 110 E2
North Battleford, *Canada* 105 C7
North Bay, *Canada* 102 C4
North Belcher Is., *Canada* 102 A4
North Bend, *Oreg., U.S.A.* 114 E1
North Bend, *Pa., U.S.A.* 110 E7
North Bend, *Wash., U.S.A.* 116 C5
North Bennington, *U.S.A.* 111 D11
North Berwick, *U.K.* 14 E6
North Berwick, *U.S.A.* 111 C14
North C., *Canada* 103 C7
North C., *N.Z.* 91 F4
North Canadian →, *U.S.A.* 113 H7
North Canton, *U.S.A.* 110 F3
North Cape = Nordkapp, *Norway* 8 A21
North Cape = Nordkapp, *Svalbard* 4 A9
North Caribou L., *Canada* 102 B1
North Carolina □, *U.S.A.* 109 H6
North Cascades National Park, *U.S.A.* 114 B3
North Channel, *Canada* 102 C3
North Channel, *U.K.* 14 F3
North Charleston, *U.S.A.* 109 J6
North Chicago, *U.S.A.* 108 D2
North Creek, *U.S.A.* 111 C11
North Dakota □, *U.S.A.* 112 B5
North Downs, *U.K.* 13 F8
North East, *U.S.A.* 110 D5
North East Frontier Agency = Arunachal Pradesh □, *India* 67 F19
North East Lincolnshire □, *U.K.* 12 D7
North Eastern □, *Kenya* 86 B5
North Esk →, *U.K.* 14 E6
North European Plain, *Europe* 6 E10
North Foreland, *U.K.* 13 F9
North Fork, *U.S.A.* 116 H7
North Fork American →, *U.S.A.* 116 G5
North Fork Feather →, *U.S.A.* 116 F5
North Fork Grand →, *U.S.A.* 112 C3
North Fork Red →, *U.S.A.* 113 H5
North Frisian Is. = Nordfriesische Inseln, *Germany* 24 A4
North Gower, *Canada* 111 A9
North Hd., *Australia* 93 F1
North Henik L., *Canada* 105 A9
North Highlands, *U.S.A.* 116 G5
North Horr, *Kenya* 86 B4
North I., *Kenya* 86 B4
North I., *N.Z.* 91 H5
North Kingsville, *U.S.A.* 110 E4
North Knife →, *Canada* 105 B10
North Koel →, *India* 69 G10
North Korea ■, *Asia* 57 E14
North Lakhimpur, *India* 67 F19
North Lanarkshire □, *U.K.* 14 F5
North Las Vegas, *U.S.A.* 117 J11
North Lincolnshire □, *U.K.* 12 D7
North Little Rock, *U.S.A.* 113 H8
North Loup →, *U.S.A.* 112 E5
North Magnetic Pole, *Canada* 4 B2
North Minch, *U.K.* 14 C3
North Moose L., *Canada* 105 C8
North Myrtle Beach, *U.S.A.* 109 J6
North Nahanni →, *Canada* 104 A4
North Olmsted, *U.S.A.* 110 E3
North Ossetia □, *Russia* 49 J7
North Pagai, I. = Pagai Utara, Pulau, *Indonesia* 62 E2
North Palisade, *U.S.A.* 116 H8
North Platte, *U.S.A.* 112 E4
North Platte →, *U.S.A.* 112 E4
North Pole, *Arctic* 4 A
North Portal, *Canada* 105 D8
North Powder, *U.S.A.* 114 D5
North Pt., *U.S.A.* 110 A1
North Rhine Westphalia = Nordrhein-Westfalen □, *Germany* 24 D3
North River, *Canada* 103 B8
North Ronaldsay, *U.K.* 14 B6
North Saskatchewan →, *Canada* 105 C7
North Sea, *Europe* 6 D6
North Seal →, *Canada* 105 B9
North Somerset □, *U.K.* 13 F5
North Sporades = Vóriai Sporádhes, *Greece* 38 B5
North Sydney, *Canada* 103 C7
North Syracuse, *U.S.A.* 111 C8
North Taranaki Bight, *N.Z.* 91 H5
North Thompson →, *Canada* 104 C4
North Tonawanda, *U.S.A.* 110 C6
North Troy, *U.S.A.* 111 B12
North Truchas Pk., *U.S.A.* 115 J11
North Twin I., *Canada* 102 B4
North Tyne →, *U.K.* 12 B5
North Uist, *U.K.* 14 D1
North Vancouver, *Canada* 104 D4
North Vernon, *U.S.A.* 108 F3

North Wabasca L., *Canada* 104 B6
North Walsham, *U.K.* 12 E9
North-West □, *S. Africa* 88 D4
North West C., *Australia* 92 D1
North West Christmas I. Ridge, *Pac. Oc.* 97 G11
North West Frontier □, *Pakistan* 68 C4
North West Highlands, *U.K.* 14 D4
North West River, *Canada* 103 B7
North Western □, *Zambia* 87 E2
North Wildwood, *U.S.A.* 108 F8
North York Moors, *U.K.* 12 C7
North Yorkshire □, *U.K.* 12 C6
Northallerton, *U.K.* 12 C6
Northam, *Australia* 93 F2
Northam, *S. Africa* 88 C4
Northampton, *Australia* 93 E1
Northampton, *U.K.* 13 E7
Northampton, *Mass., U.S.A.* 111 D12
Northampton, *Pa., U.S.A.* 111 F9
Northamptonshire □, *U.K.* 13 E7
Northbridge, *U.S.A.* 111 D13
Northcliffe, *Australia* 93 F2
Northeast Providence Chan., *W. Indies* 120 A4
Northeim, *Germany* 24 D6
Northern □, *Ghana* 83 D4
Northern □, *Malawi* 87 E3
Northern □, *Uganda* 86 B3
Northern □, *Zambia* 87 E3
Northern Cape □, *S. Africa* 88 D3
Northern Circars, *India* 67 L13
Northern Indian L., *Canada* 105 B9
Northern Ireland □, *U.K.* 15 B5
Northern Light L., *Canada* 102 C1
Northern Marianas ■, *Pac. Oc.* 96 F6
Northern Province □, *S. Leone* 82 D2
Northern Province □, *S. Africa* 89 C4
Northern Territory □, *Australia* 92 D5
Northfield, *Minn., U.S.A.* 112 C8
Northfield, *Vt., U.S.A.* 111 B12
Northland □, *N.Z.* 91 F4
Northome, *U.S.A.* 112 B7
Northport, *Ala., U.S.A.* 109 J2
Northport, *Wash., U.S.A.* 114 B5
Northumberland □, *U.K.* 12 B6
Northumberland, C., *Australia* 95 F3
Northumberland Is., *Australia* 94 C4
Northumberland Str., *Canada* 103 C7
Northville, *U.S.A.* 111 C10
Northwest Providence Channel, *W. Indies* 120 A4
Northwest Territories □, *Canada* 100 B9
Northwood, *Iowa, U.S.A.* 112 D8
Northwood, *N. Dak., U.S.A.* 112 B6
Norton, *U.S.A.* 112 F5
Norton, *Zimbabwe* 87 F3
Norton Sd., *U.S.A.* 100 B3
Nortorf, *Germany* 24 A5
Norwalk, *Calif., U.S.A.* 117 M8
Norwalk, *Conn., U.S.A.* 111 E11
Norwalk, *Iowa, U.S.A.* 112 E8
Norwalk, *Ohio, U.S.A.* 110 E2
Norway, *Maine, U.S.A.* 109 C10
Norway, *Mich., U.S.A.* 108 C2
Norway ■, *Europe* 8 E14
Norway House, *Canada* 105 C9
Norwegian Sea, *Atl. Oc.* 4 C8
Norwich, *Canada* 110 D4
Norwich, *U.K.* 13 E9
Norwich, *Conn., U.S.A.* 111 E12
Norwich, *N.Y., U.S.A.* 111 D9
Norwood, *Canada* 110 B7
Norwood, *U.S.A.* 111 B10
Noshiro, *Japan* 54 D10
Nosivka, *Ukraine* 47 G6
Nosovka = Nosivka, *Ukraine* 47 G6
Noşratābād, *Iran* 71 D8
Noss Hd., *U.K.* 14 C5
Nossebro, *Sweden* 11 F6
Nossob →, *S. Africa* 88 D3
Nossombougou, *Mali* 82 C3
Nosy Barren, *Madag.* 85 H8
Nosy Be, *Madag.* 85 G9
Nosy Boraha, *Madag.* 89 B8
Nosy Lava, *Madag.* 89 A8
Nosy Varika, *Madag.* 89 C8
Noteć →, *Poland* 45 F2
Notikewin →, *Canada* 104 B5
Notios Evvoïkos Kólpos, *Greece* 38 C5
Noto, *Italy* 31 F8
Noto, G. di, *Italy* 31 F8
Notodden, *Norway* 9 G13
Notre Dame B., *Canada* 103 C8
Notre Dame de Koartac = Quaqtaq, *Canada* 101 B13
Notre-Dame-des-Bois, *Canada* 111 A13
Notre Dame d'Ivugivic = Ivujivik, *Canada* 101 B12
Notre-Dame-du-Nord, *Canada* 102 C4
Notsé, *Togo* 83 D5
Nottawasaga B., *Canada* 110 B4
Nottaway →, *Canada* 102 B4
Nottingham, *U.K.* 12 E6
Nottingham, City of □, *U.K.* 12 E6
Nottingham I., *Canada* 101 B12
Nottinghamshire □, *U.K.* 12 D6
Nottoway →, *U.S.A.* 108 G7
Notwane →, *Botswana* 88 C4
Nouâdhibou, *Mauritania* 78 D2
Nouâdhibou, Ras, *Mauritania* 78 D2
Nouakchott, *Mauritania* 82 B1
Nouâmghâr, *Mauritania* 82 B1
Nouméa, *N. Cal.* 96 K8
Nouna, *Burkina Faso* 82 C4
Noupoort, *S. Africa* 88 E3
Nouveau Comptoir = Wemindji, *Canada* 102 B4
Nouvelle-Amsterdam, I., *Ind. Oc.* 3 F13
Nouvelle-Calédonie = New Caledonia ■, *Pac. Oc.* 96 K8
Nouzonville, *France* 19 C11
Nová Baňa, *Slovak Rep.* 27 C11
Nová Bystřice, *Czech Rep.* 26 B8
Nova Casa Nova, *Brazil* 125 E10
Nova Esperança, *Brazil* 127 A5
Nova Friburgo, *Brazil* 127 A7
Nova Gaia = Cambundi-Catembo, *Angola* 84 G3
Nova Gorica, *Slovenia* 29 C10
Nova Gradiška, *Croatia* 42 E2
Nova Iguaçu, *Brazil* 127 A7
Nova Iorque, *Brazil* 125 E10
Nova Kakhovka, *Ukraine* 47 J7
Nova Lamego, *Guinea-Biss.* 82 C2
Nova Lima, *Brazil* 127 A7
Nova Lisboa = Huambo, *Angola* 85 G3
Nova Lusitânia, *Mozam.* 87 F3
Nova Mambone, *Mozam.* 89 C6
Nova Odesa, *Ukraine* 47 J6
Nová Paka, *Czech Rep.* 26 A8
Nova Pavova, *Serbia, Yug.* 42 F5
Nova Scotia □, *Canada* 103 C7
Nova Siri, *Italy* 31 B9
Nova Sofala, *Mozam.* 89 C5
Nova Varoš, *Serbia, Yug.* 40 C3
Nova Venécia, *Brazil* 125 G10
Nova Zagora, *Bulgaria* 41 D10
Novaci, *Macedonia* 40 E5
Novaci, *Romania* 43 E8
Novaféltria, *Italy* 29 E9
Novaleksandrovskaya = Novoaleksandrovsk, *Russia* 49 H5
Novannenskiy = Novoannenskiy, *Russia* 48 E6
Novar, *Canada* 110 A5
Novara, *Italy* 28 C5
Novato, *U.S.A.* 116 G4
Novaya Kakhovka = Nova Kakhovka, *Ukraine* 47 J7
Novaya Kazanka, *Kazakstan* 49 F9
Novaya Ladoga, *Russia* 46 B7
Novaya Lyalya, *Russia* 50 D7
Novaya Sibir, Ostrov, *Russia* 51 B16
Novaya Zemlya, *Russia* 50 B6
Nové Město, *Slovak Rep.* 27 C10
Nové Město na Moravě, *Czech Rep.* 26 B9
Nové Město nad Metují, *Czech Rep.* 27 A9
Nové Zámky, *Slovak Rep.* 27 C11
Novelda, *Spain* 33 G4
Novellara, *Italy* 28 D7
Noventa Vicentina, *Italy* 29 C8
Novgorod, *Russia* 46 C6
Novgorod-Severskiy = Novhorod-Siverskyy, *Ukraine* 47 G7
Novhorod-Siverskyy, *Ukraine* 47 G7
Novi Bečej, *Serbia, Yug.* 42 E5
Novi Iskar, *Bulgaria* 40 D7
Novi Kneževac, *Serbia, Yug.* 42 D5
Novi Lígure, *Italy* 28 D5
Novi Pazar, *Bulgaria* 41 C11
Novi Pazar, *Serbia, Yug.* 40 C4
Novi Sad, *Serbia, Yug.* 42 E4
Novi Slankamen, *Serbia, Yug.* 42 E5
Novi Travnik, *Bos.-H.* 42 F2
Novi Vinodolski, *Croatia* 29 C11
Novigrad, *Istra, Croatia* 29 C10
Novigrad, *Zadar, Croatia* 29 D12
Novigradsko More, *Croatia* 29 D12
Nôvo Hamburgo, *Brazil* 127 B5
Novo Mesto, *Slovenia* 29 C12
Novo Miloševo, *Serbia, Yug.* 42 E5
Novo Remanso, *Brazil* 125 E10
Novoaleksandrovsk, *Russia* 49 H5
Novoannenskiy, *Russia* 48 E6
Novoataysk, *Russia* 50 D9
Novoazovsk, *Ukraine* 47 J10
Novocheboksarsk, *Russia* 48 B8
Novocherkassk, *Russia* 49 G5
Novodevichye, *Russia* 48 D9
Novogrudok = Navahrudak, *Belarus* 46 F3
Novohrad-Volynskyy, *Ukraine* 47 G4
Novokachalinsk, *Russia* 54 B6
Novokazalinsk = Zhangaqazaly, *Kazakstan* 50 E7
Novokhopersk, *Russia* 48 E5
Novokuybyshevsk, *Russia* 48 D9
Novokuznetsk, *Russia* 50 D9
Novomirgorod, *Ukraine* 47 H6
Novomoskovsk, *Russia* 46 E10
Novomoskovsk, *Ukraine* 47 H8
Novopolotsk = Navapolatsk, *Belarus* 46 E5
Novorossiysk, *Russia* 47 K9
Novorybnoye, *Russia* 51 B11
Novorzhev, *Russia* 46 D5
Novosej, *Albania* 40 E4
Novoselytsya, *Ukraine* 47 H4
Novoshakhtinsk, *Russia* 47 J10
Novosibirsk, *Russia* 50 D9
Novosibirskiye Ostrova, *Russia* 51 B15
Novosil, *Russia* 47 F9
Novosokolniki, *Russia* 46 D6
Novotitarovskaya, *Russia* 49 H4
Novotroitsk, *Russia* 50 D6
Novoukrayinka, *Ukraine* 47 H6
Novouljanovsk, *Russia* 48 C9
Novouzensk, *Russia* 48 E9
Novovolynsk, *Ukraine* 47 G3
Novovoronezhskiy, *Russia* 47 G10
Novozybkov, *Russia* 47 F6
Novska, *Croatia* 29 C14
Novvy Urengoy, *Russia* 50 C8
Nový Bor, *Czech Rep.* 26 A7
Novy Bug = Novyy Buh, *Ukraine* 47 J7
Nový Bydžov, *Czech Rep.* 26 A8
Novy Dwór Mazowiecki, *Poland* 45 F7
Nový Jičín, *Czech Rep.* 27 B11
Novyy Afon, *Georgia* 49 J5
Novyy Buh, *Ukraine* 47 J7
Novyy Oskol, *Russia* 47 G9
Novyy Port, *Russia* 50 C8
Now Shahr, *Iran* 71 B6
Nowa Deba, *Poland* 45 H8
Nowa Ruda, *Poland* 45 H3
Nowa Sarzyna, *Poland* 45 H9
Nowa Sól, *Poland* 45 G2
Nowata, *U.S.A.* 113 G7
Nowbarān, *Iran* 71 C6
Nowe, *Poland* 44 E5
Nowe Miasteczko, *Poland* 45 G2
Nowe Miasto, *Poland* 45 G7
Nowe Miasto Lubawskie, *Poland* 44 E6
Nowe Skalmierzyce, *Poland* 45 G4
Nowe Warpno, *Poland* 44 E1
Nowghāb, *Iran* 71 C8
Nowgong, *Assam, India* 67 F18
Nowgong, *Mad. P., India* 69 G8
Nowogard, *Poland* 44 E2
Nowogród, *Poland* 45 E8
Nowogród Bobrzanski, *Poland* 45 G2
Nowogrodziec, *Poland* 45 G2
Nowra-Bomaderry, *Australia* 95 E5
Nowshera, *Pakistan* 66 C8
Nowy Dwór Gdański, *Poland* 44 D6
Nowy Sącz, *Poland* 45 J7
Nowy Staw, *Poland* 44 D6
Nowy Targ, *Poland* 45 J7
Nowy Tomyśl, *Poland* 45 F3
Nowy Wiśnicz, *Poland* 45 J7
Noxen, *U.S.A.* 111 E8
Noxon, *U.S.A.* 114 C6
Noyabr'sk, *Russia* 50 C8
Noyant, *France* 18 E7
Noyers, *France* 19 E10
Noyon, *France* 19 C9
Noyon, *Mongolia* 56 C2
Nozay, *France* 18 E5
Nqutu, *S. Africa* 89 D5
Nsanje, *Malawi* 87 F4
Nsawam, *Ghana* 83 D4
Nsomba, *Zambia* 87 E2
Nsukka, *Nigeria* 83 D6
Ntui, *Cameroon* 83 E7
Nu Jiang →, *China* 58 E2
Nu Shan, *China* 58 E2
Nuba Mts. = Nubah, Jibalan, *Sudan* 81 E3
Nubah, Jibalan, *Sudan* 81 E3
Nubia, *Africa* 76 D7
Nubian Desert = Nûbîya, Es Sahrâ en, *Sudan* 80 C3
Nûbîya, Es Sahrâ en, *Sudan* 80 C3
Nubledo, *Spain* 34 B5
Nuboai, *Indonesia* 63 E9
Nubra →, *India* 69 B7
Nucet, *Romania* 42 D7
Nueces →, *U.S.A.* 113 M6
Nueltin L., *Canada* 105 A9
Nueva Asunción □, *Paraguay* 126 A3
Nueva Carteya, *Spain* 35 H6
Nueva Gerona, *Cuba* 120 B3
Nueva Palmira, *Uruguay* 126 C4
Nueva Rosita, *Mexico* 118 B4
Nueva San Salvador, *El Salv.* 120 D2
Nueva Tabarca, *Spain* 33 G4
Nuéve de Julio, *Argentina* 126 D3
Nuevitas, *Cuba* 120 B4
Nuevo, G., *Argentina* 128 E4
Nuevo Casas Grandes, *Mexico* 118 A3
Nuevo Guerrero, *Mexico* 119 B5
Nuevo Laredo, *Mexico* 119 B5
Nuevo León □, *Mexico* 118 C5
Nuevo Rocafuerte, *Ecuador* 124 D3
Nugget Pt., *N.Z.* 91 M2
Nugrus, Gebel, *Egypt* 80 C3
Nuhaka, *N.Z.* 91 H6
Nuits-St-Georges, *France* 19 E11
Nukey Bluff, *Australia* 95 E2
Nukheila, *Sudan* 80 D2
Nukhuyb, *Iraq* 70 C4
Nuku'alofa, *Tonga* 91 E12
Nukus, *Uzbekistan* 50 E6
Nules, *Spain* 32 F4
Nullagine, *Australia* 92 D3
Nullagine →, *Australia* 92 D3
Nullarbor, *Australia* 93 F5
Nullarbor Plain, *Australia* 93 F4
Numalla, L., *Australia* 95 D3
Numan, *Nigeria* 83 D7
Numata, *Japan* 55 F9
Numatinna →, *Sudan* 81 F2
Numazu, *Japan* 55 G9
Numbulwar, *Australia* 94 A2
Numfoor, *Indonesia* 63 E8
Numurkah, *Australia* 95 F4
Nunaksaluk I., *Canada* 103 A7
Nunap Isua, *Greenland* 4 D5
Nunavut □, *Canada* 101 B11
Nunda, *U.S.A.* 110 D7
Nungarin, *Australia* 93 F2
Nungo, *Mozam.* 87 E4
Nungwe, *Tanzania* 86 C3
Nunivak I., *U.S.A.* 100 B3
Nunkun, *India* 69 C7
Núoro, *Italy* 30 B2
Nūrābād, *Iran* 71 E8
Nure →, *Italy* 28 C6
Nuremberg = Nürnberg, *Germany* 25 F7
Nuri, *Mexico* 118 B3
Nuriootpa, *Australia* 95 E2
Nurlat, *Russia* 48 C10
Nurmes, *Finland* 8 E23
Nürnberg, *Germany* 25 F7
Nurpur, *Pakistan* 68 D4
Nurra, La, *Italy* 30 B1
Nurran, L. = Terewah, L., *Australia* 95 D4
Nurrari Lakes, *Australia* 93 E5
Nurri, *Italy* 30 C2
Nürtingen, *Germany* 25 G5
Nurzec →, *Poland* 45 F9
Nus, *Italy* 28 C4
Nusa Barung, *Indonesia* 63 H15
Nusa Kambangan, *Indonesia* 63 G13
Nusa Tenggara Barat □, *Indonesia* 62 F5
Nusa Tenggara Timur □, *Indonesia* 63 F6
Nusaybin, *Turkey* 73 D9
Nushki, *Pakistan* 68 E2
Nuuk, *Greenland* 101 B14
Nuwakot, *Nepal* 69 E10
Nuweiba', *Egypt* 70 D2
Nuwerus, *S. Africa* 88 E2
Nuweveldberge, *S. Africa* 88 E3
Nuyts, C., *Australia* 93 F5
Nuyts, Pt., *Australia* 93 G2
Nuyts Arch., *Australia* 95 E1
Nxau-Nxau, *Botswana* 88 B3
Nyaake, *Liberia* 82 E3
Nyabing, *Australia* 93 F2
Nyack, *U.S.A.* 111 E11
Nyagan, *Russia* 50 C7
Nyahanga, *Tanzania* 86 C3
Nyahua, *Tanzania* 86 D3
Nyahururu, *Kenya* 86 B4
Nyainqentanglha Shan, *China* 60 C4
Nyakanazi, *Tanzania* 86 C3
Nyakrom, *Ghana* 83 D4
Nyâlâ, *Sudan* 81 E1
Nyamandhlovu, *Zimbabwe* 87 F2
Nyambiti, *Tanzania* 86 C3
Nyamlell, *Sudan* 81 F2
Nyamwaga, *Tanzania* 86 C3
Nyandekwa, *Tanzania* 86 C3
Nyanding →, *Sudan* 81 F3
Nyandoma, *Russia* 46 B11
Nyangana, *Namibia* 88 B3
Nyanguge, *Tanzania* 86 C3
Nyankpala, *Ghana* 83 D4
Nyanza, *Rwanda* 86 C2
Nyanza □, *Kenya* 86 C3
Nyanza-Lac, *Burundi* 86 C2
Nyaponges, *Sudan* 81 F3
Nyasa, L., *Africa* 87 E3
Nyasvizh, *Belarus* 47 F4
Nyazura, *Zimbabwe* 87 F3
Nyazwidzi →, *Zimbabwe* 87 G3
Nyborg, *Denmark* 11 J4
Nybro, *Sweden* 11 H9
Nyda, *Russia* 50 C8
Nyeri, *Kenya* 86 C4
Nyerol, *Sudan* 81 F3
Nyhammar, *Sweden* 10 D8
Nyinahin, *Ghana* 82 D4
Nyíradony, *Hungary* 42 C6
Nyírbátor, *Hungary* 42 C7
Nyíregyháza, *Hungary* 42 C6
Nykøbing, *Storstrøm, Denmark* 11 K5
Nykøbing, *Vestsjælland, Denmark* 11 J5
Nykøbing, *Viborg, Denmark* 11 H2
Nyköping, *Sweden* 11 F11
Nykroppa, *Sweden* 10 E8
Nykvarn, *Sweden* 10 E11
Nyland, *Sweden* 10 A11
Nylstroom, *S. Africa* 89 C4
Nymagee, *Australia* 95 E4
Nymburk, *Czech Rep.* 26 A8
Nynäshamn, *Sweden* 11 F11
Nyngan, *Australia* 95 E4
Nyoma Rap, *India* 69 C8
Nyoman = Neman →, *Lithuania* 9 J20
Nyon, *Switz.* 25 J2
Nyong →, *Cameroon* 83 E6
Nyons, *France* 21 D9
Nyou, *Burkina Faso* 83 C4
Nýrsko, *Czech Rep.* 26 B6
Nysa, *Poland* 45 H4
Nysa →, *Europe* 24 C10
Nysa Kłodzka →, *Poland* 45 H4
Nysäter, *Sweden* 10 E6
Nyssa, *U.S.A.* 114 E5
Nysted, *Denmark* 11 K5
Nyunzu, *Dem. Rep. of the Congo* 86 D2
Nyurba, *Russia* 51 C12
Nyzhnohirskyy, *Ukraine* 47 K8
Nzébéla, *Guinea* 82 D3
Nzega, *Tanzania* 86 C3
Nzérékoré, *Guinea* 82 D3
Nzeto, *Angola* 84 F2
Nzilo, Chutes de, *Dem. Rep. of the Congo* 87 E2
Nzo →, *Ivory C.* 82 D3
Nzubuka, *Tanzania* 86 C3

O

O Barco, *Spain* 34 C4
O Carballiño, *Spain* 34 C2
O Corgo, *Spain* 34 C3
O Pino, *Spain* 34 C2
O Porriño, *Spain* 34 C2
Ō-Shima, *Japan* 55 G9
Oa, Mull of, *U.K.* 14 F2
Oacoma, *U.S.A.* 112 D5
Oahe, L., *U.S.A.* 112 C4
Oahe Dam, *U.S.A.* 112 C4
Oahu, *U.S.A.* 106 H16
Oak Harbor, *U.S.A.* 116 B4
Oak Hill, *U.S.A.* 108 G5
Oak Ridge, *U.S.A.* 109 G3
Oak View, *U.S.A.* 117 L7
Oakan-Dake, *Japan* 54 C12
Oakdale, *Calif., U.S.A.* 116 H6
Oakdale, *La., U.S.A.* 113 K8
Oakes, *U.S.A.* 112 B5
Oakesdale, *U.S.A.* 114 C5
Oakey, *Australia* 95 D5
Oakfield, *U.S.A.* 110 C6
Oakham, *U.K.* 13 E7
Oakhurst, *U.S.A.* 116 H7
Oakland, *U.S.A.* 116 H4
Oakley, *Idaho, U.S.A.* 114 E7
Oakley, *Kans., U.S.A.* 112 F4
Oakover →, *Australia* 92 D3
Oakridge, *U.S.A.* 114 E2
Oakville, *Canada* 110 C5
Oakville, *U.S.A.* 116 D3
Oamaru, *N.Z.* 91 L3
Oancea, *Romania* 43 E12
Oasis, *Calif., U.S.A.* 117 M10
Oasis, *Nev., U.S.A.* 116 H9
Oates Land, *Antarctica* 5 C11
Oatlands, *Australia* 94 G4
Oatman, *U.S.A.* 117 K12
Oaxaca, *Mexico* 119 D5
Oaxaca □, *Mexico* 119 D5
Ob →, *Russia* 50 C7
Oba, *Canada* 102 C3
Obala, *Cameroon* 83 E7
Obama, *Japan* 55 G7
Oban, *Nigeria* 83 D6
Oban, *U.K.* 14 E3
Obbia, *Somali Rep.* 74 F4
Obera, *Argentina* 127 B4
Oberammergau, *Germany* 25 H7
Oberasbach, *Germany* 25 F6
Oberbayern □, *Germany* 25 G7
Oberdrauburg, *Austria* 26 E5
Oberfranken □, *Germany* 25 E7
Oberhausen, *Germany* 24 D2
Oberkirch, *Germany* 25 G4
Oberlausitz, *Germany* 24 D10
Oberlin, *Kans., U.S.A.* 112 F4
Oberlin, *La., U.S.A.* 113 K8
Oberlin, *Ohio, U.S.A.* 110 E2
Obernai, *France* 19 D14
Oberndorf, *Germany* 25 G4
Oberon, *Australia* 95 E4
Oberösterreich □, *Austria* 26 C7
Oberpfalz □, *Germany* 25 F8
Oberpfälzer Wald, *Germany* 25 F8
Oberstdorf, *Germany* 25 H6
Oberursel, *Germany* 25 E4
Oberwart, *Austria* 27 D9
Obi, Kepulauan, *Indonesia* 63 E7
Obi Is. = Obi, Kepulauan, *Indonesia* 63 E7
Obiaruku, *Nigeria* 83 D6
Óbidos, *Brazil* 125 D7
Óbidos, *Portugal* 35 F1
Obihiro, *Japan* 54 C11
Obilatu, *Indonesia* 63 E7
Obilnoye, *Russia* 49 G7
Obing, *Germany* 25 G8
Objat, *France* 20 C5
Obluchye, *Russia* 51 E14
Obninsk, *Russia* 46 E9
Obo, *C.A.R.* 86 A2
Oboa, Mt., *Uganda* 86 B3
Obock, *Djibouti* 81 E5
Oborniki, *Poland* 45 F3
Oborniki Śląskie, *Poland* 45 G3
Oboyan, *Russia* 47 G9
Obozerskaya = Obozerskiy, *Russia* 50 C5
Obozerskiy, *Russia* 50 C5
Obrenovac, *Serbia, Yug.* 40 B4
Obrovac, *Croatia* 29 D12
Obruk, *Turkey* 72 C5
Obrzycko, *Poland* 45 F3
Observatory Inlet, *Canada* 104 B3
Obshchi Syrt, *Russia* 6 E16
Obskaya Guba, *Russia* 50 C8
Obuasi, *Ghana* 83 D4
Obubra, *Nigeria* 83 D6
Obudu, *Nigeria* 83 D6
Obwalden □, *Switz.* 25 J4
Obzor, *Bulgaria* 41 D11
Ocala, *U.S.A.* 109 L4
Ocampo, *Chihuahua, Mexico* 118 B3
Ocampo, *Tamaulipas, Mexico* 119 C5
Ocaña, *Spain* 34 F7
Ocanomowoc, *U.S.A.* 112 D10

Orbisonia

Occidental, Cordillera, *Colombia* 122 C3
Ocean City, *Md., U.S.A.* 108 F8
Ocean City, *N.J., U.S.A.* 108 F8
Ocean City, *Wash., U.S.A.* 116 C2
Ocean Falls, *Canada* 104 C3
Ocean I. = Banaba, *Kiribati* 96 H8
Ocean Park, *U.S.A.* 116 D2
Oceano, *U.S.A.* 117 K6
Oceanport, *U.S.A.* 111 F10
Oceanside, *U.S.A.* 117 M9
Ochagavía, *Spain* 32 C3
Ochakiv, *Ukraine* 47 J6
Ochamchira, *Georgia* 49 J5
Ochil Hills, *U.K.* 14 E5
Ochsenfurt, *Germany* 25 F6
Ochsenhausen, *Germany* 25 G5
Ocilla, *U.S.A.* 109 K4
Ockelbo, *Sweden* 10 D10
Ocmulgee →, *U.S.A.* 109 K4
Ocna Mureş, *Romania* 43 D8
Ocna Sibiului, *Romania* 43 E9
Ocnele Mari, *Romania* 43 E9
Ocniţa, *Moldova* 43 B12
Oconee →, *U.S.A.* 109 K4
Oconto, *U.S.A.* 108 C2
Oconto Falls, *U.S.A.* 108 C1
Ocosingo, *Mexico* 119 D6
Ocotal, *Nic.* 120 D2
Ocotlán, *Mexico* 118 C4
Ocotlán de Morelos, *Mexico* 119 D5
Ocreza →, *Portugal* 35 F3
Ócsa, *Hungary* 42 C4
Octeville, *France* 18 C5
Oda, *Ghana* 83 D4
Ōda, *Japan* 55 G6
Oda, J., *Sudan* 80 C4
Ódáðahraun, *Iceland* 8 D5
Ödåkra, *Sweden* 11 H6
Odate, *Japan* 54 D10
Odawara, *Japan* 55 G9
Odda, *Norway* 9 F12
Odder, *Denmark* 11 J4
Odei →, *Canada* 105 B9
Odemira, *Portugal* 35 H2
Ödemiş, *Turkey* 39 C9
Odendaalsrus, *S. Africa* 88 D4
Odensbacken, *Sweden* 10 E9
Odense, *Denmark* 11 J4
Odenwald, *Germany* 25 F5
Oder →, *Europe* 24 B10
Oder-Havel Kanal, *Germany* 24 C10
Oderzo, *Italy* 29 C9
Odesa, *Ukraine* 47 J6
Ödeshög, *Sweden* 11 F8
Odessa = Odesa, *Ukraine* 47 J6
Odessa, *Canada* 111 B8
Odessa, *Tex., U.S.A.* 113 K3
Odessa, *Wash., U.S.A.* 114 C4
Odiakwe, *Botswana* 88 C4
Odiel →, *Spain* 35 H4
Odienné, *Ivory C.* 82 D3
Odintsovo, *Russia* 46 E9
Odiongan, *Phil.* 61 E4
Odobeşti, *Romania* 43 E12
Odolanów, *Poland* 45 G4
O'Donnell, *U.S.A.* 113 J4
Odorheiu Secuiesc, *Romania* 43 D10
Odoyevo, *Russia* 46 F9
Odra = Oder →, *Europe* 24 B10
Odra →, *Spain* 34 C6
Odžaci, *Serbia, Yug.* 42 E4
Odžak, *Bos.-H.* 42 E3
Odzi, *Zimbabwe* 89 B5
Odzi →, *Zimbabwe* 89 B5
Oebisfelde, *Germany* 24 C6
Oeiras, *Brazil* 125 E10
Oeiras, *Portugal* 35 G1
Oelrichs, *U.S.A.* 112 D3
Oelsnitz, *Germany* 25 E8
Oelwein, *U.S.A.* 112 D9
Oenpelli, *Australia* 92 B5
Oetz, *Austria* 26 D3
Of, *Turkey* 73 B9
Ofanto →, *Italy* 31 A9
Offa, *Nigeria* 83 D5
Offaly □, *Ireland* 15 C4
Offenbach, *Germany* 25 E4
Offenburg, *Germany* 25 G3
Offida, *Italy* 29 F10
Ofidhousa, *Greece* 39 E8
Ofotfjorden, *Norway* 8 B17
Ōfunato, *Japan* 54 E10
Oga, *Japan* 54 E9
Oga-Hantō, *Japan* 54 E9
Ogaden, *Ethiopia* 74 F3
Ōgaki, *Japan* 55 G8
Ogallala, *U.S.A.* 112 E4
Ogasawara Gunto, *Pac. Oc.* 52 G18
Ogbomosho, *Nigeria* 83 D5
Ogden, *U.S.A.* 114 F7
Ogdensburg, *U.S.A.* 111 B9
Ogeechee →, *U.S.A.* 109 K5
Ogilby, *U.S.A.* 117 N12
Oglio →, *Italy* 28 C7
Ogmore, *Australia* 94 C4
Ognon →, *France* 19 E12
Ogoja, *Nigeria* 83 D6
Ogoki, *Canada* 102 B2
Ogoki →, *Canada* 102 B2
Ogoki L., *Canada* 102 B2
Ogoki Res., *Canada* 102 B2
Ogooué →, *Gabon* 84 E1
Ogosta →, *Bulgaria* 40 C7
Ogowe = Ogooué →, *Gabon* 84 E1
Ogr = Sharafa, *Sudan* 81 E2
Ograźden, *Macedonia* 40 E6
Ogre, *Latvia* 9 H21
Ogrein, *Sudan* 80 D3
Ogulin, *Croatia* 29 C12
Ogun □, *Nigeria* 83 D5
Ogurchinskiy, Ostrov, *Turkmenistan* 71 B7
Oguta, *Nigeria* 83 D6
Ogwashi-Uku, *Nigeria* 83 D6
Ogwe, *Nigeria* 83 E6
Ohai, *N.Z.* 91 L2
Ohakune, *N.Z.* 91 H5
Ohata, *Japan* 54 D10
Ohau, L., *N.Z.* 91 L2
Ohio □, *U.S.A.* 110 F2
Ohio →, *U.S.A.* 108 G1
Ohře →, *Czech Rep.* 26 A7
Ohre →, *Germany* 24 C7
Ohrid, *Macedonia* 40 E4
Ohridsko Jezero, *Macedonia* 40 E4
Ohrigstad, *S. Africa* 89 C5
Öhringen, *Germany* 25 F5
Oi Qu, *China* 58 C2
Oiapoque, *Brazil* 125
Oikou, *China* 57 E9
Oil City, *U.S.A.* 110 E5
Oil Springs, *Canada* 110 D2
Oildale, *U.S.A.* 117 K7
Oinousa, *Greece* 39 C8
Oise □, *France* 19 C9
Oise →, *France* 19 C9
Ōita, *Japan* 55 H5
Ōita □, *Japan* 55 H5
Oiticica, *Brazil* 125 E10
Ojacaliente, *Mexico* 118 C4
Ojai, *U.S.A.* 117 L7
Ojinaga, *Mexico* 118 B4
Ojiya, *Japan* 55 F9
Ojos del Salado, Cerro, *Argentina* 126 B2
Oka →, *Russia* 48 B7
Okaba, *Indonesia* 63 F9
Okahandja, *Namibia* 88 C2
Okahukura, *N.Z.* 91 H5
Okanagan L., *Canada* 104 D5
Okanogan, *U.S.A.* 114 B4
Okanogan →, *U.S.A.* 114 B4
Okány, *Hungary* 42 D6
Okaputa, *Namibia* 88 C2
Okara, *Pakistan* 68 D5
Okarito, *N.Z.* 91 K3
Okaukuejo, *Namibia* 88 B2
Okavango Swamps, *Botswana* 88 B3
Okaya, *Japan* 55 F9
Okayama, *Japan* 55 G6
Okayama □, *Japan* 55 G6
Okazaki, *Japan* 55 G8
Oke-Iho, *Nigeria* 83 D5
Okeechobee, *U.S.A.* 109 M5
Okeechobee, L., *U.S.A.* 109 M5
Okefenokee Swamp, *U.S.A.* 109 K4
Okehampton, *U.K.* 13 G4
Okene, *Nigeria* 83 D6
Oker →, *Germany* 24 C6
Okha, *India* 68 H3
Okha, *Russia* 51 D15
Ókhi Óros, *Greece* 38 C6
Okhotsk, *Russia* 51 D15
Okhotsk, Sea of, *Asia* 51 D15
Okhotskiy Perevoz, *Russia* 51 C14
Okhtyrka, *Ukraine* 47 G8
Oki-Shotō, *Japan* 55 F6
Okiep, *S. Africa* 88 D2
Okigwi, *Nigeria* 83 D6
Okija, *Nigeria* 83 D6
Okinawa □, *Japan* 55 L4
Okinawa-Guntō, *Japan* 55 L4
Okinawa-Jima, *Japan* 55 L4
Okino-erabu-Shima, *Japan* 55 L4
Okitipupa, *Nigeria* 83 D5
Oklahoma □, *U.S.A.* 113 H6
Oklahoma City, *U.S.A.* 113 H6
Okmulgee, *U.S.A.* 113 H7
Oknitsa = Ocniţa, *Moldova* 43 B12
Oko, W. →, *Sudan* 80 C4
Okolo, *Uganda* 86 B3
Okolona, *U.S.A.* 113 J10
Okombahe, *Namibia* 88 C2
Okonek, *Poland* 44 E3
Okotoks, *Canada* 104 C6
Okrika, *Nigeria* 83 E6
Oksibil, *Indonesia* 63 E10
Oktabrsk = Oktyabrsk, *Kazakstan* 50 E6
Oktyabrsk, *Kazakstan* 50 E6
Oktyabrsk, *Russia* 48 D9
Oktyabrskiy = Aktsyabrski, *Belarus* 47 F5
Oktyabrskiy, *Russia* 49 G5
Oktyabrskoy Revolyutsii, Ostrov, *Russia* 51 B10
Oktyabrskoye = Zhovtneve, *Ukraine* 47 J7
Okulovka, *Russia* 46 C7
Okuru, *N.Z.* 91 K2
Okushiri-Tō, *Japan* 54 C9
Okuta, *Nigeria* 83 D5
Okwa →, *Botswana* 88 C3
Ola, *U.S.A.* 113 H8
Ólafsfjörður, *Iceland* 8 C4
Ólafsvík, *Iceland* 8 D2
Olaine, *Latvia* 44 B10
Olancha, *U.S.A.* 117 J8
Olancha Pk., *U.S.A.* 117 J8
Olanchito, *Honduras* 120 C2
Öland, *Sweden* 11 H10
Ölands norra udde, *Sweden* 11 G11
Ölands södra udde, *Sweden* 11 H10
Olargues, *France* 20 E6
Olary, *Australia* 95 E3
Olascoaga, *Argentina* 126 D3
Olathe, *U.S.A.* 112 F7
Olavarría, *Argentina* 126 D3
Oława, *Poland* 45 H4
Olbernhau, *Germany* 24 E9
Ólbia, *Italy* 30 B2
Ólbia, G. di, *Italy* 30 B2
Olching, *Germany* 25 G7
Olcott, *U.S.A.* 110 C6
Old Bahama Chan. = Bahama, Canal Viejo de, *W. Indies* 120 B4
Old Baldy Pk. = San Antonio, Mt., *U.S.A.* 117 L9
Old Castile = Castilla y Leon □, *Spain* 34 D6
Old Crow, *Canada* 100 B6
Old Dale, *U.S.A.* 117 L11
Old Dongola, *Sudan* 80 D3
Old Forge, *N.Y., U.S.A.* 111 C10
Old Forge, *Pa., U.S.A.* 111 E9
Old Perlican, *Canada* 103 C9
Old Shinyanga, *Tanzania* 86 C3
Old Speck Mt., *U.S.A.* 111 B14
Old Town, *U.S.A.* 109 C11
Old Washington, *U.S.A.* 110 F3
Old Wives L., *Canada* 105 C7
Oldbury, *U.K.* 13 F5
Oldcastle, *Ireland* 15 C4
Oldeani, *Tanzania* 86 C4
Oldenburg, *Niedersachsen, Germany* 24 B4
Oldenburg, *Schleswig-Holstein, Germany* 24 A6
Oldenzaal, *Neths.* 17 B6
Oldham, *U.K.* 12 D5
Oldman →, *Canada* 104 D6
Oldmeldrum, *U.K.* 14 D6
Olds, *Canada* 104 C6
Oldziyt, *Mongolia* 56 B5
Olean, *U.S.A.* 110 D6
Olecko, *Poland* 44 D9
Oléggio, *Italy* 28 C5
Oleiros, *Portugal* 34 F3
Oleiros, *Spain* 34 B2
Olekma →, *Russia* 51 C13
Olekminsk, *Russia* 51 C13
Oleksandriya, *Kirovohrad, Ukraine* 47 H7
Oleksandriya, *Rivne, Ukraine* 47 G4
Oleksandrovka, *Ukraine* 47 H7
Olema, *U.S.A.* 116 G4
Olenek, *Russia* 51 C12
Olenek →, *Russia* 51 B13
Olenino, *Russia* 46 D7
Oléron, Î. d', *France* 20 C2
Oleśnica, *Poland* 45 G4
Olesno, *Poland* 45 H5
Olevsk, *Ukraine* 47 G4
Olga, *Russia* 51 E14
Olga, L., *Canada* 102 C4
Olga, Mt., *Australia* 93 E5
Ølgod, *Denmark* 11 J2
Olhão, *Portugal* 35 H3
Olib, *Croatia* 29 D11
Oliena, *Italy* 30 B2
Oliete, *Spain* 32 D4
Olifants →, *Africa* 89 C5
Olifants →, *Namibia* 88 C2
Olifantshoek, *S. Africa* 88 D3
Ólimbos, *Greece* 39 F9
Ólimbos, Óros, *Greece* 40 F6
Olímpia, *Brazil* 127 A6
Olinda, *Brazil* 125 E12
Olite, *Spain* 32 C3
Oliva, *Argentina* 126 C3
Oliva, *Spain* 33 G4
Oliva, Punta del, *Spain* 34 B5
Oliva de la Frontera, *Spain* 35 G4
Olivares, *Spain* 32 F2
Olivehurst, *U.S.A.* 116 F5
Oliveira de Azeméis, *Portugal* 34 E2
Oliveira do Douro, *Portugal* 34 D2
Olivenza, *Spain* 35 G3
Oliver, *Canada* 104 D5
Oliver L., *Canada* 105 B8
Olivet, *France* 19 E8
Olkhovka, *Russia* 48 F7
Olkusz, *Poland* 45 H6
Ollagüe, *Chile* 126 A2
Olmedo, *Spain* 34 D6
Olmeto, *France* 21 G12
Olney, *Ill., U.S.A.* 108 F1
Olney, *Tex., U.S.A.* 113 J5
Olofström, *Sweden* 11 H8
Oloma, *Cameroon* 83 E7
Olomane →, *Canada* 103 B7
Olomouc, *Czech Rep.* 27 B10
Olonets, *Russia* 46 B7
Olongapo, *Phil.* 61 D4
Olonne-sur-Mer, *France* 20 B2
Oloron, Gave d' →, *France* 20 E2
Oloron-Ste-Marie, *France* 20 E3
Olot, *Spain* 32 C7
Olovo, *Bos.-H.* 42 F3
Olovyannaya, *Russia* 51 D12
Oloy →, *Russia* 51 C16
Olsberg, *Germany* 24 D4
Olshammar, *Sweden* 11 F8
Olshanka, *Ukraine* 47 H6
Olshany, *Ukraine* 47 G8
Olsztyn, *Poland* 44 E7
Olsztynek, *Poland* 44 E7
Olt □, *Romania* 43 F9
Olt →, *Romania* 43 G9
Olten, *Switz.* 25 H3
Olteniţa, *Romania* 43 F11
Olton, *U.S.A.* 113 H3
Oltu, *Turkey* 73 B9
Oluanpi, *Taiwan* 59 G13
Olula del Rio, *Spain* 33 H2
Olur, *Turkey* 73 B10
Olutanga, *Phil.* 61 H5
Olvega, *Spain* 32 D2
Olvera, *Spain* 35 J5
Olymbos, *Cyprus* 36 D12
Olympia, *Greece* 38 D3
Olympia, *U.S.A.* 116 D4
Olympic Dam, *Australia* 95 E2
Olympic Mts., *U.S.A.* 116 C3
Olympic Nat. Park, *U.S.A.* 116 C3
Olympus, *Cyprus* 36 E11
Olympus, Mt. = Ólimbos, Óros, *Greece* 40 F6
Olympus, Mt. = Uludağ, *Turkey* 41 F13
Olympus, Mt., *U.S.A.* 116 C3
Olyphant, *U.S.A.* 111 E9
Om →, *Russia* 50 D8
Om Hajer, *Eritrea* 81 E4
Om Koi, *Thailand* 64 D2
Ōma, *Japan* 54 D10
Ōmachi, *Japan* 55 F8
Omae-Zaki, *Japan* 55 G9
Ōmagari, *Japan* 54 E10
Omagh, *U.K.* 15 B4
Omagh □, *U.K.* 15 B4
Omaha, *U.S.A.* 112 E7
Omak, *U.S.A.* 114 B4
Omalos, *Greece* 36 D5
Oman ■, *Asia* 74 C6
Oman, G. of, *Asia* 71 E8
Omaruru, *Namibia* 88 C2
Omaruru →, *Namibia* 88 C1
Omate, *Peru* 124 G4
Ombai, Selat, *Indonesia* 63 F6
Omboué, *Gabon* 84 E1
Ombrone →, *Italy* 28 F8
Omdurmân, *Sudan* 81 D3
Omegna, *Italy* 28 C5
Omemee, *Canada* 110 B6
Omeo, *Australia* 95 F4
Omeonga, *Dem. Rep. of the Congo* 86 C1
Ometepe, I. de, *Nic.* 120 D2
Ometepec, *Mexico* 119 D5
Ominato, *Japan* 54 D10
Omineca →, *Canada* 104 B4
Omiš, *Croatia* 29 E13
Omišalj, *Croatia* 29 C11
Omitara, *Namibia* 88 C2
Ōmiya, *Japan* 55 G9
Omme Å →, *Denmark* 11 J2
Ommen, *Neths.* 17 B6
Ömnögovĭ □, *Mongolia* 56 C3
Omo →, *Ethiopia* 81 F4
Omodeo, L., *Italy* 30 B1
Omodhos, *Cyprus* 36 E11
Omoko, *Nigeria* 83 D6
Omolon →, *Russia* 51 C16
Omono-Gawa →, *Japan* 54 E10
Omsk, *Russia* 50 D8
Omsukchan, *Russia* 51 C16
Ōmu, *Japan* 54 B11
Omul, Vf., *Romania* 43 E10
Omulew →, *Poland* 45 E8
Ōmura, *Japan* 55 H4
Omuramba Omatako →, *Namibia* 88 B2
Omuramba Ovambo →, *Namibia* 88 B2
Omurtag, *Bulgaria* 41 C10
Ōmuta, *Japan* 55 H5
Oña, *Spain* 34 C7
Onaga, *U.S.A.* 112 F6
Onalaska, *U.S.A.* 112 D9
Onancock, *U.S.A.* 108 G8
Onang, *Indonesia* 63 E5
Onaping L., *Canada* 102 C3
Oñati, *Spain* 32 B2
Onavas, *Mexico* 118 B3
Onawa, *U.S.A.* 112 D6
Oncócua, *Angola* 88 B1
Onda, *Spain* 32 F4
Ondaejin, *N. Korea* 57 D15
Ondangua, *Namibia* 88 B2
Ondarroa, *Spain* 32 B2
Ondava →, *Slovak Rep.* 27 C14
Ondjiva, *Angola* 88 B2
Ondo, *Nigeria* 83 D5
Ondo □, *Nigeria* 83 D6
Öndörshil, *Mongolia* 56 B5
Öndverðarnes, *Iceland* 8 D1
One Tree, *Australia* 95 E3
Onega, *Russia* 50 C4
Onega →, *Russia* 6 C13
Onega, L. = Onezhskoye Ozero, *Russia* 46 B8
Onehunga, *N.Z.* 91 G5
Oneida, *U.S.A.* 111 C9
Oneida L., *U.S.A.* 111 C9
O'Neill, *U.S.A.* 112 D5
Onekotan, Ostrov, *Russia* 51 E16
Onema, *Dem. Rep. of the Congo* 86 C1
Oneonta, *U.S.A.* 111 D9
Oneşti, *Romania* 43 D11
Onezhskoye Ozero, *Russia* 46 B8
Ongarue, *N.Z.* 91 H5
Ongers →, *S. Africa* 88 E3
Ongerup, *Australia* 93 F2
Ongjin, *N. Korea* 57 F13
Ongkharak, *Thailand* 64 E3
Ongniud Qi, *China* 57 C10
Ongoka, *Dem. Rep. of the Congo* 86 C2
Ongole, *India* 66 M12
Ongon = Havirga, *Mongolia* 56 B7
Oni, *Georgia* 49 J6
Onida, *U.S.A.* 112 C4
Onilahy →, *Madag.* 89 C7
Onitsha, *Nigeria* 83 D6
Onoda, *Japan* 55 G5
Onpyŏng-ni, *S. Korea* 57 H14
Ons, I. de, *Spain* 34 C2
Onslow, *Australia* 92 D2
Onslow B., *U.S.A.* 109 H7
Ontake-San, *Japan* 55 G8
Ontario, *Calif., U.S.A.* 117 L9
Ontario, *Oreg., U.S.A.* 114 D5
Ontario □, *Canada* 102 B2
Ontario, L., *N. Amer.* 102 D4
Ontinyent, *Spain* 33 G4
Ontonagon, *U.S.A.* 112 B10
Ontur, *Spain* 33 G3
Onyx, *U.S.A.* 117 K8
Oodnadatta, *Australia* 95 D2
Ooldea, *Australia* 93 F5
Oombulgurri, *Australia* 92 C4
Oorindi, *Australia* 94 C3
Oost-Vlaanderen □, *Belgium* 17 C3
Oostende, *Belgium* 17 C2
Oosterhout, *Neths.* 17 C4
Oosterschelde →, *Neths.* 17 C4
Oosterwolde, *Neths.* 17 B6
Ootacamund = Udagamandalam, *India* 66 P10
Ootsa L., *Canada* 104 C3
Opaka, *Bulgaria* 41 C10
Opala, *Dem. Rep. of the Congo* 86 C1
Opalenica, *Poland* 45 F3
Opan, *Bulgaria* 41 D9
Opanake, *Sri Lanka* 66 R12
Opasatika, *Canada* 102 C3
Opasquia Prov. Park, *Canada* 102 B1
Opatija, *Croatia* 29 C11
Opatów, *Poland* 45 H8
Opava, *Czech Rep.* 27 B10
Opelika, *U.S.A.* 109 J3
Opelousas, *U.S.A.* 113 K8
Opémisca, L., *Canada* 102 C5
Opheim, *U.S.A.* 114 B10
Ophthalmia Ra., *Australia* 92 D2
Opi, *Nigeria* 83 D6
Opinaca →, *Canada* 102 B4
Opinaca, Rés., *Canada* 102 B4
Opinnagau →, *Canada* 102 B3
Opiscoteo, L., *Canada* 103 B6
Opobo, *Nigeria* 83 E6
Opochka, *Russia* 46 D5
Opoczno, *Poland* 45 G7
Opol, *Phil.* 61 G6
Opole, *Poland* 45 H4
Opole Lubelskie, *Poland* 45 G8
Opolskie □, *Poland* 45 H5
Oponono L., *Namibia* 88 B2
Oporto = Porto, *Portugal* 34 D2
Opotiki, *N.Z.* 91 H6
Opp, *U.S.A.* 109 K2
Oppdal, *Norway* 9 E13
Óppido Mamertina, *Italy* 31 D8
Opportunity, *U.S.A.* 114 C5
Oprişor, *Romania* 42 F8
Oprtalj, *Croatia* 29 C10
Opua, *N.Z.* 91 F5
Opunake, *N.Z.* 91 H4
Opuwo, *Namibia* 88 B1
Opuzen, *Croatia* 29 E14
Ora, *Cyprus* 36 E12
Oracle, *U.S.A.* 115 K8
Oradea, *Romania* 42 C6
Öræfajökull, *Iceland* 8 D5
Orahovac, *Kosovo, Yug.* 40 D4
Orahovica, *Croatia* 42 E2
Orai, *India* 69 G8
Oraison, *France* 21 E9
Oral = Zhayyq →, *Kazakstan* 50 E6
Oral, *Kazakstan* 48 E10
Oran, *Algeria* 78 A5
Orange, *Australia* 95 E4
Orange, *France* 21 D8
Orange, *Calif., U.S.A.* 117 M9
Orange, *Mass., U.S.A.* 111 D12
Orange, *Tex., U.S.A.* 113 K8
Orange, *Va., U.S.A.* 108 F6
Orange →, *S. Africa* 88 D2
Orange, C., *Brazil* 122 C5
Orange Cove, *U.S.A.* 116 J7
Orange Free State = Free State □, *S. Africa* 88 D4
Orange Grove, *U.S.A.* 113 M6
Orange Walk, *Belize* 119 D7
Orangeburg, *U.S.A.* 109 J5
Orangeville, *Canada* 102 D3
Orango, *Guinea-Biss.* 82 C1
Orani, *Phil.* 61 D4
Oranienburg, *Germany* 24 C9
Oranje = Orange →, *S. Africa* 88 D2
Oranje Vrystaat = Free State □, *S. Africa* 88 D4
Oranjemund, *Namibia* 88 D2
Oranjerivier, *S. Africa* 88 D3
Orapa, *Botswana* 85 J5
Orarak, *Sudan* 81 F3
Oras, *Phil.* 61 E6
Orašje, *Bos.-H.* 42 E3
Orăştie, *Romania* 43 E8
Oraşul Stalin = Braşov, *Romania* 43 E10
Orava →, *Slovak Rep.* 27 B12
Orava, Vodna nádrž, *Slovak Rep.* 27 B12
Oraviţa, *Romania* 42 E6
Orb →, *France* 20 E7
Orba →, *Italy* 28 D5
Ørbæk, *Denmark* 11 J4
Orbe, *Switz.* 25 J2
Orbec, *France* 18 C7
Orbetello, *Italy* 29 F8
Órbigo →, *Spain* 34 C5
Orbisonia, *U.S.A.* 110 F7

Orbost, *Australia* 95 F4
Örbyhus, *Sweden* 10 D11
Orcas I., *U.S.A.* 116 B4
Orce, *Spain* 33 H2
Orce →, *Spain* 33 H2
Orchard City, *U.S.A.* 115 G10
Orchies, *France* 19 B10
Orchila, I., *Venezuela* 121 D6
Órcia →, *Italy* 29 F8
Orco →, *Italy* 28 C4
Orcutt, *U.S.A.* 117 L6
Ord, *U.S.A.* 112 E5
Ord →, *Australia* 92 C4
Ord, Mt., *Australia* 92 C4
Ordenes = Ordes, *Spain* 34 B2
Orderville, *U.S.A.* 115 H7
Ordes, *Spain* 34 B2
Ording = St-Peter-Ording, *Germany* 24 A4
Ordos = Mu Us Shamo, *China* 56 E5
Ordu, *Turkey* 72 B7
Ordubad, *Azerbaijan* 73 C12
Orduña, *Álava, Spain* 32 C2
Orduña, *Granada, Spain* 35 H7
Ordway, *U.S.A.* 112 F3
Ordzhonikidze = Vladikavkaz, *Russia* 49 J7
Ordzhonikidze, *Ukraine* 47 J8
Ore, *Dem. Rep. of the Congo* 86 B2
Ore Mts. = Erzgebirge, *Germany* 24 E8
Orebić, *Croatia* 29 F14
Örebro, *Sweden* 10 E9
Örebro län □, *Sweden* 10 E8
Oregon, *U.S.A.* 112 D10
Oregon □, *U.S.A.* 114 E3
Oregon City, *U.S.A.* 116 E4
Öregrund, *Sweden* 10 D12
Öregrundsgrepen, *Sweden* 10 D12
Orekhov = Orikhiv, *Ukraine* 47 J8
Orekhovo-Zuyevo, *Russia* 46 E10
Orel, *Russia* 47 F9
Orel →, *Ukraine* 47 H8
Orellana, *Spain* 35 F5
Orellana, Canal de, *Spain* 35 F5
Orellana, Embalse de, *Spain* 35 F5
Orem, *U.S.A.* 114 F8
Ören, *Turkey* 39 D9
Orenburg, *Russia* 50 D6
Örencik, *Turkey* 39 B11
Orense = Ourense, *Spain* 34 C3
Orense □, *Spain* 34 C3
Orepuki, *N.Z.* 91 M1
Orestiás, *Greece* 41 E10
Orestos Pereyra, *Mexico* 118 B3
Øresund, *Europe* 11 J6
Orford Ness, *U.K.* 13 E9
Organà = Organyà, *Spain* 32 C6
Organos, Pta. de los, *Canary Is.* 37 F2
Organyà, *Spain* 32 C6
Orgaz, *Spain* 35 F7
Orgeyev = Orhei, *Moldova* 43 C13
Orhaneli, *Turkey* 41 G12
Orhaneli →, *Turkey* 41 G12
Orhangazi, *Turkey* 41 F13
Orhei, *Moldova* 43 C13
Orhon Gol →, *Mongolia* 60 A5
Ória, *Italy* 31 B10
Oriental, Cordillera, *Colombia* 122 C3
Orientale □, *Dem. Rep. of the Congo* 86 B2
Oriente, *Argentina* 126 D3
Orihuela, *Spain* 33 G4
Orihuela del Tremedal, *Spain* 32 E3
Orikhiv, *Ukraine* 47 J8
Oriku, *Albania* 40 F3
Orillia, *Canada* 102 D4
Orinoco →, *Venezuela* 122 C4
Orion, *Canada* 105 D6
Oriskany, *U.S.A.* 111 C9
Orissa □, *India* 67 K14
Orissaare, *Estonia* 9 G20
Oristano, *Italy* 30 C1
Oristano, G. di, *Italy* 30 C1
Orizaba, *Mexico* 119 D5
Orizare, *Bulgaria* 41 D11
Orjen, *Bos.-H.* 40 D2
Orjiva, *Spain* 35 J7
Orkanger, *Norway* 8 E13
Örkelljunga, *Sweden* 11 H7
Örken, *Sweden* 11 G9
Örkény, *Hungary* 42 C4
Orkla →, *Norway* 8 E13
Orkney, *S. Africa* 88 D4
Orkney □, *U.K.* 14 B5
Orkney Is., *U.K.* 14 B6
Orland, *U.S.A.* 116 F4
Orlando, *U.S.A.* 109 L5
Orlando, C. d', *Italy* 31 D7
Orléanais, *France* 19 E9
Orléans, *France* 19 E8
Orleans, *U.S.A.* 111 B12
Orléans, I. d', *Canada* 103 C5
Orlice →, *Czech Rep.* 26 A8
Orlov, *Slovak Rep.* 27 B13
Orlov Gay, *Russia* 48 E9
Orlová, *Czech Rep.* 27 B11
Orlovat, *Serbia, Yug.* 42 E5
Ormara, *Pakistan* 66 G4
Ormea, *Italy* 28 D4
Ormília, *Greece* 40 F7
Ormoc, *Phil.* 61 F6
Ormond, *N.Z.* 91 H6
Ormond Beach, *U.S.A.* 109 L5
Ormož, *Slovenia* 29 B13
Ormskirk, *U.K.* 12 D5
Ormstown, *Canada* 111 A11
Ornans, *France* 19 E13
Orne □, *France* 18 D7
Orne →, *France* 18 C6
Orneta, *Poland* 44 D7
Ornö, *Sweden* 10 E12
Örnsköldsvik, *Sweden* 10 A12
Oro, *N. Korea* 57 D14
Oro →, *Mexico* 118 B3
Oro Grande, *U.S.A.* 117 L9
Oro Valley, *U.S.A.* 115 K8
Orobie, Alpi, *Italy* 28 B6
Orocué, *Colombia* 124 C4
Orodara, *Burkina Faso* 82 C4
Orodo, *Nigeria* 83 D6
Orofino, *U.S.A.* 114 C5
Orol Dengizi = Aral Sea, *Asia* 50 E7
Oromocto, *Canada* 103 C6
Oron, *Nigeria* 83 E6
Orono, *Canada* 110 C6
Orono, *U.S.A.* 109 C11
Oronsay, *U.K.* 14 E2
Oropesa, *Spain* 34 F5
Oroquieta, *Phil.* 61 G5
Orosei, *Italy* 30 B2
Orosei, G. di, *Italy* 30 B2
Orosháza, *Hungary* 42 D5
Oroszlány, *Hungary* 42 C3
Orotukan, *Russia* 51 C16
Oroville, *Calif., U.S.A.* 116 F5
Oroville, *Wash., U.S.A.* 114 B4
Oroville, L., *U.S.A.* 116 F5
Orrefors, *Sweden* 11 H9
Orroroo, *Australia* 95 E2
Orrviken, *Sweden* 10 A8
Orrville, *U.S.A.* 110 F3
Orsa, *Sweden* 10 C8
Orsara di Púglia, *Italy* 31 A8
Orsasjön, *Sweden* 10 C8
Orsha, *Belarus* 46 E6
Örsjö, *Sweden* 11 H9
Orsk, *Russia* 50 D6
Orşova, *Romania* 42 F7
Ørsted, *Denmark* 11 H4
Örsundsbro, *Sweden* 10 E11
Orta, L. d', *Italy* 28 C5
Orta Nova, *Italy* 31 A8
Ortaca, *Turkey* 39 E10
Ortakent, *Turkey* 39 D9
Ortaklar, *Turkey* 39 D9
Ortaköy, *Çorum, Turkey* 72 B6
Ortaköy, *Niğde, Turkey* 72 C6
Orte, *Italy* 29 F9
Ortegal, C., *Spain* 34 B3
Orthez, *France* 20 E3
Ortigueira, *Spain* 34 B3
Orting, *U.S.A.* 116 C4
Ortisei, *Italy* 29 B8
Ortles, *Italy* 28 B7
Ortón →, *Bolivia* 124 F5
Ortona, *Italy* 29 F11
Ortonville, *U.S.A.* 112 C6
Orūmīyeh, *Iran* 70 B5
Orūmīyeh, Daryācheh-ye, *Iran* 70 B5
Orune, *Italy* 30 B2
Oruro, *Bolivia* 124 G5
Orust, *Sweden* 11 F5
Oruzgān □, *Afghan.* 66 C5
Orvault, *France* 18 E5
Orvieto, *Italy* 29 F9
Orwell, *N.Y., U.S.A.* 111 C9
Orwell, *Ohio, U.S.A.* 110 E4
Orwell →, *U.K.* 13 F9
Orwigsburg, *U.S.A.* 111 F8
Oryakhovo, *Bulgaria* 40 C7
Orzinuovi, *Italy* 28 C6
Orzyc →, *Poland* 45 F8
Orzysz, *Poland* 44 E8
Osa →, *Poland* 44 E5
Osa, Pen. de, *Costa Rica* 120 E3
Osage, *U.S.A.* 112 D8
Osage →, *U.S.A.* 112 F9
Osage City, *U.S.A.* 112 F7
Ōsaka, *Japan* 55 G7
Osan, *S. Korea* 57 F14
Osawatomie, *U.S.A.* 112 F7
Osborne, *U.S.A.* 112 F5
Osby, *Sweden* 11 H7
Osceola, *Ark., U.S.A.* 113 H10
Osceola, *Iowa, U.S.A.* 112 E8
Oschatz, *Germany* 24 D9
Oschersleben, *Germany* 24 C7
Óschiri, *Italy* 30 B2
Oscoda, *U.S.A.* 110 B1
Osečina, *Serbia, Yug.* 40 B3
Ösel = Saaremaa, *Estonia* 9 G20
Osery, *Russia* 46 E10
Osgoode, *Canada* 111 A9
Osh, *Kyrgyzstan* 50 E8
Oshakati, *Namibia* 85 H3
Oshawa, *Canada* 102 D4
Oshigambo, *Namibia* 88 B2
Oshkosh, *Nebr., U.S.A.* 112 E3
Oshkosh, *Wis., U.S.A.* 112 C10
Oshmyany = Ashmyany, *Belarus* 9 J21
Oshnovīyeh, *Iran* 70 B5
Oshogbo, *Nigeria* 83 D5
Oshtorīnān, *Iran* 71 C6
Oshwe, *Dem. Rep. of the Congo* 84 E3
Osi, *Nigeria* 83 D6
Osieczna, *Poland* 45 G3
Osijek, *Croatia* 42 E3
Ósilo, *Italy* 30 B1
Ósimo, *Italy* 29 E10
Osintorf, *Belarus* 46 E6
Osipenko = Berdyansk, *Ukraine* 47 J9
Osipovichi = Asipovichy, *Belarus* 46 F5
Osiyan, *India* 68 F5
Osizweni, *S. Africa* 89 D5
Oskaloosa, *U.S.A.* 112 E8
Oskarshamn, *Sweden* 11 G10
Oskarström, *Sweden* 11 H6
Oskélanéo, *Canada* 102 C4
Öskemen, *Kazakstan* 50 E9
Oskol →, *Ukraine* 47 H9
Oslo, *Norway* 9 G14
Oslob, *Phil.* 61 G5
Oslofjorden, *Norway* 9 G14
Osmanabad, *India* 66 K10
Osmancık, *Turkey* 72 B6
Osmaniye, *Turkey* 70 B3
Osmanlı, *Turkey* 41 E10
Ösmo, *Sweden* 10 F11
Osnabrück, *Germany* 24 C4
Ośno Lubuskie, *Poland* 45 F1
Osoblaha, *Czech Rep.* 27 A10
Osogovska Planina, *Macedonia* 40 D6
Osor, *Italy* 29 D11
Osorio, *Brazil* 127 B5
Osorno, *Chile* 128 E2
Osorno, *Spain* 34 C6
Osoyoos, *Canada* 104 D5
Osøyro, *Norway* 9 F11
Ospika →, *Canada* 104 B4
Osprey Reef, *Australia* 94 A4
Oss, *Neths.* 17 C5
Ossa, Mt., *Australia* 94 G4
Óssa, Óros, *Greece* 38 B4
Ossa de Montiel, *Spain* 33 G2
Ossabaw I., *U.S.A.* 109 K5
Osse →, *France* 20 D4
Osse →, *Nigeria* 83 D6
Ossi, *Italy* 30 B1
Ossining, *U.S.A.* 111 E11
Ossipee, *U.S.A.* 111 C13
Ossokmanuan L., *Canada* 103 B7
Ossora, *Russia* 51 D17
Ostashkov, *Russia* 46 D7
Östavall, *Sweden* 10 B9
Oste →, *Germany* 24 B5
Ostend = Oostende, *Belgium* 17 C2
Oster, *Ukraine* 47 G6
Osterburg, *Germany* 24 C7
Osterburg, *U.S.A.* 110 F6
Osterburken, *Germany* 25 F5
Österbybruk, *Sweden* 10 D11
Österbymo, *Sweden* 11 G9
Österdalälven, *Sweden* 10 C7
Østerdalen, *Norway* 9 F14
Österfärnebo, *Sweden* 10 D10
Österforse, *Sweden* 10 A11
Östergötlands län □, *Sweden* 11 F9
Osterholz-Scharmbeck, *Germany* 24 B4
Østerild, *Denmark* 11 G2
Osterode, *Germany* 24 D6
Östersund, *Sweden* 10 A8
Östervåla, *Sweden* 10 D11
Ostfriesische Inseln, *Germany* 24 B3
Ostfriesland, *Germany* 24 B3
Östhammar, *Sweden* 10 D12
Óstia, Lido di, *Italy* 29 G9
Ostíglia, *Italy* 29 C8
Östmark, *Sweden* 10 D6
Östra Husby, *Sweden* 11 F10
Ostrava, *Czech Rep.* 27 B11
Ostróda, *Poland* 44 E6
Ostrogozhsk, *Russia* 47 G10
Ostroh, *Ukraine* 47 G4
Ostrołęka, *Poland* 45 E8
Ostrov, *Bulgaria* 41 C8
Ostrov, *Czech Rep.* 26 A5
Ostrov, *Romania* 43 F12
Ostrov, *Russia* 46 D5
Ostrów Lubelski, *Poland* 45 G9
Ostrów Mazowiecka, *Poland* 45 F8
Ostrów Wielkopolski, *Poland* 45 G4
Ostrowiec-Świętokrzyski, *Poland* 45 H8
Ostrožac, *Bos.-H.* 42 G2
Ostrzeszów, *Poland* 45 G4
Ostseebad Kühlungsborn, *Germany* 24 A7
Osttirol □, *Austria* 26 E5
Ostuni, *Italy* 31 B10
Osŭm →, *Bulgaria* 41 C8
Osumi →, *Albania* 40 F4
Ōsumi-Kaikyō, *Japan* 55 J5
Ōsumi-Shotō, *Japan* 55 J5
Osun □, *Nigeria* 83 D5
Osuna, *Spain* 35 H5
Oswegatchie →, *U.S.A.* 111 B9
Oswego, *U.S.A.* 111 C8
Oswego →, *U.S.A.* 111 C8
Oswestry, *U.K.* 12 E4
Oświęcim, *Poland* 45 H6
Otaci, *Moldova* 43 B12
Otago □, *N.Z.* 91 L2
Otago Harbour, *N.Z.* 91 L3
Ōtake, *Japan* 55 G6
Otaki, *N.Z.* 91 J5
Otaru, *Japan* 54 C10
Otaru-Wan = Ishikari-Wan, *Japan* 54 C10
Otava →, *Czech Rep.* 26 B7
Otavalo, *Ecuador* 124 C3
Otavi, *Namibia* 88 B2
Otchinjau, *Angola* 88 B1
Otelec, *Romania* 42 E5
Otelnuk L., *Canada* 103 A6
Oţelu Roşu, *Romania* 42 E7
Otero de Rey = Outeiro de Rei, *Spain* 34 B3
Othello, *U.S.A.* 114 C4
Othonoí, *Greece* 38 B1
Óthris, Óros, *Greece* 38 B4
Otira Gorge, *N.Z.* 91 K3
Otjiwarongo, *Namibia* 88 C2
Otmuchów, *Poland* 45 H4
Otočac, *Croatia* 29 D12
Otoineppu, *Japan* 54 B11
Otok, *Croatia* 29 E13
Otorohanga, *N.Z.* 91 H5
Otoskwin →, *Canada* 102 B2
Otra →, *Norway* 9 G13
Otradnyy, *Russia* 48 D10
Otranto, *Italy* 31 B11
Otranto, C. d', *Italy* 31 B11
Otranto, Str. of, *Italy* 31 B11
Otrokovice, *Czech Rep.* 27 B10
Otse, *S. Africa* 88 D4
Ōtsu, *Japan* 55 G7
Ōtsuki, *Japan* 55 G9
Ottawa = Outaouais →, *Canada* 102 C5
Ottawa, *Canada* 102 C4
Ottawa, *Ill., U.S.A.* 112 E10
Ottawa, *Kans., U.S.A.* 112 F7
Ottawa Is., *Canada* 101 C11
Ottélé, *Cameroon* 83 E7
Ottensheim, *Austria* 26 C7
Otter Cr. →, *U.S.A.* 111 B11
Otter L., *Canada* 105 B8
Otterndorf, *Germany* 24 B4
Otterup, *Denmark* 11 J4
Otterville, *Canada* 110 D4
Ottery St. Mary, *U.K.* 13 G4
Otto Beit Bridge, *Zimbabwe* 87 F2
Ottosdal, *S. Africa* 88 D4
Ottumwa, *U.S.A.* 112 E8
Otu, *Nigeria* 83 D5
Otukpa, *Nigeria* 83 D6
Oturkpo, *Nigeria* 83 D6
Otway, B., *Chile* 128 G2
Otway, C., *Australia* 95 F3
Otwock, *Poland* 45 F8
Ötztaler Ache →, *Austria* 26 D3
Ötztaler Alpen, *Austria* 26 E3
Ou →, *Laos* 64 B4
Ou Neua, *Laos* 58 F3
Ou-Sammyaku, *Japan* 54 E10
Ouachita →, *U.S.A.* 113 K9
Ouachita, L., *U.S.A.* 113 H8
Ouachita Mts., *U.S.A.* 113 H7
Ouagadougou, *Burkina Faso* 83 C4
Ouahigouya, *Burkina Faso* 82 C4
Ouahran = Oran, *Algeria* 78 A5
Oualâta, *Mauritania* 82 B3
Ouallam, *Niger* 83 C5
Ouallene, *Algeria* 78 D6
Ouargaye, *Burkina Faso* 83 C5
Ouargla, *Algeria* 78 B7
Ouarkoye, *Burkina Faso* 82 C4
Ouarzazate, *Morocco* 78 B4
Ouassouas, *Mali* 83 B5
Ouatagouna, *Mali* 83 B5
Oubangi →, *Dem. Rep. of the Congo* 84 E3
Ouche →, *France* 19 E12
Ouddorp, *Neths.* 17 C3
Oude Rijn →, *Neths.* 17 B4
Oudeïka, *Mali* 83 B4
Oudenaarde, *Belgium* 17 D3
Oudon →, *France* 18 E6
Oudtshoorn, *S. Africa* 88 E3
Ouellé, *Ivory C.* 82 D4
Ouémé →, *Benin* 83 D5
Ouessa, *Burkina Faso* 82 C4
Ouessant, Î. d', *France* 18 D1
Ouesso, *Congo* 84 D3
Ouest, Pte. de l', *Canada* 103 C7
Ouezzane, *Morocco* 78 B4
Ougarou, *Burkina Faso* 83 C5
Oughterard, *Ireland* 15 C2
Ouidah, *Benin* 83 D5
Ouidi, *Niger* 83 C7
Ouistreham, *France* 18 C6
Oujda, *Morocco* 78 B5
Oujeft, *Mauritania* 82 A2
Oulainen, *Finland* 8 D21
Ould Yenjé, *Mauritania* 82 B2
Oullins, *France* 21 C8
Oulu, *Finland* 8 D21
Oulujärvi, *Finland* 8 D22
Oulujoki →, *Finland* 8 D21
Oulx, *Italy* 28 C3
Oum Chalouba, *Chad* 79 E10
Oum Hadjer, *Chad* 79 F9
Oumé, *Ivory C.* 82 D3
Ounasjoki →, *Finland* 8 C21
Ounguati, *Namibia* 88 C2
Ounianga Sérir, *Chad* 79 E10
Our →, *Lux.* 17 E6
Ouranópolis, *Greece* 40 F7
Ourârene, *Niger* 83 B6
Ouray, *U.S.A.* 115 G10
Ourcq →, *France* 19 C10
Ourense, *Spain* 34 C3
Ouricuri, *Brazil* 125 E10
Ourinhos, *Brazil* 127 A6
Ourique, *Portugal* 35 H2
Ouro Fino, *Brazil* 127 A6
Ouro-Ndia, *Mali* 82 B4
Ouro Prêto, *Brazil* 127 A7
Ouro Sogui, *Senegal* 82 B2
Oursi, *Burkina Faso* 83 C4
Ourthe →, *Belgium* 17 D5
Ouse →, *E. Susx., U.K.* 13 G8
Ouse →, *N. Yorks., U.K.* 12 D7
Oust, *France* 20 F5
Oust →, *France* 18 E4
Outaouais →, *Canada* 102 C5
Outardes →, *Canada* 103 C6
Outeiro de Rei, *Spain* 34 B3
Outer Hebrides, *U.K.* 14 D1
Outes = Serra de Outes, *Spain* 34 C2
Outjo, *Namibia* 88 C2
Outlook, *Canada* 105 C7
Outokumpu, *Finland* 8 E23
Outreau, *France* 19 B8
Ouvèze →, *France* 21 E8
Ouyen, *Australia* 95 F3
Ouzouer-le-Marché, *France* 19 E8
Ovada, *Italy* 28 D5
Ovalau, *Fiji* 91 C8
Ovalle, *Chile* 126 C1
Ovamboland, *Namibia* 88 B2
Ovar, *Portugal* 34 E2
Overath, *Germany* 24 E3
Overflakkee, *Neths.* 17 C4
Overijssel □, *Neths.* 17 B6
Overland Park, *U.S.A.* 112 F7
Overton, *U.S.A.* 117 J12
Övertorneå, *Sweden* 8 C20
Överum, *Sweden* 11 F10
Ovid, *U.S.A.* 111 D8
Ovidiopol, *Ukraine* 47 J6
Ovidiu, *Romania* 43 F13
Oviedo, *Spain* 34 B5
Oviksfjällen, *Sweden* 10 A7
Oviši, *Latvia* 9 H19
Ovoot, *Mongolia* 56 B7
Övör Hangay □, *Mongolia* 56 B2
Ovoro, *Nigeria* 83 D6
Øvre Årdal, *Norway* 9 F12
Övre Fryken, *Sweden* 10 E7
Ovruch, *Ukraine* 47 G5
Owaka, *N.Z.* 91 M2
Owambo = Ovamboland, *Namibia* 88 B2
Owasco L., *U.S.A.* 111 D8
Owase, *Japan* 55 G8
Owatonna, *U.S.A.* 112 C8
Owbeh, *Afghan.* 66 B3
Owego, *U.S.A.* 111 D8
Owen Falls Dam, *Uganda* 86 B3
Owen Sound, *Canada* 102 D3
Owens →, *U.S.A.* 116 J9
Owens L., *U.S.A.* 117 J9
Owensboro, *U.S.A.* 108 G2
Owerri, *Nigeria* 83 D6
Owl →, *Canada* 105 B10
Owo, *Nigeria* 83 D6
Owosso, *U.S.A.* 108 D3
Owyhee, *U.S.A.* 114 F5
Owyhee →, *U.S.A.* 114 E5
Owyhee, L., *U.S.A.* 114 E5
Ox Mts. = Slieve Gamph, *Ireland* 15 B3
Öxarfjörður, *Iceland* 8 C5
Oxbow, *Canada* 105 D8
Oxelösund, *Sweden* 11 F11
Oxford, *N.Z.* 91 K4
Oxford, *U.K.* 13 F6
Oxford, *Mass., U.S.A.* 111 D13
Oxford, *Miss., U.S.A.* 113 H10
Oxford, *N.C., U.S.A.* 109 G6
Oxford, *N.Y., U.S.A.* 111 D9
Oxford, *Ohio, U.S.A.* 108 F3
Oxford L., *Canada* 105 C9
Oxfordshire □, *U.K.* 13 F6
Oxía, *Greece* 38 C3
Oxie, *Sweden* 11 J7
Oxílithos, *Greece* 38 C6
Oxnard, *U.S.A.* 117 L7
Oxsjövålen, *Sweden* 10 B7
Oxus = Amudarya →, *Uzbekistan* 50 E6
Oya, *Malaysia* 62 D4
Oyama, *Japan* 55 F9
Oyem, *Gabon* 84 D2
Oyen, *Canada* 105 C6
Oykel →, *U.K.* 14 D4
Oymyakon, *Russia* 51 C15
Oyo, *Nigeria* 83 D5
Oyo □, *Nigeria* 83 D5
Oyonnax, *France* 19 F12
Oyster Bay, *U.S.A.* 111 F11
Ōyūbari, *Japan* 54 C11
Özalp, *Turkey* 73 C10
Ozamiz, *Phil.* 61 G5
Ozark, *Ala., U.S.A.* 109 K3
Ozark, *Ark., U.S.A.* 113 H8
Ozark, *Mo., U.S.A.* 113 G8
Ozark Plateau, *U.S.A.* 113 G9
Ozarks, L. of the, *U.S.A.* 112 F8
Ożarów, *Poland* 45 H8
Ózd, *Hungary* 42 B5
Ozernoye, *Russia* 48 E10
Ozette L., *U.S.A.* 116 B2
Ozieri, *Italy* 30 B2
Ozimek, *Poland* 45 H5
Ozinki, *Russia* 48 E9
Ozona, *U.S.A.* 113 K4
Ozorków, *Poland* 45 G6
Ozren, *Bos.-H.* 42 G3
Ozuluama, *Mexico* 119 C5
Ozun, *Romania* 43 E10
Ozurgeti, *Georgia* 49 K5

P

Pa, *Burkina Faso* 82 C4
Pa-an, *Burma* 67 L20
Pa Mong Dam, *Thailand* 64 D4
Pa Sak →, *Thailand* 62 B2
Paamiut, *Greenland* 4 C5
Paar →, *Germany* 25 G7
Paarl, *S. Africa* 88 E2
Paauilo, *U.S.A.* 106 H17
Pab Hills, *Pakistan* 68 F2
Pabbay, *U.K.* 14 D1

Pabianice, *Poland* 45 G6
Pabna, *Bangla.* 67 G16
Pabo, *Uganda* 86 B3
Pacaja →, *Brazil* 125 D8
Pacaraima, Sa., *S. Amer.* 122 C4
Pacasmayo, *Peru* 124 E3
Paceco, *Italy* 30 E5
Pachhar, *India* 68 G7
Pachino, *Italy* 31 F8
Pachitea →, *Peru* 124 E4
Pachmarhi, *India* 69 H8
Pachpadra, *India* 66 G8
Pachuca, *Mexico* 119 C5
Pacific, *Canada* 104 C3
Pacific-Antarctic Ridge, *Pac. Oc.* 97 M16
Pacific Grove, *U.S.A.* 116 J5
Pacific Ocean, *Pac. Oc.* 97 G14
Pacific Rim Nat. Park, *Canada* 116 B2
Pacifica, *U.S.A.* 116 H4
Pacitan, *Indonesia* 63 H14
Packwood, *U.S.A.* 116 D5
Pacov, *Czech Rep.* 26 B8
Pacy-sur-Eure, *France* 18 C8
Padaido, Kepulauan, *Indonesia* 63 E9
Padang, *Indonesia* 62 E2
Padang Endau, *Malaysia* 65 L4
Padangpanjang, *Indonesia* 62 E2
Padangsidempuan, *Indonesia* 62 D1
Padborg, *Denmark* 11 K3
Paddle Prairie, *Canada* 104 B5
Paddockwood, *Canada* 105 C7
Paderborn, *Germany* 24 D4
Padeş, Vf., *Romania* 42 E7
Padina, *Romania* 43 F12
Padma, *India* 69 G11
Pádova, *Italy* 29 C8
Padra, *India* 68 H5
Padrauna, *India* 69 F10
Padre I., *U.S.A.* 113 M6
Padrón, *Spain* 34 C2
Padstow, *U.K.* 13 G3
Padua = Pádova, *Italy* 29 C8
Paducah, *Ky., U.S.A.* 108 G1
Paducah, *Tex., U.S.A.* 113 H4
Padul, *Spain* 35 H7
Paengnyŏng-do, *S. Korea* 57 F13
Paeroa, *N.Z.* 91 G5
Paesana, *Italy* 28 D4
Pafúri, *Mozam.* 89 C5
Pag, *Croatia* 29 D12
Paga, *Ghana* 83 C4
Pagadian, *Phil.* 61 H5
Pagai Selatan, Pulau, *Indonesia* 62 E2
Pagai Utara, Pulau, *Indonesia* 62 E2
Pagalu = Annobón, *Atl. Oc.* 77 G4
Pagara, *India* 69 G9
Pagastikós Kólpos, *Greece* 38 B5
Pagatan, *Indonesia* 62 E5
Page, *U.S.A.* 115 H8
Pagėgiai, *Lithuania* 44 C8
Pago Pago, *Amer. Samoa* 91 B13
Pagosa Springs, *U.S.A.* 115 H10
Pagwa River, *Canada* 102 B2
Pahala, *U.S.A.* 106 J17
Pahang →, *Malaysia* 65 L4
Pahiatua, *N.Z.* 91 J5
Pahokee, *U.S.A.* 109 M5
Pahrump, *U.S.A.* 117 J11
Pahute Mesa, *U.S.A.* 116 H10
Pai, *Thailand* 64 C2
Paia, *U.S.A.* 106 H16
Paicines, *U.S.A.* 116 J5
Paide, *Estonia* 9 G21
Paignton, *U.K.* 13 G4
Paiho, *Taiwan* 59 F13
Päijänne, *Finland* 9 F21
Pailani, *India* 69 G9
Pailin, *Cambodia* 64 F4
Paimpol, *France* 18 D3
Painan, *Indonesia* 62 E2
Painesville, *U.S.A.* 110 E3
Paint Hills = Wemindji, *Canada* 102 B4
Paint L., *Canada* 105 B9
Painted Desert, *U.S.A.* 115 J8
Paintsville, *U.S.A.* 108 G4
País Vasco □, *Spain* 32 C2
Paisley, *Canada* 110 B3
Paisley, *U.K.* 14 F4
Paisley, *U.S.A.* 114 E3
Paita, *Peru* 124 E2
Paiva →, *Portugal* 34 D2
Paizhou, *China* 59 B9
Pajares, *Spain* 34 B5
Pajares, Puerto de, *Spain* 34 C5
Pajęczno, *Poland* 45 G5
Pak Lay, *Laos* 64 C3
Pak Phanang, *Thailand* 65 H3
Pak Sane, *Laos* 64 C4
Pak Song, *Laos* 64 E6
Pak Suong, *Laos* 58 H4
Pakaur, *India* 69 G12
Pakenham, *Canada* 111 A8
Pákhnes, *Greece* 36 D6
Pakhuis, *S. Africa* 88 E2
Pakistan ■, *Asia* 68 E4
Pakkading, *Laos* 64 C4
Pakokku, *Burma* 67 J19
Pakość, *Poland* 45 F5
Pakowki L., *Canada* 105 D6
Pakpattan, *Pakistan* 68 D5
Pakrac, *Croatia* 42 E2
Pakruojis, *Lithuania* 44 C10
Paks, *Hungary* 42 D3
Paktīā □, *Afghan.* 66 C6
Pakwach, *Uganda* 86 B3
Pakxe, *Laos* 64 E5
Pal Lahara, *India* 69 J11
Pala, *Chad* 79 G9
Pala, *Dem. Rep. of the Congo* 86 D2
Pala, *U.S.A.* 117 M9
Palabek, *Uganda* 86 B3
Palacios, *U.S.A.* 113 L6
Palafrugell, *Spain* 32 D8
Palagiano, *Italy* 31 B10
Palagonía, *Italy* 31 E7
Palagruža, *Croatia* 29 F13
Palaiókastron, *Greece* 36 D8
Palaiokhóra, *Greece* 36 D5
Pálairos, *Greece* 38 C2
Palaiseau, *France* 19 D9
Palam, *India* 66 K10
Palamás, *Greece* 38 B4
Palamòs, *Spain* 32 D8
Palampur, *India* 68 C7
Palamut, *Turkey* 39 C9
Palana, *Australia* 94 F4
Palana, *Russia* 51 D16
Palanan, *Phil.* 61 C5
Palanan Pt., *Phil.* 61 C5
Palandri, *Pakistan* 69 C5
Palanga, *Lithuania* 9 J19
Palangkaraya, *Indonesia* 62 E4
Palani Hills, *India* 66 P10
Palanpur, *India* 68 G5
Palapye, *Botswana* 88 C4
Palas, *Pakistan* 69 B5
Palas de Rei, *Spain* 34 C3
Palashi, *India* 69 H13
Palasponga, *India* 69 J11
Palatka, *Russia* 51 C16
Palatka, *U.S.A.* 109 L5
Palau, *Italy* 30 A2
Palau ■, *Pac. Oc.* 63 C8
Palauk, *Burma* 64 F2
Palawan, *Phil.* 61 G3
Palayankottai, *India* 66 Q10
Palazzo, Pte., *France* 21 F12
Palazzo San Gervásio, *Italy* 31 B8
Palazzolo Acréide, *Italy* 31 E7
Paldiski, *Estonia* 9 G21
Pale, *Bos.-H.* 42 G3
Paleleh, *Indonesia* 63 D6
Palembang, *Indonesia* 62 E2
Palencia, *Spain* 34 C6
Palencia □, *Spain* 34 C6
Palenque, *Mexico* 119 D6
Paleokastrítsa, *Greece* 36 A3
Paleometokho, *Cyprus* 36 D12
Palermo, *Italy* 30 D6
Palermo, *U.S.A.* 114 G3
Palestina, *Chile* 128 A3
Palestine, *Asia* 75 D4
Palestine, *U.S.A.* 113 K7
Palestrina, *Italy* 29 G9
Paletwa, *Burma* 67 J18
Palghat, *India* 66 P10
Palgrave, Mt., *Australia* 92 D2
Pali, *India* 68 G5
Palikir, *Micronesia* 96 G7
Palinuro, *Italy* 31 B8
Palinuro, C., *Italy* 31 B8
Palioúrion, Ákra, *Greece* 40 G7
Palisades Reservoir, *U.S.A.* 114 E8
Paliseul, *Belgium* 17 E5
Palitana, *India* 68 J4
Palizada, *Mexico* 119 D6
Palk Bay, *Asia* 66 Q11
Palk Strait, *Asia* 66 Q11
Palkānah, *Iraq* 70 C5
Palkot, *India* 69 H11
Palla Road = Dinokwe, *Botswana* 88 C4
Pallanza = Verbánia, *Italy* 28 C5
Pallarenda, *Australia* 94 B4
Pallasovka, *Russia* 48 E8
Pallës, Bishti i, *Albania* 40 E3
Pallinup →, *Australia* 93 F2
Pallisa, *Uganda* 86 B3
Pallu, *India* 68 E6
Palm Bay, *U.S.A.* 109 L5
Palm Beach, *U.S.A.* 109 M6
Palm Coast, *U.S.A.* 109 L5
Palm Desert, *U.S.A.* 117 M10
Palm Is., *Australia* 94 B4
Palm Springs, *U.S.A.* 117 M10
Palma, *Mozam.* 87 E5
Palma, B. de, *Spain* 37 B9
Palma de Mallorca, *Spain* 37 B9
Palma del Río, *Spain* 35 H5
Palma di Montechiaro, *Italy* 30 E6
Palma Soriano, *Cuba* 120 B4
Palmares, *Brazil* 125 E11
Palmarola, *Italy* 30 B5
Palmas, *Brazil* 127 B5
Palmas, C., *Liberia* 82 E3
Pálmas, G. di, *Italy* 30 D1
Palmdale, *U.S.A.* 117 L8
Palmeira das Missões, *Brazil* 127 B5
Palmeira dos Índios, *Brazil* 125 E11
Palmela, *Portugal* 35 G2
Palmer, *U.S.A.* 100 B5
Palmer →, *Australia* 94 B3
Palmer Arch., *Antarctica* 5 C17
Palmer Lake, *U.S.A.* 112 F2
Palmer Land, *Antarctica* 5 D18
Palmerston, *Canada* 110 C4
Palmerston, *N.Z.* 91 L3
Palmerston North, *N.Z.* 91 J5
Palmerton, *U.S.A.* 111 F9
Palmetto, *U.S.A.* 109 M4
Palmi, *Italy* 31 D8
Palmira, *Argentina* 126 C2
Palmira, *Colombia* 124 C3
Palmyra = Tudmur, *Syria* 70 C3
Palmyra, *Mo., U.S.A.* 112 F9
Palmyra, *N.J., U.S.A.* 111 F9
Palmyra, *N.Y., U.S.A.* 110 C7
Palmyra, *Pa., U.S.A.* 111 F8
Palmyra Is., *Pac. Oc.* 97 G11
Palo Alto, *U.S.A.* 116 H4
Palo Verde, *U.S.A.* 117 M12
Paloich, *Sudan* 81 E3
Palompon, *Phil.* 61 F6
Palopo, *Indonesia* 63 E6
Palos, C. de, *Spain* 33 H4
Palos de la Frontera, *Spain* 35 H4
Palos Verdes, *U.S.A.* 117 M8
Palos Verdes, Pt., *U.S.A.* 117 M8
Pålsboda, *Sweden* 10 E9
Palu, *Indonesia* 63 E5
Palu, *Turkey* 70 B3
Paluke, *Liberia* 82 D3
Paluzza, *Italy* 29 B10
Palwal, *India* 68 E7
Pama, *Burkina Faso* 83 C5
Pamanukan, *Indonesia* 63 G12
Pamiers, *France* 20 E5
Pamir, *Tajikistan* 50 F8
Pamlico →, *U.S.A.* 109 H7
Pamlico Sd., *U.S.A.* 109 H8
Pampa, *U.S.A.* 113 H4
Pampa de las Salinas, *Argentina* 126 C2
Pampanua, *Indonesia* 63 E6
Pampas, *Argentina* 126 D3
Pampas, *Peru* 124 F4
Pamphylia, *Turkey* 72 D4
Pamplona, *Colombia* 124 B4
Pamplona, *Spain* 32 C3
Pampoenpoort, *S. Africa* 88 E3
Pamukçu, *Turkey* 39 B9
Pamukkale, *Turkey* 39 D11
Pan Xian, *China* 58 E5
Pana, *U.S.A.* 112 F10
Panabo, *Phil.* 61 H6
Panaca, *U.S.A.* 115 H6
Panagyurishte, *Bulgaria* 41 D8
Panaitan, *Indonesia* 63 G11
Panaji, *India* 66 M8
Panamá, *Panama* 120 E4
Panama ■, *Cent. Amer.* 120 E4
Panamá, G. de, *Panama* 120 E4
Panama Canal, *Panama* 120 E4
Panama City, *U.S.A.* 109 K3
Panamint Range, *U.S.A.* 117 J9
Panamint Springs, *U.S.A.* 117 J9
Panão, *Peru* 124 E3
Panaon I., *Phil.* 61 F6
Panare, *Thailand* 65 J3
Panarea, *Italy* 31 D8
Panaro →, *Italy* 29 D8
Panay, *Phil.* 61 F5
Panay, G., *Phil.* 63 B6
Pančevo, *Serbia, Yug.* 42 F5
Panch'iao, *Taiwan* 59 E13
Panciu, *Romania* 43 E12
Pancorbo, Desfiladero, *Spain* 34 C7
Pâncota, *Romania* 42 D6
Panda, *Mozam.* 89 C5
Pandan, *Antique, Phil.* 61 F5
Pandan, *Catanduanes, Phil.* 61 D6
Pandegelang, *Indonesia* 63 G12
Pandhana, *India* 68 J7
Pandharpur, *India* 66 L9
Pando, *Uruguay* 127 C4
Pando, L. = Hope, L., *Australia* 95 D2
Pandokrátor, *Greece* 36 A3
Pandora, *Costa Rica* 120 E3
Pandrup, *Denmark* 11 G3
Panevėžys, *Lithuania* 9 J21
Panfilov, *Kazakstan* 50 E8
Panfilovo, *Russia* 48 E6
Pang-Long, *Burma* 67 H21
Pang-Yang, *Burma* 67 H21
Panga, *Dem. Rep. of the Congo* 86 B2
Pangaíon Óros, *Greece* 41 F8
Pangalanes, Canal des = Ampangalana, Lakandranon', *Madag.* 89 C8
Pangani, *Tanzania* 86 D4
Pangani →, *Tanzania* 86 D4
Pangfou = Bengbu, *China* 57 H9
Pangil, *Dem. Rep. of the Congo* 86 C2
Pangkah, Tanjung, *Indonesia* 63 G15
Pangkajene, *Indonesia* 63 E5
Pangkalanbrandan, *Indonesia* 62 D1
Pangkalanbuun, *Indonesia* 62 E4
Pangkalpinang, *Indonesia* 62 E3
Pangnirtung, *Canada* 101 B13
Pangong Tso, *India* 68 B8
Panguitch, *U.S.A.* 115 H7
Pangutaran Group, *Phil.* 61 H4
Panhandle, *U.S.A.* 113 H4
Pani Mines, *India* 68 H5
Pania-Mutombo, *Dem. Rep. of the Congo* 86 D1
Panikota I., *India* 68 J4
Panipat, *India* 68 E7
Panjal Range, *India* 68 C7
Panjang, Hon, *Vietnam* 65 H4
Panjgur, *Pakistan* 66 F4
Panjim = Panaji, *India* 66 M8
Panjin, *China* 57 D12
Panjinad Barrage, *Pakistan* 66 E7
Panjnad →, *Pakistan* 68 E4
Panjwai, *Afghan.* 68 D1
Pankshin, *Nigeria* 83 D6
Panmunjŏm, *N. Korea* 57 F14
Panna, *India* 69 G9
Panna Hills, *India* 69 G9
Pannawonica, *Australia* 92 D2
Pano Akil, *Pakistan* 68 F3
Pano Lefkara, *Cyprus* 36 E12
Pano Panayia, *Cyprus* 36 E11
Panorama, *Brazil* 127 A5
Pánormon, *Greece* 36 D6
Pansemal, *India* 68 J6
Panshan = Panjin, *China* 57 D12
Panshi, *China* 57 C14
Pantanal, *Brazil* 124 H7
Pantar, *Indonesia* 63 F6
Pante Macassar, *Indonesia* 63 F6
Pantelleria, *Italy* 30 F4
Pantón, *Spain* 34 C3
Pánuco, *Mexico* 119 C5
Panyam, *Nigeria* 83 D6
Panyu, *China* 59 F9
Panzhihua, *China* 58 D3
Páola, *Italy* 31 C9
Paola, *Malta* 36 D2
Paola, *U.S.A.* 112 F7
Paonia, *U.S.A.* 115 G10
Paoting = Baoding, *China* 56 E8
Paot'ou = Baotou, *China* 56 D6
Paoua, *C.A.R.* 84 C3
Pápa, *Hungary* 42 C2
Papa Stour, *U.K.* 14 A7
Papa Westray, *U.K.* 14 B6
Papagayo →, *Mexico* 119 D5
Papagayo, G. de, *Costa Rica* 120 D2
Papakura, *N.Z.* 91 G5
Papantla, *Mexico* 119 C5
Papar, *Malaysia* 62 C5
Pápas, Ákra, *Greece* 38 C3
Papeete, *Tahiti* 97 J13
Papenburg, *Germany* 24 B3
Paphlagonia, *Turkey* 72 B5
Paphos, *Cyprus* 36 E11
Papien Chiang = Da →, *Vietnam* 58 G5
Papigochic →, *Mexico* 118 B3
Paposo, *Chile* 126 B1
Papoutsa, *Cyprus* 36 E12
Papua New Guinea ■, *Oceania* 96 H6
Papudo, *Chile* 126 C1
Papuk, *Croatia* 42 E2
Papun, *Burma* 67 K20
Papunya, *Australia* 92 D5
Pará = Belém, *Brazil* 125 D9
Pará □, *Brazil* 125 D8
Paraburdoo, *Australia* 92 D2
Paracale, *Phil.* 61 D5
Paracatu, *Brazil* 125 G9
Paracel Is., *S. China Sea* 62 A4
Parachilna, *Australia* 95 E2
Parachinar, *Pakistan* 68 C4
Paraćin, *Serbia, Yug.* 40 C5
Paradas, *Spain* 35 H5
Paradela, *Spain* 34 C3
Paradhísi, *Greece* 36 C10
Paradip, *India* 67 J15
Paradise, *Calif., U.S.A.* 116 F5
Paradise, *Nev., U.S.A.* 117 J11
Paradise →, *Canada* 103 B8
Paradise Hill, *Canada* 105 C7
Paradise River, *Canada* 103 B8
Paradise Valley, *U.S.A.* 114 F5
Parado, *Indonesia* 63 F5
Paragould, *U.S.A.* 113 G9
Paragua →, *Venezuela* 124 B6
Paraguaçu →, *Brazil* 125 F11
Paraguaçu Paulista, *Brazil* 127 A5
Paraguaná, Pen. de, *Venezuela* 124 A5
Paraguarí, *Paraguay* 126 B4
Paraguarí □, *Paraguay* 126 B4
Paraguay ■, *S. Amer.* 126 A4
Paraguay →, *Paraguay* 126 B4
Paraíba = João Pessoa, *Brazil* 125 E12
Paraíba □, *Brazil* 125 E11
Paraíba do Sul →, *Brazil* 127 A7
Parainen, *Finland* 9 F20
Paraiso, *Mexico* 119 D6
Parak, *Iran* 71 E7
Parakhino Paddubye, *Russia* 46 C7
Parakou, *Benin* 83 D5
Paralimni, *Cyprus* 36 D12
Parálion-Astrous, *Greece* 38 D4
Paramaribo, *Surinam* 125 B7
Paramithiá, *Greece* 38 B2
Paramushir, Ostrov, *Russia* 51 D16
Paran →, *Israel* 75 E4
Paraná, *Argentina* 126 C3
Paranã, *Brazil* 125 F9
Paraná □, *Brazil* 127 A5
Paraná →, *Argentina* 126 C4
Paranaguá, *Brazil* 127 B6
Paranaíba, *Brazil* 125 G8
Paranaíba →, *Brazil* 125 H8
Paranapanema →, *Brazil* 127 A5
Paranapiacaba, Serra do, *Brazil* 127 A6
Paranas, *Phil.* 61 F6
Paranavaí, *Brazil* 127 A5
Parang, *Maguindanao, Phil.* 63 C6
Parang, *Sulu, Phil.* 61 J4
Parângul Mare, Vf., *Romania* 43 E8
Parapóla, *Greece* 38 E5
Paraspóri, Ákra, *Greece* 39 F9
Paray-le-Monial, *France* 19 F11
Parbati →, *Mad. P., India* 68 G7
Parbati →, *Raj., India* 68 F7
Parbhani, *India* 66 K10
Parchim, *Germany* 24 B7
Parczew, *Poland* 45 G9
Pardes Hanna-Karkur, *Israel* 75 C3
Pardilla, *Spain* 34 D7
Pardo →, *Bahia, Brazil* 125 G11
Pardo →, *Mato Grosso, Brazil* 127 A5
Pardubice, *Czech Rep.* 26 A8
Pare, *Indonesia* 63 G15
Pare Mts., *Tanzania* 86 C4
Parecis, Serra dos, *Brazil* 124 F7
Paredes de Nava, *Spain* 34 C6
Paren, *Russia* 51 C17
Parent, *Canada* 102 C5
Parent, L., *Canada* 102 C4
Parentis-en-Born, *France* 20 D2
Parepare, *Indonesia* 63 E5
Parfino, *Russia* 46 D6
Párga, *Greece* 38 B2
Pargo, Pta. do, *Madeira* 37 D2
Pariaguán, *Venezuela* 124 B6
Paricutín, Cerro, *Mexico* 118 D4
Parigi, *Indonesia* 63 E6
Parika, *Guyana* 124 B7
Parikkala, *Finland* 46 B5
Parima, Serra, *Brazil* 124 C6
Parinari, *Peru* 124 D4
Pariñas, Pta., *S. Amer.* 122 D2
Parincea, *Romania* 43 D12
Parintins, *Brazil* 125 D7
Pariparit Kyun, *Burma* 67 M18
Paris, *Canada* 110 C4
Paris, *France* 19 D9
Paris, *Idaho, U.S.A.* 114 E8
Paris, *Ky., U.S.A.* 108 F3
Paris, *Tenn., U.S.A.* 109 G1
Paris, *Tex., U.S.A.* 113 J7
Paris, Ville de □, *France* 19 D9
Parish, *U.S.A.* 111 C8
Parishville, *U.S.A.* 111 B10
Park, *U.S.A.* 116 B4
Park City, *U.S.A.* 113 G6
Park Falls, *U.S.A.* 112 C9
Park Head, *Canada* 110 B3
Park Hills, *U.S.A.* 113 G9
Park Range, *U.S.A.* 114 G10
Park Rapids, *U.S.A.* 112 B7
Park River, *U.S.A.* 112 A6
Park Rynie, *S. Africa* 89 E5
Parkā Bandar, *Iran* 71 E8
Parkano, *Finland* 9 E20
Parker, *Ariz., U.S.A.* 117 L12
Parker, *Pa., U.S.A.* 110 E5
Parker Dam, *U.S.A.* 117 L12
Parkersburg, *U.S.A.* 108 F5
Parkes, *Australia* 95 E4
Parkfield, *U.S.A.* 116 K6
Parkhill, *Canada* 110 C3
Parkland, *U.S.A.* 116 C4
Parkston, *U.S.A.* 112 D6
Parksville, *Canada* 104 D4
Parla, *Spain* 34 E7
Pârliţa, *Moldova* 43 C12
Parma, *Italy* 28 D7
Parma, *Idaho, U.S.A.* 114 E5
Parma, *Ohio, U.S.A.* 110 E3
Parma →, *Italy* 28 D7
Parnaguá, *Brazil* 125 F10
Parnaíba, *Brazil* 125 D10
Parnaíba →, *Brazil* 122 D6
Parnassós, *Greece* 38 C4
Párnis, *Greece* 38 C5
Párnon Óros, *Greece* 38 D4
Pärnu, *Estonia* 9 G21
Paroo →, *Australia* 95 E3
Páros, *Greece* 39 D7
Parowan, *U.S.A.* 115 H7
Parpaillon, *France* 21 D10
Parral, *Chile* 126 D1
Parras, *Mexico* 118 B4
Parrett →, *U.K.* 13 F4
Parris I., *U.S.A.* 109 J5
Parrsboro, *Canada* 103 C7
Parry I., *Canada* 110 A4
Parry Is., *Canada* 4 B2
Parry Sound, *Canada* 102 C4
Parsberg, *Germany* 25 F7
Parsęta →, *Poland* 44 D2
Parsnip →, *Canada* 104 B4
Parsons, *U.S.A.* 113 G7
Parsons Ra., *Australia* 94 A2
Partanna, *Italy* 30 E5
Parthenay, *France* 18 F6
Partinico, *Italy* 30 D6
Partizánske, *Slovak Rep.* 27 C11
Partridge I., *Canada* 102 A2
Paru →, *Brazil* 125 D8
Parvān □, *Afghan.* 66 B6
Parvatipuram, *India* 67 K13
Parvatsar, *India* 68 F6
Påryd, *Sweden* 11 H9
Parys, *S. Africa* 88 D4
Pas, Pta. des, *Spain* 37 C7
Pas-de-Calais □, *France* 19 B9
Pasada, *Spain* 34 B5
Pasadena, *Canada* 103 C8
Pasadena, *Calif., U.S.A.* 117 L8
Pasadena, *Tex., U.S.A.* 113 L7
Pasaje →, *Argentina* 126 B3
Paşalimanı, *Turkey* 41 F11
Pasay, *Phil.* 61 D4
Pascagoula, *U.S.A.* 113 K10
Pascagoula →, *U.S.A.* 113 K10
Paşcani, *Romania* 43 C11
Pasco, *U.S.A.* 114 C4
Pasco, Cerro de, *Peru* 124 F3
Pasco I., *Australia* 92 D2
Pascoag, *U.S.A.* 111 E13
Pascua, I. de, *Pac. Oc.* 97 K17
Pasewalk, *Germany* 24 B9
Pasfield L., *Canada* 105 B7
Pasha →, *Russia* 46 B7
Pashiwari, *Pakistan* 69 B6
Pashmakli = Smolyan, *Bulgaria* 41 E8
Pasinler, *Turkey* 73 C9
Pasir Mas, *Malaysia* 65 J4
Pasir Putih, *Malaysia* 65 K4
Pasirian, *Indonesia* 63 H15

Pasirkuning

Pasirkuning, *Indonesia* **62 E2**
Påskallavik, *Sweden* **11 G10**
Pasküh, *Iran* **71 E9**
Pasłęk, *Poland* **44 D6**
Pasłęka →, *Poland* **44 D6**
Pasley, C., *Australia* **93 F3**
Pašman, *Croatia* **29 E12**
Pasni, *Pakistan* **66 G3**
Paso Cantinela, *Mexico* **117 N11**
Paso de Indios, *Argentina* **128 E3**
Paso de los Libres, *Argentina* **126 B4**
Paso de los Toros, *Uruguay* **126 C4**
Paso Robles, *U.S.A.* **115 J3**
Paspébiac, *Canada* **103 C6**
Pasrur, *Pakistan* **68 C6**
Passage West, *Ireland* **15 E3**
Passaic, *U.S.A.* **111 F10**
Passau, *Germany* **25 G9**
Passero, C., *Italy* **31 F8**
Passo Fundo, *Brazil* **127 B5**
Passos, *Brazil* **125 H9**
Passow, *Germany* **24 B10**
Passy, *France* **21 C10**
Pastavy, *Belarus* **9 J22**
Pastaza →, *Peru* **124 D3**
Pasto, *Colombia* **124 C3**
Pastrana, *Spain* **32 E2**
Pasuruan, *Indonesia* **63 G15**
Pasym, *Poland* **44 E7**
Pásztó, *Hungary* **42 C4**
Patagonia, *Argentina* **122 H4**
Patagonia, *U.S.A.* **115 L8**
Patambar, *Iran* **71 D9**
Patan, *Gujarat, India* **66 H8**
Patan, *Maharashtra, India* **68 H5**
Patan, *Nepal* **67 F14**
Patani, *Indonesia* **63 D7**
Pătârlagele, *Romania* **43 E11**
Pataudi, *India* **68 E7**
Patchewollock, *Australia* **95 F3**
Patchogue, *U.S.A.* **111 F11**
Patea, *N.Z.* **91 H5**
Pategi, *Nigeria* **83 D6**
Patensie, *S. Africa* **88 E3**
Paterna, *Spain* **33 F4**
Paternion, *Austria* **26 E6**
Paternò, *Italy* **31 E7**
Pateros, *U.S.A.* **114 B4**
Paterson, *U.S.A.* **111 F10**
Paterson Ra., *Australia* **92 D3**
Pathankot, *India* **68 C6**
Pathfinder Reservoir, *U.S.A.* **114 E10**
Pathiu, *Thailand* **65 G2**
Pathum Thani, *Thailand* **64 E3**
Pati, *Indonesia* **63 G14**
Patía →, *Colombia* **124 C3**
Patiala, *Punjab, India* **68 D7**
Patiala, *Ut. P., India* **69 F8**
Patine Kouka, *Senegal* **82 C2**
Patitírion, *Greece* **38 B5**
Patkai Bum, *India* **67 F19**
Pátmos, *Greece* **39 D8**
Patna, *India* **69 G11**
Patnos, *Turkey* **73 C10**
Pato Branco, *Brazil* **127 B5**
Patonga, *Uganda* **86 B3**
Patos, *Brazil* **125 E11**
Patos, L. dos, *Brazil* **127 C5**
Patos, Río de los →, *Argentina* **126 C2**
Patos de Minas, *Brazil* **125 G9**
Patosi, *Albania* **40 F3**
Patquía, *Argentina* **126 C2**
Pátrai, *Greece* **38 C3**
Pátraikós Kólpos, *Greece* **38 C3**
Patras = Pátrai, *Greece* **38 C3**
Patrocínio, *Brazil* **125 G9**
Patta, *Kenya* **86 C5**
Pattada, *Italy* **30 B2**
Pattani, *Thailand* **65 J3**
Pattaya, *Thailand* **62 B2**
Patten, *U.S.A.* **109 C11**
Patterson, *Calif., U.S.A.* **116 H5**
Patterson, *La., U.S.A.* **113 L9**
Patterson, Mt., *U.S.A.* **116 G7**
Patti, *Punjab, India* **68 D6**
Patti, *Ut. P., India* **69 G10**
Patti, *Italy* **31 D7**
Pattoki, *Pakistan* **68 D5**
Patton, *U.S.A.* **110 F6**
Patuakhali, *Bangla.* **67 H17**
Patuanak, *Canada* **105 B7**
Patuca →, *Honduras* **120 C3**
Patuca, Punta, *Honduras* **120 C3**
Pătulele, *Romania* **42 F7**
Pátzcuaro, *Mexico* **118 D4**
Pau, *France* **20 E3**
Pau, Gave de →, *France* **20 E2**
Pauillac, *France* **20 C3**
Pauk, *Burma* **67 J19**
Paul I., *Canada* **103 A7**
Paul Smiths, *U.S.A.* **111 B10**
Paulatuk, *Canada* **100 B7**
Paulhan, *France* **20 E7**
Paulis = Isiro, *Dem. Rep. of the Congo* **86 B2**
Paulistana, *Brazil* **125 E10**
Paulo Afonso, *Brazil* **125 E11**
Paulpietersburg, *S. Africa* **89 D5**
Pauls Valley, *U.S.A.* **113 H6**
Pauma Valley, *U.S.A.* **117 M10**
Pauri, *India* **69 D8**
Pāveh, *Iran* **70 C5**
Pavelets, *Russia* **46 F10**
Pavia, *Italy* **28 C6**
Pavilion, *U.S.A.* **110 D6**
Pavilly, *France* **18 C7**
Pāvilosta, *Latvia* **9 H19**
Pavlikeni, *Bulgaria* **41 C9**
Pavlodar, *Kazakstan* **50 D8**
Pavlograd = Pavlohrad, *Ukraine* **47 H8**
Pavlohrad, *Ukraine* **47 H8**
Pavlovo, *Russia* **48 C6**
Pavlovsk, *Russia* **48 E5**
Pavlovskaya, *Russia* **49 G4**
Pavlovskiy-Posad, *Russia* **46 E10**
Pavullo nel Frignano, *Italy* **28 D7**
Pawayan, *India* **69 E9**
Pawhuska, *U.S.A.* **113 G6**
Pawling, *U.S.A.* **111 E11**
Pawnee, *U.S.A.* **113 G6**
Pawnee City, *U.S.A.* **112 E6**
Pawtucket, *U.S.A.* **111 E13**
Paximádhia, *Greece* **36 E6**
Paxoí, *Greece* **38 B2**
Paxton, *Ill., U.S.A.* **108 E1**
Paxton, *Nebr., U.S.A.* **112 E4**
Payakumbuh, *Indonesia* **62 E2**
Payerne, *Switz.* **25 J2**
Payette, *U.S.A.* **114 D5**
Paymogo, *Spain* **35 H3**
Payne Bay = Kangirsuk, *Canada* **101 B13**
Payne L., *Canada* **101 C12**
Paynes Find, *Australia* **93 E2**
Paynesville, *Liberia* **82 D2**
Paynesville, *U.S.A.* **112 C7**
Pays de la Loire □, *France* **18 E6**
Paysandú, *Uruguay* **126 C4**
Payson, *U.S.A.* **115 J8**
Paz →, *Guatemala* **120 D1**
Paz, B. la, *Mexico* **118 C2**
Pāzanān, *Iran* **71 D6**
Pazar, *Turkey* **73 B9**
Pazarcık, *Turkey* **72 D7**
Pazardzhik, *Bulgaria* **41 D8**
Pazarköy, *Turkey* **39 B9**
Pazarlar, *Turkey* **39 C11**
Pazaryeri, *Turkey* **39 B11**
Pazaryolu, *Turkey* **73 B9**
Pazin, *Croatia* **29 C10**
Pčinja →, *Macedonia* **40 E5**
Pe Ell, *U.S.A.* **116 D3**
Peabody, *U.S.A.* **111 D14**
Peace →, *Canada* **104 B6**
Peace Point, *Canada* **104 B6**
Peace River, *Canada* **104 B5**
Peach Springs, *U.S.A.* **115 J7**
Peachland, *Canada* **104 D5**
Peachtree City, *U.S.A.* **109 J3**
Peak, The = Kinder Scout, *U.K.* **12 D6**
Peak District, *U.K.* **12 D6**
Peak Hill, *N.S.W., Australia* **95 E4**
Peak Hill, *W. Austral., Australia* **93 E2**
Peak Ra., *Australia* **94 C4**
Peake Cr. →, *Australia* **95 D2**
Peal de Becerro, *Spain* **35 H7**
Peale, Mt., *U.S.A.* **115 G9**
Pearblossom, *U.S.A.* **117 L9**
Pearl →, *U.S.A.* **113 K10**
Pearl City, *U.S.A.* **106 H16**
Pearl Harbor, *U.S.A.* **106 H16**
Pearl River, *U.S.A.* **111 E10**
Pearsall, *U.S.A.* **113 L5**
Peary Land, *Greenland* **4 A6**
Pease →, *U.S.A.* **113 H5**
Peawanuck, *Canada* **101 C11**
Pebane, *Mozam.* **87 F4**
Pebas, *Peru* **124 D4**
Pebble Beach, *U.S.A.* **116 J5**
Peć, *Kosovo, Yug.* **40 D4**
Péccioli, *Italy* **28 E7**
Pechea, *Romania* **43 E12**
Pechenga, *Russia* **50 C4**
Pechenizhyn, *Ukraine* **47 H3**
Pechiguera, Pta., *Canary Is.* **37 F6**
Pechnezhskoye Vdkhr., *Ukraine* **47 G9**
Pechora, *Russia* **50 C6**
Pechora →, *Russia* **50 C6**
Pechorskaya Guba, *Russia* **50 C6**
Pecica, *Romania* **42 D6**
Pecka, *Serbia, Yug.* **40 B3**
Pécora, C., *Italy* **30 C1**
Pečory, *Russia* **9 H22**
Pecos, *U.S.A.* **113 K3**
Pecos →, *U.S.A.* **113 L3**
Pécs, *Hungary* **42 D3**
Pedder, L., *Australia* **94 G4**
Peddie, *S. Africa* **89 E4**
Pédernales, *Dom. Rep.* **121 C5**
Pedieos →, *Cyprus* **36 D12**
Pedirka, *Australia* **95 D2**
Pedra Azul, *Brazil* **125 G10**
Pedreguer, *Spain* **33 G5**
Pedreiras, *Brazil* **125 D10**
Pedro Afonso, *Brazil* **125 E9**
Pedro Cays, *Jamaica* **120 C4**
Pedro de Valdivia, *Chile* **126 A2**
Pedro Juan Caballero, *Paraguay* **127 A4**
Pedro Muñoz, *Spain* **35 F8**
Pedrógão Grande, *Portugal* **34 F2**
Pee Dee →, *U.S.A.* **109 J6**
Peebinga, *Australia* **95 E3**
Peebles, *U.K.* **14 F5**
Peekskill, *U.S.A.* **111 E11**
Peel, *U.K.* **12 C3**
Peel →, *Australia* **95 E5**
Peel →, *Canada* **100 B6**
Peel Sound, *Canada* **100 A10**
Peene →, *Germany* **24 A9**
Peera Peera Poolanna L., *Australia* **95 D2**
Peerless Lake, *Canada* **104 B6**
Peers, *Canada* **104 C5**
Pegasus Bay, *N.Z.* **91 K4**
Peggau, *Austria* **26 D8**
Pegnitz, *Germany* **25 F7**
Pegnitz →, *Germany* **25 F6**
Pego, *Spain* **33 G4**
Pegu, *Burma* **67 L20**
Pegu Yoma, *Burma* **67 K20**
Pehčevo, *Macedonia* **40 E6**
Pehlivanköy, *Turkey* **41 E10**
Pehuajó, *Argentina* **126 D3**
Pei Xian = Pizhou, *China* **56 G9**
Peine, *Chile* **126 A2**
Peine, *Germany* **24 C6**
Peip'ing = Beijing, *China* **56 E9**
Peipus, L. = Chudskoye, Ozero, *Russia* **9 G22**
Peissenberg, *Germany* **25 H7**
Peitz, *Germany* **24 D10**
Peixe, *Brazil* **125 F9**
Peixe →, *Brazil* **125 H8**
Pek →, *Serbia, Yug.* **40 B5**
Pekalongan, *Indonesia* **63 G13**
Pekan, *Malaysia* **65 L4**
Pekanbaru, *Indonesia* **62 D2**
Pekang, *Taiwan* **59 F13**
Pekin, *U.S.A.* **112 E10**
Peking = Beijing, *China* **56 E9**
Péla, *Guinea* **82 D3**
Pelabuhan Kelang, *Malaysia* **65 L3**
Pelabuhan Ratu, Teluk, *Indonesia* **63 G12**
Pelabuhanratu, *Indonesia* **63 G12**
Pélagos, *Greece* **38 B6**
Pelaihari, *Indonesia* **62 E4**
Pelat, Mt., *France* **21 D10**
Pełczyce, *Poland* **45 E2**
Peleaga, Vf., *Romania* **42 E7**
Pelée, Mt., *Martinique* **121 D7**
Pelee, Pt., *Canada* **102 D3**
Pelee I., *Canada* **102 D3**
Pelekech, *Kenya* **86 B4**
Peleng, *Indonesia* **63 E6**
Pélézi, *Ivory C.* **82 D3**
Pelhřimov, *Czech Rep.* **26 B8**
Pelican, *U.S.A.* **104 B1**
Pelican L., *Canada* **105 C8**
Pelican Narrows, *Canada* **105 B8**
Pelješac, *Croatia* **29 F14**
Pelkosenniemi, *Finland* **8 C22**
Pella, *Greece* **40 F6**
Pella, *S. Africa* **88 D2**
Pella, *U.S.A.* **112 E8**
Pélla □, *Greece* **40 F6**
Pello, *Finland* **8 C21**
Pellworm, *Germany* **24 A4**
Pelly →, *Canada* **100 B6**
Pelly Bay, *Canada* **101 B11**
Peloponnese = Pelopónnisos □, *Greece* **38 D4**
Pelopónnisos □, *Greece* **38 D4**
Peloritani, Monti, *Italy* **31 D8**
Pelorus Sd., *N.Z.* **91 J4**
Pelotas, *Brazil* **127 C5**
Pelotas →, *Brazil* **127 B5**
Pelovo, *Bulgaria* **41 C8**
Pelplin, *Poland* **44 E5**
Pelvoux, Massif du, *France* **21 D10**
Pemalang, *Indonesia* **63 G13**
Pemanggil, Pulau, *Malaysia* **65 L5**
Pematangsiantar, *Indonesia* **62 D1**
Pemba, *Mozam.* **87 E5**
Pemba, *Zambia* **87 F2**
Pemba Channel, *Tanzania* **86 D4**
Pemba I., *Tanzania* **86 D4**
Pemberton, *Australia* **93 F2**
Pemberton, *Canada* **104 C4**
Pembina, *U.S.A.* **112 A6**
Pembroke, *Canada* **102 C4**
Pembroke, *U.K.* **13 F3**
Pembrokeshire □, *U.K.* **13 F3**
Pen-y-Ghent, *U.K.* **12 C5**
Peña, Sierra de la, *Spain* **32 C4**
Peña de Francia, Sierra de la, *Spain* **34 E4**
Penafiel, *Portugal* **34 D2**
Peñafiel, *Spain* **34 D6**
Peñaflor, *Spain* **35 H5**
Peñalara, *Spain* **34 E7**
Penamacôr, *Portugal* **34 E3**
Penang = Pinang, *Malaysia* **65 K3**
Penápolis, *Brazil* **127 A6**
Peñaranda de Bracamonte, *Spain* **34 E5**
Peñarroya, *Spain* **32 E4**
Peñarroya-Pueblonuevo, *Spain* **35 G5**
Penarth, *U.K.* **13 F4**
Peñas, C. de, *Spain* **34 B5**
Penas, G. de, *Chile* **122 H3**
Peñas de San Pedro, *Spain* **33 G3**
Peñas del Chache, *Canary Is.* **37 E6**
Peñausende, *Spain* **34 D5**
Pench'i = Benxi, *China* **57 D12**
Pend Oreille →, *U.S.A.* **114 B5**
Pend Oreille, L., *U.S.A.* **114 C5**
Pendálofon, *Greece* **40 F5**
Pendembu, *Eastern, S. Leone* **82 D2**
Pendembu, *Northern, S. Leone* **82 D2**
Pender B., *Australia* **92 C3**
Pendik, *Turkey* **41 F13**
Pendjari →, *Benin* **83 C5**
Pendleton, *U.S.A.* **114 D4**
Pendra, *India* **69 H9**
Penedo, *Brazil* **125 F11**
Penetanguishene, *Canada* **102 D4**
Penfield, *U.S.A.* **110 E6**
Pengalengan, *Indonesia* **63 G12**
Penge, *Kasai-Or., Dem. Rep. of the Congo* **86 D1**
Penge, *Sud-Kivu, Dem. Rep. of the Congo* **86 C2**
Penghu, *Taiwan* **59 F12**
Penglai, *China* **57 F11**
Pengshan, *China* **58 B4**
Pengshui, *China* **58 C7**
Penguin, *Australia* **94 G4**
Pengxi, *China* **58 B5**
Pengze, *China* **59 C11**
Penhalonga, *Zimbabwe* **87 F3**
Peniche, *Portugal* **35 F1**
Penicuik, *U.K.* **14 F5**
Penida, *Indonesia* **62 F5**
Peninnes, Alpes = Pennine, Alpi, *Alps* **25 J3**
Peninsular Malaysia □, *Malaysia* **65 L4**
Peñíscola, *Spain* **32 E5**
Penitente, Serra do, *Brazil* **125 E9**
Penkridge, *U.K.* **12 E5**
Penmarch, *France* **18 E2**
Penmarch, Pte. de, *France* **18 E2**
Penn Hills, *U.S.A.* **110 F5**
Penn Yan, *U.S.A.* **110 D7**
Penna, Punta della, *Italy* **29 F11**
Pennant, *Canada* **105 C7**
Penne, *Italy* **29 F10**
Penner →, *India* **66 M12**
Pennine, Alpi, *Alps* **25 J3**
Pennines, *U.K.* **12 C5**
Pennington, *U.S.A.* **116 F5**
Pennington →, *Nigeria* **83 E6**
Pennino, Mte., *Italy* **29 E9**
Pennsburg, *U.S.A.* **111 F9**
Pennsylvania □, *U.S.A.* **108 E7**
Penny, *Canada* **104 C4**
Peno, *Russia* **46 D7**
Penobscot →, *U.S.A.* **109 C11**
Penobscot B., *U.S.A.* **109 C11**
Penola, *Australia* **95 F3**
Penong, *Australia* **93 F5**
Penonomé, *Panama* **120 E3**
Penrith, *Australia* **95 E5**
Penrith, *U.K.* **12 C5**
Penryn, *U.K.* **13 G2**
Pensacola, *U.S.A.* **109 K2**
Pensacola Mts., *Antarctica* **5 E1**
Pense, *Canada* **105 C8**
Penshurst, *Australia* **95 F3**
Penticton, *Canada* **104 D5**
Pentland, *Australia* **94 C4**
Pentland Firth, *U.K.* **14 C5**
Pentland Hills, *U.K.* **14 F5**
Penza, *Russia* **48 D7**
Penzance, *U.K.* **13 G2**
Penzberg, *Germany* **25 H7**
Penzhino, *Russia* **51 C17**
Penzhinskaya Guba, *Russia* **51 C17**
Penzhou, *China* **58 B4**
Penzlin, *Germany* **24 B9**
Peoria, *Ariz., U.S.A.* **115 K7**
Peoria, *Ill., U.S.A.* **112 E10**
Pepacton Reservoir, *U.S.A.* **111 D10**
Pepani →, *S. Africa* **88 D3**
Pepel, *S. Leone* **82 D2**
Peqini, *Albania* **40 E3**
Pera Hd., *Australia* **94 A3**
Perabumulih, *Indonesia* **62 E2**
Perak →, *Malaysia* **65 K3**
Perakhóra, *Greece* **38 C4**
Perales de Alfambra, *Spain* **32 E4**
Perales del Puerto, *Spain* **34 E4**
Pérama, *Kérkira, Greece* **36 A3**
Pérama, *Kríti, Greece* **36 D6**
Peräpohjola, *Finland* **8 C22**
Perast, *Montenegro, Yug.* **40 D2**
Percé, *Canada* **103 C7**
Perche, *France* **18 D8**
Perchtoldsdorf, *Austria* **27 C9**
Percival Lakes, *Australia* **92 D4**
Percy, *France* **18 D5**
Percy Is., *Australia* **94 C5**
Perdido, Mte., *Spain* **32 C5**
Perdu, Mt. = Perdido, Mte., *Spain* **32 C5**
Pereira, *Colombia* **124 C3**
Perelazovskiy, *Russia* **49 F6**
Perenjori, *Australia* **93 E2**
Peresecina, *Moldova* **43 C13**
Pereslavl-Zalesskiy, *Russia* **46 D10**
Peretu, *Romania* **43 F10**
Pereyaslav-Khmelnytskyy, *Ukraine* **47 G6**
Pérez, I., *Mexico* **119 C7**
Perg, *Austria* **26 C7**
Pergamino, *Argentina* **126 C3**
Pergau →, *Malaysia* **65 K3**
Pérgine Valsugana, *Italy* **29 B8**
Pérgola, *Italy* **29 E9**
Perham, *U.S.A.* **112 B7**
Perhentian, Kepulauan, *Malaysia* **62 C2**
Periam, *Romania* **42 D5**
Péribonca →, *Canada* **103 C5**
Péribonca, L., *Canada* **103 B5**
Perico, *Argentina* **126 A2**
Pericos, *Mexico* **118 B3**
Périers, *France* **18 C5**
Périgord, *France* **20 D4**
Périgueux, *France* **20 C4**
Perijá, Sierra de, *Colombia* **124 B4**
Peristéra, *Greece* **38 B5**
Peristerona →, *Cyprus* **36 D12**
Perito Moreno, *Argentina* **128 F2**
Perivol = Dragovishtitsa, *Bulgaria* **40 D6**
Perkasie, *U.S.A.* **111 F9**
Perković, *Croatia* **29 E13**
Perlas, Arch. de las, *Panama* **120 E4**
Perlas, Punta de, *Nic.* **120 D3**
Perleberg, *Germany* **24 B7**
Perlez, *Serbia, Yug.* **42 E5**
Perm, *Russia* **50 D6**
Përmeti, *Albania* **40 F4**
Pernambuco = Recife, *Brazil* **125 E12**
Pernambuco □, *Brazil* **125 E11**
Pernatty Lagoon, *Australia* **95 E2**
Pernik, *Bulgaria* **40 D7**
Peron Is., *Australia* **92 B5**
Peron Pen., *Australia* **93 E1**
Péronne, *France* **19 C9**
Perosa Argentina, *Italy* **28 D4**
Perow, *Canada* **104 C3**
Perpendicular Pt., *Australia* **95 E5**
Perpignan, *France* **20 F6**
Perris, *U.S.A.* **117 M9**
Perros-Guirec, *France* **18 D3**
Perry, *Fla., U.S.A.* **109 K4**
Perry, *Ga., U.S.A.* **109 J4**
Perry, *Iowa, U.S.A.* **112 E7**
Perry, *Okla., U.S.A.* **113 G6**
Perryton, *U.S.A.* **113 G4**
Perryville, *U.S.A.* **113 G10**
Persan, *France* **19 C9**
Persberg, *Sweden* **10 E8**
Perşembe, *Turkey* **72 B7**
Persepolis, *Iran* **71 D7**
Pershotravensk, *Ukraine* **47 G4**
Persia = Iran ■, *Asia* **71 C7**
Persian Gulf = Gulf, The, *Asia* **71 E6**
Perstorp, *Sweden* **11 H7**
Pertek, *Turkey* **73 C8**
Perth, *Australia* **93 F2**
Perth, *Canada* **102 D4**
Perth, *U.K.* **14 E5**
Perth & Kinross □, *U.K.* **14 E5**
Perth Amboy, *U.S.A.* **111 F10**
Perth-Andover, *Canada* **103 C6**
Pertuis, *France* **21 E9**
Pertusato, C., *France* **21 G13**
Peru, *Ind., U.S.A.* **108 E2**
Peru, *N.Y., U.S.A.* **111 B11**
Peru ■, *S. Amer.* **124 D4**
Peru-Chile Trench, *Pac. Oc.* **124 G3**
Perúgia, *Italy* **29 E9**
Perušić, *Croatia* **29 D12**
Pervomaysk, *Russia* **48 C6**
Pervomaysk, *Ukraine* **47 H6**
Pervouralsk, *Russia* **50 D6**
Pésaro, *Italy* **29 E9**
Pescadores = Penghu, *Taiwan* **59 F12**
Pescara, *Italy* **29 F11**
Pescara →, *Italy* **29 F11**
Peschanokopskoye, *Russia* **49 G5**
Péscia, *Italy* **28 E7**
Pescina, *Italy* **29 F10**
Peshawar, *Pakistan* **68 B4**
Peshkopi, *Albania* **40 E4**
Peshtera, *Bulgaria* **41 D8**
Peshtigo, *U.S.A.* **108 C2**
Peski, *Russia* **48 E6**
Pêso da Régua, *Portugal* **34 D3**
Pesqueira, *Brazil* **125 E11**
Pessac, *France* **20 D3**
Pest □, *Hungary* **42 C4**
Pestovo, *Russia* **46 C8**
Pestravka, *Russia* **48 D9**
Péta, *Greece* **38 B3**
Petah Tiqwa, *Israel* **75 C3**
Petalídhion, *Greece* **38 E3**
Petaling Jaya, *Malaysia* **65 L3**
Petaloudhes, *Greece* **36 C10**
Petaluma, *U.S.A.* **116 G4**
Pétange, *Lux.* **17 E5**
Petaro, *Pakistan* **68 G3**
Petatlán, *Mexico* **118 D4**
Petauke, *Zambia* **87 E3**
Petawawa, *Canada* **102 C4**
Petén Itzá, L., *Guatemala* **120 C2**
Peter I.s Øy, *Antarctica* **5 C16**
Peter Pond L., *Canada* **105 B7**
Peterbell, *Canada* **102 C3**
Peterborough, *Australia* **95 E2**
Peterborough, *Canada* **102 D4**
Peterborough, *U.K.* **13 E7**
Peterborough, *U.S.A.* **111 D13**
Peterborough □, *U.K.* **13 E7**
Peterculter, *U.K.* **14 D6**
Peterhead, *U.K.* **14 D7**
Peterlee, *U.K.* **12 C6**
Petermann Bjerg, *Greenland* **98 B17**
Petermann Ranges, *Australia* **92 E5**
Petersburg, *Alaska, U.S.A.* **100 C6**
Petersburg, *Pa., U.S.A.* **110 F6**
Petersburg, *Va., U.S.A.* **108 G7**
Petersburg, *W. Va., U.S.A.* **108 F6**
Petersfield, *U.K.* **13 F7**
Petershagen, *Germany* **24 C4**
Petília Policastro, *Italy* **31 C9**
Petit Goâve, *Haiti* **121 C5**
Petit Jardin, *Canada* **103 C8**
Petit Lac Manicouagan, *Canada* **103 B6**
Petit-Mécatina →, *Canada* **103 B8**
Petit-Mécatina, I. du, *Canada* **103 B8**
Petit Saint Bernard, Col du, *Italy* **21 C10**
Petitcodiac, *Canada* **103 C6**
Petite Baleine →, *Canada* **102 A4**
Petite Saguenay, *Canada* **103 C5**
Petitot →, *Canada* **104 A4**
Petitsikapau L., *Canada* **103 B6**
Petlad, *India* **68 H5**
Peto, *Mexico* **119 C7**
Petone, *N.Z.* **91 J5**
Petorca, *Chile* **126 C1**
Petoskey, *U.S.A.* **108 C3**
Petra, *Jordan* **75 E4**
Petra, *Spain* **37 B10**
Petra, Ostrova, *Russia* **4 B13**
Petra Velikogo, Zaliv, *Russia* **54 C6**

Petrel = Petrer, *Spain* 33 G4
Petrella, Monte, *Italy* 30 A6
Petrer, *Spain* 33 G4
Petreto-Bicchisano, *France* 21 G12
Petrich, *Bulgaria* 40 E7
Petrified Forest National Park, *U.S.A.* 115 J9
Petrijanec, *Croatia* 29 B13
Petrikov = Pyetrikaw, *Belarus* 47 F5
Petrila, *Romania* 43 E8
Petrinja, *Croatia* 29 C13
Petrodvorets, *Russia* 46 C5
Petrograd = Sankt-Peterburg, *Russia* 46 C6
Petrolândia, *Brazil* 125 E11
Petrolia, *Canada* 102 D3
Petrolina, *Brazil* 125 E10
Petropavl, *Kazakstan* 50 D7
Petropavlovsk = Petropavl, *Kazakstan* 50 D7
Petropavlovsk-Kamchatskiy, *Russia* 51 D16
Petropavlovskiy = Akhtubinsk, *Russia* 49 F8
Petrópolis, *Brazil* 127 A7
Petroşani, *Romania* 43 E8
Petrova Gora, *Croatia* 29 C12
Petrovac, *Montenegro, Yug.* 40 D2
Petrovac, *Serbia, Yug.* 40 B5
Petrovaradin, *Serbia, Yug.* 42 E4
Petrovsk, *Russia* 48 D7
Petrovsk-Zabaykalskiy, *Russia* 51 D11
Petrovskaya, *Russia* 47 K9
Petrovskoye = Svetlograd, *Russia* 49 H6
Petrozavodsk, *Russia* 46 B8
Petrus Steyn, *S. Africa* 89 D4
Petrusburg, *S. Africa* 88 D4
Petzeck, *Austria* 26 E5
Peumo, *Chile* 126 C1
Peureulak, *Indonesia* 62 D1
Pevek, *Russia* 51 C18
Peveragno, *Italy* 28 D4
Peyrehorade, *France* 20 E2
Peyruis, *France* 21 D9
Pézenas, *France* 20 E7
Pezinok, *Slovak Rep.* 27 C10
Pfaffenhofen, *Germany* 25 G7
Pfarrkirchen, *Germany* 25 G8
Pfeffenhausen, *Germany* 25 G7
Pforzheim, *Germany* 25 G4
Pfullendorf, *Germany* 25 H5
Pfungstadt, *Germany* 25 F4
Phagwara, *India* 66 D9
Phaistós, *Greece* 36 D6
Phala, *Botswana* 88 C4
Phalera = Phulera, *India* 68 F6
Phalodi, *India* 68 F5
Phalsbourg, *France* 19 D14
Phan, *Thailand* 64 C2
Phan Rang, *Vietnam* 65 G7
Phan Ri = Hoa Da, *Vietnam* 65 G7
Phan Thiet, *Vietnam* 65 G7
Phanae, *Greece* 39 C7
Phanat Nikhom, *Thailand* 64 F3
Phangan, Ko, *Thailand* 65 H3
Phangnga, *Thailand* 65 H2
Phanh Bho Ho Chi Minh, *Vietnam* 65 G6
Phanom Sarakham, *Thailand* 64 F3
Phaphund, *India* 69 F8
Pharenda, *India* 69 F10
Pharr, *U.S.A.* 113 M5
Phatthalung, *Thailand* 65 J3
Phayao, *Thailand* 64 C2
Phelps, *U.S.A.* 110 D7
Phelps L., *Canada* 105 B8
Phenix City, *U.S.A.* 109 J3
Phet Buri, *Thailand* 64 F2
Phetchabun, *Thailand* 64 D3
Phetchabun, Thiu Khao, *Thailand* 64 E3
Phetchaburi = Phet Buri, *Thailand* 64 F2
Phi Phi, Ko, *Thailand* 65 J2
Phiafay, *Laos* 64 E6
Phibun Mangsahan, *Thailand* 64 E5
Phichai, *Thailand* 64 D3
Phichit, *Thailand* 64 D3
Philadelphia, *Miss., U.S.A.* 113 J10
Philadelphia, *N.Y., U.S.A.* 111 B9
Philadelphia, *Pa., U.S.A.* 111 G9
Philip, *U.S.A.* 112 C4
Philippeville, *Belgium* 17 D4
Philippi, *Greece* 41 E8
Philippi, *U.S.A.* 108 F5
Philippi L., *Australia* 94 C2
Philippines ■, *Asia* 61 F5
Philippolis, *S. Africa* 88 E4
Philippopolis = Plovdiv, *Bulgaria* 41 D8
Philipsburg, *Canada* 111 A11
Philipsburg, *Mont., U.S.A.* 114 C7
Philipsburg, *Pa., U.S.A.* 110 F6
Philipstown = Daingean, *Ireland* 15 C4
Philipstown, *S. Africa* 88 E3
Phillip I., *Australia* 95 F4
Phillips, *U.S.A.* 112 C9
Phillipsburg, *Kans., U.S.A.* 112 F5
Phillipsburg, *N.J., U.S.A.* 111 F9
Philmont, *U.S.A.* 111 D11
Philomath, *U.S.A.* 114 D2
Phimai, *Thailand* 64 E4
Phitsanulok, *Thailand* 64 D3
Phnom Dangrek, *Thailand* 62 B2
Phnom Penh, *Cambodia* 65 G5
Phnum Penh = Phnom Penh, *Cambodia* 65 G5
Phoenicia, *U.S.A.* 111 D10
Phoenix, *Ariz., U.S.A.* 115 K7
Phoenix, *N.Y., U.S.A.* 111 C8
Phoenix Is., *Kiribati* 96 H10
Phoenixville, *U.S.A.* 111 F9
Phon, *Thailand* 64 E4
Phon Tiou, *Laos* 64 D5
Phong →, *Thailand* 64 D4
Phong Saly, *Laos* 58 G4
Phong Tho, *Vietnam* 64 A4
Phonhong, *Laos* 64 C4
Phonum, *Thailand* 65 H2
Phosphate Hill, *Australia* 94 C2
Photharam, *Thailand* 64 F2
Phra Nakhon Si Ayutthaya, *Thailand* 64 E3
Phra Thong, Ko, *Thailand* 65 H2
Phrae, *Thailand* 64 C3
Phrom Phiram, *Thailand* 64 D3
Phrygia, *Turkey* 72 C4
Phu Dien, *Vietnam* 64 C5
Phu Loi, *Laos* 64 B4
Phu Ly, *Vietnam* 58 G5
Phu Quoc, Dao, *Vietnam* 65 G4
Phu Tho, *Vietnam* 58 G5
Phuc Yen, *Vietnam* 58 G5
Phuket, *Thailand* 65 J2
Phuket, Ko, *Thailand* 65 J2
Phul, *India* 68 D6
Phulad, *India* 68 G5
Phulchari, *Bangla.* 69 G13
Phulera, *India* 68 F6
Phulpur, *India* 69 G10
Phun Phin, *Thailand* 65 H2
Piacenza, *Italy* 28 C6
Pian Cr. →, *Australia* 95 E4
Piana, *France* 21 F12
Pianella, *Italy* 29 F11
Pianosa, *Puglia, Italy* 29 F12
Pianosa, *Toscana, Italy* 28 F7
Piapot, *Canada* 105 D7
Pias, *Portugal* 35 G3
Piaseczno, *Poland* 45 F8
Piaski, *Poland* 45 G9
Piastów, *Poland* 45 F7
Piatra, *Romania* 43 G10
Piatra Neamţ, *Romania* 43 D11
Piatra Olt, *Romania* 43 F9
Piauí □, *Brazil* 125 E10
Piaui →, *Brazil* 125 E10
Piave →, *Italy* 29 C9
Piazza Ármerina, *Italy* 31 E7
Pibor →, *Sudan* 81 F3
Pibor Post, *Sudan* 81 F3
Picardie, *France* 19 C10
Picardie, Plaine de, *France* 19 C9
Picardy = Picardie, *France* 19 C10
Picayune, *U.S.A.* 113 K10
Picerno, *Italy* 31 B8
Pichhor, *India* 69 G8
Pichilemu, *Chile* 126 C1
Pichor, *India* 68 G8
Pickerel L., *Canada* 102 C1
Pickering, *U.K.* 12 C7
Pickering, Vale of, *U.K.* 12 C7
Pickle Lake, *Canada* 102 B1
Pickwick L., *U.S.A.* 109 H1
Pico Truncado, *Argentina* 128 F3
Picos, *Brazil* 125 E10
Picton, *Australia* 95 E5
Picton, *Canada* 102 D4
Picton, *N.Z.* 91 J5
Pictou, *Canada* 103 C7
Picture Butte, *Canada* 104 D6
Picún Leufú, *Argentina* 128 D3
Pidurutalagala, *Sri Lanka* 66 R12
Piechowice, *Poland* 45 H2
Piedmont = Piemonte □, *Italy* 28 D5
Piedmont, *Ala., U.S.A.* 109 J3
Piedmont, *S.C., U.S.A.* 107 D10
Piedmonte Matese, *Italy* 31 A7
Piedra →, *Spain* 32 D3
Piedrabuena, *Spain* 35 G6
Piedrahita, *Spain* 34 E5
Piedralaves, *Spain* 34 E6
Piedras Blancas, *Spain* 34 B5
Piedras Negras, *Mexico* 118 B4
Piekary Śląskie, *Poland* 45 H5
Pieksämäki, *Finland* 9 E22
Piemonte □, *Italy* 28 D5
Pienaarsrivier, *S. Africa* 89 D4
Pieniężno, *Poland* 44 D7
Pieńsk, *Poland* 45 G2
Piercefield, *U.S.A.* 111 B10
Pierceland, *Canada* 105 C7
Piería □, *Greece* 40 F6
Pierpont, *U.S.A.* 110 E4
Pierre, *U.S.A.* 112 C4
Pierre-Buffière, *France* 20 C5
Pierre-de-Bresse, *France* 19 F12
Pierrefontaine-les-Varans, *France* 19 E13
Pierrefort, *France* 20 D6
Pierrelatte, *France* 21 D8
Piešťany, *Slovak Rep.* 27 C10
Piesting →, *Austria* 27 C9
Pieszyce, *Poland* 45 H3
Piet Retief, *S. Africa* 89 D5
Pietarsaari, *Finland* 8 E20
Pietermaritzburg, *S. Africa* 89 D5
Pietersburg, *S. Africa* 89 C4
Pietragalla, *Italy* 31 B8
Pietrasanta, *Italy* 28 E7
Pietroşiţa, *Romania* 43 E10
Pietrosul, Vf., *Maramureş, Romania* 43 C9
Pietrosul, Vf., *Suceava, Romania* 43 C10
Pieve di Cadore, *Italy* 29 B9
Pieve di Teco, *Italy* 28 D4
Pievepélago, *Italy* 28 D7
Pigadhítsa, *Greece* 40 G5
Pigeon L., *Canada* 110 B6
Piggott, *U.S.A.* 113 G9
Pigna, *Italy* 28 E4
Pigüe, *Argentina* 126 D3
Pihani, *India* 69 F9
Pihlajavesi, *Finland* 9 F23
Pijijiapan, *Mexico* 119 D6
Pikalevo, *Russia* 46 C8
Pikangikum Berens, *Canada* 105 C10
Pikes Peak, *U.S.A.* 112 F2
Piketberg, *S. Africa* 88 E2
Pikeville, *U.S.A.* 108 G4
Pikou, *China* 57 E12
Pikwitonei, *Canada* 105 B9
Piła, *Poland* 45 E3
Pila, *Spain* 33 G3
Pilaía, *Greece* 40 F6
Pilani, *India* 68 E6
Pilar, *Paraguay* 126 B4
Pilar de la Horadada, *Spain* 33 H4
Pilawa, *Poland* 45 G8
Pilaya →, *Bolivia* 124 H6
Pilbara, *Australia* 92 D2
Pilcomayo →, *Paraguay* 126 B4
Pilgrim's Rest, *S. Africa* 89 C5
Pilgrimstad, *Sweden* 10 B9
Píli, *Greece* 39 E9
Pilibhit, *India* 69 E8
Pilica →, *Poland* 45 G8
Pilion, *Greece* 38 B5
Pilis, *Hungary* 42 C4
Pilisvörösvár, *Hungary* 42 C3
Pilkhawa, *India* 68 E7
Pilliga, *Australia* 95 E4
Pílos, *Greece* 38 E3
Pilot Mound, *Canada* 105 D9
Pilot Point, *U.S.A.* 113 J6
Pilot Rock, *U.S.A.* 114 D4
Pilsen = Plzeň, *Czech Rep.* 26 B6
Pilštanj, *Slovenia* 29 B12
Piltene, *Latvia* 44 A8
Pilzno, *Poland* 45 J8
Pima, *U.S.A.* 115 K9
Pimba, *Australia* 95 E2
Pimenta Bueno, *Brazil* 124 F6
Pimentel, *Peru* 124 E3
Pina de Ebro, *Spain* 32 D4
Pinamalayan, *Phil.* 61 E4
Pinang, *Malaysia* 65 K3
Pinar, C. des, *Spain* 37 B10
Pinar del Río, *Cuba* 120 B3
Pınarbaşı, *Çanakkale, Turkey* 39 B8
Pınarbaşı, *Kayseri, Turkey* 72 C7
Pınarhisar, *Turkey* 41 E11
Pinatubo, Mt., *Phil.* 61 D3
Pincehely, *Hungary* 42 D3
Pinchang, *China* 58 B6
Pincher Creek, *Canada* 104 D6
Pinchi L., *Canada* 104 C4
Pinckneyville, *U.S.A.* 112 F10
Pińczów, *Poland* 45 H7
Pindar, *Australia* 93 E2
Pindi Gheb, *Pakistan* 68 C5
Pindiga, *Nigeria* 83 D7
Pindos Óros, *Greece* 38 B3
Pindus Mts. = Pindos Óros, *Greece* 38 B3
Pine →, *B.C., Canada* 104 B4
Pine →, *Sask., Canada* 105 B7
Pine, C., *Canada* 103 C9
Pine Bluff, *U.S.A.* 113 H9
Pine Bluffs, *U.S.A.* 112 E2
Pine City, *U.S.A.* 112 C8
Pine Cr. →, *U.S.A.* 110 E7
Pine Creek, *Australia* 92 B5
Pine Falls, *Canada* 105 C9
Pine Flat Res., *U.S.A.* 116 J7
Pine Grove, *U.S.A.* 111 F8
Pine Pass, *Canada* 104 B4
Pine Point, *Canada* 104 A6
Pine Ridge, *U.S.A.* 112 D3
Pine River, *Canada* 105 C8
Pine River, *U.S.A.* 112 B7
Pine Valley, *U.S.A.* 117 N10
Pinecrest, *U.S.A.* 116 G6
Pineda de Mar, *Spain* 32 D7
Pinedale, *Calif., U.S.A.* 116 J7
Pinedale, *Wyo., U.S.A.* 114 E9
Pinega →, *Russia* 50 C5
Pinehill, *Australia* 94 C4
Pinehouse L., *Canada* 105 B7
Pineimuta →, *Canada* 102 B1
Pinerolo, *Italy* 28 D4
Pineto, *Italy* 29 F11
Pinetop, *U.S.A.* 115 J9
Pinetown, *S. Africa* 89 D5
Pineville, *U.S.A.* 113 K8
Piney, *France* 19 D11
Ping →, *Thailand* 64 E3
Pingaring, *Australia* 93 F2
Pingba, *China* 58 D6
Pingbian, *China* 58 F4
Pingchuan, *China* 58 D3
Pingding, *China* 56 F7
Pingdingshan, *China* 56 H7
Pingdong, *Taiwan* 59 F13
Pingdu, *China* 57 F10
Pingelly, *Australia* 93 F2
Pingguo, *China* 58 F6
Pinghe, *China* 59 E11
Pinghu, *China* 59 B13
Pingjiang, *China* 59 C9
Pingle, *China* 59 E8
Pingli, *China* 58 A7
Pingliang, *China* 56 G4
Pinglu, *China* 56 E7
Pingluo, *China* 56 E4
Pingnan, *Fujian, China* 59 D12
Pingnan, *Guangxi Zhuangzu, China* 59 F8
Pingquan, *China* 57 D10
Pingrup, *Australia* 93 F2
Pingshan, *China* 58 C5
Pingtan, *China* 59 E12
Pingtang, *China* 58 E6
P'ingtung, *Taiwan* 59 F13
Pingwu, *China* 56 H3
Pingxiang, *Guangxi Zhuangzu, China* 58 F6
Pingxiang, *Jiangxi, China* 59 D9
Pingyao, *China* 56 F7
Pingyi, *China* 57 G9
Pingyin, *China* 56 F9
Pingyuan, *Guangdong, China* 59 E10
Pingyuan, *Shandong, China* 56 F9
Pingyuanjie, *China* 58 F4
Pinhal, *Brazil* 127 A6
Pinhal Novo, *Portugal* 35 G2
Pinheiro, *Brazil* 125 D9
Pinheiro Machado, *Brazil* 127 C5
Pinhel, *Portugal* 34 E3
Pini, *Indonesia* 62 D1
Piniós →, *Ilía, Greece* 38 D3
Piniós →, *Tríkkala, Greece* 38 B4
Pinjarra, *Australia* 93 F2
Pink Mountain, *Canada* 104 B4
Pinkafeld, *Austria* 27 D9
Pinnacles, *U.S.A.* 116 J5
Pinnaroo, *Australia* 95 F3
Pinneberg, *Germany* 24 B5
Pínnes, Ákra, *Greece* 41 F8
Pinon Hills, *U.S.A.* 117 L9
Pinos, *Mexico* 118 C4
Pinos, Mt., *U.S.A.* 117 L7
Pinos Pt., *U.S.A.* 115 H3
Pinos Puente, *Spain* 35 H7
Pinotepa Nacional, *Mexico* 119 D5
Pinrang, *Indonesia* 63 E5
Pins, Pte. aux, *Canada* 110 D3
Pinsk, *Belarus* 47 F4
Pintados, *Chile* 124 H5
Pinyang, *China* 59 D13
Pinyug, *Russia* 50 C5
Pioche, *U.S.A.* 115 H6
Piombino, *Italy* 28 F7
Piombino, Canale di, *Italy* 28 F7
Pioner, Ostrov, *Russia* 51 B10
Pionki, *Poland* 45 G8
Piorini, L., *Brazil* 124 D6
Piotrków Trybunalski, *Poland* 45 G6
Piove di Sacco, *Italy* 29 C9
Pīp, *Iran* 71 E9
Pipar, *India* 68 F5
Pipar Road, *India* 68 F5
Piparia, *Mad. P., India* 68 H8
Piparia, *Mad. P., India* 68 J7
Pipéri, *Greece* 38 B6
Pipestone, *U.S.A.* 112 D6
Pipestone →, *Canada* 102 B2
Pipestone Cr. →, *Canada* 105 D8
Piplan, *Pakistan* 68 C4
Piploda, *India* 68 H6
Pipmuacan, Rés., *Canada* 103 C5
Pippingarra, *Australia* 92 D2
Pipriac, *France* 18 E5
Piqua, *U.S.A.* 108 E3
Piquiri →, *Brazil* 127 A5
Pīr Sohrāb, *Iran* 71 E9
Pira, *Benin* 83 D5
Piracicaba, *Brazil* 127 A6
Piracuruca, *Brazil* 125 D10
Piræus = Piraiévs, *Greece* 38 D5
Piraiévs, *Greece* 38 D5
Pirajuí, *Brazil* 127 A6
Piram I., *India* 68 J5
Piran, *Slovenia* 29 C10
Pirané, *Argentina* 126 B4
Pirano = Piran, *Slovenia* 29 C10
Pirapora, *Brazil* 125 G10
Pirawa, *India* 68 G7
Pirdop, *Bulgaria* 41 D8
Pírgos, *Ilía, Greece* 38 D3
Pírgos, *Kríti, Greece* 39 F7
Pirgovo, *Bulgaria* 41 C9
Piribebuy, *Paraguay* 126 B4
Pirimapun, *Indonesia* 63 F9
Pirin Planina, *Bulgaria* 40 E7
Pírineos = Pyrénées, *Europe* 20 F4
Piripiri, *Brazil* 125 D10
Pirmasens, *Germany* 25 F3
Pirna, *Germany* 24 E9
Pirot, *Serbia, Yug.* 40 C6
Piru, *Indonesia* 63 E7
Piru, *U.S.A.* 117 L8
Piryatin = Pyryatyn, *Ukraine* 47 G7
Piryí, *Greece* 39 C7
Pisa, *Italy* 28 E7
Pisa →, *Poland* 45 E8
Pisagne, *Italy* 28 C7
Pisagua, *Chile* 124 G4
Pisarovina, *Croatia* 29 C12
Pisco, *Peru* 124 F3
Piscu, *Romania* 43 E12
Písek, *Czech Rep.* 26 B7
Pishan, *China* 60 C2
Pīshīn, *Iran* 71 E9
Pishin, *Pakistan* 68 D2
Pishin Lora →, *Pakistan* 68 E1
Pisidia, *Turkey* 72 D4
Pising, *Indonesia* 63 F6
Pismo Beach, *U.S.A.* 117 K6
Piso, L., *Liberia* 82 D2
Pissila, *Burkina Faso* 83 C4
Pissis, Cerro, *Argentina* 126 B2
Pissos, *France* 20 D3
Pissouri, *Cyprus* 36 E11
Pisticci, *Italy* 31 B9
Pistóia, *Italy* 28 E7
Pistol B., *Canada* 105 A10
Pisuerga →, *Spain* 34 D6
Pisz, *Poland* 44 E8
Pit →, *U.S.A.* 114 F2
Pita, *Guinea* 82 C2
Pitarpunga, L., *Australia* 95 E3
Pitcairn I., *Pac. Oc.* 97 K14
Pite älv →, *Sweden* 8 D19
Piteå, *Sweden* 8 D19
Piterka, *Russia* 48 E8
Piteşti, *Romania* 43 F9
Pithapuram, *India* 67 L13
Pithara, *Australia* 93 F2
Píthion, *Greece* 41 E10
Pithiviers, *France* 19 D9
Pithoragarh, *India* 69 E9
Pithoro, *Pakistan* 68 G3
Pitigliano, *Italy* 29 F8
Pitkyaranta, *Russia* 46 B6
Pitlochry, *U.K.* 14 E5
Pitsilia □, *Cyprus* 36 E12
Pitt I., *Canada* 104 C3
Pittsburg, *Calif., U.S.A.* 116 G5
Pittsburg, *Kans., U.S.A.* 113 G7
Pittsburg, *Tex., U.S.A.* 113 J7
Pittsburgh, *U.S.A.* 110 F5
Pittsfield, *Ill., U.S.A.* 112 F9
Pittsfield, *Maine, U.S.A.* 109 C11
Pittsfield, *Mass., U.S.A.* 111 D11
Pittsfield, *N.H., U.S.A.* 111 C13
Pittston, *U.S.A.* 111 E9
Pittsworth, *Australia* 95 D5
Pituri →, *Australia* 94 C2
Piura, *Peru* 124 E2
Piva →, *Montenegro, Yug.* 40 C2
Piwniczna, *Poland* 45 J7
Pixley, *U.S.A.* 116 K7
Piyai, *Greece* 38 B3
Pizarra, *Spain* 35 J6
Pizhou, *China* 56 G9
Pizzo, *Italy* 31 D9
Placentia, *Canada* 103 C9
Placentia B., *Canada* 103 C9
Placer, *Masbate, Phil.* 61 F5
Placer, *Surigao N., Phil.* 61 G6
Placerville, *U.S.A.* 116 G6
Placetas, *Cuba* 120 B4
Plačkovica, *Macedonia* 40 E6
Plainfield, *N.J., U.S.A.* 111 F10
Plainfield, *Ohio, U.S.A.* 110 F3
Plainfield, *Vt., U.S.A.* 111 B12
Plains, *Mont., U.S.A.* 114 C6
Plains, *Tex., U.S.A.* 113 J3
Plainview, *Nebr., U.S.A.* 112 D6
Plainview, *Tex., U.S.A.* 113 H4
Plainwell, *U.S.A.* 108 D3
Plaisance, *France* 20 E4
Plaistow, *U.S.A.* 111 D13
Pláka, *Greece* 39 B7
Pláka, Ákra, *Greece* 36 D8
Plakenska Planina, *Macedonia* 40 E5
Planá, *Czech Rep.* 26 B5
Plana Cays, *Bahamas* 121 B5
Planada, *U.S.A.* 116 H6
Plancoët, *France* 18 D4
Plandište, *Serbia, Yug.* 42 E6
Plano, *U.S.A.* 113 J6
Plant City, *U.S.A.* 109 M4
Plaquemine, *U.S.A.* 113 K9
Plasencia, *Spain* 34 E4
Plaški, *Croatia* 29 C12
Plaster City, *U.S.A.* 117 N11
Plaster Rock, *Canada* 103 C6
Plastun, *Russia* 54 B8
Plasy, *Czech Rep.* 26 B6
Plata, Río de la, *S. Amer.* 126 C4
Plátani →, *Italy* 30 E6
Plátanos, *Greece* 36 D5
Plateau □, *Nigeria* 83 D6
Platí, Ákra, *Greece* 41 F8
Platte, *U.S.A.* 112 D5
Platte →, *Mo., U.S.A.* 112 F7
Platte →, *Nebr., U.S.A.* 112 E7
Platteville, *U.S.A.* 112 D9
Plattling, *Germany* 25 G8
Plattsburgh, *U.S.A.* 111 B11
Plattsmouth, *U.S.A.* 112 E7
Plau, *Germany* 24 B8
Plauen, *Germany* 24 E8
Plauer See, *Germany* 24 B8
Plav, *Montenegro, Yug.* 40 D3
Plavinas, *Latvia* 9 H21
Plavnica, *Montenegro, Yug.* 40 D3
Plavno, *Croatia* 29 D13
Plavsk, *Russia* 46 F9
Playa Blanca, *Canary Is.* 37 F6
Playa Blanca Sur, *Canary Is.* 37 F6
Playa de las Americas, *Canary Is.* 37 F3
Playa de Mogán, *Canary Is.* 37 G4
Playa del Inglés, *Canary Is.* 37 G4
Playa Esmerelda, *Canary Is.* 37 F5
Playgreen L., *Canada* 105 C9
Pleasant Bay, *Canada* 103 C7
Pleasant Hill, *U.S.A.* 116 H4
Pleasant Mount, *U.S.A.* 111 E9
Pleasanton, *Calif., U.S.A.* 116 H5
Pleasanton, *Tex., U.S.A.* 113 L5
Pleasantville, *N.J., U.S.A.* 108 F8
Pleasantville, *Pa., U.S.A.* 110 E5
Pléaux, *France* 20 C6
Plei Ku, *Vietnam* 64 F7
Plélan-le-Grand, *France* 18 D4
Pléneuf-Val-André, *France* 18 D4
Pleniţa, *Romania* 43 F8
Plenty →, *Australia* 94 C2
Plenty, B. of, *N.Z.* 91 G6
Plentywood, *U.S.A.* 112 A2
Plérin, *France* 18 D4
Plessisville, *Canada* 103 C5

Plestin-les-Grèves, *France* 18 D3
Pleszew, *Poland* 45 G4
Pleternica, *Croatia* 42 E2
Plétipi, L., *Canada* 103 B5
Pleven, *Bulgaria* 41 C8
Plevlja, *Montenegro, Yug.* 40 C3
Plevna, *Canada* 110 B8
Plješevica, *Croatia* 29 D12
Ploaghe, *Italy* 30 B1
Plo'ana, *Slovak Rep.* 27 C12
Ploče, *Croatia* 29 E14
Płock, *Poland* 45 F6
Plöckenpass, *Italy* 29 B9
Plöckenstein, *Germany* 25 G9
Ploemeur, *France* 18 E3
Ploërmel, *France* 18 E4
Ploieşti, *Romania* 43 F11
Plomárion, *Greece* 39 C8
Plombières-les-Bains, *France* 19 E13
Plomin, *Croatia* 29 C11
Plön, *Germany* 24 A6
Plonge, Lac la, *Canada* 105 B7
Płońsk, *Poland* 45 F7
Plopeni, *Romania* 43 E10
Plopişului, Munţii, *Romania* 42 C7
Płoty, *Poland* 44 E2
Plouaret, *France* 18 D3
Plouay, *France* 18 E3
Ploučnice →, *Czech Rep.* 26 A7
Ploudalmézeau, *France* 18 D2
Plouescat, *France* 18 D2
Plougasnou, *France* 18 D3
Plougastel-Daoulas, *France* 18 D2
Plouguerneau, *France* 18 D2
Plouha, *France* 18 D4
Plouhinec, *France* 18 E2
Plovdiv, *Bulgaria* 41 D8
Plovdiv □, *Bulgaria* 41 D8
Plum, *U.S.A.* 110 F5
Plum I., *U.S.A.* 111 E12
Plumas, *U.S.A.* 116 F7
Plummer, *U.S.A.* 114 C5
Plumtree, *Zimbabwe* 87 G2
Plungė, *Lithuania* 9 J19
Pluvigner, *France* 18 E3
Plymouth, *U.K.* 13 G3
Plymouth, *Calif., U.S.A.* 116 G6
Plymouth, *Ind., U.S.A.* 108 E2
Plymouth, *Mass., U.S.A.* 111 E14
Plymouth, *N.C., U.S.A.* 109 H7
Plymouth, *N.H., U.S.A.* 111 C13
Plymouth, *Pa., U.S.A.* 111 E9
Plymouth, *Wis., U.S.A.* 108 D2
Plynlimon = Pumlumon Fawr, *U.K.* 13 E4
Plyusa, *Russia* 46 C5
Plyusa →, *Russia* 46 C5
Plyussa = Plyusa, *Russia* 46 C5
Plyussa → = Plyusa →, *Russia* 46 C5
Plzeň, *Czech Rep.* 26 B6
Pniewy, *Poland* 45 F3
Pô, *Burkina Faso* 83 C4
Po →, *Italy* 29 D9
Po, Foci del, *Italy* 29 D9
Po Hai = Bo Hai, *China* 57 E10
Pobé, *Benin* 83 D5
Pobé, *Burkina Faso* 83 C4
Pobeda, *Russia* 51 C15
Pobedy, Pik, *Kyrgyzstan* 50 E8
Pobiedziska, *Poland* 45 F4
Pobla de Segur, *Spain* 32 C5
Pobladura del Valle, *Spain* 34 C5
Pobra de Trives, *Spain* 34 C3
Pocahontas, *Ark., U.S.A.* 113 G9
Pocahontas, *Iowa, U.S.A.* 112 D7
Pocatello, *U.S.A.* 114 E7
Počátky, *Czech Rep.* 26 B8
Pochep, *Russia* 47 F7
Pochinki, *Russia* 48 C7
Pochinok, *Russia* 46 E7
Pöchlarn, *Austria* 26 C8
Pochutla, *Mexico* 119 D5
Pocito Casas, *Mexico* 118 B2
Pocking, *Germany* 25 G9
Pocomoke City, *U.S.A.* 108 F8
Poços de Caldas, *Brazil* 127 A6
Podbořany, *Czech Rep.* 26 A6
Poddębice, *Poland* 45 G5
Poděbrady, *Czech Rep.* 26 A8
Podensac, *France* 20 D3
Podenzano, *Italy* 28 D6
Podgorač, *Croatia* 42 E3
Podgorica, *Montenegro, Yug.* 40 D3
Podgorie, *Albania* 40 F4
Podilska Vysochyna, *Ukraine* 47 H4
Podkarpackie □, *Poland* 45 H9
Podkova, *Bulgaria* 41 E9
Podlapača, *Croatia* 29 D12
Podlaskie □, *Poland* 45 E10
Podoleni, *Romania* 43 D11
Podolínec, *Slovak Rep.* 27 B13
Podolsk, *Russia* 46 E9
Podor, *Senegal* 82 B1
Podporozhye, *Russia* 46 B8
Podu Iloaiei, *Romania* 43 C12
Podu Turcului, *Romania* 43 D12
Podujevo, *Kosovo, Yug.* 40 D5
Poel, *Germany* 24 B6
Pofadder, *S. Africa* 88 D2
Poggiardo, *Italy* 31 B11
Poggibonsi, *Italy* 28 E8
Póggio Mirteto, *Italy* 29 F9
Pogoanele, *Romania* 43 F12
Pogorzela, *Poland* 45 G4
Pogradeci, *Albania* 40 F4
Pogranitšnyi, *Russia* 54 B5
Poh, *Indonesia* 63 E6
P'ohang, *S. Korea* 57 F15
Pohjanmaa, *Finland* 8 E20
Pohnpei, *Micronesia* 96 G7
Pohorelá, *Slovak Rep.* 27 C13
Pohořelice, *Czech Rep.* 27 C9
Pohorje, *Slovenia* 29 B12
Pohri, *India* 68 G6
Poiana Mare, *Romania* 42 G8
Poiana Ruscăi, Munţii, *Romania* 42 E7
Poiana Stampei, *Romania* 43 C10
Poinsett, C., *Antarctica* 5 C8
Point Arena, *U.S.A.* 116 G3
Point Baker, *U.S.A.* 104 B2
Point Edward, *Canada* 102 D3
Point Hope, *U.S.A.* 100 B3
Point L., *Canada* 100 B8
Point Pedro, *Sri Lanka* 66 Q12
Point Pleasant, *N.J., U.S.A.* 111 F10
Point Pleasant, *W. Va., U.S.A.* 108 F4
Pointe-à-Pitre, *Guadeloupe* 121 C7
Pointe-Claire, *Canada* 111 A11
Pointe-Gatineau, *Canada* 111 A9
Pointe-Noire, *Congo* 84 E2
Poio, *Spain* 34 C2
Poirino, *Italy* 28 D4
Poisonbush Ra., *Australia* 92 D3
Poissonnier Pt., *Australia* 92 C2
Poitiers, *France* 18 F7
Poitou, *France* 20 B3
Poitou-Charentes □, *France* 20 B4
Poix-de-Picardie, *France* 19 C8
Poix-Terron, *France* 19 C11
Pojoaque, *U.S.A.* 115 J11
Pokaran, *India* 66 F7
Pokataroo, *Australia* 95 D4
Pokhara, *Nepal* 69 E10
Pokhvistnevo, *Russia* 48 D11
Poko, *Dem. Rep. of the Congo* 86 B2
Poko, *Sudan* 81 F3
Pokrov, *Russia* 46 E10
Pokrovsk = Engels, *Russia* 48 E8
Pokrovsk, *Russia* 51 C13
Pokrovskoye, *Russia* 47 J10
Pola = Pula, *Croatia* 29 D10
Pola, *Russia* 46 D7
Pola de Allande, *Spain* 34 B4
Pola de Lena, *Spain* 34 B5
Pola de Siero, *Spain* 34 B5
Pola de Somiedo, *Spain* 34 B4
Polacca, *U.S.A.* 115 J8
Polan, *Iran* 71 E9
Poland ■, *Europe* 45 G3
Polanica-Zdrój, *Poland* 45 H3
Połaniec, *Poland* 45 H8
Polanów, *Poland* 44 D3
Polar Bear Prov. Park, *Canada* 102 A2
Polatlı, *Turkey* 72 C5
Polatsk, *Belarus* 46 E5
Polcura, *Chile* 126 D1
Połczyn-Zdrój, *Poland* 44 E3
Polessk, *Russia* 9 J19
Polesye = Pripet Marshes, *Europe* 47 F5
Polgar, *Hungary* 42 C6
Pŏlgyo-ri, *S. Korea* 57 G14
Poli, *Cameroon* 83 C7
Políaigos, *Greece* 38 E6
Policastro, G. di, *Italy* 31 C8
Police, *Poland* 44 E1
Polička, *Czech Rep.* 27 B9
Policoro, *Italy* 31 B9
Polignano a Mare, *Italy* 31 A9
Poligny, *France* 19 F12
Políkhnitas, *Greece* 39 B8
Polillo Is., *Phil.* 61 D4
Polillo Strait, *Phil.* 61 D4
Polis, *Cyprus* 36 D11
Polístena, *Italy* 31 D9
Políyiros, *Greece* 40 F7
Polk, *U.S.A.* 110 E5
Polkowice, *Poland* 45 G3
Polla, *Italy* 31 B8
Pollachi, *India* 66 P10
Pollença, *Spain* 37 B10
Pollença, B. de, *Spain* 37 B10
Póllica, *Italy* 31 B8
Pollino, Mte., *Italy* 31 C9
Polna, *Russia* 46 C5
Polnovat, *Russia* 50 C7
Pology, *Ukraine* 47 J9
Polonne, *Ukraine* 47 G4
Polonnoye = Polonne, *Ukraine* 47 G4
Polski Trŭmbesh, *Bulgaria* 41 C9
Polsko Kosovo, *Bulgaria* 41 C9
Polson, *U.S.A.* 114 C6
Poltár, *Slovak Rep.* 27 C12
Poltava, *Ukraine* 47 H8
Põltsamaa, *Estonia* 9 G21
Polunochnoye, *Russia* 50 C7
Põlva, *Estonia* 9 G22
Polynesia, *Pac. Oc.* 97 J11
Polynésie française = French Polynesia ■, *Pac. Oc.* 97 K13
Pomarance, *Italy* 28 E7
Pomaro, *Mexico* 118 D4
Pombal, *Portugal* 34 F2
Pómbia, *Greece* 36 E6
Pomene, *Mozam.* 89 C6
Pomeroy, *Ohio, U.S.A.* 108 F4
Pomeroy, *Wash., U.S.A.* 114 C5
Pomézia, *Italy* 30 A5
Pomichna, *Ukraine* 47 H6
Pomona, *Australia* 95 D5
Pomona, *U.S.A.* 117 L9
Pomorie, *Bulgaria* 41 D11
Pomorskie □, *Poland* 44 D5
Pomorskie, Pojezierze, *Poland* 44 E3
Pomos, *Cyprus* 36 D11
Pomos, C., *Cyprus* 36 D11
Pompano Beach, *U.S.A.* 109 M5
Pompei, *Italy* 31 B7
Pompey, *France* 19 D13
Pompeys Pillar, *U.S.A.* 114 D10
Pompton Lakes, *U.S.A.* 111 F10
Ponape = Pohnpei, *Micronesia* 96 G7
Ponask L., *Canada* 102 B1
Ponca, *U.S.A.* 112 D6
Ponca City, *U.S.A.* 113 G6
Ponce, *Puerto Rico* 121 C6
Ponchatoula, *U.S.A.* 113 K9
Poncheville, L., *Canada* 102 B4
Pond, *U.S.A.* 117 K7
Pond Inlet, *Canada* 101 A12
Pondicherry, *India* 66 P11
Ponds, I. of, *Canada* 103 B8
Ponferrada, *Spain* 34 C4
Pongo, Wadi →, *Sudan* 81 F2
Poniatowa, *Poland* 45 G9
Poniec, *Poland* 45 G3
Ponikva, *Slovenia* 29 B12
Ponnani, *India* 66 P9
Ponnyadaung, *Burma* 67 J19
Ponoka, *Canada* 104 C6
Ponorogo, *Indonesia* 63 G14
Pons = Ponts, *Spain* 32 D6
Pons, *France* 20 C3
Ponsul →, *Portugal* 34 F3
Pont-à-Mousson, *France* 19 D13
Pont-Audemer, *France* 18 C7
Pont-Aven, *France* 18 E3
Pont Canavese, *Italy* 28 C4
Pont-d'Ain, *France* 19 F12
Pont-de-Roide, *France* 19 E13
Pont-de-Salars, *France* 20 D6
Pont-de-Vaux, *France* 19 F11
Pont-de-Veyle, *France* 19 F11
Pont-du-Château, *France* 19 G10
Pont-l'Abbé, *France* 18 E2
Pont-l'Évêque, *France* 18 C7
Pont-St-Esprit, *France* 21 D8
Pont-St-Martin, *Italy* 28 C4
Pont-Ste-Maxence, *France* 19 C9
Pont-sur-Yonne, *France* 19 D10
Ponta do Sol, *Madeira* 37 D2
Ponta Grossa, *Brazil* 127 B5
Ponta Pora, *Brazil* 127 A4
Pontacq, *France* 20 E3
Pontailler-sur-Saône, *France* 19 E12
Pontarlier, *France* 19 F13
Pontassieve, *Italy* 29 E8
Pontaumur, *France* 20 C6
Pontcharra, *France* 21 C10
Pontchartrain L., *U.S.A.* 113 K10
Pontchâteau, *France* 18 E4
Ponte da Barca, *Portugal* 34 D2
Ponte de Sor, *Portugal* 35 F2
Ponte dell'Ólio, *Italy* 28 D6
Ponte di Legno, *Italy* 28 B7
Ponte do Lima, *Portugal* 34 D2
Ponte do Pungué, *Mozam.* 87 F3
Ponte-Leccia, *France* 21 F13
Ponte nelle Alpi, *Italy* 29 B9
Ponte Nova, *Brazil* 127 A7
Ponteareas, *Spain* 34 C2
Pontebba, *Italy* 29 B10
Ponteceso, *Spain* 34 B2
Pontecorvo, *Italy* 30 A6
Pontedeume, *Spain* 34 B2
Ponteix, *Canada* 105 D7
Pontevedra, *Spain* 34 C2
Pontevedra □, *Spain* 34 C2
Pontevedra, R. de →, *Spain* 34 C2
Pontevico, *Italy* 28 C7
Pontiac, *Ill., U.S.A.* 112 E10
Pontiac, *Mich., U.S.A.* 108 D4
Pontian Kecil, *Malaysia* 65 M4
Pontianak, *Indonesia* 62 E3
Pontine Is. = Ponziane, Ísole, *Italy* 30 B5
Pontine Mts. = Kuzey Anadolu Dağları, *Turkey* 72 B7
Pontínia, *Italy* 30 A6
Pontivy, *France* 18 D4
Pontoise, *France* 19 C9
Ponton →, *Canada* 104 B5
Pontorson, *France* 18 D5
Pontrémoli, *Italy* 28 D6
Pontrieux, *France* 18 D3
Ponts, *Spain* 32 D6
Pontypool, *Canada* 110 B6
Pontypool, *U.K.* 13 F4
Ponza, *Italy* 30 B5
Ponziane, Ísole, *Italy* 30 B5
Poochera, *Australia* 95 E1
Poole, *U.K.* 13 G6
Poole □, *U.K.* 13 G6
Poona = Pune, *India* 66 K8
Pooncarie, *Australia* 95 E3
Poopelloe L., *Australia* 95 E3
Poopó, L. de, *Bolivia* 122 E4
Popayán, *Colombia* 124 C3
Poperinge, *Belgium* 17 D2
Popilta L., *Australia* 95 E3
Popina, *Bulgaria* 41 B10
Popio L., *Australia* 95 E3
Poplar, *U.S.A.* 112 A2
Poplar →, *Canada* 105 C9
Poplar Bluff, *U.S.A.* 113 G9
Poplarville, *U.S.A.* 113 K10
Popocatépetl, Volcán, *Mexico* 119 D5
Popokabaka, *Dem. Rep. of the Congo* 84 F3
Pópoli, *Italy* 29 F10
Popovača, *Croatia* 29 C13
Popovo, *Bulgaria* 41 C10
Poppberg, *Germany* 25 F7
Poppi, *Italy* 29 E8
Poprad, *Slovak Rep.* 27 B13
Poprad →, *Slovak Rep.* 27 B13
Porali →, *Pakistan* 68 G2
Porbandar, *India* 66 J6
Porcher I., *Canada* 104 C2
Porcuna, *Spain* 35 H6
Porcupine →, *Canada* 105 B8
Porcupine →, *U.S.A.* 100 B5
Pordenone, *Italy* 29 C9
Pordim, *Bulgaria* 41 C8
Poreč, *Croatia* 29 C10
Poretskoye, *Russia* 48 C8
Pori, *Finland* 9 F19
Porí, *Greece* 38 F5
Porkhov, *Russia* 46 D5
Porlamar, *Venezuela* 124 A6
Porlezza, *Italy* 28 B6
Porma →, *Spain* 34 C5
Pornic, *France* 18 E4
Poronaysk, *Russia* 51 E15
Póros, *Greece* 38 D5
Poroshiri-Dake, *Japan* 54 C11
Poroszló, *Hungary* 42 C5
Poroto Mts., *Tanzania* 87 D3
Porpoise B., *Antarctica* 5 C9
Porquerolles, Î. de, *France* 21 F10
Porrentruy, *Switz.* 25 H3
Porreres, *Spain* 37 B10
Porsangen, *Norway* 8 A21
Porsgrunn, *Norway* 9 G13
Port Alberni, *Canada* 104 D4
Port Alfred, *S. Africa* 88 E4
Port Alice, *Canada* 104 C3
Port Allegany, *U.S.A.* 110 E6
Port Allen, *U.S.A.* 113 K9
Port Alma, *Australia* 94 C5
Port Angeles, *U.S.A.* 116 B3
Port Antonio, *Jamaica* 120 C4
Port Aransas, *U.S.A.* 113 M6
Port Arthur = Lüshun, *China* 57 E11
Port Arthur, *Australia* 94 G4
Port Arthur, *U.S.A.* 113 L8
Port au Choix, *Canada* 103 B8
Port au Port B., *Canada* 103 C8
Port-au-Prince, *Haiti* 121 C5
Port Augusta, *Australia* 95 E2
Port Austin, *U.S.A.* 110 B2
Port Bell, *Uganda* 86 B3
Port Bergé Vaovao, *Madag.* 89 B8
Port Blandford, *Canada* 103 C9
Port-Bouët, *Ivory C.* 82 D4
Port Bradshaw, *Australia* 94 A2
Port Broughton, *Australia* 95 E2
Port Burwell, *Canada* 110 D4
Port Campbell, *Australia* 95 F3
Port Canning, *India* 69 H13
Port-Cartier, *Canada* 103 B6
Port Chalmers, *N.Z.* 91 L3
Port Charlotte, *U.S.A.* 109 M4
Port Chester, *U.S.A.* 111 F11
Port Clements, *Canada* 104 C2
Port Clinton, *U.S.A.* 108 E4
Port Colborne, *Canada* 102 D4
Port Coquitlam, *Canada* 104 D4
Port Credit, *Canada* 110 C5
Port Curtis, *Australia* 94 C5
Port d'Alcúdia, *Spain* 37 B10
Port Dalhousie, *Canada* 110 C5
Port Darwin, *Australia* 92 B5
Port Darwin, *Falk. Is.* 128 G5
Port Davey, *Australia* 94 G4
Port-de-Bouc, *France* 21 E8
Port-de-Paix, *Haiti* 121 C5
Port de Pollença, *Spain* 37 B10
Port de Sóller, *Spain* 37 B9
Port Dickson, *Malaysia* 65 L3
Port Douglas, *Australia* 94 B4
Port Dover, *Canada* 110 D4
Port Edward, *Canada* 104 C2
Port Elgin, *Canada* 102 D3
Port Elizabeth, *S. Africa* 88 E4
Port Ellen, *U.K.* 14 F2
Port-en-Bessin, *France* 18 C6
Port Erin, *U.K.* 12 C3
Port Essington, *Australia* 92 B5
Port Etienne = Nouâdhibou, *Mauritania* 78 D2
Port Ewen, *U.S.A.* 111 E11
Port Fairy, *Australia* 95 F3
Port Fouâd = Bûr Fuad, *Egypt* 80 H8
Port Gamble, *U.S.A.* 116 C4
Port-Gentil, *Gabon* 84 E1
Port Germein, *Australia* 95 E2
Port Gibson, *U.S.A.* 113 K9
Port Glasgow, *U.K.* 14 F4
Port Harcourt, *Nigeria* 83 E6
Port Hardy, *Canada* 104 C3
Port Harrison = Inukjuak, *Canada* 101 C12
Port Hawkesbury, *Canada* 103 C7
Port Hedland, *Australia* 92 D2
Port Henry, *U.S.A.* 111 B11
Port Hood, *Canada* 103 C7
Port Hope, *Canada* 102 D4
Port Hope, *U.S.A.* 110 C2
Port Hope Simpson, *Canada* 103 B8
Port Hueneme, *U.S.A.* 117 L7
Port Huron, *U.S.A.* 110 D2
Port Iliç, *Azerbaijan* 73 C13
Port Jefferson, *U.S.A.* 111 F11
Port Jervis, *U.S.A.* 111 E10
Port-Joinville, *France* 18 F4
Port Katon, *Russia* 47 J10
Port Kelang = Pelabuhan Kelang, *Malaysia* 65 L3
Port Kenny, *Australia* 95 E1
Port-la-Nouvelle, *France* 20 E7
Port Lairge = Waterford, *Ireland* 15 D4
Port Laoise, *Ireland* 15 C4
Port Lavaca, *U.S.A.* 113 L6
Port Leyden, *U.S.A.* 111 C9
Port Lincoln, *Australia* 95 E2
Port Loko, *S. Leone* 82 D2
Port Louis, *France* 18 E3
Port Louis, *Mauritius* 77 H9
Port Lyautey = Kenitra, *Morocco* 78 B4
Port MacDonnell, *Australia* 95 F3
Port McNeill, *Canada* 104 C3
Port Macquarie, *Australia* 95 E5
Port Maria, *Jamaica* 120 C4
Port Matilda, *U.S.A.* 110 F6
Port Mellon, *Canada* 104 D4
Port-Menier, *Canada* 103 C7
Port Moody, *Canada* 116 A4
Port Morant, *Jamaica* 120 C4
Port Moresby, *Papua N. G.* 96 H6
Port Musgrave, *Australia* 94 A3
Port-Navalo, *France* 18 E4
Port Neches, *U.S.A.* 113 L8
Port Nolloth, *S. Africa* 88 D2
Port Nouveau-Québec = Kangiqsualujjuaq, *Canada* 101 C13
Port of Spain, *Trin. & Tob.* 121 D7
Port Orange, *U.S.A.* 109 L5
Port Orchard, *U.S.A.* 116 C4
Port Orford, *U.S.A.* 114 E1
Port Pegasus, *N.Z.* 91 M1
Port Perry, *Canada* 102 D4
Port Phillip B., *Australia* 95 F3
Port Pirie, *Australia* 95 E2
Port Radium = Echo Bay, *Canada* 100 B8
Port Renfrew, *Canada* 104 D4
Port Roper, *Australia* 94 A2
Port Rowan, *Canada* 110 D4
Port Safaga = Bûr Safâga, *Egypt* 70 E2
Port Said = Bûr Sa'îd, *Egypt* 80 H8
Port St. Joe, *U.S.A.* 109 L3
Port St. Johns = Umzimvubu, *S. Africa* 89 E4
Port-St-Louis-du-Rhône, *France* 21 E8
Port St. Lucie, *U.S.A.* 109 M5
Port-Ste-Marie, *France* 20 D4
Port Sanilac, *U.S.A.* 110 C2
Port Severn, *Canada* 110 B5
Port Shepstone, *S. Africa* 89 E5
Port Simpson, *Canada* 104 C2
Port Stanley = Stanley, *Falk. Is.* 128 G5
Port Stanley, *Canada* 102 D3
Port Sudan = Bûr Sûdân, *Sudan* 80 D4
Port Sulphur, *U.S.A.* 113 L10
Port-sur-Saône, *France* 19 E13
Port Talbot, *U.K.* 13 F4
Port Taufiq = Bûr Taufiq, *Egypt* 80 J8
Port Townsend, *U.S.A.* 116 B4
Port-Vendres, *France* 20 F7
Port Vila, *Vanuatu* 96 J8
Port Wakefield, *Australia* 95 E2
Port Washington, *U.S.A.* 108 D2
Port Weld = Kuala Sepetang, *Malaysia* 65 K3
Portadown, *U.K.* 15 B5
Portaferry, *U.K.* 15 B6
Portage, *Pa., U.S.A.* 110 F6
Portage, *Wis., U.S.A.* 112 D10
Portage La Prairie, *Canada* 105 D9
Portageville, *U.S.A.* 113 G10
Portalegre, *Portugal* 35 F3
Portalegre □, *Portugal* 35 F3
Portales, *U.S.A.* 113 H3
Portarlington, *Ireland* 15 C4
Portbou, *Spain* 32 C8
Portel, *Portugal* 35 G3
Porter L., *N.W.T., Canada* 105 A7
Porter L., *Sask., Canada* 105 B7
Porterville, *S. Africa* 88 E2
Porterville, *U.S.A.* 116 J8
Portes-lès-Valence, *France* 21 D8
Porthcawl, *U.K.* 13 F4
Porthill, *U.S.A.* 114 B5
Porthmadog, *U.K.* 12 E3
Portile de Fier, *Europe* 42 F7
Portimão, *Portugal* 35 H2
Portishead, *U.K.* 13 F5
Portiţei, Gura, *Romania* 43 F14
Portknockie, *U.K.* 14 D6
Portland, *N.S.W., Australia* 95 E5
Portland, *Vic., Australia* 95 F3
Portland, *Canada* 111 B8
Portland, *Conn., U.S.A.* 111 E12
Portland, *Maine, U.S.A.* 101 D12
Portland, *Mich., U.S.A.* 108 D3
Portland, *Oreg., U.S.A.* 116 E4
Portland, *Pa., U.S.A.* 111 F9
Portland, *Tex., U.S.A.* 113 M6
Portland, I. of, *U.K.* 13 G5
Portland B., *Australia* 95 F3
Portland Bill, *U.K.* 13 G5
Portland Canal, *U.S.A.* 104 B2
Portmadoc = Porthmadog, *U.K.* 12 E3
Porto, *France* 21 F12
Porto, *Portugal* 34 D2
Porto □, *Portugal* 34 D2
Porto, G. de, *France* 21 F12
Pôrto Alegre, *Brazil* 127 C5
Porto Amboim = Gunza, *Angola* 84 G2
Porto Azzurro, *Italy* 28 F7
Porto Cristo, *Spain* 37 B10
Pôrto de Móz, *Brazil* 125 D8
Porto Empédocle, *Italy* 30 E6
Pôrto Esperança, *Brazil* 124 G7

Pôrto Franco, *Brazil* 125 E9
Pórto Lágos, *Greece* 41 E9
Porto Mendes, *Brazil* 127 A5
Porto Moniz, *Madeira* 37 D2
Pôrto Murtinho, *Brazil* 124 H7
Pôrto Nacional, *Brazil* 125 F9
Porto-Novo, *Benin* 83 D5
Porto Petro, *Spain* 37 B10
Porto San Giórgio, *Italy* 29 E10
Porto Sant' Elpídio, *Italy* 29 E10
Porto Santo, *Madeira* 78 B2
Porto Santo Stéfano, *Italy* 28 F8
Pôrto São José, *Brazil* 127 A5
Pôrto Seguro, *Brazil* 125 G11
Porto Tolle, *Italy* 29 D9
Porto Tórres, *Italy* 30 B1
Pôrto União, *Brazil* 127 B5
Pôrto Válter, *Brazil* 124 E4
Porto-Vecchio, *France* 21 G13
Pôrto Velho, *Brazil* 124 E6
Portobelo, *Panama* 120 E4
Portoferráio, *Italy* 28 F7
Portogruaro, *Italy* 29 C9
Portola, *U.S.A.* 116 F6
Portomaggiore, *Italy* 29 D8
Portoscuso, *Italy* 30 C1
Portovénere, *Italy* 28 D6
Portoviejo, *Ecuador* 124 D2
Portpatrick, *U.K.* 14 G3
Portree, *U.K.* 14 D2
Portrush, *U.K.* 15 A5
Portsmouth, *Domin.* 121 C7
Portsmouth, *U.K.* 13 G6
Portsmouth, *N.H., U.S.A.* 109 D10
Portsmouth, *Ohio, U.S.A.* 108 F4
Portsmouth, *R.I., U.S.A.* 111 E13
Portsmouth, *Va., U.S.A.* 108 G7
Portsmouth □, *U.K.* 13 G6
Portsoy, *U.K.* 14 D6
Portstewart, *U.K.* 15 A5
Porttipahtan tekojärvi, *Finland* 8 B22
Portugal ■, *Europe* 34 F3
Portugalete, *Spain* 32 B1
Portumna, *Ireland* 15 C3
Portville, *U.S.A.* 110 D6
Porvenir, *Chile* 128 G2
Porvoo, *Finland* 9 F21
Porzuna, *Spain* 35 F6
Posada, *Italy* 30 B2
Posada →, *Italy* 30 B2
Posadas, *Argentina* 127 B4
Posadas, *Spain* 35 H5
Poschiavo, *Switz.* 25 J6
Posets, *Spain* 32 C5
Poshan = Boshan, *China* 57 F9
Posht-e-Badam, *Iran* 71 C7
Posídhion, Ákra, *Greece* 40 G7
Posidium, *Greece* 39 F9
Poso, *Indonesia* 63 E6
Posong, *S. Korea* 57 G14
Posse, *Brazil* 125 F9
Possession I., *Antarctica* 5 D11
Pössneck, *Germany* 24 E7
Possum Kingdom L., *U.S.A.* 113 J5
Post, *U.S.A.* 113 J4
Post Falls, *U.S.A.* 114 C5
Postavy = Pastavy, *Belarus* 9 J22
Poste-de-la-Baleine = Kuujjuarapik, *Canada* 102 A4
Postmasburg, *S. Africa* 88 D3
Postojna, *Slovenia* 29 C11
Poston, *U.S.A.* 117 M12
Postville, *Canada* 103 B8
Potamós, *Andikíthira, Greece* 38 F5
Potamós, *Kíthira, Greece* 38 E4
Potchefstroom, *S. Africa* 88 D4
Potcoava, *Romania* 43 F9
Poteau, *U.S.A.* 113 H7
Poteet, *U.S.A.* 113 L5
Potenza, *Italy* 31 B8
Potenza →, *Italy* 29 E10
Potenza Picena, *Italy* 29 E10
Poteriteri, L., *N.Z.* 91 M1
Potgietersrus, *S. Africa* 89 C4
Poti, *Georgia* 49 J5
Potiskum, *Nigeria* 83 C7
Potlogi, *Romania* 43 F10
Potomac →, *U.S.A.* 108 G7
Potosí, *Bolivia* 124 G5
Potosi Mt., *U.S.A.* 117 K11
Pototan, *Phil.* 61 F5
Potrerillos, *Chile* 126 B2
Potsdam, *Germany* 24 C9
Potsdam, *U.S.A.* 111 B10
Pottenstein, *Germany* 25 F7
Pottersville, *U.S.A.* 111 C11
Pottery Hill = Abu Ballas, *Egypt* 80 C2
Pottstown, *U.S.A.* 111 F9
Pottsville, *U.S.A.* 111 F8
Pottuvil, *Sri Lanka* 66 R12
P'otzu, *Taiwan* 59 F13
Pouancé, *France* 18 E5
Pouce Coupé, *Canada* 104 B4
Poughkeepsie, *U.S.A.* 111 E11
Pouilly-sur-Loire, *France* 19 E9
Poulaphouca Res., *Ireland* 15 C5
Poulsbo, *U.S.A.* 116 C4
Poultney, *U.S.A.* 111 C11
Poulton-le-Fylde, *U.K.* 12 D5
Pouso Alegre, *Brazil* 127 A6
Pout, *Senegal* 82 C1
Pouthisat, *Cambodia* 64 F4
Pouzauges, *France* 18 F6
Pova de Sta. Iria, *Portugal* 35 G1
Považská Bystrica, *Slovak Rep.* 27 B11
Poverty B., *N.Z.* 91 H7
Povlen, *Serbia, Yug.* 40 B3
Póvoa de Lanhosa, *Portugal* 34 D2
Póvoa de Varzim, *Portugal* 34 D2
Povorino, *Russia* 48 E6
Povungnituk = Puvirnituq, *Canada* 101 B12
Powassan, *Canada* 102 C4
Poway, *U.S.A.* 117 N9
Powder →, *U.S.A.* 112 B2
Powder River, *U.S.A.* 114 E10
Powell, *U.S.A.* 114 D9
Powell, L., *U.S.A.* 115 H8
Powell River, *Canada* 104 D4
Powers, *U.S.A.* 108 C2
Powys □, *U.K.* 13 E4
Poyang Hu, *China* 59 C11
Poyarkovo, *Russia* 51 E13
Poysdorf, *Austria* 27 C9
Poza de la Sal, *Spain* 34 C7
Poza Rica, *Mexico* 119 C5
Pozanti, *Turkey* 72 D6
Požarevac, *Serbia, Yug.* 40 B5
Pozazal, Puerto, *Spain* 34 C6
Požega, *Croatia* 42 E2
Požega, *Serbia, Yug.* 40 C4
Poznań, *Poland* 45 F3
Pozo, *U.S.A.* 117 K6
Pozo Alcón, *Spain* 35 H8
Pozo Almonte, *Chile* 124 H5
Pozo Colorado, *Paraguay* 126 A4
Pozoblanco, *Spain* 35 G6
Pozzallo, *Italy* 31 F7
Pozzomaggiore, *Italy* 30 B1
Pozzuoli, *Italy* 31 B7
Pra →, *Ghana* 83 D4
Prabuty, *Poland* 44 E6
Prača, *Bos.-H.* 42 G3
Prachatice, *Czech Rep.* 26 B6
Prachin Buri, *Thailand* 64 E3
Prachuap Khiri Khan, *Thailand* 65 G2
Pradelles, *France* 20 D7
Prades, *France* 20 F6
Prado, *Brazil* 125 G11
Prado del Rey, *Spain* 35 J5
Præstø, *Denmark* 11 J6
Pragersko, *Slovenia* 29 B12
Prague = Praha, *Czech Rep.* 26 A7
Praha, *Czech Rep.* 26 A7
Prahecq, *France* 20 B3
Prahova □, *Romania* 43 E10
Prahova →, *Romania* 43 F10
Prahovo, *Serbia, Yug.* 40 B6
Praia, *C. Verde Is.* 77 E1
Práia a Mare, *Italy* 31 C8
Praid, *Romania* 43 D10
Prainha, *Amazonas, Brazil* 124 E6
Prainha, *Pará, Brazil* 125 D8
Prairie, *Australia* 94 C3
Prairie City, *U.S.A.* 114 D4
Prairie Dog Town Fork →, *U.S.A.* 113 H5
Prairie du Chien, *U.S.A.* 112 D9
Prairies, L. of the, *Canada* 105 C8
Pramánda, *Greece* 38 B3
Prampram, *Ghana* 83 D5
Pran Buri, *Thailand* 64 F2
Prang, *Ghana* 83 D4
Prapat, *Indonesia* 62 D1
Prasonísi, Ákra, *Greece* 36 D9
Prästmon, *Sweden* 10 A11
Praszka, *Poland* 45 G5
Prata, *Brazil* 125 G9
Pratabpur, *India* 69 H10
Pratapgarh, *Raj., India* 68 G6
Pratapgarh, *Ut. P., India* 69 G9
Prato, *Italy* 28 E8
Prátola Peligna, *Italy* 29 F10
Prats-de-Mollo-la-Preste, *France* 20 F6
Pratt, *U.S.A.* 113 G5
Prattville, *U.S.A.* 109 J2
Pravdinsk, *Russia* 48 B6
Pravets, *Bulgaria* 40 D7
Pravia, *Spain* 34 B4
Praya, *Indonesia* 62 F5
Pré-en-Pail, *France* 18 D6
Precordillera, *Argentina* 126 C2
Predáppio, *Italy* 29 D8
Predazzo, *Italy* 29 B8
Predeal, *Romania* 43 E10
Predejane, *Serbia, Yug.* 40 D6
Preeceville, *Canada* 105 C8
Preetz, *Germany* 24 A6
Pregrada, *Croatia* 29 B12
Preiļi, *Latvia* 9 H22
Preko, *Croatia* 29 D12
Prelog, *Croatia* 29 B13
Prémery, *France* 19 E10
Premià de Mar, *Spain* 32 D7
Premont, *U.S.A.* 113 M5
Premuda, *Croatia* 29 D11
Prenjasi, *Albania* 40 E4
Prentice, *U.S.A.* 112 C9
Prenzlau, *Germany* 24 B9
Preobrazheniye, *Russia* 54 C6
Preparis North Channel, *Ind. Oc.* 67 M18
Preparis South Channel, *Ind. Oc.* 67 M18
Přerov, *Czech Rep.* 27 B10
Prescott, *Canada* 102 D4
Prescott, *Ariz., U.S.A.* 115 J7
Prescott, *Ark., U.S.A.* 113 J8
Prescott Valley, *U.S.A.* 115 J7
Preservation Inlet, *N.Z.* 91 M1
Preševo, *Serbia, Yug.* 40 D5
Presho, *U.S.A.* 112 D4
Presicce, *Italy* 31 C11
Presidencia de la Plaza, *Argentina* 126 B4
Presidencia Roque Saenz Peña, *Argentina* 126 B3
Presidente Epitácio, *Brazil* 125 H8
Presidente Hayes □, *Paraguay* 126 A4
Presidente Prudente, *Brazil* 127 A5
Presidio, *Mexico* 118 B4
Presidio, *U.S.A.* 113 L2
Preslav, *Bulgaria* 41 C10
Preslavska Planina, *Bulgaria* 41 C10
Prešov, *Slovak Rep.* 27 B14
Prešovský □, *Slovak Rep.* 27 B13
Prespa, *Bulgaria* 41 E8
Prespa, L. = Prespansko Jezero, *Macedonia* 40 F5
Prespansko Jezero, *Macedonia* 40 F5
Presque I., *U.S.A.* 110 D4
Presque Isle, *U.S.A.* 109 B12
Prestatyn, *U.K.* 12 D4
Prestea, *Ghana* 82 D4
Presteigne, *U.K.* 13 E5
Přeštice, *Czech Rep.* 26 B6
Preston, *Canada* 110 C4
Preston, *U.K.* 12 D5
Preston, *Idaho, U.S.A.* 114 E8
Preston, *Minn., U.S.A.* 112 D8
Preston, C., *Australia* 92 D2
Prestonburg, *U.S.A.* 108 G4
Prestwick, *U.K.* 14 F4
Pretoria, *S. Africa* 89 D4
Preuilly-sur-Claise, *France* 18 F7
Préveza, *Greece* 38 C2
Préveza □, *Greece* 38 B2
Prey Veng, *Cambodia* 65 G5
Priazovskoye, *Ukraine* 47 J8
Pribilof Is., *U.S.A.* 100 C2
Priboj, *Serbia, Yug.* 40 C3
Příbram, *Czech Rep.* 26 B7
Price, *U.S.A.* 114 G8
Price I., *Canada* 104 C3
Prichard, *U.S.A.* 109 K1
Priego, *Spain* 32 E2
Priego de Córdoba, *Spain* 35 H6
Priekule, *Latvia* 9 H19
Prien, *Germany* 25 H8
Prienai, *Lithuania* 9 J20
Prieska, *S. Africa* 88 D3
Priest L., *U.S.A.* 114 B5
Priest River, *U.S.A.* 114 B5
Priest Valley, *U.S.A.* 116 J6
Prievidza, *Slovak Rep.* 27 C11
Prignitz, *Germany* 24 B7
Prijedor, *Bos.-H.* 29 D13
Prijepolje, *Serbia, Yug.* 40 C3
Prikaspiyskaya Nizmennost = Caspian Depression, *Eurasia* 49 G9
Prikro, *Ivory C.* 82 D4
Prikubanskaya Nizmennost, *Russia* 49 H4
Prilep, *Macedonia* 40 E5
Priluki = Pryluky, *Ukraine* 47 G7
Prime Seal I., *Australia* 94 G4
Primorsk, *Russia* 46 B5
Primorsko, *Bulgaria* 41 D11
Primorsko-Akhtarsk, *Russia* 47 J10
Primorskoye, *Ukraine* 47 J9
Primrose L., *Canada* 105 C7
Prince Albert, *Canada* 105 C7
Prince Albert, *S. Africa* 88 E3
Prince Albert Mts., *Antarctica* 5 D11
Prince Albert Nat. Park, *Canada* 105 C7
Prince Albert Pen., *Canada* 100 A8
Prince Albert Sd., *Canada* 100 A8
Prince Alfred, C., *Canada* 4 B1
Prince Charles I., *Canada* 101 B12
Prince Charles Mts., *Antarctica* 5 D6
Prince Edward I. □, *Canada* 103 C7
Prince Edward Is., *Ind. Oc.* 3 G11
Prince Edward Pt., *Canada* 110 C8
Prince George, *Canada* 104 C4
Prince of Wales, C., *U.S.A.* 98 C3
Prince of Wales I., *Australia* 94 A3
Prince of Wales I., *Canada* 100 A10
Prince of Wales I., *U.S.A.* 100 C6
Prince Patrick I., *Canada* 4 B2
Prince Regent Inlet, *Canada* 4 B3
Prince Rupert, *Canada* 104 C2
Princess Charlotte B., *Australia* 94 A3
Princess May Ranges, *Australia* 92 C4
Princess Royal I., *Canada* 104 C3
Princeton, *Canada* 104 D4
Princeton, *Calif., U.S.A.* 116 F4
Princeton, *Ill., U.S.A.* 112 E10
Princeton, *Ind., U.S.A.* 108 F2
Princeton, *Ky., U.S.A.* 108 G2
Princeton, *Mo., U.S.A.* 112 E8
Princeton, *N.J., U.S.A.* 111 F10
Princeton, *W. Va., U.S.A.* 108 G5
Principe, I. de, *Atl. Oc.* 76 F4
Principe da Beira, *Brazil* 124 F6
Prineville, *U.S.A.* 114 D3
Prins Harald Kyst, *Antarctica* 5 D4
Prinsesse Astrid Kyst, *Antarctica* 5 D3
Prinsesse Ragnhild Kyst, *Antarctica* 5 D4
Prinzapolca, *Nic.* 120 D3
Prior, C., *Spain* 34 B2
Priozersk, *Russia* 46 B6
Pripet = Prypyat →, *Europe* 47 G6
Pripet Marshes, *Europe* 47 F5
Pripyat Marshes = Pripet Marshes, *Europe* 47 F5
Pripyats = Prypyat →, *Europe* 47 G6
Prislop, Pasul, *Romania* 43 C9
Pristen, *Russia* 47 G9
Priština, *Kosovo, Yug.* 40 D5
Pritzwalk, *Germany* 24 B8
Privas, *France* 21 D8
Priverno, *Italy* 30 A6
Privolzhsk, *Russia* 48 B5
Privolzhskaya Vozvyshennost, *Russia* 48 E7
Privolzhskiy, *Russia* 48 E8
Privolzhye, *Russia* 48 D9
Priyutnoye, *Russia* 49 G6
Prizren, *Kosovo, Yug.* 40 D4
Prizzi, *Italy* 30 E6
Prnjavor, *Bos.-H.* 42 F2
Probolinggo, *Indonesia* 63 G15
Prochowice, *Poland* 45 G3
Proctor, *U.S.A.* 111 C11
Proddatur, *India* 66 M11
Prodhromos, *Cyprus* 36 E11
Proença-a-Nova, *Portugal* 34 F3
Profítis Ilías, *Greece* 36 C9
Profondeville, *Belgium* 17 D4
Progreso, *Coahuila, Mexico* 118 B4
Progreso, *Yucatán, Mexico* 119 C7
Prokhladnyy, *Russia* 49 J7
Prokletije, *Albania* 40 D3
Prokopyevsk, *Russia* 50 D9
Prokuplje, *Serbia, Yug.* 40 C5
Proletarsk, *Russia* 49 G5
Proletarskaya = Proletarsk, *Russia* 49 G5
Prome = Pyè, *Burma* 67 K19
Prophet →, *Canada* 104 B4
Prophet River, *Canada* 104 B4
Propriá, *Brazil* 125 F11
Propriano, *France* 21 G12
Proserpine, *Australia* 94 C4
Prosna →, *Poland* 45 F4
Prospect, *U.S.A.* 111 C9
Prosser, *U.S.A.* 114 C4
Prostějov, *Czech Rep.* 27 B10
Prostki, *Poland* 44 E9
Proston, *Australia* 95 D5
Proszowice, *Poland* 45 H7
Próti, *Greece* 38 D3
Provadiya, *Bulgaria* 41 C11
Provence, *France* 21 E9
Provence-Alpes-Côte d'Azur □, *France* 21 D10
Providence, *Ky., U.S.A.* 108 G2
Providence, *R.I., U.S.A.* 111 E13
Providence Bay, *Canada* 102 C3
Providence Mts., *U.S.A.* 117 K11
Providencia, I. de, *Colombia* 120 D3
Provideniya, *Russia* 51 C19
Provins, *France* 19 D10
Provo, *U.S.A.* 114 F8
Provost, *Canada* 105 C6
Prozor, *Bos.-H.* 42 G2
Prudhoe Bay, *U.S.A.* 100 A5
Prudhoe I., *Australia* 94 C4
Prud'homme, *Canada* 105 C7
Prudnik, *Poland* 45 H4
Prüm, *Germany* 25 E2
Prundu, *Romania* 43 F11
Pruszcz Gdański, *Poland* 44 D5
Pruszków, *Poland* 45 F7
Prut →, *Romania* 43 E13
Pruzhany, *Belarus* 47 F3
Prvič, *Croatia* 29 D11
Prydz B., *Antarctica* 5 C6
Pryluky, *Ukraine* 47 G7
Pryor, *U.S.A.* 113 G7
Prypyat →, *Europe* 47 G6
Przasnysz, *Poland* 45 E7
Przedbórz, *Poland* 45 G6
Przedecz, *Poland* 45 F5
Przemków, *Poland* 45 G2
Przemyśl, *Poland* 45 J9
Przeworsk, *Poland* 45 H9
Przewóz, *Poland* 45 G1
Przhevalsk, *Kyrgyzstan* 50 E8
Przysucha, *Poland* 45 G7
Psakhná, *Greece* 38 C5
Psará, *Greece* 39 C7
Psathoúra, *Greece* 38 B6
Psel →, *Ukraine* 47 H7
Pserimos, *Greece* 39 E9
Psíra, *Greece* 36 D7
Pskov, *Russia* 46 D5
Pskovskoye, Ozero, *Russia* 9 H22
Psunj, *Croatia* 42 E2
Pteleón, *Greece* 38 B4
Ptich = Ptsich →, *Belarus* 47 F5
Ptolemaís, *Greece* 40 F5
Ptsich →, *Belarus* 47 F5
Ptuj, *Slovenia* 29 B12
Ptujska Gora, *Slovenia* 29 B12
Pu Xian, *China* 56 F6
Pua, *Thailand* 64 C3
Puán, *Argentina* 126 D3
Pu'an, *China* 58 E5
Puan, *S. Korea* 57 G14
Pubei, *China* 58 F7
Pucallpa, *Peru* 124 E4
Pucheng, *China* 59 D12
Pucheni, *Romania* 43 E10
Puchheim, *Germany* 25 G7
Púchov, *Slovak Rep.* 27 B11
Pucioasa, *Romania* 43 E10
Pučišća, *Croatia* 29 E13
Puck, *Poland* 44 D5
Pucka, Zatoka, *Poland* 44 D5
Puçol, *Spain* 33 F4
Pudasjärvi, *Finland* 8 D22
Puding, *China* 58 D5
Pudozh, *Russia* 46 B9
Pudukkottai, *India* 66 P11
Puebla, *Mexico* 119 D5
Puebla □, *Mexico* 119 D5
Puebla de Alcocer, *Spain* 35 G5
Puebla de Don Fadrique, *Spain* 33 H2
Puebla de Don Rodrigo, *Spain* 35 F6
Puebla de Guzmán, *Spain* 35 H3
Puebla de la Calzada, *Spain* 35 G4
Puebla de Sanabria, *Spain* 34 C4
Puebla de Trives = Pobra de Trives, *Spain* 34 C3
Pueblo, *U.S.A.* 112 F2
Pueblo Hundido, *Chile* 126 B1
Puelches, *Argentina* 126 D2
Puelén, *Argentina* 126 D2
Puente Alto, *Chile* 126 C1
Puente-Genil, *Spain* 35 H6
Puente la Reina, *Spain* 32 C3
Puenteareas = Ponteareas, *Spain* 34 C2
Puentedeume = Pontedeume, *Spain* 34 B2
Puentes de Garcia Rodriguez = As Pontes de García Rodríquez, *Spain* 34 B3
Pu'er, *China* 58 F3
Puerco →, *U.S.A.* 115 J10
Puerto, *Canary Is.* 37 F2
Puerto Aisén, *Chile* 128 F2
Puerto Ángel, *Mexico* 119 D5
Puerto Arista, *Mexico* 119 D6
Puerto Armuelles, *Panama* 120 E3
Puerto Ayacucho, *Venezuela* 124 B5
Puerto Barrios, *Guatemala* 120 C2
Puerto Bermejo, *Argentina* 126 B4
Puerto Bermúdez, *Peru* 124 F4
Puerto Bolívar, *Ecuador* 124 D3
Puerto Cabello, *Venezuela* 124 A5
Puerto Cabezas, *Nic.* 120 D3
Puerto Cabo Gracias á Dios, *Nic.* 120 D3
Puerto Carreño, *Colombia* 124 B5
Puerto Castilla, *Honduras* 120 C2
Puerto Chicama, *Peru* 124 E3
Puerto Coig, *Argentina* 128 G3
Puerto Cortés, *Costa Rica* 120 E3
Puerto Cortés, *Honduras* 120 C2
Puerto Cumarebo, *Venezuela* 124 A5
Puerto de Alcudia = Port d'Alcúdia, *Spain* 37 B10
Puerto de Andraitx, *Spain* 37 B9
Puerto de Cabrera, *Spain* 37 B9
Puerto de Gran Tarajal, *Canary Is.* 37 F5
Puerto de la Cruz, *Canary Is.* 37 F3
Puerto de Mazarrón, *Spain* 33 H3
Puerto de Pozo Negro, *Canary Is.* 37 F6
Puerto de Sóller = Port de Sóller, *Spain* 37 B9
Puerto de Somosierra, *Spain* 34 D7
Puerto del Carmen, *Canary Is.* 37 F6
Puerto del Rosario, *Canary Is.* 37 F6
Puerto Deseado, *Argentina* 128 F3
Puerto Escondido, *Mexico* 119 D5
Puerto Heath, *Bolivia* 124 F5
Puerto Inírida, *Colombia* 124 C5
Puerto Juárez, *Mexico* 119 C7
Puerto La Cruz, *Venezuela* 124 A6
Puerto Leguízamo, *Colombia* 124 D4
Puerto Limón, *Colombia* 124 C4
Puerto Lobos, *Argentina* 128 E3
Puerto Lumbreras, *Spain* 33 H3
Puerto Madryn, *Argentina* 128 E3
Puerto Maldonado, *Peru* 124 F5
Puerto Manotí, *Cuba* 120 B4
Puerto Mazarrón = Puerto de Mazarrón, *Spain* 33 H3
Puerto Montt, *Chile* 128 E2
Puerto Morazán, *Nic.* 120 D2
Puerto Morelos, *Mexico* 119 C7
Puerto Natales, *Chile* 128 G2
Puerto Padre, *Cuba* 120 B4
Puerto Páez, *Venezuela* 124 B5
Puerto Peñasco, *Mexico* 118 A2
Puerto Pinasco, *Paraguay* 126 A4
Puerto Plata, *Dom. Rep.* 121 C5
Puerto Pollensa = Port de Pollença, *Spain* 37 B10
Puerto Princesa, *Phil.* 61 G3
Puerto Quepos, *Costa Rica* 120 E3
Puerto Real, *Spain* 35 J4
Puerto Rico, *Canary Is.* 37 G4
Puerto Rico ■, *W. Indies* 121 C6
Puerto Rico Trench, *Atl. Oc.* 121 C6
Puerto San Julián, *Argentina* 128 F3
Puerto Sastre, *Paraguay* 126 A4
Puerto Serrano, *Spain* 35 J5
Puerto Suárez, *Bolivia* 124 G7
Puerto Vallarta, *Mexico* 118 C3
Puerto Wilches, *Colombia* 124 B4
Puertollano, *Spain* 35 G6
Pueyrredón, L., *Argentina* 128 F2
Puffin I., *Ireland* 15 E1
Pugachev, *Russia* 48 D9
Pugal, *India* 68 E5
Puge, *China* 58 D4
Puge, *Tanzania* 86 C3
Puget Sound, *U.S.A.* 114 C2
Puget-Théniers, *France* 21 E10
Púglia □, *Italy* 31 A9
Pugŏdong, *N. Korea* 57 C16
Pugu, *Tanzania* 86 D4
Pūgūnzī, *Iran* 71 E8
Pui, *Romania* 42 E8
Puiești, *Romania* 43 D12
Puig Major, *Spain* 37 B9
Puigcerdà, *Spain* 32 C6
Puigmal, *Spain* 32 C7
Puigpunyent, *Spain* 37 B9
Puijiang, *China* 58 B4

Puisaye, Collines de la, *France* 19 E10
Puiseaux, *France* 19 D9
Pujehun, *S. Leone* 82 D2
Pujiang, *China* 59 C12
Pujols, *France* 20 D3
Pujon-chŏsuji, *N. Korea* 57 D14
Puka, *Albania* 40 D3
Pukaki L., *N.Z.* 91 L3
Pukapuka, *Cook Is.* 97 J11
Pukaskwa Nat. Park, *Canada* 102 C2
Pukatawagan, *Canada* 105 B8
Pukchin, *N. Korea* 57 D13
Pukch'ŏng, *N. Korea* 57 D15
Pukekohe, *N.Z.* 91 G5
Pukhrayan, *India* 69 F8
Pukou, *China* 59 A12
Pula, *Croatia* 29 D10
Pula, *Italy* 30 C1
Pulacayo, *Bolivia* 124 H5
Pulandian, *China* 57 E11
Pularumpi, *Australia* 92 B5
Pulaski, *N.Y., U.S.A.* 111 C8
Pulaski, *Tenn., U.S.A.* 109 H2
Pulaski, *Va., U.S.A.* 108 G5
Pulau →, *Indonesia* 63 F9
Puławy, *Poland* 45 G8
Pulga, *U.S.A.* 116 F5
Pulicat L., *India* 66 N12
Pullman, *U.S.A.* 114 C5
Pulo-Anna, *Pac. Oc.* 63 D8
Pulog, Mt., *Phil.* 61 C4
Pułtusk, *Poland* 45 F8
Pülümür, *Turkey* 73 C8
Pumlumon Fawr, *U.K.* 13 E4
Puná, I., *Ecuador* 124 D2
Punakha, *Bhutan* 67 F16
Punasar, *India* 68 F5
Punata, *Bolivia* 124 G5
Punch, *India* 69 C6
Punch →, *Pakistan* 68 C5
Punda Maria, *S. Africa* 89 C5
Pune, *India* 66 K8
P'ungsan, *N. Korea* 57 D15
Pungue, Ponte de, *Mozam.* 87 F3
Puning, *China* 59 F11
Punjab □, *India* 68 D7
Punjab □, *Pakistan* 68 E6
Puno, *Peru* 124 G4
Punpun →, *India* 69 G11
Punta Alta, *Argentina* 128 D4
Punta Arenas, *Chile* 128 G2
Punta de Díaz, *Chile* 126 B1
Punta Gorda, *Belize* 119 D7
Punta Gorda, *U.S.A.* 109 M5
Punta Prieta, *Mexico* 118 B2
Punta Prima, *Spain* 37 B11
Punta Umbría, *Spain* 35 H4
Puntarenas, *Costa Rica* 120 E3
Punto Fijo, *Venezuela* 124 A4
Punxsatawney, *U.S.A.* 110 F6
Puqi, *China* 59 C9
Puquio, *Peru* 124 F4
Pur →, *Russia* 50 C8
Purace, Vol., *Colombia* 124 C3
Puračić, *Bos.-H.* 42 F3
Puralia = Puruliya, *India* 69 H12
Puranpur, *India* 69 E9
Purbeck, Isle of, *U.K.* 13 G6
Purcell, *U.S.A.* 113 H6
Purcell Mts., *Canada* 104 D5
Puri, *India* 67 K14
Purmerend, *Neths.* 17 B4
Purnia, *India* 69 G12
Pursat = Pouthisat, *Cambodia* 64 F4
Purukcahu, *Indonesia* 62 E4
Puruliya, *India* 69 H12
Purus →, *Brazil* 122 D4
Puruvesi, *Finland* 46 B5
Purvis, *U.S.A.* 113 K10
Pŭrvomay, *Bulgaria* 41 D9
Purwa, *India* 69 F9
Purwakarta, *Indonesia* 63 G12
Purwodadi, *Indonesia* 63 G14
Purwokerto, *Indonesia* 63 G13
Puryŏng, *N. Korea* 57 C15
Pusa, *India* 69 G11
Pusan, *S. Korea* 57 G15
Pushkin, *Russia* 46 C6
Pushkino, *Moskva, Russia* 46 D9
Pushkino, *Saratov, Russia* 48 E8
Püspökladány, *Hungary* 42 C6
Pustoshka, *Russia* 46 D5
Puszczykowo, *Poland* 45 F3
Putahow L., *Canada* 105 B8
Putao, *Burma* 67 F20
Putaruru, *N.Z.* 91 H5
Putbus, *Germany* 24 A9
Puthein Myit →, *Burma* 67 M19
Putian, *China* 59 E12
Putignano, *Italy* 31 B10
Puting, Tanjung, *Indonesia* 62 E4
Putlitz, *Germany* 24 B8
Putna, *Romania* 43 C10
Putna →, *Romania* 43 E12
Putnam, *U.S.A.* 111 E13
Putnok, *Hungary* 42 B5
Putorana, Gory, *Russia* 51 C10
Puttalam, *Sri Lanka* 66 Q11
Puttgarden, *Germany* 24 A7
Püttlingen, *Germany* 25 F2
Putumayo →, *S. Amer.* 122 D4
Putuo, *China* 59 C14
Putussibau, *Indonesia* 62 D4
Puvirnituq, *Canada* 101 B12
Puy-de-Dôme, *France* 20 C6
Puy-de-Dôme □, *France* 20 C7
Puy-l'Évêque, *France* 20 D5
Puyallup, *U.S.A.* 116 C4
Puyang, *China* 56 G8
Puylaurens, *France* 20 E6
Pūzeh Rīg, *Iran* 71 E8
Pwani □, *Tanzania* 86 D4
Pweto, *Dem. Rep. of the Congo* 87 D2
Pwllheli, *U.K.* 12 E3
Pyana →, *Russia* 48 C8
Pyapon, *Burma* 67 L19
Pyasina →, *Russia* 51 B9
Pyatigorsk, *Russia* 49 H6
Pyatykhatky, *Ukraine* 47 H7
Pydna, *Greece* 40 F6
Pyè, *Burma* 67 K19
Pyetrikaw, *Belarus* 47 F5
Pyhäjoki, *Finland* 8 D21
Pyinmana, *Burma* 67 K20
Pyla, C., *Cyprus* 36 E12
Pymatuning Reservoir, *U.S.A.* 110 E4
Pyŏktong, *N. Korea* 57 D13
Pyŏnggang, *N. Korea* 57 E14
P'yŏngt'aek, *S. Korea* 57 F14
P'yŏngyang, *N. Korea* 57 E13
Pyote, *U.S.A.* 113 K3
Pyramid L., *U.S.A.* 114 G4
Pyramid Pk., *U.S.A.* 117 J10
Pyramids, *Egypt* 80 J7
Pyrénées, *Europe* 20 F4
Pyrénées-Atlantiques □, *France* 20 E3
Pyrénées-Orientales □, *France* 20 F6
Pyryatyn, *Ukraine* 47 G7
Pyrzyce, *Poland* 45 E1
Pyskowice, *Poland* 45 H5
Pytalovo, *Russia* 46 D4
Pyu, *Burma* 67 K20
Pyzdry, *Poland* 45 F4

Q

Qaanaaq, *Greenland* 4 B4
Qabirri →, *Azerbaijan* 49 K8
Qachasnek, *S. Africa* 89 E4
Qa'el Jafr, *Jordan* 75 E5
Qa'emābād, *Iran* 71 D9
Qā'emshahr, *Iran* 71 B7
Qagan Nur, *China* 56 C8
Qahar Youyi Zhongqi, *China* 56 D7
Qahremānshahr = Bākhtarān, *Iran* 70 C5
Qaidam Pendi, *China* 60 C4
Qajarīyeh, *Iran* 71 D6
Qala, Ras il, *Malta* 36 C1
Qala-i-Jadid = Spīn Búldak, *Afghan.* 68 D2
Qala Viala, *Pakistan* 68 D2
Qala Yangi, *Afghan.* 68 B2
Qal'at al Akhḍar, *Si. Arabia* 70 E3
Qal'at Dīzah, *Iraq* 70 B5
Qal'at Ṣaliḥ, *Iraq* 70 D5
Qal'at Sukkar, *Iraq* 70 D5
Qal'eh Shaharak, *Afghan.* 66 B4
Qalyûb, *Egypt* 80 H7
Qamdo, *China* 58 B1
Qamruddin Karez, *Pakistan* 68 D3
Qandahār, *Afghan.* 66 D4
Qandahār □, *Afghan.* 66 D4
Qapān, *Iran* 71 B7
Qapshaghay, *Kazakstan* 50 E8
Qaqortoq, *Greenland* 4 C5
Qâra, *Egypt* 80 B2
Qara Qash →, *India* 69 B8
Qarabutaq, *Kazakstan* 50 E7
Qaraçala, *Azerbaijan* 49 L9
Qaraghandy, *Kazakstan* 50 E8
Qārah, *Si. Arabia* 70 D4
Qarataū, *Kazakstan* 50 E8
Qardud, *Sudan* 81 E2
Qareh →, *Iran* 70 B5
Qareh Tekān, *Iran* 71 B6
Qarqan He →, *China* 60 C3
Qarqaraly, *Kazakstan* 50 E8
Qarrasa, *Sudan* 81 E3
Qarshi, *Uzbekistan* 50 F7
Qartabā, *Lebanon* 75 A4
Qaryat al Gharab, *Iraq* 70 D5
Qaryat al 'Ulyā, *Si. Arabia* 70 E5
Qasr 'Amra, *Jordan* 70 D3
Qaşr-e Qand, *Iran* 71 E9
Qasr Farâfra, *Egypt* 80 B2
Qatanā, *Syria* 75 B5
Qatar ■, *Asia* 71 E6
Qatlīsh, *Iran* 71 B8
Qattâra, *Egypt* 80 A2
Qattâra, Munkhafed el, *Egypt* 80 B2
Qattâra Depression = Qattâra, Munkhafed el, *Egypt* 80 B2
Qawām al Ḥamzah, *Iraq* 70 D5
Qāyen, *Iran* 71 C8
Qazaqstan = Kazakstan ■, *Asia* 50 E7
Qazimämmäd, *Azerbaijan* 49 K9
Qazvin, *Iran* 71 B6
Qeissan, *Sudan* 81 E3
Qena, *Egypt* 80 B3
Qena, W. →, *Egypt* 80 B3
Qeqertarsuaq, *Greenland* 4 C5
Qeqertarsuaq, *Greenland* 4 C5
Qeshlāq, *Iran* 70 C5
Qeshm, *Iran* 71 E8
Qeys, *Iran* 71 E7
Qezel Owzen →, *Iran* 71 B6
Qezi'ot, *Israel* 75 E3
Qi Xian, *China* 56 G8
Qian Gorlos, *China* 57 B13
Qian Xian, *China* 56 G5
Qiancheng, *China* 58 D7
Qianjiang, *Guangxi Zhuangzu, China* 58 F7
Qianjiang, *Hubei, China* 59 B9
Qianjiang, *Sichuan, China* 58 C7
Qianshan, *China* 59 B11
Qianwei, *China* 58 C4
Qianxi, *China* 58 D6
Qianyang, *Hunan, China* 59 D8
Qianyang, *Shaanxi, China* 56 G4
Qianyang, *Zhejiang, China* 59 B12
Qiaojia, *China* 58 D4
Qibā', *Si. Arabia* 70 E5
Qichun, *China* 59 B10
Qidong, *Hunan, China* 59 D9
Qidong, *Jiangsu, China* 59 B13
Qijiang, *China* 58 C6
Qikiqtarjuaq, *Canada* 101 B13
Qila Safed, *Pakistan* 66 E2
Qila Saifullāh, *Pakistan* 68 D3
Qilian Shan, *China* 60 C4
Qimen, *China* 59 C11
Qin He →, *China* 56 G7
Qin Jiang →, *Guangxi Zhuangzu, China* 58 F7
Qin Jiang →, *Jiangxi, China* 59 D10
Qin Ling = Qinling Shandi, *China* 56 H5
Qin'an, *China* 56 G3
Qing Xian, *China* 56 E9
Qingcheng, *China* 57 F9
Qingdao, *China* 57 F11
Qingfeng, *China* 56 G8
Qinghai □, *China* 60 C4
Qinghai Hu, *China* 60 C5
Qinghecheng, *China* 57 D13
Qinghemen, *China* 57 D11
Qingjian, *China* 56 F6
Qingjiang = Huaiyin, *China* 57 H10
Qingliu, *China* 59 D11
Qinglong, *China* 58 E5
Qingping, *China* 58 D6
Qingpu, *China* 59 B13
Qingshui, *China* 56 G4
Qingshuihe, *China* 56 E6
Qingtian, *China* 59 C13
Qingtongxia Shuiku, *China* 56 F3
Qingxi, *China* 58 D7
Qingxu, *China* 56 F7
Qingyang, *Anhui, China* 59 B11
Qingyang, *Gansu, China* 56 F4
Qingyi Jiang →, *China* 58 C4
Qingyuan, *Guangdong, China* 59 F9
Qingyuan, *Liaoning, China* 57 C13
Qingyuan, *Zhejiang, China* 59 D12
Qingyun, *China* 57 F9
Qingzhen, *China* 58 D6
Qinhuangdao, *China* 57 E10
Qinling Shandi, *China* 56 H5
Qinshui, *China* 56 G7
Qinyang = Jiyuan, *China* 56 G7
Qinyuan, *China* 56 F7
Qinzhou, *China* 58 G7
Qionghai, *China* 64 C8
Qionglai, *China* 58 B4
Qionglai Shan, *China* 58 B4
Qiongzhou Haixia, *China* 64 B8
Qiqihar, *China* 51 E13
Qirâiya, W. →, *Egypt* 75 E3
Qiryat Ata, *Israel* 75 C4
Qiryat Gat, *Israel* 75 D3
Qiryat Mal'akhi, *Israel* 75 D3
Qiryat Shemona, *Israel* 75 B4
Qiryat Yam, *Israel* 75 C4
Qishan, *China* 56 G4
Qitai, *China* 60 B3
Qiubei, *China* 58 E5
Qixia, *China* 57 F11
Qiyang, *China* 59 D8
Qızılağac Körfäzi, *Azerbaijan* 71 B6
Qojūr, *Iran* 70 B5
Qom, *Iran* 71 C6
Qomolangma Feng = Everest, Mt., *Nepal* 69 E12
Qomsheh, *Iran* 71 D6
Qorveh, *Iran* 73 E12
Qostanay, *Kazakstan* 50 D7
Qoṭūr, *Iran* 73 C11
Qu Jiang →, *China* 58 B6
Qu Xian, *China* 58 B6
Quabbin Reservoir, *U.S.A.* 111 D12
Quairading, *Australia* 93 F2
Quakenbrück, *Germany* 24 C3
Quakertown, *U.S.A.* 111 F9
Qualicum Beach, *Canada* 104 D4
Quambatook, *Australia* 95 F3
Quambone, *Australia* 95 E4
Quamby, *Australia* 94 C3
Quan Long = Ca Mau, *Vietnam* 65 H5
Quanah, *U.S.A.* 113 H5
Quang Ngai, *Vietnam* 64 E7
Quang Tri, *Vietnam* 64 D6
Quang Yen, *Vietnam* 58 G6
Quannan, *China* 59 E10
Quantock Hills, *U.K.* 13 F4
Quanzhou, *Fujian, China* 59 E12
Quanzhou, *Guangxi Zhuangzu, China* 59 E8
Qu'Appelle, *Canada* 105 C8
Quaqtaq, *Canada* 101 B13
Quaraí, *Brazil* 126 C4
Quarré-les-Tombes, *France* 19 E11
Quarteira, *Portugal* 35 H2
Quartu Sant'Élena, *Italy* 30 C2
Quartzsite, *U.S.A.* 117 M12
Quatsino Sd., *Canada* 104 C3
Quba, *Azerbaijan* 49 K9
Qūchān, *Iran* 71 B8
Queanbeyan, *Australia* 95 F4
Québec, *Canada* 103 C5
Québec □, *Canada* 103 C6
Quedlinburg, *Germany* 24 D7
Queen Alexandra Ra., *Antarctica* 5 E11
Queen Charlotte City, *Canada* 104 C2
Queen Charlotte Is., *Canada* 104 C2
Queen Charlotte Sd., *Canada* 104 C3
Queen Charlotte Strait, *Canada* 104 C3
Queen Elizabeth Is., *Canada* 98 B10
Queen Elizabeth Nat. Park, *Uganda* 86 C3
Queen Mary Land, *Antarctica* 5 D7
Queen Maud G., *Canada* 100 B9
Queen Maud Land, *Antarctica* 5 D3
Queen Maud Mts., *Antarctica* 5 E13
Queens Chan., *Australia* 92 C4
Queenscliff, *Australia* 95 F3
Queensland □, *Australia* 94 C3
Queenstown, *Australia* 94 G4
Queenstown, *N.Z.* 91 L2
Queenstown, *S. Africa* 88 E4
Queets, *U.S.A.* 116 C2
Queguay Grande →, *Uruguay* 126 C4
Queimadas, *Brazil* 125 F11
Quelimane, *Mozam.* 87 F4
Quellón, *Chile* 128 E2
Quelpart = Cheju do, *S. Korea* 57 H14
Queluz, *Portugal* 35 G1
Quemado, *N. Mex., U.S.A.* 115 J9
Quemado, *Tex., U.S.A.* 113 L4
Quemoy = Chinmen, *Taiwan* 59 E13
Quemú-Quemú, *Argentina* 126 D3
Quequén, *Argentina* 126 D4
Querétaro, *Mexico* 118 C4
Querétaro □, *Mexico* 118 C5
Querfurt, *Germany* 24 D7
Quérigut, *France* 20 F6
Querqueville, *France* 18 C5
Quesada, *Spain* 35 H7
Queshan, *China* 56 H8
Quesnel, *Canada* 104 C4
Quesnel →, *Canada* 104 C4
Quesnel L., *Canada* 104 C4
Questa, *U.S.A.* 115 H11
Questembert, *France* 18 E4
Quetico Prov. Park, *Canada* 102 C1
Quetta, *Pakistan* 68 D2
Quezaltenango, *Guatemala* 120 D1
Quezon City, *Phil.* 61 D4
Qufār, *Si. Arabia* 70 E4
Qui Nhon, *Vietnam* 64 F7
Quibaxe, *Angola* 84 F2
Quibdo, *Colombia* 124 B3
Quiberon, *France* 18 E3
Quiberon, Presqu'île de, *France* 18 E3
Quickborn, *Germany* 24 B5
Quiet L., *Canada* 104 A2
Quiindy, *Paraguay* 126 B4
Quila, *Mexico* 118 C3
Quilán, C., *Chile* 128 E2
Quilcene, *U.S.A.* 116 C4
Quilimarí, *Chile* 126 C1
Quilino, *Argentina* 126 C3
Quill Lakes, *Canada* 105 C8
Quillabamba, *Peru* 124 F4
Quillagua, *Chile* 126 A2
Quillaicillo, *Chile* 126 C1
Quillan, *France* 20 F6
Quillota, *Chile* 126 C1
Quilmes, *Argentina* 126 C4
Quilon, *India* 66 Q10
Quilpie, *Australia* 95 D3
Quilpué, *Chile* 126 C1
Quilua, *Mozam.* 87 F4
Quimilí, *Argentina* 126 B3
Quimper, *France* 18 E2
Quimperlé, *France* 18 E3
Quinault →, *U.S.A.* 116 C2
Quincy, *Calif., U.S.A.* 116 F6
Quincy, *Fla., U.S.A.* 109 K3
Quincy, *Ill., U.S.A.* 112 F9
Quincy, *Mass., U.S.A.* 111 D14
Quincy, *Wash., U.S.A.* 114 C4
Quines, *Argentina* 126 C2
Quinga, *Mozam.* 87 F5
Quingey, *France* 19 E12
Quinns Rocks, *Australia* 93 F2
Quintana de la Serena, *Spain* 35 G5
Quintana Roo □, *Mexico* 119 D7
Quintanar de la Orden, *Spain* 35 F7
Quintanar de la Sierra, *Spain* 32 D2
Quintanar del Rey, *Spain* 33 F3
Quintero, *Chile* 126 C1
Quintin, *France* 18 D4
Quinto, *Spain* 32 D4
Quípar →, *Spain* 33 G3
Quirihue, *Chile* 126 D1
Quirindi, *Australia* 95 E5
Quirinópolis, *Brazil* 125 G8
Quiroga, *Spain* 34 C3
Quissac, *France* 21 E8
Quissanga, *Mozam.* 87 E5
Quissico, *Mozam.* 89 C5
Quitilipi, *Argentina* 126 B3
Quitman, *U.S.A.* 109 K4
Quito, *Ecuador* 124 D3
Quixadá, *Brazil* 125 D11
Quixaxe, *Mozam.* 87 F5
Qujing, *China* 58 E4
Qul'ân, Jazâ'ir, *Egypt* 70 E2
Qumbu, *S. Africa* 89 E4
Quneitra, *Syria* 75 B4
Qŭnghirot, *Uzbekistan* 50 E6
Qu'nyido, *China* 58 B2
Quoin I., *Australia* 92 B4
Quoin Pt., *S. Africa* 88 E2
Quorn, *Australia* 95 E2
Qŭqon, *Uzbekistan* 50 E8
Qurein, *Sudan* 81 E3
Qurnat as Sawdā', *Lebanon* 75 A5
Qûs, *Egypt* 80 B3
Qusar, *Azerbaijan* 49 K9
Quşaybā', *Si. Arabia* 70 E4
Qusaybah, *Iraq* 70 C4
Quseir, *Egypt* 70 E2
Qūshchī, *Iran* 70 B5
Quthing, *Lesotho* 89 E4
Qūṭīābād, *Iran* 71 C6
Quwo, *China* 56 G6
Quyang, *China* 56 E8
Quynh Nhai, *Vietnam* 64 B4
Quyon, *Canada* 111 A8
Quzhou, *China* 59 C12
Quzi, *China* 56 F4
Qvareli, *Georgia* 49 K7
Qytet Stalin = Kuçovë, *Albania* 40 F3
Qyzylorda, *Kazakstan* 50 E7

R

Ra, Ko, *Thailand* 65 H2
Raab, *Austria* 26 C6
Raahe, *Finland* 8 D21
Raalte, *Neths.* 17 B6
Raasay, *U.K.* 14 D2
Raasay, Sd. of, *U.K.* 14 D2
Rab, *Croatia* 29 D11
Raba, *Indonesia* 63 F5
Rába →, *Hungary* 42 C2
Raba →, *Poland* 45 H7
Rabaçal →, *Portugal* 34 D3
Rabah, *Nigeria* 83 C6
Rabai, *Kenya* 86 C4
Rabak, *Sudan* 81 E3
Rabastens, *France* 20 E5
Rabastens-de-Bigorre, *France* 20 E4
Rabat, *Malta* 36 D1
Rabat, *Morocco* 78 B4
Rabaul, *Papua N. G.* 96 H7
Rābigh, *Si. Arabia* 74 C2
Rabka, *Poland* 45 J6
Râbniţa, *Moldova* 43 C14
Rābor, *Iran* 71 D8
Rača, *Serbia, Yug.* 40 B4
Răcăciuni, *Romania* 43 D11
Răcăşdia, *Romania* 42 F6
Racconigi, *Italy* 28 D4
Race, C., *Canada* 103 C9
Rach Gia, *Vietnam* 65 G5
Rachid, *Mauritania* 82 B2
Raciąż, *Poland* 45 F7
Racibórz, *Poland* 45 H5
Racine, *U.S.A.* 108 D2
Rackerby, *U.S.A.* 116 F5
Radama, Nosy, *Madag.* 89 A8
Radama, Saikanosy, *Madag.* 89 A8
Radan, *Serbia, Yug.* 40 D5
Rădăuţi, *Romania* 43 C10
Rădăuţi-Prut, *Romania* 43 B11
Radbuza →, *Czech Rep.* 26 B6
Radcliff, *U.S.A.* 108 G3
Radebeul, *Germany* 24 D9
Radeburg, *Germany* 24 D9
Radeče, *Slovenia* 29 B12
Radekhiv, *Ukraine* 47 G3
Radekhov = Radekhiv, *Ukraine* 47 G3
Radenthein, *Austria* 26 E6
Radew →, *Poland* 44 D2
Radford, *U.S.A.* 108 G5
Radhanpur, *India* 68 H4
Radhwa, Jabal, *Si. Arabia* 70 E3
Radika →, *Macedonia* 40 E4
Radisson, *Qué., Canada* 102 B4
Radisson, *Sask., Canada* 105 C7
Radium Hot Springs, *Canada* 104 C5
Radlje ob Dravi, *Slovenia* 29 B12
Radnevo, *Bulgaria* 41 D9
Radnice, *Czech Rep.* 26 B6
Radnor Forest, *U.K.* 13 E4
Radolfzell, *Germany* 25 H4
Radom, *Poland* 45 G8
Radomir, *Bulgaria* 40 D6
Radomka →, *Poland* 45 G8
Radomsko, *Poland* 45 G6
Radomyshl, *Ukraine* 47 G5
Radomyśl Wielki, *Poland* 45 H8
Radoszyce, *Poland* 45 G7
Radoviš, *Macedonia* 40 E6
Radovljica, *Slovenia* 29 B11
Radstadt, *Austria* 26 D6
Radstock, C., *Australia* 95 E1
Răducăneni, *Romania* 43 D12
Raduša, *Macedonia* 40 D5
Radviliškis, *Lithuania* 9 J20
Radville, *Canada* 105 D8
Radwa, J., *Si. Arabia* 80 C4
Radymno, *Poland* 45 J9
Radzanów, *Poland* 45 F7
Radziejów, *Poland* 45 F5
Radzyń Chełmiński, *Poland* 44 E5
Radzyń Podlaski, *Poland* 45 G9
Rae, *Canada* 104 A5
Rae Bareli, *India* 69 F9
Rae Isthmus, *Canada* 101 B11
Raeren, *Belgium* 17 D6

Raeside, L., *Australia* 93 E3
Raetihi, *N.Z.* 91 H5
Rafaela, *Argentina* 126 C3
Rafah, *Gaza Strip* 75 D3
Rafai, *C.A.R.* 86 B1
Raffadali, *Italy* 30 E6
Raffili, *Sudan* 81 F2
Rafḩā, *Si. Arabia* 70 D4
Rafsanjān, *Iran* 71 D8
Raft Pt., *Australia* 92 C3
Râgâ, *Sudan* 81 F2
Raga →, *Sudan* 81 F2
Ragachow, *Belarus* 47 F6
Ragag, *Sudan* 81 E1
Ragama, *Sri Lanka* 66 R11
Ragged, Mt., *Australia* 93 F3
Raghunathpalli, *India* 69 H11
Raghunathpur, *India* 69 H12
Raglan, *N.Z.* 91 G5
Ragusa, *Italy* 31 F7
Raha, *Indonesia* 63 E6
Rahad, Nahr ed →, *Sudan* 81 E3
Rahaeng = Tak, *Thailand* 64 D2
Rahatgarh, *India* 69 H8
Rahden, *Germany* 24 C4
Raheita, *Eritrea* 81 E5
Raḩīmah, *Si. Arabia* 71 E6
Rahimyar Khan, *Pakistan* 68 E4
Rāhjerd, *Iran* 71 C6
Rahon, *India* 68 D7
Raichur, *India* 66 L10
Raiganj, *India* 69 G13
Raigarh, *India* 67 J13
Raijua, *Indonesia* 63 F6
Raikot, *India* 68 D6
Railton, *Australia* 94 G4
Rainbow Lake, *Canada* 104 B5
Rainier, *U.S.A.* 116 D4
Rainier, Mt., *U.S.A.* 116 D5
Rainy L., *Canada* 105 D10
Rainy River, *Canada* 105 D10
Raippaluoto, *Finland* 8 E19
Raipur, *India* 67 J12
Ra'is, *Si. Arabia* 80 C4
Raisen, *India* 68 H8
Raisio, *Finland* 9 F20
Raj Nandgaon, *India* 67 J12
Raj Nilgiri, *India* 69 J12
Raja, Ujung, *Indonesia* 62 D1
Raja Ampat, Kepulauan, *Indonesia* 63 E7
Rajahmundry, *India* 67 L12
Rajang →, *Malaysia* 62 D4
Rajanpur, *Pakistan* 68 E4
Rajapalaiyam, *India* 66 Q10
Rajasthan □, *India* 68 F5
Rajasthan Canal, *India* 68 F5
Rajauri, *India* 69 C6
Rajgarh, *Mad. P., India* 68 G7
Rajgarh, *Raj., India* 68 F7
Rajgarh, *Raj., India* 68 E6
Rajgir, *India* 69 G11
Rajgród, *Poland* 44 E9
Rajkot, *India* 68 H4
Rajmahal Hills, *India* 69 G12
Rajpipla, *India* 66 J8
Rajpur, *India* 68 H6
Rajpura, *India* 68 D7
Rajshahi, *Bangla.* 67 G16
Rajshahi □, *Bangla.* 69 G13
Rajula, *India* 68 J4
Rakaia, *N.Z.* 91 K4
Rakaia →, *N.Z.* 91 K4
Rakan, Ra's, *Qatar* 71 E6
Rakaposhi, *Pakistan* 69 A6
Rakata, Pulau, *Indonesia* 62 F3
Rakhiv, *Ukraine* 47 H3
Rakhni, *Pakistan* 68 D3
Rakhni →, *Pakistan* 68 E3
Rakitnoye, *Russia* 54 B7
Rakitovo, *Bulgaria* 41 E8
Rakoniewice, *Poland* 45 F3
Rakops, *Botswana* 88 C3
Rakovica, *Croatia* 29 D12
Rakovník, *Czech Rep.* 26 A6
Rakovski, *Bulgaria* 41 D8
Rakvere, *Estonia* 9 G22
Raleigh, *U.S.A.* 109 H6
Raleigh B., *U.S.A.* 107 D11
Ralja, *Serbia, Yug.* 40 B4
Ralls, *U.S.A.* 113 J4
Ralston, *U.S.A.* 110 E8
Ram →, *Canada* 104 A4
Rām Allāh, *West Bank* 75 D4
Ram Hd., *Australia* 95 F4
Rama, *Nic.* 120 D3
Ramacca, *Italy* 31 E7
Ramakona, *India* 69 J8
Ramales de la Victoria, *Spain* 34 B7
Raman, *Thailand* 65 J3
Ramanathapuram, *India* 66 Q11
Ramanetaka, B. de, *Madag.* 89 A8
Ramanujganj, *India* 69 H10
Ramat Gan, *Israel* 75 C3
Ramatlhabama, *S. Africa* 88 D4
Ramban, *India* 69 C6
Rambervillers, *France* 19 D13
Rambipuji, *Indonesia* 63 H15
Rambouillet, *France* 19 D8
Ramechhap, *Nepal* 69 F12
Ramenskoye, *Russia* 46 E10
Ramganga →, *India* 69 F8
Ramgarh, *Bihar, India* 69 H11
Ramgarh, *Raj., India* 68 F6
Ramgarh, *Raj., India* 68 F4
Rāmhormoz, *Iran* 71 D6
Ramīān, *Iran* 71 B7
Ramingining, *Australia* 94 A2
Ramla, *Israel* 75 D3
Ramlu, *Eritrea* 81 E5
Râmna →, *Romania* 43 E12
Ramnad = Ramanathapuram, *India* 66 Q11
Ramnagar, *Jammu & Kashmir, India* 69 C6
Ramnagar, *Ut. P., India* 69 E8
Ramnäs, *Sweden* 10 E10
Râmnicu Sărat, *Romania* 43 E12
Râmnicu Vâlcea, *Romania* 43 E9
Ramon, *Russia* 47 G10
Ramona, *U.S.A.* 117 M10
Ramonville-St-Agne, *France* 20 E5
Ramore, *Canada* 102 C3
Ramos →, *Nigeria* 83 D6
Ramotswa, *Botswana* 88 C4
Rampur, *H.P., India* 68 D7
Rampur, *Mad. P., India* 68 H5
Rampur, *Ut. P., India* 69 E8
Rampur Hat, *India* 69 G12
Rampura, *India* 68 G6
Ramrama Tola, *India* 69 J8
Ramree I. = Ramree Kyun, *Burma* 67 K19
Ramree Kyun, *Burma* 67 K19
Rāmsar, *Iran* 71 B6
Ramsey, *U.K.* 12 C3
Ramsey, *U.S.A.* 111 E10
Ramsey L., *Canada* 102 C3
Ramsgate, *U.K.* 13 F9
Ramsjö, *Sweden* 10 B9
Ramstein, *Germany* 25 F3
Ramtek, *India* 66 J11
Ramvik, *Sweden* 10 B11
Rana Pratap Sagar Dam, *India* 68 G6
Ranaghat, *India* 69 H13
Ranahu, *Pakistan* 68 G3
Ranau, *Malaysia* 62 C5
Rancagua, *Chile* 126 C1
Rance →, *France* 18 D5
Rancheria →, *Canada* 104 A3
Ranchester, *U.S.A.* 114 D10
Ranchi, *India* 69 H11
Rancho Cucamonga, *U.S.A.* 117 L9
Randalstown, *U.K.* 15 B5
Randan, *France* 19 F10
Randazzo, *Italy* 31 E7
Randers, *Denmark* 11 H4
Randers Fjord, *Denmark* 11 H4
Randfontein, *S. Africa* 89 D4
Randle, *U.S.A.* 116 D5
Randolph, *Mass., U.S.A.* 111 D13
Randolph, *N.Y., U.S.A.* 110 D6
Randolph, *Utah, U.S.A.* 114 F8
Randolph, *Vt., U.S.A.* 111 C12
Randsburg, *U.S.A.* 117 K9
Råne älv →, *Sweden* 8 D20
Rangae, *Thailand* 65 J3
Rangaunu B., *N.Z.* 91 F4
Rangeley, *U.S.A.* 111 B14
Rangeley L., *U.S.A.* 111 B14
Rangely, *U.S.A.* 114 F9
Ranger, *U.S.A.* 113 J5
Rangia, *India* 67 F17
Rangiora, *N.Z.* 91 K4
Rangitaiki →, *N.Z.* 91 G6
Rangitata →, *N.Z.* 91 K3
Rangkasbitung, *Indonesia* 63 G12
Rangon →, *Burma* 67 L20
Rangoon, *Burma* 67 L20
Rangpur, *Bangla.* 67 G16
Rangsit, *Thailand* 64 F3
Ranibennur, *India* 66 M9
Raniganj, *Ut. P., India* 69 F9
Raniganj, *W. Bengal, India* 67 H15
Ranikhet, *India* 69 E8
Raniwara, *India* 66 G8
Rāniyah, *Iraq* 70 B5
Ranka, *India* 69 H10
Ranken →, *Australia* 94 C2
Rankin, *U.S.A.* 113 K4
Rankin Inlet, *Canada* 100 B10
Rankins Springs, *Australia* 95 E4
Rankweil, *Austria* 26 D2
Rannoch, L., *U.K.* 14 E4
Rannoch Moor, *U.K.* 14 E4
Ranobe, Helodranon' i, *Madag.* 89 C7
Ranohira, *Madag.* 89 C8
Ranomafana, *Toamasina, Madag.* 89 B8
Ranomafana, *Toliara, Madag.* 89 C8
Ranomena, *Madag.* 89 C8
Ranong, *Thailand* 65 H2
Ranotsara Nord, *Madag.* 89 C8
Rānsa, *Iran* 71 C6
Ransiki, *Indonesia* 63 E8
Rantabe, *Madag.* 89 B8
Rantauprapat, *Indonesia* 62 D1
Rantemario, *Indonesia* 63 E5
Rantoul, *U.S.A.* 108 E1
Ranum, *Denmark* 11 H3
Ranyah, W. →, *Si. Arabia* 80 C5
Raon l'Étape, *France* 19 D13
Raoping, *China* 59 F11
Raoyang, *China* 56 E8
Rapa, *Pac. Oc.* 97 K13
Rapallo, *Italy* 28 D6
Rapar, *India* 68 H4
Rāpch, *Iran* 71 E8
Raper, C., *Canada* 101 B13
Rapid City, *U.S.A.* 112 D3
Rapid River, *U.S.A.* 108 C2
Rapla, *Estonia* 9 G21
Rapti →, *India* 69 F10
Rapu Rapu I., *Phil.* 61 E6
Raqaba ez Zarqa →, *Sudan* 81 F2
Raquette →, *U.S.A.* 111 B10
Raquette Lake, *U.S.A.* 111 C10
Rarotonga, *Cook Is.* 97 K12
Ra's al 'Ayn, *Syria* 70 B4
Ra's al Khaymah, *U.A.E.* 71 E7
Râs el Mâ, *Mali* 82 B4
Ras Ghârib, *Egypt* 80 B3
Ras Mallap, *Egypt* 80 B3
Râs Timirist, *Mauritania* 82 B1
Rasca, Pta. de la, *Canary Is.* 37 G3
Râşcani, *Moldova* 43 C12
Raseiniai, *Lithuania* 9 J20
Rashad, *Sudan* 81 E3
Rashîd, *Egypt* 80 H7
Rashîd, Masabb, *Egypt* 80 H7
Rashmi, *India* 68 G6
Rasht, *Iran* 71 B6
Rasi Salai, *Thailand* 64 E5
Raška, *Serbia, Yug.* 40 C4
Râsnov, *Romania* 43 E10
Rason L., *Australia* 93 E3
Raşova, *Romania* 43 F12
Rasovo, *Bulgaria* 40 C7
Rasra, *India* 69 G10
Rasskazovo, *Russia* 48 D5
Rast, *Romania* 43 G8
Rastatt, *Germany* 25 G4
Rastede, *Germany* 24 B4
Răstoliţa, *Romania* 43 D9
Rasul, *Pakistan* 68 C5
Raszków, *Poland* 45 G4
Rat Buri, *Thailand* 64 F2
Rat Islands, *U.S.A.* 100 C1
Rat L., *Canada* 105 B9
Ratangarh, *India* 68 E6
Rätansbyn, *Sweden* 10 B8
Raṭāwī, *Iraq* 70 D5
Ratcatchers L., *Australia* 95 E3
Rath, *India* 69 G8
Rath Luirc, *Ireland* 15 D3
Rathdrum, *Ireland* 15 D5
Rathenow, *Germany* 24 C8
Rathkeale, *Ireland* 15 D3
Rathlin I., *U.K.* 15 A5
Rathmelton, *Ireland* 15 A4
Ratibor = Racibórz, *Poland* 45 H5
Rätikon, *Austria* 26 D2
Ratingen, *Germany* 24 D2
Ratlam, *India* 68 H6
Ratnagiri, *India* 66 L8
Ratodero, *Pakistan* 68 F3
Raton, *U.S.A.* 113 G2
Rattaphum, *Thailand* 65 J3
Ratten, *Austria* 26 D8
Rattray Hd., *U.K.* 14 D7
Rättvik, *Sweden* 10 D9
Ratz, Mt., *Canada* 104 B2
Ratzeburg, *Germany* 24 B6
Raub, *Malaysia* 65 L3
Rauch, *Argentina* 126 D4
Raudales de Malpaso, *Mexico* 119 D6
Raufarhöfn, *Iceland* 8 C6
Raufoss, *Norway* 9 F14
Raukumara Ra., *N.Z.* 91 H6
Rauma, *Finland* 9 F19
Raurkela, *India* 69 H11
Rausu-Dake, *Japan* 54 B12
Răut →, *Moldova* 43 C14
Rava-Ruska, *Poland* 47 G2
Rava Russkaya = Rava-Ruska, *Poland* 47 G2
Ravalli, *U.S.A.* 114 C6
Ravānsar, *Iran* 70 C5
Ravanusa, *Italy* 30 E6
Rāvar, *Iran* 71 D8
Ravena, *U.S.A.* 111 D11
Ravenna, *Italy* 29 D9
Ravenna, *Nebr., U.S.A.* 112 E5
Ravenna, *Ohio, U.S.A.* 110 E3
Ravensburg, *Germany* 25 H5
Ravenshoe, *Australia* 94 B4
Ravensthorpe, *Australia* 93 F3
Ravenswood, *Australia* 94 C4
Ravenswood, *U.S.A.* 108 F5
Ravi →, *Pakistan* 68 D4
Ravna Gora, *Croatia* 29 C11
Ravna Reka, *Serbia, Yug.* 40 B5
Ravne na Koroškem, *Slovenia* 29 B11
Rawa Mazowiecka, *Poland* 45 G7
Rawalpindi, *Pakistan* 68 C5
Rawāndūz, *Iraq* 70 B5
Rawang, *Malaysia* 65 L3
Rawene, *N.Z.* 91 F4
Rawicz, *Poland* 45 G3
Rawka →, *Poland* 45 F7
Rawlinna, *Australia* 93 F4
Rawlins, *U.S.A.* 114 F10
Rawlinson Ra., *Australia* 93 D4
Rawson, *Argentina* 128 E3
Raxaul, *India* 69 F11
Ray, *U.S.A.* 112 A3
Ray, C., *Canada* 103 C8
Rayadurg, *India* 66 M10
Rayagada, *India* 67 K13
Raychikhinsk, *Russia* 51 E13
Rāyen, *Iran* 71 D8
Rayleigh, *U.K.* 13 F8
Raymond, *Canada* 104 D6
Raymond, *Calif., U.S.A.* 116 H7
Raymond, *N.H., U.S.A.* 111 C13
Raymond, *Wash., U.S.A.* 116 D3
Raymond Terrace, *Australia* 95 E5
Raymondville, *U.S.A.* 113 M6
Raymore, *Canada* 105 C8
Rayón, *Mexico* 118 B2
Rayong, *Thailand* 64 F3
Rayville, *U.S.A.* 113 J9
Raz, Pte. du, *France* 18 D2
Razan, *Iran* 71 C6
Ražana, *Serbia, Yug.* 40 B3
Ražanj, *Serbia, Yug.* 40 C5
Razdelna, *Bulgaria* 41 C11
Razdel'naya = Rozdilna, *Ukraine* 47 J6
Razdolnoye, *Russia* 54 C5
Razdolnoye, *Ukraine* 47 K7
Razeh, *Iran* 71 C6
Razgrad, *Bulgaria* 41 C10
Razim, Lacul, *Romania* 43 F14
Razlog, *Bulgaria* 40 E7
Razmak, *Pakistan* 68 C3
Ré, Î. de, *France* 20 B2
Reading, *U.K.* 13 F7
Reading, *U.S.A.* 111 F9
Reading □, *U.K.* 13 F7
Realicó, *Argentina* 126 D3
Réalmont, *France* 20 E6
Ream, *Cambodia* 65 G4
Reata, *Mexico* 118 B4
Reay Forest, *U.K.* 14 C4
Rebais, *France* 19 D10
Rebi, *Indonesia* 63 F8
Rebiana, *Libya* 79 D10
Rebun-Tō, *Japan* 54 B10
Recanati, *Italy* 29 E10
Recaş, *Romania* 42 E6
Recco, *Italy* 28 D6
Recherche, Arch. of the, *Australia* 93 F3
Rechna Doab, *Pakistan* 68 D5
Rechytsa, *Belarus* 47 F6
Recife, *Brazil* 125 E12
Recklinghausen, *Germany* 17 C7
Reconquista, *Argentina* 126 B4
Recreo, *Argentina* 126 B2
Recz, *Poland* 45 E2
Red →, *La., U.S.A.* 113 K9
Red →, *N. Dak., U.S.A.* 100 C10
Red Bank, *U.S.A.* 111 F10
Red Bay, *Canada* 103 B8
Red Bluff, *U.S.A.* 114 F2
Red Bluff L., *U.S.A.* 113 K3
Red Cliffs, *Australia* 95 E3
Red Cloud, *U.S.A.* 112 E5
Red Creek, *U.S.A.* 111 C8
Red Deer, *Canada* 104 C6
Red Deer →, *Alta., Canada* 105 C7
Red Deer →, *Man., Canada* 105 C8
Red Deer L., *Canada* 105 C8
Red Hook, *U.S.A.* 111 E11
Red Indian L., *Canada* 103 C8
Red L., *Canada* 105 C10
Red Lake, *Canada* 105 C10
Red Lake Falls, *U.S.A.* 112 B6
Red Lake Road, *Canada* 105 C10
Red Lodge, *U.S.A.* 114 D9
Red Mountain, *U.S.A.* 117 K9
Red Oak, *U.S.A.* 112 E7
Red Rock, *Canada* 102 C2
Red Rock, L., *U.S.A.* 112 E8
Red Rocks Pt., *Australia* 93 F4
Red Sea, *Asia* 74 C2
Red Slate Mt., *U.S.A.* 116 H8
Red Sucker L., *Canada* 102 B1
Red Tower Pass = Turnu Roşu, P., *Romania* 43 E9
Red Wing, *U.S.A.* 112 C8
Reda, *Poland* 44 D5
Redang, *Malaysia* 62 C2
Redange, *Lux.* 17 E5
Redcar, *U.K.* 12 C6
Redcar & Cleveland □, *U.K.* 12 C7
Redcliff, *Canada* 105 C6
Redcliffe, *Australia* 95 D5
Redcliffe, Mt., *Australia* 93 E3
Reddersburg, *S. Africa* 88 D4
Redding, *U.S.A.* 114 F2
Redditch, *U.K.* 13 E6
Redfield, *U.S.A.* 112 C5
Redford, *U.S.A.* 111 B11
Redkino, *Russia* 46 D9
Redlands, *U.S.A.* 117 M9
Redmond, *Oreg., U.S.A.* 114 D3
Redmond, *Wash., U.S.A.* 116 C4
Redon, *France* 18 E4
Redonda, *Antigua* 121 C7
Redondela, *Spain* 34 C2
Redondo, *Portugal* 35 G3
Redondo Beach, *U.S.A.* 117 M8
Redruth, *U.K.* 13 G2
Redvers, *Canada* 105 D8
Redwater, *Canada* 104 C6
Redwood, *U.S.A.* 111 B9
Redwood City, *U.S.A.* 116 H4
Redwood Falls, *U.S.A.* 112 C7
Redwood National Park, *U.S.A.* 114 F1
Ree, L., *Ireland* 15 C3
Reed, L., *Canada* 105 C8
Reed City, *U.S.A.* 108 D3
Reedley, *U.S.A.* 116 J7
Reedsburg, *U.S.A.* 112 D9
Reedsport, *U.S.A.* 114 E1
Reedsville, *U.S.A.* 110 F7
Reefton, *N.Z.* 91 K3
Rees, *Germany* 24 D2
Reese →, *U.S.A.* 114 F5
Refahiye, *Turkey* 73 C8
Reftele, *Sweden* 11 G7
Refugio, *U.S.A.* 113 L6
Rega →, *Poland* 44 D2
Regalbuto, *Italy* 31 E7
Regen, *Germany* 25 G9
Regen →, *Germany* 25 F8
Regensburg, *Germany* 25 F8
Regenstauf, *Germany* 25 F8
Reggello, *Italy* 29 E8
Réggio di Calábria, *Italy* 31 D8
Réggio nell'Emília, *Italy* 28 D7
Reghin, *Romania* 43 D9
Regina, *Canada* 105 C8
Regina Beach, *Canada* 105 C8
Registro, *Brazil* 127 A6
Reguengos de Monsaraz, *Portugal* 35 G3
Rehar →, *India* 69 H10
Rehli, *India* 69 H8
Rehoboth, *Namibia* 88 C2
Rehovot, *Israel* 75 D3
Reichenbach, *Germany* 24 E8
Reid, *Australia* 93 F4
Reidsville, *U.S.A.* 109 G6
Reigate, *U.K.* 13 F7
Reillo, *Spain* 32 F3
Reims, *France* 19 C11
Reina Adelaida, Arch., *Chile* 128 G2
Reinbek, *Germany* 24 B6
Reindeer →, *Canada* 105 B8
Reindeer I., *Canada* 105 C9
Reindeer L., *Canada* 105 B8
Reinga, C., *N.Z.* 91 F4
Reinosa, *Spain* 34 B6
Reitz, *S. Africa* 89 D4
Reivilo, *S. Africa* 88 D3
Rejaf, *Sudan* 81 G3
Rejmyre, *Sweden* 11 F9
Rejowiec Fabryczny, *Poland* 45 G10
Reka →, *Slovenia* 29 C11
Rekovac, *Serbia, Yug.* 40 C5
Reliance, *Canada* 105 A7
Rémalard, *France* 18 D7
Remarkable, Mt., *Australia* 95 E2
Rembang, *Indonesia* 63 G14
Remedios, *Panama* 120 E3
Remeshk, *Iran* 71 E8
Remetea, *Romania* 43 D10
Remich, *Lux.* 17 E6
Remiremont, *France* 19 D13
Remo, *Ethiopia* 81 F5
Remontnoye, *Russia* 49 G6
Remoulins, *France* 21 E8
Remscheid, *Germany* 17 C7
Ren Xian, *China* 56 F8
Rende, *Italy* 31 C9
Rendína, *Greece* 38 B3
Rendsburg, *Germany* 24 A5
Renfrew, *Canada* 102 C4
Renfrewshire □, *U.K.* 14 F4
Rengat, *Indonesia* 62 E2
Rengo, *Chile* 126 C1
Renhua, *China* 59 E9
Renhuai, *China* 58 D6
Reni, *Ukraine* 47 K5
Renk, *Sudan* 81 E3
Renmark, *Australia* 95 E3
Rennell Sd., *Canada* 104 C2
Renner Springs, *Australia* 94 B1
Rennes, *France* 18 D5
Rennie L., *Canada* 105 A7
Reno, *U.S.A.* 116 F7
Reno →, *Italy* 29 D9
Renovo, *U.S.A.* 110 E7
Renqiu, *China* 56 E9
Rens, *Denmark* 11 K3
Renshou, *China* 58 C5
Rensselaer, *Ind., U.S.A.* 108 E2
Rensselaer, *N.Y., U.S.A.* 111 D11
Rentería, *Spain* 32 B3
Renton, *U.S.A.* 116 C4
Réo, *Burkina Faso* 82 C4
Reocín, *Spain* 34 B6
Reotipur, *India* 69 G10
Répcelak, *Hungary* 42 C2
Republic, *Mo., U.S.A.* 113 G8
Republic, *Wash., U.S.A.* 114 B4
Republican →, *U.S.A.* 112 F6
Repulse Bay, *Canada* 101 B11
Requena, *Peru* 124 E4
Requena, *Spain* 33 F3
Réquista, *France* 20 D6
Reşadiye = Datça, *Turkey* 39 E9
Reşadiye, *Turkey* 72 B7
Reşadiye Yarımadası, *Turkey* 39 E9
Resavica, *Serbia, Yug.* 40 B5
Resen, *Macedonia* 40 E5
Reserve, *U.S.A.* 115 K9
Resht = Rasht, *Iran* 71 B6
Resistencia, *Argentina* 126 B4
Reşiţa, *Romania* 42 E6
Resko, *Poland* 44 E2
Resolution I., *Canada* 101 B13
Resolution I., *N.Z.* 91 L1
Ressano Garcia, *Mozam.* 89 D5
Reston, *Canada* 105 D8
Reszel, *Poland* 44 D8
Retalhuleu, *Guatemala* 120 D1
Retenue, L. de, *Dem. Rep. of the Congo* 87 E2
Retezat, Munţii, *Romania* 42 E8
Retford, *U.K.* 12 D7
Rethel, *France* 19 C11
Rethem, *Germany* 24 C5
Réthímnon, *Greece* 36 D6
Réthímnon □, *Greece* 36 D6
Reti, *Pakistan* 68 E3
Retiche, Alpi, *Switz.* 25 J6
Retiers, *France* 18 E5
Retortillo, *Spain* 34 E4
Retournac, *France* 21 C8
Rétság, *Hungary* 42 C4
Réunion ■, *Ind. Oc.* 77 J9
Reus, *Spain* 32 D6
Reuterstadt Stavenhagen, *Germany* 24 B8
Reutlingen, *Germany* 25 G5
Reutte, *Austria* 26 D3
Reval = Tallinn, *Estonia* 9 G21
Revel, *France* 20 E6
Revelganj, *India* 69 G11
Revelstoke, *Canada* 104 C5
Reventazón, *Peru* 124 E2
Revigny-sur-Ornain, *France* 19 D11
Revillagigedo, Is. de, *Pac. Oc.* 118 D2

Revin, *France* 19 C11
Revúca, *Slovak Rep.* 27 C13
Revuè →, *Mozam.* 87 F3
Rewa, *India* 69 G9
Rewari, *India* 68 E7
Rexburg, *U.S.A.* 114 E8
Rey, *Iran* 71 C6
Rey, I. del, *Panama* 120 E4
Rey, Rio del →, *Nigeria* 83 E6
Rey Malabo, *Eq. Guin.* 83 E6
Reyðarfjörður, *Iceland* 8 D6
Reyes, Pt., *U.S.A.* 116 H3
Reyhanlı, *Turkey* 72 D7
Reykjahlið, *Iceland* 8 D5
Reykjanes, *Iceland* 8 E2
Reykjavík, *Iceland* 8 D3
Reynolds Ra., *Australia* 92 D5
Reynoldsville, *U.S.A.* 110 E6
Reynosa, *Mexico* 119 B5
Rēzekne, *Latvia* 9 H22
Rezina, *Moldova* 43 C13
Rezovo, *Bulgaria* 41 D12
Rezvān, *Iran* 71 E8
Rgotina, *Serbia, Yug.* 40 B6
Rhamnus, *Greece* 38 C6
Rhayader, *U.K.* 13 E4
Rheda-Wiedenbrück, *Germany* 24 D4
Rhede, *Germany* 24 D2
Rhein →, *Europe* 17 C6
Rhein-Main-Donau-Kanal, *Germany* 25 F7
Rheinbach, *Germany* 24 E2
Rheine, *Germany* 24 C3
Rheinfelden, *Germany* 25 H3
Rheinhessen-Pfalz □, *Germany* 25 F3
Rheinland-Pfalz □, *Germany* 25 E2
Rheinsberg, *Germany* 24 B8
Rhin = Rhein →, *Europe* 17 C6
Rhine = Rhein →, *Europe* 17 C6
Rhinebeck, *U.S.A.* 111 E11
Rhineland-Palatinate = Rheinland-Pfalz □, *Germany* 25 E2
Rhinelander, *U.S.A.* 112 C10
Rhinns Pt., *U.K.* 14 F2
Rhino Camp, *Uganda* 86 B3
Rhir, Cap, *Morocco* 78 B4
Rho, *Italy* 28 C6
Rhode Island □, *U.S.A.* 111 E13
Rhodes = Ródhos, *Greece* 36 C10
Rhodesia = Zimbabwe ■, *Africa* 87 F3
Rhodope Mts. = Rhodopi Planina, *Bulgaria* 41 E8
Rhodopi Planina, *Bulgaria* 41 E8
Rhön, *Germany* 24 E5
Rhondda, *U.K.* 13 F4
Rhondda Cynon Taff □, *U.K.* 13 F4
Rhône □, *France* 21 C8
Rhône →, *France* 21 E8
Rhône-Alpes □, *France* 21 C9
Rhum, *U.K.* 14 E2
Rhyl, *U.K.* 12 D4
Ri-Aba, *Eq. Guin.* 83 E6
Riachão, *Brazil* 125 E9
Riangnom, *Sudan* 81 F3
Riaño, *Spain* 34 C6
Rians, *France* 21 E9
Riansáres →, *Spain* 35 F7
Riasi, *India* 69 C6
Riau □, *Indonesia* 62 D2
Riau, Kepulauan, *Indonesia* 62 D2
Riau Arch. = Riau, Kepulauan, *Indonesia* 62 D2
Riaza, *Spain* 34 D7
Riaza →, *Spain* 34 D7
Riba de Saelices, *Spain* 32 E2
Riba-Roja de Turia, *Spain* 33 F4
Ribadavia, *Spain* 34 C2
Ribadeo, *Spain* 34 B3
Ribadesella, *Spain* 34 B5
Ribado, *Nigeria* 83 D7
Ribao, *Cameroon* 83 D7
Ribas = Ribes de Freser, *Spain* 32 C7
Ribas do Rio Pardo, *Brazil* 125 H8
Ribble →, *U.K.* 12 D5
Ribe, *Denmark* 11 J2
Ribe Amtskommune □, *Denmark* 11 J2
Ribeauvillé, *France* 19 D14
Ribécourt-Dreslincourt, *France* 19 C9
Ribeira = Santa Uxía, *Spain* 34 C2
Ribeira Brava, *Madeira* 37 D2
Ribeirão Prêto, *Brazil* 127 A6
Ribemont, *France* 19 C10
Ribera, *Italy* 30 E6
Ribérac, *France* 20 C4
Riberalta, *Bolivia* 124 F5
Ribes de Freser, *Spain* 32 C7
Ribnica, *Slovenia* 29 C11
Ribnitz-Damgarten, *Germany* 24 A8
Říčany, *Czech Rep.* 26 B7
Riccarton, *N.Z.* 91 K4
Riccia, *Italy* 31 A7
Riccione, *Italy* 29 E9
Rice, *U.S.A.* 117 L12
Rice L., *Canada* 110 B6
Rice Lake, *U.S.A.* 112 C9
Rich, C., *Canada* 110 B4
Richard Toll, *Senegal* 82 B1
Richards Bay, *S. Africa* 89 D5
Richardson →, *Canada* 105 B6
Richardson Lakes, *U.S.A.* 108 C10
Richardson Springs, *U.S.A.* 116 F5
Riche, C., *Australia* 93 F2
Richelieu, *France* 18 E7
Richey, *U.S.A.* 112 B2
Richfield, *U.S.A.* 115 G8
Richfield Springs, *U.S.A.* 111 D10
Richford, *U.S.A.* 111 B12
Richibucto, *Canada* 103 C7
Richland, *Ga., U.S.A.* 109 J3
Richland, *Wash., U.S.A.* 114 C4
Richland Center, *U.S.A.* 112 D9
Richlands, *U.S.A.* 108 G5
Richmond, *Australia* 94 C3
Richmond, *N.Z.* 91 J4
Richmond, *U.K.* 12 C6
Richmond, *Calif., U.S.A.* 116 H4
Richmond, *Ind., U.S.A.* 108 F3
Richmond, *Ky., U.S.A.* 108 G3
Richmond, *Mich., U.S.A.* 110 D2
Richmond, *Mo., U.S.A.* 112 F8
Richmond, *Tex., U.S.A.* 113 L7
Richmond, *Utah, U.S.A.* 114 F8
Richmond, *Va., U.S.A.* 108 G7
Richmond, *Vt., U.S.A.* 111 B12
Richmond Hill, *Canada* 110 C5
Richmond Ra., *Australia* 95 D5
Richwood, *U.S.A.* 108 F5
Ricla, *Spain* 32 D3
Ridder = Leninogorsk, *Kazakstan* 50 D9
Riddlesburg, *U.S.A.* 110 F6
Ridgecrest, *U.S.A.* 117 K9
Ridgefield, *Conn., U.S.A.* 111 E11
Ridgefield, *Wash., U.S.A.* 116 E4
Ridgeland, *U.S.A.* 109 J5
Ridgetown, *Canada* 102 D3
Ridgewood, *U.S.A.* 111 F10
Ridgway, *U.S.A.* 110 E6
Riding Mountain Nat. Park, *Canada* 105 C9
Ridley, Mt., *Australia* 93 F3
Riebeek-Oos, *S. Africa* 88 E4
Ried, *Austria* 26 C6
Riedlingen, *Germany* 25 G5
Riedstadt, *Germany* 25 F4
Rienza →, *Italy* 29 B8
Riesa, *Germany* 24 D9
Riesi, *Italy* 31 E7
Riet →, *S. Africa* 88 D3
Rietavas, *Lithuania* 44 C8
Rietbron, *S. Africa* 88 E3
Rietfontein, *Namibia* 88 C3
Rieti, *Italy* 29 F9
Rieupeyroux, *France* 20 D6
Riez, *France* 21 E10
Riffe L., *U.S.A.* 116 D4
Rifle, *U.S.A.* 114 G10
Rift Valley □, *Kenya* 86 B4
Rīga, *Latvia* 9 H21
Riga, G. of, *Latvia* 9 H20
Rigacikun, *Nigeria* 83 C6
Rīgān, *Iran* 71 D8
Rīgas Jūras Līcis = Riga, G. of, *Latvia* 9 H20
Rigaud, *Canada* 111 A10
Rigby, *U.S.A.* 114 E8
Rīgestān □, *Afghan.* 66 D4
Riggins, *U.S.A.* 114 D5
Rignac, *France* 20 D6
Rigolet, *Canada* 103 B8
Rihand Dam, *India* 69 G10
Riihimäki, *Finland* 9 F21
Riiser-Larsen-halvøya, *Antarctica* 5 C4
Rijau, *Nigeria* 83 C6
Rijeka, *Croatia* 29 C11
Rijeka Crnojevića, *Montenegro, Yug.* 40 D3
Rijssen, *Neths.* 17 B6
Rike, *Ethiopia* 81 E4
Rikuzentakada, *Japan* 54 E10
Rila, *Bulgaria* 40 D7
Rila Planina, *Bulgaria* 40 D7
Riley, *U.S.A.* 114 E4
Rima →, *Nigeria* 83 C6
Rimah, Wadi ar →, *Si. Arabia* 70 E4
Rimavská Sobota, *Slovak Rep.* 27 C13
Rimbey, *Canada* 104 C6
Rimbo, *Sweden* 10 E12
Rimersburg, *U.S.A.* 110 E5
Rimforsa, *Sweden* 11 F9
Rimi, *Nigeria* 83 C6
Rímini, *Italy* 29 D9
Rimouski, *Canada* 103 C6
Rimrock, *U.S.A.* 116 D5
Rinca, *Indonesia* 63 F5
Rincón de la Victoria, *Spain* 35 J6
Rincón de Romos, *Mexico* 118 C4
Rinconada, *Argentina* 126 A2
Rind →, *India* 69 G9
Ringarum, *Sweden* 11 F10
Ringas, *India* 68 F6
Ringe, *Denmark* 11 J4
Ringim, *Nigeria* 83 C6
Ringkøbing, *Denmark* 11 H2
Ringkøbing Amtskommune □, *Denmark* 11 H2
Ringkøbing Fjord, *Denmark* 11 H2
Ringsjön, *Sweden* 11 J7
Ringsted, *Denmark* 11 J5
Ringvassøy, *Norway* 8 B18
Ringwood, *U.S.A.* 111 E10
Rinía, *Greece* 39 D7
Rinjani, *Indonesia* 62 F5
Rinteln, *Germany* 24 C5
Río, Punta del, *Spain* 33 J2
Rio Branco, *Brazil* 124 E5
Río Branco, *Uruguay* 127 C5
Río Bravo del Norte →, *Mexico* 119 B5
Rio Brilhante, *Brazil* 127 A5
Rio Claro, *Brazil* 127 A6
Rio Claro, *Trin. & Tob.* 121 D7
Río Colorado, *Argentina* 128 D4
Río Cuarto, *Argentina* 126 C3
Rio das Pedras, *Mozam.* 89 C6
Rio de Janeiro, *Brazil* 127 A7
Rio de Janeiro □, *Brazil* 127 A7
Rio do Sul, *Brazil* 127 B6
Río Gallegos, *Argentina* 128 G3
Rio Grande = Grande, Rio →, *U.S.A.* 113 N6
Río Grande, *Argentina* 128 G3
Rio Grande, *Brazil* 127 C5
Río Grande, *Mexico* 118 C4
Río Grande, *Nic.* 120 D3
Rio Grande City, *U.S.A.* 113 M5
Río Grande de Santiago →, *Mexico* 118 C3
Rio Grande do Norte □, *Brazil* 125 E11
Rio Grande do Sul □, *Brazil* 127 C5
Río Hato, *Panama* 120 E3
Rio Lagartos, *Mexico* 119 C7
Rio Largo, *Brazil* 125 E11
Rio Maior, *Portugal* 35 F2
Rio Marina, *Italy* 28 F7
Río Mulatos, *Bolivia* 124 G5
Río Muni = Mbini □, *Eq. Guin.* 84 D2
Rio Negro, *Brazil* 127 B6
Rio Pardo, *Brazil* 127 C5
Rio Rancho, *U.S.A.* 115 J10
Río Segundo, *Argentina* 126 C3
Río Tercero, *Argentina* 126 C3
Rio Tinto, *Portugal* 34 D2
Rio Verde, *Brazil* 125 G8
Río Verde, *Mexico* 119 C5
Rio Vista, *U.S.A.* 116 G5
Ríobamba, *Ecuador* 124 D3
Ríohacha, *Colombia* 124 A4
Riom, *France* 20 C7
Riom-ès-Montagnes, *France* 20 C6
Rion-des-Landes, *France* 20 E3
Rionero in Vúlture, *Italy* 31 B8
Rioni →, *Georgia* 49 J5
Riós, *Spain* 34 D3
Ríosucio, *Colombia* 124 B3
Riou L., *Canada* 105 B7
Rioz, *France* 19 E13
Ripatransone, *Italy* 29 F10
Ripley, *Canada* 110 B3
Ripley, *Calif., U.S.A.* 117 M12
Ripley, *N.Y., U.S.A.* 110 D5
Ripley, *Tenn., U.S.A.* 113 H10
Ripley, *W. Va., U.S.A.* 108 F5
Ripoll, *Spain* 32 C7
Ripon, *U.K.* 12 C6
Ripon, *Calif., U.S.A.* 116 H5
Ripon, *Wis., U.S.A.* 108 D1
Riposto, *Italy* 31 E8
Risan, *Montenegro, Yug.* 40 D2
Riscle, *France* 20 E3
Rishā', W. ar →, *Si. Arabia* 70 E5
Rishiri-Tō, *Japan* 54 B10
Rishon le Ziyyon, *Israel* 75 D3
Risle →, *France* 18 C7
Rison, *U.S.A.* 113 J8
Risør, *Norway* 9 G13
Rita Blanca Cr. →, *U.S.A.* 113 H3
Riti, *Nigeria* 83 D6
Ritter, Mt., *U.S.A.* 116 H7
Rittman, *U.S.A.* 110 F3
Ritzville, *U.S.A.* 114 C4
Riva del Garda, *Italy* 28 C7
Riva Lígure, *Italy* 28 E4
Rivadavia, *Buenos Aires, Argentina* 126 D3
Rivadavia, *Mendoza, Argentina* 126 C2
Rivadavia, *Salta, Argentina* 126 A3
Rivadavia, *Chile* 126 B1
Rivarolo Canavese, *Italy* 28 C4
Rivas, *Nic.* 120 D2
Rive-de-Gier, *France* 21 C8
River Cess, *Liberia* 82 D3
River Jordan, *Canada* 116 B2
Rivera, *Argentina* 126 D3
Rivera, *Uruguay* 127 C4
Riverbank, *U.S.A.* 116 H6
Riverdale, *U.S.A.* 116 J7
Riverhead, *U.S.A.* 111 F12
Riverhurst, *Canada* 105 C7
Rivers, *Canada* 105 C8
Rivers □, *Nigeria* 83 E6
Rivers Inlet, *Canada* 104 C3
Riversdale, *S. Africa* 88 E3
Riverside, *U.S.A.* 117 M9
Riverton, *Australia* 95 E2
Riverton, *Canada* 105 C9
Riverton, *N.Z.* 91 M2
Riverton, *U.S.A.* 114 E9
Riverton Heights, *U.S.A.* 116 C4
Rives, *France* 21 C9
Rivesaltes, *France* 20 F6
Riviera, *U.S.A.* 117 K12
Riviera di Levante, *Italy* 28 D6
Riviera di Ponente, *Italy* 28 D5
Rivière-au-Renard, *Canada* 103 C7
Rivière-du-Loup, *Canada* 103 C6
Rivière-Pentecôte, *Canada* 103 C6
Rivière-Pilote, *Martinique* 121 D7
Rivière St. Paul, *Canada* 103 B8
Rivne, *Ukraine* 47 G4
Rívoli, *Italy* 28 C4
Rivoli B., *Australia* 95 F3
Rixheim, *France* 19 E14
Riyadh = Ar Riyāḍ, *Si. Arabia* 70 E5
Rize, *Turkey* 73 B9
Rizhao, *China* 57 G10
Rizokarpaso, *Cyprus* 36 D13
Rizzuto, C., *Italy* 31 D10
Rjukan, *Norway* 9 G13
Ro, *Greece* 39 E11
Roa, *Spain* 34 D7
Road Town, *Virgin Is.* 121 C7
Roan Plateau, *U.S.A.* 114 G9
Roanne, *France* 19 F11
Roanoke, *Ala., U.S.A.* 109 J3
Roanoke, *Va., U.S.A.* 108 G6
Roanoke →, *U.S.A.* 109 H7
Roanoke I., *U.S.A.* 109 H8
Roanoke Rapids, *U.S.A.* 109 G7
Roatán, *Honduras* 120 C2
Robāt Sang, *Iran* 71 C8
Robbins I., *Australia* 94 G4
Róbbio, *Italy* 28 C5
Robe, *Australia* 95 F2
Robe →, *Australia* 92 D2
Röbel, *Germany* 24 B8
Robert Lee, *U.S.A.* 113 K4
Robertsdale, *U.S.A.* 110 F6
Robertsganj, *India* 69 G10
Robertson, *S. Africa* 88 E2
Robertson I., *Antarctica* 5 C18
Robertson Ra., *Australia* 92 D3
Robertsport, *Liberia* 82 D2
Robertstown, *Australia* 95 E2
Roberval, *Canada* 103 C5
Robeson Chan., *Greenland* 4 A4
Robesonia, *U.S.A.* 111 F8
Robi, *Ethiopia* 81 F4
Robinson, *U.S.A.* 108 F2
Robinson →, *Australia* 94 B2
Robinson Ra., *Australia* 93 E2
Robinvale, *Australia* 95 E3
Robledo, *Spain* 33 G2
Roblin, *Canada* 105 C8
Roboré, *Bolivia* 124 G7
Robson, *Canada* 104 D5
Robson, Mt., *Canada* 104 C5
Robstown, *U.S.A.* 113 M6
Roca, C. da, *Portugal* 35 G1
Roca Partida, I., *Mexico* 118 D2
Rocamadour, *France* 20 D5
Rocas, I., *Brazil* 125 D12
Rocca San Casciano, *Italy* 29 D8
Roccadáspide, *Italy* 31 B8
Roccastrada, *Italy* 29 F8
Roccella Iónica, *Italy* 31 D9
Rocha, *Uruguay* 127 C5
Rochdale, *U.K.* 12 D5
Rochechouart, *France* 20 C4
Rochefort, *Belgium* 17 D5
Rochefort, *France* 20 C3
Rochefort-en-Terre, *France* 18 E4
Rochelle, *U.S.A.* 112 E10
Rocher River, *Canada* 104 A6
Rocheservière, *France* 18 F5
Rochester, *U.K.* 13 F8
Rochester, *Ind., U.S.A.* 108 E2
Rochester, *Minn., U.S.A.* 112 C8
Rochester, *N.H., U.S.A.* 111 C14
Rochester, *N.Y., U.S.A.* 110 C7
Rociu, *Romania* 43 F10
Rock →, *Canada* 104 A3
Rock Creek, *U.S.A.* 110 E4
Rock Falls, *U.S.A.* 112 E10
Rock Hill, *U.S.A.* 109 H5
Rock Island, *U.S.A.* 112 E9
Rock Rapids, *U.S.A.* 112 D6
Rock Sound, *Bahamas* 120 B4
Rock Springs, *Mont., U.S.A.* 114 C10
Rock Springs, *Wyo., U.S.A.* 114 F9
Rock Valley, *U.S.A.* 112 D6
Rockall, *Atl. Oc.* 6 D3
Rockdale, *Tex., U.S.A.* 113 K6
Rockdale, *Wash., U.S.A.* 116 C5
Rockefeller Plateau, *Antarctica* 5 E14
Rockford, *U.S.A.* 112 D10
Rockglen, *Canada* 105 D7
Rockhampton, *Australia* 94 C5
Rockingham, *Australia* 93 F2
Rockingham, *U.S.A.* 109 H6
Rockingham B., *Australia* 94 B4
Rocklake, *U.S.A.* 112 A5
Rockland, *Canada* 111 A9
Rockland, *Idaho, U.S.A.* 114 E7
Rockland, *Maine, U.S.A.* 109 C11
Rockland, *Mich., U.S.A.* 112 B10
Rocklin, *U.S.A.* 116 G5
Rockport, *Mass., U.S.A.* 111 D14
Rockport, *Mo., U.S.A.* 112 E7
Rockport, *Tex., U.S.A.* 113 L6
Rocksprings, *U.S.A.* 113 K4
Rockville, *Conn., U.S.A.* 111 E12
Rockville, *Md., U.S.A.* 108 F7
Rockwall, *U.S.A.* 113 J6
Rockwell City, *U.S.A.* 112 D7
Rockwood, *Canada* 110 C4
Rockwood, *Maine, U.S.A.* 109 C11
Rockwood, *Tenn., U.S.A.* 109 H3
Rocky Ford, *U.S.A.* 112 F3
Rocky Gully, *Australia* 93 F2
Rocky Harbour, *Canada* 103 C8
Rocky Island L., *Canada* 102 C3
Rocky Lane, *Canada* 104 B5
Rocky Mount, *U.S.A.* 109 H7
Rocky Mountain House, *Canada* 104 C6
Rocky Mountain National Park, *U.S.A.* 114 F11
Rocky Mts., *N. Amer.* 114 G10
Rocky Point, *Namibia* 88 B2
Rocroi, *France* 19 C11
Rod, *Pakistan* 66 E3
Rødby, *Denmark* 11 K5
Rødbyhavn, *Denmark* 11 K5
Roddickton, *Canada* 103 B8
Rødding, *Denmark* 11 J3
Rödeby, *Sweden* 11 H9
Rødekro, *Denmark* 11 J3
Rodenkirchen, *Germany* 24 B4
Rodez, *France* 20 D6
Rodholívas, *Greece* 40 F7
Rodhópi □, *Greece* 41 E9
Rodhopoú, *Greece* 36 D5
Ródhos, *Greece* 36 C10
Rodi Gargánico, *Italy* 29 G12
Rodna, *Romania* 43 C9
Rodnei, Munţii, *Romania* 43 C9
Rodney, *Canada* 110 D3
Rodney, C., *N.Z.* 91 G5
Rodniki, *Russia* 48 B5
Rodonit, Kepi i, *Albania* 40 E3
Rodriguez, *Ind. Oc.* 3 E13
Roe →, *U.K.* 15 A5
Roebling, *U.S.A.* 111 F10
Roebourne, *Australia* 92 D2
Roebuck B., *Australia* 92 C3
Roermond, *Neths.* 17 C6
Roes Welcome Sd., *Canada* 101 B11
Roeselare, *Belgium* 17 D3
Rogachev = Ragachow, *Belarus* 47 F6
Rogačica, *Serbia, Yug.* 40 B3
Rogagua, L., *Bolivia* 124 F5
Rogaška Slatina, *Slovenia* 29 B12
Rogatec, *Slovenia* 29 B12
Rogatica, *Bos.-H.* 42 G4
Rogatyn, *Ukraine* 47 H3
Rogdhia, *Greece* 36 D7
Rogers, *U.S.A.* 113 G7
Rogers City, *U.S.A.* 108 C4
Rogersville, *Canada* 103 C6
Roggan →, *Canada* 102 B4
Roggan L., *Canada* 102 B4
Roggeveldberge, *S. Africa* 88 E3
Roggiano Gravina, *Italy* 31 C9
Rogliano, *France* 21 F13
Rogliano, *Italy* 31 C9
Rogoaguado, L., *Bolivia* 124 F5
Rogoźno, *Poland* 45 F3
Rogue →, *U.S.A.* 114 E1
Rohan, *France* 18 D4
Róhda, *Greece* 36 A3
Rohnert Park, *U.S.A.* 116 G4
Rohri, *Pakistan* 68 F3
Rohri Canal, *Pakistan* 68 F3
Rohtak, *India* 68 E7
Roi Et, *Thailand* 64 D4
Roja, *Latvia* 9 H20
Rojas, *Argentina* 126 C3
Rojişte, *Romania* 43 F8
Rojo, C., *Mexico* 119 C5
Rokan →, *Indonesia* 62 D2
Rokel →, *S. Leone* 82 D2
Rokiškis, *Lithuania* 9 J21
Rokitno, *Russia* 47 G8
Rokycany, *Czech Rep.* 26 B6
Rolândia, *Brazil* 127 A5
Rolla, *U.S.A.* 113 G9
Rolleston, *Australia* 94 C4
Rollingstone, *Australia* 94 B4
Rom, *Sudan* 81 F3
Roma, *Australia* 95 D4
Roma, *Italy* 29 G9
Roma, *Sweden* 11 G12
Roma, *U.S.A.* 113 M5
Romain C., *U.S.A.* 109 J6
Romaine, *Canada* 103 B7
Romaine →, *Canada* 103 B7
Roman, *Bulgaria* 40 C7
Roman, *Romania* 43 D11
Roman-Kosh, Gora, *Ukraine* 47 K8
Romanche →, *France* 21 C9
Romang, *Indonesia* 63 F7
Români, *Egypt* 75 E1
Romania ■, *Europe* 43 D10
Romanija, *Bos.-H.* 42 G3
Romano, Cayo, *Cuba* 120 B4
Romanovka = Basarabeasca, *Moldova* 43 D13
Romans-sur-Isère, *France* 21 C9
Romanshorn, *Switz.* 25 H5
Rombari, *Sudan* 81 G3
Romblon, *Phil.* 61 E5
Rome = Roma, *Italy* 29 G9
Rome, *Ga., U.S.A.* 109 H3
Rome, *N.Y., U.S.A.* 111 C9
Rome, *Pa., U.S.A.* 111 E8
Rometta, *Italy* 31 D8
Romilly-sur-Seine, *France* 19 D10
Romney, *U.S.A.* 108 F6
Romney Marsh, *U.K.* 13 F8
Romny, *Ukraine* 47 G7
Rømø, *Denmark* 11 J2
Romodan, *Ukraine* 47 G7
Romodanovo, *Russia* 48 C7
Romont, *Switz.* 25 J2
Romorantin-Lanthenay, *France* 19 E8
Romsdalen, *Norway* 9 E12
Romsey, *U.K.* 13 G6
Ron, *Vietnam* 64 D6
Rona, *U.K.* 14 D3
Ronan, *U.S.A.* 114 C6
Roncador, Cayos, *Caribbean* 120 D3
Roncador, Serra do, *Brazil* 125 F8
Ronciglione, *Italy* 29 F9
Ronco →, *Italy* 29 D9
Ronda, *Spain* 35 J5
Ronda, Serranía de, *Spain* 35 J5
Rondane, *Norway* 9 F13
Rondônia □, *Brazil* 124 F6
Rondonópolis, *Brazil* 125 G8
Rong, Koh, *Cambodia* 65 G4
Rong Jiang →, *China* 58 E7
Rong Xian, *Guangxi Zhuangzu, China* 59 F8
Rong Xian, *Sichuan, China* 58 C5

Rong'an, *China* 58 E7
Rongchang, *China* 58 C5
Ronge, L. la, *Canada* 105 B7
Rongjiang, *China* 58 E7
Rongshui, *China* 58 E7
Rønne, *Denmark* 11 J8
Ronne Ice Shelf, *Antarctica* 5 D18
Ronneby, *Sweden* 11 H9
Ronnebyån →, *Sweden* 11 H9
Rönneshytta, *Sweden* 11 F9
Ronsard, C., *Australia* 93 D1
Ronse, *Belgium* 17 D3
Roodepoort, *S. Africa* 89 D4
Roof Butte, *U.S.A.* 115 H9
Rooiboklaagte →, *Namibia* 88 C3
Roorkee, *India* 68 E7
Roosendaal, *Neths.* 17 C4
Roosevelt, *U.S.A.* 114 F8
Roosevelt →, *Brazil* 122 D4
Roosevelt, Mt., *Canada* 104 B3
Roosevelt I., *Antarctica* 5 D12
Ropczyce, *Poland* 45 H8
Roper →, *Australia* 94 A2
Roper Bar, *Australia* 94 A1
Roque Pérez, *Argentina* 126 D4
Roquefort, *France* 20 D3
Roquemaure, *France* 21 D8
Roquetas de Mar, *Spain* 33 J2
Roquetes, *Spain* 32 E5
Roquevaire, *France* 21 E9
Roraima □, *Brazil* 124 C6
Roraima, Mt., *Venezuela* 122 C4
Røros, *Norway* 9 E14
Rorschach, *Switz.* 25 H5
Rosa, *Zambia* 87 D3
Rosa, L., *Bahamas* 121 B5
Rosa, Monte, *Italy* 28 C4
Rosal de la Frontera, *Spain* 35 H3
Rosalia, *U.S.A.* 114 C5
Rosamond, *U.S.A.* 117 L8
Rosans, *France* 21 D9
Rosario, *Argentina* 126 C3
Rosário, *Brazil* 125 D10
Rosario, *Baja Calif., Mexico* 118 B1
Rosario, *Sinaloa, Mexico* 118 C3
Rosario, *Paraguay* 126 A4
Rosario de la Frontera, *Argentina* 126 B3
Rosario de Lerma, *Argentina* 126 A2
Rosario del Tala, *Argentina* 126 C4
Rosário do Sul, *Brazil* 127 C5
Rosarito, *Mexico* 117 N9
Rosarno, *Italy* 31 D8
Rosas = Roses, *Spain* 32 C8
Roscoe, *U.S.A.* 111 E10
Roscoff, *France* 18 D3
Roscommon, *Ireland* 15 C3
Roscommon □, *Ireland* 15 C3
Roscrea, *Ireland* 15 D4
Rose →, *Australia* 94 A2
Rose Blanche, *Canada* 103 C8
Rose Pt., *Canada* 104 C2
Rose Valley, *Canada* 105 C8
Roseau, *Domin.* 121 C7
Roseau, *U.S.A.* 112 A7
Rosebery, *Australia* 94 G4
Rosebud, *S. Dak., U.S.A.* 112 D4
Rosebud, *Tex., U.S.A.* 113 K6
Roseburg, *U.S.A.* 114 E2
Rosedale, *U.S.A.* 113 J9
Roseland, *U.S.A.* 116 G4
Rosemary, *Canada* 104 C6
Rosenberg, *U.S.A.* 113 L7
Rosendaël, *France* 19 A9
Rosenheim, *Germany* 25 H8
Roses, *Spain* 32 C8
Roses, G. de, *Spain* 32 C8
Roseto degli Abruzzi, *Italy* 29 F11
Rosetown, *Canada* 105 C7
Rosetta = Rashîd, *Egypt* 80 H7
Roseville, *Calif., U.S.A.* 116 G5
Roseville, *Mich., U.S.A.* 110 D2
Rosewood, *Australia* 95 D5
Roshkhvār, *Iran* 71 C8
Rosières-en-Santerre, *France* 19 C9
Rosignano Maríttimo, *Italy* 28 E7
Rosignol, *Guyana* 124 B7
Roşiori de Vede, *Romania* 43 F10
Rositsa, *Bulgaria* 41 C11
Rositsa →, *Bulgaria* 41 C9
Roskilde, *Denmark* 11 J6
Roskilde Amtskommune □, *Denmark* 11 J6
Roskovec, *Albania* 40 F3
Roslavl, *Russia* 46 F7
Rosmaninhal, *Portugal* 34 F3
Rosmead, *S. Africa* 88 E4
Røsnæs, *Denmark* 11 J4
Rosolini, *Italy* 31 F7
Rosporden, *France* 18 E3
Ross, *Australia* 94 G4
Ross, *N.Z.* 91 K3
Ross Béthio, *Mauritania* 82 B1
Ross I., *Antarctica* 5 D11
Ross Ice Shelf, *Antarctica* 5 E12
Ross L., *U.S.A.* 114 B3
Ross-on-Wye, *U.K.* 13 F5
Ross River, *Australia* 94 C1
Ross River, *Canada* 104 A2
Ross Sea, *Antarctica* 5 D11
Rossall Pt., *U.K.* 12 D4
Rossan Pt., *Ireland* 15 B3
Rossano, *Italy* 31 C9
Rossburn, *Canada* 105 C8
Rosseau, *Canada* 110 A5
Rosseau L., *Canada* 110 A5
Rosses, The, *Ireland* 15 A3
Rossignol, L., *Canada* 102 D6
Rossignol Res., *Canada* 103 D6
Rossland, *Canada* 104 D5
Rosslare, *Ireland* 15 D5
Rosslau, *Germany* 24 D8
Rosso, *Mauritania* 82 B1
Rosso, C., *France* 21 F12
Rossosh, *Russia* 47 G10
Røssvatnet, *Norway* 8 D16
Røst, *Norway* 8 C15
Rosthern, *Canada* 105 C7
Rostock, *Germany* 24 A8
Rostov, *Don, Russia* 47 J10
Rostov, *Yaroslavl, Russia* 46 D10
Rostrenen, *France* 18 D3
Roswell, *Ga., U.S.A.* 109 H3
Roswell, *N. Mex., U.S.A.* 113 J2
Rota, *Spain* 35 J4
Rotan, *U.S.A.* 113 J4
Rotenburg, *Hessen, Germany* 24 E5
Rotenburg, *Niedersachsen, Germany* 24 B5
Roth, *Germany* 25 F7
Rothaargebirge, *Germany* 24 D4
Rothenburg ob der Tauber, *Germany* 25 F6
Rother →, *U.K.* 13 G8
Rotherham, *U.K.* 12 D6
Rothes, *U.K.* 14 D5
Rothesay, *Canada* 103 C6
Rothesay, *U.K.* 14 F3
Roti, *Indonesia* 63 F6
Rotja, Pta., *Spain* 33 G6
Roto, *Australia* 95 E4
Rotoroa, L., *N.Z.* 91 J4
Rotorua, *N.Z.* 91 H6
Rotorua, L., *N.Z.* 91 H6
Rott →, *Germany* 25 G9
Rottenburg, *Germany* 25 G4
Rottenmann, *Austria* 26 D7
Rotterdam, *Neths.* 17 C4
Rotterdam, *U.S.A.* 111 D10
Rottne, *Sweden* 11 G8
Rottnest I., *Australia* 93 F2
Rottumeroog, *Neths.* 17 A6
Rottweil, *Germany* 25 G4
Rotuma, *Fiji* 96 J9
Roubaix, *France* 19 B10
Roudnice nad Labem, *Czech Rep.* 26 A7
Rouen, *France* 18 C8
Rouergue, *France* 20 D5
Rouillac, *France* 20 C3
Rouleau, *Canada* 105 C8
Round Mountain, *U.S.A.* 114 G5
Round Mt., *Australia* 95 E5
Round Rock, *U.S.A.* 113 K6
Roundup, *U.S.A.* 114 C9
Rousay, *U.K.* 14 B5
Rouses Point, *U.S.A.* 111 B11
Rouseville, *U.S.A.* 110 E5
Roussillon, *Isère, France* 21 C8
Roussillon, *Pyrénées-Or., France* 20 F6
Rouxville, *S. Africa* 88 E4
Rouyn-Noranda, *Canada* 102 C4
Rovaniemi, *Finland* 8 C21
Rovato, *Italy* 28 C7
Rovenki, *Ukraine* 47 H10
Rovereto, *Italy* 28 C8
Rovigo, *Italy* 29 C8
Rovinj, *Croatia* 29 C10
Rovno = Rivne, *Ukraine* 47 G4
Rovnoye, *Russia* 48 E8
Rovuma = Ruvuma →, *Tanzania* 87 E5
Row'ān, *Iran* 71 C6
Rowena, *Australia* 95 D4
Rowley Shoals, *Australia* 92 C2
Roxa, *Guinea-Biss.* 82 C1
Roxas, *Capiz, Phil.* 61 F5
Roxas, *Isabela, Phil.* 61 C4
Roxas, *Mind. Or., Phil.* 61 E4
Roxboro, *U.S.A.* 109 G6
Roxburgh, *N.Z.* 91 L2
Roxbury, *U.S.A.* 110 F7
Roxen, *Sweden* 11 F9
Roy, *Mont., U.S.A.* 114 C9
Roy, *N. Mex., U.S.A.* 113 H2
Roy, *Utah, U.S.A.* 114 F7
Royal Canal, *Ireland* 15 C4
Royal Leamington Spa, *U.K.* 13 E6
Royal Tunbridge Wells, *U.K.* 13 F8
Royan, *France* 20 C2
Roye, *France* 19 C9
Royston, *U.K.* 13 E7
Rožaj, *Montenegro, Yug.* 40 D4
Różan, *Poland* 45 F8
Rozay-en-Brie, *France* 19 D9
Rozdilna, *Ukraine* 47 J6
Rozhyshche, *Ukraine* 47 G3
Rožmitál pod Třemšínem, *Czech Rep.* 26 B6
Rožňava, *Slovak Rep.* 27 C13
Rozogi, *Poland* 44 E8
Rozoy-sur-Serre, *France* 19 C11
Rozzano, *Italy* 28 C6
Rrësheni, *Albania* 40 E3
Rrogozhino, *Albania* 40 E3
Rtanj, *Serbia, Yug.* 40 C5
Rtishchevo, *Russia* 48 D6
Rúa = A Rúa, *Spain* 34 C3
Ruacaná, *Angola* 88 B1
Ruahine Ra., *N.Z.* 91 H6
Ruapehu, *N.Z.* 91 H5
Ruapuke I., *N.Z.* 91 M2
Ruâq, W. →, *Egypt* 75 F2
Rub' al Khālī, *Si. Arabia* 74 D4
Rubeho Mts., *Tanzania* 86 D4
Rubezhnoye = Rubizhne, *Ukraine* 47 H10
Rubh a' Mhail, *U.K.* 14 F2
Rubha Hunish, *U.K.* 14 D2
Rubha Robhanais = Lewis, Butt of, *U.K.* 14 C2
Rubi, *Spain* 32 D7
Rubicon →, *U.S.A.* 116 G5
Rubicone →, *Italy* 29 D9
Rubik, *Albania* 40 E3
Rubino, *Ivory C.* 82 D4
Rubio, *Venezuela* 124 B4
Rubizhne, *Ukraine* 47 H10
Rubtsovsk, *Russia* 50 D9
Ruby L., *U.S.A.* 114 F6
Ruby Mts., *U.S.A.* 114 F6
Rubyvale, *Australia* 94 C4
Rucheng, *China* 59 E9
Ruciane-Nida, *Poland* 44 E8
Rūd Sar, *Iran* 71 B6
Ruda, *Sweden* 11 G10
Ruda Śląska, *Poland* 45 H5
Rudall, *Australia* 95 E2
Rudall →, *Australia* 92 D3
Rüdersdorf, *Germany* 24 C9
Rudewa, *Tanzania* 87 E3
Rudkøbing, *Denmark* 11 K4
Rudna, *Poland* 45 G3
Rudnik, *Bulgaria* 41 D11
Rudnik, *Poland* 45 H9
Rudnik, *Serbia, Yug.* 40 B4
Rudnya, *Russia* 46 E6
Rudnyy, *Kazakstan* 50 D7
Rudo, *Bos.-H.* 42 G4
Rudolfa, Ostrov, *Russia* 50 A6
Rudolstadt, *Germany* 24 E7
Rudong, *China* 59 A13
Rudozem, *Bulgaria* 41 E8
Rudyard, *U.S.A.* 108 B3
Rue, *France* 19 B8
Rufa'a, *Sudan* 81 E3
Rufiji →, *Tanzania* 86 D4
Rufino, *Argentina* 126 C3
Rufisque, *Senegal* 82 C1
Rufunsa, *Zambia* 87 F2
Rugao, *China* 59 A13
Rugby, *U.K.* 13 E6
Rugby, *U.S.A.* 112 A5
Rügen, *Germany* 24 A9
Rugles, *France* 18 D7
Ruhengeri, *Rwanda* 86 C2
Ruhla, *Germany* 24 E6
Ruhland, *Germany* 24 D9
Ruhnu, *Estonia* 9 H20
Ruhr →, *Germany* 24 D2
Ruhuhu →, *Tanzania* 87 E3
Rui'an, *China* 59 D13
Ruichang, *China* 59 C10
Ruidoso, *U.S.A.* 115 K11
Ruijin, *China* 59 E10
Ruili, *China* 58 E1
Ruivo, Pico, *Madeira* 37 D3
Ruj, *Bulgaria* 40 D6
Rujen, *Macedonia* 40 D6
Rujm Tal'at al Jamā'ah, *Jordan* 75 E4
Ruk, *Pakistan* 68 F3
Rukhla, *Pakistan* 68 C4
Ruki →, *Dem. Rep. of the Congo* 84 E3
Rukwa □, *Tanzania* 86 D3
Rukwa, L., *Tanzania* 86 D3
Rulhieres, C., *Australia* 92 B4
Rum = Rhum, *U.K.* 14 E2
Rum Cay, *Bahamas* 121 B5
Rum Jungle, *Australia* 92 B5
Ruma, *Serbia, Yug.* 42 E4
Rumāḥ, *Si. Arabia* 70 E5
Rumania = Romania ■, *Europe* 43 D10
Rumaylah, *Iraq* 70 D5
Rumbêk, *Sudan* 81 F2
Rumburk, *Czech Rep.* 26 A7
Rumford, *U.S.A.* 109 C10
Rumia, *Poland* 44 D5
Rumilly, *France* 21 C9
Rumoi, *Japan* 54 C10
Rumonge, *Burundi* 86 C2
Rumson, *U.S.A.* 111 F11
Rumuruti, *Kenya* 86 B4
Runan, *China* 56 H8
Runanga, *N.Z.* 91 K3
Runaway, C., *N.Z.* 91 G6
Runcorn, *U.K.* 12 D5
Rundu, *Namibia* 88 B2
Rungwa, *Tanzania* 86 D3
Rungwa →, *Tanzania* 86 D3
Rungwe, *Tanzania* 87 D3
Rungwe, Mt., *Tanzania* 84 F6
Runka, *Nigeria* 83 C6
Runn, *Sweden* 10 D9
Runton Ra., *Australia* 92 D3
Ruokolahti, *Finland* 46 B5
Ruoqiang, *China* 60 C3
Rupa, *India* 67 F18
Rupar, *India* 68 D7
Rupat, *Indonesia* 62 D2
Rupea, *Romania* 43 D10
Rupen →, *India* 68 H4
Rupert, *U.S.A.* 114 E7
Rupert →, *Canada* 102 B4
Rupert B., *Canada* 102 B4
Rupert House = Waskaganish, *Canada* 102 B4
Rupsa, *India* 69 J12
Rur →, *Germany* 24 D1
Rurrenabaque, *Bolivia* 124 F5
Rus →, *Spain* 33 F2
Rusambo, *Zimbabwe* 87 F3
Rusape, *Zimbabwe* 87 F3
Ruschuk = Ruse, *Bulgaria* 41 C9
Ruse, *Bulgaria* 41 C9
Ruse □, *Bulgaria* 41 C10
Ruşeţu, *Romania* 43 F12
Rush, *Ireland* 15 C5
Rushan, *China* 57 F11
Rushden, *U.K.* 13 E7
Rushmore, Mt., *U.S.A.* 112 D3
Rushville, *Ill., U.S.A.* 112 E9
Rushville, *Ind., U.S.A.* 108 F3
Rushville, *Nebr., U.S.A.* 112 D3
Russas, *Brazil* 125 D11
Russell, *Canada* 105 C8
Russell, *Kans., U.S.A.* 112 F5
Russell, *N.Y., U.S.A.* 111 B9
Russell, *Pa., U.S.A.* 110 E5
Russell L., *Man., Canada* 105 B8
Russell L., *N.W.T., Canada* 104 A5
Russellkonda, *India* 67 K14
Russellville, *Ala., U.S.A.* 109 H2
Russellville, *Ark., U.S.A.* 113 H8
Russellville, *Ky., U.S.A.* 109 G2
Rüsselsheim, *Germany* 25 F4
Russi, *Italy* 29 D9
Russia ■, *Eurasia* 51 C11
Russian →, *U.S.A.* 116 G3
Russkoye Ustie, *Russia* 4 B15
Rust, *Austria* 27 D9
Rustam, *Pakistan* 68 B5
Rustam Shahr, *Pakistan* 68 F2
Rustavi, *Georgia* 49 K7
Rustenburg, *S. Africa* 88 D4
Ruston, *U.S.A.* 113 J8
Rutana, *Burundi* 86 C3
Rute, *Spain* 35 H6
Ruteng, *Indonesia* 63 F6
Ruth, *U.S.A.* 110 C2
Rutherford, *U.S.A.* 116 G4
Rutland, *U.S.A.* 111 C12
Rutland □, *U.K.* 13 E7
Rutland Water, *U.K.* 13 E7
Rutledge →, *Canada* 105 A6
Rutledge L., *Canada* 105 A6
Rutqa, W. →, *Syria* 73 E9
Rutshuru, *Dem. Rep. of the Congo* 86 C2
Ruvo di Púglia, *Italy* 31 A9
Ruvu, *Tanzania* 86 D4
Ruvu →, *Tanzania* 86 D4
Ruvuma □, *Tanzania* 87 E4
Ruvuma →, *Tanzania* 87 E5
Ruwais, *U.A.E.* 71 E7
Ruwenzori, *Africa* 86 B2
Ruya →, *Zimbabwe* 89 B5
Ruyigi, *Burundi* 86 C3
Ruyuan, *China* 59 E9
Ruzayevka, *Russia* 48 C7
Rŭzhevo Konare, *Bulgaria* 41 D8
Ružomberok, *Slovak Rep.* 27 B12
Rwanda ■, *Africa* 86 C3
Ryakhovo, *Bulgaria* 41 C10
Ryan, L., *U.K.* 14 G3
Ryazan, *Russia* 46 E10
Ryazhsk, *Russia* 46 F11
Rybache = Rybachye, *Kazakstan* 50 E9
Rybachye, *Kazakstan* 50 E9
Rybinsk, *Russia* 46 C10
Rybinskoye Vdkhr., *Russia* 46 C10
Rybnik, *Poland* 45 H5
Rybnitsa = Râbniţa, *Moldova* 43 C14
Rybnoye, *Russia* 46 E10
Rychnov nad Kněžnou, *Czech Rep.* 27 A9
Rychwał, *Poland* 45 F5
Rycroft, *Canada* 104 B5
Ryd, *Sweden* 11 H8
Rydaholm, *Sweden* 11 H8
Ryde, *U.K.* 13 G6
Ryderwood, *U.S.A.* 116 D3
Rydzyna, *Poland* 45 G3
Rye, *U.K.* 13 G8
Rye →, *U.K.* 12 C7
Rye Bay, *U.K.* 13 G8
Rye Patch Reservoir, *U.S.A.* 114 F4
Ryegate, *U.S.A.* 114 C9
Ryki, *Poland* 45 G8
Ryley, *Canada* 104 C6
Rylsk, *Russia* 47 G8
Rylstone, *Australia* 95 E4
Rymanów, *Poland* 45 J8
Ryn, *Poland* 44 E8
Ryn Peski, *Kazakstan* 49 G9
Ryōtsu, *Japan* 54 E9
Rypin, *Poland* 45 E6
Ryssby, *Sweden* 11 H8
Ryūgasaki, *Japan* 55 G10
Ryūkyū Is. = Ryūkyū-rettō, *Japan* 55 M3
Ryūkyū-rettō, *Japan* 55 M3
Rzepin, *Poland* 45 F1
Rzeszów, *Poland* 45 H8
Rzhev, *Russia* 46 D8

S

Sa, *Thailand* 64 C3
Sa Canal, *Spain* 37 C7
Sa Conillera, *Spain* 37 C7
Sa Dec, *Vietnam* 65 G5
Sa Dragonera, *Spain* 37 B9
Sa Mesquida, *Spain* 37 B11
Sa Pobla, *Spain* 32 F8
Sa Savina, *Spain* 37 C7
Sa'ādatābād, *Fārs, Iran* 71 D7
Sa'ādatābād, *Hormozgān, Iran* 71 D7
Sa'ādatābād, *Kermān, Iran* 71 D7
Saale →, *Germany* 24 D7
Saaler Bodden, *Germany* 24 A8
Saalfeld, *Germany* 24 E7
Saalfelden, *Austria* 26 D5
Saane →, *Switz.* 25 H3
Saar →, *Europe* 17 E6
Saarbrücken, *Germany* 25 F2
Saarburg, *Germany* 25 F2
Saaremaa, *Estonia* 9 G20
Saarijärvi, *Finland* 9 E21
Saariselkä, *Finland* 8 B23
Saarland □, *Germany* 25 F2
Saarlouis, *Germany* 25 F2
Sab 'Ābar, *Syria* 70 C3
Saba, *W. Indies* 121 C7
Šabac, *Serbia, Yug.* 40 B3
Sabadell, *Spain* 32 D7
Sabah □, *Malaysia* 62 C5
Sabak Bernam, *Malaysia* 65 L3
Sabalān, Kūhhā-ye, *Iran* 70 B5
Sabalana, Kepulauan, *Indonesia* 63 F5
Sábana de la Mar, *Dom. Rep.* 121 C6
Sábanalarga, *Colombia* 124 A4
Sabang, *Indonesia* 62 C1
Săbăoani, *Romania* 43 C11
Sabará, *Brazil* 125 G10
Sabarmati →, *India* 68 H5
Sabattis, *U.S.A.* 111 B10
Sabáudia, *Italy* 30 A6
Saberania, *Indonesia* 63 E9
Sabhah, *Libya* 79 C8
Sabi →, *India* 68 E7
Sabidana, J., *Sudan* 80 D4
Sabie, *S. Africa* 89 D5
Sabinal, *Mexico* 118 A3
Sabinal, *U.S.A.* 113 L5
Sabiñánigo, *Spain* 32 C4
Sabinar, Punta del, *Spain* 33 J2
Sabinas, *Mexico* 118 B4
Sabinas →, *Mexico* 118 B4
Sabinas Hidalgo, *Mexico* 118 B4
Sabine →, *U.S.A.* 113 L8
Sabine L., *U.S.A.* 113 L8
Sabine Pass, *U.S.A.* 113 L8
Sabinov, *Slovak Rep.* 27 B14
Sabinsville, *U.S.A.* 110 E7
Sabirabad, *Azerbaijan* 49 K9
Sabkhet el Bardawîl, *Egypt* 75 D2
Sablayan, *Phil.* 61 E4
Sable, *Canada* 103 A6
Sable, C., *Canada* 103 D6
Sable, C., *U.S.A.* 107 E10
Sable I., *Canada* 103 D8
Sablé-sur-Sarthe, *France* 18 E6
Sabonkafi, *Niger* 83 C6
Sabor →, *Portugal* 34 D3
Sabou, *Burkina Faso* 82 C4
Sabres, *France* 20 D3
Sabrina Coast, *Antarctica* 5 C9
Sabugal, *Portugal* 34 E3
Sabulubbek, *Indonesia* 62 E1
Sabuncu, *Turkey* 39 B12
Sabzevār, *Iran* 71 B8
Sabzvārān, *Iran* 71 D8
Sac City, *U.S.A.* 112 D7
Sacedón, *Spain* 32 E2
Săcele, *Romania* 43 E10
Sachigo →, *Canada* 102 A2
Sachigo, L., *Canada* 102 B1
Sachkhere, *Georgia* 49 J6
Sachsen □, *Germany* 24 E9
Sachsen-Anhalt □, *Germany* 24 D7
Sacile, *Italy* 29 C9
Sackets Harbor, *U.S.A.* 111 C8
Sackville, *Canada* 103 C7
Saco, *Maine, U.S.A.* 109 D10
Saco, *Mont., U.S.A.* 114 B10
Sacramento, *U.S.A.* 116 G5
Sacramento →, *U.S.A.* 116 G5
Sacramento Mts., *U.S.A.* 115 K11
Sacramento Valley, *U.S.A.* 116 G5
Sacratif, C., *Spain* 35 J7
Săcueni, *Romania* 42 C7
Sada, *Spain* 34 B2
Sada-Misaki, *Japan* 55 H6
Sádaba, *Spain* 32 C3
Sadabad, *India* 68 F8
Sadani, *Tanzania* 86 D4
Sadao, *Thailand* 65 J3
Sadd el Aali, *Egypt* 80 C3
Saddle Mt., *U.S.A.* 116 E3
Sade, *Nigeria* 83 C7
Sadimi, *Dem. Rep. of the Congo* 87 D1
Sadiola, *Mali* 82 C2
Sa'dīyah, Hawr as, *Iraq* 73 F12
Sado, *Japan* 54 F9
Sado →, *Portugal* 35 G2
Sadon, *Burma* 67 G20
Sadon, *Russia* 49 J6
Sadra, *India* 68 H5
Sadri, *India* 68 G5
Sæby, *Denmark* 11 G4
Saegertown, *U.S.A.* 110 E4
Saelices, *Spain* 32 F2
Safaalan, *Turkey* 41 E12
Safaga, *Egypt* 80 B3
Şafājah, *Si. Arabia* 70 E3
Šafárikovo = Tornal'a, *Slovak Rep.* 27 C13
Säffle, *Sweden* 10 E6
Safford, *U.S.A.* 115 K9
Saffron Walden, *U.K.* 13 E8
Safi, *Morocco* 78 B4
Şafīābād, *Iran* 71 B8
Safīd Dasht, *Iran* 71 C6
Safīd Kūh, *Afghan.* 66 B3
Safīd Rūd →, *Iran* 71 B6
Safipur, *India* 69 F9
Safonovo, *Russia* 46 E7
Safranbolu, *Turkey* 72 B5
Saft Rashîn, *Egypt* 80 J7
Safwān, *Iraq* 70 D5
Sag Harbor, *U.S.A.* 111 F12
Saga, *Japan* 55 H5

Saga □, Japan 55 H5
Sagae, Japan 54 E10
Sagala, Mali 82 C3
Sagamore, U.S.A. 110 F5
Sagar, Karnataka, India 66 M9
Sagar, Mad. P., India 69 H8
Sagara, L., Tanzania 86 D3
Sagay, Phil. 61 F5
Saginaw, U.S.A. 108 D4
Saginaw →, U.S.A. 108 D4
Saginaw B., U.S.A. 108 D4
Sagleipie, Liberia 82 D3
Saglouc = Salluit, Canada 101 B12
Sagŏ-ri, S. Korea 57 G14
Sagone, France 21 F12
Sagone, G. de, France 21 F12
Sagres, Portugal 35 J2
Sagua la Grande, Cuba 120 B3
Saguache, U.S.A. 115 G10
Saguaro Nat. Park, U.S.A. 115 K8
Saguenay →, Canada 103 C5
Sagunt, Spain 32 F4
Sagunto = Sagunt, Spain 32 F4
Sagwara, India 68 H6
Sahaba, Sudan 80 D3
Sahagún, Spain 34 C5
Saḩam al Jawlān, Syria 75 C4
Sahamandrevo, Madag. 89 C8
Sahand, Kūh-e, Iran 70 B5
Sahara, Africa 78 D6
Saharan Atlas = Saharien, Atlas, Algeria 78 B6
Saharanpur, India 68 E7
Saharien, Atlas, Algeria 78 B6
Saharsa, India 69 G12
Sahasinaka, Madag. 89 C8
Sahaswan, India 69 E8
Sahel, Africa 78 E5
Sahel, Canal du, Mali 82 C3
Sahibganj, India 69 G12
Sāḩilīyah, Iraq 70 C4
Sahiwal, Pakistan 68 D5
Şahneh, Iran 70 C5
Sahuaripa, Mexico 118 B3
Sahuarita, U.S.A. 115 L8
Sahuayo, Mexico 118 C4
Šahy, Slovak Rep. 27 C11
Sai →, India 69 G10
Sai Buri, Thailand 65 J3
Sa'id Bundâs, Sudan 81 F1
Sa'īdābād, Kermān, Iran 71 D7
Sa'īdābād, Semnān, Iran 71 B7
Sa'īdīyeh, Iran 71 B6
Saidpur, Bangla. 67 G16
Saidpur, India 69 G10
Saidu, Pakistan 69 B5
Saignes, France 20 C6
Saigon = Phanh Bho Ho Chi Minh, Vietnam 65 G6
Saijō, Japan 55 H6
Saikanosy Masoala, Madag. 89 B9
Saikhoa Ghat, India 67 F19
Saiki, Japan 55 H5
Sailana, India 68 H6
Saillans, France 21 D9
Sailolof, Indonesia 63 E8
Saimaa, Finland 9 F23
Saimbeyli, Turkey 72 D7
Şa'in Dezh, Iran 70 B5
St. Abb's Head, U.K. 14 F6
St-Affrique, France 20 E6
St-Agrève, France 21 C8
St-Aignan, France 18 E8
St. Alban's, Canada 103 C8
St. Albans, U.K. 13 F7
St. Albans, Vt., U.S.A. 111 B11
St. Albans, W. Va., U.S.A. 108 F5
St. Alban's Head, U.K. 13 G5
St. Albert, Canada 104 C6
St-Amand-en-Puisaye, France 19 E10
St-Amand-les-Eaux, France 19 B10
St-Amand-Montrond, France 19 F9
St-Amarin, France 19 E14
St-Amour, France 19 F12
St-André-de-Cubzac, France 20 D3
St-André-les-Alpes, France 21 E10
St. Andrew's, Canada 103 C8
St. Andrews, U.K. 14 E6
St-Anicet, Canada 111 A10
St. Ann B., Canada 103 C7
St. Ann's Bay, Jamaica 120 C4
St. Anthony, Canada 103 B8
St. Anthony, U.S.A. 114 E8
St. Antoine, Canada 103 C7
St-Antonin-Noble-Val, France 20 D5
St. Arnaud, Australia 95 F3
St-Astier, France 20 C4
St-Aubin-du-Cormier, France 18 D5
St-Augustin →, Canada 103 B8
St-Augustin-Saguenay, Canada 103 B8
St. Augustine, U.S.A. 109 L5
St-Aulaye, France 20 C4
St. Austell, U.K. 13 G3
St-Avold, France 19 C13
St. Barbe, Canada 103 B8
St-Barthélemy, W. Indies 121 C7
St-Béat, France 20 F4
St. Bees Hd., U.K. 12 C4
St-Benoît-du-Sault, France 20 B5
St-Bonnet, France 21 D10
St-Brévin-les-Pins, France 18 E4
St-Brice-en-Coglès, France 18 D5
St. Bride's, Canada 103 C9
St. Brides B., U.K. 13 F2
St-Brieuc, France 18 D4
St-Calais, France 18 E7
St-Cast-le-Guildo, France 18 D4
St. Catharines, Canada 102 D4
St. Catherines I., U.S.A. 109 K5
St. Catherine's Pt., U.K. 13 G6
St-Céré, France 20 D5
St-Cergue, Switz. 25 J2
St-Cernin, France 20 C6
St-Chamond, France 21 C8
St. Charles, Ill., U.S.A. 108 E1
St. Charles, Mo., U.S.A. 112 F9
St. Charles, Va., U.S.A. 108 F7
St-Chély-d'Apcher, France 20 D7
St-Chinian, France 20 E6
St. Christopher-Nevis = St. Kitts & Nevis ■, W. Indies 121 C7
St-Ciers-sur-Gironde, France 20 C3
St. Clair, Mich., U.S.A. 110 D2
St. Clair, Pa., U.S.A. 111 F8
St. Clair →, U.S.A. 110 D2
St. Clair, L., Canada 102 D3
St. Clair, L., U.S.A. 110 D2
St. Clairsville, U.S.A. 110 F4
St-Claud, France 20 C4
St. Claude, Canada 105 D9
St-Claude, France 19 F12
St-Clet, Canada 111 A10
St. Cloud, Fla., U.S.A. 109 L5
St. Cloud, Minn., U.S.A. 112 C7
St. Cricq, C., Australia 93 E1
St. Croix, Virgin Is. 121 C7
St. Croix →, U.S.A. 112 C8
St. Croix Falls, U.S.A. 112 C8
St-Cyprien, France 20 F7
St-Cyr-sur-Mer, France 21 E9
St. David's, Canada 103 C8
St. David's, U.K. 13 F2
St. David's Head, U.K. 13 F2
St-Denis, France 19 D9
St-Dié, France 19 D13
St-Dizier, France 19 D11
St-Égrève, France 21 C9
St. Elias, Mt., U.S.A. 100 B5
St. Elias Mts., Canada 104 A1
St. Elias Mts., U.S.A. 100 C6
St-Éloy-les-Mines, France 19 F9
St-Émilion, France 20 D3
St-Étienne, France 21 C8
St-Étienne-de-Tinée, France 21 D10
St-Étienne-du-Rouvray, France 18 C8
St. Eugène, Canada 111 A10
St. Eustatius, W. Indies 121 C7
St-Fargeau, France 19 E10
St-Félicien, Canada 102 C5
St-Florent, France 21 F13
St-Florent, G. de, France 21 F13
St-Florent-sur-Cher, France 19 F9
St-Florentin, France 19 E10
St-Flour, France 20 C7
St. Francis, U.S.A. 112 F4
St. Francis →, U.S.A. 113 H9
St. Francis, C., S. Africa 88 E3
St. Francisville, U.S.A. 113 K9
St-François, L., Canada 111 A10
St-Fulgent, France 18 F5
St-Gabriel, Canada 102 C5
St. Gallen = Sankt Gallen, Switz. 25 H5
St-Galmier, France 19 G11
St-Gaudens, France 20 E4
St-Gaultier, France 18 F8
St-Gengoux-le-National, France 19 F11
St-Geniez-d'Olt, France 20 D6
St. George, Australia 95 D4
St. George, Canada 103 C6
St. George, S.C., U.S.A. 109 J5
St. George, Utah, U.S.A. 115 H7
St. George, C., Canada 103 C8
St. George, C., U.S.A. 109 L3
St. George Ra., Australia 92 C4
St. George's, Canada 103 C8
St-Georges, Canada 103 C5
St. George's, Grenada 121 D7
St. George's B., Canada 103 C8
St. Georges Basin, N.S.W., Australia 95 F5
St. Georges Basin, W. Austral., Australia 92 C4
St. George's Channel, Europe 15 E6
St. Georges Hd., Australia 95 F5
St-Georges-lès-Baillargeaux, France 20 B4
St-Germain-de-Calberte, France 20 D7
St-Germain-en-Laye, France 19 D9
St-Germain-Lembron, France 20 C7
St-Gervais-d'Auvergne, France 19 F9
St-Gervais-les-Bains, France 21 C10
St-Gildas, Pte. de, France 18 E4
St-Gilles, France 21 E8
St-Girons, Ariège, France 20 F5
St-Girons, Landes, France 20 E2
St. Gotthard P. = San Gottardo, P. del, Switz. 25 J4
St. Helena, U.S.A. 114 G2
St. Helena ■, Atl. Oc. 76 H3
St. Helena, Mt., U.S.A. 116 G4
St. Helena B., S. Africa 88 E2
St. Helens, Australia 94 G4
St. Helens, U.K. 12 D5
St. Helens, U.S.A. 116 E4
St. Helens, Mt., U.S.A. 116 D4
St. Helier, U.K. 13 H5
St-Herblain, France 18 E5
St-Hilaire-du-Harcouët, France 18 D5
St-Hippolyte, France 19 E13
St-Hippolyte-du-Fort, France 20 E7
St-Honoré-les-Bains, France 19 F10
St-Hubert, Belgium 17 D5
St-Hyacinthe, Canada 102 C5
St. Ignace, U.S.A. 108 C3
St. Ignace I., Canada 102 C2
St. Ignatius, U.S.A. 114 C6
St-Imier, Switz. 25 H2
St. Ives, U.K. 13 G2
St-James, France 18 D5
St. James, U.S.A. 112 D7
St-Jean →, Canada 103 B7
St-Jean, L., Canada 103 C5
St-Jean-d'Angély, France 20 C3
St-Jean-de-Braye, France 19 E8
St-Jean-de-Luz, France 20 E2
St-Jean-de-Maurienne, France 21 C10
St-Jean-de-Monts, France 18 F4
St-Jean-du-Gard, France 20 D7
St-Jean-en-Royans, France 21 C9
St-Jean-Pied-de-Port, France 20 E2
St-Jean-Port-Joli, Canada 103 C5
St-Jean-sur-Richelieu, Canada 102 C5
St-Jérôme, Canada 102 C5
St. John, Canada 103 C6
St. John, U.S.A. 113 G5
St. John →, Liberia 82 D2
St. John →, U.S.A. 109 C12
St. John, C., Canada 103 C8
St. John's, Antigua 121 C7
St. John's, Canada 103 C9
St. Johns, Ariz., U.S.A. 115 J9
St. Johns, Mich., U.S.A. 108 D3
St. Johns →, U.S.A. 109 K5
St. John's Pt., Ireland 15 B3
St. Johnsbury, U.S.A. 111 B12
St. Johnsville, U.S.A. 111 D10
St. Joseph, La., U.S.A. 113 K9
St. Joseph, Mo., U.S.A. 112 F7
St. Joseph →, U.S.A. 108 D2
St. Joseph, I., Canada 102 C3
St. Joseph, L., Canada 102 B1
St-Jovite, Canada 102 C5
St-Juéry, France 20 E6
St-Julien-Chapteuil, France 21 C8
St-Julien-de-Vouvantes, France 18 E5
St-Julien-en-Genevois, France 19 F13
St-Junien, France 20 C4
St-Just-en-Chaussée, France 19 C9
St-Just-en-Chevalet, France 20 C7
St. Kilda, N.Z. 91 L3
St. Kitts & Nevis ■, W. Indies 121 C7
St. Laurent, Canada 105 C9
St-Laurent-de-la-Salanque, France 20 F6
St-Laurent-du-Pont, France 21 C9
St-Laurent-en-Grandvaux, France 19 F12
St-Laurent-et-Benon, France 20 C3
St. Lawrence, Australia 94 C4
St. Lawrence, Canada 103 C8
St. Lawrence →, Canada 103 C6
St. Lawrence, Gulf of, Canada 103 C7
St. Lawrence I., U.S.A. 100 B3
St. Leonard, Canada 103 C6
St-Léonard-de-Noblat, France 20 C5
St. Lewis →, Canada 103 B8
St-Lô, France 18 C5
St-Louis, France 19 E14
St. Louis, Senegal 82 B1
St. Louis, U.S.A. 112 F9
St. Louis →, U.S.A. 112 B8
St-Loup-sur-Semouse, France 19 E13
St. Lucia ■, W. Indies 121 D7
St. Lucia, L., S. Africa 89 D5
St. Lucia Channel, W. Indies 121 D7
St. Maarten, W. Indies 121 C7
St. Magnus B., U.K. 14 A7
St-Maixent-l'École, France 20 B3
St-Malo, France 18 D4
St-Malo, G. de, France 18 D4
St-Mandrier-sur-Mer, France 21 E9
St-Marc, Haiti 121 C5
St-Marcellin, France 21 C9
St-Marcouf, Is., France 18 C5
St. Maries, U.S.A. 114 C5
St-Martin, W. Indies 121 C7
St. Martin, L., Canada 105 C9
St-Martin-de-Crau, France 21 E8
St-Martin-de-Ré, France 20 B2
St-Martin-d'Hères, France 21 C9
St-Martin-Vésubie, France 21 D11
St-Martory, France 20 E4
St. Mary Pk., Australia 95 E2
St. Marys, Australia 94 G4
St. Marys, Canada 110 C3
St. Mary's, Corn., U.K. 13 H1
St. Mary's, Orkney, U.K. 14 C6
St. Marys, Ga., U.S.A. 109 K5
St. Marys, Pa., U.S.A. 110 E6
St. Mary's, C., Canada 103 C9
St. Mary's B., Canada 103 C9
St. Marys Bay, Canada 103 D6
St-Mathieu, Pte., France 18 D2
St. Matthew I., U.S.A. 100 B2
St. Matthews, I. = Zadetkyi Kyun, Burma 65 G1
St-Maurice →, Canada 102 C5
St-Maximin-la-Ste-Baume, France 21 E9
St-Médard-en-Jalles, France 20 D3
St-Méen-le-Grand, France 18 D4
St-Mihiel, France 19 D12
St. Moritz, Switz. 25 J5
St-Nazaire, France 18 E4
St. Neots, U.K. 13 E7
St-Nicolas-de-Port, France 19 D13
St-Niklaas, Belgium 17 C4
St-Omer, France 19 B9
St-Palais-sur-Mer, France 20 C2
St-Pamphile, Canada 103 C6
St-Pardoux-la-Rivière, France 20 C4
St. Pascal, Canada 103 C6
St. Paul, Canada 104 C6
St-Paul, France 21 D10
St. Paul, Minn., U.S.A. 112 C8
St. Paul, Nebr., U.S.A. 112 E5
St-Paul →, Canada 103 B8
St. Paul →, Liberia 82 D2
St. Paul, I., Ind. Oc. 3 F13
St-Paul-de-Fenouillet, France 20 F6
St. Paul I., Canada 103 C7
St-Paul-lès-Dax, France 20 E2
St-Péray, France 21 D8
St. Peter, U.S.A. 112 C8
St-Peter-Ording, Germany 24 A4
St. Peter Port, U.K. 13 H5
St. Peters, N.S., Canada 103 C7
St. Peters, P.E.I., Canada 103 C7
St. Petersburg = Sankt-Peterburg, Russia 46 C6
St. Petersburg, U.S.A. 109 M4
St-Philbert-de-Grand-Lieu, France 18 E5
St-Pie, Canada 111 A12
St-Pierre, St- P. & M. 103 C8
St-Pierre, L., Canada 102 C5
St-Pierre-d'Oléron, France 20 C2
St-Pierre-en-Port, France 18 C7
St-Pierre et Miquelon □, St- P. & M. 103 C8
St-Pierre-le-Moûtier, France 19 F10
St-Pierre-sur-Dives, France 18 C6
St-Pol-de-Léon, France 18 D3
St-Pol-sur-Mer, France 19 A9
St-Pol-sur-Ternoise, France 19 B9
St-Pons, France 20 E6
St-Pourçain-sur-Sioule, France 19 F10
St-Priest, France 21 C8
St-Quay-Portrieux, France 18 D4
St. Quentin, Canada 103 C6
St-Quentin, France 19 C10
St-Rambert-d'Albon, France 21 C8
St-Raphaël, France 21 E10
St. Regis, U.S.A. 114 C6
St-Renan, France 18 D2
St-Saëns, France 18 C8
St-Savin, France 20 B4
St-Savinien, France 20 C3
St. Sebastien, Tanjon' i, Madag. 89 A8
St-Seine-l'Abbaye, France 19 E11
St-Sernin-sur-Rance, France 20 E6
St-Sever, France 20 E3
St-Siméon, Canada 103 C6
St. Simons I., U.S.A. 109 K5
St. Simons Island, U.S.A. 109 K5
St. Stephen, Canada 103 C6
St-Sulpice, France 20 E5
St-Sulpice-Laurière, France 20 B5
St-Sulpice-les-Feuilles, France 20 B5
St-Syprien = St-Cyprien, France 20 F7
St-Thégonnec, France 18 D3
St. Thomas, Canada 102 D3
St. Thomas I., Virgin Is. 121 C7
St-Tite, Canada 102 C5
St-Tropez, France 21 E10
St. Troud = St. Truiden, Belgium 17 D5
St. Truiden, Belgium 17 D5
St-Vaast-la-Hougue, France 18 C5
St-Valery-en-Caux, France 18 C7
St-Valéry-sur-Somme, France 19 B8
St-Vallier, France 19 F11
St-Vallier-de-Thiey, France 21 E10
St-Varent, France 18 F6
St-Vaury, France 20 B5
St. Vincent, Italy 28 C4
St. Vincent, G., Australia 95 F2
St. Vincent & the Grenadines ■, W. Indies 121 D7
St-Vincent-de-Tyrosse, France 20 E2
St. Vincent Passage, W. Indies 121 D7
St-Vith, Belgium 17 D6
St-Vivien-de-Médoc, France 20 C2
St. Walburg, Canada 105 C7
St-Yrieix-la-Perche, France 20 C5
Ste-Adresse, France 18 C7
Ste-Agathe-des-Monts, Canada 102 C5
Ste-Anne, L., Canada 103 B6
Ste-Anne-des-Monts, Canada 103 C6
Ste-Croix, Switz. 25 J2
Ste-Enimie, France 20 D7
Ste-Foy-la-Grande, France 20 D4
Ste. Genevieve, U.S.A. 112 G9
Ste-Hermine, France 20 B2
Ste-Livrade-sur-Lot, France 20 D4
Ste-Marguerite →, Canada 103 B6
Ste-Marie, Martinique 121 D7
Ste-Marie-aux-Mines, France 19 D14
Ste-Marie de la Madeleine, Canada 103 C5
Ste-Maure-de-Touraine, France 18 E7
Ste-Maxime, France 21 E10
Ste-Menehould, France 19 C11
Ste-Mère-Église, France 18 C5
Ste-Rose, Guadeloupe 121 C7
Ste. Rose du Lac, Canada 105 C9
Ste-Savine, France 19 D11
Ste-Sigolène, France 21 C8
Saintes, France 20 C3
Saintes, I. des, Guadeloupe 121 C7
Stes-Maries-de-la-Mer, France 21 E8
Saintfield, U.K. 15 B6
Saintonge, France 20 C3
Saipan, Pac. Oc. 96 F6
Sairang, India 67 H18
Sairecábur, Cerro, Bolivia 126 A2
Saitama □, Japan 55 F9
Saiteli = Kadınhanı, Turkey 72 C5
Saiţi, Moldova 43 D14
Saiyid, Pakistan 68 C5
Sajama, Bolivia 124 G5
Sajan, Serbia, Yug. 42 E5
Sajó →, Hungary 42 C6
Sajószentpéter, Hungary 42 B5
Sajum, India 69 C8
Sak →, S. Africa 88 E3
Sakaba, Nigeria 83 C6
Sakai, Japan 55 G7
Sakaide, Japan 55 G6
Sakaiminato, Japan 55 G6
Sakākah, Si. Arabia 70 D4
Sakakawea, L., U.S.A. 112 B4
Sakami →, Canada 102 B4
Sakami, L., Canada 102 B4
Sâkâne, 'Erg i-n, Mali 83 A4
Sakania, Dem. Rep. of the Congo 87 E2
Sakaraha, Madag. 89 C7
Sakarya, Turkey 72 B4
Sakarya →, Turkey 72 B4
Sakashima-Guntō, Japan 55 M2
Sakassou, Ivory C. 82 D3
Sakata, Japan 54 E9
Sakchu, N. Korea 57 D13
Sakeny →, Madag. 89 C8
Sakété, Benin 83 D5
Sakha □, Russia 51 C13
Sakhalin, Russia 51 D15
Sakhalinskiy Zaliv, Russia 51 D15
Şaki, Azerbaijan 49 K8
Šakiai, Lithuania 9 J20
Sakon Nakhon, Thailand 64 D5
Sakrand, Pakistan 68 F3
Sakri, India 69 F12
Sakrivier, S. Africa 88 E3
Sakskøbing, Denmark 11 K5
Sakti, India 69 H10
Sakuma, Japan 55 G8
Sakurai, Japan 55 G7
Saky, Ukraine 47 K7
Sal →, Russia 49 G5
Sala, Eritrea 81 D4
Šal'a, Slovak Rep. 27 C10
Sala, Sweden 10 E10
Sala →, Eritrea 81 D4
Sala Consilina, Italy 31 B8
Sala-y-Gómez, Pac. Oc. 97 K17
Salaberry-de-Valleyfield, Canada 102 C5
Saladas, Argentina 126 B4
Saladillo, Argentina 126 D4
Salado →, Buenos Aires, Argentina 126 D4
Salado →, La Pampa, Argentina 128 D3
Salado →, Santa Fe, Argentina 126 C3
Salado →, Mexico 113 M5
Salaga, Ghana 83 D4
Salāh, Syria 75 C5
Sălaj □, Romania 42 C8
Sálakhos, Greece 36 C9
Salala, Liberia 82 D2
Salala, Sudan 80 C4
Salālah, Oman 74 D5
Salamanca, Chile 126 C1
Salamanca, Spain 34 E5
Salamanca, U.S.A. 110 D6
Salamanca □, Spain 34 E5
Salāmatābād, Iran 70 C5
Salamis, Cyprus 36 D12
Salamís, Greece 38 D5
Salar de Atacama, Chile 126 A2
Salar de Uyuni, Bolivia 124 H5
Sălard, Romania 42 C7
Salas, Spain 34 B4
Salas de los Infantes, Spain 34 C7
Salatiga, Indonesia 63 G14
Salaverry, Peru 124 E3
Salawati, Indonesia 63 E8
Salaya, India 68 H3
Salayar, Indonesia 63 F6
Salazar →, Spain 32 C3
Salbris, France 19 E9
Salcia, Romania 43 G9
Sălciua, Romania 43 D8
Salcombe, U.K. 13 G4
Saldaña, Spain 34 C6
Saldanha, S. Africa 88 E2
Saldanha B., S. Africa 88 E2
Saldus, Latvia 9 H20
Saldus □, Latvia 44 B9
Sale, Australia 95 F4
Sale, Italy 28 D5
Salé, Morocco 78 B4
Sale, U.K. 12 D5
Salekhard, Russia 50 C7
Salem, India 66 P11
Salem, Ill., U.S.A. 108 F1
Salem, Ind., U.S.A. 108 F2
Salem, Mass., U.S.A. 111 D14
Salem, Mo., U.S.A. 113 G9
Salem, N.H., U.S.A. 111 D13
Salem, N.J., U.S.A. 108 F8
Salem, N.Y., U.S.A. 111 C11
Salem, Ohio, U.S.A. 110 F4
Salem, Oreg., U.S.A. 114 D2
Salem, S. Dak., U.S.A. 112 D6
Salem, Va., U.S.A. 108 G5
Salemi, Italy 30 E5

Sälen, *Sweden* 10 C7
Salernes, *France* 21 E10
Salerno, *Italy* 31 B7
Salerno, G. di, *Italy* 31 B7
Salford, *U.K.* 12 D5
Salgir →, *Ukraine* 47 K8
Salgótarján, *Hungary* 42 B4
Salgueiro, *Brazil* 125 E11
Salibabu, *Indonesia* 63 D7
Salida, *U.S.A.* 106 C5
Salies-de-Béarn, *France* 20 E3
Salihli, *Turkey* 72 C3
Salihorsk, *Belarus* 47 F4
Salima, *Malawi* 85 G6
Salina, *Italy* 31 D7
Salina, *Kans., U.S.A.* 112 F6
Salina, *Utah, U.S.A.* 115 G8
Salina Cruz, *Mexico* 119 D5
Salinas, *Brazil* 125 G10
Salinas, *Chile* 126 A2
Salinas, *Ecuador* 124 D2
Salinas, *U.S.A.* 116 J5
Salinas →, *Guatemala* 119 D6
Salinas →, *U.S.A.* 116 J5
Salinas, B. de, *Nic.* 120 D2
Salinas, Pampa de las, *Argentina* 126 C2
Salinas Ambargasta, *Argentina* 126 B3
Salinas de Hidalgo, *Mexico* 118 C4
Salinas Grandes, *Argentina* 126 C3
Saline →, *Ark., U.S.A.* 113 J8
Saline →, *Kans., U.S.A.* 112 F6
Salines, *Spain* 37 B10
Salines, C. de ses, *Spain* 37 B10
Salinópolis, *Brazil* 125 D9
Salins-les-Bains, *France* 19 F12
Salir, *Portugal* 35 H2
Salisbury = Harare, *Zimbabwe* 87 F3
Salisbury, *U.K.* 13 F6
Salisbury, *Md., U.S.A.* 108 F8
Salisbury, *N.C., U.S.A.* 109 H5
Salisbury I., *Canada* 101 B12
Salisbury Plain, *U.K.* 13 F6
Şamaxi, *Azerbaijan* 49 K9
Săliște, *Romania* 43 E8
Salka, *Nigeria* 83 C5
Şalkhad, *Syria* 75 C5
Salla, *Finland* 8 C23
Sallanches, *France* 21 C10
Sallent, *Spain* 32 D6
Salles, *France* 20 D3
Salles-Curan, *France* 20 D6
Salling, *Denmark* 11 H2
Salliq, *Canada* 101 B11
Sallisaw, *U.S.A.* 113 H7
Sallom Junction, *Sudan* 80 D4
Salluit, *Canada* 101 B12
Salmās, *Iran* 70 B5
Salmerón, *Spain* 32 E2
Salmo, *Canada* 104 D5
Salmon, *U.S.A.* 114 D7
Salmon →, *Canada* 104 C4
Salmon →, *U.S.A.* 114 D5
Salmon Arm, *Canada* 104 C5
Salmon Gums, *Australia* 93 F3
Salmon River Mts., *U.S.A.* 114 D6
Salo, *Finland* 9 F20
Salò, *Italy* 28 C7
Salobreña, *Spain* 35 J7
Salome, *U.S.A.* 117 M13
Salon, *India* 69 F9
Salon-de-Provence, *France* 21 E9
Salonica = Thessaloníki, *Greece* 40 F6
Salonta, *Romania* 42 D6
Salor →, *Spain* 35 F3
Salou, *Spain* 32 D6
Salou, C. de, *Spain* 32 D6
Saloum →, *Senegal* 82 C1
Salpausselkä, *Finland* 9 F22
Salsacate, *Argentina* 126 C2
Salses, *France* 20 F6
Salsk, *Russia* 49 G5
Salso →, *Italy* 30 E6
Salsomaggiore Terme, *Italy* 28 D6
Salt, *Spain* 32 D7
Salt →, *Canada* 104 B6
Salt →, *U.S.A.* 115 K7
Salt Lake City, *U.S.A.* 114 F8
Salt Range, *Pakistan* 68 C5
Salta, *Argentina* 126 A2
Salta □, *Argentina* 126 A2
Saltara, *Italy* 29 E9
Saltash, *U.K.* 13 G3
Saltburn by the Sea, *U.K.* 12 C7
Saltcoats, *U.K.* 14 F4
Saltee Is., *Ireland* 15 D5
Saltfjellet, *Norway* 8 C16
Saltfjorden, *Norway* 8 C16
Saltholm, *Denmark* 11 J6
Saltillo, *Mexico* 118 B4
Salto, *Argentina* 126 C3
Salto, *Uruguay* 126 C4
Salto del Guaíra, *Paraguay* 127 A5
Salton City, *U.S.A.* 117 M11
Salton Sea, *U.S.A.* 117 M11
Saltpond, *Ghana* 83 D4
Saltsburg, *U.S.A.* 110 F5
Saltsjöbaden, *Sweden* 10 E12
Saluda →, *U.S.A.* 109 J5
Salûm, *Egypt* 80 A2
Salûm, Khâlig el, *Egypt* 80 A2
Salur, *India* 67 K13
Saluzzo, *Italy* 28 D4
Salvador, *Brazil* 125 F11
Salvador, *Canada* 105 C7
Salvador, L., *U.S.A.* 113 L9
Salvaterra de Magos, *Portugal* 35 F2
Sálvora, I. de, *Spain* 34 C2
Salween →, *Burma* 67 L20
Salyan, *Azerbaijan* 50 F5
Salza →, *Austria* 26 D7
Salzach →, *Austria* 26 C5
Salzburg, *Austria* 26 D6
Salzburg □, *Austria* 26 D6
Salzgitter, *Germany* 24 C6
Salzkotten, *Germany* 24 D4
Salzwedel, *Germany* 24 C7
Sam, *India* 68 F4
Sam Neua, *Laos* 58 G5
Sam Ngao, *Thailand* 64 D2
Sam Rayburn Reservoir, *U.S.A.* 113 K7
Sam Son, *Vietnam* 64 C5
Sam Teu, *Laos* 64 C5
Sama de Langreo = Langreo, *Spain* 34 B5
Samagaltay, *Russia* 51 D10
Samales Group, *Phil.* 61 J4
Samâlût, *Egypt* 80 B3
Samana, *India* 68 D7
Samaná □, *Dom. Rep.* 121 C6
Samana Cay, *Bahamas* 121 B5
Samandağı, *Turkey* 72 D6
Samandıra, *Turkey* 41 F13
Samanga, *Tanzania* 87 D4
Samangwa, *Dem. Rep. of the Congo* 86 C1
Samani, *Japan* 54 C11
Samanli Dağları, *Turkey* 41 F13
Samar, *Phil.* 61 F6
Samara, *Russia* 48 D10
Samara →, *Russia* 48 D10
Samara →, *Ukraine* 47 H8
Samaria = Shōmrōn, *West Bank* 75 C4
Samariá, *Greece* 36 D5
Samarinda, *Indonesia* 62 E5
Samarkand = Samarqand, *Uzbekistan* 50 F7
Samarqand, *Uzbekistan* 50 F7
Sāmarrā, *Iraq* 70 C4
Samastipur, *India* 69 G11
Şamaxi, *Azerbaijan* 49 K9
Samba, *Dem. Rep. of the Congo* 86 C2
Samba, *India* 69 C6
Sambalpur, *India* 67 J14
Sambar, Tanjung, *Indonesia* 62 E4
Sambas, *Indonesia* 62 D3
Sambava, *Madag.* 89 A9
Sambawizi, *Zimbabwe* 87 F2
Sambhal, *India* 69 E8
Sambhar, *India* 68 F6
Sambhar L., *India* 68 F6
Sambiase, *Italy* 31 D9
Sambir, *Ukraine* 47 H2
Sambor, *Cambodia* 64 F6
Samborombón, B., *Argentina* 126 D4
Sambuca di Sicília, *Italy* 30 E6
Samch'ŏk, *S. Korea* 57 F15
Samch'onp'o, *S. Korea* 57 G15
Same, *Tanzania* 86 C4
Samer, *France* 19 B8
Samfya, *Zambia* 87 E2
Sámi, *Greece* 38 C2
Şämkir, *Azerbaijan* 49 K8
Şamlı, *Turkey* 39 B9
Samnah, *Si. Arabia* 70 E3
Samo Alto, *Chile* 126 C1
Samoa = Western Samoa ■, *Pac. Oc.* 91 B13
Samobor, *Croatia* 29 C12
Samoëns, *France* 19 F13
Samokov, *Bulgaria* 40 D7
Šamorín, *Slovak Rep.* 27 C10
Samorogouan, *Burkina Faso* 82 C4
Sámos, *Greece* 39 D8
Samoš, *Serbia, Yug.* 42 E5
Samos, *Spain* 34 C3
Sámos □, *Greece* 39 D8
Samothráki = Mathráki, *Greece* 36 A3
Samothráki, *Greece* 41 F9
Samothráki, *Évros, Greece* 41 F9
Samoylovka, *Russia* 48 E6
Sampa, *Ghana* 82 D4
Sampacho, *Argentina* 126 C3
Sampang, *Indonesia* 63 G15
Samper de Calanda, *Spain* 32 D4
Sampéyre, *Italy* 28 D4
Sampit, *Indonesia* 62 E4
Sampit, Teluk, *Indonesia* 62 E4
Samrong, *Cambodia* 64 E4
Samrong, *Thailand* 64 E3
Samsø, *Denmark* 11 J4
Samsø Bælt, *Denmark* 11 J4
Samsun, *Turkey* 72 B7
Samtredia, *Georgia* 49 J6
Samui, Ko, *Thailand* 65 H3
Samur →, *Russia* 49 K9
Samurskiy Khrebet, *Russia* 49 K8
Samusole, *Dem. Rep. of the Congo* 87 E1
Samut Prakan, *Thailand* 64 F3
Samut Songkhram →, *Thailand* 62 B1
Samwari, *Pakistan* 68 E2
San, *Mali* 82 C4
San →, *Cambodia* 64 F5
San →, *Poland* 45 H8
San Adrián, *Spain* 32 C3
San Adrián, C. de, *Spain* 34 B2
San Agustin, C., *Phil.* 61 H7
San Agustín de Valle Fértil, *Argentina* 126 C2
San Ambrosio, *Pac. Oc.* 122 F3
San Andreas, *U.S.A.* 116 G6
San Andres, *Phil.* 61 E6
San Andrés, I. de, *Caribbean* 120 D3
San Andrês del Rabanedo, *Spain* 34 C5
San Andres Mts., *U.S.A.* 115 K10
San Andrés Tuxtla, *Mexico* 119 D5
San Angelo, *U.S.A.* 113 K4
San Anselmo, *U.S.A.* 116 H4
San Antonio, *Belize* 119 D7
San Antonio, *Chile* 126 C1
San Antonio, *Phil.* 61 D4
San Antonio, *N. Mex., U.S.A.* 115 K10
San Antonio, *Tex., U.S.A.* 113 L5
San Antonio →, *U.S.A.* 113 L6
San Antonio, C., *Argentina* 126 D4
San Antonio, C., *Cuba* 120 B3
San Antonio, C. de, *Spain* 33 G5
San Antonio, Mt., *U.S.A.* 117 L9
San Antonio de los Baños, *Cuba* 120 B3
San Antonio de los Cobres, *Argentina* 126 A2
San Antonio Oeste, *Argentina* 128 E4
San Arcángelo, *Italy* 31 B9
San Ardo, *U.S.A.* 116 J6
San Augustín, *Canary Is.* 37 G4
San Augustine, *U.S.A.* 113 K7
San Bartolomé, *Canary Is.* 37 F6
San Bartolomé de Tirajana, *Canary Is.* 37 G4
San Bartolomeo in Galdo, *Italy* 31 A8
San Benedetto del Tronto, *Italy* 29 F10
San Benedetto Po, *Italy* 28 C7
San Benedicto, I., *Mexico* 118 D2
San Benito, *U.S.A.* 113 M6
San Benito →, *U.S.A.* 116 J5
San Benito Mt., *U.S.A.* 116 J6
San Bernardino, *U.S.A.* 117 L9
San Bernardino Mts., *U.S.A.* 117 L10
San Bernardino Str., *Phil.* 61 E6
San Bernardo, *Chile* 126 C1
San Bernardo, I. de, *Colombia* 124 B3
San Blas, *Mexico* 118 B3
San Blas, Arch. de, *Panama* 120 E4
San Blas, C., *U.S.A.* 109 L3
San Bonifacio, *Italy* 29 C8
San Borja, *Bolivia* 124 F5
San Buenaventura, *Mexico* 118 B4
San Carlos = Butuku-Luba, *Eq. Guin.* 83 E6
San Carlos = Sant Carles, *Spain* 37 B8
San Carlos, *Argentina* 126 C2
San Carlos, *Chile* 126 D1
San Carlos, *Baja Calif. S., Mexico* 118 C2
San Carlos, *Coahuila, Mexico* 118 B4
San Carlos, *Nic.* 120 D3
San Carlos, *Neg. Occ., Phil.* 61 F5
San Carlos, *Pangasinan, Phil.* 61 D4
San Carlos, *Uruguay* 127 C5
San Carlos, *U.S.A.* 115 K8
San Carlos, *Venezuela* 124 B5
San Carlos de Bariloche, *Argentina* 128 E2
San Carlos de Bolívar, *Argentina* 128 D4
San Carlos de la Rápita = Sant Carles de la Ràpita, *Spain* 32 E5
San Carlos del Zulia, *Venezuela* 124 B4
San Carlos L., *U.S.A.* 115 K8
San Cataldo, *Italy* 30 E6
San Celoni = Sant Celoni, *Spain* 32 D7
San Clemente, *Chile* 126 D1
San Clemente, *Spain* 33 F2
San Clemente, *U.S.A.* 117 M9
San Clemente I., *U.S.A.* 117 N8
San Cristóbal = Es Migjorn Gran, *Spain* 37 B11
San Cristóbal, *Argentina* 126 C3
San Cristóbal, *Dom. Rep.* 121 C5
San Cristóbal, *Venezuela* 124 B4
San Cristóbal de la Casas, *Mexico* 119 D6
San Damiano d'Asti, *Italy* 28 D5
San Daniele del Friuli, *Italy* 29 B10
San Diego, *Calif., U.S.A.* 117 N9
San Diego, *Tex., U.S.A.* 113 M5
San Diego, C., *Argentina* 128 G3
San Diego de la Unión, *Mexico* 118 C4
San Dimitri, Ras, *Malta* 36 C1
San Donà di Piave, *Italy* 29 C9
San Estanislao, *Paraguay* 126 A4
San Esteban de Gormaz, *Spain* 32 D1
San Felice Circeo, *Italy* 30 A6
San Felice sul Panaro, *Italy* 29 D8
San Felipe, *Chile* 126 C1
San Felipe, *Mexico* 118 A2
San Felipe, *Venezuela* 124 A5
San Felipe →, *U.S.A.* 117 M11
San Felix, *Chile* 126 B1
San Félix, *Pac. Oc.* 122 F2
San Fernando = Sant Ferran, *Spain* 37 C7
San Fernando, *Chile* 126 C1
San Fernando, *Baja Calif., Mexico* 118 B1
San Fernando, *Tamaulipas, Mexico* 119 C5
San Fernando, *La Union, Phil.* 61 C4
San Fernando, *Pampanga, Phil.* 61 D4
San Fernando, *Spain* 35 J4
San Fernando, *Trin. & Tob.* 121 D7
San Fernando, *U.S.A.* 117 L8
San Fernando de Apure, *Venezuela* 124 B5
San Fernando de Atabapo, *Venezuela* 124 C5
San Fernando di Púglia, *Italy* 31 A9
San Francisco, *Argentina* 126 C3
San Francisco, *U.S.A.* 116 H4
San Francisco →, *U.S.A.* 115 K9
San Francisco, Paso de, *S. Amer.* 126 B2
San Francisco de Macorís, *Dom. Rep.* 121 C5
San Francisco del Monte de Oro, *Argentina* 126 C2
San Francisco del Oro, *Mexico* 118 B3
San Francisco Javier = Sant Francesc de Formentera, *Spain* 37 C7
San Francisco Solano, Pta., *Colombia* 122 C3
San Fratello, *Italy* 31 D7
San Gabriel, *Chile* 126 C1
San Gabriel Mts., *U.S.A.* 117 L9
San Gavino Monreale, *Italy* 30 C1
San Gimignano, *Italy* 28 E8
San Giórgio di Nogaro, *Italy* 29 C10
San Giórgio Iónico, *Italy* 31 B10
San Giovanni Bianco, *Italy* 28 C6
San Giovanni in Fiore, *Italy* 31 C9
San Giovanni in Persiceto, *Italy* 29 D8
San Giovanni Rotondo, *Italy* 29 G12
San Giovanni Valdarno, *Italy* 29 E8
San Giuliano Terme, *Italy* 28 E7
San Gorgonio Mt., *U.S.A.* 117 L10
San Gottardo, P. del, *Switz.* 25 J4
San Gregorio, *Uruguay* 127 C4
San Gregorio, *U.S.A.* 116 H4
San Guiseppe Jato, *Italy* 30 E6
San Ignacio, *Belize* 119 D7
San Ignacio, *Bolivia* 124 G6
San Ignacio, *Mexico* 118 B2
San Ignacio, *Paraguay* 120 C2
San Ignacio, L., *Mexico* 118 B2
San Ildefonso, C., *Phil.* 61 C5
San Isidro, *Argentina* 126 C4
San Isidro, *Phil.* 61 H7
San Jacinto, *U.S.A.* 117 M10
San Jaime = Sant Jaume, *Spain* 37 B11
San Javier, *Misiones, Argentina* 127 B4
San Javier, *Santa Fe, Argentina* 126 C4
San Javier, *Bolivia* 124 G6
San Javier, *Chile* 126 D1
San Javier, *Spain* 33 H4
San Jeronimo Taviche, *Mexico* 119 D5
San Joaquin, *U.S.A.* 116 J6
San Joaquin →, *U.S.A.* 116 G5
San Joaquin Valley, *U.S.A.* 116 J6
San Jon, *U.S.A.* 113 H3
San Jordi = Sant Jordi, *Spain* 37 B9
San Jorge, *Argentina* 126 C3
San Jorge, *Spain* 37 C7
San Jorge, B. de, *Mexico* 118 A2
San Jorge, G., *Argentina* 128 F3
San Jorge, G. of, *Argentina* 122 H4
San José = San Josep, *Spain* 37 C7
San José, *Costa Rica* 120 E3
San José, *Guatemala* 120 D1
San José, *Mexico* 118 C2
San Jose, *Mind. Occ., Phil.* 61 E4
San Jose, *Nueva Ecija, Phil.* 61 D4
San Jose, *U.S.A.* 116 H5
San Jose →, *U.S.A.* 115 J10
San Jose de Buenavista, *Phil.* 63 B6
San José de Chiquitos, *Bolivia* 124 G6
San José de Feliciano, *Argentina* 126 C4
San José de Jáchal, *Argentina* 126 C2
San José de Mayo, *Uruguay* 126 C4
San José del Cabo, *Mexico* 118 C3
San José del Guaviare, *Colombia* 124 C4
San Josep, *Spain* 37 C7
San Juan, *Argentina* 126 C2
San Juan, *Mexico* 118 C4
San Juan, *Phil.* 61 F6
San Juan, *Puerto Rico* 121 C6
San Juan □, *Argentina* 126 C2
San Juan □, *Dom. Rep.* 121 C5
San Juan →, *Argentina* 126 C2
San Juan →, *Nic.* 120 D3
San Juan →, *U.S.A.* 115 H8
San Juan Bautista = Sant Joan Baptista, *Spain* 37 B8
San Juan Bautista, *Paraguay* 126 B4
San Juan Bautista, *U.S.A.* 116 J5
San Juan Bautista Valle Nacional, *Mexico* 119 D5
San Juan Capistrano, *U.S.A.* 117 M9
San Juan Cr. →, *U.S.A.* 116 J5
San Juan de Alicante, *Spain* 33 G4
San Juan de Guadalupe, *Mexico* 118 C4
San Juan de la Costa, *Mexico* 118 C2
San Juan de los Morros, *Venezuela* 124 B5
San Juan del Norte, *Nic.* 120 D3
San Juan del Norte, B. de, *Nic.* 120 D3
San Juan del Río, *Mexico* 119 C5
San Juan del Sur, *Nic.* 120 D2
San Juan I., *U.S.A.* 116 B3
San Juan Mts., *U.S.A.* 115 H10
San Just, Sierra de, *Spain* 32 E4
San Justo, *Argentina* 126 C3
San Kamphaeng, *Thailand* 64 C2
San Lázaro, C., *Mexico* 118 C2
San Lázaro, Sa., *Mexico* 118 C3
San Leandro, *U.S.A.* 116 H4
San Leonardo de Yagüe, *Spain* 32 D1
San Lorenzo = Sant Llorenç des Cardassar, *Spain* 37 B10
San Lorenzo, *Argentina* 126 C3
San Lorenzo, *Ecuador* 124 C3
San Lorenzo, *Paraguay* 126 B4
San Lorenzo →, *Mexico* 118 C3
San Lorenzo, I., *Mexico* 118 B2
San Lorenzo, Mte., *Argentina* 128 F2
San Lorenzo de la Parrilla, *Spain* 32 F2
San Lorenzo de Morunys = Sant Llorenç de Morunys, *Spain* 32 C6
San Lucas, *Bolivia* 124 H5
San Lucas, *Baja Calif. S., Mexico* 118 C3
San Lucas, *Baja Calif. S., Mexico* 118 B2
San Lucas, *U.S.A.* 116 J5
San Lucas, C., *Mexico* 118 C3
San Lúcido, *Italy* 31 C9
San Luis, *Argentina* 126 C2
San Luis, *Cuba* 120 B3
San Luis, *Guatemala* 120 C2
San Luis, *Ariz., U.S.A.* 115 K6
San Luis, *Colo., U.S.A.* 115 H11
San Luis □, *Argentina* 126 C2
San Luis, I., *Mexico* 118 B2
San Luis, Sierra de, *Argentina* 126 C2
San Luis de la Paz, *Mexico* 118 C4
San Luis Obispo, *U.S.A.* 117 K6
San Luis Potosí, *Mexico* 118 C4
San Luis Potosí □, *Mexico* 118 C4
San Luis Reservoir, *U.S.A.* 116 H5
San Luis Río Colorado, *Mexico* 118 A2
San Manuel, *U.S.A.* 115 K8
San Marco, C., *Italy* 30 C1
San Marco Argentano, *Italy* 31 C9
San Marco in Lámis, *Italy* 29 G12
San Marcos, *Guatemala* 120 D1
San Marcos, *Mexico* 118 B2
San Marcos, *Calif., U.S.A.* 117 M9
San Marcos, *Tex., U.S.A.* 113 L6
San Marino, *San Marino* 29 E9
San Marino ■, *Europe* 29 E9
San Martín, *Argentina* 126 C2
San Martín →, *Bolivia* 124 F6
San Martín, L., *Argentina* 128 F2
San Martín de la Vega, *Spain* 34 E7
San Martin de los Andes, *Argentina* 128 E2
San Martín de Valdeiglesias, *Spain* 34 E6
San Mateo = Sant Mateu, *Baleares, Spain* 37 B7
San Mateo = Sant Mateu, *Valencia, Spain* 32 E5
San Mateo, *Phil.* 61 C4
San Mateo, *U.S.A.* 116 H4
San Matías, *Bolivia* 124 G7
San Matías, G., *Argentina* 122 H4
San Miguel = Sant Miquel, *Spain* 37 B7
San Miguel, *El Salv.* 120 D2
San Miguel, *Panama* 120 E4
San Miguel, *U.S.A.* 116 K6
San Miguel →, *Bolivia* 124 F6
San Miguel de Tucumán, *Argentina* 126 B2
San Miguel del Monte, *Argentina* 126 D4
San Miguel I., *U.S.A.* 117 L6
San Miniato, *Italy* 28 E7
San Nicolás, *Canary Is.* 37 G4
San Nicolas, *Phil.* 61 B4
San Nicolás de los Arroyas, *Argentina* 126 C3
San Nicolas I., *U.S.A.* 117 M7
San Onofre, *U.S.A.* 117 M9
San Pablo, *Bolivia* 126 A2
San Pablo, *Phil.* 61 D4
San Pablo, *U.S.A.* 116 H4
San Pàolo di Civitate, *Italy* 29 G12
San Pedro, *Buenos Aires, Argentina* 126 C4
San Pedro, *Misiones, Argentina* 127 B5
San Pedro, *Chile* 126 C1
San Pédro, *Ivory C.* 82 E3
San Pedro, *Mexico* 118 C2
San Pedro □, *Paraguay* 126 A4
San Pedro →, *Chihuahua, Mexico* 118 B3
San Pedro →, *Nayarit, Mexico* 118 C3
San Pedro →, *U.S.A.* 115 K8
San Pedro, Pta., *Chile* 126 B1
San Pedro, Sierra de, *Spain* 35 F4
San Pedro Channel, *U.S.A.* 117 M8
San Pedro de Atacama, *Chile* 126 A2
San Pedro de Jujuy, *Argentina* 126 A3
San Pedro de las Colonias, *Mexico* 118 B4

San Pedro de Macorís

San Pedro de Macorís, *Dom. Rep.* 121 C6
San Pedro del Norte, *Nic.* 120 D3
San Pedro del Paraná, *Paraguay* 126 B4
San Pedro del Pinatar, *Spain* 33 H4
San Pedro Mártir, Sierra, *Mexico* 118 A1
San Pedro Mixtepec, *Mexico* 119 D5
San Pedro Ocampo = Melchor Ocampo, *Mexico* 118 C4
San Pedro Sula, *Honduras* 120 C2
San Pietro, *Italy* 30 C1
San Pietro Vernótico, *Italy* 31 B11
San Quintín, *Mexico* 118 A1
San Rafael, *Argentina* 126 C2
San Rafael, *Calif., U.S.A.* 116 H4
San Rafael, *N. Mex., U.S.A.* 115 J10
San Rafael Mt., *U.S.A.* 117 L7
San Rafael Mts., *U.S.A.* 117 L7
San Ramón de la Nueva Orán, *Argentina* 126 A3
San Remo, *Italy* 28 E4
San Roque, *Argentina* 126 B4
San Roque, *Spain* 35 J5
San Rosendo, *Chile* 126 D1
San Saba, *U.S.A.* 113 K5
San Salvador, *El Salv.* 120 D2
San Salvador, *Spain* 37 B10
San Salvador de Jujuy, *Argentina* 126 A3
San Salvador I., *Bahamas* 121 B5
San Salvo, *Italy* 29 F11
San Sebastián = Donostia-San Sebastián, *Spain* 32 B3
San Sebastián, *Argentina* 128 G3
San Sebastian de la Gomera, *Canary Is.* 37 F2
San Serra = Son Serra, *Spain* 37 B10
San Serverino Marche, *Italy* 29 E10
San Severo, *Italy* 29 G12
San Simeon, *U.S.A.* 116 K5
San Simon, *U.S.A.* 115 K9
San Stéfano di Cadore, *Italy* 29 B9
San Stino di Livenza, *Italy* 29 C9
San Telmo = Sant Telm, *Spain* 37 B9
San Telmo, *Mexico* 118 A1
San Tiburcio, *Mexico* 118 C4
San Valentin, Mte., *Chile* 122 H3
San Vicente de Alcántara, *Spain* 35 F3
San Vicente de la Barquera, *Spain* 34 B6
San Vincente del Raspeig, *Spain* 33 G4
San Vincenzo, *Italy* 28 E7
San Vito, *Costa Rica* 120 E3
San Vito, *Italy* 30 C2
San Vito, C., *Italy* 30 D5
San Vito al Tagliamento, *Italy* 29 C9
San Vito Chietino, *Italy* 29 F11
San Vito dei Normanni, *Italy* 31 B10
Sana', *Yemen* 74 D3
Sana →, *Bos.-H.* 29 C13
Sanaba, *Burkina Faso* 82 C4
Şanāfīr, *Si. Arabia* 80 B3
Sanaga →, *Cameroon* 83 E6
Sanaloa, Presa, *Mexico* 118 C3
Sanana, *Indonesia* 63 E7
Sanand, *India* 68 H5
Sanandaj, *Iran* 70 C5
Sanandita, *Bolivia* 126 A3
Sanary-sur-Mer, *France* 21 E9
Sanawad, *India* 68 H7
Sancellas = Sencelles, *Spain* 37 B9
Sancergues, *France* 19 E9
Sancerre, *France* 19 E9
Sancerrois, Collines du, *France* 19 E9
Sancha He →, *China* 58 D6
Sanchahe, *China* 57 B14
Sánchez, *Dom. Rep.* 121 C6
Sanchor, *India* 68 G4
Sancoins, *France* 19 F9
Sancti Spíritus, *Cuba* 120 B4
Sancy, Puy de, *France* 20 C6
Sand →, *S. Africa* 89 C5
Sand Hills, *U.S.A.* 112 D4
Sand Springs, *U.S.A.* 113 G6
Sanda, *Japan* 55 G7
Sandakan, *Malaysia* 62 C5
Sandan = Sambor, *Cambodia* 64 F6
Sandanski, *Bulgaria* 40 E7
Sandaré, *Mali* 82 C2
Sandared, *Sweden* 11 G6
Sandarne, *Sweden* 10 C11
Sanday, *U.K.* 14 B6
Sandefjord, *Norway* 9 G14
Sanders, *U.S.A.* 115 J9
Sanderson, *U.S.A.* 113 K3
Sandersville, *U.S.A.* 109 J4
Sandfire Roadhouse, *Australia* 92 C3
Sandfly L., *Canada* 105 B7
Sandfontein, *Namibia* 88 C2
Sandhammaren, C., *Sweden* 11 J8
Sandía, *Peru* 124 F5
Sandıklı, *Turkey* 39 C12
Sandila, *India* 69 F9
Sandnes, *Norway* 9 G11
Sandnessjøen, *Norway* 8 C15
Sandoa, *Dem. Rep. of the Congo* 84 F4
Sandomierz, *Poland* 45 H8
Sândominic, *Romania* 43 D10
Sandover →, *Australia* 94 C2
Sandoway, *Burma* 67 K19
Sandoy, *Færoe Is.* 8 F9
Sandpoint, *U.S.A.* 114 B5
Sandray, *U.K.* 14 E1
Sandringham, *U.K.* 12 E8
Sandstone, *Australia* 93 E2
Sandu, *China* 58 E6
Sandusky, *Mich., U.S.A.* 110 C2
Sandusky, *Ohio, U.S.A.* 110 E2
Sandvig, *Sweden* 11 J8
Sandviken, *Sweden* 10 D10
Sandwich, C., *Australia* 94 B4
Sandwich B., *Canada* 103 B8
Sandwich B., *Namibia* 88 C1
Sandwip Chan., *Bangla.* 67 H17
Sandy, *Oreg., U.S.A.* 116 E4
Sandy, *Pa., U.S.A.* 110 E6
Sandy, *Utah, U.S.A.* 114 F8
Sandy Bay, *Canada* 105 B8
Sandy Bight, *Australia* 93 F3
Sandy C., *Queens., Australia* 94 C5
Sandy C., *Tas., Australia* 94 G3
Sandy Cay, *Bahamas* 121 B4
Sandy Cr. →, *U.S.A.* 114 F9
Sandy L., *Canada* 102 B1
Sandy Lake, *Canada* 102 B1
Sandy Valley, *U.S.A.* 117 K11
Sanford, *Fla., U.S.A.* 109 L5
Sanford, *Maine, U.S.A.* 109 D10
Sanford, *N.C., U.S.A.* 109 H6
Sanford →, *Australia* 93 E2
Sanford, Mt., *U.S.A.* 100 B5
Sang-i-Masha, *Afghan.* 68 C2
Sanga, *Mozam.* 87 E4
Sanga →, *Congo* 84 E3
Sangamner, *India* 66 K9
Sangar, *Afghan.* 68 C1
Sangar, *Russia* 51 C13
Sangar Sarai, *Afghan.* 68 B4
Sangaredi, *Guinea* 82 C2
Sangarh →, *Pakistan* 68 D4
Sangasso, *Mali* 82 C3
Sangatte, *France* 19 B8
Sangay, *Ecuador* 124 D3
Sange, *Dem. Rep. of the Congo* 86 D2
Sangeang, *Indonesia* 63 F5
Sângeorz-Băi, *Romania* 43 C9
Sanger, *U.S.A.* 116 J7
Sângera, *Moldova* 43 D13
Sangerhausen, *Germany* 24 D7
Sanggan He →, *China* 56 E9
Sanggau, *Indonesia* 62 D4
Sanghar, *Pakistan* 68 F3
Sangihe, Kepulauan, *Indonesia* 63 D7
Sangihe, Pulau, *Indonesia* 63 D7
Sangju, *S. Korea* 57 F15
Sangkapura, *Indonesia* 62 F4
Sangkhla, *Thailand* 64 E2
Sangkulirang, *Indonesia* 62 D5
Sangla, *Pakistan* 68 D5
Sangli, *India* 66 L9
Sangmélima, *Cameroon* 83 E7
Sangod, *India* 68 G7
Sangre de Cristo Mts., *U.S.A.* 113 G2
Sangro →, *Italy* 29 F11
Sangrur, *India* 68 D6
Sangudo, *Canada* 104 C6
Sangue →, *Brazil* 124 F7
Sangüesa, *Spain* 32 C3
Sanguinaires, Îs., *France* 21 G12
Sangzhi, *China* 59 C8
Sanhala, *Ivory C.* 82 C3
Sanibel, *U.S.A.* 109 M4
Sanirajak, *Canada* 101 B11
Sanjawi, *Pakistan* 68 D3
Sanje, *Uganda* 86 C3
Sanjiang, *China* 58 E7
Sanjo, *Japan* 54 F9
Sankh →, *India* 69 H11
Sankt Andrä, *Austria* 26 E7
Sankt Augustin, *Germany* 24 E3
Sankt Blasien, *Germany* 25 H4
Sankt Gallen, *Switz.* 25 H5
Sankt Gallen □, *Switz.* 25 H5
Sankt Goar, *Germany* 25 E3
Sankt Ingbert, *Germany* 25 F3
Sankt Johann im Pongau, *Austria* 26 D6
Sankt Johann in Tirol, *Austria* 26 D5
Sankt-Peterburg, *Russia* 46 C6
Sankt Pölten, *Austria* 26 C8
Sankt Ulrich = Ortisei, *Italy* 29 B8
Sankt Valentin, *Austria* 26 C7
Sankt Veit an der Glan, *Austria* 26 E7
Sankt Wendel, *Germany* 25 F3
Sankt Wolfgang, *Austria* 26 D6
Sankuru →, *Dem. Rep. of the Congo* 84 E4
Sanliurfa, *Turkey* 70 B3
Sanlúcar de Barrameda, *Spain* 35 J4
Sanluri, *Italy* 30 C1
Sânmartin, *Romania* 43 D10
Sanmen, *China* 59 C13
Sanmenxia, *China* 56 G6
Sanming, *China* 59 D11
Sannaspos, *S. Africa* 88 D4
Sannicandro Gargánico, *Italy* 29 G12
Sânnicolau Mare, *Romania* 42 D5
Sannieshof, *S. Africa* 88 D4
Sannīn, J., *Lebanon* 75 B4
Sanniquellie, *Liberia* 82 D3
Sannûr, W. →, *Egypt* 80 B3
Sanok, *Poland* 45 J9
Sanquhar, *U.K.* 14 F5
Sansanding, *Mali* 82 C3
Sansepolcro, *Italy* 29 E9
Sansha, *China* 59 D13
Sanshui, *China* 59 F9
Sanski Most, *Bos.-H.* 29 D13
Sansui, *China* 58 D7
Sant Antoni Abat, *Spain* 37 C7
Sant Boi de Llobregat, *Spain* 32 D7
Sant Carles, *Spain* 37 B8
Sant Carles de la Ràpita, *Spain* 32 E5
Sant Celoni, *Spain* 32 D7
Sant Feliu de Guíxols, *Spain* 32 D8
Sant Feliu de Llobregat, *Spain* 32 D7
Sant Ferran, *Spain* 37 C7
Sant Francesc de Formentera, *Spain* 37 C7
Sant Jaume, *Spain* 37 B11
Sant Joan Baptista, *Spain* 37 B8
Sant Jordi, *Spain* 37 B9
Sant Jordi, G. de, *Spain* 32 E6
Sant Llorenç de Morunys, *Spain* 32 C6
Sant Llorenç des Cardassar, *Spain* 37 B10
Sant Mateu, *Baleares, Spain* 37 B7
Sant Mateu, *Valencia, Spain* 32 E5
Sant Miquel, *Spain* 37 B7
Sant Telm, *Spain* 37 B9
Sant' Ágata Militello, *Italy* 31 D7
Santa Agnés, *Spain* 37 B7
Santa Ana, *Bolivia* 124 F5
Santa Ana, *El Salv.* 120 D2
Santa Ana, *Mexico* 118 A2
Santa Ana, *U.S.A.* 117 M9
Sant' Ángelo Lodigiano, *Italy* 28 C6
Sant' Antíoco, *Italy* 30 C1
Santa Barbara, *Chile* 126 D1
Santa Barbara, *Honduras* 120 D2
Santa Bárbara, *Mexico* 118 B3
Santa Bárbara, *Spain* 32 E5
Santa Barbara, *U.S.A.* 117 L7
Santa Bárbara, Mt., *Spain* 33 H2
Santa Barbara Channel, *U.S.A.* 117 L7
Santa Barbara I., *U.S.A.* 117 M7
Santa Catalina, Gulf of, *U.S.A.* 117 N9
Santa Catalina, I., *Mexico* 118 B2
Santa Catalina I., *U.S.A.* 117 M8
Santa Catarina □, *Brazil* 127 B6
Santa Catarina, I. de, *Brazil* 127 B6
Santa Caterina di Pittinuri, *Italy* 30 B1
Santa Caterina Villarmosa, *Italy* 31 E7
Santa Cecília, *Brazil* 127 B5
Santa Clara, *Cuba* 120 B4
Santa Clara, *Calif., U.S.A.* 116 H5
Santa Clara, *Utah, U.S.A.* 115 H7
Santa Clara, El Golfo de, *Mexico* 118 A2
Santa Clara de Olimar, *Uruguay* 127 C5
Santa Clarita, *U.S.A.* 117 L8
Santa Clotilde, *Peru* 124 D4
Santa Coloma de Farners, *Spain* 32 D7
Santa Coloma de Gramenet, *Spain* 32 D7
Santa Comba, *Spain* 34 B2
Santa Croce Camerina, *Italy* 31 F7
Santa Croce di Magliano, *Italy* 29 G11
Santa Cruz, *Argentina* 128 G3
Santa Cruz, *Bolivia* 124 G6
Santa Cruz, *Chile* 126 C1
Santa Cruz, *Costa Rica* 120 D2
Santa Cruz, *Madeira* 37 D3
Santa Cruz, *Phil.* 61 D4
Santa Cruz, *U.S.A.* 116 J4
Santa Cruz →, *Argentina* 128 G3
Santa Cruz de la Palma, *Canary Is.* 37 F2
Santa Cruz de Mudela, *Spain* 35 G7
Santa Cruz de Tenerife, *Canary Is.* 37 F3
Santa Cruz del Norte, *Cuba* 120 B3
Santa Cruz del Retamar, *Spain* 34 E6
Santa Cruz del Sur, *Cuba* 120 B4
Santa Cruz do Rio Pardo, *Brazil* 127 A6
Santa Cruz do Sul, *Brazil* 127 B5
Santa Cruz I., *U.S.A.* 117 M7
Santa Cruz Is., *Solomon Is.* 96 J8
Santa Domingo, Cay, *Bahamas* 120 B4
Sant' Egídio alla Vibrata, *Italy* 29 F10
Santa Elena, *Argentina* 126 C4
Santa Elena, C., *Costa Rica* 120 D2
Sant' Eufémia, G. di, *Italy* 31 D9
Santa Eulàlia des Riu, *Spain* 37 C8
Santa Fe, *Argentina* 126 C3
Santa Fe, *Spain* 35 H7
Santa Fe, *U.S.A.* 115 J11
Santa Fé □, *Argentina* 126 C3
Santa Fé do Sul, *Brazil* 125 H8
Santa Filomena, *Brazil* 125 E9
Santa Fiora, *Italy* 29 F8
Santa Gertrudis, *Spain* 37 C7
Santa Giustina, *Italy* 29 B9
Santa Inês, *Brazil* 125 F11
Santa Inés, *Spain* 35 G5
Santa Inés, I., *Chile* 122 J3
Santa Isabel = Rey Malabo, *Eq. Guin.* 83 E6
Santa Isabel, *Argentina* 126 D2
Santa Isabel, Pico, *Eq. Guin.* 83 E6
Santa Isabel do Morro, *Brazil* 125 F8
Santa Lucía, *Corrientes, Argentina* 126 B4
Santa Lucía, *San Juan, Argentina* 126 C2
Santa Lucía, *Spain* 33 H4
Santa Lucia, *Uruguay* 126 C4
Santa Lucia Range, *U.S.A.* 116 K5
Santa Magdalena, I., *Mexico* 118 C2
Santa Margarita, *Argentina* 126 D3
Santa Margarita, *Spain* 37 B10
Santa Margarita, *U.S.A.* 116 K6
Santa Margarita →, *U.S.A.* 117 M9
Santa Margarita, I., *Mexico* 118 C2
Santa Margherita, *Italy* 30 D1
Santa Margherita Ligure, *Italy* 28 D6
Santa María, *Argentina* 126 B2
Santa Maria, *Brazil* 127 B5
Santa Maria, *Phil.* 61 C4
Santa Maria, *U.S.A.* 117 L6
Santa María →, *Mexico* 118 A3
Santa María, B. de, *Mexico* 118 B3
Santa Maria, C. de, *Portugal* 35 J3
Santa Maria Cápua Vétere, *Italy* 31 A7
Santa Maria da Feira, *Portugal* 34 E2
Santa Maria da Vitória, *Brazil* 125 F10
Santa Maria del Camí, *Spain* 37 B9
Santa Maria di Léuca, C., *Italy* 31 C11
Santa María la Real de Nieva, *Spain* 34 D6
Santa Marinella, *Italy* 29 F8
Santa Marta, *Colombia* 124 A4
Santa Marta, Sierra Nevada de, *Colombia* 122 B3
Santa Marta de Tormes, *Spain* 34 E5
Santa Marta Grande, C., *Brazil* 127 B6
Santa Marta Ortigueira, Ría de, *Spain* 34 B3
Santa Maura = Levkás, *Greece* 38 C2
Santa Monica, *U.S.A.* 117 M8
Santa Olalla, *Huelva, Spain* 35 H4
Santa Olalla, *Toledo, Spain* 34 E6
Santa Paula, *U.S.A.* 117 L7
Santa Pola, *Spain* 33 G4
Santa Ponsa, *Spain* 37 B9
Santa Rita, *U.S.A.* 115 K10
Santa Rosa, *La Pampa, Argentina* 126 D3
Santa Rosa, *San Luis, Argentina* 126 C2
Santa Rosa, *Brazil* 127 B5
Santa Rosa, *Calif., U.S.A.* 116 G4
Santa Rosa, *N. Mex., U.S.A.* 113 H2
Santa Rosa de Copán, *Honduras* 120 D2
Santa Rosa de Río Primero, *Argentina* 126 C3
Santa Rosa del Sara, *Bolivia* 124 G6
Santa Rosa I., *U.S.A.* 117 M6
Santa Rosa Range, *U.S.A.* 114 F5
Santa Rosalía, *Mexico* 118 B2
Santa Sylvina, *Argentina* 126 B3
Santa Tecla = Nueva San Salvador, *El Salv.* 120 D2
Santa Teresa, *Argentina* 126 C3
Santa Teresa, *Australia* 94 C1
Santa Teresa, *Mexico* 119 B5
Santa Teresa di Riva, *Italy* 31 E8
Santa Teresa Gallura, *Italy* 30 A2
Santa Uxía, *Spain* 34 C2
Santa Vitória do Palmar, *Brazil* 127 C5
Santa Ynez →, *U.S.A.* 117 L6
Santa Ynez Mts., *U.S.A.* 117 L6
Santa Ysabel, *U.S.A.* 117 M10
Santadi, *Italy* 30 C1
Santaella, *Spain* 35 H6
Santai, *China* 58 B5
Santana, *Madeira* 37 D3
Sântana, *Romania* 42 D6
Santana, Coxilha de, *Brazil* 127 C4
Santana do Livramento, *Brazil* 127 C4
Santander, *Spain* 34 B7
Santander Jiménez, *Mexico* 119 C5
Santanyí, *Spain* 37 B10
Santaquin, *U.S.A.* 114 G8
Santarcángelo di Romagna, *Italy* 29 D9
Santarém, *Brazil* 125 D8
Santarém, *Portugal* 35 F2
Santarém □, *Portugal* 35 F2
Santaren Channel, *W. Indies* 120 B4
Santee, *U.S.A.* 117 N10
Santee →, *U.S.A.* 109 J6
Santéramo in Colle, *Italy* 31 B9
Santerno →, *Italy* 29 D8
Santhià, *Italy* 28 C5
Santiago, *Brazil* 127 B5
Santiago, *Chile* 126 C1
Santiago, *Panama* 120 E3
Santiago, *Phil.* 61 C4
Santiago □, *Chile* 126 C1
Santiago →, *Mexico* 98 G9
Santiago →, *Peru* 124 D3
Santiago, Punta de, *Eq. Guin.* 83 E6
Santiago de Compostela, *Spain* 34 C2
Santiago de Cuba, *Cuba* 120 C4
Santiago de los Cabelleros, *Dom. Rep.* 121 C5
Santiago del Estero, *Argentina* 126 B3
Santiago del Estero □, *Argentina* 126 B3
Santiago del Teide, *Canary Is.* 37 F3
Santiago do Cacém, *Portugal* 35 G2
Santiago Ixcuintla, *Mexico* 118 C3
Santiago Papasquiaro, *Mexico* 118 C3
Santiaguillo, L. de, *Mexico* 118 C4
Santiguila, *Mali* 82 C3
Santillana, *Spain* 34 B6
Santisteban del Puerto, *Spain* 35 G7
Santo Amaro, *Brazil* 125 F11
Santo Anastácio, *Brazil* 127 A5
Santo André, *Brazil* 127 A6
Santo Ângelo, *Brazil* 127 B5
Santo Antônio do Içá, *Brazil* 124 D5
Santo Antônio do Leverger, *Brazil* 125 G7
Santo Domingo, *Dom. Rep.* 121 C6
Santo Domingo, *Baja Calif., Mexico* 118 A1
Santo Domingo, *Baja Calif. S., Mexico* 118 B2
Santo Domingo, *Nic.* 120 D3
Santo Domingo de la Calzada, *Spain* 32 C2
Santo Domingo de los Colorados, *Ecuador* 124 D3
Santo Domingo Pueblo, *U.S.A.* 115 J10
Santo Stéfano di Camastro, *Italy* 31 D7
Santo Tirso, *Portugal* 34 D2
Santo Tomás, *Mexico* 118 A1
Santo Tomás, *Peru* 124 F4
Santo Tomé, *Argentina* 127 B4
Santo Tomé de Guayana = Ciudad Guayana, *Venezuela* 124 B6
Santomera, *Spain* 33 G3
Santoña, *Spain* 34 B7
Santoríni = Thíra, *Greece* 39 E7
Santos, *Brazil* 127 A6
Santos, Sierra de los, *Spain* 35 G5
Santos Dumont, *Brazil* 127 A7
Sanwer, *India* 68 H6
Sanxenxo, *Spain* 34 C2
Sanyuan, *China* 56 G5
São Bartolomeu de Messines, *Portugal* 35 H2
São Bernardo do Campo, *Brazil* 127 A6
São Borja, *Brazil* 127 B4
São Brás de Alportel, *Portugal* 35 H3
São Carlos, *Brazil* 127 A6
São Cristóvão, *Brazil* 125 F11
São Domingos, *Brazil* 125 F9
São Domingos, *Guinea-Biss.* 82 C1
São Francisco, *Brazil* 125 G10
São Francisco →, *Brazil* 122 E7
São Francisco do Sul, *Brazil* 127 B6
São Gabriel, *Brazil* 127 C5
São Gonçalo, *Brazil* 127 A7
Sao Hill, *Tanzania* 87 D4
São João, *Guinea-Biss.* 82 C1
São João da Boa Vista, *Brazil* 127 A6
São João da Madeira, *Portugal* 34 E2
São João da Pesqueira, *Portugal* 34 D3
São João del Rei, *Brazil* 127 A7
São João do Araguaia, *Brazil* 125 E9
São João do Piauí, *Brazil* 125 E10
São Joaquim, *Brazil* 127 B6
São Jorge, Pta. de, *Madeira* 37 D3
São José, *Brazil* 127 B5
São José do Norte, *Brazil* 127 C5
São José do Rio Prêto, *Brazil* 127 A6
São José dos Campos, *Brazil* 127 A6
São Leopoldo, *Brazil* 127 B5
São Lourenço, *Brazil* 127 A6
São Lourenço →, *Brazil* 125 G7
São Lourenço, Pta. de, *Madeira* 37 D3
São Lourenço do Sul, *Brazil* 127 C5
São Luís, *Brazil* 125 D10
São Luís Gonzaga, *Brazil* 127 B5
São Marcos →, *Brazil* 125 G9
São Marcos, B. de, *Brazil* 125 D10
São Martinho da Cortiça, *Portugal* 34 E2
São Mateus, *Brazil* 125 G11
São Mateus do Sul, *Brazil* 127 B5
São Miguel do Oeste, *Brazil* 127 B5
São Paulo, *Brazil* 127 A6
São Paulo □, *Brazil* 127 A6
São Paulo, I., *Atl. Oc.* 2 D8
São Paulo de Olivença, *Brazil* 124 D5
São Pedro do Sul, *Portugal* 34 E2
São Roque, *Madeira* 37 D3
São Roque, C. de, *Brazil* 122 D7
São Sebastião, I. de, *Brazil* 127 A6
São Sebastião do Paraíso, *Brazil* 127 A6
São Teotónio, *Portugal* 35 H2
São Tomé, *Atl. Oc.* 76 F4
São Tomé, C. de, *Brazil* 127 A7
São Tomé & Principe ■, *Africa* 77 F4
São Vicente, *Brazil* 127 A6
São Vicente, *Madeira* 37 D2
São Vicente, C. de, *Portugal* 35 H1
Saona, I., *Dom. Rep.* 121 C6
Saône →, *France* 19 G11
Saône-et-Loire □, *France* 19 F11
Saonek, *Indonesia* 63 E8

Sápai, *Greece* 41 E9
Sapanca, *Turkey* 72 B4
Saparua, *Indonesia* 63 E7
Sapele, *Nigeria* 83 D6
Sapelo I., *U.S.A.* 109 K5
Şaphane, *Turkey* 39 B11
Sapiéntza, *Greece* 38 E3
Sapone, *Burkina Faso* 83 C4
Saposoa, *Peru* 124 E3
Sapouy, *Burkina Faso* 83 C4
Sapozhok, *Russia* 48 D5
Sapphire, *Australia* 94 C4
Sappho, *U.S.A.* 116 B2
Sapporo, *Japan* 54 C10
Sapri, *Italy* 31 B8
Sapulpa, *U.S.A.* 113 H6
Saqqez, *Iran* 70 B5
Sar Dasht, *Iran* 71 C6
Sar Gachīneh, *Iran* 71 D6
Sar Planina, *Macedonia* 40 E4
Sara, *Burkina Faso* 82 C4
Sara, *Phil.* 61 F5
Sara Buri = Saraburi, *Thailand* 64 E3
Sarāb, *Iran* 70 B5
Sarabadi, *Iraq* 70 C5
Saraburi, *Thailand* 64 E3
Sarada →, *India* 67 F12
Saradiya, *India* 68 J4
Sarafére, *Mali* 82 B4
Saragossa = Zaragoza, *Spain* 32 D4
Saraguro, *Ecuador* 124 D3
Sarai Naurang, *Pakistan* 68 C4
Saraikela, *India* 69 H11
Saraiu, *Romania* 43 F13
Sarajevo, *Bos.-H.* 42 G3
Sarakhs, *Turkmenistan* 71 B9
Saran, Gunung, *Indonesia* 62 E4
Saranac L., *U.S.A.* 111 B10
Saranac Lake, *U.S.A.* 111 B10
Saranda, *Tanzania* 86 D3
Sarandë, *Albania* 40 G3
Sarandí del Yi, *Uruguay* 127 C4
Sarandí Grande, *Uruguay* 126 C4
Sarangani B., *Phil.* 61 J6
Sarangani Is., *Phil.* 61 J6
Sarangarh, *India* 67 J13
Saransk, *Russia* 48 C7
Sarapul, *Russia* 50 D6
Sarasota, *U.S.A.* 109 M4
Saratoga, *Calif., U.S.A.* 116 H4
Saratoga, *Wyo., U.S.A.* 114 F10
Saratoga Springs, *U.S.A.* 111 C11
Saratok, *Malaysia* 62 D4
Saratov, *Russia* 48 E7
Saravane, *Laos* 64 E6
Sarawak □, *Malaysia* 62 D4
Saray, *Tekirdağ, Turkey* 41 E11
Saray, *Van, Turkey* 73 C11
Saraya, *Guinea* 82 C2
Saraya, *Senegal* 82 C2
Saraycık, *Turkey* 39 B11
Sarayköy, *Turkey* 39 D10
Saraylar, *Turkey* 41 F11
Sarayönü, *Turkey* 72 C5
Sarbāz, *Iran* 71 E9
Sarbīsheh, *Iran* 71 C8
Sárbogárd, *Hungary* 42 D3
Sarca →, *Italy* 28 C7
Sarcelles, *France* 19 D9
Sarda = Sarada →, *India* 67 F12
Sardarshahr, *India* 68 E6
Sardegna □, *Italy* 30 B1
Sardhana, *India* 68 E7
Sardina, Pta., *Canary Is.* 37 F4
Sardinia = Sardegna □, *Italy* 30 B1
Sardis, *Turkey* 39 C10
Sārdūīyeh = Dar Mazār, *Iran* 71 D8
S'Arenal, *Spain* 37 B9
Sarentino, *Italy* 29 B8
Saréyamou, *Mali* 82 B4
Sargasso Sea, *Atl. Oc.* 97 D20
Sargodha, *Pakistan* 68 C5
Sarh, *Chad* 79 G9
Sarhala, *Ivory C.* 82 D3
Sārī, *Iran* 71 B7
Sari d'Orcino, *France* 21 F12
Sária, *Greece* 39 F9
Saria, *India* 69 J10
Sariab, *Pakistan* 68 D2
Sarıbeyler, *Turkey* 39 B9
Sarıgöl, *Turkey* 72 C3
Sarikamiş, *Turkey* 73 B10
Sarıkaya, *Turkey* 72 C6
Sarikei, *Malaysia* 62 D4
Sarıköy, *Turkey* 41 F11
Sarila, *India* 69 G8
Sarina, *Australia* 94 C4
Sariñena, *Spain* 32 D4
Sarita, *U.S.A.* 113 M6
Sariwŏn, *N. Korea* 57 E13
Sariyar Baraji, *Turkey* 72 B4
Sarıyer, *Turkey* 41 E13
Sarju →, *India* 69 F9
Sark, *U.K.* 13 H5
Sarkad, *Hungary* 42 D6
Sarkari Tala, *India* 68 F4
Şarkışla, *Turkey* 72 C7
Şarköy, *Turkey* 41 F11
Sarlat-la-Canéda, *France* 20 D5
Sărmăşag, *Romania* 42 C7
Sărmaşu, *Romania* 43 D9
Sarmi, *Indonesia* 63 E9
Sarmiento, *Argentina* 128 F3
Sarmizegetusa, *Romania* 42 E7
Särna, *Sweden* 10 C7
Sarnano, *Italy* 29 E10
Sarnen, *Switz.* 25 J4
Sarnia, *Canada* 102 D3
Sarno, *Italy* 31 B7
Sarnthein = Sarentino, *Italy* 29 B8
Särö, *Sweden* 11 G5
Sarolangun, *Indonesia* 62 E2
Saronikós Kólpos, *Greece* 38 D5
Saronno, *Italy* 28 C6
Saros Körfezi, *Turkey* 41 F10
Sárospatak, *Hungary* 42 B6
Sarpsborg, *Norway* 9 G14
Sarracín, *Spain* 34 C7
Sarralbe, *France* 19 D14
Sarre = Saar →, *Europe* 17 E6
Sarre, *Italy* 28 C4
Sarre-Union, *France* 19 D14
Sarrebourg, *France* 19 D14
Sarreguemines, *France* 19 C14
Sarria, *Spain* 34 C3
Sarrión, *Spain* 32 E4
Sarro, *Mali* 82 C3
Sarstedt, *Germany* 24 C5
Sartène, *France* 21 G12
Sarthe □, *France* 18 D7
Sarthe →, *France* 18 E6
Sartilly, *France* 18 D5
Saruhanlı, *Turkey* 39 C9
Sărulești, *Romania* 43 F11
Saruna →, *Pakistan* 68 F2
Sárvár, *Hungary* 42 C1
Sarvar, *India* 68 F6
Sarvestān, *Iran* 71 D7
Särvfjället, *Sweden* 10 B7
Sárviz →, *Hungary* 42 D3
Sary-Tash, *Kyrgyzstan* 50 F8
Sarych, Mys, *Ukraine* 47 K7
Saryshagan, *Kazakstan* 50 E8
Sarzana, *Italy* 28 D6
Sarzeau, *France* 18 E4
Sasan Gir, *India* 68 J4
Sasaram, *India* 69 G11
Sasebo, *Japan* 55 H4
Saser, *India* 69 B7
Saskatchewan □, *Canada* 105 C7
Saskatchewan →, *Canada* 105 C8
Saskatoon, *Canada* 105 C7
Saskylakh, *Russia* 51 B12
Sasolburg, *S. Africa* 89 D4
Sasovo, *Russia* 48 C5
Sassandra, *Ivory C.* 82 E3
Sassandra →, *Ivory C.* 82 E3
Sássari, *Italy* 30 B1
Sassnitz, *Germany* 24 A9
Sasso Marconi, *Italy* 29 D8
Sassocorvaro, *Italy* 29 E9
Sassoferrato, *Italy* 29 E9
Sasstown, *Liberia* 82 E3
Sassuolo, *Italy* 28 D7
Sástago, *Spain* 32 D4
Sasumua Dam, *Kenya* 86 C4
Sasyk, Ozero, *Ukraine* 47 K5
Sata-Misaki, *Japan* 55 J5
Satadougou, *Mali* 82 C2
Satakunta, *Finland* 9 F20
Satama-Soukoura, *Ivory C.* 82 D4
Satara, *India* 66 L8
Satara, *S. Africa* 89 C5
Satbarwa, *India* 69 H11
Såtenäs, *Sweden* 11 F6
Säter, *Sweden* 10 D9
Satevó, *Mexico* 118 B3
Satilla →, *U.S.A.* 109 K5
Satmala Hills, *India* 66 J9
Satna, *India* 69 G9
Šator, *Bos.-H.* 29 D13
Sátoraljaújhely, *Hungary* 42 B6
Satpura Ra., *India* 66 J10
Satrup, *Germany* 24 A5
Satsuna-Shotō, *Japan* 55 K5
Sattahip, *Thailand* 64 F3
Satu Mare, *Romania* 42 C7
Satu Mare □, *Romania* 42 C8
Satui, *Indonesia* 62 E5
Satun, *Thailand* 65 J3
Saturnina →, *Brazil* 124 F7
Sauce, *Argentina* 126 C4
Sauceda, *Mexico* 118 B4
Saucillo, *Mexico* 118 B3
Sauda, *Norway* 9 G12
Sauðarkrókur, *Iceland* 8 D4
Saudi Arabia ■, *Asia* 74 B3
Saugeen →, *Canada* 110 B3
Saugerties, *U.S.A.* 111 D11
Saugues, *France* 20 D7
Saugus, *U.S.A.* 117 L8
Saujon, *France* 20 C3
Sauk Centre, *U.S.A.* 112 C7
Sauk Rapids, *U.S.A.* 112 C7
Saulgau, *Germany* 25 G5
Saulieu, *France* 19 E11
Sault, *France* 21 D9
Sault Ste. Marie, *Canada* 102 C3
Sault Ste. Marie, *U.S.A.* 101 D11
Saumlaki, *Indonesia* 63 F8
Saumur, *France* 18 E6
Saunders C., *N.Z.* 91 L3
Saunders I., *Antarctica* 5 B1
Saunders Point, *Australia* 93 E4
Sauri, *Nigeria* 83 C6
Saurimo, *Angola* 84 F4
Sausalito, *U.S.A.* 116 H4
Sauveterre-de-Béarn, *France* 20 E3
Sauzé-Vaussais, *France* 20 B4
Savá, *Honduras* 120 C2
Sava, *Italy* 31 B10
Sava →, *Serbia, Yug.* 42 F5
Savage, *U.S.A.* 112 B2
Savage I. = Niue, *Cook Is.* 97 J11
Savage River, *Australia* 94 G4
Savai'i, *W. Samoa* 91 A12
Savalou, *Benin* 83 D5
Savane, *Mozam.* 87 F4
Savanna, *U.S.A.* 112 D9
Savanna-la-Mar, *Jamaica* 120 C4
Savannah, *Ga., U.S.A.* 109 J5
Savannah, *Mo., U.S.A.* 112 F7
Savannah, *Tenn., U.S.A.* 109 H1
Savannah →, *U.S.A.* 109 J5
Savannakhet, *Laos* 64 D5
Savant L., *Canada* 102 B1
Savant Lake, *Canada* 102 B1
Savanur, *India* 66 M9
Săvârşin, *Romania* 42 D7
Savaştepe, *Turkey* 39 B9
Savé, *Benin* 83 D5
Save →, *France* 20 E5
Save →, *Mozam.* 89 C5
Sāveh, *Iran* 71 C6
Savelugu, *Ghana* 83 D4
Savenay, *France* 18 E5
Săveni, *Romania* 43 C11
Saverdun, *France* 20 E5
Saverne, *France* 19 D14
Savigliano, *Italy* 28 D4
Savigny-sur-Braye, *France* 18 E7
Sávio →, *Italy* 29 D9
Šavnik, *Montenegro, Yug.* 40 D3
Savo, *Finland* 8 E22
Savoie □, *France* 21 C10
Savona, *Italy* 28 D5
Savona, *U.S.A.* 110 D7
Savonlinna, *Finland* 46 B5
Savoy = Savoie □, *France* 21 C10
Şavşat, *Turkey* 73 B10
Sävsjö, *Sweden* 11 G8
Savur, *Turkey* 70 B4
Sawahlunto, *Indonesia* 62 E2
Sawai, *Indonesia* 63 E7
Sawai Madhopur, *India* 68 G7
Sawang Daen Din, *Thailand* 64 D4
Sawankhalok, *Thailand* 64 D2
Sawara, *Japan* 55 G10
Sawatch Range, *U.S.A.* 115 G10
Sawel Mt., *U.K.* 15 B4
Sawi, *Thailand* 65 G2
Sawla, *Ghana* 82 D4
Sawmills, *Zimbabwe* 87 F2
Sawtooth Range, *U.S.A.* 114 E6
Sawu, *Indonesia* 63 F6
Sawu Sea, *Indonesia* 63 F6
Saxby →, *Australia* 94 B3
Saxmundham, *U.K.* 13 E9
Saxony = Sachsen □, *Germany* 24 E9
Saxony, Lower = Niedersachsen □, *Germany* 24 C4
Saxton, *U.S.A.* 110 F6
Say, *Mali* 82 C4
Say, *Niger* 83 C5
Saya, *Nigeria* 83 D5
Sayabec, *Canada* 103 C6
Sayaboury, *Laos* 64 C3
Sayán, *Peru* 124 F3
Sayan, Vostochnyy, *Russia* 51 D10
Sayan, Zapadnyy, *Russia* 51 D10
Saydā, *Lebanon* 75 B4
Sayhandulaan = Oldziyt, *Mongolia* 56 B5
Sayhūt, *Yemen* 74 D5
Saykhin, *Kazakstan* 49 F8
Saynshand, *Mongolia* 56 B6
Sayre, *Okla., U.S.A.* 113 H5
Sayre, *Pa., U.S.A.* 111 E8
Sayreville, *U.S.A.* 111 F10
Sayula, *Mexico* 118 D4
Sayward, *Canada* 104 C3
Sazanit, *Albania* 40 F3
Sázava →, *Czech Rep.* 26 B7
Sazin, *Pakistan* 69 B5
Sazlika →, *Bulgaria* 41 E9
Scaër, *France* 18 D3
Scafell Pike, *U.K.* 12 C4
Scalea, *Italy* 31 C8
Scalloway, *U.K.* 14 A7
Scalpay, *U.K.* 14 D3
Scandia, *Canada* 104 C6
Scandiano, *Italy* 28 D7
Scandicci, *Italy* 29 E8
Scandinavia, *Europe* 6 C8
Scansano, *Italy* 29 F8
Scapa Flow, *U.K.* 14 C5
Scappoose, *U.S.A.* 116 E4
Scarámia, Capo, *Italy* 31 F7
Scarba, *U.K.* 14 E3
Scarborough, *Trin. & Tob.* 121 D7
Scarborough, *U.K.* 12 C7
Scariff I., *Ireland* 15 E1
Scarp, *U.K.* 14 C1
Scebeli, Wabi →, *Somali Rep.* 74 G3
Šćedro, *Croatia* 29 E13
Schaal See, *Germany* 24 B6
Schaffhausen, *Switz.* 25 H4
Schagen, *Neths.* 17 B4
Schaghticoke, *U.S.A.* 111 D11
Schärding, *Austria* 26 C6
Scharhörn, *Germany* 24 B4
Scheessel, *Germany* 24 B5
Schefferville, *Canada* 103 B6
Scheibbs, *Austria* 26 C8
Schelde →, *Belgium* 17 C4
Schell Creek Ra., *U.S.A.* 114 G6
Schellsburg, *U.S.A.* 110 F6
Schenectady, *U.S.A.* 111 D11
Schenevus, *U.S.A.* 111 D10
Scherfede, *Germany* 24 D5
Schesslitz, *Germany* 25 F7
Schiedam, *Neths.* 17 C4
Schiermonnikoog, *Neths.* 17 A6
Schiltigheim, *France* 19 D14
Schio, *Italy* 29 C8
Schladming, *Austria* 26 D6
Schlanders = Silandro, *Italy* 28 B7
Schlei →, *Germany* 24 A5
Schleiden, *Germany* 24 E2
Schleiz, *Germany* 24 E7
Schleswig, *Germany* 24 A5
Schleswig-Holstein □, *Germany* 24 A5
Schlüchtern, *Germany* 25 E5
Schmalkalden, *Germany* 24 E6
Schmölln, *Germany* 24 E8
Schneeberg, *Austria* 26 D8
Schneeberg, *Germany* 24 E8
Schneverdingen, *Germany* 24 B5
Schoharie, *U.S.A.* 111 D10
Schoharie →, *U.S.A.* 111 D10
Scholls, *U.S.A.* 116 E4
Schönberg, *Mecklenburg-Vorpommern, Germany* 24 B6
Schönberg, *Schleswig-Holstein, Germany* 24 A6
Schönebeck, *Germany* 24 C7
Schongau, *Germany* 25 H6
Schöningen, *Germany* 24 C6
Schopfheim, *Germany* 25 H3
Schorndorf, *Germany* 25 G5
Schortens, *Germany* 24 B3
Schouten I., *Australia* 94 G4
Schouten Is. = Supiori, *Indonesia* 63 E9
Schouwen, *Neths.* 17 C3
Schramberg, *Germany* 25 G4
Schrankogel, *Austria* 26 D4
Schreiber, *Canada* 102 C2
Schrems, *Austria* 26 C8
Schrobenhausen, *Germany* 25 G7
Schroffenstein, *Namibia* 88 D2
Schroon Lake, *U.S.A.* 111 C11
Schruns, *Austria* 26 D2
Schuler, *Canada* 105 C6
Schumacher, *Canada* 102 C3
Schurz, *U.S.A.* 114 G4
Schuyler, *U.S.A.* 112 E6
Schuylerville, *U.S.A.* 111 C11
Schuylkill →, *U.S.A.* 111 G9
Schuylkill Haven, *U.S.A.* 111 F8
Schwabach, *Germany* 25 F7
Schwaben □, *Germany* 25 G6
Schwäbisch Gmünd, *Germany* 25 G5
Schwäbisch Hall, *Germany* 25 F5
Schwäbische Alb, *Germany* 25 G5
Schwabmünchen, *Germany* 25 G6
Schwalmstadt, *Germany* 24 E5
Schwandorf, *Germany* 25 F8
Schwaner, Pegunungan, *Indonesia* 62 E4
Schwanewede, *Germany* 24 B4
Schwarmstedt, *Germany* 24 C5
Schwarze Elster →, *Germany* 24 D8
Schwarzenberg, *Germany* 24 E8
Schwarzrand, *Namibia* 88 D2
Schwarzwald, *Germany* 25 G4
Schwaz, *Austria* 26 D4
Schwechat, *Austria* 27 C9
Schwedt, *Germany* 24 B10
Schweinfurt, *Germany* 25 E6
Schweizer-Reneke, *S. Africa* 88 D4
Schwenningen = Villingen-Schwenningen, *Germany* 25 G4
Schwerin, *Germany* 24 B7
Schweriner See, *Germany* 24 B7
Schwetzingen, *Germany* 25 F4
Schwyz, *Switz.* 25 H4
Schwyz □, *Switz.* 25 H4
Sciacca, *Italy* 30 E6
Scicli, *Italy* 31 F7
Scilla, *Italy* 31 D8
Scilly, Isles of, *U.K.* 13 H1
Ścinawa, *Poland* 45 G3
Scione, *Greece* 40 G7
Scioto →, *U.S.A.* 108 F4
Scituate, *U.S.A.* 111 D14
Scobey, *U.S.A.* 112 A2
Scone, *Australia* 95 E5
Scordia, *Italy* 31 E7
Scoresbysund = Illoqqortoormiit, *Greenland* 4 B6
Scorniceşti, *Romania* 43 F9
Scotia, *Calif., U.S.A.* 114 F1
Scotia, *N.Y., U.S.A.* 111 D11
Scotia Sea, *Antarctica* 5 B18
Scotland, *Canada* 110 C4
Scotland □, *U.K.* 14 E5
Scott, C., *Australia* 92 B4
Scott City, *U.S.A.* 112 F4
Scott Glacier, *Antarctica* 5 C8
Scott I., *Antarctica* 5 C11
Scott Is., *Canada* 104 C3
Scott L., *Canada* 105 B7
Scott Reef, *Australia* 92 B3
Scottburgh, *S. Africa* 89 E5
Scottdale, *U.S.A.* 110 F5
Scottish Borders □, *U.K.* 14 F6
Scottsbluff, *U.S.A.* 112 E3
Scottsboro, *U.S.A.* 109 H3
Scottsburg, *U.S.A.* 108 F3
Scottsdale, *Australia* 94 G4
Scottsdale, *U.S.A.* 115 K7
Scottsville, *Ky., U.S.A.* 109 G2
Scottsville, *N.Y., U.S.A.* 110 C7
Scottville, *U.S.A.* 108 D2
Scranton, *U.S.A.* 111 E9
Scugog, L., *Canada* 110 B6
Sculeni, *Moldova* 43 C12
Scunthorpe, *U.K.* 12 D7
Scuol Schuls, *Switz.* 25 J6
Scutari = Üsküdar, *Turkey* 41 F13
Seabrook, L., *Australia* 93 F2
Seaford, *U.K.* 13 G8
Seaford, *U.S.A.* 108 F8
Seaforth, *Australia* 94 C4
Seaforth, *Canada* 110 C3
Seaforth, L., *U.K.* 14 D2
Seagraves, *U.S.A.* 113 J3
Seaham, *U.K.* 12 C6
Seal →, *Canada* 105 B10
Seal L., *Canada* 103 B7
Sealy, *U.S.A.* 113 L6
Searchlight, *U.S.A.* 117 K12
Searcy, *U.S.A.* 113 H9
Searles L., *U.S.A.* 117 K9
Seascale, *U.K.* 12 C4
Seaside, *Calif., U.S.A.* 116 J5
Seaside, *Oreg., U.S.A.* 116 E3
Seaspray, *Australia* 95 F4
Seattle, *U.S.A.* 116 C4
Seaview Ra., *Australia* 94 B4
Sebago L., *U.S.A.* 111 C14
Sebago Lake, *U.S.A.* 111 C14
Sebastián Vizcaíno, B., *Mexico* 118 B2
Sebastopol = Sevastopol, *Ukraine* 47 K7
Sebastopol, *U.S.A.* 116 G4
Sebba, *Burkina Faso* 83 C5
Sebderat, *Eritrea* 81 D4
Sébékoro, *Mali* 82 C3
Seben, *Turkey* 72 B4
Sebeş, *Romania* 43 E8
Sebeşului, Munţii, *Romania* 43 E8
Sebewaing, *U.S.A.* 108 D4
Sebezh, *Russia* 46 D5
Sebha = Sabhah, *Libya* 79 C8
Sébi, *Mali* 82 B4
Şebinkarahisar, *Turkey* 73 B8
Sebiş, *Romania* 42 D7
Sebnitz, *Germany* 24 E10
Sebring, *Fla., U.S.A.* 109 M5
Sebring, *Ohio, U.S.A.* 110 F3
Sebringville, *Canada* 110 C3
Sebta = Ceuta, *N. Afr.* 78 A4
Sebuku, *Indonesia* 62 E5
Sebuku, Teluk, *Malaysia* 62 D5
Sečanj, *Serbia, Yug.* 42 E5
Secchia →, *Italy* 28 C8
Sechelt, *Canada* 104 D4
Sechura, Desierto de, *Peru* 124 E2
Seclin, *France* 19 B10
Secondigny, *France* 18 F6
Sečovce, *Slovak Rep.* 27 C14
Secretary I., *N.Z.* 91 L1
Secunderabad, *India* 66 L11
Security-Widefield, *U.S.A.* 112 F2
Sedalia, *U.S.A.* 112 F8
Sedan, *France* 19 C11
Sedan, *U.S.A.* 113 G6
Sedano, *Spain* 34 C7
Seddon, *N.Z.* 91 J5
Seddonville, *N.Z.* 91 J4
Sedé Boqér, *Israel* 75 E3
Sedeh, *Fārs, Iran* 71 D7
Sedeh, *Khorāsān, Iran* 71 C8
Séderon, *France* 21 D9
Sederot, *Israel* 75 D3
Sédhiou, *Senegal* 82 C1
Sedico, *Italy* 29 B9
Sedlčany, *Czech Rep.* 26 B7
Sedley, *Canada* 105 C8
Sedona, *U.S.A.* 115 J8
Sedova, Pik, *Russia* 50 B6
Sedro Woolley, *U.S.A.* 116 B4
Šeduva, *Lithuania* 44 C10
Sędziszów, *Poland* 45 H7
Sędziszów Małapolski, *Poland* 45 H8
Seebad Ahlbeck, *Germany* 24 B10
Seefeld in Tirol, *Austria* 26 D4
Seehausen, *Germany* 24 C7
Seeheim, *Namibia* 88 D2
Seeheim-Jugenheim, *Germany* 25 F4
Seeis, *Namibia* 88 C2
Seekoei →, *S. Africa* 88 E4
Seeley's Bay, *Canada* 111 B8
Seelow, *Germany* 24 C10
Sées, *France* 18 D7
Seesen, *Germany* 24 D6
Seevetal, *Germany* 24 B6
Sefadu, *S. Leone* 82 D2
Seferihisar, *Turkey* 39 C8
Séfeto, *Mali* 82 C3
Sefwi Bekwai, *Ghana* 82 D4
Segamat, *Malaysia* 65 L4
Şegarcea, *Romania* 43 F8
Ségbana, *Benin* 83 C5
Segbwema, *S. Leone* 82 D2
Seget, *Indonesia* 63 E8
Segonzac, *France* 20 C3
Segorbe, *Spain* 32 F4
Ségou, *Mali* 82 C3
Segovia = Coco →, *Cent. Amer.* 120 D3
Segovia, *Spain* 34 E6
Segovia □, *Spain* 34 E6
Segré, *France* 18 E6
Segre →, *Spain* 32 D5
Séguéla, *Ivory C.* 82 D3
Séguénéga, *Burkina Faso* 83 C4
Seguin, *U.S.A.* 113 L6
Segundo →, *Argentina* 126 C3
Segura →, *Spain* 33 G4
Segura, Sierra de, *Spain* 33 G2
Seh Konj, Kūh-e, *Iran* 71 D8
Seh Qal'eh, *Iran* 71 C8
Sehitwa, *Botswana* 88 C3
Sehore, *India* 68 H7
Sehwan, *Pakistan* 68 F2
Şeica Mare, *Romania* 43 D9
Seil, *U.K.* 14 E3
Seiland, *Norway* 8 A20

Seilhac, *France* 20 C5
Seiling, *U.S.A.* 113 G5
Seille →, *Moselle, France* 19 C13
Seille →, *Saône-et-Loire, France* 19 F11
Sein, Î. de, *France* 18 D2
Seinäjoki, *Finland* 9 E20
Seine →, *France* 18 C7
Seine, B. de la, *France* 18 C6
Seine-et-Marne □, *France* 19 D10
Seine-Maritime □, *France* 18 C7
Seine-St-Denis □, *France* 19 D9
Seini, *Romania* 43 C8
Seirijai, *Lithuania* 44 D10
Sejerø, *Denmark* 11 J5
Sejerø Bugt, *Denmark* 11 J5
Sejny, *Poland* 44 D10
Seka, *Ethiopia* 81 F4
Sekayu, *Indonesia* 62 E2
Seke, *Tanzania* 86 C3
Sekenke, *Tanzania* 86 C3
Seki, *Turkey* 39 E11
Sekondi-Takoradi, *Ghana* 82 E4
Sekota, *Ethiopia* 81 E4
Seksna, *Russia* 46 C10
Sekuma, *Botswana* 88 C3
Selah, *U.S.A.* 114 C3
Selama, *Malaysia* 65 K3
Selárgius, *Italy* 30 C2
Selaru, *Indonesia* 63 F8
Selb, *Germany* 25 E8
Selby, *U.K.* 12 D6
Selby, *U.S.A.* 112 C4
Selca, *Croatia* 29 E13
Selçuk, *Turkey* 39 D9
Selden, *U.S.A.* 112 F4
Sele →, *Italy* 31 B7
Selebi-Pikwe, *Botswana* 89 C4
Selemdzha →, *Russia* 51 D13
Selendi, *Manisa, Turkey* 39 C10
Selendi, *Manisa, Turkey* 39 C9
Selenga = Selenge Mörön →, *Asia* 60 A5
Selenge Mörön →, *Asia* 60 A5
Selenica, *Albania* 40 F3
Selenter See, *Germany* 24 A6
Sélestat, *France* 19 D14
Seletan, Tanjung, *Indonesia* 62 E4
Selevac, *Serbia, Yug.* 40 B4
Sélibabi, *Mauritania* 82 B2
Seliger, Ozero, *Russia* 46 D7
Seligman, *U.S.A.* 115 J7
Şelim, *Turkey* 73 B10
Selîma, El Wâhât el, *Sudan* 80 C2
Selimiye, *Turkey* 39 D9
Selinda Spillway →, *Botswana* 88 B3
Selinoús, *Greece* 38 D3
Selinsgrove, *U.S.A.* 110 F8
Selizharovo, *Russia* 46 D7
Selkirk, *Canada* 105 C9
Selkirk, *U.K.* 14 F6
Selkirk I., *Canada* 105 C9
Selkirk Mts., *Canada* 100 C8
Sellama, *Sudan* 81 E2
Selliá, *Greece* 36 D6
Sellières, *France* 19 F12
Sells, *U.S.A.* 115 L8
Sellye, *Hungary* 42 E2
Selma, *Ala., U.S.A.* 109 J2
Selma, *Calif., U.S.A.* 116 J7
Selma, *N.C., U.S.A.* 109 H6
Selmer, *U.S.A.* 109 H1
Selongey, *France* 19 E12
Selowandoma Falls, *Zimbabwe* 87 G3
Selpele, *Indonesia* 63 E8
Selsey Bill, *U.K.* 13 G7
Seltso, *Russia* 46 F8
Seltz, *France* 19 D15
Selu, *Indonesia* 63 F8
Sélune →, *France* 18 D5
Selva = La Selva del Camp, *Spain* 32 D6
Selva, *Argentina* 126 B3
Selvas, *Brazil* 122 D4
Selwyn L., *Canada* 105 B8
Selwyn Mts., *Canada* 100 B6
Selwyn Ra., *Australia* 94 C3
Semani →, *Albania* 40 F3
Semarang, *Indonesia* 63 G14
Sembabule, *Uganda* 86 C3
Şemdinli, *Turkey* 73 D11
Sémé, *Senegal* 82 B2
Semeih, *Sudan* 81 E3
Semenov, *Russia* 48 B7
Semenovka, *Chernihiv, Ukraine* 47 F7
Semenovka, *Kremenchuk, Ukraine* 47 H7
Semeru, *Indonesia* 63 H15
Semey, *Kazakstan* 50 D9
Semikarakorskiy, *Russia* 49 G5
Semiluki, *Russia* 47 G10
Seminoe Reservoir, *U.S.A.* 114 F10
Seminole, *Okla., U.S.A.* 113 H6
Seminole, *Tex., U.S.A.* 113 J3
Seminole Draw →, *U.S.A.* 113 J3
Semipalatinsk = Semey, *Kazakstan* 50 D9
Semirara Is., *Phil.* 61 F4
Semitau, *Indonesia* 62 D4
Semiyarka, *Kazakstan* 50 D8
Semiyarskoye = Semiyarka, *Kazakstan* 50 D8
Semmering P., *Austria* 26 D8
Semnān, *Iran* 71 C7
Semnān □, *Iran* 71 C7
Semporna, *Malaysia* 63 D5
Semuda, *Indonesia* 62 E4
Semur-en-Auxois, *France* 19 E11
Sen →, *Cambodia* 62 B3
Senā, *Iran* 71 D6
Sena, *Mozam.* 87 F4
Sena Madureira, *Brazil* 124 E5
Senador Pompeu, *Brazil* 125 E11
Senaki, *Georgia* 49 J6
Senanga, *Zambia* 88 B3
Senatobia, *U.S.A.* 113 H10
Sencelles, *Spain* 37 B9
Sendafa, *Ethiopia* 81 F4
Sendai, *Kagoshima, Japan* 55 J5
Sendai, *Miyagi, Japan* 54 E10
Sendai-Wan, *Japan* 54 E10
Senden, *Bayern, Germany* 25 G6
Senden, *Nordrhein-Westfalen, Germany* 24 D3
Sendhwa, *India* 68 J6
Sene →, *Ghana* 83 D4
Senec, *Slovak Rep.* 27 C10
Seneca, *U.S.A.* 109 H4
Seneca Falls, *U.S.A.* 111 D8
Seneca L., *U.S.A.* 110 D8
Senecaville L., *U.S.A.* 110 G3
Senegal ■, *W. Afr.* 82 C2
Sénégal →, *W. Afr.* 82 B1
Senegambia, *Africa* 76 E2
Senekal, *S. Africa* 89 D4
Senftenberg, *Germany* 24 D10
Senga Hill, *Zambia* 87 D3
Senge Khambab = Indus →, *Pakistan* 68 G2
Sengiley, *Russia* 48 D9
Sengua →, *Zimbabwe* 87 F2
Senhor-do-Bonfim, *Brazil* 125 F10
Senica, *Slovak Rep.* 27 C10
Senigállia, *Italy* 29 E10
Senio →, *Italy* 29 D9
Senirkent, *Turkey* 39 C12
Senise, *Italy* 31 B9
Senj, *Croatia* 29 D11
Senja, *Norway* 8 B17
Senkaku-Shotō, *Japan* 55 L1
Senlis, *France* 19 C9
Senmonorom, *Cambodia* 64 F6
Sennâr, *Sudan* 81 E3
Sennar □, *Sudan* 81 E3
Senneterre, *Canada* 102 C4
Senno, *Belarus* 46 E5
Sènnori, *Italy* 30 B1
Seno, *Laos* 64 D5
Senonches, *France* 18 D8
Senorbì, *Italy* 30 C2
Senožeče, *Slovenia* 29 C11
Sens, *France* 19 D10
Senta, *Serbia, Yug.* 42 E5
Sentani, *Indonesia* 63 E10
Sentery, *Dem. Rep. of the Congo* 86 D2
Sentinel, *U.S.A.* 115 K7
Šentjur, *Slovenia* 29 B12
Senya Beraku, *Ghana* 83 D4
Seo de Urgel = La Seu d'Urgell, *Spain* 32 C6
Seohara, *India* 69 E8
Seonath →, *India* 69 J10
Seondha, *India* 69 F8
Seoni, *India* 69 H8
Seoni Malwa, *India* 68 H8
Seoul = Sŏul, *S. Korea* 57 F14
Sepīdān, *Iran* 71 D7
Sepo-ri, *N. Korea* 57 E14
Sępólno Krajeńskie, *Poland* 44 E4
Sepone, *Laos* 64 D6
Sępopol, *Poland* 44 D8
Sept-Îles, *Canada* 103 B6
Septemvri, *Bulgaria* 41 D8
Sepúlveda, *Spain* 34 D7
Sequeros, *Spain* 34 E4
Sequim, *U.S.A.* 116 B3
Sequoia National Park, *U.S.A.* 116 J8
Serafimovich, *Russia* 48 F6
Seraing, *Belgium* 17 D5
Seraja, *Indonesia* 65 L7
Serakhis →, *Cyprus* 36 D11
Seram, *Indonesia* 63 E7
Seram Sea, *Indonesia* 63 E7
Seranantsara, *Madag.* 89 B8
Serang, *Indonesia* 63 G12
Serasan, *Indonesia* 65 L7
Seravezza, *Italy* 28 E7
Şerbettar, *Turkey* 41 E10
Serbia □, *Yugoslavia* 40 C5
Şercaia, *Romania* 43 E10
Serdo, *Ethiopia* 81 E5
Serdobsk, *Russia* 48 D7
Sered', *Slovak Rep.* 27 C10
Seredka, *Russia* 46 C5
Şereflikoçhisar, *Turkey* 72 C5
Seregno, *Italy* 28 C6
Seremban, *Malaysia* 65 L3
Serengeti Plain, *Tanzania* 86 C4
Serenje, *Zambia* 87 E3
Sereth = Siret →, *Romania* 43 E12
Sergach, *Russia* 48 C7
Sergen, *Turkey* 41 E11
Sergino, *Russia* 50 C7
Sergipe □, *Brazil* 125 F11
Sergiyev Posad, *Russia* 46 D10
Seria, *Brunei* 62 D4
Serian, *Malaysia* 62 D4
Seriate, *Italy* 28 C6
Seribu, Kepulauan, *Indonesia* 62 F3
Sérifontaine, *France* 19 C8
Sérifos, *Greece* 38 D6
Sérignan, *France* 20 E7
Sérigny →, *Canada* 103 A6
Serik, *Turkey* 72 D4
Seringapatam Reef, *Australia* 92 B3
Serinhisar, *Turkey* 39 D11
Sermaize-les-Bains, *France* 19 D11
Sermata, *Indonesia* 63 F7
Sérmide, *Italy* 29 D8
Sernovodsk, *Russia* 48 D10
Sernur, *Russia* 48 B9
Serock, *Poland* 45 F8
Serón, *Spain* 33 H2
Serós, *Spain* 32 D5
Serov, *Russia* 50 D7
Serowe, *Botswana* 88 C4
Serpa, *Portugal* 35 H3
Serpeddí, Punta, *Italy* 30 C2
Serpentara, *Italy* 30 C2
Serpentine Lakes, *Australia* 93 E4
Serpis →, *Spain* 33 G4
Serpukhov, *Russia* 46 E9
Serra de Outes, *Spain* 34 C2
Serra do Navio, *Brazil* 125 C8
Serra San Bruno, *Italy* 31 D9
Serradilla, *Spain* 34 F4
Sérrai, *Greece* 40 E7
Sérrai □, *Greece* 40 E7
Serramanna, *Italy* 30 C1
Serravalle Scrívia, *Italy* 28 D5
Serre-Ponçon, L. de, *France* 21 D10
Serres, *France* 21 D9
Serrezuela, *Argentina* 126 C2
Serrinha, *Brazil* 125 F11
Sersale, *Italy* 31 C9
Sertã, *Portugal* 34 F2
Sertanópolis, *Brazil* 127 A5
Sêrtar, *China* 58 A3
Serua, *Indonesia* 63 F8
Serui, *Indonesia* 63 E9
Serule, *Botswana* 88 C4
Sérvia, *Greece* 40 F6
Serzedelo, *Portugal* 34 D2
Sese Is., *Uganda* 86 C3
Sesepe, *Indonesia* 63 E7
Sesfontein, *Namibia* 88 B1
Sesheke, *Zambia* 88 B3
Sésia →, *Italy* 28 C5
Sesimbra, *Portugal* 35 G1
S'Espalmador, *Spain* 37 C7
S'Espardell, *Spain* 37 C7
Sessa Aurunca, *Italy* 30 A6
S'Estanyol, *Spain* 37 B9
Sestao, *Spain* 32 B2
Sesto Calende, *Italy* 28 C5
Sesto San Giovanni, *Italy* 28 C6
Sestri Levante, *Italy* 28 D6
Sestriere, *Italy* 28 D3
Sestroretsk, *Russia* 46 B6
Sestrunj, *Croatia* 29 D11
Sestu, *Italy* 30 C2
Setana, *Japan* 54 C9
Sète, *France* 20 E7
Sete Lagôas, *Brazil* 125 G10
Sétif, *Algeria* 78 A7
Seto, *Japan* 55 G8
Setonaikai, *Japan* 55 G6
Settat, *Morocco* 78 B4
Séttimo Torinese, *Italy* 28 C4
Setting L., *Canada* 105 C9
Settle, *U.K.* 12 C5
Settlement Pt., *Bahamas* 109 M6
Settlers, *S. Africa* 89 C4
Setúbal, *Portugal* 35 G2
Setúbal □, *Portugal* 35 G2
Setúbal, B. de, *Portugal* 35 G2
Seugne →, *France* 20 C3
Seul, Lac, *Canada* 100 C10
Seurre, *France* 19 F12
Sevan, *Armenia* 49 K7
Sevan, Ozero = Sevana Lich, *Armenia* 49 K7
Sevana Lich, *Armenia* 49 K7
Sevastopol, *Ukraine* 47 K7
Seven Sisters, *Canada* 104 C3
Sever →, *Spain* 35 F3
Sévérac-le-Château, *France* 20 D7
Severn →, *Canada* 102 A2
Severn →, *U.K.* 13 F5
Severn L., *Canada* 102 B1
Severnaya Zemlya, *Russia* 51 B10
Severo-Kurilsk, *Russia* 51 D16
Severo-Yeniseyskiy, *Russia* 51 C10
Severočeský □, *Czech Rep.* 26 A7
Severodonetsk = Syeverodonetsk, *Ukraine* 47 H10
Severodvinsk, *Russia* 50 C4
Severomoravský □, *Czech Rep.* 27 B10
Sevier, *U.S.A.* 115 G7
Sevier →, *U.S.A.* 115 G7
Sevier Desert, *U.S.A.* 114 G7
Sevier L., *U.S.A.* 114 G7
Sevilla, *Spain* 35 H5
Sevilla □, *Spain* 35 H5
Seville = Sevilla, *Spain* 35 H5
Sevlievo, *Bulgaria* 41 C9
Sevnica, *Slovenia* 29 B12
Sèvre-Nantaise →, *France* 18 E5
Sèvre-Niortaise →, *France* 20 B3
Sevsk, *Russia* 47 F8
Sewa →, *S. Leone* 82 D2
Sewani, *India* 68 E6
Seward, *Alaska, U.S.A.* 100 B5
Seward, *Nebr., U.S.A.* 112 E6
Seward, *Pa., U.S.A.* 110 F5
Seward Peninsula, *U.S.A.* 100 B3
Sewell, *Chile* 126 C1
Sewer, *Indonesia* 63 F8
Sewickley, *U.S.A.* 110 F4
Sexsmith, *Canada* 104 B5
Seychelles ■, *Ind. Oc.* 52 K9
Seyðisfjörður, *Iceland* 8 D6
Seydişehir, *Turkey* 72 D4
Seydvān, *Iran* 70 B5
Seyhan →, *Turkey* 70 B2
Seyhan Barajı, *Turkey* 72 D6
Seyitgazi, *Turkey* 39 B12
Seyitömer, *Turkey* 39 B11
Seym →, *Ukraine* 47 G7
Seymen, *Turkey* 41 E11
Seymour, *Australia* 95 F4
Seymour, *S. Africa* 89 E4
Seymour, *Conn., U.S.A.* 111 E11
Seymour, *Ind., U.S.A.* 108 F3
Seymour, *Tex., U.S.A.* 113 J5
Seyne, *France* 21 D10
Seyssel, *France* 21 C9
Sežana, *Slovenia* 29 C10
Sézanne, *France* 19 D10
Sezze, *Italy* 30 A6
Sfântu Gheorghe, *Covasna, Romania* 43 E10
Sfântu Gheorghe, *Tulcea, Romania* 43 F14
Sfântu Gheorghe, Braţul →, *Romania* 43 F14
Sfax, *Tunisia* 79 B8
Sha Xi →, *China* 59 D12
Sha Xian, *China* 59 D11
Shaanxi □, *China* 56 G5
Shaba = Katanga □, *Dem. Rep. of the Congo* 86 D2
Shabla, *Bulgaria* 41 C12
Shabogamo L., *Canada* 103 B6
Shabunda, *Dem. Rep. of the Congo* 86 C2
Shache, *China* 60 C2
Shackleton Ice Shelf, *Antarctica* 5 C8
Shackleton Inlet, *Antarctica* 5 E11
Shādegān, *Iran* 71 D6
Shadi, *China* 59 D10
Shadi, *India* 69 C7
Shadrinsk, *Russia* 50 D7
Shadyside, *U.S.A.* 110 G4
Shaffa, *Nigeria* 83 C7
Shafter, *U.S.A.* 117 K7
Shaftesbury, *U.K.* 13 F5
Shagamu, *Nigeria* 83 D5
Shagram, *Pakistan* 69 A5
Shah Alizai, *Pakistan* 68 E2
Shah Bunder, *Pakistan* 68 G2
Shahabad, *Punjab, India* 68 D7
Shahabad, *Raj., India* 68 G7
Shahabad, *Ut. P., India* 69 F8
Shahadpur, *Pakistan* 68 G3
Shahba, *Syria* 75 C5
Shahdād, *Iran* 71 D8
Shahdād, Namakzār-e, *Iran* 71 D8
Shahdadkot, *Pakistan* 68 F2
Shahdol, *India* 69 H9
Shahe, *China* 56 F8
Shahganj, *India* 69 F10
Shahgarh, *India* 66 F6
Shahjahanpur, *India* 69 F8
Shahpur, *India* 68 H7
Shahpur, *Baluchistan, Pakistan* 68 E3
Shahpur, *Punjab, Pakistan* 68 C5
Shahpur Chakar, *Pakistan* 68 F3
Shahpura, *Mad. P., India* 69 H9
Shahpura, *Raj., India* 68 G6
Shahr-e Bābak, *Iran* 71 D7
Shahr-e Kord, *Iran* 71 C6
Shāhrakht, *Iran* 71 C9
Shahrig, *Pakistan* 68 D2
Shahukou, *China* 56 D7
Shaikhabad, *Afghan.* 68 B3
Shajapur, *India* 68 H7
Shakargarh, *Pakistan* 68 C6
Shakawe, *Botswana* 88 B3
Shaker Heights, *U.S.A.* 110 E3
Shakhty, *Russia* 49 G5
Shakhunya, *Russia* 48 B8
Shaki, *Nigeria* 83 D5
Shākir, *Egypt* 80 B3
Shala, L., *Ethiopia* 81 F4
Shali, *Russia* 49 J7
Shallow Lake, *Canada* 110 B3
Shalqar, *Kazakstan* 50 E6
Shalskiy, *Russia* 46 B8
Shaluli Shan, *China* 58 B2
Shām, *Iran* 71 E8
Shām, Bādiyat ash, *Asia* 70 C3
Shamâl Bahr el Ghazal □, *Sudan* 81 F2
Shamâl Dârfûr □, *Sudan* 81 E2
Shamâl Kordofân □, *Sudan* 81 E3
Shamattawa, *Canada* 102 A1
Shamattawa →, *Canada* 102 A2
Shambe, *Sudan* 81 F3
Shambu, *Ethiopia* 81 F4
Shamīl, *Iran* 71 E8
Shamkhor = Şämkir, *Azerbaijan* 49 K8
Shāmkūh, *Iran* 71 C8
Shamli, *India* 68 E7
Shammar, Jabal, *Si. Arabia* 70 E4
Shamo = Gobi, *Asia* 56 C6
Shamo, L., *Ethiopia* 81 F4
Shamokin, *U.S.A.* 111 F8
Shamrock, *U.S.A.* 113 H4
Shamva, *Zimbabwe* 87 F3
Shan □, *Burma* 67 J21
Shan Xian, *China* 56 G9
Shanan →, *Ethiopia* 81 F5
Shanchengzhen, *China* 57 C13
Shāndak, *Iran* 71 D9
Shandon, *U.S.A.* 116 K6
Shandong □, *China* 57 G10
Shandong Bandao, *China* 57 F11
Shang Xian = Shangzhou, *China* 56 H5
Shanga, *Nigeria* 78 F6
Shangalowe, *Dem. Rep. of the Congo* 87 E2
Shangani, *Zimbabwe* 89 B4
Shangani →, *Zimbabwe* 87 F2
Shangbancheng, *China* 57 D10
Shangcheng, *China* 59 B10
Shangchuan Dao, *China* 59 G9
Shangdu, *China* 56 D7
Shanggao, *China* 59 C10
Shanghai, *China* 59 B13
Shanghai □, *China* 59 B13
Shanghai Shi □, *China* 59 B13
Shanghang, *China* 59 E11
Shanghe, *China* 57 F9
Shanglin, *China* 58 F7
Shangnan, *China* 56 H6
Shangqiu, *China* 56 G8
Shangrao, *China* 59 C11
Shangshui, *China* 56 H8
Shangsi, *China* 58 F6
Shangyou, *China* 59 E10
Shangyu, *China* 59 B13
Shangzhi, *China* 57 B14
Shangzhou, *China* 56 H5
Shanhetun, *China* 57 B14
Shani, *Nigeria* 83 C7
Shannon, *N.Z.* 91 J5
Shannon →, *Ireland* 15 D2
Shannon, Mouth of the, *Ireland* 15 D2
Shannon Airport, *Ireland* 15 D3
Shansi = Shanxi □, *China* 56 F7
Shantar, Ostrov Bolshoy, *Russia* 51 D14
Shantipur, *India* 69 H13
Shantou, *China* 59 F11
Shantung = Shandong □, *China* 57 G10
Shanwei, *China* 59 F10
Shanxi □, *China* 56 F7
Shanyang, *China* 56 H5
Shanyin, *China* 56 E7
Shaodong, *China* 59 D8
Shaoguan, *China* 59 E9
Shaoshan, *China* 59 D9
Shaowu, *China* 59 D11
Shaoxing, *China* 59 C13
Shaoyang, *Hunan, China* 59 D8
Shaoyang, *Hunan, China* 59 D8
Shap, *U.K.* 12 C5
Shapinsay, *U.K.* 14 B6
Shaqq el Gi'eifer →, *Sudan* 81 D2
Shaqra', *Si. Arabia* 70 E5
Shaqrā', *Yemen* 74 E4
Sharafa, *Sudan* 81 E2
Sharafkhāneh, *Iran* 70 B5
Sharbot Lake, *Canada* 111 B8
Shari, *Japan* 54 C12
Sharjah = Ash Shāriqah, *U.A.E.* 71 E7
Shark B., *Australia* 93 E1
Sharm el Sheikh, *Egypt* 80 B3
Sharon, *Mass., U.S.A.* 111 D13
Sharon, *Pa., U.S.A.* 110 E4
Sharon Springs, *Kans., U.S.A.* 112 F4
Sharon Springs, *N.Y., U.S.A.* 111 D10
Sharp Pt., *Australia* 94 A3
Sharpe L., *Canada* 102 B1
Sharpsville, *U.S.A.* 110 E4
Sharq el Istiwa'iya □, *Sudan* 81 G3
Sharya, *Russia* 48 A7
Shasha, *Ethiopia* 81 F4
Shashemene, *Ethiopia* 81 F4
Shashi, *Botswana* 89 C4
Shashi, *China* 59 B9
Shashi →, *Africa* 87 G2
Shasta, Mt., *U.S.A.* 114 F2
Shasta L., *U.S.A.* 114 F2
Shatawi, *Sudan* 81 E3
Shatsk, *Russia* 48 C5
Shatt al'Arab →, *Iraq* 71 D6
Shatura, *Russia* 46 E10
Shaumyani = Shulaveri, *Georgia* 49 K7
Shaunavon, *Canada* 105 D7
Shaver L., *U.S.A.* 116 H7
Shaw →, *Australia* 92 D2
Shaw I., *Australia* 94 C4
Shawanaga, *Canada* 110 A4
Shawangunk Mts., *U.S.A.* 111 E10
Shawano, *U.S.A.* 108 C1
Shawinigan, *Canada* 102 C5
Shawnee, *U.S.A.* 113 H6
Shay Gap, *Australia* 92 D3
Shayang, *China* 59 B9
Shaybārā, *Si. Arabia* 70 E3
Shayib el Banat, Gebel, *Egypt* 80 B3
Shaykh, J. ash, *Lebanon* 75 B4
Shaykh Miskīn, *Syria* 75 C5
Shaykh Sa'īd, *Iraq* 70 C5
Shchekino, *Russia* 46 E9
Shcherbakov = Rybinsk, *Russia* 46 C10
Shchigry, *Russia* 47 G9
Shchors, *Ukraine* 47 G6
Shchuchinsk, *Kazakstan* 50 D8
She Xian, *Anhui, China* 59 C12
She Xian, *Hebei, China* 56 F7
Shebekino, *Russia* 47 G9
Shebele = Scebeli, Wabi →, *Somali Rep.* 74 G3
Sheboygan, *U.S.A.* 108 D2
Shebshi Mts., *Nigeria* 83 D7
Shediac, *Canada* 103 C7
Sheelin, L., *Ireland* 15 C4
Sheep Haven, *Ireland* 15 A4
Sheerness, *U.K.* 13 F8
Sheet Harbour, *Canada* 103 D7
Sheffield, *U.K.* 12 D6
Sheffield, *Ala., U.S.A.* 109 H2
Sheffield, *Mass., U.S.A.* 111 D11

Sheffield, *Pa., U.S.A.* 110 E5
Shehojele, *Ethiopia* 81 E4
Shehong, *China* 58 B5
Sheikh Idris, *Sudan* 81 E3
Sheikhpura, *India* 69 G11
Shek Hasan, *Ethiopia* 81 E4
Shekhupura, *Pakistan* 68 D5
Sheki = Şaki, *Azerbaijan* 49 K8
Shelburne, *N.S., Canada* 103 D6
Shelburne, *Ont., Canada* 102 D3
Shelburne, *U.S.A.* 111 B11
Shelburne B., *Australia* 94 A3
Shelburne Falls, *U.S.A.* 111 D12
Shelby, *Mich., U.S.A.* 108 D2
Shelby, *Miss., U.S.A.* 113 J9
Shelby, *Mont., U.S.A.* 114 B8
Shelby, *N.C., U.S.A.* 109 H5
Shelby, *Ohio, U.S.A.* 110 F2
Shelbyville, *Ill., U.S.A.* 112 F10
Shelbyville, *Ind., U.S.A.* 108 F3
Shelbyville, *Ky., U.S.A.* 108 F3
Shelbyville, *Tenn., U.S.A.* 109 H2
Sheldon, *U.S.A.* 112 D7
Sheldrake, *Canada* 103 B7
Shelengo, K. →, *Sudan* 81 E2
Shelikhova, Zaliv, *Russia* 51 D16
Shell Lakes, *Australia* 93 E4
Shellbrook, *Canada* 105 C7
Shellharbour, *Australia* 95 E5
Shelon →, *Russia* 46 C6
Shelter I, *U.S.A.* 111 E12
Shelton, *Conn., U.S.A.* 111 E11
Shelton, *Wash., U.S.A.* 116 C3
Shemakha = Şamaxi, *Azerbaijan* 49 K9
Shemsi, *Sudan* 80 D2
Shen Xian, *China* 56 F8
Shenandoah, *Iowa, U.S.A.* 112 E7
Shenandoah, *Pa., U.S.A.* 111 F8
Shenandoah, *Va., U.S.A.* 108 F6
Shenandoah →, *U.S.A.* 108 F7
Shenandoah National Park, *U.S.A.* 108 F6
Shenchi, *China* 56 E7
Shendam, *Nigeria* 83 D6
Shendî, *Sudan* 81 D3
Shenge, *S. Leone* 82 D2
Shengfang, *China* 56 E9
Shëngjergji, *Albania* 40 E4
Shëngjin, *Albania* 40 E3
Shengzhou, *China* 59 C13
Shenjingzi, *China* 57 B13
Shenmëria, *Albania* 40 D4
Shenmu, *China* 56 E6
Shennongjia, *China* 59 B8
Shenqiu, *China* 56 H8
Shenqiucheng, *China* 56 H8
Shensi = Shaanxi □, *China* 56 G5
Shenyang, *China* 57 D12
Shenzhen, *China* 59 F10
Sheo, *India* 68 F4
Sheopur Kalan, *India* 66 G10
Shepetivka, *Ukraine* 47 G4
Shepetovka = Shepetivka, *Ukraine* 47 G4
Shepparton, *Australia* 95 F4
Sheppey, I. of, *U.K.* 13 F8
Shepton Mallet, *U.K.* 13 F5
Sheqi, *China* 56 H7
Sher Qila, *Pakistan* 69 A6
Sherab, *Sudan* 81 E1
Sherborne, *U.K.* 13 G5
Sherbro →, *S. Leone* 82 D2
Sherbro I., *S. Leone* 82 D2
Sherbrooke, *N.S., Canada* 103 C7
Sherbrooke, *Qué., Canada* 103 C5
Sherburne, *U.S.A.* 111 D9
Shereik, *Sudan* 80 D3
Shergarh, *India* 68 F5
Sherghati, *India* 69 G11
Sheridan, *Ark., U.S.A.* 113 H8
Sheridan, *Wyo., U.S.A.* 114 D10
Sheringham, *U.K.* 12 E9
Sherkin I., *Ireland* 15 E2
Sherkot, *India* 69 E8
Sherman, *U.S.A.* 113 J6
Sherpur, *India* 69 G10
Sherridon, *Canada* 105 B8
Sherwood Forest, *U.K.* 12 D6
Sherwood Park, *Canada* 104 C6
Sheslay →, *Canada* 104 B2
Shethanei L., *Canada* 105 B9
Shetland □, *U.K.* 14 A7
Shetland Is., *U.K.* 14 A7
Shetrunji →, *India* 68 J5
Shewa □, *Ethiopia* 81 F4
Shewa Gimira, *Ethiopia* 81 F4
Sheyenne →, *U.S.A.* 112 B6
Shibām, *Yemen* 74 D4
Shibata, *Japan* 54 F9
Shibecha, *Japan* 54 C12
Shibetsu, *Japan* 54 B11
Shibîn el Kôm, *Egypt* 80 H7
Shibîn el Qanâtir, *Egypt* 80 H7
Shibing, *China* 58 D7
Shibogama L., *Canada* 102 B2
Shibushi, *Japan* 55 J5
Shicheng, *China* 59 D11
Shickshinny, *U.S.A.* 111 E8
Shickshock Mts. = Chic-Chocs, Mts., *Canada* 103 C6
Shidao, *China* 57 F12
Shidian, *China* 58 E2
Shido, *Japan* 55 G7
Shiel, L., *U.K.* 14 E3
Shield, C., *Australia* 94 A2
Shifang, *China* 58 B5
Shiga □, *Japan* 55 G8
Shigu, *China* 58 D2
Shiguaigou, *China* 56 D6
Shihchiachuangi = Shijiazhuang, *China* 56 E8
Shijaku, *Albania* 40 E3
Shijiazhuang, *China* 56 E8
Shijiu Hu, *China* 59 B12
Shikarpur, *India* 68 E8
Shikarpur, *Pakistan* 68 F3
Shikohabad, *India* 69 F8
Shikoku □, *Japan* 55 H6
Shikoku-Sanchi, *Japan* 55 H6
Shiliguri, *India* 67 F16
Shilka, *Russia* 51 D12
Shilka →, *Russia* 51 D13
Shillelagh, *Ireland* 15 D5
Shillington, *U.S.A.* 111 F9
Shillong, *India* 67 G17
Shilo, *West Bank* 75 C4
Shilong, *China* 59 F9
Shilou, *China* 56 F6
Shilovo, *Russia* 48 C5
Shimabara, *Japan* 55 H5
Shimada, *Japan* 55 G9
Shimane □, *Japan* 55 G6
Shimanovsk, *Russia* 51 D13
Shimen, *China* 59 C8
Shimenjie, *China* 59 C11
Shimian, *China* 58 C4
Shimizu, *Japan* 55 G9
Shimodate, *Japan* 55 F9
Shimoga, *India* 66 N9
Shimoni, *Kenya* 86 C4
Shimonoseki, *Japan* 55 H5
Shimpuru Rapids, *Angola* 88 B2
Shimsk, *Russia* 46 C6
Shin, L., *U.K.* 14 C4
Shinan, *China* 58 F7
Shinano-Gawa →, *Japan* 55 F9
Shināş, *Oman* 71 E8
Shīndand, *Afghan.* 66 C3
Shinglehouse, *U.S.A.* 110 E6
Shingū, *Japan* 55 H7
Shingwidzi, *S. Africa* 89 C5
Shinjō, *Japan* 54 E10
Shinkafe, *Nigeria* 83 C6
Shinshār, *Syria* 75 A5
Shinyanga, *Tanzania* 86 C3
Shinyanga □, *Tanzania* 86 C3
Shio-no-Misaki, *Japan* 55 H7
Shiogama, *Japan* 54 E10
Shiojiri, *Japan* 55 F8
Shipchenski Prokhod, *Bulgaria* 41 D9
Shiping, *China* 58 F4
Shipki La, *India* 66 D11
Shippegan, *Canada* 103 C7
Shippensburg, *U.S.A.* 110 F7
Shippenville, *U.S.A.* 110 E5
Shiprock, *U.S.A.* 115 H9
Shiqian, *China* 58 D7
Shiqma, N. →, *Israel* 75 D3
Shiquan, *China* 56 H5
Shiquan He = Indus →, *Pakistan* 68 G2
Shīr Kūh, *Iran* 71 D7
Shiragami-Misaki, *Japan* 54 D10
Shirakawa, *Fukushima, Japan* 55 F10
Shirakawa, *Gifu, Japan* 55 F8
Shirane-San, *Gumma, Japan* 55 F9
Shirane-San, *Yamanashi, Japan* 55 G9
Shiraoi, *Japan* 54 C10
Shīrāz, *Iran* 71 D7
Shirbīn, *Egypt* 80 H7
Shire →, *Africa* 87 F4
Shiretoko-Misaki, *Japan* 54 B12
Shirinab →, *Pakistan* 68 D2
Shiriya-Zaki, *Japan* 54 D10
Shiroishi, *Japan* 54 F10
Shīrvān, *Iran* 71 B8
Shirwa, L. = Chilwa, L., *Malawi* 87 F4
Shishi, *China* 59 E12
Shishou, *China* 59 C9
Shitai, *China* 59 B11
Shivpuri, *India* 68 G7
Shixian, *China* 57 C15
Shixing, *China* 59 E10
Shiyan, *China* 59 A8
Shiyata, *Egypt* 80 B2
Shizhu, *China* 58 C7
Shizong, *China* 58 E5
Shizuishan, *China* 56 E4
Shizuoka, *Japan* 55 G9
Shizuoka □, *Japan* 55 G9
Shklov = Shklow, *Belarus* 46 E6
Shklow, *Belarus* 46 E6
Shkoder = Shkodra, *Albania* 40 D3
Shkodra, *Albania* 40 D3
Shkumbini →, *Albania* 40 E3
Shmidta, Ostrov, *Russia* 51 A10
Shō-Gawa →, *Japan* 55 F8
Shoal L., *Canada* 105 D9
Shoal Lake, *Canada* 105 C8
Shōdo-Shima, *Japan* 55 G7
Sholapur = Solapur, *India* 66 L9
Shologontsy, *Russia* 51 C12
Shōmrōn, *West Bank* 75 C4
Shoreham by Sea, *U.K.* 13 G7
Shori →, *Pakistan* 68 E3
Shorkot Road, *Pakistan* 68 D5
Shoshone, *Calif., U.S.A.* 117 K10
Shoshone, *Idaho, U.S.A.* 114 E6
Shoshone L., *U.S.A.* 114 D8
Shoshone Mts., *U.S.A.* 114 G5
Shoshong, *Botswana* 88 C4
Shoshoni, *U.S.A.* 114 E9
Shostka, *Ukraine* 47 G7
Shou Xian, *China* 59 A11
Shouchang, *China* 59 C12
Shouguang, *China* 57 F10
Shouning, *China* 59 D12
Shouyang, *China* 56 F7
Show Low, *U.S.A.* 115 J9
Shpola, *Ukraine* 47 H6
Shreveport, *U.S.A.* 113 J8
Shrewsbury, *U.K.* 13 E5
Shri Mohangarh, *India* 68 F4
Shrirampur, *India* 69 H13
Shropshire □, *U.K.* 13 E5
Shu, *Kazakstan* 50 E8
Shu →, *Kazakstan* 52 E10
Shuangbai, *China* 58 E3
Shuangcheng, *China* 57 B14
Shuangfeng, *China* 59 D9
Shuanggou, *China* 57 G9
Shuangjiang, *China* 58 F2
Shuangliao, *China* 57 C12
Shuangshanzi, *China* 57 D10
Shuangyang, *China* 57 C13
Shuangyashan, *China* 60 B8
Shubra Khit, *Egypt* 80 H7
Shucheng, *China* 59 B11
Shugozero, *Russia* 46 C8
Shuguri Falls, *Tanzania* 87 D4
Shuiji, *China* 59 D12
Shuiye, *China* 56 F8
Shujalpur, *India* 68 H7
Shukpa Kunzang, *India* 69 B8
Shulan, *China* 57 B14
Shulaveri, *Georgia* 49 K7
Shule, *China* 60 C2
Shumagin Is., *U.S.A.* 100 C4
Shumen, *Bulgaria* 41 C10
Shumerlya, *Russia* 48 C8
Shumikha, *Russia* 50 D7
Shunchang, *China* 59 D11
Shunde, *China* 59 F9
Shungay, *Kazakstan* 49 F8
Shuo Xian = Shuozhou, *China* 56 E7
Shuozhou, *China* 56 E7
Shūr →, *Fārs, Iran* 71 D7
Shūr →, *Kermān, Iran* 71 D8
Shūr →, *Yazd, Iran* 71 D7
Shūr Āb, *Iran* 71 C6
Shūr Gaz, *Iran* 71 D8
Shūrāb, *Iran* 71 C8
Shūrjestān, *Iran* 71 D7
Shurugwi, *Zimbabwe* 87 F3
Shūsf, *Iran* 71 D9
Shūsh, *Iran* 73 F13
Shūshtar, *Iran* 71 D6
Shuswap L., *Canada* 104 C5
Shuya, *Russia* 48 B5
Shuyang, *China* 57 G10
Shūzū, *Iran* 71 D7
Shwebo, *Burma* 67 H19
Shwegu, *Burma* 67 G20
Shweli →, *Burma* 67 H20
Shymkent, *Kazakstan* 50 E7
Shyok, *India* 69 B8
Shyok →, *Pakistan* 69 B6
Si Chon, *Thailand* 65 H2
Si Kiang = Xi Jiang →, *China* 59 F9
Si-ngan = Xi'an, *China* 56 G5
Si Prachan, *Thailand* 64 E3
Si Racha, *Thailand* 64 F3
Si Xian, *China* 57 H9
Siahaf →, *Pakistan* 68 E3
Siahan Range, *Pakistan* 66 F4
Siaksriindrapura, *Indonesia* 62 D2
Sialkot, *Pakistan* 68 C6
Siam = Thailand ■, *Asia* 64 E4
Sian = Xi'an, *China* 56 G5
Sianów, *Poland* 44 D3
Siantan, *Indonesia* 62 D3
Sīāreh, *Iran* 71 D9
Siargao I., *Phil.* 61 G7
Siari, *Pakistan* 69 B7
Siasi, *Phil.* 63 C6
Siasi I., *Phil.* 61 J4
Siátista, *Greece* 40 F5
Siau, *Indonesia* 63 D7
Šiauliai, *Lithuania* 9 J20
Šiauliai □, *Lithuania* 44 C10
Siazan = Siyäzän, *Azerbaijan* 49 K9
Sibâi, Gebel el, *Egypt* 70 E2
Sibayi, L., *S. Africa* 89 D5
Şibdu, *Sudan* 81 E2
Šibenik, *Croatia* 29 E12
Siberia, *Russia* 4 D13
Siberut, *Indonesia* 62 E1
Sibi, *Pakistan* 68 E2
Sibil = Oksibil, *Indonesia* 63 E10
Sibiti, *Congo* 84 E2
Sibiu, *Romania* 43 E9
Sibiu □, *Romania* 43 E9
Sibley, *U.S.A.* 112 D7
Sibolga, *Indonesia* 62 D1
Sibsagar, *India* 67 F19
Sibu, *Malaysia* 62 D4
Sibuco, *Phil.* 61 H5
Sibuguey B., *Phil.* 61 H5
Sibut, *C.A.R.* 84 C3
Sibutu, *Phil.* 63 D5
Sibutu Group, *Phil.* 61 J3
Sibutu Passage, *E. Indies* 63 D5
Sibuyan I., *Phil.* 61 E5
Sibuyan Sea, *Phil.* 61 E5
Sic, *Romania* 43 D8
Sicamous, *Canada* 104 C5
Siccus →, *Australia* 95 E2
Sichuan □, *China* 58 B5
Sichuan Pendi, *China* 58 B5
Sicilia, *Italy* 31 E7
Sicilia □, *Italy* 31 E7
Sicily = Sicilia, *Italy* 31 E7
Sicuani, *Peru* 124 F4
Šid, *Serbia, Yug.* 42 E4
Sidamo □, *Ethiopia* 81 G4
Sidaouet, *Niger* 83 B6
Sidári, *Greece* 36 A3
Siddhapur, *India* 68 H5
Siddipet, *India* 66 K11
Sidensjö, *Sweden* 10 A12
Sidéradougou, *Burkina Faso* 82 C4
Siderno, *Italy* 31 D9
Sidhauli, *India* 69 F9
Sídheros, Ákra, *Greece* 36 D8
Sidhi, *India* 69 G9
Sidhirókastron, *Greece* 40 E7
Sîdi Abd el Rahmân, *Egypt* 80 A2
Sîdi Barrâni, *Egypt* 80 A2
Sidi-bel-Abbès, *Algeria* 78 A5
Sidi Haneish, *Egypt* 80 A2
Sidi Omar, *Egypt* 80 A1
Sidlaw Hills, *U.K.* 14 E5
Sidley, Mt., *Antarctica* 5 D14
Sidmouth, *U.K.* 13 G4
Sidmouth, C., *Australia* 94 A3
Sidney, *Canada* 104 D4
Sidney, *Mont., U.S.A.* 112 B2
Sidney, *N.Y., U.S.A.* 111 D9
Sidney, *Nebr., U.S.A.* 112 E3
Sidney, *Ohio, U.S.A.* 108 E3
Sidney Lanier L., *U.S.A.* 109 H4
Sido, *Mali* 82 C3
Sidoarjo, *Indonesia* 63 G15
Sidon = Saydā, *Lebanon* 75 B4
Sidra, G. of = Surt, Khalīj, *Libya* 79 B9
Siedlce, *Poland* 45 F9
Sieg →, *Germany* 24 E3
Siegburg, *Germany* 24 E3
Siegen, *Germany* 24 E4
Siem Pang, *Cambodia* 64 E6
Siem Reap = Siemreab, *Cambodia* 64 F4
Siemiatycze, *Poland* 45 F9
Siemreab, *Cambodia* 64 F4
Siena, *Italy* 29 E8
Sieniawa, *Poland* 45 H9
Sieradz, *Poland* 45 G5
Sieraków, *Poland* 45 F3
Sierck-les-Bains, *France* 19 C13
Sierning, *Austria* 26 C7
Sierpc, *Poland* 45 F6
Sierra Blanca, *U.S.A.* 115 L11
Sierra Blanca Peak, *U.S.A.* 115 K11
Sierra City, *U.S.A.* 116 F6
Sierra Colorada, *Argentina* 128 E3
Sierra de Yeguas, *Spain* 35 H6
Sierra Gorda, *Chile* 126 A2
Sierra Leone ■, *W. Afr.* 82 D2
Sierra Madre, *Mexico* 119 D6
Sierra Mojada, *Mexico* 118 B4
Sierra Nevada, *U.S.A.* 116 H8
Sierra Vista, *U.S.A.* 115 L8
Sierraville, *U.S.A.* 116 F6
Sierre, *Switz.* 25 J3
Sifani, *Ethiopia* 81 E5
Sifié, *Ivory C.* 82 D3
Sífnos, *Greece* 38 E6
Sifton, *Canada* 105 C8
Sifton Pass, *Canada* 104 B3
Sigean, *France* 20 E6
Sighetu-Marmației, *Romania* 43 C8
Sighișoara, *Romania* 43 D9
Sigli, *Indonesia* 62 C1
Siglufjörður, *Iceland* 8 C4
Sigmaringen, *Germany* 25 G5
Signa, *Italy* 28 E8
Signakhi = Tsnori, *Georgia* 49 K7
Signal, *U.S.A.* 117 L13
Signal Pk., *U.S.A.* 117 M12
Signy-l'Abbaye, *France* 19 C11
Sigsig, *Ecuador* 124 D3
Sigüenza, *Spain* 32 D2
Siguiri, *Guinea* 82 C3
Sigulda, *Latvia* 9 H21
Sihanoukville = Kampong Saom, *Cambodia* 65 G4
Sihora, *India* 69 H9
Sihui, *China* 59 F9
Siikajoki →, *Finland* 8 D21
Siilinjärvi, *Finland* 8 E22
Siirt, *Turkey* 73 D9
Sijarira Ra., *Zimbabwe* 87 F2
Sika, *India* 68 H3
Sikao, *Thailand* 65 J2
Sikar, *India* 68 F6
Sikasso, *Mali* 82 C3
Sikeston, *U.S.A.* 113 G10
Sikhote Alin, Khrebet, *Russia* 51 E14
Sikhote Alin Ra. = Sikhote Alin, Khrebet, *Russia* 51 E14
Sikiá, *Greece* 40 F7
Síkinos, *Greece* 39 E7
Sikkani Chief →, *Canada* 104 B4
Sikkim □, *India* 67 F16
Siklós, *Hungary* 42 E3
Sikotu-Ko, *Japan* 54 C10
Sil →, *Spain* 34 C3
Silacayoapan, *Mexico* 119 D5
Šilalė, *Lithuania* 44 C9
Silandro, *Italy* 28 B7
Silawad, *India* 68 J6
Silay, *Phil.* 61 F5
Silba, *Croatia* 29 D11
Silchar, *India* 67 G18
Şile, *Turkey* 41 E13
Siler City, *U.S.A.* 109 H6
Silgarhi Doti, *Nepal* 69 E9
Silghat, *India* 67 F18
Sili, *Burkina Faso* 82 C4
Silifke, *Turkey* 70 B2
Siliguri = Shiliguri, *India* 67 F16
Siling Co, *China* 60 C3
Silistea Nouă, *Romania* 43 F10
Silistra, *Bulgaria* 41 B11
Silivri, *Turkey* 41 E12
Siljan, *Sweden* 10 D8
Siljansnäs, *Sweden* 10 D8
Silkeborg, *Denmark* 11 H3
Silkwood, *Australia* 94 B4
Silla, *Spain* 33 F4
Sillajhuay, Cordillera, *Chile* 124 G5
Sillamäe, *Estonia* 9 G22
Sillé-le-Guillaume, *France* 18 D6
Silleda, *Spain* 34 C2
Silloth, *U.K.* 12 C4
Sílo, *Greece* 41 E9
Siloam Springs, *U.S.A.* 113 G7
Silopi, *Turkey* 73 D10
Silsbee, *U.S.A.* 113 K7
Siluko, *Nigeria* 83 D6
Šilutė, *Lithuania* 9 J19
Silva Porto = Kuito, *Angola* 85 G3
Silvan, *Turkey* 73 C9
Silvani, *India* 69 H8
Silver City, *U.S.A.* 115 K9
Silver Cr. →, *U.S.A.* 114 E4
Silver Creek, *U.S.A.* 110 D5
Silver L., *U.S.A.* 116 G6
Silver Lake, *Calif., U.S.A.* 117 K10
Silver Lake, *Oreg., U.S.A.* 114 E3
Silverdalen, *Sweden* 11 G9
Silverton, *Colo., U.S.A.* 115 H10
Silverton, *Tex., U.S.A.* 113 H4
Silves, *Portugal* 35 H2
Silvi Marina, *Italy* 29 F11
Silvies →, *U.S.A.* 114 E4
Silvrettahorn, *Switz.* 28 B7
Silwa Bahari, *Egypt* 80 C3
Silz, *Austria* 26 D3
Simaltala, *India* 69 G12
Simanggang = Bandar Sri Aman, *Malaysia* 62 D4
Simao, *China* 58 F3
Simard, L., *Canada* 102 C4
Şīmareh →, *Iran* 73 F12
Simav, *Turkey* 39 B10
Simav →, *Turkey* 41 F12
Simav Dağları, *Turkey* 39 B10
Simba, *Tanzania* 86 C4
Simbach, *Germany* 25 G9
Simbirsk, *Russia* 48 C9
Simbo, *Tanzania* 86 C2
Simcoe, *Canada* 102 D3
Simcoe, L., *Canada* 102 D4
Simdega, *India* 69 H11
Simeonovgrad, *Bulgaria* 41 D9
Simeria, *Romania* 42 E8
Simeto →, *Italy* 31 E8
Simeulue, *Indonesia* 62 D1
Simferopol, *Ukraine* 47 K8
Sími, *Greece* 39 E9
Simi Valley, *U.S.A.* 117 L8
Simikot, *Nepal* 69 E9
Simitli, *Bulgaria* 40 E7
Simla, *India* 68 D7
Simlångsdalen, *Sweden* 11 H7
Şimleu-Silvaniei, *Romania* 42 C7
Simmern, *Germany* 25 F3
Simmie, *Canada* 105 D7
Simmler, *U.S.A.* 117 K7
Simnas, *Lithuania* 44 D10
Simojoki →, *Finland* 8 D21
Simojovel, *Mexico* 119 D6
Simonette →, *Canada* 104 B5
Simonstown, *S. Africa* 88 E2
Simontornya, *Hungary* 42 D3
Simplonpass, *Switz.* 25 J4
Simplontunnel, *Switz.* 25 J4
Simpson Desert, *Australia* 94 D2
Simpson Pen., *Canada* 101 B11
Simpungdong, *N. Korea* 57 D15
Simrishamn, *Sweden* 11 J8
Simsbury, *U.S.A.* 111 E12
Simushir, Ostrov, *Russia* 51 E16
Sin Cowe I., *S. China Sea* 62 C4
Sinabang, *Indonesia* 62 D1
Sinadogo, *Somali Rep.* 74 F4
Sinai = Es Sînâ', *Egypt* 75 F3
Sinai, Mt. = Mûsa, Gebel, *Egypt* 70 D2
Sinai Peninsula, *Egypt* 75 F3
Sinaia, *Romania* 43 E10
Sinaloa □, *Mexico* 118 C3
Sinaloa de Leyva, *Mexico* 118 B3
Sinalunga, *Italy* 29 E8
Sinan, *China* 58 D7
Sînandrei, *Romania* 42 E6
Sinarádhes, *Greece* 36 A3
Sincan, *Turkey* 72 B5
Sincanlı, *Turkey* 39 C12
Sincelejo, *Colombia* 124 B3
Sinch'ang, *N. Korea* 57 D15
Sinchang-ni, *N. Korea* 57 E14
Sinclair, *U.S.A.* 114 F10
Sinclair Mills, *Canada* 104 C4
Sinclair's B., *U.K.* 14 C5
Sinclairville, *U.S.A.* 110 D5
Sincorá, Serra do, *Brazil* 125 F10
Sind, *Pakistan* 68 G3
Sind □, *Pakistan* 68 G3
Sind →, *Jammu & Kashmir, India* 69 B6
Sind →, *Mad. P., India* 69 F8
Sind Sagar Doab, *Pakistan* 68 D4
Sindal, *Denmark* 11 G4
Sindangan, *Phil.* 61 G5
Sindangbarang, *Indonesia* 63 G12
Sinde, *Zambia* 87 F2
Sindelfingen, *Germany* 25 G4
Sındırgı, *Turkey* 39 B10
Sindou, *Burkina Faso* 82 C3
Sindri, *India* 69 H12
Sine →, *Senegal* 82 C1
Sinegorskiy, *Russia* 49 G5

Sinekli, *Turkey* 41 E12
Sinelnikovo = Synelnykove, *Ukraine* 47 H8
Sinendé, *Benin* 83 C5
Sines, *Portugal* 35 H2
Sines, C. de, *Portugal* 35 H2
Sineu, *Spain* 37 B10
Sinfra, *Ivory C.* 82 D3
Sing Buri, *Thailand* 64 E3
Singa, *Sudan* 81 E3
Singapore ■, *Asia* 65 M4
Singapore, Straits of, *Asia* 65 M5
Singaraja, *Indonesia* 62 F5
Singen, *Germany* 25 H4
Singida, *Tanzania* 86 C3
Singida □, *Tanzania* 86 D3
Singitikós Kólpos, *Greece* 40 F7
Singkaling Hkamti, *Burma* 67 G19
Singkang, *Indonesia* 63 E6
Singkawang, *Indonesia* 62 D3
Singkep, *Indonesia* 62 E2
Singleton, *Australia* 95 E5
Singleton, Mt., *N. Terr., Australia* 92 D5
Singleton, Mt., *W. Austral., Australia* 93 E2
Singö, *Sweden* 10 D12
Singoli, *India* 68 G6
Singora = Songkhla, *Thailand* 65 J3
Singosan, *N. Korea* 57 E14
Sinhung, *N. Korea* 57 D14
Sînî □, *Egypt* 75 F3
Siniátsikon, Óros, *Greece* 40 F5
Siniscóla, *Italy* 30 B2
Sinj, *Croatia* 29 E13
Sinjai, *Indonesia* 63 F6
Sinjajevina, *Montenegro, Yug.* 40 D3
Sinjār, *Iraq* 70 B4
Sinkat, *Sudan* 80 D4
Sinkiang Uighur = Xinjiang Uygur Zizhiqu □, *China* 60 B3
Sinmak, *N. Korea* 57 E14
Sînnai, *Italy* 30 C2
Sinnamary, *Fr. Guiana* 125 B8
Sinni →, *Italy* 31 B9
Sinnuris, *Egypt* 80 J7
Sinoie, Lacul, *Romania* 43 F13
Sinop, *Turkey* 72 A6
Sinor, *India* 68 J5
Sinp'o, *N. Korea* 57 E15
Sinsheim, *Germany* 25 F4
Sinsk, *Russia* 51 C13
Sintang, *Indonesia* 62 D4
Sinton, *U.S.A.* 113 L6
Sintra, *Portugal* 35 G1
Sinŭiju, *N. Korea* 57 D13
Sinyukha →, *Ukraine* 47 H6
Sinzig, *Germany* 24 E3
Sio →, *Hungary* 42 D3
Siocon, *Phil.* 61 H5
Siófok, *Hungary* 42 D3
Sioma, *Zambia* 88 B3
Sion, *Switz.* 25 J3
Sion Mills, *U.K.* 15 B4
Sioux City, *U.S.A.* 112 D6
Sioux Falls, *U.S.A.* 112 D6
Sioux Lookout, *Canada* 102 B1
Sioux Narrows, *Canada* 105 D10
Sipalay, *Phil.* 61 G5
Šipan, *Croatia* 40 D1
Siping, *China* 57 C13
Sipiwesk L., *Canada* 105 B9
Šipovo, *Bos.-H.* 42 F2
Sipra →, *India* 68 H6
Sipura, *Indonesia* 62 E1
Siquia →, *Nic.* 120 D3
Siquijor, *Phil.* 61 G5
Siquirres, *Costa Rica* 120 D3
Şīr Banī Yās, *U.A.E.* 71 E7
Sir Edward Pellew Group, *Australia* 94 B2
Sir Graham Moore Is., *Australia* 92 B4
Sir James MacBrien, Mt., *Canada* 100 B7
Sira →, *Norway* 9 G12
Siracusa, *Italy* 31 E8
Sirajganj, *Bangla.* 69 G13
Sirakoro, *Mali* 82 C3
Şiran, *Turkey* 73 B8
Sirasso, *Ivory C.* 82 D3
Sirathu, *India* 69 G9
Sīrdān, *Iran* 71 B6
Sirdaryo = Syrdarya →, *Kazakstan* 50 E7
Sire, *Ethiopia* 81 F4
Siren, *U.S.A.* 112 C8
Sirer, *Spain* 37 C7
Siret, *Romania* 43 C11
Siret →, *Romania* 43 E12
Sirghāyā, *Syria* 75 B5
Şiria, *Romania* 42 D6
Sirino, Mte., *Italy* 31 B8
Sirmaur, *India* 69 G9
Sírna, *Greece* 39 E8
Şirnak, *Turkey* 73 D10
Sirohi, *India* 68 G5
Sironj, *India* 68 G7
Síros, *Greece* 38 D6
Sirretta Pk., *U.S.A.* 117 K8
Sīrrī, *Iran* 71 E7
Sirsa, *India* 68 E6
Sirsa →, *India* 69 F8
Siruela, *Spain* 35 G5
Sisak, *Croatia* 29 C13
Sisaket, *Thailand* 64 E5
Sisante, *Spain* 33 F2
Sisargas, Is., *Spain* 34 B2
Sishen, *S. Africa* 88 D3
Sishui, *Henan, China* 56 G7
Sishui, *Shandong, China* 57 G9
Sisipuk L., *Canada* 105 B8
Sisophon, *Cambodia* 64 F4
Sisseton, *U.S.A.* 112 C6
Sissonne, *France* 19 C10
Sīstān, *Asia* 71 D9
Sīstān, Daryācheh-ye, *Iran* 66 D2
Sīstān va Balūchestān □, *Iran* 71 E9
Sisteron, *France* 21 D9
Sisters, *U.S.A.* 114 D3
Siswa Bazar, *India* 69 F10
Sitakili, *Mali* 82 C2
Sitamarhi, *India* 69 F11
Sitampiky, *Madag.* 89 B8
Sitapur, *India* 69 F9
Siteki, *Swaziland* 89 D5
Sitges, *Spain* 32 D6
Sithoniá, *Greece* 40 F7
Sitía, *Greece* 36 D8
Sitka, *U.S.A.* 104 B1
Sitoti, *Botswana* 88 C3
Sitra, *Egypt* 80 B2
Sittang Myit →, *Burma* 67 L20
Sittard, *Neths.* 17 C5
Sittensen, *Germany* 24 B5
Sittingbourne, *U.K.* 13 F8
Sittona, *Eritrea* 81 E4
Sittoung = Sittang Myit →, *Burma* 67 L20
Sittwe, *Burma* 67 J18
Situbondo, *Indonesia* 63 G16
Siuna, *Nic.* 120 D3
Siuri, *India* 69 H12
Siutghiol, Lacul, *Romania* 43 F13
Sīvand, *Iran* 71 D7
Sivas, *Turkey* 70 B3
Sivaslı, *Turkey* 39 C11
Siverek, *Turkey* 70 B3
Sivrihisar, *Turkey* 72 C4
Sîwa, *Egypt* 80 B2
Sîwa, El Wâhât es, *Egypt* 80 B2
Siwa Oasis, *Egypt* 76 D6
Siwalik Range, *Nepal* 69 F10
Siwan, *India* 69 F11
Siwana, *India* 68 G5
Sixmilebridge, *Ireland* 15 D3
Sixth Cataract, *Sudan* 81 D3
Siyâl, Jazâ'ir, *Egypt* 80 C4
Siyäzän, *Azerbaijan* 49 K9
Siziwang Qi, *China* 56 D6
Sjælland, *Denmark* 11 J5
Sjællands Odde, *Denmark* 11 J5
Sjenica, *Serbia, Yug.* 40 C3
Sjöbo, *Sweden* 11 J7
Sjötofta, *Sweden* 11 G7
Sjötorp, *Sweden* 11 F8
Sjumen = Shumen, *Bulgaria* 41 C10
Sjuntorp, *Sweden* 11 F6
Skadarsko Jezero, *Montenegro, Yug.* 40 D3
Skadovsk, *Ukraine* 47 J7
Skælskør, *Denmark* 11 J5
Skærbæk, *Denmark* 11 J2
Skaftafell, *Iceland* 8 D5
Skagafjörður, *Iceland* 8 D4
Skagastølstindane, *Norway* 9 F12
Skagaströnd, *Iceland* 8 D3
Skagen, *Denmark* 11 G4
Skagern, *Sweden* 11 F8
Skagerrak, *Denmark* 11 G2
Skagit →, *U.S.A.* 116 B4
Skagway, *U.S.A.* 100 C6
Skala-Podilska, *Ukraine* 47 H4
Skala Podolskaya = Skala-Podilska, *Ukraine* 47 H4
Skalat, *Ukraine* 47 H3
Skalbmierz, *Poland* 45 H7
Skälderviken, *Sweden* 11 H6
Skalica, *Slovak Rep.* 27 C10
Skallingen, *Denmark* 11 J2
Skalni Dol = Kamenyak, *Bulgaria* 41 C10
Skanderborg, *Denmark* 11 H3
Skåne, *Sweden* 11 J7
Skåne län □, *Sweden* 11 H7
Skaneateles, *U.S.A.* 111 D8
Skaneateles L., *U.S.A.* 111 D8
Skänninge, *Sweden* 11 F9
Skanör med Falsterbo, *Sweden* 11 J6
Skantzoúra, *Greece* 38 B6
Skara, *Sweden* 11 F7
Skaraborgs län □, *Sweden* 11 F7
Skärblacka, *Sweden* 11 F9
Skardu, *Pakistan* 69 B6
Skåre, *Sweden* 10 E7
Skärhamn, *Sweden* 11 G5
Skarszewy, *Poland* 44 D5
Skaryszew, *Poland* 45 G8
Skarżysko-Kamienna, *Poland* 45 G7
Skattkärr, *Sweden* 10 E7
Skattungbyn, *Sweden* 10 C8
Skawina, *Poland* 45 J6
Skebobruk, *Sweden* 10 E12
Skeena →, *Canada* 104 C2
Skeena Mts., *Canada* 104 B3
Skegness, *U.K.* 12 D8
Skeldon, *Guyana* 124 B7
Skeleton Coast Park, *Namibia* 88 C1
Skellefte älv →, *Sweden* 8 D19
Skellefteå, *Sweden* 8 D19
Skelleftehamn, *Sweden* 8 D19
Skender Vakuf, *Bos.-H.* 42 F2
Skerries, The, *U.K.* 12 D3
Skhíza, *Greece* 38 E3
Skhoinoúsa, *Greece* 39 E7
Ski, *Norway* 9 G14
Skíathos, *Greece* 38 B5
Skibbereen, *Ireland* 15 E2
Skiddaw, *U.K.* 12 C4
Skidegate, *Canada* 104 C2
Skídhra, *Greece* 40 F6
Skien, *Norway* 9 G13
Skierniewice, *Poland* 45 G7
Skikda, *Algeria* 78 A7
Skillingaryd, *Sweden* 11 G8
Skillinge, *Sweden* 11 J8
Skilloura, *Cyprus* 36 D12
Skinári, Ákra, *Greece* 38 D2
Skinnskatteberg, *Sweden* 10 E9
Skipton, *U.K.* 12 D5
Skirmish Pt., *Australia* 94 A1
Skiropoúla, *Greece* 38 C6
Skíros, *Greece* 38 C6
Skivarp, *Sweden* 11 J7
Skive, *Denmark* 11 H3
Skjálfandafljót →, *Iceland* 8 D5
Skjálfandi, *Iceland* 8 C5
Skjern, *Denmark* 11 J2
Skoczów, *Poland* 45 J5
Škofja Loka, *Slovenia* 29 B11
Skoghall, *Sweden* 10 E7
Skogstorp, *Sweden* 10 E10
Skoki, *Poland* 45 F4
Skole, *Ukraine* 47 H2
Skópelos, *Greece* 38 B5
Skopí, *Greece* 36 D8
Skopin, *Russia* 46 F10
Skopje, *Macedonia* 40 D5
Skórcz, *Poland* 44 E5
Skørping, *Denmark* 11 H3
Skövde, *Sweden* 11 F7
Skovorodino, *Russia* 51 D13
Skowhegan, *U.S.A.* 109 C11
Skradin, *Croatia* 29 E12
Skrea, *Sweden* 11 H6
Skrunda, *Latvia* 44 B9
Skrwa →, *Poland* 45 F6
Skull, *Ireland* 15 E2
Skultorp, *Sweden* 11 F7
Skultuna, *Sweden* 10 E10
Skunk →, *U.S.A.* 112 E9
Skuodas, *Lithuania* 9 H19
Skurup, *Sweden* 11 J7
Skutskär, *Sweden* 10 D11
Skvyra, *Ukraine* 47 H5
Skwierzyna, *Poland* 45 F2
Skye, *U.K.* 14 D2
Skykomish, *U.S.A.* 114 C3
Skyros = Skíros, *Greece* 38 C6
Skyttorp, *Sweden* 10 D11
Slættaratindur, *Færoe Is.* 8 E9
Slagelse, *Denmark* 11 J5
Slamet, *Indonesia* 63 G13
Slaney →, *Ireland* 15 D5
Slangberge, *S. Africa* 88 E3
Slănic, *Romania* 43 E10
Slano, *Croatia* 40 D1
Slantsy, *Russia* 46 C5
Slaný, *Czech Rep.* 26 A7
Śląskie □, *Poland* 45 H6
Slätbaken, *Sweden* 11 F10
Slate Is., *Canada* 102 C2
Slatina, *Croatia* 42 E2
Slatina, *Romania* 43 F9
Slatina Timiş, *Romania* 42 E7
Slatington, *U.S.A.* 111 F9
Slaton, *U.S.A.* 113 J4
Slave →, *Canada* 104 A6
Slave Coast, *W. Afr.* 83 D5
Slave Lake, *Canada* 104 B6
Slave Pt., *Canada* 104 A5
Slavgorod, *Russia* 50 D8
Slavinja, *Serbia, Yug.* 40 C6
Slavkov u Brna, *Czech Rep.* 27 B9
Slavonija, *Europe* 42 E2
Slavonski Brod, *Croatia* 42 E3
Slavuta, *Ukraine* 47 G4
Slavyanka, *Russia* 54 C5
Slavyanovo, *Bulgaria* 41 C8
Slavyansk = Slovyansk, *Ukraine* 47 H9
Slavyansk-na-Kubani, *Russia* 47 K10
Sława, *Poland* 45 G3
Slawharad, *Belarus* 46 F6
Sławno, *Poland* 44 D3
Sławoborze, *Poland* 44 E2
Sleaford, *U.K.* 12 D7
Sleaford B., *Australia* 95 E2
Sleat, Sd. of, *U.K.* 14 D3
Sleeper Is., *Canada* 101 C11
Sleepy Eye, *U.S.A.* 112 C7
Slemon L., *Canada* 104 A5
Ślesin, *Poland* 45 F5
Slide Mt., *U.S.A.* 111 E10
Slidell, *U.S.A.* 113 K10
Sliema, *Malta* 36 D2
Slieve Aughty, *Ireland* 15 C3
Slieve Bloom, *Ireland* 15 C4
Slieve Donard, *U.K.* 15 B6
Slieve Gamph, *Ireland* 15 B3
Slieve Gullion, *U.K.* 15 B5
Slieve Mish, *Ireland* 15 D2
Slievenamon, *Ireland* 15 D4
Sligeach = Sligo, *Ireland* 15 B3
Sligo, *Ireland* 15 B3
Sligo, *U.S.A.* 110 E5
Sligo □, *Ireland* 15 B3
Sligo B., *Ireland* 15 B3
Slippery Rock, *U.S.A.* 110 E4
Slite, *Sweden* 11 G12
Sliven, *Bulgaria* 41 D10
Slivnitsa, *Bulgaria* 40 D7
Sljeme, *Croatia* 29 C12
Sloan, *U.S.A.* 117 K11
Sloansville, *U.S.A.* 111 D10
Slobozia, *Moldova* 43 D14
Slobozia, *Argeş, Romania* 43 F10
Slobozia, *Ialomiţa, Romania* 43 F12
Slocan, *Canada* 104 D5
Słomniki, *Poland* 45 H7
Slonim, *Belarus* 47 F3
Slough, *U.K.* 13 F7
Slough □, *U.K.* 13 F7
Sloughhouse, *U.S.A.* 116 G5
Slovak Rep. ■, *Europe* 27 C13
Slovakia = Slovak Rep. ■, *Europe* 27 C13
Slovakian Ore Mts. = Slovenské Rudohorie, *Slovak Rep.* 27 C12
Slovenia ■, *Europe* 29 C11
Slovenija = Slovenia ■, *Europe* 29 C11
Slovenj Gradec, *Slovenia* 29 B12
Slovenska Bistrica, *Slovenia* 29 B12
Slovenske Konjice, *Slovenia* 29 B12
Slovenské Rudohorie, *Slovak Rep.* 27 C12
Slovyansk, *Ukraine* 47 H9
Słubice, *Poland* 45 F1
Sluch →, *Ukraine* 47 G4
Sluis, *Neths.* 17 C3
Slŭnchev Bryag, *Bulgaria* 41 D11
Slunj, *Croatia* 29 C12
Słupca, *Poland* 45 F4
Słupia →, *Poland* 44 D3
Słupsk, *Poland* 44 D4
Slurry, *S. Africa* 88 D4
Slutsk, *Belarus* 47 F4
Slyne Hd., *Ireland* 15 C1
Slyudyanka, *Russia* 51 D11
Småland, *Sweden* 11 G9
Smålandsfarvandet, *Denmark* 11 J5
Smålandsstenar, *Sweden* 11 G7
Smalltree L., *Canada* 105 A8
Smallwood Res., *Canada* 103 B7
Smara, *Morocco* 78 B4
Smarhon, *Belarus* 46 E4
Smarje, *Slovenia* 29 B12
Smartt Syndicate Dam, *S. Africa* 88 E3
Smartville, *U.S.A.* 116 F5
Smeaton, *Canada* 105 C8
Smedby, *Sweden* 11 H10
Smederevo, *Serbia, Yug.* 40 B4
Smederevska Palanka, *Serbia, Yug.* 40 B4
Smedjebacken, *Sweden* 10 D9
Smela = Smila, *Ukraine* 47 H6
Smerwick Harbour, *Ireland* 15 D1
Smethport, *U.S.A.* 110 E6
Smidovich, *Russia* 51 E14
Śmigiel, *Poland* 45 F3
Smila, *Ukraine* 47 H6
Smilyan, *Bulgaria* 41 E8
Smith, *Canada* 104 B6
Smith Center, *U.S.A.* 112 F5
Smith Sund, *Greenland* 4 B4
Smithburne →, *Australia* 94 B3
Smithers, *Canada* 104 C3
Smithfield, *S. Africa* 89 E4
Smithfield, *N.C., U.S.A.* 109 H6
Smithfield, *Utah, U.S.A.* 114 F8
Smiths Falls, *Canada* 102 D4
Smithton, *Australia* 94 G4
Smithville, *Canada* 110 C5
Smithville, *U.S.A.* 113 K6
Smoky →, *Canada* 104 B5
Smoky Bay, *Australia* 95 E1
Smoky Hill →, *U.S.A.* 112 F6
Smoky Hills, *U.S.A.* 112 F5
Smoky Lake, *Canada* 104 C6
Smøla, *Norway* 8 E13
Smolensk, *Russia* 46 E7
Smolikas, Óros, *Greece* 40 F4
Smolník, *Slovak Rep.* 27 C13
Smolyan, *Bulgaria* 41 E8
Smooth Rock Falls, *Canada* 102 C3
Smoothstone L., *Canada* 105 C7
Smorgon = Smarhon, *Belarus* 46 E4
Smulţi, *Romania* 43 E12
Smyadovo, *Bulgaria* 41 C11
Smygehamn, *Sweden* 11 J7
Smyrna = İzmir, *Turkey* 39 C9
Smyrna, *U.S.A.* 108 F8
Snæfell, *Iceland* 8 D6
Snaefell, *U.K.* 12 C3
Snæfellsjökull, *Iceland* 8 D2
Snake →, *U.S.A.* 114 C4
Snake I., *Australia* 95 F4
Snake Range, *U.S.A.* 114 G6
Snake River Plain, *U.S.A.* 114 E7
Snasahögarna, *Sweden* 10 A6
Snåsavatnet, *Norway* 8 D14
Snedsted, *Denmark* 11 H2
Sneek, *Neths.* 17 A5
Sneeuberge, *S. Africa* 88 E3
Snejbjerg, *Denmark* 11 H2
Snelling, *U.S.A.* 116 H6
Snezhnoye, *Ukraine* 47 J10
Snežnik, *Slovenia* 29 C11
Śniadowo, *Poland* 45 E8
Śniardwy, Jezioro, *Poland* 44 E8
Śnieżka, *Europe* 26 A8
Snigirevka = Snihurivka, *Ukraine* 47 J7
Snihurivka, *Ukraine* 47 J7
Snina, *Slovak Rep.* 27 C15
Snizort, L., *U.K.* 14 D2
Snøhetta, *Norway* 9 E13
Snohomish, *U.S.A.* 116 C4
Snoul, *Cambodia* 65 F6
Snow Hill, *U.S.A.* 108 F8
Snow Lake, *Canada* 105 C8
Snow Mt., *Calif., U.S.A.* 116 F4
Snow Mt., *Maine, U.S.A.* 111 A14
Snow Shoe, *U.S.A.* 110 E7
Snowbird L., *Canada* 105 A8
Snowdon, *U.K.* 12 D3
Snowdrift →, *Canada* 105 A6
Snowflake, *U.S.A.* 115 J8
Snowshoe Pk., *U.S.A.* 114 B6
Snowtown, *Australia* 95 E2
Snowville, *U.S.A.* 114 F7
Snowy →, *Australia* 95 F4
Snowy Mt., *U.S.A.* 111 C10
Snowy Mts., *Australia* 95 F4
Snug Corner, *Bahamas* 121 B5
Snyatyn, *Ukraine* 47 H3
Snyder, *Okla., U.S.A.* 113 H5
Snyder, *Tex., U.S.A.* 113 J4
Soahanina, *Madag.* 89 B7
Soalala, *Madag.* 89 B8
Soaloka, *Madag.* 89 B8
Soamanonga, *Madag.* 89 C7
Soan →, *Pakistan* 68 C4
Soanierana-Ivongo, *Madag.* 89 B8
Soanindraniny, *Madag.* 89 B8
Şoarş, *Romania* 43 E9
Soavina, *Madag.* 89 C8
Soavinandriana, *Madag.* 89 B8
Soba, *Nigeria* 83 C6
Sobat, Nahr →, *Sudan* 81 F3
Soběslav, *Czech Rep.* 26 B7
Sobhapur, *India* 68 H8
Sobinka, *Russia* 46 E11
Sobótka, *Poland* 45 H3
Sobra, *Croatia* 29 F14
Sobradinho, Reprêsa de, *Brazil* 125 E10
Sobral, *Brazil* 125 D10
Sobrance, *Slovak Rep.* 27 C15
Sobreira Formosa, *Portugal* 34 F3
Soc Giang, *Vietnam* 58 F6
Soc Trang, *Vietnam* 65 H5
Soča →, *Europe* 26 E6
Socastee, *U.S.A.* 109 J6
Sochaczew, *Poland* 45 F7
Soch'e = Shache, *China* 60 C2
Sochi, *Russia* 49 J4
Société, Is. de la, *Pac. Oc.* 97 J12
Society Is. = Société, Is. de la, *Pac. Oc.* 97 J12
Socompa, Portezuelo de, *Chile* 126 A2
Socorro, *N. Mex., U.S.A.* 115 J10
Socorro, *Tex., U.S.A.* 115 L10
Socorro, I., *Mexico* 118 D2
Socotra, *Ind. Oc.* 74 E5
Socovos, *Spain* 33 G3
Socuéllamos, *Spain* 33 F2
Soda L., *U.S.A.* 115 J5
Soda Plains, *India* 69 B8
Soda Springs, *U.S.A.* 114 E8
Sodankylä, *Finland* 8 C22
Soddy-Daisy, *U.S.A.* 109 H3
Söderala, *Sweden* 10 C10
Söderbärke, *Sweden* 10 D9
Söderfors, *Sweden* 10 D11
Söderhamn, *Sweden* 10 C11
Söderköping, *Sweden* 11 F10
Södermanland, *Sweden* 9 G17
Södermanlands län □, *Sweden* 10 E10
Södertälje, *Sweden* 10 E11
Sodiri, *Sudan* 81 E2
Sodo, *Ethiopia* 81 F4
Södra Dellen, *Sweden* 10 C10
Södra Finnskoga, *Sweden* 10 D6
Södra Sandby, *Sweden* 11 J7
Södra Ulvön, *Sweden* 10 B12
Södra Vi, *Sweden* 11 G9
Sodražica, *Slovenia* 29 C11
Sodus, *U.S.A.* 110 C7
Soekmekaar, *S. Africa* 89 C4
Soest, *Germany* 24 D4
Soest, *Neths.* 17 B5
Sofádhes, *Greece* 38 B4
Sofala □, *Mozam.* 89 B5
Sofara, *Mali* 82 C4
Sofia = Sofiya, *Bulgaria* 40 D7
Sofia →, *Madag.* 89 B8
Sofievka, *Ukraine* 47 H7
Sofikón, *Greece* 38 D5
Sofiya, *Bulgaria* 40 D7
Sofiya □, *Bulgaria* 40 D7
Sōfu-Gan, *Japan* 55 K10
Sogakofe, *Ghana* 83 D5
Sogamoso, *Colombia* 124 B4
Sogār, *Iran* 71 E8
Sögel, *Germany* 24 C3
Sogndalsfjøra, *Norway* 9 F12
Søgne, *Norway* 9 G12
Sognefjorden, *Norway* 9 F11
Söğüt, *Bilecik, Turkey* 39 A12
Söğüt, *Burdur, Turkey* 39 D11
Söğüt Dağı, *Turkey* 39 D11
Söğütköy, *Turkey* 39 E10
Sŏgwipo, *S. Korea* 57 H14
Soh, *Iran* 71 C6
Sohâg, *Egypt* 80 B3
Sohagpur, *India* 68 H8
Sŏhori, *N. Korea* 57 D15
Soignies, *Belgium* 17 D4
Soin, *Burkina Faso* 82 C4
Soira, *Eritrea* 81 E4
Soissons, *France* 19 C10
Sōja, *Japan* 55 G6
Sojat, *India* 68 G5
Sok →, *Russia* 48 D10
Sokal, *Ukraine* 47 G3
Söke, *Turkey* 39 D9
Sokelo, *Dem. Rep. of the Congo* 87 D1
Sokhós, *Greece* 40 F7
Sokhumi, *Georgia* 49 J5
Soko Banja, *Serbia, Yug.* 40 C5
Sokodé, *Togo* 83 D5
Sokol, *Russia* 46 C11

Sokolac, Bos.-H. 42 G3
Sokółka, Poland 44 E10
Sokolo, Mali 82 C3
Sokolo, Mali 82 C3
Sokolov, Czech Rep. 26 A5
Sokołów Małpolski, Poland 45 H9
Sokołów Podlaski, Poland 45 F9
Sokoły, Poland 45 F9
Sokoto, Nigeria 83 C6
Sokoto □, Nigeria 83 C6
Sokoto →, Nigeria 83 C5
Sol Iletsk, Russia 50 D6
Sola →, Poland 45 H6
Solai, Kenya 86 B4
Solan, India 68 D7
Solano, Phil. 61 C4
Solapur, India 66 L9
Solca, Romania 43 C10
Solda Gölü, Turkey 39 D11
Soldănești, Moldova 43 C13
Soldotna, U.S.A. 100 B4
Soléa □, Cyprus 36 D12
Solec Kujawski, Poland 45 E5
Soledad, Colombia 124 A4
Soledad, U.S.A. 116 J5
Soledad, Venezuela 124 B6
Solent, The, U.K. 13 G6
Solenzara, France 21 G13
Solesmes, France 19 B10
Solfonn, Norway 9 F12
Solhan, Turkey 70 B4
Soligorsk = Salihorsk, Belarus 47 F4
Solihull, U.K. 13 E6
Solikamsk, Russia 50 D6
Solila, Madag. 89 C8
Solimões = Amazonas →, S. Amer. 122 D5
Solin, Croatia 29 E13
Solingen, Germany 24 D3
Sollebrunn, Sweden 11 F6
Sollefteå, Sweden 10 A11
Sollentuna, Sweden 10 E11
Sóller, Spain 37 B9
Sollerön, Sweden 10 D8
Solling, Germany 24 D5
Solnechnogorsk, Russia 46 D9
Solo →, Indonesia 63 G15
Solofra, Italy 31 B7
Sologne, France 19 E8
Solok, Indonesia 62 E2
Sololá, Guatemala 120 D1
Solomon, N. Fork →, U.S.A. 112 F5
Solomon, S. Fork →, U.S.A. 112 F5
Solomon Is. ■, Pac. Oc. 96 H7
Solon, China 60 B7
Solon Springs, U.S.A. 112 B9
Solor, Indonesia 63 F6
Solotcha, Russia 46 E10
Solothurn, Switz. 25 H3
Solothurn □, Switz. 25 H3
Solsona, Spain 32 C6
Solt, Hungary 42 D4
Šolta, Croatia 29 E13
Solṭānābād, Khorāsān, Iran 71 C8
Solṭānābād, Khorāsān, Iran 71 B8
Soltau, Germany 24 C5
Soltsy, Russia 46 C6
Solunska Glava, Macedonia 40 E5
Solvang, U.S.A. 117 L6
Solvay, U.S.A. 111 C8
Sölvesborg, Sweden 11 H8
Solway Firth, U.K. 12 C4
Solwezi, Zambia 87 E2
Sōma, Japan 54 F10
Soma, Turkey 39 B9
Somabhula, Zimbabwe 89 B4
Somali Pen., Africa 76 F8
Somali Rep. ■, Africa 74 F4
Somalia = Somali Rep. ■, Africa 74 F4
Sombernon, France 19 E11
Sombor, Serbia, Yug. 42 E4
Sombra, Canada 110 D2
Sombrerete, Mexico 118 C4
Sombrero, Anguilla 121 C7
Şomcuta Mare, Romania 43 C8
Somdari, India 68 G5
Somers, U.S.A. 114 B6
Somerset, Ky., U.S.A. 108 G3
Somerset, Mass., U.S.A. 111 E13
Somerset, Pa., U.S.A. 110 F5
Somerset □, U.K. 13 F5
Somerset East, S. Africa 88 E4
Somerset I., Canada 100 A10
Somerset West, S. Africa 88 E2
Somersworth, U.S.A. 111 C14
Somerton, U.S.A. 115 K6
Somerville, U.S.A. 111 F10
Someş →, Romania 42 C7
Someşul Mare →, Romania 43 C8
Somme □, France 19 C9
Somme →, France 19 B8
Somme, B. de la, France 18 B8
Sommen, Jönköping, Sweden 11 F8
Sommen, Östergötland, Sweden 11 F9
Sommepy-Tahure, France 19 C11
Sömmerda, Germany 24 D7
Sommesous, France 19 D11
Sommières, France 21 E8
Somnath, India 68 J4
Somogy □, Hungary 42 D2
Somogyszob, Hungary 42 D2
Somoto, Nic. 120 D2
Sompolno, Poland 45 F5
Somport, Puerto de, Spain 32 C4
Son →, India 69 G11
Son Ha, Vietnam 64 E7
Son Hoa, Vietnam 64 F7
Son La, Vietnam 58 G4
Son Serra, Spain 37 B10
Son Servera, Spain 32 F8
Son Tay, Vietnam 58 G5
Soná, Panama 120 E3
Sonamarg, India 69 B6
Sonamukhi, India 69 H12
Sonar →, India 69 G8
Sŏnch'ŏn, N. Korea 57 E13
Sondags →, S. Africa 88 E4
Sóndalo, Italy 28 B7
Sondar, India 69 C6
Sønder Felding, Denmark 11 J2
Sønder Omme, Denmark 11 J2
Sønderborg, Denmark 11 K3
Sønderjyllands Amtskommune □, Denmark 11 J3
Sondershausen, Germany 24 D6
Sóndrio, Italy 28 B6
Sone, Mozam. 87 F3
Sonepur, India 67 J13
Song, Nigeria 83 D7
Song, Thailand 64 C3
Song Cau, Vietnam 64 F7
Song Xian, China 56 G7
Songch'ŏn, N. Korea 57 E14
Songea, Tanzania 87 E4
Songeons, France 19 C8
Songhua Hu, China 57 C14
Songhua Jiang →, China 60 B8
Songjiang, China 59 B13
Songjin, N. Korea 57 D15
Songjŏng-ni, S. Korea 57 G14
Songkan, China 58 C6
Songkhla, Thailand 65 J3
Songming, China 58 E4
Songnim, N. Korea 57 E13
Songo, Mozam. 85 H6
Songo, Sudan 79 G10
Songpan, China 58 A4
Songtao, China 58 C7
Songwe, Dem. Rep. of the Congo 86 C2
Songwe →, Africa 87 D3
Songxi, China 59 D12
Songzi, China 59 B8
Sonhat, India 69 H10
Sonid Youqi, China 56 C7
Sonipat, India 68 E7
Sonkach, India 68 H7
Sonkovo, Russia 46 D9
Sonmiani, Pakistan 68 G2
Sonmiani B., Pakistan 68 G2
Sonnino, Italy 30 A6
Sono →, Brazil 125 E9
Sonoma, U.S.A. 116 G4
Sonora, Calif., U.S.A. 116 H6
Sonora, Tex., U.S.A. 113 K4
Sonora □, Mexico 118 B2
Sonora →, Mexico 118 B2
Sonoran Desert, U.S.A. 117 L12
Sonoyta, Mexico 118 A2
Sonqor, Iran 73 E12
Sŏnsan, S. Korea 57 F15
Sonseca, Spain 35 F7
Sonsonate, El Salv. 120 D2
Sonsorol Is., Pac. Oc. 63 C8
Sonstorp, Sweden 11 F9
Sonthofen, Germany 25 H6
Soochow = Suzhou, China 59 B13
Sooke, Canada 116 B3
Sop Hao, Laos 58 G5
Sop Prap, Thailand 64 D2
Sopelana, Spain 32 B2
Sopi, Indonesia 63 D7
Sopo, Nahr →, Sudan 81 F2
Sopot, Bulgaria 41 D8
Sopot, Poland 44 D5
Sopot, Serbia, Yug. 40 B4
Sopotnica, Macedonia 40 E5
Sopron, Hungary 42 C1
Sopur, India 69 B6
Sør-Rondane, Antarctica 5 D4
Sora, Italy 29 G10
Sorah, Pakistan 68 F3
Soråker, Sweden 10 B11
Sorano, Italy 29 F8
Soraon, India 69 G9
Sorbas, Spain 33 H2
Sörbygden, Sweden 10 B10
Sore, France 20 D3
Sorel, Canada 102 C5
Soresina, Italy 28 C6
Sörforsa, Sweden 10 C10
Sórgono, Italy 30 B2
Sorgues, France 21 D8
Sorgun, Turkey 72 C6
Soria, Spain 32 D2
Soria □, Spain 32 D2
Soriano, Uruguay 126 C4
Soriano nel Cimino, Italy 29 F9
Sorkh, Kuh-e, Iran 71 C8
Sorø, Denmark 11 J5
Soro, Guinea 82 C3
Soroca, Moldova 43 B13
Sorocaba, Brazil 127 A6
Soroki = Soroca, Moldova 43 B13
Sorol Atoll, Pac. Oc. 63 C10
Sorong, Indonesia 63 E8
Soroní, Greece 36 C10
Soroti, Uganda 86 B3
Sørøya, Norway 8 A20
Sørøysundet, Norway 8 A20
Sorraia →, Portugal 35 G2
Sorrell, Australia 94 G4
Sorrento, Italy 31 B7
Sorsele, Sweden 8 D17
Sörsjön, Sweden 10 C7
Sorso, Italy 30 B1
Sorsogon, Phil. 61 E6
Sortavala, Russia 46 B6
Sortino, Italy 31 E8
Sortland, Norway 8 B16
Sorvizhi, Russia 48 B9
Sos = Sos del Rey Católico, Spain 32 C3
Sos del Rey Católico, Spain 32 C3
Sŏsan, S. Korea 57 F14
Soscumica, L., Canada 102 B4
Sösdala, Sweden 11 H7
Sosna →, Russia 47 F10
Sosnovka, Kirov, Russia 48 B10
Sosnovka, Tambov, Russia 48 D5
Sosnovyy Bor, Russia 46 C5
Sosnowiec, Poland 45 H6
Sospel, France 21 E11
Sossus Vlei, Namibia 88 C2
Šoštanj, Slovenia 29 B12
Sŏsura, N. Korea 57 C16
Sot →, India 69 F8
Sotkamo, Finland 8 D23
Soto del Barco, Spain 34 B4
Soto la Marina →, Mexico 119 C5
Soto y Amío, Spain 34 C5
Sotrondio, Spain 34 B5
Sotuta, Mexico 119 C7
Souanké, Congo 84 D2
Soubré, Ivory C. 82 D3
Souderton, U.S.A. 111 F9
Soúdha, Greece 36 D6
Soúdhas, Kólpos, Greece 36 D6
Souflíon, Greece 41 E10
Soufrière, St. Lucia 121 D7
Souillac, France 20 D5
Souilly, France 19 C12
Soukhouma, Laos 64 E5
Sŏul, S. Korea 57 F14
Soulac-sur-Mer, France 20 C2
Soulougou, Burkina Faso 83 C5
Soultz-sous-Forêts, France 19 D14
Sound, The = Øresund, Europe 11 J6
Sound, The, U.K. 13 G3
Soúnion, Ákra, Greece 38 D6
Sources, Mt. aux, Lesotho 89 D4
Soure, Brazil 125 D9
Soure, Portugal 34 E2
Souris, Man., Canada 105 D8
Souris, P.E.I., Canada 103 C7
Souris →, Canada 112 A5
Sourou →, Africa 82 C4
Soúrpi, Greece 38 B4
Sousa, Brazil 125 E11
Sousel, Portugal 35 G3
Sousse, Tunisia 79 A8
Soustons, France 20 E2
Sout →, S. Africa 88 E2
South Africa ■, Africa 88 E3
South America 122 E5
South Atlantic Ocean 122 H7
South Aulatsivik I., Canada 103 A7
South Australia □, Australia 95 E2
South Ayrshire □, U.K. 14 F4
South Baldy, U.S.A. 115 J10
South Bass I., U.S.A. 110 E2
South Bend, Ind., U.S.A. 108 E2
South Bend, Wash., U.S.A. 116 D3
South Boston, U.S.A. 109 G6
South Branch, Canada 103 C8
South Brook, Canada 103 C8
South Carolina □, U.S.A. 109 J5
South Charleston, U.S.A. 108 F5
South China Sea, Asia 62 C4
South Dakota □, U.S.A. 112 C5
South Deerfield, U.S.A. 111 D12
South Downs, U.K. 13 G7
South East C., Australia 94 G4
South East Is., Australia 93 F3
South Esk →, U.K. 14 E6
South Foreland, U.K. 13 F9
South Fork American →, U.S.A. 116 G5
South Fork Feather →, U.S.A. 116 F5
South Fork Grand →, U.S.A. 112 C3
South Fork Republican →, U.S.A. 112 E4
South Georgia, Antarctica 122 J7
South Gloucestershire □, U.K. 13 F5
South Hadley, U.S.A. 111 D12
South Haven, U.S.A. 108 D2
South Henik, L., Canada 105 A9
South Honshu Ridge, Pac. Oc. 96 E6
South Horr, Kenya 86 B4
South I., Kenya 86 B4
South I., N.Z. 91 L3
South Indian Lake, Canada 105 B9
South Invercargill, N.Z. 91 M2
South Knife →, Canada 105 B10
South Koel →, India 69 H11
South Korea ■, Asia 57 G15
South Lake Tahoe, U.S.A. 116 G6
South Lanarkshire □, U.K. 14 F5
South Loup →, U.S.A. 112 E5
South Magnetic Pole, Antarctica 5 C9
South Milwaukee, U.S.A. 108 D2
South Molton, U.K. 13 F4
South Moose L., Canada 105 C8
South Nahanni →, Canada 104 A4
South Nation →, Canada 111 A9
South Natuna Is. = Natuna Selatan, Kepulauan, Indonesia 65 L7
South Negril Pt., Jamaica 120 C4
South Orkney Is., Antarctica 5 C18
South Ossetia □, Georgia 49 J7
South Pagai, I. = Pagai Selatan, Pulau, Indonesia 62 E2
South Paris, U.S.A. 111 B14
South Pittsburg, U.S.A. 109 H3
South Platte →, U.S.A. 112 E4
South Pole, Antarctica 5 E
South Porcupine, Canada 102 C3
South Portland, U.S.A. 109 D10
South Pt., U.S.A. 110 B1
South River, Canada 102 C4
South River, U.S.A. 111 F10
South Ronaldsay, U.K. 14 C6
South Sandwich Is., Antarctica 5 B1
South Saskatchewan →, Canada 105 C7
South Seal →, Canada 105 B9
South Shetland Is., Antarctica 5 C18
South Shields, U.K. 12 C6
South Sioux City, U.S.A. 112 D6
South Taranaki Bight, N.Z. 91 H5
South Thompson →, Canada 104 C4
South Twin I., Canada 102 B4
South Tyne →, U.K. 12 C5
South Uist, U.K. 14 D1
South West Africa = Namibia ■, Africa 88 C2
South West C., Australia 94 G4
South West Rocks, Australia 95 E5
South Williamsport, U.S.A. 110 E8
South Yorkshire □, U.K. 12 D6
Southampton, Canada 102 D3
Southampton, U.K. 13 G6
Southampton, U.S.A. 111 F12
Southampton □, U.K. 13 G6
Southampton I., Canada 101 B11
Southaven, U.S.A. 113 H9
Southbank, Canada 104 C3
Southbridge, N.Z. 91 K4
Southbridge, U.S.A. 111 D12
Southend, Canada 105 B8
Southend-on-Sea, U.K. 13 F8
Southend-on-Sea □, U.K. 13 F8
Southern □, Malawi 87 F4
Southern □, S. Leone 82 D2
Southern □, Uganda 86 C3
Southern □, Zambia 87 F2
Southern Alps, N.Z. 91 K3
Southern Cross, Australia 93 F2
Southern Indian L., Canada 105 B9
Southern Ocean, Antarctica 5 C6
Southern Pines, U.S.A. 109 H6
Southern Uplands, U.K. 14 F5
Southington, U.S.A. 111 E12
Southold, U.S.A. 111 E12
Southport, Australia 95 D5
Southport, U.K. 12 D4
Southport, Fla., U.S.A. 109 K3
Southport, N.Y., U.S.A. 110 D8
Southwest C., N.Z. 91 M1
Southwold, U.K. 13 E9
Soutpansberg, S. Africa 89 C4
Souvigny, France 19 F10
Sovata, Romania 43 D10
Soverato, Italy 31 D9
Sovetsk, Kaliningd., Russia 9 J19
Sovetsk, Kirov, Russia 48 B9
Sovetskaya Gavan = Vanino, Russia 51 E15
Sovicille, Italy 29 E8
Soweto, S. Africa 89 D4
Sōya-Kaikyō = La Perouse Str., Asia 54 B11
Sōya-Misaki, Japan 54 B10
Soyaux, France 20 C4
Sozh →, Belarus 47 F6
Sozopol, Bulgaria 41 D11
Spa, Belgium 17 D5
Spain ■, Europe 7 H5
Spalding, Australia 95 E2
Spalding, U.K. 12 E7
Spangler, U.S.A. 110 F6
Spanish, Canada 102 C3
Spanish Fork, U.S.A. 114 F8
Spanish Town, Jamaica 120 C4
Sparks, U.S.A. 116 F7
Sparreholm, Sweden 10 E10
Sparta = Spárti, Greece 38 D4
Sparta, Mich., U.S.A. 108 D3
Sparta, N.J., U.S.A. 111 E10
Sparta, Wis., U.S.A. 112 D9
Spartanburg, U.S.A. 109 H5
Spartansburg, U.S.A. 110 E5
Spárti, Greece 38 D4
Spartivento, C., Calabria, Italy 31 E9
Spartivento, C., Sard., Italy 30 D1
Sparwood, Canada 104 D6
Spas-Demensk, Russia 46 E7
Spas-Klepiki, Russia 46 E11
Spassk Dalniy, Russia 51 E14
Spassk-Ryazanskiy, Russia 46 E11
Spátha, Ákra, Greece 36 D5
Spatsizi →, Canada 104 B3
Spatsizi Plateau Wilderness Park, Canada 104 B3
Spean →, U.K. 14 E4
Spearfish, U.S.A. 112 C3
Spearman, U.S.A. 113 G4
Speculator, U.S.A. 111 C10
Speia, Moldova 43 D14
Speightstown, Barbados 121 D8
Speke Gulf, Tanzania 86 C3
Spello, Italy 29 F9
Spencer, Idaho, U.S.A. 114 D7
Spencer, Iowa, U.S.A. 112 D7
Spencer, N.Y., U.S.A. 111 D8
Spencer, Nebr., U.S.A. 112 D5
Spencer, C., Australia 95 F2
Spencer B., Namibia 88 D1
Spencer G., Australia 95 E2
Spencerville, Canada 111 B9
Spences Bridge, Canada 104 C4
Spennymoor, U.K. 12 C6
Spenser Mts., N.Z. 91 K4
Spentrup, Denmark 11 H4
Sperkhiós →, Greece 38 C4
Sperrin Mts., U.K. 15 B5
Spessart, Germany 25 F5
Spétsai, Greece 38 D5
Spey →, U.K. 14 D5
Speyer, Germany 25 F4
Spezand, Pakistan 68 E2
Spezzano Albanese, Italy 31 C9
Spiekeroog, Germany 24 B3
Spiez, Switz. 25 J3
Spíli, Greece 36 D6
Spilimbergo, Italy 29 B9
Spīn Būldak, Afghan. 68 D2
Spinalónga, Greece 36 D7
Spinazzola, Italy 31 B9
Spineni, Romania 43 F9
Spirit Lake, U.S.A. 116 D4
Spirit River, Canada 104 B5
Spiritwood, Canada 105 C7
Spišská Nová Ves, Slovak Rep. 27 C13
Spišské Podhradie, Slovak Rep. 27 B13
Spital, Austria 26 D7
Spithead, U.K. 13 G6
Spittal an der Drau, Austria 26 E6
Spitzbergen = Svalbard, Arctic 4 B8
Spjelkavik, Norway 9 E12
Split, Croatia 29 E13
Split L., Canada 105 B9
Split Lake, Canada 105 B9
Splitski Kanal, Croatia 29 E13
Splügenpass, Switz. 25 J5
Spofford, U.S.A. 113 L4
Spokane, U.S.A. 114 C5
Spoleto, Italy 29 F9
Spooner, U.S.A. 112 C9
Sporyy Navolok, Mys, Russia 50 B7
Sprague, U.S.A. 114 C5
Spratly I., S. China Sea 62 C4
Spratly Is., S. China Sea 62 C4
Spray, U.S.A. 114 D4
Spreča →, Bos.-H. 42 F3
Spree →, Germany 24 C9
Spreewald, Germany 24 D9
Spremberg, Germany 24 D10
Sprengisandur, Iceland 8 D5
Spring City, U.S.A. 111 F9
Spring Creek, U.S.A. 114 F6
Spring Garden, U.S.A. 116 F6
Spring Hill, U.S.A. 109 L4
Spring Mts., U.S.A. 115 H6
Spring Valley, U.S.A. 117 N10
Springbok, S. Africa 88 D2
Springboro, U.S.A. 110 E4
Springdale, Canada 103 C8
Springdale, U.S.A. 113 G7
Springe, Germany 24 C5
Springer, U.S.A. 113 G2
Springerville, U.S.A. 115 J9
Springfield, Canada 110 D4
Springfield, N.Z. 91 K3
Springfield, Colo., U.S.A. 113 G3
Springfield, Ill., U.S.A. 112 F10
Springfield, Mass., U.S.A. 111 D12
Springfield, Mo., U.S.A. 113 G8
Springfield, Ohio, U.S.A. 108 F4
Springfield, Oreg., U.S.A. 114 D2
Springfield, Tenn., U.S.A. 109 G2
Springfield, Vt., U.S.A. 111 C12
Springfontein, S. Africa 88 E4
Springhill, Canada 103 C7
Springhill, U.S.A. 113 J8
Springhouse, Canada 104 C4
Springs, S. Africa 89 D4
Springsure, Australia 94 C4
Springvale, U.S.A. 111 C14
Springville, Calif., U.S.A. 116 J8
Springville, N.Y., U.S.A. 110 D6
Springville, Utah, U.S.A. 114 F8
Springwater, U.S.A. 110 D7
Spruce-Creek, U.S.A. 110 F6
Spruce Mt., U.S.A. 111 B12
Spur, U.S.A. 113 J4
Spurn Hd., U.K. 12 D8
Spuž, Montenegro, Yug. 40 D3
Spuzzum, Canada 104 D4
Squam L., U.S.A. 111 C13
Squamish, Canada 104 D4
Square Islands, Canada 103 B8
Squillace, G. di, Italy 31 D9
Squinzano, Italy 31 B11
Squires, Mt., Australia 93 E4
Srbac, Bos.-H. 42 E2
Srbica, Kosovo, Yug. 40 D4
Srbija = Serbia □, Yugoslavia 40 C5
Srbobran, Serbia, Yug. 42 E4
Sre Ambel, Cambodia 65 G4
Sre Khtum, Cambodia 65 F6
Sre Umbell = Sre Ambel, Cambodia 65 G4
Srebrenica, Bos.-H. 42 F4
Sredinny Ra. = Sredinnyy Khrebet, Russia 51 D16
Sredinnyy Khrebet, Russia 51 D16
Središče, Slovenia 29 B13
Sredna Gora, Bulgaria 41 D8
Srednekolymsk, Russia 51 C16
Sredni Rodopi, Bulgaria 41 E8
Srednogorie, Bulgaria 41 D8
Śrem, Poland 45 F4

Sremska Mitrovica, *Serbia, Yug.* 42 F4
Sremski Karlovci, *Serbia, Yug.* 42 E4
Srepok →, *Cambodia* 64 F6
Sretensk, *Russia* 51 D12
Sri Lanka ■, *Asia* 66 R12
Srikakulam, *India* 67 K13
Srinagar, *India* 69 B6
Środa Śląska, *Poland* 45 G3
Środa Wielkopolski, *Poland* 45 F4
Srpska Crnja, *Serbia, Yug.* 42 E5
Srpski Itebej, *Serbia, Yug.* 42 E5
Staaten →, *Australia* 94 B3
Staberhuk, *Germany* 24 A7
Stade, *Germany* 24 B5
Stadskanaal, *Neths.* 17 A6
Stadtallendorf, *Germany* 24 E5
Stadthagen, *Germany* 24 C5
Stadtlohn, *Germany* 24 D2
Stadtroda, *Germany* 24 E7
Staffa, *U.K.* 14 E2
Staffanstorp, *Sweden* 11 J7
Stafford, *U.K.* 12 E5
Stafford, *U.S.A.* 113 G5
Stafford Springs, *U.S.A.* 111 E12
Staffordshire □, *U.K.* 12 E5
Stagnone, *Italy* 30 E5
Staines, *U.K.* 13 F7
Stainz, *Austria* 26 E8
Stakhanov, *Ukraine* 47 H10
Stalać, *Serbia, Yug.* 40 C5
Stalingrad = Volgograd, *Russia* 49 F7
Staliniri = Tskhinvali, *Georgia* 49 J7
Stalino = Donetsk, *Ukraine* 47 J9
Stalinogorsk = Novomoskovsk, *Russia* 46 E10
Stalis, *Greece* 36 D7
Stallarholmen, *Sweden* 10 E11
Ställdalen, *Sweden* 10 E8
Stalowa Wola, *Poland* 45 H9
Stalybridge, *U.K.* 12 D5
Stamford, *Australia* 94 C3
Stamford, *U.K.* 13 E7
Stamford, *Conn., U.S.A.* 111 E11
Stamford, *N.Y., U.S.A.* 111 D10
Stamford, *Tex., U.S.A.* 113 J5
Stampriet, *Namibia* 88 C2
Stamps, *U.S.A.* 113 J8
Stančevo = Kalipetrovo, *Bulgaria* 41 B11
Standerton, *S. Africa* 89 D4
Standish, *U.S.A.* 108 D4
Stanford, *S. Africa* 88 E2
Stanford, *U.S.A.* 114 C8
Stånga, *Sweden* 11 G12
Stanger, *S. Africa* 89 D5
Stanišić, *Serbia, Yug.* 42 E4
Stanislaus →, *U.S.A.* 116 H5
Stanislav = Ivano-Frankivsk, *Ukraine* 47 H3
Stanisławów, *Poland* 45 F8
Stanley, *Australia* 94 G4
Stanley, *Canada* 105 B8
Stanley, *Falk. Is.* 128 G5
Stanley, *U.K.* 12 C6
Stanley, *Idaho, U.S.A.* 114 D6
Stanley, *N. Dak., U.S.A.* 112 A3
Stanley, *N.Y., U.S.A.* 110 D7
Stanovoy Khrebet, *Russia* 51 D13
Stanovoy Ra. = Stanovoy Khrebet, *Russia* 51 D13
Stansmore Ra., *Australia* 92 D4
Stanthorpe, *Australia* 95 D5
Stanton, *U.S.A.* 113 J4
Stanwood, *U.S.A.* 116 B4
Staples, *U.S.A.* 112 B7
Stąporków, *Poland* 45 G7
Star City, *Canada* 105 C8
Star Lake, *U.S.A.* 111 B9
Stará L'ubovňa, *Slovak Rep.* 27 B13
Stara Moravica, *Serbia, Yug.* 42 E4
Stara Pazova, *Serbia, Yug.* 42 F5
Stara Planina, *Bulgaria* 40 C7
Stará Turá, *Slovak Rep.* 27 C10
Stara Zagora, *Bulgaria* 41 D9
Starachowice, *Poland* 45 G8
Staraya Russa, *Russia* 46 D6
Starbuck I., *Kiribati* 97 H12
Starchiojd, *Romania* 43 E11
Stargard Szczeciński, *Poland* 44 E2
Stari Bar, *Montenegro, Yug.* 40 D3
Stari Trg, *Slovenia* 29 C12
Staritsa, *Russia* 46 D8
Starke, *U.S.A.* 109 L4
Starnberg, *Germany* 25 H7
Starnberger See, *Germany* 25 H7
Starobilsk, *Ukraine* 47 H10
Starodub, *Russia* 47 F7
Starogard Gdański, *Poland* 44 E5
Starokonstantinov = Starokonstyantyniv, *Ukraine* 47 H4
Starokonstyantyniv, *Ukraine* 47 H4
Starominskaya, *Russia* 47 J10
Staroshcherbinovskaya, *Russia* 47 J10
Start Pt., *U.K.* 13 G4
Stary Sącz, *Poland* 45 J7
Staryy Biryuzyak, *Russia* 49 H8
Staryy Chartoriysk, *Ukraine* 47 G3
Staryy Krym, *Ukraine* 47 K8
Staryy Oskol, *Russia* 47 G9
Stassfurt, *Germany* 24 D7
Staszów, *Poland* 45 H8
State College, *U.S.A.* 110 F7
Stateline, *U.S.A.* 116 G7
Staten, I. = Estados, I. de Los, *Argentina* 122 J4
Staten I., *U.S.A.* 111 F10
Statesboro, *U.S.A.* 109 J5
Statesville, *U.S.A.* 109 H5
Stauffer, *U.S.A.* 117 L7
Staunton, *Ill., U.S.A.* 112 F10
Staunton, *Va., U.S.A.* 108 F6
Stavanger, *Norway* 9 G11
Staveley, *N.Z.* 91 K3
Stavelot, *Belgium* 17 D5
Stavern, *Norway* 9 G14
Stavoren, *Neths.* 17 B5
Stavropol, *Russia* 49 H6
Stavros, *Cyprus* 36 D11
Stavrós, *Greece* 36 D6
Stavrós, Ákra, *Greece* 36 D6
Stavroúpolis, *Greece* 41 E8
Stawell, *Australia* 95 F3
Stawell →, *Australia* 94 C3
Stawiski, *Poland* 44 E9
Stawiszyn, *Poland* 45 G5
Stayner, *Canada* 110 B4
Stayton, *U.S.A.* 114 D2
Steamboat Springs, *U.S.A.* 114 F10
Stebleva, *Albania* 40 E4
Steele, *U.S.A.* 112 B5
Steelton, *U.S.A.* 110 F8
Steen River, *Canada* 104 B5
Steenkool = Bintuni, *Indonesia* 63 E8
Steens Mt., *U.S.A.* 114 E4
Steenwijk, *Neths.* 17 B6
Steep Pt., *Australia* 93 E1
Steep Rock, *Canada* 105 C9
Ştefan Vodă, *Moldova* 43 D14
Ştefăneşti, *Romania* 43 C12
Stefanie L. = Chew Bahir, *Ethiopia* 81 G4
Stefansson Bay, *Antarctica* 5 C5
Stege, *Denmark* 11 K6
Ştei, *Romania* 42 D7
Steiermark □, *Austria* 26 D8
Steigerwald, *Germany* 25 F6
Steilacoom, *U.S.A.* 116 C4
Steilrandberge, *Namibia* 88 B1
Steinbach, *Canada* 105 D9
Steinfurt, *Germany* 24 C3
Steinhausen, *Namibia* 88 C2
Steinheim, *Germany* 24 D5
Steinhuder Meer, *Germany* 24 C5
Steinkjer, *Norway* 8 D14
Steinkopf, *S. Africa* 88 D2
Stellarton, *Canada* 103 C7
Stellenbosch, *S. Africa* 88 E2
Stelvio, Paso dello, *Italy* 28 B7
Stenay, *France* 19 C12
Stendal, *Germany* 24 C7
Stende, *Latvia* 44 A9
Stenhamra, *Sweden* 10 E11
Stenstorp, *Sweden* 11 F7
Stenungsund, *Sweden* 11 F5
Steornabhaigh = Stornoway, *U.K.* 14 C2
Stepanakert = Xankändi, *Azerbaijan* 70 B5
Stepanavan, *Armenia* 49 K7
Stephens Creek, *Australia* 95 E3
Stephens I., *Canada* 104 C2
Stephens L., *Canada* 105 B9
Stephenville, *Canada* 103 C8
Stephenville, *U.S.A.* 113 J5
Stepnica, *Poland* 44 E1
Stepnoi = Elista, *Russia* 49 G7
Steppe, *Asia* 52 D9
Stereá Ellas □, *Greece* 38 C4
Sterkstroom, *S. Africa* 88 E4
Sterling, *Colo., U.S.A.* 112 E3
Sterling, *Ill., U.S.A.* 112 E10
Sterling, *Kans., U.S.A.* 112 F5
Sterling City, *U.S.A.* 113 K4
Sterling Heights, *U.S.A.* 108 D4
Sterling Run, *U.S.A.* 110 E6
Sterlitamak, *Russia* 50 D6
Sternberg, *Germany* 24 B7
Šternberk, *Czech Rep.* 27 B10
Stérnes, *Greece* 36 D6
Sterzing = Vipiteno, *Italy* 29 B8
Stettin = Szczecin, *Poland* 44 E1
Stettiner Haff, *Germany* 24 B10
Stettler, *Canada* 104 C6
Steubenville, *U.S.A.* 110 F4
Stevenage, *U.K.* 13 F7
Stevens Point, *U.S.A.* 112 C10
Stevenson, *U.S.A.* 116 E5
Stevenson L., *Canada* 105 C9
Stevensville, *U.S.A.* 114 C6
Stevns Klint, *Denmark* 11 J6
Stewart, *B.C., Canada* 104 B3
Stewart, *N.W.T., Canada* 100 B6
Stewart, *U.S.A.* 116 F7
Stewart, C., *Australia* 94 A1
Stewart, I., *Chile* 128 G2
Stewart I., *N.Z.* 91 M1
Stewarts Point, *U.S.A.* 116 G3
Stewartville, *U.S.A.* 112 D8
Stewiacke, *Canada* 103 C7
Steynsburg, *S. Africa* 88 E4
Steyr, *Austria* 26 C7
Steyr →, *Austria* 26 C7
Steytlerville, *S. Africa* 88 E3
Stia, *Italy* 29 E8
Stigler, *U.S.A.* 113 H7
Stigliano, *Italy* 31 B9
Stigtomta, *Sweden* 11 F10
Stikine →, *Canada* 104 B2
Stilfontein, *S. Africa* 88 D4
Stilís, *Greece* 38 C4
Stillwater, *N.Z.* 91 K3
Stillwater, *Minn., U.S.A.* 112 C8
Stillwater, *N.Y., U.S.A.* 111 D11
Stillwater, *Okla., U.S.A.* 113 G6
Stillwater Range, *U.S.A.* 114 G4
Stillwater Reservoir, *U.S.A.* 111 C9
Stilo, Pta., *Italy* 31 D9
Stilwell, *U.S.A.* 113 H7
Štip, *Macedonia* 40 E6
Stíra, *Greece* 38 C6
Stirling, *Canada* 110 B7
Stirling, *U.K.* 14 E5
Stirling □, *U.K.* 14 E4
Stirling Ra., *Australia* 93 F2
Stittsville, *Canada* 111 A9
Stjernøya, *Norway* 8 A20
Stjørdalshalsen, *Norway* 8 E14
Stockach, *Germany* 25 H5
Stockaryd, *Sweden* 11 G8
Stockerau, *Austria* 27 C9
Stockholm, *Sweden* 10 E12
Stockholms län □, *Sweden* 10 E12
Stockport, *U.K.* 12 D5
Stocksbridge, *U.K.* 12 D6
Stockton, *Calif., U.S.A.* 116 H5
Stockton, *Kans., U.S.A.* 112 F5
Stockton, *Mo., U.S.A.* 113 G8
Stockton-on-Tees, *U.K.* 12 C6
Stockton-on-Tees □, *U.K.* 12 C6
Stockton Plateau, *U.S.A.* 113 K3
Stoczek Łukowski, *Poland* 45 G8
Stöde, *Sweden* 10 B10
Stoeng Treng, *Cambodia* 64 F5
Stoer, Pt. of, *U.K.* 14 C3
Stogovo, *Macedonia* 40 E4
Stoholm, *Denmark* 11 H3
Stoke-on-Trent, *U.K.* 12 D5
Stoke-on-Trent □, *U.K.* 12 D5
Stokes Pt., *Australia* 94 G3
Stokes Ra., *Australia* 92 C5
Stokksnes, *Iceland* 8 D6
Stokmarknes, *Norway* 8 B16
Stolac, *Bos.-H.* 40 C1
Stolberg, *Germany* 24 E2
Stolbovoy, Ostrov, *Russia* 51 D17
Stolbtsy = Stowbtsy, *Belarus* 46 F4
Stolin, *Belarus* 47 G4
Stöllet, *Sweden* 10 D7
Stolnici, *Romania* 43 F9
Stomíon, *Greece* 36 D5
Ston, *Croatia* 29 F14
Stone, *U.K.* 12 E5
Stoneboro, *U.S.A.* 110 E4
Stonehaven, *U.K.* 14 E6
Stonehenge, *Australia* 94 C3
Stonehenge, *U.K.* 13 F6
Stonewall, *Canada* 105 C9
Stony L., *Man., Canada* 105 B9
Stony L., *Ont., Canada* 110 B6
Stony Point, *U.S.A.* 111 E11
Stony Pt., *U.S.A.* 111 C8
Stony Rapids, *Canada* 105 B7
Stony Tunguska = Tunguska, Podkamennaya →, *Russia* 51 C10
Stonyford, *U.S.A.* 116 F4
Stopnica, *Poland* 45 H7
Storå, *Sweden* 10 E9
Storå →, *Denmark* 11 H2
Stora Gla, *Sweden* 10 E6
Stora Le, *Sweden* 10 E5
Stora Lulevatten, *Sweden* 8 C18
Storavan, *Sweden* 8 D18
Stord, *Norway* 9 G11
Store Bælt, *Denmark* 11 J4
Store Heddinge, *Denmark* 11 J6
Storebro, *Sweden* 11 G9
Storfors, *Sweden* 10 E8
Storlien, *Sweden* 10 A6
Storm B., *Australia* 94 G4
Storm Lake, *U.S.A.* 112 D7
Stormberge, *S. Africa* 88 E4
Stormsrivier, *S. Africa* 88 E3
Stornoway, *U.K.* 14 C2
Storo, *Italy* 28 C7
Storozhinets = Storozhynets, *Ukraine* 47 H3
Storozhynets, *Ukraine* 47 H3
Storrs, *U.S.A.* 111 E12
Storsjön, *Gävleborg, Sweden* 10 D10
Storsjön, *Jämtland, Sweden* 10 B7
Storsjön, *Jämtland, Sweden* 10 A8
Storstrøms Amtskommune □, *Denmark* 11 J5
Storuman, *Sweden* 8 D17
Storuman, sjö, *Sweden* 8 D17
Storvätteshågna, *Sweden* 10 B6
Storvik, *Sweden* 10 D10
Storvreta, *Sweden* 10 E11
Stouffville, *Canada* 110 C5
Stoughton, *Canada* 105 D8
Stour →, *Dorset, U.K.* 13 G6
Stour →, *Kent, U.K.* 13 F9
Stour →, *Suffolk, U.K.* 13 F9
Stourbridge, *U.K.* 13 E5
Stout L., *Canada* 105 C10
Stove Pipe Wells Village, *U.S.A.* 117 J9
Støvring, *Denmark* 11 H3
Stow, *U.S.A.* 110 E3
Stowbtsy, *Belarus* 46 F4
Stowmarket, *U.K.* 13 E9
Strabane, *U.K.* 15 B4
Stracin, *Macedonia* 40 D6
Stradella, *Italy* 28 C6
Strahan, *Australia* 94 G4
Strajitsa, *Bulgaria* 41 C9
Strakonice, *Czech Rep.* 26 B6
Straldzha, *Bulgaria* 41 D10
Stralsund, *Germany* 24 A9
Strand, *S. Africa* 88 E2
Stranda, *Møre og Romsdal, Norway* 9 E12
Stranda, *Nord-Trøndelag, Norway* 8 E14
Strandby, *Denmark* 11 G4
Strangford L., *U.K.* 15 B6
Strängnäs, *Sweden* 10 E11
Stranraer, *U.K.* 14 G3
Strasbourg, *Canada* 105 C8
Strasbourg, *France* 19 D14
Strasburg, *Germany* 24 B9
Străşeni, *Moldova* 43 C13
Stråssa, *Sweden* 10 E9
Stratford, *Canada* 102 D3
Stratford, *N.Z.* 91 H5
Stratford, *Calif., U.S.A.* 116 J7
Stratford, *Conn., U.S.A.* 111 E11
Stratford, *Tex., U.S.A.* 113 G3
Stratford-upon-Avon, *U.K.* 13 E6
Strath Spey, *U.K.* 14 D5
Strathalbyn, *Australia* 95 F2
Strathaven, *U.K.* 14 F4
Strathcona Prov. Park, *Canada* 104 D3
Strathmore, *Canada* 104 C6
Strathmore, *U.K.* 14 E5
Strathmore, *U.S.A.* 116 J7
Strathnaver, *Canada* 104 C4
Strathpeffer, *U.K.* 14 D4
Strathroy, *Canada* 102 D3
Strathy Pt., *U.K.* 14 C4
Strattanville, *U.S.A.* 110 E5
Stratton, *U.S.A.* 111 A14
Stratton Mt., *U.S.A.* 111 C12
Straubing, *Germany* 25 G8
Straumnes, *Iceland* 8 C2
Strausberg, *Germany* 24 C9
Strawberry →, *U.S.A.* 114 F8
Strážnice, *Czech Rep.* 27 C10
Streaky B., *Australia* 95 E1
Streaky Bay, *Australia* 95 E1
Streator, *U.S.A.* 112 E10
Středočeský □, *Czech Rep.* 26 B7
Streetsboro, *U.S.A.* 110 E3
Streetsville, *Canada* 110 C5
Strehaia, *Romania* 43 F8
Strelcha, *Bulgaria* 41 D8
Strelka, *Russia* 51 D10
Streng →, *Cambodia* 64 F4
Stresa, *Italy* 28 C5
Streymoy, *Færoe Is.* 8 E9
Strezhevoy, *Russia* 50 C8
Stříbro, *Czech Rep.* 26 A6
Strimón →, *Greece* 40 F7
Strimonikós Kólpos, *Greece* 40 F7
Strofádhes, *Greece* 38 D3
Stroma, *U.K.* 14 C5
Strómboli, *Italy* 31 D8
Stromeferry, *U.K.* 14 D3
Stromness, *U.K.* 14 C5
Strömsbruk, *Sweden* 10 C11
Stromsburg, *U.S.A.* 112 E6
Strömsnäsbruk, *Sweden* 11 H7
Strömstad, *Sweden* 11 F5
Strömsund, *Sweden* 8 E16
Strongilí, *Greece* 39 E11
Strongoli, *Italy* 31 C10
Strongsville, *U.S.A.* 110 E3
Stronie Śląskie, *Poland* 45 H3
Stronsay, *U.K.* 14 B6
Stropkov, *Slovak Rep.* 27 B14
Stroud, *U.K.* 13 F5
Stroud Road, *Australia* 95 E5
Stroudsburg, *U.S.A.* 111 F9
Stroumbi, *Cyprus* 36 E11
Struer, *Denmark* 11 H2
Struga, *Macedonia* 40 E4
Strugi Krasnyye, *Russia* 46 C5
Strumica, *Macedonia* 40 E6
Strumica →, *Europe* 40 E7
Struthers, *Canada* 102 C2
Struthers, *U.S.A.* 110 E4
Stryama, *Bulgaria* 41 D8
Stryker, *U.S.A.* 114 B6
Stryków, *Poland* 45 G6
Stryy, *Ukraine* 47 H2
Strzegom, *Poland* 45 H3
Strzelce Krajeńskie, *Poland* 45 F2
Strzelce Opolskie, *Poland* 45 H5
Strzelecki Cr. →, *Australia* 95 D2
Strzelin, *Poland* 45 H4
Strzelno, *Poland* 45 F5
Strzybnica, *Poland* 45 H5
Strzyżów, *Poland* 45 J8
Stuart, *Fla., U.S.A.* 109 M5
Stuart, *Nebr., U.S.A.* 112 D5
Stuart →, *Canada* 104 C4
Stuart Bluff Ra., *Australia* 92 D5
Stuart L., *Canada* 104 C4
Stuart Ra., *Australia* 95 D1
Stubbekøbing, *Denmark* 11 K6
Stuben, *Austria* 26 D3
Studen Kladenets, Yazovir, *Bulgaria* 41 E9
Studenka, *Czech Rep.* 27 B11
Stugun, *Sweden* 10 A9
Stuhr, *Germany* 24 B4
Stull L., *Canada* 102 B1
Stung Treng = Stoeng Treng, *Cambodia* 64 F5
Stupart →, *Canada* 102 A1
Stupava, *Slovak Rep.* 27 C10
Stupino, *Russia* 46 E10
Sturgeon B., *Canada* 105 C9
Sturgeon Bay, *U.S.A.* 108 C2
Sturgeon Falls, *Canada* 102 C4
Sturgeon L., *Alta., Canada* 104 B5
Sturgeon L., *Ont., Canada* 102 C1
Sturgeon L., *Ont., Canada* 110 B6
Sturgis, *Canada* 105 C8
Sturgis, *Mich., U.S.A.* 108 E3
Sturgis, *S. Dak., U.S.A.* 112 C3
Sturkö, *Sweden* 11 H9
Štúrovo, *Slovak Rep.* 27 D11
Sturt Cr. →, *Australia* 92 C4
Stutterheim, *S. Africa* 88 E4
Stuttgart, *Germany* 25 G5
Stuttgart, *U.S.A.* 113 H9
Stuyvesant, *U.S.A.* 111 D11
Stykkishólmur, *Iceland* 8 D2
Styria = Steiermark □, *Austria* 26 D8
Styrsö, *Sweden* 11 G5
Su Xian = Suzhou, *China* 56 H9
Suakin, *Sudan* 80 D4
Suan, *N. Korea* 57 E14
Suaqui, *Mexico* 118 B3
Suar, *India* 69 E8
Subang, *Indonesia* 63 G12
Subansiri →, *India* 67 F18
Subarnarekha →, *India* 69 H12
Subayhah, *Si. Arabia* 70 D3
Subcetate, *Romania* 42 E8
Subi, *Indonesia* 65 L7
Subiaco, *Italy* 29 G10
Subotica, *Serbia, Yug.* 42 D4
Suca, *Ethiopia* 81 F4
Suceava, *Romania* 43 C11
Suceava □, *Romania* 43 C10
Suceava →, *Romania* 43 C11
Sucha-Beskidzka, *Poland* 45 J6
Suchań, *Poland* 45 E2
Suchan, *Russia* 54 C6
Suchedniów, *Poland* 45 G7
Suchitoto, *El Salv.* 120 D2
Suchou = Suzhou, *China* 59 B13
Süchow = Xuzhou, *China* 57 G9
Suchowola, *Poland* 44 E10
Suck →, *Ireland* 15 C3
Sucre, *Bolivia* 124 G5
Sućuraj, *Croatia* 29 E14
Sucuriú →, *Brazil* 125 H8
Sud, Pte. du, *Canada* 103 C7
Sud-Kivu □, *Dem. Rep. of the Congo* 86 C2
Sud-Ouest, Pte. du, *Canada* 103 C7
Suda →, *Russia* 46 C9
Sudak, *Ukraine* 47 K8
Sudan, *U.S.A.* 113 H3
Sudan ■, *Africa* 81 E3
Sudbury, *Canada* 102 C3
Sudbury, *U.K.* 13 E8
Sûdd, *Sudan* 81 F3
Süderbrarup, *Germany* 24 A5
Süderlügum, *Germany* 24 A4
Süderoogsand, *Germany* 24 A4
Sudeten Mts. = Sudety, *Europe* 27 A9
Sudety, *Europe* 27 A9
Suðuroy, *Færoe Is.* 8 F9
Sudi, *Tanzania* 87 E4
Sudirman, Pegunungan, *Indonesia* 63 E9
Sudiţi, *Romania* 43 F12
Sudogda, *Russia* 48 C5
Sudr, *Egypt* 80 B3
Sudzha, *Russia* 47 G8
Sue →, *Sudan* 81 F2
Sueca, *Spain* 33 F4
Suedinenie, *Bulgaria* 41 D8
Suemez I., *U.S.A.* 104 B2
Suez = El Suweis, *Egypt* 80 J8
Suez, G. of = Suweis, Khalîg el, *Egypt* 80 J8
Suez Canal = Suweis, Qanâ es, *Egypt* 80 H8
Suffield, *Canada* 104 C6
Suffolk, *U.S.A.* 108 G7
Suffolk □, *U.K.* 13 E9
Şugag, *Romania* 43 E8
Sugargrove, *U.S.A.* 110 E5
Sugarive →, *India* 69 F12
Suğla Gölü, *Turkey* 72 D5
Sugluk = Salluit, *Canada* 101 B12
Suhaia, Lacul, *Romania* 43 G10
Şuḥār, *Oman* 71 E8
Sühbaatar □, *Mongolia* 56 B8
Suhl, *Germany* 24 E6
Şuhut, *Turkey* 39 C12
Sui, *Pakistan* 68 E3
Sui Xian, *China* 56 G8
Šuica, *Bos.-H.* 42 G2
Suichang, *China* 59 C12
Suichuan, *China* 59 D10
Suide, *China* 56 F6
Suifenhe, *China* 57 B16
Suihua, *China* 60 B7
Suijiang, *China* 58 C4
Suining, *Hunan, China* 59 D8
Suining, *Jiangsu, China* 57 H9
Suining, *Sichuan, China* 58 B5
Suiping, *China* 56 H7
Suippes, *France* 19 C11
Suir →, *Ireland* 15 D4
Suisun City, *U.S.A.* 116 G4
Suixi, *China* 59 G8
Suiyang, *Guizhou, China* 58 D6
Suiyang, *Heilongjiang, China* 57 B16
Suizhong, *China* 57 D11
Suizhou, *China* 59 B9
Sujangarh, *India* 68 F6
Sukabumi, *Indonesia* 63 G12
Sukadana, *Indonesia* 62 E3
Sukagawa, *Japan* 55 F10
Sukaraja, *Indonesia* 62 E4
Sukarnapura = Jayapura, *Indonesia* 63 E10
Sukch'ŏn, *N. Korea* 57 E13
Sukhindol, *Bulgaria* 41 C9
Sukhinichi, *Russia* 46 E8
Sukhona →, *Russia* 50 D4
Sukhothai, *Thailand* 64 D2
Sukhumi = Sokhumi, *Georgia* 49 J5
Sukkur, *Pakistan* 68 F3
Sukkur Barrage, *Pakistan* 68 F3

Sukovo, *Serbia, Yug.* 40 C6
Sukri →, *India* 68 G4
Sukumo, *Japan* 55 H6
Sukunka →, *Canada* 104 B4
Sula →, *Ukraine* 47 H7
Sula, Kepulauan, *Indonesia* 63 E7
Sulaco →, *Honduras* 120 C2
Sulaiman Range, *Pakistan* 68 D3
Sulak →, *Russia* 49 J8
Sūlār, *Iran* 71 D6
Sulawesi Sea = Celebes Sea, *Indonesia* 63 D6
Sulawesi Selatan □, *Indonesia* 63 E6
Sulawesi Utara □, *Indonesia* 63 D6
Sulechów, *Poland* 45 F2
Sulęcin, *Poland* 45 F2
Sulejów, *Poland* 45 G6
Sulejówek, *Poland* 45 F8
Süleymanlı, *Turkey* 39 C9
Sulima, *S. Leone* 82 D2
Sulina, *Romania* 43 E14
Sulina, Braţul →, *Romania* 43 E14
Sulingen, *Germany* 24 C4
Suliţa, *Romania* 43 C11
Sulitjelma, *Norway* 8 C17
Sułkowice, *Poland* 45 J6
Sullana, *Peru* 124 D2
Süller, *Turkey* 39 C11
Sullivan, *Ill., U.S.A.* 112 F10
Sullivan, *Ind., U.S.A.* 108 F2
Sullivan, *Mo., U.S.A.* 112 F9
Sullivan Bay, *Canada* 104 C3
Sullivan I. = Lambi Kyun, *Burma* 65 G2
Sully-sur-Loire, *France* 19 E9
Sulmierzyce, *Poland* 45 G4
Sulmona, *Italy* 29 F10
Süloğlu, *Turkey* 41 E10
Sulphur, *La., U.S.A.* 113 K8
Sulphur, *Okla., U.S.A.* 113 H6
Sulphur Pt., *Canada* 104 A6
Sulphur Springs, *U.S.A.* 113 J7
Sultan, *Canada* 102 C3
Sultan, *U.S.A.* 116 C5
Sultan Dağları, *Turkey* 72 C4
Sultanhisar, *Turkey* 39 D10
Sultaniça, *Turkey* 41 F10
Sultaniye, *Turkey* 41 F12
Sultanpur, *Mad. P., India* 68 H8
Sultanpur, *Punjab, India* 68 D6
Sultanpur, *Ut. P., India* 69 F10
Sulu Arch., *Phil.* 61 J4
Sulu Sea, *E. Indies* 61 G4
Sülüklü, *Turkey* 72 C5
Sululta, *Ethiopia* 81 F4
Suluova, *Turkey* 72 B6
Suluq, *Libya* 79 B10
Sulzbach, *Germany* 25 F3
Sulzbach-Rosenberg, *Germany* 25 F7
Sulzberger Ice Shelf, *Antarctica* 5 D10
Sumalata, *Indonesia* 63 D6
Sumampa, *Argentina* 126 B3
Sumatera □, *Indonesia* 62 D2
Sumatera Barat □, *Indonesia* 62 E2
Sumatera Utara □, *Indonesia* 62 D1
Sumatra = Sumatera □, *Indonesia* 62 D2
Sumba, *Indonesia* 63 F5
Sumba, Selat, *Indonesia* 63 F5
Sumbawa, *Indonesia* 62 F5
Sumbawa Besar, *Indonesia* 62 F5
Sumbawanga □, *Tanzania* 84 F6
Sumbe, *Angola* 84 G2
Sumburgh Hd., *U.K.* 14 B7
Sumdeo, *India* 69 D8
Sumdo, *India* 69 B8
Sumedang, *Indonesia* 63 G12
Sümeg, *Hungary* 42 D2
Sumeih, *Sudan* 81 F2
Šumen = Shumen, *Bulgaria* 41 C10
Sumenep, *Indonesia* 63 G15
Sumgait = Sumqayıt, *Azerbaijan* 49 K9
Summer L., *U.S.A.* 114 E3
Summerland, *Canada* 104 D5
Summerside, *Canada* 103 C7
Summersville, *U.S.A.* 108 F5
Summerville, *Ga., U.S.A.* 109 H3
Summerville, *S.C., U.S.A.* 109 J5
Summit Lake, *Canada* 104 C4
Summit Peak, *U.S.A.* 115 H10
Sumner, *Iowa, U.S.A.* 112 D8
Sumner, *Wash., U.S.A.* 116 C4
Sumoto, *Japan* 55 G7
Šumperk, *Czech Rep.* 27 B9
Sumqayıt, *Azerbaijan* 49 K9
Sumter, *U.S.A.* 109 J5
Sumy, *Ukraine* 47 G8
Sun City, *Ariz., U.S.A.* 115 K7
Sun City, *Calif., U.S.A.* 117 M9
Sun City Center, *U.S.A.* 109 M4
Sun Lakes, *U.S.A.* 115 K8
Sun Valley, *U.S.A.* 114 E6
Sunagawa, *Japan* 54 C10
Sunan, *N. Korea* 57 E13
Sunart, L., *U.K.* 14 E3
Sunburst, *U.S.A.* 114 B8
Sunbury, *Australia* 95 F3
Sunbury, *U.S.A.* 111 F8
Sunchales, *Argentina* 126 C3
Suncho Corral, *Argentina* 126 B3
Sunch'ŏn, *S. Korea* 57 G14
Suncook, *U.S.A.* 111 C13
Sunda, Selat, *Indonesia* 62 F3
Sunda Is., *Indonesia* 52 K14
Sunda Str. = Sunda, Selat, *Indonesia* 62 F3
Sundance, *Canada* 105 B10
Sundance, *U.S.A.* 112 C2
Sundar Nagar, *India* 68 D7
Sundarbans, The, *Asia* 67 J16
Sundargarh, *India* 67 H14
Sundays = Sondags →, *S. Africa* 88 E4
Sunderland, *Canada* 110 B5
Sunderland, *U.K.* 12 C6
Sundre, *Canada* 104 C6
Sunds, *Denmark* 11 H3
Sundsvall, *Sweden* 10 B11
Sundsvallsbukten, *Sweden* 10 B11
Sung Hei, *Vietnam* 65 G6
Sungai Kolok, *Thailand* 65 J3
Sungai Lembing, *Malaysia* 65 L4
Sungai Petani, *Malaysia* 65 K3
Sungaigerong, *Indonesia* 62 E2
Sungailiat, *Indonesia* 62 E3
Sungaipenuh, *Indonesia* 62 E2
Sungari = Songhua Jiang →, *China* 60 B8
Sunghua Chiang = Songhua Jiang →, *China* 60 B8
Sungikai, *Sudan* 81 E2
Sungurlu, *Turkey* 72 B6
Sunja, *Croatia* 29 C13
Sunland Park, *U.S.A.* 115 L10
Sunnansjö, *Sweden* 10 D8
Sunndalsøra, *Norway* 9 E13
Sunne, *Sweden* 10 E7
Sunnemo, *Sweden* 10 E7
Sunnyside, *U.S.A.* 114 C3
Sunnyvale, *U.S.A.* 116 H4
Suntar, *Russia* 51 C12
Sunyani, *Ghana* 82 D4
Suomenselkä, *Finland* 8 E21
Suomussalmi, *Finland* 8 D23
Suoyarvi, *Russia* 46 A7
Supai, *U.S.A.* 115 H7
Supaul, *India* 69 F12
Superior, *Ariz., U.S.A.* 115 K8
Superior, *Mont., U.S.A.* 114 C6
Superior, *Nebr., U.S.A.* 112 E5
Superior, *Wis., U.S.A.* 112 B8
Superior, L., *N. Amer.* 102 C2
Supetar, *Croatia* 29 E13
Suphan Buri, *Thailand* 64 E3
Suphan Dağı, *Turkey* 70 B4
Supiori, *Indonesia* 63 E9
Supraśl, *Poland* 45 E10
Supraśl →, *Poland* 45 E9
Supung Shuiku, *China* 57 D13
Sūq Suwayq, *Si. Arabia* 70 E3
Suqian, *China* 57 H10
Sūr, *Lebanon* 75 B4
Sūr, *Oman* 74 C6
Sur, Pt., *U.S.A.* 116 J5
Sura →, *Russia* 48 C8
Surab, *Pakistan* 68 E2
Surabaja = Surabaya, *Indonesia* 63 G15
Surabaya, *Indonesia* 63 G15
Surahammar, *Sweden* 10 E10
Suraia, *Romania* 43 E12
Surakarta, *Indonesia* 63 G14
Şurakhany, *Azerbaijan* 49 K10
Šurany, *Slovak Rep.* 27 C11
Surat, *Australia* 95 D4
Surat, *India* 66 J8
Surat Thani, *Thailand* 65 H2
Suratgarh, *India* 68 E5
Suraż, *Poland* 45 F9
Surazh, *Belarus* 46 E6
Surazh, *Russia* 47 F7
Surduc, *Romania* 43 C8
Surduc Pasul, *Romania* 43 E8
Surdulica, *Serbia, Yug.* 40 D6
Surendranagar, *India* 68 H4
Surf, *U.S.A.* 117 L6
Surgères, *France* 20 B3
Surgut, *Russia* 50 C8
Sùria, *Spain* 32 D6
Suriapet, *India* 66 L11
Surigao, *Phil.* 61 G6
Surigao Strait, *Phil.* 61 F6
Surin, *Thailand* 64 E4
Surin Nua, Ko, *Thailand* 65 H1
Surinam ■, *S. Amer.* 125 C7
Suriname = Surinam ■, *S. Amer.* 125 C7
Suriname →, *Surinam* 125 B7
Sūrmaq, *Iran* 71 D7
Sürmene, *Turkey* 73 B9
Surovikino, *Russia* 49 F6
Surrey □, *U.K.* 13 F7
Sursand, *India* 69 F11
Sursar →, *India* 69 F12
Sursee, *Switz.* 25 H4
Sursk, *Russia* 48 D7
Surskoye, *Russia* 48 C8
Surt, *Libya* 79 B9
Surt, Khalīj, *Libya* 79 B9
Surtanahu, *Pakistan* 68 F4
Surte, *Sweden* 11 G6
Surtsey, *Iceland* 8 E3
Sürüç, *Turkey* 73 D8
Suruga-Wan, *Japan* 55 G9
Susa, *Italy* 28 C4
Susā →, *Denmark* 11 J5
Sušac, *Croatia* 29 F13
Susak, *Croatia* 29 D11
Susaki, *Japan* 55 H6
Sūsangerd, *Iran* 71 D6
Susanville, *U.S.A.* 114 F3
Susch, *Switz.* 25 J6
Suşehri, *Turkey* 73 B8
Sušice, *Czech Rep.* 26 B6
Susleni, *Moldova* 43 C13
Susner, *India* 68 H7
Susong, *China* 59 B11
Susquehanna, *U.S.A.* 111 E9
Susquehanna →, *U.S.A.* 111 G8
Susques, *Argentina* 126 A2
Sussex, *Canada* 103 C6
Sussex, *U.S.A.* 111 E10
Sussex, E. □, *U.K.* 13 G8
Sussex, W. □, *U.K.* 13 G7
Sustut →, *Canada* 104 B3
Susuman, *Russia* 51 C15
Susunu, *Indonesia* 63 E8
Susurluk, *Turkey* 39 B10
Susuz, *Turkey* 73 B10
Susz, *Poland* 44 E6
Sütçüler, *Turkey* 72 D4
Şuţeşti, *Romania* 43 E12
Sutherland, *S. Africa* 88 E3
Sutherland, *U.S.A.* 112 E4
Sutherland Falls, *N.Z.* 91 L1
Sutherlin, *U.S.A.* 114 E2
Suthri, *India* 68 H3
Sutlej →, *Pakistan* 68 E4
Sutter, *U.S.A.* 116 F5
Sutter Creek, *U.S.A.* 116 G6
Sutton, *Canada* 111 A12
Sutton, *Nebr., U.S.A.* 112 E6
Sutton, *W. Va., U.S.A.* 108 F5
Sutton →, *Canada* 102 A3
Sutton Coldfield, *U.K.* 13 E6
Sutton in Ashfield, *U.K.* 12 D6
Sutton L., *Canada* 102 B3
Suttor →, *Australia* 94 C4
Suttsu, *Japan* 54 C10
Suva, *Fiji* 91 D8
Suva Gora, *Macedonia* 40 E5
Suva Planina, *Serbia, Yug.* 40 C6
Suva Reka, *Kosovo, Yug.* 40 D4
Suvorov, *Russia* 46 E9
Suvorov Is. = Suwarrow Is., *Cook Is.* 97 J11
Suvorovo, *Bulgaria* 41 C11
Suwałki, *Poland* 44 D9
Suwannaphum, *Thailand* 64 E4
Suwannee →, *U.S.A.* 109 L4
Suwanose-Jima, *Japan* 55 K4
Suwarrow Is., *Cook Is.* 97 J11
Suwayq aş Şuqban, *Iraq* 70 D5
Suweis, Khalîg el, *Egypt* 80 J8
Suweis, Qanâ es, *Egypt* 80 H8
Suwŏn, *S. Korea* 57 F14
Suzdal, *Russia* 46 D11
Suzhou, *Anhui, China* 56 H9
Suzhou, *Jiangsu, China* 59 B13
Suzu, *Japan* 55 F8
Suzu-Misaki, *Japan* 55 F8
Suzuka, *Japan* 55 G8
Suzzara, *Italy* 28 D7
Svalbard, *Arctic* 4 B8
Svalöv, *Sweden* 11 J7
Svaneke, *Denmark* 11 J9
Svängsta, *Sweden* 11 H8
Svanskog, *Sweden* 10 E6
Svappavaara, *Sweden* 8 C19
Svärdsjö, *Sweden* 10 D9
Svartå, *Sweden* 10 E8
Svartisen, *Norway* 8 C15
Svartvik, *Sweden* 10 B11
Svatove, *Ukraine* 47 H10
Svatovo = Svatove, *Ukraine* 47 H10
Svay Chek, *Cambodia* 64 F4
Svay Rieng, *Cambodia* 65 G5
Svealand □, *Sweden* 10 D9
Svedala, *Sweden* 11 J7
Sveg, *Sweden* 10 B8
Svendborg, *Denmark* 11 J4
Svenljunga, *Sweden* 11 G7
Svenstavik, *Sweden* 10 B8
Svenstrup, *Denmark* 11 H3
Sverdlovsk = Yekaterinburg, *Russia* 50 D7
Sverdlovsk, *Ukraine* 47 H10
Sverdrup Is., *Canada* 4 B3
Svetac, *Croatia* 29 E12
Sveti Nikola, Prokhad, *Europe* 40 C6
Sveti Nikole, *Macedonia* 40 E5
Sveti Rok, *Croatia* 29 D12
Svetlaya, *Russia* 54 A9
Svetlogorsk = Svyetlahorsk, *Belarus* 47 F5
Svetlograd, *Russia* 49 H6
Svetlovodsk = Svitlovodsk, *Ukraine* 47 H7
Svidník, *Slovak Rep.* 27 B14
Svilaja Planina, *Croatia* 29 E13
Svilajnac, *Serbia, Yug.* 40 B5
Svilengrad, *Bulgaria* 41 E10
Svir →, *Russia* 46 B7
Sviritsa, *Russia* 46 B7
Svishtov, *Bulgaria* 41 C9
Svislach, *Belarus* 47 F3
Svitava →, *Czech Rep.* 27 B9
Svitavy, *Czech Rep.* 27 B9
Svitlovodsk, *Ukraine* 47 H7
Svobodnyy, *Russia* 51 D13
Svoge, *Bulgaria* 40 D7
Svolvær, *Norway* 8 B16
Svratka →, *Czech Rep.* 27 B9
Svrljig, *Serbia, Yug.* 40 C6
Svyetlahorsk, *Belarus* 47 F5
Swabian Alps = Schwäbische Alb, *Germany* 25 G5
Swainsboro, *U.S.A.* 109 J4
Swakop →, *Namibia* 88 C2
Swakopmund, *Namibia* 88 C1
Swale →, *U.K.* 12 C6
Swan →, *Australia* 93 F2
Swan →, *Canada* 105 C8
Swan Hill, *Australia* 95 F3
Swan Hills, *Canada* 104 C5
Swan Is., *W. Indies* 120 C3
Swan L., *Canada* 105 C8
Swan Peak, *U.S.A.* 114 C7
Swan Ra., *U.S.A.* 114 C7
Swan Reach, *Australia* 95 E2
Swan River, *Canada* 105 C8
Swanage, *U.K.* 13 G6
Swansea, *Australia* 94 G4
Swansea, *Canada* 110 C5
Swansea, *U.K.* 13 F4
Swansea □, *U.K.* 13 F3
Swar →, *Pakistan* 69 B5
Swartberge, *S. Africa* 88 E3
Swartmodder, *S. Africa* 88 D3
Swartnossob →, *Namibia* 88 C2
Swartruggens, *S. Africa* 88 D4
Swarzędz, *Poland* 45 F4
Swastika, *Canada* 102 C3
Swatow = Shantou, *China* 59 F11
Swaziland ■, *Africa* 89 D5
Sweden ■, *Europe* 9 G16
Swedru, *Ghana* 83 D4
Sweet Home, *U.S.A.* 114 D2
Sweetgrass, *U.S.A.* 114 B8
Sweetwater, *Nev., U.S.A.* 116 G7
Sweetwater, *Tenn., U.S.A.* 109 H3
Sweetwater, *Tex., U.S.A.* 113 J4
Sweetwater →, *U.S.A.* 114 E10
Swellendam, *S. Africa* 88 E3
Świder →, *Poland* 45 F8
Świdnica, *Poland* 45 H3
Świdnik, *Poland* 45 G9
Świdwin, *Poland* 44 E2
Świebodzice, *Poland* 45 H3
Świebodzin, *Poland* 45 F2
Świecie, *Poland* 44 E5
Świerzawa, *Poland* 45 G2
Świętokrzyskie □, *Poland* 45 H7
Świętokrzyskie, Góry, *Poland* 45 H7
Swift Current, *Canada* 105 C7
Swiftcurrent →, *Canada* 105 C7
Swilly, L., *Ireland* 15 A4
Swindon, *U.K.* 13 F6
Swindon □, *U.K.* 13 F6
Swinemünde = Świnoujście, *Poland* 44 E1
Swinford, *Ireland* 15 C3
Świnoujście, *Poland* 44 E1
Switzerland ■, *Europe* 25 J4
Swords, *Ireland* 15 C5
Swoyerville, *U.S.A.* 111 E9
Syasstroy, *Russia* 46 B7
Sychevka, *Russia* 46 E8
Syców, *Poland* 45 G4
Sydenham →, *Canada* 110 D2
Sydney, *Australia* 95 E5
Sydney, *Canada* 103 C7
Sydney L., *Canada* 105 C10
Sydney Mines, *Canada* 103 C7
Sydprøven = Alluitsup Paa, *Greenland* 4 C5
Sydra, G. of = Surt, Khalīj, *Libya* 79 B9
Syeverodonetsk, *Ukraine* 47 H10
Syke, *Germany* 24 C4
Sykesville, *U.S.A.* 110 E6
Syktyvkar, *Russia* 50 C6
Sylacauga, *U.S.A.* 109 J2
Sylarna, *Sweden* 8 E15
Sylhet, *Bangla.* 67 G17
Sylt, *Germany* 24 A4
Sylvan Beach, *U.S.A.* 111 C9
Sylvan Lake, *Canada* 104 C6
Sylvania, *U.S.A.* 109 J5
Sylvester, *U.S.A.* 109 K4
Sym, *Russia* 50 C9
Symón, *Mexico* 118 C4
Synelnykove, *Ukraine* 47 H8
Synnott Ra., *Australia* 92 C4
Syracuse, *Kans., U.S.A.* 113 G4
Syracuse, *N.Y., U.S.A.* 111 C8
Syracuse, *Nebr., U.S.A.* 112 E6
Syrdarya →, *Kazakstan* 50 E7
Syria ■, *Asia* 70 C3
Syrian Desert = Shām, Bādiyat ash, *Asia* 70 C3
Sysslebäck, *Sweden* 10 D6
Syzran, *Russia* 48 D9
Szabolcs-Szatmár-Bereg □, *Hungary* 42 B6
Szadek, *Poland* 45 G5
Szamocin, *Poland* 45 E4
Szamos →, *Hungary* 42 B7
Szamotuły, *Poland* 45 F3
Száraz →, *Hungary* 42 D6
Szarvas, *Hungary* 42 D5
Százhalombatta, *Hungary* 42 C3
Szczawnica, *Poland* 45 J7
Szczebrzeszyn, *Poland* 45 H9
Szczecin, *Poland* 44 E1
Szczecinek, *Poland* 44 E3
Szczeciński, Zalew = Stettiner Haff, *Germany* 24 B10
Szczekociny, *Poland* 45 H6
Szczucin, *Poland* 45 H8
Szczuczyn, *Poland* 44 E9
Szczyrk, *Poland* 45 J6
Szczytna, *Poland* 45 H3
Szczytno, *Poland* 44 E7
Szechwan = Sichuan □, *China* 58 B5
Szécsény, *Hungary* 42 B4
Szeged, *Hungary* 42 D5
Szeghalom, *Hungary* 42 C6
Székesfehérvár, *Hungary* 42 C3
Szekszárd, *Hungary* 42 D3
Szendrő, *Hungary* 42 B5
Szentendre, *Hungary* 42 C4
Szentes, *Hungary* 42 D5
Szentgotthárd, *Hungary* 42 D1
Szentlőrinc, *Hungary* 42 D3
Szerencs, *Hungary* 42 B6
Szigetszentmiklós, *Hungary* 42 C4
Szigetvár, *Hungary* 42 D2
Szikszó, *Hungary* 42 B5
Szklarska Poreba, *Poland* 45 H2
Szkwa →, *Poland* 45 E8
Szlichtyngowa, *Poland* 45 G3
Szob, *Hungary* 42 C3
Szolnok, *Hungary* 42 C5
Szombathely, *Hungary* 42 C1
Szprotawa, *Poland* 45 G2
Sztum, *Poland* 44 E6
Sztutowo, *Poland* 44 D6
Szubin, *Poland* 45 E4
Szydłowiec, *Poland* 45 G7
Szypliszki, *Poland* 44 D10

T

Ta Khli Khok, *Thailand* 64 E3
Ta Lai, *Vietnam* 65 G6
Tab, *Hungary* 42 D3
Tabacal, *Argentina* 126 A3
Tabaco, *Phil.* 61 E5
Tabagné, *Ivory C.* 82 D4
Ţābah, *Si. Arabia* 70 E4
Tabankort, *Niger* 83 B5
Ţabas, *Khorāsān, Iran* 71 C9
Ţabas, *Khorāsān, Iran* 71 C8
Tabasará, Serranía de, *Panama* 120 E3
Tabasco □, *Mexico* 119 D6
Tabāsīn, *Iran* 71 D8
Tabatinga, Serra da, *Brazil* 125 F10
Taber, *Canada* 104 D6
Taberg, *Sweden* 11 G8
Taberg, *U.S.A.* 111 C9
Tabla, *Niger* 83 C5
Tablas I., *Phil.* 61 E5
Tablas Strait, *Phil.* 61 E4
Table B. = Tafelbaai, *S. Africa* 88 E2
Table B., *Canada* 103 B8
Table Mt., *S. Africa* 88 E2
Table Rock L., *U.S.A.* 113 G8
Tabletop, Mt., *Australia* 94 C4
Tábor, *Czech Rep.* 26 B7
Tabora, *Tanzania* 86 D3
Tabora □, *Tanzania* 86 D3
Tabou, *Ivory C.* 82 E3
Tabrīz, *Iran* 70 B5
Tabuaeran, *Pac. Oc.* 97 G12
Tabuenca, *Spain* 32 D3
Tabūk, *Si. Arabia* 70 D3
Täby, *Sweden* 10 E12
Tacámbaro de Codallos, *Mexico* 118 D4
Tacheng, *China* 60 B3
Tach'i, *Taiwan* 59 E13
Tachia, *Taiwan* 59 E13
Tach'ing Shan = Daqing Shan, *China* 56 D6
Tachov, *Czech Rep.* 26 B5
Tácina →, *Italy* 31 D9
Tacloban, *Phil.* 61 F6
Tacna, *Peru* 124 G4
Tacoma, *U.S.A.* 116 C4
Tacuarembó, *Uruguay* 127 C4
Tademaït, Plateau du, *Algeria* 78 C6
Tadio, L., *Ivory C.* 82 D3
Tadjoura, *Djibouti* 81 E5
Tadjoura, Golfe de, *Djibouti* 81 E5
Tadmor, *N.Z.* 91 J4
Tadoule, L., *Canada* 105 B9
Tadoussac, *Canada* 103 C6
Tadzhikistan = Tajikistan ■, *Asia* 50 F8
Taechŏn-ni, *S. Korea* 57 F14
Taegu, *S. Korea* 57 G15
Taegwan, *N. Korea* 57 D13
Taejŏn, *S. Korea* 57 F14
Tafalla, *Spain* 32 C3
Tafar, *Sudan* 81 F2
Tafelbaai, *S. Africa* 88 E2
Tafermaar, *Indonesia* 63 F8
Tafí Viejo, *Argentina* 126 B2
Tafīhān, *Iran* 71 D7
Tafiré, *Ivory C.* 82 D3
Tafo, *Ghana* 83 D4
Tafresh, *Iran* 71 C6
Taft, *Iran* 71 D7
Taft, *Phil.* 61 F6
Taft, *U.S.A.* 117 K7
Taftān, Kūh-e, *Iran* 71 D9
Taga Dzong, *Bhutan* 67 F16
Taganrog, *Russia* 47 J10
Taganrogskiy Zaliv, *Russia* 47 J10
Tagânt, *Mauritania* 82 B2
Tagatay, *Phil.* 61 D4
Tagbilaran, *Phil.* 61 G5
Tággia, *Italy* 28 E4
Tagish, *Canada* 104 A2
Tagish L., *Canada* 104 A2
Tagliacozzo, *Italy* 29 F10
Tagliamento →, *Italy* 29 C10
Táglio di Po, *Italy* 29 D9
Tago, *Phil.* 61 G7
Tagomago, *Spain* 37 B8
Tagourāret, *Mauritania* 82 B3
Taguatinga, *Brazil* 125 F10
Tagudin, *Phil.* 61 C4
Tagum, *Phil.* 61 H6
Tagus = Tejo →, *Europe* 35 F2
Tahakopa, *N.Z.* 91 M2
Tahan, Gunong, *Malaysia* 65 K4
Tahat, *Algeria* 78 D7
Tāherī, *Iran* 71 E7
Tahiti, *Pac. Oc.* 97 J13
Tahlequah, *U.S.A.* 113 H7

Tahoe, L., *U.S.A.* 116 G6
Tahoe City, *U.S.A.* 116 F6
Tahoka, *U.S.A.* 113 J4
Taholah, *U.S.A.* 116 C2
Tahoua, *Niger* 83 C6
Tahrūd, *Iran* 71 D8
Tahsis, *Canada* 104 D3
Tahta, *Egypt* 80 B3
Tahtaköprü, *Turkey* 41 G13
Tahtalı Dağları, *Turkey* 72 C7
Tahulandang, *Indonesia* 63 D7
Tahuna, *Indonesia* 63 D7
Taï, *Ivory C.* 82 D3
Tai Hu, *China* 59 B12
Tai Shan, *China* 57 F9
Tai'an, *China* 57 F9
Taibei = T'aipei, *Taiwan* 59 E13
Taibique, *Canary Is.* 37 G2
Taibus Qi, *China* 56 D8
Taicang, *China* 59 B13
T'aichung, *Taiwan* 59 E13
Taieri →, *N.Z.* 91 M3
Taigu, *China* 56 F7
Taihang Shan, *China* 56 G7
Taihape, *N.Z.* 91 H5
Taihe, *Anhui, China* 56 H8
Taihe, *Jiangxi, China* 59 D10
Taihu, *China* 59 B11
Taijiang, *China* 58 D7
Taikang, *China* 56 G8
Tailem Bend, *Australia* 95 F2
Tailfingen, *Germany* 25 G5
Tailuko, *Taiwan* 59 E13
Taimyr Peninsula = Taymyr, Poluostrov, *Russia* 51 B11
Tain, *U.K.* 14 D4
T'ainan, *Taiwan* 59 F13
Taínaron, Ákra, *Greece* 38 E4
Taining, *China* 59 D11
T'aipei, *Taiwan* 59 E13
Taiping, *China* 59 B12
Taiping, *Malaysia* 65 K3
Taipingzhen, *China* 56 H6
Tairbeart = Tarbert, *U.K.* 14 D2
Taishan, *China* 59 F9
Taishun, *China* 59 D12
Taita Hills, *Kenya* 86 C4
Taitao, Pen. de, *Chile* 122 H3
T'aitung, *Taiwan* 59 F13
Taivalkoski, *Finland* 8 D23
Taiwan ■, *Asia* 59 F13
Taiwan Strait, *Asia* 59 E12
Taixing, *China* 59 A13
Taiyara, *Sudan* 81 E3
Taïyetos Óros, *Greece* 38 D4
Taiyiba, *Israel* 75 C4
Taiyuan, *China* 56 F7
Taizhong = T'aichung, *Taiwan* 59 E13
Taizhou, *China* 59 A12
Taizhou Liedao, *China* 59 C13
Ta'izz, *Yemen* 74 E3
Tājābād, *Iran* 71 D7
Tajikistan ■, *Asia* 50 F8
Tajima, *Japan* 55 F9
Tajo = Tejo →, *Europe* 35 F2
Tajrīsh, *Iran* 71 C6
Tak, *Thailand* 64 D2
Takāb, *Iran* 70 B5
Takachiho, *Japan* 55 H5
Takachu, *Botswana* 88 C3
Takada, *Japan* 55 F9
Takahagi, *Japan* 55 F10
Takaka, *N.Z.* 91 J4
Takamatsu, *Japan* 55 G7
Takaoka, *Japan* 55 F8
Takapuna, *N.Z.* 91 G5
Takasaki, *Japan* 55 F9
Takatsuki, *Japan* 55 G7
Takaungu, *Kenya* 86 C4
Takayama, *Japan* 55 F8
Take-Shima, *Japan* 55 J5
Takefu, *Japan* 55 G8
Takengon, *Indonesia* 62 D1
Takeo, *Japan* 55 H5
Tåkern, *Sweden* 11 F8
Tākestān, *Iran* 71 C6
Taketa, *Japan* 55 H5
Takev, *Cambodia* 65 G5
Takh, *India* 69 C7
Takht-Sulaiman, *Pakistan* 68 D3
Takikawa, *Japan* 54 C10
Takla L., *Canada* 104 B3
Takla Landing, *Canada* 104 B3
Takla Makan = Taklamakan Shamo, *China* 52 F12
Taklamakan Shamo, *China* 52 F12
Taku →, *Canada* 104 B2
Takum, *Nigeria* 83 D6
Tal Halāl, *Iran* 71 D7
Tala, *Uruguay* 127 C4
Talachyn, *Belarus* 46 E5
Talacogan, *Phil.* 61 G6
Talagang, *Pakistan* 68 C5
Talagante, *Chile* 126 C1
Talak, *Niger* 83 B6
Talamanca, Cordillera de, *Cent. Amer.* 120 E3
Talant, *France* 19 E11
Talara, *Peru* 124 D2
Talas, *Kyrgyzstan* 50 E8
Talas, *Turkey* 72 C6
Talâta, *Egypt* 75 E1
Talata Mafara, *Nigeria* 83 C6
Talaud, Kepulauan, *Indonesia* 63 D7
Talaud Is. = Talaud, Kepulauan, *Indonesia* 63 D7
Talavera de la Reina, *Spain* 34 F6
Talavera la Real, *Spain* 35 G4
Talayan, *Phil.* 61 H6
Talayuela, *Spain* 34 F5
Talbandh, *India* 69 H12
Talbert, Sillon de, *France* 18 D3
Talbot, C., *Australia* 92 B4
Talbragar →, *Australia* 95 E4
Talca, *Chile* 126 D1
Talcahuano, *Chile* 126 D1
Talcher, *India* 67 J14
Talcho, *Niger* 83 C5
Taldy Kurgan = Taldyqorghan, *Kazakstan* 50 E8
Taldyqorghan, *Kazakstan* 50 E8
Tālesh, *Iran* 71 B6
Tālesh, Kūhhā-ye, *Iran* 71 B6
Talguharai, *Sudan* 80 D4
Tali Post, *Sudan* 81 F3
Taliabu, *Indonesia* 63 E6
Talibon, *Phil.* 63 B6
Talibong, Ko, *Thailand* 65 J2
Talihina, *U.S.A.* 113 H7
Talisayan, *Phil.* 61 G6
Taliwang, *Indonesia* 62 F5
Tall 'Afar, *Iraq* 70 B4
Tall Kalakh, *Syria* 75 A5
Talla, *Egypt* 80 B3
Talladega, *U.S.A.* 109 J2
Tallahassee, *U.S.A.* 109 K3
Tallangatta, *Australia* 95 F4
Tallard, *France* 21 D10
Tällberg, *Sweden* 10 D9
Tallering Pk., *Australia* 93 E2
Talli, *Pakistan* 68 E3
Tallinn, *Estonia* 9 G21
Tallmadge, *U.S.A.* 110 E3
Tallulah, *U.S.A.* 113 J9
Tălmaciu, *Romania* 43 E9
Talmont-St-Hilaire, *France* 20 B2
Talne, *Ukraine* 47 H6
Talnoye = Talne, *Ukraine* 47 H6
Talodi, *Sudan* 81 E3
Talovaya, *Russia* 48 E5
Taloyoak, *Canada* 100 B10
Talpa de Allende, *Mexico* 118 C4
Talsi, *Latvia* 9 H20
Talsi □, *Latvia* 44 A9
Taltal, *Chile* 126 B1
Taltson →, *Canada* 104 A6
Talwood, *Australia* 95 D4
Talyawalka →, *Australia* 95 E3
Tam Chau, *Vietnam* 65 G5
Tam Ky, *Vietnam* 64 E7
Tam Quan, *Vietnam* 64 E7
Tama, *U.S.A.* 112 E8
Tamale, *Ghana* 83 D4
Taman, *Russia* 47 K9
Tamani, *Mali* 82 C3
Tamano, *Japan* 55 G6
Tamanrasset, *Algeria* 78 D7
Tamaqua, *U.S.A.* 111 F9
Tamar →, *U.K.* 13 G3
Tamarinda, *Spain* 37 B10
Tamarite de Litera, *Spain* 32 D5
Tamashima, *Japan* 55 G6
Tamási, *Hungary* 42 D3
Tamaské, *Niger* 83 C6
Tamaulipas □, *Mexico* 119 C5
Tamaulipas, Sierra de, *Mexico* 119 C5
Tamazula, *Mexico* 118 C3
Tamazunchale, *Mexico* 119 C5
Tamba-Dabatou, *Guinea* 82 C2
Tambacounda, *Senegal* 82 C2
Tambelan, Kepulauan, *Indonesia* 62 D3
Tambellup, *Australia* 93 F2
Tambo, *Australia* 94 C4
Tambo de Mora, *Peru* 124 F3
Tambohorano, *Madag.* 89 B7
Tambora, *Indonesia* 62 F5
Tambov, *Russia* 48 D5
Tambre →, *Spain* 34 C2
Tambuku, *Indonesia* 63 G15
Tamburâ, *Sudan* 81 F2
Tâmchekket, *Mauritania* 82 B2
Tâmega →, *Portugal* 34 D2
Tamenglong, *India* 67 G18
Tamgué, Massif du, *Guinea* 82 C2
Tamiahua, L. de, *Mexico* 119 C5
Tamil Nadu □, *India* 66 P10
Tamis →, *Serbia, Yug.* 42 F5
Tamluk, *India* 69 H12
Tammerfors = Tampere, *Finland* 9 F20
Tammisaari, *Finland* 9 F20
Tämnaren, *Sweden* 10 D11
Tamo Abu, Pegunungan, *Malaysia* 62 D5
Tampa, *U.S.A.* 109 M4
Tampa B., *U.S.A.* 109 M4
Tampere, *Finland* 9 F20
Tampico, *Mexico* 119 C5
Tampin, *Malaysia* 65 L4
Tamsweg, *Austria* 26 D6
Tamu, *Burma* 67 G19
Tamuja →, *Spain* 35 F4
Tamworth, *Australia* 95 E5
Tamworth, *Canada* 110 B8
Tamworth, *U.K.* 13 E6
Tamyang, *S. Korea* 57 G14
Tan An, *Vietnam* 65 G6
Tan-Tan, *Morocco* 78 C3
Tana →, *Kenya* 86 C5
Tana →, *Norway* 8 A23
Tana, L., *Ethiopia* 81 E4
Tana River, *Kenya* 86 C4
Tanabe, *Japan* 55 H7
Tanafjorden, *Norway* 8 A23
Tanaga, Pta., *Canary Is.* 37 G1
Tanahbala, *Indonesia* 62 E1
Tanahgrogot, *Indonesia* 62 E5
Tanahjampea, *Indonesia* 63 F6
Tanahmasa, *Indonesia* 62 E1
Tanahmerah, *Indonesia* 63 F10
Tanakpur, *India* 69 E9
Tanakura, *Japan* 55 F10
Tanami, *Australia* 92 C4
Tanami Desert, *Australia* 92 C5
Tanana →, *U.S.A.* 100 B4
Tananarive = Antananarivo, *Madag.* 89 B8
Tánaro →, *Italy* 28 D5
Tancheng, *China* 57 G10
Tanch'ŏn, *N. Korea* 57 D15
Tanda, *Ut. P., India* 69 F10
Tanda, *Ut. P., India* 69 E8
Tanda, *Ivory C.* 82 D4
Tandag, *Phil.* 61 G7
Tandaia, *Tanzania* 87 D3
Tăndărei, *Romania* 43 F12
Tandaué, *Angola* 88 B2
Tandil, *Argentina* 126 D4
Tandil, Sa. del, *Argentina* 126 D4
Tandlianwala, *Pakistan* 68 D5
Tando Adam, *Pakistan* 68 G3
Tando Allahyar, *Pakistan* 68 G3
Tando Bago, *Pakistan* 68 G3
Tando Mohommed Khan, *Pakistan* 68 G3
Tandou L., *Australia* 95 E3
Tandragee, *U.K.* 15 B5
Tandsjöborg, *Sweden* 10 C8
Tane-ga-Shima, *Japan* 55 J5
Taneatua, *N.Z.* 91 H6
Tanen Tong Dan, *Burma* 64 D2
Tanew →, *Poland* 45 H9
Tanezrouft, *Algeria* 78 D6
Tang, Koh, *Cambodia* 65 G4
Tang, Ra's-e, *Iran* 71 E8
Tang Krasang, *Cambodia* 64 F5
Tanga, *Tanzania* 86 D4
Tanga □, *Tanzania* 86 D4
Tanganyika, L., *Africa* 86 D3
Tangaza, *Nigeria* 83 C5
Tanger = Tangier, *Morocco* 78 A4
Tangerang, *Indonesia* 63 G12
Tangerhütte, *Germany* 24 C7
Tangermünde, *Germany* 24 C7
Tanggu, *China* 57 E9
Tanggula Shan, *China* 60 C4
Tanghe, *China* 56 H7
Tangier, *Morocco* 78 A4
Tangorin, *Australia* 94 C3
Tangorombohitr'i Makay, *Madag.* 89 C8
Tangshan, *China* 57 E10
Tangtou, *China* 57 G10
Tanguiéta, *Benin* 83 C5
Tangxi, *China* 59 C12
Tangyan He →, *China* 58 C7
Tanimbar, Kepulauan, *Indonesia* 63 F8
Tanimbar Is. = Tanimbar, Kepulauan, *Indonesia* 63 F8
Taninthari = Tenasserim □, *Burma* 64 F2
Tanjay, *Phil.* 61 G5
Tanjong Malim, *Malaysia* 65 L3
Tanjore = Thanjavur, *India* 66 P11
Tanjung, *Indonesia* 62 E5
Tanjungbalai, *Indonesia* 62 D1
Tanjungbatu, *Indonesia* 62 D5
Tanjungkarang Telukbetung, *Indonesia* 62 F3
Tanjungpandan, *Indonesia* 62 E3
Tanjungpinang, *Indonesia* 62 D2
Tanjungredeb, *Indonesia* 62 D5
Tanjungselor, *Indonesia* 62 D5
Tank, *Pakistan* 68 C4
Tankhala, *India* 68 J5
Tännäs, *Sweden* 10 B6
Tannersville, *U.S.A.* 111 E9
Tannis Bugt, *Denmark* 11 G4
Tannu-Ola, *Russia* 51 D10
Tannum Sands, *Australia* 94 C5
Tano →, *Ghana* 82 D4
Tanon Str., *Phil.* 61 F5
Tanout, *Niger* 83 C6
Tanshui, *Taiwan* 59 E13
Tansilla, *Burkina Faso* 82 C4
Tanta, *Egypt* 80 H7
Tantoyuca, *Mexico* 119 C5
Tantung = Dandong, *China* 57 D13
Tanumshede, *Sweden* 11 F5
Tanunda, *Australia* 95 E2
Tanus, *France* 20 D6
Tanzania ■, *Africa* 86 D3
Tanzilla →, *Canada* 104 B2
Tao, Ko, *Thailand* 65 G2
Tao'an = Taonan, *China* 57 B12
Tao'er He →, *China* 57 B13
Taohua Dao, *China* 59 C14
Taolanaro, *Madag.* 89 D8
Taole, *China* 56 E4
Taonan, *China* 57 B12
Taormina, *Italy* 31 E8
Taos, *U.S.A.* 115 H11
Taoudenni, *Mali* 78 D5
Taoyuan, *China* 59 C8
T'aoyüan, *Taiwan* 59 E13
Tapa, *Estonia* 9 G21
Tapa Shan = Daba Shan, *China* 58 B7
Tapachula, *Mexico* 119 E6
Tapah, *Malaysia* 65 K3
Tapajós →, *Brazil* 122 D5
Tapaktuan, *Indonesia* 62 D1
Tapanahoni →, *Surinam* 125 C8
Tapanui, *N.Z.* 91 L2
Tapauá →, *Brazil* 124 E6
Tapes, *Brazil* 127 C5
Tapeta, *Liberia* 82 D3
Taphan Hin, *Thailand* 64 D3
Tapia de Casariego, *Spain* 34 B4
Tapirapecó, Serra, *Venezuela* 124 C6
Tapolca, *Hungary* 42 D2
Tapuaenuku, Mt., *N.Z.* 91 K4
Tapul Group, *Phil.* 61 J4
Tapurucuará, *Brazil* 124 D5
Ţaqţaq, *Iraq* 70 C5
Taquara, *Brazil* 127 B5
Taquari →, *Brazil* 124 G7
Tara, *Australia* 95 D5
Tara, *Canada* 110 B3
Tara, *Russia* 50 D8
Tara, *Zambia* 87 F2
Tara →, *Montenegro, Yug.* 40 C2
Taraba □, *Nigeria* 83 D7
Taraba →, *Nigeria* 83 D7
Tarabagatay, Khrebet, *Kazakstan* 50 E9
Tarābulus, *Lebanon* 75 A4
Tarābulus, *Libya* 79 B8
Taraclia, *Moldova* 43 D14
Taraclia, *Moldova* 43 E13
Taradehi, *India* 69 H8
Tarajalejo, *Canary Is.* 37 F5
Tarakan, *Indonesia* 62 D5
Tarakit, Mt., *Kenya* 86 B4
Tarama-Jima, *Japan* 55 M2
Taran, Mys, *Russia* 9 J18
Taranagar, *India* 68 E6
Taranaki □, *N.Z.* 91 H5
Tarancón, *Spain* 32 E1
Taranga Hill, *India* 66 H8
Taransay, *U.K.* 14 D1
Táranto, *Italy* 31 B10
Táranto, G. di, *Italy* 31 B10
Tarapacá, *Colombia* 124 D5
Tarapacá □, *Chile* 126 A2
Tarapoto, *Peru* 124 E3
Tarare, *France* 21 C8
Tararua Ra., *N.Z.* 91 J5
Tarascon, *France* 21 E8
Tarascon-sur-Ariège, *France* 20 F5
Tarashcha, *Ukraine* 47 H6
Tarauacá, *Brazil* 124 E4
Tarauacá →, *Brazil* 124 E5
Taravo →, *France* 21 G12
Tarawa, *Kiribati* 96 G9
Tarawera, *N.Z.* 91 H6
Tarawera L., *N.Z.* 91 H6
Tarazona, *Spain* 32 D3
Tarazona de la Mancha, *Spain* 33 F3
Tarbat Ness, *U.K.* 14 D5
Tarbela Dam, *Pakistan* 68 B5
Tarbert, *Arg. & Bute, U.K.* 14 F3
Tarbert, *W. Isles, U.K.* 14 D2
Tarbes, *France* 20 E4
Tarboro, *U.S.A.* 109 H7
Tărcău, Munţii, *Romania* 43 D11
Tarcento, *Italy* 29 B10
Tarcoola, *Australia* 95 E1
Tarcoon, *Australia* 95 E4
Tardets-Sorholus, *France* 20 E3
Tardoire →, *France* 20 C4
Taree, *Australia* 95 E5
Tarfa, W. el →, *Egypt* 80 B3
Tarfaya, *Morocco* 78 C3
Târgovişte, *Romania* 43 F10
Târgu Bujor, *Romania* 43 E12
Târgu Cărbuneşti, *Romania* 43 F8
Târgu Frumos, *Romania* 43 C12
Târgu-Jiu, *Romania* 43 E8
Târgu Lăpuş, *Romania* 43 C8
Târgu Mureş, *Romania* 43 D9
Târgu Neamţ, *Romania* 43 C11
Târgu Ocna, *Romania* 43 D11
Târgu Secuiesc, *Romania* 43 E11
Târguşor, *Romania* 43 F13
Târhăus, Vf., *Romania* 43 D11
Ţarif, *U.A.E.* 71 E7
Tarifa, *Spain* 35 J5
Tarija, *Bolivia* 126 A3
Tarija □, *Bolivia* 126 A3
Tariku →, *Indonesia* 63 E9
Tarim Basin = Tarim Pendi, *China* 60 C3
Tarim He →, *China* 60 C3
Tarim Pendi, *China* 60 C3
Taritatu →, *Indonesia* 63 E9
Tarka →, *S. Africa* 88 E4
Tarkastad, *S. Africa* 88 E4
Tarkhankut, Mys, *Ukraine* 47 K7
Tarko Sale, *Russia* 50 C8
Tarkwa, *Ghana* 82 D4
Tarlac, *Phil.* 61 D4
Tarm, *Denmark* 11 J2
Tarma, *Peru* 124 F3
Tarn □, *France* 20 E6
Tarn →, *France* 20 D5
Tarn-et-Garonne □, *France* 20 D5
Tarna →, *Hungary* 42 C4
Târnava Mare →, *Romania* 43 D8
Târnava Mică →, *Romania* 43 D8
Târnăveni, *Romania* 43 D9
Tarnica, *Poland* 45 J9
Tarnobrzeg, *Poland* 45 H8
Tarnogród, *Poland* 45 H9
Tarnos, *France* 20 E2
Târnova, *Moldova* 43 B12
Târnova, *Romania* 42 E6
Tarnów, *Poland* 45 H8
Tarnowskie Góry, *Poland* 45 H5
Tärnsjö, *Sweden* 10 D10
Táro →, *Italy* 28 C7
Ţārom, *Iran* 71 D7
Taroom, *Australia* 95 D4
Taroudannt, *Morocco* 78 B4
Tarp, *Germany* 24 A5
Tarpon Springs, *U.S.A.* 109 L4
Tarquínia, *Italy* 29 F8
Tarragona, *Spain* 32 D6
Tarragona □, *Spain* 32 D6
Tarraleah, *Australia* 94 G4
Tarrasa = Terrassa, *Spain* 32 D7
Tàrrega, *Spain* 32 D6
Tarrytown, *U.S.A.* 111 E11
Târs, *Denmark* 11 G4
Tarshiha = Me'ona, *Israel* 75 B4
Tarso Emissi, *Chad* 79 D9
Tarsus, *Turkey* 70 B2
Tartagal, *Argentina* 126 A3
Tärtär, *Azerbaijan* 49 K8
Tärtär →, *Azerbaijan* 49 K8
Tartas, *France* 20 E3
Tartu, *Estonia* 9 G22
Ţarţūs, *Syria* 70 C2
Tarumizu, *Japan* 55 J5
Tarussa, *Russia* 46 E9
Tarutao, Ko, *Thailand* 65 J2
Tarutung, *Indonesia* 62 D1
Tarvísio, *Italy* 29 B10
Taseko →, *Canada* 104 C4
Tash-Kömür, *Kyrgyzstan* 50 E8
Tash-Kumyr = Tash-Kömür, *Kyrgyzstan* 50 E8
Tashauz = Dashhowuz, *Turkmenistan* 50 E6
Tashi Chho Dzong = Thimphu, *Bhutan* 67 F16
Ţashk, Daryācheh-ye, *Iran* 71 D7
Tashkent = Toshkent, *Uzbekistan* 50 E7
Tashtagol, *Russia* 50 D9
Tasiilaq, *Greenland* 4 C6
Tasikmalaya, *Indonesia* 63 G13
Tåsinge, *Denmark* 11 J4
Tåsjön, *Sweden* 8 D16
Taskan, *Russia* 51 C16
Tasker, *Niger* 83 C7
Taşköprü, *Turkey* 72 B6
Taşlâc, *Moldova* 43 C14
Tasman B., *N.Z.* 91 J4
Tasman Mts., *N.Z.* 91 J4
Tasman Pen., *Australia* 94 G4
Tasman Sea, *Pac. Oc.* 96 L8
Tasmania □, *Australia* 94 G4
Tăşnad, *Romania* 42 C7
Tassili n'Ajjer, *Algeria* 78 C7
Tassili Tin-Rerhoh, *Algeria* 83 A5
Tata, *Hungary* 42 C3
Tatabánya, *Hungary* 42 C3
Tatahouine, *Tunisia* 79 B8
Tatar Republic = Tatarstan □, *Russia* 48 C10
Tatarbunary, *Ukraine* 47 K5
Tatarsk, *Russia* 50 D8
Tatarstan □, *Russia* 48 C10
Tateyama, *Japan* 55 G9
Tathlina L., *Canada* 104 A5
Tathra, *Australia* 95 F4
Tati →, *India* 66 J8
Tatinnai L., *Canada* 105 A9
Tatla L., *Canada* 104 C4
Tatlısu, *Turkey* 41 F11
Tatnam, C., *Canada* 105 B10
Tatra = Tatry, *Slovak Rep.* 27 B13
Tatry, *Slovak Rep.* 27 B13
Tatshenshini →, *Canada* 104 B1
Tatsuno, *Japan* 55 G7
Tatta, *Pakistan* 68 G2
Tatuī, *Brazil* 127 A6
Tatum, *U.S.A.* 113 J3
Tat'ung = Datong, *China* 56 D7
Tatvan, *Turkey* 70 B4
Taubaté, *Brazil* 127 A6
Tauberbischofsheim, *Germany* 25 F5
Taucha, *Germany* 24 D8
Tauern-tunnel, *Austria* 26 D6
Taufikia, *Sudan* 81 F3
Taulé, *France* 18 D3
Taumarunui, *N.Z.* 91 H5
Taumaturgo, *Brazil* 124 E4
Taung, *S. Africa* 88 D3
Taungdwingyi, *Burma* 67 J19
Taunggyi, *Burma* 67 J20
Taungup, *Burma* 67 K19
Taungup Pass, *Burma* 67 K19
Taungup Taunggya, *Burma* 67 K18
Taunsa, *Pakistan* 68 D4
Taunsa Barrage, *Pakistan* 68 D4
Taunton, *U.K.* 13 F4
Taunton, *U.S.A.* 111 E13
Taunus, *Germany* 25 E4
Taupo, *N.Z.* 91 H6
Taupo, L., *N.Z.* 91 H5
Tauragė, *Lithuania* 9 J20
Tauragė □, *Lithuania* 44 C9
Tauranga, *N.Z.* 91 G6
Tauranga Harb., *N.Z.* 91 G6
Taureau, Rés., *Canada* 102 C5
Taurianova, *Italy* 31 D9
Taurus Mts. = Toros Dağları, *Turkey* 70 B2
Tauste, *Spain* 32 D3
Tauz = Tovuz, *Azerbaijan* 49 K7
Tavas, *Turkey* 39 D11
Tavda, *Russia* 50 D7
Tavda →, *Russia* 50 D7
Tavernes de la Valldigna, *Spain* 33 F4
Taveta, *Tanzania* 86 C4
Taveuni, *Fiji* 91 C9
Taviano, *Italy* 31 C11
Tavignano →, *France* 21 F13
Tavira, *Portugal* 35 H3
Tavistock, *Canada* 110 C4
Tavistock, *U.K.* 13 G3
Tavolara, *Italy* 30 B2
Távora →, *Portugal* 34 D3
Tavoy = Dawei, *Burma* 64 E2
Tavşanlı, *Turkey* 39 B11

Taw →, U.K. 13 F3
Tawa →, India 68 H8
Tawas City, U.S.A. 108 C4
Tawau, Malaysia 62 D5
Taweisha, Sudan 81 E2
Tawitawi, Phil. 63 B6
Tawu, Taiwan 59 F13
Taxco de Alarcón, Mexico 119 D5
Taxila, Pakistan 68 C5
Tay →, U.K. 14 E5
Tay, Firth of, U.K. 14 E5
Tay, L., Australia 93 F3
Tay, L., U.K. 14 E4
Tay Ninh, Vietnam 65 G6
Tayabamba, Peru 124 E3
Tayabas Bay, Phil. 61 E4
Taylakova, Russia 50 D8
Taylakovy = Taylakova, Russia 50 D8
Taylor, Canada 104 B4
Taylor, Nebr., U.S.A. 112 E5
Taylor, Pa., U.S.A. 111 E9
Taylor, Tex., U.S.A. 113 K6
Taylor, Mt., U.S.A. 115 J10
Taylorville, U.S.A. 112 F10
Taymā, Si. Arabia 70 E3
Taymyr, Oz., Russia 51 B11
Taymyr, Poluostrov, Russia 51 B11
Tayport, U.K. 14 E6
Tayshet, Russia 51 D10
Taytay, Phil. 61 F3
Taz →, Russia 50 C8
Taza, Morocco 78 B5
Tāzah Khurmātū, Iraq 70 C5
Tazawa-Ko, Japan 54 E10
Tazin, Canada 105 B7
Tazin L., Canada 105 B7
Tazovskiy, Russia 50 C8
Tbilisi, Georgia 49 K7
Tchad = Chad ■, Africa 79 E9
Tchad, L., Chad 79 F8
Tchaourou, Benin 83 D5
Tch'eng-tou = Chengdu, China 58 B5
Tchentlo L., Canada 104 B4
Tchetti, Benin 83 D5
Tchibanga, Gabon 84 E2
Tchien, Liberia 82 D3
Tchin Tabaraden, Niger 83 B6
Tch'ong-k'ing = Chongqing, China 58 C6
Tczew, Poland 44 D5
Te Anau, L., N.Z. 91 L1
Te Aroha, N.Z. 91 G5
Te Awamutu, N.Z. 91 H5
Te Kuiti, N.Z. 91 H5
Te-n-Dghâmcha, Sebkhet, Mauritania 82 B1
Te Puke, N.Z. 91 G6
Te Waewae B., N.Z. 91 M1
Teaca, Romania 43 D9
Teague, U.S.A. 113 K6
Teano, Italy 31 A7
Teapa, Mexico 119 D6
Teba, Spain 35 J6
Tebakang, Malaysia 62 D4
Teberda, Russia 49 J5
Tébessa, Algeria 78 A7
Tebicuary →, Paraguay 126 B4
Tebingtinggi, Indonesia 62 D1
Tebintingii, Indonesia 62 E2
Tebulos, Georgia 49 J7
Tecate, Mexico 117 N10
Tecer Dağları, Turkey 72 C7
Tech →, France 20 F7
Techiman, Ghana 82 D4
Techirghiol, Romania 43 F13
Tecka, Argentina 128 E2
Tecomán, Mexico 118 D4
Tecopa, U.S.A. 117 K10
Tecoripa, Mexico 118 B3
Tecuala, Mexico 118 C3
Tecuci, Romania 43 E12
Tecumseh, Canada 110 D2
Tecumseh, Mich., U.S.A. 108 D4
Tecumseh, Okla., U.S.A. 113 H6
Tedzhen = Tejen, Turkmenistan 50 F7
Tees →, U.K. 12 C6
Tees B., U.K. 12 C6
Teeswater, Canada 110 C3
Tefé, Brazil 124 D6
Tefenni, Turkey 39 D11
Tegal, Indonesia 63 G13
Tegernsee, Germany 25 H7
Teggiano, Italy 31 B8
Tegid, L. = Bala, L., U.K. 12 E4
Tegina, Nigeria 83 C6
Tegucigalpa, Honduras 120 D2
Teguidda i-n-Tessoum, Niger 83 B6
Tehachapi, U.S.A. 117 K8
Tehachapi Mts., U.S.A. 117 L8
Tehamiyam, Sudan 80 D4
Tehilla, Sudan 80 D4
Téhini, Ivory C. 82 D4
Tehoru, Indonesia 63 E7
Tehrān, Iran 71 C6
Tehri, India 69 D8
Tehuacán, Mexico 119 D5
Tehuantepec, Mexico 119 D5
Tehuantepec, G. de, Mexico 119 D5
Tehuantepec, Istmo de, Mexico 119 D6
Teide, Canary Is. 37 F3
Teifi →, U.K. 13 E3
Teign →, U.K. 13 G4
Teignmouth, U.K. 13 G4
Teiuş, Romania 43 D8
Teixeira Pinto, Guinea-Biss. 82 C1
Tejam, India 69 E9
Tejen, Turkmenistan 50 F7
Tejen →, Turkmenistan 71 B9
Tejo →, Europe 35 F2
Tejon Pass, U.S.A. 117 L8
Tekamah, U.S.A. 112 E6
Tekapo, L., N.Z. 91 K3
Tekax, Mexico 119 C7
Teke, Turkey 41 E13
Tekeli, Kazakstan 50 E8
Tekeze →, Ethiopia 81 E4
Tekija, Serbia, Yug. 40 B6
Tekirdağ, Turkey 41 F11
Tekirdağ □, Turkey 41 E11
Tekirova, Turkey 39 E12
Tekkali, India 67 K14
Tekke, Turkey 72 B7
Tekman, Turkey 73 C9
Tekoa, U.S.A. 114 C5
Tel Aviv-Yafo, Israel 75 C3
Tel Lakhish, Israel 75 D3
Tel Megiddo, Israel 75 C4
Tela, Honduras 120 C2
Telanaipura = Jambi, Indonesia 62 E2
Telavi, Georgia 49 J7
Telč, Czech Rep. 26 B8
Telciu, Romania 43 C9
Telde, Canary Is. 37 G4
Telegraph Creek, Canada 104 B2
Telekhany = Tsyelyakhany, Belarus 47 F3
Telemark, Norway 9 G12
Telén, Argentina 126 D2
Teleneşti, Moldova 43 C13
Teleng, Iran 71 E9
Teleño, Spain 34 C4
Teleorman □, Romania 43 G10
Teleorman →, Romania 43 G10
Teles Pires →, Brazil 122 D5
Telescope Pk., U.S.A. 117 J9
Teletaye, Mali 83 B5
Telfer Mine, Australia 92 C3
Telford, U.K. 13 E5
Telford and Wrekin □, U.K. 12 E5
Telfs, Austria 26 D4
Télimélé, Guinea 82 C2
Teljo, J., Sudan 81 E2
Telkwa, Canada 104 C3
Tell City, U.S.A. 108 G2
Tellicherry, India 66 P9
Telluride, U.S.A. 115 H10
Teloloapán, Mexico 119 D5
Telpos Iz, Russia 6 C17
Telsen, Argentina 128 E3
Telšiai, Lithuania 9 H20
Telšiai □, Lithuania 44 C9
Teltow, Germany 24 C9
Teluk Anson = Teluk Intan, Malaysia 65 K3
Teluk Betung = Tanjungkarang Telukbetung, Indonesia 62 F3
Teluk Intan, Malaysia 65 K3
Telukbutun, Indonesia 65 K7
Telukdalem, Indonesia 62 D1
Tema, Ghana 83 D5
Temax, Mexico 119 C7
Temba, S. Africa 89 D4
Tembagapura, Indonesia 63 E9
Tembe, Dem. Rep. of the Congo 86 C2
Tembleque, Spain 34 F7
Temblor Range, U.S.A. 117 K7
Teme →, U.K. 13 E5
Temecula, U.S.A. 117 M9
Temerloh, Malaysia 62 D2
Teminabuan, Indonesia 63 E8
Temir, Kazakstan 50 E6
Temirtau, Kazakstan 50 D8
Temirtau, Russia 50 D9
Temiscamie →, Canada 103 B5
Témiscaming, Canada 102 C4
Témiscamingue, L., Canada 102 C4
Temnikov, Russia 48 C6
Temo →, Italy 30 B1
Temosachic, Mexico 118 B3
Tempe, U.S.A. 115 K8
Témpio Pausánia, Italy 30 B2
Tempiute, U.S.A. 116 H11
Temple, U.S.A. 113 K6
Temple B., Australia 94 A3
Templemore, Ireland 15 D4
Templeton, U.S.A. 116 K6
Templeton →, Australia 94 C2
Templin, Germany 24 B9
Tempoal, Mexico 119 C5
Temryuk, Russia 47 K9
Temska →, Serbia, Yug. 40 C6
Temuco, Chile 128 D2
Temuka, N.Z. 91 L3
Tenabo, Mexico 119 C6
Tenaha, U.S.A. 113 K7
Tenakee Springs, U.S.A. 104 B1
Tenali, India 66 L12
Tenancingo, Mexico 119 D5
Tenango, Mexico 119 D5
Tenasserim, Burma 65 F2
Tenasserim □, Burma 64 F2
Tenby, U.K. 13 F3
Tenda, Colle di, France 21 D11
Tendaho, Ethiopia 81 E5
Tende, France 21 D11
Tendelti, Sudan 81 E3
Tendrovskaya Kosa, Ukraine 47 J6
Tendukhera, India 69 H8
Teneida, Egypt 80 B2
Tenenkou, Mali 82 C4
Ténéré, Niger 83 B7
Tenerife, Canary Is. 37 F3
Tenerife, Pico, Canary Is. 37 G1
Teng Xian, Guangxi Zhuangzu, China 59 F8
Teng Xian, Shandong, China 57 G9
Tengah □, Indonesia 63 E6
Tengah, Kepulauan, Indonesia 62 F5
Tengchong, China 58 E2
Tengchowfu = Penglai, China 57 F11
Tenggara □, Indonesia 63 E6
Tenggarong, Indonesia 62 E5
Tenggol, Pulau, Malaysia 65 K4
Tengiz, Ozero, Kazakstan 50 D7
Tenhult, Sweden 11 G8
Tenino, U.S.A. 116 D4
Tenkasi, India 66 Q10
Tenke, Katanga, Dem. Rep. of the Congo 87 E2
Tenke, Katanga, Dem. Rep. of the Congo 87 E2
Tenkodogo, Burkina Faso 83 C4
Tenna →, Italy 29 E10
Tennant Creek, Australia 94 B1
Tennessee □, U.S.A. 109 H2
Tennessee →, U.S.A. 108 G1
Teno, Pta. de, Canary Is. 37 F3
Tenom, Malaysia 62 C5
Tenosique, Mexico 119 D6
Tenryū-Gawa →, Japan 55 G8
Tenterden, U.K. 13 F8
Tenterfield, Australia 95 D5
Teo, Spain 34 C2
Teófilo Otoni, Brazil 125 G10
Tepa, Indonesia 63 F7
Tepalcatepec →, Mexico 118 D4
Tepecik, Bursa, Turkey 41 F12
Tepecik, Kütahya, Turkey 39 B11
Tepehuanes, Mexico 118 B3
Tepelena, Albania 40 F4
Tepetongo, Mexico 118 C4
Tepic, Mexico 118 C4
Teplá, Czech Rep. 26 B5
Teplice, Czech Rep. 26 A6
Tepoca, C., Mexico 118 A2
Tequila, Mexico 118 C4
Ter →, Spain 32 C8
Ter Apel, Neths. 17 B7
Téra, Niger 83 C5
Tera →, Spain 34 D5
Teraina, Kiribati 97 G11
Terakeka, Sudan 81 F3
Téramo, Italy 29 F10
Terang, Australia 95 F3
Terazit, Massif de, Niger 83 A6
Tercan, Turkey 73 C9
Tercero →, Argentina 126 C3
Terebovlya, Ukraine 47 H3
Teregova, Romania 42 E7
Tereida, Sudan 81 E3
Terek →, Russia 49 J8
Tereshka →, Russia 48 E8
Teresina, Brazil 125 E10
Terespol, Poland 45 F10
Terewah, L., Australia 95 D4
Terges →, Portugal 35 H3
Tergnier, France 19 C10
Teridgerie Cr. →, Australia 95 E4
Terlizzi, Italy 31 A9
Terme, Turkey 72 B7
Termez = Termiz, Uzbekistan 50 F7
Términi Imerese, Italy 30 E6
Términos, L. de, Mexico 119 D6
Termiz, Uzbekistan 50 F7
Térmoli, Italy 29 F12
Ternate, Indonesia 63 D7
Terneuzen, Neths. 17 C3
Terney, Russia 51 E14
Terni, Italy 29 F9
Ternitz, Austria 26 D9
Ternopil, Ukraine 47 H3
Ternopol = Ternopil, Ukraine 47 H3
Terowie, Australia 95 E2
Terpní, Greece 40 F7
Terra Bella, U.S.A. 117 K7
Terra Nova Nat. Park, Canada 103 C9
Terrace, Canada 104 C3
Terrace Bay, Canada 102 C2
Terracina, Italy 30 A6
Terralba, Italy 30 C1
Terranova = Ólbia, Italy 30 B2
Terrasini, Italy 30 D6
Terrassa, Spain 32 D7
Terrasson-la-Villedieu, France 20 C5
Terre Haute, U.S.A. 108 F2
Terrebonne B., U.S.A. 113 L9
Terrell, U.S.A. 113 J6
Terrenceville, Canada 103 C9
Terry, U.S.A. 112 B2
Terryville, U.S.A. 111 E11
Terschelling, Neths. 17 A5
Tersko-Kumskiy Kanal →, Russia 49 H7
Tertenía, Italy 30 C2
Terter → = Tärtär →, Azerbaijan 49 K8
Teruel, Spain 32 E3
Teruel □, Spain 32 E4
Tervel, Bulgaria 41 C11
Tervola, Finland 8 C21
Teryaweyna L., Australia 95 E3
Tešanj, Bos.-H. 42 F3
Teseney, Eritrea 81 D4
Tesha →, Russia 48 C6
Teshio, Japan 54 B10
Teshio-Gawa →, Japan 54 B10
Tešica, Serbia, Yug. 40 C5
Tesiyn Gol →, Mongolia 60 A4
Teslić, Bos.-H. 42 F2
Teslin, Canada 104 A2
Teslin →, Canada 104 A2
Teslin L., Canada 104 A2
Tessalit, Mali 83 A5
Tessaoua, Niger 83 C6
Tessin, Germany 24 A8
Tessit, Mali 83 B5
Test →, U.K. 13 G6
Testa del Gargano, Italy 29 G13
Testigos, Is. Las, Venezuela 121 D7
Tét, Hungary 42 C2
Têt →, France 20 F7
Tetachuck L., Canada 104 C3
Tetas, Pta., Chile 126 A1
Tete, Mozam. 87 F3
Tete □, Mozam. 87 F3
Teterev →, Ukraine 47 G6
Teterow, Germany 24 B8
Teteven, Bulgaria 41 D8
Tethul →, Canada 104 A6
Tetiyev, Ukraine 47 H5
Teton →, U.S.A. 114 C8
Tétouan, Morocco 78 A4
Tetovo, Macedonia 40 D4
Tetyushi, Russia 48 C9
Teuco →, Argentina 126 B3
Teulada, Italy 30 D1
Teulon, Canada 105 C9
Teun, Indonesia 63 F7
Teutoburger Wald, Germany 24 C4
Tevere →, Italy 29 G9
Teverya, Israel 75 C4
Teviot →, U.K. 14 F6
Tewantin, Australia 95 D5
Tewkesbury, U.K. 13 F5
Texada I., Canada 104 D4
Texarkana, Ark., U.S.A. 113 J8
Texarkana, Tex., U.S.A. 113 J7
Texas, Australia 95 D5
Texas □, U.S.A. 113 K5
Texas City, U.S.A. 113 L7
Texel, Neths. 17 A4
Texline, U.S.A. 113 G3
Texoma, L., U.S.A. 113 J6
Teykovo, Russia 46 D11
Teza →, Russia 48 B5
Tezin, Afghan. 68 B3
Teziutlán, Mexico 119 D5
Tezpur, India 67 F18
Tezzeron L., Canada 104 C4
Tha-anne →, Canada 105 A10
Tha Deua, Laos 64 D4
Tha Deua, Laos 64 C3
Tha Pla, Thailand 64 D3
Tha Rua, Thailand 64 E3
Tha Sala, Thailand 65 H2
Tha Song Yang, Thailand 64 D1
Thaba Putsoa, Lesotho 89 D4
Thabana Ntlenyana, Lesotho 89 D4
Thabazimbi, S. Africa 89 C4
Thādiq, Si. Arabia 70 E5
Thai Binh, Vietnam 58 G6
Thai Muang, Thailand 65 H2
Thai Nguyen, Vietnam 58 G5
Thailand ■, Asia 64 E4
Thailand, G. of, Asia 65 G3
Thakhek, Laos 64 D5
Thal, Pakistan 68 C4
Thal Desert, Pakistan 68 D4
Thala La, Burma 67 E20
Thalabarivat, Cambodia 64 F5
Thallon, Australia 95 D4
Thalwil, Switz. 25 H4
Thames, N.Z. 91 G5
Thames →, Canada 102 D3
Thames →, U.K. 13 F8
Thames →, U.S.A. 111 E12
Thames Estuary, U.K. 13 F8
Thamesford, Canada 110 C4
Thamesville, Canada 110 D3
Than, India 68 H4
Than Uyen, Vietnam 64 B4
Thana Gazi, India 68 F7
Thandla, India 68 H6
Thane, India 66 K8
Thanesar, India 68 D7
Thanet, I. of, U.K. 13 F9
Thangool, Australia 94 C5
Thanh Hoa, Vietnam 64 C5
Thanh Hung, Vietnam 65 H5
Thanh Pho Ho Chi Minh = Phanh Bho Ho Chi Minh, Vietnam 65 G6
Thanh Thuy, Vietnam 64 A5
Thanjavur, India 66 P11
Thann, France 19 E14
Thano Bula Khan, Pakistan 68 G2
Thaolinta L., Canada 105 A9
Thaon-les-Vosges, France 19 D13
Thap Sakae, Thailand 65 G2
Thap Than, Thailand 64 E2
Thar Desert, India 68 F5
Tharad, India 68 G4
Thargomindah, Australia 95 D3
Tharrawaddy, Burma 67 L19
Tharthār, Mileh, Iraq 70 C4
Tharthār, W. ath →, Iraq 70 C4
Thasopoúla, Greece 41 F8
Thásos, Greece 41 F8
That Khe, Vietnam 58 F6
Thatcher, Ariz., U.S.A. 115 K9
Thatcher, Colo., U.S.A. 113 G2
Thaton, Burma 67 L20
Thau, Bassin de, France 20 E7
Thaungdut, Burma 67 G19
Thayer, U.S.A. 113 G9
Thayetmyo, Burma 67 K19
Thazi, Burma 67 J20
The Alberga →, Australia 95 D2
The Bight, Bahamas 121 B4
The Coorong, Australia 95 F2
The Dalles, U.S.A. 114 D3
The English Company's Is., Australia 94 A2
The Frome →, Australia 95 D2
The Great Divide = Great Dividing Ra., Australia 94 C4
The Hague = 's-Gravenhage, Neths. 17 B4
The Hamilton →, Australia 95 D2
The Macumba →, Australia 95 D2
The Neales →, Australia 95 D2
The Officer →, Australia 93 E5
The Pas, Canada 105 C8
The Range, Zimbabwe 87 F3
The Rock, Australia 95 F4
The Salt L., Australia 95 E3
The Sandheads, India 69 J13
The Stevenson →, Australia 95 D2
The Warburton →, Australia 95 D2
The Woodlands, U.S.A. 113 K7
Thebes = Thívai, Greece 38 C5
Thebes, Egypt 80 B3
Thedford, Canada 110 C3
Thedford, U.S.A. 112 E4
Theebine, Australia 95 D5
Thekulthili L., Canada 105 A7
Thelon →, Canada 105 A8
Thénezay, France 18 F6
Thenon, France 20 C5
Theodore, Australia 94 C5
Theodore, Canada 105 C8
Theodore, U.S.A. 109 K1
Theodore Roosevelt National Memorial Park, U.S.A. 112 B3
Theodore Roosevelt Res., U.S.A. 115 K8
Thepha, Thailand 65 J3
Thérain →, France 19 C9
Theresa, U.S.A. 111 B9
Thermaïkós Kólpos, Greece 40 F6
Thermí, Greece 39 B8
Thermopolis, U.S.A. 114 E9
Thermopylae P., Greece 38 C4
Thesprotía □, Greece 38 B2
Thessalía □, Greece 38 B4
Thessalon, Canada 102 C3
Thessaloníki, Greece 40 F6
Thessaloníki □, Greece 40 F7
Thessaloniki, Gulf of = Thermaïkós Kólpos, Greece 40 F6
Thessaly = Thessalía □, Greece 38 B4
Thetford, U.K. 13 E8
Thetford Mines, Canada 103 C5
Theun →, Laos 64 C5
Theunissen, S. Africa 88 D4
Thevenard, Australia 95 E1
Thiámis →, Greece 38 B2
Thiberville, France 18 C7
Thibodaux, U.S.A. 113 L9
Thicket Portage, Canada 105 B9
Thief River Falls, U.S.A. 112 A6
Thiel Mts., Antarctica 5 E16
Thiene, Italy 29 C8
Thiérache, France 19 C10
Thiers, France 20 C7
Thiès, Senegal 82 C1
Thiesi, Italy 30 B1
Thiet, Sudan 81 F2
Thika, Kenya 86 C4
Thikombia, Fiji 91 B9
Thille-Boubacar, Senegal 82 B1
Thimphu, Bhutan 67 F16
þingvallavatn, Iceland 8 D3
Thionville, France 19 C13
Thíra, Greece 39 E7
Thirasía, Greece 39 E7
Third Cataract, Sudan 80 D3
Thirsk, U.K. 12 C6
Thisted, Denmark 11 H2
Thistle I., Australia 95 F2
Thívai, Greece 38 C5
Thiviers, France 20 C4
Thizy, France 19 F11
þjórsá →, Iceland 8 E3
Thlewiaza →, Man., Canada 105 B8
Thlewiaza →, N.W.T., Canada 105 A10
Thmar Puok, Cambodia 64 F4
Tho Vinh, Vietnam 64 C5
Thoa →, Canada 105 A7
Thoen, Thailand 64 D2
Thoeng, Thailand 64 C3
Thohoyandou, S. Africa 85 J6
Tholdi, Pakistan 69 B7
Thomas, U.S.A. 113 H5
Thomas, L., Australia 95 D2
Thomaston, U.S.A. 109 J3
Thomasville, Ala., U.S.A. 109 K2
Thomasville, Ga., U.S.A. 109 K4
Thomasville, N.C., U.S.A. 109 H5
Thompson, Canada 105 B9
Thompson, U.S.A. 111 E9
Thompson →, Canada 104 C4
Thompson →, U.S.A. 112 F8
Thompson Falls, U.S.A. 114 C6
Thompson Pk., U.S.A. 114 F2
Thompson Springs, U.S.A. 115 G9
Thompsontown, U.S.A. 110 F7
Thomson, U.S.A. 109 J4
Thomson →, Australia 94 C3
Thomson's Falls = Nyahururu, Kenya 86 B4
Thônes, France 21 C10
Thonon-les-Bains, France 19 F13
Thorez, Ukraine 47 H10
þórisvatn, Iceland 8 D4
Thornaby on Tees, U.K. 12 C6
Thornbury, Canada 110 B4
Thorne, U.K. 12 D7
Thornhill, Canada 104 C3

Thorold, *Canada* 110 C5
Þórshöfn, *Iceland* 8 C6
Thouarcé, *France* 18 E6
Thouars, *France* 18 F6
Thouet →, *France* 18 E6
Thouin, C., *Australia* 92 D2
Thousand Oaks, *U.S.A.* 117 L8
Thrace, *Turkey* 41 F10
Thrakikón Pélagos, *Greece* 41 F8
Three Forks, *U.S.A.* 114 D8
Three Gorges Dam, *China* 59 B8
Three Hills, *Canada* 104 C6
Three Hummock I., *Australia* 94 G3
Three Points, C., *Ghana* 82 E4
Three Rivers, *Calif., U.S.A.* 116 J8
Three Rivers, *Tex., U.S.A.* 113 L5
Three Sisters, *U.S.A.* 114 D3
Three Springs, *Australia* 93 E2
Throssell, L., *Australia* 93 E3
Throssell Ra., *Australia* 92 D3
Thuan Hoa, *Vietnam* 65 H5
Thubun Lakes, *Canada* 105 A6
Thueyts, *France* 21 D8
Thuin, *Belgium* 17 D4
Thuir, *France* 20 F6
Thule = Qaanaaq, *Greenland* 4 B4
Thun, *Switz.* 25 J3
Thunder B., *U.S.A.* 110 B1
Thunder Bay, *Canada* 102 C2
Thunersee, *Switz.* 25 J3
Thung Song, *Thailand* 65 H2
Thunkar, *Bhutan* 67 F17
Thuong Tra, *Vietnam* 64 D6
Thur →, *Switz.* 25 H5
Thurgau □, *Switz.* 25 H5
Thüringen □, *Germany* 24 D6
Thüringer Wald, *Germany* 24 E6
Thurles, *Ireland* 15 D4
Thurn P., *Austria* 26 D5
Thurrock □, *U.K.* 13 F8
Thursday I., *Australia* 94 A3
Thurso, *Canada* 102 C4
Thurso, *U.K.* 14 C5
Thurso →, *U.K.* 14 C5
Thurston I., *Antarctica* 5 D16
Thury-Harcourt, *France* 18 D6
Thutade L., *Canada* 104 B3
Thy, *Denmark* 11 H2
Thyborøn, *Denmark* 11 H2
Thyolo, *Malawi* 87 F4
Thysville = Mbanza Ngungu, *Dem. Rep. of the Congo* 84 F2
Ti-n-Amzi →, *Niger* 83 B5
Ti-n-Barraouene, O. →, *Africa* 83 B5
Ti-n-Zaouatène, *Algeria* 83 B5
Ti Tree, *Australia* 94 C1
Tiadiaye, *Senegal* 82 C1
Tian Shan, *Asia* 60 B3
Tianchang, *China* 59 A12
Tiandeng, *China* 58 F6
Tiandong, *China* 58 F6
Tian'e, *China* 58 E6
Tianhe, *China* 58 E7
Tianjin, *China* 57 E9
Tiankoura, *Burkina Faso* 82 C4
Tianlin, *China* 58 E6
Tianmen, *China* 59 B9
Tianquan, *China* 58 B4
Tianshui, *China* 56 G3
Tiantai, *China* 59 C13
Tianyang, *China* 58 F6
Tianzhen, *China* 56 D8
Tianzhu, *China* 58 D7
Tianzhuangtai, *China* 57 D12
Tiaret, *Algeria* 78 A6
Tiassalé, *Ivory C.* 82 D4
Tibagi, *Brazil* 127 A5
Tibagi →, *Brazil* 127 A5
Tibati, *Cameroon* 83 D7
Tibe, *Ethiopia* 81 F4
Tiber = Tevere →, *Italy* 29 G9
Tiberias = Teverya, *Israel* 75 C4
Tiberias, L. = Yam Kinneret, *Israel* 75 C4
Tibesti, *Chad* 79 D9
Tibet = Xizang Zizhiqu □, *China* 60 C3
Tibet, Plateau of, *Asia* 52 F12
Tibiao, *Phil.* 61 F5
Tibiri, *Niger* 83 C6
Ţibleş, Vf., *Romania* 43 C9
Ţibleşului, Munţii, *Romania* 43 C9
Tibnī, *Syria* 70 C3
Tibooburra, *Australia* 95 D3
Tibro, *Sweden* 11 F8
Tiburón, I., *Mexico* 118 B2
Ticao I., *Phil.* 61 E5
Tîchît, *Mauritania* 82 B3
Ticho, *Ethiopia* 81 F4
Ticino □, *Switz.* 25 J4
Ticino →, *Italy* 25 K5
Ticleni, *Romania* 43 F8
Ticonderoga, *U.S.A.* 111 C11
Ticul, *Mexico* 119 C7
Tidaholm, *Sweden* 11 F7
Tidan, *Sweden* 11 F8
Tiddim, *Burma* 67 H18
Tidioute, *U.S.A.* 110 E5
Tidjikja, *Mauritania* 82 B2
Tidore, *Indonesia* 63 D7
Tiébissou, *Ivory C.* 82 D3
Tiel, *Neths.* 17 C5
Tiel, *Senegal* 82 C1
Tieling, *China* 57 C12
Tielt, *Belgium* 17 C3
Tien Shan = Tian Shan, *Asia* 60 B3
Tien-tsin = Tianjin, *China* 57 E9
Tien Yen, *Vietnam* 64 B6
T'ienching = Tianjin, *China* 57 E9
Tienen, *Belgium* 17 D4
Tiénigbé, *Ivory C.* 82 D3
Tientsin = Tianjin, *China* 57 E9
Tieri, *Australia* 94 C4
Tierp, *Sweden* 10 D11
Tierra Amarilla, *Chile* 126 B1
Tierra Amarilla, *U.S.A.* 115 H10
Tierra Colorada, *Mexico* 119 D5
Tierra de Barros, *Spain* 35 G4
Tierra de Campos, *Spain* 34 C6
Tierra del Fuego, I. Gr. de, *Argentina* 122 J4
Tiétar →, *Spain* 34 F4
Tieté →, *Brazil* 127 A5
Tiffin, *U.S.A.* 108 E4
Tiflis = Tbilisi, *Georgia* 49 K7
Tifton, *U.S.A.* 109 K4
Tifu, *Indonesia* 63 E7
Tighina, *Moldova* 43 D14
Tigil, *Russia* 51 D16
Tignish, *Canada* 103 C7
Tigray □, *Ethiopia* 81 E4
Tigre →, *Peru* 124 D4
Tigre →, *Venezuela* 124 B6
Tigris = Dijlah, Nahr →, *Asia* 70 D5
Tigveni, *Romania* 43 E9
Tigyaing, *Burma* 67 H20
Tîh, Gebel el, *Egypt* 80 B3
Tijara, *India* 68 F7
Tijuana, *Mexico* 117 N9
Tikal, *Guatemala* 120 C2
Tikamgarh, *India* 69 G8
Tikaré, *Burkina Faso* 83 C4
Tikhoretsk, *Russia* 49 H5
Tikhvin, *Russia* 46 C7
Tiko, *Cameroon* 83 E6
Tikrīt, *Iraq* 70 C4
Tiksi, *Russia* 51 B13
Tilamuta, *Indonesia* 63 D6
Tilburg, *Neths.* 17 C5
Tilbury, *Canada* 102 D3
Tilbury, *U.K.* 13 F8
Tilcara, *Argentina* 126 A2
Tilden, *U.S.A.* 112 D6
Tilemses, *Niger* 83 B5
Tilemsi, Vallée du, *Mali* 83 B5
Tilhar, *India* 69 F8
Tilichiki, *Russia* 51 C17
Tílissos, *Greece* 36 D7
Till →, *U.K.* 12 B5
Tillabéri, *Niger* 83 C5
Tillamook, *U.S.A.* 114 D2
Tillberga, *Sweden* 10 E10
Tillia, *Niger* 83 B5
Tillsonburg, *Canada* 102 D3
Tillyeria □, *Cyprus* 36 D11
Tilogne, *Senegal* 82 B2
Tílos, *Greece* 39 E9
Tilpa, *Australia* 95 E3
Tilsit = Sovetsk, *Russia* 9 J19
Tilt →, *U.K.* 14 E5
Tilton, *U.S.A.* 111 C13
Tiltonsville, *U.S.A.* 110 F4
Tim, *Denmark* 11 H2
Timagami, L., *Canada* 102 C3
Timaru, *N.Z.* 91 L3
Timashevo, *Russia* 48 D10
Timashevsk, *Russia* 49 H4
Timau, *Kenya* 86 B4
Timbákion, *Greece* 36 D6
Timbedgha, *Mauritania* 82 B3
Timber Creek, *Australia* 92 C5
Timber Lake, *U.S.A.* 112 C4
Timber Mt., *U.S.A.* 116 H10
Timbo, *Guinea* 82 C2
Timbo, *Liberia* 82 D3
Timbuktu = Tombouctou, *Mali* 82 B4
Timeiaouine, *Algeria* 83 A5
Timétrine, Mts., *Mali* 83 B4
Timfi Óros, *Greece* 38 B2
Timfristós, Óros, *Greece* 38 C3
Timi, *Cyprus* 36 E11
Tîmia, *Niger* 83 B6
Timimoun, *Algeria* 78 C6
Timiş = Tamis →, *Serbia, Yug.* 42 F5
Timiş □, *Romania* 42 E6
Timişoara, *Romania* 42 E6
Timmersdala, *Sweden* 11 F7
Timmins, *Canada* 102 C3
Timok →, *Serbia, Yug.* 40 B6
Timor, *Indonesia* 63 F7
Timor Sea, *Ind. Oc.* 92 B4
Timor Timur □, *Indonesia* 63 F7
Timrå, *Sweden* 10 B11
Tin Can Bay, *Australia* 95 D5
Tin Ethisane, *Mali* 83 B4
Tin Gornai, *Mali* 83 B4
Tin Mt., *U.S.A.* 116 J9
Tina →, *S. Africa* 89 E4
Tîna, Khalîg el, *Egypt* 80 A3
Tinaca Pt., *Phil.* 61 J6
Tinajo, *Canary Is.* 37 E6
Tinca, *Romania* 42 D6
Tindal, *Australia* 92 B5
Tindouf, *Algeria* 78 C4
Tinée →, *France* 21 E11
Tineo, *Spain* 34 B4
Ting Jiang →, *China* 59 E11
Tinggi, Pulau, *Malaysia* 65 L5
Tinglev, *Denmark* 11 K3
Tingo Maria, *Peru* 124 E3
Tingrela, *Ivory C.* 82 C3
Tingsryd, *Sweden* 11 H9
Tingstäde, *Sweden* 11 G12
Tinh Bien, *Vietnam* 65 G5
Tinnevelly = Tirunelveli, *India* 66 Q10
Tinogasta, *Argentina* 126 B2
Tínos, *Greece* 39 D7
Tiñoso, C., *Spain* 33 H3
Tinpahar, *India* 69 G12
Tintina, *Argentina* 126 B3
Tintinara, *Australia* 95 F3
Tintioulé, *Guinea* 82 C3
Tinto →, *Spain* 35 H4
Tioga, *N. Dak., U.S.A.* 112 A3
Tioga, *Pa., U.S.A.* 110 E7
Tioman, Pulau, *Malaysia* 65 L5
Tione di Trento, *Italy* 28 B7
Tionesta, *U.S.A.* 110 E5
Tior, *Sudan* 81 F3
Tipongpani, *India* 67 F19
Tipperary, *Ireland* 15 D3
Tipperary □, *Ireland* 15 D4
Tipton, *Calif., U.S.A.* 116 J7
Tipton, *Iowa, U.S.A.* 112 E9
Tipton Mt., *U.S.A.* 117 K12
Tiptonville, *U.S.A.* 113 G10
Tīrān, *Iran* 71 C6
Tīrān, *Si. Arabia* 80 B3
Tirana, *Albania* 40 E3
Tiranë = Tirana, *Albania* 40 E3
Tirano, *Italy* 28 B7
Tiraspol, *Moldova* 43 D14
Tirdout, *Mali* 83 B4
Tire, *Turkey* 39 C9
Tirebolu, *Turkey* 73 B8
Tiree, *U.K.* 14 E2
Tiree, Passage of, *U.K.* 14 E2
Tîrgovişte = Târgovişte, *Romania* 43 F10
Tîrgu-Jiu = Târgu-Jiu, *Romania* 43 E8
Tîrgu Mureş = Târgu Mureş, *Romania* 43 D9
Tirich Mir, *Pakistan* 66 A7
Tiriolo, *Italy* 31 D9
Tiriro, *Guinea* 82 C3
Tírnavos, *Greece* 38 B4
Tirodi, *India* 66 J11
Tirol □, *Austria* 26 D3
Tirschenreuth, *Germany* 25 F8
Tirso →, *Italy* 30 C1
Tirstrup, *Denmark* 11 H4
Tiruchchirappalli, *India* 66 P11
Tirunelveli, *India* 66 Q10
Tirupati, *India* 66 N11
Tiruppur, *India* 66 P10
Tiruvannamalai, *India* 66 N11
Tisa, *India* 68 C7
Tisa →, *Serbia, Yug.* 42 E5
Tisdale, *Canada* 105 C8
Tishomingo, *U.S.A.* 113 H6
Tisjön, *Sweden* 10 D7
Tisnaren, *Sweden* 11 F9
Tišnov, *Czech Rep.* 27 B9
Tisovec, *Slovak Rep.* 27 C12
Tisza = Tisa →, *Serbia, Yug.* 42 E5
Tiszaföldvár, *Hungary* 42 D5
Tiszafüred, *Hungary* 42 C5
Tiszalök, *Hungary* 42 B6
Tiszavasvári, *Hungary* 42 C6
Tit-Ary, *Russia* 51 B13
Titaguas, *Spain* 32 F3
Titao, *Burkina Faso* 83 C4
Titel, *Serbia, Yug.* 42 E5
Tithwal, *Pakistan* 69 B5
Titicaca, L., *S. Amer.* 122 E4
Titisee, *Germany* 25 H4
Titiwa, *Nigeria* 83 C7
Tito, *Italy* 31 B8
Titograd = Podgorica, *Montenegro, Yug.* 40 D3
Titova Korenica, *Croatia* 29 D12
Titu, *Romania* 43 F10
Titule, *Dem. Rep. of the Congo* 86 B2
Titusville, *Fla., U.S.A.* 109 L5
Titusville, *Pa., U.S.A.* 110 E5
Tivaouane, *Senegal* 82 C1
Tivat, *Montenegro, Yug.* 40 D2
Tiverton, *U.K.* 13 G4
Tívoli, *Italy* 29 G9
Tiyo, *Eritrea* 81 E5
Tizi-Ouzou, *Algeria* 78 A6
Tizimín, *Mexico* 119 C7
Tjæreborg, *Denmark* 11 J2
Tjällmo, *Sweden* 11 F9
Tjeggelvas, *Sweden* 8 C17
Tjirebon = Cirebon, *Indonesia* 63 G13
Tjörn, *Sweden* 11 F5
Tkibuli = Tqibuli, *Georgia* 49 J6
Tkvarcheli = Tqvarcheli, *Georgia* 49 J5
Tlacotalpan, *Mexico* 119 D5
Tlahualilo, *Mexico* 118 B4
Tlaquepaque, *Mexico* 118 C4
Tlaxcala, *Mexico* 119 D5
Tlaxcala □, *Mexico* 119 D5
Tlaxiaco, *Mexico* 119 D5
Tlemcen, *Algeria* 78 B5
Tłuszcz, *Poland* 45 F8
Tlyarata, *Russia* 49 J8
To Bong, *Vietnam* 64 F7
Toad →, *Canada* 104 B4
Toad River, *Canada* 104 B3
Toamasina, *Madag.* 89 B8
Toamasina □, *Madag.* 89 B8
Toay, *Argentina* 126 D3
Toba, *China* 58 B1
Toba, *Japan* 55 G8
Toba, Danau, *Indonesia* 62 D1
Toba Kakar, *Pakistan* 68 D3
Toba Tek Singh, *Pakistan* 68 D5
Tobago, *W. Indies* 121 D7
Tobarra, *Spain* 33 G3
Tobelo, *Indonesia* 63 D7
Tobermory, *Canada* 102 C3
Tobermory, *U.K.* 14 E2
Tobi, *Pac. Oc.* 63 D8
Tobin, *U.S.A.* 116 F5
Tobin, L., *Australia* 92 D4
Tobin L., *Canada* 105 C8
Toblach = Dobbiaco, *Italy* 29 B9
Toboali, *Indonesia* 62 E3
Tobol →, *Russia* 50 D7
Toboli, *Indonesia* 63 E6
Tobolsk, *Russia* 50 D7
Tobor, *Senegal* 82 C1
Tobruk = Tubruq, *Libya* 79 B10
Tobyhanna, *U.S.A.* 111 E9
Tobyl = Tobol →, *Russia* 50 D7
Tocantinópolis, *Brazil* 125 E9
Tocantins □, *Brazil* 125 F9
Tocantins →, *Brazil* 122 D6
Toccoa, *U.S.A.* 109 H4
Toce →, *Italy* 28 C5
Tochi →, *Pakistan* 68 C4
Tochigi, *Japan* 55 F9
Tochigi □, *Japan* 55 F9
Tocina, *Spain* 35 H5
Töcksfors, *Sweden* 10 E5
Toconao, *Chile* 126 A2
Tocopilla, *Chile* 126 A1
Tocumwal, *Australia* 95 F4
Tocuyo →, *Venezuela* 124 A5
Todd →, *Australia* 94 C2
Todeli, *Indonesia* 63 E6
Todenyang, *Kenya* 86 B4
Todgarh, *India* 68 G5
Todi, *Italy* 29 F9
Todos os Santos, B. de, *Brazil* 125 F11
Todos Santos, *Mexico* 118 C2
Todtnau, *Germany* 25 H3
Toe Hd., *U.K.* 14 D1
Toecé, *Burkina Faso* 83 C4
Tofield, *Canada* 104 C6
Tofino, *Canada* 104 D3
Tofua, *Tonga* 91 D11
Tōgane, *Japan* 55 G10
Togba, *Mauritania* 82 B2
Togian, Kepulauan, *Indonesia* 63 E6
Togliatti, *Russia* 48 D9
Togo ■, *W. Afr.* 83 D5
Togtoh, *China* 56 D6
Tohma →, *Turkey* 72 C7
Tōhoku □, *Japan* 54 E10
Töhöm, *Mongolia* 56 B5
Toinya, *Sudan* 81 F2
Toiyabe Range, *U.S.A.* 114 G5
Tojikiston = Tajikistan ■, *Asia* 50 F8
Tojo, *Indonesia* 63 E6
Tōjō, *Japan* 55 G6
Tok, *U.S.A.* 100 B5
Tok-do, *Japan* 55 F5
Tokachi-Dake, *Japan* 54 C11
Tokachi-Gawa →, *Japan* 54 C11
Tokaj, *Hungary* 42 B6
Tokala, *Indonesia* 63 E6
Tōkamachi, *Japan* 55 F9
Tokanui, *N.Z.* 91 M2
Tokar, *Sudan* 80 D4
Tokara-Rettō, *Japan* 55 K4
Tokarahi, *N.Z.* 91 L3
Tokashiki-Shima, *Japan* 55 L3
Tokat, *Turkey* 72 B7
Tŏkch'ŏn, *N. Korea* 57 E14
Tokeland, *U.S.A.* 116 D3
Tokelau Is., *Pac. Oc.* 96 H10
Tokmak, *Kyrgyzstan* 50 E8
Tokmak, *Ukraine* 47 J8
Toko Ra., *Australia* 94 C2
Tokoro-Gawa →, *Japan* 54 B12
Tokuno-Shima, *Japan* 55 L4
Tokushima, *Japan* 55 G7
Tokushima □, *Japan* 55 H7
Tokuyama, *Japan* 55 G5
Tōkyō, *Japan* 55 G9
Tolaga Bay, *N.Z.* 91 H7
Tolbukhin = Dobrich, *Bulgaria* 41 C11
Toledo, *Brazil* 127 A5
Toledo, *Spain* 34 F6
Toledo, *Ohio, U.S.A.* 108 E4
Toledo, *Oreg., U.S.A.* 114 D2
Toledo, *Wash., U.S.A.* 114 C2
Toledo, Montes de, *Spain* 35 F6
Toledo Bend Reservoir, *U.S.A.* 113 K8
Tolentino, *Italy* 29 E10
Tolfa, *Italy* 29 F8
Tolga, *Australia* 94 B4
Toliara, *Madag.* 89 C7
Toliara □, *Madag.* 89 C8
Tolima, *Colombia* 124 C3
Tolitoli, *Indonesia* 63 D6
Tolkmicko, *Poland* 44 D6
Tollarp, *Sweden* 11 J7
Tollensesee, *Germany* 24 B9
Tollhouse, *U.S.A.* 116 H7
Tolmachevo, *Russia* 46 C5
Tolmezzo, *Italy* 29 B10
Tolmin, *Slovenia* 29 B10
Tolna, *Hungary* 42 D3
Tolna □, *Hungary* 42 D3
Tolo, Teluk, *Indonesia* 63 E6
Tolochin = Talachyn, *Belarus* 46 E5
Tolosa, *Spain* 32 B2
Tolox, *Spain* 35 J6
Toluca, *Mexico* 119 D5
Tom Burke, *S. Africa* 89 C4
Tom Price, *Australia* 92 D2
Toma, *Burkina Faso* 82 C4
Tomah, *U.S.A.* 112 D9
Tomahawk, *U.S.A.* 112 C10
Tomai, *Moldova* 43 D13
Tomakomai, *Japan* 54 C10
Tomales, *U.S.A.* 116 G4
Tomales B., *U.S.A.* 116 G3
Tomar, *Portugal* 35 F2
Tómaros, Óros, *Greece* 38 B2
Tomarza, *Turkey* 72 C6
Tomaszów Lubelski, *Poland* 45 H10
Tomaszów Mazowiecki, *Poland* 45 G7
Tomatlán, *Mexico* 118 D3
Tombadonkéa, *Guinea* 82 C2
Tombador, Serra do, *Brazil* 124 F7
Tombe, *Sudan* 81 F3
Tombigbee →, *U.S.A.* 109 K2
Tombouctou, *Mali* 82 B4
Tombstone, *U.S.A.* 115 L8
Tombua, *Angola* 88 B1
Tomé, *Chile* 126 D1
Tomelilla, *Sweden* 11 J7
Tomelloso, *Spain* 35 F7
Tomini, *Indonesia* 63 D6
Tomini, Teluk, *Indonesia* 63 E6
Tominian, *Mali* 82 C4
Tomiño, *Spain* 34 D2
Tomintoul, *U.K.* 14 D5
Tomislavgrad, *Bos.-H.* 42 G2
Tomkinson Ranges, *Australia* 93 E4
Tommot, *Russia* 51 D13
Tomnop Ta Suos, *Cambodia* 65 G5
Tomo →, *Colombia* 124 B5
Toms Place, *U.S.A.* 116 H8
Toms River, *U.S.A.* 111 G10
Tomsk, *Russia* 50 D9
Tomtabacken, *Sweden* 11 G8
Tona, *Spain* 32 D7
Tonalá, *Mexico* 119 D6
Tonale, Passo del, *Italy* 28 B7
Tonantins, *Brazil* 124 D5
Tonasket, *U.S.A.* 114 B4
Tonawanda, *U.S.A.* 110 D6
Tonbridge, *U.K.* 13 F8
Tondano, *Indonesia* 63 D6
Tondela, *Portugal* 34 E2
Tønder, *Denmark* 11 K2
Tondi Kiwindi, *Niger* 83 C5
Tondibi, *Mali* 83 B4
Tondoro, *Namibia* 88 B2
Tone →, *Australia* 93 F2
Tone-Gawa →, *Japan* 55 F9
Tonekābon, *Iran* 71 B6
Tong Xian, *China* 56 E9
Tongā, *Sudan* 81 F3
Tonga ■, *Pac. Oc.* 91 D11
Tonga Trench, *Pac. Oc.* 96 J10
Tongaat, *S. Africa* 89 D5
Tong'an, *China* 59 E12
Tongareva, *Cook Is.* 97 H12
Tongatapu, *Tonga* 91 E12
Tongbai, *China* 59 A9
Tongcheng, *Anhui, China* 59 B11
Tongcheng, *Hubei, China* 59 C9
Tongchŏn-ni, *N. Korea* 57 E14
Tongchuan, *China* 56 G5
Tongdao, *China* 58 D7
Tongeren, *Belgium* 17 D5
Tonggu, *China* 59 C10
Tongguan, *China* 56 G6
Tonghai, *China* 58 E4
Tonghua, *China* 57 D13
Tongjiang, *China* 58 B6
Tongjosŏn Man, *N. Korea* 57 E15
Tongkin, G. of, *Asia* 64 B7
Tongking, G. of = Tongkin, G. of, *Asia* 64 B7
Tongliang, *China* 58 C6
Tongliao, *China* 57 C12
Tongling, *China* 59 B11
Tonglu, *China* 59 C12
Tongnae, *S. Korea* 57 G15
Tongnan = Anyue, *China* 58 B5
Tongobory, *Madag.* 89 C7
Tongoy, *Chile* 126 C1
Tongren, *China* 58 D7
Tongres = Tongeren, *Belgium* 17 D5
Tongsa Dzong, *Bhutan* 67 F17
Tongue, *U.K.* 14 C4
Tongue →, *U.S.A.* 112 B2
Tongwei, *China* 56 G3
Tongxiang, *China* 59 B13
Tongxin, *China* 56 F3
Tongyang, *N. Korea* 57 E14
Tongyu, *China* 57 B12
Tongzi, *China* 58 C6
Tonj, *Sudan* 81 F2
Tonj →, *Sudan* 81 F2
Tonk, *India* 68 F6
Tonkawa, *U.S.A.* 113 G6
Tonkin = Bac Phan, *Vietnam* 64 B5
Tonle Sap, *Cambodia* 64 F4
Tonnay-Charente, *France* 20 C3
Tonneins, *France* 20 D4
Tonnerre, *France* 19 E10
Tönning, *Germany* 24 A4
Tono, *Japan* 54 E10
Tonopah, *U.S.A.* 115 G5
Tonosí, *Panama* 120 E3
Tons →, *Haryana, India* 68 D7
Tons →, *Ut. P., India* 69 F10
Tønsberg, *Norway* 9 G14
Tonya, *Turkey* 73 B8
Toobanna, *Australia* 94 B4
Toodyay, *Australia* 93 F2
Tooele, *U.S.A.* 114 F7
Toompine, *Australia* 95 D3
Toora, *Australia* 95 F4
Toora-Khem, *Russia* 51 D10
Toowoomba, *Australia* 95 D5

Top Springs, *Australia* 92 C5
Topalu, *Romania* 43 F13
Topaz, *U.S.A.* 116 G7
Topeka, *U.S.A.* 112 F7
Topl'a →, *Slovak Rep.* 27 C14
Topley, *Canada* 104 C3
Toplica →, *Serbia, Yug.* 40 C5
Toplița, *Romania* 43 D10
Topocalma, Pta., *Chile* 126 C1
Topock, *U.S.A.* 117 L12
Topola, *Serbia, Yug.* 40 B4
Topolčani, *Macedonia* 40 E5
Topoľčany, *Slovak Rep.* 27 C11
Topolnitsa →, *Bulgaria* 41 D8
Topolobampo, *Mexico* 118 B3
Topoloveni, *Romania* 43 F10
Topolovgrad, *Bulgaria* 41 D10
Topolvățu Mare, *Romania* 42 E6
Toppenish, *U.S.A.* 114 C3
Topraisar, *Romania* 43 F13
Topusko, *Croatia* 29 C12
Torà, *Spain* 32 D6
Tora Kit, *Sudan* 81 E3
Toraka Vestale, *Madag.* 89 B7
Torata, *Peru* 124 G4
Torbalı, *Turkey* 39 C9
Torbat-e Heydārīyeh, *Iran* 71 C8
Torbat-e Jām, *Iran* 71 C9
Torbay, *Canada* 103 C9
Torbay □, *U.K.* 13 G4
Torbjörntorp, *Sweden* 11 F7
Tordesillas, *Spain* 34 D6
Töreboda, *Sweden* 11 F8
Torekov, *Sweden* 11 H6
Torellò, *Spain* 32 C7
Toreno, *Spain* 34 C4
Torfaen □, *U.K.* 13 F4
Torgau, *Germany* 24 D8
Torgelow, *Germany* 24 B10
Torhamn, *Sweden* 11 H9
Torhout, *Belgium* 17 C3
Tori, *Ethiopia* 81 F3
Tori-Shima, *Japan* 55 J10
Torigni-sur-Vire, *France* 18 C6
Torija, *Spain* 32 E1
Torin, *Mexico* 118 B2
Torino, *Italy* 28 C4
Torit, *Sudan* 81 G3
Torkamān, *Iran* 70 B5
Torkovichi, *Russia* 46 C6
Tormac, *Romania* 42 E6
Tormes →, *Spain* 34 D4
Tornado Mt., *Canada* 104 D6
Tornal'a, *Slovak Rep.* 27 C13
Torne älv →, *Sweden* 8 D21
Torneå = Tornio, *Finland* 8 D21
Torneträsk, *Sweden* 8 B18
Tornio, *Finland* 8 D21
Tornionjoki →, *Finland* 8 D21
Tornquist, *Argentina* 126 D3
Toro, *Baleares, Spain* 37 B11
Toro, *Zamora, Spain* 34 D5
Torö, *Sweden* 11 F11
Toro, Cerro del, *Chile* 126 B2
Toro Pk., *U.S.A.* 117 M10
Törökszentmiklós, *Hungary* 42 C5
Toronîos Kólpos, *Greece* 40 F7
Toronto, *Canada* 102 D4
Toronto, *U.S.A.* 110 F4
Toropets, *Russia* 46 D6
Tororo, *Uganda* 86 B3
Toros Dağları, *Turkey* 70 B2
Torpa, *India* 69 H11
Torquay, *Australia* 95 F3
Torquay, *U.K.* 13 G4
Torquemada, *Spain* 34 C6
Torrance, *U.S.A.* 117 M8
Torrão, *Portugal* 35 G2
Torre Annunziata, *Italy* 31 B7
Torre de Moncorvo, *Portugal* 34 D3
Torre del Campo, *Spain* 35 H7
Torre del Greco, *Italy* 31 B7
Torre del Mar, *Spain* 35 J6
Torre-Pacheco, *Spain* 33 H4
Torre Péllice, *Italy* 28 D4
Torreblanca, *Spain* 32 E5
Torrecampo, *Spain* 35 G6
Torrecilla en Cameros, *Spain* 32 C2
Torredembarra, *Spain* 32 D6
Torredonjimeno, *Spain* 35 H7
Torrejón de Ardoz, *Spain* 34 E7
Torrejoncillo, *Spain* 34 F4
Torrelaguna, *Spain* 34 E7
Torrelavega, *Spain* 34 B6
Torremaggiore, *Italy* 29 G12
Torremolinos, *Spain* 35 J6
Torrens, L., *Australia* 95 E2
Torrens Cr. →, *Australia* 94 C4
Torrens Creek, *Australia* 94 C4
Torrent, *Spain* 33 F4
Torrenueva, *Spain* 35 G7
Torreón, *Mexico* 118 B4
Torreperogil, *Spain* 35 G7
Torres, *Brazil* 127 B5
Torres, *Mexico* 118 B2
Torres Novas, *Portugal* 35 F2
Torres Strait, *Australia* 96 H6
Torres Vedras, *Portugal* 35 F1
Torrevieja, *Spain* 33 H4
Torrey, *U.S.A.* 115 G8
Torridge →, *U.K.* 13 G3
Torridon, L., *U.K.* 14 D3
Torrijos, *Spain* 34 F6
Tørring, *Denmark* 11 J3
Torrington, *Conn., U.S.A.* 111 E11
Torrington, *Wyo., U.S.A.* 112 D2
Torroella de Montgrì, *Spain* 32 C8
Torrox, *Spain* 35 J7
Torsås, *Sweden* 11 H9
Torsby, *Sweden* 10 D6
Torshälla, *Sweden* 10 E10
Tórshavn, *Færoe Is.* 8 E9
Torslanda, *Sweden* 11 G5
Torsö, *Sweden* 11 F7
Tortola, *Virgin Is.* 121 C7
Tórtoles de Esgueva, *Spain* 34 D6
Tortolì, *Italy* 30 C2
Tortona, *Italy* 28 D5
Tortorici, *Italy* 31 D7
Tortosa, *Spain* 32 E5
Tortosa, C., *Spain* 32 E5
Tortosendo, *Portugal* 34 E3
Tortue, I. de la, *Haiti* 121 B5
Tortum, *Turkey* 73 B9
Ţorūd, *Iran* 71 C7
Torul, *Turkey* 73 B8
Toruń, *Poland* 45 E5
Tory I., *Ireland* 15 A3
Torysa →, *Slovak Rep.* 27 C14
Torzhok, *Russia* 46 D8
Torzym, *Poland* 45 F2
Tosa, *Japan* 55 H6
Tosa-Shimizu, *Japan* 55 H6
Tosa-Wan, *Japan* 55 H6
Toscana □, *Italy* 28 E8
Toscano, Arcipelago, *Italy* 28 F7
Toshkent, *Uzbekistan* 50 E7
Tosno, *Russia* 46 C6
Tossa de Mar, *Spain* 32 D7
Tösse, *Sweden* 11 F6
Tostado, *Argentina* 126 B3
Tostedt, *Germany* 24 B5
Tostón, Pta. de, *Canary Is.* 37 F5
Tosu, *Japan* 55 H5
Tosya, *Turkey* 72 B6
Toszek, *Poland* 45 H5
Totana, *Spain* 33 H3
Totebo, *Sweden* 11 G10
Toteng, *Botswana* 88 C3
Tôtes, *France* 18 C8
Tótkomlós, *Hungary* 42 D5
Totma, *Russia* 50 C5
Totnes, *U.K.* 13 G4
Totness, *Surinam* 125 B7
Toto, *Nigeria* 83 D6
Totonicapán, *Guatemala* 120 D1
Totten Glacier, *Antarctica* 5 C8
Tottenham, *Australia* 95 E4
Tottenham, *Canada* 110 B5
Tottori, *Japan* 55 G7
Tottori □, *Japan* 55 G7
Touaret, *Niger* 83 A6
Touba, *Ivory C.* 82 D3
Touba, *Senegal* 82 C1
Toubkal, Djebel, *Morocco* 78 B4
Toucy, *France* 19 E10
Tougan, *Burkina Faso* 82 C4
Touggourt, *Algeria* 78 B7
Tougouri, *Burkina Faso* 83 C4
Tougué, *Guinea* 82 C2
Toukoto, *Mali* 82 C3
Toul, *France* 19 D12
Toulepleu, *Ivory C.* 82 D3
Toulon, *France* 21 E9
Toulouse, *France* 20 E5
Toummo, *Niger* 79 D8
Toumodi, *Ivory C.* 82 D3
Tounan, *Taiwan* 59 F13
Toungo, *Nigeria* 83 D7
Toungoo, *Burma* 67 K20
Touques →, *France* 18 C7
Touraine, *France* 18 E7
Tourane = Da Nang, *Vietnam* 64 D7
Tourcoing, *France* 19 B10
Touriñán, C., *Spain* 34 B1
Tournai, *Belgium* 17 D3
Tournan-en-Brie, *France* 19 D9
Tournay, *France* 20 E4
Tournon-St-Martin, *France* 18 F7
Tournon-sur-Rhône, *France* 21 C8
Tournus, *France* 19 F11
Tours, *France* 18 E7
Tousidé, Pic, *Chad* 79 D9
Toussora, Mt., *C.A.R.* 84 C4
Touws →, *S. Africa* 88 E3
Touwsrivier, *S. Africa* 88 E3
Tovarkovskiy, *Russia* 46 F10
Tovuz, *Azerbaijan* 49 K7
Towada, *Japan* 54 D10
Towada-Ko, *Japan* 54 D10
Towanda, *U.S.A.* 111 E8
Towang, *India* 67 F17
Tower, *U.S.A.* 112 B8
Towerhill Cr. →, *Australia* 94 C3
Towner, *U.S.A.* 112 A4
Townsend, *U.S.A.* 114 C8
Townshend I., *Australia* 94 C5
Townsville, *Australia* 94 B4
Towson, *U.S.A.* 108 F7
Towuti, Danau, *Indonesia* 63 E6
Toya-Ko, *Japan* 54 C10
Toyama, *Japan* 55 F8
Toyama □, *Japan* 55 F8
Toyama-Wan, *Japan* 55 F8
Toyohashi, *Japan* 55 G8
Toyokawa, *Japan* 55 G8
Toyonaka, *Japan* 55 G7
Toyooka, *Japan* 55 G7
Toyota, *Japan* 55 G8
Tozeur, *Tunisia* 78 B7
Tqibuli, *Georgia* 49 J6
Tqvarcheli, *Georgia* 49 J5
Trá Li = Tralee, *Ireland* 15 D2
Tra On, *Vietnam* 65 H5
Trabancos →, *Spain* 34 D5
Traben-Trarbach, *Germany* 25 F3
Trabzon, *Turkey* 73 B8
Tracadie, *Canada* 103 C7
Tracy, *Calif., U.S.A.* 116 H5
Tracy, *Minn., U.S.A.* 112 C7
Tradate, *Italy* 28 C5
Trade Town, *Liberia* 82 D3
Trafalgar, C., *Spain* 35 J4
Traian, *Brăila, Romania* 43 E12
Traian, *Tulcea, Romania* 43 E13
Trail, *Canada* 104 D5
Trainor L., *Canada* 104 A4
Trákhonas, *Cyprus* 36 D12
Tralee, *Ireland* 15 D2
Tralee B., *Ireland* 15 D2
Tramore, *Ireland* 15 D4
Tramore B., *Ireland* 15 D4
Tran Ninh, Cao Nguyen, *Laos* 64 C4
Tranås, *Sweden* 11 F8
Tranbjerg, *Denmark* 11 H4
Trancas, *Argentina* 126 B2
Trancoso, *Portugal* 34 E3
Tranebjerg, *Denmark* 11 J4
Tranemo, *Sweden* 11 G7
Trang, *Thailand* 65 J2
Trangahy, *Madag.* 89 B7
Trangan, *Indonesia* 63 F8
Trangie, *Australia* 95 E4
Trångsviken, *Sweden* 10 A7
Trani, *Italy* 31 A9
Tranoroa, *Madag.* 89 C8
Tranqueras, *Uruguay* 127 C4
Transantarctic Mts., *Antarctica* 5 E12
Transilvania, *Romania* 43 D9
Transilvanian Alps = Carpații Meridionali, *Romania* 43 E9
Transtrand, *Sweden* 10 C7
Transtrandsfjällen, *Sweden* 10 C6
Transvaal, *S. Africa* 85 K5
Transylvania = Transilvania, *Romania* 43 D9
Trápani, *Italy* 30 D5
Trapper Pk., *U.S.A.* 114 D6
Traralgon, *Australia* 95 F4
Trarza, *Mauritania* 82 B2
Trasacco, *Italy* 29 G10
Trăscău, Munții, *Romania* 43 D8
Trasimeno, L., *Italy* 29 E9
Träslövsläge, *Sweden* 11 G6
Trasvase Tajo-Segura, Canal de, *Spain* 32 E2
Trat, *Thailand* 65 F4
Tratani →, *Pakistan* 68 E3
Traun, *Austria* 26 C7
Traunreut, *Germany* 25 H8
Traunsee, *Austria* 26 D6
Traunstein, *Germany* 25 H8
Travellers L., *Australia* 95 E3
Travemünde, *Germany* 24 B6
Travers, Mt., *N.Z.* 91 K4
Traverse City, *U.S.A.* 108 C3
Travis, L., *U.S.A.* 113 K5
Travnik, *Bos.-H.* 42 F2
Trbovlje, *Slovenia* 29 B12
Trébbia →, *Italy* 28 C6
Trebel →, *Germany* 24 B9
Trébeurden, *France* 18 D3
Třebíč, *Czech Rep.* 26 B8
Trebinje, *Bos.-H.* 40 D2
Trebisacce, *Italy* 31 C9
Trebišnjica →, *Bos.-H.* 40 D2
Trebišov, *Slovak Rep.* 27 C14
Trebižat →, *Bos.-H.* 29 E14
Trebnje, *Slovenia* 29 C12
Třeboň, *Czech Rep.* 26 B7
Trebonne, *Australia* 94 B4
Trebujena, *Spain* 35 J4
Trecate, *Italy* 28 C5
Tregaron, *U.K.* 13 E4
Tregnago, *Italy* 29 C8
Tregrosse Is., *Australia* 94 B5
Tréguier, *France* 18 D3
Trégunc, *France* 18 E3
Treherne, *Canada* 105 D9
Tréia, *Italy* 29 E10
Treignac, *France* 20 C5
Treinta y Tres, *Uruguay* 127 C5
Treis-karden, *Germany* 25 E3
Treklyano, *Bulgaria* 40 D6
Trelawney, *Zimbabwe* 89 B5
Trélazé, *France* 18 E6
Trelew, *Argentina* 128 E3
Trélissac, *France* 20 C4
Trelleborg, *Sweden* 11 J7
Tremadog Bay, *U.K.* 12 E3
Trémiti, *Italy* 29 F12
Tremonton, *U.S.A.* 114 F7
Tremp, *Spain* 32 C5
Trenche →, *Canada* 102 C5
Trenčiansky □, *Slovak Rep.* 27 C11
Trenčín, *Slovak Rep.* 27 C11
Trenggalek, *Indonesia* 63 H14
Trenque Lauquen, *Argentina* 126 D3
Trent →, *Canada* 110 B7
Trent →, *U.K.* 12 D7
Trentino-Alto Adige □, *Italy* 29 B8
Trento, *Italy* 28 B8
Trenton, *Canada* 102 D4
Trenton, *Mo., U.S.A.* 112 E8
Trenton, *N.J., U.S.A.* 111 F10
Trenton, *Nebr., U.S.A.* 112 E4
Trepassey, *Canada* 103 C9
Trepuzzi, *Italy* 31 B11
Tres Arroyos, *Argentina* 126 D3
Três Corações, *Brazil* 127 A6
Três Lagoas, *Brazil* 125 H8
Tres Lomas, *Argentina* 126 D3
Tres Marías, Islas, *Mexico* 118 C3
Tres Montes, C., *Chile* 128 F1
Tres Pinos, *U.S.A.* 116 J5
Três Pontas, *Brazil* 127 A6
Tres Puentes, *Chile* 126 B1
Tres Puntas, C., *Argentina* 128 F3
Três Rios, *Brazil* 127 A7
Tres Valles, *Mexico* 119 D5
Tresco, *U.K.* 13 H1
Treska →, *Macedonia* 40 E5
Treskavica, *Bos.-H.* 42 G3
Trespaderne, *Spain* 34 C7
Trets, *France* 21 E9
Treuchtlingen, *Germany* 25 G6
Treuenbrietzen, *Germany* 24 C8
Trevi, *Italy* 29 F9
Trevíglio, *Italy* 28 C6
Trevínca, Peña, *Spain* 34 C4
Treviso, *Italy* 29 C9
Trévoux, *France* 21 C8
Trgovište, *Serbia, Yug.* 40 D6
Triabunna, *Australia* 94 G4
Triánda, *Greece* 36 C10
Triangle, *Zimbabwe* 89 C5
Triaucourt-en-Argonne, *France* 19 D12
Tribsees, *Germany* 24 A8
Tribulation, C., *Australia* 94 B4
Tribune, *U.S.A.* 112 F4
Tricárico, *Italy* 31 B9
Tricase, *Italy* 31 C11
Trichinopoly = Tiruchchirappalli, *India* 66 P11
Trichur, *India* 66 P10
Trida, *Australia* 95 E4
Trier, *Germany* 25 F2
Trieste, *Italy* 29 C10
Trieste, G. di, *Italy* 29 C10
Trieux →, *France* 18 D3
Triggiano, *Italy* 31 A9
Triglav, *Slovenia* 29 B10
Trigno →, *Italy* 29 F11
Trigueros, *Spain* 35 H4
Tríkeri, *Greece* 38 B5
Trikhonis, Límni, *Greece* 38 C3
Tríkkala, *Greece* 38 B3
Tríkkala □, *Greece* 38 B3
Trikomo, *Cyprus* 36 D12
Trikora, Puncak, *Indonesia* 63 E9
Trilj, *Croatia* 29 E13
Trillo, *Spain* 32 E2
Trim, *Ireland* 15 C5
Trincomalee, *Sri Lanka* 66 Q12
Trindade, *Brazil* 125 G9
Trindade, I., *Atl. Oc.* 2 F8
Třinec, *Czech Rep.* 27 B11
Trinidad, *Bolivia* 124 F6
Trinidad, *Cuba* 120 B4
Trinidad, *Uruguay* 126 C4
Trinidad, *U.S.A.* 113 G2
Trinidad, *W. Indies* 121 D7
Trinidad →, *Mexico* 119 D5
Trinidad & Tobago ■, *W. Indies* 121 D7
Trinitápoli, *Italy* 31 A9
Trinity, *Canada* 103 C9
Trinity, *U.S.A.* 113 K7
Trinity →, *Calif., U.S.A.* 114 F2
Trinity →, *Tex., U.S.A.* 113 L7
Trinity B., *Canada* 103 C9
Trinity Is., *U.S.A.* 100 C4
Trinity Range, *U.S.A.* 114 F4
Trinkitat, *Sudan* 80 D4
Trino, *Italy* 28 C5
Trinway, *U.S.A.* 110 F2
Trionto, C., *Italy* 31 C9
Triora, *Italy* 28 D4
Tripoli = Tarābulus, *Lebanon* 75 A4
Tripoli = Tarābulus, *Libya* 79 B8
Trípolis, *Greece* 38 D4
Tripolitania, *Libya* 76 C5
Tripolitania, *N. Afr.* 79 B8
Tripura □, *India* 67 H18
Tripylos, *Cyprus* 36 E11
Trischen, *Germany* 24 A4
Tristan da Cunha, *Atl. Oc.* 77 K2
Trisul, *India* 69 D8
Trivandrum, *India* 66 Q10
Trivento, *Italy* 29 G11
Trnava, *Slovak Rep.* 27 C10
Trnavský □, *Slovak Rep.* 27 C10
Troarn, *France* 18 C6
Trochu, *Canada* 104 C6
Trodely I., *Canada* 102 B4
Troezen, *Greece* 38 D5
Trogir, *Croatia* 29 E13
Troglav, *Croatia* 29 E13
Tróia, *Italy* 31 A8
Troilus, L., *Canada* 102 B5
Troina, *Italy* 31 E7
Trois-Pistoles, *Canada* 103 C6
Trois-Rivières, *Canada* 102 C5
Troisdorf, *Germany* 24 E3
Troitsk, *Russia* 50 D7
Troitsko Pechorsk, *Russia* 50 C6
Trölladyngja, *Iceland* 8 D5
Trollhättan, *Sweden* 11 F6
Trollheimen, *Norway* 8 E13
Trombetas →, *Brazil* 125 D7
Tromsø, *Norway* 8 B18
Trona, *U.S.A.* 117 K9
Tronador, Mte., *Argentina* 128 E2
Trøndelag, *Norway* 8 D14
Trondheim, *Norway* 8 E14
Trondheimsfjorden, *Norway* 8 E14
Trönninge, *Sweden* 11 H6
Tronto →, *Italy* 29 F10
Troodos, *Cyprus* 36 E11
Troon, *U.K.* 14 F4
Tropea, *Italy* 31 D8
Tropic, *U.S.A.* 115 H7
Tropoja, *Albania* 40 D4
Trosa, *Sweden* 11 F11
Trostan, *U.K.* 15 A5
Trostberg, *Germany* 25 G8
Trostyanets, *Ukraine* 47 G8
Trout →, *Canada* 104 A5
Trout L., *N.W.T., Canada* 104 A4
Trout L., *Ont., Canada* 105 C10
Trout Lake, *Canada* 104 B6
Trout Lake, *U.S.A.* 116 E5
Trout River, *Canada* 103 C8
Trout Run, *U.S.A.* 110 E7
Trouville-sur-Mer, *France* 18 C7
Trowbridge, *U.K.* 13 F5
Troy, *Turkey* 39 B8
Troy, *Ala., U.S.A.* 109 K3
Troy, *Kans., U.S.A.* 112 F7
Troy, *Mo., U.S.A.* 112 F9
Troy, *Mont., U.S.A.* 114 B6
Troy, *N.Y., U.S.A.* 111 D11
Troy, *Ohio, U.S.A.* 108 E3
Troy, *Pa., U.S.A.* 111 E8
Troyan, *Bulgaria* 41 D8
Troyes, *France* 19 D11
Trpanj, *Croatia* 29 E14
Trstenik, *Serbia, Yug.* 40 C5
Trubchevsk, *Russia* 47 F7
Truchas Peak, *U.S.A.* 113 H2
Trucial States = United Arab Emirates ■, *Asia* 71 F7
Truckee, *U.S.A.* 116 F6
Trudfront, *Russia* 49 H8
Trudovoye, *Russia* 54 C6
Trujillo, *Honduras* 120 C2
Trujillo, *Peru* 124 E3
Trujillo, *Spain* 35 F5
Trujillo, *U.S.A.* 113 H2
Trujillo, *Venezuela* 124 B4
Truk, *Micronesia* 96 G7
Trumann, *U.S.A.* 113 H9
Trumansburg, *U.S.A.* 111 D8
Trumbull, Mt., *U.S.A.* 115 H7
Trŭn, *Bulgaria* 40 D6
Trun, *France* 18 D7
Trundle, *Australia* 95 E4
Trung-Phan = Annam, *Vietnam* 64 E7
Truro, *Canada* 103 C7
Truro, *U.K.* 13 G2
Truskavets, *Ukraine* 47 H2
Trŭstenik, *Bulgaria* 41 C8
Trustrup, *Denmark* 11 H4
Trutch, *Canada* 104 B4
Truth or Consequences, *U.S.A.* 115 K10
Trutnov, *Czech Rep.* 26 A8
Truxton, *U.S.A.* 111 D8
Truyère →, *France* 20 D6
Tryavna, *Bulgaria* 41 D9
Tryonville, *U.S.A.* 110 E5
Trzcianka, *Poland* 45 E3
Trzciel, *Poland* 45 F2
Trzcińsko Zdrój, *Poland* 45 F1
Trzebiatów, *Poland* 44 D2
Trzebiez, *Poland* 44 E1
Trzebnica, *Poland* 45 G4
Trzemeszno, *Poland* 45 F4
Tržič, *Slovenia* 29 B11
Tsagan Aman, *Russia* 49 G8
Tsamandás, *Greece* 38 B2
Tsandi, *Namibia* 88 B1
Tsaratanana, *Madag.* 89 B8
Tsaratanana, Mt. de, *Madag.* 89 A8
Tsarevo = Michurin, *Bulgaria* 41 D11
Tsarevo, *Bulgaria* 41 D9
Tsaritsáni, *Greece* 38 B4
Tsau, *Botswana* 88 C3
Tsebrykove, *Ukraine* 47 J6
Tselinograd = Astana, *Kazakstan* 50 D8
Tses, *Namibia* 88 D2
Tsetserleg, *Mongolia* 60 B5
Tsévié, *Togo* 83 D5
Tshabong, *Botswana* 88 D3
Tshane, *Botswana* 88 C3
Tshela, *Dem. Rep. of the Congo* 84 E2
Tshesebe, *Botswana* 89 C4
Tshibeke, *Dem. Rep. of the Congo* 86 C2
Tshibinda, *Dem. Rep. of the Congo* 86 C2
Tshikapa, *Dem. Rep. of the Congo* 84 F4
Tshilenge, *Dem. Rep. of the Congo* 86 D1
Tshinsenda, *Dem. Rep. of the Congo* 87 E2
Tshofa, *Dem. Rep. of the Congo* 86 D2
Tshwane, *Botswana* 88 C3
Tsigara, *Botswana* 88 C4
Tsihombe, *Madag.* 89 D8
Tsiigehtchic, *Canada* 100 B6
Tsimlyansk, *Russia* 49 G6
Tsimlyansk Res. = Tsimlyanskoye Vdkhr., *Russia* 49 F6
Tsimlyanskoye Vdkhr., *Russia* 49 F6
Tsinan = Jinan, *China* 56 F9
Tsineng, *S. Africa* 88 D3
Tsínga, *Greece* 41 E8
Tsinghai = Qinghai □, *China* 60 C4
Tsingtao = Qingdao, *China* 57 F11
Tsinjoarivo, *Madag.* 89 B8
Tsinjomitondraka, *Madag.* 89 B8
Tsiroanomandidy, *Madag.* 89 B8
Tsiteli-Tsqaro, *Georgia* 49 K8
Tsitondroina, *Madag.* 89 C8
Tsivilsk, *Russia* 48 C8
Tsivory, *Madag.* 89 C8
Tskhinvali, *Georgia* 49 J7
Tsna →, *Russia* 48 C6
Tsnori, *Georgia* 49 K7
Tso Moriri, L., *India* 69 C8

Tsobis, *Namibia*	88	B2
Tsodilo Hill, *Botswana*	88	B3
Tsogttsetsiy = Baruunsuu, *Mongolia*	56	C3
Tsolo, *S. Africa*	89	E4
Tsomo, *S. Africa*	89	E4
Tsu, *Japan*	55	G8
Tsu L., *Canada*	104	A6
Tsuchiura, *Japan*	55	F10
Tsuen Wan, *H.K.*	59	F10
Tsugaru-Kaikyō, *Japan*	54	D10
Tsumeb, *Namibia*	88	B2
Tsumis, *Namibia*	88	C2
Tsuruga, *Japan*	55	G8
Tsurugi-San, *Japan*	55	H7
Tsuruoka, *Japan*	54	E9
Tsushima, *Gifu, Japan*	55	G8
Tsushima, *Nagasaki, Japan*	55	G4
Tsuyama, *Japan*	55	G7
Tsvetkovo, *Ukraine*	47	H6
Tsyelyakhany, *Belarus*	47	F3
Tua →, *Portugal*	34	D3
Tual, *Indonesia*	63	F8
Tuam, *Ireland*	15	C3
Tuamotu Arch. = Tuamotu Is., *Pac. Oc.*	97	J13
Tuamotu Is., *Pac. Oc.*	97	J13
Tuamotu Ridge, *Pac. Oc.*	97	K14
Tuanfeng, *China*	59	B10
Tuanxi, *China*	58	D6
Tuao, *Phil.*	61	C4
Tuapse, *Russia*	49	H4
Tuatapere, *N.Z.*	91	M1
Tuba City, *U.S.A.*	115	H8
Tuban, *Indonesia*	63	G15
Tubani, *Botswana*	88	C3
Tubarão, *Brazil*	127	B6
Tūbās, *West Bank*	75	C4
Tubas →, *Namibia*	88	C2
Tübingen, *Germany*	25	G5
Tubruq, *Libya*	79	B10
Tubuai Is., *Pac. Oc.*	97	K13
Tuc Trung, *Vietnam*	65	G6
Tucacas, *Venezuela*	124	A5
T'uch'ang, *Taiwan*	59	E13
Tuchodi →, *Canada*	104	B4
Tuchola, *Poland*	44	E4
Tuchów, *Poland*	45	J8
Tuckanarra, *Australia*	93	E2
Tucson, *U.S.A.*	115	K8
Tucumán □, *Argentina*	126	B2
Tucumcari, *U.S.A.*	113	H3
Tucupita, *Venezuela*	124	B6
Tucuruí, *Brazil*	125	D9
Tucuruí, Reprêsa de, *Brazil*	125	D9
Tuczno, *Poland*	45	E3
Tudela, *Spain*	32	C3
Tudmur, *Syria*	70	C3
Tudor, L., *Canada*	103	A6
Tudora, *Romania*	43	C11
Tuella →, *Portugal*	34	D3
Tugela →, *S. Africa*	89	D5
Tuguegarao, *Phil.*	61	C4
Tugur, *Russia*	51	D14
Tui, *Spain*	34	C2
Tuineje, *Canary Is.*	37	F5
Tukangbesi, Kepulauan, *Indonesia*	63	F6
Tukarak I., *Canada*	102	A4
Tukayyid, *Iraq*	70	D5
Tûkh, *Egypt*	80	H7
Tukobo, *Ghana*	82	D4
Tuktoyaktuk, *Canada*	100	B6
Tukums, *Latvia*	9	H20
Tukums □, *Latvia*	44	B10
Tukuyu, *Tanzania*	87	D3
Tula, *Hidalgo, Mexico*	119	C5
Tula, *Tamaulipas, Mexico*	119	C5
Tula, *Nigeria*	83	D7
Tula, *Russia*	46	E9
Tulancingo, *Mexico*	119	C5
Tulare, *Serbia, Yug.*	40	D5
Tulare, *U.S.A.*	116	J7
Tulare Lake Bed, *U.S.A.*	116	K7
Tularosa, *U.S.A.*	115	K10
Tulbagh, *S. Africa*	88	E2
Tulcán, *Ecuador*	124	C3
Tulcea, *Romania*	43	E13
Tulcea □, *Romania*	43	E13
Tulchyn, *Ukraine*	47	H5
Tüleh, *Iran*	71	C7
Tulemalu L., *Canada*	105	A9
Tulgheş, *Romania*	43	D10
Tuli, *Zimbabwe*	87	G2
Tulia, *U.S.A.*	113	H4
Tuliszków, *Poland*	45	F5
Tulita, *Canada*	100	B7
Tülkarm, *West Bank*	75	C4
Tulla, *Ireland*	15	D3
Tullahoma, *U.S.A.*	109	H2
Tullamore, *Australia*	95	E4
Tullamore, *Ireland*	15	C4
Tulle, *France*	20	C5
Tulln, *Austria*	26	C9
Tullow, *Ireland*	15	D5
Tullus, *Sudan*	81	E1
Tully, *Australia*	94	B4
Tully, *U.S.A.*	111	D8
Tulnici, *Romania*	43	E11
Tulovo, *Bulgaria*	41	D9
Tulsa, *U.S.A.*	113	G7
Tulsequah, *Canada*	104	B2
Tulu Milki, *Ethiopia*	81	F4
Tulu Welel, *Ethiopia*	81	F3
Tulua, *Colombia*	124	C3
Tuluceşti, *Romania*	43	E13
Tulun, *Russia*	51	D11
Tulungagung, *Indonesia*	63	H14
Tuma →, *Russia*	46	E11
Tuma →, *Nic.*	120	D3
Tumaco, *Colombia*	124	C3
Tumatumari, *Guyana*	124	B7
Tumba, *Sweden*	10	E11
Tumba, L., *Dem. Rep. of the Congo*	84	E3
Tumbarumba, *Australia*	95	F4
Tumbaya, *Argentina*	126	A2
Tumbes, *Peru*	124	D2
Tumbur, *Sudan*	81	G3
Tumbwe, *Dem. Rep. of the Congo*	87	E2
Tumby Bay, *Australia*	95	E2
Tumd Youqi, *China*	56	D6
Tumen, *China*	57	C15
Tumen Jiang →, *China*	57	C16
Tumeremo, *Venezuela*	124	B6
Tumkur, *India*	66	N10
Tump, *Pakistan*	66	F3
Tumpat, *Malaysia*	65	J4
Tumu, *Ghana*	82	C4
Tumucumaque, Serra, *Brazil*	122	C5
Tumut, *Australia*	95	F4
Tumwater, *U.S.A.*	116	C4
Tuna, *India*	68	H4
Tunadal, *Sweden*	10	B11
Tunas de Zaza, *Cuba*	120	B4
Tunbridge Wells = Royal Tunbridge Wells, *U.K.*	13	F8
Tunçbilek, *Turkey*	39	B11
Tunceli, *Turkey*	73	C8
Tuncurry-Forster, *Australia*	95	E5
Tundla, *India*	68	F8
Tundubai, *Sudan*	80	D2
Tunduru, *Tanzania*	87	E4
Tundzha →, *Bulgaria*	41	E10
Tunga Pass, *India*	67	E19
Tungabhadra →, *India*	66	M11
Tungaru, *Sudan*	81	E3
Tungla, *Nic.*	120	D3
Tungsha Tao, *Taiwan*	59	G11
Tungshih, *Taiwan*	59	E13
Tungsten, *Canada*	104	A3
Tunguska, Nizhnyaya →, *Russia*	51	C9
Tunguska, Podkamennaya →, *Russia*	51	C10
Tunica, *U.S.A.*	113	H9
Tunis, *Tunisia*	79	A8
Tunisia ■, *Africa*	79	A7
Tunja, *Colombia*	124	B4
Tunkhannock, *U.S.A.*	111	E9
Tunliu, *China*	56	F7
Tunnsjøen, *Norway*	8	D15
Tunø, *Denmark*	11	J4
Tunungayualok I., *Canada*	103	A7
Tunuyán, *Argentina*	126	C2
Tunuyán →, *Argentina*	126	C2
Tuo Jiang →, *China*	58	C5
Tuolumne, *U.S.A.*	116	H6
Tuolumne →, *U.S.A.*	116	H5
Tūp Āghāj, *Iran*	70	B5
Tupã, *Brazil*	127	A5
Tupelo, *U.S.A.*	109	H1
Tupik, *Russia*	46	E7
Tupinambaranas, *Brazil*	124	D7
Tupiza, *Bolivia*	126	A2
Tupižnica, *Serbia, Yug.*	40	C6
Tupman, *U.S.A.*	117	K7
Tupper, *Canada*	104	B4
Tupper Lake, *U.S.A.*	111	B10
Tupungato, Cerro, *S. Amer.*	126	C2
Túquerres, *Colombia*	124	C3
Tura, *Russia*	51	C11
Turabah, *Si. Arabia*	70	D4
Turabah, *Si. Arabia*	80	C5
Tūrān, *Iran*	71	C8
Turan, *Russia*	51	D10
Turayf, *Si. Arabia*	70	D3
Turbacz, *Poland*	45	J7
Turbe, *Bos.-H.*	42	F2
Turčianske Teplice, *Slovak Rep.*	27	C11
Turcoaia, *Romania*	43	E13
Turda, *Romania*	43	D8
Turek, *Poland*	45	F5
Turen, *Venezuela*	124	B5
Turfan = Turpan, *China*	60	B3
Turfan Depression = Turpan Hami, *China*	52	E12
Turgeon →, *Canada*	102	C4
Türgovishte, *Bulgaria*	41	C10
Turgut, *Turkey*	39	D10
Turgutlu, *Turkey*	39	C9
Turgwe →, *Zimbabwe*	89	C5
Turhal, *Turkey*	72	B7
Turia →, *Spain*	33	F4
Turiaçu, *Brazil*	125	D9
Turiaçu →, *Brazil*	125	D9
Turiec →, *Slovak Rep.*	27	B11
Turin = Torino, *Italy*	28	C4
Turkana, L., *Africa*	86	B4
Türkeli, *Turkey*	41	F11
Turkestan = Türkistan, *Kazakhstan*	50	E7
Türkeve, *Hungary*	42	C5
Turkey ■, *Eurasia*	72	C7
Turkey Creek, *Australia*	92	C4
Turki, *Russia*	48	D6
Türkistan, *Kazakhstan*	50	E7
Türkmenbashi, *Turkmenistan*	50	E6
Turkmenistan ■, *Asia*	50	F6
Türkmenli, *Turkey*	39	B8
Türkoğlu, *Turkey*	72	D7
Turks & Caicos Is. ■, *W. Indies*	121	B5
Turks Island Passage, *W. Indies*	121	B5
Turku, *Finland*	9	F20
Turkwel →, *Kenya*	86	B4
Turlock, *U.S.A.*	116	H6
Turnagain →, *Canada*	104	B3
Turnagain, C., *N.Z.*	91	J6
Turneffe Is., *Belize*	119	D7
Turner, *U.S.A.*	114	B9
Turner Pt., *Australia*	94	A1
Turner Valley, *Canada*	104	C6
Turners Falls, *U.S.A.*	111	D12
Turnhout, *Belgium*	17	C4
Turnor L., *Canada*	105	B7
Turnov, *Czech Rep.*	26	A8
Tǔrnovo = Veliko Tǔrnovo, *Bulgaria*	41	C9
Turnu Măgurele, *Romania*	43	G9
Turnu Roşu, P., *Romania*	43	E9
Turobin, *Poland*	45	H9
Turpan, *China*	60	B3
Turpan Hami, *China*	52	E12
Turrës, Kalaja e, *Albania*	40	E3
Turriff, *U.K.*	14	D6
Tursāq, *Iraq*	70	C5
Tursi, *Italy*	31	B9
Turtle Head I., *Australia*	94	A3
Turtle Is., *S. Leone*	82	D2
Turtle L., *Canada*	105	C7
Turtle Lake, *U.S.A.*	112	B4
Turtleford, *Canada*	105	C7
Turukhansk, *Russia*	51	C9
Turzovka, *Slovak Rep.*	27	B11
Tuscaloosa, *U.S.A.*	109	J2
Tuscánia, *Italy*	29	F8
Tuscany = Toscana □, *Italy*	28	E8
Tuscarawas →, *U.S.A.*	110	F3
Tuscarora Mt., *U.S.A.*	110	F7
Tuscola, *Ill., U.S.A.*	108	F1
Tuscola, *Tex., U.S.A.*	113	J5
Tuscumbia, *U.S.A.*	109	H2
Tuskegee, *U.S.A.*	109	J3
Tustin, *U.S.A.*	117	M9
Tuszyn, *Poland*	45	G6
Tutak, *Turkey*	73	C10
Tutayev, *Russia*	46	D10
Tuticorin, *India*	66	Q11
Tutin, *Serbia, Yug.*	40	D4
Tutóia, *Brazil*	125	D10
Tutong, *Brunei*	62	D4
Tutova →, *Romania*	43	D12
Tutrakan, *Bulgaria*	41	B10
Tuttle Creek L., *U.S.A.*	112	F6
Tuttlingen, *Germany*	25	H4
Tutuala, *Indonesia*	63	F7
Tutuila, *Amer. Samoa*	91	B13
Tutume, *Botswana*	85	J5
Tutun, *Egypt*	80	J7
Tututepec, *Mexico*	119	D5
Tuva □, *Russia*	51	D10
Tuvalu ■, *Pac. Oc.*	96	H9
Tuxer Alpen, *Austria*	26	D4
Tuxpan, *Mexico*	119	C5
Tuxtla Gutiérrez, *Mexico*	119	D6
Tuy = Tui, *Spain*	34	C2
Tuy An, *Vietnam*	64	F7
Tuy Duc, *Vietnam*	65	F6
Tuy Hoa, *Vietnam*	64	F7
Tuy Phong, *Vietnam*	65	G7
Tuya L., *Canada*	104	B2
Tuyen Hoa, *Vietnam*	64	D6
Tuyen Quang, *Vietnam*	58	G5
Tūysarkān, *Iran*	71	C6
Tuz Gölü, *Turkey*	72	C5
Tūz Khurmātū, *Iraq*	70	C5
Tuzi, *Montenegro, Yug.*	40	D3
Tuzla, *Bos.-H.*	42	F3
Tuzlov →, *Russia*	47	J10
Tuzluca, *Turkey*	73	B10
Tvååker, *Sweden*	11	G6
Tvardiţa, *Moldova*	43	D13
Tver, *Russia*	46	D8
Tvrdošín, *Slovak Rep.*	27	B12
Tvrdošovce, *Slovak Rep.*	27	C11
Tvǔrditsa, *Bulgaria*	41	D9
Twain, *U.S.A.*	116	E5
Twain Harte, *U.S.A.*	116	G6
Twardogóra, *Poland*	45	G4
Tweed, *Canada*	110	B7
Tweed →, *U.K.*	14	F6
Tweed Heads, *Australia*	95	D5
Tweedsmuir Prov. Park, *Canada*	104	C3
Twentynine Palms, *U.S.A.*	117	L10
Twillingate, *Canada*	103	C9
Twin Bridges, *U.S.A.*	114	D7
Twin Falls, *Canada*	103	B7
Twin Falls, *U.S.A.*	114	E6
Twin Valley, *U.S.A.*	112	B6
Twinsburg, *U.S.A.*	110	E3
Twistringen, *Germany*	24	C4
Twitchell Reservoir, *U.S.A.*	117	L6
Two Harbors, *U.S.A.*	112	B9
Two Hills, *Canada*	104	C6
Two Rivers, *U.S.A.*	108	C2
Two Rocks, *Australia*	93	F2
Twofold B., *Australia*	95	F4
Tyachiv, *Ukraine*	47	H2
Tychy, *Poland*	45	H5
Tyczyn, *Poland*	45	J9
Tykocin, *Poland*	45	E9
Tyler, *Minn., U.S.A.*	112	C6
Tyler, *Tex., U.S.A.*	113	J7
Tyligul →, *Ukraine*	47	J6
Týn nad Vltavou, *Czech Rep.*	26	B7
Tynda, *Russia*	51	D13
Tyndall, *U.S.A.*	112	D6
Tyne →, *U.K.*	12	C6
Tyne & Wear □, *U.K.*	12	B6
Týnec nad Sázavou, *Czech Rep.*	26	B7
Tynemouth, *U.K.*	12	B6
Tyre = Sūr, *Lebanon*	75	B4
Tyrifjorden, *Norway*	9	F14
Tyringe, *Sweden*	11	H7
Tyrnyauz, *Russia*	49	J6
Tyrol = Tirol □, *Austria*	26	D3
Tyrone, *U.S.A.*	110	F6
Tyrone □, *U.K.*	15	B4
Tyrrell →, *Australia*	95	F3
Tyrrell, L., *Australia*	95	F3
Tyrrell L., *Canada*	105	A7
Tyrrhenian Sea, *Medit. S.*	6	G8
Tysfjorden, *Norway*	8	B17
Tystberga, *Sweden*	11	F11
Tytuvènai, *Lithuania*	44	C10
Tyub Karagan, Mys, *Kazakhstan*	49	H10
Tyuleni, Ostrova, *Kazakstan*	49	H10
Tyuleniy, *Russia*	49	H8
Tyuleniy, Mys, *Azerbaijan*	49	K10
Tyumen, *Russia*	50	D7
Tywi →, *U.K.*	13	F3
Tywyn, *U.K.*	13	E3
Tzaneen, *S. Africa*	89	C5
Tzermiádhes, *Greece*	36	D7
Tzoumérka, Óros, *Greece*	38	B3
Tzukong = Zigong, *China*	58	C5

U

U Taphao, *Thailand*	64	F3
U.S.A. = United States of America ■, *N. Amer.*	106	C7
Uatumã →, *Brazil*	124	D7
Uaupés, *Brazil*	124	D5
Uaupés →, *Brazil*	124	C5
Uaxactún, *Guatemala*	120	C2
Ub, *Serbia, Yug.*	40	B4
Ubá, *Brazil*	127	A7
Uba, *Nigeria*	83	C7
Ubaitaba, *Brazil*	125	F11
Ubangi = Oubangi →, *Dem. Rep. of the Congo*	84	E3
Ubauro, *Pakistan*	68	E3
Ubaye →, *France*	21	D10
Ubayyid, W. al →, *Iraq*	70	C4
Ube, *Japan*	55	H5
Úbeda, *Spain*	35	G7
Uberaba, *Brazil*	125	G9
Uberlândia, *Brazil*	125	G9
Überlingen, *Germany*	25	H5
Ubiaja, *Nigeria*	83	D6
Ubolratna Res., *Thailand*	64	D4
Ubombo, *S. Africa*	89	D5
Ubon Ratchathani, *Thailand*	64	E5
Ubondo, *Dem. Rep. of the Congo*	86	C2
Ubort →, *Belarus*	47	F5
Ubrique, *Spain*	35	J5
Ubundu, *Dem. Rep. of the Congo*	86	C2
Ucayali →, *Peru*	122	D3
Uchab, *Namibia*	88	B2
Uchiura-Wan, *Japan*	54	C10
Uchquduq, *Uzbekistan*	50	E7
Uchte, *Germany*	24	C4
Uchur →, *Russia*	51	D14
Uckermark, *Germany*	24	B9
Ucluelet, *Canada*	104	D3
Uda →, *Russia*	51	D14
Udagamandalam, *India*	66	P10
Udainagar, *India*	68	H7
Udaipur, *India*	68	G5
Udaipur Garhi, *Nepal*	69	F12
Udala, *India*	69	J12
Udbina, *Croatia*	29	D12
Uddeholm, *Sweden*	10	D7
Uddevalla, *Sweden*	11	F5
Uddjaur, *Sweden*	8	D17
Uden, *Neths.*	17	C5
Udgir, *India*	66	K10
Udhampur, *India*	69	C6
Udi, *Nigeria*	83	D6
Údine, *Italy*	29	B10
Udmurtia □, *Russia*	50	D6
Udon Thani, *Thailand*	64	D4
Udupi, *India*	66	N9
Udvoy Balkan, *Bulgaria*	41	D10
Udzungwa Range, *Tanzania*	87	D4
Ueckermünde, *Germany*	24	B10
Ueda, *Japan*	55	F9
Uedineniya, Os., *Russia*	4	B12
Uele →, *Dem. Rep. of the Congo*	84	D4
Uelen, *Russia*	51	C19
Uelzen, *Germany*	24	C6
Uetersen, *Germany*	24	B5
Uetze, *Germany*	24	C6
Ufa, *Russia*	50	D6
Uffenheim, *Germany*	25	F6
Ugab →, *Namibia*	88	C1
Ugalla →, *Tanzania*	86	D3
Uganda ■, *Africa*	86	B3
Ugento, *Italy*	31	C11
Ugep, *Nigeria*	83	D6
Ughelli, *Nigeria*	83	D6
Ugie, *S. Africa*	89	E4
Ugíjar, *Spain*	35	J7
Ugine, *France*	21	C10
Uglegorsk, *Russia*	51	E15
Uglich, *Russia*	46	D10
Ugljan, *Croatia*	29	D12
Ugljane, *Croatia*	29	E13
Ugra →, *Russia*	46	E9
Ugǔrchin, *Bulgaria*	41	C8
Uh →, *Slovak Rep.*	27	C15
Uherské Hradiště, *Czech Rep.*	27	B10
Uherský Brod, *Czech Rep.*	27	B10
Úhlava →, *Czech Rep.*	26	B6
Uhlenhorst, *Namibia*	88	C2
Uhrichsville, *U.S.A.*	110	F3
Uibhist a Deas = South Uist, *U.K.*	14	D1
Uibhist a Tuath = North Uist, *U.K.*	14	D1
Uig, *U.K.*	14	D2
Uíge, *Angola*	84	F2
Uijòngbu, *S. Korea*	57	F14
Uiju, *N. Korea*	57	D13
Uinta Mts., *U.S.A.*	114	F8
Uis, *Namibia*	88	B2
Uitenhage, *S. Africa*	88	E4
Uithuizen, *Neths.*	17	A6
Ujazd, *Poland*	45	H5
Újfehértó, *Hungary*	42	C6
Ujh →, *India*	68	C6
Ujhani, *India*	69	F8
Uji-guntō, *Japan*	55	J4
Ujjain, *India*	68	H6
Ujście, *Poland*	45	E3
Újszász, *Hungary*	42	C5
Ujung Pandang, *Indonesia*	63	F5
Uka, *Russia*	51	D17
Ukara I., *Tanzania*	86	C3
Uke-Shima, *Japan*	55	K4
Ukerewe I., *Tanzania*	86	C3
Ukholovo, *Russia*	48	D5
Ukhrul, *India*	67	G19
Ukhta, *Russia*	50	C6
Ukiah, *U.S.A.*	116	F3
Ukki Fort, *India*	69	C7
Ukmergé, *Lithuania*	9	J21
Ukraine ■, *Europe*	47	H7
Ukwi, *Botswana*	88	C3
Ulaan-Uul, *Mongolia*	56	B6
Ulaanbaatar, *Mongolia*	51	E11
Ulaangom, *Mongolia*	60	A4
Ulaanjirem, *Mongolia*	56	B3
Ulamba, *Dem. Rep. of the Congo*	87	D1
Ulan Bator = Ulaanbaatar, *Mongolia*	51	E11
Ulan Erge, *Russia*	49	G7
Ulan Khol, *Russia*	49	H8
Ulan Ude, *Russia*	51	D11
Ulanów, *Poland*	45	H9
Ulaş, *Sivas, Turkey*	72	C7
Ulaş, *Tekirdağ, Turkey*	41	E11
Ulaya, *Morogoro, Tanzania*	86	D4
Ulaya, *Tabora, Tanzania*	86	C3
Ulcinj, *Montenegro, Yug.*	40	E3
Ulco, *S. Africa*	88	D3
Ulefoss, *Norway*	9	G13
Uléza, *Albania*	40	E3
Ulfborg, *Denmark*	11	H2
Ulhasnagar, *India*	66	K8
Uliastay, *Mongolia*	60	B4
Ulithi Atoll, *Pac. Oc.*	63	B9
Uljma, *Serbia, Yug.*	42	E6
Ulla →, *Spain*	34	C2
Ulladulla, *Australia*	95	F5
Ullapool, *U.K.*	14	D3
Ullared, *Sweden*	11	G6
Ulldecona, *Spain*	32	E5
Ullswater, *U.K.*	12	C5
Ullŭng-do, *S. Korea*	55	F5
Ulm, *Germany*	25	G5
Ulmarra, *Australia*	95	D5
Ulmeni, *Buzău, Romania*	43	E11
Ulmeni, *Maramureş, Romania*	43	C8
Ulongué, *Mozam.*	87	E3
Ulricehamn, *Sweden*	11	G7
Ulrika, *Sweden*	11	F9
Ulsan, *S. Korea*	57	G15
Ulsta, *U.K.*	14	A7
Ulster □, *U.K.*	15	B5
Ulstrem, *Bulgaria*	41	D10
Ulubat Gölü, *Turkey*	41	F12
Ulubey, *Turkey*	39	C11
Uluborlu, *Turkey*	39	C12
Uluçinar, *Turkey*	72	D6
Uludağ, *Turkey*	41	F13
Uludere, *Turkey*	73	D10
Uluguru Mts., *Tanzania*	86	D4
Ulukışla, *Turkey*	72	D6
Ulungur He →, *China*	60	B3
Uluru = Ayers Rock, *Australia*	93	E5
Uluru Nat. Park, *Australia*	93	E5
Ulutau, *Kazakhstan*	50	E7
Ulva, *U.K.*	14	E2
Ulverston, *U.K.*	12	C4
Ulverstone, *Australia*	94	G4
Ulya, *Russia*	51	D15
Ulyanovsk = Simbirsk, *Russia*	48	C9
Ulyasutay = Uliastay, *Mongolia*	60	B4
Ulysses, *U.S.A.*	113	G4
Umag, *Croatia*	29	C10
Umala, *Bolivia*	124	G5
Uman, *Ukraine*	47	H6
Umaria, *India*	67	H12
Umarkot, *Pakistan*	68	G3
Umarpada, *India*	68	J5
Umatilla, *U.S.A.*	114	D4
Umba, *Russia*	50	C5
Umbakumba, *Australia*	94	A2
Umbértide, *Italy*	29	E9
Umbrella Mts., *N.Z.*	91	L2
Umbria □, *Italy*	29	F9
Ume älv →, *Sweden*	8	E19
Umeå, *Sweden*	8	E19
Umera, *Indonesia*	63	E7
Umfuli →, *Zimbabwe*	87	F2
Umgusa →, *Zimbabwe*	87	F2
Umim Urūmah, *Si. Arabia*	80	B4

Umka, *Serbia, Yug.* 40 B4
Umkomaas, *S. Africa* 89 E5
Umlazi, *S. Africa* 85 L6
Umm ad Daraj, J., *Jordan* 75 C4
Umm al Qaywayn, *U.A.E.* 71 E7
Umm al Qittayn, *Jordan* 75 C5
Umm Arda, *Sudan* 81 D3
Umm Bāb, *Qatar* 71 E6
Umm Badr, *Sudan* 81 E2
Umm Baiyud, *Sudan* 81 E3
Umm Bel, *Sudan* 81 E2
Umm Birkah, *Si. Arabia* 80 B4
Umm Boim, *Sudan* 81 E2
Umm Dam, *Sudan* 81 E3
Umm Debi, *Sudan* 81 E3
Umm Dubban, *Sudan* 81 D3
Umm el Fahm, *Israel* 75 C4
Umm Gafala, *Sudan* 81 E2
Umm Gimala, *Sudan* 81 E2
Umm Inderaba, *Sudan* 80 D3
Umm Keddada, *Sudan* 81 E2
Umm Koweika, *Sudan* 81 E3
Umm Lajj, *Si. Arabia* 70 E3
Umm Merwa, *Sudan* 80 D3
Umm Qantur, *Sudan* 81 E3
Umm Qurein, *Sudan* 81 F2
Umm Ruwaba, *Sudan* 81 E3
Umm Saiyala, *Sudan* 81 E3
Umm Shanqa, *Sudan* 81 E2
Umm Shutur, *Sudan* 81 F3
Umm Sidr, *Sudan* 81 E2
Umm Zehetir, *Egypt* 80 J8
Umnak I., *U.S.A.* 100 C3
Umniati →, *Zimbabwe* 87 F2
Umpqua →, *U.S.A.* 114 E1
Umreth, *India* 68 H5
Umtata, *S. Africa* 89 E4
Umuahia, *Nigeria* 83 D6
Umuarama, *Brazil* 127 A5
Umurbey, *Turkey* 41 F10
Umvukwe Ra., *Zimbabwe* 87 F3
Umzimvubu, *S. Africa* 89 E4
Umzingwane →, *Zimbabwe* 87 G2
Umzinto, *S. Africa* 89 E5
Una, *India* 68 J4
Una →, *Bos.-H.* 29 D13
Unac →, *Bos.-H.* 29 D13
Unadilla, *U.S.A.* 111 D9
Unalakleet, *U.S.A.* 100 B3
Unalaska, *U.S.A.* 100 C3
Unalaska I., *U.S.A.* 100 C3
'Unayzah, *Si. Arabia* 70 E4
'Unāzah, J., *Asia* 70 C3
Uncastillo, *Spain* 32 C3
Uncía, *Bolivia* 124 G5
Uncompahgre Peak, *U.S.A.* 115 G10
Uncompahgre Plateau, *U.S.A.* 115 G9
Unden, *Sweden* 11 F8
Underbool, *Australia* 95 F3
Undersaker, *Sweden* 10 A7
Unecha, *Russia* 47 F7
Ungarie, *Australia* 95 E4
Ungarra, *Australia* 95 E2
Ungava, Pén. d', *Canada* 101 C12
Ungava B., *Canada* 101 C13
Ungeny = Ungheni, *Moldova* 43 C12
Unggi, *N. Korea* 57 C16
Ungheni, *Moldova* 43 C12
Unguala →, *Ethiopia* 81 F5
Ungwatiri, *Sudan* 81 D4
Uni, *Russia* 48 B10
União da Vitória, *Brazil* 127 B5
Uničov, *Czech Rep.* 27 B10
Uniejów, *Poland* 45 G5
Unije, *Croatia* 29 D11
Unimak I., *U.S.A.* 100 C3
Union, *Miss., U.S.A.* 113 J10
Union, *Mo., U.S.A.* 112 F9
Union, *S.C., U.S.A.* 109 H5
Union City, *Calif., U.S.A.* 116 H4
Union City, *N.J., U.S.A.* 111 F10
Union City, *Pa., U.S.A.* 110 E5
Union City, *Tenn., U.S.A.* 113 G10
Union Gap, *U.S.A.* 114 C3
Union Springs, *U.S.A.* 109 J3
Uniondale, *S. Africa* 88 E3
Uniontown, *U.S.A.* 108 F6
Unionville, *U.S.A.* 112 E8
Unirea, *Romania* 43 F12
United Arab Emirates ■, *Asia* 71 F7
United Kingdom ■, *Europe* 7 E5
United States of America ■, *N. Amer.* 106 C7
Unity, *Canada* 105 C7
Universales, Mtes., *Spain* 32 E3
University Park, *U.S.A.* 115 K10
Unjha, *India* 68 H5
Unna, *Germany* 24 D3
Unnao, *India* 69 F9
Uno, Ilha, *Guinea-Biss.* 82 C1
Unst, *U.K.* 14 A8
Unstrut →, *Germany* 24 D7
Unterfranken □, *Germany* 25 F5
Unterschleissheim, *Germany* 25 G7
Unuk →, *Canada* 104 B2
Ünye, *Turkey* 72 B7
Unzha, *Russia* 48 A7
Unzha →, *Russia* 48 B6
Uozu, *Japan* 55 F8
Upata, *Venezuela* 124 B6
Upemba, L., *Dem. Rep. of the Congo* 87 D2
Upernavik, *Greenland* 4 B5
Upington, *S. Africa* 88 D3
Upleta, *India* 68 J4
Upolu, *W. Samoa* 91 A13
Upper □, *Ghana* 83 C4
Upper Alkali L., *U.S.A.* 114 F3
Upper Arrow L., *Canada* 104 C5
Upper Austria = Oberösterreich □, *Austria* 26 C7
Upper Foster L., *Canada* 105 B7
Upper Hutt, *N.Z.* 91 J5
Upper Klamath L., *U.S.A.* 114 E3
Upper Lake, *U.S.A.* 116 F4
Upper Musquodoboit, *Canada* 103 C7
Upper Red L., *U.S.A.* 112 A7
Upper Sandusky, *U.S.A.* 108 E4
Upper Volta = Burkina Faso ■, *Africa* 82 C4
Upphärad, *Sweden* 11 F6
Uppland, *Sweden* 10 E11
Upplands-Väsby, *Sweden* 10 E11
Uppsala, *Sweden* 10 E11
Uppsala län □, *Sweden* 10 D11
Upshi, *India* 69 C7
Upstart, C., *Australia* 94 B4
Upton, *U.S.A.* 112 C2
Ur, *Iraq* 70 D5
Urad Qianqi, *China* 56 D5
Urakawa, *Japan* 54 C11
Ural = Zhayyq →, *Kazakstan* 50 E6
Ural, *Australia* 95 E4
Ural Mts. = Uralskie Gory, *Eurasia* 50 D6
Uralla, *Australia* 95 E5
Uralsk = Oral, *Kazakstan* 48 E10
Uralskie Gory, *Eurasia* 50 D6
Urambo, *Tanzania* 86 D3
Urana, *Australia* 95 F4
Urandangi, *Australia* 94 C2
Uranium City, *Canada* 105 B7
Uraricoera →, *Brazil* 124 C6
Urawa, *Japan* 55 G9
Uray, *Russia* 50 C7
'Uray'irah, *Si. Arabia* 71 E6
Urbana, *Ill., U.S.A.* 108 E1
Urbana, *Ohio, U.S.A.* 108 E4
Urbánia, *Italy* 29 E9
Urbel →, *Spain* 34 C7
Urbino, *Italy* 29 E9
Urbión, Picos de, *Spain* 32 C2
Urcos, *Peru* 124 F4
Urdinarrain, *Argentina* 126 C4
Urdos, *France* 20 F3
Urdzhar, *Kazakstan* 50 E9
Ure →, *U.K.* 12 C6
Uren, *Russia* 48 B7
Ures, *Mexico* 118 B2
Urfa = Sanliurfa, *Turkey* 70 B3
Urganch, *Uzbekistan* 50 E7
Urgench = Urganch, *Uzbekistan* 50 E7
Ürgüp, *Turkey* 70 B2
Uri, *India* 69 B6
Uri □, *Switz.* 25 J4
Uribia, *Colombia* 124 A4
Uricani, *Romania* 42 E8
Uriondo, *Bolivia* 126 A3
Urique, *Mexico* 118 B3
Urique →, *Mexico* 118 B3
Urk, *Neths.* 17 B5
Urla, *Turkey* 39 C8
Urlați, *Romania* 43 F11
Urmia = Orūmīyeh, *Iran* 70 B5
Urmia, L. = Orūmīyeh, Daryācheh-ye, *Iran* 70 B5
Uroševac, *Kosovo, Yug.* 40 D5
Urshult, *Sweden* 11 H8
Uruaçu, *Brazil* 125 F9
Uruapan, *Mexico* 118 D4
Urubamba →, *Peru* 124 F4
Uruçara, *Brazil* 124 D7
Uruçuí, *Brazil* 125 E10
Uruguai →, *Brazil* 127 B5
Uruguaiana, *Brazil* 126 B4
Uruguay ■, *S. Amer.* 126 C4
Uruguay →, *S. Amer.* 126 C4
Urumchi = Ürümqi, *China* 50 E9
Ürümqi, *China* 50 E9
Urup →, *Russia* 49 H5
Urup, Ostrov, *Russia* 51 E16
Uryupinsk, *Russia* 48 E5
Urzhum, *Russia* 48 B9
Urziceni, *Romania* 43 F11
Usa →, *Russia* 50 C6
Uşak, *Turkey* 39 C11
Uşak □, *Turkey* 39 C11
Usakos, *Namibia* 88 C2
Ušće, *Serbia, Yug.* 40 C4
Usedom, *Germany* 24 B10
Useless Loop, *Australia* 93 E1
'Usfān, *Si. Arabia* 80 C4
Ush-Tobe, *Kazakstan* 50 E8
Ushakova, Ostrov, *Russia* 4 A12
Ushant = Ouessant, Î. d', *France* 18 D1
Ushashi, *Tanzania* 86 C3
Ushat, *Sudan* 81 F2
'Ushayrah, *Si. Arabia* 80 C5
Ushibuka, *Japan* 55 H5
Ushuaia, *Argentina* 128 G3
Ushumun, *Russia* 51 D13
Usk, *Canada* 104 C3
Usk →, *U.K.* 13 F5
Uska, *India* 69 F10
Üsküdar, *Turkey* 41 F13
Uslar, *Germany* 24 D5
Usman, *Russia* 47 F10
Usoke, *Tanzania* 86 D3
Usolye Sibirskoye, *Russia* 51 D11
Usoro, *Nigeria* 83 D6
Uspallata, P. de, *Argentina* 126 C2
Uspenskiy, *Kazakstan* 50 E8
Ussel, *France* 20 C6
Usson-du-Poitou, *France* 20 B4
Ussuri →, *Asia* 54 A7
Ussuriysk, *Russia* 51 E14
Ussurka, *Russia* 54 B6
Ust-Aldan = Batamay, *Russia* 51 C13
Ust-Amginskoye = Khandyga, *Russia* 51 C14
Ust-Bolsheretsk, *Russia* 51 D16
Ust-Buzulukskaya, *Russia* 48 E6
Ust-Chaun, *Russia* 51 C18
Ust-Donetskiy, *Russia* 49 G5
Ust-Ilimpeya = Yukta, *Russia* 51 C11
Ust-Ilimsk, *Russia* 51 D11
Ust-Ishim, *Russia* 50 D8
Ust-Kamchatsk, *Russia* 51 D17
Ust-Kamenogorsk = Öskemen, *Kazakstan* 50 E9
Ust-Khayryuzovo, *Russia* 51 D16
Ust-Kut, *Russia* 51 D11
Ust-Kuyga, *Russia* 51 B14
Ust-Labinsk, *Russia* 49 H4
Ust-Luga, *Russia* 46 C5
Ust-Maya, *Russia* 51 C14
Ust-Mil, *Russia* 51 D14
Ust-Nera, *Russia* 51 C15
Ust-Nyukzha, *Russia* 51 D13
Ust-Olenek, *Russia* 51 B12
Ust-Omchug, *Russia* 51 C15
Ust-Port, *Russia* 50 C9
Ust-Tsilma, *Russia* 50 C6
Ust Urt = Ustyurt Plateau, *Asia* 50 E6
Ustaritz, *France* 20 E2
Uster, *Switz.* 25 H4
Ústí nad Labem, *Czech Rep.* 26 A7
Ústí nad Orlicí, *Czech Rep.* 27 B9
Ústica, *Italy* 30 D6
Ustinov = Izhevsk, *Russia* 50 D6
Ustka, *Poland* 44 D3
Ustroń, *Poland* 45 J5
Ustrzyki Dolne, *Poland* 45 J9
Ustyurt Plateau, *Asia* 50 E6
Ustyuzhna, *Russia* 46 C9
Usu, *China* 60 B3
Usuki, *Japan* 55 H5
Usulután, *El Salv.* 120 D2
Usumacinta →, *Mexico* 119 D6
Usumbura = Bujumbura, *Burundi* 86 C2
Usure, *Tanzania* 86 C3
Usutuo →, *Mozam.* 89 D5
Uta, *Indonesia* 63 E9
Utah □, *U.S.A.* 114 G8
Utah L., *U.S.A.* 114 F8
Utansjö, *Sweden* 10 B11
Utarni, *India* 68 F4
Utatlan, *Guatemala* 120 C1
Ute Creek →, *U.S.A.* 113 H3
Utebo, *Spain* 32 D3
Utena, *Lithuania* 9 J21
Utete, *Tanzania* 86 D4
Uthai Thani, *Thailand* 64 E3
Uthal, *Pakistan* 68 G2
Utiariti, *Brazil* 124 F7
Utica, *N.Y., U.S.A.* 111 C9
Utica, *Ohio, U.S.A.* 110 F2
Utiel, *Spain* 33 F3
Utikuma L., *Canada* 104 B5
Utö, *Sweden* 10 F12
Utopia, *Australia* 94 C1
Utraula, *India* 69 F10
Utrecht, *Neths.* 17 B5
Utrecht, *S. Africa* 89 D5
Utrecht □, *Neths.* 17 B5
Utrera, *Spain* 35 H5
Utsjoki, *Finland* 8 B22
Utsunomiya, *Japan* 55 F9
Uttar Pradesh □, *India* 69 F9
Uttaradit, *Thailand* 64 D3
Uttoxeter, *U.K.* 12 E6
Uummannarsuaq = Nunap Isua, *Greenland* 4 D5
Uusikaarlepyy, *Finland* 8 E20
Uusikaupunki, *Finland* 9 F19
Uva, *Russia* 48 B11
Uvac →, *Serbia, Yug.* 40 C3
Uvalde, *U.S.A.* 113 L5
Uvarovo, *Russia* 48 E6
Uvat, *Russia* 50 D7
Uvinza, *Tanzania* 86 D3
Uvira, *Dem. Rep. of the Congo* 86 C2
Uvs Nuur, *Mongolia* 60 A4
'Uwairidh, Harrat al, *Si. Arabia* 70 E3
Uwajima, *Japan* 55 H6
Uweinat, Jebel, *Sudan* 80 C1
Uxbridge, *Canada* 110 B5
Uxin Qi, *China* 56 E5
Uxmal, *Mexico* 119 C7
Üydzin, *Mongolia* 56 B4
Uyo, *Nigeria* 83 D6
Üyüklü Tepe, *Turkey* 39 D9
Uyûn Mûsa, *Egypt* 75 F1
Uyuni, *Bolivia* 124 H5
Uzbekistan ■, *Asia* 50 E7
Uzen, Bolshoi →, *Kazakstan* 49 F9
Uzen, Mal →, *Kazakstan* 49 F9
Uzerche, *France* 20 C5
Uzès, *France* 21 D8
Uzh →, *Ukraine* 47 G6
Uzhgorod = Uzhhorod, *Ukraine* 47 H2
Uzhhorod, *Ukraine* 47 H2
Užice, *Serbia, Yug.* 40 C3
Uzlovaya, *Russia* 46 F10
Üzümlü, *Turkey* 39 E11
Uzunköprü, *Turkey* 41 E10
Uzunkuyu, *Turkey* 39 C8

V

Vaal →, *S. Africa* 88 D3
Vaal Dam, *S. Africa* 89 D4
Vaalwater, *S. Africa* 89 C4
Vaasa, *Finland* 8 E19
Vabre, *France* 20 E6
Vác, *Hungary* 42 C4
Vacaria, *Brazil* 127 B5
Vacaville, *U.S.A.* 116 G5
Vaccarès, Étang de, *France* 21 E8
Vach = Vakh →, *Russia* 50 C8
Vache, Î. à, *Haiti* 121 C5
Väckelsång, *Sweden* 11 H8
Väddö, *Sweden* 10 D12
Väderstad, *Sweden* 11 F8
Vadnagar, *India* 68 H5
Vado Lígure, *Italy* 28 D5
Vadodara, *India* 68 H5
Vadsø, *Norway* 8 A23
Vadstena, *Sweden* 11 F8
Vaduz, *Liech.* 25 H5
Værøy, *Norway* 8 C15
Vágar, *Færoe Is.* 8 E9
Vaggeryd, *Sweden* 11 G8
Vagney, *France* 19 D13
Vagnhärad, *Sweden* 11 F11
Vagos, *Portugal* 34 E2
Vågsfjorden, *Norway* 8 B17
Váh →, *Slovak Rep.* 27 D11
Vahsel B., *Antarctica* 5 D1
Váï, *Greece* 36 D8
Vaigach, *Russia* 50 B6
Vaiges, *France* 18 D6
Vaihingen, *Germany* 25 G4
Vail, *U.S.A.* 106 C5
Vailly-sur-Aisne, *France* 19 C10
Vaisali →, *India* 69 F8
Vaison-la-Romaine, *France* 21 D9
Vakarel, *Bulgaria* 40 D7
Vakfikebir, *Turkey* 73 B8
Vakh →, *Russia* 50 C8
Vakhtan, *Russia* 48 B8
Vál, *Hungary* 42 C3
Val-de-Marne □, *France* 19 D9
Val-d'Isère, *France* 21 C10
Val-d'Oise □, *France* 19 C9
Val-d'Or, *Canada* 102 C4
Val Marie, *Canada* 105 D7
Valaam, *Russia* 46 B6
Valadares, *Portugal* 34 D2
Valahia, *Romania* 43 F9
Valais □, *Switz.* 25 J3
Valais, Alpes du, *Switz.* 25 J3
Valandovo, *Macedonia* 40 E6
Valašské Meziříčí, *Czech Rep.* 27 B10
Valáxa, *Greece* 38 C6
Vålberg, *Sweden* 10 E7
Valbo, *Sweden* 10 D10
Valbondione, *Italy* 28 B7
Vâlcani, *Romania* 42 D5
Vâlcea □, *Romania* 43 F9
Valcheta, *Argentina* 128 E3
Valdagno, *Italy* 29 C8
Valdahon, *France* 19 E13
Valday, *Russia* 46 D7
Valdayskaya Vozvyshennost, *Russia* 46 D7
Valdeazogues →, *Spain* 35 G6
Valdecañas, Embalse de, *Spain* 34 F5
Valdemarsvik, *Sweden* 11 F10
Valdemoro, *Spain* 34 E7
Valdepeñas, *Spain* 35 G7
Valderaduey →, *Spain* 34 D5
Valdérice, *Italy* 30 D5
Valderrobres, *Spain* 32 E5
Valdés, Pen., *Argentina* 122 H4
Valdez, *U.S.A.* 100 B5
Valdivia, *Chile* 128 D2
Valdobbiádene, *Italy* 29 C8
Valdosta, *U.S.A.* 109 K4
Valdoviño, *Spain* 34 B2
Valdres, *Norway* 9 F13
Vale, *Georgia* 49 K6
Vale, *U.S.A.* 114 E5
Vale of Glamorgan □, *U.K.* 13 F4
Valea lui Mihai, *Romania* 42 C7
Valea Mărului, *Romania* 43 E12
Valemount, *Canada* 104 C5
Valença, *Brazil* 125 F11
Valença, *Portugal* 34 C2
Valença do Piauí, *Brazil* 125 E10
Valençay, *France* 19 E8
Valence = Valence d'Agen, *France* 20 D4
Valence, *France* 21 D8
Valence d'Agen, *France* 20 D4
Valencia, *Spain* 33 F4
Valencia, *U.S.A.* 115 J10
Valencia, *Venezuela* 124 A5
Valencia □, *Spain* 33 F4
Valencia, G. de, *Spain* 33 F5
Valencia de Alcántara, *Spain* 35 F3
Valencia de Don Juan, *Spain* 34 C5
Valencia I., *Ireland* 15 E1
Valenciennes, *France* 19 B10
Văleni, *Romania* 43 F9
Vălenii de Munte, *Romania* 43 E11
Valensole, *France* 21 E9
Valentigney, *France* 19 E13
Valentim, Sa. do, *Brazil* 125 E10
Valentin, *Russia* 54 C7
Valentine, *U.S.A.* 113 K2
Valenza, *Italy* 28 C5
Valera, *Venezuela* 124 B4
Valga, *Estonia* 9 H22
Valguarnera Caropepe, *Italy* 31 E7
Valier, *U.S.A.* 114 B7
Valinco, G. de, *France* 21 G12
Valjevo, *Serbia, Yug.* 40 B3
Valka, *Latvia* 9 H21
Valkeakoski, *Finland* 9 F20
Valkenswaard, *Neths.* 17 C5
Vall de Uxó = La Vall d'Uixó, *Spain* 32 F4
Valla, *Sweden* 10 E10
Valladolid, *Mexico* 119 C7
Valladolid, *Spain* 34 D6
Valladolid □, *Spain* 34 D6
Vallata, *Italy* 31 A8
Valldemossa, *Spain* 37 B9
Valle d'Aosta □, *Italy* 28 C4
Valle de Arán, *Spain* 32 C5
Valle de la Pascua, *Venezuela* 124 B5
Valle de las Palmas, *Mexico* 117 N10
Valle de Santiago, *Mexico* 118 C4
Valle de Suchil, *Mexico* 118 C4
Valle de Zaragoza, *Mexico* 118 B3
Valle Fértil, Sierra del, *Argentina* 126 C2
Valle Hermoso, *Mexico* 119 B5
Valledupar, *Colombia* 124 A4
Vallehermoso, *Canary Is.* 37 F2
Vallejo, *U.S.A.* 116 G4
Vallenar, *Chile* 126 B1
Vallentuna, *Sweden* 10 E12
Valleraugue, *France* 20 D7
Vallet, *France* 18 E5
Valletta, *Malta* 36 D2
Valley Center, *U.S.A.* 117 M9
Valley City, *U.S.A.* 112 B6
Valley Falls, *Oreg., U.S.A.* 114 E3
Valley Falls, *R.I., U.S.A.* 111 E13
Valley Springs, *U.S.A.* 116 G6
Valley View, *U.S.A.* 111 F8
Valley Wells, *U.S.A.* 117 K11
Valleyview, *Canada* 104 B5
Valli di Comácchio, *Italy* 29 D9
Vallimanca, Arroyo, *Argentina* 126 D4
Vallo della Lucánia, *Italy* 31 B8
Vallon-Pont-d'Arc, *France* 21 D8
Vallorbe, *Switz.* 25 J2
Valls, *Spain* 32 D6
Valmaseda = Balmaseda, *Spain* 32 B1
Valmiera, *Latvia* 9 H21
Valnera, *Spain* 34 B7
Valognes, *France* 18 C5
Valona = Vlóra, *Albania* 40 F3
Valongo, *Portugal* 34 D2
Valozhyn, *Belarus* 46 E4
Valpaços, *Portugal* 34 D3
Valparaíso, *Chile* 126 C1
Valparaíso, *Mexico* 118 C4
Valparaiso, *U.S.A.* 108 E2
Valparaíso □, *Chile* 126 C1
Valpovo, *Croatia* 42 E3
Valréas, *France* 21 D9
Vals, *Switz.* 25 J5
Vals →, *S. Africa* 88 D4
Vals, Tanjung, *Indonesia* 63 F9
Vals-les-Bains, *France* 21 D8
Valsad, *India* 66 J8
Valtellina, *Italy* 28 B6
Valuyki, *Russia* 47 G10
Valverde, *Canary Is.* 37 G2
Valverde del Camino, *Spain* 35 H4
Valverde del Fresno, *Spain* 34 E4
Vama, *Romania* 43 C10
Vamdrup, *Denmark* 11 J3
Våmhus, *Sweden* 10 C8
Vammala, *Finland* 9 F20
Vámos, *Greece* 36 D6
Van, *Turkey* 70 B4
Van, L. = Van Gölü, *Turkey* 70 B4
Van Alstyne, *U.S.A.* 113 J6
Van Blommestein Meer, *Surinam* 125 C7
Van Buren, *Canada* 103 C6
Van Buren, *Ark., U.S.A.* 113 H7
Van Buren, *Maine, U.S.A.* 109 B11
Van Buren, *Mo., U.S.A.* 113 G9
Van Canh, *Vietnam* 64 F7
Van Diemen, C., *N. Terr., Australia* 92 B5
Van Diemen, C., *Queens., Australia* 94 B2
Van Diemen G., *Australia* 92 B5
Van Gölü, *Turkey* 70 B4
Van Horn, *U.S.A.* 113 K2
Van Ninh, *Vietnam* 64 F7
Van Rees, Pegunungan, *Indonesia* 63 E9
Van Wert, *U.S.A.* 108 E3
Van Yen, *Vietnam* 58 G5
Vanadzor, *Armenia* 49 K7
Vanavara, *Russia* 51 C11
Vancouver, *Canada* 104 D4
Vancouver, *U.S.A.* 116 E4
Vancouver, C., *Australia* 93 G2
Vancouver I., *Canada* 104 D3
Vandalia, *Ill., U.S.A.* 112 F10
Vandalia, *Mo., U.S.A.* 112 F9
Vandenburg, *U.S.A.* 117 L6
Vanderbijlpark, *S. Africa* 89 D4
Vandergrift, *U.S.A.* 110 F5
Vanderhoof, *Canada* 104 C4
Vanderkloof Dam, *S. Africa* 88 E3
Vanderlin I., *Australia* 94 B2
Vänern, *Sweden* 11 F7
Vänersborg, *Sweden* 11 F6
Vang Vieng, *Laos* 64 C4
Vanga, *Kenya* 86 C4
Vangaindrano, *Madag.* 89 C8
Vanguard, *Canada* 105 D7
Vanino, *Russia* 51 E15
Vânju Mare, *Romania* 42 F7

Vanna

Vanna, *Norway* 8 A18
Vännäs, *Sweden* 8 E18
Vannes, *France* 18 E4
Vanoise, *France* 21 C10
Vanrhynsdorp, *S. Africa* 88 E2
Vansbro, *Sweden* 10 D8
Vansittart B., *Australia* 92 B4
Vantaa, *Finland* 9 F21
Vanua Levu, *Fiji* 91 C8
Vanua Mbalavu, *Fiji* 91 C9
Vanuatu ■, *Pac. Oc.* 96 J8
Vanwyksvlei, *S. Africa* 88 E3
Vanzylsrus, *S. Africa* 88 D3
Vapnyarka, *Ukraine* 47 H5
Var □, *France* 21 E10
Var →, *France* 21 E11
Vara, *Sweden* 11 F6
Varades, *France* 18 E5
Varáita →, *Italy* 28 D4
Varallo, *Italy* 28 C5
Varanasi, *India* 69 G10
Varanger-halvøya, *Norway* 8 A23
Varangerfjorden, *Norway* 8 A23
Varano, Lago di, *Italy* 29 G12
Varaždin, *Croatia* 29 B13
Varazze, *Italy* 28 D5
Varberg, *Sweden* 11 G6
Vardar = Axiós →, *Greece* 40 F6
Varde, *Denmark* 11 J2
Varde Å →, *Denmark* 11 J2
Vardø, *Norway* 8 A24
Varel, *Germany* 24 B4
Varella, Mui, *Vietnam* 64 F7
Varėna, *Lithuania* 9 J21
Varennes-sur-Allier, *France* 19 F10
Varennes-Vauzelles, *France* 19 E10
Vareš, *Bos.-H.* 42 F3
Varese, *Italy* 28 C5
Vârfurile, *Romania* 42 D7
Vårgårda, *Sweden* 11 F6
Varginha, *Brazil* 127 A6
Vargön, *Sweden* 11 F6
Varillas, *Chile* 126 A1
Varkaus, *Finland* 9 E22
Värmdölandet, *Sweden* 10 E12
Värmeln, *Sweden* 10 E6
Värmlands Bro, *Sweden* 10 E7
Värmlands län □, *Sweden* 10 E6
Varna, *Bulgaria* 41 C11
Varna □, *Bulgaria* 41 C11
Värnamo, *Sweden* 11 G8
Varnsdorf, *Czech Rep.* 26 A7
Várpalota, *Hungary* 42 C3
Vars, *Canada* 111 A9
Vars, *France* 21 D10
Varto, *Turkey* 73 C9
Varvarin, *Serbia, Yug.* 40 C5
Varysburg, *U.S.A.* 110 D6
Varzaneh, *Iran* 71 C7
Varzi, *Italy* 28 D6
Varzo, *Italy* 28 B5
Varzy, *France* 19 E10
Vas □, *Hungary* 42 C1
Vasa Barris →, *Brazil* 125 F11
Vásárosnamény, *Hungary* 42 B7
Vascão →, *Portugal* 35 H3
Vaşcău, *Romania* 42 D7
Vascongadas = País Vasco □, *Spain* 32 C2
Vasht = Khāsh, *Iran* 66 E2
Vasilevichi, *Belarus* 47 F5
Vasilikón, *Greece* 38 C5
Vasilkov = Vasylkiv, *Ukraine* 47 G6
Vaslui, *Romania* 43 D12
Vaslui □, *Romania* 43 D12
Väsman, *Sweden* 10 D9
Vassar, *Canada* 105 D9
Vassar, *U.S.A.* 108 D4
Västerås, *Sweden* 10 E10
Västerbotten, *Sweden* 8 D18
Västerdalälven →, *Sweden* 10 D8
Västergötland, *Sweden* 11 F7
Västerhaninge, *Sweden* 10 E12
Västervik, *Sweden* 11 G10
Västmanland, *Sweden* 9 G16
Västmanlands län □, *Sweden* 10 E10
Vasto, *Italy* 29 F11
Vasvár, *Hungary* 42 C1
Vasylkiv, *Ukraine* 47 G6
Vatan, *France* 19 E8
Vatersay, *U.K.* 14 E1
Váthia, *Greece* 38 E4
Vatican City ■, *Europe* 29 G9
Vaticano, C., *Italy* 31 D8
Vatili, *Cyprus* 36 D12
Vatin, *Serbia, Yug.* 42 E6
Vatnajökull, *Iceland* 8 D5
Vatoa, *Fiji* 91 D9
Vatólakkos, *Greece* 36 D5
Vatoloha, *Madag.* 89 B8
Vatomandry, *Madag.* 89 B8
Vatra-Dornei, *Romania* 43 C10
Vatrak →, *India* 68 H5
Vättern, *Sweden* 11 F8
Vaucluse □, *France* 21 E9
Vaucouleurs, *France* 19 D12
Vaud □, *Switz.* 25 J2
Vaughn, *Mont., U.S.A.* 114 C8
Vaughn, *N. Mex., U.S.A.* 115 J11
Vaujours L., *Canada* 102 A5
Vaupés = Uaupés →, *Brazil* 124 C5
Vaupes □, *Colombia* 124 C4
Vauvert, *France* 21 E8
Vauxhall, *Canada* 104 C6
Vav, *India* 68 G4
Vavatenina, *Madag.* 89 B8
Vava'u, *Tonga* 91 D12
Vavoua, *Ivory C.* 82 D3
Vawkavysk, *Belarus* 47 F3
Vaxholm, *Sweden* 10 E12
Växjö, *Sweden* 11 H8
Våxtorp, *Sweden* 11 H7
Vaygach, Ostrov, *Russia* 50 C6
Váyia, *Greece* 38 C5
Váyia, Ákra, *Greece* 36 C10
Vechelde, *Germany* 24 C6
Vechta, *Germany* 24 C4
Vechte →, *Neths.* 17 B6
Vecsés, *Hungary* 42 C4
Veddige, *Sweden* 11 G6
Vedea →, *Romania* 43 G10
Vedia, *Argentina* 126 C3
Vedum, *Sweden* 11 F7
Veendam, *Neths.* 17 A6
Veenendaal, *Neths.* 17 B5
Vefsna →, *Norway* 8 D15
Vega, *Norway* 8 D14
Vega, *U.S.A.* 113 H3
Vegadeo, *Spain* 34 B3
Vegorrítis, Límni, *Greece* 40 F5
Vegreville, *Canada* 104 C6
Veinge, *Sweden* 11 H7
Veisiejai, *Lithuania* 44 D10
Vejbystrand, *Sweden* 11 H6
Vejen, *Denmark* 11 J3
Vejer de la Frontera, *Spain* 35 J5
Vejle, *Denmark* 11 J3
Vejle Amtskommune □, *Denmark* 11 J3
Vejle Fjord, *Denmark* 11 J3
Vela Luka, *Croatia* 29 F13
Velas, C., *Costa Rica* 120 D2
Velasco, Sierra de, *Argentina* 126 B2
Velay, Mts. du, *France* 20 D7
Velbert, *Germany* 24 D3
Velddrif, *S. Africa* 88 E2
Velebit Planina, *Croatia* 29 D12
Velebitski Kanal, *Croatia* 29 D11
Veleka →, *Bulgaria* 41 D11
Velencei-tó, *Hungary* 42 C3
Velenje, *Slovenia* 29 B12
Veles, *Macedonia* 40 E5
Velestínon, *Greece* 38 B4
Vélez-Málaga, *Spain* 35 J6
Vélez Rubio, *Spain* 33 H2
Velhas →, *Brazil* 125 G10
Velika, *Croatia* 42 E2
Velika Gorica, *Croatia* 29 C13
Velika Kapela, *Croatia* 29 C12
Velika Kladuša, *Bos.-H.* 29 C12
Velika Kruša, *Kosovo, Yug.* 40 D4
Velika Morava →, *Serbia, Yug.* 40 B5
Velika Plana, *Serbia, Yug.* 40 B5
Velikaya →, *Russia* 46 D5
Velikaya Kema, *Russia* 54 B8
Velikaya Lepetikha, *Ukraine* 47 J7
Veliké Kapušany, *Slovak Rep.* 27 C15
Velike Lašče, *Slovenia* 29 C11
Veliki Jastrebac, *Serbia, Yug.* 40 C5
Veliki Kanal, *Serbia, Yug.* 42 E4
Veliki Popović, *Serbia, Yug.* 40 B5
Velikiye Luki, *Russia* 46 D6
Veliko Gradište, *Serbia, Yug.* 40 B5
Veliko Tŭrnovo, *Bulgaria* 41 C9
Velikonda Range, *India* 66 M11
Vélingara, *Senegal* 82 C2
Vélingara, *Senegal* 82 B2
Velingrad, *Bulgaria* 40 D7
Velino, Mte., *Italy* 29 F10
Velizh, *Russia* 46 E6
Velké Karlovice, *Czech Rep.* 27 B11
Velké Meziříčí, *Czech Rep.* 26 B9
Vel'ký Javorník, *Slovak Rep.* 27 B11
Vel'ký Krtíš, *Slovak Rep.* 27 C12
Vel'ký Meder, *Slovak Rep.* 27 D10
Vel'ký Tribeč, *Slovak Rep.* 27 C11
Velletri, *Italy* 30 A5
Vellinge, *Sweden* 11 J6
Vellmar, *Germany* 24 D5
Vellore, *India* 66 N11
Velsk, *Russia* 46 B11
Velten, *Germany* 24 C9
Velva, *U.S.A.* 112 A4
Velvendós, *Greece* 40 F6
Vemb, *Denmark* 11 H2
Vemdalen, *Sweden* 10 B7
Ven, *Sweden* 11 J6
Venaco, *France* 21 F13
Venado Tuerto, *Argentina* 126 C3
Venafro, *Italy* 31 A7
Venarey-les-Laumes, *France* 19 E11
Venaría, *Italy* 28 C4
Venčane, *Serbia, Yug.* 40 B4
Vence, *France* 21 E11
Vendas Novas, *Portugal* 35 G2
Vendée □, *France* 18 F5
Vendée →, *France* 18 F5
Vendéen, Bocage, *France* 20 B2
Vendeuvre-sur-Barse, *France* 19 D11
Vendôme, *France* 18 E8
Vendrell = El Vendrell, *Spain* 32 D6
Vendsyssel, *Denmark* 11 G4
Venelles, *France* 21 E9
Véneta, L., *Italy* 29 C9
Véneto □, *Italy* 29 C9
Venev, *Russia* 46 E10
Venézia, *Italy* 29 C9
Venézia, G. di, *Italy* 29 C10
Venezuela ■, *S. Amer.* 124 B5
Venezuela, G. de, *Venezuela* 122 B3
Vengurla, *India* 66 M8
Venice = Venézia, *Italy* 29 C9
Venice, *U.S.A.* 109 M4
Vénissieux, *France* 21 C8
Venjansjön, *Sweden* 10 D8
Venkatapuram, *India* 67 K12
Venlo, *Neths.* 17 C6
Vennesla, *Norway* 9 G12
Venosa, *Italy* 31 B8
Venray, *Neths.* 17 C6
Venta, *Lithuania* 44 B9
Venta →, *Latvia* 44 A8
Venta de Baños, *Spain* 34 D6
Venta de Cardeña = Cardeña, *Spain* 35 G6
Ventana, Punta de la, *Mexico* 118 C3
Ventana, Sa. de la, *Argentina* 126 D3
Ventersburg, *S. Africa* 88 D4
Venterstad, *S. Africa* 88 E4
Ventimíglia, *Italy* 28 E4
Ventnor, *U.K.* 13 G6
Ventoténe, *Italy* 30 B6
Ventoux, Mt., *France* 21 D9
Ventspils, *Latvia* 9 H19
Ventspils □, *Latvia* 44 A8
Ventuarí →, *Venezuela* 124 C5
Ventucopa, *U.S.A.* 117 L7
Ventura, *U.S.A.* 117 L7
Venus B., *Australia* 95 F4
Vera, *Argentina* 126 B3
Vera, *Spain* 33 H3
Veracruz, *Mexico* 119 D5
Veracruz □, *Mexico* 119 D5
Veraval, *India* 68 J4
Verbánia, *Italy* 28 C5
Verbicaro, *Italy* 31 C8
Verbier, *Switz.* 25 J3
Vercelli, *Italy* 28 C5
Verchovchevo, *Ukraine* 47 H8
Verdalsøra, *Norway* 8 E14
Verde →, *Argentina* 128 E3
Verde →, *Goiás, Brazil* 125 G8
Verde →, *Mato Grosso do Sul, Brazil* 125 H8
Verde →, *Chihuahua, Mexico* 118 B3
Verde →, *Oaxaca, Mexico* 119 D5
Verde →, *Veracruz, Mexico* 118 C4
Verde →, *Paraguay* 126 A4
Verde →, *U.S.A.* 106 D4
Verde, Cay, *Bahamas* 120 B4
Verde Island Pass, *Phil.* 61 E4
Verden, *Germany* 24 C5
Verdhikoúsa, *Greece* 38 B3
Verdi, *U.S.A.* 116 F7
Verdon →, *France* 21 E9
Verdun, *France* 19 C12
Verdun-sur-le-Doubs, *France* 19 F12
Vereeniging, *S. Africa* 89 D4
Verga, C., *Guinea* 82 C2
Vergara, *Uruguay* 127 C5
Vergato, *Italy* 28 D8
Vergemont Cr. →, *Australia* 94 C3
Vergennes, *U.S.A.* 111 B11
Vergt, *France* 20 C4
Verín, *Spain* 34 D3
Verkhnedvinsk = Vyerkhnyadzvinsk, *Belarus* 46 E4
Verkhnevilyuysk, *Russia* 51 C13
Verkhniy Baskunchak, *Russia* 49 F8
Verkhovye, *Russia* 47 F9
Verkhoyansk, *Russia* 51 C14
Verkhoyansk Ra. = Verkhoyanskiy Khrebet, *Russia* 51 C13
Verkhoyanskiy Khrebet, *Russia* 51 C13
Vermenton, *France* 19 E10
Vermilion, *Canada* 105 C6
Vermilion, *U.S.A.* 110 E2
Vermilion →, *Alta., Canada* 105 C6
Vermilion →, *Qué., Canada* 102 C5
Vermilion, B., *U.S.A.* 113 L9
Vermilion Bay, *Canada* 105 D10
Vermilion L., *U.S.A.* 112 B8
Vermillion, *U.S.A.* 112 D6
Vermont □, *U.S.A.* 111 C12
Vermosh, *Albania* 40 D3
Vernal, *U.S.A.* 114 F9
Vernalis, *U.S.A.* 116 H5
Vernazza, *Italy* 28 D6
Verner, *Canada* 102 C3
Verneuil-sur-Avre, *France* 18 D7
Verneukpan, *S. Africa* 88 E3
Vernier, *Switz.* 25 J2
Vérnio, *Italy* 28 D8
Vernon, *Canada* 104 C5
Vernon, *France* 18 C8
Vernon, *U.S.A.* 113 H5
Vernonia, *U.S.A.* 116 E3
Vernouillet, *France* 18 D8
Vero Beach, *U.S.A.* 109 M5
Véroia, *Greece* 40 F6
Véroli, *Italy* 29 G10
Verona, *Canada* 111 B8
Verona, *Italy* 28 C7
Verona, *U.S.A.* 112 D10
Verrès, *Italy* 28 C4
Versailles, *France* 19 D9
Versmold, *Germany* 24 C4
Vert, C., *Senegal* 82 C1
Vertou, *France* 18 E5
Vertus, *France* 19 D11
Verulam, *S. Africa* 89 D5
Verviers, *Belgium* 17 D5
Vervins, *France* 19 C10
Veržej, *Slovenia* 29 B13
Verzy, *France* 19 C11
Vescovato, *France* 21 F13
Veselí nad Lužnicí, *Czech Rep.* 26 B7
Veselie, *Bulgaria* 41 D11
Veselovskoye Vdkhr., *Russia* 49 G5
Veshenskaya, *Russia* 48 F5
Vesle →, *France* 19 C10
Vesoul, *France* 19 E13
Vessigebro, *Sweden* 11 H6
Vesterålen, *Norway* 8 B16
Vestfjorden, *Norway* 8 C15
Vestmannaeyjar, *Iceland* 8 E3
Vestsjællands Amtskommune □, *Denmark* 11 J5
Vestspitsbergen, *Svalbard* 4 B8
Vestvågøy, *Norway* 8 B15
Vesuvio, *Italy* 31 B7
Vesuvius, Mt. = Vesuvio, *Italy* 31 B7
Vesyegonsk, *Russia* 46 C9
Veszprém, *Hungary* 42 C2
Veszprém □, *Hungary* 42 C2
Vésztő, *Hungary* 42 D6
Vetlanda, *Sweden* 11 G9
Vetluga, *Russia* 48 B7
Vetlugu →, *Russia* 48 B8
Vetluzhskiy, *Kostroma, Russia* 48 A7
Vetluzhskiy, *Nizhniy Novgorod, Russia* 48 B7
Vetovo, *Bulgaria* 41 C10
Vetralla, *Italy* 29 F9
Vetren, *Bulgaria* 41 D8
Vettore, Mte., *Italy* 29 F10
Veurne, *Belgium* 17 C2
Veveno →, *Sudan* 81 F3
Vevey, *Switz.* 25 J2
Vévi, *Greece* 40 F5
Veynes, *France* 21 D9
Veys, *Iran* 71 D6
Vézelay, *France* 19 E10
Vézelise, *France* 19 D13
Vézère →, *France* 20 D4
Vezhen, *Bulgaria* 41 D8
Vezirköprü, *Turkey* 72 B6
Vezzani, *France* 21 F13
Vi Thanh, *Vietnam* 65 H5
Viacha, *Bolivia* 124 G5
Viadana, *Italy* 28 D7
Viamão, *Brazil* 127 C5
Viana, *Brazil* 125 D10
Viana, *Spain* 32 C2
Viana do Alentejo, *Portugal* 35 G3
Viana do Bolo, *Spain* 34 C3
Viana do Castelo, *Portugal* 34 D2
Viana do Castelo □, *Portugal* 34 D2
Vianden, *Lux.* 17 E6
Vianópolis, *Brazil* 125 G9
Viar →, *Spain* 35 H5
Viaréggio, *Italy* 28 E7
Viaur →, *France* 20 D5
Vibble, *Sweden* 11 G12
Vibo Valéntia, *Italy* 31 D9
Viborg, *Denmark* 11 H3
Viborg Amtskommune □, *Denmark* 11 H3
Vibraye, *France* 18 D7
Vic, *Spain* 32 D7
Vic, Étang de, *France* 20 E7
Vic-en-Bigorre, *France* 20 E4
Vic-Fézensac, *France* 20 E4
Vic-le-Comte, *France* 19 G10
Vic-sur-Cère, *France* 20 D6
Vícar, *Spain* 33 J2
Vicenza, *Italy* 29 C8
Vich = Vic, *Spain* 32 D7
Vichada →, *Colombia* 124 C5
Vichuga, *Russia* 48 B5
Vichy, *France* 19 F10
Vicksburg, *Ariz., U.S.A.* 117 M13
Vicksburg, *Miss., U.S.A.* 113 J9
Vico, *France* 21 F12
Vico, L. di, *Italy* 29 F9
Vico del Gargano, *Italy* 29 G12
Vicovu de Sus, *Romania* 43 C10
Victor, *India* 68 J4
Victor, *U.S.A.* 110 D7
Victor Harbor, *Australia* 95 F2
Victoria = Labuan, *Malaysia* 62 C5
Victoria, *Argentina* 126 C3
Victoria, *Canada* 104 D4
Victoria, *Chile* 128 D2
Victoria, *Guinea* 82 C2
Victoria, *Malta* 36 C1
Victoria, *Phil.* 61 D4
Victoria, *Romania* 43 E9
Victoria, *Kans., U.S.A.* 112 F5
Victoria, *Tex., U.S.A.* 113 L6
Victoria □, *Australia* 95 F3
Victoria →, *Australia* 92 C4
Victoria, Grand L., *Canada* 102 C4
Victoria, L., *Africa* 86 C3
Victoria, L., *Australia* 95 E3
Victoria Beach, *Canada* 105 C9
Victoria de Durango = Durango, *Mexico* 118 C4
Victoria de las Tunas, *Cuba* 120 B4
Victoria Falls, *Zimbabwe* 87 F2
Victoria Harbour, *Canada* 110 B5
Victoria I., *Canada* 100 A8
Victoria L., *Canada* 103 C8
Victoria Ld., *Antarctica* 5 D11
Victoria Nile →, *Uganda* 86 B3
Victoria River, *Australia* 92 C5
Victoria Str., *Canada* 100 B9
Victoria Taungdeik, *Burma* 67 J18
Victoria West, *S. Africa* 88 E3
Victorias, *Phil.* 61 F5
Victoriaville, *Canada* 103 C5
Victorica, *Argentina* 126 D2
Victorville, *U.S.A.* 117 L9
Vicuña, *Chile* 126 C1
Vicuña Mackenna, *Argentina* 126 C3
Vidal, *U.S.A.* 117 L12
Vidal Junction, *U.S.A.* 117 L12
Vidalia, *U.S.A.* 109 J4
Vidauban, *France* 21 E10
Videbæk, *Denmark* 11 H2
Videle, *Romania* 43 F10
Vídho, *Greece* 36 A3
Vidigueira, *Portugal* 35 G3
Vidin, *Bulgaria* 40 C6
Vidio, C., *Spain* 34 B4
Vidisha, *India* 68 H7
Vidra, *Romania* 43 E11
Viduša, *Bos.-H.* 40 D2
Vidzy, *Belarus* 9 J22
Viechtach, *Germany* 25 F8
Viedma, *Argentina* 128 E4
Viedma, L., *Argentina* 128 F2
Vieira do Minho, *Portugal* 34 D2
Vielha, *Spain* 32 C5
Viella = Vielha, *Spain* 32 C5
Vielsalm, *Belgium* 17 D5
Vienenburg, *Germany* 24 D6
Vieng Pou Kha, *Laos* 58 G3
Vienna = Wien, *Austria* 27 C9
Vienna, *Ill., U.S.A.* 113 G10
Vienna, *Mo., U.S.A.* 112 F9
Vienne, *France* 21 C8
Vienne □, *France* 20 B4
Vienne →, *France* 18 E7
Vientiane, *Laos* 64 D4
Vientos, Paso de los, *Caribbean* 121 C5
Viernheim, *Germany* 25 F4
Viersen, *Germany* 24 D2
Vierwaldstättersee, *Switz.* 25 J4
Vierzon, *France* 19 E9
Vieste, *Italy* 29 G13
Vietnam ■, *Asia* 64 C6
Vieux-Boucau-les-Bains, *France* 20 E2
Vif, *France* 21 C9
Vigan, *Phil.* 61 C4
Vigévano, *Italy* 28 C5
Vigia, *Brazil* 125 D9
Vigía Chico, *Mexico* 119 D7
Víglas, Ákra, *Greece* 36 D9
Vignemale, *France* 20 F3
Vigneulles-lès-Hattonchâtel, *France* 19 D12
Vignola, *Italy* 28 D8
Vigo, *Spain* 34 C2
Vigo, Ría de, *Spain* 34 C2
Vigsø Bugt, *Denmark* 11 G2
Vihiers, *France* 18 E6
Vihowa, *Pakistan* 68 D4
Vihowa →, *Pakistan* 68 D4
Vijayawada, *India* 67 L12
Vík, *Iceland* 8 E4
Vika, *Sweden* 10 D8
Vikarbyn, *Sweden* 10 D9
Vikeke, *Indonesia* 63 F7
Viken, *Skåne, Sweden* 11 H6
Viken, *Skaraborg, Sweden* 11 F8
Viking, *Canada* 104 C6
Vikmanshyttan, *Sweden* 10 D9
Vikna, *Norway* 8 D14
Vila da Maganja, *Mozam.* 87 F4
Vila de João Belo = Xai-Xai, *Mozam.* 89 D5
Vila de Rei, *Portugal* 34 F2
Vila do Bispo, *Portugal* 35 H2
Vila do Conde, *Portugal* 34 D2
Vila Franca de Xira, *Portugal* 35 G2
Vila Gamito, *Mozam.* 87 E3
Vila Gomes da Costa, *Mozam.* 89 C5
Vila Machado, *Mozam.* 87 F3
Vila Mouzinho, *Mozam.* 87 E3
Vila Nova de Famalicão, *Portugal* 34 D2
Vila Nova de Fos Côa, *Portugal* 34 D3
Vila Nova de Foscôa = Vila Nova de Fos Côa, *Portugal* 34 D3
Vila Nova de Gaia, *Portugal* 34 D2
Vila Nova de Ourém, *Portugal* 34 F2
Vila Pouca de Aguiar, *Portugal* 34 D3
Vila Real, *Portugal* 34 D3
Vila Real □, *Portugal* 34 D3
Vila-real de los Infantes, *Spain* 32 F4
Vila Real de Santo António, *Portugal* 35 H3
Vila Vasco da Gama, *Mozam.* 87 E3
Vila Velha, *Brazil* 127 A7
Vila Viçosa, *Portugal* 35 G3
Vilafranca del Maestrat, *Spain* 32 E4
Vilafranca del Penedès, *Spain* 32 D6
Vilagarcía de Arousa, *Spain* 34 C2
Vilaine →, *France* 18 E4
Vilanandro, Tanjona, *Madag.* 89 B7
Vilanculos, *Mozam.* 89 C6
Vilanova de Castelló, *Spain* 33 F4
Vilanova i la Geltrú, *Spain* 32 D6
Vilar Formosa, *Portugal* 34 E4
Vilaseca, *Spain* 32 D6
Vilaseca-Salou = Vilaseca, *Spain* 32 D6
Vilbjerg, *Denmark* 11 H2
Vilches, *Spain* 35 G7
Vileyka, *Belarus* 46 E4
Vilhelmina, *Sweden* 8 D17
Vilhena, *Brazil* 124 F6
Viliga, *Russia* 51 C16
Viliya →, *Lithuania* 9 J21

Viljandi, Estonia 9 G21
Vilkaviškis, Lithuania 44 D10
Vilkija, Lithuania 44 C10
Vilkitskogo, Proliv, Russia 51 B11
Vilkovo = Vylkove, Ukraine 47 K5
Villa Abecia, Bolivia 126 A2
Villa Ahumada, Mexico 118 A3
Villa Ana, Argentina 126 B4
Villa Ángela, Argentina 126 B3
Villa Bella, Bolivia 124 F5
Villa Bens = Tarfaya, Morocco 78 C3
Villa Cañás, Argentina 126 C3
Villa Cisneros = Dakhla, W. Sahara 78 D2
Villa Colón, Argentina 126 C2
Villa Constitución, Argentina 126 C3
Villa de María, Argentina 126 B3
Villa del Rio, Spain 35 H6
Villa Dolores, Argentina 126 C2
Villa Frontera, Mexico 118 B4
Villa Guillermina, Argentina 126 B4
Villa Hayes, Paraguay 126 B4
Villa Iris, Argentina 126 D3
Villa Juárez, Mexico 118 B4
Villa María, Argentina 126 C3
Villa Mazán, Argentina 126 B2
Villa Minozzo, Italy 28 D7
Villa Montes, Bolivia 126 A3
Villa Ocampo, Argentina 126 B4
Villa Ocampo, Mexico 118 B3
Villa Ojo de Agua, Argentina 126 B3
Villa San Giovanni, Italy 31 D8
Villa San José, Argentina 126 C4
Villa San Martín, Argentina 126 B3
Villa Santina, Italy 29 B9
Villa Unión, Mexico 118 C3
Villablino, Spain 34 C4
Villacarlos, Spain 37 B11
Villacarriedo, Spain 34 B7
Villacarrillo, Spain 35 G7
Villacastín, Spain 34 E6
Villach, Austria 26 E6
Villacidro, Italy 30 C1
Villada, Spain 34 C6
Villadiego, Spain 34 C6
Villadóssola, Italy 28 B5
Villafeliche, Spain 32 D3
Villafranca, Spain 32 C3
Villafranca de los Barros, Spain 35 G4
Villafranca de los Caballeros, Baleares, Spain 37 B10
Villafranca de los Caballeros, Toledo, Spain 35 F7
Villafranca del Cid = Vilafranca del Maestrat, Spain 32 E4
Villafranca del Panadés = Vilafranca del Penedès, Spain 32 D6
Villafranca di Verona, Italy 28 C7
Villafranca Tirrena, Italy 31 D8
Villagrán, Mexico 119 C5
Villaguay, Argentina 126 C4
Villaharta, Spain 35 G6
Villahermosa, Mexico 119 D6
Villahermosa, Spain 33 G2
Villaines-la-Juhel, France 18 D6
Villajoyosa, Spain 33 G4
Villalba, Spain 34 B3
Villalba de Guardo, Spain 34 C6
Villalón de Campos, Spain 34 C5
Villalpando, Spain 34 D5
Villaluenga, Spain 34 E7
Villamanán, Spain 34 C5
Villamartín, Spain 35 J5
Villamayor de Santiago, Spain 32 F2
Villamblard, France 20 C4
Villanova Monteleone, Italy 30 B1
Villanueva, U.S.A. 113 H2
Villanueva de Castellón = Vilanova de Castelló, Spain 33 F4
Villanueva de Córdoba, Spain 35 G6
Villanueva de la Fuente, Spain 33 G2
Villanueva de la Serena, Spain 35 G5
Villanueva de la Sierra, Spain 34 E4
Villanueva de los Castillejos, Spain 35 H3
Villanueva de los Infantes, Spain 35 G7
Villanueva del Arzobispo, Spain 33 G2
Villanueva del Fresno, Spain 35 G3
Villanueva y Geltrú = Vilanova i la Geltrú, Spain 32 D6
Villaputzu, Italy 30 C2
Villaquilambre, Spain 34 C5
Villar del Arzobispo, Spain 32 F4
Villar del Rey, Spain 35 F4
Villard-de-Lans, France 21 C9
Villarramiel, Spain 34 C6
Villarreal = Vila-real de los Infantes, Spain 32 F4
Villarrica, Chile 128 D2
Villarrica, Paraguay 126 B4
Villarrobledo, Spain 33 F2
Villarroya de la Sierra, Spain 32 D3
Villarrubia de los Ojos, Spain 35 F7
Villars-les-Dombes, France 19 F12
Villasayas, Spain 32 D2
Villaseca de los Gamitos = Villaseco de los Gamitos, Spain 34 D4
Villaseco de los Gamitos, Spain 34 D4
Villasimíus, Italy 30 C2
Villastar, Spain 32 E3
Villatobas, Spain 34 F7
Villavicencio, Argentina 126 C2
Villavicencio, Colombia 124 C4
Villaviciosa, Spain 34 B5
Villazón, Bolivia 126 A2
Ville-Marie, Canada 102 C4
Ville Platte, U.S.A. 113 K8
Villedieu-les-Poêles, France 18 D5
Villefort, France 20 D7
Villefranche-de-Lauragais, France 20 E5
Villefranche-de-Rouergue, France 20 D6
Villefranche-du-Périgord, France 20 D5
Villefranche-sur-Saône, France 21 C8
Villel, Spain 32 E3
Villemur-sur-Tarn, France 20 E5
Villena, Spain 33 G4
Villenauxe-la-Grande, France 19 D10
Villenave-d'Ornon, France 20 D3
Villeneuve-d'Ascq, France 19 B10
Villeneuve-l'Archevêque, France 19 D10
Villeneuve-lès-Avignon, France 21 E8
Villeneuve-sur-Allier, France 19 F10
Villeneuve-sur-Lot, France 20 D4
Villeneuve-sur-Yonne, France 19 D10
Villeréal, France 20 D4
Villers-Bocage, France 18 C6
Villers-Cotterêts, France 19 C10
Villers-sur-Mer, France 18 C6
Villersexel, France 19 E13
Villerupt, France 19 C12
Villeurbanne, France 21 C8
Villiers, S. Africa 89 D4
Villingen-Schwenningen, Germany 25 G4
Vilna, Canada 104 C6
Vilnius, Lithuania 9 J21
Vils, Austria 26 D3
Vils →, Bayern, Germany 25 G9
Vils →, Bayern, Germany 25 F7
Vilsbiburg, Germany 25 G8
Vilshofen, Germany 25 G9
Vilusi, Montenegro, Yug. 40 D2
Vilvoorde, Belgium 17 D4
Vilyuy →, Russia 51 C13
Vilyuysk, Russia 51 C13
Vimianzo, Spain 34 B1
Vimioso, Portugal 34 D4
Vimmerby, Sweden 11 G9
Vimoutiers, France 18 D7
Vimperk, Czech Rep. 26 B6
Viña del Mar, Chile 126 C1
Vinarós, Spain 32 E5
Vincennes, U.S.A. 108 F2
Vincent, U.S.A. 117 L8
Vinchina, Argentina 126 B2
Vindelälven →, Sweden 8 E18
Vindeln, Sweden 8 D18
Vinderup, Denmark 11 H2
Vindhya Ra., India 68 H7
Vineland, U.S.A. 108 F8
Vineuil, France 18
Vinga, Romania 42 D6
Vingåker, Sweden 10 E9
Vinh, Vietnam 64 C5
Vinh Linh, Vietnam 64 D6
Vinh Long, Vietnam 65 G5
Vinh Yen, Vietnam 58 G5
Vinhais, Portugal 34 D3
Vinica, Croatia 29 B13
Vinica, Macedonia 40 E6
Vinica, Slovenia 29 C12
Vinita, U.S.A. 113 G7
Vinkovci, Croatia 42 E3
Vinnitsa = Vinnytsya, Ukraine 47 H5
Vinnytsya, Ukraine 47 H5
Vinslöv, Sweden 11 H7
Vintjärn, Sweden 10 D10
Vinton, Calif., U.S.A. 116 F6
Vinton, Iowa, U.S.A. 112 D8
Vinton, La., U.S.A. 113 K8
Vinţu de Jos, Romania 43 D8
Viöl, Germany 24 A5
Vipava, Slovenia 29 C10
Vipiteno, Italy 29 B8
Vir, Croatia 29 D12
Virac, Phil. 61 E6
Virachei, Cambodia 64 F6
Virago Sd., Canada 104 C2
Viramgam, India 68 H5
Viranşehir, Turkey 70 B3
Virawah, Pakistan 68 G4
Virbalis, Lithuania 44 D9
Virden, Canada 105 D8
Vire, France 18 D6
Vire →, France 18 C5
Vírgenes, C., Argentina 128 G3
Virgin →, U.S.A. 115 H6
Virgin Gorda, Virgin Is. 121 C7
Virgin Is. (British) ■, W. Indies 121 C7
Virgin Is. (U.S.) ■, W. Indies 121 C7
Virginia, S. Africa 88 D4
Virginia, U.S.A. 112 B8
Virginia □, U.S.A. 108 G7
Virginia Beach, U.S.A. 108 G8
Virginia City, Mont., U.S.A. 114 D8
Virginia City, Nev., U.S.A. 116 F7
Virginia Falls, Canada 104 A3
Virginiatown, Canada 102 C4
Virje, Croatia 29 B13
Viroqua, U.S.A. 112 D9
Virovitica, Croatia 42 E2
Virpazar, Montenegro, Yug. 40 D3
Virpur, India 68 J4
Virserum, Sweden 11 G9
Virton, Belgium 17 E5
Virudunagar, India 66 Q10
Vis, Croatia 29 E13
Visalia, U.S.A. 116 J7
Visayan Sea, Phil. 61 F5
Visby, Sweden 11 G12
Viscount Melville Sd., Canada 4 B2
Visé, Belgium 17 D5
Višegrad, Bos.-H. 42 G4
Viseu, Brazil 125 D9
Viseu, Portugal 34 E3
Viseu □, Portugal 34 E3
Vişeu de Sus, Romania 43 C9
Vishakhapatnam, India 67 L13
Vişina, Romania 43 G9
Vişineşti, Moldova 43 D13
Visingsö, Sweden 11 F8
Viskafors, Sweden 11 G6
Viskan →, Sweden 11 G6
Viški Kanal, Croatia 29 E13
Vislanda, Sweden 11 H8
Visnagar, India 68 H5
Višnja Gora, Slovenia 29 C11
Viso, Mte., Italy 28 D4
Viso del Marqués, Spain 35 G7
Visoko, Bos.-H. 42 G3
Visokoi I., Antarctica 5 B1
Visp, Switz. 25 J3
Vissefjärda, Sweden 11 H9
Visselhövede, Germany 24 C5
Vissenbjerg, Denmark 11 J4
Vista, U.S.A. 117 M9
Vistonikos, Ormos = Vistonís, Límni, Greece 41 E9
Vistonís, Límni, Greece 41 E9
Vistula = Wisła →, Poland 44 D5
Vit →, Bulgaria 41 C8
Vitanje, Slovenia 29 B12
Vitebsk = Vitsyebsk, Belarus 46 E6
Viterbo, Italy 29 F9
Vitez, Bos.-H. 42 F2
Viti Levu, Fiji 91 C7
Vitigudino, Spain 34 D4
Vitim, Russia 51 D12
Vitim →, Russia 51 D12
Vitina, Bos.-H. 29 E14
Vitína, Greece 38 D4
Vítkov, Czech Rep. 27 B10
Vitória, Brazil 125 H10
Vitória da Conquista, Brazil 125 F10
Vitória de São Antão, Brazil 125 E11
Vitoria-Gasteiz, Spain 32 C2
Vitré, France 18 D5
Vitry-le-François, France 19 D11
Vitry-sur-Seine, France 19 D9
Vitsand, Sweden 10 D7
Vitsi, Óros, Greece 40 F5
Vitsyebsk, Belarus 46 E6
Vittaryd, Sweden 11 H7
Vitteaux, France 19 E11
Vittel, France 19 D12
Vittória, Italy 31 F7
Vittório Véneto, Italy 29 C9
Vittsjö, Sweden 11 H7
Viveiro, Spain 34 B3
Vivian, U.S.A. 113 J8
Viviers, France 21 D8
Vivonne, France 20 B4
Vizcaíno, Desierto de, Mexico 118 B2
Vizcaíno, Sierra, Mexico 118 B2
Vizcaya □, Spain 32 B2
Vize, Turkey 41 E11
Vizianagaram, India 67 K13
Vizille, France 21 C9
Viziñada, Croatia 29 C10
Viziru, Romania 43 E12
Vizzini, Italy 31 E7
Vjosa →, Albania 40 F3
Vlaardingen, Neths. 17 C4
Vlădeasa, Vf., Romania 42 D7
Vladičin Han, Serbia, Yug. 40 D6
Vladikavkaz, Russia 49 J7
Vladimir, Russia 46 D11
Vladimir Volynskiy = Volodymyr-Volynskyy, Ukraine 47 G3
Vladimirci, Serbia, Yug. 40 B3
Vladimirovac, Serbia, Yug. 42 E5
Vladimirovka, Russia 49 F8
Vladimirovo, Bulgaria 40 C7
Vladimorvka, Kazakstan 48 E10
Vladislavovka, Ukraine 47 K8
Vladivostok, Russia 51 E14
Vlăhiţa, Romania 43 D10
Vlakhiótis, Greece 38 E4
Vlasenica, Bos.-H. 42 F3
Vlašić, Bos.-H. 42 F2
Vlašim, Czech Rep. 26 B7
Vlasinsko Jezero, Serbia, Yug. 40 D6
Vlasotince, Serbia, Yug. 40 D6
Vlieland, Neths. 17 A4
Vlissingen, Neths. 17 C3
Vlóra, Albania 40 F3
Vlorës, Gjiri i, Albania 40 F3
Vltava →, Czech Rep. 26 A7
Vo Dat, Vietnam 65 G6
Vobarno, Italy 28 C7
Voćin, Croatia 42 E2
Vöcklabruck, Austria 26 C6
Vodice, Croatia 29 E12
Vodňany, Czech Rep. 26 B7
Vodnjan, Croatia 29 D10
Voe, U.K. 14 A7
Vogel Pk., Nigeria 83 D7
Vogelkop = Doberai, Jazirah, Indonesia 63 E8
Vogelsberg, Germany 24 E5
Voghera, Italy 28 D6
Vohibinany, Madag. 89 B8
Vohilava, Madag. 89 C8
Vohimarina = Iharana, Madag. 89 A9
Vohimena, Tanjon' i, Madag. 89 D8
Vohipeno, Madag. 89 C8
Voi, Kenya 86 C4
Void-Vacon, France 19 D12
Voineşti, Iaşi, Romania 43 C12
Voineşti, Prahova, Romania 43 E10
Voiotía □, Greece 38 C5
Voiron, France 21 C9
Voisey B., Canada 103 A7
Voitsberg, Austria 26 D8
Vojens, Denmark 11 J3
Vojmsjön, Sweden 8 D17
Vojnić, Croatia 29 C12
Vojnik, Italy 29 B12
Vojvodina □, Serbia, Yug. 42 E5
Vokhtoga, Russia 46 C11
Volary, Czech Rep. 26 C6
Volborg, U.S.A. 112 C2
Volcano Is. = Kazan-Rettō, Pac. Oc. 96 E6
Volchansk = Vovchansk, Ukraine 47 G9
Volchya →, Ukraine 47 H8
Volda, Norway 9 E12
Volga, Russia 46 C10
Volga →, Russia 49 G9
Volga Hts. = Privolzhskaya Vozvyshennost, Russia 48 E7
Volgo-Baltiyskiy Kanal, Russia 46 B9
Volgo-Donskoy Kanal, Russia 49 F7
Volgodonsk, Russia 49 G6
Volgograd, Russia 49 F7
Volgogradskoye Vdkhr., Russia 48 E8
Volgorechensk, Russia 48 B5
Volimai, Greece 38 D2
Volintiri, Moldova 43 D14
Volissós, Greece 39 C7
Volkach, Germany 25 F6
Völkermarkt, Austria 26 E7
Volkhov, Russia 46 C7
Volkhov →, Russia 46 B7
Völklingen, Germany 25 F2
Volkovysk = Vawkavysk, Belarus 47 F3
Volksrust, S. Africa 89 D4
Volnansk, Ukraine 47 H8
Volnovakha, Ukraine 47 J9
Volochanka, Russia 51 B10
Volodarsk, Russia 48 B6
Volodymyr-Volynskyy, Ukraine 47 G3
Vologda, Russia 46 C10
Volokolamsk, Russia 46 D8
Volokonovka, Russia 47 G9
Vólos, Greece 38 B4
Volosovo, Russia 46 C5
Volovets, Ukraine 47 H2
Volovo, Russia 46 F10
Volozhin = Valozhyn, Belarus 46 E4
Volsk, Russia 48 D8
Volta □, Ghana 83 D5
Volta →, Ghana 83 D5
Volta, L., Ghana 83 D5
Volta Blanche = White Volta →, Ghana 83 D4
Volta Redonda, Brazil 127 A7
Voltaire, C., Australia 92 B4
Volterra, Italy 28 E7
Voltri, Italy 28 D5
Volturno →, Italy 30 A6
Vólvi, L., Greece 40 F7
Volyně, Czech Rep. 26 B6
Volzhsk, Russia 48 C9
Volzhskiy, Russia 49 F7
Vondrozo, Madag. 89 C8
Vónitsa, Greece 38 C2
Vopnafjörður, Iceland 8 D6
Vorarlberg □, Austria 26 D2
Vóras Óros, Greece 40 F5
Vorbasse, Denmark 11 J3
Vorchdorf, Austria 26 C6
Vorderrhein →, Switz. 25 J5
Vordingborg, Denmark 11 J5
Vorë, Albania 40 E3
Voreppe, France 21 C9
Vóriai Sporádhes, Greece 38 B5
Vórios Aiyaíon □, Greece 39 C7
Vórios Evvoïkos Kólpos, Greece 38 C5
Vorkuta, Russia 50 C7
Vormsi, Estonia 9 G20
Vorona →, Russia 48 E6
Voronezh, Russia 47 G10
Voronezh, Ukraine 47 G7
Voronezh →, Russia 47 G10
Vorontsovo-Aleksandrovskoye = Zelenokumsk, Russia 49 H6
Voroshilovgrad = Luhansk, Ukraine 47 H10
Voroshilovsk = Alchevsk, Ukraine 47 H10
Vórroi, Greece 38 F6
Vorskla →, Ukraine 47 H8
Võrts Järv, Estonia 9 G22
Võru, Estonia 9 H22
Vosges, France 19 D14
Vosges □, France 19 D13
Voskopoja, Albania 40 F4
Voskresensk, Russia 46 E10
Voskresenskoye, Russia 48 B7
Voss, Norway 9 F12
Vostok I., Kiribati 97 J12
Votice, Czech Rep. 26 B7
Votsuri-Shima, Japan 55 M1
Vouga →, Portugal 34 E2
Vouillé, France 18 F7
Voúxa, Ákra, Greece 36 D5
Vouzela, Portugal 34 E2
Vouziers, France 19 C11
Vovchansk, Ukraine 47 G9
Vozhe, Ozero, Russia 46 B10
Vozhega, Russia 46 B11
Voznesensk, Ukraine 47 J6
Voznesenye, Russia 46 B8
Vrå, Denmark 11 G3
Vráble, Slovak Rep. 27 C11
Vraćevšnica, Serbia, Yug. 40 B4
Vrakhnéïka, Greece 38 C3
Vrancea □, Romania 43 E11
Vrancei, Munţii, Romania 43 E11
Vrangelya, Ostrov, Russia 51 B19
Vranica, Bos.-H. 42 G2
Vranje, Serbia, Yug. 40 D5
Vranjska Banja, Serbia, Yug. 40 D6
Vranov nad Topľou, Slovak Rep. 27 C14
Vransko, Slovenia 29 B11
Vransko Jezero, Croatia 29 E12
Vrapčište, Macedonia 40 E4
Vratsa, Bulgaria 40 C7
Vrbas, Serbia, Yug. 42 E4
Vrbas →, Bos.-H. 42 E2
Vrbnik, Croatia 29 C11
Vrbovec, Croatia 29 C13
Vrbovsko, Croatia 29 C12
Vrchlabí, Czech Rep. 26 A8
Vrede, S. Africa 89 D4
Vredefort, S. Africa 88 D4
Vreden, Germany 24 C2
Vredenburg, S. Africa 88 E2
Vredendal, S. Africa 88 E2
Vretstorp, Sweden 10 E8
Vrgorac, Croatia 29 E14
Vrhnika, Slovenia 29 C11
Vridi, Ivory C. 82 D4
Vrigstad, Sweden 11 G8
Vrindavan, India 68 F7
Vríses, Greece 36 D6
Vrnograč, Bos.-H. 29 C12
Vrondádhes, Greece 39 C8
Vrpolje, Croatia 42 E3
Vršac, Serbia, Yug. 42 E6
Vrsacki Kanal, Serbia, Yug. 42 E5
Vrútky, Slovak Rep. 27 B11
Vryburg, S. Africa 88 D3
Vryheid, S. Africa 89 D5
Vsetín, Czech Rep. 27 B11
Vu Liet, Vietnam 64 C5
Vŭcha →, Bulgaria 41 D8
Vučitrn, Kosovo, Yug. 40 D4
Vukovar, Croatia 42 E3
Vulcan, Canada 104 C6
Vulcan, Romania 43 E8
Vulcaneşti, Moldova 43 E13
Vulcano, Italy 31 D7
Vŭlchedruma, Bulgaria 40 C7
Vulkaneshty = Vulcaneşti, Moldova 43 E13
Vunduzi →, Mozam. 87 F3
Vung Tau, Vietnam 65 G6
Vŭrbitsa, Bulgaria 41 D10
Vurshets, Bulgaria 40 C7
Vutcani, Romania 43 D12
Vuya, Sudan 81 F2
Vyartsilya, Russia 46 A6
Vyatka = Kirov, Russia 50 D5
Vyatka →, Russia 48 C10
Vyatskiye Polyany, Russia 48 B10
Vyazemskiy, Russia 51 E14
Vyazma, Russia 46 E8
Vyazniki, Russia 48 B6
Vyborg, Russia 46 B5
Vychegda →, Russia 50 C5
Východné Beskydy, Europe 27 B15
Východočeský □, Czech Rep. 26 E8
Vyerkhnyadzvinsk, Belarus 46 E4
Vyksa, Russia 48 C6
Vylkove, Ukraine 47 K5
Vynohradiv, Ukraine 47 H2
Vyrnwy, L., U.K. 12 E4
Vyshniy Volochek, Russia 46 D8
Vyshzha = imeni 26 Bakinskikh Komissarov, Turkmenistan 71 B7
Vyškov, Czech Rep. 27 B9
Vysoké Mýto, Czech Rep. 27 B9
Vysokovsk, Russia 46 D9
Vyšší Brod, Czech Rep. 26 C7
Vytegra, Russia 46 B9

W

W.A.C. Bennett Dam, Canada 104 B4
Wa, Ghana 82 C4
Waal →, Neths. 17 C5
Waalwijk, Neths. 17 C5
Waat, Sudan 81 F3
Wabana, Canada 103 C9
Wabasca →, Canada 104 B5
Wabasca-Desmarais, Canada 104 B6

Wabash, *U.S.A.* 108 E3
Wabash →, *U.S.A.* 108 G1
Wabi →, *Ethiopia* 81 F5
Wabigoon L., *Canada* 105 D10
Wabowden, *Canada* 105 C9
Wąbrzeźno, *Poland* 45 E5
Wabu Hu, *China* 59 A11
Wabuk Pt., *Canada* 102 A2
Wabush, *Canada* 103 B6
Wąchock, *Poland* 45 G8
Wächtersbach, *Germany* 25 E5
Waco, *U.S.A.* 113 K6
Waconichi, L., *Canada* 102 B5
Wad Ban Naqa, *Sudan* 81 D3
Wad Banda, *Sudan* 81 E2
Wad el Haddad, *Sudan* 81 E3
Wad en Nau, *Sudan* 81 E3
Wad Hamid, *Sudan* 81 D3
Wad Medanî, *Sudan* 81 E3
Wad Thana, *Pakistan* 68 F2
Wadai, *Africa* 76 E5
Wadayama, *Japan* 55 G7
Waddeneilanden, *Neths.* 17 A5
Waddenzee, *Neths.* 17 A5
Waddington, *U.S.A.* 111 B9
Waddington, Mt., *Canada* 104 C3
Waddy Pt., *Australia* 95 C5
Wadebridge, *U.K.* 13 G3
Wadena, *Canada* 105 C8
Wadena, *U.S.A.* 112 B7
Wädenswil, *Switz.* 25 H4
Wadern, *Germany* 25 F2
Wadeye, *Australia* 92 B4
Wadhams, *Canada* 104 C3
Wādī as Sīr, *Jordan* 75 D4
Wadi Gemâl, *Egypt* 80 C4
Wadi Halfa, *Sudan* 80 C3
Wadian, *China* 59 A9
Wadlew, *Poland* 45 G6
Wadowice, *Poland* 45 J6
Wadsworth, *Nev., U.S.A.* 114 G4
Wadsworth, *Ohio, U.S.A.* 110 E3
Waegwan, *S. Korea* 57 G15
Wafangdian, *China* 57 E11
Wafrah, *Si. Arabia* 70 D5
Wageningen, *Neths.* 17 C5
Wager B., *Canada* 101 B11
Wagga Wagga, *Australia* 95 F4
Waghete, *Indonesia* 63 E9
Wagin, *Australia* 93 F2
Wagner, *U.S.A.* 112 D5
Wagon Mound, *U.S.A.* 113 G2
Wagoner, *U.S.A.* 113 H7
Wagrowiec, *Poland* 45 F4
Wah, *Pakistan* 68 C5
Wahai, *Indonesia* 63 E7
Wahiawa, *U.S.A.* 106 H15
Wâḥid, *Egypt* 75 E1
Wahnai, *Afghan.* 68 C1
Wahni, *Ethiopia* 81 E4
Wahoo, *U.S.A.* 112 E6
Wahpeton, *U.S.A.* 112 B6
Wai, Koh, *Cambodia* 65 H4
Waiau →, *N.Z.* 91 K4
Waibeem, *Indonesia* 63 E8
Waiblingen, *Germany* 25 G5
Waidhofen an der Thaya, *Austria* 26 C8
Waidhofen an der Ybbs, *Austria* 26 D7
Waigeo, *Indonesia* 63 E8
Waihi, *N.Z.* 91 G5
Waihou →, *N.Z.* 91 G5
Waika, *Dem. Rep. of the Congo* 86 C2
Waikabubak, *Indonesia* 63 F5
Waikari, *N.Z.* 91 K4
Waikato →, *N.Z.* 91 G5
Waikerie, *Australia* 95 E3
Waikokopu, *N.Z.* 91 H6
Waikouaiti, *N.Z.* 91 L3
Wailuku, *U.S.A.* 106 H16
Waimakariri →, *N.Z.* 91 K4
Waimate, *N.Z.* 91 L3
Wainganga →, *India* 66 K11
Waingapu, *Indonesia* 63 F6
Waini →, *Guyana* 124 B7
Wainwright, *Canada* 105 C6
Waiouru, *N.Z.* 91 H5
Waipara, *N.Z.* 91 K4
Waipawa, *N.Z.* 91 H6
Waipiro, *N.Z.* 91 H7
Waipu, *N.Z.* 91 F5
Waipukurau, *N.Z.* 91 J6
Wairakei, *N.Z.* 91 H6
Wairarapa, L., *N.Z.* 91 J5
Wairoa, *N.Z.* 91 H6
Waitaki →, *N.Z.* 91 L3
Waitara, *N.Z.* 91 H5
Waitsburg, *U.S.A.* 114 C5
Waiuku, *N.Z.* 91 G5
Wajima, *Japan* 55 F8
Wajir, *Kenya* 86 B5
Waka, *Ethiopia* 81 F4
Wakasa, *Japan* 55 G7
Wakasa-Wan, *Japan* 55 G7
Wakatipu, L., *N.Z.* 91 L2
Wakaw, *Canada* 105 C7
Wakayama, *Japan* 55 G7
Wakayama □, *Japan* 55 H7
Wake Forest, *U.S.A.* 109 H6
Wake I., *Pac. Oc.* 96 F8
WaKeeney, *U.S.A.* 112 F5
Wakefield, *N.Z.* 91 J4
Wakefield, *U.K.* 12 D6
Wakefield, *Mass., U.S.A.* 111 D13
Wakefield, *Mich., U.S.A.* 112 B10
Wakema, *Burma* 67 L19
Wakkanai, *Japan* 54 B10
Wakkerstroom, *S. Africa* 89 D5
Wakool, *Australia* 95 F3
Wakool →, *Australia* 95 F3
Wakre, *Indonesia* 63 E8
Wakuach, L., *Canada* 103 A6
Walamba, *Zambia* 87 E2
Wałbrzych, *Poland* 45 H3
Walbury Hill, *U.K.* 13 F6
Walcha, *Australia* 95 E5
Walcheren, *Neths.* 17 C3
Walcott, *U.S.A.* 114 F10
Wałcz, *Poland* 45 E3
Waldbröl, *Germany* 24 E3
Waldburg Ra., *Australia* 93 D2
Waldeck, *Germany* 24 D5
Walden, *Colo., U.S.A.* 114 F10
Walden, *N.Y., U.S.A.* 111 E10
Waldkirch, *Germany* 25 G3
Waldkirchen, *Germany* 25 G9
Waldkraiburg, *Germany* 25 G8
Waldport, *U.S.A.* 114 D1
Waldron, *U.S.A.* 113 H7
Waldviertel, *Austria* 26 C8
Walebing, *Australia* 93 F2
Walembele, *Ghana* 82 C4
Walensee, *Switz.* 25 H5
Wales □, *U.K.* 13 E3
Walewale, *Ghana* 83 C4
Walgett, *Australia* 95 E4
Walgreen Coast, *Antarctica* 5 D15
Walker, *U.S.A.* 112 B7
Walker, L., *Canada* 103 B6
Walker L., *Canada* 105 C9
Walker L., *U.S.A.* 114 G4
Walkerston, *Australia* 94 C4
Walkerton, *Canada* 102 D3
Wall, *U.S.A.* 112 D3
Walla Walla, *U.S.A.* 114 C4
Wallace, *Idaho, U.S.A.* 114 C6
Wallace, *N.C., U.S.A.* 109 H7
Wallaceburg, *Canada* 102 D3
Wallachia = Valahia, *Romania* 43 F9
Wallal, *Australia* 95 D4
Wallam Cr. →, *Australia* 95 D4
Wallambin, L., *Australia* 93 F2
Wallan, *Australia* 95 F3
Wallangarra, *Australia* 95 D5
Wallaroo, *Australia* 95 E2
Walldürn, *Germany* 25 F5
Wallenhorst, *Germany* 24 C4
Wallenpaupack, L., *U.S.A.* 111 E9
Wallingford, *U.S.A.* 111 E12
Wallis & Futuna, Is., *Pac. Oc.* 96 J10
Wallowa, *U.S.A.* 114 D5
Wallowa Mts., *U.S.A.* 114 D5
Walls, *U.K.* 14 A7
Wallula, *U.S.A.* 114 C4
Wallumbilla, *Australia* 95 D4
Walmsley, L., *Canada* 105 A7
Walney, I. of, *U.K.* 12 C4
Walnut Creek, *U.S.A.* 116 H4
Walnut Ridge, *U.S.A.* 113 G9
Walpole, *Australia* 93 F2
Walpole, *U.S.A.* 111 D13
Wals, *Austria* 26 D5
Walsall, *U.K.* 13 E6
Walsenburg, *U.S.A.* 113 G2
Walsh, *U.S.A.* 113 G3
Walsh →, *Australia* 94 B3
Walsrode, *Germany* 24 C5
Walterboro, *U.S.A.* 109 J5
Walters, *U.S.A.* 113 H5
Waltershausen, *Germany* 24 E6
Waltham, *U.S.A.* 111 D13
Waltman, *U.S.A.* 114 E10
Walton, *U.S.A.* 111 D9
Walton-on-the-Naze, *U.K.* 13 F9
Walvis Bay, *Namibia* 88 C1
Walvisbaai = Walvis Bay, *Namibia* 88 C1
Wamba, *Dem. Rep. of the Congo* 86 B2
Wamba, *Kenya* 86 B4
Wamba, *Nigeria* 83 D6
Wamego, *U.S.A.* 112 F6
Wamena, *Indonesia* 63 E9
Wamsutter, *U.S.A.* 114 F9
Wamulan, *Indonesia* 63 E7
Wan Xian, *China* 56 E8
Wana, *Pakistan* 68 C3
Wanaaring, *Australia* 95 D3
Wanaka, *N.Z.* 91 L2
Wanaka L., *N.Z.* 91 L2
Wan'an, *China* 59 D10
Wanapitei L., *Canada* 102 C3
Wandel Sea = McKinley Sea, *Arctic* 4 A7
Wandérama, *Ivory C.* 82 D4
Wanderer, *Zimbabwe* 87 F3
Wandhari, *Pakistan* 68 F2
Wanding, *China* 58 E2
Wandoan, *Australia* 95 D4
Wanfu, *China* 57 D12
Wang →, *Thailand* 64 D2
Wang Kai, *Sudan* 81 F2
Wang Noi, *Thailand* 64 E3
Wang Saphung, *Thailand* 64 D3
Wang Thong, *Thailand* 64 D3
Wanga, *Dem. Rep. of the Congo* 86 B2
Wangal, *Indonesia* 63 F8
Wanganella, *Australia* 95 F3
Wanganui, *N.Z.* 91 H5
Wangaratta, *Australia* 95 F4
Wangary, *Australia* 95 E2
Wangcang, *China* 58 A6
Wangcheng, *China* 59 C9
Wangdu, *China* 56 E8
Wangen, *Germany* 25 H5
Wangerooge, *Germany* 24 B3
Wangi, *Kenya* 86 C5
Wangiwangi, *Indonesia* 63 F6
Wangjiang, *China* 59 B11
Wangmo, *China* 58 E6
Wangolodougou, *Ivory C.* 82 D3
Wangqing, *China* 57 C15
Wankaner, *India* 68 H4
Wanless, *Canada* 105 C8
Wannian, *China* 59 C11
Wanning, *Taiwan* 64 C8
Wanon Niwat, *Thailand* 64 D4
Wanquan, *China* 56 D8
Wanrong, *China* 56 G6
Wanshan, *China* 58 D7
Wanshengchang, *China* 58 C6
Wantage, *U.K.* 13 F6
Wanyuan, *China* 58 A7
Wanzai, *China* 59 C10
Wapakoneta, *U.S.A.* 108 E3
Wapato, *U.S.A.* 114 C3
Wapawekka L., *Canada* 105 C8
Wapikopa L., *Canada* 102 B2
Wapiti →, *Canada* 104 B5
Wappingers Falls, *U.S.A.* 111 E11
Wapsipinicon →, *U.S.A.* 112 E9
Warab □, *Sudan* 81 F2
Warangal, *India* 66 L11
Waraseoni, *India* 69 J9
Waratah, *Australia* 94 G4
Waratah B., *Australia* 95 F4
Warburg, *Germany* 24 D5
Warburton, *Vic., Australia* 95 F4
Warburton, *W. Austral., Australia* 93 E4
Warburton Ra., *Australia* 93 E4
Ward, *N.Z.* 91 J5
Ward →, *Australia* 95 D4
Ward Mt., *U.S.A.* 116 H8
Warden, *S. Africa* 89 D4
Wardha, *India* 66 J11
Wardha →, *India* 66 K11
Ware, *Canada* 104 B3
Ware, *U.S.A.* 111 D12
Waregem, *Belgium* 17 D3
Wareham, *U.S.A.* 111 E14
Waremme, *Belgium* 17 D5
Waren, *Germany* 24 B8
Warendorf, *Germany* 24 D4
Warialda, *Australia* 95 D5
Wariap, *Indonesia* 63 E8
Warin Chamrap, *Thailand* 64 E5
Warka, *Poland* 45 G8
Warkopi, *Indonesia* 63 E8
Warm Springs, *U.S.A.* 115 G5
Warman, *Canada* 105 C7
Warmbad, *Namibia* 88 D2
Warmbad, *S. Africa* 89 C4
Warmińsko-Mazurskie □, *Poland* 44 D8
Warminster, *U.K.* 13 F5
Warminster, *U.S.A.* 111 F9
Warnemünde, *Germany* 24 A8
Warner Mts., *U.S.A.* 114 F3
Warner Robins, *U.S.A.* 109 J4
Warnow →, *Germany* 24 A8
Waroona, *Australia* 93 F2
Warracknabeal, *Australia* 95 F3
Warragul, *Australia* 95 F4
Warrego →, *Australia* 95 E4
Warrego Ra., *Australia* 94 C4
Warren, *Australia* 95 E4
Warren, *Ark., U.S.A.* 113 J8
Warren, *Mich., U.S.A.* 108 D4
Warren, *Minn., U.S.A.* 112 A6
Warren, *Ohio, U.S.A.* 110 E4
Warren, *Pa., U.S.A.* 110 E5
Warrenpoint, *U.K.* 15 B5
Warrensburg, *Mo., U.S.A.* 112 F8
Warrensburg, *N.Y., U.S.A.* 111 C11
Warrenton, *S. Africa* 88 D3
Warrenton, *U.S.A.* 116 D3
Warri, *Nigeria* 83 D6
Warrina, *Australia* 95 D2
Warrington, *U.K.* 12 D5
Warrington, *U.S.A.* 109 K2
Warrington □, *U.K.* 12 D5
Warrnambool, *Australia* 95 F3
Warroad, *U.S.A.* 112 A7
Warruwi, *Australia* 94 A1
Warsa, *Indonesia* 63 E9
Warsak Dam, *Pakistan* 68 B4
Warsaw = Warszawa, *Poland* 45 F8
Warsaw, *Ind., U.S.A.* 108 E3
Warsaw, *N.Y., U.S.A.* 110 D6
Warsaw, *Ohio, U.S.A.* 110 F3
Warstein, *Germany* 24 D4
Warszawa, *Poland* 45 F8
Warta, *Poland* 45 G5
Warta →, *Poland* 45 F1
Warthe = Warta →, *Poland* 45 F1
Waru, *Indonesia* 63 E8
Warwick, *Australia* 95 D5
Warwick, *U.K.* 13 E6
Warwick, *N.Y., U.S.A.* 111 E10
Warwick, *R.I., U.S.A.* 111 E13
Warwickshire □, *U.K.* 13 E6
Wasaga Beach, *Canada* 110 B4
Wasagaming, *Canada* 105 C9
Wasatch Ra., *U.S.A.* 114 F8
Wasbank, *S. Africa* 89 D5
Wasco, *Calif., U.S.A.* 117 K7
Wasco, *Oreg., U.S.A.* 114 D3
Wase, *Nigeria* 83 D6
Waseca, *U.S.A.* 112 C8
Wasekamio L., *Canada* 105 B7
Wash, The, *U.K.* 12 E8
Washago, *Canada* 110 B5
Washburn, *N. Dak., U.S.A.* 112 B4
Washburn, *Wis., U.S.A.* 112 B9
Washim, *India* 66 J10
Washington, *U.K.* 12 C6
Washington, *D.C., U.S.A.* 108 F7
Washington, *Ga., U.S.A.* 109 J4
Washington, *Ind., U.S.A.* 108 F2
Washington, *Iowa, U.S.A.* 112 E9
Washington, *Mo., U.S.A.* 112 F9
Washington, *N.C., U.S.A.* 109 H7
Washington, *N.J., U.S.A.* 111 F10
Washington, *Pa., U.S.A.* 110 F4
Washington, *Utah, U.S.A.* 115 H7
Washington □, *U.S.A.* 114 C3
Washington, Mt., *U.S.A.* 111 B13
Washington Court House, *U.S.A.* 108 F4
Washington I., *U.S.A.* 108 C2
Washougal, *U.S.A.* 116 E4
Wasian, *Indonesia* 63 E8
Wasilków, *Poland* 45 E10
Wasilla, *U.S.A.* 100 B5
Wasior, *Indonesia* 63 E8
Waskaganish, *Canada* 102 B4
Waskaiowaka, L., *Canada* 105 B9
Waskesiu Lake, *Canada* 105 C7
Wasserburg, *Germany* 25 G8
Wasserkuppe, *Germany* 24 E5
Wassy, *France* 19 D11
Waswanipi, *Canada* 102 C4
Waswanipi, L., *Canada* 102 C4
Watampone, *Indonesia* 63 E6
Water Park Pt., *Australia* 94 C5
Water Valley, *U.S.A.* 113 H10
Waterberge, *S. Africa* 89 C4
Waterbury, *Conn., U.S.A.* 111 E11
Waterbury, *Vt., U.S.A.* 111 B12
Waterbury L., *Canada* 105 B8
Waterdown, *Canada* 110 C5
Waterford, *Canada* 110 D4
Waterford, *Ireland* 15 D4
Waterford, *Calif., U.S.A.* 116 H6
Waterford, *Pa., U.S.A.* 110 E5
Waterford □, *Ireland* 15 D4
Waterford Harbour, *Ireland* 15 D5
Waterhen L., *Canada* 105 C9
Waterloo, *Belgium* 17 D4
Waterloo, *Ont., Canada* 102 D3
Waterloo, *Qué., Canada* 111 A12
Waterloo, *S. Leone* 82 D2
Waterloo, *Ill., U.S.A.* 112 F9
Waterloo, *Iowa, U.S.A.* 112 D8
Waterloo, *N.Y., U.S.A.* 110 D8
Watersmeet, *U.S.A.* 112 B10
Waterton Lakes Nat. Park, *U.S.A.* 114 B7
Watertown, *Conn., U.S.A.* 111 E11
Watertown, *N.Y., U.S.A.* 111 C9
Watertown, *S. Dak., U.S.A.* 112 C6
Watertown, *Wis., U.S.A.* 112 D10
Waterval-Boven, *S. Africa* 89 D5
Waterville, *Canada* 111 A13
Waterville, *Maine, U.S.A.* 109 C11
Waterville, *N.Y., U.S.A.* 111 D9
Waterville, *Pa., U.S.A.* 110 E7
Waterville, *Wash., U.S.A.* 114 C3
Watervliet, *U.S.A.* 111 D11
Wates, *Indonesia* 63 G14
Watford, *Canada* 110 D3
Watford, *U.K.* 13 F7
Watford City, *U.S.A.* 112 B3
Wathaman →, *Canada* 105 B8
Wathaman L., *Canada* 105 B8
Watheroo, *Australia* 93 F2
Wating, *China* 56 G4
Watkins Glen, *U.S.A.* 110 D8
Watling I. = San Salvador I., *Bahamas* 121 B5
Watonga, *U.S.A.* 113 H5
Watrous, *Canada* 105 C7
Watrous, *U.S.A.* 113 H2
Watsa, *Dem. Rep. of the Congo* 86 B2
Watseka, *U.S.A.* 108 E2
Watson, *Australia* 93 F5
Watson, *Canada* 105 C8
Watson Lake, *Canada* 104 A3
Watsontown, *U.S.A.* 110 E8
Watsonville, *U.S.A.* 116 J5
Wattiwarriganna Cr. →, *Australia* 95 D2
Wattwil, *Switz.* 25 H5
Watuata = Batuata, *Indonesia* 63 F6
Watubela, Kepulauan, *Indonesia* 63 E8
Watubela Is. = Watubela, Kepulauan, *Indonesia* 63 E8
Wau, *Sudan* 77 F6
Waubamik, *Canada* 110 A4
Waubay, *U.S.A.* 112 C6
Wauchope, *N.S.W., Australia* 95 E5
Wauchope, *N. Terr., Australia* 94 C1
Waukarlycarly, L., *Australia* 92 D3
Waukegan, *U.S.A.* 108 D2
Waukesha, *U.S.A.* 108 D1
Waukon, *U.S.A.* 112 D9
Waupaca, *U.S.A.* 112 C10
Waupun, *U.S.A.* 112 D10
Waurika, *U.S.A.* 113 H6
Wausau, *U.S.A.* 112 C10
Wautoma, *U.S.A.* 112 C10
Wauwatosa, *U.S.A.* 108 D2
Waveney →, *U.K.* 13 E9
Waverley, *N.Z.* 91 H5
Waverly, *Iowa, U.S.A.* 112 D8
Waverly, *N.Y., U.S.A.* 111 E8
Wavre, *Belgium* 17 D4
Wâw, *Sudan* 81 F2
Wāw al Kabīr, *Libya* 79 C9
Wawa, *Canada* 102 C3
Wawa, *Nigeria* 83 D5
Wawa, *Sudan* 80 C3
Wawanesa, *Canada* 105 D9
Wawona, *U.S.A.* 116 H7
Waxahachie, *U.S.A.* 113 J6
Way, L., *Australia* 93 E3
Waycross, *U.S.A.* 109 K4
Wayi, *Sudan* 81 F3
Wayland, *U.S.A.* 110 D7
Wayne, *Nebr., U.S.A.* 112 D6
Wayne, *W. Va., U.S.A.* 108 F4
Waynesboro, *Ga., U.S.A.* 109 J4
Waynesboro, *Miss., U.S.A.* 109 K1
Waynesboro, *Pa., U.S.A.* 108 F7
Waynesboro, *Va., U.S.A.* 108 F6
Waynesburg, *U.S.A.* 108 F5
Waynesville, *U.S.A.* 109 H4
Waynoka, *U.S.A.* 113 G5
Wazirabad, *Pakistan* 68 C6
Wda →, *Poland* 44 E5
We, *Indonesia* 62 C1
Weald, The, *U.K.* 13 F8
Wear →, *U.K.* 12 C6
Weatherford, *Okla., U.S.A.* 113 H5
Weatherford, *Tex., U.S.A.* 113 J6
Weaverville, *U.S.A.* 114 F2
Webb City, *U.S.A.* 113 G7
Webequie, *Canada* 102 B2
Webo = Nyaake, *Liberia* 82 E3
Webster, *Mass., U.S.A.* 111 D13
Webster, *N.Y., U.S.A.* 110 C7
Webster, *S. Dak., U.S.A.* 112 C6
Webster City, *U.S.A.* 112 D8
Webster Springs, *U.S.A.* 108 F5
Weda, *Indonesia* 63 D7
Weda, Teluk, *Indonesia* 63 D7
Weddell I., *Falk. Is.* 128 G4
Weddell Sea, *Antarctica* 5 D1
Wedderburn, *Australia* 95 F3
Wedel, *Germany* 24 B5
Wedemark, *Germany* 24 C5
Wedgeport, *Canada* 103 D6
Wedza, *Zimbabwe* 87 F3
Wee Waa, *Australia* 95 E4
Weed, *U.S.A.* 114 F2
Weed Heights, *U.S.A.* 116 G7
Weedsport, *U.S.A.* 111 C8
Weedville, *U.S.A.* 110 E6
Weenen, *S. Africa* 89 D5
Weener, *Germany* 24 B3
Weert, *Neths.* 17 C5
Węgierska-Górka, *Poland* 45 J6
Węgliniec, *Poland* 45 G2
Węgorzewo, *Poland* 44 D8
Węgorzyno, *Poland* 44 E2
Węgrów, *Poland* 45 F9
Wehda □, *Sudan* 81 F3
Wei He →, *Hebei, China* 56 F8
Wei He →, *Shaanxi, China* 56 G6
Weichang, *China* 57 D9
Weichuan, *China* 56 G7
Weida, *Germany* 24 E8
Weiden, *Germany* 25 F8
Weifang, *China* 57 F10
Weihai, *China* 57 F12
Weil, *Germany* 25 H3
Weilburg, *Germany* 24 E4
Weilheim, *Germany* 25 H7
Weimar, *Germany* 24 E7
Weinan, *China* 56 G5
Weingarten, *Germany* 25 F4
Weinheim, *Germany* 25 F4
Weining, *China* 58 D5
Weipa, *Australia* 94 A3
Weir →, *Australia* 95 D4
Weir →, *Canada* 105 B10
Weir River, *Canada* 105 B10
Weirton, *U.S.A.* 110 F4
Weiser, *U.S.A.* 114 D5
Weishan, *Shandong, China* 57 G9
Weishan, *Yunnan, China* 58 E3
Weissenburg, *Germany* 25 F6
Weissenfels, *Germany* 24 D7
Weisswasser, *Germany* 24 D10
Weitra, *Austria* 26 C7
Weixi, *China* 58 D2
Weixin, *China* 58 D5
Weiyuan, *China* 56 G3
Weiz, *Austria* 26 D8
Weizhou Dao, *China* 58 G7
Wejherowo, *Poland* 44 D5
Wekusko L., *Canada* 105 C9
Welch, *U.S.A.* 108 G5
Weldya, *Ethiopia* 81 E4
Welega □, *Ethiopia* 81 F3
Welkite, *Ethiopia* 81 F4
Welkom, *S. Africa* 88 D4
Welland, *Canada* 102 D4
Welland →, *U.K.* 13 E7
Wellesley Is., *Australia* 94 B2
Wellingborough, *U.K.* 13 E7
Wellington, *Australia* 95 E4
Wellington, *Canada* 110 C7
Wellington, *N.Z.* 91 J5
Wellington, *S. Africa* 88 E2
Wellington, *Somst., U.K.* 13 G4
Wellington, *Telford & Wrekin, U.K.* 13 E5
Wellington, *Colo., U.S.A.* 112 E2
Wellington, *Kans., U.S.A.* 113 G6
Wellington, *Nev., U.S.A.* 116 G7
Wellington, *Ohio, U.S.A.* 110 E2
Wellington, *Tex., U.S.A.* 113 H4
Wellington, I., *Chile* 122 H3
Wellington, L., *Australia* 95 F4
Wells, *U.K.* 13 F5
Wells, *Maine, U.S.A.* 111 C14
Wells, *N.Y., U.S.A.* 111 C10
Wells, *Nev., U.S.A.* 114 F6
Wells, L., *Australia* 93 E3
Wells, Mt., *Australia* 92 C4
Wells Gray Prov. Park, *Canada* 104 C4

Wells-next-the-Sea, *U.K.*	12 E8	West Mifflin, *U.S.A.*	110 F5	Wheeler, *Tex., U.S.A.*

Wells-next-the-Sea, *U.K.* 12 E8
Wells River, *U.S.A.* 111 B12
Wellsboro, *U.S.A.* 110 E7
Wellsburg, *U.S.A.* 110 F4
Wellsville, *N.Y., U.S.A.* 110 D7
Wellsville, *Ohio, U.S.A.* 110 F4
Wellsville, *Utah, U.S.A.* 114 F8
Wellton, *U.S.A.* 115 K6
Welmel, Wabi →, *Ethiopia* 81 F5
Welo □, *Ethiopia* 81 E4
Wels, *Austria* 26 C7
Welshpool, *U.K.* 13 E4
Welwyn Garden City, *U.K.* 13 F7
Wem, *U.K.* 12 E5
Wembere →, *Tanzania* 86 C3
Wemindji, *Canada* 102 B4
Wen Xian, *China* 56 G7
Wenatchee, *U.S.A.* 114 C3
Wenchang, *China* 64 C8
Wencheng, *China* 59 D13
Wenchi, *Ghana* 82 D4
Wenchow = Wenzhou, *China* 59 D13
Wenchuan, *China* 58 B4
Wenden, *U.S.A.* 117 M13
Wendeng, *China* 57 F12
Wendesi, *Indonesia* 63 E8
Wendo, *Ethiopia* 81 F4
Wendover, *U.S.A.* 114 F6
Weng'an, *China* 58 D6
Wengcheng, *China* 59 E9
Wengyuan, *China* 59 E10
Wenjiang, *China* 58 B4
Wenling, *China* 59 C13
Wenlock →, *Australia* 94 A3
Wenshan, *China* 58 F5
Wenshang, *China* 56 G9
Wenshui, *Guizhou, China* 58 C6
Wenshui, *Shanxi, China* 56 F7
Wensleydale, *U.K.* 12 C6
Wensu, *China* 60 B3
Wensum →, *U.K.* 12 E8
Wentworth, *Australia* 95 E3
Wentzel L., *Canada* 104 B6
Wenut, *Indonesia* 63 E8
Wenxi, *China* 56 G6
Wenxian, *China* 56 H3
Wenzhou, *China* 59 D13
Weott, *U.S.A.* 114 F2
Wepener, *S. Africa* 88 D4
Werda, *Botswana* 88 D3
Werdau, *Germany* 24 E8
Werder, *Germany* 24 C8
Werdohl, *Germany* 24 D3
Wereilu, *Ethiopia* 81 E4
Weri, *Indonesia* 63 E8
Werneck, *Germany* 25 F6
Wernigerode, *Germany* 24 D6
Werra →, *Germany* 24 D5
Werrimull, *Australia* 95 E3
Werris Creek, *Australia* 95 E5
Wertach →, *Germany* 25 G6
Wertheim, *Germany* 25 F5
Wertingen, *Germany* 25 G6
Wesel, *Germany* 24 D2
Weser →, *Germany* 24 B4
Weser-Ems □, *Germany* 24 C3
Weserbergland, *Germany* 24 C5
Wesiri, *Indonesia* 63 F7
Weslemkoon L., *Canada* 110 A7
Wesleyville, *Canada* 103 C9
Wesleyville, *U.S.A.* 110 D4
Wessel, C., *Australia* 94 A2
Wessel Is., *Australia* 94 A2
Wesselburen, *Germany* 24 A4
Wessington Springs, *U.S.A.* 112 C5
West, *U.S.A.* 113 K6
West →, *U.S.A.* 111 D12
West Baines →, *Australia* 92 C4
West Bank □, *Asia* 75 C4
West Bend, *U.S.A.* 108 D1
West Bengal □, *India* 69 H13
West Berkshire □, *U.K.* 13 F6
West Beskids = Západné Beskydy, *Europe* 27 B12
West Branch, *U.S.A.* 108 C3
West Branch Susquehanna →, *U.S.A.* 111 F8
West Bromwich, *U.K.* 13 E6
West Burra, *U.K.* 14 A7
West Canada Cr. →, *U.S.A.* 111 C10
West Cape Howe, *Australia* 93 G2
West Chazy, *U.S.A.* 111 B11
West Chester, *U.S.A.* 111 G9
West Columbia, *U.S.A.* 113 L7
West Covina, *U.S.A.* 117 L9
West Des Moines, *U.S.A.* 112 E8
West Dunbartonshire □, *U.K.* 14 F4
West End, *Bahamas* 120 A4
West Falkland, *Falk. Is.* 122 J4
West Fargo, *U.S.A.* 112 B6
West Farmington, *U.S.A.* 110 E4
West Fjord = Vestfjorden, *Norway* 8 C15
West Fork Trinity →, *U.S.A.* 113 J6
West Frankfort, *U.S.A.* 112 G10
West Hartford, *U.S.A.* 111 E12
West Haven, *U.S.A.* 111 E12
West Hazleton, *U.S.A.* 111 F9
West Helena, *U.S.A.* 113 H9
West Hurley, *U.S.A.* 111 E10
West Ice Shelf, *Antarctica* 5 C7
West Indies, *Cent. Amer.* 121 D7
West Jordan, *U.S.A.* 114 F8
West Lorne, *Canada* 110 D3
West Lothian □, *U.K.* 14 F5
West Lunga →, *Zambia* 87 E1
West Memphis, *U.S.A.* 113 H9
West Midlands □, *U.K.* 13 E6

West Mifflin, *U.S.A.* 110 F5
West Milton, *U.S.A.* 110 E8
West Monroe, *U.S.A.* 113 J8
West Newton, *U.S.A.* 110 F5
West Nicholson, *Zimbabwe* 87 G2
West Palm Beach, *U.S.A.* 109 M5
West Plains, *U.S.A.* 113 G9
West Point, *N.Y., U.S.A.* 111 E11
West Point, *Nebr., U.S.A.* 112 E6
West Point, *Va., U.S.A.* 108 G7
West Pt. = Ouest, Pte. de l', *Canada* 103 C7
West Pt., *Australia* 95 F2
West Road →, *Canada* 104 C4
West Rutland, *U.S.A.* 111 C11
West Schelde = Westerschelde →, *Neths.* 17 C3
West Seneca, *U.S.A.* 110 D6
West Siberian Plain, *Russia* 52 C11
West Sussex □, *U.K.* 13 G7
West-Terschelling, *Neths.* 17 A5
West Valley City, *U.S.A.* 114 F8
West Virginia □, *U.S.A.* 108 F5
West-Vlaanderen □, *Belgium* 17 D2
West Walker →, *U.S.A.* 116 G7
West Wyalong, *Australia* 95 E4
West Yellowstone, *U.S.A.* 114 D8
West Yorkshire □, *U.K.* 12 D6
Westall Pt., *Australia* 95 E1
Westbrook, *U.S.A.* 109 D10
Westbury, *Australia* 94 G4
Westby, *U.S.A.* 112 A2
Westend, *U.S.A.* 117 K9
Westerland, *Germany* 9 J13
Westerly, *U.S.A.* 111 E13
Western □, *Ghana* 82 D4
Western □, *Kenya* 86 B3
Western □, *S. Leone* 82 D2
Western □, *Uganda* 86 B3
Western □, *Zambia* 87 F1
Western Australia □, *Australia* 93 E2
Western Cape □, *S. Africa* 88 E3
Western Dvina = Daugava →, *Latvia* 9 H21
Western Ghats, *India* 66 N9
Western Isles □, *U.K.* 14 D1
Western Sahara ■, *Africa* 78 D3
Western Samoa ■, *Pac. Oc.* 91 B13
Westernport, *U.S.A.* 108 F6
Westerschelde →, *Neths.* 17 C3
Westerstede, *Germany* 24 B3
Westerwald, *Germany* 24 E3
Westfield, *Mass., U.S.A.* 111 D12
Westfield, *N.Y., U.S.A.* 110 D5
Westfield, *Pa., U.S.A.* 110 E7
Westhill, *U.K.* 14 D6
Westhope, *U.S.A.* 112 A4
Westland Bight, *N.Z.* 91 K3
Westlock, *Canada* 104 C6
Westmar, *Australia* 95 D4
Westmeath □, *Ireland* 15 C4
Westminster, *U.S.A.* 108 F7
Westmont, *U.S.A.* 110 F6
Westmorland, *U.S.A.* 117 M11
Weston, *Oreg., U.S.A.* 114 D4
Weston, *W. Va., U.S.A.* 108 F5
Weston I., *Canada* 102 B4
Weston-super-Mare, *U.K.* 13 F5
Westover, *U.S.A.* 110 F6
Westport, *Canada* 111 B8
Westport, *Ireland* 15 C2
Westport, *N.Z.* 91 J3
Westport, *N.Y., U.S.A.* 111 B11
Westport, *Oreg., U.S.A.* 116 D3
Westport, *Wash., U.S.A.* 116 D2
Westray, *Canada* 105 C8
Westray, *U.K.* 14 B5
Westree, *Canada* 102 C3
Westville, *U.S.A.* 116 F6
Westwood, *U.S.A.* 114 F3
Wetar, *Indonesia* 63 F7
Wetaskiwin, *Canada* 104 C6
Wete, *Tanzania* 84 F7
Wetherby, *U.K.* 12 D6
Wethersfield, *U.S.A.* 111 E12
Wetteren, *Belgium* 17 D3
Wetzlar, *Germany* 24 E4
Wewoka, *U.S.A.* 113 H6
Wexford, *Ireland* 15 D5
Wexford □, *Ireland* 15 D5
Wexford Harbour, *Ireland* 15 D5
Weyburn, *Canada* 105 D8
Weyer Markt, *Austria* 26 D7
Weyhe, *Germany* 24 C4
Weyib →, *Ethiopia* 81 F5
Weymouth, *Canada* 103 D6
Weymouth, *U.K.* 13 G5
Weymouth, *U.S.A.* 111 D14
Weymouth, C., *Australia* 94 A3
Wha Ti, *Canada* 100 B8
Whakatane, *N.Z.* 91 G6
Whale →, *Canada* 103 A6
Whale Cove, *Canada* 105 A10
Whales, B. of, *Antarctica* 5 D12
Whalsay, *U.K.* 14 A8
Whangamomona, *N.Z.* 91 H5
Whangarei, *N.Z.* 91 F5
Whangarei Harb., *N.Z.* 91 F5
Wharfe →, *U.K.* 12 D6
Wharfedale, *U.K.* 12 C5
Wharton, *N.J., U.S.A.* 111 F10
Wharton, *Pa., U.S.A.* 110 E6
Wharton, *Tex., U.S.A.* 113 L6
Wheatland, *Calif., U.S.A.* 116 F5
Wheatland, *Wyo., U.S.A.* 112 D2
Wheatley, *Canada* 110 D2
Wheaton, *Md., U.S.A.* 108 F7
Wheaton, *Minn., U.S.A.* 112 C6
Wheelbarrow Pk., *U.S.A.* 116 H10
Wheeler, *Oreg., U.S.A.* 114 D2

Wheeler, *Tex., U.S.A.* 113 H4
Wheeler →, *Canada* 103 A6
Wheeler L., *U.S.A.* 109 H2
Wheeler Pk., *N. Mex., U.S.A.* 115 H11
Wheeler Pk., *Nev., U.S.A.* 115 G6
Wheeler Ridge, *U.S.A.* 117 L8
Wheeling, *U.S.A.* 110 F4
Whernside, *U.K.* 12 C5
Whiskey Jack L., *Canada* 105 B8
Whistleduck Cr. →, *Australia* 94 C2
Whistler, *Canada* 104 C4
Whitby, *Canada* 110 C6
Whitby, *U.K.* 12 C7
White →, *Ark., U.S.A.* 113 J9
White →, *Ind., U.S.A.* 108 F2
White →, *S. Dak., U.S.A.* 112 D5
White →, *Tex., U.S.A.* 113 J4
White →, *Utah, U.S.A.* 114 F9
White →, *Vt., U.S.A.* 111 C12
White →, *Wash., U.S.A.* 116 C4
White, L., *Australia* 92 D4
White B., *Canada* 103 C8
White Bird, *U.S.A.* 114 D5
White Butte, *U.S.A.* 112 B3
White City, *U.S.A.* 112 E2
White Cliffs, *Australia* 95 E3
White Hall, *U.S.A.* 112 F9
White Haven, *U.S.A.* 111 E9
White Horse, Vale of, *U.K.* 13 F6
White I., *N.Z.* 91 G6
White L., *Canada* 111 A8
White L., *U.S.A.* 113 L8
White Mountain Peak, *U.S.A.* 115 G4
White Mts., *Calif., U.S.A.* 116 H8
White Mts., *N.H., U.S.A.* 111 B13
White Nile = Nîl el Abyad →, *Sudan* 81 D3
White Nile Dam = Khazzân Jabal al Awliyâ, *Sudan* 81 D3
White Otter L., *Canada* 102 C1
White Pass, *U.S.A.* 116 D5
White Plains, *U.S.A.* 111 E11
White River, *Canada* 102 C2
White River, *S. Africa* 89 D5
White River, *U.S.A.* 112 D4
White Rock, *Canada* 116 A4
White Russia = Belarus ■, *Europe* 46 F4
White Sea = Beloye More, *Russia* 50 C4
White Sulphur Springs, *Mont., U.S.A.* 114 C8
White Sulphur Springs, *W. Va., U.S.A.* 108 G5
White Swan, *U.S.A.* 116 D6
White Volta →, *Ghana* 83 D4
Whitecliffs, *N.Z.* 91 K3
Whitecourt, *Canada* 104 C5
Whiteface Mt., *U.S.A.* 111 B11
Whitefield, *U.S.A.* 111 B13
Whitefish, *U.S.A.* 114 B6
Whitefish L., *Canada* 105 A7
Whitefish Point, *U.S.A.* 108 B3
Whitegull, L., *Canada* 103 A7
Whitehall, *Mich., U.S.A.* 108 D2
Whitehall, *Mont., U.S.A.* 114 D7
Whitehall, *N.Y., U.S.A.* 111 C11
Whitehall, *Wis., U.S.A.* 112 C9
Whitehaven, *U.K.* 12 C4
Whitehorse, *Canada* 104 A1
Whitemark, *Australia* 94 G4
Whiteplains, *Liberia* 82 D2
Whiteriver, *U.S.A.* 115 K9
Whitesand →, *Canada* 104 A5
Whitesands, *S. Africa* 88 E3
Whitesboro, *N.Y., U.S.A.* 111 C9
Whitesboro, *Tex., U.S.A.* 113 J6
Whiteshell Prov. Park, *Canada* 105 D9
Whitesville, *U.S.A.* 110 D7
Whiteville, *U.S.A.* 109 H6
Whitewater, *U.S.A.* 108 D1
Whitewater Baldy, *U.S.A.* 115 K9
Whitewater L., *Canada* 102 B2
Whitewood, *Australia* 94 C3
Whitewood, *Canada* 105 C8
Whithorn, *U.K.* 14 G4
Whitianga, *N.Z.* 91 G5
Whitman, *U.S.A.* 111 D14
Whitney, *Canada* 102 C4
Whitney, Mt., *U.S.A.* 116 J8
Whitney Point, *U.S.A.* 111 D9
Whitstable, *U.K.* 13 F9
Whitsunday I., *Australia* 94 C4
Whittier, *U.S.A.* 117 M8
Whittlesea, *Australia* 95 F4
Wholdaia L., *Canada* 105 A8
Whyalla, *Australia* 95 E2
Wiarton, *Canada* 102 D3
Wiawso, *Ghana* 82 D4
Wiay, *U.K.* 14 D1
Wiązów, *Poland* 45 H4
Wibaux, *U.S.A.* 112 B2
Wichian Buri, *Thailand* 64 E3
Wichita, *U.S.A.* 113 G6
Wichita Falls, *U.S.A.* 113 J5
Wick, *U.K.* 14 C5
Wicked Pt., *Canada* 110 C7
Wickenburg, *U.S.A.* 115 K7
Wickepin, *Australia* 93 F2
Wickham, *Australia* 92 D2
Wickham, C., *Australia* 94 F3
Wickliffe, *U.S.A.* 110 E3
Wicklow, *Ireland* 15 D5
Wicklow □, *Ireland* 15 D5
Wicklow Hd., *Ireland* 15 D6
Wicklow Mts., *Ireland* 15 C5
Widawa →, *Poland* 45 G5

Widawka →, *Poland* 45 G5
Widgeegoara Cr. →, *Australia* 95 D4
Widgiemooltha, *Australia* 93 F3
Widnes, *U.K.* 12 D5
Wiehl, *Germany* 24 E3
Wiek, *Germany* 24 A9
Wielbark, *Poland* 44 E7
Wieleń, *Poland* 45 F3
Wielichowo, *Poland* 45 F3
Wieliczka, *Poland* 45 J7
Wielkopolskie □, *Poland* 45 F4
Wieluń, *Poland* 45 G5
Wien, *Austria* 27 C9
Wiener Neustadt, *Austria* 27 D9
Wieprz →, *Poland* 45 G8
Wieprza →, *Poland* 44 D3
Wieruszów, *Poland* 45 G5
Wiesbaden, *Germany* 25 E4
Wiesental, *Germany* 25 F4
Wiesloch, *Germany* 25 F4
Wiesmoor, *Germany* 24 B3
Wieżyca, *Poland* 44 D5
Wigan, *U.K.* 12 D5
Wiggins, *Colo., U.S.A.* 112 E2
Wiggins, *Miss., U.S.A.* 113 K10
Wight, I. of □, *U.K.* 13 G6
Wigry, Jezioro, *Poland* 44 D10
Wigston, *U.K.* 13 E6
Wigton, *U.K.* 12 C4
Wigtown, *U.K.* 14 G4
Wigtown B., *U.K.* 14 G4
Wil, *Switz.* 25 H5
Wilamowice, *Poland* 45 J6
Wilber, *U.S.A.* 112 E6
Wilberforce, *Canada* 110 A6
Wilberforce, C., *Australia* 94 A2
Wilburton, *U.S.A.* 113 H7
Wilcannia, *Australia* 95 E3
Wilcox, *U.S.A.* 110 E6
Wildbad, *Germany* 25 G4
Wildeshausen, *Germany* 24 C4
Wildon, *Austria* 26 E8
Wildrose, *U.S.A.* 117 J9
Wildspitze, *Austria* 26 E3
Wilga →, *Poland* 45 G8
Wilge →, *S. Africa* 89 D4
Wilhelm II Coast, *Antarctica* 5 C7
Wilhelmsburg, *Austria* 26 C8
Wilhelmshaven, *Germany* 24 B4
Wilhelmstal, *Namibia* 88 C2
Wilkes-Barre, *U.S.A.* 111 E9
Wilkie, *Canada* 105 C7
Wilkinsburg, *U.S.A.* 110 F5
Wilkinson Lakes, *Australia* 93 E5
Willandra Creek →, *Australia* 95 E4
Willapa B., *U.S.A.* 114 C2
Willapa Hills, *U.S.A.* 116 D3
Willard, *N.Y., U.S.A.* 110 D8
Willard, *Ohio, U.S.A.* 110 E2
Willcox, *U.S.A.* 115 K9
Willemstad, *Neth. Ant.* 121 D6
Willet, *U.S.A.* 111 D9
William →, *Canada* 105 B7
William 'Bill' Dannelly Res., *U.S.A.* 109 J2
William Creek, *Australia* 95 D2
Williams, *Australia* 93 F2
Williams, *Ariz., U.S.A.* 115 J7
Williams, *Calif., U.S.A.* 116 F4
Williams Harbour, *Canada* 103 B8
Williams Lake, *Canada* 104 C4
Williamsburg, *Ky., U.S.A.* 109 G3
Williamsburg, *Pa., U.S.A.* 110 F6
Williamsburg, *Va., U.S.A.* 108 G7
Williamson, *N.Y., U.S.A.* 110 C7
Williamson, *W. Va., U.S.A.* 108 G4
Williamsport, *U.S.A.* 110 E7
Williamston, *U.S.A.* 109 H7
Williamstown, *Australia* 95 F3
Williamstown, *Ky., U.S.A.* 108 F3
Williamstown, *Mass., U.S.A.* 111 D11
Williamstown, *N.Y., U.S.A.* 111 C9
Willimantic, *U.S.A.* 111 E12
Willingboro, *U.S.A.* 108 E8
Willis Group, *Australia* 94 B5
Williston, *S. Africa* 88 E3
Williston, *Fla., U.S.A.* 109 L4
Williston, *N. Dak., U.S.A.* 112 A3
Williston L., *Canada* 104 B4
Willits, *U.S.A.* 114 G2
Willmar, *U.S.A.* 112 C7
Willoughby, *U.S.A.* 110 E3
Willow Bunch, *Canada* 105 D7
Willow Wall, The, *China* 57 C12
Willowick, *U.S.A.* 110 E3
Willowlake →, *Canada* 104 A4
Willowmore, *S. Africa* 88 E3
Willows, *U.S.A.* 116 F4
Willowvale = Gatyana, *S. Africa* 89 E4
Wills, L., *Australia* 92 D4
Wills Cr. →, *Australia* 94 C3
Willsboro, *U.S.A.* 111 B11
Willunga, *Australia* 95 F2
Wilmette, *U.S.A.* 108 D2
Wilmington, *Australia* 95 E2
Wilmington, *Del., U.S.A.* 108 F8
Wilmington, *N.C., U.S.A.* 109 H7
Wilmington, *Ohio, U.S.A.* 108 F4
Wilmington, *Vt., U.S.A.* 111 D12
Wilmslow, *U.K.* 12 D5
Wilpena →, *Australia* 95 E2
Wilsall, *U.S.A.* 114 D8
Wilson, *N.C., U.S.A.* 109 H7
Wilson, *N.Y., U.S.A.* 110 C6
Wilson, *Pa., U.S.A.* 111 F9
Wilson →, *Australia* 92 C4

Wilson Bluff, *Australia* 93 F4
Wilson Inlet, *Australia* 93 G2
Wilsons Promontory, *Australia* 95 F4
Wilster, *Germany* 24 B5
Wilton, *U.S.A.* 112 B4
Wilton →, *Australia* 94 A1
Wiltshire □, *U.K.* 13 F6
Wiltz, *Lux.* 17 E5
Wiluna, *Australia* 93 E3
Wimborne Minster, *U.K.* 13 G6
Wimereux, *France* 19 B8
Wimmera →, *Australia* 95 F3
Winam G., *Kenya* 86 C3
Winburg, *S. Africa* 88 D4
Winchendon, *U.S.A.* 111 D12
Winchester, *U.K.* 13 F6
Winchester, *Conn., U.S.A.* 111 E11
Winchester, *Idaho, U.S.A.* 114 C5
Winchester, *Ind., U.S.A.* 108 E3
Winchester, *Ky., U.S.A.* 108 G3
Winchester, *N.H., U.S.A.* 111 D12
Winchester, *Nev., U.S.A.* 117 J11
Winchester, *Tenn., U.S.A.* 109 H2
Winchester, *Va., U.S.A.* 108 F6
Wind →, *U.S.A.* 114 E9
Wind River Range, *U.S.A.* 114 E9
Windau = Ventspils, *Latvia* 9 H19
Windber, *U.S.A.* 110 F6
Winder, *U.S.A.* 109 J4
Windermere, *U.K.* 12 C5
Windhoek, *Namibia* 88 C2
Windischgarsten, *Austria* 26 D7
Windom, *U.S.A.* 112 D7
Windorah, *Australia* 94 D3
Window Rock, *U.S.A.* 115 J9
Windrush →, *U.K.* 13 F6
Windsor, *Australia* 95 E5
Windsor, *N.S., Canada* 103 D7
Windsor, *Ont., Canada* 102 D3
Windsor, *U.K.* 13 F7
Windsor, *Colo., U.S.A.* 112 E2
Windsor, *Conn., U.S.A.* 111 E12
Windsor, *Mo., U.S.A.* 112 F7
Windsor, *N.Y., U.S.A.* 111 D9
Windsor, *Vt., U.S.A.* 111 C12
Windsor & Maidenhead □, *U.K.* 13 F7
Windsorton, *S. Africa* 88 D3
Windward Is., *W. Indies* 121 D7
Windward Passage = Vientos, Paso de los, *Caribbean* 121 C5
Winefred L., *Canada* 105 B6
Winejok, *Sudan* 81 F2
Winfield, *U.S.A.* 113 G6
Wingate Mts., *Australia* 92 B5
Wingham, *Australia* 95 E5
Wingham, *Canada* 102 D3
Winisk, *Canada* 102 A2
Winisk →, *Canada* 102 A2
Winisk L., *Canada* 102 B2
Wink, *U.S.A.* 113 K3
Winkler, *Canada* 105 D9
Winklern, *Austria* 26 E5
Winlock, *U.S.A.* 116 D4
Winneba, *Ghana* 83 D4
Winnebago, L., *U.S.A.* 108 D1
Winnecke Cr. →, *Australia* 92 C5
Winnemucca, *U.S.A.* 114 F5
Winnemucca L., *U.S.A.* 114 F4
Winnett, *U.S.A.* 114 C9
Winnfield, *U.S.A.* 113 K8
Winnibigoshish, L., *U.S.A.* 112 B7
Winnipeg, *Canada* 105 D9
Winnipeg →, *Canada* 105 C9
Winnipeg, L., *Canada* 105 C9
Winnipeg Beach, *Canada* 105 C9
Winnipegosis, *Canada* 105 C9
Winnipegosis L., *Canada* 105 C9
Winnipesaukee, L., *U.S.A.* 111 C13
Winnisquam L., *U.S.A.* 111 C13
Winnsboro, *La., U.S.A.* 113 J9
Winnsboro, *S.C., U.S.A.* 109 H5
Winnsboro, *Tex., U.S.A.* 113 J7
Winokapau, L., *Canada* 103 B7
Winona, *Minn., U.S.A.* 112 C9
Winona, *Miss., U.S.A.* 113 J10
Winooski, *U.S.A.* 111 B11
Winooski →, *U.S.A.* 111 B11
Winschoten, *Neths.* 17 A7
Winsen, *Germany* 24 B6
Winsford, *U.K.* 12 D5
Winslow, *Ariz., U.S.A.* 115 J8
Winslow, *Wash., U.S.A.* 116 C4
Winsted, *U.S.A.* 111 E11
Winston-Salem, *U.S.A.* 109 G5
Winter Garden, *U.S.A.* 109 L5
Winter Haven, *U.S.A.* 109 M5
Winter Park, *U.S.A.* 109 L5
Winterberg, *Germany* 24 D4
Winterhaven, *U.S.A.* 117 N12
Winters, *U.S.A.* 116 G5
Wintersville, *U.S.A.* 110 F4
Winterswijk, *Neths.* 17 C6
Winterthur, *Switz.* 25 H4
Winthrop, *U.S.A.* 114 B3
Winton, *Australia* 94 C3
Winton, *N.Z.* 91 M2
Wipper →, *Germany* 24 D7
Wirrulla, *Australia* 95 E1
Wisbech, *U.K.* 13 E8
Wisconsin □, *U.S.A.* 112 C10
Wisconsin →, *U.S.A.* 112 D9
Wisconsin Rapids, *U.S.A.* 112 C10
Wisdom, *U.S.A.* 114 D7
Wishaw, *U.K.* 14 F5
Wishek, *U.S.A.* 112 B5
Wisła, *Poland* 45 J5
Wisła →, *Poland* 44 D5
Wisłok →, *Poland* 45 H9

Wisłoka →, *Poland* 45 H8
Wismar, *Germany* 24 B7
Wisner, *U.S.A.* 112 E6
Wissant, *France* 19 B8
Wissembourg, *France* 19 C14
Wisznice, *Poland* 45 G10
Witbank, *S. Africa* 89 D4
Witdraai, *S. Africa* 88 D3
Witham, *U.K.* 13 F8
Witham →, *U.K.* 12 E7
Withernsea, *U.K.* 12 D8
Witkowo, *Poland* 45 F4
Witney, *U.K.* 13 F6
Witnica, *Poland* 45 F1
Witnossob →, *Namibia* 88 D3
Wittdün, *Germany* 24 A4
Witten, *Germany* 24 D3
Wittenberge, *Germany* 24 B7
Wittenburg, *Germany* 24 B7
Wittenheim, *France* 19 E14
Wittenoom, *Australia* 92 D2
Wittingen, *Germany* 24 C6
Wittlich, *Germany* 25 F2
Wittmund, *Germany* 24 B3
Wittow, *Germany* 24 A9
Wittstock, *Germany* 24 B8
Witvlei, *Namibia* 88 C2
Witzenhausen, *Germany* 24 D5
Wkra →, *Poland* 45 F7
Władysławowo, *Poland* 44 D5
Wleń, *Poland* 45 G2
Wlingi, *Indonesia* 63 H15
Włocławek, *Poland* 45 F6
Włodawa, *Poland* 45 G10
Włoszczowa, *Poland* 45 H6
Woburn, *U.S.A.* 111 D13
Wodian, *China* 56 H7
Wodzisław Śląski, *Poland* 45 H5
Wœrth, *France* 19 D14
Woinbogoin, *China* 58 A2
Woippy, *France* 19 C13
Wojcieszów, *Poland* 45 H2
Wokam, *Indonesia* 63 F8
Woking, *U.K.* 13 F7
Wokingham □, *U.K.* 13 F7
Wolbrom, *Poland* 45 H6
Wołczyn, *Poland* 45 G5
Woldegk, *Germany* 24 B9
Wolf →, *Canada* 104 A2
Wolf Creek, *U.S.A.* 114 C7
Wolf L., *Canada* 104 A2
Wolf Point, *U.S.A.* 112 A2
Wolfe I., *Canada* 102 D4
Wolfeboro, *U.S.A.* 111 C13
Wolfen, *Germany* 24 D8
Wolfenbüttel, *Germany* 24 C6
Wolfratshausen, *Germany* 25 H7
Wolfsberg, *Austria* 26 E7
Wolfsburg, *Germany* 24 C6
Wolgast, *Germany* 24 A9
Wolhusen, *Switz.* 25 H4
Wolin, *Poland* 44 E1
Wollaston, Is., *Chile* 128 H3
Wollaston L., *Canada* 105 B8
Wollaston Lake, *Canada* 105 B8
Wollaston Pen., *Canada* 100 B8
Wollongong, *Australia* 95 E5
Wolmaransstad, *S. Africa* 88 D4
Wolmirstedt, *Germany* 24 C7
Wołomin, *Poland* 45 F8
Wołów, *Poland* 45 G3
Wolseley, *S. Africa* 88 E2
Wolsey, *U.S.A.* 112 C5
Wolstenholme, C., *Canada* 98 C12
Wolsztyn, *Poland* 45 F3
Wolvega, *Neths.* 17 B6
Wolverhampton, *U.K.* 13 E5
Wondai, *Australia* 95 D5
Wongalarroo L., *Australia* 95 E3
Wongan Hills, *Australia* 93 F2
Wŏnju, *S. Korea* 57 F14
Wonosari, *Indonesia* 63 G14
Wonosobo, *Indonesia* 63 G13
Wonowon, *Canada* 104 B4
Wŏnsan, *N. Korea* 57 E14
Wonthaggi, *Australia* 95 F4
Wood Buffalo Nat. Park, *Canada* 104 B6
Wood Is., *Australia* 92 C3
Wood L., *Canada* 105 B8
Woodah I., *Australia* 94 A2
Woodbourne, *U.S.A.* 111 E10
Woodbridge, *Canada* 110 C5
Woodbridge, *U.K.* 13 E9
Woodburn, *U.S.A.* 114 D2
Woodenbong, *Australia* 95 D5
Woodend, *Australia* 95 F3
Woodford, *Australia* 95 D5
Woodfords, *U.S.A.* 116 G7
Woodlake, *U.S.A.* 116 J7
Woodland, *Calif., U.S.A.* 116 G5
Woodland, *Maine, U.S.A.* 109 C12
Woodland, *Pa., U.S.A.* 110 F6
Woodland, *Wash., U.S.A.* 116 E4
Woodland Caribou Prov. Park, *Canada* 105 C10
Woodridge, *Canada* 105 D9
Woodroffe, Mt., *Australia* 93 E5
Woods, L., *Australia* 94 B1
Woods, L. of the, *Canada* 105 D10
Woodside, *Australia* 95 F4
Woodstock, *Australia* 94 B4
Woodstock, *N.B., Canada* 103 C6
Woodstock, *Ont., Canada* 102 D3
Woodstock, *U.K.* 13 F6
Woodstock, *Ill., U.S.A.* 112 D10
Woodstock, *Vt., U.S.A.* 111 C12
Woodsville, *U.S.A.* 111 B13
Woodville, *N.Z.* 91 J5
Woodville, *Miss., U.S.A.* 113 K9
Woodville, *Tex., U.S.A.* 113 K7
Woodward, *U.S.A.* 113 G5
Woody, *U.S.A.* 117 K8
Woody →, *Canada* 105 C8
Woolamai, C., *Australia* 95 F4
Wooler, *U.K.* 12 B5
Woolgoolga, *Australia* 95 E5
Woomera, *Australia* 95 E2
Woonsocket, *R.I., U.S.A.* 111 E13
Woonsocket, *S. Dak., U.S.A.* 112 C5
Wooramel →, *Australia* 93 E1
Wooramel Roadhouse, *Australia* 93 E1
Wooster, *U.S.A.* 110 F3
Worcester, *S. Africa* 88 E2
Worcester, *U.K.* 13 E5
Worcester, *Mass., U.S.A.* 111 D13
Worcester, *N.Y., U.S.A.* 111 D10
Worcestershire □, *U.K.* 13 E5
Wörgl, *Austria* 26 D5
Workington, *U.K.* 12 C4
Worksop, *U.K.* 12 D6
Workum, *Neths.* 17 B5
Worland, *U.S.A.* 114 D10
Wormhout, *France* 19 B9
Worms, *Germany* 25 F4
Worsley, *Canada* 104 B5
Wörth, *Germany* 25 F8
Wortham, *U.S.A.* 113 K6
Wörther See, *Austria* 26 E7
Worthing, *U.K.* 13 G7
Worthington, *Minn., U.S.A.* 112 D7
Worthington, *Pa., U.S.A.* 110 F5
Wosi, *Indonesia* 63 E7
Wou-han = Wuhan, *China* 59 B10
Wousi = Wuxi, *China* 59 B13
Wowoni, *Indonesia* 63 E6
Wrangel I. = Vrangelya, Ostrov, *Russia* 51 B19
Wrangell, *U.S.A.* 104 B2
Wrangell Mts., *U.S.A.* 100 B5
Wrath, C., *U.K.* 14 C3
Wray, *U.S.A.* 112 E3
Wrekin, The, *U.K.* 13 E5
Wrens, *U.S.A.* 109 J4
Wrexham, *U.K.* 12 D4
Wrexham □, *U.K.* 12 D5
Wriezen, *Germany* 24 C10
Wright = Paranas, *Phil.* 61 F6
Wright, *U.S.A.* 112 D2
Wright Pt., *Canada* 110 C3
Wrightson Mt., *U.S.A.* 115 L8
Wrightwood, *U.S.A.* 117 L9
Wrigley, *Canada* 100 B7
Wrocław, *Poland* 45 G4
Wronki, *Poland* 45 F3
Września, *Poland* 45 F4
Wschowa, *Poland* 45 G3
Wu Jiang →, *China* 58 C6
Wu'an, *China* 56 F8
Wubin, *Australia* 93 F2
Wubu, *China* 56 F6
Wuchang, *China* 57 B14
Wucheng, *China* 56 F9
Wuchuan, *Guangdong, China* 59 G8
Wuchuan, *Guizhou, China* 58 C7
Wuchuan, *Nei Mongol Zizhiqu, China* 56 D6
Wudi, *China* 57 F9
Wuding, *China* 58 E4
Wuding He →, *China* 56 F6
Wudinna, *Australia* 95 E2
Wudu, *China* 56 H3
Wufeng, *China* 59 B8
Wugang, *China* 59 D8
Wugong Shan, *China* 59 D9
Wuhan, *China* 59 B10
Wuhe, *China* 57 H9
Wuhsi = Wuxi, *China* 59 B13
Wuhu, *China* 59 B12
Wujiang, *China* 59 B13
Wukari, *Nigeria* 83 D6
Wulajie, *China* 57 B14
Wulanbulang, *China* 56 D6
Wular L., *India* 69 B6
Wulehe, *Ghana* 83 D5
Wulian, *China* 57 G10
Wuliang Shan, *China* 58 E3
Wuliaru, *Indonesia* 63 F8
Wuling Shan, *China* 58 C7
Wulong, *China* 58 C6
Wulumuchi = Ürümqi, *China* 50 E9
Wum, *Cameroon* 83 D7
Wuming, *China* 58 F7
Wun Rog, *Sudan* 81 F2
Wundowie, *Australia* 93 F2
Wuning, *China* 59 C10
Wunnummin L., *Canada* 102 B2
Wunsiedel, *Germany* 25 E8
Wunstorf, *Germany* 24 C5
Wuntho, *Burma* 67 H19
Wuping, *China* 59 E11
Wuppertal, *Germany* 24 D3
Wuppertal, *S. Africa* 88 E2
Wuqing, *China* 57 E9
Wurtsboro, *U.S.A.* 111 E10
Würzburg, *Germany* 25 F5
Wurzen, *Germany* 24 D8
Wushan, *China* 56 G3
Wushishi, *Nigeria* 83 D6
Wusuli Jiang = Ussuri →, *Asia* 54 A7
Wutach →, *Germany* 25 H4
Wutai, *China* 56 E7
Wuting = Huimin, *China* 57 F9
Wutong, *China* 59 E8
Wutonghaolai, *China* 57 C11
Wutongqiao, *China* 58 C4
Wuwei, *Anhui, China* 59 B11
Wuwei, *Gansu, China* 60 C5
Wuxi, *Jiangsu, China* 59 B13
Wuxi, *Sichuan, China* 58 B7
Wuxiang, *China* 56 F7
Wuxuan, *China* 58 F7
Wuxue, *China* 59 C10
Wuyang, *China* 56 H7
Wuyi, *Hebei, China* 56 F8
Wuyi, *Zhejiang, China* 59 C12
Wuyi Shan, *China* 59 D11
Wuyishan, *China* 59 D12
Wuyo, *Nigeria* 83 C7
Wuyuan, *Jiangxi, China* 59 C11
Wuyuan, *Nei Mongol Zizhiqu, China* 56 D5
Wuzhai, *China* 56 E6
Wuzhi Shan, *China* 64 C7
Wuzhong, *China* 56 E4
Wuzhou, *China* 59 F8
Wyaaba Cr. →, *Australia* 94 B3
Wyalkatchem, *Australia* 93 F2
Wyalusing, *U.S.A.* 111 E8
Wyandotte, *U.S.A.* 108 D4
Wyandra, *Australia* 95 D4
Wyangala Res., *Australia* 95 E4
Wyara, L., *Australia* 95 D3
Wycheproof, *Australia* 95 F3
Wye →, *U.K.* 13 F5
Wyemandoo, *Australia* 93 E2
Wyk, *Germany* 24 A4
Wymondham, *U.K.* 13 E9
Wymore, *U.S.A.* 112 E6
Wyndham, *Australia* 92 C4
Wyndham, *N.Z.* 91 M2
Wynne, *U.S.A.* 113 H9
Wynyard, *Australia* 94 G4
Wynyard, *Canada* 105 C8
Wyola L., *Australia* 93 E5
Wyoming, *Canada* 110 D2
Wyoming □, *U.S.A.* 114 E10
Wyomissing, *U.S.A.* 111 F9
Wyong, *Australia* 95 E5
Wyrzysk, *Poland* 45 E4
Wyśmierzyce, *Poland* 45 G7
Wysoka, *Poland* 45 E4
Wysokie, *Poland* 45 H9
Wysokie Mazowieckie, *Poland* 45 F9
Wyszków, *Poland* 45 F8
Wyszogród, *Poland* 45 F7
Wytheville, *U.S.A.* 108 G5
Wyżyna Małopolska, *Poland* 45 H7

X

Xaçmaz, *Azerbaijan* 49 K9
Xai-Xai, *Mozam.* 89 D5
Xainza, *China* 60 C3
Xangongo, *Angola* 88 B2
Xankändi, *Azerbaijan* 70 B5
Xanlar, *Azerbaijan* 49 K8
Xanten, *Germany* 24 D2
Xánthi, *Greece* 41 E8
Xánthi □, *Greece* 41 E8
Xanthos, *Turkey* 39 E11
Xanxerê, *Brazil* 127 B5
Xapuri, *Brazil* 124 F5
Xar Moron He →, *China* 57 C11
Xarrë, *Albania* 40 G4
Xátiva, *Spain* 33 G4
Xau, L., *Botswana* 88 C3
Xavantina, *Brazil* 127 A5
Xenia, *U.S.A.* 108 F4
Xeropotamos →, *Cyprus* 36 E11
Xertigny, *France* 19 D13
Xhora, *S. Africa* 89 E4
Xhumo, *Botswana* 88 C3
Xi Jiang →, *China* 59 F9
Xi Xian, *Henan, China* 59 A10
Xi Xian, *Shanxi, China* 56 F6
Xia Xian, *China* 56 G6
Xiachengzi, *China* 57 B16
Xiachuan Dao, *China* 59 G9
Xiaguan, *China* 58 E3
Xiajiang, *China* 59 D10
Xiajin, *China* 56 F9
Xiamen, *China* 59 E12
Xi'an, *China* 56 G5
Xian Xian, *China* 56 E9
Xianfeng, *China* 58 C7
Xiang Jiang →, *China* 59 C9
Xiangcheng, *Henan, China* 56 H8
Xiangcheng, *Henan, China* 56 H7
Xiangcheng, *Sichuan, China* 58 C2
Xiangdu, *China* 58 F6
Xiangfan, *China* 59 A9
Xianggang = Hong Kong □, *China* 59 F10
Xianghuang Qi, *China* 56 C7
Xiangning, *China* 56 G6
Xiangquan, *China* 56 F7
Xiangquan He = Sutlej →, *Pakistan* 68 E4
Xiangshan, *China* 59 C13
Xiangshui, *China* 57 G10
Xiangtan, *China* 59 D9
Xiangxiang, *China* 59 D9
Xiangyin, *China* 59 C9
Xiangyun, *China* 58 E3
Xiangzhou, *China* 58 F7
Xianju, *China* 59 C13
Xianning, *China* 59 C10
Xianshui He →, *China* 58 B3
Xiantao, *China* 59 B9
Xianyang, *China* 56 G5
Xianyou, *China* 59 E12
Xiao Hinggan Ling, *China* 60 B7
Xiao Xian, *China* 56 G9
Xiaofeng, *China* 59 B12
Xiaogan, *China* 59 B9
Xiaojin, *China* 58 B4
Xiaolan, *China* 59 F9
Xiaoshan, *China* 59 B13
Xiaoyi, *China* 56 F6
Xiapu, *China* 59 D12
Xiawa, *China* 57 C11
Xiayi, *China* 56 G9
Xichang, *China* 58 D4
Xichong, *China* 58 B5
Xichou, *China* 58 E5
Xichuan, *China* 56 H6
Xide, *China* 58 C4
Xiemahe, *China* 59 B8
Xieng Khouang, *Laos* 64 C4
Xifei He →, *China* 56 H9
Xifeng, *Gansu, China* 56 G4
Xifeng, *Guizhou, China* 58 D6
Xifeng, *Liaoning, China* 57 C13
Xifengzhen = Xifeng, *China* 56 G4
Xigazê, *China* 60 D3
Xihe, *China* 56 G3
Xihua, *China* 56 H8
Xilaganí, *Greece* 41 F9
Xiliao He →, *China* 57 C12
Xilin, *China* 58 E5
Xilókastron, *Greece* 38 C4
Xime, *Guinea-Biss.* 82 C2
Ximeng, *China* 58 F2
Xin Jiang →, *China* 59 C11
Xin Xian = Xinzhou, *China* 56 E7
Xinavane, *Mozam.* 89 D5
Xinbin, *China* 57 D13
Xincai, *China* 59 A10
Xinchang, *China* 59 C13
Xincheng, *Guangxi Zhuangzu, China* 58 E7
Xincheng, *Jiangxi, China* 59 D10
Xindu, *China* 58 B5
Xinfeng, *Guangdong, China* 59 E10
Xinfeng, *Jiangxi, China* 59 D11
Xinfeng, *Jiangxi, China* 59 E10
Xinfengjiang Skuiku, *China* 59 F10
Xing Xian, *China* 56 E6
Xing'an, *Guangxi Zhuangzu, China* 59 E8
Xingan, *Jiangxi, China* 59 D10
Xingcheng, *China* 57 D11
Xingguo, *China* 59 D10
Xinghe, *China* 56 D7
Xinghua, *China* 57 H10
Xinghua Wan, *China* 59 E12
Xinglong, *China* 57 D9
Xingning, *China* 59 E10
Xingping, *China* 56 G5
Xingren, *China* 58 E5
Xingshan, *China* 59 B8
Xingtai, *China* 56 F8
Xingu →, *Brazil* 122 D5
Xingwen, *China* 58 C5
Xingyang, *China* 56 G7
Xinhe, *China* 56 F8
Xinhua, *China* 59 D8
Xinhuang, *China* 58 D7
Xinhui, *China* 59 F9
Xining, *China* 60 C5
Xinjian, *China* 59 C10
Xinjiang, *China* 56 G6
Xinjiang Uygur Zizhiqu □, *China* 60 B3
Xinjie, *China* 58 D3
Xinjin = Pulandian, *China* 57 E11
Xinjin, *China* 58 B4
Xinkai He →, *China* 57 C12
Xinle, *China* 56 E8
Xinlitun, *China* 57 D12
Xinlong, *China* 58 B3
Xinmin, *China* 57 D12
Xinning, *China* 59 D8
Xinping, *China* 58 E3
Xinshao, *China* 59 D8
Xintai, *China* 57 G9
Xintian, *China* 59 E9
Xinxian, *China* 59 B10
Xinxiang, *China* 56 G7
Xinxing, *China* 59 F9
Xinyang, *China* 59 A10
Xinye, *China* 59 A9
Xinyi, *China* 59 F8
Xinyu, *China* 59 D10
Xinzhan, *China* 57 C14
Xinzheng, *China* 56 G7
Xinzhou, *Hubei, China* 59 B10
Xinzhou, *Shanxi, China* 56 E7
Xinzo de Limia, *Spain* 34 C3
Xiong Xian, *China* 56 E9
Xiongyuecheng, *China* 57 D12
Xiping, *Henan, China* 56 H8
Xiping, *Henan, China* 56 H6
Xiping, *Zhejiang, China* 59 C12
Xique-Xique, *Brazil* 125 F10
Xisha Qundao = Paracel Is., *S. China Sea* 62 A4
Xishui, *Guizhou, China* 58 C6
Xishui, *Hubei, China* 59 B10
Xitole, *Guinea-Biss.* 82 C2
Xiu Shui →, *China* 59 C10
Xiuning, *China* 59 C12
Xiuren, *China* 59 E8
Xiushan, *China* 58 C7
Xiushui, *China* 59 C10
Xiuwen, *China* 58 D6
Xiuyan, *China* 57 D12
Xixabangma Feng, *China* 67 E14
Xixia, *China* 56 H6
Xixiang, *China* 56 H4
Xiyang, *China* 56 F7
Xizang Zizhiqu □, *China* 60 C3
Xlendi, *Malta* 36 C1
Xu Jiang →, *China* 59 D11
Xuan Loc, *Vietnam* 65 G6
Xuan'en, *China* 58 C7
Xuanhan, *China* 58 B6
Xuanhua, *China* 56 D8
Xuanwei, *China* 58 C5
Xuanzhou, *China* 59 B12
Xuchang, *China* 56 G7
Xudat, *Azerbaijan* 49 K9
Xuefeng Shan, *China* 59 D8
Xuejiaping, *China* 59 B8
Xun Jiang →, *China* 59 F8
Xun Xian, *China* 56 G8
Xundian, *China* 58 E4
Xunwu, *China* 59 E10
Xunyang, *China* 56 H5
Xunyi, *China* 56 G5
Xupu, *China* 59 D8
Xúquer →, *Spain* 33 F4
Xushui, *China* 56 E8
Xuwen, *China* 59 G8
Xuyen Moc, *Vietnam* 65 G6
Xuyong, *China* 58 C5
Xuzhou, *China* 57 G9
Xylophagou, *Cyprus* 36 E12

Y

Ya Xian, *China* 64 C7
Yaamba, *Australia* 94 C5
Ya'an, *China* 58 C4
Yaapeet, *Australia* 95 F3
Yabassi, *Cameroon* 83 E6
Yabelo, *Ethiopia* 81 G4
Yablanitsa, *Bulgaria* 41 C8
Yablonovy Ra. = Yablonovyy Khrebet, *Russia* 51 D12
Yablonovyy Khrebet, *Russia* 51 D12
Yabrai Shan, *China* 56 E2
Yabrūd, *Syria* 75 B5
Yacheng, *China* 64 C7
Yacuiba, *Bolivia* 126 A3
Yacuma →, *Bolivia* 124 F5
Yadgir, *India* 66 L10
Yadkin →, *U.S.A.* 109 H5
Yadrin, *Russia* 48 C8
Yaeyama-Rettō, *Japan* 55 M1
Yagaba, *Ghana* 83 C4
Yağcılar, *Turkey* 39 B10
Yagodnoye, *Russia* 51 C15
Yahila, *Dem. Rep. of the Congo* 86 B1
Yahk, *Canada* 104 D5
Yahotyn, *Ukraine* 47 G6
Yahuma, *Dem. Rep. of the Congo* 84 D4
Yahyalı, *Turkey* 72 C6
Yaita, *Japan* 55 F9
Yaiza, *Canary Is.* 37 F6
Yajiang, *China* 58 B3
Yajua, *Nigeria* 83 C7
Yakima, *U.S.A.* 114 C3
Yakima →, *U.S.A.* 114 C3
Yako, *Burkina Faso* 82 C4
Yakobi I., *U.S.A.* 104 B1
Yakoruda, *Bulgaria* 40 D7
Yakovlevka, *Russia* 54 B6
Yaku-Shima, *Japan* 55 J5
Yakumo, *Japan* 54 C10
Yakutat, *U.S.A.* 100 C6
Yakutia = Sakha □, *Russia* 51 C13
Yakutsk, *Russia* 51 C13
Yala, *Thailand* 65 J3
Yale, *U.S.A.* 110 C2
Yalgoo, *Australia* 93 E2
Yalinga, *C.A.R.* 84 C4
Yalkubul, Punta, *Mexico* 119 C7
Yalleroi, *Australia* 94 C4
Yalobusha →, *U.S.A.* 113 J9
Yalong Jiang →, *China* 58 D3
Yalova, *Turkey* 41 F13
Yalta, *Ukraine* 47 K8
Yalu Jiang →, *China* 57 E13
Yalvaç, *Turkey* 72 C4
Yam Ha Melaḥ = Dead Sea, *Asia* 75 D4
Yam Kinneret, *Israel* 75 C4
Yamada, *Japan* 55 H5
Yamagata, *Japan* 54 E10
Yamagata □, *Japan* 54 E10
Yamaguchi, *Japan* 55 G5
Yamaguchi □, *Japan* 55 G5
Yamal, Poluostrov, *Russia* 50 B8
Yamal Pen. = Yamal, Poluostrov, *Russia* 50 B8
Yamanashi □, *Japan* 55 G9
Yamba, *Australia* 95 D5
Yambarran Ra., *Australia* 92 C5
Yambéring, *Guinea* 82 C2
Yâmbiô, *Sudan* 81 G2
Yambol, *Bulgaria* 41 D10
Yamdena, *Indonesia* 63 F8
Yame, *Japan* 55 H5
Yamethin, *Burma* 67 J20
Yamma-Yamma, L., *Australia* 95 D3
Yamoussoukro, *Ivory C.* 82 D3
Yampa →, *U.S.A.* 114 F9
Yampi Sd., *Australia* 92 C3
Yampil, *Moldova* 47 H5
Yampol = Yampil, *Moldova* 47 H5
Yamrat, *Nigeria* 83 C6
Yamrukchal = Botev, *Bulgaria* 41 D8